*The Consumer Credit and Sales
Legal Practice Series*

STUDENT LOAN LAW

Fourth Edition

See *page ix* for information about the companion website.

Deanne Loonin

Contributing Author: Geoff Walsh

National Consumer Law Center®

7 Winthrop Square, 4th Floor   Boston, MA 02110

www.consumerlaw.org

About NCLC®	The National Consumer Law Center®, a nonprofit corporation founded in 1969, assists consumers, advocates, and public policy makers nationwide who use the powerful and complex tools of consumer law to ensure justice and fair treatment for all, particularly those whose poverty renders them powerless to demand accountability from the economic marketplace. For more information, go to www.consumerlaw.org.
Ordering NCLC Publications	Order securely online at www.consumerlaw.org, or contact Publications Department, National Consumer Law Center, 7 Winthrop Square, 4th Floor, Boston, MA 02110, (617) 542-9595, fax: (617) 542-8028, e-mail: publications@nclc.org.
Training and Conferences	NCLC participates in numerous national, regional, and local consumer law trainings. Its annual fall conference is a forum for consumer rights attorneys from legal services programs, private practice, government, and nonprofit organizations to share insights into common problems and explore novel and tested approaches that promote consumer justice in the marketplace. Contact NCLC for more information or see our website.
Case Consulting	Case analysis, consulting and co-counseling for lawyers representing vulnerable consumers are among NCLC's important activities. Administration on Aging funds allow us to provide free consulting to legal services advocates representing elderly consumers on many types of cases. Massachusetts Legal Assistance Corporation funds permit case assistance to advocates representing low-income Massachusetts consumers. Other funding may allow NCLC to provide very brief consultations to other advocates without charge. More comprehensive case analysis and research is available for a reasonable fee. See our website for more information at www.consumerlaw.org.
Charitable Donations and Cy Pres Awards	NCLC's work depends in part on the support of private donors. Tax-deductible donations should be made payable to National Consumer Law Center, Inc. For more information, contact Suzanne Cutler of NCLC's Development Office at (617) 542-8010 or scutler@nclc.org. NCLC has also received generous court-approved *cy pres* awards arising from consumer class actions to advance the interests of class members. For more information, contact Robert Hobbs (rhobbs@nclc.org) or Rich Dubois (rdubois@nclc.org) at (617) 542-8010.
Comments and Corrections	Write to the above address to the attention of the Editorial Department or e-mail consumerlaw@nclc.org.
About This Volume	This is the Fourth Edition of *Student Loan Law*. Discard all prior editions and supplements. This book includes a companion website. Continuing developments can be found in periodic supplements to this volume and in NCLC REPORTS.
Cite This Volume As	National Consumer Law Center, Student Loan Law (4th ed. 2010).
Attention	*This publication is designed to provide authoritative information concerning the subject matter covered. Always use the most current edition and supplement, and use other sources for more recent developments or for special rules for individual jurisdictions. This publication cannot substitute for the independent judgment and skills of an attorney or other professional. Non-attorneys are cautioned against using these materials to conduct a lawsuit without advice from an attorney and are cautioned against engaging in the unauthorized practice of law.*
Copyright	© 2010 by National Consumer Law Center, Inc. National Consumer Law Center and NCLC are registered trademarks of National Consumer Law Center, Inc. All rights reserved. ISBN: 978-1-60248-078-0 (this volume) ISBN: 0-943116-10-4 (Series) Library of Congress Control Number: 2010941050

About the Authors

Deanne Loonin is an NCLC staff attorney focusing on student loan law. She is the director of NCLC's Student Loan Borrower Assistance Project. She also works more generally on consumer credit issues. She was formerly a legal services attorney in Los Angeles specializing in consumer fraud cases. She is the author of *Surviving Debt* and co-author of *Credit Discrimination* (4th ed. 2005).

Geoff Walsh has been a legal services attorney for over twenty-five years. He is presently a staff attorney with NCLC, and before that he worked with the housing and consumer units of Community Legal Services in Philadelphia and was a staff attorney with Vermont Legal Aid in its Springfield, Vermont office. His practice has focused upon housing and bankruptcy issues. He is a contributing author to *Consumer Bankruptcy Law and Practice* and *Foreclosures*.

Acknowledgments

We are particularly grateful to Dorothy Tan for editorial supervision; Kim Calvi for editorial assistance; Shirlron Williams for cite checking; Allen Agnitti, Emily Green Caplan, and Nathanael Player for legal research; Shannon Halbrook for the companion website; Mary McLean for indexing; and Xylutions for typesetting services. Thanks also to NCLC colleagues Jon Sheldon and Diane Thompson for reviewing various sections. We would also like to thank Department of Education staff, particularly ombudsman Debra Wiley and her office, for generously answering questions and clarifying department policies. We very much appreciate the many attorneys, too numerous to name here, who have contributed pleadings and other information to this and prior editions. Special thanks to Jon Sheldon for authoring the student loan chapter in *Unfair and Deceptive Acts and Practices*, which provided the springboard for this volume.

What Your Library Should Contain

The Consumer Credit and Sales Legal Practice Series contains 18 titles, updated annually, arranged into four libraries, and designed to be an attorney's primary practice guide and legal resource in all 50 states. Each title includes free access to a companion website, containing the treatise's appendices, sample pleadings, primary sources, and other practice aids, allowing pinpoint searches and the pasting of text into a word processor. Access remains free as long as purchasers keep their titles current.

Debtor Rights Library

2009 Ninth Edition (Two Volumes), 2010 Supplement, and Companion Website, Including NCLC's Bankruptcy Forms Software

Consumer Bankruptcy Law and Practice: the definitive personal bankruptcy manual, from the initial interview to final discharge, including consumer rights when a company files for bankruptcy. The updated ninth edition contains the latest case law interpreting the 2005 Act, and includes such practice aids as the latest Bankruptcy Code, Rules, and fee schedules, a date calculator, over 150 pleadings and forms, software to compute the initial forms, means test data, and a client questionnaire and handout.

2008 Sixth Edition, 2010 Supplement, and Companion Website

Fair Debt Collection: the basic reference, covering the Fair Debt Collection Practices Act and common law, state statutory and other federal debt collection protections. Unique case summaries cover reported and unreported FDCPA cases by category. The companion website contains sample pleadings and discovery, the FTC Commentary, an index to and the full text of *all* FTC staff opinion letters, and other practice aids.

2010 Third Edition and Companion Website

Foreclosures: examines RESPA and other federal and state rights to challenge servicer abuses, as well as details on workout options, loan modification, and mediation programs implemented by federal and state governments. The volume also covers standing and substantive and procedural defenses to foreclosure and tactics after the foreclosure sale. Special chapters cover tax liens, land installment sales contracts, manufactured home foreclosures, and other topics.

2010 Seventh Edition and Companion Website

Repossessions: a unique guide to motor vehicle and mobile home repossessions, threatened seizures of household goods, statutory liens, and automobile lease and rent-to-own default remedies. The volume examines UCC Article 9 and hundreds of other federal and state statutes regulating repossessions.

2010 Fourth Edition and Companion Website

Student Loan Law: collection harassment; closed school, disability, and other discharges; tax intercepts, wage garnishment, and offset of social security benefits; and repayment plans, consolidation loans, deferments, and non-payment of loan based on school fraud.

2008 Fourth Edition, 2010 Supplement, and Companion Website

Access to Utility Service: consumer rights as to regulated and unregulated utilities, including telecommunications, terminations, billing errors, low-income payment plans, utility allowances in subsidized housing, LIHEAP, and weatherization.

National Consumer Law Center ■ (617) 542-9595 ■ FAX (617) 542-8028 ■ publications@nclc.org
Order securely online at www.consumerlaw.org

Credit and Banking Library

2010 Seventh Edition (Two Volumes) and Companion Website

Truth in Lending: detailed analysis of *all* aspects of TILA, the Consumer Leasing Act, the Fair Credit Billing Act, the Home Ownership and Equity Protection Act (HOEPA), and the Credit CARD Act, including the major 2010 amendments. Appendices and the website contain the Acts, Reg. Z, Reg. M, and their official staff commentaries, numerous sample pleadings, rescission notices, two programs to compute APRs, TIL legislative history, and a unique compilation of *all Federal Register* notices and supplementary information on Regulation Z since 1969.

2010 Seventh Edition and Companion Website

Fair Credit Reporting: the key resource for handling any type of credit reporting issue, from cleaning up blemished credit records to suing reporting agencies and creditors for inaccurate reports. Covers the new FACTA changes, identity theft, creditor liability for failing to properly reinvestigate disputed information, credit scoring, privacy issues, the Credit Repair Organizations Act, state credit reporting and repair statutes, and common law claims.

2009 Fourth Edition, 2010 Supplement, and Companion Website

Consumer Banking and Payments Law: covers checks, telechecks, electronic fund transfers, electronic check conversions, money orders, and credit, debit, payroll, and stored value cards. The title also covers banker's right of setoff, electronic transfers of federal and state benefit payments, and a special chapter on electronic records and signatures.

2009 Fourth Edition, 2010 Supplement, and Companion Website

The Cost of Credit: Regulation, Preemption, and Industry Abuses: a one-of-a-kind resource detailing state and federal regulation of consumer credit in all 50 states, examines numerous types of predatory lending, federal preemption of state law, credit math calculations, excessive credit charges, credit insurance, and numerous other topics.

2009 Fifth Edition, 2010 Supplement, and Companion Website

Credit Discrimination: analysis of the Equal Credit Opportunity Act, Fair Housing Act, Civil Rights Acts, and state credit discrimination statutes, including reprints of all relevant federal interpretations, government enforcement actions, and numerous sample pleadings.

Consumer Litigation Library

2008 First Edition, 2010 Supplement, and Companion Website

Collection Actions: a complete guide to consumer defenses and counterclaims to collection lawsuits filed in court or in arbitration, with extensive discussion of setting aside default judgments and limitations on a collector's post-judgment remedies. Special chapters include the rights of active duty military, and unique issues involving medical debt, government collections, collector's attorney fees, and bad check laws.

2007 Fifth Edition, 2010 Supplement, and Companion Website

Consumer Arbitration Agreements: successful approaches to challenge arbitration agreements' enforceability and waivers of class arbitration, the interrelation of the Federal Arbitration Act and state law, class actions and punitive damages in arbitration, implications of NAF's withdrawal from consumer arbitrations, the right to discovery, and other topics.

2010 Seventh Edition and Companion Website

Consumer Class Actions: makes class litigation manageable even for small offices, including numerous sample pleadings, class certification memoranda, discovery, class notices, settlement materials, and much more. Includes a detailed analysis of the Class Action Fairness Act, class arbitration, state class action rules and case law, and other topics.

Website and 2010 Index Guide: ALL pleadings from ALL NCLC treatises, including Consumer Law Pleadings Numbers One through Sixteen

Consumer Law Pleadings: over *2000* notable pleadings from all types of consumer cases, including predatory lending, foreclosures, automobile fraud, lemon laws, debt collection, fair credit reporting, home improvement fraud, student loans, and lender liability. Finding aids pinpoint desired pleading in seconds, ready to paste into a word processor.

National Consumer Law Center ■ (617) 542-9595 ■ FAX (617) 542-8028 ■ publications@nclc.org
Order securely online at www.consumerlaw.org

Deception and Warranties Library

2008 Seventh Edition, 2010 Supplement, and Companion Website

Unfair and Deceptive Acts and Practices: the only practice manual covering all aspects of a deceptive practices case in every state. Special sections on automobile sales, the federal racketeering (RICO) statute, unfair insurance practices, the FTC Holder Rule, telemarketing fraud, attorney fees, and many other topics.

2007 Third Edition, 2010 Supplement, and Companion Website

Automobile Fraud: examination of title law, "yo-yo" sales, odometer tampering, lemon laundering, sale of salvage and wrecked cars, undisclosed prior use, and prior damage to new cars. The website contains numerous sample pleadings and title search techniques.

2010 Fourth Edition and Companion Website

Consumer Warranty Law: comprehensive treatment of new and used car lemon laws, the Magnuson-Moss Warranty Act, UCC Articles 2 and 2A, mobile home, new home, and assistive device warranty laws, FTC Used Car Rule, tort theories, car repair and home improvement statutes, service contract and lease laws, with numerous sample pleadings.

NCLC's Companion Websites

Every NCLC manual includes a companion website, allowing rapid access to appendices, pleadings, primary sources, and other practice aids. Search for documents by category, or with a table of contents or various keyword search options. All documents can be downloaded, printed, and pasted into a word processing document. Pleadings are also available in Word format. Web access is free with each title ordered and remains free as long as a title is kept current.

Website continually subject to update

Consumer Law on the Web: combines *everything* from the 18 other NCLC companion websites. Using *Consumer Law on the Web,* instead of multiple individual companion websites, is often the fastest and most convenient way to pinpoint and retrieve key documents among the thousands available on our individual companion websites.

Other NCLC Publications for Lawyers

Issued 24 times a year

NCLC REPORTS, a four-page newsletter, keeps you up to date 24 times a year with the latest consumer law developments. It is also an essential practice tool, with novel ideas, innovative tactics, and key insights from NCLC's experienced consumer law attorneys. Learn the practice implications of new statutes, regulations, cases and trends.

2009 Second Edition and Companion Website

Foreclosure Prevention Counseling: Preserving the American Dream: explains how to obtain a workout, with advice specifically tailored for Fannie Mae, Freddie Mac, subprime, FHA-insured, VA, and Rural Housing Service loans. The book also details new loan modification initiatives from federal and state governments and industry.

2007 First Edition and Companion Website

Bankruptcy Basics: A Step-by-Step Guide for Pro Bono Attorneys, General Practitioners, and Legal Services Offices: provides everything attorneys new to bankruptcy need to file their first case, with a companion website that contains software, sample pleadings, and other practice aids that greatly simplify handling a bankruptcy case.

2007 Second Edition with CD-Rom

STOP Predatory Lending: A Guide for Legal Advocates: provides a roadmap and practical legal strategy for litigating predatory lending abuses, from small loans to mortgage loans. How to analyze the documents, spot issues, raise legal claims, select defendants, and even craft a community response.

National Consumer Law Center ■ (617) 542-9595 ■ FAX (617) 542-8028 ■ publications@nclc.org

Order securely online at www.consumerlaw.org

2009 First Edition

Instant Evidence: A Quick Guide to Federal Evidence and Objections: facilitates objection by rule number and includes common objections and motions at every stage of a case—all in under 20 pages! Spiral-bound to lay flat, all pages are laminated, allowing new notations for each trial with a dry-erase pen.

2006 Second Edition with CD-Rom

The Practice of Consumer Law: Seeking Economic Justice: contains an essential overview to consumer law and explains how to get started in a private or legal services consumer practice. Packed with invaluable sample pleadings and practice pointers for even experienced consumer attorneys.

National Consumer Law Center Guide Series are books designed for consumers, counselors, and attorneys new to consumer law:

2010 Edition

NCLC Guide to Surviving Debt: a great overview of consumer law. Everything a paralegal, new attorney, or client needs to know about home foreclosures and mortgage modifications, debt collectors, managing credit card debt, whether to refinance, credit card problems, evictions, repossessions, credit reporting, utility terminations, student loans, budgeting, and bankruptcy.

First Edition

NCLC Guide to the Rights of Utility Consumers: explains consumer rights concerning electric, gas, and other utility services: shut off protections, rights to restore terminated service, bill payment options, weatherization tips, rights to government assistance, and much more.

First Edition

NCLC Guide to Consumer Rights for Domestic Violence Survivors: provides practical advice to help survivors get back on their feet financially and safely establish their economic independence.

First Edition

NCLC Guide to Mobile Homes: what consumers and their advocates need to know about mobile home dealer sales practices and an in-depth look at mobile home quality and defects, with 35 photographs and construction details.

First Edition

Return to Sender: Getting a Refund or Replacement for Your Lemon Car: find how lemon laws work, what consumers and their lawyers should know to evaluate each other, investigative techniques and discovery tips, how to handle both informal dispute resolution and trials, and more.

Visit **www.consumerlaw.org** to order securely online or for more information on all NCLC publications and companion websites, including the full tables of contents, indices, and **web-based searches of the publications' full text**.

National Consumer Law Center ■ (617) 542-9595 ■ FAX (617) 542-8028 ■ publications@nclc.org
Order securely online at www.consumerlaw.org

About the Companion Website, Other Search Options

The Companion Website

Purchase of any title in NCLC's consumer law practice series includes free access to its companion website. Access remains free with continued subscription to that title. Frequently updated, NCLC companion websites offer the treatises' appendices plus hundreds of additional documents in PDF and Microsoft Word formats—pleadings, forms, statutes, regulations, agency interpretations, legislative and regulatory history, and much more—all easily located with flexible, powerful search tools. Documents can be electronically searched, printed, downloaded, and copy-pasted into a word processor.

Accessing the Companion Website

One-time registration is required to access NCLC companion websites. Once registered, users logging in are granted access to all websites they are authorized to use, with only one username and password required.

Subscribers do *not* need to register more than once.[1] Subscribers purchasing additional NCLC titles are automatically given access to the new websites under their existing username and password. Registering a second time with the same registration number overrides a prior username and password.

To register, go to www.consumerlaw.org/webaccess, and click "New users click here to register." Enter the Companion Website Registration Number found on the packing statement or invoice accompanying this publication.[2] Then enter the requested information and click Enter. An email address may be used for the username or a different username may be chosen.

Once registered, go to **www.consumerlaw.org/webaccess**, enter your username and password, and select the desired companion website from the list of authorized sites.

---

[1] If all your subscriptions to NCLC treatises are allowed to lapse, your account may be deleted; if this happens, you must re-register if you subsequently purchase a book.

[2] If you cannot locate this number, contact NCLC Publications at (617) 542-9595 or publications@nclc.org.

Libraries and others subscribing to the entire 18-volume set can arrange "IP access" so that a username and password are *not* required. Email publications@nclc.org with a list or range of static IP addresses for which access should be permitted *without* the need to enter a username and password.

We encourage users who find mistakes to notify us using the "Report Errors" button, on the left toolbar. Also on the left toolbar, users can click "My Account" to change personal information.

Use of the companion websites with Internet Explorer requires Adobe Reader 7.0 or later or Adobe Acrobat 7.0 or later. Users of other browsers, or those experiencing problems with the websites, should download the latest version of the free Adobe Reader **(currently 9.4) from Adobe's website at www.adobe.com.** A link to Adobe's site is provided on the NCLC companion website login page.

Locating Documents on the Companion Website

The companion website provides three options to locate documents.

1. The search page (the home page) offers keyword searches to find documents—either full-text searches of all documents on the website or of only the documents' titles.

- Narrow the search to documents of a certain type (such as federal statutes or pleadings) by making a selection from the "Document Type" menu, and then perform a full text or document title search.
- If unsure of a keyword's spelling, type the first few letters and click "See choices."
- To locate a specific appendix section, select the appendix section number (e.g., A.2.3) or a partial identifier (e.g., A) in the search page's "Appendix" drop-down fields.
- Click Search Hints for a quick reference to special search operators, wildcards, shortcuts, and complex searches. Read this closely, as syntax and search operators may be slightly different from those of other websites.

2. The contents page (click on the "Contents" tab at the top of the page) is a traditional "branching" table of contents. Click a branch to expand it into a list of sub-branches or documents. Each document appears once on this contents tree.

3. The pleading finder page (click on the "Pleading Finder" tab at the top of the page, *if available*) allows pleadings to be located using one or more menus, such as "Type of Pleading" or "Subject." **Select more than one item from one menu, or deselect items, by holding the Ctrl key while clicking.** For example, make one selection from "Type of Pleading–General," one from "Subject," and three from "Legal Claims" to locate all pleadings of that type and subject that contain one or more of the three legal claims selected. If this search produces insufficient results, simply broaden the search by deselecting "Subject" and/or "Legal Claims" to find pleadings of that type in any subject area or based upon any legal claim. This page also includes optional fields to specify terms to be found in the documents' text or titles, to further narrow search results.

Additional software, related websites, and other information can be located by clicking on links found at the left hand toolbar or on the "Search" page. These links bring you to credit math software, search tips, other websites, tables of contents and indices of all NCLC publications, and other practice aids. Some companion websites have "Software" or "Links" tabs at the top of the page, where this material may also be found.

Finding Word Versions of Website Documents

All documents on the website are in PDF format, and can be copied and pasted into a word processor. Pleadings and certain other documents also are available in Word format, facilitating the opening of entire documents in a word processor. After opening the selected PDF file, click at the top of the page on "Word Version, if available." If a Word version is listed as available, click "DOC Download Document" to save the Word file to your computer.

Documents Found on the Website

The *Student Loan Law* companion website is packed with up-to-date information, including key federal statutes and regulations, such as the College Cost Reduction Act of 2007, and Department of Education forms and policy guidance letters, many of which are newly updated for 2011. The site also includes dozens of letters, complaints and discovery pleadings useful in collection abuse, garnishment, and fraud cases. Numerous reports and helpful student guides are also available.

Locating Topics in This Treatise

Go to www.consumerlaw.org/keyword to electronically search the full text of every chapter and appendix of this title's main volume and supplement. While the chapters' complete text is not available online, this web-based search engine specifies each page of this title where a word or phrase is found. Select this title, enter a search term or combination of search terms—such as a case name, a regulation cite, or other keywords—and the page numbers containing those terms are listed. Search results are shown with the surrounding text ("hits in context"), facilitating selection of the most relevant pages.

Locating Topics in Other NCLC Manuals or **NCLC REPORTS**

The full text of all NCLC treatises and supplements, *NCLC REPORTS*, and other publications can be electronically searched to locate relevant topics as described above. Go to www.consumerlaw.org/keyword, and enter a search term or combination of search terms in a similar fashion to performing a keyword search on one title.

Current tables of contents, indices, and other information for all NCLC titles can be found at www.consumerlaw.org/shop. Click *Publications for Lawyers* and scroll down to the book you want. The PDF documents found there can be quickly searched for a word or phrase.

The Quick Reference at the back of this volume lets you pinpoint the correct treatise and treatise sections or appendices that discuss over 1000 different subject areas. These subject areas are listed in alphabetical order and can also be electronically searched at www.consumerlaw.org/qr.

Finding Pleadings

Pleadings relating to this title are found in PDF and Word format on the companion website; search options are discussed above at "Locating Documents on the Website." Over 2000 pleadings are also available at NCLC's *Consumer Law Pleadings* website using the same search techniques discussed above. Pleadings can also be located using *Consumer Law Pleadings*' index guide, which organizes pleadings by type, subject area, legal claim, title, and other categories identical to those on the website.

Summary Contents

	About the Companion Website, Other Search Options	ix
	Contents	xiii
Chapter 1	Getting Started	1
Chapter 2	Taking Out a Federal Student Loan: Basic Terms and Conditions	27
Chapter 3	Pre-Default Repayment Options	39
Chapter 4	Postponing Repayment on Federal Student Loans	51
Chapter 5	Implications of Student Loan Defaults	63
Chapter 6	Repayment Strategies for Getting Out of Default	69
Chapter 7	Federal Student Loan Collection: Due Diligence Requirements, Private Collection Agencies, and Defenses to Collection Actions	83
Chapter 8	Property and Asset Seizures to Collect Federal Student Loans	117
Chapter 9	Statutory Discharges of Federal Student Loans	139
Chapter 10	Discharging Student Loans in Bankruptcy	175
Chapter 11	Private Student Loans	217
Chapter 12	Proprietary School and Other Student Loan Litigation	237
Appendix A	Federal Student Loan Statutes	273

Appendix B	Federal Regulations	323
Appendix C	Department of Education Policy Guidance Letters	453
Appendix D	Student Assistance Forms	476
Appendix E	Sample Pleadings and Letters	591
Appendix F	Sample Discovery and Freedom of Information Act Requests	621
Appendix G	Directory of Guaranty Agencies	635
Appendix H	Student Loan Collection Agencies	641
Appendix I	Federal Student Financial Assistance: Frequently Asked Questions	643
Appendix J	NCLC's Student Loan Borrower Assistance Website	647
Appendix K	Finding Pleadings, Primary Sources on the Companion Website	649
Appendix L	Student Loans on the Web	655
	Index	657
	Quick Reference to Consumer Credit and Sales Legal Practice Series	679

Contents

About the Companion Website, Other Search Options ix

Chapter 1   Getting Started

1.1 Introduction. 1
1.2 Using This Manual. 2
    1.2.1 Road Map. 2
    1.2.2 Clearinghouse Documents 3
    1.2.3 Web-Based Text Search Feature 3
1.3 Introduction to Federal Student Assistance 3
    1.3.1 Brief History. 3
    1.3.2 The End of the FFEL Program. 4
1.4. Types of Federal Student Assistance. 5
    1.4.1 Student Loans 5
        1.4.1.1 Stafford Loans 5
        1.4.1.2 PLUS Loans. 5
        1.4.1.3 Consolidation Loans 6
            1.4.1.3.1 General 6
            1.4.1.3.2 Limits on reconsolidation 6
            1.4.1.3.3 Pros and cons of consolidation. 7
        1.4.1.4 Perkins Loans. 8
        1.4.1.5 Older Loans 8
    1.4.2 Federal Grants. 8
        1.4.2.1 General 8
        1.4.2.2 Pell Grants. 9
            1.4.2.2.1 Basics about Pell grants 9
            1.4.2.2.2 Pell grant overpayments 9
        1.4.2.3 TEACH Grants. 9
        1.4.2.4 ACG and Smart Grants 10
    1.4.3 Seizure of Student Loan Funds Generally Prohibited 11
    1.4.4 11Educational Benefits for Military Service Members 11
        1.4.4.1 The Post 9/11 G.I. Bill. 11
        1.4.4.2 Other Protections and Programs for Service Members 11
1.5 Financial Need; Applying for Federal Student Loans 12
    1.5.1 General. 12
    1.5.2 Dependent and Independent Students. 12
1.6 Individual Eligibility for Federal Student Loans. 13
    1.6.1 Academic Requirements 13
    1.6.2 Satisfactory Academic Progress 13
    1.6.3 Citizenship Requirements 13
    1.6.4 Drug Convictions. 14
    1.6.5 Incarcerated Students 14
    1.6.6 Prior Student Aid History 14
1.7 Institutional Eligibility. 14

  1.7.1 Eligibility Criteria ... 14
    1.7.1.1 Different Types of Schools ... 14
    1.7.1.2 Gainful Employment ... 15
    1.7.1.3 Admissions Standards ... 16
    1.7.1.4 Distance Education ... 16
  1.7.2 Program Participation Agreements ... 17
    1.7.2.1 General ... 17
    1.7.2.2 The "90/10" Rule for Proprietary Schools ... 17
    1.7.2.3 Limits on Incentive Compensation ... 17
    1.7.2.4 Code of Conduct and Prohibited Inducement Requirements ... 18
    1.7.2.5 Private Education Loan Certification ... 18
    1.7.2.6 Misrepresentation ... 18
  1.7.3 Consumer Information Requirements ... 18
  1.7.4 Administrative Capability ... 20
    1.7.4.1 General ... 20
    1.7.4.2 Cohort Default-Rate Requirements ... 20
      1.7.4.2.1 General ... 20
      1.7.4.2.2 School appeals process ... 20
1.8 Private Student Loans ... 21
1.9 Determining What Type of Loan a Client Has ... 21
1.10 Student Loan and Tax Deductions ... 22
1.11 Checklist for Handling Student Loan Issues ... 22
  1.11.1 First Steps ... 22
  1.11.2 Loan Cancellation ... 23
  1.11.3 Postponing Payment ... 24
  1.11.4 Repayment Options ... 24
  1.11.5 Challenging Collection ... 24
1.12 Assistance for Student Loan Borrowers ... 24
  1.12.1 Ombudsman Programs ... 24
    1.12.1.1 Federal Student Loan Ombudsman ... 24
    1.12.1.2 Other Ombudsman Programs for Federal Student Loans ... 25
    1.12.1.3 Private Student Loan Ombudsman ... 25
  1.12.2 Additional Department of Education Resources ... 25
  1.12.3 NCLC's Student Loan Borrower Assistance Project ... 25
  1.12.4 Potential Problems with For-Profit Counselors ... 26

Chapter 2   Taking Out a Federal Student Loan: Basic Terms and Conditions

2.1 Introduction ... 27
2.2 Loan Limits ... 27
  2.2.1 General ... 27
  2.2.2 Stafford Loan Limits ... 27
  2.2.3 PLUS Loan Limits ... 28
  2.2.4 Perkins Loan Limits ... 28
2.3 Federal Student Loan Interest Rates ... 28
  2.3.1 General ... 28
  2.3.2 Capitalization of Interest ... 29
  2.3.3 Stafford Loan Interest Rates ... 29
  2.3.4 PLUS and Perkins Interest Rates ... 30
  2.3.5 Consolidation Interest Rates ... 30
2.4 Loan Fees ... 30
  2.4.1 Origination Fees ... 30
  2.4.2 Late Charges and Other Fees ... 30
2.5 Disclosures ... 31
  2.5.1 General ... 31

Contents

        2.5.2 Federal Loan Disclosures. 31
        2.5.3 Consolidation Loan Disclosures 33
  2.6 Disbursement of Federal Student Loans 33
  2.7 Cancellations and Refunds 34
  2.8 Master Promissory Notes 34
  2.9 Counseling Requirements. 35

Chapter 3   Pre-Default Repayment Options

  3.1 Pre-Default Repayment Plans 39
        3.1.1 General. 39
        3.1.2 Standard, Graduated, and Extended Repayment Plans 39
        3.1.3 Repayment Plans Tied to Borrower's Income 40
            3.1.3.1 General 40
            3.1.3.2 Income-Based Repayment (IBR) 40
                3.1.3.2.1 Eligibility. 40
                3.1.3.2.2 IBR repayment formula 42
                3.1.3.2.3 Applying for IBR. 42
                3.1.3.2.4 Leaving IBR 43
                3.1.3.2.5 IBR forgiveness. 43
            3.1.3.3 Income-Contingent Repayment Plans (ICR). 45
                3.1.3.3.1 ICR eligibility 45
                3.1.3.3.2 Calculating the monthly payment under ICR plan 45
                3.1.3.3.3 ICR forgiveness. 46
            3.1.3.4 Comparing IBR and ICR 46
            3.1.3.5 Income-Sensitive Plans. 47
        3.1.4 Perkins Loan Repayment. 47
        3.1.5 How Payments Are Applied. 48
  3.2 Loan Servicing. 48
        3.2.1 Performance-Based System 48
        3.2.2 Loan Servicing Requirements. 48

Chapter 4   Postponing Repayment on Federal Student Loans

  4.1 Introduction 51
  4.2 Grace Periods. 51
  4.3 Deferments 51
        4.3.1 Benefits of Deferment. 51
        4.3.2 Borrower's Default Limits Eligibility for Deferment 52
        4.3.3 General Eligibility Requirements for Deferments. 52
        4.3.4 Applying for Deferments. 53
        4.3.5 Grounds for Direct Loans, FFELs, and Consolidation Loans Extended
            After July 1, 1993 53
            4.3.5.1 General 53
            4.3.5.2 FFEL and Direct Loan Economic Hardship Deferments. 53
            4.3.5.3 Unemployment Deferment 55
            4.3.5.4 Military Deferment 55
            4.3.5.5 Post-Active Duty Deferment 56
        4.3.6 PLUS Deferments 56
        4.3.7 Grounds for FFEL Deferments Extended Before July 1, 1993 57
        4.3.8 Grounds for Perkins Loans Deferments 57
  4.4 Forbearances 58
        4.4.1 General. 58
        4.4.2 Applying for Forbearances. 59
        4.4.3 Discretionary Forbearances 59

	4.4.4 Mandatory Forbearances	60
	4.4.5 Perkins Loan Program Provisions	61

Chapter 5 Implications of Student Loan Defaults

5.1 The Problem of Federal Student Loan Defaults	63
5.1.1 Introduction	63
5.1.2 The Causes of Default	63
5.1.3 How School Default Rates Are Calculated	64
5.1.4 Federal Student Loan Default Triggers	66
5.1.5 Consequences of Default on Federal Loans	66
5.2 Private Student Loan Defaults	66
5.2.1 The Problem of Private Student Loan Defaults	66
5.2.2 Default Triggers for Private Loans	67
5.2.3 Consequences of Private Loan Defaults	67

Chapter 6 Repayment Strategies for Getting Out of Default

6.1 Introduction	69
6.2 Consolidation As a Way Out of Default	69
6.2.1 General	69
6.2.2 Payments Are Not Required to Get Out of Default Through Consolidation	70
6.2.3 Selecting IBR	71
6.2.4 Eligible Loans	71
6.2.5 How to Apply for a Direct Consolidation Loan	72
6.3 Loan Rehabilitation	73
6.3.1 General	73
6.3.2 Rehabilitation Payment Requirements	74
6.3.3 Formalizing the Rehabilitation Agreement	74
6.3.4 Determining the Reasonable and Affordable Payment Amount	75
6.3.5 Loan Sale	76
6.3.6 Limits on Rehabilitation	77
6.3.7 Perkins Rehabilitation	78
6.4 Advantages and Disadvantages of Loan Rehabilitation and Consolidation	78
6.5 Renewing Eligibility for Federal Student Aid	79
6.6 Compromise and Write-Off Authority	79

Chapter 7 Federal Student Loan Collection: Due Diligence Requirements, Private Collection Agencies, and Defenses to Collection Actions

7.1 Introduction to Federal Student Loan Collections	83
7.2 The Federal Student Loan Collection Process	83
7.2.1 The Various Collection Entities: Figuring Out Who Is Collecting the Loan	83
7.2.2 Pre-Default Collection (Delinquency)	85
7.2.3 Post-Default Collections	86
7.2.4 Credit Bureau Reporting	87
7.2.4.1 General	87
7.2.4.2 How Long Does Information Remain in the Consumer's File?	88
7.2.4.3 Cleaning Up the Consumer's Credit Record	88
7.3 Collection Fees and Penalties	90
7.3.1 General	90
7.3.2 Amount of Collection Fees and How Fees Are Calculated	91
7.3.2.1 "Reasonable" Collection Fees	91
7.3.2.2 Fees for Rehabilitation and Consolidation	93
7.3.2.3 Perkins Collection Fees	93

Contents

      7.3.3 Avoiding Collection Fees 94
      7.3.4 United States Collection of Other Fees and Penalties 95
  7.4 Deceptive and Abusive Debt Collection Tactics and Legal Violations 95
      7.4.1 Factors That Foster Deception and Abuse in Student Loan Collections 95
            7.4.1.1 General 95
            7.4.1.2 Commission Structure Fosters Abuses 96
      7.4.2 Common Student Loan Debt Collection Abuses 97
            7.4.2.1 Violations Unique to Student Loans 97
            7.4.2.2 Illegal Debt Collection Activity Not Unique to Student Loans 99
      7.4.3 Applicability of the FDCPA to Student Loan Collection Activity 100
            7.4.3.1 General 100
            7.4.3.2 Independent Collection Agencies and Attorneys 101
            7.4.3.3 Department of Education Employees 102
            7.4.3.4 Secondary Market Lenders and Servicing Agencies 103
            7.4.3.5 FDCPA Applicability to Guaranty Agencies 104
      7.4.4 Applicability of State Debt Collection Law to Student Loans 105
      7.4.5 Other Remedies for Government Agency Debt Collection Abuse 107
            7.4.5.1 Other Federal Claims 107
            7.4.5.2 Submitting Complaints About Collection Agencies 108
  7.5 Defenses to Federal Student Loan Collection Actions 109
      7.5.1 General 109
      7.5.2 Standing and Other Procedural Issues 109
      7.5.3 Statute of Limitations Is Not a Defense to Federal Student Loan
           Collection Action 110
            7.5.3.1 Statute of Limitations Generally Eliminated 110
            7.5.3.2 Exclusions from the General Rule Eliminating the Statute of
                   Limitations 111
            7.5.3.3 Laches 111
                  7.5.3.3.1 Barriers to applying the laches doctrine in student loan
                           cases 111
                  7.5.3.3.2 Exceptions to the rule barring laches 112
                  7.5.3.3.3 FISL collection 113
      7.5.4 Other Defenses to Loan Enforceability 113
            7.5.4.1 Forgery, Mistake, Infancy, and Other Contract Defenses 113
            7.5.4.2 Connection Between Contract Defenses and Statutory Discharges . . 114
            7.5.4.3 Raising Defenses When FFELs Have Lost Their Guaranteed
                   Status 114
            7.5.4.4 Raising Defenses After a Loan Has Been Consolidated 115
            7.5.4.5 Defenses for Service Members 115
  7.6 Vacating Collection Judgments 116

Chapter 8   Property and Asset Seizures to Collect Federal Student Loans

  8.1 Introduction 117
  8.2 Tax Refund Offsets 117
      8.2.1 General 117
      8.2.2 Notice Requirements 118
      8.2.3 Grounds to Contest a Tax Offset 118
      8.2.4 Repayment Plan in Lieu of Offset 119
      8.2.5 The Review Process 119
      8.2.6 Due Process Challenges to Tax Offset 120
      8.2.7 Post-Offset Challenges 120
      8.2.8 Preventing Tax Offsets 121
      8.2.9 Bankruptcy and Tax Offsets 121
      8.2.10 Rights of Non-Obligated Spouses 122

8.3 Non-Judicial Wage Garnishment 122
    8.3.1 Introduction 122
    8.3.2 DCIA Garnishment by the Department of Education 123
        8.3.2.1 Allowable Garnishment Amounts 123
        8.3.2.2 Notice of Garnishment 124
        8.3.2.3 Borrower Defenses and Objections 124
        8.3.2.4 Repayment in Lieu of Garnishment 126
        8.3.2.5 The Hearing Process 127
    8.3.3 Guaranty Agency Wage Garnishment Program 128
        8.3.3.1 General 128
        8.3.3.2 Guaranty Agency Garnishment Hearing 129
    8.3.4 Participation of Private Collection Agencies in Garnishment .. 130
    8.3.5 Due Process Challenges to Garnishment 132
8.4 Seizure of Federal Benefits 133
    8.4.1 General 133
    8.4.2 Amount of Offset 134
    8.4.3 Challenges to Offset 134
        8.4.3.1 Notice and Hearing Rights 134
        8.4.3.2 Hardship Reductions 135
        8.4.3.3 No Time Limit on Administrative Offsets 136
        8.4.3.4 Due Process Challenges to Offsets 136
8.5 Federal Salary Offsets 136
8.6 Professional License Suspensions and Revocations 137
8.7 Seizure of Student Loan Funds Generally Prohibited 137

Chapter 9 Statutory Discharges of Federal Student Loans

9.1 Introduction 139
9.2 Loans Eligible for Discharge 139
9.3 Closed-School Discharge 140
    9.3.1 General 140
    9.3.2 The Official School Closure Date 141
    9.3.3 Correspondence Schools 141
    9.3.4 Teach-Outs 142
    9.3.5 Relief Available for Those Obtaining a Closed-School Discharge ... 142
    9.3.6 How to Obtain a Closed-School Discharge 143
        9.3.6.1 General 143
        9.3.6.2 Written Application for Discharge 143
        9.3.6.3 Oral Applications 143
        9.3.6.4 Time Limits and Appeal Rights 144
    9.3.7 Effect of School Closure on FISLs and Older FFELs 144
9.4 False-Certification Discharge 144
    9.4.1 General 144
    9.4.2 Discharge Based on Ability-to-Benefit (ATB) Falsification 145
        9.4.2.1 ATB Falsification Defined 145
        9.4.2.2 Using Independent Evidence to Prove ATB Falsification ... 147
            9.4.2.2.1 Challenging Department denials based on lack of corroborating evidence 147
            9.4.2.2.2 Obtaining investigatory files through Freedom of Information Act requests 149
            9.4.2.2.3 School files 149
            9.4.2.2.4 Testing company information 149
            9.4.2.2.5 Information on specific schools 150
            9.4.2.2.6 Other evidence of ATB fraud 150
        9.4.2.3 Group Discharges 151

Contents

        9.4.3 Discharge Based on Student's Inability to Meet Minimum State Job Requirements (Disqualifying Status) 152
        9.4.4 Discharge Based on Forgery.. 152
        9.4.5 Discharge Based on Identity Theft.................................... 153
        9.4.6 Relief Available for Those Obtaining a False-Certification Discharge 154
        9.4.7 How to Apply for a False-Certification Discharge 154
   9.5 Discharge for Unpaid Refunds 155
        9.5.1 General... 155
        9.5.2 Criteria for Unpaid-Refund Discharge 155
        9.5.3 Determining Amount of Discharge 155
        9.5.4 Applying for the Discharge 156
        9.5.5 Relief Available for Those Obtaining a Discharge 156
   9.6 Relationship Between Closed-School, False-Certification, and Unpaid-Refund Discharges... 157
   9.7 Disability Discharge 157
        9.7.1 General... 157
        9.7.2 Eligible Loans 158
        9.7.3 Definition of Total and Permanent Disability........................ 159
            9.7.3.1 Definition As of July 1, 2010 159
            9.7.3.2 Definition for Applications Submitted Prior to July 1, 2010 159
        9.7.4 Applying For Disability Discharge 159
            9.7.4.1 General 159
            9.7.4.2 Process for Certain Veterans 162
        9.7.5 Reinstatement Period.. 163
            9.7.5.1 General 163
            9.7.5.2 Notice of Reinstatement 164
        9.7.6 When Work Is Allowed.. 164
        9.7.7 Effect of Final Discharge... 164
        9.7.8 Potential Roadblocks.. 165
   9.8 Discharge Based on Death 166
   9.9 Profession-Related Loan Cancellations 166
        9.9.1 General... 166
        9.9.2 Public Service Cancellation 167
            9.9.2.1 General 167
            9.9.2.2 Eligible Borrowers.................................... 167
            9.9.2.3 Eligible Jobs.. 168
            9.9.2.4 Applying for Public Service Cancellation 168
   9.10 Teacher Loan Forgiveness.. 169
   9.11 Other Profession-Related Cancellations.. 169
   9.12 Perkins Loan Discharges... 169
   9.13 Cancellation for Certain Relatives of September 11 Victims..................... 170
   9.14 Income Tax Issues... 171
   9.15 Appealing Adverse Discharge Decisions 172

Chapter 10   Discharging Student Loans in Bankruptcy

   10.1 Student Loans and Bankruptcy 175
        10.1.1 About the Bankruptcy Option.................................... 175
        10.1.2 The Benefit of the Automatic Stay................................ 176
   10.2 When Can a Student Loan Be Discharged in Bankruptcy?..................... 176
        10.2.1 The Special Restriction on Dischargeability Applies to Most Student Loans 176
        10.2.2 Exceptions to Nondischargeability 178
            10.2.2.1 Private Student Loans................................. 178
            10.2.2.2 Some Education Debts Should be Dischargeable 179

    10.2.2.3 Refinanced Student Loans in Bankruptcy................. 180
    10.2.2.4 Pre-BAPCPA Covered Loans—The Role of Programs
        Guaranteed or Insured by a Nonprofit or Government Entity.... 181
    10.2.2.5 Discharging Student Loans over Seven Years Old No Longer
        Allowed for Cases Filed After October 7, 1998 182
 10.3 Burden of Proof and the Student Loan Dischargeability Exception 183
   10.3.1 General.. 183
   10.3.2 Parents and Other Co-Signors............................. 185
 10.4 Undue Hardship As Basis for Discharging Student Loan 185
   10.4.1 General.. 185
   10.4.2 Applying the *Brunner* "Undue Hardship" Test 187
    10.4.2.1 The First Prong: The Debtor's current Income and Expenses ... 187
    10.4.2.2 The Second *Brunner* Prong: Additional Circumstances Indicate
        Current Hardship Likely to Continue...................... 190
      10.4.2.2.1 General................................... 190
      10.4.2.2.2 Proof of health-related impairments as an "additional
          circumstances"............................ 192
    10.4.2.3 The Third *Brunner* Prong—Good Faith 193
      10.4.2.3.1 General................................... 193
      10.4.2.3.2 "Good faith" and participation in affordable
          repayment plans........................... 194
   10.4.3 Other Hardship Factors 199
 10.5 Partial Discharge or Modification of Student Loan 200
 10.6 Special Rule for HEAL Loans..................................... 202
 10.7 The Dischargeability Determination 202
   10.7.1 Procedure for Determining Dischargeability of Student Loan 202
   10.7.2 Undue Hardship Determination in Chapter 13 204
   10.7.3 Use of Older Dischargeability Standards Today When Student's Pre-1998
       Bankruptcy Did Not Determine Student Loan's Dischargeability 206
 10.8 Discharge of Student Loans Owed to State Agencies 206
 10.9 Advantages of a Chapter 13 Bankruptcy When Student Loan Cannot Be
   Discharged.. 209
   10.9.1 Separate Classification................................... 209
   10.9.2 Co-Debtor Stay.. 210
   10.9.3 Raising Defenses in Response to Creditor Claims 211
 10.10 Student Loan Payments As "Special Circumstances" Under the BAPCPA
   Means Test 211
 10.11 Student's Rights After Bankruptcy Discharge 214

Chapter 11   Private Student Loans

 11.1 The Private Student Loan Market................................. 217
   11.1.1 General.. 217
   11.1.2 State Private Loan Products 218
   11.1.3 School Products 219
   11.1.4 Who Borrows Private Student Loans and Why 219
 11.2 Private Loan Terms and Conditions 220
   11.2.1 Comparing Private Loans and Federal Loans...................... 220
   11.2.2 How to Tell If a Loan Is Federal or Private...................... 221
 11.3 Oversight of Private Student Loans 221
 11.4 Disclosures and Private Student Loans 222
   11.4.1 Truth in Lending Disclosures 222
    11.4.1.1 Introduction.. 222
    11.4.1.2 Definitions and Scope............................... 223
    11.4.1.3 Timing of Disclosures............................... 224

Contents

      11.4.1.4 Form and Content of Disclosures 224
        11.4.1.4.1 Application disclosures 224
        11.4.1.4.2 Approval disclosures 225
        11.4.1.4.3 Final disclosures. 225
      11.4.1.5 Self-Certification 225
      11.4.1.6 Cancellation and Thirty-Day Waiting Period. 226
      11.4.1.7 Remedies 226
   11.4.2 HEA Disclosures and Private Loans. 226
11.5 Fair Billing and Other Servicing Issues. 226
11.6 Default and Delinquency and Private Student Loans 227
   11.6.1 The Problem of Private Student Loan Defaults 227
   11.6.2 Default Triggers for Private Loans. 227
   11.6.3 Collection of Defaulted Private Student Loans. 227
11.7 Relief for Private Student Loan Borrowers 228
   11.7.1 General. 228
   11.7.2 Private Loan Deferments and Forbearances 228
   11.7.3 Cancellations 229
   11.7.4 Private Student Loan Ombudsman 229
11.8 Defenses in Private Student Loan Collection Actions 229
   11.8.1 General Contract Defenses 229
   11.8.2 Infancy 230
   11.8.3 Statute of Limitations Is A Defense in Private Student Loan Cases. 231
   11.8.4 Defenses for Service Members 231
11.9 School-Related Claims and Defenses 231
   11.9.1 General. 231
   11.9.2 FTC Holder Rule 232
      11.9.2.1 General. 232
      11.9.2.2 When the Credit Agreement Contradicts the FTC Holder Notice . . 232
      11.9.2.3 When Notice Is Improperly Omitted from the Credit Agreement . . 232
      11.9.2.4 National Bank Act Preemption of State Law Related to FTC
        Holder Rule Violations 234
11.10 Direct Claims Against Private Lenders 234

Chapter 12 **Proprietary School and Other Student Loan Litigation**

12.1 Introduction to Student Loan-Related Litigation 237
12.2 Oversight of Schools Participating in Federal Assistance Programs 237
   12.2.1 General. 237
   12.2.2 Accreditation Agency Concerns. 238
   12.2.3 Gaps in Federal Enforcement 238
12.3 Proprietary School Issues 239
   12.3.1 Brief History 239
   12.3.2 Recent Growth in Proprietary Higher Education and Current Concerns . . 239
   12.3.3 Common Abuses and Problems with Proprietary Schools 240
      12.3.3.1 Excessive Student Loan Default Rates. 240
      12.3.3.2 Aggressive Recruiting and Marketing Practices. 241
      12.3.3.3 Failure to Meet "Gainful Employment" Requirement 242
      12.3.3.4 Manipulation of Outcome Measures 242
      12.3.3.5 Reliance on Federal Aid 244
      12.3.3.6 Distance Education. 244
      12.3.3.7 Increased Private Loan Borrowing and Internal Loan Products . . 245
      12.3.3.8 Admission Abuses 245
12.4 Other Student Loan and Higher Education Industry Problems. 246
   12.4.1 Scholarship Scams 246
   12.4.2 Diploma Mills 246

12.5 Legal Claims to Get Relief for Students and Borrowers. 247
    12.5.1 Introduction 247
    12.5.2 Federal Claims 247
        12.5.2.1 Higher Education Act and RICO 247
        12.5.2.2 False Claims Act 248
        12.5.2.3 FTC Guides and Rule 249
        12.5.2.4 Other Federal Claims 250
        12.5.2.5 Federal Statutory Discharges 251
    12.5.3 State Claims. 251
        12.5.3.1 UDAP Theories 251
        12.5.3.2 State Education Laws 252
        12.5.3.3 Other State Claims 253
        12.5.3.4 Preemption of State Laws 253
    12.5.4 Common Law Claims 254
        12.5.4.1 General. 254
        12.5.4.2 Contract Claims 255
        12.5.4.3 Fiduciary Duty 257
12.6 Affirmative Litigation. 257
    12.6.1 General 257
    12.6.2 Potential Defendants 257
        12.6.2.1 Suing the Department of Education. 257
        12.6.2.2 Claims Against Private Accrediting Agencies 258
        12.6.2.3 Claims Against State Licensing Agencies. 259
        12.6.2.4 Suing the School and Individual Owners and Operators 259
    12.6.3 Deciding Between Class and Individual Actions 260
    12.6.4 Developing a Case 261
    12.6.5 Proving Actual Damages 261
12.7 Raising School-Related Claims and Defenses. 262
    12.7.1 General 262
    12.7.2 The Clearer Picture: Loans for Which School-Related Claims or
           Defenses Should Be Available 262
        12.7.2.1 Defenses in Perkins Loans Collection 262
        12.7.2.2 Defenses in Direct Loan Collection. 262
        12.7.2.3 FFELs Extended After January 1, 1994 263
        12.7.2.4 Federally Insured Student Loans 264
        12.7.2.5 When Loan Note Contains FTC Holder Rule Notice 264
    12.7.3 Pre-1994 FFELs, Other Loans When There Is Less Clarity As to
           Availability of School-Related Claims or Defenses 264
        12.7.3.1 General. 264
        12.7.3.2 Agency and Other Common Law Theories. 265
        12.7.3.3 State Lender Liability Statutes 266
        12.7.3.4 Private Remedy for Failure to Include FTC Holder Notice 267
        12.7.3.5 Origination Theory 269
12.8 Student Claims Against Tuition Recovery Funds 270
    12.8.1 General 270
    12.8.2 Relationship of STRF to School-Related Discharges 271

Appendix A   Federal Student Loan Statutes

A.1 Direct Loans 273
A.2 FFEL 280
A.3 Perkins Loans 290
A.4 General Provisions 298
A.5 Selected Debt Collection Statutes 316
A.6 Private Loans. 320

Contents

Appendix B	Federal Regulations	
	B.1 Direct Loan Regulations	323
	B.2 FFEL Regulations	345
	B.3 Perkins Loan Regulations	396
	B.4 Other Federal Financial Assistance Regulations	407
	B.4.1 Selected Institutional Eligibility Requirements	407
	B.4.2 Selected Student Assistance General Provisions	412
	B.5 Selected Debt Collection Procedures	439
	B.5.1 Administrative Offset	439
	B.5.2 Tax Refund Offset	441
	B.5.3 Administrative Wage Garnishment	442
	B.5.4 Collection Costs and Penalties	447
	B.5.5 Compromise of Debts	448
	B.5.6 Department of Treasury Debt Collection Regulations	448
	B.6 Selected Private Student Loan Regulations	451
Appendix C	Department of Education Policy Guidance Letters	
	C.1 Discharges	453
	C.2 Consolidation Loans	468
	C.3 Borrower Assistance	470
	C.4 Eligibility for Federal Aid	471
Appendix D	Student Assistance Forms	
	D.1 Applications for Loans and Federal Aid	476
	D.1.1 The Free Application for Federal Student Aid (FAFSA)	476
	D.1.2 Direct Consolidation Loan Application and Instructions	486
	D.1.3 Repayment Plan Selection Form	496
	D.1.4 ICR and IBR Consent to Disclosure of Tax Information	502
	D.1.5 ICR and IBR Alternative Documentation of Income	504
	D.2 Deferment and Forbearance Forms	506
	D.2.1 Economic Hardship Deferment	506
	D.2.1.1 FFEL Economic Hardship Deferment Form	506
	D.2.1.2 Direct Loan Economic Hardship Deferment Form	510
	D.2.2 Direct Unemployment Deferment Form	513
	D.2.3 FFEL/Direct Loans Military Deferment Form	516
	D.2.4 Direct Loan Parent PLUS Borrower Deferment Request	519
	D.2.5 Direct Loan General Forbearance Request	521
	D.3 Discharge Forms and Letters	523
	D.3.1 Closed School	523
	D.3.2 False Certification of Ability to Benefit	525
	D.3.3 False Certification (Disqualifying Status)	527
	D.3.4 False Certification (Unauthorized Signature/Unauthorized Payment)	529
	D.3.5 Letter from Department of Education Granting False Certification Discharge	531
	D.3.6 Certification/Agreement of Cooperation for Identity Theft Claims	532
	D.3.7 Unpaid Refund Discharge	533
	D.3.8 Total and Permanent Disability Discharge	535
	D.3.8.1 Application Form	535
	D.3.8.2 Letters from Department of Education Regarding Disability Discharges	539
	D.4 Collection Letters and Hearing Forms	542
	D.4.1 Department of Education's Request for Administrative Wage Garnishment Hearing Form	542

	D.4.2 Department of Education Financial Disclosure Statement for Wage Garnishment Hearings Only	545
	D.4.3 Department of Education Statement of Financial Status	548
	D.4.4 Private Collection Agency Complaint Form	551
	D.4.5 Sample Treasury Notice of Offset	552
D.5	Additional Forms	553
	D.5.1 FFEL Compromise and Write-Off Procedures for Guaranty Agencies	553
	D.5.2 Direct Loan Compromise Authority (April 1, 2005)	555
	D.5.3 Sample Rehabilitation Agreement	556
	D.5.3.1 Repayment Agreement Under the Loan Rehabilitation Program	556
	D.5.3.2 Perkins Loan Rehabilitation	557
	D.5.4 Authorization to Release Information	559
	D.5.5 Department of Education Ombudsman Privacy Release Statement	560
	D.5.6 Third-Party Consent Form	561
	D.5.7 Direct Loan Master Promissory Note	562
	D.5.8 Direct Loan Sample Disclosure Statement	570
	D.5.9 Direct Loan Plain Language Disclosure	572
	D.5.10 Direct Loan Notice of Disbursement Made	574
	D.5.11 Perkins Master Promissory Note	576
D.6	Private Loan Disclosures and Forms	583
	D.6.1 Application and Solicitation Model Form	583
	D.6.2 Loan Approval Model Form	585
	D.6.3 Final Disclosure Model Form	587
	D.6.4 Private Education Loan Applicant Self-Certification Form	589

Appendix E — Sample Pleadings and Letters

E.1	Sample Letter and Request for Relief	591
E.2	Discharge-Related Pleadings	591
	E.2.1 Request for Discharge of All Students	591
	E.2.2 Class Action Complaint Challenging Department of Education's False Certification Discharge Procedures	596
	E.2.3 Individual Complaint Challenging Disability Discharge Denial	600
E.3	Challenge to Student Loan Collection Letters	603
	E.3.1 Complaint	603
	E.3.2 Motion for Class Certification	604
	E.3.3 Memorandum in Support of Class Certification	605
	E.3.4 Individual State and Federal Fair Debt Action Challenging Collection Agency's Improper Threats to Garnish SSI	609
E.4	Cases Challenging Trade School Abuses	612
E.5	Raising School's Fraud in Bankruptcy Proceeding	612
	E.5.1 Dischargeability Complaint Raising School's Fraud	612
	E.5.2 Complaint to Determine Dischargeability of Student Loan	613
E.6	Private Student Loan Cases	614
	E.6.1 Class Action Complaint Against Private Student Loan Servicer, Lender, and Bank	614
	E.6.2 Private Student Loan Borrower's Complaint Against Proprietary School and Lender	618

Appendix F — Sample Discovery and Freedom of Information Act Requests

F.1	Discovery in Student Loan Collection Cases	621
F.2	Discovery Directed to For-Profit/Proprietary Schools	624
	F.2.1 First Interrogatories and Requests for Production of Documents from a School	624

Contents

	F.2.2 Additional Interrogatories and Request for Production of Documents from a School	627
	F.2.3 Production of Documents from a School (Transferability of Credits Case)	629
	F.3 Discovery in Bankruptcy Proceeding to Determine Dischargeability of Student Loan	630
	F.4 Freedom of Information Act Sample Requests	632
Appendix G	Directory of Guaranty Agencies	635
Appendix H	Student Loan Collection Agencies	641
Appendix I	Federal Student Financial Assistance: Frequently Asked Questions	643
Appendix J	NCLC's Student Loan Borrower Assistance Website	647
Appendix K	Finding Pleadings, Primary Sources on the Companion Website	
	K.1 Pleadings and Primary Sources Found on the Companion Website	649
	K.2 How to Access the Website	650
	K.3 Locating Documents on the Website	651
	K.4 How to Use the Documents, Find Word Versions, and Locate Additional Features	654
	K.5 Electronic Searches of This and Other NCLC Titles' Chapters	654
	K.6 Finding Additional Pleadings	654
Appendix L	Student Loans on the Web	655
	Index	657
	Quick Reference to Consumer Credit and Sales Legal Practice Series	679

Chapter 1 Getting Started

1.1 Introduction

As the cost of financing our nation's higher education system falls increasingly on students and families, student loan debt is rising at alarming rates. By the time they graduate, more than two-thirds of students at four-year colleges and universities have student loan debt.[1] The average debt levels for graduating seniors with student loans increased to $23,200 in 2008, a 24% increase from 2004.[2] Nearly 100% of graduates from private for-profit universities had student loans compared to about 85% in 2004.[3] These statistics refer only to federal student loan debt. The problem is exacerbated by growing rates of private student loan borrowing.

Student loan debt is different than other types of debt on the one hand because individuals incur the debt to purchase education, a truly unique commodity. If all goes well, education leads to economic rewards. College graduates earn significantly more money than those without degrees and are more likely to be employed.[4] There is also evidence of other benefits to a more educated population, such as less reliance on public assistance and better health.[5] However, this is not always the result. A bachelor's degree may be just the beginning of a student's educational journey. In addition, some college graduates may find that their professions are not as lucrative as they hoped or may lose their jobs as the economy changes. Others will confront unexpected life traumas such as disability, divorce, or death of a family member. Still others will choose career paths—such as teaching and social work—wherein success is not measured in dollars but in satisfaction and promoting social good.

Other students, including many lower-income individuals, fall victim to the practices of unscrupulous proprietary schools (also known as for-profit schools). These practices are a tremendous source of frustration, financial loss, and loss of opportunity for consumers, particularly low-income consumers hoping to break out of poverty. Attracted by the financing provided by government student loan and grant programs, many proprietary school scams and ill-conceived schools have exploited federally funded student assistance programs.[6]

Education is particularly critical for people entering the job force for the first time. This group includes many welfare-to-work clients, domestic violence survivors, and new immigrants. In addition, those re-entering the job force after layoffs or hoping to transition into other types of work because of unemployment or disability also often look to education to move ahead. Although student loan debt is a problem that crosses class lines, low-income students are much more likely to borrow and to borrow more.[7]

In many cases, borrowers experiencing problems with student loan debt will also have problems with other types of debt, particularly credit card debt. Many students use credit cards to cover some tuition and fees. According to a 2009 study by Sallie Mae, nearly one-third of students in their study charged tuition on their credit cards.[8]

The growing student loan default problem is discussed in detail in Chapter 5, *infra*. In general, the consequences of student loan defaults have grown enormously over time as the government's collection powers have steadily increased. The government has collection powers far beyond those of most unsecured creditors. As discussed in detail in Chapter 8, *infra*, the government can garnish a borrower's wages without a judgment, seize the borrower's tax refund (even an earned income tax credit), seize portions of federal benefits such as Social Security, and deny the borrower

---

1 The Project on Student Debt, *Quick Facts About Student Debt* (Jan. 2010) (citing statistics from 2007–08).
2 *Id.*
3 *Id.*
4 *See generally* Sandy Baum, Jennifer Ma, & Kathleen Payea, College Bd. Advocacy & Policy Ctr., Education Pays: The Benefits of Higher Education for Individuals and Society (2010).
5 *Id.*
6 The scope of the problem and legal claims are discussed in Chapter 12, *infra*.
7 The Project on Student Debt, Quick Facts About Student Debt (Jan. 2010), at http://projectonstudentdebt.org/files/File/Debt_Facts_and_Sources.pdf.
8 Sallie Mae, How Undergraduate Students Use Credit Cards (Apr. 2009).

The Credit Card Accountability Responsibility and Disclosure Act of 2009 included protections for consumers under the age of twenty-one. Among other provisions, the Act requires that these consumers have a co-signer over age twenty-one or show they have an independent means of repaying the proposed extension of credit. Pub. L. No. 111-24, § 301 (May 22, 2009), *codified at* 15 U.S.C. § 1637(c)(8). *See generally* National Consumer Law Center, The Cost of Credit: Regulation, Preemption, and Industry Abuses § 11.8.6.2 (4th ed. 2009 and Supp.).

eligibility for new education grants or loans. To compound the problem, collectors are allowed to charge fees that create ballooning balances.[9] Even in bankruptcy, most student loans must be paid.[10] Unlike any other type of debt, there is no statute of limitations.[11] The government can pursue borrowers to the grave.

For borrowers in default, education, initially seen as a way out of poverty, instead often leads them into a cycle of endless debt. They find themselves in a trap. Student loan debt from the past keeps them from going back to school and moving into higher-paying jobs. On the other hand, most cannot afford to go back to school and get additional training without some type of financial assistance.

It is critical for advocates to understand how best to counsel and represent student loan borrowers. An important first step is to learn about local educational options, particularly low-cost community colleges and other affordable programs. Advocates should also familiarize themselves with the range of government and private financing available.

Unfortunately, most clients do not seek legal help until long after they take out loans and are having trouble with repayment. This manual focuses on assisting these clients, reviewing in detail the primary cancellation, repayment, bankruptcy, and other options available to challenge government collection efforts and help borrowers get out of default.

The good news is that there is almost always something that borrowers can do to challenge federal student loan collection actions and either cancel a loan or set up an affordable monthly payment plan. Understanding borrower cancellation and repayment rights is the key to assisting clients with student loan problems. Resolving these problems is often a critical step in helping clients get back on their feet financially. Options for private student loan debt are more limited, but there is some relief available for these borrowers as discussed in Chapter 11, *infra*.

1.2 Using This Manual

1.2.1 Road Map

This manual is designed to help advocates negotiate the world of student financial assistance, specifically federal student loan programs. The primary focus is on federal loan programs. However, due to the increased importance of private student lending, there is a separate chapter on private student loan issues. Chapter 11, *infra*, includes a general summary of private student loan issues, collection defenses, and other possible remedies.

This chapter reviews the primary types of student assistance and how to help clients find out what types of loans they have. This chapter also reviews basic eligibility criteria for federal loans, including student and institutional eligibility. Although this manual concentrates on repayment issues and how to help borrowers after they have taken out loans, this chapter also contains information about prerequisites that all students must meet to borrow through the federal loan programs, including application requirements and eligibility criteria. It includes a checklist for advocates to follow in assisting clients with student loan problems.

Chapter 2, *infra*, describes the terms of the various federal loan programs, including loan limits and interest rates that are set by law. The Higher Education Act (HEA) also establishes limits on the fees federal student lenders can charge, including origination fees, late charges, and collection fees. Chapter 2 discusses origination and late fees, while collection fees are covered in Chapter 7, *infra*. Chapter 2 also includes information about the process for borrowers in taking out a loan, including master promissory notes, required disclosures, disbursement and cancellation rights, and counseling requirements.

Chapter 3, *infra*, reviews all of the federal student loan pre-default repayment options, including the income-based repayment plans. This chapter also includes information about federal student loan servicing. Chapter 4, *infra*, includes detailed information about deferment and forbearance rights.

Chapter 5, *infra*, describes in greater detail the problem and consequences of student loan defaults in both the federal and private contexts. It also discusses the way federal defaults are measured and problems with the cohort default rate calculation. Chapter 6, *infra*, is an essential guide to the ways borrowers can get out of default through repayment. The main options are loan consolidation, rehabilitation, compromise, and settlement.

The federal student loan collection process is described in Chapter 7, *infra*, including information about steps collectors must take during delinquency and those that are required once a loan goes into default. This chapter also reviews typical problems with collection, including fair debt collection violations, and permissible collection fees. This chapter also includes information about defenses to collection actions.

The major government extra-judicial collection tools for federal student loans, including tax offsets, garnishment, and benefits offsets, are discussed in Chapter 8, *infra*.

Chapter 9, *infra*, presents the primary cancellation options available for federal student loan borrowers, including closed-school, false-certification, unpaid-refund, disability, death, and career-related (including public service) cancellations. Cancellation of student loans may also be pursued in bankruptcy. The ways in which student loans can be discharged in bankruptcy are discussed in Chapter 10, *infra*.

---

9 *See* § 7.3, *infra*.
10 *See* Ch. 10, *infra*.
11 *See* § 7.5.3, *infra*.

Chapter 11, *infra*, summarizes the history of private student loans and reviews the problems with these products. This chapter also describes possible remedies for borrowers and laws, such as those promulgated under the Truth in Lending Act, that apply only to private student loans. Collection defenses that are most relevant in private student loan cases are also covered in this chapter.

Chapter 12, *infra*, primarily includes information about proprietary school abuses and how to challenge them. This includes a discussion of ways to hold lenders liable for school-related claims. The chapter also reviews general legal claims that borrowers may bring against other entities in the student loan industry, such as servicers and accreditation agencies.

The appendices to this manual reprint key student loan statutes and regulations and contain various practice aids. Appendix A, *infra*, includes critical federal student loan statutes. Key regulations can be found in Appendix B, *infra*. Selected Department of Education policy guidance letters are included in Appendix C, *infra*.

Appendices D, E, and F, *infra*, contain a number of useful forms and pleadings for practitioners. Appendix G, *infra*, includes a current list of state guaranty agencies along with addresses and telephone numbers. Appendix H, *infra*, contains a current list of collection agencies that contract with the Department of Education, and Appendix I, *infra*, includes basic consumer education information. Appendix J, *infra*, has basic information about NCLC's Student Loan Borrower Assistance Project website (www.studentloan borrowerassistance.org).

This manual also includes a companion website containing the statutes, regulations, forms, and pleadings from the appendices, the index to this volume, and the quick reference to the entire National Consumer Law Center's Consumer Credit and Sales Legal Practices Series. The website has numerous student loan-related pleadings as well as the latest regulations and proposed regulations issued by the Department of Education. See Appendix K, *infra*, for more information about the companion website. Finally, Appendix L, *infra*, lists useful websites on student loan issues.

This manual will be supplemented, usually on an annual basis. Between supplements, new developments are reported in NCLC REPORTS, *Deceptive Practices and Warranties Edition*, published bimonthly. For subscription information, contact the Publications Department at National Consumer Law Center, 7 Winthrop Square, 4th Floor, Boston, MA 02110, (617) 542-9595.

1.2.2 Clearinghouse Documents

Certain documents are referred to in this manual and cited by a "Clearinghouse" number. These documents may be ordered from the Sargent Shriver National Center on Poverty Law (formerly known as the National Clearinghouse for Legal Services) by writing to 111 N. Wabash St., Suite 500, Chicago, Illinois 60602, by calling (800) 621-3256 or (312) 263-3830, by sending a facsimile to (312) 263-3846, or by sending an e-mail to admin@povertylaw.org. Many documents are available on the organization's website, www.povertylaw.org. Non-subscribers can order individual documents for $10.00 plus shipping.

1.2.3 Web-Based Text Search Feature

NCLC offers a unique web-based text search feature for this manual and all its other manuals. The search engine is located at www.consumerlaw.org. Clicking on "Keyword Search" brings up a screen that allows the user to search for any term or phrase in this or any other NCLC manual. The search can be confined to a single manual or can extend to all of NCLC's manuals. The search engine will indicate the pages in the manual where the term or phrase appears. The user can then refer to the applicable book in hard copy.

This function is not only the best way to locate the discussion of a particular topic, but it is also an excellent way to find out where a particular case, statute, or regulation is discussed in NCLC's manuals. The search instructions explain how to use wildcards, how to search for phrases and the proximity of one term to another term (for either of the two terms), and how to search for one term that is not on the same page as another term.

1.3 Introduction to Federal Student Assistance

1.3.1 Brief History

Before World War II, American colleges historically provided financial aid directly to their students. The 1944 Servicemen's Readjustment Act ("G.I. Bill") signaled a new type of government involvement in education aid as well as a recognition of the connection between higher education and economic productivity.[12] The G.I. Bill guaranteed military personnel a year of education for ninety days of service, plus one month for each month of active combat duty, with a maximum award of forty-eight months of benefits.

The G.I. Bill was even more popular than its drafters envisioned. To keep up with demand, the government added the College Scholarship Service, a prelude to National Defense Student Loans, which later became the Perkins Loan Program.

The Federal Family Education Loan Program (FFELP), also known as the guaranteed loan program, was created in

---

12 John R. Thelin, *Higher Education's Student Financial Aid Enterprise in Historical Perspective, in* Footing the Tuition Bill 19, 22–24 (Frederick M. Hess ed., 2007).

the Higher Education Act of 1965. The 1965 legislation also created the Federal Insured Student Loan (FISL) program, which provided federal insurance for loans. The FISL was eventually phased out. The Higher Education Act Amendments of 1992 created a new generic name, Federal Family Education Loans (FFELs), for the major forms of federal student loans.[13]

Banks were initially reluctant to participate in the guaranteed loan program. Congress encouraged participation by covering a large percentage of any losses through loan guarantees. When banks were still reluctant to join the program, Congress created a government-sponsored enterprise—the Student Loan Marketing Association (known as SLMA or Sallie Mae) as a secondary market for guaranteed student loans.[14]

Over time, the focus in the federal loan program shifted toward providing more benefits for middle-income students. In the 1992 Higher Education Act, among other changes Congress created the unsubsidized loan program. This allowed students of any income level to get federally guaranteed student loans.[15]

Although the FFEL student loan program is a federal program, it is mostly administered through state or private nonprofit agencies called guaranty agencies. Guaranty agencies pay off the lenders when borrowers default and, in turn, are reinsured by the Department of Education. When a loan held by a lender or other servicer goes into default, it is typically turned over to a guaranty agency for collection. At a later date, the United States, as an insurer on the loan, can take over the collection effort.[16]

The guaranty agencies may be stand-alone entities, may serve dual roles in both the FFEL program and as a state higher education authority that administers scholarship programs and other activities, or may serve as a one-stop financial entity that performs guaranty agency functions and also acts as a lender.[17]

The Student Loan Reform Act of 1993 significantly changed the student loan landscape by creating a new Federal Direct Loan Program.[18] This program issues loans (referred to throughout this manual as "Direct loans") directly from the federal government to the student, with the assistance of the school or other entity that originates the loan. Lenders and guaranty agencies are cut out of the process. The landscape changed even more dramatically in 2010 when the FFEL program was eliminated, as discussed in the next subsection.

1.3.2 The End of the FFEL Program

The FFEL program was eliminated as part of the Health Care and Education Reconciliation Act of 2010.[19] The Perkins Loan Program was not affected by this legislation. Although the FFEL Program is over as of July 2010, there are many existing FFEL loans that will be held, serviced, and collected by FFEL lenders, servicers, and guaranty agencies for many more years.

The Department has issued guidance on the transition from FFEL to Direct loans.[20] Among other information, the Department advised that students who had previously received FFEL loans were required to complete new promissory notes to receive loans under the Direct Loan Program.

The elimination of the FFEL Program came about due to many factors. The credit crisis and economic recession had a huge impact. Private lenders in the FFEL Program faced increases in funding costs during the financial crisis. Beginning in 2007, many student lenders decided to leave the student loan business.

Fears of private lenders pulling out led many schools to transition to Direct loans even before the FFEL Program was eliminated. For example, from the beginning of 2008 through May 2008, 288 colleges had applied to join the Direct lending program as opposed to 80 colleges during all of 2007.[21] By the 2008–2009 fiscal year, about 88% of the total dollar amount of federal student loans was funded by the government.[22]

Before eliminating the program completely, Congress acted throughout 2008 to alleviate the market turmoil. The Ensuring Continued Access to Student Loans Act of 2008 temporarily injected liquidity into the FFEL market.[23] The law was extended for the 2009–2010 year.[24] The Department of Education also enhanced the lender-of-last-resort

---

13 Pub. L. No. 102-325, 106 Stat. 448 (July 23, 1992).
14 John R. Thelin, *Higher Education's Student Financial Aid Enterprise in Historical Perspective*, in Footing the Tuition Bill 19, 32–35 (Frederick M. Hess ed., 2007).
15 *Id.* at 38.
16 A list of state guaranty agencies can be found at Appendix G, *infra*.
17 *See generally* Ben Miller, New America Found., Rethinking the Middleman (July 2009).
18 Student Loan Reform Act of 1993, 107 Stat. 340 (enacted as § 4021 of the Omnibus Budget Reconciliation Act of 1993, Pub. L. No. 103-66, 107 Stat. 312 (Aug. 10 1993)).

19 Pub. L. No. 111-152, 124 Stat. 1029 (Mar. 30, 2010).
20 *See, e.g.*, U.S. Dep't of Educ., Implementation Guidance for the Deadline for Making Loans Under the Federal Family Education Loan (FFEL) Program, Dear Colleague Letter GEN-10-10 (June 15, 2010).
21 Beckie Supiano, *Colleges Scramble To Help Students Find New Lenders*, Chron. of Higher Educ., May 23, 2008.
22 U.S. Cong. Budget Office, Costs and Policy Options for Federal Student Loan Programs (Mar. 2010).
23 Pub. L. No. 110-227, 122 Stat. 740 (May 7, 2008).
24 The Department reported purchasing about $50 billion in FFELs through this program through the end of fiscal year 2009. The Department estimates that it will buy another $62 billion in loans under the extended authority that ended on July 1, 2010. U.S. Congressional Budget Office, Costs and Policy Options for Federal Student Loan Programs (Mar. 2010).

program, designed to provide access to FFEL loans for those students who faced difficulty obtaining conventional loans.[25]

Although the credit crisis helped accelerate the switch to Direct loans, there were even earlier concerns, particularly about the costs of compensating the FFEL private lenders and guaranty agencies. There were also concerns about conflicts of interest. The guaranty agencies provide a number of services that may be in potential conflict, including providing default insurance for lenders, default prevention, and collecting or rehabilitating loans.

The FFEL Program had become costly. Payments to lenders are set by law and, according to the Congressional Budget Office, are only weakly related to the actual costs that lenders incur.[26] Under the FFEL Program, lenders receive regular quarterly payments from the government, known as special allowance payments that are a percentage of the principal value of their outstanding guaranteed loans. That percentage equals the prevailing interest rate plus an additional amount, called a spread, minus the interest rate that borrowers contractually pay on the loans. This program, according to the Congressional Budget Office, effectively transfers to the government the interest payments that lenders receive from borrowers.[27] In return, the commercial-paper rate plus a small portion of the spread is intended to cover lenders' regular costs of acquiring funds to make loans. The rest of the spread goes toward covering administrative costs and other expenses.

When borrowers default, the government pays FFEL lenders a fixed fraction, currently set at 97% of the principal and accrued interest owed.[28] When defaults occur, the loans are usually transferred to guaranty agencies, which hold and seek to collect.

1.4. Types of Federal Student Assistance

1.4.1 Student Loans

1.4.1.1 Stafford Loans

Stafford loans are available to both undergraduate and graduate students.[29] As of July 1, 2010, federal Stafford loans are made to students through the Direct Loan Program only. Prior to July 2010, there were FFEL Stafford loans as well. Direct Stafford and FFEL Stafford loans have identical loan limits and identical deferment and cancellation provisions. The major difference is that Direct loans are originated by the government and FFEL loans by private lenders. There are also some differences in repayment options.[30]

Stafford loans are either subsidized or unsubsidized. Borrowers can receive a subsidized and an unsubsidized loan for the same enrollment period. A subsidized Stafford loan is awarded on the basis of financial need. The key difference between the two types of Stafford loans is that, for subsidized loans, borrowers are not charged any interest before the repayment period begins or during authorized periods of deferment. In essence, the government "subsidizes" the interest during these periods.

Unsubsidized loans are not awarded on the basis of financial need. Interest is charged from the time the loan is disbursed until it is paid in full. Annual and aggregate loan limits are set out in the Department of Education regulations.[31]

1.4.1.2 PLUS Loans

As of July 1, 2010, PLUS loans are available only through the Direct Loan Program.[32] Prior to that time, there were also FFEL PLUS loans. There are both parent PLUS and graduate/professional student PLUS loans. The program was extended to graduate/professional students in July 2006.

Parent PLUS loans allow parents to borrow to pay for the education of dependent undergraduate children enrolled in school at least half-time. To be eligible for PLUS loans, parents are generally required to pass a credit check.[33] Student PLUS loan borrowers are also required to pass a credit check.[34]

A graduate or professional student's maximum annual Stafford loan eligibility must be determined before the student applies for a PLUS loan.[35] The yearly limit on PLUS loans is equal to the student's cost of attendance minus any other financial aid received.[36]

PLUS loan borrowers with adverse credit histories may still get loans if they enlist an endorser who has been determined not to have an adverse credit history.[37] The lender must find that an adverse credit history exists based on a credit report if the applicant is considered delinquent for ninety days or more on the repayment of a debt or if the applicant has been the subject of a default determination, bankruptcy discharge, foreclosure, repossession, tax lien,

---

25 Pub. L. No. 110-227, 122 Stat. 740 (May 7, 2008). *See also* U.S. Dep't of Educ., The Ensuring Continued Access to Student Loans Act of 2008, Dear Colleague Letter GEN-08-08 (June 18, 2008).
26 U.S. Cong. Budget Office, Costs and Policy Options for Federal Student Loan Programs (Mar. 2010).
27 *Id.*
28 20 U.S.C. § 1078.
29 *See* Ch. 2, *infra* (Stafford Terms and Loan Limits).
30 *See* § 3.1.3, *infra* (income-based repayment)
31 *See* § 2.2, *infra*.
32 *See* § 2.2.3, *infra* (PLUS terms and limits).
33 34 C.F.R. §§ 682.201(c)(2), 685.200(c)(1)(vii) (Direct Loan).
34 34 C.F.R. §§ 682.201(b)(4), 685.200(b)(5).
35 34 C.F.R. §§ 682.201(b)(3); 685.200(b)(4).
36 34 C.F.R. § 685.203(f).
37 34 C.F.R. §§ 682.201(c)(1)(vii), 685.200(c)(1)(vii) (parent PLUS), 682.201(b)(4), 685.200(b)(5) (student PLUS).

wage garnishment, or write-off of a student loan debt during the five years preceding the date of the credit report.[38] Creditors may establish more restrictive standards.[39] However, the absence of any credit history cannot be considered an indication of an adverse credit history and is not to be used as a reason for denial.[40] The lender may waive these requirements if extenuating circumstances exist.[41]

There are standard letters that creditors use when approving or denying PLUS loans. The denial letter states that the lender (as of July 1, 2010, all PLUS loans are Direct loans) has reviewed the application and is unable to approve it due to adverse credit information obtained in a credit report. The letter lists the source of this information as well as the specific reason for the denial, for example, wage garnishment within the last five years or tax liens. The consumer is given information about Fair Credit Reporting Act rights. The letter also explains that, if the consumer believes that extenuating circumstances exist, the consumer may send documentation directly to the Applicant Services Department explaining the situation. In addition, the consumer may qualify by obtaining an eligible endorser.

In 2008, to help facilitate PLUS loan borrowing, Congress gave lenders additional discretion to find extenuating circumstances for parents or graduate/professional students applying for PLUS loans from January 1, 2007, through December 31, 2009.[42]

Initial data shows that the PLUS loan program has grown since graduate and professional students became eligible. Borrowing by parents through the PLUS loan program overall constituted 9% of education borrowing in 1998–1999 and 8% in 2008–2009, but this rose to 11% from 2003–2004 through 2005–2006.[43]

1.4.1.3 Consolidation Loans

1.4.1.3.1 General

As of July 1, 2010, Direct consolidation loans are the only type of federal consolidation loans available. All federal loan borrowers may obtain Direct consolidation loans. However, they must have at least one FFEL or Direct loan to qualify for consolidation.[44]

Prior to July 1, 2006, borrowers could even obtain a Direct consolidation loan when they were still in school. In-school consolidation was eliminated by the Higher Education Reconciliation Act.[45] However, in-school consolidation will be temporarily allowed for certain loans only from July 1, 2010, through July 1, 2011. Borrowers who meet the following requirements are eligible for these temporary consolidations:

> 1. The borrower has one or more loans from two or more of the following categories: (i) FFEL Program Loans that are held by an eligible lender; (ii) FFEL Program loans that have been purchased by the Department . . . ; and (iii) Direct Loan Program Loans.
>
> 2. The borrower has not yet entered repayment on one or more of the loans in any of the categories in #1.
>
> 3. The borrower is not consolidating any loans other than loans from the categories listed in #1.[46]

Prior to July 1, 2006, married borrowers could choose to consolidate loans from both spouses or jointly consolidate the loans of either spouse. Both borrowers had to agree to be jointly and severally liable for repayment. In addition, the borrowers had to agree to repay the joint loan regardless of any change in marital status. Perhaps because of the dubious advantages of this program, Congress eliminated it as of July 1, 2006.[47]

Borrowers have the option to consolidate all, some, or even just one of their existing student loans. There is no minimum or maximum size for a Direct consolidation loan. More information about applying for consolidation loans can be found in Chapter 6, *infra*.[48]

Borrowers can consolidate if they are out of school but in repayment or, most importantly for many low-income borrowers, if they are already in default.[49]

1.4.1.3.2 Limits on reconsolidation

A borrower who already has a consolidation loan with either the FFEL or Direct Loan program is not able to "reconsolidate" with either program, except in the following limited circumstances:

- If the borrower includes at least one other eligible loan in the new consolidation.[50] The loan added may be another consolidation loan.

---

38 34 C.F.R. §§ 682.201(c)(2)(ii)(A), (B) (FFEL), 685.200(c)(1)(vii)(B) (Direct Loan).
39 34 C.F.R. § 682.201(c)(2)(iii).
40 34 C.F.R. §§ 682.201(c)(2)(iv) (FFEL), 685.200(c)(1)(vii)(C) (Direct Loan).
41 34 C.F.R. §§ 682.201(c)(2)(ii), (v) (FFEL), 685.200(c)(1)(vii)(A) (Direct Loan).
42 Pub. L. No. 110-227, 122 Stat 740 (May 7, 2008) (amending 20 U.S.C. § 1078-2(a)(3)(B)). *See also* Pub. L. No. 110-315, § 424, 122 Stat. 3078 (Aug. 14, 2008).
43 College Bd., Trends in Student Aid 2009.
44 34 C.F.R. § 685.220(d). *See* Ch. 2, *infra* (consolidation loan interest rates and other terms).

45 Pub. L. No. 109-171, 120 Stat. 4 (Feb. 8, 2006).
46 *See* U.S. Dep't of Educ., Temporary Authority for the Consolidation of Loans in an In-School Status, Dear Colleague Letter GEN-10-13 (June 29, 2010).
47 Pub. L. No. 109-171, 120 Stat. 4 (Feb. 8, 2006).
48 *See* § 6.2.5, *infra*.
49 *See* § 6.2, *infra*.
50 34 C.F.R. § 685.220(d)(2).

- If FFEL consolidation loan borrowers have loans that have been submitted to guaranty agencies for default aversion and they want to consolidate into Direct loans for the purpose of obtaining an income-contingent repayment (ICR) or income-based repayment (IBR) plan.[51]

Borrowers may also consolidate an FFEL consolidation loan into a Direct consolidation loan if the FFEL consolidation loan is held by a guaranty agency as a result of a bankruptcy claim. This is similar to the situation in which the claim has been submitted for default aversion assistance. However, because the bankruptcy proceeding precludes the submission of a default aversion request, the Department acknowledges that borrowers in this situation should also be allowed to consolidate with the Direct Loan Program.[52]

Borrowers may also add loans received prior to the date of a consolidation loan during the 180-day period following the making of the consolidation loan. Any new loans received during this period may also be added to the consolidation loan.[53] After the 180-day period is over, the borrower may no longer add loans to the existing consolidation loan.

FFEL consolidation and non-consolidation loan borrowers may also reconsolidate in order to switch to Direct loans and use the public service forgiveness program or, if they are qualified military service members, to get the Direct Loan Program interest accrual benefit.[54] According to the Department, joint consolidation borrowers with FFEL loans cannot reconsolidate with Direct loans to get into the public service forgiveness program.

The Department has clarified that, even though borrowers with defaulted Direct consolidation loans are no longer eligible to reconsolidate except in the circumstances described above, they may enter into rehabilitation agreements that provide for reasonable and affordable payments.[55]

Financially distressed borrowers will often use consolidation as a way out of default. This is discussed in detail in Chapter 6, *infra*, including information on applying for consolidation and getting into income-based repayment. These same procedures are relevant for borrowers consolidating when they are not in default.

1.4.1.3.3 Pros and cons of consolidation

The following are the main disadvantages to consolidation:

1. Borrowers with relatively new loans will not save as much on interest through consolidation. This is because interest rates on federal loans made after July 1, 2006, are fixed. The interest rates for consolidation loans are calculated based on the average interest rates of the loans being consolidated. Borrowers with variable-rate loans from before July 1, 2006, may be able to get very significant interest rate reductions by consolidating.
2. Consolidation extends repayment, often lowering monthly payments, but creates more overall costs in interest over the life of the loan and extends loan obligations further into the future. If borrowers are close to paying off their loans, consolidation may not be worthwhile.
3. Borrowers may lose some rights by consolidating. This is most clearly a problem if the borrower consolidates federal loans into a private consolidation loan (they would lose the rights associated with federal loans). Borrowers may also lose some options and protections if they consolidate certain federal loans, particularly Perkins loans, into other federal loan programs. Parent PLUS loan borrowers also have to be careful when consolidating if they hope to repay through income-based repayment (IBR).[56] Parent PLUS loan borrowers who also have other federal student loans and choose to consolidate with Direct loans will find that the PLUS loan taints the entire consolidation loan and will mean that they will not be eligible to repay the consolidation loan using IBR.[57] If they wish to consolidate, parent PLUS loan borrowers may exclude the PLUS loans from the consolidation and pay them separately.[58] These borrowers should also be able to consolidate and choose ICR.[59]

The following are the main advantages of consolidation:

1. Consolidation allows borrowers to put all of their loans together and make just one monthly payment.
2. Consolidation might help if borrowers need to reduce payments through an extension of the repayment period. (Extending the length of repayment increases the total amount borrowers have to repay over the life of the loan.)
3. Borrowers may get an interest rate break, especially if they have variable rate loans.

There are also a growing number of private consolidation loan products. Many of these lenders went out of business during the credit crisis or stopped making these loans, but these products are likely to return as the economy recovers. Many of these lenders encouraged or even pressured gov-

---

51 34 C.F.R. § 685.220(d)(1)(i)(B)(4); § 3.1.3, *infra*.
52 This provision is not explicit in the regulation but is described in the summary of the final rules. 71 Fed. Reg. 64378 (Nov. 1, 2006); U.S. Dep't of Educ., Update on Consolidation Loan Issues, Dear Colleague Letter GEN-06-20 (Dec. 1, 2006).
53 34 C.F.R. § 685.220(e).
54 34 C.F.R. § 685.220(d)(1)(i)(B)(3) (public service), § 685.220(d)(1)(i)(B)(5) (military interest accrual program). *See* § 9.9.2, *infra* (public service forgiveness).
55 *See* § 6.3, *infra*.
56 *See* § 3.1.3.2.1, *infra*.
57 34 C.F.R. § 685.221(a)(2) provides that parent PLUS loans and consolidation loans that repaid a parent PLUS loan cannot be repaid using IBR. *See* § 3.1.3.2.1, *infra*.
58 34 C.F.R. § 685.208(a)(4)(i).
59 *See* § 3.1.3.3.1, *infra*.

ernment loan borrowers to consolidate into a private consolidation loan. In these cases, borrowers will lose their right to flexible repayment and other benefits available through the government loan programs.

1.4.1.4 Perkins Loans

The Perkins Loan Program (formerly called National Direct Student Loans and, before that, National Defense Student Loans) provides low-interest loans (hereafter "Perkins loans") to both undergraduate and graduate students with exceptional financial need.[60] Perkins loans are originated and serviced by participating schools and repaid to the school. The government does not insure the loans but instead provides initial contributions to eligible institutions to partially capitalize a loan fund. Perkins loans are administered by the school itself, at interest rates generally below those for Stafford loans.

If the student defaults, the school can seek collection through a lawsuit or otherwise. Perkins Loan Program schools may assign loans to the United States when they cannot collect.[61] The United States will then seek collection from the defaulted borrower, using the full range of collection tools available.[62] However, the schools can no longer receive any of the funds collected after assignment.[63] In a few cases, such as in reviews of disability discharges, schools are required to assign loans to the Department of Education.[64]

Since Perkins loans have different regulations than FFELs and Direct loans, student rights and obligations are often different. However, the 1998 Higher Education Act contained a number of provisions that made the Perkins Loan Program regulations much more similar to the FFEL and Direct Loan Program regulations. In particular, the closed-school discharge for loans made on or after January 1, 1986, applies to Perkins loans as well.[65] In addition, Perkins loan borrowers who make nine consecutive monthly payments may rehabilitate defaulted loans.[66]

1.4.1.5 Older Loans

Prior to 1994, borrowers could also receive loans under the Supplemental Loans for Students (SLS) program. Effective July 1, 1994, SLS loans were no longer issued. The SLS program was merged into the unsubsidized component of the Stafford Loan Program. However, many students obtained SLS loans before that date, and the conditions and benefits of those earlier loans remain unchanged.[67]

Many older loans are insured directly by the federal government, with no guaranty agency acting as intermediary. These loans are called Federally Insured Student Loans (FISLs). FISLs were made from 1966 to 1984. Unless specified otherwise, the term FFEL in this section includes FISLs.

1.4.2 Federal Grants

1.4.2.1 General

The federal grant programs are critical for low-income students, particularly the Pell grant program described below. There are also a number of "specialty" federal grant programs that require students to study certain fields or work in careers such as teaching.

In 2008–2009, 39% of undergraduate grant aid came from colleges and universities and 36% came from the federal government. The average annual rate of growth in total federal grants declined from 9% between 1998–1999 and 2003–2004 to 3% over the next five years. The average annual rate of growth in total state grants declined from 8% to 3%.[68]

A Basic Educational Opportunity Grant (BEOG)—also called a Pell grant[69]—and a Supplemental Educational Opportunity Grant (FSEOG)[70] are not loans and require no repayment (unless there is an overpayment).[71] The College Work Study program provides salaries for students in exchange for work.[72] All of these assistance programs are administered by the school. Students can have more than one form of student assistance so that, for example, a student may participate in work-study, have a Pell grant, a Stafford loan, and a PLUS loan signed by his or her parents.

---

60 Statutory authority can be found at 20 U.S.C. §§ 1087aa–1087*ii*.
61 34 C.F.R. § 674.50.
62 The Department claims to have collection tools, such as administrative wage garnishment, federal offset, and Department of Justice litigation, that are not available to schools. It is unclear whether this statement accurately reflects current practice. Perkins Loan Program schools can presumably refer accounts to the government for tax refund intercepts. They would seem to have authority to also refer accounts for federal benefits offset. However, the Department claims this is not current practice. *See* U.S. Dep't of Educ., Dear Colleague Letter CB-02-05 (Apr. 2002). *See also* 34 C.F.R. § 674.41 (Perkins loan lender due diligence requirements).
    The situation is clearer for FFELs when guaranty agencies, in most cases, have specific authority to collect on behalf of the Department prior to assignment. *See generally* Ch. 8, *infra*.
63 *See* U.S. Dep't of Educ., Dear Colleague Letter CB-02-05 (Apr. 2002).
64 *See* § 9.7, *infra* (disability discharges).
65 *See* § 9.3, *infra*.
66 34 C.F.R. § 674.39. *See* § 6.3.7, *infra*.
67 SLS loans were considered a part of the FFEL category of loans. Therefore FFEL regulations should apply to these loans as well.
68 College Bd., Trends in Student Aid 2009 (2009).
69 20 U.S.C. § 1070a; 34 C.F.R. § 690.
70 20 U.S.C. § 1070b; 34 C.F.R. § 676.
71 *Id.*
72 42 U.S.C. §§ 2751–2756b; 34 C.F.R. § 675.

1.4.2.2 Pell Grants

1.4.2.2.1 Basics about Pell grants

The Federal Pell Grant Program provides need-based grants (hereafter "Pell grants") to low-income undergraduate and certain post-baccalaureate students. As of 2010, students may use their grants at any one of approximately 5400 participating post-secondary institutions. Grant amounts are dependent on: the student's expected family contribution; the cost of attendance (as determined by the institution); the student's enrollment status (full-time or part-time); and whether the student attends for a full academic year or less. Students may not receive Federal Pell Grant Program funds from more than one school at a time.

The Health Care and Education Act of 2010 provides for more stable and predictable funding for the Federal Pell Grant Program. It also modifies, beginning with the 2010–2011 award year, the calculation for determining a Pell grant award. The maximum award for the 2010–2011 award year is $5550.[73] The grants will remain at that level for the following two years and will then increase by the rate of inflation in each of the next five years.[74]

Despite the attempts to increase Pell grant awards and keep up with costs, in 2009–2010 the maximum Pell grants covered only 35% of average tuition, fees, room, and board at public four-year colleges and 15% of total charges at private four-year colleges. Only about 25% of recipients qualified for the maximum grant in 2007–2008.[75]

Students may receive up to two Pell grants in a single academic year as long as they are enrolled at least half-time and meet certain other criteria.[76] The rules are intended to encourage a student to accelerate the completion of a program of study within a shorter time period than the regularly scheduled completion time. Students may receive Pell grants only up to eighteen semesters or the equivalent.[77]

1.4.2.2.2 Pell grant overpayments

Grants do not usually have to be repaid unless there is an overpayment. The school is liable for an overpayment if it occurred because the school failed to follow proper procedures.[78] If the school is not liable, they must notify students of the overpayment and request repayment. Once a grantee is notified of a grant repayment, he or she must either pay the grant back in full or enter into a satisfactory repayment arrangement.[79] Failure to respond will lead to lost eligibility for further federal financial aid, and the school will assign the debt to the Department of Education for collection.[80] Grant overpayment debts are not eligible for either consolidation or rehabilitation. A student who owes a grant overpayment of $50 or less that is not a remaining balance is eligible to receive additional federal student aid.[81] Students are not liable for overpayments less than $25.[82]

In addition, the amount of a grant overpayment due from a student is limited to the amount by which the original overpayment exceeds 50% of the total grant funds received by the student for the payment period or period of enrollment.[83]

The requirement to repay is waived for students who withdraw from a school because of their status as an "affected individual," defined to include those serving on active duty during a war or other military operation or during a national emergency, performing qualifying National Guard duty during a war or other military operation or during a national emergency, residing or employed in an area that is declared a disaster area by any federal, state, or local official in connection with a national emergency, or suffering direct economic hardship as a result of a war or other military operation or a national emergency, as determined by the Secretary of Education (hereafter "the Secretary").[84]

The Secretary is also permitted to waive a student's Title IV grant repayment if the student withdraws from an institution because of a major disaster.[85] An otherwise eligible student qualifies for the waiver if he or she withdraws during the award year in which the major disaster designation occurred or during the next succeeding award year, if the student withdrew because of the major disaster.[86]

1.4.2.3 TEACH Grants

The TEACH Grant Program is not tied to financial need and provides up to $4000 annually to students who are enrolled in an eligible program and who agree to teach full-time in a high-need field at a public or private elementary or secondary school that serves low-income students.[87]

---

73 Pub. L. No. 111-152, § 2101, 124 Stat. 1029 (Mar. 30, 2010).
74 *Id. See* U.S. Dep't of Educ., Revised 2010-2011 Federal Pell Grant Payment and Disbursement Schedules (Apr. 8, 2010).
75 College Bd., Trends in Student Aid 2009 (2009).
76 20 U.S.C. § 1070a(b)(5); 34 C.F.R. § 690.67.
77 20 U.S.C. § 1070a.
78 34 C.F.R. § 690.79(a)(2).
79 34 C.F.R. § 690.79(b), (c).
80 34 C.F.R. §§ 668.32(g)(4), 690.79(c).
81 34 C.F.R. § 668.22(h)(3)(ii)(B).
82 34 C.F.R. § 690.79(a)(3).
83 34 C.F.R. § 668.22(h)(3)(ii)(A).
84 68 Fed. Reg. 69312 (Dec. 12, 2003).
    This waiver was extended through September 30, 2012. 72 Fed. Reg. 72947 (Dec. 26, 2007).
85 *See* Pub. L. No. 109-66, 119 Stat. 1999 (Sept. 21, 2005) (Pell Grant Hurricane and Disaster Relief Act); Pub. L. No. 109-67, 119 Stat. 2001 (Sept. 21, 2005) (Student Grant Hurricane and Disaster Relief Act). *See also* 34 C.F.R. § 668.22(h)(5); U.S. Dep't of Educ., Reminder of Guidance for Helping Title IV Participants Affected by a Disaster, Dear Colleague Letter GEN-08-10 (June 24, 2008).
86 34 C.F.R. § 668.22(h)(5).
87 20 U.S.C. § 1070g.
    "High need" fields include bilingual education and English language acquisition, foreign language, math, reading specialist, science and special education, and any other field docu-

Recipients of these grants must teach for at least four years within a period of eight years after completing the program for which the TEACH grant was awarded. Although it is not tied to financial need, an applicant must file the Free Application for Federal Student Aid (FAFSA) form. Students who wish to participate must complete and submit an application, including an agreement to serve and promise to repay. Students must also maintain a 3.25 grade point average while in school.[88]

There are a number of potential problems with this program, including the requirement that students who do not complete the four years of qualified teaching within the eight-year time frame, fail to maintain satisfactory academic progress while in school, change their minds about teaching, or are unable to find jobs in "high need" areas must repay any grant amounts received as unsubsidized Direct Stafford loans. Due to a change in the law that went into effect on July 1, 2010, a grant recipient who obtained a degree or expertise in a field that was a high-need subject area at the time of application for the grant, but is no longer designated as "high need" at some point, may fulfill the service obligation by continuing to teach in that field.[89] However, because this change to the law only went into effect on July 1, 2010, any teaching service performed prior to the 2010-2011 school year will count toward the requirement only if the field is designated as "high need" by the state in which the grant recipient is teaching at the time he or she begins qualifying teaching service.[90]

There is no partial credit if an individual teaches for less than four years. The eight-year period can be suspended under certain limited circumstances.[91] For example, a TEACH grant recipient who is called or ordered to active military duty may request a suspension of the eight-year period in increments not to exceed three years. The request for suspension may be granted in one-year increments.[92]

A discharge from the agreement to serve as a teacher can be obtained if a student dies or becomes totally and permanently disabled.[93] Students may also qualify for a proportional discharge due an extended call or order to active-duty military status.[94]

The grant will convert to a Direct unsubsidized loan if the borrower fails or refuses to carry out the teaching service obligation.[95] Interest will accrue from the date that each grant disbursement was made.[96] Once converted, there will be a six-month grace period prior to entering repayment, and the borrower is eligible for all of the benefits of the Direct Loan Program.[97] Converted grants are not counted against annual or aggregate loan limits.[98]

The Department has a number of on-line tools to assist TEACH grant recipients. There is an on-line TEACH Grant Program certification form and "life circumstance tracking suspension" form.[99]

1.4.2.4 ACG and Smart Grants

In 2006, Congress created two new student grant programs—the Academic Competitiveness Grant Program and National Science and Mathematics Access to Retain Talent (SMART) Grant Program.[100]

The Academic Competitiveness grant was made available for the first time for the 2006–2007 school year to first-year college students who graduated from high school after January 1, 2006, and to second-year college students who graduated from high school after January 1, 2005. The Academic Competitiveness grant award is in addition to the student's Pell grant award. An Academic Competitiveness grant provides up to $750 for the first year of undergraduate study and up to $1300 for the second year of undergraduate study to full-time students who are eligible for a federal Pell grant and who had successfully completed a rigorous high school program, as determined by the state or local education agency and recognized by the Secretary of Education. Second-year students must maintain a cumulative grade point average (GPA) of at least 3.0.

The National Science and Mathematics Access to Retain Talent grant, also known as the National SMART grant, is available during the third and fourth years of undergraduate study to full-time students who are eligible for the federal Pell grant and who are majoring in physical, life, or computer sciences; mathematics; technology; engineering; or a foreign language determined critical to national security.[101] The student must also be enrolled in the courses necessary to complete the degree program and to fulfill the requirements of the intended eligible major in addition to maintaining a cumulative GPA of at least 3.0 in coursework required for the major. The National SMART grant award is in addition to the student's Pell grant award.

---

mented as high-need by the federal government or a state government and approved by the Secretary. 34 C.F.R. § 686.2.

88 34 C.F.R. § 686.11.
89 See U.S. Dep't of Educ., Teaching in a High Need Field in Order to Satisfy the TEACH Grant Program Agreement to Serve, Dear Colleague Letter GEN-09-10 (Aug. 13, 2009).
90 Id.
91 34 C.F.R. § 686.41.
92 34 C.F.R. § 686.41(a)(2).
93 Id. § 686.42.
94 34 C.F.R. § 686.42(c).
95 34 C.F.R. § 686.12(e), 686.43.
96 Id. § 686.43.
97 Id. § 686.43(c).
98 Id. § 682.204(m). See § 2.2, infra.
99 See www.dl.ed.gov/borrower/QctrHelpIndex.do?SectionId=FAQU&APageID=QctrFaquA211.
100 Pub. L. No. 109-171, 120 Stat. 4 (2006) (codified at 20 U.S.C. § 1070a-1); 34 C.F.R. §§ 691.1–691.17.
101 See U.S. Dep't of Educ., National SMART Grant-Designation of Additional Eligible Majors, Dear Colleague Letter GEN-10-04 (Apr. 2, 2010); U.S. Dep't of Educ., National SMART Grant Program: List of Eligible Majors for Award Year 2010–2011, Dear Colleague Letter GEN-10-12 (June 18, 2010).

The Obama Administration has signaled that it will not renew the Academic Competitiveness Grant Program or SMART Grant Program beyond their 2011 expiration date.[102]

1.4.3 Seizure of Student Loan Funds Generally Prohibited

Student assistance funds, including loans, grants, and work assistance may be garnished to collect debts owed to the Department of Education.[103] However, these funds (or property traceable to them) cannot be garnished by other collectors.[104] For example, a private collection agency pursuing a student for credit card debt cannot garnish or attach that student's federal student loan funds to collect the debt. These student assistance funds also cannot be seized through administrative offset.[105]

1.4.4 Educational Benefits for Military Service Members

1.4.4.1 The Post 9/11 G.I. Bill

The "Post 9/11 G.I. Bill," signed by President Bush in June 2008, provides significant educational benefits for service members on active duty and after their duty is over.[106] In general, veterans with thirty-six months or more active duty service after September 10, 2001, or veterans with thirty consecutive days or more active duty service after September 10, 2001, who are medically discharged for service-connected disability are entitled to educational assistance equal to thirty-six months.[107] The duration of service is generally based on aggregate service, not a single continuous period of service.

Service must have occurred on or after September 11, 2001. Service members who are serving on active duty are eligible as well as those who completed their service or were discharged or released. However, only certain types of discharges and releases qualify, including honorable discharges or discharges or releases for certain medical conditions or hardships. Those still on active duty may be better served using existing benefits. The Department of Veterans Affairs has information to help service members choose the best options.[108]

In order to qualify, the students must be pursuing an approved program of education. The amounts to be received are equal to the charges for the program of education, except that the amount may not exceed the maximum amount of established charges that in-state undergraduate students are regularly charged in the state in which the individual is enrolled. Students receive money not only for tuition but in many cases are also eligible for a housing allowance, an annual stipend for books and supplies, and in some cases even a relocation payment. Some assistance is also available for students pursuing education on a half-time basis or less. In some situations, this benefit may be transferred to the service member's spouse or children. Benefits are prorated for those with less than thirty-six months of active duty service. Those who served for thirty-six months are eligible for 100% of benefits.

The time period to use these benefits expires at the end of the fifteen-year period beginning on the date of the individual' last discharge or release from active duty. The sections became effective on August 1, 2009, and the Department of Defense issued regulations.[109] The Department of Veterans Affairs has posted an on-line chart with maximum in-state tuition and fees.[110]

Military service members also have new benefits due to passage of the 2008 Military Construction, Veterans' Affairs, and Related Agencies Appropriations Bill ("Post 9/11 G.I. Bill").[111]

1.4.4.2 Other Protections and Programs for Service Members

The HEA provides unique deferment, forbearance, and other rights for active-duty service members.[112] There may be state claims as well to protect service members attending school. For example, Ohio requires that institutions of higher education grant active duty military students a leave of absence without academic penalty while the student is serving on active duty. There are also provisions for refunds or credits of tuition.[113]

---

102 Austin Wright, *An Experiment in Merit-Based Student Aid Is Likely to End*, Chron. of Higher Educ., June 26, 2009.
103 20 U.S.C. § 1095a(d).
104 *Id.*
105 31 U.S.C. § 3716(c)(1)(C).
106 Pub. L. No. 110-252, Ch. 33, 122 Stat. 2323 (June 30, 2008).
107 Pub. L. No. 110-252, §§ 3311, 3312, 122 Stat. 2323 (2008) (indicating any education discontinued due to active service does not count against thirty-six-month maximum).
108 The Department of Veterans Affairs has information about the program on its website at www.gibill.va.gov. For background information about veterans education benefits, see Katherine Kiemle Buckley & Bridgid Cleary, *The Restoration and Modernization of Education Benefits Under the Post-9/11 Veterans Assistance Act of 2008*, 2 Veterans L. Rev. 185 (2010).
109 38 C.F.R. §§ 21.1029–1034.
110 *See* www.gibill.va.gov/GI_Bill_Info/CH33/Tuition_and_fees.htm.
111 Pub. L. No. 110-252, Ch. 33, 122 Stat. 2323 (June 30, 2008).
112 *See* §§ 4.3.5.4 (deferments), 4.4 (forbearance), *infra*.
113 Ohio Rev. Code Ann. § 3345.53 (West) (includes private right of enforcement); Ohio Rev. Code Ann. § 3332.20 (West) (leave of absence and other requirements apply to career colleges and schools). *See generally* U.S. Gov't Accountability Office, Higher Education: More Information Could Help Education Determine the Extent to Which Eligible Servicemembers Serving on Active Duty Benefited from Relief Provided by Lenders and Schools 17, Report No. GAO-07-11 (Nov. 2006).

In addition, Congress in 2008 passed new provisions, including re-admission requirements for service members and prohibitions on interest accrual in the Direct Loan Program.[114]

The Servicemember Civil Relief Act (SCRA) limits collection tactics and enforcement of claims against active-duty military personnel.[115] These protections, as well as SCRA interest rate benefits, are discussed in Chapter 7, *infra*.

These issues are becoming more important as military members are increasingly seeking education, often on-line, while serving. The University of Phoenix on-line, for example, has a separate division that handles military students.[116] In addition, many schools, including large proprietary schools, target those leaving the service.[117]

Military service members may also have claims against the military in cases involving false promises or misrepresentations about educational benefits. These are difficult cases because of the judicial deference to the military and because recruiting violations are generally considered to be internal disciplinary matters with no recourse available for recruits.[118] Limited judicial oversight may be allowed, particularly if the individual has not completed his or her military service and is seeking to rescind the enlistment agreement.[119]

1.5 Financial Need; Applying for Federal Student Loans

1.5.1 General

There are general eligibility criteria that apply to most federal student loan programs. In some cases, students must show financial need. The expected family contribution (EFC) is a measure of the borrower's family's financial situation and indicates how much of the borrower's (and family's, if the borrower is a dependent) resources should be available to help pay for education.

The EFC formula is calculated according to a statutory formula.[120] There is some flexibility to consider special circumstances. In addition, financial aid administrators have the discretion to use their professional judgment to make adjustments on a case-by-case basis to the data items that are used in determining a student's eligibility.[121]

Individuals who wish to apply on-line for aid must first get a personal identification number that allows them to apply on-line. They must then complete the free application for federal student aid (FAFSA).[122] As a result of the information provided on the FAFSA, a student aid report (SAR) is generated. The SAR includes the expected family contribution, the number used to determine federal student aid eligibility.

There has been a great deal of debate over how to improve the EFC, particularly with respect to assessing the financial position of independent students.[123]

Information about applying for consolidation loans is in Chapter 6, *infra*.

1.5.2 Dependent and Independent Students

In general, a borrower's responses on the application for federal assistance will determine whether he or she is considered dependent or independent. The main difference is that dependents must also report parents' income and assets, and parents are expected to contribute to their children's education.

Among other provisions, borrowers are considered independent if they:

- Are twenty-four years of age or older by December of the award year;
- Are orphans, in foster care, or wards of the court, at any time when borrowers are thirty years of age or older;
- Are emancipated minors or those in legal guardianship;
- Are Armed Forces veterans or those currently serving on active duty for other than training purposes;
- Are graduate or professional students;

---

114 Pub. L. No. 110-315, § 484C, 122 Stat. 3078 (Aug. 14, 2008) (re-admission requirements). See § 2.3.2, *infra* (interest accrual prohibition).

115 50 U.S.C. App. §§ 501–596. *See generally* National Consumer Law Center, Collection Actions Ch. 7 (2008 and Supp.).

116 *See* Dan Carnevale, *Be All You Can Be—Online*, Chron. of Higher Educ., July 7, 2006, at A31.

117 *See* § 12.3.3.2, *infra*.

118 *See generally* Anna M. Schleelin, *The Legal Implications of Unauthorized Promises and Other Military Recruiter Misconduct*, B.U. Pub. Int. L.J. 141 (Fall 2007).

119 *Id.* The main obstacle is that military enlistment agreements generally do not give rise to contract rights. *See, e.g.*, Sonnenfeld v. United States, 62 Fed. Cl. 336 (Fed. Cl. 2004).

120 20 U.S.C. § 1087nn.
   The revisions for the 2010–2011 award year can be found at 74 Fed. Reg. 26379 (June 2, 2009). For 2011–2012, see 75 Fed. Reg. 29744 (May 27, 2010).

121 20 U.S.C. § 1087tt.
   Additional flexibility is given in cases involving "affected individuals," defined to include those serving on active duty during a war or other military operation or national emergency, performing qualifying National Guard duty during a war or other military operation or during a national emergency, residing or employed in an area that is declared a disaster area, or suffering direct economic hardship as a result of a war or other military operation or national emergency. 68 Fed. Reg. 69312 (Dec. 12, 2003).
   This waiver was extended through September 30, 2012. 72 Fed. Reg. 72947 (Dec. 26, 2007).

122 A copy of the FAFSA form is reprinted at Appendix D, *infra*, and on the companion website to this manual.

123 *See, e.g.*, Sandy Baum, Lumina Found. for Educ., National Ass'n of Student Fin. Aid Administrators, Fixing the Formula: A New Approach to Determining Independent Students' Ability to Pay for College (May 2006).

- Are married on the day of application;
- Have dependents other than a spouse;
- Have been verified during the school year in which the application is submitted as either an unaccompanied youth who is a homeless child or youth or as unaccompanied, at risk of homelessness, and self-supporting; or
- Have been verified as independent by a financial aid administrator by reason of other unusual circumstances.[124]

Not living with parents or not being claimed by them on tax forms does not determine dependency status.

1.6 Individual Eligibility for Federal Student Loans

1.6.1 Academic Requirements

To be eligible for federal student assistance, individuals must be enrolled as regular students in eligible programs.[125] This means, for example, that the student cannot also be enrolled in elementary or secondary school.[126] Students must be enrolled in a degree, certificate, or other approved program at an eligible school.[127] They must also be enrolled at least half-time.[128]

Potential borrowers must have a high school diploma or General Education Certificate (GED), complete an approved home school education, or pass a test approved by the Department of Education.[129] The Department-approved tests are known as "ability to benefit" tests.[130] Students may meet this standard not only by taking a valid test under valid testing conditions but also upon completing six credit hours or the equivalent coursework that is applicable toward a degree or certificate offered by the institution of higher education.[131]

1.6.2 Satisfactory Academic Progress

A student must maintain satisfactory progress in the course of study in order to remain eligible for assistance.[132] Schools must have a published policy for monitoring that progress. There are requirements describing how often a school must check satisfactory academic progress (SAP).

In general, for programs longer than two academic years, students must have a "C" average or its equivalent by the end of the second year (regardless of how many credits they have accrued) or have an academic standing consistent with the requirements for graduation.[133]

For programs of two years or less, schools must have a qualitative standard at least as stringent as described in the standards above.

There is also a quantitative standard. Otherwise, a student could, for example, maintain a high GPA by withdrawing from every course he or she attempts after the first year. This student would have a high GPA but would not be progressing towards graduation. The SAP therefore also includes a quantitative measure to determine the number or percentage of courses, credit hours, or clock hours completed.[134]

Schools must explain how they handle course repetitions and how students may appeal determinations that they are not making satisfactory academic progress.

In June 2010, the Department issued proposed regulations that would restructure the SAP requirements. The proposed rules also specify the elements that an institution's SAP policy must contain to be considered reasonable.[135]

1.6.3 Citizenship Requirements

Prospective borrowers must be United States citizens or eligible non-citizens.[136] Eligible non-citizens primarily include permanent residents, refugees, and asylees.[137] Victims of human trafficking have the same eligibility for federal benefits as refugees. In addition, immigrants who are victims of domestic violence by their U.S. citizen or permanent resident spouses may, with their designated children, be eligible for federal public benefits, including federal student aid.[138]

All borrowers must have valid Social Security numbers and must register with the Selective Service if required.[139]

---

124 20 U.S.C. § 1087vv(d).
125 20 U.S.C. § 1091; 34 C.F.R. § 668.32.
126 34 C.F.R. § 668.32(b).
127 20 U.S.C. § 1091(a)(1), (2).
128 20 U.S.C. § 1078(b)(1)(A); 34 C.F.R. § 668.2 (definition of half-time status).
   There are a number of issues related to how "time" is counted for purposes of determining full-time and half-time status. See 34 C.F.R. § 668.2 for definitions.
129 20 U.S.C. § 1091(d); 34 C.F.R. § 668.32(e).
130 For more on ability-to-benefit tests and false-certification discharges, see § 9.4.2, infra.
131 20 U.S.C. § 1091(d)(4). See § 9.4.2, infra (ATB discharge).
132 20 U.S.C. § 1091(a)(2), (c); 34 C.F.R. §§ 668.16(e), 668.32(f), 668.34.
133 34 C.F.R. § 668.34.
134 34 C.F.R. § 668.16(e).
135 75 Fed. Reg. 34806 (June 18, 2010).
136 20 U.S.C. § 1091(a)(5).
137 34 C.F.R. § 668.33.
   Other eligible immigration categories include those on indefinite parole and/or humanitarian parole, Cuban/Haitian entrants with status pending, and conditional entrants (only if authorization was issued before April 1, 1980). Students in the United States with student visas only are not eligible for federal aid.
138 For more information, see U.S. Dep't of Educ., Eligibility for Title IV Aid for Battered Immigrants-Qualified Aliens As Provided For in the Violence Against Women Act, Dear Colleague Letter GEN-10-07 (June 4, 2010).
139 20 U.S.C. § 1091(a)(4)(B) (SSN); 34 C.F.R. § 668.32(i).

1.6.4 Drug Convictions

Students convicted under federal or state law of sale or possession of illegal drugs are suspended from federal financial assistance programs.[140] Eligibility may be suspended for one year from the date of a first conviction on a drug possession charge, two years from the date of a second conviction, and indefinitely for a third.[141] Students convicted of selling drugs lose eligibility for two years from the date of a first conviction and indefinitely for a second.[142]

Eligibility can be restored if the student satisfactorily completes a drug rehabilitation program or if the conviction is reversed or set aside.[143] A 2006 study found that, overall, nearly 200,000 would-be college students had been declared ineligible to receive financial aid because of drug convictions.[144]

Prior to July 1, 2006, borrowers were denied aid not only if they were convicted while in school but also if they were convicted of drug offenses prior to enrolling in higher education. As of July 1, 2006, however, a student will become ineligible for aid only if the conviction is for conduct that occurred during a period of enrollment for which the student was receiving Title IV program assistance.[145]

In 2006, a South Dakota district court rejected a constitutional challenge to the drug-related eligibility standard.[146] The advocacy group, Students for Sensible Drug Policy, argued unsuccessfully that the policy violated the equal protection clause of the Constitution and subjected individuals to double jeopardy.[147]

1.6.5 Incarcerated Students

Incarcerated students are not eligible for federal student loans, but they are eligible for certain grants.[148] A student is considered to be incarcerated if he or she is serving a criminal sentence in a federal, state or local penitentiary, prison, jail, reformatory, work farm, or similar correctional institution.[149]

An otherwise eligible institution may become ineligible if, in its latest complete award year, more than 25% of its regular students are incarcerated.[150]

1.6.6 Prior Student Aid History

Students are generally not eligible for federal aid if they are in default on federal student loans or if they owe overpayments on federal grants or loans.[151] In addition, students who have been convicted of, or have pleaded *nolo contendere* or guilty to, a crime involving fraud in obtaining Title IV HEA program assistance are not eligible for additional Title IV assistance unless they have repaid the fraudulently obtained funds.[152]

1.7 Institutional Eligibility

1.7.1 Eligibility Criteria

1.7.1.1 Different Types of Schools

Only students who are enrolled at an "eligible institution" may receive federal aid.[153] There are different eligibility requirements for public or private nonprofit institutions and proprietary institutions.[154] Under the three definitions (institutions of higher education, proprietary institutions of higher education, and post-secondary vocational institutions), a school is eligible to participate in all federal student aid programs as long as it offers the appropriate type of eligible program.

An institution of higher education or a post-secondary vocational institute can be either private or public but must be nonprofit. A proprietary institution is always a private, for-profit institution. The HEA defines a proprietary institution as a school that:

For selective service requirements, see 34 C.F.R. § 668.32(j), 668.37.

140 20 U.S.C. § 1091(r); 34 C.F.R. § 668.40.
141 34 C.F.R. § 668.40(b)(1).
142 34 C.F.R. § 668.40(b)(2).
143 34 C.F.R. §§ 668.40(c) (rehabilitation programs); 668.40(a)(2) (definition of "conviction").
144 Students for Sensible Drug Policy, Harmful Drug Law Hits Home: How Many College Students in Each State Lost Financial Aid Due to Drug Convictions? (Apr. 17, 2006).
  The Advisory Committee on Student Financial Assistance has also recommended elimination of the requirement. *See* Advisory Comm. on Student Fin. Assistance, The Student Aid Gauntlet: Making Access to College Simple and Certain 16 (Jan. 23, 2005), *available at* www.ed.gov/about/bdscomm/list/acsfa/gauntletcorrected.pdf.
  In addition, the GAO was unable to find any evidence that the provision actually helped to deter drug use. *See* U.S. Gen. Accountability Office, Drug Offenders: Various Factors May Limit the Impact of Federal Laws that Provide for Denial of Selected Benefits, Report No. GAO-05-238 (Sept. 26, 2005).
  Detailed information, including updated advocacy efforts about this issue can be found on the website for Students for Sensible Drug Policy, www.ssdp.org.
145 20 U.S.C. § 1091(r); 34 C.F.R. § 668.40(a)(1).
146 Students for Sensible Drug Policy Found. v. Spellings, 523 F.3d 896 (8th Cir. 2008).
147 *Id.*

148 20 U.S.C. § 1091(b)(5).
149 34 C.F.R. § 600.2.
150 20 U.S.C. § 1002(a)(3)(C).
151 20 U.S.C. § 1091(a)(3).
152 20 U.S.C. § 1091(a)(6).
153 20 U.S.C. §§ 1091(a), 1094.
154 20 U.S.C. §§ 1001 (general definition of institution of higher education), 1002 (definition for purposes of student assistance programs); 34 C.F.R. §§ 600.4 (public or private nonprofit institutions), 600.5 (proprietary institutions).

1A. Provides an eligible program of training to prepare students for gainful employment in a recognized occupation; *or*
1B. Provides a program leading to a baccalaureate degree in liberal arts and has provided such a program since January 1, 2009, and is accredited by a recognized regional accrediting agency or association, and has continuously held such accreditation since October 1, 2007, or earlier; *and*
2. Admits as regular students only persons having a certificate of graduation from a school providing secondary education, or the recognized equivalent, or those who meet the home-schooling requirements;
3. Is legally authorized within the state to provide a program of education beyond secondary education;[155]
4. Is not a public or other nonprofit institution;
5. is accredited by a nationally recognized accrediting agency or association recognized by the Department; and
6. has been in existence for at least two years.[156]

The category also includes institutions that admit students who are beyond the age of compulsory school attendance or who will be dually or concurrently enrolled in the institution and a secondary school.[157]

Institutions of higher education may offer associate, bachelor's, graduate, or professional degrees; at least a two-year program that is acceptable for full credit toward a bachelors' degree; or at least a one-year training program that leads to a degree or certificate (or other recognized educational credential) and prepares students for gainful employment in a recognized occupation.[158]

Proprietary institutions, in contrast, must only have programs that provide training for gainful employment in a recognized occupation and must meet at least one of the following categories:

1. 600 clock hours of instruction, 16 semester hours, or 24 quarter hours, offered during a minimum of 15 weeks, in the case of a program that—
   A. Provides a program of training to prepare students for gainful employment in a recognized profession; *and*
   B. Admits students who have not completed the equivalent of an associate degree; *or*
2. 300 clock hours of instruction, 8 semester hours, or 12 hours, offered during a minimum of 10 weeks, in the case of—
   A. An undergraduate program that requires the equivalent of an associate degree for admissions; *or*
   B. A graduate or professional program.

A program is also eligible if it at least 300 clock hours of instruction, but less than 600 clock hours of instruction, offered during a minimum of 10 weeks, and it has:

1. A verified completion rate of at least 70 percent, as determined in accordance with the regulations of the Secretary;
2. a verified placement rate of at least 70 percent, as determined in accordance with the regulations of the Secretary; and
3. satisfies such further criteria as the Secretary may prescribe by regulation.[159]

The calculation of clock hours and credit hours has generated considerable controversy. The Department issued proposed regulations in June 2010 that would define "credit hour."[160]

Because a school's eligibility does not necessarily extend to all its programs, the school must ensure that a program is eligible before awarding federal aid funds to students in that program. The school is responsible for determining that a program is eligible. For example, the program must be included in the notice of accreditation and must be authorized by the appropriate state to offer the program.

1.7.1.2 Gainful Employment

As described above, proprietary schools (as well as certain public or nonprofit shorter-term training programs) must provide training for gainful employment in a recognized occupation.[161]

The term "gainful employment," however, is not defined. In July 2010, the Department of Education issued proposed rules that define "gainful employment."[162] Under the proposed framework, to determine whether particular programs provide training that leads to gainful employment, the Department would take into consideration repayment rates on federal student loans, the relationship between total student loan debt and earnings and, in some cases, whether employers endorse program content.

The proposed rules, if enacted, should become effective in July 2012 with some transition periods built in. However, in September 2010, the Department announced that they would delay publication of final rules until early 2011. It was unclear at the time this manual was written whether this would impact the July 2012 effective date.

This proposal has met considerable opposition from the industry and has been the focus of tremendous controversy. An additional set of proposed rules, issued in June 2010, would require schools to annually submit information about

---

155 The Department issued proposed regulations in June 2010 to refine the definition of "state authorization." *See* 75 Fed. Reg. 34806 (June 18, 2010).
156 20 U.S.C. § 1002(b)(1).
157 20 U.S.C. § 1002(b)(2).
158 20 U.S.C. § 1001.
159 20 U.S.C. § 1088(b).
160 75 Fed. Reg. 34806 (June 18, 2010).
161 20 U.S.C. § 1002(b).
162 75 Fed. Reg. 43616 (July 26, 2010).

students who complete a program that leads to gainful employment.[163]

1.7.1.3 Admissions Standards

With a few exceptions, eligible institutions may admit as regular students only persons who have high school diplomas or recognized equivalents.[164] A recognized equivalent of a high school diploma is either a GED or a state certificate.[165]

For verification of high school status, schools are not required to keep copies of diplomas or GEDs. Rather, under current rules, the school is allowed to rely on the student's certification, including on the FAFSA, that he or she has received the credential, and a copy of the certification must be kept on file. Furthermore, the regulations do not currently define "high school diploma." This has caused some concern due to the proliferation of diploma mills.[166]

The Department of Education issued proposed rules in June 2010 that would require schools to develop and follow procedures to evaluate the validity of a student's high school diploma.[167]

In addition, students who do not have high school diplomas or GEDs may receive aid if they meet ability-to-benefit criteria.[168] Unless a school provides a four-year bachelor's degree program or a two-year associate degree program, it will not qualify as an eligible institution if, in its latest complete award year, more than 50% of its regular enrolled students had neither high school diplomas nor the equivalent.[169]

1.7.1.4 Distance Education

Prior to Congressional changes in 2006, schools that offered primarily distance education courses had their participation in federal assistance programs limited in a number of ways. These limits were removed for the most part and currently apply only to "correspondence courses." Correspondence courses are not considered to be "distance education."[170]

Due to the changes in the law, distance education courses are treated in the same way as traditional residential programs. "Distance education" is generally defined as education that uses one or more of the following technologies to deliver instruction to students who are separated from the instructor and to support regular and substantive interaction between the students and the instructor, either synchronously or asynchronously. The technologies may include:

1. The Internet;
2. One-way and two-way transmissions through open broadcast, closed circuit, cable, microwave, broadband lines, fiber optics, satellite, or wireless communication devices;
3. Audio conferencing; or
4. Video cassettes, DVDs, and CD-Roms, if they are used in a course in conjunction with any of the technologies listed above.[171]

These courses are eligible for federal financial aid if the program is offered by an institution (other than a foreign institution) that has been evaluated and is accredited for its effective delivery of distance education programs by an accrediting agency or association that is recognized by the Secretary and has accreditation of distance education within the scope of its recognition.[172]

Schools are, however, limited in correspondence course offerings. Correspondence courses are defined as courses provided by an institution under which the institution provides instructional materials, by mail or electronic transmission, including examinations on the materials, to students who are separated from the instructor. Interaction between the instructor and student is limited, is not regular and substantive, and is primarily initiated by the student. Correspondence courses are typically self-paced. If a course is part correspondence and part residential training, the Secretary considers the course to be a correspondence course.[173]

A school does not qualify as eligible if for the latest complete award year:

1. More than 50% of the school's courses were correspondence courses, or
2. 50% or more of the school's regular enrolled students were enrolled in correspondence courses.[174]

This limit may be waived for a school for good cause in some cases.[175]

Congress passed the legislation eliminating the restrictions on the broader range of distance education courses despite a U.S. General Accounting Office (GAO) study showing that eliminating the restrictions with no additional monitoring would trigger a medium to high risk of fraud and abuse and could lead to substantial cost increases.[176] The GAO also found significant variation in accrediting agen-

---

163 75 Fed. Reg. 34806 (June 18, 2010).
164 20 U.S.C. §§ 1001(a), 1002.
165 34 C.F.R. § 600.2.
166 See § 12.4.2, infra.
167 75 Fed. Reg. 34806 (June 18, 2010).
168 20 U.S.C. § 1091(d); 34 C.F.R. § 668.32(e). See §§ 1.6.1, supra, 9.4.2, infra (ATB discharge).
169 20 U.S.C. § 1002(a)(3)(D); 34 C.F.R. § 600.7(a).
170 34 C.F.R. § 600.2.

171 Id.
172 34 C.F.R. § 668.8(m) (referring to the prior term "telecommunications").
    Distance education is defined at 34 C.F.R. § 600.2.
173 34 C.F.R. § 600.2.
174 20 U.S.C. § 1002(a)(3)(B).
175 Id.
176 See U.S. Gen. Accounting Office, Distance Education: Improved Data on Program Costs and Guidelines on Quality Assessments Needed to Inform Federal Policy, Report No. GAO-04-279 (Feb. 2004).

cies' oversight of distance education programs. This is particularly troubling since the accrediting agencies are given substantial flexibility by the Department to determine standards and monitor schools.

In extreme cases, such as natural disasters, the Department may waive certain eligibility requirements, such as the requirement that a proprietary institution derive at least 10% of its revenues from non-Title IV sources.[177]

1.7.2 Program Participation Agreements

1.7.2.1 General

To participate in federal student aid programs, schools must have a current program participation agreement (PPA) signed by the school's President or CEO and an authorized representative of the Department of Education.[178] Under the PPA, the school agrees to comply with the laws, regulations, and policies governing the federal aid programs. The PPAs also require schools to certify that they have certain policies, such as drug abuse prevention policies, and that they will comply with anti-discrimination laws. Schools also certify that they will not charge for processing or handling any application, form, or data used to determine eligibility for federal aid. The PPA also includes standards of financial responsibility and administrative capacity.[179]

1.7.2.2 The "90/10" Rule for Proprietary Schools

The "90/10" rule applies only to proprietary schools. The 90/10 rule requires each proprietary school to limit the percentage of revenues it receives from Department of Education federal financial assistance (Title IV funds) to no more than 90%. The rule refers only to HEA federal assistance. This means that other types of federal student aid, such as Department of Defense G.I. assistance, is not counted toward the 90%.

The main problem, according to a GAO study, is that proprietary schools that rely more heavily on student assistance tend to have poorer student outcomes, including lower completion and placement rates and higher default rates.[180] These schools are also more likely to push students into taking out loans that they will not be able to repay.

The 90/10 rule was previously an institutional eligibility requirement but is now part of the PPA.[181] As a result of this change to the PPA, an institution that does not meet the 90/10 requirement no longer loses its eligibility to participate in the federal assistance programs. Instead, the institution's participation becomes provisional for two fiscal years. If the institution does not satisfy the requirement for two consecutive fiscal years, it will then lose its eligibility for at least two fiscal years.

Schools may consider as revenue for the 10% portion only those funds generated by the school from tuition, fees, and other institutional charges for students enrolled in eligible programs; from activities conducted by the school that are necessary for the education and training of the school's students, if those activities are conducted on campus or at a facility under the control of the school and meet other requirements; and from funds paid by, or on behalf of, a student by a party other than the school for an education or training program that is not eligible for federal assistance funds, if the program is approved or licensed by the appropriate state agency, accredited by a recognized accreditation agency, or provides an industry-recognized credential or certification.[182] An appendix to the August 2009 proposed regulations illustrates how an institution should calculate 90/10 revenue percentages.[183]

1.7.2.3 Limits on Incentive Compensation

The PPAs also require schools to agree to certain "incentive compensation" rules.[184] This provision is meant to curb the risk that recruiters will sign up poorly qualified students who will derive little benefit from the subsidy and may be unable or unwilling to repay federally guaranteed loans.[185]

The limits on incentive compensation have been significantly diluted over the years. The previous regulations generally followed the statutory language in prohibiting commissions, bonuses, and other incentive payments by school recruiters when those payments were tied directly or indirectly to success in securing enrollments or financial aid.[186] Legislation pending in Congress in 2002 would have taken much of the bite out of this law.[187] However, the Department of Education bypassed the legislative process by enacting new regulations that contained many of the provisions in the Congressional bill.[188] In a positive devel-

---

177 See, e.g., U.S. Dep't of Educ., Dear Colleague Letter GEN-06-07 (May 2006) (notification and extension of guidance to assist Title IV participants affected by Hurricanes Katrina and Rita).
178 20 U.S.C. § 1094; 34 C.F.R. § 668.14.
179 20 U.S.C. § 1094(a)(24).
180 U.S. Gen. Accounting Office, Proprietary Schools: Poorer Student Outcomes at Schools That Rely More on Federal Student Aid, Report No. GAO/HEHS-97-103 (June 1997). See § 12.3.3.5, infra.

181 20 U.S.C. § 1094 (a)(24); 34 C.F.R. §§ 668.14(b)(16), 668.28.
182 34 C.F.R. § 668.28.
183 74 Fed. Reg. 42380 (Aug. 21, 2009).
184 20 U.S.C. § 1094(a)(20).
185 See § 12.3.3.2, infra.
186 20 U.S.C. § 1094(a)(20); 34 C.F.R. § 668.24.
187 Internet Equity and Education Act of 2001, S. 1445, 107th Cong. (2001).
188 67 Fed. Reg. 67048 (Nov. 1, 2002) (amending 34 C.F.R. § 668.14(b)(22)).

opment for borrowers, in 2010 the Department proposed eliminating the safe harbors.[189]

Until the proposed regulations go into effect (July 2011 at the earliest), the safe harbors are still in the regulations. For example, the following are exempted from the definition of "incentive compensation":

- The payment of fixed compensation, such as a fixed annual salary or a fixed hourly wage, as long as that compensation is not adjusted up or down more than twice during any twelve-month period and any adjustment is not based solely on the number of students recruited, admitted, enrolled, or awarded financial aid. For this purpose, an increase in fixed compensation resulting from a cost-of-living increase that is paid to all or substantially all full-time employees is not considered an adjustment.[190]
- Compensation to recruiters based upon their recruitment of students who enroll only in programs that are not eligible for Title IV, HEA program funds.[191]
- Compensation paid to employees who perform clerical "pre-enrollment" activities, such as answering telephone calls, referring inquiries, or distributing institutional materials.[192]
- Compensation to managerial or supervisory employees who do not directly manage or supervise employees who are directly involved in recruiting or admissions activities or the awarding of Title IV, HEA program funds.[193]
- Compensation paid for Internet-based recruitment and admission activities that provide information about the institution to prospective students, refer prospective students to the institution, or permit prospective students to apply for admission on-line.[194]

1.7.2.4 Code of Conduct and Prohibited Inducement Requirements

Improper ties between lenders and schools have generated considerable controversy in recent years. The key concern has been lenders offering inducements in exchange for schools recommending the lender's products and services to students. This concern may be primarily in the past now that the FFEL Program has been eliminated.

Much of the controversy centered on school preferred-lender lists. These are lists of recommended lenders that many schools used prior to the elimination of the FFEL Program. Until recently, there was little enforcement activity in this area.[195] As noted above, the concern should be less relevant now that there are no longer FFEL loans. However, the Department is sanctioning some lenders for past violations. For example, in August 2010 the Department found that agreements between the for-profit education company Corinthian and certain lenders, including SLX (Student Loan Express) and Sallie Mae, violated the HEA improper inducement provisions.[196]

The Department has issued a number of new regulations that address this issue, including guidelines for preferred-lender lists.[197] Institutions must also establish a code of conduct as part of the PPA. The statute sets out in detail the required elements of the code of conduct, including gift bans and bans on revenue-sharing arrangements.[198]

1.7.2.5 Private Education Loan Certification

As part of the PPA, schools must also provide the Truth in Lending private education self-certification form upon request from a student or parent applying for a private education loan.[199]

1.7.2.6 Misrepresentation

The PPA states that that an eligible institution that has engaged in substantial misrepresentation of the nature of its educational program, its financial charges, or the employability of its graduates may face suspension or termination of the eligibility status for any or all programs.[200] The Department proposed significant changes to the misrepresentation regulations in June 2010.[201]

1.7.3 Consumer Information Requirements

Schools have a number of student information requirements, including information about:[202]

- The student financial assistance programs available to students who enroll at such institutions;
- The methods by which such assistance is distributed among student recipients who enroll at such institutions;

---

189 75 Fed. Reg. 34806 (June 18, 2010).
190 34 C.F.R. § 668.14(b)(22)(ii)(A).
191 34 C.F.R. § 668.14(b)(22)(ii)(B).
192 34 C.F.R. § 668.14(b)(22)(ii)(F).
193 34 C.F.R. § 668.14(b)(22)(ii)(G).
194 34 C.F.R. § 668.14(b)(22)(ii)(J).
195 U.S. Gov't Accountability Office, Federal Family Education Loan Program: Increased Department of Education Oversight of Lender and School Activities Needed to Help Ensure Program Compliance, Report No. GAO-07-750 (July 2007).
196 U.S. Dep't of Educ., Office of Inspector General, Everest Institute's Lender Agreements, Control No. ED-OIG/A02J001 (Aug. 4, 2010).
197 See 34 C.F.R. §§ 601.21, 682.212 (prohibited transactions), 682.401.
198 20 U.S.C. § 1094(e).
199 20 U.S.C. § 1094(a)(27). See § 11.4.1.5, infra.
200 20 U.S.C. § 1094(c)(3); 34 C.F.R. §§ 668.71–668.75 (misrepresentation).
201 75 Fed. Reg. 34806 (June 18, 2010).
202 20 U.S.C. § 1092.

- Any means, including forms, by which application for student financial assistance is made and requirements for accurately preparing such application;
- The rights and responsibilities of students receiving federal financial assistance;
- The cost of attending the institution, including (i) tuition and fees; (ii) books and supplies; (iii) estimates of typical student room-and-board costs or typical commuting costs; and (iv) any additional cost of the program in which the student is enrolled or expresses a specific interest;
- A statement of—
  - The requirements of any refund policy with which the institution is required to comply;
  - The requirements for return of grant or loan assistance; and
  - The requirements for officially withdrawing from the institution;
- The academic program of the institution, including (i) the current degree programs and other educational and training programs; (ii) the instructional, laboratory, and other physical plant facilities that relate to the academic program; (iii) the faculty and other instructional personnel; and (iv) any plans by the institution for improving the academic program of the institution;
- Each person designated as financial assistance personnel and the methods by which and locations in which any person so designated may be contacted by students and prospective students who are seeking information required by this subsection;
- Special facilities and services available to students with disabilities;
- The names of associations, agencies, or governmental bodies that accredit, approve, or license the institution and its programs, and the procedures under which any current or prospective student may obtain or review upon request a copy of the documents describing the institution's accreditation, approval, or licensing;
- The standards that the student must maintain in order to be considered to be making satisfactory progress;[203]
- The completion or graduation rate of certificate- or degree-seeking, full-time, undergraduate students entering such institutions;[204]
- The terms and conditions of the federal loans that students receive;
- The placement in employment of, and types of employment obtained by, graduates of the institution's degree or certificate programs, gathered from such sources as alumni surveys, student satisfaction surveys, the National Survey of Student Engagement, the Community College Survey of Student Engagement, State data systems, or other relevant sources;
- The types of graduate and professional education in which graduates of the institution's four-year-degree programs enrolled, gathered from such sources as alumni surveys, student satisfaction surveys, the National Survey of Student Engagement, State data systems, or other relevant sources; and
- The retention rate of certificate- or degree-seeking, first-time, full-time, undergraduate students entering such institutions.

Despite the required information about placement rates, the statute is silent on whether a school is required to calculate a placement rate. The Department decided in the regulations to require schools to disclose this information only if they calculate placement rates.[205] The information may be gathered from the institution's placement rate, if it calculates such a rate, and from state data systems, alumni or student satisfaction surveys, or other relevant sources. The school must identify the source of the information and must disclose any placement rates it calculates.[206]

The Department proposed in June 2010 to require schools to disclose on its website information about the occupations that its programs prepare students to enter, the on-time graduation rate of students entering a program, and the cost of each program including costs for tuition and fees. In addition, beginning June 30, 2010, schools will also have to post information about the placement rate for students completing each of the programs and the median loan debt incurred by the students who completed the program.[207]

There are additional requirements for schools to report outcome data. For example, institutions that advertise job placement rates as a means of attracting students to enroll must make available to prospective students, at or before the time that these students apply for enrollment, the most recent available data concerning employment statistics, graduation statistics, and any other information necessary to substantiate the truthfulness of the advertisements.[208]

All institutions must, on request, make available to any enrolled student or prospective student—through appropriate publications, mailings, or electronic media—information concerning financial assistance and the institution's completion or graduation rate and, if applicable, its transfer-out rate. In the case of a prospective student, the information must be made available prior to the student's enrolling or entering into any financial obligation with the institution.[209] Institutions must make completion or graduation rates available annually.[210]

---

203 See § 1.6.2, supra.
204 See 34 C.F.R. § 668.45 for requirements for calculating these rates.
205 34 C.F.R. § 668.41(d)(5).
206 Id.
207 75 Fed. Reg. 34806 (June 18, 2010).
208 34 C.F.R. § 668.14.
209 34 C.F.R. § 668.41.
210 34 C.F.R. § 668.45.

The manipulation of these rates has been a problem, particularly in the proprietary sector, as discussed in Chapter 12, *infra*.

1.7.4 Administrative Capability

1.7.4.1 General

There are a number of administrative capability requirements, including maintaining a satisfactory academic progress policy and various recordkeeping requirements.[211] This includes designating a capable individual to be responsible for administering the funds. The schools must also have sufficient internal controls for administering the funds and maintaining records as required.

1.7.4.2 Cohort Default-Rate Requirements

1.7.4.2.1 General

Schools are not considered administratively capable when their cohort default rates (CDR) rise above certain limits. The cohort default rate is a specific way of measuring federal student loan defaults. Problems with the calculation method are discussed in Chapter 5, *infra*.

A school is not administratively capable and therefore will be terminated from the federal aid program if the CDR for FFELs and Direct loans equals or exceeds 25% for the three most recent fiscal years or if the most recent CDR is greater than 40%.[212] The 2008 HEA reauthorization law increased the percentage from 25% to 30% for fiscal year 2012 and any succeeding year.[213] Perkins loans have separate cohort default-rate calculations.[214]

Under the CDR sanctions program, the Department has the authority to terminate high-default schools from the federal student aid programs.[215] According to the Department, since the inception of the program in 1991 more than 1100 schools have lost student loan program eligibility.[216] The number of schools subject to sanctions has dropped dramatically since the peak of 642 in 1994. The highest number sanctioned since the millennium is four in 2000. In September 2009, the Secretary of Education announced that two schools, Healthy Hair Academy of Dallas and Jay's Technical Institute of Houston, were subject to cohort default-rate sanctions that year.[217]

The default-rate programs apply to all institutions. However, due to higher default rates in the proprietary sector, these schools have historically been more likely to face sanctions or the threat of sanctions.

1.7.4.2.2 School appeals process

Schools have the right to appeal disciplinary action. Over the years, Congress has steadily expanded the grounds for appeal. In particular, provisions in the 1998 HEA allowed schools to appeal based on mitigating circumstances.[218] The "mitigating circumstance" most relevant for low-income clients is the exemption from sanctions for schools serving primarily low-income students. This is known as the "economically disadvantaged appeal."[219]

There are two types of economically disadvantaged appeals. The first applies to non-degree-granting schools and is based on the percentage of low-income students at the school ("low income rate") and employment placement rate.[220] These schools must show that the low-income rate and the school's placement rate (generally, the percentage of students who became employed in the occupation for which the school trained them) is 44% or more.[221]

The second, applying to degree-granting schools, is based on low-income rate and program completion rate.[222] Degree-granting schools must show that the school's low-income rate is two-thirds or more and the school's completion rate (generally, the percentage of students who completed their program) is 70% or more.[223]

The low-income rate is defined as the percentage of students who are eligible to receive a federal Pell grant of at least one-half the maximum award or have an adjusted gross income that, if added to the student's parents' income (unless the student is an independent student) or added to the spouse's income if the student is a married independent student, is less than the poverty level for the student's family size.[224] Schools can also appeal based on errors or inaccuracies in the calculation of the default rate.[225] There are also "loan servicing" appeals.[226]

---

211 34 C.F.R. § 668.16.
212 34 C.F.R. § 668.187(a)(2).
   Historically black colleges or universities and tribally controlled community colleges or Navajo community colleges are not subject to loss of eligibility as long as they meet certain requirements such as submission of a default management plan. 20 U.S.C. § 1085(a)(6).
213 Pub. L. No. 110-314, § 436(a), 122 Stat. 3078 (Aug. 14, 2008). See 34 C.F.R. § 668.16(m).
214 34 C.F.R. § 674.5.
215 20 U.S.C. § 1085.
216 Press Release, U.S. Dep't of Educ., Accountability for Results Works: College Loan Default Rates Continue to Decline (Sept. 19, 2001).
217 Press Release, U.S. Dep't of Educ., Student Loan Default Rates Increase (Sept. 14, 2009).
218 20 U.S.C. § 1085(a)(4)–(6).
219 34 C.F.R. § 668.194.
220 34 C.F.R. § 668.194(b), (d).
221 *Id*. The regulation explicitly states that a former student is not considered to have been employed based on any employment by the institution. 34 C.F.R. § 668.194(d)(2).
222 34 C.F.R. § 668.194(b), (c).
223 *Id*.
224 34 C.F.R. § 668.194(b).
225 34 C.F.R. § 668.192 (erroneous data appeals).
226 34 C.F.R. § 668.193.

It is important for advocates representing low-income clients to understand the cohort default appeals process. Vocational schools, particularly those in low-income communities, rely almost exclusively on federal assistance to stay in business.[227] They are very aware of the need to stay below the cohort default triggers. As a result, they may push borrowers into certain repayment options (such as consolidation) that may not make sense for a particular borrower. They also may try to mischaracterize certain types of employment as related to the student's program of study at the school. At a minimum, understanding these incentives is likely to give advocates additional leverage when negotiating with schools on behalf of low-income clients. It is also a good idea to check on a current school's default rate for a client who is complaining of problems with a particular school. A high default rate is usually a tip-off that there are serious problems with the school.

1.8 Private Student Loans

Banks and other financial institutions make private student loans without any direct financial backing from the federal government. They are not subsidized, meaning that interest starts to accrue at the time the loans are obtained. There are many different types of private loans, each program with specific rules and requirements. Private loans are also known as private-label or alternative loans.

Private student loans grew throughout the 1990s and early 2000s, as described in Chapter 11, *infra*. During the heyday of easy credit, many private lenders steered borrowers to these products even if they were eligible for federal student loans.

Unfortunately, much of the lending targeted low-income borrowers with subprime loans. Too many of these risky, high cost loans were destined to fail. There have been huge private student loan write-off and default rates, especially since the credit crisis began. As of early 2009, thirty-nine lenders had stopped making private student loans.[228] In addition, as the remaining lenders pulled out of the subprime market, many proprietary schools began offering their own loan products.[229]

There are some signs that the market might be slowly recovering. The remaining lenders seem to have learned some lessons. Most have reduced their origination volume and reevaluated underwriting criteria.[230] However, other players have come in to fill the gap. It is also likely that these products will make a comeback. In any case, there are countless borrowers left in financial distress because of these products.

Private loan terms and conditions, including interest rates and fees, are generally determined by an individual's or a co-signer's credit history. Thus, low-income students and/or those with negative credit histories are more likely to receive loans on less favorable terms. Federal student loan borrowers, in contrast, must meet eligibility requirements but do not have to prove creditworthiness. All eligible federal loan borrowers are subject to the same rules regarding interest rates and other terms.

A critical difference between federal and private loans is the lack of certain protections for private loan borrowers. For example, students with private loans are not eligible for the same types of discharge options discussed in Chapter 9, *infra*. The same is true with regard to deferment and forbearance rights, all of which depend on the lender's policies and the terms of the loan contracts rather than on federal regulations.

On the other hand, there are certain advantages for private loan borrowers. Unlike federal loan collections, there should be a statute of limitations for collection of private loans.[231] Private lenders have fewer collection tools. Previously, private loan borrowers were generally able to discharge their loans in bankruptcy. Due to changes in the bankruptcy law effective October 2005, the bankruptcy rules are now generally just as restrictive for private loans as for government loans.[232]

Unfortunately, private lenders have been generally inflexible in trying to assist financially distressed borrowers.[233] In the past, forbearance was the only option offered to these financially distressed borrowers. However, such policies have changed radically in recent months as most creditors have sharply restricted forbearance availability. Many lenders have also increased collection activity.

1.9 Determining What Type of Loan a Client Has

The most efficient way to find out about a client's government loan is through the National Student Loan Data System (NSLDS). The NSLDS is the Department of Education's central database for student aid. It receives data from schools, agencies that guarantee loans, the Direct Loan Program, the Federal Pell Grant Program, and other United

---

227 The main barrier keeping schools from relying exclusively on student assistance revenue is the 90/10 (previously 85/15) rule. 34 C.F.R. § 600.5. See § 1.7.2.2, *supra*.
228 Robert Tomsho, *Tuition Ammunition: A Happy Lesson on Lending*, Wall St. J., Jan. 6, 2009.
229 *See* §§ 11.1.3, 12.3.3.7, *infra*.
230 *See* § 11.1.1, *infra*.

231 *See* § 7.5.3, *infra*.
  The elimination of the statute of limitations in the Higher Education Act applies only to federal loans. 20 U.S.C. § 1091a.
232 *See* § 10.2.2.1, *infra*.
233 *See generally* National Consumer Law Center, Too Small to Help: The Plight of Financially Distressed Private Student Loan Borrowers (Apr. 9, 2009), available at www.studentloanborrower assistance.org/uploads/File/TooSmalltoHelp.pdf; § 11.7, *infra*.

States Department of Education programs. This information is available on the Internet at www.nslds.ed.gov.

Borrowers can use the NSLDS to make inquiries about loans and grants using a personal identification number (PIN). The site displays information on loan and/or grant amounts, outstanding balances, loan status, and disbursements.

A September 2004 Dear Colleague letter clarifies the requirements for requesting and using a PIN for use in the federal student aid programs. First, the person initiating a request for a PIN must be the person identified in the submission who then becomes the owner of the PIN. Second, the person to whom the PIN is sent (either by e-mail or regular mail) must be this same person. Third, the person using the PIN, for any purpose, must be the PIN owner. Finally, the owner of the PIN must not share it with any other person or transfer any of his or her rights or responsibilities to another person or entity. Advocates should note that the Department states that it is contrary to the requirements of the process for anyone to use another person's PIN, even in an attempt to provide assistance. This is true regardless of whether the PIN owner has been informed of the activity or even if he or she voluntarily agrees to provide the PIN to the other party.[234]

Borrowers can also call the Federal Student Aid Information Center at 1-800-4-FED-AID or 1-800-730-8913 (TDD). The Center's counselors can help borrowers, over the phone, to figure out what types of loans they have. There is a Direct loan service center specifically for Direct loan borrowers. Borrowers should call 1-800-848-0979 (1-800-557-7392 for Direct consolidation loans). The collection process, including the major collection players, is discussed in more detail in Chapter 7, *infra*. Information about comparing private and government loans can be found on NCLC's Student Loan Borrower Assistance Project website at www.studentloanborrowerassistance.org and in Chapter 11, *infra*.

1.10 Student Loan and Tax Deductions

Beginning in 1998, taxpayers with qualified loans to pay certain costs of attending higher education have been allowed to take tax deductions from gross income for the interest they pay on these loans.[235] Qualified loans are loans taken out solely to pay qualified education expenses for an individual, his or her spouse, or a dependent. The loans must also be for education provided during an academic period for an eligible student. Loans from related persons and qualified employer plans do not qualify.

The maximum deductible interest on a qualified student loan is $2500 per return. The amount of the student loan interest deduction is phased out (that is, gradually reduced) if the modified adjusted gross income is between $60,000 and $75,000 ($120,000 and $150,000 if borrowers file a joint return). Borrowers cannot take a student loan interest deduction if their modified adjusted gross income is $75,000 or more ($150,000 or more if you file a joint return). Parents may also deduct interest for loans taken out to pay their children's education as long as the children was dependents when the parents received the loan.

There are additional tax benefits for education, including (1) certain tax-free scholarships and fellowships; (2) non-refundable American Opportunity Tax credits (up to $2500 for the first four years of post-secondary education), Hope and Lifetime Learning credits of up to $1500 for qualified education expenses paid for each eligible student;[236] (3) limited deductions for tuition and related expenses; and (4) deductions for work-related education. It is unclear how effective these programs have been in increasing access to higher education, particularly for the neediest students.[237]

1.11 Checklist for Handling Student Loan Issues

1.11.1 First Steps

This checklist should help advocates organize and review a student loan case. Extensive information about each topic in the checklist can be found in this manual.

Before reviewing the various options below, advocates should first determine:

- The type of student loan;
- Loan origination date;
- Whether the client is already in default;
- Whether collection has begun (and, if so, the time deadlines for responding to the collection action);[238] and
- The client's goals and financial situation.

Some clients will have a number of different types of loans. If the loan is a private loan, the rest of this checklist is not relevant. In private-loan cases, borrowers should request copies of their loan agreements to determine whether

---

234 U.S. Dep't of Educ., Dear Colleague Letter GEN-04-10 (Sept. 2004).

235 For more information, see Internal Revenue Serv., Publication 970, Tax Benefits for Education; Internal Revenue Serv., Tax Topic 456, Student Loan Interest Deduction. The IRS regularly updates Publication 970. More information is available on the IRS website at www.irs.gov.

236 The American Opportunity Tax credit has replaced the Hope credit for most taxpayers. *See* Internal Revenue Serv., Publication 970, Tax Benefits for Education.

237 *See, e.g.*, Michael Arnone, *Education Tax Credits Fall Short, Study Finds*, Chron. of Higher Educ., Oct. 24, 2003, at A27.

238 *See* Chs. 7 (possible fair debt violations), 8 (defenses to tax refund intercepts, wage garnishments, and federal benefits offsets), 12 (defenses to collection lawsuits), *infra*.

the lender promised particular benefits. The next step is generally to try to negotiate with the lender unless the borrower has a legal claim or defense as discussed in Chapter 11, *infra*.

Throughout this analysis, it is important to speak with clients about their goals. Do they want to go back to school? If so, getting out of default as soon as possible is critical. If instead they are primarily interested in stopping the collection efforts, it is then important to focus on challenging collection efforts, as discussed in Chapters 7 and 8, *infra*, and, if there is a school-related defense, as discussed in Chapter 12, *infra*. In addition, possible fair debt collection violations, discussed in Chapter 7 should also be considered.

It is important to get a sense of the client's overall budget and in particular to determine whether the client is collection-proof. A client is collection-proof if he or she does not have any money or property that can legally be taken to pay the debt.

It is difficult, although not impossible, for a client to be completely protected from government student loan collection. Clients without significant federal benefits, without wages, without tax refunds, and with no other significant assets will most likely be safe from student loan collection, at least temporarily. However, as discussed in Chapter 7, *infra*, the elimination of a statute of limitations for student loan collections means that the debt may come back to haunt the client in the future.

1.11.2 Loan Cancellation

Regardless of whether the client is in default, loan cancellation is the first option to consider. Cancellation provides the most complete remedy for student loan borrowers. Advocates should always review all of the various cancellation remedies for all clients. Clients may be eligible for more than one type of cancellation, but they can recover only once.

If eligible, the client's loan will not only be canceled but also all payments made to date, including monies seized, will be returned and the client's credit report should be cleared. Cancellation options are discussed in detail in Chapter 9, *infra*.

Before reviewing cancellation options, it is important to know what type of loan the client has. Cancellation and other rights vary depending on the type of loan. After considering these issues, advocates should determine whether the client is eligible for loan cancellation. The following are the main cancellation programs:

1. *Closed school.* The closed-school cancellation applies to FFELs, federal Direct loans, and Perkins loans (including NDSLs) received at least in part on or after January 1, 1986.[239]

---

239 See § 9.3, *infra*.

2. *False certification.* Borrowers are entitled to a loan cancellation if they received at least part of an FFEL or Direct loan after January 1, 1986, and if their eligibility to borrow was falsely certified by the school.[240] The cancellation does not apply to Perkins loans, but students should be able to raise the school's misconduct as a defense to loan repayment because the school is the original lender.[241]

The Department recognizes four bases for a false-certification discharge:
   A. The school falsifies a non-high-school graduate's ability to benefit from the program;[242]
   B. The school enrolls a student unable to meet minimum state employment requirements for the job for which the student is being trained;[243]
   C. The school forges or alters the student loan note or check endorsements;[244] or
   D. The borrower is a victim of identity theft.[245]

3. *Disability cancellation.* The borrower's permanent and total disability is grounds for a student loan discharge.[246]

4. *Death.* The borrower's death is a defense to collection actions on Stafford, SLS, Perkins, and Federal Direct loans.[247] The deaths of both parents (assuming both parents are obligated) or the death of the student discharges PLUS loans.[248]

5. *Unpaid refund.* Provides for discharge based on the school's failure to make an owed refund to the student.[249] State tuition recovery funds should also be considered.[250]

6. *Public service and other job-related cancellations.* These cancellations are tied to the borrower's profession and generally require a minimum number of years of full-time employment in various fields. There are special provisions in some loan programs for military service members as well.[251]

7. *Cancellation for repayment.* Borrowers may also be able to cancel loan balances after twenty-five years of repayment through income-based or income-contingent repayment plans.[252]

---

240 See § 9.4, *infra*.
241 See § 10.7.2.1, *infra*.
242 See § 9.4.2, *infra*.
243 See § 9.4.3, *infra*.
244 See § 9.4.4, *infra*.
245 See § 9.4.5, *infra*.
246 See § 9.7, *infra*.
   For a PLUS loan on which both parents are obligated, the disability of only one parent does not discharge the loan. *See* § 9.7.2, *infra*.
247 See § 9.8, *infra*.
248 See § 9.8, *infra*.
   Assuming the parents are co-borrowers, the death of only one of the two obligated parents does not discharge a PLUS loan.
249 See § 9.5, *infra*.
250 See § 12.8.1, *infra*.
251 See §§ 9.10–9.12, *infra* (Perkins).
252 See §§ 3.1.3.2, *infra* (income-based repayment); 3.1.3.3.2, *infra* (income-contingent repayment).

§ 1.11.3 Student Loan Law

8. *Bankruptcy.* Some student loans may be discharged in bankruptcy.[253]

Obtaining a statutory loan cancellation can take a long time. In the meantime, advocates should request administrative forbearances to stop the collection efforts pending a decision.[254] If the client wants to go back to school before a decision on the cancellation is made, advocates should consider reviewing the repayment, loan rehabilitation, and consolidation options discussed in Chapter 6, *infra*, and summarized below. It may best serve the client's goals to move forward with repayment, at least temporarily, while the cancellation application is pending.

1.11.3 Postponing Payment

The question of how and whether a borrower may postpone payment depends on whether the client is already in default. Borrowers who are not yet in default are eligible for deferments. The various deferment programs detailed in Chapter 4, *infra*, should be reviewed at this point. Forbearance, available both before and after default, should also be considered. Both deferment and forbearance options are discussed in Chapter 4, *infra*.

1.11.4 Repayment Options

If a client is not yet in default, he or she should consider the range of affordable payment options described in Chapter 3, *infra*. If the client is in default and not eligible for a cancellation or cannot wait for a decision on a cancellation application, the next step is to consider the various repayment options. The following are primary strategies to get out of default through repayment:

- *Loan Consolidation.* Particularly for low-income clients, a Direct loan consolidation with an income-based repayment plan is an excellent strategy to get out of default and pay only minimal (or even no) payments each month.[255]
- *Loan Rehabilitation.* After making nine payments, each within twenty days of the due date, during a period of ten consecutive months, a borrower can get out of default by rehabilitating a loan.[256] The pros and cons of consolidation and rehabilitation are discussed in Chapter 6, *infra*.
- *Reasonable and Affordable Payment Plans.* Borrowers can renew eligibility by setting up reasonable and affordable payment plans. Six consecutive on-time monthly payments will renew eligibility but will not get the borrower out of default.[257]
- Settlement or compromise may also be an option, as discussed in Chapter 8, *infra*.

Once out of default, clients are not only eligible to return to school but are also eligible for the deferment programs discussed in Chapter 4, *infra*.

1.11.5 Challenging Collection

Many defenses can be raised specifically in response to certain types of collection such as tax refund intercepts or administrative wage garnishments. Timing for these challenges is critical. At this point, advocates should be sure to check all notices and determine whether it is still possible to file a response to a collection action. The specific time deadlines for responding to extra-judicial collection actions are discussed in Chapter 8, *infra*. Borrowers may generally request hearings after the deadlines expire, but the collection action will not be stayed pending a hearing.

The response date for lawsuits can be found on the summons. Possible defenses to student loan collection lawsuits are discussed in Chapter 12, *infra*. In addition, possible fair debt collection violations, discussed in Chapter 7, *infra*, should also be considered.

1.12 Assistance for Student Loan Borrowers

1.12.1 Ombudsman Programs

1.12.1.1 Federal Student Loan Ombudsman

An ombudsman office has been established in the Department of Education specifically to help borrowers with difficult problems. The student loan ombudsman has a website, and borrowers can submit problems on-line at www.fsahelp.ed.gov or www.ombudsman.ed.gov. The toll-free phone number is (877) 557-2575. The e-mail address is fsaombudsmanoffice@ed.gov; the fax number is (202) 275-0549; and the mail address is U.S. Department of Education, FSA Ombudsman, 830 First Street, N.E., Washington, D.C. 20202-5144.[258]

The ombudsman's stated goal is to facilitate and provide creative options for borrowers needing assistance with federal loans, Direct loans, FFELs, SLS loans, and Perkins loans. The ombudsman will research problems and determine if borrowers have been treated fairly. He or she will also contact other offices within the Department of Education, private lenders, and guaranty agencies to assist bor-

---

253 *See* Ch. 10, *infra*.
254 Forbearances are discussed at Chapter 4, *infra*.
255 *See* § 6.2, *infra*.
256 *See* § 6.3, *infra*.
257 *See* § 6.5, *infra*.
258 *See* U.S. Dep't of Educ., Dear Colleague Letter GEN-04-07 (July 2004).

rowers. However, the ombudsman office strongly emphasizes that it serves as a last resort, to be consulted only after a borrower has tried to resolve a problem on his or her own. The ombudsman does not assist with private loans and will only contact private lenders if they are part of the government loan programs.[259]

1.12.1.2 Other Ombudsman Programs for Federal Student Loans

Many guaranty agencies and private lenders have their own customer service or ombudsman programs. Some, such as Sallie Mae, describe these programs on their websites or in other materials. Sallie Mae's program is called "Customer Advocate Unit." Others are more reluctant to publicize the availability of these resources. NCLC's Student Loan Borrower Assistance website (www.studentloanborrowerassistance.org) includes information about various guaranty agency ombudsman programs.

1.12.1.3 Private Student Loan Ombudsman

The Dodd-Frank financial reform legislation of 2010 includes a provision creating a new private education loan ombudsman.[260] This program is intended to provide timely assistance to borrowers of private education loans.

The office is required to disseminate information about the availability and functions of the ombudsman to borrowers and potential borrowers as well as institutions of higher education, lenders, guaranty agencies, loan servicers, and other participants in private education student loan programs. The private loan ombudsman's functions include:

1. Receive, review, and attempt to resolve informal complaints from borrowers of loans, including, as appropriate, attempts to resolve such complaints in collaboration with the Department of Education and with institutions of higher education, lenders, guaranty agencies, loan servicers, and other participants in private education loan programs;
2. Not later than ninety days after the designated transfer date, establish a memorandum of understanding with the federal student loan ombudsman to ensure coordination in providing assistance to and serving borrowers seeking to resolve complaints related to their private education or Federal student loans;
3. Compile and analyze data on borrower complaints regarding private education loans; and
4. Make appropriate recommendations to the Director; the Secretary; the Secretary of Education; the Committee on Banking, Housing, and Urban Affairs; the Committee on Health, Education, Labor, and Pensions of the Senate; the Committee on Financial Services; and the Committee on Education and Labor of the House of Representatives.

The private loan ombudsman is also required to prepare an annual report that describes the activities and evaluates the effectiveness of the ombudsman during the preceding year.

1.12.2 Additional Department of Education Resources

The Department of Education's website is extensive and contains a great deal of useful information. For all of the various plans, borrowers and advocates will find the Department of Education's on-line calculators to be a useful resource. These include calculators for the income-based repayment plans.[261] The Information for Financial Aid Professionals (IFAP) website at http://ifap.ed.gov/ifap consolidates guidance, resource, and information related to the administration and processing of the financial assistance programs. The Department's private collection agency (PCA) website was a primary resource for information about private collection agencies. However, as of the spring of 2010, the Department took the site off-line.[262] The Department also has set up Federal Student Aid customer service centers.[263]

The Department has created a website at www.eddataexpress.ed.gov with data collected by many of the Department's program offices, including the National Center for Education Statistics and the College Board.

The Department of Education also publishes very useful guides, including *Funding Education Beyond High School* and *Your Federal Student Loans: Learn the Basics and Manage Your Debt*. The guides are updated each year and are available in English and Spanish on-line or by calling the Federal Student Aid Information Center at (800) 4-FED-AID.[264]

1.12.3 NCLC's Student Loan Borrower Assistance Project

In 2007, NCLC established a Student Loan Borrower Assistance Project (SLBA). SLBA is focused on providing information about student loan rights and responsibilities

---

259 The 2010 financial reform litigation, however, will create a new private student loan ombudsman. *See* § 1.12.1.3, *infra*.
260 Pub. L. No. 111-203, § 1035, 124 Stat. 1376 (2010).
261 *See* www2.ed.gov/offices/OSFAP/DirectLoan/calc.html. For another on-line IBR calculator, see www.ibrinfo.org.
262 *See generally* Ariel Wittenberg, Center for Pub. Integrity, Education Department Pulls Student Debt Collectors Guide Off Web Site (June 16, 2010).
263 *See* http://ifap.ed.gov/ifap/helpContactInformationList.jsp?group=2.
264 The two guides are available on the companion CD-Rom to this manual.

for borrowers and advocates. SLBA also seeks to increase public understanding of student lending issues and to identify policy solutions to promote access to education, lessen student debt burdens, and make loan repayment more manageable.

The project has a website that can be accessed through the NCLC site (www.nclc.org) or at www.studentloan borrowerassistance.org. The website contains extensive information about student loan borrower rights. The site includes a number of "self-help" packets in English and Spanish on topics such as applying for disability discharges and for Direct loan consolidation. Appendix J, *infra*, has basic information about NCLC's Student Loan Borrower Assistance Project website.

1.12.4 Potential Problems with For-Profit Counselors

There is a growing industry of for-profit companies claiming to help student loan borrowers stay out of default and successfully repay student loans.

In some cases, these counselors appear to act mainly as brokers, claiming that they can help arrange loan consolidation for a borrower. The companies may require the borrower to sign a statement indicating awareness that these sources may be available without the use of the company's services but that the borrower has determined it is in his or her best interest to hire the company. Generally, these companies make no guarantees. In some cases, they will assist only with federal loans and in some cases will not assist borrowers if their loans were previously in default.

These companies often charge high fees. In many cases, they are only offering to do work that the borrower can do on his or her own. Despite disclaimers to the contrary, these non-attorney counselors may very well be crossing over the line and engaging in the unauthorized practice of law.[265] There is also a thriving business of "default management" companies hired by schools to track down former students and get them into forbearances or other programs that will not impact the school's default rates and help them avoid sanctions.[266]

---

265 *See generally* National Consumer Law Center, Unfair and Deceptive Acts and Practices 10.4.2 (7th ed. 2008 and Supp.)
266 *See, e.g.*, Goldie Blumenstyk, Business Is Up in Keeping Default Rates Down, Chron. of Higher Educ., July 11, 2010.

Chapter 2 Taking Out a Federal Student Loan: Basic Terms and Conditions

2.1 Introduction

There are many different types of federal student loans, as described generally in Chapter 1, *supra*. As of July 1, 2010, all new Stafford, consolidation, and Direct PLUS loans will be originated through the government's Direct Loan Program. There is still a Perkins Loan program. Loans from the Perkins Loan Program ("Perkins loans") are made by schools with funding from the Department of Education.

Chapter 1, *supra*, reviews ways to ascertain what type of loan a particular borrower has. Chapter 1 also contains information about prerequisites that all students must meet in order to borrow through the federal loan programs, including application requirements and eligibility criteria.

The terms of the various federal loan programs are described in this chapter, including loan limits and interest rates that are set by law. The Higher Education Act (HEA) also establishes limits on the fees federal student lenders can charge, including origination fees, late charges, and collection fees. Origination and late fees are discussed in this chapter. Collection fees are covered in Chapter 7, *infra*. This chapter also includes information about the borrower experience in taking out a loan, including information about master promissory notes, required disclosures, disbursement and cancellation rights, and counseling requirements.

2.2 Loan Limits

2.2.1 General

The HEA includes limits on the amounts student are allowed to borrow. Student groups and some college and university associations have generally opposed increases in these loan limits. They argue that higher limits will only exacerbate students' unmanageable debt burdens. Opponents of increased loan limits argue that the real problem, is skyrocketing tuition costs. They also point to the federal trend toward funding loans rather than grants for needy students.

Advocates for higher limits also point to the increases in educational costs, but they argue that this is exactly why loan limits should be raised. The current limits are simply too low, they claim, to fund most higher education programs. These advocates also caution that, without increases in loan limits, more and more students will turn to private loan products, which carry fewer consumer protections than federal loans.[1]

Congress raised loan limits during the credit crisis, but only incrementally. Critics continue to claim that the limits are too low. Others counter that the more financial aid available, the more schools will raise tuition.

The sections below describe the limits for each type of loan as of fiscal year 2010.

2.2.2 Stafford Loan Limits

Limits on Direct Stafford loans vary depending on whether the borrower is financially dependent or independent. If a borrower is considered dependent, the borrower's parents' as well as his or her own income and assets will be considered in determining the level of financial aid.[2]

Under current regulations as of 2010, dependent undergraduate students, except those whose parents are unable to obtain Direct PLUS loans ("PLUS loans"), are allowed to borrow a maximum amount of up to $5500 in Stafford loans in the first year of study. No more than $3500 of this amount may be in subsidized loans.[3] Stafford loan borrowers may get up to $6500 for the second year, with no more than $4500 in subsidized loans, and up to $7500 in the third year and beyond, with no more than $5500 in subsidized loans.[4] The maximum total debt for dependent undergraduate borrowers is $31,000, with no more than $23,000 in subsidized loans.[5]

Independent and dependent undergraduate students whose parents are unable to obtain PLUS loans may borrow up to $9500 in the first year in Stafford loans, $10,500 in the second year, and up to $12,500 in the third year and

---
1 See Ch. 11, *infra*.
2 See § 1.5.2, *supra* (dependent versus independent student criteria).
3 34 C.F.R. § 685.203(a)–(b) (Direct subsidized and unsubsidized loans).
4 *Id.*
5 34 C.F.R. § 685.203(d)–(e).

beyond.[6] For purposes of determining whether a dependent undergraduate's parents are unable to borrow PLUS loans, the financial aid administrator must determine, after review of the family's financial information and consideration of the student's debt burden, that the student's parents likely will be precluded by exceptional circumstances from borrowing under the PLUS program and the student's family is otherwise unable to provide the student's expected family contribution.[7] Exceptional circumstances include, for example, denial of a PLUS loan to a parent based on adverse credit, on the student's parent receiving only public assistance or disability benefits, on the student's parent being incarcerated, or on his or her whereabouts being unknown. The limits on subsidized Stafford loans for these students are the same as for dependent students. The aggregate allowable limit is $57,500, with no more than $23,000 in subsidized loans.[8]

With limited exceptions, an undergraduate enrolled in a program that is one academic year or less may not borrow an amount for any academic year that exceeds the amounts allowed for borrowers in their first year of undergraduate study.[9]

Graduate and professional degree students may borrow no more than $20,500 a year in Stafford loans, consisting of no more than $8500 a year in subsidized loans.[10] In total, graduate students may borrow $138,500 in Stafford loans, with no more than $65,500 in subsidized loans.[11] The graduate debt limit includes Stafford loans received for undergraduate study.[12]

In 2008, the Department eliminated the maximum twelve-month loan period for annual loan limits in the Federal Family Education Loan (FFEL) Program and Direct Loan Program.[13] As a result, borrowers may have loan periods that span more than the typical "academic year."[14] According to the Department, these changes were intended to allow a school to certify a single loan for students in shorter non-term or nonstandard-term programs, such as a fifteen-month program when the school's academic year encompasses ten months.[15]

2.2.3 PLUS Loan Limits

A graduate or professional student's maximum annual Stafford loan eligibility under either the Direct Loan or FFEL program must be determined before the student applies for a PLUS loan.[16] The yearly limit on PLUS loans is equal to the student's cost of attendance minus any other financial aid received.[17]

2.2.4 Perkins Loan Limits

The 2008 HEA reauthorization law increased Perkins loan limits. The annual limit for undergraduates was increased from $4000 to $5500. For graduate or professional students, the annual limits were increased from $6000 to $8000.[18] The aggregate limits were increased from $40,000 to $60,000 for graduate or professional students and from $20,000 to $27,500 for students who have successfully completed two years of education leading to a bachelor's degree. The aggregate limit increased from $8000 to $11,000 for all other students.[19]

A borrower may not be able to borrow the maximum amount, depending on whether the school has depleted its Perkins loan reserves.

2.3 Federal Student Loan Interest Rates

2.3.1 General

The Higher Education Act sets fixed interest rate limits for federal student loans. Prior to July 1, 2006, the rates for most student loans were variable with an upper limit of 8.25%.[20] The variable rate era, at least for now, ended on July 1, 2006.

Most government student loan interest rates are fixed below the limits generally found in any state or federal usury laws. Regardless, the HEA expressly preempts usury laws, except for the limits in the Servicemember Civil Relief Act (SCRA) discussed below.[21] In contrast, usury laws should apply to private student loans.[22]

---

6 34 C.F.R. § 685.203(b)–(c).
7 34 C.F.R. §§ 682.201(a)(3), 685.203(c)(1)(ii)–(iii).
8 34 C.F.R. § 685.203(e)(2).
9 34 C.F.R. § 685.203.
10 34 C.F.R. § 685.203(a)(5), (c)(2)(v).
11 34 C.F.R. § 685.203(d)(2), (e)(3).
12 34 C.F.R. § 685.203(d)(2).
13 72 Fed. Reg. 61960 (Nov. 1, 2007) (amending 34 C.F.R. §§ 682.401, 682.603, and 675.301).
14 34 C.F.R. § 668.3 (defining "academic year").
15 72 Fed. Reg. 61960 (Nov. 1, 2007) (amending 34 C.F.R. §§ 682.401, 682.603, and 685.301).

16 34 C.F.R. §§ 682.201(b)(3), 685.200(b)(4).
17 34 C.F.R. § 685.203(f).
18 Pub. L. No. 110-315, § 464, 122 Stat. 3078 (Aug. 14, 2008); 20 U.S.C. § 1087dd(a).
19 34 C.F.R. § 674.12.
20 20 U.S.C. § 1077a (FFEL); 20 U.S.C. § 1087e (Direct Loan). For any twelve-month period beginning on July 1 and ending on June 30, the variable rate is determined on the preceding June 1 and is equal to the bond equivalent rate of ninety-one-day Treasury bills auctioned at the final auction held prior to June 1 plus an additional amount.
21 20 U.S.C. § 1078(d).
22 See § 11.10, infra.

The interest rate protections in the Servicemember Civil Relief Act apply to federal and private student loans.[23] The SCRA requires that creditors reduce the interest rate to 6% on an obligation incurred by a service member before active duty.[24] Prior to 2008, these protections applied only to private student loans. As of August 2008, these protections apply to federal student loans as well.[25]

The interest rate under the SCRA includes service charges, renewal charges, fees, or any other charges (except bona fide insurance) with respect to an obligation or liability.[26] The law applies to loans made prior to the borrower's entering active duty military status and is applicable while the borrower is on active duty.[27] The Department has clarified that the SCRA interest rate cap applies to the loan, not to the borrower.[28] According to the Department, the interest rate caps applies to any joint consolidation loan or other co-borrowed loan; it also applies to a PLUS loan made to a borrower with an endorser even if only one of the individuals is performing active duty military service.[29]

There is also a program, established in 2008, that prohibits interest accrual while eligible military service members are serving on active duty during a war, military mobilization, or national emergency.[30] This benefit applies only to Direct loan borrowers and only for loans first disbursed on or after October 1, 2008. Borrowers with FFEL Program loans ("FFELs") may consolidate into the Direct Loan Program to take advantage of this benefit.[31]

2.3.2 Capitalization of Interest

The Department will capitalize unpaid interest in certain circumstances. For example, the Department will capitalize interest that accrues on unsubsidized loans during deferment or forbearance periods. Capitalization occurs upon the expiration of the deferment or forbearance.[32] The Department will annually capitalize unpaid interest when the borrower is repaying under ICR or an alternative repayment plan.[33] There are special rules that limit capitalization on subsidized loans while a borrower is repaying through IBR.[34] The Department may also capitalize unpaid interest when the borrower defaults on the loan.[35]

2.3.3 Stafford Loan Interest Rates

Stafford loans are either subsidized or unsubsidized. Students can receive a subsidized and an unsubsidized loan for the same enrollment period.

A subsidized loan is awarded on the basis of financial need. The key difference between the two types of Stafford loans is that, for subsidized loans, borrowers are not charged any interest before the repayment period begins or during authorized periods of deferment. In essence, the government "subsidizes" the interest during these periods.

Unsubsidized loans are not awarded on the basis of financial need. Interest is charged from the time the loan is disbursed until it is paid in full. Interest rates vary depending on whether the loan is subsidized.

As of July 1, 2006, and for loans for which disbursement is made on or after July 1, 2006, *unsubsidized* Stafford loans generally have a fixed 6.8% interest rate. In 2007, Congress passed legislation that phased in reduced rates for subsidized Stafford loans through 2012.[36] These rates apply to subsidized loans for undergraduates only. Unsubsidized Stafford loans and loans made to all graduate students have a fixed rate of 6.8%.

For subsidized Stafford loans first disbursed on or after July 1, 2008, and before July 1, 2009, the interest rate was 6%. The rates were then reduced to 5.6% for loans first disbursed on or after July 1, 2009, and before July 1, 2010; 4.5% for loans first disbursed on or after July 1, 2010, and before July 1, 2011; and 3.4% for loans first disbursed on or after July 1, 2011, and before July 1, 2012.[37]

Variable rates for the pre-2006 loans have fluctuated. For example, in July 2008, the variable rate decreased about three percentage points to 4.21%. The rates declined even more for borrowers consolidating their loans during their grace periods. In July 2009, the variable rate decreased to 2.48%. By fiscal year 2010–2011, the rate decreased again slightly to 2.47%. Rates are even lower for loans in in-school, grace period, or deferment status.[38]

Each loan program has various repayment incentives that allow lenders to reduce interest rates for borrowers who make payments electronically and under other circumstances.[39]

---

23 50 U.S.C. App. § 527. *See generally* National Consumer Law Center, Collection Actions Ch. 7 (2008 and Supp.).
24 *Id.*
25 Pub. L. No. 110-315, § 422, 122 Stat. 3078 (Aug. 14, 2008); 34 C.F.R. §§ 682.202(a)(8), 685.202(a)(4).
26 50 U.S.C. App. § 527(d).
27 34 C.F.R. § 685.202(a)(4).
28 74 Fed. Reg. 36555 (July 23, 2009).
29 74 Fed. Reg. 36555 (July 23, 2009) (amending 34 C.F.R. § 682.202 (FFEL) and 34 C.F.R. § 685.202 (Direct Loan)). *See also* 74 Fed. Reg. 37698 (July 29, 2009) (Direct Loan).
30 Pub. L. No. 110-315, § 451(d), 122 Stat. 3078 (Aug. 14, 2008).
31 34 C.F.R. § 685.220(d)(5).
32 34 C.F.R. § 685.202(b)(3).
33 34 C.F.R. § 685.202(b)(4). *See* § 3.1.3.3.2, *infra* (limits on total amount of capitalization during ICR).
34 *See* § 3.1.3.2.2, *infra*.

35 34 C.F.R. § 685.202(b)(5).
36 Pub. L. No. 110-84, 121 Stat. 784 (Sept. 27, 2007) (amending 20 U.S.C. § 1077a(l)).
37 20 U.S.C. § 1087e(b)(7)(D).
38 Updated federal student loan interest rate information is available on-line at http://studentaid.ed.gov/PORTALSWebApp/students/english/FFEL_DL_InterestRates.jsp.
39 *See, e.g.*, 34 C.F.R. §§ 685.211(b), 674.33(f) (Perkins Loan Program allows reduction of interest rates for borrowers who make forty-eight consecutive monthly repayments and reduc-

2.3.4 PLUS and Perkins Interest Rates

PLUS loan interest rates for most loans incurred before July 1, 2006, are variable and capped at 9%.[40] PLUS loans incurred after July 1, 2006, have fixed interest rates. Probably due to Congressional error, there was a difference in the maximum fixed rates between the FFEL and Direct Loan programs. The fixed rate for Direct PLUS after July 1, 2006, is 7.9%[41] while the fixed rate for FFEL PLUS is 8.5%.[42] However, there are no more FFEL PLUS loans as of July 1, 2010.

Perkins loan interest rates are fixed, currently at 5%.[43]

2.3.5 Consolidation Interest Rates

Consolidation loans have fixed interest rates. The fixed rate is based on the weighted average of the interest rates on the loans at the time of consolidation, rounded up to the nearest one-eighth of a percentage point. The interest rate must not exceed 8.25%.[44]

During periods of low interest rates, borrowers have sought to consolidate their variable-rate loans and obtain low fixed-rate consolidation loans. The switch to fixed interest rates for Stafford and PLUS loans in 2006 changed the equation in terms of interest rate reductions. Since the underlying loan rates are generally the same, consolidation loan rates have become more standardized over time.

The interest rates are slightly different for the temporary in-school consolidation loans currently allowed only from July 1, 2010, through July 1, 2011.[45] For the temporary in-school consolidations, unless the borrower is consolidating certain loans with variable interest rates, the interest rates on these loans will be the lesser of (a) the weighted average of the interest rates on the loans being consolidated or (b) 8.25%. This is the same calculation as for "regular" consolidation loans except that there is no rounding up to the nearest higher one-eighth of one percent. If one or more of the loans is a federal Stafford loan (subsidized or unsubsidized), Direct subsidized loan or Direct unsubsidized loan with a variable interest rate that is lower during the in-school, grace, and deferment periods, the interest rate is calculated in the same manner as a "regular" consolidation loan.[46]

2.4 Loan Fees

2.4.1 Origination Fees

The Higher Education Reconciliation Act of 2005 made changes to reduce and eventually eliminate Stafford loan origination fees. Beginning with FFELs for which the first disbursement of principal was made on or after July 1, 2006, and before July 1, 2007, the maximum origination fee was 2%. The maximum fee dropped to 1.5% on July 1, 2007, 1.0% on July 1, 2008, and 0.5% on July 1, 2009. The fee was eliminated as of July 1, 2010.[47] The FFEL Program was also eliminated as of this date.

Similar changes were made to Direct Stafford loans, beginning with loans for which the first disbursement of principal was made on or after February 8, 2006, and before July 1, 2007. The origination fee for these loans was no more than 3%. This fee dropped to 2.5% on July 1, 2007, 2.0% on July 1, 2008, 1.5% on July 1, 2009, and 1.0% on July 1, 2010.[48]

Lenders are required to disclose the amount and method of calculating the origination fee.[49] In addition, borrowers should not be charged for any costs related to the processing or handling of any applications or data required to determine a student's eligibility to borrow.[50] The fee is deducted from the proceeds of the loan.[51]

The origination fees for PLUS loans are up to 4%.[52] There are no origination fees for Perkins or consolidation loans.

2.4.2 Late Charges and Other Fees

Borrowers may be required to pay a late charge of up to six cents for each dollar of each installment that is late.[53] The charge may be assessed if the borrower fails to pay all or a portion of a required installment payment within thirty days after it is due.[54]

There are no prepayment penalties allowed.[55] There are collection fees that may be charged before default, not including routine collection costs associated with preparing letters or notices.[56] Collection fees are also charged after default, as discussed in Chapter 7, *infra*.

---

tions on balances for loans paid before end of repayment period).
40 20 U.S.C. §§ 1077a (FFEL), 1087e (Direct Loan); 34 C.F.R. §§ 682.202(a)(2)(v) (FFEL), 685.202(a)(2) (Direct Loan).
41 20 U.S.C. § 1087e(b)(7)(B); 34 C.F.R. § 685.203(a)(2)(iii).
42 20 U.S.C. § 1077a(l)(2); 34 C.F.R. § 682.202 (FFEL).
43 20 U.S.C. § 1087dd(c)(1)(D); 34 C.F.R. § 674.31(b)(1).
44 20 U.S.C. § 1077a(l)(3); 34 C.F.R. §§ 682.202(a)(4)(iv) (FFEL), 685.202(a)(3)(i)(E) (Direct Loan).
45 U.S. Dep't of Educ., Temporary Authority for the Consolidation of Loans in an In-School Status, Dear Colleague Letter GEN-10-13 (June 29, 2010). *See also* § 1.4.1.3, *supra*.
46 *Id.*

47 20 U.S.C. § 1087-1(c); 34 C.F.R. § 682.202(c) (FFEL).
48 20 U.S.C. § 1087e(c); 34 C.F.R. § 685.202(c). *See* U.S. Dep't of Educ., Origination Fee and Up-Front Interest Rebate Reductions for Direct Subsidized Loans and Direct Unsubsidized Loans (Feb. 4, 2010).
49 20 U.S.C. § 1087-1(c)(4).
50 20 U.S.C. § 1094(a)(2).
51 34 C.F.R. § 685.202(c)(2).
52 20 U.S.C. § 1087e(c).
53 34 C.F.R. § 685.202(d)(1).
54 34 C.F.R. § 685.202(d)(2).
55 34 C.F.R. § 685.211(a)(2).
56 34 C.F.R. § 685.202(e)(1).

2.5 Disclosures

2.5.1 General

The Truth in Lending Act (TILA) does not apply to student loans made, insured, or guaranteed by the United States or a state guaranty agency under the provisions of Title IV of the Higher Education Act.[57] These Department of Education student loans are also exempted from all state disclosure laws.[58] There are, however, disclosure provisions in the Higher Education Act that apply to these loans, as discussed in this section. Government loans made to students in the health professions, under the separately enacted Health Education Assistance Loan program, remain subject to TILA, although there are numerous regulatory carve-outs with respect to the actual disclosures.[59]

The HEA requirements are different from Truth in Lending requirements in important ways. First, initial HEA disclosures must be given in "simple and understandable" terms before or at the time of first disbursement.[60] Additional disclosures are required before and during repayment.[61] Truth in Lending disclosures, in contrast, must be given before the credit is extended.[62]

In contrast to TILA, remedies for violations of HEA disclosures rules are severely limited. HEA explicitly states that failure to comply with its loan disclosure requirements does *not* provide a basis for a claim for civil damages.[63] Failure to provide the required information also does not relieve a borrower of the obligation to repay the loan.[64]

2.5.2 Federal Loan Disclosures

Borrowers may not be charged for disclosures and they may be provided through written or electronic means.[65]

The information that must be provided before or at the time of the first disbursement on a Stafford or PLUS loan includes:

- The lender's name;
- A toll-free telephone number accessible from within the United States that the borrower can use to obtain additional information;
- The principal amount of the loan;
- The address to which correspondence with the lender and payments should be sent;
- Notice that the lender may sell or transfer the loan to another party and, if it does, that the address and identity of the party to which correspondence and payments should be sent may change;
- The amount of any charges, including the origination fee and the default fee if applicable, and an explanation of whether those charges are to be deducted from the proceeds of the loan or paid separately by the borrower or by the lender;
- The actual interest rate;
- The annual and aggregate maximum amounts that may be borrowed;
- A statement that information concerning the loan, including the date of disbursement and the amount of the loan, will be reported to each nationwide consumer reporting agency;
- An explanation of when repayment of the loan is required and when the borrower is required to pay the interest that accrues on the loan, and a description of the types of repayment plans available;
- The minimum and maximum number of years in which the loan must be repaid and the minimum amount of required annual payments;
- An explanation for any special options the borrower may have for consolidating or refinancing;
- A statement that the borrower has the right to prepay all or part of the loan at any time, without penalty;
- Deferment rights;
- A statement about the availability of the Department of Defense program for repayment of loans on the basis of military service;[66]
- Consequences of default and the definition of "default";
- Explanation of the possible effects of accepting the loan on the student's eligibility for other forms of student financial assistance;
- Possible costs the borrower may incur during repayment or during collection;
- In the case of a Stafford or student PLUS loan, a statement that the loan proceeds will be transmitted to the school for delivery to the borrower;
- A statement of the total cumulative balance, including the loan applied for and owed to that lender, and an estimate of (or information that will allow the borrower to estimate) the projected monthly payment amount based on the cumulative or outstanding balance;
- For unsubsidized or student PLUS borrowers, an explanation that the borrower may pay the interest while in school and, if the interest is not paid while the borrower is in school, when and how often the interest will be capitalized;

---

57 15 U.S.C. § 1603(7).
　TILA does apply to private student loans. See § 11.4.1, *infra*.
58 20 U.S.C. § 1098g ("shall not be subject to any disclosure requirements of any State law").
59 United States v. Petroff-Kline, 557 F.3d 285 (6th Cir. 2009).
60 20 U.S.C. § 1083(a); 34 C.F.R. § 682.205(a).
61 20 U.S.C. § 1083(b)–(e); 34 C.F.R. § 682.205(c).
62 15 U.S.C. § 1638(b)(1). *See generally* National Consumer Law Center, Truth in Lending § 4.3 (6th ed. 2007 and Supp.).
63 20 U.S.C. § 1083(f).
64 *Id.*
65 34 C.F.R. § 682.205(e).

66 This is provided for in 10 U.S.C. § 2171.

§ 2.5.2   Student Loan Law

- For parent PLUS loan borrowers, an explanation that the parent may defer payment on the loan in certain circumstances;
- A statement summarizing the circumstances in which a borrower may obtain forbearance on the loan; and
- A description of the options available for forgiveness of the loan and the requirement to obtain forgiveness.[67]

Borrowers must also be given a separate statement of rights and responsibilities.[68] There is a form approved by the Department that satisfies this requirement. For subsequent loans taken out under a pre-signed master promissory note, the borrower must receive the plain language disclosure approved by the Department.[69]

Additional disclosures are required at or prior to the beginning of the repayment period.[70] These disclosures include some of the same disclosures as above, including the lender's name, prepayment rights, and actual interest rate. In addition, the lender must disclose:

- The scheduled date the repayment period is to begin or, if a deferment is applicable, when the deferment will end;
- The estimated balance, including the estimated amount of interest to be capitalized;
- An explanation of any fees that may accrue during the repayment period;
- The borrower's repayment schedule, including the due date of the first installment and the number, amount, and frequency of payments;
- Except in the case of a consolidation loan, an explanation of any special options the borrower may have for consolidating or refinancing the loan;
- The estimated total amount of interest to be paid on the loan, assuming that payments are made in accordance with the repayment schedule and, if interest has been paid, the amount of interest paid;
- Information on any special loan repayment benefits offered on the loan;
- If the lender provides a repayment benefit, any limitations on that benefit;
- A description of all the repayment plans available to the borrower and a statement that the borrower may change plans during the repayment period at least annually;
- A description of the options available to the borrower to avoid or be removed from default, as well as any fees associated with those options; and
- Any additional resources the lender is aware of through which the borrower may obtain advice and assistance on loan repayment.[71]

Yet more disclosures are required during repayment.[72] The lenders must provide borrowers with a bill or statement, corresponding to each payment installment time period in which a payment is due, that includes, in simple and understandable terms: the original principal balance; the borrower's current balance; the interest rate; the total amount of interest for the preceding installment paid by the borrower; the aggregate amount paid by the borrower on the loan, separating the amount paid in interest, the amount of fees, and the amount paid against the balance; a description of each fee the borrower has been charged for the most recent installment; the date by which a payment must be made to avoid additional fees and the amount of that payment and the fees; the lender's or servicer's address and toll-free phone number; and a reminder that the borrower may change repayment plans, together with a list of the plans and a link to the Department of Education's website.[73]

There are even more disclosures for borrowers having difficulty making payments.[74] If the borrower notifies the lender that he or she is having difficulty making payments, the lender must provide a description of the available repayment plans and how the borrower may request a change in repayment plans; a description of the requirements for obtaining forbearance and any costs associated with forbearance; and a description of the options available to the borrower to avoid default as well as any fees or costs associated with these options.

The lender must also make disclosures to borrowers who are sixty days delinquent informing the borrower of the date on which the loan will default if no payment is made; the minimum payment the borrower must make, as of the date of the notice, to avoid default; a description of the options available to avoid default; options for discharging the loan; and any additional resources through which the borrower may obtain advice and assistance.[75]

In the case of an unsubsidized Stafford loan or a PLUS loan, there are some exceptions to the disclosure requirements about the estimated total amount of interest to be paid. In these cases, instead of that disclosure, the lender may provide the borrower with sample projections of the monthly repayment amounts, assuming different levels of borrowing and interest accruals.[76]

At the time of offering a loan and at the time of offering repayment options, the lender must also provide notice about the availability of the various income-based repayment options and the procedures for obtaining these options.[77]

---

67   34 C.F.R. § 682.205(a)(2).
68   34 C.F.R. § 682.205(b).
69   34 C.F.R. § 682.205(g).
     The form is available in Appendix D, *infra*, and on the companion website to this manual.
70   34 C.F.R. § 682.205(c).

71   34 C.F.R. § 682.205(c)(2).
72   34 C.F.R. § 682.205(c)(3).
73   *Id.*
74   34 C.F.R. § 682.205(c)(4).
75   34 C.F.R. § 682.205(c)(5).
76   34 C.F.R. § 682.205(d).
77   34 C.F.R. § 682.205(h).

There are similar provisions for Perkins loans.[78]

2.5.3 Consolidation Loan Disclosures

There are separate disclosure requirements for consolidation loans. These borrowers must receive disclosures about whether consolidation will result in a loss of loan benefits and, if the borrower is repaying a Perkins loan, that the borrower will lose the interest-free periods available to Perkins loan borrowers as well as any Perkins cancellation benefits.[79]

Consolidation borrowers must also receive disclosures about repayment plans, options to repay the consolidation loan on a shorter schedule and to change repayment plans, and the consequences of default on the consolidation loan. There must be a disclosure that applying for the consolidation loan does not obligate the borrower to agree to take the loan.[80]

Lenders must provide consolidation loan borrowers a period of no fewer than ten days (from the date the borrower is notified by the lender that it is ready to make the consolidation loan) to cancel the loan.[81]

2.6 Disbursement of Federal Student Loans

Schools either pay borrowers directly, usually by check, or by crediting the borrower's account.[82] In general, borrowers receive at least two loan payments during the academic year. For Stafford loans, no installment can be greater than half of the amount of the loan.[83] For first-year undergraduate and first-time borrowers, the first disbursement cannot be made until thirty days after the first day of enrollment.[84] This is to ensure that students do not have to repay if they do not begin classes or if they withdraw during the first thirty days. There is an exception to this provision for schools with consistently lower cohort default rates.[85] A disbursement is made on the date the school credits the student's account or pays the student directly.[86]

A school may establish a policy requiring students to provide bank account information or open an account at a bank of the school's choosing as long as this policy does not delay the disbursement of financial aid funds to students. If a student does not comply with the policy, the school must still disburse the funds by releasing a check or notifying the student that the check is available for immediate pick up at a specified location.[87]

Before disbursement, a school must notify a student of the amount of funds that he or she can expect to receive under each federal government program and how and when those funds will be disbursed. The notice must indicate which funds are from subsidized loans and which are unsubsidized, if relevant.[88]

There are some issues to consider during the transition from FFELs to Direct loans. In the past, FFEL lenders that made a first disbursement of FFELs were obligated to make all subsequent disbursements. This policy continues for loans for which the first disbursement was made on or before June 30, 2010. In such cases, the FFEL lender must make the second and any subsequent disbursements of that loan, even if the subsequent disbursement(s) are made after June 30, 2010, when the FFEL Program no longer exists.[89] The Department had advised schools to check with FFEL lenders to see whether these lenders had established any policies that limited the making of new FFELs even if the first disbursement of the loan were to take place prior to July 1, 2010. In those instances, the school could originate a Direct loan instead, notify the borrower of the change, or discuss the situation with the borrower and suggest that the borrower select another FFEL lender that is willing to make the loan regardless of the date on which the final disbursement is scheduled to occur. This is a temporary problem during the transition in 2010 to Direct Lending.

In June 2010, the Department issued proposed regulations to allow interim disbursements under certain circumstances and to allow disbursements in order to ensure that certain students can obtain or purchase books and supplies by the seventh day of a payment period.[90]

Student loan funds must first be used to pay for tuition, fees, and room and board. If funds remain, the borrower will

---

78 34 C.F.R. § 674.16(a) (Perkins Loan).
79 34 C.F.R. § 682.205(i).
80 *Id.*
81 34 C.F.R. § 682.206(f) (FFEL).
    This should apply to Direct consolidation loans as well because of the provision in the Direct Loan Program statute, 20 U.S.C. § 1087e, that unless otherwise specified Direct loans have the same terms and conditions as FFELs.
82 34 C.F.R. § 668.164(c).
83 34 C.F.R. §§ 682.207(c), 685.301(b)(5).
84 34 C.F.R. § 668.164(f)(3).
85 34 C.F.R. §§ 668.164(f)(3), 685.303(b)(4).
86 34 C.F.R. § 668.164(a)(1).
    There are different timing requirements if schools make early disbursements. 34 C.F.R. § 668.164(a)(2).

    For general information about student loan disbursement regulations and practices, see U.S. Dep't of Educ., Federal Student Aid Handbook (2010), which is available on-line at http://ifap.ed.gov/ifap/byAwardYear.jsp?type=fsahandbook&awardyear=2010-2011.
87 34 C.F.R. § 668.164(c)(3).
88 34 C.F.R. § 668.165(a).
    A copy of a disbursement notice is in Appendix D, *infra*, and on the companion website to this manual.
89 U.S. Dep't of Educ., Implementation Guidance for the Deadline for Making Loans Under the Federal Family Education Loan (FFEL) Program, Dear Colleague Letter GEN-10-10 (June 15, 2010).
90 75 Fed. Reg. 34806 (June 18, 2010).

receive them by check or in cash unless the borrower gives the school written permission to hold the funds until later in the enrollment period.[91]

2.7 Cancellations and Refunds

Borrowers have the right to cancel all or a portion of a loan if they inform the school by the first day of the payment period or within fourteen days after the date that the school notifies the borrower that it has credited the borrower's account with loan funds, whichever is later.[92]

Lenders must provide consolidation loan borrowers a period of no fewer than ten days (from the date the borrower is notified by the lender that it is ready to make the consolidation loan) to cancel the loan.[93]

If a borrower officially withdraws, drops out, or is expelled before the first day of class during a payment period, all funds paid to the borrower for that period are an overpayment and must be returned to the government. No additional disbursements may be made.[94] The funds must be returned as soon as possible, but no later than forty-five days after the institution's determination that the student has withdrawn.[95]

Requirements to return most grant funds upon withdrawal are waived for certain military service members serving on active duty during a war or other military operation or national emergency, individuals residing in or employed in an area that is declared a disaster area in connection with a national emergency, or those who suffered direct economic hardship as a direct result of war or other military operation or national emergency.[96]

There is the possibility of post-withdrawal or late disbursements. A student generally becomes ineligible for loan funds on the date that the student is no longer enrolled at least half-time. However, there are some conditions that necessitate a late disbursement. Such would be the case if, before the date the student became ineligible (except in the case of a parent PLUS loan), the Department processed a student aid report (SAR) with an official expected family contribution and the school certified or originated the loan.[97] Post-withdrawal disbursements must be made from available grant funds before loan funds.[98]

2.8 Master Promissory Notes

Master promissory notes (MPN) allow borrowers to receive loans for a single period of enrollment or multiple periods of enrollment.[99] Borrowers may receive more than one loan under each MPN over a period of ten years, as long as the school is authorized to make multiple loans and chooses to do so. Borrowers may elect not to receive more than one loan under an MPN. If so, they must sign new MPNs for each loan received and must notify the school or the Direct Loan Servicing Center in writing of this choice.

The MPNs include a Borrower's Rights and Responsibilities Statement that contains information about loan limits and interest rates. The MPN provides that the interest rates are those specified in the HEA, unless the lender notifies the borrower in writing of a lower rate.[100] Students

---

91 *See* U.S. Dep't of Educ., Funding Education Beyond High School: 2010–11, at 19 (Mar. 2010).

This publication is available on the Department of Education website, www.ed.gov, and on the companion website to this manual. *See also* 34 C.F.R. § 668.164(d).

92 34 C.F.R. § 668.165(a)(4).

93 34 C.F.R. § 682.206(f) (FFEL).

This should apply to Direct consolidation loans as well because of the provision in the Direct Loan Program statute, 20 U.S.C. § 1087e, that unless otherwise specified Direct loans have the same terms and conditions as FFELs.

94 34 C.F.R. § 668.22.

95 34 C.F.R. § 668.22(j)(1).

The time frame for returning funds is further described in 34 C.F.R. § 668.173(b). In a disciplinary action against a school, the Department of Education argued that, in cases in which students do not notify the school of their withdrawal, the school must make a determination, within fourteen days of the student's last day of academic attendance, as to whether a student has withdrawn. In fact, in such cases, the regulations at the time gave the schools thirty days to make this determination. 34 C.F.R. § 668.22(j)(2).

In an effort to sanction the school, the Department relied on the shorter standard cited in Dear Colleague letters and in final program review determinations. The school, College America—Denver, successfully challenged the Department's position. *In re* College America—Denver, No. 06-24-SP (U.S. Dep't of Educ. Apr. 3, 2007).

The Department's Inspector General (IG) has found comparable problems with the "return of funds" policies at other schools. For example, in May 2008, the IG found that Technical Career Institute incorrectly calculated the return of federal student aid. U.S. Dep't of Educ., Office of Inspector Gen., Final Audit Report, Control No. ED-OIG/A02H0007 (May 19, 2008).

Specifically, the IG noted that an institution may not artificially create a withdrawal date that is beyond the midpoint of the period by simply choosing to withdraw the student after the midpoint. *See also* U.S. Dep't of Educ., Return of Title IV Aid-Volume 1, Dear Colleague Letter GEN-00-24 (Dec. 2000).

More information is available at U.S. Dep't of Educ., Federal Student Aid Handbook (2010), *available at* http://ifap.ed.gov/ifap/byAwardYear.jsp?type=fsahandbook&awardyear=2010-2011.

96 68 Fed. Reg. 69312 (Dec. 12, 2003).

This waiver was extended through September 30, 2012. 72 Fed. Reg. 72947 (Dec. 26, 2007).

97 34 C.F.R. § 668.164(g)(2).

98 34 C.F.R. § 668.22(a)(5).

99 34 C.F.R. § 685.102 (definitions).

Sample MPNs can be found at the companion website to this manual and at Appendix D, *infra*. For additional background, see U.S. Dep't of Educ., Dear Colleague Letter GEN-98-25 (Nov. 1, 1998).

100 *See generally* Fantetti v. Access Group, Inc., 2007 WL 1057383 (S.D. Ohio Apr. 5, 2007) (rejecting borrower's claim that lender had to wait until July 1 of following year to raise interest rate; borrower went from grace period to repayment before July 1 and was charged the applicable HEA rate).

may borrow additional funds under the same MPN regardless of any changes in school or guarantor, provided that the new school qualifies to offer MPNs.[101]

According to the Department, it is expected that the borrower's obligation to repay any loan made under an MPN would, if challenged, be ultimately established by when the loan was disbursed and when the student received the loan.[102] Each loan is separately enforceable. Disclosure statements must be sent at or before the time of the first disbursement for *each loan*, identifying the amount of the loan and additional terms.[103] The Department of Education's 2-0 PCA Procedures manual includes a section to help collectors find promissory notes.[104] A failure to produce the note may be an issue in collection litigation.[105]

MPNs may be used for students and parents for attendance at four-year or graduate/professional schools and for student and parents at other institutions otherwise designated by the Secretary of the Department of Education.[106] The Secretary may prohibit use of MPNs at specific schools. If an MPN is not authorized, borrowers must complete a new promissory note each academic year.[107]

A lender's ability to make additional loans under an MPN automatically expires upon the earliest of:

> (A) The date the lender receives written notification from the borrower requesting that the MPN no longer be used;
>
> (B) Twelve months after the date the borrower signed the MPN if no disbursements are issued by the lender under that MPN; or
>
> (C) Ten years from the date the borrower signed the MPN or the date the lender receives the MPN. However, if a portion of a loan is made on or before ten years from the signature date, remaining disbursements of that loan may be made.[108]

There are separate MPNs for Perkins loans.[109]

2.9 Counseling Requirements

The HEA includes counseling requirements when borrowers first incur loans and after they withdraw or graduate. Initial counseling is supposed to occur prior to the release of the first loan disbursement.[110]

In general, schools must ensure that entrance counseling is conducted with each Direct subsidized or unsubsidized loan student borrower prior to making the first disbursement unless the borrower has received a prior federal loan.[111] Schools must also provide entrance counseling for student PLUS loan borrowers unless that borrower has received a prior PLUS loan.[112]

The counseling must include comprehensive information on the terms and conditions of the loan and on borrower responsibilities. The session may be conducted in person, on a separate written form provided to the borrower that the borrower signs and returns, or on-line or by interactive electronic means with the borrower acknowledging receipt of the information.[113]

The school must also ensure that an individual with expertise in the Title IV programs is reasonably available after the counseling to answer questions.[114]

The entrance counseling for subsidized and unsubsidized loan borrowers must:

- Explain the use of a MPN;
- Emphasize to the borrower the seriousness and importance of the repayment obligations;
- Describe the likely consequences of default;
- Emphasize that the borrower is obligated to repay the full amount of the loan even if the borrower does not complete the program, is unable to obtain employment after completion, or is otherwise dissatisfied with or does not receive the educational or other services that the student borrower purchased from the school;
- Inform the borrower of sample monthly repayment amounts based on a range of student levels of indebtedness or the average indebtedness of other borrowers in the same program at the same school;
- To the extent practicable, explain the effect of accepting the loan on the eligibility of the borrower for other forms of student financial assistance;

---

101 See FFEL Stafford Loan Master Promissory Note, *available on* the companion website to this manual.
    In April 2009, the Department issued revised promissory note addenda and plain language disclosures for FFEL Stafford and PLUS loans. See U.S. Dep't of Educ., Dear Colleague Letter FP-09-04 (Apr. 24, 2009).
    The Direct Loan MPN is reprinted at Appendix D, *infra*, and available on the companion website to this manual.
102 34 C.F.R. § 668.165(a) (notice of disbursement).
103 See § 2.6, *supra*.
104 U.S. Dep't of Educ., PCA Procedures Manual: 2009 ED Collections Contract Ch. 11 (Sept. 2009).
    The Department had posted the manual on-line in spring 2010 but took it off-line after a month or so. The manual is available on the companion website to this manual and, as of summer 2010, is available on the website for the Center for Public Integrity. See Ariel Wittenberg, Center for Pub. Integrity, Education Department Pulls Student Debt Collectors Guide Off Website (June 16, 2010).
105 See § 7.5.2, *infra*.
106 34 C.F.R. § 682.401(d)(4)(i).
107 34 C.F.R. § 682.401(d)(4)(ii).
108 34 C.F.R. §§ 682.401(d)(4)(v), 685.102.
109 These forms are available on-line, at Appendix D, *infra*, and on the companion website to this manual. See also U.S. Dep't of Educ., Change in Implementation Date for Revised Federal Perkins Loan Program Master Promissory Note (Perkins MPN) and Guidance on Electronic Version of Perkins MPN, Dear Colleague Letter CB-09-07 (Oct. 2, 2009).
110 34 C.F.R. §§ 682.604(f) (FFEL), 685.304 (Direct Loan).
111 34 C.F.R. § 685.304(a)(1).
112 34 C.F.R. § 685.304(a)(2).
113 34 C.F.R. § 685.304(a)(3).
114 34 C.F.R. § 685.304(a)(5).

- Provide information about how interest accrues and is capitalized;
- Inform the borrower of the option to pay the interest on an unsubsidized loan while the borrower is in school;
- Explain the definition of half-time enrollment at the school and the consequences of not maintaining half-time enrollment;
- Explain the importance of contacting the appropriate offices at the school if the borrower withdraws prior to completion;
- Provide information on the National Student Loan Data System; and
- Provide the name of and contact information for the individual the borrower may contact if the borrower has any question about rights and responsibilities or the terms and conditions of the loan.[115]

There are also entrance counseling requirements for graduate or professional student PLUS borrowers.[116] These requirements vary depending on whether the borrower has previously received a Stafford loan.

The Direct Loan Program allows schools to adopt alternative approaches for initial counseling. These alternatives must be designed to target borrowers who are most likely to default on repayment and to provide them with more intensive counseling and support services.[117]

There are separate requirements for exit counseling.[118] A school must ensure that this counseling occurs shortly before the student borrower ceases at least half-time study at the school. The counseling must be in person, by audiovisual presentation, or by interactive electronic means.[119] In each case, the school must ensure that an individual with expertise in Title IV student aid is reasonably available to answer questions.[120]

If a student borrower withdraws without the school's prior knowledge or fails to complete the exit counseling as required, counseling must be provided either through interactive electronic means or by mailing written materials to the borrower's last known address within thirty days after the school learns that the borrower has withdrawn or failed to complete the counseling.[121]

Exit counseling must be provided to each subsidized or unsubsidized loan borrower and student PLUS borrowers. The exit counseling must:

- Inform the borrower of the average anticipated monthly repayment amount based on the borrower's indebtedness or on the average indebtedness of student borrowers who have obtained subsidized and unsubsidized loans, only PLUS loans, or all types of loans, depending on the types of loans the student borrower has obtained;
- Review the available repayment plan options and the difference in interest paid and total payments under each plan;
- Explain the options to prepay;
- Provide information on the effects of loan consolidation;
- Include debt management strategies;
- Explain how to contact the party servicing the loans;
- Explain the use of an MPN;
- Emphasize the seriousness and importance of the repayment obligation;
- Emphasize that the borrower is obligated to repay the full amount of the loan even if the borrower does not complete the program, is unable to obtain employment after completion. or is otherwise dissatisfied with or does not receive the educational or other services that the student borrower purchased from the school;
- Describe the likely consequences of default;
- Provide a general description of the terms and conditions under which a borrower may obtain full or partial forgiveness of loans;
- Review the information about the availability of the Student Loan Ombudsman's office;
- Inform the borrower of the availability of loan information in the National Student Loan Data System;
- A general description of the types of tax benefits that may be available; and
- Require the borrower to provide current contact information.[122]

By most accounts, counseling is no more than a formality, one of many hoops students jump through to get their student aid checks. Some guaranty agencies and schools have attempted to develop models to predict which borrowers are most at risk of defaulting and will thus require more intensive counseling. Many focus on reaching borrowers immediately after drop-out since this is clearly a predictor of default.[123] In a July 2007 report, Consumers Union concluded that entrance counseling was even less meaningful for most borrowers than exit counseling. Some recent graduates reported that exit counseling was useful, although generally too late to affect their decisions about borrowing.[124]

---

115 34 C.F.R. § 685.304(a)(6).
116 34 C.F.R. § 685.304(a)(7).
117 34 C.F.R. § 685.304(a)(8).
118 34 C.F.R. § 685.304(b).
119 34 C.F.R. § 685.304(b)(2).
120 *Id.*
121 34 C.F.R. § 675.304(b)(3).
122 34 C.F.R. § 685.304(b)(4).
123 *See* Deanne Loonin, National Consumer Law Center, No Way Out: Student Loans, Financial Distress, and The Need for Policy Reform (June 2006); Lawrence Gladieux & Laura Perna, National Ctr. for Pub. Policy & Higher Educ., Borrowers Who Drop Out: A Neglected Aspect of the College Student Loan Trend (May 2005), *available at* www.highereducation.org/reports/borrowing/borrowers.pdf; Texas Guar. Student Loan Corp., Predicting Which Borrowers Are Most Likely to Default (1998). *See also* § 5.1.2, *infra*.
124 Consumers Union, Helping Families Finance College: Im-

In 2006 and 2007, the New York Attorney General and others began to challenge abusive practices in the student lending industry. The investigations focused on improper inducements given by lenders to schools in order to increase the lender's business at that school. Provision of entrance and exit counseling by lenders was a key concern in these investigations.[125] The Department has since issued regulations prohibiting some of these activities.[126]

---

proved Student Loan Disclosures and Counseling 18 (July 2007), *available at* www.consumersunion.org/pdf/CU-College.pdf.

125 *See generally* U.S. Senate Comm. on Health, Educ., Labor & Pensions, Report on Marketing Practices in the Federal Family Education Loan Program 21–22 (June 14, 2007).
126 34 C.F.R. § 601.21.

Chapter 3 Pre-Default Repayment Options

3.1 Pre-Default Repayment Plans

3.1.1 General

Federal student loan borrowers may choose from an array of flexible and affordable repayment options. Only borrowers who are not in default can select these plans.

The repayment rules vary for different federal loan programs. However, the repayment rules for Direct Loan Program loans ("Direct loans") are generally the same as for Federal Family Education Loan Program loans ("FFELs"). There are a few exceptions, including the income-contingent repayment plan, which is available only in the Direct Loan program.

The FFEL Program was eliminated as of July 1, 2010. However, the FFEL regulations continue to apply to the large volume of outstanding FFEL loans still being serviced and held by FFEL lenders or guaranty agencies.[1] Perkins Loan Program loans ("Perkins loans") have their own set of repayment options, also discussed in this chapter.

For all of the various plans, borrowers and advocates will find the Department of Education's on-line calculators to be a useful resource. These include calculators for the income-based repayment plans.[2]

3.1.2 Standard, Graduated, and Extended Repayment Plans

Standard repayment plans are the typical repayment plans that borrowers will get if they fail to choose another option. FFEL borrowers will automatically be assigned a standard plan if they do not select a different option within forty-five days of being notified by the lender to choose a repayment plan.[3] If a Direct loan borrower does not select a plan, the Department of Education ("the Department") may choose either a standard, graduated, or extended plan.[4]

Standard plans carry the highest monthly payments, and borrowers generally pay the same amount for each installment period. The monthly amount may vary if there is a variable interest rate. Borrowers have a minimum of five years, but not more than ten years, to repay under a standard plan.[5]

Graduated repayment plans are also available. Under these plans, payments start out low and increase during the course of the repayment period. Although payments vary over time, the loan still must be paid over a period of ten years.[6] This ten-year limit should not apply to Direct loan borrowers who entered repayment prior to July 1, 2006.[7] Graduated plans tend to work best for borrowers who are likely to see relatively quick increases in earnings over time.

Extended repayment plans are another option for borrowers with total outstanding principal and interest exceeding $30,000. These borrowers may repay on a fixed or graduated payment schedule for a period not to exceed twenty-five years.[8] Prior to July 1, 2006, the Direct Loan Program allowed up to thirty years for repayment, depending on the amount owed.[9] These borrowers may still get plans of up to thirty years for repayment.[10] The periods allowed for consolidation loan repayment depend on the amount of the loan, up to thirty years.[11]

Extended plan monthly payments usually will be less than under the standard repayment plan. However, borrowers will also usually pay more interest because the repayment period is longer.

Unless the borrower and lenders otherwise agree, FFEL borrowers must pay at least $600 annually.[12] Borrowers and

---

1 See § 1.3.2, supra.
2 See www2.ed.gov/offices/OSFAP/DirectLoan/calc.html. For another on-line IBR calculator, see www.ibrinfo.org.
3 34 C.F.R. § 682.209(a)(6)(v).
4 20 U.S.C. § 1087e(d)(2).
5 34 C.F.R. §§ 682.209(a)(7)(i) (FFEL), 685.208(b)(1) (Direct Loan).
    Borrowers may request to repay in fewer than five years.
6 20 U.S.C. § 1078(b)(9)(A)(ii); 34 C.F.R. §§ 682.209(a)(7)(i), 685.208(g).
7 34 C.F.R. § 685.208(f).
8 20 U.S.C. § 1078(b)(9)(A)(iv); 34 C.F.R. §§ 682.209(a)(6)(ix), 685.208(e).
    These plans are available for borrowers who have no outstanding principal or interest balance on their loans as of October 7, 1998, or on the date they obtained the loans after October 7, 1998.
9 34 C.F.R. § 685.208(d), (i).
10 Id.
11 34 C.F.R. §§ 682.209(h), 685.208(j).
12 20 U.S.C. § 1078(b)(1)(L)(i).
    The Direct Loan Program statute refers to this provision only for extended repayment plans. 20 U.S.C. § 1087e(d)(1)(C).

lenders may agree to lower payments.[13] However, except for income-based repayment (IBR) and income-contingent repayment (ICR) of Direct loans, the Direct Loan and FFEL plans must cover at least the amount of interest due and payable.[14] The Direct Loan Program also allows some discretion to create alternative plans to accommodate a borrower's "exceptional circumstances."[15] These plans can be no more than thirty years.[16]

FFEL lenders must permit borrowers to change plans at least once a year, although they may allow it more frequently at their discretion.[17] Direct loan borrowers may change repayment plans at any time after the loan has entered repayment.[18] However, Direct Loan borrowers may not change to a repayment plan that has a maximum repayment period of less than the number of years the loan has already been in repayment, except that borrowers may switch to an ICR or IBR at any time.[19]

3.1.3 Repayment Plans Tied to Borrower's Income

3.1.3.1 General

There are three separate repayment plans tied to a borrower's income. The newest program, the IBR plan, went into effect for Direct Loan and FFEL borrowers on July 1, 2009.[20] The Direct Loan income-contingent repayment plan (ICRP) is still available for Direct loan borrowers.[21] However, because the IBR formula is more favorable for most borrowers, the ICRP will likely become less relevant over time. The FFEL income-sensitive repayment (ISR) plan will also become less relevant, if not obsolete, since it is also less favorable than IBR and because there are no new FFEL loans as of July 1, 2010.

The ICRP was a precursor to IBR. It was designed not only to benefit low-income borrowers, but also, according to Senator Kennedy in 1993, to "provide borrowers with a variety of repayment plans, including an income-contingent repayment plan, so that borrowers['] . . . obligations do not foreclose community service-oriented career choices."[22] The drafters believed that a payment plan linked to income could be best administered through the direct lending program.

For various reasons, including the slow growth of the Direct Loan Program and competition with FFEL, the ICRP never caught on as expected.[23] The IBR plan is in many ways a new and improved ICRP. The formula is more generous to borrowers and more straightforward. It is also available in both the FFEL and Direct Loan programs. The Department has publicized IBR in ways that it never publicized ICR.

It is important to counsel borrowers about the pros and cons of payment plans tied to income. Both IBR and ICR may lead to negative amortization. The lower payments in general under these plans mean that borrowers will usually take more time to pay off their loans. However, paying a minimal amount is preferable to default. The income-based plans are also very useful for low-income borrowers who may have limited hopes of paying off their loans but can use these plans to avoid the severe consequences of default.

Borrowers should be counseled that the low monthly payments may not last forever. Payment amounts are reviewed annually. If a borrower's financial situation improves, the borrower will be required to make higher payments.

Borrowers who repay through ICR and IBR (or a combination of both) will have any remaining balances forgiven after twenty-five years.[24] However, at least under current law, this amount may be taxable.[25]

These repayment plans are not as complete as bankruptcy or administrative discharges. A discharge is the end of the loan. In contrast, borrowers with IBR or ICR plans must keep up to date with the Department of Education and provide information about changes in income or address. A missed communication could lead to delinquency or default.

3.1.3.2 Income-Based Repayment (IBR)

3.1.3.2.1 Eligibility

Borrowers with FFELs or Direct loans may select IBR. The only government loans that are not eligible for IBR are Federal parent PLUS and Perkins loans. However, Perkins loans borrowers may still access the program if they have other loans and can consolidate with Direct loans. Private

---

13 34 C.F.R. § 682.209(c)(1)(ii).
14 34 C.F.R. §§ 682.209(a)(6)(iv), 685.208(a)(iv).
15 20 U.S.C. § 1087e(d)(4); 34 C.F.R. § 685.208(l).
16 34 C.F.R. § 685.208(l)(4).
  Alternative plans also do not have to cover all accrued interest.
17 34 C.F.R. § 682.209(a)(6)(xi).
18 34 C.F.R. § 685.210(b).
19 34 C.F.R. § 685.210(b)(2)(i).
20 20 U.S.C. §§ 1098e (FFEL), 1087e(d)(1)(E). See 34 C.F.R. §§ 682.215 (FFEL), 685.221 (Direct Loan).
21 See § 3.1.3.3, infra.
22 Staff of S. Comm. on the Budget, 103d Cong., Reconciliation Submissions of the Instructed Committee Pursuant to the Concurrent Resolution on the Budget (H.R. Con. Res. 64) 453 (Comm. Print 1993) (reprinting report by Senate Committee on Labor and Human Resources to accompany Title XII of the Budget Reconciliation Act).
23 See generally Susan P. Choy & Xiaojie Li, U.S. Dep't of Educ. National Ctr. for Educ. Statistics, Dealing with Debt: 1992–93 Bachelor's Degree Recipients 10 Years Later (June 2006), available at http://nces.ed.gov/pubs2006/2006156.pdf.
24 For IBR, the limit will be twenty years for borrowers who take out loans on or after July 1, 2014. See Pub. L. No. 111-152, § 2213, 124 Stat. 1029 (Mar. 30, 2010).
25 See § 3.1.3.2.5, infra.

loan borrowers are also not eligible for IBR.

Consolidation loans may be repaid through IBR unless the proceeds of the loan were used to discharge the liability on a parent PLUS loan. This is critically important for parent PLUS borrowers. Parent PLUS borrowers who also have other federal student loans and choose to consolidate with Direct loans will find that the PLUS loan taints the entire consolidation loan and will mean that they will not be eligible to repay the consolidation loan using IBR.[26] If they wish to consolidate, Parent PLUS borrowers may exclude the PLUS loans from the consolidation and pay them separately.[27]

Although this is not explicit in the regulations, the Department states on its website and application forms that borrowers with joint consolidation loans may repay under the IBR plan as long as both spouses qualify with partial financial hardships.[28] Both spouses are jointly liable for the loan and both must request IBR. The repayment plan selection form states that spouses with joint consolidation loans may repay under IBR.[29]

Borrowers in default are not eligible for IBR.[30] These borrowers may access IBR by getting out of default. However, as described in greater detail in Chapter 6, *infra*, as of summer 2010 the Department had not yet created a process to allow "forced IBR" borrowers to immediately get into IBR.[31]

Unlike income-contingent repayment (ICR), there is a threshold requirement that borrowers must meet in order to qualify for IBR. Borrowers must have a partial financial hardship to repay through IBR. Partial financial hardship (PFH) means that a borrower's annual federal student loan payments calculated under a ten-year standard repayment plan are greater than 15% of the difference between the borrower's adjusted gross income (and that of a spouse, if applicable) and 150% of the poverty guideline for the borrower's family size and state.[32] The federal loan debt amount includes all loans eligible for IBR.[33] The IBR definition of family size includes a borrower's children if the child receives more than half of their support from the borrower, regardless of who claims the child for tax purposes or who has physical custody.[34]

The borrower's federal loan amount is calculated under a standard repayment plan based on the greater of the amount due at the time the borrower initially entered repayment *or* at the time the borrower elects IBR.[35] Adjusted gross income (AGI), as defined by the IRS, is taxable income from all sources minus specific deductions, including the IRA deduction, student loan interest deduction, and alimony paid by the individual, but not standard or itemized deductions.

The Department has had at least some initial problems with respect to calculating AGI.[36] In some cases, the Department mistakenly based IBR payments on gross (or total) income, which is higher than AGI and results in a higher payment. Although the Department claims it has fixed this problem, borrowers should check the tax information they used when applying for IBR and make sure that the AGI amount on the tax return is the amount used in the IBR calculation.

The borrower's and spouse's income and federal student loan debt will be considered if they are married and file taxes jointly. This is due to a change in the regulations effective July 1, 2010, which provides that, when a married borrower and his or her spouse have eligible loans, the joint AGI and the total amount of the borrower's and spouse's eligible loans will be used in determining whether each borrower has a partial financial hardship.[37] This ensures that, if both borrowers qualify for IBR, their combined payment amounts will not exceed the 15% threshold. The payment amount is then adjusted based on the percentage of the combined total eligible loan debt attributable to each individual borrower, with a further adjustment if the borrower has multiple loan holders. Only the individual's income will be considered, however, for those married borrowers filing separately.[38]

The Department gives these examples:

Example 1: You are single and you owed a total of $40,000 in eligible student loans when the loans initially entered repayment; you now owe $45,000 on those loans. Your monthly repayment amount under a ten-year standard repayment plan would be $518, based on $45,000 and using an interest rate of 6.8%. If your IBR payment amount is less than $518, you would be eligible to repay under IBR.

---

26 34 C.F.R. § 685.221(a)(2) (providing that parent PLUS loans and consolidation loans that repaid a parent PLUS loan cannot be repaid using IBR).

27 34 C.F.R. § 685.208(a)(4)(i).

28 U.S. Dep't of Educ., Federal Student Aid, Income-Based Repayment Program Questions and Answers (Q&As) 7 (July 1, 2010), *available at* http://studentaid.ed.gov/students/attachments/siteresources/IBR_QA_2010-07-01_FINAL.pdf (see question 26).

29 The form is available at Appendix D, *infra*, and on the companion website to this manual.

30 34 C.F.R. §§ 682.215(a)(2), 685.221(a)(2).

Because the Direct Loan and FFEL regulations generally refer to the same sections, subsequent citations are to Direct loans only. FFEL citations are included if the numbering is different than for Direct loans.

31 *See* § 6.2.3, *infra*.

32 34 C.F.R. § 685.221(a)(4).

The limit will be 10% for loans taken out on or after July 1, 2014. Pub. L. No. 111-152, § 2213, 124 Stat. 1029 (Mar. 30, 2010).

33 34 C.F.R. § 685.221(a)(4)(i).

34 34 C.F.R. § 685.221(a)(3).

35 34 C.F.R. § 685.221(a)(4)(i).

36 *See* David K. Randall, *Federal Program Overcharging Some Repaying Student Loans*, Forbes.com (Mar. 22, 2010), *at* www.forbes.com/2010/03/22/income-based-repayment-overpay-personal-finance-student-loan-income.html.

37 34 C.F.R. § 685.221(a)(4)(ii).

38 34 C.F.R. § 685.221(a)(4)(i).

Example 2: You are married and you and your spouse file a joint federal income tax return. You owed a total of $60,000 in eligible student loans when the loans initially entered repayment; you now owe $55,000 on those loans. Your spouse owed a total of $40,000 in eligible student loans when the loans initially entered repayment and currently owes the same amount. The combined monthly payment amount of your loans and your spouse's loans under a ten-year standard repayment plan would be $1151 (based on $100,000 and using an interest rate of 6.8%). If your IBR payment amount is less than $1151, you and your spouse would be eligible to repay under IBR.[39]

Higher-income borrowers are less likely to have a partial financial hardship, but many middle-income borrowers will qualify as well as all borrowers with very high student loan balances. These larger balances are more common since the PLUS program was extended to graduate and professional students in 2006. This is not only because graduate school is often expensive but also because there are no limits on PLUS loans, as there are for Direct Stafford and Perkins loans.[40]

3.1.3.2.2 IBR repayment formula

If the borrower has a partial financial hardship, the aggregate monthly student loan payment is capped at 15% of adjusted gross income above 150% of the Department of Health and Human Services' (HHS) poverty guideline divided by twelve.[41]

The Department of Education gives this example:

Example: 150% of the 2009 HHS poverty guideline for a family of three is $27,465. If your AGI was $40,000, the difference would be $12,535. Fifteen percent of that is $1880; dividing this amount by twelve results in a monthly IBR payment amount of $157. This compares with a monthly payment amount of $518 under a ten-year standard repayment plan (based on an eligible loan debt amount of $45,000).[42] As in an ICRP plan, IBR payments can be zero. Under IBR, if a calculated payment is less than $5, the payment will be zero.[43] If it is equal to or greater than $5 but less than $10, the payment will be $10.[44] The zero-dollar and $10-monthly-payment regulations also apply when the borrower has multiple FFEL loan holders.[45]

If the borrower's monthly payment is not sufficient to pay the accrued interest on subsidized Stafford loans or the subsidized portion of a consolidation loan, the Department pays to the loan holder the remaining accrued interest for a period not to exceed three consecutive years from the established repayment start date on each loan repaid under IBR.[46] The Department has affirmed that this benefit applies only for the first three consecutive years beginning on the date the borrower entered IBR.[47] The three-year period does not include any period during which the borrower receives an economic hardship deferment but does include any other type of deferment or forbearance.[48]

The loan repayment period may be more than ten years. IBR payments must be applied first to interest, then to collection costs, then to late charges, and finally to principal.[49] As with ICR, the loan holder reviews the IBR amount each year.[50] If the borrower fails to certify family size, the Department will assign a family size of one for that year.[51]

3.1.3.2.3 Applying for IBR

Borrowers must contact each servicer to apply for IBR. Servicers have their own documentation processes. All borrowers are required to submit either copies of the most recent IRS tax returns or releases for the loan servicer to obtain that information.[52] In June 2010, the Department released an FFEL IBR plan request form.[53] The Department has stated that, if the borrower is providing a tax return, the

---

39 U.S. Dep't of Educ., Federal Student Aid, Income-Based Repayment Program Questions and Answers (Q&As)2 (July 1, 2010), *available at* http://studentaid.ed.gov/students/attachments/siteresources/IBR_QA_2010-07-01_FINAL.pdf (see question 4).
40 *See* § 1.4.1.1, 1.4.1.2, *supra*.
41 34 C.F.R. § 685.221(b)(i).
  The HHS poverty guidelines are published every year. The 2010 poverty guideline is $14,570 for a family of two living in the contiguous states and the District of Columbia. *See* http://aspe.hhs.gov/poverty.
42 U.S. Dep't of Educ., Federal Student Aid, Income-Based Repayment Program Questions and Answers (Q&As) 4 (July 1, 2010), *available at* http://studentaid.ed.gov/students/attachments/siteresources/IBR_QA_2010-07-01_FINAL.pdf (see question 11).
43 34 C.F.R. § 685.221(b)(1)(iii).
44 34 C.F.R. § 685.221 (b)(1)(iv).
45 34 C.F.R. § 682.215(b)(2) (FFEL)).
46 34 C.F.R. §§ 682.215(b)(4), 685.221(b)(3).
47 U.S. Dep't of Educ., Federal Student Aid, Income-Based Repayment Program Questions and Answers (Q&As) 9 (July 1, 2010), *available at* http://studentaid.ed.gov/students/attachments/siteresources/IBR_QA_2010-07-01_FINAL.pdf (see question 36).
48 34 C.F.R. §§ 682.215(b)(4) (FFEL), 685.221(b)(3).
49 34 C.F.R. § 685.221(c).
50 34 C.F.R. § 685.221(e).
51 34 C.F.R. § 685.221(e)(ii).
52 34 C.F.R. § 682.215(e)(1).
53 U.S. Dep't of Educ., Income-Based Repayment Plan Request and Alternative Documentation of Income Forms, Dear Colleague Letter GEN-10-11 (June 17, 2010).
  The Direct Loan form is available on the Department's website, Appendix D, *infra*, and on the companion website to this manual. The ibrinfo.org website has IBR application forms and instructions for a number of different lenders, including Nelnet and Citibank as well as a link to Sallie Mae's packet of information.

return does not have to include an original signature. Photocopies are acceptable.[54]

Borrowers must use an alternative documentation of income form if they are in their first year of repayment on a Direct loan, are in the second year and have been notified that alternative documentation is required, or have been notified that the IRS is unable to provide the Department with the borrower's AGI.[55] Borrowers may also choose to use this form if the AGI does not reasonably reflect current income. For example, borrowers receiving public assistance benefits that are not part of AGI should generally use this form. The Department may also use other documentation provided by the borrower to verify income.[56]

3.1.3.2.4 Leaving IBR

If a borrower chooses to leave or no longer qualifies for IBR, the borrower's payments at that point must not exceed the amount the borrower would have paid each month under a standard plan before he or she chose IBR.[57] This means that it may take more than ten years to repay the loan because the balance will be higher if any interest is capitalized.[58]

A borrower must repay under a standard plan if he or she terminates IBR. However, the borrower is not required to stay in this plan for the remaining life of the loan. In these circumstances, the borrower may request a change in repayment plan.[59] Since the maximum repayment period under most other FFEL and Direct Loan plans is ten years, in most circumstances the repayment options will be limited depending on the period of time the borrower was in the IBR plan.[60] The Department has said that borrowers can switch plans, but this does not provide additional time to repay.[61]

Loan holders should treat borrowers who are already in IBR plans but who fail to renew consent for income verification in the same way as borrowers who no longer have partial financial hardships.[62]

If a borrower is repaying under an IBR plan, and the borrower's income increases so that he or she no longer has a partial financial hardship, the borrower may remain on the IBR plan, but the monthly payments will no longer be based on income.[63] As long as the borrower is still in an IBR plan, even if making standard plan payments, he or she is still eligible for forgiveness if a balance remains after twenty-five years.[64] If the borrower later becomes eligible again, he or she will return to IBR.[65]

3.1.3.2.5 IBR forgiveness

The government will forgive any remaining loan balances after borrowers repay through an IBR plan for a period not to exceed twenty-five years.[66] This period will be twenty years for borrowers with loans taken out on July 1, 2014, or after that date.[67] To qualify for forgiveness, the borrower must have participated in the IBR program and satisfied at least one of the following conditions during that period:[68]

1. Made reduced monthly payments under a partial financial hardship (the regulations state that payments of zero qualify);
2. Made reduced monthly payments after the borrower no longer had a partial financial hardship or stopped making IBR payments;
3. Made monthly payments under any repayment plan that were not less than the amount required under the standard plan;
4. Made monthly payments under the standard ten-year repayment plan for the amount of the borrower's loans that was outstanding at the time the borrower first selected IBR;
5. Made ICR payments if in Direct Loan Program;[69] or

---

54 U.S. Dep't of Educ., Federal Student Aid, Income-Based Repayment Program Questions and Answers (Q&As) 8 (July 1, 2010), *available at*: http://studentaid.ed.gov/students/attachments/siteresources/IBR_QA_2010-07-01_FINAL.pdf (see question 32).
55 The form is available in Appendix D, *infra*, and on the companion website to this manual.
56 34 C.F.R. § 685.221(e)(i)(B).
57 34 C.F.R. § 685.221(d).
58 34 C.F.R. § 685.221(d)(ii).
59 73 Fed. Reg. 63232 (Oct. 23, 2008).
60 *Id.*
61 *Id.* (since the maximum repayment period under other FFEL and Direct Loans repayment plans, except extended repayment and consolidation, is ten years, in most circumstances the repayment options for the borrower will be severely limited depending on the period of time the borrower remained in the IBR plan).
62 34 C.F.R. § 685.221 (e)(2).

63 U.S. Dep't of Educ., Federal Student Aid, Income-Based Repayment Program Questions and Answers (Q&As) 4 (July 1, 2010), *available at* http://studentaid.ed.gov/students/attachments/siteresources/IBR_QA_2010-07-01_FINAL.pdf (see question 15).
64 *Id.* at 5 (see question 16). See § 3.1.3.2.5, *infra*.
65 U.S. Dep't of Educ., Federal Student Aid, Income-Based Repayment Program Questions and Answers (Q&As) 5 (July 1, 2010), *available at* http://studentaid.ed.gov/students/attachments/siteresources/IBR_QA_2010-07-01_FINAL.pdf (see question 17).
66 34 C.F.R. § 685.221(f).
67 Pub. L. No. 111-152, § 2213, 124 Stat. 1029 (Mar. 30, 2010).
68 34 C.F.R. § 685.221(f)(1).
69 The regulations state that ICR payments count toward forgiveness but that the borrower must also have participated in IBR. 34 C.F.R. § 685.221(f)(1).
    This could be a problem for borrowers repaying entirely through ICR. Department staff has informed NCLC that this was an error and that the ICR forgiveness regulations were inadvertently deleted. The Department plans to correct this in future technical amendments. In the meantime, they have clarified that borrowers in ICR can repay only under ICR and be subject to loan forgiveness without any participation in IBR. See § 3.1.3.3.3, *infra*.

§ 3.1.3.2.5   Student Loan Law

6. Received an economic hardship deferment.[70]

The Department will cancel any outstanding balance of principal and accrued interest in these circumstances as long as the borrower meets the conditions above each year for a twenty-year period.[71] This may be a combination of monthly payment and economic hardship deferments.[72]

If the borrower made payments under the income-contingent repayment plan, the beginning date for the twenty-five-year period is the date the borrower made a payment on the loan under that plan at any time after July 1, 1994.[73]

If the borrower did not make ICR payments, the beginning date of the twenty-five-year period is:[74]

1. For borrowers with consolidation loans, the date the borrower made a payment or received an economic hardship deferment on that loan, before the date the borrower qualified for IBR. The beginning date is the date the borrower made the payment or received the deferment, but no earlier than July 1, 2009;
2. For a borrower who has one or more other eligible loans, the date the borrower made a payment or received an economic hardship deferment on that loan. The beginning date is the date the borrower made that payment or received the deferment, but no earlier than July 1, 2009;
3. For borrowers who did not make payments or received economic hardship deferments, the date the borrower made a payment under the IBR plan;
4. If the borrower consolidates eligible loans, the date the borrower made a payment on the Direct consolidation loan after qualifying for IBR; or
5. If the borrower did not make a payment or receive an economic hardship deferment as described above, determining the date the borrower made an IBR payment on the loan.[75]

For FFEL loans, loan holders must request payment from the guaranty agency for FFELs no later than sixty days after the loan holder determines that the borrower qualifies for loan forgiveness.[76] Loan holders must also promptly return any payments received on a loan after the guaranty agency pays the loan holder the amount of loan forgiveness.[77] A loan holder is also required to make a general disclosure to the borrower on how to handle the forgiven amount.[78] If a guarantor does not pay an IBR loan forgiveness claim, the borrower continues in repayment. Unless the denial was due to lender error, the lender is deemed to have exercised forbearance from the date repayment was suspended until a new payment date is established.[79]

The regulations provide that forgiveness occurs if the Secretary or an FFEL holder determines that the borrower satisfies the conditions.[80] It is unclear to what extent the borrower can apply for forgiveness as opposed to waiting for the lender to inform them that they qualify. It is a good idea for borrowers to try to keep records of payments, but twenty-five years is a long time!

As with the ICR program, the twenty-five-year period should not have to be consecutive[81]—that is, as long as twenty-five years' worth of payments are made, the repayments do not have be paid in consecutive years. When the balance of the loan is forgiven, under current tax law the amount forgiven will be taxable income for the borrower.[82] This is a legitimate concern for many advocates and their clients. At a minimum, clients should be counseled about the potential problems that may arise in the future. In addition, borrowers should be counseled that they may be able to avoid future tax consequences. In particular, they will not have to report the cancelled debt as income to the extent they are insolvent at the time the debt is written off.[83] To establish insolvency, a borrower must send the IRS a statement concerning the discharged debt along with a list that shows that, at the time of forgiveness, the borrower had more debts (including the forgiven debt) than assets.[84]

For example, after twenty-five years, Borrower A receives a loan cancellation worth $10,000. Immediately before the cancellation, Borrower A's liabilities totaled $20,000 and the fair market value of her assets was $15,000. The amount of the insolvency in this case is $20,000 $15,000 = $5000. Borrower A can exclude up to $5000 of the $10,000 debt cancellation from taxable income because that is the amount by which Borrower A was insolvent. The remaining $5000 must be included in income. If Borrower A's liabilities totaled $30,000, the insolvency would be $15,000 ($30,000 − $15,000), and Borrower A would be able to exclude all of the $10,000 cancellation from income.

---

70 34 C.F.R. §§ 682.215(f), 685.221(f) (Direct Loan).
    There is a time limit of three years for economic hardship deferments. See § 4.3.5.2, infra.
71 34 C.F.R. § 685.221(f)(2)(ii).
72 34 C.F.R. § 685.221(f)(2).
73 34 C.F.R. § 685.221(f)(3)(i).
74 34 C.F.R. § 685.221(f)(3)(ii).
75 34 C.F.R. § 685.221(f)(3).
76 34 C.F.R. § 682.215(g)(1).
77 34 C.F.R. § 682.215(g)(7).
78 34 C.F.R. § 682.215(g)(4).
79 34 C.F.R. § 682.215(g)(6).
80 34 C.F.R. § 685.221(f)(4).
81 34 C.F.R. § 685.221(f)(2)(ii)(A) (requiring that borrowers make payments each year for a twenty-five-year period).
82 In 2009, Representative Levin sponsored a bill, H.R. 2492, that would exclude from taxable income cancellations due to twenty-five years of ICR or IBR repayments. The bill was introduced on May 19, 2009.
83 26 U.S.C. § 108.
    "Insolvent" is defined as the excess of liabilities over the fair market value of assets. The determination is made based on the taxpayer's assets and liabilities immediately before the discharge. 26 U.S.C. § 108(d)(3).
84 More information about reporting cancelled debts is available on the IRS website at www.irs.gov. In particular, see *Publication 908: Bankruptcy Tax Guide*, available at www.irs.gov/pub/irs-pdf/p908.pdf.

Even borrowers who are not insolvent may be able to escape the post-twenty-five-year negative tax consequences. In particular, some borrowers may have only temporary financial difficulties that require them to repay loans using an ICR or IBR plan. As their financial circumstances improve, they will be able to move to a different repayment plan that allows them to pay off their loans more quickly.

In addition, in most transactions, only principal amounts canceled are considered taxable income. Cancelled interest and fees are generally not counted as income. Such amounts were never available as income to the consumer. Advocates should consult a tax professional if advising borrowers on these issues.[85]

Although it is possible that the tax code will be amended before many clients reach the twenty-five-year mark, it is still important to counsel clients on the drawbacks of payment plans tied to income.

3.1.3.3 Income-Contingent Repayment Plans (ICR)

3.1.3.3.1 ICR eligibility

The ICR plan is available to Direct loan borrowers who are not in default. As of July 1, 2009, both FFEL and Direct loan borrowers not in default may also select the income-based repayment (IBR) plan. Borrowers in default may access ICR by getting out of default.[86]

Under the ICR plan, borrowers make minimal payments if they are below the poverty line in income, taking family size into account. The payments can be zero. Payments increase incrementally as income increases. The required payments are capped at 20% of any earnings above the poverty level.[87] If borrowers continue making payments for twenty-five years, any debt that remains is forgiven.[88] However, the amount forgiven may be taxable income.[89]

Borrowers with ICR plans cannot change plans unless they were required to and made payments under the plan in each of the prior three months or were not required to make payments but made three reasonable and affordable payments in the prior three months.[90] The borrower must also request the change to an ICR plan.

The ICR plan is available for Direct loan borrowers only. It does not apply to parent PLUS loans but does apply to graduate PLUS loans.[91] Unlike IBR, the regulations do not state that Parent PLUS borrowers who consolidate will taint the entire loan and be ineligible for ICR. The Department of Education has confirmed with NCLC and on its website that any Direct consolidation loan (other than Direct PLUS consolidation loans, which have not been made since July 1, 2006) may be repaid under an ICR plan. In an online questions-and-answers section, the Department states that "[p]arent PLUS loans are not eligible to be repaid under IBR or ICR. However, a parent PLUS borrower could consolidate the PLUS loans and then choose ICR for the new Direct Consolidation Loan. While a Direct Consolidation Loan that repaid a parent PLUS loan may not be repaid under IBR, it can be repaid under ICR."[92]

3.1.3.3.2 Calculating the monthly payment under ICR plan

The ICR plan payment for a Direct consolidation loan can go up or down over time as the borrower's income changes. The monthly payment is based on annual income and the loan amount. The payments should be zero for families living at the poverty line or below.[93] There is a minimum of $5 required only if the monthly payment is calculated to be greater than zero but less than or equal to $5.[94]

The exact formulae for determining the ICRP are set out in Department regulations.[95]

In general, the annual amount payable under an ICR plan is the lesser of:

(1) The amount the borrower would repay annually over twelve years using standard amortization multiplied by an income percentage factor that corresponds to the borrower's adjusted gross income (AGI) as shown in the income percentage factor table in a notice published annually by the Secretary in the Federal Register;[96] or
(2) Twenty percent of discretionary income. Discretionary income is defined as a borrower's AGI minus the amounts in the poverty guidelines. If a borrower provides acceptable documentation that the borrower has more than one person in his or her family, the Secretary

---

85 *See generally* National Consumer Law Center, Foreclosures 14.7.3.4 (3d ed. 2010) (discussing exceptions to the general rule that forgiven debt is income).
86 *See* Ch. 6, *infra*.
87 34 C.F.R. § 685.209(a)(2).
88 *See* § 3.1.3.3.3, *infra*.
89 *See* § 3.1.3.2.5, *supra*.
90 34 C.F.R. § 685.210(b).
91 34 C.F.R. § 685.208(a)(2)(ii)(A), (B).
92 U.S. Dep't of Educ., Public Service Forgiveness Program: Questions and Answers (Feb. 2010), *available at* http://studentaid.ed.gov/students/attachments/siteresources/PSLF_QAs_final_02%2012%2010.pdf.
93 The HHS poverty guidelines are published every year. The 2010 poverty guideline is $14,570 for a family of two living in the contiguous states and the District of Columbia. See http://aspe.hhs.gov/poverty.
94 34 C.F.R. § 685.209(a)(6).
95 Each year, in an annual notice to the Federal Register, the Department publishes the income percentage factors, case examples of calculations, a constant multiplier chart, and sample first-year monthly repayment tables for various income and debt levels. 34 C.F.R. § 685.209(a)(8).
96 34 C.F.R. § 685.209(a)(2).

should apply the poverty guidelines for the borrower's family size.[97]

A married borrower who wants to make payments under the ICR plan and who has filed a separate income tax return must provide his or her spouse's written consent to disclosure of tax information.[98] This requirement does not apply if the borrower and the borrower's spouse are separated. Unlike IBR, even if the married borrower files taxes separately, the adjustable gross income for both spouses is used to calculate the monthly payment.[99] If both have loans, married borrowers may also choose to repay jointly.[100] The outstanding balance on the loans of each borrower are added together to determine the repayment rate. The amount applied to each borrower's debt is the proportion of the payment equaling that of the borrower's debt to the total outstanding balance, except that the payment is credited toward outstanding interest on any loan before any payment is credited toward principal.[101]

As with IBR, an ICR plan can create negative amortization. Interest is then charged on the accrued interest (capitalization), resulting in the loan balance increasing beyond the original amount due.[102] Unlike IBR, the government does not pay the accrued interest for any period of time. However, interest capitalization is limited to 10% of the loan amount.[103] Unpaid interest is capitalized until the outstanding principal amount is 10% greater than the original principal amount. After that point, interest continues to accrue but is not capitalized. Eligible borrowers may seek deferment to avoid interest accrual, at least for a time, if the loans are subsidized.[104]

3.1.3.3.3 ICR forgiveness

The HEA states that ICR payments can be made over no more than twenty-five years.[105] Congress did not change the twenty-five-year period for borrowers repaying with ICR.

For borrowers with loans made on July 1, 2014, the forgiveness period will decrease to twenty years *for IBR only*.[106]

Prior to publication of the IBR regulations, the ICR regulations stated explicitly that borrowers repaying through ICR would have their loans forgiven after twenty-five years.[107] However, since IBR went into effect, the ICR forgiveness regulations were transferred from the section on ICR to the section on IBR forgiveness.[108] Borrowers who made ICR payments at any time after July 1, 1994, should qualify for forgiveness.[109] The problem is that the IBR forgiveness section also states that borrowers must have participated in IBR.[110] This could be a problem for borrowers repaying entirely through ICR. Department staff have informed NCLC that this was an error and that the ICR forgiveness regulations were inadvertently deleted. The Department plans to correct this problem in future technical amendments. In the meantime, they have clarified that borrowers in ICR can repay only under ICR and be subject to loan forgiveness without any participation in IBR.

The Department has consistently stated that borrowers are eligible for forgiveness whether repaying through IBR or ICR. Borrowers repaying entirely through ICR should not have to enter IBR just to complete forgiveness eligibility. However, this issue requires clarification to ensure that ICR borrowers are fully eligible for forgiveness. As with IBR, as long as twenty-five years' worth of payments are made, the repayments do not have be paid in consecutive years.[111]

Borrowers currently repaying through ICR may want to switch to IBR. They may do this without losing credit for previous payments. This may not be worth it for borrowers with very low incomes who have zero-payment plans. If their payments are zero in ICR, they will also be zero in IBR. However, working borrowers with low incomes are likely to see significant reductions in their monthly payments by switching to IBR.

3.1.3.4 Comparing IBR and ICR

There are many similarities between ICR and IBR. For a variety of reasons, the ICR plan that was created in the mid-1990s was underutilized.[112] One of the reasons was that ICR was available only for Direct loans. Until the credit crisis, the guaranteed loan program (FFEL) was significantly larger than the Direct Loans Program. The FFEL was eliminated as of July 1, 2010.

---

97 34 C.F.R. § 685.209(a)(3).
98 34 C.F.R. § 685.209(b)(1).
99 *Id.*
100 34 C.F.R. § 685.209(b)(2).
101 34 C.F.R. § 685.209(b)(3).
102 *See, e.g.*, Pfeiffer v. Duncan, 659 F. Supp. 2d 160 (D.D.C. 2009) (finding that, even though Department is authorized to capitalize interest during ICR payment plan, Department's practice of capitalizing interest that accrues between a borrower's June payment and June 30 was improper because not authorized by promissory note or regulations).
103 34 C.F.R. § 685.209(c)(5).
104 This is the case for that portion of the consolidation loan whose underlying loans were GSLs, Stafford loans, FISLs, Perkins loans, Direct loans, or other subsidized loans. Interest continues to accrue during a deferment period for that portion of the consolidation loan that derives from an unsubsidized loan, such as an SLS or unsubsidized Stafford loan. See Chapter 2, *supra*, for more information on deferments.
105 20 U.S.C. § 1087e(d)(1)(D).
106 Pub. L. No. 111-152 § 2213.
107 34 C.F.R. § 685.209(c)(4)(iv) (prior regulation).
108 34 C.F.R. § 685.221(f). *See* § 3.1.3.2.5, *supra*.
109 34 C.F.R. § 685.221(f)(3)(i).
110 34 C.R.R. § 685.221(f)(1).
111 34 C.F.R. § 685.221(f)(2)(ii)(A) (requiring that borrowers make payments each year for a twenty-five-year period).
112 *See generally* Susan P. Choy & Xiaojie Li, U.S. Dep't of Educ., Dealing with Debt: 1992–93 Bachelor's Degree Recipients 10 Years Later (June 2006), *available at* http://nces.ed.gov/pubs2006/2006156.pdf.

Overall, the IBR formula is more favorable than the formula found in the ICR plan, which caps payments at no more than 20% of the amount above 100% of poverty. As with the ICR plan, IBR payments can be zero.

According to the Department of Education, IBR and ICR share certain features, but there are also important differences between the two repayment plans. The following are similarities:

- Both plans are intended to provide borrowers with an affordable monthly payment amount based on income and family size.
- Under both plans, any remaining loan balance is forgiven after twenty-five years.[113]
- Parent PLUS loans may not be repaid under either IBR or ICR.[114]
- Payments made by a Direct loan borrower under both IBR and ICR count toward the 120 payments that are required for public service loan forgiveness.
- In both IBR and ICR, monthly payment amounts may be adjusted annually based on changes in income.

According to the Department, the following are major differences:

- IBR is available in both the FFEL and Direct Loan programs. ICR is available only under the Direct Loan Program.
- To initially qualify for IBR, a borrower must have a "partial financial hardship." There is no comparable requirement for ICR. Any Direct loan borrower (other than a parent PLUS loan borrower) may choose ICR.
- The amount of loan debt is not considered in determining the IBR payment amount during any period when there is a partial financial hardship. The monthly IBR payment amount is determined based only on income and family size. In contrast, the monthly payment under ICR takes into account the total Direct Loan debt in addition to income and family size. The required monthly payment under ICR is generally higher than under IBR, and in some cases it may be higher than the monthly payment amount under a ten-year standard repayment plan.
- With both IBR and ICR, the calculated monthly payment may not cover the full amount of interest that accrues on the loan each month. Under IBR, the government pays the remaining unpaid accrued interest on the subsidized loans for up to three consecutive years from the date the borrower begin repaying the loans under IBR. This benefit is not available under ICR.

Under ICR, the borrower is responsible for paying all of the interest that accrues on his or her loans.
- Under IBR, unpaid interest is capitalized (added to principal loan balance) only if the borrower is determined to no longer have "partial financial hardship" or if the borrower chooses to leave the IBR plan. Under ICR, unpaid interest is capitalized annually.[115]

3.1.3.5 Income-Sensitive Plans

The FFEL program offers borrowers income-sensitive repayment (ISR) plans.[116] With these plans, the amount of the borrower's installment payment is adjusted annually based on the borrower's expected total monthly gross income.

Borrowers are required to submit income information to the lender in order to establish an ISR plan. If the documentation shows that the borrower will be unable to repay the loan within the maximum ten-year repayment period, the lender is required to grant forbearance to the borrower for up to five years.[117]

The ISR plans with FFELs are generally less affordable than the income-contingent repayment plan (ICR) for Direct loans and income-based repayment (IBR) plan for Direct loans and FFELs. This is because monthly payments under an ISR plan, unlike an ICR or IBR plan, must cover at least accruing interest.[118]

3.1.4 Perkins Loan Repayment

Perkins repayment plans vary from FFEL and Direct loan repayment plans in several significant ways. The regulations set out minimum monthly repayment rates. For example, the rate is $30 for an NDSL or Perkins loan made before October 1, 1992, and $40 after that date.[119] Schools are allowed to extend the repayment period due to a borrower's prolonged illness or unemployment.[120] This extension can be up to an additional ten years if the borrower qualifies as a low-income individual.[121] Interest continues to accrue during any extension of a repayment period.

---

113 This is an example of the Department's assumption that borrowers repaying through either IBR or ICR are eligible for forgiveness. See § 3.1.3.3.3, *supra*, for a discussion of one problem with the regulations in this area.
114 However, parent PLUS loan borrowers may consolidate with Direct loans and then choose ICR. See § 3.1.3.3.1, *supra*.

115 U.S. Dep't of Educ., Federal Student Aid, Income-Based Repayment Program Questions and Answers (Q&As) 1 (July 1, 2010), *available at* http://studentaid.ed.gov/students/attachments/siteresources/IBR_QA_2010-07-01_FINAL.pdf (see question 3).
116 34 C.F.R. § 682.209(a)(6)(viii).
117 34 C.F.R. § 682.209(a)(6)(viii)(D).
118 20 U.S.C. § 1078(b)(9)(A)(iii); 34 C.F.R. § 682.209(a)(6)(iv).
119 34 C.F.R. § 674.33(b)(6)(ii), (iii).
120 34 C.F.R. § 674.33(c).
121 34 C.F.R. § 674.33(c)(2).

3.1.5 How Payments Are Applied

Borrowers who are able to make partial monthly payments are often discouraged that those payments are rarely applied to principal. This is because loan holders are allowed to credit any payment received first to accrued late charges or collection costs, then to any outstanding interest, and then to outstanding principal.[122] For IBR, the order is interest, collection fees, late charges, and then principal.[123] There are similar provisions for schools collecting Perkins loans.[124]

This means, for example, that, if the collection rate for a particular year is 24%, then 24% of each payment made by a borrower is applied to collection costs, the balance to interest. and then, if the payment is sufficient, to the reduction in the principal.[125]

Borrowers may repay the entire loan or any part of a loan at any time without penalty.[126] If the prepayment amounts equals or exceeds the monthly payment amount, the lender must apply the prepayment to future installments by advancing the next payment due date, unless the borrower requests otherwise. The lender must inform the borrower that any additional full payments submitted without instructions to the lender as to their handling will be applied to the borrower's future scheduled payments.[127]

3.2 Loan Servicing

3.2.1 Performance-Based System

In June 2009, the Department announced that four companies—AES/PHEAA, Great Lakes Education Loan Services, Nelnet, and Sallie Mae—were awarded contracts to service a portion of the approximately $550 billion outstanding federal student loan portfolio held by the Department.[128]

Each company has a new performance-based contract with a base period of five years, with a five-year option after that. The minimum contract award is valued at $5 million, with a maximum assignment to service up to fifty million student loan borrowers over the five-year period.

The Department said that revenues would be driven by contractor performance as measured by customer satisfaction and default aversion. The performance criteria include percentage of in-repayment dollars that go into default, percentage of unique "in-repayment" borrowers that go into default, borrower surveys, school surveys, and surveys of Department personnel. An independent vendor will conduct these surveys.[129] The incentives are intended to reward servicers for keeping borrowers out of default, but it is unclear how this will work in practice and whether the servicers will have adequate incentives to help borrowers who are already in default and want to get out. It is also unclear how the surveys will be designed and used.

The Department began assigning FFEL-purchased loans in September 2009 to PHEAA, Great Lakes, Nelnet and Sallie Mae.[130] Nelnet began servicing Direct loans on June 23, 2010; PHEAA, on June 30, 2010; Great Lakes, on July 7, 2010; and Sallie Mae, on July 14.

According to an analysis by Student Lending Analytics, the Department's servicing contract is worth between $1.3 to $1.5 billion over the initial five-year period.[131] The contract value grows as the cumulative number of borrowers increase. The compensation per borrower doubles when the borrower enters repayment. The compensation decreases as borrowers become increasingly delinquent. This could cause problems if servicers ignore those who become seriously delinquent. Other incentives reward servicers for placing these borrowers in deferment or forbearance even in cases in which this is not the optimal option. It is also unclear how the surveys will be used to measure performance.[132]

3.2.2 Loan Servicing Requirements

The FFEL regulations in the Higher Education Act describe loan servicing as including reporting to national credit bureaus, responding to borrower inquiries, establishing the terms of repayment, and reporting a borrower's enrollment and loan status information.[133] Lenders are required to respond, within thirty days after receipt, to any

---

122 34 C.F.R. § 682.209(b).
123 34 C.F.R. § 685.221(c).
124 34 C.F.R. § 674.33(a)(4).
125 See § 7.3, infra (collection fees).
126 34 C.F.R. § 682.209(b)(2) (FFEL). See also Pfeiffer v. Duncan, 659 F. Supp. 2d 160 (D.D.C. 2009) (finding that, even though Department is authorized to capitalize interest during ICR payment plan, Department's practice of capitalizing interest that accrues between a borrower's June payment and June 30 was improper because not authorized by promissory note or regulations).
127 34 C.F.R. § 682.209(b)(2)(ii). See, e.g., Bomhoff v. Nelnet Loan Servs., Inc., 109 P. 3d 1241 (Kan. 2005) (rejecting plaintiff's UDAP, conversion, and fraud claims that lender failed to properly apply partial student loan payments).
128 Press Release, U.S. Dep't of Educ., U.S. Department of Education Expands Its Student Loan Servicing Capacity (June 17, 2009).

129 See U.S. Dep't of Educ., Loan Servicing Information-Quarterly Customer Satisfaction Surveys Begin March 1, 2010 (Feb. 23, 2010).
130 Id.
131 SLA Values DL Servicing Contract at $1.3–$1.5 Billion over Initial 5 Year Contract Period, Student Lending Analytics Blog (June 28, 2009), at http://studentlendinganalytics.typepad.com/student_lending_analytics/2009/06/sla-values-dl-servicing-contract-at-13-15-billion-over-initial-5-year-contract-period.html.
132 See § 7.4.1.2, infra, for a discussion of the new servicing system and default prevention.
133 34 C.F.R. § 682.208(a).

inquiry from a borrower or any endorser on a loan.[134]

If a borrower disputes the terms of the loan in writing and the lender does not resolve the dispute, the lender's response must provide the borrower with an appropriate contact at the guaranty agency for resolution of the dispute.[135] Guaranty agencies that cannot resolve the dispute must provide the borrower with information about the Department of Education Student Loan Ombudsman's office.

If a loan assignment results in a change in the identity of the party to whom the borrower must send payments, the assignor and assignee of the loan must, no later than forty-five days from the date the assignee acquires a legally enforceable right to receive payment, provide either jointly or separately a notice to the borrower of the assignment, the identity of the assignee, the name and address of the party to whom subsequent payments or communications must be sent, and the telephone numbers of both the assignor and assignee.[136] If a loan has not been assigned, but there is a change in the identity of the party to whom the borrower must send payments, the holder of the loan must, no later than forty-five days after the change, provide notice to the borrower of the name, telephone number, and address of the party to whom subsequent payments or communications must be sent.[137]

The regulations also specify that guaranty agencies must be able to receive and respond to written, electronic, and telephone inquiries.[138] Borrowers must be notified of the effective date of the assignment or transfer, the date that the current loan servicer will stop accepting the borrower's payments, and the date the new servicer will begin accepting payments.[139]

---

134 34 C.F.R. § 682.208(c)(1).
135 34 C.F.R. § 682.208(c)(3). A number of guaranty agencies have their own ombudsman programs. *See* § 1.12.1.2, *supra*.
136 34 C.F.R. § 682.208(e)(1).
137 34 C.F.R. § 682.208(h).
138 34 C.F.R. § 682.401(b)(11).
139 34 C.F.R. § 682.208(e).

Chapter 4 — Postponing Repayment on Federal Student Loans

4.1 Introduction

This chapter covers the primary ways to postpone repayment on federal student loans. Grace periods give borrowers a short break after they complete or leave school and before repayment begins. Deferments allow eligible borrowers to postpone paying back their loans under certain circumstances. This is an extremely useful option, particularly since, for subsidized loans, interest does not accrue on the loan during the deferment period. However, only borrowers who have not yet defaulted on their loans are eligible for deferments.

Also discussed in this chapter are forbearances. Like deferments, forbearances allow borrowers to temporarily postpone repayment. They are less optimal than deferments because interest continues to accrue during the forbearance period. Unlike deferments, forbearances should be available to borrowers already in default.

Forbearances can be used to help borrowers avoid default in the first place. Administrative forbearances are also available for borrowers who are waiting for decisions on cancellations, consolidation loan applications, or other matters.

4.2 Grace Periods

Repayment for Direct Stafford loans begins after graduation or after a student leaves school or becomes enrolled in a half-time or shorter capacity. After one of these events, a borrower has six months to begin repayment.[1] Interest accrues for unsubsidized loans during the grace period. The grace period for Perkins loans is nine months.[2]

Repayment on Direct PLUS Program loans ("PLUS loans") generally must begin within sixty days after the final loan disbursement for the period of enrollment for which the loan was borrowed.[3] However, there are some exceptions, including deferments for PLUS loans disbursed on or after July 1, 2008.[4] These borrowers may defer repayment, generally for six months after they complete or leave school.

Grace periods do not include any period, not to exceed three years, during which a borrower who is a member of an Armed Forces reserve component is called or ordered to active duty for a period of more than thirty days.[5] Any single excluded period may not exceed three years and must include the time necessary for the borrower to resume enrollment at the next available regular enrollment period. Borrowers are entitled to another full six- or nine-month grace period, as applicable, upon completion of the excluded period of service.[6]

4.3 Deferments

4.3.1 Benefits of Deferment

Student loan borrowers are legally entitled to defer payments in certain situations. Deferment rights vary depending on the type of loan and when the loan obligation was incurred. For subsidized loans, a deferment not only postpones when a borrower must make payments, but interest obligations do not accrue during the deferment period. Instead, the federal government pays the interest portion of the loan and the student's payments on the principal are postponed until after the deferment expires.[7]

For unsubsidized loans, borrowers remain obligated for accrued interest during the deferment period. In this situation, lenders may forbear and capitalize interest payments until after the deferment period.[8] A lender may capitalize accrued interest no more frequently than on a quarterly

---

1 34 C.F.R. §§ 682.209 (FFEL), 685.207 (Direct Loan).
2 34 C.F.R. §§ 674.2, 674.31.
3 34 C.F.R. §§ 682.209(a)(2)(i)(FFEL), 685.207(d) (Direct Loan).
4 See § 4.3.6, infra.

5 34 C.F.R. §§ 682.209(a)(6) (FFEL), 685.207 (Direct Loan), 674.31 (Perkins Loan).
6 Id. See generally U.S. Gov't Accountability Office, Higher Education: More Information Could Help Education Determine the Extent to Which Eligible Servicemembers Serving on Active Duty Benefit from Relief Provided by Lenders and Schools, Report No. GAO-07-11 (Nov. 2006).
   This waiver was extended through September 30, 2012. 72 Fed. Reg. 72947 (Dec. 26, 2007).
7 See § 1.4.1.1, supra (subsidized and unsubsidized loans).
8 20 U.S.C. §§ 1077, 1078; 34 C.F.R. § 682.211(a)(4). See also 34 C.F.R. § 682.202(b).
   Capitalization refers to the adding of accrued interest and unpaid insurance premiums to the borrower's unpaid principal balance.

basis.[9] Capitalization is again permitted when repayment is required to begin or resume.

At or before the time the deferment is granted, loan holders must send a notice informing borrowers who are responsible for paying the interest during a deferment period[10] that they have the option to pay the accruing interest or cancel the deferment and continue paying on the loan. The loan holder must also provide additional information, including an example of the impact of capitalization of accrued unpaid interest on loan principal and on the total amount of interest to be paid over the life of the loan.[11]

If a loan is being deferred, the loan is not in default, and the borrower will not be subject to debt collection attempts or lawsuits and will be eligible for additional educational assistance.

4.3.2 Borrower's Default Limits Eligibility for Deferment

An important limitation to the usefulness of the borrower's deferment right is that the right exists only when borrowers are current or "delinquent" on the loan obligation, not when they are in "default."[12] If a borrower cannot qualify for a deferment because the loan is in default, the borrower can re-establish eligibility for a deferment by consolidating the loan into a new loan or by rehabilitating the defaulted loan.[13] The borrower can then apply for a deferment under the new loan. The borrower may also be eligible if he or she makes satisfactory repayment arrangements with the loan holder.[14] For FFELs, the arrangements must be made prior to the payment of a default claim by a guaranty agency.[15]

There is a period of 270 days (or nine months) in most cases before federal loans go into default. This period does not include the time a borrower is in deferment.[16] Unless the borrower obtains forbearance at the end of the deferment period, any delinquency status that existed for the borrower when the deferment period began will be reinstated.[17]

There may be some situations in which a default should not have occurred because of a back-dated deferment. For most deferments, the time period begins on the date that the condition entitling the borrower to the deferment first existed.[18] For example, if a borrower has been delinquent since January 1, experienced the condition justifying the deferment (for example, economic hardship) in June, and then applied for a deferment on December 1, the 270-day period (or nine months) before the borrower's loan goes into default would not be expired. It is the date of onset of the condition, not the application date, that is critical.

There is an exception to this general rule for FFEL unemployment deferments: an initial unemployment deferment cannot begin more than six months before the date the loan holder receives a request and supporting documentation for the deferment.[19]

4.3.3 General Eligibility Requirements for Deferments

The various student loan programs have different rules about when the borrower qualifies for a deferment. Rules differ not only by the type of loan—for example, Perkins Loan Program loans ("Perkins loans"), Direct Loan Program loans ("Direct loans"), or FFEL Program loans ("FFELs")—but also by when the loan was extended.

Most deferments carry maximum time limits, and each deferment has recertification requirements, generally every six months or one year, for the borrower to remain eligible.

In the FFEL regulations, the Department of Education ("the Department") takes the position that the maximum length of deferments applies to the borrower, not just to his or her specific loan. Consequently, a borrower may not receive more than the maximum deferment period under any given deferment category regardless of the number of different types of loans owned or the amount of time elapsed since the borrower last sought a deferment.[20] For example, if a borrower is entitled to three years of unemployment deferments and uses that time up, the borrower may not later take out new loans and seek an additional unemployment deferment on those new loans. The regulations for the Direct Loan Program state only that economic hardship and unemployment deferments may not exceed three years.[21] However, the Direct Loan regulations refer back to FFEL provisions for both the unemployment and economic hardship deferments.[22]

For most deferments, the time period starts on the date that the condition first began that entitled the borrower to the deferment.[23] There is an exception to this general rule for FFEL unemployment deferments: an initial unemployment deferment cannot begin more than six months before the date the loan holder receives a request and supporting documentation for the deferment.[24]

---

9 34 C.F.R. § 682.202(b)(3).
10 34 C.F.R. § 682.210(a)(3)(ii).
11 *Id.*
12 34 C.F.R. §§ 682.210(a)(8) (FFEL), 685.204(h).
13 Consolidation and rehabilitation are discussed in §§ 6.2 (consolidation), 6.3 (rehabilitation), *infra*.
14 34 C.F.R. §§ 682.210(a)(8) (FFEL), 685.204(h).
15 34 C.F.R. § 682.210(a)(8).
16 34 C.F.R. § 682.210(a)(7).
17 *Id.*
18 34 C.F.R. § 682.210(a)(5).

19 34 C.F.R. § 682.210(a)(5).
20 34 C.F.R. § 682.210(a)(1)(ii).
21 34 C.F.R. § 685.204(c).
22 34 C.F.R. § 685.204(b)(2)(ii), (b)(3)(ii).
23 34 C.F.R. § 682.210(a)(5).
24 34 C.F.R. § 682.210(a)(5).

4.3.4 Applying for Deferments

Except for in-school deferments, borrowers must request deferments and provide the documentation necessary to establish eligibility.[25] Borrowers may request in-school deferments in writing, but the deferment may also be granted when the lender receives eligibility information from the school.[26]

Loan holders may also grant graduate fellowship, rehabilitation training program, unemployment, military service, and economic hardship deferments if the borrower received a deferment from a different federal loan program for the same reason and the same time period.[27] Loan holders may rely in good faith on these other determinations However, they may not grant a deferment based on a determination by another loan holder if they have evidence indicating that the borrower does not qualify for the deferment.[28] The decision on whether to rely on another loan holder's granting of a deferment is optional.[29] If the loan holder grants a deferment based on a determination by another program, the loan holder must notify the borrower that the deferment has been granted and that the borrower has the option of cancelling the deferment and resuming payment.[30]

For military deferments only, a borrower's representative may request the deferment and provide the required information on behalf of the borrower.[31] In these circumstances, the loan holder must notify the borrower that the deferment has been granted and that the borrower has the option of cancelling the deferment. The loan holder may also notify the representative of the outcome of the deferment request.[32] The term "borrower's representative" is not defined, in order to allow maximum flexibility for borrowers on active duty.[33] Without supporting documentation, a military service deferment may be granted for a period not to exceed the initial twelve months from the date on which the qualifying eligible service began.[34]

4.3.5 Grounds for Direct Loans, FFELs, and Consolidation Loans Extended After July 1, 1993

4.3.5.1 General

One set of criteria for deferment applies to Direct loans, FFELs, and most consolidation loans first disbursed on or after July 1, 1993. With respect to FFEL consolidation loans, the post-July-1993 rules apply to borrowers who obtain an FFEL consolidation loan on or after July 1, 1993, and have no other outstanding FFELs at that time.[35] The following are available deferments for these loans:

- Student deferments for at least half-time study[36]
- Graduate fellowship deferments[37]
- Rehabilitation training program deferment[38]
- Unemployment deferment not to exceed three years[39]
- Economic hardship deferment, granted one year at a time for a maximum of three years[40]
- Military service and post-active-duty deferments[41]

4.3.5.2 FFEL and Direct Loan Economic Hardship Deferments

The economic hardship deferment is usually the most important one for low-income borrowers. The first three qualification categories automatically qualify the borrower for deferment as long as the borrower can provide supporting documentation. The three categories are as follows:

1. Previous qualification for economic hardship deferment under another federal loan program.[42]

---

25 34 C.F.R. §§ 685.204(i) (Direct Loan), 682.210(a)(4) (FFEL).
26 34 C.F.R. § 682.210(c).
27 34 C.F.R. §§ 682.210(s)(1)(iii) (FFEL), 685.204(i)(2) (Direct Loan).
28 34 C.F.R. §§ 682.210(s)(1)(iv), 685.204(i)(3).
29 72 Fed. Reg. 61960, 61962 (Nov. 1, 2007).
30 34 C.F.R. §§ 682.210(s)(v), 685.204(i)(4).
31 34 C.F.R. §§ 682.210(t)(7) (FFEL), 685.204(i)(1). See 4.3.5.4, infra.
32 34 C.F.R. §§ 682.210(t)(8), 685.204(i)(5).
33 72 Fed. Reg. 61960 (Nov. 1, 2007).
34 34 C.F.R. § 682.210(t)(9).

35 34 C.F.R. § 682.210(s)(1).
36 34 C.F.R. §§ 682.210(s)(2) (FFEL), 685.204(b)(1)(i)(A) (Direct Loan).
   The rules for this deferment are set out at 34 C.F.R. § 682.210(c).
37 34 C.F.R. §§ 682.210(s)(3) (FFEL), 685.204(b)(1)(i)(B) (Direct Loan).
   The rules for this deferment are set out at 34 C.F.R. § 682.210(d).
38 34 C.F.R. §§ 682.210(s)(4) (FFEL), 685.204(b)(1)(i)(C) (Direct Loan).
   The rules for this deferment are set out at 34 C.F.R. § 682.210(e).
39 34 C.F.R. §§ 682.210(s)(5) (FFEL), 685.204(b)(2)(i) (Direct Loan).
   The rules for this deferment are set out at 34 C.F.R. § 682.210(h). See § 4.3.5.3, infra.
40 34 C.F.R. §§ 682.210(s)(6) (FFEL), 685.204(b)(3)(i) (Direct Loan).
   The rules for economic hardship deferments are set out at 34 C.F.R. § 682.210(s)(6). See § 4.3.5.2, infra.
41 34 C.F.R. § 682.210(t), (u). See §§ 4.3.5.4, 4.3.5.5, supra.
42 34 C.F.R. §§ 682.210(s)(6)(i) (FFEL), 685.204(b)(3)(i) (Direct Loan).

2. *Receipt of federal or state public assistance benefits.*[43] This includes anyone receiving payments under a federal or state public assistance program, such as TANF, SSI, Food Stamps, or state general public assistance.[44]
3. *Peace Corps.* The borrower qualifies if he or she is serving as a Peace Corps volunteer.[45] Peace Corps volunteers are entitled to deferments for the lesser of their full terms of service in the Peace Corps or the remaining period of economic hardship deferment eligibility under the three-year maximum if they provide documentation proving eligibility under any of the other economic hardship categories.[46]

There is also an income/employment eligibility category. Prior to July 1, 2009, there were three ways to qualify under this category. All three continue to apply to borrowers who applied for economic hardship deferments prior to July 1, 2009, or for those who applied after July 1, 2009, for a deferment period that began prior to that date.[47] The three tests are described below (as of July 1, 2009, however, there is only one income/employment based test):

1. An individual qualifies for an economic hardship deferment under the remaining income/employment test if he or she is working full-time and the earnings from this full-time job do not exceed the greater of the minimum wage or 150% of the federal poverty level applicable to the borrower's family size and state.[48]
2. *Income* is defined as the gross amount of income received by the borrower from employment and from other sources or the borrower's adjusted gross income, as recorded on the borrower's most recently filed federal income tax return.[49] A borrower is assumed to be working full-time if the borrower is expected to be employed for at least three consecutive months at thirty hours per week.[50]
3. *Family size* is defined as the number that is determined by counting the borrower, the borrower's spouse, and the borrower's children, including unborn children who will be born during the period covered by the deferment, if the children receive more than half their support from the borrower.[51] A borrower's family size could include other individuals if, at the time the borrower requests the deferment, the other individuals reside with the borrower and receive more than half of their support from the borrower and if they will continue to receive that support from the borrower.[52] Support includes money, gifts, loans, housing, food, clothes, car, medical and dental care, and payment of college costs.[53]

Prior to July 2009, there were two other tests, described briefly below.

1. *Full-time workers with high student loan debt burdens.* Prior to July 1, 2009, a borrower working full-time also qualified for a deferment if (A) the borrower's "federal education debt burden" was at least 20% of the borrower's total monthly income and (B) after subtracting the federal education debt burden, the borrower's monthly income was less than 220% of either the minimum wage or 150% of the federal poverty level applicable to the borrower's family size and state.[54] This was often called the 20/220 test.
2. *Those not working full-time with high student loan debt burdens.* Prior to July 1, 2009, this test applied only to a borrower whose income did not exceed two times the minimum wage level or two times 150% of the poverty line for the borrower's family size and state (whichever was higher) *and*, after subtracting an amount equal to the federal student loan debt burden, the remaining amount of income did not exceed the minimum wage rate or 150% of the poverty line for the borrower's family size (whichever was higher).[55]

The income-based repayment program (IBR) that went into effect in July 2009 was in some ways intended to replace the previous complete range of income/employment eligibility categories.[56] This should not adversely affect the lowest-income borrowers. Those receiving public assistance will remain eligible for the economic hardship deferment. Anyone working full-time, but earning a very low income, should continue to meet the remaining income/employment test. If a low-income borrower is not eligible for the deferment because she is not working full-time and not receiving public assistance, she can still choose to repay through IBR. If she earns an amount below 150% of the poverty level for her family size, the payment under IBR will be zero.

In addition, the remaining income/employment test is more generous to borrowers. Previously a borrower qualified under this test if his income did not exceed the greater of the minimum wage or the federal poverty level for a family of two, regardless of family size. The current test is now the greater of the minimum wage or 150% of the federal poverty level for the borrower's actual family size

---

The Direct Loan Program economic hardship deferment regulations specifically refer to the requirements in the FFEL regulations. The standards are the same for both loan programs. This deferment is also available for Perkins Loans Program borrowers. 34 C.F.R. § 674.34(e).

43 34 C.F.R. § 682.210(s)(6)(ii).
44 34 C.F.R. § 682.210(s)(6)(ii) (FFEL).
45 34 C.F.R. § 682.210(s)(6)(iv).
46 34 C.F.R. § 682.210(s)(6).
47 73 Fed. Reg. 63232, 63235 (Oct. 23, 2008).
48 34 C.F.R. § 682.210(s)(6)(iii).
49 34 C.F.R. § 682.210(s)(6)(vii).
50 34 C.F.R. § 682.210(s)(6)(viii).
51 34 C.F.R. § 682.210(s)(6)(ix).
52 *Id.*
53 *Id.*
54 34 C.F.R. § 682.210(s)(iv) (previous regulation).
55 34 C.F.R. § 682.210(s)(v) (previous regulation).
56 *See* § 3.1.3.2, *supra*.

and state. The test was changed to mirror the standard that is used to determine partial financial hardships under IBR.

4.3.5.3 Unemployment Deferment

There are two ways to qualify for an unemployment deferment. The simpler route is for a borrower to provide proof of eligibility to receive unemployment insurance benefits.[57] Alternatively, the borrower must show that he or she has registered with an employment agency, if one is available within a fifty mile radius of the borrower's current address, and has made at least six diligent attempts during the preceding six-month period to secure full-time employment (defined as at least thirty hours per week and expected to last at least three months).[58] Borrowers may qualify for this deferment under the second "employment agency registration" category whether or not they have been previously employed.[59]

Evidence of registration with an agency may be submitted in writing or in an equivalent format.[60] The borrower will not qualify if he or she refuses to seek or accept employment in the kinds of positions or at the salary and responsibility levels for which he or she feels overqualified.[61]

In the second route to an unemployment deferment, the initial period of deferment can be granted for a period of unemployment that begins up to six months before the lender receives the borrower's request and can be granted for up to six months after that date.[62]

For either eligibility category, the lender may not grant a deferment beyond the date that is six months after the borrower provided evidence of eligibility for unemployment insurance benefits or the date the borrower provided written certification under the "employment agency registration" category.[63]

4.3.5.4 Military Deferment

The 2005 Deficit Reduction Act included a military deferment for all three loan programs: FFEL, Direct Loan, and Perkins Loan.[64]

The three-year limit on this deferment was eliminated as of October 1, 2007.[65] For a borrower whose active duty service included October 1, 2007, or began on or after that date, the deferment ends 180 days after the demobilization date for each period of service.[66] This 180-day "extension" is available each time a borrower is demobilized at the conclusion of eligible active duty service.[67]

The military deferment may not be granted for a period that will result in a refund of previous payments made by the borrower.[68] Furthermore, it applies only to periods during which borrowers are serving on active duty during a war or other military operation, serving during a national emergency, or performing qualifying National Guard duty during a war or other military operation or national emergency.[69]

"National emergency" is defined as the emergency declared by the President on September 14, 2001, due to the terrorist attacks or subsequent national emergencies declared by the President for reason of terrorist attacks.[70]

Documentation establishing eligible active duty service may include a copy of the borrower's military orders or a written statement from the borrower's commanding officer or personnel officer that the borrower is serving on active duty during a war or other military operation, serving during a national emergency, or performing qualifying National Guard duty.

Effective October 1, 2007, the deferment was extended to all federal loans in repayment at that time, regardless of when the loans were first disbursed.[71] Previously it was available only if the first loan disbursement was made on or after July 1, 2001.

Some lenders have additional policies or practices to assist military service members with deferments and forbearances. For example, some lenders have reported that they do not capitalize the interest on loans in forbearance as a result of active-duty military service.[72]

---

57 34 C.F.R. §§ 682.210(h)(1) (FFEL), 685.204(b)(2)(i),(ii) (Direct Loan).
 The Direct Loan regulations specifically refer to the standards in the FFEL deferment regulations.
58 34 C.F.R. § 682.210(h)(2).
59 34 C.F.R. § 682.210(h)(3)(i).
60 34 C.F.R. § 682.210(h)(2).
 The Secretary must approve this "equivalent" proof. The Department left open the possibility that borrowers will have registered, for example, by phone or on-line. See 67 Fed. Reg. 51036 (Aug. 6, 2002).
61 34 C.F.R. § 682.210(h)(3)(ii).
62 34 C.F.R. § 682.210(h)(3)(iv).
63 34 C.F.R. § 682.210(h)(4).
64 Pub. L. No. 109-171 § 8007, 120 Stat. 4 (Feb. 8, 2006) (amending 20 U.S.C. § 1078(b)(1)(M)).
65 Pub. L. No. 110-84, 121 Stat. 784 (Sept. 27, 2007).
66 34 C.F.R. §§ 682.210(t)(2) (FFEL), 685.203(e)(2) (Direct Loan).
67 U.S. Dep't of Educ., Dear Colleague Letter GEN-08-01 (Jan. 8, 2008); U.S. Dep't of Educ., The College Cost Reduction and Access Act of 2007 (CCRAA), Public Law 110-84, at 5 (Jan. 8, 2008).
68 34 C.F.R. §§ 682.210(t)(5), 685.204(e)(5).
69 34 C.F.R. §§ 682.210(t)(1), 685.204(e)(1). See also U.S. Dep't of Educ., Enactment of the Higher Education Reconciliation Act of 2005, Dear Colleague Letter GEN-06-02 (Mar. 2006).
 A copy is available at the Department's website, www.ed.gov, and on the companion website to this manual. "Active duty" is defined at 10 U.S.C. § 101(d)(1).
70 34 C.F.R. §§ 682.210(t)(6), 685.204(e)(6)(iii).
71 Pub. L. No. 110-84, 121 Stat. 784 (Sept. 27, 2007).
72 U.S. Gov't Accountability Office, Higher Education: More Information Could Help Education Determine the Extent to which Eligible Service members Serving on Active Duty Benefited from Relief Provided by Lenders and Schools 17, Report No. GAO-07-11 (Nov. 2006).

4.3.5.5 Post-Active-Duty Deferment

The College Cost Reduction and Access Act of 2007 included a deferment for members of the National Guard or other reserve components of the Armed Forces or members of such forces in retired status.[73] This deferment is available for FFEL, Direct loan, and Perkins loan borrowers.[74] The deferment is available to borrowers who were serving on active duty on October 1, 2007, or began serving on or after that date.[75]

The deferment is available for thirteen months following the conclusion of the borrower's active duty military service and any applicable grace period if the borrower was enrolled in a program of instruction at an eligible institution at the time, or within six months prior to the time, the borrower was called to active duty.[76] If the borrower returns to enrolled student status during the thirteen-month period on at least a half-term basis, the deferment expires at the time of that return.[77]

Borrowers must be members of the National Guard or other reserve components of the Armed Forces or service members in retired status.[78] "Active duty" includes (1) active state duty for members of the National Guard activated by a governor under state statute or policy and whose activities are paid for with state funds and (2) full-time National Guard duty activated by a governor authorized, with the approval of the President or U.S. Secretary of Defense, to order members to state active duty whose activities are paid for with federal funds.[79] If a borrower is eligible for both the thirteen-month post-active-duty deferment and the extended 180 days for demobilization through the military deferment, the borrower's eligibility for these separate deferments runs concurrently.[80]

Not all borrowers will qualify for both the military service and post-active-duty deferments. The military service deferment is available only to certain service members serving on active duty during a war, other military operation, or national emergency. This includes reserve forces ordered to active duty and retired forces ordered to active duty for service in connection with a war, military operation, or national emergency.[81] "National emergency" is defined as the emergency declared by the President on September 14, 2001, due to the terrorist attacks or subsequent national emergencies declared by the President for reason of terrorist attacks.[82] The post-active-duty deferment, in contrast, is available only to members of the National Guard or other reserve forces or retired forces called to active duty while enrolled in school. Active duty for this deferment does not have to be in connection with a war, military operation, or national emergency.

As a result, some borrowers called to active duty will not be eligible for military service deferments. Unless they are eligible for another deferment or are in a grace period, they will be obligated to make payments on their loans while on active duty. There is a mandatory forbearance to help address this issue.[83] The forbearance is available to members of the National Guard who qualify for post-active-duty deferments but do not qualify for military or other deferments. The National Guard member must be engaged in active state duty for a period of more than thirty consecutive days beginning on the day after the grace period ends for loans that have not entered repayment or on the day after the borrower ceases at least half-time enrollment for a loan in repayment.[84]

4.3.6 PLUS Deferments

FFEL and Direct PLUS loan borrowers are generally eligible for the same deferments as other borrowers. The borrower must qualify for the deferment. If the loan is a parent PLUS loan, the parent borrower must qualify for the deferment. Because PLUS loans are unsubsidized, interest will accrue during the deferment period.

There are also deferments available in some circumstances to allow PLUS loan borrowers to postpone repayment after completing or leaving school. Repayment for PLUS loans generally begins on the date the loan is fully disbursed.[85] There is no grace period. However, deferments are allowed for borrowers with PLUS loans first disbursed on or after July 1, 2008. Graduate PLUS loan borrowers may defer repayment on these loans during the six-month period that begins on the day after the student ceases to be enrolled on at least a half-time basis at an eligible institution.[86] The additional six months will automatically be applied when the graduate PLUS loan borrower requests an in-school deferment.

Parent PLUS loan borrowers with loans first disbursed on or after July 1, 2008, may also defer payment while the student on whose behalf the loan was obtained is in school.[87] The parent borrower must request this deferment. This is in addition to the parent borrower's ability to request a defer-

---

73 Pub. L. No. 110-84, 121 Stat. 784 (Sept. 27, 2007).
74 34 C.F.R. §§ 674.34(i) (Perkins Loan), 682.210(u) (FFEL), 685.204(f) (Direct Loan).
75 34 C.F.R. § 682.210(u)(1).
76 34 C.F.R. §§ 682.210(u)(1) (FFEL), 685.204(f)(1).
77 34 C.F.R. §§ 682.210(u)(3) (FFEL), 685.204(f)(3).
78 34 C.F.R. §§ 682.210(u)(1)(i), 685.204(f)(1)(i).
79 34 C.F.R. §§ 682.210(u)(2)(ii), (iii) (FFEL), 685.204(f)(2).
80 34 C.F.R. §§ 682.210(u)(4) (FFEL), 685.204(f)(4).
81 See § 4.3.5.4, supra.
82 34 C.F.R. § 682.210(t)(6).
83 34 C.F.R. §§ 682.211(h)(2)(iii) (FFEL), 685.205(a)(7) (Direct Loan). See § 4.4.4, infra.
84 Id.
85 See § 4.2, supra.
86 34 C.F.R. §§ 682.210(c)(2)(v), 685.204(g)(1).
87 34 C.F.R. §§ 682.210(c)(2)(v), 685.204(g)(2).

ment while the parent is in school and qualifies for an in-school deferment based on his or her own enrollment.

Parent borrowers may also defer repayment during the six-month period that begins on the later of the day after the student on whose behalf the loan was obtained ceases to be enrolled on at least a half-time basis or, if the parent borrower is also a student, the day after the parent borrower ceases to be enrolled on at least a half-time basis.[88]

Parent PLUS loan borrowers must request these deferments. In July 2009, the Department issued a new parent PLUS loan borrower deferment request form.[89]

There is an administrative forbearance allowed for borrowers with PLUS loans disbursed before July 1, 2008, in order to align repayment with a borrower's PLUS loans first disbursed on or after July 1, 2008, or with a borrower's Stafford loans that are subject to a grace period. The lender must notify the borrower that the borrower has the option to cancel the forbearance and to continue paying on the loan.[90]

FFEL parent PLUS loan borrowers with older loans have additional deferment rights.[91]

4.3.7 Grounds for FFEL Deferments Extended Before July 1, 1993

A different set of rules applies to those with FFELs extended before July 1, 1993. Although loans incurred in 1993 and before are now quite old, advocates will still see clients with these loans. The elimination of the statute of limitations for student loan collections makes it very difficult to escape a student loan, no matter how old it is.

The grounds for deferment under these loans include:

- Unemployment for up to two years;
- Full-time student at a participating school;[92]
- Active-duty status in the United States Armed Forces;[93]

- The receipt of or the scheduled receipt of service under a program designed to rehabilitate disabled individuals;
- Temporary total disability for up to three years;
- The provision of nursing or similar services to a spouse who is temporarily totally disabled;
- Parental leave; and
- Mothers of pre-school children starting work at no more than one dollar above the minimum wage.[94]

The regulations set out detailed standards as to when a student is eligible for a deferment based on these grounds, particularly for unemployment, rehabilitation, temporary total disability, and a spouse's temporary total disability.[95] Maximum deferment periods vary for each type of deferment.[96] Some can last indefinitely so long as the qualifying conditions or circumstances still apply.

The temporary total disability deferment can be especially critical for borrowers with disabilities that are not sufficiently permanent or severe to meet the requirements for a disability discharge.[97] However, it is only available to borrowers with these older loans.

Although disabled borrowers with older loans may apply for the temporary disability deferment, they are not entitled to the more comprehensive economic hardship deferment. The hardship deferment is available only for borrowers with loans incurred after July 1, 1993. The economic hardship deferment is broad enough to include low-income borrowers, whether disabled or not.[98] The temporary disability deferment, in contrast, applies only to those borrowers who can certify a temporary total disability or, in some cases, certify that a dependent is disabled.[99]

4.3.8 Grounds for Perkins Loans Deferments

Borrowers are entitled to defer Perkins loan principal payments without accruing interest under certain situations. As with FFELs, the specific qualifying circumstances depend on when the loan was made. For Perkins loans made after July 1, 1993, deferments are available based on a number of grounds, including:

- Qualifying in-school status;[100]
- Full-time teaching in certain schools and in Head Start;[101]

---

88 *Id.*
89 U.S. Dep't of Educ., Approval of FFEL Program Deferment Request Forms, Dear Colleague Letter FP-09-06 (July 30, 2009).
90 34 C.F.R. §§ 682.211(f)(15), 685.205(b)(10).
91 34 C.F.R. § 682.210(B)(6).
92 A borrower whose loan was obtained on or after July 1, 1987, and who has no outstanding FFEL balance on that date may obtain an in-school deferment for half-time study if the borrower also received or will receive a Stafford or SLS loan for the period during which deferment is sought. 34 C.F.R. § 682.210(c)(iii).
93 34 C.F.R. § 682.210(i).
Borrowers on active duty in the United States Armed Forces are eligible for this deferment. "Armed Forces" is defined as the U.S. Army, Navy, Air Force, Marine Corps, and the Coast Guard. 34 C.F.R. § 682.210(i)(2).
Borrowers enlisted in the reserves may qualify for the military deferment only for service on a full-time basis that is expected to last for a period of at least one year in length. Borrowers enlisted in the National Guard qualify for this deferment only while they are on active-duty status as a member of the U.S. Army or Air Force Reserves and meet the other

requirements of § 682.210(i). There is also a military deferment for newer loans. *See* § 4.3.5.4, *supra*.
94 20 U.S.C. § 1077(a)(2)(c); 34 C.F.R. § 682.210(b), (c), (e)–(i), (o), (r).
95 *See* 34 C.F.R. § 682.210(e)–(h).
96 34 C.F.R. § 682.210(b).
97 *See* § 9.7, *infra* (disability discharges).
98 *See* § 4.3.5.2, *supra*.
99 "Temporary total disability" is defined at 34 C.F.R. § 682.200(b). *See also* 34 C.F.R. § 682.210(b)(1)(iv).
100 34 C.F.R. § 674.34(b)(1)(i).
101 34 C.F.R. § 674.34(c).

- Full-time service in law enforcement or as correction officers under certain circumstances;[102]
- Certain military service;[103]
- Certain volunteer service such as the Peace Corps;[104]
- Inability to find, despite seeking, full-time employment for a period not to exceed three years;[105] and
- Qualifying economic hardship conditions for a period not to exceed three years.[106] The Perkins Loan economic hardship requirements are similar to those for FFEL and Direct Loan.[107]

In addition to the previous Perkins Loan military service deferment cited above, Perkins loan borrowers are also eligible for the newer military service and post-active-duty deferments. The rules for these deferments are the same as in the Direct Loan and FFEL programs.[108]

There are different criteria for Perkins loans made before July 1, 1993.[109] Borrowers with these older loans are not eligible for economic hardship or unemployment deferments but are eligible for temporary disability deferments, among others.

4.4 Forbearances

4.4.1 General

The Department of Education encourages the granting of forbearances to prevent borrowers from defaulting on their loans or to permit borrowers in default to resume "honoring" their loan obligations.[110] Forbearance involves a loan holder agreeing to a temporary stoppage of payments, an extension of time for making payments, or acceptance of smaller payments.[111]

Forbearance is not as helpful for a borrower as a deferment because interest will continue to accrue while the loan payments are reduced or postponed. Consequently, the size of the outstanding obligation may actually increase during a forbearance period. A borrower not yet in default can use a forbearance agreement to delay going into default.

Forbearance should be available even if the borrower is in default. The FFEL statute provides that guaranty agencies shall not be precluded from permitting forbearance solely because the loan is in default.[112] According to the FFEL regulations, loan holders are encouraged to grant forbearance in order to prevent the borrower from defaulting on a repayment obligation or to permit the borrower to resume honoring that obligation after default.[113] This is important because loan holders and collection agencies will often erroneously tell borrowers that they are not eligible for forbearances after default.

Many lenders, guaranty agencies, and state agencies will insist that borrowers are only eligible for forbearance prior to default. In some cases, this is a matter of semantics. These agencies will grant "cessations of payment" as opposed to "forbearances." This is even though, as noted above, forbearances may involve an extension of time for making payments or acceptance of smaller payments in addition to temporary cessations of payments. Regardless, there should be no practical difference between a "cessation" and "forbearance."

In general, forbearances will not remove students from default status. However, loan holders that grant forbearances or cessation of payments generally have the discretion to halt collection actions such as tax refund intercepts, collection contacts, and garnishments.

Many loan holders and servicers automatically place borrowers in forbearance or encourage forbearances even in cases in which more favorable options are available. A guaranty agency report found that servicers have used a high rate of forbearances to cure loans.[114] The agency noted that forbearances are often the simplest tool available. Furthermore, applications for forbearance are usually more readily available and can be granted through a verbal request without all the documentation required for deferments.[115] There is also a growing problem with proprietary schools placing borrowers in forbearance to help avoid defaults during the window of time in which default rates are counted against the schools.[116]

---

102 *Id.*
103 *Id.*
104 34 C.F.R. § 674.34(e).
105 34 C.F.R. § 674.34(d).
    The Perkins Loan Program unemployment deferment does not have the same documentation requirements as the FFEL and Direct Loan Programs. However, Perkins loan holders will require borrowers to provide certification supporting their applications.
106 34 C.F.R. § 674.34(e).
107 *See* § 4.3.5.2, *supra*.
108 34 C.F.R. §§ 674.34(h) (military), 674.34(i) (post-active duty). *See* §§ 4.3.5.4, 4.3.5.5, *supra*.
109 34 C.F.R. § 674.35.
110 34 C.F.R. § 682.211(a)(1).
111 34 C.F.R. §§ 674.33(d) (Perkins Loan), 682.211(a)(1) (FFEL), 685.205(a) (Direct Loan).

112 20 U.S.C. § 1078(c)(3)(D).
113 34 C.F.R. § 682.211(a)(1).
    The Direct Loan regulations are less explicit on the possibility of forbearance after default. 34 C.F.R. § 685.205(a).
114 Texas Guaranteed Student Loan Corp., White Paper: Crisis Averted or Merely Postponed?: Examining Long-term Cohort Default Rates, Resolving Defaults, and Curing Delinquencies (July 2010), *available at* www.tgslc.org/pdf/crisis_averted.pdf.
115 *Id.*
116 *See* § 12.3.3.1, *infra*.

4.4.2 Applying for Forbearances

Forbearances may be granted under certain circumstances without written documentation or written application. This category of verbal forbearance includes the Direct Loan administrative forbearances.[117] The FFEL regulations allow oral forbearances, but the loan holder in these circumstances must send a notice to the borrower within thirty days confirming the forbearance.[118] However, some of the FFEL mandatory forbearances require written documentation.[119]

If the request is made in writing, it is a good idea to use the general forbearance request form issued by the Department and by many loan holders.[120]

There are a number of regulatory requirements imposed on lenders and loan holders to inform borrowers periodically about the status of their loans in forbearance. Specifically, if a forbearance involves the postponement of all payments, the lender must contact the borrower at least once every six months to inform the borrower of the outstanding obligation to repay, the amount of unpaid principal balance, any unpaid interest that has accrued, the fact that interest will accrue on the loan for the full term of the forbearance, and the borrower's option to discontinue the forbearance at any time.[121]

4.4.3 Discretionary Forbearances

The FFEL regulations make a distinction between discretionary and mandatory forbearances. The Direct Loan Program does not make this distinction. If a Direct loan borrower qualifies for forbearance, the regulations provide that the Secretary of the Department of Education ("the Secretary") will grant forbearance, with no reference to discretion on the Secretary's part.[122] The grounds for forbearance vary between the two programs in some respects.

Both the FFEL and Direct Loan regulations provide for forbearances if borrowers are in poor health or have other personal problems that affect the ability of the borrower to make the scheduled payments.[123] Forbearance for these reasons is discretionary under FFEL regulations.[124] The forbearance is granted up to a year at a time, but there are no limits to the number of years this type of forbearance may be granted.[125]

Both FFEL and Direct Loan regulations provide for administrative forbearances under various circumstances, for example, while the lender is resolving a change in the loan's status or pending the resolution of a discharge application.[126] With a few limited exceptions, such as local or national emergencies, the FFEL administrative forbearances are discretionary.[127]

Both programs provide for forbearances during:

- A properly granted period of deferment for which the lender learns the borrower did not qualify.[128]
- At the beginning of an authorized deferment period or an administrative forbearance period for FFEL loans.[129]
- For Direct loans, the period in which payments are overdue at the beginning of an authorized deferment period.[130]
- The period beginning when the borrower entered repayment until the first payment due date was established.[131]
- The period prior to the borrower's filing of a bankruptcy petition.[132]
- For FFELs, a period not to exceed an additional sixty days after the lender has suspended collection for the initial sixty-day period and receives reliable information that the borrower (or student in the case of a PLUS loan) has died.[133]
- For FFELs, the periods described in the disability discharge regulations in regard to the borrower's total and permanent disability.[134]
- For Direct loans, a period after the Secretary receives reliable information indicating that the borrower (or the student, in the case of a Direct PLUS loan) has died or the borrower has become totally and permanently disabled, until the Secretary receives documentation of death or total and permanent disability.[135]
- Periods necessary for the Secretary or the guaranty agency to determine the borrower's eligibility for discharge of the loan because of an unpaid refund, attendance at a closed school, false certification of loan eligibility, or the borrower's or, if applicable, endorser's bankruptcy.[136] The Direct Loan Program regulations specifically include teacher loan forgiveness pro-

---

117 34 C.F.R. § 685.205(b).
118 34 C.F.R. § 682.211(b)(1).
119 34 C.F.R. § 682.211(h)(4).
120 The form is available at the Department's website, www.ed.gov. A sample form can also be found at Appendix D, *infra*.
121 34 C.F.R. § 682.211(e).
122 34 C.F.R. § 685.205(a).
123 34 C.F.R. §§ 682.211(a)(2)(i) (FFEL), 685.205(a)(1) (Direct Loan).
124 34 C.F.R. § 682.211(a)(2)(i).
125 34 C.F.R. §§ 682.211(c) (FFEL), 685.205(c) (Direct Loan).

126 34 C.F.R. §§ 682.211(f) (FFEL), 685.205(b) (Direct Loan).
127 The regulations for mandatory administrative forbearances are set out at 34 C.F.R. § 682.211(i). See § 4.4.4, *infra*.
128 34 C.F.R. §§ 682.211(f)(1), 685.205(b)(1).
129 34 C.F.R. § 682.211(f)(2).
130 34 C.F.R. §§ 685.205(b)(2) (FFEL), 685.205(b)(2) (Direct Loan).
131 34 C.F.R. §§ 682.211(f)(3) (FFEL), 685.205(b)(3) (Direct Loan).
132 34 C.F.R. §§ 682.211(f)(4) (FFEL), 685.205(b)(4) (Direct Loan).
133 34 C.F.R. § 682.211(f)(7).
134 34 C.F.R. § 682.211(f)(5).
    A similar provision for Direct loans can be found at 34 C.F.R. § 685.205(b)(5).
135 34 C.F.R. § 685.205(b)(5) (Direct Loan).
136 34 C.F.R. §§ 682.211(f)(8), 685.205(b)(6).

grams.[137] The FFEL regulations also allow for forbearances for borrower who are performing the type of service that would qualify the borrower for loan forgiveness and associated forbearance under the requirements of the teacher loan forgiveness program. However, these forbearances are mandatory rather than discretionary.[138]

- Periods not to exceed sixty days while the lender collects and processes documentation supporting the borrower's request for a deferment, forbearance, change in repayment plan, or consolidation loan.[139]
- For a period not to exceed 120 days after a borrower has submitted a valid identity theft report as defined in the Fair Credit Reporting Act or notification from a credit bureau that information furnished by the lender is a result of an alleged identity theft.[140] This time period is intended to allow lenders to determine the enforceability of the loan. The regulations specify certain actions the lender must take if the lender determines that the borrower is not eligible for an identity theft discharge but that the loan is nonetheless unenforceable.[141]

Administrative forbearances are particularly important to request when a borrower has applied for a consolidation loan or loan discharge and it is likely that considerable time will pass before the application is resolved. In some cases, the loan holder may agree to cease collection while applications are pending but may prefer to call this cessation something other than a forbearance. It is important to advocate aggressively in these cases since the Department clearly has the discretion to grant forbearances in these circumstances.

If two individuals are jointly liable for repayment of a PLUS loan or a consolidation loan, the lender may grant forbearance on repayment only if both individuals cannot make the scheduled payments based on the same or different conditions.[142]

4.4.4 Mandatory Forbearances

The FFEL Program provides for mandatory forbearances based on a statutory right.[143] To obtain mandatory forbearance, the borrower must request a forbearance from the holder of the loan and provide sufficient supporting documentation.[144] The terms of a mandatory forbearance do not have to be in writing, but the lender is required to send a confirming notice to the borrower and record the terms in the borrower's file.[145]

Most relevant for low-income borrowers are mandatory administrative forbearances for up to five years in cases in which the borrower will not be able to repay the loan within the maximum repayment term.[146] For example, the FFEL Standard Plan, Graduated Plan, and Income Sensitive Plan all generally require that the loan be repaid in no more than ten years.[147] If the documentation shows that the borrower will be unable to repay the loan within the maximum ten-year repayment period, the lender is required to grant forbearance to the borrower for up to five years.[148]

In addition, FFEL and Direct Loan forbearances are mandatory in increments of up to one year for periods that collectively do not exceed three years if the amount of the borrower's monthly student loan payments collectively is equal to or greater than 20% of the borrower's total monthly income.[149] Borrowers are required to submit documentation of income and other relevant information. FFEL forbearances are also mandatory for teachers who are performing teaching service that would qualify them for teacher loan forgiveness.[150]

The Department may also issue special forbearance guidance in disaster situations, such as after the September 11 terrorist attacks or after natural disasters. In general, the Department may grant discretionary administrative forbearances for up to three months to borrowers affected by military mobilizations.[151] Extensions beyond the three-month limit require supporting documentation and a written agreement. For example, the Department provided for automatic administrative forbearances on loan repayments for a limited period for victims of hurricanes Katrina and Rita.[152] The Department was specifically allowed flexibility to grant forbearances to borrowers on a case-by-case basis after the period for automatic forbearance eligibility ended.

There is a mandatory forbearance for borrowers who are called to active military duty for more than a thirty-day period and who do not qualify for a military service deferment during the active duty period but do qualify for the post-active-duty deferment.[153] The forbearance is available

---

137 34 C.F.R. § 685.205(b)(6)(iv).
138 34 C.F.R. § 682.211(h)(2)(ii)(C).
139 34 C.F.R. §§ 682.211(f)(11), 685.205(b)(9) (Direct Loan).
140 34 C.F.R. § 682.211(f)(6).
141 *Id. See also* § 9.4.5, *infra*.
142 34 C.F.R. § 682.211(a)(3).
143 20 U.S.C. § 1078(c)(3).
144 34 C.F.R. § 682.211(h)(3).
145 34 C.F.R. § 682.211(h)(3).
146 34 C.F.R. § 682.211(i)(5)(ii).
147 *See* § 3.1.2, *supra* (pre-default repayment plans).
148 34 C.F.R. §§ 682.211(i)(5).
149 34 C.F.R. §§ 682.211(h)(2)(i) (FFEL), 685.205(a)(6)(ii) (Direct Loan).
150 34 C.F.R. § 682.211(h)(2)(ii)(C).
  Partial teacher loan forgiveness is available for FFEL and Direct loan borrowers. Full and partial forgiveness is available for Perkins loan borrowers. *See* § 9.9, *infra* (teacher loan forgiveness).
151 Dear Colleague Letter GEN-03-06 (Mar. 2003).
152 *See* U.S. Dep't of Educ., Notification and Extension of Guidance to Assist Title IV Participants Affected by Hurricanes Katrina and Rita, Dear Colleague Letter GEN-06-07 (May 2006).
153 34 C.F.R. §§ 682.211(h)(2)(iii), 685.205(a)(7).

to members of the National Guard who qualify for a post-active-duty deferment but do not qualify for a military or other deferment. The National Guard member must be engaged in active state duty for a period of more than thirty consecutive days beginning on the day after the grace period ends for loans that have not entered repayment or on the day after the borrower ceases at least half-time enrollment for a loan in repayment.[154]

4.4.5 Perkins Loan Program Provisions

Forbearances must be granted for Perkins loan borrowers under the following circumstances:

1. If the amount of the borrower's loan payments (for all Title IV loans) are equal to or greater than 20% of the borrower's total monthly income;[155]
2. The borrower qualifies for a forbearance due to poor health or other "acceptable reasons";[156] or
3. The Secretary authorizes forbearances due to a national military mobilization or other national emergency.[157]

To qualify under the first category, a borrower is required to submit documentation of his or her most recent total monthly gross income and evidence of the monthly loan payment amounts.[158]

There is generally a three-year cumulative limit on the length of Perkins loan forbearances.[159] The Department has waived this limit for forbearances based on military service.[160] For qualified borrowers in the military, the Department has also waived the requirement that a borrower must send a written request and supporting documentation to apply for a Perkins loan forbearance. Instead, the school must grant a forbearance based on the borrower's status as an "affected individual"[161] for a one-year period, including a three-month "transition period" that immediately follows that period. These forbearances may be granted without supporting documentation or a written agreement, based on the written or oral request of the borrower, a member of the borrower's family, or another reliable source. The purpose of the three-month transition period is to assist borrowers so that they will not be required to reenter repayment immediately after they are no longer "affected individuals." In order for the borrower to receive forbearance beyond the initial period, supporting documentation from the borrower, a member of the borrower's family, or another reliable source is required. In addition, affected individuals do not have to provide the loan holder with documentation showing that they are subject to a military mobilization. The borrower, a member of his or her family, or another reliable source may request the forbearance for one year, including a three-month transition period, without providing the loan holder with documentation. Documentation must be submitted to support a forbearance beyond this period.[162]

---

154 34 C.F.R. § 682.211(h)(2)(iii).
155 34 C.F.R. § 674.33(d)(5)(i).
156 34 C.F.R. § 674.33(d)(5)(ii).
157 34 C.F.R. § 674.33(d)(5)(iii).
158 34 C.F.R. § 674.33(d)(6).
159 34 C.F.R. § 674.33(d)(2).

160 See 68 Fed. Reg. 25821 (May 14, 2003); 68 Fed. Reg. 69312 (Dec. 12, 2003).
161 "Affected individuals" are those who are serving on active duty during a war or other military operation or national emergency; are performing qualifying National Guard duty during a war or other military operation or national emergency; reside or are employed in an area that is declared a disaster area by any federal, state, or local official in connection with a national emergency; or suffered direct economic hardship as a direct result of a war or other military operation or national emergency, as determined by the Secretary.
162 68 Fed. Reg. 69312 (Dec. 12, 2003).

Chapter 5 Implications of Student Loan Defaults

5.1 The Problem of Federal Student Loan Defaults

5.1.1 Introduction

Default rates on both federal and private loans have skyrocketed in recent years. The problem is particularly acute for borrowers attending for-profit schools. For example, borrowers who attended for-profit/proprietary four-year colleges were more than twice as likely to default on their federal student loans in fiscal year 2007 than those from other four-year colleges.[1] The cohort default rate was 9.8% at for-profit four-year colleges, 3.6% at private non-profit four-year colleges, and 4.3% at public four-year colleges.[2]

While rates are much higher at for-profit schools, the problem is not confined to this sector. Defaults are a serious problem for borrowers attending all types of institutions.

Student loan defaults are a concern for taxpayers as well. In 1968, the government paid $2 million to cover loan defaults; in 1987, default payments exceeded $1 billion; and, by 1991, default claim payments reached $3.2 billion.[3] By the end of fiscal year 2008, $39.1 billion worth of loans were in default; by the end of fiscal year 2009, the total had increased to $50.8 billion.[4]

The overall default rate peaked at 22.4% in fiscal year 1990.[5] This rate decreased all the way to 5.6% in 1999 but has started climbing again in recent years.

The data for fiscal year 2007, released in September 2009, indicates persistently higher cohort default rates for proprietary school student borrowers. The rate in fiscal year 2007 for all proprietary schools was 11% compared to 3.7% for other private schools and 5.9% for public schools.[6]

The draft rates for fiscal year 2008 show a cohort default rate of 7.2%. This is an increase from 6.7% in fiscal year 2007.[7] The rates for proprietary schools generally increased to 11.9% compared to 4.1% for private institutions and 6.2% for public institutions.[8]

An August 2009 U.S. Government Accountability Office (GAO) report highlighted this troubling trend, noting that students at for-profit colleges and universities are more likely to default on federal loans. Students at these colleges receive 19% of federal student aid.[9] Four years into repayment, 23.3% of students at proprietary schools were defaulting on federal loans, a higher rate than students at either public colleges (where 9.5% were defaulting) or private ones (where 6.5% were in default).[10]

Data based on the new cohort default rates show even higher rates.[11] The "three-year rates" are 93% higher than the two-year rates for for-profit colleges, 63% higher for public two-year institutions, and 70% higher for private four-year colleges.[12]

5.1.2 The Causes of Default

Some guaranty agencies and schools have attempted to develop models to predict which borrowers are most at risk of defaulting and target more intensive efforts at these

---

1 The Project on Student Debt, High Hopes, Big Debts (Class of 2008) (May 2010) (citing data from U.S. Department of Education, National Student Loan Default Rates, *available at* www.ed.gov/offices/OSFAP/defaultmanagement/cdr.html).
2 *Id.*
3 U.S. Gen. Accounting Office, Higher Education: Ensuring Quality Education from Proprietary Institutions, GAO/T-HEHS-96-158 (June 1996).
4 Kelly Field, *Government Vastly Undercounts Defaults*, Chron. of Higher Educ. (July 11, 2010).
5 Information on default rates is available on the Department of Education's website at www.ed.gov/offices/OSFAP/defaultmanagement/cdr.html. *See* § 5.1.3, *infra*.

6 Press Release, U.S. Dep't of Educ., Student Loan Default Rates Increase (Sept. 14, 2009).
7 U.S. Dep't of Educ., FY 2008 Draft Student Loan Cohort Default Rates (May 2, 2010), *available at* http://ifap.ed.gov/eannouncements/043010FY08DraftStuLoanCDR.html.
8 *Id.* As discussed in § 5.1.3, *infra*, these cohort default rates do not give a full picture of the default problem.
9 U.S. Gov't Accountability Office, Proprietary Schools: Stronger Department of Education Oversight Needed to Help Ensure Only Eligible Students Receive Federal Student Aid, Report No. GAO-09-600 (Aug. 2009).
10 *Id.*
11 *See* § 5.1.3, *infra* (how the rate is calculated).
12 Doug Lederman, *Defaults Nearly Double*, Inside Higher Ed (Dec. 14, 2009), *at* www.insidehighered.com/news/2009/12/14/default.

The Department published these trial three-year rates on-line at http://federalstudentaid.ed.gov/datacenter/library/TrialYearCDR.xls.

borrowers. Many focus on reaching borrowers immediately after drop-out, since this is clearly a predictor of default.[13]

In a phone survey of student loan borrowers, the Texas guaranty agency, Texas Guaranteed Student Loan Corporation, found that repayers were likely to have jobs related to their training both during school and afterwards, while defaulters did not. Repayers were also more knowledgeable about their repayment options. Those who were predicted not to, but did, default faced the highest number of combined life traumas. They also frequently had bad experiences with loan servicers. They generally reported that the counseling they received was unclear or not helpful, and most had not thought about flexible options such as deferments.[14] The importance of information and communication with borrowers is reinforced by a profile conducted by the University of Illinois, Chicago, of student loan defaulters. The most commonly cited reason for defaults was lack of information.[15]

The Texas Guaranteed Student Loan Corporation provided more recent data on this issue in a 2010 report.[16] According to the report, borrowing more money is not the primary determinant of whether a borrower will default.[17] The Texas agency analyzed longer-term data to assess whether other common assumptions about default causes hold true over the long term. For example, they found that borrowers who withdraw from school are more likely to default soon after departure. However, graduates tend to default as well in significant numbers, but generally beyond the two-year cohort window.[18]

In a 2006 report, the Department of Education ("the Department") followed a group of federal student loan borrowers for ten years.[19] The Department found a correlation between the amount borrowed and default. Twenty percent of the borrowers in the study with $15,000 or more in loans received under the Stafford loans program defaulted at some point, compared to 7%–8% of those who borrowed less than $10,000. Not surprisingly, the percentage of borrowers who still owed student loans after ten years was also related to the borrowers' salaries. Thirty-three percent of the borrowers in the lowest income group still owed loans compared with 19% of those in the highest income group.[20] In addition, those who were still repaying were more likely to be female, black, and from the lowest-income families and to have parents who did not go to college.[21]

5.1.3 How School Default Rates Are Calculated

The cohort default rate is important for understanding the scope of the default problem and because it is the measure used to sanction schools with persistently high rates.[22] For schools with thirty borrowers or more, the rate tracks a cohort of current and former students who entered repayment on federal loans during that fiscal year.[23] The school must identify which borrowers in the cohort are in default, defined until 2009 as those who default before the end of the following fiscal year.[24] As of fiscal year 2009, borrowers are tracked for an additional year.[25] Loans received under the Federal Family Education Loans (FFEL), Direct PLUS, Federal Insured Student Loans (FISL), and Perkins Loan programs are not included in the calculations. Perkins Loan Program loans ("Perkins loans") have separate cohort default-rate calculations.[26]

Both the GAO and Department of Education Inspector General (IG) have released reports describing the ways in which these default rates are understated.[27] The Inspector

---

13 *See* Lawrence Gladieuz & Laura Perna, National Ctr. for Pub. Policy & Higher Educ., Borrowers Who Drop Out: A Neglected Aspect of the College Student Loan Trend (May 2005); Michael Podgursky, Mark Ehlert, Ryan Monroe, & Donald Watson, Student Loan Defaults and Enrollment Persistence" (2000), *available at* http://web.missouri.edu/~podgurskym/papers_presentations/wp/Student_Loan_default.pdf; Texas Guar. Student Loan Corp., *Predicting Which Borrowers Are Most Likely to Default* (1998), *available at* www.tgslc.org/publications/reports/defaults_texas/ins_intro.cfm.

14 Texas Guar. Student Loan Corp., Predicting Which Borrowers Are Most Likely to Default (1998), *available at* www.tgslc.org/publications/reports/defaults_texas/ins_intro.cfm.

15 U.S. Dep't of Educ., Office of Student Financial Assistance, Ensuring Loan Repayment: A National Handbook of Best Practices Ch. 3 (2000).

16 Texas Guaranteed Student Loan Corp., White Paper: Crisis Averted or Merely Postponed?: Examining Long-term Cohort Default Rates, Resolving Defaults, and Curing Delinquencies (July 2010), *available at* www.tgslc.org/pdf/crisis_averted.pdf.

17 *Id.* at 17.

18 Texas Guaranteed Student Loan Corp., White Paper: Crisis Averted or Merely Postponed?: Examining Long-term Cohort Default Rates, Resolving Defaults, and Curing Delinquencies (July 2010), *available at* www.tgslc.org/pdf/crisis_averted.pdf.

19 Susan P. Choy & Xiaojie Li, U.S. Dep't of Educ. National Ctr. for Educ. Statistics, Dealing with Debt: 1992–93 Bachelor's Degree Recipients 10 Years Later (June 2006), *available at* http://nces.ed.gov/pubs2006/2006156.pdf. *See also* Erin Dillon, Education Sector, Hidden Details: A Closer Look at Student Loan Default Rates (Oct. 23, 2007).

20 Susan P. Choy & Xiaojie Li, U.S. Dep't of Educ. National Ctr. for Educ. Statistics, Dealing with Debt: 1992–93 Bachelor's Degree Recipients 10 Years Later 24 (June 2006), *available at* http://nces.ed.gov/pubs2006/2006156.pdf.

21 *Id.* at 28.

22 *See* § 1.7.4.2, *supra*.

23 34 C.F.R. § 668.183(b).

24 34 C.F.R. § 668.183(c).

25 34 C.F.R. § 668.200, 202(c).

26 34 C.F.R. § 674.5.

27 U.S. Dep't of Educ., Office of the Inspector Gen., Audit to Determine If Cohort Default Rates Provide Sufficient Information on Defaults in the Title IV Loan Programs, Control No. ED-OIG/A03-C0017 (Dec. 2003); U.S. Gen. Accounting Office, Federal Student Aid: Timely Performance Plans and Reports Would Help Guide and Assess Achievement of Default Management Goals, Report No. GAO-03-348 (Feb. 2003); U.S. Gen. Accounting Office, Student Loans: Default Rates Need to

General Report, for example, cited a number of problems, including that the rates reflected defaults during a two-year cohort period and not the life of the loan, that PLUS loans and certain consolidation loans are excluded, and that the rates are calculated based on the number of borrowers in a cohort and not on the number of loans or the loan amount.[28]

A Department of Education IG 2008 audit highlights the ways in which schools attempt to manipulate these rates. The IG found that Technical Career Institute, based in New York, improperly paid lenders to keep the school's FFEL students out of default. The school made payments to the lenders to pay off the students' loans but then, in many cases, attempted to collect from the students.[29] Given the possible loss of participation in federal aid programs due to default rate sanctions, schools have also started hiring "default management" companies to track down former students and get them into forbearances or other programs that will not impact the school's default rates and will help them avoid sanctions.[30]

The Higher Education Act reauthorization law, known as the Higher Education Opportunity Act (HEOA), included some improvements to the cohort default rate calculation. The HEOA increased the period used to calculate the cohort default rate.[31] Under the new method, the cohort default rate is the percentage of borrowers who default on their FFEL Program loans ("FFELs") or Direct Loan Program loans ("Direct loans") before the end of the second fiscal year (instead of the first fiscal year) following the fiscal year in which the borrowers entered repayment.[32] This method is effective for cohort default rates calculated for fiscal year 2009 and subsequent years. However, the law provided for a transition period, during which sanctions will continue to be imposed based on the prior rates, until rates based on the new method are calculated for three consecutive years.[33] During the transition period, the Department will issue annually two sets of draft and official cohort default rates for fiscal years 2009, 2010, and 2011.[34]

Initial data based on the new three-year cohort default rates show that adding just one year makes a big difference. The three-year rates are 93% higher than the standard two-year rates for for-profit colleges, 63% higher for public two-year institutions and 70% higher for private four-year colleges.[35]

Despite the longer tracking period, there are still serious problems with undercounting of defaults. The rate still counts borrowers with deferments and forbearances among those who are successfully repaying their loans. This means that the number of borrowers in default is divided by a number larger than the total number of borrowers who are actually repaying their loans. As a result, the default rate is understated.[36] Further distorting the statistics, these borrowers are not placed in subsequent cohorts and are thus never included in calculations of a school's default rate even if they default on their loans after the deferment or forbearance period is over. The numbers of borrowers in deferment and forbearance continues to grow. The Chronicle of Higher Education reported in July 2010 that the proportion of borrowers in deferment and forbearances grew from 10% in fiscal year 1996 to 22% in fiscal year 2007.[37]

Both the GAO and the Department of Education's Inspector General found that excluding these borrowers from the denominator of the calculation rate would significantly increase the cohort default rates in all school sectors. Both agencies concluded that these borrowers should be excluded from the cohort default rate calculation. They concluded further that the borrowers should be added to subsequent default cohorts in the year in which their deferments or forbearances end and they have begun repaying their loans.[38]

A July 2010 article in the Chronicle of Higher Education gives some sense of the extent of undercounting due to the way the cohort default rate is calculated. The article notes that the official rates capture "only a sliver of the loans that eventually lapse."[39] The article cites unpublished data show-

---

be Computed More Appropriately, GAO/HEHS-99-135 (July 1999).

28 U.S. Dep't of Educ., Office of the Inspector Gen., Audit to Determine If Cohort Default Rates Provide Sufficient Information on Defaults in the Title IV Loan Programs, Control No. ED-OIG/A03-C0017 (Dec. 2003).

29 U.S. Dep't of Educ. Office of Inspector General, Technical Career Institutes, Inc.'s Administration of the Federal Pell Grant and Federal Family Education Loan Programs, Control No. ED-OIG/A02H0007 (May 19, 2008).

30 See, e.g., Goldie Blumenstyk, Business is Up in Keeping Default Rates Down, Chron. of Higher Educ. (July 11, 2010).

31 Pub. L. No. 110-315, § 436, 122 Stat. 3078 (Aug. 14, 2008); 20 U.S.C. § 1085.

32 34 C.F.R. § 668.202(c).

33 Pub. L. No. 110-315, § 436, 122 Stat. 3078 (Aug. 14, 2008); 20 U.S.C. § 1085. See § 1.7.4.2, supra (sanctions).

34 34 C.F.R. §§ 668.181, 668.200(b).

35 Doug Lederman, Defaults Nearly Double, Inside Higher Ed (Dec. 14, 2009), at www.insidehighered.com/news/2009/12/14/default.

The Department published these trial three-year rates on-line at http://federalstudentaid.ed.gov/datacenter/library/TrialYearCDR.xls.

36 U.S. Dep't of Educ., Office of the Inspector Gen., Audit to Determine If Cohort Default Rates Provide Sufficient Information on Defaults in the Title IV Loan Programs, Control No. ED-OIG/A03-C0017 (Dec. 2003).

37 Kelly Field, Government Vastly Undercounts Defaults, Chron. of Higher Educ. (July 11, 2010).

38 Dep't of Educ., Office of the Inspector Gen., Audit to Determine If Cohort Default Rates Provide Sufficient Information on Defaults in the Title IV Loan Programs, Control No. ED-OIG/A03-C0017 (Dec. 2003); U.S. Gen. Accounting Office, Federal Student Aid: Timely Performance Plans and Reports Would Help Guide and Assess Achievement of Default Management Goals, Report No. GAO-03-348 (Feb. 2003); U.S. Gen. Accounting Office, Student Loans: Default Rates Need to be Computed More Appropriately, Report No. GAO/HEHS-99-135 (July 1999).

39 Kelly Field, Government Vastly Undercounts Defaults, Chron. of Higher Educ. (July 11, 2010).

ing that one in every five government loans entering repayment in 1995 has gone into default.[40] The rate was higher for loans made to students from two-year colleges and higher still, reaching 40%, for those who attended for-profit institutions. For loans made to community college students, the fifteen-year default rate was 31%. However, in general, fewer community colleges students borrow.[41] Proprietary school students tend to have the highest rate of both federal and private loan borrowing.[42]

5.1.4 Federal Student Loan Default Triggers

Borrowers are in default on FFELs or Direct loans if they fail to make required payments for 270 days for loans repayable in monthly installments or 330 days for loans repayable less frequently than monthly.[43] This nine-month period is a relatively long time for borrowers to seek alternatives to default, such as more affordable repayment plans, cancellation, deferment, and/or forbearance.[44] The rules are different for Perkins loans. Perkins loan defaults are defined as the failure of a borrower to make an installment payment when due or to comply with other terms of the promissory note or written repayment agreement.[45]

The Department may also accelerate the loan and consider the borrower in default if the borrower fails to meet other terms of the promissory note and the Department or loan holder finds it reasonable to conclude that the borrower no longer intends to honor the repayment obligation.[46]

5.1.5 Consequences of Default on Federal Loans

The consequences of student loan defaults have grown enormously over time as the government's collection powers have steadily increased. The government has collection powers far beyond those of most unsecured creditors. As discussed in detail in Chapter 8, *infra*, the government can garnish a borrower's wages without a judgment, seize the borrower's tax refund (even an earned income tax credit), seize portions of federal benefits such as Social Security, and deny the borrower eligibility for new education grants or loans. To compound the problem, collectors are allowed to charge fees that create ballooning balances.[47] Even in bankruptcy, most student loans must be paid.[48] Unlike any other type of debt, there is no statute of limitations.[49] The government can pursue borrowers to the grave.

For borrowers in default, education, initially seen as a way out of poverty, instead often leads them into a cycle of endless debt. They find themselves in a trap. Student loan debt from the past keeps them from going back to school and moving into higher-paying jobs. On the other hand, most cannot afford to go back to school and get additional training without some type of financial assistance.

The federal student loan collection process is described in detail in Chapter 7, *infra*, including information about steps collectors must take during delinquency and those that are required once a loan goes into default. Chapter 7 also reviews typical problems with collection, including fair debt collection violations, and permissible collection fees. Chapter 7 also includes information about defenses to collection actions.

The major government collection tools for federal student loans, including tax offsets, garnishment, and benefits offsets are discussed in Chapter 8, *infra*.

5.2 Private Student Loan Defaults

5.2.1 The Problem of Private Student Loan Defaults

Private student loan default rates were relatively low for a number of years. Among other reasons, many companies had liberal forbearance policies that hid the extent of borrower repayment problems.[50] Fitch Ratings stated in a 2007 report that the low charge-off rates in the industry would be unsustainable over the long term. According to Fitch Ratings, lenders should have been making appropriate allowances for loan losses. They noted with concern that one of the largest lenders, Sallie Mae, had instead reduced allowances over time.[51]

Fitch Rating's belated warnings were on target. The private student loan industry began to crash in 2008 as defaults ballooned and overall economic conditions deteriorated. Lenders began reporting huge increases in delinquency and default rates. For example, in October 2008, Sallie Mae reported a loss of $159 million in the most recent quarter,

---

40 *Id.*
41 *See, e.g.*, Project on Student Debt, Issue Brief: Getting with the Program: Community College Students Need Access to Federal Loans (Oct. 2009), *available at* http://projectonstudentdebt.org/files/pub/getting_with_the_program.pdf.
42 *See* § 12.3.3.1, *infra*.
43 34 C.F.R. §§ 682.200 (FFEL definition of default), 685.102(b) (Direct Loan).
44 *See* § 3.1.2, *supra* (pre-default repayment plans); Ch. 4, *supra* (deferments and forbearances); Ch. 9, *infra* (loan cancellations).
45 34 C.F.R. § 674.2.
46 34 C.F.R. §§ 682.200 (FFEL definitions), 685.102 (Direct Loan).

47 *See* § 7.3, *infra*.
48 *See* Ch. 10, *infra*.
49 *See* § 7.5.3.1, *infra*.
50 *See generally* National Consumer Law Center, Too Small to Help: The Plight of Financially Distressed Private Student Loan Borrowers (Apr. 2009), *available at* www.studentloanborrowerassistance.org/blogs/wp-content/www.studentloanborrowerassistance.org/uploads/File/TooSmalltoHelp.pdf.
51 Fitch Ratings, An Education in Student Lending (Feb. 5, 2007).

fueled by the acceleration of delinquent private loans.[52] In 2009, Fitch Ratings stated that, from a net-charge-off perspective, the default rates had been deteriorating for the main private student lenders since 2006.[53]

Moody's Corporation acknowledged in early 2010 that the high default rates for private loan securitizations reflected weak underwriting, referring in this case to the 2006–2007 period.[54] Fitch Ratings stated in 2010 that it expects private student loan trust performance to remain under pressure until the economy shows significant signs of recovery.[55] In July 2010, Sallie Mae acknowledged that the charge-offs for private loans remained high and that the company had raised loan loss provisions for 2010 by $100 million to $1.3 billion, reflecting higher than expected defaults.[56]

Since the credit crisis, many for-profit schools in particular have begun making their own student loans. The charge-off rates for these loans can be even higher than charge-offs for private loans made by banks and finance companies. For example, two publicly owned college chains set aside roughly half their internal lending amount in 2009 as a loss reserve, essentially telling investors they do not expect students to repay more than half of what they borrow.[57]

5.2.2 Default Triggers for Private Loans

Default conditions for private student loans are specified in the loan contracts. In most cases, borrowers will not have the luxury of a nine-month period if they miss payments on a private student loan. Private loans may go into default as soon as one payment is missed.

The loan contract may specify other conditions for default. A promissory note used by Key Bank, for example, listed the following default triggers:

You are in default if you:
- Fail to make monthly payments when due, or
- Die, or
- Break other promises in the Loan Note, or
- Begin a bankruptcy proceeding, or assign assets for the benefit of creditors, or
- Provide any false written statement in applying for any Loan subject to the terms of this Note or at any time during the term of the Loan, or
- Become insolvent, or
- In the lender's judgment, experience a significant lessening of your ability to repay the Loan, or
- Are in default on any Loan you already have with this lender, or any Loan you might have in the future.[58]

5.2.3 Consequences of Private Loan Defaults

Unfortunately for borrowers, most private student lenders have not been willing to cancel or modify loans.[59] Rather than focusing on working with borrowers, lenders have ratcheted up collection. Sallie Mae, for example, has announced steps to resolve higher risk accounts, including a more aggressive use of collection efforts.[60]

Private student loan creditors do not have the same range of powerful collection tools as the government. Generally, they hire third-party debt collectors to pressure borrowers to pay. If unsuccessful, the creditors can sue and attempt to obtain judgments. If this occurs, borrowers have exemption rights under state laws.[61] The main difference between private student loans and other unsecured debts is the heightened bankruptcy dischargeability standards for private loans.[62] Potential claims in private student loan collection and other cases are discussed in Chapter 11, *infra*.

---

52 Paul Basken, *Sallie Mae Reports $159-Million Loss and More Delinquencies by Borrowers*, Chron. of Higher Educ. (Oct. 23, 2008). *See generally* National Consumer Law Center, Too Small to Help: The Plight of Financially Distressed Private Student Loan Borrowers (Apr. 2009), *available at* www.studentloanborrowerassistance.org/blogs/wp-content/www.studentloanborrowerassistance.org/uploads/File/TooSmalltoHelp.pdf.

53 Fitch Ratings, Private Education Loans: Time for a Re-Education 7 (Jan. 28, 2009).

54 *Moody's Outlook for Student Loan Securities: Expect Negative Credit Trends for Private Loans in 2010*, Student Lending Analytics Blog (Jan. 29, 2010), *at* http://studentlendinganalytics.typepad.com/student_lending_analytics/2010/01/moodys-outlook-for-student-loan-securities-expect-negative-credit-trends-for-private-loans-in-2010.html.

55 Fitch Ratings, The Student Loan Report Card (July 2010).

56 *What Ails Sallie Mae*, Student Lending Analytics Blog (July 21, 2010), *at* http://studentlendinganalytics.typepad.com/student_lending_analytics/2010/07/what-ails-sallie-mae.html.

57 Justin Pope, *For Profit Colleges' Increased Lending Prompts Concerns*, Associated Press (Aug. 15, 2009). *See* § 11.1.3, *infra*.

58 National Consumer Law Center, Paying the Price: The High Cost of Private Student Loans and the Dangers for Student Borrowers (Mar. 2008), *available at* www.studentloanborrowerassistance.org/blogs/wp-content/www.studentloanborrowerassistance.org/uploads/File/Report_PrivateLoans.pdf.

59 *See generally* National Consumer Law Center, Too Small to Help: The Plight of Financially Distressed Private Student Loan Borrowers (Apr. 2009), *available at* www.studentloanborrowerassistance.org/blogs/wp-content/www.studentloanborrowerassistance.org/uploads/File/TooSmalltoHelp.pdf.

60 Paul Basken, *Sallie Mae Reports $159-Million Loss and More Delinquencies by Borrowers*, Chron. of Higher Educ. (Oct. 23, 2008). *See* § 11.7, *infra*.

61 For more information about exemption laws, see National Consumer Law Center, Collection Actions Ch. 12 (2008 and Supp.).

62 *See* Ch. 10, *infra*.

Chapter 6 Repayment Strategies for Getting Out of Default

6.1 Introduction

Federal student loan borrowers in default not only face severe collection consequences but are also barred from obtaining new federal aid to go back to school. The primary goal for most of these borrowers is to get out of default and, in some cases, go back to school. Others simply want to stop the government collection onslaught. Whatever the reasons, there are numerous options for borrowers to get out of default by making payments on their loans. In many cases, the payments will be very low and affordable.

This chapter reviews the primary repayment options for borrowers in default. This chapter also discusses the discretionary authority that the Department of Education ("the Department") has to compromise or even write off all or part of a loan. Pre-default repayment options are covered in Chapter 3, *supra*.

Statutory discharges and bankruptcy will also renew eligibility for federal aid and allow borrowers to get out of default through complete cancellation of loans. These options should be considered before attempting to set up payment plans. Discharge rights are discussed in Chapter 9, *infra*. Victims of proprietary school fraud will often qualify for discharges. State tuition recovery funds, discussed in Chapter 12, *infra*, should also be considered when available. Bankruptcy, as discussed in Chapter 10, *infra*, is a more remote possibility due to restrictions on when student loans can be discharged in bankruptcy. However, many borrowers will be able to meet the undue hardship test required to discharge student loans in bankruptcy.

The best option for those who cannot discharge their loans is often to get out of default through repayment. The two primary ways to do this are through consolidation and rehabilitation. Both are discussed in detail in this chapter. Consolidation is also available for current borrowers, as discussed in Chapters 1 and 2, *supra*.

6.2 Consolidation As a Way Out of Default

6.2.1 General

Borrowers can consolidate their defaulted student loans into a new Direct consolidation loan with a repayment plan tied to their income. After obtaining a consolidation loan, the borrower gets a fresh start with a new loan. After consolidation, borrowers are eligible for new federal student loans, grants, and even deferments. They will no longer be listed as currently in default on their credit records and no longer subject to tax intercepts, garnishments, or other collection efforts.

As of July 1, 2010, Direct consolidation loans are the only type of federal consolidation loans available. These Direct consolidation loans may include up to three separate components representing subsidized, unsubsidized, and PLUS loans.

All federal loan borrowers may obtain Direct consolidation loans. However, they must have at least one Federal Family Education Loan (FFEL) Program loan or Direct Loan Program loan ("Direct loan") to qualify for consolidation.[1]

Previously, if the borrower was in default on an FFEL and wanted to consolidate with a Direct loan, the borrower had to show that he or she was unable to obtain FFEL consolidation or an FFEL consolidation loan with acceptable income-sensitive repayment terms.[2] These rules still apply on paper but not in practice, since there no longer are FFEL Program loans ("FFELs") as of July 1, 2010.

There are drawbacks and limits to consolidation as a way out of default, as discussed throughout this section. Among other considerations, borrowers should understand that the balance will increase after consolidation due to the addition of collection fees. In addition, not all loans are eligible for consolidation.[3] One of the most important limits is that defaulted Direct consolidation loans may not be re-consolidated. In effect, this means that borrowers have only one shot at consolidating as a way out of default. Borrowers

---

1 34 C.F.R. § 685.220(d).
2 34 C.F.R. § 685.220(d)(1)(i)(B).
3 *See* § 6.2.4, *infra*.

6.2.2 Payments Are Not Required to Get Out of Default Through Consolidation

To obtain a Direct consolidation loan, borrowers in default *either* have to make three consecutive reasonable and affordable payments based on their total financial circumstances *or* agree to select an income-contingent repayment plan (ICRP) or income-based repayment (IBR) plan and consent to the IRS disclosing to the Department certain tax return information for the purposes of calculating a monthly repayment amount.[4] If they choose to make three payments, the payments must be reasonable and affordable, on-time and voluntary. "On-time" means a payment received within fifteen days of the scheduled due date.[5] The Department has acknowledged that this is shorter than the twenty days allowed in the rehabilitation program.[6]

The three payments need not be consecutive if the borrower is an "affected individual," defined to include those who are serving on active duty during a war or other military operation or national emergency, are performing qualifying National Guard duty during a war or other military operation or national emergency, reside or are employed in an area that is declared a disaster area by any federal, state, or local official in connection with a national emergency, or suffered economic hardship as a direct result of a war or other military operation or national emergency, as determined by the Secretary of the Department of Education ("the Secretary").[7]

Borrowers may make the three reasonable and affordable payments *or* select ICR or IBR. The Department generally refers to the latter option as "forced ICR/IBR." The regulations are clear that these are alternative paths for borrowers in default. Unfortunately, however, the Department and collectors often claim inaccurately that all borrowers must make preliminary payments (sometimes three, sometimes six) in order to consolidate out of default.

This misinformation derives from the Department's incentive system, which disproportionately rewards collectors if borrowers make payments prior to consolidation. In a 2009 manual for private collection agencies ("2009 PCA manual"), the Department explained that collectors must obtain six preliminary payments prior to processing a consolidation loan for borrowers in default.[8] This is more than the three payments required in the regulations for those who choose to make preliminary payments. The Department acknowledges that in many cases the requirements discussed in the manual are more restrictive than those described in the regulations.[9]

The requirements in the manual are not regulatory mandates, according to the Department, but instead are heightened requirements that collectors must meet in order to earn commissions or administrative resolution fees.[10] Many collection agencies not surprisingly pressure borrowers into the choices that are most profitable for the agencies but not necessarily optimal for borrowers. In addition, some collectors fail to inform borrowers of the range of options. Furthermore, if borrowers apply directly to the Direct Loan Program for consolidation and do not use the collection agency as a middleperson, the agency will generally not earn any fee.[11]

The 2009 PCA manual states further that payments equal to at least 1% of the final consolidation payoff balances are automatically considered reasonable and affordable.[12] This is not in the regulations but is apparently a Department policy created to incentivize agencies to get as much as possible from borrowers. Collectors must justify accepting payments less than the 1% amount with a statement of financial status form completed by the borrower.[13]

The 2009 PCA manual lists procedures that collectors must follow in processing forced ICR/IBR consolidations.[14] If the procedures are followed, the collectors are paid administrative resolution fees only for these forced consolidations.[15] The Department reserves the right to withhold fees if the borrower's ICR or IBR payments end up exceeding the payment amount approved by the collection agency by more than $25 or if the borrower fails to fill out the required consolidation forms.[16] Once again, these provisions are more than what is required under the regulations. Pursuant to the regulations, borrowers in default can choose the forced ICR/IBR option regardless of the amount of the final ICR or IBR payment.[17]

---

4 34 C.F.R. § 685.220(d)(1)(ii)(C), (D).

5 34 C.F.R. § 682.200 (definition of satisfactory repayment arrangement).

6 71 Fed. Reg. 64378 (Nov. 1, 2006).

7 68 Fed. Reg. 69312 (Dec. 12, 2003).
   This waiver was extended through September 30, 2012. 72 Fed. Reg. 72947 (Dec. 26, 2007).

8 U.S. Dep't of Educ., PCA Procedures Manual: 2009 ED Collections Contract 117 (Sept. 2009).
   The Department had posted the manual on-line in spring 2010 but took it off-line after a month or so. The manual is available on the companion website and, as of summer 2010, on the website for the Center for Public Integrity. *See* Ariel Wittenberg, Center for Pub. Integrity, Education Department Pulls Student Debt Collectors Guide Off Web Site (June 16, 2010).

9 U.S. Dep't of Educ., PCA Procedures Manual: 2009 ED Collections Contract 116 (Sept. 2009).

10 *Id.*

11 *Id.*

12 *Id.* at 117.

13 *Id.*

14 *Id.* at 118–120.

15 *Id.* at 118.

16 *Id.* at 119.

17 34 C.F.R. § 685.220(d)(ii)(D).

There are numerous problems with the Department's policies. The Department admits that the requirements in the manual may go beyond the regulations. Although they state in the manual that agencies may not tell a borrower that the borrower is ineligible for consolidation unless he or she does not meet the regulatory requirements, they specifically allow agencies to refuse to assist borrowers with consolidation or to choose not to mention consolidation as a resolution option.[18]

Prior to certifying an account for consolidation, agencies are required to counsel borrowers and send a Department-approved letter. This letter has its own set of problems.[19] For example, the letter advises borrowers to wait to consolidate if they think they may qualify for a disability discharge. It is unclear why the Department would give this advice since borrowers with consolidation loans are eligible for disability discharges.[20] Furthermore, the letter states that bankruptcy law may make it more difficult to obtain a discharge of the consolidated loan than of current debts. Again, it is unclear why this would be the case.[21]

6.2.3 Selecting IBR

The Direct Loan Program repayment plan selection form for consolidation includes both the ICR and IBR plans.[22] However, as of summer 2010, the Department does not have a process in place to ensure that all borrowers consolidating out of default can actually get IBR. According to the Department, borrowers in default who make the preliminary three payments may immediately select IBR, but the Department has not yet set up a system to allow borrowers in the "forced ICR/IBR" situation to select IBR. The Department has acknowledged that these borrowers have the right to select IBR, but that they have not updated their systems to process "forced IBR applications.[23]

This is a huge problem that will hopefully be resolved soon. In the interim, borrowers may select ICR. This is most effective for borrowers with very low incomes who will have zero payments under either ICR or IBR. These borrowers will not need to switch to IBR if they have zero payments under ICR. However, most borrowers will want to be in IBR plans because their payments will be lower under this plan. Department staff has told NCLC that, until they fix this problem, borrowers who want IBR should go ahead and select IBR on the repayment plan selection form. They should fill out the IBR section only, not both the ICR and IBR sections. However, until the problem is resolved, these borrowers will be placed in the ICR, not IBR, plan. In general, borrowers choosing ICR must stay in that plan unless they make three reasonable and affordable payments in each of the prior three months and then request a change of repayment plan.[24] This is what will happen for borrowers who select ICR from the outset. However, borrowers who select IBR, but are placed in ICR only because of the Department's process issues, should not have to make three payments in order to switch to IBR.

6.2.4 Eligible Loans

Not all borrowers in default will be able to use the consolidation option to get out of default. First, there are some limits on which loans can be consolidated. Under the Direct consolidation loan program, borrowers can consolidate subsidized and unsubsidized loans received under the Direct Stafford loans program, supplemental loans for students (SLSs), federally insured student loans (FISLs), PLUS loans, Direct loans, Perkins Loan Program loans ("Perkins loans"), Health Education Assistance loans (HEALs), and just about any other type of federal student loan.[25] Loans that are not eligible for consolidation include state or private loans that are not federally guaranteed; law, medical, and graduate access loans; and graduate extension loans.

Although all of these different loans may be consolidated, the borrower must have at least one outstanding FFEL or Direct loan to obtain a Direct consolidation loan.[26] This means, for example, that a Perkins loan on its own cannot be consolidated into a Direct loan.

A second limit is that borrowers in default on a Direct consolidation loan are not eligible to reconsolidate. These borrowers must rehabilitate to get out of default through repayment.[27] They have only one chance at rehabilitation as well, so borrowers should be counseled that consolidation and rehabilitation are not unlimited options.[28] It is possible that a borrower will rehabilitate a loan and then consolidate it. In that case, the consolidation loan is a new loan, so it would be possible for the borrower to rehabilitate that loan if it went into default.[29]

---

18 U.S. Dep't of Educ., PCA Procedures Manual: 2009 ED Collections Contract 120 (Sept. 2009).
19 Id. at 43.
20 See § 9.7.2, infra.
21 See § Ch 10, infra (discharging student loans in bankruptcy).
22 The form is reprinted at Appendix D, infra. It is also available on the companion website and at www.ed.gov, the Department of Education's website.
23 The regulations clearly state that borrowers in default may consolidate as long as they agree to repay the consolidation loan under an ICR or IBR plan. 34 C.F.R. § 685.220(d)(1)(ii)(D).
24 34 C.F.R. § 685.220(h).
   This regulation should be updated because it refers only to the ICR option for borrowers consolidating out of default.
25 34 C.F.R. § 685.220(b).
26 34 C.F.R. § 685.220(d).
27 The Department has stated that the regulations do not prohibit reconsolidation in all circumstances, specifically mentioning the possibility of rehabilitating a defaulted consolidation loan. 71 Fed. Reg. 64378 (Nov. 1, 2006).
28 See § 6.3.6, infra.
29 See 74 Fed. Reg. 55972 (Oct. 29, 2009).

Borrowers with defaulted FFEL consolidation loans may re-consolidate under certain circumstances.[30] Such borrowers may consolidate with Direct loans if their loans are in default or have been submitted to guaranty agencies for default aversion and they want to consolidate into Direct loans for the purpose of obtaining an ICR or IBR plan.[31]

Furthermore, loans that have been reduced to judgment may be consolidated with Direct loans only if the judgment has been vacated.[32] If the borrower is facing wage garnishment, he or she may consolidate only if the garnishment order is lifted.[33] According to the Department, borrowers with joint consolidation loans are not allowed to re-consolidate.[34]

Although allowed to consolidate, some borrowers may have other reasons to leave certain loans out of a new consolidation loan. Borrowers who consolidate Perkins loans, for example, lose the unique Perkins cancellation rights if they consolidate with Direct loans.[35] Parent PLUS loan borrowers should also be careful. Since they are not eligible for IBR, having one parent PLUS loan as part of a new consolidation loan will mean that the borrower cannot repay that new loan using IBR.[36]

6.2.5 How to Apply for a Direct Consolidation Loan

There is no charge to obtain a Direct consolidation loan. Borrowers may apply by regular mail, on-line, or by phone under certain circumstances. Borrowers may request an application by calling the current toll-free number, 1-800-557-7392 or, for TDD, 1-800-557-7395. Borrowers can also apply for Direct consolidation loans on-line.[37] The Department claims that applications are processed more quickly if borrowers apply on-line.

It is important for Direct consolidation loan applicants to include accurate information about all loans to be consolidated.[38] If the loan balances on the borrower's application are incorrect, the Department notifies the borrower of the correct amount.

Once the information about the borrower's loans is compiled, the next step is to complete the application. Among other information, the application calls for two references. These individuals will not be financially obligated on the loan and do not have to possess good credit records. The references are used only if the Department cannot locate the borrower.

All "forced IBR/ICR" defaulters must select an ICR or IBR plan. Others may choose these plans as well. Borrowers requesting ICRP or IBR plans must complete the *Repayment Plan Selection* and *ICR Plan and IBR Plan Consent to Disclosure of Tax Information* forms that accompany the application and promissory note.[39]

In some cases, borrowers will be required to fill out an *Alternative Documentation of Income* form.[40] This is required if the borrower is repaying Direct loans under the ICRP or IBR plan and:

- Is in his or her first year of repayment;
- Is in his or her second year of repayment and has been notified that alternative documentation of income is required; or
- Has been notified that the Internal Revenue Service is unable to provide the Department with adjusted gross income (AGI) information for the borrower or the borrower's spouse.

A borrower may also, at the borrower's discretion, choose to use the alternative documentation form if the borrower chooses ICR and his AGI or his spouse's AGI, as reported on the most recently filed federal tax return, does not reasonably reflect current income and/or ability to repay in circumstances such as loss or change of employment. A borrower selecting IBR may also use this form if her AGI (and her spouse's AGI if they file taxes jointly) does not reasonably reflect their current income. It is a good idea for borrowers receiving public assistance to use the alternative documentation of income form and include proof of the assistance income and amount.

Within about two months (sometimes less) of the borrower sending in all the application papers or applying on-line and returning the signed documents, the borrower will receive information from the Department. The first communication is a Direct consolidation loan program summary sheet that lists the loans eligible for consolidation and provides estimates of repayment options. In many cases, the repayment information may be incomplete, especially with respect to IBR or ICR payments. Borrowers will also receive confirmation that the prior loan holder was paid off. The letter with the summary sheet advises the borrower that

---

30 34 C.F.R. § 685.220(d)(1)(i)(B)(4).
31 *Id.*
32 34 C.F.R. § 685.220(d)(1)(ii)(E).
33 34 C.F.R. § 685.220(d)(1)(ii)(F).
   The judgment and wage garnishment eligibility requirements for both FFEL and Direct consolidation loans must be met at the time the loans are made rather than at the time of the borrower's application. *See* 71 Fed. Reg. 64378 (Nov. 1, 2006).
34 *See, e.g.,* U.S. Dep't of Educ., Dear Colleague Letter FP-09-03 (Apr. 3, 2009) (stating that a joint consolidation loan may not be included in a subsequent consolidation loan under any circumstances).
35 *See* § 9.12, *infra* (Perkins cancellations).
36 34 C.F.R. § 685.221 (providing that parent PLUS loans and consolidation loans that repaid a parent PLUS loan cannot be repaid using IBR). *See* § 3.1.3.2.1, *supra*.
37 *See* https://loanconsolidation.ed.gov/AppEntry/apply-online/appindex.jsp.
38 To find out more about how to get a list of all federal loans from the National Student Loan Data System, see § 1.9, *supra*.
39 These forms are included in Appendix D, *infra*, and on the companion website to this manual.
40 A copy of this form is reprinted at Appendix D, *infra*, and included on the companion website to this manual.

the Department will consolidate the loan within ten days of the date of the letter if they do not hear otherwise from the borrower. The letter also confirms the borrower's repayment plan selection.

The next communication is usually a billing statement. This statement is often confusing for borrowers selecting ICR or IBR. The statement will often correctly state that the borrower has selected one of these plans but will then include a monthly payment amount that is higher than the ICR or IBR amount. This is generally because it takes the Department some time to calculate the ICR or IBR payment. Borrowers that face this situation should consider requesting a forbearance or deferment.[41]

Another possible roadblock is if the borrower is consolidating FFELs and the FFEL lender refuses or is slow to release the loan. The Office of the Inspector General documented this problem in 2005, finding that many FFEL lenders were either intentionally or unintentionally preventing borrowers from consolidating with Direct loans or unduly delaying the process.[42]

According to the Department, a loan holder or servicer that fails to comply with the requirement to complete and return a loan verification certificate (LVC) within ten business days of its receipt could be subject to fines or other sanctions.[43] The Department has provided a list of approved "excuses" that lenders may use in limited circumstances. In some cases, the lender must still complete the LVC but may need more time. For example, the lender may not be able to comply with the ten-day period because of a technical problem. In that situation, the lender must provide a written explanation within the ten-day time frame of the problem and comply with the request as soon as the problem is resolved.[44]

In other cases, there may be a permissible reason why the lender does not have to complete the LVC. For example, if a judgment has been entered against the borrower on a loan he or she wants to consolidate or if the borrower is subject to collection by wage garnishment, the lender or loan holder must provide a written explanation as to why it cannot complete and return the LVC.[45] Borrowers should contact Direct Loan Program servicing and their former FFEL lender if the application is taking a long time.

When a borrower in default consolidates a loan, presently up to 18.5% is added to the amount due for collection fees.[46]

The Department stated in 2009 that it would charge collection fees totaling 11.1% of the current outstanding principal and interest.[47] Lenders automatically add the fees to the consolidation. It is theoretically possible to request a waiver of collection fees before consolidation, but a waiver is very unlikely to occur in practice. After the consolidation, the fees become part of the principal amount due on the new loan.

6.3 Loan Rehabilitation

6.3.1 General

A borrower can renew eligibility for new loans and grants and cure the loan default by "rehabilitating" the defaulted loan.

Rehabilitation has become the favored tool among collectors. In fiscal year 2009, the trend of increasing collections from rehabilitations and declining collections from consolidation continued. Rehabilitations comprised about 51% of collections in fiscal year 2009 compared to about 11% for consolidation.[48] This is attributable at least in part to the standards established in 2005 to limit guaranty agency compensation when an "excessive" proportion of collections are through consolidation.[49] Agencies will often claim that this is a limit to how many consolidations they can process. On the contrary, it is not a limit, but agencies are not compensated if the proceeds of collections of defaulted loans exceed 45% of total collections in that year.[50]

As will be discussed in this section, rehabilitation is problematic for numerous reasons. Compared to consolidation, there is more discretion for loan holders and collectors to pressure borrowers to make payments beyond what they can afford. In addition, collectors routinely violate the Higher Education Act rehabilitation requirements. Although these violations could be grounds for FDCPA cases in many circumstances, as discussed in chapter 7, *infra*, an FDCPA

---

41 Forbearances are specifically allowed for up to sixty days while the Department is processing the borrower's request for a consolidation loan. 34 C.F.R. §§ 682.211(f)(11) (FFEL), 685.205(b)(9) (Direct Loan).
42 U.S. Dep't of Educ., Office of the Inspector Gen., Final Audit Report ED-OIG/A07-D0027 (Feb. 10, 2005).
43 U.S. Dep't of Educ., Update on Consolidation Loan Issues, Attachment C, Dear Colleague Letter GEN-06-20 (Dec. 1, 2006).
44 *Id.*
45 *Id.*
46 20 U.S.C. § 1078(c)(6)(B); 34 C.F.R. § 685.220(f)(iii) (Direct

Loan) (using amount in 34 C.F.R. § 682.401(b)(27) (FFEL)).
47 U.S. Dep't of Educ., PCA Procedures Manual: 2009 ED Collections Contract, 43 (Sept. 2009).43.
48 U.S. Dep't of the Treasury, U.S. Government Receivables and Debt Collection Activities of Federal Agencies: Fiscal Year 2009 Report to the Congress 14 (Mar. 2010), *available at* http://fmsq.treas.gov/news/reports/debt09.pdf.

This data includes collections on the Department of Education's defaulted portfolio, including FFELs assigned to the Department. The percentage of collections attributable to rehabilitations increased from fiscal year 2008, but the percentage of consolidations also increased. The Treasury Department attributed this increase in consolidations to the problems with the sale of rehabilitated loans. *See* § 6.3.5, *infra*.

Previously, there was a steady decline in the percentage of collections from consolidation.

49 20 U.S.C. § 1078(c)(6)(B), (C).
50 *Id.*

§ 6.3.2 Student Loan Law

case does not resolve the underlying loan situation, nor does it ensure that the borrower can use rehabilitation as a way out of default.

6.3.2 Rehabilitation Payment Requirements

Loan rehabilitation for FFELs and Direct loans may be requested after the borrower has made nine payments within twenty days of the due date during a period of ten consecutive months.[51] The rules are slightly different for Perkins loans.[52]

The Department has acknowledged that the twenty-day period is longer than the fifteen days allowed in order to regain eligibility for federal aid through reasonable and affordable payments.[53] The Department explained this discrepancy, noting that the standard for on-time payments for purposes of regaining eligibility for federal financial aid should be stricter than the standard for rehabilitation.[54]

To assist borrowers serving in the military, the Department has waived the consecutive payment requirement for "affected individuals," defined to include those who are serving on active duty during a war or other military operation or national emergency; are performing qualifying National Guard duty during a war or other military operation or national emergency; reside or are employed in an area that is declared a disaster area by any federal, state, or local official in connection with a national emergency; or suffered economic hardship as a direct result of a war or other military operation or national emergency, as determined by the Secretary.[55] Loan holders should not treat any payment missed during the time that a borrower is an affected individual, or a payment missed during the three-month transition period, as an interruption in the number of consecutive monthly on-time payments required for loan rehabilitation.[56]

Borrowers are required to make on-time payments nine times within a ten-month period. This means that they may still qualify for rehabilitation if they miss one payment. In response to questions from contractors, the Department has stated that a borrower may, for example, make eight consecutive payments on time, miss a ninth, but still qualify by making an on-time payment for the next (tenth consecutive) month.[57] The Department has also stated that borrowers must make nine *separate* payments. If two payments post on the same date, they must be separate payments. This means that a borrower must submit two separate checks, or two separate credit card transactions must be processed.[58] This situation is most likely to arise if a borrower makes a payment after the due date in one month, but still within the twenty-day window, and then makes the next month's payment on or around the due date. In addition to the rehabilitation application form, borrowers will generally be required to provide financial information to support reasonable and affordable payment requests.[59]

6.3.3 Formalizing the Rehabilitation Agreement

The FFEL regulations require agencies to provide the borrower with a written statement confirming the reasonable and affordable payment amount and explaining any other terms and conditions.[60] The statement must inform borrowers of the effects of having their loans rehabilitated and the collection costs that will be added.[61] The Department has issued a standard rehabilitation agreement form for its contractors to use.[62]

Despite this regulatory requirement, some agencies refuse to provide a written agreement. In addition, they may set up payment plans that are never formalized as rehabilitation agreements. Borrowers in these circumstances may end up paying for years without getting out of default. Agencies may use as an excuse the Department's position that borrowers must request or in some fashion initiate rehabilitation.[63]

Collection does not necessarily cease during the rehabilitation period. The Department has explained in response to questions from NCLC and other advocates that collection will stop only if the rehabilitation agreement specifically provides for a cessation. Otherwise, borrowers will continue to face the usual range of collection tactics, including tax offset, even though they have made a repayment commitment and are in the process of rehabilitating their loans. This seems particularly counterproductive since borrowers are likely to quickly get discouraged from making payments if they continue to face collection efforts.

---

51 See 34 C.F.R. §§ 682.405(a)(2) (FFEL), 685.211(f) (Direct Loan).
52 See § 6.3.7, *infra*.
53 71 Fed. Reg. 64378 (Nov. 1, 2006).
54 *Id.*
55 68 Fed. Reg. 69312 (Dec. 12, 2003).
    This waiver was extended through September 30, 2012. 72 Fed. Reg. 72947 (Dec. 26, 2007).
56 *Id.*
57 See U.S. Dep't of Educ., HERA Rehab Changes (June 28, 2006).

58 See U.S. Dep't of Educ., Answers to HERA Rehab Questions (Apr. 27, 2006).
59 See § 6.3.4, *infra*.
60 34 C.F.R. § 682.405(b)(1)(vi).
61 *Id.*
62 See U.S. Dep't of Educ., PCA Procedures Manual: 2009 ED Collections Contract 42 (Sept. 2009).
    The form is also reprinted at Appendix D, *infra*, and on the companion website to this manual.
63 71 Fed. Reg. 64378 (Nov. 1, 2006) (referring to the need to clarify when the payment period begins).

6.3.4 Determining the Reasonable and Affordable Payment Amount

The HEA states that neither guaranty agencies nor the Secretary shall demand from a borrower as monthly payment amounts more than what is reasonable and affordable based on the borrower's total financial circumstances.[64] The regulations for both FFEL and Direct loans affirm that borrowers must only pay what is reasonable and affordable.[65] The FFEL regulations go even further by prohibiting the imposition of a minimum payment. Documentation is required if the payment is below $50, but these payments are clearly allowed if that is what is reasonable and affordable for a particular borrower.[66] Regulations effective on July 1, 2010, provide that the guaranty agency *and* its agents must comply with the requirements of the rehabilitation program when determining a borrower's reasonable and affordable repayment amount.[67]

The regulations provide that the determination of reasonable and affordable must include a consideration of the borrower's and borrower's spouse's disposable income and reasonable and necessary expenses including, but not limited to, housing, utilities, food, medical costs, work-related expenses, dependent care costs, and other student assistance repayment.[68] The amount must be based on the documentation provided by the borrower or other sources, including evidence of current income, current expenses, and a statement of unpaid balances on other student loans.[69] Most agencies will require borrowers to fill out a financial status form.[70]

Despite the clarity in the law, borrowers are routinely told that they must make payments beyond what they can afford. The right to a reasonable and affordable payment is often denied. Some Department officials claim that the law is ambiguous because it means "affordable" to the borrower but "reasonable" to the government. This argument is contrary to the statutory authority stating that the payment must be reasonable and affordable based on the borrower's total financial circumstances.

This problem derives in part from a system established by the Department which provides compensation to collectors for setting up rehabilitation plans only if the plans require borrowers to make certain minimum payments. In addition, the Department states in the 2009 PCA manual that the payments must be reasonable and affordable based on the *amount owed* and on the borrower's total financial circumstances.[71] The "amount owed" criteria is not in the regulations.

The Department's system sets up payments that they will consider to be presumptively reasonable and affordable. These amounts are based on a certain percentage of the loan balance. According to the 2009 PCA manual, if the balance to be rehabilitated is less than $7500, the "minimum payment" (or the automatically qualifying reasonable and affordable payment) percentage is 1.29%.[72] The following percentages apply for higher balances:[73]

Balance ($)	Minimum %
7,500 to 9,999.99	1.14
10,000 to 19,999.99	1.00
20,000 to 39,999.99	0.87
40,000 and up	0.76

The Department has also set out minimum payment percentages in order for private collection agencies to earn a commission on Direct loan rehabilitations.[74] These are:

Balance ($)	Minimum %
Up to 7,499	1.29
7,500 to 9,999.99	1.14
10,000 to 19,999.99	1.00
20,000 to 39,999.99	0.87
40,000 and up	0.76

In its requirements for collection agencies, the Department states that payments below these "minimum payments" must be documented with financial status information. Furthermore, if the agency approves monthly payments that are less than the minimum percentages, the agency will be paid an administrative fee rather than a commission.[75]

To compound the problem, the Department terms these lower payment amounts "balance sensitive rehabilitations" (BSR) and states that, in general, these borrowers must consolidate their loans immediately after rehabilitation in order to take advantage of the longer-term repayment plans that are available on FFEL consolidation loans.[76] This is wrong because there are no more FFEL consolidation loans.

The Department reasons that it is because the borrowers agree to consolidation that they can qualify for rehabilitation with smaller monthly payments.[77] In fact, according to the regulations, borrowers must pay only what is reasonable and affordable based on their total financial circumstances with no minimum amount. Once they rehabilitate, they can select an income-based repayment plan. They do not have to consolidate in order to get a longer-term repayment plan.

---

64 20 U.S.C. § 1078-6(a)(1)(B).
65 34 C.F.R. §§ 682.405(b) (FFEL), 685.211(f)(1) (Direct Loan).
66 34 C.F.R. § 682.405(b)(1)(iii)(B).
67 34 C.F.R. § 682.405(b)(1)(iii).
68 34 C.F.R. § 682.405(b)(iii)(A).
69 34 C.F.R. § 682.405(b)(iii)(C).
70 A copy of the most commonly used form can be found at Appendix D, *infra*, and on the companion website.
71 U.S. Dep't of Educ., PCA Procedures Manual: 2009 ED Collections Contract 103 (Sept. 2009).
72 *Id.* at 112.
73 *Id.*
74 *Id.* at 94.
75 *Id.* at 104.
76 *Id.* at 105. The Department states a minimum payoff balance for a BSR of $7500.
77 *Id.*

Collectors often pressure buyers to pay more during rehabilitation, claiming that their payments will increase after the process is completed. This advice is inaccurate, most likely a relic of the pre-IBR era. In fact, borrowers coming out of default should be able to select any available payment plan, including IBR. In those cases, their IBR payments could be even lower than what they were paying under rehabilitation. This is most likely to occur if their IBR payment is zero dollars but the rehabilitation payment is a nominal amount. To date, agencies have refused to accept zero dollars as a payment during the rehabilitation period, claiming that zero dollars is not in fact a "payment."

An eligible lender purchasing a rehabilitated loan must establish a repayment schedule which meets the same requirements that are applicable to other FFELs of the same loan type as the rehabilitated loan and must permit the borrower to choose any statutorily available repayment plan for that loan type.[78] The lender must treat the first payment on the nine-payment schedule as the first payment under the applicable maximum repayment term.[79]

Collection agencies may also have their own incentive system for employees. A 2007 wage and hour case describes these compensation systems. In the case, the collection agency awarded front-end goals or bonuses to collectors that were earned when collectors met quotas for the amount of debt and number of debtors they were was able to convince to commit to a particular type of repayment program, including rehabilitation.[80] There was a second category of back-end bonuses that were awarded after a certain number of payments on new rehabilitations or consolidations were made by the debtor or funded by the Department of Education.[81]

These systems conflict with the statutory and regulatory provisions that give borrowers the right to make reasonable and affordable repayments. The FFEL collectors justify the minimum payment requirement by pointing to the statutory provision that requires guaranty agencies not only to establish rehabilitation programs with reasonable and affordable payments but also, if practicable, to sell the loans to eligible lenders.[82] This same section also states explicitly that neither the guaranty agency nor the Secretary shall demand from a borrower as monthly payments more than what is reasonable and affordable based on the borrower's total financial circumstances.[83] The FFEL collectors claim that lenders will only purchase the rehabilitated loans if the balance is paid down sufficiently. They may also claim that negative amortization is prohibited. However, there is no explicit ban on negative amortization in the rehabilitation regulations. Furthermore, it is not clear that buyers choose loans based on the amount of monthly payments.[84]

6.3.5 Loan Sale

For FFELs, after the borrower makes the required timely monthly payments under the new plan and requests rehabilitation, the guarantor or the Department of Education must sell the loan to an eligible lender if practicable.[85] The Department takes the position that FFEL lenders must sell the loans in order to complete the rehabilitation. This argument is ripe for legal challenge for a number of reasons. Most importantly, the FFEL statute provides that the loans must be sold if practicable. It does not say that borrowers should be denied rehabilitation if a sale is not practicable.[86] The FFEL regulations are more explicit, requiring a sale as a condition of rehabilitation.[87]

Even if a sale is required, the Department should be challenged on whether barriers truly exist to resale of loans when borrowers are making very low reasonable and affordable payments. The argument is even weaker in the Direct loans context since the Department does not resell rehabilitated Direct loans. This problem should be less relevant going forward since all new loans as of July 1, 2010, are Direct loans. However, there are many FFELs that will be in the pipeline for a long time that will be serviced and collected by FFEL loan holders based on FFEL regulations.

During the recession, lenders have had problems selling rehabilitated loans. Many borrowers who had completed their rehabilitation payments were stuck in limbo because of the lack of buyers. Despite this problem, the Department insisted that resale was required in order to complete rehabilitation. Among other actions, Department contractors were instructed to send a letter to borrowers who had pending-rehabilitation status. The letter stated:

> Due to current conditions in the student loan financial market, the rehabilitation of defaulted Federal Family Education Loans (FFEL), which are owned by the Department of Education will be delayed for an undetermined length of time. The U.S. Department of Education is working toward a solution that will allow affected borrowers to earn all the benefits of rehabilitation. At this point the Department does not know how quickly this new solution will be in place, so in order to remain eligible for the benefits of rehabilitation, borrowers must continue to make their monthly payments each month until this new solution is in place.[88]

---

78 34 C.F.R. 682.405(b)(4).
79 Id.
80 Rumler v. General Revenue Corp., 2007 WL 1266747 (S.D. Ind. May 1, 2007).
81 Id.
82 20 U.S.C. § 1078-6(a)(1).
83 Id.
84 See § 6.3.5, infra.
85 20 U.S.C. § 1078-6(a)(1)(A)(ii); 34 C.F.R. § 682.405(a)(1), (2)(ii).
86 20 U.S.C. § 1078-6(a)(1)(A)(i).
87 34 C.F.R. § 682.405(a)(2)(ii).
88 Dep't of Educ. Fin. Student Assistance, Language for "New" Interruption of FFEL Rehab Letter (Dec. 18, 2008).

During the economic crisis, a few agencies were able to continue rehabilitating loans without interruption. Others agreed to ease the burden for borrowers in various ways, including ceasing most collection efforts as long as borrowers continued to make their rehabilitation payments. For example, the National Council of Higher Education Loan Program (NCHELP) announced in March 2009 that borrowers making the required rehabilitation payments would no longer have their state tax rebates offset.[89] A few state governments provided assistance. For example, Illinois passed a bill that allowed the state guaranty agency to designate certain bonds as guaranteed by the state. This freed up funds and allowed the guaranty agency to rehabilitate additional loans.[90]

The market improved in 2009 and, according to reports, most agencies have been able to find buyers, although the buyers are paying lower prices. There is some question as to whether the law requires lenders to sell the loans if buyers are available regardless of whether the lenders lose money on the deal.

In addition, to ease the problem, Congress passed technical amendments in June 2009 that allow guaranty agencies to sell rehabilitated loans to the Department under certain circumstances.[91] President Obama signed the bill on July 1, 2009. The legislation authorizes the Secretary of Education to purchase, or enter into forward commitments to purchase, rehabilitated FFELs that eligible lenders purchased under the FFEL default reduction program from October 2003 through June 2010, provided such purchase does not result in any net cost to the federal government.[92] The lenders that sell these loans must agree to use the funds from such purchases to originate new federal loans to students or to purchase rehabilitated loans under the default reduction program. However, as of summer 2010, the Obama Administration has yet to exercise this authority.

Collectors may claim inability to resell in cases in which they just do not want to sell the loans. The statute requires agencies to sell the loans if practicable but does not define "practicable." Clearly, there was a time when there were no buyers and so it was not practical to sell. As of summer 2010, however, there are buyers, though these buyers may not be paying top dollar. It is unclear in such cases whether these buyers are choosing which loans to buy based on the monthly payment amount. If this is in fact true, borrowers should be advised early in the process so they do not waste their time in a rehabilitation program that will not be completed. These borrowers can usually select consolidation instead.

Once the loan is resold, there will be a new servicer. In addition, collection fees of up to 18.5% of the unpaid principal and accrued interest at the time of sale are added to the new loan.[93]

For FFELs, after a rehabilitation sale, guaranty agencies must within forty-five days of sale provide notice to the prior holder of the sale and request that any consumer reporting agency to which the default was reported remove the record of default from the borrower's credit history.[94] This benefit, however, is often oversold. The default notation is removed from the credit report, but any other negative history remains until it becomes obsolete. Borrowers can request that the entire trade line be deleted or that all negative history be deleted, but not all loan holders will comply.

6.3.6 Limits on Rehabilitation

The 2008 Higher Education Act reauthorization law limits FFEL and Direct loan borrowers to only one rehabilitation per loan.[95] This limit applies to loans rehabilitated on or after August 14, 2008, and applies only if the loan returns to default status following the rehabilitation.[96]

Loans that have been reduced to judgment may not be rehabilitated.[97] However, borrowers in this situation may be able to renew eligibility under certain circumstances.[98]

The payments made under the rehabilitation agreement must be "voluntary." Voluntary payments are those made directly by the borrower and do not include payments obtained by federal offset, garnishment, income or asset execution, or after a judgment has been entered on a loan.[99] Garnishment or other involuntary payments will not count toward the required nine rehabilitation payments.[100] However, many guaranty agencies, when pressed, will work with borrowers to resolve this impasse. For example, in 2009 meetings with the guaranty agency trade association (National Council of Higher Education Loan Programs), the association reported that the majority of its guaranty agency members were willing to release garnishments for borrowers who showed a willingness to make voluntary reasonable and affordable payments. All others agreed to accept a token voluntary payment and subtract that amount from the garnishment amount so that the gross monthly payment does not change for the borrower. Although this latter scenario means that the garnishment will continue, the borrower will

---

89 Press Release, National Council of Higher Educ. Loan Programs, Nation's Student Loan Guarantors Provide Borrower Relief (Mar. 13, 2009).
90 Pub. Act 96-0009 (creating 110 Ill. Comp. Stat. § 947-152 (May 7, 2009)).
91 Pub. L. No. 111-039, § 404, 123 Stat. 1932 (June 30, 2009).
92 Id.

93 20 U.S.C. § 1078-6(a)(1)(D)(i)(II); 34 C.F.R. § 682.405(b)(1)(vi).
94 20 U.S.C. § 1078-6(b)(3); 34 C.F.R. § 682.405(b)(3).
    There are similar provisions for Direct loans, 34 C.F.R. § 685.211(f)(1).
95 Pub. L. No. 110-315 § 426, 122 Stat. 3078 (Aug. 14, 2008).
96 34 C.F.R. §§ 682.405(a)(3), 685.211(f)(4).
97 34 C.F.R. § 682.405(a).
98 See § 6.5, infra.
99 34 C.F.R. § 682.405(b)(2).
100 Id.

also be on the way to getting out of default through rehabilitation. This scenario can only work if the borrower can make it through nine months of garnishment.

The Department states in the 2009 PCA manual that borrowers must make voluntary payments in addition to garnishment.[101] The Department also claims that it can start garnishment again without additional notice if a borrower agrees to a repayment plan but then stops paying.[102]

6.3.7 Perkins Rehabilitation

Perkins loan borrowers may also rehabilitate defaulted loans.[103] Borrowers must make on-time payments for nine consecutive months.[104] The Perkins Loan Program regulations do not explicitly state that the payments must be reasonable and affordable but rather that they must be determined by the school.[105] Loans reduced to judgment may not be consolidated.[106] Borrowers are also ineligible if they pleaded *nolo contendere* or guilty to a crime involving fraud in obtaining the federal assistance.[107]

As is true for FFEL and Direct loans after August 2008, Perkins Loan Program regulations specify that defaulted loans may be rehabilitated only once.[108] A borrower may rehabilitate only once, but there should not be a limit to the number of times a borrower is permitted to attempt rehabilitation. Collection costs related to Perkins loan rehabilitations cannot exceed 24%.[109]

Under the Perkins Loan Program, schools have thirty days after receiving a borrower's last on-time monthly payment to instruct any credit bureau to which the default was reported to remove the default from the borrower's credit history.[110]

6.4 Advantages and Disadvantages of Loan Rehabilitation and Consolidation

Unfortunately, few collectors neutrally explain the pros and cons of each option to borrowers in default. Among other reasons, as described above, collectors have financial incentives that often discourage them from providing accurate information.

Consolidation overall is much faster mainly because a borrower in default does not have to make any preliminary payments to qualify. Furthermore, there is no resale requirement. Consolidation produces a new loan, while the Department views a loan in rehabilitation as the same loan sold to a new lender. The faster process is especially important for borrowers seeking to return to school quickly. In addition, with consolidation, borrowers do not have to make preliminary payments and so are not forced to negotiate "reasonable and affordable" payments with a collector. These borrowers can consolidate and obtain income-base repayments (IBR). In this way, their payments are determined by a specific formula rather than through negotiation with collectors during which they must provide documentation and justify every expense.

With both options, collection fees of up to 18.5% are added to the principal balance.

The main advantage to rehabilitation relates to credit reporting. Consolidation results in a notation on a borrower's credit report that the defaulted loan was paid in full. In contrast, rehabilitation removes the default notation completely.[111] This may be of concern to some clients. This benefit, however, is often oversold. The default notation is removed from the credit report, but any other negative history remains until it becomes obsolete. Borrowers can request that the entire trade line be deleted or that all negative history be deleted, but not all loan holders will comply.

There are some indications that borrowers who consolidate out of default may be more likely to default again.[112] However, there has been limited study on this issue. A Texas guaranty agency study found that the cohort default rate for rehabilitated loans was 25%, lower than for consolidations.[113] However, they also found a decline in the default rate more recently for consolidation loans with underlying defaulted loans.[114]

Consolidation can also be a disadvantage for certain borrowers who may lose rights by consolidating.[115] For example, Perkins loan borrowers lose the unique Perkins cancellation rights if they consolidate with Direct loans.[116]

---

101 U.S. Dep't of Educ., PCA Procedures Manual: 2009 ED Collections Contract 104 (Sept. 2009).
102 *Id.* at 49–50.
103 34 C.F.R. § 674.39.
104 34 C.F.R. § 674.39(a)(2).
105 34 C.F.R. § 674.39(a)(2).
106 34 C.F.R. § 674.39(a).
107 34 C.F.R. § 674.39(a).
108 34 C.F.R. § 674.39(e).
109 34 C.F.R. § 674.39(c)(1).
110 34 C.F.R. § 674.39(b)(3).
111 *See* § 6.3.5, *supra*.
112 *See, e.g.*, U.S. Gen. Accounting Office, Direct Loan Default Rates, Report No. GAO-01-68 (Oct. 2000), *available at* www.gao.gov.
113 Texas Guaranteed Student Loan Corp., Crisis Averted or Merely Postponed? Examining Long-term Cohort Default Rates, Resolving Defaults, and Curing Delinquencies 12 (July 2010), *available at* www.tgslc.org/pdf/crisis_averted.pdf.
114 *Id.*
115 *See* § 1.4.1.3.3, *supra*.
116 *See* § 9.12, *infra* (Perkins cancellations).

6.5 Renewing Eligibility for Federal Student Aid

Borrowers can reinstate eligibility for federal financial aid through a process similar to rehabilitation. Only six instead of nine payments are required. This is useful for those seeking to go back to school. However, these borrowers should be cautioned that the six payments reinstates eligibility for aid but does not get them out of default. They must complete the rehabilitation process in order to get out of default.

Whether the Department or a guaranty agency holds the loan, the borrower, to renew eligibility, must enter a satisfactory repayment arrangement, defined as six consecutive on-time monthly payments.[117] "On-time" payments are defined as payments received within fifteen days of the scheduled due date.[118] The Department has acknowledged that this is shorter than the twenty days required in the rehabilitation program. The Department explained this discrepancy, noting that the standard for on-time payments for purposes of regaining eligibility for federal financial aid should be stricter than the standard for rehabilitation.[119]

The requirements for the payment amount are in separate regulations but generally mirror the requirements for rehabilitation.[120] The guarantor must provide the borrower with a written statement of the monthly payment amount and provide the borrower with an opportunity to object to its terms.[121]

Borrowers who previously set up reasonable and affordable payment plans and became delinquent on their payments cannot renew eligibility through a new reasonable and affordable plan. Therefore, a borrower has only one chance to renew eligibility with a reasonable and affordable repayment agreement.[122]

Borrowers have only one chance to renew eligibility, but they will have more than one chance to *try* to renew eligibility. For example, if the borrower successfully makes six consecutive on-time payments, renews eligibility and then defaults, the borrower is not eligible under the regulations for another chance at a reasonable and affordable payment plan. However, if the borrower makes five payments and then stops paying, the borrower never actually renewed eligibility and should thus be able to try again in the future to renew eligibility through reasonable and affordable payments.[123]

Borrowers with loans subject to a judgment for failure to repay may also be eligible to renew eligibility as long as the borrower repays the debt in full or makes repayment arrangements that are satisfactory to the holder.[124] The "one-time" requirement applies here as well.[125]

The Department has stated that a judgment holder may require more stringent repayment arrangements that it considers appropriate. The benefits that the judgment holder may offer the borrower include the return of eligibility and removal of a borrower's negative credit history.[126] Alternatively, the holder may offer to vacate the judgment and allow the borrower to sign a new promissory note after the borrower complies with the conditions of the agreement.[127]

Borrowers who stay current on the reasonable and affordable plan apparently can remain on the plan indefinitely at that level of payment. The level will change if the borrower's financial circumstances change. This could be a problem if the borrower is not informed that he or she can rehabilitate the loan and get out of default through this process.

6.6 Compromise and Write-Off Authority

The Department has authority to compromise FFELs or Perkins loans of any amount or to suspend or terminate collection of these loans.[128] The regulations state that the Department will use the standard set out by the Department of Treasury for compromise of federal claims.[129]

The Treasury regulations give federal agencies discretion to compromise debts if they cannot collect the full amount because:

(1) The debtor is unable to pay the full amount in a reasonable time, as verified through credit reports or other financial information;[130]

---

117 The regulation that provides for reinstatement of borrower eligibility, 34 C.F.R. § 682.401(b)(4) (FFEL), requires the borrower to make satisfactory repayment arrangements as defined in section 682.200. Section 682.200 provides that the borrower must make six timely payments and that the amount must be reasonable and affordable. *See also* 34 C.F.R. §§ 685.102 (definition of satisfactory repayment arrangement for purposes of regaining eligibility), 685.200(d).
118 34 C.F.R. § 682.200 (FFEL).
119 71 Fed. Reg. 64378 (Nov. 1, 2006).
120 34 C.F.R. §§ 682.200 (definition of "satisfactory repayment arrangement"), 682.401(b)(4)(i).
121 34 C.F.R. § 682.401(b)(4)(iii).
122 34 C.F.R. §§ 682.200 (FFEL) (definition of "satisfactory repayment arrangement"), 685.102 (Direct Loan).

123 The regulations at 34 C.F.R. § 682.200 (definition of "satisfactory repayment arrangement") state that a borrower may only obtain the benefit of a reasonable and affordable payment plan *with respect to renewed eligibility once*" (emphasis added).
124 34 C.F.R. § 668.35(b).
125 34 C.F.R. § 668.35(c).
126 67 Fed. Reg. 67048, 67061 (Nov. 1, 2002).
127 *Id.*
128 34 C.F.R. § 30.70(h).
  Compromises for other types of debts are set out at 34 C.F.R. § 30.70(a)–(f).
129 34 C.F.R. § 30.70(a) (referring to 4 C.F.R. § 103; regulations now found at 31 C.F.R. § 902).
130 Debtors are required to submit a current financial statement executed under penalty of perjury showing assets, liabilities, income, and expenses. 31 C.F.R. § 902.2(g).

§ 6.6   Student Loan Law

(2) The government is unable to collect the debt in full within a reasonable time by enforced collection proceedings;

(3) The cost of collecting the debt does not justify the enforced collection of the full amount;[131] or

(4) There is significant doubt concerning the government's ability to prove its case in court.[132]

Agencies are discouraged from accepting compromises payable in installments.[133] However, this is allowed as long as the agency obtains a legally enforceable written agreement providing that, in the event of default, the full original principal balance of the debt prior to compromise, less sums paid, is reinstated.[134] Agencies are also encouraged to obtain security for repayment.

The Department has also approved standardized compromise and write-off procedures, described below, for use by all guaranty agencies for FFELs.[135] The compromise standards relate to a negotiated agreement between the guaranty agency and the student loan borrower for the agency to accept less than full payment as full liquidation of the entire debt.

This compromise is often, but not always, binding on the Department of Education. It is important for borrowers to secure written verification of this point to ensure that the United States will not demand the student's balance at a later date.

1. *Collection costs* can be waived to obtain payment of all principal and interest in full. Guaranty agencies can make this determination through the supervisor directly charged with collections. In practice, many guaranty agencies will quickly agree to waive collection fees.

2. *30% of principal and interest owing* also can be waived to recover the remaining 70%. If the amount waived only involves interest, the determination can be made by the supervisor directly charged with collections. If the principal is to be waived, then the next level of management must make the determination. Guaranty agencies are less likely to agree to compromise interest and principal because the amounts compromised apparently will be taken out of the 30% that guaranty agencies make on a loan collection. On the other hand, guaranty agencies still have an incentive to compromise up to 30%. If the guaranty agencies do not collect anything, they will eventually turn the loan over to the United States and keep none of the 30%.

3. *Compromises involving more than 30%* of outstanding principal and interest will bind only the guaranty agency, *not* the United States. Such compromises cannot waive the Secretary's right to collect the remaining balance due. The guaranty agency can compromise this larger amount as long as it can document the reasons for the action, the guaranty agency director approves the compromise, and the compromise does not bind the United States.

The write-off procedures for FFELs are intended only to stop guaranty agency collection activity. In general, write-off does not relieve the debtor of the debt. This is in contrast to Perkins loan write-offs, wherein the borrower can be relieved of all repayment obligations.[136] The rules for Perkins loan write-offs differ depending on whether the school or the Department holds the loan. The Department may take a restrictive interpretation of the regulations if the school is holding the loan. In those cases, the Department may find that the school cannot write off a loan unless the borrower has a very low balance.[137] In contrast, if the school has assigned the loan to the Department, borrowers should be entitled to request a write-off, and the Department has discretion to grant one regardless of the loan amount.[138]

Once a guaranty agency has written off an FFEL loan, it must permanently assign the loan to the Department of Education.[139] The exception to this policy is that guaranty agencies have the authority to write off loans with principal balances of less than $100 and a total balance of less than $1000, and any loans in which the remaining balance represents only interest, attorney fees, court costs, or collection costs, without requiring the permanent assignment of the loan to the Department.[140]

The Department sets out guidelines for guaranty agencies to consider in deciding whether to write off loans and cease collection activity. Agencies are required to consider the

---

131 In these circumstances, agencies may impose an appropriate discount on the amount accepted in compromise for the administrative and litigative costs of collection, with consideration given to the time it will take to effect collection. The regulations state that collection costs may be a substantial factor in the settlement of small debts. 31 C.F.R. § 902.2(e).

132 31 C.F.R. § 902.2(a).

133 31 C.F.R. § 902.2(f).

134 *Id.*

135 *See* Letter from Jean Frohlicher, President of the National Council of Higher Education Loan Programs, Inc., to Robert W. Evans, Director of Policy and Program Development, U.S. Department of Educ. (Nov. 7, 1993) (regarding compromise and write-off procedures, with attached approval by Robert W. Evans on November 24, 1993, and Standardized Compromise and Write-Off Procedures). The letter is reprinted at Appendix D, *infra*, and is included on the companion website to this manual.

136 34 C.F.R. § 674.47(h)(3).

137 34 C.F.R. § 674.47(h) (schools may write off accounts with balances less than $25 or $50 if a borrower has been billed, but has not paid, the balance for a period of at least two years).

138 34 C.F.R. § 30.70(h).

139 *See* Letter from Jean Frohlicher, President of the National Council of Higher Education Loan Programs, Inc., to Robert W. Evans, Director of Policy and Program Development, U.S. Department of Educ. (Nov. 7, 1993) (regarding compromise and write-off procedures, with attached approval by Robert W. Evans on November 24, 1993, and Standardized Compromise and Write-Off Procedures). The letter is reprinted at Appendix D, *infra*, and is included on the companion website to this manual.

140 *Id.*

debtor's and, if applicable, an endorser's current inability to repay the debt. Examples of borrowers who might qualify include borrowers who are repeatedly unemployed and have no prospects for future employment; borrowers who repeatedly are public assistance recipients; borrowers who are chronically ill, partially disabled, or of an age that results in their inability to work; borrowers whose potential for future earnings is limited or non-existent; and borrowers who have no other funds available to them from other sources, such as inheritance. Borrowers who receive a compromise or write-off must reaffirm the amount compromised or written off if they later want to receive an FFEL loan.[141]

The Department has told NCLC that it offers compromises only when they conclude that it is in the best federal fiscal interest to do so. They might also offer a compromise if there are mitigating circumstances in favor of a settlement. They have said that they do not publicize compromise standards "externally," since doing so could prejudice negotiations and make it more difficult for the government to obtain the amount that is deemed reasonable for any particular borrower.

However, the Department did for a brief time post a 2009 PCA procedures manual detailing compromise standards. Unfortunately, the Department decided to take the manual off-line, apparently because of media reports publicizing the standards.[142]

The Department in the 2009 PCA manual described standard, discretionary, and nonstandard compromises. Standard compromises are those wherein the borrower pays only the current principal and interest (waiver of projected collection costs/fees), at least the current principal and half the interest, or at least 90% of the current principal and interest balance.

The manual includes the following examples:[143]

Waiver of Collection Costs
Borrower owes $2500 Principal, $1000 Interest, and $875 projected collection fees. The collector may offer a settlement as low as $3500 (principal + interest) to fully satisfy the account.

Principal and half interest
Borrower owes $2000 Principal, $1000 Interest, and $730.20 projected collection costs. The collector may offer the borrower a settlement as low as $2500 (principal + 50% interest) to fully satisfy the account.

90% principal and interest
Borrower owes $2000 Principal, $400 Interest and $584.16 projected collection costs. The collector may offer the borrower a settlement as low as $2160 (90% of principal + interest) to fully satisfy the account.

Discretionary compromises are made when the borrower offers less than the standard amount described above. These compromises require prior approval by the Department of Education. Collectors must obtain a letter from the borrower justifying the offer and, if the basis is financial hardship, the borrower's financial statement, pay stubs, most current tax return and W-2s, and other supporting documentation.[144]

Nonstandard compromises are those that the collector offers but are not approved by the Department. Collectors are limited in how many nonstandard compromises they may offer in any single quarter.[145] If the collector sets up a nonstandard compromise, the net loss to the government between the amounts the government would have collected through a standard compromise will be deducted from the collector's next commission payment.

The PCA manual includes this example:[146]

Borrower's total balance is $13,125. The Contractor compromises in conflict with the Government's current compromise standards and collects $8000 and is initially paid a commission fee of $1400 (17.5%). The Government recovers $6600.

Under the applicable compromise standards, the Contractor would only have accepted a compromise agreement under which the borrower pays $10,500. The resultant netback to the Government would have been $8,662.50. The Government has lost $2025 ($8662.50 − $6600 = $2,062.50); therefore, the Government will deduct $2,062.50 from the Contractor's next commission payment.

---

141 *Id.*
142 *See generally* Ariel Wittenberg, Center for Pub. Integrity, Education Department Pulls Student Debt Collectors Guide Off Web Site (June 16, 2010).
    The Center for Public Integrity has posted a copy of the handbook on their website. The manual is also available on the companion website to this manual.
143 U.S. Dep't of Educ., PCA Procedures Manual: 2009 ED Collections Contract 72 (Sept. 2009).
144 *Id.* at 71.
145 *Id.* at 73 (no more than six in any quarter).
146 *Id.*

Chapter 7   # Federal Student Loan Collection: Due Diligence Requirements, Private Collection Agencies, and Defenses to Collection Actions

7.1 Introduction to Federal Student Loan Collections

The government has extraordinary powers to collect student loan debt. Federal student loan collection powers have grown so much over time that the government rarely sues borrowers, opting instead for an array of extra-judicial collection tools.[1] These extra-judicial collection tools are discussed in detail in Chapter 8, *infra*.

In addition to these powerful collection tools, the government has expanded its use of private collection agencies and other more "traditional" collection efforts. In fiscal year 2009, about 10.3% of federal student loan collections occurred through private collection agency actions.[2]

Total defaulted student loan receivables (principal and interest) serviced by the Department of Education's Default Resolution Group increased from $17.4 billion at the end of fiscal year 2005 to $24.4 billion at the end of fiscal year 2009.[3] Collections increased from $2.082 billion in fiscal year 2005 to $3.074 billion in fiscal year 2009.

According to estimates in 2009, the government is expected to collect roughly $111 on every $100 of defaulted Direct Loan Program loans ("Direct loans") and $122 on every $100 of defaulted guaranteed loans in 2011.[4] These estimates, however, do not take into account collection costs or inflation. In 2009, the government paid about $258.3 million to collection agencies.

This chapter focuses on the ways in which student loans are collected, including information on the entities that do the collecting. During the relatively long period of delinquency prior to default, the government engages in a number of mandated collection efforts, including delinquency reports to credit bureaus. These "due diligence" requirements are discussed in this chapter.

This chapter also reviews the federal student loan collection system, including information about collector compensation and collection fees. The chapter also details the problem of unfair, deceptive, and abusive collection of student loans and includes legal claims to challenge these practices. In addition, the chapter discusses key claims that borrowers can raise defensively in response to federal student loan collection actions, including a number of unique rights for military service members. Collection defenses related to proprietary schools can be found in Chapter 12, *infra*.

A general description of student loan default and the consequences of default can be found in Chapter 5, *supra*. Chapter 6, *supra*, focuses on the ways in which borrowers can get out of default through repayment. Chapter 8, *infra*, covers the primary non-judicial collection efforts such as wage garnishment and tax offsets. Collection issues for private student loans can be found in Chapter 11, *infra*. This chapter covers federal student loan issues only.

7.2 The Federal Student Loan Collection Process

7.2.1 The Various Collection Entities: Figuring Out Who Is Collecting the Loan

The Department of Education ("the Department") sets standards and supervises the collection of student loans held by other entities such as guarantors, schools, and lenders. The Department also directly collects on loans that it holds. Due to the elimination of the Federal Family Education Loan (FFEL) Program as of July 1, 2010, an increasing number of loans will be held by the Department.[5]

---

1 *See* Ch 8, *infra*.
2 U.S. Dep't of the Treasury, U.S. Government Receivables and Debt Collection Activities of Federal Agencies: Fiscal Year 2009 Report to the Congress 15 (Mar. 2010), *available at* http://fmsq.treas.gov/news/reports/debt09.pdf.
   This data includes collections on the Department of Education's defaulted portfolio, including FFELs assigned to the Department.
3 U.S. Dep't of the Treasury, U.S. Government Receivables and Debt Collection Activities of Federal Agencies: Fiscal Year 2009 Report to the Congress 15 (Mar. 2010), *available at* http://fmsq.treas.gov/news/reports/debt09.pdf.
4 Kelly Field, *Government Vastly Undercounts Defaults*, Chron. of Higher Educ., July 11, 2010.

5 *See* § 1.3.2, *supra*.

Federal student aid debt collection activities are centralized in the Department of Education's Default Resolution Group (DRG). The Atlanta regional office is the main contact for private collection agency issues.[6] The Chicago office handles treasury offset and garnishment hearings as well as escalated issues.[7] The San Francisco office handles litigation review, closed-school requests, ability-to-benefit requests, and oversees bankruptcy issues.[8]

Guaranty agencies or schools hold other defaulted student loans.[9] The Department generally does not collect on these loans, and it is important to distinguish between the Department's collection on a loan and its supervision of a guarantor or school's collection on the loan.

Schools are required to collect Perkins Loan Program loans ("Perkins loans") but are also encouraged to assign defaulted loans to the Department.[10] The Department will then seek collection from the defaulted borrower, using the full range of collection tools available. The Department claims to have collection tools, such as wage garnishment, federal offset, and Department of Justice litigation, that are not available to schools.[11] It is unclear to what extent this statement reflects actual practice.[12]

The Department, state guaranty agencies, and schools also contract with private collection agencies to fulfill many of their collection responsibilities.[13] According to a report by the Department of Treasury, the Department of Education relies heavily on private collection agencies and refers every eligible debt to one of its collection agencies.[14] The Department of Education awarded a new collection contract to a total of twenty-two agencies in early 2009.

The types of activities that third parties can engage in to collect student loans are different for different types of loans. The rules also vary depending on which collection tool they use. For example, third parties acting as agents for the federal government are explicitly covered by the tax offset statute.[15] The collection agencies also initiate the Department's use of administrative wage garnishment.[16] The Department's private collection agency (PCA) website was a primary resource for information about private collection agencies. However, as of the spring of 2010, the Department took the site off-line.[17]

The widespread use of private collection agencies to pursue student loan defaulters, combined with significant expansions in the government's arsenal of collection tools, has completely changed the landscape of student loan collections. Because the Department and its agents routinely send defaulted loan portfolios to these agencies, many borrowers seeking to get out of default or otherwise address student loan problems end up dealing with the least sympathetic of all actors, a private collection agency.

If the Department is not holding a loan, it is generally *not* appropriate to initiate inquiries or make applications to the Department. Instead, borrowers should contact the party holding the loan—usually a guaranty agency on an FFEL loan and the school itself on a Perkins Loan. The guaranty agency or school may have hired a collector or servicer to deal with the loan.

Even though it is best to contact the holder directly, if problems arise, borrowers should also contact the Department. The Department has the responsibility for supervising the actions of guaranty agencies and setting standards for their conduct. Much of what guarantors do has first been approved by the Department.

The federal student aid information center, which can be contacted at 1-800-4-FED-AID (800-433-3243), is a good place for borrowers to start the process of finding out which entity is collecting. The information center staff should be able to give borrowers the address and telephone number of the agency holding a defaulted loan. The information is also available on-line through the national student loan data system.[18] Borrowers with Direct loans should contact the Direct Loan Servicing Center at 1-800-848-0979. More

---

6 The address is: U.S. Department of Education, Federal Student Aid, 61 Forsyth St., SW, Room 19T89, Atlanta, GA 30303. The phone number is 404-562-6012.

7 The address is: U.S. Department of Education, Federal Student Aid, 500 W. Madison St., Suite 1520, Chicago, IL 60661. The phone number is 312-730-1477.

8 The address is: U.S. Department of Education, Federal Student Aid, 50 Beale St., Room 8601, San Francisco, CA 94105. The phone number is 415-486-5633.

9 For a list of guaranty agencies and addresses, see Appendix G, *infra*.

10 34 C.F.R. § 674.50 (assignment regulations).

11 See U.S. Dep't of Educ., Dear Colleague Letter CB-02-05 (Apr. 2002).

12 By many accounts, schools in the Perkins Loan Program do in fact refer debts to the Department of Treasury for tax offset. Presumably they could do the same for federal benefits offsets. However, the Department claims, at least with respect to benefits offsets, that this is not current practice.

13 The Department of Education website (www.ed.gov) lists the collection agencies with Department contracts. This list is also reprinted at Appendix H, *infra*.

14 U.S. Dep't of the Treasury, U.S. Government Receivables and Debt Collection Activities of Federal Agencies: Fiscal Year 2008 Report to the Congress 15 (July 2009).

15 31 U.S.C. § 3720A.

This is significant because, prior to the legislative change allowing offset of debts owed to agents of the federal government, authorization to offset loans held by guaranty agencies was accomplished by the guarantors assigning the loans to the United States prior to offset. This posed practical problems for obligations that guarantors had already reduced to judgments, particularly since the offset program was not used to collect loans postjudgment. The offset program is now utilized to recover on debts pre- and postjudgment. See § 8.2, *infra*.

16 See § 8.3.4, *infra*.

17 *See generally* Ariel Wittenberg, Center for Pub. Integrity, Education Department Pulls Student Debt Collectors Guide Off Web Site (June 16, 2010).

18 For information about using the national student loan database to find out how many loans and what types of loans a borrower has, see § 1.9, *supra*.

information is also available at the Department's website at www.ed.gov.

It is best to contact the Federal Student Aid Ombudsman ("FSA Ombudsman") for help only after these other options have been exhausted. The toll-free phone number for the ombudsman is 1-877-557-2575.[19]

7.2.2 Pre-Default Collection (Delinquency)

Borrowers are in default on FFEL Program loans (FFELs) or Direct loans if they fail to make required payments for 270 days for loans repayable in monthly installments or 330 days for loans repayable less frequently than monthly.[20] This nine-month period is a relatively long time for borrowers to seek alternatives to default such as more affordable repayment plans, cancellation, deferment, and/or forbearance.[21]

Delinquency begins on the first day after the due date of the first missed payment.[22] Once a loan becomes delinquent, lenders are required to provide the borrower with information about the availability of the FSA Ombudsman's office.[23]

Lenders are also required to engage in at least the following collection activities, depending on how long the borrower has been delinquent:

- 1–15 days delinquent: The lender must send at least one written notice or collection letter during this period informing the borrower of the delinquency and urging the borrower to make payments.[24] The notice or collection letter must at a minimum include a lender or servicer contact, a telephone number, and a prominent statement informing borrowers that assistance may be available if they are experiencing difficulty in making scheduled payments.[25]
- 16–180 days delinquent: During this period, the lender must make at least four diligent efforts to contact the borrower by telephone and send at least four collection letters.[26] At least one attempt to contact the borrower by phone must occur on or before, and another attempt must occur after, the 90th day of delinquency. Collection letters sent during this period must include, at a minimum, information regarding deferment, forbearance, income-sensitive repayment, loan consolidation, and other available options to avoid default.[27]

At least two of the collection letters during this period must warn the borrower that, if the loan is not paid, the lender will assign the loan to the guaranty agency. These letters must also inform the borrower that, if assigned to a guaranty agency, a defaulted loan will be reported to all national credit bureaus and that the agency may institute tax refund offsets, offsets of other federal payments, wage garnishment, or assignment of the loan to the federal government for litigation.[28] Receipt of any payments from the borrower during this period allows the lender to hold off on some of the required collection activity.[29]

- 181–270 days delinquent: At a minimum, the lender during this period must provide information to the borrower regarding options to avoid default and the consequences of default.[30] On or after the 241st day of delinquency, the lender must send a final demand letter to the borrower.[31] The lender must give the borrower at least thirty days after the date the letter is mailed to respond and to bring the loan out of default.[32]

The lender is required to ensure that there is no gap in collection activity of more than forty-five days at any point during this delinquency period.[33] In addition, loan holders must provide disclosures for borrowers having difficulty repaying and those who have been delinquent for sixty days.[34]

The Department also allows agencies to limit contact to incarcerated borrowers.[35] If the borrower is to be confined

---

19 For more information about the ombudsman program, see § 1.9.9.1, *supra*.
20 34 C.F.R. §§ 682.200 (FFEL definition of default), 685.102(b) (Direct Loans).
21 See § 3.1.2, *supra* (pre-default repayment plans); Ch. 4, *supra* (deferments and forbearances); Ch. 9, *infra* (loan cancellations).
22 34 C.F.R. § 682.411(b).
   The regulatory references in this section apply to FFELs. However, unless otherwise noted, Direct Loans have the same terms and conditions as FFELs. 20 U.S.C. § 1087e(a)(1).
   For general Perkins Loan due diligence requirements, see 34 C.F.R. § 674.41.
23 34 C.F.R. § 682.411(b)(3).
24 34 C.F.R. § 682.411(c).
25 *Id.*
26 34 C.F.R. § 682.411(d).
   Lenders are excused from further telephone attempts if, after making diligent effort, they are unable to obtain the correct telephone number of a borrower. 34 C.F.R. § 682.411(g).
27 *Id.*
28 34 C.F.R. § 682.411(d)(2).
   These collection methods are discussed in detail in Chapter 8, *infra*.
29 34 C.F.R. § 682.411(d)(3).
   The obligations differ if the lender receives a payment on the loan. 34 C.F.R. § 682.411(d)(3), (4).
30 34 C.F.R. § 682.411(e).
31 34 C.F.R. § 682.411(f).
32 *Id.*
33 34 C.F.R. § 682.411(b)(2).
   In 2004, the Department clarified that the forty-five-day rule includes any gap between previously required collection activities and the final demand letter. U.S. Dep't of Educ., Application of the Lender Due Diligence 45-Day Gap Rule, Dear Colleague Letter FP-04-08 (Nov. 2004).
34 See § 2.5.2, *supra*.
35 U.S. Dep't of Educ., PCA Procedures Manual: 2009 ED Collections Contract 201 (Sept. 2009).
   The Department had posted the manual on-line in the spring of 2010 but took it off-line after a month or so. The manual is available on the companion website to this manual and, as of the summer of 2010, on the website for the Center for Public

for nine months or less, the agency should suspend collection and perform follow-up after the borrower's parole or earliest release date. Loans for borrowers incarcerated for ten years or more should be written off.

7.2.3 Post-Default Collections

The regulations specify the efforts that guaranty agencies must make to collect defaulted FFELs. These options include tax refund offsets, federal benefit offsets, wage garnishment, and litigation.[36] There are similar regulations that apply when the Department is collecting loans that it holds.[37] The Perkins Loan Program has its own set of regulations.[38]

Until 2001, the regulations prescribed specific behavior that guaranty agencies were required to follow. The rules were very detailed, listing specific collection activities for the first forty-five days through 181 days after default. The rules also restricted a guaranty agency's use of litigation in collecting defaulted loans.

Effective in 2001, the Department made a number of significant changes to these rules. In particular, guaranty agencies were no longer required to perform routine collection activities such as collection letters and phone calls.[39] Instead, the agencies are given discretion to design their own collection strategies as long as they perform at least one activity every 180 days to collect the debt, locate the borrower (if necessary), or determine if the borrower has the means to repay the debt.[40] The 2001 regulatory changes also eliminated the general prohibition against guaranty agencies suing borrowers.[41]

Although guaranty agencies have more freedom to develop collection strategies, certain requirements are still in place.

Prior to reporting the default and assessing any collection costs, the agency must provide written notice containing the information described below. Although agencies have sixty days to report the default claim to the credit bureaus, they only have forty-five days after paying a lender's default claim to send this notice.[42]

The notice must:

- Advise the borrower that the agency has paid a default claim filed by the lender and has taken assignment of the loan;
- Identify the lender that made the loan and the school at which the loan was made;
- List the outstanding principal, accrued interest, and any other charges owing on the loan;
- Demand that the borrower immediately repay the loan;
- Explain the rate of interest that will accrue on the loan, that all costs incurred to collect the loan will be charged to the borrower, the authority for assessing these costs, and the manner in which the agency will calculate the amount of these costs;
- Notify the borrower that the agency will report the default to all nationwide consumer reporting agencies;[43] and
- Explain the opportunities available to the borrower to request access to the agency's records on the loan, to request an administrative review of the legal enforceability or past-due status of the loan, and to reach a satisfactory repayment agreement as well as the methods for requesting this relief.[44]

Unless the agency uses a separate notice to advise the borrower of proposed enforcement actions, the notice with the information discussed above must also describe any other enforcement action, such as tax offsets or wage garnishment, that the agency intends to use to collect the debt and explain the procedures available to the borrower prior to these actions to access records, request administrative review, or set up a payment plan.[45]

The initial notice must also describe the grounds on which the borrower may object that the loan obligation is not a legally enforceable debt and must describe any appeal and judicial rights available to the borrower from an adverse decision regarding the legal enforceability or past-due status of the loan.[46] In addition, the notice must describe collection actions that the agency may take in the future, including the filing of a lawsuit by the agency or by the Department of Education.[47]

During the first forty-five days after filing a default claim, agencies have the option of including even more information in the notice described above or sending a separate notice explaining that, if the borrower does not make acceptable repayment arrangements, the agency will promptly initiate collection procedures.[48] The various scenarios such as wage garnishment or civil suits must be listed.[49]

Given the volume of information in these collection notices, it is not surprising that borrowers are often confused about their rights. Recognizing this problem (although not

---

Integrity. *See* Ariel Wittenberg, Center for Pub. Integrity, Education Department Pulls Student Debt Collectors Guide Off Web Site (June 16, 2010).

36 These collection methods are all discussed in detail in Chapter 8, *infra*.
37 34 C.F.R. § 685.211(d)(3).
38 34 C.F.R. § 674.45.
39 *See* 65 Fed. Reg. 46316, 46318 (July 27, 2000).
40 34 C.F.R. § 682.410(b)(6)(i).
41 *See generally* 65 Fed. Reg. 65621, 65650 (Nov. 1, 2000) (final rules).
42 34 C.F.R. § 682.410(b)(5)(ii), (6)(ii).

43 "Nationwide consumer reporting agencies" are defined as consumer reporting agencies as defined in 15 U.S.C. § 1681a (Fair Credit Reporting Act). 34 C.F.R. § 682.200.
44 34 C.F.R. § 682.410(b)(5)(vi).
45 34 C.F.R. § 682.410(b)(5)(vi)(H).
46 34 C.F.R. § 682.410(b)(5)(vi)(I), (J), (K).
47 34 C.F.R. § 682.410(b)(5)(vi)(L).
48 34 C.F.R. § 682.410(b)(6)(ii).
49 *Id.*

necessarily solving it), the Department requires that the agency notify the borrower within forty-five days of paying a default claim that "borrowers may have certain rights in the collection of debts, and that borrowers may wish to contact counselors or lawyers regarding those rights."[50] Within a reasonable time after all of this information is sent, the agency is also required to send borrowers at least one additional notice informing the borrower that the default has been reported to all nationwide consumer reporting agencies (if that is the case) and that the borrower's credit rating may thereby have been damaged.[51]

During the initial sixty-day period before the agency reports the claim to credit reporting agencies, borrowers must also be given an opportunity to inspect and copy agency records pertaining to the loan obligation, to have an administrative review of the legal enforceability of the debt, and to enter into a repayment agreement on terms "satisfactory to the agency."[52]

A collection agency's failure to follow these collection rules may violate the Fair Debt Collection Practices Act (FDCPA).[53] Violations by guaranty agencies may also be actionable under the FDCPA.[54]

Agencies are required to attempt an annual federal offset, including tax refund offsets as well as offsets of other federal payments.[55] However, before attempting offset, agencies must wait at least sixty days after sending the required collection notices described above.

The agencies are also required to initiate administrative wage garnishment against all eligible borrowers.[56] The only exception to this requirement arises if the agency determines that litigation would be more effective in collecting the debt. In these circumstances, the agency may instead file a lawsuit against a borrower.[57]

7.2.4 Credit Bureau Reporting

7.2.4.1 General

The Higher Education Act (HEA) requires that guaranty agencies, lenders, and the Secretary of the Department of Education ("the Secretary") regularly exchange information with credit reporting agencies about outstanding student loans.[58] The statute provides that the Department, guaranty agencies, and lenders must enter into agreements with each consumer credit reporting agency to exchange information concerning student borrowers.[59] Although the regulations explicitly specify that student loan default information must be reported to all national credit bureaus, there is no similar requirement with respect to the reporting of all repayment information.[60]

The Department transmits loan information electronically to national credit reporting agencies on a monthly basis. The Department currently reports to TransUnion, Equifax, and Experian.[61] The information must not be disclosed unless its accuracy and completeness have been verified.[62]

The regulations specify the information to be supplied to all nationwide consumer reporting agencies. The guaranty agency supplies—for that borrower—the total amount of loans extended, the remaining balance, the date of default, information concerning collection of the loan (including the repayment status of the loan), changes and corrections based on information after the initial report, and the date the loan is fully repaid or discharged by reason of death, bankruptcy, disability, closed school or false certification.[63]

Schools that are holding Perkins loans are required to report any updated information to any nationwide credit agency to which it reported the account.[64] A March 1999 Federal Trade Commission staff letter clarified that, pursuant to the Fair Credit Reporting Act, schools must report information to the original credit bureau even if the school no longer has a contractual relationship with that bureau.[65]

A defaulted student loan will be listed as a current debt that is in default. The default will also be listed in the historical section of the report, specifying the length of the default. If the borrower repays the debt in full, the debt will no longer be listed as a current debt in default, but the debt will still be listed on the report (for up to seven years) as a debt that was at one time in default. Perkins loan defaults, however, can be reported until the loan is paid in full.[66]

The industry has developed a standardized format, called the Metro 2 format, for creditors and others who furnish information to consumer reporting agencies.[67] The Metro 2

---

50 34 C.F.R. § 682.210(b)(6)(ii).
51 34 C.F.R. § 682.410(b)(6)(iii).
52 34 C.F.R. § 682.410(b)(5)(ii).
53 See § 7.4.3.2, infra.
54 See § 7.4.3.5, infra.
55 34 C.F.R. § 682.410(b)(6)(v). See §§ 8.2, 8.4, infra.
56 34 C.F.R. § 682.410(b)(6)(vi). See § 8.3, infra.
57 34 C.F.R. § 682.410(b)(6)(vii).
58 20 U.S.C. § 1080a.

59 20 U.S.C. § 1080a(a).
60 No later than sixty days after defaulting, the guaranty agency is required to report default claims to all nationwide consumer reporting agencies. 34 C.F.R. § 682.410(b)(5) (reporting of defaulted student loans).
61 U.S. Dep't of Educ., PCA Procedures Manual: 2009 ED Collections Contract 22 (Sept. 2009).
62 20 U.S.C. § 1080a(c)(1). But see DiNello v. U.S. Dep't of Educ., 2006 WL 3783010 (N.D. Ill. Dec. 21, 2006) (20 U.S.C. § 1080a(c)(1) requires that the information be verified for accuracy and completeness prior to disclosure but does not directly require that the report be accurate).
63 34 C.F.R. § 682.410(b)(5)(i).
64 20 U.S.C. § 1087cc(c)(4); 34 C.F.R. § 674.45(b)(1).
65 Staff Letter from David Medine to Lee S. Harris, U.S. Dep't of Educ. (Mar. 22, 1999), available on the companion website to this manual.
66 See § 7.2.4.2, infra.
67 The format and instructions for the Metro 2 format are available, at www.cdiaonline.org, from the Consumer Data Industry

format has several special provisions for student loans, analyzed in NCLC's *Fair Debt Reporting*.[68] In general, a loan that has been paid or settled in full is reported by most credit bureaus as a "paid collection account."[69] A loan that is paid off by a consolidation loan will also be reported by most bureaus as a paid collection account.

7.2.4.2 How Long Does Information Remain in the Consumer's File?

The HEA sets out special rules as to when reports on student loans become obsolete. With the notable exception of Perkins loans, reports for most student loan defaults may be included in consumer reports for seven years from the later of three dates:

(1) When the Secretary or the guaranty agency pays a claim to the loan holder on the guaranty;
(2) When the Secretary, guaranty agency, lender, or any other loan holder first reported the account to the consumer reporting agency; or
(3) If a borrower re-enters repayment after defaulting on a loan, from the date the student subsequently goes into default again on the loan.[70]

Due to a change in the 1998 HEA, Perkins loans, in contrast, may be reported until the loan is paid in full.[71] A small consolation for borrowers, passed at the same time, requires Perkins institutions to report to credit bureaus when a borrower has made six consecutive monthly payments on a defaulted loan and to disclose promptly any changes to information previously disclosed.[72]

7.2.4.3 Cleaning Up the Consumer's Credit Record

Consumers can use various tactics to clean up credit files containing reports of defaulted student loans. As discussed above, a defaulted student loan will be listed as a current debt that is in default. The default will also be listed in the historical section of the report, specifying the length of the default. If the borrower repays the debt in full, the debt will no longer be listed as a current debt in default, but the debt will still be listed on the report (for up to seven years) as a debt that was at one time in default. Perkins loan defaults, however, can be reported until the loan is paid in full.[73]

Most creditors (such as mortgage companies or banks) will look more carefully at the current status of debts than the historical information in a file. For example, some mortgage lenders will not make loans to applicants that have any current loan defaults. Nevertheless, the historical information is reported to creditors and others authorized to see the consumer's file, and derogatory information there can prove harmful to the consumer.[74]

Shopping for student loans should not have a significant impact on a consumer's credit score. Fair Isaac has said that student loan inquiries made during a focused time period (for example, thirty days) will have little to no impact on a consumer's credit score.[75]

If the borrower is eligible, the clearest way to remove the student loan default from *both* the current account information and the historical portion of the report is to obtain a closed-school, false-certification, or unpaid-refund discharge.[76] The regulations state that the discharge should be reported to all credit reporting agencies to which the holder previously reported the status of the loan "so as to delete all adverse credit history assigned to the loan."[77] Consequently, the guarantor or the Department should tell the reporting agency not only that the loan is no longer in default but that the reporting of the loan as ever being in default was in error.

Borrowers can follow up a discharge by obtaining a copy of their credit report and determining if the current and historical information on the loan has been corrected.[78] If it has not been corrected, the borrower should first request that the guarantor or the Department report the debt's correct status to the reporting agency. They should also dispute the accuracy of the default with the reporting agency. The reporting agency will be required to verify the default with the loan holder.[79] The loan holder, in turn, should refuse to verify to the reporting agency that a default ever existed.

Association in its *Credit Reporting Resource Guide* (also called *Metro 2 Manual*). *See generally* National Consumer Law Center, Fair Credit Reporting, § 6.3.2 (6th ed. 2006 and Supp.).

68 National Consumer Law Center, Fair Credit Reporting § 6.3.3.9 (6th ed. 2006 and Supp.).
69 U.S. Dep't of Educ., PCA Procedures Manual: 2009 ED Collections Contract 21 (Sept. 2009).
70 20 U.S.C. § 1080a(f).
71 Pub. L. No. 105-244, § 463(b), 112 Stat. 1581 (Oct. 7, 1998) (amending 20 U.S.C. § 1087cc(c)(3)).
   The Secretary was given specific statutory authority to promulgate regulations establishing criteria under which a school can cease reporting the information before the loan is paid in full. 20 U.S.C. § 1087cc(c)(4)(B).
72 20 U.S.C. § 1087cc(c)(5); 34 C.F.R. § 674.45(b)(1).
73 *See* § 7.2.4.2, *supra*.
74 For more on clearing up credit, see generally National Consumer Law Center, Guide to Surviving Debt Ch. 3 (2010); National Consumer Law Center, Fair Credit Reporting (6th ed. 2006 and Supp.).
75 See Fair Isaac's statement at www.myfico.com/creditEducation/Questions/Student-Loan-Shopping-FICO-Score.aspx.
76 For unpaid-refund discharges, it is possible that only a portion of the loan may be paid off. The credit report therefore may still show that the borrower is delinquent on a portion of the loan. *See* § 9.5, *infra*.
77 34 C.F.R. §§ 682.402(d)(2)(iv), 682.402(e)(2)(iv).
78 For detailed information on how to obtain a copy of a credit report, see National Consumer Law Center, Fair Credit Reporting (6th ed. 2006 and Supp.).
79 For detailed information on how to dispute the accuracy of a credit report, and the reporting agency's responsibilities, see

Loan rehabilitation is another useful tool.[80] For FFELs, guaranty agencies must, within forty-five days of the sale of the rehabilitated loan, provide notice of the sale to the prior holder and request that any consumer reporting agency to which the default was reported remove the record of default from the borrower's credit history.[81] The prior holder must, within thirty days of receiving the notification, request that any consumer reporting agency to which the default claim payment or other equivalent record was reported remove such record from the borrower's credit history.[82] For Direct loans, the Department, after rehabilitation, instructs any consumer reporting agency to which the default was reported to remove the default from the borrower's credit history.[83] Under the Perkins Loan rehabilitation program, schools have thirty days after receiving the borrower's last on-time monthly payment to instruct any credit bureau to which the default was reported to remove the default from the borrower's credit history.[84]

Contrary to claims made by many guaranty agencies and other collectors, rehabilitation does not provide complete credit report relief. Loan holders are required to remove only the record of default after a successful rehabilitation.[85] Other negative history generally remains until it becomes obsolete. In July 2009, the Department stated that the government and guaranty agencies do not have the authority to request deletion of other information.[86]

The Consumer Data Industry Association (CDIA) issued revised reporting guidelines for rehabilitated student loans in May 2010.[87] The CDIA instructs the original lender, when the loan is purchased by another lender, to report certain codes in order to remove the default.[88] There are slightly different options when the original lender repurchases the rehabilitated loan. In either case, the newly rehabilitated loan should be reported with a new account number and new data opened. Prior payment history should not be reported. The guaranty agencies report Account Status Code "DA" to delete the account. This reflects a greater benefit than the minimum legal requirement of removing the record of default.

An alternative method of removing both the current and historical information on a student loan default is to dispute whether the debt is owed, using as a basis forgery, fraud, school-related claims, or other defenses that go to the loan's enforceability.[89] As part of a settlement of such a claim, the loan holder may be willing to request that the reporting agency correct both the current and historical status of the debt.[90]

It is easier to improve only the "current status" section of a credit report. By taking any of the following steps, a borrower can have the loan's current status changed so that it no longer indicates a default:

- Repay the debt;
- Obtain a consolidation loan;[91] or
- Obtain a discharge based on total and permanent disability.[92]

The current status of the debt on a credit report will *not* be changed if the borrower merely enters into a reasonable and affordable payment plan, even after making six payments to renew eligibility for new loans.[93] A payment agreement with a note holder will *not* remove a default from a student's credit record unless the loan holder explicitly agrees that it will take the loan out of default.

If a student loan is discharged in bankruptcy, the debt will no longer be treated as currently in default in the consumer's credit file. On the other hand, the fact that the consumer filed bankruptcy will be on the consumer's credit record for ten years.[94] Nevertheless, many experts believe that filing for bankruptcy will generally help a consumer's credit record in the long run. Certainly, the possibility of bankruptcy should not be rejected solely because of potential damage to the debtor's credit record.[95]

Borrowers may also want to consider legal action in cases in which a lender or other furnisher of student loan payment information provides inaccurate or obsolete information to a credit reporting agency.[96] Claims under state laws, however,

---

National Consumer Law Center, Fair Credit Reporting (6th ed. 2006 and Supp.).

80 See § 6.3, *supra*.
81 34 C.F.R. § 682.405(b)(3)(i).
82 34 C.F.R. § 682.405(b)(3)(ii).
83 34 C.F.R. § 685.211(f).
84 34 C.F.R. § 674.39(b)(3).
85 20 U.S.C. § 1078-6(a)(1)(C).
86 74 Fed. Reg. 36555 (July 23, 2009).
87 The information is available to subscribers at www.cdiaonline.org/Metro2/content.cfm?ItemNumber=853&pnItemNumber=506.
88 Loan holders should report Account Status = 05 (Account Transferred) and Payment Rating = 0 (Current Account), For the months when there was an Account Status 88 (claim filed with government on defaulted loan), Payment History Profile = D, which indicates no payment history. They may, at their option, also use the code "AH" to indicate that the account was purchased by another company.
89 See § 7.5.4, *infra*.
90 For detailed information on how to handle credit reporting issues as part of a settlement, including sample creditor letters to a reporting agency, see National Consumer Law Center, Fair Credit Reporting (6th ed. 2006 and Supp.).
91 See § 6.2, *supra*.
92 See § 9.7, *infra*.
93 See § 6.5, *supra*.
94 *See* National Consumer Law Center, Fair Credit Reporting (6th ed. 2006 and Supp.).
95 For a discussion of bankruptcy's positive and negative impact on a consumer's credit rating, see National Consumer Law Center, Fair Credit Reporting (6th ed. 2006 and Supp.). For a discussion of the dischargeability of student loans in bankruptcy, see generally Chapter 10, *infra*.
96 *See, e.g.*, Ellis v. Pennsylvania Higher Educ. Assistance Agency, 2008 WL 4351746 (C.D. Cal. Sept. 23, 2009) (denying KeyBank's motion for reconsideration and allowing plaintiff's FCRA claim based on vicarious liability); Jordan v. Equifax Info. Servs. et al., 410 F. Supp. 2d 1349 (N.D. Ga. 2006) (FCRA

7.3 Collection Fees and Penalties

7.3.1 General

The collector payment system is structured so that the contractors keep a portion of the money they collect. Collection contractors charge the Department a contingent fee for any payments made by the borrower on a loan placed with the contractor by the Department. The Department passes these costs to borrowers to the extent allowed by law.[98] Because the Department applies borrower payments first to defray collection costs, the outstanding balance owed on the loans it holds consists almost exclusively of unpaid principal and accrued interest.

In addition to "special" incentives for good performance, the collector receives a commission on a payment as long as the collector has been assigned the file, whether or not the borrower's payment was instigated by that collector's actions.[99] The Department then deducts an amount roughly equal to the commission it has paid its collector from the borrower's payment. Only the amount left over after the commission is paid is applied to interest and then principal, in that order.[100]

The collector cannot assess an amount in advance for collection fees but must instead apportion a percentage of each *payment* toward collection fees.[101] In an effort to prevent up-front loading of collection costs, the Department has clarified that the borrower is not legally obligated to pay costs that have not been incurred. The Department has recognized that the practice of loading fees up-front can actually discourage repayment and in any case does not reflect actual costs.[102]

Consider the following example. Assume a borrower's current obligation on a loan, including principal and interest, is $10,000 and that the commission paid to collectors is 30% of the amount collected. Even if the borrower immediately pays the full $10,000, the Department will first apply the funds to pay the collection commission, leaving only $7000 to apply to the outstanding balance. The borrower's obligation is thus not paid off but only lowered to $3000. To pay off the $10,000 balance, the borrower must immediately pay $14,285.71. The Department will apply 30% of that amount (30% of $14,285.71 is $4285.71) to collection costs. The remainder ($10,000) pays off the loan.

Collection costs should be recalculated each year after a loan goes into default. As to each loan in default, the amount of the previous year's collection costs should be removed from the balance of the loan and the newly calculated rate should be applied. Rates should also be recalculated each time the loan is transferred from one entity to another.[103]

The Department will show projected collection agency fees on the total balance of the account if the account is assigned to a collection agency. *However, fees are actually earned and charged only if the borrower makes payments.*

The Department's regulations require guaranty agencies to charge collection fees, whether or not provided for in the borrower's promissory note. The method of allocating students' payments to the fees must be the same as for Department-held loans.[104]

The rules for FFEL *lenders* are different. The FFEL regulations set out what collection costs the lender can seek (that is, before the loan is turned over to the guarantor).[105] The lender can seek no collection costs unless such charges are authorized in the promissory note and such costs are actually incurred by the lender or its agent.[106] Even if incurred and authorized by contract, the regulation prohibits

---

claim against loan servicer SLM for improper furnishing of information about student loans in identity theft case allowed to proceed); Pirouzian v. SLM Corp., 396 F. Supp. 2d 1124 (S.D. Cal. 2005) (student loan borrower's FCRA claims partially preempted, but claim under section 1681s-2(b) allowed to proceed); Hinton v. USA Funds, 2005 WL 730963 (N.D. Ill. Mar. 30, 2005) (summary judgment granted in part and denied in part in case brought by student loan borrower raising FCRA claims); Potter v. Illinois Student Assistance Comm'n, 2004 WL 1203156 (Cal. App. 4 Dist. June 2, 2004) (unpublished decision) (borrower's state credit reporting act claims preempted by the HEA and FCRA). *See generally* National Consumer Law Center, Fair Credit Reporting Chs. 10, 11 (6th ed. 2006 and Supp.).

97 *See, e.g.*, Pirouzian v. SLM Corp., 396 F. Supp. 2d 1124 (S.D. Cal. 2005). *See* § 12.5.3.4, *infra*.

98 The Department states that it has passed costs on to borrowers only since 1986 and only those costs incurred after the change in the law at that time. U.S. Dep't of Educ., PCA Procedures Manual: 2009 ED Collections Contract 23 (Sept. 2009).

99 For information on Department of Education performance rankings, see *Department of Education Releases First Performance Reports for New Collection Contract* (Feb. 5, 2010).

100 34 C.F.R. § 682.404(f) (payments are applied first to collection costs and then to other incidental charges such as late charges, then to interest and principal). *See* Padilla v. Payco Gen. Am. Credits, Inc., 161 F. Supp. 2d 264 (S.D.N.Y. 2001) (defendant's summary judgment motion denied on plaintiff's claim that debt collector induced borrower to make a down payment by agreeing to apply, in violation of federal law, the payment toward principal only).

101 The Department has taken the position that a borrower is not legally obligated to pay costs that have not been incurred. Memorandum of Points and Authorities Supporting Motion to Dismiss, Hutchins v. U.S. Dep't of Educ., No. CV-F-02-6256-OWW-DLB, at 31 (E.D. Cal. filed Apr. 25, 2003) (citing H.R. Res. 300, 99th Cong. at 396 (1986), *reprinted in* 1986 U.S.C.C.A.N. 977).

The agencies can charge the borrower only those costs that have been incurred as allocated to the particular payment.

102 *See* 61 Fed. Reg. 60482 (Nov. 27, 1996).

103 *See generally In re* Evans, 322 B.R. 429 (Bankr. W.D. Wash. 2005).

104 34 C.F.R. § 682.410(b)(2).

105 34 C.F.R. § 682.202(g).

106 34 C.F.R. § 682.202(g)(1).

assessment of charges for "normal collection costs associated with preparing letters or notices or with making personal contacts with the borrower."[107]

7.3.2 Amount of Collection Fees and How Fees Are Calculated

7.3.2.1 "Reasonable" Collection Fees

The HEA provides only that collection fees must be "reasonable."[108] The Department claims that this provision applies to all loans, whenever made.[109] Promissory notes for many, but not all, student loans contain terms obligating borrowers to pay collection costs as well.[110]

In determining what is "reasonable," the regulations allow collection charges equaling the costs associated with the collection of a *particular* debt.[111] These costs may include salaries for employees, costs for computer operations and records maintenance, court costs, and attorney costs.[112]

The regulations also set out a formula for computing collection fees as a percentage of the debt *if* a collection agency is hired, based on the contingency-fee arrangement contracted with that collection agency. The regulation does *not* authorize a percentage formula if the Department or guaranty agency does not hire an independent collection agency.

If a contingency-fee arrangement is used, the regulations allow the Department to compensate collection agencies based on the average cost per borrower rather than the actual fees incurred in collecting from any particular borrower.[113] This percentage or average approach often leads to unfair results since the small number of defaulting consumers from whom recovery is made bear the brunt of all of a creditor's collection expenses. The Department has argued that the "make whole" (making the collection agencies whole) approach is fair because it allows agencies to charge enough to sustain both successful and unsuccessful collections.

A number of bankruptcy cases provide additional insight into student loan collection fee calculations.[114] According to a guaranty agency official's testimony in one of these cases, the Department has taken the position that it is more efficient for guaranty agencies to assess percentage-based collection costs than to keep track of every letter and other collection contacts.[115] According to the guaranty agency official, the Secretary has determined that tracking costs of collection of each defaulted loan would create too onerous a system, such a level of specificity would be untenable and inefficient, and such detailed record-keeping would result in far higher collection costs for debtors than percentage-based collection costs. Each dollar recovered by the agency, according to the testimony, is divided between the agency's operating fund and the reserve fund of the federal government. The amounts in the reserve fund are remitted on a regular basis back to the Secretary to fund additional student loans.[116]

The Department of Education has provided a rationale for its collection costs computation methods. The Department argues that "reasonable" collection costs mean an amount that covers all federal collection costs, recovered by a flat rate charge to all paying defaulters.[117] The "make whole" collection method defended by the Department directs guaranty agencies to charge enough for collection costs to sustain both successful and unsuccessful collection activities on all the loans held by the agency.[118] Furthermore, the Department argues that the regulations are reasonable because they impose costs only on borrowers who require effort to collect.[119] According to the Department, borrowers can avoid collection costs by entering into repayment or applying for deferments or forbearances.

In general, the Department argues that estimating costs based on "analyses establishing an average of actual additional costs incurred by the agency in processing and handling claims against other debtors in similar states of delinquency" is a time-honored and reasonable way to determine those estimated costs.[120] According to the Department, averaging eliminates expense tracking and the billing of spe-

---

107 34 C.F.R. § 682.202(g)(2).
108 20 U.S.C. § 1091a(b)(1); 34 C.F.R. § 682.410(b)(2).
109 U.S. Dep't of Educ., PCA Procedures Manual: 2009 ED Collections Contract 22 (Sept. 2009).
110 *Id.*
111 34 C.F.R. § 30.60(a).
112 34 C.F.R. §§ 682.410(b)(2) (FFEL), 674.31(b)(5)(iii)(B)(9) (Perkins promissory note must state that the borrower shall pay all attorney fees and other collection costs and charges). *See also* United States v. Estrada, 2007 WL 295604 (E.D.N.Y. Jan. 29, 2007) (collector entitled to reasonable costs, including reasonable attorney fees).
113 34 C.F.R. § 30.60(d).
114 *See, e.g.*, Educational Credit Mgmt. Corp. v. Barnes, 318 B.R. 482 (S.D. Ind. 2004), *aff'd*, Black v. Educational Credit Mgmt.,

459 F.3d 796 (7th Cir. 2006); *In re* Schlehr, 290 B.R. 387 (Bankr. D. Mont. 2003); *In re* Evans, 322 B.R. 429 (Bankr. W.D. Wash. 2005).
115 *In re* Schlehr, 290 B.R. 387 (Bankr. D. Mont. 2003).
116 *Id.*
117 Memorandum of Points and Authorities Supporting Motion to Dismiss, Hutchins v. U.S. Dep't of Educ., No. CV-F-02-6256-OWW-DLB (E.D. Cal. filed Apr. 25, 2003) (citing H.R. Res. 300, 99th Cong. at 396 (1986), *reprinted in* 1986 U.S.C.C.A.N. 977). *See also* U.S. v. Larson, 2010 WL 76433 (D. Minn. Jan. 5, 2010) (acknowledging that the flat rate method could be unfair, but finding that this is a public policy issue, not to be resolved judicially); H.R. 146, 99th Cong. at 494 (1986), *reprinted in* 1986 U.S.C.C.A.N. 453, *available on* the companion website to this manual.
118 Memorandum of Points and Authorities Supporting Motion to Dismiss, Hutchins v. U.S. Dep't of Educ., No. CV-F-02-6256-OWW-DLB, at 22–23 (E.D. Cal. filed Apr. 25, 2003).
119 *Id.* at 25.
120 *Id.* at 27.

cific costs to individual debts thus reducing costs for all debtors.[121] The Department acknowledges that averaging may still result in some charges that may exceed the actual costs incurred to collect a debt owed by a particular individual. However, the Department claims that this does not make averaging unreasonable. According to the Department, some differences are *de minimis*. In other cases, below-average costs incurred for some payments will be offset by above-average costs incurred by other recoveries.[122] In sum, the Department argues that the make-whole method solves a very practical problem: "collection action costs money; many debtors are not paying now, and may never pay. The GA cannot cover costs for these non-payers unless it charges those costs to paying debtors. Unless the GA recovers enough to meet its collection costs *and* the principal and interest on the debt, the taxpayer ends up bearing those costs."[123]

This rationale and the Department's approach seem ripe for legal challenge. In particular, a number of bankruptcy trustees have brought actions claiming that student loan collection costs are unreasonable because they are not related to actual costs incurred in the particular borrower's case. To date, these cases have been unsuccessful, and the courts have upheld the Department's regulations.[124] One court concluded that Congress intended that borrowers, not taxpayers, should foot student loan collection bills.[125]

State laws that prohibit or limit calculating fees based on an entire portfolio of debts rather than fees incurred in each case may be useful for comparison purposes.[126] For example, Iowa allows a collection agency to collect a fee from the debtor only if the fee is reasonably related to the actions taken by the collector and the collector is legally authorized to collect it.[127]

Assuming that the Department continues to use the "make whole" method, at least until legal challenges are successful, there is still a question as to how much is reasonable for collection agencies to charge. There is no numerical limit on collection fees outside of consolidation and rehabilitation.[128] As of 2010, the Department's policy is to charge no more than 25% of outstanding principal and interest as collection fees. In the 2009 Private Collection Agency manual ("2009 PCA manual"), the Department stated that collection costs at that time on accounts assigned to collection agencies were 24.34%.[129] The percentage taken out of each regular payment is 19.58%. For example, a $100 payment will reflect a collection cost of $19.58.

The Department has emphasized that the percentage is calculated on principal and interest only. It should not include any existing fee balances. Collectors may be calculating this incorrectly, leading to even higher fees.[130]

As of 2010, this policy was affirmed on the Department's website:

> Pursuant to the Higher Education Act and the terms of most borrowers' promissory notes, you are liable for the costs of collecting your defaulted Federally-financed student loans. The largest of these costs is usually the cost of contingent fees that may be incurred to collect the loan. The Department gives you repeated warnings before it refers a debt to a collection contractor. If those warnings do not persuade you to reach repayment terms on defaulted loans, the Department refers those loans to collection contractors. The contractors earn a commission, or contingent fee, for any payments then made on those loans. The Department charges each borrower the cost of the commission earned by the contractor, and applies payments from that borrower first to defray the contingent fee earned for that payment, and then to interest and principal owed on the debt. As a result, the amount needed to satisfy a student loan debt collected by the Department's contractors will be up to 25 percent more than the principal and interest repaid by the borrower. On each billing statement, the Department projects an estimate of the total amount needed to satisfy the debt on the date of the statement, including collection costs that would be incurred by payment in full of that amount.[131]

The 25% ceiling is not a limit set by statute but a result of a settlement in a case, *Gibbons v. Riley*, in which the Department was sued for charging fees beyond those stated in promissory notes.[132] In 1995, borrowers sued the Department for assessing up to 43% collection fees on certain student loan borrowers whose loan notes specified 25% collection fees.[133] The Department admitted that it was in error to systematically charge the higher collection costs to those with the 25% provision in their notes.[134] The Depart-

---

121 *Id.* at 29.
122 *Id.*
123 *Id.* at 32.
124 *See, e.g.*, Educational Credit Mgmt. Corp. v. Barnes, 318 B.R. 482 (S.D. Ind. 2004), *aff'd*, Black v. Educational Credit Mgmt., 459 F.3d 796 (7th Cir. 2006); *In re* Evans, 322 B.R. 429 (Bankr. W.D. Wash. 2005).
125 Educational Credit Mgmt. Corp. v. Barnes, 318 B.R. 482 (S.D. Ind. 2004), *aff'd*, Black v. Educational Credit Mgmt., 459 F.3d 796 (7th Cir. 2006).
126 These are discussed in detail in National Consumer Law Center, Collection Actions § 6.2.1 (2008 and Supp.).
127 Iowa Code § 537.7103(5)(c).
128 *See* § 7.3.2.2, *infra* (rehabilitation and consolidation collection fees).
129 U.S. Dep't of Educ., PCA Procedures Manual: 2009 ED Collections Contract 23 (Sept. 2009).
130 *Id.*
131 *Available at* http://www2.ed.gov/offices/OSFAP/DCS/collection.costs.html.
132 Gibbons v. Riley (E.D.N.Y. Nov. 9, 1994), *available on* the companion website to this manual (complaint filed).
133 *Id.*
134 Gibbons v. Riley, Clearinghouse No. 50,432 (E.D.N.Y. 1995).

ment also admitted that it had no method for easily distinguishing borrowers with the 25% collection provision from other borrowers.

Under the terms of the settlement agreement, the Department agreed to temporarily assess no more than 25% collection fees on all student loan payments. The agreement specified that this system would stay in place until the Department developed a way of distinguishing between collection fee limits in different loans.

The settlement agreement does not directly bind state guaranty agencies in their assessment of collection fees. However, federal regulations provide that guaranty agencies cannot charge more in collection fees than the Department can charge.[135]

To date, the Department has abided by the *Gibbons* settlement and has not publicly announced or implemented an alternative system.

Regardless of the settlement agreement, the information posted on the Department's website, described above, and testimony of Department officials indicate that the Department sets a collection fee ceiling at 25%.[136]

7.3.2.2 Fees for Rehabilitation and Consolidation

There are some limits on the amounts of collection fees that can be charged when a borrower rehabilitates or consolidates loans. When loans are rehabilitated, collection fees of up to 18.5% of the unpaid principal and accrued interest at the time of sale are added to the new loan.[137] Collection costs should be added to the unpaid principal at the time of sale. The implication is that collection costs should not be added prior to the sale while the borrower is making the required consecutive monthly payments.[138]

Up to 18.5% is added to the amount due for collection fees when a borrower in default consolidates a loan.[139] The Department stated in 2009 that it would charge collection fees totaling 11.1% of the current outstanding principal and interest in these circumstances.[140] Lenders automatically add the fees to the consolidation. It is theoretically possible to request a waiver of collection fees before consolidation, but a waiver is very unlikely to occur in practice. After the consolidation, the fees become part of the principal amount due on the new loan.

In an effort to minimize the pressure many collection agencies were placing on borrowers to consolidate, Congress in 2005 set new standards to ensure that consolidation loans are not an excessive proportion of a guaranty agency's recoveries on defaulted loans.[141] These rules apply to FFEL consolidation loans, which are no longer being made as of July 1, 2010.

7.3.2.3 Perkins Collection Fees

There are distinct collection fee provisions for schools collecting Perkins loans. Schools participating in the Perkins Loan Program must charge all reasonable costs with regard to a loan obligation.[142] The amount of collection costs charged must be based on either the actual costs incurred for collection actions with regard to the individual borrower's loan or average costs incurred for similar actions taken to collect loans in similar stages of delinquency.[143]

The collection costs must not exceed:

- For first collection efforts, 30% of the amount of principal, interest, and late charges collected;
- For second and subsequent collection efforts, 40% of the amount of principal, interest, and late charges collected; and
- For collection efforts resulting from litigation, 40% of the amount of principal, interest, and late charges collected, plus court costs.[144]

In establishing these limits in 2008, the Department specifically chose not to set the collection cost caps at the same level as in the FFEL Program. According to the Department, Perkins loans are low-balance loans compared to FFELs, but the cost of collection is about the same. The Department reasoned that higher collection limits are war-

---

(stipulated extension of time for defendants to respond to complaint). *See also* Letter of Fred J. Marinucci, Deputy Assistant General Counsel, to Andrew J. Cohen, Legal Assistance Found. of Chicago (Oct. 18, 1994), *available on* the companion website to this manual (Department does not intend to collect any amount in excess of what is allowed by the loan agreement).

135 34 C.F.R. § 682.410(b)(2).

136 *See, e.g., In re* Schlehr, 290 B.R. 387 (Bankr. D. Mont. 2003) (guaranty agency official testified that DOE has set market for contracting out collection to private collection agencies at rate of 25%; according to official, 25% rate is ceiling under regulations at 34 C.F.R. § 30.60, against which all other guaranty agencies are capped; each guaranty agency has to come up with own percentage-based collection costs based on actual expenses, which cannot exceed Department's own 25% ceiling). *See also* 61 Fed. Reg. 47398 (Sept. 6, 1996); Educational Credit Mgmt. Corp. v. Barnes, 318 B.R. 482 (S.D. Ind. 2004), *aff'd*, Black v. Educational Credit Mgmt., 459 F.3d 796 (7th Cir. 2006); *In re* Evans, 322 B.R. 429 (Bankr. W.D. Wash. 2005).

137 20 U.S.C. § 1078-6(a)(1)(D)(i)(II); 34 C.F.R. § 682.405(b)(1)(vi).

138 *See generally* § 6.3, *supra*.

139 20 U.S.C. § 1078(c)(6)(B); 34 C.F.R. § 685.220(f)(iii) (Direct) (using amount in 34 C.F.R. § 682.401(b)(27) (FFEL)).

140 U.S. Dep't of Educ., PCA Procedures Manual: 2009 ED Collections Contract 43 (Sept. 2009).

141 Pub. L. No. 109-171, 120 Stat. 4 (Feb. 8, 2006) (amending 20 U.S.C. § 1078. 34 C.F.R. § 682.410(b)(27)).

142 34 C.F.R. § 674.45(e)(1). *See* Franklin College v. Turner, 844 N.E.2d 99 (Ind. Ct. App. 2006) (the regulations set out at 34 C.F.R. § 30.60 do not apply if school is collecting Perkins loan and loan has not been assigned to the Department).

143 34 C.F.R. § 674.45(e)(2).

144 34 C.F.R. § 674.45(e)(3).

ranted because the return on collecting Perkins loans is smaller.[145] In responding to comments from consumer groups and others, the Department rejected charging only actual costs to borrowers. This practice is "administratively burdensome and not cost effective," according to the Department.[146]

Before filing suit on a loan, a school collecting a Perkins loan may waive collection costs as follows:

1. The school may waive the percentage of collection costs applicable to the amount then past due on a loan equal to the percentage of that past-due balance that the borrower pays within thirty days after the date on which the borrower and the school enter into a written repayment agreement, or
2. The school may waive all collection costs in return for a lump-sum payment of the full amount of principal and interest outstanding.[147]

Schools are required to apply payments on loans in the following order: (i) collection costs; (ii) late charges; (iii) accrued interest; and (iv) principal.[148]

7.3.3 Avoiding Collection Fees

There is no easy way to take an account away from a collection agency and avoid the collection fees. The fees will be assessed even if a borrower attempts to pay the Department directly. One exception is that no collection fees are assessed on amounts seized from tax refunds.[149] Consequently, a borrower may be better off arranging to have a large tax refund due, and having that amount intercepted, rather than paying off the loan directly to a collection agency.

In general, funds from tax offsets should be applied to principal and interest, not to collection fees.[150] Thus, the balance will decrease more rapidly through tax offsets than through low monthly payment plans. Borrowers choosing this strategy should wait until the funds taken from the tax intercepts leave them with a small balance left on their loans. Once the borrower has paid down to a small balance, exclusive of collection fees, the Department will frequently agree at this point to compromise the remaining balance and accept a lump sum payment.[151] The Department will usually waive the collection fees when the principal and interest is paid in full. This strategy saves borrowers from paying the huge collection fees that accrue once an account is turned over to a collection agency.[152]

However, collection fees may even show up in offset notices. In fact, only minimal administrative fees should be charged in connection with offsets. The Department may, however, continue to seek voluntary payments by assigning files to collection agencies even when involuntary collection methods, such as offsets, are in place.

There are a number of potential challenges to this practice. First, at least as a policy matter, the Department should not continue to send accounts to private collection agencies when involuntary collection methods are in place. This is particularly true for low-income borrowers who have no other assets or income. Second, even if the account is placed with a private agency, the collection fees should not show up on an offset notice because collection fees are not applied to the offset amount.

There are at least three other strategies a borrower can use to avoid paying collection costs once a loan has been turned over to a collection agency. The most complete remedy is to try to cancel the borrower's obligation on the loan. This can be done through a false-certification, unpaid-refund, or closed-school discharge; through a bankruptcy discharge; through raising school-related defenses on the loan; or if the student is totally and permanently disabled.[153] Making payments through a chapter 13 bankruptcy plan may also prevent collection fees.[154]

If the borrower is not eligible for cancellation, another possible solution is to consolidate the defaulted loan into a new Direct or FFEL loan. The consolidation loan will include an 18.5% collection fee from the old loan, but no further amounts will go to collection fees unless the consolidated loan goes into default.[155] Rehabilitation should also be considered.[156]

---

145 72 Fed. Reg. 69960 (Nov. 1, 2007).
146 Id.
147 34 C.F.R. § 674.47(d).
148 34 C.F.R. § 674.33(a)(4).
149 The Department affirmed in the 2009 PCA manual that agencies do not receive a commission for treasury offsets. U.S. Dep't of Educ., PCA Procedures Manual: 2009 ED Collections Contract 79 (Sept. 2009).
150 The Department of Treasury regulations on tax offsets specify only that offsets can be allocated for past-due debts, less fees charged under 31 C.F.R. § 285.2(i). This section allows fees charged by the IRS and the Financial Management Service of the Department of Treasury to be deducted from the amount collected. To the extent allowed by law, federal agencies may add these fees to the debt. Still, the fees deducted, if any, should be less than those charged by collection agencies.
151 See §§ 7.3.1, 7.3.2, 7.3.2.1, supra. See also U.S. Dep't of Educ., Amendment to Agreement Pursuant to Section 428(b) of the Higher Education Act of 1965, as amended, with a State or Private Non-Profit Institution or Organization for Coverage of its Student Loan Insurance Program under the Interest Benefits Provision of Section 428(a) of the Act, App. I § 5.1 (July 11, 1994), available on the companion website to this manual (if borrower agrees to pay principal within thirty days, agency may enter into a repayment agreement that includes the compromise of interest owed).
152 See § 7.3.2, supra.
153 See generally Chs. 9 (loan cancellations), 10 (bankruptcy), infra.
154 See § 10.9, infra.
155 See §§ 6.2.5 (consolidation), 6.3.5 (rehabilitation), 7.3.2.2 (collection fees for rehabilitation and consolidation), supra.
156 See §§ 6.2.5 (consolidation), 6.3.5 (rehabilitation), 7.3.2.2 (collection fees for rehabilitation and consolidation), supra.

Third, the borrower can complain about the collection agency's illegal or improper conduct to the Department. The Department will sometimes take the loan away from the collector.[157]

7.3.4 United States Collection of Other Fees and Penalties

In some cases, the United States or private attorneys hired by the United States to collect on student loans attempt to collect court filing fees and penalties in addition to attorney fees and collection costs.[158] Because such collection actions are usually uncontested, those fees are rarely questioned. The reality is that the United States may lack statutory authority to collect these amounts. For example, the United States need not pay filing fees, so any attempt to collect this amount, even by a private attorney collecting on behalf of the government, should be improper.[159]

Another dubious fee is a 6%-per-year penalty. Authority for this fee is explicitly found in federal regulations that allow the Secretary to impose a 6%-per-year penalty on the amount delinquent if the debtor does not make at least a partial payment on a debt within ninety days of the Secretary's demand for payment.[160]

However, the 6% penalty should not be a factor in the student loan context because it does not apply to obligations when either federal regulations or the loan agreement explicitly fixes the interest.[161] Since student loans are charged interest while they are in default, the 6% penalty does not apply.[162] In addition, the penalty does not apply to loans executed before October 25, 1982.[163]

The Department appears to agree that it does not have authority to seek this fee because the promissory note limits the fees that may be charged the student. Nevertheless, certain pre-1986 NDSLs, the predecessor to the Perkins Loan Program, did specify a certain penalty or late charge in the promissory note.

Another federal statute, the Federal Debt Collection Procedures Act, authorizes the United States to recover a surcharge of 10% of the amount of the debt when collecting on the debt using pre-judgment remedies (such as attachment) or postjudgment remedies (such as writs of execution).[164] However, the statute does not apply when litigation is used to obtain a judgment on the debt, and the United States cannot assess the surcharge based on such litigation.[165]

7.4 Deceptive and Abusive Debt Collection Tactics and Legal Violations

7.4.1 Factors That Foster Deception and Abuse in Student Loan Collections

7.4.1.1 General

The Department has turned over almost all student loans it holds to private collection agencies. In a 2009 report, the Treasury Department stated that the Department of Education uses private collection agencies heavily to collect defaulted student loans and refers every eligible debt to these agencies as quickly as possible.[166]

Student loan debt collection contacts, both by private collectors and guarantors, involve a remarkable amount of deceptive, unfair, and illegal conduct. There are several reasons for the extent of these abusive collection actions:

1. Millions of student loan obligations are being handled on a "wholesale" basis, with little or no attention being paid to the facts of the individual borrower being dunned.
2. Remedies available to collect on student loans are often both unique and misunderstood (for example, federal tax refund offsets, federal benefits offsets, and non-judicial garnishments), and collectors often misrepresent the exact nature of these remedies when they send collection letters. By all reports, much false information is provided.
3. The complexity of the student loan programs leads to much confusion about who is collecting on a debt and makes it easy for an independent collector to misrepresent itself as the government.[167] This complexity is likely

---

157 *See* § 7.4.5.2, *infra*.
158 *See* United States v. Singer, 943 F. Supp. 9 (D.D.C. 1996), *aff'd in part, rev'd in part*, 132 F.3d 1482 (D.C. Cir. 1997) (Department confessed error and the district court's ordering of 10% surcharge to Department as fees was reversed on appeal); United States v. Smith, 862 F. Supp. 257 (D. Haw. 1994); United States v. Spann, 797 F. Supp. 980 (S.D. Fla. 1992).
159 United States v. Spann, 797 F. Supp. 980 (S.D. Fla. 1992).
160 34 C.F.R. § 30.61(a). The authority for this regulation is 31 U.S.C. § 3717(e)(2).
161 31 U.S.C. § 3717(g)(1).
162 *See* United States v. Spann, 797 F. Supp. 980 (S.D. Fla. 1992).
163 31 U.S.C. § 3717(g)(2).

164 28 U.S.C. § 3011.
165 United States v. Singer, 943 F. Supp. 9 (D.D.C. 1996), *aff'd in part, rev'd in part*, 132 F.3d 1482 (D.C. Cir. 1997) (Department confessed error and the district court's ordering of 10% surcharge to Department as fees was reversed on appeal); United States v. Smith, 862 F. Supp. 257 (D. Haw. 1994) (proceeding did not involve pre- or postjudgment remedies and therefore government not entitled to 10% surcharge); United States v. Mauldin, 805 F. Supp. 35 (N.D. Ala. 1992).
166 U.S. Dep't of the Treasury, U.S. Government Receivables and Debt Collection Activities of Federal Agencies: Fiscal Year 2008 Report to the Congress 14 (July 2009).
167 *See* Peter v. GC Serv., L.P., 310 F.3d 344 (5th Cir. 2002) (debt collector's use of a Department of Education return address on a student loan collection letter violated the Fair Debt Collection Practices Act); Brider v. Nationwide Credit, 1998 WL 729747

to persist despite the elimination of the FFEL Program in July 2010. Most federal loans will be originated by the government through the Direct Loan Program, but private servicers and collection agents will continue in their previous roles.[168]

4. Private collection agencies are delegated the responsibility for determining the size of a reasonable and affordable payment plan. In addition, these collection agencies help determine if students have defenses to wage garnishments and tax refund offsets, even though the collection agencies' financial incentive is not to offer reasonable and affordable plans or to acknowledge defenses.[169]

5. There appears to be minimal government oversight of collection agencies unrelated to amounts recovered.

For example, in a December 2003 audit report, the Department of Education's Office of Inspector General (OIG) found that the Department's Federal Student Aid Division needed to improve its monitoring of private collection agencies.[170] The OIG reviewed five of the Department's private collection agency contracts and found that the Department did not perform effective monitoring in the following five key areas: (1) tracking complaints; (2) performing desk audits; (3) conducting site visits for technical assistance and trainings; (4) reviewing deliverables; and (5) maintaining contract files. As a result, according to the OIG, the Department was not able to determine whether the contractors complied with the Federal Debt Collection Practices Act (FDCPA) and Department policies, practices, and contract terms.[171]

A 2005 Department of Education OIG report focused on the Department's incentive payments to third-party collection agencies. The OIG found that the Department made incentive payments totaling almost $950,000 that were not consistent with the terms of the task orders. The OIG also noted that FSA needed to improve its internal controls.[172]

The Department frequently cites a low volume of complaints to support its claims of effective oversight. This is troubling in light of the OIG's findings that the Department is not doing an effective job of collecting and tracking complaints. Furthermore, the OIG was unable to determine the resolutions for about 98% of the complaints that were actually logged. The Department claims to be addressing these problems.[173]

7.4.1.2 Commission Structure Fosters Abuses

Much of the collector-related problems stem from the government's collector compensation system. Because of this system, collectors tend to steer borrowers toward the most lucrative options for the agencies. In the process, collectors may violate the FDCPA and other laws by misrepresenting borrower rights or otherwise providing inaccurate information.

Some organizations, like Sallie Mae, have purchased companies involved in all aspects of the student loan business in order to profit from the fees and services at each point.[174] For example, Sallie Mae purchased USA Group, the largest guaranty agency in the country and a nonprofit lender involved in servicing, loan origination, enrollment management, and debt collection. Although Sallie Mae could not own USA Funds—the guaranty agency arm of USA Group—as part of the deal, USA Funds agreed to contract all of its guaranty servicing to Sallie Mae.[175] Since the purchase of USA Group, Sallie Mae has also acquired other debt management and collection companies, including General Revenue Corporation, Pioneer Credit Recovery, Arrow Financial Services, and GRP Financial Services Corporation.

Most commonly, collection agencies will insist, in violation of the federal statute and regulations, that borrowers must pay certain minimum amounts.[176] This problem is exacerbated by internal collection agency incentive systems for employees. One compensation system was described in a 2007 wage-and-hour case brought by an employee of a collection agency. In this case, the collection agency awarded front-end goals or bonuses to collectors that were earned when a collector met quotas for the amount of debt and number of debtors he or she was able to convince to commit to a particular type of repayment program, including consolidation and rehabilitation.[177] There was a second category of back-end bonuses that were awarded after a certain

---

(N.D. Ill. Oct. 14, 1998) (denying motion to dismiss of collector whose collection letter had large bold heading "U.S. Department of Education").

168 See § 1.3.2, supra.
169 See, e.g., Arroyo v. Solomon & Solomon, 2001 U.S. Dist. LEXIS 21908 (E.D.N.Y. Nov. 16, 2001) (defendant's summary judgment motion denied in case alleging that, among other FDCPA violations, defendants demanded payments in amount more than borrower could reasonably afford).
170 U.S. Dep't of Educ., Office of Inspector Gen., Control No. ED-OIG/A19-D0002, Final Audit Report, (Dec. 23, 2003).
171 Id.
172 U.S. Dep't of Educ., Office of Inspector Gen., Control No. ED-OIG/A19-D0005, Final Audit Report (Feb. 18, 2005).

173 Id.
174 See generally Erin Dillon, Education Sector, Leading Lady: Sallie Mae and the Origins of Today's Student Loan Controversy (May 2007), available at www.educationsector.org/usr_doc/SallieMae.pdf.
175 Id. at 10.
176 Misrepresentations about reasonable and affordable payment plans may violate the FDCPA. See Arroyo v. Solomon & Solomon, 2001 U.S. Dist. LEXIS 21908 (E.D.N.Y. Nov. 16, 2001) (defendant's summary judgment motion denied in case alleging that, among other FDCPA violations, defendants demanded payments in amounts more than borrower could reasonably afford).
177 Rumler v. General Revenue Corp., 2007 WL 1266747 (S.D. Ind. May 1, 2007).

number of payments on new rehabilitations or consolidations were made by the debtor or funded by the Department of Education. Under consolidation, the collector was eligible for a bonus if the loan was successfully "funded" by the Department. At the point the loan was funded, the debt collector was eligible for a bonus based on the amount of the loan at the time of funding.[178]

With respect to rehabilitations, the problem is also caused by a system established by the Department that provides compensation to collectors for setting up rehabilitation plans only if the plans require borrowers to make certain minimum payments.[179] Similarly, agencies generally do not earn fees when borrowers apply directly to Direct Loans to consolidate.[180]

In June 2009, the Department announced a new performance-based servicer system.[181] The Department announced that four companies—AES/PHEAA, Great Lakes Education Loan Services, Nelnet, and Sallie Mae—were awarded contracts to service a portion of the approximately $550 billion outstanding federal student loan portfolio held by the Department.[182] Under the new contracts, performance is measured by customer satisfaction and default aversion. The performance criteria include percentage of in-repayment dollars that go into default, percentage of unique "in-repayment" borrowers that go into default, borrower surveys, school surveys, and surveys of Department personnel. An independent vendor will conduct these surveys.[183]

The incentives are to avoid defaults, but it is unclear how this will work in practice and whether the servicers will have adequate incentives to help borrowers who are already in default and want to get out. It is also unclear how the surveys will be designed and used.[184]

7.4.2 Common Student Loan Debt Collection Abuses

7.4.2.1 Violations Unique to Student Loans

The special rules governing student loan collections lead to a number of collection abuses. This section discusses common fair debt collection violations, followed by a discussion of whether the FDCPA and state debt collection laws apply in the student loan context.

Student loan borrowers may receive dunning letters threatening that the Department will garnish their wages without "legal action." These letters imply that the former student will receive no notice before the wage garnishment and that there will be no opportunity either to contest the validity of the student loan or to present defenses. In truth, the statute and regulations require both notice and an opportunity for an administrative hearing before an employer may be ordered to withhold any wages.[185]

Failure to comply with HEA regulations with respect to garnishment hearing, notice, and venue requirements are all possible federal and state fair debt or UDAP violations.[186] Collectors may also misrepresent a borrower's ability to obtain a closed-school, unpaid-refund, or false-certification discharge.

There is considerable confusion as well with respect to federal benefits offsets.[187] For example, borrowers have reported numerous instances of collectors threatening to offset benefits even if the borrower receives Supplemental Security Income (SSI) payments only. In fact, SSI benefits are completely exempt from offset.[188]

In May 2005, in response to complaints about collection agency threats to seize SSI benefits, the Department sent the following e-mail message to collection contract administrators:

> This is to remind you that Supplement Security Income (SSI) benefits are NOT subject to Treasury offset. These are different from the Social Security Disability benefits that may be subject to offset, under certain conditions. If a borrower advises that their only source of income is SSI, you should not be advising them that this may be offset.
>
> It has been reported that PCA collectors have been misinforming borrowers that their SSI benefits will be offset. This is causing anxiety and distress

---

178 *Id.*
179 *See* § 6.3.4, *infra.*
180 *See generally* U.S. Dep't of Educ., PCA Procedures Manual: 2009 ED Collections Contract (Sept. 2009).
181 *See* § 3.2.1, *supra.*
182 Press Release, U.S. Dep't of Educ., U.S. Dep't of Education Expands Its Student Loan Servicing Capacity (June 17, 2009) (on file with author).
183 *See* U.S. Dep't of Educ., Loan Servicing Information—Quarterly Customer Satisfaction Surveys Begin March 1, 2010 (Feb. 23, 2010).
184 *See* § 3.2.1, *supra.*

185 Cliff v. Payco Gen. Am. Credits, Inc., 363 F.3d 1113 (11th Cir. 2004) (student loan borrowers allowed to bring claims under state and federal fair debt laws that, among other violations, collection agency falsely represented claim, amount, or status of debt; falsely represented or implied that non-payment would result in garnishment; and failed to provide pre-garnishment hearing).
   The district court granted summary judgment to the collection agency on plaintiff's claim that the agency's notice contained misinformation about the HEA unemployment exemption. The court found that the agency was insulated from liability under the FDCPA's bona fide error defense. The Seventh Circuit agreed. Kort v. Diversified Collection Servs., Inc., 270 F. Supp. 2d 1017 (N.D. Ill. 2003), *aff'd*, 394 F.3d 530 (7th Cir. 2005). *See* § 8.3.3.1, *infra. See also* Sanders v. OSI Educ. Servs., Inc., 2001 WL 883608 (N.D. Ill. Aug. 3, 2001) (granting class certification based on borrowers' allegations that student loan debt collector violated Fair Debt Collection Practices Act).
186 *See, e.g.*, Cliff v. Payco Gen. Am. Credits, Inc., 363 F.3d 1113 (11th Cir. 2004).
187 *See* § 8.4, *infra.*
188 *See* § 8.4.1, *infra.*

for these borrowers and has also resulted in complaints due to this misinformation. Please remind your staff immediately concerning this issue.

Borrowers have also reported that the Department routinely continues collection even after borrowers have submitted disability discharge applications. This practice also clearly violates Department regulations.[189]

In addition, collection agencies frequently mislead borrowers with respect to repayment options. In particular, agencies are often very aggressive in steering borrowers into loan consolidation or loan rehabilitation programs.[190] These repayment strategies, as described in detail in Chapter 6, *supra*, benefit many, but not all, borrowers.

Collectors that charge excessive collection fees may also violate the FDCPA.[191] Collectors that use the Department of Education's name and/or address on the envelope or otherwise deceive borrowers into thinking they are receiving communications from the Department have also been found to be in violation of the FDCPA.[192] Collectors may also claim falsely that they will publish names of debtors.[193]

False representation of the amount of any debt should also be grounds for state and/or federal fair debt collection practices violations. These claims may arise in a number of ways, including the improper calculation of collection fees and the improper crediting of payments. In one case, borrowers successfully argued that the collector's crediting of payments to debtors' accounts on dates after the date of receipt of payment or after the date judgment was entered violated fair debt laws.[194] Borrowers argued that, among other violations, the collector's notices contained false statements because the amount listed as due contained improper interest charges attributable to improper crediting practices.[195]

An April 2007 press release from the office of Senator Edward Kennedy includes a letter sent to the CEOs of Sallie Mae and Nelnet regarding harsh and inappropriate collection tactics. According to the release, Senator Kennedy's office obtained information that these companies may have engaged in the following practices:

- Telling a borrower's spouse that the borrower would go to jail if he did not pay—a blatantly false assertion;
- Putting a borrower into default who lost his home in a natural disaster, adding substantial default and collection fees to his loan balance, taking tax refunds, and garnishing his wages—all in violation of guidance from the Secretary of Education;
- Harassing a widower about illegitimate, forged loans under the name of his deceased spouse;
- Refusing to negotiate with borrowers about deferment;
- Regularly calling borrowers at their job after being instructed to stop;
- Harassing borrowers' neighbors, family, and co-workers;
- Using abusive and profane language to intimidate borrowers;
- Attempting to collect debts not owed;
- Attempting to collect from deceased borrowers' families and relatives;
- Attempting to collect from elderly, disabled borrowers;
- Firing employees who attempt to help borrowers obtain information about their loan status;
- Instructing employees to give borrowers the "run around" rather than provide them with correct information on their loan status; and
- Intentionally sending loan payment notices to an incorrect address in order to force a borrower's account into default.[196]

Widespread complaints about student loan collection activity are leading to more litigation. For example, one debt collector was required to pay the maximum $1000 FDCPA statutory damages and, under state law claims, another $1153 in actual damages and $60,000 in punitive damages for contacting the borrower even after the borrower and the borrower's attorney had advised the collector that the debt had been discharged in bankruptcy.[197] In addition, a number

---

189 34 C.F.R. § 682.402(c)(1)(iii)(C)(2). See § 9.7.4.1, *infra*.

190 See § 7.4.1.2, *supra* (collection incentive system).

191 *See, e.g.*, Padilla v. Payco Gen. Am. Credits, Inc., 161 F. Supp. 2d 264 (S.D.N.Y. 2001) (plaintiff's summary judgment motion granted on claim that collection agency charged fees above the 18.5% allowable limit). See § 7.3, *supra*.

192 *See* Peter v. GC Serv., L.P., 310 F.3d 344 (5th Cir. 2002) (debt collector's use of a Department of Education return address on a student loan collection letter violated Fair Debt Collection Practices Act).

193 At one point in 2006, the Department of Education was using a collection letter in which was claimed that, for the purposes of locating debtors and/or securing full satisfaction of the outstanding debt amount, the Department could publish names of debtors in any newspaper, magazine, media tabloid, or other publication intended for public consumption. When brought to their attention, Department staff claimed that they do not engage in this practice and would review this provision.

194 Asch v. Teller, Levit & Silvertrust, P.C., 2003 WL 22232801 (N.D. Ill. Sept. 26, 2003) (borrowers granted summary judgment under federal and state fair debt collection practices laws).

In a later ruling, the court granted plaintiff's request for an injunction to prohibit defendants from collecting on accounts affected by defendants' failure to credit payments. Asch v. Teller, Levit & Silvertrust, P.C., 2004 WL 2967441 (N.D. Ill. Nov. 24, 2004) (granting in part and denying in part plaintiff's motion for further summary judgment).

195 *Id.*

196 Press Release, Kennedy Questions Student Loan Lenders' Collection Tactics (Apr. 26, 2007). *See generally* Josh Keller, *Senator Kennedy Accuses Sallie Mae and Nelnet of Abusive Treatment of Borrowers*, Chron. of Higher Educ., Apr. 26, 2007.

197 Miele v. Sid Bailey, Inc., 192 B.R. 611 (S.D.N.Y. 1996). *See also* Padilla v. Payco Gen. Am. Credits, Inc., 161 F. Supp. 2d 264 (S.D.N.Y. 2001) (numerous FDCPA violations raised, including charging of excessive collection fees and illegal contacts with borrower).

of class actions have been brought in this area.[198]

Private FDCPA actions are in many cases the only way borrowers can raise legal claims when collectors violate Department of Education collection regulations. Borrowers generally do not have a private right of action under the HEA.[199] However, a collector's failure to follow the law or a collector's misrepresentation of applicable law may violate the FDCPA.

There are limits to using fair debt claims to resolve student loan disputes. The FDCPA is an indirect way of obtaining relief. It is intended to address collection abuses. A collection agency's failure to offer a particular repayment plan or otherwise comply with the HEA is a violation. However, the available remedies are monetary damages. Damages include up to $1000 statutory damages.[200] These cases can be useful, but they do not help borrowers get the repayment plans or discharges to which they are entitled. Advocates who bring these cases should try to directly assist borrowers using the other strategies discussed in this manual or refer borrowers for assistance.

7.4.2.2 Illegal Debt Collection Activity Not Unique to Student Loans

The previous subsection outlined some special forms of illegal debt collection conduct relating solely to student loans. In addition, collectors may engage in a number of other basic forms of illegal debt collection that apply to collection of any type of consumer debt.

This subsection briefly lists a number of practices that are prohibited under the federal Fair Debt Collection Practices Act and can lead to actions for actual damages, up to $1000 in statutory damages, plus attorney fees.[201]

One example of a fair debt collection standard is that the collection agency must stop contacting the borrower if the borrower so requests in writing.[202] The Department claims in the 2009 PCA manual that the agency is allowed one final contact.[203] This could be a violation of the FDCPA if the contact is used to do more than advise the consumer that the collector's further efforts are being terminated or to notify the consumer that the collector may invoke specified remedies.[204]

Another fair debt collection standard requires the collection agency, in its initial communication or within five days of that communication, to send the borrower a written notice identifying the debt and the creditor and giving the borrower the right to dispute the debt or to request the name and address of the original creditor, if different from the current one. If the borrower raises a dispute, the collector must suspend collection efforts on the disputed portion of the debt until the collector responds to the request.[205]

The following collection agency conduct also violates the FDCPA:

- Communicating with third parties, such as relatives, employers, friends, or neighbors, about a debt unless the borrower or a court has given the collector permis-

---

198 *See, e.g.*, Kort v. Diversified Collection Servs., Inc., 2001 WL 881449 (N.D. Ill. Aug. 2, 2001), *class cert. granted in part*, 2001 WL 1617213 (N.D. Ill. Dec. 17, 2001) (collector allegedly violated FDCPA by giving borrowers insufficient time to respond to wage garnishment notices and by requiring affirmative proof of unemployment exception to garnishment).

The court granted summary judgment on plaintiff's claim that the collection letter in this case would cause an unsophisticated consumer to believe that a wage garnishment could occur before expiration of the thirty-day notice period required by the HEA. Kort v. Diversified Collection Servs., Inc., 270 F. Supp. 2d 1017 (N.D. Ill. 2003).

The district court granted summary judgment to the collection agency on plaintiff's claim that the agency's notice contained misinformation about the HEA unemployment exemption. The court found that the agency was insulated from liability under the FDCPA's bona fide error defense. The Seventh Circuit agreed. Kort v. Diversified Collection Servs., Inc., 270 F. Supp. 2d 1017 (N.D. Ill. 2003), *aff'd*, 394 F.3d 530 (7th Cir. 2005); Sanders v. OSI, 2001 WL 883608 (N.D. Ill. Aug. 3, 2001) (similar FDCPA violations alleged as those in *Kort*); Cliff v. Payco Gen. Am. Credits, Inc. (M.D. Fla. 1998) (class action complaint), *available on* the companion website to this manual (suit alleged violation of due process rights in collection agencies' administration of wage garnishment procedures); Mitchell v. Educational Credit Mgmt. Corp., Clearinghouse No. 52,038 (N.D. Ill. Oct. 14, 1997) (class action complaint); Sibley v. Diversified Collection Servs. (N.D. Tex. Apr. 26, 1996), *available on* the companion website to this manual (first amended class action complaint).

Sample pleadings in cases challenging private collection agency conduct can be found at Appendix E, *infra*.

199 *See* § 12.5.2.1, *infra*.
200 15 U.S.C. § 1692k(a)(2).

These damages may be very minimal in cases in which the court views the violations as "technical." *See, e.g.*, Jackson v. Diversified Collection Servs., 2010 WL 1931013 (D. Colo. May 13, 2010) (awarding FDCPA statutory damages of $10 in student loan collection case).

201 For more detail, the best resource is National Consumer Law Center's *Fair Debt Collection* (6th ed. 2008 and Supp.), which discusses what general collection practices are prohibited and the available consumer remedies for such violations.

202 15 U.S.C. § 1692c(c).

This provision, in particular, has been cited by collection agencies lobbying Congress to exempt student loan collectors from FDCPA coverage. They point out the conflict between federal student assistance due diligence provisions that require minimum contacts and the FDCPA prohibition against contacting borrowers in certain circumstances. Consumer advocates have responded with alternatives, including exempting collectors from the due diligence contact requirements in these cases in lieu of wholesale exemption from the FDCPA. This issue is likely to arise again in future legislative sessions.

203 U.S. Dep't of Educ., PCA Procedures Manual: 2009 ED Collections Contract 32 (Sept. 2009).

204 15 U.S.C. § 1692c(c). *See generally* National Consumer Law Center, Fair Debt Collection, § 5.3.8 (6th ed. 2008 and Supp.).

205 15 U.S.C. § 1692g. *See* Avila v. Rubin, 84 F.3d 222 (7th Cir. 1996) (student loan collector liable when other language overshadowed validation notice).

sion to do so. Several narrow exceptions to this prohibition apply. Collectors may contact creditors, attorneys, credit reporting agencies, co-signers, spouses, and parents if the borrower is a minor. Third-party contacts are also permitted if the contacts are solely for the purpose of locating the borrower and do not reveal in any way the contact's underlying purpose.[206]

- Communicating with the borrower at unusual or inconvenient times or places. Times from 8:00 a.m. to 9:00 p.m. are generally considered convenient, but daytime contacts with a consumer known to work a night shift may be inconvenient.[207]
- Contacting a borrower at work if the collector should know that the employer prohibits personal calls, or contacting the borrower at other inconvenient places, such as at a friend's house or the hospital.[208]
- Contacting a borrower represented by a lawyer, unless the lawyer gives permission for the communication or fails to respond to the collector's communications.[209]
- Using obscene, profane, or abusive language.[210]
- Telephoning repeatedly and frequently with intent to annoy, abuse, or harass the borrower or other persons at the called number.[211]
- Telephoning without disclosing the collector's identity.[212]
- Making false, misleading, or deceptive representations in collecting debts, such as pretending that letters carry legal authority or are from the government.[213]
- Falsely representing the character, amount, or legal status of a debt or of services rendered or compensation owed.[214]
- Falsely stating or implying a lawyer's involvement, such as using form letters written on an attorney's letterhead and bearing an attorney's signature that in fact came from a collection agency and were not reviewed by a lawyer.[215]

- Stating that nonpayment will result in arrest, garnishment, or seizure of property or wages, unless such actions are lawful and unless the loan holder fully intends to take such action.[216]
- Using any false representation or other deception to collect or attempt to collect any debt or to obtain information about the borrower.[217]
- Failing to disclose in the initial written communication with the debtor that the collector is attempting to collect a debt.[218]
- Using unfair or unconscionable means to collect debts.[219]
- Collecting fees or charges unless expressly authorized by the agreement creating the debt or permitted by law.[220]

7.4.3 Applicability of the FDCPA to Student Loan Collection Activity

7.4.3.1 General

The federal Fair Debt Collection Practices Act (FDCPA) is the main statute offering student borrowers protection from debt collection harassment.[221] The statute specifies numerous prohibited collection techniques, provides debtors with certain rights, and provides students with statutory and actual damages and attorney fees for violations.[222]

The key FDCPA issue for students is whether the FDCPA applies to student loan collection activities. If it does, a student's attorney will often be able to pinpoint FDCPA violations, leading to significant recoveries.

The FDCPA applies to collection of "debts" by "debt collectors." "Debt" is defined as "any obligation or alleged obligation of a consumer to pay money arising out of a transaction in which the money, property, insurance, or

---

206 15 U.S.C. §§ 1692b, 1692c(b).
    The Department claims in the 2009 PCA manual that a request to discontinue phone calls to the employer or the home telephone number is not considered a request to cease collection activities. U.S. Dep't of Educ., PCA Procedures Manual: 2009 ED Collections Contract 32 (Sept. 2009).
207 15 U.S.C. § 1692c(a)(1).
208 15 U.S.C. § 1692c(a)(3).
209 15 U.S.C. § 1692c(a)(2). *See* Alger v. Ganick, O'Brien & Sarin, 35 F. Supp. 2d 148 (D. Mass. 1999) (contact with represented student loan debtor would be FDCPA violation).
210 15 U.S.C. § 1692d(2).
211 15 U.S.C. § 1692d(5).
212 15 U.S.C. § 1692d(6).
213 15 U.S.C. § 1692e(1), (4), (9), (10), (13). *See* Brider v. Nationwide Credit, 1998 U.S. Dist. LEXIS 22535 (N.D. Ill. June 24, 1998) (denying motion to dismiss of a collector whose collection letter had large bold heading "U.S. Department of Education").
214 15 U.S.C. § 1692e(2)(A), (10).
215 15 U.S.C. § 1692e(3), (10). *See* Avila v. Rubin, 84 F.3d 222 (2d

Cir. 1996) (collection letters on attorney's letterhead to student loan debtor misrepresented attorney's involvement).
216 *See* Avila v. Rubin, 84 F.3d 222 (2d Cir. 1996).
217 15 U.S.C. § 1692e(10). *See* Alger v. Ganick, O'Brien & Sarin, 35 F. Supp. 2d 148 (D. Mass. 1999) (false statements to court that student loan debtor had not been making payments).
218 15 U.S.C. § 1692e(11).
219 15 U.S.C. § 1692f. *See* Alger v. Ganick, O'Brien & Sarin, 35 F. Supp. 2d 148 (D. Mass. 1999) (falsely telling process server that student loan debt was unpaid and instructing him to notify debtor to appear in court would be violation).
220 15 U.S.C. § 1692f(1). *See* Padilla v. Payco Gen. Am. Credits, Inc., 161 F. Supp. 2d 264 (S.D.N.Y. 2001) (plaintiff's summary judgment motion granted on claim that collection agency charged fees above the 18.5% allowable limit); Alger v. Ganick, O'Brien & Sarin, 35 F. Supp. 2d 148 (D. Mass. 1999) (instructing process server to demand inflated amount on student loan debt would be violation).
221 15 U.S.C. §§ 1692–1692o.
222 The FDCPA is examined in **great detail** in another NCLC manual, Fair Debt Collection (6th ed. 2008 and Supp.).

services that are the subject of the transaction are primarily for personal, family, or household purposes, whether or not such obligation has been reduced to judgment."[223] There is no question that student loan debts fall within this definition.[224]

More controversial, however, is the question of whether an entity seeking to collect a student loan debt meets the FDCPA definition of "debt collector." The basic definition of "debt collector" is "any person who uses any instrumentality of interstate commerce or the mails in any business the principal purpose of which is the collection of any debts, or who regularly collects or attempts to collect, directly or indirectly, debts owed or due or asserted to be owed or due another."[225] There are many qualifications and exceptions to this definition. The analysis varies significantly depending on whether the entity is a private collector or attorney, a nonprofit guarantor, a state agency, or the Department of Education.

If any of these entities are considered "debt collectors," the FDCPA should apply. As one court noted, there is no reason to assume that, given the congressional interest in student loan collection (in this case through wage garnishment), Congress would want to see collection efforts proceeding in an abusive and unfair manner that would otherwise run afoul of the FDCPA.[226]

Another key issue is whether an entity may evade liability by arguing that a violation occurred due to a bona fide error.[227] Debt collectors are not liable under the FDCPA if they can show by a preponderance of evidence that the violation was not intentional and resulted from a bona fide error, notwithstanding the maintenance of procedures reasonably adapted to avoid any such error.[228]

7.4.3.2 Independent Collection Agencies and Attorneys

There should be little question that an independent collection agency is covered by the FDCPA.[229] The Department affirms in the 2009 manual for collection agencies that the FDCPA applies to these agencies.[230] The FDCPA also applies to attorneys hired to sue or collect on student loans.[231] The FDCPA exception for "any officer or employee of the United States or any State"[232] does not apply to these collectors, since they are not governmental employees but private parties who have governmental contracts.[233]

Although they may acknowledge that they are generally covered by the FDCPA, private collectors may also claim that they are not subject to the FDCPA in cases in which the

---

223 15 U.S.C. § 1692a(5).
224 Brannan v. United Student Aid Funds, Inc., 94 F.3d 1260 (9th Cir. 1996); Juras v. Aman Collection Serv., Inc., 829 F.2d 739 (9th Cir. 1987); McComas v. Financial Collection Agencies, 1997 U.S. Dist. LEXIS 2725 (S.D. W. Va. Mar. 7, 1997); Beaulieu v. American Nat'l Educ. Corp., No. CV 79-L-271, Clearinghouse No. 30,892 (D. Neb. 1981); Carrigan v. Central Adjustment Bureau, Inc., 494 F. Supp. 824 (N.D. Ga. 1980); Statements of General Policy or Interpretation Staff Commentary on the Fair Debt Collection Practices Act , 53 Fed. Reg. 50097, 50102 § 803(5) (Dec. 13, 1988), *reprinted in* National Consumer Law Center, Fair Debt Collection Appx. C (6th ed. 2008 and Supp.).
225 15 U.S.C. § 1692a(6).
226 Kort v. Diversified Collection Servs., Inc., 270 F. Supp. 2d 1017 (N.D. Ill. 2003).
227 Beck v. Maximus, Inc., 457 F.3d 291 (3d Cir. 2006) (effect of debt collector's alleged bona fide error defense had to be considered in determining plaintiff's typicality and adequacy as class representative in case challenging Department of Education contractor's routine mailing of employment verification requests to employers); Kort v. Diversified Collection Servs., Inc., 394 F.3d 530 (7th Cir. 2005).
228 15 U.S.C. § 1692k(c). *See* National Consumer Law Center, Fair Debt Collection § 7.2 (6th ed. 2008 and Supp.).

229 31 U.S.C. § 3718(a)(2); Cliff v. Payco Gen. Am. Credits, Inc., 363 F.3d 1113 (11th Cir. 2004) (Secretary of Education expressed belief that third-party debt collectors acting on behalf of guaranty agencies to collect federal student loans come within the FDCPA); Kort v. Diversified Collection Servs., 270 F. Supp. 2d 1017 (N.D. Ill. 2003).

The district court granted summary judgment to the collection agency on plaintiff's claim that the agency's notice contained misinformation about the HEA unemployment exemption. The court found that the agency was insulated from liability under the FDCPA's bona fide error defense. The Seventh Circuit agreed. Kort v. Diversified Collection Servs., Inc., 270 F. Supp. 2d 1017 (N.D. Ill. 2003), *aff'd*, 394 F.3d 530 (7th Cir. 2005); Richardson v. Baker, 663 F. Supp. 651 (S.D.N.Y. 1987) (FDCPA applies to collector servicing a tax intercept for the Department of Education); Marritz, FTC Informal Staff Letter (Nov. 6, 1978), *reprinted in* National Consumer Law Center, Fair Debt Collection B (6th ed. 2008 and Supp.), *available on* the companion website to this manual.

For a good discussion on using the FDCPA in student loan cases, see Arroyo v. Solomon & Solomon, 2001 U.S. Dist. LEXIS 21908 (E.D.N.Y. Nov. 16, 2001).

230 U.S. Dep't of Educ., PCA Procedures Manual: 2009 ED Collections Contract 19 (Sept. 2009).
231 Asch v. Teller, Levit & Silvertrust, P.C., 2003 WL 22232801 (N.D. Ill. Sept. 26, 2003) (borrowers granted summary judgment under federal and state fair debt collection practices laws).

Defendant law firm collectors were collaterally estopped from contesting liability in a later lawsuit brought under the federal False Claims Act. Alger v. Ganick, O'Brien & Sarin, 35 F. Supp. 2d 148 (D. Mass. 1999); Knight v. Schulman, 102 F. Supp. 2d 867 (S.D. Ohio 1999). *See* Memorandum Opinion and Order, United States v. Teller, Levit & Silvertrust, P.C., No. 00 C 3290 (N.D. Ill., May 7, 2004).

In a later ruling, the court granted plaintiff's request for an injunction to prohibit defendants from collecting on accounts affected by defendants' failure to credit payments. Asch v. Teller, Levit & Silvertrust, P.C., 2004 WL 2967441 (N.D. Ill. Nov. 24, 2004) (granting in part and denying in part plaintiff's motion for further summary judgment). *See also* 31 U.S.C. § 3718. *See generally* Heintz v. Jenkins, 514 U.S. 291, 115 S. Ct. 1489, 131 L. Ed. 2d 395 (1995).

232 15 U.S.C. § 1692a(6)(C).
233 Knight v. Schulman, 102 F. Supp. 2d 867 (S.D. Ohio 1999). *See also* Richardson v. Baker, 663 F. Supp. 651 (S.D.N.Y. 1987) (fact that collector sent letters at behest of Department of Education does not exempt it from FDCPA).

FDCPA prohibits behavior that is required pursuant to HEA due diligence collection rules.[234] At least one court concluded that it may be appropriate for specific provisions of the HEA to qualify specific provisions of the FDCPA. However, where the HEA is silent, the court gave full effect to the FDCPA.[235] However, the court also found that the collection agency was not liable for one of the FDCPA violations because it was a bona fide error.[236] The key issue is whether a collector can comply with both the HEA and debt collection laws simultaneously. If so, there should be no conflict with the FDCPA and no preemption of state laws.[237] In cases in which conflicts may arise, the courts are likely to find that the HEA requirements take precedence.[238]

7.4.3.3 Department of Education Employees

The FDCPA specifically excludes any officer or employee of the United States or any state to the extent that their activities are in the performance of their official duties.[239] A court may also find that the Department is not a debt collector within the FDCPA definition because the collection of debts is not a principal purpose of its business and the Department is arguably collecting its own debts and not the debts of another.[240] The Department also includes a clause in its agreements with private collection agencies that hold the Department harmless for the acts of the collection agency.[241]

Guaranty agencies should not be exempt from liability under this "government actor" exemption to the FDCPA.[242] However, guaranty agencies may be exempt on other grounds.[243]

Although the law should be clear that the Department's own actions are not covered while actions by private collectors are, the problem in many cases is determining who in fact engaged in the deceptive conduct—the private collector or the Department. While the Department has turned over almost all its defaulted loans to private collectors, the Department continues to assist those collectors.

Even if the Department is partially responsible for deceptive collection practices, the debt collection agency doing the actual collection may still be liable under the FDCPA. For example, even if the Department actually sent deceptive dunning notices that instruct borrowers to make payments to a private debt collector, the letter may be viewed as an "indirect" attempt by the collection agency to collect a debt, which is within the scope of the FDCPA.[244] In some cases, private collectors use the Department of Education's name and/or address on the envelope or otherwise deceive borrowers into thinking they are receiving communications from the Department. These actions should be violations of the FDCPA.[245]

---

234 Kort v. Diversified Collection Servs., 270 F. Supp. 2d 1017 (N.D. Ill. 2003).

235 Id. (defendant collection agency pointed to the following alleged conflicts between the FDCPA and HEA: HEA regulations require collection agency to send several written notices the borrower, while the FDCPA requires debt collectors to terminate communications at borrower's request; the HEA requires an agency to make diligent attempts to trace borrower while the FDCPA limits contacts that debt collectors may make with third parties; the HEA requires contractor performing garnishment services to contact debtor's employer, an impermissible third-party contact under the FDCPA).

236 Kort v. Diversified Collection Servs., Inc., 394 F.3d 530 (7th Cir. 2005).

Debt collectors are not liable under the FDCPA if they can show by a preponderance of evidence that the violation was not intentional and resulted from a bona fide error notwithstanding the maintenance of procedures reasonably adapted to avoid any such error. 15 U.S.C. § 1692k(c).

237 See Cliff v. Payco Gen. Am. Credits, Inc., 363 F.3d 1113 (11th Cir. 2004) (claims brought under both federal and state laws); Kort v. Diversified Collection Servs., Inc., 270 F. Supp. 2d 1017 (N.D. Ill. 2003) (claims brought under FDCPA only).

238 Cliff v. Payco Gen. Am. Credits, Inc., 363 F.3d 1113 (11th Cir. 2004). See § 7.4.4, infra.

239 15 U.S.C. § 1692a(6)(C); Wagstaff v. U.S. Dep't of Educ., 509 F.3d 661 (5th Cir. 2007) (FDCPA does not contain an unequivocal and express waiver of sovereign immunity); Nelson v. U.S. Dep't of Educ., 680 F. Supp. 2d 45 (D.D.C. 2010); Greenland v. Van Ru Credit Corp., 2007 WL 4245409 (W.D. Mich. Nov. 29, 2007); DiNello v. U.S. Dep't of Educ., 2006 WL 3783010 (N.D. Ill. Dec. 21, 2006) (DOE is not a debt collector under FDCPA); Frew v. Van Ru Credit Corp., 2006 WL 2261624 (E.D. Pa. Aug. 7, 2006). See, e.g., Chatmon v. U.S. Dep't of Educ., 2003 WL 21501919 (N.D. Tex. June 24, 2003) (Department of Education official does not fall within FDCPA definition of debt collector because the Department was collecting debt owed to it and because official was acting within the scope of her employment).

240 See Chatmon v. U.S. Dep't of Educ., 2003 WL 21501919 (N.D. Tex. June 24, 2003) (Department had already reimbursed guaranty agencies when loans were assigned to it and thus Department was attempting to collect for itself).

The FDCPA does not apply to creditors collecting their own debts. 15 U.S.C. § 1692a(6)(A). See generally National Consumer Law Center, Fair Debt Collection § 4.2 (6th ed. 2008 and Supp.).

241 U.S. Dep't of Educ., PCA Procedures Manual: 2009 ED Collections Contract 9 (Sept. 2009) (referring to FDCPA violations).

242 See Brannan v. United Student Aid Funds, 94 F.3d 1260 (9th Cir. 1996); Virgen v. Mae, 2007 WL 1521553 (E.D. Cal. May 23, 2007) (guaranty agency not exempt from FDCPA under "government actor" exemption but exempt under "fiduciary exemption"); Rowe v. Educational Credit Mgmt. Corp., 465 F. Supp. 2d 1101 (D. Or. 2006), report and recommendation adopted by 2007 WL 1821414 (E.D. Cal. June 25, 2007), rev'd in part, 559 F.3d 1028 (9th Cir. 2009).

243 See § 7.4.3.5, infra.

244 See 15 U.S.C. § 1692a(6) (" 'debt collector' means any person who ... attempts to collect ... indirectly, debts owed ... another")

245 See Peter v. GC Serv., L.P., 310 F.3d 344 (5th Cir. 2002) (debt collector's use of a Department of Education return address on a student loan collection letter violated the Fair Debt Collection Practices Act).

7.4.3.4 Secondary Market Lenders and Servicing Agencies

The FDCPA does not apply to creditors collecting their own debts but only to collection agencies and collection attorneys.[246] If a lender has not yet turned an FFEL loan over to the guarantor or a school is collecting on a Perkins loan, and if the lender or school is doing the collection activity through its own in-house staff, the FDCPA does not apply. Furthermore, the FDCPA only applies if the third-party collector obtained the debt after it had gone into default.[247] On the other hand, if the lender or school turns a defaulted loan over to a third party for collection, that third party is liable under the FDCPA.

Particularly before the credit crisis and before the elimination of the FFEL Program, an FFEL-originating lender would sell the loan *before* default to a secondary market lender. In other situations, an FFEL lender will hire a servicing company *before* default to service the loan payments for the lender. In these situations, the secondary market lender and servicer are not covered by the FDCPA, because they are not assigned the loan post-default and are not taking the loan to collect on a default.[248]

Some advocates have argued that collection agencies should be covered by the FDCPA if they acquired the debt after it became "delinquent" as defined by the student loan regulations, even if it was not yet in "default" as defined by those same regulations.[249] The ambiguity arises because the FDCPA does not provide a definition of "default."[250]

The default period in the student loan regulations (previously 180 days, now 270) is unusually long. Borrower advocates argue that allowing such a long period without FDCPA coverage is inconsistent with the purposes of the FDCPA. According to this argument, the definition of "default" in the FDCPA should be the same as "delinquent" in the student loan regulations. The Federal Trade Commission's official staff commentary on the FDCPA lends support to this argument, as the commentary states that the exemption "applies to parties such as mortgage service companies whose business is servicing *current* accounts."[251] Courts have, however, rejected these arguments and interpreted the definition of "default" for FDCPA coverage to be the same as the definition of "default" in the student loan regulations.[252] These courts exempt servicers from the FDCPA even if they acquire the loan for servicing after the borrower is delinquent (according to federal student loan regulations) but before default.[253]

---

246 15 U.S.C. § 1692a(6)(A); Sparrow v. SLM Corp., 2009 WL 77462 (D. Md. Jan. 7, 2009) (as a creditor collecting its own debts in this case, Sallie Mae was subject to the FDCPA). *Cf.* Fischer v. Unipac Serv. Corp., 519 N.W.2d 793 (Iowa 1994) (FDCPA does not apply to loan servicer hired before default). *See generally* Pelfrey v. Educational Credit Mgmt. Corp., 71 F. Supp. 2d 1161 (N.D. Ala. 1999), *aff'd*, 208 F.3d 945 (11th Cir. 2000).

247 15 U.S.C. § 1692a(6)(F)(iii); Gibbs v. SLM Corp., 336 F. Supp. 2d 1 (D. Mass. 2004) (FDCPA does not apply when loan was obtained before borrower was in default).

248 15 U.S.C. § 1692a(6)(F)(iii); Johnson v. Sallie Mae Servicing Corp., 102 Fed. Appx. 484 (7th Cir. 2004) (servicing corporation was not a "debt collector" subject to FDCPA liability because debtor's student loans clearly were not in default when servicing corporation acquired them); Brumberger v. Sallie Mae Servicing Corp., 2003 WL 1733548 (E.D. La. Mar. 28, 2003), *aff'd*, 84 Fed. Appx. 458 (5th Cir. 2004) (FDCPA did not apply to loan servicer because borrower was not in default at the time servicer began servicing the loan); Fischer v. Unipac Serv. Corp., 519 N.W.2d 793 (Iowa 1994) (FDCPA does not apply to loan servicer hired before default). *See* National Consumer Law Center, Fair Debt Collection § 4.3.10 (6th ed. 2008 and Supp.). *See also* Coppola v. Connecticut Student Loan Found., 1989 U.S. Dist. LEXIS 3415 (D. Conn. Mar. 21, 1989).

249 15 U.S.C. § 1692a(6)(F)(iii).

250 The lack of a definition for the term "default" in the FDCPA has led courts to come up with inconsistent interpretations. At least one court, however, concluded that all the decisions agree that default does not occur until well after a debt becomes outstanding. *See* Alibrandi v. Financial Outsourcing Serv., Inc., 333 F.3d 82, 87 (2d Cir. 2003) (rejecting debtor's argument that default occurs immediately after a debt becomes due; in interpreting "default," court looked to underlying purpose of the FDCPA; concluding that the FDCPA's "pro-debtor" purposes would not be served if it adopted plaintiff's argument that default occurs immediately after payment becomes due, which, according to the court would have the paradoxical effect of immediately exposing debtors to the sort of adverse collection measures from which the FDCPA intended to protect them).

251 Statements of General Policy or Interpretation Staff Commentary On the Fair Debt Collection Practices Act, 53 Fed. Reg. 50097, 50103 § 803-4(f) (Dec. 13, 1988) (emphasis added).

252 *See* Brannan v. United Student Aid Funds, 94 F.3d 1260, 1262 n.3 (9th Cir. 1996) (holding limited to guaranty agency not fitting within government actor exception, and debt in this case obtained after default); Seals v. National Student Loan Program, 2004 WL 3314948 (N.D. W. Va. Aug. 16, 2004), *aff'd*, 124 Fed. Appx. 182 (4th Cir. 2005) (per curiam); Brumberger v. Sallie Mae Servicing Corp., 2003 WL 1733548 (E.D. La. Mar. 28, 2003), *aff'd*, 84 Fed. Appx. 458 (5th Cir. 2004) (citing Skerry v. Massachusetts Higher Educ. Assistance Corp. with approval; finding found no viable federal claims under FDCPA, Fair Credit Reporting Act, or Consumer Credit Protection Act); Skerry v. Massachusetts Higher Educ. Assistance Corp., 73 F. Supp. 2d 47 (D. Mass. 1999); Jones v. Intuition, Inc., 12 F. Supp. 2d 775 (W.D. Tenn. 1998). *See also* Pelfrey v. Educational Credit Mgmt. Corp., 71 F. Supp. 2d 1161 (N.D. Ala. 1999), *aff'd*, 208 F.3d 945 (11th Cir. 2000) (discussing issue but finding collector exempt for other reasons); Games v. Cavazos, 737 F. Supp. 1368 (D. Del. 1990) (decision based on government actor exception); Coppola v. Connecticut Student Loan Found., 1989 U.S. Dist. LEXIS 3415 (D. Conn. Mar. 21, 1989) (servicing agency not covered because note not in default when transferred to secondary lender for whom agency serviced loan; facts suggest that plaintiff was current on payments at the time so loan was neither "delinquent" nor in "default").

253 *See, e.g.*, Skerry v. Massachusetts, 73 F. Supp. 2d 47 (D. Mass. 1999); Mondonedo v. Sallie Mae Inc., 2009 WL 801784 (D. Kan. Mar. 25, 2009).

7.4.3.5 FDCPA Applicability to Guaranty Agencies

Much of the collection on FFEL Program loans (FFELs) is conducted by guaranty agencies or collection agencies hired by the guarantor. If a guaranty agency hires a private collector, that collector is covered by the FDCPA just as a collector hired by the Department is covered. Despite the elimination of the FFEL Program in 2010, most guaranty agencies have not yet closed. They continue to collect on their existing portfolios of FFELs.[254]

Nevertheless, the guarantor itself still engages in a significant amount of collection activity. State-created guaranty agencies may be exempt under the FDCPA's exclusion of state employees, depending on the structure and authority given the agency by the state legislature.[255]

Private guaranty agencies should clearly fall under the general definition of "collector" as defined in the FDCPA.[256] The governmental exemption does not apply to these agencies, and a guaranty agency meets the other criteria for a debt collector under the FDCPA.[257] To be a debt collector, the guaranty agency's principal purpose must be the collection of debts or it must regularly collect debts owed another,[258] interpreted to mean *originally* owed another.[259]

Historically, guaranty agencies have devoted most of their resources to collecting on defaulted loans, and their other functions are relatively minor. There is thus a strong argument that collection of debts is their principal purpose.[260] Even if this argument is unsuccessful, it is clear that guaranty agencies regularly collect debts owed another and are therefore covered by the FDCPA.[261]

Consequently, the key initial issue in bringing an FDCPA action against a guarantor is determining whether the guarantor is a state or a private entity. Private agencies should clearly fall within the FDCPA's definition of "collector." State agencies, on the other hand, will likely be exempted under the FDCPA's exclusion of state employees.[262]

Advocates should not rely on an agency's name or prior status to indicate that it is a state agency but should verify this independently. A number of guarantors recently have switched from being state entities to private one or have formed separate subsidiaries.[263] Agencies that appear to be public at first glance may in fact be private and therefore covered by the FDCPA.

A private guaranty agency may try to avoid coverage by arguing that it obtained the debt at the time the agency became the guarantor of the debt (that is, at the initiation of the loan, when the loan was not in default) and that it is therefore exempt.[264] Courts have rejected this specious argument, holding that merely acting as guarantor does not amount to "obtaining" a debt.[265]

---

254 See § 1.3.2, *supra*.
255 15 U.S.C. § 1692a(6)(C).
   State guaranty agencies will likely argue that FDCPA claims against them are barred by Eleventh Amendment sovereign immunity. *See, e.g.*, Sorrell v. Illinois Student Assistance Comm'n, 314 F. Supp. 2d 813 (C.D. Ill. 2004) (plaintiff's FDCPA claims in student loan case barred by Eleventh Amendment). *See also* Codar, Inc. v. Arizona, 168 F.3d 498 (9th Cir. 1999) (in non-student-loan case, plaintiff's FDCPA claims were barred by the Eleventh Amendment).
   See § 10.8, *infra*, for discussion of sovereign immunity in bankruptcy context.
256 Brannan v. United Student Aid Funds, Inc., 94 F.3d 1260 (9th Cir. 1996); Sibley v. Diversified Collection Servs., Inc., 1997 U.S. Dist. LEXIS 23583 (N.D. Tex. June 10, 1997) (ruling on defendants' motion to dismiss).
   See Appendix G, *infra*, for a complete list of state guaranty agencies and contact information.
257 Brannan v. United Student Aid Funds, Inc., 94 F.3d 1260 (9th Cir. 1996); Student Loan Fund, Inc. v. Duerner, 951 P.2d 1272 (Idaho 1997) (court held that guaranty agency was a collector within meaning of FDCPA; guaranty agency "did not become a governmental employee by virtue of its contract with a government agency"). *See also* Spears v. Bowman, 875 F.2d 867 (6th Cir. 1989) (unpublished, full text available at 1989 U.S. App. LEXIS 6208) (reversing ruling that collection agency was exempt as de facto state employee; remanding for factual determination of legal relationship between it and state). *But see* Games v. Cavazos, 737 F. Supp. 1368 (D. Del. 1990) (USA Funds was performing essentially a governmental function in assisting the United States in tax intercept process and, because other state guaranty agencies were in fact state entities, it made no sense to the court to distinguish between guaranty agencies that were private entities and those that were state agencies).
258 15 U.S.C. § 1692a(6).
   The guaranty agency is not a creditor because it is assigned the debt for the purposes of collecting the debt. *Id.* § 1692a(4).
259 *See* Games v. Cavazos, 737 F. Supp. 1368 (D. Del. 1990); Student Loan Fund, Inc. v. Duerner, 951 P.2d 1272 (Idaho 1997). *But see* Trubek, FTC Informal Staff Letter (Sept. 12, 1988) (Great Lakes Higher Education Corporation not covered because it is a servicing company; it is also a creditor because it owns the loans it guarantees). *See generally* Kimber v. Federal Fin. Corp., 668 F. Supp. 1480 (M.D. Ala. 1987).
260 *See* Games v. Cavazos, 737 F. Supp. 1368 (D. Del. 1990); Student Loan Fund, Inc. v. Duerner, 951 P.2d 1272 (Idaho 1997) (holding that bank, not the guaranty agency, was originator of the loans after agency argued unsuccessfully that the agency should be excluded from FDCPA coverage because it was collecting a debt that it originated). *But see* Trubek, FTC Informal Staff Letter (Sept. 12, 1988) (Great Lakes Higher Education Corporation not covered because it is a servicing company; it is also a creditor because it owns the loans it guarantees).
261 Games v. Cavazos, 737 F. Supp. 1368 (D. Del. 1990); Student Loan Fund, Inc. v. Duerner, 951 P.2d 1272 (Idaho 1997).
262 15 U.S.C. § 1692a(6)(C).
263 For example, in 1997 the California Student Aid Commission (CSAC) set up EDFUND as a separate nonprofit corporation. For a complete list of state guaranty agencies, see Appendix G, *infra*. This information is also available on the Department of Education's website at www.ed.gov.
264 See the exemption at 15 U.S.C. § 1692a(6)(F)(iii).
265 Sibley v. Diversified Collection Servs., Inc., 1997 U.S. Dist. LEXIS 23583 (N.D. Tex. June 10, 1997). *See also* Games v. Cavazos, 737 F. Supp. 1368 (D. Del. 1990) (fact that guaranty agency once held the debt does not exempt it when it had

To avoid FDCPA coverage, state and private guaranty agencies may also argue that the numerous relationships and connections between the United States government and guaranty agencies place agencies in the position of fiduciaries for the government and, thus, such agencies fall within the exemption for bona fide fiduciaries. This provision of the FDCPA excludes from the definition of "debt collector" any person or agency attempting to collect a debt to the extent such activity is incidental to a bona fide fiduciary obligation or a bona fide escrow arrangement.[266] At least a few courts have exempted nonprofit and private guaranty agencies on this basis.[267]

The Ninth Circuit addressed this issue in a 2009 case.[268] In this case, the guaranty agency Educational Credit Management Corp. (ECMC) presented three possible grounds for FDCPA exemption: that its collection activities were incidental to a bona fide fiduciary obligation, its collection activity concerned a debt which it originated, and it was a "creditor" rather than a "debt collector." The Ninth Circuit addressed the first ground only, finding that ECMC was not exempt under this category and remanding to the lower court to consider the other grounds. The court agreed that the agency had a fiduciary obligation to the Department of Education but that the collection activity was not incidental to this obligation. Although the court noted that the collection of defaulted loans is generally incidental to a guaranty agency's primary function, in this case the court accepted the borrower's evidence that the loan was assigned to ECMC by a different guarantor and acted as a collection agent.[269] The court found that such collection activity was not incidental to the guaranty agency's fiduciary duty to the Department of Education. The court also acknowledged that ECMC may turn out to have had a broader role than merely acting as a collector.

7.4.4 Applicability of State Debt Collection Law to Student Loans

While the FDCPA exempts creditors and government agencies from its scope, state law often does not. Thus, it is important to explore whether state debt collection laws apply to student loan collection.[270] In addition, state law may specifically prohibit certain collection activity not explicitly restricted by the FDCPA.

State laws that may apply include state debt collection statutes, state UDAP statutes, and common law tort theories. These legal challenges are described in detail in other NCLC manuals.[271]

In any state law challenge to student loan collection practices, advocates should expect a defense that the Higher Education Act's scheme of student loan collection preempts the state debt collection law. There can be no question that state law that directly conflicts with federal law is preempted. However, collectors even argue further that the federal scheme preempts *any* state regulation of student loan collectors.

There is a split in the circuit courts with respect to whether all state debt collection regulation is preempted or whether only those state provisions that conflict with the federal scheme are preempted.[272]

---

transferred debt to Department of Education at time of collection activities).

266 15 U.S.C. § 1692a(6)(F)(i).
267 Kirk v. ED Fund, 2007 WL 2226046 (W.D. Mo. Aug. 1, 2007) (as an auxiliary corporation of a state agency, defendant falls within FDCPA's bona fide fiduciary exception); Virgen v. Mae, 2007 WL 1521553 (E.D. Cal. May 23, 2007), *report and recommendation adopted by* 2007 WL 1821414 (E.D. Cal. June 25, 2007); Rowe v. Educational Credit Mgmt. Corp., 465 F. Supp. 2d 1101, 1103 (D. Or. 2006) (nonprofit guaranty agency is fiduciary to the United States Department of Education), *rev'd in part*, 559 F.3d 1028 (9th Cir. 2009); Seals v. National Student Loan Program, 2004 WL 3314948 (N.D. W. Va. Aug. 16, 2004), *aff'd*, 124 Fed. Appx. 182 (4th Cir. 2005) (per curiam). *See* Pelfrey v. Educational Credit Mgmt. Corp., 71 F. Supp. 2d 1161 (N.D. Ala. 1999), *aff'd*, 208 F.3d 945 (11th Cir. 2000); Davis v. United Student Aid Funds, Inc., 45 F. Supp. 2d 1104 (D. Kan. 1998) (in granting motion to dismiss, court found that nonprofit student loan guaranty agency was a fiduciary and therefore not a debt collector).

The *Pelfrey* court repeatedly cited a declaration filed with the court by Larry Oxendine, Director of Guarantor and Lender Oversight Service with the Department of Education. This declaration is a useful summary of the various arguments guaranty agencies will use to support their position that they are exempt from the FDCPA. For a copy of the Oxendine declaration from another case, see Declaration of Larry Oxendine, Mitchell v. Educational Credit Mgmt. Corp. (N.D. Ill. 1997), *available on* the companion website to this manual.

268 Rowe v. Educational Credit Mgmt. Corp., 559 F.3d 1028 (9th Cir. 2009).

269 *Id.* ECMC acknowledged in this case that it was a guaranty agency. This may not always occur since ECMC is part of the larger ECMC Group, a private nonprofit corporation and guaranty agency. *See, e.g.*, Manalansan-Lord v. Direct Loan Servicing Ctr., 2008 WL 4693410 (E.D. Mo. Oct. 22, 2008) (in motion to dismiss, ECMC stated that it was not a guaranty agency and not a debt collector). *See also* Gruen v. EdFund, 2009 WL 2136785 (N.D. Cal. July 15, 2009). *But see* Murungi v. Texas Guaranteed, 693 F. Supp. 2d 597 (E.D. La. 2010) (guaranty agency's central function is to guarantee student loans made by other entities and manage funds on behalf of government; debt collection activities are secondary).

270 Patzka v. Viterbo Coll., 917 F. Supp. 654 (W.D. Wis. 1996) (school barred from collecting interest when student not informed of interest rate; FDCPA and Wisconsin UDAP violations claimed); Sibley v. Firstcollect, Inc., 913 F. Supp. 469 (M.D. La. 1995).

For a general discussion of federal preemption in student loan cases, see § 12.5.3.4, *infra*.

271 National Consumer Law Center, Fair Debt Collection Chs. 8, 10, 11 (6th ed. 2008 and Supp.); National Consumer Law Center, Unfair and Deceptive Acts and Practices §§ 2.2.2, 5.1.1 (7th ed. 2008 and Supp.).

272 *See* § 12.5.3.4, *infra*.

§ 7.4.4

In the earlier case, *Brannan v. United Student Aid Funds*, the Ninth Circuit concluded that the federal scheme "totally occupies the field" and thus all state regulation is preempted.[273] The Ninth Circuit held that state law was preempted in any circumstances under which state law regulates pre-litigation collection activity.[274] The dissent, however, puts forth the better argument that the whole Oregon statute should not be preempted but only those prohibitions that specifically preempt a federal requirement.[275]

In 2004, the Eleventh Circuit disagreed with the *Brannan* decision.[276] In *Cliff v. Payco*, the plaintiffs claimed that the collection agency violated state and federal fair debt laws, mainly with respect to its administration of the wage garnishment program.[277] The plaintiffs argued that the "notwithstanding any provision of state law" language in the wage garnishment section of the HEA explicitly preempts only those state laws that regulate garnishment. The court agreed.

In finding that the state debt collection law was not preempted by the HEA, the court disagreed with the defendant's argument that the state law actually conflicted with the HEA. The court found that the agency could comply with the HEA and the state debt collection law simultaneously.[278] However, the court cautioned that this might not always be the case. For example, the court cited the HEA regulation that requires lenders to complete due diligence requirements when attempting to collect a student loan. State laws, the court noted, might be construed to prohibit one or more of these required contacts. In that case, in the view of other courts that have confronted this issue, a claim brought under state law would be preempted.

The *Cliff* court explained in a footnote why it came to a different conclusion than the Ninth Circuit in *Brannan*.[279] This discussion provides a guide for practitioners seeking to raise state law claims against student loan collectors. First, the court pointed out that the *Brannan* majority failed to analyze conflict preemption on a provision-by-provision basis. More importantly, the court also distinguished the two cases. In *Brannan*, the plaintiff alleged that a guaranty agency threatened to cause her to lose her job, communicated with third parties about her debt, and refused to communicate with her about her debt through her attorney. Although it is not entirely clear, according to the *Cliff* court, the HEA regulations might have required the guaranty agency to engage in some or all of these actions. In contrast, *Cliff*'s allegations are based upon a provision of state law that does not hinder the completion of the sequence of contacts.[280]

It is important to note that the plaintiffs in *Cliff* did not argue that the HEA gave them a private right of action, conceding that this issue had previously been decided against them.[281] Furthermore, the plaintiffs argued that enforcing state debt collection law against the collector is not tantamount to giving borrowers a private right of action. If that were the case, according to the plaintiffs, then the HEA should have preclusive effect on claims under the FDCPA, but courts have consistently held otherwise.[282]

The *Cliff* court also dismissed the defendant's arguments that allowing plaintiffs to proceed under state law would undermine the HEA's enforcement scheme. Finally, the court rejected the defendant's argument that the four-year statute of limitations under state law would discourage lenders from participating in federal loan programs. The court noted that collection agencies are already subject to the one-year statute under the FDCPA and that there is no evidence to suggest that the four-year statute discourages lenders in any way.[283]

A number of district court decisions took this position as well.[284] These courts held that the HEA preempts only those state debt collection provisions that specifically conflict with the federal scheme.[285]

---

273 94 F.3d 1260 (9th Cir. 1996).

274 *Id.* at 1263. *See also* Pirouzian v. SLM Corp., 396 F. Supp. 2d 1124 (S.D. Cal. 2005) (*Brannan* holding applies to lenders as well as private collection agencies).

275 Brannan v. United Student Aid Funds, 94 F.3d 1260, 1266 (9th Cir. 1996) (opinion of J. Fletcher, concurring and dissenting). *See also* Seals v. National Student Loan Program, 2004 WL 3314948 (N.D. W. Va. Aug. 16, 2004), *aff'd*, 124 Fed. Appx. 182 (4th Cir. 2005) (per curiam).

276 Cliff v. Payco Gen. Am. Credits, Inc., 363 F.3d 1113 (11th Cir. 2004).

277 Cliff v. Payco Gen. Am. Credits, Inc., 363 F.3d 1113 (11th Cir. 2004).

   The issue of HEA preemption was raised as part of the plaintiff's interlocutory appeal of the district court's denial of class certification.

278 *Id.*

279 *Id.* at n.12.

280 *Id.*

281 *See* Reply Brief for Appellant, Cliff v. OSI Collection Servs., Inc., f/k/a Payco Gen. Am. Credits, Inc., Case No. 02-12462 (Oct. 24, 2002).

   The plaintiffs noted that the 11th Circuit had recently held that there is no private right of action under the HEA in McCulloch v. PNC Bank, Inc., 298 F.3d 1217 (11th Cir. 2002). This brief, as well as other pleadings in the case, are included on the companion website to this manual. For a discussion of actions under the HEA, see § 12.5.2.1, *infra*.

282 Reply Brief for Appellant, Cliff v. OSI Collection Servs., Inc., f/k/a Payco Gen. Am. Credits, Inc., Case No. 02-12462 (Oct. 24, 2002)

283 Cliff v. Payco Gen. Am. Credits, Inc., 363 F.3d 1113 (11th Cir. 2004).

284 *See, e.g.*, McComas v. Financial Collection Agencies, 1997 U.S. Dist. LEXIS 2725 (S.D. W. Va. Mar. 7, 1997); Sibley v. Diversified Collection Servs., Inc., 1997 U.S. Dist. LEXIS 23583 (N.D. Tex. June 10, 1997) (ruling on defendants' motion to dismiss) (court declined to follow majority in *Brannan* to the extent it holds that any state statute regulating debt collection practices is per se inconsistent with collection requirements placed on guarantors by federal regulations).

285 McComas v. Financial Collection Agencies, 1997 U.S. Dist. LEXIS 2725 (S.D. W. Va. Mar. 7, 1997); Sibley v. Diversified Collection Servs., Inc., 1997 U.S. Dist. LEXIS 23583 (N.D. Tex. June 10, 1997).

There are a number of reasons why the Eleventh Circuit and the district courts are correct. Federal law specifically requires that, when the Department contracts with debt collectors to recover indebtedness, the contract shall provide that the collector is subject to "the laws and regulations of the United States Government and State governments related to debt collection practices."[286] That is, private debt collectors agree in their own contracts to be subject to state debt collection laws.

In addition, the Department's own regulation preempts only state laws "that would conflict with or hinder satisfaction of the requirements of or frustrate the purposes of this section."[287] A subsequent notice of interpretation states that the Secretary "intended these provisions ... to preempt contrary or inconsistent State law to the extent necessary to permit compliance with the Federal regulations."[288] *Brannan* found other portions of this notice of interpretation to support its conclusion that the federal scheme occupies the field.[289] But the courts rejecting *Brannan* explain how *Brannan* took a particular passage out of context and that the notice of interpretation relied on by *Brannan* actually says the exact opposite—that state law is preempted only to the extent it conflicts with the federal scheme.[290]

7.4.5 Other Remedies for Government Agency Debt Collection Abuse

7.4.5.1 Other Federal Claims

In addition to the FDCPA and state debt collection law, borrowers may have other remedies for debt collection abuse. When the United States is the collector, potential claims include the Federal Tort Claims Act,[291] the Privacy Act, the Administrative Procedure Act, and the Civil Rights Act.[292] The Dodd-Frank financial reform legislation signed into law in July 2010 creates a new Consumer Financial Protection Bureau (CFPB).[293] The CFPB will have new rule writing authority for the FDCPA.[294] In general, the CFPB has rule writing authority over debt collectors.[295]

A good, but old, example of a constitutional challenge to government student loan collection practices is *Williams v. Illinois State Scholarship Commission*,[296] in which the Illinois Supreme Court ruled that an Illinois statute[297] requiring guaranty agencies to sue only in Cook County violated the Due Process Clause. *Williams* also found violative of due process the guaranty agency's practice, even prior to the passage of the Illinois *special* venue statute, of bringing all its collection actions in Cook County.[298] However, in such cases, the plaintiffs will have to prove that the guaranty agency is a state actor in order to invoke constitutional due process protections.[299]

The guaranty agency in the Illinois case argued that it could bring its collection actions in Cook County because the state's *general* venue statute allows suit in any county with sufficient contacts with the transaction. The guaranty agency claimed it approved student loans from its Cook County offices. The court analyzed the loan process and found there to be insufficient contacts with Cook County.[300] Finally, the Illinois Supreme Court in *Williams* ruled that a venue waiver or forum selection clause found in the actual student loan agreement was against public policy and void.[301]

Similarly, if the Department is responsible for sending dunning letters that mislead students concerning the legal garnishment process (failing to disclose the right to a hearing and failing to disclose various limits to that garnishment right), an argument could be made that those who are misled into making a payment to avoid the garnishment are deprived of that property without notice of their right to a hearing, as required by the HEA and by the Due Process Clause of the Fifth Amendment. Such an argument could form the basis of a civil rights claim against the Department.

If a private collector is involved, advocates should also consider raising claims other than federal and state debt collection laws to challenge abusive collection behavior. There are numerous federal, state, and tort remedies that may apply.[302]

---

286 31 U.S.C. § 3718(a)(2)(B).
287 34 C.F.R. § 682.411(o).
288 55 Fed. Reg. 40120, 40121 (Oct. 1, 1990).
289 Brannan v. United Student Aid Funds, Inc., 94 F.3d 1260 (9th Cir. 1996). *But see* Cliff v. Payco Gen. Am. Credits, Inc., 363 F.3d 1113 (11th Cir. 2004).
290 *See, e.g.*, McComas v. Financial Collection Agencies, 1997 U.S. Dist. LEXIS 2725 (S.D. W. Va. Mar. 7, 1997).
     The *Cliff* court also found the language in the notice of interpretation unpersuasive and allowed plaintiffs to proceed with state claims. Cliff v. Payco Gen. Am. Credits, Inc., 363 F.3d 1113 (11th Cir. 2004).
291 *See, e.g.*, Burgess v. U.S. Dep't of Educ., 2006 WL 1047064 (D. Vt. Apr. 17, 2006) (FTCA claim for conversion of tax return through tax offset dismissed because of plaintiff's failure to comply with FTCA notice requirements).
292 National Consumer Law Center, Fair Debt Collection § 11.2 (6th ed. 2008 and Supp.).
293 Pub. L. No. 111-203, 124 Stat. 1376 (July 21, 2010).

294 *Id.* § 1089.
295 These changes were not yet in effect at the time this manual was written.
296 563 N.E.2d 465 (1990).
297 Ill. Rev. Stat. 1988 Supp. 1, para. 12.
298 Williams v. Illinois State Scholarship Comm'n, 563 N.E.2d 465 (1990). *But see* United States v. Frisk, 675 F.2d 1079 (9th Cir. 1982).
299 *See, e.g.*, George W. v. U.S. Dep't of Educ., 149 F. Supp. 2d 1195 (E.D. Cal. 2000) (in case raising constitutional violations for alleged unreasonable charging of collection fees, court found guaranty agency was not a state actor required to afford borrower due process).
300 Williams v. Illinois State Scholarship Comm'n, 563 N.E.2d 465 (1990).
301 *Id.*
302 *See generally* National Consumer Law Center, Fair Debt Collection (6th ed. 2008 and Supp.).

7.4.5.2 Submitting Complaints About Collection Agencies

Another response to debt collection abuse is to complain to the entity that hired the collection agency. This may or may not provide any direct relief to the borrower, but it may help others.

If a guaranty agency holds a loan, the first place to complain about collection agency misconduct is the state guaranty agency. If the collection misconduct is by an employee of the guaranty agency, it is best to contact an official at a higher level of the agency. If a guaranty agency appears to be systematically failing to follow federal policy, advocates should send the Department or ombudsman the particulars of the complaint. Many guaranty agencies have their own ombudsman offices.[303] They claim to welcome complaints about the agencies that work for them.

The Department claims that it takes complaints about collection agencies very seriously and will handle them as expeditiously as possible.

Borrowers may file complaints about the Department's private collection agencies through an on-line process.[304] Written complaints should be sent, along with any evidence to: Chief of Contract Analysis and Compliance, U.S. Department of Education, 61 Forsyth St., SW 19T89, Atlanta, GA 30303.

The Department also requires collection agencies to provide a specific fax number to which complaints can be sent and to have at least one backup person designated to receive and handle complaints.[305] The agency must have at least two personnel designated to receive and manage complaints.[306] Each of the agencies holding contracts with the Department of Education is required to set up a Special Assistance Unit to address borrower concerns. The Default Resolution Group call center (1-800-621-3115) at the Department of Education is supposed to direct borrowers to the correct Special Assistance Unit personnel.

When the Department receives calls in which the borrower complains that the agency is making unreasonable demands, the contractor uses the following script:

> When your loan went into default it became due in full immediately. Therefore, the Department of Education requires its collection agencies to demand the largest amount that you can afford (or payment in full). If you cannot afford what they are demanding, the collection agency will work with you to negotiate an affordable payment arrangement, but they will need you to provide proof of your financial situation. They may require you to provide copies of your pay stubs, bank statements and bills. . . . I'm going to give you the number for a special contact person at the collection agency who is specially trained to help borrowers like yourself. You can ask this person what information you must provide them to prove what you can afford to pay."[307]

Collection agencies are supposed to suspend collection activity after receiving notice from the Department that a complaint has been received and to forward a copy to the Atlanta Regional Office.[308] The Department instructs collection agencies to immediately suspend collection activity and, if necessary or if requested by the Department, refer the issue to the Department for resolution within five calendar days after any of the following occur:

- The borrower disputes the amount owed.
- The borrower raises a legal defense against repayment.
- The borrower requests a written review or hearing in response to notice of offset or garnishment.
- The borrower files a written or verbal complaint against the collection activities of the agency.[309]

The Department does not require the agency to return the account to the Department but does require referral.

Once the Department reviews the file, the agency will be notified to resume collection activity or close and return the account. The Department claims that an agency's failure to suspend collection activity in these circumstances will result in the recall of the account.

The initial suspension should be for sixty calendar days unless a decision is made before then. After sixty days, the agency may request the return of the account.

Borrowers should also consider complaining to state authorities. For example, the Minnesota Department of Commerce issued a civil penalty in 2005 against a collection agency owned by Sallie Mae.[310] The investigation alleged that the collection agency engaged in more than fifteen violations of Minnesota law, including:

- Withdrawing money electronically from a debtor's checking account without authorization;
- Contacting debtors at employment after receiving notification to stop; and
- Disclosing debtor's information to third parties.

---

303 See § 1.12.1.2, supra.
304 As of September 2010, the link is https://secure37.softcomca.com/1800iwillpay_com/secure/piclog/index.asp.
305 U.S. Dep't of Educ., PCA Procedures Manual: 2009 ED Collections Contract 37 (Sept. 2009).
306 Id. A copy of the PCA complaint form can be found at Appendix D, infra, and on the companion website to this manual.
307 U.S. Dep't of Educ., PCA Procedures Manual: 2009 ED Collections Contract 69–70 (Sept. 2009).
308 Id. at 36.
309 Id. at 31.
310 See Press Release, Minnesota Department of Commerce, Commerce Commissioner Takes Action Against Collection Agency (Nov. 28, 2005).

7.5 Defenses to Federal Student Loan Collection Actions

7.5.1 General

This section reviews the primary defenses to federal student loan collection actions. These defenses should be available in most cases to private student loan borrowers as well. More information about private student loan collection can be found in Chapter 11, *infra*. Defenses that are based on problems with the school, particularly with proprietary schools, are covered in Chapter 12, *infra*. Chapter 12 also discusses the possibility of impleading the school in student loan collection actions.

As collection powers have grown over time, the government is less likely to sue and more likely to use its extra-judicial powers to collect student loans.[311] Litigation accounted for less than 1% of federal student loan collection in fiscal year 2009.[312] However, there will still be cases in which borrowers face collection litigation. In addition, most of the defenses discussed in this section can be raised in response to other collection actions as well.[313]

In general, the Department views a case as a "candidate for litigation" if the following conditions are met: a minimum principal balance of $2500 for Department of Justice cases, $600 for private counsel; home address verification within last thirty days; employment and/or property verification within thirty days; no payments posted within sixty days and no Treasury offset in the last two years, with some exceptions; debts must have been on the Department's system for a minimum of three years, with some exceptions; and no unresolved disputes.[314] Effective May 15, 2009, the minimum principal balance for referrals to the U.S. Attorneys offices increased to $10,000. The minimum principal balance for referrals to the districts that use private counsels remains at $600.[315] The Department also published a new litigation support manual in March 2009.[316]

7.5.2 Standing and Other Procedural Issues

There are different issues to consider depending on which entity is suing to collect the loan. If the loan is a Perkins loan, the school may be bringing the action. Alternatively, the loan may have been assigned to the Department.

In some cases, a collection agency may be the party suing to collect. In these cases, advocates will want to explore whether the collection agency is in fact the owner of the loan. Borrowers can seek through discovery the original instrument and the originals of all evidence of assignment or transfer. There may also be questions about unauthorized practice of law. States have taken very different positions as to what activities of a collection agency constitute unauthorized practice of law.[317] Some states, for example, prohibit a contingent-fee collector from filing suit in its own name.

Federal student loan borrowers generally cannot raise the statute of limitations as a defense.[318] However, the statute does apply in private loan cases. In addition, there may be some collectors that are not covered by the general elimination of the statute of limitations for federal student loans.[319]

There also may be a question about which party has the burden of proof, particularly in cases in which the borrower is claiming that he or she repaid the loan.[320] To recover on a note, the entity holding the note and suing to collect must prove that (1) the defendant signed the note; (2) the plaintiff is the present owner or holder of the note; and (3) the note is in default.[321]

The Department has acknowledged that the use of electronic promissory notes has affected the Department's ability to provide evidence necessary to prove cases in court. To address this issue, schools that participate in the Perkins Loan Program are required to retain records showing the date and amount of each disbursement of each loan made under a master promissory note (MPN).[322] Schools are also

---

311 *See* Ch. 8, *infra* (extra-judicial collection).
312 U.S. Dep't of the Treasury, U.S. Government Receivables and Debt Collection Activities of Federal Agencies: Fiscal Year 2009 Report to the Congress 14 (Mar. 2010), *available at* http://fmsq.treas.gov/news/reports/debt09.pdf.
 This data includes collections on the Department of Education's defaulted portfolio, including FFEL loans assigned to the Department.
313 More specific information about defenses to extra-judicial collection, such as wage garnishment and offset, can be found in Chapter 8, *infra*.
314 U.S. Dep't of Educ., Federal Student Aid, Litig. Support Branch, Litigation Package Manual (Oct. 2007).
315 U.S. Dep't of Educ., Financial Student Assistance, New Litigation Minimum Balances (Mar. 31, 2009).
316 U.S. Dep't of Educ., Federal Student Aid Operations Servs., Litigation Support: Litigation Package Manual (Mar. 2009), *available on* the companion website to this manual. *See also* U.S. Dep't of Educ., PCA Procedures Manual: 2009 ED Collections Contract 229 (Sept. 2009).
317 *See generally* National Consumer Law Center, Fair Debt Collection § 11.5.2 (6th ed. 2008 and Supp.).
318 See § 7.5.3, *infra*.
319 See § 7.5.3.2, *infra*.
320 *See, e.g.*, Proctor v. U.S. Dep't of Educ., 196 Fed. Appx. 345 (6th Cir. 2006) (the Department satisfied its initial burden by showing that borrower signed promissory notes, received loans, and defaulted; borrower then had to present evidence supporting his repayment defense).
321 *See, e.g.*, United States v. Elliott, 2006 WL 3759857 (N.D. Tex. Dec. 19, 2006).
 The burden then shifts to the defendant to set forth specific facts showing that there is a genuine issue for trial. Courts have found an affidavit from the borrower, without other evidence, to be insufficient to defeat a summary judgment motion. *See, e.g.*, United States v. Lawrence, 276 F.3d 193 (5th Cir. 2001); United States v. Hargrove, 2007 WL 2811832 (W.D. Pa. Sept. 24, 2007); United States v. Lawrence, 2007 WL 1675305 (E.D. Mich. June 11, 2007).
322 34 C.F.R. § 674.19(e)(2)(i).

required to retain disbursement records for each loan until the loan is canceled, repaid, or otherwise satisfied. There are additional requirements for documents submitted to the Department as part of the assignment process.[323]

For FFELs, guaranty agencies must retain required records for each loan for no less than three years following the date the loan is repaid in full by the borrower or for no less than five years following the date the agency receives payment in full from any other source.[324] Among other documentation, agencies must maintain copies of the loan application and signed promissory notes as well as documentation of any MPN confirmation process.[325] If the promissory note was signed electronically, the agency or lender must store it electronically and it must be retrievable in a coherent format.[326]

Borrowers may seek to enjoin the Department or other loan holder from collecting. There are limits, however, to a borrower's ability to enjoin the Department, as discussed in Chapter 12, *infra*.[327]

7.5.3 Statute of Limitations Is Not a Defense to Federal Student Loan Collection Action

7.5.3.1 Statute of Limitations Generally Eliminated

The Higher Education Technical Amendments of 1991, which made technical amendments to the Higher Education Act (HEA), eliminated all statutes of limitation for any collection action by a school, guaranty agency, or the United States under a federal loan program.[328] These amendments also eliminated all limitation periods for tax intercepts, wage garnishments, and other collection efforts.[329] Unfortunately for borrowers, a lingering argument to apply a time limit to Social Security offsets was finally put to rest by the U.S. Supreme Court in 2005.[330] The only end point is that collection must cease when a borrower dies. Under those circumstances, the borrower's estate or his or her family's estate is not liable for federal financial assistance debts.[331]

The lack of a statute of limitations for student loan collections places student borrowers in the unenviable company of murderers, traitors, and only a few violators of civil laws. Despite the governmental and social interest in pursuing criminals, statutes of limitation apply to nearly all federal criminal actions. The rare exceptions exist for those crimes that are punishable by death, including espionage and treason.[332] Other exceptions apply to the prosecution of persons charged with absence without leave or missing in time of war and for individuals fleeing from justice.[333]

The legislative history for this unprecedented retroactive elimination of the statute of limitations is sparse, but the elimination appears to have been derived at least in part from the unsubstantiated premise that student loan defaulters' ability to repay increases over time.[334] Furthermore, because student loans are made without considerations of creditworthiness, some in Congress argued that the benefit for the borrower far outweighs any burden resulting from the government's right to collect *forever*. Savings in the student loan program were also mentioned.

The provision eliminating the statute of limitations applies retroactively, so loans whose limitations period had expired even before 1991 are revived.[335] The statute applies without regard to any state or federal statutory, regulatory, or administrative limitation.[336]

Courts have repeatedly rejected borrowers' due process and equal protection challenges to this retroactive change, finding that statutes of limitation are legislatively created defenses and not constitutionally protected property rights.[337]

---

323 34 C.F.R. § 674.50.
324 34 C.F.R. § 682.414(a)(2).
325 34 C.F.R. § 682.414(a)(4)(ii).
326 34 C.F.R. § 682.414(a)(5)(ii).
327 *See* § 12.6.2.1, *infra*.
328 Public Law 102-26 eliminated the statute of limitations set out in 20 U.S.C. § 1091a(a). While the elimination of the limitations period was to have sunset on November 15, 1992, the Higher Education Amendments of 1992 § 1551, codified at 20 U.S.C. § 1091a, extended indefinitely the abolition of the statute of limitations for student loan collections.
329 Pub. L. No. 102-26, 105 Stat. 123 (Apr. 9, 1991).
330 *See* Lockhart v. United States, 546 U.S. 142, 126 S. Ct. 699 (2005); § 8.4.3.3, *infra*.
331 20 U.S.C. § 1091a(d).

This provision, added in the 2008 HEA reauthorization, may alleviate the need to apply for a death discharge. However, it may still be preferable to apply for a death discharge rather than to raise this defense later in a collection action. *See* § 9.8, *infra* (death discharge).
332 18 U.S.C. § 3281; 18 U.S.C. §§ 794(a), 2381.
333 10 U.S.C. § 843; 18 U.S.C. § 3290.
334 137 Cong. Rec. S7291-02 (June 6, 1991).
335 *See, e.g.*, United States v. Distefano, 279 F.3d 1241 (10th Cir. 2002); United States v. Phillips, 20 F.3d 1005 (9th Cir. 1994); United States v. Hodges, 999 F.2d 341 (8th Cir. 1993); Chatmon v. U.S. Dep't of Educ., 2003 WL 21501919 (N.D. Tex. June 24, 2003); United States v. McLaughlin, 7 F. Supp. 2d 90 (D. Mass. 1998).
336 20 U.S.C. § 1091a. *See, e.g.*, New York State Higher Educ. Servs. Corp. v. Fabrizio, 900 N.Y.S.2d 159 (N.Y. App. Div. 2010) (New York law providing that a money judgment is paid and satisfied after twenty years was preempted by HEA provision eliminating statute of limitations for student loan collection even though the state law was not a "suspend the remedy" type of statute of limitations).
337 *See, e.g.*, United States v. Phillips, 20 F.3d 1005 (9th Cir. 1994); United States v. Hodges, 999 F.2d 341 (8th Cir. 1993); United States v. Glockson, 998 F.2d 896 (11th Cir. 1993); Gaddy v. U.S. Dep't of Educ., 2010 WL 1049576 (E.D.N.Y. Mar. 22, 2010) (although Second Circuit has not ruled on whether statute applies retroactively, all circuits that have addressed this question have found that it does); Greenland v. Van Ru Credit Corp., 2007 WL 4245409 (W.D. Mich. Nov. 29, 2007); United States v. Tuerk, 2007 WL 916866 (E.D. Pa. Mar. 20, 2007), *aff'd*, 317

Courts have also rejected claims based on lack of consideration or because of the *ex post facto* effect of the elimination of the statute of limitations.[338]

In a 2002 decision, a North Carolina district court noted the "obvious difficulty" that the retroactive application of the statutory change causes for students.[339] The borrower in this case was sued in 1998 for a student loan she had incurred between 1970 and 1972 and that she claimed to have repaid in 1973. The court initially granted summary judgment for the borrower but reversed itself in response to the government's motion to alter or amend the judgment. The problem, as discussed by the court, is that "people do not keep records indefinitely, especially when there is no apparent purpose to do so."[340] Even so, the court found that the borrower needed to show more than a bare assertion of payment in order to present sufficient evidence that her due process rights had been violated. This case at least leaves open the possibility that a borrower with a better memory of the circumstances surrounding payment and a more credible explanation of repayment might be able to present sufficient evidence to prove a due process violation.

7.5.3.2 Exclusions from the General Rule Eliminating the Statute of Limitations

Borrowers should consider whether the statute of limitations applies to government student loan collectors that are not specifically listed in the statute. The elimination of the statute of limitations applies only to enforcement actions (which include lawsuits) initiated or taken by certain entities, including guaranty agencies that have agreements with the Secretary or institutions that have agreements with the Secretary pursuant to the Direct Loan or Perkins Loan programs, or by the Secretary of Education, Attorney General, or administrative head of another federal agency.[341] Assignees or debt buyers are not specifically listed and are thus arguably subject to a statute of limitations defense. However, at least one court found that the elimination of the statute of limitations in the HEA preempted a state statute of limitations in a collection action brought by an assignee of the lender.[342]

Collection of private student loans is not covered. Thus, statutes of limitations should apply in these cases. The relevant statute in these cases depends on state law.[343]

The elimination of the statute of limitations also does not specifically apply to state agencies or state loans. However, state entities suing to collect student loans may also be able to avoid statutes of limitations if state law or state constitutions provide such protection. A state entity may not be able to escape time limits if it is merely administering a private loan fund rather than collecting a public debt.[344]

At least one court has held that a borrower's action against the government remains covered by the applicable six-year time limit specified in 28 U.S.C. § 2401(a).[345] Thus, according to this court, only the government gets the benefit of bringing actions without time limits.

7.5.3.3 Laches

7.5.3.3.1 Barriers to applying the laches doctrine in student loan cases

One possible defense to a collection action instituted many years after a default is that the equitable doctrine of laches applies. There are a number of barriers to applying this doctrine in the student loan context.

First, it is possible that Congress eliminated equitable defenses when it eliminated the statute of limitations in student loan collections. This is unclear. The Congressional amendments eliminating the statute of limitations state that Congress' purpose was to ensure that obligations to repay loans would be enforced without regard to any "statutory, regulatory, or administrative limitations."[346] Equitable defenses are not specifically mentioned. However, a number of courts have found that Congress did in fact intend to eliminate equitable defenses as well.[347]

Fed. Appx. 251 (3d Cir. 2009); United States v. Mateu, 2007 WL 196855 (S.D. Fla. Jan. 23, 2007); Johnson v. U.S. Dep't of Educ., 2005 WL 2266109 (W.D. Pa. Sept. 13, 2005); United States v. Dwelley, 59 F. Supp. 2d 115 (D. Me. 1999); United States v. McLaughlin, 7 F. Supp. 2d 90 (D. Mass. 1998); Sibley v. U.S. Dep't of Educ., 913 F. Supp. 1181 (N.D. Ill. 1995), *aff'd without op.*, 111 F.3d 133 (7th Cir. 1997), *reprinted in full at* 1997 U.S. App. LEXIS 6395 (7th Cir. 1997); United States v. Davis, 817 F. Supp. 926 (M.D. Ala. 1993).

338 *See, e.g.*, United States v. Brown, 7 Fed. Appx. 353, 354 (6th Cir. 2001); United States v. Gould, 2006 WL 1522071 (E.D. Mich. May 30, 2006); United States v. Durbin, 64 F. Supp. 2d 635, 637 (S.D. Tex. 1999); United States v. Dwelley, 59 F. Supp. 2d 115 (D. Me. 1999) (*ex post facto* clause applies only to criminal or penal measures that are applied retroactively); United States v. Davis, 817 F. Supp. 926 (M.D. Ala. 1993), *aff'd*, 17 F.3d 1439 (11th Cir. 1994) (table).

339 United States v. Charles, 240 F. Supp. 2d 488 (M.D.N.C. 2002).

340 *Id.* at 490.

341 20 U.S.C. § 1091a(a). *See generally* Glenn E. Roper, *Eternal Student Loan Liability: Who Can Sue Under 20 U.S.C. § 1091A*, 20 B.Y.U. J. Pub. L. 35 (2005).

342 Mountain Peaks Fin. Services, Inc. v. Roth-Steffen, 778 N.W.2d 380 (Ct. App. Minn. 2010) (because Congress legislated with full knowledge of the common law of assignment, all contractual rights of the named lenders, including protection from state statutes of limitations, should transfer to their assignees).

343 *See* § 11.8.3, *infra*.

344 *See* State ex. rel. Bd. of Regents for the Univ. of Okla. v. Livingston, 111 P. 3d 734 (Okla. Civ. App. 2005) (holding that, although state constitution provides that no statute of limitations applies when state is collecting a debt, university was merely administering private loan fund, not enforcing public right, and was thus subject to a statute of limitations defense).

345 Corum v. Paige, 2005 WL 1214598 (W.D. Tenn. May 20, 2005).

346 20 U.S.C. § 1091a(a)(1).

347 *See, e.g.*, United States v. Sullivan, 68 Fed. Appx. 811 (9th Cir.

§ 7.5.3.3.2 Student Loan Law

Even if a court were to decide that Congress did not eliminate equitable defenses when it eliminated the statute of limitations, a second barrier is that the laches doctrine is generally inapplicable against the United States on the grounds of sovereign immunity.[348] Many courts hold to this rule absent a clear manifestation of congressional intent to the contrary. In student loan cases, these courts have found not only that there was no congressional intent to the contrary but also that Congress' retroactive elimination of all statutes of limitations appears to indicate the opposite intent.[349]

7.5.3.3.2 Exceptions to the rule barring laches

A few courts have been willing to look beyond the traditional rule that the doctrine of laches is inapplicable against the United States. In a 1985 non-student-loan case, *S.E.R. Jobs for Progress, Inc.*, the court noted that some relaxation of the principle that laches is not a defense against the government may be developing and that exceptions to the rule might be approved in certain cases.[350]

To invoke the doctrine of laches, a borrower must show (1) a delay in asserting a right or claim; (2) that the delay was not excusable; and (3) that there was undue prejudice to the party against whom the claim is asserted.[351] Most courts that have considered this issue in the student loan context have found that the facts did not justify invoking an exception to the rule.[352]

Courts have rejected borrowers' claims for a variety of reasons. At least one court relied on the fact that, prior to 1991, the government was bound by a six-year statute of limitations for student loan collections.[353] This court speculated that, prior to the complete elimination of the statute, it was possible that the government was not actively collecting certain loans because they were barred by the existing statute of limitations. This argument should be considerably weaker now that more time has passed since the elimination of the student loan statute of limitations.

Even if borrowers can successfully persuade a court that the government was neglectful, they must also show that they were materially prejudiced by the delay. Borrowers have argued that they were prejudiced by years of inactivity on their student loan accounts, which allowed interest, penalties, and collection fees to pile up. Unfortunately for borrowers, most courts that have examined these arguments have found a lack of prejudice to borrowers.[354]

On a bright note for borrowers, at least one court, in *United States v. Rhodes*, found the doctrine of laches applicable in a student loan case.[355] The loan in this case was due in 1974. The government began collection seventeen years later. The court found this to be a "blatant and unreasonable delay on the part of the lender and its assignees."[356] The court found further prejudice to the borrower as the school had closed during the seventeen-year period of inactivity and the borrower no longer had access to any school records. The borrower had long since destroyed his own records.

Other courts have tended to distinguish the facts in *Rhodes*. A key distinction noted by other courts is that the borrower in *Rhodes* was defending the collection action on the grounds that he had already paid back the loan in full. Courts have tended to find this more sympathetic than "shakier" defenses such as lack of consideration or breach of contract.[357] Courts have also found it notable that, because of the government's delay in collecting the loan in *Rhodes*, records were no longer available from the school or from the borrower, making it impossible for either side to show

---

2003); United States v. Lawrence, 276 F.3d 193 (5th Cir. 2001) (citing Millard v. U.S. Funds, 66 F.3d 252 (9th Cir. 1995)); United States v. Phillips, 20 F.3d 1005, 1007 (9th Cir. 1994); United States v. Glockson, 998 F.2d 896, 897 (11th Cir. 1993); United States v. Hodges, 999 F.2d 341 (8th Cir. 1993); Chatmon v. U.S. Dep't of Educ., 2003 WL 21501919 (N.D. Tex. June 24, 2003). *See also* United States v. Robbins, 819 F. Supp. 672 (E.D. Mich. 1993).

The *Robbins* court also speculated that, in eliminating equitable defenses, Congress might have been swayed by the fact that student loans are not collectable after a borrower's disability or death. The court noted that this may have been sufficient to assuage any Congressional fears of a completely open-ended student loan collection process. United States v. Robbins, 819 F. Supp. 676 (E.D. Mich. 1993).

This is ironic given the restrictive stance taken in recent years by the Department toward disability, and even death, cancellations. *See* §§ 9.7 (disability), 9.8 (death), *infra*.

348 United States v. Summerlin, 310 U.S. 414, 60 S. Ct. 1019, 84 L. Ed. 2d 1283 (1940).
349 *See, e.g.*, United States v. McLaughlin, 7 F. Supp. 2d 90 (D. Mass. 1998); United States v. Davis, 817 F. Supp. 926 (M.D. Ala. 1993); United States v. Robbins, 819 F. Supp. 672 (E.D. Mich. 1993).
350 S.E.R., Jobs for Progress, Inc. v. United States, 759 F.2d 1, 7 (Fed. Cir. 1985).
351 United States v. Davis, 817 F. Supp. 926, 929 (M.D. Ala. 1993) (citing Environmental Defense Fund. V. Alexander, 614 F.2d 474, 477–78 (5th Cir.)).
352 *See, e.g.*, United States v. Durbin, 64 F. Supp. 2d 635 (S.D. Tex. 1999); United States v. Smith, 862 F. Supp. 257 (D. Haw. 1994);

United States v. Davis, 817 F. Supp. 926 (M.D. Ala. 1993); United States v. Robbins, 819 F. Supp. 672 (E.D. Mich. 1993).
353 United States v. Davis, 817 F. Supp. 926 (M.D. Ala. 1993).
354 United States v. Durbin, 64 F. Supp. 2d 635 (S.D. Tex. 1999) (laches requires reliance on failure to enforce the right; in student loan cases, borrowers do all their "relying" shortly after signing the note; in the years government has not collected the debt, borrower has done nothing with money or about debt); United States v. Dwelley, 59 F. Supp. 2d 115 (D. Me. 1999); United States v. McLaughlin, 7 F. Supp. 2d 90 (D. Mass. 1998) (no special hardship demonstrated sufficient to relax the laches rule); United States v. Robbins, 819 F. Supp. 672 (E.D. Mich. 1993).
355 United States v. Rhodes, 788 F. Supp. 339 (E.D. Mich. 1992).
356 *Id.* at 343.
357 *See, e.g.*, United States v. Davis, 817 F. Supp. 926, 930 (M.D. Ala. 1993) (distinguishing between borrower's defense of lack of consideration and borrower in *Rhodes* who alleged he had already repaid the loan).

whether the debt was still owed.³⁵⁸ At least one court simply referred to the *Rhodes* case as an anomaly.³⁵⁹

7.5.3.3.3 FISL collection

Another possible use of the doctrine of laches involves Department of Education attempts to collect loans issued under the Federally Insured Student Loans (FISL) Program. Congress' elimination of the statute of limitations for student loan collections has resulted in collection attempts for some very old FISL loans, going back to the early 1970s. Many students subjected to such collection attempts will have a solid defense—that federal law at the time allowed students to raise school-related claims.³⁶⁰

7.5.4 Other Defenses to Loan Enforceability

7.5.4.1 Forgery, Mistake, Infancy, and Other Contract Defenses

A borrower's obligation to pay a student loan is conditioned upon the loan agreement being enforceable under basic contract principles—in which forgery, mistake, and fraud are defenses—that affect a borrower's obligation on any note. This is relevant for both federal and private loans.

The only common law contract defense not available to federal student loan borrowers is infancy, that is, that the student was under age when signing the loan document. The HEA specifies that the United States and guaranty agencies, irrespective of state law on the issue, shall *not* be subject to a claim of infancy.³⁶¹ The 2008 HEA reauthorization law states that infancy may also not be raised as a defense by Perkins loan borrowers.³⁶² However, this defense is available for private loan borrowers. There are also state laws that specifically apply to infancy and educational loans. These laws are preempted by the HEA for federal loans but should apply to other types of loans.³⁶³

The HEA does not limit other contract defenses. These defenses should therefore apply to student loans just as they do to any other type of loan. Borrowers have, for example, successfully raised duress as a defense.³⁶⁴ However, courts have held that lack of consideration is not a defense to student loan cases because the student received money in exchange for a promise to repay the money.³⁶⁵ According to one court, "neither the bank nor the government guarantees satisfaction with schools or educations" and the responsibility for a bad choice lies with the student.³⁶⁶

The Department on numerous occasions has stated that the borrower does not owe on a loan, and guaranty agencies should not seek payment, to the extent to which the loan obligation is not enforceable under state law.³⁶⁷

If a borrower did not sign a student loan note, and the student's signature was forged or altered, the student should have no liability under that note. It should make no difference whether the forger is the school or lender.

Borrowers must endorse or otherwise certify any disbursements made by check or other means, except that checks may be made co-payable to the school and borrower.³⁶⁸ Forgery of that endorsement or failure to obtain that endorsement should also void the student's liability for that check.

A 1993 letter from the Department of Education spells out student rights when a check lacks the student's endorsement or the endorsement is forged.³⁶⁹ A student is not liable for the amount of a check when the student did not endorse the check, unless under state law the holder can show that the borrower is legally obligated for the amount disbursed. Holders cannot presume that a borrower who remained enrolled at a school after a check was cashed thereby received its proceeds or condoned the school's action in cashing the check.

---

358 *Id.*
359 Hamilton v. U.S.A., 2005 WL 2671373 (S.D. Ohio Oct. 19, 2005).
360 *See* § 12.7.2.4, *infra*.
    It may also be possible to argue that the statute of limitations should not be eliminated for FFELs that have lost their guaranteed status, since neither a school, guaranty agency, nor the United States will be collecting on such a loan. *See also* § 12.7.3.2, *infra*.
361 20 U.S.C. § 1091a(b)(2).
    This provision only applies explicitly to FFELs and not to Perkins loans. While the provision does not mention Direct loans, it will apply to Direct loans because, unless otherwise specified, Direct loans "shall have the same terms, conditions, and benefits" as FFELs. 20 U.S.C. § 1087e(a)(1).
362 20 U.S.C. § 1091a(b).
363 *See* § 11.8.2, *infra* (infancy defense and private student loans).
364 *See, e.g., In re* Mason, 300 B.R. 160 (Bankr. D. Conn. 2003) (consolidation loan was obtained through duress and was therefore null and void under state law). *But see* Gibbs v. SLM Corp., 336 F. Supp. 2d 1 (D. Mass. 2004) (duress claim dismissed because plaintiff failed to show that (1) one side involuntarily accepted the terms of another, (2) circumstances permitted no other alternative, and (3) said circumstances were the result of coercive acts of opposing party).
365 Cotton v. U.S. Dep't of Educ., 2006 WL 3313753 (M.D. Fla. Nov. 13, 2006); United States v. Durbin, 64 F. Supp. 2d. 635 (S.D. Tex. 1999). *See also* § 12.5.4.2, *infra*.
366 United States v. Durbin, 64 F. Supp. 2d 635 (S.D. Tex. 1999).
367 A good enunciation of this policy is found in a letter from Acting Assistant Secretary Whitehead to Congressman Stephen Solarz (May 19, 1988), *available on* the companion website to this manual. *See also* 71 Fed. Reg. 45666, 45676–77 (Aug. 9, 2006).
368 20 U.S.C. § 1077(a)(3).
    Additional disbursement requirements can be found at 20 U.S.C. § 1078-7.
369 Letter of William Morant, Acting Deputy Assistant Secretary for Student Financial Assistance, Nos. 93-L-156, 93-G-236 (July 1993), *available on* the companion website to this manual.

According to the Department letter, if a student is not obligated to pay the amount on a check that is not properly endorsed, the guarantor should correct the student's credit record to reflect that fact, must make sure that the failure to pay that amount is not causing the student to be ineligible for future loans and grants, and must return any amount collected on that check, including any tax intercept.

In 2006 regulations related to false certifications due to identity theft, the Department affirmed that a person is ordinarily not liable on an instrument, such as a promissory note or check, unless that person signed that instrument or authorized another to sign on his or her behalf.[370] The Department cited FFEL regulations providing that FFEL program benefits are payable to the holder of the loan only when the lender obtained a legally enforceable promissory note to evidence the loan and also cited regulations providing that re-insurance may be received only with respect to a claim on a legally enforceable loan.[371]

When a promissory note or check endorsement is forged, the student may have two different approaches to discharging the loan. One is to apply for a false-certification discharge based on the forgery.[372] The other is to claim that the obligation is unenforceable under common law principles. In the appropriate case, both of these strategies should work, and the student can choose which way to proceed first. Department regulations state that the false-certification discharge based on forgery applies only if the *school* signed the borrower's name without authorization.[373] If the forgery was done by someone else, relief is available under the common law or state law defense of forgery.

Fraud in obtaining the consumer's signature should also be a defense. For example, there are many reported cases of consumers who signed promissory notes unaware that they were obligating themselves on a loan. Those consumers typically thought they were simply applying to a school or applying for a grant. The student never went to the school or realized the existence of the debt until much later when a lender tried to collect on the loan. While such facts should provide a valid defense on the note, advocates should be prepared for the Department and guaranty agencies to give little credibility to such claims.

7.5.4.2 Connection Between Contract Defenses and Statutory Discharges

Many borrowers entitled to statutory discharges attempt to raise those issues as defenses. With respect to school-related claims, this issue is discussed in Chapter 12, *infra*.

Borrowers often attempt to raise other issues, such as disability, in response to collection actions. This is ineffective, however, because borrowers cannot initiate the discharge process in court.[374] A discharge-related issue may be resolved in court, but only after a borrower has exhausted the administrative process and is seeking judicial review.[375] A district court in North Carolina summarized the problem for borrowers.[376] In a case pending before that court, the borrower sought to enjoin the government from collecting on loans that the borrower alleged were paid for instruction he never received. The court noted that the plaintiff's claims appealed to the equities found in the law.[377] The court also noted that Congress had addressed the problem by passing the various administrative discharges.[378] However, these claims must be presented using the administrative process and not as defensive claims in civil litigation.[379]

The safest course is always to raise the discharge claim first. If borrowers are sued for collection, they should file an answer to the collection suit asserting the right to a discharge as a defense. The court should be asked not to enter judgment until the discharge application has been ruled on. If the Department of Education is suing, the United States Attorney will usually agree to stay the litigation until the Department rules on the discharge request.

7.5.4.3 Raising Defenses When FFELs Have Lost Their Guaranteed Status

A loan issued under the Federal Family Education Loans Program may lose its guaranteed status if a lender does not exercise due diligence, if the school was not an eligible institution, or for some other reason. While the promissory note between the lender and student will not be automatically cancelled, the guaranty agency and the United States no longer back up the loan. Typically the lender will sell the loan to a private entity, and that entity (not a guaranty agency) will try to collect from the student on the loan.

---

370 71 Fed. Reg. 45666, 45676–77 (Aug. 9, 2006).
371 *Id.* (citing 34 C.F.R. § 682.402(e)(1)(i)(B), 682.406(a)(1)). *See also* 72 Fed. Reg. 61960 (Nov. 1, 2007) (final regulations).
372 *See* § 9.4.4, *infra*.
373 34 C.F.R. § 682.402(e)(1)(i)(B). *See* § 9.4.4, *infra*.
374 Courts have consistently found that only the Department of Education has the discretion to discharge the loans based on the various discharge programs. *See, e.g.*, Haddad v. Dominican Univ., 2007 WL 809685 (N.D. Ill. Mar. 15, 2007); United States v. Levreau, 2001 WL 1690059 (D. Minn. Dec. 14, 2001) (discharge claims must be pursued administratively and may not be asserted as a defense in a collection action); United States v. Bertucci, 2000 WL 1234560 (E.D. La. 2000); United States v. Wright, 87 F. Supp. 2d 464 (D. Md. 2000); *In re* Bega, 180 B.R. 642 (Bankr. D. Kan. 1995).
375 *See* § 9.15, *infra* (APA appeals).
376 Green v. United States, 163 F. Supp. 2d 593 (W.D.N.C. 2000).
377 *Id.* at 597.
378 *Id.* at 597–598.
379 *See, e.g.*, United States v. White, 2009 WL 3872342 (E.D.N.C. Nov. 18, 2009) (only the Secretary has discretion to discharge loan; possibility of discharge does not prevent court from ruling on government's motion for summary judgment in student loan collection case).

When this private entity collects on what is now a private loan, state laws should apply as to the loan's enforceability. The state's applicable statute of limitations should apply. State common law and statutory theories of lender liability should also apply. There can no longer be any issue of preemption of state law because of a conflict with the HEA, since the loan is no longer part of the federal program.

The FTC Holder Rule should be inserted in the loan as well. Thus state remedies for failure to comply with the Holder Notice should apply as well. This is particularly important in cases raising school-related claims.[380] In these cases, as discussed in Chapter 12, *infra*, if the FFEL lost its guaranteed status because the school was never an eligible program, the fact that the loan should never have been guaranteed in the first place should be raised as a defense on any collection of the now non-guaranteed loan.[381]

Moreover, if the loan lost its guaranteed status because of the lender's lack of due diligence, it may be possible to argue that this lack of due diligence also acts as a defense to the student's obligation to pay the loan.[382] Such loans may also be dischargeable in bankruptcy, even though the loan does not meet the substantial hardship test, because the loan is not insured by a government unit.[383] The Department has stated that, even though a loan has lost its guaranteed status, the student is still eligible for a closed-school or false-certification discharge.[384]

7.5.4.4 Raising Defenses After a Loan Has Been Consolidated

A loan consolidation has significant benefits for most student loan borrowers in default.[385] However, one problem is that consolidating a student loan may make it more difficult to raise defenses on that loan. The lender may argue that the new consolidated loan is a novation and that defenses to the old loan do not apply to the new loan.

At least one federal court has rejected this argument, holding instead that a student does not waive his or her defenses to an original student loan by exchanging that loan for a federal consolidation loan.[386] The court found insufficient policy grounds to rule as a matter of law that the consolidation was a new loan extinguishing defenses to the old loan. The court also found unpersuasive the language in the loan consolidation that explicitly stated that the borrower was waiving all defenses on the original loan. The court found the waiver language not sufficiently conspicuous and not based on a knowing and voluntary agreement. The court found that there was no novation because there was no mutual agreement that the student was waiving defenses.

Another argument for why a consolidation loan does not waive student defenses is that the Department has stated that the student can continue, despite the consolidation, to apply for a closed-school, unpaid-refund, or false-certification discharge.[387] The policy grounds for the ability to continue raising school-related defenses should apply with equal force.[388] The Direct Loan consolidation promissory note affirms that borrowers may in some cases assert school-related defenses.

7.5.4.5 Defenses for Service Members

The Servicemember Civil Relief Act (SCRA) limits collection tactics and enforcement of claims against active duty military personnel.[389] In general, everyone on active duty is entitled to the benefit of the SCRA, whether or not they are stationed in a war zone and whether they enlisted or were called up. Active duty includes full-time training duty, annual training duty, and attendance at a military school while in active military service.[390]

The interest rate protections under the SCRA also apply to student loans.[391] The SCRA requires that creditors reduce the interest rate to 6% on any obligation incurred by a service member before active duty.[392] The reduction lasts as long as the service member is on active duty.

The protections in civil judicial and administrative proceedings should apply to student loan collection proceedings.[393] The SCRA also restricts execution upon assets of the service member.

---

380 See § 12.7, *infra*.
381 See § 12.7.3.2, *infra*.
382 *See* United States v. Rhodes, 788 F. Supp. 339 (E.D. Mich. 1992). *But see* United States v. Gould, 2006 WL 1522071 (E.D. Mich. May 30, 2006); United States v. Lewis 2001 WL 789224 (D. Kan. June 29, 2001) (borrower may not invoke lender's due diligence obligations against the United States on her own behalf); Vanderbilt Univ. v. Henderson, 2001 WL 1216980 (Tenn. Ct. App. Oct. 12, 2001) (borrowers cannot use statutes and regulations governing administration of NDSL program to defend against University's collection efforts). Also see the discussion in 71 Fed. Reg. 45777, 45677 (Aug. 9, 2006).
383 *Id.*
384 Dear Colleague Letter 94-G-256 (Sept. 1994), *available on* the companion website to this manual.
385 *See* § 6.2, *supra*.
386 Crawford v. American Inst. of Prof'l Careers, Inc. (D. Ariz. Feb. 8, 1996), *available at* www.consumerlaw.org/unreported.
387 *See, e.g.*, Ch. 9, *infra*.
388 See § 12.7, *infra*.
389 50 U.S.C. App. §§ 501–596. *See generally* National Consumer Law Center, Collection Actions Ch. 7 (2008 and Supp.).
390 For a discussion of service members protected by the Act, see National Consumer Law Center, Collection Actions § 7.4 (2008 and Supp.).
391 20 U.S.C. § 1078(d). *See* § 2.3.1, *supra*.
392 Pub. L. No. 108-189, § 207, 117 Stat. 2835 (Dec. 19, 2003); 50 U.S.C. App. § 527.
393 Pub. L. No. 108-189, § 2(2), 117 Stat. 2835 (Dec. 19, 2003) (referring to administrative proceedings in purpose clause); *id.* § 101(5) (defining "court" to include state and federal administrative agencies); Pub. L. No. 108-189, § 102(b), 117 Stat.

§ 7.6 Student Loan Law

The protections in judicial and administrative procedures are divided into two main categories: cases in which the service member has not been notified of the proceeding and cases in which the service member has been notified. In cases in which the service member has not been notified and has not appeared, courts are prohibited from entering default judgments unless the plaintiff files an affidavit stating whether or not the defendant is in military service and showing facts in support of the statement. If it appears that the defendant is in military service, the court may not enter a judgment until it appoints an attorney to represent the defendant, and there are special provisions for stays.[394] The SCRA also gives a service member who has been notified of an action or proceeding (other than an eviction) the right to an automatic, non-discretionary ninety-day stay upon request.[395] The service member may seek an additional stay, but this extension is not automatic. In addition, the SCRA allows the court to stay execution of any judgment against a service member and to vacate or stay any pre- or post-judgment attachment or garnishment of property.[396] There are also provisions tolling statutes of limitations during the period of active duty.[397]

7.6 Vacating Collection Judgments

Borrowers may already have judgments entered against them. In these cases, advocates should consider attempting to vacate the judgments. This is especially critical because borrowers have fewer rights if judgments have already been entered against them. For example, they may not consolidate or rehabilitate loans in these circumstances.[398] Advocates may negotiate with creditors to vacate judgments or file motions in court.[399]

A motion to set aside a default judgment is governed by Federal Rule of Civil Procedure 60(b), which allows relief from a final judgment upon motion for the following reasons: (1) mistake, inadvertence, surprise, or excusable neglect; (2) newly discovered evidence that by due diligence could not have been discovered in time to move for a new trial; (3) fraud, misrepresentation, or other misconduct of an adverse party; (4) the judgment is void; (5) the judgment has been satisfied, released, or discharged, or a prior judgment upon which it is based has been reversed or otherwise vacated, or it is no longer equitable that the judgment should have prospective application; or (6) any other reason justifying relief from the operation of the judgment. The motion must be made within a reasonable time and, for reasons (1), (2), and (3), not more than one year after the judgment, order, or proceeding was entered or taken. In addition, the party seeking to set aside the judgment must present a meritorious defense, a key factor in the Rule 60(b) analysis.[400]

2835 (Dec. 19, 2003) (SCRA applies to any judicial or administrative proceeding commenced in any court or agency).

394 See National Consumer Law Center, Collection Actions § 7.5.2 (2008 and Supp.).
395 Id. § 9.12.3.3.
396 50 U.S.C. App. § 524.
397 50 U.S.C. App. § 526(a).
398 See §§ 6.2.4 (consolidation), 6.3.6 (rehabilitation), supra.
399 See, e.g., United States v. Murphy, 2007 WL 2973584 (E.D.N.Y. Sept. 28, 2007) (vacating default judgment for improper service; rejecting argument that borrower's failure to maintain a current address on file with loan holder constituted a waiver of notice); U.S. v. Williams, 2007 WL 2463349 (E.D. Mich. Aug. 30, 2007) (setting aside default judgment when plaintiff failed to demonstrate proper service and defendant borrower submitted evidence denying liability); United States v. Cagle, 235 F.R.D. 641 (E.D. Mich. 2006) (vacating default judgment; default was grossly unfair and inequitable because it was entered only three weeks after borrower was served and borrower alleged a meritorious defense that debt had been paid and account closed).

Who bears the burden of proof depends on whether the court treats the issue of payment as one involving damages (the loan holder has the burden of proof) or as a defense to repayment (the borrower should have the burden). See, e.g., United States v. McCain, 2007 WL 2421471 (E.D. Mich. Aug. 22, 2007) (denying plaintiff's motion for summary judgment, except on liability), summary judgment granted, 2007 WL 4557700 (E.D. Mich. Dec. 20, 2007). See also United States v. Cagle, 2007 WL 1695912 (E.D. Mich. June 12, 2007) (granting government's motion for summary judgment). See generally National Consumer Law Center, Collection Actions Ch. 13 (2008 and Supp.) (setting aside or discharging a judgment).

400 See, e.g., United States v. Brown, 2010 WL 55469 (S.D. Fla. Jan. 7, 2010); United States v. Brunette, 2007 WL 201164 (E.D.N.Y. Jan. 23, 2007) (denying motion to set aside default judgment); United States v. Estrada, 2006 WL 3050886 (E.D.N.Y. Oct. 20, 2006) (absence of a meritorious defense is sufficient to support the denial of motion to vacate default judgment).

Chapter 8   Property and Asset Seizures to Collect Federal Student Loans

8.1 Introduction

Federal student loan collection powers have grown so much over time that the government rarely sues borrowers, opting instead for an array of extra-judicial collection tools. Litigation accounted for less than 1% of federal student loan collection in fiscal year 2009.[1] In contrast, collection through Department of Treasury offset (tax and benefit offsets) accounted for about 16% of collections, while collection through administrative garnishment accounted for about 10.5%. About 10.3% of collections occurred through private collection agency actions.[2] As with all federal student loan collections, there is no statute of limitations on these extra-judicial collection tools.[3]

These collection methods often break the budgets of low-income households. Those living on or near the poverty line simply cannot afford to lose a tax refund or hard-earned wages. It is therefore critical for advocates to explore possible ways to cancel, defer, or forebear clients' loans.[4] There may also be affordable repayment options available.[5] Borrowers may also have defenses to non-judicial seizures if they are serving in the military or are merchant seamen.[6]

It is important for advocates to understand the strategies available to challenge property seizures. This chapter focuses on such strategies, highlighting tax refund intercepts, administrative wage garnishments, and federal benefits offsets. In some cases, even if other options are not available, borrowers can suspend or even terminate extra-judicial collection because of hardship or other factors.

8.2 Tax Refund Offsets

8.2.1 General

The tax refund offset program involves a blanket seizure of almost all tax refunds due to debtors who are in default on their student loans.[7] Amounts offset may include "special" payments such as economic stimulus refunds.

In addition, a number of states have laws that authorize guaranty agencies to offset state income tax refunds. This subsection focuses primarily on the federal tax refund offset program.

The federal statute requires tax offset when a debt is owed to a federal agency, including a debt administered by a third party acting as an agent for the federal government.[8] The Department of Education ("the Department") uses this federal statute to delegate to guaranty agencies the authority to initiate offsets for loans still held by the guaranty agency.[9] In its 2009 Private Collection Agency (PCA) Procedures Manual ("2009 PCA Manual"), the Department describes its role as a "middle man" between the guaranty agencies and the Department of Treasury.[10]

---

1 U.S. Dep't of the Treasury, U.S. Government Receivables and Debt Collection Activities of Federal Agencies: Fiscal Year 2009 Report to the Congress 14 (Mar. 2010), *available at* http://fmsq.treas.gov/news/reports/debt09.pdf.
   This data includes collections on the Department of Education's defaulted portfolio, including FFELs assigned to the Department.
2 *Id.*
3 20 U.S.C. § 1091a(a). *See* §§ 7.5.3, *supra*, 8.4.3.3, *infra* (no time limit on federal benefits offsets).
4 *See* Ch. 4, *supra* (deferments and forbearances), Ch. 9, *infra* (cancellations).
5 *See* Ch. 6, *supra*.
6 *See* § 7.5.4.5, *supra* (Servicemember Civil Relief Act Protections).

7 31 U.S.C. § 3720A.
8 31 U.S.C. § 3720A(a).
   These rules should also apply to Perkins Loan Program loans ("Perkins loans") that have been assigned to the Department. However, if a school is collecting a Perkins loan, the regulations provide only that the school must attempt to recover the loan through litigation, assign the loan to the United States, or write off the loan. *See* 34 C.F.R. § 674.45(d).
9 *But see* McAfee v. Unger & Assocs. Inc., 730 So. 2d 623 (Ala. Civ. App. 1998) (federal regulations provide that attachment of an income tax refund can be carried out only by federal government agencies; borrower's attempt to sue collection agency employed by Department of Education failed because agency could not have been involved in the tax intercept process).
10 U.S. Dep't of Educ., PCA Procedures Manual: 2009 ED Collections Contract 79 (Sept. 2009).
   The Department had posted the manual on-line in spring 2010 but took it off-line after a short time. The manual is available on the companion website and, as of summer 2010, on the website for the Center for Public Integrity. *See* Ariel Wittenberg, Center for Pub. Integrity, Education Department Pulls Student Debt Collectors Guide Off Web Site (June 16, 2010), *available at* http://www.publicintegrity.org/data_mine/entry/2162.

Whether the debt is owed to the Department or to the guarantor, the decision of which refunds to offset is not done on an individual basis. Computer records of *all* borrowers in default meeting certain general criteria are sent to the Internal Revenue Service and anyone on that list owed a refund will have that refund offset.

The federal authority to offset tax refunds is allowed, at least according to one court, even if a state exemption arguably applies. The Eleventh Circuit overturned a federal district court determination that Alabama's personal exemption applied to tax refund intercepts.[11] The borrower had argued that the Federal Debt Collection Procedures Act (FDCPA) allows debtors to raise state exemptions to federal collection actions.[12]

8.2.2 Notice Requirements

The Secretary of the Department of Education ("the Secretary") can refer a debt for offset only after complying with certain procedures.[13] The loan holder must mail to the borrower a written notice of the Secretary's intent to seek the tax offset, using the borrower's current address, as determined from the guarantor or Department records.[14] The notice informs the borrower of the intent to refer a past-due debt to the Secretary of the Treasury for offset and provides the borrower with the opportunity to inspect and copy the records on the borrower's debt, obtain a review of the existence, amount, enforceability, or past-due status of the debt, or enter into a written repayment agreement.[15] Courts have held that actual notice is not required, so long as reasonable means are used to provide notice.[16] If the borrower was previously notified of the Department's intent to offset, the offset may occur without a new notice.[17]

---

11 Bosarge v. U.S. Dep't of Educ., 5 F.3d 1414 (11th Cir. 1993).
12 28 U.S.C. §§ 3001–3308 (Debt Collection Procedures Act).
13 31 U.S.C. § 3720A(b); 34 C.F.R. § 30.33(a), (b).
14 34 C.F.R. § 30.22(a). *See also* Glover v. Brady, 1994 U.S. Dist. LEXIS 13211 (S.D.N.Y. 1994) (no due process violation found when letter was mailed twice to last known address); Setlech v. United States, 816 F. Supp. 161 (E.D.N.Y. 1993), *aff'd*, 17 F.3d 390 (1994) (notice need not be received; reasonable efforts must be made in sending the notice; if reasonable efforts are not made, the court would require the Department to provide the borrower with a hearing as to whether the debt was due).
   A copy of a sample offset notice is available at Appendix D, *infra*, and on the companion website to this manual.
15 34 C.F.R. § 30.33(b).
16 *See, e.g.*, United States v. Hunter, 2007 WL 2122052 (E.D.N.Y. July 23, 2007); Savage v. Scales, 310 F. Supp. 2d 122 (D.D.C. 2004); Shabtai v. U.S. Dep't of Educ., 2003 WL 21983025 (S.D.N.Y. Aug. 20, 2003); Nelson v. Diversified Collection Servs., Inc., 961 F. Supp. 863 (D. Md. 1997); Setlech v. United States, 816 F. Supp. 161, 167 (E.D.N.Y. 1992) (using an address most recently in the agency's database or an address obtained from plaintiff's most recent tax return has been held to be "reasonably calculated to notify the vast majority of debtors of the intended referral and proposed offset"), *aff'd*, 17 F.3d 390 (2d Cir. 1993) (table).
17 34 C.F.R. § 30.22(d).

8.2.3 Grounds to Contest a Tax Offset

Borrowers may request review regarding the existence, amount, enforceability, or past-due status of the debt.[18]

While many borrowers report frustration in raising even the most meritorious defenses to a tax offset, the Department's stated policy is to consider the following types of defenses:[19]

- The borrower has repaid the loan or the Social Security number is incorrect and the borrower does not owe the loan.
- The borrower has entered into a repayment agreement with the guaranty agency or the Department, and the borrower is making payments as required.
- The borrower has filed for bankruptcy and the case is still open or the loan was discharged in bankruptcy.[20]
- The borrower is totally and permanently disabled.[21]
- The loan is not enforceable. The Department will apparently recognize forgery or alteration of the loan documents as a defense. It should also recognize school-related defenses on Perkins Loan Program loans ("Perkins loans"), Direct Loan Program loans ("Direct loans"), and many Federal Family Education Loan Program loans ("FFELs") issued after January 1, 1994.[22] It is less clear whether the Department will consider school-related defenses (other than the failure to pay an owed refund) for FFELs issued before that date.
- The borrower is eligible for an unpaid refund discharge and the borrower has enclosed a completed discharge form.[23]
- The borrower is eligible for a closed-school discharge and the borrower has enclosed a completed discharge form.[24]
- The borrower is eligible for a false-certification discharge based on ability to benefit, disqualifying condition, or unauthorized signature, and the borrower has enclosed a completed discharge form.[25]

Review based on financial hardship is not specifically listed in the regulations. However, the Department and

---

18 31 U.S.C. § 3720A(b); 34 C.F.R. § 30.22(b)(3)(ii), 30.33(b)(3)(ii).
19 A sample Treasury offset notice listing these defenses is available at Appendix D, *infra*, and on the companion website to this manual. *See also* U.S. Dep't of Educ., Amendment to Agreement Pursuant to Section 428(b) of the Higher Education Act of 1965, as Amended, with a State or Private Non-profit Institution or Organization for Coverage of Its Student Loan Insurance Program under the Interest Benefits Provision of Section 428(a) of the Act (July 11, 1994), *available on* the companion website to this manual.
20 *See* Ch. 10, *infra*.
21 *See* § 9.7, *infra*.
22 *See* § 12.7.2, *infra*.
23 *See* § 9.5, *infra*.
24 *See* § 9.3, *infra*.
25 *See* § 9.4, *infra*.

guaranty agencies will consider this defense at their discretion. The Department has stated that it rarely refunds a tax offset due to extreme hardship.[26]

Although not explicitly recognized by the Department as a defense, the enabling statute explicitly states that an offset cannot take place unless the Department has certified that reasonable efforts have been made by the agency to obtain payment of the debt.[27]

The failure to consider evidence should also be grounds to undo a tax offset. The enabling statute explicitly states that no offset can take place until the Department "considers any evidence presented by such person and determines that an amount of such debt is past due and legally enforceable."[28]

8.2.4 Repayment Plan in Lieu of Offset

Borrowers can request written agreements to repay debts if they do so within twenty days of receiving the notice of intent to offset.[29] The Secretary or guarantor provides a repayment schedule, and, to avoid the offset, the borrower must make the first payment within the later of the seventh day after the date of decision if a review is requested, the sixty-fifth day after the date of the notice if the borrower did not request review or an opportunity to inspect and copy records, or the fifteenth day after the date on which the Department made available relevant records if the borrower filed a timely request.[30]

Once the account is certified, according to the Department, it must remain certified until the account is resolved or inactivated as legally required by law.[31] Once certified, borrowers may not avoid offset simply by making voluntary payments. They may, however, avoid offset by paying the account in full or through compromise, rehabilitation, consolidation, or discharge. The Department has stated that the most common complaint received against collection agencies is that agencies tell borrowers that offset can be avoided by making payments.[32]

The regulations provide that the repayment agreement must be on terms acceptable to the Secretary.[33] It does not specifically require that the Secretary offer a reasonable and affordable payment plan. However, borrowers may be able to argue that a reasonable and affordable plan should be available in these circumstances. They can certainly argue this if they set up a rehabilitation plan.[34]

As long as borrowers are otherwise eligible prior to certification of the offset, borrowers have the right to get out of default through consolidation and to select income-based repayment plans.[35] They also may choose to rehabilitate their loans and, if so, have the right to "reasonable and affordable" payments.[36] If a borrower chooses to set up a payment plan rather than consolidate, the borrower should be sure to follow the rehabilitation procedures so that he or she is on the path to getting out of default.

Once an account is satisfied due to payment, rehabilitation, discharge, or consolidation, the Department of Education will notify the Department of Treasury to inactivate the account. According to the Department of Education, there is about a three-week delay between when an account is inactivated on the Department of Education's database and when the Department of Treasury's system is updated. Borrowers should wait at least three weeks, if possible, before filing taxes and to confirm with the Department of Treasury that offset will not occur. The Department of Education advises borrowers to call the Department of Treasury at 800-304-3107.[37]

By entering into a repayment agreement, the borrower waives any right to future review of issues related to the original debt.[38]

8.2.5 The Review Process

The borrower must make a written request to inspect a loan file within twenty days of the notice of offset.[39] To obtain a review, the borrower must file a request for review at the address specified in the notice by the *later* of sixty-five days after the date of the notice or fifteen days after the borrower's loan file is provided, if requested.[40] A borrower can request a later hearing, but only a timely hearing request will stop the offset pending the hearing.

When requesting review, the borrower must file identifying information and information about the particular debt, including the borrower's Social Security number and the name of the loan program. Borrowers must also explain their reasons for contesting the debts and file any documents they wish to submit.[41]

It is important for borrowers to send the guarantor or the Department of Education all relevant documentation. Even though the Department's file may not contain much useful information, it is still a good practice for borrowers to also request the Department or guaranty agency file.

---

26 U.S. Dep't of Educ., PCA Procedures Manual: 2009 ED Collections Contract 82 (Sept. 2009).
27 31 U.S.C. § 3720A(b)(5).
28 31 U.S.C. § 3720A(b)(3).
29 34 C.F.R. § 30.27(a)(1).
30 34 C.F.R. § 30.33(f).
31 U.S. Dep't of Educ., PCA Procedures Manual: 2009 ED Collections Contract 81 (Sept. 2009).
32 Id.
33 34 C.F.R. § 30.27(a).
34 See § 6.3, supra.
35 See § 6.2.3, supra.
36 See § 6.3.4, supra.
37 U.S. Dep't of Educ., PCA Procedures Manual: 2009 ED Collections Contract 82 (Sept. 2009).
38 34 C.F.R. § 30.27(e)(1).
39 34 C.F.R. § 30.33(c)(1).
40 34 C.F.R. § 30.33(d).
41 34 C.F.R. § 30.24(b)(1)–(2).

If the decision is based on documentary evidence only, the Department will review the documents submitted by the borrower and other relevant evidence and notify the borrower in writing of a decision.[42]

If the borrower wants an oral hearing, the borrower must submit the reasons why the review cannot be limited to a review of the documentary evidence and also submit a list of the witnesses the borrower wishes to call, the issues they will testify about, and the reasons why the testimony is necessary.[43]

The Secretary has established detailed standards in the regulation about when an oral hearing will be granted and the rules to follow in that hearing.[44] If granted, the oral hearing is not a formal evidentiary hearing.[45] The Department will notify the borrower of the time and place for the hearing. The Department will also designate an official to conduct the hearing, review evidence, and notify the borrower in writing of the decision.[46]

If the review is not by the Department, the borrower can request a subsequent review by the Department after receiving the guaranty agency decision. This request for further review must be made within seven days after the agency's initial determination.[47]

The timely request for a hearing stops the offset until the hearing and any further requests for review have been exhausted. The statute specifies that no offset can occur until there is a determination that a debt is owed.[48]

8.2.6 Due Process Challenges to Tax Offset

Unfortunately, there are widespread allegations that guarantors, or contractors hired by the Department, ignore borrower requests for hearings, deny requests on inadequate grounds, ignore valid defenses, or simply fail to respond in any way to student requests concerning pending intercepts. At a minimum, borrowers should be prepared for delays and should be sure to send all correspondence return receipt requested.

When hearings are offered, they often fail to meet even minimum due process standards. In-person hearings are arranged for the convenience of the guarantor or Department and consequently can be thousands of miles from the borrower's residence. The Department has responded to this problem by offering telephone hearings in lieu of in-person hearings.[49] The due process implications of preventing borrowers from presenting their cases in person have not been challenged to date.

However, there have been challenges to some of the other features of the tax refund offset program.[50] There have been mixed results and few recent cases in the area of due process challenges to all aspects of the tax offset program.

8.2.7 Post-Offset Challenges

The Internal Revenue Service (IRS) takes the position that there is no right to an administrative review of the intercept within the IRS and courts do not have jurisdiction to hear challenges against the IRS based on the intercept.[51] In denying a borrower's attempt to appeal an offset, one court stated that, although the plaintiff could not seek review of his tax offset against the Department of Treasury, he is "free to pursue any and all remedies he may have against 'the Federal agency . . . to which the amount of such [income tax refund] reduction was paid.' 26 U.S.C. § 6402(f). 'He may not, however, point the guns of this lawsuit against the Treasury.'"[52] However, in another district court case,

---

42 34 C.F.R. § 30.24(e).
43 34 C.F.R. § 30.25.
44 34 C.F.R. §§ 30.25, 30.26.
45 34 C.F.R. § 30.26(a).
46 34 C.F.R. § 30.26(c).
47 34 C.F.R. § 30.33(d)(3).
48 31 U.S.C. § 3720A(b)(3).
49 U.S. Dep't of Educ., Amendment to Agreement Pursuant to Section 428(b) of the Higher Education Act of 1965, as Amended, with a State or Private Non-profit Institution or Organization for Coverage of Its Student Loan Insurance Program under the Interest Benefits Provision of Section 428(a) of the Act, Appx. I § 2.3.1 (July 11, 1994), *available on* the companion website to this manual.
50 *See, e.g.*, Jones v. Cavazos, 889 F.2d 1043 (11th Cir. 1989) (throwing out due process challenge because plaintiff had no meritorious defense to the intercept and so lacked standing); Richardson v. Baker, 663 F. Supp. 651 (S.D.N.Y. June 22, 1987). A settlement was reached whereby the government modified offset procedures for New York borrowers. Games v. Cavazos, 737 F. Supp. 1368 (D. Del. 1990) (upholding offset notice even though it did not list potential defenses or the right to an attorney).
51 26 C.F.R. § 301.6402-6(l). *See, e.g.*, Lepelletier v. U.S. Dep't of Educ., 2009 WL 4840153 (D.D.C. Dec. 14, 2009) (it is incumbent upon creditor agency, not Treasury, to afford the debtor due process with respect to disputing outstanding debt); United States v. Hunter, 2007 WL 2122052 (E.D.N.Y. July 23, 2007); Johnson v. Internal Revenue Serv., 2001 WL 1175151 (E.D. Pa. Aug. 21, 2001); Setlech v. United States, 816 F. Supp. 161 (E.D.N.Y. 1993), *aff'd*, 17 F.3d 390 (2d Cir. 1994); Richardson v. Baker, 663 F. Supp. 651 (S.D.N.Y. 1987); Sartorious v. U.S. Dep't of Treasury, 671 F. Supp. 592 (E.D. Wis. 1987); *In re* Blake, 235 B.R. 568 (Bankr. Md. 1998) (although action against Department of Treasury prohibited, borrower could bring suit against the Department of Education; Department ordered to return refund).
52 Greenland v. Van Ru Corp., 2006 WL 2884458 (W.D. Mich. Oct. 10, 2006) (noting that 26 U.S.C. § 6402(f) prohibits suits against Department of Treasury to review offsets but allows recovery from federal agency to which the offset was paid). The *Greenland* court also found that the Administrative Procedure Act does not provide for suits against the Department of Treasury in this instance. The court specifically declined to follow a contrary unpublished decision in the *Omegbu* case. Omegbu v. U.S. Dep't of Treasury, 118 Fed. Appx. 989 (7th Cir. Dec. 16, 2004); Albert v. OSI Educ. Serv., Inc., 2004 WL 483166 (D. Minn. Mar. 11, 2004). *See also* Thomas v. Bennett, 856 F.2d 1165 (8th Cir. 1988).

the court dismissed a case against the Department of Education when a borrower's wife alleged that her tax refund was improperly seized.[53]

The Department has not set out a formal administrative procedure to review offsets after they have occurred but has indicated that it will follow the pre-offset hearing procedure even for hearings requested post-intercept. The only difference is that the offset is not stayed pending the review.

Whether in fact guarantors or the Department will actually review such post-offset requests is an open question. Such an administrative appeal may be prudent before filing suit so as to forestall the Department's argument that the borrower must first exhaust administrative remedies.[54]

If a post-offset request is ignored, the remaining approach, when the student loan is not owed, is to sue the Department of Education for return of the refund.[55] Such a challenge is generally advisable only if the borrower has a complete defense, because the Department can counterclaim on the student loan note.

8.2.8 Preventing Tax Offsets

The only surefire method of avoiding a tax refund intercept for a borrower currently in default is to lower federal income tax withholding from earnings and any estimated tax payments. Then, at the end of the year, the taxpayer is not owed a refund and there can be no interception.

This approach is partially available even for those receiving Earned Income Tax Credits (EITC).[56] Employees who are eligible for the EITC *and* who have a qualifying child are entitled to receive EITC payments in their pay during the year if they provide their employer with a completed IRS Form W-5, Earned Income Credit Advance Payment Certificate. The employee, though, can only have a portion of the EITC paid during the year.[57] A riskier strategy is to delay filing a refund. However, clients should be counseled on possible penalties associated with this option.

While most borrowers want to avoid offset of their tax refunds, borrowers who want to immediately pay off their loans may actually be better off having their tax refunds offset. Funds from tax offsets should be applied to principal and interest, not to collection fees.[58] Thus, the balance will decrease more rapidly through tax intercepts than through low monthly payment plans. Borrowers choosing this strategy should wait until the funds taken from the tax offsets leave them with a small balance left on their loans. Once the borrower has paid down to a small balance, exclusive of collection fees, the Department will frequently agree at this point to compromise the remaining balance and accept a lump sum payment.[59] The Department will usually waive the collection fees when the principal and interest are paid in full. This strategy saves borrowers from paying the huge collection fees that accrue once an account is turned over to a collection agency.[60]

8.2.9 Bankruptcy and Tax Offsets

Filing a personal bankruptcy petition *before* the offset activates the United States Bankruptcy Code automatic stay provision.[61] The stay prohibits virtually all actions against the debtor's property, including intercepts of owed tax refunds based on a student loan default.[62] The Department claims it will always readily and promptly return any amount taken by an offset during a pending bankruptcy.

It may also be possible to file bankruptcy to protect an impending return and claim any Earned Income Tax Credit due as exempt. The majority of courts have found tax credits to be part of the bankruptcy estate under federal law, available for distribution to creditors, but there is some

---

53 Burgess v. U.S. Dep't of Educ., 2006 WL 1047064 (D. Vt. Apr. 17, 2006) ("It is the Treasury Department that performs the tax refund offset, and only at that stage would a government agency become aware of the existence of a joint filer"; Department of Education also had no obligation to provide a non-debtor spouse with notice).

54 *Cf.* Bolden v. Equifax Accounts Receivable Servs., 838 F. Supp. 507 (D. Kan. 1993) (suggesting, over the Department's objection, that administrative remedies need not first be exhausted).

55 *See, e.g., In re* Blake, 235 B.R. 568 (Bankr. Md. 1998).

56 Courts have found that offsets may include the amount of an EITC owed. *See* Sorenson v. Secretary of Treasury, 475 U.S. 851 (1986) (U.S. has authority to seize earned income tax refund); Bosarge v. United States Dep't of Educ., 5 F.3d 1414 (11th Cir. 1993).

57 More information about the EITC is available on the IRS website, www.irs.treas.gov, and from the Center on Budget and Policy Priorities, www.cbpp.org, 1-202-408-1080.

58 The Department of Treasury regulations specify only that offsets can be allocated for past-due debts, less fees charged under 31 C.F.R. § 285.2(h).

This section allows fees charged by the Financial Management Service (FMS) of the Department of Treasury and the IRS to be deducted from the amount collected. To the extent allowed by law, federal agencies may add these fees to the debt. Still, the fees deducted, if any, should be less than those charged by collection agencies. *See* § 7.3, *supra*.

59 *See* §§ 7.3.1, 7.3.2, 7.3.2.3, *supra*. *See also* U.S. Dep't of Educ., Amendment to Agreement Pursuant to Section 428(b) of the Higher Education Act of 1965, as Amended, with a State or Private Non-profit Institution or Organization for Coverage of Its Student Loan Insurance Program under the Interest Benefits Provision of Section 428(a) of the Act, Appx. I § 5.1 (July 11, 1994), *available on* the companion website to this manual (if borrower agrees to pay principal within thirty days, agency may enter into a repayment agreement that includes the compromise of interest owed).

60 *See* §§ 7.3.1, 7.3.2, 7.3.2.3, *supra*.

61 11 U.S.C. § 362. *See generally* National Consumer Law Center, Consumer Bankruptcy Law and Practice § 2.5.5, Ch. 9, §§ 10.4.2.6.4, 10.4.2.6.6, 10.4.2.6.7 (9th ed. 2009 and Supp.).

62 An exception to the stay permits the IRS or another taxing authority to set off a pre-petition tax refund against a pre-petition tax debt. 11 U.S.C. § 362(b)(26).

precedent for distinguishing the right to an EITC.[63] The EITC might also be exempt under various state exemption schemes, particularly if a state exemption for "public benefits" is interpreted to include EITCs.[64]

If the offset has already occurred, borrowers can still recover that amount if they act quickly. The preference, postpetition transfer, and setoff provisions of the Bankruptcy Code may apply in some cases, enabling the borrower to reverse the transfer.[65]

8.2.10 Rights of Non-Obligated Spouses

When the United States intercepts a tax refund due on a joint return, the non-obligated spouse can recover *part* of the seized refund by filing an "injured spouse" claim with the IRS.[66] IRS regulations require that the United States notify any person who has filed a joint return with the obligated borrower of the steps that a non-obligated person can take to secure a proper partial refund.[67] If the non-obligated spouse files a separate return, the United States will seize no portion of a refund due on that return.

8.3 Non-Judicial Wage Garnishment

8.3.1 Introduction

Both the Higher Education Act and the Debt Collection Improvement Act authorize administrative wage garnishment.[68] Prior to 1996, the Department of Education was the only federal agency with this authority. However, the Debt Collection Improvement Act of 1996 (DCIA) extended the "privilege" to other federal agencies collecting debts owed to those agencies.[69] The DCIA authority should apply only when the Department is initiating garnishment. This is because the DCIA, unlike the Higher Education Act (HEA), applies only to garnishment by the "heads" of executive, judicial, or legislative agencies.[70] It does not specifically apply to agents of the federal departments.

For a time, there was some question as to whether the Department would continue operating under the authority of the HEA or whether it would try to conform to other agencies and operate under the authority of the DCIA. The mystery was cleared up when the Department published rules to operate garnishment procedures under the authority of the DCIA.[71] As discussed in detail below, these rules should apply only when the Department initiates garnishment. Since nearly all federal loans are now originated through the government Direct Loan Program and many FFELs have been assigned to the Department, over time the vast majority of garnishments will be through the Department and DCIA authority. However, the previous rules authorized by the Higher Education Act should continue to apply to guaranty agency garnishment actions.

Many states place even greater restrictions on wage garnishment or prohibit the practice outright. These state law limitations on garnishment do not apply to garnishments to satisfy student loan obligations.[72] State procedural requirements prior to garnishment are not likely to apply either.[73] On the other hand, certain tribal law restrictions on garnishment should apply.[74]

At least one court has held that the federal wage garnishment provisions do not apply to a state's garnishment efforts.[75] Thus, a state agency was not required to comply

---

63 *See generally* National Consumer Law Center, Consumer Bankruptcy Law and Practice § 2.5.5 (9th ed. 2009 and Supp.).
64 *Id.*
65 *Id.*
66 IRS forms are available on-line at www.irs.treas.gov. The injured-spouse form is Form 8379.
67 26 C.F.R. § 301.6402-6(i). *See* Burgess v. U.S. Dep't of Educ., 2006 WL 1047064 (D. Vt. Apr. 17, 2006) ("It is the Treasury Department that performs the tax refund offset, and only at that stage would a government agency become aware of the existence of a joint filer"; Department of Education also had no obligation to provide a non-debtor spouse with notice).
68 20 U.S.C. § 1095a (HEA); 31 U.S.C. § 3720D (DCIA).
69 Pub. L. No. 104-134, § 31001(o)(1), 110 Stat. 1321 (Apr. 26, 1996) (codified at 31 U.S.C. § 3720D).
70 31 U.S.C. § 3720D(a).
  The HEA, in contrast, specifically applies to guaranty agencies as well as the Secretary of Education. 20 U.S.C. § 1095a(a). *See* § 8.3.3.1, 8.3.2.4, *infra*.
71 The final rules were published in February 2003 and became effective on March 21, 2003. 68 Fed. Reg. 8142 (Feb. 19, 2003) (adding 34 C.F.R. §§ 34.1–34.30).
  The switch to the DCIA occurred because of criticism of the Department in a 2002 General Accounting Office (GAO) report, among other reasons. The GAO criticized the Department of Education and other federal agencies for failing to implement a wage garnishment program under the DCIA. In a letter to the GAO, the Department of Education complained that the report was misleading as it left the impression that no agency was conducting administrative wage garnishment. In fact, the Department of Education began garnishing wages under the authority of the HEA in 1993. *See* U.S. Gen. Accounting Office, Debt Collection Improvement Act of 1996: Status of Selected Agencies' Implementation of Administrative wage Garnishment, Report No. GAO-02-313 (Feb. 2002).
72 20 U.S.C. § 1095a(a) (garnishment requirements are allowed notwithstanding any provisions of state law). *See, e.g.*, Catto v. Duncan, 2009 WL 928094 (S.D.N.Y. Mar. 31, 2009); Frew v. Van Ru Credit Corp., 2006 WL 2261624 (E.D. Pa. Aug. 7, 2006); Educational Credit Mgmt. Corp. v. Wilson, 2005 WL 1263027 (E.D. Tenn. May 27, 2005) (guaranty agency seeking to garnish pursuant to the HEA need not comply with state laws governing garnishment orders); Nelson v. Diversified Collection Servs. Inc., 961 F. Supp. 863 (D. Md. 1997); Clear v. Missouri Coordinating Bd. for Higher Educ., 23 S.W.3d 896 (Mo. App. 2000).
73 *See* Nelson v. Diversified Collection Servs., Inc., 961 F. Supp. 863 (D. Md. 1997).
74 *See* 59 Fed. Reg. 22,473, cmt. 63 (Apr. 29, 1994).
75 United Student Aid Funds, Inc. v. South Carolina Dep't of Health & Envtl. Control, 561 S.E.2d 650 (App. S.C. 2002), *aff'd*, 588 S.E.2d 599 (S.C. 2003).

with a federal student loan garnishment order against a state employee. The court interpreted the federal wage garnishment statute so as not to interfere with the state's sovereign immunity.[76]

Section 8.3.2, *infra*, presents detailed information about the DCIA garnishment program, noting if the rules are the same for HEA garnishment by guaranty agencies. Section 8.3.3, *infra*, highlights key ways in which the HEA garnishment rules differ from the DCIA.

8.3.2 DCIA Garnishment by the Department of Education

8.3.2.1 Allowable Garnishment Amounts

Unless the borrower agrees in writing to a higher amount, the DCIA allows garnishment of disposable pay up to 15%.[77] Federal law also limits total garnishments to 25% of disposable earnings, so a student loan garnishment and other garnishments should not exceed 25% of earnings.[78]

"Disposable pay" is defined in the DCIA as compensation remaining after deducting amounts required by law to be withheld.[79] The Department's regulations follow the Department of Treasury's implementing regulations in defining "disposable pay" as amounts of a borrower's pay remaining after the deduction of health insurance premiums and any amounts required by law to be withheld, including deductions such as Social Security taxes and withholding taxes but not including any amounts withheld under a court order.[80] It includes but is not limited to salary, bonuses, commissions, or vacation pay.[81]

The statute provides only that the amount deducted may not exceed 15%.[82] The Department's regulations specify that the amount that can be garnished is the *lesser* of 15% of disposable income or the amount exceeding thirty times the prevailing minimum wage (the amount permitted by 15 U.S.C. § 1673).[83] This means that, no matter what, borrowers can keep an amount equal to thirty times the minimum wage. For example, Borrower A has a weekly disposable pay of $300. Borrower A definitely gets to keep $217.50 (30 x the current minimum wage of $7.25/hour, as of July 2009). The government can then take the lesser of the amount by which Borrower A's income exceeds $217.50 ($300 $217.50 = $82.50) or 15% of Borrower As income (15% of $300 = $45). Since $45 is less than $82.50, this is the amount the government can take each week from Borrower As wages.

The regulations explicitly grant the Department authority to issue multiple garnishment orders even though there is no provision in the DCIA allowing this practice.[84] Although it can issue multiple garnishment orders, the total amount may not exceed the lesser of the amount in the garnishment orders, the amount over thirty times the minimum wage, or 15% of disposable pay.[85]

In examining garnishment authority under the HEA, the Eleventh Circuit concluded that the maximum deduction applies to holders of student loan notes individually rather than collectively.[86] The court allowed each holder of a defaulted loan to garnish up to the maximum 10% allowed at that time as long as the total garnishments by all note holders did not exceed 25%.[87] Other courts have disagreed with this interpretation.[88]

These cases examined HEA authority. As noted above, the Department's regulations for implementing the DCIA garnishment authority explicitly allow multiple garnishment orders, but the total amount garnished under the multiple orders may be no more than 15% of disposable pay.[89] This is contrary to the Eleventh Circuit decision, which allowed the maximum amount per garnishment up to the 25% cumulative federal limit.

In a 2007 administrative wage garnishment guide for private collection agencies, the Department lists some examples to illustrate garnishment priority:

Example 1:

Creditor	Date Order Served on Employer	Requested Garnishment %
Child Recovery Service	1/15/03	20%
USAF (guaranty agency)	2/10/01	10%
DOE	11/30/03	15%

Answer: Employer should pay Child Recovery Service first 20% of the employee's disposable pay and the remaining 5% of wages available for withholding to USAF. This

---

76 *Id.* (interpreting 20 U.S.C. § 1095a).
77 31 U.S.C. § 3720D(b)(1).
78 15 U.S.C. § 1673.
79 31 U.S.C. § 3720D(g).
80 34 C.F.R. § 34.3(a)(1)–(2).
81 34 C.F.R. § 34.3(b).
82 31 U.S.C. § 3720D(b)(1).
83 34 C.F.R. § 34.19(b).
  The minimum wage can be found at 29 U.S.C. § 206(a)(1). The current minimum wage, as of July 23, 2009, is $7.25/hour. Therefore, $217.50 is protected per week (30 x $7.25 = $217.50).
84 34 C.F.R. § 34.20 (c).
85 34 C.F.R. § 34.20(c)(2).
86 Halperin v. Regional Adjustment Bureau, Inc., 206 F.3d 1063 (11th Cir. 2000).
87 *Id.*
88 *See* United States v. George, 144 F. Supp. 2d 161 (E.D.N.Y. 2001) (because plaintiff had only one loan, case was distinguishable from *Halperin*; however, criticizing reasoning in *Halperin* as "somewhat forced"; stating in a footnote that a fair reading of the legislative history "even as recounted in *Halperin*, supports an inference that any limitations on garnishment in the HEA . . . were intended to protect potential garnishees, who were often likely to be poor, from 'severe hardships.' "); Green v. Kentucky Higher Educ. Ass'n, 78 F. Supp. 2d 1259 (S.D. Ala. 1999) (interpreting 20 U.S.C. § 1095a to prevent multiple note holders from collectively garnishing more than 10%).
89 34 C.F.R. § 34.20(c)(2).

exhausts the 25% available for withholding. The employer cannot honor any part of the Department of Education (DOE) order until either of the prior orders are satisfied or cancelled.

Example 2:

Creditor	Date Order Served on Employer	Requested Garnishment %
Ford Motor	12/02/03	Full amount available under law
DOE	12/02/03	15%
Sears	3/18/02	Full amount available under law

Answer: Sears' order is first in time, thus the employer should pay Sears the full 25% of disposable pay until the order expires or the debt is paid in full. The employer should then pay the DOE 15% and Ford Motor the remaining 10% of disposable pay subject to withholding.[90]

In a 2009 manual, the Department explains that garnishments for family support take precedence over orders for student aid debts, regardless of when the latter are issued.[91]

8.3.2.2 Notice of Garnishment

The DCIA requires notice to the borrower before garnishment.[92] Notice must be sent by mail to the last known address a minimum of thirty days before the initiation of garnishment procedures.[93] The notice must inform the borrower of the nature and amount of the debt, the agency's intention to initiate garnishment, and an explanation of the borrower's rights.[94] Failure to follow these notice requirements as well as misrepresentations about the process may violate the Fair Debt Collection Practices Act (FDCPA) as long as a third-party collector is involved.[95]

If the borrower requests a hearing on or before the thirtieth day following notice of garnishment, the garnishment should not proceed until after the hearing.[96] Borrowers can still request hearings after that date, but garnishment may proceed pending a hearing decision.[97]

The regulations specify the borrower rights that must be revealed in the notice. These are the (1) right to inspect and copy records; (2) right to enter into a repayment agreement; and (3) right to request a hearing about the existence, amount, or current enforceability of the debt, the rate of withholding, and whether the borrower has been continuously employed less than twelve months after an involuntary separation from employment.[98]

8.3.2.3 Borrower Defenses and Objections

The regulations allow borrowers to raise objections to garnishment concerning the existence, amount, or current enforceability of the debt, the rate of garnishment, and whether the borrower has been continuously employed less than twelve months after involuntary separation from employment.[99] Objections to the rate or amount are considered only if they rest on claims of financial hardship.[100] The Department has the burden of proving the existence and amount of a debt.[101] Borrowers disputing the existence or amount must prove by a preponderance of the credible evidence that no debt exists, the amount is incorrect, or the borrower is not delinquent.[102]

---

90 *See* Administrative Wage Garnishment Compliance Branch, U.S. Dep't of Educ., Private Collection Agencies (PCA) Procedures Guide 62 (July 25, 2007). The guide is available on the companion website to this manual.

91 U.S. Dep't of Educ., Employer's Garnishment Handbook (Feb. 10, 2009).

92 31 U.S.C. § 3720D(b)(2).

93 31 U.S.C. § 3720D(b)(2); 34 C.F.R. § 34.4(c).

94 34 C.F.R. § 34.5.

95 *See, e.g.*, Kort v. Diversified Collection Servs., Inc., 2001 WL 881449 (N.D. Ill. Aug. 2, 2001), *class cert. granted in part*, 2001 WL 1617213 (N.D. Ill. Dec. 17, 2001) (alleging that collector violated FDCPA by giving borrowers insufficient time to respond to garnishment notices and by requiring affirmative proof of unemployment exception); Sanders v. OSI Educ. Servs., Inc., 2001 WL 883608 (N.D. Ill. Aug. 3, 2001), *plaintiff's motion for summary judgment granted in part, denied in part*, 270 F. Supp. 2d 1017 (N.D. Ill. July 8, 2003) (if a deadline for establishing a repayment plan or other response to garnishment is gratuitously established, it must not be misleading to the unsophisticated consumer; FDCPA violation found on this count).

The district court granted summary judgment for the collection agency on plaintiff's claim that the agency's notice contained misinformation about the HEA unemployment exemption. The court found that the agency was insulated from liability under the FDCPA's bona fide error defense. The Seventh Circuit agreed. Kort v. Diversified Collection Serv., Inc., 270 F. Supp. 2d 1017 (N.D. Ill. 2003), *aff'd*, 394 F.3d 530 (7th Cir. 2005). *See also* § 7.4, *supra*.

96 31 U.S.C. § 3720D(c)(1); 34 C.F.R. § 34.11(a). A copy of the AWG request for hearing form can be found at Appendix D, *infra*, and on the companion website to this manual.

97 31 U.S.C. § 3720D(c)(2).

It is unclear whether borrowers requesting hearings after the thirty days may also request in-person hearings. This issue was raised in comments submitted by the National Consumer Law Center, Community Legal Services, and Legal Aid Foundation of Los Angeles. *See* Comments to the Department of Education on proposed Administrative Wage Garnishment Regulations (submitted on June 11, 2002), *available on* the companion website to this manual.

The final rules did not directly address this issue. However, the Department reaffirmed that it provides hearings even if the request for hearing is untimely, regardless of the type of hearing sought. 68 Fed. Reg. 8142, 8149 (Feb. 19, 2003).

The "Request for Hearing" form allows a borrower to choose between a written record, in-person hearing, or telephone hearing. It does not state that only borrowers requesting hearings within thirty days are entitled to in-person hearings.

98 34 C.F.R. § 34.6(c). *See* § 8.3.2.3 (borrower defenses), *infra*.

99 34 C.F.R. § 34.6(c).

100 34 C.F.R. § 34.7.

101 34 C.F.R. § 34.14(a).

102 34 C.F.R. § 34.14(b).

Borrowers must inform loan holders that they qualify for the unemployment exception either by checking the appropriate box on the hearing form or by providing other written notice. The hearing request form issued by the Department requires that borrowers attach proof of unemployment. Guaranty agencies may also use this form. The Department's garnishment regulations implementing the DCIA garnishment authority require credible evidence of involuntary separation from employment but do not specify that evidence must be provided by the borrower.[103] There is some question as to whether borrowers should have to provide documentation or other proof that they qualify for the exception. If documentation is not required, collection letters requiring borrowers to submit affirmative proof of eligibility may violate the FDCPA.[104]

Borrowers may also raise eligibility for the statutory discharges, such as for a closed school and for total and permanent disability. This issue must be raised in the manner prescribed by the regulations, including, for example, the proper application form.

In the guidelines for HEA garnishment, which should also apply for DCIA hearings, the Department states that, if these prerequisites have not been met, the hearing official may want to adjourn the hearing to accommodate the discharge determination. The Department notes further that the federal regulations generally require the guarantor to suspend collection action on a loan when the guarantor receives reliable information indicating that the borrower may be eligible for discharge relief.[105] A favorable decision on the discharge should moot the garnishment.

The Department has issued a "Request for Hearing" form, similar to the form for guaranty agencies, that includes a list of specific defenses. These defenses include the various discharge programs, such as for disability, death, closed school, false certification, and unpaid refund.

The completed form must be sent to the address listed on the form. As of 2010, the correct address is: U.S. Department of Education, AWG Hearings Unit, P.O. Box 617547, Chicago, IL 60661. The phone number for the Chicago hearing office, as of the summer of 2010, is 312-730-1477. When calling for this purpose, borrowers or advocates should ask to speak to an AWG hearing official.[106]

The Department's form includes a check box for "hardship" immediately after spaces for identifying information. Borrowers asserting hardship may fill out the Department's Financial Disclosure Form or a form of the borrower's choosing that includes the same information.[107] According to the Department, the overwhelming majority of objections to proposed garnishment are based on hardship.[108] Borrowers bear the burden of proving by a preponderance of the credible evidence that withholding the amount of wages proposed would leave the borrower unable to meet his or her own basic living expenses and those of dependents.[109]

Borrowers may object based on hardship at any time. However, the Department will only consider these objections to an outstanding garnishment order after the order has been outstanding for at least six months.[110] In extraordinary circumstances, the Department may provide an earlier hearing if the borrower can show that his or her financial circumstances have substantially changed after the notice of proposed garnishment because of an event such as injury, divorce, or catastrophic illness.[111]

Borrowers should provide as much documentation as possible to support hardship claims. The regulations require documentation of the amount of costs incurred by the borrower, spouse, and any dependents for basic living expenses and the income available to meet expenses.[112] Examples include copies of monthly bills for all expenses, copies of income tax returns, and any recent leave and/or earnings statements for the borrower, borrower's spouse, and any employed dependents.[113] Borrowers listing credit card payments should provide details about the types of expenses paid with the cards. The Department may decide to withhold a lesser percentage of the borrower's wages or to completely stop withholding. The Department may reinstate garnishment if the borrower's financial circumstances improve.

The Department will compare the borrower's expenses and income against the amounts spent for basic living expenses by families of the same size and similar income

---

103 34 C.F.R. § 34.23.

104 However, at least one court found that a collection agency was not liable under the FDCPA even if the information in the notice about the unemployment exception was incorrect. The court agreed with the collection agency's argument that the error was inadvertent because it used the notice form required by the Department of Education and any errors in the form were the responsibility of the Department. Kort v. Diversified Collection Servs., Inc., 2001 WL 881449 (N.D. Ill. Aug. 2, 2001), *cert. granted in part*, 2001 WL 1617213 (N.D. Ill. Dec. 17, 2001) (alleging that collector violated FDCPA by giving borrowers insufficient time to respond to garnishment notices and by requiring affirmative proof of unemployment exception), *plaintiff's motion for summary judgment granted in part, denied in part*, 270 F. Supp. 2d 1017 (N.D. Ill. 2003), *aff'd*, 394 F.3d 530 (7th Cir. 2005); Sanders v. OSI Educ. Serv., Inc., 2001 WL 883608 (N.D. Ill. Aug. 3, 2001).

105 U.S. Dep't of Educ., AWG Hearing Guidelines (rev. Mar. 1, 2004).

106 U.S. Dep't of Educ., PCA Procedures Manual: 2009 ED Collections Contract 228 (Sept. 2009).

107 The financial disclosure form is reprinted at Appendix D.4.2, *infra*, and is also available on the companion website to this manual.

108 68 Fed. Reg. 8142, 8151 (Feb. 19, 2003).

109 34 C.F.R. § 34.14(c)(1).

110 34 C.F.R. § 34.24(c)(1).

111 34 C.F.R. § 34.24(c)(2).

112 34 C.F.R. § 34.24(d)(2).

113 *See, e.g.*, Harrill v. U.S. Dep't of Educ., 2009 WL 230126 (S.D. Ohio Jan. 30, 2009) (not irrational for Department to require current financial information before determining whether garnishment would create a financial hardship).

§ 8.3.2.4 Student Loan Law

using the national standards published by the Internal Revenue Service establishing the average amounts spent for basic living expenses.[114] A borrower must prove that any amount in excess of the national standards is reasonable and necessary.[115] For example, the borrower may contend that above-average expenses are needed for housing costs, retirement savings, and tuition for private schools, charitable contributions, vehicles, utilities, and telephone costs.[116]

In contrast, the FFEL regulations for guaranty agencies do not contain any provision that expressly allocates the burden of proof for financial hardship. The HEA regulations also do not require agencies to use national standards to compare borrower expenses. However, the Department encouraged guaranty agency decision makers to use these same standards.[117]

In a training manual for private collection agencies, the Department set out more specifically the type of information borrowers should submit to support the various defenses. For discharge-related defenses, borrowers should submit the required discharge forms and relevant supporting information. For borrowers claiming that they were entitled to a full or partial refund of their loans, the Department requests that borrowers answer the following questions and provide documentation to support these answers:

- What procedures did you follow to enroll in the school?
- How long after you enrolled did you first attend the school?
- What course did you enroll in?
- What was the cost of the course?
- What did the school charge for tuition, board, and fees?
- Did you receive any other loans or grants to pay for this training?
- What was the refund policy of the school?
- Did the school give you any money from loan(s), or were all loan proceeds used for tuition, board, and fee charges?
- Did you receive any mail-order lessons?
- If so, how many of these lessons did you complete?
- How many days did you attend the school?
- Why did you leave the school?
- What procedures did you follow when you withdrew from the school?
- What was your last day of attendance?
- What steps if any did you take to see if the school issued a refund to the lender?
- Did you notify your lender that you had withdrawn from the school? If so, how did you notify them?[118]

Active service members have certain rights to stay collection proceedings.[119] In addition, the Merchant Seaman Protection and Relief Act prohibits attachment of the wages of "masters" or "seamen."[120] The Department of Education acknowledges the "seamen" exception in its wage garnishment guide for private collection agencies.

The borrower, not the employer that receives a garnishment order, must assert any defenses to garnishment.[121] Guaranty agencies and the Department have the authority to sue employers refusing to comply with garnishment orders to recover amounts the employer has refused to withhold plus attorney fees, costs, and punitive damages in the court's discretion.[122] Employers in some cases have tried to litigate on behalf of their employees. However, the statutes allow borrowers, not employers, to raise defenses to garnishment.[123]

8.3.2.4 Repayment in Lieu of Garnishment

Borrowers may enter into written repayment agreements to repay under terms the Department considers acceptable.[124] As with tax offsets, the regulations do not explicitly require "reasonable and affordable repayment plans." However, assuming they are otherwise eligible, borrowers have a right to such plans through the rehabilitation process.[125] Borrowers should also consider consolidation as a way out of default or settlement.[126]

Borrowers are often confused about these options because of misleading collection letters. For example, a com-

---

114 34 C.F.R. § 34.24(e)(2) (citing 26 U.S.C. § 7122(c)(2)).
115 34 C.F.R. § 34.24(e)(4).
116 68 Fed. Reg. 8142, 8151 (Feb. 19, 2003).
117 Id. at 8152. See § 8.3.3.2, infra.
118 Student Fin. Assistance, U.S. Dep't of Educ., Administrative Wage Garnishment, Hearings Support Manual, Private Collection Agencies (Jan. 2005).
  These questions and requirements should apply to the DCIA-authorized garnishment process as well. See § 8.3.3.2, infra.
119 See § 7.5.4.5, supra.
120 46 U.S.C. § 11109.
  Definitions of these terms can be found at 46 U.S.C. § 10101.
121 Educational Credit Mgmt. Corp. v. Wilson, 2005 WL 1263027 (E.D. Tenn. May 27, 2005) (employer prohibited from asserting that borrower did not owe loan).
122 20 U.S.C. § 1095a(a)(6); Educational Credit Mgmt. Corp. v. Central Equip. Co., 477 F. Supp. 2d 788 (E.D. Ky. 2007) (ordering employer to pay actual attorney fees of guaranty agency, even though those fees amounted to more than the amount of the employee's defaulted loan). See Educational Credit Mgmt. Corp. v. Wilson, 2006 WL 4608614 (E.D. Tenn. Oct. 3, 2006) (denying compensatory damages but awarding attorney fees for collector in a case in which borrower's employer challenged wage garnishment order and borrower was eventually able to obtain a closed-school discharge of her loans; awarding attorney fees for efforts expended by collector to pursue garnishment while borrower "inexplicably" delayed applying for discharge; collector had requested higher fees, but court rejected collector's argument that it must automatically award full amount of fees claimed); Education Credit Mgmt. Corp. v. Cherish Prods., Inc., 312 F. Supp. 2d 1183 (D. Minn. 2004).
123 20 U.S.C. § 1095a(a)(5); 31 U.S.C. § 3720D.
124 31 U.S.C. § 3720D(b)(4); 34 C.F.R. § 34.6(b).
125 See § 6.3, supra.
126 See §§ 6.2 (consolidation), 6.6 (settlement/compromise), supra.

monly used student loan debt collection letter first informs borrowers that they may face wage garnishment to collect the loan. The letter then states: "However, if your financial situation warrants such consideration, we have been authorized to substantially reduce the amount on the above-referenced account and cease any further collection efforts if your account is paid in full or assist you in establishing a possible repayment program on your loan." This is misleading because, prior to garnishment, most borrowers are eligible for either consolidation or rehabilitation to get out of default. Both of these options require borrowers to make only reasonable, affordable, or income-based repayments. They do not have to prove that their financial situations "warrant consideration" nor should they pay more than what is reasonable and affordable.

Accounts should not be submitted to garnishment while a borrower is still negotiating repayment. A 2006 bankruptcy case cites a statement in the Department's publication, *Options for Financially-Challenged Borrowers in Default*, that the Department is generally willing to accept an installment payment plan under which the borrower pays 15% of disposable pay.[127]

It is unclear why a borrower would agree to voluntary payments in the same amount as would be garnished. Presumably the only advantage to the borrower would be if the payments are counted toward rehabilitation and ultimately helps the borrower get out of default. Borrowers may also attempt to negotiate a settlement agreement with the Department to avoid garnishment.

The standard agreement that the Department and its agents use for borrowers setting up rehabilitation plans in lieu of garnishment require borrowers to agree that, if they do not honor their agreements, the Department can start garnishing without giving the borrower a new opportunity for a hearing. The letter that borrowers receive clarifies that they can still request hearings but that garnishment will not be delayed or suspended pending the hearing.[128]

The Department has standard letters for collectors to use when borrowers settle debts prior to repayment or set up rehabilitation plans.[129] The letter for rehabilitation requires borrowers to acknowledge, by signing, that they have been given the opportunity for a hearing to object to garnishment and are withdrawing any such requests.[130] The borrower agrees that he or she may request a hearing again in the future but that this request will not delay or suspend garnishment. However, borrowers must acknowledge by signing that they owe the amount stated in the notice and waive any future objections based on amount. Hardship may still be raised.

Once garnishment begins, the borrower's options are more limited. Consolidation is prohibited if a garnishment order is in place. If the borrower is facing wage garnishment, he or she may consolidate only if the garnishment order is lifted.[131] In addition, payments taken through garnishment are not considered to be "voluntary payments" for purposes of rehabilitation. However, many guaranty agencies will work with borrowers, when pressed, in these circumstances.

For example, in 2009 meetings with the guaranty agency trade association (National Council of Higher Education Loan Programs), the association reported that the majority of its guaranty agency members were willing to release garnishments for borrowers who showed a willingness to make voluntary reasonable and affordable payments. All others agreed to accept a token voluntary payment and subtract that amount from the garnishment amount so that the gross monthly payment does not change for the borrower. Although this latter scenario means that the garnishment will continue, the borrower will also be on the way to getting out of default through rehabilitation. This scenario will only work if the borrower can make it through nine months of garnishment. There also may be a delay, as discussed in Chapter 6, *supra*, in completing the rehabilitation even after the required payments are made.

8.3.2.5 The Hearing Process

Borrowers who want an oral hearing must request one and also must show good reason why the issues cannot be resolved "on paper."[132] The oral hearing may be in person or by telephone.[133] Although the Department pays for telephone calls to conduct oral hearings, it does not pay for travel expenses for in-person hearings.[134]

The HEA regulations for guaranty agencies entitle borrowers to a hearing with an independent official from within the Department.[135] In contrast, the DCIA regulations allow the hearing officer to be any "qualified employee" of the

---

127 Bender v. Van Ru Corp., 338 B.R. 62 (Bankr. W.D. Mo. 2006). The publication is available on-line at www.ed.gov/offices/OSFAP/DCS/forms/2004.Borrower.Options.pdf (Oct. 2004).

128 Financial Student Assistance, U.S. Dep't of Educ., Revised Guidance for Rehab. Accounts Where AWG Has Been Initiated (Jan. 29, 2008).

129 U.S. Dep't of Educ., PCA Procedures Manual: 2009 ED Collections Contract 45–51 (Sept. 2009).

130 *Id.* at 49.

131 34 C.F.R. § 685.220(d)(1)(ii)(F). See § 6.2.4, *supra*.

In early 2007, the Department of Education's Financial Student Assistance agency sent a note to contract administrators on this issue. They acknowledged at that point that the Department had no systematic way to determine whether a borrower requesting Direct consolidation was in active garnishment status. They set up an interim process to try to deny these consolidation requests. They noted that, if a consolidation goes through, the accounts would be reviewed for a possible reversal. (Jan. 23, 2007).

132 34 C.F.R. § 34.9.

133 34 C.F.R. § 34.9(c)(1).

134 34 C.F.R. § 34.9(c).

135 34 C.F.R. § 682.410(b)(9)(i)(M). See §§ 8.3.3.1, 8.3.3.2, *supra*.

Department whom the Department designates.[136] Unfortunately for borrowers, the Department does not provide any definition of "qualified employee" and does not explicitly state that the hearing officer must be independent or neutral. The National Consumer Law Center and other advocacy groups have argued that, at minimum, employees of the collections division should not serve as hearing officers.

In its final rules issued in 2003, the Department clarified the role of Department contractors in the hearing process.[137] Department contractors cannot conduct hearings or rule on objections to garnishment because those are inherently governmental functions. The Department itself must provide a hearing and decide debtor objections. This does not, according to the Department, preclude use of contractors to analyze debtor objections and propose resolutions on objections.[138] The Department specifically acknowledged that contractors used to prepare recommendations should be trained to properly analyze debtor objections. The Department also addressed consumer advocates' requests that it adopt guidelines and training procedures for any Department staff designated to conduct hearings. In rejecting these suggestions, the Department merely affirmed that its decisions are subject to judicial review under the Administrative Procedure Act.[139]

The hearing officer is required to maintain a summary record and issue a written opinion.[140] The hearing decision must rest on evidence in the hearing record and must include a description of the evidence considered in making that decision.[141] The hearing official will consider evidence that was not included in records made available for inspection before the hearing only after the Department has notified the borrower, made the evidence available to the borrower, and provided a reasonable period for rebuttal evidence and argument by the borrower.[142] A written decision must be issued as soon as possible, but in any case no later than sixty days after the date the Department received the request for hearing.[143] If this deadline is not met, the Department must not issue a garnishment order until a hearing is held and decision rendered. Garnishment orders already issued will be suspended until a hearing is held and decision issued.[144]

Borrowers may submit evidence after sending in a request for hearing. The regulations require that the borrower make a specific request that the record be held open for consideration of such evidence, describe the evidence, and explain why it is relevant. There is a provision for a brief extension of time, upon request, for the borrower to then submit any evidence not previously presented.[145]

Borrowers who object to the decision have the right to request reconsideration.[146] The hearing decision must include a statement not only informing the borrower that he or she may appeal the ruling in federal court but also explaining the reconsideration rights available.[147] Garnishment will continue pending a decision on reconsideration.[148]

The regulations state that the Department will consider a request for reconsideration only if it determines that:

- The borrower's request is based on grounds of financial hardship and the borrower's financial circumstances, as shown by evidence submitted with the request, have materially changed since issuance of the decision so that the amount to be garnished should be reduced[149] or
- The borrower submitted evidence that was not previously submitted and this evidence demonstrates that the Department should reconsider an objection to the existence, amount, or enforceability of the debt.[150]

The Department may offer a hearing for reconsideration.[151] Appeals of reconsiderations may be made to federal court under the Administrative Procedures Act.[152]

8.3.3 Guaranty Agency Wage Garnishment Program

8.3.3.1 General

Prior to Congressional changes in 2005, the Higher Education Act administrative wage garnishment statute and regulations allowed garnishment of up to 10% of "disposable pay." As of July 1, 2006, the limit was increased to 15%.[153]

There are some differences between the HEA and DCIA program, and these differences are described below. If not discussed below, then the HEA rules are the same as under

---

136 34 C.F.R. § 34.13(a)(2).
137 68 Fed. Reg. 8142, 8149 (Feb. 19, 2003).
138 Id. at 8149–50.
   The Department also explained that it intended no inference that guaranty agencies could not use contractors as hearing officials.
139 Id. at 8150.
   APA appeal rights, however, may not be available if the guaranty agency makes the decision. See § 8.3.5, infra.
140 34 C.F.R. §§ 34.13(b)(3), 34.16.
141 34 C.F.R. § 34.17(a).
142 34 C.F.R. § 34.13(c).
143 34 C.F.R. § 34.16(a).
144 34 C.F.R. § 34.16(b).
145 34 C.F.R. § 34.13(d)(4)(iii).
146 34 C.F.R. § 34.12.
147 34 C.F.R. § 34.17(a)(4).
148 34 C.F.R. § 34.12(b).
149 34 C.F.R. § 34.12(c)(1).
150 34 C.F.R. § 34.12(c)(2).
151 34 C.F.R. § 34.12(d)(2)(ii). See, e.g., Kelly v. Aman Collection Servs. et al., 2007 WL 909547 (D. Minn. Mar. 23, 2007) (upholding hearing officer's decision in wage garnishment hearing). See § 9.15, infra.
152 See, e.g., Kelly v. Aman Collection Servs. et al., 2007 WL 909547 (D. Minn. Mar. 23, 2007) (upholding hearing officer's decision in wage garnishment hearing). See § 9.15, infra.
153 20 U.S.C. § 1095a(a)(1); 34 C.F.R. § 682.410(b)(9)(i)(A).

the DCIA, as described above.[154] The notice requirements are similar to those under the DICA.[155]

Guaranty agencies are under a general mandate to garnish wages of all eligible borrowers.[156] The only exception to this requirement arises if the agency determines that litigation would be more effective in collecting the debt.[157] The regulations clarify that agencies have the discretion to file lawsuits instead of garnishing wages only if the borrower has no wages that can be garnished or the agency determines that the borrower has sufficient attachable assets or income that is not subject to administrative wage garnishment and litigation would be more effective.[158]

The borrower must be given the opportunity for a hearing to contest the existence or amount of the debt and the terms of the repayment schedule.[159] As with the DCIA, the guarantor is required to offer the borrower an opportunity to enter into a repayment agreement, in lieu of the garnishment, on terms agreeable to the guarantor.[160]

If the borrower's written request for a hearing is received within fifteen days of the borrower's receipt of the garnishment notice (receipt is presumed within five days of mailing of the notice), no garnishment can issue until the hearing is provided.[161] The Department regulations allow thirty days.[162] Guaranty agencies must issue the hearing decision within sixty days.[163]

The defenses and objections to garnishment are similar to those allowed under the DCIA authority. For example, if the borrower has been involuntarily separated from employment, garnishment is prohibited until the borrower has been re-employed continuously for twelve months. The HEA regulations depart from the statute in authorizing garnishment unless the guarantor has *knowledge* that this exception applies to a particular borrower.[164] This places the burden on the borrower to notify the guarantor of the lack of continuous employment. In contrast, the Department's DCIA regulations require that the borrower present credible evidence of involuntary separation from employment.[165] In either case, some of the burden falls on borrowers to notify the loan holder of their unemployment status and to prove that they qualify for the unemployment exception. The regulations also do not provide notice of the twelve-months-continuous-employment requirement to the employer in the withholding order.[166]

The Department has also developed an administrative wage garnishment calculator for its contractors to use in making hardship determinations.[167] The instructions for data input clarify that pay stubs are the preferred method for verifying income. A copy of the borrower's previous year's income tax returns may also be required. Unusually high expenses require documentation of the monthly amount paid and a justification as to why they should be included as necessary living expenses. Reasonable expenses for housing, utilities, and transportation do not need documentation. Although only the borrower's wages may be garnished, the agencies will evaluate total household income and expenses in making a decision on the hardship defense.

The Department has issued instructions for agencies to follow up with borrowers who have been granted six-month hardship suspensions. During the six-month period, agencies must update and maintain current information on borrowers and seek to establish an acceptable reasonable and affordable payment plan.[168] If the borrower cannot be reached or refuses to discuss the account, the Department claims that agencies can immediately send the pre-garnishment notices and initiate procedures to garnish the account. This includes a "special" letter that explains that the temporary suspension of garnishment is about to expire or has recently expired.[169]

8.3.3.2 Guaranty Agency Garnishment Hearing

The borrower is entitled to a hearing with an independent official within the agency. "Independent official" is defined as someone not under the supervision or control of the head of the agency.[170]

---

154 *See generally* National Council of Higher Education Loan Programs, AWG Hearing Guidelines Manual (July 2005) (industry manual), *available at* www.nchelp.org/elibrary/Manuals&Guides/IndustryManualsandGuides/AWG%20Hearing%20Manual%20-%20July%202005.pdf.
155 34 C.F.R. § 682.410(b)(9)(i)(B).
156 34 C.F.R. § 682.410(b)(6)(vi).
157 34 C.F.R. § 682.410(b)(6)(vii).
158 *Id.*
159 34 C.F.R. § 682.410(b)(9)(i)(E).
160 20 U.S.C. § 1095a(a)(4); 34 C.F.R. § 682.410(b)(9)(i)(D).
161 34 C.F.R. § 682.410(b)(9)(i)(K).
162 34 C.F.R. § 34.11(a). *See* § 8.3.2.2, *supra*.
163 34 C.F.R. § 682.410(b)(9)(i)(N).
164 20 U.S.C. § 1095a(a)(d)(7); 34 C.F.R. § 682.410(b)(9)(i)(G).
165 *See* § 8.3.2.3, *supra*.

166 *See* 59 Fed. Reg. 22,474, cmts. 72, 73 (Apr. 29, 1994); 34 C.F.R. § 682.410(b)(10)(i)(I) (notice to employer must contain only the information necessary for employer to comply with withholding order).
167 The calculator was available on-line on the Department's PCA website but, as of 2010, the Department took this site off-line. The manual is available on the companion website to this manual and, as of the summer of 2010, on the website for the Center for Public Integrity. *See* Ariel Wittenberg, Center for Pub. Integrity, Education Department Pulls Student Debt Collectors Guide Off Web Site (June 16, 2010), *available at* http://www.publicintegrity.org/data_mine/entry/2162.
168 Financial Student Assistance, U.S. Dep't of Educ., Requirements for Post Hearing Administrative Wage Garnishment (AWG) Account(s) (July 9, 2008).
169 *Id.*
170 34 C.F.R. § 682.410(b)(9)(i)(M). *See, e.g.*, Kelly v. Aman Collection Servs. et al., 2007 WL 909547 (D. Minn. Mar. 23, 2007) (rejecting borrower's claims that hearing officer was under the control of a guaranty agency and so not independent).

The regulations allow the agency to establish the time and location of the hearing or to hold the hearing by telephone conference.[171]

At the hearing, the agency must provide evidence establishing the existence and amount of the debt and the agency's right to administratively garnish the borrower's wages. The case should not be allowed to proceed if, for example, the agency does not have a copy of the loan application and/or promissory note. After the agency has presented this information, the burden shifts to the borrower to provide the facts necessary to support the objection raised. In *2004 AWG Handbook*, a 2004 handbook for guaranty agencies, the Department states that the HEA does not specifically address the issue of burdens of proof. According to the Department, however, under the DCIA, the facts necessary to establish objection(s) to the existence of the debt amount, that the proposed garnishment rate would cause financial hardship, or that applicable law bars the Department from collecting the debt by garnishment must be proven by the borrower by a preponderance of the credible evidence.[172] According to the handbook, a similar standard applies to financial hardship claims.[173]

The Department also states that a favorable decision by the guaranty agency on a discharge claim generally moots the garnishment action.[174] If the agency denies the discharge claim, the hearing official then must consider the guarantor's determination by applying the same standards that a court applies in reviewing other informal administrative agency determinations.[175] Under these standards, the hearing official should uphold the denial if he concludes that the decision is "rationally based" and "founded upon a consideration of relevant factors and does not exhibit clear error of judgment."[176] If the hearing official finds that the decision does not meet this test, the case should be remanded to the guarantor for further consideration.[177]

In some cases, agencies will be unprepared to offer borrowers proper hearings. As a result, in some cases, when borrowers have pushed for hearings, agencies have simply agreed to withdraw the garnishment order. Advocates should not rely on this possibility. However, borrowers are entitled to at least the procedural rights required in the regulations and should be prepared to aggressively advocate for these rights.[178]

If the borrower does not request a hearing, or if the borrower's objection is denied, the employer is notified to deduct the garnishment amount from the borrower's paycheck. If the borrower is late in requesting a hearing on the garnishment, the garnishment order will proceed, but the borrower should still receive a hearing and a decision within sixty days.[179] If the borrower prevails, the garnishment should be ordered to cease and, if appropriate, amounts garnished should be returned. In addition, the guaranty agency has discretion to postpone a garnishment pending a hearing, even if the borrower's request for a hearing is late, if the borrower's delay was caused by factors over which the borrower had no control or if the agency receives information that the agency believes justifies a delay.[180]

Guaranty agencies have the authority to adjudicate disputes and make binding decisions.[181] However, unlike federal agency hearings, borrowers have no explicit right to judicial review of guaranty agency actions. This lack of review has been challenged, unsuccessfully to date, on constitutional due process grounds.[182] In 2003 court pleadings, the Department of Education acknowledged the problem and supported implying a private right of action under the HEA for judicial review of guaranty agency administrative wage garnishment hearing decisions.[183] Borrowers should clearly be able to appeal denials when the Department is garnishing.[184]

8.3.4 Participation of Private Collection Agencies in Garnishment

Under the HEA program, the Department has issued guidance to guaranty agencies on the extent to which collection agencies can participate in the garnishment pro-

---

171 34 C.F.R. § 682.410(b)(9)(i)(J).
  The telephone charges are the responsibility of the guaranty agency. In at least one case, a borrower challenged a collection agency's scheduling of a garnishment hearing in another state as a violation of the Fair Debt Collection Practices Act. *See* Lawson v. Management Adjustment Bureau, 1997 U.S. Dist. LEXIS 7275 (N.D. Ill. May 15, 1997) (plaintiff claimed that the scheduling of the hearing in another state violated 15 U.S.C. § 1692i(a)(2), the provision of the FDCPA that requires a collector to bring legal actions on a debt only in the judicial district in which the consumer signed the contract or where the consumer resides; court granted defendant's motion to dismiss this claim, finding that an administrative wage garnishment hearing is not a "legal action" for purposes of the FDCPA venue requirement).
172 *Id.* (citing 34 C.F.R. § 34.14(b)–(d)).
173 *Id.*
174 *Id.*
175 *Id.*
176 *Id.* (citing Lee v. Riley, No. 3:96CV-719-H (D.D.C. Feb. 29, 1998)).
177 *Id.* (citing Most v. U.S. Dep't of Educ., No. 98CV2910 (D.D.C. Dec. 21, 1999)).
178 Whether these procedures comport with due process is discussed in § 8.3.5, *infra*.
179 34 C.F.R. § 684.410(b)(9)(i)(L).
180 *Id.*
181 20 U.S.C. § 1095a.
182 *See* § 8.3.5, *infra*.
183 *See* Hutchins v. U.S. Dep't of Educ., CV-F-02-6256-OWW-DLB (E.D. Cal. filed Apr. 25, 2003) (U.S. Department of Education Memorandum of Points and Authorities Supporting Motion to Dismiss), *available on* the companion website to this manual.
184 *See, e.g.*, Gorka v. U.S. Dep't of Educ., 2004 WL 2658071 (N.D. Ill. Oct. 13, 2004) (allowing borrower's claim for improper garnishment but finding that the Department's administrative denial was reasonable). *See* § 9.15, *infra*.

cess.[185] The Department prohibits collection personnel from conducting hearings and requires that hearing officers must be independent not only of the guarantor but also of the collector. The collector cannot issue withholding orders to employers and the order cannot appear to come from the collector. Collection agencies therefore cannot issue garnishment decisions.[186]

Guaranty agencies may employ collection agencies to assist them with various aspects of the garnishment process. For example, employers receiving wage garnishment orders may be directed to send withheld amounts to collection agencies working on behalf of the guaranty agencies. In a case in which employers were directed to send payments to a collection agency but the notice was printed on the guaranty agency's stationery, at least one court found that it was not a violation of the FDCPA . According to the court, the document clearly stated that the order was issued pursuant to authority granted by federal law to the guaranty agency.[187] Collection agencies that contact employers may, however, violate the FDCPA. The FDCPA has an exception to the general prohibition against communication with third parties that allows collectors to do so as reasonably necessary to effectuate a postjudgment judicial remedy.[188] An administrative wage garnishment, however, should not be considered a postjudgment remedy. Yet the Department of Education explicitly instructs collection agencies to make contact with borrowers at their places of employment and residences. The instructions go further and require agencies, in cases in which contact cannot be made directly with the borrower at the work place, to leave at least two messages at the place of employment.[189]

For Department-held loans, the Department authorizes collectors to send out the notice of garnishment, respond to debtor inquiries, negotiate repayment arrangements (consumers have a statutory right to avoid garnishment by entering into a repayment arrangement), and receive payments from employers. The contractor may assist in finding independent hearing officers, recommend that garnishment orders be issued, prepare the orders for review, and mail out the orders executed by the guarantor.[190]

In final rules implementing the DCIA authority, the Department clarified its role in the hearing process.[191] Department contractors cannot conduct hearings or rule on objections to garnishment because those are inherently governmental functions. The Department itself must provide a hearing and decide debtor objections. This does not, according to the Department, preclude use of contractors to analyze debtor objections and propose resolutions on objections.[192] The Department specifically acknowledged that contractors used to prepare recommendations should be trained to properly analyze debtor objections. The Department also explained that it did not object to guaranty agencies using contractors as hearing officials.[193] Just because the Department allows such involvement by collectors does not mean that the involvement complies with due process requirements.[194]

According to the Department's 2009 PCA manual, the minimum requirements for selection or consideration for garnishment are:[195]

1. The balance must be greater than $200, with no negative balances and no unusually large fees requiring adjustments.
2. No accounts should be submitted while the borrower is attempting to negotiate or establish some type of reasonable and affordable repayment plan.[196] A minimum of sixty days must elapse or the borrower must clearly refuse to cooperate with the agency in establishing "reasonable and affordable repayment terms acceptable to [the collection agency]."
3. There should be no outstanding disputes concerning the validity, enforceability, financial hardship hearing, or past-due status of the debt(s).
4. Borrower's income is thirty times the federal minimum wage.[197]
5. Borrower is not a federal or military employee.
6. Borrower is not a merchant seaman.
7. Borrower is not self-employed (for example, independent contractor, real estate agent, sole proprietor).
8. Borrower is not a seasonal employee with no constant employer (that is, farm laborers). However, borrowers whose terms of employment include extended periods of leave followed by a return to service (for example,

---

185 Letter from Pamela Moran, Chief of the Loans Branch, to Guaranty Agency Directors (Nov. 1, 1994), *available on* the companion website to this manual. *See also* U.S. Dep't of Educ., PCA Procedures Manual: 2009 ED Collections Contract Ch. 13 (Sept. 2009).
186 *See, e.g.,* Sanon v. Department of Higher Educ., 2010 WL 1049264 (E.D.N.Y. Mar. 18, 2010) (claim against private collection agency dismissed because no evidence that agency was responsible for garnishment decision).
187 Greenland v. Van Ru Corp., 2007 WL 4245409 (W.D. Mich. Nov. 29, 2007).
188 15 U.S.C. § 1692c(b).
189 U.S. Dep't of Educ., Garnishment Selection and Validation Requirements (Aug. 1, 2007).
190 Letter from Pamela Moran, Chief of the Loans Branch, to Guaranty Agency Directors (Nov. 1, 1994), *available on* the companion website to this manual.

191 68 Fed. Reg. 8142, 8149 (Feb. 19, 2003).
192 *Id.* at 8149–50.
193 *Id.*
194 *See* Sibley v. Diversified Collection Servs. (N.D. Tex. Apr. 26, 1996) (first amended complaint—class action), *available at* www.consumerlaw.org/unreported (example of challenge to collection agency participation in garnishment process wherein some aspects of participation appear to exceed—and some aspects appear to be consistent with—Department guidelines).
195 U.S. Dep't of Educ., PCA Procedures Manual: 2009 ED Collections Contract Ch. 225 (Sept. 2009).
196 *See also* §§ 8.3.2.4, 8.3.3.1, *supra.*
197 *See also* § 8.3.2.1, *supra.*

teachers) are eligible for administrative wage garnishment consideration.
9. Borrower is not an employee of a sovereign foreign nation, United Nations, or the World Bank.

Prior to initiating administrative wage garnishment, the collection agency must verify the name, address, and place of employment, attempt to make contact with the borrower, and verify employment within thirty days prior to initiating administrative wage garnishment.[198] Collection agencies cannot require an employer to verify employment.

8.3.5 Due Process Challenges to Garnishment

Serious due process questions are raised regardless of whether garnishment is authorized by the DCIA or HEA. This is particularly true when one considers these procedures in conjunction with the extraordinary statutory authorization for a state, or even a private guaranty agency, to conduct its own hearing and seize wages without judicial review.

One set of due process issues relates to the notices of hearing. Prior to the Department's issuance of standard notices for garnishment, borrowers challenged a number of misleading and confusing aspects of the withholding and request-for-hearing notices.[199] These challenges have been unsuccessful to date. For example, one court found that the failure to notify plaintiffs of several possible defenses to garnishment in the pre-hearing notice was not a violation of constitutional due process.[200] Even so, the Department later issued new notices that define more clearly the defenses available to borrowers.[201]

Courts have rejected borrowers' due process claims in cases in which actual notice was allegedly not received, but the courts found that the Department had made reasonable efforts to notify the borrowers of offset or other collection processes.[202] Despite the fact that the hearing is likely to be inadequate or even unfair, borrowers seeking to raise due process claims should first request hearings in order to avoid a ruling that the borrower has "slept" on his or her constitutional claims.[203]

There are also many possible challenges to other aspects of the process, including (among other possible violations) the failure to provide in-person hearings and questions about whether an official provided by the agency is truly an independent arbiter. It is also very troubling that the Department does not seek to ensure that all hearing officers are qualified by, for example, publishing minimum qualifications.

In one case, the plaintiffs' due process challenges to the administrative hearing process based on absence of judicial review, inadequacy of hearing procedures, and failure to ensure impartiality of hearing officers were ruled not ripe and dismissed.[204] The court found the claims not ripe because the hearings were not actually held for either plaintiff. The court did consider plaintiffs' other due process claims, finding that the failure to offer borrowers the opportunity to appear in person at the hearing did not violate constitutional due process standards.[205]

---

198 U.S. Dep't of Educ., PCA Procedures Manual: 2009 ED Collections Contract 225–226 (Sept. 2009).

199 *See, e.g.*, Nelson v. Diversified Collection Servs., Inc., 961 F. Supp. 863 (D. Md. 1997) (USA funds was guarantor; finding the notice adequate and existence of pre- and post-intercept hearings before "neutral" officer sufficient to meet procedural due process concerns; upholding the notice and hearing procedures without addressing the issue that administrative hearing procedure was entrusted to a non-governmental guaranty agency with direct financial interest in the hearing's outcome); Lawson v. Management Adjustment Bureau, 1997 U.S. Dist. LEXIS 7275 (N.D. Ill. May 15, 1997) (collection agency notice not only stated valid defenses to garnishment but also invalid defenses; finding borrower stated a claim for relief under Fair Debt Collection Practices Act (FDCPA) and denied defendant's motion for summary judgment); Sibley v. Diversified Collection Servs., Inc., 1997 U.S. Dist. LEXIS 23583 (N.D. Tex. June 10, 1997) (ruling on defendants' motion to dismiss).

Class certification was denied on the remaining claims in the *Sibley* case. *See* Sibley v. Diversified Collection Servs., 1998 U.S. Dist. LEXIS 9969 (N.D. Tex. June 30, 1998).

200 Gaddy v. U.S. Dep't of Educ., 2010 WL 1049576 (E.D.N.Y. Mar. 22, 2010) (rejecting due process argument under HEA garnishment authority because HEA provided protections); Sibley v. Diversified Collection Servs., Inc., 1997 U.S. Dist. LEXIS 23583 (N.D. Tex. June 10, 1997) (ruling on defendant's motion to dismiss).

Class certification was denied on the remaining claims. *See* Sibley v. Diversified Collection Servs., 1998 U.S. Dist. LEXIS 9969 (N.D. Tex. June 30, 1998).

201 *See* § 8.3.2.2, *supra*.

202 *See, e.g.*, Savage v. Scales, 310 F. Supp. 2d 122 (D.D.C. 2004); Shabtai v. U.S. Dep't of Educ., 2003 WL 21983025 (S.D.N.Y. Aug. 20, 2003); Nelson v. Diversified Collection Servs., Inc., 961 F. Supp. 863 (D. Md. 1997); Setlech v. United States, 816 F. Sup. 161, 167 (E.D.N.Y. 1992) (using an address most recently in the agency's database or an address obtained from the IRS from plaintiff's most recent tax return has been held to be "reasonably calculated to notify the vast majority of debtors of the intended referral and proposed offset"), *aff'd*, 17 F.3d 390 (2d Cir. 1993) (table).

203 Nelson v. Diversified Collection Servs., Inc., 961 F. Supp. 863 (D. Md. 1997).

204 Sibley v. Diversified Collection Servs., Inc., 1997 U.S. Dist. LEXIS 23583 (N.D. Tex. June 10, 1997) (ruling on defendants' motion to dismiss).

Class certification was denied on the remaining claims in the *Sibley* case. *See* Sibley v. Diversified Collection Servs., 1998 U.S. Dist. LEXIS 9969 (N.D. Tex. June 30, 1998).

205 Sibley v. Diversified Collection Servs., Inc., 1997 U.S. Dist. LEXIS 23583 (N.D. Tex. June 10, 1997) (ruling on defendants' motion to dismiss).

For a more recent complaint challenging a collection agency's administration of the wage garnishment process, see Cliff v. Payco Gen. Am. Credits, Inc., (M.D. Fla. 1998) (class action complaint), *available on* the companion website to this manual.

The Department has addressed the judicial review problem, suggesting that it supports implying a private right of action under the HEA to allow borrowers to seek review of guaranty agency garnishment decisions.[206] Borrowers should clearly be able to appeal denials when the Department is garnishing.[207]

8.4 Seizure of Federal Benefits

8.4.1 General

In 1996, Congress further strengthened the debt collection powers of federal agencies.[208] Federal government agencies were given the authority to offset formerly exempt federal benefits to collect debts, such as student loans, owed to the government.[209]

Offset is explicitly allowed against Social Security benefits, benefits under Part B of the Black Lung Act, and some Railroad Retirement benefits.[210] Subsequent regulations specifically exempted SSI payments.[211] The legislation also exempted an annual amount of $9000.[212]

Only monthly covered payments may be offset, defined as "a covered benefit payment payable to a payee on a recurring basis at monthly intervals that is not expressly limited in duration, at the time the first payment is made, to a period of less than 12 months."[213]

The DCIA and other federal laws *prohibit* offset against numerous benefits, including Department of Education payments under Title IV of the Higher Education Act,[214] veterans benefits, benefits under Part C of the Black Lung Act, and "tier 2" Railroad Retirement benefits. The Secretary of the Department of Treasury also has general authority to exempt any means-tested payments from offset, when so requested by the agency administering the program, and may also exempt other benefits if offset would substantially interfere with or defeat the purposes of the program.[215]

The Department of Treasury and Social Security Administration began implementing the offset process for Social Security payments in 2001.[216] Recipients of Social Security retirement benefits have been among the most affected by the offset program. These older consumers may have student loan debt, often from many years ago. Some may have incurred loans on behalf of children.

Although this manual focuses on the Department of Education's use of this authority to collect student loan debt, federal benefits recipients may also face offsets for collection of debts owed to other federal agencies. For example, the Department of Housing and Urban Development (HUD) began using the program to collect debts. In addition, the Social Security Administration is using this power to collect Social Security overpayments.

The DCIA also allows for offset of certain state payments to repay federal debts, including student loans.[217] In addition, federal non-tax payments may be offset to collect certain debts owed to states.[218]

With respect to offset of state payments to repay federal debts, states must prescribe procedures governing the col-

---

206 *See* Hutchins v. U.S. Dep't of Educ., CV-F-02-6256-OWW-DLB (E.D. Cal. filed Apr. 25, 2003) (U.S. Department of Education Memorandum of Points and Authorities Supporting Motion to Dismiss), *available on* the companion website to this manual.

207 *See, e.g.*, Gorka v. U.S. Dep't of Educ., 2004 WL 2658071 (N.D. Ill. Oct. 13, 2004) (allowing borrower's claim for improper garnishment but finding that the Department's administrative denial was reasonable). *See* § 9.15, *infra*.

208 Debt Collection Improvement Act of 1996, Pub. L. No. 104-134, 110 Stat. 1321 (1996) (chapter 10).

209 31 U.S.C. § 3716.

210 31 U.S.C. § 3716(c)(3)(A)(i).

211 31 C.F.R. § 285.4(b) (definition of "covered benefit payment").
In May 2005, in response to complaints about collection agency threats to seize SSI, the Department sent the following e-mail message to collection contract administrators:

> This is to remind you that Supplement Security Income (SSI) benefits are NOT subject to Treasury offset. These are different from the Social Security Disability benefits that may be subject to offset, under certain conditions. If a borrower advises that their only source of income is SSI, you should not be advising them that this may be offset. It has been reported that PCA collectors have been misinforming borrowers that their SSI benefits will be offset. This is causing anxiety and distress for these borrowers and has also resulted in complaints due to this misinformation. Please remind your staff immediately concerning this issue.

See §§ 7.4.1.1, 7.4.2.1, *supra*.

212 31 U.S.C. § 3716(c)(3)(A)(ii).

213 31 C.F.R. § 285.4(b).
The statute, however, states only that all payments due to an individual may be offset. 31 U.S.C. § 3716(c)(3).

214 31 U.S.C. § 3716(c)(1)(C).

215 31 U.S.C. § 3716(c)(3)(B).
A list of exempted benefits can be found on-line at www.fms.treas.gov/debt/dmexmpt.pdf. For example, as of 2010, the list of benefits exempted by action of the Department of Treasury (as opposed to explicitly exempted by federal laws) included SSI; food stamp benefits and most other Department of Agriculture nutrition programs; a number of FEMA programs, including the individual and family grant program disaster housing, and community disaster loans; Department of Justice payments to eligible claimants of the September 11th Victims Compensation Fund; and numerous HUD programs, including Section 8 low-income housing assistance, Indian homeownership grants, and Direct Loans for the Elderly or Handicapped under Section 202. As of the summer of 2010, the latest list of exempt benefits posted on the website was last revised in May 2010.

216 Information about the benefit payment offset program is available on the Department of Treasury website at www.fms.treas.gov/news/factsheets/dcia.html.

217 31 U.S.C. § 3716(h); 31 C.F.R. § 285.6.

218 *Id.*

lection of delinquent state debts that are substantially similar to the offset requirements for federal agencies.[219] Offset of state payment is pursuant to state law.[220] This should mean that payments exempt from collection under state law may not be offset.

In addition to offset of state payments to collect federal debts, federal payments may be offset to collect state debts. Certain federal payments, such as Department of Veterans Affairs (VA) benefits are exempted.[221] Social Security payments and federal tax refunds are also exempted from offset to collect state debts.[222] Federal payments subject to offset to collect state debts must be set forth in the reciprocal agreements.[223]

According to the Department of Treasury, the program allowing administrative offset of federal payments to collect debts owed to states, and the corresponding offset of state payments to collect debts owed to federal agencies, began on a pilot basis in Maryland, New Jersey, and Kentucky.[224] In 2006, the Department of Education changed the language in the sixty-five-day offset notice to reference both federal and state payments.[225] The Department acknowledged that the state payments to be offset will vary from state to state. Prior to this change, the notice only referred to offset of federal payments.

8.4.2 Amount of Offset

The amount of the federal offset is the lesser of:

- The amount of the debt;
- An amount equal to 15% of the monthly benefit payment; or
- The amount, if any, by which the monthly benefit exceeds $750.[226]

The maximum amount that will be offset under any circumstances is 15% of the recipient's income. The Financial Management Service (FMS) of the Department of the Treasury provided the following examples:

Example 1:

A debtor receives a monthly benefit payment of $850. The amount that is offset is the lesser of $127.50 (15% of 850) or $100 (the amount by which $850 exceeds $750). In this example, $100 would be offset.[227]

Example 2:

A debtor receives a monthly benefit of $1250. The amount that is offset is the lesser of $187.50 (15% of 1250) or $500 (the amount by which 1250 exceeds 750). In this example, the offset amount is $187.50 (assuming the debt is $187.50 or more).[228]

If the recipient receives $750 or less, nothing will be offset.[229]

8.4.3 Challenges to Offset

8.4.3.1 Notice and Hearing Rights

The offset process is managed by the Financial Management Service (FMS) of the Department of Treasury. Before referring a debt to FMS for collection, the federal agency is required to provide the debtor with a notice of intent to offset and an opportunity to review the basis for the debt.[230]

The Department of Education regulations require borrowers to request a review within twenty days of receiving a notice of offset.[231] However, according to the Treasury regulations, the offset remains legal even if the debtor does not receive the notices.[232]

The borrower has the opportunity to first request the opportunity to review and copy relevant documents.[233] Borrowers have the right to request an oral hearing in lieu of a written review but must submit an explanation of why a written review is insufficient.[234] As with other offsets, borrowers should have the right to set up a repayment plan acceptable to the Secretary prior to offset.[235] Borrowers also have a right to request a temporary hardship waiver, as discussed in the next subsection.

Borrowers are likely to be confused regarding which agency to contact if they wish to challenge offsets or simply

---

219 32 C.F.R. § 285.6(d).
220 31 C.F.R. § 285.6(a)(1).
221 31 C.F.R. § 285.6(g) (referring to list of exempt benefits in 31 C.F.R. § 285.5(e)(2)).
222 31 C.F.R. § 285.6(g).
223 31 C.F.R. § 285.6(g). Payments described in 31 C.F.R. § 285.5(e)(2), are excluded from offset.
224 *Medicare Doctors Who Cheat on Their Taxes and What Should Be Done About It: Hearing Before the U.S. Senate Homeland Security and Governmental Affairs Permanent Subcommittee on Investigations*, 110th Cong. (Mar. 20, 2007) (statement of Commissioner Kenneth R. Papaj).
225 Financial Student Assistance, U.S. Dep't of Educ., State Offset Payments (Mar. 14, 2008).
226 31 C.F.R. § 285.4(e).
227 31 C.F.R. § 285.4(e)(3)(i).
228 31 C.F.R. § 285.4(e)(3)(ii).
229 31 C.F.R. § 285.4(e)(3)(iii).
230 31 U.S.C. § 3716(a).
231 34 C.F.R. § 30.24(a)(1).
   Review is with the Department of Education, not the Department of Treasury. *See, e.g.*, Lepelletier v. U.S. Dep't of Educ., 2009 WL 4840153 (D.D.C. Dec. 14, 2009) (incumbent upon the creditor agency, not Treasury, to afford the debtor due process with respect to disputing the outstanding debt).
232 31 C.F.R. § 285.4(f)(3).
233 34 C.F.R. § 30.22(B)(3).
234 34 C.F.R. § 30.25(b)(1).
   The rules for oral hearings are set out at 34 C.F.R. § 30.26.
235 34 C.F.R. § 30.22(b)(3)(iii).
   Due process challenges to these review procedures are discussed at § 8.2.6 (tax refund intercepts) and § 8.3.5 (garnishment), *supra*.

have questions about the offsets. The Department of Treasury explicitly requires borrowers to contact the "originating" agency (the Department of Education in student loan cases). The FMS notices for student loan administrative offsets list a number at the Department of Education for borrowers to call. Borrowers can contact the FMS at 1-800-304-3107 but only to find out which agency to contact, particularly if they find that their benefits are being offset but they never received notice.

8.4.3.2 Hardship Reductions

The Department of Education's policy is to allow borrowers to request full or partial reductions of offset based on financial hardship. The Department makes the determinations regarding financial hardship for student loan administrative offsets. However, the availability of this "program" is not specified on the hearing request form.

The Department requires borrowers to submit the following documents before they will review a claim of hardship:

- The notification of offset.
- The notification letter showing the amount of benefit.
- Proof of yearly income.
- A completed financial statement returned to DOE within ten days.[236] If the situation is an emergency, a borrower may submit equivalent information such as an eviction notice or a court order of foreclosure in writing with the completed financial statement.
- A letter explaining the exceptional circumstances that caused the financial hardship along with any other supporting documents.[237]

The Department set up a review unit in the Chicago Service Center. This unit will examine the documents to determine whether the offset should be reduced partially or fully. Refunds may be granted as well. Documents should be sent to:

United States Department of Education
Attn: Federal Offset Review Unit
P.O. Box 618064
Chicago, IL 60601-8064[238]

The Department claims that it will notify borrowers of decisions within ten days and that it will send disability discharge applications to borrowers who appear to be eligible.

The unit will determine whether the borrower is entitled to a waiver and, if so, whether the offset amount should be partially or fully reduced. If the Department denies the waiver, they will notify the borrower of the denial and continue offsetting. If the waiver is granted, the borrower may be entitled to a limited refund. The refund will only be for amounts offset above the newly determined offset amount and only for periods during which financial hardship can be shown.

Unfortunately for borrowers, the right to a hardship reduction is not listed in the notices sent by either DOE or FMS. Instead, borrowers may find out about the availability of the hardship reduction when they call the Department of Education number indicated on the notice of federal offset. If borrowers call that number, they will enter into a telephone menu requesting first that they provide identifying information such as name and social security number. After entering this information, borrowers are asked to press a number if they are disputing an offset or administrative wage garnishment. Once a borrower presses this option, they will at some point be asked if the offset is causing severe financial hardship. If the borrower is able to get this far in the process, the borrower will receive information about how to submit an appeal of the offset in writing.

It is unclear how flexible the Department will be in granting these reductions or waivers, particularly with respect to the fifth "exceptional circumstances" category. Exceptional circumstances should clearly include pending evictions or foreclosures but might also include disability status or other "non-temporary" exceptional circumstances. The precise standards to prove financial hardship are also unclear at this point.

In response to an inquiry from NCLC about hardship waiver/reduction policies, the Department replied:

> We use the cost of living standards published annually by the Internal Revenue Service to determine baseline allowable expenses for housing, transportation *etc.* (These standards can be found at the IRS.gov website.) We also consider the borrower's circumstances and may make reasonable modifications to the baseline standards accordingly. Borrowers can request hardship consideration at any point in the collection process, with the following provisos:
> — Except in the case of social security benefits, we will not prevent offset of any federal payment based on any hardship claim; once we know the amount of the offset (that is, after it has occurred) we will consider a hardship request for refund.
> — In the case of social security benefits, we will consider either a reduction or suspension of the offset due to hardship even before the offset begins.
> — We will not protect an account from assignment to a collection agency based on total hardship; only entering a reasonable and affordable payment plan will prevent assignment.

---

236 A copy of this form is included at Appendix D, *infra*, and on the companion website to this manual. The Department requests, but does not require, that the form be returned within ten days.

237 A sample letter requesting a hardship reduction is included at Appendix E, *infra*.

238 This address is subject to change.

§ 8.4.3.3   *Student Loan Law*

The Department states that it is much more lenient about reducing benefit offsets than tax refund offsets.[239] The Department may also temporarily suspend offset while the borrower pursues a disability or other discharge.

8.4.3.3 No Time Limit on Administrative Offsets

As with the other extra-judicial collection tools, there is no statute of limitations for federal benefit offsets. This was unclear for some time because the Debt Collection Improvement Act previously prohibited offset for claims that were "outstanding" for more than ten years. The issue of whether the ten-year statute of limitations in the DCIA applied to offsets for collection of student loans was litigated beginning in 2001. The U.S. Supreme Court ultimately decided the issue in the government's favor in late 2005.[240] This decision affirmed the Ninth Circuit but overruled contrary decisions (favorable to borrowers) by a 2002 Michigan district court and by the Eighth Circuit in 2004.[241]

It is now clear that the government will not be bound by any time limits when attempting to collect student loans through Social Security offset. This makes it more important than ever for borrowers to assert their rights and for advocates to track the Department's record in enforcing those rights. For example, Department of Education policy allows borrowers to request hardship reductions.[242] The Treasury Department stated in 2006 that about $8 million is collected annually by offsetting Social Security payments to collect student loans over ten years old. They expect this amount to grow.[243]

In 2008, Congress addressed the statute of limitations issue more generally by eliminating it for all types of government debts rather than restoring a limit for student loans. Two laws in 2008 amended the Debt Collection Improvement Act to eliminate the ten-year limit.[244] The interim final rules provide that all non-tax debts, including debts that were outstanding for ten years or longer prior to June 11, 2009, may be collected by offset.[245] For debts outstanding for more than ten years on or before June 11, 2009, the federal agency collecting the debt must certify that a notice of intent to offset was sent to the debtor after the debt became delinquent for ten years. This additional notice requirement, however, applies only to debts that previously had a ten-year limit. Since the statute of limitations was already eliminated for student loans, this additional notice requirement does not apply to student loans.

8.4.3.4 Due Process Challenges to Offsets

Borrowers' attempts to challenge the offset procedures on constitutional grounds have been unsuccessful to date. In one case, the court concluded that there was no constitutional due process violation when the Department of Education sent written notice to the borrower's last known address and provided him the opportunity for a hearing.[246] A district court also found the offset notices and procedures to be constitutionally adequate.[247]

8.5 Federal Salary Offsets

The Department has authority to offset salaries of federal government employees to collect federal debts.[248] This authority applies to federal employees and members of the Armed Forces or Reserves.[249] Deductions may be made from basic pay, special pay, incentive pay, retired pay, retainer pay, or other authorized pay.[250]

An amount of up to 15% of disposable pay may be offset.[251] This includes current and former federal employees.[252] As with other types of offset, there are notice requirements, and borrowers have the right to request hearings.[253] The regulations specifically provide a "defense" of extreme financial hardship.[254] Borrowers may also set up repayment arrangements in lieu of offset under terms acceptable to the Department.[255]

The Department also has the authority to use a data match system with the Department of Health and Human Services National Directory of New Hires, a database of all persons employed in the United States.[256] The Department suspended this program in March 2009, which was the end of the period covered by the memorandum of understanding between the two agencies.[257]

---

239 U.S. Dep't of Educ., PCA Procedures Manual: 2009 ED Collections Contract 82 (Sept. 2009).
240 Lockhart v. United States, 546 U.S. 142, 126 S. Ct. 699 (2005).
241 *See* Lee v. Paige, 376 F.3d 1179 (8th Cir. 2004); Guillermety v. Secretary of Educ., 241 F. Supp. 2d 727 (E.D. Mich. 2002).
242 *See* § 8.4.3.2, *supra*.
243 U.S. Dep't of Treasury, FY 2005 Report to the Congress, U.S. Government Receivables and Debt Collection Activities of Federal Agencies 4 (Mar. 2006).
244 Pub. L. No. 110-234, § 14219(a), 122 Stat. 923 (May 22, 2008); Pub. L. No. 110-246, § 12129(a), 122 Stat. 1651 (June 18, 2008).
    The Department of Treasury issued an interim final rule effective June 11, 2009. 74 Fed. Reg. 27707 (June 11, 2009).
245 74 Fed. Reg. 27707 (June 11, 2009).
246 Omgebu v. U.S. Dep't of Treasury, 118 Fed. Appx. 989, 2004 WL 3049825 (7th Cir. Dec. 16, 2004) (unpublished order).
247 Stover v. Illinois Student Assistance Comm'n, 2005 WL 3597743 (C.D. Ill. Apr. 21, 2005).
248 5 U.S.C. § 5514.
249 5 U.S.C. § 5514(a)(1).
250 *Id.*
251 5 U.S.C. § 5514(a)(1).
252 5 U.S.C. § 5514(a)(1); 34 C.F.R. § 31.2.
253 34 C.F.R. § 31.3
254 34 C.F.R. §§ 31.8–31.9.
255 34 C.F.R. § 31.10.
256 See 71 Fed. Reg. 26934 (May 9, 2006).
257 *See also* Doug Lederman, *$1.2 Billion, Forgone?*, InsideHigherEd.com, Mar. 17, 2010, *at* www.insidehighered.com/news/2010/03/17/ndnh.

8.6 Professional License Suspensions and Revocations

Many state laws[258] allow professional and vocational boards to refuse to certify, certify with restrictions, suspend or revoke a member's professional or vocational license, and, in some cases, impose a fine[259] when a member defaults on state[260] and/or federally[261] guaranteed student loans.

While some states' provisions apply to particular professions or vocations—attorneys,[262] health care professionals,[263] teachers,[264] insurance professionals,[265] state officers,[266] and commercial fishermen[267]—others apply more generally to anyone whose profession or vocation requires its members to be licensed.[268] Louisiana's catch-all provision is typical. It provides that "default on the repayment of *any* loan guaranteed by the Louisiana Student Financial Assistance Commission . . . shall be grounds for denying an application for, or an application for the renewal of, any license, permit, or certificate required by the state of Louisiana."[269]

Laws that suspend or revoke professional licenses because of student loan defaults typically afford affected individuals notice of the impending action and an opportunity for a hearing. Some states' laws also allow for license reissuance once a licensee in default enters into a loan repayment plan. With the exception of at least one state,[270] all of these laws mandate that the applicable board or department responsible for issuing the license take action, in some cases provisional action, once it receives notice of a member's default.

8.7 Seizure of Student Loan Funds Generally Prohibited

Student assistance funds, including loans, grants, and work assistance may be garnished to collect debts owed to the Department of Education.[271] However, these funds (or property traceable to them) cannot be garnished by other collectors.[272] For example, a private collection agency pursuing a student for credit card debt cannot garnish or attach that student's federal student loan funds to collect the debt. These student assistance funds also cannot be seized through administrative offset.[273]

---

258 Alaska Stat. § 14.43.148 (general); Cal. Bus. & Prof. Code § 685 (West) (health care practitioners); Fla. Stat. §§ 456.072, 456.074 (Health Professions and Occupations); Ga. Code Ann. §§ 7-1-707.1 (check cashers), 12-6-49.2 (professional forestry), 20-3-295 (general), 43-1-29 (general); Haw. Rev. Stat. §§ 436B-19.6 (general), 436C-2 (general), 189-2(f) (commercial marine licenses), 302A-807(e) (school personnel), 321-15 (Department of Health), 431:9-235 (insurance adjusters and bill reviewers), 431:9A-112 (insurance producers), 457-9 (nurses), 466J-8 (radiological technology); 20 Ill. Comp. Stat. §§ 2105/2105-15 (general); 215 Ill. Comp. Stat. § 5/500-70 (insurance producers); 225 Ill. Comp. Stat. §§ 30/95 (dietetic and nutrition servicers), 37/35 (environmental health practitioners), 55/85 (marriage and family therapists), 107/80 (professional counselors), 110/16 (speech-language pathology and audiology), 135/95 (genetic counselors), 335/9.1 (roofing), 410/4-7 (barbers, cosmetologists), 425/9 (debt collectors), 441/15-45 (home inspectors), 447/40-35 (private detectives, security, locksmiths), 450/20.01 (certified public accountants), 458/15-45 (real estate appraiser); 420 Ill. Comp. Stat. § 44/45 (radon industry); 2005 Iowa Court Order 05-03: Rule 35.13 (attorneys); Iowa Code §§ 261.121–261.127 (general); Ky. Rev. Stat. Ann. §§ 164.772 (West) (general), 314.091(l)(i) (West) (nurses); La. Rev. Stat. Ann. § 37:2951 (general); Mass. Gen. Laws Ann. chs. 30A § 13 (general), 112 § 61 (Department of Public Health); Minn. Stat. § 147.091(1)(y) (physicians), § 214.105 (health professions); N.J. Rule of Court 1:20-11B (attorneys); N.J. Stat. Ann. §§ 2A:13-12 (same), 18A:71C-19 (general), 45:1-21.2 (same) (West); N.M. Stat. § 61-17A-21 (barbers and cosmetologists); N.D. Cent. Code § 28-25-11 (general—judgment debtors); Okla. Stat. tit. 70 § 623.1 (general); Okla. Admin. Code § 595: 10-1-80 (commercial drivers); Tenn. Code. Ann. §§ 23-3-111 (authorizing Supreme Court to establish guidelines for attorneys), § 49-5-108 (authorizing State Board of Education to establish guidelines for teachers), 56-1-312 (general), 63-1-141 (healing arts professionals); Tex. Educ. Code Ann. § 57.491 (Vernon) (general); Tex. Gov't Code Ann. §§ 82.022(c) (Vernon) (lawyers), 466.155(a)(3)(B), (C) (Vernon) (state lottery agents); Tex. Occ. Code Ann. § 56.001–56.006 (Vernon) (chiropractic examiners, dental examiners, podiatric medical examiners, medical examiners); Order of the Supreme Court of Texas, June 18, 1996, 59 Tex. B.J. 844 (1996) (lawyers); Va. Code Ann. § 54.1-2400.5 (health professions); Wash. Rev. Code §§ 2.48.165 (lawyers), § 18.04.420 (accountants), 18.08.470 (architects), 18.11.270 (auctioneers), 18.16.230 (cosmetologists, barbers and manicurists), 18.20.200 (boarding homes), 18.27.360 (contractors), 18.39.465 (embalmers, funeral directors), 18.43.160 (engineers and land surveyors), 18.44.460 (escrow agents), 18.46.055 (birthing centers), 18.76.100 (poison center directors or specialists), 18.85.225 (real estate brokers and salespersons), 18.96.190 (landscape architects), 18.104.115 (water well construction), 18.106.290 (plumbers), 18.130.125 (health professionals), 18.140.200 (real estate appraisers), 18.160.085 (fire system sprinkler contractors), 18.165.280 (private investigators), 18.170.163 (security guards), 18.185.055 (bail bond agents). *Cf.* Miss. Code Ann. §§ 37-101-291, 37-101-293 (paid educational leave for health care professionals), 37-101-292 (same for civil engineers), 41-9-37 (same for hospital employees).

259 Fla. Stat. §§ 456.072, 456.074.
260 Florida, Hawaii, Iowa, Louisiana, Massachusetts, New Jersey, North Dakota, and Tennessee.
261 Florida, Hawaii, New Jersey, North Dakota, Oklahoma, and Tennessee.
262 Hawaii, New Jersey, and Tennessee.
263 Florida, Hawaii, Massachusetts, and Tennessee.
264 Hawaii and Tennessee.
265 Hawaii, Illinois, and Tennessee.
266 Massachusetts.
267 Hawaii.
268 Iowa, Louisiana, New Jersey, North Dakota, and Oklahoma.
269 La. Rev. Stat. Ann. § 37:2951 (emphasis added).
270 *See, e.g.*, N.D. Cent. Code § 28-25-11 (2) (providing court with discretion to suspend a judgment debtor's certificate, license, or permit based on principles of fairness).
271 20 U.S.C. § 1095a(d).
272 *Id.*
273 31 U.S.C. § 3716(c)(1)(C).

Chapter 9 Statutory Discharges of Federal Student Loans

9.1 Introduction

Statutory discharges (or cancellations) provide the most powerful remedies for federal student loan borrowers. They offer complete relief as opposed to simply delaying the repayment obligation. After a cancellation, the borrower no longer owes anything on the loan and becomes eligible for new student loans and grants. In some cases, borrowers are also entitled to refunds of past loan payments, deletion of all negative references on their credit records, and renewed eligibility for federal financial aid.

Because these are such powerful remedies, advocates should always consider the various discharges first when evaluating a student loan case, regardless of whether a client is in default. Victims of proprietary school fraud, in particular, may be eligible for at least one of these discharges.

The main ways to discharge or cancel a student loan through the Higher Education Act (HEA) are:

- The school's closure while the student was still enrolled;
- The school's false certification of the student's eligibility (including false certification due to forgery or identity theft);
- The school's failure to pay a refund owed to a student;
- The borrower's permanent and total disability;
- The borrower's death; and
- The borrower's profession, such as teaching or military service in limited circumstances and public service jobs.

In addition, there are discharges for victims of the September 11 attacks. The government also offers loan cancellations after borrowers have completed twenty-five years of repayment through an income-contingent or income-based repayment plan. These plans are discussed in Chapter 3, *supra*.

This chapter considers all the statutory bases for discharges. Borrowers may also discharge student loans in bankruptcy under certain circumstances, as discussed in Chapter 10, *infra*. Common law grounds for raising defenses in student loan collection actions, including claims to cancel student loan obligations, are covered in Chapters 10–13, *infra*.

The HEA statutory discharges can be difficult to obtain due to restrictive regulations and bureaucratic roadblocks. However, they are attainable! The Department of Education ("the Department") reported the following volume of loans discharged for fiscal years 2007–2009:[1]

	Type	Total Count	Total Dollar
2009:	Closed School	5230	$27,059,844.30
	Disqualifying Status	147	$ 1,325,944.19
	Ability to Benefit	1424	$11,273,535.29
	Unauthorized Signature	121	$ 1,062,366.29
	Unpaid Refund	1547	$ 9,923,165.38
2008:	Closed School	5231	$26,203,373.62
	Disqualifying Status	68	$ 547,887.54
	Ability to Benefit	988	$ 7,468,885.11
	Unauthorized Signature	114	$ 978,467.73
	Unpaid Refund	1657	$10,903,116.21
2007:	Closed School	5072	$26,713,863.54
	Disqualifying Status	94	$ 817,946.42
	Ability to Benefit	1081	$ 7,852,542.14
	Unauthorized Signature	74	$ 556,435.57
	Unpaid Refund	2210	$13,878,338.85

9.2 Loans Eligible for Discharge

There are three "school-related" discharges: closed school, false certification, and unpaid refund. The closed school discharge applies to Federal Family Education Loan Program loans ("FFELs"), federal Direct Loan Program loans ("Direct loans"), and Perkins Loan Program loans, including NDSLs ("Perkins loans") received at least in part on or after January 1, 1986.[2] Borrowers are entitled to a

---

[1] This data is derived from information requested under the Freedom of Information Act and published at *How Can Federal Student Loans Be Discharged?*, Student Lending Analytics Blog (Mar. 29, 2010).

[2] 20 U.S.C. § 1087(c)(1); 34 C.F.R. §§ 682.402(d)(1)(i) (FFEL), 685.214 (Direct Loan), 674.33(g).

Most of the citations in this chapter refer to FFEL rules. With the exception of public service cancellations and Perkins-specific cancellations, the rules for the main HEA discharges are the same for the different loan programs. In particular,

false certification loan discharge if they received at least part of an FFEL loan or Direct loan after January 1, 1986, and if their eligibility to borrow was falsely certified by the school.[3] The false certification discharge does not apply to Perkins loans, but students should be able to raise the school's misconduct as a defense to loan repayment because the school is the original lender.[4] The unpaid refund discharge applies to FFELs and Direct loans disbursed in whole or in part on or after January 1, 1986.[5] Students already can raise an unpaid refund as a defense to a Perkins loan collection action.[6]

Borrowers with FFELs, Direct loans, and Perkins loans may apply for death and disability discharges. There are also a number of discharges available only in the Perkins Loan Program, as discussed in § 9.12, *infra*. The public service forgiveness discharge is only available to Direct loan borrowers.

The discharges can be more complicated for Direct Consolidation Loan Program loans ("Direct consolidation loans"). For consolidation loan borrowers who receive school-related discharges (closed school, false certification, and unpaid refund), only the portion of the consolidation attributable to the discharge-eligible loan(s) will be discharged.[7] The entire consolidation loan should be dischargeable for those who receive disability or death discharges.[8] However, borrowers who consolidate Perkins loans into a Direct consolidation loan lose access to the Perkins-specific discharges.[9]

Borrowers with loans from the Direct PLUS Loans Program ("PLUS loans") are eligible for school-related discharges if the student on whose behalf the loan was taken out qualifies.[10] PLUS loan borrowers may also get discharges if they die or if the student on whose behalf they borrowed the loan dies.[11] If only one parent PLUS loan borrower dies, the other parent remains obligated to repay.[12]

Parents with PLUS loans may apply for discharges based on their own disabilities, not those of their children. If only one Parent PLUS loan borrower becomes disabled, the other borrower remains obligated to repay the loan.[13]

There are different rules for joint consolidation loans. If one of the borrowers dies or becomes disabled, the portion of the joint consolidation loan attributable to any of that borrower's loans will be discharged.[14] The same result occurs if one of the borrowers qualifies for a school-related discharge or for teacher loan forgiveness.[15] The rules for joint consolidation loans and public service forgiveness are discussed in § 9.9.2, *infra*.

9.3 Closed-School Discharge

9.3.1 General

The HEA requires the Secretary of the Department of Education ("the Secretary") to discharge a specified loan if the borrower was unable to complete the program due to the school's closure.[16] The regulations provide this discharge if the branch of the school which the student attended closed.[17] For example, if the student goes to branch "A," there is no right to a discharge if only the main campus or branch "B" closed. On the other hand, if branch "A" closes, the student has a right to a discharge even if all other branches stay open. The closed-school discharge applies to any school at which the student obtained a qualified loan, whether or not the school or branch was in fact an eligible institution under the program.[18]

The regulations provide for a discharge if the borrower was still enrolled at the time of the school's closure or if the student withdrew from the school not more than ninety days before the school's closure.[19] The ninety-day period may be

---

unless otherwise specified, Direct loans have the same terms and conditions as FFELs. 20 U.S.C. § 1087e(a)(10).

For a general description of the different loan programs, see § 1.3, *supra*.

3   20 U.S.C. § 1087(c)(1); 34 C.F.R. §§ 682.402(e), 685.215.
4   See § 12.7.2.1, *infra*.
5   20 U.S.C. § 1087(c); 34 C.F.R. §§ 682.402(l) (FFEL), 685.216.
6   See § 12.7.2.1, *infra*.
7   34 C.F.R. § 685.212(d)–(f). See also U.S. Dep't of Educ., Dear Colleague Letter 94-G-256 (Sept. 1994) (guidance on discharges in the FFEL Program).
8   34 C.F.R. §§ 682.402(k)(2)(iii), 685.212(b), 685.213(a) (Direct Loan Program provisions refer to all Direct loans).

There are a few exceptions, such as if the consolidation loan consists of loans taken out after a borrower had previously received a disability discharge or loans that were reinstated under the reinstatement regulations effective as of July 1, 2010. See § 9.7.7, *infra*.

9   See § 9.12, *infra*.

The Department cautions borrowers about this potential problem in a discussion on the Department website about the pros and cons of consolidation.

10 34 C.F.R. §§ 682.402(d)(1)(i), 685.214(a)(1) (closed school); 682.402(e)(1), 685.215(a)(1) (false certification); 682.402(l)(2), 685.216(a)(2) (unpaid refund).

11 34 C.F.R. §§ 682.402(b)(2), 685.212(a)(1).
12 34 C.F.R. § 682.402(a)(3).
13 34 C.F.R. § 682.402(a)(3).
14 34 C.F.R. §§ 682.402(a)(2), 685.220(l)(3)(i), (ii).
15 34 C.F.R. § 685.220(l)(3)(k)(iii).
16 20 U.S.C. § 1087(c)(1).
17 See 34 C.F.R. §§ 682.402(d)(1)(ii)(C) (FFEL), 685.214(a)(2)(ii) (Direct Loan).
18 See 34 C.F.R. § 682.402(d)(1)(ii)(C) (FFEL).
19 34 C.F.R. §§ 682.402(d)(1)(i) (FFEL), 685.214(c)(1)(ii) (Direct Loan), 674.33(g)(4)(i)(B) (Perkins Loan).

The "90 day rule" is not in the statute, only in the regulations. The statute provides for discharges under certain circumstances if the borrower is unable to complete the program due to the closure of the institution. 20 U.S.C. § 1087(c).

At least one court found that the plain language of the statute allowed for a closed-school discharge even if the borrower was not enrolled at the time of closure or had not withdrawn within ninety days. See Sandler v. U.S. Dep't of Educ., 2001 WL 884552 (E.D. Pa. July 19, 2001).

extended if the Secretary determines that exceptional circumstances related to the school's closing would justify an extension.[20] It also may be extended under some circumstances for students who attended correspondence schools.[21]

A student on an approved leave of absence is treated as still enrolled.[22] Until July 2003, with only a few exceptions, each student was allowed only one leave of absence annually. Since that date, schools are allowed to grant multiple leaves of absence at their discretion, as long as the total number of days for all leave does not exceed 180 within a twelve-month period.[23] Students must provide a written, signed, and dated request for a leave that includes the reason for the request.[24] If unforeseen circumstances prevent a student from providing a written request, the school may grant the request as long as it documents the decision and collects the written request at a later date.[25] If the student does not return to school after a leave of absence, the withdrawal date will be the date that the school determines the student began the leave of absence.[26] For purposes of a closed-school discharge, a borrower on an approved leave of absence who tried but could not return to the school because it was closed should still be eligible for the closed-school discharge.

A school's closure date is the date at which it ceases offering *all* programs at a particular branch, not when it stops offering the particular program in which the student is enrolled.[27] Nevertheless, when a particular program at a location ceases four or five months before the branch closes, this would seem to be an appropriate situation for the Secretary to extend the ninety-day period because of the exceptional circumstances related to the school's closing.

Borrowers can obtain closed-school discharges if the school closed before they completed a program, even if the school issued the borrower a diploma or other certificate.[28] On the other hand, if a student completes a program, there is no discharge even if the borrower never received a diploma or certificate.[29]

9.3.2 The Official School Closure Date

The Secretary determines the closure date, and, for most situations, the borrower should rely on the Secretary's cumulative list of closed schools to find out the official closure date. The Department periodically updates this list. The easiest way to access the list is through the Department of Education's website.[30]

Initially, numerous errors were reported concerning this list. This is less common now, but errors still appear. For this reason, advocates should not necessarily give up if their client has evidence of a different closing date that would affect eligibility.

Possible sources of evidence of a school's earlier closing date include dated newspaper articles or other media reports about the school's closure and declarations from other students, state regulators, or former school employees regarding the closure date. Advocates may submit to the Department of Education's Closed School Section a request to change a school closing date.[31] A change in a school closing date must be determined by the Department regardless of who holds the loan.

Official closure dates have been challenged both informally and in court.[32] In at least one case, the Department entered into a settlement agreeing to change the closure date, discharge the named plaintiff's loans, and provide notice of the new date to borrowers enrolled within 150 days of the new closure date.[33]

9.3.3 Correspondence Schools

There have been many problems over the years with correspondence schools. Most have closed or morphed into Internet or distance education schools. This section describes potential claims for borrowers who attended the "old-fashioned" correspondence schools. As problems have also arisen with distance education through the Internet, advocates and borrowers will need to pursue similar rem-

---

Advocates should consider continuing to challenge this regulation in court.

20 34 C.F.R. §§ 682.402(d)(1)(i) (FFEL), 685.214(c)(1)(ii) (Direct Loan).
21 See § 9.3.3, infra.
22 34 C.F.R. § 682.402(d)(3)(ii)(B).
     The definition of an approved leave of absence is found at 34 C.F.R. § 668.22(d).
23 34 C.F.R. § 668.22(d)(vi).
24 34 C.F.R. § 668.22(d)(3)(iii)(B).
25 Id.
26 34 C.F.R. § 668.22(d)(2).
27 See 34 C.F.R. §§ 682.402(d)(1)(ii)(A) (FFEL), 685.214(a)(2)(i) (Direct Loan).
28 See U.S. Dep't of Educ., Dear Colleague Letter GEN-94-256 (Sept. 1994), reprinted at Appx. C, infra.
29 Id.

30 The website allows advocates to search for a specific school's closure date. The general Department website is www.ed.gov. The specific site for the list is http://wdcrobcolp01.ed.gov/CFAPPS/FSA/closedschool/searchpage.cfm.
31 U.S. Dep't of Educ., SFAP/Closed School Unit, P.O. Box 23800, L'Enfant Plaza Station, Washington, D.C. 20026; 1-800-4FED-AID. A list of regional closed-school unit contacts is available at http://studentaid.ed.gov/PORTALSWebApp/students/english/closedinfo.jsp?tab=attending.
32 See Moorer v. Secretary of Educ. (D.D.C. June 7, 1996) (complaint for declaratory and injunctive relief), available on the companion website to this manual.
33 Settlement Agreement and Stipulation of Dismissal, Tello v. Secretary of Educ., (D. Md. Aug. 1998), available on the companion website to this manual; Class Action Complaint, Tello v. Secretary of Educ., (D. Md. 1997), available on the companion website to this manual.

edies to better align the closed-school remedy for these newer schools.

In an attempt to address some of the problems associated with correspondence schools, the Department in July 1997 released a "Dear Colleague" letter extending the ninety-day period for students who attended and withdrew from specified correspondence schools.[34] These extended periods apply only to the ten closed correspondence schools listed below:

1. American Career Training Travel/Hart Secretarial School (ACT) (Pompano Beach, Florida, main location). Borrowers who enrolled in ACT and took out a loan with a loan period that began on or after March 1, 1988, may be eligible for the closed-school discharge if they meet all other requirements.

For the other nine schools listed below, borrowers who took out loans with loan periods that began within twelve months of the closure date may be eligible for the closed-school discharge.

2. AMS College, Home Study Division (Alpine, California).
3. Columbia School of Broadcasting (Las Vegas, Nevada).
4. County Schools (Bridgeport, Connecticut).
5. Global Academy (Atlanta, Georgia).
6. National Training Systems (Laurel, Maryland).
7. Northwest Schools (Portland, Oregon).
8. Superior Training Services (Phoenix, Arizona).
9. United Schools (Clearwater, Florida).
10. USA Training Academy Home Study (Newark, Delaware).[35]

The "Dear Colleague" Letter provides that guaranty agencies and lenders must review records to identify borrowers with loan periods that would qualify them for discharges under these extended periods. Agencies must re-evaluate previously denied applications for borrowers identified in this process and mail out applications to all others. Previously denied applicants who meet all the other closed-school-discharge requirements should be granted discharges without the submission of new applications.

9.3.4 Teach-Outs

Students are barred from receiving a discharge if they completed the program through a "teach-out" at another school or through transfer of credits or hours earned at the closed school to another school.[36]

A "teach-out" agreement is defined as a written agreement that provides for the equitable treatment of students and a reasonable opportunity for students to complete their program of study if an institution, or an institutional location that provides one hundred percent of at least one program offered, ceases to operate before all enrolled students have completed their course of study.[37] Regulations that went into effect in July 2010 also include a definition of a "teach-out" plan.[38] The plan must be submitted to accrediting agencies in certain circumstances.[39]

The HEA does not include this "teach-out" limit to the closed-school discharge.[40] However, in a February 1998 decision in the *McComas* case, the United States District Court for the Southern District of West Virginia rejected the argument that the "teach out" bar to discharge contravened the meaning and purpose of the governing statute. The court granted the Department's summary judgment motion.[41]

9.3.5 Relief Available for Those Obtaining a Closed-School Discharge

When a borrower receives a closed-school discharge, the borrower (and any other obligor on the note) is no longer obligated to repay the loan or any charges or costs associated with the loan.[42] That is, the loan principal, interest charges, collection costs, and all other charges are forgiven.

In addition, the borrower is reimbursed all amounts paid to date on the loan, whether those payments were voluntary or involuntary, such as through tax intercepts or garnishments.[43] The borrower is no longer regarded in default and is immediately eligible for new loans and grants.[44] The discharge of an FFEL loan must also be reported to all credit reporting agencies to which the holder previously reported the loan's status "so as to delete all adverse credit history assigned to the loan."[45]

---

34 U.S. Dep't of Educ., Dear Colleague Letter 97-G-300, Clearinghouse No. 52,043 (July 1997).

35 All locations listed here are the main locations. Closure dates are not listed because many of these schools had numerous locations, and closure dates vary by location. Closure dates are listed in Dear Colleague Letter 97-G-300 (July 1997) and the Secretary's cumulative list of closed schools. *See* § 9.3.2, *supra*.

36 34 C.F.R. § 682.402(d)(3)(ii)(c).
37 34 C.F.R. § 602.3.
38 *Id.*
39 34 C.F.R. § 602.24(c).
40 20 U.S.C. § 1087(c)(1).
41 McComas v. Riley, (S.D. W. Va. Feb. 27, 1998), *available at* www.consumerlaw.org/unreported (opinion and order granting defendants' renewed motion for summary judgment).
42 *See* 34 C.F.R. §§ 682.402(d)(2)(i) (FFEL), 685.214(b)(1) (Direct Loan), 674.33(g)(2)(i) (Perkins Loan).
43 *See* 34 C.F.R. §§ 682.402(d)(2)(ii) (FFEL), 685.214(b)(2) (Direct Loan), 674.33(g)(2)(ii) (Perkins Loan).
44 *See* 34 C.F.R. §§ 682.402(d)(2)(iii) (FFEL), 685.214(b)(3) (Direct Loan), 674.33(g)(2)(iii) (Perkins Loan).
45 *See* 34 C.F.R. § 682.402(d)(2)(iv) (FFEL).
  The language in 34 C.F.R. § 685.214(b)(4) (Direct Loan) is not so extensive, solely requiring the Secretary to report the loan discharge to all credit bureaus to which the Secretary previously reported the status of the loan.

The regulations for most of the discharges explicitly provide that both past and current loan obligations may be cancelled.[46] Thus, a borrower should be allowed to seek a discharge even if the borrower's loans are already paid off, possibly through involuntary payments such as tax offsets. Although the current obligation is already extinguished, the borrower should still be able to get a refund and other appropriate relief such as elimination of negative notations on credit reports. However, at least with respect to disability discharges, the Department has indicated that it will not grant discharges for paid-in-full loans.[47]

Revocation of a closed-school discharge is contemplated in the regulations only if the borrower provides testimony, sworn statements, or documentation that does not support the material representations made to obtain the discharge.[48] It is unclear how the Department interprets this provision.

9.3.6 How to Obtain a Closed-School Discharge

9.3.6.1 General

Borrowers must apply for the discharge. Guarantors are required to provide notice informing borrowers who appear to be eligible for the discharge of their right to apply, together with an application form. The guarantors must forbear collecting from these individuals.[49] Presumably, the Department does the same on the loans it is collecting.

If a guaranty agency is holding a loan, borrowers should deal with the guaranty agency in obtaining a discharge. Only if the Department is holding the loan should the student apply directly to the Department.

9.3.6.2 Written Application for Discharge

With a few exceptions discussed below, a written application is required. To apply for a discharge, borrowers will typically fill out forms created by the loan holder and submit the application to the loan holder. For example, if the Department holds the loan, the borrower should use the Department's closed-school-discharge application form and submit the form to the Department.[50] If a guaranty agency holds the loan, that guaranty agency's form or the general FFEL form should be used. The Department has also instructed guaranty agencies to process all requests for a closed-school discharge even if the request is not on the agency's standard form.[51] In practice, however, it is generally most efficient to use the official agency form whenever possible.

The regulations contain no requirement that borrowers, in applying for a discharge, reaffirm their debt or waive other rights. The borrower only needs to provide the minimum information required by the regulations, including:

- Whether the borrower has made a claim relating to the loan with a third party such as a state tuition recovery program or surety for the school, and, if so, the amount of any recovery;
- That the borrower received the loan proceeds after January 1, 1986;
- That the borrower did not complete the program because of the school's closing while the borrower was enrolled, the borrower was on an approved leave of absence, or the borrower withdrew within ninety days of the school's closure;
- That the borrower did not complete the program through a "teach-out" at another school or by transferring credits to another school (presumably this would only apply if the borrower received a credit toward tuition at the new school because of attendance at the closed school);
- That the borrower agrees to provide, if requested, other related documentation reasonably available to the borrower;
- That the borrower agrees to cooperate with the Secretary in any action to recover money relating to the loan from third parties, such as the school owners and the school's affiliates.[52]

9.3.6.3 Oral Applications

The Department and guaranty agencies may grant closed-school discharges without a written application in limited circumstances.[53] Specifically, a discharge may be granted without an application if (1) the borrower received a discharge of a different type of loan for the same program of study or (2) the Department or guaranty agency determines that the borrower qualifies for a discharge based on information in the Secretary or guaranty agency's possession.

---

46 34 C.F.R. §§ 682.402(d)(2)(i) (closed-school discharge), 682.402(e)(2)(i) (false-certification discharge).
47 See § 9.7.2, infra.
48 34 C.F.R. § 682.402(d)(4)(ii).
49 34 C.F.R. § 682.402(d)(6).
  The guaranty agency requirements are slightly different for schools that closed between 1986 and 1994.
50 See Appx. D, infra. The form is also available on the Department of Education website at www.ed.gov.
  If the address to which the borrower is requested to send payments is the National Payment Center in Greenville, Texas, borrowers should submit completed forms to U.S. Department of Education, William D. Ford Direct Loan Program, Direct Loan Servicing Center, P.O. Box 5609, Greenville, TX 75403-5609.
51 U.S. Dep't of Educ., Dear Colleague Letter 94-G-256, (Sept. 1994), reprinted at Appx. C, infra, and available on the companion website to this manual.
52 34 C.F.R. § 682.402(d)(3).
53 34 C.F.R. §§ 682.402(d)(8) (FFEL), 674.33(g)(3) (Perkins Loan).

§ 9.3.6.4 Time Limits and Appeal Rights

There is no time limit on a borrower's eligibility for a discharge.[54] Guaranty agencies must respond to discharge requests within ninety days.[55] The Department has not set any time limits for its own response to discharge requests. Decisions may take years to process. For this reason, advocates should be prepared to request administrative forbearances for borrowers so that collection activities will cease until the discharge has been granted or denied.[56] Guaranty agencies collecting FFELs should affirmatively suspend collection if the agency has reliable information that a school has closed.[57] A borrower's request for a discharge must not be denied solely on the basis of failure to meet any time limits set by the lender, guaranty agency, or the Secretary.[58]

The regulations do not set out a right to review for denial of a closed-school discharge application. For a discussion on how to appeal an adverse decision, see § 9.15, *infra*.

9.3.7 Effect of School Closure on FISLs and Older FFELs

The closed-school discharge applies only to loans disbursed after January 1, 1986. Consequently, students whose loans were disbursed *in full* before that date will have to pursue other avenues.

Many loans from the 1970s and early 1980s were Federally Insured Student Loans (FISLs). There was no guaranty agency involvement with these loans. Instead, the lender or even a school acting as lender made the loan, and the loan was directly insured by the United States. Department FISL regulations through 1986 stated that the school's closure while the student was enrolled provided a defense to repayment on the loan.[59]

Regulations governing Direct Stafford loans never had such an explicit provision. Nevertheless, before the closed-school-discharge provision was enacted by Congress, the Department had stated a policy encouraging guaranty agencies to excuse a portion or all of a student's Stafford loan when the school closed while the student was still enrolled.[60]

Borrowers are excused from paying the percentage of the debt that equals the percentage of the loan period during which the borrower was prevented from attending school because of the school closing. However, the borrower must agree to pay the remainder of the loan and assign to the guaranty agency any right to receive a refund from the school. In addition, the policy does not apply when a borrower has a "teach-out" available from another school.

Apparently, the Department agrees that this policy still applies to pre-1986 loans, although it is unlikely that collection agencies or most personnel hired by the Department or guarantors will be aware of it. Advocates may have to educate these personnel or find a knowledgeable person in the General Counsel's office or elsewhere, such as the Ombudsman office, in the Department.

Another option for pre-1986 Stafford loans is to raise the school's closure as a school-related claim that the student asserts as a defense to the loan.[61] A loan made directly by the school, such as a Perkins loan, is subject to a straight-forward breach-of-contract defense if the school closed before the educational services were provided.[62]

9.4 False-Certification Discharge

9.4.1 General

Borrowers are entitled to a loan discharge if they received at least part of an FFEL or Direct loan after January 1, 1986,[63] and if their eligibility to borrow was falsely certified by the school.[64] The discharge does not apply to Perkins loans, but students should be able to raise the school's misconduct as a defense to loan repayment because the school is the original lender.[65]

The Department recognizes four bases for a false-certification discharge:

- The school falsifies a non-high-school graduate's ability to benefit from the program;[66]
- The school enrolls a student unable to meet minimum state employment requirements for the job for which the student is being trained;[67]
- The school forges or alters the student loan note or check endorsements;[68] or
- The borrower is a victim of identity theft.[69]

---

54 34 C.F.R. § 682.402(d)(6)(I).
55 34 C.F.R. § 682.402(d)(6)(ii)(G).
56 34 C.F.R. § 682.211(f)(8). *See also* § 4.4.3, *supra*.
57 34 C.F.R. §§ 682.402(d)(6)(ii)(B), 685.214(f)(2) (Direct Loan).
58 34 C.F.R. § 682.402(d)(6)(ii)(I).
59 34 C.F.R. § 518 (since rescinded). *See also* United States v. Griffin, 707 F.2d 1477 (D.C. Cir. 1983).
60 Letter, U.S. Dep't of Educ., Compromise and Write-off Procedures 89-G-159, Clearinghouse No. 44,338 (May 1989).
61 *See* § 12.7.3.1, *infra*.
62 *See* § 12.7.2.1, *infra*.
63 A loan is dischargeable even if part of it was disbursed in 1985, as long as part of it was disbursed in 1986. 20 U.S.C. § 1087(c); 34 C.F.R. § 682.402(e)(3)(ii)(A).
64 20 U.S.C. § 1087(c)(1).
65 *See* § 12.7.2.1, *infra*.
66 *See* § 9.4.2, *infra*.
67 *See* § 9.4.3, *infra*.
68 *See* § 9.4.4, *infra*.
69 *See* § 9.4.5, *infra*.

9.4.2 Discharge Based on Ability-to-Benefit (ATB) Falsification

9.4.2.1 ATB Falsification Defined

Department regulations authorize a false-certification discharge if the student was admitted to a school and the school falsified the student's ability to benefit from the program.[70] The school is required to test a student's ability to benefit only if the student did not have a high school diploma or its recognized equivalent prior to enrollment.[71] Therefore, borrowers who had high school diplomas or equivalencies at the time they enrolled will not be eligible for this type of false-certification discharge.

The Higher Education Opportunity Act (HEOA) added a new "ability to benefit" category. Students may be shown to have the ability to benefit from the education or training upon satisfactory completion of six credit hours or the equivalent coursework that are applicable toward a degree or certificate offered by the institution of higher education.[72] In June 2010, the Department issued proposed regulations to implement this provision.[73] The proposed regulations allow a school to determine ability to benefit based on the student's satisfactory completion of six semester hours, six trimester hours, six quarter hours, or 225 clock hours that are applicable toward a degree or certificate offered by the institution.[74]

In the proposed regulations, the Department stated that the coursework to meet this standard does not have to be in the intended program of study. However, the Department expects that the credit hours completed will be part of an eligible program offered by the institution and will show that the student has the ability to benefit from the program in which the student is enrolled or intends to enroll.[75] The Department also stated that a student who establishes eligibility by passing an ATB test during a payment period may be paid for the entire payment period. However, if a student establishes eligibility through the six hours provision, the student may not be paid for the payment period during which the student took the requisite coursework.[76]

For enrollments between July 1, 1987, and June 30, 1991, only, both borrowers who had general education diplomas (GEDs) at the time of enrolling *and* those who received the diplomas before completing the program are deemed to have the ability to benefit from the program.[77]

The rules for schools to admit "ability to benefit" students changed in 1987, 1991, and 1996. For a school *not* to have falsified the ability of a student enrolled between July 1, 1987, and June 30, 1996,[78] to benefit from the school, the student must have done at least one of the following:

- Passed an ATB test, the test being approved by the accrediting agency (or, for enrollments after July 1, 1991, by the Secretary) and administered substantially in accordance with the test publisher's or accreditor's requirements for use of the test[79] or
- Successfully completed a program of developmental or remedial education provided by the school.[80]

For periods of enrollment after July 1, 1996, and before June 30, 2000, the student must have done at least one of the following:

- Obtained a passing score on an independently administered test[81] or
- Enrolled in an eligible institution that participates in an alternative admissions process.[82]

The institution must obtain the results of an approved ATB test directly from either the test publisher or the assessment center that administered the test. There are a number of requirements for independently administered tests, including that the test be given at an assessment center by a test administrator who has no financial or ownership interest in the school.[83] In addition, the test is not independently administered if the school pays a test administrator a bonus or other incentive.[84]

Alternative processes can be implemented by the states for some or all schools in that state. These processes must be approved by the Secretary. In order to gain approval, the state must present certain information, including proof of a

---

70 34 C.F.R. §§ 682.402(e)(1)(i)(A), 685.215 (Direct Loan).
   A previous regulatory requirement that borrowers certify that they did not find employment after attending school was struck down in 1999. *See* Jordan v. Secretary of Educ., 194 F.3d 169 (D.C. Cir. 1999), *rev'g* 26 F. Supp. 2d 173 (D.D.C. 1998).
   The Department agreed to extend the benefits of the ruling to borrowers nationwide. *See* U.S. Dep't of Educ., Dear Colleague Letter G-00-327 (July 2000).
71 34 C.F.R. § 682.402(e), (e)(13)(iv) (citing student eligibility regulations at 34 C.F.R. § 668.32(e)(1) and ATB test requirements at 34 C.F.R. § 668.141–.156).
72 20 U.S.C. § 1091(d)(4).
73 75 Fed. Reg. 34806 (June 18, 2010).
74 *Id.* (adding 34 C.F.R. § 668.32(e)(5)).
75 75 Fed. Reg. 34806 (June 18, 2010).
76 75 Fed. Reg. 34806, 34838 (June 18, 2010).
77 34 C.F.R. § 682.402(e)(13)(i).
78 For students enrolled before that date, the school had to have developed and consistently applied criteria for determining whether students had the ability to benefit, and the school had to have been able to demonstrate this to the Secretary. *See* 34 C.F.R. § 682.402(e)(13)(ii)(A).
79 34 C.F.R. § 682.402(e)(13)(ii)(B)(1)–(2).
80 34 C.F.R. § 682.402(e)(13)(ii)(C).
81 34 C.F.R. §§ 682.402(e)(13)(ii)(D)(1), 668.32(e)(2).
82 34 C.F.R. § 682.402(e)(13)(D)(2) (citing regulations for approved state processes at 34 C.F.R. § 668.156).
83 The regulations for independently administered tests are set out at 34 C.F.R. § 668, Subpart J. 34 C.F.R. § 668.151 relates to the administration of tests. The Department proposed extensive changes to these regulations in June 2010, including a definition of "independent test administrator." *See* 75 Fed. Reg. 34806 (June 18, 2010).
84 34 C.F.R. § 668.151(c).

minimum success rate.[85] The Department proposed extensive changes to these provisions in June 2010.[86]

For periods of enrollment beginning on or after July 1, 2000, the student must meet one of the two conditions discussed above for July 1, 1996, through June 30, 2000, or meet the requirements for valid home schooling.[87]

A school not administering a valid test when one is required is a clear example of ATB fraud. The Department also considers the following testing errors, even if unintentional, as proof of ATB falsification:[88]

- A test requiring an independent test administrator was not so administered.
- The school allowed a student to retake the test earlier than the minimum prescribed waiting period or more frequently than allowed.
- The school allowed more time than permitted to take the test, did not use all required portions of the test, supplied answers to students, allowed students to discuss the answers among themselves, or passed a student whose score did not meet minimum standards.
- Starting after July 1, 1991, the test was not approved by the Department of Education.

Even if an approved ATB test is used, a false-certification discharge may still be granted if the student was not given the appropriate portion of the approved test.[89] In *Pellot v. Riley*, a nursing assistant student who was given only the clerical portion of an approved test was found eligible on appeal for a false-certification discharge. The accreditor guidelines and test publisher instructions made clear that a school should test aptitudes related to the course. In the case of a nursing assistant, this would include verbal and math ability, not just clerical matching skills.

Audit reports and other investigative reports by the Office of the Inspector General (OIG) demonstrate the range of possible ATB fraud. For example, in one case, the OIG uncovered numerous instances of altered ATB test results. School officials in this case admitted changing some test answers.[90]

In an August 2009 report, the Government Accountability Office (GAO) reported that weaknesses in the Department of Education's oversight of the ATB requirements places students and federal funds at risk.[91] For example, when GAO analysts posing as prospective students took the basic skills test at a local proprietary school, the "independent" test administrator gave out answers to some of the test questions. In addition, the test forms were tampered with.[92] The Department issued proposed regulations in June 2010 that would impose a number of new requirements for schools and test publishers to follow. In making these proposals, the Department cited recommendations from the August 2009 GAO report to strengthen control over ATB testing.[93]

Another common abuse occurs when schools improperly enroll students who are unable to benefit from the coursework because of limited English language skills. The regulations allow schools to give admission tests in non-English languages only in specific situations. If a student is not a native English speaker and is not fluent in English, the school may give a test in that person's language only if the coursework is conducted entirely in that language. The test must be linguistically accurate and culturally sensitive.[94]

If the coursework is in English with an English as a Second Language (ESL) component, and the student is enrolled in both the coursework and the ESL component, students may be given an approved ESL test or an approved test in their native language.[95] If the course is in English without an ESL component or if the student is not enrolled in the ESL component, he or she must be given an approved test in English.[96]

---

85 34 C.F.R. § 668.156(b).
86 75 Fed. Reg. 34806 (June 18, 2010).
87 34 C.F.R. § 682.402(e)(13)(ii)(E)(1)–(2). The home schooling regulations can be found at 34 C.F.R. § 668.32(e)(4).
88 U.S. Dep't of Educ., Dear Colleague Letter Gen-95-42, at 5–6, (Sept. 1995) (from Elizabeth M. Hicks, Deputy Assistant Secretary for Student Financial Assistance), *reprinted at* Appx. C, *infra*, and *available on* the companion website to this manual.
89 Order, Pellot v. Riley, (E.D. Pa 1998), *available on* the companion website to this manual; Memorandum of Law in Support of Plaintiff's Motion for Summary Judgment, Pellot v. Riley, (E.D. Pa. 1998), *available on* the companion website to this manual.

  The Secretary provides a list of approved "ability to benefit" (ATB) tests and passing scores. See, e.g., 71 Fed. Reg. 29135 (May 19, 2006).
90 *In re* Maurice Charles Academy of Hair Styling, No. 91-18-ST (Office of Inspector Gen. 1991). *See also In re* Roswell Beauty College of Cosmetology Arts & Sciences, No. 03-16-SP (U.S. Dep't of Educ. Sept. 15, 2003) (finding, among other problems, failure to meet ability-to-benefit testing requirements); *In re* Nationwide Beauty Sch., No. 02-63-SP (U.S. Dep't of Educ. Office Jan. 15, 2003) (findings included routine practice of falsifying or fabricating documents used to support proof of eligibility for federal student financial assistance); *In re* Hamilton Prof'l Sch., No. 02-49-SP (U.S. Dep't of Educ. June 11, 2003) (finding that the school falsified ability-to-benefit tests to obtain federal assistance funds for ineligible students); Office of Inspector Gen., Advanced Career Training Institute's Administration of the Title IV Higher Education Act Programs, Control No. ED-OIG/A04-B0019, Final Audit Report (Sept. 2003) (finding that the school had disbursed aid to students who did not pass ability-to-benefit tests); Office of Inspector Gen., Audit of Lincoln Technical Institute, Control No. ED-OIG/A03-BC0013, Final Audit Report (May 2002) (finding that the school compromised the security of ability-to-benefit tests).
91 U.S. Gov't Accountability Office (GAO) Proprietary Schools: Stronger Department of Education Oversight Needed to Help Ensure Only Eligible Students Receive Federal Student Aid, Report No. GAO-09-600 (Aug. 2009).
92 *Id.*
93 75 Fed. Reg. 34806 (June 18, 2010).
94 34 C.F.R. § 668.153(a)(1).
95 34 C.F.R. § 668.153(a)(2).
96 34 C.F.R. § 668.153(a)(3).

In June 2010, the Department proposed revisions to this section.[97] The proposals would require that individuals who are enrolled or plan to enroll in a program that is taught in English with an ESL component must take an approved English language proficiency assessment *before* beginning the portion of the program taught in English.[98] There are also specific testing requirements for students with disabilities.[99]

9.4.2.2 Using Independent Evidence to Prove ATB Falsification

9.4.2.2.1 Challenging Department denials based on lack of corroborating evidence

Often, the borrower's own statement on the discharge application form is the only available evidence of ATB falsification (for example, the student certifying that no test was given or that the school helped the student pass the test). The Department is skeptical of such applications and requires the presentation of additional independent evidence of ATB falsification, such as a finding by an entity that had oversight responsibility, statements by school officials, or statements by other students, including statements made in other claims for discharge relief.[100] This is a huge obstacle for borrowers seeking false-certification discharges.

The Department's practices in this area are ripe for legal challenge. One key issue is the level of review required once the Department receives a borrower's discharge application. The FFEL regulations provide that, when a borrower applies for a false-certification discharge, the guaranty agency shall "review the borrower's request and supporting sworn statement in light of information available from the records of the agency and from other sources, including other guaranty agencies, state authorities, and cognizant accrediting associations."[101] However, in a 1995 "Dear Colleague" letter, the Department directed guaranty agencies that an absence of findings of improper ATB practices by authorities with oversight powers "raises an inference that no improper practices were reported because none were taking place."[102] The Department's reasoning in the "Dear Colleague" letter is that responsible authorities should have discovered ATB fraud, and the fact that these agencies did not issue such a report implies that no ATB fraud occurred. This is truly incredible. In fact, Congress in 1992 provided for the false-certification discharge and overhauled the student loan system because such supervising authorities (including the Department) had failed to do their job.[103]

The Department's practices have been challenged in court in at least two separate cases.[104] There were two main issues raised in these cases. First, plaintiffs challenged the Department's assertion that the regulations require them only to look for *findings* from oversight agencies. The Department, at least in some cases, has stated that this means they do not need to examine other materials, such as student complaints.[105]

A second issue relates to Department practices after investigating a complaint. Even if the Department looks beyond investigative "findings," they will often not find evidence to support the borrower's statements. In these cases, the Department will deny the discharge and generally allow the borrower to respond by submitting any corroborating evidence. A typical Department denial under these circumstances states:

> This office has reviewed information from entities responsible for overseeing the school's compliance with ability-to-benefit regulations, and has concluded that either no evidence of ability-benefit-violations exist[s] or the evidence does not support the issues raised in your discharge request. If you wish to contest this decision, it is your responsibility to present corroborating evidence that the school improperly determined your ability-to-benefit.[106]

In at least one case, the plaintiffs argued that, if the Department does not find evidence to contradict the borrower's statement, the Department must grant the discharge.[107] The first district court to consider these issues rejected most of the plaintiffs' arguments.[108] The court found that requiring additional evidence beyond a borrower's sworn statement

---

97 75 Fed. Reg. 34806 (June 18, 2010).
98 *Id.*
99 34 C.F.R. § 668.153(b).
   The Department issued proposed regulations to revise this section in June 2010. *See* 75 Fed. Reg. 34806 (June 18, 2010).
100 U.S. Dep't of Educ., Dear Colleague Letter Gen-95-42, (Sept. 1995) (from Elizabeth M. Hicks, Deputy Assistant Secretary for Student Financial Assistance), *reprinted at* Appx. C, *infra*, and *available on* the companion website to this manual.
101 34 C.F.R. § 682.402(e)(6)(iv).
102 U.S. Dep't of Educ., Dear Colleague Letter GEN-95-42 (Sept. 1995), *reprinted at* Appx. C, *infra*.

103 *See, e.g.*, *Abuses in Federal Student Grant Programs: Hearings Before the Permanent Subcomm. on Investigations of the Comm. on Governmental Affairs*, 103d Cong. S. Hearing 103-491 (Oct. 1993). *See generally* Ch. 12, *infra* (challenging vocational school fraud).
104 Two of these complaints, Cofan v. Paige, No. CV-01-4239 (E.D. Pa. 2001), and Gill v. Riley, No. CV-00-5453 (E.D.N.Y. 2000), are reprinted at Appendix E, *infra*. The complaints and other documents from these cases are also available on the companion website to this manual.
105 Gill v. Riley, CV-00-5453 (E.D.N.Y. 2000), *reprinted at* Appx. E, *infra*.
106 This was the notice received by the plaintiff in the *Cofan* case. Cofan v. Paige, Civil Action No. 01-4239 (E.D. Pa. complaint filed 2001). This notice is available on the companion website to this manual.
107 Gill v. Riley, CV-00-5453 (E.D.N.Y. 2000), *reprinted at* Appx. E, *infra*.
108 Gill v. Paige, 226 F. Supp. 2d 366 (E.D.N.Y. 2002).

was not in conflict with the false-certification statute.[109] The court also rejected the plaintiffs' argument that the Department's policy conflicted with the regulations.[110] The plaintiffs' procedural arguments, based on the Department's announcement of the policy in a "Dear Colleague" letter rather than on formal regulations, were also rejected.[111] According to the court, the notice and comment requirements do not apply to interpretive rules, general statements of policy, or rules of agency organizations, procedure, or practice.

There was one issue left outstanding in the case. The plaintiffs requested additional discovery to develop the record regarding their claim that the adoption of the "Dear Colleague" letter was arbitrary and capricious. The plaintiffs alleged that the Department should have known that agencies it relied upon to make ATB findings provided inadequate oversight.[112] The court agreed that the facts were not sufficiently developed to determine whether the Secretary considered and rejected or entirely failed to consider the performance of accrediting agencies at policing proprietary schools. Summary judgment for the Department was denied on this issue only.[113]

In September 2007, the Department issued additional guidance to guaranty agencies for evaluating false-certification ATB discharge applications.[114] This guidance addresses the common situation in which borrowers have no evidence of fraud other than their own statements.

The 2007 guidance requires guaranty agencies to check for the availability of evidence and to make inferences in certain circumstances that fraud has occurred. Even if findings of improper ATB admission practices have been reported by oversight agencies, guaranty agencies must not grant a discharge if the guaranty agency has other information that directly contradicts material facts or contentions in the discharge application.[115]

The previous guidance in the 1995 Dear Colleague letter required guaranty agencies to obtain existing documentation of ATB findings from any public or private agency that reviewed or had oversight responsibility for the school.[116] The 2007 letter clarifies that, as a result of this responsibility, each guaranty agency must maintain, on a school-by-school basis, all oversight material it obtains in evaluating ATB discharge applications and investigating allegations of ATB violations, and it must promptly make the information available on request to the Secretary and any other guaranty agency that requests it.[117] Guaranty agencies are also required to maintain a school-by-school record of the number of discharge applications received, the campus to which each application pertains if relevant, the date of attendance of the student applying for discharge, and whether the discharge was granted or denied. The agency must share this information with the Secretary and other guaranty agencies on request. As part of obtaining necessary documentation, guaranty agencies must, among other things, either check the Department's Postsecondary Education Participants System (PEPS) for such findings or contact each oversight agency that enters data into PEPS to obtain that information.

The 1995 letter states that borrowers must provide evidence that goes beyond assertions that they meet the qualifications. The 2007 letter explains that there is more that the guaranty agencies must do in these circumstances. In addition to considering the student's allegations and any other information the student submits, guaranty agencies must consider the incidence of discharge applications filed regarding that school by students who attended the school during the same time frame as the applicant, as well as the possibility that there may have been collusion among the students in submitting the applications received. It is unclear what evidence of collusion would be. If there is a high incidence of submissions and no evidence of collusion, the guaranty agency may determine that the school's ATB practices were defective during that time frame. Agencies should give heightened weight to a high incidence of applications with regard to schools for which no oversight reports or data of any kind are available. If an agency comes to the conclusion that discharges should be granted based on incidence of discharge applications received for a particular school, the Department's letter states that it should also re-evaluate application claims previously denied for students who attended that school during the same time period.[118]

In addition, if there is no evidence that ATB requirements were met other than the absence of ATB oversight report findings and no evidence that the borrower does not qualify, credible evidence of the following provides an adequate basis for granting a discharge and should be given added weight with regard to schools for which no oversight reports are available:

- Withdrawal rates exceeding 33% at the school at the relevant time; or
- For students who entered repayment on their loans during or after fiscal year 1993, an annual loan default rate exceeding 40%; for students who entered repayment during fiscal year 1992, an annual loan default rate exceeding 45%; for students who entered repayment during fiscal year 1991, an annual loan default

---

109 *Id.* at 372.
110 *Id.* at 373.
111 *Id.* at 374.
112 *Id.* at 375.
113 *Id.* at 376.
114 U.S. Dep't of Educ., Dear Colleague Letter No. FP-07-09 (Sept. 20, 2007).
115 *Id.*
116 U.S. Dep't of Educ., Dear Colleague Letter No. 95-42 (Sept. 1995), *reprinted in* Appx. C, *infra.*
117 U.S. Dep't of Educ., Dear Colleague Letter No. FP-07-09 (Sept. 20, 2007).
118 *Id.*

rate exceeding 50%; for students who entered repayment during fiscal year 1990, an annual loan default rate exceeding 55%; and, for students who entered repayment during or before fiscal year 1989, an annual loan default rate exceeding 60%.

If there are reports that contain specific findings of violations at some campuses but not others, the Department states that agencies should consider incidence, withdrawal, and loan default rates on a campus-by-campus basis.[119]

9.4.2.2.2 Obtaining investigatory files through Freedom of Information Act requests

Lack of documentation has been the primary obstacle to the granting of false-certification discharges. There is no magic solution to gathering evidence, but there are a number of sources to try.

One good source of information is state or federal regulators' investigatory files. The Department of Education's files on a school may be obtained through a Freedom of Information Act (FOIA) request. Important documents include the school's application for eligibility with accompanying documents, any program reviews, or reviews shared with the Department by guaranty agencies, state agencies, or accreditors.[120]

A separate request should be made to the Department's Inspector General for audit and investigations concerning the school. State licensing agencies may also have files on schools, including investigation reports, which may be available under state sunshine laws. Private accrediting agencies will not usually share files on schools without a subpoena.

The Freedom of Information Act contains standards for waiver of fees for search and duplication under the statute.[121] There is also a provision that the agency should not charge for the first 100 pages of copying.[122] The following language should be included in requests to obtain a wavier of fees:

> These records are not requested for any commercial purpose but to gather information on [how the agency has carried out its obligations in the area covered by the records]. Accordingly, I request that any fees be waived as disclosure of this information is in the public interest because it is likely to contribute significantly to public understanding of the operations or activities of the government. 5 U.S.C. § 552(a)(4)(A)(iii). If there are any proposed charges which are not waived and they exceed [Fill in amount], please notify me before they are incurred.

For advocates seeking records to expose the misconduct of a school operating under the loan program, it is important to emphasize the public benefit of disclosure concerning what the Department knew about the school's operations and whether it acted effectively in enforcing HEA standards.

In addition, both the Department of Education's Office of Hearings and Appeals (OHA) and Office of Inspector General have investigative and audit reports on-line.[123]

9.4.2.2.3 School files

Advocates should try to obtain copies of all the school's files on the student. This information is generally difficult to obtain directly from the school if it has already closed. In that case, students can often obtain the schools' student records from the state agency responsible for regulating the schools. Typically, a student has an academic file and a financial aid file. The academic file will be the more important.

Advocates should look for a copy of an admission test in the file or a description of the type of test used. The absence of a test or any reference to a test is evidence that the test was never given. In fact, for independent testing done after 1991, the Department regulations state that the school is liable to the Department for all funds disbursed if the school is unable to *document* that the student received a passing score on an approved test.[124]

9.4.2.2.4 Testing company information

If the file (or the school or state licensing agency) can identify the company giving the test, consider contacting the testing agency. The Wonderlic Company tests were widely used by trade schools for ATB testing. Wonderlic can provide appropriate information on whether a particular social security number matches one of its registered test results.[125] If the student was to have received the Wonderlic test, but the test score is not registered, this may provide evidence that a proper test was not given. Wonderlic may also provide additional information about the validity of test scores at a particular school that administered the Wonderlic test for ATB purposes.

---

119 *Id.*
120 Sample FOIA requests can be found at Appendix F, *infra*.
121 5 U.S.C. § 552(a)(4)(A)(iii).
122 *Id.*

123 The Office of Inspector General website is at www.ed.gov/about/offices/list/oig/index.html?src=mr. The Office of Hearings and Appeals website is at www.ed-oha.org.
124 34 C.F.R. § 668.154(c).
125 Call Wonderlic at 888-397-8519 and ask to talk to the ATB Department; mail a request to Wonderlic Personnel Test, Inc., 1795 N. Butterfield Rd., Libertyville, IL 60048; or visit www.wonderlic.com. *See also* Buros Inst., Tests in Print 7 (Jan. 2006) (providing a description of most tests and their appropriate uses, along with the addresses of the publishers).

9.4.2.2.5 Information on specific schools

The National Consumer Law Center has compiled information on a few schools (unfortunately just a small fraction of those involved in ATB falsification). Advocates should contact the Center if they need more information on any of the following schools:

- Academy of Court Reporting (Cleveland, Ohio)—2006 report obtained in an FOIA request for investigations, inquiries, and other actions from 1985–2006.
- American Business Institute (Chicago, Illinois; closed in 1990)—1989 Illinois State Board of Education findings.
- Austin School of Beauty Culture (Chicago, Illinois; closed on July 3, 1990)—1988 Department of Education review.
- Chicago Institute of Technology, Inc. (closed in 1990)—Higher Education Assistance Foundation, Accrediting Bureau of Health Education Schools reviews.
- County Schools—information about ATB testing.
- Debbie's School of Beauty Culture (Chicago, four locations; closed between 1989 and 1993)—Higher Education Assistance Foundation and Department of Education review.
- Hausman Computer School (New York)—copy of federal court decision finding the school guilty of criminal conduct, including ATB fraud, and imprisoning the owners. United States v. Grundhofer, 916 F.2d 788 (2d Cir. 1990).
- IADE American Schools (various locations in southern California; all schools closed by 1995)—Student Financial Assistance proceeding finding that, from July 1989 through June 1991, IADE disbursed student assistance funds to students who had failed the ATB test; copy of 1997 news release with information about the indictment of IADE's owner and financial aid director.
- Illinois School of Commerce (Chicago, Illinois; closed in 1988)—Department of Education reports and copies of complaints against former president and owner.
- Marion Adult Education and Career Training Center, (Chicago, Illinois; closed in 1990)—1990 Department of Education audit report.
- Metropolitan Business College (Evergreen Park, Illinois; closed in 1992)—1987 and 1990 Department of Education audits.
- Molder Hairstyling College (Chicago, Illinois).
- National Business Academy (California, accredited by ACCET)—State attorney general office submitted compilation of materials to California guaranty agency showing ATB fraud.
- National Technical College (accredited by ABHES and ACCT)—Evidence shows, among other violations, that NTC routinely falsely certified students as having the ability to benefit from the training.
- Phillips Junior College (Augusta and Columbus, Georgia; Spokane, Washington; Campbell, California; Georgia locations closed in 1993, Washington location in 1995, and Campbell in 1996)—Department of Education audit reports.
- PTC Career Institute (Philadelphia, Atlanta, Chicago, Baltimore, Newark, Cleveland, District of Columbia; accredited by ACCSCT/CCATTS (NATTS))—Department's Office of Inspector General audit report finds ATB problems, as does an affidavit from Wonderlic Personnel Test, Inc., and an affidavit used to support application by Community Legal Services in Philadelphia for false-certification discharges. The Department has authorized false-certification discharges to PTC Philadelphia students during the audit period.
- Rome Academy of Cosmetology (Chicago, Illinois; closed in 1992)—1993 Department of Education program review.
- SCS Business and Technical Institute (Jamaica, New York)
- Tarkio College (Tarkio, Missouri)—Information obtained from Missouri Department of Higher Education, including numerous newspaper articles about the school.
- Trainco Business School (Chicago, Illinois; two locations; closed in 1990)—Illinois Attorney General complaint.
- United Business Institute (New York, Florida, Georgia, and New Jersey; accredited by SACCOE)—New York State Education Department found ATB fraud.
- United Education and Software (UES) Schools (California; includes National Technical Schools—Home Study, Pacific Coast Technical Institutes, and Pacific Coast Colleges; all accredited by CCATTS (NATTS))—Court found systematic ATB fraud, as did two Department Office of Inspector General audits.
- Wilfred Academy of Hair and Beauty (Illinois; two locations; closed in 1991 and 1992)—Audited Financial Statements 1985–1987.

In addition, advocates should check the Department of Education's Office of Hearings and Appeals website and the Office of Inspector General website.[126] Many schools have also faced state and federal investigations and lawsuits. The lawsuits are mainly a combination of whistleblower, wrongful-termination, and shareholder suits.[127]

9.4.2.2.6 Other evidence of ATB fraud

Additional information can be provided by obtaining affidavits of other students who attended the same school as the client and who can testify that they were not tested or were improperly tested. In cases in which the client did not

---

126 See § 9.4.2.2.2, supra.
127 See §§ 12.3.3, 12.5, infra.

speak English at the time of enrollment or had a low reading aptitude, advocates should consider getting an official evaluation of the client's reading level.

For example, a monolingual Spanish-speaking client who dropped out of school in the fifth or sixth grade in the client's home country should submit an affidavit regarding his or her inability to speak English at the time of enrollment, that he or she dropped out of school, and that he or she was never tested or was improperly tested. This testimony, along with an official assessment of the client's reading level, should be strong evidence for an ATB discharge, even in the absence of official investigatory records.[128]

9.4.2.3 Group Discharges

The Department will provide false-certification discharges upon proper application *without* independent evidence for a particular cohort of students (such as non-high-school graduates who were admitted at a particular branch of a school during a certain time period) if *the Department* determines that a school committed pervasive and serious violations of ATB regulations.[129]

A partial list of group discharges provided by the Department in 1998 included the following schools:

1. 10/31/96, Draughon College (Oklahoma City)—Approval of ATB borrowers enrolled from 7/1/87 through 6/30/91.[130]
2. 12/20/96, National Technical Schools Home Study Division—Approval of ATB borrowers enrolled from 8/18/87 through 11/15/88.
3. 12/20/96, six branches of UES/Pacific Coast College—Approval of ATB borrowers enrolled from 2/1/87 through 5/31/89.[131]
4. 5/20/97, Andover Tractor Trailer School—Approval of ATB borrowers enrolled from 6/1/86 through 4/30/89. This limited time period was successfully challenged in subsequent litigation. The group discharge should apply to any Andover borrower during any time period who did not have a high school diploma or GED at the time of enrollment and who otherwise meets the criteria for a false-certification discharge.[132]

Another cohort of students includes all those with loans currently or subsequently held by the Department related to enrollments at any PTC Career Institute[133] or USA Training Academy. The Department has also granted a group discharge for Cambridge Technical School students.[134] The Department also granted a group ATB discharge for certain former students who enrolled in Programming Systems Incorporated (PSI). The group discharge covers ATB students who attended any PSI school from January 1, 1986, until the school's closing. It applies to every campus of PSI, including those in New York, Baltimore, Silver Spring (Maryland), Columbus, Cleveland, Southfield (Michigan), Indianapolis, Philadelphia, Miami, Charlotte, and Flint. Loans are held by at least sixteen different guaranty agencies in addition to the Department. The Department was supposed to notify all these agencies of the group discharge.[135]

This list is not exhaustive because to date the Department has not made a list of approved false-certification group discharges widely available. There may be other schools for which group discharges have been granted by the Department.

Another way to prove ATB falsification without evidence from an independent entity is to aggregate a number of students with ATB claims against the same school and then send those applications in as a group with a cover letter. An alternative approach is to send in only one application but refer to other previously filed applications in a cover letter. Each application should then serve as independent evidence for each of the other applications.

---

128 See § 9.4.2.1, *supra*, for a discussion of ATB testing of non-English-speaking students.

129 Requests to have schools treated in this way should be sent, with accompanying evidence, to U.S. Department of Education, Union Center Plaza, 830 First Street, NE, Washington, D.C. 20202-5345, Attn: Dan Klock. Mail sent by UPS or FedEx should be sent to U.S. Department of Education, 830 First Street, NE, Room 113E2, Washington, D.C. 20202, Attn: Dan Klock. This address is current as of August 2010. It is a good idea to check with the Department for any changes.

130 *See* Letter from Carney M. McCollough to Glendon Forgey, Oklahoma Guaranteed Student Loan Program (July 31, 1996) (on file with the U.S. Department of Education), *available on* the companion website to this manual.

131 *See* Letter from Carney M. McCollough to Susan Donald, California Student Aid Comm'n (Dec. 20, 1996) (on file with the U.S. Department of Education), *available on* the companion website to this manual.

132 Letter from Carney M. McCollough to Irv Ackelsberg, Community Legal Services, (May 20, 1997), *available on* the companion website to this manual.

The deadline and other issues were challenged in White v. Riley, (E.D. Pa. 1998), *available on* the companion website to this manual (class action complaint). The letter to Irv Ackelsberg is available on the companion website to this manual.

133 PTC had schools in Philadelphia, Atlanta, Chicago, Baltimore, Newark, Cleveland, and the District of Columbia. The group discharge applies to students whose first day of attendance occurred from July 1, 1987, through June 30, 1990. *See* Letter from Pamela A. Moran to Irv Ackelsberg, Community Legal Services (June 30, 1995) (on file with the U.S. Department of Education), *available on* the companion website to this manual.

134 Letter from Carney M. McCollough to Stephen Olden, Legal Aid Soc'y of Cincinnati, (Apr. 30, 1999), *available on* the companion website to this manual

135 A copy of the application for group discharge submitted by Legal Aid Society of Cleveland is available on the companion website to this volume. Community Legal Services in Philadelphia also submitted a group discharge application on behalf of former PSI students. The Department's letter approving the group discharge is available on the companion website to this manual.

9.4.3 Discharge Based on Student's Inability to Meet Minimum State Job Requirements (Disqualifying Status)

Even students with a high school diploma can receive a false-certification discharge if, *at the time of the student's enrollment*, the school certified the student's eligibility, and "the student would not meet the requirements for employment (in the student's state of residence) in the occupation for which the training program supported by the loan was intended because of a physical or mental condition, age, or criminal record or other reason accepted by the Secretary."[136] According to the Department, "[t]hose provisions apply to all categories of students at all schools, including students for whom the school was not required to make ability-to-benefit determinations or for whom the school made such determinations properly."[137]

Student borrowers with less than a tenth-grade education should receive a false-certification discharge if they attended a cosmetology school in one of a number of states that requires licensed cosmetologists to have at least a tenth-grade education. Other examples of disqualifying status include students with felony records being trained as security guards or visually impaired students being trained as truck-drivers when state law disqualifies those individuals from those occupations. A borrower with a felony record may also be able to file a certificate of good conduct or find other relief to remove this bar to employment or licensing.[138]

Yet another example involves monolingual Spanish students who were taught exclusively in Spanish when the state licensing test was given only in English. Even absent a licensing exam requirement, it may be that a Spanish-speaking student would not "meet the requirements for employment" if the employment requires the employee to be English speaking. The fact that the program was allegedly in English would not affect the fact that the student could only speak Spanish "at the time of the student's enrollment." The equities of this argument are even stronger when the school failed to provide promised English-as-a-second-language training. However, according to anecdotal reports from advocates, the Department has generally, but not always, rejected this argument. To date, these denials have not been appealed.

The discharge should also apply when the school's program, instead of the student, does not meet minimum state requirements. For example, a discharge should be available when a program was not certified by the state and graduation from a certified program is a precondition under state law for employment.

The Department explained in a denial letter that the concept behind this discharge is the narrow focus applied to specific occupations by certain training programs that, for persons who are legally disqualified from employment in that occupation, provides no benefit of any kind, either in terms of transferable educational credit or transferable occupational skills. This discharge, according to the Department, is not targeted at borrowers who enroll in programs that lead to academic or advanced degrees, such as in law or medicine. In this case, the Department denied an application of a borrower who alleged that he had a condition that prevented him from successfully completing his medical school exams and thus finding employment as a licensed medical doctor. Among other factors, the Department also stated that not everyone who attends medical school goes on to practice medicine or even intends to do so, nor is repayment of student loan obligations contingent upon the successful completion of the program of study.

In a 2008 appeal of a false-certification denial, the Department argued that, in order to qualify, a borrower must show that the loan was for a course that specifically and exclusively prepared the borrower for a particular occupation and that the borrower must be unable to work in this occupation because of one of the numerated factors. The borrower's appeal was denied when he had a criminal record and obtained loans to attend the University of Maryland University College. The borrower took several courses in the paralegal studies program. As a convicted felon, he asserted that he was unable to meet the requirements in that state to be admitted to the bar or to work in law enforcement.[139]

Borrowers should submit detailed documentation of the status or condition that prevents them from working in the particular field. In addition, the Department will generally require a copy of the state statute or regulation showing the requirements for employment in the particular field and that the condition or status would prevent the student from meeting those requirements.

9.4.4 Discharge Based on Forgery

A third important basis for a false-certification discharge is if the school signed the borrower's name without authorization on the loan application, promissory note, loan check endorsement, or authorization for an electronic funds transfer.[140]

---

136 34 C.F.R. §§ 682.402(e)(13)(iii)(B), 685.215(a)(iii).

137 U.S. Dep't of Educ., Dear Colleague Letter Gen-95-42, at 9 (Sept. 1995) (from Elizabeth M. Hicks, Deputy Assistant Secretary for Student Financial Assistance), *reprinted at* Appx. C, *infra*.

The letter does state that a defense to the discharge would be evidence that the school asked the student about such a disqualifying condition and the student did not divulge it.

138 *See generally* Margaret Colgate Love, The Sentencing Project, Relief From the Collateral Consequences of a Criminal Conviction: A State-by-State Resource Guide (June 2008), *available at* www.sentencingproject.org/PublicationDetails.aspx?PublicationID=486.

139 Johnson v. U.S. Dep't of Educ., 580 F. Supp. 2d 154 (D.D.C. 2008).

140 34 C.F.R. § 682.402(e)(1)(i)(B), (ii).

A limitation to this cancellation is that it only applies if the school forged the borrower's signature or endorsed the borrower's loan without authorization. If someone else committed the forgery, a borrower may still qualify for a cancellation by either applying for a discharge based on identity theft or by challenging the enforceability of the loan due to forgery.[141]

It is essential to obtain copies not only of the loan application and promissory note but of all canceled checks evidencing the indebtedness. If the borrower's signature appears forged, the student must submit five specimens of the student's own signature, two of which had to have been within one year of the forgery.[142]

A false-certification discharge for a forged check is only available if the proceeds of the forged check went toward tuition payments that the student was not obligated to pay, such as that portion of tuition not owed under the applicable refund formula after the student had dropped out.[143] The regulations and a "Dear Colleague" letter appear to place the burden not on the student but on the guaranty agency to determine whether or not the forged check proceeds went toward a legitimate student obligation.[144] The Department will not grant a discharge based on forgery if the student received the proceeds of the loan through actual delivery or application of charges.[145]

9.4.5 Discharge Based on Identity Theft

The Higher Education Reconciliation Act of 2005 included a discharge of FFELs or Direct loans if the borrower's eligibility to borrow was falsely certified due to identity theft.[146] This basis for a discharge became effective on July 1, 2006.

A borrower seeking this discharge must:

- Certify that the borrower did not sign the promissory note or that any other means of identification used to obtain the loan was used without the borrower's authorization;
- Certify that the borrower did not receive or benefit from the proceeds of the loan with knowledge that the loan had been made without the borrower's authorization; and
- Provide a copy of a local, state, or federal court verdict or judgment that conclusively determines that the borrower was a victim of the crime of identity theft by a perpetrator named in the verdict or judgment.[147]

If the judicial determination of the crime does not expressly state that the loan was obtained as a result of the crime, the borrower must provide authentic samples of his or her signature or other means of identification and a statement of facts that demonstrate that the borrower's eligibility for the loan in question was falsely certified as a result of identity theft.[148]

The Department clarified in the final regulations that it is not suggesting in any way that borrowers are liable for loans they did not execute or authorize when there is no crime of identity theft. According to the Department, an individual who claims that a signature was forged is not required to delay asserting that claim until a criminal prosecution occurs and nothing in the regulations requires such a delay.[149]

Lenders may also suspend credit bureau reporting on a loan for 120 days while the lender investigates a borrower's claim of identity theft.[150] Lenders may grant a 120-day administrative forbearance upon receipt of a valid identity theft report or notification from a credit bureau of an allegation of identity theft.[151] The FTC has issued regulations that define the term "identity theft report" under the Fair Credit Reporting Act.[152] To qualify as an identity theft report, the report must (1) allege identity theft with as much specificity as the consumer can provide, (2) be a copy of an official, valid report filed by the consumer with a law enforcement agency, and, (3) by its filing, must expose the person to criminal penalties relating to the filing of false information if the information in the report is false.[153] Although this definition imposes some significant burdens on consumers, it does not rise to the level of the student loan identity theft discharge, which requires a verdict or judgment of identity theft.

The government does not pay the interest subsidy or special allowance payments if the lender finds that the loan is unenforceable based on an identity theft report.[154] However, the lender has a three-year period to submit the claims and receive interest subsidies and special allowance payments if within that time period the lender receives from the borrower a verdict of judgment conclusively proving identity theft.[155] The regulations clarify that the Higher Education Act does not preempt provisions of the Fair Credit Reporting Act that provide for the suspension of credit bureau reporting and collection on a loan after a lender receives a valid identity theft report or notification from a credit bureau.[156]

---

141 *See* §§ 7.5.4 (defenses to loan enforceability), *supra*, 9.4.5 (identity theft cancellation), *infra*.
142 34 C.F.R. § 682.402(e)(3)(iii)–(iv).
143 34 C.F.R. § 682.402(e)(1)(ii).
144 U.S. Dep't of Educ., Dear Colleague Letter 94-G-256, item 11 (Sept. 1994).
145 34 C.F.R. §§ 682.402(e)(1)(ii), 685.215(a)92).
146 Pub. L. No. 109-171, 120 Stat. 4 (Feb. 8, 2006).
147 34 C.F.R. § 682.402(e)(3)(v).

148 34 C.F.R. § 682.402(e)(3)(v)(D).
149 71 Fed. Reg. 64378, 64388–89 (Nov. 1, 2006).
150 34 C.F.R. § 682.208(b)(3).
151 34 C.F.R. § 682.211(f)(6).
152 16 C.F.R. § 603.3. *See generally* National Consumer Law Center, Fair Credit Reporting § 9.2.2.3.2 (6th ed. 2006 and Supp.).
153 *Id.*
154 34 C.F.R. §§ 682.300(b)(2)(ix), 682.302(d)(1)(viii).
155 34 C.F.R. § 682.208(b)(4).
156 34 C.F.R. § 682.411(o)(2).

The Department has issued a form letter, reprinted in Appendix D, *infra*, for borrowers seeking false certification discharge based on identity theft. This is not an application form but rather a letter in which borrowers certify that they agree to cooperate with the Department of Education and the Department of Justice in investigating the allegations of identity theft. Borrowers must also include with the letter a court judgment that "conclusively" finds that they were victims of identity theft, a written statement explaining how the identity theft relates to the student loans, and a clear copy of a government-issued identification card. The letter and statement must be notarized.

Borrowers that cannot meet the standards for the identity theft discharge may be eligible for false-certification discharges due to forgery.[157] In addition, they may have common law contract defenses or other defenses derived from HEA regulations. For example, FFEL program regulations provide that benefits are payable to loan holders only when the lender obtained a legally enforceable promissory note to evidence the loan.[158] The Department emphasized that, with very limited exceptions, FFEL program benefits are payable only if the holder has a legally enforceable promissory note to evidence the loan. Because a forged promissory note is ordinarily not an enforceable obligation, a party holding a forged note cannot claim FFEL program benefits on that loan. Holders should not be continuing to enforce such obligations.[159] Lender rights are also subject to the obligation of the lender to exercise due diligence in making the loan.[160]

9.4.6 Relief Available for Those Obtaining a False-Certification Discharge

The relief available is identical to that for a closed-school discharge, as detailed in § 9.3.5, *supra*. Revocation of a false-certification discharge is contemplated in the regulations only if the borrower provides testimony, sworn statements, or documentation that does not support the material representations made to obtain the discharge.[161]

9.4.7 How to Apply for a False-Certification Discharge

A borrower's request may not be denied solely on the basis of failing to meet any time limits set by the lender, Secretary, or guaranty agency.[162] Whether a borrower seeks a discharge based on a disqualifying condition, ATB falsification, or a forged check, the application should be directed to the entity holding the loan. For a defaulted loan, the holder is almost always either a guaranty agency or the Department of Education. Guaranty agencies have their own forms, and the Department has three different false-certification-discharge forms for loans it is holding, one relating to claims of a disqualifying condition, one for ATB fraud, and one for forgery claims.[163]

The Department has also instructed guaranty agencies to process all requests for a discharge, even if the request is not on the agency's standard form.[164] In practice, however, it is generally expeditious to use the official agency form whenever possible. In addition, the loan may be discharged without a written application if the guaranty agency, with the Secretary's permission, determines that the borrower qualifies for a discharge based on information in its possession.[165]

While it is important to fill out the forms in their entirety, it is useful to know what the regulations say is required of an application. According to the regulations, the student must submit a written request for a discharge and a sworn statement (not notarized, but sworn under the penalty of perjury) stating:

(1) Whether the borrower has made a claim against another party on the loan (for example, with regard to a state tuition recovery fund);

(2) That at least part of the loan was disbursed after January 1, 1986;

(3) That the borrower agrees to provide, at the Secretary's request, additional information concerning the student's eligibility for a discharge; and

(4) That the borrower will cooperate with the Secretary in enumerated enforcement actions and to assign to the Secretary certain rights possessed by the student to recover from third parties.[166]

For ATB falsification applications, borrowers must also state that they had not graduated from high school before being admitted and that they did not have the ability to benefit from the course.

For false-certification discharges based on the school's forging of the student's signature on the loan application, the promissory note, a check endorsement, or electronic funds transfer authorization, the student must also state that a signature on one of these documents is not the student's and

---

157 See § 9.4.4, *supra*.
158 71 Fed. Reg. 45666 (Aug. 9, 2006) (citing 34 C.F.R. §§ 682.402(e)(1)(i)(B), 682.406(a)(1)). See § 7.5.4, *supra*.
159 72 Fed. Reg. 61960 (Nov. 1, 2007).
160 *Id.* (citing 34 C.F.R. § 682.206(a)(2)).
161 34 C.F.R. § 682.402(e)(4)(ii).
162 34 C.F.R. § 682.402(e)(6)(v).
163 The Department of Education forms are reprinted at Appendix D, *infra*. They are also available on the Department's website at www.ed.gov.
164 U.S. Dep't of Educ., Dear Colleague Letter 94-G-256, (Sept. 1994), *reprinted at* Appx. C, *infra*, and *available on* the companion website to this manual.
165 34 C.F.R. § 682.402(e)(15).
166 34 C.F.R. § 682.402 (e)(3)–(e)(4).
There is questionable statutory authority for this requirement since the statute provides for assignment of rights only against the school and its affiliates and principals.

provide five signature specimens (two of which are within one year of the disputed signature).[167] When the forgery is on a check endorsement or transfer authorization, the student must state that the student never received the loan proceeds and those proceeds were never credited to amounts owed to the school for that portion of the program that the student completed.[168]

In general, borrowers will find it difficult to obtain a false-certification discharge. It will often be necessary to continue following up on applications and to dispute denials. Since discharge applications often take many years to process, advocates should be prepared to request administrative forbearances for students so that collection activities will cease until the discharge has been granted or denied.[169] The regulations do not specifically grant borrowers an automatic collection stay after applying for a discharge. Stays are granted only if the holder of the loan receives information it believes to be reliable indicating that a borrower is eligible for a discharge.[170] The borrower must respond within sixty days of receiving this notice in order to suspend collection.[171]

The Department expects guaranty agencies to respond to discharge requests within ninety days, although the Department has not set any time limits for its own response to discharge requests.[172] The Department's delays in making decisions on false-certification discharges were among the issues raised in a 1998 class action complaint. The complaint alleged that the Secretary had not assigned adequate staff to administer the program, resulting in a backlog of over 10,000 undecided applications, some of which had been pending for years.[173]

The student has a right to seek review by the Secretary of a guaranty agency denial of a false-certification discharge application.[174]

9.5 Discharge for Unpaid Refunds

9.5.1 General

The unpaid-refund discharge fills in some of the gaps left by the closed-school and false-certification discharges. This provides relief for many, but not all, victims of trade school abuses. The unpaid-refund discharge provides for discharge based on the school's failure to make an owed refund to the student.[175]

9.5.2 Criteria for Unpaid-Refund Discharge

The discharge applies to FFELs and Direct loans disbursed n whole or in part on or after January 1, 1986.[176] Students already can raise an unpaid refund as a defense to the Perkins loan collection action.[177]

The unpaid-refund discharge applies to students who signed up for a school but never attended, who withdrew, or who terminated within a time frame that entitled them to a refund but never received the refund from the school. Students who completed 60% or more of the loan period are not entitled to refunds and therefore not entitled to the discharge.[178] A student should not have to show written proof or other formal proof of withdrawal or termination in order to qualify.

9.5.3 Determining Amount of Discharge

The amount of the unpaid refund will be determined based on information the holder of the loan has or the borrower can provide or by applying the appropriate refund formula to information that the borrower provides or that is otherwise available to the agency. If the actual school refund formula is not available, the regulations set out a substitute formula to determine the amount eligible for discharge.[179]

In these circumstances, the guaranty agency is required to use the following formula to determine the amount eligible for discharge:

- In the case of a student who fails to attend or whose withdrawal or termination date is before October 7, 2000, and who completes less than 60% of the loan period, the guaranty agency discharges the lesser of the institutional charges unearned or the loan amount.[180] The guaranty agency determines the amount of the institutional charges unearned by (A) calculating the ratio of the amount of time in the loan period after the student's last day of attendance to the actual length of the loan period and (B) multiplying the resulting factor by the institutional charges assessed the student for the loan period.[181]
- In the case of a student who fails to attend or whose

---

167 34 C.F.R. § 682.402(e)(3)(iii)–(iv).
168 34 C.F.R. § 682.402(e)(3)(iv).
169 34 C.F.R. § 682.211(f)(8). See also § 4.4.3, supra.
170 34 C.F.R. § 682.402(e)(6)(ii).
171 34 C.F.R. § 682.402(e)(6)(iii).
172 34 C.F.R. § 682.402(e)(6)(iv).
173 White v. Riley, (E.D. Pa. 1998), available on the companion website to this manual (class action complaint).
   A copy of a letter from the Department in a successful false-certification discharge case is reprinted at Appendix D, infra.
174 See 34 C.F.R. § 682.402(e)(11); § 9.15, infra (appeals).

175 20 U.S.C. § 1087(c); 34 C.F.R. §§ 682.402(l) (FFEL), 685.216 (Direct Loan).
176 20 U.S.C. § 1087(c); 34 C.F.R. §§ 682.402(l), 685.216.
177 See § 12.7.2.1, infra.
178 34 C.F.R. § 682.402(o)(2)(iii).
179 34 C.F.R. § 682.402(o)(2).
180 34 C.F.R. § 682.402(o)(2)(i).
181 Id.

withdrawal or termination date is on or after October 7, 2000, and who completes less than 60% of the loan period, the guaranty agency discharges the loan amount unearned. This is determined by (A) calculating the ratio of the amount of time remaining in the loan period after the student's last day of attendance to the actual length of the loan period and (B) multiplying the resulting factor by the total amount of Title IV grants and loans received by the student or, if unknown, the loan amount.[182]

The borrower needs three pieces of information to calculate a refund: the tuition, the school's refund formula, and the percentage of the course or term the borrower completed. The school catalog or the written enrollment agreement will have the tuition, refund policy, and number of weeks per term. State licensing agencies sometimes have school catalogs and/or enrollment contract forms in their files for closed schools. The student must supply the enrollment date and last date of attendance to calculate the percentage of the course completed. A refund is calculated based on the student's last date of attendance (LDA), regardless of whether the student notified the school of his or her withdrawal.

Federal rules have generally required that schools apply refunds of unearned tuition to loans first and then to grants. This rule benefits the borrower because even a partial tuition refund may eliminate the loan balance in full. For example, if the student was entitled to a 50% refund of $5000 in tuition and had a $2500 loan and $2500 in grants, the entire loan should have been refunded by the school. The unpaid refund should be for 100% of the loan amount.

Students who completed 60% or more of the loan period are not entitled to refunds and therefore not entitled to the discharge.[183] On the other hand, most students who never attended classes at all were entitled to a full refund of their loan amount and therefore should get a full discharge of their loans.

9.5.4 Applying for the Discharge

The procedures and timing for a loan discharge are slightly different depending on whether the school is currently open or closed. To qualify for the discharge if the school is still open, the borrower and guarantor must document that they attempted to resolve the problem within 120 days from the date that the borrower submitted a completed application for discharge.[184] This requirement does not apply if the school is closed.

Except when the guaranty agency (with the Department's approval) determines, based on information in its possession, that the borrower qualifies for a discharge, borrowers must submit written discharge applications.[185] Applications should be sent to the holder or guaranty agency. In most cases the holder will be the guaranty agency.[186]

The Department has developed a uniform application form.[187] In addition, the regulations require agencies to send discharge applications to potentially eligible borrowers.[188] Once they do so, they must cease collection until the application is resolved.[189] If the borrower does not return the application within sixty days, collection actions can resume.[190]

There is no time limit for the agency to make a decision. However, once an application is granted, the holder must suspend collection within thirty days, discharge the appropriate amount, and inform the borrower of the determination.[191]

If the application is denied, the holder must notify the borrower in writing of the reason for the determination and of the borrower's right to request review within thirty days of the borrower's submission of additional documentation. Collection must be suspended during the review period.[192]

9.5.5 Relief Available for Those Obtaining a Discharge

Eligible borrowers will be granted a discharge in the amount of the unpaid refund, including any accrued interest and any other charges or fees relating to the amount of the unpaid refund.[193] If the borrower has already paid off part of the loan, and the amount still owing on the loan is less than the unpaid refund, part of the unpaid refund will be used to fully discharge the loan. The rest of the unpaid refund will be paid the borrower in cash to the extent the borrower has made payments of that amount on the loan. The holder of the loan is also required to report the discharge to all credit reporting agencies to which the holder previously reported the status of the loan.[194]

---

182   34 C.F.R. § 682.402(o)(2)(ii).
183   34 C.F.R. § 682.402(o)(2)(iii).
184   34 C.F.R. § 682.402(l)(2)(ii).
185   34 C.F.R. § 682.402(l)(5)(iv).
186   The regulations are slightly different if the lender holds the loan. In such cases, lenders are required to provide the guaranty agency with documentation related to the borrower's qualification for discharge. 34 C.F.R. § 682.402(m).
187   *See* U.S. Dep't of Educ., Dear Guaranty Agency Director Letter Gen-01-15 (Nov. 2001), *available at* www.ed.gov.
188   34 C.F.R. § 682.402(l)(5).
189   34 C.F.R. § 682.402(l)(5)(ii).
190   34 C.F.R. § 682.402(l)(5)(iii).
191   34 C.F.R. § 682.402(l)(5)(vi).
192   34 C.F.R. § 682.402(l)(5)(vii). *See* § 9.15, *infra* (administrative appeals).
193   34 C.F.R. § 682.402(l)(3)(i).
194   34 C.F.R. § 682.402(l)(3)(ii).

9.6 Relationship Between Closed-School, False-Certification, and Unpaid-Refund Discharges

Many victims of proprietary school fraud will be eligible for multiple discharges. The same borrower can apply for more than one discharge but cannot obtain duplicate relief.

However, many victims of fraud will not meet the criteria for one or more of the discharges. For this reason, it is always critical to consider all three kinds of discharges. For example, many borrowers attended schools that were then closed, but these borrowers may not have been, or cannot show that they were, in attendance at the time the school closed or within ninety days of the closure. If a particular borrower is also a high school graduate, he or she may not be eligible for either a closed-school or false-certification-of-ability-to-benefit discharge even if the schooling was worthless. The borrower may, however, be eligible to get at least partial relief from an unpaid-refund discharge. Similarly, a borrower who withdrew from a school within a short period of enrolling or who never attended classes may have both a false-certification-by-forgery and an unpaid-refund claim.

Another avenue to consider, discussed in § 9.7, *infra*, is a disability discharge. In addition, some states have tuition recovery funds that may reimburse all or part of a student's obligation.[195] Bankruptcy, discussed in detail in Chapter 10, *infra*, may also be a viable option, particularly for borrowers with bleak long-term financial prospects.

9.7 Disability Discharge

9.7.1 General

The borrower's permanent and total disability is grounds for a student loan discharge.[196] Prior to 1999, a disabled borrower simply had a licensed physician certify that the borrower was permanently disabled, with an onset date after the date of the loan. This had to be done on the proper form, and the discharge was generally granted.

In 1999, the Department's Inspector General (IG) conducted a study that led to a Department crackdown on alleged fraud. The IG found that 23% of borrowers who received disability discharges in a specified time period worked and earned money after the disability determination was made or the loan was discharged.[197]

In response to these findings, the Department in November 1999 sent out a "Dear Colleague" letter detailing a more aggressive approach to the existing regulation.[198] It then made the disability discharge a focus of the 2000 round of negotiated rulemaking. Some of the new regulations that resulted from rulemaking went into effect on July 1, 2001, although the most significant changes became effective on July 1, 2002.

Most importantly, the Department established a conditional discharge system. Under this program, borrowers who applied for a discharge first obtained preliminary approval from their loan holder. If approved, borrowers had to go through a three-year "waiting period."

The 2008 changes stemmed from a 2005 Inspector General report that highlighted problems with the "retroactive conditional discharge."[199] The IG was especially concerned with circumstances in which a borrower's disability onset date occurred more than three years before the application for disability discharge.

The Department adopted most of the suggestions in the 2005 Inspector General report despite the lack of evidence that there were problems with borrowers receiving retroactive discharges. The 2005 IG report included a limited study of about 2500 borrowers who had received disability discharges, finding that about 54% of these borrowers filed applications more than three years after their reported disability dates.[200] The mere fact that certain borrowers received retroactive discharges, however, does not prove that there were problems with these discharges. Unfortunately, the IG did not dig much deeper.

The process changed yet again on July 1, 2010. The conditional discharge period is eliminated as of this date. Eligible borrowers will get final discharges, but the Department will continue to monitor these borrowers for three years. The evaluation criteria during the three-year period will be the same as the criteria used to monitor borrowers in a conditional discharge period. The difference is that, under the conditional discharge system, if the borrower did not meet the criteria during the three years, he or she would no longer be in a conditional discharge status and would be back in repayment; interest did not accrue during the conditional period.[201] In contrast, under the system effective July 1, 2010, a borrower who does not meet the criteria during the three-year period will have his or her loan reinstated.[202]

---

195 *See* § 12.8, *infra*.
196 20 U.S.C. § 1087(a); 34 C.F.R. §§ 674.61 (Perkins Loan), 682.402(c) (FFEL), 685.213 (Direct Loan).
197 U.S. Dep't of Educ., Office of the Inspector Gen., Final Audit Report: Improving the Process for Forgiving Student Loans, Audit Control No. A06-80001 (June 7, 1999).
198 U.S. Dep't of Educ., Dear Colleague Letter No. GEN-99-36, (Nov. 1999), *available on* the companion website to this manual.
199 U.S. Dep't of Educ., Office of Inspector General, Final Audit Report: Death and Total and Permanent Disability Discharges of FFEL and Direct Loan Program Loans, Audit Control No. ED-OIG/A04E0006 (Nov. 14, 2005).
200 *Id.* at 6.
201 34 C.F.R. § 682.402(c)(4)(iv) (previous regulation).
202 *See* § 9.7.5, *infra*.

The definition of disability has also changed as of July 1, 2010. The new definition, as discussed below, is less restrictive. Advocates have been pushing Congress and the Department to tie the definition of disability to the standard used in other government programs. The Department considered but ultimately dropped this proposal in the 2002 final rules, finding that there was no documentation issued by the Social Security Administration that would effectively establish disability under the Department's standards.[203] The post-July 1, 2010, definition of disability is closer to the Social Security Administration's standard. However, the Department will still not accept proof of Social Security disability as presumptive proof of eligibility for a student loan discharge. In contract, in certain circumstances, the Department will accept a Department of Veterans Affairs (VA) determination as conclusive.[204]

9.7.2 Eligible Loans

Borrowers with FFELs, Direct loans, and Perkins loans are eligible for this discharge.[205] This includes consolidation loans. Parents with PLUS loans may apply for discharges based on their own disabilities, not those of their children. For a PLUS loan, the disability of only one of two obligated parents does not discharge the debt.[206]

Partial discharges are explicitly allowed for borrowers with joint consolidation loans and when one of the borrowers becomes disabled but the other does not qualify for a discharge.[207] The amount discharged is equal to the portion of the outstanding balance of the consolidation loan attributable to the eligible borrower's loans. However, partial discharge of a joint consolidation loan under any of the discharge programs other than the death discharge does not eliminate joint and several liability for the remaining balance of the loan.[208] This issue will be less relevant over time because of the elimination of joint consolidation loans effective July 1, 2006.[209]

There are also separate regulations allowing disability discharges for Health Education Assistance Loan Program (HEAL) loan borrowers. The Secretary of Health and Human Services (HHS) has the authority to discharge HEAL loans based on a finding of total and permanent disability.[210]

Borrowers must provide HHS with medical evidence no more than four months old to substantiate disability claims.[211] The definition of total and permanent disability for HEAL loans is similar to, but not precisely the same as, the definition for most other federal loans. HEAL loans may be discharged if the borrower is "unable to engage in any substantial gainful activity because of a medically determinable impairment, which the Secretary expects to continue for a long and indefinite period of time or to result in death."[212]

There is some question as to whether loans paid in full are eligible to be discharged. The Department apparently has a policy that a loan that has already been paid in full may not be discharged based on the borrower's total and permanent disability.[213] The reasons cited for this policy are, first, that the regulations do not specifically provide for discharge of paid-in-full loans. Second, according to the Department, a paid-in-full loan no longer exists and borrowers cannot claim benefits related to a "non-existent" debt. Third, the Department argues that a borrower who is able to repay the loan after the date he or she is determined to be totally and permanently discharged is presumably not truly disabled.

There are a number of holes in the Department's logic, and this may be an issue that can be successfully challenged. The third rationale is particularly problematic. There are many ways that a borrower can pay off a loan other than through the borrower's own work earnings. For example, a borrower may not have voluntarily paid off his or her loan. Instead, the loan could have been repaid through offsets and other involuntary collection methods.[214] It is also possible that someone else, such as the borrower's parents, may have paid off the loan. The Department appears to take the position that the borrower is solely responsible for discovering the availability of the disability discharge and that the borrower is out of luck if he or she learns of the discharge after the loan is paid off. In contrast, most of the other discharges explicitly allow discharge of both past and current loan obligations.[215]

However, loans reduced to judgment should be eligible for discharge.[216]

---

203 65 Fed. Reg. 65678, 65684 (Nov. 1, 2000).
204 See § 9.7.4.2, infra.
205 34 C.F.R. §§ 674.61 (Perkins Loan), 682.402(c) (FFEL), 685.213 (Direct Loan).
206 34 C.F.R. § 682.402(a)(3).
207 34 C.F.R. §§ 682.402(a)(2), 685.220(l)(3)(ii).
208 67 Fed. Reg. 67048, 67068 (Nov. 1, 2002).
For a death discharge, the lender may not collect from a borrower's estate or from any endorser post-discharge. 34 C.F.R. § 682.402(b)(4).
209 Pub. L. No. 109-171, 120 Stat. 4 (Feb. 8, 2006).
210 42 C.F.R. § 60.39(b)(1). See, e.g., Student Loan Mktg. Ass'n v. Herdman, 2005 WL 648143 (Cal. Ct. App. Mar. 22, 2005) (unpublished).
211 42 C.F.R. § 60.39(b)(2).
212 42 C.F.R. § 60.39(b)(1).
213 This policy is described in copies of e-mail messages obtained in an FOIA request by NCLC.
214 In an e-mail from the Department obtained in an FOIA request, a Department employee states that there may be rare exceptions to the policy against discharges for paid-in-full loans when a final offset that pays a loan in full could not be stopped in time before a disability application was processed.
215 See, e.g., 34 C.F.R. § 682.402(d)(2)(i) (closed school).
216 Borrowers with loans reduced to judgment should also qualify for the closed-school and other federal discharges. This issue came up during spring 2002 negotiated rulemaking sessions with the Department of Education. Among other changes coming out of these sessions, the negotiators agreed to eliminate the rehabilitation right for borrowers with loans reduced to judgment. The Department stated in its explanation in the Federal

9.7.3 Definition of Total and Permanent Disability

9.7.3.1 Definition As of July 1, 2010

The 2008 HEA reauthorization law amended the definition of total and permanent disability in a number of important ways. These amendments became effective on July 1, 2010.[217]

This definition is more favorable for borrowers because it allows discharges to be granted to borrowers who are unable to engage in any substantial gainful activity by reason of any medically determinable physical or mental impairment that can be expected to result in death, can be expected to last for a continuous period of 60 months, or has lasted for a continuous period of 60 months.[218] The definition also covers borrowers that have been determined by the Secretary of Veterans Affairs to be unemployable due to a service-connected condition.[219]

"Substantial gainful activity" is defined as a level of work performed for pay or profit that involves significant physical or mental activities or a combination of both.[220] The Department has explained that the term "work performed for profit" used in this context was borrowed from the Social Security Administration's definition and is intended to cover self-employed individuals who are not paid by an employer. It does not refer to income from sources other than employment. Non-employment income will not be considered, according to the Department, when determining whether a borrower is capable of substantial gainful activity.[221]

The Department explained that the new definition of total and permanent disability is based, in part, on the Social Security Administration's definition of substantial gainful activity.[222] However, the Department stated that its definition relies solely on a medical determination and, unlike the Social Security Administration's standard, does not require a physician to consider whether a borrower can earn more than a specified amount.

9.7.3.2 Definition for Applications Submitted Prior to July 1, 2010

For applications submitted prior to July 1, 2010, borrowers must prove they are unable to work and earn money because of an illness or injury that is expected to continue indefinitely or result in death.[223]

At least one court recognized the difficulty of meeting this definition.[224] The court affirmed that the physician's statements in this case were sufficient to show that the borrower was totally and permanently disabled even though, in the court's word, the doctor could not say flatly and unequivocally as a matter of medical certainty, "I can't salvage him."

Due to advances in modern medicine, it is rare for a physician to be able to state with absolute certainty that a debilitating condition will continue indefinitely or result in death. Doctors should be more comfortable certifying disabilities under the new definition.

9.7.4 Applying For Disability Discharge

9.7.4.1 General

The disability procedures under the post-July 1, 2010, rules are discussed below.

The borrower applies to the loan holder for a discharge. If a borrower has different loan holders, the borrower should submit a separate application to each. The form that was used until August 2010 was developed to incorporate the regulatory changes that went into effect on July 1, 2008.[225] Prior to July 1, 2008, a borrower was not considered disabled based on a condition that existed at the time the borrower applied for the loan unless the condition substantially deteriorated after the loan was made.[226] Thus, the onset date of the disability is relevant only for applications submitted prior to July 1, 2008. As of April 1, 2010, the Department stated that loan holders could no longer accept the previous version of the form.

The Department issued yet another new form in August 2010 to incorporate the regulatory changes that became effective on July 1, 2010.[227] Borrowers who applied after July 1, 2010, but before the new form was available or who otherwise used the old form, should be evaluated under the post-July 1, 2010, standards.[228] Beginning November 1, 2010, only the new form may be provided to borrowers. However, the previous form will be accepted until January

---

Register that this change would not affect other rights for borrowers with judgments, including discharge rights. 67 Fed. Reg. 51036, 51038 (Aug. 6, 2002).

217 Pub. L. No. 110-315, § 437, 122 Stat. 3078 (Aug. 14, 2008).
218 34 C.F.R. § 682.200.
219 *Id. See* § 9.7.4.2, *infra*.
220 34 C.F.R. § 682.200.
221 *Id.*
222 74 Fed. Reg. 36559 (July 23, 2009).
223 34 C.F.R. § 682.200 (previous regulation).
224 United States v. Norton, 2002 WL 1774238 (N.D. Iowa Feb. 5, 2002) (unreported).
225 The form was released in February 2009. The new form, issued on August 16, 2010, is available in Appendix D, *infra*, and on the companion website.
226 34 C.F.R. § 682.402(c)(1)(iii) (previous regulation). A sample complaint in a case in which the Department failed to consider substantial deterioration is available on the companion website to this manual.
227 U.S. Dep't of Educ., Revised Total and Permanent Disability Discharge Application, Dear Colleague Letter GEN-10-15 (Aug. 16, 2010), *reprinted at* Appendix D, *infra*, and *available on* the companion website to this manual.
228 *Id.*

31, 2011.[229] The Department stated that, because the old definition was more restrictive, any borrowers who meet the pre-July 1, 2010, standard as certified on the prior version of the form should be considered totally and permanently disabled in accordance with the revised definition.[230] If the borrower did not meet the prior standards and submitted the prior form, the loan holder should follow up with the doctor to see if the borrower meets the revised definition.

The form gives doctors additional space not only to provide a diagnosis and summary of the borrower's disability but to explain how the borrower's disabilities prevent the borrower from working and earning money.

The form is to be used for both the "special" veterans' application process and for all other applications. Veterans with appropriate VA documentation only have to complete sections one and three on the first page. The August 2010 version of the discharge form has a separate explanation in section 6 with respect to the process for veterans.

Borrowers must submit separate forms to each loan holder. Copies of the original form should be acceptable.[231] However, each copy must have an original borrower signature. Original physician signatures are not required on each copy.

Borrowers are required to submit the form to their loan holders within ninety days of the date the doctor certifies the application.[232] The Department has stated that it will allow five days for mailing so that lenders may stamp the date up to five days earlier than the actual receipt date.[233] If the application is incomplete or the lender needs to clarify the diagnosis or other information, the Department has stated that the lender/loan holder can still use the original submission date in determining whether the borrower met the ninety-day time limit.[234] If the borrower misses the ninety-day deadline, he or she can submit a new application.[235]

Borrowers with Direct loans should send application forms to the address given to them by their servicers. The Department states on its website that the process can take anywhere from a couple of days to several months.

The loan holder makes a preliminary determination as to whether the borrower meets the criteria for a disability discharge. For Perkins loans, the school makes this determination. In the FFEL program, the current holder makes the determination. For Direct loans, the Department's direct loan staff makes the decision.

The Department intends for this preliminary determination to be a rigorous process. The Department's expectations were initially set out in the November 1999 "Dear Colleague" letter and affirmed in the May 2002 letter.

The Department requires guaranty agencies and others making preliminary disability determinations to do the following, at a minimum:

- Require additional information to support the borrower's application when the information provided is not definitive, is illegible, or incomplete.
- Reaffirm the physician's certification if the diagnosis and prognosis do not appear to reach the standard of total and permanent disability. (The Department emphasized that guaranty agencies should ensure that physicians understand that the FFEL definition of total and permanent disability is generally a higher standard than that used by other federal or state agencies for disability.)
- Assist borrowers to obtain deferments or forbearances in cases in which it does not appear that the borrower is totally and permanently disabled.[236]

The Department also suggests that agencies may want to seek the assistance of a qualified physician to evaluate discharge requests.[237]

This is a cumbersome process even in the best of circumstances. Therefore, it is critical that borrowers submit completed applications. Common problems include failure to fill in the onset-of-disability date, failure to sign the application, illegible applications, and failure to provide sufficient supporting documentation. It is critical for the borrower to provide information from the physician that explains the borrower's condition and why this condition is disabling. It is not enough for doctors to list the diagnosis. They must also describe the reasons why the disability prevents the borrower from working. The new form, once it is available, should be more specific about the information required.

In order to help ensure a more efficient process, borrowers should follow these guidelines from the Department:

1. Be sure to sign the application. A photocopy must contain an original signature.
2. Separate applications must be submitted to each loan holder. Copies may be submitted. However, each copy must have an original borrower signature. Original physician signatures are not required on each copy.
3. The application must be signed by a doctor of medicine or osteopathy who is licensed to practice in the United States.
4. The doctor must complete the application.
5. Doctors should not use medical abbreviations or insur-

---

229 *Id.*
230 *Id.*
231 The form states that originals or copies are acceptable.
232 34 C.F.R. § 682.402(c)(2).
233 U.S. Dep't of Educ., Changes in Assignment Procedures for Conditional Disability Discharge (July 9, 2008) (see attachment entitled "Questions and Answers Related to Regulatory Changes Effective 07/01/2008"), *available at* http://ifap.ed.gov/eannouncements/070908CondDisability.html.
234 *Id.*
235 *Id.*

236 U.S. Dep't of Educ., Dear Colleague Letter GEN-02-03 (May 2002), *reprinted at* Appx. C, *infra*; U.S. Dep't of Educ., Dear Colleague Letter No. GEN-99-36, (Nov. 1999), *reprinted at* Appx. C, *infra*, and *available on* the companion website to this manual.
237 U.S. Dep't of Educ., Dear Colleague Letter GEN-02-03 (May 2002).

ance codes on the application.
6. The doctor must provide more than a diagnosis. The doctor must also identify the medical condition and clearly and fully explain how the condition prevents the borrower from working and earning money.
7. The doctor may submit additional information with the application.
8. Any alterations by the doctor must be initialed by the doctor.

According to 2008 guidance from the Department, prior to accepting assignment from a loan holder, the Department will check to ensure that the doctor has provided sufficient responses to the medical questions on the application.[238] The Department claims that it is developing guidelines to help loan holders ensure that the doctor's responses are complete. The key point is that doctors must not only provide a diagnosis but also explain how the disability prevents the borrower from working and earning money. The Department has instructed loan holders that they must get this additional information from the doctors in writing and that they may not prepare a letter for the doctor to sign.[239] The Department claims that it now gives physicians reasonable time periods to respond to requests for additional information. The Department has also created a new website (disabilitydischarge.ed.gov) pertaining to disability discharges that includes different sections for borrowers, loan holders, and physicians.

The lender may continue collection until it receives the certification of disability.[240] After receiving the certification, the lender must cease collection efforts.[241]

Lenders are required to provide guaranty agencies with disability claims within sixty days of the date on which they determine that a borrower is totally and permanently disabled.[242]

Guaranty agencies must review disability claims not later than ninety days after the lender files the claim.[243] For veteran discharges, guaranty agencies must review the claims promptly and submit them to the Department not later than forty-five days after the lender submits the claim to the agency.[244]

If the guaranty agency does not approve the claim, it must return it to the lender with an explanation of the basis for the denial.[245] The lender must then notify the borrower that the application has been denied, provide the basis for the denial, and inform the borrower that the lender will resume collection.[246]

If the guaranty agency makes a preliminary determination of eligibility, the agency should stop all collection efforts. Even though it may take three or four months for the agency to assign the account to the Department, the borrower should not be facing collection efforts during this time.

For FFELs, the loan is assigned to the Disability Discharge Unit if both the loan holder and the guaranty agency, if different, decide that the borrower is eligible for discharge.[247] The guaranty agency must notify the borrower that the loan is being assigned to the Department and that no payments are due on the loan.

In cases in which preliminary approval is granted, Perkins loans holders (schools) are required to assign the loans to the Department's Disability Discharge Unit and notify borrowers of the assignment.[248]

The Department will review all preliminarily approved loans to affirm that the borrower meets the disability discharge criteria. The Department reserves the right to require the borrower to submit additional medical evidence.[249] As part of this review, the Department may arrange for an additional medical review by an independent doctor at no expense to the borrower.[250]

A 2005 report by the Department's Inspector General contains different estimates of the percentage of physicians contacted after disability applications are received. A nurse in the Conditional Disability Discharge Unit reported that physicians are contacted for approximately half of the disability discharge applications the unit receives. The Department responded that its contractor follows up with physicians for approximately 70% of cancellation applications received.[251]

In the case of Direct loans, there is no deadline for the Department to make a determination once it receives an application from a guaranty agency or a borrower. However, during this review period, all collection activity should cease and interest should not be accruing on the borrower's loans.[252]

The Department provided NCLC with the following explanation of the procedures for disability discharges for

---

238 U.S. Dep't of Educ., Changes in Assignment Procedures for Conditional Disability Discharge (July 9, 2008), *available at* http://ifap.ed.gov/eannouncements/070908CondDisability.html.
239 U.S. Dep't of Educ., Financial Student Assistance, Clarification of Previous Disability Notice (Apr. 7, 2008).
240 34 C.F.R. § 682.402(c)(7).
241 Id.
242 34 C.F.R. § 682.402(g)(2)(i).
243 34 C.F.R. § 682.402(h)(1)(i)(B).
244 34 C.F.R. § 682.402(h)(1)(v).
245 34 C.F.R. § 682.402(c)(7)(v).

246 Id.
247 34 C.F.R. § 682.402(c)(2),(7).
248 34 C.F.R. § 674.61(b)(2)(v),(vi).
249 34 C.F.R. § 682.402(c)(3)(iv).
250 Id.
251 U.S. Dep't of Educ., Office of Inspector Gen., Final Audit Report: Death and Total and Permanent Disability Discharges of FFEL and Direct Loan Program Loans, Audit Control No. ED-OIG/A04E006, at 15 (Nov. 14, 2005).
252 Department staff confirmed in a July 2003 conversation with NCLC that it would not continue to collect while still reviewing loans. They did not cite regulatory authority, but the Department should be bound by 34 C.F.R. § 682.402(c)(7)(i), which requires that lenders cease collection activity after receiving the disability certification.

borrowers who are already facing collection. According to the Department:

> If certain collection activities are in place when a borrower applies for a total and permanent disability discharge, it would be administratively burdensome and costly to require the loan holder to cease those collection activities only to restart them if the borrower does not qualify for the discharge. Therefore, in cases in which a judgment against the borrower has already been obtained, the loan holder is not required to suspend enforcement of the judgment or vacate the judgment during the review period.[253] If the loan holder approves the discharge claim, the judgment should be transferred to the Department when the loan is assigned. Similarly, if an AWG [administrative wage garnishment] wage withholding order was already in place when the borrower submitted the application for disability discharge, the loan holder is not required to withdraw the wage withholding order during the review period. If Federal or State Offset has already been initiated by the Federal or State government, the loan holder is not required to halt the Offset during the review process. After a loan holder makes a preliminary determination that the borrower meets the criteria for a total and permanent disability discharge, the loan holder must withdraw the wage withholding order, halt State Offset, or send a record on its next Weekly Update tape to inactivate the account from the Treasury Offset Program. If a loan holder makes a preliminary determination that the borrower does not meet the criteria for a total and permanent disability discharge, the loan holder should resume routine collection activity. Borrowers that receive a favorable preliminary determination are assigned to the Department for further review. If the Department finds such a borrower ineligible at any point in the conditional discharge process, the Department will reinstate that borrower to servicing and collection activity will resume.

If there is a delay after submission of a completed application, the borrower may request an administrative forbearance to stop collection during the review period. Loan holders may grant discretionary forbearances to disabled borrowers. The regulations are slightly different for FFELs and Direct loans. For Direct loans, forbearances may be granted for a period after the Secretary receives reliable information indicating that the borrower has become totally and permanently disabled and until the Secretary receives documentation confirming total and permanent disability.[254]

There may be conflicting interpretations of this provision within the Department. Although the Department acknowledges that it will sometimes cease collection upon receipt of a disability discharge request, staff may be reluctant to call this cessation a "forbearance." However, the regulation cited above clearly gives the Department discretion to grant a forbearance in these circumstances. A similar provision applies to FFELs.[255]

If the Department agrees with the preliminary determination, the borrower as of July 1, 2010 will get a final discharge *beginning on the date the doctor signed and completed the form*.[256] The Department must notify the borrower of discharge.[257] Any payments received after the date the doctor certified the application must be returned. The notice must also explain the terms and conditions under which the borrower's obligation to repay may be reinstated.[258]

The Department may also deny the discharge. In these circumstances, the Department must send a notice that the discharge application has been denied and that the loan is due and payable.[259] Such denials may be appealed under the judicial review provision of the Administrative Procedure Act.[260]

9.7.4.2 Process for Certain Veterans

The post-July 1, 2010, definition of total and permanent disability includes borrowers who have been determined by the Secretary of Veterans Affairs to be unemployable due to service-connected conditions and who provide documentation of such determination.[261] These borrowers are not required to present additional documentation.

The veteran "exception" to the typical disability discharge process went into effect on August 14, 2008.[262] Veterans must submit the same disability discharge application as other borrowers. However, if the application includes documentation from the Department of Veterans Affairs (VA) showing that the veteran is unemployable due to a service-connected disability, the veteran will not be required to provide any additional documentation related to

---

253 *See, e.g.*, U.S. v. Emanuel, 2009 WL 4884482 (D.N.H. Dec. 10, 2009) (administrative discharge provisions make no distinction between loans that are in process of being collected and those reduced to judgment).
254 34 C.F.R. § 685.205(b)(5).
255 34 C.F.R. § 682.211(f)(5).
  The Department may argue that these regulations apply only after the discharge application is submitted to the disability discharge unit. Borrowers should challenge this restrictive reading of the regulation. However, borrowers may get the same result by requesting an agreement to cease collection rather than a forbearance.
256 34 C.F.R. §§ 674.61(b) (Perkins Loan), 682.402(c)(3) (FFEL), 685.213(b)(2) (Direct Loan).
257 34 C.F.R. § 682.402(c)(3)(ii).
258 *Id.*
259 34 C.F.R. § 682.402(c)(3)(iii).
260 *See* § 9.15, *infra*.
261 34 C.F.R. § 682.200.
262 34 C.F.R. §§ 682.402(c)(8), 685.213(c).

the veteran's disability.²⁶³ Furthermore, the reinstatement period does not apply to veterans qualifying for discharge under this section.²⁶⁴ The August 2010 version of the discharge form has a separate explanation in section 6 with respect to the process for veterans.

The Department issued a Dear Colleague letter in May 2009 summarizing these procedures.²⁶⁵ The letter describes two types of VA determinations that qualify a veteran for the student loan discharge: (1) A determination that the veteran has a service-connected disability or service-connected disabilities that are 100% disabling or (2) a determination that the veteran is totally disabled based on an individual unemployability determination.

According to the Department of Education's letter, the VA grants individual unemployability only for service-connected conditions. However, in the case of a determination that a veteran is 100% disabled, the determination must specify that the disabilities are service-connected.

The documentation from different VA offices may use different terminology. For example, acceptable documentation might say that a borrower has been granted "entitlement to individual unemployability" or that a borrower is "permanently and totally disabled" or "unable to work and earn money." There is no specific language that must be included in the VA determination in order for a veteran to qualify for the Department of Education discharge.²⁶⁶

If a veteran's application is denied because the disabilities are not service-connected, the loan holder must advise the borrower to re-apply through the "standard" disability discharge process.²⁶⁷ The borrower may include the VA documentation as well as any other supporting documentation with this application and must get a doctor to sign the application. The Department also promised to review applications already in the pipeline to identify veterans who might qualify for immediate discharge under this standard. Eligible veterans in a three-year conditional discharge period may also qualify for immediate discharge. These veterans will generally need to contact the Department to request immediate discharge.

9.7.5 Reinstatement Period

9.7.5.1 General

Although the conditional discharge period is eliminated as of July 1, 2010, the Department has the authority to reinstate a loan after a discharge based on the same disqualifying grounds as in the prior conditional program. The medical review process will be the same.²⁶⁸

The two main factors that the Department will consider during the three-year period are whether the borrower has earnings beyond a minimally acceptable amount and whether the borrower has incurred new federal student loans.

With respect to earnings, borrowers will have their loans reinstated during the three years if their annual earnings from employment during that time exceed 100% of the poverty line for a family of two.²⁶⁹ The Department's disability discharge website includes a table describing the notification used for verifying employment earnings.²⁷⁰ The Department generally sends borrowers a notice with the most recent poverty line information.

The second requirement is that borrowers may not incur new federal student loans during the three-year period. The regulations only prohibit borrowers from receiving new loans under the Perkins Loan, FFEL, or Direct Loan Programs.²⁷¹ This also includes TEACH grants.²⁷² These borrowers should be able to go to school without jeopardizing eligibility for a discharge and they can even take out non-federal loans or grants.

An exception to the federal loan prohibition is that the borrower is permitted to receive an FFEL or Direct consolidation loan during the three-year period as long as it does not include any loans that were discharged.²⁷³

Another exception is if the borrower received a loan disbursement after the date the doctor signed the application, as long as the disbursement is returned within 120 days of the disbursement.²⁷⁴

During the three-year period, the loan is discharged, so the borrower is not required to make any payments. Under the previous conditional discharge system, borrowers were also not required to make any payments on the loan. The loan is not considered past due or in default. Borrowers are required to notify the Department if their annual earnings exceed the poverty line limit.²⁷⁵

If, at any time during the three-year period, the Department finds that the borrower has earnings above the allowable limit or takes out a new federal loan, the Department

---

263 *Id.*
264 34 C.F.R. §§ 682.402(c)(5)(i), 685.213(b)(4). *See* § 9.7.5, *infra.*
265 U.S. Dep't of Educ., Procedures for Discharging Title IV Loans Based on a Determination by the Department of Veterans Affairs That a Veteran Is Unemployable Due to a Service-Connected Condition or Disability, Dear Colleague Letter GEN-09-07 (May 15, 2009). The letter is reprinted at Appendix C, *infra*, and available on the companion website to this manual as well as on the Department of Education's website.
266 *Id.*
267 34 C.F.R. §§ 682.402(c)(8)(ii)(C), 685.213(c)(2)(ii)(B).

268 34 C.F.R. § 682.402(c)(5).
269 34 C.F.R. § 682.402(c)(5)(i).
270 *See* disabilitydischarge.ed.gov.
271 34 C.F.R. § 682.402(c)(5)(i)(B).
272 *Id. See* § 1.4.2.3, *supra.*
273 34 C.F.R. § 682.402(c)(5)(ii)(B).
274 34 C.F.R. § 682.402(c)(5)(i)(C).
275 34 C.F.R. § 682.402(c)(6)(ii).

will reinstate the loan and resume collection. As with the conditional discharge, borrowers are not required to pay interest on the loan from when the loan was discharged until the date of reinstatement.[276]

The advantages to borrowers under the new system are that the definition of disability is less restrictive and they will be able to get final discharges as soon as the Department approves applications. The main problem is that the consequences of reinstatement can be more severe than losing eligibility during a conditional period. Borrowers who lose eligibility for a conditional discharge can reapply for disability discharge at a later date. This is presumably not the case if a loan is reinstated. In response to questions from NCLC, the Department states that a reinstated loan will not be considered a new loan. The Department claims that this reinstated loan will be treated like any new loan taken out by the borrower in that the loan will only be dischargeable again if there is substantial deterioration in the borrower's condition.[277]

9.7.5.2 Notice of Reinstatement

To help ensure that borrowers know the consequences of reinstatement, the Department is required to notify the borrower of reinstatement, including the reason or reasons for reinstatement, an explanation that the first loan payment following reinstatement will be due no earlier than sixty days after the date of the notice, and information on how the borrower may contact the Department if the borrower has questions about the reinstatement or believes that the loan was reinstated based on incorrect information.[278]

When negotiating these regulations, the Department did not agree to provide similar notice requirements in the regulations for the application approval and denial process. They acknowledged that there are problems with the notices and that they would take steps to further improve notices to borrowers who have applied for or received disability discharges.[279] In particular, the Department intends to take steps to develop a process to acknowledge receipt of a borrower's submission of a request that the Department reconsider its determination and to provide borrowers with information on the process for considering such requests.

9.7.6 When Work Is Allowed

The question of whether a "disabled" borrower can work and, if so, when, is particularly confusing. There are numerous contradictions in Department regulations and policy in this area.

According to the Department, a physician may not certify that a borrower has a total and permanent disability if, at the time of the physician's certification, the borrower is currently able or is expected to be able to work and earn money. Minimal earnings are allowed during the three-year reinstatement period (and previously during the three-year conditional discharge period), but the borrower must not be working and earning money at the time the doctor signed the discharge application form.

The regulations are contradictory in at least two fundamental ways. First, the borrower is allowed to have minimal earnings during the reinstatement period. Second, the borrower may get new loans, go back to school, and presumably earn money after the reinstatement period is over and after he or she has received a final discharge. There are certain requirements that the borrower must meet to get a new loan under these circumstances.[280]

The Department has acknowledged that advances in medical treatment may result in an improvement in the borrower's condition that could not be predicted at the time of the physician's certification.[281] In addition, changes in employment conditions may allow a borrower to return to work despite his or her condition. The Department has stated that it does not wish to discourage disabled individuals from attempting employment. Accordingly, the regulations do not disqualify borrowers who have minimal earnings during the reinstatement period. However, at least at the time the physician makes the determination, the borrower should not be working, even minimally.

The elimination of the conditional discharge period may have particular implications in this area. Previously, borrowers who earned above the allowable limit during the conditional discharge period faced the prospect of losing the conditional discharge. These borrowers, however, could clearly reapply for disability discharge. In contrast, if a borrower's loan is reinstated, it is unclear whether they can reapply for a discharge.[282]

9.7.7 Effect of Final Discharge

If the borrower obtains a final discharge, the balance of the loan is discharged.[283] For applications received before July 1, 2008, any payments received after the date the borrower became disabled are to be returned.[284] For applications received after July 1, 2008, only payments received after the doctor signed the form are to be returned.[285]

Borrowers who have received final discharges but wish to take out new loans must, first, obtain certification from a

---

276 34 C.F.R. § 682.402(c)(5)(ii).
277 *See* § 9.7.7, *infra*.
278 34 C.F.R. §§ 682.402(c)(5)(ii)–(iii), 685.213(b)(4)(iii).
279 74 Fed. Reg. 36559 (July 23, 2009).

280 *See* § 9.7.7, *infra*.
281 *See* 65 Fed. Reg. 65681, 65687 (Nov. 1, 2000).
282 *See* § 9.7.7, *infra*.
283 34 C.F.R. § 682.402(c)(3)(ii).
284 34 C.F.R. § 682.402(c)(1)(i), (r)(2), (3) (previous regulations).
285 34 C.F.R. § 682.402(c)(3)(ii).

physician that they are able to engage in substantial gainful activity and, second, sign a statement acknowledging that the loans they receive cannot be discharged in the future on the basis of any impairment present when the new loans were obtained, unless that impairment substantially deteriorates.[286] A third requirement applies only to borrowers who received final discharges on or after July 1, 2001, and before July 1, 2002. These borrowers must meet the two other requirements discussed above. In addition, if they apply for another loan within three years from the disability onset date, they must reaffirm the previously discharged loan before receiving the new loan.[287] This provision mirrors the requirements in the conditional discharge program that became effective in July 2002 but was eliminated as of July 1, 2010.

In response to questions from NCLC, the Department stated that it would apply the standards described to loans reinstated under the post-July 1, 2010, regulations.[288] The provisions for new loans after discharge refer to borrowers who discharged "prior" loans. The Department concedes that they do not view reinstated loans as new loans but will use the "new loan" standards in deciding whether to grant subsequent requests for discharge.

Borrowers who applied prior to July 1, 2010, and received only a conditional discharge must obtain certification from a physician that they are able to engage in substantial gainful activity and sign a statement acknowledging that the loan they receive cannot be discharged in the future on the basis of any impairment present when they applied for a total and permanent disability discharge or when the new loan is made unless the impairment substantially deteriorates. In addition, these borrowers must sign a statement acknowledging that the loan which has been conditionally discharged cannot be discharged in the future on the basis of any impairment present when the borrower applied for a total and permanent disability discharge or when the new loan is made, unless the impairment substantially deteriorates, and that collection activity will resume on any loans in a conditional discharge period.[289] This is confusing because the regulations refer to loans that have been placed in a conditional-discharge period prior to a final determination of total and permanent disability. In fact, the borrower is required to obtain a determination of total and permanent disability before the borrower can get a conditional discharge. Perhaps the Department is referring to borrowers who have obtained conditional discharges but have not yet waited the required period of time in order to qualify for a final discharge.

9.7.8 Potential Roadblocks

Doctors often express confusion about the standards required for discharge. The problem is exacerbated by potentially misleading forms that the Department routinely sends to physicians. In communicating with doctors, advocates should emphasize the regulatory definition rather than the questions asked in follow-up forms.

The Department claims that it has changed its system and now gives physicians reasonable time periods to respond to requests for additional information. The Department has also created a website about disability discharges (disabilitydischarge.ed.gov) that includes different sections for borrowers, loan holders, and physicians.

Regardless, advocates and borrowers will often face problems when doctors are required to fill out follow-up requests for information. The application may be denied if a doctor does not respond. Unfortunately, the borrower may not know that a doctor's non-response is the reason for denial because denial letters do not include adequate explanations. This is another area that the Department claims it will improve.

Data collected by guaranty agencies, as well as anecdotal information, points to a very high rate of denials due to "medical review failures." This is likely because of the arbitrariness of the Department's review process. Among other problems, follow-up letters are sent to physicians requesting very short response times, often only three days. In addition, questions on the follow-up forms can be misleading.

Borrowers should not assume that a denial based on "medical review failure" is necessarily tied to an actual medical review. Instead, this is a generic denial category that can mean anything from a missing license number to an actual medical review failure.

The lack of information, particularly reasons for denials, is likely to remain a problem and should be subject to legal challenge. A March 2009 federal district court decision agreed with a borrower's claims that the Department's current disability discharge process violates constitutional due process rights.[290] This was an appeal of a disability discharge decision under the Administrative Procedure Act.[291] The borrowers in this case had received preliminary determinations of eligibility. The Department later denied the applications based on "medical review failure."

The court found that there is a property right at stake in this process sufficient to trigger constitutional due process rights. The court then found that the current process does not meet constitutional due process standards. The court agreed that a trial-type hearing is not required but that borrowers must still be given an opportunity to be heard at a meaningful time and in a meaningful manner. In this case,

---

286 34 C.F.R. § 682.201(a)(6)(i)–(ii).
287 34 C.F.R. § 682.201(a)(6)(iii).
288 See § 9.7.5, supra.
289 34 C.F.R. § 682.201(a)(7).

290 Higgins v. Spellings, 663 F. Supp. 2d 788 (W.D. Mo. 2009).
291 See § 9.15, infra.

the borrowers were not given a minimal opportunity to submit additional information, and they had no knowledge of what evidence was being considered with regard to their claims. The court also disagreed with the Department's claims that additional procedural requirements would create significant burdens for the agency.

One of the court's greatest concerns was the lack of adequate notice of the reasons for the denial. The court noted that the term "medical review failure" was not defined in the letter. The court also disapproved of the Department's regular practice of telling borrowers to simply start over again and to reapply. Among other reasons, the court noted that there is no guarantee that the outcome will be different upon re-application. Re-application is also detrimental to borrowers because it moves up the date on which the three-year conditional period begins, affecting the date for possible refunds.

To address some of these problems, the Department has begun to provide minimal explanations of the reasons for disability discharge denials. However, they continue to routinely deny applications even for technical problems such as a doctor's failure to properly check one box in an otherwise complete application. NCLC has seen notices that advise borrowers to reapply in these circumstances. In an August 2009 denial letter, an application was denied because the doctor failed to check one box on the form. There was no indication that anyone at the Department had tried to contact the doctor to resolve the problem. Instead, the Department rejected the application. In a sign of improvement, the letter included a basic reason for denial. However, the borrower was not advised of any opportunity to resolve the existing application. Instead, the letter included a copy of a new application, and the borrower was advised that he had thirty days to send in the new application. Advocates should contact the Department under these types of circumstances and insist on resolving any errors in the original application rather than reapplying, especially if it will be difficult for the borrower to get another form from the doctor or if reapplying will otherwise prejudice the borrower.

The Department has set up a Disability Discharge Loan Servicing Center. The center can be contacted by phone at 1-888-869-4169, by e-mail at disability_discharge@acs-inc.com, or by regular mail at U.S. Department of Education Disability Discharge Loan Servicing Center, P.O. Box 5200, Greenville, TX 75403-5200. Hearing-impaired individuals with access to a TDD can call 1-888-636-6401.

9.8 Discharge Based on Death

The borrower's death is a defense to collection actions on Stafford, SLS, Perkins, and Federal Direct loans.[292] The death of both parents (assuming both parents are obligated) or the death of the student discharges PLUS loans.[293] The death of only one of two obligated parents does not discharge a PLUS loan.[294]

Partial discharges are explicitly allowed for borrowers with joint consolidation loans if one of the borrowers dies.[295] The amount discharged is equal to the portion of the outstanding balance of the consolidation loan attributable to the eligible borrower's loans.

Even the death discharge has been controversial. In the same Inspector General report that found alleged disability discharge abuse, the Department of Education concluded that some borrowers were continuing to live and work after receiving death discharges.[296] The Department expressed concern that documentation used to support death discharges may be easily forged or may not provide definitive proof of death. To address this issue, the Department required an original or certified copy of a death certificate in most circumstances.[297] The regulations were later changed to allow use of an accurate and complete photocopy of the original or certified copy of the borrower's death certificate, in addition to the original or certified copy, to support the death discharge.[298]

9.9 Profession-Related Loan Cancellations

9.9.1 General

Congress routinely considers various proposals to grant loan forgiveness to borrowers in socially desirable professions. In response to claims that these borrowers are unable to work in professions such as teaching, public interest law, and social work, Congress in 2007 also passed a loan forgiveness program for public service employees.[299]

Despite the numerous proposals to expand loan-forgiveness programs, there has been very little assessment of the effectiveness of these programs. A 2004 report funded by

---

292 20 U.S.C. § 1087; 34 C.F.R. §§ 674.61(a), 682.402(b), 685.212(a).
293 34 C.F.R. § 682.402(b)(1).
294 20 U.S.C. § 1087(a); 34 C.F.R. § 682.402(a)(3).
295 34 C.F.R. §§ 682.402(a)(2), 685.220(l)(3)(ii).
296 *See* U.S. Dep't of Educ., Dear Colleague Letter GEN-99-36 (Nov. 1999), *available on* the companion website to this manual (citing Office of Inspector General study that found that 2% of borrowers who received death discharges were working and earning money after loans were discharged).
 In a 2005 report, the Inspector General concluded that the new controls over the death-discharge process were adequate. U.S. Dep't of Educ., Office of Inspector Gen., Final Audit Report: Death and Total and Permanent Disability Discharges of FFEL and Direct Loan Program Loans, Control No. ED-OIG/A04E0006 (Nov. 14, 2005).
297 34 C.F.R. §§ 682.402(b)(2) (FFEL), 685.212(a)(3) (Direct Loan).
298 34 C.F.R. § 682.402(b)(2)–(3).
299 This program was part of the College Cost Reduction and Access Act of 2007. Pub. L. No. 110-84, 121 Stat 784 (Sept. 27, 2007).

the Lumina Foundation examined state and federal loan-forgiveness programs.[300] The scope of the report was limited, as the researchers gathered data on only 100 of the approximately 161 programs. About 75% of these programs were loan-forgiveness programs and the others were loan-repayment programs that repay existing education debt in exchange for specified work. Teaching, nursing, and medicine were the three fields most likely to be covered by such programs.

Only 48 of the 122 loan-forgiveness programs were able to provide any data about how many students had fulfilled their work commitments. Those programs reported that, on average, 63% of participants had completed at least some job service.[301]

This report provides a starting point for measuring the effectiveness of these programs with respect to the numbers of borrowers who drop out of the programs, the extent to which the programs help address labor shortages, and whether the programs attract students who otherwise might not have entered the targeted occupations.

The need for relief for borrowers who work in low-paying professions is clear. These programs are intended to address the concern that, if the cost of education continues to grow at its current pace, lower- and middle-income students will simply be unable to work as teachers, social workers, doctors, or lawyers serving under-privileged communities. This is a very serious issue. However, many of these borrowers are receiving some income and are able to make some payments. The problem is that their monthly payments are often too high and the total amount to be repaid is unaffordable. The State PIRGs found, for example, that 23% of public college and 38% of private college graduates would have unmanageable debt as starting teachers. The percentages are even higher for social workers, with 37% of public college and 55% of private college graduates facing unmanageable debt.[302]

9.9.2 Public Service Cancellation

9.9.2.1 General

This program is available to borrowers who work in public service jobs for ten years and repay their loans through an eligible repayment plan. The remaining balance is then forgiven after the ten years of service is completed.

There is a danger of overselling this program. Only borrowers with Direct loans qualify and only payments made after October 2007 in the Direct Loan Program count toward the ten-year forgiveness. Many borrowers will not complete ten years of public service. A larger group is likely to pay off their loans before the ten-years period of public service expires.

Borrowers with low-paying jobs repaying through an income-based plan and with high loan balances are most likely to qualify. Higher loan balances are more likely to occur in the federal loan programs now that graduate and professional students may take out PLUS loans. There are no loan limits in the Direct PLUS Loans program.[303]

9.9.2.2 Eligible Borrowers

The public service program applies only to Direct loan borrowers, but it covers all types of Direct loans, including Stafford, PLUS, and consolidation loans. Most borrowers with other federal government loans can consolidate with Direct loans in order to obtain this benefit.[304]

Parent PLUS loan borrowers are eligible based on their own public service jobs. However, because parent PLUS loan borrowers are not eligible for income-based repayment (IBR) or income-contingent repayment (ICR), it is unclear how they would have a balance left after ten years.[305]

Borrowers with other types of government loans who think they might be eligible for this program should seriously consider consolidating with Direct loans as soon as possible because only payments made through the Direct Loan Program count toward the ten-year forgiveness period. Borrowers who have previously consolidated their loans are specifically allowed to reconsolidate to use the public service program.[306]

According to the Department, joint consolidation loan borrowers are also eligible. However, if only one of the borrowers meets the criteria, the forgiveness after ten years will apply only to the balance attributable to that borrower's loans.[307]

---

300 Andrea R. Berger, Elana Benatar, Rita J. Kirshstein, & David Rhodes, American Inst. for Research, *Workforce Contingent Financial Aid: How States Link Financial Aid to Employment* (Feb. 2004), *available at* www.luminafoundation.org/research/Workforce.pdf. *See also* Peter Schmidt, *Programs That Pay Tuition in Exchange for Work Are Unproved, Report Says*, Chron. of Higher Educ., Feb. 27, 2004, at A20.

301 Andrea R. Berger, Elana Benatar, Rita J. Kirshstein, & David Rhodes, American Inst. for Research, *Workforce Contingent Financial Aid: How States Link Financial Aid to Employment* (Feb. 2004), *available at* www.luminafoundation.org/research/Workforce.pdf.

302 State PIRGS' Higher Educ. Project, Paying Back, Not Giving Back: Student Debt's Negative Impact on Public Service Career Opportunities (Apr. 2006), *available at* http://pirg.org/highered/payingback.pdf.

303 *See* § 2.2.3, *supra*.
304 *See* § 6.2, *supra*.
305 *See* § 6.2, *supra*.
306 34 C.F.R. § 685.220(d)(1)(i)(B)(3), (5).
307 U.S. Dep't of Educ., Questions and Answers about Public Service Loan Forgiveness (Feb. 3, 2010), *available at* http://studentaid.ed.gov/students/attachments/siteresources/PSLF_QAs_final_02%2012%2010.pdf.

In order to qualify, borrowers must not be in default and must have made 120 monthly payments (ten years of payments) on their loans *after* October 1, 2007. Payments can be made through any one or combination of eligible repayment plans—including the IBR, ICR, ten-year standard, or any other plan—if the monthly payment amount is not less than what the borrower would have to pay under the standard plan.[308]

Borrowers must be employed in a public service job at the time of the forgiveness and must have been employed in a public service job during the period in which they made each of the 120 payments.

9.9.2.3 Eligible Jobs

Jobs with federal, state, local, or tribal government organizations, public child or family service agencies, 501(c)(3) nonprofit organizations, or tribal colleges or universities should be considered "public service jobs."[309] Government employers should include the military, public schools, and colleges but does not include members of Congress. Time spent serving in a full-time AmeriCorps position also counts toward fulfilling the ten-year repayment requirement.[310]

Some borrowers who work in certain jobs but not for an employer in one of the categories discussed above should also qualify. Borrowers who are working for organizations that provide any of the following services should qualify:

- Emergency management
- Military service
- Public safety
- Law enforcement
- Public interest law services
- Early childhood education (including licensed or regulated child care, Head Start, and state-funded pre-kindergarten)
- Public service for individuals with disabilities and the elderly, public health (including nurses, nurse practitioners, nurses in a clinical setting, and full-time professionals engaged in health care practitioner occupations and health care support occupations, as such terms are defined by the Bureau of Labor Statistics)
- Public education
- Public library services, school library or other school-based services[311]

These employers must not be organized for profit, a labor union, a partisan political organization, or an organization engaged in religious activities, unless the qualifying activities are unrelated to religious instruction, worship services, or any form of proselytizing.[312]

The discharge is based on the employer's eligibility, not the type of job. Anyone working full-time for a qualifying employer, regardless of his or her job, may qualify.

The law also states that the public service job must be "full-time." This is defined as working in qualifying employment in one or more jobs for the greater of an annual average of at least thirty hours per week; or, for a contractual or employment period of at least eight months, an average of thirty hours per week; or, unless the qualifying employment is with two or more employers, the number of hours the employer considers full-time.[313] There is no requirement that borrowers must work in the same public service job for the entire ten-year period. There is also no requirement that the ten years of public service be consecutive.

According to the Department, borrowers employed by private companies doing work under contract with state government or nonprofits do not qualify.[314] In addition, borrowers must be hired and paid by a qualifying employer.[315] This means, for example, that unpaid internships are not covered. Borrowers may be working in more than one job as long as the multiple jobs meet the full-time definition.

9.9.2.4 Applying for Public Service Cancellation

The regulations do not explain what type of information will be required at the end of the ten-year period to prove eligibility. The Department has stated that it will not accept annual borrower submissions of eligibility information, claiming that tracking and reviewing documents on an annual basis is too complex and costly. The Department said that it is the borrower's responsibility to gather and maintain the documents to support eligibility.[316]

In a February 2010 document listing questions and answers, the Department reiterated that it is the borrower's responsibility to have documentation that supports a request for loan forgiveness. This includes documentation from the borrower's employer or employers.[317] The Department states that it is developing an application that borrowers may use to document qualifying employment during the ten years. Until the form becomes available, the Department advises

---

308 34 C.F.R. § 685.219(c)(iv)).
309 34 C.F.R. § 685.219(b).
310 34 C.F.R. § 685.219(c)(iii).
311 34 C.F.R. § 685.219(b).
312 *Id.*

313 *Id.*
314 U.S. Dep't of Educ., Questions and Answers about Public Service Loan Forgiveness (Feb. 3, 2010), *available at* http://studentaid.ed.gov/students/attachments/siteresources/PSLF_QAs_final_02%2012%2010.pdf.
315 34 C.F.R. § 685.219(b) (definition of "employee" or "employed").
316 73 Fed. Reg. 37694, 37705 (July 1, 2008).
317 U.S. Dep't of Educ., Questions and Answers about Public Service Loan Forgiveness (Feb. 3, 2010), *available at* http://studentaid.ed.gov/students/attachments/siteresources/PSLF_QAs_final_02%2012%2010.pdf.

borrowers to keep records that clearly identify employers, show that the employer meets the definition of a public service employer, show dates of employment, and demonstrate full-time employment.

9.10 Teacher Loan Forgiveness

Teacher loan forgiveness or cancellation under the FFEL Program and Direct Loan Program includes repayment of up to a maximum of $5000 to individuals who are full-time teachers over five consecutive years in certain schools that serve low-income families.[318] The $5000 limit represents the combined total eligible for forgiveness on the borrower's eligible FFELs and Direct loans.[319] For borrowers who teach five consecutive years as highly qualified math or science teachers in eligible secondary schools or as special education teachers in eligible elementary or secondary schools, the limit is $17,500.[320] Borrowers may not receive more than $5000 or $17,500 in forgiveness under both the FFEL Program and Direct Loan Program.[321]

Teacher loan forgiveness under the FFEL Program and Direct Loan Program apply only to borrowers with no outstanding loan balances as of October 1, 1998, or later. Unlike Perkins loan borrowers, FFEL and Direct loan borrowers are not eligible for teacher-loan forgiveness for defaulted loans unless they first make satisfactory repayment arrangements and reestablish loan eligibility.[322] A joint Direct Consolidation loan may be partially discharged if one of the borrowers qualifies for teacher-loan forgiveness.[323] Whether or not they are working in low-income communities, teachers can also apply for loan forgiveness through the public service forgiveness program.[324]

Borrowers may also qualify for the program based on teaching service performed at a location operated by certain educational service agencies. However, only service performed at educational services agencies after the 2007–2008 academic year is counted.

The requirement of uninterrupted service is waived for borrowers who are serving on active duty during a war or other military operation and other "affected individuals" as described above.[325]

9.11 Other Profession-Related Cancellations

The Department administers a loan-forgiveness-demonstration program for certain child care providers with FFELs or Direct loans.[326] This program is contingent upon annual appropriations. Under this program, borrowers who have received an associate's or bachelor's degree in early childhood education or child care and who are providing full-time child care services in child care facilities that serve certain low-income communities are eligible for forgiveness of up to 100% of their total eligible loans. Only loans made after October 7, 1998, qualify. This program is available on a first-come, first-served basis. The Secretary has not yet issued regulations to implement this program. In January 2004, the Department published the application for this cancellation program.[327]

The 2008 HEA reauthorization law created a number of new job-related cancellation programs, including loan forgiveness for service in areas of national need and limited loan repayment for civil legal assistance attorneys. Under the civil legal attorney program, attorneys may be awarded up to $6000 in repayment assistance in 2010 and may be prioritized to receive assistance in future years if Congress continues to fund the program.[328] It is very possible that the program will not be funded in subsequent years. The funds for 2010 will be committed on a first-come, first served basis.[329]

9.12 Perkins Loan Discharges

The Perkins Loan Program was the first to provide for cancellations of loans for teachers in low-income school districts and for other service, including military and volunteer service.

Perkins loans may be canceled under certain circumstances, including for:

- Full-time teachers in designated elementary or secondary schools serving students from low-income families[330]. This applies to a teaching service period that includes August 14, 2008—or begins on or after that date—at an educational service agency.[331]

---

318 34 C.F.R. §§ 682.216 (FFEL), 685.217 (Direct Loan).
319 34 C.F.R. §§ 682.216(a)(3), 685.217(a)(3).
320 34 C.F.R. § 682.216(a)(4) (FFEL).
321 34 C.F.R. §§ 682.216(d)(2), 685.217(d)(2).
322 34 C.F.R. §§ 682.216 (c)(10), 685.217 (c)(10).
323 34 C.F.R. § 685.220(l)(3)(iv).
324 See § 9.9.2, supra.
325 68 Fed. Reg. 25821 (May 14, 2003).
    This waiver was extended through September 30, 2012. 72 Fed. Reg. 72947 (Dec. 26, 2007).

326 See 67 Fed. Reg. 55385 (Aug. 29, 2002).
327 U.S. Dep't of Educ., Dear Colleague Letter GEN-04-01 (Jan. 2004). The form is available on the Department of Education's website at www.ed.gov. The forms are frequently updated. The most recent form should be posted on the Department of Education website.
328 For requirements and application procedures, see 75 Fed. Reg. 38999 (July 7, 2010).
329 More information about this program and other public and private attorney loan forgiveness programs is available on the Equal Justice Works website, www.equaljusticeworks.org.
330 34 C.F.R. § 674.53(a).
331 34 C.F.R. § 674.53(a)(1)(iii).

- Full-time special education teachers (includes teaching children with disabilities in a public or other nonprofit elementary or secondary school).[332]
- Full-time qualified professional providers or early intervention services for the disabled.[333]
- Full-time teachers of math, science, foreign languages, bilingual education, or other fields designated as teacher-shortage areas.[334]
- Full-time employees of public or nonprofit child or family services agencies providing services to high-risk children and their families from low-income communities.[335]

A 2005 Second Circuit decision examined the eligibility criteria for this discharge.[336] The court found that, based on the criteria listed in the statute, the plaintiffs qualified for cancellation of their Perkins loans even though the Department had denied discharges. Since the Second Circuit decision, the Department has clarified its position in a Dear Colleague letter and in regulations.[337]

- Full-time nurses or medical technicians.[338]
- Full-time law enforcement or correction officers.[339]
- Full-time staff members in the education component of Head Start.[340]
- VISTA or Peace Corps volunteers.[341]
- Military service.[342]
- Full-time staff members in a pre-kindergarten or child care program that is licensed or regulated by a state.[343]
- Full-time fire fighters to local, state, or federal fire departments.[344]
- Full-time faculty members at a Tribal College or University.[345]
- Full-time speech pathologists with master's degrees working in certain elementary or secondary schools.[346]
- Certain librarians working in certain schools[347].
- Full-time attorneys employed in public or community defender organizations.[348]

---

332 34 C.F.R. § 674.53(b).
333 34 C.F.R. §§ 674.55(c), 674.56(c).
334 34 C.F.R. § 674.53(c).
335 34 C.F.R. § 674.56(b).
336 De la Mota v. U.S. Dep't of Educ., 412 F.3d 71 (2d Cir. 2005).
337 U.S. Dep't of Educ., Child or Family Service Loan Cancellation Benefit in the Federal Perkins Loan Program, Dear Colleague Letter GEN-05-15 (Oct. 19, 2005); 34 C.F.R. § 674.56(b).
338 34 C.F.R. § 674.56(a).
339 34 C.F.R. § 674.57(a).
340 34 C.F.R. § 674.58.
341 34 C.F.R. § 674.60.
342 34 C.F.R. § 674.59.
343 34 C.F.R. § 674.58.
344 34 C.F.R. § 674.56(d).
345 34 C.F.R. § 674.56(e).
346 34 C.F.R. § 674.56(g).
347 34 C.F.R. § 674.56(f).
348 34 C.F.R. § 674.57(b).

Under certain circumstances, Perkins loan cancellations are available even for borrowers in default.[349] In general, to qualify for a Perkins loan discharge, borrowers must perform uninterrupted service for a specific length of time. The Department has waived this requirement of uninterrupted and/or consecutive service for borrowers who are members of the military reserves called or ordered to active duty for a period of more than thirty days or who are regular active duty members of the Armed Forces reassigned to a different duty station for more than thirty days as a result of a military mobilization.[350] Subsequent waivers were given to a broader group of service members and others affected by national emergencies or military operations.

"Affected individuals" includes borrowers serving on active duty during a war or other military operation or national emergency; performing qualifying National Guard duty during a war or other military operation or national emergency; residing or employed in an area that is declared a disaster area by any federal, state, or local official in connection with a national emergency; or suffering direct economic hardship as a direct result of a war or other military operation or national emergency, as determined by the Secretary.[351] The reason for the interruption in service must be related to the borrower's status as an "affected individual."[352]

Borrowers should obtain forms from the schools holding their loans. Borrowers should also be advised that they will lose access to these Perkins-specific cancellations if they consolidate their loans with Direct loans.

9.13 Cancellation for Certain Relatives of September 11 Victims

Congress passed a cancellation program for certain relatives of victims of the September 11 attacks.[353] The program applies to Perkins, FFEL, and Direct loan borrowers. There are two categories of discharges. The first is for spouses of eligible public servants. Eligible public servants include police officers, firefighters, other safety or rescue personnel, or members of the Armed Forces who died or became permanently and totally disabled due to injuries suffered in the September 11 attacks.[354]

---

349 34 C.F.R. § 674.52(c).
350 68 Fed. Reg. 25821 (May 14, 2003).
351 68 Fed. Reg. 69312 (Dec. 12, 2003).
   This waiver was extended through September 30, 2012. 72 Fed. Reg. 72947 (Dec. 26, 2007).
352 Id.
353 The provisions were passed as part of the Third Higher Education Extension Act of 2006, Pub. L. 109-292 (Sept. 30, 2006). See 34 C.F.R. §§ 674.64 (Perkins Loan), 682.407 (FFEL), 685.218 (Direct Loan).
354 34 C.F.R. § 682.407(a)(1) (FFEL) (definition of eligible public servant).
   The definition of total and permanent disability is a disability

Spouses of public servants are eligible for discharges of FFELs, Direct loans, or Perkins loans, including any portion of a joint consolidation loan that was used to repay the spouse's government student loans. If the public servant survived, the eligible spouse must have been married to the public servant at the time of the attacks and must still be married. If the public servant died, the spouse must have been married to the public servant at the time of the attacks and until the date the public servant died.[355] Parents with PLUS loans may also discharge loans incurred on behalf of their eligible public servant children.[356]

The second category is for spouses and parents of eligible victims. Eligible victims are individuals who died or became permanently and totally disabled due to injuries suffered in the September 11 attacks.[357] Parents of eligible victims may discharge parent PLUS loans incurred on behalf of eligible victims or consolidation loans that repaid such a loan.[358]

Spouses may apply to discharge the portion of a joint consolidation loan that was incurred on behalf of the eligible victim.[359] Spouses of eligible victims who became disabled must still be married to the victim.[360]

Borrowers must have owed the loan amounts as of September 11, 2001.[361] Borrowers may also discharge consolidation loans that were taken out to pay loans that were owed as of September 11, 2001. However, borrowers must still owe something on the loans at the time they apply for discharges. There are no refunds for payments already made.[362]

The Department has developed a discharge application form.[363] The Department asserts that about one thousand borrowers will be eligible for discharges under these provisions.[364]

9.14 Income Tax Issues

The Internal Revenue Code specifically allows tax-free treatment for loans that are cancelled through programs tied to work for certain amounts of time in certain professions, such as teaching and medicine, including nursing.[365] In September 2008, the Department of Treasury issued a letter outlining the Department's treatment of student loan discharges and taxes.[366] The letter states that teacher loan forgiveness and public service loan forgiveness satisfy the requirements for income exclusion under the Internal Revenue Code because these programs are conditioned on the borrower working for a certain period of time in qualifying public service positions.[367] Some loan repayment assistance programs have also been found not to generate taxable income.[368]

Other debt forgiveness programs may result in taxable income.[369] The Department of Treasury's 2008 letter noted that death and disability, closed-school, false-certification,

---

that is the result of a physical injury to the individual that was treated by a medical professional within seventy-two hours of the injury having been sustained or within seventy-two hours of the rescue; the physical injury is verified by contemporaneous medical records created by or at the direction of the medical professional who provided the care; and the individual is unable to work and earn money due to the disability and the disability is expected to continue indefinitely or result in death. Borrowers may also qualify if the medical condition has deteriorated to the extent that they are now permanently and totally disabled. 34 C.F.R. § 682.407(a)(5)(i)–(ii) (FFEL).

Note that this definition was not changed to reflect the changes in the disability discharge program. *See* § 9.7.3.1, *supra*.

355 34 C.F.R. § 682.407(b).
356 34 C.F.R. § 682.407(b)(4) (FFEL).
357 34 C.F.R. § 682.407(a)(2).
358 34 C.F.R. § 682.407(a)(3).
359 34 C.F.R. § 682.407(c)(1)(iv).
360 34 C.F.R. § 682.407(b)(1)–(2).
361 34 C.F.R. § 682.407(g).
362 34 C.F.R. § 682.407(g)(2).
363 U.S. Dep't of Educ., Dear Colleague Letter GEN-07-08 (Nov. 9, 2007).
364 71 Fed. Reg. 78075, 78077 (Dec. 28, 2006).

365 26 U.S.C. 108(f)(2). *See* I.R.S. Info. Ltr. 2009-0126, 2009 WL 1833452 (June 26, 2009) (discussing taxable status of debt discharged pursuant to Direct Loan and FFEL public service loan forgiveness programs); Internal Revenue Serv., Tax Benefits for Education, Publication 970 (2009).
366 The letter dated September 18, 2008, and addressed to Representative Sander Levin can be found at www.ibrinfo.org/files/Treasury_response_levin.pdf and on the companion website to this manual.
367 *Cf.* I.R.S. Serv. Ctr. Adv. 2000-38-044, 2000 WL 33116350 (Sept. 22, 2000) (finding as income, not student loans, forgiven penalties imposed on Indian Health Scholarship recipients for failing to complete pledged work; even if student loans, not excludable under 26 U.S.C. § 108(f)(2), since "Section 108(f) is intended to exclude from income amounts that are forgiven when an individual works in the required professions; not when an individual fails to fulfill a work requirement").
368 *See* Rev. Rul. 2008-34, 2008-28 I.R.B. 76 (finding that law school's loan repayment assistance program which refinanced law school debt for graduates working for specified government and public interest employers met student loan definition under 26 U.S.C. § 108(f)(1)–(2) and was therefore excludable from income); I.R.S. Priv. Ltr. Rul. 10-16-043 (Apr. 23, 2010) (loan repayment assistance program for employees of community health services centers excludable from income); Internal Revenue Serv., Tax Benefits for Education, Publication 970 (2009) (listing National Health Service Corps repayment assistance, state public health repayment assistance, and law school loan repayment assistance). *Cf.* Moloney v. Commissioner, T.C. Summ. Op. 2006-53, 2006 WL 995393 (T.C. Apr. 17, 2006) (state loan repayment assistance program for attorneys working for governmental entities or nonprofits qualified as taxable income); I.R.S. Field Serv. Advisory, 1992 WL 1466143 (June 25, 1992) (finding Washington State's loan repayment assistance program for health professionals not a student loan and includible in income).
369 *See* Porten v. Commissioner, 65 T.C.M. (CCH) 1994 (1993) (finding student loan debt forgiven due to borrower's residence in Alaska, under state statute, did not qualify for the 26 U.S.C. § 108(f) exclusion from taxable income); I.R.S. Priv. Ltr. Rul. 87-14-035 (Jan. 2, 1986) (tuition loan indebtedness forgiven for employees of university includible as income).

and unpaid-refund discharges are not based on the borrower working in certain professions and are thus not excluded from income under the statute per se. Forgiveness after twenty-five years of income-contingent or income-based repayment is also not automatically excluded from income.[370]

In general, however, debt forgiven when a borrower is insolvent or in bankruptcy is not income.[371] Forgiveness of interest income is also not income,[372] provided that, if a borrower took a prior deduction for student loan interest payments, the amount previously taken as a deduction may become income in the year the interest is forgiven under the "tax benefit" rule.[373] Other common law exceptions may also apply, particularly the "disputed debt" doctrine, which excludes from income debt forgiven as the result of a bona fide dispute over its legitimacy.[374]

Lenders and guaranty agencies are not subject to penalties for failure to report amounts forgiven pursuant to the terms of a debt obligation. This specifically includes forgiveness upon a stated event such as death, disability, or service as a teacher.[375] The IRS has, however, made clear that the Department is required to issue 1099-Cs upon debt forgiveness, whether or not the forgiven debt is subject to tax.[376]

Borrowers who receive a 1099-C should seek competent tax advice. Borrowers and their counsel should not assume that the debt discharged is taxable since one of the generally applicable exclusions, such as insolvency, may apply.

9.15 Appealing Adverse Discharge Decisions

Before seeking judicial review of a discharge denial, student loan borrowers should be certain that they have presented a complete and fully documented application. If a discharge was denied for want of evidence that is now available or on the basis of erroneous facts, the borrower should resubmit an accurate and complete application rather than seeking judicial review. The Department will generally reconsider a prior discharge denial, particularly if circumstances have changed.

In addition, for false-certification and unpaid-refund discharges only, FFEL borrowers should first seek administrative review from the Department.[377] The closed-school and disability discharge regulations do not provide for this type of "internal" review.

The Administrative Procedure Act (APA) is available only after borrowers have exhausted administrative remedies. Borrowers cannot initiate the discharge process in court.[378] A district court in North Carolina summarized the problem for borrowers.[379] In a case pending before that court, the borrower sought to enjoin the government from collecting on loans that the borrower alleged were paid for instruction he never received. The court noted that the plaintiff's claims appealed to the equities found in the law.[380] The court also noted that Congress had addressed the problem by passing the various administrative discharges.[381] However, these claims must be presented through the administrative process and not as defensive claims in civil litigation.

The APA governs judicial review of any informal agency adjudication, including denial of a student loan discharge by the Department of Education. The pertinent section provides that the court shall hold unlawful and set aside agency action, findings, and conclusions found to be "arbitrary, capricious, an abuse of discretion, or otherwise not in accordance with law...."[382] Section 706 "require[s] the reviewing court to engage in a substantial inquiry."[383] In determining whether an agency's action was unlawful under section 706(2)(A), the court must "consider whether the decision was based on a consideration of the relevant factors and whether there has been a clear error in judgment."[384] If

---

370 In 2009, Representative Levin sponsored a bill, H.R. 2492, that would exclude from taxable income cancellations due to twenty-five years of ICR or IBR repayments. The bill was introduced on May 19, 2009.
371 26 U.S.C. § 108(a)(1)(B) (insolvency); 26 U.S.C. § 108(a)(1)(A).
372 26 U.S.C. § 108(a)(e)(2). See 26 C.F.R. § 1.221-1 (providing for the deductibility of some interest on student loans).
373 See Schlifke v. Commissioner, 61 T.C.M. (CCH) 1697 (1991) (home mortgage interest).
374 See Zarin v. Commissioner, 916 F.2d 110 (3d Cir. 1990). See generally National Consumer Law Center, Foreclosures § 14.7.3.4 (3d ed. 2010) (discussing exceptions to the general rule that forgiven debt is income).
375 69 Fed. Reg. 62181 (Oct. 25, 2004).
376 See, e.g., I.R.S. Info. Ltr. 2009-0126, 2009 WL 1833452 (June 26, 2009) (discussing Department of Education's duty to report debt discharged pursuant to Direct Loan and FFEL public service loan forgiveness programs that result in nontaxable income).
377 34 C.F.R. §§ 682.402(e)(11)(ii) (false-certification administrative appeals), 682.402(l)(5)(vii) (unpaid-refund administrative appeals).
378 Courts have consistently found that only the Department of Education has the discretion to discharge the loans based on the various discharge programs. See, e.g., Carlin v. CBE, 2008 WL 2113255 (E.D.N.Y. May 19, 2008); Haddad v. Dominican Univ., 2007 WL 809685 (N.D. Ill. Mar. 15, 2007); United States v. Levreau, 2001 WL 1690059 (D. Minn. Dec. 14, 2001) (discharge claims must be pursued administratively and may not be asserted as a defense in a collection action); United States v. Bertucci, 2000 WL 1234560 (E.D. La. 2000); United States v. Wright, 87 F. Supp. 2d 464 (D. Md. 2000); In re Bega, 180 B.R. 642 (Bankr. D. Kan. 1995).
379 Green v. United States, 163 F. Supp. 2d 593 (W.D.N.C. 2000).
380 Id. at 597.
381 Id. at 597–598.
382 5 U.S.C. § 706(2)(A). See also Jordan v. Secretary of Educ. of the U.S., 194 F.3d 169 (D.C. Cir. 1999).
383 Citizens to Preserve Overton Park, Inc. v. Volpe, 401 U.S. 402, 415 (1971); C.K. v. New Jersey Dep't of Health & Human Servs., 92 F.3d 171, 182 (3d Cir. 1996).
384 Citizens to Preserve Overton Park, Inc. v. Volpe, 401 U.S. 416

the court determines that the agency relied on factors Congress did not intend for it to consider, or has failed to consider an important aspect of the problem, the action should be set aside as arbitrary and capricious.[385]

An agency is bound by its own regulations.[386] If an agency's action does not comport with its regulations, the action is contrary to law and should be reversed by a reviewing court.[387]

In many cases, the Department may not even be relying on regulations to set policy. The Department frequently sets standards for student loan discharges and other programs through informal "Dear Colleague" letters or other informal methods such as staff interpretations or communications. Courts should be persuaded that these types of informal decisions are not due the same type of deference as regulations that have been issued through the public notice and comment process.[388]

Because the Department of Education's decision to deny a student loan discharge is an informal adjudication, there is no formal record. The district court will consider all material that was presented to the Department by the borrower and should also consider any other information or documents the Department relied upon. The government will typically prepare and submit what it considers to be the administrative record. The borrower, however, is free to present to the court any additional evidence that had a bearing on the agency's decision. The guaranty agencies act as agents for the Department in reviewing discharge requests. Material submitted to the guaranty agencies should also be submitted as part of the agency record.[389]

An action for APA review is filed in federal district court. There is no time limit in the APA for seeking judicial review. Most courts have looked to 28 U.S.C. § 2401(a) as the relevant statute of limitations for appeals of agency decisions.[390] This section requires that civil actions against the United States be filed within six years after the right of action first accrued.

The APA provides for relief pending review.[391] When an agency finds that justice so requires, it may postpone the effective date of action taken by it, pending judicial review. The test is generally similar to that required for preliminary injunctions.

There are limits to APA relief. Monetary damages are not available under the APA.[392] However, plaintiffs may argue that the government has waived sovereign immunity on claims for monetary relief in certain circumstances.[393] The APA does create a potential cause of action for declaratory relief.[394] Regardless of the relief sought, review under the APA is available only when there is no other adequate remedy in a court.[395] However, the Supreme Court has held that this limitation should not be construed to defeat the central purpose of providing a broad spectrum of judicial review of agency action. The restriction is designed primarily to ensure that federal courts do not duplicate the previously established statutory procedures relating to specific agencies.[396] The agency action challenged must also be final.[397]

(1971) (citations omitted); C.K. v. New Jersey Dep't of Health & Human Servs., 92 F.3d 182 (3d Cir. 1996).

385 Frisby v. U.S. Dep't of Hous. & Urban Dev., 755 F.2d 1052, 1055 (3d Cir. 1985) (citing Motor Vehicle Mfrs. Ass'n v. State Farm Mut. Auto. Ins. Co., 463 U.S. 29, 43 (1983)).

386 *See* United States v. Nixon, 418 U.S. 683, 696 (1974).

387 *See* Frisby v. U.S. Dep't of Hous. & Urban Dev., 755 F.2d 1055–56 (3d Cir. 1985); Kelly v. Railroad Ret. Bd., 625 F.2d 486, 491–92 (3d Cir. 1980).

388 *See, e.g.*, De La Mota v. U.S. Dep't of Educ., 412 F.3d 71 (2d Cir. 2005).

389 A sample APA appeal can be found at Appendix E, *infra*. See §§ 8.3.3.1, 8.3.3.2, *supra*, for a discussion of APA claims when a guaranty agency, rather than the Department, makes the underlying decision.

390 *See, e.g.*, Southwest Williamson County Cmty. Ass'n, Inc. v. Slater, 173 F.3d 1033, 1036 (6th Cir. 1999); Chemical Weapons Work Group v. Department of Army, 111 F.3d 1485 (10th Cir. 1997); Elk Grove Vill. v. Evans, 997 F.2d 328, 331 (7th Cir. 1993); Impro Prods., Inc. v. Block, 722 F.2d 845 (D.C. Cir. 1983); Lewis v. Glickman, 104 F. Supp. 2d 1311 (D. Kan. 2000), *aff'd sub nom.* Jones v. Glickman, 2002 WL 1435904, 42 Fed. Appx. 292 (10th Cir. 2002); Kelly v. Aman Collection Servs. et al, 2007 WL 909547 (D. Minn. Mar. 23, 2007) (denying plaintiff's challenges to tax offsets and wage garnishment due to expiration of six-year APA statute of limitations).

391 5 U.S.C. § 705.

392 5 U.S.C. § 702 ("An action in a court of the United States seeking relief other than money damages and stating a claim that an agency or an officer or employee thereof acted or failed to act in an official capacity or under color of legal authority shall not be dismissed nor relief therein be denied on the ground that it is against the United States or that the United States is an indispensable party. The United States may be named as a defendant in any such action, and a judgment or decree may be entered against the United States.").

393 *See, e.g.*, De La Mota v. U.S. Dep't of Educ., 2003 WL 21919774 (S.D.N.Y. Aug. 12, 2003) (discussing and rejecting various theories to waive sovereign immunity on claims for monetary relief).

394 *See id*. (HEA anti-injunction provision waives the Secretary's immunity from suit seeking declaratory relief). *See also* § 12.6.2.1, *infra*.

395 5 U.S.C. § 704. *See* Marlow v. U.S. Dep't of Educ., 820 F.2d 581, 583 n.3 (2d Cir. 1987); Infante v. Drug Enforcement Admin., 938 F. Supp. 1149 (E.D.N.Y. 1996).

396 *See* Bowen v. Massachusetts, 487 U.S. 879, 108 S. Ct. 2722, 101 L. Ed. 2d 749 (1988). *See also* De La Mota U.S. Dep't of Educ., 2003 WL 21919774 (S.D.N.Y. Aug. 12, 2003) (court allowed APA action to proceed in case in which alternative remedy of breach-of-contact action against the plaintiffs' law schools was not an adequate remedy), *rev'd on other grounds*, 412 F.3d 71 (2d Cir. 2005).

397 5 U.S.C. § 704.

Chapter 10   Discharging Student Loans in Bankruptcy

10.1 Student Loans and Bankruptcy

10.1.1 About the Bankruptcy Option

Discharging student loans in bankruptcy is an important strategy for low-income consumers, either through a chapter 7 ("straight") or a chapter 13 ("wage earner plan") bankruptcy filing.[1] Although the 2005 amendments have made bankruptcy a more cumbersome process for debtors, it is still an option consumers struggling with debt may consider.[2] In addition, even when a student loan cannot be discharged in bankruptcy, a chapter 13 bankruptcy filing offers other important options for the student loan borrower.

Deciding whether to file for bankruptcy to deal with a student loan requires at least two decisions. The first decision—whether bankruptcy can effectively deal with a student loan—is described later in this chapter. The other issue is whether bankruptcy makes sense for a consumer in light of the consumer's total debt picture. This question is detailed in another NCLC manual[3] and will only be briefly summarized here.

The 2005 Bankruptcy Abuse Prevention and Consumer Protection Act (BAPCPA) amendments to the Bankruptcy Code limit consumers' access to bankruptcy relief in a number of ways. Generally effective for cases filed as of October 17, 2005, the amendments created new paperwork and counseling requirements for consumer debtors. The scope of bankruptcy relief has been restricted in specific areas, and important new limits on repeat filings are now in effect.[4] However, the 2005 amendments did not change the general standards and procedures applicable to student loan discharge determinations.[5] The extensive pre-BAPCPA case law construing the "undue hardship" dischargeability standard under section 523(a)(8) of the Code remains pertinent under the new regime.

In a chapter 7 bankruptcy, virtually all of a consumer's debts are eliminated (discharged) with no obligation to make payments, and the consumer will be able to keep exempt property. Non-exempt property, however, may be liquidated to pay creditors. It is therefore critical for a consumer's attorney to study carefully the consumer's exemption, redemption, and other rights if the consumer wishes to retain a home, car, or other significant asset. Nevertheless, exemption statutes will permit many low-income individuals to retain all their assets in a chapter 7 proceeding.

If a consumer is concerned about his or her ability to retain a home, car, or other asset, a chapter 13 filing will often be a successful approach. In a chapter 13 bankruptcy, a debtor pays some portion (even if only 5% or 10%) of his or her unsecured debts in accordance with a court-approved ("confirmed") plan, usually over a three- to five-year period.[6] At the conclusion of the plan, the remaining obligations on any unsecured debts are discharged.[7] The opportunity to cure defaults on, or to restructure, secured debt is also available in a chapter 13 case.[8]

Currently, the fee is $299 for filing a chapter 7 bankruptcy and $274 for filing a chapter 13 bankruptcy.[9] Debtors in chapter 7 may now seek wavier of the filing fee through the *in forma pauperis* provisions enacted with BAPCPA.[10] The filing fees generally cannot be waived in a chapter 13 case but may be paid in installments in both chapter 13 and chapter 7 cases.[11]

---

1 For a general introduction to bankruptcy law, see National Consumer Law Center, Consumer Bankruptcy Law and Practice Chs. 1–6 (9th ed. 2009 and Supp.).
2 In 1998, student loan debtors suffered a major setback to their ability to discharge student loans. For all bankruptcy cases filed on or after October 7, 1998, the discharge of student loans that first became due more than seven years prior to the bankruptcy filing is no longer allowed. Pub. L. No. 105-244, § 971, 112 Stat. 1581 (Oct. 7, 1998) (Higher Education Programs Authorization Extension Act).
3 National Consumer Law Center, Consumer Bankruptcy Law and Practice (9th ed. 2009 and Supp.).
4 *Id.*
5 The primary area related to student loans in bankruptcy affected by the BACPA amendments is the expanded definition of entities covered by the exception from discharge for educational loans. These changes are discussed at § 10.2.1, *infra*.
6 National Consumer Law Center, Consumer Bankruptcy Law and Practice Ch. 4 (9th ed. 2009 and Supp.).
7 11 U.S.C. § 1328(c).
8 *See* National Consumer Law Center, Consumer Bankruptcy Law and Practice Ch. 11 (9th ed. 2009 and Supp.).
9 Fees effective April 9, 2006.
10 28 U.S.C. § 1930(f)(1).
11 Part of each fee is a mandatory noticing fee rather than a filing fee. That part of the fee is waivable in most jurisdictions. For more information about bankruptcy court fee waivers, see National Consumer Law Center, Consumer Bankruptcy Law and

10.1.2 The Benefit of the Automatic Stay

Another consideration is that filing a chapter 7 or chapter 13 bankruptcy instantly protects the student from most collection actions on claims arising before the bankruptcy. For example, the "automatic stay" prevents a student loan creditor from continuing with an administrative wage garnishment.[12] The fact that a particular student loan debt may be nondischargeable has no bearing on the creditor's duty to comply with the automatic stay. The stay bars both direct and indirect actions by the creditor to collect a prebankruptcy debt, regardless of the debt's dischargeability status. Most courts agree that, upon notice of a bankruptcy filing, a university must cease any practice of withholding transcripts because the debtor is in default on loans owed to the institution.[13]

After the bankruptcy case has closed and the automatic stay is no longer in effect, the creditor may resume collection activity on a nondischargeable student loan. This action will not violate the discharge order entered at the close of the bankruptcy case.[14] Typically, the bankruptcy court will not have made a specific determination as to the nondischargeability of the educational debt during the pendency of the case. If the creditor believes that the loan was covered by the dischargeability exception of section 523(a)(8), the creditor will resume collection efforts after the close of the case. The creditor, of course, assumes the risk that the debt may not have been a loan covered by the dischargeability exception. For example, sanctions may be imposed on a creditor who resumes postbankruptcy collection on a debt it believed was a nondischargeable student loan but a court later construes to have been merely an agreement to pay tuition.[15]

An obligation to pay tuition, absent any formal agreement on repayment terms, is a dischargeable debt. The automatic stay and the discharge order bar creditor actions to collect unpaid tuition during and after the bankruptcy case. A common device used by educational institutions to coerce payment of unpaid tuition bills is to withhold transcripts and other certifications of course completion. When used to compel payment of tuition debts listed on the debtor's bankruptcy schedules, these collection actions violate the automatic stay and discharge order.[16]

10.2 When Can a Student Loan Be Discharged in Bankruptcy?

10.2.1 The Special Restriction on Dischargeability Applies to Most Student Loans

A chapter 7 or 13 discharge eliminates all of a debtor's unsecured debts, with certain statutory exceptions. While student loans are technically unsecured debts subject to discharge, the Bankruptcy Code limits their dischargeability. Educational loans can only be discharged upon a finding by a court that repayment of the debt "will impose an undue hardship on the debtor and the debtor's dependents."[17]

However, before the undue hardship standard comes into play, there may be a preliminary question that must be addressed. This is whether the obligation in question is covered by section 523(a)(8) of the Code at all. Although amendments to the Code over the past three decades have extended the reach of the undue hardship discharge limitation to cover more types of loans, not every obligation related to payment for educational services is subject to the discharge exception today. For example, to be covered by the exception the loan must have been for an appropriate educational purpose. Particularly relevant in the case of private loans, the indebtedness must have been incurred to pay for statutorily defined "qualified higher educational expenses."[18] In other cases, the obligation may not be a "loan" at all.[19] Any of these circumstances will affect whether the dischargeability exception applies to the obligation. In addition, bankruptcy cases filed while prior versions of section 523(a)(8) were in effect remain subject to the older versions of the Code in force at the time the case was filed.[20] These and other exceptions to the scope of section 523(a)(8) are discussed below.

Under the current wording of section 523(a)(8), applicable to chapter 7 and chapter 13 bankruptcy cases filed

---

Practice §§ 7.2, 14.6 (9th ed. 2009 and Supp.).

12 See 11 U.S.C. § 362.
 The automatic stay remains in effect while the bankruptcy case is pending or until such time as it is lifted by the court upon request by a creditor based on grounds specified in section 362 of the Bankruptcy Code. See § 8.2.9, *supra*, for a discussion of the automatic stay in relation to tax intercepts.
13 *See, e.g., In re* Mu'Min, 374 B.R. 149, 155 n.15 (Bankr. E.D. Pa. 2007) (rejecting university's "good faith" defense to bankruptcy debtor's action for damages based on university's violation of automatic stay in refusing to release transcript because debtor's student loan was in default); *In re* Parker, 334 B.R. 529, 536 (Bankr. D. Mass. 2005) (nondischargeable nature of student loan debt does not affect university's obligation to comply with automatic stay).
14 11 U.S.C. § 524(a).
15 *In re* Parker, 334 B.R. 5290 (Bankr. D. Mass. 2005). *See generally* note 44, *infra* (collecting cases distinguishing student loan debts from obligations to pay tuition).

16 *In re* Kuehn, 563 F.3d 289 (7th Cir. 2009) (withholding transcript unless former student pays dischargeable tuition debt is an act to collect the debt prohibited by the automatic stay); *In re* Moore, 407 B.R. 855 (Bankr. E.D. Va. 2009) (unpaid tuition, absent signed note and advance of funds, is not an educational loan; school held in contempt of discharge order for withholding transcript).
17 11 U.S.C. § 523(a)(8).
18 *See* § 10.2.2.1, *infra*.
19 *See* § 10.2.2.2, *infra*.
20 *See* § 10.2.2.4, *infra*.

after the BAPCPA effective date of October 17, 2005, the debtor must satisfy the undue hardship standard if the debt falls within any of the following categories:

(A)(i) an educational benefit overpayment or loan made, insured, or guaranteed by a governmental unit, or made under any program funded in whole or in part by a governmental unit or nonprofit institution; or

(ii) an obligation to repay funds received as an educational benefit, scholarship, or stipend; or

(B) any other educational loan that is a qualified education loan, as defined in section 221(d)(1) of the Internal Revenue Code of 1986, incurred by a debtor who is an individual.[21]

Both before and after the 2005 amendments, the undue hardship restriction on dischargeability applied to educational loans "made, insured or guaranteed by any governmental unit, or made under any program funded in whole or in part by a government unit or a nonprofit institution."[22] Consequently, the dischargeability of Stafford loans, supplemental student loans (SLS), Federal Direct loans, and Perkins loans has been restricted for many years. The exception from discharge also applied to loans made by state agencies and nonprofit organizations.[23] Beginning with 1990 amendments, the dischargeability exception was extended to educational benefit overpayments (such as Pell grant overpayments) and obligations to repay funds received as educational benefits, scholarships, or stipends.[24] The general restriction on dischargeability applies to loans incurred to pay for secondary school expenses as well as costs of post-secondary education.[25] As discussed below, under pre-BAPCPA law, loans made by for-profit institutions remained dischargeable.[26] The 2005 amendments expanded the scope of the discharge exception to encompass most loans by private for-profit lenders as well.

The 2005 amendments made two major structural changes to section 523(a)(8). First, newly renumbered subsection (A)(i) of section 523(a)(8) provides that an educational benefit overpayment or loan made, insured, or guaranteed by a government unit—or made under any program funded in whole or in part by a government unit or nonprofit institution—is nondischargeable unless there has been a showing of undue hardship. Subsection (A)(ii) provides separately that an obligation to repay funds received as an education benefit, scholarship, or stipend is nondischargeable without the undue hardship finding. Current subsections (A)(i) and (A)(ii) essentially incorporate the pre-

---

21 *Id.*

22 11 U.S.C. §§ 523(a)(8)(A)(i), 1328(a)(2); *In re* O'Brien, 419 F.3d 104 (2d Cir. 2005) (the term "funded," as used in bankruptcy statute excepting student loans from discharge "made under any program funded in whole or in part by a governmental unit or non-profit institution," modified the word "program" rather than the word "loan" and did not require nonprofit institution that guaranteed debtor's student loans to actually supply any portion of funding for the loans in order for discharge exception to apply).

In general, it is the purpose for which the loan was made that controls rather than the use of the loan proceeds. *In re* Murphy, 282 F.3d 868 (5th Cir. 2002) (student loans nondischargeable even if portion used by debtor to purchase car, housing, food, and other living expenses). *See also* National Consumer Law Center, Consumer Bankruptcy Law and Practice § 14.4.3.8 (9th ed. 2009 and Supp.) (discussing dischargeability of student loans).

23 *See* TI Fed. Credit Union v. DelBonis, 72 F.3d 921 (1st Cir. 1995) (federally chartered credit union is a governmental unit for purposes of exception to discharge); *In re* Merchant, 958 F.2d 738 (6th Cir. 1992) (loan guaranteed by nonprofit institution was nondischargeable); *In re* Roberts, 149 B.R. 547 (C.D. Ill. 1993) (loan from nonprofit credit union nondischargeable). *Cf. In re* Reis, 274 B.R.46 (Bankr. D. Mass. 2002) (private student loan made by grandparents not excepted from discharge because not made pursuant to student loan program of governmental unit or by nonprofit entity).

24 11 U.S.C. § 523(a)(8); *In re* Burks, 244 F.3d 1245 (11th Cir. 2001) (obligation to repay stipend due to failure to fulfill stipend agreement to teach in "other race" institution after receiving degree was nondischargeable); U.S. Dep't of Health & Human Servs. v. Smith, 807 F.2d 122 (8th Cir. 1986) (scholarship grants received to finance medical training in exchange for agreement to practice in designated physician shortage area nondischargeable). *See also In re* Coole, 202 B.R. 518 (Bankr. D.N.M. 1996) (an "educational benefit overpayment" involves a program like the GI Bill, wherein students receive payments based on their attendance at school and overpayment occurs when student continues to receive payments after leaving school).

25 *In re* Rosen, 179 B.R. 935, 938 (Bankr. D. Or. 1995) (1984 amendments to section 523(a)(8) deleted limitation to loans related to institutions of "higher" education). *But see In re* Davis, 316 B.R. 610 (Bankr. S.D.N.Y. 2004) (tuition debt for parochial secondary school tuition is dischargeable because not a loan).

However, the discharge exception for private student loans, set forth in subsection (B) of section 523(a)(8) and incorporating the IRS student loan definition, is limited to loans incurred "solely to pay for qualified *higher* education expenses." 26 U.S.C. § 221(d)(1) (emphasis added).

26 *In re* Scott, 287 B.R. 470 (Bankr. E.D. Mo. 2002) (loan made by for-profit truck driving school dischargeable); *In re* Jones, 242 B.R. 441 (Bankr. W.D. Tenn. 1999) (debt to for-profit trade school was not within scope of section 523(a)(8)); *In re* Shorts, 209 B.R. 818 (Bankr. D.R.I. 1997) (same); *In re* Simmons, 175 B.R. 624 (Bankr. E.D. Va. 1994) (credit union was not a nonprofit institution and loan was not made pursuant to a program within meaning of section 523(a)(8)); *In re* Sinclair-Ganos, 133 B.R. 382 (Bankr. W.D. Mich. 1991) (credit union not a nonprofit institution within meaning of section 523(a)(8)). *But see In re* Pilcher, 149 B.R. 595 (B.A.P. 9th Cir. 1993) (private loan received from for-profit lender as part of Law Access program involving two nonprofit institutions was covered by exception to discharge); *In re* O'Brien, 299 B.R. 725 (Bankr. S.D.N.Y. 2003) (same), *aff'd*, 419 F.3d 104 (2d Cir. 2005); *In re* Bolen, 287 B.R. 127 (Bankr. D. Vt. 2002) (same).

§ 10.2.2 Student Loan Law

BAPCPA language of section 523(a)(8) defining the scope of the student loan discharge exception.

The 2005 amendments added new subsection (B) to section 523(a)(8). Subsection (B) is a kind of catch-all category. It provides that, in addition to the student loans described in subsection (A), any other obligation that is a qualified educational loan as defined in section 221(d)(1) of the Internal Revenue Code is also nondischargeable. This is especially significant because it means most private loans, which before the 2005 amendments were dischargeable unless the lender proved that the loan was made or funded by a government unit or nonprofit institution, are now nondischargeable unless the debtor can prove hardship.

10.2.2 Exceptions to Nondischargeability

10.2.2.1 Private Student Loans

There are a few limits to new subsection (B). These limits are derived from the Internal Revenue Code definition of a "qualified education loan," which is now explicitly referenced by section 523(a)(8).[27] Only "qualified education loans" are nondischargeable under new subsection (B). This means that the scope of section 523(a)(8) now includes those student loans for which the taxpayer may claim the deduction for interest paid on the student loan. Certain key limitations on the scope of the IRS deduction focus on the types of expenses for which the loan was incurred, the timing of the loan, and the type of institution attended.

According to section 221(d)(1) of the Internal Revenue Code ("IRS Code"), loans qualifying for the tax deduction must be incurred solely to pay for "qualified higher education expenses." The definition of these expenses is a broad one.[28] The term "qualified higher education expenses" as used in section 221(d)(1) of the IRS Code incorporates the definition of "cost of attendance" at an educational institution from the Higher Education Act of 1965.[29] These costs include a variety of non-tuition items such as room and board, supplies, books, and a computer. The IRS Code does not set specific limits on these costs, referring instead to the Higher Education Act and its definition of appropriate costs "as determined by the institution."[30] These educational expenses must be incurred on behalf of the taxpayer, the taxpayer's spouse, or any dependent of the taxpayer.[31] The debtor must have been a "taxpayer" at the time the educational debt was incurred.[32]

Significantly, to qualify for the tax deduction, the indebtedness must be "incurred by the taxpayer *solely* to pay qualified higher education expenses."[33] The Treasury De-

---

27 26 U.S.C. § 221(d).
28 Section 221(d) provides:

(d) Definitions—For purposes of this section—
(1) Qualified education loan.—The term "qualified education loan" means any indebtedness incurred by the taxpayer solely to pay for qualified higher education expenses—
(A) which are incurred on behalf of the taxpayer, the taxpayer's spouse, or any dependent of the taxpayer as of the time the indebtedness was incurred,
(B) which are paid or incurred within a reasonable period of time before or after the indebtedness is incurred, and
(C) which are attributable to education furnished during a period during which the recipient was an eligible student.

Note that the expenses must be incurred on behalf of the taxpayer, the taxpayer's spouse, or any dependent of the taxpayer and must be paid or incurred within a reasonable period of time before or after the indebtedness is incurred and attributable to education furnished during a period in which the recipient was an eligible student.

29 26 U.S.C. § 221(d)(2) (incorporating the terms of the HEA); 20 U.S.C. § 1087*ll*.

Section 1087*ll* defines the pertinent "cost of attendance" for a student as:

(1) tuition and fees normally assessed a student carrying the same academic workload as determined by the institution, and including costs for rental or purchase of any equipment, materials, or supplies required of all students in the same course of study;
(2) an allowance for books, supplies, transportation, and miscellaneous personal expenses, including a reasonable allowance for the documented rental or purchase of a personal computer, for a student attending the institution on at least a half-time basis, as determined by the institution;
(3) an allowance (as determined by the institution) for room and board costs incurred by the student which—
(A) shall be an allowance determined by the institution for a student without dependents residing at home with parents;
(B) for students without dependents residing in institutionally owned or operated housing, shall be a standard allowance determined by the institution based on the amount normally assessed most of its residents for room and board; and
(C) for all other students shall be an allowance based on the expenses reasonably incurred by such students for room and board[.] . . .

30 20 U.S.C. § 1087*ll*(1) (referenced in IRS Code at 26 U.S.C. § 221(d)(2)).
31 *But see In re* Willis, 2010 WL 1688221, at *7 (S.D. Ind. Apr. 23, 2010) (incorrectly finding that private trade school loan that debtor incurred on behalf of his grandson was a qualified educational loan under 26 U.S.C. § 221(d)(1)).
32 *In re* LeBlanc, 404 B.R. 793 (Bankr. M.D. Pa. 2009) (nonresident alien who did not file a tax return during relevant time period was a not a "taxpayer"; loan extended to her did not qualify as a student loan under 26 U.S.C. § 221(d) and 11 U.S.C. § 523(a)(8)).
33 26 U.S.C. § 221(d)(1).

Note that, unlike the more expansive coverage of section 523(a)(8)(A), which encompasses loans to pay for secondary school education, private loans covered by the section 523(a)

partment regulations implementing section 221(d)(1) explain what is meant by the term "solely to pay qualified higher education expenses." Loans meeting this standard are distinguished from "mixed-use" loans:

> Mixed–use loans. Student J signs a promissory note for a loan secured by Student J's personal residence. Student J will use part of the loan proceeds to pay for certain improvements to Student J's residence and part of the loan proceeds to pay qualified higher education expenses of Student J's spouse. Because Student J obtains the loan not solely to pay qualified higher education expenses, the loan is not a qualified education loan.[34]

Consistent with the above example, cash advances, revolving lines of credit, and credit card debt should not be considered qualified education loans unless the total debt consists of credit incurred solely to pay for qualifying education expenses.[35] There has been little litigation to date over the scope of this "mixed use" limitation under the IRS guidelines. Under the pre-BAPCPA Bankruptcy Code the courts were not sympathetic to arguments that attempted to avoid the reach of section 523(a)(8) by focusing on the use of the proceeds from government-related loan programs for non-academic purposes.[36] For private loans covered by the new subsection (B), there should be stronger arguments for consideration of how the loan proceeds were used. The IRS guidelines defer to educational institutions in how they define costs of attendance. Private loans that fund expenses beyond what the educational institution determines to be the reasonable costs of attendance should be considered "mixed use" loans and therefore wholly dischargeable. Typically, educational institutions develop these cost estimates for use in financial aid programs and for other purposes, so the reasonable cost of attendance information should be publicly available.[37]

In order to be considered a qualified education loan under subsection (B) of section 523(a)(8), the loan must have been taken out to pay expenses for education furnished during a period in which the recipient was an eligible student.[38] The expenses must be paid or incurred within a reasonable period of time before or after the indebtedness is incurred.[39] There are circumstances under which a student may take out a loan to attend school but may not necessarily be an eligible student. For example, aggressive proprietary schools in some cases enroll non-high-school graduates without properly administering the required "ability to benefit" test.[40] Students improperly enrolled in this way are eligible to administratively cancel their loans and should also be categorized as "ineligible" students.

Another requirement for a "qualified higher educational expense" under the IRS Code is that the expenses be for attendance at an "eligible education institution." Eligible institutions are defined as institutions that are eligible to participate in a Title IV program.[41] Title IV refers to the title of the HEA that governs federal financial assistance programs. Most, but not all, schools are eligible to participate in these programs. For example, numerous unaccredited schools have gone in and out of business in recent years. These unaccredited schools are not eligible to participate in the Title IV programs. Other scam programs such as "diploma mills" are also not eligible to participate in Title IV programs. Borrowers with student loans from these schools should be able to discharge the loans without having to prove hardship.

10.2.2.2 Some Education Debts Should be Dischargeable

In addition to covering certain lenders, section 523(a)(8) is directed toward loan transactions with an educational purpose. In some instances, the purpose of a loan may place it outside of the dischargeability exception. For example, an employer may pay off the costs associated with an employee's education and training as part of a hiring agreement. The courts have held that these payments were dischargeable debts because the employer paid the expenses for business purposes, as a hiring incentive, and not primarily as educational loans.[42] The educational purpose requirement

---

(8)(B) must have been taken out to pay for *higher* education expenses.

34 26 C.F.R. § 1.221-1(e)(4) ex. 6.
35 *See* 26 C.F.R. § 1.221-1; 64 Fed. Reg. 3257, 3258 (Jan. 21, 1999) (see "Explanation of Provisions" in preamble to proposed Treasury Regulations) ("Accordingly, mixed use loans are not qualified education loans. Similarly, revolving lines of credit (e.g., credit card debt) generally are not qualified education loans, unless the borrower uses the line of credit solely to pay qualified higher education expenses.").
36 Murphy v. Pennsylvania Higher Educ. Assistance Agency, 282 F.3d 868, 873 (5th Cir. 2002) (suggesting that allowing ultimate use of loan funds to determine dischargeability would encourage students to seek discharge of loans when the money went toward "social uses, alcohol, or even drugs").
37 *But see In re* Rogers, 374 B.R. 510 (Bankr. E.D.N.Y. 2007) (suggesting that debtor has burden of proof to show which portion of private loan proceeds exceeded the institution's costs of attendance).

38 26 U.S.C. § 221(d)(1)(C).
39 *But see In re* Willis, 2010 WL 1688221, at *7 (S.D. Ind. Apr. 23, 2010) (incorrectly finding that private trade school loan that debtor incurred on behalf of his grandson was a qualified educational loan under 26 U.S.C. § 221(d)(1)).
40 *See* § 9.4.2, *supra*.
41 26 U.S.C. § 221(d)(2) (referring to 26 U.S.C. § 25A(f)(2)(B)).
42 *See In re* Segal, 57 F.3d 342 (3d Cir. 1995) (when nonprofit hospital paid off debtor's student loans, replacing it with new loans, those new loans were dischargeable because they were not made under a "program" of giving educational loans); *In re* Hawkins, 317 B.R. 104 (B.A.P. 9th Cir. 2004) (tuition subsidy related to continued medical practice in Ohio was not an educational loan subject to section 523(a)(8)), aff'd, 469 F.3d 1316 (9th Cir. 2006); *In re* Rezendez, 324 B.R. 689 (N.D. Ind.

applies to government-related and private loans, and to cases filed before and after the 2005 amendments. However, obligations to fulfill military service duties in return for education subsidies give rise to nondischargeable debts if the military service is not completed.[43]

Finally, courts routinely hold that bankruptcy debtors may discharge tuition debts when creditors fail to establish the existence of a "loan" involving a transfer of funds and a formal agreement specifying repayment terms.[44]

10.2.2.3 Refinanced Student Loans in Bankruptcy

For any number of reasons, a borrower may decide to refinance a student loan, replacing an obligation that originated as a student loan with a new and different obligation. This may occur through one of the student loan consolidation options offered under various federal programs or through a private consolidation product.[45] The refinancing could be accomplished through completely private sources of credit. For example, a student with a private educational loan may wish to take advantage of a lower interest rate offered by a different lender. This may appear to be an attractive option for borrowers with high-rate private loans seeking to get better deals. A problem, however, is that private lenders are increasingly encouraging or even pressuring borrowers with government loans to consolidate into private consolidation loans. Borrowers who choose this option will lose the unique flexible repayment and other borrower-friendly provisions associated with the government loan programs.

The restriction on dischargeability generally applies in the same way to consolidation loans.[46] However, as students turn with increasing frequency to various options, including conventional bank loans, cash advances, and even credit card debt, in order to deal with oppressive student loan debt, what is the status of these new forms of debt when the student files for bankruptcy relief? In part, it depends upon the context in which the refinancing occurs. Loan consolidations under the Higher Education Act, for example, take place in the context of a federally insured program. These consolidations are simply new student loans that fit squarely

---

2004) (cost of plumbers' union apprentice program was dischargeable because not an educational loan and not subject to agreement to pay any fixed amount); *In re* Nies, 334 B.R. 495 (Bankr. D. Mass. 2005) (hospital recruitment program that paid doctor's student loans as a hiring incentive was not an educational loan); *In re* McFadyan, 192 B.R. 328 (Bankr. N.D.N.Y. 1995) (hospital's funding of nurse's training course in return for commitment to continue employment with hospital was a transaction intended to further employer's business objectives, not a loan for educational purposes). *But see In re* Kesler, 401 B.R. 356 (Bankr. S.D. Ill. 2009) (apprentice's written agreement that he would repay cost of carpentry apprenticeship program if he later worked for non-member employer treated as nondischargeable educational loan); *In re* Baiocchi, 389 B.R. 828 (Bankr. E.D. Wis. 2008) (upon premature termination of employment, employee's obligation to repay former employer for funds it paid toward her law school attendance was an "educational benefit, scholarship, or stipend" under section 523(a)(8)(A)(ii)).

43 *In re* Udell, 454 F.3d 180 (3d Cir. 2006) (dismissed cadet's obligation to repay costs of Air Force Academy attendance must be treated as education loan subject to section 523(a)(8) after initial five-year period of absolute nondischargeability under 19 U.S.C. § 2005(d) has passed); *In re* Dunn, 325 B.R. 807 (Bankr. N.D. Iowa 2005) (same rule applies to obligations to repay private college subsidy under ROTC program).

44 *In re* Chambers, 348 F.3d 650 (7th Cir. 2003) (tuition debt and related charges held dischargeable, as no evidence parties entered into loan arrangement prior to services being provided); *In re* Mehta, 310 F.3d 308 (3d Cir. 2002) (student's unilateral decision not to pay tuition does not create a loan); Cazenovia College v. Renshaw, 222 F.3d 82 (2d Cir. 2000) (tuition debt not a loan); *In re* Nelson, 188 B.R. 32 (D.S.D. 1995) (debt for tuition, room, and board to university was not a loan); *In re* Navarro, 284 B.R. 727 (Bankr. C.D. Cal. 2002) (agreement that student would be responsible for tuition and fees was not a promissory note for sum certain and therefore was dischargeable); *In re* Ray, 262 B.R. 544 (Bankr. D. Okla. 2001) (tuition debt was neither "loan" nor "obligation to repay funds received as an educational benefit"); *In re* Pelzman, 233 B.R. 575 (Bankr. D.D.C. 1999) (room and board for first semester nondischargeable because pursuant to program but not for remaining semesters when extension of credit violated school policy); *In re* Gordon, 231 B.R. 459 (Bankr. D. Conn. 1999) (residency program assistance not student loan); *In re* Feyes, 228 B.R. 887 (Bankr. N.D. Ohio 1998) (credit extension was dischargeable when school allowed student to attend classes on a credit basis and pay for them when he could and no promissory note was signed); *In re* Johnson, 222 B.R. 783 (Bankr. E.D. Va. 1998) (debt for tuition was not obligation for funds received on a loan and there was no "program"); *In re* Meinhart, 211 B.R. 750 (Bankr. D. Colo. 1997) (debt to school was not an obligation to repay "funds received" as required by statute); *In re* Coole, 202 B.R. 518 (Bankr. D.N.M. 1996) (debt to school for services rendered was not a loan); *In re* Alibatya, 178 B.R. 335 (Bankr. E.D.N.Y. 1995) (no loan when debtor failed to pay student housing rent under lease with university). *See also In re Gamble*, 388 B.R. 877 (Bankr. C.D. Ill. 2008) (open student debit account for tuition and other charges not a student loan); *In re* Parker, 334 B.R. 529 (Bankr. D. Mass. 2005) (university violated automatic stay and discharge injunction by refusing to allow student to register for class unless she paid past tuition bill discharged in bankruptcy); *In re* Davis, 316 B.R. 610 (Bankr. S.D.N.Y. 2004) (debtor's failure to comply with tuition payment plan schedule did not constitute a student loan obligation under discharge exception); *In re* Van Ess, 186 B.R. 375 (Bankr. D.N.J. 1994) (unpaid law school tuition bill was not a student loan debt). *Cf. In re* DePasquale, 225 B.R. 830 (B.A.P. 1st Cir. 1998) (payment agreement for overdue tuition constituted "loan"); *In re* Johnson, 218 B.R. 449 (B.A.P. 8th Cir. 1998) (debtor who signed promissory note to college for unpaid tuition had student loan).

For a more extensive summary of cases on the subject of distinguishing student loans from student tuition account debts, see Matthew C. Welnicki, *Dischargeability of Student Financial Obligations: Student Loans Versus Student Tuition Account Debts*, 31 J.C. & U.L. 665 (2005).

45 *See* § 6.2, *supra*.
46 *See In re* Flint, 238 B.R. 676 (E.D. Mich. 1999), *rev'g* 231 B.R. 611 (Bankr. E.D. Mich. 1999); *In re* Shaffer, 237 B.R. 617 (Bankr. N.D. Tex. 1999); *In re* Cobb, 196 B.R. 34 (Bankr. E.D. Va. 1996).

within the definition of nondischargeable student loans made under any program funded by governmental and nonprofit entities.[47] To date there has been little reported litigation addressing the application of section 523(a)(8) to purely private refinancings that take place outside of the federally insured consolidation programs.

The IRS Code addresses this question in part. IRS Code section 221(d)(1) defines a "qualified education loan" as including "indebtedness used to refinance indebtedness which qualifies as a qualified education loan."[48] Therefore, under the IRS definition, a subsequent loan that does nothing more than pay off and replace an earlier student loan with a new one will be a "qualified education loan." This will entitle the taxpayer to an interest deduction for the new loan payments, but it will preclude the same taxpayer from discharging the consolidated loan debt in bankruptcy absent the showing of undue hardship. Use of mixed-use private loans to refinance, however, may produce a different result. As discussed above, for the private loan to be included in the new discharge prohibition enacted as part of BAPCPA, the loan must comply with the IRS definition in section 221(d)(1). This means that the debtor must have incurred the loan solely to pay for qualified education expenses. A completely private refinancing for mixed-use purposes potentially will produce a dischargeable debt.

The Treasury Department regulations applicable to private educational loans make clear that the "solely to pay for qualified higher education expenses" limitation applies in exactly the same fashion to refinancing transactions. To qualify as an educational loan, the new indebtedness must be incurred solely to refinance a qualified education loan.[49] Likewise, a consolidation loan will not be a "qualified education loan" unless incurred solely to refinance two or more qualified education loans.[50] Cash advances, revolving lines of credit, and credit card debt should not be considered qualified education loans unless the total debt consists of credit incurred solely to pay for qualifying education expenses.[51]

10.2.2.4 Pre-BAPCPA Covered Loans—The Role of Programs Guaranteed or Insured by a Nonprofit or Government Entity

The pre-BAPCPA language of section 523(a)(8) remains controlling for bankruptcy cases filed before BAPCPA's effective date of October 17, 2005. The key language of the pre-BAPCPA version of section 523(a)(8) excepted from discharge a "loan made, insured or guaranteed by a governmental unit, or made under any program funded in whole or in party by a governmental unit or nonprofit institution."[52] This phrase contains two distinct provisions. The first excludes from discharge loans "made, insured or guaranteed by a governmental unit." The second excludes from discharge loans "made under any program funded in whole or in part by a governmental unit or nonprofit institution." The second phrase, with its reference to a student loan "program" funded by a nonprofit or by a government unit, has inspired the most litigation. Identifying the pertinent "program" for purposes of this discharge exception has not always been a simple task. For example, the players in a student loan transaction may have included a private lending bank, a nonprofit guarantor of the loan, and a third entity serving as a loan broker to bring the parties together. Determining which of these is the pertinent student loan "program" and how that program is funded can be critical issues in determining whether a particular loan is excepted from discharge under the pre-2005 Code.

In applying the pre-BAPCPA version of section 523(a)(8), several courts held that a for-profit bank's relationship with a nonprofit entity that guaranteed the bank's student loans created a unitary student loan "program," making the for-profit bank's loans nondischargeable.[53] These courts viewed the nonprofit guarantor's obligation to pay the loan in the event of default as equivalent to the nonprofit's "funding" of a student loan program. Other courts viewed private banks' relationships with "nonprofit" loan brokers in a similar way. Loan brokers may have financial ties with nonprofit institutions, or they may be nonprofit organizations themselves. According to some courts, the activities of these brokers affiliated with nonprofits created a student loan "program" for purposes of section 523(a)(8).[54] In

---

47 *See, e.g., In re* Lapusan, 244 B.R. 423 (Bankr. S.D. Ill. 2000) (consolidation loan under HEA is an educational loan that is nondischargeable for purposes of section 523(a)(8)); *In re* Shaffer, 237 B.R. 617 (Bankr. N.D. Tex. 1999) (same). *But see In re* Lakemaker, 241 B.R. 577 (Bankr. N.D. Ill. 1999) (loan repayment not involving government or nonprofit program did not create an education loan under section 523(a)(8)).
48 26 U.S.C. § 221(d)(1).
49 26 C.F.R. § 1.221-1(e)(3)(v) ("Refinanced and consolidated indebtedness—(A) In general. A qualified education loan includes indebtedness incurred solely to refinance a qualified education loan. A qualified education loan includes a single, consolidated indebtedness incurred solely to refinance two or more qualified education loans of a borrower.").
50 *Id.*
51 *See* 26 C.F.R. § 1.221-1; 64 Fed. Reg. 3257, 3258 (Jan. 21, 1999) (see "Explanation of Provisions" in preamble to proposed Treasury Regulations) ("Accordingly, mixed use loans are not qualified education loans. Similarly, revolving lines of credit (e.g., credit card debt) generally are not qualified education loans, unless the borrower uses the line of credit solely to pay qualified higher education expenses.").
52 11 U.S.C. § 523(a)(8)(2004).
  This same language now appears in subsection (A)(i) of section 523(a)(8). Subsection A(ii) of section 523(a)(8) now incorporates the other, less utilized, category of nondischargeable obligations under the pre-BAPCPA text: "an obligation to repay funds received as an educational benefit, scholarship or stipend."
53 *In re* Merchant, 958 F.2d 738 (6th Cir. 1992); *In re* McLain, 272 B.R. 42 (Bankr. D.N.H. 2002); *In re* Hammarstrom, 95 B.R. 160 (Bankr. N.D. Cal. 1989).
54 *In re* O'Brien, 419 F.3d 104 (2d Cir. 2005); *In re* Pilcher, 149

these rulings the courts construed the "program" requirement of section 523(a)(8) broadly and found the discharge exception to be applicable even though private for-profit banks made the loans and disbursed the funds to the debtor.

The status of credit unions as student loan creditors produced conflicting rulings under the pre-BAPCPA version of section 523(a)(8). A number of courts held that credit unions that made loans for educational purposes were "governmental units."[55] These courts considered factors such as the legislative history of the Federal Credit Union Act and concluded that credit unions performed a governmental function in making loans to needy students.[56] Other courts rejected this view, noting that credit unions competed with other private banks, had shareholders, and paid dividends.[57] This approach would appear to comport better with the plain language of the definition of a "governmental unit" in Bankruptcy Code section 101(27).[58] This definition requires that the entity be a "department, agency, or instrumentality" of the government. Typically, this standard is not met merely by a showing that the entity is subject to government regulation or receives regular funding from the government.[59] However, regardless of the "governmental unit" status of the credit union itself, if the credit union made the educational loan under a program funded by some other agency that was clearly a nonprofit or governmental unit, then the loan is within the scope of section 523(a)(8), under either the pre- or post-BAPCPA version of the section.[60]

The language in the pre-BAPCPA version of section 523(a)(8), which remains in current subpart (i) of section 523(a)(8)(A), was intended to protect government agencies and nonprofit organizations that operate student loan programs.[61] As described above, cases decided under the pre-BAPCPA version of section 523(a)(8) did not always turn on the for-profit versus nonprofit status of the original lender.[62] The courts' construction of the term "program" brought a wide range of loan transactions within the discharge exception and excluded others. What the 2005 BAPCPA amendment accomplished by adding new subsection (B) to section 523(a)(8) was to exclude the "program" affiliation requirement for nearly all private student loans, without regard to whether they were originated by a for-profit or nonprofit entity. The amendments make all student loans presumptively nondischargeable so long as they qualify for the student loan interest deduction under federal tax law.

10.2.2.5 Discharging Student Loans over Seven Years Old No Longer Allowed for Cases Filed After October 7, 1998

In 1998, student loan debtors suffered a major setback to their ability to discharge student loans. For all bankruptcy cases filed after October 7, 1998, the discharge of student loans that first became due more than seven years prior to the bankruptcy filing will no longer be allowed.[63] Cases filed before October 7, 1998, are not affected by the change in law. The following discussion of discharges under the seven-year rule is still relevant for consumers who filed before the change in law, and there remains a question as to whether a student loan was discharged.

For cases filed before October 7, 1998, if the first student loan installment became due more than seven years prior to the bankruptcy filing, then the entire loan and not just the first installment is discharged.[64] The most important issue in counting the seven-year period is that the seven years are "exclusive of any applicable suspension of the repayment period."[65] This means that a deferment or forbearance may

---

B.R. 595 (B.A.P. 9th Cir. 1993); *In re* Bolen, 287 B.R. 127 (Bankr. D. Vt. 2002). *See also In re* Johnson, 2008 WL 5120913 (Bankr. M.D. Pa. Dec. 3, 2008) (under pre-BAPCPA Code, Law Access loan by private lender funded through nonprofit program is nondischargeable).

55 *See, e.g.*, TI Fed. Credit Union v. DelBonis, 72 F.3d 921 (1st Cir. 1995); *In re* Trusko, 212 B.R. 819 (Bankr. D. Md. 1997).

56 TI Fed. Credit Union v. DelBonis, 72 F.3d 921, 935 (1st Cir. 1995).

57 *In re* Simmons, 175 B.R. 624 (Bankr. E.D. Va. 1994) (credit union was not a nonprofit and its loans were not made in connection with a nonprofit or governmental program); *In re* Sinclair-Ganos, 133 B.R. 382 (Bankr. W.D. Mich. 1991) (same).

58 11 U.S.C. § 101(27).

59 *See, e.g.*, *In re* Merriweather, 185 B.R. 235 (Bankr. S.D. Tex. 1995) (private mortgage company approved by HUD to participate in federal mortgage insurance program is not a "governmental unit"); *In re* Liggins, 145 B.R. 227 (Bankr. E.D. Va. 1992) (private landlord receiving subsidies under federally assisted housing program is not a "governmental unit"); *In re* Lutz, 82 B.R. 699 (Bankr. M.D. Pa. 1988) (same); *In re* Brown, 49 B.R. 558 (Bankr. M.D. Pa. 1985) (credit union is not "governmental unit" for purposes of Bankruptcy Code § 525(a) anti-discrimination provision).

60 *See In re* Roberts, 149 B.R. 547 (C.D. Ill. 1993) (credit union as nonprofit organization made loans pursuant to its established student loan program). *But see In re* Simmons, 175 B.R. 624 (Bankr. E.D. Va. 1994) (credit union failed to show that it was a nonprofit and did not have an established program though which it made student loans).

61 TI Fed. Credit Union v. DelBonis, 72 F.3d 921, 937 (1st Cir. 1995); *In re* Segal, 57 F.3d 342, 348 (3d Cir. 1995).

62 *See, e.g.*, *In re* O'Brien 419 F.3d 104 (2d Cir. 2005); *In re* Merchant, 958 F.2d 738 (6th Cir. 1992); *In re* Pilcher, 149 B.R. 595 (B.A.P. 9th Cir. 1993); *In re* Segal, 57 F.3d 342, 348 (3d Cir. 1995) (nonprofit did not make loan as part of any distinct educational loan program); *In re* Lakemaker, 241 B.R. 577, 580–581 (Bankr. N.D. Ill. 1999) (rejecting medical center's claim that its salary advances were loans under an educational program); *In re* LaFlamme, 188 B.R. 867 (Bankr. D.N.H. 1995); Seton Hall Univ. v. Van Ess, 186 B.R. 375, 380 (Bankr. D.N.J. 1994) (law school did not give extension of credit pursuant to a loan program).

63 Pub. L. No. 105-244, § 971, 112 Stat. 1581 (Oct. 7, 1998) (Higher Education Programs Authorization Extension Act).

64 *See, e.g.*, *In re* Nunn, 788 F.2d 617 (9th Cir. 1986).

65 11 U.S.C. § 523(a)(8)(A); U.S. Dep't of Educ. v. Scott (*In re* Scott), 147 F.3d 788 (8th Cir. 1998) (loan first became due after six-month grace period expired, not when student left school). *See also* National Consumer Law Center, Consumer Bank-

lengthen the seven-year period if repayments were suspended during that period.[66] On the other hand, the seven-year period should not be lengthened just because the consumer was allowed to make reduced payments or entered into a reasonable and affordable repayment agreement, because payments were not suspended.[67] Consolidating one or more student loans, though, will likely start the seven-year period running all over again as of the date of the consolidated loan.[68]

10.3 Burden of Proof and the Student Loan Dischargeability Exception

10.3.1 General

Courts sometimes refer to the discharge exception for student loans in section 523(a)(8) as "presumptive" or "self-executing."[69] However, this general rule obscures an important qualification. The rule assumes that the underlying obligation is actually a "student loan" within the scope of the education-related obligations defined in section 523(a)(8). If, contrary to this assumption, the obligation does not fall within one of the categories of debts defined by section 523(a)(8), the discharge order will cover the obligation.[70]

There are many reasons why an educational obligation may not qualify for the exception from discharge under section 523(a)(8). The creditor may be unable to establish the existence of a "loan" that involved a transfer of funds and a formal agreement specifying repayment terms.[71] In cases under the pre-BAPCPA version of section 523(a)(8), creditors failed to establish an educational purpose or benefit related to certain loans.[72] In other cases governed by the pre-BAPCPA version of section 523(a)(8), creditors were left unprotected by section 523(a)(8) when they could not prove that the funds had been advanced through a "program" funded by a nonprofit institution or governmental entity.[73] In still other pre-BAPCPA cases, courts rejected creditors' claims that the debts were "for an obligation to repay funds received as an education benefit, scholarship or stipend" because the transactions were entirely unrelated to any governmental or nonprofit entity.[74]

Identifying an obligation as falling outside the scope of section 523(a)(8) does not answer the question of how best to protect the debtor from future collection activity based on the transaction. In a clear case, the debtor may refrain from seeking a judicial determination of the status of the debt during the bankruptcy case and later assert the bankruptcy discharge as a defense if the creditor attempts postbankruptcy collection. In response to future collection efforts, the debtor can also reopen the bankruptcy case and bring a proceeding in bankruptcy court for contempt against the creditor for violation of the discharge order.[75] However, when there is any doubt about the status of an educational debt under the statutory definition, the debtor's better option will always be to seek a determination of the dischargeability of the debt during the bankruptcy case. There is no tactical advantage to be gained by a delay of the determination. Unlike the facts underlying an undue hardship claim, the status of the debt under the relevant statutory definition will not change in the future.

---

ruptcy Law and Practice § 15.4.3.8 (9th ed. 2009 and Supp.).

66 *In re* Huber, 169 B.R. 82 (Bankr. W.D.N.Y. 1994) (deferment period counts even when debtor eventually found not eligible for deferment when repayment requirement was suspended); *In re* Barciz, 123 B.R. 771 (Bankr. N.D. Ohio 1990) (forbearance tolls running of period). *But see In re* Flynn, 190 B.R. 139 (Bankr. D.N.H. 1995) (a reference to a period of forbearance did not refer to a suspension of payment).

67 *In re* Salter, 207 B.R. 272 (Bankr. M.D. Fla. 1997) (stipulation changing amount of payments did not constitute a new obligation that would restart the seven-year time period); *In re* Marlewski, 168 B.R. 378 (Bankr. E.D. Wis. 1994) (repayment agreement does not toll period when agreement did not call for suspension of payments or lengthening of repayment period). *See also In re* Manriquez, 207 B.R. 890 (B.A.P. 9th Cir. 1996) (retroactive forbearance agreement signed after the seven years had already run did not render loan nondischargeable).

68 *See, e.g.*, Hiatt v. Indiana State Student Assistance Comm'n, 36 F.3d 21 (7th Cir. 1994); United States v. McGrath, 143 B.R. 820 (D. Md. 1992), *aff'd without op.*, 8 F.3d 821 (4th Cir. 1993); *In re* Burns, 334 B.R. 521 (Bankr. D. Mass. 2005) (debtor had initially filed for chapter 7 relief in 1988; five-year limit not met because loans were consolidated in 1984); *In re* Cobb, 196 B.R. 34 (Bankr. E.D. Va. 1996); *In re* Hasselgrave, 177 B.R. 681 (Bankr. D. Or. 1995); *In re* Menendez, 151 B.R. 972 (Bankr. M.D. Fla. 1993); *In re* Martin, 137 B.R. 770 (Bankr. W.D. Mo. 1992).

One court has held that a consolidation loan obtained by duress was void, permitting the debtor to obtain a discharge under the former seven-year rule. *In re* Mason, 300 B.R. 160 (Bankr. D. Conn. 2003).

69 United Student Funds, Inc. v. Espinosa, 130 S. Ct. 1367, 1379–80 (2010) (citing to Tennessee Student Assistance Corp. v. Hood, 541 U.S. 440, 450 (2004) ("[u]nless the debtor affirmatively secures a hardship determination, the discharge order will not include the student loan debt")).

70 Procedural issues related to the dischargeability determination, if the obligation is a covered student loan, are addressed in § 10.7, *infra*.

71 *See generally* § 10.2.2.2, *supra*.

72 *See* § 10.2.2.4, *supra*.

73 *Id.*

74 11 U.S.C. § 523(a)(8). *See* London-Marable v. Sterling, 2008 WL 2705374 (D. Ariz. July 9, 2008) (third clause of pre-BAPCPA § 523(a)(8) required that loan have some relation to governmental or nonprofit organization; clause not applicable to loan from family member); *In re* Scott, 287 B.R. 470 (Bankr. E.D. Mo. 2002) (loan from wholly private truck driving school not an "educational benefit" under former version of section 523(a)(8)); *In re* Jones, 242 B.R. 441 (Bankr. W.D. Tenn. 1999) (same); *In re* Meinhart, 211 B.R. 750 (Bankr. D. Colo. 1997) (education loan from family members is outside scope of existing dischargeability exception).

75 *See* 11 U.S.C. § 524(a).

§ 10.3.1

The procedural mechanism for obtaining a ruling on an obligation's status under the statutory student loan definition is the same one the debtor would use when seeking an undue hardship determination. The debtor files an adversary action in the bankruptcy court to obtain a declaration from the court as to whether the debt is dischargeable. The debtor may file this action either during the initial bankruptcy case or in a reopened bankruptcy case. When it is foreseeable that there will be a dispute about the status of an educational loan under the statutory definition, the creditor often files the adversary action.

In terms of burden of proof, there is a significant difference between a bankruptcy adversary action seeking an undue hardship determination and an action seeking a declaration of whether the underlying obligation is a student loan covered by section 523(a)(8). In any proceeding that involves a determination of the loan's status under the statutory student loan definition, the creditor must establish by a preponderance of the evidence that the debt is a loan or similar obligation that falls within the scope of one of the provisions of section 523(a)(8).[76] This burden of proof falls upon the creditor regardless of who files the action. As with all claims asserting an exception to discharge, the evidence must be narrowly construed against the creditor.[77] The burden of proof will not shift to the debtor to establish undue hardship unless the creditor first meets the "condition precedent to nondischargeability" of proving that its debt falls within the statutory definition of a presumptively nondischargeable student loan.[78] Once it is established that the obligation is covered by section 523(a)(8), the initial burden then shifts to the debtor to make out a prima facie showing that would support a determination of undue hardship.[79]

The 2005 Code amendments applying the discharge exception to private loans create some additional burden of proof tests for creditors. For example, creditors claiming the protection for a private student loan must show that the loan was given solely for costs of attendance at an "eligible educational institution."[80] Similarly, it should be the creditor's, not the debtor's, burden of proof to establish what the "costs of attendance" were as determined by the educational institution.[81]

---

76 *In re* Mehta, 310 F.3d 308, 311 (3d Cir. 2002) (student loan creditor opposing discharge has burden of establishing that the obligation is an educational loan under section 523(a)(8)); *In re* Renshaw, 222 F.3d 82, 86 (2d Cir. 2000) (same); *In re* Nies, 334 B.R. 495 (Bankr. D. Mass. 2005) (hospital did not demonstrate by preponderance of evidence that loan under physician recruitment program was for an educational purpose); *In re* Davis, 316 B.R. 610 (Bankr. S.D.N.Y. 2004) (creditor did not meet burden of establishing existence of educational loan resulting from unpaid tuition); *In re* Pelzman, 233 B.R. 575 (Bankr. D.D.C. 1999) (the statute is not satisfied by a simple showing of an educational loan without creditor establishing existence of program to grant loan); Navy Fed. Credit Union v. Burton, 1997 WL 33344247 (Bankr. D.S.C. July 7, 1997) (creditor failed to meet burden of proving loan consolidations were either completely used for or intended for an educational benefit); *In re* McFayden, 192 B.R. 328, 331 (Bankr. N.D.N.Y. 1995) (creditor must establish by preponderance of evidence that debt was an educational loan and that it was made as part of program funded by nonprofit entity); *In re* Doyle, 106 B.R. 272 (Bankr. N.D. Ala. 1989) (party in interest who asserts that "student loan" is excepted from discharge has burden of proving that debt, in fact, is obligation of type described in section 523(a)(8)); *In re* Ealy, 78 B.R. 897 (Bankr. C.D. Ill. 1987) (not reaching undue hardship determination because creditor did not meet its burden of establishing that loan proceeds were used for educational purposes); *In re* Keenan, 53 B.R. 913 (Bankr. D. Conn 1985) (postdischarge student loan creditor who asserts right to payment on basis that debt was not discharged has burden of proving that debt came within definition of student loan that was not discharged); *In re* Norman, 25 B.R. 545 (Bankr. S.D. Cal. 1982) (under pre-1998 version of section 523(a)(8), creditor's burden of proof in dischargeability action included proving that loan came due during five- or seven-year period before bankruptcy filing). *See generally* Raymond L. Woodcock, *Burden of Proof, Undue Hardship, and Other Arguments for the Student Debtor Under 11 U.S.C. § 523(a)(8)(B)*, 24 J. of Coll. & Univ. L. 377 (Winter 1998).

77 *In re* Chambers, 348 F.3d 650, 654 (7th Cir. 2003) (definition of educational loan under section 523(a)(8), like other exceptions to discharge, is to be narrowly construed in favor of debtor); *In re* Mehta, 310 F.3d 308, 311 (3d Cir. 2002) (same); *In re* Renshaw, 222 F.3d 82, 86 (2d Cir. 2000) (scope of obligations under section 523(a)(8) to be narrowly construed); *In re* Davis, 316 B.R. 610, 613 (Bankr. S.D.N.Y. 2004) (scope of student loan exception to discharge should be construed narrowly against creditor and in favor of debtor); *In re* Johnson, 222 B.R. 783, 786 (Bankr. E.D. Va. 1998) (exceptions to discharge should be narrowly construed; tuition and fees debt did not fall within any category of section 523(a)(8)); *In re* Alibatya, 178 B.R. 335, 338 (Bankr. E.D.N.Y. 1995) (student charges were not educational loan; scope of section 523(a)(8) should be strictly construed against creditor and liberally in favor of debtor); *In re* Van Ess, 186 B.R. 375, 377–78 (Bankr. D.N.J. 1994) (rule of narrow construction against creditor applies in determining whether transaction was educational loan under section 523(a)(8)).

78 *In re* Keenan, 53 B.R. 913, 916 (Bankr. D. Conn. 1985) (burden of proof in student loan dischargeability action is shifting burden, with creditor having initial burden of proof on status of obligation as one covered by dischargeability exception). *See also In re* Norman, 25 B.R. 545 (Bankr. S.D. Cal. 1982) (after creditor proves status of loan as within dischargeability exception, burden of proof on undue hardship shifts to debtor, who has best access to evidence of his or her particular financial difficulties).

79 *See, e.g., In re* Traversa, 2010 WL 1541443, at *6 (Bankr. D. Conn. Apr. 15, 2010) (discussing burden of production and moving forward in undue hardship action).

80 26 U.S.C. § 221(d)(2). *See* §§ 10.2.1, 10.2.2.1, *supra*. *See generally In re* Willis, 2010 WL 1688221 (S.D. Ind. Apr. 23, 2010) (creditor provided certification that truck driving school had certification under Title IV of Higher Education Act).

81 26 U.S.C. § 221(d)(1), (2); 20 U.S.C. § 1087*ll*. *In re* Rogers, 374 B.R. 510 (Bankr. E.D.N.Y. 2007) (incorrectly suggesting that debtor had burden of proof as to what educational institution determined were its "costs of attendance"). *See* § 10.2.2.1, *supra*.

10.3.2 Parents and Other Co-Signors

Most courts find the exception to discharge for student loans applies not only to student borrowers but also to parents, spouses, or non-relatives who co-sign a student loan.[82] Early on, the courts were divided over this question.[83] The arguments in favor of excluding co-obligors from the discharge exception focused on several rationales. First, several courts held that the co-obligors' debts were not "educational loans" because the co-obligors did not use the loan proceeds for their own educational benefit. Second, granting discharge for co-obligors furthers the "fresh start" goal of bankruptcy. Third, the legislative history of the discharge exception focused on students about to embark on lucrative careers and the perception that these recent graduates might abuse the bankruptcy discharge option to the detriment of the loan programs. Presumably, these abuse considerations would not be as compelling in cases involving middle-aged parents.[84]

Only one court of appeals has addressed the issue of the dischargeability of student loans by co-obligors.[85] The court in *In re Pelkowski* considered and rejected all of the arguments mentioned above. The court found no basis for status-based distinctions in either the legislative history or in the plain language of the student loan discharge exception. Since *Pelkowski*, no reported decisions have allowed a co-obligor to discharge a student loan unless the co-obligor met the undue hardship test. Furthermore, when parents are the sole obligors on student loans for their children—for example, on PLUS loans—no courts have allowed the parents to discharge their student loan debt without meeting the undue hardship standard.[86] Parents who were solely liable for their children's student loans have certainly prevailed in their own hardship discharge actions.[87]

Married bankruptcy debtors may be co-obligors on student loans or may seek discharge of their individual loans. Joint liability may arise from either the initial loan transactions or from later consolidations. In hardship discharge actions brought in joint bankruptcy cases, spousal debtors have met with inconsistent outcomes. The results vary depending on the financial prospects and resources of each spouse.[88]

10.4 Undue Hardship As Basis for Discharging Student Loan

10.4.1 General

A student loan may be discharged if payment of the debt "will impose an undue hardship on the debtor and the debtor's dependents."[89] There is no statutory definition of "undue hardship." Generally, it means the consumer's present income is inadequate to pay the loan and this situation is not likely to change even after considering the consumer's future earning potential.

All courts of appeals except the First and Eighth circuits have adopted the three-prong test for determining undue hardship set forth in the Second Circuit decision in *Brunner*

---

82   *See In re* Pelkowski, 990 F.2d 737 (3d Cir. 1993); *In re* Varma, 149 B.R. 817 (N.D. Tex. 1992); *In re* Wilcon, 143 B.R. 4 (D. Mass. 1992); Uterhark v. Great Lakes Higher Educ. Corp. (*In re* Uterhark), 185 B.R. 39 (Bankr. N.D. Ohio 1995); Owens v. Nebraska Higher Educ. Loan Program, Inc. (*In re* Owens), 161 B.R. 829 (Bankr. D. Neb. 1993). *But see* Cockels v. Sallie Mae, 414 B.R. 149 (E.D. Mich. 2009) (debtor liable for student loan debt she co-signed for ex-fiancé); *In re* Cownden, 2008 WL 6192256 (Bankr. N.D. Ohio Nov. 13, 2008) (absent debtor showing her own undue hardship, court cannot use equitable powers to grant partial discharge of portion of consolidated loan used for educational expenses of non-debtor ex-spouse); *In re* Kirkish, 144 B.R. 367 (Bankr. W.D. Mich. 1992); *In re* Behr, 80 B.R. 124 (Bankr. N.D. Iowa 1987).

    Courts have been less willing to find that the exception to discharge applies to co-signers who are not the student's parents. *See, e.g., In re* Pryor, 234 B.R. 716 (Bankr. W.D. Tenn. 1999) (exception not applicable to non-student co-signer); *In re* Meier, 85 B.R. 805 (Bankr. W.D. Wis. 1986) (exception not applicable to accommodation party).

83   *See In re* Votruba, 310 B.R. 698 (Bankr. N.D. Ohio 2004) (discussing split, collecting cases); *In re* Hamblin, 277 B.R. 676, 679–80 (Bankr. S.D. Miss. 2002) (collecting cases).

84   *See generally In re* Kirkish, 144 B.R. 367 (Bankr. W.D. Mich 1992); *In re* Behr, 80 B.R. 124 (Bankr. N.D. Iowa 1987); *In re* Meier, 85 B.R. 805 (Bankr. W.D. Wis. 1986); *In re* Washington, 41 B.R. 211 (Bankr. E.D. Va. 1984); *In re* Boylen, 29 B.R. 924 (Bankr. N.D. Ohio 1983).

85   *In re* Pelkowski, 990 F.2d 737 (3d Cir. 1993) (brought by parent debtor).

86   *See In re* Wells, 380 B.R. 652, 658–59 (Bankr. N.D.N.Y. 2007) (under prevailing view, a parent must establish own undue hardship in order to discharge student loan debt incurred for child's education); *In re* Votruba, 310 B.R. 698 (Bankr. N.D. Ohio 2004); *In re* James, 226 B.R. 885 (Bankr. S.D. Cal. 1998); *In re* Uterhark, 185 B.R. 39 (Bankr. N.D. Ohio 1995).

87   *See, e.g., In re* Gordon, 2008 WL 5159783 (Bankr. N.D. Ga. Oct. 10, 2008) (62-year-old parent with limited earnings and future work span granted discharge of liability on loans incurred for her children's education); *In re* Wilkinson-Bell, 2007 WL 1021969 (Bankr. C.D. Ill. Apr. 2, 2007) (debtor/mother solely liable on PLUS loan for daughter; debt dischargeable in spite of mother's disabled condition at time she incurred loan); *In re* Hamilton, 361 B.R. 532 (Bankr. D. Mont. 2007) (retired debtor with health problems who is sole signatory on his children's student loans meets undue hardship standard for discharge).

88   *See, e.g., In re* De Cecco, 2007 WL 1970258 (Bankr. N.D. Cal. July 3, 2007) (co-debtor husband denied discharge of his student loan debt; co-debtor wife granted discharge of all but $10,000 of her $107,000 student loan debt in view of marked psychological impairments that limited her employability); *In re* Loftus, 371 B.R. 402 (Bankr. N.D. Iowa 2007) (divorced couple with consolidated student loans; former wife granted discharge, while former husband failed to show undue hardship due to his more marketable job skills); *In re* Wilcox, 265 B.R. 864 (Bankr. N.D. Ohio 2001) (debtors jointly liable on wife's student loan; wife granted full hardship discharge, husband partial discharge).

89   11 U.S.C. § 523(a)(8)(B).

v. *New York State Higher Education Services Corporation*.[90] The *Brunner* test requires a showing that (1) the debtor cannot maintain, based on current income and expenses, a "minimal" standard of living for the debtor and the debtor's dependents if forced to repay the student loans; (2) additional circumstances exist indicating that this state of affairs is likely to persist for a significant portion of the repayment period of the student loans; and (3) the debtor has made good faith efforts to repay the loans.[91]

The Eighth Circuit has endorsed a "totality of circumstances" test for determining undue hardship.[92] This test considers (1) the debtor's past, current, and reasonably reliable future financial resources; (2) the debtor's and the debtor's dependents' reasonable necessary living expenses; and (3) any other relevant facts and circumstances applicable to the bankruptcy case.[93] In addition to allowing courts to consider a greater range of factors, the "totality of the circumstances" test does not require that the court review the debtor's past conduct for "good faith."[94] There is no basis in the Bankruptcy Code for imposition of *Brunner's* "good faith" test.[95] The "good faith" criterion inserts another highly subjective element into a standard that is already quite discretionary. Under the "totality of the circumstances" test the court may also consider the hardship that the existence of the debt itself creates for the debtor, for example by exacerbating a mental illness or preventing effective treatment.[96]

In the First Circuit, lower courts may apply either the *Brunner* or the "totality of circumstances" tests for undue hardship.[97] Most First Circuit courts have gravitated toward the "totality of circumstances" test.[98] Nationwide, the *Brunner* and "totality of circumstances" tests have displaced other less prevalent standards articulated by various courts in the past.[99]

---

90 831 F.2d 395 (2d Cir. 1987).

91 The Second Circuit's *Brunner* test has been adopted by the Third, Fourth, Fifth, Sixth, Seventh, Ninth, Tenth, and Eleventh Circuits. *See In re* Frushour, 433 F.3d. 393 (4th Cir. 2005); *In re* Oyler, 397 F.3d 382 (6th Cir. 2005); Educational Credit Mgmt. Corp. v. Polleys, 356 F.3d 1302 (10th Cir. 2004); *In re* Gerhardt, 348 F.3d 89 (5th Cir. 2003); *In re* Cox, 338 F.3d 1238 (11th Cir. 2003); Goulet v. Educational Credit Mgmt. Corp., 284 F.3d 773 (7th Cir. 2002); *In re* Brightful, 267 F.3d 324 (3d Cir. 2001); *In re* Rifino, 245 F.3d 1083 (9th Cir. 2001).

An interesting study of the development of the "undue hardship" standard under § 523(a)(8) can be found in Rafael I Pardo & Michelle R. Lacey, *Undue Hardship in the Bankruptcy Courts: An Empirical Assessment of the Discharge of Educational Debt*, 74 U. Cin. L. Rev. 405 (Winter 2005). From an evaluation of hundreds of published undue-hardship decisions applying the *Brunner* standard, the authors conclude that the rule has become useless as a predictable and reliable legal standard. Debtors similarly situated by demographics and financial circumstances are typically not treated the same when different courts apply the standard. The authors conclude that "those debtors granted a discharge and those denied a discharge predominantly resemble one another and that there are few statistically significant differences in the factual circumstances of the two groups." *Id*. at 412.

Furthermore, the authors find that the extensive body of judicial interpretation built upon the "good faith" and "additional circumstances" prongs of *Brunner* have no concrete support in the legislative history of the "undue hardship" exception in section 523(a)(8). In practice, the *Brunner* "good faith" test has allowed courts to apply personal value judgments to conduct that are irrelevant to the "undue hardship" concept referenced in the statute. *Id.* at 514–19.

Future ability to pay meant something quite different when *Brunner* was decided in 1987. At that time, all student loan debts that had been due for five years were dischargeable without reference to hardship. Thus, predicting the duration of future financial hardship was a more reasonable undertaking under the Code as it existed in 1987. Since then, with changes to the statute that ended fixed-time-period discharges and with the advent of income-contingent repayment plans extending loan payments for up to twenty-five years, the requirement to predict the debtor's financial future has become an open field for the exercise of unlimited judicial discretion. *Id.* at 512–13, n.415.

92 *In re* Long, 322 F.3d 549 (8th Cir. 2003).

93 322 F.3d 549, 554–55 (8th Cir. 2003).

94 *In re* Kelly, 312 B.R. 200, 206 (B.A.P. 1st Cir. 2004).

95 *In re* Hicks, 331 B.R. 18 (Bankr. D. Mass. 2005); *In re* Kopf, 245 B.R. 731 (Bankr. D. Me. 2000).

96 *In re* Reynolds, 425 F.3d 526, 532–34 (8th Cir. 2005); *In re* Brooks, 406 B.R. 382 (Bankr. D. Minn. 2009).

97 *In re* Nash, 446 F.3d 188 (1st Cir. 2006) (court declines to mandate either the *Brunner* or the Eighth Circuit's "totality of circumstances" test); *In re* Lorenz, 337 B.R. 423 (B.A.P. 1st Cir. 2006) (debtor's household income did not establish undue hardship under either major standard).

98 *In re* Paul, 337 B.R. 730 (Bankr. D. Mass. 2006) (courts in First Circuit free to chose their own approach in determining undue hardship; noting that most courts within First Circuit have adopted "totality of the circumstances" test); *In re* Hicks, 331 B.R. 18 (Bankr. D. Mass. 2005) (developing own test after analyzing *Brunner* and "totality of the circumstances" standards: "Can the debtor now, and in the foreseeable future, maintain a reasonable, minimal standard of living for the debtor and the debtor's dependents and still afford to make payments on the debtor's student loans?").

99 Another commonly used test that preceded *Brunner* and is similar in some ways is the *Johnson* test. In re Johnson, 1979 U.S. Dist. LEXIS 11428, 5 B.C.D. 532 (Bankr. E.D. Pa. June 27, 1979).

Like *Brunner*, the *Johnson* test has three parts:

(1) The Mechanical Test: Courts will ask whether the debtor's future financial resources will be sufficient to support the debtor and dependents (similar to steps one and two of *Brunner*).

(2) The Good Faith Test: Here the courts ask whether the debtor was negligent or irresponsible in his or her efforts to maximize income and minimize expenses and, if so, whether the absence of such negligence would have altered the answer to the mechanical test (similar to step three in *Brunner*).

(3) The Policy Test: The courts ask whether the circumstances, particularly the amount and percentage of total indebtedness of the student loan, indicate that the dominant purpose of the bankruptcy petition was to discharge the student debt. Courts will favor debtors who have truly fallen on hard

Regardless of the test used, courts must ultimately engage in the discretionary determination of when "hardship" becomes "undue." Courts are generally in agreement that "ordinary" or "garden variety" hardship, however defined, is simply not sufficient. On the other extreme are courts that require extraordinary circumstances such as the total physical incapacity of the debtor.[100]

10.4.2 Applying the Brunner "Undue Hardship" Test

10.4.2.1 The First Prong: The Debtor's current Income and Expenses

The three-part *Brunner* test begins by reviewing the debtor's current financial condition. While the second *Brunner* prong focuses on expectations for the future and the third prong examines past conduct, this initial test examines the debtor's circumstances at the time of trial.[101] The debtor must be unable to maintain a "minimal" standard of living for herself and her dependents and still repay the student loan.

Most courts agree that the minimal standard of living contemplated by *Brunner* allows the debtor to purchase basic necessities. These include food, clothing, decent housing, utilities, communication services, transportation, and health insurance or the ability to pay for medical and dental expenses. There is little agreement among the courts as to what levels of expenditures for these items are consistent with a minimal standard of living. Nor have courts agreed on what additional categories of expenditures can be part of this minimal standard.

Courts often reiterate that the *Brunner* "minimal standard of living" does not require the debtor to live in poverty.[102] Nevertheless, in proving that the debtor is maintaining a minimal standard of living, it may be helpful in some cases to present evidence that the debtor's actual living expenses are below certain national standards for allowable living expenses.[103] On the other hand, debtors should be able to show reasonable and necessary expenses that may exceed those used for IRS collection purposes.[104] The basic purpose of the first *Brunner* prong is to ensure that, after borrowers have provided for their basic needs, they do not allocate discretionary income to the detriment of the student loan creditor.[105]

Courts have generally refused to find ordinary household expenses, if not excessive, to be inconsistent with a minimal standard of living. A wide range of expenditures for food[106]

---

times after incurring student loan debt and are unlikely to derive future benefits from the education financed with the loan.

See *In re* Roe, 226 B.R. 258 (Bankr. N.D. Ala. 1998); *In re* Taylor, 198 B.R. 700 (Bankr. N.D. Ohio 1996).

For decisions comparing the *Brunner* and *Johnson* tests, see *In re* Kopf, 245 B.R. 731 (Bankr. D. Me. 2000); *In re* Lehman, 226 B.R. 805 (Bankr. D. Vt. 1998) (court chooses *Brunner* test and denies discharge); *In re* Holtorf, 204 B.R. 567 (Bankr. S.D. Cal. 1997); *In re* Hawkins, 187 B.R. 294 (Bankr. N.D. Iowa 1995) (*Brunner* test applied after discussing both *Brunner* and *Johnson* tests).

100 E.g., *In re* Frushour, 433 F.3d 393, 401 (4th Cir. 2005) (only "rare" circumstances will satisfy "additional circumstances" test of *Brunner*); *In re* Oyler, 397 F.3d 382, 386 (6th Cir. 2005) (facts indicating a "certainty of hopelessness" "may include illness, disability, a lack of usable job skills, or the existence of a large number of dependents"); *In re* Gerhardt, 348 F.3d 89 (5th Cir. 2003) (exceptional circumstances necessary to satisfy second prong of *Brunner* test). See also *In re* Spence, 541 F.3d 538 (4th Cir. 2008) (debtor in her mid-sixties with advanced education, student loans totaling $161,000, and currently in low-paying clerical job failed to show "certainty of hopelessness" because she failed to show that she had tried to find higher-paying jobs).

101 United Student Aid Funds v. Pena, 155 F.3d 1108 (9th Cir. 1998) (focus should be on time of trial, but court has some discretion to average out income and expenses when there is evidence of fluctuation); *In re* Cota, 298 B.R. 408 (Bankr. D. Ariz. 2003) ("current" income and expenses means at time of trial).

102 *In re* Hornsby, 144 F.3d 433 (6th Cir. 1998) (debtors did not need to be at poverty level to show undue hardship); *In re* Faish, 72 F.3d 298 (3d Cir. 1995). See also *In re* Lebovits, 223 B.R. 265 (Bankr. E.D.N.Y. 1998) (rejecting creditor contention that debtors with income over HHS poverty guideline are precluded from discharge under *Brunner* standard).

103 *In re* Brown, 378 B.R. 623, 628 (Bankr. W.D. Mo. 2007) (income significantly above HHS Poverty Guidelines does not preclude undue hardship discharge); *In re* McGinnis, 289 B.R. 257 (Bankr. M.D. Ga. 2003) (debtor's income can exceed poverty level and still satisfy *Brunner* test); *In re* Ivory, 269 B.R. 890 (Bankr. N.D. Ala. 2001) (applying both a subjective and objective evaluation of debtor's income and expenses and citing studies showing that income far higher than poverty level needed for minimal standard of living).

104 See *In re* Howe, 319 B.R. 886 (B.A.P. 9th Cir. 2005) (reversing bankruptcy court for adhering to IRS guidelines when debtor had reasonable medical expenses over guideline amounts); *In re* Albee, 338 B.R. 407 (Bankr. W.D. Mo. 2006) (lender cannot rely on IRS guidelines only to show certain expenses over guidelines and ignore those below guidelines); Internal Revenue Serv., U.S. Dep't of Treasury, National Standards for Allowable Living Expenses, at www.irs.gov/individuals/article/0,id=96543,00.html. See also *In re* Miller, 409 B.R. 299 (Bankr. E.D. Pa. 2009) (IRS local standards and means testing methodology are useful frames of reference in assessing expenses for minimal standard of living but are not determinative).

For information about food budgets, also visit the U.S. website of the Department of Agriculture, Center for Nutrition Policy and Promotion, at www.usda.gov/cnpp/using3.html.

105 *In re* Mitcham, 293 B.R. 138 (Bankr. N.D. Ohio 2003). See, e.g., *In re* Neeson, 2008 WL 379699 (Bankr. W.D. Mo. Feb. 12, 2008) (debtor's demonstrated need to draw on credit card debt to pay for daily necessities indicated lack of excess income to pay toward student loan).

106 *In re* Brooks, 406 B.R. 382, 390–91 (Bankr. D. Minn. 2009) (summarizing Eighth Circuit's range of findings on reasonable food expenses; $275 monthly food expense for one person consistent with minimal standard); *In re* Lebovits, 223 B.R. 265

and vehicles[107] have been considered in line with the standard. Most courts have recognized reasonable expenditures for Internet service, cell phones, and cable television as components of a minimal standard of living.[108] A modest amount allocated for entertainment is appropriate.[109] A higher expense for an item such as cable television or Internet may be particularly appropriate when the debtor has listed minimal or no other expenses for entertainment.[110] Other expenses, such as cigarettes, have met with a mixed reception.[111] In making this review, courts should give some leeway to an unusually high expense when debtor omitted other expenses for necessities that would exhaust financial resources if considered.[112]

Modest contributions to a retirement account are consistent with a minimal standard of living.[113] Reasonable allow-

---

(Bankr. E.D.N.Y. 1998) ($1600 monthly food expense for family of nine not prohibitive).

107 *In re* Naylor, 348 B.R. 680 (Bankr. W.D. Pa. 2006) ($235 monthly car payment is minimal, particularly given bankruptcy debtors' limited ability to finance a car loan on better terms); *In re* Myers, 280 B.R. 416 (Bankr. S.D. Ohio 2002) (expenses for maintaining three vehicles were within minimum standards of living for family with nine children); *In re* Lewis, 276 B.R. 912 (Bankr. C.D. Ill. 2002) (debtor not required to purchase less expensive auto).

108 *In re* Frushour, 433 F.3d 393 (4th Cir. 2005) ($95.00 monthly expense for cable and Internet not unreasonable, but debt found nondischargeable on other grounds); *In re* Lorenz, 337 B.R. 423 (B.A.P. 1st Cir. 2006) ($53 monthly for cable); *In re* Cline, 248 B.R. 347 (8th Cir. B.A.P. 2000) ($30 monthly for cable; dissent finds expense unnecessary); *In re* McLaney, 375 B.R. 666 (M.D. Ala. 2007) ($65 monthly for cable television, $50 for land phone, and $50 for cell phone were reasonable); *In re* Vargas, 2010 WL 148632 (Bankr. C.D. Ill. Jan. 12, 2010) ($127.91 per month for cable television and Internet service was reasonable); *In re* Zook, 2009 WL 512436 (Bankr. S.D. Cal. Feb. 27, 2009) ($140 monthly reasonable for cable television and home phone, plus $35 for cell phone service; debtor's mental illness left her home bound much of the time); *In re* Brooks, 406 B.R. 382 (Bankr. D. Minn. 2009) ($130 monthly is reasonable expense for cell phone service for debtor and daughter); *In re* Douglas, 366 B.R. 241, 255 (Bankr. M.D. Ga. 2007) ($48 monthly for cable and Internet "extremely reasonable" and $100 monthly for cell phone service necessary for working parents to keep in touch with children); *In re* Durrani, 311 B.R. 496 (Bankr. N.D. Ill. 2004), *aff'd*, 320 B.R. 357 (N.D. Ill. 2005) ($52 monthly for cable television); *In re* Ivory, 269 B.R. 890 (Bankr. N.D. Ala. 2001) ($100 monthly for phone and Internet service meets minimal standard); *In re* Garybush, 265 B.R. 587 (Bankr. S.D. Ohio 2001) ($32 monthly for cable television); *In re* Thomson, 234 B.R. 506 (Bankr. D. Mont. 1999) ($30 monthly for cable television); *In re* Young, 225 B.R. 312 (Bankr. E.D. Pa. 1998) ($50 monthly for cable television); *In re* McLeod, 197 B.R. 624 (Bankr. N.D. Ohio 1996) ($22.50 monthly for cable television).

109 *In re* Cline, 248 BR. 347 (B.A.P. 8th Cir. 2000) (discharge granted when single debtor with no dependents allocated $50 monthly for recreation); *In re* Innes, 284 B.R. 496, 505 (D. Kan. 2002) (reasonable to allocate expenses for "modest Christmas gifts" for debtors' children, a "single frugal summer vacation," and participation in a bowling league); *In re* Nary, 253 B.R. 752 (N.D. Tex. 2000) (undue hardship found when married debtor with two children spent $95 monthly for recreation); *In re* Larson, 426 B.R. 782 (Bankr. N.D. Ill. 2010) (discharge granted when married disabled debtor with no children allocated $108 for recreation and an additional $76 for participation in Lions' Club); *In re* Vargas, 2010 WL 148632, at *3 (Bankr. C.D. Ill. Jan. 12, 2010) (discharge granted when debtor listed $50 recreation expense for lottery tickets in addition to $130 for cable and Internet: "In the Court's view, $50 per month for recreation is neither excessive nor unreasonable. Whether used for dining out or movies or bowling or gambling is of no consequence."); *In re* Miller, 409 B.R. 299 (Bankr. E.D. Pa. 2009); *In re* Zook, 2009 WL 512436, at *8–9 (Bankr. S.D. Cal. Feb. 27, 2009)

(expenses of $35 per month for cellular phone services, $140 per month for cable television, Internet, and home telephone service, and $50 per month for books, rental movies, and other miscellaneous entertainment, were not unreasonable given that debtor suffered from bipolar disorder that made it difficult for her to socialize or venture from her apartment); *In re* Myers, 280 B.R. 416 (Bankr. N.D. Ohio 2002); *In re* Ivory, 269 B.R. 890 (Bankr. N.D. Ala. 2001); *In re* Thomson, 234 B.R. 506 (Bankr. S.D. Mont. 1999) ($50 monthly for recreation for debtors with three children; discharge granted); *In re* Lebovits, 223 B.R. 265, 273 (Bankr. E.D.N.Y. 1998) ($50 recreation expense for large family is "minimal, at most"). *But see In re* Murphy, 305 B.R. 780 (Bankr. E.D. Va. 2004) (rejecting as excessive $128 for therapeutic horseback riding for daughter in addition to $135 monthly for other family recreation); *In re* Koch, 144 B.R. 959 (Bankr. W.D. Pa. 1992) ($60 monthly recreation expense for debtor with two dependents deemed excessive).

110 *In re* McLaney, 375 B.R. 666 (M.D. Ala. 2007).

111 *In re* Vargas, 2010 WL 148632 (Bankr. C.D. Ill. Jan. 12, 2010) (long time smoker reducing expense to $40 monthly is appropriate); *In re* Gharavi, 335 B.R. 492 (Bankr. D. Mass. 2006) ($175 monthly cigarette expense not per se unreasonable particularly when debtor's expense otherwise very moderate); *In re* Doherty, 219 B.R. 665 (Bankr. W.D.N.Y. 1998) (debtor with bipolar disorder satisfies standard with $40 monthly tobacco expense). *But see In re* Hornsby, 144 F.3d 433 (6th Cir. 1998) (remand when lower court did not consider certain expenses of debtors, including their $100 monthly cigarette expense); *In re* Brooks, 406 B.R. 382 (Bankr. D. Minn. 2009) (debtor may discharge loan debt under totality of circumstances test when, disregarding debtor's $100 monthly cigarette expense, her income still would not cover basic necessities).

112 *In re* McLaney, 375 B.R. 666 (M.D. Ala. 2007).

113 *In re* Craig, 579 F.3d 1040 (9th Cir. 2009) (reversing bankruptcy court's application of per se rule that debtor's $68 monthly 401(k) contribution was inconsistent with minimal standard of living; bankruptcy courts must evaluate debtor's overall financial circumstances, such as income, amount of contributions, and age before treating contribution amount as income available to pay toward student loan); *In re* Larson, 426 B.R. 782 (Bankr. N.D. Ill. 2010) (58-year-old debtor's $86 monthly contribution to employee retirement plan is reasonable expense); *In re* Carson-Callow, 2008 WL 2357012 (Bankr. D. Idaho June 6, 2008) (contribution to 401(k) plan equal to 8% of debtor's gross income does not preclude discharge); *In re* Allen, 329 B.R. 544 (Bankr. W.D. Pa. 2005) ($111.67 monthly payment to retirement account is reasonable expense). *See generally* James Winston Kim, *Saving Our Future: Why Voluntary Contributions to Retirement Accounts Are Reasonable Expenses*, 26 Emory Bankr. Dev. J. (2010) (arguing for exclusion of reasonable retirement account contributions under chapter 7 abuse standard and test for disposable income for chapter 13 plan payments).

ances for savings to cover emergencies typically pass muster.[114] Various amounts listed for charitable donations and tithing have not prevented discharge of student loan debts.[115]

The first *Brunner* prong looks at whether the debtor can repay the loan and provide a minimal standard of living not only for the debtor but also for the debtor's dependents. The term "dependent" as used in section 523(a)(8) is not limited to individuals, such as children, who are financially dependent on the debtor.[116] For example, a hardship related to a dependent can arise when the debtor provides home-based care for an infirm parent and this obligation limits the debtor's earnings outside the home.[117] Certain expenses for education of the debtors' children have raised recurring disputes in hardship discharge cases. In particular, courts have scrutinized private school tuition expenses for minor children and allowed various amounts depending on the circumstances.[118] Some courts have looked askance at debtors' expenditures for adult children whom the debtor has no legal obligation to support.[119]

In cases in which the student does not file bankruptcy with his or her spouse, courts frequently consider the non-filing spouse's income and contributions to household expenses.[120] There can be a basic unfairness in this approach,

---

114 *In re* McLaney, 375 B.R. 666 (M.D. Ala. 2007) (debtors' allowance of $200 monthly for unexpected contingencies related to home and vehicle maintenance was consistent with minimal standard of living); *In re* Zook, 2009 WL 512436 (Bankr. D.D.C. Feb. 27, 2009) (setting aside some funds for emergencies related to job loss and medical expenses is reasonable to maintain minimal standard of living). *See also In re* Alston, 297 B.R. 410 (Bankr. E.D. Pa. 2003) (debtor's use of Earned Income Tax Credit refunds of approximately $3000 to $5000 for necessary home repairs and furniture, expenses normally part of a monthly budget, did not establish debtor was living beyond minimal standard of living).

115 *In re* Cline, 248 B.R. 347 (B.A.P. 8th Cir. 2000) ($25 monthly charitable contribution for single debtor reasonable under totality of circumstances test); *In re* McLaney, 375 B.R. 666 (M.D. Ala. 2007) (declining to apply Religious Liberty and Charitable Donation Protection Act, but finding church tithing of $220 monthly reasonable); *In re* Nary, 253 B.R. 752 (N.D. Tex. 2000) (partial discharge granted; debtors listed monthly charitable contribution of $65); *In re* Larson, 426 B.R. 782 (Bankr. N.D. Ill. 2010) (church tithing of $80 monthly, equivalent to 3% of debtors' gross monthly income was reasonable for minimal standard of living); *In re* Halverson, 401 B.R. 378 (Bankr. D. Minn. 2009) (partial discharge granted under totality of circumstances test for debtors contributing $209 monthly—10% of gross income—to church); *In re* Durrani, 311 B.R. 496 (Bankr. N.D. Ill. 2004), *aff'd*, 320 B.R. 357 (N.D. Ill. 2005) (granting discharge, applying standard under Religious Liberty and Charitable Donation Protection Act of 1997, finding monthly tithing of $226 consistent with Act's allowing contributions of up to 15% of gross income). *See also In re* Windland, 201 B.R. 178 (Bankr. N.D. Ohio 1996) (payroll deductions of $19 monthly for Christmas gifts for debtors' children are consistent with undue hardship finding. *But see In re* Fullbright, 319 B.R. 650 (Bankr. D. Mont. 2005) ($430 monthly church tithing expense is excessive).

116 11 U.S.C. § 523(a)(8) (exception to discharge applies "unless excepting such debt from discharge under this paragraph would impose an undue hardship *on the debtor and the debtor's dependents*") (emphasis added).

117 *See In re* Santamassino, 373 B.R. 807 (Bankr. D. Vt. 2007) (well-documented obligation to care for mother is additional circumstance limiting future repayment ability); *In re* Doe, 325 B.R. 69 (Bankr. S.D.N.Y. 2005); *In re* Rutherford, 317 B.R. 865 (Bankr. N.D. Ala. 2004) (debtor caring for mother). *See also In re* Torres, 2009 WL 4591085 (Bankr. D. Mass. Dec. 1, 2009) (limitations imposed on debtor's earnings due to need to care for disabled non-debtor spouse must be taken into account just as court would consider income from non-debtor spouse if non-debtor spouse worked).

118 *In re* Cheesman, 25 F.3d 360 (6th Cir. 1994) (debtors satisfied first *Brunner* prong while including $100 monthly private school tuition as expense for daughter); *In re* Russ, 365 B.R. 640 (Bankr. N.D. Tex. 2007) (debtor could not satisfy *Brunner* first prong when she was paying private school tuition of $405 monthly for son while making no payments on her own student loans); *In re* Ivory, 269 B.R. 890 (Bankr. N.D. Ala. 2001) ($500 monthly private school tuition was necessary expenditure given manner in which school met children's medical needs); *In re* Grawey, 2001 WL 34076376 (Bankr. C.D. Ill. Oct. 11, 2001) ($277 monthly parochial school tuition expense for debtors' two children does not preclude hardship discharge when debtor cut back on other necessary expenses to send children to the school); *In re* Lebovits, 223 B.R. 265 (Bankr. E.D.N.Y. 1998) ($100-per-child monthly private school expense for debtors with seven children was reasonable in view of family's orthodox religious beliefs). *See generally In re* Cleary, 357 B.R. 369 (Bankr. D.S.C. 2006) (discussing private school tuition treatment under BAPCPA chapter 13 projected disposable income standard); *In re* Lynch, 299 B.R. 776, 779–80 (Bankr. W.D.N.C. 2003) (summarizing private school tuition cases under pre-BAPCA chapter 13 disposable income standard).

119 *In re* Bray, 332 B.R. 186, 194–95 (Bankr. W.D. Mo. 2005) (collecting cases which held that expenditures related to support of emancipated adult children should not be considered in undue hardship analysis); *In re* Gill, 326 B.R. 611 (Bankr. E.D. Va. 2005) (necessary medical expenses for an emancipated 24-year-old excluded as relevant household expense; *In re* Williams, 301 B.R. 62 (Bankr. N.D. Cal. 2003) (finding no support for consideration of expenses for support of adult children in *Brunner* first prong review). *But see In re* Reed, 2005 WL 1398479 (Bankr D. Vt. 2005) (expenses for child in undergraduate college program were reasonable household expenditures); *In re* Doe, 325 B.R. 69 (Bankr. S.D.N.Y. 2005) (debtor's expenditures to support mother in her household treated as expenses for dependent). *See generally In re* Grove, 323 B.R. 216, 229 n.4 (Bankr. N.D. Ohio 2005) (discussing decisions addressing treatment of debtors' expenditures for adult children under section 523(a)(8)); *In re* Gonzales, 157 B.R. 604 (Bankr. E.D. Mich. 1993) (under pre-BAPCPA chapter 13 disposable income test, costs for debtor's 19- and 21-year-old children to attend college considered nondiscretionary expenses).

120 *See, e.g., In re* Davis, 373 B.R. 241, 248 (W.D.N.Y. 2007) (total household income, including that of non-debtor spouse, live-in companion, life partner, and contributing co-habitant, must be considered in conducting minimal standard of living analysis); *In re* Miller, 409 B.R. 299, 313 (Bankr. E.D. Pa. 2009) (when household has established practice of pooling resources, court takes income, needs, and expenses of non-filing spouse and debtor's disabled daughter who received SSI into account under

particularly when the debtor spouse incurred student loan debt before the marriage. In such a case, the full amount of the non-debtor spouse's discretionary income should not be committed to payment of the debtor spouse's student loan obligation. In order to mitigate this unfairness in appropriate cases, some courts have apportioned the non-debtor spouse's income so that a portion is not considered available to the debtor.[121]

10.4.2.2 The Second *Brunner* Prong: Additional Circumstances Indicate Current Hardship Likely to Continue

10.4.2.2.1 General

Under the second prong, the court evaluates any "additional circumstances" that make it more likely than not that the debtor's current state of affairs will continue for the remainder of the loan's repayment term. The court must not only evaluate a wide range of current facts but also predict whether those facts are likely to change. Needless to say, courts have differed significantly in their view of what the debtor must show under this part of the *Brunner* test.

On one extreme are courts that require the debtor to establish the "certainty of hopelessness" or extraordinary or "exceptional" circumstances beyond the current and foreseeable inability to pay. According to this view, the exceptional circumstances must be something beyond the likely persistence of the debtor's financial problems, such as proof of serious illness, psychiatric problems, or disability of a dependent.[122]

The requirement to show a "certainty of hopelessness" is troubling in two ways. First, it requires debtors to prove a negative. Second, it suggests a burden of proof much stricter than the "preponderance of the evidence" standard that applies to hardship determination cases. The test goes a long way toward eviscerating the "fresh start" potential inherent in the Code section allowing for discharge in certain circumstances.[123]

In *In re Nys*,[124] the Ninth Circuit rejected an overly restrictive construction of the second prong of the *Brunner* test. The court instead developed a non-exclusive list of twelve "additional circumstances" that courts may consider in reviewing the second prong of the *Brunner* test.[125] Significantly, these factors include the "maximized income

---

first *Brunner* prong); *In re* Wynn, 378 B.R. 140, 147–48 (Bankr. S.D. Miss. 2007) (court must consider earnings of non-filing spouse when determining minimal standard of living in context of section 523(a)(8)); *In re* Bray, 332 B.R. 186, 192–93 (Bankr. W.D. Mo. 2005) ("overwhelming authority requires that a court consider the spouse's income"); *In re* Murphy, 305 B.R. 780 (Bankr. E.D. Va. 2004) (family income must be measure of income calculation for undue hardship); *In re* Dolan, 256 B.R. 230 (Bankr. D. Mass. 2000); *In re* Greco, 251 B.R. 670 (Bankr. E.D. Pa. 2000); *In re* White, 243 B.R. 498, 509 (Bankr. N.D. Ala. 1999) (collecting cases); *In re* Koch, 144 B.R. 959 (Bankr. W.D. Pa. 1992); *In re* Albert, 25 B.R. 98 (Bankr. N.D. Ohio 1982). *See In re* Walker, 427 B.R. 471, 485 n.40 (B.A.P. 8th Cir. 2010) (proper to consider non-debtor spouse's income under Eighth Circuit "totality of circumstances" test); *In re* Lorenz, 337 B.R. 423 (B.A.P. 1st Cir. 2006) (court must consider income of debtor's long-term domestic partner). *But see In re* Kainu, 2009 WL 1033756 (Bankr. D.N.H. Apr. 14, 2009) (court will not attribute income to debtor from non-debtor spouse who had been in and out of prison and refused to contribute to household expenses when not incarcerated); *In re* Halverson, 401 B.R. 378 (Bankr. D. Minn. 2009) (non-debtor spouse's income not considered when couple in second marriage, both over sixty-five, and manage finances separately).

121 *In re* Reynolds, 425 F.3d 526, 535–36 (8th Cir. 2005) (Bright, J. concurring); *In re* Innes, 284 B.R. 496, 507–08 (D. Kan. 2002) (joint filing; co-debtor spouse's income apportioned for undue hardship analysis); *In re* Turner, 2009 WL 1035255 (Bankr. N.D. Iowa Apr. 14, 2009).

122 *E.g., In re* Frushour, 433 F.3d 393, 401 (4th Cir. 2005) (only "rare" circumstances will satisfy "additional circumstances" test of *Brunner*); *In re* Oyler, 397 F.3d 382, 386 (6th Cir. 2005) (facts indicating a "certainty of hopelessness" "may include illness, disability, a lack of usable job skills, or the existence of a large number of dependents"); *In re* Gerhardt, 348 F.3d 89 (5th Cir. 2003) (exceptional circumstances necessary to satisfy second prong of *Brunner* test). *See also In re* Spence, 541 F.3d 538 (4th Cir. 2008) (debtor in her mid-sixties with student loans totaling $161,000 and currently in low-paying clerical job failed to show "certainty of hopelessness").

123 *See* Educational Credit Mgmt. Corp. v. Polleys, 356 F.3d 1302 (10th Cir. 2004) (courts need not require a "certainty of hopelessness"); *In re* Carnduff, 367 B.R. 120 (9th Cir. B.A.P. 2007) (under second *Brunner* prong, debtors not required to prove continuation of financial hardship with certainty, but by preponderance of evidence); *In re* Jackson, 2007 WL 2295585 (Bankr. S.D.N.Y. Aug. 9, 2007) (*Brunner* test does not require a finding of "certainty of hopelessness"); *In re* King, 368 B.R. 358 (Bankr. D. Vt. 2007) ("certainty of hopelessness" standard was never adopted by court of appeals in *Brunner*; widespread use of standard by courts is based on erroneous reading of Second Circuit decision); *In re* Hicks, 331 B.R. 18, 27 n.12 (Bankr. D. Mass. 2005) (the focus of many courts on the "certainty of hopelessness" language makes it appear that "any room for optimism will result in a finding of nondischargeability"); *In re* Kopf, 245 B.R. 731, 744 (Bankr. D. Me. 2000) (rejecting "certainty of hopelessness" and "total incapacity" standards as contrary to Code's "fresh start" goal).

124 *In re* Nys, 446 F.3d 938 (9th Cir. 2006).

125 These additional circumstances are: (1) the serious mental or physical disability of the debtor or the debtor's dependents that prevents employment or advancement; (2) the debtor's obligations to care for dependents; (3) lack of, or severely limited, education; (4) poor quality of education; (5) lack of usable or marketable job skills; (6) underemployment; (7) maximized income potential in the chosen educational field, and no other more lucrative job skills; (8) limited number of years remaining in the debtor's work life to allow payment of the loan; (9) age or other factors that prevent retraining or relocation as a means for payment of the loan; (10) lack of assets, whether or not exempt, which could be used to pay the loan; (11) potentially increasing expenses that outweigh any potential appreciation in the value of the debtor's assets and/or likely increases in the debtor's income; (12) lack of better financial options elsewhere. *In re* Nys, 446 F.3d 947 (9th Cir. 2006).

potential in the chosen educational field, and no other more lucrative job skills"; "limited number of years remaining in the debtor's work life to allow payment of the loan"; and "age or other factors that prevent retraining or relocation as a means for payment of the loan."[126] There is nothing particularly "exceptional" about these circumstances. These characteristics apply to many debtors who made reasonable decisions regarding a course of study, chose reasonable career options after completing school and, despite being in good health and working hard, do not earn enough to pay for basic necessities for their family and still repay a student loan. The Ninth Circuit decision goes some distance in recognizing the hardship that these debtors face and suggests a more flexible standard for evaluating their loan discharge claims.

The Tenth Circuit has interpreted the "additional circumstances" term of the second *Brunner* prong similarly to the Ninth Circuit.[127] The approaches taken by the Ninth and Tenth Circuits offer a counterweight to those rulings that force debtors to prove a negative with respect to their future prospects. Under the second prong of *Brunner*, the debtor cannot fairly be called upon to prove to a "certainty" that every chance of improvement is impossible. Instead, the debtor should first show that he or she is unable to afford life's basic necessities: healthcare, transportation, food, decent housing, utilities, and care for oneself upon retirement. Then the debtor must show that it is more likely than not that these financial difficulties will continue for a substantial part of the loan repayment period. The court should evaluate only realistic expectation rather than speculate concerning future prospects.[128]

---

126 *Id. See, e.g., In re* Scott, 417 B.R. 623 (Bankr. W.D. Wash. 2009) (applying *Nys* factors, discharge granted for debtors aged thirty and thirty-three with $322,000 in student loans; debtors maximized earning capacity working as biologist for university and operations manager for police association and faced increased expenses for children ages two and five); *In re* Brown, 2007 WL 1747135 (Bankr. N.D. W. Va. June 15, 2007) (discharge granted for 50-year-old debtor earning $8.50 per hour as telemarketing customer service representative who had reached maximum earning capacity, did not earn enough to pay loan and support minimal family expenses, and appeared trapped in "cycle of poverty"), *aff'd sub. nom* United States v. Brown, 2007 WL 4190399 (N.D. W. Va. Nov. 21, 2007) (lack of likelihood of increased income meets Fourth Circuit's "certainty of hopelessness" standard); *In re* Hamilton, 361 B.R. 532 (Bankr. D. Mont. 2007) (age may be "additional circumstance" meeting second prong of *Brunner* analysis, particularly when record includes evidence of age discrimination); *In re* Renville, 2006 WL 3206126 (D. Mont. Nov. 3, 2006) (under *Nys*, debtor's lack of assets is an additional circumstance to be considered with second *Brunner* prong; discharge granted). *See also In re* Gordon, 2008 WL 5159783 (Bankr. N.D. Ga. Oct. 10, 2008) (62-year-old debtor's low income and limited future work capacity sufficient to show undue hardship); *In re* Greenwood, 349 B.R. 795 (Bankr. D. Ariz. 2006) (forty-three-year old social worker satisfied "additional circumstances" second *Brunner* prong by meeting several *Nys* factors, including lack of college degree, no accessible assets, past attempts to increase income from other jobs, maximized earning capacity in field, and lack of any better financial options).

127 Educational Credit Mgmt. Corp. v. Polleys, 356 F.3d 1302, 1310 (10th Cir. 2004) (rejecting "certainty of hopelessness" standard; courts must consider "ascertainable facts" indicating debtor's ability to provide adequate shelter, nutrition, and healthcare for remainder of loan term).

128 *In re* Mosley, 494 F.3d 1320, 1326 (11th Cir. 2007) (second *Brunner* prong satisfied by debtor's evidence of lack of marketable job skills, depression, chronic back pain, and long-term difficulties providing himself with basic necessities); *In re* Cline, 248 B.R. 347 (B.A.P. 8th Cir. 2000) (single woman unable to increase income would need decades to repay $53,000 in loans); Queen v. Pennsylvania Higher Educ. Assistance Agency, 210 B.R. 677 (E.D. Pa. 1997), *aff'd without op. sub nom. In re* Mayer, 156 F.3d 1225 (3d Cir. 1998) (discharge granted to single-parent manual laborer with uncompleted masters degree; any salary increase from full-time work would be offset by day-care costs); *In re* Carson-Callow, 2008 WL 2357012 (Bankr. D. Idaho June 6, 2008) (60-year-old debtor, in poor health and earning $30 hourly at research projects, not likely to see increased income); *In re* Lavy (Bankr. W.D. Wash. Nov. 14, 2008) (partial discharge; all but $38,563 of total $121,135 of student loan debt granted debtor attorney, age 60, whose heart condition likely to prevent future full-time work); *In re* Thomson, 234 B.R. 506 (Bankr. D. Mont. 1999) (discharge granted to veteran with permanent and total disability); *In re* Kasey, 227 B.R. 473 (Bankr. W.D. Va. 1998) (discharge granted for single mother suffering from depression with three young children, unlikely to finish education, who had attempted payments), *aff'd in unpublished op.*, 187 F.3d 630 (4th Cir. 1999); *In re* Bessette, 226 B.R. 103 (Bankr. D. Idaho 1998) (chapter 7 debtor had two minor dependents, limited job skills, and limited potential for increasing income); *In re* Young, 225 B.R. 312 (Bankr. E.D. Pa. 1998) (discharge granted when court also considered race and age as factors in determining whether hardship conditions were likely to persist); *In re* Lebovits, 223 B.R. 265 (Bankr. E.D.N.Y. 1998) (discharge granted to parent with Master of Social Work degree with seven children when religious convictions required parochial schooling); *In re* Doherty, 219 B.R. 665 (Bankr. W.D.N.Y. 1998) (chapter 7 debtor satisfied her burden of proving that her present inability to repay the debt was likely to continue, presenting undisputed evidence of an incurable mental illness that was the cause of present inability to earn a sufficient wage); *In re* Doherty, 219 B.R. 665 (Bankr. W.D.N.Y. 1998) (court took judicial notice of prognosis for debtor suffering from bipolar disorder); *In re* Shankwiler, 208 B.R. 701 (Bankr. C.D. Cal. 1997); *In re* Dotson-Cannon, 206 B.R. 530 (Bankr. W.D. Mo. 1997) (student loans discharged when single 51-year-old woman with Bachelor of Science degree in public administration was only able to obtain $7-per-hour clerical work); *In re* Coats, 214 B.R. 397 (Bankr. N.D. Okla. 1997); *In re* Windland, 201 B.R. 178 (Bankr. N.D. Ohio 1996); *In re* Derby, 199 B.R. 328 (Bankr. W.D. Pa. 1996); Hoyle v. Pennsylvania Higher Educ. Assistance Agency, 199 B.R. 518 (Bankr. E.D. Pa. 1996); *In re* Fuertes, 198 B.R. 379 (Bankr. S.D. Fla. 1996). *But see In re* Garybush, 265 B.R. 587 (Bankr. S.D. Ohio 2001) (no discharge when family income should improve because debtor can resume part-time employment when youngest child enters school); *In re* Vinci, 232 B.R. 644 (Bankr. E.D. Pa. 1999); *In re* Pantelis, 229 B.R. 716 (Bankr. N.D. Ohio 1999) (no discharge when no documentation of physical disability and no showing of effective job search); *In re* Elmore, 230 B.R. 22 (Bankr. D. Conn. 1999); *In re* McLeod,

Although it sometimes turns up as part of the "good faith" analysis under the third *Brunner* prong, the issue of voluntary underemployment has become a factor in the "additional circumstances" analysis as well. In considering whether a debtor's current hardship will continue, some courts have evaluated the debtor's career choices to date. If the debtor appears to have chosen to work in a low-paying field instead and disregarded more lucrative endeavors, the court may refrain from finding that the debtor's current difficult circumstances will continue. Ministers, musicians, artists, and public interest lawyers have not fared well under this analysis.[129]

In several recent cases, student loan creditors have raised a kind of "pre-existing condition" challenge in undue hardship actions. According to this argument, if the debtor knew he or she had a medical impairment or similar limitation on future employment when the debtor took out the student loans, the courts should not consider the condition as contributing to any hardship. This would exclude the condition as an "additional circumstance" tending to show continuation of the debtor's current financial hardship. The courts have routinely rejected this argument, finding that it has no basis under the *Brunner* undue hardship standard.[130]

Finally, the relevant time frame for the court's evaluation of the debtor's future prospects under the second *Brunner* prong is the remaining period established for repayment under the loan documents, not a hypothetical decades-long income-based repayment plan suggested by the creditor.[131] One court has held that a consolidation loan that effectively restructured a student loan with the same lender at the end of the original ten-year term did not "restart the clock" on a new fifteen-year repayment period for purposes of considering future inability to repay.[132]

10.4.2.2.2 Proof of health-related impairments as an "additional circumstances"

Medical and mental health-related impairments often appear as the "additional circumstances" that will prolong a debtor's current financial hardship. Unfortunately, many bankruptcy debtors are unable to pay for development of medical evidence in connection with undue hardship litigation. The bankruptcy courts have shown an appreciation for this problem facing debtors in undue hardship cases.[133] The courts' decisions indicate a number of ways in which debtors have brought this important information into the record without significant expense.

For example, many courts have not required the introduction of expert testimony to prove that a debtor's earning potential is impaired by a psychological, emotional, or substance dependency problem.[134] In other instances, courts

---

197 B.R. 624 (Bankr. N.D. Ohio 1996).

129 *In re* Frushour, 433 F.3d 393 (4th Cir. 2005) (no discharge for debtor who pursued low-paying artistic interior design career for which she incurred educational debt); *In re* Oyler, 397 F.3d 382 (6th Cir. 2005) (pastor failed to meet *Brunner* test because his decision not to maximize his earnings, though commendable, was voluntarily made); *In re* Gerhardt, 348 F.3d 89 (5th Cir. 2003) (debtor failed second prong of *Brunner* test by choosing to work only as a cellist in the low-paying field in which he was trained); *In re* Evans-Lambert, 2008 WL 1734123 (Bankr. N.D. Ga. Mar. 25, 2008) (federal public defender had credentials and experience to choose higher-salaried work); *In re* Bender, 338 B.R. 62 (Bankr. W.D. Mo. 2006) (public defender could leave position and earn higher income elsewhere). *But see In re* Avant, 2006 WL 3782168 (Bankr. W.D. Mo. Dec. 21, 2006) (debtor with significant medical needs cannot be expected to leave low-paying government attorney position that provides health insurance when there is no evidence she can find higher-paying jobs with similar health insurance benefits).

130 *In re* Mason, 464 F.3d 878 (9th Cir. 2006) (debtor's learning disability that pre-dated her decision to take out student loans may be considered in assessing likely persistence of undue hardship); *In re* Renville, 2006 WL 3206126 (D. Mont. Nov. 3, 2006); *In re* Walrond-Rogers, 2008 WL 2478389 (Bankr. D. Mass. June 17, 2008) (applying "totality of circumstances" standard and rejecting creditor's preexisting-condition argument related to debtor's prior knowledge of her daughter's severe disability); *In re* Wilkinson-Bell, 2007 WL 1021969 (Bankr. C.D. Ill. Apr. 2, 2007) (debtor met good faith standard although her blindness pre-dated her decision to take out student loan for daughter); Educational Credit Mgmt. Corp. v. Curiston, 351 B.R. 22 (Bankr. D. Conn. 2006) (no basis under Second Circuit *Brunner* decision for excluding debtor's preexisting mental impairment as "additional circumstance" indicating continuation of financial hardship). *See also In re* Walker, 406 B.R. 840, 863 (Bankr. D. Minn. 2009), *aff'd*, 427 B.R. 471 (B.A.P. 8th Cir. 2010) (rejecting as "beyond the pale" creditor's argument that debtor's "planned" births of five children after taking out student loans precluded her claiming child-related circumstances as basis for undue hardship).

131 Educational Credit Mgmt. Corp. v. Polleys, 356 F.3d 1302, 1310 (10th Cir. 2004) (under second *Brunner* prong, "inquiry into future circumstances should be limited to the foreseeable future, at most over the term of the loan").

132 *In re* Ordaz, 287 B.R. 912 (Bankr. C.D. Ill. 2002). *See also In re* Coatney, 345 B.R. 905 (Bankr. C.D. Ill. 2006) (deferring ruling on dischargeability because debtor did not present evidence of original loan term; time frame under income-contingent repayment plan not relevant to second prong of *Brunner* test).

133 *In re* Richardson, 2008 WL 3911075, at *3 n.3 (Bankr. E.D. N.C. Aug. 14, 2008) (court notes it has established pro bono panel of mental health experts available at no cost to debtors to evaluate and provide testimony on mental health issues related to section 523(a)(8) dischargeability issues), *aff'd*, 326 Fed. Appx. 173 (4th Cir. 2009).

134 *See also In re* Mosley, 494 F.3d 1320 (11th Cir. 2007) (debtor not required to submit independent medical evidence to corroborate his testimony about impact of psychiatric disorder on ability to work); *In re* Barrett, 487 F.3d 353 (6th Cir. 2007) (medical bills, letters from treating physicians, and other indicia of medical treatment may corroborate debtor's testimony regarding undue hardship based on health condition); *In re* Brightful, 267 F.3d 324 (3d Cir. 2001) (bankruptcy judge may make reasonable conclusions concerning debtor's emotional state without expert testimony); *In re* Pena, 155 F.3d 1108 (9th Cir. 1998) (debtor's testimony about mental impairment, combined with evidence of her Social Security disability award related to

have freely taken judicial notice of treatises and other publicly available information about the debtor's condition in order to make findings about the likely effect on future employment.[135] The court may consider a finding by the Social Security Administration that a debtor is disabled or not disabled, but the agency finding should not be preclusive one way or another on the ultimate undue hardship determination.[136] Particularly when the creditor fails to present rebuttal evidence, the court should give decisive weight to the debtor's evidence of a limiting impairment.[137]

When the debtor is able to present direct corroborating testimony about his or her condition, either from friends, family members or treating professionals, this greatly improves the likelihood of obtaining a hardship discharge and having it survive on appeal.[138]

10.4.2.3 The Third *Brunner* Prong—Good Faith

10.4.2.3.1 General

The third prong of the *Brunner* test requires that the borrower show a good faith attempt to repay the loan. This requirement looks to the debtor's past conduct. As a legal standard it has been particularly controversial, primarily due to its subjectivity, and also because it is not based on any specific Congressional authority.[139] The test ostensibly considers whether the debtor made efforts to obtain employment, maximize income, and minimize expenses in the

---

condition, are sufficient evidence to establish medical condition); *In re* Hertzel, 329 B.R. 221 (B.A.P. 6th Cir. 2005) (court takes judicial notice of well-known medical facts about debtor's condition of multiple sclerosis); *In re* Cline, 248 B.R. 347 (B.A.P. 8th Cir. 2000) (court's findings were not unreliable simply because no expert testimony was presented that debtor was clinically disabled); *In re* Cheney, 280 B.R. 648 (N.D. Iowa 2002) (debtor not required to submit expert evidence of clinical diagnoses of depression or mental disability, particularly when debtor's testimony about her condition was not rebutted); *In re* Cekic-Torres, 431 B.R. 75 (Bankr. N.D. Ohio 2010) (no expert corroborating testimony or medical records, but relying on debtor's testimony, observation of her morbid obesity, and photos of visible leg wounds to establish impairments limiting employment); *In re* Walker, 406 B.R. 840 (Bankr. D. Minn. 2009), *aff'd*, 427 B.R. 471 (B.A.P. 8th Cir. 2010) (referring to treatises on autism to elucidate limits parent of autistic child faces in sustaining employment outside home); *In re* Jackson, 2007 WL 2295585 (Bankr. S.D.N.Y. Aug. 9, 2007) (no requirement that debtor provide corroborating medical testimony on effect of disability on work efforts); *In re* Hamilton, 361 B.R. 532 (Bankr. D. Mont. 2007) (creditor's vocational expert, who was not medical doctor, failed to rebut evidence of work-related health limitations established by debtor's medical records and by testimony of debtor and his wife). *But see In re* Nash, 446 F.3d 188 (1st Cir. 2006) (bankruptcy court properly held debtor needed opinion of qualified expert to show expected duration of her psychological disorders); *In re* Burton, 339 B.R. 856 (Bankr. E.D. Va. 2006) (collecting cases on use of medical evidence in dischargeability cases; declining to give corroborating weight to Social Security disability determination); *In re* Pobiner, 309 B.R. 405 (Bankr. E.D.N.Y. 2004) (debtor must provide corroborating evidence from his physician or psychotherapist to support claim on second *Brunner* prong); *In re* Burkhead, 304 B.R. 560 (Bankr. D. Mass. 2004) (although debtor documented through medical records that her medical condition was serious, she failed to testify or provide expert testimony that her condition would persist).

135 *In re* Denittis, 362 B.R. 57 (Bankr. D. Mass. 2007) (parties stipulated to debtor's diagnosis of multiple sclerosis; court may take judicial notice of published resources on long-term effects of condition); *In re* Jara, 2006 WL 2806556 (Bankr. D.N.J. Sept. 27, 2006) (taking judicial notice of National Institute of Mental Health publication describing chronic nature of bi-polar disorder); *In re* Gobin, 2006 WL 3885136 (Bankr. E.D. Ky. May 15, 2006) (taking judicial notice of National Institute of Mental Health publication on symptoms of depression).

136 *See In re* Traversa, 2008 WL 4681844 (Bankr. D. Conn. Sept. 24, 2008) (Social Security Administration finding that debtor disabled not determinative of undue hardship under section 523(a)(8)); *In re* Benjumen, 408 B.R. 2 (Bankr. E.D.N.Y. July 20, 2009) (Social Security Administration denial of debtor's disability claim not determinative on undue hardship issue).

137 *See, e.g., In re* Barrett, 487 F.3d 353, 363 (6th Cir. 2007) (noting creditor's failure to subpoena any medical records or otherwise rebut debtor's evidence of impairments); *In re* Tucker, 2009 WL 2877906 (Bankr. D.N.H. Sept. 3, 2009) (creditor failed to meet burden of production by not offering rebuttal evidence against debtor's uncorroborated testimony about mental impairment).

138 *In re* Benjumen, 408 B.R. 9 (Bankr. E.D.N.Y. 2009) (applying Federal Rule of Evidence 702 in rejecting creditor's attempt to exclude testimony of licensed psychologist/certified rehabilitation counselor regarding effect of debtor's bipolar disorder on likely future employment). *See In re* Reynolds, 425 F.3d 526 (8th Cir. 2005) (extensive testimony of debtor corroborated by testimony of psychiatric expert witness as to her medical and psychological condition and by attorney expert as to debtor's inability to gain admission to the Minnesota bar); *In re* Kelsey, 287 B.R. 132 (Bankr. D. Vt. 2001) (treating psychiatrist testified at length and established that it was more likely than not that debtor's debilitating condition would persist for a significant portion of repayment period).

139 Ulm v. Educational Credit Mgmt. Corp., 304 B.R. 915, 921 n.2 (S.D. Ga. 2004) (questioning relevance of "good faith" prong where debtor has met first two tests); *In re* Cummings, 2007 WL 3445912, at *1 (Bankr. N.D. Cal. Nov. 13, 2007) (finding good faith on part of individual debtor and criticizing good faith test in general, noting that good faith prong of *Brunner* test "was made up out of whole cloth and is in no way related to the language of the statute"). *See In re* Brunner, 46 B.R. 752, 755 (S.D.N.Y. 1985) (good faith requirement "inferred" from Commission on the Bankruptcy Law's concern over regulating discharges during initial five-year repayment period of loan term, after which discharge would be automatic under the early Code provision). *See also* Rafael I Pardo & Michelle R. Lacey, *Undue Hardship in the Bankruptcy Courts: An Empirical Assessment of the Discharge of Educational Debt*, 74 U. Cin. L. Rev. 405, 514–17 (Winter 2005) (concluding after review of extensive body of "undue hardship" decisions that "good faith" test has allowed courts to apply personal value judgments to conduct that is irrelevant to "undue hardship" concept referenced in statute).

past.[140] Under this standard, a court may also assess whether the debtor willfully or negligently caused the default.[141] Similarly, the court may consider whether the debtor fell into default due to conditions that were reasonably beyond the debtor's control. In order to satisfy the "good faith" test, it is not essential that the debtor have actually made any payments.[142] Debtors who clearly lacked sufficient income to make minimal payments may still qualify for a discharge.[143]

Judicial construction of the good faith test has strayed far from the context of the original *Brunner* case. The *Brunner* court found bad faith when a debtor filed to discharge her student loan debt within a month of the due date for her first loan payment.[144] Under the Bankruptcy Code at the time, all student loans were automatically dischargeable after payments had been due for five years. The court was concerned about students who were seeking discharges quickly after graduation and without making any effort to pay on the loan during the five-year period before the loan could be discharged automatically without an undue hardship determination. Today, borrowers who are seeking discharge of student loan debts are not jumping the gun on a future automatic discharge. On the contrary, many have already been burdened by the obligations for decades and, if denied a discharge, face future decades of crushing debt.

As part of a concerted litigation strategy over the past two decades, student loan creditors have often succeeded in shifting the courts' attention under the "good faith" analysis to the question of whether the debtor considered various alternative loan repayment options.[145] As discussed in the following subsection, these options can extend loan repayment terms for up to twenty-five years, often with little concrete benefit to the creditor or the debtor. Although these options have little to do with the good faith test announced by the *Brunner* court, they provide student loan creditors with a tool for deflecting courts away from making undue hardship determinations under section 523(a)(8) of the Bankruptcy Code.

10.4.2.3.2 "Good faith" and participation in affordable repayment plans

Student loan authorities and the Department of Education routinely argue that courts need not find that repayment will impose an undue hardship on students because the Department's regulations provide for payment relief in the form of repayment plans tied to income. Prior to 2009, courts generally focused on the income-contingent repayment plan (ICRP).[146] This plan is still available, only in the Direct Loan Program. As of July 1, 2009, there is a more advantageous plan for borrowers. This income-based repayment (IBR) plan is available in both the Direct Loan Program and FFEL Program.[147] This section refers to both plans as "income-based" plans. However, most court decisions to date refer to ICR.

Several courts of appeals have ruled that the debtor's response to the availability of an income-based plan may be treated as an important factor in the "undue hardship" evaluation, particularly under the "good faith" test.[148] At

---

140 *In re* Mosley, 494 F.3d 1320, 1327 (11th Cir. 2007); *In re* O'Hearn, 339 F.3d 559, 564 (7th Cir. 2003); *In re* Birrane, 287 B.R. 490, 497 (B.A.P. 9th Cir. 2002).

141 *In re* Faish, 72 F.3d 298, 305 (3d Cir. 1995); *In re* Roberson, 999 F.2d 1132, 1136 (7th Cir. 1993).

142 *In re* Mosley, 494 F.3d 1320, 1327 (11th Cir. 2007) (failure to make any payments, by itself, does not establish lack of good faith); Educational Credit Mgmt. Corp. v. Polleys, 356 F.3d 1302 (10th Cir. 2004) (same); *In re* Innes, 284 B.R. 496 (D. Kan. 2002) (finding of good faith effort not precluded by debtor's failure to make payments, as debtor lacked sufficient income to make minimum monthly payments); *In re* Nary, 253 B.R. 752 (N.D. Tex. 2000) (good faith measured by efforts to obtain employment and maximize income, and absence of payments does not preclude discharge); *In re* Grove, 323 B.R. 216, 225 (Bankr. N.D. Ohio 2005) (good faith found although debtor filed adversary action shortly after loan became due and never made a payment); *In re* Norasteh, 311 B.R. 671, 676 (Bankr. S.D.N.Y. 2004) (no payments does not end good faith inquiry); *In re* Alston, 297 B.R. 410 (Bankr. E.D. Pa. 2003); *In re* McGinnis, 289 B.R. 257 (Bankr. M.D. Ga. 2003) (actual payments not required to show good faith; requests for forbearances not evidence of bad faith); *In re* Ivory, 269 B.R. 890 (Bankr. N.D. Ala. 2001) (no bad faith when debtor never had ability to repay loan); *In re* Coats, 214 B.R. 397 (Bankr. N.D. Okla. 1997); *In re* Maulin, 190 B.R. 153 (Bankr. W.D.N.Y. 1995). *See also In re* Lewis, 276 B.R. 912 (Bankr. C.D. Ill. 2002) (consolidation does not prevent court from finding good faith based on debtor's loan payments prior to consolidation).

143 *In re* Coco, 335 Fed. Appx. 224 (3d Cir. 2009) (unpublished) (summary judgment for creditor vacated when bankruptcy court gave too much weight to debtor's past lack of payments and evidence indicated debtor's earnings were likely never sufficient to make loan payments); *In re* Naylor, 348 B.R. 680 (Bankr. W.D. Pa. 2006) (involuntary payments by seizure of debtor's tax refunds and portions of his Social Security checks effectively deprived debtor of ability to make voluntary payments on student loans; involuntary payments should be considered as loan payments for good faith determination).

144 Brunner v. New York State Higher Educ. Servs. Corp., 831 F.2d 395, 397.

145 *See, e.g., In re* Frushour, 433 F.3d 393, 402 (4th Cir. 2005) (finding lack of good faith when debtor did not "seriously consider" income-contingent repayment plan that would have extended payments up to twenty-five years); *In re* Tirch, 409 F.3d 677 (6th Cir. 2005) (failure to enter into income-contingent repayment plan indicated bad faith).

146 *See* § 3.1.3.3, *supra.*

147 *See* § 3.1.3.2, *supra.*

148 *In re* Nys, 446 F.3d 938, 947 (9th Cir. 2005) (debtor's consideration of ICRP option is an important indicator of good faith); *In re* Frushour, 433 F.3d 393, 402 (4th Cir. 2005) (important component of good faith inquiry); *In re* Alderete, 412 F.3d 1200, 1206 (10th Cir. 2005) (carries "significant weight" in evaluating good faith); *In re* Tirch, 409 F.3d 677, 682 (6th Cir. 2005) (decision not to take advantage of ICRP probative of debtor's intent to repay); Educational Credit Mgmt. Corp. v. Bronsdon, 421 B.R. 27 (D. Mass. 2009) (bankruptcy court erred

the same time, courts agree that participation in an income-based plan is not required to satisfy the "good faith" standard.[149] Courts applying "totality of the circumstances" test recognize the option to participate in an income-based plan as a factor in determining undue hardship, but not a determining one.[150]

While some courts may embrace arguments relating to the availability of these payment plans, the Bankruptcy Code undeniably provides an opportunity for a debtor to obtain an absolute and immediate discharge of student loans if the statutory conditions are met.[151] No comparable discharge is available under the Department's regulations and administrative collection programs.[152] There is thus an in-

---

in not considering availability of ICRP as factor in undue hardship determination); *In re* Kehler, 326 B.R. 142 (Bankr. N.D. Ind. 2005) (discharge denied; finding that 62-year-old debtor can make monthly $87.97 ICRP payments on a $62,000 educational loan over next twenty-five years); *In re* DeRose, 316 B.R. 606 (Bankr. W.D.N.Y. 2004) (debtor did not prove undue hardship because she could repay through an ICRP); *In re* Hollins, 286 B.R. 310 (Bankr. N.D. Tex. 2002) (debtor's eligibility for ICRP precluded her from satisfying *Brunner* test); *In re* Douglass, 237 B.R. 652 (Bankr. N.D. Ohio 1999) (debtor who failed to make any payments on student loans or negotiate an ICRP denied discharge based on lack of good faith effort to repay). *See also* U.S. Dep't of Health & Human Servs. v. Smitley, 347 F.3d 109 (4th Cir. 2003) (the availability of an ICRP should be considered under the "unconscionability" standard for HEAL loans).

149 *In re* Mosley, 494 F.3d 1320 (11th Cir. 2007) (rejecting a per se rule that debtor cannot show good faith if debtor did not enroll in ICRP); *In re* Barrett, 487 F.3d 353, 364 (6th Cir. 2007); *In re* Nys, 446 F.3d 938, 947 (9th Cir. 2006); *In re* Alderete, 412 F.3d 1200, 1206 (10th Cir. 2005); *In re* Frushour, 433 F.3d 393, 402 (4th Cir. 2005). *See In re* Rutherford, 317 B.R. 865, 880-81 (Bankr. N.D. Ala. 2004) (collecting cases on lack of per se ICRP participation requirement). *See also In re* Jesperson, 571 F.3d 775 (8th Cir. 2009) (plurality of panel expressly rejects consideration of ICRP as threshold test for dischargeability).

150 *In re* Jesperson, 571 F.3d 775 (8th Cir. 2009) (debtor who, according to court's calculation, had $900 monthly surplus income to pay toward ICRP precluded from discharge); *In re* Cumberworth, 347 B.R. 652 (B.A.P. 8th Cir. 2006) (recognizing that standards for eligibility for an ICRP and test for "undue hardship" under section 523(a)(8) as two separate and distinct determinations); *In re* Groves, 398 B.R. 673 (Bankr. W.D. Mo. 2008) (after imputing income as if debtor employed at work for which she was qualified, payment required by ICRP would still create undue hardship); *In re* Wallace, 2007 WL 4210450, at *7 (Bankr. E.D. Mo. Nov. 27, 2007) (ICRP option irrelevant because its baseline is a poverty level income, while "totality of circumstances" analysis must consider debtor's reasonably necessary living expenses); *In re* Standfuss, 245 B.R. 356 (Bankr. E.D. Mo. 2000) ("flexibility" of ICRP plan considered in determining debtors' ability to repay student loan). *See also In re* Lee, 352 B.R. 91 (B.A.P. 8th Cir. 2006) (placing too much weight on ICRP factor can be viewed as inimical to fresh start); *In re* Ford, 269 B.R. 673 (B.A.P. 8th Cir. 2001) (availability of ICRP is merely one factor considered in "totality of circumstances" test and not determinative in case in which ICRP would result in 62-year-old woman with arthritic condition carrying large and increasing debt that would not be forgiven until she is eighty-seven- years old); *In re* Denittis, 362 B.R. 57 (Bankr. D Mass. 2007) (undue hardship found despite ICRP option, noting that "good faith" prong of *Brunner* is not a requirement in "totality of circumstances" analysis followed by many First Circuit courts).

151 *See In re* Barrett, 487 F.3d 353 (6th Cir. 2007) (no evidence of Congressional intent that ICRP program eliminates discharge option, particularly when there is no reasonable likelihood that debtor will ever be able to repay loan); *In re* Durrani, 311 B.R. 496 (Bankr. N.D. Ill. 2004), aff'd, 320 B.R. 357 (N.D. Ill. 2005) (first prong of *Brunner* test looks at whether debtor can maintain minimal standard of living and "repay this loan," not whether debtor has some surplus income available to pay accruing interest or some portion of loan); *In re* Marshall, 430 B.R. 809, 815 (Bankr. S.D. Ohio 2010) (creditor's insistence on IBR participation has improper effect of creating a "fourth prong to the *Brunner* test—the IBR prong"); *In re* Alston, 297 B.R. 410 (Bankr. E.D. Pa. 2003) (requiring debtor to wait twenty-five years to obtain discharge under ICRP is contrary to "fresh start" purpose of the Bankruptcy Code). *See generally In re* Walker, 406 B.R. 840 (Bankr. D. Minn. 2009), aff'd, 427 B.R. 471 (B.A.P. 8th Cir. 2010) (discussing importance of student loan discharge in context of broader "fresh start" goals of bankruptcy legislation).

152 *In re* Dufresne, 341 B.R. 391 (Bankr. D. Mass. 2006) (unlike discharge, ICRP "simply condemns a debtor whose honesty and efforts are not otherwise in question to privation beyond reasonable limits—to an ever-present and ever-growing mountain of debt which, given her reasonably foreseeable financial prospects (derived from her actual past and present circumstances), will not likely ever be repaid"); Limkemann v. U.S. Dep't of Educ., 314 B.R. 190, 195–96 (Bankr. N.D. Iowa 2004) (DOE's arguments focused on ICRP, if accepted, would deprive courts of role in making hardship discharge determinations); *In re* Kopf, 245 B.R. 731 (Bankr. D. Me. 2000) (no matter how flexible or "humanely executed" such programs may be, they simply are not the equivalent of a discharge).

The *Kopf* court noted that, even when a debtor's monthly payment obligation is reduced to zero under an ICRP, this will only "postpone repayment indefinitely and, unless interest is abated, permit additional interest accruals." *In re* Kopf, 245 B.R. 735 (Bankr. D. Me. 2000). *See* Educational Credit Mgmt. Corp. v. Durrani, 320 B.R. 357 (N.D. Ill. 2005) ("[c]ourts must not turn to the ICRP as a substitute for the thoughtful and considered exercise of . . . discretion" required under the *Brunner* test); *In re* Korhonen, 296 B.R. 492, 496 (Bankr. D. Minn. 2003) ("[ICRP] cannot trump the Congressionally mandated individualized determination of undue hardship"); *In re* Nanton-Marie, 303 B.R. 228 (Bankr. S.D. Fla. 2003) (nothing in Bankruptcy Code requires consideration of ICRP as condition precedent to undue hardship discharge); *In re* Johnson, 299 B.R. 676, 682 (Bankr. M.D. Ga. 2003) ("If Congress had intended the question of dischargeability of student loans to be delegated to a non-judicial entity, no matter how fair its formulas or intentions, it could have provided for such."); *In re* Thomsen, 234 B.R. 506, 514 (Bankr. D. Mont. 1999) (under ICRP, debtors will simply replace nondischargeable student loans with another nondischargeable debt in form of income taxes). *See generally* §§ 3.1.3.2.5, 3.1.3.3.3, *supra* (discussing long-term consequences for borrowers making small payments under an ICRP).

For a thorough discussion of the relationship between section 523(a)(8)'s discharge provision and the ICRP option, see Terrence L. Michael & Janie M. Phelps, *Judges?!—We Don't Need No Stinking Judges!!!: The Discharge of Student Loans in Bankruptcy Cases and the Income Contingent Repayment Plan*,

herent conflict between the "fresh start" goal of the Bankruptcy Code and the mounting long-term debt burden often associated with an income-based plan.[153]

Often the student loan creditor's argument really boils down to the contention that the income-based plan operates as a kind of implicit repeal of the Code's authorization for courts to grant a complete discharge of a student loan upon a finding of undue hardship. Congressional action in amending the Code in 2005 belies this argument. Despite extensive amendments to the Code, including revisions to section 523(a)(8), Congress in enacting BAPCPA left intact the provision for full discharge of student loan debts in appropriate cases.[154]

These long-term repayment extensions subvert the "fresh start" goal in a number of ways. Student loan creditors tout the purported advantage to the debtor of reduced, long-term payments that are "affordable." Payments under an income-based plan may be twenty, ten, or even zero dollars per month. While little or no portion of the payments is applied to principal under these long-term plans, interest increases and compounds.[155] At the end of twenty-five years, the amount due may far exceed the original loan amount. The regulations permit the debt to be written off at the end of the twenty-five-year repayment period.[156] However, the IRS Code allows assessment of taxes against the forgiven amount. In the end, a debtor may end up worse off at an advanced age, facing a significant non-dischargeable tax burden.[157]

The stress of the debt will have burdened the debtor for a lifetime, often with no real benefit to the creditor.[158] There are also numerous administrative requirements that the borrower must meet during the twenty-five years in order to remain in the income-based plan. Many borrowers lose eligibility if they fail to return a form or if they move without alerting the government.

---

38 Tex. Tech. L. Rev. 73 (Fall 2005) (one of the authors is a bankruptcy judge).

153 *In re* Barrett, 487 F.3d 353, 364 (6th Cir. 2007); *In re* Lee, 352 B.R. 91, 96 (B.A.P. 8th Cir. 2006); *In re* Booth, 410 B.R. 672 (Bankr. E.D. Wash. 2009) (focus of the ICRP is on deferral not discharge and thus is the antithesis of a fresh start); *In re* Waldron-Rogers, 2008 WL 2478389 (Bankr. D. Mass. June 17, 2008) (Congress never directed that zero-dollar payment plans be sole option for debtors with payment hardships); *In re* King, 368 B.R. 358 (Bankr. D. Vt. 2007).

154 *In re* Barrett, 487 F.3d 353, 364 (6th Cir. 2007); *In re* Denittis, 362 B.R. 57, 64 (Bankr. D. Mass. 2007).

155 *In re* Vargas, 2010 WL 148632 (Bankr. C.D. Ill. Jan. 12, 2010) (ICRP plans may work for debtors facing short-term hardship, but bankruptcy discharge provides relief for those facing long-term inability to pay); *In re* Brooks, 406 B.R. 382, 393 (Bankr. D. Minn. 2009) (repayment options that do not reduce loan principal miss the focus of "undue hardship" analysis, which looks at the burden that actually paying off loan will impose on debtor); *In re* Fahrer, 308 B.R. 27 (Bankr. W.D. Mo. 2004) (reasonable for debtor to refuse ICRP when term would exceed her expected working life); *In re* Kopf, 245 B.R. 731, 735 (Bankr. D. Me. 2000) (even when debtor's monthly payment obligation is reduced to zero under an ICRP, this will only "postpone repayment indefinitely and, unless interest is abated, permit additional interest accruals").

156 See §§ 3.1.3.1, 3.1.3.2, *supra*.

For loans first incurred in July 2014 and afterwards, the repayment limit will be twenty years for those borrowers repaying through IBR.

157 *In re* Coco, 335 Fed. Appx. 224, 2009 WL 1426757, at *4 (3d Cir. May 22, 2009) (unpublished decision) (reversing finding of nondischargeability and ruling, *inter alia*, that lower court gave too much weight to debtor's refusal to enroll in ICRP, noting "her participation in the ICRP could ultimately result in her simply trading a student loan debt for an IRS debt"); *In re* Brooks, 406 B.R. 382, 394–95 (Bankr. D. Minn. 2009) (potential tax liability after extended repayment period is a significant drawback to ICRP option); *In re* Durrani, 311 B.R. 496, 508 (Bankr. N.D. Ill. 2005), *aff'd*, 320 B.R. 357 (N.D. Ill. 2005) (court must take into account considerable tax burden debtor will face at end of twenty-five-year repayment period); *In re* Brunell, 356 B.R. 567 (Bankr. D. Mass. 2006) (refusing to grant discharge of student loan debt but allowing discharge of tax debt from loan forgiveness at end of ICRP term); *In re* Allen, 324 B.R. 278, 282 (Bankr. W.D. Pa. 2005) (tax consequences of ICRP can be particularly disastrous for debtors who begin plans at or near retirement age). *See also In re* Coatney, 345 B.R. 905 (Bankr. C.D. Ill. 2006). *But see* Educational Credit Mgmt. Corp. v. Bronsdon, 421 B.R. 27 (D. Mass. 2009) (reversing bankruptcy court for, *inter alia*, giving too much weight to tax consequences of ICRP when impact not clear).

The court in *Coatney* noted that the debtor's participation in an ICRP would be extremely problematic. With a current loan balance of $120,000, the indebtedness could grow to hundreds of thousands of dollars by the end of the eighteen-year ICRP term. This could leave the debtor with tens of thousands of dollars in nondischargeable income taxes due. *In re* Coatney, 345 B.R. 911 (Bankr. C.D. Ill. 2006).

However, rather than finding the underlying debt dischargeable, the court granted the debtor a four-year deferment, after which he could seek another dischargeability determination based on a more complete record.

In another decision, the court focused upon the "undue hardship" that would arise from assessment of taxes at the time of loan forgiveness at the end of a twenty-five-year ICRP. *In re* Grove, 323 B.R. 216, 230 (Bankr. N.D. Ohio 2005).

Here, rather than discharging the debt, the court granted a partial discharge to the extent of any indebtedness remaining at the end of the ICRP term, thus precluding assessment of taxes against the forgiven indebtedness. While addressing one problem, the *Grove* decision unfortunately left the debtor, at age 57, with the full burden of growing indebtedness for the future twenty-five-year term of the ICRP.

158 *In re* Marshall, 430 B.R. 809, 815 (Bankr. S.D. Ohio 2010) (even though no payments would be required under IBR, debtor faces long-term emotional harm from heavy debt burden extending into her advanced age); *In re* Larson, 426 B.R. 782 (Bankr. N.D. Ill. 2010) (psychological and emotional toll of extending minimal payments for debtor over twenty-five years subverts "fresh start" goal of Bankruptcy Code); *In re* Durrani, 311 B.R. 496, 508 (Bankr. N.D. Ill. 2004), *aff'd*, 320 B.R. 357 (N.D. Ill. 2005) (noting emotional toll taken by long-term deferral of mounting debt); Educational Credit Mgmt. Corp. v. Porrazzo, 307 B.R. 345 (Bankr. D. Conn. 2004) (no lack of good faith as debtor's decision to reject ICRP was appropriate given that regular status reviews over twenty-five-year period would exacerbate his anxiety disorder).

By considering a debtor's ability to pay under an income-based plan for a period of up to twenty-five years, courts following the *Brunner* test may misapply its second prong, which looks to whether the debtor's inability to repay will persist for a significant portion of the remaining repayment period under the original loan obligations.[159] Again, it should not be overlooked that *Brunner* was decided in 1987. At that time, *any* student loan could be discharged after it had been due for five years. As a practical matter, the loan repayment periods within the court's contemplation in 1987 were always subject to this potential for automatic discharge. Therefore, creditors should not rely on *Brunner* to support arguments that a twenty-five-year loan repayment period should be imposed upon a debtor in lieu of discharging the debt.[160] Similarly, courts should not require that students apply for an income-based plan as an "exhaustion of administrative remedies" threshold before seeking a hardship discharge in bankruptcy.[161] There is no requirement to this effect in the Code.

In addition, student borrowers should present evidence of any obstacles they have faced in attempting to negotiate an affordable plan. An agency's claim of flexible payment arrangements will be undercut by testimony that the agency failed to cooperate with the borrower and ultimately demanded payments in excess of the student's ability to pay or that the student was told that affordable payment plans simply do not exist.[162]

Even when the borrower intends to argue that an income-based plan should not be a substitute for a bankruptcy discharge, the debtor should review available payment options before the discharge hearing[163] and be prepared to present evidence when an income-based plan is not feasible, particularly when the accrual of interest will effectively prevent any meaningful repayment of the loan.[164] The IBR plan limits interest accrual, but only for subsidized loans and only for a three-year period.[165]

Since payments must be made under an income-based plan if the debtor's income is even slightly above poverty level (150% of poverty level in the case of IBR), the debtor should present evidence that making these payments will prevent the debtor from maintaining a minimal standard of living.[166]

---

159 *See, e.g., In re* Ordaz, 287 B.R. 912 (Bankr. C.D. Ill. 2002) (consolidation loan that effectively restructured student loan with same lender at end of original ten-year term did not "restart the clock" on new fifteen-year repayment period for purposes of considering future inability to repay).

However, applying a "totality of circumstances" test, the Eighth Circuit Bankruptcy Appellate Panel has concluded that a twenty-five-year repayment period under an ICRP would not impose an undue hardship on a debtor under the circumstances of that case. *See* Long v. Educational Credit Mgmt. Corp., 292 B.R. 635 (B.A.P. 8th Cir. 2003). *See also In re* Coatney, 345 B.R. 905 (Bankr. C.D. Ill. 2006) (declining to rule on dischargeability when only evidence before court was duration of ICRP and no facts presented regarding original loan repayment period).

160 *See* Rafael I. Pardo & Michelle R. Lacey, *Undue Hardship in the Bankruptcy Courts: An Empirical Assessment of the Discharge of Educational Debt*, 74 U. Cin. L. Rev. 405 n.415 (Winter 2005).

161 However, in a case that did not involve an ICRP, one court denied a hardship discharge adversary complaint without prejudice because the student had failed to exhaust administrative remedies by first seeking an unpaid-refund discharge. *See In re* Scholl, 259 B.R. 345 (Bankr. N.D. Iowa 2001).

162 *In re* Cheney, 280 B.R. 648 (N.D. Iowa 2002) (student loan creditor failed to prove that it had properly advised debtor of availability of ICRP and other programs or to assist debtor in pursuing them); *In re* Lee, 345 B.R. 911, 918 (Bankr. W.D. Ark. 2006) (court will not fault debtor who was never advised of various options such as ICRP), *aff'd*, 352 B.R. 91 (B.A.P. 9th Cir. 2006); *In re* McMullin, 316 B.R. 70 (Bankr. E.D. La. 2004) (no evidence debtor was ever actually informed of repayment options); *In re* Carlson, 273 B.R. 481 (Bankr. D.S.C. 2001) (no evidence debtor was advised of ICRP); *In re* Thomsen, 234 B.R. 506, 514 (Bankr. D. Mont. 1999) (debtor made three separate requests for affordable payment plans, but DOE never sent application and instead demanded excessive payments contrary to rule for "satisfactory payment arrangements").

Some courts have rejected generalized statements made by student loan creditors about the availability of ICRPs and other payment programs without proof that the debtor would in fact be eligible for such programs. Educational Credit Mgmt. Corp. v. Porrazzo, 307 B.R. 345 (Bankr. D. Conn. 2004) (student loan creditor failed to prove that debtor was eligible for Ford Program); *In re* Strand, 298 B.R. 367 (Bankr. D. Minn. 2003).

163 *See In re* Chambers, 239 B.R. 767 (Bankr. N.D. Ohio 1999) (debtor admitted on cross-examination that she was unaware of availability of ICRP before filing bankruptcy and that she would have participated in the payment program had she known). *See also In re* Shilling, 333 B.R. 716 (Bankr. W.D. Pa. 2005) (debtor fails *Brunner* "good faith" test when she did not articulate any reason for deciding not to pursue an ICRP).

164 *In re* Barrett, 337 B.R. 896 (B.A.P. 6th Cir. 2006) (lender's emphasis on ICRP "fails to take account of the additional worry and anxiety that the Debtor is likely to suffer if he is compelled to watch his debt steadily increase knowing that he does not have the ability to repay it for reasons beyond his control"), *aff'd*, 487 F.3d 353 (6th Cir. 2007); *In re* Dufresne, 341 B.R. 391 (Bankr. D. Mass. 2006) (rejecting ICRP alternative and noting that lender's calculus ignored "the indefinite and perhaps decades-long duration of the forbearance, the ongoing accruals of interest added to current debt, the public credit reporting of a large and growing debt in a perpetual default status, the tax consequences of a debt forgiven many years hence"); *In re* Strand, 298 B.R. 367 (Bankr. D. Minn. 2003) (interest accruing over twenty-five-year period under ICRP will leave debtor "hamstrung into poverty for the rest of his life" and prevent him from obtaining credit or approval of rental applications). *See also In re* Robbins, 371 B.R. 372 (Bankr. E.D. Ark. 2007) (there is "no point" to pursuing ICRP when payments would be zero).

165 *See* § 3.1.3.3.2, *supra*.

There are also some limits on capitalization in the ICR plan.

166 *In re* Lee, 352 B.R. 91 (B.A.P. 9th Cir. 2006) (ICRP payments of $13.03 monthly not an option for debtor whose expenses for necessities already exceeded income); *In re* Curiston, 351 B.R. 22 (D. Conn. 2006) (bankruptcy court properly found participation in ICRP futile given debtor's financial situation); *In re* Kloos, 2010 WL 3089722 (Bankr. D. Neb. Aug. 5, 2010) (no

§ 10.4.2.3.2   Student Loan Law

Many bankruptcy courts that focus on the income-based plans operate on the mistaken assumption that these options are nearly universally available. This is not the case. In fact, there are a number of restrictions on these plans. It is essential for consumers and their attorneys to present evidence with respect to whether the consumer is eligible for an income-based plan.[167] Even eligible consumers should be prepared to present evidence that the plan is not affordable without causing hardship or that their current lenders have told them that the plans are not eligible.

Until July 2009, the main restriction on ICR was that it was available only through the Direct Loan Program. This is still the case, but the more affordable IBR plan is available through both the Direct Loan Program and FFEL Program. This is significant because the FFEL Program was eliminated as of July 2010. Over time, nearly all federal loans will be made through the Direct Loan Program.

Despite these changes, there are still cases in which borrowers will not be eligible for IBR or ICR. The IBR plan has a threshold requirement that borrowers must meet. Even low-income borrowers may not meet this threshold "partial financial hardship" standard. This is most likely to occur if they have relatively low loan balances.[168] These borrowers might qualify for ICR, but they would have to be in the Direct Loan Program to choose ICR. They could in most cases consolidate into the Direct Loan Program and out of the FFEL Program. However, there are some limits on this right to consolidate.[169]

Borrowers that have other types of federal loans, usually Perkins Loan Program loans ("Perkins loans"), are not eligible for the income-based plans. If they have only Perkins loans, they are also not eligible to consolidate with loans issued through the Direct Loan Program. Borrowers with private loans also have no access to the government income-based repayment plans or consolidation. This is critical since, as of 2005, most private student loans are also subject to the special student loan dischargeability restrictions.

Borrowers in default are not eligible for the income-based plans. They must first get out of default, usually through rehabilitation or consolidation, in order to qualify.[170] However, not all borrowers will be eligible to rehabilitate or consolidate out of default. For example, borrowers who have previously rehabilitated their loans in most cases cannot do so again.

Even if a borrower is eligible to rehabilitate a loan, it is important to point out that rehabilitation is not as complete as bankruptcy relief and is not even the same as getting immediately into an income-based repayment plan. Payments through rehabilitation plans must be reasonable and affordable. However, the Department of Education ("the Department") does not use the ICR or IBR formula to make the "reasonable and affordable" determination.[171] Despite the statutory and regulatory right to a reasonable and affordable payment plan, both private lenders and the Department often claim that borrowers must make minimum payments that in some cases will be more than what the borrower can reasonably afford. This is yet another flaw in the argument that borrowers seeking bankruptcy discharges can easily obtain alternative repayments options.

Borrowers in default on FFEL consolidation loans are usually eligible to "re-consolidate" with their Direct loans. Borrowers may also consolidate an FFEL consolidation loan into a Direct consolidation loan if the FFEL consolidation loan is held by a guaranty agency as a result of a bankruptcy claim. This is similar to the situation in which the claim has been submitted for default aversion assistance. However, because the bankruptcy proceeding precludes the submission of a default aversion request, the Department acknowledges that borrowers in this situation should also be allowed to consolidate with the Direct Loan Program.[172] A borrower who is in default on a Direct consolidation loan may not "re-consolidate."[173]

Borrowers who have received wage garnishment orders are not eligible for rehabilitation or consolidation unless the garnishment order is lifted. Similar to the FFEL Program,

---

bad faith when debtor already unable to make ICRP payments and depending on charity for necessities); *In re* Zook, 2009 WL 512436, at *11 (Bankr. D.D.C. Feb. 27, 2009) (ICRP would be "nothing but pointless hardship" for debtor with mental impairment who needed all available income to save for emergencies and retirement); *In re* Neeson, 2008 WL 379699 (Bankr. W.D. Mo. Feb. 12, 2008) (ICRP not option for debtor who lacks funds to purchase car and who has been using credit cards to pay for clothes, utilities, and home repairs); *In re* Douglas, 366 B.R. 241 (Bankr. M.D. Ga. 2007) (debtor diagnosed with HIV and with limited employment options due to felony conviction has reasonable basis for not considering ICRP; she could not maintain minimal standard of living under current income and expenses when paying nothing on student loan); *In re* Greenwood, 349 B.R. 795 (Bankr. D. Ariz. 2006) (no lack of good faith when debtor rejected ICRP requiring $260 monthly payments that he cannot afford); *In re* Bray, 332 B.R. 186, 198 (Bankr. W.D. Mo. 2005) (ICRP with monthly payments of $200 "not a viable option" for debtor who met undue hardship test); *In re* Carter, 295 B.R. 555 (Bankr. W.D. Pa. 2003) (loan consolidation and repayment plan not viable alternative for debtor unable to provide for basic necessities).

167 *See, e.g., In re* Cekic-Torres, 431 B.R. 785 (Bankr. N.D. Ohio 2010) (ICRP/IBR not relevant when student loan creditor is private entity and not participating in eligible federal program); *In re* Groves, 398 B.R. 673 (Bankr. W.D. Mo. 2008) (granting full discharge of debtor's student loans not eligible for ICRP; partial discharge of loans eligible for ICRP).
168 *See* § 3.1.3.2.1, *supra*.
169 *See* § 1.4.1.3.2, *supra*.

170 *See* Ch. 6, *supra*.
171 *See* § 6.3.4, *infra*.
172 This provision is not explicit in the final regulations but is described in the summary of the final rules. 71 Fed. Reg. 64378 (Nov. 1, 2006); U.S. Dep't of Educ., Dear Colleague Letter GEN-06-20 (Dec. 1, 2006).
173 *See* §§ 1.4.1.3.2, 6.2.4, *supra*.

loans that have been reduced to judgment may be consolidated with the Direct Loan Program only if the judgment has been vacated.[174]

Some of the courts that have addressed this issue have acknowledged that not all borrowers are eligible for income-contingent repayment plans (ICRPs). These courts note that borrowers must then present evidence that they inquired about the program and found out they were not eligible. The court would then treat this as evidence establishing good faith for the *Brunner* test.[175]

Judges may also start to consider the public service forgiveness program that went into effect for Direct Loan borrowers in 2008.[176] This program, however, is even more limited than IBR or ICR because borrowers must work in full-time public service jobs for ten years in order to qualify.

10.4.3 Other Hardship Factors

The student's undue hardship argument may be stronger when the student loan arose from a proprietary school that closed down or defrauded the student. Absent a meaningful educational experience, the student has no job skills and, because of the default, is ineligible for future government educational loans. If a discharge is not granted, the student will not be able to go back to school and will not be able to obtain a decent paying job, making repayment now or in the future an undue hardship.

In addition, the nature of the schooling will be relevant to whether the education enabled or would enable the debtor to obtain substantially higher income.[177] Another bankruptcy court has put it this way:

There is thus great pressure and temptation on the part of college authorities to encourage students to apply for loans and grant them when in effect it is not a sound economic thing to do. This should be a substantial factor in determining whether a student loan should be dischargeable. Was the student inveigled into obtaining the loan and taking particular courses in college when the college authorities should have known that upon graduation from college the student had little chance of obtaining employment in that field?[178]

Yet another bankruptcy court has used an investment analysis. Education is an investment with the hope that the student will obtain a higher-paying job in the future. For example, it would be inequitable for a doctor to discharge his medical school debts just before embarking on a well-paid career made possible because of his educational loans. But this exception should not apply when a student attends a cosmetology school and the schooling did not increase the student's job skills in any significant way.[179]

The Ninth Circuit's list of factors limiting future repayment ability under the second prong of the *Brunner* test includes the "poor quality of the education" received with the loan and the debtor's "lack of usable or marketable job skills."[180] There is therefore a sound basis for a court to consider the limited nature of many trade school programs in deciding an "undue hardship" action.[181] As an alternative to or in conjunction with pursuing an undue hardship action, a debtor may wish to raise issues of fraud or lack of educational benefit from a program by challenging the creditor's proof of claim or through nonbankruptcy administrative remedies.[182]

---

174 See § 6.2.4, *supra*.
175 See, e.g., *In re* Alderete, 412 F.3d 1200 (10th Cir. 2005).
176 See § 9.9.2, *supra*.
177 United Student Aid Funds v. Pena (*In re* Pena), 155 F.3d 1108 (9th Cir. 1998) (value of education relevant to future ability to pay student loans); *In re* Carter, 295 B.R. 555 (Bankr. W.D. Pa. 2003) (debtor never completed program for position as medical assistant); *In re* Lewis, 276 B.R. 912 (Bankr. C.D. Ill. 2002) (lack of benefit from uncompleted junior college program considered under second prong of *Brunner* test); *In re* Evans, 131 B.R. 372 (Bankr. S.D. Ohio 1991) (trade school education in word-processing did not improve debtor's ability to repay her student loans); *In re* Price, 25 B.R. 256, 258 (Bankr. W.D. Mo. 1982). *See also* Correll v. Union Nat'l Bank of Pittsburgh, 105 B.R. 302 (Bankr. W.D. Pa. 1989); *In re* Carter, 29 B.R. 228 (Bankr. N.D. Ohio 1983); *In re* Love, 28 B.R. 475 (Bankr. S.D. Ind. 1983); *In re* Ford, 22 B.R. 442 (Bankr. W.D.N.Y. 1982); *In re* Littell, 6 B.R. 85 (Bankr. D. Or. 1980); *In re* Johnson, 5 B.C.D. 532 (Bankr. E.D. Pa. 1979). *But see In re* Chapman, 238 B.R. 450 (Bankr. W.D. Mo. 1999) (rejecting debtor's argument that loans were not really student loans because he did not receive any educational benefit; applying *Brunner* and "totality of circumstances" tests, failed to find undue hardship); *In re* O'Flaherty, 204 B.R. 793 (Bankr. N.D. Ala. 1997) (in applying *Brunner* test, court considered debtor's current income and expenses rather than his ability to utilize education acquired through loan; debtor was unable to fulfill goal of ordination as Catholic priest).
178 *In re* Littell, 6 B.R. 85 (Bankr. D. Or. 1980). *See also* Correll v. Union Nat'l Bank of Pittsburgh, 105 B.R. 302 (Bankr. W.D. Pa. 1989).
179 Powelson v. Stewart Sch. of Hairstyling, Inc., 25 B.R. 274 (Bankr. D. Neb. 1982). *See also In re* Law, 159 B.R. 287 (Bankr. D.S.D. 1993) (debtor obtained no benefit from $20,000 student loan for two-and-a-half weeks of flight training).
180 *In re* Nys, 446 F.3d 938, 947 (9th Cir. 2006). *See also In re* Cota, 298 B.R. 408, 418–19 (Bankr. D. Ariz. 2003) (useless nature of debtor's trade school education is factor to be considered under second *Brunner* prong, rejecting creditor's argument that lender was not responsible for poor quality of education).
181 See Amy E. Sparrow, *Unduly Harsh: The Need to Examine Educational Value in the Student Loan Discharge Cases Involving For-Profit Trade Schools*, 80 Temp. L. Quarterly 329 (Spring 2007) (cogently arguing that courts need to give more weight to quality-of-education issues in hardship discharge actions).
182 See *In re* Goldberg, 297 B.R. 465 (Bankr. W.D.N.C. 2003) (striking student loan creditor's proof of claim for lack of consideration when school closed before student received any benefit from purported education program). *See also In re* Gregory, 387 B.R. 182 (Bankr. N.D. Ohio 2008) (refusing to consider untimely closing of debtor's educational institution as an undue hardship factor and noting availability of administrative remedies outside of bankruptcy for relief from obligation);

The fact that the student was swindled by the school may also be relevant to the consumer's good faith in seeking to discharge the loan. The student may not have felt that the obligation was owed in circumstances under which the school referred the consumer to the lender and the school had defrauded the student.

Courts have also considered whether there should be a different hardship test applied in chapter 13 cases. Sometimes creditors argue against a chapter 13 undue hardship discharge for a student loan on the basis that a debtor can only propose a chapter 13 plan if the debtor has disposable income. If the debtor has disposable income, can it be an undue hardship to repay the student loan? Courts generally reject this argument and apply the same undue hardship standards for chapter 13 and 7 bankruptcies.[183]

Finally, debtors seeking a hardship discharge before a sympathetic bankruptcy court that is inclined to grant a discharge must still be vigilant in proving all the elements of the appropriate hardship test.[184] Appellate courts in several cases have reversed judgments favorable to the debtors on the basis that the record evidence failed to support findings that the debtors' financial circumstances were likely to persist.[185]

10.5 Partial Discharge or Modification of Student Loan

In cases involving large student loan debts owed by middle-class debtors, courts have been exploring the possibility of offering a partial hardship discharge. The court may find that the student has future earnings potential but that the amount of debt is still excessive. In this situation, several courts have discharged only part of the debt and required the balance to be paid out over time.[186] The trend is for courts

---

In re Barton, 266 B.R. 922 (Bankr. S.D. Ga. 2001) (no private right of action to pursue closed-school discharge claim in bankruptcy court, but debtor may pursue hardship discharge under section 523(a)(8)).

School-related cancellations are discussed in Chapter 9, *supra*.

183 *In re* Strauss, 216 B.R. 638 (Bankr. N.D. Cal. 1998); *In re* Oswalt, 215 B.R. 337 (Bankr. W.D.N.Y. 1997) (chapter 13 debtor entitled to undue hardship discharge); *In re* Goranson, 183 B.R. 52 (Bankr. W.D.N.Y. 1995); *In re* Evans, 131 B.R. 372 (Bankr. S.D. Ohio 1991). *See also In re* Elebrashy, 189 B.R. 922 (Bankr. N.D. Ohio 1995).

184 The debtor has the burden of proof on all elements of the hardship test. Goulet v. Educational Credit Mgmt. Corp., 284 F.3d 773 (7th Cir. 2002); *In re* Rifino, 245 F.3d 1083 (9th Cir. 2001); *In re* Faish, 72 F.3d 298 (3d Cir. 1995). *See In re* Nys, 446 F.3d 938 (9th Cir. 2005) (in assessing debtor's future prospects, court will not presume that present inability to make payments will continue; rather, debtor has burden to provide additional evidence to show that inability to pay is likely to persist). *See generally In re* Traversa, 2010 WL 1541443, at *6 (Bankr. D. Conn. Apr. 15, 2010) (discussing shifting burden of production and moving forward in hardship discharge action).

185 *In re* Frushour, 433 F.3d 393 (4th Cir. 2005) (reversing lower courts, court of appeals opines that childcare costs and need to replace old car, among other barriers, will not deter debtor, a single mother, from finding a better-paying job; dissent strongly criticizes reversal of lower courts' fact findings); *In re* Tirch, 409 F.3d 677 (6th Cir. 2005) (debtor presented insufficient evidence of extent and duration of claimed impairments); *In re* Oyler, 397 F.3d 382 (6th Cir. 2005) (debtor fails second *Brunner* prong because he chose to work as low-paid pastor when he should have chosen work that pays more); *In re* O'Hearn, 339 F.3d 559 (7th Cir. 2003) (vacating bankruptcy court decision based on factual inferences not supported by record); Goulet v. Educational Credit Mgmt. Corp., 284 F.3d 773 (7th Cir. 2002) (record devoid of evidence that debtor's problems with alcoholism and a felony conviction, which predated several of his student loan obligations, were "insurmountable," or that they prevented debtor from being gainfully employed); *In re* Rifino, 245 F.3d 1083 (9th Cir. 2001) (debtor failed to prove that her financial circumstances were likely to persist by rebutting creditor's testimony concerning debtors' earning potential as social worker); *In re* Brightful, 267 F.3d 324 (3d Cir. 2001) (debtor failed to introduce evidence that her mental and emotional condition prevented her from using her skills as legal secretary to secure full-time employment).

Student debtors should also carefully evaluate whether to file a cross-appeal in cases in which they have been granted less than a full discharge and the student loan creditor has filed an appeal. *See In re* Alderete, 308 B.R. 495 (B.A.P. 10th Cir. 2004) (finding that entire debt should have been discharged but was compelled to affirm bankruptcy court decision not to discharge loan principal because debtor had not filed cross-appeal), *rev'd in part on other grounds*, 412 F.3d 1200 (10th Cir. 2005) (bankruptcy court cannot order partial discharge absent a finding of undue hardship).

186 *In re* Carnduff, 367 B.R. 120 (9th Cir. B.A.P. 2007) (bankruptcy court erred in failing to consider partial discharge despite finding that the only way debtors could ever repay their $350,000 student loan debt would be if one of them won the lottery). *See In re* Hornsby, 144 F.3d 433 (6th Cir. 1998) (partial discharge is permitted under court's equitable powers); *In re* Saxman, 325 F.3d 1168 (9th Cir. 2003) (bankruptcy court may exercise equitable powers to partially discharge student loan if debtor satisfies undue hardship test as to portion of debt to be discharged); *In re* Blair, 291 B.R. 514 (B.A.P. 9th Cir. 2003); *In re* Nary, 253 B.R. 752 (N.D. Tex. 2000); *In re* Kapinos, 243 B.R. 271 (W.D. Va. 2000); *In re* Brown, 239 B.R. 204 (S.D. Cal. 1999); *In re* Ammirati, 187 B.R. 902 (D.S.C. 1995), *aff'd with unpublished op.*, 85 F.3d 615 (4th Cir. 1996); *In re* Siegel, 282 B.R. 629 (Bankr. N.D. Ohio 2002) (based on debtor's $400 per month in disposable income, discharge allowed for $13,500 out of $30,000 debt, with $16,500 balance to be paid with no interest over twelve years); *In re* Barron, 264 B.R. 833 (Bankr. E.D. Tex. 2001) (bankruptcy court may use equitable power under section 105(a) of Bankruptcy Code to grant partial discharge and restructure student loan debt); *In re* Lohr, 252 B.R. 84 (Bankr. E.D. Va. 2000) (discharge allowed for $30,500 out of $35,000 in student loans; recommendation that $4500 balance be paid at 7% interest amortized over ten years); *In re* Rivers, 213 B.R. 616 (Bankr. S.D. Ga. 1997) ($40,000 out of $55,000 consolidated student loans held nondischargeable); *In re* Muto, 216 B.R. 325 (Bankr. N.D.N.Y. 1996); *In re* Wetzel, 213 B.R. 220 (Bankr. N.D.N.Y. 1996); *In re* Raimondo, 183 B.R. 677 (Bankr. W.D.N.Y. 1995); *In re* Fox, 189 B.R. 115 (Bankr. N.D. Ohio 1995); *In re* Gammoh 174 B.R. 707 (Bankr. N.D. Ohio 1994). *See also* Graves v. Myrvang, 232 F.3d 1116 (9th Cir. 2000) (Ninth Circuit applies *Hornsby* analysis to

that allow partial discharges to require the consumer to show undue hardship for the portion of the loans to be discharged.[187] Another approach is for the court to discharge some, but not all, of a debtor's individual student loans. This approach rejects a pro rata reduction but still offers the debtor some relief by applying the hardship test on a loan-by-loan basis.[188]

Other courts have used the dischargeability proceeding to restructure the loan, reducing the amount owed and establishing a modified repayment schedule. For example, courts have discharged collection fees and accrued interest and delayed for several years the obligation to make payments, during which time no further interest would accrue.[189]

Despite recent interest in partial discharges, the view most consistent with the statutory language is that courts should determine simply whether the debt is or is not dischargeable.[190] Courts that have created the middle-ground approach of a partial discharge should not apply it to low-income debtors with limited future earnings potential. The partial discharge should be relevant only to debtors with significant future earnings potential but with extremely large student loan debt loads, such as those over $100,000.[191] If repayment of a relatively small student loan will likely be a

---

dischargeability provision relating to child support).

187 See, e.g., In re Alderete, 412 F.3d 1200 (10th Cir. 2005); In re Miller, 377 F.3d 616 (6th Cir. 2004); In re Cox, 338 F.3d 1238 (11th Cir. 2003); In re Saxman, 325 F.3d 1168 (9th Cir. 2003); In re Davis, 373 B.R. 241 (W.D.N.Y. 2007) (court may consider partial discharge only upon finding that undue hardship would result if debtor required to repay entire obligation); In re Paul, 337 B.R. 730, 739 (Bankr. D. Mass. 2006) (noting that First Circuit has not addressed issue but summarizing lower court decisions within Circuit approving partial discharge subject to undue hardship finding).

188 Educational Credit Mgmt. Corp. v. Kelly, 312 B.R. 200 (B.A.P. 1st Cir. 2004) (adopting based on "such debt" language in section 523(a)(8) "hybrid approach," which provides that undue hardship test should be applied independently as to each loan, absent evidence that loans were consolidated); In re Lavy, 2008 WL 4964721 (Bankr. W.D. Wash. Nov. 14, 2008) (debtor's combined student loans totaling $121,000 reduced by partial discharge, leaving one loan with principal of $38,563, with accrued interest on remaining loan also discharged); In re Gharavi 335 B.R. 492 (Bankr. D. Mass. 2006) (discharging three of four loans of debtor who whose work hours were limited by her multiple sclerosis); In re Allen, 329 B.R. 544 (Bankr. W.D. Pa. 2005) (the larger of two loans discharged; debtor could divert her $130 monthly church tithing contribution to pay smaller loan); In re Lamanna, 285 B.R. 347 (Bankr. D R.I. 2002) (debtor with twenty-four separate loans; ordering discharge of those, based on age of loans, that could not be paid during debtor's remaining working years); In re Myers, 280 B.R. 416 (Bankr. S.D. Ohio 2002) (three loans totaling $59,438 discharged and three smaller loans totaling $5472 found nondischargeable); In re Morris, 277 B.R. 910 (Bankr. W.D. Ark. 2002) (largest student loan in amount of $65,912 discharged but not smaller loans totaling $41,741); In re Grigas, 252 B.R. 866 (Bankr. D.N.H. 2000) (based on court's finding that debtor could pay $224 per month for fifteen years, debtor's fifteen student loans should be analyzed in chronological order so that only those that can be fully repaid within fifteen years will be excepted from discharge); In re Shankwiler, 208 B.R. 701 (Bankr. C.D. Cal. 1997) (holding that each loan should be treated separately); In re Hinkle, 200 B.R. 690 (Bankr. W.D. Wash. 1996) (discharging three out of six student loans). See also State Univ. of N.Y. v. Menezes, 352 B.R. 8 (D. Mass. 2006) (reversing bankruptcy court that had granted partial discharge without considering undue hardship with regard to each loan separately).

189 In re Carlson-Callow, 2008 WL 2357012 (Bankr. D. Idaho June 6, 2008) (calculating affordable student loan payment for 60-year-old debtor at $447 monthly, setting payments at this amount until debtor's anticipated retirement in five years, with remainder of $88,000 student loan debt discharged); In re Gobin, 2006 WL 3885136 (Bankr. E.D. Ky. May 15, 2006) (granting hardship discharge as to collection costs, future interest, and any tax liability incurred at end of ICRP period); In re Grove, 323 B.R. 216 (Bankr. N.D. Ohio 2005) (any student loan debt still owing at end of twenty-five-year ICRP is discharged in order to avoid potential tax assessment); In re Shirzadi, 269 B.R. 664 (Bankr. S.D. Ind. 2001) (reducing monthly payment amount and suspending accrual of interest and late fees for nine months pending rehearing on whether debtor entitled to partial discharge); In re Garybush, 265 B.R. 587 (Bankr. S.D. Ohio 2001) (discharging all interest, costs, and fees, granting four-year deferment on payments, and setting monthly amount to be paid on principal after deferment); In re Kapinos, 253 B.R. 709 (Bankr. W.D. Va. 2000) (discharging accrued interest and future interest for period of five years, at which time debtor may reopen case to seek further discharge relief); In re Griffin, 197 B.R. 144 (Bankr. E.D. Okla. 1996) (discharging accrued interest and attorney fees on loans but not principal); In re Heckathorn, 199 B.R. 188 (Bankr. N.D. Okla. 1996) (finding debt nondischargeable but deferring repayment for five years and suspending accrual of interest for three years); In re O'Donnell, 198 B.R. 1 (Bankr. D.N.H. 1996); In re Mayes, 183 B.R. 261 (Bankr. E.D. Okla. 1995). But see In re Binder, 338 B.R. 62 (Bankr. W.D. Mo. 2006) (court does not have authority to restructure student loans, collecting cases on restructuring).

190 Courts rejecting partial discharges have done so largely based on a strict construction of section 523(a)(8)—that the statutory language does not use the phrase "to the extent" as found in other sections providing for partial discharge. In re Roach, 288 B.R. 437 (Bankr. E.D. La. 2003) (no support for partial discharge in plain language of Code); Educational Credit Mgmt. Corp. v. Carter, 279 B.R. 872 (M.D. Ga. 2002) (bankruptcy court lacks authority under section 523(a)(8) and section 105(a) to grant partial discharge). See also In re Cox, 338 F.3d 1238 (11th Cir. 2003) (bankruptcy court's equitable powers under section 105 cannot override plain language of section 523(a)(8)); In re Pincus, 280 B.R. 303 (Bankr. S.D.N.Y. 2002) (no language in section 523(a)(8) permits granting of partial discharge); In re Brown, 249 B.R. 525 (Bankr. W.D. Mo. 2000) (granting full discharge after determining that Bankruptcy Code precludes partial discharge); In re Young, 225 B.R. 312 (Bankr. E.D. Pa. 1998); In re Skaggs, 196 B.R. 865 (Bankr. W.D. Okla. 1996); In re Hawkins, 187 B.R. 294 (Bankr. N.D. Iowa 1995); In re Barrows, 182 B.R. 640 (Bankr. D.N.H. 1994). Cf. In re Richardson, 334 B.R. 316 (Bankr. D. Mass. 2005) (while court would allow discharge of separate individual loans, a single consolidated loan cannot be subject to partial discharge—so court discharges entire loan for debtor who meets undue hardship test).

191 Cf. In re Heckathorn, 199 B.R. 188 (Bankr. N.D. Okla. 1996).

hardship for the foreseeable future, the debt should be completely discharged to allow the debtor a fresh start.

10.6 Special Rule for HEAL Loans

The limits on dischargeability of loans issued through the Health Education Assistance Loan Program (HEAL) are more severe than for other student loans. They can be discharged only if the court finds denial of discharge would be "unconscionable," and the student cannot seek a discharge during the first seven years of the loan repayment period.[192] The Sixth Circuit has concluded that the unconscionability standard for HEAL loans is "significantly more stringent" than the undue hardship standard[193] and, therefore, only debtors presenting the most compelling facts will be granted a discharge.[194] This standard can be particularly harsh on students who never benefited from the HEAL loans.[195] However, under a plain language reading of 11 U.S.C. § 523(b), HEAL loans may be more easily dischargeable if the debtor receives a second bankruptcy discharge.[196]

Some students may have both HEAL and non-HEAL student loans. The Fourth Circuit has held that a bankruptcy court should first consider the dischargeability of the non-HEAL loans, since the discharge of the non-HEAL loans could affect the repayment analysis under the more stringent unconscionability standard for the remaining HEAL loans.[197]

10.7 The Dischargeability Determination

10.7.1 Procedure for Determining Dischargeability of Student Loan

Whether a student loan is discharged based on hardship is not automatically determined in the bankruptcy proceeding. The debtor must affirmatively seek such a determination. If the debtor fails to do so, and a loan holder subsequently attempts to collect on the loan, the loan's dischargeability can be resolved at that later date either by the bankruptcy court or by a state court in a proceeding relating to the note's collection. In general, it is best to resolve the loan's dischargeability in the bankruptcy court while the case is pending.

If there is no dispute about a student loan being dischargeable, it should be relatively easy to resolve this at the time of the bankruptcy. For example, if the loan was clearly over seven years old for cases filed before October 7, 1998, even accounting for all deferments, forbearances, consolidations, and the like, the guaranty agency or the Department will usually admit the loan's dischargeability.[198] A written stipulation of this sort may even make it unnecessary for the bankruptcy court to rule on the issue.

Requests for stipulations are usually fruitless when the student seeks a hardship discharge or when the seven-year period is in doubt. Guaranty agencies are strongly urged by the Department of Education to contest dischargeability.[199] Schools making Perkins loans are instructed to oppose dischargeability if they determine that legal costs are not expected to exceed one-third of the amount owed.[200]

Even when the student loan creditor intends to contest the loan's dischargeability, it is usually the best approach to resolve the loan's dischargeability at the time of the bankruptcy filing. The student may do this by bringing an adversary proceeding in the bankruptcy court seeking a declaratory judgment that a particular debt is dischargeable.[201] An adversary proceeding is a lawsuit within the

---

192 42 U.S.C. § 294f(g).
   As under section 523(a)(8), the debtor must affirmatively seek a determination that the grounds for discharge of a HEAL debt have been satisfied. *See* United States v. Rushing, 287 B.R. 343 (D.N.J. 2002). *See also In re* Burd, 2008 WL 5054247 (Bankr. D. Vt. Nov. 24, 2008) (seven-year wait period before debtor may seek discharge of HEAL loan excludes time when loan not in repayment status); *In re* Simone, 375 B.R. 481 (Bankr. C.D. Ill. 2007) (a statutory unconscionability standard similar to HEAL standard applies to determinations of dischargeability of loans under Indian Health Service Loans Repayment Program, 25 U.S.C. § 1616a(m)(4)).

193 *In re* Rice, 78 F.3d 1144, 1149 (6th Cir. 1996) (denial not unconscionable; nondischarge of loan must be "shockingly unfair, harsh, or unjust"). *See also* U.S. Dep't of Health & Human Servs. v. Smitley, 347 F.3d 109 (4th Cir. 2003); *In re* Malloy, 155 B.R. 940 (E.D. Va. 1993), *aff'd without op.*, 23 F.3d 402 (4th Cir. 1994).

194 *See In re* Buracker, 2004 WL 950771 (Bankr. C.D. Ill. May 3, 2004) (61-year-old chiropractor whose circumstances were not likely to improve granted discharge of $123,000 in HEAL loans); *In re* Ascue, 268 B.R. 739 (Bankr. W.D. Va. 2001), *aff'd with unpublished opinion*, 2002 WL 192561 (W.D. Va. Feb. 7, 2002) (partial discharge eliminating $300,000 in interest on National Health Service Corps loan for debtor whose earnings were limited).

195 *In re* Rogers, 250 B.R. 883 (Bankr. S.D. Ohio 2000) (debtor never received health education degree and employed as shipping clerk).

196 *In re* Tanski, 195 B.R. 408 (Bankr. E.D. Wis. 1996). *But see In re* Britt, 355 B.R. 427 (S.D.N.Y. 2006) (amendments to Public Health Service Act require application of 42 U.S.C. § 292f(g) unconscionability standard in all HEAL loan cases, not 11 U.S.C. § 523(a)(8) undue hardship standard).

197 U.S. Dep't of Health & Human Servs. v. Smitley, 347 F.3d 109 (4th Cir. 2003).

198 However, some prodding may be required. One or more letters requesting a stipulation that the loan is dischargeable can be followed up with a request for the court to determine the issue if no agreement is forthcoming. In any event, it is important to create a paper trail establishing the dischargeability in order to prevent later disputes.

199 34 C.F.R. § 682.402(f)–(i).

200 34 C.F.R. § 674.49(c)(4). *See also* 34 C.F.R. § 682.402(i)(2) (FFEL loan regulations).

201 The student has the burden to prove entitlement to a hardship

bankruptcy case initiated by the filing of an adversary complaint. It is subject to rules almost identical to the Federal Rules of Civil Procedure, including those relating to discovery procedure.[202] For a more detailed discussion of adversary proceedings, see National Consumer Law Center, Consumer Bankruptcy Law and Practice (9th ed. 2009 and Supp.). In addition, sample adversary complaints and related pleadings in student loan cases are provided at Appendix E, *infra*, and on the companion website to this manual.[203]

An adversary proceeding to determine dischargeability of a student loan may be brought at any time, and a bankruptcy case that has been closed may be reopened without payment of an additional filing fee in order to obtain a dischargeability determination.[204] Likewise, courts have held that, since the denial of a hardship discharge is generally made without prejudice, a student may renew a request for discharge relief when there has been a change in circumstances.[205] In some instances, the courts have expressly invited debtors to reopen and seek discharge upon the occurrence of certain future events.[206]

Since there are no time limitations on when the action can be filed, a student may consider reopening a bankruptcy case to seek a hardship discharge when the student's situation has taken a turn for the worse after the bankruptcy case is closed.[207] In some situations, a student may also defer filing the adversary proceeding until some time after the bankruptcy is closed when the student's ability to prove the elements of the hardship test may improve with time.[208] Particularly when the student needs to file bankruptcy for other reasons, but may not be in a position to prove all of the elements of the applicable hardship test, the student should attempt to avoid a premature filing of the hardship adversary proceeding.[209]

---

discharge, though the student loan creditor generally has the initial burden to establish the existence of the debt. *In re* Kopf, 245 B.R. 731 (Bankr. D. Me. 2000); *In re* Green, 238 B.R. 727 (Bankr. N.D. Ohio 1999). See § 10.3, *supra* (discussing burden of proof in student loan hardship discharge actions).

202 See Fed. R. Bankr. P. 7001–7087.

Under the present fee schedule adopted by the administrative office of the federal courts, there is no filing fee for an adversary complaint brought by a debtor in a bankruptcy case.

203 For reasons discussed in § 10.8, *infra*, concerning sovereign immunity, in preparing the adversary complaint it is generally advisable to name the director of the student loan agency as a defendant in order to invoke the *Ex parte Young* doctrine.

204 See 11 U.S.C. § 350(b); Fed. R. Bankr. P. 4007(b).

If the student is eligible for a discharge under the Higher Education Act as discussed in Chapter 9, *supra*, it is advisable that the student apply for an administrative discharge before filing a bankruptcy adversary complaint. See *In re* Scholl, 259 B.R. 345 (Bankr. N.D. Iowa 2001) (hardship discharge adversary complaint denied without prejudice when student failed to exhaust administrative remedies by first seeking an unpaid-refund discharge).

Borrowers may also be eligible for disability discharges through the Department of Education. Most borrowers found to be eligible for this discharge are given a three-year conditional discharge period. See § 9.7, *supra*.

At least one court has held that it is not fitting to adjudicate an undue hardship case during this conditional discharge period since the borrower may potentially receive complete relief outside of bankruptcy. See *In re* Furrow, 2005 WL 1397156 (Bankr. W.D. Mo. May 24, 2005). But see *In re* Pitts, 432 B.R. 866 (Bankr. M.D. Fla. 2010) (hardship discharge under section 523(a)(8) grants distinct and prompt relief from burdensome student loan obligation; debtor need not exhaust lengthy administrative discharge procedures before seeking bankruptcy discharge).

205 *In re* Andrews, 661 F.2d 702 (8th Cir. 1981) (recommending that denial of hardship discharge by bankruptcy courts should be made without prejudice to permit debtor to seek relief under Rule 4007 when there has been a change in circumstances); *In re* Walker, 427 B.R. 471 (B.A.P. 8th Cir. 2010) (in reopened chapter 7 case, bankruptcy court properly focused on debtor's circumstances at time of 2008 trial, rejecting creditor's contention that only debtor's circumstances before her 2004 discharge could be considered); *In re* Sobh, 61 B.R. 576 (E.D. Mich. 1986) (res judicata does not bar debtor from filing new complaint seeking a hardship discharge based on new facts); *In re* Revere, 2007 WL 4879279, at *3 (Bankr. N.D. Ind. Oct. 22, 2007) (denial of discharge complaint is without prejudice to debtor's raising undue hardship issue in future proceeding). But see *In re* Zygarewicz, 423 B.R. 909 (Bankr. E.D. Cal. 2010) (despite language in Code requiring court to evaluate debtor's current circumstances for undue hardship, court in reopened case refused to consider financial impact of post-discharge auto accident on debtor); *In re* Bugos, 288 B.R. 435 (Bankr. E.D. Va. 2003) (absent circumstances that are foreseeable or that relate current situation to time petition was filed, bankruptcy case should not be reopened to determine undue hardship); *In re* Kapsin, 265 B.R. 778 (Bankr. N.D. Ohio 2001) (change in circumstances one-and-one-half years later did not constitute "cause" for reopening bankruptcy).

The Bankruptcy Code also provides that a student loan that was excepted from discharge in a prior bankruptcy may be discharged in a subsequent bankruptcy case if the debtor can satisfy the undue hardship test. See 11 U.S.C. § 523(b).

206 *In re* Nash, 446 F.3d 188, 194 (1st Cir. 2006) (debtor may reopen case to bring new dischargeability action if she obtains more supportive medical evidence); *In re* Coatney, 345 B.R. 905, 911 (Bankr. C.D. Ill. 2006) (debtor may reopen and raise claims again at end of four-year deferment granted by court); *In re* Grove, 323 B.R. 216 (Bankr. N.D. Ohio 2005) (debtor may reopen case if he is turned down for ICRP). See also *In re* Richardson, 2008 WL 3911075 (Bankr. E.D.N.C. Aug. 14, 2008) (expressly providing, in order denying discharge, for opportunity to request reconsideration during specified sixty-day period in the future), aff'd, 326 Fed. Appx. 173 (4th Cir. 2009); *In re* Vujovic, 388 B.R. 684 (Bankr. E.D.N.C. 2008) (using section 105(a) power to defer final dischargeability decision and enjoin collection for two years, allowing future review of debtor's financial circumstances).

207 *In re* Fisher, 223 B.R. 377 (Bankr. M.D. Fla. 1998) (debtor may reopen bankruptcy two years later when debtor's medical condition did not manifest until after case closed).

208 See *In re* Doherty, 219 B.R. 665 (Bankr. W.D.N.Y. 1998) (good faith shown when debtor tried to make payments for a year and a half before reopening her case to bring discharge proceeding).

209 *In re* Kraft, 161 B.R. 82 (Bankr. W.D.N.Y. 1993) (hardship complaint filed too early as debtor could not prove good faith under *Brunner* test).

The right to reopen a bankruptcy case is not limitless. The court will reopen a case only for cause.[210] A court may refuse to reopen a case if the debtor does not provide sufficient facts to show cause.[211] However, even if the court denies a motion to reopen, the debtor should still be able to file a new bankruptcy case and initiate an adversary proceeding to prove undue hardship based on his or her current circumstances.[212] However, a loan consolidation obtained after a bankruptcy filing may impair the debtor's ability to seek discharge of prebankruptcy student loans through a later reopening of the bankruptcy case. A consolidation loan obtained *postpetition* may be considered a new postpetition obligation extinguishing the loans in existence before the debtor filed the bankruptcy case.[213]

If the student does not obtain a stipulation or court determination of a student loan's dischargeability at the time of the bankruptcy, then the loan's dischargeability is left in limbo—the lack of prosecution of the issue prejudices neither the debtor nor the creditor's position. If the loan's dischargeability is not determined, the guaranty agency or Department can be expected to try to collect on the loan through tax intercepts, garnishments, and collection contacts. The student would then have to argue before a collection agency or in an administrative hearing that the debt is not owed because the loan was discharged by the bankruptcy. Such arguments may not go far in such proceedings even when the student can prove the application of the seven-year rule but certainly will be of no avail when hardship is the basis for discharge.

The better approach is to apply to the bankruptcy court (even after the bankruptcy case has been closed) for a determination that the loan is discharged by the bankruptcy. Then the court determination can be presented to the collector or guarantor.

If the Department or other party is pressing a collection action on the note in state court, the student has two choices. The student can ask the state court judge to rule on the dischargeability of the debt. Alternatively, the student can seek to remove the action to the bankruptcy court for such a determination[214] (or request that the state action be stayed pending the reopening of the bankruptcy case).

10.7.2 Undue Hardship Determination in Chapter 13

Chapter 13 debtors may also file an adversary proceeding to determine the dischargeability of student loan obligations. The issue may be raised at any time during the three- to five-year period of the plan,[215] and similar timing considerations apply as discussed previously.[216] However, some courts have required that the student wait until the end of the chapter 13 plan before seeking a hardship discharge.[217]

The United States Supreme Court recently addressed an issue involving how chapter 13 plans treat student loans.[218] The Court in *United Student Aid Funds, Inc. v. Espinosa* did not examine any broad questions related to the substantive standards for discharge of student loans in bankruptcy.

However, a consolidation loan entered into after the bankruptcy case has been closed may cut off the student's right to seek a hardship discharge of the original loans. *In re* Clarke, 266 B.R. 301 (Bankr. E.D. Pa. 2001) (consolidation loan extinguishes original student loans). *See In re* Mersmann, 503 F.3d 1033(10th Cir. 2007); Whelton v. Educational Credit Management Corp., 432 F.3d 150 (2d Cir. 2005); *In re* McBurney, 357 B.R. 536 (B.A.P. 9th Cir. 2006) (postpetition consolidation paid off older loans). *See also In re* Barrett, 417 BR. 471 (Bankr. N.D. Ohio Aug. 11, 2009) (postbankruptcy consolidation of student loans creates new loan, dischargeability of which can be determined in future bankruptcy case but not by reopening the prior case). *But see In re* Smith, 2010 WL 2305302 (Bankr. S.D. Tex. June 4, 2010) (postbankruptcy consolidation that did not pay off pre-petition loans would require compliance with reaffirmation agreement provisions of 11 U.S.C. § 524(c), otherwise transaction would be void).

210 11 U.S.C. § 350(b).
211 Courts have found that the party seeking to reopen the case has the burden of demonstrating cause. *See, e.g., In re* Cloninger, 209 B.R. 125 (Bankr. E.D. Ark. 1997).
212 *See, e.g., In re* Root, 318 B.R. 851 (Bankr. W.D. Mont. 2004) (denying debtor's motion to reopen case thirteen years after case was closed).
213 *See In re* McBurney, 357 B.R. 536 (B.A.P. 9th Cir. 2006) (postpetition consolidation paid off older loans). *See also In re* Barrett, 417 BR. 471 (Bankr. N.D. Ohio Aug. 11, 2009) (postbankruptcy consolidation of student loans creates new loan, dischargeability of which can be determined in future bankruptcy case but not by reopening the prior case). *But see In re* Smith, 2010 WL 2305302 (Bankr. S.D. Tex. June 4, 2010) (postbankruptcy consolidation that did not pay off pre-petition loans would require compliance with reaffirmation agreement provisions of 11 U.S.C. § 524(c), otherwise transaction would be void).
214 28 U.S.C. § 1452; Fed. R. Bankr. P. 9027.
215 *In re* Cassim, 594 F.3d 432 (6th Cir. 2010) (no impediment under ripeness doctrine to seeking discharge by adversary action commenced three months after chapter 13 petition filed); *In re* Coleman, 560 F.3d 1000 (9th Cir. 2009) (substantial controversy satisfying ripeness doctrine arises when debtor files chapter 13 petition and needs to know whether future plan payments will lead to discharge of student loan); *In re* Ekenasi, 325 F.3d 541 (4th Cir. 2003) (although debtor need not wait until end of chapter 13 plan to bring dischargeability proceeding, debtor must demonstrate that *Brunner* factors can be predicted with sufficient certainty if seeking discharge earlier in case); *In re* Hoffer, 383 B.R. 78 (Bankr. S.D. Ohio 2008) (allowing chapter 13 debtor to proceed with dischargeability action commenced sixteen months prior to anticipated completion of plan).
216 *See* § 10.7.1, *supra*.
217 *In re* Bender, 368 F.3d 846 (8th Cir. 2004) (student loan discharge determination in chapter 13 case not ripe for adjudication until conclusion of plan at time of discharge); *In re* Pair, 269 B.R. 719 (Bankr. N.D. Ala. 2001). *See, e.g., In re* Raisor, 180 B.R. 163 (Bankr. E.D. Tex. 1995). *See generally In re* Walton, 340 B.R. 892 (Bankr. S.D. Ind. 2006) (collecting cases on timing of adversary proceeding).
218 United Student Aid Funds, Inc. v. Espinosa, 130 U.S. 1367, 130 S. Ct. 1367, 176 L. Ed.2d 158 (2010).

Rather, the Court focused narrowly on a chapter 13 procedural issue that had provoked significant disagreement among the circuit courts.

A federal rule of bankruptcy procedure requires that certain matters be brought before a bankruptcy court judge as an "adversary proceeding," rather than by motion or through some less formal procedural device.[219] An adversary proceeding in a bankruptcy case is similar to a federal court civil action.[220] Adversary proceedings have their own rules for service of a summons and complaint.[221] The bankruptcy rules list a proceeding to determine the dischargeability of a debt as one of the matters that must be brought before the court in accordance with the adversary proceeding rules.[222]

Instead of following the adversary proceeding rules, some debtors' attorneys developed a practice of including a term discharging a student loan debt in a chapter 13 plan. These attorneys argued that, while this practice did not comply with the adversary proceeding rules, creditors could object to the plan and demand that an adversary proceeding be filed. Otherwise, a student loan creditor who had notice of such a plan term and failed to object before the court confirmed the plan should be bound by the confirmation order. Substantial case law has always supported giving res judicata treatment to final bankruptcy court orders confirming a debtor's plan of reorganization.[223]

The debtors' arguments for giving preclusive effect to plan confirmation orders that discharged student loan debts met with mixed responses. Prior to the *Espinosa* Supreme Court ruling, two courts of appeals had agreed with the debtors.[224] Two circuits considered the bankruptcy court orders purporting to discharge student loan debts solely under plan terms to be void as entered in violation of mandatory procedural rules requiring the filing of an adversary complaint.[225] Three courts of appeals held that the orders were void as entered in violation of creditors' due process rights.[226] According to these latter courts, the creditors had the right to expect that a student loan discharge would never be granted absent the filing and service of an adversary complaint. Under this view, without proper service of the complaint, a creditor could ignore the plan terms purporting to discharge a student loan debt.

The debtor in *Espinosa* filed a chapter 13 case in 1992. He proposed to pay the full amount of the principal owed on his student loan over the course of his five-year plan. The plan expressly proposed to discharge any interest due on the loan. The debtor never filed an adversary proceeding to obtain findings from the court of undue hardship under section 523(a)(8). Despite receiving a copy of the debtor's plan proposing to discharge the student loan interest, the creditor did not object to confirmation. The bankruptcy court confirmed the plan in 1993. In 1997, after the debtor had made all payments owed on the loan principal, the bankruptcy court entered an order discharging the debtor of all debts, including the debt for interest on the student loan. Throughout the proceeding the bankruptcy court never made an "undue hardship" finding as to the debtor's ability to pay the debt for interest.

Ten years after the plan confirmation order had become final in Mr. Espinosa's case, the creditor for the first time sought to overturn the plan confirmation order. The creditor argued that the order was void as violative of the bankruptcy rules and statutes, which required an undue hardship finding by the court and the filing of an adversary proceeding before the court could enter an order discharging a student loan debt. The creditor also contended that the confirmation order had been entered in violation of its due process rights.

In the Supreme Court, Mr. Espinosa won his battle, but overall debtors seeking to discharge student loans solely through chapter 13 plan terms lost the war. The Court rejected the creditor's arguments that the plan confirmation order in Mr. Espinosa's case was "void."[227] The bankruptcy court had jurisdiction to enter the order. The creditor had the opportunity to raise the failure to follow procedural rules before the order was entered and could have appealed an adverse decision. Although the bankruptcy court committed legal error in entering the order confirming the plan, the debtor's failure to follow a procedural rule did not render the order void. Because the creditor had clear notice of the plan and the opportunity to object, the creditor's due process argument was meritless.[228]

As a result of the *Espinosa* court's decision, debtors who in the past followed procedures similar to those used by Mr. Espinosa to discharge all or part of a student loan debt under a chapter 13 plan should be able to rely on the finality of those orders. However, the more troubling aspects of the Supreme Court's decision focused on prospective use of the same procedure. The Ninth Circuit had ruled that bankruptcy courts must confirm similar plans when they propose to discharge student loan debts without an undue hardship determination in an adversary proceeding and the creditor

---

219 Fed. R. Bankr. P. 7001.

220 *See* National Consumer Law Center, Consumer Bankruptcy Law and Practice § 14.2.4 (9th ed. 2009 and Supp.).

221 Fed. R. Bankr. P. 7003, 7004.

222 Fed. R. Bankr. P. 7001(6).

223 *E.g.*, Travelers Indemnity Co. v. Bailey, 129 U.S. 2195, 129 S. Ct. 2195 (2009).

224 *In re* Pardee, 193 F.3d 1193 (9th Cir. 1999); *In re* Andersen, 179 F.3d 1253 (10th Cir. 1999), *overruled by In re* Mersmann, 503 F.3d 1033 (10th Cir. 2007).

225 *In re* Mersmann, 503 F.3d 1033 (10th Cir. 2007); Whelton v. Educational Credit Mgmt. Corp., 432 F.3d 150 (2d Cir. 2005).

226 *In re* Ruehle, 412 F.3d 679 (6th Cir. 2005); *In re* Hanson, 397 F.3d 482 (7th Cir. 2005); *In re* Banks, 299 F.3d 296 (4th Cir. 2002).

227 United Student Aid Funds, Inc. v. Espinosa, 130 U.S. 1367, 130 S. Ct. 1367, 176 L. Ed. 2d 158 (2010).

228 130 S. Ct. 1367, 1378 (2010).

does not object. The Supreme Court rejected this view. According to the Supreme Court, the bankruptcy court must not confirm such a plan even if the creditor does not object or even appear in the proceeding.[229] Instead, the Supreme Court implies a duty on the part of bankruptcy courts in such a case to direct the debtor to conform to the adversary proceeding rules. The bankruptcy court must make an independent determination of undue hardship before a plan proposing to discharge student loan debt may be confirmed. The court concluded by warning that attorneys who attempt to obtain a discharge of a student loan debt solely through chapter 13 plan terms and without seeking the required finding of undue hardship in an adversary proceeding may face sanctions under the bankruptcy rules equivalent to Federal Rule of Civil Procedure 11 and similar provisions.[230] The court did note that the debtors and student loan creditors may stipulate to facts necessary for the court to enter the undue hardship findings. In that unlikely event, an adversary complaint would not be necessary.

10.7.3 Use of Older Dischargeability Standards Today When Student's Pre-1998 Bankruptcy Did Not Determine Student Loan's Dischargeability

Unless the student or another party seeks a determination in the bankruptcy proceeding concerning a student loan's dischargeability, the loan's dischargeability will *not* be determined in a bankruptcy proceeding—the loan is neither ruled discharged nor enforceable. Instead, whether the loan has been discharged by the bankruptcy will not be determined until a later date, perhaps many years later, when a guarantor or the Department seeks to collect on that debt in court or when the student seeks a judicial determination of the loan's enforceability.

When a student loan's dischargeability is determined after the bankruptcy proceeding, the test will be whether the loan was dischargeable based on the Bankruptcy Code in effect at the time of the bankruptcy case, not at the time the loan's dischargeability is determined.[231] This distinction may have a significant impact on whether the debt is dischargeable.

For example, the dischargeability exception for bankruptcies filed before November 1990 was that student loans more than *five* years old were dischargeable in chapter 7 bankruptcies (compared to the subsequent seven-year standard).[232] Also, a chapter 13 discharge operated to discharge a student loan obligation, even one less than five years old (compared to the present, wherein dischargeability is treated the same for chapter 7 and 13 cases).[233]

Thus, when a loan was first due in 1983, and the loan's dischargeability was not determined in a chapter 7 bankruptcy filed in 1989, a court today should determine that the loan was discharged by that bankruptcy.[234] While the loan is not dischargeable under the present Bankruptcy Code, it is dischargeable under the five-year test in place at that time. Likewise, a loan that first became due in 1990 was discharged in a bankruptcy filed in 1998 (before October 7, 1998) under the seven-year rule.

10.8 Discharge of Student Loans Owed to State Agencies

Following the Supreme Court decision in *Seminole Tribe v. Florida*, state agencies collecting student loan debts aggressively asserted Eleventh Amendment immunity (sovereign immunity) as a way of barring debtors from discharging student loans in bankruptcy.[235] The issue of sovereign immunity arises because debtors must affirmatively seek student loan discharges through an adversary proceeding. State agencies had argued that this proceeding, which they characterized as a private suit in federal court against the state, was barred by the Eleventh Amendment.[236]

---

229 130 S. Ct. 1367, 1381 (2010).
230 130 S. Ct. 1367, 1382 (2010).
231 *See, e.g.*, Educational Credit Mgmt. Corp. v. Crockett, 2008 WL 4949048 (W.D. Va. Nov. 19, 2008) (in chapter 7 case filed in January 1979 and reopened in 2007, applying bankruptcy law in effect in January 1979, when code contained no express limitation on student loan discharge).
232 Section 523(a)(8) was amended by Pub. L. No. 101-647, § 3621, 104 Stat 4964 (Nov. 29, 1990).
233 Section 1328(a)(2) of the Bankruptcy Code was amended by Pub. L. No. 101-508, § 3007 (Nov. 5, 1990).
234 Similarly, between November 6, 1978, and August 14, 1979, there was no statutory restriction in place on the dischargeability of student loans. Thus students can argue today that any student loan listed as a debt in a bankruptcy during that period is discharged, no matter how recently the debt was first due before the bankruptcy proceeding. 20 U.S.C. § 1087-3, dealing with the discharge of student loans in bankruptcy, was repealed by the Bankruptcy Reform Act, Pub. L. No. 95-598, § 317 (1978). It was replaced as to cases filed on and after August 14, 1979, by the United States Bankruptcy Code. *See* S. Rep. No. 230 (1979), *reprinted in* 1979 U.S.C.C.A.N. 936, 938. *But see In re* Adamo, 619 F.2d 216 (2d Cir. 1980).
235 Seminole Tribe v. Florida, 517 U.S. 44 (1996). *See generally* Patricia L. Barsalou & Scott A. Stengel, *Ex Parte Young: Relativity in Practice*, 72 Am. Bankr. L.J. 455 (1998); National Consumer Law Center, Consumer Bankruptcy Law and Practice § 14.3.2.2 (9th ed. 2009 and Supp.).
236 The doctrine of sovereign immunity acts as a jurisdictional bar to suits filed by private individuals against non-consenting states. For a good summary of the doctrine in student loan cases, see *In re* Greenwood, 237 B.R. 128 (N.D. Tex. 1999) (upholding state agency's sovereign immunity claim).

For other cases in which sovereign immunity was affirmed, see, for example, Murphy v. Michigan Guar. Agency (*In re* Murphy), 271 F.3d 629 (5th Cir. 2001) (adversary proceeding seeking student loan discharge was "suit" against state barred by Eleventh Amendment); *In re* Kahl, 240 B.R. 524 (Bankr.

Fortunately for student loan debtors, the sovereign immunity issue in undue hardship cases has now been resolved favorably by the Supreme Court. In *Tennessee Student Assistance Corporation v. Hood*,[237] the Court relied upon an exception previously carved out for admiralty proceedings and held that a bankruptcy dischargeability suit brought against the state does not implicate a state's Eleventh Amendment immunity from suit.

Drawing on a distinction between *in rem* and *in personam* proceedings, the Court in *Hood* noted that a bankruptcy court's jurisdiction is "premised on the debtor and his estate, and not on the creditors," and therefore the discharge of a debt by a bankruptcy court is an *in rem* proceeding.[238] This permitted the Court to rely upon its earlier decision holding that the Eleventh Amendment does not bar federal jurisdiction over certain *in rem* admiralty proceedings.[239] Since the bankruptcy court's jurisdiction is "premised on the *res*," a state is bound by a discharge determination even if it elects not to participate in the bankruptcy proceeding.[240]

The Eleventh Circuit in *In re Crowe* applied the Supreme Court's *Hood* ruling to a debtor's dischargeability claim, finding that the Eleventh Amendment was not implicated on that claim and denying the guaranty agency's motion to dismiss.[241] However, the debtor in *Crowe* also sought damages from the state agencies for their attempts to collect the student loans after receiving notice of the bankruptcy filing. This damages claim, according to the court, was premised on the persona of the state, not on the *res* of the debtor's property, and so was not within the ambit of the *Hood* decision.[242] The court held that Congress had not abrogated the state's sovereign immunity with respect to *in personam actions in* bankruptcy cases and that the district court should have granted the state agency's motion to dismiss as to the damages claim.[243]

The Eleventh Circuit's sovereign immunity ruling in *Crow* is inconsistent with the Supreme Court's later opinion in *Central Virginia Community College v. Katz*.[244] In *Katz*, the Court held that proceedings to avoid liens or to compel turnover of preferential transfers are not suits against the state that implicate a state's sovereign immunity, because they are ancillary to a bankruptcy court's *in rem* jurisdiction. In response to *Katz*, the Eleventh Circuit abrogated the *Crowe* decision.[245] While *Katz* now appears to permit many bankruptcy proceedings against state governments, even proceedings in which damages may be sought, it is not clear whether other circuit courts will follow the Eleventh Circuit. Thus, if the debtor seeks additional relief against a state agency, such as an order to enforce the automatic stay or discharge injunction or to enjoin the agency from discriminating against the debtor based on a student loan discharge, the debtor may rely upon, in addition to *Katz*, the following three exceptions to sovereign immunity:

1. Pursuant to the *Ex Parte Young* doctrine, suits against state officials in their individual capacities seeking prospective declaratory or injunctive relief for ongoing violations of federal law are not barred.[246] A number of bankruptcy courts prior to *Hood* had dismissed discharge actions against state agencies on sovereign immunity grounds subject to the debtor's possible use of the *Young* doctrine in bringing an action against a state official.[247]

E.D. Pa. 1999); *In re* Stout, 231 B.R. 313 (Bankr. W.D. Mo. 1999); and *In re* Schmitt, 220 B.R. 68 (Bankr. W.D. Mo. 1998).

237 541 U.S. 440 (2004).

238 *Id.* at 447. *See also* Central Va. Comm. College v. Katz, 546 U.S. 356, 126 S. Ct. 990 (2006) (holding that trustee's proceeding to set aside debtor's preferential transfers to state agencies not barred by sovereign immunity).

239 California v. Deep Sea Research, Inc., 523 U.S. 491 (1998).

240 The Court in *Hood* also addressed the guaranty agency's concern that it had been served with a summons and complaint in an adversary proceeding, since the Court had previously ruled that the primary purpose of the Eleventh Amendment is to prevent the "indignity" of subjecting a state to court process. *See* Alden v. Maine, 527 U.S. 706 (1999).

The Court concluded that the Bankruptcy Rule requirement that an adversary proceeding be filed to obtain a discharge under section 523(a)(8) did not transform the substantive nature of the matter from an *in rem* to an *in personam* proceeding. The Court sensibly observed that, "[t]o conclude that the issuance of a summons, which is required only by the Rules, precludes Hood from exercising her statutory right to an undue hardship determination would give the Rules an impermissible effect." Tennessee Student Assistance Corp. v. Hood, 541 U.S. 440, 454 (2004).

241 *In re* Crow, 394 F.3d 918 (11th Cir. 2004).

242 *Id.*

243 *Id.*

244 546 U.S. 356 (2006).

245 *In re* Omine, 485 F.3d 1305, 1314 (11th Cir. 2007) (sovereign immunity does not bar chapter 13 debtor's action for damages against state to remedy violation of bankruptcy stay related to state's postpetition child support enforcement actions). *See also In re* Slayton, 409 B.R. 897 (Bankr. N.D. Ill. 2009) (in wake of *Hood* and *Katz*, debtor can pursue claims seeking injunctive relief, damages—but not punitive damages—and attorney fees against state for violation of discharge order and code's anti-discrimination provision (section 525(a))). *See generally In re* Mini, 2007 WL 2223820, at *4–5 (Bankr. N.D. Cal. July 30, 2007) (discussing effect of *Katz* on bankruptcy enforcement actions against state agencies).

246 *Ex parte* Young, 209 U.S. 123 (1908) (allowing federal court suit against state official acting *ultra vires* to proceed). *See also* Idaho v. Coeur d'Alene Tribe, 521 U.S. 261 (1997).

To invoke the *Young* doctrine, the party seeking enforcement of federal law must establish the following two elements. First, the party must allege that a state official is acting in violation of federal law. *See* Pennhurst State Sch. & Hosp. v. Halderman, 465 U.S. 89, 106 (1984).

Second, the relief sought must be prospective in that the party must seek to enjoin future violations of federal law rather than obtain monetary compensation or other retrospective relief for past violations. Green v. Mansour, 474 U.S. 64, 68 (1985); Quern v. Jordan, 440 U.S. 332, 346–49 (1979).

247 *In re* Kahl, 240 B.R. 524 (Bankr. E.D. Pa. 1999) (dismissing case without prejudice to afford debtor opportunity to invoke *Young* doctrine if relevant); *In re* Schmitt, 220 B.R. 68 (Bankr.

2. The second exception to sovereign immunity is that Congress may abrogate it by unequivocally expressing an intent to do so and acting pursuant to a valid exercise of power.[248] While courts are in general agreement that Congress clearly intended to abrogate immunity through section 106(a) of the Bankruptcy Code, they are divided on whether this provision is valid.[249] And though this was the question on which the Supreme Court granted certiorari in *Hood*, it ultimately declined to rule on whether the abrogation in section 106(a) was valid based on authority found in the Bankruptcy Clause of the Constitution (Article I, § 8, clause 4).

3. The third exception is that states may waive Eleventh Amendment immunity and therefore consent to suit in federal courts. For example, participation in the federal loan program may act as a waiver of the state's Eleventh Amendment immunity in bankruptcy or other federal proceedings.[250] Mere participation, however, is generally insufficient to waive sovereign immunity without some indication of affirmative assent to suit.[251]

Another issue that may arise in these cases is the threshold question of whether the state actor collecting the loan is truly an "arm of the state."[252] If not, the state actor should not be entitled to assert sovereign immunity.

Most circuit courts have established a multi-prong test to determine whether an agency is an "arm of the state."[253] The foremost factor under these tests is whether the state will be financially burdened by the action in question.[254] This should be a strong argument in the student loan context, within which states are usually not responsible for guaranty agencies' financial obligations,[255] because such entities typically have a legal existence distinct from the state.[256] Moreover, based on their contractual arrangement

---

W.D. Mo. 1998); *In re* Morrell, 218 B.R. 87 (Bankr. C.D. Cal. 1997) (granting debtors leave to amend in state franchise tax case to invoke *Young* doctrine). *But see In re* Stout, 231 B.R. 313 (Bankr. W.D. Mo. 1999) (*Young* doctrine does not give blanket authorization for suits against state officials to obtain injunctive relief).

248 For a good discussion of this exception, see Hood v. Tennessee Student Assistance Corp., 319 F.3d 755 (6th Cir. 2003), *aff'd on other grounds*, 541 U.S. 440 (2004).

249 *See* Nelson v. La Crosse County Dist. Att'y (State of Wis.), 301 F.3d 820 (7th Cir. 2002) (Constitution's Bankruptcy Clause not valid authority for abrogating states' sovereign immunity); *In re* Sacred Heart Hosp. of Norristown, 133 F.3d 237 (3d Cir. 1997) (section 106 not valid abrogation); *In re* Estate of Fernandez, 123 F.3d 241 (5th Cir. 1997) (section 106(a) violates Eleventh Amendment and therefore unconstitutional); *In re* Creative Goldsmiths, 119 F.3d 1140 (4th Cir. 1997). *Cf. In re* Wilson, 258 B.R. 303 (Bankr. S.D. Ga. 2001) (section 108 valid abrogation as enacted pursuant to privileges and immunities clause of Fourteenth Amendment); *In re* Lees, 252 B.R. 441 (Bankr. W.D. Tenn. 2000), *aff'd on other grounds*, 264 B.R. 884 (W.D. Tenn. 2001).

A few courts have held that the issue of whether immunity had been waived or abrogated need not be considered in regard to dischargeability proceedings because the states, in ratifying the Constitution, ceded their sovereignty over discharge matters to Congress. Hood v. Tennessee Student Assistance Corp., 319 F.3d 755 (6th Cir. 2003) (Congress validly abrogated states' sovereign immunity under Constitution's Bankruptcy Clause and Fourteenth Amendment), *aff'd on other grounds*, 541 U.S. 440 (2004); *In re* Bleimeister, 251 B.R. 383 (Bankr. D. Ariz. 2000), *aff'd on other grounds*, 296 F.3d 858 (9th Cir. 2002).

250 *See In re* Innes, 184 F.3d 1275 (10th Cir. 1999); *In re* Rose, 187 F.3d 926 (8th Cir. 1999); *In re* Huffine, 246 B.R. 405 (Bankr. E.D. Wash. 2000) (waiver found based on review of Perkins Loan Program as a whole, including statute, participation contract, and governing regulations). *But see In re* Janc, 251 B.R. 525 (Bankr. W.D. Mo. 2000) (state guaranty agency did not waive sovereign immunity by participating in student loan program).

251 *See also In re* Innes, 184 F.3d 1275 (10th Cir. 1999); *In re* Rose, 187 F.3d 926 (8th Cir. 1999); *In re* Phelps, 237 B.R. 527 (Bankr.

D.R.I. 1999) (waiver found when, among other actions, creditor acknowledged it was party to discharge proceeding and only raised immunity issue after unfavorable decision on hardship). *See generally* College Sav. Bank v. Florida Prepaid Postsecondary Educ. Expense Bd., 527 U.S. 666 (1999) (rejecting doctrine of "constructive waiver"); Atascadero v. Scanlon, 473 U.S. 234 (1985).

While sovereign immunity may be raised for the first time on appeal, it is not an ordinary limitation on subject matter jurisdiction and therefore federal courts are not required to *sua sponte* consider a possible immunity defense. Wisconsin Dep't of Corrections v. Schacht, 524 U.S. 381, 389–391 (1998); Toll v. Moreno, 458 U.S. 1, 17–19 (1982). *See also* Parella v. Retirement Bd. of Rhode Island Employee Ret. Sys., 173 F.3d 46 (1st Cir. 1999).

252 *See* Lake County Estates, Inc. v. Tahoe Reg'l Planning Agency, 440 U.S. 391 (1979).

253 *See, e.g.*, Duke v. Grady Muni. Schs., 127 F.3d 972 (10th Cir. 1997); Mancuso v. New York State Thruway Auth., 86 F.3d 289 (2d Cir. 1996); Hadley v. North Ark. Cmty. Technical Coll., 76 F.3d 1437 (8th Cir. 1996); Harter v. C.D. Vernon, 101 F.3d 334 (4th Cir. 1996); Christy v. Pennsylvania Turnpike Comm'n, 54 F.3d 1140 (3d Cir. 1995); Metcalf & Eddy v. Puerto Rico Aqueduct & Sewer Auth., 991 F.2d 935 (1st. Cir. 1993).

For a more detailed discussion of this topic, see NCLC REPORTS, *Bankruptcy and Foreclosures Ed.* (Nov./Dec. 2000).

254 *See* Metcalf & Eddy v. Puerto Rico Aqueduct & Sewer Auth., 991 F.2d 935 (1st Cir. 1993).

255 The enabling statutes of guaranty agencies often provide that their bonds and loan guaranties are not an obligation of the state. *See, e.g.*, Iowa Code § 261.38; Mich. Comp. Laws § 390.1154; N.J. Stat. Ann. § 18A:71A-18 (West) (same for New Jersey Higher Education Student Assistance Authority); N.C. Gen. Stat. § 116-202; 24 Pa. Cons. Stat. § 5105.1(b) (bonds and notes of Pennsylvania Higher Education Assistance Authority not debt of Pennsylvania); R.I. Gen. Laws § 16-57-12.

256 *See In re* Muir, 239 B.R. 213 (Bankr. D. Mont. 1999) (student loan guaranty agency failed to satisfy burden of demonstrating that it was an arm of the state and entitled to Eleventh Amendment immunity). *But see In re* Kahl, 240 B.R. 524 (Bankr. E.D. Pa. 1999) (finding Texas agency to be an arm of the state, but no waiver of sovereign immunity). *See generally* Duke v. Grady Muni. Schs., 127 F.3d 972 (10th Cir. 1997) (court must focus on legal liability for a judgment rather than practical or indirect impact a judgment would have on a state's treasury); Metcalf & Eddy v. Puerto Rico Aqueduct & Sewer Auth., 991 F.2d 935 (1st Cir. 1993) (rejecting among other arguments the state agency's claim that it could claim immunity solely on basis that judgments against it might absorb unrestricted funds donated by

with the Department of Education, guaranty agencies are reimbursed by the federal government for most of the indebtedness on discharged loans.[257] One court has applied the various factors of the "arm of the state" test to a student loan authority and found that it was not entitled to claim sovereign immunity.[258]

Finally, it is important to keep in mind that the filing of a proof of claim by a college or guaranty agency can itself be a waiver of sovereign immunity.[259] In addition, the federal guaranteed loan program (FFEL) was eliminated as of July 1, 2010. As time goes on, there will be fewer loans serviced, collected, and funded by state agencies.[260]

10.9 Advantages of a Chapter 13 Bankruptcy When Student Loan Cannot Be Discharged

10.9.1 Separate Classification

If a student loan cannot be discharged based on undue hardship in a chapter 7 or 13 bankruptcy filing, there are still strategic advantages to filing a chapter 13 bankruptcy.[261] One advantage is that the student's chapter 13 plan, not the loan holder, determines the size of a student's loan payments. For the three- to five-year life of the chapter 13 plan, the plan will determine how much the student pays each unsecured creditor, including student loan creditors.

For many plans, this would mean that only 5% or 10% of the outstanding loan would be paid off over those three to five years. At the end of the plan, the student could seek a determination that repayment of the balance would cause an undue hardship. During the three- to five-year pendency of the plan, no collection action, garnishment, or tax intercepts can be taken against the student, though interest on the debt will continue to accrue.[262]

Nevertheless, if the remainder of the debt is not dischargeable after the plan has terminated, the student is then obligated to pay the remainder. When that is the case, it is in the student's interest to pay off as much of the student loan in the chapter 13 plan as possible, at the expense of other unsecured creditors—creditors whose remaining balance *will* be dischargeable after the plan is completed.

One way to pay more on the student loan than on other unsecured debts is to separately classify the student loan for payments at a higher percentage than other unsecured debts pursuant to 11 U.S.C. § 1322(b)(1). Recent cases have been divided, both in the means of analysis and the result, as to whether students can separately classify student loans, some allowing separate classification[263] and some not.[264] Some

---

state and in that way lead indirectly to depletion of the state's treasury).

257 See 10 U.S.C. § 1087(b).

258 *In re* Lees, 264 B.R. 884 (W.D. Tenn. 2001).

259 See Gardner v. New Jersey, 329 U.S. 565 (1947); Rose v. U.S. Dep't of Educ., 187 F.3d 926 (8th Cir. 1999); *In re* Straight, 143 F.3d 1387 (10th Cir. 1998); *In re* Burke, 146 F.3d 1313 (11th Cir. 1998); *In re* Diaz, 2009 WL 3584517 (Bankr. M.D. Fla. Sept. 30, 2009) (by filing proof of claim, state agency voluntarily waived all forms of sovereign immunity, including protections under Code section 106(a)(3), which otherwise limits punitive damages and attorney fees awards against states); *In re* Stanley, 273 B.R. 907 (Bankr. N.D. Fla. 2002) (state guaranty agency that waived sovereign immunity by filing proof of claim could not reinstate immunity defense by later withdrawing claim).

260 See § 1.3.2, *supra*.

261 For more details, see National Consumer Law Center, Consumer Bankruptcy Law and Practice § 15.4.3.8.5 (9th ed. 2009 and Supp.).

262 If the student loan debt is nondischargeable, postpetition interest will not be discharged. See *In re* Kielisch, 258 F.3d 315 (4th Cir. 2001); *In re* Pardee, 218 B.R. 916 (B.A.P. 9th Cir. 1998), aff'd, 187 F.3d 648 (9th Cir. 1999); *In re* Jordan, 146 B.R. 31 (D. Colo. 1992).

In addition, section 502(b)(2) of the Code provides that general unsecured creditors such as student loan creditors may not include unmatured, postpetition interest in their bankruptcy claims. Leeper v. Pennsylvania Higher Educ. Assistance Agency, 49 F.3d 98 (3d Cir. 1995) (interest accruing during pendency of plan not discharged, even though debtor paid pre-petition debt in full through chapter 13 plan). Accord *In re* Biege, 417 B.R. 697 (Bankr. M.D. Pa. 2009).

One court has held that, while unmatured, postpetition interest may not be included in the student loan creditor's claim, section 502(b) does not prevent the creditor from applying chapter 13 plan payments to accrued interest, including postpetition interest, on the nondischargeable debt. *In re* Kielisch, 258 F.3d 315 (4th Cir. 2001). See also U. S. Dep't of Educ. v. Harris, 339 B.R. 673 (W.D. Tenn. 2006) (in a second chapter 13 case, DOE can apply trustee payments first to interest and charges that accrued postpetition during earlier chapter 13 case, then to principal).

263 *In re* Kalfayan, 415 B.R. 907 (Bankr. S.D. Fla. 2009) (separate classification allowing maintenance of current payments on student loan not unfairly discriminatory because debtor must be current on student loans to keep optometrist license and thereby fund plan for all creditors); *In re* Webb, 370 B.R. 418 (Bankr. N.D. Ga. 2007); *In re* Cox, 186 B.R. 744 (Bankr. N.D. Fla. 1995); *In re* Tucker, 159 B.R. 325 (Bankr. D. Mont. 1993); *In re* Foreman, 136 B.R. 532 (Bankr. S.D. Iowa 1992); *In re* Boggan, 125 B.R. 533 (Bankr. N.D. Ill. 1991); See also *In re* Sullivan, 195 B.R. 649 (Bankr. W.D. Tex. 1996); *In re* Dodds, 140 B.R. 542 (Bankr. D. Mont. 1992).

On the analogous question of whether nondischargeable child support debts may be separately classified, many courts have concluded in the affirmative. *E.g., In re* Leser, 939 F.2d 669 (8th Cir. 1991); *In re* Husted, 142 B.R. 72 (Bankr. W.D.N.Y. 1992); *In re* Whittaker, 113 B.R. 531 (Bankr. D. Minn. 1990) (allowing a fresh start is sufficient to justify discriminatory classification in favor of nondischargeable support debt).

264 *In re* Groves, 39 F.3d 212 (8th Cir. 1994) (plan could not discriminate in favor of student loans solely due to their nondischargeability); *In re* Bentley, 266 B.R. 229 (B.A.P. 1st Cir. 2001) (chapter 13 plan that favored student loan creditor failed unfair discrimination test by altering "allocation of benefits and burdens" to detriment of other unsecured creditors); *In re* Sperna, 173 B.R. 654 (B.A.P. 9th Cir. 1994) (plan could not discriminate in favor of student loans solely due to their non-

courts have even issued opinions providing guidance as to the amount of discrimination that will be allowed.[265]

A useful alternative to separate classification, in those jurisdictions where separate classification has not been approved, is to cure a default on the student loan pursuant to 11 U.S.C. § 1322(b)(5).[266] This allows the debtor to cure an arrearage on the student loan over time while maintaining the postpetition payments during the life of the plan. A number of courts have already permitted debtors to make ongoing student loan payments from income on this basis outside the plan.[267] An added benefit of this approach is that the ongoing payments will include postpetition interest that would not otherwise be paid as part of a claim under the plan.[268] By failing to give effect to section 1322(b)(5) as a distinct plan provision, some courts have required debtors proposing to pay student loans outside the plan to satisfy the unfair discrimination test under section 1322(b)(1).[269]

A final approach might be to establish a five-year plan, not separately classify the student loan for the first three years of the plan, and then classify it for greater payment during the plan's final two years.[270] The basis for this approach is the Bankruptcy Code provision that requires disposable income only to be paid out over three years.[271] Any amount that creditors receive in the final two years would be a bonus in any event. Courts have split on whether they will allow this separate classification of student loans in years four and five of a chapter 13 plan.[272]

10.9.2 Co-Debtor Stay

Another advantage of chapter 13 is that there is an additional type of "automatic stay" that goes into effect when the case is filed. This stay prohibits any act or legal action to collect a debtor's consumer debt from a co-debtor

---

dischargeability); McCullough v. Brown, 162 B.R. 506 (N.D. Ill. 1993); *In re* Knecht, 410 B.R. 650 (Bankr. D. Mont. 2009) (denying confirmation of plan with separate classification for student loan and paying zero dollars to all other unsecured creditors); *In re* Thibodeau, 248 B.R. 699 (Bankr. D. Mass. 2000) (plan was not proposed in nondiscriminatory manner based on debtor's sizeable income and lack of good faith); *In re* Burns, 216 B.R. 945 (Bankr. S.D. Cal. 1998); *In re* Gonzalez, 206 B.R. 239 (Bankr. S.D. Fla. 1997); *In re* Coonce, 213 B.R. 344 (Bankr. S.D. Ill. 1997); *In re* Willis, 189 B.R. 203 (Bankr. N.D. Okla. 1995), *rev'd and remanded*, 197 B.R. 912 (N.D. Okla. 1996); *In re* Colfer, 159 B.R. 602 (Bankr. D. Me. 1993) (refusing to allow separate classification); *In re* Smalberger, 157 B.R. 472 (Bankr. D. Or. 1993), *aff'd*, 170 B.R. 707 (D. Or. 1994); *In re* Chapman, 146 B.R. 411 (Bankr. N.D. Ill. 1992); *In re* Scheiber, 129 B.R. 604 (Bankr. D. Minn. 1991); *In re* Furlow, 70 B.R. 973 (Bankr. E.D. Pa. 1987) (separate classification of student loan debt not allowed without further explanation of reasons). *See also In re* Pora, 353 B.R. 247 (Bankr. N.D. Cal. 2006) ("majority approach" requires debtor to show that proposed separate classification for student loan does not unfairly discriminate).

265 *In re* Simmons, 288 B.R. 737 (Bankr. N.D. Tex. 2003) (plan providing for 100% repayment of student loan and zero percent to general unsecured creditors may be confirmed when all of debtor's disposable income paid into plan for first thirty-six months and student loan creditor paid in months forty-one through forty-eight of plan); *In re* Williams, 253 B.R. 220 (Bankr. W.D. Tenn. 2000) (plan that provides for 100% repayment of student loan will be confirmed only if other unsecured creditors are paid at least 70%; debtors may show "unique circumstances" to justify confirmation of plans with more than 30% difference in repayment percentage).

266 Section 1322(b)(5) permits the curing of defaults under the plan and maintenance of ongoing payments, typically made outside the plan, on any secured or unsecured claims when the last payment on the debt is due after the final payment under the plan.

267 *In re* Webb, 370 B.R. 418 (Bankr. N.D. Ga. 2007) (debtor may pay general unsecured creditors a 1% dividend through plan payments while making regularly scheduled student loan payments directly to student loan creditor pursuant to 11 U.S.C. § 1322(b)(5); new section 1322(b)(10), added by BAPCPA, does not preclude this plan structure). *See In re* Knight, 370 B.R. 429 (Bankr. N.D. Ga. 2007) (payment of student loan under section 1322(b)(5) permitted despite BAPCPA changes to disposable income test under section 1325(b)(1)(B)); *In re* Williams, 253 B.R. 220 (Bankr. W.D. Tenn. 2000); *In re* Chandler, 210 B.R. 898 (Bankr. D.N.H. 1997); *In re* Sullivan, 195 B.R. 649 (Bankr. W.D. Tex. 1996); *In re* Cox, 186 B.R. 744 (Bankr. N.D. Fla. 1995); *In re* Christophe, 151 B.R. 475 (Bankr. N.D. Ill. 1993) (plan can propose cure of student loan default pursuant to section 1322(b)(5)); *In re* Benner, 156 B.R. 631 (Bankr. D. Minn. 1993); *In re* Saulter, 133 B.R. 148 (Bankr. W.D. Mo. 1991). *See also In re* Machado, 378 B.R. 14, 17 (Bankr. D. Mass. 2007) (in providing for cure and maintenance of payments, chapter 13 plan can allow for current payments to be paid by debtor directly to creditor, while only payments to cure prebankruptcy arrearage need be paid through trustee and subject to trustee's commission).

268 *In re* Williams, 253 B.R. 220 (Bankr. W.D. Tenn. 2000) (maintenance of ongoing payments on student loans under section 1322(b)(5) includes payment of postpetition interest). See note 262, *supra*, discussing accrual of interest during a chapter 13 case.

269 *In re* Labib-Kiyarash, 271 B.R. 189 (B.A.P. 9th Cir. 2001) (use of section 1322(b)(5) is subject to debtor showing that classification is fair under section 1322(b)(1)); *In re* Harding, 423 B.R. 568 (Bankr. S.D. Fla. 2010) (plan's cure provision with payment of student loan outside plan violated prohibition on unfair discrimination against remaining unsecured creditors); *In re* Kruse, 406 B.R. 833 (Bankr. N.D. Iowa 2009) (plan's "cure and maintain" treatment of student loan debt unfairly discriminatory); *In re* Parrott, 2009 B.R. 5216043 (Bankr. E.D. Tenn. Dec. 29, 2009); *In re* Simmons, 288 B.R. 737 (Bankr. N.D. Tex. 2003); *In re* Edwards, 263 B.R. 690 (Bankr. R.I. 2001); *In re* Thibodeau, 248 B.R. 699 (Bankr. D. Mass. 2000).

270 *In re* Strickland, 181 B.R. 598 (Bankr. N.D. Ala. 1995) (holding that nondischargeable student loan debt could not be treated more favorably than other unsecured claims for first thirty-six months of chapter 13 plan, but remaining twenty-four months could be devoted solely to payment of student loan).

271 11 U.S.C. § 1325(b)(1)(B).

272 *Compare In re* Stickland, 181 B.R. 598 (Bankr. N.D. Ala. 1995) (allowing separate treatment in years four and five), *and In re* Rudy, 1993 WL 365370 (Bankr. S.D. Ohio 1993) (same), *with In re* Sullivan, 195 B.R. 649 (Bankr. W.D. Tex. 1996) (not allowing separate classification).

or co-obligor.[273] Students who file under chapter 13 can thus protect from collection parents or other family members who may have co-signed a student loan as long as the student's plan provides for payment of the student loan.[274] In addition, the need to retain the co-debtor stay may provide an additional justification for the separate classification of a student loan in a chapter 13 plan.[275]

10.9.3 Raising Defenses in Response to Creditor Claims

The chapter 13 claim allowance process may also present an opportunity for consumers to raise defenses to a student loan obligation. In addition to the various grounds for objections to creditors' claims that may be raised under the Bankruptcy Code,[276] no claim may be allowed to the extent that it is unenforceable against the debtor.[277] This means that the student may assert as objections any defenses, counterclaims, or setoffs the debtor may have, including for instance defenses relating to the school's misconduct.[278] The objection will generally be treated by the bankruptcy court as a "contested matter."[279]

For students who are confronted with unlawful or excessive interest and collection fees or the miscrediting of payments by loan servicers, this process also provides an opportunity for the student to challenge the amount owed on the student loan. A student loan creditor is bound by a determination disallowing collection costs as part of its claim in bankruptcy regardless of whether the student loan debt is nondischargeable. Student loan creditors may be denied collection costs and fees as part of their claims when no entitlement exists under the relevant regulations or contract provisions.[280] Unfortunately, the courts have rejected several recent challenges to guarantee agency's fixed-percentage collection fees.[281] In collection actions, the Department of Education generally claims attorney fees award based on a fixed percentage of the underlying debt, typically 20%.[282] Several courts, however, have rejected these claims, requiring the government to document rates, time, and tasks consistently with a traditional lodestar calculation.[283]

10.10 Student Loan Payments As "Special Circumstances" Under the BAPCPA Means Test

The 2005 amendments to the Bankruptcy Code apply a "means test" to debtors who have primarily consumer debts and whose income exceeds their state's median. The test begins with a calculation of the debtor's "current monthly income."[284] Certain expenditures may then be deducted from this monthly income. Deductible expenditures include specified living expenses and payments for certain secured and priority debts.[285] After subtracting these deductions, the means test applies a formula to determine whether the debtor has the ability to repay unsecured creditors from any remaining disposable income. If application of the formula

---

273 See 11 U.S.C. § 1301.
 For a more detailed discussion of the co-debtor stay in chapter 13, see National Consumer Law Center, Consumer Bankruptcy Law and Practice § 9.4.4 (9th ed. 2009 and Supp.).
274 The Department of Education regulations acknowledge the chapter 13 co-debtor stay by noting that guaranty agencies must suspend all collection efforts against a "co-maker or endorser" if the student borrower has filed under chapter 13. See 34 C.F.R. § 682.402(f)(2).
275 11 U.S.C. 1322(b)(1). See § 10.9.1, supra.
276 For a detailed discussion of objections to claims, see National Consumer Law Center, Consumer Bankruptcy Law and Practice § 14.4.3 (9th ed. 2009 and Supp.).
277 11 U.S.C. § 502(b)(1).
278 See also In re Mason, 300 B.R. 160 (Bankr. D. Conn. 2003) (consolidation loan obtained by duress held void and unenforceable). See generally Ch. 12, infra.
279 Such proceedings are governed by Fed. R. Bankr. P. 9014.
280 In re Schlehr, 290 B.R. 387 (Bankr. D. Mont. 2003) (denying objection to collection fees included in student loan creditor's proofs of claim, as chapter 13 trustee failed to rebut prima facie validity of claims); In re McAlpin, 254 B.R. 449 (Bankr. D. Minn. 2000), rev'd on other grounds, 263 B.R. 881 (B.A.P. 8th Cir. 2001), aff'd, 278 F.3d 866 (8th Cir. 2002) (collection costs and fees disallowed, based on 34 C.F.R. § 674.45(e), when creditor failed to prove they were reasonable, and limited to actual or average cost incurred). But see In re Kirkland, 600 F.3d 310 (4th Cir. 2010) (bankruptcy court lacked subject matter jurisdiction to determine proper application of postpetition fees and costs in action brought by debtor after case closing).
281 Black v. Educational Credit Mgmt. Corp., 459 F.3d 796 (7th Cir. 2006), aff'g Educational Credit Mgmt. Corp. v. Barnes, 318 B.R. 482 (S.D. Ind. 2004) (DOE regulation that authorizes collection charges based on annual aggregate agency costs, up to 25% of outstanding principal and interest for individual loan, is valid exercise of statutory authority); United States v. Larson, 2010 WL 76433 (D. Minn. Jan. 5, 2010) (upholding flat-rate method of calculating collection costs); In re Belton, 337 B.R. 471 (Bankr. W.D.N.Y. 2006) (same); In re Evans, 322 B.R. 429 (Bankr. W.D. Wash. 2005) (25% fees based on agency's purported aggregate costs are authorized by federal regulation and notes). See also United States v. Vilus, 419 F. Supp. 2d 293 (E.D.N.Y. 2005) (percentage fees upheld in student loan debt collection cases, rejecting debtors' arguments that fees should be based on hourly rates for work actually performed).
282 See, e.g., United States v. Vilus, 419 F. Supp. 2d 293 (E.D.N.Y. 2005) (percentage attorney fees upheld in student loan debt collection cases, rejecting debtors' arguments that fees should be based on hourly rates for work actually performed).
283 United States v. Washington, 2009 WL 6636862 (E.D.N.Y. Dec. 14, 2009); United States v. Davis, 2007 WL 2287889 (E.D.N.Y. Aug. 8, 2007); United States v. O'Connor, 2006 WL 1419388 (E.D.N.Y. May 18, 2006).
284 "Current Monthly Income" has a specific definition in the 2005 amendments, 11 U.S.C. § 101(10A). See National Consumer Law Center, Consumer Bankruptcy Law and Practice § 13.4.3.2 (9th ed. 2009 and Supp.).
285 11 U.S.C. § 707(b)(2)(A)(i). See National Consumer Law Center, Consumer Bankruptcy Law and Practice §§ 13.4.5.2, 13.4.5.3 (9th ed. 2009 and Supp.).

shows that the debtor can make payments to unsecured creditors, a "presumption of abuse" arises.[286] The debtor's chapter 7 case is then subject to dismissal or it may be converted to chapter 13.

In order to reduce current monthly income, the above-median-income debtor will first want to show the maximum allowable expenditures and expenses. Student loan payments would appear to be an obvious choice to apply toward this reduction. Unfortunately, student loan debt payments, like most general unsecured debts, are not allowable deductions from current monthly income for the means test calculation.[287] Yet, there is still a way in which the debtor may use student loan payments to reduce current monthly income and avoid the presumption of abuse. After deductions for allowed expenditures, the Code permits the debtor to rebut the presumption of abuse by demonstrating "special circumstances" that may bring the debtor's disposable income under the presumed abuse tolerance level set by the means test formula.[288] The Code defines these "special circumstances" only generally. The circumstances must "justify additional expenses or adjustments of current monthly income for which there is no reasonable alternative."[289] As examples of acceptable "special circumstances," the Code mentions "a serious medical condition or a call or order to active duty in the Armed Forces."[290]

May an obligation to pay a nondischargeable student loan be a "special circumstance" similar to a serious medical condition or a call to military service? Several courts have said yes.[291] For example, in *In re Delbecq*, the means test left the debtor with $304 in disposable monthly income, and she faced a trustee's motion to dismiss asserting the presumption of abuse. In response, the debtor argued that her monthly student loan payment of $350 was a "special circumstance" that rebutted the presumption.[292] If her disposable income was reduced by the amount of her student loan payments, she would have no disposable income under the means test formula. The court agreed with the debtor and denied the trustee's motion to dismiss.[293]

In holding that the obligation to pay the student loans was a "special circumstance" under section 707(b)(2)(B)(i), the court in *Delbecq* looked to the legislative history of the means test. Congress intended that the means test bar from chapter 7 those debtors who had a meaningful ability to pay their debts. According to the court, forcing the debtor into chapter 13 would do nothing to further this intent. Because separate classification of student loan debts was permitted in a chapter 13 plan in the district, the non-student-loan creditors would receive nothing under any plan the debtor was likely to propose.[294] The student loan creditor would receive all disbursements under her plan. The student loan debt was presumed to be nondischargeable, so the debtor had no alternative but to pay it. Thus, the debtor did not have any meaningful ability to repay her non-student-loan debts either inside or outside of bankruptcy. This amounted to special circumstances that placed the debtor in clear need of chapter 7 relief and required adjustments to her income and expenses based upon the student loan debt. The obligation to make significant student loan payments may also be a basis for opposing a motion to dismiss a chapter 7 case under a claim of general abuse of chapter 7 or lack of bad faith.[295]

A similar issue involving student loans and the debtor's projected disposable income has arisen in chapter 13 cases. Under BAPCPA, above-median-income debtors must pay their projected disposable income to creditors under a chapter 13 plan. The calculation of disposable income for this purpose uses the same standards under section 707(b)(2)(A) and (B) that apply in determining the presumption of abuse under the chapter 7 means test.

The chapter 13 debtor will often prefer to make regular monthly payments on a nondischargeable student loan debt directly to student loan creditors rather than as part of the plan payment disbursed by the chapter 13 trustee. This will maximize payments toward the long-term nondischargeable student loan debt, and the debtor will be less likely to fall into default on the student loan. Paying the student loan creditor only a pro rata share of the total disbursement to unsecured creditors under the plan is likely to fall far short of the full installments due each month on the student loan debt. Thus, the requirement under BAPCPA that the above-median-income debtor pay all of his or her projected disposable income to unsecured creditors under the plan exposes the debtor to a heightened risk of default and the accrual of unpaid interest during the plan.[296] However, if the

---

286 11 U.S.C. § 707(b)(1).
287 11 U.S.C. § 707(b)(2)(A)(ii)(I) ("other necessary expenses" "shall not include any payments for debts").
288 11 U.S.C. § 707(b)(2)(B)(i). *See* National Consumer Law Center, Consumer Bankruptcy Law and Practice § 13.4.6.2 (9th ed. 2009 and Supp.).
289 11 U.S.C. § 707(b)(2)(B)(i).
290 *Id.*
291 *In re* Martin, 371 B.R. 347 (Bankr. C.D. Ill. 2007); *In re* Delbecq, 368 B.R. 754 (Bankr. S.D. Ind. 2007); *In re* Haman, 366 B.R. 307 (Bankr. D. Del. 2007) (debtor's obligation to pay as co-signor on son's student loan is "special circumstance"); *In re* Templeton, 365 B.R. 213 (Bankr. W.D. Okla. 2007). *See* Anthony P. Cali, *The "Special Circumstance" of Student Loan Debt Under the Bankruptcy Abuse Prevention and Consumer Protection Act of 2005*, 52 Ariz. L. Rev. 473 (Summer 2010) (reviewing decisions and policies related to issue and generally supporting treatment of student loans payments as "special circumstance").
292 *In re* Delbecq, 368 B.R. 754 (Bankr. S.D. Ind. 2007).
293 *Id.*
294 *See* § 10.9.1, *supra* (discussing chapter 13 plan classification issues related to student loans).
295 11 U.S.C. § 707(b)(1) and (3). *See In re* Thurston, 2008 WL 3414138 (Bankr. N.D. Ohio Aug. 8, 2008).
296 If the student loan debt is nondischargeable, postpetition interest will not be discharged. *See In re* Kielisch, 258 F.3d 315 (4th

student loan payments can be excluded from projected disposable income as a "special circumstance," the payment of the regular monthly installments on the long-term debt outside of the plan would be appropriate. This should be allowed, because the same "special circumstances" standard of section 707(b)(2)(B)(i) that reduces current monthly income under the means test for chapter 7 applies to adjustments to disposable income in chapter 13. Therefore, the chapter 13 debtor should be able to argue for the same "special circumstances" exclusion of student loan payments from income as the court allowed in *Delbecq*.

At least one court has agreed with this analysis in the context of chapter 13.[297] Finding that monthly payments of $450 toward a nondischargeable student loan were "special circumstances," the court in *In re Knight* held that a downward adjustment of the debtor's projected disposable income in the full amount of his scheduled student loan payments was appropriate. The court found that the debtor had no reasonable alternative to payment of his student loans. There would be a demonstrable economic unfairness to the debtor if completion of a chapter 13 plan left him in default on his student loans and subject to garnishment or tax offsets.[298] This would be inconsistent with the intent of BAPCPA to encourage debtors to complete chapter 13 repayment plans. As an alternative basis for its decision, the court in *In re Knight* found that the debtor was permitted to make payments on the student loans under section 1322(b)(5).[299]

Some courts have rejected the view that the obligation to pay a nondischargeable student loan debt is, per se, a "special circumstance" that justifies additional deductions from monthly income under the means test.[300] A per se rule that any specific debt within a general category of expenditures will always qualify for the "special circumstances" deduction is not a tenable position, and it is not one that any courts have endorsed. Under a fair reading of the statute, the debtor must make some particularized showing that, in his or her case, there is no alternative to payment of the student loan debt.[301] However, in rejecting debtors' arguments that student loan payments were "special circumstances," some recent decisions endorsed a line of reasoning that deviates from the statutory language as widely as does the view that student loans should always be treated as a "special circumstances." These courts adopted the position that "special circumstances" must be the result of some involuntary hardship that befell the debtor.[302] According to these courts, student loans are a routine obligation that individuals take on voluntarily. Under this view, payments toward a nondischargeable student loan would almost never be a special circumstance reducing disposable income under section 707(b)(2)(B).

The decisions that give substantial weight to the reasons why the debtor incurred a particular debt, such as a student loan, ignore the relevant statutory language.[303] By its terms, the statute requires only that the debtor demonstrate that certain circumstances are "special" to the extent that they require additional expenditures from current monthly income and there is no reasonable alternative to payment for these expenditures. There is nothing in the statutory language suggesting that anything about the past circumstances which created the obligation is relevant. The only criterion is that there presently be no reasonable alternative to the expenditure.[304] The standard should be met when there is nothing within the debtor's power to reduce or otherwise avoid the additional expense of the student loan.[305] The means testing system was intended to be a process to direct debtors with some truly discretionary income or an extravagant lifestyle into some form of debt repayment. The lack of alternatives for repayment of student loan debt should focus on the debtors' resources and expenses and not on whether student loans are a common or "voluntary" form of debt.[306]

The means testing provisions of the Bankruptcy Code have their own requirements for evidentiary support to back

---

Cir. 2001); Leeper v. Pennsylvania Higher Educ. Assistance Agency, 49 F.3d 98 (3d Cir. 1995) (interest accruing during pendency of plan not discharged even though debtor paid pre-petition debt in full through chapter 13 plan).

297 *In re* Knight, 370 B.R. 429 (Bankr. N.D. Ga. 2007).

298 *Id.* at 437.

299 *See* § 10.9.1, *supra*.

300 *In re* Conlee, 2010 WL 3210974 (Bankr. N.D. Ohio Aug. 11, 2010); *In re* Siler, 426 B.R. 167 (Bankr. W.D.N.C. 2010); *In re* Carillo, 421 B.R. 540 (Bankr. D. Ariz. 2009); *In re* Pageau, 383 B.R. 221 (Bankr. D.N.H. 2008); *In re* Lightsey, 374 B.R. 377, 382 n.3 (Bankr. S.D. Ga. 2007).

301 *See In re* Champagne, 389 B.R. 191 (Bankr. D. Kan. 2008) (emphasizing fact-intensive nature of special circumstances determination; rejecting view that nondischargeable student loan obligation is per se a special circumstance but also rejecting view that student loan debt burden can never satisfy this requirement).

302 *In re* Zahringer (Bankr. E.D. Wis. May 30, 2008); *In re* Pageau, 383 B.R. 221 (Bankr. D.N.H. 2008) (there must be "special circumstances" in the reasons that led debtor to incur education loan).

303 11 U.S.C. § 707(b)(2)(B).

304 *See In re* Haman, 366 B.R. 307, 313–14 (Bankr. D. Del. 2007) (rejecting view that circumstances must result from events outside debtor's control).

305 *In re* Hammock, 2010 WL 2723730 (Bankr. E.D. N.C. July 8, 2010) (need for education credentials for job advancement not sufficient to show "special circumstances" and lack of reasonable alternatives); *In re* Templeton, 365 B.R. 213 (Bankr. W.D. Okla. 2007). *See also In re* Knight, 370 BR. 429, 439–40 (Bankr. N.D. Ga. 2007) (a "reasonable alternative" is not to pay a miniscule percentage to student loan creditor along with all general unsecured creditors in chapter 13 plan and have debtor owe more on student loan after bankruptcy than before). *But see In re* Pageau, 383 B.R. 221 (Bankr. D.N.H. 2008) (in districts that allow separate classification of student loans in chapter 13 plans, treatment of student loan debt in this manner under a plan is reasonable alternative for dealing with expense, precluding finding of special circumstances for chapter 7 debtor); *In re* Lightsey, 374 B.R. 377, 382 n.3 (Bankr. S.D. Ga. 2007) (same).

306 *In re* Delbecq, 368 B.R. 754 (Bankr. S.D. Ind. 2007).

up a "special circumstances" claim. This requirement is consistent with the view that there is no automatic exclusion or inclusion of particular expenditures and that claims for special circumstances deductions must be reviewed on a case-by-case basis. Clauses (ii) and (iii) of section 707(b)(2)(B) require that the debtor document and verify the basis for a claim of special circumstances. In several recent decisions involving student loans as the basis for the deduction, the courts held debtors strictly to these requirements.[307]

The means testing calculation can work to the benefit of an above-median-income chapter 13 debtor who wishes to continue making regular payments on a nondischargeable student loan. This was the conclusion of the bankruptcy court in In re Orawsky.[308] Based on her Form 22C, the debtor in Orawsky had a negative monthly disposable income. However, according to her income and expense schedules (I and J), she had $104.83 in disposable monthly income after expenses. Among her regular monthly expenses listed on Schedule J was the debtor's $217 student loan payment. Under her chapter 13 plan, she proposed to pay $100 monthly, to be distributed pro rata to all her unsecured creditors. The plan provided that she would continue to make her monthly $217 student loan payments directly to the student loan creditor. After considering the policies behind the means testing formula, the bankruptcy court concluded that the debtor's obligation to pay the "monthly disposable income" amount from her Form 22C (that is, $0) controlled. She was therefore free to fund her plan with what were essentially "optional" or "voluntary" contributions from income, and she was under no obligation to use these funds for plan payments to non-student-loan unsecured creditors. Use of these "optional" funds to stay current on student loan payments and to provide some benefit to all general unsecured creditors in the form of $100 monthly plan payments from earnings effectively disposed of the trustee's unfair classification objection.

---

307 In re Zahringer, 2008 WL 2245864 (Bankr. E.D. Wis. May 30, 2008); In re Wagner, 2008 WL 706616 (Bankr. D. Neb. Mar. 14, 2008); In re Vaccariello, 375 B.R. 809 (Bankr. N.D. Ohio 2007). See also In re Fonash, 401 B.R. 143 (Bankr. M.D. Pa. 2008) (listing student loan information on schedules does not satisfy documentation and attestation requirements for "special circumstances" under section 707(b)(2)(B)(ii)(I) and (II)). Cf. In re Knight, 370 B.R. 429, 440 (Bankr. N.D. Ga. 2007) (allowing debtor twenty days to correct initial failure to supply documentation and attestation required under section 707(b)(2)(B)). See generally In re Womer, 427 B.R. 334 (Bankr. M.D. Pa. 2010) (debtors failed to meet burden of proving lack of alternatives to payment, including whether loans were dischargeable under section 523(a)(8)).

308 387 B.R. 128 (Bankr. E.D. Pa. 2008). See also In re Sharp, 415 B.R. 803 (2009) (following Orawsky, above-median-income chapter 13 debtor's discretionary payments to student loan creditors not unfairly discriminatory).

10.11 Student's Rights After Bankruptcy Discharge

If there has been a judicial determination that a student loan is discharged in bankruptcy, the debtor is no longer liable for the obligation and is protected from any attempt to collect the debt.[309] The lender should not accept any further payments on the loan, such as payments the lender may receive through a tax intercept program or even those voluntarily made by the debtor. Department of Education regulations provide that, if a guaranty agency receives payments on a discharged loan on which the Department previously paid a claim to the agency, the agency must return the payments to the sender and notify the borrower that there is no obligation to pay the loan.[310]

Similarly, a school cannot withhold a former student's transcripts just because the debt has been discharged in bankruptcy.[311] The 1994 amendments to the Bankruptcy Code clarified this principle, prohibiting discrimination with respect to student loans or grants based upon discharge of a prior debt. Prior to this time, courts had split on whether schools could deny transcripts after discharge and also on whether schools could deny transcripts to students who filed for bankruptcy but had not yet received a discharge.[312] Some courts have continued to allow denial of transcripts in

---

309 11 U.S.C. § 524(a)(2).
    Damages and attorney fees are available if improper collection activities occur. See National Consumer Law Center, Consumer Bankruptcy Law and Practice § 15.5.1.4 (9th ed. 2009).
310 34 C.F.R. § 682.402(r)(1).
311 Id. See also National Consumer Law Center, Consumer Bankruptcy Law and Practice § 15.5.5.2 (9th ed. 2009).
312 In re Merchant, 958 F.2d 738 (6th Cir. 1992); Juras v. Aman Collection, 829 F.2d 739 (9th Cir. 1987) (institutions cannot withhold transcripts from students who have had their loans discharged, who are making payments under chapter 13 plan, or who have filed for bankruptcy but not yet received a discharge); In re Gustafson, 111 B.R. 282 (B.A.P. 9th Cir. 1990), rev'd on other grounds, 934 F.2d 216 (9th Cir. 1991); In re Carson, 150 B.R. 228 (Bankr. E.D. Mo. 1993) (protections of automatic stay override creditor's ability to collect student loan debt until such time as debt is determined to be nondischargeable; therefore no withholding of transcripts until debt is found to be nondischargeable). But see In re Joyner, 171 B.R. 759 (Bankr. E.D. Pa. 1994); In re Najafi, 154 B.R. 185 (Bankr. E.D. Pa. 1993) (rejecting Gustafson, reasoning that it is unfair to creditor if students can get transcripts up until the moment debt is found to be nondischargeable; finding college had right comparable to a "security interest" in the transcript).
    Both the Najafi and Joyner courts ordered the colleges to release transcripts upon payment of $300 in each case by the students to the colleges. Both cases involved private colleges and, in both cases, the student debts were found nondischargeable. See generally Ana Kellia Ramares, Annotation: Validity, Constructions, and Application of Statutes, Regulations, or Policies Allowing Denial of Student Loans, Student Loan Guarantees, or Educational Services to Debtors Who Have Had Student Loans Scheduled in Bankruptcy, 107 A.L.R. Fed. 192 (1998).

the latter situation (in which a debtor filed for bankruptcy but has not yet been granted a discharge). The debtor's response in this situation should be that, as soon as a bankruptcy is filed, acts such as withholding of transcripts are prohibited by the automatic stay.[313]

While the Department of Education in the early 1990s stated that students who discharged student loans in bankruptcy would not be eligible for new student loans,[314] the question of a student's eligibility for new loans and grants after discharging a student loan in bankruptcy has now been resolved by Congressional action. The Bankruptcy Reform Act of 1994 specifies that those discharging student loans in bankruptcy remain eligible for new loans and grants. The United States, guarantors, and lenders cannot discriminate against those who have not paid their student loans when those loans were discharged in bankruptcy.[315]

The Bankruptcy Reform Act's legislative history states that the "section clarifies the anti-discrimination provisions of the Bankruptcy Code to ensure that applicants for student loans or grants are not denied those benefits due to a prior bankruptcy. The section overrules *In re Goldrich*. . . ."[316]

The Department responded by changing its regulations so that students no longer have to reaffirm student loans discharged in bankruptcy to be eligible for new loans or grants. The Department states that such a reaffirmation requirement is no longer permissible because the Bankruptcy Reform Act prohibits denial of a loan or loan guarantee based on a bankruptcy discharge.[317] Consequently, the offending language has been deleted from the regulations.[318]

Nevertheless, the Department will look to a prior bankruptcy in considering an applicant's future creditworthiness in applying for PLUS loans. A PLUS loan is a specialized type of loan taken out by parents of the student, during the application for which, by statute, the Department is required to consider the parent(s)' creditworthiness. Thus applicants for PLUS loans will be required to explain the bankruptcy or secure a credit-worthy endorser. The PLUS regulations that allow a lender to consider past bankruptcies in assessing a borrower's creditworthiness may be challenged as violating the nondiscrimination provisions in the Bankruptcy Code.[319]

---

313 Loyola v. McClarty, 234 B.R. 386 (E.D. La. 1999).

314 Its position was that the Bankruptcy Code's prohibition of governmental discrimination at 11 U.S.C. § 525(a) did not apply to the granting of credit, such as a student loan. *See, e.g.*, *In re Goldrich*, 771 F.2d 28 (2d Cir. 1985) (student loan not within scope of section 525(a)).

Of course, the Code discrimination prohibition will clearly apply to Pell and other student *grants*.

315 11 U.S.C. § 525(c). *See* Pub. L. No. 103-394, § 313, 108 Stat. 4106 (amending 11 U.S.C. § 525 (Oct. 22, 1994)). *See also* 140 Cong. Rec. H10, 7771 (daily ed. Oct. 4, 1994).

While the Bankruptcy Reform Act applies to bankruptcies filed after October 22, 1994, unless otherwise noted the language of section 313 makes clear a Congressional intent to apply that section to any student loan discharged in bankruptcy, even to student loans discharged under the Bankruptcy Act— that is, discharged before 1979.

316 H.R. Rep. No. 103-835 at 58 (Judiciary Comm.) (1994), *reprinted in* 1994 U.S.C.C.A.N. 3340, 3367.

317 59 Fed. Reg. 61212 (Nov. 29, 1994) (FFEL loans). *See also* 59 Fed. Reg. 61667 (Dec. 1, 1994) (FDSL loans).

318 59 Fed. Reg. 61215 (Nov. 29, 1994) (amending 34 C.F.R. § 682.201(4)(i)).

319 *See* 34 C.F.R. § 682.201(c)(2)(ii)(B) (PLUS loan regulations).

Chapter 11   Private Student Loans

11.1 The Private Student Loan Market

11.1.1 General

Banks and other financial institutions make private student loans without any direct financial backing from the federal government. They are not subsidized, meaning that interest starts to accrue at the time the loans are obtained. There are many different types of private loans, each program with specific rules and requirements. Private loans are also known as private-label or alternative loans.

The private student loan industry grew throughout the 1990s and early 2000s. During this time, many private lenders steered borrowers to these products even if they were eligible for federal student loans. Unfortunately, much of the lending targeted low-income borrowers with subprime loans. Too many of these risky, high-cost loans were destined to fail and have been failing at astronomical rates, especially since the credit crisis began.

The market grew steadily throughout the "easy credit" era. In 2007–2008, private loan volume, including private-sector and state-sponsored loans, totaled $19 billion, up from $3 billion in 1997–1998.[1] The rapid growth in the private student loan market slowed in 2006–2007 and, in 2007–2008, the volume of private loans declined by about 1% in constant dollars.[2] As the credit crisis hit, lenders began reporting huge increases in delinquency and default rates. In October 2008, Sallie Mae reported a loss of $159 million in the most recent quarter, fueled by the acceleration of delinquent private loans[3] Fitch Ratings in 2009 stated that, from a net-charge-off perspective, the rates had been deteriorating for the main private student lenders since 2006.[4] As of early 2009, thirty-nine lenders had stopped making private student loans.[5] As the remaining lenders pulled out of the subprime market, many proprietary schools began offering their own loan products.[6]

Sallie Mae and others have attributed much of the poor performance to their "non-traditional" loan portfolio. These loans are described as loans to borrowers that are expected to have a high default rate due to numerous factors, among them lower-tier credit ratings or low program completion and graduation rates usually at "non-traditional schools." Even when the borrower is expected to graduate, non-traditional loans tend to go to borrowers with low expected incomes relative to the cost of attendance.[7] Both Sallie Mae and Citi's Student Loan Corporation have identified lending to students who attend schools having lower graduation rates and lower earning potential as the main source of credit deterioration.[8]

According to Sallie Mae, at the end of 2009, 18.6% of the company's non-traditional loans had been charged off, compared to 3.2% of traditional loans. About 31.4% of the non-traditional loans were delinquent compared to 9.5% of traditional loans. Interestingly, only 28% of non-traditional loans had co-signers compared to 61% of traditional loans.[9] Overall, Sallie Mae executives noted in 2010 that, of the $6 billion in non-traditional private loans they had made, they projected 40% would default. These loans, they claim, made up about 11% of their private student loan portfolio.[10]

Many of the most expensive private student loans were made to proprietary school students. A general discussion of raising school-related claims against lenders can be found in Chapter 12, *infra*. Issues specific to private loans are discussed in this chapter.

Fitch Ratings stated in 2010 that it expects private student loan trust performance to remain under pressure until the

---

1 U.S. Gov't Accountability Office, Higher Education: Factors Lenders Consider in Making Lending Decisions for Private Education Loans, Report No. GAO-10-86R (Nov. 17, 2009).
2 College Bd., Trends in Student Aid (2008), *available at* http://professionals.collegeboard.com/profdownload/trends-in-student-aid-2008.pdf.
3 Paul Basken, *Sallie Mae Reports $159-Million Loss and More Delinquencies by Borrowers*, Chron. of Higher Educ., Oct. 23, 2008.
4 Fitch Ratings, Private Education Loans: Time for a Re-Education 7 (Jan. 28, 2009).

5 Robert Tomsho, *Tuition Ammunition: A Happy Lesson on Lending*, Wall St. J., Jan. 6, 2009.
6 See § 11.1.3, *infra*.
7 Fitch Ratings, Private Education Loans: Time for a Re-Education 7 (Jan. 28, 2009).
8 *Id.* Citi sold Student Loan Corporation to Discover in 2010.
9 *In Search of Answers in Sallie Mae's 4Q Supplement: Private Loan Originations Down 55%, Delinquencies Remain High*, Student Lending Analytics Blog (Jan. 20, 2010).
10 *The $5.4 Billion Private Student Loan Problem*, Student Lending Analytics Blog (May 16, 2010.).

economy shows significant signs of recovery.[11] There are some signs that the market might be slowly recovering. However, it is unclear whether the securitization market will bounce back quickly or ever return to previous levels. Fitch Ratings, for example, stated in February 2009 that the weak job market, lack of home equity financing, and negative student loan industry performance are all leading to diminished investor interest in private student loan securitizations.[12]

Despite the changes in the sector, it is unlikely that private student loans will disappear, and they have certainly not disappeared so far. Sallie Mae representatives, for example, have said that the company expected to make the same volume of private loans in 2009 as in 2008 and may fund even more if they are able to access government funding.[13] Fitch Ratings predicts that the private loan market will remain most relevant for international graduate students with no access to federal loans and undergraduate borrowers whose parents cannot access PLUS loans.[14]

The remaining lenders seem to have learned some lessons. Most have reduced their origination volume and re-evaluated underwriting criteria.[15] Sallie Mae, the largest student lender, has tightened underwriting, terminated certain school relationships, and reduced volume.[16] In March 2009, the company announced that it would replace its existing private loan product with a shorter-term loan that requires borrowers to make payments while they are in school.[17] Yet, by 2010, there were signs that lenders were already beginning to relax at least some of these requirements, approving loans to borrowers with lower credit scores and allowing delays in repayment.[18]

In 2010, loan originations by the "traditional" private lenders were still below previous limits. For example, in 2009, Sallie Mae's private loan originations were down 55% in the fourth quarter as compared to the same period the previous year. The company provided these reasons for the decline: "continued tightening of our underwriting criteria, an increase in guaranteed student loan limits and the Company's withdrawal from certain markets."[19]

Other entities have come in to "fill the gap." Some are credit companies that are known more for other types of credit products. For example, Discover began offering a private student loan product, purchasing Student Loan Corporation in 2010.[20] Other traditional lenders are competing for specific segments of the market, such as parents. Wells Fargo, for example, introduced a student loan for parents in 2010.

Interest in making student loans will likely remain high, particularly in the proprietary sector, as these schools have incentives to steer borrowers to private loans to keep federal default rates low and to avoid having too large of a share of revenues from federal aid.[21] Other schools may rely on private loan funds because they are ineligible to participate in federal programs, in some cases due to previous disqualification.

11.1.2 State Private Loan Products

A number of states have created private loan products or offer student loans with state backing. For example, for 2010–2011, Vermont Student Assistance Corporation offered a private student loan with fixed rates ranging from 6.9% to 7.75% and fees ranging from zero percent to 5%. Maine Educational Loan Authority also offers a private student loan product.[22] Many states issue bonds to fund these programs. Iowa Student Loan Corporation, for example, issued a tax-exempt bond in late 2009 to fund private student loans for students attending colleges in Iowa as well as for Iowa residents attending out-of-state schools. Fixed rates for these loans vary from 7.7% to 7.9%, with fees ranging from zero percent to 4%.

New York also created a private loan product.[23] The New York Higher Education Financing Authority issues private bonds to purchase loans made by private lenders that participate in the program. Participating lenders must sign agreements to make loans in accordance with the program guidelines. There are numerous disclosure requirements in the law. Loan rates are set by the New York State Education

---

11 Fitch Ratings, The Student Loan Report Card (July 2010).
12 Fitch Ratings, U.S. Private Loan ABS Exhibiting Recession Strains (Feb. 25, 2009).
13 *Summary of December 16, 2008, Sallie Mae Straight Talk Conference Call*, Student Lending Analytics Blog (Dec. 17, 2008).
14 Fitch Ratings, Private Education Loans: Time for a Re-Education 3 (Jan. 28, 2009).
15 Id.
16 Id. at 4.
17 Jane J. Kim, *Sallie Mae to Revamp Private Loans*, Wall St. J., Mar. 19, 2009.
18 See generally Kim Clark, *7 Ways Private Student Loans are Getting Better*, U.S. News & World Report, June 21, 2010.
19 *In Search of Answers in Sallie Mae's 4Q Supplement: Private Loan Originations Down 55%, Delinquencies Remain High*, Student Lending Analytics Blog (Jan. 20, 2010).

20 Sean Sposito, *Discover Looking at Student Loans to Boost Growth*, American Banker, Sept. 21, 2010. Student Loan Corporation was owned mainly by CitiGroup.
21 Private loans are not included in the federal cohort default-rate calculation. See § 5.1.3, supra. In addition, proprietary schools are required to maintain at least 10% of revenues from non-Department of Education federal student assistance funds. This is known as the "90/10" rule. See § 1.7.2.2, supra.
22 *What's Happening in Private Student Loan Land?*, Student Lending Analytics Blog (Aug. 4, 2010).
23 N.Y. Educ. Law §§ 690 to 694-b; N.Y. Comp. Codes R. & Regs. Tit. 8, §§ 2231.1 to 2213.28. See also New York Higher Educ. Servs. Corp., New York Higher Education Loan Program (NYHELPS) Underwriting Manual (Aug. 25, 2010), available at www.hesc.com/content.nsf/NYHELPs/NYHELPs_Regulations/$file/AmendmentProgramManualFINAL081010.pdf.

Department and are determined by credit score. Interest rate maximums cannot exceed 16.5%.[24]

11.1.3 School Products

Since the credit crisis, many for-profit schools in particular have begun making their own student loans. Many nonprofit and public schools also offer loan products. However, these are generally short-term loans and usually have low or no interest charged. Some of these school products are not considered "private education loans" for purposes of the Truth in Lending (TILA) disclosures.[25]

The proprietary school internal loan products vary between schools that originate closed-end or open-end credit products and schools that guarantee loans for national banks or other financial companies. The charge-off rates for many of the proprietary school loans can be even higher than charge-offs for private loans made by banks and finance companies. For example, two publicly owned college chains set aside roughly half their internal lending amount in 2009 as a loss reserve, essentially telling investors that students are not expected to repay more than half of what they borrow.[26]

In some cases, schools that originate loans should be regulated under state lending laws. This was an issue in a 2009 case before an arbitration association against Alta Colleges. The complaint alleges that the school did not obtain a required license from the state Attorney General authorizing the issuance of supervised loans.[27]

11.1.4 Who Borrows Private Student Loans and Why

There are many explanations for the high rates of private borrowing, although it is difficult to know for sure given the paucity of data. There is no comprehensive data base on private loans comparable to the National Student Loan Data System.[28]

A high proportion of private loan borrowers also obtain federal loans and, in many cases, borrow up to the federal loan limits. However, according to the GAO, about 26% of students who obtained private loans in 2007–2008 did not obtain Federal Stafford loans.[29] The Project on Student Debt found that almost two-thirds of private loan borrowers in 2007–2008 borrowed less than they could have in Stafford loans, compared to less than half of private loan borrowers in 2003–2004.[30] In 2007–2008, 26% of private loan borrowers took out no Stafford loans at all and 14% did not apply for federal financial aid. Thirty eight percent of private loan borrowers had Stafford loans but borrowed less than the maximum amount. Interestingly, the majority of private loan borrowers (63%) attended schools charging $10,000 or less in tuition and fees. The percentage of African-Americans who took out private loans quadrupled between 2003–2004 and 2007–2008, from 4% to 17%.[31]

The percentage of all undergraduates with private loans rose from 5% in 2003–2004 to 14% in 2007–2008. Loan volume grew as well, from $7.2 billion in 2003–2004 to $15 billion in 2007–2008.[32] Proprietary colleges had the largest proportion of students taking out private loans and the largest increase in private loan borrowing. Forty two percent of all proprietary school students had private loans in 2007–2008, up from 12% in 2003–2004. This is compared to public two-year schools—where 4% of students had private loans in 2007–2008, up from 1% in 2003–2004—and public four-year schools, where 14% of students had private loans in 2007–2008, up from 5% in 2003–2004. Even at private nonprofit four-year schools, 25% had private loans in 2007–2008, up from 11% in 2003–2004.[33]

Some students turn to private loans because their families may not actually make the expected family contribution that is built into the federal assistance calculations. In other cases, a student may choose to borrow beyond his or her student budget (costs of tuition and estimated living expenses) to cover higher living expenses. In many cases, however, it appears that borrowers turn to private loans because of a lack of information and/or sophistication about the different government and private programs. This lack of information is particularly problematic in cases in which schools aggressively sell private loan products.

In 2008, in order to promote better understanding of private loans, Congress considered requiring companies that make private loans directly to students to notify colleges when their students take out private loans. Instead, Congress passed a provision requiring that, upon the request of a private lender, a school shall certify that a student is enrolled or is scheduled to enroll at the institution.[34]

A 2006 report presents a number of explanations for the growth of private student loans. The Institute for Higher Education Policy reported anecdotal evidence that parents may be reluctant to take on debt solely in their names to pay

---

24 N.Y. Comp. Codes R. & Regs. tit. 8, § 2213.9.
25 See § 11.4.1.2, infra.
26 Justin Pope, *For Profit Colleges' Increased Lending Prompts Concerns*, Associated Press, Aug. 15, 2009.
27 Mensch v. Alta Colleges, Before the American Arbitration Association, Denver Colorado (Nov. 19, 2009), *available on* the companion website to this manual (complaint).
28 See § 1.9, supra.
29 U.S. Gov't Accountability Office, Higher Education: Factors Lenders Consider in Making Lending Decisions for Private Education Loans, Report No. GAO-10-86R (Nov. 17, 2009).

30 The Project on Student Debt, Private Loans: Facts and Trends (Aug. 2009).
31 Id.
32 Id.
33 Id.
34 Pub. L. No. 110-315, § 493, 122 Stat. 3078 (Aug. 14, 2008). See § 11.4.1.5, infra.

for their child's post-secondary education, thus leading more students to borrow private loans. In other cases, borrowers may be attracted by initially low interest rates. There is also the suggestion that students perceive private loan borrowing to be more convenient than federal loans. Among other reasons, borrowers do not have to fill out the Free Application for Federal Student Aid (FAFSA) form to get private loans.[35] The use of private loans among graduate and professional students may decline now that these borrowers are eligible for PLUS loans.[36] However, limits on how students are able to use PLUS loans as well as aggressive private lender marketing will likely mean that many students will still turn to private loans.

The Government Accountability Office (GAO) found in 2009 that a slightly higher percentage of dependent undergraduate students borrowed private loans compared to independent students and a higher percentage of dependent students from middle- and high-income families borrowed private loans compared to dependent students from low-income families.[37] The GAO noted that private lenders may use school-related factors in deciding to lend and to establish terms and conditions. They concluded that lenders generally view longer programs of study, high graduation rates, and low cohort rates on federal loans as more favorable conditions for lending.[38] Many lenders singled out low cohort default rates as the most commonly used "non-individual" factor.

Most of these explanations for private loan borrowing tend to focus on demand and the high cost of education. These factors do not take into account the "supply side" reasons for private loan borrowing. To get the capital to make the loans, lenders must continually feed investors with new loans. As a result, private student lending, particularly prior to the credit crisis, became very much a push market in which products were offered not only in response to consumer need but also to fulfill investor demand. Loan products are developed for repackaging rather than to provide the most affordable and sustainable products for borrowers.[39]

11.2 Private Loan Terms and Conditions

11.2.1 Comparing Private Loans and Federal Loans

Private loan terms and conditions, including interest rates and fees, are generally determined by an individual's or a co-signer's credit history. Thus, low-income students and/or those with negative credit histories are more likely to receive loans on less favorable terms. Federal student loan borrowers, in contrast, must meet eligibility requirements but do not have to prove creditworthiness.[40] All eligible federal loan borrowers are subject to the same rules regarding interest rates and other terms.

Both federal and private loans can be used only to help finance post-secondary education and can be certified only up to a certain amount. For private loans, this amount often is either a set dollar amount or the cost of attendance minus aid, whichever is less. Federal loans have loan limits.[41]

The three most compelling differences relate to flexibility, the level of risk and associated interest rates, and the services and rewards attached.[42]

Private loans have traditionally had higher interest rates than government loans. There are reports of private loans with interest rates of at least 15% or higher.[43] NCLC issued a report in 2008 based on a survey of private student loans. All of the loans in the survey had variable rates. The lowest initial rate in the sample was around 5% and the highest close to 19%. The average initial disclosed annual percentage rate (APR) for the loans in the survey was 11.5%.[44]

Private lenders generally assess interest risks based on credit scores. These loans often require co-signers. Those that do not require co-signers typically have very high origination fees and higher interest rates.

Private loans allow greater flexibility with regard to origination fees, interest rates, and repayment terms. This primarily benefits generally higher-income borrowers with favorable credit scores or those who can secure a "credit-

---

35 Institute for Higher Educ. Policy, The Future of Private Loans: Who is Borrowing, and Why? 22 (Dec. 2006).
36 See § 1.4.1.2, *supra* (PLUS loans).
37 U.S. Gov't Accountability Office, Higher Education: Factors Lenders Consider in Making Lending Decisions for Private Education Loans, Report No. GAO-10-86R (Nov. 17, 2009).
38 *Id.*
39 *See generally* National Consumer Law Center, Paying the Price: The High Cost of Private Student Loans and the Dangers for Borrowers (Mar. 2008), *available at* www.studentloanborrowerassistance.org/uploads/File/Report_PrivateLoans.pdf.

40 *See* § 1.6, *supra* (federal loan eligibility requirements).
    Parent PLUS loan borrowers, in contrast, are required to meet certain creditworthiness standards.
41 *See* § 2.2, *supra*.
42 *See generally* Inst. for Higher Educ. Policy, Private Loans and Choice in Financing in Higher Education (2003), *available on* the companion website to this manual.
43 *See, e.g.*, Sam Kennedy, *School Steers Students to Backbreaking Loans*, The Morning Call, May 22, 2005, at A1.
    For a summary of 2010 rates for the major student lenders, see *Rates They Are A Changing* . . . , Student Lending Analytics Blog (July 1, 2010).
44 National Consumer Law Center, Paying the Price: The High Cost of Private Student Loans and the Dangers for Student Borrowers (Mar. 2008), *available at* www.studentloanborrowerassistance.org/uploads/File/Report_PrivateLoans.pdf.

worthy" co-signer. Private loans are also more flexible in allowing borrowers to obtain loans throughout the year as opposed to the limited time during each semester when federal loans are available.

A critical difference is the lack of certain protections for private loan borrowers. For example, students with private loans are not eligible for the same types of discharge options discussed in Chapter 9, *supra*. The same is true with regard to deferment and forbearance rights, all of which depend on the lender's policies and the terms of the loan contracts rather than on federal regulations.[45]

On the other hand, there are certain advantages for private loan borrowers. Unlike federal loan collections, there should be a statute of limitations for collection of private loans.[46] Private lenders have fewer collection tools.[47]

Private student loans are similar to most other unsecured credit products in terms of collection and consumer protections, with the very notable exception of bankruptcy rights. Previously, private loan borrowers were generally able to discharge their loans in bankruptcy. Due to changes in the bankruptcy law effective October 2005, the bankruptcy rules are now generally just as restrictive for private loans as for government loans.[48]

There are also differences in the way the products are regulated. The Higher Education Act has an extensive regulatory scheme that governs federal student loans. It is difficult, however, to find ways to privately enforce these provisions.[49]

Private student loans, in contrast, are generally regulated in the same way as most other types of credit. This means that there is a complex patchwork of federal and state oversight.[50]

In addition, because the HEA is so comprehensive, courts have found that it preempts many state laws.[51] This is not the case for private loans since the HEA does not apply to these products. However, national entities will often claim that they are not subject to state laws based on other preemption grounds.[52]

There are numerous claims that can be raised against private student lenders, such as those under the TILA, that are not available against federal lenders. However, some laws, such as the Fair Debt Collection Practices Act (FDCPA), apply equally to federal and private loans as long as third-party debt collectors are at issue.[53]

---

45 See § 11.7.2, *infra* (private student loan deferments and forbearances).
46 See § 11.8.3, *infra*.
   The elimination of the statute of limitations in the Higher Education Act applies only to federal loans. 20 U.S.C. § 1091a.
47 See § 11.6.3, *infra*.
48 See § 10.2.2.1, *supra*.
49 See § 12.5.2.1, *infra*.
50 See § 11.3, *infra*.
51 See § 12.5.3.4, *infra*.
52 See § 11.9.2.2, *infra* (preemption in the context of FTC Holder Rule claims).
53 See § 7.4.3, *supra*.

11.2.2 How to Tell If a Loan Is Federal or Private

The most reliable way to find out whether a loan is federal is to check the Department of Education's National Student Loan Data System (NSLDS).[54] Only federal loans will be listed in the data base. There is no comprehensive data base of private student loans.

There are other clues to help borrowers find out whether a loan is a private loan. A high interest rate, for example, is one clue that the loan may be a private one. Federal student loan interest rates are limited by law and, under current regulations, will not be higher than 8.5% (for Federal Family Education Loan Program PLUS loans, which are no longer being made).[55] A second clue lies in whether there is a co-signer on the loan. There are no co-signers on most federal loans. There are parent PLUS loans, which allow parents to take out loans on behalf of their children, but the parents are the primary obligors on these loans. Many private lenders, in contrast, require co-signers. If a borrower is a co-signer or knows that there is a co-signer on the loan, it is most likely a private student loan.

Another signal that it is a private loan is if a borrower has received TILA disclosures.[56] There are disclosures for federal loans, but these disclosures are not made pursuant to the TILA.[57] Sample private loan agreements can be found on the companion website to this manual.

11.3 Oversight of Private Student Loans

Oversight of private student lenders generally depends on which entity is making the loan. The most basic division at the federal level is between depository lenders, such as banks, and non-depositor lenders, such as finance companies. Depositories have traditionally been regulated by federal or state governments. Regulation of non-depositories is more recent and more limited. Another NCLC volume, *The Cost of Credit: Regulation, Preemption, and Industry Abuses*, has extensive information about the different types of creditors and regulatory entities.[58]

Until the credit crisis, when many lenders left the business, much of the private student lending was done by national banks, such as Citi and Wells Fargo. Some of these banks are still in existence and in some cases still making student loans.

---

54 See www.nslds.ed.gov; § 1.9, *supra*.
55 See § 2.3, *supra* (interest rates and federal student loans).
56 See § 11.4, *infra*.
57 See § 2.5, *supra*.
58 See generally National Consumer Law Center, The Cost of Credit: Regulation, Preemption, and Industry Abuses § 2.3 (4th ed. 2009 and Supp.).

SLM Corporation, commonly known as Sallie Mae, is one of the largest private lenders, selling products for all types of student borrowers. Congress created Sallie Mae in 1972 to provide a secondary market for student loans. Due to changes in the federal student loan industry, including the creation of the government's Direct Loan program in the 1990s, Sallie Mae ultimately won Congressional approval to become a fully private company.[59] By 2004, Sallie Mae had reached its goal of complete privatization and has dominated the federal and private student lending sectors.[60]

For many years, Sallie Mae funded much of its private lending through sales of asset-backed securities. As the securitization market dried up during the credit crisis and many Sallie Mae securitizations did not perform well, Sallie Mae began to originate an increasing number of loans through its bank. The bank was established in 2005 as a commercial bank supervised by the Federal Deposit Insurance Corporation (FDIC).[61]

The Dodd-Frank Wall Street Reform and Consumer Protection Act, effective July 21, 2011, will change the federal regulatory landscape considerably.[62] The Dodd-Frank changes are summarized in an issue of *NCLC REPORTS*[63] and will be examined in more detail in the forthcoming 2011 supplement to *The Cost of Credit: Regulation, Preemption, and Industry Abuses*.

The legislation created a new Consumer Financial Protection Bureau (CFPB) charged with protecting consumers across the board in the financial arena. The CFPB takes over rule-writing authority for all of the major consumer financial protection statutes, including the TILA and Fair Credit Reporting Act (FCRA), as well as new rule-writing authority for the FDCPA.[64] The CFPB also has authority to write rules to prevent unfair, deceptive, or abusive acts or practices (UDAAP) in connection with a broad array of consumer financial products and services, including private student loans.[65] The CFPA has specific rule-writing authority over private student lenders.[66] The Department of Education will retain jurisdiction over federal student lending.

There is no new private enforcement in the financial reform law. However, unfair and deceptive acts and practices as well as other state causes of action may be available for violations of the UDAAP rules. The CFPA rulemaking authority applies to virtually everyone in the financial services area, including private student lenders. The CFPA has full *enforcement* authority under numerous consumer protections statutes such as the TILA and the UDAAP rules over banks and credit unions with $10 billion or more in assets including all of their subsidiaries. Banking regulators will have enforcement power over smaller institutions.[67] The CFPA also has specific enforcement authority over certain non-banks, including those making private student lenders.[68]

There are also state regulatory authorities that are relevant for state lenders, including schools, in many cases. Some states have private loan programs that are regulated under specific laws and regulations and specifically exempt from other lending laws.[69] Internal school credit products may also be subject to state lending laws and regulations.[70]

11.4 Disclosures and Private Student Loans

11.4.1 Truth in Lending Disclosures

11.4.1.1 Introduction

Effective February 14, 2010, lenders making private student loans are required to provide special disclosures.[71] There are three sets of required disclosures: (1) application and solicitation; (2) loan approval; and (3) final disclosures.

---

59 *See generally* Erin Dillon, Leading Lady: Sallie Mae and the Origins of Today's Student Loan Controversy, Education Sector Reports (Educ. Sector May 2007), *available at* www.educationsector.org/usr_doc/SallieMae.pdf.

60 Sallie Mae has expanded into nearly every area of the student loan industry, often by acquiring other entities. For example, in 1999 Sallie Mae acquired Nellie Mae in order to begin originating student loans. It merged with USA Group in 2000 and acquired Student Loan Funding, increasing the company's loan portfolio by about 20%. A merger with a higher education consulting firm led to a greater presence in guarantee servicing and debt management. The company also acquired two collection agencies, General Revenue Corporation and Pioneer Credit Recovery, to help in its growing student loan collection business. For more information, see www.salliemae.com. Erin Dillon, Leading Lady: Sallie Mae and the Origins of Today's Student Loan Controversy, Education Sector Reports (Educ. Sector May 2007), *available at* www.educationsector.org/usr_doc/SallieMae.pdf.

61 For more information about the FDIC and other federal regulators, see National Consumer Law Center, The Cost of Credit: Regulation, Preemption, and Industry Abuses § 3.7 (4th ed. 2009 and Supp.).

62 Pub. L. No. 111-203, 124 Stat. 1376 (July 21, 2010).

63 29 NCLC REPORTS *Consumer Credit and Usury Ed.* 4–5 (July/Aug. 2010); 29 NCLC REPORTS, *Deceptive Practices and Warranties Editions* 4–5 (July/Aug. 2010).

64 Dodd-Frank Wall Street Reform and Consumer Protection Act Pub. L. No. 111-203, §§ 1002, 1022, 1089, 124 Stat. 1376 (July 21. 2010).

65 *Id.* § 1031.

66 Dodd-Frank Wall Street Reform and Consumer Protection Act, Pub. L. No. 111-203, § 1024, 124 Stat. 1376 (July 21. 2010).

67 *Id.* § 1026.
   As of 2010, Sallie Mae Bank had deposits well below $10 billion and so would not be under the enforcement authority of the CFPB.

68 Dodd-Frank Wall Street Reform and Consumer Protection Act, Pub. L. No. 111-203, § 1024, 124 Stat. 1376 (July 21. 2010).

69 *See, e.g.*, N.Y. Educ. Law § 694-1(1).

70 *See* § 11.1.3, *supra*.

71 15 U.S.C. § 1638(e); Reg. Z, 12 C.F.R. § 226.46. *See* § 11.4.1.2, *infra* (discussing the definition of private student loans).

Each is subject to special timing rules and detailed form and content requirements. The Federal Reserve Board ("the Board") has created model forms. Sample notices are included in the Federal Register as well as on-line.[72]

In addition to the TILA student loan disclosures discussed in these sections, the Higher Education Opportunity Act of 2008 (HEOA) included several new substantive protections.[73] These include a self-certification form, which provides an overview of the cost of the education and the student's financial resources.[74] Perhaps most significantly, private student loan borrowers now have a right of cancellation.[75] Co-branding—the use by creditors who are not specifically endorsed by the educational institution of the name of the educational institution or symbols associated with the school, such as a school mascot—is restricted.[76] Borrowers must also be given at least thirty days from loan approval to accept a loan.[77]

11.4.1.2 Definitions and Scope

The HEOA eliminated the $25,000 TILA limit for private education loans, so that "private education loans" in any amount are covered.[78] "Private education loans" are defined in the TILA as loans provided by private educational lenders that are not made, insured, or guaranteed under Title IV of the Higher Education Act and are issued expressly for post-secondary educational expenses to a borrower, regardless of whether the loan is provided through the educational institution or directly to the borrower from the lender.[79]

"Private educational lenders" are defined as financial institutions and federal credit unions that solicit, make, or extend private education loans and any other person engaged in the business of soliciting, making, or extending private education loans.[80]

In the regulations, the Board did not provide a new definition of "private educational lender." Instead, the Board chose to use Regulation Z's existing regulation, which defines "creditor" as a person (A) who regularly extends consumer credit that is subject to a finance charge or is payable by written agreement in more than four installments (not including a down payment) and (B) to whom the obligation is initially payable, either on the face of the note or contract or by agreement when there is no note or contract.[81]

The category of private education loans does not include open-end credit or any loan secured by real property.[82] In the regulations, the Board also exempted credit for which the educational institution is the creditor if the term of the extension of credit is ninety days or less or an interest rate will not be applied to the credit balance and the term of the extension of credit is one year or less, even if the credit is payable in more than four installments.[83]

The exemptions for certain loans made by institutions were not in the proposed regulations but were later included in response to comments from educational institutions that they should not have to provide "burdensome" disclosures for "emergency" loans made to students. These institution-based exceptions apply only when the covered educational institution is the creditor and not when an institution-affiliated organization is the creditor.[84]

The official staff commentary to the regulations ("the commentary") clarifies the definition of private education loan. Loans extended for post-secondary educational expense incurred while a student is enrolled as well as loans extended to consolidate a consumer's preexisting private education loans are included in the category of private education loans.[85] The category of private education loans may also include extensions of credit that will be used for multiple purposes.[86] The commentary states that, if the consumer expressly indicates that the proceeds of the loan will be used to pay for post-secondary educational expenses by indicating the loan's purpose on an application, the loan will then be considered a private education loan.[87] Because a creditor might not know that this is the intended purpose, the commentary provides that creditors are not required to provide application/solicitation disclosures for multi-purpose loans.

If the consumer indicates that the loan will be used to pay for post-secondary education expenses, the creditor must calculate the information in the required disclosures based on the entire amount of the loan, even if only a part is intended for these expenses. The creditor may rely solely on a check-box or a purpose line on a loan application to determine the applicant's intent.[88] The Board decided to include multi-purpose loans despite industry objections, expressing concern that without these provisions creditors could avoid compliance by lending more than the amount a consumer needs for educational purposes.

---

72 74 Fed. Reg. 41,194 (Aug. 14, 2009). *See* www.federalreserve.gov/newsevents/press/bcreg/20090730a.htm.
　　The samples are also available in Appendix D, *infra*, and on the companion website to this manual
73 Pub. L. No. 110-315, § 1022 (2008).
74 15 U.S.C. § 1638(e)(3). *See* § 11.4.1.5, *infra*.
75 15 U.S.C. § 1638(e)(7). *See* § 11.4.1.6, *infra*.
76 15 U.S.C. § 1650(c).
77 15 U.S.C. § 1638(e)(6). *See* § 11.4.1.6, *infra*.
78 15 U.S.C. § 1603(3).
79 15 U.S.C. § 1650(a)(7).
80 15 U.S.C. § 1650(a)(6).
81 12 C.F.R. § 226.2(a)(17). *See generally* National Consumer

---

Law Center, Truth in Lending § 2.3 (6th ed. 2007 and Supp.).
82 15 U.S.C. § 1650(a)(7); Reg. Z, 12 C.F.R. § 226.46(b)(5)(iii).
83 Reg. Z, 12 C.F.R. § 226.46(b)(5)(iv).
84 Reg. Z, 12 C.F.R. § 226.46(b)(5)(iv). *See also* 74 Fed. Reg. 41194 (Aug. 14, 2009).
85 Official Staff Interpretations to Reg. Z, 12 C.F.R. Pt. 226, Supp. I, § 226.46(b)(5)(1).
86 Official Staff Interpretations to Reg. Z, 12 C.F.R. Pt. 226, Supp. I, § 226.46(b)(5)(2).
87 *Id.*
88 *Id.*

The HEOA provided that a depository institution or federal credit union would be covered for any private education loan it makes regardless of whether or not it regularly extended credit. The Board created an exception so that depository institutions and federal credit unions will be treated the same as other creditors and will only be required to comply with the private education loan rules if they regularly extend credit and otherwise meet the definition of "creditor" in TILA.[89]

11.4.1.3 Timing of Disclosures

There are three sets of required disclosures: (1) application and solicitation; (2) loan approval; and (3) final and separate timing provisions for each. The Board eliminated the previous timing rules that were set out in the special rules for student credit plans.[90] However, these timing rules remained in place for credit extensions made before the mandatory compliance date.

This change in timing should be an improvement for borrowers. Under the rules for interim student credit extensions, complete disclosures were required only at the time the creditor and consumer agreed upon a repayment schedule for the entire obligation.

The application or solicitation disclosures may be provided on or with the application or solicitation.[91] The term "solicitation" is defined as an offer of credit that does not require the consumer to complete an application. This also includes a "firm offer of credit" as defined in the Fair Credit Reporting Act.[92] Creditors may disclose this information orally in a telephone application or solicitation.[93] If the creditor does not provide oral disclosures, the creditor must provide the disclosures or place them in the mail no later than three business days after the consumer has applied for the credit. The Board created an exception so that creditors do not have to provide the application/solicitation disclosures if they deny the application or provide or place the approval disclosures in the mail no later than three business days after the consumer requests the credit.[94] The Board explained this exception as necessary to address circumstances in which creditors communicate approval of a loan at the time of application. According to the Board, consumers might be confused by receiving both the application and approval disclosures at the same time.[95]

Before consummation, the approval disclosures must be provided on or with any notice of approval given to the consumer.[96] Creditors may make limited changes to loan terms after approval without providing another thirty-day acceptance period.[97] The final disclosures must be provided after the consumer accepts the loan.[98] The cancellation right section prohibits the creditor from disbursing the funds until at least three business days after the consumer receives the final disclosures.[99]

11.4.1.4 Form and Content of Disclosures

11.4.1.4.1 Application disclosures

The application or solicitation disclosures must include information about interest rates. This is disclosed as a rate, or range of interest rates, and actually offered by the creditor at the time of application or solicitation.[100] If the rate will depend, in part, on a later determination of the consumer's creditworthiness or other factors, the disclosure must include a statement that the rate for which the consumer may qualify will depend on these factors.[101] The disclosure must also indicate whether the rate is fixed or variable, if the interest rate may increase after consummation, and the limits on the interest rate adjustments. In addition, the disclosure must state whether the interest rates typically will be higher if the loan is not co-signed or guaranteed.[102]

The next section includes information about fees and default or late-payment costs, including an itemization of the fees or range of fees required to obtain the loan.[103] The fee information is followed by repayment terms, including a description of any payment deferral options and whether interest will accrue during deferral periods.[104] If there are no deferral options, the creditor must disclose that fact.[105] The disclosure also includes a statement that, if the consumer files for bankruptcy, the consumer may still be required to pay back the loan.[106]

---

89 74 Fed. Reg. 41194 (Aug. 14, 2009).
90 12 C.F.R. § 226.17(i); Official Staff Interpretations to Reg. Z, 12 C.F.R. § 226.17(i)–(1),(2).
91 12 C.F.R. § 226.46(d)(1)(i).
92 *Id.*
93 12 C.F.R. § 226.46(d)(1)(ii).
94 *Id.*
95 74 Fed. Reg. 41194 (Aug. 14, 2009).
96 12 C.F.R. § 226.46(d)(2).
97 See § 11.4.1.6, *infra*.
98 12 C.F.R. § 226.46(d)(3).
99 12 C.F.R. § 226.48(d). See § 11.4.1.6, *infra*.
100 Reg. Z, 12 C.F.R. § 226.47(a)(1).
101 *Id.*
102 Reg. Z, 12 C.F.R. § 226.47(a)(1)(ii)–(iv).
    The proposed rules required the creditor to state whether a co-signer was required. 74 Fed. Reg. 12464 (Mar. 24, 2009).
    The Board eliminated this provision because of the Equal Credit Opportunity Act regulation that prohibits creditors from requiring co-signers unless certain conditions are met. Instead, creditors will have to disclose in the private loan disclosures whether interest rates typically will be higher without a co-signer. This does not seem particularly useful as presumably most consumers know that rates are likely to be lower with a co-signer.
103 Reg. Z, 12 C.F.R. § 226.47(a)(2).
104 Reg. Z, 12 C.F.R. § 226.47(a)(3).
105 *Id.*
106 Reg. Z, 12 C.F.R. § 226.47(a)(3)(iv).

The disclosure includes cost estimates, including an example of the total cost of the loan calculated as the total of payments over the term of the loan using the highest rate of interest disclosed and including all finance charges applicable to loans at that rate.[107] The regulations require creditors to use an amount financed of $10,000, or $5000 if the creditor only offers loans of this type for less than $10,000, and calculations must be provided for each payment option.[108]

The second page of the sample form includes additional information about federal loan alternatives and eligibility for loans. This disclosure also informs the consumers that, before the loan may be consummated, the consumer must complete the self-certification form.[109] The creditors must provide a statement that the consumer may qualify for federal student financial assistance, the interest rates available under each program and whether the rates are fixed or variable, a statement that the consumer may obtain additional information from the school or the Department of Education website, and a statement that a school may have school-specific education loan benefits and terms not detailed on the disclosure form.[110]

Creditors are excused from providing the disclosures with application or solicitation for a multi-purpose loan.[111] Creditors also need not provide the disclosures if the loan application is made over the telephone, the loan is approved at the time of application, and the creditor timely provides the approval disclosures.[112] Creditors also need not provide the disclosures if the loan is denied.[113]

11.4.1.4.2 Approval disclosures

The approval disclosures must include information about interest rates, including whether the rate is fixed or variable and if it may increase after consummation.[114]

Despite consumer advocates' objections, the final rules exempt private student loans from the requirement under the Truth in Lending Act that the APR be more prominent than other disclosures. The Board claimed, based on limited consumer testing, that consumers were confused when the APR was presented prominently along with a less prominent disclosure of the interest rate.[115] The sample disclosures include a box at the top similar to that on other TIL disclosures, but the box usually reserved for the APR is instead a box for the interest rate. The APR is disclosed less prominently below the box with the following explanation:

"The APR is typically different than the interest rate since it considers fees and reflects the cost of your loan as a yearly rate."

The approval disclosure also must include information about fees, repayment terms, and bankruptcy limits as described above for application disclosures.[116] The fees disclosure requires an itemization of the fees or range of fees required to obtain the loan.

These disclosures must also include an estimate of the total amount of payments calculated based on the applicable interest rate and the maximum possible rate of interest for the loan. If a maximum rate cannot be determined, the rate used must be 25%.[117]

Consumer advocates argued that creditors should be required to set a maximum rate. Instead, the Board required creditors, in cases in which no maximum rate can be determined, to include a statement that there is no maximum rate and that the monthly payment amount disclosed is an estimate and will be higher if the applicable interest rate increases.[118] As with the application disclosures, the approval disclosure also includes information about consumer rights and alternatives to private loans.[119]

11.4.1.4.3 Final disclosures

The content of the final disclosures are similar to the approval disclosures, with the addition of information about cancellation rights.[120] The sample form has a box at the top titled "Right to Cancel" and includes the following statement: "You have a right to cancel this transaction, without penalty, by midnight on DATE. No funds will be disbursed to you or to your school until after this time. You may cancel by calling us at [fill in number]."

11.4.1.5 Self-Certification

The creditor must obtain a self-certification form from the consumer or the school with information about cost of attendance, the expected family contribution, and estimated financial assistance.[121] The Department of Education explained in July 2009 that the form is intended to make borrowers aware of the amount they must borrow to cover any gaps in assistance before they get a private loan.[122] This form must be signed by the consumer, in written or electronic form, before consummation. Schools must provide the form directly to the consumer upon request. If the school has information required to complete the form the school

---

107 Reg. Z, 12 C.F.R. § 226.47(a)(4).
108 Id.
109 Reg. Z, 12 C.F.R. § 226.47(a)(8). See § 11.4.1.5, infra.
110 Reg. Z, 12 C.F.R. § 226.47(a)(6).
111 Reg. Z, 12 C.F.R. § 226.46(d)(1)(iii).
112 Reg. Z, 12 C.F.R. § 226.46(d)(1)(ii).
113 Id.
114 Reg. Z, 12 C.F.R. § 226.47(b)(1).
115 74 Fed. Reg. 41194 (Aug. 14, 2009).
116 Reg. Z, 12 C.F.R. § 226.47(b).
117 Reg. Z, 12 C.F.R. § 226.47(b)(3)(vii)(B).
118 Reg. Z, 12 C.F.R. § 226.47(b)(3)(vii).
119 Reg. Z, 12 C.F.R. § 226.47(b)(4)–(5).
120 Reg. Z, 12 C.F.R. § 226.47(c).
121 Reg. Z, 12 C.F.R. § 226.48(e).
122 74 Fed. Reg. 37,432 (July 28, 2009).

must provide such information.[123] The Department of Education issued an approved self-certification form in February 2010.[124]

The commentary notes that the self-certification rule applies only to loans that will be used for post-secondary educational expenses while the student is attending an institution of higher education as defined in the Truth in Lending Act. Therefore, it does not apply to all covered educational institutions and does not apply to consolidation loans.[125]

It is unclear how useful this self-certification form will be. Initially, Congress considered a proposal that would require mandatory school certification of all private student loans.[126] The self-certification concept was adopted instead. Among other problems, the TILA specifically exempts creditors from liability for any violations related to the self-certification provisions.[127]

11.4.1.6 Cancellation and Thirty-Day Waiting Period

The borrower has the right to accept the terms of a loan at any time within thirty calendar days following the date on which the consumer receives the approval disclosures.[128] With only a few exceptions described below, the creditor may not change the disclosed terms prior to the earlier of the date of disbursement or the expiration of the thirty-day period if the consumer has not accepted the loan within that time frame.

A creditor may withdraw an offer before consummation if the credit would be prohibited by law or if the creditor has reason to believe that the consumer has committed fraud in connection with the loan application.[129] The creditor may also change the interest rate based on adjustments to the index used for a loan, change the interest rate and terms if this will unequivocally benefit the consumer, or reduce the loan amount based upon a certification or other information received from the institution or consumer that the cost of attendance has decreased or the consumer's other financial aid has increased.[130] If the creditor changes the terms under these exceptions, no new disclosures are required and there is no requirement to provide a new thirty-day period to accept. In addition, the consumer may request a change and the creditor may accommodate it. In that case, the creditor must once again provide the approval disclosures and thirty days to accept.[131]

The consumer also has a right to cancel the loan, without penalty, until midnight of the third business day following the date on which the consumer receives the final disclosures. No funds may be disbursed until the three-day period has expired.[132]

11.4.1.7 Remedies

Actions for violations involving private education loans may be brought one year from the date on which the first regular payment of principal is due under the loan.[133] There is a private right of action for several, but not all, of the approval and consummation disclosure requirements.[134] The Board also added the new private loan right of cancellation to the TILA rescission remedies section.[135] Lenders are not liable for failure to comply with the provisions regarding self-certification.[136]

11.4.2 HEA Disclosures and Private Loans

There are a number of private loan-related disclosures that schools must provide. Institutions that provide information regarding private education loans must provide these disclosures regardless of whether the school participates in a preferred-lender arrangement. Schools must provide the information required in the TILA disclosures discussed above, information about the availability of federal loans or other assistance, and a statement that the terms and conditions of federal loans or assistance may be more beneficial than the terms and conditions of private education loans.[137]

The schools are also required to provide self-certification forms to enrolled or admitted students, as discussed in § 11.4.1.5, *supra*.

11.5 Fair Billing and Other Servicing Issues

Private loan borrower rights to fair billing and accounting statements are not as clear as for federal loans. The Truth in Lending Act's (TILA) fair billing provisions apply only to open-end credit.[138] There is another TILA provision that

---

123 34 C.F.R. §§ 601.11(d), 668.14(b)(29).
124 *See* U.S. Dep't of Educ., Education Loan Applicant Self-Certification Form, Dear Colleague Letter GEN-10-01 (Feb. 14, 2010).
125 Official Staff Commentary to Reg. Z, 12 C.F.R. Pt. 226, Supp. I, § 226.48(e)(1).
126 This proposal may be considered when the new Consumer Financial Protection Bureau begins its mandate. Most private loans are under the jurisdiction of the CFPB. *See* § 11.3, *supra*.
127 15 U.S.C. § 1640(j). *See* § 11.4.1.7, *infra*.
128 12 C.F.R. § 226.48(c).
129 12 C.F.R. § 226.48(c)(3).
130 *Id.*
131 12 C.F.R. § 226.48(c)(4).
132 12 C.F.R. § 226.48(d).
133 15 U.S.C. § 1640(e).
134 The requirements are added at 15 U.S.C. § 1640(a).
135 15 U.S.C. § 1640(a)(3).
136 15 U.S.C. § 1640(j) (exemption from liability for creditors once mandatory compliance begins).
137 34 C.F.R. § 601.11(a)–(b).
138 *See generally* National Consumer Law Center, Truth in Lending § 5.8 (6th ed. 2007 and Supp.).

requires servicers to provide consumers with the name, address, and telephone number of the owner of the debt.[139] Other federal laws may apply in certain circumstances. For example, the Fair Debt Collection Practices Act requires collectors to give consumers a validation notice setting forth the consumer's right to dispute the debt or any portion of it and to require the creditor to identify the original creditor.[140] However, these rights apply after the debt has already been sent to collection. Common law claims might also be used. There may be an opportunity for additional regulations regarding private loan servicing through the new Consumer Financial Protection Bureau (CFPB).[141]

11.6 Default and Delinquency and Private Student Loans

11.6.1 The Problem of Private Student Loan Defaults

Private student loan default rates were relatively low for a number of years. Among other reasons, many companies had liberal forbearance policies that hid the extent of borrower repayment problems.[142] The private student loan industry began to crash in 2008 as defaults ballooned and overall economic conditions deteriorated.[143] Moody's acknowledged in early 2010 that the high default rates for private loan securitizations reflected weak underwriting, referring in this case to the 2006–2007 period.[144] In July 2010, Sallie Mae acknowledged that the charge-offs for private loans remained high and that the company had raised loan loss provisions for 2010 by $100 million to $1.3 billion, reflecting higher than expected defaults.[145] A large portion of the defaulted loans went to "non-traditional" students or those attending "non-traditional" schools.[146]

11.6.2 Default Triggers for Private Loans

Default conditions for private student loans are specified in the loan contracts. In most cases, borrowers will not have the luxury of a nine-month period if they miss payments on a private student loan. Private loans may go into default as soon as one payment is missed.

The loan contract may specify other conditions for default. A promissory note used by KeyBank, for example, listed the following default triggers:

> You are in default if you:
> - Fail to make monthly payments when due, or
> - Die, or
> - Break other promises in the Loan Note, or
> - Begin a bankruptcy proceeding, or assign assets for the benefit of creditors, or
> - Provide any false written statement in applying for any Loan subject to the terms of this Note or at any time during the term of the Loan, or
> - Become insolvent, or
> - In the lender's judgment, experience a significant lessening of your ability to repay.[147]

The clause triggering default if a consumer files bankruptcy is particularly troubling. It is similar to the universal default clauses previously used in many credit card agreements.[148] This should be an issue for the new CFPB to consider regulating.[149]

11.6.3 Collection of Defaulted Private Student Loans

Private student loan creditors do not have the same range of powerful collection tools as the government.[150] Generally, they hire third-party debt collectors to pressure borrowers to pay. As with collectors of federal loans, these agencies are subject to fair debt laws.[151] If unsuccessful with private debt collectors or if they choose not to use collectors, the creditors can sue and attempt to obtain judgments. If this occurs, borrowers have exemption rights under state laws.[152] The main difference between private student loans and other unsecured debts is the heightened bankruptcy dischargeability standards for private loans.[153]

---

139 15 U.S.C. § 1641(f)(2).
140 15 U.S.C. § 1692g.
141 *See* § 11.3, *supra*.
142 *See generally* National Consumer Law Center, Too Small to Help: The Plight of Financially Distressed Private Student Loan Borrowers (Apr. 2009), *available at* www.studentloanborrowerassistance.org/uploads/File/TooSmalltoHelp.pdf.
143 *See* § 11.1.1, *supra*.
144 *Moody's Outlook for Student Loan Securities: Expect Negative Credit Trends for Private Loans in 2010*, Student Lending Analytics Blog (Jan. 29, 2010).
145 *What Ails Sallie Mae*, Student Lending Analytics Blog (July 21, 2010).
146 *See* § 11.1.1, *supra*.

147 *See generally* National Consumer Law Center, Too Small to Help: The Plight of Financially Distressed Private Student Loan Borrowers (Apr. 2009), *available at* www.studentloanborrowerassistance.org/uploads/File/TooSmalltoHelp.pdf.
148 *See generally* National Consumer Law Center, The Cost of Credit: Regulation, Preemption, and Industry Abuses § 11.8.3.2.2 (4th ed. 2009 and Supp.).
149 *See* § 11.3, *supra*.
150 *See* Ch. 7, *supra*.
151 *See* § 7.4.3, *supra*.
152 For more information about exemption laws, see National Consumer Law Center, Collection Actions Ch. 12 (2008 and Supp.).
153 *See* Ch. 10, *supra*.

11.7 Relief for Private Student Loan Borrowers

11.7.1 General

Unlike the federal student loan programs, there is no comprehensive federal law requiring private student lenders to offer particular types of relief or flexible repayment. Private student loan borrowers are generally at the mercy of their creditors.

Unfortunately, private lenders have been generally inflexible in trying to assist financially distressed borrowers.[154] In the past, forbearance was the only option offered to these most distressed borrowers. However, many lenders have changed these policies more recently, sharply restricting forbearance availability.[155] Many lenders have also increased collection activity. Sallie Mae, for example, has announced steps to resolve higher risk accounts, including a more aggressive use of collection efforts.[156]

Some lenders claim that they are offering more options for financially distressed borrowers, particularly during the recession. Sallie Mae stated in 2010 that its private credit collections are conducted by a stand-alone consumer credit collections unit. They reported publicly that they had increased collection technology and practices in recent months, including policies to reduce reliance on forbearance as well as additional workout and settlement programs to help borrowers avoid default. There may be some additional flexibility, but creditors rarely if ever publicize the specific requirements for these options. They will generally consider relief only on a case-by-case basis.

Borrowers may have more explicit rights if the creditors promised particular relief in the loan agreements. This is why private student loan borrowers should be advised to get copies of their loan agreements.

Some common relief provisions are discussed in the following sections.

11.7.2 Private Loan Deferments and Forbearances

Unlike federal loans, there is no federal law requiring private student loan creditors or servicers to offer deferments or forbearances. In a 2008 study, the National Consumer Law Center surveyed private loan notes and found that most lenders provided an in-school deferment option.[157] However, interest generally accrued during this period, and borrowers were given the choice of paying the interest while in school or approving capitalization once they entered repayment. Since the economic crisis of 2008–2009, many lenders that are still offering private student loans are now requiring borrowers to pay interest while in school.

No forbearance rights were specified in nearly half of the loans in the NCLC survey.[158] Creditors may offer these plans, but they do not inform borrowers about available choices ahead of time in the loan notes. A number of lenders in the survey disclosed that they would charge fees to process forbearance and deferment requests. The fees were generally up to $50 for forbearances.

In the past, forbearance was the most common option offered to financially distressed private loan borrowers. Sallie Mae, for example, allegedly encouraged forbearance as a way of keeping delinquency rates lower.[159] These policies allowed the company to characterize loans of financially distressed borrowers as current. These policies have changed radically since 2008, as most creditors have sharply restricted forbearance availability.

In a 2009 report, Fitch Ratings described the prevalence of lenient forbearance policies throughout the industry.[160] The company noted that lenders began to impose more restrictive forbearance criteria starting in 2008 after realizing that the economic downturn would have a more prolonged impact on a borrower's ability to repay.[161]

More recently, Sallie Mae claimed that it is applying far more analysis to forbearance requests to make sure that borrowers are both committed to repaying their debt and have the actual ability to benefit from forbearance.[162] Other lenders claim to have adopted similar policies.

Student Loan Corporation announced in public filings that the Office of the Comptroller of the Currency reviewed forbearance polices on private student loans and recommended a number of proposed changes, including more rigorous requirements for participation in forbearance and loss mitigation programs, shorter forbearance periods, and

---

154 *See generally* National Consumer Law Center, Too Small to Help: The Plight of Financially Distressed Private Student Loan Borrowers (Apr. 9, 2009), *available at* www.studentloanborrowerassistance.org/uploads/File/TooSmalltoHelp.pdf.

155 *See* § 11.7.2, *infra*.

156 Paul Basken, *Sallie Mae Reports $159-Million Loss and More Delinquencies by Borrowers*, Chron. of Higher Educ., Oct. 23, 2008.

157 National Consumer Law Center, Paying the Price: The High Cost of Private Student Loans and the Dangers for Student Borrowers (Mar. 2008), *available at* www.studentloanborrowerassistance.org/uploads/File/Report_PrivateLoans.pdf.

158 *Id.*

159 *See, e.g., In re* SLM Corp. Secs. Litig., 2010 WL 3783749 (S.D.N.Y. Sept. 24, 2010) (denying Sallie Mae Corporation and Company Officer Albert Lord's motion to dismiss in shareholder litigation).

160 Fitch Ratings, Private Education Loans: Time for a Re-Education 6 (Jan. 28, 2009).

161 *Id.*

162 Paul Basken, *Sallie Mae Reports $159-Million Loss and More Delinquencies by Borrowers*, Chron. of Higher Educ., Oct. 23, 2008.

the requirement for minimum periods of payment performance between forbearance grants.[163]

11.7.3 Cancellations

Lenders, including nonprofit lenders, are generally not willing to cancel loans or offer reasonable settlements.[164] Private lenders generally do not discharge student loan debt upon death of the original borrower or co-signer. A number of loans in a 2008 NCLC study stated explicitly that there will be no cancellation if the borrower or co-signer dies or becomes disabled.[165]

At least some lenders claim to be changing these policies and offering cancellations in certain circumstances. Sallie Mae announced in 2010 that it had hired a company to administer claims under a new total and permanent disability provision on private education loans.[166] This provision applies only to the Smart Option Student Loans. The company also announced that it would forgive any unpaid balance in the event of a primary borrower's death. It is unclear whether this policy is being administered consistently.

It is also difficult to negotiate private student loan modifications. In general, rather than focusing on working with borrowers, lenders have described efforts to ratchet up collection. Sallie Mae, for example, has announced steps to resolve higher risk accounts, including a more aggressive use of collection efforts.[167] In an April 2009 report, NCLC documented increasingly aggressive private student loan collection efforts and creditor failure to offer flexible options or loan modifications to assist financially distressed borrowers.[168] Some lenders have been more flexible during the recession, but they generally do not publicly disclose these policies. Modifications are offered on a case-by-case basis.

11.7.4 Private Student Loan Ombudsman

The Dodd-Frank financial reform legislation of 2010 includes a provision creating a new private education loan ombudsman.[169] This program is intended to provide timely assistance to borrowers of private education loans.

The office is required to disseminate information about the availability and functions of the ombudsman to borrowers and potential borrowers as well as to institutions of higher education, lenders, guaranty agencies, loan servicers, and other participants in private education student loan programs. Its functions include the following:

1. Receive, review, and attempt to resolve informal complaints from borrowers of loans, including, as appropriate, attempts to resolve such complaints in collaboration with the Department of Education and with institutions of higher education, lenders, guaranty agencies, loan servicers, and other participants in private education loan programs;
2. Not later than ninety days after the designated transfer date, establish a memorandum of understanding with the federal student loan ombudsman to ensure coordination in providing assistance to and serving borrowers seeking to resolve complaints related to their private education or Federal student loans;
3. Compile and analyze data on borrower complaints regarding private education loans; and
4. Make appropriate recommendations to the Director, the Secretary, the Secretary of Education, the Committee on Banking, Housing, and Urban Affairs and the Committee on Health, Education, Labor, and Pensions of the Senate and the Committee on Financial Services and the Committee on Education and Labor of the House of Representatives.

The private loan ombudsman is also required to prepare an annual report that describes the activities and evaluates the effectiveness of the ombudsman during the preceding year.

11.8 Defenses in Private Student Loan Collection Actions

11.8.1 General Contract Defenses

The contract defenses discussed in Chapter 7, *supra*, apply in private student loan collection actions as well. A borrower's obligation to pay a student loan is conditioned upon the loan agreement being enforceable under basic contract principles—in which forgery, mistake, and fraud are defenses—that affect a borrower's obligation on any note.[170]

---

163 *See OCC Tightens Forbearance Policies on Private Student Loans*, Student Lending Analytics Blog (Jan. 19, 2010).
164 *See generally* National Consumer Law Center, Too Small to Help: The Plight of Financially Distressed Student Loan Borrowers (Apr. 2009), *available at* www.studentloanborrowerassistance.org/uploads/File/TooSmalltoHelp.pdf.
165 National Consumer Law Center, Paying the Price: The High Cost of Private Student Loans and the Dangers for Student Borrowers (Mar. 2008), *available at* www.studentloanborrowerassistance.org/uploads/File/Report_PrivateLoans.pdf.
166 *See* News Release, Securian Co., Securian Wins Contract for Administering Total and Permanent Disability Claims on Private Student Loans (Mar. 8, 2010), *available at* http://securian.mediaroom.com/index.php?s=43&item=223.
167 Paul Basken, *Sallie Mae Reports $159-Million Loss and More Delinquencies by Borrowers*, Chron. of Higher Educ., Oct. 23, 2008.
168 National Consumer Law Center, Too Small to Help: The Plight of Financially Distressed Private Student Loan Borrowers (Apr. 2009), *available at* www.studentloanborrowerassistance.org/uploads/File/TooSmalltoHelp.pdf.

169 Pub. L. No. 111-203, § 1035.
170 *See* § 7.5.4.1, *supra*.

11.8.2 Infancy

The only common law contract defense not available to federal student loan borrowers is infancy. However, this defense is available for private student loans. The defense is well entrenched in the American legal system even though it does not apply to federal student loans. However, legislative actions by states have created exceptions that limit the availability and efficacy of the affirmative defense of infancy.

While some states include contracts for necessaries within the class of contracts that may be disaffirmed,[171] a number of jurisdictions have enacted laws that prohibit minors from disaffirming contracts for necessaries.[172] In a number of states, individuals who have attained the status of emancipated minors take on the status of adults with respect to the formation of and liability for contracts.[173] Most of these provisions specifically provide that emancipated minors may enter into binding contracts and that they can sue or be sued.

A handful of states provide that minors who are married are no longer under a disability to make enforceable contracts due to minority and that such contracts are not subject to being disaffirmed or invalidated on the basis of infancy.[174] In addition, many states' laws provide that minors who have reached a certain age may contract for various types of insurance.

Some states have carved out a statutory exception to the infancy doctrine when a minor misrepresents his or her age when entering into a contract. These laws require some measure of reliance, as they state that the other party to the contract must have had "good reasons to believe" that the minor was capable of contracting.[175] Even in states that do not have statutes limiting the infancy defense, such limitation has been imposed in numerous jurisdictions.[176]

A number of states have laws that specifically address the issue of minors contracting for educational loans. Some of these provide that written obligations entered into by minors, usually at least sixteen years of age, to further education are enforceable as long as the person making the loan has a certification from the school that the minor is enrolled or has been accepted for enrollment.[177] Others have more general limits on the infancy defense for education loans. However, many of these laws apply only to specific loan programs, in some cases not to private loans, but only to loans made by the state guaranty agencies.[178]

---

171 Iowa Code Ann. § 599.2; Kan. Stat. Ann. § 38-102; Utah Code Ann. § 15-2-2; Wash. Rev. Code § 26.28.030.

172 See, e.g., Cal. Fam. Code § 6712 (West); Ga. Code Ann. § 13-3-20(b); Idaho Code Ann. § 32-104; La. Civ. Code Ann. art. 1923; Mont. Code Ann. § 41-1-305; N.D. Cent. Code § 14-10-12; Okla. Stat. tit. 15, § 20; S.C. Code Ann. § 63-5-310; S.D. Codified Laws § 26-2-4.

173 See, e.g., Alaska Stat. § 09.55.590(g); Cal. Fam. Code § 7050(e) (West); Ga. Code Ann. § 13-3-20(b); La. Civ. Code Ann. art. 1922; Nev. Rev. Stat. § 129.010; N.M. Stat. Ann. § 32A-21-5; Tenn. Code Ann. § 29-31-105; Tex. Fam. Code Ann. § 31.006 (Vernon); Va. Code Ann. § 16.1-334(2)–(3).

174 See, e.g., Ariz. Rev. Stat. Ann. § 44-131(B); Fla. Stat. Ann. § 743.01; Idaho Code Ann. § 32-101(3); Kan. Stat. Ann. § 38-101.

175 Iowa Code Ann. § 599.3; Kan. Stat. Ann. § 38-103; Utah Code Ann. § 15-2-3; Wash. Rev. Code Ann. § 26.28.040. See also La. Civ. Code Ann. art. 1924 ("The mere representation of majority by an unemancipated minor does not preclude an action for rescission of the contract. When the other party reasonably relies on the minor's representation of majority, the contract may not be rescinded.").

176 See, e.g., Carney v. Southland Loan Co., 88 S.E.2d 805 (Ga. Ct. App. 1955) (when minor induced loan company to finance purchase of automobile by fraudulently misrepresenting age as 22, and loan company relied upon such misrepresentation in good faith, buyer was estopped from repudiating contract and loan company was entitled to recover on cross-complaint for unpaid balance); Monasquan Sav. & Loan Ass'n v. Mayer, 236 A.2d 407 (N.J. Super. Ct. App. Div. 1967) (when borrower misrepresented age in application for loan, infancy was no defense in mortgage foreclosure proceedings). But see Doenges-Long Motors, Inc. v. Gillen, 328 P.2d 1077 (Colo. 1958) (minor has absolute right to disaffirm contract but is liable for damages flowing from tortious act); Gillis v. Whitley's Discount Auto Sales, Inc., 319 S.E.2d 661 (N.C. Ct. App. 1984) (minor's alleged misrepresentation of age does not bar him from disaffirming contract even when fraudulent; minor may recover whatever consideration he paid but must restore what benefit he has under contract, namely automobile). See generally Annot., Infant's misrepresentation as to his age as estopping him from disaffirming his voidable transaction, 29 A.L.R.3d 1270 (1970).

177 This provision is derived from the Model Minor Student Capacity to Borrow Act. See, e.g., Alaska Stat. § 14.43.140; Ariz. Rev. Stat. Ann. § 44-140.01; Mich. Comp. Laws § 600.1404(2); N.J. Stat. Ann. § 9:17A-2 (West); N.M. Stat. Ann. § 58-6-3(B); N.D. Cent. Code § 41-10.2-02; Okla. Stat. tit. 15, § 33; Or. Rev. Stat. § 348.105; Wash. Rev. Code Ann. § 26.30.020.

178 These laws include: Ala. Code § 26-1-5 (age of majority for purposes of contracting for educational loans for college level education and above is seventeen years of age); Ark. Code Ann. § 23-47-509; Fla. Stat.§ 743.05 (for purpose of borrowing money for their own higher educational expenses, disability of non-age of minors is removed for all persons who have reached sixteen years of age; valid only if interest rate exceeds prevailing interest rate for federal Guaranteed Student Loan Program); Ga. Code Ann. § 13-3-23; Haw. Rev. Stat. § 304A-603 (Michie); Ind. Code § 21-16-3-1 (title refers to Guaranteed Student Loans); Kan. Stat. Ann. § 72-7406 (provision is part of Higher Education Student Loan Guarantee Act and refers to certain programs administered by state board of regents); Ky. Rev. Stat. Ann. § 164.756 (West); Me. Rev. Stat. Ann. tit. 33, § 52 (refers to any minor sixteen years of age or over who receives certain aid and assistance from New England Higher Education Assistance Foundation); Me. Rev. Stat. Ann. tit. 20, § 11462 (refers to state Higher Education Loan Program); Mich. Comp. Laws § 390.958 (refers to loans guaranteed by state Higher Education Assistance Authority); Mo. Rev. Stat. § 431.067; Mont. Code Ann. § 41-1-303; N.H. Rev. Stat. Ann. § 193:26; N.Y. Educ. Law §§ 281, 681 (McKinney) (refers to loans made under state Higher Education Services Corporation), 693(11) (refers to loans made under state Higher Education Services Corporation); N.C. Gen. Stat. § 116-174.1 (applies to all minors in North Carolina seventeen years of age and upwards and only to

11.8.3 Statute of Limitations Is A Defense in Private Student Loan Cases

The elimination of the statute of limitations applies to collection by government agencies and their agents. The statute specifically applies to institutions collecting federal grant or work assistance refunds; guaranty agencies that have agreements with the Department and are collecting federal loans; institutions that have agreements with the Department and are collecting government loans; and the Secretary of Education, Attorney General, or administrative head of another federal agency to collect government grants and loans.[179]

Collection of private student loans is not covered. Thus, statutes of limitations should apply in these cases. The relevant statute depends on state law.[180] The elimination of the statute of limitations for federal loans also does not specifically apply to state agencies or state loans. However, state entities suing to collect student loans may also be able to avoid statutes of limitations if state law or state constitutions provide such protection. A state entity may not be able to escape time limits if it is merely administering a private loan fund rather than collecting a public debt.[181]

11.8.4 Defenses for Service Members

The Servicemember Civil Relief Act (SCRA) limits collection tactics and enforcement of claims against active duty military personnel.[182] In general, everyone on active duty is entitled to the benefit of the Act, whether or not they are stationed in a war zone and whether they enlisted or were called up. Active duty includes full-time training duty, annual training duty, and attendance at a military school while in active military service.[183]

The interest rate protections under the Act also apply to federal and private student loans.[184] The Act requires that creditors reduce the interest rate to 6% on any obligation incurred by a service member before active duty.[185] The reduction lasts as long as the service member is on active duty.

11.9 School-Related Claims and Defenses

11.9.1 General

For years, lenders fought to get into the largely unregulated private student loan industry. During this time, an alliance developed between unlicensed and unaccredited schools and mainstream banks and lenders.[186] The creditors did not just provide high-interest private loans to students to attend unscrupulous schools; they actually sought out the schools and partnered with them, helping to lure students into scam operations. Then, like subprime mortgage providers, these creditors made huge profits on these loans by securitizing them and shifting the risky debt onto unsuspecting investors.

Affected consumers have been hit particularly hard. They are stuck with debts they cannot repay from worthless schools. Lenders that poured resources into scamming students have spared no expense in trying to silence students who fight back by making it difficult for students to bring lawsuits in convenient forums, by mandating arbitration, and by claiming that state laws do not apply to them.

As discussed in detail in Chapter 12, *infra*, there are many claims borrowers can raise directly against schools that have harmed them. However, these cases generally do not resolve the underlying and often most important issue of loan debt. Chapter 12 reviews the claims that can be brought against proprietary schools. Chapter 12 also focuses on ways to hold federal student loan lenders liable for school-related claims and defenses. Much of this discussion, as described in Chapter 12, applies to private student loans as well. The

---

enter into written contracts of indebtedness, at a rate of interest not exceeding contract rate authorized in Chapter 24 of General Statutes); 24 Pa. Cons. Stat. Ann. § 5105 (refers to loans made by state Higher Education Assistance Agency); R.I. Gen. Laws §§ 16-57-9(a) (provision refers to loans made by state Higher Education Assistance Authority), 16-62-8 (refers to loans made by state Student Loan Authority); S.C. Code Ann. § 63-5-320; S.D. Codified Laws § 13-56-4 (refers to loans made under Higher Education Loan Guaranty Program); Vt. Stat. Ann. tit. 16, § 2866 (refers to loans made under state Education Loan Program); Va. Code Ann. § 8.01-278(B); Wis. Stat. Ann. § 39.32(4) (provision refers to loans administered by state Higher Educational Aids Board).

179 20 U.S.C. § 1091a(a).
180 *See, e.g.*, Education Res. Inst., Inc. v. Yokoyama, 2008 WL 3906834 (Cal. Ct. App. Aug. 26, 2008) (applying six-year state "promissory note" statute of limitations in private student loan case).
181 *See* State *ex. rel.* Board of Regents for the Univ. of Okla. v. Livingston, 111 P. 3d 734 (Okla. Civ. App. 2005) (although state constitution provides that no statute of limitations applies when state is collecting a debt, court held that university was merely administering a private loan fund, not enforcing a public right, and was thus subject to a statute-of-limitations defense).
182 50 U.S.C. App. §§ 501–596. *See generally* National Consumer Law Center, Collection Actions Ch. 7 (2008 and Supp.).
183 For a discussion of service members protected by the Act, see National Consumer Law Center, Collection Actions § 7.4 (2008 and Supp.). *See* § 7.5.4.5, *supra*.
184 20 U.S.C. § 1078(d). *See* § 2.3, *supra*.
185 50 U.S.C. App. § 527.
186 An example is ongoing litigation against Silver State Helicopters. *See* Pinnacle Law Group, Pinnacle Law Group Files Class Action on Behalf of Students Against Keybank for Predatory Lending Practices in Connection with Failed Vocational School, Silver State Helicopters (May 12, 2008), *available at* www.pinnaclelawgroup.com/pdf/SSH-KeyBank_PressRelease.PDF.

following sections focus on unique issues that arise in attempting to hold private student lenders liable for school-related claims and defenses.

11.9.2 FTC Holder Rule

11.9.2.1 General

The Federal Trade Commission's Rule on Preservation of Consumer Claims and Defenses[187] ("FTC Holder Rule") addresses the issue of assignee and related creditor liability for seller misconduct.[188] The FTC Holder Rule operates by way of a notice placed in consumer credit agreements whereby, as a matter of the contract itself, the parties agree that the consumer can raise seller-related claims and defenses against the holder of the note or contract. Even if a transaction is beyond the scope of the rule, if the agreement contains the notice, the holder is subject to seller-related claims and defenses. In contrast, problems may arise, as discussed below, if the notice *should* have been inserted but is not in the agreement.

In general, the seller must insert the notice in consumer credit agreements whenever the seller is the originating creditor. In addition, the seller must arrange for the lender to insert the notice in the lender's credit agreement whenever the seller refers the consumer to the lender or otherwise has a business arrangement with the lender.

The FTC's Statement of Basis and Purpose for the Rule specifically states that it applies to vocational training.[189] The FTC Holder Rule applies to "sellers," broadly defined as sellers of goods or services to consumers,[190] thus covering for-profit vocational schools. Nevertheless, only sellers within the FTC's jurisdiction are covered by the FTC Holder Rule. Public entities and truly nonprofit corporations are not within the scope of the FTC Act,[191] and so these sellers are not required to place the notice in the contract.

The language of the FTC Holder Rule notice ("FTC Holder Notice") makes clear that consumers can raise not just defenses but also affirmative claims against the holder of a credit agreement. There is no limit as to which claims can be brought, including all claims available under state and other applicable law. However, there is a cap on recovery. A consumer cannot recover under the FTC Holder Rule more than the amount the consumer has paid on the loan plus cancellation of the remaining indebtedness. But there is no limit on creditor's liability for its own conduct.[192]

The main barrier in applying the FTC Holder Rule in private student loan cases are (1) if the lender includes the notice but attempts to contradict it with other language or (2) fails to include the notice, particularly if the lender argues that it is not required to do so.

11.9.2.2 When the Credit Agreement Contradicts the FTC Holder Notice

Of the private loans surveyed in NCLC's 2008 report, 90% of the loans that included the FTC Holder Notice also had language attempting to undermine it in some way. In most cases, these contradictory clauses stated that, if the student is dissatisfied with the school or fails to complete the course, the student still must repay the note in full. This directly contradicts the FTC Holder Notice, which explicitly allows borrowers to raise claims related to school closure or other school-related claims against lenders.[193]

Such a waiver should be no more effective than if it was written by the seller, and courts in most cases will not enforce such a term in the fine print of a standard form contract. Since it directly contradicts the FTC Holder Notice, the contract meaning is ambiguous and should be interpreted against the party drafting the contract. Courts have little trouble refusing to enforce such waivers as being in conflict with the FTC Holder Notice.[194] Moreover, the very attempt to so limit the federal notice is an unfair and deceptive practice in its own right and should be in violation of a state deceptive practices statute.[195]

11.9.2.3 When Notice Is Improperly Omitted from the Credit Agreement

Of the private loans surveyed in NCLC's 2008 report, nearly 40% of the loans did not include the FTC Holder Rule notice. It is counter-intuitive that a lender would be in a stronger position by violating a federal requirement than it would be by complying. But the failure to include the notice does complicate the question of the lender's liability for the school's misconduct.

---

187 16 C.F.R. Pt. 433.
188 The rule is discussed in detail in National Consumer Law Center, Unfair and Deceptive Acts and Practices § 11.6 (7th ed. 2008 and Supp.).
189 40 Fed. Reg. 53524 (Nov. 18, 1975). See also 41 Fed. Reg. 20024 (May 14, 1976) (staff guidelines).
190 16 C.F.R. § 433(1)(j).
191 National Consumer Law Center, Unfair and Deceptive Acts and Practices § 2.3.5 (7th ed. 2008 and Supp.).
192 Id. § 11.6.3.7. See also § 11.10, infra (direct liability in private student loan cases).
193 National Consumer Law Center, Paying the Price: The High Cost of Private Student Loans and the Dangers for Borrowers (Mar. 2008), available at www.studentloanborrowerassistance.org/uploads/File/Report_PrivateLoans.pdf.
   This issue was raised in a class action, Barnes v. SLM Financial Corp. The complaint is included in Appendix E, infra, and on the companion website to this manual.
194 See Alvarez v. Union Mortgage Co., 747 S.W.2d 484 (Tex. Ct. App. 1988). See also Mahaffey v. Investor's Nat'l Sec. Co., 747 P.2d 890 (Nev. 1987).
195 Heastie v. Community Bank, 727 F. Supp. 1133 (N.D. Ill. 1989).

There should be no question of the lender's liability when the school is the originating creditor that assigns the note to the lender.[196] UCC Article 9, adopted in all fifty states, makes the omitted FTC Holder Notice part of the contract as a matter of law, allowing the consumer to utilize the notice as if it were included.[197] Moreover, under the basic law of assignment, the assignee lender steps into the shoes of the assignor school and is subject to all school-related defenses.

Matters are more complicated when the school arranges a direct loan from a lender to the student. Revised UCC Article 3 has the same provision as Article 9, making the lender liable when the FTC Holder Notice is improperly omitted. Unfortunately, only Arkansas, Minnesota, South Carolina, and Texas have adopted this provision. However, a number of other states have statutes that allow consumers to raise seller-related claims and defenses against related lenders even if the FTC Holder Notice is omitted.[198]

In a few cases, the existence of the required FTC Holder Notice has been implied into the credit agreement,[199] but a number of courts in the context of guaranteed student loan programs have held otherwise.[200] These cases can be distinguished because the Department of Education had approved the loan agreements and was otherwise closely involved with the credit transaction. That is not the case with private student loans.

The FTC Holder Notice requires the seller, not the lender, to arrange the inclusion of the notice in the credit agreement. In addition, there is no private right of action for a violation of the FTC Act.[201] But it should be a violation of a state deceptive practices statute for a lender to draft a note knowing that it involves a violation of federal law, even if the violation is by a related seller.[202] Nevertheless, in some states issues around coverage may arise as to whether the lender's practice is within the scope of the deceptive practices statute.[203] Failing to comply with the FTC Holder Notice requirement may also lead to RICO liability,[204] or the lender's liability may be based upon the theory of agency, aiding and abetting, co-conspiracy, or close-connectedness.[205]

Thus in one case a federal court found that a national bank aided and abetted a for-profit school's state deceptive practices act violation when the bank was complicit in the school's failure to arrange for the FTC Holder Notice to be in the bank's credit agreement.[206] The students showed not only that the bank knew about the FTC Holder Rule violations but that it also provided substantial assistance or encouragement to the school. The court relied on allegations that the bank was aware that, if it permitted the notice to be included in the contracts, the bank would be unable to sell the loans in the secondary market. The plaintiffs alleged that the bank consciously avoided the FTC Holder Rule. The bank also provided substantial assistance to the school because it was the school's preferred lender and the bank helped create, review and approve the school's marketing regarding the loan product.

Nevertheless, the court found that the National Bank Act preempted this state law cause of action as brought against

---

196 See § 11.1.3, *supra*, for a discussion of school loan products.
197 U.C.C. §§ 9-403(d), 9-404(d).
198 *See* National Consumer Law Center, Unfair and Deceptive Acts and Practices § 11.6.5.2 (7th ed. 2008 and Supp.).
199 Gonzalez v. Old Kent Mortgage Co., 2000 U.S. Dist. LEXIS 14530 (E.D. Pa. Sept. 19, 2000); Anderson v. Central States Waterproofing (Minn. Dist. Ct. Hennepin Cnty. 1982), *available at* www.consumerlaw.org/unreported; Associates Home Equity Servs., Inc. v. Troup, 778 A.2d 529 (N.J. Super. Ct. App. Div. 2001). *See also* Xerographic Supplies Corp. v. Hertz Commercial Leasing Corp., 386 So. 2d 299 (Fla. Dist. Ct. App. 1980) (appellate court does not reach trial court's holding that FTC Holder Notice must be implied into contract). *But see* Vietnam Veterans of Am., Inc. v. Guerdon Indus., 644 F. Supp. 951 (D. Del. 1986) (declining to read absent FTC Holder Notice into contract); Crisomia v. Parkway Mortgage, Inc., 2001 Bankr. LEXIS 1469 (Bankr. E.D. Pa. Aug. 21, 2001); Hayner v. Old Kent Bank, 2002 Mich. App. LEXIS 190 (Mich. Ct. App. Feb. 12, 2002) (FTC Holder Rule places no duty upon lender who accepted contract without notice); Pratt v. North Dixie Manufactured Hous., Ltd., 2003 WL 21040658 (Ohio Ct. App. May 9, 2003) (unpublished) (finding no basis for holder liability when assigned contract did not include FTC Holder Notice).
200 Keams v. Tempe Technical Inst., Inc., 993 F. Supp. 714 (D. Ariz. 1997); Bartels v. Alabama Commercial Coll., 918 F. Supp. 1565 (S.D. Ga. 1995), *aff'd in part, rev'd in part, and remanded without op.*, 189 F.3d 483 (11th Cir. 1999); Armstrong v. Accrediting Council for Continuing Educ. & Training, Inc., 832 F. Supp. 419 (D.D.C. 1993), *vacated and remanded*, 84 F.3d 1452 (D.C. Cir. 1996) (table, text available at 1996 U.S. App. LEXIS 12241) (remanding for further consideration of whether to exercise jurisdiction over state claims), *on remand*, 950 F. Supp. 1 (D.D.C. 1996) (maintaining jurisdiction of pendent claims and finding case appropriate for declaratory relief), *on further remand*, 980 F. Supp. 53 (D.D.C. 1997) (determining that California law controls and inviting plaintiff to amend complaint to assert claims and defenses under California consumer protection laws), *aff'd*, 168 F.3d 1362 (D.C. Cir. 1999) (affirming district court's dismissal of claims); Jackson v. Culinary Sch. of Wash., 788 F. Supp. 1233 (D.D.C. 1992), *aff'd in part, rev'd and remanded in part*, 27 F.3d 573 (D.C. Cir. 1994) (on *de novo* review, reversing district court's decision to issue declaratory judgment on state law issues), *vacated*, 515 U.S. 1139 (1995) (appellate court should have used abuse of discretion standard to review district court's decision to issue declaratory judgment on state law issues), *on remand*, 59 F.3d 254 (D.C. Cir. 1995) (remanding for district court to exercise its discretion about whether to issue declaratory judgment on state law issues); Hernandez v. Alexander, 1992 U.S. Dist. LEXIS 21930 (D. Nev. May 18, 1992). *See* § 12.7.3, *infra*.
201 *See* National Consumer Law Center, Unfair and Deceptive Acts and Practices § 14.1 (7th ed. 2008 and Supp).
202 *See id.* § 11.6.4.4.
203 *Id.* § 11.6.4.4.4.
204 *Id.* § 11.6.4.5.
205 These theories are discussed in Chapter 12, *infra*, and in National Consumer Law Center, Unfair and Deceptive Acts and Practices § 11.6.5 (7th ed. 2008 and Supp.).
206 Kilgore v. Keybank, 2010 WL 1461577 (N.D. Cal. Apr. 12, 2010).

§ 11.9.2.4   Student Loan Law

a national bank. Section 11.9.2.4, *infra*, examines federal preemption issues when state law claims are brought against a national bank based upon the fact that the bank's credit agreements do not contain the required FTC Holder Notice.

11.9.2.4 National Bank Act Preemption of State Law Related to FTC Holder Rule Violations

As described in § 11.9.2.3, *supra*, the FTC Holder Rule requires that schools arrange for the FTC Holder Notice to be placed in a lender's credit agreement. When the notice is not included, there are various state law claims against the lender for this rule violation, even though the lender is not directly liable under the FTC Act for the violation. Nevertheless, national banks have claimed that the National Bank Act preempts the application of state law to the bank because the state law interferes with the bank's credit practices—in this case, its credit practice of offering credit without placing the notice in the loan agreement in violation of the FTC Holder Rule.

The issue of National Bank Act preemption of state law is a complex and evolving one beyond the scope of this manual. The Dodd-Frank Wall Street Reform and Consumer Protection Act, effective July 21, 2011, significantly limits such federal preemption of state law, effective with contracts entered into after July 21, 2010.[207] A state consumer financial law is preempted only if the law "prevents or significantly interferes with the exercise by the national bank of its powers."[208]

Federal preemption of state consumer law is examined in more detail in another NCLC manual, *National Consumer Law Center, The Cost of Credit: Regulation, Preemption, and Industry Abuses*.[209] The Dodd-Frank changes are summarized in an *NCLC REPORTS* article[210] and will be examined in more detail in *Cost of Credit*'s forthcoming 2011 supplement. This subsection examines, solely, several recent student loan cases on the topic, which may no longer be applicable to student loans consummated after July 21, 2010.[211]

Two Ohio federal district courts considered whether an Ohio statute could be applied to national banks when the statute makes lenders liable for seller-related claims and defenses even without inclusion of the required FTC Holder Notice. The more recent of the two decisions finds no preemption,[212] specifically ruling contrary to the older Ohio decision that found preemption.[213]

In a California federal court case, a national bank was found to have aided and abetted a for-profit vocational school in the school's deceptive practice of violating the FTC Holder Rule.[214] Nevertheless, the court dismissed the claim as preempted by the National Bank Act. The lender successfully argued that the injunctive relief demanded would effectively read the FTC Holder Rule notice into the promissory notes, thereby imposing a state law limitation on the terms of credit. The court stated that "it is difficult to conceive how Plaintiffs' action can survive in light of its clear interference with powers conferred on Key Bank by federal law"[215] This decision is on appeal to the Ninth Circuit.

11.10 Direct Claims Against Private Lenders

Private student lenders are subject to special TILA requirements.[216] Lenders may be sued and borrowers may obtain damages for violations of the TILA rules.[217] These lenders are also subject to Equal Credit Opportunity Act (ECOA) anti-discrimination provisions as well as ECOA notice and record-keeping requirements.[218] The U.S. Gov-

---

207 Pub. L. No. 111-203, § 1043 (July 21, 2010).
208 *Id.* § 1044.
209 National Consumer Law Center, The Cost of Credit: Regulation, Preemption, and Industry Abuses Ch. 3 (4th ed. 2009 and Supp.).
210 29 NCLC REPORTS, *Consumer Credit and Usury* 4–5 (July/Aug. 2010); 29 NCLC REPORTS, *Deceptive Practices and Warranties Editions* 4–5 (July/Aug. 2010).
211 Preemption changes go into effect on July 1, 2011, but apply to contracts entered into after July 1, 2010.
212 Blanco v. Keybank USA, 2005 WL 4135013 (N.D. Ohio Sept. 30, 2005).
213 Abel v. Keybank U.S.A., 313 F. Supp. 2d 720 (N.D. Ohio Mar. 3, 2004).
214 Kilgore v. Keybank, 2010 WL 1461577 (N.D. Cal. Apr. 12, 2010).
215 In a similar case also involving the same school, Silver State Helicopters, which closed and filed for bankruptcy, the court approved conditional certification of a class for settlement purposes. The court did not reach the substantive claims, such as NBA preemption. The settlement includes conditional and unconditional debt forgiveness based on the number of certifications that a student received, an early re-repayment refund, freeze on interest accrual, amended reports to credit reporting agency, and additional compensation to class representatives. Holman v. Student Loan Xpres, 2009 WL 4015573 (M.D. Fla. Nov. 19, 2009).
216 *See* § 11.4, *supra*.
217 *See, e.g.*, Rodriguez v. SLM Corp., 2009 WL 3769217 (D. Conn. Nov. 10, 2009) (dismissing TILA claims as beyond the statute of limitations; ruling against plaintiff's fraudulent concealment claims to toll the statute); Abel v. Keybank, 2005 WL 2216938 (N.D. Ohio Sept. 12, 2005) (awarding attorneys fees for TILA claims, the only claims that survived motion to dismiss).
  The complaint in another class action, Barnes v. SLM Financial Corp., raising TILA and other claims is included in Appendix E, *infra*, and on the companion website.
218 *See* Rodriguez v. SLM Corp., 2009 WL 598252 (D. Conn. Mar. 6, 2009) (denying SLM's motion to dismiss in ECOA discrimination case alleging that Sallie Mae charged unreasonably high private student loan interest rates and additional fees to minority borrowers compared to similarly-situated white borrowers). *See generally* National Consumer Law Center, Credit Discrimination (5th ed. 2009 and Supp.).

ernment Accountability Office found in a 2009 study that private lenders may use school-related factors in deciding on lending and to establish terms and conditions. They concluded that lenders generally view longer programs of study, high graduation rates, and low cohort rates on federal loans as more favorable conditions for lending.[219] These policies may have a disparate impact on protected classes. The federal credit reporting laws and fair debt collection practices laws also apply in private student loan cases.[220]

There are likely to be new federal provisions under the CFPB rule-making authority.[221] As part of its new authority, the CFPB has the authority to ban abusive products. To ban an act as abusive, the CFPA must find that the act or practice (1) materially interferes with a consumer's ability to understand a term or condition of a consumer financial product or service or (2) takes unreasonable advantage of (A) a consumer's lack of understanding of the material risks, costs, or conditions of the product or service; (B) a consumer's inability to protect his or her own interests when selecting or using a product or service; or (C) the consumer's reliance on someone covered under the Act.[222]

Private lenders may be held liable for engaging in deceptive marketing tactics. In 2006, for example, the United States Students Association filed a complaint with the FTC alleging that a private student loan company engaged in false and deceptive advertising practices designed to discourage customers from applying for federal grant and loan aid.[223]

Common law claims, including breach of contract, may also be raised.[224] State law claims should also be considered but, as discussed earlier in this section, national banks will likely argue that these state laws are preempted.[225] These state law claims may include usury claims. These claims are specifically preempted in federal student loan cases[226] but not in private student loan cases. State disclosure requirements are also preempted in federal student loan cases but not in private loan cases.[227]

Ensuring that assignees are liable is critical, as many private loans are assigned after origination and often securitized and sold to investor pools.[228]

---

219 U.S. Gov't Accountability Office, Higher Education: Factors Lenders Consider in Making Lending Decisions for Private Education Loans, Report No. GAO-10-86R (Nov. 17, 2009).

220 *See* §§ 7.4.3, *supra* (FDCPA), 12.5.2.4, *infra* (federal claims generally).

221 *See* § 11.3, *supra*.

222 Dodd-Frank Wall Street Reform and Consumer Protection Act, Pub. L. No. 111-203, § 1031(d), 124 Stat. 1376 (July 21. 2010).

223 A copy of the complaint is available at www.newamerica.net/files/FTC%20Complaint.pdf. *See also* Diana Jean Schemo, *Private Loans Deepen a Crisis in Student Debt*, N.Y. Times, June 10, 2007.

224 *See, e.g.*, Savedoff v. Access Group, 2007 WL 649278 (N.D. Ohio Feb. 26, 2007) (partial summary judgment granted for class of borrowers in breach of contract case against private lender alleging improper compounding of unpaid interest and improper application of payments), *aff'd in part, rev'd in part*, 524 F.3d 754 (6th Cir. 2008).

225 *See also* § 11.9.2.2, *supra* (preemption in context of FTC Holder Rule).

226 20 U.S.C. § 1078(d). *See* § 2.3.1, *supra*.

227 20 U.S.C. § 1098g.

228 For an extensive discussion of assignee liability for seller-related claims, see National Consumer Law Center, Unfair and Deceptive Acts and Practices § 11.6 (7th ed. 2008 and Supp.).

For a general discussion of assignee liability, see National Consumer Law Center, The Cost of Credit: Regulation, Preemption, and Industry Abuses §§ 10.6, 12.2 (4th ed. 2009 and Supp.).

Chapter 12   Proprietary School and Other Student Loan Litigation

12.1 Introduction to Student Loan-Related Litigation

In most cases, clients will seek legal help for student loan problems long after they have left or graduated from school. As noted above, the complete elimination of a statute of limitations for most student loans means that collection efforts can go on indefinitely.[1] Some clients may seek legal assistance for loans from ten, twenty, or even thirty years ago.

Although the majority of student loan claims will be raised defensively in response to collection actions, affirmative litigation may still be viable and useful in some cases.

This chapter focuses on key claims and defenses in cases involving abuses by proprietary schools (also referred to as for-profit schools). Although focused on proprietary schools, many of the claims discussed in this chapter may also be raised in cases against others in the student loan industry, such as servicers or accreditation agencies.

School-related claims may be brought affirmatively against the schools and in many cases against lenders that are affiliated with the schools. These issues are discussed in this chapter, including school-related affirmative claims and defenses. Many of the school-related issues discussed in this chapter are relevant for private student loans. In addition, Chapter 11, *supra*, highlights a number of school-related and other claims that are specific to private loan cases. These include not only school-related claims against lenders but also legal claims, such as Truth in Lending Act (TILA) violations, that may be brought directly against private student lenders.

Other defenses to raise in federal student loan collection cases are discussed in Chapter 7, *supra*. Most of these defenses apply to private loans as well. Defenses that are unique to private loans are discussed in Chapter 11, *supra*.

12.2 Oversight of Schools Participating in Federal Assistance Programs

12.2.1 General

The Department of Education does not review the educational quality of schools before certifying their eligibility to participate in the federal student aid programs. Instead, the Department of Education requires the schools to be licensed by a state agency, and the Department recognizes various private accrediting agencies and associations whose job it is to review the educational standards of the school.[2]

The current regulatory structure for schools participating in federal financial assistance programs is often referred to as the "triad." The three "arms" of the triad consist of the federal Department of Education, state agencies, and accrediting agencies. The Department of Education ("the Department") relies heavily on the other two arms to determine program standards.[3] The federal Department mainly plays a gate-keeping role, verifying institutions' eligibility, certifying their financial and administrative capacities, and granting recognition to accrediting agencies.

The state-based regulatory approach varies widely.[4] Some states have developed standards that set, for example, minimum qualifications for proprietary school teachers.[5] Others have created state tuition recovery funds.[6] Overall, nearly every state agency is understaffed and under-funded.

With respect to accreditors, a school must be accredited by an agency that has the authority to cover all of the institution's programs. This is considered the school's primary accreditor. There may also be other programmatic

---

1   See § 7.5.3.1, *supra*.

2   For more information on problems with accreditors, see § 12.2.2, *infra*.

3   *See generally* U.S. Gen. Accounting Office, Higher Education: Ensuring Quality Education From Proprietary Institutions, Report No. GAO/T-HEHS-96-158 (June 1996).

4   The Department issued proposed regulations in June 2010 to revise the definition of "state authorization." *See* 75 Fed. Reg. 34806 (June 18, 2010).

5   *See* § 12.5.3.2, *infra*.

6   *See* § 12.8, *infra*.

accrediting agencies. The Department periodically publishes a list of nationally recognized accrediting agencies.[7]

The general requirements for institutional eligibility are reviewed in Chapter 1, *supra*. This chapter highlights issues most relevant to proprietary schools.

12.2.2 Accreditation Agency Concerns

The role of the accrediting agencies has been particularly controversial. During Senate hearings in the early 1990s, the Senate noted the inherent conflict of interest in accreditation: once an agency approves a school for accreditation, the agency thereafter assumes the role of the school's advocate.[8] Despite these conflicts, the basic model persists, allowing for a buffer between schools and direct federal oversight.

Accreditation agencies are supposed to demonstrate that they have rigorous standards. The Higher Education Act (HEA) sets out factors that accreditation agencies must address in evaluating the quality of an institution, including success with respect to student achievement and, as appropriate, consideration of course completion, state licensing examination, and job placement rates.[9]

Agencies are required to make available to the public and the state licensing agency and Department of Education certain information about their actions, including final denials, withdrawals, suspensions, or terminations of accreditation.[10] The accreditation review must also confirm that the institution has transfer-of-credit policies that are publicly disclosed and that include a statement of the criteria established by the institution regarding the transfer of credit earned at another institution.[11]

In addition, agencies must monitor growth of programs at institutions experiencing significant enrollment growth and monitor headcount enrollment at institutions that offer distance or correspondence education.[12]

The Department has begun to pay closer attention to accreditation agency issues. In December 2009, the Department's Inspector General (IG) recommended that the Department consider limiting, suspending, or terminating an accreditor's status. In an audit of The Higher Learning Commission of the North Central Association of Colleges and Schools, the IG focused on the agency's standards for program length and creditor hours. The report found issues related to HLC's granting of accreditation to American Intercontinental University (AIU) despite having found concerns related to AIU's assignment of credit hours.[13] In the final management report, the IG found that the decision to grant accreditation to AIU even though the HLC found that the school had an "egregious" credit policy, was not in the best interests of students. The IG recommended that the Department determine whether the accrediting agency is in fact in compliance with the HEA and, if not, take appropriate action to limit, suspend, or terminate the agency's recognition.[14]

Another concern involves for-profit schools that acquire nonprofit and other schools in order to access more prestigious regional accreditations. There is some question as to whether these acquisitions violate the federal regulation requiring a two-year delay before for-profit schools can qualify to participate in federal assistance programs.[15]

12.2.3 Gaps in Federal Enforcement

The Department of Education's Inspector General has acknowledged that reducing risk in the student aid programs has been a management challenge for the Department and that it continues to find fraud and abuse by program participants as well as weaknesses in program administration.[16] The problems are particularly acute in the proprietary school sector. In a June 2010 U.S. Senate hearing, Inspector General Kathleen Tighe testified that historically the majority of post-secondary institutional audits and investigations have involved proprietary schools.[17] She stated that, since last testifying in 2005, the IG had issued thirty-seven reports on post-secondary institutions, twenty-one of which involved proprietary schools.[18]

In an August 2009 report, the Government Accountability Office (GAO) concluded that stronger Department of Education oversight is needed to address certain proprietary school problems.[19] The report noted the higher loan default

---

7 This information is also available on-line at www.ed.gov/admins/finaid/accred/index.html.
8 S. Rep. No. 102-58 (1991).
9 20 U.S.C. § 1099b; 34 C.F.R. § 602.16.
10 20 U.S.C. § 1099b(c)(7).
11 20 U.S.C. § 1099b(c)(9).
12 34 C.F.R. § 602.19.
   The Department of Education issued a Dear Colleague letter in June 2009 to collect information from agencies about their compliance with these provisions. U.S. Dep't of Educ., Dear Colleague Letter GEN-09-08 (June 5, 2009).
13 U.S. Dep't of Educ., Office of Inspector General, The Higher Learning Commission of the North Central Association of Colleges and Schools' Decision to Accredit American Inter-Continental University, Control No. ED-OIG/L13J0006 (Dec. 17, 2009).
14 *Id.* See also U.S. Dep't of Educ., Office of Inspector General, Control No. Ed-OIG/X13J0003 (May 24, 2010).
15 *See* Daniel Golden, *Your Taxes Support For-Profit as They Buy Colleges*, Businessweek (Mar. 5, 2010); § 1.7.1.1, *supra*.
16 Office of Inspector Gen., Semiannual Report to Congress: No. 48, Oct. 1, 2003–Mar. 31, 2004; Office of Inspector Gen., Semiannual Report to Congress: No. 47, Apr. 1, 2003–Sept. 30, 2003. Reports are available on the OIG website at www.ed.gov/about/offices/list/oig.
17 *Emerging Risk? An Overview of the Federal Investment in For-Profit Education: Hearing Before the U.S. Senate Comm. on Health, Educ., Labor & Pensions* (June 24, 2010) (statement of Kathleen S. Tighe, Inspector Gen., Dep't of Educ.).
18 *Id.*
19 U.S. Gov't Accountability Office, Proprietary Schools: Stronger Department of Education Oversight Needed to Help Ensure Only Eligible Students Receive Federal Student Aid, Report

rate among proprietary school students and focused particularly on the Department's lack of oversight of the "ability to benefit" requirements.[20]

The Obama Administration has begun to take a tougher stance on "program integrity" issues. Among other actions, the Administration proposed regulations in June 2010 that would revise numerous regulations that have been the sources of abuse, including the incentive compensation ban.[21]

12.3 Proprietary School Issues

12.3.1 Brief History

Unfair and deceptive vocational and correspondence school practices are a tremendous source of frustration, financial loss, and loss of opportunity for consumers, particularly low-income consumers hoping to break out of poverty. Attracted by the financing provided by government student loan and grant programs, many vocational school scams and ill-conceived schools have exploited federally funded student assistance programs.

Abuses were widespread during the 1980s and early 1990s when student financial assistance became more widely available for non-high-school graduates and for vocational training. The problem has unfortunately grown over time. The proprietary school industry is larger than ever, now consisting mainly of public companies competing to create profits for their owners and shareholders.

The abuses are generally fueled by a federal student loan system that has created a con artist's perfect dream. Schools were able to pressure vulnerable and low-income consumers into signing documents obligating them to thousands of dollars. Many schools promised that students would not have to repay loans until they found high-paying jobs. The schools then literally took the money and ran, leaving loan collection to third parties and the government.

This problem, for the most part, grew out of good intentions. In 1979, Congress amended the HEA to encourage lenders to market loans to for-profit vocational school students.[22] Congress hoped to open up the student financial assistance market, particularly to non-high-school graduates and others wishing to pursue vocational training.[23] Unfortunately, these changes not only opened the door to eager students but also to unscrupulous for-profit school operators and lenders.

The tragedy of proprietary school fraud is that it robs vulnerable people of their dreams. According to testimony given by a former owner of a truck-driver training school, "In the proprietary school business what you sell is dreams and so ninety-nine percent of the sales were made in poor, black areas, [at] welfare offices and unemployment lines, and in housing projects. My approach was that if [a prospect] could breathe, scribble his name, had a driver's license, and was over 18 years of age, he was qualified for North American's program."[24]

Unless addressed through loan cancellation, repayment, or other remedies, these problems can literally last forever because of the elimination of a statute of limitations for federal student loan collection.[25] The alliance between these schools and private student lenders adds another dimension to the problem that has increased the debt burden for vulnerable consumers.[26]

12.3.2 Recent Growth in Proprietary Higher Education and Current Concerns

Proprietary school fraud is by no means only a legacy of the past. New abuses have emerged. A number of problems are tied to the aggressive push for growth in the sector. The booming for-profit educational market is increasingly dominated by regional and even national franchises, many with stock shares traded on Wall Street.

The for-profit education publicly traded companies in the U.S. have tripled enrollment to 1.4 million students in the past decade and increased revenues to about $26 billion.[27] This is an increase from just less than 200,000 students in 1998.[28] However, these annual enrollment measures fail to show that these schools also have very high withdrawal

---

No. GAO-09-600 (Aug. 2009).

20 *Id.* See §§ 1.7.1.3, 9.4.2.1 (ability to benefit requirements), *supra*, 12.3.3.8, *infra*.

21 75 Fed. Reg. 34806 (June 18, 2010). See §§ 1.7.2.3, *supra*, 12.3.3.2, *infra*.

22 Higher Education Technical Amendments of 1979, Pub. L. No. 96-49, 93 Stat. 351 (1979).

    The 1979 amendments removed a ceiling on the federal interest subsidy paid to participating guaranteed student loan program lenders. Later amendments removed other limitations on student borrowers attending for-profit schools. *See* Education Amendments of 1980, Pub. L. No. 96-374, 94 Stat. 1367 (1980); Higher Education Amendments of 1986, Pub. L. No. 99-498, §§ 425, 1075(a), 100 Stat. 1268, 1359 (1986).

23 Although the issue was not briefed by the parties in the litigation, the *Armstrong* court on its own initiative summarized some of the changes that made federal student aid more widely available over time. *See* Armstrong v. Accrediting Council for Continuing Educ. & Training, 168 F. Rep. 3d 1362, 1364 (D.C. Cir. 1999).

24 S. Rep. No. 102-58, at 12–13 (1991) (testimony), *quoted in* Patrick F. Linehan, *Dreams Protected: A New Approach to Policing Proprietary Schools' Misrepresentations*, 89 Geo. L.J. 753 (Mar. 2001).

25 *See* § 7.5.3.1, *supra*.

26 *See* § 12.3.3.7, *infra*.

27 Daniel Golden, *Your Taxes Support For-Profit As They Buy Colleges*, Businessweek (Mar. 5, 2010).

28 U.S. Senate Comm. on Health, Educ., Labor & Pensions, Emerging Risk?: An Overview of Growth, Spending, Student Debt, and Unanswered Questions in For-Profit Higher Education (June 24, 2010).

rates. According to the U.S. Senate Committee on Health, Education, Labor and Pensions, the high withdrawal rates mean that schools must recruit large numbers of new students each year to maintain, or grow, their enrollment levels.[29]

In some cases, schools do not participate in the federal student loan programs. These schools may pressure students to take out private loans or may require direct payment. For example, in May 2007, the California Attorney General sued individual operators as well as a company that owned and managed a computer training vocational school in the state for allegedly failing to offer instruction as promised, among other violations.[30]

However, most of these schools stay in business and make enormous profits through federal student assistance sources. According to a 2010 U.S. Senate report, $4.3 billion in Pell grants and $19.6 billion in federal loans went to for-profit schools in 2008–2009, about double the share from 1999–2000.[31] In 2009, for-profit schools received almost one quarter of all Pell grants, up from just 13% in 1999.

Many for-profits have experienced enrollment surges during the economic crisis. For example, new enrollments at one of the large school companies, ITT, had increased by one-third from 2008–2009, and the company forecast that its profits would be 50% higher than the previous year. Laid-off workers returning to school and increased government aid have boosted enrollment.[32]

As the schools have grown and increased their share of federal assistance dollars, their profits have also grown. The average operating profit in fiscal year 2005 among publicly traded for-profit companies was $127 million. The same number in fiscal year 2009 was $229 million, an increase of 81%.[33] According to a 2010 U.S. Senate report, the amount of profits and other revenues spent on educating students is shrinking, while funds spent on advertisements and web marketing continue to grow.[34] Another report found that, for the sixteen companies analyzed, profits in 2009 totaled $2.7 billion. Between fiscal years 2009 and 2010, one company doubled its profits from $119 million to $241 million, while a second had profits increase from $235 million to $411 million.[35]

12.3.3 Common Abuses and Problems with Proprietary Schools

12.3.3.1 Excessive Student Loan Default Rates

The federal cohort default rate (CDR) data for fiscal year 2008, released in September 2010, indicates persistently higher cohort default rates for proprietary school borrowers. The national rate for all sectors was 7%, up from 6.7% in 2007.[36] The federal cohort default rate in fiscal year 2008 for all proprietary schools was the highest among all school sectors at 11.6%, almost double the average rate for public colleges.[37] An August 2009 GAO report highlighted this troubling trend, noting that students at for-profit colleges and universities are more likely to default on federal loans. For example, four years after borrowers entered repayment, 23.3% of proprietary school borrowers have defaulted compared to 9.5% of borrowers from public schools and 6.5% of borrowers from private nonprofit schools.[38]

Schools are not considered administratively capable when their CDRs rise above certain limits. The CDR is a specific way of measuring federal student loan defaults that clearly underestimates the scope of the problem.[39] The sanctions program, including school appeal rights, is described in Chapter 1, *supra*.[40] In general, a school is not administratively capable and therefore will be terminated from the federal aid program if the CDR for Federal Family Education Loan Program loans (FFELs) and Direct Loan Program loans ("Direct loans") equals or exceeds 25% for the three most recent fiscal years or if the most recent CDR is greater than 40%.[41] The 2008 HEA reauthorization law increased

---

29 U.S. Senate Comm. on Health, Educ., Labor & Pensions, The Return on the Federal Investment in For-Profit Education: Debt Without a Diploma (Sept. 30, 2010).
30 *See* Press Release, Office of the Cal. Att'y Gen., Brown Sues to Aid Swindled Students (May 7, 2007).
31 U.S. Senate Comm. on Health, Educ., Labor & Pensions, Emerging Risk?: An Overview of Growth, Spending, Student Debt and Unanswered Questions in For-Profit Higher Education (June 24, 2010).
32 Justin Pope, *For-Profit Colleges Boost Lending*, Associated Press: AP Impact, Aug. 14, 2009.
33 U.S. Senate Comm. on Health, Educ., Labor & Pensions, Emerging Risk?: An Overview of Growth, Spending, Student Debt and Unanswered Questions in For-Profit Higher Education (June 24, 2010).
34 *Id.*

35 U.S. Senate Comm. on Health, Educ., Labor & Pensions, The Return on the Federal Investment in For-Profit Education: Debt Without a Diploma (Sept. 30, 2010).
36 Press Release, U.S. Dep't of Educ., Student Loan Default Rates Increase (Sept. 13, 2010).
  These rates only measure federal student loans and, as described in Chapter 5, *supra*, the rate only captures defaults for a relatively short period of time. Due to problems with the formula, the cohort rate underestimates the full scope of the problem. It is also does not consider private student loan default rates.
37 *Id. See also* Press Release, The Project on Student Debt, Federal Student Loan Default Rates on the Rise (Sept. 13, 2010).
38 U.S. Gov't Accountability Office, Proprietary Schools: Stronger Department of Education Oversight Needed to Help Ensure Only Eligible Students Receive Federal Student Aid, Report No. GAO-09-600 (Aug. 2009).
39 More specific information about the calculation method can be found in § 5.1.3, *supra*.
40 *See* § 1.7.4.2.2, *supra*.
41 34 C.F.R. § 668.187(a)(2).

the percentage from 25% to 30% for fiscal year 2012 and any succeeding year.[42] Perkins Loan Program loans ("Perkins loans") have separate cohort default-rate calculations.[43]

Given the possible loss of participation in federal aid programs due to default-rate sanctions, schools have started hiring "default management" companies to track down former students and get them into forbearances or other programs that will not impact the school's default rates and help them avoid sanctions.[44]

Default rates are high at least in part because borrowing rates in this sector, as well as withdrawal rates, are disproportionately high. More than 95% of students at two-year for-profit schools and 93% at four-year for-profit schools took out federal student loans in 2007, while only 16.6% of students attending community colleges and 44.3% at public four-year institutions borrowed during the same period.[45]

Failure to complete is generally viewed as a high risk factor for default.[46] According to a 2010 report, at many schools, more than half of proprietary school students withdraw within two years of enrollment.[47] High cost also drives up loan balances.[48]

Default and write-off rates for private student loans are also disproportionately high among proprietary school students.[49] In many cases, these debts are from credit products originated by the school.[50]

12.3.3.2 Aggressive Recruiting and Marketing Practices

All institutions that wish to receive federal financial aid must enter into program participation agreements with the Department of Education. Among the requirements in these agreements are bans on paying recruiters on a per-student basis.[51] This provision is meant to curb the risk that recruiters will sign up poorly qualified students who will derive little benefit from the subsidy and may be unable or unwilling to repay federally guaranteed loans.

The limits on incentive compensation have been significantly diluted in recent years. Department of Education Inspector General Tighe testified in 2010 that the safe harbors in the current regulations have in many cases shielded schools from administrative, civil, and criminal liability.[52] In June 2010, the Department proposed to eliminate the safe harbors.[53]

In addition to possible violations of the HEA incentive compensation ban, schools often commit fraud or make misrepresentations in their advertisements and other statements when recruiting students. A 2010 GAO report using undercover testing at fifteen for-profit colleges found that four colleges encouraged fraudulent practices and that all fifteen made deceptive or otherwise questionable statements.[54]

The emphasis on growth in the proprietary school sector, particularly among the publicly traded companies, has increased competition and led schools to unleash aggressive marketing campaigns. Unfortunately, the system also creates incentives for schools to inflate or otherwise misrepresent performance data such as completion and job placement rates in order to maintain and grow profits.[55] Inspector General Kathleen Tighe testified in 2010 that, over the years, the IG's office has identified a relationship between rapid growth and failure to maintain administrative capability.[56]

Schools have taken marketing and recruitment to new levels in recent years. For example, news reports have highlighted recruitment at homeless shelters.[57] Many schools, particularly those with on-line courses, also target military service members. By 2009, for-profit schools accounted for 29% of college enrollments and 40% of the half-billion dollar annual amount of federal tuition assistance for active duty students.[58] The U.S. House Armed Services Subcom-

---

Historically black colleges or universities and tribally controlled community colleges or Navajo community colleges are not subject to loss of eligibility as long as they meet certain requirements such as submission of a default management plan. 20 U.S.C. § 1085(a)(6).

42 Pub. L. No. 110-314, § 436(a), 122 Stat. 3078 (Aug. 14, 2008). See 34 C.F.R. § 668.16(m).
43 34 C.F.R. § 674.5.
44 See, e.g., Goldie Blumenstyk, *Business Is Up in Keeping Default Rates Down*, Chron. of Higher Educ., July 11, 2010.
45 U.S. Senate Comm. on Health, Educ., Labor & Pensions, The Return on the Federal Investment in For-Profit Education: Debt Without a Diploma (Sept. 30, 2010).
46 See § 5.1.2, supra.
47 U.S. Senate Comm. on Health, Educ., Labor & Pensions, The Return on the Federal Investment in For-Profit Education: Debt Without a Diploma (Sept. 30, 2010).
48 For a description of the relatively high tuitions at for-profit schools, see generally U.S. Senate Comm. on Health, Educ., Labor & Pensions, The Return on the Federal Investment in For-Profit Education: Debt Without a Diploma (Sept. 30, 2010).
49 See Chs. 5 and 11, supra.
50 See § 11.1.3, supra.

51 20 U.S.C. § 1094(a)(20).
52 *Emerging Risk? An Overview of the Federal Investment in For-Profit Education: Hearing Before the U.S Senate Comm. on Health, Educ., Labor & Pensions* (June 24, 2010) (statement of Kathleen S. Tighe, Inspector Gen., U.S. Dep't of Educ.).
53 75 Fed. Reg. 34806 (June 18, 2010).
54 U.S. Gov't Accountability Office, For-Profit Colleges: Undercover Testing Finds Colleges Encouraged Fraud and Engaged in Deceptive and Questionable Marketing Practices, Report No. GAO-10-948T (Aug. 4, 2010).
55 See § 12.3.3.4, infra.
56 *Emerging Risk? An Overview of the Federal Investment in For-Profit Education: Hearing Before the U.S Senate Comm. on Health, Educ., Labor & Pensions* (June 24, 2010) (statement of Kathleen S. Tighe, Inspector Gen., U.S. Dep't of Educ.).
57 Daniel Golden, *Homeless Dropouts from High School Lured by For-Profit Colleges*, www.Bloomberg.com (Apr. 30, 2010).
58 Daniel Golden, *For-Profit Colleges Target the Military*, www.bloomberg.com (Dec. 30, 2009).

mittee held a hearing in 2010 about the need for higher standards for on-line education programs.

In August 2010, the U.S. Senate Committee on Health, Education, Labor, and Pensions held hearings on the "recruitment experience" at for-profit schools. A former admissions representative from Westwood College testified about the boiler room operation that required the representatives to turn "leads" into enrollees.[59]

A 2003 Department of Education program review of University of Phoenix provides a detailed look at an aggressive marketing structure and the problems this creates. The report describes extensive use of incentive compensation based on enrollments for those involved in recruiting or admission activities, in violation of the HEA requirements.[60]

A case against another school, based mainly on allegations of race discrimination, describes a system that requires admissions employees to meet enrollment targets that are set by management.[61] A Fair Labor Standards Act case against another proprietary school provides additional insight into an aggressive marketing strategy. In order to avoid paying overtime, the school argued that field representatives who engaged in a range of activities—including high school visits and calls to prospective students—were actually salespeople.[62] The court noted that college recruiters are ordinarily not engaged in selling services. In contrast, the employees in this case not only identified prospective students but also were paid based on inducing them to enroll. As discussed in the decision, the employee's potential for salary enhancements and eligibility for recognition and rewards was based primarily on the number of tuition-paying "student starts" the employee collected.[63]

12.3.3.3 Failure to Meet "Gainful Employment" Requirement

To be eligible to participate in the federal assistance programs, proprietary institutions must only offer programs that provide training for gainful employment in a recognized occupation. These same provisions apply to public or nonprofit shorter-term training programs.[64]

The term "gainful employment," however, is not defined. In July 2010, the Department issued proposed rules that define "gainful employment."[65] Under the proposed framework, to determine whether particular programs provide training that leads to gainful employment, the Department would take into consideration repayment rates on federal student loans, the relationship between total student loan debt and earnings, and in some cases whether employers endorse program content.

The proposed rules, if enacted, should become effective in July 2012, with some transition periods built in. However, in September 2010, the Department announced that they would delay publication of final rules until early 2011. It was unclear at the time this manual was written whether this would impact the July 2012 effective date.

This proposal has met considerable opposition from the industry and has been the focus of tremendous controversy. An additional set of proposed rules, issued in June 2010, would require schools to annually submit information about students who complete a program that leads to gainful employment.[66]

12.3.3.4 Manipulation of Outcome Measures

There are a number of provisions in the HEA requiring schools to disclose information about completion and job placement rates.[67] For example, institutions that advertise job placement rates as a means of attracting students to enroll must make available to prospective students, at or before the time those students apply for enrollment, the most recent available data concerning employment statistics, graduation statistics, and any other information necessary to substantiate the truthfulness of the advertisements.[68]

As with the cohort default rate, there are problems with the rules specifying how these rates are calculated. Furthermore, schools frequently misrepresent or otherwise attempt to manipulate their rates.

In a 2010 report, the U.S. Senate highlighted the wide variation in the quality of completion and job placement information, noting that it is self-reported with no auditing mechanism in place to ensure accuracy outside of the "opaque" accreditation process.[69]

The official completion rates only count first-time, full-time enrolled students.[70] This is a huge problem since so

---

59 *For-Profit Schools: The Student Recruitment Experience: Hearing Before the U.S. Senate Comm. on Health, Educ., Labor & Pensions* (Aug. 4, 2010) (testimony of Joshua Pruyn, Former Admissions Representative, Alta Coll., Inc.).

60 U.S. Dep't of Educ., Student Financial Assistance Program Review Report, PCRN 200340922254, Univ. of Phoenix, Site Visit of 8/18/03 to 8/22/03 (on file with NCLC).
  A false claims lawsuit against UOP makes similar allegations. U.S. *ex rel.* Hendow & Albertson v. University of Phoenix, No. Civ. 5-03-0457 (E.D. Ca. complaint filed Mar. 7, 2003). See § 12.5.2.2, *infra*.

61 Legrand v. New York Restaurant Sch., 2004 WL 1555102 (S.D.N.Y. July 12, 2004).

62 Nielsen v. Devry Inc., 302 F. Supp. 2d 747 (W.D. Mich. 2003).

63 *Id.*

64 20 U.S.C. § 1001(b), 1002

65 75 Fed. Reg. 43616 (July 26, 2010).

66 75 Fed. Reg. 34806 (June 18, 2010).

67 See § 1.7, *supra*.

68 34 C.F.R. § 668.14(b)(10).

69 *See generally* U.S. Senate Comm. on Health, Educ., Labor & Pensions, Emerging Risk?: An Overview of Growth, Spending, Student Debt and Unanswered Questions in For-Profit Higher Education (June 24, 2010).

70 *Id.*

many proprietary students attend part-time or have previous post-secondary experience. Despite the undercounting in this formula, in many cases, reported completion rates in the proprietary sector are very low.[71]

There is no uniform definition of how placement is calculated. There is a definition for short-term programs that are required to meet certain placement and completion standards. These standards apply to short-term programs of at least 300 clock hours of instruction but less than 600 clock hours of instruction, offered during a minimum of ten weeks, and:

(i) has a verified completion rate of at least 70%, as determined in accordance with the regulations of the Secretary;

(ii) has a verified placement rate of at least 70%, as determined in accordance with the regulations of the Secretary; and

(iii) satisfies such further criteria as the Secretary may prescribe by regulation.[72]

For purposes of these short-term programs, placement rates are calculated by first determining the number of students who, during the award year, received the degree, certificate, or other recognized educational credential awarded for successfully completing the program. Of this total, the school must determine the number of students who, within 180 days of the day they received their degree, certificate, or other recognized educational credential, obtained gainful employment in the recognized occupation for which they were trained or in a related comparable recognized occupation and, on the date of this calculation, are employed or have been employed for at least thirteen weeks following receipt of the credential.[73] The rate is the number of students placed divided by the total.

These schools are also required to collect documentation to support the numbers of students categorized as "placed" in jobs. Examples of satisfactory documentation of a student's gainful employment include but are not limited to:

(i) a written statement from the student's employer;

(ii) signed copies of State or Federal income tax forms; and

(iii) written evidence of payments of Social Security taxes.[74]

Proposed rules, issued in June 2010, would require schools to annually submit information about students who complete a program that leads to gainful employment.[75]

Many recent cases against proprietary schools and government investigations have focused on misrepresentations about job placement rates. This is a serious problem because it is almost impossible to determine the "real" rates. Although there are serious flaws with the completion data itself and the reporting of such data, as described above, the completion data is at least collected in some consistent way. This is not the case with job placement data. The Department does not collect job placement rates for any type of institution.

Because there is little or no oversight, there is ample room for schools to manipulate the placement rates.[76] A 2005 *60 Minutes* story about Career Education Corporation (CEC) described ways in which school officials pump up placement rates by including students placed in any job, not necessarily jobs they were trained for.[77]

The lack of enforcement occurs not only in the area of data reporting but also with respect to whether schools are substantiating data. As noted above, the schools are supposed to document placement information by, for example, retaining written statements from a student's employer or signed copies of state or federal income tax forms. Although not a panacea, this type of documentation at least provides one way of evaluating the types of employment reported.

A 2010 GAO report using undercover testing at fifteen for-profit colleges found that four colleges encouraged fraudulent practices and that all fifteen made deceptive or otherwise questionable statements.[78] This included misrepresentations about salaries after graduation and failure to provide clear information about costs and graduation rates.

Another problem is that even legitimate trade schools may offer courses in areas with bleak job prospects. A 1997 General Accounting Office study found that a large percentage of the federal assistance money that goes to trade school students is used to train students for low-demand jobs.[79] In some cases, the data was dramatic, with students being trained for occupations in which local supply exceeded

---

71 *Id.*
72 20 U.S.C. § 1088(b).
73 34 C.F.R. § 668.8(g).
74 *Id.*
75 75 Fed. Reg. 34806 (June 18, 2010).
76 *See, e.g.,* Brent Hunsberger, *Degrees of Risk,* Oregonian, Sept. 10, 2006.
77 Transcript of *60 Minutes: An Expensive Lesson; Career Education Corporation Schools,* CBS News Transcripts (Jan. 30, 2005).
78 U.S. Gov't Accountability Office, For-Profit Colleges: Undercover Testing Finds Colleges Encouraged Fraud and Engaged in Deceptive and Questionable Marketing Practices, Report No. GAO-10-948T (Aug. 4, 2010). *See also The Federal Investment in For-Profit Education: Are Students Succeeding?: Hearing Before the U.S. Senate Comm. on Health, Educ., Labor & Pensions* (Sept. 30, 2010) (testimony of Kathleen A. Bittel, for-profit school employee, about manipulation of job placement rates and other issues).
79 *See* U.S. Gen. Accounting Office, Proprietary Schools: Millions Spent to Train Students for Oversupplied Occupations, Report No. GAO/HEHS-97-104 (June 1997).

In contrast, several major federal job training programs restrict training to fields with favorable job projections. Most welfare-to-work programs also require welfare agencies to work with private industry councils and ensure that programs provided training for jobs likely to become available in the area. *See id.*

demand by ratios of ten to one or more. Common proprietary school courses, such as barbering/cosmetology and appliance/equipment repair were oversupplied for all states in the study.[80]

12.3.3.5 Reliance on Federal Aid

In annual reports and other information to investors, the proprietary school companies repeatedly discuss their reliance on federal student aid to stay in business and to grow. *Forbes Magazine* noted this trend, describing Career Education Corporation (CEC) as a "company built to swallow Title IV [federal student assistance] funds in the way a whale gathers up plankton."[81]

In 2002, federal assistance funds accounted for an average of 62.9% of revenues at the five largest for-profit schools. By 2009, the same companies reported that federal aid made up an average of 77.4% of their revenue.[82] The share of federal dollars is even higher because federal law allows schools to exclude many federal funding sources from the "revenue" calculation. In general, while for-profit schools enrolled close to 10% of all higher education students in 2009, they received approximately 23% of federal aid.[83]

The "90/10" rule is intended to limit the amount of revenue schools can receive from federal funds.[84] The "90/10" rule requires each proprietary school to limit the percentage of revenues it receives from Department of Education federal financial assistance ("Title IV" funds) to no more than 90%. The rule refers only to HEA federal assistance. This means that other types of federal student aid, such as Department of Defense G.I. assistance, is not counted toward the 90%.[85] When the full amount of Department of Education funds are combined with other federal dollars, the aggregate federal share of the school's revenue, according to a 2010 U.S. Senate report, is about 87.4% and can range as high as 93.1%.[86]

Due to the possibility of sanctions if the 90/10 rule is violated, the industry has pushed hard to include more revenue sources in the 10% category and to dilute the potential penalties from violations. In 2010, Department of Education Inspector General Kathleen Tighe testified about proprietary institutions that miscalculate or devise other creative accounting schemes to make it appear that they meet this rule.[87]

12.3.3.6 Distance Education

Prior to Congressional changes in 2006, schools that offered primarily distance education courses had their participation in federal assistance programs limited in a number of ways. These limits were removed for the most part and currently apply only to "correspondence courses." Correspondence courses are not considered to be "distance education."[88] Due to the changes in the law, most other distance education courses are treated in the same way as traditional residential programs.

Department of Education Inspector General Tighe has identified this issue as an area that is placing increased demands on the IG office's investigative and audit resources.[89] The key issue is determining whether distance education students are "regular students" who are actually in attendance for purposes of federal aid. The point at which a student progresses from on-line registration to actual on-line academic engagement or class attendance is often not defined by institutions and is not currently defined by federal statute or regulations, according to Tighe.[90] She noted that, since 2001, the IG has recommended amending the HEA to address cost-of-attendance calculations for on-line learners. The HEA limits the cost of attendance for students engaged in correspondence course, but not for distance education students.

The U.S. Senate 2010 report highlighted the ways in which the repeal of the 50% rule has transformed for-profit schools. Of the fourteen publicly traded schools, at least seven have more than 50% of their students in exclusively on-line curriculum. Four of these schools have more than 98% of student on-line.[91]

---

80 U.S. Gen. Accounting Office, Proprietary Schools: Millions Spent to Train Students for Oversupplied Occupations, Report No. GAO/HEHS-97-104 (June 1997).

81 Daniel Kruger, *Blackboard Jungle*, Forbes Magazine, Dec. 13, 2004.

82 U.S. Senate Comm. on Health, Educ., Labor & Pensions, Emerging Risk?: An Overview of Growth, Spending, Student Debt and Unanswered Questions in For-Profit Higher Education (June 24, 2010).

83 *Id.*

84 See § 1.7.2.2, *supra*.

85 See § 1.7.2.2, *supra*.

86 U.S. Senate Comm. on Health, Educ., Labor & Pensions, The Return on the Federal Investment in For-Profit Education: Debt Without a Diploma (Sept. 30, 2010).

  According to the report, much of this is traceable to GI bill funds, Workforce Investment Act funds, and Vocational Rehabilitation funds.

87 *Emerging Risk? An Overview of the Federal Investment in For-Profit Education: Hearing Before the U.S Senate Comm. on Health, Educ., Labor & Pensions* (June 24, 2010) (statement of Kathleen S. Tighe, Inspector Gen., U.S. Dep't of Educ.).

88 34 C.F.R. § 600.2. See § 1.7.1.4, *supra*.

89 *Emerging Risk? An Overview of the Federal Investment in For-Profit Education: Hearing Before the U.S Senate Comm. on Health, Educ., Labor & Pensions* (June 24, 2010) (statement of Kathleen S. Tighe, Inspector Gen., U.S. Dep't of Educ.).

90 *Id.*

91 U.S. Senate Comm. on Health, Educ., Labor & Pensions, Emerging Risk?: An Overview of Growth, Spending, Student Debt and Unanswered Questions in For-Profit Higher Education (June 24, 2010).

12.3.3.7 Increased Private Loan Borrowing and Internal Loan Products

Private for-profit schools thrived during the heyday of subprime private lending. In 2007–2008, students attending for-profit schools comprised about 9% of all undergraduates but 27% of those with private loans. Forty-two percent of all proprietary school students had private loans in 2007–2008, up from 12% in 2003–2004.[92] Problems with private loans and relief for borrowers are discussed in Chapter 11, *supra*.

As the credit market has tightened, many schools have begun to develop their own internal loan products. The schools that report this information have acknowledged very high write-off rates for these loans.[93]

There exists a common problem among students who seek education at an institution other than the one at which the student originally enrolled. If a debt is allegedly still owed to the former school, the school will often refuse to release transcripts or school records.[94]

12.3.3.8 Admission Abuses

There are numerous concerns about school manipulation of admissions criteria, including violations of ability-to-benefit (ATB) requirements, requirements for satisfactory academic progress, and other requirements.[95] In an August 2009 report, the GAO reported that weaknesses in the Department of Education's oversight of the ATB requirements places students and federal funds at risk.[96] For example, when GAO analysts posing as prospective students took the basic skills test at a local proprietary school, the "independent" test administrator gave out answers to some of the test questions. In addition, the test forms were tampered with.[97]

The Department issued proposed regulations in June 2010 that would impose a number of new requirements for schools and test publishers to follow. In making these proposals, the Department cited recommendations from the August 2009 GAO report to strengthen control over ATB testing.[98]

Department of Education Inspector General Kathleen Tighe identified falsification of eligibility as a main problem involving proprietary institutions. This includes falsification not only of high school diplomas but also of enrollment and attendance records and academic progress.[99]

Yet another problem area concerns the for-profit education sector's growing use of mandatory arbitration clauses in school enrollment agreements.[100]

---

92 The Project on Student Debt, Private Loans: Facts and Trends (Aug. 2009).
93 See § 11.1.3, *supra*.
94 See Vilbon v. Katharine Gibbs Coll., 76 Mass. App. Ct. 1126, 2010 WL 1559093 (Mass. App. Ct. Apr. 21, 2010) (settlement agreement with school did not extinguish student's debt, so school was entitled to withhold transcripts); *The Federal Investment in For-Profit Education: Are Students Succeeding?: Hearing Before the U.S. Senate Comm. on Health, Educ., Labor & Pensions* (Sept. 30, 2010) (testimony of Danielle Johnson).
95 See § 1.6.1, *supra*.
96 U.S. Gov't Accountability Office, Proprietary Schools: Stronger Department of Education Oversight Needed to Help Ensure Only Eligible Students Receive Federal Student Aid, Report No. GAO-09-600 (Aug. 2009).
97 *Id.*
98 75 Fed. Reg. 34806 (June 18, 2010).
99 *Emerging Risk? An Overview of the Federal Investment in For-Profit Education: Hearing Before the U.S Senate Comm. on Health, Educ., Labor & Pensions* (June 24, 2010) (statement of Kathleen S. Tighe, Inspector Gen., U.S. Dep't of Educ.).
100 Fallo v. High-Tech Inst., 559 F.3d 874 (8th Cir. 2009) (upholding arbitration clause in trade school case).

In a case involving a closed trade school, Silver State Helicopters, a California court denied KeyBank's motion to compel arbitration. Kilgore v. KeyBank Nat'l Ass'n, No. C 08-2958 THE (N.D. Ca. July 8, 2009). Pleadings for this case are available on the Pinnacle Law Group's website at http://pinnaclelawgroup.com. Selected pleadings are also available on the companion website to this manual.

Student lenders and loan servicing companies also employ mandatory arbitration clauses. *See, e.g.*, Fensterstock v. Education Fin. Partners, 618 F. Supp. 2d 276 (S.D.N.Y. 2009) (arbitration clause in promissory note, which effectively required a waiver of right to class action litigation and arbitration, was unconscionable and unenforceable under California law); Smith v. Microskills San Diego, 63 Cal. Rptr. 3d 608 (Cal. Ct. App. July 26, 2007) (school not entitled to enforce arbitration clause when clause was in student loan note, not in contract with school); Cross v. Maric College, 2006 WL 1769779 (Cal. App. June 29, 2006) (school failed to carry initial burden of proof to show a valid arbitration agreement existed); Thornton v. Career Training Ctr., 26 Cal. Rptr. 3d 723 (Cal. App. 2005) (arbitration clauses in promissory notes executed by students to obtain student loans did not apply to student action against vocational training school alleging state UDAP claims), *rev. granted*, 115 P.3d 1121 (Cal. 2005).

The review granted in Thornton v. Career Training Ctr. was dismissed and remanded (56 Cal Rptr. 3d 472 (Cal. 2007)) in light of a decision in a related case. According to one San Diego-based lawyer who represents large post-secondary education clients, "[i]f you're a proprietary school and you don't have [an arbitration provision], you're insane." Elizabeth F. Farrell, *Signer Beware*, Chron. of Higher Educ., Apr. 18, 2003, at A33 (quoting Keith Zakarin).

The Chronicle of Higher Education reports that many large for-profit college systems, including ITT Educational Services, Corinthian, Education Management Corporation, and Kaplan include arbitration provisions in their enrollment contracts. For a detailed discussion of problems with mandatory arbitration clauses and how advocates can challenge these clauses, see National Consumer Law Center, Consumer Arbitration Agreements (5th ed. 2007 and Supp.).

12.4 Other Student Loan and Higher Education Industry Problems

12.4.1 Scholarship Scams

Companies that take advance payment from consumers to find them scholarships and grants is another growing form of abuse. These companies may send high school and college students postcards advertising that, for an advance fee, the service can find "unclaimed" scholarship and grant funds from private companies. They promise to refund the fee if the student does not receive a minimum amount. Nevertheless, these companies all too often provide neither the promised financial aid nor the promised refunds.[101] Sometimes the promised refund is claimed not to be owed because onerous conditions for receiving the refund were placed in the fine print.[102] When these companies are unable to convince the student to send money up front, they may go so far as to obtain the student's checking account number and withdraw money from the account with an unauthorized demand draft or telecheck.[103]

At other times, these companies merely provide consumers with lists of financial aid sources to which the consumers must apply on their own.[104] One company agreed to stop its practice of selling employment and financial aid directories that it misrepresented as programs guaranteeing students jobs with free room, board, and transportation or free financial aid.[105]

In 2000, Congress passed legislation specifically addressing this issue. The College Scholarship Fraud Prevention Act of 2000 required the United States Sentencing Commission to provide enhanced penalties for financial aid fraud.[106] The Act also requires the Department of Education, Department of Justice, and the Federal Trade Commission to coordinate enforcement and outreach activities in this area.[107]

12.4.2 Diploma Mills

Another problem is the rise of so-called "diploma mills." "Diploma mills" and other unaccredited schools resemble the distance education programs that have managed to secure legitimate accreditation. "Diploma mills" are defined as entities that, (1) for a fee, offer degrees, diplomas, or certificates which may be used to represent to the general public that the individual possessing such a degree, diploma, or certificate has completed a program of postsecondary education or training; (2) require such individual to complete little or no education or coursework to obtain such degree, diploma, or certificate; and (3) lack accreditation by a recognized accrediting agency or association.[108] The Department is required to maintain information and resources on its website to assist students, families, and employers in understanding what a diploma mill is and how to identify and avoid diploma mills. Furthermore, the Department must collaborate with the United States Postal Service, the Federal Trade Commission, the Department of Justice (including the Federal Bureau of Investigation), the Internal Revenue Service, and the Office of Personnel Management to maximize federal efforts to "prevent, identify, and prosecute diploma mills" and "broadly disseminate to the public information about diploma mills" as well as resources to identify such diploma mills.[109]

Some states have laws providing specific penalties for entities that issue false academic degrees.[110] In addition, Federal Trade Commission rules require schools to disclose their lack of accreditation.[111] However, enforcement of these rules has generally been a low priority.

---

101 U.S. Dep't of Justice, U.S. Dep't of Educ., & Federal Trade Comm'n, College Fraud Prevention Act of 2000: Eighth Annual Report to Congress (May 2009), *available at* www.ftc.gov/os/2009/06/P094803scholarshipfraud.pdf; FTC v. National Scholarship Found., Inc., 5 Trade Reg. Rep. (CCH) ¶ 24,512 (S.D. Fla. 1998) (order for permanent injunction); FTC v. Deco Consulting Servs., Inc., 5 Trade Reg. Rep. (CCH) ¶ 24,363 (S.D. Fla. 1998) (consent decree); FTC v. National Grant Found., Inc., 5 Trade Reg. Rep. (CCH) ¶ 24,427 (S.D. Fla. 1998) (proposed consent decree); FTC v. College Assistance Servs., Inc., 5 Trade Reg. Rep. (CCH) ¶ 24,357 (S.D. Fla. 1998) (proposed consent decree); FTC v. Career Assistance Planning, Inc., 5 Trade Reg. Rep. (CCH) ¶ 24,218 (N.D. Ga. 1997) (consent decree); FTC v. Nwaigwe, 5 Trade Reg. Rep. (CCH) ¶ 24,253 (D. Md. 1997) (proposed consent decree).
102 FTC v. Student Aid Inc., 5 Trade Reg. Rep. (CCH) ¶ 24,312 (S.D.N.Y. 1997) (proposed consent decree).
103 *Id. See* National Consumer Law Center, Unfair and Deceptive Acts and Practices §§ 6.9.1–6.9.3 (7th ed. 2008 and Supp.) (discussion of demand drafts or telechecks).
104 FTC v. National Grant Found., Inc., 5 Trade Reg. Rep. (CCH) ¶ 24,427 (S.D. Fla. 1998) (proposed consent decree).
105 FTC v. Progressive Media, Inc., 5 Trade Reg. Rep. (CCH) ¶ 24,304 (W.D. Wash. 1997) (proposed consent decree).
   More information can be found on the Department of Education's website at www.ed.gov.
106 Scholarship Fraud Prevention Act, Pub. L. No. 106-420, 114 Stat. 1867 (Nov. 1, 2000). *See* 20 U.S.C. § 1092d.
   Many of the FTC enforcement actions are against individuals falsely applying for financial aid.
107 Project Scholarscam is the FTC's ongoing project to prevent and prosecute scholarship fraud. For more information, see www.ftc.gov/scholarshipscams. The Department of Education also has consumer education information to help borrowers avoid scholarship scams, available at http://studentaid.ed.gov or by calling 1-800-4FED-AID (1-800-433-3243).
108 20 U.S.C. § 1003.
109 20 U.S.C. § 1011l.
110 *See, e.g.*, Haw. Rev. Stat. § 446E-5; Me. Rev. Stat. Ann. tit. 20-A, § 10802; Or. Rev. Stat. § 348.603. *See generally* Creola Johnson, *Degrees of Deception: Are Consumers and Employers Being Duped by Online Universities and Diploma Mills*, 32 J.C. & U.L. 411 (2006).
111 16 C.F.R. § 254.3.

The Department issued proposed rules in June 2010 that would require schools to develop and follow procedures to evaluate the validity of a student's high school diploma.[112]

12.5 Legal Claims to Get Relief for Students and Borrowers

12.5.1 Introduction

As described throughout this manual, there are many provisions in the Higher Education Act (HEA) governing the practices of collectors, lenders, servicers, and schools. The problem is that it is very difficult for borrowers to get relief when these HEA provisions are violated. Possible options for relief are discussed in the following sections.

Borrowers harmed by proprietary school practices may wish to raise school-related claims either in response to a collection action or, if possible, affirmatively. The ways to hold lenders liable for school-related violations are discussed in the following sections. For federal loans, there are specific regulatory provisions allowing borrowers to raise school-related claims. For private loans, borrowers have to find a theory of derivative liability based on the FTC Holder Rule or other laws. These options are also relevant for pre-1994 FFELs and some other federal loans, as discussed below.

Other defenses to raise in federal student loan collection cases are discussed in Chapter 7, *supra*. Most of these defenses apply to private loans as well. Defenses that are unique to private loans are discussed in Chapter 11, *supra*, as well as direct liability claims against private student lenders.

Borrowers may also be faced with collection suits brought by schools seeking to collect loans or other money allegedly owed to the school. The various claims discussed in this section may be brought directly against the school in these cases. For example, a school may seek money beyond what is allowed under state refund laws. Schools will often withhold transcripts or records until a borrower pays debts allegedly owed.[113] Many schools have also created their own internal credit products, as discussed in Chapter 11, *supra*. These are private student loans and, in some cases, open-ended (revolving) credit products.

12.5.2 Federal Claims

12.5.2.1 Higher Education Act and RICO

There are serious drawbacks with bringing claims under the Racketeer Influenced and Corrupt Organizations Act (RICO) and, in particular, under the HEA. A RICO claim requires consumers to prove various technical elements, which will significantly complicate a case.[114] Nevertheless, RICO claims have proved successful in a number of proprietary school cases.[115] The RICO claim has the benefit of treble damages and attorney fees, and its structure is well-suited to bringing in as defendants the school, school personnel, lenders, accrediting associations, and other parties.

There are many possible HEA claims, including violations of the HEA misrepresentation regulations.[116] The problem is that HEA claims will almost certainly be dismissed outright because the vast majority of courts find that there is no implied private right of action under the statute.[117] More

---

112 75 Fed. Reg. 34806 (June 18, 2010). *See* § 1.7.1.3, *supra*.
113 *See, e.g.*, Vilbon v. Katharine Gibbs Coll., 76 Mass. App. Ct. 1126, 2010 WL 1559093 (Mass. App. Ct. Apr. 21, 2010) (settlement agreement with school did not extinguish student's debt, so school was entitled to withhold transcripts).
114 18 U.S.C. §§ 1961–1968. *See* National Consumer Law Center, Unfair and Deceptive Acts and Practices § 14.2 (7th ed. 2008 and Supp.).
115 *See* Rosario v. Livaditis, 963 F.2d 1013 (7th Cir. 1992); Rodriguez v. McKinney, 878 F. Supp. 744 (E.D. Pa. 1995); Moy v. Adelphi Inst., Inc., 866 F. Supp. 696 (E.D.N.Y. 1994), *ex rel.* Moy v. Terranova, 1999 WL 118773 (E.D.N.Y. Mar. 2, 1999); Gonzalez v. North Am. Coll., 700 F. Supp. 362 (S.D. Tex. 1988) (students sufficiently alleged RICO claim). *See also* Johnson v. Sallie Mae Servicing, 2006 WL 3541855 (D.S.C. Dec. 7, 2006), *aff'd without op.*, 258 Fed. Appx. 567 (4th Cir. 2007) (denying defendant's motion to dismiss). *But see* Johnson v. Midland Career Inst., 1996 U.S. Dist. LEXIS 1308 (N.D. Ill. 1996).
116 *See* § 12.5.3.1, *infra* (misrepresentation).
117 To date, the following circuit courts have ruled on this issue: Thomas M. Cooley Law Sch. v. American Bar Ass'n, 459 F.3d 705 (6th Cir. 2006); Slovinec v. DePaul Univ., 332 F.3d 1068 (7th Cir. 2003); McColloch v. PNC Bank Inc., 298 F.3d 1217 (11th Cir. 2002) (in enacting the HEA, Congress expressly provided detailed regulatory scheme which confers on Secretary of Education the exclusive authority to monitor and enforce provisions of the HEA); Labickas v. Arkansas State Univ., 78 F.3d 333 (8th Cir. 1996); Parks Sch. Of Bus. Inc. v. Symington, 51 F.3d 1480 (9th Cir. 1995); L'ggrke v. Benkula, 966 F.2d 1346 (10th Cir. 1992). *See also* Gruen v. Edfund, 2009 WL 2136785 (N.D. Cal. July 15, 2009); Hiwassee Coll. Inc. v. Southern Ass'n of Colls. & Schs., Inc., 2007 WL 433098 (N.D. Ga. Feb. 5, 2007), *aff'd*, 531 F.3d 1333 (11th Cir. 2008) (no implied private right of action under HEA for school challenging accreditor's decision); Brown v. Louisiana Office of Student Fin. Assistance, 2007 WL 496658 (N.D. Tex. Feb. 15, 2007); Nehorai v. United State Dep't of Educ. Direct Loans, 2008 WL 1767072 (E.D.N.Y. Apr. 14, 2008); Gibbs v. SLM Corp., 336 F. Supp. 2d 1 (D. Mass. 2004); White v. Apollo Group, 241 F. Supp. 2d 710 (W.D. Tex. 2003); Robinett v. Delgado Cmty. Coll., 2000 WL 798407 (E.D. La. June 19, 2000); Waugh v. Connecticut Student Loan Found., 966 F. Supp. 141 (D. Conn. 1997); Morgan v. Markerdowne Corp., 976 F. Supp. 301 (D.N.J. 1997); Bartels v. Alabama Commercial Coll., 918 F. Supp. 1565 (S.D. Ga. 1995), *aff'd without published op.*, 189 F.3d 483 (11th Cir. 1999); Moy v. Adelphi Inst., Inc., 866 F. Supp. 696

accurately, according to one court, "nearly every court that has examined this issue has found that there is no implied private right of action under the HEA."[118]

Federal court jurisdiction is the only benefit of an HEA claim. No multiple or statutory damages or attorney fees will be available. In addition, anything that violates the HEA should also be a UDAP, contract, or tort violation. This may be the only way most borrowers can privately enforce the HEA. HEA violations may also form the basis of federal or possibly state claims brought under the Fair Debt Collection Practices Act.[119]

12.5.2.2 False Claims Act

The federal False Claims Act may be used against schools that violate federal regulations. The Act is intended to reach all types of fraud that might result in financial loss to the government. It makes liable anyone who "knowingly makes, uses or causes to be made or used, a false record or statement to get a false or fraudulent claim paid or approved by the Government."[120] The Act authorizes the United States to institute a civil action against an alleged false claimant as well as grants individuals the right to act as private attorneys general to bring a civil action in the United State's name as a realtor.[121]

False Claims Act cases against various schools have survived motions to dismiss. In one case, former enrollment counselors sued the University of Phoenix alleging that the university knowingly made false promises to comply with the incentive compensation ban.[122] The Ninth Circuit agreed with the realtors that a claim could be made based either on the theory of false certification or promissory fraud. The owner of University of Phoenix agreed to settle this case in December 2009. The two former recruiters bringing the litigation received nearly $19 million or about 30% of the reported $67.5 million settlement.[123]

In order to state a claim under the False Claims Act, the statement alleged to be false must have been false when made and must be material to the government's decision to

---

(E.D.N.Y. 1994); Spinner v. Chesapeake Bus. Inst. of Va., Clearinghouse No. 49,131A (E.D. Va. Feb. 5, 1993); Jackson v. Culinary Sch. of Wash., 811 F. Supp. 714 (D.D.C. 1993) (claim dismissed based on summary judgment motion that students had not presented evidence of origination relationship), *aff'd on other grounds*, 27 F.3d 573 (D.C. Cir. 1994) (origination theory not enforceable against the Secretary), *vacated on other grounds*, 115 S. Ct. 2573 (1995) (appellate court used *de novo* instead of abuse of discretion standard to review district court's decision to decide state law issues in declaratory judgment action), *remanded to district court on state law claims, aff'g own ruling on origination*, 59 F.3d 254 (D.C. Cir. 1995) (to determine on what basis federal court decided to rule on state law issues), *motion dismissed*, 1995 U.S. App. LEXIS 22304 (D.C. Cir. 1995); Keams v. Tempe Tech. Inst., 807 F. Supp. 569 (D. Ariz. 1992); Graham v. Security Sav. & Loan, 125 F.R.D. 687 (N.D. Ind. 1989), *aff'd sub nom.* Veal v. First Am. Sav. Bank, 914 F.2d 909 (7th Cir. 1990); Davies v. Sallie Mae., Inc., 86 Cal. Rptr. 3d 136 (Ct. App. Cal. 2008). *But see* Tipton v. Northeastern Bus. Coll. (S.D. W. Va. Jan. 8, 1988), *available at* www.consumerlaw.org/unreported (private right of action); Chavez v. LTV Aerospace Corp., 412 F. Supp. 4 (N.D. Tex. 1976) (private cause of action when school allegedly imposed illegal charges on students).

In 2003 court pleadings, the Department of Education suggested that it supports implying a private right of action under the HEA in very limited circumstances. Specifically, the Department supported a private right for borrowers to seek judicial review of guaranty agency administrative wage garnishment hearing decisions. Borrowers already have this right in cases in which the Department conducts the hearing. *See* Memorandum of Points and Authorities in Support of Motion to Dismiss, Hutchins et al. v. USA et al., No. 02-CV-6256 (E.D. Ca. memorandum filed Apr. 25, 2003).

118 Gruen v. Edfund, 2009 WL 2136785 (N.D. Cal. July 15, 2009).
119 *See* § 7.4.3, *supra*.
120 31 U.S.C. § 3729(a)(2).
121 31 U.S.C. § 3730(b)(1).
122 United States *ex rel.* Hendow v. University of Phoenix, 461 F.3d 1166 (9th Cir. 2006). *See also* United States *ex rel.* Main v. Oakland City Univ., 426 F.3d 914 (7th Cir. 2005), *cert. denied*, 547 U.S. 1071 (U.S. 2006) (former university recruiter brought False Claims Act case, contending that university falsely represented that it would not pay recruiters fees for enrolling students); United States v. Chapman Univ., 2006 WL 1562231 (C.D. Cal. May 23, 2006) (False Claims Act claim survived motion to dismiss except for claims based on student applications for state licensing). *See* § 9.2.6, *supra* (incentive compensation).

Oakland City University settled the false claims act case against it in 2007. The university denied liability but agreed to pay $5.3 million to the federal government and to the whistle-blower bringing the suit. *See* Elizabeth Quill, *University Will Pay $5.3-Million to Settle Whistle-Blower's Lawsuit*, Chron. of Higher Educ., Aug. 10, 2007, at A20.

A False Claims Act lawsuit was filed against Kaplan University in 2008. Former academic officers of the school allege that Kaplan enrolled unqualified students, inflated grades, and falsified documents. *See* Goldie Blumenstyk, *3 Former Employees Accuse Kaplan U of Bilking Government Out of Billions*, Chron. of Higher Educ., Mar. 21, 2008, at A12.

In 2009, four false claim suits against Kaplan Higher Education were consolidated in Florida. The four lawsuits had been filed in Florida in April 2007, Illinois in October 2007, Pennsylvania in November 2006, and Nevada in November 2007. Goldie Blumenstyk, *4 False-Claims Lawsuits Against Kaplan are Consolidated*, Chron. of Higher Educ., June 11, 2009.

The Justice Department also settled a false claims lawsuit against Alta Colleges in April 2009. The lawsuit alleged that the company and its Westwood College campuses obtained a state license to operate in Texas by falsely stating that they observed state requirements on job placement reporting and that their interior design programs complied with the requirements for a professional license in the field. Andrew Mytelka, *Proprietary College to Pay $7-Million to Settle Federal Student-Aid Charges*, Chron. of Higher Educ., Apr. 20, 2009.

123 *See* Goldie Blumenstyk, *Whistle–Blowers Will Get $19-Million in U. of Phoenix Settlement*, Chron. of Higher Educ., Dec. 14, 2009.

False Claims Act claims in a case with similar allegations was dismissed under the "first to file" bar at 31 U.S.C. § 3730(b)(5). U.S. v. Apollo Group, 2009 WL 3756623 (S.D. Cal. Nov. 6, 2009).

pay money. Furthermore, there must be an actual claim on the government's fisc. The "promissory fraud" theory holds defendants liable for each claim submitted to the government under a contract, when the contract or extension of government benefit was originally obtained through false statements or fraudulent conduct.

A plaintiff seeking to bring a False Claims Act case against a company collecting student loans was dismissed on the grounds that there was a prior public disclosure of the collection company's abusive actions.[124] The prior disclosures included previous lawsuits and media reports. Plaintiffs may still bring a case under these circumstances if they were the original source of the public disclosure.

A plaintiff was allowed to proceed in a case alleging that a university repeatedly violated the incentive compensation ban. The plaintiff alleged more than twenty separate instances in which the school violated the ban by compensating enrollment counselors directly based on securing enrollments, by ranking counselors against each other based on the number of enrollments they secured, and by providing incentive trips, lunches, dinners, gift certificates, and paid days off based on the number of enrollments secured. The plaintiff-realtor had worked at the school as an enrollment counselor.[125] The key issue, according to the court, was whether the school made a false statement or record in order to get the government to pay or approve the claim. In this case, the plaintiff alleged that this occurred when the school falsely certified that it complied with the incentive compensation ban with the intent that the government pay or approve the claim for student loan funds.

12.5.2.3 FTC Guides and Rule

The FTC has issued guides concerning unfair and deceptive private vocational school practices.[126] The guides specify that schools cannot misrepresent, through their name or otherwise, that they are connected with government agencies or civil service commissions or that they are an employment agency or employer.[127]

Among other provisions, the FTC guides require that schools disclose if the course is offered through correspondence.[128] It is deceptive for a school to misrepresent the nature of its approval or accreditation or the extent to which former students, employers, or counselors recommend a course.[129]

The FTC updated its vocational school guides in 1998, renaming them "Guides for Private Vocational and Distance Education Schools."[130] The most significant change was a provision addressing misrepresentations about a school's placement success following training. The guides now specifically state that it is deceptive for a school, in promoting a course of training, to misrepresent the availability of employment after graduation from a course, the success that the member's graduates have realized in obtaining such employment, or the salary that the member's graduates will receive in such employment.[131] The guides also state that it is deceptive for a school to misrepresent that the lack of a high school education or prior training is not an impediment to successful completion of a course or obtaining employment.[132]

In July 2009, the FTC issued a request for public comment on the overall costs, benefits, necessity, and regulatory and economic impact of the vocational and distance education school guides.[133] The FTC specifically requested comments on the need for the guides as well as evidence of any benefits for consumers.

---

124 Schultz v. Devry Inc., 2009 WL 562286 (N.D. Ill. Mar. 4, 2009) (granting Devry's motion to dismiss and holding that former employee did not have direct and independent knowledge of information on which allegations were based); United States v. Diversified Collection Servs., Inc., 2006 WL 3834407 (S.D. Ohio Dec. 29, 2006).

125 U.S. v. Significant Educ., 2009 WL 322875 (D. Ariz. Feb. 10, 2009).

126 Guides for Private Vocational and Distance Education Schools, 16 C.F.R. §§ 254.0–254.10.

In 1978, the FTC also promulgated a rule related to private trade school activities. Trade Regulation Rule Concerning Proprietary Vocational and Home-Study Schools, 43 Fed. Reg. 60795 (Dec. 18, 1978).

The FTC withdrew the vocational school rule's effective date pending further FTC action and, in 1988, finally terminated the rule. 53 Fed. Reg. 29482 (Aug. 5, 1988).

Nevertheless, the rule's statement of basis and purpose, 43 Fed. Reg. 60791 (Dec. 18, 1978), and the FTC staff report recommending the rule still provide a useful factual and legal background to vocational school issues. Bureau of Consumer Protection, Proprietary Vocational and Home-Study Schools, Final Report and Proposed Trade Regulation Rule, Clearinghouse No. 31,041 (1976).

127 16 C.F.R. § 254.2. *See also* FTC v. Couture Sch. of Modeling, 5 Trade Reg. Rep. (CCH) ¶ 22,815 (D. Md. 1990) (injunction); United States v. Eyler, 5 Trade Reg. Rep. (CCH) ¶ 22,891 (M.D. Fla. 1990) (consent decree); People v. Wilshire Computer Coll. (Cal. Super. Ct. 1991), *available at* www.consumerlaw.org/unreported (preliminary injunction pursuant to stipulation).

128 16 C.F.R. § 254.2(c).

129 16 C.F.R. § 254.3. *See also* Malone v. Academy of Court Reporting, 582 N.E.2d 54 (Ohio Ct. App. 1990) (concealment of fact that school was not certified or accredited to issue promised associate degree violates UDAP); Cavaliere v. Duff's Bus. Inst., 605 A.2d 397 (Pa. Super. Ct. 1992); Webster College v. Speier, 605 S.W.2d 712 (Tex. App. 1980). *But see* Lidecker v. Kendall Coll., 550 N.E.2d 1121 (Ill. App. Ct. 1990) (failure to inform prospective students of nursing school's lack of accreditation not a UDAP violation when school did not intend that students rely on omission, and lack of accreditation did not cause student harm).

130 63 Fed. Reg. 42570 (Aug. 10, 1998) (amending 16 C.F.R. pt. 254); 63 Fed. Reg. 72350 (Dec. 31, 1998) (corrections).

131 16 C.F.R. § 254.4(d).

132 16 C.F.R. § 254.5.

133 74 Fed. Reg. 37973 (July 30, 2009).

§ 12.5.2.4   *Student Loan Law*

12.5.2.4 Other Federal Claims

Another potential claim in the typical proprietary school/student loan case is that the Department of Education failed to adequately supervise the school and improperly recognized the accrediting agency. The Federal Tort Claims Act[134] sharply limits a party's ability to recover *damages* from a federal agency, but the Act does not prevent the student from receiving reimbursement of amounts improperly paid or otherwise receiving money to be made whole.[135] Before initiating an action, the borrower must first exhaust administrative remedies.[136]

The Secretary of the Department of Education ("the Secretary") is likely to argue that the Department has no responsibility to review the educational quality of the school. The counter-argument is that the Secretary has an obligation under the Higher Education Act to evaluate the fiscal responsibility of the school.[137]

At least one federal court decision found that students could proceed on this theory.[138] The court allowed the students to proceed to trial to try to prove any of the following: (1) that the Secretary acted arbitrarily and capriciously in certifying branch campuses to participate in the loan program; (2) that certain campuses were not affiliated with any other eligible school and thus were never approved for participation in the program; or (3) that the courses did not provide education for a recognized occupation or "useful employment." The court also allowed the students to proceed in their mandamus action against the Secretary to force the school to repay program funds when the program failed to satisfy federal standards.[139]

There are other federal claims to consider as well. The federal Fair Debt Collections Practices Act (FDCPA) is essential in challenging abusive student loan collection practices. Private FDCPA actions are in many cases the only way borrowers can get relief when collectors violate Department of Education collection regulations.[140]

There are limits, however, to using fair debt claims to resolve student loan disputes. The FDCPA is an indirect way of obtaining relief. It is intended to address collection abuses. A collection agency's failure to offer a particular repayment plan or otherwise comply with the HEA is a violation. However, the available remedies are monetary damages. These can be extremely useful, but they do not help borrowers get the repayment plans or discharges to which they are entitled.

The federal Fair Credit Reporting Act (FCRA) may also be used to challenge problems related to the reporting of student loans on credit reports.[141] Claims relating to credit reporting under state laws, however, may be preempted by the HEA or the FCRA.[142]

Federal student loan lenders are not subject to Truth in Lending Act (TILA) disclosure requirements.[143] However, the Sixth Circuit affirmed in 2009 that the TILA federal student loan exemption applies only to government student loan programs promulgated under the Higher Education Act. The TILA should apply to other federal student loan programs.[144] In addition, the TILA does apply to private student loans, as discussed in Chapter 11, *supra*.[145]

---

134 28 U.S.C. § 1346(b).
135 Florence County Sch. Dist. Four v. Carter, 510 U.S. 7 (1993); Burlington Sch. Comm. v. Massachusetts Dep't of Educ., 471 U.S. 359 (1985); Army & Air Force Exch. Serv. v. Sheehan, 456 U.S. 728, 739 n.11 (1982); United States v. Testan, 424 U.S. 392, 401–02 (1976); Porter v. Warner Holding Co., 328 U.S. 395 (1946); Muller v. Committee on Special Educ., 145 F.3d 95 (2d Cir. 1998); Gadsby by Gadsby v. Grasmick, 109 F.3d 940 (4th Cir. 1997); Whayne v. U.S. Dep't of Educ., 915 F. Supp. 1143 (D. Kan. 1996) (Federal Tort Claims cause of action dismissed due to plaintiff's failure to exhaust administrative remedies).
136 *See, e.g.*, Sanon v. Department of Higher Educ., 2010 WL 1049264 (E.D.N.Y. Mar. 18, 2010); Shabtai v. U.S. Dep't of Educ., 2003 WL 21983025 (S.D.N.Y. Aug. 20, 2003) (borrower's federal tort claim alleging that the Department had failed to grant loan cancellation and other issues dismissed due to failure to exhaust administrative remedies).
137 *See* 34 C.F.R. §§ 668.14, 668.15.
     The ineligibility of the school may also be a defense. See § 7.5.4.3, *supra*.
138 Hernandez v. Alexander (D. Nev. May 18, 1992), *available at* www.consumerlaw.org/unreported. *But see* Armand v. Secretary of Educ. (S.D. Fla. July 19, 1995), *available at* www.consumerlaw.org/unreported.
139 For a discussion of declaratory relief and injunctive actions against the Department, see § 12.6.2.1, *infra*. In general, the HEA states that no injunction shall be issued against the Secretary. 20 U.S.C. § 1082(a)(2).
     Strategies to address this prohibition are discussed in § 12.6.2.1, *infra*.
140 *See* § 7.4, *supra*.
141 *See, e.g.*, Ellis v. Pennsylvania Higher Educ. Assistance Agency, 2008 WL 4351746 (C.D. Cal. Sept. 23, 2008) (denying KeyBank's motion for reconsideration and allowing plaintiff's FCRA claim based on vicarious liability); Jordan v. Equifax Info. Servs. et al., 410 F. Supp. 2d 1349 (N.D. Ga. 2006) (FCRA claim against loan servicer SLM for improper furnishing of information about student loans in identity theft case allowed to proceed); Pirouzian v. SLM Corp., 396 F. Supp. 2d 1124 (S.D. Cal. 2005) (student loan borrower's FCRA claims partially preempted, but claim under section 1681s-2(b) allowed to proceed); Hinton v. USA Funds, 2005 WL 730963 (N.D. Ill. Mar. 30, 2005) (summary judgment granted in part and denied in part in case brought by student loan borrower raising FCRA claims); Potter v. Illinois Student Assistance Comm'n, 2004 WL 1203156 (Cal. App. 4 Dist. June 2, 2004) (borrower's state credit reporting act claims preempted by HEA and FCRA). *See generally* National Consumer Law Center, Fair Credit Reporting Chs. 10, 11 (6th ed. 2006 and Supp.).
142 *See, e.g.*, Pirouzian v. SLM Corp., 396 F. Supp. 2d 1124 (S.D. Cal. 2005). See § 12.5.3.4, *infra*.
143 15 U.S.C. § 1603(7).
144 *See* U.S. v. Petroff-Kline, 557 F.3d 285 (6th Cir. 2009) (applying TILA to borrower's Health Education (HEAL) loans).
145 *See* § 11.4.1, *supra*.

12.5.2.5 Federal Statutory Discharges

The most efficient and complete way to get relief for school-related problems is often through a statutory discharge program. These discharges, however, are limited. Only borrowers who qualify for closed-school, false-certification, or unpaid-refund discharges can get this relief. Eligibility and application procedures are discussed in detail in Chapter 9, *supra*. Borrowers may also qualify for discharges unrelated to school problems, if they are totally and permanently disabled or meet the criteria for public service or other job-related discharge programs.[146]

12.5.3 State Claims

12.5.3.1 UDAP Theories

Unfair and deceptive acts and practices (UDAP) claims are generally well-suited to challenge trade school abuses. Oral and print misrepresentations can be deceptive; the failure to disclose can be deceptive; and enrolling students unable to benefit from a program can be unfair or unconscionable.[147] Using a deceptive name for an educational program or making changes to a program without proper disclosures may also give rise to UDAP claims.[148] Misrepresentations about a school's ability to grant degrees should also be actionable.[149]

School program participation agreements state that an eligible institution that has engaged in substantial misrepresentation of the nature of its educational program, its financial charges, or the employability of its graduates, may face suspension or termination of the eligibility status for any or all programs.[150] These HEA misrepresentation provisions may form the basis of UDAP claims. The Department proposed significant changes to the misrepresentation regulations in June 2010.[151]

The student's proof burden is simplified with a UDAP claim because the student normally need not prove intent, scienter, or other components of a common law fraud claim.[152] Some states do, however, require proof of reliance on the deceptive statement or conduct.[153] UDAP remedies often offer multiple or punitive damages and attorney fees.[154] State UDAP laws have various exclusions that may apply in these cases. For example, community colleges or other public colleges may be excluded from various UDAP laws that have government entity exemptions.[155]

Schools may not deceive students with respect to the nature, terms, or conditions of contractual obligations, veterans' educational benefits, and federally insured student loans.[156] A school may not misrepresent its refund policy or deceive students into attending additional classes before dropping out with the result that their contractual obligation is significantly increased under the refund formula.[157] Schools must also pay all owed refunds.[158]

---

146 *See* Ch. 9, *supra*.

147 *See generally* National Consumer Law Center, Unfair and Deceptive Acts and Practices §§ 4.3, 4.4 (7th ed. 2008 and Supp.).

148 *See, e.g.*, Deen v. New Sch. Univ., 2007 WL 1032295 (S.D.N.Y. Mar. 27, 2007), *cert. denied*, 2008 WL 331366 (S.D.N.Y. Feb. 4, 2008).

149 *See, e.g.*, Bobbitt v. Academy of Court Reporting, Inc., 249 F.R.D. 488 (E.D. Mich. May 1, 2008), *op. corrected and superseded*, Bobbitt v. Academy of Court Reporting, Inc., 252 F.R.D. 327 (E.D. Mich. June 25, 2008) (granting motion for class certification in case challenging school's misrepresentations about ability to grant degrees).

  A settlement agreement was approved in this case. *See* Bobbitt v. Academy of Court Reporting, Inc., 2009 WL 2168833 (E.D. Mich. July 21, 2009), *amended in part by* 2009 WL 2413629 (E.D. Mich. Aug. 6, 2009).

150 20 U.S.C. § 1094(c)(3); 34 C.F.R. §§ 668.71–668.75 (misrepresentation).

151 75 Fed. Reg. 34806 (June 18, 2010).

152 *See* National Consumer Law Center, Unfair and Deceptive Acts and Practices § 4.2 (7th ed. 2008 and Supp.).

153 *See id.* §§ 7.5.2, 10.5.2. *See, e.g.*, Finstad v. Washburn Univ. of Topeka, 845 P.2d 685 (Kan. 1993) (finding, in UDAP case, that students failed to demonstrate causation between school's false statement regarding accreditation and students' injuries; students did not claim they were induced to enroll by the false statement).

154 *See* National Consumer Law Center, Unfair and Deceptive Acts and Practices Ch. 13 (7th ed. 2008 and Supp.).

155 *See, e.g.*, Meyer v. Community Coll. of Beaver County, 965 A.2d 406 (Pa. Commw. Ct. 2009) (community college that had its certification revoked was immune from UDAP statutory and treble damages), *review granted*, 978 A.2d 348 (Pa. 2009); Barr v. Community Coll. of Beaver County, 968 A.2d 235 (Pa. Commw. Ct. 2009), *review granted*, 978 A.2d 347 (Pa. 2009).

156 Bell & Howell Co., 95 F.T.C. 761 (1980) (consent order); People v. Wilshire Computer Coll. (Cal. Super. Ct. 1991), *available at* www.consumerlaw.org/unreported (preliminary injunction pursuant to stipulation); Manley v. Wichita Bus. Coll., 701 P.2d 893 (Kan. 1985). *But see* Finstad v. Washburn Univ. of Topeka, 845 P.2d 685 (Kan. 1993) (overruling holding in *Manley* that actual damages are not required in Kansas UDAP cases); Gamble v. University Sys. of N.H., 610 A.2d 357 (N.H. 1992) (university's imposition of mid-semester tuition increase due to fiscal crisis not a UDAP violation when it notified almost all affected students of possible increase in letter accompanying initial billing for semester).

157 People v. Wilshire Computer Coll. (Cal. Super. Ct. 1991) (preliminary injunction pursuant to stipulation), *available at* www.consumerlaw.org/unreported; Manley v. Wichita Bus. Coll., 701 P.2d 893 (Kan. 1985); Reynolds v. Sterling Coll., Inc., 750 A.2d 1020 (Vt. 2000) (awarding summary judgment to student on contractual claim; remanding consumer fraud claim; finding change in refund policy after substantial tuition payments had been made is a unilateral modification of specific contractual term for which no consideration had been received). *But see* Finstad v. Washburn Univ. of Topeka, 845 P.2d 685 (Kan. 1993) (overruling holding in *Manley* that actual damages are not required in Kansas UDAP cases).

158 United States v. Eyler, 5 Trade Reg. Rep. (CCH) ¶ 22,891 (M.D. Fla. 1990) (consent decree); People v. Wilshire Computer Coll.

Also deceptive are misrepresentations concerning the nature of school placement services.[159] For example, in one UDAP case, consumer recovery was based on the school's "admissions officers" (who worked on commission and made as much as $56,000 a year) promising 90% to 95% job placement when in fact the school was reporting to its accrediting agency job placement rates averaging only 47%. The school's higher 90%–95% figure was derived only from students who kept in touch with the school's placement office, not the total number of the school's graduates.[160]

UDAP claims based on violations of HEA or other federal claims should be heard in state court. Basing a UDAP claim on a federal legal violation does not make it a federal cause of action.[161]

12.5.3.2 State Education Laws

A state's education statutes may provide another source of precedent on unfair or deceptive trade school practices.[162] In some cases, these statutes will provide for a private right of action. If not, a violation of these standards may be actionable under a state UDAP statute.

Statutes regulating professions or occupations may also apply to proprietary institutions of higher education. A Hawaii law, for example, requires unaccredited degree-granting institutions to make certain disclosures in catalogs, promotional materials, and contracts.[163]

A few states set minimum standards for schools, in some cases only for vocational or "career" schools.[164] Others prohibit false statements or misrepresentations or require schools to provide certain disclosures.[165]

(Cal. Super. Ct. 1991), *available at* www.consumerlaw.org/unreported (preliminary injunction pursuant to stipulation).

In addition, there is now a federal discharge program to reimburse students for unpaid refunds. *See* § 9.5, *supra*.

159 Fla. Admin. Code Ann. r. 2-18.002 (Contracts for Future Consumer Services); Control Data Corp., 97 F.T.C. 84 (1981) (consent order); Bell & Howell Co., 95 F.T.C. 761 (1980) (consent order); Universal Training Serv. Inc., 94 F.T.C. 167 (1979) (consent order); Art Instruction Schs. Inc., 93 F.T.C. 32 (1979) (consent order); Driver Training Inst. Inc., 92 F.T.C. 235 (1978) (consent order); Commercial Programming Unlimited Inc., 88 F.T.C. 913 (1976) (consent order); Lafayette United Corp., 88 F.T.C. 683 (1976) (consent order); Lear Siegler Inc., 86 F.T.C. 860 (1975) (consent order); Weaver Airline Personnel Sch., 85 F.T.C. 237 (1975) (consent order); Eastern Detective Academy Inc., 78 F.T.C. 1428 (1971); Missouri Coll. of Automation, 67 F.T.C. 258 (1965) (consent order).

160 Beckett v. Computer Career Inst., Inc. (Or. Cir. Ct. July 2, 1990), *aff'd in part and rev'd in part*, 852 P.2d 840 (Or. Ct. App. 1993).

161 *See, e.g.*, Brooks v. Sallie Mae, 2009 WL 4038467 (D. Conn. Nov. 19, 2009) (mere presence of a federal law defense does not give rise to federal jurisdiction).

162 Cal. Educ. Code §§ 94800–94800.5 (West). *See* Daghlian v. DeVry Univ., Inc., 461 F. Supp. 2d 1121 (C.D. Cal. 2006) (accepting plaintiff's argument that drafting error in California education law unfairly restricts private right of action and extending right to a longer list of violations; plaintiff sued private university for misrepresentations regarding transfer of academic units; UDAP claim also included). *See also* Ohio Rev. Code Ann. § 3332.16 (West) (consumer transactions with career schools and colleges are subject to state UDAP statute).

The California legislature passed a bill (AB 48) on September 28, 2009, and the Private Postsecondary Education Act became effective on January 1, 2010. Although this legislation appears to re-regulate the proprietary school industry, consumer advocates have highlighted many flaws. Among other problems, there is no review in determining eligibility for state approval; the bill would also exempt all regionally accredited schools. The bill delegates authority to the Department of Consumer Affairs and provides inadequate enforcement resources. *See* Betsy Imholz, *Guest Post: California Dreamin' Becoming Proprietary Students' Nightmare*, New America Higher Ed Watch Blog (Aug. 13, 2009), *at* www.newamerica.net/blog/higher-ed-watch/2009/guest-post-california-dreamin-becoming-proprietary-students-nightmare-13914.

163 Haw. Rev. Stat. § 446E-2; Killian v. Pacific Educ. Servs. Co., 2007 WL 1303023 (D. Haw. May 3, 2007) (awarding former student's judgment for damages and attorney fees for school's failure to make mandatory disclosures under Hawaii law regarding accreditation status and for other misrepresentations).

164 *See, e.g.*, Alaska Stat. § 14.48.060 (post-secondary educational institutions); Colo. Rev. Stat. Ann. § 12-59-106 (private occupational school standards); Del. Code Ann. tit. 14, § 8504 (private business and trade schools); Ga. Code Ann. § 20-3-250.6 (non-public post-secondary educational institutions); Idaho Code Ann. §§ 33-2402 (public post-secondary educational institutions), 33-2403 (proprietary schools); Ind. Code § 21-17-3-13 (post-secondary proprietary educational institutions); Ky. Rev. Stat. Ann. § 165A.370 (West) (proprietary schools); La. Rev. Stat. Ann. § 17:3141.5 (proprietary schools); Md. Code Ann., Educ. § 11-202 (post-secondary educational institutions); Mich. Comp. Laws § 390.771 (non-incorporated private educational institutions); Mich. Admin. Code r. 390.564 (proprietary schools); Minn. Stat. Ann. § 141.25 (private career schools); Miss. Code Ann. § 75-60-11 (proprietary schools and colleges); Mo. Rev. Stat. § 173.604 (proprietary schools); Neb. Rev. Stat. §§ 85-1608, 85-1635 (private post-secondary career schools (includes private right of enforcement); Nev. Rev. Stat. Ann. § 394.450 (private post-secondary educational institutions); N.H. Rev. Stat. Ann. § 188-D:20 (private post-secondary career schools); N.M. Stat. §§ 21-23-6.2 (post-secondary educational institutions), 21-25-3 (non-proprietary out-of-state institutions); N.Y. Educ. Law § 5002 (McKinney) (licensed private trade schools and registered business schools); N.C. Gen. Stat. § 116-15(f) (non-public post-secondary educational institutions); Ohio Rev. Code Ann. § 3332.05 (West) (career schools and colleges); Or. Rev. Stat. § 345.325 (career schools); 24 Pa. Cons. Stat. § 6502 (private colleges, universities, and seminaries); Tenn. Code Ann. §§ 49-7-2006, 49-7-2011 (post-secondary educational institutions) (includes private right of enforcement); Tex. Educ. Code Ann. § 132.0551 (Vernon) (career schools and colleges); Utah Code Ann. § 13-34-104 (post-secondary proprietary schools); Vt. Stat. Ann. tit. 16, § 176(c) (post-secondary schools chartered in Vermont), 176a(c) (post-secondary schools not chartered in Vermont); 8 Va. Admin. Code §§ 40-31-140 (institutions of higher education), 40-31-150 (career technical schools), 40-31-160 (all post-secondary schools); Wyo. Stat. Ann. § 21-2-401 (private post-secondary education).

165 *See, e.g.*, Ala. Code § 16-46-4 (proprietary post-secondary

12.5.3.3 Other State Claims

In some states, a state RICO claim may provide superior remedies to a UDAP claim, or the two together may provide more relief than just a UDAP claim. For example, in Oregon, one UDAP and state RICO case against a school resulted in a jury verdict of $320,000 in multiple and punitive damages for nine former computer school students.[166] On appeal, the state RICO recovery was reversed on technical grounds, but all the UDAP actual and punitive damages were affirmed, as was the award of attorney fees to the consumers.[167] State debt collection claims, including possible preemption issues, are discussed in Chapter 7, *supra*.

12.5.3.4 Preemption of State Laws

Despite the existence of federal regulation of the student loan program, the Higher Education Act should generally not preempt all UDAP or other state claims against a school. Specifically, only state claims that conflict with the purposes or provisions of the HEA should be preempted.[168] Conflict preemption may arise under two circumstances: from a direct conflict between state and federal law, such that compliance with both is impossible (called "direct conflict"), or because a state law "stands as an obstacle to the accomplishment and execution of the full purposes and objectives of Congress" (called "obstacle preemption").[169] Courts have found conflicts in numerous cases and preempted state claims.[170]

A few sections of the HEA expressly preempt certain state law claims. These include state usury laws,[171] state statutes of limitations,[172] state infancy defenses,[173] and state disclosure requirements.[174] The fact that certain provisions are expressly preempted bolsters the argument that Congress did not intend the HEA to so "occupy the field" that it would automatically preempt all state laws.[175] However, if the court characterizes particular claims as fitting within these categories, the claim may be preempted. For example, the Ninth Circuit ruled in 2010 that a number of plaintiffs' claims against Sallie Mae were not misrepresentation claims, but rather disclosure claims, and therefore explicitly preempted.[176]

The Fourth Circuit addressed preemption of state claims in student loan cases, overturning a district court's ruling that the plaintiff's state claims were preempted based on "obstacle preemption."[177] According to the court, the ex-

---

schools); Fla. Stat. Ann. § 1005.04 (non-public post-secondary education); Haw. Rev. Stat. §§ 446E-2, 446E-5; 105 Ill. Comp. Stat. Ann. § 425/26 (Private Business and Vocational School Act includes private right of action); Ind. Code §§ 21-17-3-7 (post-secondary proprietary educational institutions; required disclosures), 21-17-3-18 (same; (prohibited actions); Iowa Code § 261B.9 (post-secondary schools); La. Rev. Stat. Ann. § 17:3141.14 (proprietary schools); Mass. Gen. Laws ch. 75C, §§ 5, 10 (private correspondent schools) (includes private right of action); Mass. Gen. Laws ch. 75D, §§ 10, 14 (private business schools; includes private right of action); Mass. Gen. Laws Ann. ch. 93 § 21 (private trade schools; includes private enforcement right); Mich. Admin. Code r. 390.566 (proprietary schools); Minn. Stat. Ann §§ 141.265,141.28 (private career schools); Miss. Code Ann. §§ 75-60-19(1)(f), 75-60-33 (proprietary schools and colleges); Nev. Rev. Stat. §§ 394.441, 394.445, 394.520 (private post-secondary educational institutions; includes private right of enforcement); N.M. Stat. §§ 21-23-7, 21-23-10 (post-secondary educational institutions; includes private right of enforcement), 21-24-4 (out-of-state proprietary schools); N.Y. Educ. Law § 5005 (McKinney) (licensed private trade schools and registered business schools); N.D. Cent. Code § 15-20.4-09 (post-secondary educational institutions, private enforcement right); Ohio Rev. Code Ann. §§ 3332.09(F) (West) (career schools and colleges), 3332.16 (West) (consumer transactions subject to state UDAP statute); Ohio Admin. Code 3332-1-12; Or. Rev. Stat. § 345.325 (career schools); R.I. Gen. Laws § 16-50-4 (correspondence schools and home study courses); Tex. Educ. Code § 132.151 (Vernon) (career schools or colleges); Utah Code Ann. § 13-34-104(5), 13-34-107, 13-34-108 (post-secondary proprietary schools); Vt. Stat. Ann. tit. 16, § 176(c)(1) (post-secondary schools chartered in Vermont), 176a(e)(2) (post-secondary schools not chartered in Vermont); Wash. Rev. Code Ann. § 28C.10.110 (unfair practices of private vocational schools).

166 Beckett v. Computer Career Inst., Inc. (Or. Cir. Ct. July 2, 1990), *aff'd in part and rev'd in part*, 852 P.2d 840 (Or. Ct. App. 1993).

167 Beckett v. Computer Career Inst., Inc., 852 P.2d 840 (Or. Ct. App. 1993).

168 Courts have consistently concluded that the HEA does not occupy the field of higher education loans, so "field preemption" is not appropriate in these cases. *See, e.g.*, College Loan Corp. v. SLM Corp., 396 F.3d 588 (4th Cir. 2005). *See* Cliff v. Payco Gen. Am. Credits, 363 F.3d 1113 (11th Cir. 2004) (HEA does not occupy the field of student loan debt collection, and state fair debt collection claims not preempted); Morgan v. Markerdowne Corp., 976 F. Supp. 301 (D.N.J. 1997) (HEA preempts only those state laws which are in conflict with it); Williams v. National Sch. of Health Tech., Inc., 836 F. Supp. 273 (E.D. Pa. 1993), *aff'd*, 37 F.3d 1491 (3d Cir. 1994).

169 See the discussion in College Loan Corp. v. SLM Corp., 396 F.3d 588 (4th Cir. 2005).

170 *See, e.g.*, Armstrong v. Accrediting Council for Continuing Educ. & Training, Inc., 168 F.3d 1362 (D.C. Cir. 1999) (federal student loan policy preempted student loan recipient's state law mistake and illegality claims as well as assertion of vocational school misconduct as a defense to collection); Washkoviak v. Student Loan Mktg. Ass'n, 849 A.2d 37 (D.C. Ct. App. 2004) (UDAP claims based on lenders failure to disclose information about late fees and for improper charging of late fees preempted by HEA), *on subsequent appeal*, 900 A.2d 168 (D.C. Ct. App. 2006).

For a detailed discussion of whether the HEA preempts state debt collection claims, see § 7.4.4, *supra*.

171 20 U.S.C. § 1078(d). *See* § 2.3.1, *supra*.

172 20 U.S.C. § 1091a(a).

173 20 U.S.C. § 1091a(b)(2).

174 20 U.S.C. § 1098g. *See* § 2.5.1, *supra*.

175 *See, e.g.*, College Loan Corp. v. SLM Corp., 396 F.3d 588 (4th Cir. 2005).

176 Chae v. SLM Corp., 593 F.3d 936 (9th Cir. 2010). This is problematic as it conflates disclosure with fraud.

177 College Loan Corp. v. SLM, 396 F.3d 588 (4th Cir. 2005).

istence of extensive regulations pursuant to the HEA does not automatically mean that non-conflicting state law is preempted.[178] Furthermore, the fact that there is no private right of action to enforce the HEA does not lead to the conclusion that the plaintiff's pursuit of state law claims would obstruct the federal scheme.[179] To the contrary, the court emphasized that the Supreme Court has recognized that the availability of a state law claim is even more important in an area where no federal private right of action exists.[180] In this case, the plaintiff sought redress under state law for the defendant's alleged violation of the HEA provision requiring lenders who receive loan verification certificates to complete and return these certificates within ten days.[181]

However, a 2010 Ninth Circuit court disagreed with the Fourth Circuit. In distinguishing its case, the Ninth Circuit referred to the Fourth Circuit case as a suit between two lenders. The Fourth Circuit found that it was unable to confirm that the creation of uniformity was actually an important goal of the HEA. The Ninth Circuit, in contrast, found that permitting varying state law challenges across the country will almost certainly be harmful to the FFEL Program. The court found further that the claims based on miscalculation of interest rates would if successful create an actual conflict with federal law.[182]

The Ninth Circuit decision is troubling for a number of reasons. It could mean that student borrowers with HEA claims will have no means of judicial recourse.[183] At a minimum, the state law contract and fraud (common law) claims should have been allowed to proceed. Fulfillment of contract obligations and avoidance of deception are fundamental underpinnings of commerce, and federal student lenders should not be immunized or above the rule of law. Dismissing these claims also conflicts with the HEA, which states that "FFEL loan agreements shall be enforceable in all federal and state courts . . . in accordance with the terms of the master promissory note."[184] In general, the Ninth Circuit decision is contrary to established principles for determining congressional intent for purposes of preemption. Among other reasons, the Ninth Circuit ruled earlier that the express provisions of the HEA for preemption of some state laws imply that Congress intentionally did not preempt state law generally or in respects other than those it addressed.[185]

The Ninth Circuit also noted that borrowers do have recourse because they can complain to the servicer and to the Department of Education and ask them to intervene.[186] Even the court describes this as an informal process. Regardless, it is not a true remedy. Even if the agency takes action, the action is against the servicer and there is no relief for individual borrowers.

Issues related to preemption of state laws also arise in cases against private student lenders. National banks frequently argue that they are not subject to state law, as discussed in Chapter 11, *supra*.

12.5.4 Common Law Claims

12.5.4.1 General

State UDAP claims are key to school cases, but other theories should also be considered. Common law fraud, in particular, should not be overlooked because of the possibility of punitive damages.[187] The HEA should not preempt state law claims of fraud or infliction of emotional distress.[188]

---

178 *Id.* (citing Abbott by Abbott v. American Cyanamid Co., 844 F.2d at 1108 (4th Cir. 1988)).
See § 7.4.4, *supra*, for a discussion of possible conflicts with the FDCPA.
179 College Loan Corp. v. SLM Corp., 396 F.3d 588 (4th Cir. 2005). See also § 12.7.3.3, *infra*.
180 College Loan Corp. v. SLM Corp., 396 F.3d 588 (4th Cir. 2005) (citing Silkwood v. Kerr-McGee Corp., 464 U.S. 238, 104 S. Ct. 615 (1984), *cited in* Worm v. American Cyanamid Co., 970 F.2d 1301 (4th Cir. 1992)), *on appeal after remand*, 5 F.3d 744 (4th Cir. 1993).
The *College Loan Corporation* court noted in its opinion that defendant Salle Mae's argument boils down to a contention that "it was free to enter into a contract that invoked a federal standard as the indicator of compliance, then to proceed to breach its duties thereunder and to shield its breach by pleading preemption. In this case at least, federal supremacy does not mandate such a result." *See also* Career Care Inst. v. Accrediting Bureau of Health Educ. Schs., Inc., 2009 WL 742532 (E.D. Va. Mar. 18, 2009) (citing College Loan Corp. v. Sallie Mae with approval); Muringi v. Texas Guaranteed, 646 F. Supp. 2d 804 (E.D. La. 2009).
181 34 C.F.R. § 682.209(j). *See* § 6.2.5, *supra*.
182 Chae v. SLM Corp., 593 F.3d 936 (9th Cir. 2010).
183 A copy of an amicus brief filed by NCLC and other consumer groups can be found on the companion website to this manual.
184 20 U.S.C. § 1082(m).
185 Keams v. Tempe Technical Inst., 39 F.3d 222 (9th Cir. 1994).
186 Chae v. SLM Corp., 593 F.3d 936 n.6 (9th Cir. 2010).
187 *See* Bobbitt v. Academy of Court Reporting, Inc., 249 F.R.D. 488 (E.D. Mich. 2008), *corrected and superseded by* 252 F.R.D. 327 (E.D. Mich. 2008) (granting motion for class certification in case challenging school's misrepresentations about ability to grant degrees); Harman v. Sullivan Univ. Sys., Inc., 2005 WL 1353752 (W.D. Ky. June 6, 2005) (sufficient evidence for plaintiff to proceed on fraudulent misrepresentation claim); Moy v. Adelphi Inst., Inc., 866 F. Supp. 696 (E.D.N.Y. 1994) (misrepresentation and fraud claims survived motion to dismiss, but not claim for negligent misrepresentation or breach of fiduciary duty), *ex rel.* Moy v. Terranova, 1999 WL 118773 (E.D.N.Y. Mar. 2 1999); Phillips Coll. of Ala., Inc. v. Lester, 622 So. 2d 308 (Ala. 1993) (a valid fraud claim asserted against school that had promised in written materials but failed to provide a specific number of hours of practical training); Craig v. Forest Inst. of Prof'l Psychology, 713 So. 2d 967 (Ala. Civ. App. 1997). *But see* Spafford v. Cuyahoga Cmty. Coll., 2005 WL 797936 (Ohio. App. Apr. 7, 2005) (upholding trial court's directed verdict for defendant on fraud, breach of contract, and UDAP claims).
188 Muringi v. Texas Guaranteed, 646 F. Supp. 2d 804 (E.D. La. 2009).

However, fraud and negligence claims may be difficult to prove in proprietary school cases. To prove fraudulent misrepresentation, for example, plaintiffs must show that (1) the defendant made a false representation; (2) the defendant acted with an intent to deceive; (3) the defendant made a representation directed at a particular person; (4) the plaintiff relied on the representation; and (5) the plaintiff was damaged as a result.

The first element may be particularly difficult as many proprietary school employees make representations that are clearly misleading but often difficult to prove as false. For example, representations about job placement made before a student enrolls may be different when the student graduates due to many factors, including the student's academic performance and unexpected changes in the labor market.[189] The Department issued proposed regulations in June 2010 stating that misrepresentations include statements concerning the school's knowledge about the current or likely future conditions, compensation, or employment opportunities in the industry or occupation for which the students are being prepared.[190]

Proving causation can also be a problem if the plaintiff is trying to prove that his or her failure to learn marketable skills is the schools' fault.[191]

Similarly, a common problem with negligence claims is showing that the school had a duty of care to the plaintiff student. The main barrier to these claims is the judicial academic abstention doctrine.[192] This doctrine developed from judicial concern that decisions about educational quality are often subjective. In addition, courts are hesitant to appear to be creating educational policy, preferring to leave this to educational experts.[193]

Courts have also, on a variety of legal theories, rescinded enrollment agreements and directed schools to reimburse students for their tuition payments or student loan debts.[194]

12.5.4.2 Contract Claims

The threshold question in contract claims against schools is whether there is an enforceable contractual promise. Courts are reluctant to enforce a school's representations that it will provide a "quality education" or other assertions about the value of the school's diploma because of the subjective inquiry involved.

In general, courts are more likely to find a breach of a contractual obligation if the student's claim is based, at least in part, on objective promises or guarantees, particularly if they are set forth in written materials, such as catalogs or advertisements.[195] School catalogs, bulletins, and regulations should be considered part of the contract between the school and its students.[196]

The general rule is that courts will not allow a claim for educational malpractice but may allow a contract claim based on failure to provide any instruction or a specific service.[197] This view is based on the belief that there is no clear standard of care in education.

---

189 *See generally* Patrick F. Linehan, *Dreams Protected: A New Approach to Policing Proprietary Schools' Misrepresentations*, 89 Geo. L. J. 753 (Mar. 2001).
190 75 Fed. Reg. 34806 (June 18, 2010).
191 *See, e.g.*, Idrees v. American Univ. of the Caribbean, 546 F. Supp. 1342 (S.D.N.Y. 1982).
192 *See, e.g.*, Alsides v. Brown Inst., Ltd., 592 N.W.2d 468 (Minn. App. 1999) (rejecting claims against educational institutions outside of a contractual relationship). *See also* § 12.5.4.2, *infra* (educational malpractice claims). *See generally* Patrick F. Linehan, *Dreams Protected: A New Approach to Policing Proprietary Schools' Misrepresentations*, 89 Geo. L. J. 753 (Mar. 2001).
193 *Id. See also* Diallo v. American Intercontinental Univ., Inc., 687 S.E.2d 278 (Ga. Ct. App. Ga. 2009) (denying class certification in fraud action brought by students against private college alleging that the education they received was not worth the cost).
194 André v. Pace Univ., 655 N.Y.S.2d 777 (N.Y. App. Term 1996), *rev'g* 618 N.Y.S.2d 975 (N.Y. City Ct. 1994) (school's complete failure to provide course at promised level allows damages and rescission); Brown v. Hambric, 638 N.Y.S.2d 873 (N.Y. City Ct. 1995) (travel agent school found to be a deceptive pyramid scheme; rescission of contract warranted and failure to deliver promised support and training was unconscionable and deceptive business practice); James v. SCS Bus. & Technical Inst., 595 N.Y.S.2d 885 (Civ. Ct. County of N.Y. 1992) (unconscionability and lack of consideration); Cavaliere v. Duff's Bus. Inst., 605 A.2d 397 (Pa. Super. Ct. 1992) (general claim of lack of quality education not actionable, but misrepresentation or breach of contract would be).
195 A student handbook is another good source with which to establish a contractual relationship. *See generally* Idrees v. American Univ. of the Caribbean, 546 F. Supp. 1342 (S.D.N.Y. 1982) (inaccurate and misleading statements in a university brochure about facilities, equipment, and faculty constituted fraudulent misrepresentation); Claudia G. Catalano, *Liability of Private School or Educational Institution for Breach of Contract Arising from Provision of Deficient Educational Instruction*, 46 A.L.R.5th 581 (1997); Ralph D. Mawdsley, *Litigation Involving Higher Education Employee and Student Handbooks*, 109 Educ. L. Report 1031 (1996).
196 Ross v. Creighton Univ., 957 F.2d 410 (7th Cir. 1992) (basic legal relationship between student and school is contractual in nature); Harman v. Sullivan Univ. Sys., Inc., 2005 WL 1353752 (W.D. Ky. June 6, 2005) (sufficient evidence for plaintiff to proceed on breach-of-contract claim when school's handbook falsely claimed that program met certain accreditation standards and that graduates would be eligible to take the national certifying exam in radiology). *See also* Gally v. Columbia Univ., 22 F. Supp. 2d 199 (S.D.N.Y. 1998) (implied contract between students and school required university to act in good faith and students to satisfy academic requirements and comply with school procedures); Zumbrun v. University of S. Cal., 101 Cal. Rptr. 499 (Cal. Ct. App. 1972); Wickstrom v. North Idaho Coll., 725 P.2d 155 (Idaho 1986).
197 Jamieson v. Vatterott Educ. Ctr., Inc., 473 F. Supp. 2d 1153 (D. Kan. 2007) (dismissing former students' breach of contract claims that were not based on promises in the enrollment agreement); United States v. Brooks, 2007 WL 3244724 (E.D. Mich. Nov. 2, 2007) (courts have rejected the assertion that misconduct by a school absolves a borrower of obligation to repay student loans); Ambrose v. New England Ass'n of Schs.

For example, in reviewing student claims of breach of contract based on alleged unsuitable computer courses, the court in one case held that an inquiry into whether the courses were appropriate was "best left to the educational community. A different situation might be presented if defendants were to provide 'no educational services' or failed to meet its contractual obligation to provide certain specified services, such as a designated number of hours of instruction. . . ."[198]

The difference between educational malpractice and a contract claim is not always clear. In general, the more limited the claim (for example, a school's failure to offer a particular promised course) and the more the claim is tied to written promises, the stronger the case.[199] Some courts have allowed an implied contract theory.[200]

Courts have found a lack of consideration in some education cases. For example, failure of consideration was found when the school accepted the student's tuition and failed to provide the promised educational services.[201] In another case, the court awarded summary judgment to a student, agreeing that a change in the school's refund policy after substantial tuition payments had been made was a unilateral modification of a specific contractual term for which no consideration had been received.[202] However, other courts have held that lack of consideration is not a defense in student loan cases because the student received money in exchange for a promise to repay the money.[203] According to one court, "neither the bank nor the government guarantees satisfaction with schools or educations" and the responsibility for a bad choice lies with the student.[204] It is also possible to raise contract defenses such as duress when appropriate.[205]

A 2010 Ninth Circuit decision, however, is troubling in finding that a contract claim was preempted by the HEA.[206]

Chapter 7, *supra*, reviews other contract defenses that may be raised in response to collection actions. Many of these claims may also be raised affirmatively in breach of contract actions. For example, forgery is a common claim in proprietary school cases. There may be some problems

---

& Colls., Inc., 2000 WL 1195363 (D. Me. Aug. 7, 2000), *aff'd*, 252 F.3d 488 (1st Cir. 2001); Whayne v. U.S. Dep't of Educ., 915 F. Supp. 1143 (D. Kan. 1996) (allegation that education simply was not good enough insufficient to state a claim for breach of contract; educational malpractice claim rejected as a matter of state law); Cencor Inc. v. Tolman, 868 P.2d 396 (Colo. 1994) (although no claim for educational malpractice, plaintiff may have a claim for failure to provide a specific service); Page v. Klein Tools, Inc., 610 N.W.2d 900 (Mich. 2000) (explaining policy considerations underlying various courts' rejection of educational malpractice claims); Alsides v. Brown Inst., 592 N.W.2d 468 (Minn. Ct. App. 1999) (courts may consider contract, fraud, and misrepresentation claims only if they do not require inquiry into nuances of educational processes and theories); Andre v. Pace Univ., 655 N.Y.S.2d 777 (N.Y. App. Term 1996), *rev'g* 618 N.Y.S.2d 975 (N.Y. City Ct. 1994); Cavaliere v. Duff's Bus. Inst., 605 A.2d 397 (Pa. Super. Ct. 1992) (if contract with school were to provide for certain specified services such as, for example, a designated number of hours of instruction and school failed to meet its obligation, then contract action with appropriate consequential damages might be viable).

198 Andre v. Pace Univ., 655 N.Y.S.2d 777 (N.Y. App. Term 1996), *rev'g* 618 N.Y.S.2d 975 (N.Y. City Ct. 1994).

199 Dillon v. Ultrasound Diagnostic Schs., 1997 U.S. Dist. LEXIS 20795 (E.D. Pa. 1997) (plaintiff's complaints identified specific alleged benefits and services which defendants promised and failed to provide so as to state a claim for breach of educational contract); Gundlach v. Reinstein, 924 F. Supp. 684 (E.D. Pa. 1996) (no written contract between law school and student; student failed to identify specific manner in which school breached contract), *aff'd*, 114 F.3d 1172 (3d Cir. 1997); Cencor Inc. v. Tolman, 868 P.2d 396 (Colo. 1994) (agreeing that enrollment agreement and school catalog constituted express terms of contract and that students showed specific services which had not been provided; also finding failure to provide qualified teacher); Wickstrom v. North Idaho Coll., 725 P.2d 155 (Idaho 1986); Collins v. Minnesota Sch. of Bus., Inc., 655 N.W.2d 320 (Minn. 2003); Alsides v. Brown Inst., 592 N.W.2d 468 (Minn. Ct. App. 1999) (allowing students to proceed with claims involving a computer school's promises to provide instruction on a particular software program and particular types of computers; frequent absences or tardiness of instructors; insufficient operable computers; outdated hardware and software; and failure to deliver number of hours of instruction promised); Squires v. Sierra Nevada Educ. Found., 823 P.2d 256 (Nev. 1991); Brown v. Hambric, 638 N.Y.S.2d 873 (N.Y. City Ct. 1995); Ryan v. University of N.C. Hosps., 494 S.E.2d 789 (N.C. App. 1998) (upholding claim for breach of contract); Britt v. Chestnut Hill Coll., 632 A.2d 557 (Pa. Super. Ct. 1993); Thomas v. French, 638 P.2d 613 (Wash. Ct. App. 1981), *rev'd on other grounds*, 659 P.2d 1097 (Wash. 1983) (viable contract claim when private cosmetology school's contract expressly required school to prepare students to take a state cosmetology exam).

200 *See, e.g.*, Gally v. Columbia Univ., 22 F. Supp. 2d 199 (S.D.N.Y. 1998); Gupta v. New Britain Gen. Hosp., 687 A.2d 111 (Conn. 1996) (residency contract is an educational contract carrying an implied covenant of good faith and fair dealing, but resident failed to prove bad faith or arbitrary action); Wickstrom v. North Idaho Coll., 725 P.2d 155 (Idaho 1986) (valid cause of action based on breach of implied contract when school failed to satisfy "objective criteria" such as number of hours). *But see* Harris v. Adler Sch. of Prof'l Psychology, 723 N.E.2d 717 (Ill. App. Ct. 1999) (no cause of action in Illinois for breach of implied provision of good faith; students dismissed from doctoral program on basis of failed exam had alleged that school breached implied term in failing to have objective and articulable criteria for grading exams).

201 595 N.Y.S.2d 885 (N.Y. Civ. Ct. 1992) (withdrawn from publication). *But see* Cotton v. U.S. Dep't of Educ., 2006 WL 3313753 (M.D. Fla. Nov. 13, 2006) (failure of consideration is not a defense in student loan cases because student received money in exchange for his promise to repay the money); United States v. Durbin, 64 F. Supp. 2d. 635 (S.D. Tex. 1999).

202 Reynolds v. Sterling Coll., Inc., 750 A.2d 1020 (Vt. 2000).

203 Cotton v. U.S. Dep't of Educ., 2006 WL 3313753 (M.D. Fla. Nov. 13, 2006); United States v. Durbin, 64 F. Supp. 2d. 635 (S.D. Tex. 1999).

204 United States v. Durbin, 64 F. Supp. 2d 635 (S.D. Tex. 1999).

205 *See* § 7.5.4.1, *supra*.

206 Chae v. SLM Corp., 593 F.3d 936 (9th Cir. 2010). *See* § 12.5.3.4, *supra*.

raising these defenses and claims if the loan has been consolidated.²⁰⁷

In addition to the contract defenses discussed in Chapter 7, *supra*, when a guaranty agency or the Department is seeking collection on a guaranteed loan, a possible defense is that the loan never should have been guaranteed and that the guarantor or the Department should not be collecting on the loan. In certain cases, the school was not an eligible institution when the loan was extended, so under federal law the loan was not eligible for a federal guarantee. More common is the situation in which the Department recognized a school as eligible when the school should not in fact have been found to be eligible. No court has yet found this as a basis to refuse to enforce an FFEL.²⁰⁸

12.5.4.3 Fiduciary Duty

A fiduciary duty is generally understood as a "duty of utmost good faith, trust, confidence, and candor owed by a fiduciary to the beneficiary; a duty to act with the highest degree of honesty and loyalty toward another person and in the best interests of the other person."²⁰⁹

There are few if any reported decisions finding a fiduciary relationship related to educational institutions and financial aid. A number of cases raising this claim have not been successful to date.²¹⁰ However, this could be a promising theory. In most of these cases, courts have found that plaintiff borrowers did not plead sufficient facts to establish a fiduciary duty.²¹¹ Courts have found fiduciary duties in other areas of university and student interaction, such as in the context of sexual harassment and other faculty misconduct.²¹²

12.6 Affirmative Litigation

12.6.1 General

The following sections focus on cases involving federal student loans. Private loan cases are discussed in Chapter 11, *supra*. Possible defenses to collection actions are discussed in Chapter 7, *supra*, including procedural issues such as standing that may be relevant to ensure that the loan holder that is suing to collect can prove the case.

12.6.2 Potential Defendants

12.6.2.1 Suing the Department of Education

The HEA contains an explicit grant of federal jurisdiction for suits against the Secretary of Education.²¹³ In general, courts will not allow injunctive relief against the Secretary except when the Secretary exercises powers that are clearly outside his or her statutory authority.²¹⁴ This is a high standard. For example, according to one court, the anti-injunction provision may not be overcome merely because the Secretary exercised poor judgment or even if the Secretary violated the specific mandates of another statutory scheme.²¹⁵ An anti-injunction provision may also be overruled if the court finds that the plaintiff has no alternative

---

207 *See* § 7.5.4.4, *supra*.
208 *See, e.g.*, Pageus v. U.S. Dep't of Educ., 2010 WL731590 (N.D. Ga. Feb. 25, 2010) (even if court was to assume that school had been deemed ineligible, this would not have an impact on borrower's liability for the student loans). *See also* § 7.5.4.3, *supra*. *But see* Hernandez v. Alexander, 1992 U.S. Dist. LEXIS 21930 (D. Nev. May 18, 1992) (appearing to accept argument that loan could be unenforceable because school was improperly certified as eligible).
209 DiPasquale v. Costas, 926 N.E.2d 682, 706 (Ohio Ct. App. 2010). *See generally* National Consumer Law Center, The Cost of Credit: Regulation, Preemption, and Industry Abuses § 12.9 (4th ed. 2009 and Supp.).
210 *See, e.g.*, Moy v. Adelphi Inst., Inc., 866 F. Supp. 696 (E.D.N.Y. 1994) (finding that plaintiffs—students in a class action against proprietary school alleging that defendant and its directors acted as fiduciaries by enrolling students and accepting government funds on their behalf—did not allege sufficient facts to suggest fiduciary relationship but merely described a business relationship); Fernandez v. Medical College of Wisconsin, Inc., 549 N.W.2d 792 (Wis. Ct. App. 1996) (summary judgment for school in case brought by medical student after being dismissed from the program).
211 *See generally* Kent Weeks & Rich Haglund, *Fiduciary Duties of College and University Faculty and Administrators*, 29 J.C. & U.L. 153 (2002).
212 *See, e.g.*, Schneider v. Plymouth State Coll., 144 N.H. 458 (1999); Johnson v. Scmitz, 119 F. Supp. 2d 90 (D. Conn. 2000). *But see* Hendricks v. Clemson Univ. 578 S.E.2d 711 (S.C. 2003) (no duty of care in case involving faculty advisor and athlete); Ho v. University of Tex., 984 S.W.2d 672 (Tex. App. 1998) (no duty in case involving faculty advisor).
213 20 U.S.C. § 1082(a).
214 *See, e.g.*, Lepelletier v. U.S. Dep't of Educ., 2009 WL 3416265 (D.D.C. Oct. 22, 2009); Shabtai v. U.S. Dep't of Educ., 2003 WL 21983025 (S.D.N.Y. Aug. 20, 2003); De La Mota v. U.S. Dep't of Educ., 2003 WL 21919774 (S.D.N.Y. Aug. 12, 2003) (plaintiffs did not point to a specific provision of the HEA that overrides the explicit and express prohibition against injunctive relief), *rev'd on other grounds*, 412 F.3d 71 (2d Cir. 2005); Kitchen v. U.S. Dep't of Educ., 1998 WL 167325 (S.D.N.Y. Apr. 9, 1998) (collection of student loans within Secretary's statutory authority; borrower's motion for preliminary injunctive relief denied); Advanced Career Training v. Riley, 1997 WL 214863 (E.D. Pa. Apr. 25, 1997) (plaintiff schools failed to show that the Secretary acted clearly outside of his statutory authority); Coalition of N.Y. State Private Career Sch. Inc. v. Riley, 1996 WL 678453 (N.D.N.Y. Nov. 15, 1996); Calise Beauty Sch., Inc. v. Riley, 941 F. Supp. 425 (S.D.N.Y. Sept. 30, 1996) (denying injunctive relief to vocational schools that were removed from federal loan programs; the Secretary did not exceed his HEA authority by allegedly violating non-discretionary duties in calculating and publishing cohort default rates and ruling on appeals; even if the Secretary did violate these duties, such violations would at most constitute wrongful exercise of proper administrative functions).
215 Advanced Career Training v. Riley, 1997 WL 214863 (E.D. Pa. Apr. 25, 1997).

legal remedy.²¹⁶ Courts have generally rejected this argument in the student loan context, finding that plaintiff schools or borrowers bringing actions against the Secretary have an available alternative in the Administrative Procedures Act (APA).²¹⁷

Although injunction actions are subject to these restrictions, actions for declaratory relief should not be similarly barred.²¹⁸ Thus, even courts that have accepted the view that an agency or officer is immune from injunction have held that declaratory relief is available.²¹⁹ The key difference, according to one court, is that an injunction is a coercive order by a court directing a party to do or refrain from doing something and applies to future actions. A declaratory judgment states the existing legal rights in a controversy but does not, in itself, coerce any party or enjoin any future action.²²⁰ A declaratory judgment is a milder remedy that is frequently available in situations in which an injunction is unavailable or inappropriate.²²¹ However, a court may find declaratory relief to be barred as well if such relief would produce the same effect as an injunction.²²²

The limit on injunctive actions is not always fatal. In some collection cases, the guaranty agency will be the loan holder and an injunction can generally be crafted to fully protect students without naming the Secretary. In other cases, additional agencies, such as the Department of Treasury, will be involved in collection efforts. These agencies should be named in cases seeking injunctive relief.

In bringing affirmative actions against the Department, borrowers should also be prepared that the Department or other loan holder might file a suit to collect on the loan.

Borrowers might also use the Administrative Procedures Act claims to challenge Department decisions in garnishment or offset hearings or other matters. Appellate review is discussed in Chapter 8, *supra*.

Contract claims may also be brought against the Department as long as the claims satisfy the requirements of 28 U.S.C. § 1346, which governs cases in which the United States is a defendant.²²³

12.6.2.2 Claims Against Private Accrediting Agencies

Attorneys representing defrauded student borrowers may want to consider adding as a party to the lawsuit the private accrediting agency that accredited the defendant school. Although usually nonprofit organizations, these agencies may be an important alternative source of assets, particularly when schools are bankrupt or insolvent.

The Department of Education does not review the educational quality of private vocational schools before certifying their eligibility to participate in the federal aid program. Instead the Department of Education recognizes various private accrediting agencies and associations whose

---

216 South Carolina v. Regan, 465 U.S. 367, 104 S. Ct. 1107, 79 L. Ed. 2d 372 (1984) (holding, in tax case, that Anti-Injunction Act was not intended to bar action when Congress has not provided plaintiff with alternative legal way to challenge validity of tax).

217 *See, e.g.*, Advanced Career Training v. Riley, 1997 WL 214863 (E.D. Pa. Apr. 25, 1997) (APA claim allows plaintiff to obtain either declaratory relief or remand to the Department for further evaluation).

218 Section 1082(a)(2) does not by its terms exclude declaratory relief from the forms of relief as to which the Secretary may "sue and be sued." A number of such class actions seeking declaratory relief have been certified. *See* Keams v. Tempe Technical Inst., 39 F.3d 222 (9th Cir. 1994), *appeal after remand*, 103 F.3d 138 (9th Cir. 1996), *redesignated as op.*, 110 F.3d 44 (9th Cir. 1997), *claims against all defendants dismissed*, 16 F. Supp. 2d 1119 (D. Ariz. 1998); Shorter v. Riley, Clearinghouse No. 47,950B (N.D. Ga. Nov. 18, 1993); Genzale v. Zenzi's Beauty Coll., Clearinghouse No. 49,931 (Cal. Super. Ct. Apr. 19, 1993) (order certifying the class).

219 There are several higher education cases. *See, e.g.*, American Ass'n of Cosmetology Sch. v. Riley, 170 F.3d 1250 (9th Cir. 1999); Thomas v. Bennett, 856 F.2d 1165, 1168 (8th Cir. 1988) (affirming denial of Secretary's motion to dismiss plaintiff's declaratory relief complaint in which individual taxpayer challenged a student-loan-related tax offset, notwithstanding anti-injunction provision); OneSimpleLoan v. U.S. Secretary of Educ., 2006 WL 1596768 (S.D.N.Y. June 9, 2006), *aff'd*, 496 F.3d 197 (2d Cir. 2007); De La Mota v. U.S. Dep't of Educ., 2003 WL 21919774 (S.D.N.Y. Aug. 12, 2003), *summary judgment granted*, 2003 WL 22038741 (S.D.N.Y. Aug. 29, 2003), *rev'd on other grounds*, 412 F.3d 71 (2d Cir. 2005); Bank of America NT & SA v. Riley, 940 F. Supp. 348, 350–51 (D.D.C. 1996), *aff'd*, 132 F.3d 1480 (D.C. Cir. 1997); Student Loan Mktg. Ass'n v. Riley, 907 F. Supp. 464 (D.D.C. 1995) (refusing to dismiss, for lack of jurisdiction, Salle Mae's declaratory relief action challenging Secretary's announced intention to apply a statutory offset fee to certain assets), *aff'd*, 104 F.3d 397 (D.C. Cir.); Pro Schs., Inc. v. Riley, 824 F. Supp. 1314–16 (E.D. Wis. 1993) (allowing cosmetology schools operator to challenge Secretary's termination of its FFEL eligibility in an action for declaratory relief).

220 Ulstein Maritime, Ltd. v. United States, 833 F.2d 1052 (1st Cir. 1987).

221 *Id.*

222 American Ass'n of Cosmetology Schs. v. Riley, 170 F.3d 1250 (9th Cir. 1999) (the anti-injunction bar cannot be skirted by simple expedient of labeling an action that really seeks injunctive relief as an action for "declaratory relief").

Courts have on occasion refused to grant declaratory relief in cases in which the effect would be identical to a legally impermissible injunction. Samuels v. Mackell, 401 U.S. 66, 91 S. Ct. 764, 27 L. Ed. 2d 688 (1971), *cited in* Ulstein Maritime, Ltd. v. United States, 833 F.2d 1052 (1st Cir. 1987); Great Lakes Co. v. Huffman, 319 U.S. 293, 63 S. Ct. 1070, 87 L. Ed. 1407 (1943).

223 Valentino v. U.S. Dep't of Educ., 2009 WL 2985686 (S.D. Cal. Sept. 16, 2009) (finding no subject matter jurisdiction to hear breach of contract claim against government); DiNello v. U.S. Dep't of Educ., 2006 WL 3783010 (N.D. Ill. Dec. 21, 2006) (citing Powe v. U.S. Dep't of Educ., 2005 WL 2045781 (S.D. Ala. Aug. 25, 2005)); De La Mota v. U.S. Dep't of Educ., 2003 WL 21919774 (S.D.N.Y. Aug. 12, 2003), *rev'd on other grounds*, 412 F.3d 71 (2d Cir. 2005).

job it is to review the educational standards of the schools.[224] The school's accreditation makes a school eligible for government assistance programs, and the failure to adequately examine a school may be directly connected to the student's injury.

Accreditation agencies are required to demonstrate that they have rigorous standards. The regulations set out factors that accreditation agencies must address in evaluating the quality of an institution, including success with respect to student achievement and, as appropriate, consideration of course completion, state licensing examination, and job placement rates.[225]

In general, the agency must have the administrative and fiscal capacity to carry out accrediting activities.[226] The agency is required to demonstrate that it has standards for accreditation that are sufficiently rigorous to ensure that the agency is a reliable authority on the quality of education or training in institutions it accredits.[227]

Inspector General audit reports have concluded, however, that many accreditation agencies have not followed through on these responsibilities.[228]

Advocates have met with mixed success in their attempts to hold agencies liable for the bad acts of schools they accredit. Most courts have found that accrediting agencies are not responsible for students damaged by inferior schools accredited by these agencies. For example, the Ninth Circuit found that accrediting agencies owed no tort law duty under state law to students who attended the schools accredited by those agencies.[229]

Students in another federal court action in the District of Columbia presented UDAP and common law claims against an accrediting agency. The court found that the District of Columbia UDAP statute did not apply to accrediting agencies but did allow the students to pursue common law claims for misrepresentation and fraud against the accrediting agency.[230]

Both sides sought summary judgment in the case. The students claimed that the accreditor fraudulently provided accreditation even though the accreditor had no knowledge of whether the school met the accreditor's standards. The court found that the students could go forward with their case to trial, having met all the prima facie elements of fraud.[231]

A settlement was reached with the accreditor in this case.[232] Without admitting any liability or fault, the accreditor agreed to make payments to members of the class. The amount paid to each class member varied depending on the total number of claims received.

A claim of negligence against an accrediting agency is even more difficult. The borrower has to show a duty of the accreditor to the student, the borrower's reliance on the accreditor's certification, and the accreditor's negligence in the accreditation process in causing proximate injury to the consumer. The little case law in this area generally involves personal injury relating to products that received independent certification.[233] At least a few courts have considered the issue in the student loan context and found that an accrediting agency did not owe a duty to the students upon which a negligence action could be brought.[234] Courts have also found that accreditation agencies are not state actors for purposes of constitutional claims.[235]

12.6.2.3 Claims Against State Licensing Agencies

Claims may be available against state licensing agencies that have responsibility to review a school's operation. For example, a New York appellate court allowed a claim to proceed when the students sought declaratory and injunctive relief in having the state education department fulfill its statutory obligation to supervise private vocational schools.[236]

12.6.2.4 Suing the School and Individual Owners and Operators

A major obstacle to affirmative litigation against schools is that, in many cases, the school will already be closed by the time the client seeks assistance. This is especially a

---

224 See § 12.2.2, supra.
225 34 C.F.R. § 602.16.
226 34 C.F.R. § 602.15.
227 34 C.F.R. § 602.16.
228 See § 12.2.2, supra.
229 Keams v. Tempe Technical Inst., 39 F.3d 222 (9th Cir. 1994), appeal after remand, 103 F.3d 138 (9th Cir. 1996), redesignated as op., 110 F.3d 44 (9th Cir. 1997) (students failed to identify a single decision in which any court has held that accrediting agencies owe a tort law duty to students), claims against all defendants dismissed, 16 F. Supp. 2d 1119 (D. Ariz. 1998).
230 Armstrong v. Accrediting Council for Continuing Educ. & Training, Inc., 832 F. Supp. 419 (D.D.C. 1993).
231 Armstrong v. Accrediting Council for Continuing Educ. & Training, Inc., 961 F. Supp. 305 (D.D.C. 1997).
232 Armstrong v. Accrediting Council for Continuing Educ. & Training, Inc. (D.D.C. Mar. 30, 1998), available at www.consumerlaw.org/unreported (settlement agreement and order approving settlement).
233 See Jerald A. Jacobs & Jefferson Caffery Glassie, American Soc'y of Ass'n Execs., Certification and Accreditation Law Handbook Ch. 3 (1992).
234 Keams v. Tempe Technical Inst., 39 F.3d 222 (9th Cir. 1994), appeal after remand, 103 F.3d 138 (9th Cir. 1996), redesignated as op., 110 F.3d 44 (9th Cir. 1997), claims against all defendants dismissed, 16 F. Supp. 2d 1119 (D. Ariz. 1998); Ambrose v. New England Ass'n of Schs. & Colls., 2000 WL 1195363 (D. Me. Aug. 7, 2000) (analogizing negligent accreditation claims to educational malpractice; finding it improper for courts to make these subjective determinations; summary judgment granted to defendant accrediting organization), aff'd, 252 F.3d 488 (1st Cir. 2001).
235 See, e.g., Hiwassee Coll., Inc. v. Southern Ass'n Of Colls. & Schs., 531 F.3d 1333 (11th Cir. Apr. 14, 2008); McKeesport Hosp. v. Accreditation Council for Graduate Med. Educ., 24 F.3d 519 (3d Cir. 1994).
236 Figueroa v. Market Training Inst., Inc., 167 A.D.2d 503 (N.Y. App. Div. 1990).

problem in cases against smaller schools that are not part of a large corporation. These schools may close during the course of litigation. As a result, relying on a recovery from the school can be frustrating. In these circumstances, the borrower will be forced to raise the school-related claim, by way of recoupment, to an action to collect on the debt or as a declaratory action that the debt is not owed.[237] However, affirmative claims against schools should still be considered, especially in cases in which the school is still open.

If the school is already in bankruptcy, advocates should consider recovering a judgment in bankruptcy. Students may have a consumer priority, giving them first crack at any school assets ahead of unsecured creditors.[238] Another benefit arises if the student's attorney serves on a creditor's committee. In these cases, the attorney fees for that service will be paid out of the school's assets.[239]

Another possible approach to recovering from a bankrupt school is to jump ahead of other creditors by means of a criminal restitution order. *United States v. Grundhoefer*[240] affirms an order of almost $1 million in criminal restitution to students victimized by a private vocational school. Brooklyn and Bronx Legal Services suggested to two different federal judges sentencing several principals of the school that all the criminal restitution go to defrauded students and not to the school's other creditors. The judges agreed, instructing the government and the legal services attorneys to work out a restitution plan. The school's bankruptcy trustee, representing the school's other creditors, appealed. The Second Circuit found no abuse of discretion in the restitution plan and no standing by the other creditors to object to the courts' orders.[241]

When dealing with an insolvent school, advocates should also explore the following potential alternative defendants:

- *A bonding company or state tuition recovery fund* is a potential defendant, since schools are licensed by many states, and a bond or contribution to a state tuition recovery fund is usually a precondition to licensure.[242]
- *The parent company or franchisor* is often a deep pocket and may aid or abet the school's misrepresentations.
- *Owners, officers,*[243] *and employees* are responsible for their own actions, even if they are acting as a corporate agent. Individuals dealing directly with a student and supervisors of these individuals are potential defendants, as is a school's owner to the extent the owner supervises the school or to the extent the corporate veil can be pierced.
- *Advertising agencies, accountants, lawyers, or others aiding and abetting a fraudulent scheme* are individually liable for their own misconduct.[244]

12.6.3 Deciding Between Class and Individual Actions

An individual action is one way to pursue a proprietary school case. A second, and often more efficient, approach is to join a number of individual students as plaintiffs. Sometimes it is easier to obtain punitive damages on behalf of a limited number of students than on behalf of a class. The case can easily be brought before a jury, when sympathetic facts on each individual plaintiff can be presented directly to the jury. A class action, in contrast, might not allow as effective a presentation of each student's case and might not result in a punitive damages award.

The most common problem with class actions against the schools is that they fail to redress the borrowers' loan problems. Advocates must be careful and should consider joining the lenders in these cases using theories of derivative liability, discussed below. At a minimum, any settlement agreements should not limit borrowers' future rights to resolve loan issues.

It may be possible to bring a class action seeking a declaration that the student does not owe on a loan because of school-related defenses. It usually makes sense to do so on behalf of a class of students who were victimized by the same program and who took out loans to attend. To proceed as a class, it will be necessary to convince the court that the class action requirements have been met.

In theory, if an action meets that test, then issues of lender liability should be sufficiently common to the class that the class should be certified. In fact, the standards may even be easier for a declaratory judgment action than in a damage action against a school. At least one court has ruled that an

---

237 See § 12.7, *infra*.
238 *See, e.g., In re* Longo, 144 B.R. 305 (Bankr. Md. 1992) (granting consumer deposit priority pursuant to 11 U.S.C. § 507(a)(6) in case in which Maryland Higher Education Commission brought tuition recovery claims on behalf of student borrowers; school president argued unsuccessfully that school's services were business and not consumer in nature).
239 More detailed analyses of a consumer creditor's rights when a company has filed for bankruptcy can be found in National Consumer Law Center, Unfair and Deceptive Acts and Practices § 11.9 (7th ed. 2008 and Supp.), and National Consumer Law Center, Consumer Bankruptcy Law and Practice Ch. 17 (9th ed. 2009 and Supp.).
240 916 F.2d 788 (2d Cir. 1990).
241 *Id.*
242 *See* § 12.8, *infra* (student tuition recovery funds).
243 *See* Hawley v. Business Computer Training Inst., 2008 WL 2048325 (W.D. Wash. May 9, 2008) (plaintiff's allegations sufficient to justify piercing of the corporate veil), *cert. denied*, 2008 WL 2492343 (W.D. Wash. June 18, 2008); Goldsmith v. Rodano (Cal. Super. Ct. Aug. 21, 1995), *available at* www.consumerlaw.org/unreported (former president agrees to pay $100,000 to seventy-five students and $30,000 to student's attorney).
244 *See* National Consumer Law Center, Unfair and Deceptive Acts and Practices § 11.5 (7th ed. 2008 and Supp.).

action seeking to declare loans unenforceable is not a damage action and that only the requirements of Rule 23(b)(2), not (b)(3), need be met.[245]

Class actions seeking damages may provide significant relief in some cases. However, there may be problems with showing commonality for the class. For example, if the case involves marketing, the Rule 23(b)(2) commonality requirement may be a problem in proprietary school class action litigation because each student may be subjected to a different sales or marketing presentation. However, courts may find that each of these individual presentations is sufficiently close to the school's standard sales script to present common issues of fact, and the core issue in question may be whether the school operated pursuant to an ongoing scheme to defraud and deceive students.[246]

For example, one federal court certified a class of about 400 Native Americans recruited to attend the TTI trade school by one particular salesperson over a fifteen-month period.[247] Although the bulk of the evidence related to oral sales presentations, the court found enough commonality in the salesman's presentations to justify the class action.

12.6.4 Developing a Case

One of the best ways to develop evidence of school malfeasance is to find disgruntled former employees—both commissioned sales representatives and faculty. The names, addresses, and dates of employment of present and past school employees can be obtained through discovery. The names of disgruntled sales representatives may also be obtained from court records, since many of them must sue the school for their back commissions or wrongful termination. Not only can these people provide crucial evidence, but the "educational" institution's use of commissioned enrollment officers probably will have an impact on the jury or judge. Clients may also remember instructors' names and/or be able to provide a school catalog with this information.

Advocates should also be sure to obtain the school's sales manuals, marketing memos, other advertisements, and sales training materials. It is critical to find out how the student was enrolled—for example, outside an unemployment office or in another high-pressure environment.

Other information can be found on file with private accrediting associations, state licensing agencies, and the Department of Education. Advocates may want to focus on drop-out and job placement rates.[248] Although data on completion and job placement can be very useful in developing a case, it is also very difficult to find reliable data. In many cases, schools are required to keep this information and in some cases meet minimum standards for completion and job placement.[249]

Some of this data is available through the National Center for Education Statistics (NCES), which administers the Integrated Postsecondary Education Data System (IPEDS). This is an on-line data collection program that compiles information on all postsecondary institutions in the U.S. The Department has also created a website at www.eddataexpress.ed.gov with data collected by many of the Department's program offices, including the National Center for Education Statistics and the College Board. The most recent cohort enrollments and completion data can be found here as well. However, NCES does not collect job placement rates for any type of institution.

Freedom of Information Act requests sent to federal and state agencies are also useful in collecting information, particularly with respect to possible investigations against schools.[250]

12.6.5 Proving Actual Damages

Student plaintiffs may have suffered a variety of actual damages as a result of proprietary school fraud. In one case, the plaintiffs successfully argued that they would never have attended had they known of the school's actual placement rate, which was lower than represented. The students' actual damages were found to be their *total* tuition (even though most had graduated from the school) plus the students' lost wages incurred when they left their jobs to attend the school.[251]

---

245 Shorter v. Riley, Clearinghouse No. 47,950B (N.D. Ga. Nov. 18, 1993). *See generally* National Consumer Law Center, Unfair and Deceptive Acts and Practices § 13.5 (7th ed. 2008 and Supp.); National Consumer Law Center, Consumer Class Actions (7th ed. 2010).

246 *See* Shorter v. Riley, Clearinghouse No. 47,950B (N.D. Ga. Nov. 18, 1993).

247 Keams v. Tempe Technical Inst., 807 F. Supp. 569 (D. Ariz. 1992), *rev'd*, 39 F.3d 222 (9th Cir. 1994), *appeal after remand*, 103 F.3d 138 (9th Cir. 1996), *redesignated as op.*, 110 F.3d 44 (9th Cir. 1997), *claims against all defendants dismissed*, 16 F. Supp. 2d 1119 (D. Ariz. 1998).

248 For information on gathering evidence from state licensing agencies, including Freedom of Information Act requests, see § 9.4.2.2, *supra*.

249 *See* §§ 1.7, 12.3.3.4, *supra*.

250 *See* § 9.4.2.2.2, *supra*.
    Sample FOIA requests are included in Appendix F, *infra*. Advocates should be prepared to respond if agencies deny fee waivers for FOIA requests. *See* James, Hoyer et al. v. State of New York, 2010 WL 1949120 (N.Y. Sup. Ct. Mar. 31, 2010) (granting law firm's application for judgment pursuant to state FOIA law and requiring state to provide most documents requested regarding Attorney General investigation of student loan industry); Students for Sensible Drug Policy, Harmful Drug Law Hits Home (Apr. 17, 2006) (describing battle with the federal Department of Education regarding FOIA requests and fee waivers; the group and Public Citizen filed lawsuit against the Department in January 2006 and the Department settled the case and provided data free of charge), *available at* www.ssdp.org/states/ssdp-state-report.pdf.

251 Beckett v. Computer Career Inst., Inc. (Or. Cir. Ct. July 2,

Other damage claims to consider in these cases include child care and transportation expenses incurred while students attended school. In addition, many students were encouraged or required by schools to purchase equipment or materials.

A number of sample complaints against proprietary schools are included on the companion website to this manual. Claims for damages in these cases include damages due to payment of fraudulently obtained tuition, payment for textbooks, overcharges for equipment and educational aids, payments for equipment and educational aids, exhausting federal aid limits, making it impossible or difficult to afford alternative education, loss of earnings, loss of educational opportunity, loss of time due to attending a worthless program, damage to credit rating, and fees and charges incurred in fighting off collection actions.

12.7 Raising School-Related Claims and Defenses

12.7.1 General

As discussed above, suing schools may be a problem not only because schools close or become insolvent but also because these cases generally do not resolve loan problems. Including lenders in lawsuits or separately suing lenders for school-related claims can lead to relief such as loan cancellations and reimbursement for payments made. These school-related claims and defenses are discussed in this section. There may also be direct claims that can be raised against lenders, as discussed in Chapter 11, *supra*. These claims are generally relevant in private student loan cases.

These sections apply mainly to federal student loan cases. There are unique regulations for federal loans, discussed below, that specifically allow school-related defenses. The issues that are most relevant for private loan cases are discussed in Chapter 11, *supra*. There is some overlap, however, as noted in this chapter and in Chapter 11.

Raising school-related defenses on their student loans is critical for student loan borrowers. The same right to raise seller-related claims on loans has proven essential for other defrauded consumers as well, such as those victimized by home improvement contractors or used-car dealers. In most cases, when the seller refers the consumer to the lender or when the seller and lender have a business arrangement, consumers can successfully raise as a defense to their loans all claims and defenses they have against the seller.[252] This is generally accomplished through the FTC Holder Rule.[253]

This section sets out existing standards for raising school-related defenses for all these types of loans. Advocates must properly match their client's type of loan with the appropriate discussion below.[254]

12.7.2 The Clearer Picture: Loans for Which School-Related Claims or Defenses Should Be Available

12.7.2.1 Defenses in Perkins Loans Collection

Schools are the lender for Perkins loans. In these cases, the lender (that is, the school) should be subject to school-related defenses. In addition, the lender may *assign* the note to the United States for collection.[255] The United States, as assignee, should be subject to all defenses that could be raised against the assignor.[256]

12.7.2.2 Defenses in Direct Loan Collection

The HEA specifies that, notwithstanding any other provision of state or federal law, the Secretary shall, for Direct loans, specify in regulations when school misconduct may be asserted as a defense to loan repayment, but the student's recovery pursuant to such a defense cannot exceed the amount the student has repaid on the loan.[257] This is increasingly critical since, as of July 1, 2010, the guaranteed loan program was eliminated and most federal loans will be Direct loans. The smaller Perkins program still exists.

The regulations state that, in any proceeding to collect on a Direct loan, the borrower may assert as a defense against repayment any act or omission of the school attended by the student that would give rise to a cause of action against the school under applicable state law.[258] These defenses can be raised not only in litigation but also in tax offset, wage garnishment, and other salary offset proceedings.[259] If the defense is successful, the borrower is relieved of the obligation to repay all or part of the loan and associated costs and fees and obtains any other appropriate relief, including reimbursment to the borrower of amounts paid voluntarily or through enforced collection, a determination that the borrower is not in default on the loan and is eligible for

---

1990), aff'd in part and rev'd in part, 852 P.2d 840 (Or. Ct. App. 1993).
252 *See generally* National Consumer Law Center, Unfair and Deceptive Acts and Practices § 11.6 (7th ed. 2008 and Supp.).
253 *See* § 12.7.2.5, *infra*.

254 For information on how to find out what type of loan a client has, see § 1.9, *supra*.
255 *See* 34 C.F.R. §§ 674.8(d), 674.50 (assignment of defaulted loans).
256 The note is not a negotiable instrument, so the United States cannot be a holder in due course. *See generally* National Consumer Law Center, Unfair and Deceptive Acts and Practices § 11.6 (7th ed. 2008 and Supp.).
257 20 U.S.C. § 1087e(h).
258 34 C.F.R. § 685.206(c)(1).
259 34 C.F.R. § 685.206(c)(1).

federal assistance, and updated reports to credit bureaus to which the Department previously made adverse credit reports.[260]

The Direct loan master promissory note (MPN) restates this provision, providing that, "[i]n some cases, you may assert, as a defense against collection of your loan, that the school did something wrong or failed to do something that it should have done. You can make such a defense against repayment only if the school's act or omission directly relates to your loan or to the educational services that the loan was intended to pay for, and if what the school did or did not do would give rise to a legal cause of action against the school under applicable state law. If you believe that you have a defense against repayment of your loan, contact the Direct Loan Servicing Center."[261] The next section of the MPN explains that the government does not guarantee the quality of the academic programs provided by schools that participate in federal student aid programs. The note warns: "You must repay your loan even if you do not complete the education paid for with the loan, are unable to obtain employment in the field of study for which your school provided training, or are dissatisfied with or do not receive, the education you paid for with the loan."[262]

The Department has the authority to initiate an appropriate proceeding to require the school whose act or omission resulted in the borrowers successful defense to pay to the Department the amount of the loan to which the defense applies.[263]

Unlike the FTC Holder Rule, the Direct Loan regulation is not limited to for-profit schools. However, the regulation is more restrictive in other ways. Unlike both the FTC Holder Rule and the FFEL regulation, the Direct Loan regulation is limited to defensive actions. Further, claims are limited to those available under state law. However, the Direct Loan regulation applies even if the regulation is omitted from the loan agreement. This would only be an issue if the Department ceased putting the language in the MPN.

12.7.2.3 FFELs Extended After January 1, 1994

Starting on January 1, 1994, all FFELs use a common promissory note that is drafted by the United States Department of Education. In the MPN version that expires on July 31, 2011, the language is as follows:

Any lender holding a loan made under this MPN is subject to all claims and defenses that I could assert against the school with respect to that loan if (i) the loan was made by the school or a school-affiliated organization, (ii) the lender who made the loan provided an improper inducement (as defined by the Act) to the school or to any other party in connection with the making of the loan, (iii) the school refers loan applicants (borrowers) to the lender, or (iv) the school is affiliated with the lender by common control, contract, or business arrangement. My recovery under this provision will not exceed the amount I paid on the loan.[264]

The MPN language was codified in the FFEL regulations in 2007, although the limit on recovery is not in the regulations.[265] In adopting the regulations, the Department stated that it would eliminate the existing difference in legal rights between borrowers attending for-profit institutions (who are covered by the FTC Holder Rule under the FTC's own authority and the FFEL Program promissory note) and those attending nonprofit institutions.[266] The previous language in the MPN applied only to claims against for-profit schools.

According to the Department, the change was also consistent with a long line of court decisions finding that the HEA does not preempt state laws that allow borrowers to raise state law claims as a defense against collection of an FFEL Program loan, unless the state laws actually conflict with the objectives of the HEA.[267] The Department also noted that it did not anticipate a significant increase in risk or costs to lenders, since the principles of the FTC Holder Rule have been part of the FFEL Program since 1994 and there has not been significant litigation based on this language since that time.[268]

The regulations allow borrowers to raise claims and defenses. One of the "triggers" is the existence of a referral relationship between the school and lender. The Department had previously issued a letter stating when referral relationship exists.[269] A referral relationship does not exist if the only relationship between school and lender is based on certain specific duties required of the school and lender by the Higher Education Act or regulations. Moreover, simply giving students a list of available lenders does not create a referral relationship. The Department statement concludes that FTC interpretations will ordinarily be dispositive as to

---

260 34 C.F.R. § 685.206(c)(2).
261 This MPN expires on May 31, 2011. A copy can be found at Appendix D, *infra*, and on the companion website to this manual.
262 *Id.*
263 34 C.F.R. § 685.206(c)(3).
    The Department has additional authority to require reimbursement from schools due to a school's violation of a federal statute or regulation or the school's negligent or willful false certification. 34 C.F.R. § 685.308.

264 Copies of the most recent MPNs can be found on the Department of Education website and on the companion website to this manual.
265 34 C.F.R. § 682.209(k).
266 72 Fed. Reg. 32410 (June 12, 2007).
267 *Id.* (citing Armstrong v. Accrediting Council for Continuing Educ. & Training, Inc., 168 F.3d 1362 (D.C. Cir. 1999)).
268 *Id.*
269 Division of Policy Dev., Office of the Assistant Sec'y for Postsecondary Educ., Overview of the Federal Trade Commission Holder Rule (July 2, 1993), *available on* the companion website to this manual.

whether a referral relationship exists. Interested parties should consider statements from the FTC staff on the FTC Holder Rule's application.[270]

12.7.2.4 Federally Insured Student Loans

Federally insured student loans (FISLs) usually date back to the 1970s or early 1980s. Loans from a bank or even from a school were insured directly by the United States. Students can raise many school-related defenses to FISLs because, until 1986 (when it was dropped without comment), an FISL regulation explicitly stated that the United States would not collect an FISL to the extent that a school had closed or students had certain school-related defenses.[271] This regulation should apply at least to FISLs entered into before 1986. Moreover, when the school was the originating lender, students should also be able to raise all defenses against the assignee (the United States) based on the same rationale that applies to Perkins loans.[272]

12.7.2.5 When Loan Note Contains FTC Holder Rule Notice

Federal FFELs and Direct loans do not include the FTC Holder Rule notice ("FTC Holder Notice"). Instead, as described above, the promissory notes for both programs restate the applicable regulation regarding school-related claims. Private student loans, however, should contain the FTC Holder Notice language. Possible remedies if the notice is not included are discussed below and in Chapter 11, *supra*.

Although most relevant in the private student loan context, there is at least a policy argument that the broader language of the FTC Holder Notice should be included with federal student loans as well.

The FTC's Rule on Preservation of Consumer Claims and Defenses[273] ("FTC Holder Rule") addresses the issue of assignee and related creditor liability for seller misconduct.[274] The rule operates by way of a notice being placed in consumer credit agreements whereby, as a matter of the contract itself, the parties agree that the consumer can raise seller-related claims and defenses against the holder of the note or contract. Even if a transaction is beyond the scope of the rule, if the agreement contains the notice, the holder is subject to seller-related claims and defenses. In contrast, problems may arise, as discussed below, if the notice *should* have been inserted but is not in the agreement.

In general, the seller must insert the notice in consumer credit agreements whenever the seller is the originating creditor. In addition, the seller must arrange for the lender to insert the notice in the lender's credit agreement whenever the seller refers the consumer to the lender or otherwise has a business arrangement with the lender.

The FTC's Statement of Basis and Purpose for the rule specifically states that it applies to vocational training.[275] The rule applies to "sellers," broadly defined as sellers of goods or services to consumers,[276] thus covering for-profit vocational schools. Nevertheless, only sellers within the FTC's jurisdiction are covered by the FTC Holder Rule. Public entities and truly nonprofit corporations are not within the scope of the FTC Act,[277] so these sellers are not required to place the notice in the contract.

The language of the FTC Holder Notice makes clear that consumers can raise not just defenses but also affirmative claims against the holder of a credit agreement. There is no limit as to which claims can be brought, including all claims available under state and other applicable law. However, there is a cap on recovery. A consumer cannot recover under the FTC Holder Rule no more than the amount the consumer has paid on the loan plus cancellation of the remaining indebtedness. But there is no limit on creditor's liability for its own conduct.[278]

12.7.3 Pre-1994 FFELs, Other Loans When There Is Less Clarity As to Availability of School-Related Claims or Defenses

12.7.3.1 General

Common problems arise in private student loan cases if the lender does not include the notice or in some cases argues that it is not required to do so. These issues are discussed in Chapter 11, *supra*. Failure to include the notice may also be an issue for pre-1994 FFELs, before it was clear that the Department agreed to include its version of the FTC Holder Notice in the loan agreements and codified the notice

---

270 The Department statement particularly references 40 Fed. Reg. 53506 (Nov. 18, 1975), 41 Fed. Reg. 43594 (Aug. 16, 1976), and 57 Fed. Reg. 28814 (June 29, 1992).
271 34 C.F.R. § 518 (1985) (since rescinded). *See also* United States v. Griffin, 707 F.2d 1477 (D.C. Cir. 1983).
272 *See* § 12.7.2.1, *supra*. *Cf.* United States v. Griffin, 707 F.2d 1477 (D.C. Cir. 1983) (not ruling on whether the United States was an assignee or surety because Department regulations authorized students to raise defenses).
273 16 C.F.R. Pt. 433.
274 The rule is discussed in detail in National Consumer Law Center, Unfair and Deceptive Acts and Practices § 11.6 (7th ed. 2008 and Supp.).

275 40 Fed. Reg. 53524 (Nov. 18, 1975). *See also* Federal Trade Commission Guidelines on Trade Regulation Rule Concerning Preservation of Consumers' Claims and Defenses, 41 Fed. Reg. 20024 (May 14, 1976).
276 16 C.F.R. § 433.1(j).
277 National Consumer Law Center, Unfair and Deceptive Acts and Practices § 2.3.5 (7th ed. 2008 and Supp.).
278 *Id.* § 11.6.3.7. *See also* § 11.10, *supra* (direct creditor liability in private student loan cases).

in regulations.[279] The sections below focus on other options for derivative liability under these circumstances, mainly in the federal student loan context. Chapter 11, *supra*, expands on this issue for private loans.

It is quite frustrating to students that lenders, guaranty agencies, and the Department still, in large part, refuse to recognize legitimate school-related defenses for FFELs entered into before 1994. For these loans, the only undisputed right to relief is through a closed-school, unpaid-refund, or false-certification discharge.[280]

The key question in determining whether students can raise school-related defenses to FFELs extended before 1994 is whether the originating lender (usually a bank) is subject to the student's claims against the school. If the bank is subject to the student's claims, so are its assignees—the secondary market lender, the guaranty agency, and the United States.[281]

One way to address this problem is to bring an affirmative action in state or federal court for declaratory relief specifying that the borrower does not owe the loan. The borrower can then use the declaration as a defense in any tax intercept or other administrative collection action. An action for declaratory relief should not violate the HEA's anti-injunction provision.[282] Other options are discussed in the following sections.[283]

12.7.3.2 Agency and Other Common Law Theories

One ground for lender liability for school-related claims is that the lender has appointed the school its agent for certain functions and that, under *respondeat superior*, the principal is liable for the actions of its agent within the actual or apparent scope of the agent's authority. Typically, in many proprietary school enrollments, the school acts as the lender's agent in giving the loan papers to the student, filling out the lender's portion of the loan paperwork, helping the student fill out the student portion, and forwarding that paperwork to the lender.[284]

This argument is relevant in private and federal student loan cases. The key question in federal student loan cases is whether the federal regulatory scheme preempts application of the state or federal common law of *respondeat superior*. Unfortunately for borrowers, the current judicial trend favors federal preemption in these circumstances.[285]

Even if the claim survives preemption, a weakness of the agency approach is that the principal will only be liable for acts within the actual or apparent authority of the agent. This will usually relate to the student's enrollment in the school and not to the school's quality of teaching, equipment, or placement services.

However, the principal should also be responsible for misrepresentations made by the agency. The strength of the agency approach therefore lies in misrepresentation, rather than contract, claims against the school. If the school makes misrepresentations to induce the student to enroll and sign the forms, those misrepresentations can be raised against the lender if the school had actual or apparent authority to make such representations.

Another agency argument in federal student loan cases is that the school was acting as the Department of Education's agent in administering the HEA and that the Department should thus be estopped from collecting on a loan involving misconduct by its agent.[286] Other common law theories that may apply in some states include close connectedness and

---

279 See § 12.7.2.3, *supra*.
280 See Ch. 9, *supra* (discharges).
281 There may be additional issues that arise in trying to hold secondary market purchasers liable for a school's fraud or negligence. *See* Crawford v. American Inst. of Prof'l Careers, Inc., 934 F. Supp. 335 (D. Ariz. 1996) (deeming state law claims against secondary purchasers preempted by the HEA; agreeing that purchasers could not comply with state law and anti-discrimination provisions of the HEA, which require purchasers to purchase certain loans without any independent oversight or control over school programs; no separate fraud or wrongdoing alleged against purchaser in this case).
282 Bank of America, NT & SA v. Riley, 940 F. Supp. 348 (D.D.C. 1996) (HEA's anti-injunctive provision does not apply to a declaratory judgment action against the Secretary), *aff'd*, 132 F.3d 1480 (D.C. Cir. 1997). *See also* Thomas v. Bennett, 856 F.2d 1165 (8th Cir. 1988); Student Loan Mktg. Ass'n v. Riley, 907 F. Supp. 464 (D.D.C. 1995), *aff'd and remanded*, 104 F.3d 397 (D.C. 1997); Pro Schools, Inc. v. Riley, 824 F. Supp. 1314 (E.D. Wis. 1993).

   A number of briefs filed on behalf of students have also persuasively countered the argument that the anti-injunctive provision applies to actions for declaratory relief. *See* § 12.6.2.1, *supra*.
283 This issue is discussed more extensively in National Consumer Law Center, Unfair and Deceptive Acts and Practices § 11.6.5 (7th ed. 2008 and Supp.).
284 *See* Shorter v. Riley, Clearinghouse No. 47,950B (N.D. Ga. Nov. 18, 1993); Hicks v. Riley, Clearinghouse No. 49,133 (N.D. Ga. May 27, 1993) (plaintiff's motion to approve settlement and brief in support thereof); Tillis v. Bank of America, Clearinghouse No. 49,932 (Cal. Super. Ct. Nov. 17, 1993).
285 *See, e.g.*, Keams v. Tempe Technical Inst., 39 F.3d 222 (9th Cir. 1994), *appeal after remand*, 103 F.3d 138 (9th Cir. 1996), *redesignated as op.*, 110 F.3d 44 (9th Cir. 1997), *claims against all defendants dismissed*, 16 F. Supp. 2d 1119 (D. Ariz. 1998); Morgan v. Markerdowne Corp., 976 F. Supp. 301 (D.N.J. 1997) (New Jersey's law of agency and close connectedness preempted to the extent they would hold lenders and guarantors liable for alleged misrepresentations by school); Crawford v. American Inst. of Prof'l Careers, 934 F. Supp. 335 (D. Ariz. 1996); Bartels v. Alabama Commercial Coll., Inc., 918 F. Supp. 1565 (N.D. Ga. 1995), *aff'd without published op.*, 189 F.3d 483 (11th Cir. Ga. 1999); Bogart v. Nebraska Student Loan Program, 858 S.W.2d 78 (Ark. 1993) (finding that federal law preempts state law claim based on agency, the students apparently not bringing to court's attention various federal court rulings limiting preemption).
286 Spinner v. Chesapeake Bus. Inst. of Va., Clearinghouse No. 49,131A (E.D. Va. Feb. 5, 1993).

joint enterprise,[287] and that the enrollment contract and loan papers were integrated contracts, making the breach of the enrollment contract a defense as to enforcement of the loan.[288]

12.7.3.3 State Lender Liability Statutes

A number of states have enacted statutes specifically requiring that lenders be liable for the actions of their related sellers, specifying in some detail the type of relationship between the seller and lender that is sufficient to allow the consumer to raise seller-related defenses on the loan.[289] While these statutes in some states are vague,[290] they still may provide a basis for a student raising school-related defenses.[291]

The major obstacle in federal student loan cases yet again is federal preemption of the state statutes. In theory, the HEA should not preempt state laws because the Department of Education requires that student loans provide for the same or similar protection specified in these state laws.[292] Specifically, in post-1994 student loans containing the FTC Holder Notice, lenders should be liable for school-related claims.

Courts have generally agreed that the HEA does not expressly preempt state lender liability statutes and that it does not implicitly preempt the field of lender liability.[293] Therefore, these state statutes should be preempted only if they are in actual conflict with federal requirements or objectives.[294]

The problem for students is that courts have generally found that some federal requirements or objectives are in conflict with state statutory provisions. For example, state statutes finding lenders liable when the loan is conditioned on the proceeds going to a particular purpose or when the lender provides forms to the seller have been considered preempted.[295] These judicial interpretations have far-reaching consequences, since the HEA requires all lenders to

---

287 Tillis v. Bank of America, Clearinghouse No. 49,932 (Cal. Super. Ct. Nov. 17, 1993).

288 *But see* Bartels v. Alabama Commercial College, Inc., 918 F. Supp. 1565 (S.D. Ga. 1995), *aff'd without published op.*, 189 F.3d 483 (11th Cir. 1999); Shorter v. Alexander, Clearinghouse No. 47,950 (N.D. Ga. Dec. 8, 1992).

289 *See generally* National Consumer Law Center, Unfair and Deceptive Acts and Practices § 11.6.5.2 (7th ed. 2008 and Supp.).

290 Armstrong v. Accrediting Council for Continuing Educ. & Training, Inc., 84 F.3d 1452 (D.C. Cir. 1996), *on remand*, 950 F. Supp. 1 (D.D.C. 1996) (court maintained jurisdiction of pendent claims and found case to be appropriate for declaratory relief), *on further remand*, 980 F. Supp. 53 (D.D.C. 1997), *aff'd*, 168 F.3d 1362 (D.C. Cir. 1999) (state law claims preempted by pre-1992 federal policy to protect lenders; in essence, all state law claims prior to 1993 preempted unless there is an origination relationship); Jackson v. Culinary Sch. of Wash., Ltd., 811 F. Supp. 714 (D.D.C. 1993) (summary judgment) (state statute required that lender act at express request of seller and seller receive compensation from lender; finding insufficient facts to establish such compensation), *aff'd on other grounds*, 27 F.3d 573 (D.C. Cir. 1994) (declining to consider complex state law issues in declaratory judgment action), *affirmance vacated*, 115 S. Ct. 2573 (1995) (appellate court used de novo instead of abuse of discretion standard to review district court's decision to decide state law issues in declaratory judgment action), *remanded to district court on state law claims*, 59 F.3d 254 (D.C. Cir. 1995) (to determine on what basis federal court decided to rule on state law issues), *motion dismissed*, 1995 U.S. App. LEXIS 22304 (D.C. Cir. July 25, 1995); Williams v. National Sch. of Health Tech., Inc., 836 F. Supp. 273 (E.D. Pa. 1993) (state retail installment sales act applies to loans directly from a seller, not to loans directly from a lender; student loan directly from lender was not structured to avoid this Pennsylvania law but was structured pursuant to federal scheme; consequently, installment sales act does not apply by its very terms and there is no reason to extend statute to third-party student loans).

291 *See* Tipton v. Secretary of Educ., 768 F. Supp. 540 (S.D. W. Va. 1991).

292 *See* § 12.7.2.2, 12.7.2.3, *supra*.

293 *See, e.g.*, Armstrong v. Accrediting Council for Continuing Educ. & Training, Inc., 84 F.3d 1452 (D.C. Cir. 1996), *on remand*, 950 F. Supp. 1 (D.D.C. 1996) (maintaining jurisdiction of pendent claims and finding case to be appropriate for declaratory relief), *on further remand*, 980 F. Supp. 53 (D.D.C. 1997), *aff'd*, 168 F.3d 1362 (D.C. Cir. 1999) (state law claims preempted by pre-1992 federal policy to protect lenders; in essence, all state law claims prior to 1993 preempted unless there is an origination relationship); Keams v. Tempe Technical Inst., 39 F.3d 222 (9th Cir. 1994), *appeal after remand*, 103 F.3d 138 (9th Cir. 1996), *redesignated as op.*, 110 F.3d 44 (9th Cir. 1997), *claims against all defendants dismissed*, 16 F. Supp. 2d 1119 (D. Ariz. 1998); Jackson v. Culinary Sch. of Wash., Ltd., 27 F.3d 573 (D.C. Cir. 1994), *vacated on other grounds*, 115 S. Ct. 2573 (1995) (appellate court used de novo instead of abuse of discretion standard to review district court's decision to decide state law issues in declaratory judgment action), *remanded to district court on state law claims*, 59 F.3d 254 (D.C. Cir. 1995) (to determine on what basis federal court decided to rule on state law issues), *motion dismissed*, 1995 U.S. App. LEXIS 22304 (D.C. Cir. 1995); Spinner v. Chesapeake Bus. Inst. of Va., Clearinghouse No. 49,131A (E.D. Va. Feb. 5, 1993); Jackson v. Culinary Sch. of Wash., Ltd., 811 F. Supp. 714 (D.D.C. 1993) (claim dismissed based on summary judgment motion that students had not presented evidence of origination relationship), *aff'd on other grounds*, 27 F.3d 573 (D.C. Cir. 1994) (origination theory not enforceable against the Secretary), *vacated on other grounds*, 115 S. Ct. 2573 (1995) (appellate court used de novo instead of abuse of discretion standard to review district court's decision to decide state law issues in declaratory judgment action), *remanded to district court on state law claims, aff'g own ruling on origination*, 59 F.3d 254 (D.C. Cir. 1995) (to determine on what basis federal court decided to rule on state law issues), *motion dismissed*, 1995 U.S. App. LEXIS 22304 (D.C. Cir. July 25, 1995); Hernandez v. Alexander (D. Nev. May 18, 1992), *available at* www.consumerlaw.org/unreported; Tipton v. Secretary of Educ. (S.D. W. Va. Mar. 31, 1992), *available at* www.consumerlaw.org/unreported (denial of permission for an interlocutory appeal); Tipton v. Secretary of Educ., 768 F. Supp. 540 (S.D. W. Va. 1991); Wilson v. Manufacturers Hanover Trust Co., Clearinghouse No. 45,921 (4th Cir. Sept. 25, 1990). *See* § 9.3.2.1.1, *supra*.

294 *See* § 12.5.3.4, *supra*.

295 Tipton v. Secretary of Educ., 768 F. Supp. 540 (S.D. W. Va. 1991).

condition the loan on the student using the money to go to school and all lenders must supply forms to schools.

Even more troubling for student litigants, though, is courts finding certain state statutory provisions to conflict with federal "objectives" that are not embodied in any statute or regulation. The 1999 *Armstrong* decision is illustrative of this trend. The loan at issue in that case was made in 1988. The *Armstrong* court refused to imply the FTC Holder Rule terms and concluded that state law claims were preempted.[296] The court found that state laws that would allow school-related defenses to be raised against lenders were preempted during the period that the FTC had decided not to enforce the Holder Rule with respect to student loans.[297]

In a blow to student advocates, the court stuck to this position even while acknowledging that the FTC and the Secretary of Education have since concluded that the FTC Holder Rule does apply and that it did apply during this period of non-enforcement.[298] The *Armstrong* court seemed uneasy about the result, acknowledging that students with these older loans are left "holding the bag" but claimed it had no authority to protect the students.[299]

The key question in private student loan cases is whether certain lenders, generally national banks, are subject to state law.[300]

12.7.3.4 Private Remedy for Failure to Include FTC Holder Notice

As described above, all FFEL student loans extended on or after January 1, 1994, include a provision based on the FTC Holder Rule allowing students to raise school-related defenses when certain conditions are met.[301] Direct loans restate the relevant regulation for those products. Unfortunately for students, virtually no federal student loans before that date contained such a provision.

Federal law is clear that many of those pre-1994 FFELs should have included the FTC Holder Notice. The FTC Holder Rule specifies that, when a for-profit seller (such as a proprietary trade school) refers the consumer to a particular lender, then the FTC Holder Notice must be included in the promissory note.

The FTC staff in charge of enforcing the Holder Rule has unambiguously stated that the Holder Rule applies to FFELs.[302] The Secretary of Education[303] and a 1993 congressional conference report[304] reach the same conclusion. These 1991, 1992, and 1993 interpretations supersede a few earlier courts that ruled otherwise.[305] Subsequent court rulings are in line with the FTC, the Department, and congressional interpretation that the FTC Holder Rule does apply to FFELs.[306]

---

296 Armstrong v. Accrediting Counsel for Continuing Educ. & Training, Inc., 168 F.3d 1362 (D.C. Cir. 1999).

297 This period was from 1982 to 1993, or possibly from 1982 to 1991, depending on a court's historical interpretation. The court noted that a common promissory note with the FTC Holder Rule was instituted in 1993, although the FTC began enforcing the Rule again in 1991. Armstrong v. Accrediting Counsel for Continuing Educ. & Training, Inc., 168 F.3d 1362, 1365 (D.C. Cir. 1999).

298 Armstrong v. Accrediting Council for Continuing Educ. & Training, Inc., 168 F.3d 1362, 1368 (D.C. Cir. 1999).

299 *Id.* at 1370.
As discussed below in § 12.7.3.5, *supra*, the *Armstrong* court indicated that state law claims were not preempted, even during the period of FTC non-enforcement, when the school and lender had an "origination relationship" under federal law.

300 *See* § 11.9.2.4, *supra*.

301 *See* § 12.7.2.3, *supra*.
The Federal Trade Commission Trade Regulation Rule Concerning the Preservation of Consumers' Claims and Defenses, 16 C.F.R. § 433, is discussed in detail at National Consumer Law Center, Unfair and Deceptive Acts and Practices § 11.6 (7th ed. 2008 and Supp.).

302 *See* F.T.C. Staff Letter from David Medine, Associate Director for Credit Practices (Feb. 11, 1993), *available on* the companion website to this manual; F.T.C. Staff Opinion Letter to Jonathan Sheldon, National Consumer Law Center (July 24, 1991), *available on* the companion website to this manual.
These letters reverse a prior letter on the subject, F.T.C. Informal Staff Letter (Esposito) (Jan. 9, 1989), *available on* the companion website to this manual. The full Federal Trade Commission, while not formally adopting the 1991 staff opinion, did refer to that opinion with apparent approval in 1992. In an FTC decision not to amend the Holder Rule, the FTC stated that "the Commission staff has provided NCLC with an opinion letter stating that such educational loans are not exempt from the Rule." 57 Fed. Reg. 28815 n.11 (June 29, 1992). *But see* Armstrong v. Accrediting Council for Continuing Educ. & Training, Inc., 168 F.3d 1362 (D.C. Cir. 1999).

303 The introductory material to the Department's common promissory note, at page 7, states: "The Secretary of Education has determined that the Governing Law and Notices section of the common promissory note must include the Federal Trade Commission (FTC) consumer defense clause as required by the FTC regulations, 16 C.F.R. Section 433.2." *See* Common Application Material and Promissory Note (Apr. 16, 1993), *available on* the companion website to this manual.

304 "The Holder Rule applies to student loan borrowers attending for-profit institutions, and the new Federal Family Education Loan promissory note includes the required notice." Omnibus Budget Reconciliation Act of 1993, H.R. 2264 (Conf. Rep.), H.R. Rep. No. 213, 455, 103d Cong. (1st Sess. Aug. 4, 1993).
In addition, Congress, in the Higher Education Amendments of 1992, had an opportunity, by adopting the House version, to limit significantly the FTC Holder Rule's applicability to GSLs. Instead, Congress decided to adopt the Senate version that would not limit the FTC Holder Rule's applicability.

305 Veal v. First Am. Savs. Bank, 914 F.2d 909 (7th Cir. 1990). *See also* McVey v. U.S. Training Acad. (Bankr. E.D. Ky. Aug. 25, 1988), *available at* www.consumerlaw.org/unreported.

306 *See, e.g.*, Morgan v. Markerdowne Corp., 976 F. Supp. 301 (D.N.J. 1997); Jackson v. Culinary Sch. of Wash., Ltd., 788 F. Supp. 1233 (D.D.C. 1992). *See also* Spinner v. Chesapeake Bus. Inst. of Va., Clearinghouse No. 49,131A (E.D. Va. Feb. 5, 1993); C. Mansfield, *The Federal Trade Commission Holder Rule and Its Applicability to Student Loans—Re-Allocating the Risk of Proprietary School Failure*, 26 Wake Forest L. Rev. 635

§ 12.7.3.4 Student Loan Law

The problem for students, however, is that, while courts may assume that the FTC Holder Notice should have been included in the Guaranteed Student Loans Program note, courts are leery of providing consumers with a *remedy* for the lenders' failure to include that notice. There is no direct private right of action for violation of the FTC Holder Rule.[307] As a result, consumers must use state law theories to claim violations of the FTC Holder Rule. To date, such state law claims have met with limited success.

In other contexts, courts have had little difficulty finding a violation of an FTC Holder Rule to be a state UDAP violation.[308] Yet, in the federal student loan context, courts have usually found ways to avoid UDAP liability for FFELs violating the rule.[309] Borrowers may also claim liability based on state "holder" laws.[310] For a discussion of these claims in private loan cases, see Chapter 11, *supra*.

Despite this judicial reluctance, in many states a consumer should be able to challenge a lender's systematic failure to comply with the FTC Holder Rule as a state UDAP violation.[311] This is particularly the case for loans entered into after April 16, 1993, when the Department of Education announced to lenders and guarantors that the FTC Holder Rule applies to student loans.[312] Lenders after that date had no excuse not to include the FTC Holder Notice in their promissory notes, when applicable.

Another approach is to seek to enforce the FTC Holder Rule language as an implied term in the note even though the notice is not present.[313] This approach has not been successful in the federal student loan context.[314] Also not successful to date has been the argument that the lender should be estopped from taking advantage of the illegality in the note or that an illegal note cannot be enforced.[315]

It may also be possible to argue that the note without the FTC Holder Rule is unconscionable and thus unenforceable

---

(1991). *But cf.* Hernandez v. Alexander (D. Nev. May 18, 1992), *available at* www.consumerlaw.org/unreported.

307 *See* National Consumer Law Center, Unfair and Deceptive Acts and Practices § 11.6.2 (7th ed. 2008 and Supp.).

308 *See generally* National Consumer Law Center, Unfair and Deceptive Acts and Practices § 11.6.4.4 (7th ed. 2008 and Supp.).

309 *See, e.g.*, Armstrong v. Accrediting Council for Continuing Educ. & Training, Inc., 84 F.3d 1452 (D.C. Cir. 1996), *on remand*, 950 F. Supp. 1 (D.D.C. 1996) (maintaining jurisdiction of pendent claims and finding case to be appropriate for declaratory relief), *on further remand*, 980 F. Supp. 53 (D.D.C. 1997) (determining that California law controls and inviting plaintiff to amend complaint to assert claims and defenses under California consumer protection laws), *aff'd*, 168 F.3d 1362 (D.C. Cir. 1999) (affirming district court's dismissal of claims); Keams v. Tempe Technical Inst., Inc., 993 F. Supp. 714 (D. Ariz. 1997) (since student loan contracts did not include terms of Holder Rule, former vocational school students were not able to assert claims and defenses arising from school's behavior against assignee), *claims against all defendants dismissed*, 16 F. Supp. 2d 1119 (D. Ariz. 1998); Morgan v. Markerdowne Corp., 976 F. Supp. 301 (D.N.J. 1997); United States v. Ornecipe (S.D. Fla. 1995), *available at* www.consumerlaw.org/unreported (Florida UDAP statute does not apply to banks); Jackson v. Culinary Sch. of Wash., Ltd., 811 F. Supp. 714 (D.D.C. 1993) (summary judgment) (finding insufficient facts to find UDAP liability), *aff'd on other grounds*, 27 F.3d 573 (D.C. Cir. 1994) (declining to consider complex state law issue in declaratory judgment action), *vacated*, 115 S. Ct. 2573 (1995) (appellate court used de novo instead of abuse of discretion standard to review district court's decision to decide state law issues in declaratory judgment action), *remanded to district court on state law claims*, 59 F.3d 254 (D.C. Cir. 1995) (to determine on what basis federal court decided to rule on state law issues), *motion dismissed*, 1995 U.S. App. LEXIS 22304 (D.C. Cir. July 25, 1995); Williams v. National Sch. of Health Tech., Inc., 836 F. Supp. 273 (E.D. Pa. 1993) (United States committed no wrongdoing, so no UDAP violation; failing to consider that lender did engage in wrongdoing and that the United States is an assignee of the lender); Spinner v. Chesapeake Bus. Inst. of Va., Clearinghouse No. 49,131A (E.D. Va. Feb. 5, 1993) (UDAP statute exempted practices authorized by federal laws or regulations; determining that student loan contracts were authorized); Hernandez v. Alexander (D. Nev. May 18, 1992), *available at* www.consumerlaw.org/unreported. *See* Ch. 11, *supra* (private loans). *But see* Keams v. Tempe Technical Inst., Inc. (D. Ariz. Oct. 19, 1995), *available at* www.consumerlaw.org/unreported.

310 *See generally* National Consumer Law Center, Unfair and Deceptive Acts and Practices § 11.6.5.2 (7th ed. 2008 and Supp).

311 *See* Keams v. Tempe Technical Inst., 39 F.3d 222 (9th Cir. 1994), *appeal after remand*, 103 F.3d 138 (9th Cir. 1996), *redesignated as op.*, 110 F.3d 44 (9th Cir. 1997), *claims against all defendants dismissed*, 16 F. Supp. 2d 1119 (D. Ariz. 1998); Jackson v. Culinary Sch. of Wash., Ltd., 788 F. Supp. 1233 (D.D.C. 1992) (see note 145, *supra*, for the subsequent history in this case); Shorter v. Alexander (N.D. Ga. Dec. 8, 1992), *available at* www.consumerlaw.org/unreported; Ch. 11, *supra* (private loans). *But see* Armand v. Secretary of Educ. (S.D. Fla. July 19, 1995), *available at* www.consumerlaw.org/unreported (Florida UDAP statute does not apply to banks).

312 Common Application Material and Promissory Note (Apr. 16, 1993), *available on* the companion website to this manual.

313 *See* Anderson v. Central States Waterproofing (Minn. Dist. Ct. Hennepin Cnty. 1982), *available at* www.consumerlaw.org/unreported.

314 Armstrong v. Accrediting Council for Continuing Educ. & Training, Inc., 84 F.3d 1452 (D.C. Cir. 1996), *on remand*, 950 F. Supp. 1 (D.D.C. 1996), *on further remand*, 980 F. Supp. 53 (D.D.C. 1997), *aff'd*, 168 F.3d 1362 (D.C. Cir. 1999); Lee v. Riley (W.D. Ky. Feb. 27, 1998), *available at* www.consumerlaw.org/unreported (memorandum opinion); Bartels v. Alabama Commercial Coll., Inc., 918 F. Supp. 1565 (S.D. Ga. 1995), *rev'd on other grounds*, 54 F.3d 702 (11th Cir. 1995); Spinner v. Chesapeake Bus. Inst. of Va., Clearinghouse No. 49,131A (E.D. Va. Feb. 5, 1993); Jackson v. Culinary Sch. of Wash., Ltd., 788 F. Supp. 1233 (D.D.C. 1992) (see note 145, for subsequent history in this case); Hernandez v. Alexander (D. Nev. May 18, 1992), *available at* www.consumerlaw.org/unreported; Shorter v. Alexander (N.D. Ga. Dec. 8, 1992), *available at* www.consumerlaw.org/unreported.

For a discussion of this issue in private loan cases, see § 11.9.2, *supra*.

315 Armstrong v. Accrediting Council for Continuing Educ. & Training, Inc., 84 F.3d 1452 (D.C. Cir. 1996), *on remand*, 950 F. Supp. 1 (D.D.C. 1996), *on further remand*, 980 F. Supp. 53 (D.D.C. 1997), *aff'd*, 168 F.3d 1362 (D.C. Cir. 1999); Spinner v. Chesapeake Bus. Inst. of Va., Clearinghouse No. 49,131A (E.D. Va. Feb. 5, 1993).

or that the Department, guaranty agency, or the lender had a fiduciary duty to the borrower or were engaged in constructive fraud. At least one federal court rejected the fiduciary duty argument in a federal student loan case but let go to trial both the arguments that the note involved constructive fraud and was unconscionable.[316] A RICO claim is another possibility.[317] Failure to include the FTC Holder Notice is a growing problem among private student lenders, as discussed in Chapter 11, *supra*.[318]

12.7.3.5 Origination Theory

The Secretary of Education recognizes that students can raise school-related defenses to FFEL collection actions when the school is in an "origination relationship" with the lender.[319] Therefore, if an origination relationship can be proven, even loans from the period prior to the inclusion of the FTC Holder Notice should be subject to school-related defenses as well as private student loans.

The *Armstrong* court affirmed this concept, citing the origination relationship as a major exception to lenders' protection from student suits prior to re-enforcement of the FTC Holder Rule.[320]

Unfortunately for students, the District of Columbia Circuit ruled that the Secretary has not sufficiently communicated an intention to be bound by the origination policy so as to create a legally enforceable right grounded in federal law.[321] The *Armstrong* decision, however, indicates that, if there was an origination relationship, a state law theory of lender liability would not be preempted even during the period of FTC non-enforcement.[322]

Some courts have found the origination theory binding on the Department and guarantors,[323] based on the Department's statements that it expects guaranty agencies not to collect unenforceable loans when an origination relationship exists.[324] Other courts find that, even if the Department's statements are binding on the Department, the statements have never been promulgated as a rule and are not binding on guarantors.[325]

If a court allows a consumer to raise defenses when there is an origination relationship, the next step is to present sufficient proof of the relationship. Department regulations define origination as a special relationship in which the lender delegates to the school substantial functions normally

---

316 Spinner v. Chesapeake Bus. Inst. of Va., Clearinghouse No. 49,131A (E.D. Va. Feb. 5, 1993).
317 *See* §§ 12.5.2.1, 12.5.3.3 (federal RICO claims), 12.5.4.1(state RICO claims), *supra*.
318 *See* § 12.5.3.3, *supra*.
319 A good enunciation of this policy is found in a letter from Acting Assistant Secretary Whitehead to Congressman Stephen Solarz (May 19, 1988), *available on* the companion website to this manual.

In addition, a recent Department of Education regulation requires schools to warn students that students cannot raise school-related defenses against lenders "other than a loan made or originated by the school." 34 C.F.R. § 682.604(f)(2)(iii). *See also* 41 Fed. Reg. 4496 (Jan. 29, 1976) (explanation of the origins of this policy).

One early case dismissed the origination theory as applied to GSL because the plaintiffs had mistakenly relied on FISL regulations. *See* Veal v. First Am. Savs. Bank, 914 F.2d 909 (7th Cir. 1990).

The Department itself has stated that, while the FISL regulations do not regulate GSLs, the origination theory is independently applicable to GSLs. Letter from Fred J. Marinucci, U.S. Department of Educ. Office of General Counsel, to the Honorable John T. Copenhaver, Jr., federal district court judge, Clearinghouse No. 45,919 (Nov. 9, 1990).
320 Armstrong v. Accrediting Council for Continuing Educ. & Training, 168 F.3d 1362, 1365 (D.C. Cir. 1999) (as long as lenders avoided school origination relationships, they could make and sell loans without fear that students could assert school misconduct as a defense against repaying their loans); Morgan v. Markerdowne Corp., 976 F. Supp. 301 (D.N.J. 1997) (origination relationship between lender and school subjects lenders and guarantors to school-related defenses).
321 Jackson v. Culinary Sch. of Wash., Ltd., 27 F.3d 573 (D.C. Cir. 1994), *vacated on other grounds*, 115 S. Ct. 2573 (1995) (appellate court used de novo instead of abuse of discretion standard to review district court's decision to decide state law issues in declaratory judgment action), *remanded to district court on state law claims, aff'g ruling on origination*, 59 F.3d 254 (D.C. Cir. 1995) (to determine on what basis federal court decided to rule on state law issues), *motion dismissed*, 1995 U.S. App. LEXIS 22304 (D.C. Cir. July 25, 1995); Williams v. National Sch. of Health Tech., Inc. 836 F. Supp. 273 (E.D. Pa. 1993), *aff'd without op.*, 37 F.3d 1491 (3d Cir. 1994). *See also* Bartels v. Alabama Commercial Coll., Inc., 918 F. Supp. 1565 (S.D. Ga. 1995), *aff'd without published op.*, 189 F.3d 483 (11th Cir. Ga. 1999).
322 *See* Armstrong v. Accrediting Council for Continuing Educ. & Training, Inc., 168 F.3d 1362 (D.C. Cir. 1999); § 12.7.3.3, *supra*.
323 Morgan v. Markerdowne Corp., 976 F. Supp. 301 (D.N.J. 1997); Tipton v. Secretary of Educ., 768 F. Supp. 540 (S.D. W. Va. 1991). *See also* Hernandez v. Alexander (D. Nev. May 18, 1992), *available at* www.consumerlaw.org/unreported; Alberto v. School of Bus. Machs., Clearinghouse No. 46,755 (N.J. Super. Ct. July 26, 1991). *Cf.* Plaintiff's Opposition to Motions to Dismiss of Defendants Bank of America, California Student Loan Finance Corp., the Higher Education Assistance Found., and the Secretary of Educ., Armstrong v. Accrediting Council for Continuing Educ. & Training, Inc. (D.D.C. filed Apr. 1, 1992), *available at* www.consumerlaw.org/unreported.
324 *See, e.g.*, Letter from Acting Assistant Secretary Whitehead to Congressman Stephen Solarz (May 19, 1988), *available at* the companion website to this manual.
325 Armstrong v. Accrediting Council for Continuing Educ. & Training, Inc., 84 F.3d 1452 (D.C. Cir. 1996), *on remand*, 950 F. Supp. 1 (D.D.C. 1996), *on further remand*, 980 F. Supp. 53 (D.D.C. 1997), *aff'd*, 168 F.3d 1362 (D.C. Cir. 1999) (affirming district court's dismissal of claims); Bartels v. Alabama Commercial Coll., Inc., 918 F. Supp. 1565 (S.D. Ga. 1995), *aff'd without published op.*, 189 F.3d 483 (11th Cir. 1999); Williams v. National Sch. of Health Tech., Inc., 836 F. Supp. 273 (E.D. Pa. 1993); Spinner v. Chesapeake Bus. Inst. of Va., Clearinghouse No. 49,131A (E.D. Va. Feb. 5, 1993); Shorter v. Alexander (N.D. Ga. Dec. 8, 1992), *available at* www.consumerlaw.org/unreported.

performed by lenders.[326] The regulations also, until 1994, gave three examples in which the Secretary determined that an origination relationship exists:

- The school determines who receives a loan and the amount of the loan;
- The lender has the school verify the identity of the borrower; *or*
- The lender has the school complete forms normally completed by the lender.[327]

The burden of proving this relationship is on the student.[328]

12.8 Student Claims Against Tuition Recovery Funds

12.8.1 General

State tuition recovery funds (STRFs) can be a valuable source of relief for defrauded students when a school is insolvent and when the student cannot obtain a HEA statutory discharge. STRFs contain deposits of money collected from schools approved to operate in the state. The funds are disbursed to victimized students under specified conditions.

Many states have either an STRF or a bond program to reimburse defrauded students. States with STRFs tend to have two different funds—one for degree-granting institutions and one for schools that offer non-degree-granting vocational programs.[329]

---

326 34 C.F.R. § 682.200(b) ("Origination").

327 *Id.* Morgan v. Markerdowne Corp., 976 F. Supp. 301 (D.N.J. 1997) (origination relationship existed when school chose banks from which borrowers would obtain financing, obtained all of necessary financial papers, either completed papers or assisted borrowers in completing papers, verified borrowers' information, and had borrowers sign documents).

328 Jackson v. Culinary Sch. of Wash., Ltd., 811 F. Supp. 714 (D.D.C. 1993) (dismissing claim based on summary judgment motion that students had not presented evidence of origination relationship), *aff'd on other grounds*, 27 F.3d 573 (D.C. Cir. 1994) (origination theory not enforceable against the Secretary), *vacated on other grounds*, 115 S. Ct. 2573 (1995) (appellate court used de novo instead of abuse of discretion standard to review district court's decision to decide state law issues in declaratory judgment action), *remanded to district court on state law claims, aff'g own ruling on origination*, 59 F.3d 254 (D.C. Cir. 1995) (to determine on what basis federal court decided to rule on state law issues), *motion dismissed*, 1995 U.S. App. LEXIS 22304 (D.C. Cir. July 25, 1995); Hernandez v. Alexander, 845 F. Supp. 1417 (D. Nev. 1993) (not sufficient to allege that school determined amount of loan requested but not of loan actually lent, verified identity of borrower—there being no requirement that lender verify borrower's identity—and filled in portions of note normally filled in by student and school but not by lender). *See also* Armand v. Secretary of Educ. (S.D. Fla. July 19, 1995), *available at* www.consumerlaw.org/unreported. *But cf.* Shorter v. Riley, Clearinghouse No. 47,950B (N.D. Ga. Nov. 18, 1993) (question of whether there is origination relationship must be decided at trial and not based on either sides' summary judgment motions).

329 The following is a fairly current list of states that have STRFs, including contact information:

Arizona: Student Tuition Recovery Fund, Arizona State Board for Private Postsecondary Education, 1400 W. Washington Street, Room 260, Phoenix, AZ 85007; 602-542-5709, 602-542-1253 (fax); http://azppse.gov.

Arkansas: State Board of Higher Education, Surety Bonds for Certified Institutions, 114 E. Capitol Avenue, Little Rock, Ark. 72201; 501-371-2000; www.adhe.edu.

Arkansas State Board of Private Career Education, Student Protection Fund, 501 Woodlane, Suite 312 South, Little Rock, AR 72201; 501-683-8000, 501-683-8050 (fax); www.sbpce.org.

California: Bureau for Private Postsecondary Education, 1625 North Market Boulevard, Suite S-202, Sacramento, CA 95834; P.O. Box 980818, West Sacramento, CA 95798-0818; 916-574-7720, 916-574-8648 (fax); www.bppe.ca.gov.

Connecticut: Department of Higher Education, Private Occupational School Student Protection Account, 61 Woodland Street, Hartford, CT 06105-2326; 860-947-1800; www.ctdhe.org.

Florida: Florida Student Protection Fund, Florida Department of Education, Commission for Independent Education, 1414 Turlington Bldg., 325 W. Gaines St., Suite 1414, Tallahassee, FL 32399-0400; 850-245-3200, 850-245-3233 (fax); www.fldoe.org/cie.

Georgia: Non-Public Post Secondary Commission, Tuition Guaranteed Trust Fund, 2082 E. Exchange Place, Suite 220, Tucker, GA 30084-5305; 770-414-3300, 770-414-3309 (fax); www.gnpec.org.

Idaho: Private Surety Bond, Board of Education, P.O. Box 83720, Boise, ID 83720; 208-429-5536; www.pte.idaho.gov.

Kentucky: Student Protection Fund, State Board for Proprietary Education, P.O. Box 1360, Frankfort, KY 40602; 502-564-3296, ext. 228; http://bpe.ky.gov.

Maryland: Guaranty Student Tuition Fund, Maryland Higher Education Commission, 839 Bestgate Rd., Suite 400, Annapolis, MD 21401; 410-260-4500; www.mhec.state.md.us.

Massachusetts: Board of Cosmetology, 239 Causeway Street, Boston, MA 02114; 617-727-3074; www.mass.gov/dpl.

Board of Higher Education, One Ashburton Place, Suite 1401, Boston, MA 02108; 617-994-6950; www.mass.edu.

Private Postsecondary Schools, 350 Main St., Malden, MA 02148.

Nebraska: Department of Education, 301 Centennial Mall South, Lincoln, NE 68509; 402-471-4827; www.nde.state.ne.us.

Nevada: Student Indemnification Account, Nevada Commission on Postsecondary Education, 3663 East Sunset Road, Suite 202, Las Vegas, NV 89120; 702-486-7330; www.doe.nv.gov.

New Mexico: This state does not have a Student Tuition Recovery Fund. However, the New Mexico Higher Education Department does require all licensed in-state institutions and registered out-of-state institutions to have a surety bond. New Mexico Higher Education Department, 2048 Galisteo, Santa Fe, NM 87505; 505-476-8400; www.hed.state.nm.us.

The STRF is an important student remedy because it will provide relief in situations in which defrauded students cannot obtain a closed-school, unpaid-refund, or false-certification discharge. The operation of STRFs varies significantly by state. Advocates will need to contact their own state regulatory agency concerning detailed information on their STRF.

New York: Tuition Reimbursement Account, 116 W. 32d St., 5th Floor, New York, NY 10001; 212-643-4760; www.highered.nysed.gov/bpss.

Ohio: Student Tuition Recovery Fund, Student Tuition Recovery Authority, c/o State Board of Career Colleges and Schools, 35 East Gay St., Suite 403, Columbus, OH 43215; 614-466-2752, 877-275-4219; http://scr.ohio.gov/ConsumerInformation/StudentTuitionRecoveryFund/tabid/67/Default.aspx.

Oregon: Tuition Protection Fund, Education Department, 255 Capitol Street, NE, Salem, OR 97310-0203; 503-947-5600; www.lawserver.com/law/state/oregon/or-statutes/oregon_statutes_345-110.

Tennessee: Tuition Guaranty Fund, Tennessee Higher Education Commission, Division of Postsecondary School Authorization, Parkway Towers, Suite 1900, 404 James Robertson Parkway, Nashville, TN 37219; 615-741-5293; www.tennessee.gov/thec/Divisions/LRA/PostsecondaryAuth/academic_transcripts.html.

Texas: Tuition Trust Account, Texas Workforce Commission, Career Schools and Colleges, 101 East 15th St., Austin, TX 78778; 512-936-3100; http://law.onecle.com/texas/education/132.2415.00.html.

Virginia: State Council of Higher Education for Virginia, Student Tuition Guaranty Fund, 101 N. 14th Street, James Monroe Building, Richmond, VA 23218; 804-225-2600, 804-371-2938; www.schev.edu.

Washington: Tuition Recovery Trust Fund, Workforce Training and Education Coordinating Board, 128 10th Ave., S.W., P.O. Box 43105, Olympia, WA 98504-3105; 360-753-5662; www.wtb.wa.gov/whattoknowifschoolcloses.asp.

12.8.2 Relationship of STRF to School-Related Discharges

Quite often students entitled to relief from an STRF are also entitled under federal law to a school-related discharge.[330] Students entitled to recovery from the STRF and a federal discharge provision can expect to be placed in the middle of a tug-a-war between the state agency and the Department, as each agency tries to have the other pay for the student's loss. For example, the Department's closed-school regulations require students to specify whether they have applied to an STRF and what payment they received from the STRF.[331] The applicant for a closed-school discharge also assigns to the government, upon discharge, all the student's rights to a loan received, including STRF funds received from a private party.[332]

State agencies often respond by delaying processing on an STRF application until the closed-school or false-certification application is resolved. As a result, STRF applications are often held in limbo for long periods of time. Despite these delays, it is important for students to apply to the STRF in any case and keep records of application dates as the state STRF, unlike the federal discharge programs, may limit the time period for applications. Students who do not apply to the STRF pending decisions on their federal discharge applications risk losing the tuition fund remedy. Students should also contact the STRF periodically to check on the status of their recovery fund applications.

---

330 *See* Ch. 9, *supra* (loan cancellations).
331 34 C.F.R. § 682.402(d)(3)(i).
332 34 C.F.R. § 682.402(d)(5)(i).

Appendix A Federal Student Loan Statutes

Most of the statutory authority for federal student assistance can be found at 20 U.S.C. §§ 1070–1099e. Section 1070a (not reprinted here) relates to Pell grants. The Federal Family Education Loan Program (FFEL) statutory authority begins at section 1071. This appendix includes most of the relevant authority from these sections. It also includes selected authority for the Federal Direct Loan Program (§§ 1087a–1087j) and the Perkins Loan Program (§§ 1087aa–1087*ii*). These and additional statutory sections for all these programs can be found on the companion website to this manual.

A.1 Direct Loans

20 U.S.C. sec.

* * *

1087d. Agreements with institutions
1087e. Terms and conditions of loans

* * *

§ 1087d. Agreements with institutions

(a) Participation agreements
An agreement with any institution of higher education for participation in the direct student loan program under this part shall—
  (1) provide for the establishment and maintenance of a direct student loan program at the institution under which the institution will—
    (A) identify eligible students who seek student financial assistance at such institution in accordance with section 1091 of this title;
    (B) estimate the need of each such student as required by part E of this subchapter for an academic year, except that, any loan obtained by a student under this part with the same terms as loans made under section 1078-8 of this title (except as otherwise provided in this part), or a loan obtained by a parent under this part with the same terms as loans made under section 1078-2 of this title (except as otherwise provided in this part), or obtained under any State-sponsored or private loan program, may be used to offset the expected family contribution of the student for that year;
    (C) provide a statement that certifies the eligibility of any student to receive a loan under this part that is not in excess of the annual or aggregate limit applicable to such loan, except that the institution may, in exceptional circumstances identified by the Secretary, refuse to certify a statement that permits a student to receive a loan under this part, or certify a loan amount that is less than the student's determination of need (as determined under part E of this subchapter), if the reason for such action is documented and provided in written form to such student;
    (D) set forth a schedule for disbursement of the proceeds of the loan in installments, consistent with the requirements of section 1078-7 of this title; and
    (E) provide timely and accurate information—
      (i) concerning the status of student borrowers (and students on whose behalf parents borrow under this part) while such students are in attendance at the institution and concerning any new information of which the institution becomes aware for such students (or their parents) after such borrowers leave the institution, to the Secretary for the servicing and collecting of loans made under this part; and
      (ii) if the institution does not have an agreement with the Secretary under subsection (b) of this section, concerning student eligibility and need, as determined under subparagraphs (A) and (B), to the Secretary as needed for the alternative origination of loans to eligible students and parents in accordance with this part;
  (2) provide assurances that the institution will comply with requirements established by the Secretary relating to student loan information with respect to loans made under this part;
  (3) provide that the institution accepts responsibility and financial liability stemming from its failure to perform its functions pursuant to the agreement;
  (4) provide that students at the institution and their parents (with respect to such students) will be eligible to participate in the programs under part B of this subchapter at the discretion of the Secretary for the period during which such institution participates in the direct student loan program under this part, except that a student or parent may not receive loans under both this part and part B of this subchapter for the same period of enrollment;
  (5) provide for the implementation of a quality assurance system, as established by the Secretary and developed in consultation with institutions of higher education, to ensure that the institution is complying with program requirements and meeting program objectives;
  (6) provide that the institution will not charge any fees of any kind, however described, to student or parent borrowers for origination activities or the provision of any information necessary for a student or parent to receive a loan under this part, or any benefits associated with such loan; and

(7) include such other provisions as the Secretary determines are necessary to protect the interests of the United States and to promote the purposes of this part.

(b) Origination

An agreement with any institution of higher education, or consortia thereof, for the origination of loans under this part shall—

(1) supplement the agreement entered into in accordance with subsection (a) of this section;

(2) include provisions established by the Secretary that are similar to the participation agreement provisions described in paragraphs (1)(E)(ii), (2), (3), (4), (5), (6), and (7) of subsection (a) of this section, as modified to relate to the origination of loans by the institution or consortium;

(3) provide that the institution or consortium will originate loans to eligible students and parents in accordance with this part; and

(4) provide that the note or evidence of obligation on the loan shall be the property of the Secretary.

(c) Withdrawal and termination procedures

The Secretary shall establish procedures by which institutions or consortia may withdraw or be terminated from the program under this part.

[Pub. L. No. 89-329, Title IV, § 454, *as added by* Pub. L. No. 99-498, Title IV, § 404, 100 Stat. 1438 (Oct. 17, 1986), *and amended by* Pub. L. No. 100-50, § 12, June 3, 1987, 101 Stat. 348; Pub. L. 102-325, Title IV, § 451, 106 Stat. 571 (July 23, 1992); Pub. L. No. 103-66, Title IV, § 4021, 107 Stat. 345 (Aug. 10, 1993)]

§ 1087e. Terms and conditions of loans

(a) In general

(1) Parallel terms, conditions, benefits, and amounts

Unless otherwise specified in this part, loans made to borrowers under this part shall have the same terms, conditions, and benefits, and be available in the same amounts, as loans made to borrowers under sections 1078, 1078-2, 1078-3, and 1078-8 of this title.

(2) Designation of loans

Loans made to borrowers under this part that, except as otherwise specified in this part, have the same terms, conditions, and benefits as loans made to borrowers under—

(A) section 1078 of this title shall be known as "Federal Direct Stafford Loans";

(B) section 1078-2 of this title shall be known as "Federal Direct PLUS Loans";

(C) section 1078-3 of this title shall be known as "Federal Direct Consolidation Loans"; and

(D) section 1078-8 of this title shall be known as "Federal Direct Unsubsidized Stafford Loans".

(b) Interest rate

(1) Rates for FDSL and FDUSL

For Federal Direct Stafford Loans and Federal Direct Unsubsidized Stafford Loans for which the first disbursement is made on or after July 1, 1994, the applicable rate of interest shall, during any 12-month period beginning on July 1 and ending on June 30, be determined on the preceding June 1 and be equal to—

(A) the bond equivalent rate of 91-day Treasury bills auctioned at the final auction held prior to such June 1; plus

(B) 3.1 percent,

except that such rate shall not exceed 8.25 percent.

(2) In school and grace period rules

(A) Notwithstanding the provisions of paragraph (1), but subject to paragraph (3), with respect to any Federal Direct Stafford Loan or Federal Direct Unsubsidized Stafford Loan for which the first disbursement is made on or after July 1, 1995, the applicable rate of interest for interest which accrues—

(i) prior to the beginning of the repayment period of the loan; or

(ii) during the period in which principal need not be paid (whether or not such principal is in fact paid) by reason of a provision described in section 1078(b)(1)(M) or 1077(a)(2)(C) of this title,

shall not exceed the rate determined under subparagraph (B).

(B) For the purpose of subparagraph (A), the rate determined under this subparagraph shall, during any 12-month period beginning on July 1 and ending on June 30, be determined on the preceding June 1 and be equal to—

(i) the bond equivalent rate of 91-day Treasury bills auctioned at the final auction prior to such June 1; plus

(ii) 2.5 percent,

except that such rate shall not exceed 8.25 percent.

(3) Out-year rule

Notwithstanding paragraphs (1) and (2), for Federal Direct Stafford Loans and Federal Direct Unsubsidized Stafford Loans made on or after July 1, 1998, the applicable rate of interest shall, during any 12-month period beginning on July 1 and ending on June 30, be determined on the preceding June 1 and be equal to—

(A) the bond equivalent rate of the security with a comparable maturity as established by the Secretary; plus

(B) 1.0 percent,

except that such rate shall not exceed 8.25 percent.

(4) Rates for FDPLUS

(A)(i) For Federal Direct PLUS Loans for which the first disbursement is made on or after July 1, 1994, the applicable rate of interest shall, during any 12-month period beginning on July 1 and ending on or before June 30, 2001, be determined on the preceding June 1 and be equal to—

(I) the bond equivalent rate of 52-week Treasury bills auctioned at final auction held prior to such June 1; plus

(II) 3.1 percent,

except that such rate shall not exceed 9 percent.

(ii) For any 12-month period beginning on July 1 of 2001 or any succeeding year, the applicable rate of interest determined under this subparagraph shall be determined on the preceding June 26 and be equal to—

(I) the weekly average 1-year constant maturity Treasury yield, as published by the Board of Governors of the Federal Reserve System, for the last calendar week ending on or before such June 26; plus

(II) 3.1 percent,

except that such rate shall not exceed 9 percent.

(B) For Federal Direct PLUS loans made on or after July 1, 1998, the applicable rate of interest shall, during any 12-month period beginning on July 1 and ending on June 30, be determined on the preceding June 1 and be equal to—

(i) the bond equivalent rate of the security with a comparable maturity as established by the Secretary; plus

(ii) 2.1 percent,

except that such rate shall not exceed 9 percent.

(5) Temporary interest rate provision

(A) **Rates for FDSL and FDUSL**

Notwithstanding the preceding paragraphs of this subsection, for Federal Direct Stafford Loans and Federal Direct Unsubsidized Stafford Loans for which the first disbursement is made on or after July 1, 1998, and before October 1, 1998, the applicable rate of interest shall, during any 12-month period beginning on July 1 and ending on June 30, be determined on the preceding June 1 and be equal to—

(i) the bond equivalent rate of 91-day Treasury bills auctioned at the final auction held prior to such June 1; plus

(ii) 2.3 percent,

except that such rate shall not exceed 8.25 percent.

(B) **In school and grace period rules**

Notwithstanding the preceding paragraphs of this subsection, with respect to any Federal Direct Stafford Loan or Federal Direct Unsubsidized Stafford Loan for which the first disbursement is made on or after July 1, 1998, and before October 1, 1998, the applicable rate of interest for interest which accrues—

(i) prior to the beginning of the repayment period of the loan; or

(ii) during the period in which principal need not be paid (whether or not such principal is in fact paid) by reason of a provision described in section 1078(b)(1)(M) or 1077(a)(2)(C) of this title,

shall be determined under subparagraph (A) by substituting "1.7 percent" for "2.3 percent".

(C) **PLUS loans**

Notwithstanding the preceding paragraphs of this subsection, with respect to Federal Direct PLUS Loan for which the first disbursement is made on or after July 1, 1998, and before October 1, 1998, the applicable rate of interest shall be determined under subparagraph (A)—

(i) by substituting "3.1 percent" for "2.3 percent"; and

(ii) by substituting "9.0 percent" for "8.25 percent".

(6) Interest rate provision for new loans on or after October 1, 1998, and before July 1, 2006

(A) **Rates for FDSL and FDUSL**

Notwithstanding the preceding paragraphs of this subsection, for Federal Direct Stafford Loans and Federal Direct Unsubsidized Stafford Loans for which the first disbursement is made on or after October 1, 1998, and before July 1, 2006, the applicable rate of interest shall, during any 12-month period beginning on July 1 and ending on June 30, be determined on the preceding June 1 and be equal to—

(i) the bond equivalent rate of 91-day Treasury bills auctioned at the final auction held prior to such June 1; plus

(ii) 2.3 percent,

except that such rate shall not exceed 8.25 percent.

(B) **In school and grace period rules**

Notwithstanding the preceding paragraphs of this subsection, with respect to any Federal Direct Stafford Loan or Federal Direct Unsubsidized Stafford Loan for which the first disbursement is made on or after October 1, 1998, and before July 1, 2006, the applicable rate of interest for interest which accrues—

(i) prior to the beginning of the repayment period of the loan; or

(ii) during the period in which principal need not be paid (whether or not such principal is in fact paid) by reason of a provision described in section 1078(b)(1)(M) or 1077(a)(2)(C) of this title,

shall be determined under subparagraph (A) by substituting "1.7 percent" for "2.3 percent".

(C) **PLUS loans**

Notwithstanding the preceding paragraphs of this subsection, with respect to Federal Direct PLUS Loan for which the first disbursement is made on or after October 1, 1998, and before July 1, 2006, the applicable rate of interest shall be determined under subparagraph (A)—

(i) by substituting "3.1 percent" for "2.3 percent"; and

(ii) by substituting "9.0 percent" for "8.25 percent".

(D) **Consolidation loans**

Notwithstanding the preceding paragraphs of this subsection, any Federal Direct Consolidation loan for which the application is received on or after February 1, 1999, and before July 1, 2006, shall bear interest at an annual rate on the unpaid principal balance of the loan that is equal to the lesser of—

(i) the weighted average of the interest rates on the loans consolidated, rounded to the nearest higher one-eighth of one percent; or

(ii) 8.25 percent.

(E) **Temporary rules for consolidation loans**

Notwithstanding the preceding paragraphs of this subsection, any Federal Direct Consolidation loan for which the application is received on or after October 1, 1998, and before February 1, 1999, shall bear interest at an annual rate on the unpaid principal balance of the loan that is equal to—

(i) the bond equivalent rate of 91-day Treasury bills auctioned at the final auction held prior to such June 1; plus

(ii) 2.3 percent,

except that such rate shall not exceed 8.25 percent.

(7) Interest rate provision for new loans on or after July 1, 2006

(A) **Rates for FDSL and FDUSL**

Notwithstanding the preceding paragraphs of this subsection, for Federal Direct Stafford Loans and Federal Direct Unsubsidized Stafford Loans for which the first disbursement is made on or after July 1, 2006, the applicable rate of interest shall be 6.8 percent on the unpaid principal balance of the loan.

(B) **PLUS loans**

Notwithstanding the preceding paragraphs of this subsection, with respect to any Federal Direct PLUS loan for which the first disbursement is made on or after July 1, 2006, the applicable rate of interest shall be 7.9 percent on the unpaid principal balance of the loan.

(C) **Consolidation loans**

Notwithstanding the preceding paragraphs of this subsection, any Federal Direct Consolidation loan for which the application is received on or after July 1, 2006, shall bear interest at an annual rate on the unpaid principal balance of the loan that is equal to the lesser of—

(i) the weighted average of the interest rates on the loans consolidated, rounded to the nearest higher one-eighth of one percent; or

(ii) 8.25 percent.

(D) Reduced rates for undergraduate FDSL

Notwithstanding the preceding paragraphs of this subsection and subparagraph (A) of this paragraph, for Federal Direct Stafford Loans made to undergraduate students for which the first disbursement is made on or after July 1, 2006, and before July 1, 2012, the applicable rate of interest shall be as follows:

(i) For a loan for which the first disbursement is made on or after July 1, 2006, and before July 1, 2008, 6.8 percent on the unpaid principal balance of the loan.

(ii) For a loan for which the first disbursement is made on or after July 1, 2008, and before July 1, 2009, 6.0 percent on the unpaid principal balance of the loan.

(iii) For a loan for which the first disbursement is made on or after July 1, 2009, and before July 1, 2010, 5.6 percent on the unpaid principal balance of the loan.

(iv) For a loan for which the first disbursement is made on or after July 1, 2010, and before July 1, 2011, 4.5 percent on the unpaid principal balance of the loan.

(v) For a loan for which the first disbursement is made on or after July 1, 2011, and before July 1, 2012, 3.4 percent on the unpaid principal balance of the loan.

(8) Repayment incentives

(A) In general

Notwithstanding any other provision of this part, the Secretary is authorized to prescribe by regulation such reductions in the interest rate or origination fee paid by a borrower of a loan made under this part as the Secretary determines appropriate to encourage on-time repayment of the loan. Such reductions may be offered only if the Secretary determines the reductions are cost neutral and in the best financial interest of the Federal Government. Any increase in subsidy costs resulting from such reductions shall be completely offset by corresponding savings in funds available for the William D. Ford Federal Direct Loan Program in that fiscal year from section 1087h of this title and other administrative accounts.

(B) Accountability

Prior to publishing regulations proposing repayment incentives, the Secretary shall ensure the cost neutrality of such reductions. The Secretary shall not prescribe such regulations in final form unless an official report from the Director of the Office of Management and Budget to the Secretary and a comparable report from the Director of the Congressional Budget Office to the Congress each certify that any such reductions will be completely cost neutral. Such reports shall be transmitted to the authorizing committees not less than 60 days prior to the publication of regulations proposing such reductions.

(9) Publication

The Secretary shall determine the applicable rates of interest under this subsection after consultation with the Secretary of the Treasury and shall publish such rate in the Federal Register as soon as practicable after the date of determination.

(c) Loan fee

(1) In general

The Secretary shall charge the borrower of a loan made under this part an origination fee of 4.0 percent of the principal amount of loan.

(2) Subsequent reduction

Paragraph (1) shall be applied to loans made under this part, other than Federal Direct Consolidation loans and Federal Direct PLUS loans—

(A) by substituting "3.0 percent" for "4.0 percent" with respect to loans for which the first disbursement of principal is made on or after February 8, 2006, and before July 1, 2007;

(B) by substituting "2.5 percent" for "4.0 percent" with respect to loans for which the first disbursement of principal is made on or after July 1, 2007, and before July 1, 2008;

(C) by substituting "2.0 percent" for "4.0 percent" with respect to loans for which the first disbursement of principal is made on or after July 1, 2008, and before July 1, 2009;

(D) by substituting "1.5 percent" for "4.0 percent" with respect to loans for which the first disbursement of principal is made on or after July 1, 2009, and before July 1, 2010; and

(E) by substituting "1.0 percent" for "4.0 percent" with respect to loans for which the first disbursement of principal is made on or after July 1, 2010.

(d) Repayment plans

(1) Design and selection

Consistent with criteria established by the Secretary, the Secretary shall offer a borrower of a loan made under this part a variety of plans for repayment of such loan, including principal and interest on the loan. The borrower shall be entitled to accelerate, without penalty, repayment on the borrower's loans under this part. The borrower may choose—

(A) a standard repayment plan, consistent with subsection (a)(1) of this section and with section 1078(b)(9)(A)(i) of this title;

(B) a graduated repayment plan, consistent with section 1078(b)(9)(A)(ii) of this title;

(C) an extended repayment plan, consistent with section 1078(b)(9)(A)(iv) of this title, except that the borrower shall annually repay a minimum amount determined by the Secretary in accordance with section 1078(b)(1)(L) of this title;

(D) an income contingent repayment plan, with varying annual repayment amounts based on the income of the borrower, paid over an extended period of time prescribed by the Secretary, not to exceed 25 years, except that the plan described in this subparagraph shall not be available to the borrower of a Federal Direct PLUS loan made on behalf of a dependent student; and

(E) beginning on July 1, 2009, an income-based repayment plan that enables borrowers who have a partial financial hardship to make a lower monthly payment in accordance with section 1098e of this title, except that the plan described in this subparagraph shall not be available to the borrower of a Federal Direct PLUS Loan made on behalf of a dependent student or a Federal Direct Consolidation Loan, if the proceeds of such loan were used to discharge the liability on such Federal Direct PLUS Loan or a loan under section 1078-2 of this title made on behalf of a dependent student.

(2) Selection by Secretary

If a borrower of a loan made under this part does not select a repayment plan described in paragraph (1), the Secretary may provide the borrower with a repayment plan described in subparagraph (A), (B), or (C) of paragraph (1).

(3) Changes in selections

The borrower of a loan made under this part may change the borrower's selection of a repayment plan under paragraph (1), or the Secretary's selection of a plan for the borrower under paragraph (2), as the case may be, under such terms and conditions as may be established by the Secretary.

(4) Alternative repayment plans

The Secretary may provide, on a case by case basis, an alternative repayment plan to a borrower of a loan made under this part who demonstrates to the satisfaction of the Secretary that the terms and conditions of the repayment plans available under paragraph (1) are not adequate to accommodate the borrower's exceptional circumstances. In designing such alternative repayment plans, the Secretary shall ensure that such plans do not exceed the cost to the Federal Government, as determined on the basis of the present value of future payments by such borrowers, of loans made using the plans available under paragraph (1).

(5) Repayment after default

The Secretary may require any borrower who has defaulted on a loan made under this part to—

(A) pay all reasonable collection costs associated with such loan; and

(B) repay the loan pursuant to an income contingent repayment plan.

(e) Income contingent repayment

(1) Information and procedures

The Secretary may obtain such information as is reasonably necessary regarding the income of a borrower (and the borrower's spouse, if applicable) of a loan made under this part that is, or may be, repaid pursuant to income contingent repayment, for the purpose of determining the annual repayment obligation of the borrower. Returns and return information (as defined in section 6103 of Title 26) may be obtained under the preceding sentence only to the extent authorized by section 6103(l)(13) of Title 26. The Secretary shall establish procedures for determining the borrower's repayment obligation on that loan for such year, and such other procedures as are necessary to implement effectively income contingent repayment.

(2) Repayment based on adjusted gross income

A repayment schedule for a loan made under this part and repaid pursuant to income contingent repayment shall be based on the adjusted gross income (as defined in section 62 of Title 26) of the borrower or, if the borrower is married and files a Federal income tax return jointly with the borrower's spouse, on the adjusted gross income of the borrower and the borrower's spouse.

(3) Additional documents

A borrower who chooses, or is required, to repay a loan made under this part pursuant to income contingent repayment, and for whom adjusted gross income is unavailable or does not reasonably reflect the borrower's current income, shall provide to the Secretary other documentation of income satisfactory to the Secretary, which documentation the Secretary may use to determine an appropriate repayment schedule.

(4) Repayment schedules

Income contingent repayment schedules shall be established by regulations promulgated by the Secretary and shall require payments that vary in relation to the appropriate portion of the annual income of the borrower (and the borrower's spouse, if applicable) as determined by the Secretary.

(5) Calculation of balance due

The balance due on a loan made under this part that is repaid pursuant to income contingent repayment shall equal the unpaid principal amount of the loan, any accrued interest, and any fees, such as late charges, assessed on such loan. The Secretary may promulgate regulations limiting the amount of interest that may be capitalized on such loan, and the timing of any such capitalization.

(6) Notification to borrowers

The Secretary shall establish procedures under which a borrower of a loan made under this part who chooses or is required to repay such loan pursuant to income contingent repayment is notified of the terms and conditions of such plan, including notification of such borrower—

(A) that the Internal Revenue Service will disclose to the Secretary tax return information as authorized under section 6103(l)(13) of Title 26; and

(B) that if a borrower considers that special circumstances, such as a loss of employment by the borrower or the borrower's spouse, warrant an adjustment in the borrower's loan repayment as determined using the information described in subparagraph (A), or the alternative documentation described in paragraph (3), the borrower may contact the Secretary, who shall determine whether such adjustment is appropriate, in accordance with criteria established by the Secretary.

(7) Maximum repayment period

In calculating the extended period of time for which an income contingent repayment plan under this subsection may be in effect for a borrower, the Secretary shall include all time periods during which a borrower of loans under part B, part C, or part D of this subchapter—

(A) is not in default on any loan that is included in the income contingent repayment plan; and

(B)(i) is in deferment due to an economic hardship described in section 1085(o) of this title;

(ii) makes monthly payments under paragraph (1) or (6) of section 1098e(b) of this title;

(iii) makes monthly payments of not less than the monthly amount calculated under section 1078(b)(9)(A)(i) of this title or subsection (d)(1)(A), based on a 10-year repayment period, when the borrower first made the election described in section 1098e(b)(1) of this title;

(iv) makes payments of not less than the payments required under a standard repayment plan under section 1078(b)(9)(A)(i) of this title or subsection (d)(1)(A) with a repayment period of 10 years; or

(v) makes payments under an income contingent repayment plan under subsection (d)(1)(D).

(f) Deferment

(1) Effect on principal and interest

A borrower of a loan made under this part who meets the requirements described in paragraph (2) shall be eligible for a deferment, during which periodic installments of principal need not be paid, and interest—

(A) shall not accrue, in the case of a—

(i) Federal Direct Stafford Loan; or

(ii) a Federal Direct Consolidation Loan that consolidated only Federal Direct Stafford Loans, or a combination of such loans and Federal Stafford Loans for which the student borrower received an interest subsidy under section 1078 of this title; or

(B) shall accrue and be capitalized or paid by the borrower, in the case of a Federal Direct PLUS Loan, a Federal Direct Unsubsidized Stafford Loan, or a Federal Direct Consolidation Loan not described in subparagraph (A)(ii).

(2) Eligibility

A borrower of a loan made under this part shall be eligible for a deferment during any period—

(A) during which the borrower—

(i) is carrying at least one-half the normal full-time work load for the course of study that the borrower is pursuing, as determined by the eligible institution (as such term is defined in section 1085(a) of this title) the borrower is attending; or

(ii) is pursuing a course of study pursuant to a graduate fellowship program approved by the Secretary, or pursuant to a rehabilitation training program for individuals with disabilities approved by the Secretary,

except that no borrower shall be eligible for a deferment under this subparagraph, or a loan made under this part (other than a Federal Direct PLUS Loan or a Federal Direct Consolidation Loan), while serving in a medical internship or residency program;

(B) not in excess of 3 years during which the borrower is seeking and unable to find full-time employment;

(C) during which the borrower—

(i) is serving on active duty during a war or other military operation or national emergency; or

(ii) is performing qualifying National Guard duty during a war or other military operation or national emergency,

and for the 180-day period following the demobilization date for the service described in clause (i) or (ii); or

(D) not in excess of 3 years during which the Secretary determines, in accordance with regulations prescribed under section 1085(o) of this title, that the borrower has experienced or will experience an economic hardship.

(3) "Borrower" defined

For the purpose of this subsection, the term "borrower" means an individual who is a new borrower on the date such individual applies for a loan under this part for which the first disbursement is made on or after July 1, 1993.

(4) Deferments for previous part B loan borrowers

A borrower of a loan made under this part, who at the time such individual applies for such loan, has an outstanding balance of principal or interest owing on any loan made, insured, or guaranteed under part B of this subchapter prior to July 1, 1993, shall be eligible for a deferment under section 1077(a)(2)(C) of this title or section 1078(b)(1)(M) of this title as such sections were in effect on July 22, 1992.

(g) Federal Direct Consolidation Loans

A borrower of a loan made under this part may consolidate such loan with the loans described in section 1078-3(a)(4) of this title. To be eligible for a consolidation loan under this part, a borrower shall meet the eligibility criteria set forth in section 1078-3(a)(3) of this title. The Secretary, upon application for such a loan, shall comply with the requirements applicable to a lender under section 1078-3(b)(1)(G) of this title.

(h) Borrower defenses

Notwithstanding any other provision of State or Federal law, the Secretary shall specify in regulations which acts or omissions of an institution of higher education a borrower may assert as a defense to repayment of a loan made under this part, except that in no event may a borrower recover from the Secretary, in any action arising from or relating to a loan made under this part, an amount in excess of the amount such borrower has repaid on such loan.

(i) Loan application and promissory note

The common financial reporting form required in section 1090(a)(1) of this title shall constitute the application for loans made under this part (other than a Federal Direct PLUS loan). The Secretary shall develop, print, and distribute to participating institutions a standard promissory note and loan disclosure form.

(j) Loan disbursement

(1) In general

Proceeds of loans to students under this part shall be applied to the student's account for tuition and fees, and, in the case of institutionally owned housing, to room and board. Loan proceeds that remain after the application of the previous sentence shall be delivered to the borrower by check or other means that is payable to and requires the endorsement or other certification by such borrower.

(2) Payment periods

The Secretary shall establish periods for the payments described in paragraph (1) in a manner consistent with payment of Federal Pell Grants under subpart 1 of part A of this subchapter.

(k) Fiscal control and fund accountability

(1) In general

(A) An institution shall maintain financial records in a manner consistent with records maintained for other programs under this subchapter.

(B) Except as otherwise required by regulations of the Secretary an institution may maintain loan funds under this part in the same account as other Federal student financial assistance.

(2) Payments and refunds

Payments and refunds shall be reconciled in a manner consistent with the manner set forth for the submission of a payment summary report required of institutions participating in the program under subpart 1 of part A of this subchapter, except that nothing in this paragraph shall prevent such reconciliations on a monthly basis.

(3) Transaction histories

All transaction histories under this part shall be maintained using the same system designated by the Secretary for the provision of Federal Pell Grants under subpart 1 of part A of this subchapter.

(*l*) Armed Forces student loan interest payment program

(1) Authority

Using funds received by transfer to the Secretary under section 2174 of Title 10 for the payment of interest on a loan made under this part to a member of the Armed Forces, the Secretary shall pay the interest on the loan as due for a period not in excess of 36 consecutive months. The Secretary may not pay interest on such a loan out of any funds other than funds that have been so transferred.

(2) Forbearance

During the period in which the Secretary is making payments on a loan under paragraph (1), the Secretary shall grant the borrower forbearance, in the form of a temporary cessation of all payments on the loan other than the payments of interest on the loan that are made under that paragraph.

(m) Repayment plan for public service employees
(1) In general
The Secretary shall cancel the balance of interest and principal due, in accordance with paragraph (2), on any eligible Federal Direct Loan not in default for a borrower who—
  (A) has made 120 monthly payments on the eligible Federal Direct Loan after October 1, 2007, pursuant to any one or a combination of the following—
    (i) payments under an income-based repayment plan under section 1098e of this title;
    (ii) payments under a standard repayment plan under subsection (d)(1)(A), based on a 10-year repayment period;
    (iii) monthly payments under a repayment plan under subsection (d)(1) or (g) of this section of not less than the monthly amount calculated under subsection (d)(1)(A), based on a 10-year repayment period; or
    (iv) payments under an income contingent repayment plan under subsection (d)(1)(D); and
  (B)(i) is employed in a public service job at the time of such forgiveness; and
    (ii) has been employed in a public service job during the period in which the borrower makes each of the 120 payments described in subparagraph (A).
(2) Loan cancellation amount
After the conclusion of the employment period described in paragraph (1), the Secretary shall cancel the obligation to repay the balance of principal and interest due as of the time of such cancellation, on the eligible Federal Direct Loans made to the borrower under this part.
(3) Definitions
In this subsection:
  (A) Eligible Federal Direct Loan
  The term "eligible Federal Direct Loan" means a Federal Direct Stafford Loan, Federal Direct PLUS Loan, or Federal Direct Unsubsidized Stafford Loan, or a Federal Direct Consolidation Loan.
  (B) Public service job
  The term "public service job" means—
    (i) a full-time job in emergency management, government (excluding time served as a member of Congress), military service, public safety, law enforcement, public health (including nurses, nurse practitioners, nurses in a clinical setting, and full-time professionals engaged in health care practitioner occupations and health care support occupations, as such terms are defined by the Bureau of Labor Statistics), public education, social work in a public child or family service agency, public interest law services (including prosecution or public defense or legal advocacy on behalf of low-income communities at a nonprofit organization), early childhood education (including licensed or regulated childcare, Head Start, and State funded prekindergarten), public service for individuals with disabilities, public service for the elderly, public library sciences, school-based library sciences and other school-based services, or at an organization that is described in section 501(c)(3) of Title 26 and exempt from taxation under section 501(a) of such title; or
    (ii) teaching as a full-time faculty member at a Tribal College or University as defined in section 1059c(b) of this title and other faculty teaching in high-needs subject areas or areas of shortage (including nurse faculty, foreign language faculty, and part-time faculty at community colleges), as determined by the Secretary.
(4) Ineligibility for double benefits
No borrower may, for the same service, receive a reduction of loan obligations under both this subsection and section 1078-10, 1078-11, 1078-12, or 1087j of this title.

(n) Identity fraud protection
The Secretary shall take such steps as may be necessary to ensure that monthly Federal Direct Loan statements and other publications of the Department do not contain more than four digits of the Social Security number of any individual.

(o) No accrual of interest for active duty service members
(1) In general
Notwithstanding any other provision of this part and in accordance with paragraphs (2) and (4), interest shall not accrue for an eligible military borrower on a loan made under this part for which the first disbursement is made on or after October 1, 2008.
(2) Consolidation loans
In the case of any consolidation loan made under this part that is disbursed on or after October 1, 2008, interest shall not accrue pursuant to this subsection only on such portion of such loan as was used to repay a loan made under this part for which the first disbursement is made on or after October 1, 2008.
(3) Eligible military borrower
In this subsection, the term "eligible military borrower" means an individual who—
  (A)(i) is serving on active duty during a war or other military operation or national emergency; or
    (ii) is performing qualifying National Guard duty during a war or other military operation or national emergency; and
  (B) is serving in an area of hostilities in which service qualifies for special pay under section 310 of Title 37.
(4) Limitation
An individual who qualifies as an eligible military borrower under this subsection may receive the benefit of this subsection for not more than 60 months.

(p) Disclosures
Each institution of higher education with which the Secretary has an agreement under section 1087c of this title, and each contractor with which the Secretary has a contract under section 1087f of this title, shall, with respect to loans under this part and in accordance with such regulations as the Secretary shall prescribe, comply with each of the requirements under section 1083 of this title that apply to a lender with respect to a loan under part B of this subchapter.

[Pub. L. No. 89-329, Title IV, § 455, *as added by* Pub. L. No. 99-498, Title IV, § 404, 100 Stat. 1439 (Oct. 17, 1986), *and amended by* Pub. L. No. 102-325, Title IV, § 451, 106 Stat. 572 (July 23, 1992); Pub. L. No. 103-66, Title IV, § 4021, 107 Stat. 346 (Aug. 10, 1993); Pub. L. No. 103-382, Title III, § 359, 108 Stat. 3968 (Oct. 20, 1994); Pub. L. No. 105-178, Title VIII, § 8301(c), 112 Stat. 498 (June 9, 1998); Pub. L. No. 105-244, Title IV, §§ 401(g)(6), 452(a)(1), (b), (c), 112 Stat. 1652, 1715 to 1717 (Oct. 7, 1998); Pub. L. No. 106-554, § 1(a)(1) [Title III, § 318(b)], 114 Stat. 2763, 2763A-49 (Dec. 21, 2000); Pub. L. No. 107-139,

§ 1(b), (c), 116 Stat. 9 (Feb. 8, 2002); Pub. L. No. 107-314, Div. A, Title VI, § 651(c), 116 Stat. 2580 (Dec. 2, 2002); Pub. L. No. 109-171, Title VIII, §§ 8007(b), 8008(b), (c)(2), (3), 8009(d), 120 Stat. 160, 162 to 164 (Feb. 8, 2006); Pub. L. No. 110-84, Title II, §§ 201(b), 202(b), 203(b)(3), 205, Title IV, § 401, 121 Stat. 791, 792, 795, 800 (Sept. 27, 2007); Pub. L. No. 110-315, Title I, § 103(b)(8), Title IV, §§ 425(b)(3), 451, 122 Stat. 3089, 3234, 3261 (Aug. 14, 2008); Pub. L. No. 111-39, Title IV, § 404(b)(2), 123 Stat. 1946 (July 1, 2009)]

* * *

A.2 FFEL

20 U.S.C. sec.

* * *

1077. Eligibility of student borrowers and terms of federally insured student loans

* * *

1078-3. Federal consolidation loans.

* * *

1080a. Reports to consumer reporting agencies and institutions of higher education

* * *

1083. Student loan information by eligible lenders

* * *

1087. Repayment by Secretary of loans of bankrupt, deceased, or disabled borrowers; treatment of borrowers attending closed schools or falsely certified as eligible to borrow

* * *

§ 1077. Eligibility of student borrowers and terms of federally insured student loans

(a) List of requirements
Except as provided in section 1078-3 of this title, a loan by an eligible lender shall be insurable by the Secretary under the provisions of this part only if—
  (1) made to a student who (A) is an eligible student under section 1091 of this title, (B) has agreed to notify promptly the holder of the loan concerning any change of address, and (C) is carrying at least one-half the normal full-time academic workload for the course of study the student is pursuing (as determined by the institution); and
  (2) evidenced by a note or other written agreement which—
    (A) is made without security and without endorsement;
    (B) provides for repayment (except as provided in subsection (c) of this section) of the principal amount of the loan in installments over a period of not less than 5 years (unless sooner repaid or unless the student, during the 6 months preceding the start of the repayment period, specifically requests that repayment be made over a shorter period) nor more than 10 years beginning 6 months after the month in which the student ceases to carry at an eligible institution at least one-half the normal full-time academic workload as determined by the institution, except—
      (i) as provided in subparagraph (C);
      (ii) that the note or other written instrument may contain such reasonable provisions relating to repayment in the event of default in the payment of interest or in the payment of the cost of insurance premiums, or other default by the borrower, as may be authorized by regulations of the Secretary in effect at the time the loan is made; and
      (iii) that the lender and the student, after the student ceases to carry at an eligible institution at least one-half the normal full-time academic workload as determined by the institution, may agree to a repayment schedule which begins earlier, or is of shorter duration, than required by this subparagraph, but in the event a borrower has requested and obtained a repayment period of less than 5 years, the borrower may at any time prior to the total repayment of the loan, have the repayment period extended so that the total repayment period is not less than 5 years;
    (C) provides that periodic installments of principal need not be paid, but interest shall accrue and be paid, during any period—
      (i) during which the borrower—
        (I) is pursuing at least a half-time course of study as determined by an eligible institution; or
        (II) is pursuing a course of study pursuant to a graduate fellowship program approved by the Secretary, or pursuant to a rehabilitation training program for individuals with disabilities approved by the Secretary,
    except that no borrower shall be eligible for a deferment under this clause, or a loan made under this part (other than a loan made under section 1078-2 or 1078-3 of this title), while serving in a medical internship or residency program;
      (ii) not in excess of 3 years during which the borrower is seeking and unable to find full-time employment; or
      (iii) not in excess of 3 years for any reason which the lender determines, in accordance with regulations prescribed by the Secretary under section 1085(o) of this title, has caused or will cause the borrower to have an economic hardship;
    and provides that any such period shall not be included in determining the 10-year period described in subparagraph (B);
    (D) provides for interest on the unpaid principal balance of the loan at a yearly rate, not exceeding the applicable maximum rate prescribed in section 1077a of this title, which interest shall be payable in installments over the period of the loan except that, if provided in the note or other written agreement, any interest payable by the student may be deferred until not later than the date upon which repayment of the first installment of principal falls due, in which case interest accrued during that period may be added on that date to the principal;
    (E) provides that the lender will not collect or attempt to collect from the borrower any portion of the interest on the note which is payable by the Secretary under this part, and that the lender will enter into such agreements with the Secretary as may be necessary for the purpose of section 1087 of this title;
    (F) entitles the student borrower to accelerate without penalty repayment of the whole or any part of the loan;

(G)(i) contains a notice of the system,[1] of disclosure of information concerning such loan to consumer reporting agencies under section 1080a of this title, and (ii) provides that the lender on request of the borrower will provide information on the repayment status of the note to such consumer reporting agencies;

(H) provides that, no more than 6 months prior to the date on which the borrower's first payment on a loan is due, the lender shall offer the borrower the option of repaying the loan in accordance with a graduated or income-sensitive repayment schedule established by the lender and in accordance with the regulations of the Secretary; and

(I) contains such other terms and conditions, consistent with the provisions of this part and with the regulations issued by the Secretary pursuant to this part, as may be agreed upon by the parties to such loan, including, if agreed upon, a provision requiring the borrower to pay the lender, in addition to principal and interest, amounts equal to the insurance premiums payable by the lender to the Secretary with respect to such loan;

(3) the funds borrowed by a student are disbursed to the institution by check or other means that is payable to and requires the endorsement or other certification by such student, except—

(A) that nothing in this subchapter and part C of subchapter I of chapter 34 of Title 42 shall be interpreted—

(i) to allow the Secretary to require checks to be made copayable to the institution and the borrower; or

(ii) to prohibit the disbursement of loan proceeds by means other than by check; and

(B) in the case of any student who is studying outside the United States in a program of study abroad that is approved for credit by the home institution at which such student is enrolled, the funds shall, at the request of the borrower, be delivered directly to the student and the checks may be endorsed, and fund transfers authorized, pursuant to an authorized power-of-attorney; and

(4) the funds borrowed by a student are disbursed in accordance with section 1078-7 of this title.

(b) Special rules for multiple disbursement

For the purpose of subsection (a)(4) of this section—

(1) all loans issued for the same period of enrollment shall be considered as a single loan; and

(2) the requirements of such subsection shall not apply in the case of a loan made under section 1078-2 or 1078-3 of this title, or made to a student to cover the cost of attendance at an eligible institution outside the United States.

(c) Special repayment rules

Except as provided in subsection (a)(2)(H) of this section, the total of the payments by a borrower during any year of any repayment period with respect to the aggregate amount of all loans to that borrower which are insured under this part shall not, unless the **borrower** and the lender otherwise agree, be less than $600 or the balance of all such loans (together with interest thereon), whichever amount is less (but in no instance less than the amount of interest due and payable).

---

1 *Editor's note:* So in original. The comma probably should not appear.

(d) Borrower information

The lender shall obtain the borrower's driver's license number, if any, at the time of application for the loan.

[Pub. L. No. 89-329, Title IV, § 427, *as added by* Pub. L. No. 99-498, Title IV, § 402(a), 100 Stat. 1361 (Oct. 17, 1986), *and amended by* Pub. L. No. 100-50, § 10(b), (c), 101 Stat. 341 (June 3, 1987); Pub. L. No. 100-369, §§ 5(b)(1), 7(c), 11(a), 102 Stat. 836–838 (July 18, 1988); Pub. L. No. 101-239, Title II, §§ 2002(a)(1), 2004(b)(2), 103 Stat. 2111, 2116 (Dec. 19, 1989); Pub. L. No. 102-164, Title VI, §§ 601(a), 602(a), 105 Stat. 1065, 1066 (Nov. 15, 1991); Pub. L. No. 102-325, Title IV, § 414, 106 Stat. 513 (July 23, 1992); Pub. L. No. 103-208, § 2(c)(4), 107 Stat. 2461 (Dec. 20, 1993); Pub. L. No. 110-315, Title IV, § 432(b)(1), 122 Stat. 3246 (Aug. 14, 2008)]

* * *

§ 1078-3. Federal consolidation loans

(a) Agreements with eligible lenders

(1) Agreement required for insurance coverage

For the purpose of providing loans to eligible borrowers for consolidation of their obligations with respect to eligible student loans, the Secretary or a guaranty agency shall enter into agreements in accordance with subsection (b) of this section with the following eligible lenders:

(A) the Student Loan Marketing Association or the Holding Company of the Student Loan Marketing Association, including any subsidiary of the Holding Company, created pursuant to section 1087-3 of this title;

(B) State agencies described in subparagraphs (D) and (F) of section 1085(d)(1) of this title; and

(C) other eligible lenders described in subparagraphs (A), (B), (C), (E), and (J) of such section.

(2) Insurance coverage of consolidation loans

Except as provided in section 1079(e) of this title, no contract of insurance under this part shall apply to a consolidation loan unless such loan is made under an agreement pursuant to this section and is covered by a certificate issued in accordance with subsection (b)(2) of this section. Loans covered by such a certificate that is issued by a guaranty agency shall be considered to be insured loans for the purposes of reimbursements under section 1078(c) of this title, but no payment shall be made with respect to such loans under section 1078(f) of this title to any such agency.

(3) Definition of eligible borrower

(A) For the purpose of this section, the term "eligible borrower" means a borrower who—

(i) is not subject to a judgment secured through litigation with respect to a loan under this subchapter and part C of subchapter I of chapter 34 of Title 42 or to an order for wage garnishment under section 1095a of this title; and

(ii) at the time of application for a consolidation loan—

(I) is in repayment status as determined under section 1078(b)(7)(A) of this title;

(II) is in a grace period preceding repayment; or

(III) is a defaulted borrower who has made arrangements to repay the obligation on the defaulted loans satisfactorily to the holders of the defaulted loans.

(B)(i)[2] An individual's status as an eligible borrower under this section or under section 1087e(g) of this title terminates under both sections upon receipt of a consolidation loan under this section or under section 1087e(g) of this title, except that—

(I) an individual who receives eligible student loans after the date of receipt of the consolidation loan may receive a subsequent consolidation loan;

(II) loans received prior to the date of the consolidation loan may be added during the 180-day period following the making of the consolidation loan;

(III) loans received following the making of the consolidation loan may be added during the 180-day period following the making of the consolidation loan;

(IV) loans received prior to the date of the first consolidation loan may be added to a subsequent consolidation loan; and

(V) an individual may obtain a subsequent consolidation loan under section 1087e(g) of this title only—

(aa) for the purposes of obtaining income contingent repayment or income-based repayment, and only if the loan has been submitted to the guaranty agency for default aversion or if the loan is already in default;

(bb) for the purposes of using the public service loan forgiveness program under section 1087e(m) of this title; or

(cc) for the purpose of using the no accrual of interest for active duty service members benefit offered under section 1087e(o) of this title.

(4) "Eligible student loans" defined

For the purpose of paragraph (1), the term "eligible student loans" means loans—

(A) made, insured, or guaranteed under this part, including loans on which the borrower has defaulted (but has made arrangements to repay the obligation on the defaulted loans satisfactory to the Secretary or guaranty agency, whichever insured the loans).

(B) made under part D of this subchapter;

(C) made under part C of this subchapter;

(D) made under subpart II of part A of title VII of the Public Health Service Act; or

(E) made under part E of title VIII of the Public Health Service Act.

(b) Contents of agreements, certificates of insurance, and loan notes

(1) Agreements with lenders

Any lender described in subparagraph (A), (B), or (C) of subsection (a)(1) of this section who wishes to make consolidation loans under this section shall enter into an agreement with the Secretary or a guaranty agency which provides—

(A) that, in the case of all lenders described in subsection (a)(1) of this section, the lender will make a consolidation loan to an eligible borrower (on request of that borrower) only if the borrower certifies that the borrower has no other application pending for a loan under this section;

(B) that each consolidation loan made by the lender will bear interest, and be subject to repayment, in accordance with subsection (c) of this section;

---

[2] *Editor's note:* So in original. There is no subd. (ii).

(C) that each consolidation loan will be made, notwithstanding any other provision of this part limiting the annual or aggregate principal amount for all insured loans made to a borrower, in an amount (i) which is not less than the minimum amount required for eligibility of the borrower under subsection (a)(3) of this section, and (ii) which is equal to the sum of the unpaid principal and accrued unpaid interest and late charges of all eligible student loans received by the eligible borrower which are selected by the borrower for consolidation;

(D) that the proceeds of each consolidation loan will be paid by the lender to the holder or holders of the loans so selected to discharge the liability on such loans;

(E) that the lender shall offer an income-sensitive repayment schedule, established by the lender in accordance with the regulations promulgated by the Secretary, to the borrower of any consolidation loan made by the lender on or after July 1, 1994;

(F) that the lender shall disclose to a prospective borrower, in simple and understandable terms, at the time the lender provides an application for a consolidation loan—

(i) whether consolidation would result in a loss of loan benefits under this part or part C of this subchapter, including loan forgiveness, cancellation, and deferment;

(ii) with respect to Federal Perkins Loans under part D of this subchapter—

(I) that if a borrower includes a Federal Perkins Loan under part D of this subchapter in the consolidation loan, the borrower will lose all interest-free periods that would have been available for the Federal Perkins Loan, such as—

(aa) the periods during which no interest accrues on such loan while the borrower is enrolled in school at least half-time;

(bb) the grace period under section 1087dd(c)(1)(A) of this title; and

(cc) the periods during which the borrower's student loan repayments are deferred under section 1087dd(c)(2) of this title;

(II) that if a borrower includes a Federal Perkins Loan in the consolidation loan, the borrower will no longer be eligible for cancellation of part or all of the Federal Perkins Loan under section 1087ee(a) of this title; and

(III) the occupations listed in section 1087ee of this title that qualify for Federal Perkins Loan cancellation under section 1087ee(a) of this title;

(iii) the repayment plans that are available to the borrower;

(iv) the options of the borrower to prepay the consolidation loan, to pay such loan on a shorter schedule, and to change repayment plans;

(v) that borrower benefit programs for a consolidation loan may vary among different lenders;

(vi) the consequences of default on the consolidation loan; and

(vii) that by applying for a consolidation loan, the borrower is not obligated to agree to take the consolidation loan; and

(G) such other terms and conditions as the Secretary or the guaranty agency may specifically require of the lender to carry out this section.

(2) Issuance of certificate of comprehensive insurance coverage

The Secretary shall issue a certificate of comprehensive insurance coverage under section 1079(b) of this title to a lender which has entered into an agreement with the Secretary under paragraph (1) of this subsection. The guaranty agency may issue a certificate of comprehensive insurance coverage to a lender with which it has an agreement under such paragraph. The Secretary shall not issue a certificate to a lender described in subparagraph (B) or (C) of subsection (a)(1) of this section unless the Secretary determines that such lender has first applied to, and has been denied a certificate of insurance by, the guaranty agency which insures the preponderance of its loans (by value).

(3) Contents of certificate

A certificate issued under paragraph (2) shall, at a minimum, provide—

> **(A)** that all consolidation loans made by such lender in conformity with the requirements of this section will be insured by the Secretary or the guaranty agency (whichever is applicable) against loss of principal and interest;
>
> **(B)** that a consolidation loan will not be insured unless the lender has determined to its satisfaction, in accordance with reasonable and prudent business practices, for each loan being consolidated—
>
>> **(i)** that the loan is a legal, valid, and binding obligation of the borrower;
>>
>> **(ii)** that each such loan was made and serviced in compliance with applicable laws and regulations; and
>>
>> **(iii)** in the case of loans under this part, that the insurance on such loan is in full force and effect;
>
> **(C)** the effective date and expiration date of the certificate;
>
> **(D)** the aggregate amount to which the certificate applies;
>
> **(E)** the reporting requirements of the Secretary on the lender and an identification of the office of the Department of Education or of the guaranty agency which will process claims and perform other related administrative functions;
>
> **(F)** the alternative repayment terms which will be offered to borrowers by the lender;
>
> **(G)** that, if the lender prior to the expiration of the certificate no longer proposes to make consolidation loans, the lender will so notify the issuer of the certificate in order that the certificate may be terminated (without affecting the insurance on any consolidation loan made prior to such termination); and
>
> **(H)** the terms upon which the issuer of the certificate may limit, suspend, or terminate the lender's authority to make consolidation loans under the certificate (without affecting the insurance on any consolidation loan made prior to such limitation, suspension, or termination).

(4) Terms and conditions of loans

A consolidation loan made pursuant to this section shall be insurable by the Secretary or a guaranty agency pursuant to paragraph (2) only if the loan is made to an eligible borrower who has agreed to notify the holder of the loan promptly concerning any change of address and the loan is evidenced by a note or other written agreement which—

> **(A)** is made without security and without endorsement, except that if the borrower is a minor and such note or other written agreement executed by him or her would not, under applicable law, create a binding obligation, endorsement may be required;
>
> **(B)** provides for the payment of interest and the repayment of principal in accordance with subsection (c) of this section;
>
> **(C)(i)** provides that periodic installments of principal need not be paid, but interest shall accrue and be paid in accordance with clause (ii), during any period for which the borrower would be eligible for a deferral under section 1078(b)(1)(M) of this title, and that any such period shall not be included in determining the repayment schedule pursuant to subsection (c)(2) of this section; and
>
> **(ii)** provides that interest shall accrue and be paid during any such period—
>
>> **(I)** by the Secretary, in the case of a consolidation loan for which the application is received by an eligible lender before November 13, 1997 that consolidated only Federal Stafford Loans for which the student borrower received an interest subsidy under section 1078 of this title;
>>
>> **(II)** by the Secretary, in the case of a consolidation loan for which the application is received by an eligible lender on or after November 13, 1997, except that the Secretary shall pay such interest only on that portion of the loan that repays Federal Stafford Loans for which the student borrower received an interest subsidy under section 1078 of this title or Federal Direct Stafford Loans for which the borrower received an interest subsidy under section 1087e of this title; or
>>
>> **(III)** by the borrower, or capitalized, in the case of a consolidation loan other than a loan described in subclause (I) or (II);
>
> **(D)** entitles the borrower to accelerate without penalty repayment of the whole or any part of the loan; and
>
> **(E)(i)** contains a notice of the system of disclosure concerning such loan to consumer reporting agencies under section 1080a of this title, and
>
> **(ii)** provides that the lender on request of the borrower will provide information on the repayment status of the note to such consumer reporting agencies.

(5) Direct loans

In the event that a borrower is unable to obtain a consolidation loan from a lender with an agreement under subsection (a)(1) of this section, or is unable to obtain a consolidation loan with income-sensitive repayment terms or income-based repayment terms acceptable to the borrower from such a lender, or chooses to obtain a consolidation loan for the purposes of using the public service loan forgiveness program offered under section 1087e(m) of this title, the Secretary shall offer any such borrower who applies for it, a Federal Direct Consolidation loan. In addition, in the event that a borrower chooses to obtain a consolidation loan for the purposes of using the no accrual of interest for active duty service members program offered under section 1087e(o) of this title, the Secretary shall offer a Federal Direct Consolidation loan to any such borrower who applies for participation in such program. A direct consolidation loan offered under this paragraph shall, as requested by the borrower, be repaid either pursuant to income contingent repayment under part C of this subchapter, pursuant to income-based repayment under section 1098e of this title, or pursuant to any other repayment provisions under this section, except that if a borrower intends to be eligible to use the public service loan forgiveness program under section 1087e(m) of this title, such loan shall be repaid using one of the repayment options described in section 1087e(m)(1)(A) of this title. The Secretary shall not offer such loans if, in the Secretary's judgment, the Department of Education does not have the necessary origination and servicing arrangements in place for such loans.

(6) Nondiscrimination in loan consolidation

An eligible lender that makes consolidation loans under this section shall not discriminate against any borrower seeking such a loan—

(A) based on the number or type of eligible student loans the borrower seeks to consolidate, except that a lender is not required to consolidate loans described in subparagraph (D) or (E) of subsection (a)(4) of this section or subsection (d)(1)(C)(ii) of this section;

(B) based on the type or category of institution of higher education that the borrower attended;

(C) based on the interest rate to be charged to the borrower with respect to the consolidation loan; or

(D) with respect to the types of repayment schedules offered to such borrower.

(c) Payment of principal and interest

(1) Interest rate

(A) Notwithstanding subparagraphs (B) and (C), with respect to any loan made under this section for which the application is received by an eligible lender—

(i) on or after October 1, 1998, and before July 1, 2006, the applicable interest rate shall be determined under section 1077a(k)(4) of this title; or

(ii) on or after July 1, 2006, the applicable interest rate shall be determined under section 1077a(l)(3) of this title.

(B) A consolidation loan made before July 1, 1994, shall bear interest at an annual rate on the unpaid principal balance of the loan that is equal to the greater of—

(i) the weighted average of the interest rates on the loans consolidated, rounded to the nearest whole percent; or

(ii) 9 percent.

(C) A consolidation loan made after on or July 1, 1994, shall bear interest at an annual rate on the unpaid principal balance of the loan that is equal to the weighted average of the interest rates on the loans consolidated, rounded upward to the nearest whole percent.

(D) A consolidation loan for which the application is received by an eligible lender on or after November 13, 1997 and before October 1, 1998, shall bear interest at an annual rate on the unpaid principal balance of the loan that is equal to the rate specified in section 1077a(f) of this title, except that the eligible lender may continue to calculate interest on such a loan at the rate previously in effect and defer, until not later than April 1, 1998, the recalculation of the interest on such a loan at the rate required by this subparagraph if the recalculation is applied retroactively to the date on which the loan is made.

(2) Repayment schedules

(A) Notwithstanding any other provision of this part, to the extent authorized by its certificate of insurance under subsection (b)(2) of this section and approved by the issuer of such certificate, the lender of a consolidation loan shall establish repayment terms as will promote the objectives of this section, which shall include the establishment of graduated, income-sensitive, or income-based repayment schedules, established by the lender in accordance with the regulations of the Secretary. Except as required by such income-sensitive or income-based repayment schedules, or by the terms of repayment pursuant to income contingent repayment offered by the Secretary under subsection (b)(5) of this section, such repayment terms shall require that if the sum of the consolidation loan and the amount outstanding on other student loans to the individual—

(i) is less than $7,500, then such consolidation loan shall be repaid in not more than 10 years;

(ii) is equal to or greater than $7,500 but less than $10,000, then such consolidation loan shall be repaid in not more than 12 years;

(iii) is equal to or greater than $10,000 but less than $20,000, then such consolidation loan shall be repaid in not more than 15 years;

(iv) is equal to or greater than $20,000 but less than $40,000, then such consolidation loan shall be repaid in not more than 20 years;

(v) is equal to or greater than $40,000 but less than $60,000, then such consolidation loan shall be repaid in not more than 25 years; or

(vi) is equal to or greater than $60,000, then such consolidation loan shall be repaid in not more than 30 years.

(B) The amount outstanding on other student loans which may be counted for the purpose of subparagraph (A) may not exceed the amount of the consolidation loan.

(3) Additional repayment requirements

Notwithstanding paragraph (2)—

(A) except in the case of an income-based repayment schedule under section 1098e of this title, a repayment schedule established with respect to a consolidation loan shall require that the minimum installment payment be an amount equal to not less than the accrued unpaid interest;

(B) except as required by the terms of repayment pursuant to income contingent repayment offered by the Secretary under subsection (b)(5) of this section, the lender of a consolidation loan may, with respect to repayment on the loan, when the amount of a monthly or other similar payment on the loan is not a multiple of $5, round the payment to the next highest whole dollar amount that is a multiple of $5; and

(C) an income-based repayment schedule under section 1098e of this title shall not be available to a consolidation loan borrower who used the proceeds of the loan to discharge the liability on a loan under section 1078-2 of this title, or a Federal Direct PLUS loan, made on behalf of a dependent student.

(4) Commencement of repayment

Repayment of a consolidation loan shall commence within 60 days after all holders have, pursuant to subsection (b)(1)(D) of this section, discharged the liability of the borrower on the loans selected for consolidation.

(5) Insurance premiums prohibited

No insurance premium shall be charged to the borrower on any consolidation loan, and no insurance premium shall be payable by the lender to the Secretary with respect to any such loan, but a fee may be payable by the lender to the guaranty agency to cover the costs of increased or extended liability with respect to such loan.

(d) Special program authorized

(1) General rule and definition of eligible student loan

(A) In general
Subject to the provisions of this subsection, the Secretary or a guaranty agency shall enter into agreements with eligible lenders described in subparagraphs (A), (B), and (C) of subsection (a)(1) of this section for the consolidation of eligible student loans.

(B) Applicability rule
Unless otherwise provided in this subsection, the agreements entered into under subparagraph (A) and the loans made under such agreements for the consolidation of eligible student loans under this subsection shall have the same terms, conditions, and benefits as all other agreements and loans made under this section.

(C) Definition
For the purpose of this subsection, the term "eligible student loans" means loans—

(i) of the type described in subparagraphs (A), (B), and (C) of subsection (a)(4) of this section; and

(ii) made under subpart I of part A of title VII of the Public Health Service Act.

(2) Interest rate rule

(A) In general
The portion of each consolidated loan that is attributable to an eligible student loan described in paragraph (1)(C)(ii) shall bear interest at a rate not to exceed the rate determined under subparagraph (B).

(B) Determination of the maximum interest rate
For the 12-month period beginning after July 1, 1992, and for each 12-month period thereafter, beginning on July 1 and ending on June 30, the interest rate applicable under subparagraph (A) shall be equal to the average of the bond equivalent rates of the 91-day Treasury bills auctioned for the quarter prior to July 1, for each 12-month period for which the determination is made, plus 3 percent.

(C) Publication of maximum interest rate
The Secretary shall determine the applicable rate of interest under subparagraph (B) after consultation with the Secretary of the Treasury and shall publish such rate in the Federal Register as soon as practicable after the date of such determination.

(3) Special rules

(A) No special allowance rule
No special allowance under section 1087-1 of this title shall be paid with respect to the portion of any consolidated loan under this subsection that is attributable to any loan described in paragraph (1)(C)(ii).

(B) No interest subsidy rule
No interest subsidy under section 1078(a) of this title shall be paid on behalf of any eligible borrower for any portion of a consolidated loan under this subsection that is attributable to any loan described in paragraph (1)(C)(ii).

(C) Additional reserve rule
Notwithstanding any other provision of this chapter, additional reserves shall not be required for any guaranty agency with respect to a loan made under this subsection.

(D) Insurance rule
Any insurance premium paid by the borrower under subpart I of part A of title VII of the Public Health Service Act with respect to a loan made under that subpart and consolidated under this subsection shall be retained by the student loan insurance account established under section 710 of the Public Health Service Act.

(4) Regulations
The Secretary is authorized to promulgate such regulations as may be necessary to facilitate carrying out the provisions of this subsection.

(e) Termination of authority
The authority to make loans under this section expires at the close of September 30, 2014. Nothing in this section shall be construed to authorize the Secretary to promulgate rules or regulations governing the terms or conditions of the agreements and certificates under subsection (b) of this section. Loans made under this section which are insured by the Secretary shall be considered to be new loans made to students for the purpose of section 1074(a) of this title.

(f) Interest payment rebate fee

(1) In general
For any month beginning on or after October 1, 1993, each holder of a consolidation loan under this section for which the first disbursement was made on or after October 1, 1993, shall pay to the Secretary, on a monthly basis and in such manner as the Secretary shall prescribe, a rebate fee calculated on an annual basis equal to 1.05 percent of the principal plus accrued unpaid interest on such loan.

(2) Special rule
For consolidation loans based on applications received during the period from October 1, 1998 through January 31, 1999, inclusive, the rebate described in paragraph (1) shall be equal to 0.62 percent of the principal plus accrued unpaid interest on such loan.

(3) Deposit
The Secretary shall deposit all fees collected pursuant to this subsection into the insurance fund established in section 1081 of this title.

[Pub. L. No. 89-329, Title IV, § 428C, *as added by* Pub. L. No. 99-498, Title IV, § 402(a), 100 Stat. 1388 (Oct. 17, 1986), *and amended by* Pub. L. No. 100-50, § 10(s), 101 Stat. 345 (June 3, 1987); Pub. L. No. 102-325, Title IV, § 419, 106 Stat. 532 (July 23, 1992); Pub. L. No. 102-408, Title III, § 306(a), (b), 106 Stat. 2084, 2086 (Oct. 13, 1992); Pub. L. No. 103-66, Title IV, §§ 4046(a), (b)(2), 4106(a), 107 Stat. 360, 363, 368 (Aug. 10, 1993); Pub. L. No. 103-208, § 2(c)(33) to (37), 107 Stat. 2466 (Dec. 20, 1993); Pub. L. No. 103-382, Title III, § 356, 108 Stat. 3967 (Oct. 20, 1994); Pub. L. No. 104-208, Div. A, Title I, § 101(e) [Title VI, § 602(b)(1)(A)(ii)], 110 Stat. 3009-283 (Sept. 30, 1996); Pub. L. No. 105-33, Title VI, § 6104(3), 111 Stat. 652 (Aug. 5, 1997); Pub. L. No. 105-78, Title VI, § 609(b) to (e), 111 Stat. 1522, 1523 (Nov. 13, 1997); Pub. L. No. 105-244, Title IV, §§ 416(b)(2), 420, 112 Stat. 1682, 1695 (Oct. 7, 1998); Pub. L. No. 107-139, § 1(a)(2), 116 Stat. 8 (Feb. 8, 2002); Pub. L. No. 109-171, Title VIII, §§ 8004(b)(3), 8009(a), (b)(2), (c), 120 Stat. 158, 163, 164 (Feb. 8, 2006); Pub. L. No. 109-234, Title VII, § 7015(a), (c), (d), 120 Stat. 485 (June 15, 2006); Pub. L. No. 110-84, Title II, § 203(b)(1), (2), 121 Stat. 794 (Sept. 27, 2007); Pub. L. No. 110-315, Title IV, §§ 425(a) to (b)(2), (c), (d)(1), (e), 432(b)(3), 122 Stat. 3233 to 3235, 3246 (Aug. 14, 2008); Pub. L. No. 111-39, Title IV, § 402(c)(1), (f)(3), 123 Stat. 1940, 1943 (July 1, 2009)]

* * *

§ 1080a. Reports to consumer reporting agencies and institutions of higher education

(a) Agreements to exchange information
For the purpose of promoting responsible repayment of loans covered by Federal loan insurance pursuant to this part or covered by a guaranty agreement pursuant to section 1078 of this title, the Secretary and each guaranty agency, eligible lender, and subsequent holder shall enter into an agreement with each consumer reporting agency to exchange information concerning student borrowers, in accordance with the requirements of this section. For the purpose of assisting such consumer reporting agencies in complying with the Fair Credit Reporting Act [15 U.S.C.A. § 1681 et seq.], such agreements may provide for timely response by the Secretary (concerning loans covered by Federal loan insurance) or by a guaranty agency, eligible lender, or subsequent holder (concerning loans covered by a guaranty agreement), or to requests from such consumer reporting agencies for responses to objections raised by borrowers. Subject to the requirements of subsection (c) of this section, such agreements shall require the Secretary or the guaranty agency, eligible lender, or subsequent holder, as appropriate, to disclose to such consumer reporting agencies, with respect to any loan under this part that has not been repaid by the borrower—

(1) that the loan is an education loan (as such term is defined in section 1019 of this title);

(2) the total amount of loans made to any borrower under this part and the remaining balance of the loans;

(3) information concerning the repayment status of the loan for inclusion in the file of the borrower, except that nothing in this subsection shall be construed to affect any otherwise applicable provision of the Fair Credit Reporting Act (15 U.S.C. 1681 et seq.);

(4) information concerning the date of any default on the loan and the collection of the loan, including information concerning the repayment status of any defaulted loan on which the Secretary has made a payment pursuant to section 1080(a) of this title or the guaranty agency has made a payment to the previous holder of the loan; and

(5) the date of cancellation of the note upon completion of repayment by the borrower of the loan or payment by the Secretary pursuant to section 1087 of this title.

(b) Additional information
Such agreements may also provide for the disclosure by such consumer reporting agencies to the Secretary or a guaranty agency, whichever insures or guarantees a loan, upon receipt of a notice under subsection (a)(4) of this section that such a loan is in default, of information concerning the borrower's location or other information which may assist the Secretary, the guaranty agency, the eligible lender, or the subsequent holder in collecting the loan.

(c) Contents of agreements
Agreements entered into pursuant to this section shall contain such provisions as may be necessary to ensure that—

(1) no information is disclosed by the Secretary or the guaranty agency, eligible lender, or subsequent holder unless its accuracy and completeness have been verified and the Secretary or the guaranty agency has determined that disclosure would accomplish the purpose of this section;

(2) as to any information so disclosed, such consumer reporting agencies will be promptly notified of, and will promptly record, any change submitted by the Secretary, the guaranty agency, eligible lender, or subsequent holder with respect to such information, or any objections by the borrower with respect to any such information, as required by section 611 of the Fair Credit Reporting Act (15 U.S.C. 1681i);

(3) no use will be made of any such information which would result in the use of collection practices with respect to such a borrower that are not fair and reasonable or that involve harassment, intimidation, false or misleading representations, or unnecessary communication concerning the existence of such loan or concerning any such information; and

(4) with regard to notices of default under subsection (a)(4) of this section, except for disclosures made to obtain the borrower's location, the Secretary, or the guaranty agency, eligible lender, or subsequent holder whichever is applicable

(A) shall not disclose any such information until the borrower has been notified that such information will be disclosed to consumer reporting agencies unless the borrower enters into repayment of his or her loan, but

(B) shall, if the borrower has not entered into repayment within a reasonable period of time, but not less than 30 days, from the date such notice has been sent to the borrower, disclose the information required by this subsection.

(d) Contractor status of participants
A guaranty agency, eligible lender, or subsequent holder or consumer reporting agency which discloses or receives information under this section shall not be considered a Government contractor within the meaning of section 552a of Title 5.

(e) Disclosure to institutions
The Secretary and each guaranty agency, eligible lender, and subsequent holder of a loan are authorized to disclose information described in subsections (a) and (b) of this section concerning student borrowers to the eligible institutions such borrowers attend or previously attended. To further the purpose of this section, an eligible institution may enter into an arrangement with any or all of the holders of delinquent loans made to borrowers who attend or previously attended such institution for the purpose of providing current information regarding the borrower's location or employment or for the purpose of assisting the holder in contacting and influencing borrowers to avoid default.

(f) Duration of authority
Notwithstanding paragraphs (4) and (5) of subsection (a) of section 605 of the Fair Credit Reporting Act (15 U.S.C. 1681c(a)(4), (a)(5)), a consumer reporting agency may make a report containing information received from the Secretary or a guaranty agency, eligible lender, or subsequent holder regarding the status of a borrower's defaulted account on a loan guaranteed under this part until—

(1) 7 years from the date on which the Secretary or the agency paid a claim to the holder on the guaranty;

(2) 7 years from the date the Secretary, guaranty agency, eligible lender, or subsequent holder first reported the account to the consumer reporting agency; or

(3) in the case of a borrower who reenters repayment after defaulting on a loan and subsequently goes into default on such loan, 7 years from the date the loan entered default such subsequent time.

[Pub. L. No. 89-329, Title IV, § 430A, *as added by* Pub. L. 99-498, Title IV, § 402(a), 100 Stat. 1398 (Oct. 17, 1986), *and amended by* Pub. L. No. 100-50, § 10(v), 101 Stat. 346 (June 3, 1987); Pub. L. No. 102-325, Title IV, § 424, 106 Stat. 543 (July 23, 1992); Pub. L. No. 103-208, § 2(c)(52), 107 Stat. 2467 (Dec. 20, 1993); Pub. L. No. 110-315, Title IV, § 432(a), 122 Stat. 3245 (Aug. 14, 2008); Pub. L. No. 111-39, Title IV, § 402(f)(8), 123 Stat. 1944 (July 1, 2009)]

* * *

§ 1083. Student loan information by eligible lenders

(a) Required disclosure before disbursement
Each eligible lender, at or prior to the time such lender disburses a loan that is insured or guaranteed under this part (other than a loan made under section 1078-3 of this title), shall provide thorough and accurate loan information on such loan to the borrower in simple and understandable terms. Any disclosure required by this subsection may be made by an eligible lender by written or electronic means, including as part of the application material provided to the borrower, as part of the promissory note evidencing the loan, or on a separate written form provided to the borrower. Each lender shall provide to each borrower a telephone number, and may provide an electronic address, through which additional loan information can be obtained. The disclosure shall include—
   (1) a statement prominently and clearly displayed and in bold print that the borrower is receiving a loan that must be repaid;
   (2) the name of the eligible lender, and the address to which communications and payments should be sent;
   (3) the principal amount of the loan;
   (4) the amount of any charges, such as the origination fee and Federal default fee, and whether those fees will be—
      (A) collected by the lender at or prior to the disbursal of the loan;
      (B) deducted from the proceeds of the loan;
      (C) paid separately by the borrower; or
      (D) paid by the lender;
   (5) the stated interest rate on the loan;
   (6) for loans made under section 1078-8 of this title or to a student borrower under section 1078-2 of this title, an explanation—
      (A) that the borrower has the option to pay the interest that accrues on the loan while the borrower is a student at an institution of higher education; and
      (B) if the borrower does not pay such interest while attending an institution, when and how often interest on the loan will be capitalized;
   (7) for loans made to a parent borrower on behalf of a student under section 1078-2 of this title, an explanation—
      (A) that the parent has the option to defer payment on the loan while the student is enrolled on at least a half-time basis in an institution of higher education;
      (B) if the parent does not pay the interest on the loan while the student is enrolled in an institution, when and how often interest on the loan will be capitalized; and
      (C) that the parent may be eligible for a deferment on the loan if the parent is enrolled on at least a half-time basis in an institution of higher education;
   (8) the yearly and cumulative maximum amounts that may be borrowed;
   (9) a statement of the total cumulative balance, including the loan being disbursed, owed by the borrower to that lender, and an estimate of the projected monthly payment, given such cumulative balance;
   (10) an explanation of when repayment of the loan will be required and when the borrower will be obligated to pay interest that accrues on the loan;
   (11) a description of the types of repayment plans that are available for the loan;
   (12) a statement as to the minimum and maximum repayment terms which the lender may impose, and the minimum annual payment required by law;
   (13) an explanation of any special options the borrower may have for loan consolidation or other refinancing of the loan;
   (14) a statement that the borrower has the right to prepay all or part of the loan, at any time, without penalty;
   (15) a statement summarizing circumstances in which repayment of the loan or interest that accrues on the loan may be deferred;
   (16) a statement summarizing the circumstances in which a borrower may obtain forbearance on the loan;
   (17) a description of the options available for forgiveness of the loan, and the requirements to obtain loan forgiveness;
   (18) a definition of default and the consequences to the borrower if the borrower defaults, including a statement that the default will be reported to a consumer reporting agency; and
   (19) an explanation of any cost the borrower may incur during repayment or in the collection of the loan, including fees that the borrower may be charged, such as late payment fees and collection costs.

(b) Required disclosure before repayment
Each eligible lender shall, at or prior to the start of the repayment period on a loan made, insured, or guaranteed under section 1078, 1078-2, or 1078-8 of this title, disclose to the borrower by written or electronic means the information required under this subsection in simple and understandable terms. Each eligible lender shall provide to each borrower a telephone number, and may provide an electronic address, through which additional loan information can be obtained. The disclosure required by this subsection shall be made not less than 30 days nor more than 150 days before the first payment on the loan is due from the borrower. The disclosure shall include—
   (1) the name of the eligible lender or loan servicer, and the address to which communications and payments should be sent;
   (2) the scheduled date upon which the repayment period is to begin or the deferment period under section 1078-2(d)(1) of this title is to end, as applicable;
   (3) the estimated balance owed by the borrower on the loan or loans covered by the disclosure (including, if applicable, the estimated amount of interest to be capitalized) as of the scheduled date on which the repayment period is to begin or the deferment period under 1078-2(d)(1) of this title is to end, as applicable;
   (4) the stated interest rate on the loan or loans, or the combined interest rate of loans with different stated interest rates;
   (5) information on loan repayment benefits offered for the loan or loans, including—

(A) whether the lender offers any benefits that are contingent on the repayment behavior of the borrower, such as—
(i) a reduction in interest rate if the borrower repays the loan by automatic payroll or checking account deduction;
(ii) a reduction in interest rate if the borrower makes a specified number of on-time payments; and
(iii) other loan repayment benefits for which the borrower could be eligible that would reduce the amount of repayment or the length of the repayment period;
(B) if the lender provides a loan repayment benefit—
(i) any limitations on such benefit;
(ii) explicit information on the reasons a borrower may lose eligibility for such benefit;
(iii) for a loan repayment benefit that reduces the borrower's interest rate—
(I) examples of the impact the interest rate reduction would have on the length of the borrower's repayment period and the amount of repayment; and
(II) upon the request of the borrower, the effect the reduction in interest rate would have with respect to the borrower's payoff amount and time for repayment; and
(iv) whether and how the borrower can regain eligibility for a benefit if a borrower loses a benefit;
(6) a description of all the repayment plans that are available to the borrower and a statement that the borrower may change from one plan to another during the period of repayment;
(7) the repayment schedule for all loans covered by the disclosure, including—
(A) the date the first installment is due; and
(B) the number, amount, and frequency of required payments, which shall be based on a standard repayment plan or, in the case of a borrower who has selected another repayment plan, on the repayment plan selected by the borrower;
(8) an explanation of any special options the borrower may have for loan consolidation or other refinancing of the loan and of the availability and terms of such other options;
(9) except as provided in subsection (d)—
(A) the projected total of interest charges which the borrower will pay on the loan or loans, assuming that the borrower makes payments exactly in accordance with the repayment schedule; and
(B) if the borrower has already paid interest on the loan or loans, the amount of interest paid;
(10) the nature of any fees which may accrue or be charged to the borrower during the repayment period;
(11) a statement that the borrower has the right to prepay all or part of the loan or loans covered by the disclosure at any time without penalty;
(12) a description of the options by which the borrower may avoid or be removed from default, including any relevant fees associated with such options; and
(13) additional resources, including nonprofit organizations, advocates, and counselors (including the Student Loan Ombudsman of the Department) of which the lender is aware, where borrowers may receive advice and assistance on loan repayment.

(c) Separate notification
Each eligible lender shall, at the time such lender notifies a borrower of approval of a loan which is insured or guaranteed under this part, provide the borrower with a separate notification which summarizes, in simple and understandable terms, the rights and responsibilities of the borrower with respect to the loan, including a statement of the consequences of defaulting on the loan and a statement that each borrower who defaults will be reported to a consumer reporting agency. The requirement of this subsection shall be in addition to the information required by subsection (a) of this section.

(d) Special disclosure rules on plus loans, and unsubsidized loans
Loans made under sections 1078-2 and 1078-8 of this title shall not be subject to the disclosure of projected monthly payment amounts required under subsection (b)(7) if the lender, in lieu of such disclosure, provides the borrower with sample projections of monthly repayment amounts, assuming different levels of borrowing and interest accruals resulting from capitalization of interest while the borrower, or the student on whose behalf the loan is made, is in school, in simple and understandable terms. Such sample projections shall disclose the cost to the borrower of—
(1) capitalizing the interest; and
(2) paying the interest as the interest accrues.

(e) Required disclosures during repayment
(1) Pertinent information about a loan provided on a periodic basis
Each eligible lender shall provide the borrower of a loan made, insured, or guaranteed under this part with a bill or statement (as applicable) that corresponds to each payment installment time period in which a payment is due and that includes, in simple and understandable terms—
(A) the original principal amount of the borrower's loan;
(B) the borrower's current balance, as of the time of the bill or statement, as applicable;
(C) the interest rate on such loan;
(D) the total amount the borrower has paid in interest on the loan;
(E) the aggregate amount the borrower has paid for the loan, including the amount the borrower has paid in interest, the amount the borrower has paid in fees, and the amount the borrower has paid against the balance;
(F) a description of each fee the borrower has been charged for the most recently preceding installment time period;
(G) the date by which the borrower needs to make a payment in order to avoid additional fees and the amount of such payment and the amount of such fees;
(H) the lender's or loan servicer's address and toll-free phone number for payment and billing error purposes; and
(I) a reminder that the borrower has the option to change repayment plans, a list of the names of the repayment plans available to the borrower, a link to the appropriate page of the Department's website to obtain a more detailed description of the repayment plans, and directions for the borrower to request a change in repayment plan.
(2) Information provided to a borrower having difficulty making payments
Each eligible lender shall provide to a borrower who has notified the lender that the borrower is having difficulty making payments on a loan made, insured, or guaranteed under this part with the following information in simple and understandable terms:

(A) A description of the repayment plans available to the borrower, including how the borrower should request a change in repayment plan.

(B) A description of the requirements for obtaining forbearance on a loan, including expected costs associated with forbearance.

(C) A description of the options available to the borrower to avoid defaulting on the loan, and any relevant fees or costs associated with such options.

(3) Required disclosures during delinquency

Each eligible lender shall provide to a borrower who is 60 days delinquent in making payments on a loan made, insured, or guaranteed under this part with a notice, in simple and understandable terms, of the following:

(A) The date on which the loan will default if no payment is made.

(B) The minimum payment the borrower must make to avoid default.

(C) A description of the options available to the borrower to avoid default, and any relevant fees or costs associated with such options, including a description of deferment and forbearance and the requirements to obtain each.

(D) Discharge options to which the borrower may be entitled.

(E) Additional resources, including nonprofit organizations, advocates, and counselors (including the Student Loan Ombudsman of the Department), of which the lender is aware, where the borrower can receive advice and assistance on loan repayment.

(f) Cost of disclosure and consequences of nondisclosure

(1) No cost to borrowers

The information required under this section shall be available without cost to the borrower.

(2) Consequences of nondisclosure

The failure of an eligible lender to provide information as required by this section shall not—

(A) relieve a borrower of the obligation to repay a loan in accordance with the loan's terms; or

(B) provide a basis for a claim for civil damages.

(3) Rule of construction

Nothing in this section shall be construed as subjecting the lender to the Truth in Lending Act with regard to loans made under this part.

(4) Actions by the Secretary

The Secretary may limit, suspend, or terminate the continued participation of an eligible lender in making loans under this part for failure by that lender to comply with this section.

[Pub. L. No. 89-329, Title IV, § 433, *as added by* Pub. L. No. 99-498, Title IV, § 402(a), 100 Stat. 1406 (Oct. 17, 1986), *and amended by* Pub. L. No. 100-50, § 10(z), 101 Stat. 346 (June 3, 1987); Pub. L. No. 102-325, Title IV, § 426, 106 Stat. 548 (July 23, 1992); Pub. L. No. 103-208, § 2(c)(53), (54), (k)(4), 107 Stat. 2468, 2485 (Dec. 20, 1993); Pub. L. No. 105-244, Title IV, § 428, 112 Stat. 1704 (Oct. 7, 1998); Pub. L. No. 110-315, Title IV, § 434(a), 122 Stat. 3247 (Aug. 14, 2008)]

* * *

§ 1087. Repayment by Secretary of loans of bankrupt, deceased, or disabled borrowers; treatment of borrowers attending schools that fail to provide a refund, attending closed schools, or falsely certified as eligible to borrow

(a) Repayment in full for death and disability

(1) In general.

If a student borrower who has received a loan described in subparagraph (A) or (B) of section 1078(a)(1) of this title dies or becomes permanently and totally disabled (as determined in accordance with regulations of the Secretary), or if a student borrower who has received such a loan is unable to engage in any substantial gainful activity by reason of any medically determinable physical or mental impairment that can be expected to result in death, has lasted for a continuous period of not less than 60 months, or can be expected to last for a continuous period of not less than 60 months) then the Secretary shall discharge the borrower's liability on the loan by repaying the amount owed on the loan. The Secretary may develop such safeguards as the Secretary determines necessary to prevent fraud and abuse in the discharge of liability under this subsection. Notwithstanding any other provision of this subsection, the Secretary may promulgate regulations to reinstate the obligation of, and resume collection on, loans discharged under this subsection in any case in which—

(A) a borrower received a discharge of liability under this subsection and after the discharge the borrower—

(i) receives a loan made, insured, or guaranteed under this title; or

(ii) has earned income in excess of the poverty line; or

(B) the Secretary determines necessary.

(2) Disability determinations.

A borrower who has been determined by the Secretary of Veterans Affairs to be unemployable due to a service-connected condition and who provides documentation of such determination to the Secretary of Education, shall be considered permanently and totally disabled for the purpose of discharging such borrower's loans under this subsection, and such borrower shall not be required to present additional documentation for purposes of this subsection.

(b) Payment of claims on loans in bankruptcy

The Secretary shall pay to the holder of a loan described in section 1078(a)(1)(A) or (B), 1078-1, 1078-2, 1078-3, or 1078-8 of this title, the amount of the unpaid balance of principal and interest owed on such loan—

(1) when the borrower files for relief under chapter 12 or 13 of Title 11;

(2) when the borrower who has filed for relief under chapter 7 or 11 of such title commences an action for a determination of dischargeability under section 523(a)(8)(B) of such title; or

(3) for loans described in section 523(a)(8)(A) of such title, when the borrower files for relief under chapter 7 or 11 of such title.

(c) Discharge

(1) In general

If a borrower who received, on or after January 1, 1986, a loan made, insured, or guaranteed under this part and the student borrower, or the student on whose behalf a parent borrowed, is unable to complete the program in which such student is enrolled due to the closure of the institution or if such student's eligibility to borrow under this part was falsely certified by the eligible institution or was falsely certified as a result of a crime of identity theft, or if the institution failed to make a refund of loan proceeds which the institution owed to such student's lender, then the Secretary shall discharge the borrower's liability on the loan (including interest and collection fees) by repaying the amount owed on the loan and shall subsequently pursue any claim available to such borrower against the institution and its affiliates and principals or settle the loan obligation pursuant to the financial responsibility authority under subpart 3 of part G of this subchapter. In the case of a discharge based upon a failure to refund, the amount of the discharge shall not exceed that portion of the loan which should have been refunded. The Secretary shall report to the authorizing committees annually as to the dollar amount of loan discharges attributable to failures to make refunds.

(2) Assignment

A borrower whose loan has been discharged pursuant to this subsection shall be deemed to have assigned to the United States the right to a loan refund up to the amount discharged against the institution and its affiliates and principals.

(3) Eligibility for additional assistance

The period of a student's attendance at an institution at which the student was unable to complete a course of study due to the closing of the institution shall not be considered for purposes of calculating the student's period of eligibility for additional assistance under this subchapter and part C of subchapter I of chapter 34 of Title 42.

(4) Special rule

A borrower whose loan has been discharged pursuant to this subsection shall not be precluded from receiving additional grants, loans, or work assistance under this subchapter and part C of subchapter I of chapter 34 of Title 42 for which the borrower would be otherwise eligible (but for the default on such discharged loan). The amount discharged under this subsection shall be treated the same as loans under section 1087ee(a)(5) of this title.

(5) Reporting

The Secretary shall report to consumer reporting agencies with respect to loans which have been discharged pursuant to this subsection.

(d) Repayment of loans to parents

If a student on whose behalf a parent has received a loan described in section 1078-2 of this title dies, then the Secretary shall discharge the borrower's liability on the loan by repaying the amount owed on the loan.

[Pub. L. No. 89-329, Title IV, § 437, *as added by* Pub. L. No. 99-498, Title IV, § 402(a), 100 Stat. 1414 (Oct. 17, 1986), *and amended by* Pub. L. No. 102-325, Title IV, § 428, 106 Stat. 551 (July 23, 1992); Pub. L. No. 103-208, § 2(c)(63) to (65), 107 Stat. 2469 (Dec. 20, 1993); Pub. L. No. 105-244, Title IV, § 431, 112 Stat. 1709 (Oct. 7, 1998); Pub. L. No. 109-171, Title VIII, § 8012, 120 Stat. 166 (Feb. 8, 2006); Pub. L. No. 110-315, Title I, § 103(b)(7), Title IV, §§ 432(b)(4), 437(b), 122 Stat. 3089, 3246, 3258 (Aug. 14, 2008); Pub. L. No. 111-39, 123 Stat 1934 (July 1, 2009)]

* * *

A.3 Perkins Loans

20 U.S.C. sec.

* * *

1087bb. Allocation of funds.
1087cc. Agreements with institutions of higher education.
1087dd. Terms of loans.

* * *

§ 1087bb. Allocation of funds

(a) Allocation based on previous allocation

(1) From the amount appropriated pursuant to section 1087aa(b) of this title for each fiscal year, the Secretary shall first allocate to each eligible institution an amount equal to—

(A) 100 percent of the amount received under subsections (a) and (b) of this section for fiscal year 1999 (as such subsections were in effect with respect to allocations for such fiscal year), multiplied by

(B) the institution's default penalty, as determined under subsection (e) of this section,

except that if the institution has a cohort default rate in excess of the applicable maximum cohort default rate under subsection (f) of this section, the institution may not receive an allocation under this paragraph.

(2)(A) From the amount so appropriated, the Secretary shall next allocate to each eligible institution that began participation in the program under this part after fiscal year 1999 but is not a first or second time participant, an amount equal to the greater of—

(i) $5,000; or

(ii) 100 percent of the amount received and expended under this part for the first year it participated in the program.

(B) From the amount so appropriated, the Secretary shall next allocate to each eligible institution that began participation in the program under this part after fiscal year 1999 and is a first or second time participant, an amount equal to the greatest of—

(i) $5,000;

(ii) an amount equal to (I) 90 percent of the amount received and used under this part in the second preceding fiscal year by eligible institutions offering comparable programs of instruction, divided by (II) the number of students enrolled at such comparable institutions in such fiscal year, multiplied by (III) the number of students enrolled at the applicant institution in such fiscal year; or

(iii) 90 percent of the institution's allocation under this part for the preceding fiscal year.

(C) Notwithstanding subparagraphs (A) and (B) of this paragraph, the Secretary shall allocate to each eligible institution which—

(i) was a first-time participant in the program in fiscal year 2000 or any subsequent fiscal year, and

(ii) received a larger amount under this subsection in the second year of participation,

an amount equal to 90 percent of the amount it received under this subsection in its second year of participation.

(D) For any fiscal year after a fiscal year in which an institution receives an allocation under subparagraph (A),

(B), or (C), the Secretary shall allocate to such institution an amount equal to the product of—
  (i) the amount determined under subparagraph (A), (B), or (C), multiplied by
  (ii) the institution's default penalty, as determined under subsection (e) of this section,
except that if the institution has a cohort default rate in excess of the applicable maximum cohort default rate under subsection (f) of this section, the institution may not receive an allocation under this paragraph.

(3)(A) If the amount appropriated for any fiscal year is less than the amount required to be allocated to all institutions under paragraph (1) of this subsection, then the amount of the allocation to each such institution shall be ratably reduced.

(B) If the amount appropriated for any fiscal year is more than the amount required to be allocated to all institutions under paragraph (1) but less than the amount required to be allocated to all institutions under paragraph (2), then—
  (i) the Secretary shall allot the amount required to be allocated to all institutions under paragraph (1), and
  (ii) the amount of the allocation to each institution under paragraph (2) shall be ratably reduced.

(C) If additional amounts are appropriated for any such fiscal year, such reduced amounts shall be increased on the same basis as they were reduced (until the amount allocated equals the amount required to be allocated under paragraphs (1) and (2) of this subsection).

(b) Allocation of excess based on share of excess eligible amounts

(1) From the remainder of the amount appropriated pursuant to section 1087aa(b) of this title after making the allocations required by subsection (a) of this section, the Secretary shall allocate to each eligible institution which has an excess eligible amount an amount which bears the same ratio to such remainder as such excess eligible amount bears to the sum of the excess eligible amounts of all such eligible institutions (having such excess eligible amounts).

(2) For any eligible institution, the excess eligible amount is the amount, if any, by which—
  (A)(i) that institution's eligible amount (as determined under paragraph (3)), divided by (ii) the sum of the eligible amounts of all institutions (as so determined), multiplied by (iii) the amount appropriated pursuant to section 1087aa(b) of this title for the fiscal year; exceeds
  (B) the amount required to be allocated to that institution under subsection (a) of this section,
except that an eligible institution which has a cohort default rate in excess of the applicable maximum cohort default rate under subsection (f) of this section may not receive an allocation under this paragraph.

(3) For any eligible institution, the eligible amount of that institution is equal to—
  (A) the amount of the institution's self-help need, as determined under subsection (c) of this section; minus
  (B) the institution's anticipated collections; multiplied by
  (C) the institution's default penalty, as determined under subsection (e) of this section;
except that, if the institution has a cohort default rate in excess of the applicable maximum cohort default rate under subsection (f) of this section, the eligible amount of that institution is zero.

(c) Determination of institution's self-help need

(1) The amount of an institution's self-help need is equal to the sum of the self-help need of the institution's eligible undergraduate students and the self-help need of the institution's eligible graduate and professional students.

(2) To determine the self-help need of an institution's eligible undergraduate students, the Secretary shall—
  (A) establish various income categories for dependent and independent undergraduate students;
  (B) establish an expected family contribution for each income category of dependent and independent undergraduate students, determined on the basis of the average expected family contribution (computed in accordance with part E of this subchapter) of a representative sample within each income category for the second preceding fiscal year;
  (C) compute 25 percent of the average cost of attendance for all undergraduate students;
  (D) multiply the number of eligible dependent students in each income category by the lesser of—
    (i) 25 percent of the average cost of attendance for all undergraduate students determined under subparagraph (C); or
    (ii) the average cost of attendance for all undergraduate students minus the expected family contribution determined under subparagraph (B) for that income category, except that the amount computed by such subtraction shall not be less than zero;
  (E) add the amounts determined under subparagraph (D) for each income category of dependent students;
  (F) multiply the number of eligible independent students in each income category by the lesser of—
    (i) 25 percent of the average cost of attendance for all undergraduate students determined under subparagraph (C); or
    (ii) the average cost of attendance for all undergraduate students minus the expected family contribution determined under subparagraph (B) for that income category, except that the amount computed by such subtraction for any income category shall not be less than zero;
  (G) add the amounts determined under subparagraph (F) for each income category of independent students; and
  (H) add the amounts determined under subparagraphs (E) and (G).

(3) To determine the self-help need of an institution's eligible graduate and professional students, the Secretary shall—
  (A) establish various income categories for graduate and professional students;
  (B) establish an expected family contribution for each income category of graduate and professional students, determined on the basis of the average expected family contribution (computed in accordance with part E of this subchapter) of a representative sample within each income category for the second preceding fiscal year;
  (C) determine the average cost of attendance for all graduate and professional students;
  (D) subtract from the average cost of attendance for all graduate and professional students (determined under subparagraph (C)), the expected family contribution (determined under subparagraph (B)) for each income category, except

that the amount computed by such subtraction for any income category shall not be less than zero;

(E) multiply the amounts determined under subparagraph (D) by the number of eligible students in each category;

(F) add the amounts determined under subparagraph (E) for each income category.

(4)(A) For purposes of paragraphs (2) and (3), the term "average cost of attendance" means the average of the attendance costs for undergraduate students and for graduate and professional students, which shall include (i) tuition and fees determined in accordance with subparagraph (B), (ii) standard living expenses determined in accordance with subparagraph (C), and (iii) books and supplies determined in accordance with subparagraph (D).

(B) The average undergraduate and graduate and professional tuition and fees described in subparagraph (A)(i) shall be computed on the basis of information reported by the institution to the Secretary, which shall include (i) total revenue received by the institution from undergraduate and graduate tuition and fees for the second year preceding the year for which it is applying for an allocation, and (ii) the institution's enrollment for such second preceding year.

(C) The standard living expense described in subparagraph (A)(ii) is equal to 150 percent of the difference between the income protection allowance for a family of five with one in college and the income protection allowance for a family of six with one in college for a single independent student.

(D) The allowance for books and supplies described in subparagraph (A)(iii) is equal to $600.

(d) Anticipated collections

(1) An institution's anticipated collections are equal to the amount which was collected during the second year preceding the beginning of the award period, multiplied by 1.21.

(2) The Secretary shall establish an appeals process by which the anticipated collections required in paragraph (1) may be waived for institutions with low cohort default rates in the program assisted under this part.

(e) Default penalties

(1) Years preceding fiscal year 2000

For any fiscal year preceding fiscal year 2000, any institution with a cohort default rate that—

(A) equals or exceeds 15 percent, shall establish a default reduction plan pursuant to regulations prescribed by the Secretary, except that such plan shall not be required with respect to an institution that has a default rate of less than 20 percent and that has less than 100 students who have loans under this part in such academic year;

(B) equals or exceeds 20 percent, but is less than 25 percent, shall have a default penalty of 0.9;

(C) equals or exceeds 25 percent, but is less than 30 percent, shall have a default penalty of 0.7; and

(D) equals or exceeds 30 percent shall have a default penalty of zero.

(2) Years following fiscal year 2000

For fiscal year 2000 and any succeeding fiscal year, any institution with a cohort default rate (as defined under subsection (g) of this section) that equals or exceeds 25 percent shall have a default penalty of zero.

(3) Ineligibility

(A) In general

For fiscal year 2000 and any succeeding fiscal year, any institution with a cohort default rate (as defined in subsection (g) of this section) that equals or exceeds 50 percent for each of the 3 most recent years for which data are available shall not be eligible to participate in a program under this part for the fiscal year for which the determination is made and the 2 succeeding fiscal years, unless, within 30 days of receiving notification from the Secretary of the loss of eligibility under this paragraph, the institution appeals the loss of eligibility to the Secretary. The Secretary shall issue a decision on any such appeal within 45 days after the submission of the appeal. Such decision may permit the institution to continue to participate in a program under this part if—

(i) the institution demonstrates to the satisfaction of the Secretary that the calculation of the institution's cohort default rate is not accurate, and that recalculation would reduce the institution's cohort default rate for any of the 3 fiscal years below 50 percent; or

(ii) there are, in the judgment of the Secretary, such a small number of borrowers entering repayment that the application of this subparagraph would be inequitable.

(B) Continued participation

During an appeal under subparagraph (A), the Secretary may permit the institution to continue to participate in a program under this part.

(C) Return of funds

Within 90 days after the date of any termination pursuant to subparagraph (A), or the conclusion of any appeal pursuant to subparagraph (B), whichever is later, the balance of the student loan fund established under this part by the institution that is the subject of the termination shall be distributed as follows:

(i) The Secretary shall first be paid an amount which bears the same ratio to such balance (as of the date of such distribution) as the total amount of Federal capital contributions to such fund by the Secretary under this part bears to the sum of such Federal capital contributions and the capital contributions to such fund made by the institution.

(ii) The remainder of such student loan fund shall be paid to the institution.

(D) Use of returned funds

Any funds returned to the Secretary under this paragraph shall be reallocated to institutions of higher education pursuant to subsection (i) of this section.

(E) Definition

For the purposes of subparagraph (A), the term "loss of eligibility" shall be defined as the mandatory liquidation of an institution's student loan fund, and assignment of the institution's outstanding loan portfolio to the Secretary.

(f) Applicable maximum cohort default rate

(1) Award years prior to 2000

For award years prior to award year 2000, the applicable maximum cohort default rate is 30 percent.

(2) Award year 2000 and succeeding award years

For award year 2000 and subsequent years, the **applicable** maximum cohort default rate is 25 percent.

(g) "Cohort default rate" defined

(1)(A) The term "cohort default rate" means, for any award year in which 30 or more current and former students at the institution enter repayment on loans under this part (received for attendance at the institution), the percentage of those current and former students who enter repayment on such loans (received for attendance at that institution) in that award year who default before the end of the following award year.

(B) For any award year in which less than 30 of the institution's current and former students enter repayment, the term "cohort default rate" means the percentage of such current and former students who entered repayment on such loans in any of the three most recent award years and who default before the end of the award year immediately following the year in which they entered repayment.

(C) A loan on which a payment is made by the institution of higher education, its owner, agency, contractor, employee, or any other entity or individual affiliated with such institution, in order to avoid default by the borrower, is considered as in default for the purposes of this subsection.

(D) In the case of a student who has attended and borrowed at more than one school, the student (and his or her subsequent repayment or default) is attributed to the school for attendance at which the student received the loan that entered repayment in the award year.

(E) In determining the number of students who default before the end of such award year, the institution, in calculating the cohort default rate, shall exclude—

(i) any loan on which the borrower has, after the time periods specified in paragraph (2)—
 (I) voluntarily made 6 consecutive payments;
 (II) voluntarily made all payments currently due;
 (III) repaid in full the amount due on the loan; or
 (IV) received a deferment or forbearance, based on a condition that began prior to such time periods;

(ii) any loan which has, after the time periods specified in paragraph (2), been rehabilitated or canceled; and

(iii) any other loan that the Secretary determines should be excluded from such determination.

(F) The Secretary shall prescribe regulations designed to prevent an institution from evading the application to that institution of a cohort default rate determination under this subsection through the use of such measures as branching, consolidation, change of ownership or control or other means as determined by the Secretary.

(2) For purposes of calculating the cohort default rate under this subsection, a loan shall be considered to be in default—

(A) 240 days (in the case of a loan repayable monthly), or

(B) 270 days (in the case of a loan repayable quarterly),

after the borrower fails to make an installment payment when due or to comply with other terms of the promissory note.

(h) Filing deadlines

The Secretary shall, from time to time, set dates before which institutions must file applications for allocations under this part.

(i) Reallocation of excess allocations

(1) In general

(A) If an institution of higher education returns to the Secretary any portion of the sums allocated to such institution under this section for any fiscal year, the Secretary shall reallocate 80 percent of such returned portions to participating institutions in an amount not to exceed such participating institution's excess eligible amounts as determined under paragraph (2).

(B) For the purpose of this subsection, the term "participating institution" means an institution of higher education that—

(i) was a participant in the program assisted under this part in fiscal year 1999; and

(ii) did not receive an allocation under subsection (a) of this section in the fiscal year for which the reallocation determination is made.

(2) Excess eligible amount

For any participating institution, the excess eligible amount is the amount, if any, by which—

(A)(i) that institution's eligible amount (as determined under subsection (b)(3) of this section), divided by (ii) the sum of the eligible amounts of all participating institutions (as determined under paragraph (3)), multiplied by (iii) the amount of funds available for reallocation under this subsection; exceeds

(B) the amount required to be allocated to that institution under subsection (b) of this section.

(3) Remainder

The Secretary shall reallocate the remainder of such returned portions in accordance with regulations of the Secretary.

(4) Allocation reductions

If under paragraph (1) of this subsection an institution returns more than 10 percent of its allocation, the institution's allocation for the next fiscal year shall be reduced by the amount returned. The Secretary may waive this paragraph for a specific institution if the Secretary finds that enforcing it is contrary to the interest of the program.

[Pub. L. No. 89-329, Title IV, § 462, *as added by* Pub. L. No. 99-498, Title IV, § 405(a), 100 Stat. 1440 (Oct. 17, 1986), *and amended by* Pub. L. No. 100-50, § 13(a) to (d), 101 Stat. 348 (June 3, 1987); Pub. L. No. 102-325, Title IV, § 462, 106 Stat. 576 (July 23, 1992); Pub. L. No. 103-208, § 2(f)(1) to (4), 107 Stat. 2470, 2471 (Dec. 20, 1993); Pub. L. No. 105-244, Title IV, § 462(a)(1), (2), (b) to (e), 112 Stat. 1720–1723 (Oct. 7, 1998); Pub. L. No. 110-315, Title IV, § 462, 122 Stat. 3266 (Aug. 14, 2008); Pub. L. No. 111-39, Title IV, § 405(1), 123 Stat. 1947 (July 1, 2009)]

§ 1087cc. Agreements with institutions of higher education

(a) Contents of agreements

An agreement with any institution of higher education for the payment of Federal capital contributions under this part shall—

(1) provide for the establishment and maintenance of a student loan fund for the purpose of this part;

(2) provide for the deposit in such fund of—

(A) Federal capital contributions from funds appropriated under section 1087aa of this title;

(B) a capital contribution by an institution in an amount equal to one-third of the Federal capital contributions described in subparagraph (A);

(C) collections of principal and interest on student loans made from deposited funds;
(D) charges collected pursuant to regulations under section 1087dd(c)(1)(H) of this title; and
(E) any other earnings of the funds;

(3) provide that such student loan fund shall be used only for—
(A) loans to students, in accordance with the provisions of this part;
(B) administrative expenses, as provided in subsection (b) of this section;
(C) capital distributions, as provided in section 1087ff of this title; and
(D) costs of litigation, and other collection costs agreed to by the Secretary in connection with the collection of a loan from the fund (and interest thereon) or a charge assessed pursuant to regulations under section 1087dd(c)(1)(H) of this title;

(4) provide that where a note or written agreement evidencing a loan has been in default despite due diligence on the part of the institution in attempting collection thereon—
(A) if the institution has knowingly failed to maintain an acceptable collection record with respect to such loan, as determined by the Secretary in accordance with criteria established by regulation, the Secretary may—
(i) require the institution to assign such note or agreement to the Secretary, without recompense; and
(ii) apportion any sums collected on such a loan, less an amount not to exceed 30 percent of any sums collected to cover the Secretary's collection costs, among other institutions in accordance with section 1087bb of this title; or
(B) if the institution is not one described in subparagraph (A), the Secretary may allow such institution to refer such note or agreement to the Secretary, without recompense, except that, once every six months, any sums collected on such a loan (less an amount not to exceed 30 percent of any such sums collected to cover the Secretary's collection costs) shall be repaid to such institution and treated as an additional capital contribution under section 1087bb of this title;

(5) provide that, if an institution of higher education determines not to service and collect student loans made available from funds under this part, the institution will assign, at the beginning of the repayment period, notes or evidence of obligations of student loans made from such funds to the Secretary and the Secretary shall apportion any sums collected on such notes or obligations (less an amount not to exceed 30 percent of any such sums collected to cover that Secretary's collection costs) among other institutions in accordance with section 1087bb of this title;

(6) provide that, notwithstanding any other provision of law, the Secretary will provide to the institution any information with respect to the names and addresses of borrowers or other relevant information which is available to the Secretary, from whatever source such information may be derived;

(7) provide assurances that the institution will comply with the provisions of section 1087cc-1 of this title;

(8) provide that the institution of higher education will make loans first to students with exceptional need; and

(9) include such other reasonable provisions as may be necessary to protect the United States from unreasonable risk of loss and as are agreed to by the Secretary and the institution, except that nothing in this paragraph shall be construed to permit the Secretary to require the assignment of loans to the Secretary other than as is provided for in paragraphs (4) and (5).

(b) Administrative expenses

An institution which has entered into an agreement under subsection (a) of this section shall be entitled, for each fiscal year during which it makes student loans from a student loan fund established under such agreement, to a payment in lieu of reimbursement for its expenses in administering its student loan program under this part during such year. Such payment shall be made in accordance with section 1096 of this title.

(c) Cooperative agreements with consumer reporting agencies

(1) For the purpose of promoting responsible repayment of loans made pursuant to this part, the Secretary and each institution of higher education participating in the program under this part shall enter into cooperative agreements with consumer reporting agencies to provide for the exchange of information concerning student borrowers concerning whom the Secretary has received a referral pursuant to section 1087gg of this title and regarding loans held by the Secretary or an institution.

(2) Each cooperative agreement made pursuant to paragraph (1) shall be made in accordance with the requirements of section 1080a of this title except that such agreement shall provide for the disclosure by the Secretary or an institution, as the case may be, to such consumer reporting agencies, with respect to any loan held by the Secretary or the institution, respectively, of—
(A) the date of disbursement and the amount of such loans made to any borrower under this part at the time of disbursement of the loan;
(B) information concerning the repayment and collection of any such loan, including information concerning the status of such loan; and
(C) the date of cancellation of the note upon completion of repayment by the borrower of any such loan, or upon cancellation or discharge of the borrower's obligation on the loan for any reason.

(3) Notwithstanding paragraphs (4) and (5) of subsection (a) of section 1681c of Title 15, a consumer reporting agency may make a report containing information received from the Secretary or an institution regarding the status of a borrower's account on a loan made under this part until the loan is paid in full.

(4)(A) Except as provided in subparagraph (B), an institution of higher education, after consultation with the Secretary and pursuant to the agreements entered into under paragraph (1), shall disclose at least annually to any consumer reporting agency with which the Secretary has such an agreement the information set forth in paragraph (2), and shall disclose promptly to such consumer reporting agency any changes to the information previously disclosed.
(B) The Secretary may promulgate regulations establishing criteria under which an institution of higher education may cease reporting the information described in paragraph (2) before a loan is paid in full.

(5) Each institution of higher education shall notify the appropriate consumer reporting agencies whenever a borrower of a loan that is made and held by the institution and that is in default makes 6 consecutive monthly payments on such loan, for the purpose of encouraging such consumer reporting agencies to update the status of information maintained with respect to that borrower.

(d) Limitation on use of interest bearing accounts
In carrying out the provisions of subsection (a)(9) of this section, the Secretary may not require that any collection agency, collection attorney, or loan servicer collecting loans made under this part deposit amounts collected on such loans in interest bearing accounts, unless such agency, attorney, or servicer holds such amounts for more than 45 days.

(e) Special due diligence rule
In carrying out the provisions of subsection (a)(5) of this section relating to due diligence, the Secretary shall make every effort to ensure that institutions of higher education may use Internal Revenue Service skip-tracing collection procedures on loans made under this part.

[Pub. L. No. 89-329, Title IV, § 463, *as added by* Pub. L. No. 99-498, Title IV, § 405(a), 100 Stat. 1444 (Oct. 17, 1986), *and amended by* Pub. L. No. 100-50, § 13(e), (f), 101 Stat. 349 (June 3, 1987); Pub. L. No. 102-325, Title IV, § 463(a), (b), 106 Stat. 579 (July 23, 1992); Pub. L. No. 103-208, Title II, § 2(f)(5) to (7), 107 Stat. 2471 (Dec. 20, 1993); Pub. L. No. 105-244, Title IV, § 463, 112 Stat. 1724 (Oct. 7, 1998); Pub. L. No. 110-315, Title IV, §§ 432(b)(5), 463, 122 Stat. 3246, 3266 (Aug. 14, 2008); Pub. L. No. 111-39, Title IV, § 405(2), 123 Stat. 1947 (July 1, 2009)]

§ 1087dd. Terms of loans

(a) Terms and conditions
(1) Loans from any student loan fund established pursuant to an agreement under section 1087cc of this title to any student by any institution shall, subject to such conditions, limitations, and requirements as the Secretary shall prescribe by regulation, be made on such terms and conditions as the institution may determine.
(2)(A) Except as provided in paragraph (4), the total of loans made to a student in any academic year or its equivalent by an institution of higher education from a loan fund established pursuant to an agreement under this part shall not exceed—
   (i) $5,500, in the case of a student who has not successfully completed a program of undergraduate education; or
   (ii) $8,000, in the case of a graduate or professional student (as defined in regulations issued by the Secretary).
(B) Except as provided in paragraph (4), the aggregate unpaid principal amount for all loans made to a student by institutions of higher education from loan funds established pursuant to agreements under this part may not exceed—
   (i) $60,000, in the case of any graduate or professional student (as defined by regulations issued by the Secretary, and including any loans from such funds made to such person before such person became a graduate or professional student);
   (ii) $27,500, in the case of a student who has successfully completed 2 years of a program of education leading to a bachelor's degree but who has not completed the work necessary for such a degree (determined under regulations issued by the Secretary), and including any loans from such funds made to such person before such person became such a student; and
   (iii) $11,000, in the case of any other student.

(3) Regulations of the Secretary under paragraph (1) shall be designed to prevent the impairment of the capital student loan funds to the maximum extent practicable and with a view toward the objective of enabling the student to complete his course of study.
(4) In the case of a program of study abroad that is approved for credit by the home institution at which a student is enrolled and that has reasonable costs in excess of the home institution's budget, the annual and aggregate loan limits for the student may exceed the amounts described in paragraphs (2)(A) and (2)(B) by 20 percent.

(b) Demonstration of need and eligibility required
(1) A loan from a student loan fund assisted under this part may be made only to a student who demonstrates financial need in accordance with part E of this subchapter, who meets the requirements of section 1091 of this title, and who provides the institution with the student's drivers license number, if any, at the time of application for the loan. A student who is in default on a loan under this part shall not be eligible for an additional loan under this part unless such loan meets one of the conditions for exclusion under section 1087bb(g)(1)(E) of this title.
(2) If the institution's capital contribution under section 1087bb of this title is directly or indirectly based in part on the financial need demonstrated by students who are (A) attending the institution less than full time, or (B) independent students, then a reasonable portion of the loans made from the institution's student loan fund containing the contribution shall be made available to such students.

(c) Contents of loan agreement
(1) Any agreement between an institution and a student for a loan from a student loan fund assisted under this part—
   (A) shall be evidenced by note or other written instrument which, except as provided in paragraph (2), provides for repayment of the principal amount of the loan, together with interest thereon, in equal installments (or, if the borrower so requests, in graduated periodic installments determined in accordance with such schedules as may be approved by the Secretary) payable quarterly, bimonthly, or monthly, at the option of the institution, over a period beginning nine months after the date on which the student ceases to carry, at an institution of higher education or a comparable institution outside the United States approved for this purpose by the Secretary, at least one-half the normal full-time academic workload, and ending 10 years and 9 months after such date except that such period may begin earlier than 9 months after such date upon the request of the borrower;
   (B) shall include provision for acceleration of repayment of the whole, or any part, of such loan, at the option of the borrower;
   (C)(i) may provide, at the option of the institution, in accordance with regulations of the Secretary, that during the repayment period of the loan, payments of principal and interest by the borrower with respect to all outstanding loans made to the student from a student loan fund assisted under this part shall be at a rate equal to not less than $40 per month, except that the institution may, subject to such regulations, permit a borrower to pay less than $40 per month for a period of not more than one year where necessary to avoid hardship to the borrower, but

without extending the 10-year maximum repayment period provided for in subparagraph (A) of this paragraph; and

(ii) may provide that the total payments by a borrower for a monthly or similar payment period with respect to the aggregate of all loans held by the institution may, when the amount of a monthly or other similar payment is not a multiple of $5, be rounded to the next highest whole dollar amount that is a multiple of $5;

(D) shall provide that the loan shall bear interest, on the unpaid balance of the loan, at the rate of 5 percent per year in the case of any loan made on or after October 1, 1981, except that no interest shall accrue (i) prior to the beginning date of repayment determined under paragraph (2)(A)(i), or (ii) during any period in which repayment is suspended by reason of paragraph (2);

(E) shall provide that the loan shall be made without security and without endorsement;

(F) shall provide that the liability to repay the loan shall be cancelled—

(i) upon the death of the borrower;

(ii) if the borrower becomes permanently and totally disabled as determined in accordance with regulations of the Secretary;

(iii) if the borrower is unable to engage in any substantial gainful activity by reason of any medically determinable physical or mental impairment that can be expected to result in death, has lasted for a continuous period of not less than 60 months, or can be expected to last for a continuous period of not less than 60 months; or

(iv) if the borrower is determined by the Secretary of Veterans Affairs to be unemployable due to a service-connected disability;

(G) shall provide that no note or evidence of obligation may be assigned by the lender, except upon the transfer of the borrower to another institution participating under this part (or, if not so participating, is eligible to do so and is approved by the Secretary for such purpose), to such institution, and except as necessary to carry out section 1087cc(a)(6) of this title;

(H) pursuant to regulations of the Secretary, shall provide for an assessment of a charge with respect to the loan for failure of the borrower to pay all or part of an installment when due, which shall include the expenses reasonably incurred in attempting collection of the loan, to the extent permitted by the Secretary, except that no charge imposed under this subparagraph shall exceed 20 percent of the amount of the monthly payment of the borrower; and

(I) shall contain a notice of the system of disclosure of information concerning default on such loan to consumer reporting agencies under section 1087cc(c) of this title.

(2)(A) No repayment of principal of, or interest on, any loan from a student loan fund assisted under this part shall be required during any period—

(i) during which the borrower—

(I) is pursuing at least a half-time course of study as determined by an eligible institution; or

(II) is pursuing a course of study pursuant to a graduate fellowship program approved by the Secretary, or pursuant to a rehabilitation training program for disabled individuals approved by the Secretary,

except that no borrower shall be eligible for a deferment under this clause, or loan made under this part while serving in a medical internship or residency program;

(ii) not in excess of 3 years during which the borrower is seeking and unable to find full-time employment;

(iii) during which the borrower—

(I) is serving on active duty during a war or other military operation or national emergency; or

(II) is performing qualifying National Guard duty during a war or other military operation or national emergency,

and for the 180-day period following the demobilization date for the service described in subclause (I) or (II);

(iv) not in excess of 3 years for any reason which the lender determines, in accordance with regulations prescribed by the Secretary under section 1085(o) of this title, has caused or will cause the borrower to have an economic hardship; or

(v) during which the borrower is engaged in service described in section 1087ee(a)(2) of this title;

and provides that any such period shall not be included in determining the 10-year period described in subparagraph (A) of paragraph (1).

(B) No repayment of principal of, or interest on, any loan for any period described in subparagraph (A) shall begin until 6 months after the completion of such period.

(C) An individual with an outstanding loan balance who meets the eligibility criteria for a deferment described in subparagraph (A) as in effect on October 7, 1998, shall be eligible for deferment under this paragraph notwithstanding any contrary provision of the promissory note under which the loan or loans were made, and notwithstanding any amendment (or effective date provision relating to any amendment) to this section made prior to the date of such deferment.

(3)(A) The Secretary is authorized, when good cause is shown, to extend, in accordance with regulations, the 10-year maximum repayment period provided for in subparagraph (A) of paragraph (1) with respect to individual loans.

(B) Pursuant to uniform criteria established by the Secretary, the repayment period for any student borrower who during the repayment period is a low-income individual may be extended for a period not to exceed 10 years and the repayment schedule may be adjusted to reflect the income of that individual.

(4) The repayment period for a loan made under this part shall begin on the day immediately following the expiration of the period, specified in paragraph (1)(A), after the student ceases to carry the required academic workload, unless the borrower requests and is granted a repayment schedule that provides for repayment to commence at an earlier point in time, and shall exclude any period of authorized deferment, forbearance, or cancellation.

(5) The institution may elect—

(A) to add the amount of any charge imposed under paragraph (1)(H) to the principal amount of the loan as of the first day after the day on which the installment was due and to notify the borrower of the assessment of the charge; or

(B) to make the amount of the charge payable to the institution not later than the due date of the next installment.

(6) Requests for deferment of repayment of loans under this part by students engaged in graduate or post-graduate fellowship-supported study (such as pursuant to a Fulbright grant) outside the United States shall be approved until completion of the period of the fellowship.

(7) There shall be excluded from the 9-month period that begins on the date on which a student ceases to carry at least one-half the normal full-time academic workload (as described in paragraph (1)(A)) any period not to exceed 3 years during which a borrower who is a member of a reserve component of the Armed Forces named in section 10101 of Title 10 is called or ordered to active duty for a period of more than 30 days (as defined in section 101(d)(2) of such title). Such period of exclusion shall include the period necessary to resume enrollment at the borrower's next available regular enrollment period.

(d) Availability of loan fund to all eligible students

An agreement under this part for payment of Federal capital contributions shall include provisions designed to make loans from the student loan fund established pursuant to such agreement reasonably available (to the extent of the available funds in such fund) to all eligible students in such institutions in need thereof.

(e) Forbearance

(1) The Secretary shall ensure that, as documented in accordance with paragraph (2), an institution of higher education shall grant a borrower forbearance of principal and interest or principal only, renewable at 12-month intervals for a period not to exceed 3 years, on such terms as are otherwise consistent with the regulations issued by the Secretary and agreed upon in writing by the parties to the loan, if—

(A) the borrower's debt burden equals or exceeds 20 percent of such borrower's gross income;

(B) the institution determines that the borrower should qualify for forbearance for other reasons; or

(C) the borrower is eligible for interest payments to be made on such loan for service in the Armed Forces under section 2174 of Title 10 and, pursuant to that eligibility, the interest on such loan is being paid under subsection (j) of this section, except that the form of a forbearance under this paragraph shall be a temporary cessation of all payments on the loan other than payments of interest on the loan that are made under subsection (j) of this section.

(2) For the purpose of paragraph (1), the terms of forbearance agreed to by the parties shall be documented by—

(A) confirming the agreement of the borrower by notice to the borrower from the institution of higher education; and

(B) recording the terms in the borrower's file.

(f) Special repayment rule authority

(1) Subject to such restrictions as the Secretary may prescribe to protect the interest of the United States, in order to encourage repayment of loans made under this part which are in default, the Secretary may, in the agreement entered into under this part, authorize an institution of higher education to compromise on the repayment of such defaulted loans in accordance with paragraph (2). The Federal share of the compromise repayment shall bear the same relation to the institution's share of such compromise repayment as the Federal capital contribution to the institution's loan fund under this part bears to the institution's capital contribution to such fund.

(2) No compromise repayment of a defaulted loan as authorized by paragraph (1) may be made unless the student borrower pays—

(A) 90 percent of the loan under this part;

(B) the interest due on such loan; and

(C) any collection fees due on such loan;

in a lump sum payment.

(g) Discharge

(1) In general

If a student borrower who received a loan made under this part on or after January 1, 1986, is unable to complete the program in which such student is enrolled due to the closure of the institution, then the Secretary shall discharge the borrower's liability on the loan (including the interest and collection fees) and shall subsequently pursue any claim available to such borrower against the institution and the institution's affiliates and principals, or settle the loan obligation pursuant to the financial responsibility standards described in section 1099c(c) of this title.

(2) Assignment

A borrower whose loan has been discharged pursuant to this subsection shall be deemed to have assigned to the United States the right to a loan refund in an amount that does not exceed the amount discharged against the institution and the institution's affiliates and principals.

(3) Eligibility for additional assistance

The period during which a student was unable to complete a course of study due to the closing of the institution shall not be considered for purposes of calculating the student's period of eligibility for additional assistance under this subchapter and part C of subchapter I of chapter 34 of Title 42.

(4) Special rule

A borrower whose loan has been discharged pursuant to this subsection shall not be precluded, because of that discharge, from receiving additional grant, loan, or work assistance under this subchapter and part C of subchapter I of chapter 34 of Title 42 for which the borrower would be otherwise eligible (but for the default on the discharged loan). The amount discharged under this subsection shall be treated as an amount canceled under section 1087ee(a) of this title.

(5) Reporting

The Secretary or institution, as the case may be, shall report to consumer reporting agencies with respect to loans that have been discharged pursuant to this subsection.

(h) Rehabilitation of loans

(1) Rehabilitation

(A) In general

If the borrower of a loan made under this part who has defaulted on the loan makes 9 on-time, consecutive, monthly payments of amounts owed on the loan, as determined by the institution, or by the Secretary in the case of a loan held by the Secretary, the loan shall be considered rehabilitated, and the institution that made that loan (or the Secretary, in the case of a loan held by the Secretary) shall request that any consumer reporting agency to which the default was reported remove the default from the borrower's credit history.

(B) Comparable conditions

As long as the borrower continues to make scheduled repayments on a loan rehabilitated under this paragraph, the rehabilitated loan shall be subject to the same terms and conditions, and qualify for the same benefits and privileges, as other loans made under this part.

(C) Additional assistance

The borrower of a rehabilitated loan shall not be precluded by section 1091 of this title from receiving additional grant, loan, or work assistance under this subchapter and part C of subchapter I of chapter 34 of Title 42 (for which the borrower is otherwise eligible) on the basis of defaulting on the loan prior to such rehabilitation.

(D) Limitations

A borrower only once may obtain the benefit of this paragraph with respect to rehabilitating a loan under this part.

(2) Restoration of eligibility

If the borrower of a loan made under this part who has defaulted on that loan makes 6 ontime, consecutive, monthly payments of amounts owed on such loan, the borrower's eligibility for grant, loan, or work assistance under this subchapter and part C of subchapter I of chapter 34 of Title 42 shall be restored to the extent that the borrower is otherwise eligible. A borrower only once may obtain the benefit of this paragraph with respect to restored eligibility.

(i) Incentive repayment program

(1) In general

Each institution of higher education may establish, with the approval of the Secretary, an incentive repayment program designed to reduce default and to replenish student loan funds established under this part. Each such incentive repayment program may—

(A) offer a reduction of the interest rate on a loan on which the borrower has made 48 consecutive, monthly repayments, but in no event may the rate be reduced by more than 1 percent;

(B) provide for a discount on the balance owed on a loan on which the borrower pays the principal and interest in full prior to the end of the applicable repayment period, but in no event may the discount exceed 5 percent of the unpaid principal balance due on the loan at the time the early repayment is made; and

(C) include such other incentive repayment options as the institution determines will carry out the objectives of this subsection.

(2) Limitation

No incentive repayment option under an incentive repayment program authorized by this subsection may be paid for with Federal funds, including any Federal funds from the student loan fund, or with institutional funds from the student loan fund.

(j) Armed Forces student loan interest payment program

(1) Authority

Using funds received by transfer to the Secretary under section 2174 of Title 10 for the payment of interest on a loan made under this part to a member of the Armed Forces, the Secretary shall pay the interest on the loan as due for a period not in excess of 36 consecutive months. The Secretary may not pay interest on such a loan out of any funds other than funds that have been so transferred.

(2) Forbearance

During the period in which the Secretary is making payments on a loan under paragraph (1), the institution of higher education shall grant the borrower forbearance in accordance with subsection (e)(1)(C) of this section.

(k) The Secretary may develop such additional safeguards as the Secretary determines necessary to prevent fraud and abuse in the cancellation of liability under subsection (c)(1)(F). Notwithstanding subsection (c)(1)(F), the Secretary may promulgate regulations to resume collection on loans cancelled under subsection (c)(1)(F) in any case in which—

(1) a borrower received a cancellation of liability under subsection (c)(1)(F) and after the cancellation the borrower—

(A) receives a loan made, insured, or guaranteed under this subchapter and part C of subchapter I of chapter 34 of Title 42; or

(B) has earned income in excess of the poverty line; or

(2) the Secretary determines necessary.

[Pub. L. No. 89-329, Title IV, § 464, *as added by* Pub. L. No. 99-498, Title IV, § 405(a), 100 Stat. 1448 (Oct. 17, 1986), *and amended by* Pub. L. No. 100-50, § 13(i), 101 Stat. 349 (June 3, 1987); Pub. L. No. 100-369, § 7(c), July 18, 1988, 102 Stat. 837; Pub. L. No. 101-239, Title II, § 2002(a)(3), 103 Stat. 2111 (Dec. 19, 1989); Pub. L. No. 102-325, Title IV, § 464, 106 Stat. 580 (July 23, 1992); Pub. L. No. 103-208, § 2(f)(9) to (11), 107 Stat. 2471 (Dec. 20, 1993); Pub. L. No. 105-244, Title IV, § 464, 112 Stat. 1725 (Oct. 7, 1998); Pub. L. No. 107-314, Div. A, Title VI, § 651(d), 116 Stat. 2580 (Dec. 2, 2002); Pub. L. No. 109-171, Title VIII, § 8007(c), 120 Stat. 160 (Feb. 8, 2006); Pub. L. No. 110-84, Title II, § 202(c), 121 Stat. 792 (Sept. 27, 2007); Pub. L. No. 110-315, Title IV, §§ 432(b)(7), 464, 122 Stat. 3246, 3266 (Aug. 14, 2008); Pub. L. No. 111-39, Title IV, § 405(4), 123 Stat. 1947 (July 1, 2009)]

* * *

A.4 General Provisions

20 U.S.C. sec.

* * *

1091. Student eligibility.
1091a. Statute of limitations, and State court judgments.
1091b. Institutional refunds.

* * *

1094. Program participation agreements

* * *

1095a. Wage garnishment requirements.

* * *

§ 1091. Student eligibility

(a) In general

In order to receive any grant, loan, or work assistance under this subchapter and part C of subchapter I of chapter 34 of Title 42, a student must—

(1) be enrolled or accepted for enrollment in a degree, certificate, or other program (including a program of study abroad

approved for credit by the eligible institution at which such student is enrolled) leading to a recognized educational credential at an institution of higher education that is an eligible institution in accordance with the provisions of section 1094 of this title, except as provided in subsections (b)(3) and (b)(4) of this section, and not be enrolled in an elementary or secondary school;

(2) if the student is presently enrolled at an institution, be maintaining satisfactory progress in the course of study the student is pursuing in accordance with the provisions of subsection (c) of this section;

(3) not owe a refund on grants previously received at any institution under this subchapter and part C of subchapter I of chapter 34 of Title 42, or be in default on any loan from a student loan fund at any institution provided for in part D of this subchapter, or a loan made, insured, or guaranteed by the Secretary under this subchapter and part C of subchapter I of chapter 34 of Title 42 for attendance at any institution;

(4) file with the Secretary, as part of the original financial aid application process, a certification, which need not be notarized, but which shall include—

(A) a statement of educational purpose stating that the money attributable to such grant, loan, or loan guarantee will be used solely for expenses related to attendance or continued attendance at such institution; and

(B) such student's social security number;

(5) be a citizen or national of the United States, a permanent resident of the United States, or able to provide evidence from the Immigration and Naturalization Service that he or she is in the United States for other than a temporary purpose with the intention of becoming a citizen or permanent resident; and

(6) if the student has been convicted of, or has pled nolo contendere or guilty to, a crime involving fraud in obtaining funds under this subchapter and part C of subchapter I of chapter 34 of Title 42, have completed the repayment of such funds to the Secretary, or to the holder in the case of a loan under this subchapter and part C of subchapter I of chapter 34 of Title 42 obtained by fraud.

(b) **Eligibility for student loans**

(1) In order to be eligible to receive any loan under this subchapter and part C of subchapter I of chapter 34 of Title 42 (other than a loan under section 1078-2 or 1078-3 of this title, or under section 1078-8 of this title pursuant to an exercise of discretion under section 1087tt of this title) for any period of enrollment, a student who is not a graduate or professional student (as defined in regulations of the Secretary), and who is enrolled in a program at an institution which has a participation agreement with the Secretary to make awards under subpart 1 of part A of this subchapter, shall—

(A)(i) have received a determination of eligibility or ineligibility for a Pell Grant under such subpart 1 for such period of enrollment; and

(ii) if determined to be eligible, have filed an application for a Pell Grant for such enrollment period; or

(B) have (i) filed an application with the Pell Grant processor for such institution for such enrollment period, and have (ii) received from the financial aid administrator of the institution a preliminary determination of the student's eligibility or ineligibility for a grant under such subpart 1.

(2) In order to be eligible to receive any loan under section 1078-1[1] of this title for any period of enrollment, a student shall—

(A) have received a determination of need for a loan under section 1078(a)(2)(B) of this title;

(B) if determined to have need for a loan under section 1078 of this title, have applied for such a loan; and

(C) has applied for a loan under section 1078-8 of this title, if such student is eligible to apply for such a loan.

(3) A student who—

(A) is carrying at least one-half the normal full-time work load for the course of study that the student is pursuing, as determined by an eligible institution, and

(B) is enrolled in a course of study necessary for enrollment in a program leading to a degree or certificate,

shall be, notwithstanding paragraph (1) of subsection (a) of this section, eligible to apply for loans under part B or C of this subchapter. The eligibility described in this paragraph shall be restricted to one 12-month period.

(4) A student who—

(A) is carrying at least one-half the normal full-time work load for the course of study the student is pursuing, as determined by the institution, and

(B) is enrolled or accepted for enrollment in a program at an eligible institution necessary for a professional credential or certification from a State that is required for employment as a teacher in an elementary or secondary school in that State,

shall be, notwithstanding paragraph (1) of subsection (a) of this section, eligible to apply for loans under part B, C, or D of this subchapter or work-study assistance under part C of subchapter I of chapter 34 of Title 42.

(5) Notwithstanding any other provision of this subsection, no incarcerated student is eligible to receive a loan under this subchapter and part C of subchapter I of chapter 34 of Title 42.

(c) **Satisfactory progress**

(1) For the purpose of subsection (a)(2) of this section, a student is maintaining satisfactory progress if—

(A) the institution at which the student is in attendance, reviews the progress of the student at the end of each academic year, or its equivalent, as determined by the institution, and

---

1 *Editor's note:* Section 1078-1 of this title, referred to in subsec. (b)(2), was repealed by Pub. L. 103-66, except with respect to loans provided under that section prior to Aug. 10, 1993. A new section 1078-1, relating to voluntary flexible agreements with guaranty agencies, was enacted by Pub. L. 105-244.

Subsec. (h) of this section, referred to in subsec. (i), was redesignated subsec. (g) of this section by Pub. L. 103-208, § 2(h)(25), Dec. 20, 1993, 107 Stat. 2477.

The Military Selective Service Act, referred to in subsec. (n), is Act June 24, 1948, c. 625, 62 Stat. 604, as amended, which is classified principally to section 451 *et seq.* of the Appendix to Title 50. For complete classification, see section 451 of the Appendix to Title 50 and Tables.

This chapter, referred to in subsec. (o), was in the original "this Act", meaning Pub. L. 89-329, as amended, known as the Higher Education Act of 1965. For complete classification of this Act to the Code, see Short Title note set out under section 1001 of this title and Tables.

(B) the student has a cumulative C average, or its equivalent or academic standing consistent with the requirements for graduation, as determined by the institution, at the end of the second such academic year.

(2) Whenever a student fails to meet the eligibility requirements of subsection (a)(2) of this section as a result of the application of this subsection and subsequent to that failure the student has academic standing consistent with the requirements for graduation, as determined by the institution, for any grading period, the student may, subject to this subsection, again be eligible under subsection (a)(2) of this section for a grant, loan, or work assistance under this subchapter and part C of subchapter I of chapter 34 of Title 42.

(3) Any institution of higher education at which the student is in attendance may waive the provisions of paragraph (1) or paragraph (2) of this subsection for undue hardship based on—

(A) the death of a relative of the student,

(B) the personal injury or illness of the student, or

(C) special circumstances as determined by the institution.

(d) Students who are not high school graduates

In order for a student who does not have a certificate of graduation from a school providing secondary education, or the recognized equivalent of such certificate, to be eligible for any assistance under subparts 1, 3, and 4 of part A and parts B, C, and D of this subchapter and part C of subchapter I of chapter 34 of Title 42, the student shall meet one of the following standards:

(1) The student shall take an independently administered examination and shall achieve a score, specified by the Secretary, demonstrating that such student can benefit from the education or training being offered. Such examination shall be approved by the Secretary on the basis of compliance with such standards for development, administration, and scoring as the Secretary may prescribe in regulations.

(2) The student shall be determined as having the ability to benefit from the education or training in accordance with such process as the State shall prescribe. Any such process described or approved by a State for the purposes of this section shall be effective 6 months after the date of submission to the Secretary unless the Secretary disapproves such process. In determining whether to approve or disapprove such process, the Secretary shall take into account the effectiveness of such process in enabling students without high school diplomas or the equivalent thereof to benefit from the instruction offered by institutions utilizing such process, and shall also take into account the cultural diversity, economic circumstances, and educational preparation of the populations served by the institutions.

(3) The student has completed a secondary school education in a home school setting that is treated as a home school or private school under State law.

(4) The student shall be determined by the institution of higher education as having the ability to benefit from the education or training offered by the institution of higher education upon satisfactory completion of six credit hours or the equivalent coursework that are applicable toward a degree or certificate offered by the institution of higher education.

(e) Certification for GSL eligibility

Each eligible institution may certify student eligibility for a loan by an eligible lender under part B of this subchapter prior to completing the review for accuracy of the information submitted by the applicant required by regulations issued under this subchapter and part C of subchapter I of chapter 34 of Title 42, if—

(1) checks for the loans are mailed to the eligible institution prior to disbursements;

(2) the disbursement is not made until the review is complete; and

(3) the eligible institution has no evidence or documentation on which the institution may base a determination that the information submitted by the applicant is incorrect.

(f) Loss of eligibility for violation of loan limits

(1) No student shall be eligible to receive any grant, loan, or work assistance under this subchapter and part C of subchapter I of chapter 34 of Title 42 if the eligible institution determines that the student fraudulently borrowed in violation of the annual loan limits under part B, part C, or part D of this subchapter in the same academic year, or if the student fraudulently borrowed in excess of the aggregate maximum loan limits under such part B, part C, or part D.

(2) If the institution determines that the student inadvertently borrowed amounts in excess of such annual or aggregate maximum loan limits, such institution shall allow the student to repay any amount borrowed in excess of such limits prior to certifying the student's eligibility for further assistance under this subchapter and part C of subchapter I of chapter 34 of Title 42.

(g) Verification of immigration status

(1) In general

The Secretary shall implement a system under which the statements and supporting documentation, if required, of an individual declaring that such individual is in compliance with the requirements of subsection (a)(5) of this section shall be verified prior to the individual's receipt of a grant, loan, or work assistance under this subchapter and part C of subchapter I of chapter 34 of Title 42.

(2) Special rule

The documents collected and maintained by an eligible institution in the admission of a student to the institution may be used by the student in lieu of the documents used to establish both employment authorization and identity under section 1324a(b)(1)(B) of Title 8 to verify eligibility to participate in work-study programs under part C of subchapter I of chapter 34 of Title 42.

(3) Verification mechanisms

The Secretary is authorized to verify such statements and supporting documentation through a data match, using an automated or other system, with other Federal agencies that may be in possession of information relevant to such statements and supporting documentation.

(4) Review

In the case of such an individual who is not a citizen or national of the United States, if the statement described in paragraph (1) is submitted but the documentation required under paragraph (2) is not presented or if the documentation required under paragraph (2)(A) is presented but such documentation is not verified under paragraph (3)—

(A) the institution—

(i) shall provide a reasonable opportunity to submit to the institution evidence indicating a satisfactory immigration status, and

(ii) may not delay, deny, reduce, or terminate the individual's eligibility for the grant, loan, or work assistance on the basis of the individual's immigration status until such a reasonable opportunity has been provided; and

(B) if there are submitted documents which the institution determines constitute reasonable evidence indicating such status—

(i) the institution shall transmit to the Immigration and Naturalization Service either photostatic or other similar copies of such documents, or information from such documents, as specified by the Immigration and Naturalization Service, for official verification,

(ii) pending such verification, the institution may not delay, deny, reduce, or terminate the individual's eligibility for the grant, loan, or work assistance on the basis of the individual's immigration status, and

(iii) the institution shall not be liable for the consequences of any action, delay, or failure of the Service to conduct such verification.

(h) Limitations of enforcement actions against institutions
The Secretary shall not take any compliance, disallowance, penalty, or other regulatory action against an institution of higher education with respect to any error in the institution's determination to make a student eligible for a grant, loan, or work assistance based on citizenship or immigration status—

(1) if the institution has provided such eligibility based on a verification of satisfactory immigration status by the Immigration and Naturalization Service,

(2) because the institution, under subsection (g)(4)(A)(i) of this section, was required to provide a reasonable opportunity to submit documentation, or

(3) because the institution, under subsection (g)(4)(B)(i) of this section, was required to wait for the response of the Immigration and Naturalization Service to the institution's request for official verification of the immigration status of the student.

(*i*) Validity of loan guarantees for loan payments made before immigration status verification completed
Notwithstanding subsection (h)[2] of this section, if—

(1) a guaranty is made under this subchapter and part C of subchapter I of chapter 34 of Title 42 for a loan made with respect to an individual,

---

2 *Editor's note:* Section 1078-1 of this title, referred to in subsec. (b)(2), was repealed by Pub. L. 103-66, except with respect to loans provided under that section prior to Aug. 10, 1993. A new section 1078-1, relating to voluntary flexible agreements with guaranty agencies, was enacted by Pub. L. 105-244.

Subsec. (h) of this section, referred to in subsec. (i), was redesignated subsec. (g) of this section by Pub. L. 103-208, § 2(h)(25), Dec. 20, 1993, 107 Stat. 2477.

The Military Selective Service Act, referred to in subsec. (n), is Act June 24, 1948, c. 625, 62 Stat. 604, as amended, which is classified principally to section 451 *et seq.* of the Appendix to Title 50. For complete classification, see section 451 of the Appendix to Title 50 and Tables.

This chapter, referred to in subsec. (o), was in the original "this Act", meaning Pub. L. 89-329, as amended, known as the Higher Education Act of 1965. For complete classification of this Act to the Code, see Short Title note set out under section 1001 of this title and Tables.

* * *

(2) at the time the guaranty is entered into, the provisions of subsection (h) of this section had been complied with,

(3) amounts are paid under the loan subject to such guaranty, and

(4) there is a subsequent determination that, because of an unsatisfactory immigration status, the individual is not eligible for the loan,

the official of the institution making the determination shall notify and instruct the entity making the loan to cease further payments under the loan, but such guaranty shall not be voided or otherwise nullified with respect to such payments made before the date the entity receives the notice.

(j) Repealed. Pub. L. No. 110-315, Title IV, § 485(a)(4), Aug. 14, 2008, 122 Stat. 3288

(k) Special rule for correspondence courses
A student shall not be eligible to receive grant, loan, or work assistance under this subchapter and part C of subchapter I of chapter 34 of Title 42 for a correspondence course unless such course is part of a program leading to an associate, bachelor or graduate degree.

(*l*) Courses offered through telecommunications
(1) Relation to correspondence courses.—
(A) In general.
A student enrolled in a course of instruction at an institution of higher education that is offered principally through distance education and leads to a recognized certificate, or recognized associate, recognized baccalaureate, or recognized graduate degree, conferred by such institution, shall not be considered to be enrolled in correspondence courses.

(B) Exception.
An institution of higher education referred to in subparagraph (A) shall not include an institution or school described in section 3(3)(C) of the Carl D. Perkins Career and Technical Education Act of 2006.

(2) Reductions of financial aid.
A student's eligibility to receive grants, loans, or work assistance under this title shall be reduced if a financial aid officer determines under the discretionary authority provided in section 479A that distance education results in a substantially reduced cost of attendance to such student.

(3) Special rule.
For award years beginning prior to July 1, 2008, the Secretary shall not take any compliance, disallowance, penalty, or other action based on a violation of this subsection against a student or an eligible institution when such action arises out of such institution's prior award of student assistance under this title if the institution demonstrates to the satisfaction of the Secretary that its course of instruction would have been in conformance with the requirements of this subsection.

(m) Students with a first baccalaureate or professional degree
A student shall not be ineligible for assistance under parts B, C, and D of this subchapter and part C of subchapter I of chapter 34 of Title 42 because such student has previously received a baccalaureate or professional degree.

(n) Data base matching
To enforce the Selective Service registration provisions of section 12(f) of the Military Selective Service Act (50 U.S.C. App. 462(f)),

the Secretary shall conduct data base matches with the Selective Service, using common demographic data elements. Appropriate confirmation, through an application output document or through other means, of any person's registration shall fulfill the requirement to file a separate statement of compliance. In the absence of a confirmation from such data matches, an institution may also use data or documents that support either the student's registration, or the absence of a registration requirement for the student, to fulfill the requirement to file a separate statement of compliance. The mechanism for reporting the resolution of nonconfirmed matches shall be prescribed by the Secretary in regulations.

(o) Study abroad
Nothing in this chapter shall be construed to limit or otherwise prohibit access to study abroad programs approved by the home institution at which a student is enrolled. An otherwise eligible student who is engaged in a program of study abroad approved for academic credit by the home institution at which the student is enrolled shall be eligible to receive grant, loan, or work assistance under this subchapter and part C of subchapter I of chapter 34 of Title 42, without regard to whether such study abroad program is required as part of the student's degree program.

(p) Verification of social security number
The Secretary of Education, in cooperation with the Commissioner of the Social Security Administration, shall verify any social security number provided by a student to an eligible institution under subsection (a)(4) of this section and shall enforce the following conditions:

(1) Except as provided in paragraphs (2) and (3), an institution shall not deny, reduce, delay, or terminate a student's eligibility for assistance under this part because social security number verification is pending.

(2) If there is a determination by the Secretary that the social security number provided to an eligible institution by a student is incorrect, the institution shall deny or terminate the student's eligibility for any grant, loan, or work assistance under this subchapter and part C of subchapter I of chapter 34 of Title 42 until such time as the student provides documented evidence of a social security number that is determined by the institution to be correct.

(3) If there is a determination by the Secretary that the social security number provided to an eligible institution by a student is incorrect, and a correct social security number cannot be provided by such student, and a loan has been guaranteed for such student under part B of this subchapter, the institution shall notify and instruct the lender and guaranty agency making and guaranteeing the loan, respectively, to cease further disbursements of the loan, but such guaranty shall not be voided or otherwise nullified with respect to such disbursements made before the date that the lender and the guaranty agency receives such notice.

(4) Nothing in this subsection shall permit the Secretary to take any compliance, disallowance, penalty, or other regulatory action against—

(A) any institution of higher education with respect to any error in a social security number, unless such error was a result of fraud on the part of the institution; or

(B) any student with respect to any error in a social security number, unless such error was a result of fraud on the part of the student.

(q) Verification of income data
(1) Matching with IRS
The Secretary, in cooperation with the Secretary of the Treasury, is authorized to obtain from the Internal Revenue Service such information reported on Federal income tax returns by applicants, or by any other person whose financial information is required to be provided on the Federal student financial aid application, as the Secretary determines is necessary for the purpose of—

(A) prepopulating the Federal student financial aid application described in section 483; or

(B) verifying the information reported on such student financial aid applications.

(2) Consent
The Secretary may require that applicants for financial assistance under this subchapter and part C of subchapter I of chapter 34 of Title 42 provide a consent to the disclosure of the data described in paragraph (1) as a condition of the student receiving assistance under this subchapter and part C of subchapter I of chapter 34 of Title 42. The parents of an applicant, in the case of a dependent student, or the spouse of an applicant, in the case of an applicant who is married but files separately, may also be required to provide consent as a condition of the student receiving assistance under this subchapter and part C of subchapter I of chapter 34 of Title 42.

(r) Suspension of eligibility for drug-related offenses
(1) In general
A student who is convicted of any offense under any Federal or State law involving the possession or sale of a controlled substance for conduct that occurred during a period of enrollment for which the student was receiving any grant, loan, or work assistance under this subchapter and part C of subchapter I of chapter 34 of Title 42 shall not be eligible to receive any grant, loan, or work assistance under this subchapter and part C of subchapter I of chapter 34 of Title 42 from the date of that conviction for the period of time specified in the following table:

If convicted of an offense involving:	
The possession of a controlled substance:	**Ineligibility period is:**
First offense	1 year
Second offense	2 years
Third offense	Indefinite
The sale of a controlled substance:	**Ineligibility period is:**
First offense	2 years
Second Offense	Indefinite

(2) Rehabilitation
A student whose eligibility has been suspended under paragraph (1) may resume eligibility before the end of the ineligibility period determined under such paragraph if—

(A) the student satisfactorily completes a drug rehabilitation program that—

(i) complies with such criteria as the Secretary shall prescribe in regulations for purposes of this paragraph; and

(ii) includes two unannounced drug tests;

(B) the student successfully passes two unannounced drug tests conducted by a drug rehabilitation program that complies with such criteria as the Secretary shall prescribe in regulations for purposes of subparagraph (A)(i); or

(C) the conviction is reversed, set aside, or otherwise rendered nugatory.

(3) Definitions

In this subsection, the term "controlled substance" has the meaning given the term in section 802(6) of Title 21.

(s) Students with intellectual disabilities

(1) Definitions

In this subsection the terms "comprehensive transition and postsecondary program for students with intellectual disabilities" and "student with an intellectual disability" have the meanings given the terms in section 1140 of this title.

(2) Requirements

Notwithstanding subsections (a), (c), and (d), in order to receive any grant or work assistance under section 1070a of this title, subpart 3 of part A of this subchapter, or part C of subchapter I of chapter 34 of Title 42, a student with an intellectual disability shall—

(A) be enrolled or accepted for enrollment in a comprehensive transition and postsecondary program for students with intellectual disabilities at an institution of higher education;

(B) be maintaining satisfactory progress in the program as determined by the institution, in accordance with standards established by the institution; and

(C) meet the requirements of paragraphs (3), (4), (5), and (6) of subsection (a).

(3) Authority

Notwithstanding any other provision of law unless such provision is enacted with specific reference to this section, the Secretary is authorized to waive any statutory provision applicable to the student financial assistance programs under section 1070a of this title, subpart 3 of part A of this subchapter, or part C of subchapter I of chapter 34 of Title 42 (other than a provision of part E of this subchapter related to such a program), or any institutional eligibility provisions of this subchapter and part C of subchapter I of chapter 34 of Title 42, as the Secretary determines necessary to ensure that programs enrolling students with intellectual disabilities otherwise determined to be eligible under this subsection may receive such financial assistance.

(4) Regulations

Notwithstanding regulations applicable to grant or work assistance awards made under section 1070a of this title, subpart 3 of part A of this subchapter, and part C of subchapter I of chapter 34 of Title 42 (other than a regulation under part E of this subchapter related to such an award), including with respect to eligible programs, instructional time, credit status, and enrollment status as described in section 1088 of this title, the Secretary shall promulgate regulations allowing programs enrolling students with intellectual disabilities otherwise determined to be eligible under this subsection to receive such awards.

(t) Data analysis on access to federal student aid for certain populations

(1) Development of the system.

Within one year of August 14, 2008, the Secretary shall analyze data from the FAFSA containing information regarding the number, characteristics, and circumstances of students denied Federal student aid based on a drug conviction while receiving Federal aid.

(2) Results from analysis.

The results from the analysis of such information shall be made available on a continuous basis via the Department website and the Digest of Education Statistics.

(3) Data updating.

The data analyzed under this subsection shall be updated at the beginning of each award year and at least one additional time during such award year.

(4) Report to Congress.

The Secretary shall prepare and submit to the authorizing committees, in each fiscal year, a report describing the results obtained by the establishment and operation of the data system authorized by this subsection.

[Pub. L. No. 89-329, Title IV, § 484, *as added by* Pub. L. No. 99-498, Title IV, § 407(a), 100 Stat. 1479 (Oct. 17, 1986), *and amended by* Pub. L. No. 99-603, Title I, § 121(a)(3), 100 Stat. 3388 (Nov. 6, 1986); Pub. L. No. 100-50, § 15(7) to (9), 101 Stat. 356, 357 (June 3, 1987); Pub. L. No. 100-369, §§ 1, 2, 6, 102 Stat. 835, 836 (July 18, 1988); Pub. L. No. 100-525, § 2(g), 102 Stat. 2611 (Oct. 24, 1988); Pub. L. No. 101-508, Title III, § 3005(a), 104 Stat. 1388-27 (Nov. 5, 1990); Pub. L. No. 102-26, § 2(b), (c)(2), (d)(2)(A), 105 Stat. 123, 124 (Apr. 9, 1991); Pub. L. No. 102-73, Title VIII, § 801(a), 105 Stat. 359 (July 25, 1991); Pub. L. No. 102-325, Title IV, § 484(a), (b)(1), (c) to (h), 106 Stat. 615 to 619 (July 23, 1992); Pub. L. No. 103-208, § 2(h)(13) to (25), 107 Stat. 2476, 2477 (Dec. 20, 1993); Pub. L. No. 103-382, Title III, § 360A, 108 Stat. 3969 (Oct. 20, 1994); Pub. L. No. 104-208, Div. C, Title V, § 507(b), 110 Stat. 3009-673 (Sept. 30, 1996); Pub. L. No. 105-244, Title IV, § 483(a) to (f)(1), 112 Stat. 1735, 1736 (Oct. 7, 1998); Pub. L. No. 109-171, Title VIII, §§ 8020(c), 8021, 120 Stat. 178 (Feb. 8, 2006); Pub. L. No. 109-270, § 2(c)(2), 120 Stat. 746 (Aug. 12, 2006); Pub. L. No. 110-315, Title IV, § 485(a)(3), (4), (8), 122 Stat. 3287, 3288, 3289 (Aug. 14, 2008); Pub. L. No. 111-39, Title IV, § 407(b)(4), 123 Stat. 1950 (July 1, 2009)]

§ 1091a. Statute of limitations, and State court judgments

(a) In general

(1) It is the purpose of this subsection to ensure that obligations to repay loans and grant overpayments are enforced without regard to any Federal or State statutory, regulatory, or administrative limitation on the period within which debts may be enforced.

(2) Notwithstanding any other provision of statute, regulation, or administrative limitation, no limitation shall terminate the period within which suit may be filed, a judgment may be enforced, or an offset, garnishment, or other action initiated or taken by—

(A) an institution that receives funds under this subchapter and part C of subchapter I of chapter 34 of Title 42 that is seeking to collect a refund due from a student on a grant made, or work assistance awarded, under this subchapter and part C of subchapter I of chapter 34 of Title 42;

(B) a guaranty agency that has an agreement with the Secretary under section 1078(c) of this title that is seeking the repayment of the amount due from a borrower on a loan made under part B of this subchapter after such guaranty agency reimburses the previous holder of the loan for its loss on account of the default of the borrower;

(C) an institution that has an agreement with the Secretary pursuant to section 1087c or 1087cc(a) of this title that is seeking the repayment of the amount due from a borrower on a loan made under part C or D of this subchapter after the default of the borrower on such loan; or

(D) the Secretary, the Attorney General, or the administrative head of another Federal agency, as the case may be, for payment of a refund due from a student on a grant made under this subchapter and part C of subchapter I of chapter 34 of Title 42, or for the repayment of the amount due from a borrower on a loan made under this subchapter and part C of subchapter I of chapter 34 of Title 42 that has been assigned to the Secretary under this subchapter and part C of subchapter I of chapter 34 of Title 42.

(b) Assessment of costs and other charges
Notwithstanding any provision of State law to the contrary—

(1) a borrower who has defaulted on a loan made under this subchapter and part C of subchapter I of chapter 34 of Title 42 shall be required to pay, in addition to other charges specified in this subchapter and part C of subchapter I of chapter 34 of Title 42 reasonable collection costs;

(2) in collecting any obligation arising from a loan made under part B of this subchapter, a guaranty agency or the Secretary shall not be subject to a defense raised by any borrower based on a claim of infancy; and

(3) in collecting any obligation arising from a loan made under part D of this subchapter, an institution of higher education that has an agreement with the Secretary pursuant to section 1087cc(a) of this title shall not be subject to a defense raised by any borrower based on a claim of infancy.

(c) State court judgments
A judgment of a State court for the recovery of money provided as grant, loan, or work assistance under this subchapter and part C of subchapter I of chapter 34 of Title 42 that has been assigned or transferred to the Secretary under this subchapter and part C of subchapter I of chapter 34 of Title 42 may be registered in any district court of the United States by filing a certified copy of the judgment and a copy of the assignment or transfer. A judgment so registered shall have the same force and effect, and may be enforced in the same manner, as a judgment of the district court of the district in which the judgment is registered.

(d) Special rule
This section shall not apply in the case of a student who is deceased, or to a deceased student's estate or the estate of such student's family. If a student is deceased, then the student's estate or the estate of the student's family shall not be required to repay any financial assistance under this subchapter and part C of subchapter I of chapter 34 of Title 42, including interest paid on the student's behalf, collection costs, or other charges specified in this subchapter and part C of subchapter I of chapter 34 of Title 42.

[Pub. L. No. 89-329, Title IV, § 484A, *as added by* Pub. L. No. 99-498, Title IV, § 407(a), 100 Stat. 1482 (Oct. 17, 1986), *and amended by* Pub. L. No. 102-26, § 3(a), 105 Stat. 124 (Apr. 9, 1991); Pub. L. No. 105-244, Title IV, § 484, 112 Stat. 1737 (Oct. 7, 1998); Pub. L. No. 110-315, Title IV, § 486, 122 Stat. 3290 (Aug. 14, 2008)]

§ 1091b. Institutional refunds

(a) Return of title IV funds

(1) In general
If a recipient of assistance under this subchapter and part C of subchapter I of chapter 34 of Title 42 withdraws from an institution during a payment period or period of enrollment in which the recipient began attendance, the amount of grant or loan assistance (other than assistance received under part C of subchapter I of chapter 34 of Title 42) to be returned to the title IV programs is calculated according to paragraph (3) and returned in accordance with subsection (b) of this section.

(2) Leave of absence

(A) Leave not treated as withdrawal
In the case of a student who takes 1 or more leaves of absence from an institution for not more than a total of 180 days in any 12-month period, the institution may consider the student as not having withdrawn from the institution during the leave of absence, and not calculate the amount of grant and loan assistance provided under this subchapter and part C of subchapter I of chapter 34 of Title 42 that is to be returned in accordance with this section if—

(i) the institution has a formal policy regarding leaves of absence;

(ii) the student followed the institution's policy in requesting a leave of absence; and

(iii) the institution approved the student's request in accordance with the institution's policy.

(B) Consequences of failure to return
If a student does not return to the institution at the expiration of an approved leave of absence that meets the requirements of subparagraph (A), the institution shall calculate the amount of grant and loan assistance provided under this subchapter and part C of subchapter I of chapter 34 of Title 42 that is to be returned in accordance with this section based on the day the student withdrew (as determined under subsection (c) of this section).

(3) Calculation of amount of title IV assistance earned

(A) In general
The amount of grant or loan assistance under this subchapter and part C of subchapter I of chapter 34 of Title 42 that is earned by the recipient for purposes of this section is calculated by—

(i) determining the percentage of grant and loan assistance under this subchapter and part C of subchapter I of chapter 34 of Title 42 that has been earned by the student, as described in subparagraph (B); and

(ii) applying such percentage to the total amount of such grant and loan assistance that was disbursed (and that could have been disbursed) to the student, or on the student's behalf, for the payment period or period of enrollment for which the assistance was awarded, as of the day the student withdrew.

(B) Percentage earned
For purposes of subparagraph (A)(i), the percentage of grant or loan assistance under this subchapter and part C of subchapter I of chapter 34 of Title 42 that has been earned by the student is—

(i) equal to the percentage of the payment period or period of enrollment for which assistance was awarded that was completed (as determined in accordance with subsection (d)) of this section as of the day the student withdrew, provided that such date occurs on or before the completion of 60 percent of the payment period or period of enrollment; or

(ii) 100 percent, if the day the student withdrew occurs after the student has completed (as determined in accordance with subsection (d) of this section) 60 percent of the payment period or period of enrollment.

(C) **Percentage and amount not earned**

For purposes of subsection (b) of this section, the amount of grant and loan assistance awarded under this subchapter and part C of subchapter I of chapter 34 of Title 42 that has not been earned by the student shall be calculated by—

(i) determining the complement of the percentage of grant assistance under subparts 1 and 3 of part A of this subchapter, or loan assistance under parts B, C, and D of this subchapter, that has been earned by the student described in subparagraph (B); and

(ii) applying the percentage determined under clause (i) to the total amount of such grant and loan assistance that was disbursed (and that could have been disbursed) to the student, or on the student's behalf, for the payment period or period of enrollment, as of the day the student withdrew.

(4) **Differences between amounts earned and amounts received**

(A) **In general**

After determining the eligibility of the student for a late disbursement or post-withdrawal disbursement (as required in regulations prescribed by the Secretary), the institution of higher education shall contact the borrower and obtain confirmation that the loan funds are still required by the borrower. In making such contact, the institution shall explain to the borrower the borrower's obligation to repay the funds following any such disbursement. The institution shall document in the borrower's file the result of such contact and the final determination made concerning such disbursement.

(B) **Return**

If the student has received more grant or loan assistance than the amount earned as calculated under paragraph (3)(A), the unearned funds shall be returned by the institution or the student, or both, as may be required under paragraphs (1) and (2) of subsection (b) of this section, to the programs under this subchapter and part C of subchapter I of chapter 34 of Title 42 in the order specified in subsection (b)(3) of this section.

(b) **Return of title IV program funds**

(1) **Responsibility of the institution**

The institution shall return not later than 45 days from the determination of withdrawal, in the order specified in paragraph (3), the lesser of—

(A) the amount of grant and loan assistance awarded under this subchapter and part C of subchapter I of chapter 34 of Title 42 that has not been earned by the student, as calculated under subsection (a)(3)(C) of this section; or

(B) an amount equal to—

(i) the total institutional charges incurred by the student for the payment period or period of enrollment for which such assistance was awarded; multiplied by

(ii) the percentage of grant and loan assistance awarded under this subchapter and part C of subchapter I of chapter 34 of Title 42 that has not been earned by the student, as described in subsection (a)(3)(C)(i) of this section.

(2) **Responsibility of the student**

(A) **In general**

The student shall return assistance that has not been earned by the student as described in subsection (a)(3)(C)(ii) of this section in the order specified in paragraph (3) minus the amount the institution is required to return under paragraph (1).

(B) **Special rule**

The student (or parent in the case of funds due to a loan borrowed by a parent under part B or C of this subchapter) shall return or repay, as appropriate, the amount determined under subparagraph (A) to—

(i) a loan program under this subchapter and part C of subchapter I of chapter 34 of Title 42 in accordance with the terms of the loan; and

(ii) a grant program under this subchapter and part C of subchapter I of chapter 34 of Title 42, as an overpayment of such grant and shall be subject to—

(I) repayment arrangements satisfactory to the institution; or

(II) overpayment collection procedures prescribed by the Secretary.

(C) **Grant overpayment requirements**

(i) **In general**

Notwithstanding subparagraphs (A) and (B), a student shall only be required to return grant assistance in the amount (if any) by which—

(I) the amount to be returned by the student (as determined under subparagraphs (A) and (B)), exceeds

(II) 50 percent of the total grant assistance received by the student under this subchapter and part C of subchapter I of chapter 34 of Title 42 for the payment period or period of enrollment.

(ii) **Minimum**

A student shall not be required to return amounts of $50 or less.

(D) **Waivers of Federal Pell Grant repayment by students affected by disasters**

The Secretary may waive the amounts that students are required to return under this section with respect to Federal Pell Grants if the withdrawals on which the returns are based are withdrawals by students—

(i) who were residing in, employed in, or attending an institution of higher education that is located in an area in which the President has declared that a major disaster exists, in accordance with section 5170 of Title 42;

(ii) whose attendance was interrupted because of the impact of the disaster on the student or the institution; and

(iii) whose withdrawal ended within the academic year during which the designation occurred or during the next succeeding academic year.

(E) **Waivers of grant assistance repayment by students affected by disasters**

In addition to the waivers authorized by subparagraph (D), the Secretary may waive the amounts that students are required to return under this section with respect to any other grant assistance under this subchapter and part C of subchapter I of chapter 34 of Title 42 if the withdrawals on which the returns are based are withdrawals by students—

(i) who were residing in, employed in, or attending an institution of higher education that is located in an area in which the President has declared that a major disaster exists, in accordance with section 5170 of Title 42;

(ii) whose attendance was interrupted because of the impact of the disaster on the student or the institution; and

(iii) whose withdrawal ended within the academic year during which the designation occurred or during the next succeeding academic year.

(3) Order of return of title IV funds

(A) In general

Excess funds returned by the institution or the student, as appropriate, in accordance with paragraph (1) or (2), respectively, shall be credited to outstanding balances on loans made under this subchapter and part C of subchapter I of chapter 34 of Title 42 to the student or on behalf of the student for the payment period or period of enrollment for which a return of funds is required. Such excess funds shall be credited in the following order:

(i) To outstanding balances on loans made under section 1078-8 of this title for the payment period or period of enrollment for which a return of funds is required.

(ii) To outstanding balances on loans made under section 1078 of this title for the payment period or period of enrollment for which a return of funds is required.

(iii) To outstanding balances on unsubsidized loans (other than parent loans) made under part C of this subchapter for the payment period or period of enrollment for which a return of funds is required.

(iv) To outstanding balances on subsidized loans made under part C of this subchapter for the payment period or period of enrollment for which a return of funds is required.

(v) To outstanding balances on loans made under part D of this subchapter for the payment period or period of enrollment for which a return of funds is required.

(vi) To outstanding balances on loans made under section 1078-2 of this title for the payment period or period of enrollment for which a return of funds is required.

(vii) To outstanding balances on parent loans made under part C of this subchapter for the payment period or period of enrollment for which a return of funds is required.

(B) Remaining excesses

If excess funds remain after repaying all outstanding loan amounts, the remaining excess shall be credited in the following order:

(i) To awards under subpart 1 of part A of this subchapter for the payment period or period of enrollment for which a return of funds is required.

(ii) To awards under subpart 3 of part A of this subchapter for the payment period or period of enrollment for which a return of funds is required.

(iii) To other assistance awarded under this subchapter and part C of subchapter I of chapter 34 of Title 42 for which a return of funds is required.

(c) Withdrawal date

(1) In general

In this section, the term "day the student withdrew"—

(A) is the date that the institution determines—

(i) the student began the withdrawal process prescribed by the institution;

(ii) the student otherwise provided official notification to the institution of the intent to withdraw; or

(iii) in the case of a student who does not begin the withdrawal process or otherwise notify the institution of the intent to withdraw, the date that is the mid-point of the payment period for which assistance under this subchapter and part C of subchapter I of chapter 34 of Title 42 was disbursed or a later date documented by the institution; or

(B) for institutions required to take attendance, is determined by the institution from such attendance records.

(2) Special rule

Notwithstanding paragraph (1), if the institution determines that a student did not begin the withdrawal process, or otherwise notify the institution of the intent to withdraw, due to illness, accident, grievous personal loss, or other such circumstances beyond the student's control, the institution may determine the appropriate withdrawal date.

(d) Percentage of the payment period or period of enrollment completed

For purposes of subsection (a)(3)(B) of this section, the percentage of the payment period or period of enrollment for which assistance was awarded that was completed, is determined—

(1) in the case of a program that is measured in credit hours, by dividing the total number of calendar days comprising the payment period or period of enrollment for which assistance is awarded into the number of calendar days completed in that period as of the day the student withdrew; and

(2) in the case of a program that is measured in clock hours, by dividing the total number of clock hours comprising the payment period or period of enrollment for which assistance is awarded into the number of clock hours scheduled to be completed by the student in that period as of the day the student withdrew.

(e) Effective date

The provisions of this section shall take effect 2 years after October 7, 1998. An institution of higher education may choose to implement such provisions prior to that date.

[Pub. L. No. 89-329, Title IV, § 484B, *as added by* Pub. L. No. 102-325, Title IV, § 485(a), 106 Stat. 619 (July 23, 1992), *and amended by* Pub. L. No. 103-208, § 2(h)(26), (27), 107 Stat. 2477 (Dec. 20, 1993); Pub. L. No. 105-244, Title IV, § 485, 112 Stat. 1737 (Oct. 7, 1998); Pub. L. No. 109-66, § 2, 119 Stat. 1999 (Sept. 21, 2005); Pub. L. No. 109-67, § 2, 119 Stat. 2001 (Sept. 21, 2005); Pub. L. No. 109-171, Title VIII, § 8022, 120 Stat. 178 (Feb. 8, 2006)]

* * *

§ 1094. Program participation agreements

(a) Required for programs of assistance; contents

In order to be an eligible institution for the purposes of any program authorized under this subchapter and part C of subchapter

I of chapter 34 of Title 42, an institution must be an institution of higher education or an eligible institution (as that term is defined for the purpose of that program) and shall, except with respect to a program under subpart 4 of part A of this subchapter, enter into a program participation agreement with the Secretary. The agreement shall condition the initial and continuing eligibility of an institution to participate in a program upon compliance with the following requirements:

(1) The institution will use funds received by it for any program under this subchapter and part C of subchapter I of chapter 34 of Title 42 and any interest or other earnings thereon solely for the purpose specified in and in accordance with the provision of that program.

(2) The institution shall not charge any student a fee for processing or handling any application, form, or data required to determine the student's eligibility for assistance under this subchapter and part C of subchapter I of chapter 34 of Title 42 or the amount of such assistance.

(3) The institution will establish and maintain such administrative and fiscal procedures and records as may be necessary to ensure proper and efficient administration of funds received from the Secretary or from students under this subchapter and part C of subchapter I of chapter 34 of Title 42, together with assurances that the institution will provide, upon request and in a timely fashion, information relating to the administrative capability and financial responsibility of the institution to—

(A) the Secretary;

(B) the appropriate guaranty agency; and

(C) the appropriate accrediting agency or association.

(4) The institution will comply with the provisions of subsection (c) of this section and the regulations prescribed under that subsection, relating to fiscal eligibility.

(5) The institution will submit reports to the Secretary and, in the case of an institution participating in a program under part B or part D of this subchapter, to holders of loans made to the institution's students under such parts at such times and containing such information as the Secretary may reasonably require to carry out the purpose of this subchapter and part C of subchapter I of chapter 34 of Title 42.

(6) The institution will not provide any student with any statement or certification to any lender under part B of this subchapter that qualifies the student for a loan or loans in excess of the amount that student is eligible to borrow in accordance with sections 1075(a), 1078(a)(2), and 1078(b)(1)(A) and (B) of this title.

(7) The institution will comply with the requirements of section 1092 of this title.

(8) In the case of an institution that advertises job placement rates as a means of attracting students to enroll in the institution, the institution will make available to prospective students, at or before the time of application (A) the most recent available data concerning employment statistics, graduation statistics, and any other information necessary to substantiate the truthfulness of the advertisements, and (B) relevant State licensing requirements of the State in which such institution is located for any job for which the course of instruction is designed to prepare such prospective students.

(9) In the case of an institution participating in a program under part B or C of this subchapter, the institution will inform all eligible borrowers enrolled in the institution about the availability and eligibility of such borrowers for State grant assistance from the State in which the institution is located, and will inform such borrowers from another State of the source for further information concerning such assistance from that State.

(10) The institution certifies that it has in operation a drug abuse prevention program that is determined by the institution to be accessible to any officer, employee, or student at the institution.

(11) In the case of any institution whose students receive financial assistance pursuant to section 1091(d) of this title, the institution will make available to such students a program proven successful in assisting students in obtaining a certificate of high school equivalency.

(12) The institution certifies that—

(A) the institution has established a campus security policy; and

(B) the institution has complied with the disclosure requirements of section 1092(f) of this title.

(13) The institution will not deny any form of Federal financial aid to any student who meets the eligibility requirements of this subchapter and part C of subchapter I of chapter 34 of Title 42 on the grounds that the student is participating in a program of study abroad approved for credit by the institution.

(14)(A) The institution, in order to participate as an eligible institution under part B or C of this subchapter, will develop a Default Management Plan for approval by the Secretary as part of its initial application for certification as an eligible institution and will implement such Plan for two years thereafter.

(B) Any institution of higher education which changes ownership and any eligible institution which changes its status as a parent or subordinate institution shall, in order to participate as an eligible institution under part B or C of this subchapter, develop a Default Management Plan for approval by the Secretary and implement such Plan for two years after its change of ownership or status.

(C) This paragraph shall not apply in the case of an institution in which (i) neither the parent nor the subordinate institution has a cohort default rate in excess of 10 percent, and (ii) the new owner of such parent or subordinate institution does not, and has not, owned any other institution with a cohort default rate in excess of 10 percent.

(15) The institution acknowledges the authority of the Secretary, guaranty agencies, lenders, accrediting agencies, the Secretary of Veterans Affairs, and the State agencies under subpart 1 of part G of this subchapter to share with each other any information pertaining to the institution's eligibility to participate in programs under this subchapter and part C of subchapter I of chapter 34 of Title 42 or any information on fraud and abuse.

(16)(A) The institution will not knowingly employ an individual in a capacity that involves the administration of programs under this subchapter and part C of subchapter I of chapter 34 of Title 42, or the receipt of program funds under this subchapter and part C of subchapter I of chapter 34 of Title 42, who has been convicted of, or has pled nolo contendere or guilty to, a crime involving the acquisition, use, or expenditure of funds under this subchapter and part C of subchapter I of chapter 34 of Title 42, or has been judicially determined to have committed fraud involving funds under this subchapter and part C of subchapter I of chapter 34 of Title 42 or contract with an institution or third party servicer that has been terminated under section 1082 of this title involving the acquisition, use, or expenditure of funds under this subchapter and part C of subchapter I of chapter 34 of Title 42, or who has been judicially determined to have committed fraud involving funds under this subchapter and part C of subchapter I of chapter 34 of Title 42.

(B) The institution will not knowingly contract with or employ any individual, agency, or organization that has been, or whose officers or employees have been—

(i) convicted of, or pled nolo contendere or guilty to, a crime involving the acquisition, use, or expenditure of funds under this subchapter and part C of subchapter I of chapter 34 of Title 42; or

(ii) judicially determined to have committed fraud involving funds under this subchapter and part C of subchapter I of chapter 34 of Title 42.

(17) The institution will complete surveys conducted as a part of the Integrated Postsecondary Education Data System (IPEDS) or any other Federal postsecondary institution data collection effort, as designated by the Secretary, in a timely manner and to the satisfaction of the Secretary.

(18) The institution will meet the requirements established pursuant to section 1092(g) of this title.

(19) The institution will not impose any penalty, including the assessment of late fees, the denial of access to classes, libraries, or other institutional facilities, or the requirement that the student borrow additional funds, on any student because of the student's inability to meet his or her financial obligations to the institution as a result of the delayed disbursement of the proceeds of a loan made under this subchapter and part C of subchapter I of chapter 34 of Title 42 due to compliance with the provisions of this subchapter and part C of subchapter I of chapter 34 of Title 42, or delays attributable to the institution.

(20) The institution will not provide any commission, bonus, or other incentive payment based directly or indirectly on success in securing enrollments or financial aid to any persons or entities engaged in any student recruiting or admission activities or in making decisions regarding the award of student financial assistance, except that this paragraph shall not apply to the recruitment of foreign students residing in foreign countries who are not eligible to receive Federal student assistance.

(21) The institution will meet the requirements established by the Secretary and accrediting agencies or associations, and will provide evidence to the Secretary that the institution has the authority to operate within a State.

(22) The institution will comply with the refund policy established pursuant to section 1091b of this title.

(23)(A) The institution, if located in a State to which section 1973gg-2(b) of Title 42 does not apply, will make a good faith effort to distribute a mail voter registration form, requested and received from the State, to each student enrolled in a degree or certificate program and physically in attendance at the institution, and to make such forms widely available to students at the institution.

(B) The institution shall request the forms from the State 120 days prior to the deadline for registering to vote within the State. If an institution has not received a sufficient quantity of forms to fulfill this section from the State within 60 days prior to the deadline for registering to vote in the State, the institution shall not be held liable for not meeting the requirements of this section during that election year.

(C) This paragraph shall apply to general and special elections for Federal office, as defined in section 431(3) of Title 2, and to the elections for Governor or other chief executive within such State).

(D) The institution shall be considered in compliance with the requirements of subparagraph (A) for each student to whom the institution electronically transmits a message containing a voter registration form acceptable for use in the State in which the institution is located, or an Internet address where such a form can be downloaded, if such information is in an electronic message devoted exclusively to voter registration.

(24) In the case of a proprietary institution of higher education (as defined in section 1002(b) of this title), such institution will derive not less than ten percent of such institution's revenues from sources other than funds provided under this subchapter and part C of subchapter I of chapter 34 of Title 42, as calculated in accordance with subsection (d)(1), or will be subject to the sanctions described in subsection (d)(2).

(25) In the case of an institution that participates in a loan program under this title, the institution will—

(A) develop a code of conduct with respect to such loans with which the institution's officers, employees, and agents shall comply, that—

(i) prohibits a conflict of interest with the responsibilities of an officer, employee, or agent of an institution with respect to such loans; and

(ii) at a minimum, includes the provisions described in subsection (e);

(B) publish such code of conduct prominently on the institution's website; and

(C) administer and enforce such code by, at a minimum, requiring that all of the institution's officers, employees, and agents with responsibilities with respect to such loans be annually informed of the provisions of the code of conduct.

(26) The institution will, upon written request, disclose to the alleged victim of any crime of violence (as that term is defined in section 16 of Title 18), or a nonforcible sex offense, the report on the results of any disciplinary proceeding conducted by such institution against a student who is the alleged perpetrator of such crime or offense with respect to such crime or offense. If the alleged victim of such crime or offense is deceased as a result of such crime or offense, the next of kin of such victim shall be treated as the alleged victim for purposes of this paragraph.

(27) In the case of an institution that has entered into a preferred lender arrangement, the institution will at least annually compile, maintain, and make available for students attending the institution, and the families of such students, a list, in print or other medium, of the specific lenders for loans made, insured, or guaranteed under this subchapter and part C of subchapter I of chapter 34 of Title 42 or private education loans that the institution recommends, promotes, or endorses in accordance with such preferred lender arrangement. In making such list, the institution shall comply with the requirements of subsection (h).

(28)(A) The institution will, upon the request of an applicant for a private education loan, provide to the applicant the form required under section 1638(e)(3) of Title 15, and the information required to complete such form, to the extent the institution possesses such information.

(B) For purposes of this paragraph, the term "private education loan" has the meaning given such term in section 1650 of Title 15.

(29) The institution certifies that the institution—

(A) has developed plans to effectively combat the unauthorized distribution of copyrighted material, including through the use of a variety of technology-based deterrents; and

(B) will, to the extent practicable, offer alternatives to illegal downloading or peer-to-peer distribution of intellectual property, as determined by the institution in consultation with the chief technology officer or other designated officer of the institution.

(b) Hearings

(1) An institution that has received written notice of a final audit or program review determination and that desires to have such determination reviewed by the Secretary shall submit to the Secretary a written request for review not later than 45 days after receipt of notification of the final audit or program review determination.

(2) The Secretary shall, upon receipt of written notice under paragraph (1), arrange for a hearing and notify the institution within 30 days of receipt of such notice the date, time, and place of such hearing. Such hearing shall take place not later than 120 days from the date upon which the Secretary notifies the institution.

(c) Audits; financial responsibility; enforcement of standards

(1) Notwithstanding any other provisions of this subchapter and part C of subchapter I of chapter 34 of Title 42, the Secretary shall prescribe such regulations as may be necessary to provide for—

(A)(i) except as provided in clauses (ii) and (iii), a financial audit of an eligible institution with regard to the financial condition of the institution in its entirety, and a compliance audit of such institution with regard to any funds obtained by it under this subchapter and part C of subchapter I of chapter 34 of Title 42 or obtained from a student or a parent who has a loan insured or guaranteed by the Secretary under this subchapter and part C of subchapter I of chapter 34 of Title 42, on at least an annual basis and covering the period since the most recent audit, conducted by a qualified, independent organization or person in accordance with standards established by the Comptroller General for the audit of governmental organizations, programs, and functions, and as prescribed in regulations of the Secretary, the results of which shall be submitted to the Secretary and shall be available to cognizant guaranty agencies, eligible lenders, State agencies, and the appropriate State agency notifying the Secretary under subpart 1 of part G of this subchapter, except that the Secretary may modify the requirements of this clause with respect to institutions of higher education that are foreign institutions, and may waive such requirements with respect to a foreign institution whose students receive less than $500,000 in loans under this subchapter and part C of subchapter I of chapter 34 of Title 42 during the award year preceding the audit period;

(ii) with regard to an eligible institution which is audited under chapter 75 of Title 31, deeming such audit to satisfy the requirements of clause (i) for the period covered by such audit; or

(iii) at the discretion of the Secretary, with regard to an eligible institution (other than an eligible institution described in section 1002(a)(1)(C) of this title) that has obtained less than $200,000 in funds under this subchapter and part C of subchapter I of chapter 34 of Title 42 during each of the 2 award years that precede the audit period and submits a letter of credit payable to the Secretary equal to not less than 1/2 of the annual potential liabilities of such institution as determined by the Secretary, deeming an audit conducted every 3 years to satisfy the requirements of clause (i), except for the award year immediately preceding renewal of the institution's eligibility under section 1099c(g) of this title;

(B) in matters not governed by specific program provisions, the establishment of reasonable standards of financial responsibility and appropriate institutional capability for the administration by an eligible institution of a program of student financial aid under this subchapter and part C of subchapter I of chapter 34 of Title 42, including any matter the Secretary deems necessary to the sound administration of the financial aid programs, such as the pertinent actions of any owner, shareholder, or person exercising control over an eligible institution;

(C)(i) except as provided in clause (ii), a compliance audit of a third party servicer (other than with respect to the servicer's functions as a lender if such functions are otherwise audited under this part and such audits meet the requirements of this clause), with regard to any contract with an eligible institution, guaranty agency, or lender for administering or servicing any aspect of the student assistance programs under this subchapter and part C of subchapter I of chapter 34 of Title 42, at least once every year and covering the period since the most recent audit, conducted by a qualified, independent organization or person in accordance with standards established by the Comptroller General for the audit of governmental organizations, programs, and functions, and as prescribed in regulations of the Secretary, the results of which shall be submitted to the Secretary; or

(ii) with regard to a third party servicer that is audited under chapter 75 of Title 31, such audit shall be deemed to satisfy the requirements of clause (i) for the period covered by such audit;

(D)(i) a compliance audit of a secondary market with regard to its transactions involving, and its servicing and collection of, loans made under this subchapter and part C of subchapter I of chapter 34 of Title 42, at least once a year and covering the period since the most recent audit, conducted by a qualified, independent organization or person in accordance with standards established by the Comptroller General for the audit of governmental organizations, programs, and functions, and as prescribed in regulations of the Secretary, the results of which shall be submitted to the Secretary; or

(ii) with regard to a secondary market that is audited under chapter 75 of Title 31, such audit shall be deemed to satisfy the requirements of clause (i) for the period covered by the audit;

(E) the establishment, by each eligible institution under part B of this subchapter responsible for furnishing to the lender the statement required by section 1078(a)(2)(A)(i) of this title, of policies and procedures by which the latest known address and enrollment status of any student who has had a loan insured under this part and who has either formally terminated his enrollment, or failed to re-enroll on at least a half-time basis, at such institution, shall be furnished either to the holder (or if unknown, the insurer) of the note, not later than 60 days after such termination or failure to re-enroll;

(F) the limitation, suspension, or termination of the participation in any program under this subchapter and part C of subchapter I of chapter 34 of Title 42 of an eligible institution, or the imposition of a civil penalty under paragraph (3)(B) whenever the Secretary has determined, after reasonable notice and opportunity for hearing, that such institution has violated or failed to carry out any provision of this subchapter and part C of subchapter I of chapter 34 of Title 42, any regulation prescribed under this subchapter and part C of subchapter I of chapter 34 of Title 42, or any applicable special arrangement, agreement, or limitation, except that no period of suspension under this section shall exceed 60 days unless the institution and the Secretary agree to an extension or unless limitation or termination proceedings are initiated by the Secretary within that period of time;

(G) an emergency action against an institution, under which the Secretary shall, effective on the date on which a notice and statement of the basis of the action is mailed to the institution (by registered mail, return receipt requested), withhold funds from the institution or its students and withdraw the institution's authority to obligate funds under any program under this subchapter and part C of subchapter I of chapter 34 of Title 42, if the Secretary—

(i) receives information, determined by the Secretary to be reliable, that the institution is violating any provision of this subchapter and part C of subchapter I of chapter 34 of Title 42, any regulation prescribed under this subchapter and part C of subchapter I of chapter 34 of Title 42, or any applicable special arrangement, agreement, or limitation,

(ii) determines that immediate action is necessary to prevent misuse of Federal funds, and

(iii) determines that the likelihood of loss outweighs the importance of the procedures prescribed under subparagraph (D) for limitation, suspension, or termination,

except that an emergency action shall not exceed 30 days unless limitation, suspension, or termination proceedings are initiated by the Secretary against the institution within that period of time, and except that the Secretary shall provide the institution an opportunity to show cause, if it so requests, that the emergency action is unwarranted;

(H) the limitation, suspension, or termination of the eligibility of a third party servicer to contract with any institution to administer any aspect of an institution's student assistance program under this subchapter and part C of subchapter I of chapter 34 of Title 42, or the imposition of a civil penalty under paragraph (3)(B), whenever the Secretary has determined, after reasonable notice and opportunity for a hearing, that such organization, acting on behalf of an institution, has violated or failed to carry out any provision of this subchapter and part C of subchapter I of chapter 34 of Title 42, any regulation prescribed under this subchapter and part C of subchapter I of chapter 34 of Title 42, or any applicable special arrangement, agreement, or limitation, except that no period of suspension under this subparagraph shall exceed 60 days unless the organization and the Secretary agree to an extension, or unless limitation or termination proceedings are initiated by the Secretary against the individual or organization within that period of time; and

(I) an emergency action against a third party servicer that has contracted with an institution to administer any aspect of the institution's student assistance program under this subchapter and part C of subchapter I of chapter 34 of Title 42, under which the Secretary shall, effective on the date on which a notice and statement of the basis of the action is mailed to such individual or organization (by registered mail, return receipt requested), withhold funds from the individual or organization and withdraw the individual or organization's authority to act on behalf of an institution under any program under this subchapter and part C of subchapter I of chapter 34 of Title 42, if the Secretary—

(i) receives information, determined by the Secretary to be reliable, that the individual or organization, acting on behalf of an institution, is violating any provision of this subchapter and part C of subchapter I of chapter 34 of Title 42, any regulation prescribed under this subchapter and part C of subchapter I of chapter 34 of Title 42, or any applicable special arrangement, agreement, or limitation,

(ii) determines that immediate action is necessary to prevent misuse of Federal funds, and

(iii) determines that the likelihood of loss outweighs the importance of the procedures prescribed under subparagraph (F), for limitation, suspension, or termination,

except that an emergency action shall not exceed 30 days unless the limitation, suspension, or termination proceedings are initiated by the Secretary against the individual or organization within that period of time, and except that the Secretary shall provide the individual or organization an opportunity to show cause, if it so requests, that the emergency action is unwarranted.

(2) If an individual who, or entity that, exercises substantial control, as determined by the Secretary in accordance with the definition of substantial control in subpart 3 of part G of this subchapter, over one or more institutions participating in any program under this subchapter and part C of subchapter I of chapter 34 of Title 42, or, for purposes of paragraphs (1)(H) and (I), over one or more organizations that contract with an institution to administer any aspect of the institution's student assistance program under this subchapter and part C of subchapter I of chapter 34 of Title 42, is determined to have committed one or more violations of the requirements of any program under this subchapter and part C of subchapter I of chapter 34 of Title 42, or has been suspended or debarred in accordance with the regulations of the Secretary, the Secretary may use such determination, suspension, or debarment as the basis for imposing an emergency action on, or limiting, suspending, or terminating, in a single proceeding, the participation

of any or all institutions under the substantial control of that individual or entity.

(3)(A) Upon determination, after reasonable notice and opportunity for a hearing, that an eligible institution has engaged in substantial misrepresentation of the nature of its educational program, its financial charges, or the employability of its graduates, the Secretary may suspend or terminate the eligibility status for any or all programs under this subchapter and part C of subchapter I of chapter 34 of Title 42 of any otherwise eligible institution, in accordance with procedures specified in paragraph (1)(D) of this subsection, until the Secretary finds that such practices have been corrected.

(B)(i) Upon determination, after reasonable notice and opportunity for a hearing, that an eligible institution—

(I) has violated or failed to carry out any provision of this subchapter and part C of subchapter I of chapter 34 of Title 42 or any regulation prescribed under this subchapter and part C of subchapter I of chapter 34 of Title 42; or

(II) has engaged in substantial misrepresentation of the nature of its educational program, its financial charges, and the employability of its graduates,

the Secretary may impose a civil penalty upon such institution of not to exceed $25,000 for each violation or misrepresentation.

(ii) Any civil penalty may be compromised by the Secretary. In determining the amount of such penalty, or the amount agreed upon in compromise, the appropriateness of the penalty to the size of the institution of higher education subject to the determination, and the gravity of the violation, failure, or misrepresentation shall be considered. The amount of such penalty, when finally determined, or the amount agreed upon in compromise, may be deducted from any sums owing by the United States to the institution charged.

(4) The Secretary shall publish a list of State agencies which the Secretary determines to be reliable authority as to the quality of public postsecondary vocational education in their respective States for the purpose of determining eligibility for all Federal student assistance programs.

(5) The Secretary shall make readily available to appropriate guaranty agencies, eligible lenders, State agencies notifying the Secretary under subpart 1 of part G of this subchapter, and accrediting agencies or associations the results of the audits of eligible institutions conducted pursuant to paragraph (1)(A).

(6) The Secretary is authorized to provide any information collected as a result of audits conducted under this section, together with audit information collected by guaranty agencies, to any Federal or State agency having responsibilities with respect to student financial assistance, including those referred to in subsection (a)(15) of this section.

(7) Effective with respect to any audit conducted under this subsection after December 31, 1988, if, in the course of conducting any such audit, the personnel of the Department of Education discover, or are informed of, grants or other assistance provided by an institution in accordance with this subchapter and part C of subchapter I of chapter 34 of Title 42 for which the institution has not received funds appropriated under this subchapter and part C of subchapter I of chapter 34 of Title 42 (in the amount necessary to provide such assistance), including funds for which reimbursement was not requested prior to such discovery or information, such institution shall be permitted to offset that amount against any sums determined to be owed by the institution pursuant to such audit, or to receive reimbursement for that amount (if the institution does not owe any such sums).

(d) Implementation of non-title IV revenue requirement
(1) Calculation

In making calculations under subsection (a)(24), a proprietary institution of higher education shall—

(A) use the cash basis of accounting, except in the case of loans described in subparagraph (D)(i) that are made by the proprietary institution of higher education;

(B) consider as revenue only those funds generated by the institution from—

(i) tuition, fees, and other institutional charges for students enrolled in programs eligible for assistance under this subchapter and part C of subchapter I of chapter 34 of Title 42;

(ii) activities conducted by the institution that are necessary for the education and training of the institution's students, if such activities are—

(I) conducted on campus or at a facility under the control of the institution;

(II) performed under the supervision of a member of the institution's faculty; and

(III) required to be performed by all students in a specific educational program at the institution; and

(iii) funds paid by a student, or on behalf of a student by a party other than the institution, for an education or training program that is not eligible for funds under this subchapter and part C of subchapter I of chapter 34 of Title 42, if the program—

(I) is approved or licensed by the appropriate State agency;

(II) is accredited by an accrediting agency recognized by the Secretary; or

(III) provides an industry-recognized credential or certification;

(C) presume that any funds for a program under this subchapter and part C of subchapter I of chapter 34 of Title 42 that are disbursed or delivered to or on behalf of a student will be used to pay the student's tuition, fees, or other institutional charges, regardless of whether the institution credits those funds to the student's account or pays those funds directly to the student, except to the extent that the student's tuition, fees, or other institutional charges are satisfied by—

(i) grant funds provided by non-Federal public agencies or private sources independent of the institution;

(ii) funds provided under a contractual arrangement with a Federal, State, or local government agency for the purpose of providing job training to low-income individuals who are in need of that training;

(iii) funds used by a student from savings plans for educational expenses established by or on behalf of the student and which qualify for special tax treatment under Title 26; or

(iv) institutional scholarships described in subparagraph (D)(iii);

(D) include institutional aid as revenue to the school only as follows:
  (i) in the case of loans made by a proprietary institution of higher education on or after July 1, 2008 and prior to July 1, 2012, the net present value of such loans made by the institution during the applicable institutional fiscal year accounted for on an accrual basis and estimated in accordance with generally accepted accounting principles and related standards and guidance, if the loans—
    (I) are bona fide as evidenced by enforceable promissory notes;
    (II) are issued at intervals related to the institution's enrollment periods; and
    (III) are subject to regular loan repayments and collections;
  (ii) in the case of loans made by a proprietary institution of higher education on or after July 1, 2012, only the amount of loan repayments received during the applicable institutional fiscal year, excluding repayments on loans made and accounted for as specified in clause (i); and
  (iii) in the case of scholarships provided by a proprietary institution of higher education, only those scholarships provided by the institution in the form of monetary aid or tuition discounts based upon the academic achievements or financial need of students, disbursed during each fiscal year from an established restricted account, and only to the extent that funds in that account represent designated funds from an outside source or from income earned on those funds;
(E) in the case of each student who receives a loan on or after July 1, 2008, and prior to July 1, 2011, that is authorized under section 1078-8 of this title or that is a Federal Direct Unsubsidized Stafford Loan, treat as revenue received by the institution from sources other than funds received under this subchapter and part C of subchapter I of chapter 34 of Title 42, the amount by which the disbursement of such loan received by the institution exceeds the limit on such loan in effect on the day before May 7, 2008; and
(F) exclude from revenues—
  (i) the amount of funds the institution received under part C of subchapter I of chapter 34 of Title 42, unless the institution used those funds to pay a student's institutional charges;
  (ii) the amount of funds the institution received under subpart 4 of part A of this subchapter;
  (iii) the amount of funds provided by the institution as matching funds for a program under this subchapter and part C of subchapter I of chapter 34 of Title 42;
  (iv) the amount of funds provided by the institution for a program under this subchapter and part C of subchapter I of chapter 34 of Title 42 that are required to be refunded or returned; and
  (v) the amount charged for books, supplies, and equipment, unless the institution includes that amount as tuition, fees, or other institutional charges.

(2) Sanctions

(A) Ineligibility

A proprietary institution of higher education that fails to meet a requirement of subsection (a)(24) for two consecutive institutional fiscal years shall be ineligible to participate in the programs authorized by this subchapter and part C of subchapter I of chapter 34 of Title 42 for a period of not less than two institutional fiscal years. To regain eligibility to participate in the programs authorized by this subchapter and part C of subchapter I of chapter 34 of Title 42, a proprietary institution of higher education shall demonstrate compliance with all eligibility and certification requirements under section 1099c of this title for a minimum of two institutional fiscal years after the institutional fiscal year in which the institution became ineligible.

(B) Additional enforcement

In addition to such other means of enforcing the requirements of this subchapter and part C of subchapter I of chapter 34 of Title 42 as may be available to the Secretary, if a proprietary institution of higher education fails to meet a requirement of subsection (a)(24) for any institutional fiscal year, then the institution's eligibility to participate in the programs authorized by this subchapter and part C of subchapter I of chapter 34 of Title 42 becomes provisional for the two institutional fiscal years after the institutional fiscal year in which the institution failed to meet the requirement of subsection (a)(24), except that such provisional eligibility shall terminate—
  (i) on the expiration date of the institution's program participation agreement under this subsection that is in effect on the date the Secretary determines that the institution failed to meet the requirement of subsection (a)(24); or
  (ii) in the case that the Secretary determines that the institution failed to meet a requirement of subsection (a)(24) for two consecutive institutional fiscal years, on the date the institution is determined ineligible in accordance with subparagraph (A).

(3) Publication on College Navigator website

The Secretary shall publicly disclose on the College Navigator website—
  (A) the identity of any proprietary institution of higher education that fails to meet a requirement of subsection (a)(24); and
  (B) the extent to which the institution failed to meet such requirement.

(4) Report to Congress

Not later than July 1, 2009, and July 1 of each succeeding year, the Secretary shall submit to the authorizing committees a report that contains, for each proprietary institution of higher education that receives assistance under this subchapter and part C of subchapter I of chapter 34 of Title 42, as provided in the audited financial statements submitted to the Secretary by each institution pursuant to the requirements of subsection (a)(24)—
  (A) the amount and percentage of such institution's revenues received from sources under this subchapter and part C of subchapter I of chapter 34 of Title 42; and
  (B) the amount and percentage of such institution's revenues received from other sources.

(e) Code of conduct requirements

An institution of higher education's code of conduct, as required under subsection (a)(25), shall include the following requirements:

(1) Ban on revenue-sharing arrangements

(A) Prohibition

The institution shall not enter into any revenue-sharing arrangement with any lender.

(B) Definition

For purposes of this paragraph, the term "revenue-sharing arrangement" means an arrangement between an institution and a lender under which—

(i) a lender provides or issues a loan that is made, insured, or guaranteed under this subchapter and part C of subchapter I of chapter 34 of Title 42 to students attending the institution or to the families of such students; and

(ii) the institution recommends the lender or the loan products of the lender and in exchange, the lender pays a fee or provides other material benefits, including revenue or profit sharing, to the institution, an officer or employee of the institution, or an agent.

(2) Gift ban
(A) Prohibition

No officer or employee of the institution who is employed in the financial aid office of the institution or who otherwise has responsibilities with respect to education loans, or agent who has responsibilities with respect to education loans, shall solicit or accept any gift from a lender, guarantor, or servicer of education loans.

(B) Definition of gift
(i) In general

In this paragraph, the term "gift" means any gratuity, favor, discount, entertainment, hospitality, loan, or other item having a monetary value of more than a de minimus amount. The term includes a gift of services, transportation, lodging, or meals, whether provided in kind, by purchase of a ticket, payment in advance, or reimbursement after the expense has been incurred.

(ii) Exceptions

The term "gift" shall not include any of the following:

(I) Standard material, activities, or programs on issues related to a loan, default aversion, default prevention, or financial literacy, such as a brochure, a workshop, or training.

(II) Food, refreshments, training, or informational material furnished to an officer or employee of an institution, or to an agent, as an integral part of a training session that is designed to improve the service of a lender, guarantor, or servicer of education loans to the institution, if such training contributes to the professional development of the officer, employee, or agent.

(III) Favorable terms, conditions, and borrower benefits on an education loan provided to a student employed by the institution if such terms, conditions, or benefits are comparable to those provided to all students of the institution.

(IV) Entrance and exit counseling services provided to borrowers to meet the institution's responsibilities for entrance and exit counseling as required by subsections (b) and (l) of section 1092 of this title, as long as—

(aa) the institution's staff are in control of the counseling, (whether in person or via electronic capabilities); and

(bb) such counseling does not promote the products or services of any specific lender.

(V) Philanthropic contributions to an institution from a lender, servicer, or guarantor of education loans that are unrelated to education loans or any contribution from any lender, guarantor, or servicer that is not made in exchange for any advantage related to education loans.

(VI) State education grants, scholarships, or financial aid funds administered by or on behalf of a State.

(iii) Rule for gifts to family members

For purposes of this paragraph, a gift to a family member of an officer or employee of an institution, to a family member of an agent, or to any other individual based on that individual's relationship with the officer, employee, or agent, shall be considered a gift to the officer, employee, or agent if—

(I) the gift is given with the knowledge and acquiescence of the officer, employee, or agent; and

(II) the officer, employee, or agent has reason to believe the gift was given because of the official position of the officer, employee, or agent.

(3) Contracting arrangements prohibited
(A) Prohibition

An officer or employee who is employed in the financial aid office of the institution or who otherwise has responsibilities with respect to education loans, or an agent who has responsibilities with respect to education loans, shall not accept from any lender or affiliate of any lender any fee, payment, or other financial benefit (including the opportunity to purchase stock) as compensation for any type of consulting arrangement or other contract to provide services to a lender or on behalf of a lender relating to education loans.

(B) Exceptions

Nothing in this subsection shall be construed as prohibiting—

(i) an officer or employee of an institution who is not employed in the institution's financial aid office and who does not otherwise have responsibilities with respect to education loans, or an agent who does not have responsibilities with respect to education loans, from performing paid or unpaid service on a board of directors of a lender, guarantor, or servicer of education loans;

(ii) an officer or employee of the institution who is not employed in the institution's financial aid office but who has responsibility with respect to education loans as a result of a position held at the institution, or an agent who has responsibility with respect to education loans, from performing paid or unpaid service on a board of directors of a lender, guarantor, or servicer of education loans, if the institution has a written conflict of interest policy that clearly sets forth that officers, employees, or agents must recuse themselves from participating in any decision of the board regarding education loans at the institution; or

(iii) an officer, employee, or contractor of a lender, guarantor, or servicer of education loans from serving on a board of directors, or serving as a trustee, of an institution, if the institution has a written conflict of interest policy that the board member or trustee must recuse themselves from any decision regarding education loans at the institution.

(4) Interaction with borrowers

The institution shall not—

(A) for any first-time borrower, assign, through award packaging or other methods, the borrower's loan to a particular lender; or

(B) refuse to certify, or delay certification of, any loan based on the borrower's selection of a particular lender or guaranty agency.

(5) Prohibition on offers of funds for private loans
(A) Prohibition
The institution shall not request or accept from any lender any offer of funds to be used for private education loans (as defined in section 1650 of Title 15), including funds for an opportunity pool loan, to students in exchange for the institution providing concessions or promises regarding providing the lender with—

(i) a specified number of loans made, insured, or guaranteed under this subchapter and part C of subchapter I of chapter 34 of Title 42;

(ii) a specified loan volume of such loans; or

(iii) a preferred lender arrangement for such loans.

(B) Definition of opportunity pool loan
In this paragraph, the term "opportunity pool loan" means a private education loan made by a lender to a student attending the institution or the family member of such a student that involves a payment, directly or indirectly, by such institution of points, premiums, additional interest, or financial support to such lender for the purpose of such lender extending credit to the student or the family.

(6) Ban on staffing assistance
(A) Prohibition
The institution shall not request or accept from any lender any assistance with call center staffing or financial aid office staffing.

(B) Certain assistance permitted
Nothing in paragraph (1) shall be construed to prohibit the institution from requesting or accepting assistance from a lender related to—

(i) professional development training for financial aid administrators;

(ii) providing educational counseling materials, financial literacy materials, or debt management materials to borrowers, provided that such materials disclose to borrowers the identification of any lender that assisted in preparing or providing such materials; or

(iii) staffing services on a short-term, nonrecurring basis to assist the institution with financial aid-related functions during emergencies, including State-declared or federally declared natural disasters, federally declared national disasters, and other localized disasters and emergencies identified by the Secretary.

(7) Advisory board compensation
Any employee who is employed in the financial aid office of the institution, or who otherwise has responsibilities with respect to education loans or other student financial aid of the institution, and who serves on an advisory board, commission, or group established by a lender, guarantor, or group of lenders or guarantors, shall be prohibited from receiving anything of value from the lender, guarantor, or group of lenders or guarantors, except that the employee may be reimbursed for reasonable expenses incurred in serving on such advisory board, commission, or group.

(f) Institutional requirements for teach-outs
(1) In general
In the event the Secretary initiates the limitation, suspension, or termination of the participation of an institution of higher education in any program under this subchapter and part C of subchapter I of chapter 34 of Title 42 under the authority of subsection (c)(1)(F) or initiates an emergency action under the authority of subsection (c)(1)(G) and its prescribed regulations, the Secretary shall require that institution to prepare a teach-out plan for submission to the institution's accrediting agency or association in compliance with section 1099b(c)(3) of this title, the Secretary's regulations on teach-out plans, and the standards of the institution's accrediting agency or association.

(2) Teach-out plan defined
In this subsection, the term "teach-out plan" means a written plan that provides for the equitable treatment of students if an institution of higher education ceases to operate before all students have completed their program of study, and may include, if required by the institution's accrediting agency or association, an agreement between institutions for such a teach-out plan.

(g) Inspector General report on gift ban violations
Inspector General of the Department shall—

(1) submit an annual report to the authorizing committees identifying all violations of an institution's code of conduct that the Inspector General has substantiated during the preceding year relating to the gift ban provisions described in subsection (e)(2); and

(2) make the report available to the public through the Department's website.

(h) Preferred lender list requirements
(1) In general
In compiling, maintaining, and making available a preferred lender list as required under subsection (a)(27), the institution will—

(A) clearly and fully disclose on such preferred lender list—

(i) not less than the information required to be disclosed under section 1019b(a)(2)(A) of this title;

(ii) why the institution has entered into a preferred lender arrangement with each lender on the preferred lender list, particularly with respect to terms and conditions or provisions favorable to the borrower; and

(iii) that the students attending the institution, or the families of such students, do not have to borrow from a lender on the preferred lender list;

(B) ensure, through the use of the list of lender affiliates provided by the Secretary under paragraph (2), that—

(i) there are not less than three lenders of loans made under part B of this subchapter that are not affiliates of each other included on the preferred lender list and, if the institution recommends, promotes, or endorses private education loans, there are not less than two lenders of private education loans that are not affiliates of each other included on the preferred lender list; and

(ii) the preferred lender list under this paragraph—

(I) specifically indicates, for each listed lender, whether the lender is or is not an affiliate of each other lender on the preferred lender list; and

(II) if a lender is an affiliate of another lender on the preferred lender list, describes the details of such affiliation;

(C) prominently disclose the method and criteria used by the institution in selecting lenders with which to enter into preferred lender arrangements to ensure that such lenders are selected on the basis of the best interests of the borrowers, including—

(i) payment of origination or other fees on behalf of the borrower;

(ii) highly competitive interest rates, or other terms and conditions or provisions of loans under this subchapter and part C of subchapter I of chapter 34 of Title 42 or private education loans;

(iii) high-quality servicing for such loans; or

(iv) additional benefits beyond the standard terms and conditions or provisions for such loans;

(D) exercise a duty of care and a duty of loyalty to compile the preferred lender list under this paragraph without prejudice and for the sole benefit of the students attending the institution, or the families of such students;

(E) not deny or otherwise impede the borrower's choice of a lender or cause unnecessary delay in loan certification under this subchapter and part C of subchapter I of chapter 34 of Title 42 for those borrowers who choose a lender that is not included on the preferred lender list; and

(F) comply with such other requirements as the Secretary may prescribe by regulation.

(2) **Lender affiliates list**

(A) **In general**

The Secretary shall maintain and regularly update a list of lender affiliates of all eligible lenders, and shall provide such list to institutions for use in carrying out paragraph (1)(B).

(B) **Use of most recent list**

An institution shall use the most recent list of lender affiliates provided by the Secretary under subparagraph (A) in carrying out paragraph (1)(B).

(*i*) **Definitions**

the purpose of this section:

(1) **Agent**

The term "agent" has the meaning given the term in section 1019 of this title.

(2) **Affiliate**

The term "affiliate" means a person that controls, is controlled by, or is under common control with another person. A person controls, is controlled by, or is under common control with another person if—

(A) the person directly or indirectly, or acting through one or more others, owns, controls, or has the power to vote five percent or more of any class of voting securities of such other person;

(B) the person controls, in any manner, the election of a majority of the directors or trustees of such other person; or

(C) the Secretary determines (after notice and opportunity for a hearing) that the person directly or indirectly exercises a controlling interest over the management or policies of such other person's education loans.

(3) **Education loan**

The term "education loan" has the meaning given the term in section 1019 of this title.

(4) **Eligible institution**

The term "eligible institution" means any such institution described in section 1002 of this title.

(5) **Officer**

The term "officer" has the meaning given the term in section 1019 of this title.

(6) **Preferred lender arrangement**

The term "preferred lender arrangement" has the meaning given the term in section 1019 of this title.

(j) **Construction**

Nothing in the amendments made by the Higher Education Amendments of 1992 shall be construed to prohibit an institution from recording, at the cost of the institution, a hearing referred to in subsection (b)(2), subsection (c)(1)(D), or subparagraph (A) or (B)(i) of subsection (c)(2), of this section to create a record of the hearing, except the unavailability of a recording shall not serve to delay the completion of the proceeding. The Secretary shall allow the institution to use any reasonable means, including stenographers, of recording the hearing.

[Pub. L. No. 89-329, Title IV, § 487, *as added by* Pub. L. No. 99-498, Title IV, § 407(a), 100 Stat. 1488 (Oct. 17, 1986), *and amended by* Pub. L. No. 101-239, Title II, §§ 2003(c)(2), 2006(c), 103 Stat. 2114, 2118 (Dec. 19, 1989); Pub. L. No. 101-542, Title II, § 205, 104 Stat. 2387 (Nov. 8, 1990); Pub. L. No. 102-26, § 2(c)(3), 105 Stat. 124 (Apr. 9, 1991); Pub. L. No. 102-325, Title IV, § 490, 106 Stat. 625 (July 23, 1992); Pub. L. No. 103-208, § 2(h)(42), (43), 107 Stat. 2478 (Dec. 20, 1993); Pub. L. No. 105-244, Title I, § 102(b)(4), Title IV, § 489(a), (b)(1), (c), 112 Stat. 1622, 1750, 1751 (Oct. 7, 1998); Pub. L. No. 106-113, Div. B, §1000(a)(4) [Title III, § 314], 113 Stat. 1535, 1501A-266 (Nov. 29, 1999); Pub. L. No. 110-315, Title IV, § 493(a)(1)(A), (b) to (d), 122 Stat. 3308, 3309 (Aug. 14, 2008); Pub. L. No. 111-39, Title IV, § 407(b)(8), 123 Stat. 1952 (July 1, 2009)]

* * *

§ 1095a. Wage garnishment requirement

(a) **Garnishment requirements**

Notwithstanding any provision of State law, a guaranty agency, or the Secretary in the case of loans made, insured or guaranteed under this subchapter and part C of subchapter I of chapter 34 of Title 42 that are held by the Secretary, may garnish the disposable pay of an individual to collect the amount owed by the individual, if he or she is not currently making required repayment under a repayment agreement with the Secretary, or, in the case of a loan guaranteed under part B of this subchapter on which the guaranty agency received reimbursement from the Secretary under section 1078(c) of this title, with the guaranty agency holding the loan, as appropriate, provided that—

(1) the amount deducted for any pay period may not exceed 15 percent of disposable pay, except that a greater percentage may be deducted with the written consent of the individual involved;

(2) the individual shall be provided written notice, sent by mail to the individual's last known address, a minimum of 30 days prior to the initiation of proceedings, from the guaranty agency or the Secretary, as appropriate, informing such individual of the nature and amount of the loan obligation to be collected, the intention of the guaranty agency or the Secretary, as appropriate, to initiate proceedings to collect the debt through deductions from pay, and an explanation of the rights of the individual under this section;

(3) the individual shall be provided an opportunity to inspect and copy records relating to the debt;

(4) the individual shall be provided an opportunity to enter into a written agreement with the guaranty agency or the Secretary, under terms agreeable to the Secretary, or the head of the guaranty agency or his designee, as appropriate, to establish a schedule for the repayment of the debt;

(5) the individual shall be provided an opportunity for a hearing in accordance with subsection (b) of this section on the determination of the Secretary or the guaranty agency, as appropriate, concerning the existence or the amount of the debt, and, in the case of an individual whose repayment schedule is established other than by a written agreement pursuant to paragraph (4), concerning the terms of the repayment schedule;

(6) the employer shall pay to the Secretary or the guaranty agency as directed in the withholding order issued in this action, and shall be liable for, and the Secretary or the guaranty agency, as appropriate, may sue the employer in a State or Federal court of competent jurisdiction to recover, any amount that such employer fails to withhold from wages due an employee following receipt of such employer of notice of the withholding order, plus attorneys' fees, costs, and, in the court's discretion, punitive damages, but such employer shall not be required to vary the normal pay and disbursement cycles in order to comply with this paragraph;

(7) if an individual has been reemployed within 12 months after having been involuntarily separated from employment, no amount may be deducted from the disposable pay of such individual until such individual has been reemployed continuously for at least 12 months; and

(8) an employer may not discharge from employment, refuse to employ, or take disciplinary action against an individual subject to wage withholding in accordance with this section by reason of the fact that the individual's wages have been subject to garnishment under this section, and such individual may sue in a State or Federal court of competent jurisdiction any employer who takes such action. The court shall award attorneys' fees to a prevailing employee and, in its discretion, may order reinstatement of the individual, award punitive damages and back pay to the employee, or order such other remedy as may be reasonably necessary.

(b) Hearing requirements
A hearing described in subsection (a)(5) of this section shall be provided prior to issuance of a garnishment order if the individual, on or before the 15th day following the mailing of the notice described in subsection (a)(2) of this section, and in accordance with such procedures as the Secretary or the head of the guaranty agency, as appropriate, may prescribe, files a petition requesting such a hearing. If the individual does not file a petition requesting a hearing prior to such date, the Secretary or the guaranty agency, as appropriate, shall provide the individual a hearing under subsection (a)(5) of this section upon request, but such hearing need not be provided prior to issuance of a garnishment order. A hearing under subsection (a)(5) of this section may not be conducted by an individual under the supervision or control of the head of the guaranty agency, except that nothing in this sentence shall be construed to prohibit the appointment of an administrative law judge. The hearing official shall issue a final decision at the earliest practicable date, but not later than 60 days after the filing of the petition requesting the hearing.

(c) Notice requirements
The notice to the employer of the withholding order shall contain only such information as may be necessary for the employer to comply with the withholding order.

(d) No attachment of student assistance
Except as authorized in this section, notwithstanding any other provision of Federal or State law, no grant, loan, or work assistance awarded under this subchapter and part C of subchapter I of chapter 34 of Title 42, or property traceable to such assistance, shall be subject to garnishment or attachment in order to satisfy any debt owed by the student awarded such assistance, other than a debt owed to the Secretary and arising under this subchapter and part C of subchapter I of chapter 34 of Title 42.

(e) "Disposable pay" defined
For the purpose of this section, the term "disposable pay" means that part of the compensation of any individual from an employer remaining after the deduction of any amounts required by law to be withheld.

[Pub. L. 89-329, Title IV, § 488A, *as added by* Pub. L. 102-164, Title VI, § 605(a), Nov. 15, 1991, 105 Stat. 1066, *and amended by* Pub. L. 105-244, Title IV, § 490A, Oct. 7, 1998, 112 Stat. 1753; Pub. L. 109-171, Title VIII, § 8024, Feb. 8, 2006, 120 Stat. 180]

A.5 Selected Debt Collection Statutes

The following is selected statutory authority from the federal debt collection act. These provisions apply to all federal agencies including the Department of Education.

31 U.S.C. sec.

* * *

3716. Administrative offset.

* * *

3720A. Reduction of tax refund by amount of debt.

* * *

3720D. Garnishment.

* * *

§ 3716. Administrative offset

(a) After trying to collect a claim from a person under section 3711(a) of this title, the head of an executive, judicial, or legislative agency may collect the claim by administrative offset. The head of the agency may collect by administrative offset only after giving the debtor—

(1) written notice of the type and amount of the claim, the intention of the head of the agency to collect the claim by administrative offset, and an explanation of the rights of the debtor under this section;

(2) an opportunity to inspect and copy the records of the agency related to the claim;

(3) an opportunity for a review within the agency of the decision of the agency related to the claim; and

(4) an opportunity to make a written agreement with the head of the agency to repay the amount of the claim.

(b) Before collecting a claim by administrative offset, the head of an executive, judicial, or legislative agency must either—

(1) adopt, without change, regulations on collecting by administrative offset promulgated by the Department of Justice, the Government Accountability Office, or the Department of the Treasury; or

(2) prescribe regulations on collecting by administrative offset consistent with the regulations referred to in paragraph (1).

(c)(1)(A) Except as otherwise provided in this subsection, a disbursing official of the Department of the Treasury, the Department of Defense, the United States Postal Service, the Department of Health and Human Services, or any other government corporation, or any disbursing official of the United States designated by the Secretary of the Treasury, shall offset at least annually the amount of a payment which a payment certifying agency has certified to the disbursing official for disbursement, by an amount equal to the amount of a claim which a creditor agency has certified to the Secretary of the Treasury pursuant to this subsection.

(B) An agency that designates disbursing officials pursuant to section 3321(c) of this title is not required to certify claims arising out of its operations to the Secretary of the Treasury before such agency's disbursing officials offset such claims.

(C) Payments certified by the Department of Education under a program administered by the Secretary of Education under title IV of the Higher Education Act of 1965 shall not be subject to administrative offset under this subsection.

(2) Neither the disbursing official nor the payment certifying agency shall be liable—

(A) for the amount of the administrative offset on the basis that the underlying obligation, represented by the payment before the administrative offset was taken, was not satisfied; or

(B) for failure to provide timely notice under paragraph (8).

(3)(A)(i) Notwithstanding any other provision of law (including sections 207 and 1631(d)(1) of the Social Security Act (42 U.S.C. 407 and 1383(d)(1)), section 413(b) of Public Law 91-173 (30 U.S.C. 923(b)), and section 14 of the Act of August 29, 1935 (45 U.S.C. 231m)), except as provided in clause (ii), all payments due to an individual under—

(I) the Social Security Act,

(II) part B of the Black Lung Benefits Act, or

(III) any law administered by the Railroad Retirement Board (other than payments that such Board determines to be tier 2 benefits),

shall be subject to offset under this section.

(ii) An amount of $9,000 which a debtor may receive under Federal benefit programs cited under clause (i) within a 12-month period shall be exempt from offset under this subsection. In applying the $9,000 exemption, the disbursing official shall—

(I) reduce the $9,000 exemption amount for the 12-month period by the amount of all Federal benefit payments made during such 12-month period which are not subject to offset under this subsection; and

(II) apply a prorated amount of the exemption to each periodic benefit payment to be made to the debtor during the applicable 12-month period.

For purposes of the preceding sentence, the amount of a periodic benefit payment shall be the amount after any reduction or deduction required under the laws authorizing the program under which such payment is authorized to be made (including any reduction or deduction to recover any overpayment under such program).

(B) The Secretary of the Treasury shall exempt from administrative offset under this subsection payments under means-tested programs when requested by the head of the respective agency. The Secretary may exempt other payments from administrative offset under this subsection upon the written request of the head of a payment certifying agency. A written request for exemption of other payments must provide justification for the exemption under standards prescribed by the Secretary. Such standards shall give due consideration to whether administrative offset would tend to interfere substantially with or defeat the purposes of the payment certifying agency's program. The Secretary shall report to the Congress annually on exemptions granted under this section.

(C) The provisions of sections 205(b)(1), 809(a)(1), and 1631(c)(1) of the Social Security Act shall not apply to any administrative offset executed pursuant to this section against benefits authorized by title II, VIII, or title XVI of the Social Security Act, respectively.

(D) This section shall apply to payments made after the date which is 90 days after the enactment of this subparagraph (or such earlier date as designated by the Secretary of Health and Human Services) with respect to claims or debts, and to amounts payable, under title XVIII of the Social Security Act.

(4) The Secretary of the Treasury may charge a fee sufficient to cover the full cost of implementing this subsection. The fee may be collected either by the retention of a portion of amounts collected pursuant to this subsection, or by billing the agency referring or transferring a claim for those amounts. Fees charged to the agencies shall be based on actual administrative offsets completed. Amounts received by the United States as fees under this subsection shall be deposited into the account of the Department of the Treasury under section 3711(g)(7) of this title, and shall be collected and accounted for in accordance with the provisions of that section.

(5) The Secretary of the Treasury in consultation with the Commissioner of Social Security and the Director of the Office of Management and Budget, may prescribe such rules, regulations, and procedures as the Secretary of the Treasury considers necessary to carry out this subsection. The Secretary shall consult with the heads of affected agencies in the development of such rules, regulations, and procedures.

(6) Any Federal agency that is owed by a person a past due, legally enforceable nontax debt that is over 180 days delinquent, including nontax debt administered by a third party acting as an agent for the Federal Government, shall notify the Secretary of the Treasury of all such nontax debts for purposes of administrative offset under this subsection.

(7)(A) The disbursing official conducting an administrative offset with respect to a payment to a payee shall notify the payee in writing of—

(i) the occurrence of the administrative offset to satisfy a past due legally enforceable debt, including a description of the type and amount of the payment otherwise payable to the payee against which the offset was executed;

(ii) the identity of the creditor agency requesting the offset; and

(iii) a contact point within the creditor agency that will handle concerns regarding the offset.

(B) If the payment to be offset is a periodic benefit payment, the disbursing official shall take reasonable steps, as determined by the Secretary of the Treasury, to provide the notice to the payee not later than the date on which the payee is otherwise scheduled to receive the payment, or as soon as practical thereafter, but no later than the date of the administrative offset. Notwithstanding the preceding sentence, the failure of the debtor to receive such notice shall not impair the legality of such administrative offset.

(8) A levy pursuant to the Internal Revenue Code of 1986 shall take precedence over requests for administrative offset pursuant to other laws.

(d) Nothing in this section is intended to prohibit the use of any other administrative offset authority existing under statute or common law.

(e)(1) Notwithstanding any other provision of law, regulation, or administrative limitation, no limitation on the period within which an offset may be initiated or taken pursuant to this section shall be effective.

(2) This section does not apply when a statute explicitly prohibits using administrative offset or setoff to collect the claim or type of claim involved.

(f) The Secretary may waive the requirements of sections 552a(o) and (p) of title 5 for administrative offset or claims collection upon written certification by the head of a State or an executive, judicial, or legislative agency seeking to collect the claim that the requirements of subsection (a) of this section have been met.

(g) The Data Integrity Board of the Department of the Treasury established under 552a(u) of title 5 shall review and include in reports under paragraph (3)(D) of that section a description of any matching activities conducted under this section. If the Secretary has granted a waiver under subsection (f) of this section, no other Data Integrity Board is required to take any action under section 552a(u) of title 5.

(h)(1) The Secretary may, in the discretion of the Secretary, apply subsection (a) with respect to any past-due, legally-enforceable debt owed to a State if—

(A) the appropriate State disbursing official requests that an offset be performed; and

(B) a reciprocal agreement with the State is in effect which contains, at a minimum—

(i) requirements substantially equivalent to subsection (b) of this section; and

(ii) any other requirements which the Secretary considers appropriate to facilitate the offset and prevent duplicative efforts.

(2) This subsection does not apply to—

(A) the collection of a debt or claim on which the administrative costs associated with the collection of the debt or claim exceed the amount of the debt or claim;

(B) any collection of any other type, class, or amount of claim, as the Secretary considers necessary to protect the interest of the United States; or

(C) the disbursement of any class or type of payment exempted by the Secretary of the Treasury at the request of a Federal agency.

(3) In applying this section with respect to any debt owed to a State, subsection (c)(3)(A) shall not apply.

[*Added by* Pub. L. No. 97-452, § 1(16)(A), 96 Stat. 2471 (Jan. 12, 1983), *and amended by* Pub. L. No. 104-134, Title III, § 31001(c)(1), (d)(2), (e), (f), 110 Stat. 1321–359, 1321–362 (Apr. 26, 1996); Pub. L. No. 106-169, Title II, § 251(b)(10), 113 Stat. 1856 (Dec. 14, 1999); Pub. L. No. 108-271, § 8(b), 118 Stat. 814 (July 7, 2004); Pub. L. No. 110-234, Title XIV, § 14219(a), 122 Stat. 1482 (May 22, 2008); Pub. L. No. 110-246, § 4(a), Title XIV, § 14219(a), 122 Stat. 1664, 2244 (June 18, 2008); Pub. L. No. 110-275, Title I, § 189(b), 122 Stat. 2590 (July 15, 2008)]

* * *

§ 3720A. Reduction of tax refund by amount of debt

(a) Any Federal agency that is owed by a person a past-due, legally enforceable debt (including debt administered by a third party acting as an agent for the Federal Government) shall, and any agency subject to section 9 of the Act of May 18, 1933 (16 U.S.C. 831h), owed such a debt may, in accordance with regulations issued pursuant to subsections (b) and (d), notify the Secretary of the Treasury at least once each year of the amount of such debt.

(b) No Federal agency may take action pursuant to subsection (a) with respect to any debt until such agency—

(1) notifies the person incurring such debt that such agency proposes to take action pursuant to such paragraph with respect to such debt;

(2) gives such person at least 60 days to present evidence that all or part of such debt is not past-due or not legally enforceable;

(3) considers any evidence presented by such person and determines that an amount of such debt is past due and legally enforceable;

(4) satisfies such other conditions as the Secretary may prescribe to ensure that the determination made under paragraph (3) with respect to such debt is valid and that the agency has made reasonable efforts (determined on a government-wide basis) to obtain payment of such debt; and

(5) certifies that reasonable efforts have been made by the agency (pursuant to regulations) to obtain payment of such debt.

(c) Upon receiving notice from any Federal agency that a named person owes to such agency a past-due legally enforceable debt, the Secretary of the Treasury shall determine whether any amounts, as refunds of Federal taxes paid, are payable to such person. If the Secretary of the Treasury finds that any such amount is payable, he shall reduce such refunds by an amount equal to the amount of such debt, pay the amount of such reduction to such agency, and notify such agency of the individual's home address.

(d) The Secretary of the Treasury shall issue regulations prescribing the time or times at which agencies must submit notices of past-due legally enforceable debts, the manner in which such notices must be submitted, and the necessary information that must be contained in or accompany the notices. The regulations shall specify the minimum amount of debt to which the reduction procedure established by subsection (c) may be applied and the fee that an agency must pay to reimburse the Secretary of the Treasury for the full cost of applying such procedure. Any fee paid to the

Secretary pursuant to the preceding sentence may be used to reimburse appropriations which bore all or part of the cost of applying such procedure.

(e) Any Federal agency receiving notice from the Secretary of the Treasury that an erroneous payment has been made to such agency under subsection (c) shall pay promptly to the Secretary, in accordance with such regulations as the Secretary may prescribe, an amount equal to the amount of such erroneous payment (without regard to whether any other amounts payable to such agency under such subsection have been paid to such agency).

(f)(1) Subsection (a) shall apply with respect to an OASDI overpayment made to any individual only if such individual is not currently entitled to monthly insurance benefits under title II of the Social Security Act.

(2)(A) The requirements of subsection (b) shall not be treated as met in the case of the recovery of an OASDI overpayment from any individual under this section unless the notification under subsection (b)(1) describes the conditions under which the Commissioner of Social Security is required to waive recovery of an overpayment, as provided under section 204(b) of the Social Security Act.

(B) In any case in which an individual files for a waiver under section 204(b) of the Social Security Act within the 60-day period referred to in subsection (b)(2), the Commissioner of Social Security shall not certify to the Secretary of the Treasury that the debt is valid under subsection (b)(4) before rendering a decision on the waiver request under such section 204(b). In lieu of payment, pursuant to subsection (c), to the Commissioner of Social Security of the amount of any reduction under this subsection based on an OASDI overpayment, the Secretary of the Treasury shall deposit such amount in the Federal Old-Age and Survivors Insurance Trust Fund or the Federal Disability Insurance Trust Fund, whichever is certified to the Secretary of the Treasury as appropriate by the Commissioner of Social Security.

(g) In the case of refunds of business associations, this section shall apply only to refunds payable on or after January 1, 1995. In the case of refunds of individuals who owe debts to Federal agencies that have not participated in the Federal tax refund offset program prior to the date of enactment of this subsection, this section shall apply only to refunds payable on or after January 1, 1994.

(h)(1)[1] The disbursing official of the Department of the Treasury—
(1) shall notify a taxpayer in writing of—
(A) the occurrence of an offset to satisfy a past-due legally enforceable nontax debt;
(B) the identity of the creditor agency requesting the offset; and
(C) a contact point within the creditor agency that will handle concerns regarding the offset;
(2) shall notify the Internal Revenue Service on a weekly basis of—
(A) the occurrence of an offset to satisfy a past-due legally enforceable non-tax[2] debt;
(B) the amount of such offset; and
(C) any other information required by regulations; and
(3) shall match payment records with requests for offset by using a name control, taxpayer identifying number (as that term is used in section 6109 of the Internal Revenue Code of 1986), and any other necessary identifiers.

(h)(2)[3] The term "disbursing official" of the Department of the Treasury means the Secretary or his designee.

(i) An agency subject to section 9 of the Act of May 18, 1933 (16 U.S.C. 831h), may implement this section at its discretion.

[*Added by* Pub. L. No. 98-369, tit. VI, § 2653(a)(1), 98 Stat. 1153 (July 18, 1984), *and amended by* Pub. L. No. 101-508, tit. V, § 5129(b), 104 Stat. 1388-287 (Nov. 5, 1990); Pub. L. No. 102-589, § 3, 106 Stat. 5133 (Nov. 10, 1992); Pub. L. No. 103-296, tit. I, § 108(j)(2), 108 Stat. 1488 (Aug. 15, 1994); Pub. L. No. 104-134, tit. III, § 31001(u)(1), (v)(1), (w), 110 Stat. 1321-375 (Apr. 26, 1996)]

* * *

§ 3720D. Garnishment

(a) Notwithstanding any provision of State law, the head of an executive, judicial, or legislative agency that administers a program that gives rise to a delinquent nontax debt owed to the United States by an individual may in accordance with this section garnish the disposable pay of the individual to collect the amount owed, if the individual is not currently making required repayment in accordance with any agreement between the agency head and the individual.

(b) In carrying out any garnishment of disposable pay of an individual under subsection (a), the head of an executive, judicial, or legislative agency shall comply with the following requirements:

(1) The amount deducted under this section for any pay period may not exceed 15 percent of disposable pay, except that a greater percentage may be deducted with the written consent of the individual.

(2) The individual shall be provided written notice, sent by mail to the individual's last known address, a minimum of 30 days prior to the initiation of proceedings, from the head of the executive, judicial, or legislative agency, informing the individual of—
(A) the nature and amount of the debt to be collected;
(B) the intention of the agency to initiate proceedings to collect the debt through deductions from pay; and
(C) an explanation of the rights of the individual under this section.

(3) The individual shall be provided an opportunity to inspect and copy records relating to the debt.

(4) The individual shall be provided an opportunity to enter into a written agreement with the executive, judicial, or legislative agency, under terms agreeable to the head of the agency, to establish a schedule for repayment of the debt.

---

1 *Editor's note:* So in original. Subsec. (h) contains two pars. designated (1) and (2).

2 *Editor's note:* So in original. Probably should not be hyphenated.

3 *Editor's note:* So in original. Subsec. (h) contains two pars. designated (1) and (2).

(5) The individual shall be provided an opportunity for a hearing in accordance with subsection (c) on the determination of the head of the executive, judicial, or legislative agency concerning—

(A) the existence or the amount of the debt, and

(B) in the case of an individual whose repayment schedule is established other than by a written agreement pursuant to paragraph (4), the terms of the repayment schedule.

(6) If the individual has been reemployed within 12 months after having been involuntarily separated from employment, no amount may be deducted from the disposable pay of the individual until the individual has been reemployed continuously for at least 12 months.

(c)(1) A hearing under subsection (b)(5) shall be provided prior to issuance of a garnishment order if the individual, on or before the 15th day following the mailing of the notice described in subsection (b)(2), and in accordance with such procedures as the head of the executive, judicial, or legislative agency may prescribe, files a petition requesting such a hearing.

(2) If the individual does not file a petition requesting a hearing prior to such date, the head of the agency shall provide the individual a hearing under subsection (a)(5) [FN1] upon request, but such hearing need not be provided prior to issuance of a garnishment order.

(3) The hearing official shall issue a final decision at the earliest practicable date, but not later than 60 days after the filing of the petition requesting the hearing.

(d) The notice to the employer of the withholding order shall contain only such information as may be necessary for the employer to comply with the withholding order.

(e)(1) An employer may not discharge from employment, refuse to employ, or take disciplinary action against an individual subject to wage withholding in accordance with this section by reason of the fact that the individual's wages have been subject to garnishment under this section, and such individual may sue in a State or Federal court of competent jurisdiction any employer who takes such action.

(2) The court shall award attorneys' fees to a prevailing employee and, in its discretion, may order reinstatement of the individual, award punitive damages and back pay to the employee, or order such other remedy as may be reasonably necessary.

(f)(1) The employer of an individual—

(A) shall pay to the head of an executive, judicial, or legislative agency as directed in a withholding order issued in an action under this section with respect to the individual, and

(B) shall be liable for any amount that the employer fails to withhold from wages due an employee following receipt by such employer of notice of the withholding order, plus attorneys' fees, costs, and, in the court's discretion, punitive damages.

(2)(A) The head of an executive, judicial, or legislative agency may sue an employer in a State or Federal court of competent jurisdiction to recover amounts for which the employer is liable under paragraph (1)(B).

(B) A suit under this paragraph may not be filed before the termination of the collection action, unless earlier filing is necessary to avoid expiration of any applicable statute of limitations period.

(3) Notwithstanding paragraphs (1) and (2), an employer shall not be required to vary its normal pay and disbursement cycles in order to comply with this subsection.

(g) For the purpose of this section, the term "disposable pay" means that part of the compensation of any individual from an employer remaining after the deduction of any amounts required by any other law to be withheld.

(h) The Secretary of the Treasury shall issue regulations to implement this section.

[*Added by* Pub. L. No. 104-134, tit. III, § 31001(o)(1), 110 Stat. 1321-369 (Apr. 26, 1996)]

* * *

A.6 Private Loans

15 U.S.C. sec.

* * *

1650. Preventing unfair and deceptive private educational lending practices and eliminating conflicts of interest

* * *

§ 1650. Preventing unfair and deceptive private educational lending practices and eliminating conflicts of interest

(a) Definitions

As used in this section—

(1) the term "covered educational institution"—

(A) means any educational institution that offers a postsecondary educational degree, certificate, or program of study (including any institution of higher education); and

(B) includes an agent, officer, or employee of the educational institution;

(2) the term "gift"—

(A)(i) means any gratuity, favor, discount, entertainment, hospitality, loan, or other item having more than a de minimis monetary value, including services, transportation, lodging, or meals, whether provided in kind, by purchase of a ticket, payment in advance, or reimbursement after the expense has been incurred; and

(ii) includes an item described in clause (i) provided to a family member of an officer, employee, or agent of a covered educational institution, or to any other individual based on that individual's relationship with the officer, employee, or agent, if—

(I) the item is provided with the knowledge and acquiescence of the officer, employee, or agent; and

(II) the officer, employee, or agent has reason to believe the item was provided because of the official position of the officer, employee, or agent; and

(B) does not include—

(i) standard informational material related to a loan, default aversion, default prevention, or financial literacy;

(ii) food, refreshments, training, or informational material furnished to an officer, employee, or agent of a covered educational institution, as an integral part of a training session or through participation in an advisory council that is designed to improve the service of the private educational lender to the covered educational institution, if such training or participation contributes to the professional development of the officer, employee, or agent of the covered educational institution;
(iii) favorable terms, conditions, and borrower benefits on a private education loan provided to a student employed by the covered educational institution, if such terms, conditions, or benefits are not provided because of the student's employment with the covered educational institution;
(iv) the provision of financial literacy counseling or services, including counseling or services provided in coordination with a covered educational institution, to the extent that such counseling or services are not undertaken to secure—
 (I) applications for private education loans or private education loan volume;
 (II) applications or loan volume for any loan made, insured, or guaranteed under title IV of the Higher Education Act of 1965 (20 U.S.C. 1070 et seq.); or
 (III) the purchase of a product or service of a specific private educational lender;
(v) philanthropic contributions to a covered educational institution from a private educational lender that are unrelated to private education loans and are not made in exchange for any advantage related to private education loans; or
(vi) State education grants, scholarships, or financial aid funds administered by or on behalf of a State;
(3) the term "institution of higher education" has the same meaning as in section 102 of the Higher Education Act of 1965 (20 U.S.C. 1002);
(4) the term "postsecondary educational expenses" means any of the expenses that are included as part of the cost of attendance of a student, as defined under section 472 of the Higher Education Act of 1965 (20 U.S.C. 1087ll);
(5) the term "preferred lender arrangement" has the same meaning as in section 151 of the Higher Education Act of 1965 [20 U.S.C.A. § 1019];
(6) the term "private educational lender" means—
 (A) a financial institution, as defined in section 1813 of Title 12 that solicits, makes, or extends private education loans;
 (B) a Federal credit union, as defined in section 1752 of Title 12 that solicits, makes, or extends private education loans; and
 (C) any other person engaged in the business of soliciting, making, or extending private education loans;
(7) the term "private education loan"—
 (A) means a loan provided by a private educational lender that—
  (i) is not made, insured, or guaranteed under[1] title IV of the Higher Education Act of 1965 (20 U.S.C. 1070 et seq.); and

---

[1] *Editor's note:* So in original. The word "of" probably should not appear.

(ii) is issued expressly for postsecondary educational expenses to a borrower, regardless of whether the loan is provided through the educational institution that the subject student attends or directly to the borrower from the private educational lender; and
 (B) does not include an extension of credit under an open end consumer credit plan, a reverse mortgage transaction, a residential mortgage transaction, or any other loan that is secured by real property or a dwelling; and
(8) the term "revenue sharing" means an arrangement between a covered educational institution and a private educational lender under which—
 (A) a private educational lender provides or issues private education loans with respect to students attending the covered educational institution;
 (B) the covered educational institution recommends to students or others the private educational lender or the private education loans of the private educational lender; and
 (C) the private educational lender pays a fee or provides other material benefits, including profit sharing, to the covered educational institution in connection with the private education loans provided to students attending the covered educational institution or a borrower acting on behalf of a student.

(b) Prohibition on certain gifts and arrangements
A private educational lender may not, directly or indirectly—
(1) offer or provide any gift to a covered educational institution in exchange for any advantage or consideration provided to such private educational lender related to its private education loan activities; or
(2) engage in revenue sharing with a covered educational institution.

(c) Prohibition on co-branding
A private educational lender may not use the name, emblem, mascot, or logo of the covered educational institution, or other words, pictures, or symbols readily identified with the covered educational institution, in the marketing of private education loans in any way that implies that the covered educational institution endorses the private education loans offered by the private educational lender.

(d) Advisory board compensation
Any person who is employed in the financial aid office of a covered educational institution, or who otherwise has responsibilities with respect to private education loans or other financial aid of the institution, and who serves on an advisory board, commission, or group established by a private educational lender or group of such lenders shall be prohibited from receiving anything of value from the private educational lender or group of lenders. Nothing in this subsection prohibits the reimbursement of reasonable expenses incurred by an employee of a covered educational institution as part of their service on an advisory board, commission, or group described in this subsection.

(e) Prohibition on prepayment or repayment fees or penalty
It shall be unlawful for any private educational lender to impose a fee or penalty on a borrower for early repayment or prepayment of any private education loan.

(f) Credit card protections for college students
 (1) Disclosure required

An institution of higher education shall publicly disclose any contract or other agreement made with a card issuer or creditor for the purpose of marketing a credit card.

(2) Inducements prohibited

No card issuer or creditor may offer to a student at an institution of higher education any tangible item to induce such student to apply for or participate in an open end consumer credit plan offered by such card issuer or creditor, if such offer is made—

(A) on the campus of an institution of higher education;

(B) near the campus of an institution of higher education, as determined by rule of the Bureau; or

(C) at an event sponsored by or related to an institution of higher education.

(3) Sense of the Congress

It is the sense of the Congress that each institution of higher education should consider adopting the following policies relating to credit cards:

(A) That any card issuer that markets a credit card on the campus of such institution notify the institution of the location at which such marketing will take place.

(B) That the number of locations on the campus of such institution at which the marketing of credit cards takes place be limited.

(C) That credit card and debt education and counseling sessions be offered as a regular part of any orientation program for new students of such institution.

[Pub. L. No. 90-321, Title I, § 140, *as added by* Pub. L. No. 110-315, Title X, § 1011(a), 122 Stat. 3479 (Aug. 14, 2008), *and amended by* Pub. L. No. 111-24, Title III, § 304, 123 Stat. 1749 (May 22, 2009);]

* * *

Appendix B Federal Regulations

Reprinted below are selected regulations for the Federal Family Education Loan (FFEL), Direct Loan, and Perkins Loan programs, as well as general debt collection regulations. Additional regulations can be found on the companion website to this manual. Key proposed regulations are also available on the companion website.

B.1 Direct Loan Regulations

34 C.F.R. sec

* * *

685.102 Definitions.

* * *

685.200 Borrower eligibility.

* * *

685.204 Deferment.
685.205 Forbearance.
685.206 Borrower responsibilities and defenses.
685.207 Obligation to repay.
685.208 Repayment plans.
685.209 Income contingent repayment plan.
685.210 Choice of repayment plan.
685.211 Miscellaneous repayment provisions.
685.212 Discharge of a loan obligation.
685.213 Total and permanent disability discharge.
685.214 Closed school discharge.
685.215 Discharge for false certification of student eligibility or unauthorized payment.
685.216 Unpaid refund discharge.

* * *

685.219 Public Service Loan Forgiveness Program.
685.220 Consolidation.
685.221 Income-based repayment plan.

* * *

SOURCE: 59 Fed. Reg. 61690 (Dec. 1, 1994); 61 Fed. Reg. 29899 (June 12, 1996); 73 Fed. Reg. 35495 (June 23, 2008), unless otherwise noted.

AUTHORITY: 20 U.S.C 1070g, 1087a, *et seq.*, unless otherwise noted.

* * *

§ 685.102 Definitions.

(a)(1) The definitions of the following terms used in this part are set forth in subpart A of the Student Assistance General Provisions, 34 CFR part 668:
Academic Competitiveness Grant (ACG) Program
Academic year
Campus-based programs
Dependent student
Disburse
Eligible program
Eligible student
Enrolled
Expected family contribution
Federal Consolidation Loan Program
Federal Direct Student Loan Program (Direct Loan Program)
Federal Pell Grant Program
Federal Perkins Loan Program
Federal PLUS Program
Federal Supplemental Educational Opportunity Grant Program
Federal Work-Study Program
Full-time student
Graduate or professional student
Half-time student
Independent student
Leveraging Educational Assistance Partnership Program
National Science and Mathematics Access to Retain Talent Grant (National SMART Grant) Program
One-third of an academic year
Parent
Payment period
State
Teacher Education Assistance for College and Higher Education (TEACH) Grant Program
TEACH Grant
Two-thirds of an academic year
U.S. citizen or national
Undergraduate student

(2) The following definitions are set forth in the regulations for Institutional Eligibility under the Higher Education Act of 1965, as amended, 34 CFR Part 600:
Accredited
Clock hour
Educational program
Eligible institution
Federal Family Education Loan (FFEL) Program
Institution of higher education
Nationally recognized accrediting agency or association
Preaccredited
Program of study by correspondence
Secretary

(3) The following definitions are set forth in the regulations for the Federal Family Education Loan (FFEL) Program, 34 CFR Part 682:
Act
Endorser
Federal Insured Student Loan (FISL) Program
Federal Stafford Loan Program
Foreign school
Guaranty agency
Holder
Legal guardian
Lender
Totally and permanently disabled

(b) The following definitions also apply to this part:

Alternative originator: An entity under contract with the Secretary that originates Direct Loans to students and parents of students who attend a Direct Loan Program school that does not originate loans.

Consortium: For purposes of this part, a consortium is a group of two or more schools that interacts with the Secretary in the same manner as other schools, except that the electronic communication between the Secretary and the schools is channeled through a single point. Each school in a consortium shall sign a Direct Loan Program participation agreement with the Secretary and be responsible for the information it supplies through the consortium.

Default: The failure of a borrower and endorser, if any, to make an installment payment when due, or to meet other terms of the promissory note, if the Secretary finds it reasonable to conclude that the borrower and endorser, if any, no longer intend to honor the obligation to repay, provided that this failure persists for 270 days.

Estimated financial assistance.

(1) The estimated amount of assistance for a period of enrollment that a student (or a parent on behalf of a student) will receive from Federal, State, institutional, or other sources, such as scholarships, grants, net earnings from need-based employment, or loans, including but not limited to—

(i) Except as provided in paragraph (2)(iii) of this definition, national service education awards or post-service benefits under title I of the National and Community Service Act of 1990 (AmeriCorps).

(ii) Except as provided in paragraph (2)(vii) of this definition, veterans' education benefits;

(iii) Any educational benefits paid because of enrollment in a postsecondary education institution, or to cover postsecondary education expenses;

(iv) Fellowships or assistantships, except non-need-based employment portions of such awards;

(v) Insurance programs for the student's education; and

(vi) The estimated amount of other Federal student financial aid, including but not limited to a Federal Pell Grant, Academic Competitiveness Grant, National SMART Grant, campus-based aid, and the gross amount (including fees) of subsidized and unsubsidized Federal Stafford Loans or subsidized and unsubsidized Direct Stafford Loans and Federal PLUS or Direct PLUS Loans.

(2) Estimated financial assistance does not include—

(i) Those amounts used to replace the expected family contribution (EFC), including the amounts of any TEACH Grant, unsubsidized Federal Stafford Loans or Direct Stafford Loans, Federal PLUS or Direct PLUS Loans, and non-federal non-need-based loans, including private, state-sponsored, and institutional loans. However, if the sum of the amounts received that are being used to replace the student's EFC exceed the EFC, the excess amount must be treated as estimated financial assistance;

(ii) Federal Perkins loan and Federal Work-Study funds that the student has declined;

(iii) For the purpose of determining eligibility for a Direct Subsidized Loan, national service education awards or post-service benefits under title I of the National and Community Service Act of 1990 (AmeriCorps);

(iv) Any portion of the estimated financial assistance described in paragraph (1) of this definition that is included in the calculation of the student's EFC;

(v) Non-need-based employment earnings;

(vi) Assistance not received under a title IV, HEA program, if that assistance is designated to offset all or a portion of a specific amount of the cost of attendance and that component is excluded from the cost of attendance as well. If that assistance is excluded from either estimated financial assistance or cost of attendance, it must be excluded from both;

(vii) Federal veterans' education benefits paid under-

(A) Chapter 103 of title 10, United States Code (Senior Reserve Officers' Training Corps);

(B) Chapter 106A of title 10, United States Code (Educational Assistance for Persons Enlisting for Active Duty);

(C) Chapter 1606 of title 10, United States Code (Selected Reserve Educational Assistance Program);

(D) Chapter 1607 of title 10, United States Code (Educational Assistance Program for Reserve Component Members Supporting Contingency Operations and Certain Other Operations);

(E) Chapter 30 of title 38, United States Code (All-Volunteer Force Educational Assistance Program, also known as the "Montgomery GI Bill-active duty");

(F) Chapter 31 of title 38, United States Code (Training and Rehabilitation for Veterans with Service-Connected Disabilities);

(G) Chapter 32 of title 38, United States Code (Post-Vietnam Era Veterans' Educational Assistance Program);

(H) Chapter 33 of title 38, United States Code (Post 9/11 Educational Assistance);

(I) Chapter 35 of title 38, United States Code (Survivors' and Dependents' Educational Assistance Program);

(J) Section 903 of the Department of Defense Authorization Act, 1981 (10 U.S.C. 2141 note) (Educational Assistance Pilot Program);

(K) Section 156(b) of the "Joint Resolution making further continuing appropriations and providing for productive employment for the fiscal year 1983, and for other purposes" (42 U.S.C. 402 note) (Restored Entitlement Program for Survivors, also known as "Quayle benefits");

(L) The provisions of chapter 3 of title 37, United States Code, related to subsistence allowances for members of the Reserve Officers Training Corps; and

(M) Any program that the Secretary may determine is covered by section 480(c)(2) of the HEA; and

(viii) Iraq and Afghanistan Service Grants made under section 420R of the HEA.

Federal Direct Consolidation Loan Program:

(1) A loan program authorized by title IV, part D of the Act that provides loans to borrowers who consolidate certain Federal educational loan(s), and one of the components of the Direct Loan Program. Loans made under this program are referred to as Direct Consolidation Loans.

(2) The term "Direct Subsidized Consolidation Loan" refers to the portion of a Direct Consolidation Loan attributable to certain subsidized title IV education loans that were repaid by the consolidation loan. Interest is not charged to the borrower during deferment periods, or, for a borrower whose consolidation application was received before July 1, 2006, during in-school and grace periods.

(3) The term "Direct Unsubsidized Consolidation Loan" refers to the portion of a Direct Consolidation Loan attributable to unsubsidized title IV education loans, certain subsidized title IV education loans, and certain other Federal education loans that were repaid by the consolidation loan. The borrower is responsible for the interest that accrues during any period.

(4) The term "Direct PLUS Consolidation Loan" refers to the portion of a Direct Consolidation Loan attributable to Direct PLUS Loans, Direct PLUS Consolidation Loans, Federal PLUS Loans, and Parent Loans for Undergraduate Students that were repaid by the consolidation loan. The borrower is responsible for the interest that accrues during any period.

Federal Direct PLUS Program: A loan program authorized by title IV, Part D of the Act that is one of the components of the Federal Direct Loan Program. The Federal Direct PLUS Program provides loans to parents of dependent students attending schools that participate in the Direct Loan Program. The Federal Direct PLUS Program also provides loans to graduate or professional students attending schools that participate in the Direct Loan Program. The borrower is responsible for the interest that accrues during any period. Loans made under this program are referred to as Direct PLUS Loans.

Federal Direct Stafford/Ford Loan Program: A loan program authorized by title IV, part D of the Act that provides loans to undergraduate, graduate, and professional students attending Direct Loan Program schools, and one of the components of the Direct Loan Program. The Secretary subsidizes the interest while the borrower is in an in-school, grace, or deferment period. Loans made under this program are referred to as Direct Subsidized Loans.

Federal Direct Unsubsidized Stafford/Ford Loan Program: A loan program authorized by title IV, part D of the Act that provides loans to undergraduate, graduate, and professional students attending Direct Loan Program schools, and one of the components of the Direct Loan Program. The borrower is responsible for the interest that accrues during any period. Loans made under this program are referred to as Direct Unsubsidized Loans.

Grace period: A six-month period that begins on the day after a Direct Loan Program borrower ceases to be enrolled as at least a half-time student at an eligible institution and ends on the day before the repayment period begins.

Interest rate: The annual interest rate that is charged on a loan, under title IV, part D of the Act.

Loan fee: A fee, payable by the borrower, that is used to help defray the costs of the Direct Loan Program.

Master Promissory Note (MPN):
 (1) A promissory note under which the borrower may receive loans for a single academic year or multiple academic years.
 (2) For MPNs processed by the Secretary before July 1, 2003, loans may no longer be made under an MPN after the earliest of—
  (i) The date the Secretary or the school receives the borrower's written notice that no further loans may be disbursed;
  (ii) One year after the date of the borrower's first anticipated disbursement if no disbursement is made during that twelve-month period; or
  (iii) Ten years after the date of the first anticipated disbursement, except that a remaining portion of a loan may be disbursed after this date.
 (3) For MPNs processed by the Secretary on or after July 1, 2003, loans may no longer be made under an MPN after the earliest of—
  (i) The date the Secretary or the school receives the borrower's written notice that no further loans may be made;
  (ii) One year after the date the borrower signed the MPN or the date the Secretary receives the MPN, if no disbursements are made under that MPN; or
  (iii) Ten years after the date the borrower signed the MPN or the date the Secretary receives the MPN, except that a remaining portion of a loan may be disbursed after this date.

Period of enrollment: The period for which a Direct Subsidized, Direct Unsubsidized, or Direct PLUS Loan is intended. The period of enrollment must coincide with one or more bona fide academic terms established by the school for which institutional charges are generally assessed (e.g., a semester, trimester, or quarter in weeks of instructional time; an academic year; or the length of the program of study in weeks of instructional time). The period of enrollment is also referred to as the loan period.

Satisfactory repayment arrangement.

(1) For the purpose of regaining eligibility under section 428F(b) of the HEA, the making of six consecutive, voluntary, on-time, full monthly payments on a defaulted loan. A borrower may only obtain the benefit of this paragraph with respect to renewed eligibility once.
(2) For the purpose of consolidating a defaulted loan under 34 CFR 685.220(d)(1)(ii)(C), the making of three consecutive, voluntary, on-time, full monthly payments on a defaulted loan.
(3) The required monthly payment amount may not be more than is reasonable and affordable based on the borrower's total financial circumstances. "On-time" means a payment made within 15 days of the scheduled due date, and voluntary payments are those payments made directly by the borrower and do not include payments obtained by Federal offset, garnishment, or income or asset execution.

School origination option 1: In general, under this option the school performs the following functions: creates a loan origination record, transmits the record to the Servicer, prepares the promissory note, obtains a completed and signed promissory note from a borrower, transmits the promissory note to the Servicer, receives the funds electronically, disburses a loan to a borrower, creates a disbursement record, transmits the disbursement record to the Servicer, and reconciles on a monthly basis. The Servicer initiates the drawdown of funds for schools participating in school origination option 1. The Secretary may modify the functions performed by a particular school.

School origination option 2: In general, under this option the school performs the following functions: creates a loan origination record, transmits the record to the Servicer, prepares the promissory note, obtains a completed and signed promissory note from a borrower, transmits the promissory note to the Servicer, determines funding needs, initiates the drawdown of funds, receives the funds electronically, disburses a loan to a borrower, creates a disbursement record, transmits the disbursement record to the Servicer, and reconciles on a monthly basis. The Secretary may modify the functions performed by a particular school.

Servicer: An entity that has contracted with the Secretary to act as the Secretary's agent in providing services relating to the origination or servicing of Direct Loans.

Standard origination: In general, under this option the school performs the following functions: creates a loan origination record, transmits the record to the Servicer, receives funds electronically, disburses funds, creates a disbursement record, transmits the disbursement record to the Servicer, and reconciles on a monthly basis. The Servicer prepares the promissory note, obtains a completed and signed promissory note from a

borrower, and initiates the drawdown of funds for schools participating in standard origination. The Secretary may modify the functions performed by a particular school.

(Authority: 20 U.S.C. 1070g, 1087a, *et seq.*)

[60 Fed. Reg. 61793 (Dec. 1, 1995); 61 Fed. Reg. 29899 (June 12, 1996); 61 Fed. Reg. 60610 (Nov. 29, 1996); 64 Fed. Reg. 58965 (Nov. 1, 1999); 65 Fed. Reg. 38729 (June 22, 2000); 65 Fed. Reg. 65629 (Nov. 1, 2000); 66 Fed. Reg. 34765 (June 29, 2001); 67 Fed. Reg. 67081 (Nov. 1, 2002); 68 Fed. Reg. 75429 (Dec. 31, 2003); 69 Fed. Reg. 12276 (Mar. 16, 2004); 71 Fed. Reg. 38003 (July 3, 2006); 71 Fed. Reg. 45709 (Aug. 9, 2006); 71 Fed. Reg. 64399 (Nov. 1, 2006); 72 Fed. Reg. 62032 (Nov. 1, 2007); 73 Fed. Reg. 35495 (June 23, 2008); 74 Fed. Reg. 56000 (Oct. 29, 2009)]

* * *

§ 685.200 Borrower eligibility.

(a) *Student Direct Subsidized or Direct Unsubsidized borrower.*
 (1) A student is eligible to receive a Direct Subsidized Loan, a Direct Unsubsidized Loan, or a combination of these loans, if the student meets the following requirements:
  (i) The student is enrolled, or accepted for enrollment, on at least a half-time basis in a school that participates in the Direct Loan Program.
  (ii) The student meets the requirements for an eligible student under 34 CFR part 668.
  (iii) In the case of an undergraduate student who seeks a Direct Subsidized Loan or a Direct Unsubsidized Loan at a school that participates in the Federal Pell Grant Program, the student has received a determination of Federal Pell Grant eligibility for the period of enrollment for which the loan is sought.
  (iv) In the case of a borrower whose previous loan or TEACH Grant service obligation was cancelled due to total and permanent disability, the student—
   (A) In the case of a borrower whose prior loan under title IV of the Act or TEACH Grant service obligation was discharged after a final determination of total and permanent disability, the borrower—
    (1) Obtains a certification from a physician that the borrower is able to engage in substantial gainful activity;
    (2) Signs a statement acknowledging that the Direct Loan the borrower receives cannot be discharged in the future on the basis of any impairment present when the new loan is made, unless that impairment substantially deteriorates; and

(3) If the borrower receives a new Direct Loan, other than a Direct Consolidation Loan, within three years of the date that any previous title IV loan or TEACH Grant service obligation was discharged due to a total and permanent disability in accordance with § 685.213(b)(4), 34 CFR 674.61(b)(3)(i), 34 CFR 682.402(c), or 34 CFR 686.42(b) based on a discharge request received on or after July 1, 2010, resumes repayment on the previously discharged loan in accordance with § 685.213(b)(3)(ii)(A), 34 CFR 674.61(b)(5), or 34 CFR 682.402(c)(5), or acknowledges that he or she is once again subject to the terms of the TEACH Grant agreement to serve before receiving the new loan.

(B) In the case of a borrower whose prior loan under title IV of the Act was conditionally discharged after an initial determination that the borrower was totally and permanently disabled based on a discharge request received prior to July 1, 2010—

(1) The suspension of collection activity on the prior loan has been lifted;

(2) The borrower complies with the requirements in paragraphs (a)(1)(iv)(A)(1) and (2) of this section;

(3) The borrower signs a statement acknowledging that the loan that has been conditionally discharged prior to a final determination of total and permanent disability cannot be discharged in the future on the basis of any impairment present when the borrower applied for a total and permanent disability discharge or when the new loan is made, unless that impairment substantially deteriorates; and

(4) The borrower signs a statement acknowledging that the suspension of collection activity on the prior loan will be lifted.

(v) In the case of a student who seeks a loan but does not have a certificate of graduation from a school providing secondary education or the recognized equivalent of such a certificate, the student meets the requirements under 34 CFR 668.32(e)(2), (3), or (4).

(2)(i) A Direct Subsidized Loan borrower must demonstrate financial need in accordance with title IV, part F of the Act.

(ii) The Secretary considers a member of a religious order, group, community, society, agency, or other organization who is pursuing a course of study at an institution of higher education to have no financial need if that organization—

(A) Has as its primary objective the promotion of ideals and beliefs regarding a Supreme Being;

(B) Requires its members to forego monetary or other support substantially beyond the support it provides; and

(C)(1) Directs the member to pursue the course of study; or

(2) Provides subsistence support to its members.

(b) *Student PLUS borrower.* A graduate or professional student is eligible to receive a Direct PLUS Loan originated on or after July 1, 2006, if the student meets the following requirements—

(1) The student is enrolled, or accepted for enrollment, on at least a half-time basis in a school that participates in the Direct Loan Program.

(2) The student meets the requirements for an eligible student under 34 CFR part 668.

(3) The student meets the requirements of paragraphs (a)(1)(iv) and (a)(1)(v) of this section, if applicable.

(4) The student has received a determination of his or her annual loan maximum eligibility under the Federal Direct Stafford/Ford Loan Program and the Federal Direct Unsubsidized Stafford/Ford Loan Program or under the Federal Subsidized and Unsubsidized Stafford Loan Program, as applicable; and

(5) The student meets the requirements of paragraph (c)(1)(vii) of this section.

(c) *Parent PLUS borrower.*

(1) A parent is eligible to receive a Direct PLUS Loan if the parent meets the following requirements:

(i) The parent is borrowing to pay for the educational costs of a dependent undergraduate student who meets the requirements for an eligible student under 34 CFR part 668.

(ii) The parent provides his or her and the student's social security number.

(iii) The parent meets the requirements pertaining to citizenship and residency that apply to the student under 34 CFR 668.33.

(iv) The parent meets the requirements concerning defaults and overpayments that apply to the student in 34 CFR 668.32(g).

(v) The parent complies with the requirements for submission of a Statement of Educational Purpose that apply to the student under 34 CFR part 668, except for the completion of a Statement of Selective Service Registration Status.

(vi) The parent meets the requirements that apply to a student under paragraph (a)(1)(iv) of this section.

(vii)(A) The parent—

(1) Does not have an adverse credit history;

(2) Has an adverse credit history but has obtained an endorser who does not have an adverse credit history; or

(3) Has an adverse credit history but documents to the satisfaction of the Secretary that extenuating circumstances exist.

(B) For purposes of paragraph (c)(1)(vii)(A) of this section, an adverse credit history means that as of the date of the credit report, the applicant—

(1) Is 90 or more days delinquent on any debt; or

(2) Has been the subject of a default determination, bankruptcy discharge, foreclosure, repossession, tax lien, wage garnishment, or write-off of a debt under title IV of the Act during the five years preceding the date of the credit report.

(C) For the purposes of (c)(1)(vii)(A) of this section, the Secretary does not consider the absence of a credit history as an adverse credit history and does not deny a Direct PLUS loan on that basis.

(2) For purposes of paragraph (c)(1) of this section, a "parent" includes the individuals described in the definition of "parent" in 34 CFR 668.2 and the spouse of a parent who remarried, if that spouse's income and assets would have been taken into account when calculating a dependent student's expected family contribution.

(3) Has completed repayment of any title IV, HEA program assistance obtained by fraud, if the parent has been convicted of, or has pled nolo contendere or guilty to, a crime involving fraud in obtaining title IV, HEA program assistance.

(d) *Defaulted FFEL Program and Direct Loan borrowers.* Except as noted in § 685.220(d)(1)(ii)(D), in the case of a student or parent borrower who is currently in default on an FFEL Program or a Direct Loan Program Loan, the borrower shall make satisfactory repayment arrangements, as described in paragraph (2) of the definition of that term under § 685.102(b), on the defaulted loan.

(e) *Use of loan proceeds to replace expected family contribution.* The amount of a Direct Unsubsidized Loan, a Direct PLUS loan, or a non-federal non-need based loan, including a private, state-sponsored, or institution loan, obtained for a loan period may be used to replace the expected family contribution for that loan period.

(Authority: 20 U.S.C. 1087a *et seq.*)

[60 Fed. Reg. 61816 (Dec. 1, 1995); 61 Fed. Reg. 29900 (June 12, 1996); 65 Fed. Reg. 65629, 65693 (Nov. 1, 2000); 66 Fed. Reg. 34765 (June 29, 2001); 66 Fed. Reg. 44007 (Aug. 21, 2001); 68 Fed. Reg. 75430 (Dec. 31, 2003); 71 Fed. Reg. 45710 (Aug. 9, 2006); 71 Fed. Reg. 64399 (Nov. 1, 2006); 74 Fed. Reg. 56001 (Oct. 29, 2009)]

* * *

§ 685.204 Deferment.

(a)(1) A Direct Loan borrower whose loan is eligible for interest subsidies and who meets the requirements described in paragraphs (b) and (e) of this section is eligible for a deferment during which periodic installments of principal and interest need not be paid.

(2) A Direct Loan borrower whose loan is not eligible for interest subsidies and who meets the requirements described in paragraphs (b) and (e) of this section is eligible for a deferment during which periodic installments of principal need not be paid but interest does accrue and is capitalized or paid by the borrower.

(b) Except as provided in paragraphs (d) and (g) of this section, a Direct Loan borrower is eligible for a deferment during any period during which the borrower meets any of the following requirements:

(1)(i) The borrower—

(A) Is carrying at least one-half the normal full-time work load for the course of study that the borrower is pursuing, as determined by the eligible school the borrower is attending;

(B) Is pursuing a course of study pursuant to a graduate fellowship program approved by the Secretary; or

(C) Is pursuing a rehabilitation training program, approved by the Secretary, for individuals with disabilities; and

(ii) The borrower is not serving in a medical internship or residency program, except for a residency program in dentistry.

(iii)(A) For the purpose of paragraph (b)(1)(i)(A) of this section, the Secretary processes a deferment when—

(1) The borrower submits a request to the Secretary along with documentation verifying the borrower's eligibility;

(2) The Secretary receives information from the borrower's school indicating that the borrower is eligible to receive a new loan;

(3) The Secretary receives student status information from the borrower's school, either directly or indirectly, indicating that the borrower is enrolled on at least a half-time basis; or

(4) The Secretary confirms a borrower's half-time enrollment status through the use of the National Student Loan Data System if requested to do so by the school the borrower is attending.

(B)(1) Upon notification by the Secretary that a deferment has been granted based on paragraph (b)(1)(iii)(A)(2), (3), or (4) of this section, the borrower has the option to cancel the deferment and continue paying on the loan.

(2) If the borrower elects to cancel the deferment and continue paying on the loan, the borrower has the option to make the principal and interest payments that were deferred. If the borrower does not make the payments, the Secretary applies a deferment for the period in which payments were not made and capitalizes the interest. The Secretary will provide information, including an example, to assist the borrower in understanding the impact of capitalization of accrued, unpaid interest on the borrower's loan principal and on the total amount of interest to be paid over the life of the loan.

(2)(i) The borrower is seeking and unable to find full-time employment.

(ii) For purposes of paragraph (b)(2)(i) of this section, the Secretary determines whether a borrower is eligible for a deferment due to the inability to find full-time employment using the standards and procedures set forth in 34 CFR 682.210(h) with references to the lender understood to mean the Secretary.

(3)(i) The borrower has experienced or will experience an economic hardship.

(ii) For purposes of paragraph (b)(3)(i) of this section, the Secretary determines whether a borrower is eligible for a deferment due to an economic hardship using the standards and procedures set forth in 34 CFR 682.210(s)(6) with references to the lender understood to mean the Secretary.

(c) No deferment under paragraphs (b) (2) or (3) of this section may exceed three years.

(d) If, at the time of application for a borrower's first Direct Loan, a borrower has an outstanding balance of principal or interest owing on any FFEL Program loan that was made, insured, or guaranteed prior to July 1, 1993, the borrower is eligible for a deferment during—

(1) The periods described in paragraphs (b) and (e) of this section; and

(2) The periods described in 34 CFR 682.210(b), including those periods that apply to a "new borrower" as that term is defined in 34 CFR 682.210(b)(7).

(e) *Military service deferment.*

(1) A borrower who receives a Direct Loan Program loan may receive a military service deferment for such loan for any period during which the borrower is—

(i) Serving on active duty during a war or other military operation or national emergency; or

(ii) Performing qualifying National Guard duty during a war or other military operation or national emergency.

(2) For a borrower whose active duty service includes October 1, 2007, or begins on or after that date, the deferment period ends 180 days after the demobilization date for each period of the service described in paragraphs (e)(1)(i) and (e)(1)(ii) of this section.

(3) Serving on active duty during a war or other military operation or national emergency means service by an individual who is—

(i) A Reserve of an Armed Force ordered to active duty under 10 U.S.C. 12301(a), 12301(g), 12302, 12304, or 12306;

(ii) A retired member of an Armed Force ordered to active duty under 10 U.S.C. 688 for service in connection with a war or other military operation or national emergency, regardless of the location at which such active duty service is performed; or

(iii) Any other member of an Armed Force on active duty in connection with such emergency or subsequent actions or conditions who has been assigned to a duty station at a location other than the location at which the member is normally assigned.

(4) Qualifying National Guard duty during a war or other operation or national emergency means service as a member of the National Guard on full-time National Guard duty, as defined in 10 U.S.C. 101(d)(5) under a call to active service authorized by the President or the Secretary of Defense for a period of more than 30 consecutive days under 32 U.S.C. 502(f) in connection with a war, other military operation, or national emergency declared by the President and supported by Federal funds.

(5) These provisions do not authorize the refunding of any payments made by or on behalf of a borrower during a period for which the borrower qualified for a military service deferment.

(6) As used in this paragraph—

(i) Active duty means active duty as defined in 10 U.S.C. 101(d)(1) except that it does not include active duty for training or attendance at a service school;

(ii) Military operation means a contingency operation as defined in 10 U.S.C. 101(a)(13); and

(iii) National emergency means the national emergency by reason of certain terrorist attacks declared by the President on September 14, 2001, or subsequent national emergencies declared by the President by reason of terrorist attacks.

(7) Without supporting documentation, the military service deferment will be granted to an otherwise eligible borrower for a period not to exceed 12 months from the date of the qualifying eligible service based on a request from the borrower or the borrower's representative.

(f) *Post-active duty student deferment.*

(1) A borrower who receives a Direct Loan Program loan is entitled to receive a military active duty student deferment for 13 months

following the conclusion of the borrower's active duty military service if—

(i) The borrower is a member of the National Guard or other reserve component of the Armed Forces of the United States or a member of such forces in retired status; and

(ii) The borrower was enrolled on at least a half-time basis in a program of instruction at an eligible institution at the time, or within six months prior to the time, the borrower was called to active duty.

(2) As used in paragraph (f)(1) of this section, "Active Duty" means active duty as defined in section 101(d)(1) of title 10, United States Code, except that—

(i) Active duty includes active State duty for members of the National Guard under which a Governor activates National Guard personnel based on State statute or policy and the activities of the National Guard are paid for with State funds;

(ii) Active duty includes full-time National Guard duty under which a Governor is authorized, with the approval of the President or the U.S. Secretary of Defense, to order a member to State active duty and the activities of the National Guard are paid for with Federal funds;

(iii) Active duty does not include active duty for training or attendance at a service school; and

(iv) Active duty does not include employment in a full-time, permanent position in the National Guard unless the borrower employed in such a position is reassigned to active duty under paragraph (f)(2)(i) of this section or full-time National Guard duty under paragraph (f)(2)(ii) of this section.

(3) If the borrower returns to enrolled student status on at least a half-time basis during the grace period or the 13-month deferment period, the deferment expires at the time the borrower returns to enrolled student status on at least a half-time basis.

(4) If a borrower qualifies for both a military service deferment and a post-active duty student deferment, the 180-day post-demobilization deferment period and the 13-month post-active duty student deferment period apply concurrently.

(g) *In-school deferments for Direct PLUS Loan borrowers with loans first disbursed on or after July 1, 2008.*

(1)(i) A student Direct PLUS Loan borrower is entitled to a deferment on a Direct PLUS Loan first disbursed on or after July 1, 2008 during the 6-month period that begins on the day after the student ceases to be enrolled on at least a half-time basis at an eligible institution.

(ii) If the Secretary grants an in-school deferment to a student Direct PLUS Loan borrower based on § 682.204(b)(1)(iii)(A)

(2), (3), or (4), the deferment period for a Direct PLUS Loan first disbursed on or after July 1, 2008 includes the 6-month post-enrollment period described in paragraph (g)(1)(i) of this section.

(2) Upon the request of the borrower, an eligible parent Direct PLUS Loan borrower will receive a deferment on a Direct PLUS Loan first disbursed on or after July 1, 2008—

(i) During the period when the student on whose behalf the loan was obtained is enrolled at an eligible institution on at least a half-time basis; and

(ii) During the 6-month period that begins on the later of the day after the student on whose behalf the loan was obtained ceases to be enrolled on at least a half-time basis or, if the parent borrower is also a student, the day after the parent borrower ceases to be enrolled on at least a half-time basis.

(h) A borrower whose loan is in default is not eligible for a deferment, unless the borrower has made payment arrangements satisfactory to the Secretary.

(i)(1) To receive a deferment, except as provided under paragraph (b)(1)(i)(A) of this section, the borrower must request the deferment and provide the Secretary with all information and documents required to establish eligibility for the deferment. In the case of a deferment under paragraph (e)(1) of this section, a borrower's representative may request the deferment and provide the required information and documents on behalf of the borrower.

(2) After receiving a borrower's written or verbal request, the Secretary may grant a deferment under paragraphs (b)(1)(i)(B), (b)(1)(i)(C), (b)(2)(i), (b)(3)(i), (e)(1), and (f)(1) of this section if the Secretary confirms that the borrower has received a deferment on a Perkins or FFEL Loan for the same reason and the same time period.

(3) The Secretary relies in good faith on the information obtained under paragraph (i)(2) of this section when determining a borrower's eligibility for a deferment, unless the Secretary, as of the date of the determination, has information indicating that the borrower does not qualify for the deferment. The Secretary resolves any discrepant information before granting a deferment under paragraph (i)(2) of this section.

(4) If the Secretary grants a deferment under paragraph (i)(2) of this section, the Secretary notifies the borrower that the deferment has been granted and that the borrower has the option to cancel the deferment and continue to make payments on the loan.

(5) If the Secretary grants a military service deferment based on a request from a borrower's representative, the Secretary notifies the borrower that the deferment has been granted and that the borrower has the option to cancel the deferment and continue to make payments on the loan. The Secretary may also notify the

borrower's representative of the outcome of the deferment request.

(Approved by the Office of Management and Budget under control number 1845-0021)

(Authority: 20 U.S.C. 1087a *et seq.*)

[60 Fed. Reg. 33345 (June 28, 1995); 61 Fed. Reg. 29900 (June 12, 1996); 64 Fed. Reg. 58968 (Nov. 1, 1999); 71 Fed. Reg. 45711 (Aug. 9, 2006); 72 Fed. Reg. 62009 (Nov. 1, 2007); 73 Fed. Reg. 63254 (Oct. 23, 2008); 74 Fed. Reg. 56002 (Oct. 29, 2009)]

§ 685.205 Forbearance.

(a) *General.* "Forbearance" means permitting the temporary cessation of payments, allowing an extension of time for making payments, or temporarily accepting smaller payments than previously scheduled. The borrower has the option to choose the form of forbearance. Except as provided in paragraph (b)(9) of this section, if payments of interest are forborne, they are capitalized. The Secretary grants forbearance if the borrower or endorser intends to repay the loan but requests forbearance and provides sufficient documentation to support this request, and—

(1) The Secretary determines that, due to poor health or other acceptable reasons, the borrower or endorser is currently unable to make scheduled payments;

(2) The borrower's payments of principal are deferred under § 685.204 and the Secretary does not subsidize the interest benefits on behalf of the borrower;

(3) The borrower is in a medical or dental internship or residency that must be successfully completed before the borrower may begin professional practice or service, or the borrower is serving in a medical or dental internship or residency program leading to a degree or certificate awarded by an institution of higher education, a hospital, or a health care facility that offers postgraduate training;

(4) The borrower is serving in a national service position for which the borrower is receiving a national service education award under title I of the National and Community Service Act of 1990; or

(5) The borrower—

(i) Is performing the type of service that would qualify the borrower for loan forgiveness under the requirements of the teacher loan forgiveness program in § 685.217; and

(ii) Is required, by the Secretary, before a forbearance is granted under § 685.205(a)(5)(i) to—

(A) Submit documentation for the period of the annual forbearance request showing the beginning and ending dates that the borrower is expected to perform, for that year, the type of service described in § 685.217(c); and

(B) Certify the borrower's intent to satisfy the requirements of § 685.217(c).
(6) For not more than three years during which the borrower or endorser—
   (i) Is currently obligated to make payments on loans under title IV of the Act; and
   (ii) The sum of these payments each month (or a proportional share if the payments are due less frequently than monthly) is equal to or greater than 20 percent of the borrower's or endorser's total monthly gross income.
(7) The borrower is a member of the National Guard who qualifies for a post-active duty student deferment, but does not qualify for a military service or other deferment, and is engaged in active State duty for a period of more than 30 consecutive days, beginning—
   (i) On the day after the grace period expires for a Direct Subsidized Loan or Direct Unsubsidized Loan that has not entered repayment; or
   (ii) On the day after the borrower ceases enrollment on at least a half-time basis, for a Direct Loan in repayment.

(b) *Administrative forbearance.* In certain circumstances, the Secretary grants forbearance without requiring documentation from the borrower. These circumstances include but are not limited to—
(1) A properly granted period of deferment for which the Secretary learns the borrower did not qualify;
(2) The period for which payments are overdue at the beginning of an authorized deferment period;
(3) The period beginning when the borrower entered repayment without the Secretary's knowledge until the first payment due date was established;
(4) The period prior to a borrower's filing of a bankruptcy petition;
(5) A period after the Secretary receives reliable information indicating that the borrower (or the student in the case of a Direct PLUS Loan obtained by a parent borrower) has died, or the borrower has become totally and permanently disabled, until the Secretary receives documentation of death or total and permanent disability;
(6) Periods necessary for the Secretary to determine the borrower's eligibility for discharge—
   (i) Under § 685.214;
   (ii) Under § 685.215;
   (iii) Under § 685.216;
   (iv) Under § 685.217; or
   (v) Due to the borrower's or endorser's (if applicable) bankruptcy;
(7) A period of up to three years in cases where the effect of a variable interest rate on a fixed-amount or graduated repayment schedule causes the extension of the maximum repayment term;

(8) A period during which the Secretary has authorized forbearance due to a national military mobilization or other local or national emergency;
(9) A period of up to 60 days necessary for the Secretary to collect and process documentation supporting the borrower's request for a deferment, forbearance, change in repayment plan, or consolidation loan. Interest that accrues during this period is not capitalized; or
(10) For Direct PLUS Loans first disbursed before July 1, 2008, to align repayment with a borrower's Direct PLUS Loans that were first disbursed on or after July 1, 2008, or with Direct Subsidized Loans or Direct Unsubsidized Loans that have a grace period in accordance with § 685.207(b) or (c). The Secretary notifies the borrower that the borrower has the option to cancel the forbearance and continue paying on the loan.

(c) *Period of forbearance.*
(1) The Secretary grants forbearance for a period of up to one year.
(2) The forbearance is renewable, upon request of the borrower, for the duration of the period in which the borrower meets the condition required for the forbearance.

(Approved by the Office of Management and Budget under control number 1845-0021)

(Authority: 20 U.S.C. 1087a *et seq.*)

[61 Fed. Reg. 29900 (June 12, 1996); 64 Fed. Reg. 58968 (Nov. 1, 1999); 65 Fed. Reg. 65629 (Nov. 1, 2000); 66 Fed. Reg. 34765 (June 29, 2001); 68 Fed. Reg. 75430 (Dec. 31, 2003); 71 Fed. Reg. 45712 (Aug. 9, 2006); 73 Fed. Reg. 63255 (Oct. 23, 2008); 74 Fed. Reg. 56003 (Oct. 29, 2009)]

§ 685.206 Borrower responsibilities and defenses.

(a) The borrower shall give the school the following information as part of the origination process for a Direct Subsidized, Direct Unsubsidized, or Direct PLUS Loan:
(1) A statement, as described in 34 CFR Part 668, that the loan will be used for the cost of the student's attendance.
(2) Information demonstrating that the borrower is eligible for the loan.
(3) Information concerning the outstanding FFEL Program and Direct Loan Program loans of the borrower and, for a parent borrower, of the student, including any Federal Consolidation Loan or Direct Consolidation Loan.
(4) A statement authorizing the school to release to the Secretary information relevant to the student's eligibility to borrow or to have a parent borrow on the student's behalf (e.g., the student's enrollment status, financial assistance, and employment records).

(b)(1) The borrower shall promptly notify the Secretary of any change of name, address, student status to less than half-time, employer, or employer's address; and
(2) The borrower shall promptly notify the school of any change in address during enrollment.

(c) *Borrower defenses.*
(1) In any proceeding to collect on a Direct Loan, the borrower may assert as a defense against repayment, any act or omission of the school attended by the student that would give rise to a cause of action against the school under applicable State law. These proceedings include, but are not limited to, the following:
   (i) Tax refund offset proceedings under 34 CFR 30.33.
   (ii) Wage garnishment proceedings under section 488A of the Act.
   (iii) Salary offset proceedings for Federal employees under 34 CFR Part 31.
   (iv) Credit bureau reporting proceedings under 31 U.S.C. 3711(f).
(2) If the borrower's defense against repayment is successful, the Secretary notifies the borrower that the borrower is relieved of the obligation to repay all or part of the loan and associated costs and fees that the borrower would otherwise be obligated to pay. The Secretary affords the borrower such further relief as the Secretary determines is appropriate under the circumstances. Further relief may include, but is not limited to, the following:
   (i) Reimbursing the borrower for amounts paid toward the loan voluntarily or through enforced collection.
   (ii) Determining that the borrower is not in default on the loan and is eligible to receive assistance under title IV of the Act.
   (iii) Updating reports to credit bureaus to which the Secretary previously made adverse credit reports with regard to the borrower's Direct Loan.
(3) The Secretary may initiate an appropriate proceeding to require the school whose act or omission resulted in the borrower's successful defense against repayment of a Direct Loan to pay to the Secretary the amount of the loan to which the defense applies. However, the Secretary does not initiate such a proceeding after the period for the retention of records described in § 685.309(c) unless the school received actual notice of the claim during that period.

(Approved by the Office of Management and Budget under control number 1845-0021)

(Authority: 20 U.S.C. 1087a *et seq.*)

[60 Fed. Reg. 33345 (June 28, 1995); 64 Fed. Reg. 58972 (Nov. 1, 1999)]

§ 685.207 Obligation to repay.

(a) *Obligation of repayment in general.*

(1) A borrower is obligated to repay the full amount of a Direct Loan, including the principal balance, fees, any collection costs charged under § 685.202(e), and any interest not subsidized by the Secretary, unless the borrower is relieved of the obligation to repay as provided in this part.

(2) The borrower's repayment of a Direct Loan may also be subject to the deferment provisions in § 685.204, the forbearance provisions in § 685.205, and the discharge provisions in § 685.212.

(b) *Direct Subsidized Loan repayment.*

(1) During the period in which a borrower is enrolled at an eligible school on at least a half-time basis, the borrower is in an "in-school" period and is not required to make payments on a Direct Subsidized Loan unless—

(i) The loan entered repayment before the in-school period began; and

(ii) The borrower has not been granted a deferment under § 685.204.

(2)(i) When a borrower ceases to be enrolled at an eligible school on at least a half-time basis, a six-month grace period begins, unless the grace period has been previously exhausted.

(ii)(A) Any borrower who is a member of a reserve component of the Armed Forces named in section 10101 of title 10, United States Code and is called or ordered to active duty for a period of more than 30 days is entitled to have the active duty period excluded from the six-month grace period. The excluded period includes the time necessary for the borrower to resume enrollment at the next available regular enrollment period. Any single excluded period may not exceed 3 years.

(B) Any borrower who is in a grace period when called or ordered to active duty as specified in paragraph (b)(2)(ii)(A) of this section is entitled to a full six-month grace period upon completion of the excluded period.

(iii) During a grace period, the borrower is not required to make any principal payments on a Direct Subsidized Loan.

(3) A borrower is not obligated to pay interest on a Direct Subsidized Loan for in-school or grace periods unless the borrower is required to make payments on the loan during those periods under paragraph (b)(1) of this section.

(4) The repayment period for a Direct Subsidized Loan begins the day after the grace period ends. A borrower is obligated to repay the loan under paragraph (a) of this section during the repayment period.

(c) *Direct Unsubsidized Loan repayment.*

(1) During the period in which a borrower is enrolled at an eligible school on at least a half-time basis, the borrower is in an "in-school" period and is not required to make payments of principal on a Direct Unsubsidized Loan unless—

(i) The loan entered repayment before the in-school period began; and

(ii) The borrower has not been granted a deferment under § 685.204.

(2)(i) When a borrower ceases to be enrolled at an eligible school on at least a half-time basis, a six-month grace period begins, unless the grace period has been previously exhausted.

(ii)(A) Any borrower who is a member of a reserve component of the Armed Forces named in section 10101 of title 10, United States Code and is called or ordered to active duty for a period of more than 30 days is entitled to have the active duty period excluded from the six-month grace period. The excluded period includes the time necessary for the borrower to resume enrollment at the next available regular enrollment period. Any single excluded period may not exceed 3 years.

(B) Any borrower who is in a grace period when called or ordered to active duty as specified in paragraph (c)(2)(ii)(A) of this section is entitled to a full six-month grace period upon completion of the excluded period.

(iii) During a grace period, the borrower is not required to make any principal payments on a Direct Unsubsidized Loan.

(3) A borrower is responsible for the interest that accrues on a Direct Unsubsidized Loan during in-school and grace periods. Interest begins to accrue on the day the first installment is disbursed. Interest that accrues may be capitalized or paid by the borrower.

(4) The repayment period for a Direct Unsubsidized Loan begins the day after the grace period ends. A borrower is obligated to repay the loan under paragraph (a) of this section during the repayment period.

(d) *Direct PLUS Loan repayment.*

The repayment period for a Direct PLUS Loan begins on the day the loan is fully disbursed. Interest begins to accrue on the day the first installment is disbursed. A borrower is obligated to repay the loan under paragraph (a) of this section during the repayment period.

(e) *Direct Consolidation Loan repayment.*

(1) Except as provided in paragraphs (e)(2) and (e)(3) of this section, the repayment period for a Direct Consolidation Loan begins and interest begins to accrue on the day the loan is made. The borrower is obligated to repay the loan under paragraph (a) of this section during the repayment period.

(2) In the case of a borrower whose consolidation application was received before July 1, 2006, a borrower who obtains a Direct Subsidized Consolidation Loan during an in-school period will be subject to the repayment provisions in paragraph (b) of this section.

(3) In the case of a borrower whose consolidation application was received before July 1, 2006, a borrower who obtains a Direct Unsubsidized Consolidation Loan during an in-school period will be subject to the repayment provisions in paragraph (c) of this section.

(f) *Determining the date on which the grace period begins for a borrower in a correspondence program.*

For a borrower of a Direct Subsidized or Direct Unsubsidized Loan who is a correspondence student, the grace period specified in paragraphs (b)(2) and (c)(2) of this section begins on the earliest of—

(1) The day after the borrower completes the program;

(2) The day after withdrawal as determined pursuant to 34 CFR 668.22; or

(3) 60 days following the last day for completing the program as established by the school.

(Authority: 20 U.S.C. 1087a *et seq.*)

[64 Fed. Reg. 58968 (Nov. 1, 1999); 68 Fed. Reg. 75430 (Dec. 31, 2003); 71 Fed. Reg. 45712 (Aug. 9, 2006)]

§ 685.208 Repayment plans.

(a) *General.*

(1) Borrowers who entered repayment before July 1, 2006.

(i) A borrower may repay a Direct Subsidized Loan, a Direct Unsubsidized Loan, a Direct Subsidized Consolidation Loan, or a Direct Unsubsidized Consolidation Loan under the standard repayment plan, the extended repayment plan, the graduated repayment plan, the income contingent repayment plan, or the income-based repayment plan, in accordance with paragraphs (b), (d), (f), (k), and (m) of this section, respectively.

(ii) A borrower may repay a Direct PLUS Loan or a Direct PLUS Consolidation Loan under the standard repayment plan, the extended repayment plan, or the graduated repayment plan, in accordance with paragraphs (b), (d), and (f) of this section, respectively.

(2) Borrowers entering repayment on or after July 1, 2006.

(i) A borrower may repay a Direct Subsidized Loan or a Direct Unsubsidized Loan under the standard repayment plan, the extended repayment plan, the graduated repayment plan, the income contingent repayment plan, or the income-based repayment plan, in accordance with paragraphs (b), (e), (g), (k), and (m) of this section, respectively.

(ii)(A) A Direct PLUS Loan that was made to a graduate or professional student borrower may be repaid under the standard repayment plan, the extended repayment plan, the graduated repayment plan, the income-contingent repayment plan, or the income-based repayment plan in accordance with paragraphs (b), (e), (g), (k), and (m) of this section, respectively.

(B) A Direct PLUS Loan that was made to a parent borrower may be repaid under the standard repayment plan, the extended repayment plan, or the graduated repayment plan, in accordance with paragraphs (b), (e), and (g) of this section, respectively.

(iii) A borrower may repay a Direct Consolidation Loan under the standard repayment plan, the extended repayment plan, the graduated repayment plan, the income contingent repayment plan, or, unless the Direct Consolidation Loan repaid a parent Direct PLUS Loan or a parent Federal PLUS Loan, the income-based repayment plan, in accordance with paragraphs (c), (e), (h), (k), and (m) of this section, respectively. A Direct Consolidation Loan that repaid a parent Direct PLUS Loan or a parent Federal PLUS Loan may not be repaid under the income-based repayment plan.

(iv) No scheduled payment may be less than the amount of interest accrued on the loan between monthly payments, except under the income contingent repayment plan, the income-based repayment plan, or an alternative repayment plan.

(3) The Secretary may provide an alternative repayment plan in accordance with paragraph (l) of this section.

(4) All Direct Loans obtained by one borrower must be repaid together under the same repayment plan, except that—

(i) A borrower of a Direct PLUS Loan or a Direct Consolidation Loan that is not eligible for repayment under the income-contingent repayment plan or the income-based repayment plan may repay the Direct PLUS Loan or Direct Consolidation Loan separately from other Direct Loans obtained by the borrower; and

(ii) A borrower of a Direct PLUS Consolidation Loan that entered repayment before July 1, 2006, may repay the Direct PLUS Consolidation Loan separately from other Direct Loans obtained by that borrower.

(5) Except as provided in § 685.209 and § 685.221 for the income contingent or income-based repayment plan, the repayment period for any of the repayment plans described in this section does not include periods of authorized deferment or forbearance.

(b) *Standard repayment plan for all Direct Subsidized Loan, Direct Unsubsidized Loan, and Direct PLUS Loan borrowers, regardless of when they entered repayment, and for Direct Consolidation Loan borrowers who entered repayment before July 1, 2006.*

(1) Under this repayment plan, a borrower must repay a loan in full within ten years from the date the loan entered repayment by making fixed monthly payments.

(2) A borrower's payments under this repayment plan are at least $50 per month, except that a borrower's final payment may be less than $50.

(3) The number of payments or the fixed monthly repayment amount may be adjusted to reflect changes in the variable interest rate identified in § 685.202(a).

(c) *Standard repayment plan for Direct Consolidation Loan borrowers entering repayment on or after July 1, 2006.*

(1) Under this repayment plan, a borrower must repay a loan in full by making fixed monthly payments over a repayment period that varies with the total amount of the borrower's student loans, as described in paragraph (j) of this section.

(2) A borrower's payments under this repayment plan are at least $50 per month, except that a borrower's final payment may be less than $50.

(d) *Extended repayment plan for all Direct Loan borrowers who entered repayment before July 1, 2006.*

(1) Under this repayment plan, a borrower must repay a loan in full by making fixed monthly payments within an extended period of time that varies with the total amount of the borrower's loans, as described in paragraph (i) of this section.

(2) A borrower makes fixed monthly payments of at least $50, except that a borrower's final payment may be less than $50.

(3) The number of payments or the fixed monthly repayment amount may be adjusted to reflect changes in the variable interest rate identified in § 685.202(a).

(e) *Extended repayment plan for all Direct Loan borrowers entering repayment on or after July 1, 2006.*

(1) Under this repayment plan, a new borrower with more than $30,000 in outstanding Direct Loans accumulated on or after October 7, 1998 must repay either a fixed annual or graduated repayment amount over a period not to exceed 25 years from the date the loan entered repayment. For this repayment plan, a new borrower is defined as an individual who has no outstanding principal or interest balance on a Direct Loan as of October 7, 1998, or on the date the borrower obtains a Direct Loan on or after October 7, 1998.

(2) A borrower's payments under this plan are at least $50 per month, and will be more if necessary to repay the loan within the required time period.

(3) The number of payments or the monthly repayment amount may be adjusted to reflect changes in the variable interest rate identified in § 685.202(a).

(f) *Graduated repayment plan for all Direct Loan borrowers who entered repayment before July 1, 2006.*

(1) Under this repayment plan, a borrower must repay a loan in full by making payments at two or more levels within a period of time that varies with the total amount of the borrower's loans, as described in paragraph (i) of this section.

(2) The number of payments or the monthly repayment amount may be adjusted to reflect changes in the variable interest rate identified in § 685.202(a).

(3) No scheduled payment under this repayment plan may be less than the amount of interest accrued on the loan between monthly payments, less than 50 percent of the payment amount that would be required under the standard repayment plan described in paragraph (b) of this section, or more than 150 percent of the payment amount that would be required under the standard repayment plan described in paragraph (b) of this section.

(g) *Graduated repayment plan for Direct Subsidized Loan, Direct Unsubsidized Loan, and Direct PLUS Loan borrowers entering repayment on or after July 1, 2006.*

(1) Under this repayment plan, a borrower must repay a loan in full by making payments at two or more levels over a period of time not to exceed ten years from the date the loan entered repayment.

(2) The number of payments or the monthly repayment amount may be adjusted to reflect changes in the variable interest rate identified in § 685.202(a).

(3) A borrower's payments under this repayment plan may be less than $50 per month. No single payment under this plan will be more than three times greater than any other payment.

(h) *Graduated repayment plan for Direct Consolidation Loan borrowers entering repayment on or after July 1, 2006.*

(1) Under this repayment plan, a borrower must repay a loan in full by making monthly payments that gradually increase in stages over the course of a repayment period that varies with the total amount of the borrower's student loans, as described in paragraph (j) of this section.

(2) A borrower's payments under this repayment plan may be less than $50 per month. No single payment under this plan will be more than three times greater than any other payment.

(i) *Repayment period for the extended and graduated plans described in paragraphs (d) and (f) of this section, respectively.* Under these repayment plans, if the total amount of the borrower's Direct Loans is—

(1) Less than $10,000, the borrower must repay the loans within 12 years of entering repayment;

(2) Greater than or equal to $10,000 but less than $20,000, the borrower must repay the loans within 15 years of entering repayment;

(3) Greater than or equal to $20,000 but less than $40,000, the borrower must repay the loans within 20 years of entering repayment;

(4) Greater than or equal to $40,000 but less than $60,000, the borrower must repay the loans within 25 years of entering repayment; and

(5) Greater than or equal to $60,000, the borrower must repay the loans within 30 years of entering repayment.

(j) *Repayment period for the standard and graduated repayment plans described in paragraphs (c) and (h) of this section, respectively.* Under these repayment plans, if the total amount of the Direct Consolidation Loan and the borrower's other student loans, as defined in § 685.220(i), is—

(1) Less then $7,500, the borrower must repay the Consolidation Loan within 10 years of entering repayment;

(2) Equal to or greater than $7,500 but less than $10,000, the borrower must repay the Consolidation Loan within 12 years of entering repayment;

(3) Equal to or greater than $10,000 but less than $20,000, the borrower must repay the Consolidation Loan within 15 years of entering repayment;

(4) Equal to or greater than $20,000 but less than $40,000, the borrower must repay the Consolidation Loan within 20 years of entering repayment;

(5) Equal to or greater than $40,000 but less than $60,000, the borrower must repay the Consolidation Loan within 25 years of entering repayment; and

(6) Equal to or greater than $60,000, the borrower must repay the Consolidation Loan within 30 years of entering repayment.

(k) *Income contingent repayment plan.*

(1) Under the income contingent repayment plan, a borrower's monthly repayment amount is generally based on the total amount of the borrower's Direct Loans, family size, and Adjusted Gross Income (AGI) reported by the borrower for the most recent year for which the Secretary has obtained income information. The borrower's AGI includes the income of the borrower's spouse. A borrower must make payments on a loan until the loan is repaid in full or until the loan has been in repayment through the end of the income contingent repayment period.

(2) The regulations in effect at the time a borrower enters repayment and selects the income contingent repayment plan or changes into the income contingent repayment plan from another plan govern the method for determining the borrower's monthly repayment amount for all of the borrower's Direct Loans, unless—

(i) The Secretary amends the regulations relating to a borrower's monthly repayment amount under the income contingent repayment plan; and

(ii) The borrower submits a written request that the amended regulations apply to the repayment of the borrower's Direct Loans.

(3) Provisions governing the income contingent repayment plan are in § 685.209.

(l) *Alternative repayment.*

(1) The Secretary may provide an alternative repayment plan for a borrower who demonstrates to the Secretary's satisfaction that the terms and conditions of the repayment plans specified in paragraphs (b) through (h) of this section are not adequate to accommodate the borrower's exceptional circumstances.

(2) The Secretary may require a borrower to provide evidence of the borrower's exceptional circumstances before permitting the borrower to repay a loan under an alternative repayment plan.

(3) If the Secretary agrees to permit a borrower to repay a loan under an alternative repayment plan, the Secretary notifies the borrower in writing of the terms of the plan. After the borrower receives notification of the terms of the plan, the borrower may accept the plan or choose another repayment plan.

(4) A borrower must repay a loan under an alternative repayment plan within 30 years of the date the loan entered repayment, not including periods of deferment and forbearance.

(5) If the amount of a borrower's monthly payment under an alternative repayment plan is less than the accrued interest on the loan, the unpaid interest is capitalized until the outstanding principal amount is 10 percent greater than the original principal amount. After the outstanding principal amount is 10 percent greater than the original principal amount, interest continues to accrue but is not capitalized. For purposes of this paragraph, the original principal amount is the amount owed by the borrower when the borrower enters repayment.

(m) *Income-based repayment plan.*

(1) Under this repayment plan, the required monthly payment for a borrower who has a partial financial hardship is limited to no more than 15 percent of the amount by which the borrower's AGI exceeds 150 percent of the poverty guideline applicable to the borrower's family size, divided by 12. The Secretary determines annually whether the borrower continues to qualify for this reduced monthly payment based on the amount of the borrower's eligible loans, AGI, and poverty guideline.

(2) The specific provisions governing the income-based repayment plan are in § 685.221.

(Authority: 20 U.S.C. 1087a *et seq.*)

[61 Fed. Reg. 31359 (June 19, 1996); 62 Fed. Reg. 25515 (May 9, 1997); 66 Fed. Reg. 34765 (June 29, 2001); 71 Fed. Reg. 45666 (Sept. 8, 2006); 71 Fed. Reg. 64399 (Nov. 1, 2006); 73 Fed. Reg. 63255, 63256 (Oct. 23, 2008)]

§ 685.209 Income contingent repayment plan.

(a) *Repayment amount calculation.*

(1) The amount the borrower would repay is based upon the borrower's Direct Loan debt when the borrower's first loan enters repayment, and this basis for calculation does not change unless the borrower obtains another Direct Loan or the borrower and the borrower's spouse obtain approval to repay their loans jointly under paragraph (b)(2) of this section. If the borrower obtains another Direct Loan, the amount the borrower would repay is based on the combined amounts of the loans when the last loan enters repayment. If the borrower and the borrower's spouse repay the loans jointly, the amount the borrowers would repay is based on both borrowers' Direct Loan debts at the time they enter joint repayment.

(2) The annual amount payable under the income contingent repayment plan by a borrower is the lesser of—

(i) The amount the borrower would repay annually over 12 years using standard amortization multiplied by an income percentage factor that corresponds to the borrower's adjusted gross income (AGI) as shown in the income percentage factor table in a notice published annually by the Secretary in the Federal Register; or

(ii) 20 percent of discretionary income.

(3) For purposes of this section, discretionary income is defined as a borrower's AGI minus the amount of the "HHS Poverty Guidelines for all States (except Alaska and Hawaii) and the District of Columbia" as published by the United States Department of Health and Human Services on an annual basis.[1] For residents of Alaska and Hawaii, discretionary income is defined as a borrower's AGI minus the amounts in the "HHS Poverty Guidelines for Alaska" and the "HHS Poverty Guidelines for Hawaii" respectively. If a borrower

---

1 The HHS Poverty Guidelines are available from the Office of the Assistant Secretary for Planning and Evaluation, Department of Health and Human Services (HHS), Room 438F, Humphrey Building, 200 Independence Avenue, S.W., Washington, D.C. 20201.

provides documentation acceptable to the Secretary that the borrower has more than one person in the borrower's family, the Secretary applies the HHS Poverty Guidelines for the borrower's family size.

(4) For exact incomes not shown in the income percentage factor table in the annual notice published by the Secretary, an income percentage factor is calculated, based upon the intervals between the incomes and income percentage factors shown on the table.

(5) Each year, the Secretary recalculates the borrower's annual payment amount based on changes in the borrower's AGI, the variable interest rate, the income percentage factors in the table in the annual notice published by the Secretary, and updated HHS Poverty Guidelines (if applicable).

(6) If a borrower's monthly payment is calculated to be greater than $0 but less than or equal to $5.00, the amount payable by the borrower shall be $5.00.

(7) For purposes of the annual recalculation described in paragraph (a)(5) of this section, after periods in which a borrower makes payments that are less than interest accrued on the loan, the payment amount is recalculated based upon unpaid accrued interest and the highest outstanding principal loan amount (including amount capitalized) calculated for that borrower while paying under the income contingent repayment plan.

(8) For each calendar year after calendar year 1996, the Secretary publishes in the Federal Register a revised income percentage factor table reflecting changes based on inflation. This revised table is developed by changing each of the dollar amounts contained in the table by a percentage equal to the estimated percentage changes in the Consumer Price Index (as determined by the Secretary) between December 1995 and the December next preceding the beginning of such calendar year.

(9) Examples of the calculation of monthly repayment amounts and tables that show monthly repayment amounts for borrowers at various income and debt levels are included in the annual notice published by the Secretary.

(b) *Treatment of married borrowers.*

(1) A married borrower who wishes to repay under the income contingent repayment plan and who has filed an income tax return separately from his or her spouse must provide his or her spouse's written consent to the disclosure of certain tax return information under paragraph (c)(5) of this section (unless the borrower is separated from his or her spouse). The AGI for both spouses is used to calculate the monthly repayment amount.

(2) Married borrowers may repay their loans jointly. The outstanding balances on the loans of each borrower are added together to determine the borrowers' payback rate under (a)(1) of this section.

(3) The amount of the payment applied to each borrower's debt is the proportion of the payments that equals the same proportion as that borrower's debt to the total outstanding balance, except that the payment is credited toward outstanding interest on any loan before any payment is credited toward principal.

(c) *Other features of the income contingent repayment plan.*

(1) *Alternative documentation of income.* If a borrower's AGI is not available or if, in the Secretary's opinion, the borrower's reported AGI does not reasonably reflect the borrower's current income, the Secretary may use other documentation of income provided by the borrower to calculate the borrower's monthly repayment amount.

(2) *First and second year borrowers.* The Secretary requires alternative documentation of income from borrowers in their first and second years of repayment, when in the Secretary's opinion, the borrower's reported AGI does not reasonably reflect the borrower's current income.

(3) *Adjustments to repayment obligations.* The Secretary may determine that special circumstances, such as a loss of employment by the borrower or the borrower's spouse, warrant an adjustment to the borrower's repayment obligations.

(4) *Repayment period.*

(i) The maximum repayment period under the income contingent repayment plan is 25 years.

(ii) The repayment period includes—

(A) Periods in which the borrower makes payments under the income-contingent repayment plan on loans that are not in default;

(B) Periods in which the borrower makes reduced monthly payments under the income-based repayment plan or a recalculated reduced monthly payment after the borrower no longer has a partial financial hardship or stops making income-based payments, as provided in § 685.221(d)(1)(i);

(C) Periods in which the borrower made monthly payments under the standard repayment plan after leaving the income-based repayment plan as provided in § 685.221(d)(2);

(D) Periods in which the borrower makes payments under the standard repayment plan described in § 685.208(b);

(E) For borrowers who entered repayment before October 1, 2007, and if the repayment period is not more than 12 years, periods in which the borrower makes monthly payments under the extended repayment plans described in § 685.208(d) and (e), or the standard repayment plan described in § 685.208(c);

(F) Periods after October 1, 2007, in which the borrower makes monthly payments under any other repayment plan that are not less than the amount required under the standard repayment plan described in § 685.208(b); or

(G) Periods of economic hardship deferment after October 1, 2007.

(5) *Limitation on capitalization of interest.* If the amount of a borrower's monthly payment is less than the accrued interest, the unpaid interest is capitalized until the outstanding principal amount is ten percent greater than the original principal amount. After the outstanding principal amount is ten percent greater than the original amount, interest continues to accrue but is not capitalized. For purposes of this paragraph, the original amount is the amount owed by the borrower when the borrower enters repayment.

(6) *Notification of terms and conditions.* When a borrower elects or is required by the Secretary to repay a loan under the income contingent repayment plan, the Secretary notifies the borrower of the terms and conditions of the plan, including—

(i) That the Internal Revenue Service will disclose certain tax return information to the Secretary or the Secretary's agents; and

(ii) That if the borrower believes that special circumstances warrant an adjustment to the borrower's repayment obligations, as described in § 685.209(c)(3), the borrower may contact the Secretary and obtain the Secretary's determination as to whether an adjustment is appropriate.

(7) *Consent to disclosure of tax return information.*

(i) A borrower shall provide written consent to the disclosure of certain tax return information by the Internal Revenue Service (IRS) to agents of the Secretary for purposes of calculating a monthly repayment amount and servicing and collecting a loan under the income contingent repayment plan. The borrower shall provide consent by signing a consent form, developed consistent with 26 CFR 301.6103(c)-1 and provided to the borrower by the Secretary, and shall return the signed form to the Secretary.

(ii) The borrower shall consent to disclosure of the borrower's taxpayer identity information as defined in 26 U.S.C. 6103(b)(6), tax filing status, and AGI.

(iii) The borrower shall provide consent for a period of five years from the date the borrower signs the consent form. The Secretary provides the borrower a new consent form before that period expires. The IRS does not disclose tax return information after the IRS has processed a borrower's withdrawal of consent.

(iv) The Secretary designates the standard repayment plan for a borrower who selects the income contingent repayment plan but—

(A) Fails to provide the required written consent;
(B) Fails to renew written consent upon the expiration of the five-year period for consent; or
(C) Withdraws consent and does not select another repayment plan.
(v) If a borrower defaults and the Secretary designates the income contingent repayment plan for the borrower but the borrower fails to provide the required written consent, the Secretary mails a notice to the borrower establishing a repayment schedule for the borrower.

(Approved by the Office of Management and Budget under control number 1845-0021)

(Authority: 20 U.S.C. 1087a *et seq.*)

[60 Fed. Reg. 33345 (June 28, 1995); 60 Fed. Reg. 61823 (Dec. 1, 1995); 61 Fed. Reg. 24447 (May 15, 1996); 61 Fed. Reg. 31359 (June 19, 1996); 64 Fed. Reg. 29183 (May 28, 1999); 64 Fed. Reg. 58972 (Nov. 1, 1999); 73 Fed. Reg. 63256 (Oct. 23, 2008)]

§ 685.210 Choice of repayment plan.

(a) *Initial selection of a repayment plan.*
(1) Before a Direct Loan enters into repayment, the Secretary provides the borrower a description of the available repayment plans and requests the borrower to select one. A borrower may select a repayment plan before the loan enters repayment by notifying the Secretary of the borrower's selection in writing.
(2) If a borrower does not select a repayment plan, the Secretary designates the standard repayment plan described in § 685.208(b) for the borrower.

(b) *Changing repayment plans.*
(1) A borrower may change repayment plans at any time after the loan has entered repayment by notifying the Secretary. However, a borrower who is repaying a defaulted loan under the income contingent repayment plan under § 685.211(d)(3)(ii) may not change to another repayment plan unless—
(i) The borrower was required to and did make a payment under the income contingent repayment plan in each of the prior three (3) months; or
(ii) The borrower was not required to make payments but made three reasonable and affordable payments in each of the prior three months; and
(iii) The borrower makes and the Secretary approves a request to change plans.
(2)(i) A borrower may not change to a repayment plan that has a maximum repayment period of less than the number of years the loan has already been in repayment, except that a borrower may change to either the income contingent or income-based repayment plan at any time.
(ii) If a borrower changes plans, the repayment period is the period provided under the borrower's new repayment plan, calculated from the date the loan initially entered repayment. However, if a borrower changes to the income contingent repayment plan or the income-based repayment plan, the repayment period is calculated as described in § 685.209(c)(4) or § 685.221(b)(6), respectively.

(Authority: 20 U.S.C. 1087a *et seq.*)

[65 Fed. Reg. 65629 (Nov. 1, 2000); 68 Fed. Reg. 75430 (Dec. 31, 2003); 73 Fed. Reg. 63256 (Oct. 23, 2008)]

§ 685.211 Miscellaneous repayment provisions.

(a) *Payment application and prepayment.*
(1) Except as provided for the income-based repayment plan under § 685.221(c)(1), the Secretary applies any payment first to any accrued charges and collection costs, then to any outstanding interest, and then to outstanding principal.
(2) A borrower may prepay all or part of a loan at any time without penalty. If a borrower pays any amount in excess of the amount due, the excess amount is a prepayment.
(3) If a prepayment equals or exceeds the monthly repayment amount under the borrower's repayment plan, the Secretary—
(i) Applies the prepaid amount according to paragraph (a)(1) of this section;
(ii) Advances the due date of the next payment unless the borrower requests otherwise; and
(iii) Notifies the borrower of any revised due date for the next payment.
(4) If a prepayment is less than the monthly repayment amount, the Secretary applies the prepayment according to paragraph (a)(1) of this section.

(b) *Repayment incentives.* To encourage on-time repayment, the Secretary may reduce the interest rate for a borrower who repays a loan under a system or on a schedule that meets requirements specified by the Secretary.

(c) *Refunds and returns of title IV, HEA program funds from schools.* The Secretary applies any refund or return of title IV, HEA program funds that the Secretary receives from a school under § 668.22 against the borrower's outstanding principal and notifies the borrower of the refund or return.

(d) *Default.*
(1) *Acceleration.* If a borrower defaults on a Direct Loan, the entire unpaid balance and accrued interest are immediately due and payable.
(2) *Collection charges.* If a borrower defaults on a Direct Loan, the Secretary assesses collection charges in accordance with § 685.202(e).
(3) *Collection of a defaulted loan.*
(i) The Secretary may take any action authorized by law to collect a defaulted Direct Loan including, but not limited to, filing a lawsuit against the borrower, reporting the default to national credit bureaus, requesting the Internal Revenue Service to offset the borrower's Federal income tax refund, and garnishing the borrower's wages.
(ii) If a borrower defaults on a Direct Subsidized Loan, a Direct Unsubsidized Loan, a Direct Consolidation Loan, or a student Direct PLUS Loan, the Secretary may designate the income contingent repayment plan or the income-based repayment plan for the borrower.

(e) *Ineligible borrowers.*
(1) The Secretary determines that a borrower is ineligible if, at the time the loan was made and without the school's or the Secretary's knowledge, the borrower (or the student on whose behalf a parent borrowed) provided false or erroneous information, has been convicted of, or has pled nolo contendere or guilty to, a crime involving fraud in obtaining title IV, HEA program funds, or took actions that caused the borrower or student—
(i) To receive a loan for which the borrower is wholly or partially ineligible;
(ii) To receive interest benefits for which the borrower was ineligible; or
(iii) To receive loan proceeds for a period of enrollment for which the borrower was not eligible.
(2) If the Secretary makes the determination described in paragraph (e)(1) of this section, the Secretary sends an ineligible borrower a demand letter that requires the borrower to repay some or all of a loan, as appropriate. The demand letter requires that within 30 days from the date the letter is mailed, the borrower repay any principal amount for which the borrower is ineligible and any accrued interest, including interest subsidized by the Secretary, through the previous quarter.
(3) If a borrower fails to comply with the demand letter described in paragraph (e)(2) of this section, the borrower is in default on the entire loan.
(4) A borrower may not consolidate a loan under § 685.220 for which the borrower is wholly or partially ineligible.

(f) *Rehabilitation of defaulted loans.*
(1) A defaulted Direct Loan, except for a loan on which a judgment has been obtained, is rehabilitated if the borrower makes nine voluntary, reasonable, and affordable monthly

payments within 20 days of the due date during ten consecutive months. The amount of such a payment is determined on the basis of the borrower's total financial circumstances. If a defaulted loan is rehabilitated, the Secretary instructs any consumer reporting agency to which the default was reported to remove the default from the borrower's credit history.

(2) A defaulted Direct Loan on which a judgment has been obtained may not be rehabilitated.

(3) A Direct Loan obtained by fraud for which the borrower has been convicted of, or has pled nolo contendere or guilty to, a crime involving fraud in obtaining title IV, HEA program assistance may not be rehabilitated.

(4) Effective for any defaulted Direct Loan that is rehabilitated on or after August 14, 2008, the borrower cannot rehabilitate the loan again if the loan returns to default status following the rehabilitation.

(Authority: 20 U.S.C. 1087a et seq.)

[64 Fed. Reg. 57961 (Oct. 27, 1999); 64 Fed. Reg. 59043 (Nov. 1, 1999); 65 Fed. Reg. 65629 (Nov. 1, 2000); 66 Fed. Reg. 34765 (June 29, 2001); 67 Fed. Reg. 67081 (Nov. 1, 2002); 71 Fed. Reg. 45714 (Aug. 9, 2006); 73 Fed. Reg. 63256 (Oct. 23, 2008); 74 Fed. Reg. 56003 (Oct. 29, 2009)]

§ 685.212 Discharge of a loan obligation.

(a) *Death.*

(1) If a borrower (or a student on whose behalf a parent borrowed a Direct PLUS Loan) dies, the Secretary discharges the obligation of the borrower and any endorser to make any further payments on the loan based on an original or certified copy of the borrower's (or student's in the case of a Direct PLUS loan obtained by a parent borrower) death certificate, or an accurate and complete photocopy of the original or certified copy of the borrower's (or student's in the case of a Direct PLUS loan obtained by a parent borrower) death certificate.

(2) If an original or certified copy of the death certificate or an accurate and complete photocopy of the original or certified copy of the death certificate is not available, the Secretary discharges the loan only if other reliable documentation establishes, to the Secretary's satisfaction, that the borrower (or student) has died. The Secretary discharges a loan based on documentation other than an original or certified copy of the death certificate, or an accurate and complete photocopy of the original or certified copy of the death certificate only under exceptional circumstances and on a case-by-case basis.

(3) In the case of a Direct PLUS Consolidation Loan that repaid a Direct PLUS Loan or a Federal PLUS Loan obtained on behalf of a student who dies, the Secretary discharges an amount equal to the portion of the outstanding balance of the consolidation loan, as of the date of the student's death, attributable to that Direct PLUS Loan or Federal PLUS Loan.

(b) *Total and permanent disability.* If a borrower meets the requirements in § 685.213(c), the Secretary discharges the obligation of the borrower and any endorser to make any further payments on the loan.

(c) *Bankruptcy.* If a borrower's obligation to repay a loan is discharged in bankruptcy, the Secretary does not require the borrower to make any further payments on the loan.

(d) *Closed schools.* If a borrower meets the requirements in § 685.214, the Secretary discharges the obligation of the borrower and any endorser to make any further payments on the loan. In the case of a Direct Consolidation Loan, the Secretary discharges the portion of the consolidation loan equal to the amount of the discharge applicable to any loan disbursed, in whole or in part, on or after January 1, 1986 that was included in the consolidation loan.

(e) *False certification and unauthorized disbursement.* If a borrower meets the requirements in § 685.215, the Secretary discharges the obligation of the borrower and any endorser to make any further payments on the loan. In the case of a Direct Consolidation Loan, the Secretary discharges the portion of the consolidation loan equal to the amount of the discharge applicable to any loan disbursed, in whole or in part, on or after January 1, 1986 that was included in the consolidation loan.

(f) *Unpaid refunds.* If a borrower meets the requirements in § 685.216, the Secretary discharges the obligation of the borrower and any endorser to make any further payments on the amount of the loan equal to the unpaid refund and any accrued interest and other charges associated with the unpaid refund. In the case of a Direct Consolidation Loan, the Secretary discharges the portion of the consolidation loan equal to the amount of the unpaid refund owed on any loan disbursed, in whole or in part, on or after January 1, 1986 that was included in the consolidation loan.

(g) *Payments received after eligibility for discharge.*

(1) *For the discharge conditions in paragraphs (a), (c), (d), and (e) of this section.* Upon receipt of acceptable documentation and approval of the discharge request, the Secretary returns to the sender, or, for a discharge based on death, the borrower's estate, any payments received after the date that the eligibility requirements for discharge were met.

(2) *For the discharge condition in paragraph (b) of this section.* Upon making a final determination of eligibility for discharge based on total and permanent disability, the Secretary returns to the sender any payments received after the date the borrower became totally and permanently disabled, as certified under § 685.213(b).

(3) *For the discharge condition in paragraph (f) of this section.* Upon receipt of acceptable documentation and approval of the discharge request, the Secretary returns to the sender payments received in excess of the amount owed on the loan after applying the unpaid refund.

(h) *Teacher loan forgiveness program.* If a new borrower meets the requirements in § 685.217, the Secretary repays up to $5,000, or up to $17,500, of the borrower's Direct Subsidized Loans, Direct Unsubsidized Loans, and, in certain cases, Direct Consolidation Loans.

(i) *Public Service Loan Forgiveness Program.* If a borrower meets the requirements in § 685.219, the Secretary cancels the remaining principal and accrued interest of the borrower's eligible Direct Subsidized Loan, Direct Unsubsidized Loan, Direct PLUS Loan, and Direct Consolidation Loan.

(j) *September 11 survivors discharge.* If a borrower meets the requirements in § 685.218, the Secretary discharges the obligation of the borrower and any endorser to make any further payments—

(1) On an eligible Direct Loan if the borrower qualifies as the spouse of an eligible public servant;

(2) On the portion of a joint Direct Consolidation Loan incurred on behalf of an eligible victim, if the borrower qualifies as the spouse of an eligible victim;

(3) On a Direct PLUS Loan incurred on behalf of an eligible victim if the borrower qualifies as an eligible parent; and

(4) On the portion of a Direct Consolidation Loan that repaid a PLUS loan incurred on behalf of an eligible victim, if the borrower qualifies as an eligible parent.

(Approved by the Office of Management and Budget under control number 1845-0021)

(Authority: 20 U.S.C. 1087a et seq.)

[61 Fed. Reg. 29900 (June 12, 1996); 62 Fed. Reg. 30412 (June 3, 1997); 62 Fed. Reg. 63435 (Nov. 28, 1997); 63 Fed. Reg. 34816 (June 26, 1998); 64 Fed. Reg. 58969 (Nov. 1, 1999); 65 Fed. Reg. 65629, 65694 (Nov. 1, 2000); 66 Fed. Reg. 34765 (June 29, 2001); 67 Fed. Reg. 67081 (Nov. 1, 2002); 71 Fed. Reg. 45666 (Sept. 8, 2006); 71 Fed. Reg. 78075 (Dec. 28, 2006); 72 Fed. Reg. 62010 (Nov. 1, 2007); 73 Fed. Reg. 63256 (Oct. 23, 2008)]

§ 685.213 Total and permanent disability discharge.

(a) *General.*

(1) A borrower's Direct Loan is discharged if the borrower becomes totally and permanently disabled, as defined in 34 CFR 682.200(b), and satisfies the eligibility requirements in this section.

(2) For a borrower who becomes totally and permanently disabled as described in paragraph (1) of the definition of that term in 34 CFR 682.200(b), the borrower's loan discharge application is processed in accordance with paragraph (b) of this section.

(3) For veterans who are totally and permanently disabled as described in paragraph (2) of the definition of that term in 34 CFR 682.200(b), the veteran's loan discharge application is processed in accordance with paragraph (c) of this section.

(b) *Discharge application process for a borrower who is totally and permanently disabled as described in paragraph (1) of the definition of that term in 34 CFR 682.200(b).*

(1) *Borrower application for discharge.* To qualify for a discharge of a Direct Loan based on a total and permanent disability, a borrower must submit a discharge application to the Secretary on a form approved by the Secretary. The application must contain a certification by a physician, who is a doctor of medicine or osteopathy legally authorized to practice in a State, that the borrower is totally and permanently disabled as described in paragraph (1) of the definition of that term in 34 CFR 682.200(b). The borrower must submit the application to the Secretary within 90 days of the date the physician certifies the application. Upon receipt of the borrower's application, the Secretary notifies the borrower that no payments are due on the loan while the Secretary determines the borrower's eligibility for discharge.

(2) *Determination of eligibility.*

(i) If, after reviewing the borrower's application, the Secretary determines that the certification provided by the borrower supports the conclusion that the borrower meets the criteria for a total and permanent disability discharge, as described in paragraph (1) of the definition of that term in 34 CFR 682.200(b), the borrower is considered totally and permanently disabled as of the date the physician certifies the borrower's application.

(ii) Upon making a determination that the borrower is totally and permanently disabled, as described in paragraph (1) of the definition of that term in 34 CFR 682.200(b), the Secretary discharges the borrower's obligation to make any further payments on the loan, notifies the borrower that the loan has been discharged, and returns to the person who made the payments on the loan any payments received after the date the physician certified the borrower's loan discharge application. The notification to the borrower explains the terms and conditions under which the borrower's obligation to repay the loan will be reinstated, as specified in paragraph (b)(4)(i) of this section.

(iii) If the Secretary determines that the certification provided by the borrower does not support the conclusion that the borrower is totally and permanently disabled, as described in paragraph (1) of the definition of that term in 34 CFR 682.200(b), the Secretary notifies the borrower that the application for a disability discharge has been denied, and that the loan is due and payable to the Secretary under the terms of the promissory note.

(iv) The Secretary reserves the right to require the borrower to submit additional medical evidence if the Secretary determines that the borrower's application does not conclusively prove that the borrower is totally and permanently disabled as described in paragraph (1) of the definition of that term in 34 CFR 682.200(b). As part of the Secretary's review of the borrower's discharge application, the Secretary may arrange for an additional review of the borrower's condition by an independent physician at no expense to the borrower.

(3) *Treatment of disbursements made during the period from the date of the physician's certification until the date of discharge.* If a borrower received a title IV loan or TEACH Grant prior to the date the physician certified the borrower's discharge application and a disbursement of that loan or grant is made during the period from the date of the physician's certification until the date the Secretary grants a discharge under this section, the processing of the borrower's loan discharge request will be suspended until the borrower ensures that the full amount of the disbursement has been returned to the loan holder or to the Secretary, as applicable.

(4) *Conditions for reinstatement of a loan after a total and permanent disability discharge.*

(i) The Secretary reinstates a borrower's obligation to repay a loan that was discharged in accordance with paragraph (b)(2)(ii) of this section if, within three years after the date the Secretary granted the discharge, the borrower—

(A) Has annual earnings from employment that exceed 100 percent of the poverty guideline for a family of two, as published annually by the United States Department of Health and Human Services pursuant to 42 U.S.C. 9902(2);

(B) Receives a new TEACH Grant or a new loan under the Perkins, FFEL or Direct Loan programs, except for a FFEL or Direct Consolidation Loan that includes loans that were not discharged; or

(C) Fails to ensure that the full amount of any disbursement of a title IV loan or TEACH Grant received prior to the discharge date that is made during the three-year period following the discharge date is returned to the loan holder or to the Secretary, as applicable, within 120 days of the disbursement date.

(ii) If the borrower's obligation to repay the loan is reinstated, the Secretary—

(A) Notifies the borrower that the borrower's obligation to repay the loan has been reinstated; and

(B) Does not require the borrower to pay interest on the loan for the period from the date the loan was discharged until the date the borrower's obligation to repay the loan was reinstated.

(iii) The Secretary's notification under paragraph (b)(4)(ii)(A) of this section will include—

(A) The reason or reasons for the reinstatement;

(B) An explanation that the first payment due date on the loan following reinstatement will be no earlier than 60 days after the date of the notification of reinstatement; and

(C) Information on how the borrower may contact the Secretary if the borrower has questions about the reinstatement or believes that the obligation to repay the loan was reinstated based on incorrect information.

(5) *Borrower's responsibilities after a total and permanent disability discharge.* During the three-year period described in paragraph (b)(4)(i) of this section, the borrower or, if applicable, the borrower's representative must—

(i) Promptly notify the Secretary of any changes in address or phone number;

(ii) Promptly notify the Secretary if the borrower's annual earnings from employment exceed the amount specified in paragraph (b)(4)(i)(A) of this section; and

(iii) Provide the Secretary, upon request, with documentation of the borrower's annual earnings from employment.

(c) *Discharge application process for veterans who are totally and permanently disabled as described in paragraph (2) of the definition of that term in 34 CFR 682.200(b).*

(1) *Veteran's application for discharge.* To qualify for a discharge of a Direct Loan based on a total and permanent disability as described in paragraph (2) of the definition of that term in 34 CFR 682.200(b), a veteran must submit a discharge application to the Secretary on a form approved by the Secretary. The application must be accompanied by documentation from the Department of Veterans Affairs showing that the Department of

Veterans Affairs has determined that the veteran is unemployable due to a service-connected disability. The Secretary does not require the veteran to provide any additional documentation related to the veteran's disability. Upon receipt of the veteran's application, the Secretary notifies the veteran that no payments are due on the loan while the Secretary determines the veteran's eligibility for discharge.

(2) *Determination of eligibility.*

(i) If the Secretary determines, based on a review of the documentation from the Department of Veterans Affairs, that the veteran is totally and permanently disabled as described in paragraph (2) of the definition of that term in § 682.200(b), the Secretary discharges the veteran's obligation to make any further payments on the loan and returns to the person who made the payments on the loan any payments received on or after the effective date of the determination by the Department of Veterans Affairs that the veteran is unemployable due to a service-connected disability.

(ii)(A) If the Secretary determines, based on a review of the documentation from the Department of Veterans Affairs, that the veteran is not totally and permanently disabled as described in paragraph (2) of the definition of that term in 34 CFR 682.200(b), the Secretary notifies the veteran that the application for a disability discharge has been denied, and that the loan is due and payable to the Secretary under the terms of the promissory note.

(B) The Secretary notifies the veteran that he or she may reapply for a total and permanent disability discharge in accordance with the procedures described in paragraph (b) of this section if the documentation from the Department of Veterans Affairs does not indicate that the veteran is totally and permanently disabled as described in paragraph (2) of the definition of that term in 34 CFR 682.200(b), but indicates that the veteran may be totally and permanently disabled as described in paragraph (1) of the definition of that term.

[65 Fed. Reg. 65629, 65694 (Nov. 1, 2000); 72 Fed. Reg. 62010 (Nov. 1, 2007); 73 Fed. Reg. 35495 (June 23, 2008); 73 Fed. Reg. 36792, 36793 (June 30, 2008); 74 Fed. Reg. 56003 (Oct. 29, 2009)]

§ 685.214 Closed school discharge.

(a) *General.*

(1) The Secretary discharges the borrower's (and any endorser's) obligation to repay a Direct Loan in accordance with the provisions of this section if the borrower (or the student on whose behalf a parent borrowed) did not complete the program of study for which the loan was made because the school at which the borrower (or student) was enrolled closed, as described in paragraph (c) of this section.

(2) For purposes of this section—

(i) A school's closure date is the date that the school ceases to provide educational instruction in all programs, as determined by the Secretary; and

(ii) "School" means a school's main campus or any location or branch of the main campus.

(b) *Relief pursuant to discharge.*

(1) Discharge under this section relieves the borrower of any past or present obligation to repay the loan and any accrued charges or collection costs with respect to the loan.

(2) The discharge of a loan under this section qualifies the borrower for reimbursement of amounts paid voluntarily or through enforced collection on the loan.

(3) The Secretary does not regard a borrower who has defaulted on a loan discharged under this section as in default on the loan after discharge, and such a borrower is eligible to receive assistance under programs authorized by title IV of the Act.

(4) The Secretary reports the discharge of a loan under this section to all credit reporting agencies to which the Secretary previously reported the status of the loan.

(c) *Borrower qualification for discharge.* In order to qualify for discharge of a loan under this section, a borrower shall submit to the Secretary a written request and sworn statement, and the factual assertions in the statement must be true. The statement need not be notarized but must be made by the borrower under penalty of perjury. In the statement, the borrower shall—

(1) State that the borrower (or the student on whose behalf a parent borrowed)—

(i) Received the proceeds of a loan, in whole or in part, on or after January 1, 1986 to attend a school;

(ii) Did not complete the program of study at that school because the school closed while the student was enrolled, or the student withdrew from the school not more than 90 days before the school closed (or longer in exceptional circumstances); and

(iii) Did not complete the program of study through a teach-out at another school or by transferring academic credits or hours earned at the closed school to another school;

(2) State whether the borrower (or student) has made a claim with respect to the school's closing with any third party, such as the holder of a performance bond or a tuition recovery program, and, if so, the amount of any payment received by the borrower (or student) or credited to the borrower's loan obligation; and

(3) State that the borrower (or student)—

(i) Agrees to provide to the Secretary upon request other documentation reasonably available to the borrower that demonstrates that the borrower meets the qualifications for discharge under this section; and

(ii) Agrees to cooperate with the Secretary in enforcement actions in accordance with paragraph (d) of this section and to transfer any right to recovery against a third party to the Secretary in accordance with paragraph (e) of this section.

(d) *Cooperation by borrower in enforcement actions.*

(1) In order to obtain a discharge under this section, a borrower shall cooperate with the Secretary in any judicial or administrative proceeding brought by the Secretary to recover amounts discharged or to take other enforcement action with respect to the conduct on which the discharge was based. At the request of the Secretary and upon the Secretary's tendering to the borrower the fees and costs that are customarily provided in litigation to reimburse witnesses, the borrower shall—

(i) Provide testimony regarding any representation made by the borrower to support a request for discharge;

(ii) Produce any documents reasonably available to the borrower with respect to those representations; and

(iii) If required by the Secretary, provide a sworn statement regarding those documents and representations.

(2) The Secretary denies the request for a discharge or revokes the discharge of a borrower who—

(i) Fails to provide the testimony, documents, or a sworn statement required under paragraph (d)(1) of this section; or

(ii) Provides testimony, documents, or a sworn statement that does not support the material representations made by the borrower to obtain the discharge.

(e) *Transfer to the Secretary of borrower's right of recovery against third parties.*

(1) Upon discharge under this section, the borrower is deemed to have assigned to and relinquished in favor of the Secretary any right to a loan refund (up to the amount discharged) that the borrower (or student) may have by contract or applicable law with respect to the loan or the enrollment agreement for the program for which the loan was received, against the school, its principals, its affiliates and their successors, its sureties, and any private fund, including the portion of a public fund that represents funds received from a private party.

(2) The provisions of this section apply notwithstanding any provision of State law that would otherwise restrict transfer of those

rights by the borrower (or student), limit or prevent a transferee from exercising those rights, or establish procedures or a scheme of distribution that would prejudice the Secretary's ability to recover on those rights.

(3) Nothing in this section limits or forecloses the borrower's (or student's) right to pursue legal and equitable relief regarding disputes arising from matters unrelated to the discharged Direct Loan.

(f) *Discharge procedures.*

(1) After confirming the date of a school's closure, the Secretary identifies any Direct Loan borrower (or student on whose behalf a parent borrowed) who appears to have been enrolled at the school on the school closure date or to have withdrawn not more than 90 days prior to the closure date.

(2) If the borrower's current address is known, the Secretary mails the borrower a discharge application and an explanation of the qualifications and procedures for obtaining a discharge. The Secretary also promptly suspends any efforts to collect from the borrower on any affected loan. The Secretary may continue to receive borrower payments.

(3) If the borrower's current address is unknown, the Secretary attempts to locate the borrower and determines the borrower's potential eligibility for a discharge under this section by consulting with representatives of the closed school, the school's licensing agency, the school's accrediting agency, and other appropriate parties. If the Secretary learns the new address of a borrower, the Secretary mails to the borrower a discharge application and explanation and suspends collection, as described in paragraph (f)(2) of this section.

(4) If a borrower fails to submit the written request and sworn statement described in paragraph (c) of this section within 60 days of the Secretary's mailing the discharge application, the Secretary resumes collection and grants forbearance of principal and interest for the period in which collection activity was suspended. The Secretary may capitalize any interest accrued and not paid during that period.

(5) If the Secretary determines that a borrower who requests a discharge meets the qualifications for a discharge, the Secretary notifies the borrower in writing of that determination.

(6) If the Secretary determines that a borrower who requests a discharge does not meet the qualifications for a discharge, the Secretary notifies that borrower in writing of that determination and the reasons for the determination.

(Approved by the Office of Management and Budget under control number 1845-0021)

(Authority: 20 U.S.C. 1087a *et seq.*)

[60 Fed. Reg. 33345 (June 28, 1995); 64 Fed. Reg. 58972 (Nov. 1, 1999); 65 Fed. Reg. 65629 (Nov. 1, 2000); 66 Fed. Reg. 34765 (June 29, 2001)]

§ 685.215 Discharge for false certification of student eligibility or unauthorized payment.

(a) *Basis for discharge.*

(1) *False certification.* The Secretary discharges a borrower's (and any endorser's) obligation to repay a Direct Loan in accordance with the provisions of this section if a school falsely certifies the eligibility of the borrower (or the student on whose behalf a parent borrowed) to receive the loan. The Secretary considers a student's eligibility to borrow to have been falsely certified by the school if the school—

(i) Certified the student's eligibility for a Direct Loan on the basis of ability to benefit from its training and the student did not meet the eligibility requirements described in 34 CFR part 668 and section 484(d) of the Act, as applicable;

(ii) Signed the borrower's name on the loan application or promissory note without the borrower's authorization; or

(iii) Certified the eligibility of a student who, because of a physical or mental condition, age, criminal record, or other reason accepted by the Secretary, would not meet the requirements for employment (in the student's State of residence when the loan was originated) in the occupation for which the training program supported by the loan was intended.

(iv) Certified the individual's eligibility for a Direct Loan as a result of the crime of identity theft committed against the individual, as that crime is defined in § 682.402(e)(14).

(2) *Unauthorized payment.* The Secretary discharges a borrower's (and any endorser's) obligation to repay a Direct Loan if the school, without the borrower's authorization, endorsed the borrower's loan check or signed the borrower's authorization for electronic funds transfer, unless the proceeds of the loan were delivered to the student or applied to charges owed by the student to the school.

(b) *Relief pursuant to discharge.*

(1) Discharge for false certification under paragraph (a)(1) of this section relieves the borrower of any past or present obligation to repay the loan and any accrued charges and collection costs with respect to the loan.

(2) Discharge for unauthorized payment under paragraph (a)(2) of this section relieves the borrower of the obligation to repay the amount of the payment discharged.

(3) The discharge under this section qualifies the borrower for reimbursement of amounts paid voluntarily or through enforced collection on the discharged loan or payment.

(4) The Secretary does not regard a borrower who has defaulted on a loan discharged under this section as in default on the loan after discharge, and such a borrower is eligible to receive assistance under programs authorized by title IV of the Act.

(5) The Secretary reports the discharge under this section to all credit reporting agencies to which the Secretary previously reported the status of the loan.

(c) *Borrower qualification for discharge.* In order to qualify for discharge under this section, the borrower shall submit to the Secretary a written request and a sworn statement, and the factual assertions in the statement must be true. The statement need not be notarized but must be made by the borrower under penalty of perjury. In the statement, the borrower shall meet the requirements in paragraphs (c)(1) through (6) of this section.

(1) *Ability to benefit.* In the case of a borrower requesting a discharge based on defective testing of the student's ability to benefit, the borrower shall state that the borrower (or the student on whose behalf a parent borrowed)—

(i) Received a disbursement of a loan, in whole or in part, on or after January 1, 1986 to attend a school; and

(ii) Received a Direct Loan at that school on the basis of an ability to benefit from the school's training and did not meet the eligibility requirements described in 34 CFR Part 668 and section 484(d) of the Act, as applicable.

(2) *Unauthorized loan.* In the case of a borrower requesting a discharge because the school signed the borrower's name on the loan application or promissory note without the borrower's authorization, the borrower shall—

(i) State that he or she did not sign the document in question or authorize the school to do so; and

(ii) Provide five different specimens of his or her signature, two of which must be within one year before or after the date of the contested signature.

(3) *Unauthorized payment.* In the case of a borrower requesting a discharge because the school, without the borrower's authorization, endorsed the borrower's loan check or signed the borrower's authorization for electronic funds transfer, the borrower shall—

(i) State that he or she did not endorse the loan check or sign the authorization for electronic funds transfer or authorize the school to do so;

(ii) Provide five different specimens of his or her signature, two of which must be within one year before or after the date of the contested signature;

(iii) State that the proceeds of the contested disbursement were not delivered to the student or applied to charges owed by the student to the school.

(4) *Identity theft.* In the case of an individual whose eligibility to borrow was falsely certified because he or she was a victim of the crime of identity theft and is requesting a discharge, the individual shall—

(i) Certify that the individual did not sign the promissory note, or that any other means of identification used to obtain the loan was used without the authorization of the individual claiming relief;

(ii) Certify that the individual did not receive or benefit from the proceeds of the loan with knowledge that the loan had been made without the authorization of the individual;

(iii) Provide a copy of a local, State, or Federal court verdict or judgment that conclusively determines that the individual who is named as the borrower of the loan was the victim of a crime of identity theft; and

(iv) If the judicial determination of the crime does not expressly state that the loan was obtained as a result of the crime of identity theft, provide—

(A) Authentic specimens of the signature of the individual, as provided in paragraph (c)(2)(ii), or of other means of identification of the individual, as applicable, corresponding to the means of identification falsely used to obtain the loan; and

(B) A statement of facts that demonstrate, to the satisfaction of the Secretary, that eligibility for the loan in question was falsely certified as a result of the crime of identity theft committed against that individual.

(5) *Claim to third party.* The borrower shall state whether the borrower (or student) has made a claim with respect to the school's false certification or unauthorized payment with any third party, such as the holder of a performance bond or a tuition recovery program, and, if so, the amount of any payment received by the borrower (or student) or credited to the borrower's loan obligation.

(6) *Cooperation with Secretary.* The borrower shall state that the borrower (or student)—

(i) Agrees to provide to the Secretary upon request other documentation reasonably available to the borrower that demonstrates that the borrower meets the qualifications for discharge under this section; and

(ii) Agrees to cooperate with the Secretary in enforcement actions as described in § 685.214(d) and to transfer any right to recovery against a third party to the Secretary as described in § 685.214(e).

(7) *Discharge without an application.* The Secretary may discharge a loan under this section without an application from the borrower if the Secretary determines, based on information in the Secretary's possession, that the borrower qualifies for a discharge.

(d) *Discharge procedures.*

(1) If the Secretary determines that a borrower's Direct Loan may be eligible for a discharge under this section, the Secretary mails the borrower a disclosure application and an explanation of the qualifications and procedures for obtaining a discharge. The Secretary also promptly suspends any efforts to collect from the borrower on any affected loan. The Secretary may continue to receive borrower payments.

(2) If the borrower fails to submit the written request and sworn statement described in paragraph (c) of this section within 60 days of the Secretary's mailing the disclosure application, the Secretary resumes collection and grants forbearance of principal and interest for the period in which collection activity was suspended. The Secretary may capitalize any interest accrued and not paid during that period.

(3) If the borrower submits the written request and sworn statement described in paragraph (c) of the section, the Secretary determines whether to grant a request for discharge under this section by reviewing the request and sworn statement in light of information available from the Secretary's records and from other sources, including guaranty agencies, State authorities, and cognizant accrediting associations.

(4) If the Secretary determines that the borrower meets the applicable requirements for a discharge under paragraph (c) of this section, the Secretary notifies the borrower in writing of that determination.

(5) If the Secretary determines that the borrower does not qualify for a discharge, the Secretary notifies the borrower in writing of that determination and the reasons for the determination.

(Approved by the Office of Management and Budget under control number 1845-0021)

(Authority: 20 U.S.C. 1087a *et seq.*)

[60 Fed. Reg. 33345 (June 28, 1995); 61 Fed. Reg. 29900 (June 12, 1996); 64 Fed. Reg. 58972 (Nov. 1, 1999); 65 Fed. Reg. 65622, 65629 (Nov. 1, 2000); 66 Fed. Reg. 34765 (June 29, 2001); 71 Fed. Reg. 45714 (Aug. 9, 2006)]

§ 685.216 Unpaid refund discharge.

(a)(1) *Unpaid refunds in closed school situations.* In the case of a school that has closed, the Secretary discharges a former or current borrower's (and any endorser's) obligation to repay that portion of a Direct Loan equal to the refund that should have been made by the school under applicable law and regulations, including this section. Any accrued interest and other charges associated with the unpaid refund are also discharged.

(2) *Unpaid refunds in open school situations.*

(i) In the case of a school that is open, the Secretary discharges a former or current borrower's (and any endorser's) obligation to repay that portion of a Direct Loan equal to the refund that should have been made by the school under applicable law and regulations, including this section, if—

(A) The borrower (or the student on whose behalf a parent borrowed) is not attending the school that owes the refund;

(B) The borrower has been unable to resolve the unpaid refund with the school; and

(C) The Secretary is unable to resolve the unpaid refund with the school within 120 days from the date the borrower submits a complete application in accordance with paragraph (c)(1) of this section regarding the unpaid refund. Any accrued interest and other charges associated with the unpaid refund are also discharged.

(ii) For the purpose of paragraph (a)(2)(i)(C) of this section, within 60 days of the date notified by the Secretary, the school must submit to the Secretary documentation demonstrating that the refund was made by the school or that the refund was not required to be made by the school.

(b) *Relief to borrower following discharge.*

(1) If the borrower receives a discharge of a portion of a loan under this section, the borrower is reimbursed for any amounts paid in excess of the remaining balance of the loan (including accrued interest and other charges) owed by the borrower at the time of discharge.

(2) The Secretary reports the discharge of a portion of a loan under this section to all credit reporting agencies to which the Secretary previously reported the status of the loan.

(c) *Borrower qualification for discharge.*

(1) Except as provided in paragraph (c)(2) of this section, to receive a discharge of a portion of a loan under this section, a borrower must submit a written application to the Secretary. The application requests the information required to calculate the amount of the discharge and requires the borrower to sign a statement swearing to the accuracy of the information in the application. The statement need not be notarized but must be made by the borrower under penalty of perjury. In the statement, the borrower must—

(i) State that the borrower (or the student on whose behalf a parent borrowed)—

(A) Received the proceeds of a loan, in whole or in part, on or after January 1, 1986 to attend a school;

(B) Did not attend, withdrew, or was terminated from the school within a timeframe that entitled the borrower to a refund; and

(C) Did not receive the benefit of a refund to which the borrower was entitled either from the school or from a third party, such as the holder of a performance bond or a tuition recovery program;

(ii) State whether the borrower (or student) has any other application for discharge pending for this loan; and

(iii) State that the borrower (or student)—

(A) Agrees to provide to the Secretary upon request other documentation reasonably available to the borrower that demonstrates that the borrower meets the qualifications for discharge under this section; and

(B) Agrees to cooperate with the Secretary in enforcement actions as described in § 685.214(d) and to transfer any right to recovery against a third party to the Secretary as described in § 685.214(e).

(2) The Secretary may discharge a portion of a loan under this section without an application if the Secretary determines, based on information in the Secretary's possession, that the borrower qualifies for a discharge.

(d) *Determination of amount eligible for discharge.*

(1) The Secretary determines the amount eligible for discharge based on information showing the refund amount or by applying the appropriate refund formula to information that the borrower provides or that is otherwise available to the Secretary. For purposes of this section, all unpaid refunds are considered to be attributed to loan proceeds.

(2) If the information in paragraph (d)(1) of this section is not available, the Secretary uses the following formulas to determine the amount eligible for discharge:

(i) In the case of a student who fails to attend or whose withdrawal or termination date is before October 7, 2000 and who completes less than 60 percent of the loan period, the Secretary discharges the lesser of the institutional charges unearned or the loan amount. The Secretary determines the amount of the institutional charges unearned by—

(A) Calculating the ratio of the amount of time remaining in the loan period after the student's last day of attendance to the actual length of the loan period; and

(B) Multiplying the resulting factor by the institutional charges assessed the student for the loan period.

(ii) In the case of a student who fails to attend or whose withdrawal or termination date is on or after October 7, 2000 and who completes less than 60 percent of the loan period, the Secretary discharges the loan amount unearned. The Secretary determines the loan amount unearned by—

(A) Calculating the ratio of the amount of time remaining in the loan period after the student's last day of attendance to the actual length of the loan period; and

(B) Multiplying the resulting factor by the total amount of title IV grants and loans received by the student, or, if unknown, the loan amount.

(iii) In the case of a student who completes 60 percent or more of the loan period, the Secretary does not discharge any amount because a student who completes 60 percent or more of the loan period is not entitled to a refund.

(e) *Discharge procedures.*

(1) Except as provided in paragraph (c)(2) of this section, if the Secretary learns that a school did not make a refund of loan proceeds owed under applicable law and regulations, the Secretary sends the borrower a discharge application and an explanation of the qualifications and procedures for obtaining a discharge. The Secretary also promptly suspends any efforts to collect from the borrower on any affected loan. The Secretary may continue to receive borrower payments.

(2) If a borrower who is sent a discharge application fails to submit the application within 60 days of the Secretary's sending the discharge application, the Secretary resumes collection and grants forbearance of principal and interest for the period in which collection activity was suspended. The Secretary may capitalize any interest accrued and not paid during that period.

(3) If a borrower qualifies for a discharge, the Secretary notifies the borrower in writing. The Secretary resumes collection and grants forbearance of principal and interest on the portion of the loan not discharged for the period in which collection activity was suspended. The Secretary may capitalize any interest accrued and not paid during that period.

(4) If a borrower does not qualify for a discharge, the Secretary notifies the borrower in writing of the reasons for the determination. The Secretary resumes collection and grants forbearance of principal and interest for the period in which collection activity was suspended. The Secretary may capitalize any interest accrued and not paid during that period.

(Approved by the Office of Management and Budget under control number 1845-0021)

(Authority: 20 U.S.C. 1087a *et seq.*)

[64 Fed. Reg. 58969 (Nov. 1, 1999); 65 Fed. Reg. 65629 (Nov. 1, 2000); 66 Fed. Reg. 34765 (June 29, 2001)]

* * *

§ 685.219 Public Service Loan Forgiveness Program.

(a) *General.* The Public Service Loan Forgiveness Program is intended to encourage individuals to enter and continue in full-time public service employment by forgiving the remaining balance of their Direct loans after they satisfy the public service and loan payment requirements of this section.

(b) *Definitions.* The following definitions apply to this section:

AmeriCorps position means a position approved by the Corporation for National and Community Service under section 123 of the National and Community Service Act of 1990 (42 U.S.C. 12573).

Eligible Direct loan means a Direct Subsidized Loan, Direct Unsubsidized Loan, Direct PLUS loan, or a Direct Consolidation loan.

Employee or employed means an individual who is hired and paid by a public service organization.

Full-time

(1) means working in qualifying employment in one or more jobs for the greater of—

(i)(A) An annual average of at least 30 hours per week, or

(B) For a contractual or employment period of at least 8 months, an average of 30 hours per week; or

(ii) Unless the qualifying employment is with two or more employers, the number of hours the employer considers full-time.

(2) Vacation or leave time provided by the employer or leave taken for a condition that is a qualifying reason for leave under the Family and Medical Leave Act of 1993, 29 U.S.C. 2612(a)(1) and (3) is not considered in determining the average hours worked on an annual or contract basis.

Government employee means an individual who is employed by a local, State, Federal, or Tribal government, but does not include a member of the U.S. Congress.

Law enforcement means service performed by an employee of a public service organization that is publicly funded and whose principal activities pertain to crime prevention, control or reduction of crime, or the enforcement of criminal law.

Military service, for uniformed members of the U.S. Armed Forces or the National Guard, means "active duty" service or "full-time National Guard duty" as defined in section 101(d)(1) and (d)(5) of title 10 in the United States Code, but does not include active duty for training or attendance at a service school. For civilians, "Military service" means service on behalf of the U.S. Armed Forces or the National Guard performed by an employee of a public service organization.

Peace Corps position means a full-time assignment under the Peace Corps Act as provided for under 22 U.S.C. 2504.

Public interest law refers to legal services provided by a public service organization that are funded in whole or in part by a local, State, Federal, or Tribal government.

Public service organization means:
(1) A Federal, State, local, or Tribal government organization, agency, or entity;
(2) A public child or family service agency;
(3) A non-profit organization under section 501(c)(3) of the Internal Revenue Code that is exempt from taxation under section 501(a) of the Internal Revenue Code;
(4) A Tribal college or university; or
(5) A private organization that—
  (i) Provides the following public services: Emergency management, military service, public safety, law enforcement, public interest law services, early childhood education (including licensed or regulated child care, Head Start, and State funded prekindergarten), public service for individuals with disabilities and the elderly, public health (including nurses, nurse practitioners, nurses in a clinical setting, and full-time professionals engaged in health care practitioner occupations and health care support occupations, as such terms are defined by the Bureau of Labor Statistics), public education, public library services, school library or other school-based services; and
  (ii) Is not a business organized for profit, a labor union, a partisan political organization, or an organization engaged in religious activities, unless the qualifying activities are unrelated to religious instruction, worship services, or any form of proselytizing.

(c) *Borrower eligibility.*
(1) A borrower may obtain loan forgiveness under this program if he or she—
  (i) Is not in default on the loan for which forgiveness is requested;
  (ii) Is employed full-time by a public service organization or serving in a full-time AmeriCorps or Peace Corps position—
    (A) When the borrower makes the 120 monthly payments described under paragraph (c)(1)(iii) of this section;
    (B) At the time of application for loan forgiveness; and
    (C) At the time the remaining principal and accrued interest are forgiven;
  (iii) Makes 120 separate monthly payments after October 1, 2007, on eligible Direct loans for which forgiveness is sought. Except as provided in paragraph (c)(2) of this section for a borrower in an AmeriCorps or Peace Corps position, the borrower must make the monthly payments within 15 days of the scheduled due date for the full scheduled installment amount; and
  (iv) Makes the required 120 monthly payments under one or more of the following repayment plans—
    (A) Except for a parent PLUS borrower, an income-based repayment plan, as determined in accordance with § 685.221;
    (B) Except for a parent PLUS borrower, an income-contingent repayment plan, as determined in accordance with § 685.209;
    (C) A standard repayment plan, as determined in accordance with § 685.208(b); or
    (D) Any other repayment plan if the monthly payment amount paid is not less than what would have been paid under the Direct Loan standard repayment plan described in § 685.208(b).
(2) If a borrower makes a lump sum payment on an eligible loan for which the borrower is seeking forgiveness by using all or part of a Segal Education Award received after a year of AmeriCorps service, or by using all or part of a Peace Corps transition payment if the lump sum payment is made no later than six months after leaving the Peace Corps, the Secretary will consider the borrower to have made qualifying payments equal to the lesser of—
  (i) The number of payments resulting after dividing the amount of the lump sum payment by the monthly payment amount the borrower would have made under paragraph (c)(1)(iv) of this section; or
  (ii) Twelve payments.

(d) *Forgiveness Amount.* The Secretary forgives the principal and accrued interest that remains on all eligible loans for which loan forgiveness is requested by the borrower. The Secretary forgives this amount after the borrower makes the 120 monthly qualifying payments under paragraph (c) of this section.

(e) *Application.*
(1) After making the 120 monthly qualifying payments on the eligible loans for which loan forgiveness is requested, a borrower may request loan forgiveness on a form provided by the Secretary.
(2) If the Secretary determines that the borrower meets the eligibility requirements for loan forgiveness under this section, the Secretary—
  (i) Notifies the borrower of this determination; and
  (ii) Forgives the outstanding balance of the eligible loans.
(3) If the Secretary determines that the borrower does not meet the eligibility requirements for loan forgiveness under this section, the Secretary resumes collection of the loan and grants forbearance of payment on both principal and interest for the period in which collection activity was suspended. The Secretary notifies the borrower that the application has been denied, provides the basis for the denial, and informs the borrower that the Secretary will resume collection of the loan. The Secretary may capitalize any interest accrued and not paid during this period.

(Authority: 20 U.S.C. 1087e(m))

[73 Fed. Reg. 63256 (Oct. 23, 2008); 74 Fed. Reg. 56005 (Oct. 29, 2009)]

§ 685.220 Consolidation.

(a) *Direct Consolidation Loans.* A borrower may consolidate education loans made under certain Federal programs into a Direct Consolidation Loan. Loans consolidated into a Direct Consolidation Loan are discharged when the Direct Consolidation Loan is originated.

(b) *Loans eligible for consolidation.* The following loans may be consolidated into a Direct Consolidation Loan:
(1) Federal Subsidized Stafford Loans.
(2) Guaranteed Student Loans.
(3) Federal Insured Student Loans (FISL).
(4) Direct Subsidized Loans.
(5) Direct Subsidized Consolidation Loans.
(6) Federal Perkins Loans.
(7) National Direct Student Loans (NDSL).
(8) National Defense Student Loans (NDSL).
(9) Federal PLUS Loans.
(10) Parent Loans for Undergraduate Students (PLUS).
(11) Direct PLUS Loans.
(12) Direct PLUS Consolidation Loans.
(13) Federal Unsubsidized Stafford Loans.
(14) Federal Supplemental Loans for Students (SLS).
(15) Federal Consolidation Loans.
(16) Direct Unsubsidized Loans.
(17) Direct Unsubsidized Consolidation Loans.
(18) Auxiliary Loans to Assist Students (ALAS).
(19) Health Professions Student Loans (HPSL) and Loans for Disadvantaged Students (LDS) made under subpart II of part A of title VII of the Public Health Service Act.
(20) Health Education Assistance Loans (HEAL).
(21) Nursing loans made under subpart II of part B of title VIII of the Public Health Service Act.

(c) *Subsidized, unsubsidized, and PLUS components of Direct Consolidation Loans.*
(1) The portion of a Direct Consolidation Loan attributable to the loans identified in paragraphs (b)(1) through (5) of this section, and attributable to the portion of Federal Consolidation Loans under paragraph (b)(15) of this section that is eligible for interest benefits during a deferment period under Section 428C(b)(4)(C) of the Act, is referred to as a Direct Subsidized Consolidation Loan.

(2) Except as provided in paragraph (c)(1) of this section, the portion of a Direct Consolidation Loan attributable to the loans identified in paragraphs (b)(6) through (8) and (b)(13) through (21) of this section is referred to as a Direct Unsubsidized Consolidation Loan.

(3) The portion of a Direct Consolidation Loan attributable to the loans identified in paragraphs (b)(9) through (12) of this section is referred to as a Direct PLUS Consolidation Loan.

(d) *Eligibility for a Direct Consolidation Loan.*
(1) A borrower may obtain a Direct Consolidation Loan if the borrower meets the following requirements:
   (i) At the time the borrower applies for a Direct Consolidation Loan, the borrower either—
      (A) Has an outstanding balance on a Direct Loan; or
      (B) Has an outstanding balance on an FFEL loan and—
         (1) The borrower is unable to obtain a FFEL consolidation loan;
         (2) The borrower is unable to obtain a FFEL consolidation loan with income-sensitive repayment terms acceptable to the borrower;
         (3) The borrower wishes to use the Public Service Loan Forgiveness Program or the no accrual of interest benefit for active duty service;
      (4) The borrower has an FFEL Consolidation Loan that is in default or has been submitted to the guaranty agency by the lender for default aversion, and the borrower wants to consolidate the FFEL Consolidation Loan into the Direct Loan Program for the purpose of obtaining an income contingent repayment plan or an income-based repayment plan; or
      (5) The borrower has a FFEL Consolidation Loan and the borrower wants to consolidate that loan into the Direct Loan Program for purposes of using the Public Service Loan Forgiveness Program or the no accrual of interest benefit for active duty service.
   (ii) At the time the borrower applies for the Direct Consolidation Loan, on the loans being consolidated, the borrower is—
      (A) In the grace period;
      (B) In a repayment period but not in default;
      (C) In default but has made satisfactory repayment arrangements, as defined in applicable program regulations, on the defaulted loan; or
      (D) In default but agrees to repay the consolidation loan under the income contingent repayment plan described in § 685.208(k) or the income-based repayment plan described in § 685.208(m),

and signs the consent form described in § 685.209(d)(5) or § 685.221(e).
      (E) Not subject to a judgment secured through litigation, unless the judgment has been vacated; or
      (F) Not subject to an order for wage garnishment under section 488A of the Act, unless the order has been lifted.
   (iii) On the loans being consolidated, the borrower is—
      (A) Not subject to a judgment secured through litigation, unless the judgment has been vacated; or
      (B) Not subject to an order for wage garnishment under section 488A of the Act, unless the order has been lifted.
   (iv) The borrower certifies that no other application to consolidate any of the borrower's loans listed in paragraph (b) of this section is pending with any other lender.
   (v) The borrower agrees to notify the Secretary of any change in address.
(2) A borrower may not consolidate a Direct Consolidation Loan into a new consolidation loan under this section or under § 682.201(c) unless at least one additional eligible loan is included in the consolidation.
(3) Eligible loans received before or after the date a Direct Consolidation Loan is made may be added to a subsequent Direct Consolidation Loan.

(e) *Application for a Direct Consolidation Loan.* To obtain a Direct Consolidation Loan, a borrower shall submit a completed application to the Secretary. A borrower may add eligible loans to a Direct Consolidation Loan by submitting a request to the Secretary within 180 days after the date on which the Direct Consolidation Loan is originated.

(f) *Origination of a consolidation loan.*
(1)(i) The holder of a loan that a borrower wishes to consolidate into a Direct Loan shall complete and return the Secretary's request for certification of the amount owed within 10 business days of receipt or, if it is unable to provide the certification, provide to the Secretary a written explanation of the reasons for its inability to provide the certification.
(ii) If the Secretary approves an application for a consolidation loan, the Secretary pays to each holder of a loan selected for consolidation the amount necessary to discharge the loan.
(iii) For a Direct Loan or FFEL Program loan that is in default, the Secretary limits collection costs that may be charged to the borrower to no more than those authorized under the FFEL Program.
(2) Upon receipt of the proceeds of a Direct Consolidation Loan, the holder of a consolidated loan shall promptly apply the proceeds to fully discharge the borrower's obligation on the consolidated loan. The holder of a consolidated loan shall notify the borrower that the loan has been paid in full.
(3) The principal balance of a Direct Consolidation Loan is equal to the sum of the amounts paid to the holders of the consolidated loans.
(4) If the amount paid by the Secretary to the holder of a consolidated loan exceeds the amount needed to discharge that loan, the holder of the consolidated loan shall promptly refund the excess amount to the Secretary to be credited against the outstanding balance of the Direct Consolidation Loan.
(5) If the amount paid by the Secretary to the holder of the consolidated loan is insufficient to discharge that loan, the holder shall notify the Secretary in writing of the remaining amount due on the loan. The Secretary promptly pays the remaining amount due.

(g) *Interest rate.* The interest rate on a Direct Subsidized Consolidation Loan or a Direct Unsubsidized Consolidation Loan is the rate established in § 685.202(a)(3)(i). The interest rate on a Direct PLUS Consolidation Loan is the rate established in § 685.202(a)(3)(ii).

(h) *Repayment plans.* A borrower may choose a repayment plan for a Direct Consolidation Loan in accordance with § 685.208, except that a borrower who became eligible to consolidate a defaulted loan under paragraph (d)(1)(ii)(D) of this section must repay the consolidation loan under the income contingent repayment plan unless—
(1)(i) The borrower was required to and did make a payment under the income contingent repayment plan in each of the prior three (3) months; or
   (ii) The borrower was not required to make payments but made three reasonable and affordable payments in each of the prior three (3) months; and
(2) The borrower makes and the Secretary approves a request to change plans.

(i) *Repayment period.*
(1) Except as noted in paragraph (i)(4) of this section, the repayment period for a Direct Consolidation Loan begins on the day the loan is disbursed.
(2)(i) Borrowers who entered repayment before July 1, 2006. The Secretary determines the repayment period under § 685.208(i) on the basis of the outstanding balances on all of the borrower's loans that are eligible for consolidation and the balances on other education loans except as provided in paragraphs (i)(3)(i), (ii), and (iii) of this section.
   (ii) Borrowers entering repayment on or after July 1, 2006. The Secretary determines the repayment period under § 685.208(j) on the basis of the outstanding balances on all of the borrower's loans that are eligible for consolidation and the balances on other education loans except as provided in paragraphs (i)(3)(i) and (ii) of this section.

(3)(i) The total amount of outstanding balances on the other education loans used to determine the repayment period under §§ 685.208(i) and (j) may not exceed the amount of the Direct Consolidation Loan.
(ii) The borrower may not be in default on the other education loan unless the borrower has made satisfactory repayment arrangements with the holder of the loan.
(iii) The lender of the other educational loan may not be an individual.
(4) Borrowers whose consolidation application was received before July 1, 2006. A Direct Consolidation Loan receives a grace period if it includes a Direct Loan or FFEL Program loan for which the borrower is in an in-school period at the time of consolidation. The repayment period begins the day after the grace period ends.

(j) *Repayment schedule.*
(1) The Secretary provides a borrower of a Direct Consolidation Loan a repayment schedule before the borrower's first payment is due. The repayment schedule identifies the borrower's monthly repayment amount under the repayment plan selected.
(2) If a borrower adds an eligible loan to the consolidation loan under paragraph (e) of this section, the Secretary makes appropriate adjustments to the borrower's monthly repayment amount and repayment period.

(k) *Refunds and returns of title IV, HEA program funds received from schools.* If a lender receives a refund or return of title IV, HEA program funds from a school on a loan that has been consolidated into a Direct Consolidation Loan, the lender shall transmit the refund or return and an explanation of the source of the refund or return to the Secretary within 30 days of receipt.

(l) *Special provisions for joint consolidation loans.* The provisions of paragraphs (l)(1) through (3) of this section apply to a Direct Consolidation Loan obtained by two married borrowers in accordance with the regulations that were in effect for consolidation applications received prior to July 1, 2006.
(1) *Deferment.* To obtain a deferment on a joint Direct Consolidation Loan under § 685.204, both borrowers must meet the requirements of that section.
(2) *Forbearance.* To obtain forbearance on a joint Direct Consolidation Loan under § 685.205, both borrowers must meet the requirements of that section.
(3) *Discharge.*
(i) If a borrower dies and the Secretary receives the documentation described in § 685.212(a), the Secretary discharges an amount equal to the portion of the outstanding balance of the consolidation loan, as of the date of the borrower's death, attributable to any of that borrower's loans that were repaid by the consolidation loan.
(ii) If a borrower meets the requirements for total and permanent disability discharge under § 685.212(b), the Secretary discharges an amount equal to the portion of the outstanding balance of the consolidation loan, as of the date the borrower became totally and permanently disabled, attributable to any of that borrower's loans that were repaid by the consolidation loan.
(iii) If a borrower meets the requirements for discharge under § 685.212(d), (e), or (f) on a loan that was consolidated into a joint Direct Consolidation Loan, the Secretary discharges the portion of the consolidation loan equal to the amount of the loan that would be eligible for discharge under the provisions of § 685.212(d), (e), or (f) as applicable, and that was repaid by the consolidation loan.
(iv) If a borrower meets the requirements for loan forgiveness under § 685.212(h) on a loan that was consolidated into a joint Direct Consolidation Loan, the Secretary repays the portion of the outstanding balance of the consolidation loan attributable to the loan that would be eligible for forgiveness under the provisions of § 685.212(h), and that was repaid by the consolidation loan.

(Approved by the Office of Management and Budget under control number 1845-0021)

(Authority: 20 U.S.C. 1078-8, 1087a *et seq.*)

[60 Fed. Reg. 33345 (June 28, 1995); 61 Fed. Reg. 29900 (June 12, 1996); 64 Fed. Reg. 58969, 58970, 59044 (Nov. 1, 1999); 65 Fed. Reg. 37045 (June 13, 2000); 65 Fed. Reg. 65629 (Nov. 1, 2000); 66 Fed. Reg. 34765 (June 29, 2001); 67 Fed. Reg. 67082 (Nov. 1, 2002); 68 Fed. Reg. 75430 (Dec. 31, 2003); 71 Fed. Reg. 45716 (Aug. 9, 2006); 71 Fed. Reg. 64400 (Nov. 1, 2006); 73 Fed. Reg. 63257, 63258 (Oct. 23, 2008); 74 Fed. Reg. 56005 (Oct. 29, 2009)]

§ 685.221 Income-based repayment plan.

(a) *Definitions.* As used in this section—
(1) *Adjusted gross income* (AGI) means the borrower's adjusted gross income as reported to the Internal Revenue Service. For a married borrower filing jointly, AGI includes both the borrower's and spouse's income. For a married borrower filing separately, AGI includes only the borrower's income.
(2) *Eligible loan* means any outstanding loan made to a borrower under the FFEL or Direct Loan programs except for a defaulted loan, a FFEL or Direct PLUS Loan made to a parent borrower, or a FFEL or Direct Consolidation Loan that repaid a FFEL or Direct PLUS Loan made to a parent borrower.
(3) *Family size* means the number that is determined by counting the borrower, the borrower's spouse, and the borrower's children, including unborn children who will be born during the year the borrower certifies family size, if the children receive more than half their support from the borrower. A borrower's family size includes other individuals if, at the time the borrower certifies family size, the other individuals—
(i) Live with the borrower; and
(ii) Receive more than half their support from the borrower and will continue to receive this support from the borrower for the year the borrower certifies family size. Support includes money, gifts, loans, housing, food, clothes, car, medical and dental care, and payment of college costs.
(4) *Partial financial hardship* means a circumstance in which—
(i) For an unmarried borrower or a married borrower who files an individual Federal tax return, the annual amount due on all of the borrower's eligible loans, as calculated under a standard repayment plan based on a 10-year repayment period, using the greater of the amount due at the time the borrower initially entered repayment or at the time the borrower elects the income-based repayment plan, exceeds 15 percent of the difference between the borrower's AGI and 150 percent of the poverty guideline for the borrower's family size; or
(ii) For a married borrower who files a joint Federal tax return with his or her spouse, the annual amount due on all of the borrower's eligible loans and, if applicable, the spouse's eligible loans, as calculated under a standard repayment plan based on a 10-year repayment period, using the greater of the amount due at the time the loans initially entered repayment or at the time the borrower or spouse elects the income-based repayment plan, exceeds 15 percent of the difference between the borrower's and spouse's AGI, and 150 percent of the poverty guideline for the borrower's family size.
(5) *Poverty guideline* refers to the income categorized by State and family size in the poverty guidelines published annually by the United States Department of Health and Human Services pursuant to 42 U.S.C. 9902(2). If a borrower is not a resident of a State identified in the poverty guidelines, the poverty guideline to be used for the borrower is the poverty guideline (for the relevant family size) used for the 48 contiguous States.

(b) *Terms of the repayment plan.*
(1) A borrower may select the income-based repayment plan only if the borrower has a partial financial hardship. The borrower's aggregate monthly loan payments are limited to no more than 15 percent of the amount by which the borrower's AGI exceeds 150 percent of the poverty guideline applicable to the borrower's family size, divided by 12.

(2) The Secretary adjusts the calculated monthly payment if—
  (i) Except for borrowers provided for in paragraph (b)(2)(ii) of this section, the total amount of the borrower's eligible loans are not Direct Loans, in which case the Secretary determines the borrower's adjusted monthly payment by multiplying the calculated payment by the percentage of the total amount of eligible loans that are Direct Loans;
  (ii) Both the borrower and borrower's spouse have eligible loans and filed a joint Federal tax return, in which case the Secretary determines—
    (A) Each borrower's percentage of the couple's total eligible loan debt;
    (B) The adjusted monthly payment for each borrower by multiplying the calculated payment by the percentage determined in paragraph (b)(2)(ii)(A) of this section; and
    (C) If the borrower's loans are held by multiple holders, the borrower's adjusted monthly Direct Loan payment by multiplying the payment determined in paragraph (b)(2)(ii)(B) of this section by the percentage of the outstanding principal amount of eligible loans that are Direct Loans;
  (iii) The calculated amount under paragraph (b)(1), (b)(2)(i), or (b)(2)(ii) of this section is less than $5.00, in which case the borrower's monthly payment is $0.00; or
  (iv) The calculated amount under paragraph (b)(1), (b)(2)(i), or (b)(2)(ii) of this section is equal to or greater than $5.00 but less than $10.00, in which case the borrower's monthly payment is $10.00.
(3) If the borrower's monthly payment amount is not sufficient to pay the accrued interest on the borrower's Direct Subsidized loan or the subsidized portion of a Direct Consolidation Loan, the Secretary does not charge the borrower the remaining accrued interest for a period not to exceed three consecutive years from the established repayment period start date on that loan under the income-based repayment plan. On a Direct Consolidation Loan that repays loans on which the Secretary has not charged the borrower accrued interest, the three-year period includes the period for which the Secretary did not charge the borrower accrued interest on the underlying loans. This three-year period does not include any period during which the borrower receives an economic hardship deferment.
(4) Except as provided in paragraph (b)(3) of this section, accrued interest is capitalized at the time a borrower chooses to leave the income-based repayment plan or no longer has a partial financial hardship.
(5) If the borrower's monthly payment amount is not sufficient to pay any of the principal due, the payment of that principal is postponed until the borrower chooses to leave the income-based repayment plan or no longer has a partial financial hardship.
(6) The repayment period for a borrower under the income-based repayment plan may be greater than 10 years.

(c) *Payment application and prepayment.* The Secretary applies any payment made under an income-based repayment plan in the following order:
  (1) Accrued interest.
  (2) Collection costs.
  (3) Late charges.
  (4) Loan principal.

(d) *Changes in the payment amount.*
(1) If a borrower no longer has a partial financial hardship, the borrower may continue to make payments under the income-based repayment plan, but the Secretary recalculates the borrower's monthly payment. The Secretary also recalculates the monthly payment for a borrower who chooses to stop making income-based payments. In either case, as result of the recalculation—
  (i) The maximum monthly amount that the Secretary requires the borrower to repay is the amount the borrower would have paid under the standard repayment plan based on the amount of the borrower's eligible loans that were outstanding at the time the borrower began repayment on the loans under the income-based repayment plan; and
  (ii) The borrower's repayment period based on the recalculated payment amount may exceed 10 years.
(2) If a borrower no longer wishes to pay under the income-based payment plan, the borrower must pay under the standard repayment plan and the Secretary recalculates the borrower's monthly payment based on—
  (i) The time remaining under the maximum ten-year repayment period for the amount of the borrower's loans that were outstanding at the time the borrower discontinued paying under the income-based repayment plan; or
  (ii) For a Direct Consolidation Loan, the applicable repayment period specified in § 685.208(j) for the amount of that loan and the balance of other student loans that was outstanding at the time the borrower discontinued paying under the income-based repayment plan.

(e) *Eligibility documentation and verification.*
(1) The Secretary determines whether a borrower has a partial financial hardship to qualify for the income-based repayment plan for the year the borrower selects the plan and for each subsequent year that the borrower remains on the plan. To make this determination, the Secretary requires the borrower to—
  (i)(A) Provide written consent to the disclosure of AGI and other tax return information by the Internal Revenue Service to the Secretary. The borrower provides consent by signing a consent form and returning it to the Secretary;
    (B) If a borrower's AGI is not available, or the Secretary believes that the borrower's reported AGI does not reasonably reflect the borrower's current income, the Secretary may use other documentation provided by the borrower to verify income; and
  (ii) Annually certify the borrower's family size. If the borrower fails to certify family size, the Secretary assumes a family size of one for that year.
(2) The Secretary designates the repayment option described in paragraph (d)(1) of this section for any borrower who selects the income-based repayment plan but—
  (i) Fails to renew the required written consent for income verification; or
  (ii) Withdraws consent and does not select another repayment plan.

(f) *Loan forgiveness.*
(1) To qualify for loan forgiveness after 25 years, a borrower must have participated in the income-based repayment plan and satisfied at least one of the following conditions during that period:
  (i) Made reduced monthly payments under a partial financial hardship as provided in paragraph (b)(1) or (2) of this section, including a monthly payment amount of $0.00, as provided under paragraph (b)(2)(ii) of this section.
  (ii) Made reduced monthly payments after the borrower no longer had a partial financial hardship or stopped making income-based payments as provided in paragraph (d) of this section.
  (iii) Made monthly payments under any repayment plan, that were not less than the amount required under the Direct Loan standard repayment plan described in § 685.208(b).
  (iv) Made monthly payments under the Direct Loan standard repayment plan described in § 685.208(b) based on the amount of the borrower's loans that were outstanding at the time the borrower first selected the income-based repayment plan.
  (v) Paid Direct Loans under the income-contingent repayment plan.
  (vi) Received an economic hardship deferment on eligible Direct Loans.
(2) As provided under paragraph (f)(4) of this section, the Secretary cancels any outstanding balance of principal and accrued interest on Direct loans for which the borrower qualifies for forgiveness if the Secretary determines that—
  (i) The borrower made monthly payments under one or more of the repayment plans described in paragraph (f)(1) of this section, including a monthly payment amount

of $0.00, as provided under paragraph (b)(2)(ii) of this section; and

(ii)(A) The borrower made those monthly payments each year for a 25-year period, or

(B) Through a combination of monthly payments and economic hardship deferments, the borrower has made the equivalent of 25 years of payments.

(3) For a borrower who qualifies for the income-based repayment plan, the beginning date for the 25-year period is—

(i) If the borrower made payments under the income contingent repayment plan, the date the borrower made a payment on the loan under that plan at any time after July 1, 1994;

(ii) If the borrower did not make payments under the income contingent repayment plan—

(A) For a borrower who has a Direct Consolidation Loan, the date the borrower made a payment or received an economic hardship deferment on that loan, before the date the borrower qualified for income-based repayment. The beginning date is the date the borrower made the payment or received the deferment, but no earlier than July 1, 2009;

(B) For a borrower who has one or more other eligible Direct Loans, the date the borrower made a payment or received an economic hardship deferment on that loan. The beginning date is the date the borrower made that payment or received the deferment on that loan, but no earlier than July 1, 2009;

(C) For a borrower who did not make a payment or receive an economic hardship deferment on the loan under paragraph (f)(3)(ii)(A) or (B) of this section, the date the borrower made a payment under the income-based repayment plan on the loan;

(D) If the borrower consolidates his or her eligible loans, the date the borrower made a payment on the Direct Consolidation Loan after qualifying for the income-based repayment plan; or

(E) If the borrower did not make a payment or receive an economic hardship deferment on the loan under paragraph (f)(3)(i) or (ii) of this section, determining the date the borrower made a payment under the income-based repayment plan on the loan.

(4) If the Secretary determines that a borrower satisfies the loan forgiveness requirements, the Secretary cancels the outstanding balance and accrued interest on the Direct Consolidation Loan described in paragraph (f)(3)(i), (iii) or (iv) of this section or other eligible Direct Loans described in paragraph (f)(3)(ii) or (iv) of this section.

(Authority: 20 U.S.C. 1098e)

[73 Fed. Reg. 63258 (Oct. 23, 2008); 74 Fed. Reg. 56006 (Oct. 29, 2009)]

* * *

B.2 FFEL Regulations

34 C.F.R. sec.

* * *

682.200 Definitions.
682.201 Eligible borrowers.
682.202 Permissible charges by lenders to borrowers.

* * *

682.209 Repayment of a loan.
682.210 Deferment.
682.211 Forbearance.
682.212 Prohibited transactions.

* * *

682.215 Income-based repayment plan.

* * *

682.402 Death, disability, closed school, false certification, unpaid refunds, and bankruptcy payments.

* * *

682.405 Loan rehabilitation agreement.

* * *

682.410 Fiscal, administrative, and enforcement requirements.
682.411 Lender due diligence in collecting guaranty agency loans.

* * *

SOURCE: 57 Fed. Reg. 60323 (Dec. 18, 1992); 58 Fed. Reg. 36870 (July 9, 1993); 73 Fed. Reg. 35495 (June 23, 2008); 74 Fed. Reg. 55664 (Oct. 28, 2009), unless otherwise noted.

AUTHORITY: 20 U.S.C. 1070g, 1071 to 1087-2, unless otherwise noted.

§ 682.200 Definitions.

(a)(1) The definitions of the following terms used in this part are set forth in subpart A of the Student Assistance General Provisions, 34 CFR part 668:

Academic Competitiveness Grant (ACG) Program
Academic year
Campus-based programs
Dependent student
Eligible program
Eligible student
Enrolled
Expected family contribution
Federal Consolidation Loan Program
Federal Pell Grant Program
Federal Perkins Loan Program
Federal PLUS Program
Federal Work-Study (FWS) Program
Full-time student
Graduate and professional student
Half-time student
Independent student
Leveraging Educational Assistance Partnership (LEAP) Program
National of the United States (Referred to as U.S. Citizen or National in 34 CFR 668.2)
National Science and Mathematics Access to Retain Talent Grant (National SMART Grant) Program
Payment period
Supplemental Educational Opportunity Grant (SEOG) Program
Supplemental Loans for Students (SLS) Program
Teacher Education Assistance for College and Higher Education (TEACH) Grant Program
TEACH Grant
Undergraduate student

(2) The following definitions are set forth in the regulations for Institutional Eligibility under the Higher Education Act of 1965, as amended, 34 CFR part 600:

Accredited
Clock hour
Correspondence course
Educational program
Federal Family Education Loan Program (formerly known as the Guaranteed Student Loan (GSL) Program)
Institution of higher education (§ 600.4)
Nationally recognized accrediting agency
Postsecondary Vocational Institution
Preaccredited
Secretary
State

(3) The definition for cost of attendance is set forth in section 472 of the Act, as amended.

(b) The following definitions also apply to this part:

Act. The Higher Education Act of 1965, as amended, 20 U.S.C. 1071 *et seq.*

Actual interest rate. The annual interest rate a lender charges on a loan, which may be equal to or less than the applicable interest rate on that loan.

Applicable interest rate. The maximum annual interest rate that a lender may charge under the Act on a loan.

Authority. Any private non-profit or public entity that may issue tax-exempt obligations to obtain funds to be used for the making or purchasing of FFEL loans. The term "Authority" also includes any agency, including a State postsecondary institution or any other instrumentality of a State or local governmental unit, regardless of the designation or primary purpose of that agency, that may issue tax-exempt obligations, any party authorized to issue those obligations on behalf of a governmental agency, and any non-profit organization authorized by law to issue tax-exempt obligations.

Borrower. An individual to whom a FFEL Program loan is made.

Co-Maker: One of two married individuals who jointly borrow a Consolidation loan, each of whom are eligible and who are jointly and severally liable for repayment of the loan. The term co-maker also includes one of two parents who are joint borrowers as previously authorized in the PLUS Program.

Default. The failure of a borrower and endorser, if any, or joint borrowers on a PLUS or Consolidation loan, to make an installment payment when due, or to meet other terms of the promissory note, the Act, or regulations as applicable, if the Secretary or guaranty agency finds it reasonable to conclude that the borrower and endorser, if any, no longer intend to honor the obligation to repay, provided that this failure persists for—

(1) 270 days for a loan repayable in monthly installments; or

(2) 330 days for a loan repayable in less frequent installments.

Disbursement. The transfer of loan proceeds by a lender to a holder, in the case of a Consolidation loan, or to a borrower, a school, or an escrow agent by issuance of an individual check, a master check or by electronic funds transfer that may represent loan amounts for borrowers.

Disposable income. That part of an individual's compensation from an employer and other income from any source, including spousal income, that remains after the deduction of any amounts required by law to be withheld, or any child support or alimony payments that are made under a court order or legally enforceable written agreement. Amounts required by law to be withheld include, but are not limited, to Federal, State, and local taxes, Social Security contributions, and wage garnishment payments.

Endorser. An individual who signs a promissory note and agrees to repay the loan in the event that the borrower does not.

Escrow agent. Any guaranty agency or other eligible lender that receives the proceeds of a FFEL program loan as an agent of an eligible lender for the purpose of transmitting those proceeds to the borrower or the borrower's school.

Estimated financial assistance.

(1) The estimated amount of assistance for a period of enrollment that a student (or a parent on behalf of a student) will receive from Federal, State, institutional, or other sources, such as, scholarships, grants, the net earnings from need-based employment, or loans, including but not limited to—

(i) Except as provided in paragraph (2)(iii) of this definition, national service education awards or post-service benefits under title I of the National and Community Service Act of 1990 (AmeriCorps);

(ii) Except as provided in paragraph (2)(vii) of this definition, veterans' education benefits;

(iii) Any educational benefits paid because of enrollment in a postsecondary education institution, or to cover postsecondary education expenses;

(iv) Fellowships or assistantships, except non-need-based employment portions of such awards;

(v) Insurance programs for the student's education; and

(vi) The estimated amount of other Federal student financial aid, including but not limited to a Federal Pell Grant, Academic Competitiveness Grant, National SMART Grant, campus-based aid, and the gross amount (including fees) of subsidized and unsubsidized Federal Stafford Loans or subsidized and unsubsidized Federal Direct Stafford/Ford Loans, and Federal PLUS or Federal Direct PLUS Loans.

(2) Estimated financial assistance does not include—

(i) Those amounts used to replace the expected family contribution, including the amounts of any TEACH Grant, unsubsidized Federal Stafford or Federal Direct Stafford/Ford Loans, Federal PLUS or Federal Direct PLUS Loans, and non-federal non-need-based loans, including private, state-sponsored, and institutional loans. However, if the sum of the amounts received that are being used to replace the student's EFC exceed the EFC, the excess amount must be treated as estimated financial assistance;

(ii) Federal Perkins loan and Federal Work-Study funds that the student has declined;

(iii) For the purpose of determining eligibility for a subsidized Stafford loan, national service education awards or post-service benefits under title I of the National and Community Service Act of 1990 (AmeriCorps);

(iv) Any portion of the estimated financial assistance described in paragraph (1) of this definition that is included in the calculation of the student's expected family contribution (EFC);

(v) Non-need-based employment earnings;

(vi) Assistance not received under a title IV, HEA program, if that assistance is designated to offset all or a portion of a specific amount of the cost of attendance and that component is excluded from the cost of attendance as well. If that assistance is excluded from either estimated financial assistance or cost of attendance, it must be excluded from both;

(vii) Federal veterans' education benefits paid under—

(A) Chapter 103 of title 10, United States Code (Senior Reserve Officers' Training Corps;

(B) Chapter 106A of title 10, United States Code (Educational Assistance for Persons Enlisting for Active Duty);

(C) Chapter 1606 of title 10, United States Code (Selected Reserve Educational Assistance Program);

(D) Chapter 1607 of title 10, United States Code (Educational Assistance Program for Reserve Component Members Supporting Contingency Operations and Certain Other Operations);

(E) Chapter 30 of title 38, United States Code (All-Volunteer Force Educational Assistance Program, also known as the "Montgomery GI Bill-active duty");

(F) Chapter 31 of title 38, United States Code (Training and Rehabilitation for Veterans with Service-Connected Disabilities);

(G) Chapter 32 of title 38, United States Code (Post-Vietnam Era Veterans' Educational Assistance Program);

(H) Chapter 33 of title 38, United States Code (Post 9/11 Educational Assistance);

(I) Chapter 35 of title 38, United States Code (Survivors' and Dependents' Educational Assistance Program);

(J) Section 903 of the Department of Defense Authorization Act, 1981 (10 U.S.C. 2141 note) (Educational Assistance Pilot Program);

(K) Section 156(b) of the "Joint Resolution making further continuing appropriations and providing for productive employment for the fiscal year 1983, and for other purposes" (42 U.S.C. 402 note) (Restored Entitlement Program for Survivors, also known as "Quayle benefits");

(L) The provisions of chapter 3 of title 37, United States Code, related to subsistence allowances for members of the Reserve Officers Training Corps; and

(M) Any program that the Secretary may determine is covered by section 480(c)(2) of the HEA; and

(viii) Iraq and Afghanistan Service Grants made under section 420R of the HEA.

Federal GSL programs. The Federal Insured Student Loan Program, the Federal Supplemental Loans for Students Program, the Federal PLUS Program, and the Federal Consolidation Loan Program.

Federal Insured Student Loan Program. The loan program authorized by title IV-B of the Act under which the Secretary directly insures lenders against losses.

Foreign school. A school not located in a State.

Grace period. The period that begins on the day after a Stafford loan borrower ceases to be enrolled as at least a half-time student at an institution of higher education and ends on the day before the repayment period begins. See also "Post-deferment grace period." For an SLS borrower who also has a Federal Stafford loan on which the borrower has not yet entered repayment, the grace period is an equivalent period after the borrower ceases to be enrolled as at least a half-time student at an institution of higher education.

Guaranty agency. A State or private nonprofit organization that has an agreement with the Secretary under which it will administer a loan guarantee program under the Act.

Holder. An eligible lender owning an FFEL Program loan including a Federal or State agency or an organization or corporation acting on behalf of such an agency and acting as a conservator, liquidator, or receiver of an eligible lender.

Legal guardian. An individual appointed by a court to be a "guardian" of a person and specifically required by the court to use his or her financial resources for the support of that person.

Lender.
(1) The term "eligible lender" is defined in section 435(d) of the Act, and in paragraphs (2)-(5) of this definition.
(2) With respect to a National or State chartered bank, a mutual savings bank, a savings and loan association, a stock savings bank, or a credit union—
  (i) The phrase "subject to examination and supervision" in section 435(d) of the Act means "subject to examination and supervision in its capacity as a lender";
  (ii) The phrase "does not have as its primary consumer credit function the making or holding of loans made to students under this part" in section 435(d) of the Act means that the lender does not, or in the case of a bank holding company, the company's wholly-owned subsidiaries as a group do not at any time, hold FFEL Program loans that total more than one-half of the lender's or subsidiaries' combined consumer credit loan portfolio, including home mortgages held by the lender or its subsidiaries. For purposes of this paragraph, loans held in trust by a trustee lender are not considered part of the trustee lender's consumer credit function.
(3) A bank that is subject to examination and supervision by an agency of the United States, making student loans as a trustee, may be an eligible lender if it makes loans under an express trust, operated as a lender in the FFEL programs prior to January 1, 1975, and met the requirements of this paragraph prior to July 23, 1992.
(4) The corporate parent or other owner of a school that qualifies as an eligible lender under section 435(d) of the Act is not an eligible lender unless the corporate parent or owner itself qualifies as an eligible lender under section 435(d) of the Act.
(5)(i) The term eligible lender does not include any lender that the Secretary determines, after notice and opportunity for a hearing before a designated Department official, has, directly or through an agent or contractor—
  (A) Except as provided in paragraph (5)(ii) of this definition, offered, directly or indirectly, points, premiums, payments (including payments for referrals, finder fees or processing fees), or other inducements to any school, any employee of a school, or any individual or entity in order to secure applications for FFEL loans or FFEL loan volume. This includes but is not limited to—
    (1) Payments or offerings of other benefits, including prizes or additional financial aid funds, to a prospective borrower or to a school or school employee in exchange for applying for or accepting a FFEL loan from the lender;
    (2) Payments or other benefits, including payments of stock or other securities, tuition payments or reimbursements, to a school, a school employee, any school-affiliated organization, or to any other individual in exchange for FFEL loan applications, application referrals, or a specified volume or dollar amount of loans made, or placement on a school's list of recommended or suggested lenders;
    (3) Payments or other benefits provided to a student at a school who acts as the lender's representative to secure FFEL loan applications from individual prospective borrowers, unless the student is also employed by the lender for other purposes and discloses that employment to school administrators and to prospective borrowers;
    (4) Payments or other benefits to a loan solicitor or sales representative of a lender who visits schools to solicit individual prospective borrowers to apply for FFEL loans from the lender;
    (5) Payment to another lender or any other party, including a school, a school employee, or a school-affiliated organization or its employees, of referral fees, finder fees or processing fees, except those processing fees necessary to comply with Federal or State law;
    (6) Compensation to an employee of a school's financial aid office or other employee who has responsibilities with respect to student loans or other financial aid provided by the school or compensation to a school-affiliated organization or its employees, to serve on a lender's advisory board, commission or other group established by the lender, except that the lender may reimburse the employee for reasonable expenses incurred in providing the service;
    (7) Payment of conference or training registration, travel, and lodging costs for an employee of a school or school-affiliated organization;
    (8) Payment of entertainment expenses, including expenses for private hospitality suites, tickets to shows or sporting events, meals, alcoholic beverages, and any lodging, rental, transportation, and other gratuities related to lender-sponsored activities for employees of a school or a school-affiliated organization;
    (9) Philanthropic activities, including providing scholarships, grants, restricted gifts, or financial contributions in exchange for FFEL loan applications or application referrals, or a specified volume or dollar amount of FFEL loans made, or placement on a school's list of recommended or suggested lenders;
    (10) Performance of, or payment to another third party to perform, any school function required under title IV, except that the lender may perform entrance counseling as provided in § 682.604(f) and exit counseling as provided in § 682.604(g), and may provide services to participating foreign schools at the direction of the Secretary, as a third-party servicer; and
    (11) Any type of consulting arrangement or other contract with an employee of a financial aid office at a school, or an employee of a school who otherwise has responsibilities with respect to student loans or other financial aid provided by the school under which the employee would provide services to the lender.
  (B) Conducted unsolicited mailings, by postal or electronic means, of student loan application forms to students enrolled in secondary schools or postsecondary institutions or to family members of such students, except to a student or borrower who previously has received a FFEL loan from the lender;
  (C) Offered, directly or indirectly, a FFEL loan to a prospective borrower to induce the purchase of a policy of insurance or other product or service by the borrower or other person; or
  (D) Engaged in fraudulent or misleading advertising with respect to its FFEL loan activities.
(ii) Notwithstanding paragraph (5)(i) of this definition, a lender, in carrying out its role in the FFEL program and in attempting to provide better service, may provide—

(A) Technical assistance to a school that is comparable to the kinds of technical assistance provided to a school by the Secretary under the Direct Loan program, as identified by the Secretary in a public announcement, such as a notice in the Federal Register;
(B) Support of and participation in a school's or a guaranty agency's student aid and financial literacy-related outreach activities, including in-person entrance and exit counseling, as long as the name of the entity that developed and paid for any materials is provided to the participants and the lender does not promote its student loan or other products;
(C) Meals, refreshments, and receptions that are reasonable in cost and scheduled in conjunction with training, meeting, or conference events if those meals, refreshments, or receptions are open to all training, meeting, or conference attendees;
(D) Toll-free telephone numbers for use by schools or others to obtain information about FFEL loans and free data transmission service for use by schools to electronically submit applicant loan processing information or student status confirmation data;
(E) A reduced origination fee in accordance with § 682.202(c);
(F) A reduced interest rate as provided under the Act;
(G) Payment of Federal default fees in accordance with the Act;
(H) Purchase of a loan made by another lender at a premium;
(I) Other benefits to a borrower under a repayment incentive program that requires, at a minimum, one or more scheduled payments to receive or retain the benefit or under a loan forgiveness program for public service or other targeted purposes approved by the Secretary, provided these benefits are not marketed to secure loan applications or loan guarantees;
(J) Items of nominal value to schools, school-affiliated organizations, and borrowers that are offered as a form of generalized marketing or advertising, or to create good will; and
(K) Other services as identified and approved by the Secretary through a public announcement, such as a notice in the Federal Register.
(iii) For the purposes of this paragraph (5)—
(A) The term "school-affiliated organization" is defined in § 682.200.
(B) The term "applications" includes the Free Application for Federal Student Aid (FAFSA), FFEL loan master promissory notes, and FFEL Consolidation loan application and promissory notes.

(C) The term "other benefits" includes, but is not limited to, preferential rates for or access to the lender's other financial products, information technology equipment, or non-loan processing or non-financial aid-related computer software at below market rental or purchase cost, and printing and distribution of college catalogs and other materials at reduced or no cost.
(6) The term eligible lender does not include any lender that—
(i) Is debarred or suspended, or any of whose principals or affiliates (as those terms are defined in 34 CFR part 85) is debarred or suspended under Executive Order (E.O.) 12549 (3 CFR, 1986 Comp., p. 189) or the Federal Acquisition Regulation (FAR), 48 CFR part 9, subpart 9.4;
(ii) Is an affiliate, as defined in 34 CFR part 85, of any person who is debarred or suspended under E.O. 12549 (3 CFR, 1986 Comp., p. 189) or the FAR, 48 CFR part 9, subpart 9.4; or
(iii) Employs a person who is debarred or suspended under E.O. 12549 (3 CFR, 1986 Comp., p. 189) or the FAR, 48 CFR part 9, subpart 9.4, in a capacity that involves the administration or receipt of FFEL Program funds.
(7) An eligible lender may not make or hold a loan as trustee for a school, or for a school-affiliated organization as defined in this section, unless on or before September 30, 2006—
(i) The eligible lender was serving as trustee for the school or school-affiliated organization under a contract entered into and continuing in effect as of that date; and
(ii) The eligible lender held at least one loan in trust on behalf of the school or school-affiliated organization on that date.
(8) As of January 1, 2007, and for loans first disbursed on or after that date under a trustee arrangement, an eligible lender operating as a trustee under a contract entered into on or before September 30, 2006, and which continues in effect with a school or a school-affiliated organization, must comply with the requirements of § 682.601(a)(3), (a)(5), and (a)(7).

Master Promissory Note (MPN). A promissory note under which the borrower may receive loans for a single period of enrollment or multiple periods of enrollment.

Nationwide consumer reporting agency. A consumer reporting agency as defined in 15 U.S.C. 1681a.

Nonsubsidized Stafford loan. A Stafford loan made prior to October 1, 1992 that does not qualify for interest benefits under § 682.301(b) or special allowance payments under § 682.302.

Origination relationship. A special business relationship between a school and a lender in which the lender delegates to the school, or to an entity or individual affiliated with the school, substantial functions or responsibilities normally performed by lenders before making FFEL program loans. In this situation, the school is considered to have "originated" a loan made by the lender.

Origination fee. A fee that the lender is required to pay the Secretary to help defray the Secretary's costs of subsidizing the loan. The lender may pass this fee on to the Stafford loan borrower. The lender must pass this fee on to the SLS or PLUS borrower.

Participating school. A school that has in effect a current agreement with the Secretary under § 682.600.

Period of enrollment. The period for which a Stafford, SLS, or PLUS loan is intended. The period of enrollment must coincide with one or more bona fide academic terms established by the school for which institutional charges are generally assessed (e.g., a semester, trimester, or quarter in weeks of instructional time, an academic year, or the length of the student's program of study in weeks of instructional time). The period of enrollment is also referred to as the loan period.

Post-deferment grace period. For a loan made prior to October 1, 1981, a single period of six consecutive months beginning on the day following the last day of an authorized deferment period.

Repayment period.
(1) For a Stafford loan, the period beginning on the date following the expiration of the grace period and ending no later than 10 years, or 25 years under an extended repayment schedule, from the date the first payment of principal is due from the borrower, exclusive of any period of deferment or forbearance.
(2) For unsubsidized Stafford loans, the period that begins on the day after the expiration of the applicable grace period that follows after the student ceases to be enrolled on at least a half-time basis and ending no later than 10 years or 25 years under an extended repayment schedule, from that date, exclusive of any period of deferment or forbearance. However, payments of interest are the responsibility of the borrower during the in-school and grace period, but may be capitalized by the lender.
(3) For SLS loans, the period that begins on the date the loan is disbursed, or if the loan is disbursed in more than one installment, on the date the last disbursement is made and ending no later than 10 years from that date, exclusive of any period of deferment or forbearance. The first payment of principal is due within 60 days after the loan is fully disbursed unless a borrower who is also a Stafford loan borrower but who, has not yet

entered repayment on the Stafford loan requests that commencement of repayment on the SLS loan be delayed until the borrower's grace period on the Stafford loan expires. Interest on the loan accrues and is due and payable from the date of the first disbursement of the loan. The borrower is responsible for paying interest on the loan during the grace period and periods of deferment, but the interest may be capitalized by the lender.

(4) For Federal PLUS loans, the period that begins on the date the loan is disbursed, or if the loan is disbursed in more than one installment, on the date the last disbursement is made and ending no later than 10 years, or 25 years under an extended repayment schedule from that date, exclusive of any period of deferment or forbearance. Interest on the loan accrues and is due and payable from the date of the first disbursement of the loan.

(5) For Federal Consolidation loans, the period that begins on the date the loan is disbursed and ends no later than 10, 12, 15, 20, 25, or 30 years from that date depending upon the sum of the amount of the Consolidation loan, and the unpaid balance on other student loans, exclusive of any period of deferment or forbearance.

Satisfactory repayment arrangement.

(1) For purposes of regaining eligibility under § 682.401(b)(4), the making of six (6) consecutive, on-time, voluntary full monthly payments on a defaulted loan. A borrower may only obtain the benefit of this paragraph with respect to renewed eligibility once.

(2) For purposes of consolidating a defaulted loan under 34 CFR 682.201(c)(1)(iii)(C), the making of three (3) consecutive, on-time voluntary full monthly payments on a defaulted loan.

(3) The required full monthly payment amount may not be more than is reasonable and affordable based on the borrower's total financial circumstances. Voluntary payments are those payments made directly by the borrower, and do not include payments obtained by income tax off-set, garnishment, or income or asset execution. On-time means a payment received by the Secretary or a guaranty agency or its agent within 15 days of the scheduled due date.

School.

(1) An "institution of higher education" as that term is defined in 34 CFR 600.4.

(2) For purposes of an in-school deferment, the term includes an institution of higher education, whether or not it participates in any title IV program or has lost its eligibility to participate in the FFEL program because of a high default rate.

School-affiliated organization. A school-affiliated organization is any organization that is directly or indirectly related to a school and includes, but is not limited to, alumni organizations, foundations, athletic organizations, and social, academic, and professional organizations.

School lender. A school, other than a correspondence school, that has entered into a contract of guarantee under this part with the Secretary or, a similar agreement with a guaranty agency.

Stafford Loan Program. The loan program authorized by Title IV-B of the Act which encourages the making of subsidized and unsubsidized loans to undergraduate, graduate, and professional students and is one of the Federal Family Education Loan programs.

State lender. In any State, a single State agency or private nonprofit agency designated by the State that has entered into a contract of guarantee under this part with the Secretary, or a similar agreement with a guaranty agency.

Subsidized Stafford Loan: A Stafford loan that qualifies for interest benefits under § 682.301(b) and special allowance under § 682.302.

Substantial gainful activity. A level of work performed for pay or profit that involves doing significant physical or mental activities, or a combination of both.

Temporarily totally disabled. The condition of an individual who, though not totally and permanently disabled, is unable to work and earn money or attend school, during a period of at least 60 days needed to recover from injury or illness. With regard to a disabled dependent of a borrower, this term means a spouse or other dependent who, during a period of injury or illness, requires continuous nursing or similar services for a period of at least 90 days.

Third-party servicer. Any State or private, profit or nonprofit organization or any individual that enters into a contract with a lender or guaranty agency to administer, through either manual or automated processing, any aspect of the lender's or guaranty agency's FFEL programs required by any statutory provision of or applicable to Title IV of the HEA, any regulatory provision prescribed under that statutory authority, or any applicable special arrangement, agreement, or limitation entered into under the authority of statutes applicable to Title IV of the HEA that governs the FFEL programs, including, any applicable function described in the definition of third-party servicer in 34 CFR part 668; originating, guaranteeing, monitoring, processing, servicing, or collecting loans; claims submission; or billing for interest benefits and special allowance.

Totally and permanently disabled. The condition of an individual who—

(1) Is unable to engage in any substantial gainful activity by reason of any medically determinable physical or mental impairment that—

(i) Can be expected to result in death;

(ii) Has lasted for a continuous period of not less than 60 months; or

(iii) Can be expected to last for a continuous period of not less than 60 months; or

(2) Has been determined by the Secretary of Veterans Affairs to be unemployable due to a service-connected disability.

Unsubsidized Stafford loan. A loan made after October 1, 1992, authorized under section 428H of the Act for borrowers who do not qualify for interest benefits under § 682.301(b) but do qualify for special allowance under § 682.302.

Write-off. Cessation of collection activity on a defaulted FFEL loan due to a determination in accordance with applicable standards that no further collection activity is warranted.

(Approved by the Office of Management and Budget under control number 1845-0020)

(Authority: 8 U.S.C. 1101; 20 U.S.C. 1070 to 1087-2, 1088-1098, 1141; E.O. 12549 (3 CFR, 1986 Comp., p. 189), E.O. 12689 (3 CFR, 1989 Comp., p. 235))

[59 Fed. Reg. 22454 (Apr. 29, 1994); 59 Fed. Reg. 25744 (May 17, 1994); 59 Fed. Reg. 32656 (June 24, 1994); 59 Fed. Reg. 33348 (June 28, 1994); 59 Fed. Reg. 61215 (Nov. 29, 1994); 60 Fed. Reg. 32912 (June 26, 1995); 60 Fed. Reg. 61756 (Dec. 1, 1995); 61 Fed. Reg. 60608 (Nov. 29, 1996); 64 Fed. Reg. 18975 (Apr. 16, 1999); 64 Fed. Reg. 58952 (Nov. 1, 1999); 65 Fed. Reg. 38729 (June 22, 2000); 65 Fed. Reg. 65691 (Nov. 1, 2000); 67 Fed. Reg. 67078 (Nov. 1, 2002); 69 Fed. Reg. 12276 (Mar. 16, 2004); 71 Fed. Reg. 38003 (July 3, 2006); 71 Fed. Reg. 45699 (Aug. 9, 2006); 72 Fed. Reg. 61999, 62000 (Nov. 1, 2007); 72 Fed. Reg. 62031 (Nov. 1, 2007); 73 Fed. Reg. 35495 (June 23, 2008); 74 Fed. Reg. 55988 (Oct. 29, 2009)]

§ 682.201 Eligible borrowers.

(a) *Student Stafford borrower.* Except for a refinanced SLS/PLUS loan made under § 682.209(e) or (f), a student is eligible to receive a Stafford loan, and an independent undergraduate student, a graduate or professional student, or, subject to paragraph (a)(3) of this section, a dependent undergraduate student, is eligible to receive an unsubsidized Stafford loan, if the student who is enrolled or accepted for enrollment on at least a half-time basis at a participating school meets the requirements for an eligible student under 34 CFR part 668, and—

(1) In the case of an undergraduate student who seeks a Stafford loan or unsubsidized Stafford loan for the cost of attendance at a school that participates in the Pell Grant Program, has received a final determination, or, in the case of a student who has filed an application with the school for a Pell Grant, a preliminary determination, from the school of the student's eligibility or ineligibility for a Pell Grant and, if eligible, has applied for the period of enrollment for which the loan is sought;

(2) In the case of any student who seeks an unsubsidized Stafford loan for the cost of attendance at a school that participates in the Stafford Loan Program, the student must—
  (i) Receive a determination of need for a subsidized Stafford loan; and
  (ii) If the determination of need is in excess of $200, have made a request to a lender for a subsidized Stafford loan;
(3) For purposes of a dependent undergraduate student's eligibility for an additional unsubsidized Stafford loan amount, as described at § 682.204(d), is a dependent undergraduate student for whom the financial aid administrator determines and documents in the school's file, after review of the family financial information provided by the student and consideration of the student's debt burden, that the student's parents likely will be precluded by exceptional circumstances (e.g., denial of a PLUS loan to a parent based on adverse credit, the student's parent receives only public assistance or disability benefits, is incarcerated, or his or her whereabouts are unknown) from borrowing under the PLUS Program and the student's family is otherwise unable to provide the student's expected family contribution. A parent's refusal to borrow a PLUS loan does not constitute an exceptional circumstance;
(4)(i) Reaffirms any FFEL loan amount on which there has been a total cessation of collection activity, including all principal interest, collection costs, court costs, attorney fees, and late charges that have accrued on that amount up to the date of reaffirmation;
  (ii) For purposes of this section, reaffirmation means the acknowledgment of the loan by the borrower in a legally binding manner. The acknowledgment may include, but is not limited to, the borrower—
    (A) Signing a new promissory note that includes the same terms and conditions as the original note signed by the borrower or repayment schedule; or
    (B) Making a payment on the loan.
(5) The suspension of collection activity has been lifted from any loan on which collection activity had been suspended based on a conditional determination that the borrower was totally and permanently disabled.
(6) In the case of a borrower whose prior loan under title IV of the Act or whose TEACH Grant service obligation was discharged after a final determination of total and permanent disability, the student must—
  (i) Obtain certification from a physician that the borrower is able to engage in substantial gainful activity;
  (ii) Sign a statement acknowledging that the FFEL loan the borrower receives cannot be discharged in the future on the basis of any impairment present when the new loan is made, unless that impairment substantially deteriorates; and
  (iii) If a borrower receives a new FFEL loan, other than a Federal Consolidation Loan, within three years of the date that any previous title IV loan or TEACH Grant service obligation was discharged due to a total and permanent disability in accordance with § 682.402(c)(3)(ii), 34 CFR 674.61(b)(3)(i), 34 CFR 685.213, or 34 CFR 686.42(b) based on a discharge request received on or after July 1, 2010, resume repayment on the previously discharged loan in accordance with § 682.402(c)(5), 34 CFR 674.61(b)(5), or 34 CFR 685.213(b)(4), or acknowledge that he or she is once again subject to the terms of the TEACH Grant agreement to serve before receiving the new loan.
(7) In the case of a borrower whose prior loan under title IV of the HEA was conditionally discharged after an initial determination that the borrower was totally and permanently disabled based on a discharge request received prior to July 1, 2010, the borrower must—
  (i) Comply with the requirements of paragraphs (a)(6)(i) and (a)(6)(ii) of this section; and
  (ii) Sign a statement acknowledging that—
    (A) The loan that has been conditionally discharged prior to a final determination of total and permanent disability cannot be discharged in the future on the basis of any impairment present when the borrower applied for a total and permanent disability discharge or when the new loan is made unless that impairment substantially deteriorates; and
    (B) Collection activity will resume on any loans in a conditional discharge period.
(8) In the case of any student who seeks a loan but does not have a certificate of graduation from a school providing secondary education or the recognized equivalent of such a certificate, the student meets the requirements under 34 CFR part 668.32(e).
(9) Is not serving in a medical internship or residency program, except for an internship in dentistry.

(b) *Student PLUS borrower.* A graduate or professional student who is enrolled or accepted for enrollment on at least a half-time basis at a participating school is eligible to receive a PLUS Loan on or after July 1, 2006, if the student—
(1) Meets the requirements for an eligible student under 34 CFR 668;
(2) Meets the requirements of paragraphs (a)(4), (a)(5), (a)(6), (a)(7), (a)(8), and (a)(9) of this section, if applicable;
(3) Has received a determination of his or her annual loan maximum eligibility under the Federal Subsidized and Unsubsidized Stafford Loan Program or under the Federal Direct Subsidized Stafford/Ford Loan Program and Federal Direct Unsubsidized Stafford/Ford Loan Program, as applicable; and
(4) Does not have an adverse credit history in accordance with paragraphs (c)(2)(i) through (c)(2)(v) of this section, or obtains an endorser who has been determined not to have an adverse credit history, as provided for in paragraph (c)(1)(vii) of this section.

(c)(1) *Parent PLUS borrower.* A parent borrower, is eligible to receive a PLUS Program loan, other than a loan made under § 682.209(e), if the parent—
  (i) Is borrowing to pay for the educational costs of a dependent undergraduate student who meets the requirements for an eligible student set forth in 34 CFR part 668;
  (ii) Provides his or her and the student's social security number;
  (iii) Meets the requirements pertaining to citizenship and residency that apply to the student in 34 CFR 668.33;
  (iv) Meets the requirements concerning defaults and overpayments that apply to the student in 34 CFR 668.35 and meets the requirements of judgment liens that apply to the student under 34 CFR 668.32(g)(3);
  (v) Except for the completion of a Statement of Selective Service Registration Status, complies with the requirements for submission of a Statement of Educational Purpose that apply to the student in 34 CFR part 668;
  (vi) Meets the requirements of paragraphs (a)(4), (a)(5), (a)(6), and (a)(7) of this section, as applicable; and
  (vii) In the case of a Federal PLUS loan made on or after July 1, 1993, does not have an adverse credit history or obtains an endorser who has been determined not to have an adverse credit history as provided in paragraph (c)(2)(ii) of this section.
  (viii) Has completed repayment of any title IV, HEA program assistance obtained by fraud, if the parent has been convicted of, or has pled nolo contendere or guilty to, a crime involving fraud in obtaining title IV, HEA program assistance.
(2)(i) For purposes of this section, the lender must obtain a credit report on each applicant from at least one national credit bureau. The credit report must be secured within a timeframe that would ensure the most accurate, current representation of the borrower's credit history before the first day of the period of enrollment for which the loan is intended.
  (ii) Unless the lender determines that extenuating circumstances existed, the lender must consider each applicant to have an adverse credit history based on the credit report if—
    (A) The applicant is considered 90 or more days delinquent on the repayment of a debt; or

(B) The applicant has been the subject of a default determination, bankruptcy discharge, foreclosure, repossession, tax lien, wage garnishment, or write-off of a Title IV debt, during the five years preceding the date of the credit report.

(iii) Nothing in this paragraph precludes the lender from establishing more restrictive credit standards to determine whether the applicant has an adverse credit history.

(iv) The absence of any credit history is not an indication that the applicant has an adverse credit history and is not to be used as a reason to deny a PLUS loan to that applicant.

(v) The lender must retain a record of its basis for determining that extenuating circumstances existed. This record may include, but is not limited to, an updated credit report, a statement from the creditor that the borrower has made satisfactory arrangements to repay the debt, or a satisfactory statement from the borrower explaining any delinquencies with outstanding balances of less than $500.

(3) For purposes of paragraph (c)(1) of this section, a "parent" includes the individuals described in the definition of "parent" in 34 CFR 668.2 and the spouse of a parent who remarried, if that spouse's income and assets would have been taken into account when calculating a dependent student's expected family contribution.

(d) *Consolidation program borrower.*

(1) An individual is eligible to receive a Consolidation loan if the individual—

(i) On the loans being consolidated—

(A) Is, at the time of application for a Consolidation loan—

(1) In a grace period preceding repayment;

(2) In repayment status;

(3) In a default status and has either made satisfactory repayment arrangements as defined in applicable program regulations or has agreed to repay the consolidation loan under the income-sensitive repayment plan described in § 682.209(a)(6)(iii) or the income-based repayment plan described in § 682.215;

(B) Not subject to a judgment secured through litigation, unless the judgment has been vacated;

(C) Not subject to an order for wage garnishment under section 488A of the Act, unless the order has been lifted;

(D) Not in default status resulting from a claim filed under § 682.412.

(ii) Certifies that no other application for a Consolidation loan is pending; and

(iii) Agrees to notify the holder of any changes in address.

(2) A borrower may not consolidate a loan under this section for which the borrower is wholly or partially ineligible.

(e) A borrower's eligibility to receive a Consolidation loan terminates upon receipt of a Consolidation loan except that—

(1) Eligible loans received prior to the date a Consolidation loan was made and loans received during the 180-day period following the date a Consolidation loan was made, may be added to the Consolidation loan based on the borrower's request received by the lender during the 180-day period after the date the Consolidation loan was made;

(2) A borrower who receives an eligible loan before or after the date a Consolidation loan is made may receive a subsequent Consolidation loan;

(3) A Consolidation loan borrower may consolidate an existing Consolidation loan if the borrower has at least one other eligible loan made before or after the existing Consolidation loan that will be consolidated;

(4) If the consolidation loan is in default or has been submitted to the guaranty agency for default aversion, the borrower may obtain a subsequent consolidation loan under the Federal Direct Consolidation Loan Program for purposes of obtaining an income contingent repayment plan or an income-based repayment plan; and

(5) A FFEL borrower may consolidate his or her loans (including a FFEL Consolidation Loan) into the Federal Direct Consolidation Loan Program for the purpose of using—

(i) The Public Service Loan Forgiveness Program; or

(ii) For FFEL Program loans first disbursed on or after October 1, 2008 (including Federal Consolidation Loans that repaid FFEL or Direct Loan program Loans first disbursed on or after October 1, 2008), the no accrual of interest benefit for active duty service members.

(Authority: 20 U.S.C. 1077, 1078, 1078-1, 1078-2, 1078-3, 1082, and 1091)

[59 Fed. Reg. 25745 (May 17, 1994); 59 Fed. Reg. 33349 (June 28, 1994); 59 Fed. Reg. 61215 (Nov. 29, 1994); 60 Fed. Reg. 32912 (June 26, 1995); 60 Fed. Reg. 61756, 61815 (Dec. 1, 1995); 62 Fed. Reg. 63433 (Nov. 28, 1997); 64 Fed. Reg. 18975, 18976 (Apr. 16, 1999); 64 Fed. Reg. 58952 (Nov. 1, 1999); 65 Fed. Reg. 65619, 65691 (Nov. 1, 2000); 66 Fed. Reg. 44007 (Aug. 21, 2001); 68 Fed. Reg. 75428 (Dec. 31, 2003); 71 Fed. Reg. 45699 (Aug. 9, 2006); 71 Fed. Reg. 64397 (Nov. 1, 2006); 73 Fed. Reg. 63248 (Oct. 23, 2008); 74 Fed. Reg. 55990 (Oct. 29, 2009)]

§ 682.202 Permissible charges by lenders to borrowers.

The charges that lenders may impose on borrowers, either directly or indirectly, are limited to the following:

(a) *Interest.* The applicable interest rates for FFEL Program loans are given in paragraphs (a)(1) through (a)(4) and (a)(8) of this section.

(1) *Stafford Loan Program.*

(i) For loans made prior to July 1, 1994, if, the borrower, on the date the promissory note evidencing the loan is signed, has an outstanding balance of principal or interest on a previous Stafford loan, the interest rate is the applicable interest rate on that previous Stafford loan.

(ii) If the borrower, on the date the promissory note evidencing the loan is signed, has no outstanding balance on any FFEL Program loan, and the first disbursement is made—

(A) Prior to October 1, 1992, for a loan covering a period of instruction beginning on or after July 1, 1988, the interest rate is 8 percent until 48 months elapse after the repayment period begins, and 10 percent thereafter; or

(B) On or after October 1, 1992, and prior to July 1, 1994, the interest rate is a variable rate, applicable to each July 1–June 30 period, that equals the lesser of—

(1) The bond equivalent rate of the 91-day Treasury bills auctioned at the final auction prior to the June 1 immediately preceding the July 1–June 30 period, plus 3.10 percent; or

(2) 9 percent.

(iii) For a Stafford loan for which the first disbursement is made before October 1, 1992—

(A) If the borrower, on the date the promissory note is signed, has no outstanding balance on a Stafford loan but has an outstanding balance of principal or interest on a PLUS or SLS loan made for a period of enrollment beginning before July 1, 1988, or on a Consolidation loan that repaid a loan made for a period of enrollment beginning before July 1, 1988, the interest rate is 8 percent; or

(B) If the borrower, on the date the promissory note evidencing the loan is signed, has an outstanding balance of principal or interest on a PLUS or SLS loan made for a period of enrollment beginning on or after July 1, 1988, or on a Consolidation loan that repaid a loan made for a period of enrollment beginning on or after July 1, 1988, the interest rate is 8 percent until 48 months elapse after the repayment period begins, and 10 percent thereafter.

(iv) For a Stafford loan for which the first disbursement is made on or after October 1, 1992, but before December 20, 1993, if the borrower, on the date the promissory note evidencing the loan is signed, has no outstanding balance on a Stafford loan but has an outstanding balance of principal or interest on a PLUS, SLS, or Consolidation loan, the interest rate is 8 percent.

(v) For a Stafford loan for which the first disbursement is made on or after December 20, 1993 and prior to July 1, 1994, if the borrower, on the date the promissory note is signed, has no outstanding balance on a Stafford loan but has an outstanding balance of principal or interest on a PLUS, SLS, or Consolidation loan, the interest rate is the rate provided in paragraph (a)(1)(ii)(B) of this section.

(vi) For a Stafford loan for which the first disbursement is made on or after July 1, 1994, and prior to July 1, 1995, for a period of enrollment that includes or begins on or after July 1, 1994, the interest rate is a variable rate, applicable to each July 1–June 30 period, that equals the lesser of—

(A) The bond equivalent rate of the 91-day Treasury bills auctioned at the final auction prior to the June 1 immediately preceding the July 1–June 30 period, plus 3.10; or

(B) 8.25 percent.

(vii) For a Stafford loan for which the first disbursement is made on or after July 1, 1995 and prior to July 1, 1998 the interest rate is a variable rate applicable to each July 1–June 30 period, that equals the lesser of—

(A) The bond equivalent rate of the 91-day Treasury bills auctioned at the final auction prior to the June 1 immediately preceding the July 1–June 30 period, plus 2.5 percent during the in-school, grace and deferment period and 3.10 percent during repayment; or

(B) 8.25 percent.

(viii) For a Stafford loan for which the first disbursement is made on or after July 1, 1998 and prior to July 1, 2006, the interest rate is a variable rate, applicable to each July 1–June 30 period, that equals the lesser of—

(A) The bond equivalent rate of the 91-day Treasury bills auctioned at the final auction prior to the June 1 immediately preceding the July 1–June 30 period plus 1.7 percent during the in-school, grace and deferment periods and 2.3 percent during repayment; or

(B) 8.25 percent.

(ix) For a Stafford loan for which the first disbursement is made on or after July 1, 2006, the interest rate is 6.8 percent.

(x) For a subsidized Stafford loan made to an undergraduate student for which the first disbursement is made on or after:

(A) July 1, 2006 and before July 1, 2008, the interest rate is 6.8 percent on the unpaid principal balance of the loan.

(B) July 1, 2008 and before July 1, 2009, the interest rate is 6 percent on the unpaid principal balance of the loan.

(C) July 1, 2009 and before July 1, 2010, the interest rate is 5.6 percent on the unpaid principal balance of the loan.

(D) July 1, 2010 and before July 1, 2011, the interest rate is 4.5 percent on the unpaid principal balance of the loan.

(E) July 1, 2011 and before July 2012, the interest rate is 3.4 percent on the unpaid balance of the loan.

(2) *PLUS Program.*

(i) For a combined repayment schedule under § 682.209(d), the interest rate is the weighted average of the rates of all loans included under that schedule.

(ii) For a loan disbursed on or after July 1, 1987 but prior to October 1, 1992, and for any loan made under § 682.209(e) or (f), the interest rate is a variable rate, applicable to each July 1–June 30 period, that equals the lesser of—

(A) The bond equivalent rate of the 52-week Treasury bills auctioned at the final auction prior to the June 1 immediately preceding the July 1–June 30 period, plus 3.25 percent; or

(B) 12 percent.

(iii) For a loan disbursed on or after October 1, 1992 and prior to July 1, 1994, the interest rate is a variable rate, applicable to each July 1–June 30 period, that equals the lesser of—

(A) The bond equivalent rate of the 52-week Treasury bills auctioned at the final auction prior to the June 1 immediately preceding the July 1–June 30 period, plus 3.10 percent; or

(B) 10 percent.

(iv) For a loan for which the first disbursement is made on or after July 1, 1994 and prior to July 1, 1998, the interest rate is a variable rate applicable to each July 1–June 30 period, that equals the lesser of—

(A) The bond equivalent rate of the 52-week Treasury bills auctioned at the final auction prior to the June 1 immediately preceding the July 1–June 30 period, plus 3.10 percent; or

(B) 9 percent.

(v) For a loan for which the first disbursement is made on or after July 1, 1998, the interest rate is a variable rate, applicable to each July 1–June 30 period, that equals the lesser of—

(A) The bond equivalent rate of the 91-day Treasury bills auctioned at the final auction prior to the June 1 immediately preceding the July 1–June 30 period, plus 3.10 percent; or

(B) 9 percent.

(vi)(A) Beginning on July 1, 2001, and prior to July 1, 2006, the interest rate on the loans described in paragraphs (a)(2)(ii) through (iv) of this section is a variable rate applicable to each July 1–June 30, as determined on the preceding June 26, and is equal to the weekly average 1-year constant maturity Treasury yield, as published by the Board of Governors of the Federal Reserve System, for the last calendar week ending on or before such June 26; plus—

(1) 3.25 percent for loans described in paragraph (a)(2)(ii) of this section; or

(2) 3.1 percent for loans described in paragraphs (a)(2)(iii) and (iv) of this section.

(B) The interest rates calculated under paragraph (a)(2)(vi)(A) of this section shall not exceed the limits specified in paragraphs (a)(2)(ii)(B), (a)(2)(iii)(B), and (a)(2)(iv)(B) of this section, as applicable.

(vii) For a PLUS loan first disbursed on or after July 1, 2006, the interest rate is 8.5 percent.

(3) *SLS Program.*

(i) For a combined repayment schedule under § 682.209(d), the interest rate is the weighted average of the rates of all loans included under that schedule.

(ii) For a loan disbursed on or after July 1, 1987 but prior to October 1, 1992, and for any loan made under § 682.209(e) or (f), the interest rate is a variable rate, applicable to each July 1–June 30 period, that equals the lesser of—

(A) The bond equivalent rate of the 52-week Treasury bills auctioned at the final auction prior to the June 1 immediately preceding the July 1–June 30 period, plus 3.25 percent; or

(B) 12 percent.

(iii) For a loan disbursed on or after October 1, 1992, the interest rate is a variable rate, applicable to each July 1–June 30 period, that equals the lesser of—

(A) The bond equivalent rate of the 52-week Treasury bills auctioned at the final auction prior to the June 1 immediately preceding the July 1–June 30 period, plus 3.10 percent; or

(B) 11 percent.

(iv)(A) Beginning on July 1, 2001, the interest rate on the loans described in paragraphs (a)(3)(ii) and (iii) of this section is a variable rate applicable to each July 1–June 30, as determined on the preceding June 26, and is equal to the weekly average 1-year constant maturity Treasury yield, as published by the Board of Governors of the Federal Reserve System, for the last calendar week ending on or before such June 26; plus—

(1) 3.25 percent for loans described in paragraph (a)(3)(ii) of this section; or

(2) 3.1 percent for loans described in paragraph (a)(3)(iii) of this section.

(B) The interest rates calculated under paragraph (a)(3)(iv)(A) of this section shall not exceed the limits specified in paragraphs (a)(3)(ii)(B) and (a)(3)(iii)(B) of this section, as applicable.

(4) *Consolidation Program.*

(i) A Consolidation Program loan made before July 1, 1994 bears interest at the rate that is the greater of—

(A) The weighted average of interest rates on the loans consolidated, rounded to the nearest whole percent; or

(B) 9 percent.

(ii) A Consolidation loan made on or after July 1, 1994, for which the loan application was received by the lender before November 13, 1997, bears interest at the rate that is equal to the weighted average of interest rates on the loans consolidated, rounded upward to the nearest whole percent.

(iii) For a Consolidation loan for which the loan application was received by the lender on or after November 13, 1997 and before October 1, 1998, the interest rate for the portion of the loan that consolidated loans other than HEAL loans is a variable rate, applicable to each July 1–June 30 period, that equals the lesser of—

(A) The bond equivalent rate of the 91-day Treasury bills auctioned at the final auction held prior to June 1 of each year plus 3.10 percent; or

(B) 8.25 percent.

(iv) For a Consolidation loan for which the application was received by the lender on or after October 1, 1998, the interest rate for the portion of the loan that consolidated loans other than HEAL loans is a fixed rate that is the lesser of—

(A) The weighted average of interest rates on the loans consolidated, rounded to the nearest higher one-eighth of one percent; or

(B) 8.25 percent.

(v) For a Consolidation loan for which the application was received by the lender on or after November 13, 1997, the annual interest rate applicable to the portion of each consolidation loan that repaid HEAL loans is a variable rate adjusted annually on July 1 and must be equal to the average of the bond equivalent rates of the 91-day Treasury bills auctioned for the quarter ending June 30, plus 3 percent. There is no maximum rate on this portion of the loan.

(5) *Actual interest rates under the Stafford loan, SLS, PLUS, and Consolidation Programs.* A lender may charge a borrower an actual rate of interest that is less than the applicable interest rate specified in paragraphs (a)(1)–(4) of this section.

(6) *Refund of excess interest paid on Stafford loans.*

(i) For a loan with an applicable interest rate of 10 percent made prior to July 23, 1992, and for a loan with an applicable interest rate of 10 percent made from July 23, 1992 through September 30, 1992, to a borrower with no outstanding FFEL Program loans—

(A) If during any calendar quarter, the sum of the average of the bond equivalent rates of the 91-day Treasury bills auctioned for that quarter, plus 3.25 percent, is less than 10 percent, the lender shall calculate an adjustment and credit the adjustment as specified under paragraph (a)(6)(i)(B) of this section if the borrower's account is not more than 30 days delinquent on December 31. The amount of the adjustment for a calendar quarter is equal to—

(1) 10 percent minus the sum of the average of the bond equivalent rates of the 91-day Treasury bills auctioned for the applicable quarter plus 3.25 percent;

(2) Multiplied by the average daily principal balance of the loan (not including unearned interest added to principal); and

(3) Divided by 4;

(B) No later than 30 calendar days after the end of the calendar year, the holder of the loan shall credit any amounts computed under paragraph (a)(6)(i)(A) of this section to—

(1) The Secretary, for amounts paid during any period in which the borrower is eligible for interest benefits;

(2) The borrower's account to reduce the outstanding principal balance as of the date the holder adjusts the borrower's account, provided that the borrower's account was not more than 30 days delinquent on that December 31; or

(3) The Secretary, for a borrower who on the last day of the calendar year is delinquent for more than 30 days.

(ii) For a fixed interest rate loan made on or after July 23, 1992 to a borrower with an outstanding FFEL Program loan—

(A) If during any calendar quarter, the sum of the average of the bond equivalent rates of the 91-day Treasury bills auctioned for that quarter, plus 3.10 percent, is less than the applicable interest rate, the lender shall calculate an adjustment and credit the adjustment to reduce the outstanding principal balance of the loan as specified under paragraph (a)(6)(ii)(C) of this section if the borrower's account is not more than 30 days delinquent on December 31. The amount of an adjustment for a calendar quarter is equal to—

(1) The applicable interest rate minus the sum of the average of the bond equivalent rates of the 91-day Treasury bills auctioned for the applicable quarter plus 3.10 percent;

(2) Multiplied by the average daily principal balance of the loan (not including unearned interest added to principal); and

(3) Divided by 4;

(B) For any quarter or portion thereof that the Secretary was obligated to pay interest subsidy on behalf of the borrower, the holder of the loan shall refund to the Secretary, no later than the end of the following quarter, any excess interest calculated in accordance with paragraph (a)(6)(ii)(A) of this section;

(C) For any other quarter, the holder of the loan shall, within 30 days of the end of the calendar year, reduce the borrower's outstanding principal by the amount of excess interest calculated under paragraph (a)(6)(ii)(A) of this section, provided that the borrower's account was not more than 30 days delinquent as of December 31;

(D) For a borrower who on the last day of the calendar year is delinquent for more than 30 days, any excess interest calculated shall be refunded to the Secretary; and

(E) Notwithstanding paragraphs (a)(6)(ii)(B), (C) and (D) of this section, if the loan was disbursed during a quarter, the amount of any adjustment refunded to the Secretary or credited to the borrower for that quarter shall be prorated accordingly.

(7) *Conversion to Variable Rate.*

(i) A lender or holder shall convert the interest rate on a loan under paragraphs (a)(6)(i) or (ii) of this section to a variable rate.

(ii) The applicable interest rate for each 12-month period beginning on July 1 and ending on June 30 preceding each 12-month period is equal to the sum of—

(A) The bond equivalent rate of the 91-day Treasury bills auctioned at the final auction prior to June 1; and

(B) 3.25 percent in the case of a loan described in paragraph (a)(6)(i) of this section or 3.10 percent in the case of a loan described in paragraph (a)(6)(ii) of this section.

(iii)(A) In connection with the conversion specified in paragraph (a)(6)(ii) of this section for any period prior to the conversion for which a rebate has not been provided under paragraph (a)(6) of this section, a lender or holder shall convert the interest rate to a variable rate.

(B) The interest rate for each period shall be reset quarterly and the applicable interest rate for the quarter or portion shall equal the sum of—

(1) The average of the bond equivalent rates of 91-day Treasury bills auctioned for the preceding 3-month period; and

(2) 3.25 percent in the case of loans as specified under paragraph (a)(6)(i) of this section or 3.10 percent in the case of loans as specified under paragraph (a)(6)(ii) of this section.

(iv)(A) The holder of a loan being converted under paragraph (a)(7)(iii)(A) of this section shall complete such conversion on or before January 1, 1995.

(B) The holder shall, not later than 30 days prior to the conversion, provide the borrower with—

(1) A notice informing the borrower that the loan is being converted to a variable interest rate;

(2) A description of the rate to the borrower;

(3) The current interest rate; and

(4) An explanation that the variable rate will provide a substantially equivalent benefit as the adjustment otherwise provided under paragraph (a)(6) of this section.

(v) The notice may be provided as part of the disclosure requirement as specified under § 682.205.

(vi) The interest rate as calculated under this paragraph may not exceed the maximum interest rate applicable to the loan prior to the conversion.

(8) *Applicability of the Servicemembers Civil Relief Act (50 U.S.C 527, App. sec. 207).* Notwithstanding paragraphs (a)(1) through (a)(4) of this section, effective August 14, 2008, upon the loan holder's receipt of the borrower's written request and a copy of the borrower's military orders, the maximum interest rate, as defined in 50 U.S.C. 527, App. section 207(d), on FFEL Program loans made prior to the borrower entering active duty status is 6 percent while the borrower is on active duty military service.

(b) *Capitalization.*

(1) A lender may add accrued interest and unpaid insurance premiums to the borrower's unpaid principal balance in accordance with this section. This increase in the principal balance of a loan is called "capitalization."

(2) Except as provided in paragraph (b)(4) and (b)(5) of this section, a lender may capitalize interest payable by the borrower that has accrued—

(i) For the period from the date the first disbursement was made to the beginning date of the in-school period or, for a PLUS loan, for the period from the date the first disbursement was made to the date the repayment period begins;

(ii) For the in-school or grace periods, or for a period needed to align repayment of an SLS with a Stafford loan, if capitalization is expressly authorized by the promissory note (or with the written consent of the borrower);

(iii) For a period of authorized deferment;

(iv) For a period of authorized forbearance; or

(v) For the period from the date the first installment payment was due until it was made.

(3) A lender may capitalize accrued interest under paragraphs (b)(2)(ii) through (iv) of this section no more frequently than quarterly. Capitalization is again permitted when repayment is required to begin or resume. A lender may capitalize accrued interest under paragraph (b)(2)(i) and (v) of this section only on the date repayment of principal is scheduled to begin.

(4)(i) For unsubsidized Stafford loans disbursed on or after October 7, 1998 and prior to July 1, 2000, the lender may capitalize the unpaid interest that accrues on the loan according to the requirements of section 428H(e)(2) of the Act.

(ii) For Stafford loans first disbursed on or after July 1, 2000, the lender may capitalize the unpaid interest—

(A) When the loan enters repayment;

(B) At the expiration of a period of authorized deferment;

(C) At the expiration of a period of authorized forbearance; and

(D) When the borrower defaults.

(5) For Consolidation loans, the lender may capitalize interest as provided in paragraphs (b)(2) and (b)(3) of this section, except that the lender may capitalize the unpaid interest for a period of authorized in-school deferment only at the expiration of the deferment.

(6) For any borrower in an in-school or grace period or the period needed to align repayment, deferment, or forbearance status, during which the Secretary does not pay interest benefits and for which the borrower has agreed to make payments of interest, the lender may capitalize past due interest provided that the lender has notified the borrower that the borrower's failure to resolve any delinquency constitutes the borrower's consent to capitalization of delinquent interest and all interest that will accrue through the remainder of that period.

(c) *Fees for FFEL Program loans.*

(1)(i) For Stafford loans first disbursed prior to July 1, 2006, a lender may charge a borrower an origination fee not to exceed 3 percent of the principal amount of the loan.

(ii) For Stafford loans first disbursed on or after July 1, 2006, but before July 1, 2007, a lender may charge a borrower an origination fee not to exceed 2 percent of the principal amount of the loan.

(iii) For Stafford loans first disbursed on or after July 1, 2007, but before July 1, 2008, a lender may charge a borrower an origination fee not to exceed 1.5 percent of the principal amount of the loan.

(iv) For Stafford loans first disbursed on or after July 1, 2008, but before July 1, 2009, a lender may charge a borrower an origination fee not to exceed 1 percent of the principal amount of the loan.

(v) For Stafford loans first disbursed on or after July 1, 2009, but before July 1, 2010, a lender may charge a borrower an origination fee not to exceed .5 percent of the principal amount of the loan.

(vi) For Stafford loans first disbursed on or after July 1, 2010, a lender may not charge a borrower an origination fee.

(vii) Except as provided in paragraph (c)(2) of this section, a lender must charge all borrowers the same origination fee.

(2)(i) A lender may charge a lower origination fee than the amount specified in paragraph (c)(1) of this section to a borrower whose expected family contribution (EFC), used to determine eligibility for the loan, is equal to or less than the maximum qualifying EFC for a Federal Pell Grant at the time the loan is certified or to a borrower who qualifies for a subsidized Stafford loan. A lender must charge all such borrowers the same origination fee.

(ii) With the approval of the Secretary, a lender may use a standard comparable to that defined in paragraph (c)(2)(i) of this section.

(3) If a lender charges a lower origination fee on unsubsidized loans under paragraph (c)(1) or (c)(2) of this section, the lender must charge the same fee on subsidized loans.

(4)(i) For purposes of this paragraph (c), a lender is defined as:

(A) All entities under common ownership, including ownership by a common holding company, that make loans to borrowers in a particular state; and

(B) Any beneficial owner of loans that provides funds to an eligible lender trustee to make loans on the beneficial owner's behalf in a particular state.

(ii) If a lender as defined in paragraph (c)(4)(i) charges a lower origination fee to any borrower in a particular state under paragraphs (c)(1) or (c)(2) of this section, the lender must charge all such borrowers who reside in that state or attend school in that state the same origination fee.

(5) Shall charge a borrower an origination fee on a PLUS loan of 3 percent of the principal amount of the loan;

(6) Shall deduct a pro rata portion of the fee (if charged) from each disbursement; and

(7) Shall refund by a credit against the borrower's loan balance the portion of the origination fee previously deducted from the loan that is attributable to any portion of the loan—

(i) That is returned by a school to a lender in order to comply with the Act or with applicable regulations;

(ii) That is repaid or returned within 120 days of disbursement, unless—

(A) The borrower has no FFEL Program loans in repayment status and has requested, in writing, that the repaid or returned funds be used for a different purpose; or

(B) The borrower has a FFEL Program loan in repayment status, in which case the payment is applied in accordance with § 682.209(b) unless the borrower has requested, in writing, that the repaid or returned funds be applied as a cancellation of all or part of the loan;

(iii) For which a loan check has not been negotiated within 120 days of disbursement; or

(iv) For which loan proceeds disbursed by electronic funds transfer or master check in accordance with § 682.207(b)(1)(ii)(B) and (C) have not been released from the restricted account maintained by the school within 120 days of disbursement.

(d) *Insurance premium and Federal default fee.*
(1) For loans guaranteed prior to July 1, 2006, a lender may charge the borrower the amount of the insurance premium paid by the lender to the guarantor (up to 1 percent of the principal amount of the loan) if that charge is provided for in the promissory note.

(2) For loans guaranteed on or after July 1, 2006, other than an SLS or PLUS loan refinanced under § 682.209(e) or (f), a lender may charge the borrower the amount of the Federal default fee paid by the lender to the guarantor (up to 1 percent of the principal amount of the loan) if that charge is provided for in the promissory note.

(3) If the borrower is charged the insurance premium or the Federal default fee, the amount charged must be deducted proportionately from each disbursement of the borrower's loan proceeds, if the loan is disbursed in more than one installment.

(4) The lender shall refund the insurance premium or Federal default fee paid by the borrower in accordance with the circumstances and procedures applicable to the return of origination fees, as described in paragraph (c)(7) of this section.

(e) *Administrative charge for a refinanced PLUS or SLS Loan.* A lender may charge a borrower up to $100 to cover the administrative costs of making a loan to a borrower under § 682.209(e) for the purpose of refinancing a PLUS or SLS loan to secure a variable interest rate.

(f) *Late charge.*
(1) If authorized by the borrower's promissory note, the lender may require the borrower to pay a late charge under the circumstances described in paragraph (f)(2) of this section. This charge may not exceed six cents for each dollar of each late installment.

(2) The lender may require the borrower to pay a late charge if the borrower fails to pay all or a portion of a required installment payment within 15 days after it is due.

(g) *Collection charges.*
(1) If provided for in the borrower's promissory note, and notwithstanding any provisions of State law, the lender may require that the borrower or any endorser pay costs incurred by the lender or its agents in collecting installments not paid when due, including, but not limited to—
   (i) Attorney's fees;
   (ii) Court costs; and
   (iii) Telegrams.

(2) The costs referred to in paragraph (g)(1) of this section may not include routine collection costs associated with preparing letters or notices or with making personal contacts with the borrower (e.g., local and long-distance telephone calls).

(h) *Special allowance.* Pursuant to § 682.412(c), a lender may charge a borrower the amount of special allowance paid by the Secretary on behalf of the borrower.

(Authority: 20 U.S.C. 1077, 1078, 1078-1, 1078-2, 1078-3, 1079, 1082, 1087-1, 1091a)

[59 Fed. Reg. 22475 (Apr. 29, 1994); 59 Fed. Reg. 25745 (May 17, 1994); 59 Fed. Reg. 29543 (June 8, 1994); 59 Fed. Reg. 35625 (July 13, 1994); 59 Fed. Reg. 61427 (Nov. 30, 1994); 60 Fed. Reg. 32912 (June 26, 1995); 61 Fed. Reg. 60486 (Nov. 27, 1996); 62 Fed. Reg. 63434 (Nov. 28, 1997); 64 Fed. Reg. 18976 (Apr. 16, 1999); 64 Fed. Reg. 58953 (Nov. 1, 1999); 66 Fed. Reg. 34762 (June 29, 2001); 71 Fed. Reg. 45699, 45700 (Aug. 9, 2006); 72 Fed. Reg. 62000 (Nov. 1, 2007); 74 Fed. Reg. 55991 (Oct. 29, 2009)]

* * *

§ 682.209 Repayment of a loan.

(a) *Conversion of a loan to repayment status.*
(1) For a Consolidation loan, the repayment period begins on the date the loan is disbursed. The first payment is due within 60 days after the date the loan is disbursed.

(2)(i) For a PLUS loan, the repayment period begins on the date of the last disbursement made on the loan. Interest accrues and is due and payable from the date of the first disbursement of the loan. The first payment is due within 60 days after the date the loan is fully disbursed.

(ii) For an SLS loan, the repayment period begins on the date the loan is disbursed, or, if the loan is disbursed in multiple installments, on the date of the last disbursement of the loan. Interest accrues and is due and payable from the date of the first disbursement of the loan. Except as provided in paragraph (a)(2)(iii), (a)(2)(iv), and (a)(2)(v) of this section the first payment is due within 60 days after the date the loan is fully disbursed.

(iii) For an SLS borrower who has not yet entered repayment on a Stafford loan, the borrower may postpone payment, consistent with the grace period on the borrower's Stafford loan.

(iv) If the lender first learns after the fact that an SLS borrower has entered the repayment period, the repayment begins no later than 75 days after the date the lender learns that the borrower has entered the repayment period.

(v) The lender may establish a first payment due date that is no more than an additional 30 days beyond the period specified in paragraphs (a)(2)(i)–(a)(2)(iv) of this section in order for the lender to comply with the required deadline contained in § 682.205(c)(1).

(3)(i) Except as provided in paragraph (a)(4) of this section, for a Stafford loan the repayment period begins—

(A) For a borrower with a loan for which the applicable interest rate is 7 percent per year, not less than 9 nor more than 12 months following the date on which the borrower is no longer enrolled on at least a half-time basis at an eligible school. The length of this grace period is determined by the lender for loans made under the FISL Program, and by the guaranty agency for loans guaranteed by the agency;

(B) For a borrower with a loan for which the initial applicable interest rate is 8 or 9 percent per year, the day after 6 months following the date on which the borrower is no longer enrolled on at least a half-time basis at an institution of higher education and

(C) For a borrower with a loan with a variable interest rate, the day after 6 months following the date on which the borrower is no longer enrolled on at least a half-time basis at an institution of higher education.

(ii) The first payment on a Stafford loan is due on a date established by the lender that is no more than—

(A) 60 days following the first day that the repayment period begins;

(B) 60 days from the expiration of a deferment or forbearance period;

(C) 60 days following the end of the post deferment grace period;

(D) If the lender first learns after the fact that the borrower has entered the repayment period, no later than 75 days after the date the lender learns that the borrower has entered the repayment period; or

(E) An additional 30 days beyond the period specified in paragraphs (a)(3)(ii)(A)–(a)(3)(ii)(D) of this section in order for the lender to comply with the required deadlines contained in § 682.205(c)(1).

(iii) When determining the date that the student was no longer enrolled on at least a half-time basis, the lender must use a new date it receives from a school, unless the lender has already disclosed repayment terms to the borrower and the new date is within the same month and year as the most recent date reported to the lender.

(4) For a borrower of a Stafford loan who is a correspondence student, the grace period specified in paragraph (a)(3)(i) of this section begins on the earliest of—

(i) The day after the borrower completes the program;

(ii) The day after withdrawal as determined pursuant to 34 CFR 668.22; or

(iii) 60 days following the last day for completing the program as established by the school.

(5) For purposes of establishing the beginning of the repayment period for Stafford and SLS loans, the grace periods referenced in paragraphs (a)(2)(iii) and (a)(3)(i) of this section exclude any period during which a borrower who is a member of a reserve component of the Armed Forces named in section 10101 of title 10, United States Code is called or ordered to active duty for a period of more than 30 days. Any single excluded period may not exceed three years and includes the time necessary for the borrower to resume enrollment at the next available regular enrollment period. Any Stafford or SLS borrower who is in a grace period when called or ordered to active duty as specified in this paragraph is entitled to a full grace period upon completion of the excluded period.

(6)(i) The repayment schedule may provide for substantially equal installment payments or for installment payments that increase or decrease in amount during the repayment period. If the loan has a variable interest rate that changes annually, the lender may establish a repayment schedule that—

(A) Provides for adjustments of the amount of the installment payment to reflect annual changes in the variable interest rate; or

(B) Contains no provision for an adjustment of the amount of the installment payment to reflect annual changes in the variable interest rate, but requires the lender to grant a forbearance to the borrower (or endorser, if applicable) for a period of up to 3 years of payments in accordance with § 682.211(i)(5) in cases where the effect of a variable interest rate on a standard or graduated repayment schedule would result in a loan not being repaid within the maximum repayment term.

(ii) If a graduated or income-sensitive repayment schedule is established, it may not provide for any single installment that is more than three times greater than any other installment. An agreement as specified in paragraph (c)(1)(ii) of this section is not required if the schedule provides for less than the minimum annual payment amount specified in paragraph (c)(1)(i) of this section.

(iii) Not more than six months prior to the date that the borrower's first payment is due, the lender must offer the borrower a choice of a standard, income-sensitive, income-based, graduated, or, if applicable, an extended repayment schedule.

(iv) Except in the case of an income-based repayment schedule, the repayment schedule must require that each payment equal at least the interest that accrues during the interval between scheduled payments.

(v) The lender shall require the borrower to repay the loan under a standard repayment schedule described in paragraph (a)(6)(vi) of this section if the borrower—

(A) Does not select an income-sensitive, income-based, graduated, or, if applicable, an extended repayment schedule within 45 days after being notified by the lender to choose a repayment schedule;

(B) Chooses an income-sensitive repayment schedule, but does not provide the documentation requested by the lender under paragraph (a)(6)(viii)(C) of this section within the time period specified by the lender; or

(C) Chooses an income-based repayment schedule, but does not provide the income documentation requested by the lender under § 682.215(e)(1)(i) within the time period specified by the lender.

(vi) Under a standard repayment schedule, the borrower is scheduled to pay either—

(A) The same amount for each installment payment made during the repayment period, except that the borrower's final payment may be slightly more or less than the other payments; or

(B) An installment amount that will be adjusted to reflect annual changes in the loan's variable interest rate.

(vii) Under a graduated repayment schedule—

(A)(1) The amount of the borrower's installment payment is scheduled to change (usually by increasing) during the course of the repayment period; or

(2) If the loan has a variable interest rate that changes annually, the lender may establish a repayment schedule that may have adjustments in the payment amount as provided under paragraph (a)(6)(i) of this section; and

(B) An agreement as specified in paragraph (c)(1)(ii) of this section is not required if the schedule provides for less than the minimum annual payment amount specified in paragraph (c)(1)(i) of this section.

(viii) Under an income-sensitive repayment schedule—

(A)(1) The amount of the borrower's installment payment is adjusted annually, based on the borrower's expected total monthly gross income received by the borrower from employment and from other sources during the course of the repayment period; or

(2) If the loan has a variable interest rate that changes annually, the lender may establish a repayment schedule that may have adjustments in the payment amount as provided under paragraph (a)(6)(i) of this section; and

(B) In general, the lender shall request the borrower to inform the lender of his or her income no earlier than 90 days prior to the due date of the borrower's initial installment payment and subsequent annual payment adjustment under an income-sensitive repayment schedule. The income information must be sufficient for the lender to make a reasonable determination of what the borrower's payment amount should be. If the lender receives late notification that the borrower has dropped below half-time enrollment status at a school, the lender may request that income information earlier than 90 days prior to the due date of the borrower's initial installment payment;

(C) If the borrower reports income to the lender that the lender considers to be insufficient for establishing monthly installment payments that would repay the loan within the applicable maximum repayment period, the lender shall require the borrower to submit evidence showing the amount of the most recent total monthly gross income received by the borrower from employment and from other sources including, if applicable, pay statements from employers and documentation of any income received by the borrower from other parties;

(D) The lender shall grant a forbearance to the borrower (or endorser, if applicable) for a period of up to 5 years of payments in accordance with § 682.211(i)(5) in cases where the effect of decreased installment amounts paid under an income-sensitive repayment schedule would result in a loan not being repaid within the maximum repayment term; and

(E) The lender shall inform the borrower that the loan must be repaid within the time limits specified under paragraph (a)(7) of this section.

(ix) Under an extended repayment schedule, a new borrower whose total outstanding principal and interest in FFEL loans exceed $30,000 may repay the loan on a fixed annual repayment amount or a graduated repayment amount for a period that may not exceed 25 years. For purposes of this section, a "new borrower" is an individual who has no outstanding principal or interest balance on an FFEL Program loan as of October 7, 1998, or on the date he or she obtains an FFEL Program loan after October 7, 1998.

(x) Under an income-based repayment schedule, the borrower repays the loan in accordance with § 682.215.

(xi) A borrower may request a change in the repayment schedule on a loan. The lender must permit the borrower to change the repayment schedule no less frequently than annually, or at any time in the case of a borrower in an income-based repayment plan.

(xii) For purposes of this section, a lender shall, to the extent practicable require that all FFEL loans owed by a borrower to the lender be combined into one account and repaid under one repayment schedule. In that event, the word "loan" in this section shall mean all of the borrower's loans that were combined by the lender into that account.

(7)(i) Subject to paragraphs (a)(7)(ii) through (iv) of this section, and except as provided in paragraph (a)(6)(ix) a lender shall allow a borrower at least 5 years, but not more than 10 years, or 25 years under an extended repayment plan to repay a Stafford, SLS, or Plus loan, calculated from the beginning of the repayment period. Except in the case of a FISL loan for a period of enrollment beginning on or after July 1, 1986, the lender shall require a borrower to fully repay a FISL loan within 15 years after it is made.

(ii) If the borrower receives an authorized deferment or is granted forbearance, as described in § 682.210 or § 682.211 respectively, the periods of deferment or forbearance are excluded from determinations of the 5-, 10-, 15- and 25-year periods, and from the 10-, 12-, 15-, 20-, 25-, and 30-year periods for repayment of a Consolidation loan pursuant to § 682.209(h).

(iii) If the minimum annual repayment required in paragraph (c) of this section would result in complete repayment of the loan in less than 5 years, the borrower is not entitled to the full 5-year period.

(iv) The borrower may, prior to the beginning of the repayment period, request and be granted by the lender a repayment period of less than 5 years. Subject to paragraph (a)(7)(iii) of this section, a borrower who makes such a request may notify the lender at any time to extend the repayment period to a minimum of 5 years.

(8) If, with respect to the aggregate of all loans held by a lender, the total payment made by a borrower for a monthly or similar payment period would not otherwise be a multiple of five dollars, except in the case of payments made under an income-based repayment plan, the lender may round that periodic payment to the next highest whole dollar amount that is a multiple of five dollars.

(b) *Payment application and prepayment.*

(1) Except in the case of payments made under an income-based repayment plan, the lender may credit the entire payment amount first to any late charges accrued or collection costs and then to any outstanding interest and then to outstanding principal.

(2)(i) The borrower may prepay the whole or any part of a loan at any time without penalty.

(ii) If the prepayment amount equals or exceeds the monthly payment amount under the repayment schedule established for the loan, the lender shall apply the prepayment to future installments by advancing the next payment due date, unless the borrower requests otherwise. The lender must either inform the borrower in advance using a prominent statement in the borrower's coupon book or billing statement that any additional full payment amounts submitted without instructions to the lender as to their handling will be applied to future scheduled payments with the borrower's next scheduled payment due date advanced consistent with the number of additional payments received, or provide a notification to the borrower after the payments are received informing the borrower that the payments have been so applied and the date of the borrower's next scheduled payment due date. Information related to next scheduled payment due date need not be provided to borrower's making such prepayments while in an in-school, grace, deferment, or forbearance period when payments are not due.

(c) *Minimum annual payment.*

(1)(i) Subject to paragraph (c)(1)(ii) of this section and except as otherwise provided by a graduated, income-sensitive, extended, or income-based repayment plan selected by the borrower, during each year of the repayment period, a borrower's total payments to all holders of the borrower's FFEL Program loans must total at least $600 or the unpaid balance of all loans, including interest, whichever amount is less.

(ii) If the borrower and the lender agree, the amount paid may be less.

(2) The provisions of paragraphs (c)(1)(i) and (ii) of this section may not result in an extension of the maximum repayment period unless forbearance as described in § 682.211, or deferment described in § 682.210, has been approved.

(d) *Combined repayment of a borrower's student PLUS and SLS loans held by a lender.*

(1) A lender may, at the request of a student borrower, combine the borrower's student PLUS and SLS loans held by it into a single repayment schedule.

(2) The repayment period on the loans included in the combined repayment schedule must be calculated based on the beginning of repayment of the most recent included loan.

(3) The interest rate on the loans included in the new combined repayment schedule must be the weighted average of the rates of all included loans.

(e) *Refinancing a fixed-rate PLUS or SLS Program loan to secure a variable interest rate.*

(1) Subject to paragraph (g) of this section, a lender may, at the request of a borrower, refinance a PLUS or SLS loan with a fixed interest rate in order to permit the borrower to obtain a variable interest rate.

(2) A loan made under paragraph (e)(1) of this section—

(i) Must bear interest at the variable rate described in § 682.202(a)(2)(ii) and (3)(ii) as appropriate; and

(ii) May not extend the repayment period provided for in paragraph (a)(7)(i) of this section.

(3) The lender may not charge an additional insurance premium or Federal default fee on the loan, but may charge the borrower an administrative fee pursuant to § 682.202(e).

(f) *Refinancing of a fixed-rate PLUS or SLS Program loan to secure a variable interest rate by a discharge of previous loan.*

(1) Subject to paragraph (g) of this section, a borrower who has applied for, but been denied, a refinanced loan authorized under paragraph (e) of this section by the holder of the borrower's fixed-rate PLUS or SLS loan, may obtain a loan from another lender for the purpose of discharging the fixed-rate loan and obtaining a variable interest rate.

(2) A loan made under paragraph (f)(1) of this section—

(i) Must bear interest at the variable interest rate described in § 682.202(a)(2)(ii) and (3)(ii), as appropriate;

(ii) May not operate to extend the repayment period provided for in paragraph (a)(7)(i) of this section; and

(iii) Must be disbursed to the holder of the fixed-rate loan to discharge the borrower's obligation thereon.

(3) Upon receipt of the proceeds of a loan made under paragraph (f)(1) of this section, the holder of the fixed-rate loan shall, within five business days, apply the proceeds to discharge the borrower's obligation on the fixed-rate loan, and provide the refinancing lender with either a copy of the borrower's original promissory note evidencing the fixed-rate loan or the holder's written certification that the

borrower's obligation on the fixed-rate loan has been fully discharged.

(4) The refinancing lender may charge the borrower an insurance premium on a loan made under paragraph (f)(1) of this section, but may not charge a fee to cover administrative costs.

(5) For purposes of deferments under § 682.210, the refinancing loan—

(i) Is considered a PLUS loan if any of the included loans is a PLUS loan made to a parent;

(ii) Is considered an SLS loan if the combined loan does not include a PLUS loan made to a parent; or

(iii) Is considered a loan to a "new borrower" as defined in § 682.210(b)(7), if all the loans that were refinanced were made on or after July 1, 1987, for a period of enrollment beginning on or after that date.

(g) *Conditions for refinancing certain loans.*

(1) A lender may not refinance a loan under paragraphs (e) or (f) of this section if that loan is in default, involves a violation of a condition of reinsurance described in § 682.406, or, in the case of a Federal SLS or Federal PLUS loan, is uninsured by the Secretary.

(2)(i) Prior to refinancing a fixed-rate loan under paragraph (f) of this section, the lender shall obtain a written statement from the holder of the loan certifying that—

(A) The holder has refused to refinance the fixed-rate loan under paragraph (e) of this section; and

(B) The fixed-rate loan is eligible for insurance or reinsurance under paragraph (g)(1) of this section.

(ii) The holder of the fixed-rate loan shall, within 10 business days of receiving a lender's written request to provide a certification under paragraph (g)(2)(i) of this section, provide the lender with that certification, or provide the lender and the guarantor on the loan with a written explanation of the reasons for its inability to provide the certification to the requesting lender.

(iii) The refinancing lender may rely in good faith on the certification provided by the holder of the fixed-rate loan under paragraph (g)(2)(ii) of this section.

(h) *Consolidation loans.*

(1) For a Consolidation loan, the repayment period begins on the day of disbursement, with the first payment due within 60 days after the date of disbursement.

(2) If the sum of the amount of the Consolidation loan and the unpaid balance on other student loans to the applicant—

(i) Is less than $7,500, the borrower shall repay the Consolidation loan in not more than 10 years;

(ii) Is equal to or greater than $7,500 but less than $10,000, the borrower shall repay the Consolidation loan in not more than 12 years;

(iii) Is equal to or greater than $10,000 but less than $20,000, the borrower shall repay the Consolidation loan in not more than 15 years;

(iv) Is equal to or greater than $20,000 but less than $40,000, the borrower shall repay the Consolidation loan in not more than 20 years;

(v) Is equal to or greater than $40,000 but less than $60,000, the borrower shall repay the Consolidation loan in not more than 25 years; or

(vi) Is equal to or greater than $60,000, the borrower shall repay the Consolidation loan in not more than 30 years.

(3) For the purpose of paragraph (h)(2) of this section, the unpaid balance on other student loans—

(i) May not exceed the amount of the Consolidation loan; and

(ii) With the exception of the defaulted title IV loans on which the borrower has made satisfactory repayment arrangements with the holder of the loan, does not include the unpaid balance on any defaulted loans.

(4) A repayment schedule for a Consolidation loan—

(i) Must be established by the lender;

(ii) Must require that each payment equal at least the interest that accrues during the interval between scheduled payments.

(5) Upon receipt of the proceeds of a loan made under paragraph (h)(2) of this section, the holder of the underlying loan shall promptly apply the proceeds to discharge fully the borrower's obligation on the underlying loan, and provide the consolidating lender with the holder's written certification that the borrower's obligation on the underlying loan has been fully discharged.

(i) *Treatment by a lender of borrowers' title IV, HEA program funds received from schools if the borrower withdraws.*

(1) A lender shall treat a refund or a return of title IV, HEA program funds under § 668.22 when a student withdraws received by the lender from a school as a credit against the principal amount owed by the borrower on the borrower's loan.

(2)(i) If a lender receives a refund or a return of title IV, HEA program funds under § 668.22 when a student withdraws from a school on a loan that is no longer held by that lender, or that has been discharged by another lender by refinancing under § 682.209(f) or by a Consolidation loan, the lender must transmit the amount of the payment, within 30 days of its receipt, to the lender to whom it assigned the loan, or to the lender that discharged the prior loan, with an explanation of the source of the payment.

(ii) Upon receipt of a refund or a return of title IV, HEA program funds transmitted under paragraph (i)(2)(i) of this section, the holder of the loan promptly must provide written notice to the borrower that the holder has received the return of title IV, HEA program funds.

(j) *Certification on loans to be repaid through consolidation.*

Within 10 business days after receiving a written request for a certification from a lender under § 682.206(f), a holder shall either provide the requesting lender the certification or, if it is unable to certify to the matters described in that paragraph, provide the requesting lender and the guarantor on the loan at issue with a written explanation of the reasons for its inability to provide the certification.

(k) Any lender holding a loan is subject to all claims and defenses that the borrower could assert against the school with respect to that loan if—

(1) The loan was made by the school or a school-affiliated organization;

(2) The lender who made the loan provided an improper inducement, as described in paragraph (5)(i) of the definition of Lender in § 682.200(b), to the school or any other party in connection with the making of the loan;

(3) The school refers borrowers to the lender; or

(4) The school is affiliated with the lender by common control, contract, or business arrangement.

(Approved by the Office of Management and Budget under control number 1845-0020)

(Authority: 20 U.S.C. 1077, 1078, 1078-1, 1078-2, 1078-3, 1079, 1082, 1085)

[59 Fed. Reg. 33352 (June 28, 1994); 59 Fed. Reg. 33593 (June 29, 1994); 60 Fed. Reg. 30788 (June 12, 1995); 60 Fed. Reg. 32912 (June 26, 1995); 60 Fed. Reg. 61756 (Dec. 1, 1995); 61 Fed. Reg. 16718 (Apr. 17, 1996); 62 Fed. Reg. 63434 (Nov. 28, 1997); 64 Fed. Reg. 18977 (Apr. 16, 1999); 64 Fed. Reg. 58957, 59043 (Nov. 1, 1999); 66 Fed. Reg. 34763 (June 29, 2001); 67 Fed. Reg. 67078 (Nov. 1, 2002); 68 Fed. Reg. 75428 (Dec. 31, 2003); 71 Fed. Reg. 45701 (Aug. 9, 2006); 71 Fed. Reg. 64398 (Nov. 1, 2006); 72 Fed. Reg. 62001 (Nov. 1, 2007); 73 Fed. Reg. 63248 (Oct. 23, 2008); 74 Fed. Reg. 55994 (Oct. 29, 2009)]

§ 682.210 Deferment.

(a) *General.*

(1)(i) A borrower is entitled to have periodic installment payments of principal deferred during authorized periods after the beginning of the repayment period, pursuant to paragraph (b) and paragraphs (s) through (v) of this section.

(ii) With the exception of a deferment authorized under paragraph (o) of this section, a borrower may continue to receive a specific type of deferment that is limited to a maximum period of time only if the total amount of time that the borrower has received the deferment does not exceed the maximum time period allowed for the deferment.

(2)(i) For a loan made before October 1, 1981, the borrower is also entitled to have periodic installments of principal deferred during the six-month period (post-deferment grace period) that begins after the completion of each deferment period or combination of those periods, except as provided in paragraph (a)(2)(ii) of this section.

(ii) Once a borrower receives a post-deferment grace period following an unemployment deferment, as described in paragraph (b)(1)(v) of this section, the borrower does not qualify for additional post-deferment grace periods following subsequent unemployment deferments.

(3)(i) Interest accrues and is paid by—

(A) The Secretary during the deferment period for a subsidized Stafford loan and for all or a portion of a Consolidation loan that qualifies for interest benefits under § 682.301; or

(B) The borrower during the deferment period and, as applicable, the post-deferment grace period, on all other loans.

(ii) A borrower who is responsible for payment of interest during a deferment period must be notified by the lender, at or before the time the deferment is granted, that the borrower has the option to pay the accruing interest or cancel the deferment and continue paying on the loan. The lender must also provide information, including an example, on the impact of capitalization of accrued, unpaid interest on loan principal, and on the total amount of interest to be paid over the life of the loan.

(4) As a condition for receiving a deferment, except for purposes of paragraphs (c)(1)(ii), (iii), and (iv) of this section, the borrower must request the deferment, and provide the lender with all information and documents required to establish eligibility for a specific type of deferment.

(5) An authorized deferment period begins on the date that the holder determines is the date that the condition entitling the borrower to the deferment first existed, except that an initial unemployment deferment as described in paragraph (h)(2) of this section cannot begin more than 6 months before the date the holder receives a request and documentation required for the deferment.

(6) An authorized deferment period ends on the earlier of—

(i) The date when the condition establishing the borrower's eligibility for the deferment ends;

(ii) Except as provided in paragraph (a)(6)(iv) of this section, the date on which, as certified by an authorized official, the borrower's eligibility for the deferment is expected to end;

(iii) Except as provided in paragraph (a)(6)(iv) of this section, the expiration date of the period covered by any certification required by this section to be obtained for the deferment;

(iv) In the case of an in-school deferment, the student's anticipated graduation date as certified by an authorized official of the school; or

(v) The date when the condition providing the basis for the borrower's eligibility for the deferment has continued to exist for the maximum amount of time allowed for that type of deferment.

(7) A lender may not deny a borrower a deferment to which the borrower is entitled, even though the borrower may be delinquent, but not in default, in making required installment payments. The 270- or 330-day period required to establish default does not run during the deferment and post-deferment grace periods. Unless the lender has granted the borrower forbearance under § 682.211, when the deferment and, if applicable, the post-deferment grace period expire, a borrower resumes any delinquency status that existed when the deferment period began.

(8) A borrower whose loan is in default is not eligible for a deferment on that loan, unless the borrower has made payment arrangements acceptable to the lender prior to the payment of a default claim by a guaranty agency.

(9) The borrower promptly must inform the lender when the condition entitling the borrower to a deferment no longer exists.

(10) Authorized deferments are described in paragraph (b) of this section. Specific requirements for each deferment are set forth in paragraphs (c) through (s) of this section.

(11) If two individuals are jointly liable for repayment of a PLUS loan or a Consolidation loan, the lender shall grant a request for deferment if both individuals simultaneously meet the requirements of this section for receiving the same, or different deferments.

(b) *Authorized deferments.*

(1) Deferment is authorized for a FFEL borrower during any period when the borrower is—

(i) Except as provided in paragraph (c)(5) of this section, engaged in full-time study at a school, or at a school that is operated by the Federal Government (e.g., the service academies), unless the borrower is not a national of the United States and is pursuing a course of study at a school not located in a State;

(ii) Engaged in a course of study under an eligible graduate fellowship program;

(iii) Engaged in a rehabilitation training program for disabled individuals;

(iv) Temporarily totally disabled, or unable to secure employment because the borrower is caring for a spouse or other dependent who is disabled and requires continuous nursing or similar services for up to three years; or

(v) Conscientiously seeking, but unable to find, full-time employment in the United States, for up to two years.

(2) For a borrower of a Stafford or SLS loan, and for a parent borrower of a PLUS loan made before August 15, 1983, deferment is authorized during any period when the borrower is—

(i) On active duty status in the United States Armed Forces, or an officer in the Commissioned Corps of the United States Public Health Service, for up to three years (including any period during which the borrower received a deferment authorized under paragraph (b)(5)(i) of this section);

(ii) A full-time volunteer under the Peace Corps Act, for up to three years;

(iii) A full-time volunteer under title I of the Domestic Volunteer Service Act of 1973 (ACTION programs), for up to three years;

(iv) A full-time volunteer for a tax-exempt organization, for up to three years; or

(v) Engaged in an internship of residency program, for up to two years (including any period during which the borrower received a deferment authorized under paragraph (b)(5)(iii) of this section).

(3) For a borrower of a Stafford or SLS loan who has been enrolled on at least a half-time basis at an institution of higher education during the six months preceding the beginning of this deferment, deferment is authorized during a period of up to six months during which the borrower is—

(i)(A) Pregnant;

(B) Caring for his or her newborn child; or

(C) Caring for a child immediately following the placement of the child with the borrower before or immediately following adoption; and

(ii) Not attending a school or gainfully employed.

(4) For a "new borrower," as defined in paragraph (b)(7) of this section, deferment is authorized during periods when the borrower is engaged in at least half-time study at a school, unless the borrower is not a national of the United States and is pursuing a course of study at a school not located in a State.

(5) For a new borrower, as defined in paragraph (b)(7) of this section, of a Stafford or SLS loan, deferment is authorized during any period when the borrower is—

(i) On active duty status in the National Oceanic and Atmospheric Administration Corps, for up to three years (including any period during which the borrower received a deferment authorized under paragraph (b)(2)(i) of this section);

(ii) Up to three years of service as a full-time teacher in a public or non-profit private elementary or secondary school in a teacher shortage area designated by the Secretary under paragraph (q) of this section.

(iii) Engaged in an internship or residency program, for up to two years (including any period during which the borrower received a deferment authorized under paragraph (b)(2)(v) of this section); or

(iv) A mother who has preschool-age children (i.e., children who have not enrolled in first grade) and who is earning not more than $1 per hour above the Federal minimum wage, for up to 12 months of employment, and who began that full-time employment within one year of entering or re-entering the work force. Full-time employment involves at least 30 hours of work a week and it expected to last at least 3 months.

(6) For a parent borrower of a PLUS loan, deferment is authorized during any period when a student on whose behalf the parent borrower received the loan—

(i) Is not independent as defined in section 480(d) of the Act; and

(ii) Meets the conditions and provides the required documentation, for any of the deferments described in paragraphs (b)(1)(i)–(iii) and (b)(4) of this section.

(7) For purposes of paragraph (b)(5) of this section, a "new borrower" with respect to a loan is a borrower who, on the date he or she signs and promissory note, has no outstanding balance on—

(i) A Stafford, SLS, or PLUS loan made prior to July 1, 1987 for a period of enrollment beginning prior to July 1, 1987; or

(ii) A Consolidation loan that repaid a loan made prior to July 1, 1987 and for a period of enrollment beginning prior to July 1, 1987.

(c) *In-school deferment.*

(1) Except as provided in paragraph (c)(5) of this section, the lender processes a deferment for full-time study or half-time study at a school, when—

(i) The borrower submits a request and supporting documentation for a deferment;

(ii) The lender receives information from the borrower's school about the borrower's eligibility in connection with a new loan;

(iii) The lender receives student status information from the borrower's school, either directly or indirectly, indicating that the borrower's enrollment status supports eligibility for a deferment; or

(iv) The lender confirms a borrower's half-time enrollment status through the use of the National Student Loan Data System if requested to do so by the school the borrower is attending.

(2) The lender must notify the borrower that a deferment has been granted based on paragraphs (c)(1)(ii), (iii), or (iv) of this section and that the borrower has the option to cancel the deferment and continue paying on the loan.

(3) The lender must consider a deferment granted on the basis of a certified loan application or other information certified by the school to cover the period lasting until the anticipated graduation date appearing on the application, and as updated by notice or Student Status Confirmation Report update to the lender from the school or guaranty agency, unless and until it receives notice that the borrower has ceased the level of study (i.e., full-time or half-time) required for the deferment.

(4) In the case of a FFEL borrower, the lender shall treat a certified loan application or other form certified by the school or for multiple holders of a borrower's loans, shared data from the Student Status Confirmation Report, as sufficient documentation for an in-school student deferment for any outstanding FFEL loan previously made to the borrower that is held by the lender.

(5) A borrower serving in a medical internship or residency program, except for an internship in dentistry, is prohibited from receiving or continuing a deferment on a Stafford, or a PLUS (unless based on the dependent's status) SLS, or Consolidation loan under paragraph (c) of this section.

(d) *Graduate fellowship deferment.*

(1) To qualify for a deferment for study in a graduate fellowship program, a borrower shall provide the lender with a statement from an authorized official of the borrower's fellowship program certifying—

(i) That the borrower holds at least a baccalaureate degree conferred by an institution of higher education;

(ii) That the borrower has been accepted or recommended by an institution of higher education for acceptance on a full-time basis into an eligible graduate fellowship program; and

(iii) The borrower's anticipated completion date in the program.

(2) For purposes of paragraph (d)(1) of this section, an eligible graduate fellowship program is a fellowship program that—

(i) Provides sufficient financial support to graduate fellows to allow for full-time study for at least six months;

(ii) Requires a written statement from each applicant explaining the applicant's objectives before the award of that financial support;

(iii) Requires a graduate fellow to submit periodic reports, projects, or evidence of the fellow's progress; and

(iv) In the case of a course of study at a foreign university, accepts the course of study for completion of the fellowship program.

(e) *Rehabilitation training program deferment.*

(1) To qualify for a rehabilitation training program deferment, a borrower shall provide the lender with a statement from an authorized official of the borrower's rehabilitation training program certifying that the borrower is either receiving, or is scheduled to receive, services under an eligible rehabilitation training program for disabled individuals.

(2) For purposes of paragraph (e)(1) of this section, an eligible rehabilitation training program for disabled individuals is a program that—

(i) Is licensed, approved, certified, or otherwise recognized as providing rehabilitation training to disabled individuals by—

(A) A State agency with responsibility for vocational rehabilitation programs;

(B) A State agency with responsibility for drug abuse treatment programs;

(C) A State agency with responsibility for mental health services program;

(D) A State agency with responsibility for alcohol abuse treatment programs; or

(E) The Department of Veterans Affairs; and

(ii) Provides or will provide the borrower with rehabilitation services under a written plan that—

(A) Is individualized to meet the borrower's needs;

(B) Specifies the date on which the services to the borrower are expected to end; and

(C) Is structured in a way that requires a substantial commitment by the borrower to his or her rehabilitation. The Secretary considers a substantial commitment by the borrower to be a commitment of time and effort that normally would prevent an individual from engaging in full-time employment, either because of the number of hours that must be devoted to rehabilitation or because of the nature of the rehabilitation. For the purpose of this paragraph, full-time employment involves at least 30 hours of work per week and is expected to last at least three months.

(f) *Temporary total disability deferment.*

(1) To qualify for a temporary total disability deferment, a borrower shall provide the lender with a statement from a physician, who is a doctor of medicine or osteopathy and is legally authorized to practice, certifying that the borrower is temporarily totally disabled as defined in § 682.200(b).

(2) A borrower is not considered temporarily totally disabled on the basis of a condition that existed before he or she applied for the loan, unless the condition has substantially deteriorated so as to render the borrower temporarily totally disabled, as substantiated by

the statement required under paragraph (f)(1) of this section, after the borrower submitted the loan application.

(3) A lender may not grant a deferment based on a single certification under paragraph (f)(1) of this section beyond the date that is six months after the date of certification.

(g) *Dependent's disability deferment.*

(1) To qualify for a deferment given to a borrower whose spouse or other dependent requires continuous nursing or similar services for a period of at least 90 days, the borrower shall provide the lender with a statement—

(i) From a physician, who is a doctor of medicine or osteopathy and is legally authorized to practice, certifying that the borrower's spouse or dependent requires continuous nursing or similar services for a period of at least 90 days; and

(ii) From the borrower, certifying that the borrower is unable to secure full-time employment because he or she is providing continuous nursing or similar services to the borrower's spouse or other dependent. For the purpose of this paragraph, full-time employment involves at least 30 hours of work per week and is expected to last at least three months.

(2) A lender may not grant a deferment based on a single certification under paragraph (g)(1) of this section beyond the date that is six months after the date of the certification.

(h) *Unemployment deferment.*

(1) A borrower qualifies for an unemployment deferment by providing evidence of eligibility for unemployment benefits to the lender.

(2) A borrower also qualifies for an unemployment deferment by providing to the lender a written certification, or an equivalent as approved by the Secretary, that—

(i) The borrower has registered with a public or private employment agency, if one is available to the borrower within a 50-mile radius of the borrower's current address; and

(ii) For all requests beyond the initial request, the borrower has made at least six diligent attempts during the preceding 6-month period to secure full-time employment.

(3) For purposes of obtaining an unemployment deferment under paragraph (h)(2) of this section, the following rules apply:

(i) A borrower may qualify for an unemployment deferment whether or not the borrower has been previously employed.

(ii) An unemployment deferment is not justified if the borrower refuses to seek or accept employment in kinds of positions or at salary and responsibility levels for which the borrower feels overqualified by virtue of education or previous experience.

(iii) Full-time employment involves at least 30 hours of work a week and is expected to last at least three months.

(iv) The initial period of unemployment deferment may be granted for a period of unemployment beginning up to 6 months before the date the lender receives the borrower's request, and may be granted for up to 6 months after that date.

(4) A lender may not grant an unemployment deferment beyond the date that is 6 months after the date the borrower provides evidence of the borrower's eligibility for unemployment insurance benefits under paragraph (h)(1) of this section or the date the borrower provides the written certification, or an approved equivalent, under paragraph (h)(2) of this section.

(i) *Military deferment.*

(1) To qualify for a military deferment, a borrower or a borrower's representative shall provide the lender with—

(i) A written statement from the borrower's commanding or personnel officer certifying—

(A) That the borrower is on active duty in the Armed Forces of the United States;

(B) The date on which the borrower's service began; and

(C) The date on which the borrower's service is expected to end; or

(ii)(A) A copy of the borrower's official military orders; and

(B) A copy of the borrower's military identification.

(2) For the purpose of this section, the Armed Forces means the Army, Navy, Air Force, Marine Corps, and the Coast Guard.

(3) A borrower enlisted in a reserve component of the Armed Forces may qualify for a military deferment only for service on a full-time basis that is expected to last for a period of at least one year in length, as evidenced by official military orders, unless an order for national mobilization of reservists is issued.

(4) A borrower enlisted in the National Guard qualifies for a military deferment only while the borrower is on active duty status as a member of the U.S. Army or Air Force Reserves, and meets the requirements of paragraph (i)(3) of this section.

(5) A lender that grants a military service deferment based on a request from a borrower's representative must notify the borrower that the deferment has been granted and that the borrower has the option to cancel the deferment and continue to make payments on the loan. The lender may also notify the borrower's representative of the outcome of the deferment request.

(j) *Public Health Service deferment.* To qualify for a Public Health Service deferment, the borrower shall provide the lender with a statement from an authorized official of the United States Public Health Service (USPHS) certifying—

(1) That the borrower is engaged in full-time service as an officer in the Commissioned Corps of the USPHS;

(2) The date on which the borrower's service began; and

(3) The date on which the borrower's service is expected to end.

(k) *Peace Corps deferment.*

(1) To qualify for a deferment for service under the Peace Corps Act, the borrower shall provide the lender with a statement from an authorized official of the Peace Corps certifying—

(i) That the borrower has agreed to serve for a term of at least one year;

(ii) The date on which the borrower's service began; and

(iii) The date on which the borrower's service is expected to end.

(2) The lender must grant a deferment for the borrower's full term of service in the Peace Corps, not to exceed three years.

(*l*) *Full-time volunteer service in the ACTION programs.* To qualify for a deferment as a full-time paid volunteer in an ACTION program, the borrower shall provide the lender with a statement from an authorized official of the program certifying—

(1) That the borrower has agreed to serve for a term of at least one year;

(2) The date on which the borrower's service began; and

(3) The date on which the borrower's service is expected to end.

(m) *Deferment for full-time volunteer service for a tax-exempt organization.* To qualify for a deferment as a full-time paid volunteer for a tax-exempt organization, a borrower shall provide the lender with a statement from an authorized official of the volunteer program certifying—

(1) That the borrower—

(i) Serves in an organization that has obtained an exemption from taxation under section 501(c)(3) of the Internal Revenue Code of 1986;

(ii) Provides service to low-income persons and their communities to assist them in eliminating poverty and poverty-related human, social, and environmental conditions;

(iii) Does not receive compensation that exceeds the rate prescribed under section 6 of the Fair Labor Standards Act of 1938 (the Federal minimum wage), except that the tax-exempt organization may provide health, retirement, and other fringe benefits to the volunteer that are substantially equivalent to the benefits offered to other employees of the organization;

(iv) Does not, as part of his or her duties, give religious instruction, conduct worship services, engage in religious proselytizing, or engage in fund-raising to support religious activities; and

(v) Has agreed to serve on a full-time basis for a term of at least one year;

(2) The date on which the borrower's service began; and

(3) The date on which the borrower's service is expected to end.

(n) *Internship or residency deferment.*

(1) To qualify for an internship or residency deferment under paragraphs (b)(2)(v) or (b)(5)(iii) of this section, the borrower shall provide the lender with a statement from an authorized official of the organization with which the borrower is undertaking the internship or residency program certifying—

(i) That the internship or residency program is a supervised training program that requires the borrower to hold at least a baccalaureate degree prior to acceptance into the program;

(ii) That, except for a borrower that provides the statement from a State official described in paragraph (n)(2) of this section, the internship or residency program leads to a degree or certificate awarded by an institution of higher education, a hospital, or a health care facility that offers postgraduate training;

(iii) That the borrower has been accepted into the internship or residency program; and

(iv) The anticipated dates on which the borrower will begin and complete the internship or residency program, or, in the case of a borrower providing the statement described in paragraph (n)(2) of this section, the anticipated date on which the borrower will begin and complete the minimum period of participation in the internship program that the State requires be completed before an individual may be certified for professional practice or service.

(2) For a borrower who does not provide a statement certifying to the matters set forth in paragraph (n)(1)(ii) of this section to qualify for an internship deferment under paragraph (b)(2)(v) of this section, the borrower shall provide the lender with a statement from an official of the appropriate State licensing agency certifying that the internship or residency program, or a portion thereof, is required to be completed before the borrower may be certified for professional practice or service.

(o) *Parental-leave deferment.*

(1) To qualify for the parental-leave deferment described in paragraph (b)(3) of this section, the borrower shall provide the lender with—

(i) A statement from an authorized official of a participating school certifying that the borrower was enrolled on at least a half-time basis during the six months preceding the beginning of the deferment period;

(ii) A statement from the borrower certifying that the borrower—

(A) Is pregnant, caring for his or her newborn child, or caring for a child immediately following the placement of the child with the borrower in connection with an adoption;

(B) Is not, and will not be, attending school during the deferment period; and

(C) Is not, and will not be, engaged in full-time employment during the deferment period; and

(iii) A physician's statement demonstrating the existence of the pregnancy, a birth certificate, or a statement from the adoption agency official evidencing a pre-adoption placement.

(2) For purposes of paragraph (o)(1)(ii)(C) of this section, full-time employment involves at least 30 hours of work per week and is expected to last at least three months.

(p) *NOAA deferment.*

To qualify for a National Oceanic and Atmospheric Administration (NOAA) deferment, the borrower shall provide the lender with a statement from an authorized official of the NOAA corps, certifying—

(1) That the borrower is on active duty service in the NOAA corps;

(2) The date on which the borrower's service began; and

(3) The date on which the borrower's service is expected to end.

(q) *Targeted teacher deferment.*

(1) To qualify for a targeted teacher deferment under paragraph (b)(5)(ii) of this section, the borrower, for each school year of service for which a deferment is requested, must provide to the lender—

(i) A statement by the chief administrative officer of the public or nonprofit private elementary or secondary school in which the borrower is teaching, certifying that the borrower is employed as a full-time teacher; and

(ii) A certification that he or she is teaching in a teacher shortage area designated by the Secretary as provided in paragraphs (q)(5) through (7) of this section, as described in paragraph (q)(2) of this section.

(2) In order to satisfy the requirement for certification that a borrower is teaching in a teacher shortage area designated by the Secretary, a borrower must do one of the following:

(i) If the borrower is teaching in a State in which the Chief State School Officer has complied with paragraph (q)(3) of this section and provides an annual listing of designated teacher shortage areas to the State's chief administrative officers whose schools are affected by the Secretary's designations, the borrower may obtain a certification that he or she is teaching in a teacher shortage area from his or her school's chief administrative officer.

(ii) If a borrower is teaching in a State in which the Chief State School Officer has not complied with paragraph (q)(3) of this section or does not provide an annual listing of designated teacher shortage areas to the State's chief administrative officers whose schools are affected by the Secretary's designations, the borrower must obtain certification that he or she is teaching in a teacher shortage area from the Chief State School Officer for the State in which the borrower is teaching.

(3) In the case of a State in which borrowers wish to obtain certifications as provided for in paragraph (q)(2)(i) of this section, the State's Chief State School Officer must first have notified the Secretary, by means of a one-time written assurance, that he or she provides annually to the State's chief administrative officers whose schools are affected by the Secretary's designations and the guaranty agency for that State, a listing of the teacher shortage areas designated by the Secretary as provided for in paragraphs (q)(5) through (7) of this section.

(4) If a borrower who receives a deferment continues to teach in the same teacher shortage area as that in which he or she was teaching when the deferment was originally granted, the borrower shall, at the borrower's request, continue to receive the deferment for those subsequent years, up to the three-year maximum deferment period, even if his or her position does not continue to be within an area designated by the Secretary as a teacher shortage area in those subsequent years. To continue to receive the deferment in a subsequent year under this paragraph, the borrower shall provide the lender with a statement by the chief administrative officer of the public or nonprofit private elementary or secondary school that employs the borrower, certifying that the borrower continues to be employed as a full-time teacher in the same teacher shortage area for which the deferment was received for the previous year.

(5) For purposes of this section a teacher shortage area is—

(i)(A) A geographic region of the State in which there is a shortage of elementary or secondary school teachers; or

(B) A specific grade level or academic, instructional, subject-matter, or discipline classification in which there is a statewide shortage of elementary or secondary school teachers; and

(ii) Designated by the Secretary under paragraphs (q)(6) or (q)(7) of this section.

(6)(i) In order for the Secretary to designate one or more teacher shortage areas in a State for a school year, the Chief State School Officer shall by January 1 of the calendar year in which the school year begins, and in accordance with objective written standards, propose teacher shortage areas to the Secretary for designation. With respect to private nonprofit schools included in the recommendation, the Chief State School Officer shall consult with appropriate officials of the private nonprofit schools in the State prior to submitting the recommendation.

(ii) In identifying teacher shortage areas to propose for designation under paragraph (q)(6)(i) of this section, the Chief State School Officer shall consider data from the school year in which the recommendation is to be made, unless that data is not yet available, in which case he or she may use data from the immediately preceding school year, with respect to—

(A) Teaching positions that are unfilled;

(B) Teaching positions that are filled by teachers who are certified by irregular, provisional, temporary, or emergency certification; and

(C) Teaching positions that are filled by teachers who are certified, but who are teaching in academic subject areas other than their area of preparation.

(iii) If the total number of unduplicated full-time equivalent (FTE) elementary or secondary teaching positions identified under paragraph (q)(6)(ii) of this section in the shortage areas proposed by the State for designation does not exceed 5 percent of the total number of FTE elementary and secondary teaching positions in the State, the Secretary designates those areas as teacher shortage areas.

(iv) If the total number of unduplicated FTE elementary and secondary teaching positions identified under paragraph (q)(6)(ii) of this section in the shortage areas proposed by the State for designation exceeds 5 percent of the total number of elementary and secondary FTE teaching positions in the State, the Chief State School Officer shall submit, with the list of proposed areas, supporting documentation showing the methods used for identifying shortage areas, and an explanation of the reasons why the Secretary should nevertheless designate all of the proposed areas as teacher shortage areas. The explanation must include a ranking of the proposed shortage areas according to priority, to assist the Secretary in determining which areas should be designated. The Secretary, after considering the explanation, determines which shortage areas to designate as teacher shortage areas.

(7) A Chief State School Officer may submit to the Secretary for approval an alternative written procedure to the one described in paragraph (q)(6) of this section, for the Chief State School Officer to use to select the teacher shortage areas recommended to the Secretary for designation, and for the Secretary to use to choose the areas to be designated. If the Secretary approves the proposed alternative procedure, in writing, that procedure, once approved, may be used instead of the procedure described in paragraph (q)(6) of this section for designation of teacher shortage areas in that State.

(8) For purposes of paragraphs (q)(1) through (7) of this section—

(i) The definition of the term school in § 682.200(b) does not apply;

(ii) Elementary school means a day or residential school that provides elementary education, as determined under State law;

(iii) Secondary school means a day or residential school that provides secondary education, as determined under State law. In the absence of applicable State law, the Secretary may determine, with respect to that State, whether the term "secondary school" includes education beyond the twelfth grade;

(iv) Teacher means a professional who provides direct and personal services to students for their educational development through classroom teaching;

(v) Chief State School Officer means the highest ranking educational official for elementary and secondary education for the State;

(vi) School year means the period from July 1 of a calendar year through June 30 of the following calendar year;

(vii) Teacher shortage area means an area of specific grade, subject matter, or discipline classification, or a geographic area in which the Secretary determines that there is an inadequate supply of elementary or secondary school teachers; and

(viii) Full-time equivalent means the standard used by a State in defining full-time employment, but not less than 30 hours per week. For purposes of counting full-time equivalent teacher positions, a teacher working part of his or her total hours in a position that is designated as a teacher shortage area is counted on a pro rata basis corresponding to the percentage of his or her working hours spent in such a position.

(r) *Working-mother deferment.*

(1) To qualify for the working-mother deferment described in paragraph (b)(5)(iv) of this section, the borrower shall provide the lender with a statement certifying that she—

(i) Is the mother of a preschool-age child;

(ii) Entered or reentered the workforce not more than one year before the beginning date of the period for which the deferment is being sought;

(iii) Is currently engaged in full-time employment; and

(iv) Does not receive compensation that exceeds $1 per hour above the rate prescribed under section 6 of the Fair Labor Standards Act of 1938 (the Federal minimum wage).

(2) In addition to the certification required under paragraph (r)(1) of this section, the borrower shall provide to the lender documents demonstrating the age of her child (e.g., a birth certificate) and the rate of her compensation (e.g., a pay stub showing her hourly rate of pay).

(3) For purposes of this paragraph—

(i) A preschool-age child is one who has not yet enrolled in first grade or a higher grade in elementary school; and

(ii) Full-time employment involves at least 30 hours of work a week and is expected to last at least 3 months.

(s) *Deferments for new borrowers on or after July 1, 1993—*

(1) *General.*

(i) A new borrower who receives an FFEL Program loan first disbursed on or after July 1, 1993 is entitled to receive deferments under paragraphs (s)(2) through (s)(6) of this section. For purposes of paragraphs (s)(2) through (s)(6) of this section, a "new borrower" is an individual who has no outstanding principal or interest balance on an FFEL Program loan as of July 1, 1993 or on the date he or she obtains a loan on or after July 1, 1993. This term also includes a borrower who obtains a Federal Consolidation Loan on or after July 1, 1993 if the borrower has no other outstanding FFEL Program loan when the Consolidation Loan was made.

(ii) As a condition for receiving a deferment, except for purposes of paragraph (s)(2) of this section, the borrower must request the deferment and provide the lender with all information and documents required to establish eligibility for the deferment.

(iii) After receiving a borrower's written or verbal request, a lender may grant a deferment under paragraphs (s)(3) through (s)(6) of this section if the lender is able to confirm that the borrower has received a deferment on another FFEL loan or on a Direct Loan for the same reason and the same time period. The lender may grant the deferment based on information from the other FFEL loan holder or the Secretary or from an authoritative electronic database maintained or authorized by the Secretary that supports eligibility for the deferment for the same reason and the same time period.

(iv) A lender may rely in good faith on the information it receives under paragraph (s)(1)(iii) of this section when determining a borrower's eligibility for a deferment unless the lender, as of the date of the determination, has information indicating that the borrower does not qualify for the deferment. A lender must resolve any discrepant information before granting a deferment under paragraph (s)(1)(iii) of this section.

(v) A lender that grants a deferment under paragraph (s)(1)(iii) of this section must notify the borrower that the deferment has been granted and that the borrower has the option to pay interest that accrues on an unsubsidized FFEL loan or to cancel the deferment and continue to make payments on the loan.

(2) *In-school deferment.* An eligible borrower is entitled to a deferment based on the borrower's at least half-time study in accordance with the rules prescribed in § 682.210(c), except that the borrower is not required to obtain a Stafford or SLS loan for the period of enrollment covered by the deferment.

(3) *Graduate fellowship deferment.* An eligible borrower is entitled to a graduate fellowship deferment in accordance with the rules prescribed in § 682.210(d).

(4) *Rehabilitation training program deferment.* An eligible borrower is entitled to a rehabilitation training program deferment in accordance with the rules prescribed in § 682.210(e).

(5) *Unemployment deferment.* An eligible borrower is entitled to an unemployment deferment in accordance with the rules prescribed in § 682.210(h) for periods that, collectively, do not exceed 3 years.

(6) *Economic hardship deferment.* An eligible borrower is entitled to an economic hardship deferment for periods of up to one year at a time that, collectively, do not exceed 3 years (except that a borrower who receives a deferment under paragraph (s)(6)(vi) of this section is entitled to an economic hardship deferment for the lesser of the borrower's full term of service in the Peace Corps or the borrower's remaining period of economic hardship deferment eligibility under the 3-year maximum), if the borrower provides documentation satisfactory to the lender showing that the borrower is within any of the categories described in paragraphs (s)(6)(i) through (s)(6)(vi) of this section.

(i) Has been granted an economic hardship deferment under either the Direct Loan or Federal Perkins Loan Programs for the period of time for which the borrower has requested an economic hardship deferment for his or her FFEL loan.

(ii) Is receiving payment under a Federal or State public assistance program, such as Aid to Families with Dependent Children, Supplemental Security Income, Food Stamps, or State general public assistance.

(iii) Is working full-time and has a monthly income that does not exceed the greater of (as calculated on a monthly basis)—

(A) The minimum wage rate described in section 6 of the Fair Labor Standards Act of 1938; or

(B) An amount equal to 150 percent of the poverty guideline applicable to the borrower's family size as published annually by the Department of Health and Human Services pursuant to 42 U.S.C. 9902(2). If a borrower is not a resident of a State identified in the poverty guidelines, the poverty guideline to be used for the borrower is the poverty guideline (for the relevant family size) used for the 48 contiguous States.

(iv) Is serving as a volunteer in the Peace Corps.

(v) For an initial period of deferment granted under paragraph (s)(6)(iii) of this section, the lender must require the borrower to submit evidence showing the amount of the borrower's monthly income.

(vi) To qualify for a subsequent period of deferment that begins less than one year after the end of a period of deferment under paragraph (s)(6)(iii) of this section, the lender must require the borrower to submit evidence showing the amount of the borrower's monthly income or a copy of the borrower's most recently filed Federal income tax return.

(vii) For purposes of paragraph (s)(6) of this section, a borrower's monthly income is the gross amount of income received by the borrower from employment and from other sources, or one-twelfth of the borrower's adjusted gross income, as recorded on the borrower's most recently filed Federal income tax return.

(viii) For purposes of paragraph (s)(6) of this section, a borrower is considered to be working full-time if the borrower is expected to be employed for at least three consecutive months at 30 hours per week.

(ix) For purposes of paragraph (s)(6)(iii)(B) of this section, family size means the number that is determined by counting the borrower, the borrower's spouse, and the borrower's children, including unborn children who will be born during the period covered by the deferment, if the children receive more than half their support from the borrower. A borrower's family size includes other individuals if, at the time the borrower requests the economic hardship deferment, the other individuals—

(A) Live with the borrower; and

(B) Receive more than half their support from the borrower and will continue to receive this support from the borrower for the year the borrower certifies family size. Support includes money, gifts, loans, housing, food, clothes, car, medical and dental care, and payment of college costs.

(t) *Military service deferments—*

(1) A borrower who receives a FFEL Program loan, may receive a military service deferment for such loan for any period during which the borrower is—

(i) Serving on active duty during a war or other military operation or national emergency; or

(ii) Performing qualifying National Guard duty during a war or other military operation or national emergency.

(2) For a borrower whose active duty service includes October 1, 2007, or begins on or after that date, the deferment period ends 180 days after the demobilization date for each period of service described in paragraph (t)(1)(i) and (t)(1)(ii) of this section.

(3) Serving on active duty during a war or other military operation or national emergency means service by an individual who is—

(i) A Reserve of an Armed Force ordered to active duty under 10 U.S.C. 12301(a), 12301(g), 12302, 12304 or 12306;

(ii) A retired member of an Armed Force ordered to active duty under 10 U.S.C. 688 for service in connection with a war or other military operation or national emergency, regardless of the location at which such active duty service is performed; or

(iii) Any other member of an Armed Force on active duty in connection with such emergency or subsequent actions or conditions who has been assigned to a duty station at a location other than the location at which member is normally assigned.

(4) Qualifying National Guard duty during a war or other operation or national emergency means service as a member of the National Guard on full-time National Guard duty, as defined in 10 U.S.C. 101(d)(5), under a call to active service authorized by the President or the Secretary of Defense for a period of more than 30 consecutive days under 32 U.S.C. 502(f) in connection with a war, other military operation, or national emergency declared by the President and supported by Federal funds.

(5) Payments made by or on behalf of a borrower during a period for which the borrower qualified for a military service deferment are not refunded.

(6) As used in this paragraph—

(i) *Active duty* means active duty as defined in 10 U.S.C. 101(d)(1) except that it does not include active duty for training or attendance at a service school;

(ii) *Military operation* means a contingency operation as defined in 10 U.S.C. 101(a)(13); and

(iii) *National emergency* means the national emergency by reason of certain terrorist attacks declared by the President on September 14, 2001, or subsequent national emergencies declared by the President by reason of terrorist attacks.

(7) To receive a military service deferment, the borrower, or the borrower's representative, must request the deferment and provide the lender with all information and documents required to establish eligibility for the deferment, except that a lender may grant a borrower a military service deferment under

the procedures specified in paragraphs (s)(1)(iii) through (s)(1)(v) of this section.

(8) A lender that grants a military service deferment based on a request from a borrower's representative must notify the borrower that the deferment has been granted and that the borrower has the option to cancel the deferment and continue to make payments on the loan. The lender may also notify the borrower's representative of the outcome of the deferment request.

(9) Without supporting documentation, a military service deferment may be granted to an otherwise eligible borrower for a period not to exceed the initial 12 months from the date the qualifying eligible service began based on a request from the borrower or the borrower's representative.

(u) *Post-active duty student deferment.*

(1) Effective October 1, 2007, a borrower who receives a FFEL Program loan and is serving on active duty on that date, or begins serving on or after that date, is entitled to receive a post-active duty student deferment for 13 months following the conclusion of the borrower's active duty military service and any applicable grace period if—

(i) The borrower is a member of the National Guard or other reserve component of the Armed Forces of the United States or a member of such forces in retired status; and

(ii) The borrower was enrolled, on at least a half-time basis, in a program of instruction at an eligible institution at the time, or within six months prior to the time, the borrower was called to active duty.

(2) As used in paragraph (u)(1) of this section, "active duty" means active duty as defined in section 101(d)(1) of title 10, United States Code for at least a 30-day period, except that—

(i) Active duty includes active State duty for members of the National Guard under which a Governor activates National Guard personnel based on State statute or policy and the activities of the National Guard are paid for with State funds;

(ii) Active duty includes full-time National Guard duty under which a Governor is authorized, with the approval of the President or the U.S. Secretary of Defense, to order a member to State active duty and the activities of the National Guard are paid for with Federal funds;

(iii) Active duty does not include active duty for training or attendance at a service school; and

(iv) Active duty does not include employment in a full-time, permanent position in the National Guard unless the borrower employed in such a position is reassigned to active duty under paragraph (u)(2)(i) of this section or full-time National Guard duty under paragraph (u)(2)(ii) of this section.

(3) If the borrower returns to enrolled student status, on at least a half-time basis, during the 13-month deferment period, the deferment expires at the time the borrower returns to enrolled student status, on at least a half-time basis.

(4) If a borrower qualifies for both a military service deferment and a post-active duty student deferment, the 180-day post-demobilization military service deferment period and the 13-month post-active duty student deferment period apply concurrently.

(5) To receive a military active duty student deferment, the borrower must request the deferment and provide the lender with all information and documents required to establish eligibility for the deferment, except that a lender may grant a borrower a military active duty student deferment under the procedures specified in paragraphs (s)(1)(iii) through (s)(1)(v) of this section.

(v) *In-school deferments for PLUS loan borrowers with loans first disbursed on or after July 1, 2008.*

(1)(i) A student PLUS borrower is entitled to a deferment on a PLUS loan first disbursed on or after July 1, 2008 during the 6-month period that begins on the day after the student ceases to be enrolled on at least a half-time basis at an eligible institution.

(ii) If a lender grants an in-school deferment to a student PLUS borrower based on § 682.210(c)(1)(ii), (iii), or (iv), the deferment period for a PLUS loan first disbursed on or after July 1, 2008 includes the 6-month post-enrollment period described in paragraph (v)(1)(i) of this section. The notice required by § 682.210(c)(2) must inform the borrower that the in-school deferment on a PLUS loan first disbursed on or after July 1, 2008 will end six months after the day the borrower ceases to be enrolled on at least a half-time basis.

(2) Upon the request of the borrower, an eligible parent PLUS borrower must be granted a deferment on a PLUS loan first disbursed on or after July 1, 2008—

(i) During the period when the student on whose behalf the loan was obtained is enrolled at an eligible institution on at least a half-time basis; and

(ii) During the 6-month period that begins on the later of the day after the student on whose behalf the loan was obtained ceases to be enrolled on at least a half-time basis or, if the parent borrower is also a student, the day after the parent borrower ceases to be enrolled on at least a half-time basis.

(Approved by the Office of Management and Budget under control number 1845-0020)

(Authority: 20 U.S.C. 1077, 1078, 1078-1, 1078-2, 1078-3, 1082, 1085)

[58 Fed. Reg. 9120 (Feb. 19, 1993); 59 Fed. Reg. 25746 (May 17, 1994); 59 Fed. Reg. 33594 (June 29, 1994); 59 Fed. Reg. 61215 (Nov. 29, 1994); 60 Fed. Reg. 30788 (June 12, 1995); 60 Fed. Reg. 32912 (June 26, 1995); 60 Fed. Reg. 61756 (Dec. 1, 1995); 61 Fed. Reg. 16718 (Apr. 17, 1996); 64 Fed. Reg. 18977 (Apr. 16, 1999); 64 Fed. Reg. 57531 (Oct. 25, 1999); 64 Fed. Reg. 58626 (Oct. 29, 1999); 64 Fed. Reg. 58958 (Nov. 1, 1999); 65 Fed. Reg. 65619 (Nov. 1, 2000); 66 Fed. Reg. 34763 (June 29, 2001); 67 Fed. Reg. 67078 (Nov. 1, 2002); 68 Fed. Reg. 75429 (Dec. 31, 2003); 71 Fed. Reg. 45701 (Aug. 9, 2006); 72 Fed. Reg. 62001 (Nov. 1, 2007); 73 Fed. Reg. 63248 (Oct. 23, 2008); 74 Fed. Reg. 55994 (Oct. 29, 2009)]

§ 682.211 Forbearance.

(a)(1) The Secretary encourages a lender to grant forbearance for the benefit of a borrower or endorser in order to prevent the borrower or endorser from defaulting on the borrower's or endorser's repayment obligation, or to permit the borrower or endorser to resume honoring that obligation after default. Forbearance means permitting the temporary cessation of payments, allowing an extension of time for making payments, or temporarily accepting smaller payments than previously were scheduled.

(2) Subject to paragraph (g) of this section, a lender may grant forbearance of payments of principal and interest under paragraphs (b), (c), and (d) of this section only if—

(i) The lender reasonably believes, and documents in the borrower's file, that the borrower or endorser intends to repay the loan but, due to poor health or other acceptable reasons, is currently unable to make scheduled payments; or

(ii) The borrower's payments of principal are deferred under § 682.210 and the Secretary does not pay interest benefits on behalf of the borrower under § 682.301.

(3) If two individuals are jointly liable for repayment of a PLUS loan or a Consolidation loan, the lender may grant forbearance on repayment of the loan only if the ability of both individuals to make scheduled payments has been impaired based on the same or differing conditions.

(4) Except as provided in paragraph (f)(10) of this section, if payments of interest are forborne, they may be capitalized as provided in § 682.202(b).

(b) A lender may grant forbearance if—

(1) The lender and the borrower or endorser agree to the terms of the forbearance and, unless the agreement was in writing, the lender sends, within 30 days, a notice to the borrower or endorser confirming the terms of the forbearance and records the terms of the forbearance in the borrower's file; or

(2) In the case of forbearance of interest during a period of deferment, if the lender

informs the borrower at the time the deferment is granted that interest payments are to be forborne.

(c) A lender may grant forbearance for a period of up to one year at a time if both the borrower or endorser and an authorized official of the lender agree to the terms of the forbearance. If the lender and the borrower or endorser agree to the terms orally, the lender must notify the borrower or endorser of the terms within 30 days of that agreement.

(d) A guaranty agency may authorize a lender to grant forbearance to permit a borrower or endorser to resume honoring the agreement to repay the debt after default but prior to claim payment. The terms of the forbearance agreement in this situation must include a new signed agreement to repay the debt.

(e)(1) At the time of granting a borrower or endorser a forbearance, the lender must provide the borrower or endorser with information to assist the borrower or endorser in understanding the impact of capitalization of interest on the loan principal and total interest to be paid over the life of the loan; and

(2) At least once every 180 days during the period of forbearance, the lender must contact the borrower or endorser to inform the borrower or endorser of—

(i) The outstanding obligation to repay;

(ii) The amount of the unpaid principal balance and any unpaid interest that has accrued on the loan since the last notice provided to the borrower or endorser under this paragraph;

(iii) The fact that interest will accrue on the loan for the full term of the forbearance;

(iv) The amount of interest that will be capitalized, as of the date of the notice, and the date capitalization will occur;

(v) The option of the borrower or endorser to pay the interest that has accrued before the interest is capitalized; and

(vi) The borrower's or endorser's option to discontinue the forbearance at any time.

(f) A lender may grant forbearance, upon notice to the borrower or if applicable, the endorser, with respect to payments of interest and principal that are overdue or would be due—

(1) For a properly granted period of deferment for which the lender learns the borrower did not qualify;

(2) Upon the beginning of an authorized deferment period under § 682.210, or an administrative forbearance period as specified under paragraph (f)(11) or (i)(2) of this section;

(3) For the period beginning when the borrower entered repayment without the lender's knowledge until the first payment due date was established;

(4) For the period prior to the borrower's filing of a bankruptcy petition as provided in § 682.402(f);

(5) For the periods described in § 682.402(c) in regard to the borrower's total and permanent disability;

(6) Upon receipt of a valid identity theft report as defined in section 603(q)(4) of the Fair Credit Reporting Act (15 U.S.C. 1681a) or notification from a credit bureau that information furnished by the lender is a result of an alleged identity theft as defined in § 682.402(e)(14), for a period not to exceed 120 days necessary for the lender to determine the enforceability of the loan. If the lender determines that the loan does not qualify for discharge under § 682.402(e)(1)(i)(C), but is nonetheless unenforceable, the lender must comply with §§ 682.300(b)(2)(ix) and 682.302(d)(1)(viii).

(7) For a period not to exceed an additional 60 days after the lender has suspended collection activity for the initial 60-day period required pursuant to § 682.211(i)(6) and § 682.402(b)(3), when the lender receives reliable information that the borrower (or student on whose behalf a parent has borrowed a PLUS Loan) has died;

(8) For periods necessary for the Secretary or guaranty agency to determine the borrower's eligibility for discharge of the loan because of an unpaid refund, attendance at a closed school or false certification of loan eligibility, pursuant to § 682.402(d) or (e), or the borrower's or, if applicable, endorser's bankruptcy, pursuant to § 682.402(f);

(9) For a period of delinquency at the time a loan is sold or transferred, if the borrower or endorser is less than 60 days delinquent on the loan at the time of sale or transfer;

(10) For a period of delinquency that may remain after a borrower ends a period of deferment or mandatory forbearance until the next due date, which can be no later than 60 days after the period ends;

(11) For a period not to exceed 60 days necessary for the lender to collect and process documentation supporting the borrower's request for a deferment, forbearance, change in repayment plan, or consolidation loan. Interest that accrues during this period is not capitalized;

(12) For a period not to exceed 3 months when the lender determines that a borrower's ability to make payments has been adversely affected by a natural disaster, a local or national emergency as declared by the appropriate government agency, or a military mobilization;

(13) For a period not to exceed 60 days necessary for the lender to collect and process documentation supporting the borrower's eligibility for loan forgiveness under the income-based repayment program. The lender must notify the borrower that the requirement to make payments on the loans for which forgiveness was requested has been suspended pending approval of the forgiveness by the guaranty agency;

(14) For a period of delinquency at the time a borrower makes a change to the repayment plan; or

(15) For PLUS loans first disbursed before July 1, 2008, to align repayment with a borrower's PLUS loans that were first disbursed on or after July 1, 2008, or with Stafford Loans that are subject to a grace period under § 682.209(a)(3). The notice specified in paragraph (f) introductory text of this section must inform the borrower that the borrower has the option to cancel the forbearance and continue paying on the loan.

(g) In granting a forbearance under this section, except for a forbearance under paragraph (i)(5) of this section, a lender shall grant a temporary cessation of payments, unless the borrower chooses another form of forbearance subject to paragraph (a)(1) of this section.

(h) *Mandatory forbearance.*

(1) *Medical or dental interns or residents.* Upon receipt of a request and sufficient supporting documentation, as described in § 682.210(n), from a borrower serving in a medical or dental internship or residency program, a lender shall grant forbearance to the borrower in yearly increments (or a lesser period equal to the actual period during which the borrower is eligible) if the borrower has exhausted his or her eligibility for a deferment under § 682.210(n), or the borrower's promissory note does not provide for such a deferment—

(i) For the length of time remaining in the borrower's medical or dental internship or residency that must be successfully completed before the borrower may begin professional practice or service; or

(ii) For the length of time that the borrower is serving in a medical or dental internship or residency program leading to a degree or certificate awarded by an institution of higher education, a hospital, or a health care facility that offers postgraduate training.

(2) *Borrowers who are not medical or dental interns or residents, and endorsers.* Upon receipt of a request and sufficient supporting documentation from an endorser (if applicable), or from a borrower (other than a borrower who is serving in a medical or dental internship or residency described in paragraph (h)(1) of this section), a lender shall grant forbearance—

(i) In increments up to one year, for periods that collectively do not exceed three years, if—

(A) The borrower or endorser is currently obligated to make payments on Title IV loans; and

(B) The amount of those payments each month (or a proportional share if the payments are due less frequently than monthly) is collectively equal to or greater than 20 percent of the borrower's or endorser's total monthly income;

(ii) In yearly increments (or a lesser period equal to the actual period during which the borrower is eligible) for as long as a borrower—

(A) Is serving in a national service position for which the borrower receives a national service educational award under the National and Community Service Trust Act of 1993;

(B) Is performing the type of service that would qualify the borrower for a partial repayment of his or her loan under the Student Loan Repayment Programs administered by the Department of Defense under 10 U.S.C. 2171; or

(C) Is performing the type of service that would qualify the borrower for loan forgiveness and associated forbearance under the requirements of the teacher loan forgiveness program in § 682.215; and

(iii) In yearly increments (or a lesser period equal to the actual period for which the borrower is eligible) when a member of the National Guard who qualifies for a post-active duty student deferment, but does not qualify for a military service deferment or other deferment, is engaged in active State duty as defined in § 682.210(u)(2)(i) and (ii) for a period of more than 30 consecutive days, beginning—

(A) On the day after the grace period expires for a Stafford loan that has not entered repayment; or

(B) On the day after the borrower ceases at least half-time enrollment, for a FFEL loan in repayment.

(3) *Forbearance agreement.* After the lender determines the borrower's or endorser's eligibility, and the lender and the borrower or endorser agree to the terms of the forbearance granted under this section, the lender sends, within 30 days, a notice to the borrower or endorser confirming the terms of the forbearance and records the terms of the forbearance in the borrower's file.

(4) *Documentation.*

(i) Before granting a forbearance to a borrower or endorser under paragraph (h)(2)(i) of this section, the lender shall require the borrower or endorser to submit at least the following documentation:

(A) Evidence showing the amount of the most recent total monthly gross income received by the borrower or endorser from employment and from other sources; and

(B) Evidence showing the amount of the monthly payments owed by the borrower or endorser to other entities for the most recent month for the borrower's or endorser's Title IV loans.

(ii) Before granting a forbearance to a borrower or endorser under paragraph (h)(2)(ii)(B) of this section, the lender shall require the borrower or endorser to submit documentation showing the beginning and ending dates that the Department of Defense considers the borrower to be eligible for a partial repayment of his or her loan under the Student Loan Repayment Programs.

(iii) Before granting a forbearance to a borrower under paragraph (h)(2)(ii)(C) of this section, the lender must require the borrower to—

(A) Submit documentation for the period of the annual forbearance request showing the beginning and anticipated ending dates that the borrower is expected to perform, for that year, the type of service described in § 682.215(c); and

(B) Certify the borrower's intent to satisfy the requirements of § 682.215(c).

(i) *Mandatory administrative forbearance.*

(1) The lender shall grant a mandatory administrative forbearance for the periods specified in paragraph (i)(2) of this section until the lender is notified by the Secretary or a guaranty agency that the forbearance period no longer applies. The lender may not require a borrower who is eligible for a forbearance under paragraph (i)(2)(ii) of this section to submit a request or supporting documentation, but shall require a borrower (or endorser, if applicable) who requests forbearance because of a military mobilization to provide documentation showing that he or she is subject to a military mobilization as described in paragraph (i)(4) of this section.

(2) The lender is not required to notify the borrower (or endorser, if applicable) at the time the forbearance is granted, but shall grant a forbearance to a borrower or endorser during a period, and the 30 days following the period, when the lender is notified by the Secretary that—

(i) Exceptional circumstances exist, such as a local or national emergency or military mobilization; or

(ii) The geographical area in which the borrower or endorser resides has been designated a disaster area by the president of the United States or Mexico, the Prime Minister of Canada, or by a Governor of a State.

(3) As soon as feasible, or by the date specified by the Secretary, the lender shall notify the borrower (or endorser, if applicable) that the lender has granted a forbearance and the date that payments should resume. The lender's notification shall state that the borrower or endorser—

(i) May decline the forbearance and continue to be obligated to make scheduled payments; or

(ii) Consents to making payments in accordance with the lender's notification if the forbearance is not declined.

(4) For purposes of paragraph (i)(2)(i) of this section, the term "military mobilization" shall mean a situation in which the Department of Defense orders members of the National Guard or Reserves to active duty under sections 688, 12301(a), 12301(g), 12302, 12304, and 12306 of title 10, United States Code. This term also includes the assignment of other members of the Armed Forces to duty stations at locations other than the locations at which they were normally assigned, only if the military mobilization involved the activation of the National Guard or Reserves.

(5) The lender shall grant a mandatory administrative forbearance to a borrower (or endorser, if applicable) during a period when the borrower (or endorser, if applicable) is making payments for a period of—

(i) Up to 3 years of payments in cases where the effect of a variable interest rate on a standard or graduated repayment schedule would result in a loan not being repaid within the maximum repayment term; or

(ii) Up to 5 years of payments in cases where the effect of decreased installment amounts paid under an income-sensitive repayment schedule would result in the loan not being repaid within the maximum repayment term.

(6) The lender shall grant a mandatory administrative forbearance to a borrower for a period not to exceed 60 days after the lender receives reliable information indicating that the borrower (or student in the case of a PLUS loan) has died, until the lender receives documentation of death pursuant to § 682.402(b)(3).

(Approved by the Office of Management and Budget under control number 1845-0020)

(Authority: 20 U.S.C. 1077, 1078, 1078-1, 1078-2, 1078-3, 1080, 1082)

[58 Fed. Reg. 9120 (Feb. 19, 1993); 59 Fed. Reg. 25746 (May 17, 1994); 59 Fed. Reg. 33595 (June 29, 1994); 60 Fed. Reg. 30788 (June 12, 1995); 60 Fed. Reg. 32912 (June 26, 1995); 60 Fed. Reg. 61756 (Dec. 1, 1995); 61 Fed. Reg. 16718 (Apr. 17, 1996); 64 Fed. Reg. 18977 (Apr. 16, 1999); 64 Fed. Reg. 58626 (Oct. 29, 1999); 64 Fed. Reg. 58959 (Nov. 1, 1999); 65 Fed. Reg. 65627 (Nov. 1, 2000); 66 Fed. Reg. 34763 (June 29, 2001); 66 Fed. Reg. 44007 (Aug. 21, 2001); 67 Fed. Reg. 67079 (Nov. 1, 2002); 68 Fed. Reg. 75429 (Dec. 31, 2003); 71 Fed. Reg. 45702 (Aug. 9, 2006); 71 Fed. Reg. 64398 (Nov. 1, 2006); 72 Fed. Reg. 62001 (Nov. 1, 2007); 73 Fed. Reg. 63249 (Oct. 23, 2008); 74 Fed. Reg. 55994 (Oct. 29, 2009)]

§ 682.212 Prohibited transactions.

(a) No points, premiums, payments, or additional interest of any kind may be paid or otherwise extended to any eligible lender or other party in order to—
 (1) Secure funds for making loans; or
 (2) Induce a lender to make loans to either the students or the parents of students of a particular school or particular category of students or their parents.

(b) The following are examples of transactions that, if entered into for the purposes described in paragraph (a) of this section, are prohibited:
 (1) Cash payments by or on behalf of a school made to a lender or other party.
 (2) The maintaining of a compensating balance by or on behalf of a school with a lender.
 (3) Payments by or on behalf of a school to a lender of servicing costs on loans that the school does not own.
 (4) Payments by or on behalf of a school to a lender of unreasonably high servicing costs on loans that the school does own.
 (5) Purchase by or on behalf of a school of stock of the lender.
 (6) Payments ostensibly made for other purposes.

(c) Except when purchased by an agency of any State functioning as a secondary market or in any other circumstances approved by the Secretary, notes, or any interest in notes, may not be sold or otherwise transferred at discount if the underlying loans were made—
 (1) By a school; or
 (2) To students or parents of students attending a school by a lender having common ownership with that school.

(d) Except to secure a loan from an agency of a State functioning as a secondary market or in other circumstances approved by the Secretary, a school or lender (with respect to a loan made to a student, or a parent of a student, attending a school having common ownership with that lender), may not use a loan made under the FFEL programs as collateral for any loan bearing aggregate interest and other charges in excess of the sum of the interest rate applicable to the loan plus the rate of the most recently prescribed special allowance under § 682.302.

(e) The prohibitions described in paragraphs (a), (b), (c), and (d) of this section apply to any school, lender, or other party that would participate in a proscribed transaction.

(f) This section does not preclude a buyer of loans made by a school from obtaining from the loan seller a warranty that—
 (1) Covers future reductions by the Secretary or a guaranty agency in computing the amount of loss payable on default claims filed on the loans, if the reductions are attributable to an act, or failure to act, on the part of the seller or previous holder; and
 (2) Does not cover matters for which a purchaser is charged with responsibility under this part, such as due diligence in collecting loans.

(g) Section 490(c) of the Act provides that any person who knowingly and willfully makes an unlawful payment to an eligible lender as an inducement to make, or to acquire by assignment, a FFEL loan shall, upon conviction thereof, be fined not more than $10,000 or imprisoned not more than one year, or both.

(h) A school may, at its option, make available a list of recommended or suggested lenders, in print or any other medium or form, for use by the school's students or their parents provided that such list complies with the requirements in 34 CFR 601.10 and 668.14(a)(28).

(Approved by the Office of Management and Budget under control number 1845-0020)

(Authority: 20 U.S.C. 1077, 1078, 1078-1, 1078-2, 1078-3, 1082, 1097)

[72 Fed. Reg. 62002 (Nov. 1, 2007); 74 Fed. Reg. 55663 (Oct. 28, 2009)]

* * *

§ 682.215 Income-based repayment plan.

(a) *Definitions.* As used in this section—
 (1) *Adjusted gross income* (AGI) means the borrower's adjusted gross income as reported to the Internal Revenue Service. For a married borrower filing jointly, AGI includes both the borrower's and spouse's income. For a married borrower filing separately, AGI includes only the borrower's income.
 (2) *Eligible loan* means any outstanding loan made to a borrower under the FFEL and Direct Loan programs except for a defaulted loan, a FFEL or Direct PLUS Loan made to a parent borrower, or a FFEL or Direct Consolidation Loan that repaid a FFEL or Direct PLUS Loan made to a parent borrower.
 (3) *Family size* means the number that is determined by counting the borrower, the borrower's spouse, and the borrower's children, including unborn children who will be born during the year the borrower certifies family size, if the children receive more than half their support from the borrower. A borrower's family size includes other individuals if, at the time the borrower certifies family size, the other individuals—
  (i) Live with the borrower; and
  (ii) Receive more than half their support from the borrower and will continue to receive this support from the borrower for the year the borrower certifies family size. Support includes money, gifts, loans, housing, food, clothes, car, medical and dental care, and payment of college costs.
 (4) *Partial financial hardship* means a circumstance in which—
  (i) For an unmarried borrower or a married borrower who files an individual Federal tax return, the annual amount due on all of the borrower's eligible loans, as calculated under a standard repayment plan based on a 10-year repayment period, using the greater of the amount due at the time the borrower initially entered repayment or at the time the borrower elects the income-based repayment plan, exceeds 15 percent of the difference between the borrower's AGI and 150 percent of the poverty guideline for the borrower's family size; or
  (ii) For a married borrower who files a joint Federal tax return with his or her spouse, the annual amount due on all of the borrower's eligible loans and, if applicable, the spouse's eligible loans, as calculated under a standard repayment plan based on a 10-year repayment period, using the greater of the amount due at the time the loans initially entered repayment or at the time the borrower or spouse elects the income-based repayment plan, exceeds 15 percent of the difference between the borrower's and spouse's AGI, and 150 percent of the poverty guideline for the borrower's family size.
 (5) *Poverty guideline* refers to the income categorized by State and family size in the poverty guidelines published annually by the United States Department of Health and Human Services pursuant to 42 U.S.C. 9902(2). If a borrower is not a resident of a State identified in the poverty guidelines, the poverty guideline to be used for the borrower is the poverty guideline (for the relevant family size) used for the 48 contiguous States.

(b) *Repayment plan.*
 (1) A borrower may elect the income-based repayment plan only if the borrower has a partial financial hardship. The borrower's aggregate monthly loan payments are limited to no more than 15 percent of the amount by which the borrower's AGI exceeds 150 percent of the poverty line income applicable to the borrower's family size, divided by 12. The loan holder adjusts the calculated monthly payment if—
  (i) Except for borrowers provided for in paragraph (b)(1)(ii) of this section, the total amount of the borrower's eligible loans includes loans not held by the loan holder, in which case the loan holder determines the borrower's adjusted monthly payment by multiplying the calculated payment by the percentage of the total outstanding principal amount of eligible loans that are held by the loan holder;
  (ii) Both the borrower and the borrower's spouse have eligible loans and filed a joint

Federal tax return, in which case the loan holder determines—

(A) Each borrower's percentage of the couple's total eligible loan debt;

(B) The adjusted monthly payment for each borrower by multiplying the calculated payment by the percentage determined in paragraph (b)(1)(ii)(A) of this section; and

(C) If the borrower's loans are held by multiple holders, the borrower's adjusted monthly payment by multiplying the payment determined in paragraph (b)(1)(ii)(B) of this section by the percentage of the total outstanding principal amount of eligible loans that are held by the loan holder;

(iii) The calculated amount under paragraph (b)(1), (b)(1)(i), or (b)(1)(ii) of this section is less than $5.00, in which case the borrower's monthly payment is $0.00; or

(iv) The calculated amount under paragraph (b)(1), (b)(1)(i), or (b)(1)(ii) of this section is equal to or greater than $5.00 but less than $10.00, in which case the borrower's monthly payment is $10.00.

(2) A borrower with eligible loans held by two or more loan holders must request income-based repayment from each loan holder if the borrower wants to repay all of his or her eligible loans under an income-based repayment plan. Each loan holder must apply the payment calculation rules in paragraphs (b)(1)(iii) and (iv) of this section to loans they hold.

(3) If a borrower elects an income-based repayment plan, the loan holder must, unless the borrower requests otherwise, require that all eligible loans owed by the borrower to that holder be repaid under the income-based repayment plan.

(4) If the borrower's monthly payment amount is not sufficient to pay the accrued interest on the borrower's subsidized Stafford Loans or the subsidized portion of the borrower's Federal Consolidation loan, the Secretary pays to the holder the remaining accrued interest for a period not to exceed three consecutive years from the established repayment period start date on each loan repaid under the income-based repayment plan. On a Consolidation Loan that repays loans on which the Secretary has paid accrued interest under this section, the three-year period includes the period for which the Secretary paid accrued interest on the underlying loans. The three-year period does not include any period during which the borrower receives an economic hardship deferment.

(5) Except as provided in paragraph (b)(4) of this section, accrued interest is capitalized at the time the borrower chooses to leave the income-based repayment plan or no longer has a partial financial hardship.

(6) If the borrower's monthly payment amount is not sufficient to pay any principal due, the payment of that principal is postponed until the borrower chooses to leave the income-based repayment plan or no longer has a partial financial hardship.

(7) The special allowance payment to a lender during the period in which the borrower has a partial financial hardship under an income-based repayment plan is calculated on the principal balance of the loan and any accrued interest unpaid by the borrower.

(8) The repayment period for a borrower under an income-based repayment plan may be greater than 10 years.

(c) *Payment application and prepayment.*

(1) The loan holder shall apply any payment made under an income-based repayment plan in the following order:

(i) Accrued interest.
(ii) Collection costs.
(iii) Late charges.
(iv) Loan principal.

(2) The borrower may prepay the whole or any part of a loan at any time without penalty.

(3) If the prepayment amount equals or exceeds a monthly payment amount of $10.00 or more under the repayment schedule established for the loan, the loan holder shall apply the prepayment consistent with the requirements of § 682.209(b)(2)(ii).

(4) If the prepayment amount exceeds the monthly payment amount of $0.00 under the repayment schedule established for the loan, the loan holder shall apply the prepayment consistent with the requirements of paragraph (c)(1) of this section.

(d) *Changes in the payment amount.*

(1) If a borrower no longer has a partial financial hardship, the borrower may continue to make payments under the income-based repayment plan but the loan holder must recalculate the borrower's monthly payment. The loan holder also recalculates the monthly payment for a borrower who chooses to stop making income-based payments. In either case, as a result of the recalculation—

(i) The maximum monthly amount that the loan holder may require the borrower to repay is the amount the borrower would have paid under the FFEL standard repayment plan based on a 10-year repayment period on the borrower's eligible loans that were outstanding at the time the borrower began repayment on the loans with that holder under the income-based repayment plan; and

(ii) The borrower's repayment period based on the recalculated payment amount may exceed 10 years.

(2) If a borrower no longer wishes to pay under the income-based repayment plan, the borrower must pay under the FFEL standard repayment plan and the loan holder recalculates the borrower's monthly payment based on—

(i) The time remaining under the maximum ten-year repayment period for the amount of the borrower's loans that were outstanding at the time the borrower discontinued paying under the income-based repayment plan; or

(ii) For a Consolidation Loan, the applicable repayment period remaining specified in § 682.209(h)(2) for the total amount of that loan and the balance of other student loans that was outstanding at the time the borrower discontinued paying under the income-based repayment plan.

(e) *Eligibility documentation and verification.*

(1) The loan holder determines whether a borrower has a partial financial hardship to qualify for the income-based repayment plan for the year the borrower elects the plan and for each subsequent year that the borrower remains on the plan. To make this determination, the loan holder requires the borrower to—

(i)(A) Provide written consent to the disclosure of AGI and other tax return information by the Internal Revenue Service to the loan holder. The borrower provides consent by signing a consent form and returning it to the loan holder;

(B) If the borrower's AGI is not available, or the loan holder believes that the borrower's reported AGI does not reasonably reflect the borrower's current income, the loan holder may use other documentation provided by the borrower to verify income; and

(ii) Annually certify the borrower's family size. If the borrower fails to certify family size, the loan holder must assume a family size of one for that year.

(2) The loan holder designates the repayment option described in paragraph (d)(1) of this section for any borrower who selects the income-based repayment plan but—

(i) Fails to renew the required written consent for income verification; or

(ii) Withdraws consent and does not select another repayment plan.

(f) *Loan forgiveness.*

(1) To qualify for loan forgiveness after 25 years, the borrower must have participated in the income-based repayment plan and satisfied at least one of the following conditions during that period—

(i) Made reduced monthly payments under a partial financial hardship as provided under paragraph (b)(1) of this section. Monthly payments of $0.00 qualify as reduced monthly payments as provided in paragraph (b)(1)(ii) of this section;

(ii) Made reduced monthly payments after the borrower no longer had a partial financial hardship or stopped making income-based payments as provided in paragraph (d)(1) of this section;

(iii) Made monthly payments under any repayment plan, that were not less than the amount required under the FFEL standard repayment plan described in § 682.209(a)(6)(vi) with a 10-year repayment period;
(iv) Made monthly payments under the FFEL standard repayment plan described in § 682.209(a)(6)(vi) based on a 10-year repayment period for the amount of the borrower's loans that were outstanding at the time the borrower first selected the income-based repayment plan; or
(v) Received an economic hardship deferment on eligible FFEL loans.
(2) As provided under paragraph (f)(4) of this section, the Secretary repays any outstanding balance of principal and accrued interest on FFEL loans for which the borrower qualifies for forgiveness if the guaranty agency determines that—
(i) The borrower made monthly payments under one or more of the repayment plans described in paragraph (f)(1) of this section, including a monthly amount of $0.00 as provided in paragraph (b)(1)(ii) of this section; and
(ii)(A) The borrower made those monthly payments each year for a 25-year period; or
(B) Through a combination of monthly payments and economic hardship deferments, the borrower made the equivalent of 25 years of payments.
(3) For a borrower who qualifies for the income-based repayment plan, the beginning date for the 25-year period is—
(i) For a borrower who has a FFEL Consolidation Loan, the date the borrower made a payment or received an economic hardship deferment on that loan, before the date the borrower qualified for income-based repayment. The beginning date is the date the borrower made the payment or received the deferment, but no earlier than July 1, 2009;
(ii) For a borrower who has one or more other eligible FFEL loans, the date the borrower made a payment or received an economic hardship deferment on that loan. The beginning date is the date the borrower made that payment or received the deferment on that loan, but no earlier than July 1, 2009;
(iii) For a borrower who did not make a payment or receive an economic hardship deferment on the loan under paragraph (f)(3)(i) or (ii) of this section, the date the borrower made a payment under the income-based repayment plan on the loan; or
(iv) If the borrower consolidates his or her eligible loans, the date the borrower made a payment on the FFEL Consolidation Loan that met the conditions in (f)(1) after qualifying for the income-based repayment plan.
(4) If a borrower satisfies the loan forgiveness requirements, the Secretary repays the outstanding balance and accrued interest on the FFEL Consolidation Loan described in paragraph (f)(3)(i), (iii), or (iv) of this section or other eligible FFEL loans described in paragraph (f)(3)(ii) or (iv) of this section.
(5) A borrower repaying a defaulted loan is not considered to be repaying under a qualifying repayment plan for the purpose of loan forgiveness, and any payments made on a defaulted loan are not counted toward the 25-year forgiveness period.

(g) *Loan forgiveness processing and payment.*
(1) No later than 60 days after the loan holder determines that a borrower qualifies for loan forgiveness under paragraph (f) of this section, the loan holder must request payment from the guaranty agency.
(2) If the loan holder requests payment from the guaranty agency later than the period specified in paragraph (g)(1) of this section, interest that accrues on the discharged amount after the expiration of the 60-day filing period is ineligible for reimbursement by the Secretary, and the holder must repay all interest and special allowance received on the discharged amount for periods after the expiration of the 60-day filing period. The holder cannot collect from the borrower any interest that is not paid by the Secretary under this paragraph.
(3)(i) Within 45 days of receiving the holder's request for payment, the guaranty agency must determine if the borrower meets the eligibility requirements for loan forgiveness under this section and must notify the holder of its determination.
(ii) If the guaranty agency approves the loan forgiveness, it must, within the same 45-day period required under paragraph (g)(3)(i) of this section, pay the holder the amount of the forgiveness.
(4) After being notified by the guaranty agency of its determination of the eligibility of the borrower for loan forgiveness, the holder must, within 30 days, inform the borrower of the determination and, if appropriate, that the borrower's repayment obligation on the loans for which income-based forgiveness was requested is satisfied. The lender must also provide the borrower with information on the required handling of the forgiveness amount.
(5)(i) The holder must apply the proceeds of the income-based repayment loan forgiveness amount to satisfy the outstanding balance on those loans for which income-based forgiveness was requested; or
(ii) If the forgiveness amount exceeds the outstanding balance on the eligible loans subject to forgiveness, the loan holder must refund the excess amount to the guaranty agency.
(6) If the guaranty agency does not pay the forgiveness claim, the lender will continue the borrower in repayment on the loan. The lender is deemed to have exercised forbearance of both principal and interest from the date the borrower's repayment obligation was suspended until a new payment due date is established. Unless the denial of the forgiveness claim was due to an error by the lender, the lender may capitalize any interest accrued and not paid during this period, in accordance with § 682.202(b).
(7) The loan holder must promptly return to the sender any payment received on a loan after the guaranty agency pays the loan holder the amount of loan forgiveness.

(Authority: 20 U.S.C. 1098e)

[73 Fed. Reg. 63249 (Oct. 23, 2008); 74 Fed. Reg. 55995 (Oct. 29, 2009)]

* * *

§ 682.402 Death, disability, closed school, false certification, unpaid refunds, and bankruptcy payments.

(a) *General.*
(1) Rules governing the payment of claims based on filing for relief in bankruptcy, and discharge of loans due to death, total and permanent disability, attendance at a school that closes, false certification by a school of a borrower's eligibility for a loan, and unpaid refunds by a school are set forth in this section.
(2) If a Consolidation loan was obtained jointly by a married couple, the amount of the Consolidation loan that is discharged if one of the borrowers dies or becomes totally and permanently disabled is equal to the portion of the outstanding balance of the Consolidation loan, as of the date the borrower died or became totally and permanently disabled, attributable to any of that borrower's loans that would have been eligible for discharge.
(3) If a PLUS loan was obtained by two parents as co-makers, and only one of the borrowers dies, becomes totally and permanently disabled, has collection of his or her loan obligation stayed by a bankruptcy filing, or has that obligation discharged in bankruptcy, the other borrower remains obligated to repay the loan unless that borrower would qualify for discharge of the loan under these regulations.
(4) Except for a borrower's loan obligation discharged by the Secretary under the false certification discharge provision of paragraph (e)(1)(ii) or (iii) of this section, a loan qualifies for payment under this section and as provided in paragraph (h)(1)(iv) of this section, only to the extent that the loan is legally enforceable under applicable law by the holder of the loan.
(5) For purposes of this section—
(i) The legal enforceability of a loan is conclusively determined on the basis of a ruling by a court or administrative tribunal

of competent jurisdiction with respect to that loan, or a ruling with respect to another loan in a judgment that collaterally estops the holder from contesting the enforceability of the loan;

(ii) A loan is conclusively determined to be legally unenforceable to the extent that the guarantor determines, pursuant to an objection presented in a proceeding conducted in connection with credit bureau reporting, tax refund offset, wage garnishment, or in any other administrative proceeding, that the loan is not legally enforceable; and

(iii) If an objection has been raised by the borrower or another party about the legal enforceability of the loan and no determination has been made under paragraph (a)(5)(i) or (ii) of this section, the Secretary may authorize the payment of a claim under this section under conditions the Secretary considers appropriate. If the Secretary determines in that or any other case that a claim was paid under this section with respect to a loan that was not a legally enforceable obligation of the borrower, the recipient of that payment must refund that amount of the payment to the Secretary.

(b) *Death.*

(1) If an individual borrower dies, or the student for whom a parent received a PLUS loan dies, the obligation of the borrower and any endorser to make any further payments on the loan is discharged.

(2) A discharge of a loan based on the death of the borrower (or student in the case of a PLUS loan) must be based on an original or certified copy of the death certificate, or an accurate and complete photocopy of the original or certified copy of the death certificate. Under exceptional circumstances and on a case-by-case basis, the chief executive officer of the guaranty agency may approve a discharge based upon other reliable documentation supporting the discharge request.

(3) After receiving reliable information indicating that the borrower (or student) has died, the lender must suspend any collection activity against the borrower and any endorser for up to 60 days and promptly request the documentation described in paragraph (b)(2) of this section. If additional time is required to obtain the documentation, the period of suspension of collection activity may be extended up to an additional 60 days. If the lender is not able to obtain an original or certified copy of the death certificate, or an accurate and complete photocopy of the original or certified copy of the death certificate or other documentation acceptable to the guaranty agency, under the provisions of paragraph (b)(2) of this section, during the period of suspension, the lender must resume collection activity from the point that it had been discontinued. The lender is deemed to have exercised forbearance as to repayment of the loan during the period when collection activity was suspended.

(4) Once the lender has determined under paragraph (b)(2) of this section that the borrower (or student) has died, the lender may not attempt to collect on the loan from the borrower's estate or from any endorser.

(5) The lender shall return to the sender any payments received from the estate or paid on behalf of the borrower after the date of the borrower's (or student's) death.

(6) In the case of a Federal Consolidation Loan that includes a Federal PLUS or Direct PLUS loan borrowed for a dependent who has died, the obligation of the borrower or any endorser to make any further payments on the portion of the outstanding balance of the Consolidation Loan attributable to the Federal PLUS or Direct PLUS loan is discharged as of the date of the dependent's death.

(c)(1) *Total and permanent disability.*

(i) A borrower's loan is discharged if the borrower becomes totally and permanently disabled, as defined in § 682.200(b), and satisfies the eligibility requirements in this section.

(ii) For a borrower who becomes totally and permanently disabled as described in paragraph (1) of the definition of that term in § 682.200(b), the borrower's loan discharge application is processed in accordance with paragraphs (c)(2) through (7) of this section.

(iii) For a veteran who is totally and permanently disabled as described in paragraph (2) of the definition of that term in § 682.200(b), the veteran's loan discharge application is processed in accordance with paragraph (c)(8) of this section.

(2) Discharge application process for a borrower who is totally and permanently disabled as described in paragraph (1) of the definition of that term in § 682.200(b). After being notified by the borrower or the borrower's representative that the borrower claims to be totally and permanently disabled, the lender promptly requests that the borrower or the borrower's representative submit a discharge application to the lender on a form approved by the Secretary. The application must contain a certification by a physician, who is a doctor of medicine or osteopathy legally authorized to practice in a State, that the borrower is totally and permanently disabled as described in paragraph (1) of the definition of that term in § 682.200(b). The borrower must submit the application to the lender within 90 days of the date the physician certifies the application. If the lender and guaranty agency approve the discharge claim under the procedures described in paragraph (c)(7) of this section, the guaranty agency must assign the loan to the Secretary.

(3) Secretary's eligibility determination.

(i) If, after reviewing the borrower's application, the Secretary determines that the certification provided by the borrower supports the conclusion that the borrower is totally and permanently disabled, as described in paragraph (1) of the definition of that term in § 682.200(b), the borrower is considered totally and permanently disabled as of the date the physician certifies the borrower's application.

(ii) Upon making a determination that the borrower is totally and permanently disabled as described in paragraph (1) of the definition of that term in § 682.200(b), the Secretary discharges the borrower's obligation to make further payments on the loan and notifies the borrower that the loan has been discharged. Any payments received after the date the physician certified the borrower's loan discharge application are returned to the person who made the payments on the loan. The notification to the borrower explains the terms and conditions under which the borrower's obligation to repay the loan will be reinstated, as specified in paragraph (c)(5)(i) of this section.

(iii) If the Secretary determines that the certification provided by the borrower does not support the conclusion that the borrower is totally and permanently disabled as described in paragraph (1) of the definition of that term in § 682.200(b), the Secretary notifies the borrower that the application for a disability discharge has been denied and that the loan is due and payable to the Secretary under the terms of the promissory note.

(iv) The Secretary reserves the right to require the borrower to submit additional medical evidence if the Secretary determines that the borrower's application does not conclusively prove that the borrower is totally and permanently disabled as described in paragraph (1) of the definition of that term in § 682.200(b). As part of the Secretary's review of the borrower's discharge application, the Secretary may arrange for an additional review of the borrower's condition by an independent physician at no expense to the borrower.

(4) Treatment of disbursements made during the period from the date of the physician's certification until the date of discharge. If a borrower received a Title IV loan or TEACH Grant prior to the date the physician certified the borrower's discharge application and a disbursement of that loan or grant is made during the period from the date of the physician's certification until the date the Secretary grants a discharge under this section, the processing of the borrower's loan discharge request will be suspended until the borrower ensures that the full amount of the disbursement has been returned to the loan holder or to the Secretary, as applicable.

(5) Conditions for reinstatement of a loan after a total and permanent disability discharge.
(i) The Secretary reinstates the borrower's obligation to repay a loan that was discharged in accordance with paragraph (c)(3)(ii) of this section if, within three years after the date the Secretary granted the discharge, the borrower—
(A) Has annual earnings from employment that exceed 100 percent of the poverty guideline for a family of two, as published annually by the United States Department of Health and Human Services pursuant to 42 U.S.C. 9902(2);
(B) Receives a new TEACH Grant or a new loan under the Perkins, FFEL, or Direct Loan programs, except for a FFEL or Direct Consolidation Loan that includes loans that were not discharged; or
(C) Fails to ensure that the full amount of any disbursement of a title IV loan or TEACH Grant received prior to the discharge date that is made during the three-year period following the discharge date is returned to the loan holder or to the Secretary, as applicable, within 120 days of the disbursement date.
(ii) If a borrower's obligation to repay a loan is reinstated, the Secretary—
(A) Notifies the borrower that the borrower's obligation to repay the loan has been reinstated; and
(B) Does not require the borrower to pay interest on the loan for the period from the date the loan was discharged until the date the borrower's obligation to repay the loan was reinstated.
(iii) The Secretary's notification under paragraph (c)(5)(ii)(A) of this section will include—
(A) The reason or reasons for the reinstatement;
(B) An explanation that the first payment due date on the loan following reinstatement will be no earlier than 60 days after the date of the notification of reinstatement; and
(C) Information on how the borrower may contact the Secretary if the borrower has questions about the reinstatement or believes that the obligation to repay the loan was reinstated based on incorrect information.
(6) Borrower's responsibilities after a total and permanent disability discharge. During the three-year period described in paragraph (c)(5)(i) of this section, the borrower or, if applicable, the borrower's representative must—
(i) Promptly notify the Secretary of any changes in address or phone number;
(ii) Promptly notify the Secretary if the borrower's annual earnings from employment exceed the amount specified in paragraph (c)(5)(i)(A) of this section; and

(iii) Provide the Secretary, upon request, with documentation of the borrower's annual earnings from employment.
(7) Lender and guaranty agency actions.
(i) After being notified by a borrower or a borrower's representative that the borrower claims to be totally and permanently disabled, the lender must continue collection activities until it receives either the certification of total and permanent disability from a physician or a letter from a physician stating that the certification has been requested and that additional time is needed to determine if the borrower is totally and permanently disabled as described in paragraph (1) of the definition of that term in § 682.200(b). Except as provided in paragraph (c)(7)(iii) of this section, after receiving the physician's certification or letter the lender may not attempt to collect from the borrower or any endorser.
(ii) The lender must submit a disability claim to the guaranty agency if the borrower submits a certification by a physician and the lender makes a determination that the certification supports the conclusion that the borrower is totally and permanently disabled as described in paragraph (1) of the definition of that term in § 682.200(b).
(iii) If the lender determines that a borrower who claims to be totally and permanently disabled is not totally and permanently disabled as described in paragraph (1) of the definition of that term in § 682.200(b), or if the lender does not receive the physician's certification of total and permanent disability within 60 days of the receipt of the physician's letter requesting additional time, as described in paragraph (c)(7)(i) of this section, the lender must resume collection of the loan and is deemed to have exercised forbearance of payment of both principal and interest from the date collection activity was suspended. The lender may capitalize, in accordance with § 682.202(b), any interest accrued and not paid during that period.
(iv) The guaranty agency must pay a claim submitted by the lender if the guaranty agency has reviewed the application and determined that it is complete and that it supports the conclusion that the borrower is totally and permanently disabled as described in paragraph (1) of the definition of that term in § 682.200(b).
(v) If the guaranty agency does not pay the disability claim, the guaranty agency must return the claim to the lender with an explanation of the basis for the agency's denial of the claim. Upon receipt of the returned claim, the lender must notify the borrower that the application for a disability discharge has been denied, provide the basis for the denial, and inform the borrower that the lender will resume collection

on the loan. The lender is deemed to have exercised forbearance of both principal and interest from the date collection activity was suspended until the first payment due date. The lender may capitalize, in accordance with § 682.202(b), any interest accrued and not paid during that period.
(vi) If the guaranty agency pays the disability claim, the lender must notify the borrower that—
(A) The loan will be assigned to the Secretary for determination of eligibility for a total and permanent disability discharge and that no payments are due on the loan; and
(B) If the Secretary discharges the loan based on a determination that the borrower is totally and permanently disabled as described in paragraph (1) of the definition of that term in § 682.200(b), the Secretary will reinstate the borrower's obligation to repay the loan if, within three years after the date the Secretary granted the discharge, the borrower—
(1) Receives annual earnings from employment that exceed 100 percent of the poverty guideline for a family of two, as published annually by the United States Department of Health and Human Services pursuant to 42 U.S.C. 9902(2);
(2) Receives a new TEACH Grant or a new title IV loan, except for a FFEL or Direct Consolidation Loan that includes loans that were not discharged; or
(3) Fails to ensure that the full amount of any disbursement of a title IV loan or TEACH Grant received prior to the discharge date that is made during the three-year period following the discharge date is returned to the loan holder or to the Secretary, as applicable, within 120 days of the disbursement date.
(vii) After receiving a claim payment from the guaranty agency, the lender must forward to the guaranty agency any payments subsequently received from or on behalf of the borrower.
(viii) The Secretary reimburses the guaranty agency for a disability claim paid to the lender after the agency pays the claim to the lender.
(ix) The guaranty agency must assign the loan to the Secretary after the guaranty agency pays the disability claim.
(8) Discharge application process for veterans who are totally and permanently disabled as described in paragraph (2) of the definition of that term in § 682.200(b)—
(i) *General.* After being notified by the veteran or the veteran's representative that the veteran claims to be totally and permanently disabled, the lender promptly re-

quests that the veteran or the veteran's representative submit a discharge application to the lender, on a form approved by the Secretary. The application must be accompanied by documentation from the Department of Veterans Affairs showing that the Department of Veterans Affairs has determined that the veteran is unemployable due to a service-connected disability. The veteran will not be required to provide any additional documentation related to the veteran's disability.

(ii) *Lender and guaranty agency actions.*

(A) After being notified by a veteran or a veteran's representative that the veteran claims to be totally and permanently disabled as described in paragraph (2) of the definition of that term in § 682.200(b), the lender must continue collection activities until it receives the veteran's completed loan discharge application with the required documentation from the Department of Veterans Affairs, as described in paragraph (8)(i) of this section. Except as provided in paragraph (c)(8)(ii)(C) of this section, the lender will not attempt to collect from the veteran or any endorser after receiving the veteran's discharge application and documentation from the Department of Veterans Affairs.

(B) If the veteran submits a completed loan discharge application and the required documentation from the Department of Veterans Affairs, and the documentation indicates that the veteran is totally and permanently disabled as described in paragraph (2) of the definition of that term in § 682.200(b), the lender must submit a disability claim to the guaranty agency.

(C) If the documentation from the Department of Veterans Affairs does not indicate that the veteran is totally and permanently disabled as described in paragraph (2) of the definition of that term in § 682.200(b), the lender—

(1) Must resume collection and is deemed to have exercised forbearance of payment of both principal and interest from the date collection activity was suspended. The lender may capitalize, in accordance with § 682.202(b), any interest accrued and not paid during that period.

(2) Must inform the veteran that he or she may reapply for a total and permanent disability discharge in accordance with the procedures described in § 682.402(c)(2) through (c)(7), if the documentation from the Department of Veterans Affairs does not indicate that the veteran is totally and permanently disabled as described in paragraph (2) of the definition of that term in § 682.200(b), but indicates that the veteran may be totally and permanently disabled as described in paragraph (1) of the definition of that term.

(D) If the documentation from the Department of Veterans Affairs indicates that the borrower is totally and permanently disabled as described in paragraph (2) of the definition of that term in § 682.200(b), the guaranty agency must submit a copy of the veteran's discharge application and supporting documentation to the Secretary, and must notify the veteran that the veteran's loan discharge request has been referred to the Secretary for a determination of discharge eligibility.

(E) If the documentation from the Department of Veterans Affairs does not indicate that the veteran is totally and permanently disabled as described in paragraph (2) of the definition of that term in § 682.200(b), the guaranty agency does not pay the disability claim and must return the claim to the lender with an explanation of the basis for the agency's denial of the claim. Upon receipt of the returned claim, the lender must notify the veteran that the application for a disability discharge has been denied, provide the basis for the denial, and inform the veteran that the lender will resume collection on the loan. The lender is deemed to have exercised forbearance of both principal and interest from the date collection activity was suspended until the first payment due date. The lender may capitalize, in accordance with § 682.202(b), any interest accrued and not paid during that period.

(F) If the Secretary determines, based on a review of the documentation from the Department of Veterans Affairs, that the veteran is totally and permanently disabled as described in paragraph (2) of the definition of that term in § 682.200(b), the Secretary notifies the guaranty agency that the veteran is eligible for a total and permanent disability discharge. Upon notification by the Secretary that the veteran is eligible for a discharge, the guaranty agency pays the disability discharge claim. Upon receipt of the claim payment from the guaranty agency, the lender notifies the veteran that the veteran's obligation to make any further payments on the loan has been discharged and returns to the person who made the payments on the loan any payments received on or after the effective date of the determination by the Department of Veterans Affairs that the veteran is unemployable due to a service-connected disability.

(G) If the Secretary determines, based on a review of the documentation from the Department of Veterans Affairs, that the veteran is not totally and permanently disabled as described in paragraph (2) of the definition of that term in § 682.200(b), the Secretary notifies the guaranty agency of this determination. Upon notification by the Secretary that the veteran is not eligible for a discharge, the guaranty agency and the lender must follow the procedures described in paragraph (c)(8)(ii)(E) of this section.

(H) The Secretary reimburses the guaranty agency for a disability claim paid to the lender after the agency pays the claim to the lender.

(d) *Closed school—*

(1) *General.*

(i) The Secretary reimburses the holder of a loan received by a borrower on or after January 1, 1986, and discharges the borrower's obligation with respect to the loan in accordance with the provisions of paragraph (d) of this section, if the borrower (or the student for whom a parent received a PLUS loan) could not complete the program of study for which the loan was intended because the school at which the borrower (or student) was enrolled, closed, or the borrower (or student) withdrew from the school not more than 90 days prior to the date the school closed. This 90-day period may be extended if the Secretary determines that exceptional circumstances related to a school's closing would justify an extension.

(ii) For purposes of the closed school discharge authorized by this section—

(A) A school's closure date is the date that the school ceases to provide educational instruction in all programs, as determined by the Secretary;

(B) The term "borrower" includes all endorsers on a loan; and

(C) A "school" means a school's main campus or any location or branch of the main campus, regardless of whether the school or its location or branch is considered eligible.

(2) *Relief available pursuant to discharge.*

(i) Discharge under paragraph (d) of this section relieves the borrower of an existing or past obligation to repay the loan and any charges imposed or costs incurred by the holder with respect to the loan that the borrower is, or was otherwise obligated to pay.

(ii) A discharge of a loan under paragraph (d) of this section qualifies the borrower for reimbursement of amounts paid voluntarily or through enforced collection on a loan obligation discharged under paragraph (d) of this section.

(iii) A borrower who has defaulted on a loan discharged under paragraph (d) of this section is not regarded as in default on the loan after discharge, and is eligible to receive assistance under the Title IV, HEA programs.

(iv) A discharge of a loan under paragraph (d) of this section must be reported by the loan holder to all credit reporting agencies to which the holder previously reported the status of the loan, so as to delete all adverse credit history assigned to the loan.

(3) *Borrower qualification for discharge.* Except as provided in paragraph (d)(8) of this section, in order to qualify for a discharge of a loan under paragraph (d) of this section, a borrower must submit a written request and sworn statement to the holder of the loan. The statement need not be notarized, but must be made by the borrower under the penalty of perjury, and, in the statement, the borrower must state—

(i) Whether the student has made a claim with respect to the school's closing with any third party, such as the holder of a performance bond or a tuition recovery program, and if so, the amount of any payment received by the borrower (or student) or credited to the borrower's loan obligation;

(ii) That the borrower (or the student for whom a parent received a PLUS loan)—

(A) Received, on or after January 1, 1986, the proceeds of any disbursement of a loan disbursed, in whole or in part, on or after January 1, 1986 to attend a school;

(B) Did not complete the educational program at that school because the school closed while the student was enrolled or on an approved leave of absence in accordance with § 682.605(c), or the student withdrew from the school not more than 90 days before the school closed; and

(C) Did not complete the program of study through a teach-out at another school or by transferring academic credits or hours earned at the closed school to another school;

(iii) That the borrower agrees to provide, upon request by the Secretary or the Secretary's designee, other documentation reasonably available to the borrower that demonstrates, to the satisfaction of the Secretary or the Secretary's designee, that the student meets the qualifications in paragraph (d) of this section; and

(iv) That the borrower agrees to cooperate with the Secretary or the Secretary's designee in enforcement actions in accordance with paragraph (d)(4) of this section, and to transfer any right to recovery against a third party in accordance with paragraph (d)(5) of this section.

(4) *Cooperation by borrower in enforcement actions.*

(i) In any judicial or administrative proceeding brought by the Secretary or the Secretary's designee to recover for amounts discharged under paragraph (d) of this section or to take other enforcement action with respect to the conduct on which those claims were based, a borrower who requests or receives a discharge under paragraph (d) of this section must cooperate with the Secretary or the Secretary's designee. At the request of the Secretary or the Secretary's designee, and upon the Secretary's or the Secretary's designee's tendering to the borrower the fees and costs as are customarily provided in litigation to reimburse witnesses, the borrower shall—

(A) Provide testimony regarding any representation made by the borrower to support a request for discharge; and

(B) Produce any documentation reasonably available to the borrower with respect to those representations and any sworn statement required by the Secretary with respect to those representations and documents.

(ii) The Secretary revokes the discharge, or denies the request for discharge, of a borrower who—

(A) Fails to provide testimony, sworn statements, or documentation to support material representations made by the borrower to obtain the discharge; or

(B) Provides testimony, a sworn statement, or documentation that does not support the material representations made by the borrower to obtain the discharge.

(5) *Transfer to the Secretary of borrower's right of recovery against third parties.*

(i) Upon discharge under paragraph (d) of this section, the borrower is deemed to have assigned to and relinquished in favor of the Secretary any right to a loan refund (up to the amount discharged) that the borrower (or student) may have by contract or applicable law with respect to the loan or the enrollment agreement for the program for which the loan was received, against the school, its principals, affiliates and their successors, its sureties, and any private fund, including the portion of a public fund that represents funds received from a private party.

(ii) The provisions of paragraph (d) of this section apply notwithstanding any provision of State law that would otherwise restrict transfer of such rights by the borrower (or student), limit or prevent a transferee from exercising those rights, or establish procedures or a scheme of distribution that would prejudice the Secretary's ability to recover on those rights.

(iii) Nothing in this section shall be construed as limiting or foreclosing the borrower's (or student's) right to pursue legal and equitable relief regarding disputes arising from matters otherwise unrelated to the loan discharged.

(6) *Guaranty agency responsibilities—*

(i) *Procedures applicable if a school closed on or after January 1, 1986, but prior to June 13, 1994.*

(A) If a borrower received a loan for attendance at a school with a closure date on or after January 1, 1986, but prior to June 13, 1994, the loan may be discharged in accordance with the procedures specified in paragraph (d)(6)(i) of this section.

(B) If a loan subject to paragraph (d) of this section was discharged in part in accordance with the Secretary's "Closed School Policy" as authorized by section IV of Bulletin 89-G-159, the guaranty agency shall initiate the discharge of the remaining balance of the loan not later than August 13, 1994.

(C) A guaranty agency shall review its records and identify all schools that appear to have closed on or after January 1, 1986 and prior to June 13, 1994, and shall identify the loans made to any borrower (or student) who appears to have been enrolled at the school on the school closure date or who withdrew not more than 90 days prior to the closure date.

(D) A guaranty agency shall notify the Secretary immediately if it determines that a school not previously known to have closed appears to have closed, and, within 30 days of making that determination, notify all lenders participating in its program to suspend collection efforts against individuals with respect to loans made for attendance at the closed school, if the student to whom (or on whose behalf) a loan was made, appears to have been enrolled at the school on the closing date, or withdrew not more than 90 days prior to the date the school appears to have closed. Within 30 days after receiving confirmation of the date of a school's closure from the Secretary, the agency shall—

(1) Notify all lenders participating in its program to mail a discharge application explaining the procedures and eligibility criteria for obtaining a discharge and an explanation of the information that must be included in the sworn statement (which may be combined) to all borrowers who may be eligible for a closed school discharge; and

(2) Review the records of loans that it holds, identify the loans made to any borrower (or student) who appears to have been enrolled at the school on the school closure date or who withdrew not more than 90 days prior to the closure date, and mail a discharge

application and an explanation of the information that must be included in the sworn statement (which may be combined) to the borrower. The application shall inform the borrower of the procedures and eligibility criteria for obtaining a discharge.

(E) If a loan identified under paragraph (d)(6)(i)(D)(2) of this section is held by the guaranty agency as a defaulted loan and the borrower's current address is known, the guaranty agency shall immediately suspend any efforts to collect from the borrower on any loan received for the program of study for which the loan was made (but may continue to receive borrower payments), and notify the borrower that the agency will provide additional information about the procedures for requesting a discharge after the agency has received confirmation from the Secretary that the school had closed.

(F) If a loan identified under paragraph (d)(6)(i)(D)(2) of this section is held by the guaranty agency as a defaulted loan and the borrower's current address is unknown, the agency shall, by June 13, 1995, further refine the list of borrowers whose loans are potentially subject to discharge under paragraph (d) of this section by consulting with representatives of the closed school, the school's licensing agency, accrediting agency, and other appropriate parties. Upon learning the new address of a borrower who would still be considered potentially eligible for a discharge, the guaranty agency shall, within 30 days after learning the borrower's new address, mail to the borrower a discharge application that meets the requirements of paragraph (d)(6)(i)(E) of this section.

(G) If the guaranty agency determines that a borrower identified in paragraph (d)(6)(i)(E) or (F) of this section has satisfied all of the conditions required for a discharge, the agency shall notify the borrower in writing of that determination within 30 days after making that determination.

(H) If the guaranty agency determines that a borrower identified in paragraph (d)(6)(i)(E) or (F) of this section does not qualify for a discharge, the agency shall notify the borrower in writing of that determination and the reasons for it within 30 days after the date the agency—

(1) Made that determination based on information available to the guaranty agency;

(2) Was notified by the Secretary that the school had not closed;

(3) Was notified by the Secretary that the school had closed on a date that was more than 90 days after the borrower (or student) withdrew from the school;

(4) Was notified by the Secretary that the borrower (or student) was ineligible for a closed school discharge for other reasons; or

(5) Received the borrower's completed application and sworn statement.

(I) If a borrower described in paragraph (d)(6)(i)(E) or (F) of this section fails to submit the written request and sworn statement described in paragraph (d)(3) of this section within 60 days of being notified of that option, the guaranty agency shall resume collection and shall be deemed to have exercised forbearance of payment of principal and interest from the date it suspended collection activity. The agency may capitalize, in accordance with § 682.202(b), any interest accrued and not paid during that period.

(J) A borrower's request for discharge may not be denied solely on the basis of failing to meet any time limits set by the lender, guaranty agency, or the Secretary.

(ii) *Procedures applicable if a school closed on or after June 13, 1994.*

(A) A guaranty agency shall notify the Secretary immediately whenever it becomes aware of reliable information indicating a school may have closed. The designated guaranty agency in the state in which the school is located shall promptly investigate whether the school has closed and, within 30 days after receiving information indicating that the school may have closed, report the results of its investigation to the Secretary concerning the date of the school's closure and whether a teach-out of the closed school's program was made available to students.

(B) If a guaranty agency determines that a school appears to have closed, it shall, within 30 days of making that determination, notify all lenders participating in its program to suspend collection efforts against individuals with respect to loans made for attendance at the closed school, if the student to whom (or on whose behalf) a loan was made, appears to have been enrolled at the school on the closing date, or withdrew not more than 90 days prior to the date the school appears to have closed. Within 30 days after receiving confirmation of the date of a school's closure from the Secretary, the agency shall—

(1) Notify all lenders participating in its program to mail a discharge application explaining the procedures and eligibility criteria for obtaining a discharge and an explanation of the information that must be included in the sworn statement (which may be combined) to all borrowers who may be eligible for a closed school discharge; and

(2) Review the records of loans that it holds, identify the loans made to any borrower (or student) who appears to have been enrolled at the school on the school closure date or who withdrew not more than 90 days prior to the closure date, and mail a discharge application and an explanation of the information that must be included in the sworn statement (which may be combined) to the borrower. The application shall inform the borrower of the procedures and eligibility criteria for obtaining a discharge.

(C) If a loan identified under paragraph (d)(6)(ii)(B)(2) of this section is held by the guaranty agency as a defaulted loan and the borrower's current address is known, the guaranty agency shall immediately suspend any efforts to collect from the borrower on any loan received for the program of study for which the loan was made (but may continue to receive borrower payments), and notify the borrower that the agency will provide additional information about the procedures for requesting a discharge after the agency has received confirmation from the Secretary that the school had closed.

(D) If a loan identified under paragraph (d)(6)(ii)(B)(2) of this section is held by the guaranty agency as a defaulted loan and the borrower's current address is unknown, the agency shall, within one year after identifying the borrower, attempt to locate the borrower and further determine the borrower's potential eligibility for a discharge under paragraph (d) of this section by consulting with representatives of the closed school, the school's licensing agency, accrediting agency, and other appropriate parties. Upon learning the new address of a borrower who would still be considered potentially eligible for a discharge, the guaranty agency shall, within 30 days after learning the borrower's new address, mail to the borrower a discharge application that meets the requirements of paragraph (d)(6)(ii)(B) of this section.

(E) If the guaranty agency determines that a borrower identified in paragraph (d)(6)(ii)(C) or (D) of this section has satisfied all of the conditions required for a discharge, the agency shall notify the borrower in writing of that determination within 30 days after making that determination.

(F) If the guaranty agency determines that a borrower identified in paragraph (d)(6)(ii)(C) or (D) of this section does not qualify for a discharge, the agency shall notify the borrower in writing of that determination and the reasons for it within 30 days after the date the agency—

(1) Made that determination based on information available to the guaranty agency;

(2) Was notified by the Secretary that the school had not closed;

(3) Was notified by the Secretary that the school had closed on a date that was more than 90 days after the borrower (or student) withdrew from the school;

(4) Was notified by the Secretary that the borrower (or student) was ineligible for a closed school discharge for other reasons; or

(5) Received the borrower's completed application and sworn statement.

(G) Upon receipt of a closed school discharge claim filed by a lender, the agency shall review the borrower's request and supporting sworn statement in light of information available from the records of the agency and from other sources, including other guaranty agencies, state authorities, and cognizant accrediting associations, and shall take the following actions—

(1) If the agency determines that the borrower satisfies the requirements for discharge under paragraph (d) of this section, it shall pay the claim in accordance with § 682.402(h) not later than 90 days after the agency received the claim; or

(2) If the agency determines that the borrower does not qualify for a discharge, the agency shall, not later than 90 days after the agency received the claim, return the claim to the lender with an explanation of the reasons for its determination.

(H) If a borrower fails to submit the written request and sworn statement described in paragraph (d)(3) of this section within 60 days of being notified of that option, the lender or guaranty agency shall resume collection and shall be deemed to have exercised forbearance of payment of principal and interest from the date it suspended collection activity. The lender or guaranty agency may capitalize, in accordance with § 682.202(b), any interest accrued and not paid during that period.

(I) A borrower's request for discharge may not be denied solely on the basis of failing to meet any time limits set by the lender, guaranty agency, or the Secretary.

(7) *Lender responsibilities.*

(i) A lender shall comply with the requirements prescribed in paragraph (d) of this section. In the absence of specific instructions from a guaranty agency or the Secretary, if a lender receives information from a source it believes to be reliable indicating that an existing or former borrower may be eligible for a loan discharge under paragraph (d) of this section, the lender shall immediately notify the guaranty agency, and suspend any efforts to collect from the borrower on any loan received for the program of study for which the loan was made (but may continue to receive borrower payments).

(ii) If the borrower fails to submit the written request and sworn statement described in paragraph (d)(3) of this section within 60 days after being notified of that option, the lender shall resume collection and shall be deemed to have exercised forbearance of payment of principal and interest from the date the lender suspended collection activity. The lender may capitalize, in accordance with § 682.202(b), any interest accrued and not paid during that period.

(iii) The lender shall file a closed school claim with the guaranty agency in accordance with § 682.402(g) no later than 60 days after the lender receives the borrower's written request and sworn statement described in paragraph (d)(3) of this section. If a lender receives a payment made by or on behalf of the borrower on the loan after the lender files a claim on the loan with the guaranty agency, the lender shall forward the payment to the guaranty agency within 30 days of its receipt. The lender shall assist the guaranty agency and the borrower in determining whether the borrower is eligible for discharge of the loan.

(iv) Within 30 days after receiving reimbursement from the guaranty agency for a closed school claim, the lender shall notify the borrower that the loan obligation has been discharged, and request that all credit bureaus to which it previously reported the status of the loan delete all adverse credit history assigned to the loan.

(v) Within 30 days after being notified by the guaranty agency that the borrower's request for a closed school discharge has been denied, the lender shall resume collection and notify the borrower of the reasons for the denial. The lender shall be deemed to have exercised forbearance of payment of principal and interest from the date the lender suspended collection activity, and may capitalize, in accordance with § 682.202(b), any interest accrued and not paid during that period.

(8) *Discharge without an application.* A borrower's obligation to repay an FFEL Program loan may be discharged without an application from the borrower if the—

(i) Borrower received a discharge on a loan pursuant to 34 CFR 674.33(g) under the Federal Perkins Loan Program, or 34 CFR 685.213 under the William D. Ford Federal Direct Loan Program; or

(ii) The Secretary or the guaranty agency, with the Secretary's permission, determines that the borrower qualifies for a discharge based on information in the Secretary or guaranty agency's possession.

(e) *False certification by a school of a student's eligibility to borrow and unauthorized disbursements—*

(1) *General.*

(i) The Secretary reimburses the holder of a loan received by a borrower on or after January 1, 1986, and discharges a current or former borrower's obligation with respect to the loan in accordance with the provisions of paragraph (e) of this section, if the borrower's (or the student for whom a parent received a PLUS loan) eligibility to receive the loan was falsely certified by an eligible school. On or after July 1, 2006, the Secretary reimburses the holder of a loan, and discharges a borrower's obligation with respect to the loan in accordance with the provisions of paragraph (e) of this section, if the borrower's eligibility to receive the loan was falsely certified as a result of a crime of identity theft. For purposes of a false certification discharge, the term "borrower" includes all endorsers on a loan. A student's or other individual's eligibility to borrow shall be considered to have been falsely certified by the school if the school—

(A) Certified the student's eligibility for a FFEL Program loan on the basis of ability to benefit from its training and the student did not meet the applicable requirements described in 34 CFR part 668 and section 484(d) of the Act, as applicable and as described in paragraph (e)(13) of this section; or

(B) Signed the borrower's name without authorization by the borrower on the loan application or promissory note.

(C) Certified the eligibility of an individual for an FFEL Program loan as a result of the crime of identity theft committed against the individual, as that crime is defined in § 682.402(e)(14).

(ii) The Secretary discharges the obligation of a borrower with respect to a loan disbursement for which the school, without the borrower's authorization, endorsed the borrower's loan check or authorization for electronic funds transfer, unless the student for whom the loan was made received the proceeds of the loan either by actual delivery of the loan funds or by a credit in the amount of the contested disbursement applied to charges owed to the school for that portion of the educational program completed by the student. However, the Secretary does not reimburse the lender with respect to any amount disbursed by means of a check bearing an unauthorized endorsement unless the school also executed the application or promissory note for that loan for the named borrower without that individual's consent.

(iii) If a loan was made as a result of the crime of identity theft that was committed by an employee or agent of the lender, or if at the time the loan was made, an employee or agent of the lender knew of the identity theft of the individual named as the borrower—

(A) The Secretary does not pay reinsurance, and does not reimburse the holder, for any amount disbursed on the loan; and

(B) Any amounts received by a holder as interest benefits and special allowance payments with respect to the loan must be refunded to the Secretary, as provided in paragraphs (e)(8)(ii)(B)(4) and (e)(10)(ii)(D) of this section.

(2) *Relief available pursuant to discharge.*

(i) Discharge under paragraph (e)(1)(i) of this section relieves the borrower of an existing or past obligation to repay the loan certified by the school, and any charges imposed or costs incurred by the holder with respect to the loan that the borrower is, or was, otherwise obligated to pay.

(ii) A discharge of a loan under paragraph (e) of this section qualifies the borrower for reimbursement of amounts paid voluntarily or through enforced collection on a loan obligation discharged under paragraph (e) of this section.

(iii) A borrower who has defaulted on a loan discharged under paragraph (e) of this section is not regarded as in default on the loan after discharge, and is eligible to receive assistance under the Title IV, HEA programs.

(iv) A discharge of a loan under paragraph (e) of this section is reported by the loan holder to all credit reporting agencies to which the holder previously reported the status of the loan, so as to delete all adverse or inaccurate credit history assigned to the loan.

(v) Discharge under paragraph (e)(1)(ii) of this section qualifies the borrower for relief only with respect to the amount of the disbursement discharged.

(3) *Borrower qualification for discharge.* Except as provided in paragraph (e)(14) of this section, to qualify for a discharge of a loan under paragraph (e) of this section, the borrower must submit to the holder of the loan a written request and a sworn statement. The statement need not be notarized, but must be made by the borrower under penalty of perjury, and, in the statement, the borrower must—

(i) State whether the student has made a claim with respect to the school's false certification with any third party, such as the holder of a performance bond or a tuition recovery program, and if so, the amount of any payment received by the borrower (or student) or credited to the borrower's loan obligation;

(ii) In the case of a borrower requesting a discharge based on defective testing of the student's ability to benefit, state that the borrower (or the student for whom a parent received a PLUS loan)—

(A) Received, on or after January 1, 1986, the proceeds of any disbursement of a loan disbursed, in whole or in part, on or after January 1, 1986 to attend a school; and

(B) Was admitted to that school on the basis of ability to benefit from its training and did not meet the applicable requirements for admission on the basis of ability to benefit as described in paragraph (e)(13) of this section;

(iii) In the case of a borrower requesting a discharge because the school signed the borrower's name on the loan application or promissory note—

(A) State that the signature on either of those documents was not the signature of the borrower; and

(B) Provide five different specimens of his or her signature, two of which must be not earlier or later than one year before or after the date of the contested signature;

(iv) In the case of a borrower requesting a discharge because the school, without authorization of the borrower, endorsed the borrower's name on the loan check or signed the authorization for electronic funds transfer or master check, the borrower shall—

(A) Certify that he or she did not endorse the loan check or sign the authorization for electronic funds transfer or master check, or authorize the school to do so;

(B) Provide five different specimens of his or her signature, two of which must be not earlier or later than one year before or after the date of the contested signature; and

(C) State that the proceeds of the contested disbursement were not received either through actual delivery of the loan funds or by a credit in the amount of the contested disbursement applied to charges owed to the school for that portion of the educational program completed by the student;

(v) In the case of an individual who is requesting a discharge of a loan because the individual's eligibility was falsely certified as a result of a crime of identity theft committed against the individual—

(A) Certify that the individual did not sign the promissory note, or that any other means of identification used to obtain the loan was used without the authorization of the individual claiming relief;

(B) Certify that the individual did not receive or benefit from the proceeds of the loan with knowledge that the loan had been made without the authorization of the individual;

(C) Provide a copy of a local, State, or Federal court verdict or judgment that conclusively determines that the individual who is named as the borrower of the loan was the victim of a crime of identify theft by a perpetrator named in the verdict or judgment;

(D) If the judicial determination of the crime does not expressly state that the loan was obtained as a result of the crime, provide—

(1) Authentic specimens of the signature of the individual, as provided in paragraph (e)(3)(iii)(B), or other means of identification of the individual, as applicable, corresponding to the means of identification falsely used to obtain the loan; and

(2) A statement of facts that demonstrate, to the satisfaction of the Secretary, that eligibility for the loan in question was falsely certified as a result of the crime of identity theft committed against that individual.

(vi) That the borrower agrees to provide upon request by the Secretary or the Secretary's designee, other documentation reasonably available to the borrower, that demonstrates, to the satisfaction of the Secretary or the Secretary's designee, that the student meets the qualifications in paragraph (e) of this section; and

(vii) That the borrower agrees to cooperate with the Secretary or the Secretary's designee in enforcement actions in accordance with paragraph (e)(4) of this section, and to transfer any right to recovery against a third party in accordance with paragraph (e)(5) of this section.

(4) *Cooperation by borrower in enforcement actions.*

(i) In any judicial or administrative proceeding brought by the Secretary or the Secretary's designee to recover for amounts discharged under paragraph (e) of this section or to take other enforcement action with respect to the conduct on which those claims were based, a borrower who requests or receives a discharge under paragraph (e) of this section must cooperate with the Secretary or the Secretary's designee. At the request of the Secretary or the Secretary's designee, and upon the Secretary's or the Secretary's designee's tendering to the borrower the fees and costs as are customarily provided in litigation to reimburse witnesses, the borrower shall—

(A) Provide testimony regarding any representation made by the borrower to support a request for discharge; and

(B) Produce any documentation reasonably available to the borrower with respect to those representations and any sworn statement required by the Secretary with respect to those representations and documents.

(ii) The Secretary revokes the discharge, or denies the request for discharge, of a borrower who—

(A) Fails to provide testimony, sworn statements, or documentation to support material representations made by the borrower to obtain the discharge; or

(B) Provides testimony, a sworn statement, or documentation that does not support the material representations made by the borrower to obtain the discharge.

(5) *Transfer to the Secretary of borrower's right of recovery against third parties.*

(i) Upon discharge under paragraph (e) of this section, the borrower is deemed to have assigned to and relinquished in favor of the Secretary any right to a loan refund (up to the amount discharged) that the borrower (or student) may have by contract or applicable law with respect to the loan or the enrollment agreement for the program for which the loan was received, against the school, its principals, affiliates and their successors, its sureties, and any private fund, including the portion of a public fund that represents funds received from a private party.

(ii) The provisions of paragraph (e) of this section apply notwithstanding any provision of state law that would otherwise restrict transfer of such rights by the borrower (or student), limit or prevent a transferee from exercising those rights, or establish procedures or a scheme of distribution that would prejudice the Secretary's ability to recover on those rights.

(iii) Nothing in this section shall be construed as limiting or foreclosing the borrower's (or student's) right to pursue legal and equitable relief regarding disputes arising from matters otherwise unrelated to the loan discharged.

(6) *Guaranty agency responsibilities—general.*

(i) A guaranty agency shall notify the Secretary immediately whenever it becomes aware of reliable information indicating that a school may have falsely certified a student's eligibility or caused an unauthorized disbursement of loan proceeds, as described in paragraph (e)(3) of this section. The designated guaranty agency in the state in which the school is located shall promptly investigate whether the school has falsely certified a student's eligibility and, within 30 days after receiving information indicating that the school may have done so, report the results of its preliminary investigation to the Secretary.

(ii) If the guaranty agency receives information it believes to be reliable indicating that a borrower whose loan is held by the agency may be eligible for a discharge under paragraph (e) of this section, the agency shall immediately suspend any efforts to collect from the borrower on any loan received for the program of study for which the loan was made (but may continue to receive borrower payments), and inform the borrower of the procedures for requesting a discharge.

(iii) If the borrower fails to submit the written request and sworn statement described in paragraph (e)(3) of this section within 60 days of being notified of that option, the guaranty agency shall resume collection and shall be deemed to have exercised forbearance of payment of principal and interest from the date it suspended collection activity. The agency may capitalize, in accordance with § 682.202(b), any interest accrued and not paid during that period.

(iv) Upon receipt of a discharge claim filed by a lender or a request submitted by a borrower with respect to a loan held by the guaranty agency, the agency shall have up to 90 days to determine whether the discharge should be granted. The agency shall review the borrower's request and supporting sworn statement in light of information available from the records of the agency and from other sources, including other guaranty agencies, state authorities, and cognizant accrediting associations.

(v) A borrower's request for discharge and sworn statement may not be denied solely on the basis of failing to meet any time limits set by the lender, the Secretary or the guaranty agency.

(7) *Guaranty agency responsibilities with respect to a claim filed by a lender based on the borrower's assertion that he or she did not sign the loan application or the promissory note that he or she was a victim of the crime of identity theft, or that the school failed to test, or improperly tested, the student's ability to benefit.*

(i) The agency shall evaluate the borrower's request and consider relevant information it possesses and information available from other sources, and follow the procedures described in paragraph (e)(7) of this section.

(ii) If the agency determines that the borrower satisfies the requirements for discharge under paragraph (e) of this section, it shall, not later than 30 days after the agency makes that determination, pay the claim in accordance with § 682.402(h) and—

(A) Notify the borrower that his or her liability with respect to the amount of the loan has been discharged, and that the lender has been informed of the actions required under paragraph (e)(7)(ii)(C) of this section;

(B) Refund to the borrower all amounts paid by the borrower to the lender or the agency with respect to the discharged loan amount, including any late fees or collection charges imposed by the lender or agency related to the discharged loan amount; and

(C) Notify the lender that the borrower's liability with respect to the amount of the loan has been discharged, and that the lender must—

(1) Immediately terminate any collection efforts against the borrower with respect to the discharged loan amount and any charges imposed or costs incurred by the lender related to the discharged loan amount that the borrower is, or was, otherwise obligated to pay; and

(2) Within 30 days, report to all credit reporting agencies to which the lender previously reported the status of the loan, so as to delete all adverse credit history assigned to the loan; and

(D) Within 30 days, demand payment in full from the perpetrator of the identity theft committed against the individual, and if payment is not received, pursue collection action thereafter against the perpetrator.

(iii) If the agency determines that the borrower does not qualify for a discharge, it shall, within 30 days after making that determination—

(A) Notify the lender that the borrower's liability on the loan is not discharged and that, depending on the borrower's decision under paragraph (e)(7)(iii)(B) of this section, the loan shall either be returned to the lender or paid as a default claim; and

(B) Notify the borrower that the borrower does not qualify for discharge, and state the reasons for that conclusion. The agency shall advise the borrower that he or she remains obligated to repay the loan and warn the borrower of the consequences of default, and explain that the borrower will be considered to be in default on the loan unless the borrower submits a written statement to the agency within 30 days stating that the borrower—

(1) Acknowledges the debt and, if payments are due, will begin or resume making those payments to the lender; or

(2) Requests the Secretary to review the agency's decision.

(iv) Within 30 days after receiving the borrower's written statement described in paragraph (e)(7)(iii)(B)(1) of this section, the agency shall return the claim file to the lender and notify the lender to resume collection efforts if payments are due.

(v) Within 30 days after receiving the borrower's request for review by the Secretary, the agency shall forward the claim file to the Secretary for his review and take the actions required under paragraph (e)(11) of this section.

(vi) The agency shall pay a default claim to the lender within 30 days after the borrower fails to return either of the written statements described in paragraph (e)(7)(iii)(B) of this section.

(8) *Guaranty agency responsibilities with respect to a claim filed by a lender based only on the borrower's assertion that he or she did not sign the loan check or the authorization for the release of loan funds via electronic funds transfer or master check.*

(i) The agency shall evaluate the borrower's request and consider relevant information it possesses and information available from other sources, and follow the procedures described in paragraph (e)(8) of this section.

(ii) If the agency determines that a borrower who asserts that he or she did not endorse the loan check satisfies the requirements for discharge under paragraph (e)(3)(iv) of this section, it shall, within 30 days after making that determination—

(A) Notify the borrower that his or her liability with respect to the amount of the contested disbursement of the loan has been discharged, and that the lender has been informed of the actions required under paragraph (e)(8)(ii)(B) of this section;

(B) Notify the lender that the borrower's liability with respect to the amount of the contested disbursement of the loan has been discharged, and that the lender must—

(1) Immediately terminate any collection efforts against the borrower with respect to the discharged loan amount and any charges imposed or costs incurred by the lender related to the discharged loan amount that the borrower is, or was, otherwise obligated to pay;

(2) Within 30 days, report to all credit reporting agencies to which the lender previously reported the status of the loan, so as to delete all adverse credit history assigned to the loan;

(3) Refund to the borrower, within 30 days, all amounts paid by the borrower with respect to the loan disbursement that was discharged, including any charges imposed or costs incurred by the lender related to the discharged loan amount; and

(4) Refund to the Secretary, within 30 days, all interest benefits and special allowance payments received from the Secretary with respect to the loan disbursement that was discharged; and

(C) Transfer to the lender the borrower's written assignment of any rights the borrower may have against third parties with respect to a loan disbursement that was discharged because the borrower did not sign the loan check.

(iii) If the agency determines that a borrower who asserts that he or she did not sign the electronic funds transfer or master check authorization satisfies the requirements for discharge under paragraph (e)(3)(iv) of this section, it shall, within 30 days after making that determination, pay the claim in accordance with § 682.402(h) and—

(A) Notify the borrower that his or her liability with respect to the amount of the contested disbursement of the loan has been discharged, and that the lender has been informed of the actions required under paragraph (e)(8)(iii)(C) of this section;

(B) Refund to the borrower all amounts paid by the borrower to the lender or the agency with respect to the discharged loan amount, including any late fees or collection charges imposed by the lender or agency related to the discharged loan amount; and

(C) Notify the lender that the borrower's liability with respect to the contested disbursement of the loan has been discharged, and that the lender must—

(1) Immediately terminate any collection efforts against the borrower with respect to the discharged loan amount and any charges imposed or costs incurred by the lender related to the discharged loan amount that the borrower is, or was, otherwise obligated to pay; and

(2) Within 30 days, report to all credit reporting agencies to which the lender previously reported the status of the loan, so as to delete all adverse credit history assigned to the loan.

(iv) If the agency determines that the borrower does not qualify for a discharge, it shall, within 30 days after making that determination—

(A) Notify the lender that the borrower's liability on the loan is not discharged and that, depending on the borrower's decision under paragraph (e)(8)(iv)(B) of this section, the loan shall either be returned to the lender or paid as a default claim; and

(B) Notify the borrower that the borrower does not qualify for discharge, and state the reasons for that conclusion. The agency shall advise the borrower that he or she remains obligated to repay the loan and warn the borrower of the consequences of default, and explain that the borrower will be considered to be in default on the loan unless the borrower submits a written statement to the agency within 30 days stating that the borrower—

(1) Acknowledges the debt and, if payments are due, will begin or resume making those payments to the lender; or

(2) Requests the Secretary to review the agency's decision.

(v) Within 30 days after receiving the borrower's written statement described in paragraph (e)(8)(iv)(B)(1) of this section, the agency shall return the claim file to the lender and notify the lender to resume collection efforts if payments are due.

(vi) Within 30 days after receiving the borrower's request for review by the Secretary, the agency shall forward the claim file to the Secretary for his review and take the actions required under paragraph (e)(11) of this section.

(vii) The agency shall pay a default claim to the lender within 30 days after the borrower fails to return either of the written statements described in paragraph (e)(8)(iv)(B) of this section.

(9) *Guaranty agency responsibilities in the case of a loan held by the agency for which a discharge request is submitted by a borrower based on the borrower's assertion that he or she did not sign the loan application or the promissory note, that he or she was a victim of the crime of identity theft, or that the school failed to test, or improperly tested, the student's ability to benefit.*

(i) The agency shall evaluate the borrower's request and consider relevant information it possesses and information available from other sources, and follow the procedures described in paragraph (e)(9) of this section.

(ii) If the agency determines that the borrower satisfies the requirements for discharge under paragraph (e)(3) of this section, it shall immediately terminate any collection efforts against the borrower with respect to the discharged loan amount and any charges imposed or costs incurred by the agency related to the discharged loan amount that the borrower is, or was otherwise obligated to pay and, not later than 30 days after the agency makes the determination that the borrower satisfies the requirements for discharge—

(A) Notify the borrower that his or her liability with respect to the amount of the loan has been discharged;

(B) Report to all credit reporting agencies to which the agency previously reported the status of the loan, so as to delete all adverse credit history assigned to the loan;

(C) Refund to the borrower all amounts paid by the borrower to the lender or the agency with respect to the discharged loan amount, including any late fees or collection charges imposed by the lender or agency related to the discharged loan amount; and

(D) Within 30 days, demand payment in full from the perpetrator of the identity theft committed against the individual, and if payment is not received, pursue collection action thereafter against the perpetrator.

(iii) If the agency determines that the borrower does not qualify for a discharge, it shall, within 30 days after making that determination, notify the borrower that the borrower's liability with respect to the amount of the loan is not discharged, state the reasons for that conclusion, and if the borrower is not then making payments in accordance with a repayment arrangement with the agency on the loan, advise the borrower of the consequences of continued failure to reach such an arrangement, and that collection action will resume on the loan unless within 30 days the borrower—

(A) Acknowledges the debt and, if payments are due, reaches a satisfactory arrangement to repay the loan or resumes making payments under such an arrangement to the agency; or

(B) Requests the Secretary to review the agency's decision.

(iv) Within 30 days after receiving the borrower's request for review by the Secretary, the agency shall forward the borrower's discharge request and all relevant documentation to the Secretary for his review and take the actions required under paragraph (e)(11) of this section.

(v) The agency shall resume collection action if within 30 days of giving notice of its determination the borrower fails to seek review by the Secretary or agree to repay the loan.

(10) *Guaranty agency responsibilities in the case of a loan held by the agency for which a discharge request is submitted by a borrower based only on the borrower's assertion that he or she did not sign the loan check or the authorization for the release of loan proceeds via electronic funds transfer or master check.*

(i) The agency shall evaluate the borrower's request and consider relevant information it possesses and information available from other sources, and follow the procedures described in paragraph (e)(10) of this section.

(ii) If the agency determines that a borrower who asserts that he or she did not endorse the loan check satisfies the requirements for discharge under paragraph (e)(3)(iv) of this section, it shall refund to the Secretary the amount of reinsurance payment received with respect to the amount discharged on that loan less any repayments made by the lender under paragraph (e)(10)(ii)(D)(2) of this section, and within 30 days after making that determination—

(A) Notify the borrower that his or her liability with respect to the amount of the contested disbursement of the loan has been discharged;

(B) Report to all credit reporting agencies to which the agency previously reported the status of the loan, so as to delete all adverse credit history assigned to the loan;

(C) Refund to the borrower all amounts paid by the borrower to the lender or the agency with respect to the discharged loan amount, including any late fees or collection charges imposed by the lender or agency related to the discharged loan amount;

(D) Notify the lender to whom a claim payment was made that the lender must refund to the Secretary, within 30 days—

(1) All interest benefits and special allowance payments received from the Secretary with respect to the loan disbursement that was discharged; and

(2) The amount of the borrower's payments that were refunded to the borrower by the guaranty agency under paragraph (e)(10)(ii)(C) of this section that represent borrower payments previously paid to the lender with respect to the loan disbursement that was discharged;

(E) Notify the lender to whom a claim payment was made that the lender must, within 30 days, reimburse the agency for the amount of the loan that was discharged, minus the amount of borrower payments made to the lender that were refunded to the borrower by the guaranty agency under paragraph (e)(10)(ii)(C) of this section; and

(F) Transfer to the lender the borrower's written assignment of any rights the borrower may have against third parties with respect to the loan disbursement that was discharged.

(iii) In the case of a borrower who requests a discharge because he or she did not sign the electronic funds transfer or master check authorization, if the agency determines that the borrower meets the conditions for discharge, it shall immediately terminate any collection efforts against the borrower with respect to the discharged loan amount and any charges imposed or costs incurred by the agency related to the discharged loan amount that the borrower is, or was, otherwise obligated to pay, and within 30 days after making that determination—

(iv) The agency shall take the actions required under paragraphs (e)(9)(iii) through (v) if the agency determines that the borrower does not qualify for a discharge.

(11) *Guaranty agency responsibilities if a borrower requests a review by the Secretary.*

(i) Within 30 days after receiving the borrower's request for review under paragraph (e)(7)(iii)(B)(2), (e)(8)(iv)(B)(2), (e)(9)(iii)(B), or (e)(10)(iv) of this section, the agency shall forward the borrower's discharge request and all relevant documentation to the Secretary for his review.

(ii) The Secretary notifies the agency and the borrower of a determination on review. If the Secretary determines that the borrower is not eligible for a discharge under paragraph (e) of this section, within 30 days after being so informed, the agency shall take the actions described in paragraphs (e)(8)(iv) through (vii) or (e)(9)(iii) through (v) of this section, as applicable.

(iii) If the Secretary determines that the borrower meets the requirements for a discharge under paragraph (e) of this section, the agency shall, within 30 days after being so informed, take the actions required under paragraph (e)(7)(ii), (e)(8)(ii), (e)(8)(iii), (e)(9)(ii), (e)(10)(ii), or (e)(10)(iii) of this section, as applicable.

(12) *Lender Responsibilities.*

(i) If the lender is notified by a guaranty agency or the Secretary, or receives information it believes to be reliable from another source indicating that a current or former borrower may be eligible for a discharge under paragraph (e) of this section, the lender shall immediately suspend any efforts to collect from the borrower on any loan received for the program of study for which the loan was made (but may continue to receive borrower payments) and, within 30 days of receiving the information or notification, inform the borrower of the procedures for requesting a discharge.

(ii) If the borrower fails to submit the written request and sworn statement described in paragraph (e)(3) of this section within 60 days of being notified of that option, the lender shall resume collection and shall be deemed to have exercised forbearance of payment of principal and interest from the date the lender suspended collection activity. The lender may capitalize, in accordance with § 682.202(b), any interest accrued and not paid during that period.

(iii) The lender shall file a claim with the guaranty agency in accordance with § 682.402(g) no later than 60 days after the lender receives the borrower's written request and sworn statement described in paragraph (e)(3) of this section. If a lender receives a payment made by or on behalf of the borrower on the loan after the lender files a claim on the loan with the guaranty agency, the lender shall forward the payment to the guaranty agency within 30 days of its receipt. The lender shall assist the guaranty agency and the borrower in determining whether the borrower is eligible for discharge of the loan.

(iv) The lender shall comply with all instructions received from the Secretary or a guaranty agency with respect to loan discharges under paragraph (e) of this section.

(v) The lender shall review a claim that the borrower did not endorse and did not receive the proceeds of a loan check. The lender shall take the actions required under paragraphs (e)(8)(ii)(A) and (B) of this section if it determines that the borrower did not endorse the loan check, unless the lender secures persuasive evidence that the proceeds of the loan were received by the borrower or the student for whom the loan was made, as provided in paragraph (e)(1)(ii). If the lender determines that the loan check was properly endorsed or the proceeds were received by the borrower or student, the lender may consider the borrower's objection to repayment as a statement of intention not to repay the loan, and may file a claim with the guaranty agency for reimbursement on that ground, but shall not report the loan to credit bureaus as in default until the guaranty agency, or, as applicable, the Secretary, reviews the claim for relief. By filing such a claim, the lender shall be deemed to have agreed to the following—

(A) If the guarantor or the Secretary determines that the borrower endorsed the loan check or the proceeds of the loan were received by the borrower or the student, any failure to satisfy due diligence requirements by the lender prior to the filing of the claim that would have resulted in the loss of reinsurance on the loan in the event of default will be waived by the Secretary; and

(B) If the guarantor or the Secretary determines that the borrower did not endorse the loan check and that the proceeds of the loan were not received by the borrower or the student, the lender will comply with the requirements specified in paragraph (e)(8)(ii)(B) of this section.

(vi) Within 30 days after being notified by the guaranty agency that the borrower's request for a discharge has been denied, the lender shall notify the borrower of the reasons for the denial and, if payments are due, resume collection against the borrower. The lender shall be deemed to have exercised forbearance of payment of principal and interest from the date the lender suspended collection activity, and may capitalize, in accordance with § 682.202(b), any interest accrued and not paid during that period.

(13) *Requirements for certifying a borrower's eligibility for a loan.*

(i) For periods of enrollment beginning between July 1, 1987 and June 30, 1991, a student who had a general education diploma or received one before the scheduled completion of the program of instruction is deemed to have the ability to benefit from the training offered by the school.

(ii) A student not described in paragraph (e)(13)(i) of this section is considered to have the ability to benefit from training offered by the school if the student—

(A) For periods of enrollment beginning prior to July 1, 1987, was determined to have the ability to benefit from the school's training in accordance with the requirements of 34 CFR 668.6, as in existence at the time the determination was made;

(B) For periods of enrollment beginning between July 1, 1987 and June 30, 1996, achieved a passing grade on a test—

(1) Approved by the Secretary, for periods of enrollment beginning on or after July 1, 1991, or by the accrediting agency, for other periods; and

(2) Administered substantially in accordance with the requirements for use of the test;

(C) Successfully completed a program of developmental or remedial education provided by the school; or

(D) For periods of enrollment beginning on or after July 1, 1996 through June 30, 2000—

(1) Obtained, within 12 months before the date the student initially receives title IV, HEA program assistance, a passing score specified by the Secretary on an independently administered test in accordance with subpart J of 34 CFR part 668; or

(2) Enrolled in an eligible institution that participates in a State process approved by the Secretary under subpart J of 34 CFR part 668.

(E) For periods of enrollment beginning on or after July 1, 2000—

(1) Met either of the conditions described in paragraph (e)(13)(ii)(D) of this section; or

(2) Was home schooled and met the requirements of 34 CFR 668.32(e)(4).

(iii) Notwithstanding paragraphs (e)(13)(i) and (ii) of this section, a student did not have the ability to benefit from training offered by the school if—

(A) The school certified the eligibility of the student for a FFEL Program loan; and

(B) At the time of certification, the student would not meet the requirements for employment (in the student's State of residence) in the occupation for which the training program supported by the loan was intended because of a physical or mental condition, age, or criminal record or other reason accepted by the Secretary.

(iv) Notwithstanding paragraphs (e)(13)(i) and (ii) of this section, a student has the ability to benefit from the training offered by the school if the student received a high school diploma or its recognized equivalent prior to enrollment at the school.

(14) *Identity theft.*

(i) The unauthorized use of the identifying information of another individual that is punishable under 18 U.S.C. 1028, 1029, or 1030, or substantially comparable State or local law.

(ii) Identifying information includes, but is not limited to—

(A) Name, Social Security number, date of birth, official State or government issued driver's license or identification number, alien registration number, government passport number, and employer or taxpayer identification number;

(B) Unique biometric data, such as fingerprints, voiceprint, retina or iris image, or unique physical representation;

(C) Unique electronic identification number, address, or routing code; or

(D) Telecommunication identifying information or access device (as defined in 18 U.S.C. 1029(e)).

(15) *Discharge without an application.* A borrower's obligation to repay all or a portion of an FFEL Program loan may be discharged without an application from the borrower if the Secretary, or the guaranty agency with the Secretary's permission, determines that the borrower qualifies for a discharge based on information in the Secretary or guaranty agency's possession.

(f) *Bankruptcy*—

(1) *General.* If a borrower files a petition for relief under the Bankruptcy Code, the Secretary reimburses the holder of the loan for unpaid principal and interest on the loan in accordance with paragraphs (h) through (k) of this section.

(2) *Suspension of collection activity.*

(i) If the lender is notified that a borrower has filed a petition for relief in bankruptcy, the lender must immediately suspend any collection efforts outside the bankruptcy proceeding against the borrower and—

(A) Must suspend any collection efforts against any co-maker or endorser if the borrower has filed for relief under Chapters 12 or 13 of the Bankruptcy Code; or

(B) May suspend any collection efforts against any co-maker or endorser if the borrower has filed for relief under Chapters 7 or 11 of the Bankruptcy Code.

(ii) If the lender is notified that a co-maker or endorser has filed a petition for relief in bankruptcy, the lender must immediately suspend any collection efforts outside the bankruptcy proceeding against the co-maker or endorser and—

(A) Must suspend collection efforts against the borrower and any other parties to the note if the co-maker or endorser has filed for relief under Chapters 12 or 13 of the Bankruptcy Code; or

(B) May suspend any collection efforts against the borrower and any other parties to the note if the co-maker or endorser has filed for relief under Chapters 7 or 11 of the Bankruptcy Code.

(3) *Determination of filing.* The lender must determine that a borrower has filed a petition for relief in bankruptcy on the basis of receiving a notice of the first meeting of creditors or other proof of filing provided by the debtor's attorney or the bankruptcy court.

(4) *Proof of claim.*

(i) Except as provided in paragraph (f)(4)(ii) of this section, the holder of the loan shall file a proof of claim with the bankruptcy court within—

(A) 30 days after the holder receives a notice of first meeting of creditors unless, in the case of a proceeding under chapter 7, the notice states that the borrower has no assets; or

(B) 30 days after the holder receives a notice from the court stating that a chapter 7 no-asset case has been converted to an asset case.

(ii) A guaranty agency that is a state guaranty agency, and on that basis may assert immunity from suit in bankruptcy court, and that does not assign any loans affected by a bankruptcy filing to another guaranty agency—

(A) Is not required to file a proof of claim on a loan already held by the guaranty agency; and

(B) May direct lenders not to file proofs of claim on loans guaranteed by that agency.

(5) *Filing of bankruptcy claim with the guaranty agency.*

(i) The lender shall file a bankruptcy claim on the loan with the guaranty agency in accordance with paragraph (g) of this section, if—

(A) The borrower has filed a petition for relief under Chapters 12 or 13 of the Bankruptcy Code; or

(B) The borrower has filed a petition for relief under Chapters 7 or 11 of the Bankruptcy Code before October 8, 1998 and the loan has been in repayment for more than seven years (exclusive of any applicable suspension of the repayment period) from the due date of the first payment until the date of the filing of the petition for relief; or

(C) The borrower has begun an action to have the loan obligation determined to be dischargeable on grounds of undue hardship.

(ii) In cases not described in paragraph (f)(5)(i) of this section, the lender shall continue to hold the loan notwithstanding the bankruptcy proceeding. Once the bankruptcy proceeding is completed or dismissed, the lender shall treat the loan as if the lender had exercised forbearance as to repayment of principal and interest accrued from the date of the borrower's filing of the bankruptcy petition until the date the lender is notified that the bankruptcy proceeding is completed or dismissed.

(g) *Claim procedures for a loan held by a lender—*

(1) *Documentation.* A lender shall provide the guaranty agency with the following documentation when filing a death, disability, closed school, false certification, or bankruptcy claim:

(i) The original or a true and exact copy of the promissory note.

(ii) The loan application, if a separate loan application was provided to the lender.

(iii) In the case of a death claim, an original or certified death certificate, or other documentation supporting the discharge request that formed the basis for the determination of death.

(iv) In the case of a disability claim, a copy of the certification of disability described in paragraph (c)(2) of this section.

(v) In the case of a bankruptcy claim—

(A) Evidence that a bankruptcy petition has been filed, all pertinent documents sent to or received from the bankruptcy court by the lender, and an assignment to the guaranty agency of any proof of claim filed by the lender regarding the loan; and

(B) A statement of any facts of which the lender is aware that may form the basis for an objection or exception to the discharge of the borrower's loan obligation in bankruptcy and all documents supporting those facts.

(vi) In the case of a closed school claim, the documentation described in paragraph (d)(3) of this section, or any other documentation as the Secretary may require;

(vii) In the case of a false certification claim, the documentation described in paragraph (e)(3) of this section.

(2) *Filing deadlines.* A lender shall file a death, disability, closed school, false certification, or bankruptcy claim within the following periods:

(i) Within 60 days of the date on which the lender determines that a borrower (or the student on whose behalf a parent obtained a PLUS loan) has died, or the lender determines that the borrower is totally and permanently disabled.

(ii) In the case of a closed school claim, the lender shall file a claim with the guaranty agency no later than 60 days after the borrower submits to the lender the written request and sworn statement described in paragraph (d)(3) of this section or after the lender is notified by the Secretary or the Secretary's designee or by the guaranty agency to do so.

(iii) In the case of a false certification claim, the lender shall file a claim with the guaranty agency no later than 60 days after the borrower submits to the lender the written request and sworn statement described in paragraph (e)(3) of this section or after the lender is notified by the Secretary or the Secretary's designee or by the guaranty agency to do so.

(iv) A lender shall file a bankruptcy claim with the guaranty agency by the earlier of—

(A) 30 days after the date on which the lender receives notice of the first meeting of creditors or other information described in paragraph (f)(3) of this section; or

(B) 15 days after the lender is served with a complaint or motion to have the loan determined to be dischargeable on grounds of undue hardship, or, if the lender secures an extension of time within which an answer may be filed, 25 days before the expiration of that extended period, whichever is later.

(h) *Payment of death, disability, closed school, false certification, and bankruptcy claims by the guaranty agency.*

(1) *General.*

(i) Except as provided in paragraph (h)(1)(v) of this section, the guaranty agency shall review a death, disability, bankruptcy, closed school, or false certification claim promptly and shall pay the lender on an approved claim the amount of loss in accordance with paragraphs (h)(2) and (h)(3) of this section—

(A) Not later than 45 days after the claim was filed by the lender for death and bankruptcy claims; and

(B) Not later than 90 days after the claim was filed by the lender for disability, closed school, or false certification claims.

(ii) In the case of a bankruptcy claim, the guaranty agency shall, upon receipt of the claim from the lender, immediately take those actions required under paragraph (i) of this section to oppose the discharge of the loan by the bankruptcy court.

(iii) In the case of a closed school claim or a false certification claim based on the determination that the borrower did not sign the loan application, the promissory note, or the authorization for the electronic transfer of loan funds, or that the school failed to test, or improperly tested, the student's ability to benefit, the guaranty agency shall document its determination that the borrower is eligible for discharge under paragraphs (d) or (e) of this section and pay the borrower or the holder the amount determined under paragraph (h)(2) of this section.

(iv) In reviewing a claim under this section, the issue of confirmation of subsequent loans under an MPN will not be reviewed and a claim will not be denied based on the absence of any evidence relating to confirmation in a particular loan file. However, if a court rules that a loan is unenforceable solely because of the lack of evidence of the confirmation process or processes, insurance benefits must be repaid.

(v) In the case of a disability claim based on a veteran's discharge request processed in accordance with § 682.402(c)(8), the guaranty agency shall—

(A) Review the claim promptly and not later than 45 days after the claim was filed by the lender submit the veteran's discharge application and supporting documentation to the Secretary or return the claim to the lender in accordance with § 682.402(c)(8)(ii)(D) or (E), as applicable; and

(B) Not later than 45 days after receiving notification from the Secretary of the veteran's eligibility or ineligibility for discharge, pay the claim or return the claim to the lender in accordance with § 682.402(c)(8)(ii)(F) or (G), as applicable.

(2)(i) The amount of loss payable—

(A) On a death or disability claim is equal to the sum of the remaining principal balance and interest accrued on the loan, collection costs incurred by the lender and applied to the borrower's account within 30 days of the date those costs were actually incurred, and unpaid interest up to the date the lender should have filed the claim.

(B) On a bankruptcy claim is equal to the unpaid balance of principal and interest determined in accordance with paragraph (h)(3) of this section.

(ii) The amount of loss payable to a lender on a closed school claim or on a false certification claim is equal to the sum of the remaining principal balance and interest accrued on the loan, collection costs incurred by the lender and applied to the borrower's account within 30 days of the date those costs were actually incurred, and unpaid interest determined in accordance with paragraph (h)(3) of this section.

(iii) In the case of a closed school or false certification claim filed by a lender on an outstanding loan owed by the borrower, on the same date that the agency pays a claim to the lender, the agency shall pay the borrower an amount equal to the amount paid on the loan by or on behalf of the borrower, less any school tuition refunds or payments received by the holder or the borrower from a tuition recovery fund, performance bond, or other third-party source.

(iv) In the case of a claim filed by a lender based on a request received from a borrower whose loan had been repaid in full by, or on behalf of the borrower to the lender, on the same date that the agency notifies the lender that the borrower is eligible for a closed school or false certification discharge, the agency shall pay the borrower an amount equal to the amount paid on the loan by or on behalf of the borrower, less any school tuition refunds or payments received by the holder or the borrower from a tuition recovery fund, performance bond, or other third-party source.

(v) In the case of a loan that has been included in a Consolidation Loan, the agency shall pay to the holder of the borrower's Consolidation Loan, an amount equal to—

(A) The amount paid on the loan by or on behalf of the borrower at the time the loan was paid through consolidation;

(B) The amount paid by the consolidating lender to the holder of the loan when it was repaid through consolidation; minus

(C) Any school tuition refunds or payments received by the holder or the borrower from a tuition recovery fund, performance bond, or other third-party source if those refunds or payments were—

(1) Received by the borrower or received by the holder and applied to the borrower's loan balance before the date the loan was repaid through consolidation; or

(2) Received by the borrower or received by the Consolidation Loan holder on or after the date the consolidating lender made a payment to the former holder to discharge the borrower's obligation to that former holder.

(3) Payment of interest. If the guarantee covers unpaid interest, the amount payable on an approved claim includes the unpaid interest that accrues during the following periods:

(i) During the period before the claim is filed, not to exceed the period provided for in paragraph (g)(2) of this section for filing the claim.

(ii) During a period not to exceed 30 days following the receipt date by the lender of a claim returned by the guaranty agency for additional documentation necessary for the claim to be approved by the guaranty agency.

(iii) During the period required by the guaranty agency to approve the claim and to authorize payment or to return the claim to the lender for additional documentation not to exceed—

(A) 45 days for death or bankruptcy claims; or

(B) 90 days for disability, closed school, or false certification claims.

(*i*) *Guaranty agency participation in bankruptcy proceedings*—

(1) *Undue hardship claims.*

(i) In response to a petition filed prior to October 8, 1998 with regard to any bankruptcy proceeding by the borrower for discharge under 11 U.S.C. 523(a)(8) on the grounds of undue hardship, the guaranty agency must, on the basis of reasonably available information, determine whether the first payment on the loan was due more than 7 years (exclusive of any applicable suspension of the repayment period) before the filing of that petition and, if so, process the claim.

(ii) In all other cases, the guaranty agency must determine whether repayment under either the current repayment schedule or any adjusted schedule authorized under this part would impose an undue hardship on the borrower and his or her dependents.

(iii) If the guaranty agency determines that repayment would not constitute an undue hardship, the guaranty agency must then determine whether the expected costs of opposing the discharge petition would exceed one-third of the total amount owed on the loan, including principal, interest, late charges, and collection costs. If the guaranty agency has determined that the expected costs of opposing the discharge petition will exceed one-third of the total amount of the loan, it may, but is not required to, engage in the activities described in paragraph (i)(1)(iv) of this section.

(iv) The guaranty agency must use diligence and may assert any defense consistent with its status under applicable law to avoid discharge of the loan. Unless discharge would be more effectively opposed by not taking the following actions, the agency must—

(A) Oppose the borrower's petition for a determination of dischargeability; and

(B) If the borrower is in default on the loan, seek a judgment for the amount owed on the loan.

(v) In opposing a petition for a determination of dischargeability on the grounds of undue hardship, a guaranty agency may agree to discharge of a portion of the amount owed on a loan if it reasonably determines that the agreement is necessary in order to obtain a judgment on the remainder of the loan.

(2) *Response by a guaranty agency to plans proposed under Chapters 11, 12, and 13.* The guaranty agency shall take the following actions when a petition for relief in bankruptcy under Chapters 11, 12, or 13 is filed:

(i) The agency is not required to respond to a proposed plan that—

(A) Provides for repayment of the full outstanding balance of the loan;

(B) Makes no provision with regard to the loan or to general unsecured claims.

(ii) In any other case, the agency shall determine, based on a review of its own records and documents filed by the debtor in the bankruptcy proceeding—

(A) What part of the loan obligation will be discharged under the plan as proposed;

(B) Whether the plan itself or the classification of the loan under the plan meets the requirements of 11 U.S.C. 1129, 1225, or 1325, as applicable; and

(C) Whether grounds exist under 11 U.S.C. 1112, 1208, or 1307, as applicable, to move for conversion or dismissal of the case.

(iii) If the agency determines that grounds exist to challenge the proposed plan, the agency shall, as appropriate, object to the plan or move to dismiss the case, if—

(A) The costs of litigation of these actions are not reasonably expected to exceed one-third of the amount of the loan to be discharged under the plan; and

(B) With respect to an objection under 11 U.S.C. 1325, the additional amount that may be recovered under the plan if an objection is successful can reasonably be expected to equal or exceed the cost of litigating the objection.

(iv) The agency shall monitor the debtor's performance under a confirmed plan. If the debtor fails to make payments required under the plan or seeks but does not demonstrate entitlement to discharge under 11 U.S.C. 1328(b), the agency shall oppose any requested discharge or move to dismiss the case if the costs of litigation together with the costs incurred for objections to the plan are not reasonably expected to exceed one-third of the amount of the loan to be discharged under the plan.

(j) *Mandatory purchase by a lender of a loan subject to a bankruptcy claim.*

(1) The lender shall repurchase from the guaranty agency a loan held by the agency pursuant to a bankruptcy claim paid to that lender, unless the guaranty agency sells the loan to another lender, promptly after the earliest of the following events:

(i) The entry of an order denying or revoking discharge or dismissing a proceeding under any chapter.

(ii) A ruling in a proceeding under chapter 7 or 11 that the loan is not dischargeable under 11 U.S.C. 523(a)(8) or other applicable law.

(iii) The entry of an order granting discharge under chapter 12 or 13, or confirming a plan of arrangement under chapter 11, unless the court determined that the loan is dischargeable under 11 U.S.C. 523(a)(8) on grounds of undue hardship.

(2) The lender may capitalize all outstanding interest accrued on a loan purchased under paragraph (j) of this section to cover any periods of delinquency prior to the bankruptcy action through the date the lender purchases the loan and receives the supporting loan documentation from the guaranty agency.

(k) *Claims for reimbursement from the Secretary on loans held by guarantee agencies.*

(1)(i) The Secretary reimburses the guaranty agency for its losses on bankruptcy claims paid to lenders after—

(A) A determination by the court that the loan is dischargeable under 11 U.S.C. 523(a)(8) with respect to a proceeding initiated under chapter 7 or chapter 11; or

(B) With respect to any other loan, after the agency pays the claim to the lender.

(ii) The guaranty agency shall refund to the Secretary the full amount of reimbursement received from the Secretary on a loan that a lender repurchases under this section.

(2) The Secretary pays a death, disability, bankruptcy, closed school, or false certification claim in an amount determined under § 682.402(k)(5) on a loan held by a guaranty agency after the agency has paid a default claim to the lender thereon and received payment under its reinsurance agreement. The Secretary reimburses the guaranty agency only if—

(i) The guaranty agency determines that the borrower (or the student for whom a parent obtained a PLUS loan or each of the co-makers of a PLUS loan) has died, or the borrower (or each of the co-makers of a PLUS loan) has become totally and permanently disabled since applying for the loan, or has filed for relief in bankruptcy, in accordance with the procedures in paragraphs (b), (c), or (f) of this section, or the student was unable to complete an educational program because the school closed, or the borrower's eligibility to borrow (or the student's eligibility in the case of a PLUS loan) was falsely certified by an eligible school. For purposes of this paragraph, references to the "lender" and "guaranty agency" in paragraphs (b) through (f) of this section mean the guaranty agency and the Secretary respectively;

(ii) In the case of a Stafford, SLS, or PLUS loan, the guaranty agency determines that the borrower (or the student for whom a parent obtained a PLUS loan, or each of the co-makers of a PLUS loan) has died, or the borrower (or each of the co-makers of a PLUS loan) has become totally and permanently disabled since applying for the loan, or has filed the petition for relief in bankruptcy within 10 years of the date the borrower entered repayment, exclusive of periods of deferment or periods of forbearance granted by the lender that extended the 10-year maximum repayment period, or the borrower (or the student for whom a parent received a PLUS loan) was unable to complete an educational program because the school closed, or the borrower's eligibility to borrow (or the student's eligibility in the case of a PLUS loan) was falsely certified by an eligible school;

(iii) In the case of a Consolidation loan, the borrower (or one of the co-makers) has died, is determined to be totally and permanently disabled under § 682.402(c), or has filed the petition for relief in bankruptcy within the maximum repayment period described in § 682.209(h)(2), exclusive of periods of deferment or periods of forbearance granted by the lender that extended the maximum repayment period;

(iv) The guaranty agency has not written off the loan in accordance with the procedures established by the agency under § 682.410(b)(6)(x), except for closed school and false certification discharges; and

(v) The guaranty agency has exercised due diligence in the collection of the loan in accordance with the procedures established by the agency under § 682.410(b)(6)(x), until the borrower (or the student for whom a parent obtained a PLUS loan, or each of the co-makers of a PLUS loan) has died, or the borrower (or each of the co-makers of a PLUS loan) has become totally and permanently disabled or filed a Chapter 12 or Chapter 13 petition, or had the loan discharged in bankruptcy, or for closed school and false certification claims, the guaranty agency receives a request for discharge from the borrower or another party.

(3) [*Reserved*]

(4) Within 30 days of receiving reimbursement for a closed school or false certification claim, the guaranty agency shall pay—

(i) The borrower an amount equal to the amount paid on the loan by or on behalf of the borrower, less any school tuition refunds or payments received by the holder, guaranty agency, or the borrower from a tuition recovery fund, performance bond, or other third-party source; or

(ii) The amount determined under paragraph (h)(2)(iv) of this section to the holder of the borrower's Consolidation Loan.

(5) The Secretary pays the guaranty agency a percentage of the outstanding principal and interest that is equal to the complement of the reinsurance percentage paid on the loan. This interest includes interest that accrues during—

(i) For death or bankruptcy claims, the shorter of 60 days or the period from the date the guaranty agency determines that the borrower (or the student for whom a parent obtained a PLUS loan, or each of the co-makers of a PLUS loan) died, or filed a petition for relief in bankruptcy until the Secretary authorizes payment;

(ii) For disability claims, the shorter of 60 days or the period from the date the guaranty agency makes a preliminary determination that the borrower became totally and permanently disabled until the Secretary authorizes payment; or

(iii) For closed school or false certification claims, the period from the date on which the guaranty agency received payment from the Secretary on a default claim to the date on which the Secretary authorizes payment of the closed school or false certification claim.

(*l*) *Unpaid refund discharge.*

(1) *Unpaid refunds in closed school situations.* In the case of a school that has closed, the Secretary reimburses the guarantor of a loan and discharges a former or current borrower's (and any endorser's) obligation to repay that portion of an FFEL Program loan (disbursed, in whole or in part, on or after January 1, 1986) equal to the refund that should have been made by the school under applicable Federal law and regulations, including this section. Any accrued interest and other charges (late charges, collection costs, origination fees, and insurance premiums) associated with the unpaid refund are also discharged.

(2) *Unpaid refunds in open school situations.* In the case of a school that is open, the guarantor discharges a former or current borrower's (and any endorser's) obligation to repay that portion of an FFEL loan (disbursed, in whole or in part, on or after January 1, 1986) equal to the amount of the refund that should have been made by the school under applicable Federal law and regulations, including this section, if—

(i) The borrower (or the student on whose behalf a parent borrowed) is not attending the school that owes the refund; and

(ii) The guarantor receives documentation regarding the refund and the borrower and guarantor have been unable to resolve the unpaid refund within 120 days from the date the guarantor receives a complete application in accordance with paragraph (*l*)(4) of this section. Any accrued interest and other charges (late charges, collection costs, origination fees, and insurance premiums) associated with the amount of the unpaid refund amount are also discharged.

(3) *Relief to borrower (and any endorser) following discharge.*

(i) If a borrower receives a discharge of a portion of a loan under this section, the borrower is reimbursed for any amounts paid in excess of the remaining balance of the loan (including accrued interest, late charges, collection costs, origination fees, and insurance premiums) owed by the borrower at the time of discharge.

(ii) The holder of the loan reports the discharge of a portion of a loan under this section to all credit reporting agencies to which the holder of the loan previously reported the status of the loan.

(4) *Borrower qualification for discharge.* To receive a discharge of a portion of a loan under this section, a borrower must submit a written application to the holder or guaranty agency except as provided in paragraph (*l*)(5)(iv) of this section. The application requests the information required to calculate the amount of the discharge and requires the borrower to sign a statement swearing to the accuracy of the information in the application. The statement need not be notarized but must be made by the borrower under penalty of perjury. In the statement, the borrower must—

(i) State that the borrower (or the student on whose behalf a parent borrowed)—

(A) Received the proceeds of a loan, in whole or in part, on or after January 1, 1986 to attend a school;

(B) Did not attend, withdrew, or was terminated from the school within a timeframe that entitled the borrower to a refund; and

(C) Did not receive the benefit of a refund to which the borrower was entitled either from the school or from a third party, such as a holder of a performance bond or a tuition recovery program.

(ii) State whether the borrower has any other application for discharge pending for this loan; and

(iii) State that the borrower—

(A) Agrees to provide upon request by the Secretary or the Secretary's designee other documentation reasonably available to the borrower that demonstrates that the borrower meets the qualifications for an unpaid refund discharge under this section; and

(B) Agrees to cooperate with the Secretary or the Secretary's designee in enforcement actions in accordance with paragraph (e) of this section and to transfer any right to recovery against a third party to the Secretary in accordance with paragraph (d) of this section.

(5) *Unpaid refund discharge procedures.*

(i) Except for the requirements of paragraph (*l*)(5)(iv) of this section related to an open school, if the holder or guaranty agency learns that a school did not pay a refund of loan proceeds owed under applicable law and regulations, the holder or the guaranty agency sends the borrower a discharge application and an explanation of the qualifications and procedures for obtaining a discharge. The holder of the loan also promptly suspends any efforts to collect from the borrower on any affected loan.

(ii) If the borrower returns the application, specified in paragraph (*l*)(4) of this section, the holder or the guaranty agency must review the application to determine whether the application appears to be complete. In the case of a loan held by a lender, once the lender determines that the application appears complete, it must provide the application and all pertinent information to the guaranty agency including, if available, the borrower's last date of attendance. If the borrower returns the application within 60 days, the lender must extend the period during which efforts to collect on the affected loan are suspended to the date the lender receives either a denial of the request or the unpaid refund amount from the guaranty agency. At the conclusion of the period during which the collection activity was suspended, the lender may capitalize any interest accrued and not paid during that period in accordance with § 682.202(b).

(iii) If the borrower fails to return the application within 60 days, the holder of the loan resumes collection efforts and grants forbearance of principal and interest for the period during which the collection activity was suspended. The holder may capitalize any interest accrued and not paid during that period in accordance with § 682.202(b).

(iv) The guaranty agency may, with the approval of the Secretary, discharge a portion of a loan under this section without an application if the guaranty agency determines, based on information in the guaranty agency's possession, that the borrower qualifies for a discharge.

(v) If the holder of the loan or the guaranty agency determines that the information contained in its files conflicts with the information provided by the borrower, the guaranty agency must use the most reliable information available to it to determine eligibility for and the appropriate payment of the refund amount.

(vi) If the holder of the loan is the guaranty agency and the agency determines that the borrower qualifies for a discharge of an unpaid refund, the guaranty agency must suspend any efforts to collect on the affected loan and, within 30 days of its determination, discharge the appropriate amount and inform the borrower of its determination. Absent documentation of the exact amount of refund due the borrower, the guaranty agency must calculate the amount of the unpaid refund using the unpaid refund calculation defined in paragraph (o) of this section.

(vii) If the guaranty agency determines that a borrower does not qualify for an unpaid refund discharge, (or, if the holder is the lender and is informed by the guarantor that the borrower does not qualify for a discharge)—

(A) Within 30 days of the guarantor's determination, the agency must notify the borrower in writing of the reason for the determination and of the borrower's right to request a review of the agency's determination. The guaranty agency must make a determination within 30 days of the borrower's submission of additional documentation supporting the borrower's eligibility that was not considered in any prior determination. During the review period, collection activities must be suspended; and

(B) The holder must resume collection if the determination remains unchanged and grant forbearance of principal and interest for any period during which collection activity was suspended under this section. The holder may capitalize any interest accrued and not paid during these periods in accordance with § 682.202(b).

(viii) If the guaranty agency determines that a current or former borrower at an open school may be eligible for a discharge under this section, the guaranty agency must notify the lender and the school of the unpaid refund allegation. The notice to the school must include all pertinent facts available to the guaranty agency regarding the alleged unpaid refund. The school must, no later than 60 days after receiving the notice, provide the guaranty agency with documentation demonstrating, to the satisfaction of the guarantor, that the alleged unpaid refund was either paid or not required to be paid.

(ix) In the case of a school that does not make a refund or provide sufficient documentation demonstrating the refund was either paid or was not required, within 60 days of its receipt of the allegation notice from the guaranty agency, relief is provided to the borrower (and any endorser) if the guaranty agency determines the relief is appropriate. The agency must forward documentation of the school's failure to pay the unpaid refund to the Secretary.

(m) *Unpaid refund discharge procedures for a loan held by a lender.* In the case of an unpaid refund discharge request, the lender must provide the guaranty agency with documentation related to the borrower's qualification for discharge as specified in paragraph (l)(4) of this section.

(n) *Payment of an unpaid refund discharge request by a guaranty agency.*

(1) *General.* The guaranty agency must review an unpaid refund discharge request promptly and must pay the lender the amount of loss as defined in paragraphs (l)(1) and (l)(2) of this section, related to the unpaid refund not later than 45 days after a properly filed request is made.

(2) *Determination of the unpaid refund discharge amount to the lender.* The amount of loss payable to a lender on an unpaid refund includes that portion of an FFEL Program loan equal to the amount of the refund required under applicable Federal law and regulations, including this section, and including any accrued interest and other charges (late charges, collection costs, origination fees, and insurance premiums) associated with the unpaid refund.

(o)(1) *Determination of amount eligible for discharge.* The guaranty agency determines the amount eligible for discharge based on information showing the refund amount or by applying the appropriate refund formula to information that the borrower provides or that is otherwise available to the guaranty agency. For purposes of this section, all unpaid refunds are considered to be attributed to loan proceeds.

(2) If the information in paragraph (o)(1) of this section is not available, the guaranty agency uses the following formulas to determine the amount eligible for discharge:

(i) In the case of a student who fails to attend or whose withdrawal or termination date is before October 7, 2000 and who completes less than 60 percent of the loan period, the guaranty agency discharges the lesser of the institutional charges unearned or the loan amount. The guaranty agency determines the amount of the institutional charges unearned by—

(A) Calculating the ratio of the amount of time in the loan period after the student's last day of attendance to the actual length of the loan period; and

(B) Multiplying the resulting factor by the institutional charges assessed the student for the loan period.

(ii) In the case of a student who fails to attend or whose withdrawal or termination date is on or after October 7, 2000 and who completes less than 60 percent of the loan period, the guaranty agency discharges the loan amount unearned. The guaranty agency determines the loan amount unearned by—

(A) Calculating the ratio of the amount of time remaining in the loan period after the student's last day of attendance to the actual length of the loan period; and

(B) Multiplying the resulting factor by the total amount of title IV grants and loans received by the student, or if unknown, the loan amount.

(iii) In the case of a student who completes 60 percent or more of the loan period, the guaranty agency does not discharge any amount because a student who completes 60 percent or more of the loan period is not entitled to a refund.

(p) *Requests for reimbursement from the Secretary on loans held by guaranty agencies.* The Secretary reimburses the guaranty agency for its losses on unpaid refund request payments to lenders or borrowers in an amount that is equal to the amount specified in paragraph (n)(2) of this section.

(q) *Payments received after the guaranty agency's payment of an unpaid refund request.*

(1) The holder must promptly return to the sender any payment on a fully discharged loan, received after the guaranty agency pays an unpaid refund request unless the sender is required to pay (as in the case of a tuition recovery fund) in which case, the payment amount must be forwarded to the Secretary. At the same time that the holder returns the payment, it must notify the borrower that there is no obligation to repay a loan fully discharged.

(2) If the holder has returned a payment to the borrower, or the borrower's representative, with the notice described in paragraph (q)(1) of this section, and the borrower (or representative) continues to send payments to the holder, the holder must remit all of those payments to the Secretary.

(3) If the loan has not been fully discharged, payments must be applied to the remaining debt.

(r) *Payments received after the Secretary's payment of a death, disability, closed school, false certification, or bankruptcy claim.*

(1) If the guaranty agency receives any payments from or on behalf of the borrower on or attributable to a loan that has been discharged in bankruptcy on which the Secretary previously paid a bankruptcy claim, the guaranty agency must return 100 percent of these payments to the sender. The guaranty agency must promptly return, to the sender, any payment on a cancelled or discharged loan made by the sender and received after the Secretary pays a closed school or false certification claim. At the same time that the agency returns the payment, it must notify the borrower that there is no obligation to repay a loan discharged on the basis of death, bankruptcy, false certification, or closing of the school.

(2) If the guaranty agency receives any payments from or on behalf of the borrower on or attributable to a loan that has been assigned to the Secretary for determination of eligibility for a total and permanent disability discharge,

the guaranty agency must forward those payments to the Secretary for crediting to the borrower's account. At the same time that the agency forwards the payments, it must notify the borrower that there is no obligation to make payments on the loan while it is conditionally discharged prior to a final determination of eligibility for a total and permanent disability discharge, unless the Secretary directs the borrower otherwise.

(3) When the Secretary makes a final determination to discharge the loan, the Secretary returns to the sender any payments received on the loan after the date the borrower became totally and permanently disabled.

(4) The guaranty agency shall remit to the Secretary all payments received from a tuition recovery fund, performance bond, or other third party with respect to a loan on which the Secretary previously paid a closed school or false certification claim.

(5) If the guaranty agency has returned a payment to the borrower, or the borrower's representative, with the notice described in paragraphs (r)(1) or (r)(2) of this section, and the borrower (or representative) continues to send payments to the guaranty agency, the agency must remit all of those payments to the Secretary.

(s) *Applicable suspension of the repayment period.* For purposes of this section and 11 U.S.C. 523(a)(8)(A) with respect to loans guaranteed under the FFEL Program, an applicable suspension of the repayment period—

(1) Includes any period during which the lender does not require the borrower to make a payment on the loan;

(2) Begins on the date on which the borrower qualifies for the requested deferment as provided in § 682.210(a)(5) or the lender grants the requested forbearance;

(3) Closes on the later of the date on which—
(i) The condition for which the requested deferment or forbearance was received ends; or
(ii) The lender receives notice of the end of the condition for which the requested deferment or forbearance was received, if the condition ended earlier than represented by the borrower at the time of the request and the borrower did not notify timely the lender of the date on which the condition actually ended.

(4) Includes the period between the end of the borrower's grace period and the first payment due date established by the lender in the case of a borrower who entered repayment without the knowledge of the lender;

(5) Includes the period between the filing of the petition for relief and the date on which the proceeding is completed or dismissed, unless payments have been made during that period in amounts sufficient to meet the amount owed under the repayment schedule in effect when the petition was filed.

(Approved by the Office of Management and Budget under control number 1845-0020)

(Authority: 20 U.S.C. 1070g, 1078, 1078-1, 1078-2, 1078-3, 1082, 1087)

[58 Fed. Reg. 9120 (Feb. 19, 1993); 59 Fed. Reg. 22476 (Apr. 29, 1994); 59 Fed. Reg. 25746 (May 17, 1994); 59 Fed. Reg. 29543 (June 8, 1994); 59 Fed. Reg. 35625 (July 13, 1994); 59 Fed. Reg. 46175 (Sept. 7, 1994); 59 Fed. Reg. 61216 (Nov. 29, 1994); 59 Fed. Reg. 61428 (Nov. 30, 1994); 60 Fed. Reg. 32912 (June 26, 1995); 60 Fed. Reg. 61757 (Dec. 1, 1995); 62 Fed. Reg. 63434 (Nov. 28, 1997); 64 Fed. Reg. 18979 (Apr. 16, 1999); 64 Fed. Reg. 58628 (Oct. 29, 1999); 64 Fed. Reg. 58960 (Nov. 1, 1999); 65 Fed. Reg. 65620, 65691 (Nov. 1, 2000); 66 Fed. Reg. 34763 (June 29, 2001); 67 Fed. Reg. 67079 (Nov. 1, 2002); 68 Fed. Reg. 75429 (Dec. 31, 2003); 71 Fed. Reg. 45706 (Aug. 9, 2006); 71 Fed. Reg. 64398 (Nov. 1, 2006); 72 Fed. Reg. 62004 (Nov. 1, 2007); 73 Fed. Reg. 35495 (June 23, 2008); 73 Fed. Reg. 36793 (June 30, 2008); 74 Fed. Reg. 55997 (Oct. 29, 2009)]

* * *

§ 682.405 Loan rehabilitation agreement.

(a) *General.*

(1) A guaranty agency that has a basic program agreement must enter into a loan rehabilitation agreement with the Secretary. The guaranty agency must establish a loan rehabilitation program for all borrowers with an enforceable promissory note for the purpose of rehabilitating defaulted loans, except for loans for which a judgment has been obtained, loans on which a default claim was filed under § 682.412, and loans on which the borrower has been convicted of, or has pled nolo contendere or guilty to, a crime involving fraud in obtaining title IV, HEA program assistance, so that the loan may be purchased, if practicable, by an eligible lender and removed from default status.

(2) A loan is considered to be rehabilitated only after—
(i) The borrower has made and the guaranty agency has received nine of the ten payments required under a monthly repayment agreement.
(A) Each of which payments is—
(1) Made voluntarily;
(2) In the full amount required; and
(3) Received within 20 days of the due date for the payment, and
(B) All nine payments are received within a 10-month period that begins with the month in which the first required due date falls and ends with the ninth consecutive calendar month following that month, and

(ii) The loan has been sold to an eligible lender.

(3) After the loan has been rehabilitated, the borrower regains all benefits of the program, including any remaining deferment eligibility under section 428(b)(1)(M) of the Act, from the date of the rehabilitation. Effective for any loan that is rehabilitated on or after August 14, 2008, the borrower cannot rehabilitate the loan again if the loan returns to default status following the rehabilitation.

(b) *Terms of agreement.* In the loan rehabilitation agreement, the guaranty agency agrees to ensure that its loan rehabilitation program meets the following requirements at all times:

(1) A borrower may request rehabilitation of the borrower's defaulted loan held by the guaranty agency. In order to be eligible for rehabilitation of the loan, the borrower must voluntarily make at least nine of the ten payments required under a monthly repayment agreement.
(i) Each of which payment is—
(A) Made voluntarily,
(B) In the full amount required, and
(C) Received within 20 days of the due date for the payment, and
(ii) All nine payments are received within a ten-month period that begins with the month in which the first required due date falls and ends with the ninth consecutive calendar month following that month.
(iii) For the purposes of this section, the determination of reasonable and affordable by the guaranty agency or its agents must—
(A) Include a consideration of the borrower's and spouse's disposable income and reasonable and necessary expenses including, but not limited to, housing, utilities, food, medical costs, work-related expenses, dependent care costs and other Title IV repayment;
(B) Not be a required minimum payment amount, e.g. $50, if the agency determines that a smaller amount is reasonable and affordable based on the borrower's total financial circumstances. The agency must include documentation in the borrower's file of the basis for the determination if the monthly reasonable and affordable payment established under this section is less than $50 or the monthly accrued interest on the loan, whichever is greater. However, $50 may not be the minimum payment for a borrower if the agency determines that a smaller amount is reasonable and affordable; and
(C) Be based on the documentation provided by the borrower or other sources including, but not limited to—
(1) Evidence of current income (e.g., proof of welfare benefits, Social Security benefits, child support, veterans' benefits, Supplemental Security

Income, Workmen's Compensation, two most recent pay stubs, most recent copy of U.S. income tax return, State Department of Labor reports);
(2) Evidence of current expenses (e.g., a copy of the borrower's monthly household budget, on a form provided by the guaranty agency); and
(3) A statement of the unpaid balance on all FFEL loans held by other holders.

(iv) The agency must include any payment made under § 682.401(b)(4) in determining whether the nine out of ten payments required under paragraph (b)(1) of this section have been made.

(v) A borrower may request that the monthly payment amount be adjusted due to a change in the borrower's total financial circumstances only upon providing the documentation specified in paragraph (b)(1)(iii)(C) of this section.

(vi) A guaranty agency must provide the borrower with a written statement confirming the borrower's reasonable and affordable payment amount, as determined by the agency, and explaining any other terms and conditions applicable to the required series of payments that must be made before a borrower's account can be considered for repurchase by an eligible lender. The statement must inform borrowers of the effects of having their loans rehabilitated (e.g., credit clearing, possibility of increased monthly payments). The statement must inform the borrower of the amount of the collection costs to be added to the unpaid principal at the time of the sale. The collection costs may not exceed 18.5 percent of the unpaid principal and accrued interest at the time of the sale.

(vii) A guaranty agency must provide the borrower with an opportunity to object to terms of the rehabilitation of the borrower's defaulted loan.

(2) For the purposes of this section, payment in the full amount required means payment of an amount that is reasonable and affordable, based on the borrower's total financial circumstances, as agreed to by the borrower and the agency. Voluntary payments are those made directly by the borrower and do not include payments obtained by Federal offset, garnishment, income or asset execution, or after a judgment has been entered on a loan. A guaranty agency must attempt to secure a lender to purchase the loan at the end of the 9- or 10-month payment period as applicable.

(3) Upon the sale of a rehabilitated loan to an eligible lender—
(i) The guaranty agency must, within 45 days of the sale—
(A) Provide notice to the prior holder of such sale, and
(B) Request that any consumer reporting agency to which the default was reported remove the record of default from the borrower's credit history.
(ii) The prior holder of the loan must, within 30 days of receiving the notification from the guaranty agency, request that any consumer reporting agency to which the default claim payment or other equivalent record was reported remove such record from the borrower's credit history.
(4) An eligible lender purchasing a rehabilitated loan must establish a repayment schedule that meets the same requirements that are applicable to other FFEL Program loans of the same loan type as the rehabilitated loan and must permit the borrower to choose any statutorily available repayment plan for that loan type. The lender must treat the first payment made under the nine payments as the first payment under the applicable maximum repayment term, as defined under § 682.209(a) or (h). For Consolidation loans, the maximum repayment term is based on the balance outstanding at the time of loan rehabilitation.

(c) A guaranty agency must make available financial and economic education materials, including debt management information, to any borrower who has rehabilitated a defaulted loan in accordance with paragraph (a)(2) of this section.

(Approved by the Office of Management and Budget under control number 1845-0020)

(Authority: 20 U.S.C. 1078-6)

[59 Fed. Reg. 33355 (June 28, 1994); 60 Fed. Reg. 30788 (June 12, 1995); 64 Fed. Reg. 18980 (Apr. 16, 1999); 64 Fed. Reg. 58965 (Nov. 1, 1999); 66 Fed. Reg. 34764 (June 29, 2001); 67 Fed. Reg. 67080 (Nov. 1, 2002); 68 Fed. Reg. 75429 (Dec. 31, 2003); 71 Fed. Reg. 45707 (Aug. 9, 2006); 71 Fed. Reg. 64398 (Nov. 1, 2006); 73 Fed. Reg. 63254 (Oct. 23, 2008); 74 Fed. Reg. 56000 (Oct. 29, 2009)]

* * *

§ 682.410 Fiscal, administrative, and enforcement requirements.

(a) *Fiscal requirements*—
(1) *Reserve fund assets.* A guaranty agency shall establish and maintain a reserve fund to be used solely for its activities as a guaranty agency under the FFEL Program ("guaranty activities"). The guaranty agency shall credit to the reserve fund—
(i) The total amount of insurance premiums and Federal default fees collected;
(ii) Funds received from a State for the agency's guaranty activities, including matching funds under section 422(a) of the Act;
(iii) Federal advances obtained under sections 422(a) and (c) of the Act;
(iv) Federal payments for default, bankruptcy, death, disability, closed schools, and false certification claims;
(v) Supplemental preclaims assistance payments;
(vi) Transitional support payments received under section 458(a) of the Act;
(vii) Funds collected by the guaranty agency on FFEL Program loans on which a claim has been paid;
(viii) Investment earnings on the reserve fund; and
(ix) Other funds received by the guaranty agency from any source for the agency's guaranty activities.

(2) *Uses of reserve fund assets.* A guaranty agency may not use the assets of the reserve fund established under paragraph (a)(1) of this section to pay costs prohibited under § 682.418, but shall use the assets of the reserve fund to pay only—
(i) Insurance claims;
(ii) Costs that are reasonable, as defined under § 682.410(a)(11)(iii), and that are ordinary and necessary for the agency to fulfill its responsibilities under the HEA, including costs of collecting loans, providing preclaims assistance, monitoring enrollment and repayment status, and carrying out any other guaranty activities. Those costs must be—
(A) Allocable to the FFEL Program;
(B) Not higher than the agency would incur under established policies, regulations, and procedures that apply to any comparable non-Federal activities of the guaranty agency;
(C) Not included as a cost or used to meet cost sharing or matching requirements of any other federally supported activity, except as specifically provided by Federal law;
(D) Net of all applicable credits; and
(E) Documented in accordance with applicable legal and accounting standards;
(iii) The Secretary's equitable share of collections;
(iv) Federal advances and other funds owed to the Secretary;
(v) Reinsurance fees;
(vi) Insurance premiums and Federal default fees related to cancelled loans;
(vii) Borrower refunds, including those arising out of student or other borrower claims and defenses;
(viii)(A) The repayment, on or after December 29, 1993, of amounts credited under paragraphs (a)(1)(ii) or (a)(1)(ix) of this section, if the agency provides the Secretary 30 days prior notice of the repayment and demonstrates that—
(1) These amounts were originally received by the agency under appropriate contemporaneous documentation specifying that receipt was on a temporary basis only;

(2) The objective for which these amounts were originally received by the agency has been fully achieved; and

(3) Repayment of these amounts would not cause the agency to fail to comply with the minimum reserve levels provided by paragraph (a)(10) of this section, except that the Secretary may, for good cause, provide written permission for a payment that meets the other requirements of this paragraph (a)(2)(ix)(A).

(B) The repayment, prior to December 29, 1993, of amounts credited under paragraphs (a)(1)(ii) or (a)(1)(ix) of this section, if the agency demonstrates that—

(1) These amounts were originally received by the agency under appropriate contemporaneous documentation that receipt was on a temporary basis only; and

(2) The objective for which these amounts were originally received by the agency has been fully achieved.

(ix) Any other costs or payments ordinary and necessary to perform functions directly related to the agency's responsibilities under the HEA and for their proper and efficient administration;

(x) Notwithstanding any other provision of this section, any other payment that was allowed by law or regulation at the time it was made, if the agency acted in good faith when it made the payment or the agency would otherwise be unfairly prejudiced by the nonallowability of the payment at a later time; and

(xi) Any other amounts authorized or directed by the Secretary.

(3) *Accounting basis.* Except as approved by the Secretary, a guaranty agency shall credit the items listed in paragraph (a)(1) of this section to its reserve fund upon their receipt, without any deferral for accounting purposes, and shall deduct the items listed in paragraph (a)(2) of this section from its reserve fund upon their payment, without any accrual for accounting purposes.

(4) *Accounting records.*

(i) The accounting records of a guaranty agency must reflect the correct amount of sources and uses of funds under paragraph (a) of this section.

(ii) A guaranty agency may reverse prior credits to its reserve fund if—

(A) The agency gives the Secretary prior notice setting forth a detailed justification for the action;

(B) The Secretary determines that such credits were made erroneously and in good faith; and

(C) The Secretary determines that the action would not unfairly prejudice other parties.

(iii) A guaranty agency shall correct any other errors in its accounting or reporting as soon as practicable after the errors become known to the agency.

(iv) If a general reconstruction of a guaranty agency's historical accounting records is necessary to make a change under paragraphs (a)(4)(ii) and (a)(4)(iii) of this section or any other retroactive change to its accounting records, the agency may make this reconstruction only upon prior approval by the Secretary and without any deduction from its reserve fund for the cost of the reconstruction.

(5) *Investments.* The guaranty agency shall exercise the level of care required of a fiduciary charged with the duty of investing the money of others when it invests the assets of the reserve fund described in paragraph (a)(1) of this section. It may invest these assets only in low-risk securities, such as obligations issued or guaranteed by the United States or a State.

(6) *Development of assets.*

(i) If the guaranty agency uses in a substantial way for purposes other than the agency's guaranty activities any funds required to be credited to the reserve fund under paragraph (a)(1) of this section or any assets derived from the reserve fund to develop an asset of any kind and does not in good faith allocate a portion of the cost of developing and maintaining the developed asset to funds other than the reserve fund, the Secretary may require the agency to—

(A) Correct this allocation under paragraph (a)(4)(iii) of this section; or

(B) Correct the recorded ownership of the asset under paragraph (a)(4)(iii) of this section so that—

(1) If, in a transaction with an unrelated third party, the agency sells or otherwise derives revenue from uses of the asset that are unrelated to the agency's guaranty activities, the agency promptly shall deposit into the reserve fund described in paragraph (a)(1) of this section a percentage of the sale proceeds or revenue equal to the fair percentage of the total development cost of the asset paid with the reserve fund monies or provided by assets derived from the reserve fund; or

(2) If the agency otherwise converts the asset, in whole or in part, to a use unrelated to its guaranty activities, the agency promptly shall deposit into the reserve fund described in paragraph (a)(1) of this section a fair percentage of the fair market value or, in the case of a temporary conversion, the rental value of the portion of the asset employed for the unrelated use.

(ii) If the agency uses funds or assets described in paragraph (a)(6)(i) of this section in the manner described in that paragraph and makes a cost and maintenance allocation erroneously and in good faith, it shall correct the allocation under paragraph (a)(4)(iii) of this section.

(7) *Third-party claims.* If the guaranty agency has any claim against any other party to recover funds or other assets for the reserve fund, the claim is the property of the United States.

(8) *Related-party transactions.* All transactions between a guaranty agency and a related organization or other person that involve funds required to be credited to the agency's reserve fund under paragraph (a)(1) of this section or assets derived from the reserve fund must be on terms that are not less advantageous to the reserve fund than would have been negotiated on an arm's-length basis by unrelated parties.

(9) *Scope of definition.* The provisions of this § 682.410(a) define reserve funds and assets for purposes of sections 422 and 428 of the Act. These provisions do not, however, affect the Secretary's authority to use all funds and assets of the agency pursuant to section 428(c)(9)(F)(vi) of the Act.

(10) *Minimum reserve fund level.* The guaranty agency must maintain a current minimum reserve level of not less than—

(i) .5 percent of the amount of loans outstanding, for the fiscal year of the agency that begins in calendar year 1993;

(ii) .7 percent of the amount of loans outstanding, for the fiscal year of the agency that begins in calendar year 1994;

(iii) .9 percent of the amount of loans outstanding, for the fiscal year of the agency that begins in calendar year 1995; and

(iv) 1.1 percent of the amount of loans outstanding, for each fiscal year of the agency that begins on or after January 1, 1996.

(11) *Definitions.* For purposes of this section—

(i) *Reserve fund level* means—

(A) The total of reserve fund assets as defined in paragraph (a)(1) of this section;

(B) Minus the total amount of the reserve fund assets used in accordance with paragraphs (a)(2) and (a)(3) of this section; and

(ii) *Amount of loans outstanding* means—

(A) The sum of—

(1) The original principal amount of all loans guaranteed by the agency; and

(2) The original principal amount of any loans on which the guarantee was transferred to the agency from another guarantor, excluding loan guarantees transferred to another agency pursuant to a plan of the Secretary in response to the insolvency of the agency;

(B) Minus the original principal amount of all loans on which—
(1) The loan guarantee was cancelled;
(2) The loan guarantee was transferred to another agency;
(3) Payment in full has been made by the borrower;
(4) Reinsurance coverage has been lost and cannot be regained; and
(5) The agency paid claims.

(iii) *Reasonable cost* means a cost that, in its nature and amount, does not exceed that which would be incurred by a prudent person under the circumstances prevailing at the time the decision was made to incur the cost. The burden of proof is upon the guaranty agency, as a fiduciary under its agreements with the Secretary, to establish that costs are reasonable. In determining reasonableness of a given cost, consideration must be given to—

(A) Whether the cost is of a type generally recognized as ordinary and necessary for the proper and efficient performance and administration of the guaranty agency's responsibilities under the HEA;
(B) The restraints or requirements imposed by factors such as sound business practices, arms-length bargaining, Federal, State, and other laws and regulations, and the terms and conditions of the guaranty agency's agreements with the Secretary; and
(C) Market prices of comparable goods or services.

(b) *Administrative requirements*—
(1) *Independent audits.* The guaranty agency shall arrange for an independent financial and compliance audit of the agency's FFEL program as follows:
(i) With regard to a guaranty agency that is an agency of a State government, an audit must be conducted in accordance with 31 U.S.C. 7502 and 34 CFR part 80, appendix G.
(ii) With regard to a guaranty agency that is a nonprofit organization, an audit must be conducted in accordance with OMB Circular A-133, Audits of Institutions of Higher Education and Other Nonprofit Organizations and 34 CFR 74.61(h)(3). If a nonprofit guaranty agency meets the criteria in Circular A-133 to have a program specific audit, and chooses that option, the program specific audit must meet the following requirements:
(A) The audit must examine the agency's compliance with the Act, applicable regulations, and agreements entered into under this part.
(B) The audit must examine the agency's financial management of its FFEL program activities.
(C) The audit must be conducted in accordance with the standards for audits issued by the United States General Accounting Office's (GAO) Government Auditing Standards. Procedures for audits are contained in an audit guide developed by, and available from, the Office of the Inspector General of the Department.
(D) The audit must be conducted annually and must be submitted to the Secretary within six months of the end of the audit period. The first audit must cover the agency's activities for a period that includes July 23, 1992, unless the agency is currently submitting audits on a biennial basis, and the second year of its biennial cycle starts on or before July 23, 1992. Under these circumstances, the agency shall submit a biennial audit that includes July 23, 1992 and submit its next audit as an annual audit.

(2) *Collection charges.* Whether or not provided for in the borrower's promissory note and subject to any limitation on the amount of those costs in that note, the guaranty agency shall charge a borrower an amount equal to reasonable costs incurred by the agency in collecting a loan on which the agency has paid a default or bankruptcy claim. These costs may include, but are not limited to, all attorney's fees, collection agency charges, and court costs. Except as provided in §§ 682.401(b)(27) and 682.405(b)(1)(iv), the amount charged a borrower must equal the lesser of—
(i) The amount the same borrower would be charged for the cost of collection under the formula in 34 CFR 30.60; or
(ii) The amount the same borrower would be charged for the cost of collection if the loan was held by the U.S. Department of Education.

(3) *Interest charged by guaranty agencies.* The guaranty agency shall charge the borrower interest on the amount owed by the borrower after the capitalization required under paragraph (b)(4) of this section has occurred at a rate that is the greater of—
(i) The rate established by the terms of the borrower's original promissory note;
(ii) In the case of a loan for which a judgment has been obtained, the rate provided for by State law.

(4) *Capitalization of unpaid interest.* The guaranty agency shall capitalize any unpaid interest due the lender from the borrower at the time the agency pays a default claim to the lender.

(5) *Reports to consumer reporting agencies.*
(i) After the completion of the procedures in paragraph (b)(5)(ii) of this section, the guaranty agency shall, after it has paid a default claim, report promptly, but not less than sixty days after completion of the procedures in paragraph (b)(6)(v) of this section, and on a regular basis, to all nationwide consumer reporting agencies—

(A) The total amount of loans made to the borrower and the remaining balance of those loans;
(B) The date of default;
(C) Information concerning collection of the loan, including the repayment status of the loan;
(D) Any changes or corrections in the information reported by the agency that result from information received after the initial report; and
(E) The date the loan is fully repaid by or on behalf of the borrower or discharged by reason of the borrower's death, bankruptcy, total and permanent disability, or closed school or false certification.

(ii) The guaranty agency, after it pays a default claim on a loan but before it reports the default to a consumer reporting agency or assesses collection costs against a borrower, shall, within the timeframe specified in paragraph (b)(6)(ii) of this section, provide the borrower with—
(A) Written notice that meets the requirements of paragraph (b)(5)(vi) of this section regarding the proposed actions;
(B) An opportunity to inspect and copy agency records pertaining to the loan obligation;
(C) An opportunity for an administrative review of the legal enforceability or past-due status of the loan obligation; and
(D) An opportunity to enter into a repayment agreement on terms satisfactory to the agency.

(iii) The procedures set forth in 34 CFR 30.20-30.33 (administrative offset) satisfy the requirements of paragraph (b)(5)(ii) of this section.

(iv)(A) In response to a request submitted by a borrower, after the deadlines established under agency rules, for access to records, an administrative review, or for an opportunity to enter into a repayment agreement, the agency shall provide the requested relief but may continue reporting the debt to consumer reporting agencies until it determines that the borrower has demonstrated that the loan obligation is not legally enforceable or that alternative repayment arrangements satisfactory to the agency have been made with the borrower.

(B) The deadline established by the agency for requesting administrative review under paragraph (b)(5)(ii)(C) of this section must allow the borrower at least 60 days from the date the notice described in paragraph (b)(5)(ii)(A) of this section is sent to request that review.

(v) An agency may not permit an employee, official, or agent to conduct the administrative review required under this paragraph if that individual is—

(A) Employed in an organizational component of the agency or its agent that is charged with collection of loan obligations; or

(B) Compensated on the basis of collections on loan obligations.

(vi) The notice sent by the agency under paragraph (b)(5)(ii)(A) of this section must—

(A) Advise the borrower that the agency has paid a default claim filed by the lender and has taken assignment of the loan;

(B) Identify the lender that made the loan and the school for attendance at which the loan was made;

(C) State the outstanding principal, accrued interest, and any other charges then owing on the loan;

(D) Demand that the borrower immediately begin repayment of the loan;

(E) Explain the rate of interest that will accrue on the loan, that all costs incurred to collect the loan will be charged to the borrower, the authority for assessing these costs, and the manner in which the agency will calculate the amount of these costs;

(F) Notify the borrower that the agency will report the default to all nationwide consumer reporting agencies to the detriment of the borrower's credit rating;

(G) Explain the opportunities available to the borrower under agency rules to request access to the agency's records on the loan, to request an administrative review of the legal enforceability or past-due status of the loan, and to reach an agreement on repayment terms satisfactory to the agency to prevent the agency from reporting the loan as defaulted to consumer reporting agencies and provide deadlines and method for requesting this relief;

(H) Unless the agency uses a separate notice to advise the borrower regarding other proposed enforcement actions, describe specifically any other enforcement action, such as offset against federal or state income tax refunds or wage garnishment that the agency intends to use to collect the debt, and explain the procedures available to the borrower prior to those other enforcement actions for access to records, for an administrative review, or for agreement to alternative repayment terms;

(I) Describe the grounds on which the borrower may object that the loan obligation as stated in the notice is not a legally enforceable debt owed by the borrower;

(J) Describe any appeal rights available to the borrower from an adverse decision on administrative review of the loan obligation;

(K) Describe any right to judicial review of an adverse decision by the agency regarding the legal enforceability or past-due status of the loan obligation;

(L) Describe the collection actions that the agency may take in the future if those presently proposed do not result in repayment of the loan obligation, including the filing of a lawsuit against the borrower by the agency and assignment of the loan to the Secretary for the filing of a lawsuit against the borrower by the Federal Government; and

(M) Inform the borrower of the options that are available to the borrower to remove the loan from default, including an explanation of the fees and conditions associated with each option.

(vii) As part of the guaranty agency's response to a borrower who appeals an adverse decision resulting from the agency's administrative review of the loan obligation, the agency must provide the borrower with information on the availability of the Student Loan Ombudsman's office.

(6) *Collection efforts on defaulted loans.*

(i) A guaranty agency must engage in reasonable and documented collection activities on a loan on which it pays a default claim filed by a lender. For a non-paying borrower, the agency must perform at least one activity every 180 days to collect the debt, locate the borrower (if necessary), or determine if the borrower has the means to repay the debt.

(ii) Within 45 days after paying a lender's default claim, the agency must send a notice to the borrower that contains the information described in paragraph (b)(5)(ii) of this section. During this time period, the agency also must notify the borrower, either in the notice containing the information described in paragraph (b)(5)(ii) of this section, or in a separate notice, that if he or she does not make repayment arrangements acceptable to the agency, the agency will promptly initiate procedures to collect the debt. The agency's notification to the borrower must state that the agency may administratively garnish the borrower's wages, file a civil suit to compel repayment, offset the borrower's State and Federal income tax refunds and other payments made by the Federal Government to the borrower, assign the loan to the Secretary in accordance with § 682.409, and take other lawful collection means to collect the debt, at the discretion of the agency. The agency's notification must include a statement that borrowers may have certain legal rights in the collection of debts, and that borrowers may wish to contact counselors or lawyers regarding those rights.

(iii) Within a reasonable time after all of the information described in paragraph (b)(6)(ii) of this section has been sent, the agency must send at least one notice informing the borrower that the default has been reported to all nationwide consumer reporting agencies and that the borrower's credit rating may thereby have been damaged.

(iv) The agency must send a notice informing the borrower of the options that are available to remove the loan from default, including an explanation of the fees and conditions associated with each option. This notice must be sent within a reasonable time after the end of the period for requesting an administrative review as specified in paragraph (b)(5)(iv)(B) of this section or, if the borrower has requested an administrative review, within a reasonable time following the conclusion of the administrative review.

(v) A guaranty agency must attempt an annual Federal offset against all eligible borrowers. If an agency initiates proceedings to offset a borrower's State or Federal income tax refunds and other payments made by the Federal Government to the borrower, it may not initiate those proceedings sooner than 60 days after sending the notice described in paragraph (b)(5)(ii)(A) of this section.

(vi) A guaranty agency must initiate administrative wage garnishment proceedings against all eligible borrowers, except as provided in paragraph (b)(6)(vii) of this section, by following the procedures described in paragraph (b)(9) of this section.

(vii) A guaranty agency may file a civil suit against a borrower to compel repayment only if the borrower has no wages that can be garnished under paragraph (b)(9) of this section, or the agency determines that the borrower has sufficient attachable assets or income that is not subject to administrative wage garnishment that can be used to repay the debt, and the use of litigation would be more effective in collection of the debt.

(7) *Special conditions for agency payment of a claim.*

(i) A guaranty agency may adopt a policy under which it pays a claim to a lender on a loan under the conditions described in § 682.509(a)(1).

(ii) Upon the payment of a claim under a policy described in paragraph (b)(7)(i) of this section, the guaranty agency shall—

(A) Perform the loan servicing functions required of a lender under § 682.208, except that the agency is not required to follow the credit bureau reporting requirements of that section;

(B) Perform the functions of the lender during the repayment period of the loan, as required under § 682.209;

(C) If the borrower is delinquent in repaying the loan at the time the agency pays a claim thereon to the lender or becomes delinquent while the agency holds the loan, exercise due diligence in accordance with § 682.411 in attempting to collect the loan from the borrower and any endorser or co-maker; and

(D) After the date of default on the loan, if any, comply with paragraph (b)(6) of this section with respect to collection activities on the loan, with the date of default treated as the claim payment date for purposes of those paragraphs.

(8) *Preemption of State law.* The provisions of paragraphs (b)(2), (5), and (6) of this section preempt any State law, including State statutes, regulations, or rules, that would conflict with or hinder satisfaction of the requirements of these provisions.

(9) *Administrative Garnishment.*

(i) If a guaranty agency decides to garnish the disposable pay of a borrower who is not making payments on a loan held by the agency, on which the Secretary has paid a reinsurance claim, it shall do so in accordance with the following procedures:

(A) The employer shall deduct and pay to the agency from a borrower's wages an amount that does not exceed the lesser of 15 percent of the borrower's disposable pay for each pay period or the amount permitted by 15 U.S.C. 1673, unless the borrower provides the agency with written consent to deduct a greater amount. For this purpose, the term "disposable pay" means that part of the borrower's compensation from an employer remaining after the deduction of any amounts required by law to be withheld.

(B) At least 30 days before the initiation of garnishment proceedings, the guaranty agency shall mail to the borrower's last known address, a written notice of the nature and amount of the debt, the intention of the agency to initiate proceedings to collect the debt through deductions from pay, and an explanation of the borrower's rights.

(C) The guaranty agency shall offer the borrower an opportunity to inspect and copy agency records related to the debt.

(D) The guaranty agency shall offer the borrower an opportunity to enter into a written repayment agreement with the agency under terms agreeable to the agency.

(E) The guaranty agency shall offer the borrower an opportunity for a hearing in accordance with paragraph (b)(9)(i)(J) of this section concerning the existence or the amount of the debt and, in the case of a borrower whose proposed repayment schedule under the garnishment order is established other than by a written agreement under paragraph (b)(9)(i)(D) of this section, the terms of the repayment schedule.

(F) The guaranty agency shall sue any employer for any amount that the employer, after receipt of the garnishment notice provided by the agency under paragraph (b)(9)(i)(H) of this section, fails to withhold from wages owed and payable to an employee under the employer's normal pay and disbursement cycle.

(G) The guaranty agency may not garnish the wages of a borrower whom it knows has been involuntarily separated from employment until the borrower has been reemployed continuously for at least 12 months.

(H) Unless the guaranty agency receives information that the agency believes justifies a delay or cancellation of the withholding order, it shall send a withholding order to the employer within 20 days after the borrower fails to make a timely request for a hearing, or, if a timely request for a hearing is made by the borrower, within 20 days after a final decision is made by the agency to proceed with garnishment.

(I) The notice given to the employer under paragraph (b)(9)(i)(H) of this section must contain only the information as may be necessary for the employer to comply with the withholding order.

(J) The guaranty agency shall provide a hearing, which, at the borrower's option, may be oral or written, if the borrower submits a written request for a hearing on the existence or amount of the debt or the terms of the repayment schedule. The time and location of the hearing shall be established by the agency. An oral hearing may, at the borrower's option, be conducted either in-person or by telephone conference. All telephonic charges must be the responsibility of the guaranty agency.

(K) If the borrower's written request is received by the guaranty agency on or before the 15th day following the borrower's receipt of the notice described in paragraph (b)(9)(i)(B) of this section, the guaranty agency may not issue a withholding order until the borrower has been provided the requested hearing. For purposes of this paragraph, in the absence of evidence to the contrary, a borrower shall be considered to have received the notice described in paragraph (b)(9)(i)(B) of this section 5 days after it was mailed by the agency. The guaranty agency shall provide a hearing to the borrower in sufficient time to permit a decision, in accordance with the procedures that the agency may prescribe, to be rendered within 60 days.

(L) If the borrower's written request is received by the guaranty agency after the 15th day following the borrower's receipt of the notice described in paragraph (b)(9)(i)(B) of this section, the guaranty agency shall provide a hearing to the borrower in sufficient time that a decision, in accordance with the procedures that the agency may prescribe, may be rendered within 60 days, but may not delay issuance of a withholding order unless the agency determines that the delay in filing the request was caused by factors over which the borrower had no control, or the agency receives information that the agency believes justifies a delay or cancellation of the withholding order. For purposes of this paragraph, in the absence of evidence to the contrary, a borrower shall be considered to have received the notice described in paragraph (b)(9)(i)(B) of this section 5 days after it was mailed by the agency.

(M) The hearing official appointed by the agency to conduct the hearing may be any qualified individual, including an administrative law judge, not under the supervision or control of the head of the guaranty agency.

(N) The hearing official shall issue a final written decision at the earliest practicable date, but not later than 60 days after the guaranty agency's receipt of the borrower's hearing request.

(O) As specified in section 488A(a)(8) of the HEA, the borrower may seek judicial relief, including punitive damages, if the employer discharges, refuses to employ, or takes disciplinary action against the borrower due to the issuance of a withholding order.

(ii) References to "the borrower" in this paragraph include all endorsers on a loan.

(10) *Conflicts of interest.*

(i) A guaranty agency shall maintain and enforce written standards of conduct governing the performance of its employees, officers, directors, trustees, and agents engaged in the selection, award, and administration of contracts or agreements. The standards of conduct must, at a minimum, require disclosure of financial or other interests and must mandate disinterested decision-making. The standards must provide for appropriate disciplinary actions to be applied for violations of the standards by employees, officers, directors, trustees, or agents of the guaranty agency, and must include provisions to—

(A) Prohibit any employee, officer, director, trustee, or agent from participating in the selection, award, or decision-making related to the administration of a contract or agreement supported by the reserve fund described in paragraph (a) of this section, if that participation would create a conflict of interest. Such a conflict would arise if the employee, officer, director, trustee, or agent, or any member of his or her immediate family, his or her partner, or an organization that employs or is about to employ any of those parties has a financial or ownership interest in the organization selected for an award or would benefit from the decision made in the administration of the contract or agreement. The prohibitions described in this paragraph do not apply to employees of a State agency covered by codes of conduct established under State law;

(B) Ensure sufficient separation of responsibility and authority between its lender claims processing as a guaranty agency and its lending or loan servicing activities, or both, within the guaranty agency or between that agency and one or more affiliates, including independence in direct reporting requirements and such management and systems controls as may be necessary to demonstrate, in the independent audit required under § 682.410(b)(1), that claims filed by another arm of the guaranty agency or by an affiliate of that agency receive no more favorable treatment than that accorded the claims filed by a lender or servicer that is not an affiliate or part of the guaranty agency; and

(C) Prohibit the employees, officers, directors, trustees, and agents of the guaranty agency, his or her partner, or any member of his or her immediate family, from soliciting or accepting gratuities, favors, or anything of monetary value from contractors or parties to agreements, except that nominal and unsolicited gratuities, favors, or items may be accepted.

(ii) *Guaranty agency restructuring.* If the Secretary determines that action is necessary to protect the Federal fiscal interest because of an agency's failure to meet the requirements of § 682.410(b)(10)(i), the Secretary may require the agency to comply with any additional measures that the Secretary believes are appropriate, including the total divestiture of the agency's non-FFEL functions and the agency's interests in any affiliated organization.

(c) *Enforcement requirements.* A guaranty agency shall take such measures and establish such controls as are necessary to ensure its vigorous enforcement of all Federal, State, and guaranty agency requirements, including agreements, applicable to its loan guarantee program, including, at a minimum, the following:

(1) Conducting comprehensive biennial on-site program reviews, using statistically valid techniques to calculate liabilities to the Secretary that each review indicates may exist, of at least—

(i)(A) Each participating lender whose dollar volume of FFEL loans made or held by the lender and guaranteed by the agency in the preceding year—

(1) Equaled or exceeded two percent of the total of all loans guaranteed in that year by the agency;

(2) Was one of the ten largest lenders whose loans were guaranteed in that year by the agency; or

(3) Equaled or exceeded $10 million in the most recent fiscal year;

(B) Each lender described in section 435(d)(1)(D) or (J) of the Act that is located in any State in which the agency is the principal guarantor and, at the option of each guaranty agency, the Student Loan Marketing Association; and

(C) Each participating school, located in a State for which the guaranty agency is the principal guaranty agency, that has a cohort default rate, as described in subpart M of 34 CFR part 668, for either of the 2 immediately preceding fiscal years, as defined in 34 CFR 668.182, that exceeds 20 percent, unless the school is under a mandate from the Secretary under subpart M of 34 CFR part 668 to take specific default reduction measures or if the total dollar amount of loans entering repayment in each fiscal year on which the cohort default rate over 20 percent is based does not exceed $100,000; or

(ii) The schools and lenders selected by the agency as an alternative to the reviews required by paragraphs (c)(1)(A)–(C) of this section if the Secretary approves the agency's proposed alternative selection methodology.

(2) Demanding prompt repayment by the responsible parties to lenders, borrowers, the agency, or the Secretary, as appropriate, of all funds found in those reviews to be owed by the participants with regard to loans guaranteed by the agency, whether or not the agency holds the loans, and monitoring the implementation by participants of corrective actions, including these repayments, required by the agency as a result of those reviews.

(3) Referring to the Secretary for further enforcement action any case in which repayment of funds to the Secretary is not made in full within 60 days of the date of the agency's written demand to the school, lender, or other party for payment, together with all supporting documentation, any correspondence, and any other documentation submitted by that party regarding the repayment.

(4) Adopting procedures for identifying fraudulent loan applications.

(5) Undertaking or arranging with State or local law enforcement agencies for the prompt and thorough investigation of all allegations and indications of criminal or other programmatic misconduct by its program participants, including violations of Federal law or regulations.

(6) Promptly referring to appropriate State and local regulatory agencies and to nationally recognized accrediting agencies and associations for investigation information received by the guaranty agency that may affect the retention or renewal of the license or accreditation of a program participant.

(7) Promptly reporting all of the allegations and indications of misconduct having a substantial basis in fact, and the scope, progress, and results of the agency's investigations thereof to the Secretary.

(8) Referring appropriate cases to State or local authorities for criminal prosecution or civil litigation.

(9) Promptly notifying the Secretary of—

(i) Any action it takes affecting the FFEL program eligibility of a participating lender or school;

(ii) Information it receives regarding an action affecting the FFEL program eligibility of a participating lender or school taken by a nationally recognized accrediting agency, association, or a State licensing agency;

(iii) Any judicial or administrative proceeding relating to the enforceability of FFEL loans guaranteed by the agency or in which tuition obligations of a school's students are directly at issue, other than a proceeding relating to a single borrower or student; and

(iv) Any petition for relief in bankruptcy, application for receivership, or corporate dissolution proceeding brought by or against a school or lender participating in its loan guarantee program.

(10) Cooperating with all program reviews, investigations, and audits conducted by the Secretary relating to the agency's loan guarantee program.

(11) Taking prompt action to protect the rights of borrowers and the Federal fiscal interest respecting loans that the agency has guaranteed when the agency learns that a participating school or holder of loans is experiencing problems that threaten the solvency of the school or holder, including—

(i) Conducting on-site program reviews;

(ii) Providing training and technical assistance, if appropriate;

(iii) Filing a proof of claim with a bankruptcy court for recovery of any funds due the agency and any refunds due to borrowers on FFEL loans that it has guaranteed when the agency learns that a school has filed a bankruptcy petition;

(iv) Promptly notifying the Secretary that the agency has determined that a school or holder of loans is experiencing potential solvency problems; and

(v) Promptly notifying the Secretary of the results of any actions taken by the agency to protect Federal funds involving such a school or holder.

(Approved by the Office of Management and Budget under control number 1845-0020)

(Authority: 20 U.S.C. 1078, 1078-1, 1078-2, 1078-3, 1080a, 1082, 1087, 1091a, and 1099)

[58 Fed. Reg. 9119 (Feb. 19, 1993); 59 Fed. Reg. 22487 (Apr. 29, 1994); 59 Fed. Reg. 25747 (May 17, 1994); 59 Fed. Reg. 33357 (June 28, 1994); 59 Fed. Reg. 35625 (July 13, 1994); 59 Fed. Reg. 46175 (Sept. 7, 1994); 59 Fed. Reg. 60691 (Nov. 25, 1994); 60 Fed. Reg. 32912 (June 26, 1995); 61 Fed. Reg. 60436, 60486 (Nov. 27, 1996); 64 Fed. Reg. 18980 (Apr. 16, 1999); 64 Fed. Reg. 58630 (Oct. 29, 1999); 64 Fed. Reg. 58965 (Nov. 1, 1999); 65 Fed. Reg. 65621 (Nov. 1, 2000); 65 Fed. Reg. 65650 (Nov. 1, 2000); 66 Fed. Reg. 34764 (June 29, 2001); 68 Fed. Reg. 75429 (Dec. 31, 2003); 71 Fed. Reg. 45708 (Aug. 9, 2006); 74 Fed. Reg. 56000 (Oct. 29, 2009)]

§ 682.411 Lender due diligence in collecting guaranty agency loans.

(a) *General.* In the event of delinquency on an FFEL Program loan, the lender must engage in at least the collection efforts described in paragraphs (c) through (n) of this section, except that in the case of a loan made to a borrower who is incarcerated, residing outside a State, Mexico, or Canada, or whose telephone number is unknown, the lender may send a forceful collection letter instead of each telephone effort required by this section.

(b) *Delinquency.*

(1) For purposes of this section, delinquency on a loan begins on the first day after the due date of the first missed payment that is not later made. The due date of the first payment is established by the lender but must occur by the deadlines specified in § 682.209(a) or, if the lender first learns after the fact that the borrower has entered the repayment period, no later than 75 days after the day the lender so learns, except as provided in § 682.209(a)(2)(v) and (a)(3)(ii)(E). If a payment is made late, the first day of delinquency is the day after the due date of the next missed payment that is not later made. A payment that is within five dollars of the amount normally required to advance the due date may nevertheless advance the due date if the lender's procedures allow for that advancement.

(2) At no point during the periods specified in paragraphs (c), (d), and (e) of this section may the lender permit the occurrence of a gap in collection activity, as defined in paragraph (j) of this section, of more than 45 days (60 days in the case of a transfer).

(3) As part of one of the collection activities provided for in this section, the lender must provide the borrower with information on the availability of the Student Loan Ombudsman's office.

(c) *1–15 days delinquent.* Except in the case in which a loan is brought into this period by a payment on the loan, expiration of an authorized deferment or forbearance period, or the lender's receipt from the drawee of a dishonored check submitted as a payment on the loan, the lender during this period must send at least one written notice or collection letter to the borrower informing the borrower of the delinquency and urging the borrower to make payments sufficient to eliminate the delinquency. The notice or collection letter sent during this period must include, at a minimum, a lender or servicer contact, a telephone number, and a prominent statement informing the borrower that assistance may be available if he or she is experiencing difficulty in making a scheduled repayment.

(d) *16–180 days delinquent (16–240 days delinquent for a loan repayable in installments less frequently than monthly).*

(1) Unless exempted under paragraph (d)(4) of this section, during this period the lender must engage in at least four diligent efforts to contact the borrower by telephone and send at least four collection letters urging the borrower to make the required payments on the loan. At least one of the diligent efforts to contact the borrower by telephone must occur on or before, and another one must occur after, the 90th day of delinquency. Collection letters sent during this period must include, at a minimum, information for the borrower regarding deferment, forbearance, income-sensitive repayment, income-based repayment and loan consolidation, and other available options to avoid default.

(2) At least two of the collection letters required under paragraph (d)(1) of this section must warn the borrower that, if the loan is not paid, the lender will assign the loan to the guaranty agency that, in turn, will report the default to all national credit bureaus, and that the agency may institute proceedings to offset the borrower's State and Federal income tax refunds and other payments made by the Federal Government to the borrower or to garnish the borrower's wages, or to assign the loan to the Federal Government for litigation against the borrower.

(3) Following the lender's receipt of a payment on the loan or a correct address for the borrower, the lender's receipt from the drawee of a dishonored check received as a payment on the loan, the lender's receipt of a correct telephone number for the borrower, or the expiration of an authorized deferment or forbearance period, the lender is required to engage in only—

(i) Two diligent efforts to contact the borrower by telephone during this period, if the loan is less than 91 days delinquent (121 days delinquent for a loan repayable in installments less frequently than monthly) upon receipt of the payment, correct address, correct telephone number, or returned check, or expiration of the deferment or forbearance; or

(ii) One diligent effort to contact the borrower by telephone during this period if the loan is 91–120 days delinquent (121–180 days delinquent for a loan repayable in installments less frequently than monthly) upon receipt of the payment, correct address, correct telephone number, or returned check, or expiration of the deferment or forbearance.

(4) A lender need not attempt to contact by telephone any borrower who is more than 120 days delinquent (180 days delinquent for a loan repayable in installments less frequent than monthly) following the lender's receipt of—

(i) A payment on the loan;

(ii) A correct address or correct telephone number for the borrower;

(iii) A dishonored check received from the drawee as a payment on the loan; or

(iv) The expiration of an authorized deferment or forbearance.

(e) *181–270 days delinquent (241–330 days delinquent for a loan repayable in installments less frequently than monthly).* During this period the lender must engage in efforts to urge the borrower to make the required payments on the loan. These efforts must, at a minimum, provide information to the borrower regarding options to avoid default and the consequences of defaulting on the loan.

(f) *Final demand.* On or after the 241st day of delinquency (the 301st day for loans payable in less frequent installments than monthly) the lender must send a final demand letter to the borrower requiring repayment of the loan in full and notifying the borrower that a default will be reported to a national credit bureau. The lender must allow the borrower at least 30 days after the date the letter is mailed to respond to the final demand letter and to bring the loan out of default before filing a default claim on the loan.

(g) *Collection procedures when borrower's telephone number is not available.* Upon completion of a diligent but unsuccessful effort to ascertain the correct telephone number of a borrower as required by paragraph (m) of this section, the lender is excused from any further efforts to contact the borrower by telephone, unless the borrower's number is obtained before the 211th day of delinquency (the 271st day for loans repayable in installments less frequently than monthly).

(h) *Skip-tracing.*

(1) Unless the letter specified under paragraph (f) of this section has already been sent, within 10 days of its receipt of information indicating that it does not know the borrower's current address, the lender must begin to diligently attempt to locate the borrower through the use of effective commercial skip-tracing techniques. These efforts must include, but are not limited to, sending a letter

to or making a diligent effort to contact each endorser, relative, reference, individual, and entity, identified in the borrower's loan file, including the schools the student attended. For this purpose, a lender's contact with a school official who might reasonably be expected to know the borrower's address may be with someone other than the financial aid administrator, and may be in writing or by phone calls. These efforts must be completed by the date of default with no gap of more than 45 days between attempts to contact those individuals or entities.

(2) Upon receipt of information indicating that it does not know the borrower's current address, the lender must discontinue the collection efforts described in paragraphs (c) through (f) of this section.

(3) If the lender is unable to ascertain the borrower's current address despite its performance of the activities described in paragraph (h)(1) of this section, the lender is excused thereafter from performance of the collection activities described in paragraphs (c) through (f) and (l)(1) through (l)(3) and (l)(5) of this section unless it receives communication indicating the borrower's address before the 241st day of delinquency (the 301st day for loans payable in less frequent installments than monthly).

(4) The activities specified by paragraph (m)(1)(i) or (ii) of this section (with references to the "borrower" understood to mean endorser, reference, relative, individual, or entity as appropriate) meet the requirement that the lender make a diligent effort to contact each individual identified in the borrower's loan file.

(i) *Default aversion assistance.* Not earlier than the 60th day and no later than the 120th day of delinquency, a lender must request default aversion assistance from the guaranty agency that guarantees the loan.

(j) *Gap in collection activity.* For purposes of this section, the term gap in collection activity means, with respect to a loan, any period—

(1) Beginning on the date that is the day after—
(i) The due date of a payment unless the lender does not know the borrower's address on that date;
(ii) The day on which the lender receives a payment on a loan that remains delinquent notwithstanding the payment;
(iii) The day on which the lender receives the correct address for a delinquent borrower;
(iv) The day on which the lender completes a collection activity;
(v) The day on which the lender receives a dishonored check submitted as a payment on the loan;
(vi) The expiration of an authorized deferment or forbearance period on a delinquent loan; or
(vii) The day the lender receives information indicating it does not know the borrower's current address; and

(2) Ending on the date of the earliest of—
(i) The day on which the lender receives the first subsequent payment or completed deferment request or forbearance agreement;
(ii) The day on which the lender begins the first subsequent collection activity;
(iii) The day on which the lender receives written communication from the borrower relating to his or her account; or
(iv) Default.

(k) *Transfer.* For purposes of this section, the term transfer with respect to a loan means any action, including, but not limited to, the sale of the loan, that results in a change in the system used to monitor or conduct collection activity on a loan from one system to another.

(l) *Collection activity.* For purposes of this section, the term collection activity with respect to a loan means—

(1) Mailing or otherwise transmitting to the borrower at an address that the lender reasonably believes to be the borrower's current address a collection letter or final demand letter that satisfies the timing and content requirements of paragraph (c), (d), (e), or (f) of this section;
(2) Making an attempt to contact the borrower by telephone to urge the borrower to begin or resume repayment;
(3) Conducting skip-tracing efforts, in accordance with paragraph (h)(1) or (m)(1)(iii) of this section, to locate a borrower whose correct address or telephone number is unknown to the lender;
(4) Mailing or otherwise transmitting to the guaranty agency a request for default aversion assistance available from the agency on the loan at the time the request is transmitted; or
(5) Any telephone discussion or personal contact with the borrower so long as the borrower is apprised of the account's past-due status.

(m) *Diligent effort for telephone contact.*
(1) For purposes of this section, the term diligent effort with respect to telephone contact means—
(i) A successful effort to contact the borrower by telephone;
(ii) At least two unsuccessful attempts to contact the borrower by telephone at a number that the lender reasonably believes to be the borrower's correct telephone number; or
(iii) An unsuccessful effort to ascertain the correct telephone number of a borrower, including, but not limited to, a directory assistance inquiry as to the borrower's telephone number, and sending a letter to or making a diligent effort to contact each reference, relative, and individual identified in the most recent loan application or most recent school certification for that borrower held by the lender. The lender may contact a school official other than the financial aid administrator who reasonably may be expected to know the borrower's address or telephone number.

(2) If the lender is unable to ascertain the borrower's correct telephone number despite its performance of the activities described in paragraph (m)(1)(iii) of this section, the lender is excused thereafter from attempting to contact the borrower by telephone unless it receives a communication indicating the borrower's current telephone number before the 211th day of delinquency (the 271st day for loans repayable in installments less frequently than monthly).

(3) The activities specified by paragraph (m)(1)(i) or (ii) of this section (with references to "the borrower" understood to mean endorser, reference, relative, or individual as appropriate), meet the requirement that the lender make a diligent effort to contact each endorser or each reference, relative, or individual identified on the borrower's most recent loan application or most recent school certification.

(n) *Due diligence for endorsers.*
(1) Before filing a default claim on a loan with an endorser, the lender must—
(i) Make a diligent effort to contact the endorser by telephone; and
(ii) Send the endorser on the loan two letters advising the endorser of the delinquent status of the loan and urging the endorser to make the required payments on the loan with at least one letter containing the information described in paragraph (d)(2) of this section (with references to "the borrower" understood to mean the endorser).

(2) On or after the 241st day of delinquency (the 301st day for loans payable in less frequent installments than monthly) the lender must send a final demand letter to the endorser requiring repayment of the loan in full and notifying the endorser that a default will be reported to a national credit bureau. The lender must allow the endorser at least 30 days after the date the letter is mailed to respond to the final demand letter and to bring the loan out of default before filing a default claim on the loan.

(3) Unless the letter specified under paragraph (n)(2) of this section has already been sent, upon receipt of information indicating that it does not know the endorser's current address or telephone number, the lender must diligently attempt to locate the endorser through the use of effective commercial skip-tracing techniques. This effort must include an inquiry to directory assistance.

(o) *Preemption.* The provisions of this section—

(1) Preempt any State law, including State statutes, regulations, or rules, that would conflict with or hinder satisfaction of the requirements or frustrate the purposes of this section; and

(2) Do not preempt provisions of the Fair Credit Reporting Act that provide relief to a borrower while the lender determines the legal enforceability of a loan when the lender receives a valid identity theft report or notification from a credit bureau that information furnished is a result of an alleged identity theft as defined in § 682.402(e)(14).

(Approved by the Office of Management and Budget under control number 1845-0020)

(Authority: 20 U.S.C. 1078, 1078-1, 1078-2, 1078-3, 1080a, 1082, 1087)

[58 Fed. Reg. 9119 (Feb. 19, 1993); 59 Fed. Reg. 22489 (Apr. 29, 1994); 59 Fed. Reg. 25747 (May 17, 1994); 59 Fed. Reg. 46175 (Sept. 7, 1994); 60 Fed. Reg. 32912 (June 26, 1995); 61 Fed. Reg. 60486 (Nov. 27, 1996); 62 Fed. Reg. 13539 (Mar. 21, 1997); 64 Fed. Reg. 18981 (Apr. 16, 1999); 64 Fed. Reg. 58630 (Oct. 29, 1999); 64 Fed. Reg. 58965 (Nov. 1, 1999); 72 Fed. Reg. 62006 (Nov. 1, 2007); 73 Fed. Reg. 63254 (Oct. 23, 2008)]

* * *

B.3 Perkins Loan Regulations

34 C.F.R. sec.

* * *

674.33 Repayment.
674.34 Deferment of repayment—Federal Perkins loans, NDSLs and Defense loans.

* * *

674.38 Deferment procedures.
674.39 Loan rehabilitation.

* * *

674.50 Assignment of defaulted loans to the United States.
674.51 Special definitions.
674.52 Cancellation procedures.

* * *

674.61 Discharge for death or disability.

* * *

SOURCE: 52 Fed. Reg. 45555 (Nov. 30, 1987); 52 Fed. Reg. 45747 (Dec. 1, 1987); 52 Fed. Reg. 45754 (Dec. 1, 1987); 73 Fed. Reg. 35494 (June 23, 2008); 74 Fed. Reg. 55660 (Oct. 28, 2009), unless otherwise noted.

AUTHORITY: 20 U.S.C. 1070g, 1087aa–1087hh, unless otherwise noted.

* * *

§ 674.33 Repayment.

(a) *Repayment Plan.*

(1) The institution shall establish a repayment plan before the student ceases to be at least a half-time regular student.

(2) If the last scheduled payment would be $25 or less the institution may combine it with the next-to-last repayment.

(3) If the installment payment for all loans made to a borrower by an institution is not a multiple of $5, the institution may round that payment to the next highest dollar amount that is a multiple of $5.

(4) The institution shall apply any payment on a loan in the following order:
  (i) Collection costs.
  (ii) Late charges.
  (iii) Accrued interest.
  (iv) Principal.

(b) *Minimum monthly repayment—*

(1) *Minimum monthly repayment option.*
  (i) An institution may require a borrower to pay a minimum monthly repayment if—
    (A) The promissory note includes a minimum monthly repayment provision specifying the amount of the minimum monthly repayment; and
    (B) The monthly repayment of principal and interest for a 10-year repayment period is less than the minimum monthly repayment; or
  (ii) An institution may require a borrower to pay a minimum monthly repayment if the borrower has received loans with different interest rates at the same institution and the total monthly repayment would otherwise be less than the minimum monthly repayment.

(2) *Minimum monthly repayment of loans from more than one institution.* If a borrower has received loans from more than one institution and has notified the institution that he or she wants the minimum monthly payment determination to be based on payments due to other institutions, the following rules apply:
  (i) If the total of the monthly repayments is equal to at least the minimum monthly repayment, no institution may exercise a minimum monthly repayment option.
  (ii) If only one institution exercises the minimum monthly repayment option when the monthly repayment would otherwise be less than the minimum repayment option, that institution receives the difference between the minimum monthly repayment and the repayment owed to the other institution.
  (iii) If each institution exercises the minimum repayment option, the minimum monthly repayment must be divided among the institutions in proportion to the amount of principal advanced by each institution.

(3) *Minimum monthly repayment of both Defense and NDSL or Federal Perkins loans from one or more institutions.* If the borrower has notified the institution that he or she wants the minimum monthly payment determination to be based on payments due to other institutions, and if the total monthly repayment is less than $30 and the monthly repayment on a Defense loan is less than $15 a month, the amount attributed to the Defense loan may not exceed $15 a month.

(4) *Minimum monthly repayment of loans with differing grace periods and deferments.* If the borrower has received loans with different grace periods and deferments, the institution shall treat each note separately, and the borrower shall pay the applicable minimum monthly payment for a loan that is not in the grace or deferment period.

(5) *Hardship.* The institution may reduce the borrower's scheduled repayments for a period of not more than one year at a time if—
  (i) It determines that the borrower is unable to make the scheduled repayments due to hardship (see § 674.33(c)); and
  (ii) The borrower's scheduled repayment is the minimum monthly repayment described in paragraph (b) of this section.

(6) *Minimum monthly repayment rates.* For the purposes of this section, the minimum monthly repayment rate is—
  (i) $15 for a Defense loan;
  (ii) $30 for an NDSL Loan or for a Federal Perkins loan made before October 1, 1992, or for a Federal Perkins loan made on or after October 1, 1992, to a borrower who, on the date the loan is made, has an outstanding balance of principal or interest owing on any loan made under this part; or
  (iii) $40 for a Federal Perkins loan made on or after October 1, 1992, to a borrower who, on the date the loan is made, has no outstanding balance of principal or interest owing on any loan made under this part.

(7) The institution shall determine the minimum repayment amount under paragraph (b) of this section for loans with repayment installment intervals greater than one month by multiplying the amounts in paragraph (b) of this section by the number of months in the installment interval.

(c) *Extension of repayment period—*

(1) *Hardship.* The institution may extend a borrower's repayment period due to prolonged illness or unemployment.

(2) *Low-income individual.*
  (i) For Federal Perkins loans and NDSLs made on or after October 1, 1980, the institution may extend the borrower's repayment period up to 10 additional years beyond the 10-year maximum repayment period if the institution determines during the course of the repayment period that the borrower is a "low-income individual." The borrower qualifies for an extension of the repayment period on the basis of low-income status only during the period in

which the borrower meets the criteria described in paragraph (c)(2)(i)(A) or (B) of this section. The term low-income individual means the following:

(A) For an unmarried borrower without dependents, an individual whose total income for the preceding calendar year did not exceed 45 percent of the Income Protection Allowance for the current award year for a family of four with one in college.

(B) For a borrower with a family that includes the borrower and any spouse or legal dependents, an individual whose total family income for the preceding calendar year did not exceed 125 percent of the Income Protection Allowance for the current award year for a family with one in college and equal in size to that of the borrower's family.

(ii) The institution shall use the Income Protection Allowance published annually in accordance with section 478 of the HEA in making this determination.

(iii) The institution shall review the borrower's status annually to determine whether the borrower continues to qualify for an extended repayment period based on his or her status as a "low-income individual."

(iv) Upon determining that a borrower ceases to qualify for an extended repayment period under this section, the institution shall amend the borrower's repayment schedule. The term of the amended repayment schedule may not exceed the number of months remaining on the original repayment schedule, provided that the institution may not include the time elapsed during any extension of the repayment period granted under this section in determining the number of months remaining on the original repayment schedule.

(3) Interest continues to accrue during any extension of a repayment period.

(d) *Forbearance.*

(1) Forbearance means the temporary cessation of payments, allowing an extension of time for making payments, or temporarily accepting smaller payments than previously were scheduled.

(2) Upon receipt of a request and supporting documentation, the institution shall grant the borrower forbearance of principal and, unless otherwise indicated by the borrower, interest renewable at intervals of up to 12 months for periods that collectively do not exceed three years.

(3) The terms of forbearance must be agreed upon, in writing, by the borrower and the institution. The school confirms this agreement by notice to the borrower, and by recording the terms in the borrower's file.

(4) In granting a forbearance under this section, an institution shall grant a temporary cessation of payments, unless the borrower chooses another form of forbearance subject to paragraph (d)(1) of this section.

(5) An institution shall grant forbearance if—

(i) The amount of the payments the borrower is obligated to make on title IV loans each month (or a proportional share if the payments are due less frequently than monthly) is collectively equal to or greater than 20 percent of the borrower's total monthly gross income;

(ii) The institution determines that the borrower should qualify for the forbearance due to poor health or for other acceptable reasons; or

(iii) The Secretary authorizes a period of forbearance due to a national military mobilization or other national emergency.

(6) Before granting a forbearance to a borrower under paragraph (d)(5)(i) of this section, the institution shall require the borrower to submit at least the following documentation:

(i) Evidence showing the amount of the most recent total monthly gross income received by the borrower; and

(ii) Evidence showing the amount of the monthly payments owed by the borrower for the most recent month for the borrower's title IV loans.

(7) Interest accrues during any period of forbearance.

(8) The institution may not include the periods of forbearance described in this paragraph in determining the 10-year repayment period.

(e) *Compromise of repayment.*

(1) An institution may compromise on the repayment of a defaulted loan if—

(i) The institution has fully complied with all due diligence requirements specified in subpart C of this part; and

(ii) The student borrower pays in a single lump-sum payment—

(A) 90 percent of the outstanding principal balance on the loan under this part;

(B) The interest due on the loan; and

(C) Any collection fees due on the loan.

(2) The Federal share of the compromise repayment must bear the same relation to the institution's share of the compromise repayment as the Federal capital contribution to the institution's loan Fund under this part bears to the institution's capital contribution to the Fund.

(f)(1) *Incentive repayment program.* An institution may establish the following repayment incentives:

(i) A reduction of no more than one percent of the interest rate on a loan on which the borrower has made 48 consecutive, monthly repayments.

(ii) A discount of no more than five percent on the balance owed on a loan which the borrower pays in full prior to the end of the repayment period.

(iii) With the Secretary's approval, any other incentive the institution determines will reduce defaults and replenish its Fund.

(2) *Limitation on the use of funds.*

(i) The institution must reimburse its Fund, on at least a quarterly basis, for money lost to its Fund that otherwise would have been paid by the borrower as a result of establishing a repayment incentive under paragraphs (f)(1)(i), (ii) and (iii) of this section.

(ii) An institution may not use Federal funds, including Federal funds from the student loan fund, or institutional funds from the student loan fund to pay for any repayment incentive authorized by this section.

(g) *Closed school discharge.*

(1) *General.*

(i) The holder of an NDSL or a Federal Perkins Loan discharges the borrower's (and any endorser's) obligation to repay the loan if the borrower did not complete the program of study for which the loan was made because the school at which the borrower was enrolled closed.

(ii) For the purposes of this section—

(A) A school's closure date is the date that the school ceases to provide educational instruction in all programs, as determined by the Secretary;

(B) "School" means a school's main campus or any location or branch of the main campus; and

(C) The "holder" means the Secretary or the school that holds the loan.

(2) *Relief pursuant to discharge.*

(i) Discharge under this section relieves the borrower of any past or present obligation to repay the loan and any accrued interest or collection costs with respect to the loan.

(ii) The discharge of a loan under this section qualifies the borrower for reimbursement of amounts paid voluntarily or through enforced collection on the loan.

(iii) A borrower who has defaulted on a loan discharged under this section is not considered to have been in default on the loan after discharge, and such a borrower is eligible to receive assistance under programs authorized by title IV of the HEA.

(iv) The Secretary or the school, if the school holds the loan, reports the discharge of a loan under this section to all credit bureaus to which the status of the loan was previously reported.

(3) Determination of borrower qualification for discharge by the Secretary. The Secretary may discharge the borrower's obligation to repay an NDSL or Federal Perkins Loan without an application if the Secretary determines that—

(i) The borrower qualified for and received a discharge on a loan pursuant to 34 CFR

682.402(d) (Federal Family Education Loan Program) or 34 CFR 685.213 (Federal Direct Loan Program), and was unable to receive a discharge on an NDSL or Federal Perkins Loan because the Secretary lacked the statutory authority to discharge the loan; or

(ii) Based on information in the Secretary's possession, the borrower qualifies for a discharge.

(4) *Borrower qualification for discharge.* Except as provided in paragraph (g)(3) of this section, in order to qualify for discharge of an NDSL or Federal Perkins Loan, a borrower must submit to the holder of the loan a written request and sworn statement, and the factual assertions in the statement must be true. The statement need not be notarized but must be made by the borrower under penalty of perjury. In the statement the borrower must—

(i) State that the borrower—

(A) Received the proceeds of a loan to attend a school;

(B) Did not complete the program of study at that school because the school closed while the student was enrolled, or the student withdrew from the school not more than 90 days before the school closed (or longer in exceptional circumstances); and

(C) Did not complete and is not in the process of completing the program of study through a teachout at another school as defined in 34 CFR 602.2 and administered in accordance with 34 CFR 602.207(b)(6), by transferring academic credit earned at the closed school to another school, or by any other comparable means;

(ii) State whether the borrower has made a claim with respect to the school's closing with any third party, such as the holder of a performance bond or a tuition recovery program, and, if so, the amount of any payment received by the borrower or credited to the borrower's loan obligation; and

(iii) State that the borrower—

(A) Agrees to provide to the holder of the loan upon request other documentation reasonably available to the borrower that demonstrates that the borrower meets the qualifications for discharge under this section; and

(B) Agrees to cooperate with the Secretary in enforcement actions in accordance with paragraph (g)(6) of this section and to transfer any right to recovery against a third party to the Secretary in accordance with paragraph (g)(7) of this section.

(5) *Fraudulently obtained loans.* A borrower who secured a loan through fraudulent means, as determined by the ruling of a court or an administrative tribunal of competent jurisdiction, is ineligible for a discharge under this section.

(6) *Cooperation by borrower in enforcement actions.*

(i) In order to obtain a discharge under this section, a borrower must cooperate with the Secretary in any judicial or administrative proceeding brought by the Secretary to recover amounts discharged or to take other enforcement action with respect to the conduct on which the discharge was based. At the request of the Secretary and upon the Secretary's tendering to the borrower the fees and costs that are customarily provided in litigation to reimburse witnesses, the borrower must—

(A) Provide testimony regarding any representation made by the borrower to support a request for discharge;

(B) Provide any documents reasonably available to the borrower with respect to those representations; and

(C) If required by the Secretary, provide a sworn statement regarding those documents and representations.

(ii) The holder denies the request for a discharge or revokes the discharge of a borrower who—

(A) Fails to provide the testimony, documents, or a sworn statement required under paragraph (g)(6)(i) of this section; or

(B) Provides testimony, documents, or a sworn statement that does not support the material representations made by the borrower to obtain the discharge.

(7) *Transfer to the Secretary of borrower's right of recovery against third parties.*

(i) In the case of a loan held by the Secretary, upon discharge under this section, the borrower is deemed to have assigned to and relinquished in favor of the Secretary any right to a loan refund (up to the amount discharged) that the borrower may have by contract or applicable law with respect to the loan or the enrollment agreement for the program for which the loan was received, against the school, its principals, its affiliates and their successors, its sureties, and any private fund, including the portion of a public fund that represents funds received from a private party.

(ii) The provisions of this section apply notwithstanding any provision of State law that would otherwise restrict transfer of those rights by the borrower, limit or prevent a transferee from exercising those rights, or establish procedures or a scheme of distribution that would prejudice the Secretary's ability to recover on those rights.

(iii) Nothing in this section limits or forecloses the borrower's right to pursue legal and equitable relief regarding disputes arising from matters unrelated to the discharged NDSL or Federal Perkins Loan.

(8) *Discharge procedures.*

(i) After confirming the date of a school's closure, the holder of the loan identifies any NDSL or Federal Perkins Loan borrower who appears to have been enrolled at the school on the school closure date or to have withdrawn not more than 90 days prior to the closure date.

(ii) If the borrower's current address is known, the holder of the loan mails the borrower a discharge application and an explanation of the qualifications and procedures for obtaining a discharge. The holder of the loan also promptly suspends any efforts to collect from the borrower on any affected loan. The holder of the loan may continue to receive borrower payments.

(iii) In the case of a loan held by the Secretary, if the borrower's current address is unknown, the Secretary attempts to locate the borrower and determine the borrower's potential eligibility for a discharge under this section by consulting with representatives of the closed school or representatives of the closed school's third-party billing and collection servicers, the school's licensing agency, the school accrediting agency, and other appropriate parties. If the Secretary learns the new address of a borrower, the Secretary mails to the borrower a discharge application and explanation and suspends collection, as described in paragraph (g)(8)(ii) of this section.

(iv) In the case of a loan held by a school, if the borrower's current address is unknown, the school attempts to locate the borrower and determine the borrower's potential eligibility for a discharge under this section by taking steps required to locate the borrower under § 674.44.

(v) If the borrower fails to submit the written request and sworn statement described in paragraph (g)(4) of this section within 60 days of the holder of the loan's mailing the discharge application, the holder of the loan resumes collection and grants forbearance of principal and interest for the period during which collection activity was suspended.

(vi) If the holder of the loan determines that a borrower who requests a discharge meets the qualifications for a discharge, the holder of the loan notifies the borrower in writing of that determination.

(vii) In the case of a loan held by the Secretary, if the Secretary determines that a borrower who requests a discharge does not meet the qualifications for a discharge, the Secretary notifies that borrower, in writing, of that determination and the reasons for the determination.

(viii) In the case of a loan held by a school, if the school determines that a borrower who requests a discharge does not meet the qualifications for discharge, the school submits that determination and all supporting materials to the Secretary for approval. The Secretary reviews the materials, makes an independent determination, and notifies the borrower in writing of the determination and the reasons for the determination.

(ix) In the case of a loan held by a school and discharged by either the school or the Secretary, the school must reimburse its Fund for the entire amount of any outstanding principal and interest on the loan, and any collection costs charged to the Fund as a result of collection efforts on a discharged loan. The school must also reimburse the borrower for any amount of principal, interest, late charges or collection costs the borrower paid on a loan discharged under this section.

(Approved by the Office of Management and Budget under control number 1845-0019)

Authority: 20 U.S.C. 1087dd.

[57 Fed. Reg. 32345 (July 21, 1992); 57 Fed. Reg. 60706 (Dec. 21, 1992); 58 Fed. Reg. 36870, 36871 (July 9, 1993); 59 Fed. Reg. 61409 (Nov. 30, 1994); 60 Fed. Reg. 61814 (Dec. 1, 1995); 62 Fed. Reg. 50848 (Sept. 26, 1997); 64 Fed. Reg. 58309 (Oct. 28, 1999); 65 Fed. Reg. 18002, 18003 (Apr. 6, 2000); 65 Fed. Reg. 26136 (May 5, 2000); 67 Fed. Reg. 67076 (Nov. 1, 2002); 74 Fed. Reg. 55660 (Oct. 28, 2009)]

§ 674.34 Deferment of repayment—Federal Perkins loans, NDSLs and Defense loans.

(a) The borrower may defer making a scheduled installment repayment on a Federal Perkins loan, an NDSL, or a Defense loan, regardless of contrary provisions of the borrower's promissory note and regardless of the date the loan was made, during periods described in paragraphs (b), (c), (d), (e), (f), and (g) of this section.

(b)(1) The borrower need not repay principal, and interest does not accrue, during a period after the commencement or resumption of the repayment period on a loan, when the borrower is—

(i) Enrolled and in attendance as a regular student in at least a half-time course of study at an eligible institution;

(ii) Enrolled and in attendance as a regular student in a course of study that is part of a graduate fellowship program approved by the Secretary;

(iii) Engaged in graduate or post-graduate fellowship-supported study (such as a Fulbright grant) outside the United States; or

(iv) Enrolled in a course of study that is part of a rehabilitation training program for disabled individuals approved by the Secretary as described in paragraph (g) of this section.

(2) No borrower is eligible for a deferment under paragraph (b)(1) of this section while serving in a medical internship or residency program, except for a residency program in dentistry.

(3) The institution of higher education at which the borrower is enrolled does not need to be participating in the Federal Perkins Loan program for the borrower to qualify for a deferment.

(4) If a borrower is attending an institution of higher education as at least a half-time regular student for a full academic year and intends to enroll as at least a half-time regular student in the next academic year, the borrower is entitled to a deferment for 12 months.

(5) If an institution no longer qualifies as an institution of higher education, the borrower's deferment ends on the date the institution ceases to qualify.

(c)(1) The borrower of a Federal Perkins loan need not repay principal, and interest does not accrue, for any period during which the borrower is engaged in service described in §§ 674.53, 674.54, 674.56, 674.57, 674.58, 674.59, and 674.60.

(2) The borrower of an NDSL need not repay principal, and interest does not accrue, for any period during which the borrower is engaged in service described in §§ 674.53, 674.54, 674.56, 674.57, 674.58, and 674.59.

(d) The borrower need not repay principal, and interest does not accrue, for any period not to exceed 3 years during which the borrower is seeking and unable to find full-time employment.

(e) The borrower need not repay principal, and interest does not accrue, for periods of up to one year at a time (except that a deferment under paragraph (e)(5) of this section may be granted for the lesser of the borrower's full term of service in the Peace Corps or the borrower's remaining period of economic hardship deferment eligibility) that, collectively, do not exceed 3 years, during which the borrower is suffering an economic hardship, if the borrower provides documentation satisfactory to the institution showing that the borrower is within any of the categories described in paragraphs (e)(1) through (e)(5) of this section.

(1) Has been granted an economic hardship deferment under either the Federal Direct Loan Program or the FFEL programs for the period of time for which the borrower has requested an economic hardship deferment for his or her Federal Perkins loan.

(2) Is receiving payment under a federal or state public assistance program, such as Aid to Families with Dependent Children, Supplemental Security Income, Food Stamps, or state general public assistance.

(3) Is working full-time and earning a total monthly gross income that does not exceed the greater of—

(i) The monthly earnings of an individual earning the minimum wage described in section 6 of the Fair Labor Standards Act of 1938; or

(ii) An amount equal to 100 percent of the poverty guideline applicable to the borrower's family size as published annually by the Department of Health and Human Services pursuant to 42 U.S.C. 9902(2). If a borrower is not a resident of a State identified in the poverty guidelines, the poverty guideline to be used for the borrower is the poverty guideline (for the relevant family size) used for the 48 contiguous States.

(4) Is not receiving total monthly gross income that exceeds twice the amount specified in paragraph (e)(3) of this section and, after deducting an amount equal to the borrower's monthly payments on federal postsecondary education loans, as determined under paragraph (e)(10) of this section, the remaining amount of that income does not exceed the amount specified in paragraph (e)(3) of this section;

(5) Is serving as a volunteer in the Peace Corps.

(6) For a deferment granted under paragraph (e)(4) of this section, the institution shall require the borrower to submit at least the following documentation to qualify for an initial period of deferment—

(i) Evidence showing the amount of the borrower's most recent total monthly gross income, as defined in section 674.2; and

(ii) Evidence that would enable the institution to determine the amount of the monthly payments that would have been owed by the borrower during the deferment period to other entities for federal postsecondary education loans in accordance with paragraph (e)(9) of this section.

(7) To qualify for a subsequent period of deferment that begins less than one year after the end of a period of deferment under paragraphs (e)(3) and (e)(4) of this section, the institution shall require the borrower to submit a copy of the borrower's federal income tax return if the borrower filed a tax return within eight months prior to the date the deferment is requested.

(8)(i) For purposes of paragraph (e)(3) of this section, a borrower is considered to be working full-time if the borrower is expected to be employed for at least three consecutive months at 30 hours per week.

(ii) For purposes of paragraph (e)(3)(ii) of this section, family size means the number that is determined by counting the borrower, the borrower's spouse, and the borrower's children, including unborn children who will be born during the period covered by the deferment, if the children receive more than half their support from the borrower. A borrower's family size includes other individuals if, at the time the

borrower requests the economic hardship deferment, the other individuals—
(A) Live with the borrower; and
(B) Receive more than half their support from the borrower and will continue to receive this support from the borrower for the year the borrower certifies family size. Support includes money, gifts, loans, housing, food, clothes, car, medical and dental care, and payment of college costs.

(9) In determining a borrower's Federal education debt burden under paragraphs (e)(4) of this section, the institution shall—
(i) If the Federal postsecondary education loan is scheduled to be repaid in 10 years or less, use the actual monthly payment amount (or a proportional share if the payments are due less frequently than monthly); or
(ii) If the Federal postsecondary education loan is scheduled to be repaid in more than 10 years, use a monthly payment amount (or a proportional share if the payments are due less frequently than monthly) that would have been due on the loan if the loan had been scheduled to be repaid in 10 years.

(f) To qualify for a deferment for study as part of a graduate fellowship program pursuant to paragraph (b)(1)(ii) of this section, a borrower must provide the institution certification that the borrower has been accepted for or is engaged in full-time study in the institution's graduate fellowship program.

(g) To qualify for a deferment for study in a rehabilitation training program, pursuant to paragraph (b)(1)(iv) of this section, the borrower must be receiving, or be scheduled to receive, services under a program designed to rehabilitate disabled individuals and must provide the institution with the following documentation:
(1) A certification from the rehabilitation agency that the borrower is either receiving or scheduled to receive rehabilitation training services from the agency.
(2) A certification from the rehabilitation agency that the rehabilitation program—
(i) Is licensed, approved, certified, or otherwise recognized by one of the following entities as providing rehabilitation training to disabled individuals—
(A) A State agency with responsibility for vocational rehabilitation programs;
(B) A State agency with responsibility for drug abuse treatment programs;
(C) A State agency with responsibility for mental health services programs;
(D) A State agency with responsibility for alcohol abuse treatment programs; or
(E) The Department of Veterans Affairs; and
(ii) Provides or will provide the borrower with rehabilitation services under a written plan that—
(A) Is individualized to meet the borrower's needs;
(B) Specifies the date on which the services to the borrower are expected to end; and
(C) Is structured in a way that requires a substantial commitment by the borrower to his or her rehabilitation. The Secretary considers a substantial commitment by the borrower to be a commitment of time and effort that would normally prevent an individual from engaging in full-time employment either because of the number of hours that must be devoted to rehabilitation or because of the nature of the rehabilitation.

(h) *Military service deferment.*
(1) The borrower need not pay principal, and interest does not accrue, on a Federal Perkins Loan, an NDSL, or a Defense Loan for any period during which the borrower is—
(i) Serving on active duty during a war or other military operation or national emergency; or
(ii) Performing qualifying National Guard duty during a war or other military operation or national emergency.
(2) Serving on active duty during a war or other military operation or national emergency means service by an individual who is—
(i) A Reserve of an Armed Force ordered to active duty under 10 U.S.C. 12301(a), 12301(g), 12302, 12304, or 12306;
(ii) A retired member of an Armed Force ordered to active duty under 10 U.S.C. 688 for service in connection with a war or other military operation or national emergency, regardless of the location at which such active duty service is performed; or
(iii) Any other member of an Armed Force on active duty in connection with such emergency or subsequent actions or conditions who has been assigned to a duty station at a location other than the location at which the member is normally assigned.
(3) Qualifying National Guard duty during a war or other operation or national emergency means service as a member of the National Guard on full-time National Guard duty, as defined in 10 U.S.C. 101(d)(5), under a call to active service authorized by the President or the Secretary of Defense for a period of more than 30 consecutive days under 32 U.S.C. 502(f) in connection with a war, other military operation, or national emergency declared by the President and supported by Federal funds.
(4) As used in this paragraph—
(i) *Active duty* means active duty as defined in 10 U.S.C. 101(d)(1) except that it does not include active duty for training or attendance at a service school;
(ii) *Military operation* means a contingency operation as defined in 10 U.S.C. 101(a)(13); and
(iii) *National emergency* means the national emergency by reason of certain terrorist attacks declared by the President on September 14, 2001, or subsequent national emergencies declared by the President by reason of terrorist attacks.
(5) These provisions do not authorize the refunding of any payments made by or on behalf of a borrower during a period for which the borrower qualified for a military service deferment.
(6) For a borrower whose active duty service includes October 1, 2007, or begins on or after that date, the deferment period ends 180 days after the demobilization date for each period of service described in paragraphs (h)(1)(i) and (h)(1)(ii) of this section.
(7) Without supporting documentation, a military service deferment may be granted to an otherwise eligible borrower for a period not to exceed 12 months from the date of the qualifying eligible service based on a request from the borrower or the borrower's representative.

(i) *Post-active duty student deferment.*
(1) Effective October 1, 2007, a borrower of a Federal Perkins loan, an NDSL, or a Defense loan serving on active duty military service on that date, or who begins serving on or after that date, need not pay principal, and interest does not accrue for up to 13 months following the conclusion of the borrower's active duty military service and initial grace period if—
(i) The borrower is a member of the National Guard or other reserve component of the Armed Forces of the United States or a member of such forces in retired status; and
(ii) The borrower was enrolled, on at least a half-time basis, in a program of instruction at an eligible institution at the time, or within six months prior to the time, the borrower was called to active duty.
(2) As used in paragraph (*i*)(1) of this section "Active duty" means active duty as defined in section 101(d)(1) of title 10, United States Code, for at least a 30-day period, except that—
(i) Active duty includes active State duty for members of the National Guard under which the Governor activates National Guard personnel based on State statute or policy and the activities of the National Guard are paid for with State funds;
(ii) Active duty includes full-time National Guard duty under which the Governor is authorized, with the approval of the President or the U.S. Secretary of Defense, to order a member to State active duty and the activities of the National Guard are paid for with Federal funds;
(iii) Active duty does not include active duty for training or attendance at a service school; and

(iv) Active duty does not include employment in a full-time, permanent position in the National Guard unless the borrower employed in such a position is reassigned to active duty under paragraph (i)(2)(i) of this section or full-time National Guard duty under paragraph (i)(2)(ii) of this section.

(3) If the borrower returns to enrolled student status, on at least a half-time basis, during the 13-month deferment period, the deferment expires at the time the borrower returns to enrolled student status, on at least a half-time basis.

(4) If a borrower qualifies for both a military service deferment and a post-active duty student deferment under both paragraphs (h) and (i) of this section, the 180-day post-demobilization military service deferment period and the 13-month post-active duty student deferment period apply concurrently.

(j) The institution may not include the deferment periods described in paragraphs (b), (c), (d), (e), (f), (g), (h) and (*i*) of this section and the period described in paragraph (k) of this section in determining the 10-year repayment period.

(k) The borrower need not pay principal and interest does not accrue until six months after completion of any period during which the borrower is in deferment under paragraphs (b), (c), (d), (e), (f), (g), and (h) of this section.

(Approved by the Office of Management and Budget under control number 1845-0019)

(Authority: 20 U.S.C. 1087dd)

[59 Fed. Reg. 61410 (Nov. 30, 1994); 60 Fed. Reg. 31410 (June 15, 1995); 60 Fed. Reg. 61815 (Dec. 1, 1995); 62 Fed. Reg. 50848 (Sept. 26, 1997); 64 Fed. Reg. 57531 (Oct. 25, 1999); 64 Fed. Reg. 58311 (Oct. 28, 1999); 65 Fed. Reg. 18003 (Apr. 6, 2000); 65 Fed. Reg. 26136 (May 5, 2000); 67 Fed. Reg. 67076 (Nov. 1, 2002); 71 Fed. Reg. 45666 (Sept. 8, 2006); 72 Fed. Reg. 61996 (Nov. 1, 2007); 73 Fed. Reg. 63247 (Oct. 23, 2008)]

* * *

§ 674.38 Deferment procedures.

(a)(1) Except as provided in paragraph (a)(5) of this section, a borrower must request the deferment and provide the institution with all information and documents required by the institution by the date that the institution establishes.

(2) After receiving a borrower's written or verbal request, an institution may grant a deferment under §§ 674.34(b)(1)(ii), 674.34(b)(1)(iii), 674.34(b)(1)(iv), 674.34(d), 674.34(e), 674.34(h), and 674.34(i) if the institution is able to confirm that the borrower has received a deferment on another Perkins Loan, a FFEL Loan, or a Direct Loan for the same reason and the same time period. The institution may grant the deferment based on information from the other Perkins Loan holder, the FFEL Loan holder or the Secretary or from an authoritative electronic database maintained or authorized by the Secretary that supports eligibility for the deferment for the same reason and the same time period.

(3) An institution may rely in good faith on the information it receives under paragraph (a)(2) of this section when determining a borrower's eligibility for a deferment unless the institution, as of the date of the determination, has information indicating that the borrower does not qualify for the deferment. An institution must resolve any discrepant information before granting a deferment under paragraph (a)(2) of this section.

(4) An institution that grants a deferment under paragraph (a)(2) of this section must notify the borrower that the deferment has been granted and that the borrower has the option to cancel the deferment and continue to make payments on the loan.

(5) In the case of an in school deferment, the institution may grant the deferment based on student enrollment information showing that a borrower is enrolled as a regular student on at least a half-time basis, if the institution notifies the borrower of the deferment and of the borrower's option to cancel the deferment and continue paying on the loan.

(6) In the case of a military service deferment under §§ 674.34(h) and 674.35(c)(1), a borrower's representative may request the deferment on behalf of the borrower. An institution that grants a military service deferment based on a request from a borrower's representative must notify the borrower that the deferment has been granted and that the borrower has the option to cancel the deferment and continue to make payments on the loan. The institution may also notify the borrower's representative of the outcome of the deferment request.

(7) If the borrower fails to meet the requirements of paragraph (a)(1) of this section, the institution may declare the loan to be in default, and may accelerate the loan.

(b)(1) The institution may grant a deferment to a borrower after it has declared a loan to be a default.

(2) As a condition for a deferment under this paragraph, the institution—

(i) Shall require the borrower to execute a written repayment agreement on the loan; and

(ii) May require the borrower to pay immediately some or all of the amounts previously scheduled to be repaid before the date on which the institution determined that the borrower had demonstrated that grounds for a deferment existed, plus late charges and collection costs.

(c) If the information supplied by the borrower demonstrates that for some or all of the period for which a deferment is requested, the borrower had retained in-school status or was within the initial grace period on the loan, the institution shall—

(1) Redetermine the date on which the borrower was required to commence repayment on the loan;

(2) Deduct from the loan balance any interest accrued and late charges added before the date on which the repayment period commenced, as determined in paragraph (c)(1) of this section; and

(3) Treat in accordance with paragraph (b) of this section, the request for deferment for any remaining portion of the period for which deferment was requested.

(d) The institution must determine the continued eligibility of a borrower for a deferment at least annually, except that a borrower engaged in service described in §§ 674.34(e)(6), 674.35(c)(3), 674.36(c)(2), 674.37(c)(2), and § 674.60(a)(1) must be granted a deferment for the lesser of the borrower's full term of service in the Peace Corps, or the borrower's remaining period of eligibility for a deferment under § 674.34(e), not to exceed 3 years.

(Approved by the Office of Management and Budget under control number 1845-0019)

(Authority: 20 U.S.C. 425, 1087dd)

[53 Fed. Reg. 49147 (Dec. 6, 1988); 59 Fed. Reg. 61410, 61411 (Nov. 30, 1994); 64 Fed. Reg. 57531 (Oct. 25, 1999); 64 Fed. Reg. 58315 (Oct. 28, 1999); 72 Fed. Reg. 61996, 61997 (Nov. 1, 2007)]

§ 674.39 Loan rehabilitation.

(a) Each institution must establish a loan rehabilitation program for all borrowers for the purpose of rehabilitating defaulted loans made under this part, except for loans for which a judgment has been secured or loans obtained by fraud for which the borrower has been convicted of, or has pled nolo contendere or guilty to, a crime involving fraud in obtaining title IV, HEA program assistance. The institution's loan rehabilitation program must provide that—

(1) A defaulted borrower is notified of the option and consequences of rehabilitating a loan; and

(2) A loan is rehabilitated if the borrower makes an on-time, monthly payment, as determined by the institution, each month for nine consecutive months and the borrower requests rehabilitation.

(b) Within 30 days of receiving the borrower's last on-time, consecutive, monthly payment, the institution must—

(1) Return the borrower to regular repayment status;

(2) Treat the first payment made under the nine consecutive payments as the first payment under the 10-year repayment maximum; and

(3) Instruct any credit bureau to which the default was reported to remove the default from the borrower's credit history.

(c) Collection costs on a rehabilitated loan—

(1) If charged to the borrower, may not exceed 24 percent of the unpaid principal and accrued interest as of the date following application of the twelfth payment;

(2) That exceed the amounts specified in paragraph (c)(1) of this section, may be charged to an institution's Fund until July 1, 2002 in accordance with § 674.47(e)(5); and

(3) Are not restricted to 24 percent in the event the borrower defaults on the rehabilitated loan.

(d) After rehabilitating a defaulted loan and returning to regular repayment status, the borrower regains the balance of the benefits and privileges of the promissory note as applied prior to the borrower's default on the loan. Nothing in this paragraph prohibits an institution from offering the borrower flexible repayment options following the borrower's return to regular repayment status on a rehabilitated loan.

(e) The borrower may rehabilitate a defaulted loan only one time.

Authority: 20 U.S.C. 1087dd.

[53 Fed. Reg. 49147 (Dec. 6, 1988); 57 Fed. Reg. 32346 (July 21, 1992); 58 Fed. Reg. 36870 (July 9, 1993); 59 Fed. Reg. 61410, 61411 (Nov. 30, 1994); 64 Fed. Reg. 58311 (Oct. 28, 1999); 65 Fed. Reg. 65614 (Nov. 1, 2000); 67 Fed. Reg. 67077 (Nov. 1, 2002); 71 Fed. Reg. 45698 (Aug. 9, 2006); 74 Fed. Reg. 55661 (Oct. 28, 2009)]

* * *

§ 674.50 Assignment of defaulted loans to the United States.

(a) An institution may submit a defaulted loan note to the Secretary for assignment to the United States if—

(1) The institution has been unable to collect on the loan despite complying with the diligence procedures, including at least a first level collection effort as described in § 674.45(a) and litigation, if required under § 674.46(a), to the extent these actions were required by regulations in effect on the date the loan entered default;

(2) The amount of the borrower's account to be assigned, including outstanding principal, accrued interest, collection costs and late charges is $25.00 or greater; and

(3) The loan has been accelerated.

(b) An institution may submit a defaulted note for assignment only during the submission period established by the Secretary.

(c) The Secretary may require an institution to submit the following documents for any loan it proposes to assign—

(1) An assignment form provided by the Secretary and executed by the institution, which must include a certification by the institution that it has complied with the requirements of this subpart, including at least a first level collection effort as described in § 674.45(a) in attempting collection on the loan.

(2) The original promissory note or a certified copy of the original note.

(3) A copy of the repayment schedule.

(4) A certified copy of any judgment order entered on the loan.

(5) A complete statement of the payment history.

(6) Copies of all approved requests for deferment and cancellation.

(7) A copy of the notice to the borrower of the effective date of acceleration and the total amount due on the loan.

(8) Documentation that the institution has withdrawn the loan from any firm that it employed for address search, billing, collection or litigation services, and has notified that firm to cease collection activity on the loans.

(9) Copies of all pleadings filed or received by the institution on behalf of a borrower who has filed a petition in bankruptcy and whose loan obligation is determined to be nondischargeable.

(10) Documentation that the institution has complied with all of the due diligence requirements described in paragraph (a)(1) of this section if the institution has a cohort default rate that is equal to or greater than 20 percent as of June 30 of the second year preceding the submission period.

(11) A record of disbursements for each loan made to a borrower on an MPN that shows the date and amount of each disbursement.

(12)(i) Upon the Secretary's request with respect to a particular loan or loans assigned to the Secretary and evidenced by an electronically signed promissory note, the institution that created the original electronically signed promissory note must cooperate with the Secretary in all activities necessary to enforce the loan or loans. Such institution must provide—

(A) An affidavit or certification regarding the creation and maintenance of the electronic records of the loan or loans in a form appropriate to ensure admissibility of the loan records in a legal proceeding. This affidavit or certification may be executed in a single record for multiple loans provided that this record is reliably associated with the specific loans to which it pertains; and

(B) Testimony by an authorized official or employee of the institution, if necessary, to ensure admission of the electronic records of the loan or loans in the litigation or legal proceeding to enforce the loan or loans.

(ii) The affidavit or certification in paragraph (c)(12)(i)(A) of this section must include, if requested by the Secretary—

(A) A description of the steps followed by a borrower to execute the promissory note (such as a flowchart);

(B) A copy of each screen as it would have appeared to the borrower of the loan or loans the Secretary is enforcing when the borrower signed the note electronically;

(C) A description of the field edits and other security measures used to ensure integrity of the data submitted to the originator electronically;

(D) A description of how the executed promissory note has been preserved to ensure that it has not been altered after it was executed;

(E) Documentation supporting the institution's authentication and electronic signature process; and

(F) All other documentary and technical evidence requested by the Secretary to support the validity or the authenticity of the electronically signed promissory note.

(iii) The Secretary may request a record, affidavit, certification or evidence under paragraph (a)(6) of this section as needed to resolve any factual dispute involving a loan that has been assigned to the Secretary including, but not limited to, a factual dispute raised in connection with litigation or any other legal proceeding, or as needed in connection with loans assigned to the Secretary that are included in a Title IV program audit sample, or for other similar purposes. The institution must respond to any request from the Secretary within 10 business days.

(iv) As long as any loan made to a borrower under a MPN created by an institution is not satisfied, the institution is responsible for ensuring that all parties entitled to access to the electronic loan record, including the Secretary, have full and complete access to the electronic loan record.

(d) Except as provided in paragraph (e) of this section, and subject to paragraph (g) of this section, the Secretary accepts an assignment of a note described in paragraph (a) of this section and submitted in accordance with paragraph (c) of this section.

(e) The Secretary does not accept assignment of a loan if—

(1) The institution has not provided the Social Security number of the borrower, unless the loan is submitted for assignment under 674.8(d)(3);

(2) The borrower has received a discharge in bankruptcy, unless—
  (i) The bankruptcy court has determined that the loan obligation is nondischargeable and has entered judgment against the borrower; or
  (ii) A court of competent jurisdiction has entered judgment against the borrower on the loan after the entry of the discharge order; or
(3) The institution has initiated litigation against the borrower, unless the judgment has been entered against the borrower and assigned to the United States.

(f)(1) The Secretary provides an institution written notice of the acceptance of the assignment of the note. By accepting assignment, the Secretary acquires all rights, title, and interest of the institution in that loan.
(2) The institution shall endorse and forward to the Secretary any payment received from the borrower after the date on which the Secretary accepted the assignment, as noted in the written notice of acceptance.

(g)(1) The Secretary may determine that a loan assigned to the United States is unenforceable in whole or in part because of the acts or omissions of the institution or its agent. The Secretary may make this determination with or without a judicial determination regarding the enforceability of the loan.
(2) The Secretary may require the institution to reimburse the Fund for that portion of the outstanding balance on a loan assigned to the United States which the Secretary determines to be unenforceable because of an act or omission of that institution or its agent.
(3) Upon reimbursement to the Fund by the institution, the Secretary shall transfer all rights, title and interest of the United States in the loan to the institution for its own account.

(h) An institution shall consider a borrower whose loan has been assigned to the United States for collection to be in default on that loan for the purpose of eligibility for title IV financial assistance, until the borrower provides the institution confirmation from the Secretary that he or she has made satisfactory arrangements to repay the loan.

(Approved by the Office of Management and Budget under control number 1845-0019)

(Authority: 20 U.S.C. 424, 1087cc)

[53 Fed. Reg. 49147 (Dec. 6, 1988); 57 Fed. Reg. 32347 (July 21, 1992); 57 Fed. Reg. 60706 (Dec. 21, 1992); 58 Fed. Reg. 36870, 36871 (July 9, 1993); 59 Fed. Reg. 61412 (Nov. 30, 1994); 64 Fed. Reg. 58315 (Oct. 28, 1999); 65 Fed. Reg. 65614 (Nov. 1, 2000); 67 Fed. Reg. 67077 (Nov. 1, 2002); 72 Fed. Reg. 61997 (Nov. 1, 2007)]

§ 674.51 Special definitions.

The following definitions apply to this Subpart:

(a) *Academic year or its equivalent for elementary and secondary schools and special education:*
(1) One complete school year, or two half years from different school years, excluding summer sessions, that are complete and consecutive and generally fall within a 12-month period.
(2) If such a school has a year-round program of instruction, the Secretary considers a minimum of nine consecutive months to be the equivalent of an academic year.

(b) *Academic year or its equivalent for institutions of higher education:* A period of time in which a full-time student is expected to complete—
(1) The equivalent of 2 semesters, 2 trimesters, or 3 quarters at an institution using credit hours; or
(2) At least 900 clock hours of training for each program at an institution using clock hours.

(c) *Title I Children:* Children of ages 5 through 17 who are counted under section 1124(c)(1) of the Elementary and Secondary Education Act of 1965, as amended.

(d) *Child with a disability:* A child or youth from ages 3 through 21, inclusive, who requires special education and related services because he or she has one or more disabilities as defined in section 602(3) of the Individuals with Disabilities Education Act.

(e) *Community defender organizations:* A defender organization established in accordance with section 3006A(g)(2)(B) of title 18, United States Code.

(f) *Early intervention services:* Those services defined in section 632(4) of the Individuals with Disabilities Education Act that are provided to infants and toddlers with disabilities.

(g) *Educational service agency:* A regional public multi-service agency authorized by State law to develop, manage, and provide services or programs to local educational agencies as defined in section 9101 of the Elementary and Secondary Education Act of 1965, as amended.

(h) *Elementary school:* A school that provides elementary education, including education below grade 1, as determined by—
(1) State law; or
(2) The Secretary, if the school is not in a State.

(i) *Faculty member at a Tribal College or University:* An educator or tenured individual who is employed by a Tribal College or University, as that term is defined in section 316 of the HEA, to teach, research, or perform administrative functions. For purposes of this definition an educator may be an instructor, lecturer, lab faculty, assistant professor, associate professor, full professor, dean, or academic department head.

(j) *Federal public defender organization:* A defender organization established in accordance with section 3006A(g)(2)(A) of title 18, United States Code.

(k) *Firefighter:* A firefighter is an individual who is employed by a Federal, State, or local firefighting agency to extinguish destructive fires; or provide firefighting related services such as—
(1) Providing community disaster support and, as a first responder, providing emergency medical services;
(2) Conducting search and rescue; or
(3) Providing hazardous materials mitigation (HAZMAT).

(l) *Handicapped children:* Children of ages 3 through 21 inclusive who require special education and related services because they are—
(1) Mentally retarded;
(2) Hard of hearing;
(3) Deaf;
(4) Speech and language impaired;
(5) Visually handicapped;
(6) Seriously emotionally disturbed;
(7) Orthopedically impaired;
(8) Specific learning disabled; or
(9) Otherwise health impaired.

(m) *High-risk children:* Individuals under the age of 21 who are low-income or at risk of abuse or neglect, have been abused or neglected, have serious emotional, mental, or behavioral disturbances, reside in placements outside their homes, or are involved in the juvenile justice system.

(n) *Infant or toddler with a disability:* An infant or toddler from birth to age 2, inclusive, who needs early intervention services for specified reasons, as defined in section 632(5)(A) of the Individuals with Disabilities Education Act.

(o) *Librarian with a master's degree:* A librarian with a master's degree is an information professional trained in library or information science who has obtained a postgraduate academic degree in library science awarded after the completion of an academic program of up to six years in duration, excluding a doctorate or professional degree.

(p) *Local educational agency:*
(1) A public board of education or other public authority legally constituted within a State to administer, direct, or perform a service function for public elementary or secondary schools in a city, county, township, school district, other political subdivision of a State; or such combination of school districts of counties as are recognized in a State as an administrative agency for its public elementary or secondary schools.
(2) Any other public institution or agency having administrative control and direction of a public elementary or secondary school.

(q) *Low-income communities:* Communities in which there is a high concentration of children eligible to be counted under title I of the Elementary and Secondary Education Act of 1965, as amended.

(r) *Medical technician:* An allied health professional (working in fields such as therapy, dental hygiene, medical technology, or nutrition) who is certified, registered, or licensed by the appropriate State agency in the State in which he or she provides health care services. An allied health professional is someone who assists, facilitates, or complements the work of physicians and other specialists in the health care system.

(s) *Nurse:* A licensed practical nurse, a registered nurse, or other individual who is licensed by the appropriate State agency to provide nursing services.

(t) *Qualified professional provider of early intervention services:* A provider of services as defined in section 632 of the Individuals with Disabilities Education Act.

(u) *Secondary school:*
(1) A school that provides secondary education, as determined by—
(i) State law; or
(ii) The Secretary, if the school is not in a State.
(2) However, State laws notwithstanding, secondary education does not include any education beyond grade 12.

(v) *Speech language pathologist with a master's degree:* An individual who evaluates or treats disorders that affect a person's speech, language, cognition, voice, swallowing and the rehabilitative or corrective treatment of physical or cognitive deficits/disorders resulting in difficulty with communication, swallowing, or both and has obtained a postgraduate academic degree awarded after the completion of an academic program of up to six years in duration, excluding a doctorate or professional degree.

(w) *State education agency:*
(1) The State board of education; or
(2) An agency or official designated by the Governor or by State law as being primarily responsible for the State supervision of public elementary and secondary schools.

(x) *Substantial gainful activity:* A level of work performed for pay or profit that involves doing significant physical or mental activities, or a combination of both.

(y) *Teacher:*
(1) A teacher is a person who provides—
(i) Direct classroom teaching;
(ii) Classroom-type teaching in a non-classroom setting; or
(iii) Educational services to students directly related to classroom teaching such as school librarians or school guidance counselors.

(2) A supervisor, administrator, researcher, or curriculum specialist is not a teacher unless he or she primarily provides direct and personal educational services to students.
(3) An individual who provides one of the following services does not qualify as a teacher unless that individual is licensed, certified, or registered by the appropriate State education agency for that area in which he or she is providing related special educational services, and the services provided by the individual are part of the educational curriculum for handicapped children:
(i) Speech and language pathology and audiology;
(ii) Physical therapy;
(iii) Occupational therapy;
(iv) Psychological and counseling services; or
(v) Recreational therapy.

(z) *Teaching in a field of expertise:* The majority of classes taught are in the borrower's field of expertise.

(aa) *Total and permanent disability:* The condition of an individual who—
(1) Is unable to engage in any substantial gainful activity by reason of any medically determinable physical or mental impairment that—
(i) Can be expected to result in death;
(ii) Has lasted for a continuous period of not less than 60 months; or
(iii) Can be expected to last for a continuous period of not less than 60 months; or
(2) Has been determined by the Secretary of Veterans Affairs to be unemployable due to a service-connected disability.

(bb) *Tribal College or University:* An institution that—
(1) Qualifies for funding under the Tribally Controlled Colleges and Universities Assistance Act of 1978 (25 U.S.C. 1801 *et seq.*) or the Navajo Community College Assistance Act of 1978 (25 U.S.C. 640a note); or
(2) Is cited in section 532 of the Equity in Education Land Grant Status Act of 1994 (7 U.S.C. 301 note).

(Authority: 20 U.S.C. 1087ee(a).)

[59 Fed. Reg. 61412 (Nov. 30, 1994); 65 Fed. Reg. 65690 (Nov. 1, 2000); 74 Fed. Reg. 55661 (Oct. 28, 2009)]

§ 674.52 Cancellation procedures.

(a) *Application for cancellation.* To qualify for cancellation of a loan, a borrower shall submit to the institution to which the loan is owed, by the date that the institution establishes, both a written request for cancellation and any documentation required by the institution to demonstrate that the borrower meets the conditions for the cancellation requested.

(b) *Part-time employment.*
(1)(i) An institution may refuse a request for cancellation based on a claim of simultaneously teaching in two or more schools or institutions if it cannot determine easily from the documentation supplied by the borrower that the teaching is full-time. However, it shall grant the cancellation if one school official certifies that a teacher worked full-time for a full academic year.
(ii) An institution may refuse a request for cancellation based on a claim of simultaneous employment as a nurse or medical technician in two or more facilities if it cannot determine easily from the documentation supplied by the borrower that the combined employment is full-time. However, it shall grant the cancellation if one facility official certifies that a nurse or medical technician worked full-time for a full year.
(2) If the borrower is unable due to illness or pregnancy to complete the academic year, the borrower still qualifies for the cancellation if—
(i) The borrower completes the first half of the academic year, and has begun teaching the second half; and
(ii) The borrower's employer considers the borrower to have fulfilled his or her contract for the academic year for purposes of salary increment, tenure, and retirement.

(c) *Cancellation of a defaulted loan.*
(1) Except with regard to cancellation on account of the death or disability of the borrower, a borrower whose defaulted loan has not been accelerated may qualify for a cancellation by complying with the requirements of paragraph (a) of this section.
(2) A borrower whose defaulted loan has been accelerated—
(i) May qualify for a loan cancellation for services performed before the date of acceleration; and
(ii) Cannot qualify for a cancellation for services performed on or after the date of acceleration.
(3) An institution shall grant a request for discharge on account of the death or disability of the borrower without regard to the repayment status of the loan.

(d) *Concurrent deferment period.* The Secretary considers a Perkins Loan, NDSL or Defense Loan borrower's loan deferment under § 674.34(c) to run concurrently with any period for which cancellation under §§ 674.53, 674.54, 674.55, 674.56, 674.57, 674.58, 674.59, and 674.60 is granted.

(e) *National community service.* No borrower who has received a benefit under subtitle D of title I of the National and Community Service

Act of 1990 may receive a cancellation under this subpart.

(Approved by the Office of Management and Budget under control number 1845-0019)

(Authority: 20 U.S.C. 425, 1087ee)

[53 Fed. Reg. 49147 (Dec. 6, 1988); 57 Fed. Reg. 32347 (July 21, 1992); 58 Fed. Reg. 36870 (July 9, 1993); 59 Fed. Reg. 61413 (Nov. 30, 1994); 62 Fed. Reg: 50848 (Sept. 26, 1997); 64 Fed. Reg. 58313 (Oct. 28, 1999); 65 Fed. Reg. 18003 (Apr. 6, 2000); 65 Fed. Reg. 26136 (May 5, 2000); 72 Fed. Reg. 55053 (Sept. 28, 2007)]

* * *

§ 674.61 Discharge for death or disability.

(a) *Death.* An institution must discharge the unpaid balance of a borrower's Defense, NDSL, or Perkins loan, including interest, if the borrower dies. The institution must discharge the loan on the basis of an original or certified copy of the death certificate, or an accurate and complete photocopy of the original or certified copy of the death certificate. Under exceptional circumstances and on a case-by-case basis, the chief financial officer of the institution may approve a discharge based upon other reliable documentation supporting the discharge request.

(b) *Total and permanent disability as defined in § 674.51(aa)(1)*—

(1) *General.* A borrower's Defense, NDSL, or Perkins loan is discharged if the borrower becomes totally and permanently disabled, as defined in § 674.51(aa)(1), and satisfies the additional eligibility requirements contained in this section.

(2) *Discharge application process for borrowers who have a total and permanent disability as defined in § 674.51(aa)(1).*

(i) To qualify for discharge of a Defense, NDSL, or Perkins loan based on a total and permanent disability as defined in § 674.51(aa)(1), a borrower must submit a discharge application approved by the Secretary to the institution that holds the loan.

(ii) The application must contain a certification by a physician, who is a doctor of medicine or osteopathy legally authorized to practice in a State, that the borrower is totally and permanently disabled as defined in § 674.51(aa)(1).

(iii) The borrower must submit the application to the institution within 90 days of the date the physician certifies the application.

(iv) Upon receiving the borrower's complete application, the institution must suspend collection activity on the loan and inform the borrower that—

(A) The institution will review the application and assign the loan to the Secretary for an eligibility determination if the institution determines that the certification supports the conclusion that the borrower is totally and permanently disabled, as defined in § 674.51(aa)(1);

(B) The institution will resume collection on the loan if the institution determines that the certification does not support the conclusion that the borrower is totally and permanently disabled; and

(C) If the Secretary discharges the loan based on a determination that the borrower is totally and permanently disabled, as defined in § 674.51(aa)(1), the Secretary will reinstate the borrower's obligation to repay the loan if, within three years after the date the Secretary granted the discharge, the borrower—

(1) Has annual earnings from employment that exceed 100 percent of the poverty guideline for a family of two, as published annually by the United States Department of Health and Human Services pursuant to 42 U.S.C. 9902(2);

(2) Receives a new TEACH Grant or a new loan under the Perkins, FFEL, or Direct Loan programs, except for a FFEL or Direct Consolidation Loan that includes loans that were not discharged; or

(3) Fails to ensure that the full amount of any disbursement of a Title IV loan or TEACH Grant received prior to the discharge date that is made during the three-year period following the discharge date is returned to the loan holder or to the Secretary, as applicable, within 120 days of the disbursement date.

(v) If, after reviewing the borrower's application, the institution determines that the application is complete and supports the conclusion that the borrower is totally and permanently disabled as defined in § 674.51(aa)(1), the institution must assign the loan to the Secretary.

(vi) At the time the loan is assigned to the Secretary, the institution must notify the borrower that the loan has been assigned to the Secretary for determination of eligibility for a total and permanent disability discharge and that no payments are due on the loan.

(3) *Secretary's eligibility determination.*

(i) If the Secretary determines that the borrower is totally and permanently disabled as defined in § 674.51(aa)(1), the Secretary discharges the borrower's obligation to make further payments on the loan and notifies the borrower that the loan has been discharged. The notification to the borrower explains the terms and conditions under which the borrower's obligation to repay the loan will be reinstated, as specified in paragraph (b)(5) of this section.

(ii) If the Secretary determines that the certification provided by the borrower does not support the conclusion that the borrower is totally and permanently disabled as defined in § 674.51(aa)(1), the Secretary notifies the borrower that the application for a disability discharge has been denied, and that the loan is due and payable to the Secretary under the terms of the promissory note.

(iii) The Secretary reserves the right to require the borrower to submit additional medical evidence if the Secretary determines that the borrower's application does not conclusively prove that the borrower is totally and permanently disabled as defined in § 674.51(aa)(1). As part of the Secretary's review of the borrower's discharge application, the Secretary may arrange for an additional review of the borrower's condition by an independent physician at no expense to the borrower.

(4) *Treatment of disbursements made during the period from the date of the physician's certification until the date of discharge.* If a borrower received a Title IV loan or TEACH Grant prior to the date the physician certified the borrower's discharge application and a disbursement of that loan or grant is made during the period from the date of the physician's certification until the date the Secretary grants a discharge under this section, the processing of the borrower's loan discharge request will be suspended until the borrower ensures that the full amount of the disbursement has been returned to the loan holder or to the Secretary, as applicable.

(5) *Conditions for reinstatement of a loan after a total and permanent disability discharge.*

(i) The Secretary reinstates a borrower's obligation to repay a loan that was discharged in accordance with paragraph (b)(3)(i) of this section if, within three years after the date the Secretary granted the discharge, the borrower—

(A) Has annual earnings from employment that exceed 100 percent of the poverty guideline for a family of two, as published annually by the United States Department of Health and Human Services pursuant to 42 U.S.C. 9902(2);

(B) Receives a new TEACH Grant or a new loan under the Perkins, FFEL or Direct Loan programs, except for a FFEL or Direct Consolidation Loan that includes loans that were not discharged; or

(C) Fails to ensure that the full amount of any disbursement of a Title IV loan or TEACH Grant received prior to the discharge date that is made during the three-year period following the discharge date is returned to the loan holder or to the Secretary, as applicable, within 120 days of the disbursement date.

(ii) If a borrower's obligation to repay a loan is reinstated, the Secretary—

(A) Notifies the borrower that the borrower's obligation to repay the loan has been reinstated; and

(B) Does not require the borrower to pay interest on the loan for the period from the date the loan was discharged until the date the borrower's obligation to repay the loan was reinstated.

(iii) The Secretary's notification under paragraph (b)(5)(ii)(A) of this section will include—

(A) The reason or reasons for the reinstatement;

(B) An explanation that the first payment due date on the loan following reinstatement will be no earlier than 60 days after the date of the notification of reinstatement; and

(C) Information on how the borrower may contact the Secretary if the borrower has questions about the reinstatement or believes that the obligation to repay the loan was reinstated based on incorrect information.

(6) *Borrower's responsibilities after a total and permanent disability discharge.* During the three-year period described in paragraph (b)(5)(i) of this section, the borrower or, if applicable, the borrower's representative—

(i) Must promptly notify the Secretary of any changes in address or phone number;

(ii) Must promptly notify the Secretary if the borrower's annual earnings from employment exceed the amount specified in paragraph (b)(5)(i)(A) of this section; and

(iii) Must provide the Secretary, upon request, with documentation of the borrower's annual earnings from employment.

(7) *Payments received after the physician's certification of total and permanent disability.*

(i) If, after the date the physician certifies the borrower's loan discharge application, the institution receives any payments from or on behalf of the borrower on or attributable to a loan that was assigned to the Secretary for determination of eligibility for a total and permanent disability discharge, the institution must forward those payments to the Secretary for crediting to the borrower's account.

(ii) At the same time that the institution forwards the payment, it must notify the borrower that there is no obligation to make payments on the loan prior to the Secretary's determination of eligibility for a total and permanent disability discharge, unless the Secretary directs the borrower otherwise.

(iii) When the Secretary makes a determination to discharge the loan, the Secretary returns any payments received on the loan after the date the physician certified the borrower's loan discharge application to the person who made the payments on the loan.

(c) *Total and permanent disability discharges for veterans—*

(1) *General.* A veteran's Defense, NDSL, or Perkins loan will be discharged if the veteran is totally and permanently disabled, as defined in § 674.51(aa)(2).

(2) *Discharge application process for veterans who have a total and permanent disability as defined in § 674.51(aa)(2).*

(i) To qualify for discharge of a Defense, NDSL, or Perkins loan based on a total and permanent disability as defined in § 674.51(aa)(2), a veteran must submit a discharge application approved by the Secretary to the institution that holds the loan.

(ii) With the application, the veteran must submit documentation from the Department of Veterans Affairs showing that the Department of Veterans Affairs has determined that the veteran is unemployable due to a service-connected disability. The veteran will not be required to provide any additional documentation related to the veteran's disability.

(iii) Upon receiving the veteran's completed application and the required documentation from the Department of Veterans Affairs, the institution must suspend collection activity on the loan and inform the veteran that—

(A) The institution will review the application and submit the application and supporting documentation to the Secretary for an eligibility determination if the documentation from the Department of Veterans Affairs indicates that the veteran is totally and permanently disabled as defined in § 674.51(aa)(2);

(B) The institution will resume collection on the loan if the documentation from the Department of Veterans Affairs does not indicate that the veteran is totally and permanently disabled as defined in § 674.51(aa)(2); and

(C) If the documentation from the Department of Veterans Affairs does not indicate that the veteran is totally and permanently disabled as defined in § 674.51(aa)(2), but the documentation indicates that the veteran may be totally and permanently disabled as defined in § 674.51(aa)(1), the veteran may reapply for a total and permanent disability discharge in accordance with the procedures described in § 674.61(b).

(iv) If the documentation from the Department of Veterans Affairs indicates that the veteran is totally and permanently disabled as defined in § 674.51(aa)(2), the institution must submit a copy of the veteran's application and the documentation from the Department of Veterans Affairs to the Secretary. At the time the application and documentation are submitted to the Secretary, the institution must notify the veteran that the veteran's discharge request has been referred to the Secretary for determination of discharge eligibility and that no payments are due on the loan.

(v) If the documentation from the Department of Veterans Affairs does not indicate that the veteran is totally and permanently disabled as defined in § 674.51(aa)(2), the institution must resume collection on the loan.

(3) *Secretary's determination of eligibility.*

(i) If the Secretary determines, based on a review of the documentation from the Department of Veterans Affairs, that the veteran is totally and permanently disabled as defined in § 674.51(aa)(2), the Secretary notifies the institution of this determination, and the institution must—

(A) Discharge the veteran's obligation to make further payments on the loan; and

(B) Return to the person who made the payments on the loan any payments received on or after the effective date of the determination by the Department of Veterans Affairs that the veteran is unemployable due to a service-connected disability.

(ii) If the Secretary determines, based on a review of the documentation from the Department of Veterans Affairs, that the veteran is not totally and permanently disabled as defined in § 674.51(aa)(2), the Secretary notifies the institution of this determination, and the institution must resume collection on the loan.

(d) *No Federal reimbursement.* No Federal reimbursement is made to an institution for cancellation of loans due to death or disability.

(e) *Retroactive.* Discharge for death applies retroactively to all Defense, NDSL, and Perkins loans.

(Approved by the Office of Management and Budget under control number 1845-0019)

(Authority: 20 U.S.C. 425, 1070g, 1087dd; sec. 130(g)(2) of the Education Amendments of 1976, Pub. L. 94-482)

[53 Fed. Reg. 49147 (Dec. 6, 1988); 59 Fed. Reg. 61413, 61415 (Nov. 30, 1994); 64 Fed. Reg. 58315 (Oct. 28, 1999); 65 Fed. Reg. 18002 (Apr. 6, 2000); 65 Fed. Reg. 26136 (May 5, 2000); 65 Fed. Reg. 65690 (Nov. 1, 2000); 66 Fed. Reg. 44007 (Aug. 21, 2001); 68 Fed. Reg. 75428 (Dec. 31, 2003); 72 Fed. Reg. 61998 (Nov. 1, 2007); 73 Fed. Reg. 35494 (June 23, 2008); 73 Fed. Reg. 36793 (June 30, 2008); 74 Fed. Reg. 55663 (Oct. 28, 2009); 74 Fed. Reg. 55987 (Oct. 29, 2009)]

* * *

B.4 Other Federal Financial Assistance Regulations

B.4.1 Selected Institutional Eligibility Requirements

34 C.F.R. sec.

600.1 Scope
600.2 Definitions
600.3 [*Reserved*]
600.4 Institution of higher education
600.5 Proprietary institution of higher education
600.6 Postsecondary vocational institution
600.7 Conditions of institutional ineligibility
600.8 Treatment of a branch campus
600.9 [*Reserved*]
600.10 Date, extent, duration, and consequence of eligibility
600.11 Special rules regarding institutional accreditation or preaccreditation

* * *

SOURCE: 53 Fed. Reg. 11210 (Apr. 5, 1988); 55 Fed. Reg. 32182 (Aug. 7, 1990); 56 Fed. Reg. 36695 (July 31, 1991); 58 Fed. Reg. 13342 (Mar. 10, 1993); 59 Fed. Reg. 22335 (Apr. 29, 1994); 59 Fed. Reg. 22336 (Apr. 29, 1994); 59 Fed. Reg. 32657 (June 24, 1994); 64 Fed. Reg. 58615 (Oct. 29, 1999); 67 Fed. Reg. 67070 (Nov. 1, 2002), unless otherwise noted.

AUTHORITY: 20 U.S.C. 1001, 1002, 1003, 1088, 1091, 1094, 1099b, and 1099c, unless otherwise noted.

§ 600.1 Scope.

This part establishes the rules and procedures that the Secretary uses to determine whether an educational institution qualifies in whole or in part as an eligible institution of higher education under the Higher Education Act of 1965, as amended (HEA). An eligible institution of higher education may apply to participate in programs authorized by the HEA (HEA programs).

(Authority: 20 U.S.C. 1088, 1094, 1099b, 1099c, and 1141)

[59 Fed. Reg. 22336 (Apr. 29, 1994)]

§ 600.2 Definitions.

The following definitions apply to terms used in this part:

Accredited: The status of public recognition that a nationally recognized accrediting agency grants to an institution or educational program that meets the agency's established requirements.

Award year: The period of time from July 1 of one year through June 30 of the following year.

Branch Campus: A location of an institution that is geographically apart and independent of the main campus of the institution. The Secretary considers a location of an institution to be independent of the main campus if the location—
(1) Is permanent in nature;
(2) Offers courses in educational programs leading to a degree, certificate, or other recognized educational credential;
(3) Has its own faculty and administrative or supervisory organization; and
(4) Has its own budgetary and hiring authority.

Clock hour: A period of time consisting of—
(1) A 50- to 60-minute class, lecture, or recitation in a 60-minute period;
(2) A 50- to 60-minute faculty-supervised laboratory, shop training, or internship in a 60-minute period; or
(3) Sixty minutes of preparation in a correspondence course.

Correspondence course:
(1) A course provided by an institution under which the institution provides instructional materials, by mail or electronic transmission, including examinations on the materials, to students who are separated from the instructor. Interaction between the instructor and student is limited, is not regular and substantive, and is primarily initiated by the student. Correspondence courses are typically self-paced.
(2) If a course is part correspondence and part residential training, the Secretary considers the course to be a correspondence course.
(3) A correspondence course is not distance education.

Direct assessment program: A program as described in 34 CFR 668.10.

Distance education means education that uses one or more of the technologies listed in paragraphs (1) through (4) of this definition to deliver instruction to students who are separated from the instructor and to support regular and substantive interaction between the students and the instructor, either synchronously or asynchronously. The technologies may include—
(1) The internet;
(2) One-way and two-way transmissions through open broadcast, closed circuit, cable, microwave, broadband lines, fiber optics, satellite, or wireless communications devices;
(3) Audio conferencing; or
(4) Video cassettes, DVDs, and CD-ROMs, if the cassettes, DVDs, or CD-ROMs are used in a course in conjunction with any of the technologies listed in paragraphs (1) through (3) of this definition.

Educational program:
(1) A legally authorized postsecondary program of organized instruction or study that:
(i) Leads to an academic, professional, or vocational degree, or certificate, or other recognized educational credential, or is a comprehensive transition and postsecondary program, as described in 34 CFR part 668, subpart O; and
(ii) May, in lieu of credit hours or clock hours as a measure of student learning, utilize direct assessment of student learning, or recognize the direct assessment of student learning by others, if such assessment is consistent with the accreditation of the institution or program utilizing the results of the assessment and with the provisions of § 668.10.
(2) The Secretary does not consider that an institution provides an educational program if the institution does not provide instruction itself (including a course of independent study) but merely gives credit for one or more of the following: Instruction provided by other institutions or schools; examinations or direct assessments provided by agencies or organizations; or other accomplishments such as "life experience."

Eligible institution: An institution that—
(1) Qualifies as—
(i) An institution of higher education, as defined in § 600.4;
(ii) A proprietary institution of higher education, as defined in § 600.5; or
(iii) A postsecondary vocational institution, as defined in § 600.6; and
(2) Meets all the other applicable provisions of this part.

Federal Family Education Loan (FFEL) Programs: The loan programs (formerly called the Guaranteed Student Loan (GSL) programs) authorized by title IV-B of the HEA, including the Federal Stafford Loan, Federal PLUS, Federal Supplemental Loans for Students (Federal SLS), and Federal Consolidation Loan programs, in which lenders use their own funds to make loans to enable students or their parents to pay the costs of the students' attendance at eligible institutions. The Federal Stafford Loan, Federal PLUS, Federal SLS, and Federal Consolidation Loan programs are defined in 34 CFR part 668.

Incarcerated student: A student who is serving a criminal sentence in a Federal, State, or local penitentiary, prison, jail, reformatory, work farm, or other similar correctional institution. A student is not considered incarcerated if that student is in a half-way house or home detention or is sentenced to serve only weekends.

Legally authorized: The legal status granted to an institution through a charter, license, or other written document issued by the appropriate agency or official of the State in which the institution is physically located.

Nationally recognized accrediting agency: An agency or association that the Secretary recognizes as a reliable authority to determine the quality of education or training offered by an institution or a program offered by an institution. The Secretary recognizes these agencies and associations under the provisions of 34 CFR part 602 and publishes a list of the recognized agencies in the Federal Register.

Nonprofit institution: An institution that—

(1) Is owned and operated by one or more nonprofit corporations or associations, no part of the net earnings of which benefits any private shareholder or individual;

(2) Is legally authorized to operate as a nonprofit organization by each State in which it is physically located; and

(3) Is determined by the U.S. Internal Revenue Service to be an organization to which contributions are tax-deductible in accordance with section 501(c)(3) of the Internal Revenue Code (26 U.S.C. 501(c)(3)).

One-academic-year training program: An educational program that is at least one academic year as defined under 34 CFR 668.2.

Preaccredited: A status that a nationally recognized accrediting agency, recognized by the Secretary to grant that status, has accorded an unaccredited public or private nonprofit institution that is progressing toward accreditation within a reasonable period of time.

Recognized equivalent of a high school diploma: The following are the equivalent of a high school diploma—

(1) A General Education Development Certificate (GED);

(2) A State certificate received by a student after the student has passed a State-authorized examination that the State recognizes as the equivalent of a high school diploma;

(3) An academic transcript of a student who has successfully completed at least a two-year program that is acceptable for full credit toward a bachelor's degree; or

(4) For a person who is seeking enrollment in an educational program that leads to at least an associate degree or its equivalent and who has not completed high school but who excelled academically in high school, documentation that the student excelled academically in high school and has met the formalized, written policies of the institution for admitting such students.

Recognized occupation: An occupation that is—

(1) Listed in an "occupational division" of the latest edition of the Dictionary of Occupational Titles, published by the U.S. Department of Labor; or

(2) Determined by the Secretary in consultation with the Secretary of Labor to be a recognized occupation.

Regular student: A person who is enrolled or accepted for enrollment at an institution for the purpose of obtaining a degree, certificate, or other recognized educational credential offered by that institution.

Secretary: The Secretary of the Department of Education or an official or employee of the Department of Education acting for the Secretary under a delegation of authority.

State: A State of the Union, American Samoa, the Commonwealth of Puerto Rico, the District of Columbia, Guam, the Virgin Islands, the Commonwealth of the Northern Mariana Islands, the Republic of the Marshall Islands, the Federated States of Micronesia, and the Republic of Palau. The latter three are also known as the Freely Associated States.

Teach-out plan: A written plan developed by an institution that provides for the equitable treatment of students if an institution, or an institutional location that provides 100 percent of at least one program, ceases to operate before all students have completed their program of study, and may include, if required by the institution's accrediting agency, a teach-out agreement between institutions.

Title IV, HEA program: Any of the student financial assistance programs listed in 34 CFR 668.1(c).

(Authority: 20 U.S.C. 1071, *et seq.*, 1078-2, 1088, 1091, 1094, 1099b, 1099c, 1141; 26 U.S.C. 501(c))

[59 Fed. Reg. 32657 (June 24, 1994); 63 Fed. Reg. 40622 (July 29, 1998); 64 Fed. Reg. 58615 (Oct. 29, 1999); 71 Fed. Reg. 45692 (Aug. 9, 2006); 74 Fed. Reg. 55425 (Oct. 27, 2009); 74 Fed. Reg. 55932 (Oct. 29, 2009)]

§ 600.3 [*Reserved*]

§ 600.4 Institution of higher education.

(a) An institution of higher education is a public or private nonprofit educational institution that—

(1) Is in a State, or for purposes of the Federal Pell Grant, Federal Supplemental Educational Opportunity Grant, Federal Work-Study, and Federal TRIO programs may also be located in the Federated States of Micronesia or the Marshall Islands;

(2) Admits as regular students only persons who—

(i) Have a high school diploma;

(ii) Have the recognized equivalent of a high school diploma; or

(iii) Are beyond the age of compulsory school attendance in the State in which the institution is physically located;

(3) Is legally authorized to provide an educational program beyond secondary education in the State in which the institution is physically located;

(4)(i) Provides an educational program—

(A) For which it awards an associate, baccalaureate, graduate, or professional degree;

(B) That is at least a two-academic-year program acceptable for full credit toward a baccalaureate degree; or

(C) That is at least a one-academic-year training program that leads to a certificate, degree, or other recognized educational credential and prepares students for gainful employment in a recognized occupation; and

(ii) May provide a comprehensive transition and postsecondary program, as described in 34 CFR part 668, subpart O; and

(5) Is—

(i) Accredited or preaccredited; or

(ii) Approved by a State agency listed in the Federal Register in accordance with 34 CFR part 603, if the institution is a public postsecondary vocational educational institution that seeks to participate only in Federal student assistance programs.

(b) An institution is physically located in a State if it has a campus or other instructional site in that State.

(c) The Secretary does not recognize the accreditation or preaccreditation of an institution unless the institution agrees to submit any dispute involving the final denial, withdrawal, or termination of accreditation to initial arbitration before initiating any other legal action.

(Authority: 20 U.S.C. 1091, 1094, 1099b, 1141(a))

[64 Fed. Reg. 58615 (Oct. 29, 1999); 74 Fed. Reg. 55932 (Oct. 29, 2009)]

§ 600.5 Proprietary institution of higher education.

(a) A proprietary institution of higher education is an educational institution that—

(1) Is not a public or private nonprofit educational institution;

(2) Is in a State;

(3) Admits as regular students only persons who—

(i) Have a high school diploma;

(ii) Have the recognized equivalent of a high school diploma; or

(iii) Are beyond the age of compulsory school attendance in the State in which the institution is physically located;

(4) Is legally authorized to provide an educational program beyond secondary education in the State in which the institution is physically located;

(5)(i)(A) Provides an eligible program of training, as defined in 34 CFR 668.8, to prepare students for gainful employment in a recognized occupation; or

(B)(1) Has provided a program leading to a baccalaureate degree in liberal arts, as defined in paragraph (e) of this section, continuously since January 1, 2009; and

(2) Is accredited by a recognized regional accrediting agency or association, and has continuously held such accreditation since October 1, 2007, or earlier; and

(ii) May provide a comprehensive transition and postsecondary program for students with intellectual disabilities, as provided in 34 CFR part 668, subpart O;

(6) Is accredited; and

(7) Has been in existence for at least two years.

(b)(1) The Secretary considers an institution to have been in existence for two years only if—

(i) The institution has been legally authorized to provide, and has provided, a continuous educational program to prepare students for gainful employment in a recognized occupation during the 24 months preceding the date of its eligibility application; and

(ii) The educational program that the institution provides on the date of its eligibility application is substantially the same in length and subject matter as the program that the institution provided during the 24 months preceding the date of its eligibility application.

(2)(i) The Secretary considers an institution to have provided a continuous educational program during the 24 months preceding the date of its eligibility application even if the institution did not provide that program during normal vacation periods, or periods when the institution temporarily closed due to a natural disaster that directly affected the institution or the institution's students.

(ii) The Secretary considers an institution to have satisfied the provisions of paragraph (b)(1)(ii) of this section if the institution substantially changed the subject matter of the educational program it provided during that 24-month period because of new technology or the requirements of other Federal agencies.

(3) In determining whether an applicant institution satisfies the requirement contained in paragraph (b)(1) of this section, the Secretary—

(i) Counts any period during which the applicant institution has been certified as a branch campus; and

(ii) Except as provided in paragraph (b)(3)(i) of this section, does not count any period during which the applicant institution was a part of another eligible proprietary institution of higher education, postsecondary vocational institution, or vocational school.

(c) An institution is physically located in a State if it has a campus or other instructional site in that State.

(d) The Secretary does not recognize the accreditation of an institution unless the institution agrees to submit any dispute involving the final denial, withdrawal, or termination of accreditation to initial arbitration before initiating any other legal action.

(e) For purposes of this section, a "program leading to a baccalaureate degree in liberal arts" is a program that the institution's recognized regional accreditation agency or organization determines, is a general instructional program in the liberal arts subjects, the humanities disciplines, or the general curriculum, falling within one or more of the following generally-accepted instructional categories comprising such programs, but including only instruction in regular programs, and excluding independently-designed programs, individualized programs, and unstructured studies:

(1) A program that is a structured combination of the arts, biological and physical sciences, social sciences, and humanities, emphasizing breadth of study.

(2) An undifferentiated program that includes instruction in the general arts or general science.

(3) A program that focuses on combined studies and research in the humanities subjects as distinguished from the social and physical sciences, emphasizing languages, literatures, art, music, philosophy, and religion.

(4) Any single instructional program in liberal arts and sciences, general studies, and humanities not listed in paragraph (e)(1) through (e)(3) of this section.

(f), (g) [Reserved by 74 Fed. Reg. 55932]

(Approved by the Office of Management and Budget under control number 1845-0012)

(Authority: 20 U.S.C. 1088, 1091)

[59 Fed. Reg. 22337 (Apr. 29, 1994); 59 Fed. Reg. 32082 (June 22, 1994); 59 Fed. Reg. 47801 (Sept. 19, 1994); 59 Fed. Reg. 61177 (Nov. 29, 1994); 61 Fed. Reg. 29901 (June 12, 1996); 61 Fed. Reg. 60569 (Nov. 29, 1996); 64 Fed. Reg. 58615 (Oct. 29, 1999); 74 Fed. Reg. 55932 (Oct. 29, 2009)]

§ 600.6 Postsecondary vocational institution.

(a) A postsecondary vocational institution is a public or private nonprofit educational institution that—

(1) Is in a State;

(2) Admits as regular students only persons who—

(i) Have a high school diploma;

(ii) Have the recognized equivalent of a high school diploma; or

(iii) Are beyond the age of compulsory school attendance in the State in which the institution is physically located;

(3) Is legally authorized to provide an educational program beyond secondary education in the State in which the institution is physically located;

(4)(i) Provides an eligible program of training, as defined in 34 CFR 668.8, to prepare students for gainful employment in a recognized occupation; and

(ii) May provide a comprehensive transition and postsecondary program for students with intellectual disabilities, as provided in 34 CFR part 668, subpart O;

(5) Is—

(i) Accredited or preaccredited; or

(ii) Approved by a State agency listed in the Federal Register in accordance with 34 CFR part 603, if the institution is a public postsecondary vocational educational institution that seeks to participate only in Federal assistance programs; and

(6) Has been in existence for at least two years.

(b)(1) The Secretary considers an institution to have been in existence for two years only if—

(i) The institution has been legally authorized to provide, and has provided, a continuous education or training program to prepare students for gainful employment in a recognized occupation during the 24 months preceding the date of its eligibility application; and

(ii) The education or training program it provides on the date of its eligibility application is substantially the same in length and subject matter as the program it provided during the 24 months preceding the date of its eligibility application.

(2)(i) The Secretary considers an institution to have provided a continuous education or training program during the 24 months preceding the date of its eligibility application even if the institution did not provide that program during normal vacation periods, or periods when the institution temporarily closed due to a natural disaster that affected the institution or the institution's students.

(ii) The Secretary considers an institution to have satisfied the provisions of paragraph (b)(1)(ii) of this section if the institution substantially changed the subject matter of the educational program it provided during that 24-month period because of new technology or the requirements of other Federal agencies.

(3) In determining whether an applicant institution satisfies the requirement contained in paragraph (b)(1) of this section, the Secretary—

(i) Counts any period during which the applicant institution qualified as an eligible institution of higher education;

(ii) Counts any period during which the applicant institution was part of another eligible institution of higher education, provided that the applicant institution continues to be part of an eligible institution of higher education;

(iii) Counts any period during which the applicant institution has been certified as a branch campus; and

(iv) Except as provided in paragraph (b)(3)(iii) of this section, does not count any period during which the applicant institution was a part of another eligible proprietary institution of higher education or postsecondary vocational institution.

(c) An institution is physically located in a State or other instructional site if it has a campus or instructional site in that State.

(d) The Secretary does not recognize the accreditation or preaccreditation of an institution unless the institution agrees to submit any dispute involving the final denial, withdrawal, or termination of accreditation to initial arbitration before initiating any other legal action.

(Authority: 20 U.S.C. 1088, 1091, 1094(c)(3))

[64 Fed. Reg. 58616 (Oct. 29, 1999); 74 Fed. Reg. 55933 (Oct. 29, 2009)]

§ 600.7 Conditions of institutional ineligibility.

(a) *General rule.* For purposes of title IV of the HEA, an educational institution that otherwise satisfies the requirements contained in Secs. 600.4, 600.5, or 600.6 nevertheless does not qualify as an eligible institution under this part if—

(1) For its latest complete award year—

(i) More than 50 percent of the institution's courses were correspondence courses as calculated under paragraph (b) of this section;

(ii) Fifty percent or more of the institution's regular enrolled students were enrolled in correspondence courses;

(iii) More than twenty-five percent of the institution's regular enrolled students were incarcerated;

(iv) More than fifty percent of its regular enrolled students had neither a high school diploma nor the recognized equivalent of a high school diploma, and the institution does not provide a four-year or two-year educational program for which it awards a bachelor's degree or an associate degree, respectively;

(2) The institution, or an affiliate of the institution that has the power, by contract or ownership interest, to direct or cause the direction of the management of policies of the institution—

(A) Files for relief in bankruptcy, or

(B) Has entered against it an order for relief in bankruptcy; or

(3) The institution, its owner, or its chief executive officer—

(i) Has pled guilty to, has pled nolo contendere to, or is found guilty of, a crime involving the acquisition, use, or expenditure of title IV, HEA program funds; or

(ii) Has been judicially determined to have committed fraud involving title IV, HEA program funds.

(b) *Special provisions regarding correspondence courses and students*—

(1) *Calculating the number of correspondence courses.* For purposes of paragraphs (a)(1)(i) and (ii) of this section—

(i) A correspondence course may be a complete educational program offered by correspondence, or one course provided by correspondence in an on-campus (residential) educational program;

(ii) A course must be considered as being offered once during an award year regardless of the number of times it is offered during that year; and

(iii) A course that is offered both on campus and by correspondence must be considered two courses for the purpose of determining the total number of courses the institution provided during an award year.

(2) *Exceptions.*

(i) The provisions contained in paragraphs (a)(1)(i) and (ii) of this section do not apply to an institution that qualifies as a "technical institute or vocational school used exclusively or principally for the provision of vocational education to individuals who have completed or left high school and who are available for study in preparation for entering the labor market" under section 3(3)(C) of the Carl D. Perkins Vocational and Applied Technology Education Act of 1995.

(ii) The Secretary waives the limitation contained in paragraph (a)(1)(ii) of this section for an institution that offers a 2-year associate-degree or a 4-year bachelor's-degree program if the students enrolled in the institution's correspondence courses receive no more than 5 percent of the title IV, HEA program funds received by students at that institution.

(c) *Special provisions regarding incarcerated students*—

(1) *Exception.* The Secretary may waive the prohibition contained in paragraph (a)(1)(iii) of this section, upon the application of an institution, if the institution is a nonprofit institution that provides four-year or two-year educational programs for which it awards a bachelor's degree, an associate degree, or a postsecondary diploma.

(2) *Waiver for entire institution.* If the nonprofit institution that applies for a waiver consists solely of four-year or two-year educational programs for which it awards a bachelor's degree, an associate degree, or a postsecondary diploma, the Secretary waives the prohibition contained in paragraph (a)(1)(iii) of this section for the entire institution.

(3) *Other waivers.* If the nonprofit institution that applies for a waiver does not consist solely of four-year or two-year educational programs for which it awards a bachelor's degree, an associate degree, or a postsecondary diploma, the Secretary waives the prohibition contained in paragraph (a)(1)(iii) of this section—

(i) For the four-year and two-year programs for which it awards a bachelor's degree, an associate degree or a postsecondary diploma; and

(ii) For the other programs the institution provides, if the incarcerated regular students enrolled in those other programs have a completion rate of 50 percent or greater.

(d) *Special provision for a nonprofit institution if more than 50 percent of its enrollment consists of students who do not have a high school diploma or its equivalent.*

(1) Subject to the provisions contained in paragraphs (d)(2) and (d)(3) of this section, the Secretary waives the limitation contained in paragraph (a)(1)(iv) of this section for a nonprofit institution if that institution demonstrates to the Secretary's satisfaction that it exceeds that limitation because it serves, through contracts with Federal, State, or local government agencies, significant numbers of students who do not have a high school diploma or its recognized equivalent.

(2) *Number of critical students.* The Secretary grants a waiver under paragraph (d)(1) of this section only if no more than 40 percent of the institution's enrollment of regular students consists of students who—

(i) Do not have a high school diploma or its equivalent; and

(ii) Are not served through contracts described in paragraph (d)(3) of this section.

(3) *Contracts with Federal, State, or local government agencies.* For purposes of granting a waiver under paragraph (d)(1) of this section, the contracts referred to must be with Federal, State, or local government agencies for the purpose of providing job training to low-income individuals who are in need of that training. An example of such a contract is a job training contract under the Job Training Partnership Act (JPTA).

(e) *Special provisions.*

(1) For purposes of paragraph (a)(1) of this section, when counting regular students, the institution shall—

(i) Count each regular student without regard to the full-time or part-time nature of the student's attendance (*i.e.*, "head count" rather than "full-time equivalent");

(ii) Count a regular student once regardless of the number of times the student enrolls during an award year; and

(iii) Determine the number of regular students who enrolled in the institution during the relevant award year by—

(A) Calculating the number of regular students who enrolled during that award year; and

(B) Excluding from the number of students in paragraph (e)(1)(iii)(A) of this section, the number of regular students who enrolled but subsequently withdrew or were expelled from the institution and were entitled to receive a 100 percent refund of their tuition and fees less any administrative fee that the institution is permitted to keep under its fair and equitable refund policy.

(2) For the purpose of calculating a completion rate under paragraph (c)(3)(ii) of this section, the institution shall—

(i) Determine the number of regular incarcerated students who enrolled in the other programs during the last completed award year;

(ii) Exclude from the number of regular incarcerated students determined in paragraph (e)(2)(i) of this section, the number of those students who enrolled but subsequently withdrew or were expelled from the institution and were entitled to receive a 100 percent refund of their tuition and fees, less any administrative fee the institution is permitted to keep under the institution's fair and equitable refund policy;

(iii) Exclude from the total obtained in paragraph (e)(2)(ii) of this section, the number of those regular incarcerated students who remained enrolled in the programs at the end of the applicable award year;

(iv) From the total obtained in paragraph (e)(2)(iii) of this section, determine the number of regular incarcerated students who received a degree, certificate, or other recognized educational credential awarded for successfully completing the program during the applicable award year; and

(v) Divide the total obtained in paragraph (e)(2)(iv) of this section by the total obtained in paragraph (e)(2)(iii) of this section and multiply by 100.

(f)(1) If the Secretary grants a waiver to an institution under this section, the waiver extends indefinitely provided that the institution satisfies the waiver requirements in each award year.

(2) If an institution fails to satisfy the waiver requirements for an award year, the institution becomes ineligible on June 30 of that award year.

(g)(1) For purposes of paragraph (a)(1) of this section, and any applicable waiver or exception under this section, the institution shall substantiate the required calculations by having the certified public accountant who prepares its audited financial statement under 34 CFR 668.15 or its title IV, HEA program compliance audit under 34 CFR 668.23 report on the accuracy of those determinations.

(2) The certified public accountant's report must be based on performing an "attestation engagement" in accordance with the American Institute of Certified Public Accountants (AICPA's) Statement on Standards for Attestation Engagements. The certified public accountant shall include that attestation report with or as part of the audit report referenced in paragraph (g)(1) of this section.

(3) The certified public accountant's attestation report must indicate whether the institution's determinations regarding paragraph (a)(1) of this section and any relevant waiver or exception under paragraphs (b), (c), and (d) of this section are accurate; *i.e.*, fairly presented in all material respects.

(h) *Notice to the Secretary.* An institution shall notify the Secretary—

(1) By July 31 following the end of an award year if it falls within one of the prohibitions contained in paragraph (a)(1)of this section, or fails to continue to satisfy a waiver or exception granted under this section; or

(2) Within 10 days if it falls within one of the prohibitions contained in paragraphs (a)(2) or (a)(3) of this section.

(i) *Regaining eligibility.*

(1) If an institution loses its eligibility because of one of the prohibitions contained in paragraph (a)(1) of this section, to regain its eligibility, it must demonstrate—

(i) Compliance with all eligibility requirements;

(ii) That it did not fall within any of the prohibitions contained in paragraph (a)(1) of this section for at least one award year; and

(iii) That it changed its administrative policies and practices to ensure that it will not fall within any of the prohibitions contained in paragraph (a)(1) of this section.

(2) If an institution loses its eligibility because of one of the prohibitions contained in paragraphs (a)(2) and (a)(3) of this section, this loss is permanent. The institution's eligibility cannot be reinstated.

(Approved by the Office of Management and Budget under control number 1840-0098)

(Authority: 20 U.S.C. 1088)

[59 Fed. Reg. 22339 (Apr. 29, 1994); 59 Fed. Reg. 32082 (June 22, 1994), *as amended at* 59 Fed. Reg. 47801 (Sept. 19, 1994); 60 Fed. Reg. 34430 (June 30, 1995); 64 Fed. Reg. 58616 (Oct. 29, 1999); 71 Fed. Reg. 45692 (Aug. 9, 2006)]

§ 600.8 Treatment of a branch campus.

A branch campus of an eligible proprietary institution of higher education or a postsecondary vocational institution must be in existence for at least two years as a branch campus after the branch is certified as a branch campus before seeking to be designated as a main campus or a free-standing institution.

(Authority: 20 U.S.C. 1099c)

[59 Fed. Reg. 22340 (Apr. 29, 1994), *as amended at* 64 Fed. Reg. 58616 (Oct. 29, 1999); 67 Fed. Reg. 67070 (Nov. 1, 2002)]

§ 600.9 [*Reserved*]

[59 Fed. Reg. 22340 (Apr. 29, 1994), *as amended at* 65 Fed. Reg. 65671 (Nov. 1, 2000)]

§ 600.10 Date, extent, duration, and consequence of eligibility.

(a) *Date of eligibility.*

(1) If the Secretary determines that an applicant institution satisfies all the statutory and regulatory eligibility requirements, the Secretary considers the institution to be an eligible institution as of the date—

(i) The Secretary signs the institution's program participation agreement described in 34 CFR part 668, subpart B, for purposes of participating in any title IV, HEA program; and

(ii) The Secretary receives all the information necessary to make that determination for purposes other than participating in any title IV, HEA program.

(2) [*Reserved*]

(b) *Extent of eligibility.*

(1) If the Secretary determines that the entire applicant institution, including all its locations and all its educational programs, satisfies the applicable requirements of this part, the Secretary extends eligibility to all educational programs and locations identified on the institution's application for eligibility.

(2) If the Secretary determines that only certain educational programs or certain locations of an applicant institution satisfy the applicable requirements of this part, the Secretary extends eligibility only to those educational programs and locations that meet those requirements and identifies the eligible educational programs and locations in the eligibility notice sent to the institution under Sec. 600.21.

(3) Eligibility does not extend to any location that an institution establishes after it receives its eligibility designation if the institution pro-

vides at least 50 percent of an educational program at that location, unless—
(i) The Secretary approves that location under Sec. 600.20(e)(4); or
(ii) The location is licensed and accredited, the institution does not have to apply to the Secretary for approval of that location under Sec. 600.20(c), and the institution has reported to the Secretary that location under Sec. 600.21.

(c) *Subsequent additions of educational programs.*
(1) Except as provided in paragraph (c)(2) of this section, if an eligible institution adds an educational program after it has been designated as an eligible institution by the Secretary, the institution must apply to the Secretary to have that additional program designated as an eligible program of that institution.
(2) An eligible institution that adds an educational program after it has been designated as an eligible institution by the Secretary does not have to apply to the Secretary to have that additional program designated as an eligible program of that institution except as provided in 34 CFR 668.10 if the additional program—
(i) Leads to an associate, baccalaureate, professional, or graduate degree; or
(ii)(A) Prepares students for gainful employment in the same or related recognized occupation as an educational program that has previously been designated as an eligible program at that institution by the Secretary; and
(B) Is at least 8 semester hours, 12 quarter hours, or 600 clock hours.
(3) If an institution incorrectly determines under paragraph (c)(2) of this section that an educational program satisfies the applicable statutory and regulatory eligibility provisions without applying to the Secretary for approval, the institution is liable to repay to the Secretary all HEA program funds received by the institution for that educational program, and all the title IV, HEA program funds received by or on behalf of students who were enrolled in that educational program.

(d) *Duration of eligibility.*
(1) If an institution participates in the title IV, HEA programs, the Secretary's designation of the institution as an eligible institution under the title IV, HEA programs expires when the institution's program participation agreement, as described in 34 CFR part 668, subpart B, expires.
(2) If an institution participates in an HEA program other than a title IV, HEA program, the Secretary's designation of the institution as an eligible institution, for purposes of that non-title IV, HEA program, does not expire as long as the institution continues to satisfy the statutory and regulatory requirements governing its eligibility.

(e) *Consequence of eligibility.*
(1) If, as a part of its institutional eligibility application, an institution indicates that it wishes to participate in a title IV, HEA program and the Secretary determines that the institution satisfies the applicable statutory and regulatory requirements governing institutional eligibility, the Secretary will determine whether the institution satisfies the standards of administrative capability and financial responsibility contained in 34 CFR part 668, subpart B.
(2) If, as part of its institutional eligibility application, an institution indicates that it does not wish to participate in any title IV, HEA program and the Secretary determines that the institution satisfies the applicable statutory and regulatory requirements governing institutional eligibility, the institution is eligible to apply to participate in any HEA program listed by the Secretary in the eligibility notice it receives under Sec. 600.21. However, the institution is not eligible to participate in those programs, or receive funds under those programs, merely by virtue of its designation as an eligible institution under this part.

(Approved by the Office of Management and Budget under control number 1845-0098)

(Authority: 20 U.S.C. 1088 and 1141)

[59 Fed. Reg. 22340 (Apr. 29, 1994), *as amended at* 59 Fed. Reg. 47801 (Sept. 19, 1994); 65 Fed. Reg. 65671 (Nov. 1, 2000); 71 Fed. Reg. 45692 (Aug. 9, 2006)]

§ 600.11 Special rules regarding institutional accreditation or preaccreditation.

(a) *Change of accrediting agencies.* For purposes of Secs. 600.4(a)(5)(i), 600.5(a)(6), and 600.6(a)(5)(i), the Secretary does not recognize the accreditation or preaccreditation of an otherwise eligible institution if that institution is in the process of changing its accrediting agency, unless the institution provides to the Secretary—
(1) All materials related to its prior accreditation or preaccreditation; and
(2) Materials demonstrating reasonable cause for changing its accrediting agency.

(b) *Multiple accreditation.* The Secretary does not recognize the accreditation or preaccreditation of an otherwise eligible institution if that institution is accredited or preaccredited as an institution by more than one accrediting agency, unless the institution—
(1) Provides to each such accrediting agency and the Secretary the reasons for that multiple accreditation or preaccreditation;
(2) Demonstrates to the Secretary reasonable cause for that multiple accreditation or preaccreditation; and
(3) Designates to the Secretary which agency's accreditation or preaccreditation the institution uses to establish its eligibility under this part.

(c) *Loss of accreditation or preaccreditation.*
(1) An institution may not be considered eligible for 24 months after it has had its accreditation or preaccreditation withdrawn, revoked, or otherwise terminated for cause, unless the accrediting agency that took that action rescinds that action.
(2) An institution may not be considered eligible for 24 months after it has withdrawn voluntarily from its accreditation or preaccreditation status under a show-cause or suspension order issued by an accrediting agency, unless that agency rescinds its order.

(d) *Religious exception.*
(1) If an otherwise eligible institution loses its accreditation or preaccreditation, the Secretary considers the institution to be accredited or preaccredited for purposes of complying with the provisions of Secs. 600.4, 600.5, and 600.6 if the Secretary determines that its loss of accreditation or preaccreditation—
(i) Is related to the religious mission or affiliation of the institution; and
(ii) Is not related to its failure to satisfy the accrediting agency's standards.
(2) If the Secretary considers an unaccredited institution to be accredited or preaccredited under the provisions of paragraph (d)(1) of this section, the Secretary will consider that unaccredited institution to be accredited or preaccredited for a period sufficient to allow the institution to obtain alternative accreditation or preaccreditation, except that period may not exceed 18 months.

(Authority: 20 U.S.C. 1099b)

[59 Fed. Reg. 22341 (Apr. 29, 1994)]

* * *

B.4.2 Selected Student Assistance General Provisions

34 C.F.R. sec.

§ 668.1 Scope
§ 668.2 General definitions
§ 668.3 Academic year
§ 668.4 Payment period
§ 668.5 Written arrangements to provide educational programs
§ 668.6 [*Reserved*]
§ 668.7 [*Reserved*]
§ 668.8 Eligible program
§ 668.9 Relationship between clock hours and semester, trimester, or quarter hours in calculating Title IV, HEA program assistance

Federal Regulations Appx. B.4.2 § 668.2

* * *

§ 668.11 Scope
§ 668.12 [*Reserved*]
§ 668.13 Certification procedures
§ 668.14 Program participation agreement
§ 668.15 Factors of financial responsibility
§ 668.16 Standards of administrative capability
§ 668.17 [*Reserved*]
§ 668.18 [*Reserved*]
§ 668.19 Financial aid history
§ 668.20 Limitations on remedial coursework that is eligible for Title IV, HEA program assistance.
§ 668.21 Treatment of Federal Perkins Loan, FSEOG, and Federal Pell Grant program funds if the recipient withdraws, drops out, or is expelled before his or her first day of class.
§ 668.22 Treatment of Title IV funds when a student withdraws.

* * *

SOURCE: 45 Fed. Reg. 86855 (Dec. 31, 1980); 50 Fed. Reg. 26953 (June 28, 1985); 51 Fed. Reg. 8948 (Mar. 14, 1986); 51 Fed. Reg. 29398 (Aug. 15, 1986); 51 Fed. Reg. 41921 (Nov. 19, 1986); 56 Fed. Reg. 61337 (Dec. 2, 1991); 59 Fed. Reg. 21866 (Apr. 26, 1994); 59 Fed. Reg. 22318, 22418 (Apr. 29, 1994); 60 Fed. Reg. 61433 (Nov. 29, 1995); 64 Fed. Reg. 57358 (Oct. 22, 1999); 64 Fed. Reg. 58617 (Oct. 29, 1999); 64 Fed. Reg. 59037, 59066 (Nov. 1, 1999); 65 Fed. Reg. 38729 (June 22, 2000); 65 Fed. Reg. 65637, 65674 (Nov. 1, 2000); 68 Fed. Reg. 66615 (Nov. 26, 2003); 73 Fed. Reg. 35492 (June 23, 2008), unless otherwise noted.

AUTHORITY: 20 U.S.C. 1001, 1002, 1003, 1070g, 1085, 1088, 1091, 1092, 1094, 1099c, and 1099c-1, unless otherwise noted.

* * *

§ 668.1 Scope.

(a) This part establishes general rules that apply to an institution that participates in any student financial assistance program authorized by Title IV of the Higher Education Act of 1965, as amended (Title IV, HEA program). To the extent that an institution contracts with a third-party servicer to administer any aspect of the institution's participation in any Title IV, HEA program, the applicable rules in this part also apply to that servicer. An institution's use of a third-party servicer does not alter the institution's responsibility for compliance with the rules in this part.

(b) As used in this part, an "institution" includes—

(1) An institution of higher education as defined in 34 CFR 600.4;

(2) A proprietary institution of higher education as defined in 34 CFR 600.5; and

(3) A postsecondary vocational institution as defined in 34 CFR 600.6.

(c) The Title IV, HEA programs include—

(1) The Federal Pell Grant Program (20 U.S.C. 1070a *et seq.*; 34 CFR part 690);

(2) The Academic Competitiveness Grant (ACG) Program (20 U.S.C. 1070a-1; 34 CFR part 691);

(3) The Federal Supplemental Educational Opportunity Grant (FSEOG) Program (20 U.S.C. 1070b *et seq.*; 34 CFR parts 673 and 676);

(4) The Leveraging Educational Assistance Partnership (LEAP) Program (20 U.S.C. 1070c *et seq.*; 34 CFR part 692);

(5) The Federal Stafford Loan Program (20 U.S.C. 1071 *et seq.*; 34 CFR part 682);

(6) The Federal PLUS Program (20 U.S.C. 1078-2; 34 CFR part 682);

(7) The Federal Consolidation Loan Program (20 U.S.C. 1078-3; 34 CFR part 682);

(8) The Federal Work-Study (FWS) Program (42 U.S.C. 2751 *et seq.*; 34 CFR parts 673 and 675);

(9) The William D. Ford Federal Direct Loan (Direct Loan) Program (20 U.S.C. 1087a *et seq.*; 34 CFR part 685);

(10) The Federal Perkins Loan Program (20 U.S.C. 1087aa *et seq.*; 34 CFR parts 673 and 674);

(11) The National Science and Mathematics Access to Retain Talent Grant (National SMART Grant) Program (20 U.S.C. 1070a-1; 34 CFR part 691); and

(12) The Teacher Education Assistance for College and Higher Education (TEACH) Grant program.

(Authority: 20 U.S.C. 1070 *et seq.*)

[52 Fed. Reg. 45724 (Dec. 1, 1987), *as amended at* 56 Fed. Reg. 36696 (July 31, 1991); 59 Fed. Reg. 22418 (Apr. 29, 1994); 61 Fed. Reg. 60396 (Nov. 27, 1996); 63 Fed. Reg. 40623 (July 29, 1998); 65 Fed. Reg. 38729 (June 22, 2000); 71 Fed. Reg. 38002 (July 3, 2006); 73 Fed. Reg. 35492 (June 23, 2008)]

§ 668.2 General definitions.

(a) The following definitions are contained in the regulations for Institutional Eligibility under the Higher Education Act of 1965, as Amended, 34 CFR part 600:

Accredited
Award year
Branch campus
Clock hour
Correspondence course
Educational program
Eligible institution
Federal Family Education Loan (FFEL) programs
Incarcerated student
Institution of higher education
Legally authorized
Nationally recognized accrediting agency
Nonprofit institution
One-year training program
Postsecondary vocational institution
Preaccredited
Proprietary institution of higher education
Recognized equivalent of a high school diploma
Recognized occupation
Regular student
Secretary
State
Telecommunications course

(b) The following definitions apply to all Title IV, HEA programs:

Academic Competitiveness Grant (ACG) Program: A grant program authorized by Title IV-A-1 of the HEA under which grants are awarded during the first and second academic years of study to eligible financially needy undergraduate students who successfully complete rigorous secondary school programs of study.

Campus-based programs:

(1) The Federal Perkins Loan Program (34 CFR parts 673 and 674);

(2) The Federal Work-Study (FWS) Program (34 CFR parts 673 and 675); and

(3) The Federal Supplemental Educational Opportunity Grant (FSEOG) Program (34 CFR parts 673 and 676).

Defense loan: A loan made before July 1, 1972, under Title II of the National Defense Education Act of 1958.

(Authority: 20 U.S.C. 421–429)

Dependent student: Any student who does not qualify as an independent student (see Independent student).

Designated department official: An official of the Department of Education to whom the Secretary has delegated responsibilities indicated in this part.

Direct Loan Program loan: A loan made under the William D. Ford Federal Direct Loan Program.

(Authority: 20 U.S.C. 1087a *et seq.*)

Direct PLUS Loan: A loan made under the Federal Direct PLUS Program.

(Authority: 20 U.S.C. 1078-2 and 1087a *et seq.*)

Direct Subsidized Loan: A loan made under the Federal Direct Stafford/Ford Loan Program.

(Authority: 20 U.S.C. 1071 and 1087a *et seq.*)

Direct Unsubsidized Loan: A loan made under the Federal Direct Unsubsidized Stafford/Ford Loan Program.

(Authority: 20 U.S.C. 1087a *et seq.*)

Enrolled: The status of a student who—

(1) Has completed the registration requirements (except for the payment of tuition and fees) at the institution that he or she is attending; or

(2) Has been admitted into an educational program offered predominantly by correspondence and has submitted one lesson, com-

pleted by him or her after acceptance for enrollment and without the help of a representative of the institution.
(Authority: 20 U.S.C. 1088)

Expected family contribution (EFC): The amount, as determined under title IV, part F of the HEA, an applicant and his or her spouse and family are expected to contribute toward the applicant's cost of attendance.

Federal Consolidation Loan program: The loan program authorized by Title IV-B, section 428C, of the HEA that encourages the making of loans to borrowers for the purpose of consolidating their repayment obligations, with respect to loans received by those borrowers, under the Federal Insured Student Loan (FISL) Program as defined in 34 CFR part 682, the Federal Stafford Loan, Federal PLUS (as in effect before October 17, 1986), Federal Consolidation Loan, Federal SLS, ALAS (as in effect before October 17, 1986), Federal Direct Student Loan, and Federal Perkins Loan programs, and under the Health Professions Student Loan (HPSL) Program authorized by subpart II of part C of Title VII of the Public Health Service Act, for Federal PLUS borrowers whose loans were made after October 17, 1986, and for Higher Education Assistance Loans (HEAL) authorized by subpart I of part A of Title VII of the Public Health Services Act.
(Authority: 20 U.S.C. 1078-3)

Federal Direct PLUS Program: A loan program authorized by title IV, Part D of the HEA that is one of the components of the Direct Loan Program. The Federal Direct PLUS Program provides loans to parents of dependent students attending schools that participate in the Direct Loan Program. The Federal Direct PLUS Program also provides loans to graduate or professional students attending schools that participate in the Direct Loan Program. The borrower is responsible for the interest that accrues during any period.
(Authority: 20 U.S.C. 10782 and 1087a *et seq.*)

Federal Direct Stafford/Ford Loan Program: A loan program authorized by Title IV, Part D of the HEA that is one of the components of the Direct Loan Program. The Federal Direct Stafford/Ford Loan Program provides loans to undergraduate, graduate, and professional students attending schools that participate in the Direct Loan Program. The Secretary subsidizes the interest while the borrower is in an in-school, grace, or deferment period.
(Authority: 20 U.S.C. 1071 and 1087a *et seq.*)

Federal Direct Unsubsidized Stafford/Ford Loan Program: A loan program authorized by Title IV, Part D of the HEA that is one of the components of the Direct Loan Program. The Federal Direct Unsubsidized Stafford/Ford Loan Program provides loans to undergraduate, graduate, and professional students that participate in the Direct Loan Program. The borrower is responsible for the interest that accrues during any period.
(Authority: 20 U.S.C. 1087a *et seq.*)

Federal Pell Grant Program: A grant program authorized by Title IV-A-1 of the HEA under which grants are awarded to help financially needy students meet the cost of their postsecondary education.
(Authority: 20 U.S.C. 1070a)

Federal Perkins loan: A loan made under Title IV-E of the HEA to cover the cost of attendance for a period of enrollment beginning on or after July 1, 1987, to an individual who on July 1, 1987, had no outstanding balance of principal or interest owing on any loan previously made under Title IV-E of the HEA.
(Authority: 20 U.S.C. 1087aa *et seq.*)

Federal Perkins Loan program: The student loan program authorized by Title IV-E of the HEA after October 16, 1986. Unless otherwise noted, as used in this part, the Federal Perkins Loan Program includes the National Direct Student Loan Program and the National Defense Student Loan Program.
(Authority: 20 U.S.C. 1087aa–1087ii)

Federal PLUS loan: A loan made under the Federal PLUS Program.
(Authority: 20 U.S.C. 1078-2)

Federal PLUS program: The loan program authorized by Title IV-B, section 428B, of the HEA, that encourages the making of loans to parents of dependent undergraduate students. Before October 17, 1986, the PLUS Program also provided for making loans to graduate, professional, and independent undergraduate students. Before July 1, 1993, the PLUS Program also provided for making loans to parents of dependent graduate students. Beginning July 1, 2006, the PLUS Program provides for making loans to graduate and professional students.
(Authority: 20 U.S.C. 1078-2)

Federal SLS loan: A loan made under the Federal SLS Program.
(Authority: 20 U.S.C. 1078-1)

Federal Stafford loan: A loan made under the Federal Stafford Loan Program.
(Authority: 20 U.S.C. 1071 *et seq.*)

Federal Stafford Loan program: The loan program authorized by Title IV-B (exclusive of sections 428A, 428B, and 428C) that encourages the making of subsidized Federal Stafford and unsubsidized Federal Stafford loans as defined in 34 CFR part 682 to undergraduate, graduate, and professional students.
(Authority: 20 U.S.C. 1071 *et seq.*)

Federal Supplemental Educational Opportunity Grant (FSEOG) program: The grant program authorized by Title IV-A-2 of the HEA.
(Authority: 20 U.S.C. 1070b *et seq.*)

Federal Supplemental Loans for Students (Federal SLS) Program: The loan program authorized by Title IV-B, section 428A of the HEA, as in effect for periods of enrollment that began before July 1, 1994. The Federal SLS Program encourages the making of loans to graduate, professional, independent undergraduate, and certain dependent undergraduate students.
(Authority: 20 U.S.C. 1078-1)

Federal Work Study (FWS) program: The part-time employment program for students authorized by Title IV-C of the HEA.
(Authority: 42 U.S.C. 2751–2756b)

FFELP loan: A loan made under the FFEL programs.
(Authority: 20 U.S.C. 1071 *et seq.*)

Full-time student: An enrolled student who is carrying a full-time academic workload, as determined by the institution, under a standard applicable to all students enrolled in a particular educational program. The student's workload may include any combination of courses, work, research, or special studies that the institution considers sufficient to classify the student as a full-time student. However, for an undergraduate student, an institution's minimum standard must equal or exceed one of the following minimum requirements:

(1) For a program that measures progress in credit hours and uses standard terms (semesters, trimesters, or quarters), 12 semester hours or 12 quarter hours per academic term.

(2) For a program that measures progress in credit hours and does not use terms, 24 semester hours or 36 quarter hours over the weeks of instructional time in the academic year, or the prorated equivalent if the program is less than one academic year.

(3) For a program that measures progress in credit hours and uses nonstandard terms (terms other than semesters, trimesters or quarters) the number of credits determined by—

(i) Dividing the number of weeks of instructional time in the term by the number of weeks of instructional time in the program's academic year; and

(ii) Multiplying the fraction determined under paragraph (3)(i) of this definition by the number of credit hours in the program's academic year.

(4) For a program that measures progress in clock hours, 24 clock hours per week.

(5) A series of courses or seminars that equals 12 semester hours or 12 quarter hours in a maximum of 18 weeks.

(6) The work portion of a cooperative education program in which the amount of work performed is equivalent to the academic workload of a full-time student.

(7) For correspondence coursework, a full-time course load must be—

(i) Commensurate with the full-time definitions listed in paragraphs (1) through (6) of this definition; and

(ii) At least one-half of the coursework must be made up of non-correspondence coursework that meets one-half of the institution's requirement for full-time students.

HEA: The Higher Education Act of 1965, as amended.
(Authority: 20 U.S.C. 1070 et seq.)

Graduate or professional student: A student who—

(1) Is not receiving title IV aid as an undergraduate student for the same period of enrollment;

(2) Is enrolled in a program or course above the baccalaureate level or is enrolled in a program leading to a professional degree; and

(3) Has completed the equivalent of at least three years of full-time study either prior to entrance into the program or as part of the program itself.

(Authority: 20 U.S.C. 1082 and 1088)

Half-time student:

(1) Except as provided in paragraph (2) of this definition, an enrolled student who is carrying a half-time academic workload, as determined by the institution, that amounts to at least half of the workload of the applicable minimum requirement outlined in the definition of a full-time student.

(2) A student enrolled solely in a program of study by correspondence who is carrying a workload of at least 12 hours of work per week, or is earning at least six credit hours per semester, trimester, or quarter. However, regardless of the work, no student enrolled solely in correspondence study is considered more than a half-time student.

(Authority: 20 U.S.C. 1082 and 1088)

Independent student: A student who qualifies as an independent student under section 480(d) of the HEA.

(Authority: 20 U.S.C. 1087vv)

Initiating official: The designated department official authorized to begin an emergency action under 34 CFR 668.83.

Leveraging Educational Assistance Partnership (LEAP) Program: The grant program authorized by Title IV-A-4 of the HEA.

National Defense Student Loan program: The student loan program authorized by Title II of the National Defense Education Act of 1958.

(Authority: 20 U.S.C. 421–429)

National Direct Student Loan (NDSL) program: The student loan program authorized by Title IV-E of the HEA between July 1, 1972, and October 16, 1986.

(Authority: 20 U.S.C. 1087aa–1087ii)

National Early Intervention Scholarship and Partnership (NEISP) program: The scholarship program authorized by Chapter 2 of subpart 1 of Title IV-A of the HEA.

(Authority: 20 U.S.C. 1070a-21 et seq.)

National Science and Mathematics Access to Retain Talent Grant (National SMART Grant) Program: A grant program authorized by Title IV-A-1 of the HEA under which grants are awarded during the third and fourth academic years of study to eligible financially needy undergraduate students pursuing eligible majors in the physical, life, or computer sciences, mathematics, technology, or engineering, or foreign languages determined to be critical to the national security of the United States.

(Authority: 20 U.S.C. 1070a-1)

One-third of an academic year: A period that is at least one-third of an academic year as determined by an institution. At a minimum, one-third of an academic year must be a period that begins on the first day of classes and ends on the last day of classes or examinations and is a minimum of 10 weeks of instructional time during which, for an undergraduate educational program, a full-time student is expected to complete at least 8 semester or trimester hours or 12 quarter hours in an educational program whose length is measured in credit hours or 300 clock hours in an educational program whose length is measured in clock hours. For an institution whose academic year has been reduced under § 668.3, one-third of an academic year is the pro-rated equivalent, as measured in weeks and credit or clock hours, of at least one-third of the institution's academic year.

(Authority: 20 U.S.C. 1088)

Output document: The Student Aid Report (SAR), Electronic Student Aid Report (ESAR), or other document or automated data generated by the Department of Education's central processing system or Multiple Data Entry processing system as the result of the processing of data provided in a Free Application for Federal Student Aid (FAFSA).

Parent: A student's biological or adoptive mother or father or the student's stepparent, if the biological parent or adoptive mother or father has remarried at the time of application.

Participating institution: An eligible institution that meets the standards for participation in Title IV, HEA programs in subpart B and has a current program participation agreement with the Secretary.

Professional degree: A degree that signifies both completion of the academic requirements for beginning practice in a given profession and a level of professional skill beyond that normally required for a bachelor's degree. Professional licensure is also generally required. Examples of a professional degree include but are not limited to Pharmacy (Pharm.D.), Dentistry (D.D.S. or D.M.D.), Veterinary Medicine (D.V.M.), Chiropractic (D.C. or D.C.M.), Law (L.L.B. or J.D.), Medicine (M.D.), Optometry (O.D.), Osteopathic Medicine (D.O.), Podiatry (D.P.M., D.P., or Pod.D.), and Theology (M.Div., or M.H.L.).

(Authority: 20 U.S.C. 1082 and 1088)

Show-cause official: The designated department official authorized to conduct a show-cause proceeding for an emergency action under 34 CFR 668.83.

(Authority: 20 U.S.C. 1070c et seq.)

Teacher Education Assistance for College and Higher Education (TEACH) Grant Program: A grant program authorized by title IV of the HEA under which grants are awarded by an institution to students who are completing, or intend to complete, coursework to begin a career in teaching and who agree to serve for not less than four years as a full-time, highly-qualified teacher in a high-need field in a low-income school. If the recipient of a TEACH Grant does not complete four years of qualified teaching service within eight years of completing the course of study for which the TEACH Grant was received or otherwise fails to meet the requirements of 34 CFR 686.12, the amount of the TEACH Grant converts into a Federal Direct Unsubsidized Loan.

(Authority: 20 U.S.C. 1070g)

TEACH Grant: A grant authorized under title IV-A-9 of the HEA and awarded to students in exchange for prospective teaching service.

(Authority: 20 U.S.C. 1070g)

Third-party servicer:

(1) An individual or a State, or a private, profit or nonprofit organization that enters into a contract with an eligible institution to administer, through either manual or automated processing, any aspect of the institution's participation in any Title IV, HEA program. The Secretary considers administration of participation in a Title IV, HEA program to—

(i) Include performing any function required by any statutory provision of or applicable to Title IV of the HEA, any regulatory provision prescribed under that statutory authority, or any applicable special arrangement, agreement, or limitation entered into under the authority of statutes applicable to Title IV of the HEA, such as, but not restricted to—

(A) Processing student financial aid applications;

(B) Performing need analysis;

(C) Determining student eligibility and related activities;

(D) Certifying loan applications;

(E) Processing output documents for payment to students;

(F) Receiving, disbursing, or delivering Title IV, HEA program funds, excluding lock-box processing of loan payments and normal bank electronic fund transfers;

(G) Conducting activities required by the provisions governing student consumer information services in subpart D of this part;

(H) Preparing and certifying requests for advance or reimbursement funding;

(I) Loan servicing and collection;

(J) Preparing and submitting notices and applications required under 34 CFR part 600 and subpart B of this part; and

(K) Preparing a Fiscal Operations Report and Application to Participate (FISAP);
(ii) Exclude the following functions—
(A) Publishing ability-to-benefit tests;
(B) Performing functions as a Multiple Data Entry Processor (MDE);
(C) Financial and compliance auditing;
(D) Mailing of documents prepared by the institution;
(E) Warehousing of records; and
(F) Providing computer services or software; and
(iii) Notwithstanding the exclusions referred to in paragraph (1)(ii) of this definition, include any activity comprised of any function described in paragraph (1)(i) of this definition.
(2) For purposes of this definition, an employee of an institution is not a third-party servicer. The Secretary considers an individual to be an employee if the individual—
(i) Works on a full-time, part-time, or temporary basis;
(ii) Performs all duties on site at the institution under the supervision of the institution;
(iii) Is paid directly by the institution;
(iv) Is not employed by or associated with a third-party servicer; and
(v) Is not a third-party servicer for any other institution.
(Authority: 20 U.S.C. 1088)

Three-quarter time student: An enrolled student who is carrying a three-quarter-time academic workload, as determined by the institution, that amounts to at least three quarters of the work of the applicable minimum requirement outlined in the definition of a full-time student.
(Authority: 20 U.S.C. 1082 and 1088)

Two-thirds of an academic year: A period that is at least two-thirds of an academic year as determined by an institution. At a minimum, two-thirds of an academic year must be a period that begins on the first day of classes and ends on the last day of classes or examinations and is a minimum of 20 weeks of instructional time during which, for an undergraduate educational program, a full-time student is expected to complete at least 16 semester or trimester hours or 24 quarter hours in an educational program whose length is measured in credit hours or 600 clock hours in an educational program whose length is measured in clock hours. For an institution whose academic year has been reduced under § 668.3, two-thirds of an academic year is the pro-rated equivalent, as measured in weeks and credit or clock hours, of at least two-thirds of the institution's academic year.
(Authority: 20 U.S.C. 1088)

U.S. citizen or national: (1) A citizen of the United States; or (2) A person defined in the Immigration and Nationality Act, 8 U.S.C. 1101(a)(22), who, though not a citizen of the United States, owes permanent allegiance to the United States.
(Authority: 8 U.S.C. 1101)

Undergraduate student:
(1) A student who is enrolled in an undergraduate course of study that usually does not exceed four years, or is enrolled in a longer program designed to lead to a degree at the baccalaureate level. For purposes of 34 CFR 690.6(c)(5) students who have completed a baccalaureate program of study and who are subsequently completing a State-required teacher certification program are treated as undergraduates.
(2) In addition to meeting the definition in paragraph (1) of this definition, a student is only considered an undergraduate for purposes of the Federal Supplemental Educational Opportunity Grant (FSEOG) Program, the Federal Pell Grant Program, the Academic Competitiveness Grant (ACG) Program, National Science and Mathematics Access to Retain Talent (SMART) Grant Program, and TEACH Grant program if the student has not yet earned a baccalaureate or professional degree. However, for purposes of 34 CFR 690.6(c)(5) and 686.3(a) students who have completed a baccalaureate program of study and who are subsequently completing a State-required teacher certification program are treated as undergraduates.
(3) For purposes of dual degree programs that allow individuals to complete a bachelor's degree and either a graduate or professional degree within the same program, a student is considered an undergraduate student for at least the first three years of that program.
(4) A student enrolled in a four to five year program designed to lead to an undergraduate degree. A student enrolled in a program of any other, longer length is considered an undergraduate student for only the first four years of that program.
(Authority: 20 U.S.C. 1070g)

Valid institutional student information record (valid ISIR): A valid institutional student information record as defined in 34 CFR 690.2 for purposes of the Federal Pell Grant Program.

Valid student aid report (valid SAR): A valid student aid report (valid SAR) as defined in 34 CFR 690.2 for purposes of the Federal Pell Grant Program.
(Authority: 20 U.S.C. 1070 *et seq.*, unless otherwise noted)

William D. Ford Federal Direct Loan (Direct Loan) Program: The loan program authorized by Title IV, Part D of the HEA.
(Authority: 20 U.S.C. 1087a *et seq.*)

[52 Fed. Reg. 45725 (Dec. 1, 1987); 56 Fed. Reg. 36696 (July 31, 1991); 57 Fed. Reg. 27703 (June 22, 1992); 58 Fed. Reg. 13343 (Mar. 10, 1993); 58 Fed. Reg. 32200 (June 8, 1993); 58 Fed. Reg. 36871 (July 9, 1993); 59 Fed. Reg. 12520 (Mar. 16, 1994); 59 Fed. Reg. 21866 (Apr. 26, 1994); 59 Fed. Reg. 22418 (Apr. 29, 1994); 59 Fed. Reg. 32657 (June 24, 1994); 59 Fed. Reg. 61178 (Nov. 29, 1994); 60 Fed. Reg. 61809 (Dec. 1, 1995); 61 Fed. Reg. 60396 (Nov. 27, 1996); 63 Fed. Reg. 40623 (July 29, 1998); 65 Fed. Reg. 38729 (June 22, 2000); 65 Fed. Reg. 65674 (Nov. 1, 2000); 67 Fed. Reg. 67071 (Nov. 1, 2002); 69 Fed. Reg. 12275 (Mar. 16, 2004); 71 Fed. Reg. 38002 (July 3, 2006); 71 Fed. Reg. 45666 (Sept. 8, 2006); 71 Fed. Reg. 64397, 64418 (Nov. 1, 2006); 72 Fed. Reg. 62024, 62025 (Nov. 1, 2007); 73 Fed. Reg. 35492 (June 23, 2008)]

§ 668.3 Academic year.

(a) *General*. Except as provided in paragraph (c) of this section, an academic year for a program of study must include—
(1)(i) For a program offered in credit hours, a minimum of 30 weeks of instructional time; or
(ii) For a program offered in clock hours, a minimum of 26 weeks of instructional time; and
(2) For an undergraduate educational program, an amount of instructional time whereby a full-time student is expected to complete at least—
(i) Twenty-four semester or trimester credit hours or 36 quarter credit hours for a program measured in credit hours; or
(ii) 900 clock hours for a program measured in clock hours.

(b) *Definitions*. For purposes of paragraph (a) of this section—
(1) A week is a consecutive seven-day period;
(2) A week of instructional time is any week in which at least one day of regularly scheduled instruction or examinations occurs or, after the last scheduled day of classes for a term or payment period, at least one day of study for final examinations occurs; and
(3) Instructional time does not include any vacation periods, homework, or periods of orientation or counseling.

(c) *Reduction in the length of an academic year*.
(1) Upon the written request of an institution, the Secretary may approve, for good cause, an academic year of 26 through 29 weeks of instructional time for educational programs offered by the institution if the institution offers a two-year program leading to an associate degree or a four-year program leading to a baccalaureate degree.
(2) An institution's written request must—
(i) Identify each educational program for which the institution requests a reduction, and the requested number of weeks of instructional time for that program;
(ii) Demonstrate good cause for the requested reductions; and
(iii) Include any other information that the Secretary may require to determine whether

to grant the request.

(3)(i) The Secretary approves the request of an eligible institution for a reduction in the length of its academic year if the institution has demonstrated good cause for granting the request and the institution's accrediting agency and State licensing agency have approved the request.

(ii) If the Secretary approves the request, the approval terminates when the institution's program participation agreement expires. The institution may request an extension of that approval as part of the recertification process.

(Approved by the Office of Management and Budget under control number 1845-0022)

(Authority: 20 U.S.C. 1088)

[59 Fed. Reg. 22421 (Apr. 29, 1994); 59 Fed. Reg. 32657 (June 24, 1994); 59 Fed. Reg. 34964 (July 7, 1994); 59 Fed. Reg. 61178 (Nov. 29, 1994); 60 Fed. Reg. 42408 (Aug. 15, 1995); 67 Fed. Reg. 67071 (Nov. 1, 2002); 71 Fed. Reg. 45693 (Aug. 9, 2006)]

§ 668.4 Payment period.

(a) *Payment periods for an eligible program that measures progress in credit hours and uses standard terms or nonstandard terms that are substantially equal in length.* For a student enrolled in an eligible program that measures progress in credit hours and uses standard terms (semesters, trimesters, or quarters), or for a student enrolled in an eligible program that measures progress in credit hours and uses nonstandard terms that are substantially equal in length, the payment period is the academic term.

(b) *Payment periods for an eligible program that measures progress in credit hours and uses nonstandard terms that are not substantially equal in length.* For a student enrolled in an eligible program that measures progress in credit hours and uses nonstandard terms that are not substantially equal in length—

(1) For Pell Grant, ACG, National SMART Grant, FSEOG, Perkins Loan, and TEACH Grant program funds, the payment period is the academic term;

(2) For FFEL and Direct Loan program funds—

(i) For a student enrolled in an eligible program that is one academic year or less in length—

(A) The first payment period is the period of time in which the student successfully completes half of the number of credit hours in the program and half of the number of weeks of instructional time in the program; and

(B) The second payment period is the period of time in which the student successfully completes the program; and

(ii) For a student enrolled in an eligible program that is more than one academic year in length—

(A) For the first academic year and any subsequent full academic year—

(1) The first payment period is the period of time in which the student successfully completes half of the number of credit hours in the academic year and half of the number of weeks of instructional time in the academic year; and

(2) The second payment period is the period of time in which the student successfully completes the academic year;

(B) For any remaining portion of an eligible program that is more than half an academic year but less than a full academic year in length—

(1) The first payment period is the period of time in which the student successfully completes half of the number of credit hours in the remaining portion of the program and half of the number of weeks of instructional time remaining in the program; and

(2) The second payment period is the period of time in which the student successfully completes the remainder of the program; and

(C) For any remaining portion of an eligible program that is not more than half an academic year, the payment period is the remainder of the program.

(c) *Payment periods for an eligible program that measures progress in credit hours and does not have academic terms or for a program that measures progress in clock hours.*

(1) For a student enrolled in an eligible program that is one academic year or less in length—

(i) The first payment period is the period of time in which the student successfully completes half of the number of credit hours or clock hours, as applicable, in the program and half of the number of weeks of instructional time in the program; and

(ii) The second payment period is the period of time in which the student successfully completes the program or the remainder of the program.

(2) For a student enrolled in an eligible program that is more than one academic year in length—

(i) For the first academic year and any subsequent full academic year—

(A) The first payment period is the period of time in which the student successfully completes half of the number of credit hours or clock hours, as applicable, in the academic year and half of the number of weeks of instructional time in the academic year; and

(B) The second payment period is the period of time in which the student successfully completes the academic year;

(ii) For any remaining portion of an eligible program that is more than half an academic year but less than a full academic year in length—

(A) The first payment period is the period of time in which the student successfully completes half of the number of credit hours or clock hours, as applicable, in the remaining portion of the program and half of the number of weeks of instructional time remaining in the program; and

(B) The second payment period is the period of time in which the student successfully completes the remainder of the program; and

(iii) For any remaining portion of an eligible program that is not more than half an academic year, the payment period is the remainder of the program.

(3) For purposes of paragraphs (c)(1) and (c)(2) of this section, if an institution is unable to determine when a student has successfully completed half of the credit hours or clock hours in a program, academic year, or remainder of a program, the student is considered to begin the second payment period of the program, academic year, or remainder of a program at the later of the date, as determined by the institution, on which the student has successfully completed—

(i) Half of the academic coursework in the program, academic year, or remainder of the program; or

(ii) Half of the number of weeks of instructional time in the program, academic year, or remainder of the program.

(d) *Application of the cohort default rate exemption.* Notwithstanding paragraphs (a), (b), and (c) of this section, if 34 CFR 682.604(c)(10) or 34 CFR 685.301(b)(8) applies to an eligible program that measures progress in credit hours and uses nonstandard terms, an eligible program that measures progress in credit hours and does not have academic terms, or an eligible program that measures progress in clock hours, the payment period for purposes of FFEL and Direct Loan funds is the loan period for those portions of the program to which 34 CFR 682.604(c)(10) or 34 CFR 685.301(b)(8) applies.

(e) *Excused absences.* For purposes of this section, in determining whether a student successfully completes the clock hours in a payment period, an institution may include clock hours for which the student has an excused absence (i.e., an absence that a student does not have to make up) if—

(1) The institution has a written policy that permits excused absences; and

(2) The number of excused absences under the written policy for purposes of this paragraph (e) does not exceed the lesser of—

(i) The policy on excused absences of the institution's accrediting agency or, if the institution has more than one accrediting agency, the agency designated under 34 CFR 600.11(b);

(ii) The policy on excused absences of any State agency that licenses the institution or otherwise legally authorizes the institution to operate in the State; or

(iii) Ten percent of the clock hours in the payment period.

(f) *Re-entry within 180 days.* If a student withdraws from a program described in paragraph (c) of this section during a payment period and then reenters the same program within 180 days, the student remains in that same payment period when he or she returns and, subject to conditions established by the Secretary or by the FFEL lender or guaranty agency, is eligible to receive any title IV, HEA program funds for which he or she was eligible prior to withdrawal, including funds that were returned by the institution or student under the provisions of § 668.22.

(g) *Re-entry after 180 days or transfer.*

(1) Except as provided in paragraph (g)(3) of this section, and subject to the conditions of paragraph (g)(2) of this section, an institution calculates new payment periods for the remainder of a student's program based on paragraph (c) of this section, for a student who withdraws from a program described in paragraph (c) of this section, and—

(i) Reenters that program after 180 days;

(ii) Transfers into another program at the same institution within any time period; or

(iii) Transfers into a program at another institution within any time period.

(2) For a student described in paragraph (g)(1) of this section—

(i) For the purpose of calculating payment periods only, the length of the program is the number of credit hours and the number of weeks of instructional time, or the number of clock hours and the number of weeks of instructional time, that the student has remaining in the program he or she enters or reenters; and

(ii) If the remaining hours and weeks constitute half of an academic year or less, the remaining hours constitute one payment period.

(3) Notwithstanding the provisions of paragraph (g)(1) of this section, an institution may consider a student who transfers into another program at the same institution to remain in the same payment period if—

(i) The student is continuously enrolled at the institution;

(ii) The coursework in the payment period the student is transferring out of is substantially similar to the coursework the student will be taking when he or she first transfers into the new program;

(iii) The payment periods are substantially equal in length in weeks of instructional time and credit hours or clock hours, as applicable;

(iv) There are little or no changes in institutional charges associated with the payment period to the student; and

(v) The credits from the payment period the student is transferring out of are accepted toward the new program.

(h) *Definitions.* For purposes of this section—

(1) Terms are *substantially equal in* length if no term in the program is more than two weeks of instructional time longer than any other term in that program; and

(2) A student *successfully completes* credit hours or clock hours if the institution considers the student to have passed the coursework associated with those hours.

(Authority: 20 U.S.C. 1070 *et seq.*)

[61 Fed. Reg. (Nov. 29, 1996); 67 Fed. Reg. 67071 (Nov. 1, 2002); 72 Fed. Reg. 62025 (Nov. 1, 2007); 73 Fed. Reg. 35492 (June 23, 2008)]

§ 668.5 Written arrangements to provide educational programs.

(a) *Written arrangements between eligible institutions.* If an eligible institution enters into a written arrangement with another eligible institution, or with a consortium of eligible institutions, under which the other eligible institution or consortium provides all or part of the educational program of students enrolled in the former institution, the Secretary considers that educational program to be an eligible program if it otherwise satisfies the requirements of Sec. 668.8.

(b) *Written arrangements for study-abroad.* Under a study abroad program, if an eligible institution enters into a written arrangement with a foreign institution, or an organization acting on behalf of a foreign institution, under which the foreign institution provides part of the educational program of students enrolled in the eligible institution, the Secretary considers that educational program to be an eligible program if it otherwise satisfies the requirements of paragraphs (c)(1) through (c)(3) of this section.

(c) *Written arrangements between an eligible institution and an ineligible institution or organization.* If an eligible institution enters into a written arrangement with an institution or organization that is not an eligible institution under which the ineligible institution or organization provides part of the educational program of students enrolled in the eligible institution, the Secretary considers that educational program to be an eligible program if—

(1) The ineligible institution or organization has not had its eligibility to participate in the title IV, HEA programs terminated by the Secretary, or has not voluntarily withdrawn from participation in those programs under a termination, show-cause, suspension, or similar type proceeding initiated by the institution's State licensing agency, accrediting agency, guarantor, or by the Secretary;

(2) The educational program otherwise satisfies the requirements of Sec. 668.8; and

(3)(i) The ineligible institution or organization provides not more than 25 percent of the educational program; or

(ii)(A) The ineligible institution or organization provides more than 25 percent but not more than 50 percent of the educational program;

(B) The eligible institution and the ineligible institution or organization are not owned or controlled by the same individual, partnership, or corporation; and

(C) The eligible institution's accrediting agency, or if the institution is a public postsecondary vocational educational institution, the State agency listed in the Federal Register in accordance with 34 CFR part 603, has specifically determined that the institution's arrangement meets the agency's standards for the contracting out of educational services.

(d) *Administration of title IV, HEA programs.*

(1) If an institution enters into a written arrangement as described in paragraph (a), (b), or (c) of this section, except as provided in paragraph (d)(2) of this section, the institution at which the student is enrolled as a regular student must determine the student's eligibility for title IV, HEA program funds, and must calculate and disburse those funds to that student.

(2) In the case of a written arrangement between eligible institutions, the institutions may agree in writing to have any eligible institution in the written arrangement make those calculations and disbursements, and the Secretary does not consider that institution to be a third-party servicer for that arrangement.

(3) The institution that calculates and disburses a student's title IV, HEA program assistance under paragraph (d)(1) or (d)(2) of this section must—

(i) Take into account all the hours in which the student enrolls at each institution that apply to the student's degree or certificate when determining the student's enrollment status and cost of attendance; and

(ii) Maintain all records regarding the student's eligibility for and receipt of title IV, HEA program funds.

(Authority: 20 U.S.C. 1094)

[65 Fed. Reg. 65674 (Nov. 1, 2000)]

§ 668.6 [*Reserved*]

§ 668.7 [*Reserved*]

[60 Fed. Reg. 61809, Dec. 1995]

§ 668.8 Eligible program.

(a) *General.* An eligible program is an educational program that—
 (1) Is provided by a participating institution; and
 (2) Satisfies the other relevant requirements contained in this section.

(b) *Definitions.* For purposes of this section—
 (1) The Secretary considers the "equivalent of an associate degree" to be—
  (i) An associate degree; or
  (ii) The successful completion of at least a two-year program that is acceptable for full credit toward a bachelor's degree and qualifies a student for admission into the third year of a bachelor's degree program;
 (2) A week is a consecutive seven-day period; and
 (3)(i) The Secretary considers that an institution provides one week of instructional time in an academic program during any week the institution provides at least one day of regularly scheduled instruction or examinations, or, after the last scheduled day of classes for a term or a payment period, at least one day of study for final examinations.
  (ii) Instructional time does not include any vacation periods, homework, or periods of orientation or counseling.

(c) *Institution of higher education.* An eligible program provided by an institution of higher education must—
 (1) Lead to an associate, bachelor's, professional, or graduate degree;
 (2) Be at least a two-academic-year program that is acceptable for full credit toward a bachelor's degree; or
 (3) Be at least a one-academic-year training program that leads to a certificate, degree, or other recognized educational credential and that prepares a student for gainful employment in a recognized occupation.

(d) *Proprietary institution of higher education and postsecondary vocational institution.* An eligible program provided by a proprietary institution of higher education or postsecondary vocational institution—
 (1)(i) Must require a minimum of 15 weeks of instruction, beginning on the first day of classes and ending on the last day of classes or examinations;
  (ii) Must be at least 600 clock hours, 16 semester or trimester hours, or 24 quarter hours;
  (iii) Must provide undergraduate training that prepares a student for gainful employment in a recognized occupation; and
  (iv) May admit as regular students persons who have not completed the equivalent of an associate degree;
 (2) Must—
  (i) Require a minimum of 10 weeks of instruction, beginning on the first day of classes and ending on the last day of classes or examinations;
  (ii) Be at least 300 clock hours, 8 semester or trimester hours, or 12 quarter hours;
  (iii) Provide training that prepares a student for gainful employment in a recognized occupation; and
  (iv)(A) Be a graduate or professional program; or
   (B) Admit as regular students only persons who have completed the equivalent of an associate degree;
 (3) For purposes of the FFEL and Direct Loan programs only, must—
  (i) Require a minimum of 10 weeks of instruction, beginning on the first day of classes and ending on the last day of classes or examinations;
  (ii) Be at least 300 clock hours but less than 600 clock hours;
  (iii) Provide undergraduate training that prepares a student for gainful employment in a recognized occupation;
  (iv) Admit as regular students some persons who have not completed the equivalent of an associate degree; and
  (v) Satisfy the requirements of paragraph (e) of this section; or
 (4) For purposes of a proprietary institution of higher education only, is a program leading to a baccalaureate degree in liberal arts, as defined in 34 CFR 600.5(e), that—
  (i) Is provided by an institution that is accredited by a recognized regional accrediting agency or association, and has continuously held such accreditation since October 1, 2007, or earlier; and
  (ii) The institution has provided continuously since January 1, 2009.

(e) *Qualitative factors.*
 (1) An educational program that satisfies the requirements of paragraphs (d)(3)(i) through (iv) of this section qualifies as an eligible program only if—
  (i) The program has a substantiated completion rate of at least 70 percent, as calculated under paragraph (f) of this section;
  (ii) The program has a substantiated placement rate of at least 70 percent, as calculated under paragraph (g) of this section;
  (iii) The number of clock hours provided in the program does not exceed by more than 50 percent the minimum number of clock hours required for training in the recognized occupation for which the program prepares students, as established by the State in which the program is offered, if the State has established such a requirement, or as established by any Federal agency; and
  (iv) The program has been in existence for at least one year. The Secretary considers an educational program to have been in existence for at least one year only if an institution has been legally authorized to provide, and has continuously provided, the program during the 12 months (except for normal vacation periods and, at the discretion of the Secretary, periods when the institution closes due to a natural disaster that directly affects the institution or the institution's students) preceding the date on which the institution applied for eligibility for that program.
 (2) An institution shall substantiate the calculation of its completion and placement rates by having the certified public accountant who prepares its audit report required under § 668.23 report on the institution's calculation based on performing an attestation engagement in accordance with the Statements on Standards for Attestation Engagements of the American Institute of Certified Public Accountants (AICPA).

(f) *Calculation of completion rate.* An institution shall calculate its completion rate for an educational program for any award year as follows:
 (1) Determine the number of regular students who were enrolled in the program during the award year.
 (2) Subtract from the number of students determined under paragraph (f)(1) of this section, the number of regular students who, during that award year, withdrew from, dropped out of, or were expelled from the program and were entitled to and actually received, in a timely manner a refund of 100 percent of their tuition and fees.
 (3) Subtract from the total obtained under paragraph (f)(2) of this section the number of students who were enrolled in the program at the end of that award year.
 (4) Determine the number of regular students who, during that award year, received within 150 percent of the published length of the educational program the degree, certificate, or other recognized educational credential awarded for successfully completing the program.
 (5) Divide the number determined under paragraph (f)(4) of this section by the total obtained under paragraph (f)(3) of this section.

(g) *Calculation of placement rate.*
 (1) An institution shall calculate its placement rate for an educational program for any award year as follows:
  (i) Determine the number of students who, during the award year, received the degree, certificate, or other recognized educational credential awarded for successfully completing the program.
  (ii) Of the total obtained under paragraph (g)(1)(i) of this section, determine the number of students who, within 180 days of the day they received their degree, certificate, or other recognized educational credential, obtained gainful employment in the recognized occupation for which they were trained or in a related comparable recog-

nized occupation and, on the date of this calculation, are employed, or have been employed, for at least 13 weeks following receipt of the credential from the institution.

(iii) Divide the number of students determined under paragraph (g)(1)(ii) of this section by the total obtained under paragraph (g)(1)(i) of this section.

(2) An institution shall document that each student described in paragraph (g)(1)(ii) of this section obtained gainful employment in the recognized occupation for which he or she was trained or in a related comparable recognized occupation. Examples of satisfactory documentation of a student's gainful employment include, but are not limited to—

(i) A written statement from the student's employer;

(ii) Signed copies of State or Federal income tax forms; and

(iii) Written evidence of payments of Social Security taxes.

(h) *Eligibility for Federal Pell Grant, ACG, National SMART Grant, TEACH Grant, and FSEOG Programs.* In addition to satisfying other relevant provisions of the section—

(1) An educational program qualifies as an eligible program for purposes of the Federal Pell Grant Program only if the educational program is an undergraduate program or a postbaccalaureate teacher certificate or licensing program as described in 34 CFR 690.6(c);

(2) An educational program qualifies as an eligible program for purposes of the ACG, National SMART Grant, and FSEOG programs only if the educational program is an undergraduate program; and

(3) An educational program qualifies as an eligible program for purposes of the TEACH Grant program if it satisfies the requirements of the definition of TEACH Grant-eligible program in 34 CFR 686.2(d).

(i) *Flight training.* In addition to satisfying other relevant provisions of this section, for a program of flight training to be an eligible program, it must have a current valid certification from the Federal Aviation Administration.

(j) *English as a second language (ESL).*

(1) In addition to satisfying the relevant provisions of this section, an educational program that consists solely of instruction in ESL qualifies as an eligible program if—

(i) The institution admits to the program only students who the institution determines need the ESL instruction to use already existing knowledge, training, or skills; and

(ii) The program leads to a degree, certificate, or other recognized educational credential.

(2) An institution shall document its determination that ESL instruction is necessary to enable each student enrolled in its ESL program to use already existing knowledge, training, or skills with regard to the students that it admits to its ESL program under paragraph (j)(1)(i) of this section.

(3) An ESL program that qualifies as an eligible program under this paragraph is eligible for purposes of the Federal Pell Grant Program only.

(k) *Undergraduate educational program in credit hours.* If an institution offers an undergraduate educational program in credit hours, the institution must use the formula contained in paragraph (l) of this section to determine whether that program satisfies the requirements contained in paragraph (c)(3) or (d) of this section, and the number of credit hours in that educational program for purposes of the Title IV, HEA programs, unless—

(1) The program is at least two academic years in length and provides an associate degree, a bachelor's degree, a professional degree, or an equivalent degree as determined by the Secretary; or

(2) Each course within the program is acceptable for full credit toward that institution's associate degree, bachelor's degree, professional degree, or equivalent degree as determined by the Secretary, provided that the institution's degree requires at least two academic years of study.

(l) *Formula.* For purposes of determining whether a program described in paragraph (k) of this section satisfies the requirements contained in paragraph (c)(3) or (d) of this section, and the number of credit hours in that educational program with regard to the Title IV, HEA programs—

(1) A semester hour must include at least 30 clock hours of instruction;

(2) A trimester hour must include at least 30 clock hours of instruction; and

(3) A quarter hour must include at least 20 hours of instruction.

(m) An otherwise eligible program that is offered in whole or in part through telecommunications is eligible for title IV, HEA program purposes if the program is offered by an institution, other than a foreign institution, that has been evaluated and is accredited for its effective delivery of distance education programs by an accrediting agency or association that—

(1) Is recognized by the Secretary under subpart 2 of part H of the HEA; and

(2) Has accreditation of distance education within the scope of its recognition.

(n) For Title IV, HEA program purposes, eligible program includes a direct assessment program approved by the Secretary under § 668.10 and a comprehensive transition and postsecondary program approved by the Secretary under § 668.232.

(Authority: 20 U.S.C. 1070a, 1070a-1, 1070b, 1070c-1, 1070c-2, 1070g, 1085, 1087aa-1087hh, 1088, 1091; 42 U.S.C. 2753)

[52 Fed. Reg. 45727 (Dec. 1, 1987); 53 Fed. Reg. 49147 (Dec. 6, 1988); 58 Fed. Reg. 32202 (June 8, 1993); 58 Fed. Reg. 39620 (July 23, 1993); 58 Fed. Reg. 69594 (Dec. 30, 1993); 59 Fed. Reg. 21866 (Apr. 26, 1994); 59 Fed. Reg. 22421 (Apr. 29, 1994); 59 Fed. Reg. 32656, 32657 (June 24, 1994); 59 Fed. Reg. 34964 (July 7, 1994); 59 Fed. Reg. 61179 (Nov. 29, 1994); 60 Fed. Reg. 42408 (Aug. 15, 1995); 63 Fed. Reg. 40623 (July 29, 1998); 64 Fed. Reg. 58291 (Oct. 28, 1999); 64 Fed. Reg. 59037 (Nov. 1, 1999); 65 Fed. Reg. 65675 (Nov. 1, 2000); 67 Fed. Reg. 67072 (Nov. 1, 2002); 71 Fed. Reg. 38002 (July 3, 2006); 71 Fed. Reg. 45693 (Aug. 9, 2006); 73 Fed. Reg. 35492 (June 23, 2008); 74 Fed. Reg. 55933 (Oct. 29, 2009)]

§ 668.9 Relationship between clock hours and semester, trimester, or quarter hours in calculating Title IV, HEA program assistance.

(a) In determining the amount of Title IV, HEA program assistance that a student who is enrolled in a program described in § 668.8(k) is eligible to receive, the institution shall apply the formula contained in § 668.8(l) to determine the number of semester, trimester, or quarter hours in that program, if the institution measures academic progress in that program in semester, trimester, or quarter hours.

(b) Notwithstanding paragraph (a) of this section, a public or private nonprofit hospital-based school of nursing that awards a diploma at the completion of the school's program of education is not required to apply the formula contained in § 668.8(l) to determine the number of semester, trimester, or quarter hours in that program for purposes of calculating Title IV, HEA program assistance.

(Authority: 20 U.S.C. 1082, 1085, 1088, 1091, 1141)

[58 Fed. Reg. 39620 (July 23, 1993); 58 Fed. Reg. 69594 (Dec. 30, 1993); 59 Fed. Reg. 22423 (Apr. 29, 1994); 59 Fed. Reg. 32656, 32657 (June 24, 1994); 59 Fed. Reg. 61179 (Nov. 29, 1994)]

* * *

§ 668.11 Scope.

(a) This subpart establishes standards that an institution must meet in order to participate in any Title IV, HEA program.

(b) Noncompliance with these standards by an institution already participating in any Title IV, HEA program or with applicable standards in this subpart by a third-party servicer that contracts with the institution may subject the institution or servicer, or both, to proceedings under

subpart G of this part. These proceedings may lead to any of the following actions:
(1) An emergency action.
(2) The imposition of a fine.
(3) The limitation, suspension, or termination of the participation of the institution in a Title IV, HEA program.
(4) The limitation, suspension, or termination of the eligibility of the servicer to contract with any institution to administer any aspect of the institution's participation in a Title IV, HEA program.

(Authority: 20 U.S.C. 1094)

[59 Fed. Reg. 22423 (Apr. 29, 1994); 59 Fed. Reg. 32657 (June 24, 1994)]

§ 668.12 [Reserved]

[52 Fed. Reg. 45727 (Dec. 1, 1987), *as amended by* 65 Fed. Reg. 65675 (Nov. 11, 2000)]

§ 668.13 Certification procedures.

(a) *Requirements for certification.*
(1) The Secretary certifies an institution to participate in the title IV, HEA programs if the institution qualifies as an eligible institution under 34 CFR part 600, meets the standards of this subpart and 34 CFR part 668, subpart L, and satisfies the requirements of paragraph (a)(2) of this section.
(2) Except as provided in paragraph (a)(3) of this section, if an institution wishes to participate for the first time in the title IV, HEA programs or has undergone a change in ownership that results in a change in control as described in 34 CFR 600.31, the institution must require the following individuals to complete title IV, HEA program training provided or approved by the Secretary no later than 12 months after the institution executes its program participation agreement under § 668.14:
  (i) The individual the institution designates under § 668.16(b)(1) as its title IV, HEA program administrator.
  (ii) The institution's chief administrator or a high level institutional official the chief administrator designates.
(3)(i) An institution may request the Secretary to waive the training requirement for any individual described in paragraph (a)(2) of this section.
  (ii) When the Secretary receives a waiver request under paragraph (a)(3)(i) of this section, the Secretary may grant or deny the waiver, require another institutional official to take the training, or require alternative training.

(b) *Period of participation.*
(1) If the Secretary certifies that an institution meets the standards of this subpart, the Secretary also specifies the period for which the institution may participate in a Title IV, HEA program. An institution's period of participation expires six years after the date that the Secretary certifies that the institution meets the standards of this subpart, except that the Secretary may specify a shorter period.
(2) Provided that an institution has submitted an application for a renewal of certification that is materially complete at least 90 days prior to the expiration of its current period of participation, the institution's existing certification will be extended on a month to month basis following the expiration of the institution's period of participation until the end of the month in which the Secretary issues a decision on the application for recertification.

(c) *Provisional certification.*
(1)(i) The Secretary may provisionally certify an institution if—
  (A) The institution seeks initial participation in a Title IV, HEA program;
  (B) The institution is an eligible institution that has undergone a change in ownership that results in a change in control according to the provisions of 34 CFR part 600;
  (C) The institution is a participating institution—
    (1) That is applying for a certification that the institution meets the standards of this subpart;
    (2) That the Secretary determines has jeopardized its ability to perform its financial responsibilities by not meeting the factors of financial responsibility under § 668.15 and subpart L of this part or the standards of administrative capability under § 668.16; and
    (3) Whose participation has been limited or suspended under subpart G of this part, or voluntarily enters into provisional certification;
  (D) The institution seeks a renewal of participation in a Title IV, HEA program after the expiration of a prior period of participation in that program; or
  (E) The institution is a participating institution that was accredited or preaccredited by a nationally recognized accrediting agency on the day before the Secretary withdrew the Secretary's recognition of that agency according to the provisions contained in 34 CFR part 603.
  (ii) A proprietary institution's certification automatically becomes provisional at the start of a fiscal year after it did not derive at least 10 percent of its revenue for its preceding fiscal year from sources other than Title IV, HEA program funds, as required under § 668.14(b)(16).
(2) If the Secretary provisionally certifies an institution, the Secretary also specifies the period for which the institution may participate in a Title IV, HEA program. Except as provided in paragraphs (c)(3) and (4) of this section, a provisionally certified institution's period of participation expires—
  (i) Not later than the end of the first complete award year following the date on which the Secretary provisionally certified the institution under paragraph (c)(1)(i) of this section;
  (ii) Not later than the end of the third complete award year following the date on which the Secretary provisionally certified the institution under paragraphs (c)(1)(ii), (iii), (iv) or (e)(2) of this section; and
  (iii) If the Secretary provisionally certified the institution under paragraph (c)(1)(v) of this section, not later than 18 months after the date that the Secretary withdrew recognition from the institutions nationally recognized accrediting agency.
(3) Notwithstanding the maximum periods of participation provided for in paragraph (c)(2) of this section, if the Secretary provisionally certifies an institution, the Secretary may specify a shorter period of participation for that institution.
(4) For the purposes of this section, "provisional certification" means that the Secretary certifies that an institution has demonstrated to the Secretary's satisfaction that the institution—
  (i) Is capable of meeting the standards of this subpart within a specified period; and
  (ii) Is able to meet the institution's responsibilities under its program participation agreement, including compliance with any additional conditions specified in the institution's program participation agreement that the Secretary requires the institution to meet in order for the institution to participate under provisional certification.

(d) *Revocation of provisional certification.*
(1) If, before the expiration of a provisionally certified institution's period of participation in a Title IV, HEA program, the Secretary determines that the institution is unable to meet its responsibilities under its program participation agreement, the Secretary may revoke the institution's provisional certification for participation in that program.
(2)(i) If the Secretary revokes the provisional certification of an institution under paragraph (d)(1) of this section, the Secretary sends the institution a notice by certified mail, return receipt requested. The Secretary also may transmit the notice by other, more expeditious means, if practical.
  (ii) The revocation takes effect on the date that the Secretary mails the notice to the institution.
  (iii) The notice states the basis for the revocation, the consequences of the revocation to the institution, and that the institution may request the Secretary to reconsider the revocation. The consequences of a revocation are described in § 668.26.

(3)(i) An institution may request reconsideration of a revocation under this section by submitting to the Secretary, within 20 days of the institution's receipt of the Secretary's notice, written evidence that the revocation is unwarranted. The institution must file the request with the Secretary by hand-delivery, mail, or facsimile transmission.

(ii) The filing date of the request is the date on which the request is—

(A) Hand-delivered;

(B) Mailed; or

(C) Sent by facsimile transmission.

(iii) Documents filed by facsimile transmission must be transmitted to the Secretary in accordance with instructions provided by the Secretary in the notice of revocation. An institution filing by facsimile transmission is responsible for confirming that a complete and legible copy of the document was received by the Secretary.

(iv) The Secretary discourages the use of facsimile transmission for documents longer than five pages.

(4)(i) The designated department official making the decision concerning an institution's request for reconsideration of a revocation is different from, and not subject to supervision by, the official who initiated the revocation of the institution's provisional certification. The deciding official promptly considers an institution's request for reconsideration of a revocation and notifies the institution, by certified mail, return receipt requested, of the final decision. The Secretary also may transmit the notice by other, more expeditious means, if practical.

(ii) If the Secretary determines that the revocation is warranted, the Secretary's notice informs the institution that the institution may apply for reinstatement of participation only after the later of the expiration of—

(A) Eighteen months after the effective date of the revocation; or

(B) A debarment or suspension of the institution under Executive Order (E.O.) 12549 (3 CFR, 1986 comp., p. 189) or the Federal Acquisition Regulations, 48 CFR part 9, subpart 9.4.

(iii) If the Secretary determines that the revocation of the institution's provisional certification is unwarranted, the Secretary's notice informs the institution that the institution's provisional certification is reinstated, effective on the date that the Secretary's original revocation notice was mailed, for a specified period of time.

(5)(i) The mailing date of a notice of revocation or a request for reconsideration of a revocation is the date evidenced on the original receipt of mailing from the U.S. Postal Service.

(ii) The date on which a request for reconsideration of a revocation is submitted is—

(A) If the request was sent by a delivery service other than the U.S. Postal Service, the date evidenced on the original receipt by that service; and

(B) If the request was sent by facsimile transmission, the date that the document is recorded as received by facsimile equipment that receives the transmission.

(Approved by the Office of Management and Budget under control number 1845-0537)

(Authority: 20 U.S.C. 1099c and E.O. 12549 (3 CFR, 1989 Comp., p. 189) and E.O. 12689 (3 CFR, 1989 Comp., p. 235))

[59 Fed. Reg. 22424 (Apr. 29, 1994); 59 Fed. Reg. 32657 (June 24, 1994); 59 Fed. Reg. 34964 (July 7, 1994); 60 Fed. Reg. 34431 (June 30, 1995); 62 Fed. Reg. 62876 (Nov. 25, 1997); 63 Fed. Reg. 40623 (July 29, 1998); 64 Fed. Reg. 58617 (Oct. 29, 1999); 65 Fed. Reg. 65675 (Nov. 1, 2000); 74 Fed. Reg. 55934 (Oct. 29, 2009)]

§ 668.14 Program participation agreement.

(a)(1) An institution may participate in any Title IV, HEA program, other than the LEAP and NEISP programs, only if the institution enters into a written program participation agreement with the Secretary, on a form approved by the Secretary. A program participation agreement conditions the initial and continued participation of an eligible institution in any Title IV, HEA program upon compliance with the provisions of this part, the individual program regulations, and any additional conditions specified in the program participation agreement that the Secretary requires the institution to meet.

(2) An institution's program participation agreement applies to each branch campus and other location of the institution that meets the applicable requirements of this part unless otherwise specified by the Secretary.

(b) By entering into a program participation agreement, an institution agrees that—

(1) It will comply with all statutory provisions of or applicable to Title IV of the HEA, all applicable regulatory provisions prescribed under that statutory authority, and all applicable special arrangements, agreements, and limitations entered into under the authority of statutes applicable to Title IV of the HEA, including the requirement that the institution will use funds it receives under any Title IV, HEA program and any interest or other earnings thereon, solely for the purposes specified in and in accordance with that program;

(2) As a fiduciary responsible for administering Federal funds, if the institution is permitted to request funds under a Title IV, HEA program advance payment method, the institution will time its requests for funds under the program to meet the institution's immediate Title IV, HEA program needs;

(3) It will not request from or charge any student a fee for processing or handling any application, form, or data required to determine a student's eligibility for, and amount of, Title IV, HEA program assistance;

(4) It will establish and maintain such administrative and fiscal procedures and records as may be necessary to ensure proper and efficient administration of funds received from the Secretary or from students under the Title IV, HEA programs, together with assurances that the institution will provide, upon request and in a timely manner, information relating to the administrative capability and financial responsibility of the institution to—

(i) The Secretary;

(ii) A guaranty agency, as defined in 34 CFR part 682, that guarantees loans made under the Federal Stafford Loan and Federal PLUS programs for attendance at the institution or any of the institution's branch campuses or other locations;

(iii) The nationally recognized accrediting agency that accredits or preaccredits the institution or any of the institution's branch campuses, other locations, or educational programs;

(iv) The State agency that legally authorizes the institution and any branch campus or other location of the institution to provide postsecondary education; and

(v) In the case of a public postsecondary vocational educational institution that is approved by a State agency recognized for the approval of public postsecondary vocational education, that State agency;

(5) It will comply with the provisions of § 668.15 relating to factors of financial responsibility;

(6) It will comply with the provisions of § 668.16 relating to standards of administrative capability;

(7) It will submit reports to the Secretary and, in the case of an institution participating in the Federal Stafford Loan, Federal PLUS, or the Federal Perkins Loan Program, to holders of loans made to the institution's students under that program at such times and containing such information as the Secretary may reasonably require to carry out the purpose of the Title IV, HEA programs;

(8) It will not provide any statement to any student or certification to any lender in the case of an FFEL Program loan, or origination record to the Secretary in the case of a Direct Loan Program loan that qualifies the student or parent for a loan or loans in excess of the amount that the student or parent is eligible to borrow in accordance with sections 425(a), 428(a)(2), 428(b)(1)(A) and (B), 428B, 428H, and 455(a) of the HEA;

(9) It will comply with the requirements of subpart D of this part concerning institutional and financial assistance information for students and prospective students;

(10) In the case of an institution that advertises job placement rates as a means of attracting students to enroll in the institution, it will make available to prospective students, at or before the time that those students apply for enrollment—

(i) The most recent available data concerning employment statistics, graduation statistics, and any other information necessary to substantiate the truthfulness of the advertisements; and

(ii) Relevant State licensing requirements of the State in which the institution is located for any job for which an educational program offered by the institution is designed to prepare those prospective students;

(11) In the case of an institution participating in the FFEL program, the institution will inform all eligible borrowers, as defined in 34 CFR part 682, enrolled in the institution about the availability and eligibility of those borrowers for State grant assistance from the State in which the institution is located, and will inform borrowers from another State of the source of further information concerning State grant assistance from that State;

(12) It will provide the certifications described in paragraph (c) of this section;

(13) In the case of an institution whose students receive financial assistance pursuant to section 484(d) of the HEA, the institution will make available to those students a program proven successful in assisting students in obtaining the recognized equivalent of a high school diploma;

(14) It will not deny any form of Federal financial aid to any eligible student solely on the grounds that the student is participating in a program of study abroad approved for credit by the institution;

(15)(i) Except as provided under paragraph (b)(15)(ii) of this section, the institution will use a default management plan approved by the Secretary with regard to its administration of the FFEL or Direct Loan programs, or both for at least the first two years of its participation in those programs, if the institution—

(A) Is participating in the FFEL or Direct Loan programs for the first time; or

(B) Is an institution that has undergone a change of ownership that results in a change in control and is participating in the FFEL or Direct Loan programs.

(ii) The institution does not have to use an approved default management plan if—

(A) The institution, including its main campus and any branch campus, does not have a cohort default rate in excess of 10 percent; and

(B) The owner of the institution does not own and has not owned any other institution that had a cohort default rate in excess of 10 percent while that owner owned the institution.

(16) For a proprietary institution, the institution will derive at least 10 percent of its revenues for each fiscal year from sources other than Title IV, HEA program funds, as provided in § 668.28(a) and (b), or be subject to sanctions described in § 668.28(c);

(17) The Secretary, guaranty agencies and lenders as defined in 34 CFR part 682, nationally recognized accrediting agencies, the Secretary of Veterans Affairs, State agencies recognized under 34 CFR part 603 for the approval of public postsecondary vocational education, and State agencies that legally authorize institutions and branch campuses or other locations of institutions to provide postsecondary education, have the authority to share with each other any information pertaining to the institution's eligibility for or participation in the Title IV, HEA programs or any information on fraud and abuse;

(18) It will not knowingly—

(i) Employ in a capacity that involves the administration of the Title IV, HEA programs or the receipt of funds under those programs, an individual who has been convicted of, or has pled nolo contendere or guilty to, a crime involving the acquisition, use, or expenditure of Federal, State, or local government funds, or has been administratively or judicially determined to have committed fraud or any other material violation of law involving Federal, State, or local government funds;

(ii) Contract with an institution or third-party servicer that has been terminated under section 432 of the HEA for a reason involving the acquisition, use, or expenditure of Federal, State, or local government funds, or that has been administratively or judicially determined to have committed fraud or any other material violation of law involving Federal, State, or local government funds; or

(iii) Contract with or employ any individual, agency, or organization that has been, or whose officers or employees have been—

(A) Convicted of, or pled nolo contendere or guilty to, a crime involving the acquisition, use, or expenditure of Federal, State, or local government funds; or

(B) Administratively or judicially determined to have committed fraud or any other material violation of law involving Federal, State, or local government funds;

(19) It will complete, in a timely manner and to the satisfaction of the Secretary, surveys conducted as a part of the Integrated Postsecondary Education Data System (IPEDS) or any other Federal collection effort, as designated by the Secretary, regarding data on postsecondary institutions;

(20) In the case of an institution that is co-educational and has an intercollegiate athletic program, it will comply with the provisions of § 668.48;

(21) It will not impose any penalty, including, but not limited to, the assessment of late fees, the denial of access to classes, libraries, or other institutional facilities, or the requirement that the student borrow additional funds for which interest or other charges are assessed, on any student because of the student's inability to meet his or her financial obligations to the institution as a result of the delayed disbursement of the proceeds of a Title IV, HEA program loan due to compliance with statutory and regulatory requirements of or applicable to the Title IV, HEA programs, or delays attributable to the institution;

(22)(i) It will not provide any commission, bonus, or other incentive payment based directly or indirectly upon success in securing enrollments or financial aid to any person or entity engaged in any student recruiting or admission activities or in making decisions regarding the awarding of title IV, HEA program funds, except that this limitation does not apply to the recruitment of foreign students residing in foreign countries who are not eligible to receive title IV, HEA program funds.

(ii) Activities and arrangements that an institution may carry out without violating the provisions of paragraph (b)(22)(i) of this section include, but are not limited to:

(A) The payment of fixed compensation, such as a fixed annual salary or a fixed hourly wage, as long as that compensation is not adjusted up or down more than twice during any twelve month period, and any adjustment is not based solely on the number of students recruited, admitted, enrolled, or awarded financial aid. For this purpose, an increase in fixed compensation resulting from a cost of living increase that is paid to all or substantially all full-time employees is not considered an adjustment.

(B) Compensation to recruiters based upon their recruitment of students who enroll only in programs that are not eligible for title IV, HEA program funds.

(C) Compensation to recruiters who arrange contracts between the institution and an employer under which the employer's employees enroll in the institution, and the employer pays, directly or by reimbursement, 50 percent or more of the tuition and fees charged to its employees; provided that the compensation is not based upon the number of employees who enroll in the institution, or the revenue they generate, and the recruiters have no contact with the employees.

(D) Compensation paid as part of a profit-sharing or bonus plan, as long as those payments are substantially the same amount or the same percentage of salary or wages, and made to all or substantially all of the institution's full-time professional and administrative staff. Such payments can be limited to all, or substantially all of the full-time employees at one or more organizational level at the institution, except that an organizational level may not consist predominantly of recruiters, admissions staff, or financial aid staff.

(E) Compensation that is based upon students successfully completing their educational programs, or one academic year of their educational programs, whichever is shorter. For this purpose, successful completion of an academic year means that the student has earned at least 24 semester or trimester credit hours or 36 quarter credit hours, or has successfully completed at least 900 clock hours of instruction at the institution.

(F) Compensation paid to employees who perform clerical "pre-enrollment" activities, such as answering telephone calls, referring inquiries, or distributing institutional materials.

(G) Compensation to managerial or supervisory employees who do not directly manage or supervise employees who are directly involved in recruiting or admissions activities, or the awarding of title IV, HEA program funds.

(H) The awarding of token gifts to the institution's students or alumni, provided that the gifts are not in the form of money, no more than one gift is provided annually to an individual, and the cost of the gift is not more than $100.

(I) Profit distributions proportionately based upon an individual's ownership interest in the institution.

(J) Compensation paid for Internet-based recruitment and admission activities that provide information about the institution to prospective students, refer prospective students to the institution, or permit prospective students to apply for admission on-line.

(K) Payments to third parties, including tuition sharing arrangements, that deliver various services to the institution, provided that none of the services involve recruiting or admission activities, or the awarding of title IV, HEA program funds.

(L) Payments to third parties, including tuition sharing arrangements, that deliver various services to the institution, even if one of the services involves recruiting or admission activities or the awarding of title IV, HEA program funds, provided that the individuals performing the recruitment or admission activities, or the awarding of title IV, HEA program funds, are not compensated in a manner that would be impermissible under paragraph (b)(22) of this section.

(23) It will meet the requirements established pursuant to part H of Title IV of the HEA by the Secretary and nationally recognized accrediting agencies;

(24) It will comply with the requirements of § 668.22;

(25) It is liable for all—

(i) Improperly spent or unspent funds received under the Title IV, HEA programs, including any funds administered by a third-party servicer; and

(ii) Returns of title IV, HEA program funds that the institution or its servicer may be required to make;

(26) If the stated objectives of an educational program of the institution are to prepare a student for gainful employment in a recognized occupation, the institution will—

(i) Demonstrate a reasonable relationship between the length of the program and entry level requirements for the recognized occupation for which the program prepares the student. The Secretary considers the relationship to be reasonable if the number of clock hours provided in the program does not exceed by more than 50 percent the minimum number of clock hours required for training in the recognized occupation for which the program prepares the student, as established by the State in which the program is offered, if the State has established such a requirement, or as established by any Federal agency; and

(ii) Establish the need for the training for the student to obtain employment in the recognized occupation for which the program prepares the student.

(27) In the case of an institution participating in a Title IV, HEA loan program, the institution—

(i) Will develop, publish, administer, and enforce a code of conduct with respect to loans made, insured or guaranteed under the Title IV, HEA loan programs in accordance with 34 CFR 601.21; and

(ii) Must inform its officers, employees, and agents with responsibilities with respect to loans made, insured or guaranteed under the Title IV, HEA loan programs annually of the provisions of the code required under paragraph (b)(27) of this section;

(28) For any year in which the institution has a preferred lender arrangement (as defined in 34 CFR 601.2(b)), it will at least annually compile, maintain, and make available for students attending the institution, and the families of such students, a list in print or other medium, of the specific lenders for loans made, insured, or guaranteed under title IV of the HEA or private education loans that the institution recommends, promotes, or endorses in accordance with such preferred lender arrangement. In making such a list, the institution must comply with the requirements in 34 CFR 682.212(h) and 34 CFR 601.10;

(29)(i) It will, upon the request of an enrolled or admitted student who is an applicant for a private education loan (as defined in 34 CFR 601.2(b)), provide to the applicant the self-certification form required under 34 CFR 601.11(d) and the information required to complete the form, to the extent the institution possesses such information, including—

(A) The applicant's cost of attendance at the institution, as determined by the institution under part F of title IV of the HEA;

(B) The applicant's estimated financial assistance, including amounts of financial assistance used to replace the expected family contribution as determined by the institution in accordance with title IV, for students who have completed the Free Application for Federal Student Aid; and

(C) The difference between the amounts under paragraphs (b)(29)(i)(A) and (29)(i)(B) of this section, as applicable.

(ii) It will, upon the request of the applicant, discuss with the applicant the availability of Federal, State, and institutional student financial aid;

(30) The institution—

(i) Has developed and implemented written plans to effectively combat the unauthorized distribution of copyrighted material by users of the institution's network, without unduly interfering with educational and research use of the network, that include—

(A) The use of one or more technology-based deterrents;

(B) Mechanisms for educating and informing its community about appropriate versus inappropriate use of copyrighted material, including that described in § 668.43(a)(10);

(C) Procedures for handling unauthorized distribution of copyrighted material, including disciplinary procedures; and

(D) Procedures for periodically reviewing the effectiveness of the plans to combat the unauthorized distribution of copyrighted materials by users of the institution's network using relevant assessment criteria. No particular technology measures are favored or required for inclusion in an institution's plans, and each institution retains the authority to determine what its particular plans for compliance with paragraph (b)(30) of this section will be, including those that prohibit content monitoring; and

(ii) Will, in consultation with the chief technology officer or other designated officer of the institution—

(A) Periodically review the legal alternatives for downloading or otherwise acquiring copyrighted material;

(B) Make available the results of the review in paragraph (b)(30)(ii)(A) of this section to its students through a Web site or other means; and

(C) To the extent practicable, offer legal alternatives for downloading or otherwise acquiring copyrighted material, as determined by the institution; and

(31) The institution will submit a teach-out plan to its accrediting agency in compliance with 34 CFR 602.24(c), and the standards of the institution's accrediting agency upon the occurrence of any of the following events:

(i) The Secretary initiates the limitation, suspension, or termination of the participation of an institution in any Title IV, HEA program under 34 CFR 600.41 or subpart G of this part or initiates an emergency action under § 668.83.

(ii) The institution's accrediting agency acts to withdraw, terminate, or suspend the accreditation or preaccreditation of the institution.

(iii) The institution's State licensing or authorizing agency revokes the institution's license or legal authorization to provide an educational program.

(iv) The institution intends to close a location that provides 100 percent of at least one program.

(v) The institution otherwise intends to cease operations.

(c) In order to participate in any Title IV, HEA program (other than the LEAP and NEISP programs), the institution must certify that it—

(1) Has in operation a drug abuse prevention program that the institution has determined to be accessible to any officer, employee, or student at the institution; and

(2)(i) Has established a campus security policy in accordance with section 485(f) of the HEA; and

(ii) Has complied with the disclosure requirements of § 668.47 as required by section 485(f) of the HEA.

(d)(1) The institution, if located in a State to which section 4(b) of the National Voter Registration Act (42 U.S.C. 1973gg-2(b)) does not apply, will make a good faith effort to distribute a mail voter registration form, requested and received from the State, to each student enrolled in a degree or certificate program and physically in attendance at the institution, and to make those forms widely available to students at the institution.

(2) The institution must request the forms from the State 120 days prior to the deadline for registering to vote within the State. If an institution has not received a sufficient quantity of forms to fulfill this section from the State within 60 days prior to the deadline for registering to vote in the State, the institution is not liable for not meeting the requirements of this section during that election year.

(3) This paragraph applies to elections as defined in section 301(1) of the Federal Election Campaign Act of 1971 (2 U.S.C. 431(1)), and includes the election for Governor or other chief executive within such State.

(e)(1) A program participation agreement becomes effective on the date that the Secretary signs the agreement.

(2) A new program participation agreement supersedes any prior program participation agreement between the Secretary and the institution.

(f)(1) Except as provided in paragraphs (g) and (h) of this section, the Secretary terminates a program participation agreement through the proceedings in subpart G of this part.

(2) An institution may terminate a program participation agreement.

(3) If the Secretary or the institution terminates a program participation agreement under paragraph (f) of this section, the Secretary establishes the termination date.

(g) An institution's program participation agreement automatically expires on the date that—

(1) The institution changes ownership that results in a change in control as determined by the Secretary under 34 CFR part 600; or

(2) The institution's participation ends under the provisions of § 668.26(a)(1), (2), (4), or (7).

(h) An institution's program participation agreement no longer applies to or covers a location of the institution as of the date on which that location ceases to be a part of the participating institution.

(Approved by the Office of Management and Budget under control number 1845-0022)

(Authority: 20 U.S.C. 1085, 1088, 1091, 1092, 1094, 1099a-3, 1099c, and 1141)

[54 Fed. Reg. 46538 (Nov. 3, 1989); 55 Fed. Reg. 26200 (June 27, 1990); 57 Fed. Reg. 57310 (Dec. 3, 1992); 58 Fed. Reg. 32202 (June 8, 1993); 58 Fed. Reg. 36870 (July 9, 1993); 59 Fed. Reg. 21866 (Apr. 26, 1994); 59 Fed. Reg. 22423, 22425 (Apr. 29, 1994); 59 Fed. Reg. 32657 (June 24, 1994); 59 Fed. Reg. 34964 (July 7, 1994); 63 Fed. Reg. 40623 (July 29, 1998); 64 Fed. Reg. 58617 (Oct. 29, 1999); 64 Fed. Reg. 59038 (Nov. 1, 1999); 65 Fed. Reg. 38729 (June 22, 2000); 65 Fed. Reg. 65637 (Nov. 1, 2000); 67 Fed. Reg. 67072 (Nov. 1, 2002); 73 Fed. Reg. 35492 (June 23, 2008); 74 Fed. Reg. 55648 (Oct. 28, 2009); 74 Fed. Reg. 55934 (Oct. 29, 2009)]

§ 668.15 Factors of financial responsibility.

(a) *General.* To begin and to continue to participate in any Title IV, HEA program, an institution must demonstrate to the Secretary that the institution is financially responsible under the requirements established in this section.

(b) *General standards of financial responsibility.* In general, the Secretary considers an institution to be financially responsible only if it—

(1) Is providing the services described in its official publications and statements;

(2) Is providing the administrative resources necessary to comply with the requirements of this subpart;

(3) Is meeting all of its financial obligations, including but not limited to—

(i) Refunds that it is required to make; and

(ii) Repayments to the Secretary for liabilities and debts incurred in programs administered by the Secretary;

(4) Is current in its debt payments. The institution is not considered current in its debt payments if—

(i) The institution is in violation of any existing loan agreement at its fiscal year end, as disclosed in a note to its audited financial statement; or

(ii) the institution fails to make a payment in accordance with existing debt obligations for more than 120 days, and at least one creditor has filed suit to recover those funds;

(5) Except as provided in paragraph (d) of this section, in accordance with procedures established by the Secretary, submits to the Secretary an irrevocable letter of credit, acceptable and payable to the Secretary equal to 25 percent of the total dollar amount of Title IV, HEA program refunds paid by the institution in the previous fiscal year;

(6) Has not had, as part of the audit report for the institution's most recently completed fiscal year—

(i) A statement by the accountant expressing substantial doubt about the institution's ability to continue as a going concern; or

(ii) A disclaimed or adverse opinion by the accountant;

(7) For a for-profit institution—

(i)(A) Demonstrates at the end of its latest fiscal year, an acid test ratio of at least 1:1. For purposes of this section, the acid test ratio shall be calculated by adding cash and cash equivalents to current accounts receivable and dividing the sum by total current liabilities. The calculation of the acid test ratio shall exclude all unsecured or uncollateralized related party receivables;

(B) Has not had operating losses in either or both of its two latest fiscal years that in sum result in a decrease in tangible net worth in excess of 10 percent of the institution's tangible net worth at the beginning of the first year of the two-year period. The Secretary may calculate an operating loss for an institution by excluding from net income: extraordinary gains or losses; income or losses from discontinued operations; prior period adjustment; and, the cumulative effect of changes in accounting principle. For purposes of this section, the calculation of tangible net worth shall exclude all assets defined as intangible in accordance with generally accepted accounting principles; and

(C) Had, for its latest fiscal year, a positive tangible net worth. In applying this standard, a positive tangible net worth occurs when the institution's tangible assets exceed its liabilities. The calculation of tangible net worth shall exclude all assets classified as intangible in accordance with the generally accepted accounting principles; or

(ii) Demonstrates to the satisfaction of the Secretary that it has currently issued and outstanding debt obligations that are (without insurance, guarantee, or credit enhancement) listed at or above the second highest rating level of credit quality given by a nationally recognized statistical rating organization;

(8) For a nonprofit institution—

(i)(A) Prepares a classified statement of financial position in accordance with generally accepted accounting principles or provides the required information in notes to the audited financial statements;

(B) Demonstrates at the end of its latest fiscal year, an acid test ratio of at least 1:1. For purposes of this section, the acid test ratio shall be calculated by adding cash and cash equivalents to current accounts receivable and dividing the sum by total current liabilities. The calculation of the acid test ratio shall exclude all unsecured or uncollateralized related party receivables.

(C)(1) Has, at the end of its latest fiscal year, a positive unrestricted current fund balance or positive unrestricted net assets. In calculating the unrestricted current fund balance or the unrestricted net assets for an institution, the Secretary may include funds that are temporarily restricted in use by the institution's governing body that can be transferred to the current unrestricted fund or added to net unrestricted assets at the discretion of the governing body; or

(2) Has not had, an excess of current fund expenditures over current fund revenues over both of its 2 latest fiscal years that results in a decrease exceeding 10 percent in either the unrestricted current fund balance or the unrestricted net assets at the beginning of the first year of the 2-year period. The Secretary may exclude from net changes in fund balances for the operating loss calculation: Extraor-

dinary gains or losses; income or losses from discontinued operations; prior period adjustment; and the cumulative effect of changes in accounting principle. In calculating the institution's unrestricted current fund balance or the unrestricted net assets, the Secretary may include funds that are temporarily restricted in use by the institution's governing body that can be transferred to the current unrestricted fund or added to net unrestricted assets at the discretion of the governing body; or

(ii) Demonstrates to the satisfaction of the Secretary that it has currently issued and outstanding debt obligations which are (without insurance, guarantee, or credit enhancement) listed at or above the second highest rating level of credit quality given by a nationally recognized statistical rating organization.

(9) For a public institution—

(i) Has its liabilities backed by the full faith and credit of a State, or by an equivalent governmental entity;

(ii) Has a positive current unrestricted fund balance if reporting under the Single Audit Act;

(iii) Has a positive unrestricted current fund in the State's Higher Education Fund, as presented in the general purpose financial statements;

(iv) Submits to the Secretary, a statement from the State Auditor General that the institution has, during the past year, met all of its financial obligations, and that the institution continues to have sufficient resources to meet all of its financial obligations; or

(v) Demonstrates to the satisfaction of the Secretary that it has currently issued and outstanding debt obligations which are (without insurance, guarantee, or credit enhancement) listed at or above the second highest rating level of credit quality given by a nationally recognized statistical rating organization.

(c) *Past performance of an institution or persons affiliated with an institution.* An institution is not financially responsible if—

(1) A person who exercises substantial control over the institution or any member or members of the person's family alone or together—

(i)(A) Exercises or exercised substantial control over another institution or a third-party servicer that owes a liability for a violation of a Title IV, HEA program requirement; or

(B) Owes a liability for a violation of a Title IV, HEA program requirement; and

(ii) That person, family member, institution, or servicer does not demonstrate that

the liability is being repaid in accordance with an agreement with the Secretary; or

(2) The institution has—

(i) Been limited, suspended, terminated, or entered into a settlement agreement to resolve a limitation, suspension, or termination action initiated by the Secretary or a guaranty agency (as defined in 34 CFR part 682) within the preceding five years;

(ii) Had—

(A) An audit finding, during its two most recent audits of its conduct of the Title IV, HEA programs, that resulted in the institution's being required to repay an amount greater than five percent of the funds that the institution received under the Title IV, HEA programs for any award year covered by the audit; or

(B) A program review finding, during its two most recent program reviews, of its conduct of the Title IV, HEA programs that resulted in the institution's being required to repay an amount greater than five percent of the funds that the institution received under the Title IV, HEA programs for any award year covered by the program review;

(iii) Been cited during the preceding five years for failure to submit acceptable audit reports required under this part or individual Title IV, HEA program regulations in a timely fashion; or

(iv) Failed to resolve satisfactorily any compliance problems identified in program review or audit reports based upon a final decision of the Secretary issued pursuant to subpart G or subpart H of this part.

(d) *Exceptions to the general standards of financial responsibility.*

(1)(i) An institution is not required to meet the standard in paragraph (b)(5) of this section if the Secretary determines that the institution—

(A)(1) Is located in, and is legally authorized to operate within, a State that has a tuition recovery fund that is acceptable to the Secretary and ensures that the institution is able to pay all required refunds; and

(2) Contributes to that tuition recovery fund.

(B) Has its liabilities backed by the full faith and credit of the State, or by an equivalent governmental entity; or

(C) As determined under paragraph (g) of this section, demonstrates, to the satisfaction of the Secretary, that for each of the institution's two most recently completed fiscal years, it has made timely refunds to students in accordance with § 668.22(j), and that it has met or exceeded all of the financial responsibility standards in this section that were in effect for the corresponding periods during the two-year period.

(ii) In evaluating an application to approve a State tuition recovery fund to exempt its participating schools from the federal cash reserve requirements, the Secretary will consider the extent to which the State tuition recovery fund:

(A) Provides refunds to both in-state and out-of-state students;

(B) Allocates all refunds in accordance with the order delineated in § 668.22(i); and

(C) Provides a reliable mechanism for the State to replenish the fund should any claims arise that deplete the funds assets.

(2) The Secretary considers an institution to be financially responsible, even if the institution is not otherwise financially responsible under paragraphs (b)(1) through (4) and (b)(6) through (9) of this section, if the institution—

(i) Submits to the Secretary an irrevocable letter of credit that is acceptable and payable to the Secretary equal to not less than one-half of the Title IV, HEA program funds received by the institution during the last complete award year for which figures are available; or

(ii) Establishes to the satisfaction of the Secretary, with the support of a financial statement submitted in accordance with paragraph (e) of this section, that the institution has sufficient resources to ensure against its precipitous closure, including the ability to meet all of its financial obligations (including refunds of institutional charges and repayments to the Secretary for liabilities and debts incurred in programs administered by the Secretary). The Secretary considers the institution to have sufficient resources to ensure against precipitous closure only if—

(A) The institution formerly demonstrated financial responsibility under the standards of financial responsibility in its preceding audited financial statement (or, if no prior audited financial statement was requested by the Secretary, demonstrates in conjunction with its current audit that it would have satisfied this requirement), and that its most recent audited financial statement indicates that—

(1) All taxes owed by the institution are current;

(2) The institution's net income, or a change in total net assets, before extraordinary items and discontinued operations, has not decreased by more than 10 percent from the prior fiscal year, unless the institution demonstrates that the decreased net income shown on the current financial statement is a result of downsizing pursuant to a management-approved business plan;

(3) Loans and other advances to related parties have not increased from the prior fiscal year unless such increases were secured and collateralized, and do not exceed 10 percent of the prior fiscal year's working capital of the institution;

(4) The equity of a for-profit institution, or the total net assets of a nonprofit institution, have not decreased by more than 10 percent of the prior year's total equity;

(5) Compensation for owners or other related parties (including bonuses, fringe benefits, employee stock option allowances, 401k contributions, deferred compensation allowances) has not increased from the prior year at a rate higher than for all other employees;

(6) The institution has not materially leveraged its assets or income by becoming a guarantor on any new loan or obligation on behalf of any related party;

(7) All obligations owed to the institution by related parties are current, and that the institution has demanded and is receiving payment of all funds owed from related parties that are payable upon demand. For purposes of this section, a person does not become a related party by attending an institution as a student;

(B) There have been no material findings in the institution's latest compliance audit of its administration of the Title IV HEA programs; and

(C) There are no pending administrative or legal actions being taken against the institution by the Secretary, any other Federal agency, the institution's nationally recognized accrediting agency, or any State entity.

(3) An institution is not required to meet the acid test ratio in paragraph (b)(7)(i)(A) or (b)(8)(i)(B) of this section if the institution is an institution that provides a 2-year or 4-year educational program for which the institution awards an associate or baccalaureate degree that demonstrates to the satisfaction of the Secretary that—

(i) There is no reasonable doubt as to its continued solvency and ability to deliver quality educational services;

(ii) It is current in its payment of all current liabilities, including student refunds, repayments to the Secretary, payroll, and payment of trade creditors and withholding taxes; and

(iii) It has substantial equity in institution-occupied facilities, the acquisition of which was the direct cause of its failure to meet the acid test ratio requirement.

(4) The Secretary may determine an institution to be financially responsible even if the institution is not otherwise financially responsible under paragraph (c)(1) of this section if—

(i) The institution notifies the Secretary, in accordance with 34 CFR 600.30, that the person referenced in paragraph (c)(1) of this section exercises substantial control over the institution; and

(ii)(A) The person repaid to the Secretary a portion of the applicable liability, and the portion repaid equals or exceeds the greater of—

(1) The total percentage of the ownership interest held in the institution or third-party servicer that owes the liability by that person or any member or members of that person's family, either alone or in combination with one another;

(2) The total percentage of the ownership interest held in the institution or servicer that owes the liability that the person or any member or members of the person's family, either alone or in combination with one another, represents or represented under a voting trust, power of attorney, proxy, or similar agreement; or

(3) Twenty-five percent, if the person or any member of the person's family is or was a member of the board of directors, chief executive officer, or other executive officer of the institution or servicer that owes the liability, or of an entity holding at least a 25 percent ownership interest in the institution that owes the liability;

(B) The applicable liability described in paragraph (c)(1) of this section is currently being repaid in accordance with a written agreement with the Secretary; or

(C) The institution demonstrates why—

(1) The person who exercises substantial control over the institution should nevertheless be considered to lack that control; or

(2) The person who exercises substantial control over the institution and each member of that person's family nevertheless does not or did not exercise substantial control over the institution or servicer that owes the liability.

(e) [*Reserved*]

(f) *Definitions and terms*. For the purposes of this section—

(1)(i) An "ownership interest" is a share of the legal or beneficial ownership or control of, or a right to share in the proceeds of the operation of, an institution, institution's parent corporation, a third-party servicer, or a third-party servicer's parent corporation.

(ii) The term "ownership interest" includes, but is not limited to—

(A) An interest as tenant in common, joint tenant, or tenant by the entireties;
(B) A partnership; and
(C) An interest in a trust.
(iii) The term "ownership interest" does not include any share of the ownership or control of, or any right to share in the proceeds of the operation of—
(A) A mutual fund that is regularly and publicly traded;
(B) An institutional investor; or
(C) A profit-sharing plan, provided that all employees are covered by the plan;
(2) The Secretary generally considers a person to exercise substantial control over an institution or third-party servicer, if the person—
(i) Directly or indirectly holds at least a 25 percent ownership interest in the institution or servicer;
(ii) Holds, together with other members of his or her family, at least a 25 percent ownership interest in the institution or servicer;
(iii) Represents, either alone or together with other persons, under a voting trust, power of attorney, proxy, or similar agreement one or more persons who hold, either individually or in combination with the other persons represented or the person representing them, at least a 25 percent ownership in the institution or servicer; or
(iv) Is a member of the board of directors, the chief executive officer, or other executive officer of—
(A) The institution or servicer; or
(B) An entity that holds at least a 25 percent ownership interest in the institution or servicer; and
(3) The Secretary considers a member of a person's family to be a parent, sibling, spouse, child, spouse's parent or sibling, or sibling's or child's spouse.

(g) *Two-year performance requirement.*
(1) The Secretary considers an institution to have satisfied the requirements in paragraph (d)(1)(C) of this section if the independent certified public accountant, or government auditor who conducted the institution's compliance audits for the institution's two most recently completed fiscal years, or the Secretary or a State or guaranty agency that conducted a review of the institution covering those fiscal years—
(i)(A) For either of those fiscal years, did not find in the sample of student records audited or reviewed that the institution made late refunds to 5 percent or more of the students in that sample. For purposes of determining the percentage of late refunds under this paragraph, the auditor or reviewer must include in the sample only those title IV, HEA program recipients who received or should have received a refund under § 668.22; or

(B) The Secretary considers the institution to have satisfied the conditions in paragraph (g)(1)(i)(A) of this section if the auditor or reviewer finds in the sample of student records audited or reviewed that the institution made only one late refund to a student in that sample; and
(ii) For either of those fiscal years, did not note a material weakness or a reportable condition in the institution's report on internal controls that is related to refunds.
(2) If the Secretary or a State or guaranty agency finds during a review conducted of the institution that the institution no longer qualifies for an exemption under paragraph (d)(1)(C) of this section, the institution must—
(i) Submit to the Secretary the irrevocable letter of credit required in paragraph (b)(5) of this section no later than 30 days after the Secretary or State or guaranty agency notifies the institution of that finding; and
(ii) Notify the Secretary of the guaranty agency or State that conducted the review.
(3) If the auditor who conducted the institution's compliance audit finds that the institution no longer qualifies for an exemption under paragraph (d)(1)(C) of this section, the institution must submit to the Secretary the irrevocable letter of credit required in paragraph (b)(5) of this section no later than 30 days after the date the institution's compliance audit must be submitted to the Secretary.

(h) *Foreign institutions.* The Secretary makes a determination of financial responsibility for a foreign institution on the basis of financial statements submitted under the following requirements—
(1) If the institution received less than $500,000 U.S. in title IV, HEA program funds during its most recently completed fiscal year, the institution must submit its audited financial statement for that year. For purposes of this paragraph, the audited financial statements may be prepared under the auditing standards and accounting principles used in the institution's home country; or
(2) If the institution received $500,000 U.S. or more in title IV, HEA program funds during its most recently completed fiscal year, the institution must submit its audited financial statement in accordance with the requirements of § 668.23, and satisfy the general standards of financial responsibility contained in this section, or qualify under an alternate standard of financial responsibility contained in this section.

(Approved by the Office of Management and Budget under control number 1840-0537)

(Authority: 20 U.S.C. 1094 and 1099c and Section 4 of Pub. L. 95-452, 92 Stat. 1101–1109)

[53 Fed. Reg. 49147 (Dec. 6, 1988); 56 Fed. Reg. 36697 (July 31, 1991); 57 Fed. Reg. 27703 (June 22, 1992); 58 Fed. Reg. 32201 (June 8, 1993); 59 Fed. Reg. 21866 (Apr. 26, 1994); 59 Fed. Reg. 22423, 22428 (Apr. 29, 1994); 59 Fed. Reg. 32627 (June 24, 1994); 59 Fed. Reg. 34964 (July 7, 1994); 59 Fed. Reg. 61179 (Nov. 29, 1994); 60 Fed. Reg. 34431 (June 30, 1995); 60 Fed. Reg. 42408 (Aug. 15, 1995); 61 Fed. Reg. 29901 (June 12, 1996); 61 Fed. Reg. 60569 (Nov. 29, 1996); 62 Fed. Reg. 27128 (May 16, 1997); 71 Fed. Reg. 45694 (Aug. 9, 2006)]

§ 668.16 Standards of administrative capability.

To begin and to continue to participate in any Title IV, HEA program, an institution shall demonstrate to the Secretary that the institution is capable of adequately administering that program under each of the standards established in this section. The Secretary considers an institution to have that administrative capability if the institution—

(a) Administers the Title IV, HEA programs in accordance with all statutory provisions of or applicable to Title IV of the HEA, all applicable regulatory provisions prescribed under that statutory authority, and all applicable special arrangements, agreements, and limitations entered into under the authority of statutes applicable to Title IV of the HEA;

(b)(1) Designates a capable individual to be responsible for administering all the Title IV, HEA programs in which it participates and for coordinating those programs with the institution's other Federal and non-Federal programs of student financial assistance. The Secretary considers an individual to be "capable" under this paragraph if the individual is certified by the State in which the institution is located, if the State requires certification of financial aid administrators. The Secretary may consider other factors in determining whether an individual is capable, including, but not limited to, the individual's successful completion of Title IV, HEA program training provided or approved by the Secretary, and previous experience and documented success in administering the Title IV, HEA programs properly;

(2) Uses an adequate number of qualified persons to administer the Title IV, HEA programs in which the institution participates. The Secretary considers the following factors to determine whether an institution uses an adequate number of qualified persons—
(i) The number and types of programs in which the institution participates;
(ii) The number of applications evaluated;
(iii) The number of students who receive any student financial assistance at the institution and the amount of funds administered;
(iv) The financial aid delivery system used by the institution;

(v) The degree of office automation used by the institution in the administration of the Title IV, HEA programs;
(vi) The number and distribution of financial aid staff; and
(vii) The use of third-party servicers to aid in the administration of the Title IV, HEA programs;
(3) Communicates to the individual designated to be responsible for administering Title IV, HEA programs, all the information received by any institutional office that bears on a student's eligibility for Title IV, HEA program assistance; and
(4) Has written procedures for or written information indicating the responsibilities of the various offices with respect to the approval, disbursement, and delivery of Title IV, HEA program assistance and the preparation and submission of reports to the Secretary;

(c)(1) Administers Title IV, HEA programs with adequate checks and balances in its system of internal controls; and
(2) Divides the functions of authorizing payments and disbursing or delivering funds so that no office has responsibility for both functions with respect to any particular student aided under the programs. For example, the functions of authorizing payments and disbursing or delivering funds must be divided so that for any particular student aided under the programs, the two functions are carried out by at least two organizationally independent individuals who are not members of the same family, as defined in § 668.15, or who do not together exercise substantial control, as defined in § 668.15, over the institution;

(d)(1) Establishes and maintains records required under this part and the individual Title IV, HEA program regulations; and
(2)(i) Reports annually to the Secretary on any reasonable reimbursements paid or provided by a private education lender or group of lenders as described under section 140(d) of the Truth in Lending Act (15 U.S.C. 1631(d)) to any employee who is employed in the financial aid office of the institution or who otherwise has responsibilities with respect to education loans, including responsibilities involving the selection of lenders, or other financial aid of the institution, including—
(A) The amount for each specific instance of reasonable expenses paid or provided;
(B) The name of the financial aid official, other employee, or agent to whom the expenses were paid or provided;
(C) The dates of the activity for which the expenses were paid or provided; and
(D) A brief description of the activity for which the expenses were paid or provided.

(ii) Expenses are considered to be reasonable if the expenses—
(A) Meet the standards of and are paid in accordance with a State government reimbursement policy applicable to the entity; or
(B) Meet the standards of and are paid in accordance with the applicable Federal cost principles for reimbursement, if no State policy that is applicable to the entity exists.
(iii) The policy must be consistently applied to an institution's employees reimbursed under this paragraph;

(e) For purposes of determining student eligibility for assistance under a Title IV, HEA program, establishes, publishes, and applies reasonable standards for measuring whether an otherwise eligible student is maintaining satisfactory progress in his or her educational program. The Secretary considers an institution's standards to be reasonable if the standards—
(1) Are the same as or stricter than the institution's standards for a student enrolled in the same educational program who is not receiving assistance under a Title IV, HEA program;
(2) Include the following elements:
(i) A qualitative component which consists of grades (provided that the standards meet or exceed the requirements of § 668.34), work projects completed, or comparable factors that are measurable against a norm.
(ii) A quantitative component that consists of a maximum timeframe in which a student must complete his or her educational program. The timeframe must—
(A) For an undergraduate program, be no longer than 150 percent of the published length of the educational program measured in academic years, terms, credit hours attempted, clock hours completed, etc. as appropriate;
(B) Be divided into increments, not to exceed the lesser of one academic year or one-half the published length of the educational program;
(C) Include a schedule established by the institution designating the minimum percentage or amount of work that a student must successfully complete at the end of each increment to complete his or her educational program within the maximum timeframe; and
(D) Include specific policies defining the effect of course incompletes, withdrawals, repetitions, and noncredit remedial courses on satisfactory progress;
(3) Provide for consistent application of standards to all students within categories of students, e.g., full-time, part-time, undergraduate, and graduate students, and educational programs established by the institution;
(4) Provide for a determination at the end of each increment by the institution as to whether the student has met the qualitative and quantitative components of the standards (as provided for in paragraphs (e)(2)(i) and (ii) of this section);
(5) Provide specific procedures under which a student may appeal a determination that the student is not making satisfactory progress; and
(6) Provide specific procedures for a student to re-establish that he or she is maintaining satisfactory progress.

(f) Develops and applies an adequate system to identify and resolve discrepancies in the information that the institution receives from different sources with respect to a student's application for financial aid under Title IV, HEA programs. In determining whether the institution's system is adequate, the Secretary considers whether the institution obtains and reviews—
(1) All student aid applications, need analysis documents, Statements of Educational Purpose, Statements of Registration Status, and eligibility notification documents presented by or on behalf of each applicant;
(2) Any documents, including any copies of State and Federal income tax returns, that are normally collected by the institution to verify information received from the student or other sources; and
(3) Any other information normally available to the institution regarding a student's citizenship, previous educational experience, documentation of the student's social security number, or other factors relating to the student's eligibility for funds under the Title IV, HEA programs;

(g) Refers to the Office of Inspector General of the Department of Education for investigation—
(1) After conducting the review of an application provided for under paragraph (f) of this section, any credible information indicating that an applicant for Title IV, HEA program assistance may have engaged in fraud or other criminal misconduct in connection with his or her application. The type of information that an institution must refer is that which is relevant to the eligibility of the applicant for Title IV, HEA program assistance, or the amount of the assistance. Examples of this type of information are—
(i) False claims of independent student status;
(ii) False claims of citizenship;
(iii) Use of false identities;
(iv) Forgery of signatures or certifications; and
(v) False statements of income; and
(2) Any credible information indicating that any employee, third-party servicer, or other agent of the institution that acts in a capacity that involves the administration of the Title IV, HEA programs, or the receipt of funds under those programs, may have engaged in fraud, misrepresentation, conversion or breach of fiduciary responsibility, or other illegal

conduct involving the Title IV, HEA programs. The type of information that an institution must refer is that which is relevant to the eligibility and funding of the institution and its students through the Title IV, HEA programs;

(h) Provides adequate financial aid counseling to eligible students who apply for Title IV, HEA program assistance. In determining whether an institution provides adequate counseling, the Secretary considers whether its counseling includes information regarding—

(1) The source and amount of each type of aid offered;

(2) The method by which aid is determined and disbursed, delivered, or applied to a student's account; and

(3) The rights and responsibilities of the student with respect to enrollment at the institution and receipt of financial aid. This information includes the institution's refund policy, the requirements for the treatment of title IV, HEA program funds when a student withdraws under § 668.22, its standards of satisfactory progress, and other conditions that may alter the student's aid package;

(*i*) Has provided all program and fiscal reports and financial statements required for compliance with the provisions of this part and the individual program regulations in a timely manner;

(j) Shows no evidence of significant problems that affect, as determined by the Secretary, the institution's ability to administer a Title IV, HEA program and that are identified in—

(1) Reviews of the institution conducted by the Secretary, the Department of Education's Office of Inspector General, nationally recognized accrediting agencies, guaranty agencies as defined in 34 CFR part 682, the State agency or official by whose authority the institution is legally authorized to provide postsecondary education, or any other law enforcement agency; or

(2) Any findings made in any criminal, civil, or administrative proceeding;

(k) Is not, and does not have any principal or affiliate of the institution (as those terms are defined in 34 CFR part 85) that is—

(1) Debarred or suspended under Executive Order (E.O.) 12549 (3 CFR, 1986 Comp., p. 189) or the Federal Acquisition Regulations (FAR), 48 CFR part 9, subpart 9.4; or

(2) Engaging in any activity that is a cause under 34 CFR 85.305 or 85.405 for debarment or suspension under E.O. 12549 (3 CFR, 1986 Comp., p. 189) or the FAR, 48 CFR part 9, subpart 9.4;

(*l*) For an institution that seeks initial participation in a Title IV, HEA program, does not have more than 33 percent of its undergraduate regular students withdraw from the institution during the institution's latest completed award year. The institution must count all regular students who are enrolled during the latest completed award year, except those students who, during that period—

(1) Withdrew from, dropped out of, or were expelled from the institution;

(2) Were entitled to and actually received in a timely manner, a refund of 100 percent of their tuition and fees;

(m)(1) Has a cohort default rate—

(i) That is less than 25 percent for each of the three most recent fiscal years during which rates have been issued, to the extent those rates are calculated under subpart M of this part;

(ii) On or after 2014, that is less than 30 percent for at least two of the three most recent fiscal years during which the Secretary has issued rates for the institution under subpart N of this part; and

(iii) As defined in 34 CFR 674.5, on loans made under the Federal Perkins Loan Program to students for attendance at that institution that does not exceed 15 percent.

(2)(i) However, if the Secretary determines that an institution's administrative capability is impaired solely because the institution fails to comply with paragraph (m)(1) of this section, and the institution is not subject to a loss of eligibility under §§ 668.187(a) or 668.206(a), the Secretary allows the institution to continue to participate in the Title IV, HEA programs. In such a case, the Secretary may provisionally certify the institution in accordance with § 668.13(c) except as provided in paragraphs (m)(2)(ii), (m)(2)(iii), (m)(2)(iv), and (m)(2)(v) of this section.

(ii) An institution that fails to meet the standard of administrative capability under paragraph (m)(1)(ii) based on two cohort default rates that are greater than or equal to 30 percent but less than or equal to 40 percent is not placed on provisional certification under paragraph (m)(2)(i) of this section—

(A) If it has timely filed a request for adjustment or appeal under §§ 668.209, 668.210, or 668.212 with respect to the second such rate, and the request for adjustment or appeal is either pending or succeeds in reducing the rate below 30 percent; or

(B) If it has timely filed an appeal under §§ 668.213 or 668.214 after receiving the second such rate, and the appeal is either pending or successful.

(iii) The institution may appeal the loss of full participation in a Title IV, HEA program under paragraph (m)(2)(i) of this section by submitting an erroneous data appeal in writing to the Secretary in accordance with and on the grounds specified in §§ 668.192 or 668.211 as applicable;

(iv) If you have 30 or fewer borrowers in the three most recent cohorts of borrowers used to calculate your cohort default rate under subpart N of this part, we not provisionally certify you solely based on cohort default rates;

(v) If a rate that would otherwise potentially subject you to provisional certification under paragraph (m)(1)(ii) and (m)(2)(i) of this section is calculated as an average rate, we will not provisionally certify you solely based on cohort default rates;

(n) Does not otherwise appear to lack the ability to administer the Title IV, HEA programs competently; and

(o) Participates in the electronic processes that the Secretary—

(1) Provides at no substantial charge to the institution; and

(2) Identifies through a notice published in the Federal Register.

(Approved by the Office of Management and Budget under control number 1840-0537)

Authority: 20 U.S.C. 1082, 1085, 1092, 1094, and 1099c.

[53 Fed. Reg. 49147 (Dec. 6, 1988); 58 Fed. Reg. 32201 (June 8, 1993); 59 Fed. Reg. 22423, 22431 (Apr. 29, 1994); 59 Fed. Reg. 32657 (June 24, 1994); 59 Fed. Reg. 34964 (July 7, 1994); 59 Fed. Reg. 61180 (Nov. 29, 1994); 60 Fed. Reg. 34431 (June 30, 1995); 60 Fed. Reg. 42408 (Aug. 15, 1995); 61 Fed. Reg. 60603 (Nov. 29, 1996); 62 Fed. Reg. 27128 (May 16, 1997); 63 Fed. Reg. 40624 (July 29, 1998); 64 Fed. Reg. 59038 (Nov. 1, 1999); 65 Fed. Reg. 65637 (Nov. 1, 2000); 74 Fed. Reg. 55648 (Oct. 28, 2009)]

§ 668.17 [*Reserved*]

[65 Fed. Reg. 65637 (Nov. 1, 2000)]

§ 668.18 Readmission requirements for servicemembers.

(a) *General.*

(1) An institution may not deny readmission to a person who is a member of, applies to be a member of, performs, has performed, applies to perform, or has an obligation to perform, service in the uniformed services on the basis of that membership, application for membership, performance of service, application for service, or obligation to perform service.

(2)(i) An institution must promptly readmit to the institution a person described in paragraph (a)(1) of this section with the same academic status as the student had when the student last attended the institution or was last admitted to the institution, but did not begin attendance because of that membership, application for membership, performance of service, application for service, or obligation to perform service.

(ii) "Promptly readmit" means that the institution must readmit the student into the next class or classes in the student's program beginning after the student provides notice of his or her intent to reenroll, unless the student requests a later date of readmission or unusual circumstances require the institution to admit the student at a later date.

(iii) To readmit a person with the "same academic status" means that the institution admits the student—

(A) To the same program to which he or she was last admitted by the institution or, if that exact program is no longer offered, the program that is most similar to that program, unless the student requests or agrees to admission to a different program;

(B) At the same enrollment status that the student last held at the institution, unless the student requests or agrees to admission at a different enrollment status;

(C) With the same number of credit hours or clock hours completed previously by the student, unless the student is readmitted to a different program to which the completed credit hours or clock hours are not transferable;

(D) With the same academic standing (e.g., with the same satisfactory academic progress status) the student previously had; and

(E)(1) If the student is readmitted to the same program, for the first academic year in which the student returns, assessing—

(i) The tuition and fee charges that the student was or would have been assessed for the academic year during which the student left the institution; or

(ii) Up to the amount of tuition and fee charges that other students in the program are assessed for that academic year, if veterans' education benefits, as defined in section 480(c) of the HEA, or other service-member education benefits, will pay the amount in excess of the tuition and fee charges assessed for the academic year in which the student left the institution; or

(2) If the student is admitted to a different program, and for subsequent academic years for a student admitted to the same program, assessing no more than the tuition and fee charges that other students in the program are assessed for that academic year.

(iv)(A) If the institution determines that the student is not prepared to resume the program with the same academic status at the point where the student left off, or will not be able to complete the program, the institution must make reasonable efforts at no extra cost to the student to help the student become prepared or to enable the student to complete the program including, but not limited to, providing refresher courses at no extra cost to the student and allowing the student to retake a pretest at no extra cost to the student.

(B) The institution is not required to readmit the student on his or her return if—

(1) After reasonable efforts by the institution, the institution determines that the student is not prepared to resume the program at the point where he or she left off;

(2) After reasonable efforts by the institution, the institution determines that the student is unable to complete the program; or

(3) The institution determines that there are no reasonable efforts the institution can take to prepare the student to resume the program at the point where he or she left off or to enable the student to complete the program.

(C)(1) "Reasonable efforts" means actions that do not place an undue hardship on the institution.

(2) "Undue hardship" means an action requiring significant difficulty or expense when considered in light of the overall financial resources of the institution and the impact otherwise of such action on the operation of the institution.

(D) The institution carries the burden to prove by a preponderance of the evidence that the student is not prepared to resume the program with the same academic status at the point where the student left off, or that the student will not be able to complete the program.

(3) This section applies to an institution that has continued in operation since the student ceased attending or was last admitted to the institution but did not begin attendance, notwithstanding any changes of ownership of the institution since the student ceased attendance.

(4) The requirements of this section supersede any State law (including any local law or ordinance), contract, agreement, policy, plan, practice, or other matter that reduces, limits, or eliminates in any manner any right or benefit provided by this section for the period of enrollment during which the student resumes attendance, and continuing so long as the institution is unable to comply with such requirements through other means.

(b) *Service in the uniformed services.* For purposes of this section, service in the uniformed services means service, whether voluntary or involuntary, in the Armed Forces, including service by a member of the National Guard or Reserve, on active duty, active duty for training, or full-time National Guard duty under Federal authority, for a period of more than 30 consecutive days under a call or order to active duty of more than 30 consecutive days.

(c) *Readmission procedures.*

(1) Any student whose absence from an institution is necessitated by reason of service in the uniformed services shall be entitled to readmission to the institution if—

(i) Except as provided in paragraph (d) of this section, the student (or an appropriate officer of the Armed Forces or official of the Department of Defense) gives advance oral or written notice of such service to an office designated by the institution, and provides such notice as far in advance as is reasonable under the circumstances;

(ii) The cumulative length of the absence and of all previous absences from that institution by reason of service in the uniformed services, including only the time the student spends actually performing service in the uniformed services, does not exceed five years; and

(iii) Except as provided in paragraph (f) of this section, the student gives oral or written notice of his or her intent to return to an office designated by the institution—

(A) For a student who completes a period of service in the uniformed services, not later than three years after the completion of the period of service; or

(B) For a student who is hospitalized for or convalescing from an illness or injury incurred in or aggravated during the performance of service in the uniformed services, not later than two years after the end of the period that is necessary for recovery from such illness or injury.

(2)(i) An institution must designate one or more offices at the institution that a student may contact to provide notification of service required by paragraph (c)(1)(i) of this section and notification of intent to return required by paragraph (c)(1)(iii) of this section.

(ii) An institution may not require that the notice provided by the student under paragraph (c)(1)(i) or (c)(1)(iii) of this section follow any particular format.

(iii) The notice provided by the student under paragraph (c)(1)(i) of this section—

(A) May not be subject to any rule for timeliness; timeliness must be determined by the facts in any particular case; and

(B) Does not need to indicate whether the student intends to return to the institution.

(iv) For purposes of paragraph (c)(1)(i) of this section, an "appropriate officer" is a commissioned, warrant, or noncommissioned officer authorized to give such notice by the military service concerned.

(d) *Exceptions to advance notice.*

(1) No notice is required under paragraph (c)(1)(i) of this section if the giving of such notice is precluded by military necessity, such as—

(i) A mission, operation, exercise, or requirement that is classified; or

(ii) A pending or ongoing mission, operation, exercise, or requirement that may be compromised or otherwise adversely affected by public knowledge.

(2) Any student (or an appropriate officer of the Armed Forces or official of the Department of Defense) who did not give advance written or oral notice of service to the appropriate official at the institution in accordance with paragraph (c)(1) of this section may meet the notice requirement by submitting, at the time the student seeks readmission, an attestation to the institution that the student performed service in the uniformed services that necessitated the student's absence from the institution.

(e) *Cumulative length of absence.* For purposes of paragraph (c)(1)(ii) of this section, a student's cumulative length of absence from an institution does not include any service—

(1) That is required, beyond five years, to complete an initial period of obligated service;

(2) During which the student was unable to obtain orders releasing the student from a period of service in the uniformed services before the expiration of the five-year period and such inability was through no fault of the student; or

(3) Performed by a member of the Armed Forces (including the National Guard and Reserves) who is—

(i) Ordered to or retained on active duty under—

(A) 10 U.S.C. 688 (involuntary active duty by a military retiree);

(B) 10 U.S.C. 12301(a) (involuntary active duty in wartime);

(C) 10 U.S.C. 12301(g) (retention on active duty while in captive status);

(D) 10 U.S.C. 12302 (involuntary active duty during a national emergency for up to 24 months);

(E) 10 U.S.C. 12304 (involuntary active duty for an operational mission for up to 270 days);

(F) 10 U.S.C. 12305 (involuntary retention on active duty of a critical person during time of crisis or other specific conditions);

(G) 14 U.S.C. 331 (involuntary active duty by retired Coast Guard officer);

(H) 14 U.S.C. 332 (voluntary active duty by retired Coast Guard officer);

(I) 14 U.S.C. 359 (involuntary active duty by retired Coast Guard enlisted member);

(J) 14 U.S.C. 360 (voluntary active duty by retired Coast Guard enlisted member);

(K) 14 U.S.C. 367 (involuntary retention of Coast Guard enlisted member on active duty); or

(L) 14 U.S.C. 712 (involuntary active duty by Coast Guard Reserve member for natural or man-made disasters);

(ii) Ordered to or retained on active duty (other than for training) under any provision of law because of a war or national emergency declared by the President or the Congress, as determined by the Secretary concerned;

(iii) Ordered to active duty (other than for training) in support, as determined by the Secretary concerned, of an operational mission for which personnel have been ordered to active duty under section 12304 of title 10, United States Code;

(iv) Ordered to active duty in support, as determined by the Secretary concerned, of a critical mission or requirement of the Armed Forces (including the National Guard or Reserve); or

(v) Called into Federal service as a member of the National Guard under chapter 15 of title 10, United States Code, or section 12406 of title 10, United States Code (i.e., called to respond to an invasion, danger of invasion, rebellion, danger of rebellion, insurrection, or the inability of the President with regular forces to execute the laws of the United States).

(f) *Notification of intent to reenroll.* A student who fails to apply for readmission within the periods described in paragraph (c)(1)(iii) of this section does not automatically forfeit eligibility for readmission to the institution, but is subject to the institution's established leave of absence policy and general practices.

(g) *Documentation.*

(1) A student who submits an application for readmission to an institution under paragraph (c)(1)(iii) of this section shall provide to the institution documentation to establish that—

(i) The student has not exceeded the service limitation in paragraph (c)(1)(ii) of this section; and

(ii) The student's eligibility for readmission has not been terminated due to an exception in paragraph (h) of this section.

(2)(i) Documents that satisfy the requirements of paragraph (g)(1) of this section include, but are not limited to, the following:

(A) DD (Department of Defense) 214 Certificate of Release or Discharge from Active Duty.

(B) Copy of duty orders prepared by the facility where the orders were fulfilled carrying an endorsement indicating completion of the described service.

(C) Letter from the commanding officer of a Personnel Support Activity or someone of comparable authority.

(D) Certificate of completion from military training school.

(E) Discharge certificate showing character of service.

(F) Copy of extracts from payroll documents showing periods of service.

(G) Letter from National Disaster Medical System (NDMS) Team Leader or Administrative Officer verifying dates and times of NDMS training or Federal activation.

(ii) The types of documents that are necessary to establish eligibility for readmission will vary from case to case. Not all of these documents are available or necessary in every instance to establish readmission eligibility.

(3) An institution may not delay or attempt to avoid a readmission of a student under this section by demanding documentation that does not exist, or is not readily available, at the time of readmission.

(h) *Termination of readmission eligibility.* A student's eligibility for readmission to an institution under this section by reason of such student's service in the uniformed services terminates upon the occurrence of any of the following events:

(1) A separation of such person from the Armed Forces (including the National Guard and Reserves) with a dishonorable or bad conduct discharge.

(2) A dismissal of a commissioned officer permitted under section 1161(a) of title 10, United States Code by sentence of a general court-martial; in commutation of a sentence of a general court-martial; or, in time of war, by order of the President.

(3) A dropping of a commissioned officer from the rolls pursuant to section 1161(b) of title 10, United States Code due to absence without authority for at least three months; separation by reason of a sentence to confinement adjudged by a court-martial; or, a sentence to confinement in a Federal or State penitentiary or correctional institution.

(Approved by the Office of Management and Budget under control number 1845-NEW1)

(Authority: 20 U.S.C. 1088, *et seq.*)

[74 Fed. Reg. 55934 (Oct. 29, 2009)]

§ 668.19 Financial aid history.

(a) Before an institution may disburse title IV, HEA program funds to a student who previously attended another eligible institution, the institution must use information it obtains from the Secretary, through the National Student Loan Data System (NSLDS) or its successor system, to determine—

(1) Whether the student is in default on any title IV, HEA program loan;

(2) Whether the student owes an overpayment on any title IV, HEA program grant or Federal Perkins Loan;

(3) For the award year for which a Federal Pell Grant, an ACG, a National SMART Grant, or a TEACH Grant is requested, the student's Scheduled Federal Pell Grant, ACG, National SMART Grant, or a TEACH Grant Award and the amount of Federal Pell Grant, ACG, National SMART Grant, or a TEACH Grant funds disbursed to the student;

(4) The outstanding principal balance of loans made to the student under each of the title IV, HEA loan programs; and

(5) For the academic year for which title IV, HEA aid is requested, the amount of, and period of enrollment for, loans made to the student under each of the title IV, HEA loan programs.

(b)(1) If a student transfers from one institution to another institution during the same award year, the institution to which the student transfers must request from the Secretary, through NSLDS, updated information about that student so it can make the determinations required under paragraph (a) of this section; and

(2) The institution may not make a disbursement to that student for seven days following its request, unless it receives the information from NSLDS in response to its request or obtains that information directly by accessing NSLDS, and the information it receives allows it to make that disbursement.

(Approved by the Office of Management and Budget under control number 1845-0537)

(Authority: 20 U.S.C. 1070g, 1091, 1094)

[53 Fed. Reg. 33431 (Aug. 30, 1988); 58 Fed. Reg. 32203 (June 8, 1993); 59 Fed. Reg. 21866 (Apr. 26, 1994); 60 Fed. Reg. 61809 (Dec. 1, 1995); 63 Fed. Reg. 40624 (July 29, 1998); 65 Fed. Reg. 65675 (Nov. 1, 2000); 71 Fed. Reg. 38002 (July 3, 2006); 73 Fed. Reg. 35492 (June 23, 2008)]

§ 668.20 Limitations on remedial coursework that is eligible for Title IV, HEA program assistance.

(a) A noncredit or reduced credit remedial course is a course of study designed to increase the ability of a student to pursue a course of study leading to a certificate or degree.

(1) A noncredit remedial course is one for which no credit is given toward a certificate or degree; and

(2) A reduced credit remedial course is one for which reduced credit is given toward a certificate or degree.

(b) Except as provided in paragraphs (c) and (d) of this section, in determining a student's enrollment status and cost of attendance, an institution shall include any noncredit or reduced credit remedial course in which the student is enrolled. The institution shall attribute the number of credit or clock hours to a noncredit or reduced credit remedial course by—

(1) Calculating the number of classroom and homework hours required for that course;

(2) Comparing those hours with the hours required for nonremedial courses in a similar subject; and

(3) Giving the remedial course the same number of credit or clock hours it gives the non-remedial course with the most comparable classroom and homework requirements.

(c) In determining a student's enrollment status under the Title IV, HEA programs or a student's cost of attendance under the campus-based, FFEL, and Direct Loan programs, an institution may not take into account any noncredit or reduced credit remedial course if—

(1) That course is part of a program of instruction leading to a high school diploma or the recognized equivalent of a high school diploma, even if the course is necessary to enable the student to complete a degree or certificate program;

(2) The educational level of instruction provided in the noncredit or reduced credit remedial course is below the level needed to pursue successfully the degree or certificate program offered by that institution after one year in that remedial course; or

(3) Except for a course in English as a second language, the educational level of instruction provided in that course is below the secondary level. For purposes of this section, the Secretary considers a course to be below the secondary level if any of the following entities determine that course to be below the secondary level:

(i) The State agency that legally authorized the institution to provide postsecondary education.

(ii) In the case of an accredited or preaccredited institution, the nationally recognized accrediting agency or association that accredits or preaccredits the institution.

(iii) In the case of a public postsecondary vocational institution that is approved by a State agency recognized for the approval of public postsecondary vocational education, the State agency recognized for the approval of public postsecondary vocational education that approves the institution.

(iv) The institution.

(d) Except as set forth in paragraph (f) of this section, an institution may not take into account more than one academic year's worth of noncredit or reduced credit remedial coursework in determining—

(1) A student's enrollment status under the Title IV, HEA programs; and

(2) A student's cost of attendance under the campus-based, FFEL, and Direct Loan programs.

(e) One academic year's worth of noncredit or reduced credit remedial coursework is equivalent to—

(1) Thirty semester or 45 quarter hours; or

(2) Nine hundred clock hours.

(f) Courses in English as a second language do not count against the one-year academic limitation contained in paragraph (d) of this section.

(Authority: 20 U.S.C. 1094)

[56 Fed. Reg. 36698 (July 31, 1991); 57 Fed. Reg. 27703 (June 22, 1992); 58 Fed. Reg. 32203 (June 8, 1993); 59 Fed. Reg. 21866 (Apr. 26, 1994); 63 Fed. Reg. 40624 (July 29, 1998)]

§ 668.21 Treatment of title IV grant and loan funds if the recipient does not begin attendance at the institution.

(a) If a student does not begin attendance in a payment period or period of enrollment—

(1) The institution must return all title IV, HEA program funds that were credited to the student's account at the institution or disbursed directly to the student for that payment period or period of enrollment, for Federal Perkins Loan, FSEOG, TEACH Grant, Federal Pell Grant, ACG, and National SMART Grant program funds; and

(2) For FFEL and Direct Loan funds—

(i)(A) The institution must return all FFEL and Direct Loan funds that were credited to the student's account at the institution for that payment period or period of enrollment; and

(B) The institution must return the amount of payments made directly by or on behalf of the student to the institution for that payment period or period of enrollment, up to the total amount of the loan funds disbursed;

(ii) For remaining amounts of FFEL or Direct Loan funds disbursed directly to the student for that payment period or period of enrollment, including funds that are disbursed directly to the student by the lender for a study-abroad program in accordance with § 682.207(b)(1)(v)(C)(1) or for a student enrolled in a foreign school in accordance with § 682.207(b)(1)(v)(D), the institution is not responsible for returning the funds, but must immediately notify the lender or the Secretary, as appropriate, when it becomes aware that the student will not or has not begun attendance so that the lender or Secretary will issue a final demand letter to the borrower in accordance with 34 CFR 682.412 or 34 CFR 685.211, as appropriate; and

(iii) Notwithstanding paragraph (a)(2)(ii) of this section, if an institution knew that a student would not begin attendance prior to disbursing FFEL or Direct Loan funds directly to the student for that payment period or period of enrollment (e.g., the student notified the institution that he or she would not attend, or the institution expelled the student), the institution must return those funds.

(b) The institution must return those funds for which it is responsible under paragraph (a) of this section to the respective title IV, HEA program as soon as possible, but no later than 30 days after the date that the institution becomes aware that the student will not or has not begun attendance.

(c) For purposes of this section, the Secretary considers that a student has not begun attendance in a payment period or period of enrollment if the institution is unable to document the student's attendance at any class during the payment period or period of enrollment.

(d) In accordance with procedures established by the Secretary or FFEL Program lender, an institution returns title IV, HEA funds timely if—

(1) The institution deposits or transfers the funds into the bank account it maintains under § 668.163 as soon as possible, but no later than 30 days after the date that the institution becomes aware that the student will not or has not begun attendance;

(2) The institution initiates an electronic funds transfer (EFT) as soon as possible, but no later than 30 days after the date that the institution becomes aware that the student will not or has not begun attendance;

(3) The institution initiates an electronic transaction, as soon as possible, but no later than 30 days after the date that the institution becomes aware that the student will not or has not begun attendance, that informs an FFEL lender to adjust the borrower's loan account for the amount returned; or

(4) The institution issues a check as soon as possible, but no later than 30 days after the date that the institution becomes aware that the student will not or has not begun attendance. An institution does not satisfy this requirement if—

(i) The institution's records show that the check was issued more than 30 days after the date that the institution becomes aware that the student will not or has not begun attendance; or

(ii) The date on the cancelled check shows that the bank used by the Secretary or FFEL Program lender endorsed that check more than 45 days after the date that the institution becomes aware that the student will not or has not begun attendance.

(Authority: 20 U.S.C. 1070g, 1094)

[60 Fed. Reg. 61810 (Dec. 1, 1995); 63 Fed. Reg. 40624 (July 29, 1998); 72 Fed. Reg. 62027 (Nov. 1, 2007); 73 Fed. Reg. 35493 (June 23, 2008)]

§ 668.22 Treatment of Title IV funds when a student withdraws.

(a) *General.*

(1) When a recipient of title IV grant or loan assistance withdraws from an institution during a payment period or period of enrollment in which the recipient began attendance, the institution must determine the amount of title IV grant or loan assistance that the student earned as of the student's withdrawal date in accordance with paragraph (e) of this section.

(2) For purposes of this section, "title IV grant or loan assistance" includes only assistance from the Federal Perkins Loan, Direct Loan, FFEL, Federal Pell Grant, Academic Competitiveness Grant, National SMART Grant, TEACH Grant, and FSEOG programs, not including the non-Federal share of FSEOG awards if an institution meets its FSEOG matching share by the individual recipient method or the aggregate method.

(3) If the total amount of title IV grant or loan assistance, or both, that the student earned as calculated under paragraph (e)(1) of this section is less than the amount of title IV grant or loan assistance that was disbursed to the student or on behalf of the student in the case of a PLUS loan, as of the date of the institution's determination that the student withdrew—

(i) The difference between these amounts must be returned to the title IV programs in accordance with paragraphs (g) and (h) of this section in the order specified in paragraph (i) of this section; and

(ii) No additional disbursements may be made to the student for the payment period or period of enrollment.

(4) If the total amount of title IV grant or loan assistance, or both, that the student earned as calculated under paragraph (e)(1) of this section is greater than the total amount of title IV grant or loan assistance, or both, that was disbursed to the student or on behalf of the student in the case of a PLUS loan, as of the date of the institution's determination that the student withdrew, the difference between these amounts must be treated as a post-withdrawal disbursement in accordance with paragraph (a)(5) of this section and § 668.164(g).

(5)(i) A post-withdrawal disbursement must be made from available grant funds before available loan funds.

(ii)(A) If outstanding charges exist on the student's account, the institution may credit the student's account up to the amount of outstanding charges with all or a portion of any—

(1) Grant funds that make up the post-withdrawal disbursement in accordance with § 668.164(d)(1) and (d)(2); and

(2) Loan funds that make up the post-withdrawal disbursement in accordance with § 668.164(d)(1), (d)(2), and (d)(3) only after obtaining confirmation from the student or parent in the case of a parent PLUS loan, that they still wish to have the loan funds disbursed in accordance with paragraph (a)(5)(iii) of this section.

(B)(1) The institution must disburse directly to a student any amount of a post-withdrawal disbursement of grant funds that is not credited to the student's account. The institution must make the disbursement as soon as possible, but no later than 45 days after the date of the institution's determination that the student withdrew, as defined in paragraph (l)(3) of this section.

(2) The institution must offer to disburse directly to a student, or parent in the case of a parent PLUS loan, any amount of a post-withdrawal disbursement of loan funds that is not credited to the student's account, in accordance with paragraph (a)(5)(iii) of this section.

(3) The institution must make a direct disbursement of any loan funds that make up the post-withdrawal disbursement only after obtaining the student's, or parent's in the case of a parent PLUS loan, confirmation that the student or parent still wishes to have the loan funds disbursed in accordance with paragraph (a)(5)(iii) of this section.

(iii)(A) The institution must provide within 30 days of the date of the institution's determination that the student withdrew, as defined in paragraph (l)(3) of this section, a written notification to the student, or parent in the case of parent PLUS loan, that—

(1) Requests confirmation of any post-withdrawal disbursement of loan funds that the institution wishes to credit to the student's account in accordance with paragraph (a)(5)(ii)(A)(2) of this section, identifying the type and amount of those loan funds and explaining that a student, or parent in the case of a parent PLUS loan, may accept or decline some or all of those funds;

(2) Requests confirmation of any post-withdrawal disbursement of loan funds that the student, or parent in the case of a parent PLUS loan, can receive as a direct disbursement, identifying the type and amount of these title IV funds and explaining that the student, or parent in the case of a parent PLUS loan, may accept or decline some or all of those funds;

(3) Explains that a student, or parent in the case of a parent PLUS loan, who does not confirm that a post-withdrawal disbursement of loan funds may be credited to the student's account may not receive any of those loan funds as a direct disbursement unless the institution concurs;

(4) Explains the obligation of the student, or parent in the case of a parent PLUS loan, to repay any loan funds he or she chooses to have disbursed; and

(5) Advises the student, or parent in the case of a parent PLUS loan, that no post-withdrawal disbursement of loan funds will be made, unless the institution chooses to make a post-withdrawal disbursement based on a late response in accordance with paragraph (a)(5)(iii)(C) of this section, if the student or parent in the case of a parent PLUS loan, does not respond within 14 days of the date that the institution sent the notification, or a later deadline set by the institution.

(B) The deadline for a student, or parent in the case of a parent PLUS loan, to accept a post-withdrawal disbursement under paragraph (a)(5)(iii)(A) of this section must be the same for both a confirmation of a direct disbursement of the post-withdrawal disbursement of loan funds and a confirmation of a post-withdrawal disbursement of loan funds to be credited to the student's account.

(C) If the student, or parent in the case of a parent PLUS loan, submits a timely response that confirms that they wish to receive all or a portion of a direct disbursement of the post-withdrawal disbursement of loan funds, or confirms that a post-withdrawal disbursement of loan funds may be credited to the student's account, the institution must disburse the funds in the manner specified by the student, or parent in the case of a parent PLUS loan, as soon as possible, but no later than 180 days after the date of the institution's determination that the student withdrew, as defined in paragraph (l)(3) of this section.

(D) If a student, or parent in the case of a parent PLUS loan, submits a late response to the institution's notice requesting confirmation, the institution may make the post-withdrawal disbursement of loan funds as instructed by the student, or parent in the case of a parent PLUS loan (provided the institution disburses all the funds accepted by the student, or parent in the case of a parent PLUS loan), or decline to do so.

(E) If a student, or parent in the case of a parent PLUS loan, submits a late response to the institution and the institution does not choose to make the post-withdrawal disbursement of loan funds, the institution must inform the student, or parent in the case of a parent PLUS loan, in writing of the outcome of the post-withdrawal disbursement request.

(F) If the student, or parent in the case of a parent PLUS loan, does not respond to the institution's notice, no portion of the post-withdrawal disbursement of loan funds that the institution wishes to credit to the student's account, nor any portion of loan funds that would be disbursed directly to the student, or parent in the case of a parent PLUS loan, may be disbursed.

(iv) An institution must document in the student's file the result of any notification made in accordance with paragraph (a)(5)(iii) of this section of the student's right to cancel all or a portion of loan funds or of the student's right to accept or decline loan funds, and the final determination made concerning the disbursement.

(b) *Withdrawal date for a student who withdraws from an institution that is required to take attendance.*

(1) For purposes of this section, for a student who ceases attendance at an institution that is required to take attendance, including a student who does not return from an approved leave of absence, as defined in paragraph (d) of this section, or a student who takes a leave of absence that does not meet the requirements of paragraph (d) of this section, the student's withdrawal date is the last date of academic attendance as determined by the institution from its attendance records.

(2) An institution must document a student's withdrawal date determined in accordance with paragraph (b)(1) of this section and maintain the documentation as of the date of the institution's determination that the student withdrew, as defined in paragraph (l)(3) of this section.

(3)(i) An institution is required to take attendance if an outside entity (such as the institution's accrediting agency or a State agency) has a requirement, as determined by the entity, that the institution take attendance.

(ii) If an outside entity requires an institution to take attendance for only some students, the institution must use its attendance records to determine a withdrawal date in accordance with paragraph (b)(1) of this section for those students.

(c) *Withdrawal date for a student who withdraws from an institution that is not required to take attendance.*

(1) For purposes of this section, for a student who ceases attendance at an institution that is not required to take attendance, the student's withdrawal date is—

(i) The date, as determined by the institution, that the student began the withdrawal process prescribed by the institution;

(ii) The date, as determined by the institution, that the student otherwise provided official notification to the institution, in writing or orally, of his or her intent to withdraw;

(iii) If the student ceases attendance without providing official notification to the institution of his or her withdrawal in accordance with paragraph (c)(1)(i) or (c)(1)(ii) of this section, the mid-point of the payment period (or period of enrollment, if applicable);

(iv) If the institution determines that a student did not begin the institution's withdrawal process or otherwise provide official notification (including notice from an individual acting on the student's behalf) to the institution of his or her intent to withdraw because of illness, accident, grievous personal loss, or other such circumstances beyond the student's control, the date that the institution determines is related to that circumstance;

(v) If a student does not return from an approved leave of absence as defined in paragraph (d) of this section, the date that the institution determines the student began the leave of absence; or

(vi) If a student takes a leave of absence that does not meet the requirements of paragraph (d) of this section, the date that the student began the leave of absence.

(2)(i)(A) An institution may allow a student to rescind his or her official notification to withdraw under paragraph (c)(1)(i) or (ii) of this section by filing a written statement that he or she is continuing to participate in academically-related activities and intends to complete the payment period or period of enrollment.

(B) If the student subsequently ceases to attend the institution prior to the end of the payment period or period of enrollment, the student's rescission is negated and the withdrawal date is the student's original date under paragraph (c)(1)(i) or (ii) of this section, unless a later date is determined under paragraph (c)(3) of this section.

(ii) If a student both begins the withdrawal process prescribed by the institution and otherwise provides official notification of his or her intent to withdraw in accordance with paragraphs (c)(1)(i) and (c)(1)(ii) of this section respectively, the student's withdrawal date is the earlier date unless a later date is determined under paragraph (c)(3) of this section.

(3)(i) Notwithstanding paragraphs (c)(1) and (2) of this section, an institution that is not required to take attendance may use as the student's withdrawal date a student's last date of attendance at an academically-related activity provided that the institution documents that the activity is academically related and documents the student's attendance at the activity.

(ii) An "academically-related activity" includes, but is not limited to, an exam, a tutorial, computer-assisted instruction, academic counseling, academic advisement, turning in a class assignment or attending a study group that is assigned by the institution.

(4) An institution must document a student's withdrawal date determined in accordance with paragraphs (c)(1), (2), and (3) of this section and maintain the documentation as of the date of the institution's determination that the student withdrew, as defined in paragraph (l)(3) of this section.

(5)(i) "Official notification to the institution" is a notice of intent to withdraw that a student provides to an office designated by the institution.

(ii) An institution must designate one or more offices at the institution that a student may readily contact to provide official notification of withdrawal.

(d) *Approved leave of absence.*

(1) For purposes of this section (and, for a title IV, HEA program loan borrower, for purposes of terminating the student's in-school status), an institution does not have to treat a leave of absence as a withdrawal if it is an approved leave of absence. A leave of absence is an approved leave of absence if—

(i) The institution has a formal policy regarding leaves of absence;

(ii) The student followed the institution's policy in requesting the leave of absence;

(iii) The institution determines that there is a reasonable expectation that the student will return to the school;

(iv) The institution approved the student's request in accordance with the institution's policy;

(v) The leave of absence does not involve additional charges by the institution;

(vi) The number of days in the approved leave of absence, when added to the number of days in all other approved leaves of absence, does not exceed 180 days in any 12-month period;

(vii) Except for a clock hour or nonterm credit hour program, upon the student's return from the leave of absence, the student is permitted to complete the coursework he or she began prior to the leave of absence; and

(viii) If the student is a title IV, HEA program loan recipient, the institution explains to the student, prior to granting the leave of absence, the effects that the student's failure to return from a leave of absence may have on the student's loan repayment terms, including the exhaustion of some or all of the student's grace period.

(2) If a student does not resume attendance at the institution at or before the end of a leave of absence that meets the requirements of this section, the institution must treat the student as a withdrawal in accordance with the requirements of this section.

(3) For purposes of this paragraph—

(i) The number of days in a leave of absence is counted beginning with the first day of the student's initial leave of absence in a 12-month period.

(ii) A "12-month period" begins on the first day of the student's initial leave of absence.

(iii) An institution's leave of absence policy is a "formal policy" if the policy—

(A) Is in writing and publicized to students; and

(B) Requires students to provide a written, signed, and dated request, that includes the reason for the request, for a leave of absence prior to the leave of absence. However, if unforeseen circumstances prevent a student from providing a prior written request, the institution may grant the student's request for a leave of absence, if the institution documents its decision and collects the written request at a later date.

(e) *Calculation of the amount of title IV assistance earned by the student.*

(1) *General.* The amount of title IV grant or loan assistance that is earned by the student is calculated by—

(i) Determining the percentage of title IV grant or loan assistance that has been earned by the student, as described in paragraph (e)(2) of this section; and

(ii) Applying this percentage to the total amount of title IV grant or loan assistance that was disbursed (and that could have been disbursed, as defined in paragraph (l)(1) of this section) to the student, or on the student's behalf, for the payment period or period of enrollment as of the student's withdrawal date.

(2) *Percentage earned.* The percentage of title IV grant or loan assistance that has been earned by the student is—

(i) Equal to the percentage of the payment period or period of enrollment that the student completed (as determined in accordance with paragraph (f) of this section) as of the student's withdrawal date, if this date occurs on or before—

(A) Completion of 60 percent of the payment period or period of enrollment for a program that is measured in credit hours; or

(B) Sixty percent of the clock hours scheduled to be completed for the payment period or period of enrollment for a program that is measured in clock hours; or

(ii) 100 percent, if the student's withdrawal date occurs after—

(A) Completion of 60 percent of the payment period or period of enrollment for a program that is measured in credit hours; or

(B) Sixty percent of the clock hours scheduled to be completed for the payment period or period of enrollment for a program measured in clock hours.

(3) *Percentage unearned.* The percentage of title IV grant or loan assistance that has not been earned by the student is calculated by determining the complement of the percentage of title IV grant or loan assistance earned by the student as described in paragraph (e)(2) of this section.

(4) *Total amount of unearned title IV assistance to be returned.* The unearned amount of title IV assistance to be returned is calculated by subtracting the amount of title IV assistance earned by the student as calculated under paragraph (e)(1) of this section from the amount of title IV aid that was disbursed to the student as of the date of the institution's determination that the student withdrew.

(5) *Use of payment period or period of enrollment.*

(i) The treatment of title IV grant or loan funds if a student withdraws must be determined on a payment period basis for a student who attended a standard term-based (semester, trimester, or quarter) educational program.

(ii)(A) The treatment of title IV grant or loan funds if a student withdraws may be determined on either a payment period basis or a period of enrollment basis for a student who attended a nonterm based educational program or a nonstandard term-based educational program.

(B) An institution must consistently use either a payment period or period of enrollment for all purposes of this section for each of the following categories of students who withdraw from the same

non-term based or nonstandard term-based educational program:
  (1) Students who have attended an educational program at the institution from the beginning of the payment period or period of enrollment.
  (2) Students who re-enter the institution during a payment period or period of enrollment.
  (3) Students who transfer into the institution during a payment period or period of enrollment.
(iii) For a program that measures progress in credit hours and uses nonstandard terms that are not substantially equal in length, if the institution uses the payment period to determine the treatment of title IV grant or loan funds for a category of students found in paragraph (e)(5)(ii)(B) of this section, the institution must—
  (A)(1) For students in the category who are disbursed or could have been disbursed aid using both the payment period definition in § 668.4(b)(1) and the payment period definition in § 668.4(b)(2), use the payment period during which the student withdrew that ends later; and
  (2) If in the payment period that ends later there are funds that have been or could have been disbursed from overlapping payment periods, the institution must include in the return calculation any funds that can be attributed to the payment period that ends later; and
  (B) For students in the category who are disbursed or could have been disbursed aid using only the payment period definition in § 668.4(b)(1) or the payment period definition in § 668.4(b)(2), use the payment period definition for which title IV, HEA program funds were disbursed for a student's calculation under this section.

(f) *Percentage of payment period or period of enrollment completed.*
  (1) For purposes of paragraph (e)(2)(i) of this section, the percentage of the payment period or period of enrollment completed is determined—
  (i) In the case of a program that is measured in credit hours, by dividing the total number of calendar days in the payment period or period of enrollment into the number of calendar days completed in that period as of the student's withdrawal date; and
  (ii)(A) In the case of a program that is measured in clock hours, by dividing the total number of clock hours in the payment period or period of enrollment into the number of clock hours scheduled to be completed as of the student's withdrawal date.
  (B) The scheduled clock hours used must be those established by the institution prior to the student's beginning class date for the payment period or period of enrollment and must be consistent with the published materials describing the institution's programs, unless the schedule was modified prior to the student's withdrawal.
  (C) The schedule must have been established in accordance with requirements of the accrediting agency and the State licensing agency, if such standards exist.
  (2)(i) The total number of calendar days in a payment period or period of enrollment includes all days within the period, except that scheduled breaks of at least five consecutive days are excluded from the total number of calendar days in a payment period or period of enrollment and the number of calendar days completed in that period.
  (ii) The total number of calendar days in a payment period or period of enrollment does not include days in which the student was on an approved leave of absence.

(g) *Return of unearned aid, responsibility of the institution.*
  (1) The institution must return, in the order specified in paragraph (i) of this section, the lesser of—
  (i) The total amount of unearned title IV assistance to be returned as calculated under paragraph (e)(4) of this section; or
  (ii) An amount equal to the total institutional charges incurred by the student for the payment period or period of enrollment multiplied by the percentage of title IV grant or loan assistance that has not been earned by the student, as described in paragraph (e)(3) of this section.
  (2) For purposes of this section, "institutional charges" are tuition, fees, room and board (if the student contracts with the institution for the room and board) and other educationally-related expenses assessed by the institution.
  (3) If, for a non-term program an institution chooses to calculate the treatment of title IV assistance on a payment period basis, but the institution charges for a period that is longer than the payment period, "total institutional charges incurred by the student for the payment period" is the greater of—
  (i) The prorated amount of institutional charges for the longer period; or
  (ii) The amount of title IV assistance retained for institutional charges as of the student's withdrawal date.

(h) *Return of unearned aid, responsibility of the student.*
  (1) After the institution has allocated the unearned funds for which it is responsible in accordance with paragraph (g) of this section, the student must return assistance for which the student is responsible in the order specified in paragraph (i) of this section.
  (2) The amount of assistance that the student is responsible for returning is calculated by subtracting the amount of unearned aid that the institution is required to return under paragraph (g) of this section from the total amount of unearned title IV assistance to be returned under paragraph (e)(4) of this section.
  (3) The student (or parent in the case of funds due to a parent PLUS Loan) must return or repay, as appropriate, the amount determined under paragraph (h)(1) of this section to—
  (i) Any title IV loan program in accordance with the terms of the loan; and
  (ii) Any title IV grant program as an overpayment of the grant; however, a student is not required to return the following—
  (A) The portion of a grant overpayment amount that is equal to or less than 50 percent of the total grant assistance that was disbursed (and that could have been disbursed, as defined in paragraph (l)(1) of this section) to the student for the payment period or period of enrollment.
  (B) With respect to any grant program, a grant overpayment amount, as determined after application of paragraph (h)(3)(ii)(A) of this section, of 50 dollars or less that is not a remaining balance.
  (4)(i) A student who owes an overpayment under this section remains eligible for title IV, HEA program funds through and beyond the earlier of 45 days from the date the institution sends a notification to the student of the overpayment, or 45 days from the date the institution was required to notify the student of the overpayment if, during those 45 days the student—
  (A) Repays the overpayment in full to the institution;
  (B) Enters into a repayment agreement with the institution in accordance with repayment arrangements satisfactory to the institution; or
  (C) Signs a repayment agreement with the Secretary, which will include terms that permit a student to repay the overpayment while maintaining his or her eligibility for title IV, HEA program funds.
  (ii) Within 30 days of the date of the institution's determination that the student withdrew, an institution must send a notice to any student who owes a title IV, HEA grant overpayment as a result of the student's withdrawal from the institution in order to recover the overpayment in accordance with paragraph (h)(4)(i) of this section.
  (iii) If an institution chooses to enter into a repayment agreement in accordance with paragraph (h)(4)(i)(B) of this section with a student who owes an overpayment of title IV, HEA grant funds, it must—
  (A) Provide the student with terms that permit the student to repay the overpayment while maintaining his or her eligibility for title IV, HEA program funds; and

(B) Require repayment of the full amount of the overpayment within two years of the date of the institution's determination that the student withdrew.

(iv) An institution must refer to the Secretary, in accordance with procedures required by the Secretary, an overpayment of title IV, HEA grant funds owed by a student as a result of the student's withdrawal from the institution if—

(A) The student does not repay the overpayment in full to the institution, or enter a repayment agreement with the institution or the Secretary in accordance with paragraph (h)(4)(i) of this section within the earlier of 45 days from the date the institution sends a notification to the student of the overpayment, or 45 days from the date the institution was required to notify the student of the overpayment;

(B) At any time the student fails to meet the terms of the repayment agreement with the institution entered into in accordance with paragraph (h)(4)(i)(B) of this section; or

(C) The student chooses to enter into a repayment agreement with the Secretary.

(v) A student who owes an overpayment is ineligible for title IV, HEA program funds—

(A) If the student does not meet the requirements in paragraph (h)(4)(i) of this section, on the day following the 45-day period in that paragraph; or

(B) As of the date the student fails to meet the terms of the repayment agreement with the institution or the Secretary entered into in accordance with paragraph (h)(4)(i) of this section.

(vi) A student who is ineligible under paragraph (h)(4)(v) of this section regains eligibility if the student and the Secretary enter into a repayment agreement.

(5) The Secretary may waive grant overpayment amounts that students are required to return under this section if the withdrawals on which the returns are based are withdrawals by students—

(i) Who were residing in, employed in, or attending an institution of higher education that is located in an area in which the President has declared that a major disaster exists, in accordance with section 401 of the Robert T. Stafford Disaster Relief and Emergency Assistance Act (42 U.S.C. 5170);

(ii) Whose attendance was interrupted because of the impact of the disaster on the student or institution; and

(iii) Whose withdrawal occurred within the award year during which the designation occurred or during the next succeeding award year.

(i) *Order of return of title IV funds.*
(1) *Loans.* Unearned funds returned by the institution or the student, as appropriate, in accordance with paragraph (g) or (h) of this section respectively, must be credited to outstanding balances on title IV loans made to the student or on behalf of the student for the payment period or period of enrollment for which a return of funds is required. Those funds must be credited to outstanding balances for the payment period or period of enrollment for which a return of funds is required in the following order:

(i) Unsubsidized Federal Stafford loans.
(ii) Subsidized Federal Stafford loans.
(iii) Unsubsidized Federal Direct Stafford loans.
(iv) Subsidized Federal Direct Stafford loans.
(v) Federal Perkins loans.
(vi) Federal PLUS loans received on behalf of the student.
(vii) Federal Direct PLUS received on behalf of the student.

(2) *Remaining funds.* If unearned funds remain to be returned after repayment of all outstanding loan amounts, the remaining excess must be credited to any amount awarded for the payment period or period of enrollment for which a return of funds is required in the following order:

(i) Federal Pell Grants.
(ii) Academic Competitiveness Grants.
(iii) National SMART Grants.
(iv) FSEOG Program aid.
(v) TEACH Grants.

(j) *Timeframe for the return of title IV funds.*
(1) An institution must return the amount of title IV funds for which it is responsible under paragraph (g) of this section as soon as possible but no later than 45 days after the date of the institution's determination that the student withdrew as defined in paragraph (l)(3) of this section. The timeframe for returning funds is further described in § 668.173(b).

(2) An institution must determine the withdrawal date for a student who withdraws without providing notification to the institution no later than 30 days after the end of the earlier of the—

(i) Payment period or period of enrollment, as appropriate, in accordance with paragraph (e)(5) of this section;
(ii) Academic year in which the student withdrew; or
(iii) Educational program from which the student withdrew.

(k) *Consumer information.* An institution must provide students with information about the requirements of this section in accordance with § 668.43.

(l) *Definitions.* For purposes of this section—
(1) Title IV grant or loan funds that "could have been disbursed" are determined in accordance with the late disbursement provisions in § 668.164(g).

(2) A "period of enrollment" is the academic period established by the institution for which institutional charges are generally assessed (*i.e.*, length of the student's program or academic year).

(3) The "date of the institution's determination that the student withdrew" is—

(i) For a student who provides notification to the institution of his or her withdrawal, the student's withdrawal date as determined under paragraph (c) of this section or the date of notification of withdrawal, whichever is later;

(ii) For a student who did not provide notification of his of her withdrawal to the institution, the date that the institution becomes aware that the student ceased attendance;

(iii) For a student who does not return from an approved leave of absence, the earlier of the date of the end of the leave of absence or the date the student notifies the institution that he or she will not be returning to the institution; or

(iv) For a student whose rescission is negated under paragraph (c)(2)(i)(B) of this section, the date the institution becomes aware that the student did not, or will not, complete the payment period or period of enrollment.

(v) For a student who takes a leave of absence that is not approved in accordance with paragraph (d) of this section, the date that the student begins the leave of absence.

(4) A "recipient of title IV grant or loan assistance" is a student for whom the requirements of § 668.164(g)(2) have been met.

(5) Terms are "substantially equal in length" if no term in the program is more than two weeks of instructional time longer than any other term in that program.

(Approved by the Office of Management and Budget under control number 1845-0022)

(Authority: 20 U.S.C. 1070g, 1091b)

[53 Fed. Reg. 49147 (Dec. 6, 1988); 58 Fed. Reg. 32202 (June 8, 1993); 59 Fed. Reg. 21866 (Apr. 26, 1994); 59 Fed. Reg. 22436 (Apr. 29, 1994); 59 Fed. Reg. 32657 (June 24, 1994); 59 Fed. Reg. 34964 (July 7, 1994); 59 Fed. Reg. 61180 (Nov. 29, 1994); 60 Fed. Reg. 34431 (June 30, 1995); 60 Fed. Reg. 42408 (Aug. 15, 1995); 60 Fed. Reg. 61810 (Dec. 1, 1995); 61 Fed. Reg. 60396 (Nov. 27, 1996); 63 Fed. Reg. 40624 (July 29, 1998); 64 Fed. Reg. 59038 (Nov. 1, 1999); 67 Fed. Reg. 67073 (Nov. 1, 2002); 71 Fed. Reg. 45666 (Sept. 8, 2006); 71 Fed. Reg. 64397 (Nov. 1, 2006); 72 Fed. Reg. 62027 (Nov. 1, 2007); 73 Fed. Reg. 35493 (June 23, 2008)]

* * *

B.5 Selected Debt Collection Procedures

B.5.1 Administrative Offset

34 C.F.R. sec.

* * *

30.20 To what do Secs. 30.20–30.31 apply?
30.21 When may the Secretary offset a debt?
30.22 What notice does the debtor receive before the commencement of offset?
30.23 How must a debtor request an opportunity to inspect and copy records relating to a debt?
30.24 What opportunity does the debtor receive to obtain a review of the existence or amount of a debt?
30.25 How may a debtor obtain an oral hearing?
30.26 What special rules apply to an oral hearing?
30.27 When does the Secretary enter into a repayment agreement rather than offset?
30.28 When may the Secretary offset before completing the procedures under §§ 30.22–30.27?
30.29 What procedures apply when the Secretary offsets to collect a debt owed another agency?
30.30 What procedures apply when the Secretary requests another agency to offset a debt owed under a program or activity of the Department?
30.31 How does the Secretary apply funds recovered by offset if multiple debts are involved?

* * *

Source: 51 Fed. Reg. 24099 (July 1, 1986); 53 Fed. Reg. 33425 (Aug. 30, 1988), unless otherwise noted.

* * *

§ 30.20 To what do §§ 30.20–30.31 apply?

(a)(1)(i) Sections 30.20–30.31 establish the general procedures used by the Secretary to collect debts by administrative offset.
  (ii) The Secretary uses the procedures established under other regulations, including § 30.33, What procedures does the Secretary follow for IRS tax refund offsets?, 34 CFR part 31, Salary Offset for Federal Employees Who Are Indebted to the United States Under Programs Administrated by the Secretary of Education, and 34 CFR part 32, Salary Offset to Recover Overpayments of Pay or Allowances from Department of Education Employees, if the conditions requiring application of those special procedures exists.
  (2) The word "offset" is used in this subpart to refer to the collection of a debt by administrative offset.

(b) The Secretary does not rely on 31 U.S.C. 3716 as authority for offset if:
  (1) The debt is owed by a State or local government;
  (2) The debt, or the payment against which offset would be taken, arises under the Social Security Act;
  (3) The debt is owed under:
    (i) The Internal Revenue Code of 1954; or
    (ii) The tariff laws of the United States; or
  (4) The right to collect the debt first accrued more than ten years before initiation of the offset.

(c)(1) The Secretary may rely on 31 U.S.C. 3716 as authority for offset of a debt to which paragraph (b)(4) of this section would otherwise apply if facts material to the Government's right to collect the debt were not known and could not reasonably have been known by the official or officials of the Government who are charged with the responsibility to discover and collect the debt.
  (2) If paragraph (c)(1) of this section applies, the Secretary may rely on 31 U.S.C. 3716 as authority for offset up to 10 years after the date that the official or officials described in that paragraph first knew or reasonably should have known of the right of the United States to collect the debt.

(d) The Secretary determines when the right to collect a debt first accrued under the existing law regarding accrual of debts such as 28 U.S.C. 2415.

(Authority: 20 U.S.C. 1221e-3(a)(1) and 1226a-1, 31 U.S.C. 3716(b))

[51 Fed. Reg. 24099 (July 1, 1986), *as amended at* 51 Fed. Reg. 35646 (Oct. 7, 1986); 53 Fed. Reg. 33425 (Aug. 30, 1988); 54 Fed. Reg. 43583 (Oct. 26, 1989)]

§ 30.21 When may the Secretary offset a debt?

(a) The Secretary may offset a debt if:
  (1) The debt is liquidated or certain in amount; and
  (2) Offset is feasible and not otherwise prohibited.

(b)(1) Whether offset is feasible is determined by the Secretary in the exercise of sound discretion on a case-by-case basis, either:
  (i) For each individual debt or offset; or
  (ii) For each class of similar debts or offsets.
  (2) The Secretary considers the following factors in making this determination:
    (i) Whether offset can be practically and legally accomplished.
    (ii) Whether offset will further and protect the interests of the United States.

(c) The Secretary may switch advance funded grantees to a reimbursement payment system before initiating an offset.

(Authority: 20 U.S.C. 1221e-3(a)(1) and 1226a-1, 31 U.S.C. 3716(b))

§ 30.22 What notice does the debtor receive before the commencement of offset?

(a)(1) Except as provided in §§ 30.28 and 30.29, the Secretary provides a debtor with written notice of the Secretary's intent to offset before initiating the offset.
  (2) The Secretary mails the notice to the debtor at the current address of the debtor, as determined by the Secretary from information regarding the debt maintained by the Department.

(b) The written notice informs the debtor regarding:
  (1) The nature and amount of the debt;
  (2) The Secretary's intent to collect the debt by offset;
  (3) The debtor's opportunity to:
    (i) Inspect and copy Department records pertaining to the debt;
    (ii) Obtain a review within the Department of the existence or amount of the debt; and
    (iii) Enter into a written agreement with the Secretary to repay the debt;
  (4) The date by which the debtor must request an opportunity set forth under paragraph (b)(3) of this section; and
  (5) The Secretary's decision, in appropriate cases, to switch the debtor from advance funding to a reimbursement payment system.

(c)(1) In determining whether a debtor has requested an opportunity set forth under paragraph (b)(3) of this section in a timely manner, the Secretary relies on:
  (i) A legibly dated U.S. Postal Service postmark for the debtor's request; or
  (ii) A legibly stamped U.S. Postal service mail receipt for debtor's request.
  (2) The Secretary does not rely on either of the following as proof of mailing;
    (i) A private metered postmark.
    (ii) A mail receipt that is not dated by the U.S. Postal Service.

NOTE: The U.S. Postal Service does not uniformly provide a dated postmark. Before relying on this method for proof of mailing, a debtor should check with its local post office.

(d) If a debtor previously has been notified of the Secretary's intent to offset or offered an opportunity to take any of the actions set forth in paragraph (b)(3) of this section in connection with the same debt, the Secretary may offset without providing the debtor with an additional notice of intent or opportunity to take any of those actions under these offset procedures.

(Authority: 20 U.S.C. 1221e-3(a)(1) and 1226a-1, 31 U.S.C. 3716(b))

§ 30.23 How must a debtor request an opportunity to inspect and copy records relating to a debt?

(a) If a debtor wants to inspect and copy Department documents relating to the debt, the debtor must:

(1) File a written request to inspect and copy the documents within 20 days after the date of the notice provided under § 30.22; and

(2) File the request at the address specified in that notice.

(b) A request filed under paragraph (a) of this section must contain:

(1) All information provided to the debtor in the notice under § 30.22 or § 30.33(b) that identifies the debtor and the debt, including the debtor's Social Security number and the program under which the debt arose, together with any corrections of that identifying information; and

(2) A reasonably specific identification of the records the debtor wishes to have available for inspection and copying.

(c) The Secretary may decline to provide an opportunity to inspect and copy records if the debtor fails to request inspection and copying in accordance with this section.

(Approved by the Office of Management and Budget under control number 1880-0515)

(Authority: 20 U.S.C. 1221e-3(a)(1) and 1226a-1, 31 U.S.C. 3716(b))

[51 Fed. Reg. 24099 (July 1, 1986), *as amended at* 51 Fed. Reg. 35646 (Oct. 7, 1986)]

§ 30.24 What opportunity does the debtor receive to obtain a review of the existence or amount of a debt?

(a) If a debtor wants a review within the Department of the issues identified in the notice under § 30.22(b)(3)(ii) or § 30.33(b)(3)(ii), the debtor must:

(1) File a request for review within 20 days after the date of the notice provided under § 30.22; and

(2) File a request at the address specified in that notice.

(b) A request filed under paragraph (a) of this section must contain:

(1) All information provided to the debtor in the notice under § 30.22 or § 30.33(b) that identifies the debtor and the particular debt, including the debtor's Social Security number and the program under which the debt arose, together with any corrections of that identifying information; and

(2) An explanation of the reasons the debtor believes that the notice the debtor received under § 30.22 or § 30.33(b) inaccurately states any facts or conclusions relating to the debt.

(c) The Secretary may decline to provide an opportunity for review of a debt if the debtor fails to request the review in accordance with this section.

(d)(1) The debtor shall:

(i) File copies of any documents relating to the issues identified in the notice under § 30.22(b)(3)(ii) or § 30.33(b)(3)(ii) that the debtor wishes the Secretary to consider in the review;

(ii) File the documents at the address specified in that notice, and

(iii) File the documents no later than:

(A) 20 days after the date of the notice provided under § 30.22; or

(B) If the debtor has requested an opportunity to inspect and copy records under § 30.23 within the time period specified in that section, 15 days after the date on which the Secretary makes available to the debtor the relevant, requested records.

(2) The Secretary may decline to consider any reasons or documents that the debtor fails to provide in accordance with paragraphs (b) and (d) of this section.

(e) If the Secretary bases the review on only the documentary evidence, the Secretary:

(1) Reviews the documents submitted by the debtor and other relevant evidence; and

(2) Notifies the debtor in writing of the Secretary's decision regarding the issues identified in the notice under § 30.22(b)(3)(ii) or § 30.33(b)(3)(ii) and, if appropriate, the question of waiver of the debt.

(Approved by the Office of Management and Budget under control number 1880-0515)

(Authority: 20 U.S.C. 1221e-3(a)(1) and 1226a-1, 31 U.S.C. 3716(b))

[51 Fed. Reg. 24099 (July 1, 1986), *as amended at* 51 Fed. Reg. 35646 (Oct. 7, 1986)]

§ 30.25 How may a debtor obtain an oral hearing?

(a) If a debtor wants the Secretary to conduct the review requested under § 30.24 as an oral hearing, the debtor must file a written request for an oral hearing together with the request for review filed under § 30.24(a).

(b) A request filed under paragraph (a) of this section must contain the following in addition to the information filed under § 30.24(b):

(1) An explanation of reason(s) why the debtor believes the Secretary cannot resolve the issues identified in the notice under § 30.22(b)(3)(ii) or § 30.33(b)(3)(ii) through a review of the documentary evidence.

(2) An identification of:

(i) The individuals that the debtor wishes to have testify at the oral hearing;

(ii) The specific issues identified in the notice regarding which each individual is prepared to testify; and

(iii) The reasons why each individual's testimony is necessary to resolve the issue.

(c) The Secretary grants a debtor's request for an oral hearing regarding the issues identified in the notice under § 30.22(b)(3)(ii) or § 30.33(b)(3)(ii) only if:

(1)(i) A statute authorizes or requires the Secretary to consider waiver of the indebtedness involved;

(ii) The debtor files a request for waiver of the indebtedness with the request for review filed under paragraph (a)(1) of this section; and

(iii) The question of waiver of the indebtedness turns on an issue of credibility or veracity; or

(2) The Secretary determines that the issues identified in the notice under § 30.22(b)(3)(ii) or § 30.33(b)(3)(ii) cannot be resolved by review of only the documentary evidence.

(d) Notwithstanding paragraph (b) of this section, the Secretary may deny oral hearings for a class of similar debts if:

(1) The issues identified in the notice under § 30.22(b)(3)(ii) or 30.33(b)(3)(ii) for which an oral hearing was requested, or the issue of waiver, rarely involve issues of credibility or veracity; and

(2) The Secretary determines that review of the documentary evidence is ordinarily an adequate means to correct mistakes.

(e) The Secretary may decline to consider any reasons that the debtor fails to provide in accordance with paragraph (b)(1) of this section.

(Approved by the Office of Management and Budget under control number 1880-0515)

(Authority: 20 U.S.C. 1221e-3(a)(1) and 1226a-1, 31 U.S.C. 3716(b))

[51 Fed. Reg. 24099 (July 1, 1986), *as amended at* 51 Fed. Reg. 35647 (Oct. 7, 1986)]

§ 30.26 What special rules apply to an oral hearing?

(a) The oral hearing under § 30.25 is not a formal evidentiary hearing subject to 5 U.S.C. 554, unless required by law.

(b) If the Secretary grants an oral hearing, the Secretary notifies the debtor in writing of:
   (1) The time and place for the hearing;
   (2) The debtor's right to representation; and
   (3) The debtor's right to present and cross examine witnesses.

(c) If the Secretary grants an oral hearing, the Secretary designates an official to:
   (1) Govern the conduct of the hearing;
   (2) Take all necessary action to avoid unreasonable delay in the proceedings;
   (3) Review the evidence presented at the hearing, the documents submitted by the debtor, and other relevant evidence; and
   (4) After considering the evidence, notify the debtor in writing of the official's decision regarding the issues identified in the notice under § 30.22(b)(3)(ii) or § 30.33(b)(3)(ii) and, if appropriate, the question of waiver of the debt.

(d) The official designated under paragraph (c) of this section may decline to hear any witnesses or testimony not identified by the debtor in accordance with § 30.25(b)(2).

(e) The decision of the designated official under paragraph (c) of this section constitutes the final decision of the Secretary.

(Authority: 20 U.S.C. 1221-3(a)(1) and 1226a-1, 31 U.S.C. 3716(b))

§ 30.27 When does the Secretary enter into a repayment agreement rather than offset?

(a) If a debtor wants an opportunity to enter into a written agreement to repay a debt on terms acceptable to the Secretary, the debtor must:
   (1) File a request to enter into such agreement within 20 days after the date of the notice provided under § 30.22; and
   (2) File the request at the address specified in the notice.

(b) A request filed under paragraph (a) of this section must contain all information provided to the debtor in the notice under § 30.22 or § 30.33(b) that identifies the debtor and the debt, including the debtor's Social Security number and the program under which the debt arose, together with any corrections of that identifying information.

(c) If the Secretary receives a request filed in accordance with this section, the Secretary may enter into a written agreement requiring repayment in accordance with 4 CFR 102.11, instead of offsetting the debt.

(d) In deciding whether to enter into the agreement, the Secretary may consider:
   (1) The Government's interest in collecting the debt; and
   (2) Fairness to the debtor.

(e)(1) A debtor that enters into a repayment agreement with the Secretary under this section waives any right to further review by the Secretary of the issues relating to the original debt identified in the notice under § 30.22(b)(3)(ii) or § 30.33(b)(3)(ii).
   (2) If a debtor breaches a repayment agreement, the Secretary may offset, or, under § 30.30, refer to another agency for offset:
      (i) The amount owing under the agreement; or
      (ii) The entire original debt, to the extent not repaid.

(Authority: 20 U.S.C. 1221-3(a)(1) and 1226a-1, 31 U.S.C. 3716(b))

[51 Fed. Reg. 24099 (July 1, 1986), *as amended at* 51 Fed. Reg. 35647 (Oct. 7, 1986)]

§ 30.28 When may the Secretary offset before completing the procedures under §§ 30.22–30.27?

(a) The Secretary may offset before completing the procedures otherwise required by §§ 30.22–30.27 if:
   (1) Failure to offset would substantially prejudice the Government's ability to collect the debt; and
   (2) The amount of time remaining before the payment by the United States which is subject to offset does not reasonably permit completion of the procedures under §§ 30.22–30.27.

(b) If the Secretary offsets under paragraph (a) of this section, the Secretary:
   (1) Promptly completes the procedures under §§ 30.22–30.27 after initiating the offset; and
   (2) Refunds any amounts recovered under the offset that are later found not to be owed to the United States.

(Authority: 20 U.S.C. 1221e-3(a)(1) and 1226a-1, 31 U.S.C. 3716(b))

§ 30.29 What procedures apply when the Secretary offsets to collect a debt owed another agency?

The Secretary may initiate offset to collect a debt owed another Federal agency if:
(a) An official of that agency certifies in writing:
   (1) That the debtor owes a debt to the United States;
   (2) The amount of the debt; and
   (3) That the agency has complied with 4 CFR 102.3; and

(b) For offsets under 31 U.S.C. 3716, the Secretary makes an independent determination that the offset meets the standards under § 30.21(a)(2).

(Authority: 20 U.S.C. 1221e-3(a)(1) and 1226a-1, 31 U.S.C. 3716(b))

§ 30.30 What procedures apply when the Secretary requests another agency to offset a debt owed under a program or activity of the Department?

(a) The Secretary may request another Federal agency to offset a debt owed under a program or activity of the Department if the Secretary certifies in writing to the other Federal agency:
   (1) That the debtor owes a debt to the United States;
   (2) The amount of the debt; and
   (3) That the Secretary has complied with 4 CFR 102.3.

(b) Before providing the certification required under paragraph (a) of this section, the Secretary complies with the procedures in §§ 30.20–30.27.

(Authority: 20 U.S.C. 1221e-3(a)(1) and 1226a-1, 31 U.S.C. 3716(b))

§ 30.31 How does the Secretary apply funds recovered by offset if multiple debts are involved?

If the Secretary collects more than one debt of a debtor by administrative offset, the Secretary applies the recovered funds to satisfy those debts based on the Secretary's determination of the best interests of the United States, determined by the facts and circumstances of the particular case.

(Authority: 20 U.S.C. 1221e-3(a)(1) and 1226a-1, 31 U.S.C. 3716(b))

* * *

B.5.2 Tax Refund Offset

34 C.F.R. sec.

* * *

30.33. What procedures does the Secretary follow for IRS tax refund offsets?

* * *

SOURCE: 51 Fed. Reg. 24099 (July 1, 1986); 53 Fed. Reg. 33425 (Aug. 30, 1988), unless otherwise noted.

* * *

§ 30.33 What procedures does the Secretary follow for IRS tax refund offsets?

(a) If a named person owes a debt under a program or activity of the Department, the Secretary may refer the debt for offset to the Secretary of the Treasury after complying with the procedures in §§ 30.20–30.28, as modified by this section.

(b) Notwithstanding § 30.22(b), the notice sent to a debtor under § 30.22 informs the debtor that:
  (1) The debt is past due;
  (2) The Secretary intends to refer the debt for offset to the Secretary of Treasury;
  (3) The debtor has an opportunity to:
    (i) Inspect and copy Department records regarding the existence, amount, enforceability, or past-due status of the debt;
    (ii) Obtain a review within the Department of the existence, amount, enforceability, or past-due status of the debt;
    (iii) Enter into a written agreement with the Secretary to repay the debt; and
  (4) The debtor must take an action set forth under paragraph (b)(3) by a date specified in the notice.

(c) Notwithstanding § 30.23(a), if a debtor wants to inspect and copy Department records regarding the existence, amount, enforceability, or past-due status of the debt, the debtor must:
  (1) File a written request to inspect and copy the records within 20 days after the date of the notice provided under § 30.22; and
  (2) File the request at the address specified in that notice.

(d) Notwithstanding the time frame under § 30.24(a), if a debtor wants a review under that paragraph, the debtor must file a request for review at the address specified in the notice by the later of:
  (1) Sixty-five days after the date of the notice provided under § 30.22;
  (2) If the debtor has requested an opportunity to inspect and copy records within the time period specified in paragraph (c) of this section, 15 days after the date on which the Secretary makes available to the debtor the relevant, requested records; or
  (3) If the debtor has requested a review within the appropriate time frame under paragraph (d) (1) or (2) of this section and the Secretary has provided an initial review by a guarantee agency, seven days after the date of the initial determination by the guarantee agency.

(e) Notwithstanding the time frames under § 30.24(d), a debtor shall file the documents specified under that paragraph with the request for review.

(f) Notwithstanding the time frame under § 30.27(a), a debtor must agree to repay the debt under terms acceptable to the Secretary and make the first payment due under the agreement by the latest of:
  (1) The seventh day after the date of decision of the Secretary if the debtor requested a review under § 30.24;
  (2) The sixty-fifth day after the date of the notice under § 30.22(b), if the debtor did not request a review under § 30.24, or an opportunity to inspect and copy records of the Department under § 30.23; or
  (3) The fifteenth day after the date on which the Secretary made available relevant records regarding the debt, if the debtor filed a timely request under § 30.23(a).

(Authority: 20 U.S.C. 1221e-3(a)(1) and 1226a-1, 31 U.S.C. 3720A)

* * *

B.5.3 Administrative Wage Garnishment

34 C.F.R. sec.

34.1 Purpose of this part.
34.2 Scope of this part.
34.3 Definitions.
34.4 Notice of proposed garnishment.
34.5 Contents of a notice of proposed garnishment.
34.6 Rights in connection with garnishment.
34.7 Consideration of objection to the rate or amount of withholding.
34.8 Providing a hearing.
34.9 Conditions for an oral hearing.
34.10 Conditions for a paper hearing.
34.11 Timely request for a hearing.
34.12 Request for reconsideration.
34.13 Conduct of a hearing.
34.14 Burden of proof.
34.15 Consequences of failure to appear for an oral hearing.
34.16 Issuance of the hearing decision.
34.17 Content of decision.
34.18 Issuance of the wage garnishment order.
34.19 Amounts to be withheld under a garnishment order.
34.20 Amount to be withheld under multiple garnishment orders.
34.21 Employer certification.
34.22 Employer responsibilities.
34.23 Exclusions from garnishment.
34.24 Claim of financial hardship by debtor subject to garnishment.
34.25 Determination of financial hardship.
34.26 Ending garnishment.
34.27 Actions by employer prohibited by law.
34.28 Refunds of amounts collected in error.
34.29 Enforcement action against employer for noncompliance with garnishment order.
34.30 Application of payments and accrual of interest.

Source: 68FR 8142, Feb. 19, 2003, unless otherwise noted.

Authority: 31 U.S.C. 3720D, unless otherwise noted.

§ 34.1 Purpose of this part.

This part establishes procedures the Department of Education uses to collect money from a debtor's disposable pay by means of administrative wage garnishment to satisfy delinquent debt owed to the United States.

(Authority: 31 U.S.C. 3720D)

§ 34.2 Scope of this part.

(a) This part applies to collection of any financial obligation owed to the United States that arises under a program we administer.

(b) This part applies notwithstanding any provision of State law.

(c) We may compromise or suspend collection by garnishment of a debt in accordance with applicable law.

(d) We may use other debt collection remedies separately or in conjunction with administrative wage garnishment to collect a debt.

(e) To collect by offset from the salary of a Federal employee, we use the procedures in 34 CFR part 31, not those in this part.

(Authority: 31 U.S.C. 3720D)

§ 34.3 Definitions.

As used in this part, the following definitions apply:

Administrative debt means a debt that does not arise from an individual's obligation to repay a loan or an overpayment of a grant received under a student financial assistance program authorized under Title IV of the Higher Education Act.

Business day means a day Monday through Friday, unless that day is a Federal holiday.

Certificate of service means a certificate signed by an authorized official of the U.S. Department of Education (the Department) that indicates the nature of the document to which it pertains, the date we mail the document, and to whom we are sending the document.

Day means calendar day. For purposes of computation, the last day of a period will be included unless that day is a Saturday, a Sunday, or a Federal legal holiday; in that case, the last day of the period is the next business day after the end of the period.

Debt or *claim* means any amount of money, funds, or property that an appropriate official of the Department has determined an individual owes to the United States under a program we administer.

Debtor means an individual who owes a delinquent nontax debt to the United States under a program we administer.

Disposable pay. This term—
(a)(1) Means that part of a debtor's compensation for personal services, whether or not denominated as wages, from an employer that remains after the deduction of health insurance premiums and any amounts required by law to be withheld.
(2) For purposes of this part, "amounts required by law to be withheld include amounts for deductions such as social security taxes and withholding taxes, but do not include any amount withheld" under a court order; and
(b) Includes, but is not limited to, salary, bonuses, commissions, or vacation pay.

Employer. This term—
(a) Means a person or entity that employs the services of another and that pays the latter's wages or salary;
(b) Includes, but is not limited to, State and local governments; and
(c) Does not include an agency of the Federal Government.

Financial hardship means an inability to meet basic living expenses for goods and services necessary for the survival of the debtor and his or her spouse and dependents.

Garnishment means the process of withholding amounts from an employee's disposable pay and paying those amounts to a creditor in satisfaction of a withholding order.

We means the United States Department of Education.

Withholding order.
(a) This term means any order for withholding or garnishment of pay issued by this Department, another Federal agency, a State or private non-profit guaranty agency, or a judicial or administrative body.
(b) For purposes of this part, the terms "wage garnishment order" and "garnishment order" have the same meaning as "withholding order."

You means the debtor.

(Authority: 31 U.S.C. 3720D)

§ 34.4 Notice of proposed garnishment.

(a) We may start proceedings to garnish your wages whenever we determine that you are delinquent in paying a debt owed to the United States under a program we administer.

(b) We start garnishment proceedings by sending you a written notice of the proposed garnishment.

(c) At least 30 days before we start garnishment proceedings, we mail the notice by first class mail to your last known address.

(d)(1) We keep a copy of a certificate of service indicating the date of mailing of the notice.
(2) We may retain this certificate of service in electronic form.

(Authority: 31 U.S.C. 3720D)

§ 34.5 Contents of a notice of proposed garnishment.

In a notice of proposed garnishment, we inform you of—

(a) The nature and amount of the debt;

(b) Our intention to collect the debt through deductions from pay until the debt and all accumulated interest, penalties, and collection costs are paid in full; and

(c) An explanation of your rights, including those in § 34.6, and the time frame within which you may exercise your rights.

(Authority: 31 U.S.C. 3720D)

§ 34.6 Rights in connection with garnishment.

Before starting garnishment, we provide you the opportunity—

(a) To inspect and copy our records related to the debt;

(b) To enter into a written repayment agreement with us to repay the debt under terms we consider acceptable;

For a hearing in accordance with § 34.8 concerning—
(1) The existence, amount, or current enforceability of the debt;
(2) The rate at which the garnishment order will require your employer to withhold pay; and
(3) Whether you have been continuously employed less than 12 months after you were involuntarily separated from employment.

(Authority: 31 U.S.C. 3720D)

§ 34.7 Consideration of objection to the rate or amount of withholding.

(a) We consider objections to the rate or amount of withholding only if the objection rests on a claim that withholding at the proposed rate or amount would cause financial hardship to you and your dependents.

(b) We do not provide a hearing on an objection to the rate or amount of withholding if the rate or amount we propose to be withheld does not exceed the rate or amount agreed to under a repayment agreement reached within the preceding six months after a previous notice of proposed garnishment.

(c) We do not consider an objection to the rate or amount of withholding based on a claim that by virtue of 15 U.S.C. 1673, no amount of wages are available for withholding by the employer.

(Authority: 31 U.S.C. 3720D)

§ 34.8 Providing a hearing.

(a) We provide a hearing if you submit a written request for a hearing concerning the existence, amount, or enforceability of the debt or the rate of wage withholding.

(b) At our option the hearing may be an oral hearing under § 34.9 or a paper hearing under § 34.10.

(Authority: 31 U.S.C. 3720D)

§ 34.9 Conditions for an oral hearing.

(a) We provide an oral hearing if you—
(1) Request an oral hearing; and
(2) Show in the request a good reason to believe that we cannot resolve the issues in dispute by review of the documentary evidence, by demonstrating that the validity of the claim turns on the credibility or veracity of witness testimony.

(b) If we determine that an oral hearing is appropriate, we notify you how to receive the oral hearing.

(c)(1) At your option, an oral hearing may be conducted either in person or by telephone conference.
(2) We provide an in-person oral hearing with regard to administrative debts only in Washington D.C.
(3) We provide an in-person oral hearing with regard to debts based on student loan or grant obligations only at our regional service centers in Atlanta, Chicago, or San Francisco.
(4) You must bear all travel expenses you incur in connection with an in person hearing.
(5) We bear the cost of any telephone calls we place in order to conduct an oral hearing by telephone.

(d)(1) To arrange the time and location of the oral hearing, we ordinarily attempt to contact you first by telephone call to the number you provided to us.
(2) If we are unable to contact you by telephone, we leave a message directing you to contact us within 5 business days to arrange the time and place of the hearing.

(3) If we can neither contact you directly nor leave a message with you by telephone—
(i) We notify you in writing to contact us to arrange the time and place of the hearing; or
(ii) We select a time and place for the hearing, and notify you in writing of the time and place set for the hearing.

(e) We consider you to have withdrawn the request for an oral hearing if—
(1) Within 15 days of the date of a written notice to contact us, we receive no response to that notice; or
(2) Within five business days of the date of a telephone message to contact us, we receive no response to that message.

(Authority: 31 U.S.C. 3720D)

§ 34.10 Conditions for a paper hearing.

We provide a paper hearing—

(a) If you request a paper hearing;

(b) If you requested an oral hearing, but we determine under § 34.9(e) that you have withdrawn that request;

(c) If you fail to appear for a scheduled oral hearing, as provided in § 34.15; or

(d) If we deny a request for an oral hearing because we conclude that, by a review of the written record, we can resolve the issues raised by your objections.

(Authority: 31 U.S.C. 3720D)

§ 34.11 Timely request for a hearing.

(a) A hearing request is timely if—
(1) You mail the request to the office designated in the garnishment notice and the request is postmarked not later than the 30th day following the date of the notice; or
(2) The designated office receives the request not later than the 30th day following the date of the garnishment notice.

(b) If we receive a timely written request from you for a hearing, we will not issue a garnishment order before we—
(1) Provide the requested hearing; and
(2) Issue a written decision on the objections you raised.

(c) If your written request for a hearing is not timely—
(1) We provide you a hearing; and
(2) We do not delay issuance of a garnishment order unless—
(i) We determine from credible representations in the request that the delay in filing the request for hearing was caused by factors over which you had no control; or
(ii) We have other good reason to delay issuing a garnishment order.

(d) If we do not complete a hearing within 60 days of an untimely request, we suspend any garnishment order until we have issued a decision.

(Authority: 31 U.S.C. 3720D)

§ 34.12 Request for reconsideration.

(a) If you have received a decision on an objection to garnishment you may file a request for reconsideration of that decision.

(b) We do not suspend garnishment merely because you have filed a request for reconsideration.

(c) We consider your request for reconsideration if we determine that—
(1) You base your request on grounds of financial hardship, and your financial circumstances, as shown by evidence submitted with the request, have materially changed since we issued the decision so that we should reduce the amount to be garnished under the order; or
(2)(i) You submitted with the request evidence that you did not previously submit; and
(ii) This evidence demonstrates that we should reconsider your objection to the existence, amount, or enforceability of the debt.

(d)(1) If we agree to reconsider the decision, we notify you.
(2)(i) We may reconsider based on the request and supporting evidence you have presented with the request; or
(ii) We may offer you an opportunity for a hearing to present evidence.

(Authority: 31 U.S.C. 3720D)

§ 34.13 Conduct of a hearing.

(a)(1) A hearing official conducts any hearing under this part.
(2) The hearing official may be any qualified employee of the Department whom the Department designates to conduct the hearing.

(b)(1) The hearing official conducts any hearing as an informal proceeding.
(2) A witness in an oral hearing must testify under oath or affirmation.
(3) The hearing official maintains a summary record of any hearing.

(c) Before the hearing official considers evidence we obtain that was not included in the debt records available for inspection when we sent notice of proposed garnishment, we notify you that additional evidence has become available, may be considered by the hearing official, and is available for inspection or copying.

(d) The hearing official considers any objection you raise and evidence you submit—
(1) In or with the request for a hearing;
(2) During an oral hearing;
(3) By the date that we consider, under § 34.9(e), that a request for an oral hearing has been withdrawn; or
(4) Within a period we set, ordinarily not to exceed seven business days, after—
(i) We provide you access to our records regarding the debt, if you requested access to records within 20 days after the date of the notice under § 34.4;
(ii) We notify you that we have obtained and intend to consider additional evidence;
(iii) You request an extension of time in order to submit specific relevant evidence that you identify to us in the request; or
(iv) We notify you that we deny your request for an oral hearing.

(Authority: 31 U.S.C. 3720D)

§ 34.14 Burden of proof.

(a)(1) We have the burden of proving the existence and amount of a debt.
(2) We meet this burden by including in the record and making available to the debtor on request records that show that—
(i) The debt exists in the amount stated in the garnishment notice; and
(ii) The debt is currently delinquent.

(b) If you dispute the existence or amount of the debt, you must prove by a preponderance of the credible evidence that—
(1) No debt exists;
(2) The amount we claim to be owed on the debt is incorrect, or
(3) You are not delinquent with respect to the debt.

(c)(1) If you object that the proposed garnishment rate would cause financial hardship, you bear the burden of proving by a preponderance of the credible evidence that withholding the amount of wages proposed in the notice would leave you unable to meet the basic living expenses of you and your dependents.
(2) The standards for proving financial hardship are those in § 34.24.

(d)(1) If you object on the ground that applicable law bars us from collecting the debt by garnishment at this time, you bear the burden of proving the facts that would establish that claim.
(2) Examples of applicable law that may prevent collection by garnishment include the automatic stay in bankruptcy (11 U.S.C.

362(a)), and the preclusion of garnishment action against a debtor who was involuntarily separated from employment and has been reemployed for less than a continuous period of 12 months (31 U.S.C. 3720D(b)(6)).

(e) The fact that applicable law may limit the amount that an employer may withhold from your pay to less than the amount or rate we state in the garnishment order does not bar us from issuing the order.

(Authority: 31 U.S.C. 3720D)

§ 34.15 Consequences of failure to appear for an oral hearing.

(a) If you do not appear for an in-person hearing you requested, or you do not answer a telephone call convening a telephone hearing, at the time set for the hearing, we consider you to have withdrawn your request for an oral hearing.

(b) If you do not appear for an oral hearing but you demonstrate that there was good cause for not appearing, we may reschedule the oral hearing.

(c) If you do not appear for an oral hearing you requested and we do not reschedule the hearing, we provide a paper hearing to review your objections, based on the evidence in your file and any evidence you have already provided.

(Authority: 31 U.S.C. 3720D)

§ 34.16 Issuance of the hearing decision.

(a) *Date of decision.* The hearing official issues a written opinion stating his or her decision, as soon as practicable, but not later than 60 days after the date on which we received the request for hearing.

(b) If we do not provide you with a hearing and render a decision within 60 days after we receive your request for a hearing—
  (1) We do not issue a garnishment order until the hearing is held and a decision rendered; or
  (2) If we have already issued a garnishment order to your employer, we suspend the garnishment order beginning on the 61st day after we receive the hearing request until we provide a hearing and issue a decision.

(Authority: 31 U.S.C. 3720D)

§ 34.17 Content of decision.

(a) The written decision is based on the evidence contained in the hearing record. The decision includes—
  (1) A description of the evidence considered by the hearing official;
  (2) The hearing official's findings, analysis, and conclusions regarding objections raised to the existence or amount of the debt;
  (3) The rate of wage withholding under the order, if you objected that withholding the amount proposed in the garnishment notice would cause an extreme financial hardship; and
  (4) An explanation of your rights under this part for reconsideration of the decision.

(b) The hearing official's decision is the final action of the Secretary for the purposes of judicial review under the Administrative Procedure Act (5 U.S.C. 701 *et seq.*).

(Authority: 31 U.S.C. 3720D)

§ 34.18 Issuance of the wage garnishment order.

(a)(1) If you fail to make a timely request for a hearing, we issue a garnishment order to your employer within 30 days after the deadline for timely requesting a hearing.
  (2) If you make a timely request for a hearing, we issue a withholding order within 30 days after the hearing official issues a decision to proceed with garnishment.

(b)(1) The garnishment order we issue to your employer is signed by an official of the Department designated by the Secretary.
  (2) The designated official's signature may be a computer-generated facsimile.

(c)(1) The garnishment order contains only the information we consider necessary for your employer to comply with the order and for us to ensure proper credit for payments received from your employer.
  (2) The order includes your name, address, and social security number, as well as instructions for withholding and information as to where your employer must send the payments.

(d)(1) We keep a copy of a certificate of service indicating the date of mailing of the order.
  (2) We may create and maintain the certificate of service as an electronic record.

(Authority: 31 U.S.C. 3720D)

§ 34.19 Amounts to be withheld under a garnishment order.

(a)(1) After an employer receives a garnishment order we issue, the employer must deduct from all disposable pay of the debtor during each pay period the amount directed in the garnishment order unless this section or § 34.20 requires a smaller amount to be withheld.
  (2) The amount specified in the garnishment order does not apply if other law, including this section, requires the employer to withhold a smaller amount.

(b) The employer must comply with our garnishment order by withholding the lesser of—
  (1) The amount directed in the garnishment order; or—
  (2) The amount specified in 15 U.S.C. 1673(a) (2) (Restriction on Garnishment); that is, the amount by which a debtor's disposable pay exceeds an amount equal to 30 times the minimum wage. (See 29 CFR 870.10.)

(Authority: 31 U.S.C. 3720D)

§ 34.20 Amount to be withheld under multiple garnishment orders.

If a debtor's pay is subject to several garnishment orders, the employer must comply with our garnishment order as follows:

(a) Unless other Federal law requires a different priority, the employer must pay us the amount calculated under § 34.19(b) before the employer complies with any later garnishment orders, except a family support withholding order.

(b) If an employer is withholding from a debtor's pay based on a garnishment order served on the employer before our order, or if a withholding order for family support is served on an employer at any time, the employer must comply with our garnishment order by withholding an amount that is the smaller of—
  (1) The amount calculated under § 34.19(b); or
  (2) An amount equal to 25 percent of the debtor's disposable pay less the amount or amounts withheld under the garnishment order or orders with priority over our order.

(c)(1) If a debtor owes more than one debt arising from a program we administer, we may issue multiple garnishment orders.
  (2) The total amount withheld from the debtor's pay for orders we issue under paragraph (c)(1) of this section does not exceed the amounts specified in the orders, the amount specified in § 34.19(b)(2), or 15 percent of the debtor's disposable pay, whichever is smallest.

(d) An employer may withhold and pay an amount greater than that amount in paragraphs (b) and (c) of this section if the debtor gives the employer written consent.

(Authority: 31 U.S.C. 3720D)

§ 34.21 Employer certification.

(a) Along with a garnishment order, we send to an employer a certification in a form prescribed by the Secretary of the Treasury.

(b) The employer must complete and return the certification to us within the time stated in the instructions for the form.

(c) The employer must include in the certification information about the debtor's employment status, payment frequency, and disposable pay available for withholding.

(Authority: 31 U.S.C. 3720D)

§ 34.22 Employer responsibilities.

(a)(1) Our garnishment order indicates a reasonable period of time within which an employer must start withholding under the order.
(2) The employer must promptly pay to the Department all amounts the employer withholds according to the order.

(b) The employer may follow its normal pay and disbursement cycles in complying with the garnishment order.

(c) The employer must withhold the appropriate amount from the debtor's wages for each pay period until the employer receives our notification to discontinue wage garnishment.

(d) The employer must disregard any assignment or allotment by an employee that would interfere with or prohibit the employer from complying with our garnishment order, unless that assignment or allotment was made for a family support judgment or order.

(Authority: 31 U.S.C. 3720D)

§ 34.23 Exclusions from garnishment.

(a) We do not garnish your wages if we have credible evidence that you—
(1) Were involuntarily separated from employment; and
(2) Have not yet been reemployed continuously for at least 12 months.

(b) You have the burden of informing us of the circumstances surrounding an involuntary separation from employment.

(Authority: 31 U.S.C. 3720D)

§ 34.24 Claim of financial hardship by debtor subject to garnishment.

(a) You may object to a proposed garnishment on the ground that withholding the amount or at the rate stated in the notice of garnishment would cause financial hardship to you and your dependents. (See § 34.7.)

(b) You may, at any time, object that the amount or the rate of withholding which our order specifies your employer must withhold causes financial hardship.

(c)(1) We consider an objection to an outstanding garnishment order and provide you an opportunity for a hearing on your objection only after the order has been outstanding for at least six months.
(2) We may provide a hearing in extraordinary circumstances earlier than six months if you show in your request for review that your financial circumstances have substantially changed after the notice of proposed garnishment because of an event such as injury, divorce, or catastrophic illness.

(d)(1) You bear the burden of proving a claim of financial hardship by a preponderance of the credible evidence.
(2) You must prove by credible documentation—
(i) The amount of the costs incurred by you, your spouse, and any dependents, for basic living expenses; and
(ii) The income available from any source to meet those expenses.

(e)(1) We consider your claim of financial hardship by comparing—
(i) The amounts that you prove are being incurred for basic living expenses; against
(ii) The amounts spent for basic living expenses by families of the same size and similar income to yours.
(2) We regard the standards published by the Internal Revenue Service under 26 U.S.C. 7122(c)(2) (the "National Standards") as establishing the average amounts spent for basic living expenses for families of the same size as, and with family incomes comparable to, your family.
(3) We accept as reasonable the amount that you prove you incur for a type of basic living expense to the extent that the amount does not exceed the amount spent for that expense by families of the same size and similar income according to the National Standards.
(4) If you claim for any basic living expense an amount that exceeds the amount in the National Standards, you must prove that the amount you claim is reasonable and necessary.

(Authority: 31 U.S.C. 3720D)

§ 34.25 Determination of financial hardship.

(a)(1) If we conclude that garnishment at the amount or rate proposed in a notice would cause you financial hardship, we reduce the amount of the proposed garnishment to an amount that we determine will allow you to meet proven basic living expenses.

(2) If a garnishment order is already in effect, we notify your employer of any change in the amount the employer must withhold or the rate of withholding under the order.

(b) If we determine that financial hardship would result from garnishment based on a finding by a hearing official or under a repayment agreement we reached with you, this determination is effective for a period not longer than six months after the date of the finding or agreement.

(c)(1) After the effective period referred to in paragraph (b) of this section, we may require you to submit current information regarding your family income and living expenses.
(2) If we conclude from a review of that evidence that we should increase the rate of withholding or payment, we—
(i) Notify you; and
(ii) Provide you with an opportunity to contest the determination and obtain a hearing on the objection under the procedures in § 34.24.

(Authority: 31 U.S.C. 3720D)

§ 34.26 Ending garnishment.

(a)(1) A garnishment order we issue is effective until we rescind the order.
(2) If an employer is unable to honor a garnishment order because the amount available for garnishment is insufficient to pay any portion of the amount stated in the order, the employer must—
(i) Notify us; and
(ii) Comply with the order when sufficient disposable pay is available.

(b) After we have fully recovered the amounts owed by the debtor, including interest, penalties, and collection costs, we send the debtor's employer notification to stop wage withholding.

(Authority: 31 U.S.C. 3720D)

§ 34.27 Actions by employer prohibited by law.

An employer may not discharge, refuse to employ, or take disciplinary action against a debtor due to the issuance of a garnishment order under this part.

(Authority: 31 U.S.C. 3720D)

§ 34.28 Refunds of amounts collected in error.

(a) If a hearing official determines under §§ 34.16 and 34.17 that a person does not owe the debt described in our notice or that an administrative wage garnishment under this part was barred by law at the time of the collection action, we promptly refund any amount collected by means of this garnishment.

(b) Unless required by Federal law or contract, we do not pay interest on a refund.

(Authority: 31 U.S.C. 3720D)

§ 34.29 Enforcement action against employer for noncompliance with garnishment order.

(a) If an employer fails to comply with § 34.22 to withhold an appropriate amount from wages owed and payable to an employee, we may sue the employer for that amount.

(b)(1) We do not file suit under paragraph (a) of this section before we terminate action to enforce the debt as a personal liability of the debtor.
(2) However, the provision of paragraph (b)(1) of this section may not apply if earlier filing of a suit is necessary to avoid expiration of any applicable statute of limitations.

(c)(1) For purposes of this section, termination of an action to enforce a debt occurs when we terminate collection action in accordance with the FCCS, other applicable standards, or paragraph (c)(2) of this section.
(2) We regard termination of the collection action to have occurred if we have not received for one year any payments to satisfy the debt, in whole or in part, from the particular debtor whose wages were subject to garnishment.

(Authority: 31 U.S.C. 3720D)

§ 34.30 Application of payments and accrual of interest.

We apply payments received through a garnishment in the following order—

(a) To costs incurred to collect the debt;

(b) To interest accrued on the debt at the rate established by—
(1) The terms of the obligation under which it arises; or
(2) Applicable law; and

(c) To outstanding principal of the debt.

(Authority: 31 U.S.C. 3720D)

B.5.4 Collection Costs and Penalties

34 C.F.R. sec.

* * *

30.60 What costs does the Secretary impose on delinquent debtors?
30.61 What penalties does the Secretary impose on delinquent debtors?

* * *

Source: 51 Fed. Reg. 24099 (July 1, 1986); 53 Fed. Reg. 33425 (Aug. 30, 1988), unless otherwise noted.

* * *

§ 30.60 What costs does the Secretary impose on delinquent debtors?

(a) The Secretary may charge a debtor for the costs associated with the collection of a particular debt. These costs include, but are not limited to—
(1) Salaries of employees performing Federal loan servicing and debt collection activities;
(2) Telephone and mailing costs;
(3) Costs for reporting debts to credit bureaus;
(4) Costs for purchase of credit bureau reports;
(5) Costs associated with computer operations and other costs associated with the maintenance of records;
(6) Bank charges;
(7) Collection agency costs;
(8) Court costs and attorney fees; and
(9) Costs charged by other Governmental agencies.

(b) Notwithstanding any provision of State law, if the Secretary uses a collection agency to collect a debt on a contingent fee basis, the Secretary charges the debtor, and collects through the agency, an amount sufficient to recover—
(1) The entire amount of the debt; and
(2) The amount that the Secretary is required to pay the agency for its collection services.

(c)(1) The amount recovered under paragraph (b) of this section is the entire amount of the debt, multiplied by the following fraction:
[Graphic Omitted]
(2) In paragraph (c)(1) of this section, cr equals the commission rate the Department pays to the collection agency.

(d) If the Secretary uses more than one collection agency to collect similar debts, the commission rate (cr) described in paragraph (c)(2) of this section is calculated as a weighted average of the commission rates charged by all collection agencies collecting similar debts, computed for each fiscal year based on the formula
[Graphic Omitted]
where—
(1) X_i equals the dollar amount of similar debts placed by the Department with an individual collection agency as of the end of the preceding fiscal year;
(2) Y_i equals the commission rate the Department pays to that collection agency for the collection of the similar debts;
(3) Z equals the dollar amount of similar debts placed by the Department with all collection agencies as of the end of the preceding fiscal year; and
(4) N equals the number of collection agencies with which the Secretary has placed similar debts as of the end of the preceding fiscal year.

(e) If a debtor has agreed under a repayment or settlement agreement with the Secretary to pay costs associated with the collection of a debt at a specified amount or rate, the Secretary collects those costs in accordance with the agreement.

(f) The Secretary does not impose collection costs against State or local governments under paragraphs (a) through (d) of this section.

(Authority: 20 U.S.C. 1221e-3(a)(1) and 1226a-1, 31 U.S.C. 3711(e), 3717(e)(1), 3718)

§ 30.61 What penalties does the Secretary impose on delinquent debtors?

(a) If a debtor does not make a payment on a debt, or portion of a debt, within 90 days after the date specified in the first demand for payment sent to the debtor, the Secretary imposes a penalty on the debtor.

(b)(1) The amount of the penalty imposed under paragraph (a) of this section is 6 percent per year of the amount of the delinquent debt.
(2) The penalty imposed under this section runs from the date specified in the first demand for payment to the date the debt (including the penalty) is paid.

(c) If a debtor has agreed under a repayment or settlement agreement with the Secretary to pay a penalty for failure to pay a debt when due, or has such an agreement under a grant or contract under which the debt arose, the Secretary collects the penalty in accordance with the agreement, grant, or contract.

(d) The Secretary does not impose a penalty against State or local governments under paragraphs (a) and (b) of this section.

(Authority: 20 U.S.C. 1221e-3(a)(1) and 1226a-1, 31 U.S.C. 3711(e))

* * *

B.5.5 Compromise of Debts

34 C.F.R. sec.

* * *

30.70. How does the Secretary exercise discretion to compromise a debt or to suspend or terminate collection of a debt?

* * *

SOURCE: 51 Fed. Reg. 24099 (July 1, 1986); 53 Fed. Reg. 33425 (Aug. 30, 1988); 53 Fed. Reg. 33426 (Aug. 30, 1988), unless otherwise noted.

* * *

§ 30.70 How does the Secretary exercise discretion to compromise a debt or to suspend or terminate collection of a debt?

(a) The Secretary uses the standards in the FCCS, 4 CFR part 103, to determine whether compromise of a debt is appropriate if—
 (1) The debt must be referred to the Department of Justice under this section; or
 (2) The amount of the debt is less than or equal to $20,000 and the Secretary does not follow the procedures in paragraph (e) of this section.

(b) The Secretary refers a debt to the Department of Justice to decide whether to compromise a debt if—
 (1) The debt was incurred under a program or activity subject to section 452(f) of the General Education Provisions Act and the initial determination of the debt was more than $50,000; or
 (2) The debt was incurred under a program or activity not subject to section 452(f) of the General Education Provisions Act and the amount of the debt is more than $20,000.

(c) The Secretary may compromise the debt under the procedures in paragraph (e) of this section if—
 (1) The debt was incurred under a program or activity subject to section 452(f) of the General Education Provisions Act; and
 (2) The initial determination of the debt was less than or equal to $50,000.

(d) The Secretary may compromise a debt without following the procedure in paragraph (e) of this section if the amount of the debt is less than or equal to $20,000.

(e) The Secretary may compromise the debt pursuant to paragraph (c) of this section if—
 (1) The Secretary determines that—
  (i) Collection of any or all of the debt would not be practical or in the public interest; and
  (ii) The practice that resulted in the debt has been corrected and will not recur;
 (2) At least 45 days before compromising the debt, the Secretary publishes a notice in the Federal Register stating—
  (i) The Secretary's intent to compromise the debt; and
  (ii) That interested persons may comment on the proposed compromise; and
 (3) The Secretary considers any comments received in response to the Federal Register notice before finally compromising the debt.

(f)(1) The Secretary uses the standards in the FCCS, 4 CFR part 104, to determine whether suspension or termination of collection action is appropriate.
 (2) The Secretary—
  (i) Refers the debt to the Department of Justice to decide whether to suspend or terminate collection action if the amount of the debt at the time of the referral is more than $20,000; or
  (ii) May decide to suspend or terminate collection action if the amount of the debt at the time of the Secretary's decision is less than or equal to $20,000.

(g) In determining the amount of a debt under paragraphs (a) through (f) of this section, the Secretary excludes interest, penalties, and administrative costs.

(h) Notwithstanding paragraphs (b) through (f) of this section, the Secretary may compromise a debt, or suspend or terminate collection of a debt, in any amount if the debt arises under the Guaranteed Student Loan Program authorized under title IV, part B, of the Higher Education Act of 1965, as amended, or the Perkins Loan Program authorized under title IV, part E, of the Higher Education Act of 1965, as amended.

(i) The Secretary refers a debt to the General Accounting Office (GAO) for review and approval before referring the debt to the Department of Justice for litigation if—
 (1) The debt arose from an audit exception taken by GAO to a payment made by the Department; and
 (2) The GAO has not granted an exception from the GAO referral requirement.

(j) Nothing in this section precludes—
 (1) A contracting officer from exercising his authority under applicable statutes, regulations, or common law to settle disputed claims relating to a contract; or
 (2) The Secretary from redetermining a claim.

(Authority: 20 U.S.C. 1082(a) (5) and (6), 1087hh, 1221e-3(a)(1), 1226a-1, and 1234a(f), 31 U.S.C. 3711(e))

[51 Fed. Reg. 24099 (July 1, 1986); 53 Fed. Reg. 33425 (Aug. 30, 1988); 53 Fed. Reg. 33426 (Aug. 30, 1988)]

* * *

B.5.6 Department of Treasury Debt Collection Regulations

31 C.F.R. sec.

* * *

285.4 Offset of Federal benefit payments to collect past-due legally enforceable nontax debt.

* * *

901.3 Collection by administrative offset.

* * *

Source: 65 Fed. Reg. 70395 (Nov. 22, 2000), unless otherwise noted.

* * *

§ 285.4 Offset of Federal benefit payments to collect past-due, legally enforceable nontax debt.

(a) *Scope.*
 (1) This section sets forth special rules applicable to the offset of Federal benefit payments payable to an individual under the Social Security Act (other than Supplemental Security Income (SSI) payments), part B of the Black Lung Benefits Act, or any law administered by the Railroad Retirement Board (other than payments that such Board determines to be tier 2 benefits) to collect delinquent nontax debt owed to the United States.
 (2) As used in this section, benefit payments "due to" an individual, "payable to" an individual, and/or benefit payments "received by" an individual, refer to those benefit payments expected to be paid to an individual before any amounts are offset to satisfy the payee's delinquent debt owed to the United States. Nothing in these phrases, similar phrases, or this section is intended to imply or confer any new or additional rights or benefits on an individual with respect to his or her entitlement to benefit payments. The Financial Management Service (FMS), the Social Security Administration, the Railroad Retirement Board, and other payment agencies are not liable for the amount offset from an individual's benefit payment on the basis that the underlying obligation, represented by the payment before the offset was taken, was not satisfied. See 31 U.S.C. 3716(c)(2)(A).

(b) *Definitions.* As used in this section:

Administrative offset or *offset* means withholding funds payable by the United States (including funds payable by the United States on behalf of a State government) to, or held by the United States for, a person to satisfy a debt.

Agency or *Federal agency* means a department, agency, court, court administrative office, or instrumentality in the executive, judicial, or legislative branch of the Federal Government, including government corporations.

Covered benefit payment means a Federal benefit payment payable to an individual under the Social Security Act (other than SSI payments), part B of the Black Lung Benefits Act, or any law administered by the Railroad Retirement Board (other than payments that such Board determines to be tier 2 benefits). The amount of the covered benefit payment payable to a debtor for purposes of this section will be the amount after reduction or deduction required under the laws authorizing the program. Reductions to recover benefit overpayments are excluded from the covered benefit payment when calculating amounts available for offset.

Creditor agency means a Federal agency owed a debt that seeks to collect that debt through administrative offset.

Debt or *claim* means an amount of money, funds, or property which has been determined by an agency official to be due the United States from any person, organization, or entity except another Federal agency. Debt or claim does not include a debt or claim arising under the Internal Revenue Code of 1986 or the tariff laws of the United States.

Debtor means a person who owes a debt. The term "person" includes any individual, organization or entity, except another Federal agency.

Disbursing official means an official who has authority to disburse public money pursuant to 31 U.S.C. 3321 or another law, including an official of the Department of the Treasury, the Department of Defense, the United States Postal Service, or any other government corporation, or any official of the United States designated by the Secretary of the Treasury to disburse public money.

FMS means the Financial Management Service, a bureau of the Department of the Treasury.

Monthly covered benefit payment means a covered benefit payment payable to a payee on a recurring basis at monthly intervals that is not expressly limited in duration, at the time the first payment is made, to a period of less than 12 months.

Payee means a person who is due a payment from a disbursing official. For purposes of this section, a "payee" is a person who is entitled to the benefit of all or part of a payment from a disbursing official.

Taxpayer identifying number means the identifying number described under section 6109 of the Internal Revenue Code of 1986 (26 U.S.C. 6109). For an individual, the taxpayer identifying number generally is the individual's social security number.

(c) *Administrative offset, generally.* Disbursing officials shall offset payments to satisfy, in whole or in part, debts owed by the payee. Disbursing officials shall compare payment records with records of debts submitted to FMS for collection by administrative offset. A match will occur when the taxpayer identifying number and name of the payee (as defined in paragraph (b) of this section) on a payment record are the same as the taxpayer identifying number and name of the debtor on a debt record. When a match occurs and all other requirements for offset have been met, the disbursing official shall offset the payment to satisfy, in whole or in part, the debt. Any amounts not offset shall be paid to the payee. Covered benefit payments, i.e., payments made to individuals under the Social Security Act (other than Supplemental Security Income (SSI) payments), part B of the Black Lung Benefits Act, or any law administered by the Railroad Retirement Board (RRB) (other than tier 2 benefit payments) are among the types of payments which may be offset to collect debts owed to the United States. Offset of covered benefit payments are subject to the limitations contained in this section. Offsets of covered benefit payments will occur only if the name and taxpayer identifying number of the person who is entitled to the benefit of all or a part of the payment matches the name and taxpayer identifying number of the debtor.

(d) *Submission of debts to FMS for collection by administrative offset.* Creditor agencies must notify FMS of all past-due, legally enforceable debt delinquent for more than 180 days for purposes of collection by administrative offset. Creditor agencies may notify FMS of all debt delinquent for less than 180 days for purposes of collection by administrative offset. Prior to such notification, creditor agencies must certify to FMS that the debt is past-due, legally enforceable, and that the creditor agency has provided the debtor with notice and an opportunity for a review in accordance with the provisions of 31 U.S.C. 3716(a) and other applicable law.

(e) *Offset amount.*
(1) The amount offset from a monthly covered benefit payment shall be the lesser of:
(i) The amount of the debt, including any interest, penalties and administrative costs;
(ii) An amount equal to 15% of the monthly covered benefit payment; or
(iii) The amount, if any, by which the monthly covered benefit payment exceeds $750.
(2) A debtor shall not receive a refund of any amounts offset if the debtor's monthly covered benefit payments are reduced, suspended, terminated, or otherwise not received for a period of 12 months.
(3) *Examples.*
(i) A debtor receives monthly Social Security benefits of $850. The amount offset is the lesser of $127.50 (15% of $850) or $100 (the amount by which $850 exceeds $750). In this example, the amount offset is $100 (assuming the debt is $100 or more).
(ii) A debtor receives monthly Social Security benefits of $1250. The amount offset is the lesser of $187.50 (15% of $1250) or $500 (the amount by which $1250 exceeds $750). In this example, the amount offset is $187.50 (assuming the debt is $187.50 or more).
(iii) A debtor receives monthly Social Security payments of $650. No amount will be offset because $650 is less than $750.

(f) *Notification of offset.*
(1) Before offsetting a covered benefit payment, the disbursing official will notify the payee in writing of the date offset will commence. The notice shall inform the payee of the type of payment that will be offset; the identity of the creditor agency which requested the offset; and a contact point within the creditor agency that will handle concerns regarding the offset.
(2) The disbursing official conducting the offset will notify the payee in writing of the occurrence of the offset to satisfy, in whole or in part, a delinquent debt owed to the United States. The notice shall inform the payee of the type and amount of the payment that was offset; the identity of the creditor agency which requested the offset; and a contact point within the creditor agency that will handle concerns regarding the offset.
(3) Non-receipt by the debtor of the notices described in paragraphs (f)(1) and (f)(2) of this section shall not impair the legality of the administrative offset.

(g) *Fees.* A fee which FMS has determined to be sufficient to cover the full cost of the offset procedure, shall be deducted from each offset amount. Creditor agencies may add this fee to the debt if not otherwise prohibited by law.

(h) *Disposition of amounts collected.* The disbursing official conducting the offset will transmit amounts collected for debts, less fees charged under paragraph (g) of this section, to the appropriate creditor agency. If an erroneous offset payment is made to a creditor agency, the disbursing official will notify the creditor agency that an erroneous offset payment has been made. The disbursing official may deduct the amount of the erroneous offset payment from future amounts payable to the creditor agency. Alternatively, upon the disbursing official's request, the creditor agency shall return promptly to the disbursing official or the affected payee an amount equal to the amount of the erroneous payment. The disbursing official and the creditor agency shall adjust the debtor records appropriately.

[63 Fed. Reg. 44988 (Aug. 21, 1998); 63 Fed. Reg. 71204 (Dec. 23, 1998)]

* * *

§ 901.3 Collection by administrative offset.

(a) *Scope.*

(1) The term "administrative offset" has the meaning provided in 31 U.S.C. 3701(a)(1).

(2) This section does not apply to:

(i) Debts arising under the Social Security Act, except as provided in 42 U.S.C. 404;

(ii) Payments made under the Social Security Act, except as provided for in 31 U.S.C. 3716(c) (*see* 31 CFR 285.4, Federal Benefit Offset);

(iii) Debts arising under, or payments made under, the Internal Revenue Code (*see* 31 CFR 285.2, Tax Refund Offset) or the tariff laws of the United States;

(iv) Offsets against Federal salaries to the extent these standards are inconsistent with regulations published to implement such offsets under 5 U.S.C. 5514 and 31 U.S.C. 3716 (*see* 5 CFR part 550, subpart K, and 31 CFR 285.7, Federal Salary Offset);

(v) Offsets under 31 U.S.C. 3728 against a judgment obtained by a debtor against the United States;

(vi) Offsets or recoupments under common law, State law, or Federal statutes specifically prohibiting offsets or recoupments of particular types of debts; or

(vii) Offsets in the course of judicial proceedings, including bankruptcy.

(3) Unless otherwise provided for by contract or law, debts or payments that are not subject to administrative offset under 31 U.S.C. 3716 may be collected by administrative offset under the common law or other applicable statutory authority.

(4) Unless otherwise provided by law, administrative offset of payments under the authority of 31 U.S.C. 3716 to collect a debt may not be conducted more than 10 years after the Government's right to collect the debt first accrued, unless facts material to the Government's right to collect the debt were not known and could not reasonably have been known by the official or officials of the Government who were charged with the responsibility to discover and collect such debts. This limitation does not apply to debts reduced to a judgment.

(5) In bankruptcy cases, agencies should seek legal advice from their agency counsel concerning the impact of the Bankruptcy Code, particularly 11 U.S.C. 106, 362, and 553, on pending or contemplated collections by offset.

(b) *Mandatory centralized administrative offset.*

(1) Creditor agencies are required to refer past due, legally enforceable nontax debts which are over 180 days delinquent to the Secretary for collection by centralized administrative offset. Debts which are less than 180 days delinquent also may be referred to the Secretary for this purpose. *See* § 901.3(b)(5) for debt certification requirements.

(2) The names and taxpayer identifying numbers (TINs) of debtors who owe debts referred to the Secretary as described in paragraph (b)(1) of this section shall be compared to the names and TINs on payments to be made by Federal disbursing officials. Federal disbursing officials include disbursing officials of Treasury, the Department of Defense, the United States Postal Service, other Government corporations, and disbursing officials of the United States designated by the Secretary. When the name and TIN of a debtor match the name and TIN of a payee and all other requirements for offset have been met, the payment will be offset to satisfy the debt.

(3) Federal disbursing officials will notify the debtor/payee in writing that an offset has occurred to satisfy, in part or in full, a past due, legally enforceable delinquent debt. The notice shall include a description of the type and amount of the payment from which the offset was taken, the amount of offset that was taken, the identity of the creditor agency requesting the offset, and a contact point within the creditor agency who will respond to questions regarding the offset.

(4)(i) Before referring a delinquent debt to the Secretary for administrative offset, agencies must have prescribed administrative offset regulations consistent with this section or have adopted this section without change by cross-reference.

(ii) Such regulations shall provide that offsets may be initiated only after the debtor:

(A) Has been sent written notice of the type and amount of the debt, the intention of the agency to use administrative offset to collect the debt, and an explanation of the debtor's rights under 31 U.S.C. 3716; and

(B) The debtor has been given:

(1) The opportunity to inspect and copy agency records related to the debt;

(2) The opportunity for a review within the agency of the determination of indebtedness; and

(3) The opportunity to make a written agreement to repay the debt.

(iii) Agency regulations may provide for the omission of the procedures set forth in paragraph (a)(4)(ii) of this section when:

(A) The offset is in the nature of a recoupment;

(B) The debt arises under a contract as set forth in *Cecile Industries, Inc. v. Cheney*, 995 F.2d 1052 (Fed. Cir. 1993) (notice and other procedural protections set forth in 31 U.S.C. 3716(a) do not supplant or restrict established procedures for contractual offsets accommodated by the Contracts Disputes Act); or

(C) In the case of non-centralized administrative offsets conducted under paragraph (c) of this section, the agency first learns of the existence of the amount owed by the debtor when there is insufficient time before payment would be made to the debtor/payee to allow for prior notice and an opportunity for review. When prior notice and an opportunity for review are omitted, the agency shall give the debtor such notice and an opportunity for review as soon as practicable and shall promptly refund any money ultimately found not to have been owed to the Government.

(iv) When an agency previously has given a debtor any of the required notice and review opportunities with respect to a particular debt (*see, e.g.*, § 901.2), the agency need not duplicate such notice and review opportunities before administrative offset may be initiated.

(5) Agencies referring delinquent debts to the Secretary must certify, in a form acceptable to the Secretary, that:

(i) The debt(s) is (are) past due and legally enforceable; and

(ii) The agency has complied with all due process requirements under 31 U.S.C. 3716(a) and the agency's regulations.

(6) Payments that are prohibited by law from being offset are exempt from centralized administrative offset. The Secretary shall exempt payments under means-tested programs from centralized administrative offset when requested in writing by the head of the payment certifying or authorizing agency. Also, the Secretary may exempt other classes of payments from centralized offset upon the written request of the head of the payment certifying or authorizing agency.

(7) Benefit payments made under the Social Security Act (42 U.S.C. 301 *et seq.*), part B of the Black Lung Benefits Act (30 U.S.C. 921 *et seq.*), and any law administered by the Railroad Retirement Board (other than tier 2 benefits), may be offset only in accordance with Treasury regulations, issued in consultation with the Social Security Administration, the Railroad Retirement Board, and the Office of Management and Budget. See 31 CFR 285.4.

(8) In accordance with 31 U.S.C. 3716(f), the Secretary may waive the provisions of the Computer Matching and Privacy Protection Act of 1988 concerning matching agreements and post-match notification and verification (5 U.S.C. 552a(*o*) and (p)) for centralized administrative offset upon receipt of a certification from a creditor agency that the due process requirements enumerated in 31 U.S.C. 3716(a) have been met. The certification of a debt in accordance with paragraph (b)(5) of this section will satisfy this requirement. If such a waiver is granted, only the Data Integrity Board of the Department of the Treasury is required to oversee any matching activities, in accordance with 31 U.S.C. 3716(g).

This waiver authority does not apply to offsets conducted under paragraphs (c) and (d) of this section.

(c) *Non-centralized administrative offset.*

(1) Generally, non-centralized administrative offsets are ad hoc case-by-case offsets that an agency conducts, at the agency's discretion, internally or in cooperation with the agency certifying or authorizing payments to the debtor. Unless otherwise prohibited by law, when centralized administrative offset is not available or appropriate, past due, legally enforceable nontax delinquent debts may be collected through non-centralized administrative offset. In these cases, a creditor agency may make a request directly to a payment authorizing agency to offset a payment due a debtor to collect a delinquent debt. For example, it may be appropriate for a creditor agency to request that the Office of Personnel Management (OPM) offset a Federal employee's lump sum payment upon leaving Government service to satisfy an unpaid advance.

(2) Before requesting a payment authorizing agency to conduct a non-centralized administrative offset, agencies must adopt regulations providing that such offsets may occur only after:

(i) The debtor has been provided due process as set forth in paragraph (b)(4) of this section; and

(ii) The payment authorizing agency has received written certification from the creditor agency that the debtor owes the past due, legally enforceable delinquent debt in the amount stated, and that the creditor agency has fully complied with its regulations concerning administrative offset.

(3) Payment authorizing agencies shall comply with offset requests by creditor agencies to collect debts owed to the United States, unless the offset would not be in the best interests of the United States with respect to the program of the payment authorizing agency, or would otherwise be contrary to law. Appropriate use should be made of the cooperative efforts of other agencies in effecting collection by administrative offset.

(4) When collecting multiple debts by non-centralized administrative offset, agencies should apply the recovered amounts to those debts in accordance with the best interests of the United States, as determined by the facts and circumstances of the particular case, particularly the applicable statute of limitations.

(d) *Requests to OPM to offset a debtor's anticipated or future benefit payments under the Civil Service Retirement and Disability Fund.* Upon providing OPM written certification that a debtor has been afforded the procedures provided in paragraph (b)(4) of this section, creditor agencies may request OPM to offset a debtor's anticipated or future benefit payments under the Civil Service Retirement and Disability Fund (Fund) in accordance with regulations codified at 5 CFR 831.1801–831.1808. Upon receipt of such a request, OPM will identify and "flag" a debtor's account in anticipation of the time when the debtor requests, or becomes eligible to receive, payments from the Fund. This will satisfy any requirement that offset be initiated prior to the expiration of the time limitations referenced in paragraph (a)(4) of this section.

(e) *Review requirements.*

(1) For purposes of this section, whenever an agency is required to afford a debtor a review within the agency, the agency shall provide the debtor with a reasonable opportunity for an oral hearing when the debtor requests reconsideration of the debt and the agency determines that the question of the indebtedness cannot be resolved by review of the documentary evidence, for example, when the validity of the debt turns on an issue of credibility or veracity.

(2) Unless otherwise required by law, an oral hearing under this section is not required to be a formal evidentiary hearing, although the agency should carefully document all significant matters discussed at the hearing.

(3) This section does not require an oral hearing with respect to debt collection systems in which a determination of indebtedness rarely involves issues of credibility or veracity and the agency has determined that review of the written record is ordinarily an adequate means to correct prior mistakes.

(4) In those cases when an oral hearing is not required by this section, an agency shall accord the debtor a "paper hearing," that is, a determination of the request for reconsideration based upon a review of the written record.

[65 Fed. Reg. 70395 (Nov. 22, 2000)]

* * *

B.6 Selected Private Student Loan Regulations

12 C.F.R. sec.

* * *

226.46 Special disclosure requirements for private education loans.

* * *

SOURCE: Reg. Z, 46 Fed. Reg. 20892 (Apr. 7, 1981); 52 Fed. Reg. 43181 (Nov. 9, 1987); 54 Fed. Reg. 13864 (Apr. 6, 1989); 56 Fed. Reg. 13754 (Apr. 4, 1991); 58 Fed. Reg. 17084 (Apr. 1, 1993); 59 Fed. Reg. 40204 (Aug. 5, 1994); 73 Fed. Reg. 44599 (July 30, 2008); 74 Fed. Reg. 36094 (July 22, 2009); 74 Fed. Reg. 41232 (Aug. 14, 2009), unless otherwise noted.

AUTHORITY: 12 U.S.C. 3806; 15 U.S.C. 1604, 1637(c)(5), and 1639(l); Pub. L. No. 111-24 § 2, 123 Stat. 1734.

* * *

§ 226.46 Special disclosure requirements for private education loans.

(a) *Coverage.* The requirements of this subpart apply to private education loans as defined in § 226.46(b)(5). A creditor may, at its option, comply with the requirements of this subpart for an extension of credit subject to §§ 226.17 and 226.18 that is extended to a consumer for expenses incurred after graduation from a law, medical, dental, veterinary, or other graduate school and related to relocation, study for a bar or other examination, participation in an internship or residency program, or similar purposes.

(1) *Relation to other subparts in this part.* Except as otherwise specifically provided, the requirements and limitations of this subpart are in addition to and not in lieu of those contained in other subparts of this Part.

(b) *Definitions.* For purposes of this subpart, the following definitions apply:

(1) *Covered educational institution* means:

(i) An educational institution that meets the definition of an institution of higher education, as defined in paragraph (b)(2) of this section, without regard to the institution's accreditation status; and

(ii) Includes an agent, officer, or employee of the institution of higher education. An agent means an institution-affiliated organization as defined by section 151 of the Higher Education Act of 1965 (20 U.S.C. 1019) or an officer or employee of an institution-affiliated organization.

(2) *Institution of higher education* has the same meaning as in sections 101 and 102 of the Higher Education Act of 1965 (20 U.S.C. 1001–1002) and the implementing regulations published by the U.S. Department of Education.

(3) *Postsecondary educational expenses* means any of the expenses that are listed as part of the cost of attendance, as defined under section 472 of the Higher Education Act of 1965 (20 U.S.C. 1087ll), of a student at a covered educational institution. These expenses include tuition and fees, books, supplies, miscellaneous personal expenses, room and board, and an allowance for any loan fee, origination fee, or insurance premium charged to a student or parent for a loan incurred to cover the cost of the student's attendance.

(4) *Preferred lender arrangement* has the same meaning as in section 151 of the Higher Education Act of 1965 (20 U.S.C. 1019).

(5) *Private education loan* means an extension of credit that:

(i) Is not made, insured, or guaranteed under title IV of the Higher Education Act of 1965 (20 U.S.C. 1070 et seq.);

(ii) Is extended to a consumer expressly, in whole or in part, for postsecondary educational expenses, regardless of whether the loan is provided by the educational institution that the student attends;

(iii) Does not include open-end credit any loan that is secured by real property or a dwelling; and

(iv) Does not include an extension of credit in which the covered educational institution is the creditor if:

(A) The term of the extension of credit is 90 days or less; or

(B) an interest rate will not be applied to the credit balance and the term of the extension of credit is one year or less, even if the credit is payable in more than four installments.

(c) *Form of disclosures*—

(1) *Clear and conspicuous.* The disclosures required by this subpart shall be made clearly and conspicuously.

(2) *Transaction disclosures.*

(i) The disclosures required under §§ 226.47(b) and (c) shall be made in writing, in a form that the consumer may keep. The disclosures shall be grouped together, shall be segregated from everything else, and shall not contain any information not directly related to the disclosures required under §§ 226.47(b) and (c), which include the disclosures required under § 226.18.

(ii) The disclosures may include an acknowledgment of receipt, the date of the transaction, and the consumer's name, address, and account number. The following disclosures may be made together with or separately from other required disclosures: the creditor's identity under § 226.18(a), insurance or debt cancellation under § 226.18(n), and certain security interest charges under § 226.18(o).

(iii) The term "finance charge" and corresponding amount, when required to be disclosed under § 226.18(d), and the interest rate required to be disclosed under §§ 226.47(b)(1)(i) and (c)(1), shall be more conspicuous than any other disclosure, except the creditor's identity under § 228.18(a).

(3) *Electronic disclosures.* The disclosures required under §§ 226.47(b) and (c) may be provided to the consumer in electronic form, subject to compliance with the consumer consent and other applicable provisions of the Electronic Signatures in Global and National Commerce Act (E-Sign Act) (15 U.S.C. 7001 *et seq.*). The disclosures required by § 226.47(a) may be provided to the consumer in electronic form on or with an application or solicitation that is accessed by the consumer in electronic form without regard to the consumer consent or other provisions of the E-Sign Act. The form required to be received under § 226.48(e) may be accepted by the creditor in electronic form as provided for in that section.

(d) *Timing of disclosures*—

(1) *Application or solicitation disclosures.*

(i) The disclosures required by § 226.47(a) shall be provided on or with any application or solicitation. For purposes of this subpart, the term solicitation means an offer of credit that does not require the consumer to complete an application. A "firm offer of credit" as defined in section 603(l) of the Fair Credit Reporting Act (15 U.S.C. 1681a(l)) is a solicitation for purposes of this section.

(ii) The creditor may, at its option, disclose orally the information in § 226.47(a) in a telephone application or solicitation. Alternatively, if the creditor does not disclose orally the information in § 226.47(a), the creditor must provide the disclosures or place them in the mail no later than three business days after the consumer has applied for the credit, except that, if the creditor either denies the consumer's application or provides or places in the mail the disclosures in § 226.47(b) no later than three business days after the consumer requests the credit, the creditor need not also provide the § 226.47(a) disclosures.

(iii) Notwithstanding paragraph (d)(1)(i), for a loan that the consumer may use for multiple purposes including, but not limited to, postsecondary educational expenses, the creditor need not provide the disclosures required by § 226.47(a).

(2) *Approval disclosures.* The creditor shall provide the disclosures required by § 226.47(b) before consummation on or with any notice of approval provided to the consumer. If the creditor mails notice of approval, the disclosures must be mailed with the notice. If the creditor communicates notice of approval by telephone, the creditor must mail the disclosures within three business days of providing the notice of approval. If the creditor communicates notice of approval electronically, the creditor may provide the disclosures in electronic form in accordance with § 226.46(d)(3); otherwise the creditor must mail the disclosures within three business days of communicating the notice of approval. If the creditor communicates approval in person, the creditor must provide the disclosures to the consumer at that time.

(3) *Final disclosures.* The disclosures required by § 226.47(c) shall be provided after the consumer accepts the loan in accordance with § 226.48(c)(1).

(4) *Receipt of mailed disclosures.* If the disclosures under paragraphs (d)(1), (d)(2) or (d)(3), are mailed to the consumer, the consumer is considered to have received them three business days after they are mailed.

(e) *Basis of disclosures and use of estimates*—

(1) *Legal obligation.* Disclosures shall reflect the terms of the legal obligation between the parties.

(2) *Estimates.* If any information necessary for an accurate disclosure is unknown to the creditor, the creditor shall make the disclosure based on the best information reasonably available at the time the disclosure is provided, and shall state clearly that the disclosure is an estimate.

(f) *Multiple creditors; multiple consumers.* If a transaction involves more than one creditor, only one set of disclosures shall be given and the creditors shall agree among themselves which creditor will comply with the requirements that this part imposes on any or all of them. If there is more than one consumer, the disclosures may be made to any consumer who is primarily liable on the obligation.

(g) *Effect of subsequent events*—

(1) *Approval disclosures.* If a disclosure under § 226.47(b) becomes inaccurate because of an event that occurs after the creditor delivers the required disclosures, the inaccuracy is not a violation of Regulation Z (12 CFR part 226), although new disclosures may be required under § 226.48(c).

(2) *Final disclosures.* If a disclosure under § 226.47(c) becomes inaccurate because of an event that occurs after the creditor delivers the required disclosures, the inaccuracy is not a violation of Regulation Z (12 CFR part 226).

* * *

Appendix C — Department of Education Policy Guidance Letters

The Department of Education Office of Postsecondary Education periodically distributes "Dear Colleague" letters. These are used to communicate Department instructions and directives and to announce new forms. This appendix contains a selection of Dear Colleague letters of particular significance for low-income borrowers. The most efficient way to obtain additional copies or to search for other Dear Colleague letters is through the Department of Education website at www.ifap.ed.gov/ifap/byYear.jsp?type=dpcletters (the general website is www.ed.gov). The website also contains archived letters going back to 1997. The letters in this appendix, as well as a number of other important letters, can also be found on the companion website to this manual.

C.1 Discharges

MAY 15, 2009, GEN-09-07

Publication Date: May 15, 2009

DCL ID: GEN-09-07, FP-09-05, CB-09-04

SUBJECT: Procedures for discharging Title IV loans based on a determination by the Department of Veterans Affairs that a veteran is unemployable due to a service-connected condition or disability

SUMMARY: This letter explains the change made to § 437(a) of the Higher Education Act by the Higher Education Opportunity Act that establishes a separate standard for determining whether certain veterans are totally and permanently disabled for Title IV loan discharge purposes. This letter provides implementation guidance to FFEL lenders, guaranty agencies, and Perkins school lenders on the procedures for processing total and permanent disability discharge requests for borrowers who are covered by the new statutory provisions.

Dear Colleague:

This Dear Colleague Letter provides an overview of the procedures for processing total and permanent disability loan discharges for Federal Family Education Loan (FFEL) Program and Perkins Loan borrowers who have been determined by the Department of Veterans Affairs (VA) to be unemployable due to a service-connected condition. The Department of Education (the Department) will follow the same procedures for Direct Loan borrowers and other borrowers whose loans are held by the Department, and for Teacher Education Assistance for College and Higher Education (TEACH) Grant recipients who have applied for total and permanent disability discharge of their TEACH Grant service obligations.

I. Overview of Statutory Change

Section 437(b) of the Higher Education Opportunity Act (HEOA) amended § 437(a) of the Higher Education Act of 1965, as amended (HEA) to provide that a FFEL loan may be discharged if the borrower—

> ...has been determined by the Secretary of Veterans Affairs to be unemployable due to a service-connected condition and ... provides documentation of such determination to the Secretary of Education, [such borrower] shall be considered permanently and totally disabled for the purpose of discharging such borrower's loans under this subsection, and such borrower shall not be required to present additional documentation for purposes of this subsection.

This same standard applies to the Direct Loan Program in accordance with § 455(a)(1) of the HEA. In the Perkins Loan Program, § 464(b)(1)(A)(iv) of the HEOA amended § 464(c)(1)(F) of the HEA to provide that a borrower's liability to repay a Perkins Loan Program loan shall be cancelled "if the borrower is determined by the Secretary of Veterans Affairs to be unemployable due to a service-connected disability." These provisions became effective August 14, 2008 for the FFEL and Direct Loan programs, and July 1, 2008 for the Perkins Loan Program.

II. Department of Veterans Affairs Determinations That Qualify a Borrower for a Disability Discharge Under the New Statutory Standard

To qualify for a total and permanent disability loan discharge under the statutory standard described above, a veteran must have received a determination from the VA that he or she is unemployable due to a service-connected condition or disability.

We have consulted with the VA and gathered information about its disability determination process. We have determined that a 100% or total disability rating from the VA represents a determination that the veteran has a total impairment in earning capacity, i.e., is unemployable. In addition, a veteran with a less than 100% disability rating may qualify for total disability based on an individual unemployability determination, if the VA determines that the veteran's service-connected disabilities are sufficient to result in unemployability.

Accordingly, there are two types of VA determinations that qualify a veteran for a discharge of his or her Title IV student loans based on the statutory standard:

1. A determination that the veteran has a service-connected disability, or service connected disabilities, that are 100% disabling; or

2. A determination that the veteran is totally disabled based on an individual unemployability determination.

The VA grants individual unemployability only for service-connected conditions. Therefore, any determination of individual unemployability qualifies a veteran for discharge. In the case of a determination that a veteran is 100% disabled, the determination must specify that the disabilities are service-connected.

III. Processing Loan Discharge Applications for Veterans Who Have Been Determined to be Unemployable Due to a Service-Connected Condition or Disability

The following procedures must be followed when processing a disability discharge request for a veteran:

1. The borrower must apply to the loan holder (i.e., the current owner of the loan) for a total and permanent disability discharge. For Perkins Loans, the loan holder is the Perkins school lender. For FFEL loans, the loan holder is the lender or, if a default claim has been paid on the loan, the guaranty agency. For FFEL or Perkins Loans that have been assigned to the Department, the loan holder is the Department. To apply, a borrower who has received one of the VA disability determinations specified above completes only Sections 1 and 3 of the recently approved *Discharge Application: Total and Permanent Disability* (TPD application) [OMB No. 1845-0065, Expiration Date: 12/31/2011] and submits the application to the loan holder.

The borrower is not required to have a physician complete Section 4 of the TPD application. Instead, the borrower submits with the application documentation from the VA showing that the borrower has received a determination of individual unemployability or has been determined to be 100% disabled due to one or more service-connected disabilities. The borrower may provide a copy of the VA Rating Decision or a letter from the VA confirming that the borrower has received one of the qualifying ratings. As explained above, a rating of 100% disabled must specify that the borrower's condition is service-connected. After receiving the TPD application, the loan holder must suspend collection activity on the loan.

2. For FFEL borrowers, the loan holder (either the lender or the guaranty agency) must ensure that the TPD application has been completed and that the appropriate VA documentation has been provided and must make a preliminary determination of the borrower's eligibility. If the current loan holder is the lender and the VA documentation indicates that the borrower is eligible for a TPD discharge, the holder must then submit the application and VA documentation to the guaranty agency. At the same time the FFEL lender should file a TPD claim with the guaranty agency. For FFEL borrowers, both the FFEL lender and the guaranty agency will make preliminary determinations of eligibility. For Perkins borrowers, the Perkins school must ensure that the TPD application has been completed and the appropriate VA documentation provided and make the preliminary determination of eligibility.

3. The preliminary determination of eligibility is based on the VA documentation provided by the borrower. FFEL lenders, guaranty agencies and Perkins schools must carefully review the documentation provided by the borrower when making preliminary determinations of eligibility. If the documentation clearly demonstrates that the borrower does not qualify for a discharge under the new statutory standard for certain veterans, the TPD request must be rejected by the FFEL lender, guaranty agency or Perkins school. For example, if the VA documentation states that the borrower is 100% disabled, but also states that the borrower's disabilities are not service-connected, the TPD claim must be rejected.

4. If the borrower appears to be eligible for a total and permanent disability discharge based on the VA documentation, the guaranty agency or Perkins school must submit a copy of the TPD application and VA documentation to the Department, and notify the borrower that his or her disability discharge request has been submitted to the Department for further review. The guaranty agency or Perkins school does not need to assign the loan to the Department.

5. After receiving the TPD application and supporting documentation from the guaranty agency or Perkins school, the Department will review the VA documentation. The Department may also contact the VA for more complete information regarding the borrower's VA disability rating. If the Department determines that the borrower meets the eligibility criteria for discharge under the standard for veterans with service-connected disabilities or conditions, the Department will instruct the guaranty agency or Perkins school to discharge the loan. Borrowers who are granted a TPD discharge through this process are not placed in a three-year conditional discharge period and are not required to provide any additional medical or income information to qualify for the discharge. The outstanding balance on the loan is discharged immediately.

6. Upon notification by the Department that the borrower qualifies for a discharge, the guaranty agency must pay the discharge claim to the lender. If the guaranty agency is the loan holder, it must discharge the loan. The Perkins school discharges the loan upon notification by the Department. For both FFEL and Perkins Loans, the loan holder refunds any payments that were made on or after the effective date of the grant of disability by the VA. A Rating Decision from the VA will generally state the effective date of the grant of disability in the section of the Rating Decision titled "Decision." The effective date of the grant of disability is NOT the Date of the Rating Decision or the Effective Date of Payment. A letter from a VA Regional Office may simply confirm the borrower's VA disability status, without providing an effective date. If the documentation provided by the borrower does not include an effective date, the Department will obtain the effective date from the VA, and provide that information to the guaranty agency or Perkins school. Receipt of a Title IV loan after the effective date does not disqualify a borrower for a TPD discharge; therefore the Department will not review the borrower's National Student Loan Data System (NSLDS) records for this purpose.

7. If a borrower's application for a TPD loan discharge based on VA documentation is denied by a Perkins school after its review or by the Department, the Perkins school must notify the borrower that the discharge request has been denied, and that

the borrower must resume repayment on the loan. If the FFEL loan was held by a lender and the application is denied by a guaranty agency after its review or by the Department, the guaranty agency will return the claim to the lender. The FFEL loan holder will notify the borrower that the discharge request has been denied, and that the borrower must resume payment on the loan. The loan is deemed to have been in forbearance from the date collection activity was suspended. If the VA documentation suggests that the borrower may be totally and permanently disabled, but the borrower is not eligible for the total and permanent disability discharge process described in this letter because the borrower's disabilities are not service-connected, the FFEL loan holder or Perkins school must advise the borrower to re-apply for a TPD discharge through the standard TPD discharge process. To re-apply for a total and permanent disability discharge under the standard process, the borrower must have a physician complete the Physician's Certification Section of the TPD application and resubmit the TPD application to the loan holder. The borrower may include the VA documentation, as well as any other supporting documentation, along with the completed TPD application. The Department will take the VA documentation into consideration when conducting its medical review under the standard process for total and permanent disability discharges.

During the discharge process, loan holders must provide borrowers with a phone number they can call to speak with a loan holder representative if they have any questions about their discharge requests. The Department's Veterans Disability Discharge Unit (see contact information at the end of this letter) will assist loan holders in addressing questions about specific applications or processes for discharges on the basis of VA documentation. As with the current total and permanent disability discharge process, there is no formal appeals process for a borrower whose application for discharge has been denied.

IV. Application Availability and Effective Date For Use

We have revised the TPD application [OMB Number 1845-0065] to reflect changes to the TPD process made by final regulations that were published on November 1, 2007 [72 FR 61960], as well as the HEOA provisions described in this letter. The revised TPD application has been approved by the Office of Management and Budget and has been posted to the Department's Information for Financial Aid Professionals (IFAP) web site as an attachment to Dear Colleague Letters GEN-09-01, FP-09-01, and CB-09-01, which are available at this link:

http://ifap.ed.gov/dpcletters/GEN0901FP0901CB0901.html.

While the revised TPD application is being phased in, Perkins, FFEL, and Direct Loan borrowers may apply for TPD discharges based on VA documentation using the earlier version of the application. The borrower may leave the Physician's Certification Section of the form blank when applying for a TPD discharge based on a qualifying disability determination by the VA. The Physician's Certification is in Section 3 of the earlier version of the TPD form, and is in Section 4 of the recently approved version. In place of the information requested in the Physician's Certification Section of the TPD form, the borrower must submit to the loan holder a copy of the appropriate VA documentation as described in this letter.

V. Triggering Date for Implementation

The procedures for granting total and permanent disability discharges based on VA documentation are in effect as of the date of this Dear Colleague Letter.

For FFEL and Direct Loan borrowers, total and permanent discharge requests based on VA documentation received on or after August 14, 2008 must be processed using the new procedures described in this letter. For Perkins Loan borrowers, total and permanent disability discharge requests based on VA documentation received on or after July 1, 2008 must be processed using the new procedures. Applications that were submitted on or after these dates and that are currently being processed under the "regular" TPD procedures may now be processed under the procedures outlined in this Dear Colleague Letter, if the borrower provides the appropriate documentation from the VA.

In addition to providing for total and permanent disability discharges based on VA determinations, the HEOA also modified the criteria for qualifying for a total and permanent disability discharge under the standard procedures. These new criteria will be effective July 1, 2010, and will be addressed in regulations that the Department will develop as part of the negotiated rulemaking process.

VI. Mailing Address

Guaranty agencies and Perkins schools should send total and permanent disability discharge requests based on qualifying VA documentation to the Department at the following address:

U.S. Department of Education
FSA, Business Operations, Processing Division
Veterans Disability Discharge Unit
61 Forsyth Street, SW 19T89
Atlanta, GA 30303

Please include a contact name, phone number and e-mail address with each submission. For submission questions, please contact the Department's Veterans Disability Discharge Unit by phone at (404) 562-6012, by fax at (404) 562-6059, or by e-mail to FSAAtlantaContracts@ed.gov. When calling, request the Veterans Disability Discharge Unit. When faxing or e-mailing, include "RE: Veterans Disability Discharge" in the subject line. The attached Questions and Answers provide additional information on the procedures for processing total and permanent disability discharge requests based on disability determinations from the VA. We look forward to working with you to successfully implement these new discharge procedures.

Sincerely,

Daniel T. Madzelan

Delegated the Authority to Perform
the Functions and Duties of the
Assistant Secretary for
Postsecondary Education

ATTACHMENT

Total and Permanent Disability Discharges Based on Department of Veterans Affairs Disability Determinations

Questions and Answers

Q1. What is the trigger date for processing total and permanent disability (TPD) discharge requests from eligible veterans under the streamlined procedures described in the accompanying Dear Colleague letter?

A1. The streamlined procedures apply to all TPD discharge requests that have been or are received by the loan holder on or after August 14, 2008 (or on or after July 1, 2008, for Perkins loans) and that are accompanied by the appropriate Department of Veterans Affairs (VA) documentation, as described in the accompanying Dear Colleague Letter. In addition, an eligible veteran whose TPD discharge request is currently in process under the regular discharge procedures may receive a TPD discharge under the streamlined procedures if he or she provides the appropriate VA documentation to the loan holder or to the Department, if the borrower's loan has already been assigned to the Department.

Q2. Will eligible veterans whose TPD applications are currently in process under the regular procedures at the Department of Education be notified of their right to submit VA disability documentation to prove eligibility for a TPD discharge under the new standard?

A2. As the Department conducts reviews of borrowers whose loans have been assigned to us as part of the regular procedures, we will identify veterans who might qualify for immediate discharge under the new standard. If it appears that a borrower might qualify for a discharge based on a VA disability determination, we will attempt to obtain the necessary documentation of the disability from the borrower or directly from the VA, so that the borrower's eligibility for a discharge can be evaluated.

Q3. Will veterans currently in the three-year conditional discharge period receive final discharges without completing the rest of the three-year conditional discharge period? How will they be notified of this possibility?

Q3.* Eligible veterans currently in the three-year conditional period may qualify for an immediate discharge if the Department receives documentation of a qualifying VA disability determination. However, in most cases, the Department does not have veteran status information for borrowers who are currently in the three-year conditional discharge period. Veterans in a conditional discharge status will need to contact the Department and request consideration for immediate discharge based on the appropriate disability documentation from the VA.

Q4. What documentation is a borrower required to submit to the loan holder to receive a total and permanent disability discharge under the streamlined procedures, if the borrower is applying for a TPD discharge based on a qualifying VA disability determination?

A4. The borrower must submit to the loan holder a completed *Discharge Application: Total and Permanent Disability* (OMS No. 1845-0065) as well as the appropriate documentation from the VA. The borrower must only complete Sections 1 and 3 of the revised TPD application with the 12/31/2011 expiration date (or Sections 1 and 2 of the previous version of the TPD application with the 05/31/2008 expiration date). The borrower is not required to have a physician complete the Physician's Certification Section (Section 4 of the revised form; Section 3 of the previous version). Acceptable documentation from the VA includes, but is not limited to, a copy of a VA Rating Decision or a letter from a VA Regional Office showing that the borrower is 100% disabled due to one or more service-connected disabilities, or has received a determination of individual unemployability.

Q5. Is there specific language that will appear in any VA documentation that qualifies a borrower for discharge under the new standard for certain veterans?

A5. No. The documentation from different VA offices may use different terminology to describe a borrower's VA disability status. For example, acceptable documentation from the VA might say that a borrower has been granted "entitlement to individual unemployability" or say that, due to service-connected disabilities, the borrower is "100% disabled", or "permanently and totally disabled" or is "unable to work and earn money." FFEL lenders, guaranty agencies and Perkins schools must carefully review the VA documentation to determine if it demonstrates that the borrower is qualified for a TPD discharge under the new standard.

Q6. What is the status of a loan while a TPD claim is being processed under the new standard for eligible veterans?

A6. The loan holder must suspend collection activity on the loan during this period. If the discharge request is denied, the loan is considered to have been in forbearance during this period.

Q7. In the FFEL program, how does a guaranty agency pay a TPD claim to a FFEL loan holder under the new procedures for veterans?

A7. The loan holder will submit the total and permanent disability claim and the required documentation to the guaranty agency for review. The claim amount requested is the outstanding balance on the loan(s) if no borrower payments had been received after the effective date of the VA disability determination. If payments have been received after the effective date, the claim amount is the outstanding balance plus the amount of the payments received after the effective date. The FFEL loan holder must maintain the suspension of collection activity until the holder is notified by the guaranty agency of the status of the disability discharge request. The guaranty agency will pay the claim once the Department has approved the discharge. If the Department denies the discharge, the guaranty agency will not pay the claim and the loan holder will resume collection on the loan.

Q8. What is "the effective date of the VA disability determination"?

A8. For TPD discharge purposes, the effective date of the VA disability determination is the effective date of the grant of disability. The effective date of the grant of disability is generally reported in the section of a VA Rating Decision titled "Decision". The effective date of the grant of disability is NOT the Date of the Rating Decision or the Effective Date of Payment.

---

* *Editor's note:* So in original.

Q9. Is a guaranty agency or Perkins school required to assign a loan to the Department if the guaranty agency or school has determined that the borrower appears to be eligible for discharge based on a VA disability determination?

A9. No. However, after making a preliminary determination of the borrower's discharge eligibility, the guaranty agency or Perkins school must forward a copy of the completed TPD application and VA documentation to the Department for review. The Department will review the documentation and then notify the guaranty agency or Perkins school if the borrower qualifies for a discharge.

Q10. In the FFEL program, how are payments refunded to the borrower?

A10. Upon receipt of claim payment from the guaranty agency, the loan holder must forward to the payer the total amount of payments received after the effective date of the VA disability determination.

Q11. In the Perkins program, how are payments refunded to the borrower?

A11. Upon being notified by the Department that a borrower qualifies for a TPD discharge based on a VA disability determination, the Perkins school must return to the payer any loan payments made after the effective date of the VA disability determination. Schools may use their Perkins Funds to refund the payments.

Q12. If the discharged loan is a FFEL Consolidation Loan, how are payments that were made on the underlying loans prior to consolidation refunded to the borrower?

A12. For Consolidation Loans, the holder of the Consolidation Loan must refund any payments that were made on an underlying loan after the effective date of the VA disability determination. If the payment histories are not available from the prior lenders, the Consolidation Loan holder must make reasonable attempts to obtain the information from other sources. If the Consolidation Loan holder is unable to obtain a payment history from other sources, the holder must ask the borrower to submit evidence of payments made on the underlying loans after the effective date of the VA disability determination, and prior to the date the underlying loans were consolidated, to receive a refund of those payments.

Q13. Are all Perkins, FFEL and Direct Loan program loans made prior to the effective date of the VA disability determination eligible for discharge?

A13. Yes, all outstanding Title IV loans made prior to the effective date of the VA disability determination are eligible for discharge. In addition, receipt of Title IV loans after the effective date does not disqualify the borrower for a discharge of loans received prior to the effective date. Loans that were fully repaid or otherwise satisfied prior to the effective date of the VA disability determination are not eligible for discharge under these procedures, unless the loans were repaid by a Consolidation Loan, and there is an outstanding balance on the Consolidation Loan.

Q14. If the borrower meets the criteria for a total and permanent disability discharge based upon a VA disability determination, is the borrower subject to the three-year conditional discharge period?

A14. No. The borrower is not subject to the three-year conditional discharge period. The TPD discharge is final. A final discharge cancels the borrower's obligation (and, if applicable, any endorser's obligation) to repay the remaining balance on the outstanding FFEL, Perkins, and/or Direct Loan Program loans.

Q15. What loan status information is reported to NSLDS for a loan that has been discharged based on a VA determination of unemployability due to a service-connected condition?

A15. A new NSLDS loan status code for this discharge type is under development. In the interim, upon a guaranty agency's or Perkins school's discharge of a loan based on documentation from the VA, the guaranty agency or Perkins school must report a loan status of 'DI' to NSLDS for loans not in default and a loan status of 'DS' for defaulted loans. The guaranty agency must also make an online update of the borrower's NSLDS record, reducing the balance of all loans that were discharged to zero. Perkins schools will not report the cancellation code of "PI" for a VA discharge, but will only report the loan status code of "01" or "OS" and a zero balance. The Department will publish NSLDS Technical Updates providing further details on the implementation of the new loan status code for discharges based on VA disability determinations as needed.

Q17. How does a Perkins school report a loan cancelled under these provisions on the Fiscal Operations Report and Application to Participate (FISAP)?

A17. Perkins school must report the cancelled loan principal with other cancellations in Part III; Section A, Field 22 (disability based on VA determination) on the FISAP that will be available by August 1, 2009.

Q18. If a borrower has a loan discharged based on a VA disability determination, can the borrower later receive new Title IV loans?

A18. Yes. A borrower who has received a discharge of a prior loan based on a VA disability determination may receive a new Perkins, FFEL or Direct Loan program loan in accordance with the eligibility requirements in 34 CFR 674.9(g)(1) and (2), 682.201 (a)(6)(i) and (ii), and 34 CFR 685.200(a)(1)(iv)(A), respectively.

FEBRUARY 9, 2009, GEN-09-01

Publication Date: February 9, 2009

GEN-09-01
FP-09-01
CB-09-01

SUBJECT: Revised Total and Permanent Disability Discharge Application

SUMMARY: The letter announces the approval of a revised Discharge Application: Total and Permanent Disability for use by borrowers in the Federal Family Education Loan (FFEL), William D. Ford Federal Direct Loan (Direct Loan), and Federal Perkins Loan (Perkins Loan) programs, and by recipients of grants under the Teacher Education for College and Higher Education (TEACH) Grant Program.

[*Editor's note:* Technical note is omitted.]

Dear Colleague:

The Office of Management and Budget (OMB) has approved a revised Discharge Application: Total and Permanent Disability. The revised form will be used by FFEL, Direct Loan, and Perkins Loan program borrowers to apply for discharge of their loans based on a total and permanent disability, and by TEACH Grant recipients to apply for total and permanent disability discharges of their TEACH Grant service obligations.

The revised Discharge Application: Total and Permanent Disability incorporates the changes made to the terms of total and permanent disability discharges made by the *Title IV final regulations* for the FFEL, Direct Loan, and Perkins Loan program that were published on November 1, 2007 (effective July 1, 2008), as well as the provisions of the *TEACH Grant Program final regulations* published on June 23, 2008 that allow for the discharge of a TEACH Grant recipient's service obligation based on total and permanent disability.

The revised form also reflects one of the changes made by the Higher Education Opportunity Act (Public Law 110-315) (HEOA) to the provisions of the Higher Education Act governing total and permanent disability discharges. This change established a new standard for determining that certain veterans are totally and permanently disabled for Title IV loan discharge purposes. Specifically, a veteran who has been determined by the Secretary of Veterans Affairs to be unemployable due to a service-connected condition or disability and who provides documentation of that determination will be considered totally and permanently disabled for loan discharge purposes, and will not be required to provide any additional documentation to establish his or her eligibility for discharge. This new standard will also apply to eligible veterans who request a discharge of a TEACH Grant service obligation based on total and permanent disability.

Additional information related to the HEOA change affecting veterans that is described above may be found in *Dear Colleague Letter GEN-08-12/FP-08-10*. We will issue a separate Dear Colleague Letter that explains the new standard for veterans and provides detailed operational guidance to FFEL Program lenders, guaranty agencies, and Perkins school lenders on documentation requirements and special procedures for processing total and permanent disability discharge requests from veterans who are covered by the HEOA provision.

Other HEOA provisions affecting total and permanent disability discharges require implementing regulations and thus will necessitate further changes to the discharge application at a later date.

In addition to revising the application to reflect the necessary regulatory and statutory changes, we have also significantly revised and expanded the Physician's Certification section of the form. Our experience with the prior version of the discharge application has shown that in many cases the physician who certifies the form does not provide sufficient information to clearly establish that the discharge applicant is totally and permanently disabled in accordance with the regulatory definition. To address this issue, we have revised the questions for the physician so that they request more detailed information about the applicant's disabling condition, and we have added more space for physicians to provide the requested information.

Implementation of the Revised Discharge Application: Total and Permanent Disability

The OMB-approved revised Discharge Application: Total and Permanent Disability (expiration date 12/31/2011) is attached to this letter. In light of the new discharge standard for certain veterans, program participants are urged to begin distributing the attached revised form to borrowers as soon as possible. Beginning July 1, 2009, only the attached revised form may be provided to borrowers. However, the previous version of the form (expiration date 05/31/2008) may continue to be accepted after this date.

Imaging Technology

The attached form instructs the borrower to complete and sign the form in ink. This is to accommodate imaging technology, but a pencil signature does not invalidate a form. The blank space at the top, bottom, or sides of the form may be used for bar coding.

Printing Instructions

The attached form must be printed with black ink on white paper. The typeface, point size, and general presentation of the form may not be changed from the version that was approved by OMB. However, program participants may change the order of the program names that appear in the header of the form so that the name of the program for which the form is being used appears first. (For example, a Perkins school could change the order of the program names so that Federal Perkins Loan Program appears first.) In addition, program participants may remove bold type in section headings or may add bold or italic type to the instructions.

FFEL Program loan holders and Perkins school lenders should pre-print the address to which the completed form should be sent, along with appropriate contact information, at the bottom of Section 3 on Page 1 of the form.

Obtaining Copies for Reproduction

The revised form, in both Microsoft Word and PDF format, is provided as an attachment to this letter. The form will also be available in PDF format on the web site of the *National Council of Higher Education Loan Programs* (NCHELP).

FFEL Program guaranty agencies and Perkins school lenders are responsible for ensuring that the form used is identical to the form approved by OMB. No changes may be made to the form except as expressly authorized above.

Sincerely,

Jeff Baker, Director
Policy Liaison and Implementation

Attachments/Enclosures:

[*Editor's note:* The attachment to this letter is not reprinted herein. The updated form can be found at Appendix D.3.8.1, *infra*.]

SEPTEMBER 24, 2007, FP-07-09

Additional Guidance for False Certification Ability-to-Benefit Loan Discharge Procedures

Publication Date: September 24, 2007

DCL ID: FP-07-09

Award Year:
Update to Ability-to-Benefit Loan Discharge Procedures

SUMMARY: This letter provides additional guidance to guaranty agencies for evaluating applications for FFEL false certification loan discharges based upon a borrower's claim that an institution did not properly determine the borrower's ability-to-benefit.

Dear Guaranty Agency Director:

A portion of DCL GEN 95-42 (September 1995) (copy attached) discusses how to evaluate applications for discharges of loans made under the Federal Family Education Loan Program (FFELP) and the William D. Ford Federal Direct Loan Program (DLP) based on a school's false certification of a student's ability-to-benefit (ATB), when the borrower offers no evidence of the false certification other than his or her own statement. This letter supplements that guidance and clarifies for guaranty agencies certain responsibilities they bear in this area.

1. By regulation, guaranty agencies are required to consider ATB discharge applications "in light of information available from the records of the agency and from other sources, including other guaranty agencies, state authorities, and cognizant accrediting associations." 34 C.F.R. § 682.402(e)(6)(iv). DCL GEN 95-42 elaborates that "Because several authorities with oversight responsibilities, including the Department, accrediting agencies, guarantors, state licensing bodies, and the school's own auditor, would typically have both the opportunity and responsibility to find and report improper ATB admission practices, the absence of any such finding in reports about a school raises an inference that no improper practices were reported because none were taking place."

In applying the above regulations and guidance, guaranty agencies evaluating records of oversight that are contained solely in the Department's Institutional Data System or Postsecondary Education Participants System (PEPS), and that cannot be located in hard copy, are instructed to regard ATB violations entered into those systems as findings of improper ATB admission practices for discharge purposes, even if a "0" may be entered in the corresponding liability field. In contrast, if hard copy records of oversight findings are available, guaranty agencies must not regard ATB violations entered into those systems, with a "0" in the corresponding liability field, as findings of improper ATB admission practices for discharge purposes without examining the hard copy oversight reports and such other information as is reasonably available to determine the nature of the violations and whether there is any evidence the findings were discovered in later inquiry or proceedings to be erroneous.

In addition, even if findings of improper ATB admission practices by a school have been reported by oversight agencies, a guaranty agency must not grant a discharge if the guaranty agency has other information that directly contradicts material facts or contentions in the discharge application. Guaranty agencies must consider all information available to them regarding the sufficiency of the application, including other self-certified information provided by the student, such as the information contained in the student's Free Application for Federal Student Aid (FAFSA).

2. DCL GEN 95-42 states that guaranty agencies must "obtain existing documentation [of ATB findings] available from any public or private agency that reviewed or had oversight responsibility for the school." The regulations also impose responsibility on guaranty agencies for investigating and reporting any reliable information that a school in a state for which the guaranty agency is responsible may have falsely certified a student's eligibility. 34 C.F.R. § 682.402(e)(6)(i).

As a result of these responsibilities, and without regard to document retention policies, each guaranty agency must maintain, on a school-by-school basis, all oversight material it obtains in evaluating ATB discharge applications and in investigating allegations of ATB violations and must promptly make the information available on request to the Secretary and any other guaranty agency that requests it. This responsibility is not in lieu of any additional agency obligations as described in the regulations and DCL GEN 95-42.

As part of this recordkeeping responsibility, guaranty agencies must maintain a school-by-school record of the number of discharge applications it has received, the campus to which each application pertains if the school had or has multiple campuses, the date of attendance of the student applying for discharge, and whether the discharge was granted or denied. The agency must share this information with other guaranty agencies and the Secretary on request.

As part of obtaining the documentation necessary for determining whether a school has a relevant history of ATB oversight report findings, guaranty agencies must, among other things, either check the Department's PEPS for such findings, or contact each oversight agency that enters data into PEPS regarding the school to obtain that information.

3. DCL GEN 95-42 explains that in the absence of any ATB oversight findings about a school, the evidence provided by a student seeking an ATB discharge must go beyond the student's assertions that he or she meets the individual qualifications for discharge.

In such cases, if there is no evidence that ATB requirements were met other than the absence of ATB oversight report findings, and if there is also no borrower-specific evidence that he or she fails to qualify for a discharge, guaranty agencies must consider, in addition to the student's allegations and any other evidence the student submits, the incidence of discharge applications filed regarding that school by students who attended the school during the same time frame as the applicant, as well as the possibility that there has been collusion among the students in submitting the applications received.

In such cases, if there is a high incidence of applications submitted and no evidence of collusion, the guaranty agency may determine that the school's ATB practices were defective during that time frame. Guaranty agencies in such cases should give heightened weight to a high incidence of discharge applications with regard to schools for which no oversight reports or data of any kind are available. If a guaranty agency determines that discharges should be granted based on incidence of discharge applications received for a particular school, it should re-evaluate the discharge claims previously denied for students who attended that school during the same time period, to determine whether discharge is now warranted.

Similarly, where there is no evidence that ATB requirements were met other than the absence of ATB oversight report findings, and there is also no borrower-specific evidence that he or she fails to qualify for a discharge, credible evidence of the following provides an adequate basis for granting a discharge application, and should be given heightened weight with regard to schools for which no oversight reports are available: (i) withdrawal rates exceeding 33 percent at the school at the relevant time, or (ii) for students who entered repayment on their loans during or after federal fiscal year 1993, an annual loan default rate exceeding 40 percent; for students who entered repayment on their loans during federal fiscal year 1992, an annual loan default rate exceeding 45 percent; for students who entered repayment on their loans during federal fiscal year 1991, an annual loan default rate exceeding 50 percent; for students who entered repayment on their loans during federal fiscal year 1990, an annual loan default rate exceeding 55 percent; and for students who entered repayment on their loans during or before federal fiscal year 1989, an annual loan default rate exceeding 60 percent.

If oversight reports contain specific findings that ATB violations occurred at some of a school's campuses but not at others, consideration of incidence, withdrawal, and loan default rates should proceed on a campus-by-campus basis rather than based on data regarding the school as a whole.

Should you have questions about the information provided in this letter please contact Janet Nori by email at janet.nori@ed.gov or by phone at (415) 485-5658.

Sincerely,

Lawrence A. Warder

Acting Chief Operating Officer
Federal Student Aid

Attachments/Enclosures: [*Editor's note:* The attachment to this letter is not reprinted herein.]

SEPTEMBER 1995, GEN-95-42

Publication Date: September 1995

GEN-95-42

SUBJECT: Loan discharges based on improper determination that a student had the ability-to-benefit (ATB) from the school's training.

REFERENCE: § 34 CFR 682.402(e) and § 685.214(a)

Dear Colleague:

Section 437(c)(1) of the Higher Education Act of 1965, as amended (HEA) provides for the discharge of a borrower's loan obligation under the Federal Family Education Loan (FFEL) Program, and § 455(a)(1) makes this relief available under the William D. Ford Federal Direct Loan Program, if the student's eligibility to borrow was falsely certified by the school. In September 1994, initial guidance concerning these loan discharges was provided in "Dear Colleague" Letter 94-L-166/G-256 issued to lenders and guaranty agencies in the FFEL Program. However, in the area of discharges based on a school's defective determination of a student's ability-to-benefit (ATB), the "Dear Colleague" Letter promised more detailed guidance concerning those discharges.

This letter addresses some common questions about discharges based on improper ATB determinations that have been asked by borrowers, lenders, guaranty agencies, and other parties. The Department intends to apply the guidance in this letter to similar false certification discharges in the William D. Ford Federal Direct Loan Program.

Thank you for ensuring that the intent of the false certification discharge provision is achieved. For further information, you may contact the Department's Customer Support Inquiry Service between the hours of 9:00 AM and 5:00 PM Eastern Time, at 1-800-433-7327. After hours calls will be accepted by an automated voice response system. Callers leaving their name and phone number will receive a return call the next business day. You may FAX your inquiry to the Customer Support Inquiry Service at any time by calling (202) 260-4199.

Sincerely,

Elizabeth M. Hicks

Deputy Assistant Secretary for
Student Financial Assistance

Enclosure

Enclosure A:

SUMMARY OF ATB REQUIREMENTS[1]

For periods of enrollment beginning January 1, 1986[2] through June 30, 1987

The school could determine that the student had the ability to benefit from the school's training in accordance with the requirements of 34 CFR 668.6, as those regulations existed at that time. The school simply had to "develop and consistently apply criteria" to determine if regular students who did not have a high school diploma or GED, and who were beyond the age of compulsory attendance, had the ability to benefit from the school's training.

For periods of enrollment beginning July 1, 1987 through June 30, 1991

Schools were required to use one of the following standards for

---

1 This summary presents a brief overview of some of the major ATB requirements over time. The Department has issued several "Dear Colleague" Letters that explained ATB requirements in greater detail. The reader may find "Dear Colleague" Letters GEN-89-55 (December 1989), GEN-90-33 (September 1990), and GEN-91-20 (June 1991) to be particularly helpful.

2 Sections 437(c)(1) and 455(a)(1) of the HEA do not authorize loan discharges based on defective ATB determination for loans made before January 1, 1986.

admission of students without a high school diploma or its equivalent on the basis of ATB in accordance with 34 CFR 668.7 as it was in effect at that time: (1) the student received a GED prior to the student's completion of the program or by the end of the first year of the program, whichever was earlier; (2) the student was counseled prior to admission and successfully completed the school's program of remedial or developmental education that did not exceed one academic year or its equivalent; (3) the student passed a nationally recognized, standardized, or industry-developed ATB test, subject to criteria developed by the school's accrediting association; or (4) if the student failed the ATB test, he or she successfully completed the school's program of remedial or developmental education that did not exceed one academic year or its equivalent.

For periods of enrollment beginning July 1, 1991 through July 22, 1992

A student who was not a high school graduate or did not have a GED at the time of enrollment must have passed an independently administered ATB test approved by the Department[3] before the student's receipt of Title IV aid.

For periods of enrollment beginning on or after July 23, 1992

A student who was not a high school graduate or did not have a GED at the time of enrollment must meet one of the following standards before receiving Title IV aid: (1) achieve a score specified by the Department on an independently administered ATB test approved by the Department; or (2) be considered to have the ability to benefit from the school's training in accordance with a process prescribed by the state in which the school is located.

GENERAL RULES FOR LOAN DISCHARGES BASED ON A SCHOOL'S DEFECTIVE DETERMINATION OF A STUDENT'S ATB

1. The regulations[4] require the borrower to certify, under penalty of perjury, that the school failed to determine (or improperly determined) the student's ability-to-benefit from the school's training.
2. A student may, nevertheless, be considered to have had the ability to benefit from the school's training even though the school failed to determine the student's ability or did so improperly. The regulations recognize that a student who obtains employment in the occupation for which the school's program was designed to prepare him or her has proved, on the basis of that employment, that he or she actually possessed the ability to benefit from that training, without regard to whether the school was negligent in its implementation of the Department's ATB regulations. Therefore, the borrower must further certify that the student did not secure employment in the occupation for which the school stated its program was designed to prepare the student, or if the student completed the training program, he or she either was not able to find employment in that occupation, despite a reasonable attempt, or was able to get a job in that occupation only after receiving training from another school.
3. The regulations also recognize that a student would not be regarded as having had the ability-to-benefit from the school's training, despite a school's conclusion that the student had such ability if, at the time the school certified the student's eligibility for a loan, the student would not meet the legal requirements for employment (in the student's state of residence) in the occupation for which the training program was intended because of a physical or mental condition, age, or criminal record or other reason accepted by the Secretary.[5]

QUESTIONS AND ANSWERS

No evidence

1. If a borrower asserts in a claim for discharge that the school improperly determined the student's ATB, and the borrower presents neither documentary evidence from an oversight authority nor any other information to support that claim, and the guaranty agency has no specific information about the ATB testing practices of the school the student attended, is the statement, by itself, sufficient to qualify the borrower for a false certification discharge?

In evaluating an application for discharge, a guaranty agency must consider the statements in the application together with other evidence about the testing and admission practices of the school, and inferences that can reasonably be drawn from that other evidence. Because several authorities with oversight responsibilities, including the Department, accrediting agencies, guarantors, state licensing bodies, and the school's own auditor, would typically have both the opportunity and responsibility to find and report improper ATB admission practices, the absence of any such finding in reports about a school raises an inference that no improper practices were reported because none were taking place.

A borrower's statement must be evaluated in light of such an inference and the possibility that the borrower's statement may be motivated or affected by the borrower's financial self-interest in obtaining relief from the debt. Thus, a borrower's statement that he or she (or the student, in the case of a PLUS Loan) was "falsely certified" or "improperly tested" would not ordinarily be persuasive, and would not therefore be sufficient to establish entitlement to discharge, if it is not supported by some other evidence that as a result of improper ATB admissions practices, students were admitted on the basis of ATB who should not have been admitted. That supporting evidence can include a finding by an entity or organization that had oversight responsibility over the school's SFA administration or educational programs, statements or admissions by school officials with knowledge of the school's practices, or statements made by other students who attended the school that are both sufficiently detailed and consistent with each other to appear reliable. Those statements can include statements made in other claims for discharge relief.

---

3 Listings of approved tests were published in the Federal Register on December 19, 1990 and December 30, 1992, and in "Dear Colleague" Letter GEN-93-21 (August 1993). A comprehensive listing was published in Chapter 2 of the 1995–96 Federal Student Financial Aid Handbook.

4 34 CFR 682.402(e) for the FFEL Program, and 34 CFR 685.214(c) for the William D. Ford Federal Direct Loan Program.

5 34 CFR 682.402(e)(13)(iii)(B), published November 29, 1994, and § 685.214(a)(1)(iii), published December 1, 1994.

The Department expects a guaranty agency to obtain existing documentation available from any public or private agency that reviewed or had oversight responsibility for the school. If the guaranty agency concludes that such documentation either does not exist or does not support the borrower's assertion, it becomes the responsibility of the borrower making the claim to produce persuasive evidence that would corroborate his or her allegation of improper ATB determination.

Testing violations

2. In those instances where a school used an ATB test to determine a student's eligibility, what violations of ATB testing procedures justify discharge of a borrower's loan obligation, assuming the borrower is otherwise eligible?[6]

Discharge is warranted only in those cases where the ATB test was not "administered substantially in accordance with the requirements for use of the test."[7] For periods of enrollment beginning prior to July 1, 1991, a violation of the requirements for the use of an ATB test will be considered to have occurred if the school: (1) failed to substantially comply with the school's accrediting agency standards for ATB testing; or (2) if no such accrediting agency standards existed, the school failed to substantially comply with the test publisher's requirements for the use of the test. For periods of enrollment beginning on or after July 1, 1991, compliance with the Department's ATB requirements could only be met if the ATB test was approved by the Department and was administered substantially in accordance with the test publisher's rules for the use of the test.

The following violations of the applicable testing procedures are substantial enough to invalidate the results of the test, even though the violation may not have been knowingly committed:

— A test that was required to have been administered by an independent test administrator was not administered by such an individual.
— A school permitted a student who failed an ATB test to retake the test earlier than the minimum waiting period prescribed.
— A school permitted a student who failed an ATB test to retake the test more frequently than allowed.
— A school allowed more time for students to complete their ATB tests than was permitted.
— A school considered a student to have passed an ATB test even though the student did not achieve a minimum passing score which was permissible under the statute, regulations, and Departmental guidance in effect at the time the test was given.
— The school administered only part of a multi-part test, unless giving less than the entire test was permissible under the school's accrediting agency standards.
— For ATB tests given for periods of enrollment beginning on or after July 1, 1991, the version of the test used by the school was a version not approved by the Department.

— A school supplied answers to the ATB test, or permitted students to discuss the questions among themselves, in violation of the testing rules.

3. Even though a guaranty agency determines that a school did not completely comply with the Department's ATB regulations with respect to the use of an ATB test during periods when a test was required, are there violations of those regulations that are not sufficient to justify discharge of a borrower's loan obligation because, despite those technical regulatory violations, the test was administered substantially in accordance with the requirements for use of the test? 682.402(e)(13)(ii)(B)(2).

The Department has identified three violations of an accrediting agency's or a test publisher's requirements that, in the Department's view, do not have the effect of helping the student pass the test. These violations are not substantial enough to justify loan discharge.

— A school used photocopied versions of the ATB test.
— A school used a version of an ATB test that was obsolete by less than one year.
— A school used an ATB test that was approved by the U.S. Department of Education, but had not been approved by the school's accrediting agency.

Although some states have laws addressing the conditions under which postsecondary institutions may properly admit students who do not have a high school diploma or GED, violation of such state requirements does not make borrowers eligible for false certification loan discharge under § 437(c) of the HEA. State ATB requirements address the institution's qualification for a state license, and not whether students attending such schools are eligible for federal aid.

Section 437(c) of the HEA provides for loan discharge where a student's eligibility to borrow was falsely certified by the school. Student eligibility to borrow under the FFEL and William D. Ford Federal Direct Loan Programs is defined by the HEA and implementing regulations, and not by state laws addressing ATB admission. The regulations implementing the false certification discharge provision provide, among other things, that a borrower is eligible for false certification discharge if he or she (or the student in the case of a PLUS Loan) did not meet the requirements for admission on the basis of ability to benefit under FEDERAL law. The regulations describe FEDERAL standards for ATB admission between 1986 and the present, and explicitly refer to the FEDERAL regulatory standards in place during those periods.

Foreign language ATB test

4. A school's program was taught entirely or substantially in English. The ATB test used by the school for periods of enrollment beginning July 1, 1991 or later was given in a language other than English. The school admitted such students who passed their non-English ATB tests. Would a non-English language ATB test given to these students be considered a valid determination of their ATB?

The answer depends on whether the student was enrolled in a program with an English as a Second Language ("ESL") component, and whether the test instrument selected by the school

---

6 NOTE: A borrower who obtains employment in the occupation for which the school's training program was intended does not qualify for a loan discharge unless the borrower obtained employment only after receiving additional training at another school. See § 682.402(e)(3)(ii)(C) and § 685.214(c)(1)(iii).
7 34 CFR 682.402(e)(13)(ii)(B)(2).

was appropriate. The Department has approved examinations for testing students enrolled in ESL programs, programs with an ESL component, or for testing non-native speakers of English enrolling in regular academic or vocational programs taught in English. The approved examinations expect some degree of functional literacy in English. Before selecting an appropriate test, schools are encouraged to consider whether the examinations can determine the degree of English language proficiency necessary to succeed in the student's particular program of study. Whether a particular test used by a school could appropriately be used for a non-native English speaking student depends on the scope of approval of the test. For example, some tests were approved for use if Spanish is both the student's native language and the language of instruction, while others were approved for use where the student's native language is Spanish and the language of instruction is English.

Remedial Program

5. If a school admitted students for periods of enrollment beginning during the period July 1, 1987–July 1, 1991, and the school chose the ATB option of enrolling students in a program of remedial or developmental education, what rules applied to those programs?

For a school to be considered as having complied with the ATB requirements if it chose this option,[8] the school had to ensure that the students enrolled in, and successfully completed, the institutionally prescribed program of remedial or developmental education. In addition, students had to be either: (1) counselled before admission; or (2) fail an ATB test administered by the school. Those programs may not exceed one academic year or its equivalent. [NOTE: Extensive discussions concerning remedial programs were contained in "Dear Colleague" Letters GEN-89-55, issued December 1989, and GEN-91-20, June 1991.]

Student unable to get a job

6. What documentation is required to show that a student whose ATB was improperly determined was unable to get a job in the occupation for which he or she was trained?[9]

The answer depends on whether the student completed the school's training program. If the student DID NOT COMPLETE the program, the student must simply certify that he or she did not find employment in that occupation. The student's sworn statement that he or she could not get a job in that occupation will be considered proof that the school's defective (or non-existent) determination of the student's ability-to-benefit harmed the student to the extent that a discharge is permissible.

If the student COMPLETED the school's training program, it appears that, notwithstanding the school's improper ATB determination, the student's ability to successfully comprehend the subject matter was equivalent to a student who had a high school diploma or GED. The student obtained the degree or certificate that he or she desired, and for which the loan was obtained. However, the Department's regulations recognize that it is also important to consider whether the student was able to obtain employment after completing the school's program. For this reason, the loan discharge regulations permit a discharge if the student is unable to obtain employment in the occupation for which he or she was trained by the school, despite making a "reasonable attempt" to obtain employment in that occupation.

To fairly balance the interests of the student and the federal taxpayer, the Department believes that a student who COMPLETED the school's training program and who claims that he or she was unable to obtain employment in that occupation because of the school's defective determination of his or her ATB, should be expected to provide evidence that he or she made a "reasonable attempt" to obtain employment in that occupation. Ordinarily, a person who makes a reasonable attempt to obtain employment does not limit his or her job search to only one such effort. More commonly, an individual will try several times to obtain employment in a specific occupation. Therefore, if there were no unusual circumstances faced by a specific individual, it would be reasonable for a guaranty agency to consider three separate attempts by the student to find a job as a persuasive indication of the student's good-faith effort.

The type of information about a job search that most people could readily recall would include the basic facts, such as the name and address of the employer contacted, the date the employer was contacted, the position applied for, and the reason (if any) given by the employer for not hiring the person. Other information (for example, the employer's phone number or the name or title of the person contacted) may be remembered by the student, and would support his or her claim. In situations where an employer contacted by a student routinely declined to hire individuals who were trained by the school attended by the student, a generic statement from the employer to that effect would serve as evidence of the student's reasonable attempt to obtain employment with that employer.

Student's age, mental or physical condition, or criminal record

7. Are the regulatory provisions with respect to factors such as the student's age, mental or physical condition, or criminal record applicable to all students at all schools?

Those provisions[10] apply to all categories of students at all schools, including students for whom the school was not required to make ability-to-benefit determinations or for whom the school made such determinations properly.

8. What documentation is required from a borrower who requests a discharge on the basis that the student's age, mental or physical condition, criminal record, or other reason accepted by the Secretary prohibited the student from meeting the requirements for employment in the student's state of residence in the occupation for which the student was trained?

The borrower must provide evidence that the student had that disqualifying status at the time of enrollment, and evidence that a STATE PROHIBITION (in the student's state of residence) against employment in that occupation based on that status also existed at the time of enrollment. However, a loan discharge is

---

8 This option was not available to schools for periods of enrollment beginning on or after July 1, 1991.
9 34 CFR 682.402(e)(3)(ii)(C) and § 685.214(c)(1)(iii).

10 34 CFR 682.402(e)(13)(iii)(B), published November 29, 1994, and § 685.214(a)(1)(iii), published December 1, 1994.

not authorized if it can be shown that the school asked the student if he or she had such a disqualifying status, but the student did not divulge that information.

9. To whom should information be sent if it is believed that a possible "other reason" (in addition to the student's age, mental or physical condition, or criminal record) should be accepted by the Secretary?

Those parties that wish to provide such information should submit it to:

Ms. Carney McCullough
Chief, General Provisions Branch
Policy, Training, and Analysis Service
Policy Development Division
U.S. Department of Education
600 Independence Avenue, S.W.
Washington, DC 20202-5345

The submitted information must include unambiguous evidence that a STATE PROHIBITION based on that "other reason" existed at the time of the student's enrollment that would prohibit employment (in the student's state of residence) in the occupation for which the student was trained.

Group discharges

10. Does the Department regard as reasonable the approval of discharges for all borrowers who fall within a specified group, for example, ATB students who enrolled in a school with serious and well-documented ATB violations that could be considered to have affected every student admitted to the school based on ATB? If so, would those borrowers still be required to complete discharge applications?

In some cases, discharge may be authorized by the Department for borrowers who demonstrate that they fall within a particular cohort of students and who are otherwise eligible for false certification discharge. Such borrowers may receive discharge without individually presenting proof of improper determination of ATB or admission. All borrowers will, however, still be required to request a discharge and sign the sworn statement prescribed by the regulations. The Department will inform guaranty agencies when it has made such a determination, and notify them of the requirements and procedures for handling such discharges as they occur.

The Department invites interested parties to notify it of such special circumstances that may justify this approach. The type of documentation described in response to question #1 will be considered if it shows that a school committed pervasive and serious violations of the Department's regulations during the time period covered by the documentation. Those parties who wish to provide such documentation should submit it to Ms. Carney McCullough, at the address given in question #9.

Suspected fraud

11. What steps should a guaranty agency take if it suspects that a borrower has made false statements on a discharge request, but the agency is unable to disprove those suspected false statements?

The agency should contact the Department's Inspector General for assistance (1-800-MISUSED). Depending on the investigative strategy in a specific case, the agency will be advised whether it should grant the discharge.

Reporting school violations

12. The FFEL regulations [§ 682.402(e)(6)(i)] require a guaranty agency to notify the Department immediately whenever it becomes aware of reliable information indicating that a school may have falsely certified a student's eligibility. To what address should this notification be sent?

Guaranty agencies should notify the Guarantor and Lender Review Branch in the Department's regional office responsible for the state in which the school is located.

Former 34 CFR 668.6

13. The regulations state that for periods of enrollment beginning prior to July 1, 1987, a student's ATB was to be determined "in accordance with the requirements of 34 CFR 668.6." However, that section of the current regulations has nothing in it except the word "reserved."

The text of § 668.6 as it existed during the applicable time period follows:

> § 668.6. Ability to benefit.
>
> (a) "Ability to benefit" means that a person admitted to an institution of higher education has the ability to benefit from the education or training he or she is to receive.
>
> (b)(1) An institution that admits as regular students persons who do not have a high school diploma or the recognized equivalent of a high school diploma and who are beyond the age of compulsory school attendance in the State in which the institution is located, shall develop and consistently apply criteria for determining whether these students have the ability to benefit from the education or training offered.
>
> (2) An institution must be able to demonstrate, upon request of the Secretary, that these students have the ability to benefit.

(Authority: 20 U.S.C. 1088, 1141)

SEPTEMBER 1994

Publication Date: September 1994

SUMMARY: This letter provides guidance concerning closed school and false certification loan discharges and relief for unauthorized endorsements in the Federal Family Education Loan (FFEL) Program.

Dear Colleague:

On April 29, 1994, final regulations (effective July 1, 1994) affecting the FFEL program were published in the *Federal Register*. Sections 34 CFR 682.402(d) and (e) of those regulations prescribe the procedures for discharging the loan obligation of a borrower who received an FFEL loan on or after January 1, 1986. If the student was unable to complete his or her program of study because the school closed, or the borrower's (or the student's for whom a parent received a PLUS loan) eligibility to receive the loan was falsely certified by the school. The regulations also prescribe the procedures for providing relief for unauthorized endorsements. This letter provides guidance on implementing those regulations. Part I covers closed school loan discharges. Part II covers false certification discharges and relief for unauthorized endorsements. Part III provides guidance that applies to both types of discharges and unauthorized endorsements. Attachment A is the Department's "Cumulative List of Schools That Closed Since January 1, 1986."

The regulations give the guaranty agency initial decision-making authority on discharge claims. A formal appeal to the Department is provided under the rules only in false certification claims and unauthorized check endorsements. To review whether guarantor decisions to discharge loans comply with the regulations, the Department will use the review and audit procedures it currently uses to examine other guarantor decisions. The intent of this letter and future Department communications on this responsibility is to give guarantors an interpretation of the regulations or an explanation of the application of particular regulations to general fact patterns. In the future, more specific guidance may be given as the need arises with respect to particular schools or to specific fact patterns that come to light in litigation or otherwise.

We appreciate your assistance and cooperation as we work to implement these provisions.

Sincerely,

Leo Kornfeld

Deputy Assistant Secretary for
Student Financial Assistance Programs

Attachment

PART I. CLOSED SCHOOL DISCHARGES

1. How is a school's closure date determined?

   For purposes of the closed school discharge authorized under the regulations, a school's closure date is the date that the school ceases to provide educational instruction in all programs, as determined by the Secretary. See 34 CFR 682.402(d)(1)(ii)(A).

   Attachment A to this letter is the "Cumulative List of Schools That Closed Since January 1, 1986." It lists the schools known by the Secretary to have closed on or after January 1, 1986. The Secretary intends to update the Cumulative List with monthly supplements as new information and corrections become available. Guaranty agencies will be responsible for using the most current information. For example, if a school's closure date is revised, guaranty agencies will be expected to use the new closure date after receiving the monthly supplement containing that correction.

   For approximately two years, the Secretary has published a quarterly cumulative list of closed schools. The Secretary intends to discontinue publishing this quarterly list and give guaranty agencies and lenders access to an electronic computer database containing the information. Guaranty agencies and lenders will be able to access the computer database by modem using the telephone system, or update their records with the printed monthly supplements. Additional details will be provided at a later date.

2. What should guaranty agencies and lenders do with the listings of closed schools published by the Department?

   Guaranty agencies and lenders should review Attachment A and the subsequent lists of closed schools and notify the Department's Closed School Section immediately at (202) 401-3462 if corrections are necessary or information is missing. If the guaranty agency receives documentation that it believes will affect the Secretary's determination of a school's closure date, it should notify the Closed School Section. Evidence indicating that a school's closure date may be incorrect may include a letter from the school or state licensing agency, or a newspaper article. The Secretary will determine whether the closure date needs to be revised. In the meantime, the guaranty agency should suspend collection activity on the loan until a determination is made by the Secretary.

   It is important that the Department has the correct name, address, OPE-ID number, and closure date for each school, and that all schools are listed (including unauthorized branches and locations). Unless the Department has complete and accurate information, potentially qualifying borrowers may be prevented from receiving loan discharges, and ineligible borrowers may receive discharges to which they are not entitled. Any comments, corrections, or additions to the Cumulative List, or other information regarding closed schools, should be sent to: U.S. Department of Education, Closed School Section, P.O. Box 23800, L'Enfant Plaza Station, Washington, DC 20026, telephone number (202)708-6048.

   Within 30 days of receiving confirmation of the date of a school's closure by means of Attachment A or a supplemental listing of closed schools from the Department, or confirmation of a school's closure date by any other means, a guaranty agency must review its records and identify borrowers who appear to be eligible for a closed school loan discharge. After the eligible borrowers have been identified, the guaranty agency must follow the notification procedures prescribed in § 682.402(d)(6).

3. What should a guaranty agency do when it is notified of a revised school closure date by the Department?

   A guaranty agency must review its records to identify any borrower who received a loan discharge from that agency based on the former closure date. If the revised closure date is less than 90 days later than the closure date on which discharge decisions were made for individuals who claimed to have been in attendance on that earlier closure date, the guarantor can deem those students to have withdrawn within the qualifying 90-day pre-closure period and need not revise those decisions or demand additional information from the borrowers to confirm the discharge previously granted. For individuals who claim to have withdrawn within that 90-day period and received discharges on that basis, the agency must redetermine the borrowers' eligibility based on the new date. Within 30 days after making a determination that a previously discharged borrower does not qualify for a discharge based on the revised closure date, the agency should notify the borrower of the reasons for that determination. The agency must advise the borrower that he or she remains obligated to repay the loan, warn the borrower of the consequences of default, and explain that the borrower will be considered to be in default on the loan unless the borrower submits a written statement to the agency within 30 days stating that the borrower acknowledges the debt and, if payments are due, will begin or resume making those payments.

The Department derives the information on which it sets or revises the closure date from the most authoritative sources available, and it is unlikely that the borrower would have more reliable information about the date of the school's closure. However, because the guarantor must explain to the borrower the reasons for any reconsideration decision denying a discharge or revoking one previously given, the borrower will be able to contest that decision before being considered to be in default. If the borrower presents evidence that the guarantor considers sufficient to warrant changing the closure date, the guarantor can defer action on the loan with respect to that debtor, and should present that evidence, with its recommendation, to the Department.

Within 30 days after receiving the borrower's written statement, if the loan had been filed as a closed school claim by a lender, the agency shall treat the loan as a repurchase by the lender and return the claim file to the lender. The amount owed by the borrower will be the sum of the claim amount previously paid to the lender plus the amount of payments refunded to the borrower by the guaranty agency when it paid the claim. The lender should be instructed to resume collection efforts if payments are due. If the borrower fails to acknowledge the debt within 30 days, the agency shall consider the borrower to be in default. If the loan had been held by the agency as a defaulted loan when it was discharged, the agency should once again treat the loan as a defaulted loan owed by the borrower (including any refunded payments) to the agency. The lender or agency shall be deemed to have exercised forbearance of payment of principal and interest from the date collection activity had been suspended, and may capitalize, in accordance with § 682.202(b), any interest accrued and not paid during that period.

If an agency discovers that a borrower may have made a false certification on an application for a loan discharge, it should follow normal procedures for reporting cases of suspected fraud by contacting the Department's Office of Inspector General.

4. Does a borrower or student who attended a branch location ineligible under the Title IV programs potentially qualify for a closed school discharge?

For purposes of closed school loan discharges, a "school" means a school's main campus or any location or branch of the main campus, regardless of whether the school or its location or branch is considered eligible. *See* § 682.402(d)(1)(ii)(C). The Secretary will list closure dates for schools or locations that received funds under Title IV of the Higher Education Act, even though the school or location may have been ineligible for any of a variety of reasons, or because the location was never approved by the Secretary. In publicizing the closure date, the Secretary will use the OPE-ID number of the funding school as the OPE-ID number for ineligible locations.

5. Does a borrower or student who claims a last day of attendance that is more than 90 days prior to the school's closure date qualify for discharge?

Unless an exception has been made (see question 6), the guaranty agency should deny the claim and state the specific reasons for the denial.

6. How can a guaranty agency obtain an extension from the Department to the 90-day limit on the pre-closure withdrawal period?

The regulations provide that the Secretary may extend the 90-day period to allow a longer time period for discharge if the Secretary determines that exceptional circumstances related to a school's closing would justify an extension. Guaranty agencies that believe that exceptional circumstances justify an extension for a particular school should request an extension by contracting the Department's Closed School Section at the address previously provided. In its request, the guaranty agency should present facts it believes would justify an extension, and make whatever recommendation it deems appropriate. The Secretary will then decide whether to extend the 90-day timeframe, and notify all guaranty agencies if he determines that an extension is warranted.

7. Does a borrower or student who did not complete the program but received a diploma or a certificate qualify for discharge?

Before closing, some schools may have issued a diploma or certificate to students who did not complete the program of study. The issuance of a diploma to a student who did not complete the training program will not disqualify the borrower for discharge if the other requirements for discharge are satisfied.

8. What is a student completed the program but the school did not issue a diploma or certificate?

If a student completed the program, the issuance of a diploma or certificate is irrelevant. A borrower is eligible for a loan discharge only if the student was unable to complete a program of study.

9. How does a guaranty agency submit a request for reinsurance and report closed school activity to the Department?

The guaranty agency files a reinsurance request and reports closed school activity to the Department by using the revised Guaranty Agency Quarterly/Annual Report (ED Form 1130) and Guaranty Agency Monthly Claims and Collections Report (ED Form 1189). For guidance on completing these forms, please refer to "Dear Guaranty Agency Director" Letters 93-G-234 (June 1993), 94-G-250 (January 1994), and 94-G-253 (June 1994).

PART II. FALSE CERTIFICATION DISCHARGE AND RELIEF FOR UNAUTHORIZED ENDORSEMENTS

10. If a borrower (or student) claims that he or she did not sign the application, promissory note, loan check, or electronic funds transfer authorization, how does a guaranty agency determine if the borrower's allegation is valid?

The agency should carefully compare the contested signature(s) with the examples of signatures submitted by the borrower in accordance with § 682.402(e)(3)(iii) or (lv), and to the best of the agency's ability decide if the preponderance of evidence supports the borrower's assertion.

11. What sources of information or evidence should a guaranty agency investigate, and what actions should it take in the case of a claim for relief based on the borrower's (or student's) assertion that he or she die not sign the loan check or electronic funds transfer authorization?

If the borrower presents evidence that the guarantor finds to be credible showing that the borrower did not endorse the loan check or authorize the EFT disbursements, the guarantor must determine whether the student or borrower nevertheless received the disbursement either directly or through a credit satisfying a school charge actually due an owed by the student [*i.e.*, the tuition and other charges net of any refund owed the student]. To make that judgment, the guarantor must consider relevant evidence in its possession and other information that may be available from other sources. These sources include, in the first instance, the school records pertaining to the student's account, which may be available from State agency record custodians if not from the school itself. Where the guarantor is presented with a claim by a lender, the lender should have presented with the claim evidence to support the contention that the student received the proceeds. A guaranty agency should contact the school, the Department's regional office, the school's state licensing agency, and any other party that the guaranty agency has reason to believe would have relevant evidence and attempt to obtain documentation to show whether the student or borrower received the proceeds of the loan.

Whether the guarantor's review of evidence presented by the lender or secured by its own efforts leads it to conclude that is more probable, based on that evidence or lack of evidence, that the borrower or student did not receive the proceeds of such a disbursement, the guarantor must conclude that the loan is not enforceable, and take the actions prescribed in the regulations to give relief to the borrower and to effect the return of funds paid by the Department with respect to that loan to the lender and to the guarantor.

12. If a borrower's application for a false certification loan discharge was denied by a guaranty agency, and the borrower appeals the agency's decision to the Secretary, to what address should the guaranty agency forward the borrower's request?

Appeals should be forwarded to: U.S. Department of Education, P.O. Box 422037, San Francisco, California 94142-2037. The appeal must be clearly identified as a "false certification appeal" and must contain all the information and documentation examined by the agency when making its determination. The Department representatives in San Francisco will acknowledge receipt of the appeal to the guaranty agency and respond to the appeal request promptly. Until the appeal request is acted upon and a final decision made by the Department, the guaranty agency should cease all collections activity on the account.

13. How should guaranty agencies evaluate a borrower's claim for loan discharge based upon an alleged failure of the school to properly apply ability-to-benefit (ATB) provisions at the time the student was admitted?

Because of the complexity created by the various statutory and regulatory changes to the ATB requirements over the period covered by the false certification provisions of the regulations, the Department is still developing specific guidance which can be used by guaranty agencies to determine the validity of ATB false certification claims by borrowers seeking discharge of their FFEL loans. We will provide more detailed guidance about these ATB requirements (including guidance about what constitutes improper ATB testing) within the next few weeks.

PART III. GENERAL

14. Will the Department provide a standardized application form for borrowers to use to request a closed school (or false certification) discharge?

The Department is developing application forms for closed school and false certification student loan discharges for loans held by the Department. The Ad Hoc Standardization Committee, which is composed of members representing the Department and the student aid community, is developing standardized application forms for use by other entities holding FFEL Program loans eligible for discharge. The Department expects he forms to be available soon. Until forms are available, the Department encourages lenders and guaranty agencies either to develop and use their own forms, or to inform applicants of the regulatory requirements for discharge so that they can submit discharge requests without using application forms. A guaranty agency or lender may use one application for all discharges, or one application for closed school discharges and another for false certification discharges. Guaranty agencies must ensure that their discharge request/application forms require the borrower to provide the information and certifications specified in the regulations. Agencies using their own forms must submit them to the Department's FFEL Policy Section for review in accordance with 34 CFR 682.401(d).

The guaranty agency or lender must evaluate all discharge requests submitted by borrowers regardless of whether standardized forms are developed to determine if the applicants meet the regulatory requirements for discharge, and guarantors must ensure that sufficient information and supporting documents are secured to demonstrate whether the borrower qualifies for discharge.

15. What amount of a Federal Consolidation Loan is dischargeable?

The Federal Consolidation Loan is not itself dischargeable, but the Consolidation Loan proceeds used to pay off a loan that qualified for discharge are refunded to the borrower by means of a credit to the Consolidation Loan. The amount of the credit is the amount dischargeable on the FFEL Program loans paid off by the Consolidation Loan.

16. Is a payment history necessary to apply a discharge credit to a Federal Consolidation Loan?

Payment histories are necessary to determine that portion of the Consolidation Loan that was disbursed to pay off the discharged loan(s), and whether other payments were made reducing the discharged loan balance prior to the payoff from the Consolidation Loan. If the payment histories are not available from the prior lenders, the current lender must make reasonable attempts to obtain the information from other sources. If the lender is unable to obtain a payment history from other sources, the borrower will be required to submit evidence of payments made on the loan prior to the date of the Consolidation Loan. All payments made by the borrower on the old loan before that date are included in determining the discharge amount applied to the remaining balance of the Consolidation Loan. Post-consolidation interest should be calculated by the lender based on the balance of the closed school loan at the time the Consolidation Loan was made.

17. How should a discharge credit be applied to a Federal Consolidation Loan?

The total discharge credit amount shall fist be applied to reduce the outstanding balance of the Consolidation loan. If the entire outstanding Consolidation Loan balance is repaid by the discharge credit, any difference is returned to the borrower.

18. If the borrower fails to submit the written request and sworn statement within 60 days of being notified of this requirement, what action should the lender or guaranty agency take?

The lender or guaranty agency should resume collection activity on the loan. If the borrower submits the written request and sworn statement at a later date, the lender or guaranty agency must suspend collection activity and review the borrower's request. A borrowers' request for discharge may not be denied solely on the basis of failing to meet any time limits set by the lender, the guaranty agency, of the Department.

19. What should a lender do if a borrower's request for discharge is incomplete or contains information that would clearly make the borrower ineligible for the discharge?

The lender should not submit a claim to a guaranty agency, and must inform the borrower of the reasons why the borrower's request is inadequate within 30 days of the date the lender received the borrower's request. *See* § 682.208(c)(l). Some reasons will be more obvious than others, for example, the borrower's loan was disbursed before January 1, 1986. Because the eligibility requirements for a false certification discharge typically depend on information not generally known by the lender, it is likely that lenders will be unable to readily determine whether a borrower's request for a false certification discharge is insufficient unless the borrower's sworn statement is incomplete. In all cases where the borrower appears to meet the eligibility requirements described in the regulations, the lender must file a claim with the guaranty agency no later than 60 days after the lender received the borrower's written request and sworn statement or after the lender is notified by the Secretary or the Secretary's designee or by the guaranty agency to file a claim.

20. Can a loan that does not qualify for federal reinsurance be discharged?

Legally enforceable loans that have lost reinsurance, because of a violation of due diligence or other programmatic requirements by the lender or guaranty agency, are generally eligible for discharge if the borrower meets all of the requirements for a discharge. In such cases, the Secretary will use his authority pursuant to § 682.406(b) to waive his right to refuse to make a reinsurance payment on the loan.

C.2 Consolidation Loans

APRIL 3, 2009, FP-09-03

Publication Date: April 3, 2009

DCL ID: FP-09-03

SUBJECT: Completion of Loan Verification Certificates

SUMMARY: This letter provides updated guidance to FFEL Program loan holders concerning the completion and return of Loan Verification Certificates in connection with a borrower's application to consolidate a single FFEL Program consolidation loan into a new Federal Direct Consolidation loan.

Dear Colleague:

In a Dear Colleague Letter (DCL) dated May 17, 2007 (GEN 07-03, FP 07-07), we provided guidance that allowed the holder of a Federal Family Education Loan (FFEL) Program loan to refuse to complete and return a Loan Verification Certificate (LVC) if the loan holder believed that the only loan to be included in the new consolidation loan was a single consolidation loan held by that loan holder. That guidance continues to apply if a borrower has applied to consolidate a single FFEL Program consolidation loan with another FFEL Program lender. The earlier guidance also applies if the single consolidation loan is a joint consolidation loan, since a joint consolidation loan may not be included in a subsequent consolidation loan under any circumstances in either the FFEL Program or the William D. Ford Federal Direct Loan (Direct Loan) Program.

Statutory changes made to section 428C(a)(3) of the Higher Education Act (the HEA) by the College Cost Reduction and Access Act (the CCRAA) and the Higher Education Opportunity Act (the HEOA) allow a borrower to consolidate a single FFEL Program consolidation loan into the Direct Loan Program if:

- The FFEL consolidation loan has been submitted for default aversion or is already in default and the borrower wishes to obtain, effective July 1, 2009, an Income-Based Repayment plan on the Direct Consolidation Loan;
- The borrower wishes to use the Direct Loan Program's Public Service Loan Forgiveness Program under section 455(m) of the HEA (effective July 1, 2008); or
- The borrower wishes to take advantage of the Direct Loan Program's no interest accrual benefit for active duty service members under section 455(o) of the HEA and the FFEL Program consolidation loan is one that repaid FFEL Program loans that were first disbursed on or after October 1, 2008.

As a result of these statutory changes, all loan holders must return completed LVCs to the Direct Loan Program in accordance with 34 CFR 682.209(j) for any borrower who has applied to consolidate a single FFEL Program consolidation loan (other than a joint consolidation loan) into the Direct Loan Program. Except in the case of a joint FFEL consolidation loan, a loan holder may not refuse to complete and return an LVC for a borrower who has applied to consolidate into the Direct Loan Program based solely on the fact that the only loan to be consolidated is a single FFEL Program consolidation loan.

Please direct any questions on this letter to Pam Moran by phone to (202) 502-7732 or by e-mail to pamela.moran@ed.gov.

Sincerely,

Daniel T. Madzelan

Delegated the Authority to Perform
the Functions and Duties of the
Assistant Secretary for
Postsecondary Education

MAY 2007, GEN-07-03, FP-07-07

Publication Date: May 2007
DCL ID: GEN-07-03, FP-07-07

SUBJECT: Update on Consolidation Loan Issues

SUMMARY: This letter responds to questions we have received as a result of the Department's previous guidance concerning the completion and return of Loan Verification Certificates (LVCs).

Posted on 05-22-2007

Dear Colleague:

On December 1, 2006, the Department issued a Dear Colleague Letter (GEN-06-20; FP-0-16) to remind program participants of the rules governing the consolidation of loans following recently enacted legislation. Since we issued that letter, we have received a number of questions from borrowers and lenders on this topic. For this reason, we are providing this updated guidance.

In Attachment C to the December 1, 2006 Dear Colleague Letter, we listed the limited circumstances in which a loan holder is not required to complete a Loan Verification Certificate (LVC) and instead must provide the requesting lender with a written explanation for not completing the form. The Department's regulations at 34 C.F.R. § 682.209(j) allow a loan holder that cannot, because of certain limited reasons, provide the completed LVC within the 10 business-day period to explain in writing to the intended consolidating lender, within the same 10 business-day period, why it cannot do so. One such circumstance is the occurrence of a technical problem, such as a computer malfunction, that prevents the holder or servicer from providing the information within the 10 business-day period. In that case, the loan holder must provide the information as soon as the technical problem is resolved. The only other reasons noted in that Dear Colleague Letter for not completing an LVC were when:

- The loan holder never held the loan;
- The loan holder held the loan but has assigned it to a guaranty agency;
- The loan holder sold the loan;
- The loan the borrower wishes to consolidate is more than 270 days delinquent and a default claim has been submitted to the guaranty agency;
- The loan has not been fully disbursed or the borrower is not in grace or repayment status;
- A judgment has been entered against the borrower on the loan that the borrower wants to consolidate; or
- The loan the borrower wishes to consolidate is subject to collection by wage garnishment.

In each circumstance listed above, the loan holder must provide the requesting lender with an explanation of why the LVC is not being completed.

As a result of comments received since we issued the December letter, we have identified two additional circumstances in which a loan holder can decline to complete an LVC. These are when:

- The loan holder had within the last 90 days completed an LVC on the borrower's loan for another lender, thus indicating that the borrower may have more than one consolidation loan application outstanding.
- The borrower appears to have no eligible loans other than a single consolidation loan held by the loan holder (e.g., NSLDS or other available records indicate that the borrower has already consolidated all eligible loans).

As with the earlier listing, for each of these two additional circumstances the loan holder must provide the requesting lender, within the 10 business-day period, with an explanation of why the LVC is not being completed with payoff information. For these two additional conditions only, the loan holder must also notify our Federal Student Aid Financial Partners staff of the holder's decision not to complete the LVC. To provide this notification, the loan holder must send an email to "LVC.Referral@ed.gov" that includes a password protected Winzip file. The password protected file must include the name of the loan holder submitting the file, a contact name and phone number, the name and lender ID (LID) number of the requesting lender, the borrower's name and social security number, the type of loan held, and the reason why the LVC was not completed. When choosing to password protect the file, the Winzip software will ask what encryption algorithm to use; select AES encryption. The password must contain at least 8 characters, including numeric and alphanumeric characters, upper and lower case letters and special characters. Send the password by separate email to the same address (LVC.Referral@ed.gov).

Once the explanation is provided to the requesting lender, if the requesting lender provides additional information to the loan holder that supports the borrower's eligibility to consolidate the loan(s), the holder must complete the LVC within 10 business days of receipt of that information. For the first circumstance noted above, such information would be a written statement from the borrower stating that the borrower has cancelled any previous consolidation loan applications. For the second circumstance, the requesting lender could provide documentation showing that the borrower has one or more additional loans that will be included along with the single consolidation loan in a new consolidation loan.

The Department intends to monitor the LVC process closely and will take appropriate enforcement actions if a consolidating lender has a pattern of sending LVC requests for borrowers who are not eligible for a consolidation loan, or if a loan holder has a practice of refusing to complete LVCs for borrowers who are eligible to consolidate their loans.

On another matter, we are concerned that some LVCs sent to loan holders, particularly those sent by third-party servicers and by entities making loans under a lender trustee agreement, do not include the name of the consolidating lender to which the borrower has submitted a consolidation loan application and which will be making the consolidation loan. An LVC may not be submitted to a loan holder and cannot be completed by the holder, unless the borrower has submitted a properly completed and signed consolidation loan application to the requesting lender legally authorizing the release of the borrower-specific information noted on the LVC. The inclusion of the single consolidating lender's name and Lender ID on the LVC is considered certification by that lender that it has received a properly completed consolidation application from the borrower. Of course, if that lender cannot document to the Department's satisfaction, that it, or its authorized agent, received the completed and signed consolidation loan application before the LVC was requested, it will be subject to appropriate sanctions. Therefore, if a loan holder receives an LVC that does not include the name and lender identification (LID) number of the eligible lender or trustee lender that received the borrower's application under Item 19 of the LVC, it should not provide any information related to a borrower's loan and should instead provide a written explanation to inform the requestor as to why it is not completing the LVC. This is the only additional circumstance, beyond those noted in this letter, under which a loan holder may provide a written explanation to the requestor rather than submitting a completed LVC.

Finally, we have been advised that some consolidating lenders (or their agents) have asked borrowers to complete and sign a consolidation loan application prior to the borrower's loans being eligible for consolidation (e.g., while the loans are is still in an in-school status and have not entered the grace period). Such practices are not permitted, since the borrower certifies in the application that the loans are eligible for consolidation.

We thank you for your cooperation. If you have any questions on the issues discussed in this letter, please contact Pamela Moran by email at pamela.moran@ed.gov or by phone at (202) 502-7732.

Sincerely,

James F. Manning

Delegated the Authority for
the Assistant Secretary for
Postsecondary Education

Attachments/Enclosures:

[*Editor's note*: Attachments not reprinted herein.]

C.3 Borrower Assistance

APRIL 2005, GEN-05-06

Publication Date: April 2005

DCL ID: GEN-05-06, FP-05-04

SUBJECT: Access To and Use of NSLDS Information

SUMMARY: This letter reminds members of the financial aid community who have access to information contained in NSLDS that they are responsible for using their access properly and for protecting the sensitive data contained in the system.

Posted on 04-11-2005

Dear Colleague:

The U.S. Department of Education's National Student Loan Data System (NSLDS) is a comprehensive database containing personal and financial information related to an individual's receipt of Federal student financial aid authorized under Title IV of the Higher Education Act of 1965, as amended. The data contained in NSLDS is confidential and is protected by the Privacy Act of 1974, as amended and other applicable statutes and regulations. Access to NSLDS by postsecondary educational institutions, organizations that participate in the Federal Family Education Loan (FFEL) Program, and other approved entities is made available only for the general purpose of assisting with determining the eligibility of an applicant for Federal student aid and in the collection of Federal student loans and grant overpayments. NSLDS information may not be used for any other purpose, including the marketing of student loans or other products.

Failure to comply with NSLDS access and use requirements, as described in this letter, may result in the organization or individual user losing access to NSLDS and/or being subject to sanctions, including, but not limited to, the initiation of a limitation, suspension, or termination action or a debarment proceeding against the postsecondary institution or FFEL participant. Additionally, institutional sanctions may apply to any organization that, by sharing its institutional or FFEL Program identifiers, has provided other entities or individuals the capability to access to NSLDS information. We are specifically troubled by the use of FFEL lender ID's by organizations only minimally related to the lender of record. Such organizations include collection agencies and loan brokerage or marketing firms.

Access to NSLDS information is granted to individuals whose specific job responsibilities include at least one of the activities listed below. These individuals must not use their access to NSLDS information for any other purpose.

Under Federal law, the Department is required to publish a Notice identifying the routine uses of records maintained in a Federal system of records like NSLDS. The Notice for NSLDS was published on December 27, 1999, 64 Fed. Reg. 72384, 72395–72397. That notice makes it clear that the Department can properly disclose information from records in NSLDS to persons who are authorized to receive the information only for specific purposes. The system Notice explains that lenders, loan holders and servicers can have access to NSLDS information for limited purposes, which include only the following—

- Determining a specific student applicant's eligibility for Title IV student aid;
- Billing and collecting on a Title IV loan;
- Enforcing the terms of a Title IV loan;
- Billing and collecting on a Title IV grant overpayment;
- Submitting student enrollment information;
- Ensuring the accuracy of a financial aid or borrower record;
- Assisting with default aversion activities; and
- Obtaining default rate information.

Each organization whose employees are allowed access to NSLDS data is required to have a Destination Point Administrator (DPA) appointed by the organization's Chief Executive Officer (CEO) using a document that requires the signatures of both the DPA and the CEO. The DPA must not only monitor the use and access of NSLDS data by all of the organization's NSLDS users, but must also ensure users are aware of their responsibilities regarding access to NSLDS. The DPA must also de-activate a User-ID when the person to whom it was assigned is no longer with the organization or otherwise is no longer eligible to have access to NSLDS. Thus, all authorized NSLDS users in an organization, their DPA, and the organization's CEO are all personally responsible for prohibiting improper access to the NSLDS database or improper use of the data contained in and obtained from the NSLDS database.

Each NSLDS user is responsible for protecting his or her access to NSLDS and the data available. Each person who accesses NSLDS must use his or her own User-ID. That person is responsible for safeguarding the User-ID and password and must not allow any other person to use them. Access to the NSLDS Web site is limited to one borrower's record at a time by an individual user. Use of an automated tool to access borrowers' information or use of screen scraping technology for downloading data or pre-populating forms are prohibited. Further, sharing or providing data retrieved by an authorized person from NSLDS with persons or organizations who are not expressly authorized to receive that information for the purposes listed in the Systems Notice are also prohibited.

We are concerned that some organizations and individuals may not understand the requirements, as described in this letter, for access to and use of the private information contained in NSLDS. As noted above, access to NSLDS is restricted to the staff of an eligible Title IV participating postsecondary institution and to eligible FFEL lenders, lender servicers, and guaranty agencies. With exceptions not relevant here, no other persons or organizations can have access to NSLDS data. Federal laws and rules require the Department to take appropriate steps to ensure the confidentiality of records containing personal and confidential information. To meet this obligation, we regularly analyze NSLDS usage statistics to determine if security of the NSLDS system may be compromised and we have implemented an on-going daily monitoring of the system to track access usage. If, as result of these system activities or for any other reason, we believe that a user and/or an organization has violated the NSLDS access and use responsibilities we will discharge our duty under the Privacy Act by immediately, and without any advance notice or right to appeal, terminate that user's and organization's access to NSLDS. Additionally, depending upon the nature of the violation, we may initiate other sanctions against the organization, as noted above.

An eligible organization that allows unauthorized access to NSLDS will be considered to have violated its responsibilities and places itself at risk of losing access to NSLDS, to other Departmental systems and data, and to possible loss of eligibility to participate in the Title IV student aid programs. We urge all organizations to provide a copy of this letter to any of its staff who has access to NSLDS, to provide in its briefings and/or training sessions information on the importance of maintaining the privacy of NSLDS data, and to review its own policies, procedures, and agreements to ensure that it is in full compliance.

We look forward to working with our partner organizations to maintain both the usefulness of NSLDS data and the security of the information contained in NSLDS. If you have any questions on access to NSLDS information please contact NSLDS customer service at 1-800-999-8219.

Sincerely,

Matteo Fontana

General Manager, FSA Financial Partners Services

C.4 Eligibility for Federal Aid

JUNE 4, 2010, GEN-10-07

Publication Date: June 4, 2010

DCL ID: GEN-10-07

SUBJECT: Student Aid Eligibility—Eligibility for Title IV Aid for "Battered Immigrants-Qualified Aliens" as provided for in the Violence Against Women Act

SUMMARY: This letter describes the process by which a person who has documentation provided by the Department of Homeland Security's United States Citizenship and Immigration Service that supports a finding that the person is a "Battered Immigrant" and meets the definition of a "qualified alien" can qualify for Title IV, HEA program assistance.

Dear Colleague:

BACKGROUND:

Under certain conditions and with the documentation described below, some non-U.S. citizens who are "Battered Immigrants-Qualified Aliens" and their designated children may receive federal student financial assistance under Title IV of the Higher Education Act of 1965, as amended (HEA).

Normally, when a U.S. citizen (or lawful permanent resident) marries an alien and wishes to bring his or her spouse to the U.S., the U.S. citizen petitions the Department of Homeland Security's (DHS's) United States Citizenship and Immigration Service (USCIS) office so the alien spouse may legally reside in the U.S. However, sometimes in the case of domestic violence, the abusing citizen-spouse threatens the alien-spouse and/or controls the petitioning process. Immigrants who are spouses of U.S. citizens or spouses of lawful permanent residents, and who are victims of domestic violence, as determined by the USCIS, may be deemed "qualified aliens," which under the Violence Against Women Act (VAWA) makes them and their designated children eligible for "federal public benefits," including federal student financial assistance under Title IV of the HEA. The VAWA allows the battered immigrant to self-petition the USCIS for such a determination without the cooperation or knowledge of the abuser.

Due to confidentiality concerns,[1] information about such battered immigrants is not maintained in the Department of Homeland Security's Systematic Alien Verification for Entitlements system that is generally used for computer matching between the Department of Education (ED) and DHS. Instead, DHS has a unit separate from its central or regional offices that maintains information on VAWA Battered Immigrants.

---

1 8 USC 1367(a)(2) prohibits DHS from using or disclosing to anyone, other than a sworn officer of DHS, *any* information related to the beneficiary of a protected application, which includes all applications under VAWA.

As a result, the submission of a Free Application for Federal Student Aid (FAFSA) by a Battered Immigrant-Qualified Alien will not yield a positive match with DHS. Also, the collection from the applicant by a postsecondary educational institution of USCIS-provided documentation and its submission to the local USCIS office with a G-845S Document Verification Request form, as provided for other types of eligible noncitizens, will not provide verification of the applicant's status as a qualified alien.[2]

The guidance in this letter describes the documentation process that must be used for a person who requests Title IV eligibility based upon his or her status as a "Battered Immigrant-Qualified Alien."

Generally, a Battered Immigrant-Qualified Alien receives an Alien Registration Number (A-Number) upon arrival to the U.S. When completing the FAFSA, the Battered Immigrant will indicate on the FAFSA that they are an eligible noncitizen and provide their "A-Number." While Battered Immigrants are not "eligible noncitizens" for the purpose of the ED/DHS computer match, as indicated above, they are noncitizens who, as determined by DHS-USCIS, are eligible for federal benefits, including Title IV student assistance.

DOCUMENTATION REQUIREMENTS:

The documentation that must be provided depends on the applicant's DHS-USCIS Case Type, as described below.

1. Type of Case: Self-petitioning cases under VAWA

Description—When an immigrant self-petitions DHS-USCIS for a status of Battered Immigrant-Qualified Alien (by filing an I-360 form), the USCIS will make an initial determination to:

(1) deny the petition,

(2) approve the petition, or

(3) find that a "prima facie" case has been established.

Either the approval of the self-petition or a finding of a "prima facie" case establishes an otherwise eligible applicant's eligibility for Title IV, HEA program assistance. However, a finding of a "prima facie" case will have an expiration date. As a result, for "prima facie" cases, Title IV eligibility will end the day after the expiration date, unless the USCIS has changed the applicant's status to "approved," or has extended the expiration date of the "prima facie" case.

Documentation—The USCIS will respond to an applicant's self-petition by issuing to the applicant an I-797, Notice of Action form.

NOTE: The I-797 form is used by the USCIS for many purposes, so it is critical that it be carefully reviewed.

---

[2] ED has developed this guidance in conjunction with DHS-USCIS to establish these special procedures for an institution to verify a student's Battered Immigrant-Qualified Alien status. Due to the confidential and sensitive nature of this information, if an institution requires that the applicant information be verified, the institution must send such verification inquiries to the specific office address at the end of this guidance, rather than to its local DHS-USCIS office. Local DHS-USCIS offices will not be able to verify Battered Immigrant-Qualified Alien status.

Approval—USCIS will provide a DHS-USCIS Form I-797, Notice of Action form, indicating the applicant's status. When a self-petitioning spouse is approved, the I-797 will indicate "Notice Type: Approval Notice" and the Section reference will read, "Self-Petitioning Spouse of U.S.C. or L.P.R." In the narrative below, there will be a statement such as, "The above petition has been approved." When the I-797 has the above designations, an otherwise eligible applicant can be awarded and disbursed Title IV, HEA program assistance and no verification with DHS-USCIS is required.

In cases where the self-petitioning spouse's application has been approved, a separate I-797 form will be issued by USCIS with the names and dates of birth of any children listed by the applicant. That I-797 form will read, "Notice Type: Notice of Dependent Child(ren), Section: Self-Petitioning Spouse of U.S.C. or L.P.R." In the narrative it will state, "The following derivative children are named on the approved Petition" and then the names and birth dates of the child(ren) will be provided. These children, if otherwise eligible, may receive Title IV, HEA program assistance and no verification with DHS-USCIS is required.

The status of a child listed on a self-petitioner's notice of action when the petition has been approved by DHS-USCIS continues even after the child has reached the age of majority. In some cases, a dependent child can be the self-petitioner and therefore the I-797 form would read, "Notice Type: Approval Notice, Section: Self-Petitioning Child of U.S.C. or L.P.R." in a case where the U.S. citizen or lawful permanent resident is abusing the child.

When the I-797 form has the above designations, an otherwise eligible applicant can be awarded and disbursed Title IV, HEA program assistance and no verification with DHS-USCIS is required.

"Prima Facie" Case—The I-797, Notice of Action will sometimes indicate "Section: Self-Petitioning Spouse of U.S.C. or L.P.R. ESTABLISHMENT OF PRIMA FACIE CASE." This status is usually provided for a period of up to 180 days (as indicated on the I-797, Notice of Action form). As long as the I-797 form has not expired, an otherwise eligible applicant can be awarded and disbursed Title IV, HEA program assistance and no verification with DHS-USCIS is required. Also, at times, DHS-USCIS will extend the "prima facie" case for a specific period of time until the case is either approved or denied. As long as the expiration date has not occurred, an otherwise eligible Title IV, HEA applicant is eligible to receive Title IV, HEA program assistance. It is our understanding that a self-petitioner can submit a written request for an extension up to 15 days prior to the expiration date and receive an extension. Unless the I-360 application has been denied, the petitioner should receive an extension of the "prima facie" case on a subsequent I-797 form.

The I-797 may include a section with the names and dates of birth of any children of the self-petitioning spouse. These children are also eligible to receive Federal Title IV student aid under the "prima facie" determination of the parent with the same expiration date limitation. The child's eligibility continues even after the child has reached the age of majority, as long as the I-797 has not expired.

Other General Notes:

a. While the dependent children may be listed on the parent's self-petition approval, each of the eligible children must individually make a separate request for deferred action to DHS-USCIS.

b. If the self-petitioning spouse is ultimately denied approval, then the dependent children initially listed on the petitioner's I-797 would also be denied and therefore not be eligible for Title IV, HEA program assistance.

c. In some cases, the USCIS will initially acknowledge the receipt of the self-petition. An acknowledgment does not make the applicant (or his/her named dependent children) eligible for Title IV, HEA program assistance.

d. The USCIS may also issue a Notice of Deferred Action. This is an administrative choice to give lower priority for removal of the immigrant from the U.S. Again, because the I-797 Notice of Action can be used for a wide variety of purposes (beyond the scope of Title IV, HEA program eligibility), and as the "Case Type" heading on the form indicates, this notice of deferred action could be applicable to cases unrelated to a self-petitioning case under VAWA; therefore, the Notice of Deferred Action alone cannot be used as documentation of a self-petitioner. Instead, the self-petitioner must provide either a copy of the self-petitioner approval notice or a notice of action that establishes a "prima facie" case (that has not expired). Generally, a Notice of Deferred Action has a termination date, therefore prior to the termination date, an otherwise eligible applicant also providing a copy of the self-petitioner's approval status or that of the establishment of a "prima facie" case may be awarded and disbursed Title IV, HEA program assistance. However, after the termination date of the Notice of Deferred Action, the applicant is no longer eligible to receive Title IV, HEA funds. The applicant may request and receive a supplemental notice extending the termination date and therefore regain Title IV eligibility.

2. Type of Case: Suspension of deportation cases under VAWA

Description—An immigration judge can issue an order to suspend the deportation of the abused spouse, parent, or child under VAWA. An otherwise eligible applicant whose immigration court order has not expired may be awarded and disbursed Title IV, HEA program assistance and no verification is required with DHS-USCIS.

Documentation—The applicant receives a copy of the Immigration Court Order. If the court order clearly indicates suspension of deportation by the immigration judge, an otherwise eligible applicant may be awarded and disbursed Title IV, HEA program assistance and no verification is required with DHS-USCIS. Often, the institution may be unclear about the court's order; we suggest that the institution follow the instructions below to obtain verification from USCIS.

3. Type of Case—Cancellation of removal cases under VAWA

Description—An immigration judge can issue an order to cancel the removal of the abused spouse, parent, or child under VAWA. An otherwise eligible applicant whose immigration court order has not expired may be awarded and disbursed Title IV, HEA program assistance and no verification is required with DHS-USCIS.

Documentation—The applicant receives a copy of the Immigration Court Order. If the court order clearly indicates cancellation of removal by the immigration judge, an otherwise eligible applicant may be awarded and disbursed Title IV, HEA program assistance and no verification is required with DHS-USCIS. Often, the institution may be unclear about the court's order; we suggest that the institution follow the instructions below to obtain verification from USCIS.

FINANCIAL AID ADMINISTRATOR ACTION:

Since the applicants above will not successfully pass the computer match conducted between ED and DHS, the financial aid administrator must collect and examine a copy of the USCIS-provided documents described above and retain a copy of the documents in the student's financial assistance file. If the documents support the applicant's status under VAWA and have not expired, an otherwise eligible student can be awarded and disbursed Title IV, HEA program assistance and verification with DHS-USCIS is not required. It is important for financial aid administrators and others at the institution to bear in mind the confidential and sensitive nature of the documents establishing the student's Battered Immigrant-Qualified Alien status, and the institution's obligation to comply with the privacy requirements of the Family Educational Rights and Privacy Act (FERPA), 20 U.S.C. § 1232g and 34 CFR Part 99.

The financial aid administrator must also check the student's response to the citizenship question on the FAFSA. Most of the affected students will indicate that they are eligible noncitizens. By following the guidance in this letter, the financial aid administrator will resolve the fact that the student did not successfully pass the computer match. However, it is also possible that the student may indicate that he or she is neither a citizen, nor an eligible noncitizen. In this case, the student should correct the FAFSA and indicate that the student is an eligible noncitizen. This is an important correction needed to allow for the calculation of an Expected Family Contribution (EFC). Indicating that the student is neither a citizen, nor an eligible noncitizen, will cause the FAFSA to be rejected.

Students who apply for Title IV, HEA program assistance in a subsequent year may rely upon the original DHS-USCIS documentation provided, as long as that documentation has not expired. If the documentation has expired, the applicant is required to obtain new DHS-USCIS documentation. When the documentation has not expired, but was provided in a prior award year, the institution must have the student provide a written and dated statement indicating that their DHS-USCIS immigration status as provided under VAWA remains in effect without change. This documentation must remain in the applicant's financial assistance file at the institution.

PROCEDURES WHEN THE DOCUMENTATION IS LOST, THE INSTITUTION IS UNCLEAR ABOUT THE DOCUMENTATION, OR THE DOCUMENTATION HAS EXPIRED:

In the event that:

- The student has lost or cannot provide a copy of his or her USCIS-provided documentation,
- The institution has reservations about the documentation provided by the applicant or is unclear about the outcome reflected in the documentation, or

- The documentation has expired,

the financial aid administrator must submit a completed G-845S form and attach copies of any documentation provided by the applicant. When completing the G-845S form, check "Box 8—Other" and write-in "VAWA verification" and submit the information to DHS-USCIS for a VAWA verification determination at the following address. (NOTE: This is not the Buffalo Field Office address.)

DHS-USCIS
186 Exchange Street
Buffalo, NY 14204

Eligibility for Title IV, HEA program assistance as a Battered Immigrant—Qualified Alien will be based on the results of the G-845S submission to the Buffalo office of DHS-USCIS.

FOR FURTHER INFORMATION OR TO CONTACT THE DEPARTMENT OF EDUCATION ON THIS TOPIC:

If you have any questions regarding this letter, please contact Dan Klock via e-mail at dan.klock@ed.gov or Carney McCullough via e-mail at carney.mccullough@ed.gov.

We appreciate your cooperation and assistance in helping these applicants as we work to implement this new process.

Sincerely,

Daniel T. Madzelan

Delegated the Authority to Perform
the Functions and Duties of the
Assistant Secretary for
Postsecondary Education

Appendix D   Student Assistance Forms

The Department of Education prints forms for the various discharge programs as well as loan and deferment applications. Most of these forms are available on the Department's website at www.ed.gov. Selected forms are reprinted below. Advocates should note that many state guaranty agencies prefer that borrowers use their discharge forms instead of the federal forms printed below. State guaranty agency forms are available from the individual agencies and are not reprinted here.

D.1 Applications for Loans and Federal Aid

D.1.1 The Free Application for Federal Student Aid (FAFSA)

FREE APPLICATION FOR FEDERAL STUDENT AID
July 1, 2010 — June 30, 2011

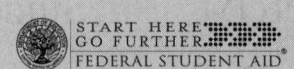

Use this form to apply free for federal and state student grants, work-study and loans.
Or apply free online at **www.fafsa.gov**.

Applying by the Deadlines

For federal aid, submit your application as early as possible, but no earlier than January 1, 2010. We must receive your application no later than June 30, 2011. Your college must have your correct, complete information by your last day of enrollment in the 2010-2011 school year.

For state or college aid, the deadline may be as early as January 2010. See the table to the right for state deadlines. You may also need to complete additional forms.

Check with your high school guidance counselor or a financial aid administrator at your college about state and college sources of student aid and deadlines.

If you are filing close to one of these deadlines, we recommend you file online at **www.fafsa.gov**. This is the fastest and easiest way to apply for aid.

Using Your Tax Return

If you are supposed to file a 2009 federal income tax return, we recommend that you complete it before filling out this form. If you have not yet completed your 2009 tax return, you can still submit your FAFSA using best estimates. After you submit your tax return, correct any income or tax information that is different from what you initially submitted on your FAFSA.

Filling Out the FAFSA

If you or your family has unusual circumstances that might affect your financial situation (such as loss of employment), complete this form to the extent you can, then submit it as instructed and consult with the financial aid office at the college you plan to attend.

For more information or help in filling out the FAFSA, go to **www.studentaid.ed.gov/completefafsa** or call 1-800-4-FED-AID (1-800-433-3243). TTY users (for the hearing impaired) may call 1-800-730-8913.

Fill the answer fields directly on your screen or print the form and complete it by hand. Your answers will be read electronically; therefore, if you complete the form by hand:

- use black ink and fill in circles completely:
- print clearly in CAPITAL letters and skip a box between words:
- report dollar amounts (such as $12,356.41) like this:

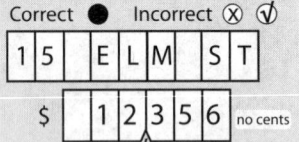

Blue is for student information and purple is for parent information.

Mailing Your FAFSA

After you complete this application, make a copy of pages 3 through 8 for your records. Then mail the original of pages 3 through 8 to:

Federal Student Aid Programs, P.O. Box 4692, Mt. Vernon, IL 62864-4692.

After your application is processed, you will receive a summary of your information in your *Student Aid Report* (SAR). If you provide an e-mail address, your SAR will be sent by e-mail within 3-5 days. If you do not provide an e-mail address, your SAR will be mailed to you within three weeks. If you would like to check the status of your FAFSA, go to **www.fafsa.gov** or call 1-800-4-FED-AID.

Let's Get Started!

Now go to page 3 of the application form and begin filling it out. Refer to the notes as instructed.

STATE AID DEADLINES

Check with your financial aid administrator for these states and territories:

AL, AS *, AZ, CO, FM *, GA, GU *, HI *, MH *, MP *, NC, NE, NM, NV *, PR, PW *, SD *, TX *, UT, VA *, VI *, VT *, WA, WI and WY *.

Pay attention to the symbols that may be listed after your state deadline.

AK	April 15, 2010 *(date received)*
AR	Academic Challenge - June 1, 2010 *(date received)*
	Workforce Grant - Contact the financial aid office.
	Higher Education Opportunity Grant
	- June 1, 2010 (fall term) *(date received)*
	- November 1, 2010 (spring term) *(date received)*
CA	Initial awards - March 2, 2010 + *
	Additional community college awards
	- September 2, 2010 *(date postmarked)* + *
CT	February 15, 2010 *(date received)* # *
DC	June 30, 2010 *(date received by state)* # *
DE	April 15, 2010 *(date received)*
FL	May 15, 2010 *(date processed)*
IA	July 1, 2010 *(date received)*
ID	Opportunity Grant - March 1, 2010 *(date received)* # *
IL	As soon as possible after 1/1/2010. Awards made until funds are depleted.
IN	March 10, 2010 *(date received)*
KS	April 1, 2010 *(date received)* # *
KY	March 15, 2010 *(date received)* #
LA	July 1, 2010 *(date received)*
MA	May 1, 2010 *(date received)* #
MD	March 1, 2010 *(date received)*
ME	May 1, 2010 *(date received)*
MI	March 1, 2010 *(date received)*
MN	30 days after term starts *(date received)*
MO	April 1, 2010 *(date received)* #
MS	MTAG and MESG Grants - September 15, 2010 *(date received)* #
	HELP Scholarship - March 31, 2010 *(date received)* #
MT	March 1, 2010 *(date received)* #
ND	March 15, 2010 *(date received)*
NH	May 1, 2010 *(date received)*
NJ	2009-2010 Tuition Aid Grant recipients - June 1, 2010 *(date received)*
	All other applicants
	- October 1, 2010, fall & spring terms *(date received)*
	- March 1, 2011, spring term only *(date received)*
NY	May 1, 2011 *(date received)* + *
OH	October 1, 2010 *(date received)*
OK	April 15, 2010 *(date received)* #
OR	OSAC Scholarship - March 1, 2010
	Oregon Opportunity Grant - Contact the financial aid office.
PA	All 2009-2010 State Grant recipients & all non-2009-2010 State Grant recipients in degree program
	- May 1, 2010 *(date received)* *
	All other applicants - August 1, 2010 *(date received)* *
RI	March 1, 2010 *(date received)* #
SC	Tuition Grants - June 30, 2010 *(date received)*
	SC Commission on Higher Education - no deadline
TN	State Grant - February 15, 2010 *(date received)* #
	State Lottery - September 1, 2010 *(date received)* #
WV	April 15, 2010 *(date received)* # *

\# For priority consideration, submit application by date specified.
\+ Applicants encouraged to obtain proof of mailing.
* Additional form may be required.

Notes for questions 14 and 15 (page 3)

If you are an eligible noncitizen, write in your eight- or nine-digit Alien Registration Number. Generally, you are an eligible noncitizen if you are (1) a permanent U.S. resident with a Permanent Resident Card (I-551); (2) a conditional permanent resident (I-551C); or (3) the holder of an Arrival-Departure Record (I-94) from the Department of Homeland Security showing any one of the following designations: "Refugee," "Asylum Granted," "Parolee" (I-94 confirms that you were paroled for a minimum of one year and status has not expired), "Victim of human trafficking," T-Visa holder (T-1, T-2, T-3, etc.) or "Cuban-Haitian Entrant."

If you are in the U.S. on an F1 or F2 student visa, a J1 or J2 exchange visitor visa, or a G series visa (pertaining to international organizations), select "No, I am not a citizen or eligible noncitizen." You will not be eligible for federal student aid; however, you should still complete the application because you may be eligible for state or college aid.

Notes for question 22 (page 3)

The Selective Service System, and the registration requirement for young men, preserves America's ability to provide manpower in an emergency to the U.S. Armed Forces. Almost all men—ages 18 through 25—must register. For more information about Selective Service, visit **www.sss.gov**.

Notes for question 30 (page 4)

For undergraduates, select the enrollment status for the college you will most likely attend.

- "Full-time" generally means taking at least 12 credit hours in a term or 24 clock hours per week.
- "Three-quarter-time" generally means taking at least 9 credit hours in a term or 18 clock hours per week.
- "Half-time" generally means taking at least 6 credit hours in a term or 12 clock hours per week.

Notes for question 32 (page 4)

The Teacher Education Assistance for College and Higher Education (TEACH) Grant Program provides grants to students enrolled in a participating college who intend to teach in a high-need field in a public or private elementary or secondary school that serves students from low-income families. Answer "**Yes**" to learn more about the TEACH Grant. Answer "**No**" if you are not interested in the TEACH Grant. Answer "**Don't know**" if you are not sure but would like more information about the TEACH Grant. Additional information about the TEACH Grant Program is available at **www.teachgrant.ed.gov**.

Notes for questions 34 (page 4) and 81 (page 6)

If you filed or will file a foreign tax return, a tax return with Puerto Rico, another U.S. territory (e.g., Guam, American Samoa, the U.S. Virgin Islands, Swain's Island or the Northern Marianas Islands) or one of the Freely Associated States (i.e., the Republic of Palau, the Republic of the Marshall Islands or the Federated States of Micronesia), use the information from that return to fill out this form. If you filed a foreign return, convert all monetary units to U.S. dollars, using the exchange rate that is in effect today. To view the daily exchange rate, go to **www.federalreserve.gov/releases/h10/update**.

Notes for questions 35 (page 4) and 82 (page 6)

In general, a person is eligible to file a 1040A or 1040EZ if he or she makes less than $100,000, does not itemize deductions, does not receive income from his or her own business or farm and does not receive alimony. A person is not eligible to file a 1040A or 1040EZ if he or she makes $100,000 or more, itemizes deductions, receives income from his or her own business or farm, is self-employed, receives alimony or is required to file Schedule D for capital gains. If you filed a 1040 only to claim Hope or Lifetime Learning credits, and you would have otherwise been eligible for a 1040A or 1040EZ, you should answer "**Yes**" to this question. If you filed a 1040 and were not required to file a tax return, you should answer "**Yes**" to this question.

Notes for questions 38 (page 4) and 86 (page 7) — Notes for those who filed a 1040EZ

On the 1040EZ, if a person didn't check either box on line 5, enter 01 if he or she is single, or 02 if he or she is married. If a person checked either the "you" or "spouse" box on line 5, use 1040EZ worksheet line F to determine the number of exemptions ($3,650 equals one exemption).

Notes for questions 42 and 43 (page 4) and 90 and 91 (page 7)

Net worth means current value minus debt. If net worth is negative, enter 0.

Investments include real estate (do not include the home you live in), trust funds, UGMA and UTMA accounts, money market funds, mutual funds, certificates of deposit, stocks, stock options, bonds, other securities, installment and land sale contracts (including mortgages held), commodities, etc.

Investments also include qualified educational benefits or education savings accounts (e.g. Coverdell savings accounts, 529 college savings plans and the refund value of 529 prepaid tuition plans). For a student who does not report parental information, the accounts owned by the student (and/or the student's spouse) are reported as student investments in question 42. For a student who must report parental information, the accounts are reported as parental investments in question 90, including all accounts owned by the student and all accounts owned by the parents for any member of the household.

Investments do not include the home you live in, the value of life insurance, retirement plans (401[k] plans, pension funds, annuities, non-education IRAs, Keogh plans, etc.) or cash, savings and checking accounts already reported in questions 41 and 89.
Investments also do not include UGMA and UTMA accounts for which you are the custodian, but not the owner.

Investment value means the current balance or market value of these investments as of today. Investment debt means only those debts that are related to the investments.

Business and/or investment farm value includes the market value of land, buildings, machinery, equipment, inventory, etc. Business and/or investment farm debt means only those debts for which the business or investment farm was used as collateral.

Business value does not include the value of a small business if your family owns and controls more than 50 percent of the business and the business has 100 or fewer full-time or full-time equivalent employees. For small business value, your family includes (1) persons directly related to you, such as a parent, sister or cousin, or (2) persons who are or were related to you by marriage, such as a spouse, stepparent or sister-in-law.

Investment farm value does not include the value of a family farm that you (your spouse and/or your parents) live on and operate.

Notes for questions 49 (page 5)

Answer "**Yes**" if you are currently serving in the U.S. Armed Forces or are a National Guard or Reserves enlistee who is on active duty for other than state or training purposes.

Answer "**No**" if you are a National Guard or Reserves enlistee who is on active duty for state or training purposes.

FREE APPLICATION FOR FEDERAL STUDENT AID
July 1, 2010 – June 30, 2011

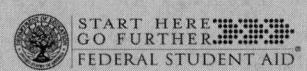

Step One (Student):
For questions 1-32, leave blank any questions that do not apply to you (the student).

OMB # 1845-0001

Your full name (**exactly as it appears on your Social Security card**)

1. Last name
2. First name
3. Middle initial

Your mailing address

4. Number and street (include apt. number)
5. City (and country if not U.S.)
6. State
7. ZIP code
8. Your Social Security Number
9. Your date of birth — MONTH DAY YEAR (19__)
10. Your permanent telephone number

Your Driver's license number (if you have one)

11. Driver's license number
12. Driver's license state

13. Your e-mail address. If you provide your e-mail address, we will communicate with you electronically. For example, when your FAFSA has been processed, you will be notified by e-mail. Your e-mail address will also be shared with your state and the colleges listed on your FAFSA to allow them to communicate with you. If you prefer to be contacted by postal mail or do not have an e-mail address, please leave this field blank.

14. Are you a U.S. citizen? Mark only one. See Notes page 2.
    - Yes, I am a U.S. citizen (U.S. national). **Skip to question 16.** ○ 1
    - No, but I am an eligible noncitizen. **Fill in question 15.** ○ 2
    - No, I am not a citizen or eligible noncitizen. **Skip to question 16.** ○ 3

15. Alien Registration Number: A

Report your marital status as of the date you sign your FAFSA.
If your marital status changes after you sign your FAFSA, you cannot change this information.

16. What is your marital status as of today?
    - I am single ○ 1
    - I am married/remarried ○ 2
    - I am separated ○ 3
    - I am divorced or widowed ○ 4

17. Month and year you were married, separated, divorced or widowed — MONTH YEAR

18. What is your state of legal residence? STATE
19. Did you become a legal resident of this state before January 1, 2005? Yes ○ 1   No ○ 2
20. If the answer to question 19 is "No," give month and year you became a legal resident. MONTH YEAR

21. Are you male or female?
    - Male ○ 1
    - Female ○ 2
    - If female, skip to question 23.

22. Most male students must register with Selective Service to receive federal aid. If you are male, age 18-25 and not registered, fill in the circle and we will register you. **See Notes page 2.**   Register me ○ 1

23. Have you been convicted for the possession or sale of illegal drugs for an offense that occurred while you were receiving federal student aid (such as grants, loans or work-study)?
    Answer "No" if you have never received federal student aid or if you have never had a drug conviction while receiving federal student aid. If you have a drug conviction for an offense that occurred while you were receiving federal student aid, answer "Yes," but complete and submit this application, and we will mail you a worksheet to help you determine if your conviction affects your eligibility for aid. If you are unsure how to answer this question, call 1-800-433-3243 for help.
    No ○ 1
    Yes ○ 3

Some states and colleges offer aid based on the level of schooling your parents completed.

24. Highest school your father completed — Middle school/Jr. high ○ 1   High school ○ 2   College or beyond ○ 3   Other/unknown ○ 4
25. Highest school your mother completed — Middle school/Jr. high ○ 1   High school ○ 2   College or beyond ○ 3   Other/unknown ○ 4

26. When you begin college in the 2010-2011 school year, what will be your high school completion status?
    - High school diploma ○ 1
    - General Educational Development (GED) certificate ○ 2
    - Homeschooled ○ 3
    - None of the above ○ 4

For Help–www.studentaid.ed.gov/completefafsa   Page 3   Step One CONTINUED on page 4

Step One CONTINUED from page 3

27. Will you have your first bachelor's degree before July 1, 2010? Yes ○ 1 No ○ 2

28. When you begin the 2010-2011 school year, what will be your grade level?
    Never attended college and 1st year undergraduate .... ○ 0
    Attended college before and 1st year undergraduate .... ○ 1
    2nd year undergraduate/sophomore .... ○ 2
    3rd year undergraduate/junior .... ○ 3
    4th year undergraduate/senior .... ○ 4
    5th year/other undergraduate .... ○ 5
    1st year graduate/professional .... ○ 6
    Continuing graduate/professional or beyond .... ○ 7

29. When you begin the 2010-2011 school year, what degree or certificate will you be working on?
    1st bachelor's degree .... ○ 1
    2nd bachelor's degree .... ○ 2
    Associate degree (occupational or technical program) .... ○ 3
    Associate degree (general education or transfer program) .... ○ 4
    Certificate or diploma (occupational, technical or education program of less than two years) .... ○ 5
    Certificate or diploma (occupational, technical or education program of two or more years) .... ○ 6
    Teaching credential (nondegree program) .... ○ 7
    Graduate or professional degree .... ○ 8
    Other/undecided .... ○ 9

30. When you begin the 2010–2011 school year, what do you expect your enrollment status to be? **See Notes page 2.**
    Full-time .... ○ 1
    Three-quarter-time .... ○ 2
    Half-time .... ○ 3
    Less than half-time .... ○ 4
    Don't know .... ○ 5

31. In addition to grants, are you interested in being considered for work-study or student loans?
    Work-study (student aid that you earn through work) .... ○ 1
    Student loans (which you must pay back) .... ○ 2
    Both work-study and student loans .... ○ 3
    Neither .... ○ 4
    Don't know .... ○ 5

32. Are you planning to complete course work necessary to become an elementary or secondary school teacher, either now or in the future? **See Notes page 2.** Yes ○ 1 No ○ 2 Don't know ○ 3

Step Two (Student): Answer questions 33–58 about yourself (the student). If you are single, separated, divorced or widowed, answer only about yourself. If you are married as of today, include information about your spouse (husband or wife).

33. For 2009, have you (the student) completed your IRS income tax return or another tax return listed in question 34?
    I have already completed my return. .... ○ 1
    I will file, but I have not yet completed my return. .... ○ 2
    I'm not going to file. **Skip to question 39.** .... ○ 3

34. What income tax return did you file or will you file for 2009?
    IRS 1040 .... ○ 1
    IRS 1040A or 1040EZ .... ○ 2
    A foreign tax return. **See Notes page 2.** .... ○ 3
    A tax return with Puerto Rico, another U.S. territory or Freely Associated State. **See Notes page 2.** .... ○ 4

35. If you have filed or will file a 1040, were you eligible to file a 1040A or 1040EZ? **See Notes page 2.** Yes ○ 1 No ○ 2 Don't know ○ 3

For questions 36–45, if the answer is zero or the question does not apply to you, enter 0. Report whole dollar amounts with no cents.

36. What was your (and spouse's) adjusted gross income for 2009? Adjusted gross income is on IRS Form 1040—line 37; 1040A—line 21; or 1040EZ—line 4. $ ☐☐☐☐☐☐

37. Enter your (and spouse's) income tax for 2009. Income tax amount is on IRS Form 1040—line 55; 1040A—line 35; or 1040EZ—line 11. $ ☐☐☐☐☐☐

38. Enter your (and spouse's) exemptions for 2009. Exemptions are on IRS Form 1040—line 6d or Form 1040A—line 6d. For Form 1040EZ, **see Notes page 2.**   ☐☐

Questions 39 and 40 ask about earnings (wages, salaries, tips, etc.) in 2009. Answer the questions whether or not a tax return was filed. This information may be on the W-2 forms, or on IRS Form 1040—lines 7 + 12 + 18 + Box 14 of IRS Schedule K-1 (Form 1065); or 1040A—line 7; or 1040EZ—line 1. If any individual earning item is negative, do not include that item in your calculation.

39. How much did you earn from working in 2009? $ ☐☐☐☐☐☐

40. How much did your spouse earn from working in 2009? $ ☐☐☐☐☐☐

41. As of today, what is your (and spouse's) total current balance of cash, savings and checking accounts? Do not include student financial aid. $ ☐☐☐☐☐☐

42. As of today, what is the net worth of your (and spouse's) investments, including real estate? **Don't include** the home you live in. Net worth means current value minus debt. **See Notes page 2.** $ ☐☐☐☐☐☐

43. As of today, what is the net worth of your (and spouse's) current businesses and/or investment farms? Don't include a family farm or family business with 100 or fewer full-time or full-time equivalent employees. **See Notes page 2.** $ ☐☐☐☐☐☐

For Help — 1-800-433-3243   Step Two CONTINUED on page 5

Step Two CONTINUED from page 4

44. **Student's 2009 Additional Financial Information** (Enter the combined amounts for you and your spouse.)

a. Education credits (American Opportunity, Hope and Lifetime Learning tax credits) from IRS Form 1040—line 49 or 1040A—line 31. $ ☐☐☐☐☐

b. Child support paid because of divorce or separation or as a result of a legal requirement. **Don't include** support for children in your household, as reported in question 94. $ ☐☐☐☐☐

c. Taxable earnings from need-based employment programs, such as Federal Work-Study and need-based employment portions of fellowships and assistantships. $ ☐☐☐☐☐

d. Student grant and scholarship aid reported to the IRS in your adjusted gross income. Includes AmeriCorps benefits (awards, living allowances and interest accrual payments), as well as grant and scholarship portions of fellowships and assistantships. $ ☐☐☐☐☐

e. Combat pay or special combat pay. Only enter the amount that was taxable and included in your adjusted gross income. Do not enter untaxed combat pay reported on the W-2 (Box 12, Code Q). $ ☐☐☐☐☐

f. Earnings from work under a cooperative education program offered by a college. $ ☐☐☐☐☐

45. **Student's 2009 Untaxed Income** (Enter the combined amounts for you and your spouse.)

a. Payments to tax-deferred pension and savings plans (paid directly or withheld from earnings), including, but not limited to, amounts reported on the W-2 forms in Boxes 12a through 12d, codes D, E, F, G, H and S. $ ☐☐☐☐☐

b. IRA deductions and payments to self-employed SEP, SIMPLE, Keogh and other qualified plans from IRS Form 1040—line 28 + line 32 or 1040A—line 17. $ ☐☐☐☐☐

c. Child support received for any of your children. **Don't include** foster care or adoption payments. $ ☐☐☐☐☐

d. Tax exempt interest income from IRS Form 1040—line 8b or 1040A—line 8b. $ ☐☐☐☐☐

e. Untaxed portions of IRA distributions from IRS Form 1040—lines (15a minus 15b) or 1040A—lines (11a minus 11b). Exclude rollovers. If negative, enter a zero here. $ ☐☐☐☐☐

f. Untaxed portions of pensions from IRS Form 1040—lines (16a minus 16b) or 1040A—lines (12a minus 12b). Exclude rollovers. If negative, enter a zero here. $ ☐☐☐☐☐

g. Housing, food and other living allowances paid to members of the military, clergy and others (including cash payments and cash value of benefits). **Don't include** the value of on-base military housing or the value of a basic military allowance for housing. $ ☐☐☐☐☐

h. Veterans noneducation benefits, such as Disability, Death Pension, or Dependency & Indemnity Compensation (DIC) and/or VA Educational Work-Study allowances. $ ☐☐☐☐☐

i. Other untaxed income not reported in items 45a through 45h, such as workers' compensation, disability, etc. **Don't include** student aid, earned income credit, additional child tax credit, welfare payments, untaxed Social Security benefits, Supplemental Security Income, Workforce Investment Act educational benefits, on-base military housing or a military housing allowance, combat pay, benefits from flexible spending arrangements (e.g., cafeteria plans), foreign income exclusion or credit for federal tax on special fuels. $ ☐☐☐☐☐

j. Money received, or paid on your behalf (e.g., bills), not reported elsewhere on this form. $ ☐☐☐☐☐

Step Three (Student): Answer all questions in this step to determine if you will need to provide parental information.

46. Were you born before January 1, 1987? .... Yes ○¹ No ○²

47. As of today, are you married? (Also answer "Yes" if you are separated but not divorced.) .... Yes ○¹ No ○²

48. At the beginning of the 2010–2011 school year, will you be working on a master's or doctorate program (such as an MA, MBA, MD, JD, PhD, EdD, graduate certificate, etc.)? .... Yes ○¹ No ○²

49. Are you currently serving on active duty in the U.S. Armed Forces for purposes other than training? **See Notes page 2.** Yes ○¹ No ○²

50. Are you a veteran of the U.S. Armed Forces? **See Notes page 9.** .... Yes ○¹ No ○²

51. Do you have children who will receive more than half of their support from you between July 1, 2010 and June 30, 2011? Yes ○¹ No ○²

52. Do you have dependents (other than your children or spouse) who live with you and who receive more than half of their support from you, now and through June 30, 2011? .... Yes ○¹ No ○²

53. At any time since you turned age 13, were both your parents deceased, were you in foster care or were you a dependent or ward of the court? **See Notes page 9.** .... Yes ○¹ No ○²

54. Are you or were you an emancipated minor as determined by a court in your state of legal residence? **See Notes page 9.** Yes ○¹ No ○²

55. Are you or were you in legal guardianship as determined by a court in your state of legal residence? **See Notes page 9.** Yes ○¹ No ○²

56. At any time on or after July 1, 2009, did your high school or school district homeless liaison determine that you were an unaccompanied youth who was homeless? **See Notes page 9.** .... Yes ○¹ No ○²

57. At any time on or after July 1, 2009, did the director of an emergency shelter or transitional housing program funded by the U.S. Department of Housing and Urban Development determine that you were an unaccompanied youth who was homeless? **See Notes page 9.** .... Yes ○¹ No ○²

58. At any time on or after July 1, 2009, did the director of a runaway or homeless youth basic center or transitional living program determine that you were an unaccompanied youth who was homeless or were self-supporting and at risk of being homeless? **See Notes page 9.** .... Yes ○¹ No ○²

For Help–www.studentaid.ed.gov/completefafsa

Student Assistance Forms Appx. D.1.1

If you (the student) answered "No" to every question in Step Three, go to Step Four.
If you answered "Yes" to any question in Step Three, skip Step Four and go to Step Five on page 8.
(Health professions students: Your college may require you to complete Step Four even if you answered "Yes" to any Step Three question.)
If you believe that you are unable to provide parental information, see Notes page 9.

Step Four (Parent Information): Complete this step if you (the student) answered "No" to all questions in Step Three.

Answer all the questions in Step Four about your parents even if you do not live with them. Grandparents, foster parents, legal guardians, aunts and uncles are not considered parents on this form unless they have legally adopted you. If your parents are living and married to each other, answer the questions about them. If your parent is single, widowed, divorced, separated or remarried, see the Notes on page 9 for additional instructions.

59. What is your parents' marital status as of today?

Married or remarried ○ 1   Divorced or separated ○ 3
Single ○ 2   Widowed ○ 4

60. Month and year they were married, separated, divorced or widowed   MONTH YEAR

What are the Social Security Numbers, names and dates of birth of the parents reporting information on this form? If your parent does not have a Social Security Number, you must enter 000-00-0000. Enter two digits for each day and month (e.g., for May 31, enter 05 31).

61. FATHER'S/STEPFATHER'S SOCIAL SECURITY NUMBER
62. FATHER'S/STEPFATHER'S LAST NAME, AND
63. FIRST INITIAL
64. FATHER'S/STEPFATHER'S DATE OF BIRTH   1 9

65. MOTHER'S/STEPMOTHER'S SOCIAL SECURITY NUMBER
66. MOTHER'S/STEPMOTHER'S LAST NAME, AND
67. FIRST INITIAL
68. MOTHER'S/STEPMOTHER'S DATE OF BIRTH   1 9

69. **Your parents' e-mail address.** If you provide your parents' e-mail address, we will let them know your FAFSA has been processed. This e-mail address will also be shared with your state and the colleges listed on your FAFSA to allow them to communicate with your parents.

70. What is your parents' state of legal residence?   STATE

71. Did your parents become legal residents of this state before January 1, 2005?   Yes ○ 1   No ○ 2

72. If the answer to question 71 is "No," give month and year legal residency began for the parent who has lived in the state the longest.   MONTH YEAR

73. How many people are in your parents' household?
Include:
• yourself, even if you don't live with your parents,
• your parents,
• your parents' other children if (a) your parents will provide more than half of their support between July 1, 2010 and June 30, 2011, or (b) the children could answer "No" to every question in Step Three on page 5 of this form, and
• other people if they now live with your parents, your parents provide more than half of their support and your parents will continue to provide more than half of their support between July 1, 2010 and June 30, 2011.

74. How many people in your parents' household will be college students between July 1, 2010 and June 30, 2011?
Always count yourself as a college student. Do not include your parents. You may include others only if they will attend, at least half-time in 2010-2011, a program that leads to a college degree or certificate.

In 2008 or 2009, did you, your parents or anyone in your parents' household (from question 73) receive benefits from any of the federal benefits programs listed? Mark all the programs that apply. Answering these questions will not reduce your eligibility for student aid or for these other benefits. Food Stamps or TANF may have a different name in your parents' state. Call 1-800-4-FED-AID to find out the name of the state's program.

75. Supplemental Security Income ○
76. Food Stamps ○
77. Free or Reduced Price Lunch ○
78. Temporary Assistance for Needy Families (TANF) ○
79. Special Supplemental Nutrition Program for Women, Infants and Children (WIC) ○

80. For 2009, have your parents completed their IRS income tax return or another tax return listed in question 81?

My parents have already completed their return .... ○ 1
My parents will file, but they have not yet completed their return .... ○ 2
My parents are not going to file. **Skip to question 87.** .... ○ 3

81. What income tax return did your parents file or will they file for 2009?

IRS 1040 .... ○ 1
IRS 1040A or 1040EZ .... ○ 2
A foreign tax return. **See Notes page 2.** .... ○ 3
A tax return with Puerto Rico, another U.S. territory or Freely Associated State. **See Notes page 2.** .... ○ 4

82. If your parents have filed or will file a 1040, were they eligible to file a 1040A or 1040EZ? **See Notes page 2.**   Yes ○ 1   No ○ 2   Don't know ○ 3

83. As of today, is either of your parents a dislocated worker? **See Notes page 9.**   Yes ○ 1   No ○ 2   Don't know ○ 3

For Help — 1-800-433-3243   Page 6   Step Four CONTINUED on page 7

481

Appx. D.1.1   *Student Loan Law*

Step Four CONTINUED from page 6

For questions 84–93, if the answer is zero or the question does not apply, enter 0. Report whole dollar amounts with no cents.

84. What was your parents' adjusted gross income for 2009? Adjusted gross income is on IRS Form 1040—line 37; 1040A—line 21; or 1040EZ—line 4. $ ☐☐☐,☐☐☐

85. Enter your parents' income tax for 2009. Income tax amount is on IRS Form 1040—line 55; 1040A—line 35; or 1040EZ—line 11. $ ☐☐☐,☐☐☐

86. Enter your parents' exemptions for 2009. Exemptions are on IRS Form 1040—line 6d or on Form 1040A—line 6d. For Form 1040EZ, **see Notes page 2**.   ☐☐

Questions 87 and 88 ask about earnings (wages, salaries, tips, etc.) in 2009. Answer the questions whether or not a tax return was filed. This information may be on the W-2 forms, on IRS Form 1040—lines 7 + 12 + 18 + Box 14 of IRS Schedule K-1 (Form 1065); on 1040A—line 7; or on 1040EZ—line 1. If any individual earning item is negative, do not include that item in your calculation.

87. How much did your father/stepfather earn from working in 2009? $ ☐☐☐,☐☐☐

88. How much did your mother/stepmother earn from working in 2009? $ ☐☐☐,☐☐☐

89. As of today, what is your parents' total current balance of cash, savings and checking accounts? $ ☐☐☐,☐☐☐

90. As of today, what is the net worth of your parents' investments, including real estate? **Don't include** the home you live in. Net worth means current value minus debt. **See Notes page 2.** $ ☐☐☐,☐☐☐

91. As of today, what is the net worth of your parents' current businesses and/or investment farms? Don't include a family farm or family business with 100 or fewer full-time or full-time equivalent employees. **See Notes page 2.** $ ☐☐☐,☐☐☐

92. **Parents' 2009 Additional Financial Information** (Enter the amounts for your parent[s].)

     a. Education credits (American Opportunity, Hope and Lifetime Learning tax credits) from IRS Form 1040—line 49 or 1040A—line 31. $ ☐☐,☐☐☐

     b. Child support paid because of divorce or separation or as a result of a legal requirement. **Don't include** support for children in your parents' household, as reported in question 73. $ ☐☐,☐☐☐

     c. Your parents' taxable earnings from need-based employment programs, such as Federal Work-Study and need-based employment portions of fellowships and assistantships. $ ☐☐,☐☐☐

     d. Student grant and scholarship aid reported to the IRS in your parents' adjusted gross income. Includes AmeriCorps benefits (awards, living allowances and interest accrual payments), as well as grant and scholarship portions of fellowships and assistantships. $ ☐☐,☐☐☐

     e. Combat pay or special combat pay. Only enter the amount that was taxable and included in your parents' adjusted gross income. Do not enter untaxed combat pay reported on the W-2 (Box 12, Code Q). $ ☐☐,☐☐☐

     f. Earnings from work under a cooperative education program offered by a college. $ ☐☐,☐☐☐

93. **Parents' 2009 Untaxed Income** (Enter the amounts for your parent[s].)

     a. Payments to tax-deferred pension and savings plans (paid directly or withheld from earnings), including, but not limited to, amounts reported on the W-2 forms in Boxes 12a through 12d, codes D, E, F, G, H and S. $ ☐☐,☐☐☐

     b. IRA deductions and payments to self-employed SEP, SIMPLE, Keogh and other qualified plans from IRS Form 1040—line 28 + line 32 or 1040A—line 17. $ ☐☐,☐☐☐

     c. Child support received for any of your parents' children. **Don't include** foster care or adoption payments. $ ☐☐,☐☐☐

     d. Tax exempt interest income from IRS Form 1040—line 8b or 1040A—line 8b. $ ☐☐,☐☐☐

     e. Untaxed portions of IRA distributions from IRS Form 1040—lines (15a minus 15b) or 1040A—lines (11a minus 11b). Exclude rollovers. If negative, enter a zero here. $ ☐☐,☐☐☐

     f. Untaxed portions of pensions from IRS Form 1040—lines (16a minus 16b) or 1040A—lines (12a minus 12b). Exclude rollovers. If negative, enter a zero here. $ ☐☐,☐☐☐

     g. Housing, food and other living allowances paid to members of the military, clergy and others (including cash payments and cash value of benefits). **Don't include** the value of on-base military housing or the value of a basic military allowance for housing. $ ☐☐,☐☐☐

     h. Veterans noneducation benefits, such as Disability, Death Pension, or Dependency & Indemnity Compensation (DIC) and/or VA Educational Work-Study allowances. $ ☐☐,☐☐☐

     i. Other untaxed income not reported in items 93a through 93h, such as workers' compensation, disability, etc. **Don't include** student aid, earned income credit, additional child tax credit, welfare payments, untaxed Social Security benefits, Supplemental Security Income, Workforce Investment Act educational benefits, on-base military housing or a military housing allowance, combat pay, benefits from flexible spending arrangements (e.g., cafeteria plans), foreign income exclusion or credit for federal tax on special fuels. $ ☐☐,☐☐☐

For Help–www.studentaid.ed.gov/completefafsa   Page 7

Student Assistance Forms Appx. D.1.1

Step Five (Student): Complete this step only if you (the student) answered "Yes" to any questions in Step Three.

94. How many people are in your household?
Include:
- yourself (and your spouse),
- your children, if you will provide more than half of their support between July 1, 2010 and June 30, 2011, and
- other people if they now live with you, you provide more than half of their support and you will continue to provide more than half of their support between July 1, 2010 and June 30, 2011.

95. How many people in your (and your spouse's) household will be college students between July 1, 2010 and June 30, 2011?
Always count yourself as a college student. Include others only if they will attend, at least half-time in 2010-2011, a program that leads to a college degree or certificate.

In 2008 or 2009, did you (or your spouse) or anyone in your household (from question 94) receive benefits from any of the federal benefits programs listed? Mark all the programs that apply. Answering these questions will not reduce your eligibility for student aid or for these other benefits. Food Stamps or TANF may have a different name in your state. Call 1-800-4-FED-AID to find out the name of the state's program.

96. Supplemental Security Income ○
97. Food Stamps ○
98. Free or Reduced Price Lunch ○
99. Temporary Assistance for Needy Families (TANF) ○
100. Special Supplemental Nutrition Program for Women, Infants and Children (WIC) ○

101. As of today, are you (or your spouse) a dislocated worker? **See Notes page 9.**   Yes ○ 1   No ○ 2   Don't know ○ 3

Step Six (Student): Indicate which colleges you want to receive your FAFSA information.

Enter the six-digit federal school code and your housing plans. You can find the school codes at **www.fafsa.gov** or you can call 1-800-4-FED-AID. If you cannot get the code, write in the complete name, address, city and state of the college. For state aid, you may wish to list your preferred college first. To have more colleges receive your FAFSA information, read *What is the FAFSA?* on page 10.

102.a 1ST FEDERAL SCHOOL CODE   OR   NAME OF COLLEGE / ADDRESS AND CITY   STATE
102.b on campus ○ 1 / with parent ○ 2 / off campus ○ 3

102.c 2ND FEDERAL SCHOOL CODE   OR   NAME OF COLLEGE / ADDRESS AND CITY   STATE
102.d on campus ○ 1 / with parent ○ 2 / off campus ○ 3

102.e 3RD FEDERAL SCHOOL CODE   OR   NAME OF COLLEGE / ADDRESS AND CITY   STATE
102.f on campus ○ 1 / with parent ○ 2 / off campus ○ 3

102.g 4TH FEDERAL SCHOOL CODE   OR   NAME OF COLLEGE / ADDRESS AND CITY   STATE
102.h on campus ○ 1 / with parent ○ 2 / off campus ○ 3

Step Seven (Student and Parent): Read, sign and date.

If you are the student, by signing this application you certify that you (1) will use federal and/or state student financial aid only to pay the cost of attending an institution of higher education, (2) are not in default on a federal student loan or have made satisfactory arrangements to repay it, (3) do not owe money back on a federal student grant or have made satisfactory arrangements to repay it, (4) will notify your college if you default on a federal student loan and (5) will not receive a Federal Pell Grant from more than one college for the same period of time.

If you are the parent or the student, by signing this application you agree, if asked, to provide information that will verify the accuracy of your completed form. This information may include U.S. or state income tax forms that you filed or are required to file. Also, you certify that you understand that **the Secretary of Education has the authority to verify information reported on this application with the Internal Revenue Service and other federal agencies**. If you sign any document related to the federal student aid programs electronically using a Personal Identification Number (PIN), you certify that you are the person identified by the PIN and have not disclosed that PIN to anyone else. If you purposely give false or misleading information, you may be fined up to $20,000, sent to prison, or both.

103. Date this form was completed   MONTH   DAY   2010 ○   or   2011 ○

104. Student (Sign below)

Parent (A parent from Step Four sign below.)

If you or your family paid a fee for someone to fill out this form or to advise you on how to fill it out, that person must complete this part.

Preparer's name, firm and address

105. Preparer's Social Security Number (or 106)

106. Employer ID number (or 105)

107. Preparer's signature and date

COLLEGE USE ONLY

D/O ○ 1

FAA Signature

DATA ENTRY USE ONLY: ○ P   ○ *   ○ L   ○ E

Federal School Code

For Help — 1-800-433-3243

Notes for question 50 (page 5)

Answer "**Yes**" (you are a veteran) if you (1) have engaged in active duty in the U.S. Armed Forces (Army, Navy, Air Force, Marines or Coast Guard) or are a National Guard or Reserve enlistee who was called to active duty for other than state or training purposes, or were a cadet or midshipman at one of the service academies, **and** (2) were released under a condition other than dishonorable. Also answer "**Yes**" if you are not a veteran now but will be one by June 30, 2011.

Answer "**No**" (you are not a veteran) if you (1) have never engaged in active duty in the U.S. Armed Forces, (2) are currently an ROTC student or a cadet or midshipman at a service academy, (3) are a National Guard or Reserve enlistee activated only for state or training purposes, or (4) were engaged in active duty in the U.S. Armed Forces but released under dishonorable conditions.

Also answer "**No**" if you are currently serving in the U.S. Armed Forces and will continue to serve through June 30, 2011.

Notes for question 53 (page 5)

Answer "**Yes**" if you had no living parent (biological or adoptive) at any time since you turned age 13, even if you are now adopted.

Answer "**Yes**" if you were in foster care at any time since you turned age 13, even if you are no longer in foster care as of today.

Answer "**Yes**" if you were a dependent or ward of the court at any time since you turned age 13, even if you are no longer a dependent or ward of the court as of today. Note that for federal student aid purposes, a ward of the court is not someone who is incarcerated.

Note that the financial aid administrator at your school may require you to provide proof that you were in foster care or a dependent or ward of the court.

Notes for questions 54 and 55 (page 5)

Answer "**Yes**" if you can provide a copy of a court's decision that as of today you are an emancipated minor or are in legal guardianship. Also answer "**Yes**" if you can provide a copy of a court's decision that you were an emancipated minor or were in legal guardianship immediately before you reached the age of being an adult in your state. The court must be located in your state of legal residence at the time the court's decision was issued.

Answer "**No**" if you are still a minor and the court decision is no longer in effect or the court decision was not in effect at the time you became an adult.

Note that the financial aid administrator at your college may require you to provide proof that you were an emancipated minor or in legal guardianship.

Notes for questions 56–58 (page 5)

Answer "**Yes**" if you received a determination at any time on or after July 1, 2009, that you were an unaccompanied youth who was homeless or, for question 58, at risk of being homeless.

- "**Homeless**" means lacking fixed, regular and adequate housing, which includes living in shelters, motels or cars, or temporarily living with other people because you had nowhere else to go.
- "**Unaccompanied**" means you are not living in the physical custody of your parent or guardian.
- "**Youth**" means you are 21 years of age or younger or you are still enrolled in high school as of the day you sign this application.

Answer "**No**" if you are not homeless, at risk of being homeless or if you do not have a determination. You should contact your financial aid office for assistance if you do not have a determination but believe you are an unaccompanied youth who is homeless or are an unaccompanied youth providing for your own living expenses who is at risk of being homeless.

Note that the financial aid administrator at your college may require you to provide a copy of the determination if you answered "**Yes**" to any of these questions.

Notes for students unable to provide parental information on pages 6 and 7

Under very limited circumstances (for example, your parents are incarcerated; you have left home due to an abusive family environment; or you do not know where your parents are and are unable to contact them), you may be able to submit your FAFSA without parental information. **If you are unable to provide parental information**, skip Steps Four and Five, and go to Step Six. Once you submit your FAFSA without parental data, **you must follow up with the financial aid office at the college you plan to attend**, in order to complete your FAFSA.

Notes for Step Four, questions 59–93 (pages 6 and 7)

Additional instructions about who is considered a parent on this form:

- If your parent is widowed or single, answer the questions about that parent.
- If your widowed parent is remarried as of today, answer the questions about that parent and your stepparent.
- If your parents are divorced or separated, answer the questions about the parent you lived with more during the past 12 months. (If you did not live with one parent more than the other, give answers about the parent who provided more financial support during the past 12 months, or during the most recent year that you actually received support from a parent.) If this parent is remarried as of today, answer the questions about that parent and your stepparent.

Notes for questions 83 (page 6) and 101 (page 8)

In general, a person may be considered a dislocated worker if he or she:

- is receiving unemployment benefits due to being laid off or losing a job and is unlikely to return to a previous occupation;
- has been laid off or received a lay-off notice from a job;
- was self-employed but is now unemployed due to economic conditions or natural disaster; or
- is a displaced homemaker. A displaced homemaker is generally a person who previously provided unpaid services to the family (e.g., a stay-at-home mom or dad), is no longer supported by the husband or wife, is unemployed or underemployed, and is having trouble finding or upgrading employment.

If a person quits work, generally he or she is not considered a dislocated worker even if, for example, the person is receiving unemployment benefits.

Answer "**Yes**" to question 83 if your parent is a dislocated worker. Answer "**Yes**" to question 101 if you or your spouse is a dislocated worker.

Answer "**No**" to question 83 if your parent is not a dislocated worker. Answer "**No**" to question 101 if neither you nor your spouse is a dislocated worker.

Answer "**Don't know**" to question 83 if you are not sure whether your parent is a dislocated worker. Answer "**Don't know**" to question 101 if you are not sure whether you or your spouse is a dislocated worker. You can contact your financial aid office for assistance in answering these questions.

Note that the financial aid administrator at your school may require you to provide proof that your parent is a dislocated worker, if you answered "**Yes**" to question 83, or that you **or** your spouse is a dislocated worker, if you answered "**Yes**" to question 101.

Student Assistance Forms   Appx. D.1.1

What is the FAFSA℠?

Why fill out a FAFSA?

The *Free Application for Federal Student Aid* (FAFSA) is the first step in the financial aid process. You use the FAFSA to apply for federal student aid, such as grants, loans and work-study. In addition, most states and colleges use information from the FAFSA to award nonfederal aid.

Why all the questions?

The questions on the FAFSA are required to calculate your Expected Family Contribution (EFC). The EFC measures your family's financial strength and determines your eligibility for federal student aid. Your state and the colleges you list may also use some of your responses. They will determine if you may be eligible for school or state aid, in addition to federal aid.

How do I find out what my Expected Family Contribution (EFC) is?

Your EFC will be listed on your *Student Aid Report* (SAR). Your SAR summarizes the information you submitted on your FAFSA. It is important to review your SAR to make sure all of your information is correct and complete. Make corrections or provide additional information, as necessary.

How much aid do I get?

Using the information on your FAFSA and your EFC, the financial aid office at your college will determine the amount of aid you will receive. The colleges use your EFC to prepare a financial aid package to help you meet your financial need. Financial need is the difference between your EFC and your college's cost of attendance (which can include living expenses), as determined by the college. If you or your family have unusual circumstances that should be taken into account, contact your college's financial aid office. Some examples of unusual circumstances are: unusual medical or dental expenses or a large change in income from last year to this year.

When do I get the aid?

Any financial aid you are eligible to receive will be paid to you through your college. Typically, your college will first use the aid to pay tuition, fees and room and board (if provided by the college). Any remaining aid is paid to you for your other educational expenses. If you are eligible for a Federal Pell Grant, you may receive it from only one college for the same period of enrollment.

How can I have more colleges receive my FAFSA information?

If you are completing a paper FAFSA, you can only list four colleges in the school code step. You may add more colleges by doing one of the following:

1. Use the Federal Student Aid PIN you will receive after your FAFSA has been processed and go to *FAFSA on the Web* at **www.fafsa.gov**. Select the "Add or Delete a School Code" link.
2. Use the *Student Aid Report* (SAR), which you will receive after your FAFSA is processed. Your Data Release Number (DRN) verifies your identity and will be listed on the first page of your SAR. You can call 1-800-4-FED-AID and provide your DRN to a customer service representative, who will add more school codes for you.
3. Provide your DRN to the financial aid administrator at the college you want added, and he or she can add their school code to your FAFSA.

Note: Your FAFSA record can only list up to ten school codes. If there are ten school codes on your record, any new school codes that you add will replace one or more of the school codes listed.

Where can I get more information on student aid?

The best place for information about student financial aid is the financial aid office at the college you plan to attend. The financial aid administrator can tell you about student aid available from your state, the college itself and other sources.

- You can also visit our web sites **www.FederalStudentAid.ed.gov** or **www.studentaid.ed.gov**.
- For information by phone you can call our Federal Student Aid Information Center at 1-800-4-FED-AID (1-800-433-3243). TTY users (for the hearing impaired) may call 1-800-730-8913.
- You can also check with your high school counselor, your state aid agency or your local library's reference section.

Information about other nonfederal assistance may be available from foundations, religious organizations, community organizations and civic groups, as well as organizations related to your field of interest, such as the American Medical or American Bar Association. Check with your parents' employers or unions to see if they award scholarships or have tuition payment plans.

Information on the Privacy Act and use of your Social Security Number

We use the information that you provide on this form to determine if you are eligible to receive federal student financial aid and the amount that you are eligible to receive. Sections 483 and 484 of the Higher Education Act of 1965, as amended, give us the authority to ask you and your parents these questions, and to collect the Social Security Numbers of you and your parents. We use your Social Security Number to verify your identity and retrieve your records, and we may request your Social Security Number again for those purposes.

State and institutional student financial aid programs may also use the information that you provide on this form to determine if you are eligible to receive state and institutional aid and the need that you have for such aid. Therefore, we will disclose the information that you provide on this form to each institution you list in questions 102a - 102h, state agencies in your state of legal residence and the state agencies of the states in which the colleges that you list in questions 102a - 102h are located.

If you are applying solely for federal aid, you must answer all of the following questions that apply to you: 1-9, 14-16, 18, 21-23, 26-28, 33-37, 39-59, 61-68, 70, 73-85, 87-101, 103-104. If you do not answer these questions, you will not receive federal aid.

Without your consent, we may disclose information that you provide to entities under a published "routine use." Under such a routine use, we may disclose information to third parties that we have authorized to assist us in administering the above programs; to other federal agencies under computer matching programs, such as those with the Internal Revenue Service, Social Security Administration, Selective Service System, Department of Homeland Security, Department of Justice and Veterans Affairs; to your parents or spouse; and to members of Congress if you ask them to help you with student aid questions.

If the federal government, the U.S. Department of Education, or an employee of the U.S. Department of Education is involved in litigation, we may send information to the Department of Justice, or a court or adjudicative body, if the disclosure is related to financial aid and certain conditions are met. In addition, we may send your information to a foreign, federal, state, or local enforcement agency if the information that you submitted indicates a violation or potential violation of law, for which that agency has jurisdiction for investigation or prosecution. Finally, we may send information regarding a claim that is determined to be valid and overdue to a consumer reporting agency. This information includes identifiers from the record; the amount, status and history of the claim; and the program under which the claim arose.

State Certification

By submitting this application, you are giving your state financial aid agency permission to verify any statement on this form and to obtain income tax information for all persons required to report income on this form.

The Paperwork Reduction Act of 1995

The Paperwork Reduction Act of 1995 says that no one is required to respond to a collection of information unless it displays a valid OMB control number, which for this form is 1845-0001. The time required to complete this form is estimated to be three hours, including time to review instructions, search data resources, gather the data needed, and complete and review the information collection. If you have comments about this estimate or suggestions for improving this form, please write to:

    U.S. Department of Education, Washington, DC 20202-4700.

We may request additional information from you to process your application more efficiently. We will collect this additional information only as needed and on a voluntary basis.

Federal Direct Consolidation Loan
Instructions for Application and Promissory Note

OMB No. 1845-0053
Form Approved
Exp. Date 11/30/2010

Before You Begin

Before beginning, you will need to gather all of your loan records, account statements, and bills so that you will have on hand all the information needed to complete the Application and Promissory Note.

Use a blue or black ball point pen to complete the Application and Promissory Note. Enter dates as month-day-year (mm-dd-yyyy). Use only numbers. Example: June 24, 1982 = 06-24-1982.

Some of the items in Sections A and C may have been completed for you. If so, review these items carefully to make sure the information is correct. Cross out any information that is incorrect and enter the correct information. Put your initials next to any information that you change.

Incorrect or incomplete information may delay processing.

Section A: Borrower Information

Item 1: Enter your last name, then your first name and middle initial.

Item 2: Enter your nine-digit Social Security Number.

Item 3: Enter your permanent address (number, street, apartment number, or rural route number and box number, then city, state, zip code). If your mailing address is post office box or general delivery, you must list **both** your permanent address and your mailing address.

Item 4: Enter the area code and telephone number at which you can most easily be reached. (Do not list your work telephone number here.) If you do not have a telephone, enter N/A.

Item 5 (optional): Enter your preferred e-mail address for receiving communications. You are not required to provide this information. If you do, we may use your e-mail address to communicate with you. If you do not have an e-mail address or do not wish to provide one, enter N/A.

Item 6: Enter any former names (such as a maiden name) under which one or more of your loans may have been made. If none, enter N/A.

Item 7: Enter your date of birth.

Item 8: Enter the two letter abbreviation for the state that issued your driver's license, followed by your driver's license number. If you do not have a driver's license, enter N/A.

Item 9: Enter your employer's name. If you are self-employed, enter the name of your business. If you are not employed, enter N/A.

Item 10: Enter your employer's address or, if you are self-employed, the address of your business (street, city, state, zip code).

Item 11: Enter your work area code and telephone number. If you are self-employed, enter the area code and telephone number of your business.

Section B: Reference Information

Item 12: Enter the requested information for two persons who do not live with you and who have known you for at least three years. References who live outside the United States are not acceptable. If a reference does not have a telephone number, enter N/A.

Section C1: Education Loan Indebtedness – Loans You Want to Consolidate
Section C2: Education Loan Indebtedness – Loans You Do Not Want to Consolidate

Section C1 asks for information about your federal education loans that you want to consolidate. Section C2 asks for information about your education loans that you are not consolidating, but want considered when calculating your maximum repayment period. If you need more space to list loans in Section C1 or C2, use the Additional Loan Listing Sheet included with your Application and Promissory Note. To find the information you will need to complete Sections C1 and C2, you can look at the last monthly billing statement you received, your quarterly interest statement or annual statement, your coupon book, or the Internet site of your loan holder or servicer. You may also obtain information about your loans by accessing the National Student Loan Data System at www.nslds.ed.gov.

Items 13-16: Enter the requested information for all of your federal education loans that you want to consolidate, including any Direct Loans that you want to consolidate. **You must consolidate at least one Direct Loan or FFEL Program loan.**

Item 13: Enter the code that corresponds to the loan type from the chart provided on this instructions page ("Loan Types and Their Codes"). If you are not sure about the loan type, leave this item blank.

Item 14: Enter the full name and mailing address of the holder of the loan or the holder's servicer. (This is the address to which you are or will be sending your payments.) You must provide at least the name, city, and state of the loan holder or servicer.

Item 15: Enter the account number for each loan (the number should be on your statement or in your payment book). If you cannot find the account number, leave this item blank.

Item 16: Enter the estimated amount needed to pay off the loan, including any unpaid interest, late fees, and collection costs.

Item 17: If you are in your grace period on any of the loans you wish to consolidate and you want to delay processing of your Direct Consolidation Loan until you have completed your grace period, enter the month and year of your expected grace period end date. If you provide this information, processing of your consolidation loan will be delayed until approximately 30-60 days before the end of your grace period. If you leave Item 17 blank, processing of your consolidation loan will begin as soon as we receive your completed Application and Promissory Note and any other required documents, and any loans listed in Section C1 that are in a grace period will enter repayment immediately upon consolidation.

Items 18-21: Enter the requested information for all of your education loans that you do not want to consolidate or that are not eligible for consolidation, but that you want considered when determining the maximum repayment period for your Direct Consolidation Loan.

Item 18: Follow the instructions for Item 13.

Item 19: Follow the instructions for Item 14.

Item 20: Follow the instructions for Item 15.

Item 21: Enter the current balance for each loan. Use the amount on your last statement or give us an approximate amount.

Section D: Repayment Plan Selection

See the instructions provided in this section.

Section E: Borrower Understandings, Certifications, and Authorizations

Items 22-24: Carefully read these items.

Section F: Promissory Note

This is a legally binding contract.

Item 25: Carefully read the Promise to Pay and the entire Application and Promissory Note, including the Borrower Understandings, Certifications, and Authorizations in Section E, the terms and conditions on page 4, and the Borrower's Rights and Responsibilities Statement on pages 5-8.

Item 26: Sign and date the Application and Promissory Note. If you do not sign the Application and Promissory Note, your application cannot be processed.

Final Notes

Review all the information on your Application and Promissory Note. When complete, make a copy for your records and mail the original pages 1, 2, and 3 to us in the envelope provided, along with the completed Repayment Plan Selection form and, if required, the Income Contingent Repayment Plan Consent to Disclosure of Tax Information form. If you no longer have the envelope, mail the Application and Promissory Note to the address shown below.

As soon as we receive your completed Application and Promissory Note and supporting documents, we will begin processing (unless you have entered your expected grace period end date in Section C1, Item 17). During this time, we might call you with questions. We will be sending you a notice before we pay off your loans.

In the meantime, if you currently are required to make payments on your loans, continue to do so. You will need to continue making payments until you receive written notification that your loans have been successfully consolidated and it is time to start paying your Direct Consolidation Loan. If you are having difficulty making payments on your loans, contact your loan holder or servicer at the correspondence address or telephone number on your current loan statements to find out ways you might be able to postpone loan payments; ask specifically about your "deferment" or "forbearance" options.

Loan Types and Their Codes (use these codes to complete Sections C1 and C2)

A	Subsidized Federal Stafford Loans	N	National Defense Student Loans (NDSL)
B	Guaranteed Student Loans (GSL)	O	Subsidized Federal Consolidation Loans
C	Federal Insured Student Loans (FISL)	P	Auxiliary Loans to Assist Students (ALAS)
D	Direct Subsidized Loans	Q	Health Professions Student Loans (HPSL)
E	Direct Subsidized Consolidation Loans	R	Health Education Assistance Loans (HEAL)
F	Federal Perkins Loans	S	Federal PLUS Loans (for parents or for graduate/professional students)
G	Unsubsidized Federal Stafford Loans (including Nonsubsidized Stafford Loans)	T	Parent Loans for Undergraduate Students (PLUS)
H	Federal Supplemental Loans for Students (SLS)	U	Direct PLUS Loans (for parents or for graduate/professional students)
J	Unsubsidized Federal Consolidation Loans	V	Direct PLUS Consolidation Loans
K	Direct Unsubsidized Consolidation Loans	Y	Nursing Student Loans (NSL)
L	Direct Unsubsidized Loans	Z	Loans for Disadvantaged Students (LDS)
M	National Direct Student Loans (NDSL)	W	Education loans ineligible for consolidation

For help completing this form, call 1-800-557-7392.

For the hearing impaired, the TDD number is 1-800-557-7395.

Mail your completed Application and Promissory Note and any other required forms (see Final Notes, above) to the following address:

U.S. Department of Education
Consolidation Department
P.O. Box 242800
Louisville, KY 40224-2800

Student Assistance Forms   Appx. D.1.2

Federal Direct Consolidation Loan Application and Promissory Note

OMB No. 1845-0053
Form Approved
Exp. Date 11/30/2010

WARNING: Any person who knowingly makes a false statement or misrepresentation on this form will be subject to penalties which may include fines, imprisonment, or both, under the U.S. Criminal Code and 20 U.S.C. 1097.

Before You Begin

Read the instructions for completing this Federal Direct Consolidation Loan Application and Promissory Note. Print using blue or black ink or type. You must sign and date this form. If you cross out anything and write in new information, put your initials beside the change.

NOTE: PAGES 1, 2, and 3 OF THIS FORM MUST BE SUBMITTED IN ORDER TO PROCESS YOUR LOAN REQUEST.

Section A: Borrower Information

1. Last Name   First Name   Middle Initial
2. Social Security Number
3. Permanent Street Address (if P.O. box or general delivery, see instructions)
   City   State   Zip Code
4. Area Code/Telephone Number ( )
5. E-Mail Address (Optional)
6. Former Name(s)
7. Date of Birth (mm-dd-yyyy)
8. Driver's License State and Number
   State --   Number
9. Employer's Name
10. Employer's Address
    City   State   Zip Code
11. Work Area Code/Telephone Number ( )

Section B: Reference Information

12. References: List two persons with different addresses who have known you for at least three years. Do not list individuals who live with you (for example, your spouse) or who live outside the United States.

	1.	2.
Name		
Permanent Address		
City, State, Zip Code		
E-Mail Address (optional)		
Area Code/Telephone Number	( )	( )
Relationship to Borrower		

Section C1: Education Loan Indebtedness – Loans You Want to Consolidate (continued on page 2)

Read the instructions before completing this section. List each federal education loan that you want to consolidate, including any William D. Ford Federal Direct Loan (Direct Loan) Program loans that you want to include in your Direct Consolidation Loan. If you need more space to list additional loans, use the Additional Loan Listing Sheet included with this package. List each loan separately. Please print. **ONLY LIST LOANS THAT YOU WANT TO CONSOLIDATE IN THIS SECTION.**

13. Loan Type (See Instructions)	14. Loan Holder's/Servicer's Name, Address, and Area Code/Telephone Number (See Instructions)	15. Loan Account Number	16. Estimated Payoff Amount

Submit pages 1, 2, and 3
Page 1 of 9

487

Borrower's Name (please print) _____ **Social Security Number** _____

Section C1: Education Loan Indebtedness – Loans You Want to Consolidate (continued from page 1)

13. Loan Type (See Instructions)	14. Loan Holder's/Servicer's Name, Address, and Area Code/Telephone Number (See Instructions)	15. Loan Account Number	16. Estimated Payoff Amount

17. Grace Period End Date. If any of the loans you want to consolidate are in a grace period, you can delay the processing of your Direct Consolidation Loan until the end of your grace period by entering your expected grace period end date in the space provided. If you leave this item blank, your Direct Consolidation Loan will be processed and any loans listed in Section C1 that are in a grace period will enter repayment immediately upon consolidation.

Expected Grace Period End Date (month/year): _____

Section C2: Education Loan Indebtedness – Loans You Do Not Want to Consolidate

Read the instructions before completing this section. List all education loans that you are not consolidating, but want to have considered when calculating your maximum repayment period. Include any Direct Loan Program loans that you do not want to consolidate. If you need more space to list additional loans, use the Additional Loan Listing Sheet included with this package. List each loan separately. Please print. **ONLY LIST LOANS THAT YOU DO NOT WANT TO CONSOLIDATE IN THIS SECTION.**

18. Loan Type (See Instructions)	19. Loan Holder's/Servicer's Name, Address, and Area Code/Telephone Number (See Instructions)	20. Loan Account Number	21. Current Balance

Section D: Repayment Plan Selection

To understand your repayment plan options, carefully read the repayment plan information in the Borrower's Rights and Responsibilities Statement on pages 5-8 of this Application and Promissory Note (Note) and in any supplemental materials you receive with this Note. Then select a repayment plan by completing the **Repayment Plan Selection** form that accompanies this Note. Please note the following:

- If you select the Income Contingent Repayment (ICR) Plan, you must also complete the **Income Contingent Repayment Plan Consent to Disclosure of Tax Information** form that is included with this Note. **Your selection of the ICR Plan cannot be processed without this form.**
- If you want to consolidate a defaulted loan(s) and you have not made a satisfactory repayment arrangement with your current holder(s), you must select the ICR Plan, or effective July 1, 2009, the Income-Based Repayment Plan. You must also select the ICR Plan or the Income-Based Repayment Plan if you are consolidating a delinquent Federal Consolidation Loan that the lender has submitted to the guaranty agency for default aversion, and you are not consolidating any additional eligible loans.

Student Assistance Forms Appx. D.1.2

Borrower's Name (please print)	Social Security Number

Section E: Borrower Understandings, Certifications, and Authorizations

22. I understand that:

A. My Direct Consolidation Loan will, to the extent used to pay off loans that I have selected for consolidation, count against the applicable aggregate loan limits under the Act. The term "the Act" is defined under "Governing Law" on page 4 of this Note.

B. The amount of my Direct Consolidation Loan is the sum of the balances of my outstanding eligible loans that I have chosen to consolidate. My outstanding balance on each loan to be consolidated includes unpaid principal, unpaid accrued interest, and late charges as defined by federal regulations and as certified by each holder. Collection costs may also be included. For a Direct Loan Program or Federal Family Education Loan (FFEL) Program loan that is in default, the U.S. Department of Education (ED) limits collection costs that may be included in the payoff balances of the loans to a maximum of 18.5 percent of the outstanding principal and interest. For any other defaulted federal education loans, all collection costs that are owed may be included in the payoff balances of the loans.

C. ED will provide me with information about the loans and payoff amounts that ED verifies with the holders of my loans before the actual payoffs occur. If I do not want to consolidate any of the loans that ED has verified, I must notify ED before the loans are paid off.

D. If the amount ED sends to my holders is more than the amount needed to pay off the balances of the selected loans, the holders will refund the excess to ED and it will be applied against the outstanding balance of my Direct Consolidation Loan. If the amount that ED sends to my holders is less than the amount needed to pay off the balances of the loans selected for consolidation, ED will include the remaining amount in my Direct Consolidation Loan.

E. Unless I am consolidating a delinquent Federal Consolidation Loan that the lender has submitted to the guaranty agency for default aversion or a defaulted Federal Consolidation Loan, or, effective July 1, 2008, I am consolidating a Federal Consolidation Loan into the Direct Loan Program to use the Public Service Loan Forgiveness Program, I may consolidate an existing Federal Consolidation Loan or Direct Consolidation Loan only if I include at least one additional eligible loan in the consolidation.

F. If I am consolidating a delinquent Federal Consolidation Loan that the lender has submitted to the guaranty agency for default aversion or a defaulted Federal Consolidation Loan, and I am not including another eligible loan, I must agree to repay my Direct Consolidation Loan under the Income Contingent Repayment Plan or, effective July 1, 2009, the Income-Based Repayment Plan.

23. Under penalty of perjury, I certify that:

A. The information that I have provided on this Note is true, complete, and correct to the best of my knowledge and belief and is made in good faith.

B. I do not have any other application pending for a Federal Consolidation Loan with any FFEL Program lender.

C. All of the loans selected for consolidation have been used to finance my education or the education of my dependent student(s).

D. All of the loans selected for consolidation are in a grace period or in repayment (including loans in deferment or forbearance).

E. Unless I am consolidating a delinquent Federal Consolidation Loan that the lender has submitted to the guaranty agency for default aversion or a defaulted Federal Consolidation Loan, or, effective July 1, 2008, I am consolidating one or more FFEL Program loans into the Direct Loan Program to use the Public Service Loan Forgiveness Program, if none of the loans I am consolidating is a Direct Loan Program loan, I have sought and been unable to obtain a Federal Consolidation Loan from a FFEL Program lender, or I have been unable to obtain a Federal Consolidation Loan with income-sensitive repayment terms or, effective July 1, 2009, income-based repayment terms that are acceptable to me.

F. If I owe an overpayment on a Federal Perkins Loan, Federal Pell Grant, Federal Supplemental Educational Opportunity Grant, Academic Competitiveness Grant (ACG), National Science or Mathematics Access to Retain Talent (SMART) Grant, or Leveraging Educational Assistance Partnership Grant, I have made satisfactory arrangements with the holder to repay the amount owed.

G. If I am in default on any loan I am consolidating (except as provided above in Item 22.F.), I have either made a satisfactory repayment arrangement with the holder of that defaulted loan, or I will repay my Direct Consolidation Loan under the income contingent repayment plan or, effective July 1, 2009, the Income-Based Repayment Plan.

H. If I have been convicted of, or pled *nolo contendere* or guilty to, a crime involving fraud in obtaining federal student aid funds under Title IV of the Higher Education Act of 1965, as amended (the Act), I have completed the repayment of those funds to ED, or to the loan holder in the case of a Title IV federal student loan.

24. I make the following authorizations:

A. I authorize ED to contact the holders of the loans selected for consolidation to determine the eligibility of the loans for consolidation and the payoff amounts. I further authorize release to ED or its agent of any information required to consolidate my education loans in accordance with the Act.

B. I authorize ED to issue the proceeds of my Direct Consolidation Loan to the holders of the selected loans to pay off the debts.

C. I authorize ED to investigate my credit record and report information about my loan status to persons and organizations permitted by law to receive that information.

D. I authorize my school(s) and ED to release information about my Direct Consolidation Loan to the references on the loan and to members of my immediate family, unless I submit written directions otherwise.

E. I authorize my school(s), ED, or their agents to verify my social security number with the Social Security Administration (SSA) and, if the number on my loan record is incorrect, then I authorize SSA to disclose my correct social security number to these parties.

Section F: Promissory Note (continued on page 4) – to be completed and signed by the borrower.

25. Promise to Pay:

I promise to pay to the U.S. Department of Education (ED) all sums disbursed under the terms of this Note to pay off my prior loan obligations, plus interest and other charges and fees that may become due as provided in this Note. If I do not make payments on this Note when due, I will also pay reasonable collection costs, including but not limited to attorney's fees, court costs, and other fees.

If ED accepts my application, I understand that ED will on my behalf send funds to the holders of the loans that I want to consolidate to pay off those loans. I further understand that the amount of my Direct Consolidation Loan will equal the sum of the amounts that the holders of the loans verified as the payoff balances on the loans selected for consolidation. My signature on this Note serves as my authorization to pay off the balances of the loans selected for consolidation as provided by the holders of the loans.

The payoff amount may be greater than or less than the estimated total balance I have indicated in Section C1. Further, I understand that if any collection costs are owed on the loans selected for consolidation, these costs may be added to the principal balance of my Direct Consolidation Loan.

I will not sign this Note before reading the entire Note, even if I am told not to read it. I am entitled to an exact copy of this Note and the Borrower's Rights and Responsibilities Statement. My signature certifies that I have read, understand, and agree to the terms and conditions of this Note, including the Borrower Understandings, Certifications, and Authorizations in Section E, and the Borrower's Rights and Responsibilities Statement.

I UNDERSTAND THAT THIS IS A LOAN THAT I MUST REPAY.

26. Borrower's Signature _____ Today's Date (mm-dd-yyyy) _____

Governing Law

The terms of this Federal Direct Consolidation Loan Application and Promissory Note (Note) will be interpreted in accordance with the Higher Education Act of 1965, as amended (20 U.S.C. 1070 et seq.), the U.S. Department of Education's (ED's) regulations, as they may be amended in accordance with their effective date, and other applicable federal laws and regulations (collectively referred to as the "Act"). Applicable state law, except as preempted by federal law, may provide for certain borrower rights, remedies, and defenses in addition to those stated in this Note.

Disclosure of Loan Terms

This Note applies to a Federal Direct Consolidation Loan (Direct Consolidation Loan). Under this Note, the principal amount that I owe, and am required to repay, will be equal to all sums disbursed to pay off my prior loan obligations, plus any unpaid interest that is capitalized and added to the principal amount.

My Direct Consolidation Loan may have up to two separate loan identification numbers depending on the loans I choose to consolidate. These loan identification numbers will represent prior subsidized loans and prior unsubsidized loans. Each applicable loan identification number is represented by this Note.

When the loans that I am consolidating are paid off, a disclosure statement will be sent to me identifying the amount of my Direct Consolidation Loan, the associated loan identification numbers, and additional terms of the loan. Important additional information is also contained in the Borrower's Rights and Responsibilities Statement. The Borrower's Rights and Responsibilities Statement and any disclosure I receive in connection with the loan made under this Note are hereby incorporated into this Note.

Interest

Interest will be calculated using a formula provided for by the Act. Unless ED notifies me in writing of a lower rate, the interest rate on my Direct Consolidation Loan will be based on the weighted average of the interest rates on the loans being consolidated, rounded to the nearest higher one-eighth of one percent, but will not exceed 8.25%. This is a fixed interest rate, which means that the rate will remain the same throughout the life of the loan.

Except for interest ED does not charge me during a deferment period on the subsidized portion of my Direct Consolidation Loan, I agree to pay interest on the principal amount of my Direct Consolidation Loan from the date of disbursement until the loan is paid in full or discharged. ED may add interest that accrues but is not paid when due to the unpaid principal balance of this loan, as provided under the Act. This is called capitalization.

Late Charges and Collection Costs

ED may collect from me: (1) a late charge of not more than six cents for each dollar of each late payment if I fail to make any part of a required installment payment within 30 days after it becomes due, and (2) any other charges and fees that are permitted by the Act related to the collection of my Direct Consolidation Loan. If I default on my loan, I will pay reasonable collection costs, plus court costs and attorney fees.

Repayment

I must repay the full amount of the Direct Consolidation Loan made under this Note, plus accrued interest. I will repay my loan in monthly installments during a repayment period that begins on the date of the first disbursement of the loan, unless it is in a deferment or forbearance period. Payments made by me or on my behalf will be applied first to late charges and collection costs that are due, then to interest that has not been paid, and finally to the principal amount of the loan, except during periods of repayment under the Income-Based Repayment Plan. Under the Income-Based Repayment Plan, payments will be applied first to interest that is due, then to fees that are due, and then to the principal amount.

ED will provide me with a choice of repayment plans. Information on these plans is included in the Borrower's Rights and Responsibilities Statement. I must select a repayment plan. If I do not select a repayment plan, ED will choose a plan for me in accordance with ED's regulations.

ED will provide me with a repayment schedule that identifies my payment amounts and due dates. My first payment will be due within 60 days of the first disbursement of my Direct Consolidation Loan unless it is in a deferment or forbearance period. If I am unable to make my scheduled loan payments, ED may allow me to temporarily stop making payments, reduce my payment amount, or extend the time for making payments, as long as I intend to repay my loan. Allowing me to temporarily delay or reduce loan payments is called forbearance.

ED may adjust payment dates on my Direct Consolidation Loan or may grant me forbearance to eliminate a delinquency that remains even though I am making scheduled installment payments.

I may prepay any part of the unpaid balance on my loan at any time without penalty. After I have repaid my Direct Consolidation Loan in full, ED will send me a notice telling me that I have paid off my loan.

Acceleration and Default

At ED's option, the entire unpaid balance of the Direct Consolidation Loan will become immediately due and payable (this is called "acceleration") if either of the following events occurs: (1) I make a false representation that results in my receiving a loan for which I am not eligible; or (2) I default on the loan.

The following events will constitute a default on my loan: (1) I fail to pay the entire unpaid balance of the loan after ED has exercised its option under the preceding paragraph; (2) I fail to make installment payments when due, provided my failure has persisted for at least 270 days; or (3) I fail to comply with other terms of the loan, and ED reasonably concludes that I no longer intend to honor my repayment obligation. If I default, ED may capitalize all outstanding interest into a new principal balance, and collection costs will become immediately due and payable.

If I default, the default will be reported to national credit bureaus and will significantly and adversely affect my credit rating. I understand that a default will have additional adverse consequences to me as disclosed in the Borrower's Rights and Responsibilities Statement. I also understand that if I default, ED may require me to repay the loan under an income contingent repayment plan in accordance with the Act.

Legal Notices

Any notice required to be given to me will be effective if mailed by first class mail to the most recent address that ED has for me. I will immediately notify ED of a change of address or status, as specified in the Borrower's Rights and Responsibilities Statement.

If ED fails to enforce or insist on compliance with any term on this Note, this does not waive any right of ED. No provision of this Note may be modified or waived except in writing by ED. If any provision of this Note is determined to be unenforceable, the remaining provisions will remain in force.

Borrower's Rights and Responsibilities Statement

Important Notice: This Borrower's Rights and Responsibilities Statement provides additional information about the terms and conditions of the loan you will receive under the accompanying Federal Direct Consolidation Loan (Direct Consolidation Loan) Application and Promissory Note (Note). **Please keep a copy of the Note and this Borrower's Rights and Responsibilities Statement for your records.**

In this document, the words "we," "us," and "our" refer to the U.S. Department of Education. The word "loan" refers to your Direct Consolidation Loan.

1. The William D. Ford Federal Direct Loan Program. The William D. Ford Federal Direct Loan (Direct Loan) Program includes the following types of loans, known collectively as "Direct Loans":

- Federal Direct Stafford/Ford Loans (Direct Subsidized Loans)
- Federal Direct Unsubsidized Stafford/Ford Loans (Direct Unsubsidized Loans)
- Federal Direct PLUS Loans (Direct PLUS Loans)
- Federal Direct Consolidation Loans (Direct Consolidation Loans)

The Direct Loan Program is authorized by Title IV, Part D, of the Higher Education Act of 1965, as amended.

Direct Loans are made by the U.S. Department of Education. Our Direct Loan Servicing Center services, answers questions about, and processes payments on Direct Loans. We will provide you with the Direct Loan Servicing Center's address and telephone number.

2. Laws that apply to this Note. The terms and conditions of loans made under this Note are determined by the Higher Education Act of 1965, as amended (20 U.S.C. 1070 et seq.) and other applicable federal laws and regulations. These laws and regulations are referred to as "the Act" throughout this Borrower's Rights and Responsibilities Statement. State law, unless it is preempted by federal law, may provide you with certain rights, remedies, and defenses in addition to those stated in the Note and this Borrower's Rights and Responsibilities Statement.

NOTE: Any change to the Act applies to loans in accordance with the effective date of the change.

3. Direct Consolidation Loan identification numbers. Depending on the type(s) of federal education loan(s) that you choose to consolidate, your loan may have up to two individual loan identification numbers. However, you will have only one Direct Consolidation Loan and will receive only one bill.

3a. the subsidized portion of your loan ("Direct Subsidized Consolidation Loan") will have one loan identification number representing the amount of the following types of loans that you consolidate:

- Subsidized Federal Stafford Loans
- Direct Subsidized Loans
- Subsidized Federal Consolidation Loans
- Direct Subsidized Consolidation Loans
- Federal Insured Student Loans (FISL)
- Guaranteed Student Loans (GSL)

3b. The unsubsidized portion of your loan ("Direct Unsubsidized Consolidation Loan") will have one identification number representing the amount of the following types of loans that you consolidate:

- Unsubsidized and Nonsubsidized Federal Stafford Loans
- Direct Unsubsidized Loans
- Unsubsidized Federal Consolidation Loans
- Direct Unsubsidized Consolidation Loans
- Federal PLUS Loans (for parents or for graduate and professional students)
- Direct PLUS Loans (for parents or for graduate and professional students)
- Direct PLUS Consolidation Loans
- Federal Perkins Loans
- National Direct Student Loans (NDSL)
- National Defense Student Loans (NDSL)
- Federal Supplemental Loans for Students (SLS)
- Parent Loans for Undergraduate Students (PLUS)
- Auxiliary Loans to Assist Students (ALAS)
- Health Professions Student Loans (HPSL)
- Health Education Assistance Loans (HEAL)
- Nursing Student Loans (NSL)
- Loans for Disadvantaged Students (LDS)

4. Adding eligible loans to your Direct Consolidation Loan. You may add eligible loans to your Direct Consolidation Loan by submitting a request to us within 180 days of the date your Direct Consolidation Loan is made. (Your Direct Consolidation Loan is "made" on the date we pay off the first loan that you are consolidating.) After we pay off any loans that you add during the 180-day period, we will notify you of the new total amount of your Direct Consolidation Loan and of any adjustments that must be made to your monthly payment amount.

If you want to consolidate an additional eligible loan after the 180-day period, you must apply for a new Direct Consolidation Loan.

5. Loans that may be consolidated. *General.* Only the federal education loans listed in Items 3a.and 3b. of this Borrower's Rights and Responsibilities Statement may be consolidated into a Direct Consolidation Loan. You may only consolidate loans that are in a grace period or in repayment (including loans in deferment or forbearance). At least one of the loans that you consolidate must be a Direct Loan Program loan or a Federal Family Education Loan (FFEL) Program loan.

Defaulted loans. You may consolidate a loan that is in default if **(a)** you first make satisfactory repayment arrangements with the holder of the defaulted loan, or **(b)** you agree to repay your Direct Consolidation Loan under the Income Contingent Repayment Plan (see Item 10).

Existing consolidation loans. Generally, you may consolidate an existing Direct Consolidation Loan or Federal Consolidation Loan into a new Direct Consolidation Loan only if you include at least one additional eligible loan in the consolidation. However, you may consolidate a Federal Consolidation Loan into a new Direct Consolidation Loan without including an additional loan if the Federal Consolidation Loan is delinquent and has been submitted by the lender to the guaranty agency for default aversion, or if the Federal Consolidation Loan is in default. In such cases, you must agree to repay the new Direct Consolidation Loan under the Income Contingent Repayment Plan or, effective July 1, 2009, the Income-Based Repayment Plan. Effective July 1, 2008, you may also consolidate a single Federal Consolidation Loan into a new Direct Consolidation Loan for purposes of using the public service loan forgiveness program described in Item 16 of this Borrower's Rights and Responsibilities Statement.

6. Information you must report to us. Until your loan is repaid, you must notify the Direct Loan Servicing Center if you:

- Change your address or telephone number;
- Change your name (for example, maiden name to married name);
- Change your employer or your employer's address or telephone number changes; or
- Have any other change in status that would affect your loan (for example, if you received a deferment while you were unemployed, but have found a job and therefore no longer meet the eligibility requirements for the deferment)

7. Interest rate. The interest rate on your Direct Consolidation Loan will be **the lesser of** the weighted average of the interest rates on the loans being consolidated, rounded to the nearest higher one-eighth of one percent, OR 8.25%. We will send you a notice that tells you the interest rate on your loan.

The interest rate on a Direct Consolidation Loan is a fixed rate. This means that the interest rate will remain the same throughout the life of your loan.

8. Payment of interest. We charge interest on a Direct Consolidation Loan from the date the loan is made until it is paid in full or discharged, including during periods of deferment or forbearance. However, we do not charge interest on the subsidized portion of a Direct Consolidation Loan ("Direct Subsidized Consolidation Loan" – see Item 3a.) during deferment periods.

If you do not pay the interest as it is charged during the periods described above, we will add the interest to the unpaid principal amount of your loan at the end of the deferment or forbearance period. This is called "capitalization." Capitalization increases the unpaid principal balance of your loan, and we will then charge interest on the increased principal amount.

The chart below shows the difference in the total amount you would repay on a $15,000 Direct Unsubsidized Consolidation Loan if you pay the interest as it is charged during a 12-month deferment or forbearance period, compared to the amount you would repay if you do not pay the interest and it is capitalized.

	If you pay the interest as it is charged...	If you do not pay the interest and it is capitalized...
Loan Amount	$15,000	$15,000
Capitalized Interest for 12 months (at the maximum rate of 8.25%)	$0	$1,238
Principal to be Repaid	$15,000	$16,238
Monthly Payment (Standard Repayment Plan)	$146	$158
Number of Payments	180	180
Total Amount Repaid	$26,209	$28,359

In this example, you would pay $12 less per month and $2,150 less altogether if you pay the interest as it is charged during a 12-month deferment or forbearance period.

You may be able to claim a federal income tax deduction for interest payments you make on Direct Loans. For further information, refer to IRS Publication 970, which is available at http://www.irs.ustreas.gov.

9. Repayment incentive programs. A repayment incentive is a benefit that we offer to encourage you to repay your loan on time. Under a repayment incentive program, the interest rate we charge on your loan may be reduced. Some repayment incentive programs require you to make a certain number of payments on time to keep the reduced interest rate. For Direct Consolidation Loans, the following repayment incentive program may be available to you:

Interest Rate Reduction for Electronic Debit Account Repayment

Under the Electronic Debit Account (EDA) repayment option, your bank automatically deducts your monthly loan payment from your checking or savings account and sends it to us. EDA helps to ensure that your payments are made on time. In addition, you receive a 0.25 percent interest rate reduction while you repay under the EDA option. We will include information about the EDA option in your first bill. You can also get this information on the Direct Loan Servicing Center's web site, or by calling the Direct Loan Servicing Center's toll-free telephone number (the web site address and telephone number are provided on all correspondence that the Direct Loan Servicing Center sends you).

The Direct Loan Servicing Center can provide you with more information on other repayment incentive programs that may be available.

Note: Another repayment incentive program, the up-front interest rebate, is available on Direct Subsidized Loans, Direct Unsubsidized Loans, and Direct PLUS Loans. The rebate is equal to a percentage of the loan amount, and is the same amount that would result if the interest rate on the loan were lowered by a specific percentage. To permanently keep an up-front interest rebate, a borrower must make each of the first 12 required monthly payments on time when the loan enters repayment. If you consolidate a Direct Loan on which you received an up-front interest rebate before you permanently earn the rebate (the correspondence you received about your loan will tell you if you received a rebate), you will have to make the first 12 required monthly payments on your Direct Consolidation Loan on time to keep the interest rebate. You will lose the rebate if you do not make all of your first 12 required monthly payments on time. If you lose the rebate, we will add the rebate amount back to the principal balance on your loan account. This will increase the amount that you must repay.

10. Repaying your loan. Your first payment will be due within 60 days of the first disbursement of your Direct Consolidation Loan unless your loan is in a deferment or forbearance period. The Direct Loan Servicing Center will notify you of the date your first payment is due.

You must make payments on your loan even if you do not receive a bill or repayment notice. Billing information is sent to you as a convenience, and you are obligated to make payments even if you do not receive a bill or notice.

You may choose one of the following repayment plans to repay your loan:

- **Standard Repayment Plan** – Under this plan, you will make fixed monthly payments and repay your loan in full within 10 to 30 years (not including periods of deferment or forbearance) from the date the loan entered repayment, depending on the amount of your Direct Consolidation Loan and the amount of your other student loan debt as listed in Section C2 of your Note (see the chart below). Your payments must be at least $50 a month and will be more, if necessary, to repay the loan within the required time period.

- **Graduated Repayment Plan** – Under this plan, your payments will be lower at first and will then increase over time, usually every two years. You will repay your loan in full within 10 to 30 years (not including periods of deferment or forbearance) from the date the loan entered repayment, depending on the total amount of your Direct Consolidation Loan and the amount of your other student loan debt as listed in Section C2 of your Note (see the chart below). No single payment under this plan will be more than three times greater than any other payment.

Maximum Repayment Periods Under the Standard and Graduated Repayment Plans	
Total Education Loan Indebtedness	Maximum Repayment Period
Less than $7,500	10 years
$7,500 to $9,999	12 years
$10,000 to $19,999	15 years
$20,000 to $39,999	20 years
$40,000 to $59,999	25 years
$60,000 or more	30 years

- **Extended Repayment Plan** – You may choose this plan only if **(1)** you had no outstanding balance on a Direct Loan Program loan as of October 7, 1998, or on the date you obtained a Direct Loan Program loan on or after October 7, 1998, and **(2)** you have an outstanding balance on Direct Loan Program Loans that exceeds $30,000. Under this plan, you may choose to make either fixed or graduated monthly payments and will repay your loan in full over a repayment period not to exceed 25 years (not including periods of deferment or forbearance) from the date your loan entered repayment. If you choose to make fixed monthly payments, your payments must be at least $50 a month and will be more, if necessary, to repay the loan within the required time period. If you choose to make graduated monthly payments, your payments will start out lower and will then increase over time, generally every two years. Under a graduated repayment schedule, your monthly payment must at least be equal to the amount of interest that accrues each month, and no single payment will be more than three times greater than any other payment.

- **Income Contingent Repayment Plan** – Under this plan, your monthly payment amount will be based on your adjusted gross income (and that of your spouse if you are married), your family size, and the total amount of your Direct Loans. Until we obtain the information needed to calculate your monthly payment amount, your payment will equal the amount of interest that has accrued on your loan unless you request a forbearance. As your income changes, your payments may change. If you do not repay your loan after 25 years under this plan, the unpaid portion will be forgiven. You may have to pay income tax on any amount forgiven.

- **Income-Based Repayment Plan (effective July 1, 2009)** – Under this plan, your required monthly payment amount will be based on your income during any period when you have a partial financial hardship. Your monthly payment amount may be adjusted annually. The maximum repayment period under this plan may exceed 10 years. If you meet certain requirements over a specified period, you may qualify for cancellation of any outstanding balance on your loans. **NOTE:** Direct Consolidation Loans that repaid parent Direct

PLUS Loans or parent Federal PLUS Loans may not be repaid under the Income-Based Repayment Plan.

If you can show to our satisfaction that the terms and conditions of these repayment plans are not adequate to meet your exceptional circumstances, we may provide you with an alternative repayment plan.

If you do not choose a repayment plan, we will choose a plan for you in accordance with the Act.

You may change repayment plans at any time after you have begun repaying your loan. There is no penalty if you make loan payments before they are due, or pay more than the amount due each month.

Except as provided by the Act for payments made under the Income-Based Repayment Plan, we apply your payments and prepayments in the following order: late charges and collection costs first, outstanding interest second, and outstanding principal last.

When you have repaid your loan in full, the Direct Loan Servicing Center will send you a notice telling you that you have paid off your loan. You should keep this notice in a safe place.

11. Late charges and collection costs. If you do not make any part of a payment within 30 days after it is due, we may require you to pay a late charge. This charge will not be more than six cents for each dollar of each late payment. If you do not make payments as scheduled, we may also require you to pay other charges and fees involved in collecting your loan.

12. Demand for immediate repayment. The entire unpaid amount of your loan becomes due and payable (on your Note this is called "acceleration") if you:

- Make a false statement that causes you to receive a loan that you are not eligible to receive; or
- Default on your loan.

13. Defaulting on your loan. Default (failing to repay your loan) is defined in detail in the "Promissory Note" section on page 4 of your Note. If you default:

- We will require you to immediately repay the entire unpaid amount of your loan.
- We may sue you, take all or part of your federal tax refund or other federal payments, and/or garnish your wages so that your employer is required to send us part of your wages to pay off your loan.
- We will require you to pay reasonable collection fees and costs, plus court costs and attorney fees.
- You will lose eligibility for other federal student aid and assistance under most federal benefit programs.
- You will lose eligibility for loan deferments.
- We will also report your default to national credit bureaus (see Item 14).

14. Credit bureau notification. We will report information about your loan to one or more national credit bureaus. This information will include the disbursement dates, amount, and repayment status of your loan (for example, whether you are current or delinquent in making payments).

If you default on a loan, we will also report this to national credit bureaus. We will notify you at least 30 days in advance that we plan to report default information to a credit bureau unless you resume making payments on the loan within 30 days. You will be given a chance to ask for a review of the debt before we report it.

If a credit bureau contacts us regarding objections you have raised about the accuracy or completeness of any information we have reported, we are required to provide the credit bureau with a prompt response.

15. Deferment and forbearance (postponing payments). If you meet certain requirements, you may receive a **deferment** that allows you to temporarily stop making payments on your loan. If you cannot make your scheduled loan payments, but do not qualify for a deferment, we may give you a **forbearance**. A forbearance allows you to temporarily stop making payments on your loan, temporarily make smaller payments, or extend the time for making payments.

Deferment

You may receive a deferment while you are:

- Enrolled at least half-time at an eligible school;
- In a full-time course of study in a graduate fellowship program;
- In an approved full-time rehabilitation program for individuals with disabilities;
- Unemployed (for a maximum of three years; you must be conscientiously seeking, but unable to find, full-time employment); or

- Experiencing an economic hardship (including Peace Corps service), as determined under the Act (for a maximum of three years).
- Serving on active duty during a war or other military operation or national emergency, or performing qualifying National Guard duty during a war or other military operation or national emergency, and if you are serving on or after October 1, 2007, for the 180-day period following the demobilization date for your qualifying service.

Effective October 1, 2007, if you are a member of the National Guard or other reserve component of the U.S. Armed Forces (current or retired) and you are called or ordered to active duty while enrolled at an eligible school, or within 6 months of having been enrolled, you are eligible for a deferment during the 13 months following the conclusion of the active duty service, or until the date you return to enrolled student status, whichever is earlier.

You may be eligible to receive additional deferments if, at the time you received your first Direct Loan, you had an outstanding balance on a loan made under the Federal Family Education Loan (FFEL) Program before July 1, 1993. If you meet this requirement, you may receive a deferment while you are:

- Temporarily totally disabled, or unable to work because you are required to care for a spouse or dependent who is disabled (for a maximum of three years);
- On active duty in the U.S. Armed Forces, on active duty in the National Oceanic and Atmospheric Administration (NOAA), or serving full-time as an officer in the Commissioned Corps of the Public Health Service (for a combined maximum of three years);
- Serving in the Peace Corps (for a maximum of three years);
- A full-time paid volunteer for a tax-exempt organization or an ACTION program (for a maximum of three years);
- In a medical internship or residency program (for a maximum of two years);
- Teaching in a designated teacher shortage area (for a maximum of three years);
- On parental leave (for a maximum of six months);
- A working mother entering or re-entering the workforce (for a maximum of one year); or
- While the student for whom you borrowed a PLUS loan is dependent and is enrolled at least half-time at an eligible school, or is in an approved full-time rehabilitation training program for individuals with disabilities.

You may receive a deferment based on your enrollment in school on at least a half-time basis if **(1)** you submit a deferment request form to the Direct Loan Servicing Center along with documentation of your eligibility for the deferment, or **(2)** the Direct Loan Servicing Center receives information from the school you are attending that indicates you are enrolled at least half-time. If the Direct Loan Servicing Center processes a deferment based on information received from your school, you will be notified of the deferment and will have the option of canceling the deferment and continuing to make payments on your loan.

For all other deferments, you (or, for a deferment based on active military duty or qualifying National Guard duty during a war or other military operation or national emergency, your representative) must submit a deferment request form to the Direct Loan Servicing Center, along with documentation of your eligibility for the deferment. In certain circumstances, you may not be required to provide documentation of your eligibility if the Direct Loan Servicing Center confirms that you have been granted the same deferment for the same period of time on a FFEL Program loan. The Direct Loan Servicing Center can provide you with a deferment request form that explains the requirements for the type of deferment you are requesting. You may also obtain deferment request forms and information on deferment eligibility requirements from the Direct Loan Servicing Center's web site at www.dl.ed.gov.

If you are in default on your loan, you are not eligible for a deferment.

You are responsible for paying the interest on a Direct Unsubsidized Consolidation Loan during a deferment period. You are not responsible for paying the interest on a Direct Subsidized Consolidation Loan during a deferment period.

Forbearance

We will give you a forbearance if: You are serving in a medical or dental internship or residency program, and you meet specific requirements;

- You are serving in a national service position for which you receive a national service education award under the National and Community Service Act of 1990 (AmeriCorps);
- You qualify for partial repayment of your loans under the Student Loan Repayment Program, as administered by the Department of Defense.
- You are performing service that would qualify you for loan forgiveness under the teacher loan forgiveness program that is available to certain Direct Loan and FFEL program borrowers; or
- The total amount you owe each month for all of the student loans you received under Title IV of the Act is 20 percent or more of your total monthly gross income (for a maximum of three years).

In addition, we may give you a forbearance if you are temporarily unable to make your scheduled loan payments for reasons including, but not limited to, financial hardship or illness.

To request a forbearance, contact the Direct Loan Servicing Center. The Direct Loan Servicing Center can provide you with a forbearance request form that explains the requirements for the type of forbearance you are requesting. You may also obtain forbearance request forms and information on forbearance eligibility requirements from the Direct Loan Servicing Center's web site at www.dl.ed.gov.

Under certain circumstances, we may also give you a forbearance without requiring you to submit a request or documentation. These circumstances include, but are not limited to, the following:

- Periods necessary for us to determine your eligibility for a loan discharge;
- A period of up to 60 days in order for us to collect and process documentation related to your request for a deferment, forbearance, change in repayment plan, or consolidation loan (we do not capitalize interest charged during this period); or
- Periods when you are involved in a military mobilization, or a local or national emergency.

You are responsible for paying the interest on your entire Direct Consolidation Loan during a forbearance period.

16. Discharge (having your loan forgiven). We will discharge (forgive) your Direct Loan Consolidation Loan if:

- The Direct Loan Servicing Center receives acceptable documentation of your death. We will also discharge the portion of a Direct Consolidation Loan that repaid one or more Direct PLUS Loans or Federal PLUS Loans obtained on behalf of a student who dies.
- Your loan is discharged in bankruptcy. However, federal student loans are not automatically discharged if you file for bankruptcy. To have your loan discharged in bankruptcy, you must prove to the bankruptcy court, in an adversary proceeding, that repaying the loan would cause undue hardship.
- We determine that you are totally and permanently disabled (as defined in the Act), based on a physician's certification, and you meet additional requirements during a 3-year conditional discharge period. During that period, your earnings from work must not exceed the poverty line amount for a family of two, and you must not receive any additional loans under the Direct Loan, FFEL, or Federal Perkins Loan programs. You may not receive a discharge due to total and permanent disability based on a condition that existed before you received any of the loans that you consolidated, unless a doctor certifies that the condition substantially deteriorated after the loan was made.

In certain cases, we may also discharge all or a portion of your Direct Consolidation Loan if:

- One or more Direct Loan Program, FFEL Program, or Federal Perkins Loan Program loans that you consolidated was used to pay for a program of study that you (or the dependent student for whom you borrowed a PLUS loan) were unable to complete because the school closed;
- Your eligibility (or the eligibility of the dependent student for whom you borrowed a PLUS loan) for one or more of the Direct Loan Program or FFEL Program loans that you consolidated was falsely certified by the school;
- Your eligibility for one or more of the Direct Loan Program or FFEL Program loans that you consolidated was falsely certified as a result of a crime of identity theft; or
- The school did not pay a required refund of one or more Direct Loan Program or FFEL Program loans that you consolidated.

We may forgive a portion of your Direct Consolidation Loan that repaid Direct Subsidized or Direct Unsubsidized Loans you received after October 1, 1998, or subsidized or unsubsidized Federal Stafford Loans you received under the FFEL program after October 1, 1998 if you teach full time for five consecutive years in certain low-income elementary and/or secondary schools and meet certain other qualifications, and if you did not owe a Direct Loan or FFEL program loan as of October 1, 1998, or as of the date you obtain a loan after October 1, 1998.

A public service loan forgiveness program is available that provides for the cancellation of the remaining balance due on your eligible Direct Loan Program loans after you have made 120 payments (after October 1, 2007) on those loans under certain repayment plans while you are employed in certain public service jobs.

To request a loan discharge based on one of the conditions described above (except for discharges due to death or bankruptcy), you must complete an application that you may obtain from the Direct Loan Servicing Center or from the Direct Loan Servicing Center's web site at www.dl.ed.gov.

In some cases, you may assert, as a defense against collection of your loan, that the school did something wrong or failed to do something that it should have done. You can make such a defense against repayment only if the school's act or omission directly relates to your loan or to the educational services that the loan was intended to pay for, and if what the school did or did not do would give rise to a legal cause of action against the school under applicable state law. If you believe that you have a defense against repayment of your loan, contact the Direct Loan Servicing Center.

We do not guarantee the quality of the academic programs provided by schools that participate in federal student financial aid programs. You must repay your loan even if you do not complete your education, are unable to obtain employment in your field of study, or are dissatisfied with, or do not receive, the education you paid for with the loan.

17. Department of Defense and other federal agency loan repayment.
Under certain circumstances, military personnel may have educational loans repaid by the Secretary of Defense. This benefit is offered as part of a recruitment program that does not apply to individuals based on their previous military service or to those who are not eligible for enlistment in the U.S. Armed Forces. For more information, contact your local military service recruitment office.

Other agencies of the federal government may also offer student loan repayment programs as an incentive to recruit and retain employees. Contact the agency's human resources department for more information.

END OF BORROWER'S RIGHTS AND RESPONSIBILITIES STATEMENT

IMPORTANT NOTICES

Gramm-Leach-Bliley Act Notice

In 1999, Congress enacted the Gramm-Leach-Bliley Act (Public Law 106-102). This Act requires that lenders provide certain information to their customers regarding the collection and use of nonpublic personal information.

We disclose nonpublic personal information to third parties only as necessary to process and service your loan and as permitted by the Privacy Act of 1974. See the Privacy Act Notice below. We do not sell or otherwise make available any information about you to any third parties for marketing purposes.

We protect the security and confidentiality of nonpublic personal information by implementing the following policies and practices. All physical access to the sites where nonpublic personal information is maintained is controlled and monitored by security personnel. Our computer systems offer a high degree of resistance to tampering and circumvention. These systems limit data access to our staff and contract staff on a "need-to-know" basis, and control individual users' ability to access and alter records within the systems. All users of these systems are given a unique user ID with personal identifiers. All interactions by individual users with the systems are recorded.

Privacy Act Notice

The Privacy Act of 1974 (5 U.S.C. 552a) requires that the following notice be provided to you:

The authority for collecting the requested information from and about you is §451 et seq. of the Higher Education Act (HEA) of 1965, as amended (20 U.S.C. 1087a et seq.) and the authorities for collecting and using your Social Security Number (SSN) are §484(a)(4) of the HEA (20 U.S.C. 1091(a)(4)) and 31 U.S.C. 7701(b). Participating in the William D. Ford Federal Direct Loan (Direct Loan) Program and giving us your SSN are voluntary, but you must provide the requested information, including your SSN, to participate.

The principal purposes for collecting the information on this form, including your SSN, are to verify your identity, to determine your eligibility to receive a loan or a benefit on a loan (such as a deferment, forbearance, discharge, or forgiveness) under the Direct Loan Program, to permit the servicing of your loan(s), and, if it becomes necessary, to locate you and to collect and report on your loan(s) if your loan(s) become delinquent or in default. We also use your SSN as an account identifier and to permit you to access your account information electronically.

The information in your file may be disclosed, on a case by case basis or under a computer matching program, to third parties as authorized under routine uses in the appropriate systems of records notices. The routine uses of this information include, but are not limited to, its disclosure to federal, state, or local agencies, to private parties such as relatives, present and former employers, business and personal associates, to consumer reporting agencies, to financial and educational institutions, and to guaranty agencies in order to verify your identity, to determine your eligibility to receive a loan or a benefit on a loan, to permit the servicing or collection of your loan(s), to enforce the terms of the loan(s), to investigate possible fraud and to verify compliance with federal student financial aid program regulations, or to locate you if you become delinquent in your loan payments or if you default. To provide default rate calculations, disclosures may be made to guaranty agencies, to financial and educational institutions, or to state agencies. To provide financial aid history information, disclosures may be made to educational institutions. To assist program administrators with tracking refunds and cancellations, disclosures may be made to guaranty agencies, to financial and educational institutions, or to federal or state agencies. To provide a standardized method for educational institutions to efficiently submit student enrollment status, disclosures may be made to guaranty agencies or to financial and educational institutions. To counsel you in repayment efforts, disclosures may be made to guaranty agencies, to financial and educational institutions, or to federal, state, or local agencies.

In the event of litigation, we may send records to the Department of Justice, a court, adjudicative body, counsel, party, or witness if the disclosure is relevant and necessary to the litigation. If this information, either alone or with other information, indicates a potential violation of law, we may send it to the appropriate authority for action. We may send information to members of Congress if you ask them to help you with federal student aid questions. In circumstances involving employment complaints, grievances, or disciplinary actions, we may disclose relevant records to adjudicate or investigate the issues. If provided for by a collective bargaining agreement, we may disclose records to a labor organization recognized under 5 U.S.C. Chapter 71. Disclosures may be made to our contractors for the purpose of performing any programmatic function that requires disclosure of records. Before making any such disclosure, we will require the contractor to maintain Privacy Act safeguards. Disclosures may also be made to qualified researchers under Privacy Act safeguards.

Financial Privacy Act Notice

Under the Right to Financial Privacy Act of 1978 (12 U.S.C. 3401-3421), ED will have access to financial records in your student loan file maintained in compliance with the administration of the Direct Loan Program.

Paperwork Reduction Notice

According to the Paperwork Reduction Act of 1995, no persons are required to respond to a collection of information unless it displays a currently valid OMB control number. The valid OMB control number for this information collection is 1845-0053. The time required to complete this information collection is estimated to average 1.0 hour (60 minutes) per response, including the time to review instructions, search existing data resources, gather and maintain the data needed, and complete and review the information collection. **If you have any comments concerning the accuracy of the time estimate(s) or suggestions for improving this form, please write to:** U.S. Department of Education, Washington, DC 20202-4700.

If you have any questions regarding the status of your individual submission of this form, write directly to:

**U.S. Department of Education
Consolidation Department
P.O. Box 242800
Louisville, KY 40224-2800**

Appx. D.1.3   Student Loan Law

D.1.3 Repayment Plan Selection Form

REPAYMENT PLAN SELECTION
William D. Ford Federal Direct Loan Program

OMB No. 1845-0014
Form Approved
Exp. Date 08/31/2010

WARNING: Any person who knowingly makes a false statement or misrepresentation on this form will be subject to penalties that may include fines, imprisonment, or both, under the U.S. Criminal Code and 20 U.S.C. 1097.

Instructions

Read the enclosed information carefully to understand your repayment options and then complete this form to select a repayment plan or to change your previous repayment plan. **Please print clearly using blue or black ink.**

If you need help completing this form, contact the Loan Consolidation Department through one of the options provided in Section 6 on the back of this form. **Return the completed form to the address shown in Section 6.** If you are selecting any repayment plan except for the Income Contingent Repayment Plan with the joint repayment option, you may do so electronically at the Direct Loan Servicing Center's Web site: www.dl.ed.gov

Section 1: Borrower Information – to be completed by ALL BORROWERS

Borrower's Last Name   Borrower's First Name   Borrower's Middle Initial   Borrower's Social Security Number:

|__|__|__|-|__|__|-|__|__|__|__|

Section 2: Repayment Plan Selection – to be completed by ALL BORROWERS

Place an "X" in the box under the repayment plan that you wish to select for each type of loan that you owe. The enclosed information describes each of the repayment plans. You must choose the same repayment plan for all of your Direct Loans, unless you have both parent Direct PLUS Loans (Direct PLUS Loans you received as a parent to pay for the education of a dependent student) and one or more of the other types of Direct Loans listed below (Direct Subsidized Loans, Direct Unsubsidized Loans, Direct Consolidation Loans, and student Direct PLUS Loans (Direct PLUS Loans you received to pay for your own graduate or professional education)), and you want to repay your Direct Subsidized Loans, Direct Unsubsidized Loans, Direct Consolidation Loans, and/or student Direct PLUS Loans under the Income Contingent Repayment (ICR) Plan or Income-Based Repayment (IBR) Plan. In that case, you must select a different repayment plan for your parent Direct PLUS Loans. You may repay any Direct Consolidation Loan (except for a Direct PLUS Consolidation Loan) under the ICR Plan, but a Direct PLUS Consolidation Loan or a Direct Consolidation that repaid parent PLUS loans may not be repaid under the IBR Plan.

- You may not repay parent Direct PLUS Loans under the ICR or IBR Plan.
- To be eligible to repay your loans under the IBR Plan, you must have a partial financial hardship (see Section 5 of this form).

Loan Types	Standard	Graduated	Extended		Income Contingent	Income-Based
Direct Subsidized Loans Direct Unsubsidized Loans Direct Consolidation Loans Student Direct PLUS Loans	☐	☐	Fixed Payments ☐	Graduated Payments ☐	☐	☐
Parent Direct PLUS Loans Direct PLUS Consolidation Loans	☐	☐	Fixed Payments ☐	Graduated Payments ☐	Not Available	Not Available

Section 3: Spouse Information – to be completed by SOME MARRIED BORROWERS

If you are married, complete this section only if you are (1) selecting the ICR Plan (unless you are separated from your spouse), (2) selecting the IBR Plan and you and your spouse file your federal income taxes jointly, or (3) selecting any repayment plan for a Direct Consolidation Loan held jointly by you and your spouse.

Spouse's Last Name   Spouse's First Name   Spouse's Middle Initial   Spouse's Social Security Number:

|__|__|__|-|__|__|-|__|__|__|__|

Section 4: Additional ICR Information – to be completed by BORROWERS WHO SELECT ICR

Complete this section *only* if you are selecting the ICR Plan.

Note: To repay under the ICR Plan, you must complete an ICR & IBR Plan Consent to Disclosure of Tax Information form. You may also be required to complete an ICR & IBR Plan Alternative Documentation of Income form. We have enclosed the required ICR & IBR Plan form(s). Please complete and return the enclosed form(s) along with this Repayment Plan Selection form. If you do not submit the required ICR & IBR form(s), you will be placed on the Standard Repayment Plan (unless you were previously on another Direct Loan repayment plan).

When you begin repaying your loan under ICR, your initial payment amount will be the full amount of interest that accumulates on your loan each month. If you cannot afford the initial interest payment, you may request a forbearance until you are notified of your actual ICR payment.

During a forbearance you are not required to make any payments of principal or interest, but interest continues to accumulate on your loan. If you are beginning repayment of your Direct Loan for the first time, interest that you do not pay during the forbearance will be capitalized (added to your outstanding principal balance) at the end of the forbearance. Capitalization increases your loan's principal amount, and therefore the total amount of interest you will repay on your loan. If you are requesting a change from another Direct Loan repayment plan to the ICR Plan, you may receive a forbearance for up to 60 days during which unpaid interest will not be capitalized. During the 60-day period, you will have to provide us with the information that we need to calculate your payment amount under ICR. To request a forbearance, contact the Direct Loan Servicing Center through one of the options provided on your billing statements.

A. Family Size. Enter your family size on the line below. Your family size number includes you and your spouse. It includes your children if they get more than half their support from you. It includes other people only if: (1) they now live with you, *and* (2) they now get more than half their support from you *and* they will continue to get this support from you. **Support** includes money, gifts, loans, housing, food, clothes, car, medical and dental care, payment of college costs, etc. **If your family size number changes, notify the Consolidation Department in writing at the mailing address or the Web site address shown in Section 6.**

Family Size: _____

B. ICR Joint Repayment Option. If you and your spouse each have Direct Loans and both of you want to repay the loans under the ICR Plan, you may choose to repay your loans jointly (see ICR Plan description in the enclosed Repayment Plan Choices sheet). If you choose to repay jointly, place an "X" in the box below and have your spouse sign and date this form.

☐ I wish to repay my loan(s) jointly with my spouse under the ICR Plan.

C. Certification. Read the certification statement below, then sign and date this form. If you selected the ICR Joint Repayment Option (see "B", above), your spouse must also sign and date this form.

All of the information I provided on this form is true and complete to the best of my knowledge. If asked by an authorized official, I agree to provide proof of the information that I have provided on this form.

Borrower's Signature _____   Date _____

Spouse's Signature (if required) _____   Date _____

Student Assistance Forms Appx. D.1.3

Section 5: Additional IBR Information – to be completed by BORROWERS WHO SELECT IBR

Complete this section *only* if you are selecting the IBR Plan.

To repay under the IBR Plan, you must have a **partial financial hardship**. You are considered to have a partial financial hardship if the annual amount due on all of your eligible loans, as calculated under a standard repayment plan with a 10-year repayment period, is more than 15% of the difference between your adjusted gross income (AGI) and 150% of the poverty guideline amount for your family size and state. (If you are married and file a joint federal tax return with your spouse, your AGI includes both your income and your spouse's income.) Eligible loans for the IBR Plan are Direct Subsidized Loans, Direct Unsubsidized Loans, Direct Consolidation Loans that did not repay parent PLUS loans, student Direct PLUS Loans, Federal Family Education Loan (FFEL) Stafford Loans, student FFEL PLUS Loans, and FFEL Consolidation Loans that did not repay parent PLUS loans. If you have both Direct Loans and FFEL loans, your total eligible loan debt will be considered when determining partial financial hardship. The following loans are **not** eligible for IBR: Direct PLUS Consolidation Loans, parent Direct PLUS Loans, parent FFEL PLUS Loans, Direct Consolidation Loans or FFEL Consolidation Loans that repaid parent PLUS loans, and loans on which you are in default.

To enroll in the IBR Plan, you must complete an ICR & IBR Plan Consent to Disclosure of Tax Information form. You may also be required to complete an ICR & IBR Plan Alternative Documentation of Income form. We have enclosed the required form(s). Please complete and return the enclosed form(s) along with this Repayment Plan Selection form. If you do not submit the required ICR & IBR form(s), you will be placed on the Standard Repayment Plan (unless you were previously on another Direct Loan repayment plan).

If you select the IBR Plan, you must continue to make payments on your loan(s) under your current repayment plan until we receive all the necessary information to determine your eligibility for the IBR Plan and your IBR payment amount. If you are unable to make your loan payments under your current repayment plan while we are determining your eligibility for IBR and your IBR payment amount, you may request a forbearance. During a forbearance you are not required to make any payments of principal or interest, but interest continues to accumulate on your loan. If you are beginning repayment of your Direct Loan for the first time, interest that you do not pay during the forbearance will be capitalized (added to your outstanding principal balance) at the end of the forbearance. Capitalization increases your loan's principal amount, and therefore the total amount of interest you will repay on your loan. If you are requesting a change from another Direct Loan repayment plan to the IBR Plan, you may receive a forbearance for up to 60 days during which unpaid interest will not be capitalized. During the forbearance, you will have to provide us with your income information that we need to calculate your payment amount under IBR. To request a forbearance, contact the Direct Loan Servicing Center at 1-800-848-0979, Monday through Friday 8:00 am to 8:30 pm (Eastern Time). Individuals who use a telecommunications device for the deaf (TDD) may call 1-800-848-0983.

A. Family Size. Enter your family size on the line below. Your family size is determined by counting you, your spouse, and your children, including children who will be born during the year you certify your family size, if your children receive more than half their support from you. Your family size also includes other individuals if, at the time you certify your family size, these other individuals (1) live with you and (2) receive more than half of their support from you and will continue to receive this support for the year you certify your family size. Support includes money, gifts, loans, housing, food, clothes, car, medical and dental care, and payment of college costs. **If you select IBR, you must notify us of your family size every year. The Department will contact you annually by mail to confirm and update family size information.**

Family Size: _____

If you have any questions regarding the IBR Plan, partial financial hardship, or your family size determination, please contact the Loan Consolidation Department (see Section 6 below).

B. Eligible Loans. Direct Subsidized Loans, Direct Unsubsidized Loans, Direct Consolidation Loans that did not repay parent PLUS loans, student Direct PLUS Loans, Federal Family Education Loan (FFEL) Stafford Loans, student FFEL PLUS Loans, and FFEL Consolidation Loans that did not repay parent PLUS loans are eligible for repayment under the IBR Plan. Direct PLUS Consolidation Loans, parent Direct PLUS Loans, parent FFEL PLUS Loans, Direct Consolidation Loans or FFEL Consolidation Loans that repaid parent PLUS loans, and loans on which you are in default are not eligible for IBR. Your IBR payment amount will be based on your total eligible loan debt.

C. IBR Joint Consolidation Loan Repayment. If you and your spouse have an eligible joint consolidation loan that you want to repay under the IBR Plan, place an "X" in the box below and have your spouse sign and date below in Section D. Both you and your spouse must have a partial financial hardship to repay an eligible joint consolidation loan under IBR (see description of partial financial hardship above).

☐ I wish to repay my joint consolidation loan(s) with my spouse under the IBR Plan.

D. Certification. Read the certification statement below, then sign and date this form. If you want to repay a joint consolidation loan under the IBR Plan (see "C", above), your spouse must also sign and date this form.

All of the information I provided on this form is true and complete to the best of my knowledge. If asked by an authorized official, I agree to provide proof of the information that I have provided on this form.

Borrower's Signature _____ **Date** _____

Spouse's Signature (if required) _____ **Date** _____

Section 6: Where to Send the Completed Form

Return this form to:

U.S. Department of Education
Loan Consolidation Department
P.O. Box 242800
Louisville, KY 40224-2800

If you need help completing this form, or if you need to report a change in your address:

- Call us at **1-800-557-7392** or, if you use a telecommunications device for the deaf (TDD), at **1-800-557-7395**.
- E-mail us by going to **www.loanconsolidation.ed.gov** and clicking on **Contact Us**.
- Write to us at the mailing address provided above.

Section 7: Important Notices

PRIVACY ACT NOTICE

The Privacy Act of 1974 (5 U.S.C. 552a) requires that the following notice be provided to you:

The authority for collecting the requested information from and about you is §451 *et seq*. of the Higher Education Act (HEA) of 1965, as amended (20 U.S.C. 1087a *et seq*.) and the authorities for collecting and using your Social Security Number (SSN) are §484(a)(4) of the HEA (20 U.S.C. 1091(a)(4)) and 31 U.S.C. 7701(b). Participating in the William D. Ford Federal Direct Loan (Direct Loan) Program and giving us your SSN are voluntary, but you must provide the requested information, including your SSN, to participate.

The principal purposes for collecting the information on this form, including your SSN, are to verify your identity, to determine your eligibility to receive a loan or a benefit on a loan (such as a deferment, forbearance, discharge, or forgiveness) under the Direct Loan Program, to permit the servicing of your loan(s), and, if it becomes necessary, to locate you and to collect and report on your loan(s) if your loan(s) become delinquent or in default. We also use your SSN as an account identifier and to permit you to access your account information electronically.

The information in your file may be disclosed, on a case-by-case basis or under a computer-matching program, to third parties as authorized under routine uses in the appropriate systems of records notices. The routine uses of this information include, but are not limited to, its disclosure to federal, state, or local agencies, to private parties such as relatives, present and former employers, business and personal associates, to consumer reporting agencies, to financial and educational institutions, and to guaranty agencies in order to verify your identity, to determine your eligibility to receive a loan or a benefit on a loan, to permit the servicing or collection of your loan(s), to enforce the terms of the loan(s), to investigate possible fraud and to verify compliance with federal student financial aid program regulations, or to locate you if you become delinquent in your loan payments or if you default. To provide default rate calculations, disclosures may be made to guaranty agencies, to financial and educational institutions, or to state agencies. To provide financial aid history information, disclosures may be made to educational institutions. To assist program administrators with tracking refunds and cancellations, disclosures may be made to guaranty agencies, to financial and educational institutions, or to federal or state agencies. To provide a standardized method for educational institutions to efficiently submit student enrollment status, disclosures may be made to guaranty agencies or to financial and educational institutions. To counsel you in repayment efforts, disclosures may be made to guaranty agencies, to financial and educational institutions, or to federal, state, or local agencies.

In the event of litigation, we may send records to the Department of Justice, a court, adjudicative body, counsel, party, or witness if the disclosure is relevant and necessary to the litigation. If this information, either alone or with other information, indicates a potential violation of law, we may send it to the appropriate authority for action. We may send information to members of Congress if you ask them to help you with federal student aid questions. In circumstances involving employment complaints, grievances, or disciplinary actions, we may disclose relevant records to adjudicate or investigate the issues. If provided for by a collective bargaining agreement, we may disclose records to a labor organization recognized under 5 U.S.C. Chapter 71. Disclosures may be made to our contractors for the purpose of performing any programmatic function that requires disclosure of records. Before making any such disclosure, we will require the contractor to maintain Privacy Act safeguards. Disclosures may also be made to qualified researchers under Privacy Act safeguards.

PAPERWORK REDUCTION NOTICE

According to the Paperwork Reduction Act of 1995, no persons are required to respond to a collection of information unless it displays a currently valid OMB control number. The valid OMB control number for this information collection is 1845-0014. The time required to complete this information collection is estimated to average .33 hours (20 minutes) per response, including the time to review instructions, search existing data resources, gather and maintain the data needed, and complete and review the information collection. **If you have comments concerning the accuracy of the time estimate(s) or suggestions for improving this form, please write to:** U.S. Department of Education, Washington, DC 20202-4537. ***Do not send the completed form to this address.***

If you have questions about the status of your individual submission of this form, contact the Loan Consolidation Department (see Section 6).

Repayment Plan Selection   Reverse

Student Assistance Forms   Appx. D.1.3

Repayment Plan Choices
William D. Ford Federal Direct Loan Program
Federal Direct Stafford/Ford Loans, Federal Direct Unsubsidized Stafford/Ford Loans, Federal Direct PLUS Loans, Federal Direct Consolidation Loans

DECIDE ON A REPAYMENT PLAN

The William D. Ford Federal Direct Loan (Direct Loan) Program offers assorted repayment plans so you can choose the one that is right for you: Standard Repayment Plan, Graduated Repayment Plan, Extended Repayment Plan, Income Contingent Repayment (ICR) Plan, and Income-Based Repayment (IBR) Plan. For each plan: (1) You can prepay your loan at any time without penalty; (2) If your loan has a variable interest rate, your monthly payment amount may be adjusted annually; and (3) The "Repayment Period" excludes periods of deferment and forbearance, except periods of economic hardship deferment after October 1, 2007, for the ICR and IBR Plans. You can select the plan you want at http://www.dl.ed.gov or by completing and submitting a Repayment Plan Selection form.

You must choose the same repayment plan for all of your Direct Loans, unless you want to repay under the ICR Plan or the IBR Plan and you have loans that may be repaid under ICR or IBR and other loans that may not be repaid under ICR or IBR. (See the descriptions of the ICR and IBR plans below for the types of Direct Loans that may not be repaid under these repayment plans.) In that case, you may choose a different repayment plan for the loans that are not eligible for ICR or IBR.

If you do not select a repayment plan, you will be assigned the Standard Repayment Plan. If you have questions about your choices, please call the Consolidation Department at 1-800-557-7392 for assistance.

CHANGING REPAYMENT PLANS

There is no limit to when or how often you may change plans. You may change to another plan as long as the new plan has a repayment term longer than the amount of time you have already spent in repayment. The new repayment term is determined by subtracting the amount of time you have spent in repayment from the term allowed under the new plan. Exceptions are: (1) If you are required to repay under the ICR plan, you must make three consecutive on-time monthly payments of a payment amount based on your income before changing to another plan; and (2) If you choose to leave the IBR Plan, your account will be placed on the Standard Repayment Plan; and (3) You may change to the ICR Plan or the IBR Plan at any time.

STANDARD REPAYMENT PLAN

Non-Consolidation Loans
(Direct Subsidized Loans, Direct Unsubsidized Loans, & Direct PLUS Loans)
Minimum Monthly Payment $50
Maximum Repayment Period   10 years

Under this plan, you will pay a fixed amount of at least $50 each month for up to 10 years. Due to its short repayment period, this plan results in the lowest total interest paid under any of the repayment plans.

Consolidation Loans
Minimum Monthly Payment $50
Maximum Repayment Period   10 - 30 years

Under this plan, you will pay a fixed amount of at least $50 each month over a repayment period of 10 to 30 years, depending on total education indebtedness. This plan may result in lower total interest paid when compared to other plans.

GRADUATED REPAYMENT PLAN

Non-Consolidation Loans
(Direct Subsidized Loans, Direct Unsubsidized Loans, & Direct PLUS Loans)
Minimum Monthly Payment   Monthly interest accrual
Maximum Repayment Period   10 years

Under this plan, you will pay a minimum payment amount equal to the amount of interest that accrues monthly for up to 10 years. Your payments start out low, and then increase every two years. No single payment under this plan will be more than three times greater than any other payment. Generally, the amount you will repay over the term of your loan will be higher under the Graduated Repayment Plan than under the Standard Repayment Plan. This plan may be beneficial if your income is low now but is likely to steadily increase.

Consolidation Loans
Minimum Monthly Payment   Monthly interest accrual
Maximum Repayment Period   10 - 30 years

Under this plan, you will pay a minimum payment amount equal to the amount of interest that accrues monthly over a repayment period of 10 to 30 years, depending on your total education indebtedness. Your payments start out low, and then increase every two years. No single payment under this plan will be more than three times greater than any other payment. Generally, the amount you will repay over the term of your loan will be higher under the Graduated Repayment Plan than under the Standard Repayment Plan. This plan may be beneficial if your income is low now but is likely to steadily increase.

Total Education Indebtedness Amounts / Number of Monthly Payments under Standard and Graduated Repayment Plans for Consolidation Loans

If your Total Education Indebtedness is		Maximum Number of Monthly Payments
At Least	Less Than	
	$7,500	120 (10 years)
$7,500	$10,000	144 (12 years)
$10,000	$20,000	180 (15 years)
$20,000	$40,000	240 (20 years)
$40,000	$60,000	300 (25 years)
$60,000		360 (30 years)

EXTENDED REPAYMENT PLAN

You may choose this plan only if (1) you had no outstanding balance on a Direct Loan on October 7, 1998 or on the date you obtained a Direct Loan after that date, and (2) you owe more than $30,000 in outstanding Direct Loans.

Fixed Monthly Payment Option (All loan types)
Minimum Monthly Payment $50
Maximum Repayment Period   25 years

Under this plan, you will pay a fixed amount of at least $50 each month over a repayment period not to exceed 25 years.

Graduated Monthly Payment Option (All loan types)
Minimum Monthly Payment   Monthly interest accrual
Maximum Repayment Period   25 years

Under this plan, you will pay a minimum amount of at least the amount of interest that accrues monthly over a repayment period not to exceed 25 years. Your payments start out low and then increase every two years. This plan may be beneficial if your income is low now but is likely to steadily increase.

Under either fixed or graduated monthly payment option, the Extended Repayment Plan will give you a lower monthly payment on your non-consolidation loans than Standard or Graduated Repayment Plans. Because of the longer repayment period, you will pay more interest over the life of your loan.

If you have a consolidation loan and owe more than $30,000 but less than $40,000, the Extended Repayment Plan will provide you with a longer repayment period than the Standard or Graduated Repayment Plans, but the total amount of interest you pay over the life of the loan may be more than under those plans.

RPC 2009

INCOME CONTINGENT REPAYMENT (ICR) PLAN

Not available for Direct PLUS Loans made to parent borrowers or Direct PLUS Consolidation Loans.

Minimum Monthly Payment $0 or $5.00
Maximum Repayment Period   25 years

Under this plan, the payment amount is based upon your income. The monthly payment amount will be the lesser of the following two calculations:

1. the amount you would pay if you repaid your loan in 12 years, multiplied by an income percentage factor (ranging from approximately 55 percent to 200 percent) that varies with your annual income, or

2. 20 percent of your monthly discretionary income. Discretionary income is your federal Adjusted Gross Income (AGI) minus the poverty level for your family size.

If you are married, both your AGI and your spouse's AGI will be used to calculate your monthly repayment amount, even if you file your income taxes separately from your spouse.

If you and your spouse each have Direct Loans and want to repay your loans under the ICR Plan, you may choose to repay your loans jointly. The outstanding balances on each of your loans will be added together to determine your repayment amount.

If your calculated monthly payment is between $0 and $5.00, you will be required to make a $5.00 monthly payment. If your income is less than or equal to the poverty level for your family size, your payment will be $0. In the event that your payment amount is less than the amount of interest accruing on your loan, the interest will be added to your loan principal (capitalized) once a year until the principal balance is 10 percent higher than the original balance. After this occurs, interest will continue to accrue but will not be added to the principal balance.

Under this plan, it is possible you will not make payments large enough to pay off your loans in 25 years. If loans are not fully repaid after 25 years of repayment, any unpaid amount will be forgiven. The maximum 25-year repayment period may include prior periods of repayment under certain other repayment plans, and periods of economic hardship deferment after October 1, 2007. The forgiven amount may be considered taxable income.

Your repayment amount is adjusted annually. It may be higher when your income is higher and lower when your income is lower.

If you select the Income Contingent Repayment Plan, we will:

1. require you to submit documentation of current income (yours and your spouse's) in the first year of repayment. You may be required to submit documentation of current income (yours and your spouse's) in your second year of repayment as well.

2. require you to complete a form that authorizes the Internal Revenue Service (IRS) to provide income information (yours and your spouse's) to the U.S. Department of Education. You must sign this form and return it to us. The AGI from the IRS will be used to calculate your monthly repayment amount in years subsequent to the year(s) in which alternative documentation is required.

In special circumstances when your federal tax return does not reflect your present income (for example, due to loss of employment), you may submit documentation of your current income. Your monthly payment will be based on this documented income information.

> NOTE: If you are repaying your loan(s) under the ICR or IBR Plan, your repayment period will be a maximum of 25 years. If loans are not fully repaid after 25 years of repayment, any unpaid amount will be forgiven. The maximum 25-year repayment period may include prior periods of repayment under certain other repayment plans, and certain periods of economic hardship deferment. The forgiven amount may be considered taxable income.

INCOME-BASED REPAYMENT (IBR) PLAN

Not available for Direct PLUS Loans made to parent borrowers (parent Direct PLUS Loans), Direct PLUS Consolidation Loans, or Direct Consolidation Loans that repaid parent Direct PLUS Loans or Federal Family Education Loan Program PLUS loans made to parent borrowers.

Minimum Monthly Payment $0 or $10.00
Maximum Repayment Period   25 years

The Income-Based Repayment (IBR) Plan bases your monthly payment on your annual income and family size. You must be experiencing a Partial Financial Hardship to initially select this plan. A Partial Financial Hardship is a circumstance in which the annual amount due on all your eligible loans (see the accompanying Repayment Plan Selection form for a definition of "eligible loans") at the time you entered repayment, as calculated under a 10-year Standard Repayment Plan, exceeds 15 percent of the difference between your Adjusted Gross Income (AGI) and 150 percent of the poverty line income for your family size.

Under this plan, your required monthly payment will be no more than 15 percent of the amount by which your AGI exceeds 150 percent of the poverty line income for your family size and state, divided by 12. In addition:

1. If the calculated payment is less than $5.00 your required monthly payment will be $0.00.

2. If the calculated payment is equal to or greater than $5.00, but less than $10.00, your required monthly payment will be $10.00.

3. If all of your loans are not Direct Loans, your monthly payment amount will be determined by multiplying the calculated monthly payment by the percentage of the total amount of your eligible loans that are Direct Loans.

If you are married and file your federal income taxes jointly with your spouse, both your AGI and your spouse's AGI will be used to calculate your monthly payment. If you and your spouse file taxes separately, only your AGI will be used to calculate your monthly payment. Under this plan, it is possible you will not make payments large enough to pay off your loans in 25 years. If loans are not fully repaid after 25 years of repayment, any unpaid amount will be forgiven. The maximum 25-year repayment period may include prior periods of repayment under certain other repayment plans, and certain periods of economic hardship deferment after October 1, 2007. The forgiven amount may be considered taxable income.

Your repayment amount may be adjusted annually. It may be higher or lower depending on changes in your income. If you select the Income-Based Repayment Plan, we will:

1. require you to submit documentation of current income (yours and your spouse's if you are married and file taxes jointly) in order to apply for the IBR plan.

2. require you to complete a form that authorizes the Internal Revenue Service (IRS) to provide income information (yours and your spouse's if you are married and files taxes jointly) to the U.S. Department of Education. You must sign this form and return it to us. The AGI from the IRS will be used to calculate your monthly repayment amount in years subsequent to the year(s) in which alternative documentation is required.

In special circumstances when your federal tax return does not reflect your present income (for example, due to loss of employment), you may submit documentation of your current income. Your monthly payment will be based on this documented income information.

If your payment does not cover all of the interest accumulating monthly on your Direct Subsidized Loans or Direct Subsidized Consolidation Loans, you will not be charged the remaining portion of the interest on those loans for a period not to exceed three consecutive years from the time you begin repayment under the IBR Plan.

If you no longer have partial financial hardship, your monthly payment amount will be adjusted. Your adjusted payment amount will not exceed the amount required to pay your loan in full under a 10-year Standard Repayment Plan based on the amount of your eligible loans that was outstanding at the time you began repayment under the IBR Plan (minimum of $50.00). The repayment period based on this recalculated payment amount may be more than 10 years.

If you choose to leave the IBR Plan, your account will be placed on the Standard Repayment Plan. Your required monthly payment will be recalculated based on (1) the time remaining under the maximum 10-year repayment period for the amount of your loans that are outstanding at the time you leave the IBR Plan, or (2) if you are a Direct Consolidation Loan borrower, the time remaining under the applicable maximum repayment period for the amount of your Direct Consolidation Loan and your other student loans that are outstanding at the time you leave the IBR Plan.

Go to Page 3 for sample payment amounts per plan. ⇨

U.S. Department of Education Direct Loan Program

REPAYMENT PLAN CHOICES

Example Payment Amounts by Repayment Plan

Non-Consolidation Borrowers *

Debt When Loan Enters Repayment	Standard		Extended Fixed		Extended Graduated		Graduated		Income Contingent ** Income = $25,000				Income-Based ** Income = $25,000			
									Single		Married/HoH***		Single		Married/HoH***	
	Per Month	Total	Per Month	Total	Per Month	Total	Per Month	Total	Per Month	Total	Per Month	Total	Per Month	Total	Per Month	Total
$5,000	$58	$6,904	N/A	N/A	N/A	N/A	$40	$7,275	$37	$8,347	$36	$11,088	N/A	N/A	$39	$8,005
10,000	115	13,809	N/A	N/A	N/A	N/A	79	14,550	75	16,699	71	22,158	110	13,672	39	16,081
25,000	288	34,524	N/A	N/A	N/A	N/A	198	36,375	186	41,748	178	55,440	110	45,014	39	60,754
50,000	575	69,048	347	104,109	284	112,678	396	72,749	247	93,322	189	122,083	110	109,623	39	92,704
100,000	1,151	138,096	694	208,217	568	225,344	792	145,498	247	187,553	189	170,153	110	118,058	39	97,020

Notes: * Payments are calculated using a fixed interest rate of 6.8% for Direct Subsidized and Unsubsidized Loans disbursed on or after July 1, 2006.
** Assumes a 5 percent annual income growth (Census Bureau).
*** HOH is Head of Household. Assumes a family size of two.

Consolidation Borrowers *

Debt When Loan Enters Repayment	Standard		Extended Fixed		Extended Graduated		Graduated		Income Contingent ** Income = $25,000				Income-Based ** Income = $25,000			
									Single		Married/HoH***		Single		Married/HoH***	
	Per Month	Total	Per Month	Total	Per Month	Total	Per Month	Total	Per Month	Total	Per Month	Total	Per Month	Total	Per Month	Total
$5,000	$61	$7,359	N/A	N/A	N/A	N/A	$38	$7,978	$40	$9,414	$38	$12,294	N/A	N/A	$39	$7,818
10,000	97	17,461	N/A	N/A	N/A	N/A	69	19,165	80	18,828	77	24,587	110	17,638	39	22,414
25,000	213	51,123	N/A	N/A	N/A	N/A	172	55,491	201	47,069	189	61,588	110	59,451	39	52,725
50,000	394	118,264	394	118,264	344	126,834	344	126,834	247	106,630	189	137,766	110	91,388	39	78,816
100,000	751	270,452	788	236,528	688	253,660	688	286,305	247	187,553	189	170,153	110	117,343	39	97,020

Notes: * Payments are calculated using the maximum interest rate for consolidation loans, 8.25%.
** Assumes a 5 percent annual income growth (Census Bureau).
*** HOH is Head of Household. Assumes a family size of two.

RPC 2009

D.1.4 ICR and IBR Consent to Disclosure of Tax Information

**William D. Ford Federal Direct Loan Program
Income Contingent Repayment Plan &
Income-Based Repayment Plan
Consent to Disclosure of Tax Information**

OMB No. 1845-0017
Form Approved
Exp. Date 06/30/2012

I (We) authorize the Internal Revenue Service (IRS) to disclose certain tax return information (for the tax years listed below) which includes my (our) name(s), address(es), Social Security Number(s), filing status, tax year, and Adjusted Gross Income(s). This information will be disclosed to the U.S. Department of Education (ED) and the William D. Ford Federal Direct Loan (Direct Loan) Program contractors and subcontractors for the sole purpose of determining the appropriate income contingent repayment (ICR) amount, or determining eligibility for income-based repayment (IBR) and the appropriate IBR amount on the Direct Loan Program loan(s) that may be repaid under the ICR or IBR Plan. ED's Direct Loan Program contractors and subcontractors may change. You may obtain the names of the current Direct Loan Program contractors and subcontractors by writing to ED at the address shown at the bottom of this page.

Request for Tax Years: 2008, 2009, 2010, 2011, and 2012.

Read the instructions on the back of this form before completing the items below.

Items 1-3: If you are repaying or want to repay your loan(s) under the Income Contingent Repayment Plan **or** the Income-Based Repayment Plan, you **must** complete Items 1-3 below:

(1) Borrower's (Taxpayer's) Name Printed *as it appears on your tax returns*

(2) Borrower's (Taxpayer's) Social Security Number

(3) Borrower's (Taxpayer's) Signature
Signature is valid for 60 days – see instructions on the back of the form.

_____-_____-_____(MM-DD-YYYY)
Date of borrower's signature

Items 4-6: Your spouse must complete Items 4-6 if:
- You are repaying under the Income Contingent Repayment Plan and you are married, OR
- You are repaying under the Income-Based Repayment Plan and you and your spouse file a joint federal income tax return.

(4) Spouse's (Taxpayer's) Name Printed *as it appears on your tax returns*

(5) Spouse's (Taxpayer's) Social Security Number

(6) Spouse's (Taxpayer's) Signature
Signature is valid for 60 days – see instructions on the back of the form.

_____-_____-_____(MM-DD-YYYY)
Date of spouse's signature

Return this form to: U.S. Department of Education
Consolidation Department
P.O. Box 242800
Louisville, KY 40224-2800

Student Assistance Forms Appx. D.1.4

William D. Ford Federal Direct Loan Program
Income Contingent Repayment Plan & Income-Based Repayment Plan – Consent to Disclosure of Tax Information

Borrower Instructions: Please complete this form using the following instructions. To be considered for the Income Contingent Repayment Plan or the Income-Based Repayment Plan, you must complete Items 1-3 for the Consent to Disclosure of Tax Information on the front of this form:

- **Item 1.** Print (or type) your name as it appears on your tax returns.
- **Item 2.** Print (or type) your Social Security Number.
- **Item 3.** Sign and date the form in blue or black ink only. Report the date as month-day-year (MM-DD-YYYY).

Items 4-6 must be completed only if:
- **You are repaying under the Income Contingent Repayment Plan and you are married (even if you file separate federal income tax returns), OR**
- **You are repaying under the Income-Based Repayment Plan and you and your spouse file a joint federal income tax return.**

(Do not complete Items 4-6 if you are repaying under the Income-Based Repayment Plan and you and your spouse file separate federal income tax returns.)

- **Item 4.** Print (or type) your spouse's name as it appears on tax returns.
- **Item 5.** Print (or type) your spouse's Social Security Number.
- **Item 6.** Have your spouse sign and date the form in blue or black ink only. Report the date as month-day-year (MM-DD-YYYY).

Make a copy of the completed form for your records. Send the original form to the U.S. Department of Education (ED) at the address shown on the front. **DO NOT SEND THIS FORM TO THE INTERNAL REVENUE SERVICE (IRS).** Once your application to participate in the Income Contingent Repayment Plan or the Income-Based Repayment Plan has been approved, ED will forward this form to the IRS. *Because the IRS will not accept this form if more than 60 days have passed since you and/or your spouse signed the form, you must return the completed form to ED promptly.*

Request to Revoke Tax Information Authorization: You and/or your spouse may revoke the Consent to Disclosure of Tax Information at any time. To revoke consent, send a copy of this completed form with the word **"REVOKE"** across the top directly to the revocation address given below. The revocation must be signed by the taxpayer(s) who signed the original Consent to Disclosure of Tax Information. If you and/or your spouse do not have a copy of the original form, a statement of revocation is acceptable. The statement must indicate that the authority to disclose tax information to the Direct Loan Program is revoked, and must be signed by the taxpayer(s) who signed the original authorization form.

NOTE: If you and/or your spouse revoke(s) the Consent to Disclosure of Tax Information, you and/or your spouse become(s) ineligible for income contingent or income-based repayment, and you and/or your spouse must contact the Direct Loan Servicing Center to select another repayment option. If you and/or your spouse fail(s) to contact the Direct Loan Servicing Center, ED will assign you and/or your spouse to the Standard Repayment Plan.

Revocation Address: Direct Loan Servicing Center
P.O. Box 5609
Greenville, TX 75403-5609

PRIVACY ACT NOTICE

The Privacy Act of 1974 (5 U.S.C. 552a) requires that the following notice be provided to you:

The authority for collecting the requested information from and about you is §451 *et seq.* of the Higher Education Act (HEA) of 1965, as amended (20 U.S.C. 1087a *et seq.*) and the authorities for collecting and using your Social Security Number (SSN) are §484(a)(4) of the HEA (20 U.S.C. 1091(a)(4)) and 31 U.S.C. 7701(b). Participating in the William D. Ford Federal Direct Loan (Direct Loan) Program and giving us your SSN are voluntary, but you must provide the requested information, including your SSN, to participate.

The principal purposes for collecting the information on this form, including your SSN, are to verify your identity, to determine your eligibility to receive a loan or a benefit on a loan (such as a deferment, forbearance, discharge, or forgiveness) under the Direct Loan Program, to permit the servicing of your loan(s), and, if it becomes necessary, to locate you and to collect and report on your loan(s) if your loan(s) become delinquent or in default. We also use your SSN as an account identifier and to permit you to access your account information electronically.

The information in your file may be disclosed, on a case-by-case basis or under a computer-matching program, to third parties as authorized under routine uses in the appropriate systems of records notices. The routine uses of this information include, but are not limited to, its disclosure to federal, state, or local agencies, to private parties such as relatives, present and former employers, business and personal associates, to consumer reporting agencies, to financial and educational institutions, and to guaranty agencies in order to verify your identity, to determine your eligibility to receive a loan or a benefit on a loan, to permit the servicing or collection of your loan(s), to enforce the terms of the loan(s), to investigate possible fraud and to verify compliance with federal student financial aid program regulations, or to locate you if you become delinquent in your loan payments or if you default. To provide default rate calculations, disclosures may be made to guaranty agencies, to financial and educational institutions, or to state agencies. To provide financial aid history information, disclosures may be made to educational institutions. To assist program administrators with tracking refunds and cancellations, disclosures may be made to guaranty agencies, to financial and educational institutions, or to federal or state agencies. To provide a standardized method for educational institutions to efficiently submit student enrollment status, disclosures may be made to guaranty agencies or to financial and educational institutions. To counsel you in repayment efforts, disclosures may be made to guaranty agencies, to financial and educational institutions, or to federal, state, or local agencies.

In the event of litigation, we may send records to the Department of Justice, a court, adjudicative body, counsel, party, or witness if the disclosure is relevant and necessary to the litigation. If this information, either alone or with other information, indicates a potential violation of law, we may send it to the appropriate authority for action. We may send information to members of Congress if you ask them to help you with federal student aid questions. In circumstances involving employment complaints, grievances, or disciplinary actions, we may disclose relevant records to adjudicate or investigate the issues. If provided for by a collective bargaining agreement, we may disclose records to a labor organization recognized under 5 U.S.C. Chapter 71. Disclosures may be made to our contractors for the purpose of performing any programmatic function that requires disclosure of records. Before making any such disclosure, we will require the contractor to maintain Privacy Act safeguards. Disclosures may also be made to qualified researchers under Privacy Act safeguards.

Paperwork Reduction Notice: According to the Paperwork Reduction Act of 1995, no persons are required to respond to a collection of information unless it displays a currently valid OMB control number. The valid OMB control number for this information collection is 1845-0017. The time required to complete this information collection is estimated to average 0.2 hours (12 minutes) per response, including the time to review instructions, search existing data resources, gather and maintain the data needed, and complete and review the information collection. **If you have comments concerning the accuracy of the time estimate(s) or suggestions for improving this form, please write to:** U.S. Department of Education, Washington, DC 20202-4537. *Do not send the completed form to this address.*

If you have questions about the status of your individual submission of this form, contact the Consolidation Department at the following address:

U.S. Department of Education
Consolidation Department
P.O Box 242800
Louisville, KY 40224-2800

Appx. D.1.5   Student Loan Law

D.1.5 ICR and IBR Alternative Documentation of Income

ADI

Direct Loans
William D. Ford Federal Direct Loan Program

Income Contingent Repayment Plan & Income-Based Repayment Plan
Alternative Documentation of Income
William D. Ford Federal Direct Loan Program
Federal Direct Stafford/Ford Loans, Federal Direct Unsubsidized Stafford/Ford Loans,
Federal Direct Subsidized Consolidation Loans, Federal Direct Unsubsidized Consolidation Loans
WARNING: Any person who knowingly makes a false statement or misrepresentation on this form shall be subject to penalties which may include fines, imprisonment, or both, under the U.S. Criminal Code and 20 U.S.C. 1097.

OMB No. 1845-0016
Form Approved
Exp. Date 06/30/2012

Section 1: Identifying Information

Before completing this form, carefully read the instructions in Section 5.

All borrowers must provide the Borrower Information below.

If you are married, you must also provide the Spouse Information below if (1) you are repaying under the ICR Plan, or (2) you are repaying under the IBR Plan and you and your spouse file a joint federal tax return.

Borrower Information:
Borrower's Name (please print clearly):

_____
Last Name   First Name   Middle Initial

Borrower's Social Security Number:

|___|___|___|-|___|___|-|___|___|___|___|

Spouse Information:
Your Spouse's Name (please print clearly):

_____
Last Name   First Name   Middle Initial

Your Spouse's Social Security Number:

|___|___|___|-|___|___|-|___|___|___|___|

Section 2: Borrower's Income Information – to be completed by ALL BORROWERS

All borrowers must complete this section.

You must list all taxable income you are currently receiving (i.e., income from employment, unemployment income, dividend income, interest income, tips, alimony). Include the amount of money received, how often you receive this money, and your employer (if any) or the source of your income if you are not employed. You must attach supporting documentation for **all income** reported in this section (e.g., pay stubs, letters from your employer stating your income, interest or bank statements, dividend statements, canceled checks, or, when these forms of documentation are unavailable, a signed statement explaining your income source(s) and giving the addresses of these sources). Copies are acceptable, but **all supporting documentation must be no more than 90 days old**. If you have more than two sources of income, provide the information requested in this section on a separate piece of paper and mail it with this form. Do not report untaxed income such as Supplemental Security Income, child support, or federal or state public assistance. If your income or the income of your spouse changes significantly after your submission of this form, you must notify the Direct Loan Servicing Center of this change (see contact information in Section 5).

Amount of Income	Frequency of Payment (Please check the appropriate box.)					Employer or Source of Income
	Weekly	Bi-weekly	Semi-monthly	Monthly	Yearly	
$	☐	☐	☐	☐	☐	
$	☐	☐	☐	☐	☐	

☐ Check this box if you do not have any taxable income and receive only untaxed income such as Supplemental Security Income, child support, or federal or state public assistance.

Section 3: Spouse's Income Information – to be completed by SOME MARRIED BORROWERS

If you are married, you must provide your spouse's income information if:
1. You are repaying under the ICR Plan, *or*
2. You are repaying under the IBR Plan and you and your spouse file a joint federal tax return.

If you are required to complete this section, you must provide the same information and supporting documentation for your spouse's income that is required for your own income, as explained above in Section 2.

Amount of Income	Frequency of Payment (Please check the appropriate box.)					Employer or Source of Income
	Weekly	Bi-weekly	Semi-monthly	Monthly	Yearly	
$	☐	☐	☐	☐	☐	
$	☐	☐	☐	☐	☐	

☐ Check this box if your spouse does not have any taxable income and receives only untaxed income such as Supplemental Security Income, child support, or federal or state public assistance.

Section 4: Certification and Signature

All borrowers must complete this section. If you are married, your spouse must sign and date below *only* if (1) you are repaying under the ICR Plan, *or* (2) you are repaying under the IBR Plan and you and your spouse file a joint federal tax return.

Certification: I certify that all of the information reported in Section 2 and, if applicable, Section 3 is true and complete to the best of my knowledge. I agree to provide to the U.S. Department of Education (the Department) on an annual basis (or as required by the Department) alternative documentation of my income for the purpose of determining my appropriate repayment amount under the ICR Plan or IBR Plan. I understand that (1) if I do not provide this information the Department will base my ICR or IBR amount on my AGI, as reported by the IRS, or, in some instances, I will not be allowed to repay my loan(s) under the ICR or IBR Plan; (2) the Department may request my income information from the IRS even if alternative documentation of my income is accepted; and (3) if I am married, my spouse's income information, documentation, and signature are also required if I am repaying under the ICR Plan, or if I am repaying under the IBR Plan and my spouse and I file a joint federal tax return.

_____   _____
Borrower's Signature   **Date of Borrower's Signature**

_____   _____
Spouse's Signature   **Date of Spouse's Signature**

Section 5: Instructions and Where to Send the Completed Form

INSTRUCTIONS:

YOU ARE REQUIRED to complete this form if you are repaying your Direct Loans under the Income Contingent Repayment (ICR) or the Income-Based Repayment (IBR) Plan and:

- You are in your first year of repayment;
- You are in your second year of repayment and have been notified that alternative documentation of your income is required; or
- You have been notified that the Internal Revenue Service (IRS) is unable to provide the U.S. Department of Education (the Department) with your Adjusted Gross Income (AGI) or that of your spouse (if applicable).

YOU MAY complete this form if:

- You are repaying your Direct Loans under the ICR Plan and your AGI (and your spouse's AGI, if you are married), as reported on your most recently filed federal tax return, does not reasonably reflect your current income (e.g., due to circumstances such as loss or change in employment by you or your spouse).
- You are repaying your Direct Loans under the IBR Plan and your AGI (and your spouse's AGI, if you and your spouse file a joint federal tax return), as reported on your most recently filed federal tax return, does not reasonably reflect your current income (e.g., due to circumstances such as loss or change in employment by you or your spouse).

In cases where alternative documentation of your income is used, the amount of your monthly payment under the ICR or IBR Plan is based on the current income information you and your spouse (if applicable) provide and is reevaluated annually. Your monthly payment may be adjusted more frequently than annually if you notify the Direct Loan Servicing Center that your AGI (or your spouse's AGI, if you file a joint federal tax return) has changed significantly since your most recent submission of this form and you provide supporting documentation showing this change. To submit alternative documentation of your income, you must attach the required documentation, complete and sign this form, and return it to the address below. If you are married, your spouse must also complete and sign the applicable sections of this form and submit the required documentation if (1) you are repaying your loans under the ICR Plan, or (2) you are repaying your loans under the IBR Plan and you and your spouse file a joint federal tax return. If you need assistance, please call 1-800-557-7392, or TDD 1-800-557-7395.

Return this form to:

U.S. Department of Education
Consolidation Department
P.O. Box 242800
Louisville, KY 40224-2800

If you need assistance in completing this form, call 1-800-557-7392. Individuals who use a telecommunications device for the deaf (TDD) may call 1-800-557-7395.

Section 6: Important Notices

PRIVACY ACT NOTICE

The Privacy Act of 1974 (5 U.S.C. 552a) requires that the following notice be provided to you:

The authority for collecting the requested information from and about you is §451 et seq. of the Higher Education Act (HEA) of 1965, as amended (20 U.S.C. 1087a et seq.) and the authorities for collecting and using your Social Security Number (SSN) are §484(a)(4) of the HEA (20 U.S.C. 1091(a)(4)) and 31 U.S.C. 7701(b). Participating in the William D. Ford Federal Direct Loan (Direct Loan) Program and giving us your SSN are voluntary, but you must provide the requested information, including your SSN, to participate.

The principal purposes for collecting the information on this form, including your SSN, are to verify your identity, to determine your eligibility to receive a loan or a benefit on a loan (such as a deferment, forbearance, discharge, or forgiveness) under the Direct Loan Program, to permit the servicing of your loan(s), and, if it becomes necessary, to locate you and to collect and report on your loan(s) if your loan(s) become delinquent or in default. We also use your SSN as an account identifier and to permit you to access your account information electronically.

The information in your file may be disclosed, on a case-by-case basis or under a computer-matching program, to third parties as authorized under routine uses in the appropriate systems of records notices. The routine uses of this information include, but are not limited to, its disclosure to federal, state, or local agencies, to private parties such as relatives, present and former employers, business and personal associates, to consumer reporting agencies, to financial and educational institutions, and to guaranty agencies in order to verify your identity, to determine your eligibility to receive a loan or a benefit on a loan, to permit the servicing or collection of your loan(s), to enforce the terms of the loan(s), to investigate possible fraud and to verify compliance with federal student financial aid program regulations, or to locate you if you become delinquent in your loan payments or if you default. To provide default rate calculations, disclosures may be made to guaranty agencies, to financial and educational institutions, or to state agencies. To provide financial aid history information, disclosures may be made to educational institutions. To assist program administrators with tracking refunds and cancellations, disclosures may be made to guaranty agencies, to financial and educational institutions, or to federal or state agencies. To provide a standardized method for educational institutions to efficiently submit student enrollment status, disclosures may be made to guaranty agencies or to financial and educational institutions. To counsel you in repayment efforts, disclosures may be made to guaranty agencies, to financial and educational institutions, or to federal, state, or local agencies.

In the event of litigation, we may send records to the Department of Justice, a court, adjudicative body, counsel, party, or witness if the disclosure is relevant and necessary to the litigation. If this information, either alone or with other information, indicates a potential violation of law, we may send it to the appropriate authority for action. We may send information to members of Congress if you ask them to help you with federal student aid questions. In circumstances involving employment complaints, grievances, or disciplinary actions, we may disclose relevant records to adjudicate or investigate the issues. If provided for by a collective bargaining agreement, we may disclose records to a labor organization recognized under 5 U.S.C. Chapter 71. Disclosures may be made to our contractors for the purpose of performing any programmatic function that requires disclosure of records. Before making any such disclosure, we will require the contractor to maintain Privacy Act safeguards. Disclosures may also be made to qualified researchers under Privacy Act safeguards.

Paperwork Reduction Notice. According to the Paperwork Reduction Act of 1995, no persons are required to respond to a collection of information unless it displays a currently valid OMB control number. The valid OMB control number for this information collection is 1845-0016. The time required to complete this information collection is estimated to average 0.33 hours (20 minutes) per response, including the time to review instructions, search existing data resources, gather and maintain the data needed, and complete and review the information collection. **If you have comments concerning the accuracy of the time estimate(s) or suggestions for improving this form, please write to:** U.S. Department of Education, Washington, DC 20202-4537. *Do not send the completed form to this address.*

If you have questions about the status of your individual submission of this form, contact the Consolidation Department at the following address:

U.S. Department of Education
Consolidation Department
P.O. Box 242800
Louisville, KY 40224-2800

D.2 Deferment and Forbearance Forms

D.2.1 Economic Hardship Deferment

D.2.1.1 FFEL Economic Hardship Deferment Form

At the time this manual was written, the Direct Loan economic hardship deferment form had not yet been updated. This FFEL form reflects the current law for economic hardship. Borrowers applying for Direct Loan deferment should use the Direct Loan form included at D.2.1.2.

Student Assistance Forms Appx. D.2.1.1

ECONOMIC HARDSHIP DEFERMENT REQUEST
Federal Family Education Loan Program

OMB No. 1845-0005
Form Approved
Exp. Date 05/31/2012

Use this form only if all of your outstanding Federal Family Education Loan Program loans were made on or after July 1, 1993, or if you had no balance on loans made before July 1, 1993, when you obtained a loan disbursed on or after July 1, 1993.

WARNING: Any person who knowingly makes a false statement or misrepresentation on this form or on any accompanying documents is subject to penalties that may include fines, imprisonment, or both, under the U.S. Criminal Code and 20 U.S.C. 1097.

HRD

SECTION 1: BORROWER IDENTIFICATION

Please enter or correct the following information.

SSN |__|__|__|-|__|__|-|__|__|__|__|
Name _____
Address _____
City, State, Zip Code _____
Telephone - Home ( ) _____
Telephone - Other ( ) _____
E-mail Address (Optional) _____

SECTION 2: DEFERMENT REQUEST

Before answering any questions, carefully read the entire form, including the instructions and other information in Sections 4, 5, and 6.

■ I meet the qualifications stated in Section 6 for the Economic Hardship Deferment checked below and request that my loan holder defer repayment of my loan(s) beginning

|__|__|-|__|__|-|__|__|__|__|. **(You must provide this date regardless of which condition you check below.)**

To qualify, I must meet **one** of the conditions listed below and must provide the required documentation, as described in Section 6, for only that condition.

Check one:

(1) ☐ I have been granted an economic hardship deferment under the William D. Ford Federal Direct Loan (Direct Loan) Program or the Federal Perkins Loan Program for the same period of time for which I am requesting this deferment. **I have attached documentation of the deferment.**

(2) ☐ I am receiving or received payments under a federal or state public assistance program, such as Temporary Assistance for Needy Families (TANF), Supplemental Security Income (SSI), Food Stamps, or state general public assistance. **I have attached documentation of these payments.**

(3) ☐ I am serving as a Peace Corps volunteer. **I have attached documentation certifying my period of service in the Peace Corps.**

(4) ☐ I work full time and my monthly income does not exceed the **larger of** (A) the Federal Minimum Wage Rate or (B) 150% of the poverty guideline for my family size and state. **I have attached documentation of this income.**

My monthly income (as defined in Section 5) is $ _____.   My family size (as defined in Section 5) is _____.

(A) Federal Minimum Wage Rate (monthly amount, based on $7.25 an hour): **$1,256.67**

(B) 150% of the poverty guideline for my family size and state: **This amount is listed in Section 6.**

SECTION 3: BORROWER UNDERSTANDINGS, CERTIFICATIONS, AND AUTHORIZATION

■ **I understand that:**

(1) I am not required to make payments of loan principal during my deferment. Interest will not be charged on my subsidized loan(s) during my deferment. However, interest will be charged on my unsubsidized loan(s).

(2) I have the option of paying the interest that accrues on my unsubsidized loan(s) during my deferment.

(3) I may choose to make interest payments by checking the box below. My loan holder may capitalize interest that I do not pay during the deferment period.

☐ I wish to make interest payments on my unsubsidized loan(s) during my deferment.

(4) My deferment will begin on the date the deferment condition began.

(5) My deferment will end on the earlier of the date that the condition that establishes my deferment eligibility ends or the certified deferment end date.

(6) My maximum cumulative eligibility for an economic hardship deferment is 36 months. Except for a deferment based on condition (3), as described in Section 2, I must reapply every 12 months if I continue to meet the criteria for an economic hardship deferment.

(7) If my deferment does not cover all my past due payments, my loan holder may grant me a forbearance for all payments due before the begin date of my deferment. If the period for which I am eligible for a deferment has ended, my loan holder may grant me a forbearance for all payments due at the time my deferment request is processed.

(8) My loan holder may grant me a forbearance on my loans for up to 60 days, if necessary, for the collection and processing of documentation related to my deferment request. Interest that accrues during this forbearance will not be capitalized.

■ **I certify that:** (1) The information I provided in Sections 1 and 2 above is true and correct. (2) I will provide additional documentation to my loan holder, as required, to support my deferment status. (3) I will notify my loan holder immediately when the condition that qualified me for the deferment ends. (4) I have read, understand, and meet the eligibility criteria of the deferment for which I have applied, as explained in Section 6.

■ **I authorize** the school, the lender, the guarantor, the Department, and their respective agents and contractors to contact me regarding my loan(s), including repayment of my loan(s), at the current or any future number that I provide for my cellular telephone or other wireless device using automated telephone dialing equipment or artificial or prerecorded voice or text messages.

Borrower's Signature _____   Date _____

507

SECTION 4: INSTRUCTIONS FOR COMPLETING THE FORM

Type or print using dark ink. Report dates as month-day-year (MM-DD-YYYY). For example, 'January 31, 2009' = '01-31- 2009'. Include your name and social security number (SSN) on any documentation that you are required to submit with this form. If you need help completing this form, contact your loan holder.

Return the completed form and any required documentation to the address shown in Section 7.

SECTION 5: DEFINITIONS

- **Capitalization** is the addition of unpaid interest to the principal balance of my loan. The principal balance of a loan increases when payments are postponed during periods of deferment or forbearance and unpaid interest is capitalized. As a result, more interest may accrue over the life of the loan, the monthly payment amount may be higher, or more payments may be required. The chart below provides estimates, for a $15,000 unsubsidized loan balance at a 9% interest rate, of the monthly payments due following a 12-month deferment. It compares the effects of paying the interest as it accrues, capitalizing the interest at the end of the deferment, and capitalizing interest quarterly and at the end of the deferment. My actual loan interest cost will depend on my interest rate, length of the deferment, and frequency of capitalization. Paying interest during the period of deferment lowers the monthly payment by about $18 and saves about $772 over the lifetime of the loan, as depicted in the chart below.

Treatment of Interest Accrued During Deferment	Loan Amount	Capitalized Interest for 12 Months	Principal to Be Repaid	Monthly Payment	Number of Payments	Total Amount Repaid	Total Interest Paid
Interest is paid	$15,000.00	$0.00	$15,000.00	$190.01	120	$24,151.64*	$9,151.64
Interest is capitalized at the end of deferment	$15,000.00	$1,350.00	$16,350.00	$207.11	120	$24,853.79	$9,853.79
Interest is capitalized quarterly during deferment and at the end of deferment	$15,000.00	$1,396.25	$16,396.25	$207.70	120	$24,924.09	$9,924.09

*Total amount repaid includes $1,350 of interest paid during the 12-month period of deferment.

- A **deferment** is a period during which I am entitled to postpone repayment of the principal balance of my loan(s). The federal government pays the interest that accrues during an eligible deferment for all subsidized Federal Stafford Loans and for Federal Consolidation Loans for which the Consolidation Loan application was received by my loan holder **(1)** on or after January 1, 1993, but before August 10, 1993, **(2)** on or after August 10, 1993, if it includes *only* Federal Stafford Loans that were eligible for federal interest subsidy, or **(3)** on or after November 13, 1997, for that portion of the Consolidation Loan that paid a subsidized FFEL Program loan or a subsidized Federal Direct Loan. I am responsible for the interest that accrues during this period on all other FFEL Program loans.

- **Family size** is determined by counting **(1)** myself, **(2)** my spouse, **(3)** my children, including unborn children who will be born during the period covered by the deferment, if they receive more than half of their support from me, and **(4)** other people if, at the time I request this deferment, they live with me, receive more than half their support from me, and will continue to receive this support from me for the year that I certify my family size. Support includes money, gifts, loans, housing, food, clothes, car, medical and dental care, and payment of college costs.

- The **Federal Family Education Loan (FFEL) Program** includes Federal Stafford Loans (both subsidized and unsubsidized), Federal Supplemental Loans for Students (SLS), Federal PLUS Loans, Federal Consolidation Loans, Guaranteed Student Loans (GSL), Federal Insured Student Loans (FISL), and Auxiliary Loans to Assist Students (ALAS).

- The **Federal Perkins Loan (Perkins Loan) Program** includes Federal Perkins Loans, National Direct Student Loans (NDSL), and National Defense Student Loans (Defense Loan).

- **Forbearance** means permitting the temporary cessation of payments, allowing for an extension of time for making payments, or temporarily accepting smaller payments than previously scheduled. I am responsible for the interest that accrues on my loan(s) during a forbearance. If I do not pay the interest that accrues, the interest may be capitalized.

- **Full-time employment** is defined as working at least 30 hours per week in a position expected to last at least 3 consecutive months.

- The **holder** of my FFEL Program loan(s) may be a lender, guaranty agency, secondary market, or the U.S. Department of Education.

- **Monthly income** is either:

  (1) the amount of my monthly income from employment and other sources before taxes and other deductions, **or**

  (2) one-twelfth of the amount of my income reported as "adjusted gross income" on my most recently filed Federal Income Tax Return.

  I may choose either of these income amounts for the purpose of reporting my monthly income on this deferment request.

- The **William D. Ford Federal Direct Loan (Direct Loan) Program** includes Federal Direct Stafford/Ford (Direct Subsidized) Loans, Federal Direct Unsubsidized Stafford/Ford (Direct Unsubsidized) Loans, Federal Direct PLUS (Direct PLUS) Loans, and Federal Direct Consolidation (Direct Consolidation) Loans. These loans are known collectively as "Direct Loans."

SECTION 6: ELIGIBILITY CRITERIA FOR ECONOMIC HARDSHIP DEFERMENT

- If I had no outstanding balance on a FFEL Program loan as of the date I obtained a loan **on or after July 1, 1993**, I may defer repayment of my loan(s) during the period that I meet one of the economic hardship deferment conditions described in Section 2.

- If my economic hardship deferment eligibility is based on condition (1), as described in Section 2, I must provide my loan holder with documentation of the deferment that has been granted under the Direct Loan Program or the Federal Perkins Loan Program (for example, correspondence from my loan holder showing that I have been granted a deferment).

- If my economic hardship deferment eligibility is based on condition (2), as described in Section 2, I must provide my loan holder with documentation confirming that I am receiving or received payments under a federal or state public assistance program.

- If my economic hardship deferment eligibility is based on condition (3), as described in Section 2, I must provide my loan holder with documentation which certifies the beginning and anticipated ending dates of my service in the Peace Corps and which is signed and dated by an authorized Peace Corps official.

- If my economic hardship deferment eligibility is based on condition (4), as described in Section 2, I must provide my loan holder with documentation of my monthly income as defined in Section 5. If I am reporting monthly income from employment and other sources, I must provide documentation such as pay stubs. If I am reporting one-twelfth of my adjusted gross income, I must provide a copy of my most recently filed Federal Income Tax Return.

- If my economic hardship deferment eligibility is based on condition (4), I must use the applicable amount based on my family size and state as shown in the chart below. If I am not currently residing in the United States, I will use the amount for the 48 contiguous states and the District of Columbia.

Borrower's Family Size (See definition in Section 5)	These monthly amounts represent 150% of the poverty guideline		
	48 Contiguous States and District of Columbia	Alaska	Hawaii
1	$1,353.75	$1,691.25	$1,557.50
2	1,821.25	2,276.25	2,095.00
3	2,288.75	2,861.25	2,632.50
4	2,756.25	3,446.25	3,170.00
For each additional person, add:	467.50	585.00	537.50

SECTION 7: WHERE TO SEND THE COMPLETED DEFERMENT REQUEST

Return the completed deferment request and any required documentation to:
(If no address is shown, return to your loan holder.)

If you need help completing this form, call:
(If no telephone number is shown, call your loan holder.)

SECTION 8: IMPORTANT NOTICES

Privacy Act Notice

The Privacy Act of 1974 (5 U.S.C. 552a) requires that the following notice be provided to you:

The authority for collecting the requested information from and about you is §421 et seq. of the Higher Education Act (HEA) of 1965, as amended (20 U.S.C. 1071 et seq.) and the authorities for collecting and using your Social Security Number (SSN) are §484(a)(4) of the HEA (20 U.S.C. 1091(a)(4)) and 31 U.S.C. 7701(b). Participating in the Federal Family Education Loan Program (FFELP) and giving us your SSN are voluntary, but you must provide the requested information, including your SSN, to participate.

The principal purposes for collecting the information on this form, including your SSN, are to verify your identity, to determine your eligibility to receive a loan or a benefit on a loan (such as a deferment, forbearance, discharge, or forgiveness) under the FFELP, to permit the servicing of your loan(s), and, if it becomes necessary, to locate you and to collect and report on your loan(s) if your loan(s) becomes delinquent or in default. We also use your SSN as an account identifier and to permit you to access your account information electronically.

The information in your file may be disclosed, on a case-by-case basis or under a computer matching program, to third parties as authorized under routine uses in the appropriate systems of records notices. The routine uses of this information include, but are not limited to, its disclosure to federal, state, or local agencies, to private parties such as relatives, present and former employers, business and personal associates, to consumer reporting agencies, to financial and educational institutions, and to guaranty agencies in order to verify your identity, to determine your eligibility to receive a loan or a benefit on a loan, to permit the servicing or collection of your loan(s), to enforce the terms of the loan(s), to investigate possible fraud and to verify compliance with federal student financial aid program regulations, or to locate you if you become delinquent in your loan payments or if you default. To provide default rate calculations, disclosures may be made to guaranty agencies, to financial and educational institutions, or to state agencies. To provide financial aid history information, disclosures may be made to educational institutions. To assist program administrators with tracking refunds and cancellations, disclosures may be made to guaranty agencies, to financial and educational institutions, or to federal or state agencies. To provide a standardized method for educational institutions to efficiently submit student enrollment status, disclosures may be made to guaranty agencies or to financial and educational institutions. To counsel you in repayment efforts, disclosures may be made to guaranty agencies, to financial and educational institutions, or to federal, state, or local agencies.

In the event of litigation, we may send records to the Department of Justice, a court, adjudicative body, counsel, party, or witness if the disclosure is relevant and necessary to the litigation. If this information, either alone or with other information, indicates a potential violation of law, we may send it to the appropriate authority for action. We may send information to members of Congress if you ask them to help you with federal student aid questions. In circumstances involving employment complaints, grievances, or disciplinary actions, we may disclose relevant records to adjudicate or investigate the issues. If provided for by a collective bargaining agreement, we may disclose records to a labor organization recognized under 5 U.S.C. Chapter 71. Disclosures may be made to our contractors for the purpose of performing any programmatic function that requires disclosure of records. Before making any such disclosure, we will require the contractor to maintain Privacy Act safeguards. Disclosures may also be made to qualified researchers under Privacy Act safeguards.

Paperwork Reduction Notice

According to the Paperwork Reduction Act of 1995, no persons are required to respond to a collection of information unless it displays a currently valid OMB control number. The valid OMB control number for this information collection is 1845-0005. The time required to complete this information collection is estimated to average 0.16 hours (10 minutes) per response, including the time to review instructions, search existing data resources, gather and maintain the data needed, and complete and review the information collection. **If you have any comments concerning the accuracy of the time estimate(s) or suggestions for improving this form, please write to:**

U.S. Department of Education, Washington, DC 20202-4537

If you have questions regarding the status of your individual submission of this form, write directly to the address shown in Section 7.

Appx. D.2.1.2   *Student Loan Law*

D.2.1.2 Direct Loan Economic Hardship Deferment Form

Direct Loans
William D. Ford Federal Direct Loan Program

ECONOMIC HARDSHIP DEFERMENT REQUEST
William D. Ford Federal Direct Loan Program

WARNING: Any person who knowingly makes a false statement or misrepresentation on this form or on any accompanying documents is subject to penalties that may include fines, imprisonment or both, under the U.S. Criminal Code and 20 U.S.C. 1097.

OMB No. 1845-0011
Form Approved
Exp. Date 05/31/2012

HRD

SECTION 1: BORROWER IDENTIFICATION

Last Name   First Name   Middle Initial   Social Security Number

Street Address   Area Code/Telephone Number (Home)
                              ( )
                              Area Code/Telephone Number (Other)
                              ( )
City   State   Zip Code   E-mail Address (optional)

SECTION 2: DEFERMENT REQUEST

Before completing this form, carefully read the entire form, including the instructions and other information in Sections 4, 5, and 6.

■ I request that the U.S. Department of Education (ED) defer repayment of my loan(s) during the period that I meet one of the conditions checked below, beginning on the following date: |__|__|-|__|__|-|__|__|__|__|. Except for deferment based on Condition (3), I must reapply every 12 months if I continue to meet the requirements for a deferment. My maximum eligibility for an economic hardship deferment is 36 months.

To qualify, I must meet **ONE** of the conditions listed below and **MUST PROVIDE THE REQUIRED DOCUMENTATION**, as described in Section 6, for only that condition.

Check one:

(1) ☐ I have been granted an economic hardship deferment under the Federal Family Education Loan (FFEL) Program or the Federal Perkins Loan Program for the same period of time for which I am requesting this deferment. **I HAVE ATTACHED DOCUMENTATION OF THE DEFERMENT (see Section 6).**

(2) ☐ I am receiving or received payments under a federal or state public assistance program, such as Temporary Assistance for Needy Families (TANF), Supplemental Security Income (SSI), Food Stamps, or state general public assistance. **I HAVE ATTACHED DOCUMENTATION OF THESE PAYMENTS (see Section 6).**

(3) ☐ I am serving as a Peace Corps volunteer. **I HAVE ATTACHED DOCUMENTATION OF MY PERIOD OF SERVICE IN THE PEACE CORPS (see Section 6).**

(4) ☐ I work full-time (as defined in Section 5) **and** my monthly income does not exceed the **larger of** (A) the Federal Minimum Wage Rate or (B) 150% of the Poverty Line income for my family size and state. **I HAVE ATTACHED DOCUMENTATION OF MY MONTHLY INCOME (see Section 6).**

My monthly income (as defined in Section 5) is $ _____.   My family size (as defined in Section 5) is _____.

(A) Federal Minimum Wage Rate (monthly amount, based on $7.25 an hour): **$1,256.67**

(B) 150% of the Poverty Line income for my family size and state: **This amount is listed in Section 6.**

SECTION 3: BORROWER UNDERSTANDINGS, CERTIFICATIONS AND AUTHORIZATION

■ **I understand** that the following terms and conditions apply to this deferment:

(1) I am not required to make payments of loan principal during my deferment. No interest will be charged on my subsidized loan(s) during my deferment. However, interest will be charged on my unsubsidized loan(s). For any unsubsidized loan(s), I will receive an interest statement, and I may pay the interest at any time. If I do not pay the interest that accrues on my unsubsidized loan(s), it will be capitalized at the end of my deferment period.

(2) My deferment will begin on the date the condition that qualifies me for the deferment began.

(3) My deferment will end on the earlier of (A) the date that the condition that qualified me for the deferment ends, or (B) the deferment end date provided to me by the Direct Loan Servicing Center.

(4) If my deferment does not cover all of my past due payments, ED may grant me a forbearance for all payments that were due before the begin date of your deferment. If the period for which you are eligible for a deferment has ended, ED may grant you a forbearance for all payments that are due at the time your deferment request is processed.

(5) ED may grant me a forbearance on my loan(s) for up to 60 days, if necessary, for the collection and processing of documentation related to my deferment request. ED will not capitalize interest that accrues during this forbearance.

■ **I certify** that: (1) The information I have provided on this form is true and correct. (2) I will provide additional documentation to the Direct Loan Servicing Center, as required, to support my eligibility for this deferment. (3) I will notify the Direct Loan Servicing Center immediately if the condition that qualifies me for this deferment ends. (4) I have read, understand, and meet the eligibility requirements of the deferment for which I have applied, as explained in Section 6.

■ **I authorize** my schools, ED, and their respective agents and contractors to contact me regarding my loan request or my loan, including repayment of my loan, at the current or any future number that I provide for my cellular telephone or other wireless device using automated dialing equipment or artificial or prerecorded voice or text messages.

BORROWER'S SIGNATURE _____   DATE _____

Page 1 of 3

REVISED 04-23-2008

Student Assistance Forms Appx. D.2.1.2

SECTION 4: INSTRUCTIONS FOR COMPLETING THE DEFERMENT REQUEST FORM

Type or print using dark ink. Report dates as month-day-year. For example, show "January 31, 2009" as "01-31-2009". Include your name and social security number (SSN) on all attached documentation. **REMEMBER TO SIGN AND DATE THE FORM AND ATTACH THE REQUIRED DOCUMENTATION.**

Send the completed form and any required documentation to:

U.S. Department of Education
Direct Loan Servicing Center
P.O. Box 5609
Greenville, TX 75403-5609

If you need help completing this form, call:
1-800-848-0979.

If you use a telecommunications device for the deaf (TDD), call:
1-800-848-0983

Direct Loan Servicing Center web site:
www.dl.ed.gov

SECTION 5: DEFINITIONS

- If unpaid interest is **capitalized**, this means that it is added to the principal balance of your loan(s). This will increase the principal amount and the total cost of your loan(s).

- A **deferment** allows you to temporarily postpone making payments on your loan(s). No interest is charged during a deferment on Direct Subsidized Loans and Direct Subsidized Consolidation Loans. Interest is charged during a deferment on all other Direct Loans.

- **Family size** is determined by counting **(1)** yourself, **(2)** your spouse, **(3)** your children, including unborn children who will be born during the period covered by the deferment, if they receive more than half of their support from you, and **(4)** other persons if, at the time you request an economic hardship deferment, they live with you, receive more than half their support from you, and will continue to receive this support from you for the year that you certify your family size. Support includes money, gifts, loans, housing, food, clothes, car, medical and dental care, and payment of college costs.

- The **Federal Family Education Loan (FFEL) Program** includes Federal Stafford Loans (subsidized and unsubsidized), Federal Supplemental Loans for Students (SLS), Federal PLUS Loans, Federal Consolidation Loans, Guaranteed Student Loans (GSL), Federal Insured Student Loans (FISL), and Auxiliary Loans to Assist Students (ALAS).

- The **Federal Perkins Loan (Perkins Loan) Program** includes Federal Perkins Loans, National Direct Student Loans (NDSL), and National Defense Student Loans (NDSL).

- A **forbearance** allows you to temporarily postpone making payments on your loan(s), gives you an extension of time for making payments, or lets you temporarily make smaller payments than previously scheduled. Interest is charged during a forbearance on all types of Direct Loans.

- **Full-time** employment is defined as working at least 30 hours per week in a position expected to last at least three consecutive months.

- **Monthly income** is either: **(1)** the amount of your monthly income from employment and other sources before taxes and other deductions, **OR (2)** one-twelfth of the amount of your income reported as "adjusted gross income" on your most recently filed Federal Income Tax Return. You may choose either of these income amounts for the purpose of reporting your monthly income on this deferment request.

- The **William D. Ford Federal Direct Loan (Direct Loan) Program** includes Federal Direct Stafford/Ford (Direct Subsidized) Loans, Federal Direct Unsubsidized Stafford/Ford (Direct Unsubsidized) Loans, Federal Direct PLUS (Direct PLUS) Loans, and Federal Direct Consolidation (Direct Consolidation) Loans. These loans are known collectively as "Direct Loans".

SECTION 6: ELIGIBILITY REQUIREMENTS

- You may defer repayment of your loan(s) during the period that you meet one of the economic hardship conditions described in Section 2.

- Except for a deferment based on **CONDITION (3)**, you must reapply every 12 months if you continue to meet the requirements for an economic hardship deferment. **You may receive an economic hardship deferment for a maximum of 36 months.**

- For **CONDITION (1)**, you must provide the Direct Loan Servicing Center with documentation of the deferment that has been granted under the FFEL Program or the Federal Perkins Loan Program (for example, correspondence from your loan holder showing that you have been granted a deferment).

- For **CONDITION (2)**, you must provide the Direct Loan Servicing Center with documentation confirming that you are receiving or received payments under a federal or state public assistance program.

- For **CONDITION (3)**, you must provide the Direct Loan Servicing Center with documentation that certifies the beginning and expected ending dates of your service in the Peace Corps and which is signed and dated by an authorized Peace Corps official.

- For **CONDITION (4)**, you must:

  - Provide the Direct Loan Servicing Center with documentation of your monthly income (as defined in Section 5). If you are reporting monthly income from employment and other sources, you must provide documentation such as pay stubs. If you are reporting one-twelfth of your adjusted gross income, you must provide a copy of your most recently filed Federal Income Tax Return.

  - Use the Poverty Line income amount for your family size and state as shown in the chart below. If you are not currently residing in the United States, use the Poverty Line amount for the 48 contiguous states.

Borrower's Family Size (see definition in Section 5)	These are monthly figures that represent 150% of the Poverty Line		
	48 Contiguous States and District of Columbia	Alaska	Hawaii
1	$1,353.75	$1,691.25	$1,557.50
2	1,821.25	2,276.25	2,095.00
3	2,288.75	2,861.25	2,632.50
4	2,756.25	3,446.25	3,170.00
For each additional person, add:	467.50	585.00	537.50

REVISED 04-23-2008

SECTION 7: IMPORTANT NOTICES

PRIVACY ACT NOTICE

The Privacy Act of 1974 (5 U.S.C. 552a) requires that the following notice be provided to you:

The authority for collecting the requested information from and about you is §451 *et seq.* of the Higher Education Act (HEA) of 1965, as amended (20 U.S.C. 1087a *et seq.*) and the authorities for collecting and using your Social Security Number (SSN) are §484(a)(4) of the HEA (20 U.S.C. 1091(a)(4)) and 31 U.S.C. 7701(b). Participating in the William D. Ford Federal Direct Loan (Direct Loan) Program and giving us your SSN are voluntary, but you must provide the requested information, including your SSN, to participate.

The principal purposes for collecting the information on this form, including your SSN, are to verify your identity, to determine your eligibility to receive a loan or a benefit on a loan (such as a deferment, forbearance, discharge, or forgiveness) under the Direct Loan Program, to permit the servicing of your loan(s), and, if it becomes necessary, to locate you and to collect and report on your loan(s) if your loan(s) become delinquent or in default. We also use your SSN as an account identifier and to permit you to access your account information electronically.

The information in your file may be disclosed, on a case-by-case basis or under a computer matching program, to third parties as authorized under routine uses in the appropriate systems of records notices. The routine uses of this information include, but are not limited to, its disclosure to federal, state, or local agencies, to private parties such as relatives, present and former employers, business and personal associates, to consumer reporting agencies, to financial and educational institutions, and to guaranty agencies in order to verify your identity, to determine your eligibility to receive a loan or a benefit on a loan, to permit the servicing or collection of your loan(s), to enforce the terms of the loan(s), to investigate possible fraud and to verify compliance with federal student financial aid program regulations, or to locate you if you become delinquent in your loan payments or if you default. To provide default rate calculations, disclosures may be made to guaranty agencies, to financial and educational institutions, or to state agencies. To provide financial aid history information, disclosures may be made to educational institutions. To assist program administrators with tracking refunds and cancellations, disclosures may be made to guaranty agencies, to financial and educational institutions, or to federal or state agencies. To provide a standardized method for educational institutions to efficiently submit student enrollment status, disclosures may be made to guaranty agencies or to financial and educational institutions. To counsel you in repayment efforts, disclosures may be made to guaranty agencies, to financial and educational institutions, or to federal, state, or local agencies.

In the event of litigation, we may send records to the Department of Justice, a court, adjudicative body, counsel, party, or witness if the disclosure is relevant and necessary to the litigation. If this information, either alone or with other information, indicates a potential violation of law, we may send it to the appropriate authority for action. We may send information to members of Congress if you ask them to help you with federal student aid questions. In circumstances involving employment complaints, grievances, or disciplinary actions, we may disclose relevant records to adjudicate or investigate the issues. If provided for by a collective bargaining agreement, we may disclose records to a labor organization recognized under 5 U.S.C. Chapter 71. Disclosures may be made to our contractors for the purpose of performing any programmatic function that requires disclosure of records. Before making any such disclosure, we will require the contractor to maintain Privacy Act safeguards. Disclosures may also be made to qualified researchers under Privacy Act safeguards.

Paperwork Reduction Notice.

According to the Paperwork Reduction Act of 1995, no persons are required to respond to a collection of information unless it displays a currently valid OMB control number. The valid OMB control number for this information collection is 1845-0011. The time required to complete this information collection is estimated to average 0.16 hours (10 minutes) per response, including the time to review instructions, search existing data resources, gather and maintain the data needed, and complete and review the information collection. **If you have comments concerning the accuracy of the time estimate(s) or suggestions for improving this form, please write to:** U.S. Department of Education, Washington, DC 20202-4537. *Do not send the completed form to this address.*

If you have questions about the status of your individual submission of this form, contact the Direct Loan Servicing Center (see Section 4).

Student Assistance Forms   Appx. D.2.2

D.2.2 Direct Unemployment Deferment Form

UNEMPLOYMENT DEFERMENT REQUEST
Federal Family Education Loan Program

WARNING: Any person who knowingly makes a false statement or misrepresentation on this form or on any accompanying documents is subject to penalties that may include fines, imprisonment, or both, under the U.S. Criminal Code and 20 U.S.C. 1097.

OMB No. 1845-0005
Form Approved
Exp. Date 05/31/2012

UNEM

SECTION 1: BORROWER IDENTIFICATION

Please enter or correct the following information.

SSN |__|__|__|-|__|__|-|__|__|__|__|
Name _____
Address _____
City, State, Zip Code _____
Telephone - Home ( ) _____
Telephone - Other ( ) _____
E-mail Address (Optional) _____

SECTION 2: DEFERMENT REQUEST

Before answering any questions, carefully read the entire form, including the instructions and other information in Sections 4, 5, and 6.

- I meet the qualifications stated in Section 6 for an Unemployment Deferment and request that my loan holder defer repayment of my loan(s). **To document eligibility, complete the following:**

    (1) I became unemployed or began working less than full time (see definition in Section 5) on |__|__|-|__|__|-|__|__|__|__|. Except as explained in Section 3, my deferment begins on this date, unless I request my deferment to begin on the following later date: |__|__|-|__|__|-|__|__|__|__|.

    (2) *Check ONE of the boxes below:*

    (A) ☐ I am diligently seeking but unable to find full-time employment in the United States (see definitions in Section 5) in any field or at any salary or responsibility level. I am registered with a public or private employment agency if there is one within 50 miles of my current address. Further, if I am requesting an extension of an existing unemployment deferment, I have made at least 6 diligent attempts to find full-time employment in the most recent 6 months.

    NOTE: School placement offices and "temporary" agencies do not qualify as public or private employment agencies.

    OR

    (B) ☐ I am eligible for unemployment benefits, and I have attached documentation of my eligibility for these benefits. The documentation includes my name, address, and social security number, and shows that I am eligible to receive unemployment benefits during the period for which I am requesting deferment.

SECTION 3: BORROWER UNDERSTANDINGS, CERTIFICATIONS, AND AUTHORIZATION

- **I understand that:**

    (1) I am not required to make payments of loan principal during my deferment. Interest will not be charged on my subsidized loan(s) during my deferment. However, interest will be charged on my unsubsidized loan(s).

    (2) I have the option of paying the interest that accrues on my unsubsidized loan(s) during my deferment.

    (3) I may choose to make interest payments by checking the box below. My loan holder may capitalize interest that I do not pay during the deferment period.

    ☐ I wish to make interest payments on my unsubsidized loan(s) during my deferment.

    (4) My deferment will begin on the date the condition that qualifies me for the deferment began, as shown in Section 2, Item (1), unless I request my deferment to begin on a later date. However, if this is my first unemployment deferment request for my current period of unemployment and I am not providing documentation of my eligibility for unemployment benefits, my deferment will begin no more than 6 months before the date my loan holder receives this request, even if I became unemployed or began working less than full time more than 6 months ago.

    (5) My deferment will end on the earlier of the date that the condition that establishes my deferment eligibility ends or the date on which I exhaust my maximum cumulative eligibility as explained in Section 6.

    (6) My deferment will last for no more than 6 months after the date my loan holder receives the deferment request. I must reapply every 6 months.

    (7) My loan holder will not grant this deferment request unless all applicable sections of this form are completed and any required additional documentation is provided.

    (8) If my deferment does not cover all my past due payments, my loan holder may grant me a forbearance for all payments due before the begin date of my deferment or—if the period for which I am eligible for a deferment has ended—a forbearance for all payments due at the time my deferment request is processed.

    (9) My loan holder may grant me a forbearance on my loans for up to 60 days, if necessary, for the collection and processing of documentation related to my deferment request. Interest that accrues during this forbearance will not be capitalized.

- **I certify that: (1)** The information I have provided in Sections 1 and 2 above is true and correct. **(2)** I will provide additional documentation to my loan holder, as required, to support my deferment status. **(3)** I will notify my loan holder immediately when the condition(s) that qualified me for the deferment ends. **(4)** I have read, understand, and meet the eligibility criteria of the deferment for which I have applied, as explained in Section 6.

- **I authorize** the school, the lender, the guarantor, the Department, and their respective agents and contractors to contact me regarding my loan(s), including repayment of my loan(s), at the current or any future number that I provide for my cellular telephone or other wireless device using automated telephone dialing equipment or artificial or prerecorded voice or text messages.

Borrower's Signature _____ Date _____

SECTION 4: INSTRUCTIONS FOR COMPLETING THE FORM

Type or print using dark ink. Report dates as month-day-year (MM-DD-YYYY). For example, 'January 31, 2009' = '01-31-2009'. If you are qualifying for this deferment by documenting your eligibility for unemployment benefits, attach the documentation to this form. If you need help completing this form, contact your loan holder.

Return the completed form and any required documentation to the address shown in Section 7.

SECTION 5: DEFINITIONS

- **Capitalization** is the addition of unpaid interest to the principal balance of my loan. The principal balance of a loan increases when payments are postponed during periods of deferment or forbearance and unpaid interest is capitalized. As a result, more interest may accrue over the life of the loan, the monthly payment amount may be higher, or more payments may be required. The chart below provides estimates, for a $15,000 unsubsidized loan balance at a 9% interest rate, of the monthly payments due following a 12-month deferment. It compares the effects of paying the interest as it accrues, capitalizing the interest at the end of the deferment, and capitalizing interest quarterly and at the end of the deferment. My actual loan interest cost will depend on my interest rate, length of the deferment, and frequency of capitalization. Paying interest during the period of deferment lowers the monthly payment by about $18 and saves about $772 over the lifetime of the loan, as depicted in the chart below.

Treatment of Interest Accrued During Deferment	Loan Amount	Capitalized Interest for 12 Months	Principal to Be Repaid	Monthly Payment	Number of Payments	Total Amount Repaid	Total Interest Paid
Interest is paid	$15,000.00	$0.00	$15,000.00	$190.01	120	$24,151.64*	$9,151.64
Interest is capitalized at the end of deferment	$15,000.00	$1,350.00	$16,350.00	$207.11	120	$24,853.79	$9,853.79
Interest is capitalized quarterly during deferment and at the end of deferment	$15,000.00	$1,396.25	$16,396.25	$207.70	120	$24,924.09	$9,924.09

*Total amount repaid includes $1,350 of interest paid during the 12-month period of deferment.

- A **deferment** is a period during which I am entitled to postpone repayment of the principal balance of my loan(s). The federal government pays the interest that accrues during an eligible deferment for all subsidized Federal Stafford Loans and for Federal Consolidation Loans for which the Consolidation Loan application was received by my loan holder **(1)** on or after January 1, 1993, but before August 10, 1993, **(2)** on or after August 10, 1993, if it includes *only* Federal Stafford Loans that were eligible for federal interest subsidy, or **(3)** on or after November 13, 1997, for that portion of the Consolidation Loan that paid a subsidized FFEL Program loan or a subsidized Federal Direct Loan. I am responsible for the interest that accrues during this period on all other FFEL Program loans.

- The **Federal Family Education Loan (FFEL) Program** includes Federal Stafford Loans (both subsidized and unsubsidized), Federal Supplemental Loans for Students (SLS), Federal PLUS Loans, and Federal Consolidation Loans.

- **Forbearance** means permitting the temporary cessation of payments, allowing an extension of time for making payments, or temporarily accepting smaller payments than previously scheduled. I am responsible for paying the interest that accrues on my loan(s) during a forbearance. If I do not pay the interest that accrues, the interest may be capitalized.

- **Full-time employment** is defined as working at least 30 hours per week in a position expected to last at least 3 months.

- The **holder** of my FFEL Program loan(s) may be a lender, guaranty agency, secondary market, or the U.S. Department of Education.

- The **United States,** for the purpose of this deferment, includes any state of the Union, the District of Columbia, the Commonwealth of Puerto Rico, American Samoa, Guam, the Virgin Islands, the Commonwealth of the Northern Mariana Islands, the Freely Associated States (the Republic of the Marshall Islands, the Federated States of Micronesia, and the Republic of Palau), and U.S. military bases and embassy compounds in foreign countries.

SECTION 6: ELIGIBILITY CRITERIA FOR UNEMPLOYMENT DEFERMENT

- I may defer (postpone) repayment of my loans while I am unemployed. If my first loans were made **before July 1, 1993**, my maximum cumulative eligibility for Unemployment Deferments is 24 months. If I did not have an outstanding FFEL Program Loan as of the date I obtained a loan **on or after July 1, 1993**, my maximum cumulative eligibility is 36 months.

- To qualify:

    (1) I am diligently seeking but unable to find full-time employment in the United States (see definitions in Section 5) in any field or at any salary or responsibility level. I am registered with a public or private employment agency if there is one within 50 miles of my current address. School placement offices and "temporary" agencies do not qualify as public or private employment agencies. Further, if I am requesting an extension of an existing unemployment deferment, I have made at least 6 diligent attempts to find full-time employment in the most recent 6 months. (Complete Item (A) in Section 2.)

    OR

    (2) I am eligible for unemployment benefits, and I have attached documentation of my eligibility for these benefits. The documentation includes my name, address, and social security number, and shows that I am eligible to receive unemployment benefits during the period for which I am requesting deferment. (Complete Item (B) in Section 2.)

SECTION 7: WHERE TO SEND THE COMPLETED DEFERMENT REQUEST

Return the completed deferment request and any required documentation to: (If no address is shown, return to your loan holder.)	If you need help completing this form, call: (If no telephone number is shown, call your loan holder.)

SECTION 8: IMPORTANT NOTICES

Privacy Act Notice

The Privacy Act of 1974 (5 U.S.C. 552a) requires that the following notice be provided to you:

The authority for collecting the requested information from and about you is §421 et seq. of the Higher Education Act (HEA) of 1965, as amended (20 U.S.C. 1071 et seq.) and the authorities for collecting and using your Social Security Number (SSN) are §484(a)(4) of the HEA (20 U.S.C. 1091(a)(4)) and 31 U.S.C. 7701(b). Participating in the Federal Family Education Loan Program (FFELP) and giving us your SSN are voluntary, but you must provide the requested information, including your SSN, to participate.

The principal purposes for collecting the information on this form, including your SSN, are to verify your identity, to determine your eligibility to receive a loan or a benefit on a loan (such as a deferment, forbearance, discharge, or forgiveness) under the FFELP, to permit the servicing of your loan(s), and, if it becomes necessary, to locate you and to collect and report on your loan(s) if your loan(s) becomes delinquent or in default. We also use your SSN as an account identifier and to permit you to access your account information electronically.

The information in your file may be disclosed, on a case-by-case basis or under a computer matching program, to third parties as authorized under routine uses in the appropriate systems of records notices. The routine uses of this information include, but are not limited to, its disclosure to federal, state, or local agencies, to private parties such as relatives, present and former employers, business and personal associates, to consumer reporting agencies, to financial and educational institutions, and to guaranty agencies in order to verify your identity, to determine your eligibility to receive a loan or a benefit on a loan, to permit the servicing or collection of your loan(s), to enforce the terms of the loan(s), to investigate possible fraud and to verify compliance with federal student financial aid program regulations, or to locate you if you become delinquent in your loan payments or if you default. To provide default rate calculations, disclosures may be made to guaranty agencies, to financial and educational institutions, or to state agencies. To provide financial aid history information, disclosures may be made to educational institutions. To assist program administrators with tracking refunds and cancellations, disclosures may be made to guaranty agencies, to financial and educational institutions, or to federal or state agencies. To provide a standardized method for educational institutions to efficiently submit student enrollment status, disclosures may be made to guaranty agencies or to financial and educational institutions. To counsel you in repayment efforts, disclosures may be made to guaranty agencies, to financial and educational institutions, or to federal, state, or local agencies.

In the event of litigation, we may send records to the Department of Justice, a court, adjudicative body, counsel, party, or witness if the disclosure is relevant and necessary to the litigation. If this information, either alone or with other information, indicates a potential violation of law, we may send it to the appropriate authority for action. We may send information to members of Congress if you ask them to help you with federal student aid questions. In circumstances involving employment complaints, grievances, or disciplinary actions, we may disclose relevant records to adjudicate or investigate the issues. If provided for by a collective bargaining agreement, we may disclose records to a labor organization recognized under 5 U.S.C. Chapter 71. Disclosures may be made to our contractors for the purpose of performing any programmatic function that requires disclosure of records. Before making any such disclosure, we will require the contractor to maintain Privacy Act safeguards. Disclosures may also be made to qualified researchers under Privacy Act safeguards.

Paperwork Reduction Notice

According to the Paperwork Reduction Act of 1995, no persons are required to respond to a collection of information unless it displays a currently valid OMB control number. The valid OMB control number for this information collection is 1845-0005. The time required to complete this information collection is estimated to average 0.16 hours (10 minutes) per response, including the time to review instructions, search existing data resources, gather and maintain the data needed, and complete and review the information collection. **If you have any comments concerning the accuracy of the time estimate(s) or suggestions for improving this form, please write to:**

U.S. Department of Education, Washington, DC 20202-4537

If you have questions regarding the status of your individual submission of this form, write directly to the address shown in Section 7.

Appx. D.2.3   Student Loan Law

D.2.3 FFEL/Direct Loans Military Deferment Form

MILITARY DEFERMENT REQUEST
Federal Family Education Loan Program / William D. Ford Federal Direct Loan Program / Federal Perkins Loan Program

OMB No. 1845-0080
Form Approved
Exp. Date 04/30/2010

MIL

Use this form only for Federal Family Education Loan Program, William D. Ford Federal Direct Loan Program, or Federal Perkins Loan Program loans first disbursed on or after July 1, 2001, and Federal Consolidation Loans or Direct Consolidation Loans only if all of the Title IV loans included in the Consolidation Loan were first disbursed on or after July 1, 2001.

WARNING: Any person who knowingly makes a false statement or misrepresentation on this form or on any accompanying documents will be subject to penalties which may include fines, imprisonment or both, under the U.S. Criminal Code and 20 U.S.C. 1097.

SECTION 1: BORROWER IDENTIFICATION

Last Name   First Name   Middle Initial   Social Security Number

Street Address   Area Code/Telephone Number (Home) ( )

City   State   Zip Code   Area Code/Telephone Number (Other) ( )

E-mail Address (optional)

SECTION 2: DEFERMENT REQUEST

Carefully read the entire form, including the instructions and other information in Sections 5, 6, and 7. A representative may complete and sign this form on your behalf if you are unable to do so.

■ I meet the qualifications stated in Section 7 for this deferment and request that my loan holder defer repayment of my eligible loan(s) for a period not to exceed three years while I am either:
- Serving on active duty during a war or other military operation or national emergency, as defined in Section 6, or
- Performing qualifying National Guard duty during a war or other military operation or national emergency, as defined in Section 6.

SECTION 3: BORROWER UNDERSTANDINGS AND CERTIFICATIONS

■ I understand that:
(1) I am not required to make payments of loan principal during my deferment. Interest will not be charged on my subsidized FFEL or Direct Loan program loan(s) or Perkins Loan Program loan(s) during my deferment. However, interest will be charged on my unsubsidized FFEL and Direct Loan program loan(s).
(2) I have the option of paying the interest on my unsubsidized FFEL or Direct Loan program loan(s) during my deferment.
(3) My loan holder may capitalize interest that I do not pay during the deferment period on my unsubsidized FFEL or Direct Loan program loan(s).
(4) My deferment will begin on the date I began performing the military service that qualifies me for the deferment, as certified by an authorized official or documented by my military orders.
(5) My deferment will end on the earlier of (a) the date that I stop performing the military service that qualifies me for the deferment, (b) the ending date of my qualifying military service, as certified by an authorized official or documented by my military orders, or (c) the date on which my loan reaches the maximum period of deferment under the law. The total military deferment period may not exceed three years for any eligible loan.
(6) If my deferment does not cover all my past due payments, my loan holder may grant me a forbearance for all payments due before the begin date of my deferment or—if the period for which I am eligible for a deferment has ended—a forbearance for all payments due at the time my deferment request is processed.
(7) During the deferment period on my eligible loans, I may request a forbearance on my other FFEL, Direct Loan or Perkins Loan program loans that are not eligible for this deferment.
(8) My loan holder may capitalize unpaid interest that accrues during a forbearance period on a FFEL or Direct Loan program loan, and this will increase the principal balance of the loan. Unpaid interest that accrues on a Perkins Loan Program loan during a forbearance period is not capitalized.
(9) My loan holder may grant me a forbearance on my FFEL or Direct Loan program loan(s) for up to 60 days, if necessary, for the collection and processing of documentation related to my deferment request. Interest that accrues during this forbearance period will not be capitalized.

■ **I certify that: (1)** The information I provided in Section 1 above is true and correct. **(2)** I will provide additional documentation to my loan holder, as required, to support my eligibility for this deferment. **(3)** I will notify my loan holder immediately if I stop performing the military duty that qualifies me for this deferment or I otherwise become ineligible for this deferment. **(4)** I have read, understand, and meet the eligibility criteria for this deferment, as stated in Section 2 and explained in Section 7.

Signature of Borrower or Borrower's Representative _____   Date _____
Printed Name of Borrower's Representative (if applicable) _____   Relationship to Borrower _____
Address of Borrower's Representative _____   Telephone ( ) _____

SECTION 4: AUTHORIZED OFFICIAL'S CERTIFICATION

Note: As an alternative to completing this section, a written statement from the commanding or personnel officer or a copy of the military orders may be attached.
I certify, to the best of my knowledge and belief, that the borrower named above is/was engaged in the service described in Sections 2, 6, and 7 that begins/began on |__|__|-|__|__|-|__|__|__|__| and ends/ended on |__|__|-|__|__|-|__|__|__|__|. Enter dates as month-day-year (mm-dd-yyyy).

Name of Military Branch or National Guard _____
Address _____   City, State, Zip _____
Name/Title of Authorized Official _____   Telephone ( ) _____
Authorized Official's Signature _____   Date _____

SECTION 5: INSTRUCTIONS FOR COMPLETING THE FORM

Type or print using dark ink. Enter dates as month-day-year (mm-dd-yyyy). Use only numbers. Example: January 1, 2008 = 01-01-2008. In order to establish your eligibility, **(1)** an authorized official must complete section 4, or **(2)** a copy of your military orders or a written statement from your commanding or personnel officer must be attached. If you need help completing this form, contact your loan holder. If you are applying for a deferment of loans that are held by different loan holders, you must submit a separate deferment request to each loan holder.

Return the completed form and any required documentation to the address shown in Section 8.

SECTION 6: DEFINITIONS

- **Active duty** means full-time duty in the active military service of the United States as defined in 10 U.S.C. 101(d)(1), but does not include training or attendance at a service school.
- An **authorized certifying official** is my commanding or personnel officer.
- **Capitalization** is the addition of unpaid interest to the principal balance of my FFEL or Direct Loan program loan. This will increase the principal and total cost of my loan.
- A **deferment** is a period during which I am entitled to temporarily postpone making payments on the principal balance of my loan(s). Interest is not charged during a deferment on subsidized FFEL or Direct Loan program loans, or on Perkins Loan Program loans. Interest is charged during a deferment on unsubsidized FFEL and Direct Loan program loans.
- The **Federal Family Education Loan (FFEL) Program** includes Federal Stafford Loans (both subsidized and unsubsidized), Federal PLUS Loans, and Federal Consolidation Loans.
- The **Federal Perkins Loan (Perkins Loan) Program** includes Federal Perkins Loans, National Direct Student Loans (NDSL), and National Defense Student Loans (Defense Loan).
- The William D. Ford **Federal Direct Loan (Direct Loan) Program** includes Federal Direct Stafford/Ford (Direct Subsidized) Loans, Federal Direct Unsubsidized Stafford/Ford (Direct Unsubsidized) Loans, Federal Direct PLUS (Direct PLUS) Loans, and Federal Direct Consolidation (Direct Consolidation) Loans.
- **Forbearance** means permitting the temporary cessation of payments, allowing an extension of time for making payments, or temporarily accepting smaller payments than scheduled. I am responsible for paying the interest that accrues on my loans during a forbearance. If I do not pay the interest that accrues on a FFEL or Direct Loan program loan during forbearance, it may be capitalized. Unpaid interest that accrues on a Perkins Loan Program loan during a forbearance is not capitalized.
- The **holder** of my FFEL Program loan(s) may be a lender, guaranty agency, secondary market, or the U.S. Department of Education (ED). The holder of my Direct Loan Program loan(s) is ED. The holder of my Perkins Loan Program loan(s) may be a school or ED.
- **Military operation** means a contingency operation as defined in 10 U.S.C. 101(a)(13). A contingency operation is a military operation that **(1)** is designated by the U.S. Secretary of Defense as an operation in which members of the Armed Forces are or may become involved in military actions, operations, or hostilities against an enemy of the U.S. or against an opposing military force; or **(2)** results in the call or order to, or retention on, active duty of members of the uniformed services under 10 U.S.C. 688, 12301(a), 12302, 12304, 12305, or 12406; 10 U.S.C. Chapter 15; or any other provision of law during a war or during a national emergency declared by the President or Congress.
- **National emergency** means the national emergency by reason of certain terrorist attacks declared by the President on September 14, 2001, or subsequent national emergencies declared by the President by reason of terrorist attacks.
- **Qualifying National Guard duty during a war or other operation or national emergency** means training or other duty, other than inactive, performed by a member of the National Guard on full-time National Guard duty, as defined in 10 U.S.C. 101(d)(5), under a call to active service authorized by the President or the Secretary of Defense. The training or other duty must be performed for more than 30 consecutive days under 32 U.S.C. 502(f) in connection with a war, other military operation, or national emergency as declared by the President and supported by federal funds.
- **Serving on active duty during a war or other military operation or national emergency** means service by an individual who is **(1)** a Reserve of an Armed Force ordered to active duty under 10 U.S.C. 12301(a), 12301(g), 12302, 12304, or 12306; or **(2)** a retired member of an Armed Force ordered to active duty under 10 U.S.C. 688 for service in connection with a war or other military operation or national emergency, regardless of the location at which the active duty service is performed; or **(3)** any other member of an Armed Force on active duty in connection with the emergency or subsequent actions or conditions who has been assigned to a duty station at a location other than the location where the member is normally assigned.
- **Title IV loans** include loans made under the FFEL, Direct Loan, and Perkins Loan programs.

SECTION 7: ELIGIBILITY CRITERIA FOR MILITARY DEFERMENT

- A military deferment is available only for:
    - Federal Stafford Loans (both subsidized and unsubsidized), Federal PLUS Loans, Direct Subsidized Loans, Direct Unsubsidized Loans, Direct PLUS Loans, and Federal Perkins Loans, that were first disbursed **on or after July 1, 2001**, and
    - Federal Consolidation Loans and Direct Consolidation Loans, only if all of my Title IV loans included in the consolidation loan were first disbursed **on or after July 1, 2001**.
- I may defer repayment of my eligible loan(s) for a maximum of 3 years while I am:
    - Serving on **active duty** during a war or other military operation or national emergency. I must provide my loan holder with a copy of my military orders or a written statement from my commanding or personnel officer, or I must have my commanding or personnel officer certify Section 4 on this form; or
    - Performing qualifying **National Guard duty** during a war or other military operation or national emergency. I must provide my loan holder with a copy of my military orders or a written statement from my commanding or personnel officer, or I must have my commanding or personnel officer certify Section 4 on this form.

SECTION 8: WHERE TO SEND THE COMPLETED DEFERMENT REQUEST

Return the completed deferment request and any required documentation to:

U.S. Department of Education
Direct Loan Servicing Center
P.O. Box 5609
Greenville, TX 75403-5609

If you need help completing this form, call: **1-800-848-0979**.

If you use a telecommunications device for the deaf (TDD), call: **1-800-848-0983**.

Direct Loan Servicing Center Web site: **www.dl.ed.gov**

SECTION 9: IMPORTANT NOTICES

Privacy Act Notice. The Privacy Act of 1974 (5 U.S.C. 552a) requires that the following notice be provided to you:

The authority for collecting the requested information from and about you is §421 *et seq.*, §451 *et seq.*, and/or §461 *et seq.* of the Higher Education Act (HEA) of 1965, as amended (20 U.S.C. 1071 *et seq.*, 20 U.S.C. 1087a *et seq.*, and/or 20 U.S.C. 1087aa *et seq.*), and the authorities for collecting and using your Social Security Number (SSN) are §484(a)(4) of the HEA (20 U.S.C. 1091(a)(4)) and 31 U.S.C. 7701(b). Participating in the Federal Family Education Loan (FFEL) Program, William D. Ford Federal Direct Loan (Direct Loan) Program, and Federal Perkins Loan (Perkins) Program and giving us your SSN are voluntary, but you must provide the requested information, including your SSN, to participate.

The principal purposes for collecting the information on this form, including your SSN, are to verify your identity, to determine your eligibility to receive a loan or a benefit on a loan (such as a deferment, forbearance, discharge, or forgiveness) under the FFEL Program, Direct Loan Program, and/or Perkins Program, to permit the servicing of your loan(s), and, if it becomes necessary, to locate you and to collect and report on your loan(s) if your loan(s) become delinquent or in default. We also use your SSN as an account identifier and to permit you to access your account information electronically.

The information in your file may be disclosed, on a case-by-case basis or under a computer matching program, to third parties as authorized under routine uses in the appropriate systems of records notices. The routine uses of this information include, but are not limited to, its disclosure to federal, state, or local agencies, to private parties such as relatives, present and former employers, business and personal associates, to consumer reporting agencies, to financial and educational institutions, and to guaranty agencies in order to verify your identity, to determine your eligibility to receive a loan or a benefit on a loan, to permit the servicing or collection of your loan(s), to enforce the terms of the loan(s), to investigate possible fraud and to verify compliance with federal student financial aid program regulations, or to locate you if you become delinquent in your loan payments or if you default. To provide default rate calculations, disclosures may be made to guaranty agencies, to financial and educational institutions, or to state agencies. To provide financial aid history information, disclosures may be made to educational institutions. To assist program administrators with tracking refunds and cancellations, disclosures may be made to guaranty agencies, to financial and educational institutions, or to federal or state agencies. To provide a standardized method for educational institutions to efficiently submit student enrollment status, disclosures may be made to guaranty agencies or to financial and educational institutions. To counsel you in repayment efforts, disclosures may be made to guaranty agencies, to financial and educational institutions, or to federal, state, or local agencies.

In the event of litigation, we may send records to the Department of Justice, a court, adjudicative body, counsel, party, or witness if the disclosure is relevant and necessary to the litigation. If this information, either alone or with other information, indicates a potential violation of law, we may send it to the appropriate authority for action. We may send information to members of Congress if you ask them to help you with federal student aid questions. In circumstances involving employment complaints, grievances, or disciplinary actions, we may disclose relevant records to adjudicate or investigate the issues. If provided for by a collective bargaining agreement, we may disclose records to a labor organization recognized under 5 U.S.C. Chapter 71. Disclosures may be made to our contractors for the purpose of performing any programmatic function that requires disclosure of records. Before making any such disclosure, we will require the contractor to maintain Privacy Act safeguards. Disclosures may also be made to qualified researchers under Privacy Act safeguards.

Paperwork Reduction Notice. According to the Paperwork Reduction Act of 1995, no persons are required to respond to a collection of information unless it displays a currently valid OMB control number. The valid OMB control number for this information collection is 1845-0080. The time required to complete this information collection is estimated to average 0.5 hours (30 minutes) per response, including the time to review instructions, search existing data resources, gather and maintain the data needed, and complete and review the information collection. *If you have any comments concerning the accuracy of the time estimate(s) or suggestions for improving this form, please write to:*

U.S. Department of Education
Washington, DC 20202-4700

If you have questions regarding the status of your individual submission of this form, contact your loan holder (see Section 8).

Student Assistance Forms   Appx. D.2.4

D.2.4 Direct Loan Parent PLUS Borrower Deferment Request

Direct Loans — William D. Ford Federal Direct Loan Program

IN-SCHOOL DEFERMENT REQUEST
William D. Ford Federal Direct Loan Program

OMB No. 1845-0011
Form Approved
Exp. Date 05/31/2012

SCH

WARNING: Any person who knowingly makes a false statement or misrepresentation on this form or on any accompanying documents is subject to penalties that may include fines, imprisonment or both, under the U.S. Criminal Code and 20 U.S.C. 1097.

SECTION 1: BORROWER IDENTIFICATION

Last Name   First Name   Middle Initial   Social Security Number

Street Address   Area Code/Telephone Number (Home) ( )

    Area Code/Telephone Number (Other) ( )

City   State   Zip Code

Email Address (optional)

SECTION 2: DEFERMENT REQUEST

Before completing this form, carefully read the entire form, including the instructions and other information in Sections 5, 6, and 7.
YOU MUST HAVE AN AUTHORIZED OFFICIAL AT YOUR SCHOOL COMPLETE SECTION 4.

■ I meet the qualifications for the deferment(s) checked below and request that the U.S. Department of Education (ED) defer repayment of my loan(s):

(1) ☐ While I am enrolled **AT LEAST HALF TIME** at an eligible school. If I am a graduate or professional student Direct PLUS Loan borrower, I will also receive a deferment on my Direct PLUS Loan(s) first disbursed on or after July 1, 2008 during the 6-month period after I cease to be enrolled on at least a half-time basis.

(2) ☐ If I am a parent borrower of a Direct PLUS Loan first disbursed on or after July 1, 2008 and I am also a student, during the 6-month period after I cease to be enrolled at least half time at an eligible school.

(3) ☐ If I am a parent borrower of a Direct PLUS Loan first disbursed on or after July 1, 2008, while the student named below on whose behalf I obtained the loan is enrolled at least half time at an eligible school. By checking the box below, I may also request a deferment of a Direct PLUS Loan first disbursed on or after July 1, 2008 during the six-month period after the student ceases to be enrolled at least half time at an eligible school:

     ☐ I request that ED defer repayment of my Direct PLUS Loan(s) first disbursed on or after July 1, 2008 during the 6-month period after the student named below on whose behalf I obtained the loan ceases to be enrolled at least half time at an eligible school.

If you are requesting a deferment based on condition (3), enter the student's name and SSN below:
STUDENT'S NAME _____   **STUDENT'S SSN** |__|__|__|-|__|__|-|__|__|__|__|

SECTION 3: BORROWER UNDERSTANDINGS, CERTIFICATIONS AND AUTHORIZATION

■ **I understand** that the following terms and conditions apply to this deferment:

(1) I am not required to make payments of loan principal during my deferment. No interest will be charged on my subsidized loan(s) during my deferment. However, interest will be charged on my unsubsidized loan(s). For any unsubsidized loan(s), I will receive an interest statement, and I may pay the interest at any time. If I do not pay the interest that accrues on my unsubsidized loan(s), it will be capitalized at the end of my deferment period.

(2) For a deferment based on condition (1) in Section 2, my deferment will begin on the date I became enrolled as at least a half-time student, and will end on the earlier of **(A)** the date that I drop below at least half time enrollment, or **(B)** the date that I am expected to complete my program requirements, as certified by an authorized official in Section 4 of this form. However, if I am a graduate or professional student Direct PLUS Loan borrower, my deferment on Direct PLUS Loans first disbursed on or after July 1, 2008 will end six months after I cease to be enrolled on at least a half-time basis.

(3) If I am a parent borrower of a Direct PLUS Loan first disbursed on or after July 1, 2008 and I request a deferment based on condition (2) in Section 2, my deferment will begin on the day after I cease to be enrolled at least half time and will end six months after that date.

(4) If I am a parent borrower of a Direct PLUS Loan first disbursed on or after July 1, 2008 and I request a deferment based on condition (3) in Section 2, my deferment will begin on the day the student on whose behalf I obtained the loan became enrolled as at least a half-time student. Unless I also request a deferment during the 6-month period after the student ceased to be enrolled on at least a half-time basis, my deferment will end on the earlier of **(A)** the date the student drops below at least half-time enrollment, or **(B)** the date the student is expected to complete his or her program requirements, as certified by an authorized official in Section 4.

(5) If my deferment does not cover all of my past due payments, ED may grant me a forbearance for all payments that were due before the begin date of my deferment. If the period for which I am eligible for a deferment has ended, ED may grant me a forbearance for all payments that are due at the time my deferment request is processed.

(6) ED may grant me a forbearance on my loans for up to 60 days, if necessary, for the collection and processing of documentation related to my deferment request. ED will not capitalize interest that accrues during this forbearance.

■ **I certify** that: **(1)** The information I have provided on this form is true and correct. **(2)** I will provide additional documentation to the Direct Loan Servicing Center, as required, to support my eligibility for this deferment. **(3)** I will notify the Direct Loan Servicing Center immediately if I drop below half-time enrollment or, for a deferment based on condition (3) in Section 2, if the student on whose behalf I obtained a Direct PLUS Loan drops below half-time enrollment. **(4)** I have read, understand, and meet the eligibility requirements of the deferment for which I have applied.

■ **I authorize** my schools, ED, and their respective agents and contractors to contact me regarding my loan request or my loan, including repayment of my loan, at the current or any future number that I provide for my cellular telephone or other wireless device using automated dialing equipment or artificial or prerecorded voice or text messages.

BORROWER'S SIGNATURE _____   **DATE** _____

SECTION 4: AUTHORIZED OFFICIAL'S CERTIFICATION

NOTE: *As an alternative to completing this section, the school may attach its own enrollment certification report listing the required information.*

I certify, to the best of my knowledge and belief, that the borrower or student named above:
(1) Is/was enrolled as at least a half-time student during the academic period from |__|__|-|__|__|-|__|__|__|__| to |__|__|-|__|__|-|__|__|__|__| and
(2) Is reasonably expected to complete his/her program requirements on |__|__|-|__|__|-|__|__|__|__|.

School's Name _____   OPE-ID _____

School's Address _____   City, State, Zip _____

Name/Title of Authorized Official _____   Telephone ( ) _____

AUTHORIZED OFFICIAL'S SIGNATURE _____   **DATE** _____

SECTION 5: INSTRUCTIONS FOR COMPLETING THE DEFERMENT REQUEST FORM

Type or print using dark ink. Report dates as month-day-year. For example, show "January 31, 2009" as "01-31-2009".

REMEMBER TO SIGN AND DATE THE FORM AND HAVE AN AUTHORIZED SCHOOL OFFICIAL COMPLETE SECTION 4.

Send the completed form and any required documentation to:

U.S. Department of Education
Direct Loan Servicing Center
P.O. Box 5609
Greenville, TX 75403-5609

If you need help completing this form, call:
1-800-848-0979.

If you use a telecommunications device for the deaf (TDD), call:
1-800-848-0983

Direct Loan Servicing Center web site:
www.dl.ed.gov

SECTION 6: DEFINITIONS

- An **authorized official** who may complete Section 4 is an authorized official of the school where you or your student are/were enrolled as at least a half-time student.

- If unpaid interest is **capitalized**, this means that it is added to the principal balance of your loan(s). This will increase the principal amount and the total cost of your loan(s).

- A **deferment** allows you to temporarily postpone making payments on your loan(s). No interest is charged during a deferment on Direct Subsidized Loans and Direct Subsidized Consolidation Loans. Interest is charged during a deferment on all other Direct Loans.

- An **eligible school** is a school that has been approved by ED to participate in ED's Federal Student Aid programs or that meets other requirements. The Direct Loan Servicing Center can tell you if the school where you are enrolled is an eligible school.

- A **forbearance** allows you to temporarily postpone making payments on your loan(s), gives you an extension of time for making payments, or lets you temporarily make smaller payments than previously scheduled. Interest is charged during a forbearance on all types of Direct Loans.

- The **William D. Ford Federal Direct Loan (Direct Loan) Program** includes Federal Direct Stafford/Ford (Direct Subsidized) Loans, Federal Direct Unsubsidized Stafford/Ford (Direct Unsubsidized) Loans, Federal Direct PLUS (Direct PLUS) Loans, and Federal Direct Consolidation (Direct Consolidation) Loans. These loans are known collectively as "Direct Loans".

SECTION 7: ELIGIBILITY REQUIREMENTS

- You may defer repayment of your loans –

  (1) While you are enrolled at least half-time at an eligible school;

  (2) For Direct PLUS Loans first disbursed on or after July 1, 2008, during the 6-month period after you cease to be enrolled at least half time at an eligible school;

  (3) For Direct PLUS Loans first disbursed on or after July 1, 2008, while the student on whose behalf you obtained the loan is enrolled at least half time at an eligible school, and during the 6-month period after the student ceases to be enrolled at least half time.

SECTION 8: IMPORTANT NOTICES

PRIVACY ACT NOTICE

The Privacy Act of 1974 (5 U.S.C. 552a) requires that the following notice be provided to you:

The authority for collecting the requested information from and about you is §451 *et seq.* of the Higher Education Act (HEA) of 1965, as amended (20 U.S.C. 1087a *et seq.*) and the authorities for collecting and using your Social Security Number (SSN) are §484(a)(4) of the HEA (20 U.S.C. 1091(a)(4)) and 31 U.S.C. 7701(b). Participating in the William D. Ford Federal Direct Loan (Direct Loan) Program and giving us your SSN are voluntary, but you must provide the requested information, including your SSN, to participate.

The principal purposes for collecting the information on this form, including your SSN, are to verify your identity, to determine your eligibility to receive a loan or a benefit on a loan (such as a deferment, forbearance, discharge, or forgiveness) under the Direct Loan Program, to permit the servicing of your loan(s), and, if it becomes necessary, to locate you and to collect and report on your loan(s) if your loan(s) become delinquent or in default. We also use your SSN as an account identifier and to permit you to access your account information electronically.

The information in your file may be disclosed, on a case-by-case basis or under a computer matching program, to third parties as authorized under routine uses in the appropriate systems of records notices. The routine uses of this information include, but are not limited to, its disclosure to federal, state, or local agencies, to private parties such as relatives, present and former employers, business and personal associates, to consumer reporting agencies, to financial and educational institutions, and to guaranty agencies in order to verify your identity, to determine your eligibility to receive a loan or a benefit on a loan, to permit the servicing or collection of your loan(s), to enforce the terms of the loan(s), to investigate possible fraud and to verify compliance with federal student financial aid program regulations, or to locate you if you become delinquent in your loan payments or if you default. To provide default rate calculations, disclosures may be made to guaranty agencies, to financial and educational institutions, or to state agencies. To provide financial aid history information, disclosures may be made to educational institutions. To assist program administrators with tracking refunds and cancellations, disclosures may be made to guaranty agencies, to financial and educational institutions, or to federal or state agencies. To provide a standardized method for educational institutions to efficiently submit student enrollment status, disclosures may be made to guaranty agencies or to financial and educational institutions. To counsel you in repayment efforts, disclosures may be made to guaranty agencies, to financial and educational institutions, or to federal, state, or local agencies.

In the event of litigation, we may send records to the Department of Justice, a court, adjudicative body, counsel, party, or witness if the disclosure is relevant and necessary to the litigation. If this information, either alone or with other information, indicates a potential violation of law, we may send it to the appropriate authority for action. We may send information to members of Congress if you ask them to help you with federal student aid questions. In circumstances involving employment complaints, grievances, or disciplinary actions, we may disclose relevant records to adjudicate or investigate the issues. If provided for by a collective bargaining agreement, we may disclose records to a labor organization recognized under 5 U.S.C. Chapter 71. Disclosures may be made to our contractors for the purpose of performing any programmatic function that requires disclosure of records. Before making any such disclosure, we will require the contractor to maintain Privacy Act safeguards. Disclosures may also be made to qualified researchers under Privacy Act safeguards.

Paperwork Reduction Notice.

According to the Paperwork Reduction Act of 1995, no persons are required to respond to a collection of information unless it displays a currently valid OMB control number. The valid OMB control number for this information collection is 1845-0011. The time required to complete this information collection is estimated to average 0.16 hours (10 minutes) per response, including the time to review instructions, search existing data resources, gather and maintain the data needed, and complete and review the information collection. **If you have comments concerning the accuracy of the time estimate(s) or suggestions for improving this form, please write to:** U.S. Department of Education, Washington, DC 20202-4537. *Do not send the completed form to this address.*

If you have questions about the status of your individual submission of this form, contact the Direct Loan Servicing Center (see Section 5).

Student Assistance Forms Appx. D.2.5

D.2.5 Direct Loan General Forbearance Request

Direct Loans
William D. Ford Federal Direct Loan Program

GENERAL FORBEARANCE REQUEST
William D. Ford Federal Direct Loan Program

OMB No. 1845-0031
Form Approved
Exp. Date 07/31/2009

WARNING: Any person who knowingly makes a false statement or misrepresentation on this form or on any accompanying documents will be subject to penalties which may include fines, imprisonment, or both, under the U.S. Criminal Code and 20 U.S.C. 1097.

GFB
General

SECTION 1: BORROWER / ENDORSER IDENTIFICATION
PLEASE PRINT LEGIBLY IN BLUE OR BLACK INK

Last Name   First Name   Middle Initial   Social Security Number

Street Address   Area Code/Telephone Number (Home)
                                                ( )
                                                Area Code/Telephone Number (Other)
City   State   Zip Code   ( )
                                                E-mail Address (optional)

SECTION 2: FORBEARANCE REQUEST

Before completing this form, carefully read the entire form, including the instructions and other information in Sections 3, 4, 5, and 6. You may complete and submit your forbearance request electronically at the Direct Loan Servicing Center's web site: **www.dl.ed.gov**.

- I am willing but unable to make my current Direct Loan payments due to a temporary financial hardship. I am requesting this forbearance because: _____

- If this forbearance request is approved, I want to (check one):
  ☐ Temporarily stop making payments; or
  ☐ Make smaller payments of $_____ per month.

- If this forbearance request is approved, I am requesting that the U.S. Department of Education (ED) grant a forbearance on my loan(s) beginning (MM-DD-YYYY) |__|__|-|__|__|-|__|__|__|__| and ending (MM-DD-YYYY) |__|__|-|__|__|-|__|__|__|__| for a period not to exceed 12 months. At the end of the forbearance, I may apply to renew the forbearance if I am still experiencing a financial hardship.

SECTION 3: BORROWER / ENDORSER UNDERSTANDINGS AND CERTIFICATIONS

I understand that the following terms and conditions apply to this forbearance request:
(1) I will continue to receive billing statements for my current payment amount which I must pay until I am notified by the Direct Loan Servicing Center that my forbearance request has been granted.
(2) ED may grant me a forbearance on my loans for up to 60 days, if necessary, for the collection and processing of documentation related to my forbearance request. ED will not capitalize interest that accrues during this forbearance.
(3) ED will not grant this forbearance request unless this form is completed and any required documentation is provided.
(4) During the forbearance period, I am not required to make payments of loan principal and interest, but interest will be charged on all of my loans.
(5) If I requested a temporary suspension of payments, I will receive a quarterly interest statement, and I may pay the interest at any time. If I do not pay the interest that accrues on my loan(s), it will be capitalized at the end of the forbearance period.
(6) If I requested a reduced payment forbearance, I will receive a monthly bill for the requested payment amount until the forbearance ends, and any unpaid interest that has accrued during the period will be capitalized at the end of the forbearance period.

I certify that:
(1) The information I have provided on this form is true and correct.
(2) I will provide additional documentation to the Direct Loan Servicing Center, as required, to support my continued forbearance status.
(3) I will notify the Direct Loan Servicing Center immediately when the condition that qualified me for the forbearance ends.
(4) I have read, understand, and meet the eligibility requirements of the forbearance for which I have applied.
(5) Upon termination of this forbearance, I will repay my loan(s) according to the terms of my promissory note and repayment schedule.

BORROWER'S OR ENDORSER'S SIGNATURE: _____ **DATE:** _____

SECTION 4: INSTRUCTIONS FOR COMPLETING THE GENERAL FORBEARANCE REQUEST FORM

- Type or print using dark ink. Report dates as month-day-year. For example, show "January 31, 2007" as "01-31-2007". **REMEMBER TO SIGN AND DATE THE FORM.**

Send the completed form and any required documentation to: **U.S. Department of Education** **Direct Loan Servicing Center** **P.O. Box 5609** **Greenville, TX 75403--5609**	If you need help completing this form, call: **1-800-848-0979** If you use a telecommunications device for the deaf (TDD), call: **1-800-848-0983** Direct Loan Servicing Center web site: **www.dl.ed.gov**

SECTION 5: DEFINITIONS

- If unpaid interest is **capitalized**, this means that it is added to the principal balance of your loan(s). This will increase the principal amount and the total cost of your loan(s).
- An **endorser** is someone who promises to repay a PLUS loan or the PLUS portion of a consolidation loan if the parent borrower does not repay it.
- A **forbearance** allows you to temporarily postpone making payments on your loan(s) or lets you temporarily make smaller payments than previously scheduled. Interest is charged during a forbearance on all types of Direct Loans.
- The **William D. Ford Federal Direct Loan (Direct Loan) Program** includes Federal Direct Stafford/Ford (Direct Subsidized) Loans, Federal Direct Unsubsidized Stafford/Ford (Direct Unsubsidized) Loans, Federal Direct PLUS (Direct PLUS) Loans, and Federal Direct Consolidation (Direct Consolidation) Loans. These loans are known collectively as "Direct Loans".

SECTION 6: IMPORTANT NOTICES

Privacy Act Notice. The Privacy Act of 1974 (5 U.S.C. 552a) requires that the following notice be provided to you:

The authority for collecting the requested information from and about you is §451 et seq. of the Higher Education Act (HEA) of 1965, as amended (20 U.S.C. 1087a et seq.) and the authorities for collecting and using your Social Security Number (SSN) are §484(a)(4) of the HEA (20 U.S.C. 1091(a)(4)) and 31 U.S.C. 7701(b). Participating in the William D. Ford Federal Direct Loan (Direct Loan) Program and giving us your SSN are voluntary, but you must provide the requested information, including your SSN, to participate.

The principal purposes for collecting the information on this form, including your SSN, are to verify your identity, to determine your eligibility to receive a loan or a benefit on a loan (such as a deferment, forbearance, discharge, or forgiveness) under the Direct Loan Program, to permit the servicing of your loan(s), and, if it becomes necessary, to locate you and to collect and report on your loan(s) if your loan(s) become delinquent or in default. We also use your SSN as an account identifier and to permit you to access your account information electronically.

The information in your file may be disclosed, on a case by case basis or under a computer matching program, to third parties as authorized under routine uses in the appropriate systems of records notices. The routine uses of this information include, but are not limited to, its disclosure to federal, state, or local agencies, to private parties such as relatives, present and former employers, business and personal associates, to consumer reporting agencies, to financial and educational institutions, and to guaranty agencies in order to verify your identity, to determine your eligibility to receive a loan or a benefit on a loan, to permit the servicing or collection of your loan(s), to enforce the terms of the loan(s), to investigate possible fraud and to verify compliance with federal student financial aid program regulations, or to locate you if you become delinquent in your loan payments or if you default. To provide default rate calculations, disclosures may be made to guaranty agencies, to financial and educational institutions, or to state agencies. To provide financial aid history information, disclosures may be made to educational institutions. To assist program administrators with tracking refunds and cancellations, disclosures may be made to guaranty agencies, to financial and educational institutions, or to federal or state agencies. To provide a standardized method for educational institutions efficiently to submit student enrollment status, disclosures may be made to guaranty agencies or to financial and educational institutions. To counsel you in repayment efforts, disclosures may be made to guaranty agencies, to financial and educational institutions, or to federal, state, or local agencies.

In the event of litigation, we may send records to the Department of Justice, a court, adjudicative body, counsel, party, or witness if the disclosure is relevant and necessary to the litigation. If this information, either alone or with other information, indicates a potential violation of law, we may send it to the appropriate authority for action. We may send information to members of Congress if you ask them to help you with federal student aid questions. In circumstances involving employment complaints, grievances, or disciplinary actions, we may disclose relevant records to adjudicate or investigate the issues. If provided for by a collective bargaining agreement, we may disclose records to a labor organization recognized under 5 U.S.C. Chapter 71. Disclosures may be made to our contractors for the purpose of performing any programmatic function that requires disclosure of records. Before making any such disclosure, we will require the contractor to maintain Privacy Act safeguards. Disclosures may also be made to qualified researchers under Privacy Act safeguards.

Paperwork Reduction Notice. According to the Paperwork Reduction Act of 1995, no persons are required to respond to a collection of information unless it displays a currently valid OMB control number. The valid OMB control number for this information collection is 1845-0031. The time required to complete this information collection is estimated to average 0.2 hours (12 minutes) per response, including the time to review instructions, search existing data resources, gather and maintain the data needed, and complete and review the information collection. **If you have comments concerning the accuracy of the time estimate(s) or suggestions for improving this form, please write to:** U.S. Department of Education, Washington, DC 20202-4651. ***Do not send the completed form to this address.***

If you have questions about the status of ***your individual submission of this form***, contact the Direct Loan Servicing Center (see Section 4).

Student Assistance Forms

Appx. D.3.1

D.3 Discharge Forms and Letters

D.3.1 Closed School

LOAN DISCHARGE APPLICATION: SCHOOL CLOSURE

OMB No. 1845-0015
Form Approved
Exp. Date 10/31/2011

Federal Family Education Loan Program / William D. Ford Federal Direct Loan Program / Federal Perkins Loan Program

WARNING: Any person who knowingly makes a false statement or misrepresentation on this form or on any accompanying documents will be subject to penalties that may include fines, imprisonment, or both, under the U.S. Criminal Code and 20 U.S.C. 1097.

SECTION 1: BORROWER IDENTIFICATION

Please enter or correct the following information.

SSN ___-__-____
Name _____
Address _____
City, State, Zip Code _____
Telephone - Home ( ) _____
Telephone - Other ( ) _____
E-mail (optional) _____

SECTION 2: STUDENT INFORMATION

Before completing this section, carefully read the entire form, including the instructions, definitions, and terms and conditions in Sections 4, 5, and 6 on this form. If you are a student borrower applying for loan discharge, begin with Item 3. If you are a parent borrower applying for a PLUS loan discharge, begin with Item 1.

1. Student Name (Last, First, MI): _____
2. Student SSN: ___-__-____
3. Closed School Name: _____
4. Date school closed (if known): __-__-____
5. Closed School Address (street, city, state, zip code): _____
6. Dates of attendance at the closed school: From __-__-____ To __-__-____
7. Name of the program of study that you (or, for parent PLUS borrowers, the student) were enrolled in at the time the school closed: _____
8. Did you (or, for parent PLUS borrowers, the student) complete the program of study at the closed school? ❑ Yes ❑ No
   If No, check all reasons that apply:
   ❑ You (or, for parent PLUS borrowers, the student) were on an approved leave of absence when the school closed:
   From __-__-____ To __-__-____
   ❑ The school closed while you (or, for parent PLUS borrowers, the student) were still enrolled.
   ❑ You (or, for parent PLUS borrowers, the student) withdrew from the school on: __-__-____
   ❑ Other (please explain): _____
9. Did you (or, for parent PLUS borrowers, the student) complete or are you in the process of completing the program of study or a comparable program of study at another school? ❑ Yes ❑ No **If Yes, complete (a) and (b) below:**
   (a) Did the other school give you (or, for parent PLUS borrowers, the student) credit for training received at the closed school by allowing transfer of credits or hours earned at the closed school, or by any other means? ❑ Yes ❑ No
   (b) Were you (or, for parent PLUS borrowers, the student) required to start the program over from the beginning at the other school? ❑ Yes ❑ No
10. Did the holder of your loan receive any money back (a refund) from the school on your behalf? ❑ Yes ❑ No ❑ Don't Know
    If Yes, give the amount and explain why the money was refunded: _____
11. Did you (or, for parent PLUS borrowers, the student) make any monetary claim with, or receive any payment from, the school or any third party (see definition in Section 5) in connection with enrollment or attendance at the school? ❑ Yes ❑ No ❑ Don't Know   If Yes, please provide the following information:
    (a) Name/address/telephone number of the party with whom the claim was made or from whom payment was received: _____
    _____
    (b) Amount/status of claim: _____   (c) Amount of payment received: $ _____
    (Write "none" if no payment was received.)

SECTION 3: BORROWER CERTIFICATION

My signature below certifies that I have read and agree to the terms and conditions that apply to this loan discharge, as specified in Section 6 on the following page. Under penalty of perjury, I certify that all of the information I have provided on this form and in any accompanying documentation is true and accurate to the best of my knowledge and belief.

Borrower's Signature: _____   Today's Date: _____

Page 1 of 2

523

SECTION 4: INSTRUCTIONS FOR COMPLETING THE APPLICATION

Type or print using dark ink. Enter dates as month-day-year (mm-dd-yyyy). Use only numbers. Example: June 24, 2006 = 06-24-2006. If you need more space to answer any of the items, continue on separate sheets of paper and attach them to this form. Indicate the number of the item(s) you are answering and include your name and social security number (SSN) on all attached pages.

Sign and date the form, then send the completed form and any attachments to the address in Section 8.

SECTION 5: DEFINITIONS

- The **Federal Family Education Loan (FFEL) Program** includes Federal Stafford Loans (both subsidized and unsubsidized), Federal Supplemental Loans for Students (SLS), Federal PLUS Loans, and Federal Consolidation Loans.
- The **William D. Ford Federal Direct Loan (Direct Loan) Program** includes Federal Direct Stafford/Ford Loans (Direct Subsidized Loans), Federal Direct Unsubsidized Stafford/Ford Loans (Direct Unsubsidized Loans), Federal Direct PLUS Loans (Direct PLUS Loans), and Federal Direct Consolidation Loans (Direct Consolidation Loans).
- The **Federal Perkins Loan (Perkins Loan) Program** includes Federal Perkins Loans and National Direct Student Loans (NDSL).
- The **date a school closed** is the date that the school stopped providing educational instruction in **all programs**, as determined by the U.S. Department of Education (the Department).
- The **holder** of a borrower's FFEL Program loan(s) may be a lender, a guaranty agency, or the Department. The holder of a borrower's Direct Loan Program loan(s) is the Department. The holder of a borrower's Perkins Loan Program loan(s) may be a school or the Department.
- **Loan discharge** due to school closure cancels the obligation of a borrower (and endorser, if applicable) to repay the remaining balance on a FFEL Program, Direct Loan Program, or Perkins Loan Program loan, and qualifies the borrower for reimbursement of any amounts paid voluntarily or through forced collection on the loan. For consolidation loans, only the amount of the underlying loans (the loans that were consolidated) that were used to pay for the program of study listed in Item 7 will be considered for discharge. The loan holder reports the discharge to all credit reporting agencies to which the holder previously reported the status of the loan.
- The **student** refers to the student for whom a parent borrower obtained a Federal PLUS Loan or Direct PLUS Loan.
- **Dates of attendance**: The "to" date means the last date that you (or, for parent PLUS borrowers, the student) actually attended the closed school.
- **Program of study** means the instructional program leading to a degree or certificate in which you (or, for parent PLUS borrowers, the student) were enrolled.
- **Third party** refers to any entity that may provide reimbursement for a refund owed by the school, such as a State or other agency offering a tuition recovery program or a holder of a performance bond.

SECTION 6: TERMS AND CONDITIONS FOR LOAN DISCHARGE BASED ON SCHOOL CLOSURE

- I received FFEL Program, Direct Loan Program, or Perkins Loan Program loan funds on or after January 1, 1986, to attend (or, if I am a parent PLUS borrower, for the student to attend) the school identified as "closed school" in Section 2 of this form. Those funds were either received by me directly, or applied as a credit to the amount owed to the school. I (or, if I am a parent PLUS borrower, the student) was enrolled at that school or on an approved leave of absence on the date that it closed, or withdrew from the school not more than 90 days before it closed (or longer if authorized by the Department). Due to the school's closure, I (or, if I am a PLUS borrower, the student) did not complete the program of study at that school. I (or, if I am a parent PLUS borrower, the student) did not complete and am not in the process of completing that program of study or a comparable program at another school by transferring credits or hours earned at the closed school to another school, or by any other means by which I (or, if I am a parent PLUS borrower, the student) benefited from the training provided by the closed school.
- I will provide, upon request, testimony, a sworn statement, or other documentation reasonably available to me that demonstrates to the satisfaction of the Department or its designee that I meet the qualifications for loan discharge based on school closure, or that supports any representation that I made on this form or on any accompanying documents.
- I agree to cooperate with the Department or its designee regarding any enforcement actions related to my request for loan discharge.
- I understand that my request for loan discharge may be denied, or my discharge may be revoked if I fail to provide testimony, a sworn statement, or documentation upon request, or if I provide testimony, a sworn statement, or documentation that does not support the material representations I have made, or if I (or, if I am a parent PLUS borrower, the student) completed or am in the process of completing the program of study or a comparable program at another school through transfer of credits or hours from the closed school or by any other means by which I (or, if I am a parent PLUS borrower, the student) benefited from the training provided by the closed school.
- I further understand that if my loan(s) is discharged based on any false, fictitious, or fraudulent statements that I knowingly made on this form or on any accompanying documents, I may be subject to civil and criminal penalties under applicable federal law.
- I hereby assign and transfer to the Department any right to a refund on the discharged loan(s) that I may have from the school identified in Section 2 of this form and/or any owners, affiliates, or assigns of the school, and from any third party that may pay claims for a refund because of the actions of the school, up to the amount discharged by the Department on my loan(s).

SECTION 7: IMPORTANT NOTICES

Privacy Act Disclosure Notice: The Privacy Act of 1974 (5 U.S.C. 552a) requires that the following notice be provided to you:

The authorities for collecting the requested information from and about you are §421 et seq., §451 et seq. and §461 et seq. of the Higher Education Act of 1965, as amended (20 U.S.C. 1071 et seq., 20 U.S.C. 1087a et seq., and 20 U.S.C. 1087aa et seq.) and the authorities for collecting and using your Social Security Number (SSN) are §§428B(f) and 484(a)(4) of the HEA (20 U.S.C. 1078-2(f) and 20 U.S.C. 1091(a)(4)) and 31 U.S.C. 7701(b). Participating in the Federal Family Education Loan (FFEL) Program, the William D. Ford Federal Direct Loan (Direct Loan) Program, or the Federal Perkins Loan (Perkins Loan) Program and giving us your SSN are voluntary, but you must provide the requested information, including your SSN, to participate.

The principal purposes for collecting the information on this form, including your SSN, are to verify your identity, to determine your eligibility to receive a loan or a benefit on a loan (such as a deferment, forbearance, discharge, or forgiveness) under the FFEL, Direct Loan, and/or Perkins Loan Programs, to permit the servicing of your loan(s), and, if it becomes necessary, to locate you and to collect and report on your loan(s) if your loan(s) become delinquent or in default. We also use your SSN as an account identifier and to permit you to access your account information electronically.

The information in your file may be disclosed, on a case-by-case basis or under a computer matching program, to third parties as authorized under routine uses in the appropriate systems of records notices. The routine uses of this information include, but are not limited to, its disclosure to federal, state, or local agencies, to private parties such as relatives, present and former employers, business and personal associates, to consumer reporting agencies, to financial and educational institutions, and to guaranty agencies in order to verify your identity, to determine your eligibility to receive a loan or a benefit on a loan, to permit the servicing or collection of your loan(s), to enforce the terms of the loan(s), to investigate possible fraud and to verify compliance with federal student financial aid program regulations, or to locate you if you become delinquent in your loan payments or if you default. To provide default rate calculations, disclosures may be made to guaranty agencies, to financial and educational institutions, or to state agencies. To provide financial aid history information, disclosures may be made to educational institutions. To assist program administrators with tracking refunds and cancellations, disclosures may be made to guaranty agencies, to financial and educational institutions, or to federal or state agencies. To provide a standardized method for educational institutions to efficiently submit student enrollment status, disclosures may be made to guaranty agencies or to financial and educational institutions. To counsel you in repayment efforts, disclosures may be made to guaranty agencies, to financial and educational institutions, or to federal, state, or local agencies.

In the event of litigation, we may send records to the Department of Justice, a court, adjudicative body, counsel, party, or witness if the disclosure is relevant and necessary to the litigation. If this information, either alone or with other information, indicates a potential violation of law, we may send it to the appropriate authority for action. We may send information to members of Congress if you ask them to help you with federal student aid questions. In circumstances involving employment complaints, grievances, or disciplinary actions, we may disclose relevant records to adjudicate or investigate the issues. If provided for by a collective bargaining agreement, we may disclose records to a labor organization recognized under 5 U.S.C. Chapter 71. Disclosures may be made to our contractors for the purpose of performing any programmatic function that requires disclosure of records. Before making any such disclosure, we will require the contractor to maintain Privacy Act safeguards. Disclosures may also be made to qualified researchers under Privacy Act safeguards.

Paperwork Reduction Notice: According to the Paperwork Reduction Act of 1995, no persons are required to respond to a collection of information unless it displays a currently valid OMB control number. The valid OMB control number for this information collection is 1845-0015. The time required to complete this information collection is estimated to average 0.5 hours (30 minutes) per response, including the time to review instructions, search existing data resources, gather and maintain the data needed, and complete and review the information collection. **If you have any comments concerning the accuracy of the time estimate(s) or suggestions for improving this application, please write to:** U.S. Department of Education, Washington, DC 20202-4537. If you have questions regarding the status of your individual submission of this application, contact your loan holder (see Section 8).

SECTION 8: WHERE TO SEND THE COMPLETED LOAN DISCHARGE APPLICATION

Send the completed loan discharge application and any attachments to:
(If no address is shown, return to your loan holder.)

If you need help completing this form, call:

Student Assistance Forms

Appx. D.3.2

D.3.2 False Certification of Ability to Benefit

**LOAN DISCHARGE APPLICATION:
FALSE CERTIFICATION (ABILITY TO BENEFIT)**

OMB No. 1845-0015
Form Approved
Exp. Date 10/31/2011

Federal Family Education Loan Program / William D. Ford Federal Direct Loan Program

WARNING: Any person who knowingly makes a false statement or misrepresentation on this form or on any accompanying documents will be subject to penalties that may include fines, imprisonment, or both, under the U.S. Criminal Code and 20 U.S.C. 1097.

SECTION 1: BORROWER IDENTIFICATION

Please enter or correct the following information.

SSN

Name

Address

City, State, Zip Code

Telephone - Home (   )

Telephone - Other (   )

E-mail (optional)

SECTION 2: STUDENT INFORMATION

Before completing this section, carefully read the entire form, including the instructions, definitions, and terms and conditions in Sections 4, 5, and 6 on this form. If you are a student borrower applying for loan discharge, begin with Item 3. If you are a parent borrower applying for a PLUS loan discharge, begin with Item 1.

1. Student Name (Last, First, MI): _____
2. Student SSN: _____
3. School Name: _____
4. School Address (street, city, state, zip code): _____
5. Dates of attendance at school: From _____ To _____
6. Name of the program of study that you (or, for parent PLUS borrowers, the student) were enrolled in at the school: _____
7. Did you (or, for parent PLUS borrowers, the student) have a high school diploma or GED at the time of enrollment at the school?
   ❑ Yes   ❑ No   NOTE: *If Yes, you are not eligible for a loan discharge based on false certification of ability to benefit.*
8. Did you (or, for parent PLUS borrowers, the student) receive a GED before completing the program of study at the school?
   ❑ Yes   ❑ No   If Yes, date GED received: _____
9. Before you (or, for parent PLUS borrowers, the student) were admitted to the school, did the school give an entrance examination to test your (or, for parent PLUS borrowers, the student's) ability to benefit from the program of study listed in Item 6?
   ❑ Yes   ❑ No   ❑ Don't Know   If No or Don't Know, go to Item 10.
   (a) Give the date of the test if you know it: (b) Give the name of the test if you know it: (c) Give the score on the test if you know it:

   (d) Did anything appear improper about the way the test was given or scored?   ❑ Yes   ❑ No
   If Yes, explain in detail what appeared improper, and provide the name, telephone number and address of anyone who can support your statement (if you need more space, see the instructions in Section 4): _____

10. Did you (or, for parent PLUS borrowers, the student) complete a developmental or remedial program at the school?
    ❑ Yes   ❑ No   ❑ Don't Know   If Yes, list the program name, dates, courses, and grades earned: _____

11. Did the holder of your loan receive any money back (a refund) from the school on your behalf?   ❑ Yes   ❑ No   ❑ Don't Know
    If Yes, give the amount and explain why the money was refunded: _____

12. Did you (or, for parent PLUS borrowers, the student) make any monetary claim with, or receive any payment from, the school or any third party (see definition in Section 5) in connection with enrollment or attendance at the school?   ❑ Yes   ❑ No   ❑ Don't Know   If Yes, please provide the following information:
    (a) Name/address/telephone number of the party with whom the claim was made or from whom payment was received: _____

    (b) Amount/status of claim: _____   (c) Amount of payment received: $ _____
    (Write "none" if no payment was received.)

SECTION 3: BORROWER CERTIFICATION

My signature below certifies that I have read and agree to the terms and conditions that apply to this loan discharge, as specified in Section 6 on the following page. Under penalty of perjury, I certify that all of the information I have provided on this form and in any accompanying documentation is true and accurate to the best of my knowledge and belief.

Borrower's Signature: _____   Today's Date: _____

SECTION 4: INSTRUCTIONS FOR COMPLETING THE APPLICATION

Type or print using dark ink. Enter dates as month-day-year (mm-dd-yyyy). Use only numbers. Example: June 24, 2006 = 06-24-2006. If you need more space to answer any of the items, continue on separate sheets of paper and attach them to this form. Indicate the number of the item(s) you are answering and include your name and social security number (SSN) on all attached pages.
Sign and date the form, then send the completed form and any attachments to the address in Section 8.

SECTION 5: DEFINITIONS

- The **Federal Family Education Loan (FFEL) Program** includes Federal Stafford Loans (both subsidized and unsubsidized), Federal Supplemental Loans for Students (SLS), Federal PLUS Loans, and Federal Consolidation Loans.
- The **William D. Ford Federal Direct Loan (Direct Loan) Program** includes Federal Direct Stafford/Ford Loans (Direct Subsidized Loans), Federal Direct Unsubsidized Stafford/Ford Loans (Direct Unsubsidized Loans), Federal Direct PLUS Loans (Direct PLUS Loans), and Federal Direct Consolidation Loans (Direct Consolidation Loans).
- The **holder** of a borrower's FFEL Program loan(s) may be a lender, a guaranty agency, or the U.S. Department of Education (the Department). The holder of a borrower's Direct Loan Program loan(s) is the Department.
- **Loan discharge** due to false certification of ability to benefit cancels the obligation of a borrower (and endorser, if applicable) to repay the remaining balance on a FFEL Program or Direct Loan Program loan, and qualifies the borrower for reimbursement of any amounts paid voluntarily or through forced collection on the loan. For consolidation loans, only the amount of the underlying loans (the loans that were consolidated) that were used to pay for the program of study listed in Item 6 will be considered for discharge. The loan holder reports the discharge to all credit reporting agencies to which the holder previously reported the status of the loan.
- The **student** refers to the student for whom a parent borrower obtained a Federal PLUS Loan or Direct PLUS Loan.
- **Program of study** means the instructional program leading to a degree or certificate in which you (or, for PLUS borrowers, the student) were enrolled.
- **Third party** refers to any entity that may provide reimbursement for a refund owed by the school, such as a State or other agency offering a tuition recovery program or a holder of a performance bond.

SECTION 6: TERMS AND CONDITIONS FOR LOAN DISCHARGE BASED ON FALSE CERTIFICATION (ABILITY TO BENEFIT)

- I received FFEL Program or Direct Loan Program loan funds on or after January 1, 1986, to attend (or, if I am a parent PLUS borrower, for the student to attend) the school identified in Section 2 of this form. Those funds were either received by me directly, or applied as a credit to the amount owed to the school.
- I will provide, upon request, testimony, a sworn statement, or other documentation reasonably available to me that demonstrates to the satisfaction of the Department or its designee that I meet the qualifications for loan discharge based on false certification of ability to benefit, or that supports any representation that I made on this form or on any accompanying documents.
- I agree to cooperate with the Department or its designee regarding any enforcement actions related to my request for loan discharge.
- I understand that my request for loan discharge may be denied, or my discharge may be revoked, if I fail to provide testimony, a sworn statement, or documentation upon request, or if I provide testimony, a sworn statement, or documentation that does not support the material representations I have made on this form or on any accompanying documents.
- I further understand that if my loan(s) is discharged based on any false, fictitious, or fraudulent statements that I knowingly made on this form or on any accompanying documents, I may be subject to civil and criminal penalties under applicable federal law.
- I hereby assign and transfer to the Department any right to a refund on the discharged loan(s) that I may have from the school identified in Section 2 of this form and/or any owners, affiliates, or assigns of the school, and from any third party that may pay claims for a refund because of the actions of the school, up to the amount discharged by the Department on my loan(s).

SECTION 7: IMPORTANT NOTICES

Privacy Act Disclosure Notice: The Privacy Act of 1974 (5 U.S.C. 552a) requires that the following notice be provided to you:

The authorities for collecting the requested information from and about you are §421 et seq. and §451 et seq. of the Higher Education Act of 1965, as amended (20 U.S.C. 1071 et seq., and 20 U.S.C. 1087a et seq.) and the authorities for collecting and using your Social Security Number (SSN) are §§428B(f) and 484(a)(4) of the HEA (20 U.S.C. 1078-2(f) and 20 U.S.C. 1091(a)(4)) and 31 U.S.C. 7701(b). Participating in the Federal Family Education Loan (FFEL) Program or the William D. Ford Federal Direct Loan (Direct Loan) Program and giving us your SSN are voluntary, but you must provide the requested information, including your SSN, to participate.

The principal purposes for collecting the information on this form, including your SSN, are to verify your identity, to determine your eligibility to receive a loan or a benefit on a loan (such as a deferment, forbearance, discharge, or forgiveness) under the FFEL and/or Direct Loan Programs, to permit the servicing of your loan(s), and, if it becomes necessary, to locate you and to collect and report on your loan(s) if your loan(s) become delinquent or in default. We also use your SSN as an account identifier and to permit you to access your account information electronically.

The information in your file may be disclosed, on a case-by-case basis or under a computer matching program, to third parties as authorized under routine uses in the appropriate systems of records notices. The routine uses of this information include, but are not limited to, its disclosure to federal, state, or local agencies, to private parties such as relatives, present and former employers, business and personal associates, to consumer reporting agencies, to financial and educational institutions, and to guaranty agencies in order to verify your identity, to determine your eligibility to receive a loan or a benefit on a loan, to permit the servicing or collection of your loan(s), to enforce the terms of the loan(s), to investigate possible fraud and to verify compliance with federal student financial aid program regulations, or to locate you if you become delinquent in your loan payments or if you default. To provide default rate calculations, disclosures may be made to guaranty agencies, to financial and educational institutions, or to state agencies. To provide financial aid history information, disclosures may be made to educational institutions. To assist program administrators with tracking refunds and cancellations, disclosures may be made to guaranty agencies, to financial and educational institutions, or to federal or state agencies. To provide a standardized method for educational institutions to efficiently submit student enrollment status, disclosures may be made to guaranty agencies or to financial and educational institutions. To counsel you in repayment efforts, disclosures may be made to guaranty agencies, to financial and educational institutions, or to federal, state, or local agencies.

In the event of litigation, we may send records to the Department of Justice, a court, adjudicative body, counsel, party, or witness if the disclosure is relevant and necessary to the litigation. If this information, either alone or with other information, indicates a potential violation of law, we may send it to the appropriate authority for action. We may send information to members of Congress if you ask them to help you with federal student aid questions. In circumstances involving employment complaints, grievances, or disciplinary actions, we may disclose relevant records to adjudicate or investigate the issues. If provided for by a collective bargaining agreement, we may disclose records to a labor organization recognized under 5 U.S.C. Chapter 71. Disclosures may be made to our contractors for the purpose of performing any programmatic function that requires disclosure of records. Before making any such disclosure, we will require the contractor to maintain Privacy Act safeguards. Disclosures may also be made to qualified researchers under Privacy Act safeguards.

Paperwork Reduction Notice: According to the Paperwork Reduction Act of 1995, no persons are required to respond to a collection of information unless it displays a currently valid OMB control number. The valid OMB control number for this information collection is 1845-0015. The time required to complete this information collection is estimated to average 0.5 hours (30 minutes) per response, including the time to review instructions, search existing data resources, gather and maintain the data needed, and complete and review the information collection.
If you have any comments concerning the accuracy of the time estimate(s) or suggestions for improving this application, please write to: U.S. Department of Education, Washington, DC 20202-4537.

If you have questions regarding the status of your individual submission of this application, contact your loan holder (see Section 8).

SECTION 8: WHERE TO SEND THE COMPLETED LOAN DISCHARGE APPLICATION

Send the completed loan discharge application and any attachments to:
(If no address is shown, return to your loan holder.)

If you need help completing this form, call:

Student Assistance Forms Appx. D.3.3

D.3.3 False Certification (Disqualifying Status)

LOAN DISCHARGE APPLICATION:
FALSE CERTIFICATION (DISQUALIFYING STATUS)
Federal Family Education Loan Program / William D. Ford Federal Direct Loan Program

WARNING: Any person who knowingly makes a false statement or misrepresentation on this form or on any accompanying documents will be subject to penalties that may include fines, imprisonment, or both, under the U.S. Criminal Code and 20 U.S.C. 1097.

OMB No. 1845-0015
Form Approved
Exp. Date 10/31/2011

SECTION 1: BORROWER IDENTIFICATION

Please enter or correct the following information.
SSN ___ - ___ - ___
Name ___
Address ___
City, State, Zip Code ___
Telephone - Home ( ) ___
Telephone - Other ( ) ___
E-mail (optional) ___

SECTION 2: STUDENT INFORMATION

Before completing this section, carefully read the entire form, including the instructions, definitions, and terms and conditions in Sections 4, 5, and 6 on this form. If you are a student borrower applying for loan discharge, begin with Item 3. If you are a parent borrower applying for a PLUS loan discharge, begin with Item 1.

1. Student Name (Last, First, MI): ___
2. Student SSN: ___ - ___ - ___
3. School Name: ___
4. School Address (street, city, state, zip code): ___
5. Dates of attendance at the school: From ___ - ___ - ___ To ___ - ___ - ___
6. Name of the program of study that you (or, for parent PLUS borrowers, the student) were enrolled in when the school certified or originated the loan that you are requesting to have discharged: ___
7. To qualify for a loan discharge based on false certification due to a disqualifying status, you (or, for parent PLUS borrowers, the student) must have been unable – at the time the school certified or originated your loan – to meet the **legal requirements for employment** in your state of residence (or, for parent PLUS borrowers, in the student's state of residence) in the occupation for which the program of study was intended because of age, a physical or mental condition, criminal record, or other reason. Indicate your disqualifying status by checking the appropriate box(es) below:
❑ Age ❑ Physical condition ❑ Mental condition ❑ Criminal record ❑ Other (please specify): ___

Important: You must provide documentation to prove that you (or, for parent PLUS borrowers, the student) had the disqualifying status at the time the school certified or originated your loan. **Also, provide as much information as possible about the state legal requirements for employment that you (or, for parent PLUS borrowers, the student) could not meet. Include the title and/or section number of the specific state law or regulation, or attach a copy of the law or regulation.** You may obtain this information from the appropriate state agency, such as the consumer protection office or department of labor and employment, from a public library, or from an Internet site that contains state laws and regulations. ___

8. (a) Before certifying or originating the loan, did the school ask you (or, for parent PLUS borrowers, the student) if the disqualifying status explained in Item 7 existed?
❑ Yes ❑ No ❑ Don't Know
(b) Did you (or, for parent PLUS borrowers, the student) inform the school of the disqualifying status before the loan was certified or originated?
❑ Yes ❑ No

9. Did the holder of your loan receive any money back (a refund) from the school on your behalf? ❑ Yes ❑ No ❑ Don't Know
If Yes, give the amount and explain why the money was refunded: ___

10. Did you (or, for parent PLUS borrowers, the student) make any monetary claim with, or receive any payment from, the school or any third party (see definition in Section 5) in connection with enrollment or attendance at the school: ❑ Yes ❑ No ❑ Don't Know If Yes, please provide the following information:
(a) Name/address/telephone number of the party with whom the claim was made or from whom payment was received: ___

(b) Amount/status of claim: ___ (c) Amount of payment received: $ ___
(Write "none" if no payment was received.)

SECTION 3: BORROWER CERTIFICATION

My signature below certifies that I have read and agree to the terms and conditions that apply to this loan discharge, as specified in Section 6 on the following page. Under penalty of perjury, I certify that all of the information I have provided on this form and in any accompanying documentation is true and accurate to the best of my knowledge and belief.

Borrower's Signature: ___ Today's Date: ___

SECTION 4: INSTRUCTIONS FOR COMPLETING THE APPLICATION

Type or print using dark ink. Enter dates as month-day-year (mm-dd-yyyy). Use only numbers. Example: June 24, 2006 = 06-24-2006. If you need more space to answer any of the items, continue on separate sheets of paper and attach them to this form. Indicate the number of the item(s) you are answering and include your name and social security number (SSN) on all attached pages.

Sign and date the form, then send the completed form and any attachments to the address in Section 8.

SECTION 5: DEFINITIONS

- The **Federal Family Education Loan (FFEL) Program** includes Federal Stafford Loans (both subsidized and unsubsidized), Federal Supplemental Loans for Students (SLS), Federal PLUS Loans, and Federal Consolidation Loans.
- The **William D. Ford Federal Direct Loan (Direct Loan) Program** includes Federal Direct Stafford/Ford Loans (Direct Subsidized Loans), Federal Direct Unsubsidized Stafford/Ford Loans (Direct Unsubsidized Loans), Federal Direct PLUS Loans (Direct PLUS Loans), and Federal Direct Consolidation Loans (Direct Consolidation Loans).
- The **holder** of a borrower's FFEL Program loan(s) may be a lender, a guaranty agency, or the U.S. Department of Education (the Department). The holder of a borrower's Direct Loan Program loan(s) is the Department.
- **Loan discharge** due to false certification (disqualifying status) cancels the obligation of a borrower (and endorser, if applicable) to repay the remaining balance on a FFEL Program or Direct Loan Program loan, and qualifies the borrower for reimbursement of any amounts paid voluntarily or through forced collection on the loan. For consolidation loans, only the amount of the underlying loans (the loans that were consolidated) that were used to pay for the program of study listed in Item 6 will be considered for discharge. The loan holder reports the discharge to all credit reporting agencies to which the holder previously reported the status of the loan.
- The **student** refers to the student for whom a parent borrower obtained a Federal PLUS Loan or Direct PLUS Loan.
- **Program of study** means the instructional program leading to a degree or certificate in which you (or, for parent PLUS borrowers, the student) were enrolled.
- **Certification and origination** are steps in a school's processing of a loan. In the FFEL Program, a loan is **certified** when the school signs a loan application or submits an electronic loan record to the lender or guaranty agency after determining that the borrower meets all loan eligibility requirements. In the Direct Loan Program, a loan is **originated** when the school creates an electronic loan origination record after determining that the borrower meets all loan eligibility requirements.
- **Third party** refers to any entity that may provide reimbursement for a refund owed by the school, such as a State or other agency offering a tuition recovery program or a holder of a performance bond.

SECTION 6: TERMS AND CONDITIONS FOR LOAN DISCHARGE BASED ON FALSE CERTIFICATION (DISQUALIFYING STATUS)

- I received FFEL or Direct Loan program loan funds on or after January 1, 1986, to attend (or, if I am a parent PLUS borrower, for the student to attend) the school identified in Section 2 of this form. Those funds were either received by me directly, or applied as a credit to the amount owed to the school.
- I will provide, upon request, testimony, a sworn statement, or other documentation reasonably available to me that demonstrates to the satisfaction of the Department or its designee that I meet the qualifications for loan discharge based on false certification (disqualifying status), or that supports any representation that I made on this form or on any accompanying documents.
- I agree to cooperate with the Department or its designee regarding any enforcement actions related to my request for loan discharge.
- I understand that my request for loan discharge may be denied, or my discharge may be revoked, if I fail to provide testimony, a sworn statement, or documentation upon request, or if I provide testimony, a sworn statement, or documentation that does not support the material representations I have made on this form or on any accompanying documents.
- I further understand that if my loan(s) is discharged based on any false, fictitious, or fraudulent statements that I knowingly made on this form or on any accompanying documents, I may be subject to civil and criminal penalties under applicable federal law.
- I hereby assign and transfer to the Department any right to a refund on the discharged loan(s) that I may have from the school identified in Section 2 of this form and/or any owners, affiliates, or assigns of the school, and from any third party that may pay claims for a refund because of the actions of the school, up to the amount discharged by the Department on my loan(s).

SECTION 7: IMPORTANT NOTICES

Privacy Act Disclosure Notice: The Privacy Act of 1974 (5 U.S.C. 552a) requires that the following notice be provided to you:

The authorities for collecting the requested information from and about you are §421 et seq. and §451 et seq. of the Higher Education Act of 1965, as amended (20 U.S.C. 1071 et seq., and 20 U.S.C. 1087a et seq.) and the authorities for collecting and using your Social Security Number (SSN) are §§428B(f) and 484(a)(4) of the HEA (20 U.S.C. 1078-2(f) and 20 U.S.C. 1091(a)(4)) and 31 U.S.C. 7701(b). Participating in the Federal Family Education Loan (FFEL) Program or the William D. Ford Federal Direct Loan (Direct Loan) Program and giving us your SSN are voluntary, but you must provide the requested information, including your SSN, to participate.

The principal purposes for collecting the information on this form, including your SSN, are to verify your identity, to determine your eligibility to receive a loan or a benefit on a loan (such as a deferment, forbearance, discharge, or forgiveness) under the FFEL and/or Direct Loan Programs, to permit the servicing of your loan(s), and, if it becomes necessary, to locate you and to collect and report on your loan(s) if your loan(s) become delinquent or in default. We also use your SSN as an account identifier and to permit you to access your account information electronically.

The information in your file may be disclosed, on a case-by-case basis or under a computer matching program, to third parties as authorized under routine uses in the appropriate systems of records notices. The routine uses of this information include, but are not limited to, its disclosure to federal, state, or local agencies, to private parties such as relatives, present and former employers, business and personal associates, to consumer reporting agencies, to financial and educational institutions, and to guaranty agencies in order to verify your identity, to determine your eligibility to receive a loan or a benefit on a loan, to permit the servicing or collection of your loan(s), to enforce the terms of the loan(s), to investigate possible fraud and to verify compliance with federal student financial aid program regulations, or to locate you if you become delinquent in your loan payments or if you default. To provide default rate calculations, disclosures may be made to guaranty agencies, to financial and educational institutions, or to state agencies. To provide financial aid history information, disclosures may be made to educational institutions. To assist program administrators with tracking refunds and cancellations, disclosures may be made to guaranty agencies, to financial and educational institutions, or to federal or state agencies. To provide a standardized method for educational institutions to efficiently submit student enrollment status, disclosures may be made to guaranty agencies or to financial and educational institutions. To counsel you in repayment efforts, disclosures may be made to guaranty agencies, to financial and educational institutions, or to federal, state, or local agencies.

In the event of litigation, we may send records to the Department of Justice, a court, adjudicative body, counsel, party, or witness if the disclosure is relevant and necessary to the litigation. If this information, either alone or with other information, indicates a potential violation of law, we may send it to the appropriate authority for action. We may send information to members of Congress if you ask them to help you with federal student aid questions. In circumstances involving employment complaints, grievances, or disciplinary actions, we may disclose relevant records to adjudicate or investigate the issues. If provided for by a collective bargaining agreement, we may disclose records to a labor organization recognized under 5 U.S.C. Chapter 71. Disclosures may be made to our contractors for the purpose of performing any programmatic function that requires disclosure of records. Before making any such disclosure, we will require the contractor to maintain Privacy Act safeguards. Disclosures may also be made to qualified researchers under Privacy Act safeguards.

Paperwork Reduction Notice: According to the Paperwork Reduction Act of 1995, no persons are required to respond to a collection of information unless it displays a currently valid OMB control number. The valid OMB control number for this information collection is 1845-0015. The time required to complete this information collection is estimated to average 0.5 hours (30 minutes) per response, including the time to review instructions, search existing data resources, gather and maintain the data needed, and complete and review the information collection. **If you have any comments concerning the accuracy of the time estimate(s) or suggestions for improving this application, please write to:** U.S. Department of Education, Washington, DC 20202-4537

If you have questions regarding the status of your individual submission of this application, contact your loan holder (see Section 8).

SECTION 8: WHERE TO SEND THE COMPLETED LOAN DISCHARGE APPLICATION

Send the completed loan discharge application and any attachments to:
(If no address is shown, return to your loan holder.)

If you need help completing this form, call:

Student Assistance Forms   Appx. D.3.4

D.3.4 False Certification (Unauthorized Signature/Unauthorized Payment)

LOAN DISCHARGE APPLICATION: FALSE CERTIFICATION (UNAUTHORIZED SIGNATURE / UNAUTHORIZED PAYMENT)

OMB No. 1845-0015
Form Approved
Exp. Date 10/31/2011

Federal Family Education Loan Program / William D. Ford Federal Direct Loan Program

WARNING: Any person who knowingly makes a false statement or misrepresentation on this form or on any accompanying documents will be subject to penalties that may include fines, imprisonment, or both, under the U.S. Criminal Code and 20 U.S.C. 1097.

SECTION 1: BORROWER IDENTIFICATION

Please enter or correct the following information.

- SSN
- Name
- Address
- City, State, Zip Code
- Telephone - Home ( )
- Telephone - Other ( )
- E-mail (optional)

SECTION 2: STUDENT INFORMATION

Before completing this section, carefully read the entire form, including the instructions, definitions, and terms and conditions in Sections 4, 5, and 6 on this form. If you are a student borrower applying for loan discharge, begin with Item 3. If you are a parent borrower applying for a PLUS loan discharge, begin with Item 1.

1. Student Name (Last, First, MI): _____
2. Student SSN: _____
3. School Name: _____
4. School Address (street, city, state, zip code): _____
5. Dates of attendance at the school: From _____ To _____
6. Did you sign the application, promissory note, master promissory note (MPN), or combined application/promissory note for your loan(s)? ❑ Yes ❑ No
   If No, on which document(s) did someone else sign your name? ❑ Application ❑ Promissory note ❑ MPN ❑ Combined application/promissory note
7. Did you endorse each loan check or sign your name on each electronic funds transfer authorization or master check authorization?
   ❑ Yes ❑ No ❑ Does Not Apply
   If No, on which document(s) did someone else sign your name? ❑ Loan check ❑ Electronic funds transfer authorization ❑ Master check authorization
   If No, did you (or, for parent PLUS borrowers, the student) ever receive any money from the school, or did the school ever reduce the amount of money that you (or, for parent PLUS borrowers, the student) owed to the school? ❑ Yes ❑ No ❑ Don't Know If Yes, explain (give dates, amounts, and circumstances):
   _____
   If No or Don't Know, explain how you (or, for parent PLUS borrowers, the student) paid the tuition and fees owed to the school:
   _____
8. If you answered No to Item 6 or Item 7, do you know who signed your name on the document(s) checked in Item 6 or 7?
   ❑ Yes ❑ No If Yes, identify the person who signed your name on the document(s).
   School employee or representative (name and position): _____
   Other person (name): _____
   Provide any other information about the circumstances under which another person signed your name:

IMPORTANT: If you did not sign your name on one of the documents listed in Item 6 or Item 7, you must attach documents containing four other samples of your signature in addition to the signature on this application. At least two of these samples must clearly show that your signatures were written within one year before or after the date of the document on which someone else signed your name. Examples of documents that would include both a signature sample and the date that the signature was written include—but are not limited to—cancelled checks, tax returns, and driver's licenses. If you do not provide these signature samples, you cannot be considered for a loan discharge.

9. Did the holder of your loan receive any money back (a refund) from the school on your behalf? ❑ Yes ❑ No ❑ Don't Know
   If Yes, give the amount and explain why the money was refunded: _____

10. Did you (or, for parent PLUS borrowers, the student) make any monetary claim with, or receive any payment from, the school or any third party (see definition in Section 5) in connection with enrollment or attendance at the school: ❑ Yes ❑ No ❑ Don't Know If Yes, please provide the following information:
    (a) Name/address/telephone number of the party with whom the claim was made or from whom payment was received:
    _____
    (b) Amount/status of claim: _____ (c) Amount of payment received: $ _____
    (Write "none" if no payment was received.)

SECTION 3: BORROWER CERTIFICATION

My signature below certifies that I have read and agree to the terms and conditions that apply to this loan discharge, as specified in Section 6 on the following page. Under penalty of perjury, I certify that all of the information I have provided on this form and in any accompanying documentation is true and accurate to the best of my knowledge and belief.

Borrower's Signature: _____   Today's Date: _____

SECTION 4: INSTRUCTIONS FOR COMPLETING THE APPLICATION

Type or print using dark ink. Enter dates as month-day-year (mm-dd-yyyy). Use only numbers. Example: June 24, 2006 = 06-24-2006. If you need more space to answer any of the items, continue on separate sheets of paper and attach them to this form. Indicate the number of the item(s) you are answering and include your name and social security number (SSN) on all attached pages.
Sign and date the form, then send the completed form and any attachments to the address in Section 8.

SECTION 5: DEFINITIONS

- The **Federal Family Education Loan (FFEL) Program** includes Federal Stafford Loans (both subsidized and unsubsidized), Federal Supplemental Loans for Students (SLS), Federal PLUS Loans, and Federal Consolidation Loans.
- The **William D. Ford Federal Direct Loan (Direct Loan) Program** includes Federal Direct Stafford/Ford Loans (Direct Subsidized Loans), Federal Direct Unsubsidized Stafford/Ford Loans (Direct Unsubsidized Loans), Federal Direct PLUS Loans (Direct PLUS Loans), and Federal Direct Consolidation Loans (Direct Consolidation Loans).
- The **holder** of a borrower's FFEL Program loan(s) may be a lender, a guaranty agency, or the U.S. Department of Education (the Department). The holder of a borrower's Direct Loan Program loan(s) is the Department.
- **Unauthorized signature** means that the school, without the borrower's authorization, signed the borrower's name on a loan application or promissory note.
- **Unauthorized payment** means that the school, without the borrower's authorization, endorsed the borrower's loan check or signed the borrower's authorization for electronic funds transfer or master check, and did not give the loan proceeds to the borrower or apply the loan proceeds to charges owed by the student to the school.
- **Loan discharge** due to an unauthorized signature on a loan application or promissory note cancels the obligation of a borrower (and endorser, if applicable) to repay the remaining balance on a FFEL Program or Direct Loan Program loan, and qualifies the borrower for reimbursement of any amounts paid voluntarily or through forced collection on the loan. Discharge due to an unauthorized signature on a loan check, electronic funds transfer authorization, or master check authorization applies only to the amount of the unauthorized payment. For consolidation loans, only the loan amounts associated with the document listed in Section 2, Item 6 or Item 7, will be considered for discharge. The loan holder reports the discharge to all credit reporting agencies to which the holder previously reported the status of the loan.
- The **student** refers to the student for whom a parent borrower obtained a Federal PLUS Loan or Direct PLUS Loan.
- **Third party** refers to any entity that may provide reimbursement for a refund owed by the school, such as a State or other agency offering a tuition recovery program or a holder of a performance bond.

SECTION 6: TERMS AND CONDITIONS FOR LOAN DISCHARGE BASED ON FALSE CERTIFICATION (UNAUTHORIZED SIGNATURE/UNAUTHORIZED PAYMENT)

- The school identified in Section 2 of this form received FFEL Program or Direct Loan Program loan funds on or after January 1, 1986 for me to attend (or, if I am a parent PLUS borrower, for the student to attend) the school. I am applying for a discharge of my FFEL Program or Direct Loan Program loan(s) because the loan application, promissory note, master promissory note, combined application/promissory note, loan disbursement check, electronic funds transfer authorization, or master check authorization were not authorized for the reasons stated in this application.
- I will provide, upon request, testimony, a sworn statement, or other documentation reasonably available to me that demonstrates to the satisfaction of the Department or its designee that I meet the qualifications for loan discharge based on unauthorized signature/unauthorized payment, or that supports any representation that I made on this form or on any accompanying documents.
- I agree to cooperate with the Department or its designee regarding any enforcement actions related to my request for loan discharge.
- I understand that my request for loan discharge may be denied, or my discharge may be revoked, if I fail to provide testimony, a sworn statement, or documentation upon request, or if I provide testimony, a sworn statement, or documentation that does not support the material representations I have made on this form or on any accompanying documents.
- I further understand that if my loan(s) is discharged based on any false, fictitious, or fraudulent statements that I knowingly made on this form or on any accompanying documents, I may be subject to civil and criminal penalties under applicable federal law.
- I hereby assign and transfer to the Department any right to a refund on the discharged loan(s) that I may have from the school identified in Section 2 of this form and/or any owners, affiliates, or assigns of the school, and from any third party that may pay claims for a refund because of the actions of the school, up to the amount discharged by the Department on my loan(s).

SECTION 7: IMPORTANT NOTICES

Privacy Act Disclosure Notice: The Privacy Act of 1974 (5 U.S.C. 552a) requires that the following notice be provided to you:

The authorities for collecting the requested information from and about you are §421 et seq. and §451 et seq. of the Higher Education Act of 1965, as amended (20 U.S.C. 1071 et seq., and 20 U.S.C. 1087a et seq.) and the authorities for collecting and using your Social Security Number (SSN) are §§428B(f) and 484(a)(4) of the HEA (20 U.S.C. 1078-2(f) and 20 U.S.C. 1091(a)(4)) and 31 U.S.C. 7701(b). Participating in the Federal Family Education Loan (FFEL) Program or the William D. Ford Federal Direct Loan (Direct Loan) Program and giving us your SSN are voluntary, but you must provide the requested information, including your SSN, to participate.

The principal purposes for collecting the information on this form, including your SSN, are to verify your identity, to determine your eligibility to receive a loan or a benefit on a loan (such as a deferment, forbearance, discharge, or forgiveness) under the FFEL and/or Direct Loan Programs, to permit the servicing of your loan(s), and, if it becomes necessary, to locate you and to collect and report on your loan(s) if your loan(s) become delinquent or in default. We also use your SSN as an account identifier and to permit you to access your account information electronically.

The information in your file may be disclosed, on a case-by-case basis or under a computer matching program, to third parties as authorized under routine uses in the appropriate systems of records notices. The routine uses of this information include, but are not limited to, its disclosure to federal, state, or local agencies, to private parties such as relatives, present and former employers, business and personal associates, to consumer reporting agencies, to financial and educational institutions, and to guaranty agencies in order to verify your identity, to determine your eligibility to receive a loan or a benefit on a loan, to permit the servicing or collection of your loan(s), to enforce the terms of the loan(s), to investigate possible fraud and to verify compliance with federal student financial aid program regulations, or to locate you if you become delinquent in your loan payments or if you default. To provide default rate calculations, disclosures may be made to guaranty agencies, to financial and educational institutions, or to state agencies. To provide financial aid history information, disclosures may be made to educational institutions. To assist program administrators with tracking refunds and cancellations, disclosures may be made to guaranty agencies, to financial and educational institutions, or to federal or state agencies. To provide a standardized method for educational institutions to efficiently submit student enrollment status, disclosures may be made to guaranty agencies or to financial and educational institutions. To counsel you in repayment efforts, disclosures may be made to guaranty agencies, to financial and educational institutions, or to federal, state, or local agencies.

In the event of litigation, we may send records to the Department of Justice, a court, adjudicative body, counsel, party, or witness if the disclosure is relevant and necessary to the litigation. If this information, either alone or with other information, indicates a potential violation of law, we may send it to the appropriate authority for action. We may send information to members of Congress if you ask them to help you with federal student aid questions. In circumstances involving employment complaints, grievances, or disciplinary actions, we may disclose relevant records to adjudicate or investigate the issues. If provided for by a collective bargaining agreement, we may disclose records to a labor organization recognized under 5 U.S.C. Chapter 71. Disclosures may be made to our contractors for the purpose of performing any programmatic function that requires disclosure of records. Before making any such disclosure, we will require the contractor to maintain Privacy Act safeguards. Disclosures may also be made to qualified researchers under Privacy Act safeguards.

Paperwork Reduction Notice: According to the Paperwork Reduction Act of 1995, no persons are required to respond to a collection of information unless it displays a currently valid OMB control number. The valid OMB control number for this information collection is 1845-0015. The time required to complete this information collection is estimated to average 0.5 hours (30 minutes) per response, including the time to review instructions, search existing data resources, gather and maintain the data needed, and complete and review the information collection. **If you have any comments concerning the accuracy of the time estimate(s) or suggestions for improving this application, please write to:** U.S. Department of Education, Washington, DC 20202-4537.

If you have questions regarding the status of your individual submission of this application, contact your loan holder (see Section 8).

SECTION 8: WHERE TO SEND THE COMPLETED LOAN DISCHARGE APPLICATION

Send the completed loan discharge application and any attachments to:
(If no address is shown, return to your loan holder.)

If you need help completing this form, call:

Student Assistant Forms   Appx. D.3.5

D.3.5 Letter from Department of Education Granting False Certification Discharge

**U. S. DEPARTMENT OF EDUCATION
STUDENT FINANCIAL ASSISTANCE**

DATE: JUNE 28, 2006

SSN:
DEBT NO.

DEAR BORROWER:

THIS LETTER ACKNOWLEDGES RECEIPT OF YOUR SWORN STATEMENT REQUESTING DISCHARGE OF FEDERAL FAMILY EDUCATION LOAN(S) DUE TO THE FALSE CERTIFICATION OF YOUR ABILITY TO BENEFIT FROM THE TRAINING OFFERED BY THE SCHOOL ATTENDED WITH THE LOAN.

THE U.S. DEPARTMENT OF EDUCATION HAS DETERMINED THAT YOU QUALIFY FOR DISCHARGE OF YOUR FEDERAL FAMILY EDUCATION LOAN(S) WHICH YOU OBTAINED TO ATTEND USA Training Academy Home Study.

AS A RESULT OF THIS DETERMINATION:

- YOU WILL BE RELIEVED OF THE OBLIGATION TO REPAY THE LOAN;

- YOU WILL BE REFUNDED ALL MONIES PAID BY YOU ON THE LOAN(S), WHICH OUR RECORDS INDICATE TO BE $729.52. A CHECK HAS BEEN REQUESTED FROM THE U.S. TREASURY. PLEASE ALLOW 4-6 WEEKS FOR DELIVERY;

- IF YOU WERE IN DEFAULT ON THE DISCHARGED LOAN(S), YOU WILL NO LONGER BE REGARDED AS IN DEFAULT ON THE LOAN(S), AND THE PAST REPORTING OF A DEFAULT WILL NOT PRECLUDE YOU FROM RECEIVING ASSISTANCE UNDER THE TITLE IV, HIGHER EDUCATION ACT PROGRAMS IN THE FUTURE;

- THE DEPARTMENT OF EDUCATION WILL REPORT THE DISCHARGE TO ALL CREDIT REPORTING AGENCIES TO WHICH IT PREVIOUSLY REPORTED SO THAT ANY ADVERSE CREDIT HISTORY ASSIGNED TO THE LOAN(S) MAY BE DELETED.

THIS DISCHARGE COVERS ONLY THE LOAN(S) HELD BY THE U.S. DEPARTMENT OF EDUCATION, LISTED ABOVE, WHICH WERE OBTAINED TO ATTEND USA Training Academy Home Study. THE DEPARTMENT HAS MADE NO DETERMINATION WITH REGARD TO LOANS HELD BY GUARANTEE AGENCIES, SERVICERS, LENDERS, OR EDUCATIONAL INSTITUTIONS.

IF YOU HAVE FURTHER QUESTIONS REGARDING THIS MATTER, YOU CAN CONTACT A DEPARTMENT REPRESENTATIVE BY CALLING 1-800-621-3115.

W70   0002064   0606270017

Appx. D.3.6   *Student Loan Law*

D.3.6 Certification/Agreement of Cooperation for Identity Theft Claims

Direct Loans
William D. Ford Federal Direct Loan Program

CERTIFICATION/AGREEMENT OF COOPERATION FOR IDENTITY THEFT CLAIMS

Purpose of this Agreement

Please complete, sign, and date this letter to certify that you agree to cooperate with the U.S. Department of Education and the U.S. Department of Justice in the investigation of your allegation of identity theft. Include with this signed agreement all of the information described below:

- A court judgment that was made in your favor that conclusively finds you were a victim of identity theft and identifies the name(s) of the individual(s) who committed the crime.
- A written statement that describes how the identity theft relates specifically to your student loan(s).
- A clear copy of a valid government-issued photo identification card (i.e. Driver's License, State-issue ID Card, or Passport) OR a clear copy of your Social Security Card.

Action You Must Take

Please return this completed letter, your written statement, and attachments to the following address:

**Direct Loan Servicing Center
P.O. Box 5609
Greenville, TX 75403-5609**

A Notary Public must notarize this letter and your written statement.

Important

Please read the following statement carefully:

I certify under penalty of perjury that my enclosed written statement and all supporting documents provided are true and correct to the best of my knowledge.

I agree to cooperate with officials of the U.S. Department of Education and the U.S. Department of Justice in the investigation of the facts and circumstances relating to the student loan obtained in my name. I further agree to testify in any administrative proceeding or criminal or civil court case relating to this matter.

I understand that providing this statement and agreeing to cooperate and provide testimony does not release me from my obligation to repay the loan obtained in my name. Until the U.S. Department of Education notifies me in writing that the investigation has been concluded and unless I choose to make payments on the loan, the loan will be placed in a suspension status. Although I will not have to make payments while this loan is in administrative forbearance, interest will continue to accrue.

_____   _____
Signature   Date

_____   _____
Notary Public   Date

Rev. 03/08   IDCert-LNS

Student Assistance Forms Appx. D.3.7

D.3.7 Unpaid Refund Discharge

LOAN DISCHARGE APPLICATION: UNPAID REFUND
Federal Family Education Loan Program/William D. Ford Federal Direct Loan Program

OMB No. 1845-0058
Form Approved
Exp. Date 04/30/2011

WARNING: Any person who knowingly makes a false statement or misrepresentation on this form or on any accompanying documents will be subject to penalties that may include fines, imprisonment, or both, under the U.S. Criminal Code and 20 U.S.C. 1097.

SECTION 1: BORROWER IDENTIFICATION

Please enter or correct the following information:
SSN ☐☐☐ – ☐☐ – ☐☐☐☐
Name _____
Address _____
City, State, Zip Code _____
Telephone – Home ( ) _____
Telephone – Other ( ) _____
E-mail (optional) _____

SECTION 2: SCHOOL AND LOAN INFORMATION

Before responding, carefully read the entire form, including the instructions, definitions, and terms and conditions in Sections 5, 6 and 7 on this form. If the school that you believe owes you a refund is currently open, you should first contact the school to attempt to resolve this issue before applying for an unpaid refund loan discharge. If you are a student borrower applying for loan discharge, begin with Item 3. If you are a parent borrower applying for a PLUS loan discharge, begin with Item 1.

1. Student Name (Last, First, MI):
2. Student SSN: ☐☐☐ – ☐☐ – ☐☐☐☐
3. School Name:
4. School Address (street, city, state, zip code):
5. Is this school still open? ☐ Yes ☐ No ☐ Don't Know
6. If this school is closed, were you (or, for parent PLUS borrowers, was the student) attending the school when it closed? ☐ Yes ☐ No
7. Do you have any other pending or approved application(s) for discharge of a loan you obtained to attend this school? ☐ Yes ☐ No
8. Has this school or any third party (see the definition of "third party" in Section 6 on the following page) made a refund or payment for any loan for which you are requesting a discharge, or is such a refund or payment being considered? ☐ Yes ☐ No

If your answers to Items 7 and 8 are "No," skip to Section 3. If your answer to Item 7 or 8 is "Yes," provide the information requested in Items 9, 10, and 11 for each discharge, refund or payment, if known. Use a separate sheet of paper if you need to report more than one discharge, refund or payment.

9. Reason for discharge, refund or payment:
10. From whom did you request or from whom did you receive the discharge, refund or payment? Include telephone number.
11. Amount you received or that you expect to receive: $_____

SECTION 3: REFUND INFORMATION

If you have documentation from the school showing the amount of the unpaid refund, attach a copy to this form. If you believe that the amount of the refund shown in the documentation from the school is correct, skip to Section 4. If you don't believe that the amount is correct or if you don't have this documentation, complete Items 12 through 17. If you are unable to provide any of the requested information, write "Don't Know."

12. What amount do you believe the school owes you? $_____
13. Why do you believe the school owes you this amount?
14. Your (or, for parent PLUS borrowers, the student's) first and last dates of attendance at the school:
☐☐–☐☐–☐☐☐☐ to ☐☐–☐☐–☐☐☐☐ OR ☐ Never Attended
15. Your (or, for parent PLUS borrowers, the student's) program of study at the school:

Items 16 and 17 request information about the amount of the school's charges or the amount of the financial aid you received for the period of enrollment for which the loan was intended. For example, if you received a loan for the spring quarter only and you left school during the spring quarter, provide an amount for that quarter only. However, if you received a loan for the winter and spring quarters, provide the total amount for both quarters. If the unpaid refund is for more than one loan and the loans were for different periods of enrollment, provide the amounts requested in Item 16 or 17 for each period of enrollment separately, using a separate sheet of paper for your additional response(s).

16. If your (or, for parent PLUS borrowers, the student's) last date of attendance was **before October 7, 2000**, enter the amount of the school's charges for the period of enrollment for which the loan was intended. Include tuition, fees, and other school charges. $_____
17. If your (or, for parent PLUS borrowers, the student's) last date of attendance was **on or after October 7, 2000**, enter the total amount of federal grants and loans received for any part of the period of enrollment for which the loan was intended. $_____

Attach a copy of any documentation that supports your responses to Items 12 through 17. Examples of documentation may include, but are not limited to, the school's catalog, refund policy, tuition bill(s), enrollment contract, student account statement, registration forms, withdrawal form, attendance records, and any correspondence from the school that contains information about the refund you believe the school owes you.

SECTION 4: BORROWER CERTIFICATION

My signature below certifies that –

- I received each loan for which I am requesting a discharge on or after January 1, 1986. I received the loan funds directly, or they were applied as a credit to my (or, for parent PLUS borrowers, the student's) school account to pay the amount owed to the school.
- I (or, for parent PLUS borrowers, the student) did not attend the school or withdrew or was terminated from the school within the time frame that would entitle me to a refund of some or all of my loan funds. Except as explained in Section 2, Items 7 through 11, I have not received this refund, or any benefit of a refund to which I am entitled, from the school or any third party.
- I have read and agree to the terms and conditions for loan discharge, as specified in Section 7 on the following page.
- Under penalty of perjury, all of the information I have provided on this application and in any accompanying documentation is true and accurate to the best of my knowledge and belief.

Borrower's Signature: _____ Today's Date: _____

SECTION 5: INSTRUCTIONS FOR COMPLETING THE FORM

Before you complete this application, you need to know the following:

- If the school is currently open, you should first contact the school and attempt to resolve the unpaid refund issue before applying for this type of discharge.
- If you (or, for parent PLUS borrowers, the student) are currently attending the school, you are not eligible for this type of discharge. You should contact the school about the refund that you believe you are owed.
- If you, (or, for parent PLUS borrowers, the student) were enrolled when the school closed or withdrew from the school within 90 days before the school closed and you (or, for parent PLUS borrowers, the student) did not complete the program of study at another school, you may wish to apply for a closed school loan discharge rather than an unpaid refund discharge. If you are unsure about which type of loan discharge is most appropriate for you, contact your loan holder at the address shown in Section 9.

When completing this form, type or print using dark ink. Enter dates as month-day-year (mm-dd-yyyy). Use only numbers. Example: June 24, 2006 = 06-24-2006. If you need more space to answer any of the Items, continue on separate sheets of paper and attach them to this form. Indicate the number of the Item(s) you are answering and include your name and social security number (SSN) on all attached pages. If a refund is owed for more than one student or from more than one school, use separate forms for each student or school.

Return the completed form and any attachments to the address shown in Section 9.

SECTION 6: DEFINITIONS

- The **Federal Family Education Loan (FFEL) Program** includes Federal Stafford Loans (both subsidized and unsubsidized), Federal Supplemental Loans for Students (SLS), Federal PLUS Loans, and Federal Consolidation Loans.
- The **William D. Ford Federal Direct Loan (Direct Loan) Program** includes Federal Direct Stafford/Ford Loans (Direct Subsidized Loans), Federal Direct Unsubsidized Stafford/Ford Loans (Direct Unsubsidized Loans), Federal Direct PLUS Loans (Direct PLUS Loans), and Federal Direct Consolidation Loans (Direct Consolidation Loans).
- **Loan discharge** due to an unpaid refund cancels your obligation (and any endorser's obligation) to repay the portion of your loan that should have been refunded. Any accrued interest and other charges on the amount of the unpaid refund will also be discharged, and you will be reimbursed for any amount that you have repaid that exceeds the remaining balance of the loan after the discharge. Your loan holder will report the discharge to all credit reporting agencies to which the loan holder previously reported the status of the loan.
- **Program of study** means the instructional program leading to a degree or certificate in which you (or, for parent PLUS borrowers, the student) were enrolled.
- The **student** (as in "or, for parent PLUS borrowers, the student") refers to the student for whom a parent borrower obtained a Federal PLUS Loan or Direct PLUS Loan.
- **Third party** refers to any entity that may provide reimbursement for a refund owed by the school, such as a State or other entity offering a tuition recovery program or a holder of a performance bond.

SECTION 7: TERMS AND CONDITIONS FOR LOAN DISCHARGE BASED ON UNPAID REFUND

- I agree to cooperate with the U.S. Department of Education (the Department) or the Department's designee in any enforcement action related to this application and to provide to the Department or the Department's designee, upon request, other documentation reasonably available to me that demonstrates that I meet the qualifications for an unpaid refund discharge.
- I assign and transfer to the Department any right to recovery on the amount discharged that I may have from the school identified in Section 2 of this form and/or any owners, affiliates or assigns of the school, and from any party that may pay claims for a refund because of the actions of the school, up to the amount discharged by the Department on my loan(s).
- I understand that this request may be denied, or my discharge may be revoked, if I fail to cooperate, provide documentation, or meet any of the other terms of my agreement on this form.
- I understand that if my loan is discharged based on any false, fictitious, or fraudulent statements that I knowingly made on this form or on any accompanying documents, I may be subject to civil and criminal penalties under applicable federal law.

SECTION 8: IMPORTANT NOTICES

Privacy Act Notice. The Privacy Act of 1974 (5 U.S.C. 552a) requires that the following notice be provided to you:

The authorities for collecting the requested information from and about you are §421 *et seq.* and §451 *et seq.* of the Higher Education Act of 1965, as amended (20 U.S.C. 1071 *et seq.* and 20 U.S.C. 1087a *et seq.*) and the authorities for collecting and using your Social Security Number (SSN) are §§428B(f) and 484(a)(4) of the HEA (20 U.S.C. 1078-2(f) and 1091(a)(4)) and 31 U.S.C. 7701(b). Participating in the Federal Family Education Loan (FFEL) Program or the William D. Ford Federal Direct Loan (Direct Loan) Program and giving us your SSN are voluntary, but you must provide the requested information, including your SSN, to participate.

The principal purposes for collecting the information on this form, including your SSN, are to verify your identity, to determine your eligibility to receive a loan or a benefit on a loan (such as a deferment, forbearance, discharge, or forgiveness) under the FFEL and/or Direct Loan Programs, to permit the servicing of your loan(s), and, if it becomes necessary, to locate you and to collect and report on your loan(s) if your loan(s) become delinquent or in default. We also use your SSN as an account identifier and to permit you to access your account information electronically.

The information in your file may be disclosed, on a case-by-case basis or under a computer matching program, to third parties as authorized under routine uses in the appropriate systems of records notices. The routine uses of this information include, but are not limited to, its disclosure to federal, state, or local agencies, to private parties such as relatives, present and former employers, business and personal associates, to consumer reporting agencies, to financial and educational institutions, and to guaranty agencies in order to verify your identity, to determine your eligibility to receive a loan or a benefit on a loan, to permit the servicing or collection of your loan(s), to enforce the terms of the loan(s), to investigate possible fraud and to verify compliance with federal student financial aid program regulations, or to locate you if you become delinquent in your loan payments or if you default. To provide default rate calculations, disclosures may be made to guaranty agencies, to financial and educational institutions, or to state agencies. To provide financial aid history information, disclosures may be made to educational institutions. To assist program administrators with tracking refunds and cancellations, disclosures may be made to guaranty agencies, to financial and educational institutions, or to federal or state agencies. To provide a standardized method for educational institutions to efficiently submit student enrollment status, disclosures may be made to guaranty agencies or to financial and educational institutions. To counsel you in repayment efforts, disclosures may be made to guaranty agencies, to financial and educational institutions, or to federal, state, or local agencies.

In the event of litigation, we may send records to the Department of Justice, a court, adjudicative body, counsel, party, or witness if the disclosure is relevant and necessary to the litigation. If this information, either alone or with other information, indicates a potential violation of law, we may send it to the appropriate authority for action. We may send information to members of Congress if you ask them to help you with federal student aid questions. In circumstances involving employment complaints, grievances, or disciplinary actions, we may disclose relevant records to adjudicate or investigate the issues. If provided for by a collective bargaining agreement, we may disclose records to a labor organization recognized under 5 U.S.C. Chapter 71. Disclosures may be made to our contractors for the purpose of performing any programmatic function that requires disclosure of records. Before making any such disclosure, we will require the contractor to maintain Privacy Act safeguards. Disclosures may also be made to qualified researchers under Privacy Act safeguards.

Paperwork Reduction Notice. According to the Paperwork Reduction Act of 1995, no persons are required to respond to a collection of information unless it displays a currently valid OMB control number. The valid OMB control number for this information collection is 1845-0058. The time required to complete this information collection is estimated to average 0.5 hours (30 minutes) per response, including the time to review instructions, search existing data resources, gather and maintain the data needed, and complete and review the information collection. **If you have comments concerning the accuracy of the time estimate(s) or suggestions for improving this form, please write to:** U.S. Department of Education, Washington, DC 20202-4537.

If you have questions regarding the status of *your individual submission of this form,* **contact your loan holder (see Section 9).**

SECTION 9: WHERE TO SEND THE COMPLETED LOAN DISCHARGE APPLICATION

Send the completed loan discharge application and any attachments to:
(If no address is shown, return to your loan holder.)

If you need help completing this form, call:

Student Assistance Forms

Appx. D.3.8.1

D.3.8 Total and Permanent Disability Discharge

D.3.8.1 Application Form

*** LOAN HOLDER USE ONLY ***
ORIGINAL RECEIPT DATE:

DISCHARGE APPLICATION:
TOTAL AND PERMANENT DISABILITY
Federal Family Education Loan Program / Federal Perkins Loan Program /
William D. Ford Federal Direct Loan Program / Teacher Education Assistance for College and Higher Education Grant Program

WARNING: Any person who knowingly makes a false statement or misrepresentation on this form or on any accompanying documents will be subject to penalties that may include fines, imprisonment, or both, under the U.S. Criminal Code and 20 U.S.C. 1097.

OMB No. 1845-0065
Form Approved
Exp. Date 12/31/2011

READ THIS FIRST: This is an application for a total and permanent disability discharge of your Federal Family Education Loan (FFEL) Program, Federal Perkins Loan (Perkins Loan) Program, and/or William D. Ford Federal Direct Loan (Direct Loan) Program loan(s), and/or your Teacher Education Assistance for College and Higher Education (TEACH) Grant Program service obligation.

To qualify for this discharge (except for certain veterans as explained below), a physician must certify in Section 4 of this form that you are unable to engage in any substantial gainful activity (see definition in Section 5) by reason of a medically determinable physical or mental impairment that **(1)** can be expected to result in death; **(2)** has lasted for a continuous period of not less than 60 months; or **(3)** can be expected to last for a continuous period of not less than 60 months. This disability standard may differ from disability standards used by other federal agencies (for example, the Social Security Administration) or state agencies. Except as noted below for certain veterans, a disability determination by another federal or state agency does not establish your eligibility for this discharge.

If you are a veteran, you will be considered totally and permanently disabled for purposes of this discharge if you provide documentation from the U.S. Department of Veterans Affairs (VA) showing that you have been determined to be **unemployable due to a service-connected disability.** If you provide this documentation, you are not required to have a physician complete Section 4 of this form or provide any additional documentation related to your disabling condition. You only need to complete Sections 1 and 3.

SECTION 1: APPLICANT IDENTIFICATION

Please enter or correct the following information.

SSN ☐☐☐ - ☐☐ - ☐☐☐☐
Name _____
Address _____
City, State, Zip Code _____
Telephone - Home ( ) _____
Telephone - Other ( ) _____
E-mail Address (Optional) _____

SECTION 2: INSTRUCTIONS FOR COMPLETING AND SUBMITTING THIS APPLICATION

- Type or print in dark ink. Enter your name and Social Security Number at the top of page 2 (if not preprinted).
- Have a doctor of medicine or osteopathy complete and sign Section 4, unless you are a qualifying veteran (see the next bullet).
- If you are a veteran who has received a determination from the VA that you are **unemployable due to a service-connected disability**, attach documentation of this determination. You are not required to have a physician complete Section 4. **If you do not have documentation showing that you are unemployable due to a service-connected disability and cannot obtain this documentation, you must have a physician complete Section 4.**
- Sign and date the application in Section 3. A representative may sign on your behalf if you are unable to do so because of your disability.
- Make sure that Sections 3 and (if applicable) 4 include all requested information. Incomplete or inaccurate information may cause your application to be delayed or rejected.
- Send the completed application with any necessary attachments to the address shown below. If no address is shown, send the application and any attachments to your loan holder or, if you are applying for discharge of a TEACH Grant Program service obligation, to the U.S. Department of Education (the Department) at the address shown on correspondence you received related to your TEACH Grant.
- If you are applying for discharge of more than one loan and your loans are held by more than one loan holder, or if you are applying for discharge of both a TEACH Grant service obligation and one or more loans, you must submit a separate discharge application (original or copy) with any necessary attachments to each loan holder and, for TEACH Grants, to the Department. A "copy" means a photocopy of the original application completed by you (or your representative) and your physician. Any copy must include an **original signature** from you or your representative.
- **IMPORTANT:** You must submit this application to your loan holder(s) and/or the Department within 90 days of the date of your physician's signature in Section 4. See Section 3 for address and contact information. (**NOTE TO VETERANS:** This requirement does not apply if you are a veteran who provides the documentation described above under "READ THIS FIRST.")

SECTION 3: APPLICANT'S DISCHARGE REQUEST, AUTHORIZATION, UNDERSTANDINGS, AND CERTIFICATIONS

Before signing, carefully read the entire application, including the instructions in Section 2 and other information on the following pages.

I request that the Department discharge my FFEL, Perkins Loan, and/or Direct Loan program loan(s), and/or my TEACH Grant service obligation.

I authorize any physician, hospital, or other institution having records about the disability that is the basis for my request for a discharge to make information from those records available to the holder(s) of my loan(s) and/or to the Department.

I understand that **(i)** I must submit a separate discharge application to each holder of the loan(s) that I want to have discharged. If I am applying for discharge of both a TEACH Grant service obligation and one or more loans, I must submit a separate discharge application to each loan holder and, for TEACH Grants, to the Department. Unless I am a veteran who provides the documentation described above under "READ THIS FIRST," I must submit a discharge application to each loan holder and/or the Department within 90 days of the date of my physician's signature in Section 4. **(ii)** Unless I am a veteran who provides the documentation described above under "READ THIS FIRST," I may be required to repay a discharged loan or satisfy a discharged TEACH Grant service obligation if I fail to meet certain requirements during a post-discharge monitoring period, as explained in Section 6. **(iii)** If I am a veteran, the certification by a physician on this form (if I am required to obtain such a certification) is only for the purposes of establishing my eligibility to receive a discharge of a FFEL Program loan, a Perkins Loan Program loan, a Direct Loan Program loan, and/or a TEACH Grant service obligation, and is not for purposes of determining my eligibility for, or the extent of my eligibility for, VA benefits.

I certify that: (i) I have a total and permanent disability, as defined in Section 5. **(ii)** I have read and understand the information on the discharge process, the terms and conditions for discharge, and the eligibility requirements to receive future loans or TEACH Grants as explained in Sections 6 and 7.

Signature of Applicant or Applicant's Representative	Date	Printed Name of Applicant's Representative (if applicable)
Address of Applicant's Representative (if applicable)		Representative's Relationship to Applicant (if applicable)

Send the completed discharge application and any attachments to: | If you need help completing this form, call:

Page 1 of 4

REVISED 7/2010

535

Appx. D.3.8.1 *Student Loan Law*

Applicant Name: _____ Applicant SSN: ☐☐☐ - ☐☐ - ☐☐☐☐

SECTION 4: PHYSICIAN'S CERTIFICATION

READ THIS FIRST: The applicant identified above is applying for a discharge of a federal student loan and/or a teaching service obligation for a federal grant on the basis that he or she has a total and permanent disability, as defined in Section 5 of this form. To qualify for a discharge, the applicant must be unable to engage in any substantial gainful activity (as defined in Section 5) by reason of a medically determinable physical or mental impairment that **(1)** can be expected to result in death; **(2)** has lasted for a continuous period of not less than 60 months; or **(3)** can be expected to last for a continuous period of not less than 60 months. This disability standard may be different from standards used under other programs in connection with occupational disability, or eligibility for social service or veterans benefits. A determination that the applicant is disabled by another federal agency (for example, the Social Security Administration) or a state agency does not establish the applicant's eligibility for this loan discharge.

Instructions for Physician:

- Complete this form only if you are a doctor of medicine or osteopathy legally authorized to practice in a state, as defined in Section 5, and only if the applicant's condition meets the definition of total and permanent disability in Section 5.
- Type or print in dark ink. All fields must be completed. If a field is not applicable, enter "N/A." Your signature date must include month, day, and year (mm-dd-yyyy).
- Provide all requested information for Items 1, 2, and 3 below, and attach additional pages if necessary. Complete the physician's certification at the bottom of this page. The applicant's loan discharge application cannot be processed if the information requested in this section is missing.
- If you make any changes to the information you provide in this section, you must initial each change.
- **Please return the completed form to the applicant or the applicant's representative.** The holder(s) of the applicant's loan(s) (as defined in Section 5) or the U.S. Department of Education may contact you for additional information or documentation.

1. **Ability to Engage in Substantial Gainful Activity.** Does the applicant have a medically determinable physical or mental impairment (as explained in Item 2 below) that **(a)** prevents the applicant from engaging in any substantial gainful activity, in any field of work, and **(b)** can be expected to result in death, *or* has lasted for a continuous period of not less than 60 months, *or* can be expected to last for a continuous period of not less than 60 months? ☐ Yes ☐ No

    Substantial gainful activity means a level of work performed for pay or profit that involves doing significant physical or mental activities, or a combination of both. *If the applicant is able to engage in any substantial gainful activity, in any field of work, you must answer "No."*

    IF THE ANSWER TO QUESTION 1 IS NO, DO NOT COMPLETE THIS APPLICATION.

2. **Disabling Condition.** Complete the following regarding the applicant's disabling physical or mental impairment. **Do not use abbreviations or insurance codes**.

    (a) Provide the diagnosis: _____

    (b) Describe the severity of the disabling physical or mental impairment, including, if applicable, the phase of the disabling condition: _____

3. **Limitations.** Explain how the disabling condition prevents the applicant from engaging in substantial gainful activity in *any* field of work by responding to Items (a) through (e) below, as relevant to the applicant's condition. Attach additional pages if more space is needed.

    In addition to what is required below, you may include any additional information that you believe would be helpful in understanding the applicant's condition, such as medications used to treat the condition, surgical and non-surgical treatments for the condition, etc.

    (a) Limitations on sitting, standing, walking, or lifting: _____

    (b) Limitations on activities of daily living: _____

    (c) Residual functionality: _____

    (d) Social/behavioral limitations, if any: _____

    (e) Current Global Assessment Function Score (for psychiatric conditions): _____

Physician's Certification

- I certify that, in my best professional judgment, the applicant identified above is unable to engage in any substantial gainful activity in *any* field of work by reason of a medically determinable physical or mental impairment that (1) can be expected to result in death, (2) has lasted for a continuous period of not less than 60 months, or (3) can be expected to last for a continuous period of not less than 60 months.
- I understand that an applicant who is currently able to engage in any substantial gainful activity in *any* field of work does not have a total and permanent disability as defined on this form.

I am a doctor of (check one) ☐ medicine ☐ osteopathy/osteopathic medicine. I am legally authorized to practice in the state of _____, and my professional license number is _____ (subject to verification through state records).

Physician's Signature (a signature stamp is not acceptable)	Date (mm-dd-yyyy)	Printed Name of Physician (first name, middle initial, last name)
Address		City, State, Zip Code
( ) Telephone	( ) Fax	E-mail Address (Optional)

REVISED 7/2010

Student Assistance Forms Appx. D.3.8.1

SECTION 5: DEFINITIONS

- If you have a **total and permanent disability**, this means that:

   (1) You are unable to engage in any substantial gainful activity by reason of a medically determinable physical or mental impairment that can be expected to result in death, that has lasted for a continuous period of not less than 60 months, or that can be expected to last for a continuous period of not less than 60 months, **OR**

   (2) You are a veteran who has been determined by the VA to be **unemployable due to a service-connected disability**.

   NOTE: This disability standard may differ from disability standards used by other federal agencies (for example, the Social Security Administration) or state agencies. Except in the case of certain veterans, a disability determination by another federal or state agency does not establish your eligibility for a discharge of your loan(s) and/or TEACH Grant service obligation due to a total and permanent disability.

- **Substantial gainful activity** means a level of work performed for pay or profit that involves doing significant physical or mental activities, or a combination of both.

- A **discharge of a loan** due to a total and permanent disability cancels your obligation (and, if applicable, an endorser's obligation) to repay the remaining balance on your FFEL, Perkins Loan, and/or Direct Loan program loans. A **discharge of a TEACH Grant service obligation** cancels your obligation to complete the teaching service that you agreed to perform as a condition for receiving a TEACH Grant.

- The **post-discharge monitoring period** begins on the date the Department grants a discharge of your loan or TEACH Grant service obligation and lasts for three years. If you fail to meet certain conditions at any time during or at the end of the post-discharge monitoring period, the Department will reinstate your obligation to repay your discharged loan or complete your TEACH Grant service obligation. See Section 6 for more information.

- The **Federal Family Education Loan (FFEL) Program** includes Federal Stafford Loans (both subsidized and unsubsidized), Federal Supplemental Loans for Students (SLS), Federal PLUS Loans, and Federal Consolidation Loans.

- The **Federal Perkins Loan (Perkins Loan) Program** includes Federal Perkins Loans, National Direct Student Loans (NDSL), and National Defense Student Loans (Defense Loans).

- The **William D. Ford Federal Direct Loan (Direct Loan) Program** includes Federal Direct Stafford/Ford Loans (Direct Subsidized Loans), Federal Direct Unsubsidized Stafford/Ford Loans (Direct Unsubsidized Loans), Federal Direct PLUS Loans (Direct PLUS Loans), and Federal Direct Consolidation Loans (Direct Consolidation Loans).

- The **Teacher Education Assistance for College and Higher Education (TEACH) Grant Program** provides grants to students who agree to teach full time for at least four years in high-need fields in low-income elementary or secondary schools as a condition for receiving the grant funds. If a TEACH Grant recipient does not complete the required teaching service within eight years after completing the program of study for which the TEACH Grant was received, the TEACH Grant funds are converted to a Direct Unsubsidized Loan that the grant recipient must repay in full, with interest, to the Department.

- The **holder** of your FFEL Program loan(s) may be a lender, a guaranty agency, or the Department. The holder of your Perkins Loan Program loan(s) may be a school you attended or the Department. The holder of your Direct Loan Program loan(s) is the Department. If you received a TEACH Grant, the Department holds your TEACH Grant Agreement to Serve.

- The term **"state"** as used on this application includes the 50 United States, the District of Columbia, American Samoa, the Commonwealth of Puerto Rico, Guam, the U.S. Virgin Islands, the Commonwealth of the Northern Mariana Islands, the Republic of the Marshall Islands, the Federated States of Micronesia, and the Republic of Palau.

SECTION 6: DISCHARGE PROCESS / ELIGIBILITY REQUIREMENTS / TERMS AND CONDITIONS FOR DISCHARGE (continues on next page)

NOTE: If you are applying for discharge of loans that are held by the Department, or are applying for discharge of a TEACH Grant service obligation, the discharge process begins with the review by the Department described below.

For veterans who have been determined by the VA to be unemployable due to a service-connected disability:

1. **Review of discharge application by your loan holder.** Your loan holder will review your completed discharge application and the required documentation you provide from the VA. If the documentation indicates that you are totally and permanently disabled in accordance with paragraph (2) of the definition of "total and permanent disability" in Section 5, your loan holder will refer your application and the accompanying documentation to the Department for further review. If the documentation from the VA does not indicate that you are totally and permanently disabled, you will be notified that you must resume payment of your loan(s). If the documentation from the VA does not indicate that you are totally and permanently disabled in accordance with paragraph (2) of the definition of "total and permanent disability," but it indicates that you may be totally and permanently disabled in accordance with paragraph (1) of the definition, you will be notified that you may reapply for discharge under the process for other applicants, as described below. For FFEL Program loans held by a lender, both the lender and the guaranty agency will review your application and accompanying documentation before sending the application and documentation to the Department.

2. **Review of discharge application by the Department.** The Department will review the documentation from the VA to determine if you are totally and permanently disabled in accordance with paragraph (2) of the definition of "total and permanent disability" in Section 5.

3. **Discharge.** If the Department determines that you are totally and permanently disabled, you will be notified that your loan(s) and/or TEACH Grant service obligation has been discharged. The discharge will be reported to national consumer reporting agencies, and any loan payments received on or after the effective date of the determination by the VA that you are unemployable due to a service-connected disability will be refunded to the person who made the payments. If the Department determines that you are not totally and permanently disabled, you will be notified that you must resume repayment of your loan(s), or if you applied for discharge of a TEACH Grant service obligation, that you must comply with all terms and conditions of your TEACH Grant Agreement to Serve.

For all other applicants:

1. **Review of discharge application by your loan holder.** Your loan holder will review your completed discharge application and any accompanying documentation to determine whether you appear to be totally and permanently disabled in accordance with paragraph (1) of the definition of "total and permanent disability" in Section 5. If applicable, your loan holder may also contact your physician for additional information. For FFEL Program loans held by a lender, this determination will be made by both the lender and the guaranty agency. If the loan holder determines that you do not appear to be totally and permanently disabled, you will be notified of that decision. You must then resume payment of your loan(s). If your loan holder determines that you appear to be totally and permanently disabled, your loan(s) will be assigned to the Department. The Department will be your new loan holder.

2. **Review of discharge application by the Department.** The Department will review the physician's certification in Section 4 and any accompanying documentation to determine if you are totally and permanently disabled in accordance with paragraph (1) of the definition of "total and permanent disability" in Section 5. The Department may also contact your physician for additional information, or may arrange for an additional review of your condition by an independent physician at the Department's expense. Based on the results of this review, the Department will determine your eligibility for discharge.

3. **Discharge.** If the Department determines that you are totally and permanently disabled, you will be notified that a discharge has been granted, and that you will be subject to a post-discharge monitoring period for three years beginning on the discharge date. The notification of discharge will explain the terms and conditions under which the Department will reinstate your obligation to repay your discharged loan or complete your discharged TEACH Grant service obligation, as described in Item 4, below. The discharge will be reported to national consumer reporting agencies, and any loan payments that were received after the date the physician certified your discharge application will be returned to the person who made the payments.

   If the Department determines that you are not totally and permanently disabled, you will be notified of that determination. You must then resume repayment of your loan(s), or if you applied for discharge of a TEACH Grant service obligation, you must comply with all terms and conditions of your TEACH Grant Agreement to Serve.

4. **Post-discharge monitoring period.** If you are granted a discharge, the Department will monitor your status during the 3-year post-discharge monitoring period that begins on the date the discharge is granted. The Department will reinstate your obligation to repay your discharged loan(s) and/or your obligation to complete your discharged TEACH Grant service obligation if, at any time during the post-discharge monitoring period, you:

   - Receive annual earnings from employment that exceed the poverty line amount (see Note below) for a family of two in your state, regardless of your actual family size;

   - Receive a new loan under the FFEL, Perkins Loan, or Direct Loan Program or a new TEACH Grant; or

   - Fail to ensure that a loan or TEACH Grant disbursement was returned to the loan holder or (for a TEACH Grant) to the Department within 120 days of the disbursement date, in the case of a FFEL, Perkins, or Direct Loan program loan or a TEACH grant that was made before the discharge date, but was disbursed during the 3-year post-discharge monitoring period.

   During the 3-year post-discharge monitoring period, you (or your representative) must:

   - Promptly notify the Department if your annual earnings from employment exceed the poverty line amount for a family of two in your state (see Note below), regardless of your actual family size;

SECTION 6: DISCHARGE PROCESS / ELIGIBILITY REQUIREMENTS / TERMS AND CONDITIONS FOR DISCHARGE (continued from previous page)

- Promptly notify the Department of any changes in your address or telephone number; and
- If requested, provide the Department with documentation of your annual earnings from employment.

Note: The poverty line amounts are updated annually and may be obtained at http://aspe.hhs.gov/poverty. The Department will notify you of the current poverty line amounts during each year of the post-discharge monitoring period.

5. Reinstatement of obligation to repay discharged loans or complete discharged TEACH Grant service obligation. If you do not meet the requirements described above in Item 4 at any time during or at the end of the post-discharge monitoring period, the Department will reinstate your obligation to repay your discharged loan(s) and/or to complete your discharged TEACH Grant service obligation. If you received a discharge of your loan(s), this means that you will be responsible for repaying your loan(s) in accordance with the terms of your promissory note(s). However, you will not be required to pay interest on your loan(s) for the period from the date of the discharge until the date your repayment obligation was reinstated. The Department will continue to be your loan holder. If you received a discharge of your TEACH Grant service obligation, you will again be subject to the requirements of your TEACH Grant Agreement to Serve. If you do not meet the terms of that agreement and the TEACH Grant funds you received are converted to a Direct Unsubsidized Loan, you must repay that loan in full, and interest will be charged from the date(s) that the TEACH Grant funds were disbursed.

If your obligation to repay a loan or complete a TEACH Grant service obligation is reinstated, the Department will notify you of the reinstatement. This notification will include:

- The reason or reasons for the reinstatement;
- For loans, an explanation that the first payment due date following the reinstatement will be no earlier than 60 days following the notification of reinstatement; and
- Information on how you may contact the Department if you have questions about the reinstatement, or if you believe that your obligation to repay a loan or complete a TEACH Grant service obligation was reinstated based on incorrect information.

SECTION 7: ELIGIBILITY REQUIREMENTS TO RECEIVE FUTURE LOANS OR TEACH GRANTS

For veterans who receive a total and permanent disability discharge based on a determination by the VA that they are unemployable due to a service-connected disability:

If you are granted a **discharge** based on a determination that you are totally and permanently disabled in accordance with paragraph (2) of the definition of "total and permanent disability" in Section 5, you are not eligible to receive future loans under the FFEL, Perkins Loan, or Direct Loan programs or TEACH Grants unless:

- You obtain a certification from a physician that you are able to engage in substantial gainful activity; and
- You sign a statement acknowledging that the new loan or TEACH Grant service obligation cannot be discharged in the future on the basis of any injury or illness present at the time the new loan or TEACH Grant is made, unless your condition substantially deteriorates so that you are again totally and permanently disabled.

For all other individuals who receive a total and permanent disability discharge:

If you are granted a **discharge** based on a determination that you are totally and permanently disabled in accordance with paragraph (1) of the definition of "total and permanent disability" in Section 5, you are not eligible to receive future loans under the FFEL, Perkins Loan, or Direct Loan programs or TEACH Grants unless:

- You obtain a certification from a physician that you are able to engage in substantial gainful activity;
- You sign a statement acknowledging that the new loan or TEACH Grant service obligation cannot be discharged in the future on the basis of any injury or illness present at the time the new loan or TEACH Grant is made, unless your condition substantially deteriorates so that you are again totally and permanently disabled; and
- If you request a FFEL, Perkins Loan, or Direct Loan program loan or a new TEACH Grant within three years of the date that a previous loan or TEACH Grant was discharged, you resume payment on the previously discharged loan or acknowledge that you are once again subject to the terms of the TEACH Grant Agreement to Serve before receiving the new loan.

SECTION 8: IMPORTANT NOTICES

Privacy Act Notice. The Privacy Act of 1974 (5 U.S.C. 552a) requires that the following notice be provided to you:

The authorities for collecting the requested information from and about you are §421 *et seq.*, §451 *et seq.*,§461 *et seq.*, and §420L *et seq.* of the Higher Education Act of 1965, as amended (the HEA) (20 U.S.C. 1071 *et seq.*, 20 U.S.C. 1087a *et seq.*, 20 U.S.C. 1087aa *et seq.*, and 20 U.S.C. 1070g *et seq.*) and the authorities for collecting and using your Social Security Number (SSN) are §§428B(f) and 484(a)(4) of the HEA (20 U.S.C. 1078-2(f) and 1091(a)(4)) and §31001(i)(1) of the Debt Collection Improvement Act of 1996 (31 U.S.C. 7701(c)). Participating in the Federal Family Education Loan (FFEL) Program, the William D. Ford Federal Direct Loan (Direct Loan) Program, the Federal Perkins Loan (Perkins Loan) Program, and/or the Teacher Education Assistance for College and Higher Education (TEACH) Grant Program and giving us your SSN are voluntary, but you must provide the requested information, including your SSN, to participate.

The principal purposes for collecting the information on this form, including your SSN, are to verify your identity, to determine your eligibility to receive a FFEL, Direct Loan, and/or Perkins Loan program loan or a TEACH Grant, to receive a benefit on a loan (such as a deferment, forbearance, discharge, or forgiveness) or a discharge of a TEACH Grant service obligation, to permit the servicing of your loan(s) or TEACH Grant(s), and, if it becomes necessary, to locate you and to collect and report on your loan(s) if your loan(s) become delinquent or in default. We also use your SSN as an account identifier and to permit you to access your account information electronically.

The information in your file may be disclosed, on a case-by-case basis or under a computer matching program, to third parties as authorized under routine uses in the appropriate systems of records notices.

For a loan or for a TEACH Grant that has not been converted to a Direct Unsubsidized Loan, the routine uses of the information that we collect about you include, but are not limited to, its disclosure to federal, state, or local agencies, to institutions of higher education, and to third party servicers to determine your eligibility to receive a loan or a TEACH Grant, to investigate possible fraud, and to verify compliance with federal student financial aid program regulations.

In the event of litigation, we may send records to the Department of Justice, a court, adjudicative body, counsel, party, or witness if the disclosure is relevant and necessary to the litigation. If this information, either alone or with other information, indicates a potential violation of law, we may send it to the appropriate authority for action. We may send information to members of Congress if you ask them to help you with federal student aid questions. In circumstances involving employment complaints, grievances, or disciplinary actions, we may disclose relevant records to adjudicate or investigate the issues. If provided for by a collective bargaining agreement, we may disclose records to a labor organization recognized under 5 U.S.C. Chapter 71. Disclosures may be made to our contractors for the purpose of performing any programmatic function that requires disclosure of records. Before making any such disclosure, we will require the contractor to maintain Privacy Act safeguards. Disclosures may also be made to qualified researchers under Privacy Act safeguards.

For a loan, including a TEACH Grant that has been converted to a Direct Unsubsidized Loan, the routine uses of this information also include, but are not limited to, its disclosure to federal, state, or local agencies, to private parties such as relatives, present and former employers, business and personal associates, to creditors, to financial and educational institutions, and to guaranty agencies to verify your identity, to determine your program eligibility and benefits, to permit making, servicing, assigning, collecting, adjusting, or discharging your loan(s), to enforce the terms of the loan(s), to investigate possible fraud and to verify compliance with federal student financial aid program regulations, to locate you if you become delinquent in your loan payments or if you default, or to verify whether your debt qualifies for discharge or cancellation. To provide default rate calculations, disclosures may be made to guaranty agencies, to financial and educational institutions, or to federal, state or local agencies. To provide financial aid history information, disclosures may be made to educational institutions. To assist program administrators with tracking refunds and cancellations, disclosures may be made to guaranty agencies, to financial and educational institutions, or to federal or state agencies. To provide a standardized method for educational institutions to efficiently submit student enrollment status, disclosures may be made to guaranty agencies or to financial and educational institutions. To counsel you in repayment efforts, disclosures may be made to guaranty agencies, to financial and educational institutions, or to federal, state, or local agencies.

Paperwork Reduction Notice. According to the Paperwork Reduction Act of 1995, no persons are required to respond to a collection of information unless it displays a currently valid OMB control number. The valid OMB control number for this information collection is 1845-0065. The time required to complete this information collection is estimated to average 0.5 hours (30 minutes) per response, including the time to review instructions, search existing data resources, gather and maintain the data needed, and complete and review the information collection.

If you have comments concerning the accuracy of the time estimate(s) or suggestions for improving this form, please write to: U.S. Department of Education, Washington, DC 20202-4537. *Do not send the completed loan discharge application to this address.*

If you have comments or concerns regarding the status of *your individual submission* of this form, contact your loan holder (see Section 3).

D.3.8.2 Letters from Department of Education Regarding Disability Discharges

1. Letter from Loan Holder Explaining Preliminary Approval of Discharge

U. S. DEPARTMENT OF EDUCATION
STUDENT FINANCIAL ASSISTANCE

DATE: OCTOBER 27, 2007

DEAR STUDENT LOAN BORROWER:

THE U.S. DEPARTMENT OF EDUCATION (ED) HAS RECEIVED AND REVIEWED YOUR APPLICATION FOR DISCHARGE OF YOUR STUDENT LOAN(S) DUE TO TOTAL AND PERMANENT DISABILITY. ED HAS MADE A PRELIMINARY DETERMINATION THAT YOUR LOAN(S) APPEARS TO MEET THE CRITERIA FOR TOTAL AND PERMANENT DISABILITY DISCHARGE. ED'S CONDITIONAL DISABILITY DISCHARGE UNIT WILL NOW REVIEW YOUR APPLICATION AND NOTIFY YOU OF THE INITIAL DETERMINATION REGARDING YOUR REQUEST FOR TOTAL AND PERMANENT DISABILITY LOAN DISCHARGE.

THOUGH YOU ARE NOT REQUIRED TO MAKE PAYMENTS AT THIS TIME, YOU SHOULD NOTE THAT ANY INTEREST THAT ACCRUES ON YOUR LOAN(S) PRIOR TO RECEIPT OF AN INITIAL DETERMINATION LETTER IS YOUR RESPONSIBILITY. IN THE EVENT YOUR REQUEST FOR LOAN DISCHARGE IS DENIED, THIS UNPAID ACCRUED INTEREST MAY BE CAPITALIZED (ADDED TO THE PRINCIPAL BALANCE) IF NOT REPAID PRIOR TO ENTERING REPAYMENT.
IF YOU HAVE GENERAL QUESTIONS REGARDING THE CHANGES IN THE TOTAL AND PERMANENT DISABILITY DISCHARGE RULES AND PROCEDURES, PLEASE CONTACT ED'S CUSTOMER SERVICE CENTER TOLL-FREE AT (800) 621-3115. IF YOU HAVE SPECIFIC QUESTIONS ABOUT THE STATUS OF YOUR DISCHARGE APPLICATION, PLEASE CONTACT ED'S DISABILITY DISCHARGE LOAN SERVICING CENTER TOLL-FREE AT (888) 869-4169 OR SEND AN EMAIL TO DISABILITY_DISCHARGE@AFSA.COM. HEARING IMPAIRED INDIVIDUALS WITH ACCESS TO A TDD (TELECOMMUNICATIONS DEVICE FOR THE DEAF) CAN CALL (888) 636-6401. SEND ALL WRITTEN CORRESPONDENCE TO:

U.S. DEPARTMENT OF EDUCATION
CONDITIONAL DISABILITY DISCHARGE UNIT
P.O. BOX 7200
UTICA, NEW YORK 13504

2. Letter from Department of Education Denying Discharge Based on Medical Review Failure

Conditional Discharge Ineligibility

12/26/2007

Account #.
Loan #(s):

Reason for Notice

Your loan discharge request for total and permanent disability submitted to
USA FUNDS
has been transferred to the U.S. Department of Education's (ED's) Disability Discharge Loan Servicing Center based on a preliminary determination that you were totally and permanently disabled.

ED is the new holder of your loan(s). The change in ownership of your loan(s) will be reported to national credit bureaus.

Important Information

Further review of your discharge application and supporting documentation indicates that you do not meet ED's definition of total and permanent disability for the following reason:

Medical Review Failure

ED will return your loan(s) to an active status. You must resume payment on the loan(s).

You will soon be informed of when and how to make payments.

Questions

If you have any questions, please contact the Disability Discharge Loan Servicing Center at 1-888-869-4169 or send an email to disability_discharge@acs-inc.com. Written correspondence can be sent to U.S. Department of Education Conditional Total and Permanent Disability Assignments PO Box 7200 Utica, NY 13504. Hearing impaired individuals with access to a TDD (Telecommunications Device for the Deaf) can call 1-888-636-6401.

Our Mission is to Ensure Equal Access to Education and to Promote Educational Excellence Throughout the Nation

Student Assistance Forms Appx. D.3.8.2

3. Letter from Department of Education Approving Final Discharge

We Help Put America Through School

Notice of Loan Discharge

03/04/2010

Account #:
Conditional Discharge Period Begin Date: 01/01/2003
Loan #:

Reason for Notice

This notice certifies you have fully met the requirements of the 3-year conditional discharge process. All loans referenced above that were assigned to the U.S. Department of Education Federal Student Aid's (FSA) Disability Discharge Loan Servicing Center by

WELLESLEY COLLEGE

have been discharged due to total and permanent disability. Your loan(s) in the amount of

$1,707.77

were discharged on

02/25/2010

Important Information

We will return to you any payments received by your previous loan holder and/or by FSA after 01/01/2003. (NOTE: If a loan listed above is a FFEL Loan obligation that is a portion of a joint consolidation loan, a co-made PLUS Loan, or an endorsed loan, FSA will instruct your loan holder to discharge your loan obligation or the applicable portion of your loan obligation. FSA is only processing your discharge eligibility. FSA is not the new holder of your loan obligation. You should contact your loan holder for further information about repayment arrangements for any remaining balance or any refund of payments for which you may be eligible.)

Questions

Please contact the Disability Discharge Loan Servicing Center from 8:00 AM to 8:30 PM Eastern Time, Monday through Friday at 1-888-869-4169 or send an e-mail to disability_discharge@acs-inc.com. Individuals with access to a TDD (Telecommunications Device for the Deaf) can call 1-888-636-6401. Written correspondence can be sent to:

U.S. Department of Education
Disability Discharge Loan Servicing Center
P.O. Box 5200
Greenville, TX 75403-5200

Appx. D.4   *Student Loan Law*

D.4 Collection Letters and Hearing Forms

D.4.1 *Department of Education's Request for Administrative Wage Garnishment Hearing Form*

REQUEST FOR HEARING

If you object to garnishment of your wages for the debt described in the notice, you can use this form to request a hearing. **Your request must be in writing and mailed or delivered to the address below**.

Your Name: _____ SSN: _____
Address: _____
_____

Telephone: _____
Employer: _____
   Address: _____
   _____

   Telephone: _____
   Beginning Date Of Current Employment: _____

( )   CHECK HERE if you object on the grounds that garnishment in amounts equal to **15%** of your disposable pay would cause financial hardship to you and your dependents. (To arrange voluntary repayment, contact customer service at the number below.)

You must complete either the enclosed **FINANCIAL DISCLOSURE FORM** or a Financial Disclosure Form of your choosing to present your hardship claim. You must enclose copies of earnings and income records, and proof of expenses, as explained on the form. If your request for an oral hearing is granted, you will be notified of the date, time, and location of your hearing. If your request for an oral hearing is denied, the Department will make its determination of the amounts you should pay based on a review of your written materials.

NOTE: You should also state below any other objections you have to garnishment to collect this debt at this time.

NOTE: IT IS IN YOUR INTEREST TO REQUEST COPIES OF ALL DOCUMENTATION HELD BY THE DEPARTMENT BY CALLING THE CUSTOMER SERVICE NUMBER LISTED ON THE ENCLOSED NOTICE PRIOR TO COMPLETING A REQUEST FOR HEARING.

I.   **HEARING REQUEST (Check ONLY ONE of the following)**

( ) I want a written records hearing of my objection(s) based on the Department's review of this written statement, the documents I have enclosed, and the records in my debt file at the Department.

( ) I want an in-person hearing at the Department hearing office to present my objection(s). I understand that I must pay my own expenses to appear for this hearing.

   I want this In-Person hearing held in: ____ Atlanta, GA, ____ Chicago, IL, ____ San Francisco, CA. (Check the location you wish for the hearing.)

( ) I want a hearing by telephone to present my objections. (You must provide a daytime telephone number at which you can be contacted between the hours of 8:00 am to 4:00 pm, Monday through Friday.) I can be reached at:( ) _____-_____

This is an attempt to collect a debt and any information obtained will be used for that purpose.

Student Assistance Forms　　　　　　　　　　　　　　　　　　　　　　　　Appx. D.4.1

REQUEST FOR HEARING

II. IF YOU WANT AN IN-PERSON OR TELEPHONE HEARING, YOU MUST COMPLETE THE FOLLOWING:

The debt records and documents I submitted to support my statement in Part III do not show all the material (important) facts about my objection to collection of this debt. I need a hearing to explain the following important facts about this debt: (**EXPLAIN** the additional facts that you believe make a hearing necessary on a separate sheet of paper. If you have already fully described these facts in your response in Part III, **WRITE HERE** the number of the objection in which you described these facts _____.)

Note: If you do not request an in-person or telephone hearing, we will review your objection based on information and documents you supply with this form and on records in your loan file. We will provide an oral hearing to a debtor who requests an oral hearing and shows in the request for the hearing, a good reason to believe that we cannot resolve the issues in dispute by reviewing the documentary evidence. An example is when the validity of the claim turns on the issue of credibility or veracity.

_____

III. Check the objections that apply. EXPLAIN any further facts concerning your objection on a separate sheet of paper. ENCLOSE the documents described here (if you do not enclose documents, the Department will consider your objection(s) based on the information on this form and records held by the Department).

For some objections you must submit a completed application. Obtain applications by contacting Customer Service at the number below, or go to the Department's Web site at:
  HTTP://WWW.ED.GOV/Offices/OSFAP/DCS, select Forms, then select the application described for that objection.

1. ( ) I do not owe the full amount shown because I repaid some or all of this debt. (ENCLOSE: copies of the front and back of all checks, money orders and any receipts showing payments made to the holder of the debt.)

2. ( ) I am making payments on this debt as required under the repayment agreement I reached with the holder of the debt. (ENCLOSE: copies of the repayment agreement and copies of the front and back of checks where you paid on the agreement.)

3. ( ) I filed for bankruptcy and my case is still open. (ENCLOSE: copies of <u>any documents from the court</u> that show the date that you filed, the name of the court, and your case number.)

4. ( ) This debt was discharged in bankruptcy. (ENCLOSE: copies of debt discharge order and the schedule of debts filed with the court.)

5. ( ) The borrower has died. (ENCLOSE: Original, certified copy, or clear, accurate, and complete photocopy of the original or certified Death Certificate.) For loans only.

6. ( ) I am totally and permanently disabled - unable to work and earn money because of an impairment that is expected to continue indefinitely or result in death. (Obtain and submit a completed Loan Discharge Application: Total and Permanent Disability form; the form must be completed by physician.) For loans only.

7. ( ) I used this loan to enroll in _____(school) on or about ___/___/___, and I withdrew from school on or about ___/___/___. I paid the school $_____ and I believe that I am owed, but have not been paid, a refund from the school in the amount of $_____. (Obtain and submit a completed Loan Discharge Application: Unpaid Refund form. ENCLOSE: any records you have showing your withdrawal date). For loans only.

This is an attempt to collect a debt and any information obtained will be used for that purpose

Appx. D.4.1 *Student Loan Law*

REQUEST FOR HEARING

8. ( ) I used this loan to enroll in _____(school) on or about ___/___/___ and I was unable to complete my education because the school closed. (Obtain and submit a completed Loan Discharge Application: School Closure form. ENCLOSE: any records you have showing your withdrawal date.) For loans only.

9. ( ) This is not my Social Security Number, and I do not owe this debt. (ENCLOSE: a copy of your driver's license or other identification issued by a federal, state or local government agency, and a copy of your Social Security Card.)

10. ( ) I believe that this debt is not an enforceable debt in the amount stated for the reason explained in the attached letter. (Attach a letter explaining any reason other than those listed above for your objection to collection of this debt amount by garnishment of your salary. ENCLOSE: any supporting records.)

11. ( ) I did not have a high school diploma or GED when I enrolled at the school I attended with this guaranteed student loan. The school did not properly test my ability to benefit from the training offered. (Obtain and submit a completed Loan Discharge Application: False Certification (Ability to Benefit) form. ENCLOSE: any records you have showing your withdrawal date.) For loans only.

12. ( ) When I borrowed this guaranteed student loan to attend _____(school), I had a condition (physical, mental, age, criminal record) that prevented me from meeting State requirements for performing the occupation for which the school trained me. (Obtain and submit completed Loan Discharge Application: False Certification (Disqualifying Status) form. For loans only.

13. ( ) I was involuntarily terminated from my last employment and I have been employed in my current job for less than twelve months. (Attach statement from employer showing date of hire in current job and statement from prior employer showing involuntary termination.)

14 ( ) I believe that _____ (school) without my permission signed my name on the loan application, promissory note, loan check, or electronic funds transfer (EFT) authorization. (Obtain and submit a completed Loan Discharge Application: False Certification (Unauthorized Signature / Unauthorized Payment) form. ENCLOSE: any records you have showing your withdrawal date). For loans only.

IV. I state under penalty of law that the statements made on this request are true and accurate to the best of my knowledge.

DATE: _____ SIGNATURE: _____

SEND THIS REQUEST FOR HEARING FORM TO: U.S. DEPARTMENT OF EDUCATION
　　　　　　　　　　　　　　　　　　　　　　　　　　　　　　AWG HEARINGS UNIT
　　　　　　　　　　　　　　　　　　　　　　　　　　　　　　P.O. BOX 617547
　　　　　　　　　　　　　　　　　　　　　　　　　　　　　　CHICAGO, IL 60661-7547

If you wish to arrange a voluntary agreement for payments in amounts equal to 15% of your disposable pay, do not use this form. Instead, call the Customer Service telephone number below:

U.S. Department of Education Customer Service
1-800-621-3115

Violation of any such agreement may result in an immediate order to your employer for garnishment of 15% of your disposable pay.

This is an attempt to collect a debt and any information obtained will be used for that purpose.

Student Assistance Forms Appx. D.4.2

D.4.2 Department of Education Financial Disclosure Statement for Wage Garnishment Hearings Only

U.S. Department of Education
Financial Disclosure Statement

To evaluate a hardship claim, ED compares the expenses you claim and support against averages spent for those expenses by families of the same size and income as yours. ED considers proven expenses as reasonable up to the amount of these averages. If you claim more for an expense than the average spent by families like yours, you must provide persuasive explanation why the amount you claim is necessary. These average amounts were determined by the IRS from different government studies. You can find the average expense amount that the Department uses under "Collection Financial Standards" at http://www.irs.gov/

- **Complete all items.** Do not leave any item blank. If the answer is zero, write zero.
- **Provide documentation of expenses.** Expenses may not be considered if you do not provide documents supporting the amounts claimed.
- **Disclose and provide documentation of household income.**
- Failure to provide this information and documentation may result in a denial of your claim of financial hardship as unproven.

Income

Your Name: _____ Your Social Security No.: _____
Address: _____
         _____ Phone: _____
         _____ County: _____

Current Employer: _____ Date Employed: _____
Employer Phone: _____   Present Position: _____

Gross Income: $_____ ❑ Weekly ❑ Bi-Weekly ❑ Monthly ❑ Other _____
Net Income: $_____ ❑ Weekly ❑ Bi-Weekly ❑ Monthly ❑ Other _____

*****ENCLOSE A COPY OF YOUR TWO MOST RECENT PAY STUBS***
ENCLOSE COPIES OF MOST RECENT W-2s AND 1040, 1040A, 1040EZ or other IRS FILING

Number of dependents: _____ (including yourself)

Marital status: ❑ Married ❑ Single ❑ Divorced

Your spouse's name: _____ Spouse SSN: _____

Gross Income: $_____ ❑ Weekly ❑ Bi-Weekly ❑ Monthly ❑ Other _____
Net Income: $_____ ❑ Weekly ❑ Bi-Weekly ❑ Monthly ❑ Other _____

*****ENCLOSE COPY OF TWO MOST RECENT PAY STUBS***
ENCLOSE COPIES OF MOST RECENT W-2s AND 1040, 1040A, 1040EZ or other IRS FILING

This is an attempt to collect a debt and any information obtained will be used for that purpose.

Other household member(s) with income: Name _____
        SSN: _____

Gross Income: $_____   ❑ Weekly ❑ Bi-Weekly ❑ Monthly ❑ Other _____
Net Income: $_____   ❑ Weekly ❑ Bi-Weekly ❑ Monthly ❑ Other _____

*****ENCLOSE COPY OF TWO MOST RECENT PAY STUBS***
ENCLOSE COPIES OF MOST RECENT W-2s AND 1040, 1040A, 1040EZ or other IRS FILING

Other Income
  Child support: $_____   ❑ Weekly ❑ Bi-Weekly ❑ Monthly ❑ Other
  Alimony: $_____   ❑ Weekly ❑ Bi-Weekly ❑ Monthly ❑ Other
  Interest: $_____   ❑ Weekly ❑ Bi-Weekly ❑ Monthly ❑ Other
  Public assistance: $_____   ❑ Weekly ❑ Bi-Weekly ❑ Monthly ❑ Other
  Other: $_____   Describe: _____

Please explain all deductions shown on pay-stubs:

Deductions	Amount	Reason
401k:	_____	_____
Retirement:	_____	_____
Union Dues:	_____	_____
Medical:	_____	_____
Credit Union:	_____	_____
Other:	_____	_____

Monthly Expenses

Shelter (SEND COPY OF MORTGAGE OR LEASE)
  Rent/Mortgage: $_____   Paid to whom: _____
  2nd home mortgage: $_____   Paid to whom: _____
  Home insurance: $_____
  Other: $_____   Describe: _____

Food and Household
Expenses: $_____
Clothing: $_____

Utilities (SEND COPIES OF BILLS)
  Electric: $_____
  Gas: $_____
  Water/Sewer $_____
  Garbage pickup: $_____
  Basic telephone: $_____
  Other: $_____   Describe: _____

This is an attempt to collect a debt and any information obtained will be used for that purpose.

Student Assistance Forms   Appx. D.4.2

Medical (SEND COPIES OF BILLS)
    Insurance $_____/per month   *(Only list payments not deducted from paycheck)*
    Bill payments $_____/per month *(Only list payments not covered by insurance)*
    Other: $_____/per month
Describe: _____

Transportation (SEND COPIES OF CAR PAYMENT AGREEMENT OR BILLS)

Of cars _____
    1st Car payment: $_____/per month
    2nd Car payment: $_____/per month
    Gas and oil: $_____/per month
    Public transportation: $_____/per month
    Car insurance: $_____/per month
    Other: $_____   Describe: _____

Child Care (SEND COPIES OF BILLS)

    Child care: $_____/per month   Number of children: _____
    Child support: $_____/per month   Number of children: _____
    Other: $_____/per month   Describe: _____

Other Insurance: $_____   Describe: _____

Other Expenses (Attach a list describing expense, monthly payment and enclose bills)

Based on this Statement, I think I can afford to pay $_____per month

I declare under penalty of perjury that the answers and statements contained herein are true and correct.

Signature _____ Date _____

Warning: 18 U.S.C. 1001 provides that "whoever…knowingly and willfully falsifies, conceals, or covers up by any trick, scheme, or device a material fact, or makes any materially false, fictitious, or fraudulent statement or representation…shall be fined up to $10,000.00 or imprisoned up to five years, or both."

Complete, sign, and return the requested information and documentation to:

           U.S. Department of Education
           AWG Hearings Unit
           P. O. Box 617547
           Chicago, Illinois 60661-7547

Privacy Act Notice

This request is authorized under 31 U.S.C. 3711, 20 U.S.C. 1078-6, and 20 U.S.C. 1095a. You are not required to provide this information. If you do not, we cannot determine your financial ability to repay your student aid debt. The information you provide will be used to evaluate your ability to pay. It may be disclosed to government agencies and their contractors, to employees, lenders, and others to enforce this debt; to third parties in audit, research, or dispute about the management of this debt; and to parties with a right to this information under the Freedom of Information Act or other federal law, or with your consent. These uses are explained in the Federal Register of June 4, 1999, Vol. 64, p.30166, revised Dec.27, 1999, Vol. 64, p. 72407. We will send a copy at your request.

This is an attempt to collect a debt and any information obtained will be used for that purpose.

D.4.3 Department of Education Statement of Financial Status

THIS IS IN RESPONSE TO YOUR REQUEST TO ESTABLISH A MONTHLY PAYMENT PLAN. IN ORDER TO DETERMINE A PAYMENT AMOUNT THAT IS BOTH AFFORDABLE FOR YOU AND REASONABLE BASED ON THE AMOUNT YOU OWE, YOU MUST COMPLETE THE FOLLOWING STATEMENT OF FINANCIAL STATUS.

INSTRUCTIONS:

1. **IMMEDIATELY BEGIN SENDING THE AMOUNT YOU PROPOSE TO PAY** EACH MONTH TO:

    U.S. DEPARTMENT OF EDUCATION
    P.O. BOX 105028
    ATLANTA, GA 30348-5028

INCLUDE YOUR SOCIAL SECURITY NUMBER ON YOUR PAYMENT INSTRUMENT AND DO NOT SEND CASH.

2. COMPLETE EVERY FIELD ON THIS FORM. IF AN ANSWER IS ZERO, WRITE ZERO.

3. INCLUDE PROOF OF YOUR HOUSEHOLD INCOME FOR BOTH YOU AND YOUR SPOUSE (TWO MOST RECENT PAY STUBS AND FEDERAL INCOME TAX RETURNS), AND PROOF OF YOUR EXPESNSES (SUCH AS COPIES OF MONTHLY BILLS).

4. DO NOT INCLUDE MONTHLY PAYMENTS ON CREDIT CARDS IF THE ITEMS PURCHASED BY THAT CREDIT CARD FIT UNDER AN EXPENSE CATEGORY LISTED HERE. INCLUDE THOSE COSTS UNDER THAT EXPENSE CATEGORY. FOR EXAMPLE, PAYMENTS REQUIRED ON DEPARTMENT STORE CREDIT CARDS USED TO PURCHASE CLOTHING SHOULD BE LISTED UNDER CLOTHING EXPENSES.

5. IF YOU ARE PAYING SOME EXPENSES QUARTERLY OR ANNUALLY, SUCH AS AUTOMOBILE INSURANCE OR PROPERTY TAXES, CALCULATE THE AMOUNT THAT WOULD BE DUE IF THESE EXPENSES WERE PAID ON A MONTHLY BASIS AND PUT THAT AMOUNT IN THE SPACE PROVIDED.

6. RETURN THE COMPLETED FORM TO: U.S. DEPARTMENT OF EDUCATION
                                    PO BOX 5609
                                    GREENVILLE, TX 75403-5609

Student Assistance Forms

STATEMENT OF FINANCIAL STATUS

AMOUNT YOU ARE PROPOSING TO PAY EACH MONTH: $ _____

COUNTY IN WHICH YOU LIVE: _____ SSN: _____

NAME, ADDRESS _____
AND PHONE
NUMBER OF YOUR _____
CURRENT
EMPLOYER(S) _____

NUMBER OF DEPENDENTS (AS DEFINED BY IRS) INCLUDING SELF: _____
MARITAL STATUS (MARRIED, SINGLE, DIVORCED)   _____
SPOUSE'S NAME AND SSN: _____

MONTHLY INCOME:

NOTE: GROSS INCOME IS INCOME BEFORE ANY DEDUCTIONS SUCH AS TAXES. NET INCOME IS YOUR TAKE-HOME PAY. INCLUDE A COPY OF RECENT PAY STUBS.

YOUR MONTHLY INCOME   GROSS $_____ NET $_____
YOUR SPOUSE'S MONTHLY INCOME   GROSS $_____ NET $_____
OTHER CONTRIBUTING RESIDENT(S) MONTHLY INCOME   NET $_____
OTHER (CHILD SUPPORT, ETC. DESCRIBE_____)NET $_____

MONTHLY EXPENSES:

RENT/MORTGAGE   (TO WHOM:_____) $_____
PROPERTY TAX   (TO WHOM:_____) $_____
HOME INSURANCE   (TO WHOM:_____) $_____

FOOD $_____   ELECTRICITY $_____   WATER/SEWER $_____
CLOTHING $_____   NATURAL GAS $_____   GARBAGE $_____
BASIC PHONE $_____   CAR PYMNT 1 $_____   CAR PYMNT 2 $_____
CAR INSURE $_____   PUBLIC TRAN $_____   GAS AND OIL $_____
MEDICAL INSURANCE PAYMENTS NOT DEDUCTED FROM PAYCHECK $_____
MEDICAL CO-PAYMENTS AND EXPENSES NOT COVERED BY INSURANCE $_____

Appx. D.4.3

CHILD CARE EXPENSES(NUMBER OF CHILDREN:_____) $_____
CHILD SUPPORT   (NUMBER OF CHILDREN:_____) $_____

LIST ANY OTHER MONTHLY EXPENSES BELOW:

1)_____ $_____
2)_____ $_____
3)_____ $_____

ASSETS:

BANK ACCOUNT 1(BANK NAME:_____) $_____
BANK ACCOUNT 2(BANK NAME:_____) $_____
BANK ACCOUNT 3(BANK NAME:_____) $_____
STOCKS/BONDS   (BANK NAME:_____) $_____
HOME   VALUE $_____ OWED $_____
OTHER REAL ESTATE   VALUE $_____ OWED $_____
CAR 1(YR,MAKE,MODEL:_____)VALUE $_____ OWED $_____
CAR 1(YR,MAKE,MODEL:_____)VALUE $_____ OWED $_____

PLEASE SIGN THE DECLARATION BELOW:

I DECLARE UNDER PENALTIES PROVIDED BY 18 U.S.C. SECTION 1001, THAT THE ANSWERS AND STATEMENTS CONTAINED HEREIN ARE TO THE BEST OF MY KNOWLEDGE AND BELIEF TRUE, CORRECT AND COMPLETE.

SIGNATURE:_____DATE:_____

WARNING:18 U.S.C. 1001 PROVIDES THAT "WHOEVER...KNOWINGLY AND WILLFULLY FALSIFIES, CONCEALS OR COVERS UP BY ANY TRICK, SCHEME, OR DEVICE A MATERIAL FACT, OR MAKES ANY FALSE, FICTITIOUS OR FRAUDULENT STATEMENTS OR REPRESENTATION.., SHALL BE FINED NOT MORE THAN $10,000.00, OR IMPRISONED NOT MORE THAN FIVE YEARS, OR BOTH".

                         PRIVACY ACT NOTICE

THIS REQUEST IS AUTHORIZED UNDER 31 U.S.C. 3711,20 U.S.C. 1078-6,AND 20 U.S.C. 1095A.YOU ARE NOT REQUIRED TO PROVIDE THIS INFORMATION. IF YOU DO NOT, WE CANNOT DETERMINE YOUR FINANCIAL ABILITY TO REPAY YOUR STUDENT AID DEBT. THE INFORMATION YOU PROVIDE WILL BE USED TO EVALUATE YOUR ABILITY TO PAY. IT MAY BE DISCLOSED TO GOVERNMENT AGENCIES AND THEIR CONTRACTORS, TO EMPLOYERS, LENDERS, AND OTHERS TO ENFORCE THIS DEBT; TO THIRD PARTIES IN AUDIT, RESEARCH, OR DISPUTE ABOUT THE MANAGEMENT OF THIS DEBT; AND TO PARTIES WITH A RIGHT TO THIS INFORMATION UNDER THE FREEDOM OF INFORMATION ACT OR OTHER FEDERAL LAW OR WITH YOUR CONSENT. THESE USES ARE EXPLAINED IN NOTICE IN THE STUDENT FINANCIAL ASSISTANCE COLLECTION FILES, NO 18-11-07; WE WILL SEND A COPY AT YOUR REQUEST.

Student Assistance Forms   Appx. D.4.4

D.4.4 Private Collection Agency Complaint Form

PCA Procedures Manual - 2009

PCA COMPLAINT FORM

AGY#:_____   Date complaint received:_____

Complaint written or verbal:_____   Date of response:_____

Respondent's name/phone #/email address: _____
_____

Borrower's Name: _____   SSN/Debt ID:_____

Borrower's phone number (if not YET updated on L103):_____

PCA employee(s) named OR responsible for complaint:_____
_____

TYPE OF COMPLAINT:
- ❑ RECEIVED BY THE PCA ADDRESSED TO THE PCA
- ❑ RECEIVED BY THE PCA ADDRESSED TO ED
- ❑ RECEIVED BY ED ADDRESSED TO ED
- ❑ VANGENT COMPLAINT

LIST BORROWER'S COMPLAINT ISSUES
- ✓ _____
- ✓ _____
- ✓ _____

PCA RESPONSE _____
- ✓ _____
- ✓ _____

PCA RESOLUTION/ PREVENTIVE MEASURES
- ✓ _____
- ✓ _____
- ✓ _____

Document the L102 with issues and responses
And provide collector notes and borrower letters with this form

Revised April 2009

Appx. D.4.5   *Student Loan Law*

D.4.5 *Sample Treasury Notice of Offset*

PCA Procedures Manual - 2009

B. Sample Treasury Notice of Offset

DEPARTMENT OF THE TREASURY
FINANCIAL MANAGEMENT SERVICE
PO BOX 1686
BIRMINGHAM, ALABAMA 35201-1686

THIS IS NOT A BILL – PLEASE RETAIN FOR YOUR RECORDS

07/03/08

JOE BORROWER
123 STREET
CITYTOWN, ST 11111-2222

Dear JOE BORROWER:

As authorized by Federal law, we applied all or part of your Federal payment to a debt you owe. The government agency (or agencies) collecting your debt is listed below.

U.S. DEPARTMENT OF EDUCATION C/O GREAT LAKES HIGHER ED GUAR CORP COLLECTION SUPPORT P.O. BOX 7859 MADISON, WI 53707-7859 (608) 246-1535 (800) 354-6980 PURPOSE: Non-Tax Federal Debt	TIN Num: 999-99-9999 TOP Trace Num: P49899999 Acct Num: WI999999999 Amount This Creditor: $146.40 Creditor: 05 Site: WI

The Agency has previously sent notice to you at the last address know to the Agency. That notice explained the amount and type of debt you owe, the rights available to you, and that the Agency intended to collect the debt by intercepting any Federal payments made to you, including tax refunds. **If you believe your payment was reduced in error or if you have questions about this debt, you must contact the Agency at the address and telephone number shown above.** The U.S. Department of the Treasury's Financial Management Service cannot resolve issues regarding debts with other agencies.

We will forward the money taken from your Federal payment to the Agency to be applied to your debt balance; however, the Agency may not receive the funds for several weeks after the payment date. If you intend to contact the Agency, please have this notice available. Please do not contact the Social Security Administration regarding this reduction made in your Federal payment.

U.S. Department of the Treasury
Financial Management Service
(800) 304-3107
TELECOMMUNICATIONS DEVICE FOR THE DEAF (TDD) (866) 297-0517

Student Assistance Forms Appx. D.5.1

D.5 Additional Forms

D.5.1 FFEL Compromise and Write-Off Procedures for Guaranty Agencies

NCHELP

National Council of Higher Education Loan Programs, Inc.

801 Pennsylvania Avenue, S.E., Suite 375
Washington, DC 20003 • (202)547-1571
FAX (202)546-8745

Clearinghouse No. 49,168
Accession No. 1095310

November 7, 1993

DEC - 8 1993

Mr. Robert W. Evans
Director of Policy and Program Development
U.S. Department of Education
Office of Student Financial Assistance
Room 4310, ROB #3
7th & D Streets, S.W.
Washington, D.C. 20202

RE: Compromise and Write-Off Procedures

Dear Bob:

Thank you for reviewing the recommendations for standardized write-off and compromise procedures submitted by the Ad Hoc Standardization Group. NCHELP has made all of the clarifications and amendments you requested.

If you have any questions regarding these revised procedures, please let me know. Your prompt approval of these revised procedures will be appreciated by the community.

Sincerely yours,

Jean S. Frohlicher
President

I hereby approve the attached Standardized Compromise and Write-Off Procedures for use by guaranty agencies in the Federal Family Education Loan Program. Agencies may use these procedures without further approval from the Department of Education. Any changes a guaranty agency wishes to make in these approved procedures must be submitted to the Department for specific approval.

Robert W. Evans 11/24/93

Robert W. Evans, Director, Division of Policy Development

cc: Woody Farber
    Art Bilski
    Fred Hasselback
    Dallas Martin

STANDARDIZED COMPROMISE AND WRITE-OFF PROCEDURES

The following guidelines are established to allow a guaranty agency to compromise amounts owing on a defaulted reinsured student loan and to write off accounts where the loan(s) is determined to be uncollectible and the agency seeks to discontinue its semi-annual reviews as required under the due diligence requirements. Write off in this context does not relate to "writing the loan off the books" but only relates to the cessation of collection activity. In all cases, the reasons for the agency's decision and actions will be documented in the borrower's file.

COMPROMISE AUTHORITY

Compromise refers to a negotiated agreement between the debtor and the guaranty agency to accept a payment of a lesser portion of the total debt as full liquidation of the entire indebtedness. A guaranty agency will be permitted in certain cases to accept a compromise amount from a debtor as full satisfaction of the debt to all parties, including the U.S. Department of Education. The authority to accept a compromise as full satisfaction of the debt is intended to maximize collections on defaulted loans. The guaranty agency may compromise a loan at any time after it pays a default claim on that loan.

A guaranty agency will be permitted to compromise under the following circumstances and in the following amounts:

1. An agency can compromise an amount up to an amount equal to all collection costs in order to obtain payment in full of all principal and interest owing on a defaulted loan(s). The agency shall consider the litigative risk of seeking a judgment on a reinsured loan, the likelihood and timing of the collection of the loan, and the borrower's current and expected financial condition.

2. An agency can compromise an amount up to 30% of all principal and interest owing in order to obtain a payment in full of the reinsured portion of a loan(s). The agency shall consider the litigative risk of seeking a judgment on a reinsured loan, the likelihood and timing of the collection of the loan, and the borrower's current and expected financial condition. Compromises of less than 70% of the total indebtedness of principal and interest do not allow the guaranty agency to waive the Secretary's right to collect the remaining balance due.

3. An agency can compromise in situations that do not meet the criteria in #1 and #2 above, provided the agency can demonstrate and document the reasons for doing so and the compromise is approved by the division/agency director.

Approval authority for compromise settlements will be determined within each guaranty agency. However, the following minimum approval authorities will exist:

1. The supervisor directly charged with collections will have the authority to compromise all collection costs and the accrued interest on the loan(s), not to exceed 30% of the principal and interest owing.

2. The next level of management will have the authority to accept compromises in #1 above and any compromise of any principal amounts, not to exceed 30% of the principal and interest owing.

3. The agency director can approve compromises described in #1 and #2 above as well as compromises which exceed the 30% threshold.

DISCRETIONARY WRITE-OFF

Write-off of a reinsured loan(s) is intended only for the purpose of the guaranty agency's ceasing required collection activity as described in 34 C.F.R. 682.410(b)(6) and (7). The write-off of the loan does not relieve the debtor of the debt. Once an agency has "written off" a loan(s), it will insure that the account is permanently assigned to the U.S. Department of Education under 34 C.F.R. 682.409 *et seq.*

Exception to the above policy will be that guaranty agencies will have the authority to write off loan(s) with principal balances of less than $100 and a total balance less than $1,000, and any loan(s) where the remaining balance represents only interest, attorney fees, court costs, or collection costs without requiring the permanent assignment of the loan(s) to the U.S. Department of Education.

In making its determination to write off a loan and to cease collection activity, an agency will consider the debtor's and, if applicable, an endorser's current and expected inability to repay the debt. Examples of this condition are:

a. Borrowers who are repeatedly unemployed and have no prospects for future employment;
b. Borrowers who are repeatedly public assistance recipients;
c. Borrowers who are chronically ill, partially disabled, or of an age that results in their inability to work;
d. Borrowers whose potential for future earnings is limited or non-existent;
e. Borrowers who have no other funds available to them from other sources, such as an inheritance.

Approval authority for the write-off of a loan(s) will be individualized within each agency. However, the following minimum guidelines will apply:

1. Balances up to $5,000 can be approved by the supervisor responsible for collection of the loan(s).

2. Balances up to $20,000 can be approved by the next level of management within the guaranty agency if the documents authorizing a write-off contain the signatures of each agency official participating or concurring in the write-off decision.

3. Balances exceeding $20,000 can be approved by the division/agency director if the documents authorizing a write-off contain the signatures of each agency official participating or concurring in the write-off decision. In each case, upon approval of the write-off, the account will be scheduled for permanent assignment to the U.S. Department of Education under the provisions in 34 C.F.R. 682.409, *et seq.* (except those previously noted).

A debtor who benefits from a compromise or write-off must reaffirm the amount compromised or written off if he or she later wants to receive an FFEL Program loan.

D.5.2 Direct Loan Compromise Authority (April 1, 2005)

The Department of Education took this information off-line in spring 2010. Advocates should check the private contractor website to see if the Department restores this information or check with the Department for other information about Direct Loan compromises).

COMPROMISES

Subject: New Compromise Authority
Date: 04/01/04

With the growth and natural maturation of the Direct Loan defaulted loan portfolio we have taken a look at our compromise authority and decided that we no longer need to exclude Direct Loan program debts from eligibility.

The new guidelines are listed below. The chart contains the limits that you are required to follow.

These new guidelines are effective as of April 1, 2004.

Proposed New Compromise and Write-Off Authority:

Type of Compromise	Borrower Pays	Account Eligibility
1. Waiver of fees	Principal and Interest (P & I)	All debts
2. 50% Interest + Fees	All principal and 50% interest	All debts
3. 10% P&I	90% P & I	All debts
4. Discretionary		All debts

Lawannah Howell
Assistant COR

D.5.3 Sample Rehabilitation Agreement

D.5.3.1 Repayment Agreement Under the Loan Rehabilitation Program

REHABILITATION LETTERS

The standard rehabilitation agreement letter must include the following language:

This letter confirms my acceptance into the loan rehabilitation program and my agreement to repayment of my defaulted Federal Family Education Loan (FFEL) program student loans held by the U.S. Department of Education. I understand that compliance with this agreement is a prerequisite to the sale of my loans to an authorized lender.

Please check the appropriate paragraph:

( ) I understand that I must make at least nine (9) monthly payments in the amount of $«Insert», beginning «Insert», with each payment due on the same day each month thereafter. I must make the full payments in the agreed amount within twenty (20) days of their monthly due dates over a ten month period. If I fail to make the required number of on-time payments in a ten (10) month period, I will need to begin a new series of agreed upon payments in order to qualify for rehabilitation of my loans.

( ) I am currently making monthly payments. I understand that these payments, if timely, will be included in the calculation of the required minimum number of monthly payments. I will continue to meet my established monthly payment due date.

I also understand and agree to the following terms and conditions:

1. I understand that this agreement is null and void if I do not honor the terms of this agreement by making a full payment within twenty (20) of the monthly due date every month for a minimum of nine (9) months. Should this occur, I will need to begin a new series of agreed-upon payments in order to qualify for rehabilitation of my loans.

2. I cannot change the monthly payment amount without ED's agreement or the agreement of the collection agency servicing my account.

3. I may have to provide a new financial statement in order to support a request to change my monthly required payment amount.

4. I must continue to make monthly payments to ED beyond the required minimum period until I am notified in writing by ED or my new lender that the sale has been completed and that I am to begin making payments directly to my lender.

5. Any interest that I owe at the time my loan(s) is sold will be capitalized by the lender. In addition, the Department may add collection costs equal to 2% of the amount of principal and interest that I owe to the loan balance. Any outstanding interest and collection costs will be capitalized by the lender. This means that the lender will add any unpaid interest and collection costs to the principal that I owe on the loan(s), and this combined amount will become the new principal balance on the loan(s). Interest will then accrue on this new higher principal balance.

6. After the sale of my loan(s), any payments made to ED will be forwarded to my lender for credit to my account. Any involuntary payment (Treasury offset) or post-dated check will be refunded to me at the address on my billing statement.

7. My new lender will establish a new due date and will calculate a new monthly payment amount based upon the balance owed at the time of sale. The amount of the required monthly installment payment may substantially increase.

I have read the above and agree to the terms and conditions of the loan rehabilitation program and this repayment agreement.

Signed: _____ Date: _____

Please return this repayment agreement to:

D.5.3.2 Perkins Loan Rehabilitation

1. REPAYMENT AGREEMENT UNDER THE PERKINS LOAN REHABILITATION PROGRAM

**Repayment Agreement Under
The Perkins Loan Rehabilitation Program**

Note: Read this entire agreement before signing. Retain a copy for your records. Return a signed copy to the address shown at the end of this agreement.

I have been given an opportunity for a hearing to object to garnishment. I now withdraw any request for a hearing that I have filed.

I agree with the U.S. Department of Education (Department) that I will repay under the terms of this agreement my defaulted Perkins Loans held by the Department. I understand that compliance with this agreement is a prerequisite to rehabilitation of my loan(s).

( ) I understand that I must make 12 consecutive payments in the amount of $<<payment amount>>, beginning <<due date>>, with each payment due on the same day each month thereafter until a minimum of twelve consecutive monthly payments have been made.

( ) I am currently making consecutive monthly payments. I understand that these payments, if consecutive and if made in amounts at least equal to the agreed-amount, will be included in the calculation of the required twelve consecutive monthly payments required for rehabilitation of the loan(s). I will continue to meet my established monthly payment due date.

I understand that I must complete a new series of twelve (12) payments in order to qualify for rehabilitation—

- If I fail to make the required number of payments over a twelve (12) month period,
- If I make any payment later than fifteen (15) days after its due date, or
- If a check is returned for insufficient funds.

I also understand and agree to the following terms and conditions.

- I cannot change the monthly payment amount without the Department's agreement or the agreement of the collection agency servicing my account.
- The department agrees to waive collection of any cost the Department incurs as a result of the rehabilitation of my loan(s) under this agreement, unless I default on the loan(s) in the future. The Department will collect as part of the debt then owed, the collection cost originally waived under this agreement. This will substantially increase the amount that will then be owed and needed to satisfy the debt to the Department.

If I do not honor this agreement, the Department can start garnishing my pay at the rate of 15% of my disposable pay or the installment payment amount then in effect, whichever is less, without giving me further notice or any new opportunity for a hearing before that garnishment starts. I understand that if the Department starts garnishing my wages in the future, I can then object to garnishment, and the Department will give me a hearing on my objection(s).

I agree that—

- The Department will give me a hearing on objections I make in the future, but it will not delay or suspend garnishment while it hears and makes a decision on my objections;
- I can object in the future that garnishment would cause financial hardship to me and my dependents;
- I owe the amount stated in the notice of proposed garnishment I have just been sent, and I waive any future objection that I do not owe that amount;
- I can object to garnishment for reasons that arise after the date of this agreement, and

- I can also object to garnishment if I believe that I am entitled to have this debt discharged or that, I am protected by law from administrative wage garnishment.

I have read the above and agree to the terms and conditions of the Perkins loan rehabilitation program and this repayment agreement.

Signature: _____ date: _____

[Sign and return this agreement to the address indicated below. Keep a copy for your records.]

Return signed agreement to: U.S. Department of Education

c/o: PCA address

Our business hours are: Monday–Thursday 8 am–9 pm, Friday 8 am–5 pm and Saturday 8 am–12 pm (CST). Our phone number is 1 888 xxx-xxxx.

This communication is from a debt collector attempting to collect a debt and any information obtained will be used for that purpose.

I understand that I cannot change the monthly payment amount without (agency name) approval.

Signature: _____ date: _____

2. GUIDANCE FOR COLLECTION CONTRACTORS REGARDING PERKINS LOAN REHABILITATIONS

Rehabilitation

Subject: New Nine Month Perkins Rehabs
Date: 02/18/09

The Higher Education Opportunity Act (HEOA) enacted in August of 2008, reduced the number of on time, consecutive, monthly payments required to rehabilitate a Perkins loan from 12 to 9. The statute however does not contain a "skip a month" provision similar to the HERA FFEL provisions.

The system edits have now been updated to process Perkins accounts for rehabilitation where nine required payments have been made. Effective with the Perkins rehab sweep for March, you can submit Perkins accounts which meet this requirement. The process for identifying these accounts has not changed. Remember that for Perkins Rehab accounts timely payments are still defined as having been made within 15 days of the due date.

Following is the language for a new Perkins Rehab letter to be sent to borrowers that are already on a 12 month repayment schedule:

> Since you entered the loan rehabilitation program Congress reduced the number of payments required for rehabilitation from twelve to nine.
>
> Therefore, if you continue making your monthly payments on-time each month, your loan will be eligible for rehabilitation three months sooner than originally planned.

You will also need to revise your current Perkins Rehab letter changing the number of required payments from 12 to 9.

Please feel free to call me or Mike Bryant if you have any questions.

Lawannah Howell
COR

D.5.4 Authorization to Release Information

<u>Example</u>
**Authorization to Release
Information to a Third Party**

Section 1: Individual Subject Information

Subject's Name: _____

Subject's Social Security Number: _____

Subject's Date of Birth: mm/dd/yy: _____

Section 2: Third Party's Information

Name(s) of individual(s) to whom the U.S. Department of Education is authorized to disclose information about the above-named subject:

_____   _____

_____   _____

_____   _____

Company name (if applicable) and address of individuals authorized to receive information about the above-named subject:

_____

_____

_____

Section 3: Subject's Authorization for Release

I _____, hereby certify that I am the individual named above as the subject of these records. I understand that the knowing and willful request for, or acquisition of, a record pertaining to an individual under false pretenses is a criminal offense under the Privacy Act subject to a $5000 fine. I hereby authorize the U.S. Department of Education (ED) to disclose information in my records regarding my student aid obligations held by ED to the individual(s) named in Section 2 above.

Signature_____ Date: _____

Completed authorizations should be faxed to:

319-665-7646   or   319-665-7647

Appx. D.5.5   Student Loan Law

D.5.5 Department of Education Ombudsman Privacy Release Statement

**Office of the Ombudsman
Privacy Release Statement**

Please fill out all pertinent information. Please print clearly:

Name_____

Address:_____City/State/Zip_____

Home Phone:_____ Work Phone:_____
              (area code)   (area code)

E-mail:_____

Soc. Sec.# _____-_____-_____ Date of Birth: _____-_____-_____

What is the best way to contact you? _____

Please describe your complaint: (Please be as detailed as possible.)

_____
_____
_____
_____
_____
_____
_____
_____

My signature on this page allows representatives of the Office of the Ombudsman, Office of Student Financial Aid, U.S. Department of Education to obtain, under the "Right to Privacy Act of 1974," any information requested and to examine and/or copy any records related to my student financial aid.

_____   _____
Signature   Date

Third-Party Authorization *(Complete only if you are designating the person named below to give or receive information about your situation.)*

NAME:_____ RELATIONSHIP TO YOU_____

Address_____PHONE:_____

Return this form to Office of the Ombudsman, U.S. Department of Education, 4th Floor, UCP-3, MS: 5144, 830 First Street, N.E. Washington, DC 20202-5144. You may fax the completed form to 202/275-0549. If you have any questions, please call 202/377-3800.

For use by Ombudsman Staff only:
Ombudsman Case # _____ Specialist _____

K:ombudsman/case management/documentation/privacy release form – includes 3rd party authorization

Student Assistance Forms   Appx. D.5.6

D.5.6 *Third-Party Consent Form*

Information Release Consent
Please complete form in ink

I authorize _____ to release to, and discuss with, the representative named below all
             Organization / Institution

activity, correspondence and payment records in connection with my student loan(s).

(Please Print)

REPRESENTATIVE'S NAME	REPRESENTATIVE'S PHONE NO. ( )
REPRESENTATIVE'S STREET ADDRESS	
REPRESENTATIVES RELATIONSHIP	Representative's E-mail

CITY	STATE	ZIP

This authorization is to continue until written revocation is given by me and received by my Organization/Institution. I release my loan holder, its officers, employees or related personnel, both individually and collectively from liability for claims arising out of disclosure to the party designated herein.

I state, under penalty of perjury, that I am the individual whose records are covered by this authorization. I am aware that it is a criminal offense to acquire under false pretenses, information in an individual's records that are subject to the Federal Privacy Act.

I further understand that a completed and signed copy of this document is as good as the original (i.e. faxed).

BORROWER'S LAST NAME	FIRST NAME	MI
BORROWER'S STREET ADDRESS		

CITY	STATE	ZIP
TELEPHONE NO. ( )	SOCIAL SECURITY NO. or ACCOUNT NUMBER	
WORK OR ALTERNATE NUMBER ( )	Borrower's e-mail	
BORROWER SIGNATURE	SIGNATURE DATE	

Information release consent_ASA_3/2008

Appx. D.5.7 *Student Loan Law*

D.5.7 Direct Loan Master Promissory Note

Direct Loans — William D. Ford Federal Direct Loan Program

Federal Direct Stafford/Ford Loan
Federal Direct Unsubsidized Stafford/Ford Loan
Master Promissory Note
William D. Ford Federal Direct Loan Program

OMB No. 1845-0007
Form Approved
Exp. Date 05/31/2011

Warning: Any person who knowingly makes a false statement or misrepresentation on this form will be subject to penalties which may include fines, imprisonment, or both, under the U.S. Criminal Code and 20 U.S.C. 1097.

SECTION A: BORROWER INFORMATION
READ THE INSTRUCTIONS IN SECTION F BEFORE COMPLETING THIS SECTION

1. Driver's License State and No.
2. Social Security No.
3. E-mail Address (optional)
4. Name and Address
5. Date of Birth
6. Area Code/Telephone No.

7. References: List two persons with different U.S. addresses who have known you for at least three years. The first reference should be a parent or legal guardian.

	1.	2.
Name		
Permanent Street Address		
City, State, Zip Code		
Area Code/Telephone No.	( )	( )
Relationship to Borrower		

SECTION B: SCHOOL INFORMATION – TO BE COMPLETED BY THE SCHOOL

8. School Name and Address
9. School Code/Branch
10. Identification No.

SECTION C: BORROWER REQUEST, CERTIFICATIONS, AUTHORIZATIONS, AND UNDERSTANDINGS – READ CAREFULLY BEFORE SIGNING BELOW

11. This is a Master Promissory Note (MPN) for one or more Federal Direct Stafford/Ford (Direct Subsidized) Loans and/or Federal Direct Unsubsidized Stafford/Ford (Direct Unsubsidized) Loans. I request a total amount of Direct Subsidized Loans and/or Direct Unsubsidized Loans under this MPN not to exceed the allowable maximums under the Act ("the Act" is defined in Section E under Governing Law). My school will notify me of the loan type and loan amount that I am eligible to receive. I may cancel a loan or request a lower amount by contacting my school. Additional information about my right to cancel a loan or request a lower amount is included in the Borrower's Rights and Responsibilities Statement and in the disclosure statements that will be provided to me.

12. Under penalty of perjury, I certify that:

A. The information I have provided on this MPN and as updated by me from time to time is true, complete, and correct to the best of my knowledge and belief and is made in good faith.

B. I will use the proceeds of loans made under this MPN for authorized educational expenses that I incur and I will immediately repay any loan proceeds that cannot be attributed to educational expenses for attendance on at least a half-time basis at the school that certified my loan eligibility.

C. If I owe an overpayment on a Federal Perkins Loan, Federal Pell Grant, Federal Supplemental Educational Opportunity Grant, Academic Competitiveness Grant (ACG), National Science or Mathematics Access to Retain Talent (SMART) Grant, or Leveraging Educational Assistance Partnership Grant, I have made satisfactory arrangements to repay the amount owed.

D. If I am in default on any loan received under the Federal Perkins Loan Program (including National Direct Student Loans), the William D. Ford Federal Direct Loan (Direct Loan) Program, or the Federal Family Education Loan (FFEL) Program, I have made satisfactory repayment arrangements with the holder to repay the amount owed.

E. If I have been convicted of, or pled *nolo contendere* (no contest) or guilty to, a crime involving fraud in obtaining funds under title IV of the Higher Education Act of 1965 (HEA), as amended, I have completed the repayment of the funds to the U.S. Department of Education (ED) or to the loan holder in the case of a Title IV federal student loan.

13. For each Direct Subsidized Loan and Direct Unsubsidized Loan I receive under this MPN, I make the following authorizations:

A. I authorize my school to certify my eligibility for the loan.

B. I authorize my school to credit my loan proceeds to my student account at the school.

C. I authorize my school to pay to ED any refund that may be due up to the full amount of the loan.

D. I authorize ED to investigate my credit record and report information about my loan status to persons and organizations permitted by law to receive that information.

E. Unless I notify ED differently, I authorize ED to defer repayment of principal on my loan while I am enrolled at least half-time at an eligible school.

F. I authorize my school and ED to release information about my loan to the references on the loan and to members of my immediate family, unless I submit written directions otherwise.

G. I authorize my schools, lenders and guarantors, ED, and their agents to release information about my loan to each other.

H. I authorize my schools, ED, and their respective agents and contractors to contact me regarding my loan request or my loan, including repayment of my loan, at the current or any future number that I provide for my cellular telephone or other wireless device using automated dialing equipment or artificial or prerecorded voice or text messages.

14. I will be given the opportunity to pay the interest that ED charges during grace, in school, deferment, forbearance, and other periods as provided under the Act, including during in-school deferment periods. Unless I pay the interest, I understand that ED may add unpaid interest that is charged on each loan made under this MPN to the principal balance of that loan (this is called "capitalization") at the end of the grace, deferment, forbearance, or other period. Capitalization will increase the principal balance on my loan and the total amount of interest I must pay.

15. I understand that ED has the authority to verify information reported on this MPN with other federal agencies.

SECTION D: PROMISE TO PAY

16. I promise to pay to ED all loan amounts disbursed under the terms of this MPN, plus interest and other charges and fees that may become due as provided in this MPN. **I understand that more than one loan may be made to me under this MPN.** I understand that by accepting any disbursement issued at any time under this MPN, I agree to repay the loan associated with that disbursement. I understand that, within certain timeframes, I may cancel or reduce the amount of a loan by refusing to accept or by returning all or a portion of any disbursement that is issued. Unless I make interest payments, interest that ED charges on my loans during grace, in-school, deferment, forbearance, and other periods will be added to the principal balance of the loan as provided under the Act. If I do not make a payment on a loan made under this MPN when it is due, I will also pay reasonable collection costs, including but not limited to attorney's fees, court costs, and other fees. I will not sign this MPN before reading the entire MPN, even if I am told not to read it, or told that I am not required to read it. I am entitled to an exact copy of this MPN and the Borrower's Rights and Responsibilities Statement. My signature certifies that I have read, understand, and agree to the terms and conditions of this MPN, including the Borrower Request, Certifications, Authorizations, and Understanding in Section C, the Notice About Subsequent Loans Made Under this MPN in Section E, and the terms and conditions described in Section E of this MPN and in the Borrower's Rights and Responsibilities Statement.

I UNDERSTAND THAT I MAY RECEIVE ONE OR MORE LOANS UNDER THIS MPN, AND THAT I MUST REPAY ALL LOANS THAT I RECEIVE UNDER THIS MPN.

17. Borrower's Signature _____
18. Today's Date (mm-dd-yyyy) _____

Revised 03/2009

Direct Subsidized Loan and Direct Unsubsidized Loan MPN *(continued)*

SECTION E: MPN TERMS AND CONDITIONS

GOVERNING LAW

The terms of this Application and Master Promissory Note (MPN) will be interpreted in accordance with the Higher Education Act of 1965, as amended (20. U.S.C. 1070 *et seq.*), the U.S. Department of Education's (ED's) regulations, as they may be amended in accordance with their effective date, and other applicable federal laws and regulations (collectively referred to as the "Act"). Applicable state law, except as preempted by federal law, may provide for certain borrower rights, remedies, and defenses in addition to those stated in this MPN.

DISCLOSURE OF LOAN TERMS

This MPN applies to Federal Direct Stafford/Ford (Direct Subsidized) Loans and Federal Direct Unsubsidized Stafford/Ford (Direct Unsubsidized) Loans. Under this MPN, the principal amount that I owe, and am required to repay, will be the sum of all disbursements that are made (unless I reduce or cancel any disbursements as explained below under Loan Cancellation), plus any unpaid interest that is capitalized and added to the principal amount.

At or before the time of the first disbursement of each loan, a disclosure statement will be sent to me identifying the amount of the loan and additional terms of the loan. Important additional information is also contained in the Borrower's Rights and Responsibilities Statement accompanying this MPN. The Borrower's Rights and Responsibilities Statement and any disclosure statement I receive in connection with any loan under this MPN are hereby incorporated into this MPN.

Loans disbursed under this MPN are subject to the annual and aggregate loan limits specified under the Act. I may request additional loan funds to pay for my educational costs up to the annual and aggregate loan limits by contacting my school's financial aid office. My school will determine if I am eligible for any additional loan funds. I will be notified of any increase or other change in the amount of my loan.

My eligibility for Direct Subsidized Loans and Direct Unsubsidized Loans may increase or decrease based on changes in my financial circumstances. My school will notify me of any changes in my eligibility. I will be notified of any increase or decrease in the amount of my loan.

I understand that each loan made under this MPN is separately enforceable based on a true and exact copy of this MPN.

LOAN CANCELLATION

I may pay back all or part of a disbursement within the timeframes set by the Act, as explained in the Borrower's Rights and Responsibilities Statement and in a disclosure statement that I will receive. If I return the full loan amount within those timeframes, I will not incur any loan fee or interest charges. If I return part of a disbursement within those timeframes, the loan fee and interest charges will be reduced in proportion to the amount returned.

INTEREST

Unless ED notifies me in writing of a lower rate, the interest rate for any loan I receive under this MPN is determined using a formula specified in the Act. As explained in the Borrower's Rights and Responsibilities Statement, I will be notified of the actual interest rate for each loan that I receive.

ED does not charge interest on a Direct Subsidized Loan during an in school, grace, or deferment period, and during certain periods of repayment under the Income-Based Repayment Plan. ED charges interest on a Direct Subsidized Loan during all other periods (including forbearance periods), starting on the day after my grace period ends. ED charges interest on a Direct Unsubsidized Loan during all periods (including in-school, grace, deferment, and forbearance periods), starting on the date of the first disbursement. I agree to pay all interest that is charged to me. I will be given the opportunity to pay the interest that accrues during grace, in school, deferment, forbearance, or other periods as provided under the Act.

If I do not pay the interest, I understand that ED may capitalize the interest at the end of the grace, deferment, forbearance, or other period.

LOAN FEE

A loan fee is charged for each Direct Subsidized Loan and Direct Unsubsidized Loan as provided by the Act, and will be deducted proportionately from each disbursement of each of my loans. The loan fee will be shown on disclosure statements that will be issued to me. I understand the loan fee may be refundable only as permitted by the Act.

LATE CHARGES AND COLLECTION COSTS

ED may collect from me: (1) a late charge of not more than six cents for each dollar of each late payment if I fail to make any part of a required installment payment within 30 days after it becomes due, and (2) any other charges and fees that are permitted by the Act related to the collection of my loans. If I default on my loans, I will pay reasonable collection costs, plus court costs and attorney fees.

GRACE PERIOD

I will receive a six-month grace period on repayment of each loan made under this MPN. The grace period begins the day after I cease to be enrolled at least half-time at an eligible school. I am not required to make any payments on my loan during the grace period. However, interest will accrue on my Direct Unsubsidized Loan during the grace period and will be capitalized if I do not repay it.

REPAYMENT

I must repay the full amount of the loans made under this MPN, plus accrued interest. I will repay each loan in monthly installments during a repayment period that begins on the day immediately following my 6-month grace period on that loan. Payments made by me or on my behalf will be applied first to late charges and collection costs that are due, then to interest that has not been paid, and finally to the principal amount of the loan, except during periods of repayment under an Income-Based Repayment Plan, when payments will be applied first to interest that is due, then to fees that are due, and then to the principal amount.

ED will provide me with a choice of repayment plans. Information on these repayment plans is included in the Borrower's Rights and Responsibilities Statement.

ED will provide me with a repayment schedule that identifies my payment amounts and due dates. If I am unable to make my scheduled loan payments, ED may allow me to temporarily stop making payments, reduce my payment amount, or extend the time for making payments, as long as I intend to repay my loan. Allowing me to temporarily delay or reduce loan payments is called forbearance.

ED may adjust payment dates on my loans or may grant me forbearance to eliminate a delinquency that remains even though I am making scheduled installment payments.

I may prepay all or any part of the unpaid balance on my loans at any time without penalty. If I do not specify which loans I am prepaying, ED will determine how to apply the prepayment in accordance with the Act. After I have repaid in full a loan made under this MPN, ED will send me a notice telling me that I have paid off my loan.

ACCELERATION AND DEFAULT

At ED's option, the entire unpaid balance of a loan made under this MPN will become immediately due and payable (this is called "acceleration") if any one of the following events occurs: (1) I do not enroll as at least a half-time student at the school that certified my loan eligibility; (2) I do not use the proceeds of the loan solely for my educational expenses; (3) I make a false representation that results in my receiving a loan for which I am not eligible; or (4) I default on the loan.

The following events will constitute a default on my loan: (1) I do not pay the entire unpaid balance of the loan after ED has exercised its option under items (1), (2), and (3) in the preceding paragraph; (2) I do not make installment payments when due, provided my failure has persisted for at least 270 days; or (3) I do not comply with other terms of the loan, and ED reasonably concludes that I no longer intend to honor my repayment obligation. If I default, ED may capitalize all the outstanding interest into a new principal balance, and collection costs will become immediately due and payable.

If I default, the default will be reported to national consumer reporting agencies and will significantly and adversely affect my credit history. I understand that a default will have additional adverse consequences to me as disclosed in the Borrower's Rights and Responsibilities Statement.

LEGAL NOTICES

Any notice required to be given to me will be effective if mailed by first class mail to the most recent address ED has for me. I will immediately notify ED of a change of address or status as specified in the Borrower's Rights and Responsibilities Statement.

If ED fails to enforce or insist on compliance with any term of this MPN, this does not waive any right of ED. No provision of this MPN may be modified or waived except in writing by ED. If any provision of this MPN is determined to be unenforceable, the remaining provisions will remain in force.

Information about my loans will be submitted to the National Student Loan Data System (NSLDS). Information in NSLDS is accessible to schools, lenders, and guarantors for specific purposes as authorized by ED.

NOTICE ABOUT SUBSEQUENT LOANS MADE UNDER THIS MPN

This MPN authorizes ED to disburse multiple loans to me to pay my educational expenses during the multi-year term of this MPN, upon my request and upon my school's annual certification of my loan eligibility.

At schools that are authorized to use the multi-year feature of the MPN and choose to do so, subsequent loans may be made under this MPN for subsequent academic years. At any school, subsequent loans may be made under this MPN for the same academic year.

I understand that no subsequent loans will be made under this MPN after the earliest of the following dates: (1) the date ED or my school receives my written notice that no further loans may be made; (2) one year after the date I sign the MPN or the date ED receives the MPN if no disbursements are made under the MPN; or (3) ten years after the date I sign the MPN or the date ED receives the MPN.

Any amendment to the Act governs the terms of any loan disbursed on or after the effective date of the amendment, and any amended terms are considered part of this MPN.

Direct Subsidized Loan and Direct Unsubsidized Loan MPN *(continued)*

SECTION F: INSTRUCTIONS FOR COMPLETING THE MPN

This is a Master Promissory Note (MPN) under which you may receive multiple Direct Subsidized Loans and/or Direct Unsubsidized Loans over a maximum ten-year period.

Print using a blue or black ink ballpoint pen or type. Do not use pencil. Report all dates as month-day-year (mm-dd-yyyy). Use only numbers. Example: June 24, 1982 = 06-24-1982.

Some of the items in Section A may have been completed for you. If so, review these items carefully to make sure that the information is correct. Cross out any information that is incorrect and enter the correct information. Put your initials next to any information that you change.

SECTION A: BORROWER INFORMATION

Item 1. Enter the two-letter abbreviation for the state that issued your current driver's license, followed by your driver's license number. If you do not have a driver's license, enter N/A.

Item 2. Enter your nine-digit Social Security Number.

Item 3. Enter your preferred e-mail address for receiving communications. You are not required to provide this information. If you do, we may use your e-mail address to communicate with you. If you do not have an e-mail address or do not wish to provide one, enter N/A.

Item 4. Enter your last name, then your first name and middle initial. Enter your permanent address (number, street, apartment number, or rural route number and box number, then city, state, zip code). If your mailing address is a post office box or general delivery, you must list **both** your street address and your mailing address. A temporary school address is not acceptable.

Item 5. Enter your date of birth.

Item 6. Enter the area code and telephone number at which you can most easily be reached. If you do not have a telephone, enter N/A.

Item 7. Enter the requested information for two adults with different U.S. addresses who have known you for at least three years. The first reference should be a parent or legal guardian. References who live outside the United States are not acceptable. If a reference does not have a telephone number, enter N/A.

SECTION B: SCHOOL INFORMATION

This section will be completed by the school that certifies your loan eligibility.

SECTION C: BORROWER REQUEST, CERTIFICATIONS, AUTHORIZATIONS, AND UNDERSTANDINGS

Items 11, 12, 13, 14, and 15. Read these items carefully.

SECTION D: PROMISE TO PAY

Item 16. Read this item carefully.

Items 17 and 18. Sign your full legal name, in blue or black ink, and enter the date you signed this MPN.

By signing this MPN, you:

(1) Acknowledge that you have read, understand, and agree to the terms and conditions of the MPN, including the Borrower Request, Certifications, Authorizations, and Understanding in Section C and the accompanying Borrower's Rights and Responsibilities Statement; and

(2) Agree to repay the loan(s) in full according to the terms and conditions of the MPN.

SECTION G: IMPORTANT NOTICES

GRAMM-LEACH-BLILEY ACT NOTICE

In 1999, Congress enacted the Gramm-Leach-Bliley Act (Public Law 106-102). This Act requires that lenders provide certain information to their customers regarding the collection and use of nonpublic personal information.

We disclose nonpublic personal information to third parties only as necessary to process and service your loan and as permitted by the Privacy Act of 1974. See the Privacy Act Notice below. We do not sell or otherwise make available any information about you to any third parties for marketing purposes.

We protect the security and confidentiality of nonpublic personal information by implementing the following policies and practices. All physical access to the sites where nonpublic personal information is maintained is controlled and monitored by security personnel. Our computer systems offer a high degree of resistance to tampering and circumvention. These systems limit data access to our staff and contract staff on a "need-to-know" basis, and control individual users' ability to access and alter records within the systems. All users of these systems are given a unique user ID with personal identifiers. All interactions by individual users with the systems are recorded.

PRIVACY ACT NOTICE

The Privacy Act of 1974 (5 U.S.C. 552a) requires that the following notice be provided to you:

The authority for collecting the requested information from and about you is §451 *et seq.* of the Higher Education Act (HEA) of 1965, as amended (20 U.S.C. 1087a *et seq.*) and the authorities for collecting and using your Social Security Number (SSN) are §484(a)(4) of the HEA (20 U.S.C. 1091(a)(4)) and 31 U.S.C. 7701(b). Participating in the William D. Ford Federal Direct Loan (Direct Loan) Program and giving us your SSN are voluntary, but you must provide the requested information, including your SSN, to participate.

The principal purposes for collecting the information on this form, including your SSN, are to verify your identity, to determine your eligibility to receive a loan or a benefit on a loan (such as a deferment, forbearance, discharge, or forgiveness) under the Direct Loan Program, to permit the servicing of your loan(s), and, if it becomes necessary, to locate you and to collect and report on your loan(s) if your loan(s) become delinquent or in default. We also use your SSN as an account identifier and to permit you to access your account information electronically.

The information in your file may be disclosed, on a case-by-case basis or under a computer matching program, to third parties as authorized under routine uses in the appropriate systems of records notices. The routine uses of this information include, but are not limited to, its disclosure to federal, state, or local agencies, to private parties such as relatives, present and former employers, business and personal associates, to consumer reporting agencies, to financial and educational institutions, and to guaranty agencies in order to verify your identity, to determine your eligibility to receive a loan or a benefit on a loan, to permit the servicing or collection of your loan(s), to enforce the terms of the loan(s), to investigate possible fraud and to verify compliance with federal student financial aid program regulations, or to locate you if you become delinquent in your loan payments or if you default. To provide default rate calculations, disclosures may be made to guaranty agencies, to financial and educational institutions, or to state agencies. To provide financial aid history information, disclosures may be made to educational institutions. To assist program administrators with tracking refunds and cancellations, disclosures may be made to guaranty agencies, to financial and educational institutions, or to federal or state agencies. To provide a standardized method for educational institutions to efficiently submit student enrollment status, disclosures may be made to guaranty agencies or to financial and educational institutions. To counsel you in repayment efforts, disclosures may be made to guaranty agencies, to financial and educational institutions, or to federal, state, or local agencies.

In the event of litigation, we may send records to the Department of Justice, a court, adjudicative body, counsel, party, or witness if the disclosure is relevant and necessary to the litigation. If this information, either alone or with other information, indicates a potential violation of law, we may send it to the appropriate authority for action. We may send information to members of Congress if you ask them to help you with federal student aid questions. In circumstances involving employment complaints, grievances, or disciplinary actions, we may disclose relevant records to adjudicate or investigate the issues. If provided for by a collective bargaining agreement, we may disclose records to a labor organization recognized under 5 U.S.C. Chapter 71. Disclosures may be made to our contractors for the purpose of performing any programmatic function that requires disclosure of records. Before making any such disclosure, we will require the contractor to maintain Privacy Act safeguards. Disclosures may also be made to qualified researchers under Privacy Act safeguards.

FINANCIAL PRIVACY ACT NOTICE

Under the Right to Financial Privacy Act of 1978 (12 U.S.C. 3401-3421), ED will have access to financial records in your student loan file maintained in compliance with the administration of the Direct Loan Program.

PAPERWORK REDUCTION NOTICE

According to the Paperwork Reduction Act of 1995, no persons are required to respond to a collection of information unless it displays a currently valid OMB control number. The valid OMB control number for this information collection is 1845-0007. The time required to complete this information collection is estimated to average 0.5 hours (30 minutes) per response, including the time to review instructions, search existing data sources, gather and maintain the data needed, and complete and review the information. **If you have any comments concerning the accuracy of the time estimate(s) or suggestions for improving the form, please write to:** U.S. Department of Education, Washington, DC 20202-4537.

If you have any comments or concerns regarding the status of *your individual submission* of this form, write directly to:

U.S. Department of Education
Common Origination and Disbursement School Relations Center
Attn: Applicant Services
PO Box 9002
Niagara Falls, NY 14302

Student Assistance Forms   Appx. D.5.7

William D. Ford Federal Direct Loan Program
Direct Subsidized Loan and Direct Unsubsidized Loan Borrower's Rights and Responsibilities Statement

Important Notice: This Borrower's Rights and Responsibilities Statement provides additional information about the terms and conditions of the loans you receive under the accompanying Master Promissory Note (MPN) for Federal Direct Stafford/Ford Loans (Direct Subsidized Loans) and Federal Direct Unsubsidized Stafford/Ford Loans (Direct Unsubsidized Loans). **Please keep this Borrower's Rights and Responsibilities Statement for your records.** You may request another copy of this Borrower's Rights and Responsibilities Statement at any time by contacting the Direct Loan Servicing Center.

Throughout this Borrower's Rights and Responsibilities Statement, the words "we," "us," and "our" refer to the U.S. Department of Education. The word "loan" refers to one or more loans made under the accompanying MPN.

1. The William D. Ford Federal Direct Loan Program. The William D. Ford Federal Direct Loan (Direct Loan) Program includes the following types of loans, known collectively as "Direct Loans":

- Federal Direct Stafford/Ford Loans (Direct Subsidized Loans)
- Federal Direct Unsubsidized Stafford/Ford Loans (Direct Unsubsidized Loans)
- Federal Direct PLUS Loans (Direct PLUS Loans)
- Federal Direct Consolidation Loans (Direct Consolidation Loans)

The Direct Loan Program is authorized by Title IV, Part D, of the Higher Education Act of 1965, as amended.

You must complete a Free Application for Federal Student Aid (FAFSA) before you receive a Direct Subsidized Loan or Direct Unsubsidized Loan.

Direct Loans are made by the U.S. Department of Education. Our Direct Loan Servicing Center services, answers questions about, and processes payments on Direct Loans. We will provide you with the address and telephone number of the Direct Loan Servicing Center after the school notifies us that the first disbursement of your loan has been made.

2. Laws that apply to this MPN. The terms and conditions of loans made under this MPN are determined by the Higher Education Act of 1965, as amended (20 U.S.C. 1070 et seq.) and other applicable federal laws and regulations. These laws and regulations are referred to as "the Act" throughout this Borrower's Rights and Responsibilities Statement. State law, unless it is preempted by federal law, may provide you with certain rights, remedies, and defenses in addition to those stated in the MPN and this Borrower's Rights and Responsibilities Statement.

NOTE: Any change to the Act applies to loans in accordance with the effective date of the change.

3. Direct Subsidized Loans and Direct Unsubsidized Loans. Direct Subsidized Loans and Direct Unsubsidized Loans are made to students to help pay for the cost of education beyond high school. To receive a Direct Subsidized Loan, you must have financial need. We do not charge interest on Direct Subsidized Loans while you are in school and during certain other periods. Direct Unsubsidized Loans are not based on financial need. We charge interest on Direct Unsubsidized Loans during all periods. For more information on interest charges, see item #9 of this Borrower's Rights and Responsibilities Statement ("Payment of interest").

4. About the MPN. You may receive more than one loan under this MPN over a period of up to 10 years to pay for your educational costs, as long as the school you are attending is authorized to use the multi-year feature of the MPN and chooses to do so.

If your school is not authorized to use the multi-year feature of the MPN or chooses not to do so, or if you do not want to receive more than one loan under this MPN,

you must sign a new MPN for each loan that you receive. If you do not want to receive more than one loan under this MPN, you must notify your school or the Direct Loan Servicing Center in writing.

5. Use of your loan money. You may use the loan money you receive only to pay for your authorized educational expenses for attendance at the school that determined you were eligible to receive the loan. Authorized expenses include the following:

- Tuition
- Room
- Board
- Institutional fees
- Books
- Supplies
- Equipment
- Dependent child care expenses
- Transportation
- Commuting expenses
- Rental or purchase of a personal computer
- Loan fees
- Other documented, authorized costs

6. Information you must report to us after you receive your loan. You must notify the Direct Loan Servicing Center and/or the financial aid office at your school about certain changes.

Until you graduate or otherwise leave school, you must notify your school's financial aid office if you:

- Change your address or telephone number;
- Change your name (for example, maiden name to married name);
- Do not enroll at least half-time for the loan period certified by the school
- Do not enroll at the school that determined you were eligible to receive the loan;
- Stop attending school or drop below half-time enrollment;
- Transfer from one school to another school; or
- Graduate.

You must also notify the Direct Loan Servicing Center if any of the above events occur at any time after you receive your loan. In addition, you must notify the Direct Loan Servicing Center if you:

- Change your employer, or your employer's address or telephone number changes; or
- Have any other change in status that would affect your loan (for example, if you received a deferment while you were unemployed, but you have found a job and therefore no longer meet the eligibility requirements for the deferment).

7. Amount you may borrow. The charts that follow show the maximum amounts of Direct Subsidized Loans and Direct Unsubsidized Loans that you may borrow for a single academic year (annual loan limits), and the maximum amounts that you may borrow in total for undergraduate and graduate study (aggregate loan limits). The annual and aggregate loan limits for independent undergraduates also apply to dependent undergraduates whose parents are unable to borrow under the PLUS program. If you are enrolled in certain health professions programs, you may qualify for higher annual and aggregate limits on Direct Unsubsidized Loans.

The actual loan amount you receive will be determined by your school, based on your academic level, dependency status, and other factors such as:

- The length of the program or the remaining portion of the program in which you are enrolled, if it is less than a full academic year;
- Your cost of attendance;
- Your Expected Family Contribution;
- Other financial aid you receive; and

- Your remaining eligibility under the annual or aggregate loan limits.

The actual amount you receive for an academic year may be less than the maximum annual amounts shown in the charts.

If you are an undergraduate student, your school must determine your eligibility for a Federal Pell Grant before you may receive a Direct Subsidized Loan or Direct Unsubsidized Loan. Your school is also required to determine your eligibility for a Direct Subsidized Loan before determining your eligibility for a Direct Unsubsidized Loan.

If you have received student loans from another federal student loan program, you are responsible for informing your school and your lender of your other student loans. In some cases, you may not be eligible for loans for which you have applied.

Annual Loan Limits for Direct Subsidized Loans and Direct Unsubsidized Loans:

Dependent Undergraduate Students (*except* students whose parents cannot borrow PLUS loans)	
First Year Total (maximum $3,500 subsidized)	$5,500
Second Year Total (maximum $4,500 subsidized)	$6,500
Third Year and Beyond (each year) (maximum $5,500 subsidized)	$7,500
Independent Undergraduate Students (and dependent students whose parents cannot borrow PLUS loans)	
First Year Total (maximum $3,500 subsidized)	$9,500
Second Year (maximum $4,500 subsidized)	$10,500
Third Year and Beyond (each year) (maximum $5,500 subsidized)	$12,500
Graduate and Professional Students	
Total Amount (each year) (maximum $8,500 subsidized)	$20,500

Aggregate Loan Limits for Direct Subsidized and Direct Unsubsidized Loans:

Dependent Undergraduate Students (*except* students whose parents cannot borrow PLUS loans)	
Total Amount Cumulative (maximum $23,000 subsidized)	$31,000
Independent Undergraduate Students (and dependent students whose parents cannot borrow PLUS loans)	
Total Amount Cumulative (maximum $23,000 subsidized)	$57,500
Graduate and Professional Students	
Total Amount Cumulative (maximum $65,500 subsidized; includes Stafford Loans received for undergraduate study)	$138,500

8. Interest rate. The interest rate on Direct Subsidized Loans and Direct Unsubsidized Loans is a fixed rate. Different fixed interest rates may apply to separate loans made under this MPN depending on whether the loan is

Revised 03/2009

William D. Ford Federal Direct Loan Program
Direct Subsidized Loan and Direct Unsubsidized Loan Borrower's Rights and Responsibilities Statement

subsidized or unsubsidized, when the loan is first disbursed, and whether you are a graduate or undergraduate student. You will be notified of the actual interest rate for each loan you receive in a disclosure statement that we send to you. If you qualify under the Servicemembers Civil Relief Act, the interest rate on your loans obtained prior to military service may be limited to 6 percent during your military service. To receive this benefit, you must contact the Direct Loan Servicing Center for information about the documentation you must provide to show that you qualify.

9. Payment of interest. We do not charge interest on a Direct Subsidized Loan while you are enrolled in school at least half-time, during your grace period, during deferment periods, and during certain periods of repayment under the Income-Based Repayment Plan. Except as provided below for certain military borrowers, we charge interest on a Direct Subsidized Loan during all other periods (starting on the day after your grace period ends), including forbearance periods.

Except as provided below for certain military borrowers, we charge interest on a Direct Unsubsidized Loan during all periods (starting on the day your loan is paid out). This includes periods while you are enrolled in school at least half-time, during your grace period, and during deferment and forbearance periods. Therefore, you will pay more interest on a Direct Unsubsidized Loan than on a Direct Subsidized Loan.

If you do not pay the interest as it is charged on either type of loan, we will add it to the unpaid principal amount of your loan. This is called "capitalization." Capitalization increases the unpaid principal balance of your loan, and we will then charge interest on the increased principal amount.

Under the no accrual of interest benefit for active duty service members, we do not charge interest on Direct Loan Program Loans first disbursed on or after October 1, 2008 during periods of qualifying active duty military service (for up to 60 months). For Direct Consolidation Loans, this benefit applies to the portion of the consolidation loan that repaid loans first disbursed on or after October 1, 2008.

The chart below shows the difference in the total amount you would repay on a $15,000 Direct Unsubsidized Loan if you pay the interest as it is charged during a 12-month deferment or forbearance period, compared to the amount you would repay if you do not pay the interest and it is capitalized.

	If you pay the interest as it is charged...	If you do not pay the interest and it is capitalized...
Loan Amount	$15,000	$15,000
Interest for 12 months (at an interest rate of 6.8%)	$1,020 (paid as accrued)	$1,020 (unpaid and capitalized)
Principal to be Repaid	$15,000	$16,020
Monthly Payment (Standard Repayment Plan)	$173	$184
Number of Payments	120	120
Total Amount Repaid	$21,734	$22,123

In this example, you would pay $11 less per month and $389 less altogether if you pay the interest as it is charged during a 12-month deferment or forbearance period.

You may be able to claim a federal income tax deduction for interest payments you make on Direct Loans. For further information, refer to IRS Publication 970, which is available at http://www.irs.ustreas.gov.

10. Loan fee. We charge a loan fee that is a percentage of the principal amount of each loan you receive. The percentage is determined by the Act and varies depending on when a loan is first disbursed. The specific loan fee that you are charged will be shown on a disclosure statement that we send to you. This fee will be subtracted proportionally from each disbursement of your loan.

11. Repayment incentive programs. A repayment incentive is a benefit that we offer to encourage you to repay your loan on time. Under a repayment incentive program, the interest rate we charge on your loan may be reduced. Some repayment incentive programs require you to make a certain number of payments on time to keep the reduced interest rate. The two repayment incentive programs described below may be available to you. The Direct Loan Servicing Center can provide you with more information on other repayment incentive programs that may be available.

(1) Interest Rate Reduction for Electronic Debit Account Repayment

Under the Electronic Debit Account (EDA) repayment option, your bank automatically deducts your monthly loan payment from your checking or savings account and sends it to us. EDA helps to ensure that your payments are made on time. In addition, you receive a 0.25 percent interest rate reduction while you repay under the EDA option. We will include information about the EDA option in your first bill. You can also get the information on the Direct Loan Servicing Center's web site, or by calling the Direct Loan Servicing Center. The Direct Loan Servicing Center's web site address and toll-free telephone number are provided on all correspondence that the Direct Loan Servicing Center sends you.

(2) Up-Front Interest Rebate

You may receive an up-front interest rebate on your loan. The rebate is equal to a percentage of the loan amount that you borrow. This is the same amount that would result if the interest rate on your loan were lowered by a specific percentage, but you receive the rebate up front. The correspondence that you receive about your loan will tell you if you received an up-front interest rebate.

To keep an up-front interest rebate that you receive on your loan, you must make all of your first 12 required monthly payments on time when your loan enters repayment. "On time" means that we must receive each payment no later than 6 days after the due date.

You will lose the rebate if you do not make all of your first 12 required monthly payments on time. If you lose the rebate, we will add the rebate amount back to the principal balance on your loan account. This will increase the amount that you must repay.

12. Disbursement (how your loan money will be paid out). Generally, your school will disburse (pay out) your loan money in more than one installment, usually at the beginning of each academic term (for example, at the beginning of each semester or quarter). If your school does not use academic terms or does not have academic terms that meet certain requirements, it will generally disburse your loan in at least two installments, one at the beginning of the period of study for which you are receiving the loan, and one at the midpoint of that period of study.

In most cases, if the Direct Subsidized Loan or Direct Unsubsidized Loan that you are receiving is your first student loan under either the Direct Loan Program or the Federal Family Education Loan (FFEL) Program, you must complete entrance counseling before your school can make the first disbursement of your loan.

Your school may disburse your loan money by crediting it to your account at the school, or may give some or all of it to you directly by check or other means. The Direct Loan Servicing Center will notify you in writing each time your school disburses part of your loan money.

If your school credits your loan money to your account and the amount credited is more than the amount of your tuition and fees, room and board, and other authorized charges, the excess amount is called a credit balance. Unless you authorize your school to hold the credit balance for you, your school must pay you the credit balance within the following timeframes:

- If the credit balance occurs after the first day of class of a payment period (your school can tell you this date), your school must pay you the credit balance no later than 14 days after the date the balance occurs.

- If the credit balance occurs on or before the first day of class of a payment period, your school must pay you the credit balance no later than 14 days after the first day of class of the payment period.

13. Canceling your loan. Before your loan money is disbursed, you may cancel all or part of your loan at any time by notifying your school. After your loan money is disbursed, there are two ways to cancel all or part of your loan:

- If your school obtains your written confirmation of the types and amounts of Title IV loans that you want to receive for an award year before crediting loan money to your account at the school, you may tell the school that you want to cancel all or part of that loan within 14 days after the date the school notifies you of your right to cancel all or part of the loan, or by the first day of your school's payment period, whichever is later (your school can tell you the first day of the payment period). If the school does not obtain your written confirmation of the types and amounts of loans you want to receive before crediting the loan money to your account, you may cancel all or part of that loan by informing the school within 30 days of the date the school notifies you of your right to cancel all or part of the loan. In either case, your school will return the cancelled loan amount to us. You do not have to pay interest or the loan fee on the part of your loan that you tell your school to cancel within these timeframes. If you received an up-front interest rebate on your loan, the rebate does not apply to the part of your loan that you tell your school to cancel. Your loan will be adjusted to eliminate any interest, loan fee, and rebate amount that applies to the amount of the loan that was cancelled.

If you ask your school to cancel all or part of your loan outside the timeframes described above, your school may process your cancellation request, but it is not required to do so.

- Within 120 days of the date your school disbursed your loan money (by crediting the loan money to your account at the school, by paying it directly to you, or both), you may return all or part of your loan to us. Contact the Direct Loan Servicing Center for guidance on how and where to return your loan money. You do not have to pay interest or the loan fee on the part of your loan that you return within 120 days of the date that part of your loan is disbursed. If you received an up-front interest rebate on your loan, the rebate does not apply to the part of your loan that you return. Your loan will be adjusted to eliminate any interest, loan fee, and rebate amount that applies to the amount of the loan that you return.

14. Grace period. You will receive a six-month grace period on repayment of each Direct Subsidized Loan and

William D. Ford Federal Direct Loan Program
Direct Subsidized Loan and Direct Unsubsidized Loan Borrower's Rights and Responsibilities Statement

Direct Unsubsidized Loan that you receive. Your six-month grace period begins the day after you stop attending school or drop below half-time enrollment. You do not have to begin making payments on your loan until after your grace period ends.

If you are called or ordered to active duty for more than 30 days from a reserve component of the U.S. Armed Forces, the period of your active duty service and the time necessary for you to re-enroll in school after your active duty ends are not counted as part of your grace period. However, the total period that is excluded from your grace period may not exceed three years. If the call or order to active duty occurs while you are in school and requires you to drop below half-time enrollment, the start of your grace period will be delayed until after the end of the excluded period. If the call or order to active duty occurs during your grace period, you will receive a full six-month grace period at the end of the excluded period.

15. Repaying your loan. The repayment period for each Direct Subsidized Loan and Direct Unsubsidized Loan that you receive begins on the day after your grace period ends. The Direct Loan Servicing Center will notify you of the date your first payment is due.

You must make payments on your loan even if you do not receive a bill or repayment notice. Billing information is sent to you as a convenience, and you are obligated to make payments even if you do not receive a notice or bill.

You may choose one of the following repayment plans to repay your loan:

- **Standard Repayment Plan** – Under this plan, you will make fixed monthly payments and repay your loan in full within 10 years (not including periods of deferment or forbearance) from the date the loan entered repayment. Your payments must be at least $50 a month and will be more, if necessary, to repay the loan within the required time period.

- **Graduated Repayment Plan** – Under this plan, you will usually make lower payments at first, and your payments will gradually increase over time. You will repay your loan in full within 10 years (not including periods of deferment or forbearance) from the date the loan entered repayment. No single payment will be more than three times greater than any other payment.

- **Extended Repayment Plan** – Under this plan, you will repay your loan in full over a period not to exceed 25 years (not including periods of deferment or forbearance) from the date the loan entered repayment. You may choose to make fixed monthly payments or graduated monthly payments that start out lower and gradually increase over time. If you make fixed monthly payments, your payments must be at least $50 a month and will be more, if necessary, to repay the loan within the required time period. You are eligible for this repayment plan only if (1) you have an outstanding balance on Direct Loan Program loans that exceeds $30,000, and (2) you had no outstanding balance on a Direct Loan Program loan as of October 7, 1998 or on the date you obtained a Direct Loan Program loan after October 7, 1998.

- **Income Contingent Repayment Plan** – Under this plan, your monthly payment amount will be based on your annual income (and that of your spouse if you are married), your family size, and the total amount of your Direct Loans. Until we obtain the information needed to calculate your monthly payment amount, your payment will equal the amount of interest that has accrued on your loan unless you request a forbearance. As your income changes, your payments may change. If you do not repay your loan after 25 years under this plan, the unpaid portion will be forgiven. You may have to pay income tax on any amount forgiven.

- **Income-Based Repayment Plan (effective July 1, 2009)** – Under this plan, your required monthly payment amount will be based on your income during any period when you have a partial financial hardship. Your monthly payment amount may be adjusted annually. The maximum repayment period under this plan may exceed 10 years. If you meet certain requirements over a 25-year period, you may qualify for cancellation of any outstanding balance on your loans.

If you can show to our satisfaction that the terms and conditions of the above repayment plans are not adequate to meet your exceptional circumstances, we may provide you with an alternative repayment plan.

If you do not choose a repayment plan, we will place you on the Standard Repayment Plan.

The chart at the end of this Borrower's Rights and Responsibilities Statement ("Repaying Your Loans") allows you to estimate the monthly and total amounts you would repay under the Standard, Graduated, Extended, and Income Contingent repayment plans based on various initial loan amounts.

You may change repayment plans at any time after you have begun repaying your loan. There is no penalty if you make loan payments before they are due, or pay more than the amount due each month.

Except as provided by the Act for payments made under the Income-Based Repayment Plan, we apply your payments and prepayments in the following order: (1) late charges and collection costs first, (2) outstanding interest second, and (3) outstanding principal last.

When you have repaid a loan in full, the Direct Loan Servicing Center will send you a notice telling you that you have paid off your loan. You should keep this notice in a safe place.

16. Late charges and collection costs. If you do not make any part of a payment within 30 days after it is due, we may require you to pay a late charge. This charge will not be more than six cents for each dollar of each late payment. If you do not make payments as scheduled, we may also require you to pay other charges and fees involved in collecting your loan.

17. Demand for immediate repayment. The entire unpaid amount of your loan becomes due and payable (on your MPN this is called "acceleration") if you:

- Receive loan money, but do not enroll at least half-time at the school that determined you were eligible to receive the loan;
- Use your loan money to pay for anything other than expenses related to your education at the school that determined you were eligible to receive the loan;
- Make a false statement that causes you to receive a loan that you are not eligible to receive; or
- Default on your loan.

18. Defaulting on your loan. Default (failing to repay your loan) is defined in detail in the Terms and Conditions section of your MPN. If you default:

- We will require you to immediately repay the entire unpaid amount of your loan.
- We may sue you, take all or part of your federal and state tax refunds and other federal or state payments, and/or garnish your wages so that your employer is required to send us part of your salary to pay off your loan.
- We will require you to pay reasonable collection fees and costs, plus court costs and attorney fees.
- You may be denied a professional license.

- You will lose eligibility for other federal student aid and assistance under most federal benefit programs.
- You will lose eligibility for loan deferments.
- We will report your default to national consumer reporting agencies (see #19, "Consumer reporting agency notification").

19. Consumer reporting agency notification. We will report information about your loan to national consumer reporting agencies. This information will include the disbursement dates, amount, and repayment status of your loan (for example, whether you are current or delinquent in making payments). Your loan will be identified as an education loan.

If you default on a loan, we will also report this to national consumer reporting agencies. We will notify you at least 30 days in advance that we plan to report default information to a consumer reporting agency unless you resume making payments on the loan within 30 days. You will be given a chance to ask for a review of the debt before we report it.

If a consumer reporting agency contacts us regarding objections you have raised about the accuracy or completeness of any information we have reported, we are required to provide the agency with a prompt response.

20. Deferment and forbearance (postponing payments)

If you meet certain requirements, you may receive a **deferment** that allows you to temporarily stop making payments on your loan. If you cannot make your scheduled loan payments, but do not qualify for a deferment, we may give you a **forbearance**. A forbearance allows you to temporarily stop making payments on your loan, temporarily make smaller payments, or extend the time for making payments.

Deferment

You may receive a deferment while you are:

- Enrolled at least half-time at an eligible school;
- In a full-time course of study in a graduate fellowship program;
- In an approved full-time rehabilitation program for individuals with disabilities;
- Unemployed (for a maximum of three years; you must be diligently seeking, but unable to find, full-time employment); or
- Experiencing an economic hardship (including Peace Corps service), as determined under the Act (for a maximum of three years).
- Serving on active duty during a war or other military operation or national emergency or performing qualifying National Guard duty during a war or other military operation or national emergency and, if you were serving on or after October 1, 2007, for an additional 180-day period following the demobilization date for your qualifying service.

If you are a member of the National Guard or other reserve component of the U.S. Armed forces (current or retired) and you are called or ordered to active duty while you are enrolled at least half-time at an eligible school or within 6 months of having been enrolled at least half-time, you are also eligible for a deferment during the 13 months following the conclusion of your active duty service, or until you return to enrolled student status on at least a half-time basis, whichever is earlier.

You may be eligible to receive additional deferments if, at the time you received your first Direct Loan, you had an outstanding balance on a loan made under the Federal Family Education Loan (FFEL) Program before July 1, 1993. If you meet this requirement, you may receive a deferment while you are:

- Temporarily totally disabled, or unable to work because you are required to care for a spouse or

William D. Ford Federal Direct Loan Program
Direct Subsidized Loan and Direct Unsubsidized Loan Borrower's Rights and Responsibilities Statement

dependent who is disabled (for a maximum of three years);
- On active duty in the U.S. Armed Forces, on active duty in the National Oceanic and Atmospheric Administration (NOAA), or serving full-time as an officer in the Commissioned Corps of the Public Health Service (for a combined maximum of three years);
- Serving in the Peace Corps (for a maximum of three years);
- A full-time paid volunteer for a tax-exempt organization or an ACTION program (for a maximum of three years);
- In a medical internship or residency program (for a maximum of two years);
- Teaching in a designated teacher shortage area (for a maximum of three years);
- On parental leave (for a maximum of six months); or
- A working mother entering or re-entering the workforce (for a maximum of one year).

You may receive a deferment based on your enrollment in school on at least a half-time basis if (1) you submit a deferment request form to the Direct Loan Servicing Center along with documentation of your eligibility for the deferment, or (2) the Direct Loan Servicing Center receives information from the school you are attending that indicates you are enrolled at least half-time. If the Direct Loan Servicing Center processes a deferment based on information received from your school, you will be notified of the deferment and will have the option of canceling the deferment and continuing to make payments on your loan.

For all other deferments, you (or, for a deferment based on active duty military service or qualifying National Guard duty during a war or other military operation or national emergency, a representative acting on your behalf) must submit a deferment request form to the Direct Loan Servicing Center, along with documentation of your eligibility for the deferment. In certain circumstances, you may not be required to provide documentation of your eligibility if the Direct Loan Servicing Center confirms that you have been granted the same deferment for the same period of time on a FFEL Program loan. The Direct Loan Servicing Center can provide you with a deferment request form that explains the eligibility and documentation requirements for the type of deferment you are requesting. You may also obtain deferment request forms and information on deferment eligibility requirements from the Direct Loan Servicing Center's web site.

If you are in default on your loan, you are not eligible for a deferment.

You are not responsible for paying the interest on a Direct Subsidized Loan during a period of deferment. However, you are responsible for paying the interest on a Direct Unsubsidized Loan during a period of deferment.

Forbearance

We may give you a forbearance if you are temporarily unable to make your scheduled loan payments for reasons including, but not limited to, financial hardship and illness.

We will give you a forbearance if:
- You are serving in a medical or dental internship or residency program, and you meet specific requirements;
- The total amount you owe each month for all of the student loans you received under Title IV of the Act is 20 percent or more of your total monthly gross income (for a maximum of three years);
- You are serving in a national service position for which you receive a national service award under the National and Community Service Trust Act of 1993. In some cases, the interest that accrues on a qualified loan during the service period will be paid by the Corporation for National and Community Service;
- You are performing service that would qualify you for loan forgiveness under the teacher loan forgiveness program that is available to certain Direct Loan and FFEL program borrowers;
- You qualify for partial repayment of your loans under the Student Loan Repayment Program, as administered by the Department of Defense; or
- You are called to active duty in the U.S. Armed Forces.

To request a forbearance, contact the Direct Loan Servicing Center. The Direct Loan Servicing Center can provide you with a forbearance request form that explains the eligibility and documentation requirements for the type of forbearance you are requesting. You may also obtain forbearance request forms and information on forbearance eligibility requirements from the Direct Loan Servicing Center's web site.

Under certain circumstances, we may also give you a forbearance without requiring you to submit a request or documentation. These circumstances include, but are not limited to, the following:

- Periods necessary for us to determine your eligibility for a loan discharge;
- A period of up to 60 days in order for us to collect and process documentation related to your request for a deferment, forbearance, change in repayment plan, or consolidation loan (we do not capitalize the interest that is charged during this period); or
- Periods when you are involved in a military mobilization, or a local or national emergency.

You are responsible for paying the interest on both Direct Subsidized Loans and Direct Unsubsidized Loans during a period of forbearance.

21. Discharge (having your loan forgiven). We will discharge (forgive) your loan if:

- You die. The Direct Loan Servicing Center must receive acceptable documentation of your death, as defined in the Act.
- Your loan is discharged in bankruptcy. However, federal student loans are not automatically discharged if you file for bankruptcy. In order to have your loan discharged in bankruptcy, you must prove to the bankruptcy court that repaying the loan would cause undue hardship.
- You become totally and permanently disabled (as defined in the Act) and meet certain other requirements.

In certain cases, we may also discharge all or a portion of your loan if:

- You could not complete a program of study because the school closed;
- Your loan eligibility was falsely certified by the school;
- A loan in your name was falsely certified as a result of a crime of identity theft; or
- The school did not pay a refund of your loan money that it was required to pay under federal regulations.

We may forgive a portion of any student loans you received under the Direct Loan or FFEL program after October 1, 1998 if you teach full time for five consecutive years in certain low-income elementary and/or secondary schools and meet certain other qualifications, and if you did not owe a Direct Loan or FFEL program loan as of October 1, 1998, or as of the date you obtain a loan after October 1, 1998.

A public service loan forgiveness program is also available. Under this program, the remaining balance due on your eligible Direct Loan Program loans may be cancelled after you have made 120 payments on those loans (after October 2, 2007) under certain repayment plans while you are employed in certain public service jobs.

The Act may provide for certain loan forgiveness or repayment benefits on your loans in addition to the benefits described above. If other forgiveness or repayment options become available, the Direct Loan Servicing Center will provide information about these benefits.

To request a loan discharge based on one of the conditions described above (except for discharges due to death or bankruptcy), you must complete an application that you may obtain from the Direct Loan Servicing Center.

In some cases, you may assert, as a defense against collection of your loan, that the school did something wrong or failed to do something that it should have done. You can make such a defense against repayment only if the school's act or omission directly relates to your loan or to the educational services that the loan was intended to pay for, and if what the school did or did not do would give rise to a legal cause of action against the school under applicable state law. If you believe that you have a defense against repayment of your loan, contact the Direct Loan Servicing Center.

We do not guarantee the quality of the academic programs provided by schools that participate in federal student financial aid programs. You must repay your loan even if you do not complete the education paid for with the loan, are unable to obtain employment in the field of study for which your school provided training, or are dissatisfied with, or do not receive, the education you paid for with the loan.

22. Loan consolidation. A Direct Consolidation Loan Program is available that allows you to consolidate (combine) one or more of your eligible federal education loans into one loan. Consolidation allows you to extend the period of time that you have to repay your loans, and to combine several loan debts into a single monthly payment. This may make it easier for you to repay your loans. However, you will pay more interest if you extend your repayment period through consolidation, since you will be making payments for a longer period of time. Contact the Direct Loan Servicing Center for more information about loan consolidation.

23. Department of Defense and other federal agency loan repayment. Under certain circumstances, military personnel may have their federal education loans repaid by the Secretary of Defense. This benefit is offered as part of a recruitment program that does not apply to individuals based on their previous military service or to those who are not eligible for enlistment in the U.S. Armed Forces. For more information, contact your local military service recruitment office.

Other agencies of the federal government may also offer student loan repayment programs as an incentive to recruit and retain employees. Contact the agency's human resources department for more information.

24. AmeriCorps program education awards. Under the National and Community Service Act of 1990, you may receive an education award that can be used to repay a Direct Subsidized Loan or Direct Unsubsidized Loan if you successfully complete a term of service in an AmeriCorps program. For more information, contact an official of your program.

William D. Ford Federal Direct Loan Program
Direct Subsidized Loan and Direct Unsubsidized Loan Borrower's Rights and Responsibilities Statement

Repaying Your Loans[1]

Initial Debt When You Enter Repayment	Standard		Extended[2,3]		Graduated		Income Contingent[5,6] Income = $15,000				Income Contingent[5,6] Income = $25,000				Income Contingent[5,6] Income = $45,000			
							Single		Married/HOH[7]		Single		Married/HOH[7]		Single		Married/HOH[7]	
	Per Month	Total	Per Month	Total	Per[4] Month	Total	Per Month	Total	Per Month	Total	Per Month	Total	Per Month	Total	Per Month	Total	Per Month	Total
3,500	50	4,471	Not Available		25	5,157	21	6,939	20	6,673	27	6,092	25	6,405	36	5,128	36	5,128
5,000	58	6,905	Not Available		40	7,278	30	9,912	29	9,533	38	8,703	36	9,150	51	7,326	51	7,326
5,500	63	7,595	Not Available		43	8,007	33	10,903	30	10,463	42	9,574	40	10,065	56	8,059	56	8,059
7,500	86	10,357	Not Available		59	10,919	45	14,868	30	14,019	57	13,055	54	13,725	76	10,989	76	10,989
10,500	121	14,500	Not Available		83	15,283	64	20,815	30	18,877	80	18,277	76	19,215	107	15,385	107	15,385
15,000	173	20,714	Not Available		119	21,834	87	29,685	30	25,229	114	26,110	108	27,451	153	21,978	153	21,978
18,500	213	25,548	Not Available		146	26,929	87	35,992	30	29,465	140	32,203	134	33,856	188	27,106	188	27,106
23,000	265	31,762	Not Available		182	33,479	87	43,141	30	34,128	174	40,036	166	42,091	234	33,699	234	33,699
30,000	345	41,429	Not Available		237	43,668	87	52,340	30	39,756	228	52,221	197	55,743	407	43,956	407	43,956
40,000	460	55,239	277	83,289	316	58,229	87	62,005	30	44,827	253	72,717	197	84,352	468	58,608	468	58,608
46,000	529	63,524	319	95,782	363	66,956	87	66,084	30	46,378	253	89,828	197	105,472	509	67,399	509	67,399
50,000	575	69,048	347	104,111	395	72,778	87	68,153	30	46,860	253	103,268	197	111,575	587	73,260	587	73,260
60,000	690	82,858	391	140,816	474	87,334	87	71,219	30	46,934	253	136,615	197	124,085	587	88,251	587	88,251
70,000	806	96,667	456	164,285	535	101,890	87	71,721	30	46,934	253	148,551	197	133,106	587	106,551	587	106,551
80,000	920	110,477	522	187,754	632	116,445	87	71,721	30	46,934	253	157,373	197	138,907	587	128,146	587	128,146
90,000	1,036	124,287	587	211,224	711	131,002	87	71,721	30	46,934	253	163,227	197	141,925	587	152,967	587	152,967
100,000	1,151	138,096	652	234,693	790	145,556	87	71,721	30	46,934	253	166,457	197	142,386	587	181,224	587	181,224
110,000	1,266	151,906	717	258,162	869	160,111	87	71,721	30	46,934	253	167,172	197	142,386	587	213,485	587	213,485
120,000	1,381	165,716	782	281,632	948	174,668	87	71,721	30	46,934	253	167,172	197	142,386	587	250,281	587	250,281
130,000	1,496	179,525	848	305,101	1,024	189,224	87	71,721	30	46,934	253	167,172	197	142,386	587	292,313	587	292,313
138,500	1,594	191,264	903	325,050	1,094	201,596	87	71,721	30	46,934	253	167,172	197	142,386	587	332,912	587	332,912

The **estimated** payments were calculated using a fixed interest rate of 6.80%.
This repayment plan is available only to borrowers who have an outstanding balance on Direct Loan Program loans that exceeds $30,000, and who had no outstanding balance on a Direct Loan Program loan as of October 7, 1998 or on the date they obtained a Direct Loan Program loan on or after October 7, 1998.
These amounts are fixed, rounded to the nearest dollar, and calculated based on a 25-year repayment term.
This is your beginning payment, which may increase during your 10-year repayment term.
Assumes a 5% annual income growth (Census Bureau).
The **estimated** payments were calculated using the formula requirements in effect during 2006.
HOH is Head of Household; assumes a family size of two.

Revised 03/2009

D.5.8 Direct Loan Sample Disclosure Statement

U.S. Department of Education
P.O. Box 9003
Niagara Falls, NY 14302-9003

Disclosure Statement
William D. Ford Federal Direct Loan Program

Direct Subsidized Loan
Direct Unsubsidized Loan

Borrower Information

1. Name and Address

2. Date of Disclosure Statement

3. Area Code/Telephone Number

School Information

4. School Name and Address

5. School Code/Branch

Loan Information

6. Loan Identification Number(s)

7. Loan Period(s)

8. Loan Fee %

9. Information about the loan(s) that your school plans to disburse (pay out) follows. This information is explained in detail on the back. The actual disbursement dates and amounts may be different than the dates and amounts shown below. The school and the servicer will notify you of the actual disbursement dates and amounts.

Direct Subsidized Loan

Gross Loan Amount − Loan Fee Amount + Interest Rebate Amount = Net Loan Amount

Your school plans to disburse the Net Loan Amount as follows:

Date	Net Disbursement Amount	Date	Net Disbursement Amount

Direct Unsubsidized Loan

Gross Loan Amount − Loan Fee Amount + Interest Rebate Amount = Net Loan Amount

Your school plans to disburse the Net Loan Amount as follows:

Date	Net Disbursement Amount	Date	Net Disbursement Amount

If there are further disbursements to be made on the loan(s) the school will inform you.

Disclosure Statement (continued)

This Disclosure Statement provides information about the Direct Subsidized Loan and/or Direct Unsubsidized Loan that your school plans to disburse (pay out) by crediting your student account, paying you directly, or both. It replaces any Disclosure Statements that you may have received previously for the same loan(s). Keep this Disclosure statement for your records.

You must have signed a Master Promissory Note (MPN) before your loan money is disbursed. The MPN, the Borrower's Rights and Responsibilities statement, and the Plain Language Disclosure explain the terms of your loan(s). If you have any questions about your MPN or this Disclosure Statement, contact your school.

Item 9 on the front of this Disclosure Statement provides the following information about the amount of each loan that your school plans to disburse to you:

- **Gross Loan Amount** - This is the total amount of the loan that you are borrowing. You will be responsible for repaying this amount.
- **Loan Fee Amount** - This is the amount of the fee that we charge on your loan. It is based on a percentage of your Gross Loan Amount. The percentage is shown in item 8. The Loan Fee Amount will be subtracted from your Gross Loan Amount.
- **Interest Rebate Amount** - This is the amount of an up-front interest rebate that you may receive as part of a program to encourage the timely repayment of Direct Loans. If you receive a rebate, the Interest Rebate Amount will be added back after the Loan Fee Amount is subtracted.

  To keep an up-front interest rebate that you receive on your loan, you must make all of your first 12 required monthly payments on time (we must receive each payment no later then 6 days after the due date) when your loan enters repayment. You will lose the rebate if you do not make all of your first 12 required monthly payments on your loan account. This will increase the amount that you must repay.

- **Net Loan Amount** - This is the amount of your loan money that remains after the Loan Fee Amount is subtracted and the Interest Rebate Amount is added. The school will disburse the Net Loan Amount to you by crediting the students account, paying you directly, or both.

  Item 9 shows the school's plan for disbursing your Net Loan Amount to you. The actual disbursement dates and amounts may be different than the dates and amounts that are shown. Your school and the servicer will notify you of the actual disbursement dates and amounts.

Before your loan money is disbursed, you may cancel all or part of your loan(s) at any time by notifying the school.

After your loan money is disbursed, there are two ways to cancel all or part of your loan(s):

- Within 14 days after the date the school notifies you that it has credited loan money to the students account, at the school or by the first day of the school's payment period, whichever is later (the school can tell you the first day of the payment period), you may tell the school that you want to cancel all or part of the loan money that was credited to the students account. The school will return the cancelled loan amount to us. You do not have to pay interest or the loan fee on the part of your loan(s) that you tell your school to cancel within this timeframe. If you received an up-front interest rebate on your loan(s), the rebate does not apply to the part of your loan(s) that you tell the school to cancel. Your loan(s) will be adjusted to eliminate any interest, loan fee, and rebate amount that applies to the amount of the loan(s) that was cancelled.

  If you ask the school to cancel all or part of your loan(s) outside the timeframe described above, the school may process your cancellation request, but it is not required to do so.

- Within 120 days of the date the school disbursed your loan money (by crediting the loan money to the student's account at the school, by paying it directly to you, or both), you may return all or part of your loan(s) to us. Contact the servicer for guidance on how and where to return within 120 days of the date that part of your loan is disbursed. If you received an up-front interest rebate on your loan(s), the rebate does not apply to the part of your loan(s) that you return. Your loan(s) will be adjusted to eliminate any interest, loan fee, and rebate amount that applies to the amount of the loan(s) that you return

Appx. D.5.9 *Student Loan Law*

D.5.9 Direct Loan Plain Language Disclosure

Plain Language Disclosure for Direct Subsidized Loans and Direct Unsubsidized Loans
William D. Ford Federal Direct Loan Program

1. General information. You are receiving a Direct Subsidized Loan and/or Direct Unsubsidized Loan to help cover the costs of your education. This Plain Language Disclosure (Disclosure) summarizes information about your loan. Please read this Disclosure carefully and keep a copy in a safe place. In this Disclosure, the words "we," "us," and "our" refer to the U.S. Department of Education (the Department). If you have questions about your loan, contact our Direct Loan Servicing Center. The Direct Loan Servicing Center's telephone number and address are shown on correspondence you will receive related to your loan.

You must repay this loan, even if you are unhappy with your education, do not complete your program of study, or cannot find work in your area of study. Borrow only the amount you can afford to repay, even if you are eligible to borrow more.

By accepting your loan proceeds, you are certifying, under penalty of perjury, that if you have been convicted of, or have pled *nolo contendere* or guilty to, a crime involving fraud in obtaining federal student aid funds under Title IV of the Higher Education Act of 1965, as amended, you have completed the repayment of those funds to the Department, or to the loan holder in the case of a Title IV federal student loan.

Information about your loans will be reported to the National Student Loan Data System (NSLDS). Information in NSLDS is accessible to schools, lenders, and guarantors for specific purposes as authorized by the Department.

2. Master Promissory Note (MPN). You are receiving a loan under an MPN that you signed previously. You may receive additional loans under that MPN for up to 10 years if the school that you attend is authorized to use the multi-year feature of the MPN and chooses to do so. If your school is not authorized to use the multi-year feature of the MPN or chooses not to do so, or if you do not want to receive more than one loan under the same MPN, you must sign a new MPN for each loan. If you do not want to receive more than one loan under the same MPN, you must notify your school or the Direct Loan Servicing Center in writing.

3. Loan terms and conditions. This Disclosure summarizes information about your loan. Please refer to your MPN and the Borrower's Rights and Responsibilities Statement that you received previously for the complete terms and conditions of your loan. If you need another copy of the Borrower's Rights and Responsibilities Statement, contact the Direct Loan Servicing Center. Unless we tell you otherwise in this Disclosure, your MPN and the Borrower's Rights and Responsibilities Statement control the terms and conditions of your loan. Loans made under your MPN are subject to the Higher Education Act of 1965, as amended, and federal regulations (collectively referred to as "the Act"). Any changes to the law or regulations apply to loans in accordance with the effective date of the changes.

4. Use of loan money. You may use your loan money only to pay for educational expenses (for example, tuition, room, board, books) at the school that determined you were eligible to receive the loan. If you accept this loan, your eligibility for other student assistance may be affected.

5. Information you must report. While you are still in school, you must notify your school if you **(i)** change your address or telephone number; **(ii)** change your name (for example, maiden name to married name); **(iii)** do not enroll at least half-time for the loan period certified by the school, or do not enroll at the school that certified your eligibility for the loan; **(iv)** stop attending school or drop below half-time enrollment; or **(v)** graduate or transfer to another school.

You must also notify the Direct Loan Servicing Center of any of the above changes at any time after you receive your loan. In addition, you must notify the Direct Loan Servicing Center if you **(i)** change employers or if your employer's address or phone number changes; or **(ii)** have any other change in status that affects your loan (for example, if you received a deferment but no longer meet the eligibility requirements for that deferment).

6. Amount you may borrow. There are limits on the amount you may borrow each academic year (annual loan limits) and in total (aggregate loan limits), as explained in the Borrower's Rights and Responsibilities Statement. You cannot borrow more than these limits.

Effective for loans first disbursed on or after July 1, 2008, the annual and aggregate loan limits are as follows:

Annual Loan Limits

Dependent Undergraduates (***except*** students whose parents cannot borrow PLUS loans)	
First Year (freshman)	$5,500 (maximum $3,500 subsidized)
Second Year (sophomore)	$6,500 (maximum $4,500 subsidized)
Third Year (junior) and Beyond	$7,500 (maximum $5,500 subsidized)
Independent Undergraduates (and dependent students whose parents cannot borrow PLUS loans)	
First Year (freshman)	$9,500 (maximum $3,500 subsidized)
Second Year (sophomore)	$10,500 (maximum $4,500 subsidized)
Third Year (junior) and Beyond	$12,500 (maximum $5,500 subsidized)
Graduate and Professional Students	
$20,500 (maximum $8,500 subsidized)	

Aggregate Loan Limits

Dependent Undergraduates (***except*** students whose parents cannot borrow PLUS loans)
$31,000 (maximum $23,000 subsidized)
Independent Undergraduates (and dependent students whose parents cannot borrow PLUS loans)
$57,500 (maximum $23,000 subsidized)
Graduate and Professional Students
$138,500 (maximum $65,500 subsidized)

7. Interest. Loans with a first disbursement date on or after July 1, 2006 have a fixed interest rate. However, different fixed interest rates may apply to separate loans made under the MPN depending on whether the loan is subsidized or unsubsidized, when the loan is first disbursed, and whether you are an undergraduate or graduate student. Loans with a first disbursement date prior to July 1, 2006 have a variable rate that is adjusted each year on July 1 but will never be more than 8.25%. Some variable interest rate loans have an interest rate that is lower during in-school, grace, and deferment periods, and higher during repayment and forbearance periods. For loans with a variable interest rate, we will notify you annually of the actual interest rate for each loan that you receive.

If you qualify under the Servicemembers Civil Relief Act, the interest rate on your loans obtained prior to military service may be limited to 6% during your military service. To receive this benefit, you must contact the Direct Loan Servicing Center for information about the documentation you must provide to show that you qualify.

We do not charge interest on Direct Subsidized Loans while you are enrolled in school at least half time, during your grace period, and during deferment periods. Except as provided below for certain military borrowers, we charge interest on Direct Subsidized Loans during all other periods (starting on the day after your grace period ends), including forbearance periods.

Except as provided below for certain military borrowers, we charge interest on Direct Unsubsidized Loans during all periods (starting on the day your loan is paid out). This includes periods while you are enrolled in school, during your grace period, and during deferment and forbearance periods. Therefore, you will pay more interest on Direct Unsubsidized Loans than on Direct Subsidized Loans.

If you do not pay the interest that is charged to you during in-school, grace, deferment, and forbearance periods, we will add it to the unpaid amount of your loan. This is called capitalization. Capitalization increases the unpaid amount of your loan, and we will then charge interest on the increased amount.

Under the no accrual of interest benefit for active duty service members, we do not charge interest on Direct Loan Program loans first disbursed on or after October 1, 2008 during periods of qualifying active duty military service (for up to 60 months). For Direct Consolidation Loans, this benefit applies to the portion of the consolidation loan that repaid loans first disbursed on or after October 1, 2008.

8. Loan fee. We charge a loan fee on your loan that is a percentage of the principal amount of the loan. The percentage is determined by the Act and varies depending on when a loan is first disbursed. The specific loan fee that you are charged will be shown on a disclosure statement that we send to you. This fee will be subtracted proportionately from each disbursement of your loan.

9. Repayment incentive programs. A repayment incentive is a benefit that we offer to encourage you to repay your loan on time. Under a repayment incentive program, the interest rate we charge on your loan may be reduced. Some repayment incentive programs require you to make a certain number of payments on time to keep the reduced interest rate. The following repayment incentive programs may be available to you: *Interest Rate Reduction for Electronic Debit Account Repayment* and *Up-Front Interest Rebate*. These repayment incentive programs are described in the Borrower's Rights and Responsibilities Statement. The Direct Loan Servicing Center can provide you with more information on other repayment incentive programs that may be available.

10. Disbursement of loan money. Generally, your school will disburse (pay out) your loan money in more than one installment, usually at the beginning of each academic term (for example, at the beginning of each semester or quarter). If your school does not use academic terms or does not have academic terms that meet certain requirements, it will generally disburse your loan in at least two installments, one at the beginning of the period of study for which you are receiving the loan and one at the midpoint of that period of study. Your school may disburse your loan money by crediting it to your student account, or may give it to you directly by check or other means. The Direct Loan Servicing Center will notify you each time your school disburses a portion of your loan.

11. Canceling your loan. Before your loan money is disbursed, you may cancel all or part of your loan at any time by notifying your school. After your loan money is disbursed, there are two ways to cancel all or part of your loan:

- If your school obtains your written confirmation of the types and amounts of Title IV loans that you want to receive for an award year before crediting loan money to your account at the school, you may tell the school that you want to cancel all or part of that loan within 14 days after the date the school notifies you of your right to cancel all or part of the loan, or by the first day of your school's payment period, whichever is later (your school can tell you the first day of the payment period). If the school does not obtain your written confirmation of the types and amounts of loans you want to receive before crediting the loan money to your account, you may cancel all or part of that loan by informing the school within 30 days of the date the school notifies you of your right to cancel all or part of the loan. In either case, your school will return the cancelled loan amount to us. You do not have to pay interest or the loan fee on the part of your loan that you tell your school to cancel within these timeframes. If you received an up-front interest rebate on your loan, the rebate does not apply to the part of your loan that you tell your school to cancel. Your loan will be adjusted to eliminate any interest, loan fee, and rebate amount that applies to the amount of the loan that was cancelled.

  If you ask your school to cancel all or part of your loan outside the timeframes described above, your school may process your cancellation request, but it is not required to do so.

Page 1 of 2
Revised 03/2009

Student Assistance Forms   Appx. D.5.9

Plain Language Disclosure for Direct Subsidized Loans and Direct Unsubsidized Loans
William D. Ford Federal Direct Loan Program

- Within 120 days of the date your school disbursed your loan money (by crediting the loan money to your account at the school, by paying it directly to you, or both), you may return all or part of your loan to us. Contact the Direct Loan Servicing Center for guidance on how and where to return your loan money. You do not have to pay interest or the loan fee on the part of your loan that you return within 120 days of the date that part of your loan is disbursed. If you received an up-front interest rebate on your loan, the rebate does not apply to the part of your loan that you return. Your loan will be adjusted to eliminate any interest, loan fee, and rebate amount that applies to the amount of the loan that you return.

12. Grace period. You will receive a 6-month grace period on repayment that starts the day after you stop attending school or drop below half-time enrollment. You do not have to begin making payments on your loan until after your grace period ends.

13. Repaying your loan. You must repay each loan that you receive according to the repayment schedule provided by the Direct Loan Servicing Center. You must begin repaying your loan after your grace period ends. The amount of time you have to repay your loan (the repayment period) will vary from 10 to 25 years, depending on the repayment plan that you choose and the total amount you have borrowed. For Direct Subsidized Loans and Direct Unsubsidized Loans that enter repayment on or after July 1, 2006, you may choose one of the following repayment plans:

Standard Repayment Plan. Refer to the Borrower's Rights and Responsibilities Statement for the terms and conditions of this plan.

Graduated Repayment Plan. If you choose this plan, your payments will usually be lower at first, and will then increase over time. No single payment will be more than 3 times greater than any other payment. Under this plan, you must repay your loan in full within 10 years (not including periods of deferment and forbearance) from the date the loan entered repayment. If your loan has a variable interest rate, we may need to adjust the number or amount of your payments to reflect changes in the interest rate.

Extended Repayment Plan. You may choose this plan only if (i) you had no outstanding balance on a Direct Loan Program loan as of October 7, 1998 or on the date you obtained a Direct Loan Program loan on or after October 7, 1998, and (ii) you have an outstanding balance on Direct Loan Program loans that exceeds $30,000. If you are eligible for and choose this plan, you will make monthly payments based on fixed annual or graduated repayment amounts and will repay your loan in full over a period not to exceed 25 years (not including periods of deferment and forbearance) from the date your loan entered repayment. Your payments must be at least $50 per month and will be more, if necessary, to repay the loan within the required time period. If your loan has a variable interest rate, we may need to adjust the number or amount of your payments to reflect changes in the interest rate.

Income Contingent Repayment Plan. Refer to the Borrower's Rights and Responsibilities Statement for the terms and conditions of this plan.

Effective July 1, 2009, if you are eligible, you may also choose an **Income-Based Repayment Plan**. Under this plan, your required monthly payment amount will be based on your income during any period when you have a partial financial hardship. The maximum repayment period under this plan may exceed 10 years. If you meet certain requirements over a 25-year period, you may qualify for cancellation of any outstanding balance on your loans.

These plans are designed to give you flexibility in meeting your obligation to repay your loan. You may change repayment plans at any time after you have begun repaying your loan. You may make loan payments before they are due, or pay more than the amount due each month, without penalty. When you have repaid a loan in full, the Direct Loan Servicing Center will send you a notice telling you that you have paid off your loan. You should keep this notice in a safe place.

14. Late charges and collection costs. We may require you to pay a late charge of not more than six cents for each dollar of each late payment if you do not make any part of a payment within 30 days after it is due. We may also require you to pay other charges and fees involved in collecting your loan.

15. Demand for immediate repayment. The entire unpaid amount of your loan becomes due and payable (on your MPN this is called "acceleration") if you (i) receive loan money but do not enroll at least half-time at the school that determined you were eligible to receive the loan; (ii) use your loan money to pay for anything other than educational expenses at the school that determined you were eligible to receive the loan; (iii) make a false statement that causes you to receive a loan that you are not eligible to receive; or (iv) default on your loan.

16. Default. You are in default on your loan if you (i) do not repay the entire unpaid amount of your loan if we require you to do so; (ii) have not made a payment on your loan for at least 270 days; or (iii) do not comply with other terms and conditions of your loan, and we conclude that you no longer intend to honor your obligation to repay your loan.

If you default on your loan, we will report your default to national consumer reporting agencies. We may sue you, take all or part of your federal tax refund, and/or garnish your wages so that your employer is required to send us part of your salary to pay off your loan. We will require you to pay reasonable collection fees and costs, plus court costs and attorney fees. You will lose eligibility for other federal student aid and assistance under most federal benefit programs. You will lose eligibility for loan deferments.

17. Consumer reporting agency notification. We will report information about your loan to national consumer reporting agencies. This information will include the disbursement dates, amount, and repayment status of your loan (for example, whether you are current or delinquent in making payments). Your loan will be identified as an education loan.

18. Deferment and forbearance (postponing payments). If you meet certain requirements, you may receive a **deferment** that allows you to temporarily stop making payments on your loan. For example:

You may receive a deferment while you are attending school at least half-time or for up to 3 years while you are unemployed.

You may receive a deferment while you are serving on active duty during a war or other military operation or national emergency, or performing qualifying National Guard duty during a war or other military operation or national emergency, and if you are serving on or after October 1, 2007, for an additional 180-day period following the demobilization date for your qualifying service.

If you are a member of the National Guard or other reserve component of the U.S. Armed Forces (current or retired) and you are called or ordered to active duty while enrolled at least half-time at an eligible school, or within 6 months after having been enrolled at least half-time, you are eligible for a deferment during the 13 months following the conclusion of your active duty service, or until the date you return to enrolled student status on at least a half-time basis, whichever is earlier.

This is not a complete list of available deferments. For a complete list, refer to the Borrower's Rights and Responsibilities Statement that you received previously.

We do not charge interest on Direct Subsidized Loans during deferment periods. However, we do charge interest on Direct Unsubsidized Loans during deferment periods.

If you cannot make your scheduled loan payments but do not qualify for a deferment, we may give you a **forbearance**. A forbearance allows you to temporarily stop making payments on your loan, temporarily make smaller payments, or extend the time for making payments. For example, we may give you a forbearance if you are temporarily unable to make scheduled loan payments because of financial hardship or illness. We may also give you a forbearance under other conditions as described in the Borrower's Rights and Responsibilities Statement. We charge interest on both Direct Subsidized Loans and Direct Unsubsidized Loans during forbearance periods.

To request a deferment or forbearance, contact the Direct Loan Servicing Center.

19. Loan discharge. We may discharge (forgive) all or part of your loan if **(i)** you die, and we receive an original or certified copy of your death certificate; **(ii)** you become totally and permanently disabled and meet certain other requirements; **(iii)** your loan is discharged in bankruptcy; **(iv)** you were unable to complete your course of study because your school closed; **(v)** your school falsely certified your eligibility; **(vi)** your school did not pay a refund of your loan money that it was required to pay under federal regulations; or, effective July 1, 2006, **(vii)** a loan in your name was falsely certified as a result of a crime of identity theft. To request a loan discharge, contact the Direct Loan Servicing Center.

We may forgive a portion of any loans you received under the Direct Loan or Federal Family Education Loan (FFEL) program after October 1, 1998 if you teach full-time for 5 consecutive years in certain low-income elementary and/or secondary schools and meet certain other qualifications, and if you did not owe a Direct Loan or FFEL program loan as of October 1, 1998, or as of the date you obtain a loan after October 1, 1998. Contact the Direct Loan Servicing Center for specific eligibility requirements.

A public service loan forgiveness program is also available. Under this program, the remaining balance due on your eligible Direct Loan Program loans may be cancelled after you have made 120 payments on those loans (after October 1, 2007) under certain repayment plans while you are employed in certain public service jobs.

The Act may provide for certain loan forgiveness or repayment benefits on your loan in addition to the benefits described above. If other forgiveness or repayment options become available, the Direct Loan Servicing Center will provide information about these benefits.

In some cases, you may assert, as a defense against collection of your loan, that your school did something wrong or failed to do something that it should have done. You can make such a defense against repayment only if what your school did or did not do would give rise to a legal cause of action under applicable state law. If you believe that you have a defense against repayment of your loan, contact the Direct Loan Servicing Center.

20. Loan consolidation. You may consolidate (combine) one or more of your eligible federal education loans into one loan. Consolidation allows you to extend the period of time that you have to repay your loans, and to combine several loan debts into a single monthly payment. This may make it easier for you to repay your loans. However, you will pay more interest if you extend your repayment period through consolidation, since you will be making payments for a longer period of time. Contact the Direct Loan Servicing Center for more information about loan consolidation.

D.5.10 Direct Loan Notice of Disbursement Made

NOTICE OF DISBURSEMENT(S) MADE

04/15/2008

A-000000001   S002531370   ACCOUNT#: XXX-XX-XXXX-1
FIRSTNAME MI LASTNAME
ADDRESS LINE 1
ADDRESS LINE 2
CITY STATE ZIP

Our records show that the following Direct Loan disbursement(s) were recently made to you or your school account.

Disbursement(s) Covered By This Notice

Loan ID	Loan Type*	School**	Net Disbursed***	Gross Disbursed	Loan Fee	Interest Rebate Type/Amount****	Most Recent Date Disbursed	Interest Rate	Interest Type
XXXXX4841S08G03937001	S	1	$1,734.00	$1,750.00	$42.00	R2 / $26.00	03/26/2008	6.800%	Fixed

*   (S)ubsidized, (U)nsubsidized, (P)LUS
**   1 = UNIVERSITY OF THE SACRED HEART
     2 =
     3 =
*** Net Disbursed equals Gross Disbursed minus Loan Fee plus any R2 Interest Rebate.
**** R1 Interest Rebate - Given to you as a reduction in your loan balance (amount owed) under a repayment incentive program in effect when you received this loan.
     R2 Interest Rebate - Given to you as an increase in your Net Disbursed amount under a repayment incentive program in effect when you received this loan.

Summary Of All Your Direct Loans
(Except Any Consolidation Loans)

Loan Type	Expected Repayment Start Date	Repayment Plan(s) If Selected	Interest Rebate Amount	Amount Owed
Subsidized	02/14/2013	Standard	$26.00	$1,750.00
Unsubsidized			$0.00	$0.00
PLUS			$0.00	$0.00
Total *(Does Not Include Any Consolidation Loans)* as of 04/15/2008			**$26.00**	**$1,750.00**

General Information

THIS IS A LOAN - This is not a grant, award, or scholarship. **It is a loan that must be repaid.** Failure to make payments on time can result in reporting you to National Credit Bureaus, garnishing your wages, withholding federal income tax refunds, taking legal action against you, and other consequences. *If you no longer need these funds, refer to the cancellation instructions on the back.*

PAYMENTS - The payment address is: U.S. Department of Education, P.O. Box 530260, Atlanta, GA 30353-0260. If you have difficulty repaying your loan(s) at any time, call us at the toll-free telephone number on the back of this Notice to discuss options such as changing your repayment plan(s) or receiving a forbearance or a deferment. You may repay this loan in full at *any time* without a prepayment penalty. For an estimated payoff amount, access our Web site or call our toll-free telephone number (both shown on the back).

CONSOLIDATION - You can consolidate your eligible federal education loans by calling the Loan Origination Center at 1-800-557-7392. The Telecommunications Device for the Deaf (TDD) number is 1-800-557-7395.

REPAYMENT PLANS - Your choice of repayment plans includes: Standard Plan (fixed payment for up to 10 years to repay), Extended Plan - Fixed Monthly Payment Option (fixed payments for up to 25 years based on current Direct Loan balances greater than $30,000), Extended Plan - Graduated Monthly Payment Option (smaller payments at first and larger payments later for up to 25 years based on current Direct Loan balances greater than $30,000), Graduated Plan (smaller payments at first and larger payments later for up to 10 years to repay), and Income Contingent Repayment (ICR) Plan (payment based on your income, family size, and loan amount; ICR is NOT available for PLUS loans).

INTEREST REBATE - You may have received an up-front interest rebate as part of a program to encourage timely repayment of Direct Loans. If you received the rebate, it is shown above. **To keep the rebate,** you must make your first 12 required monthly payments on time (within 6 days of the due date) when you begin repaying your loan(s). **If you do not make all 12 payments on time,** the rebate amount will be added back into your Amount Owed.

WEL1AV13

Our Mission is to Ensure Equal Access to Education and to Promote Educational Excellence Throughout the Nation
U.S. Department of Education

Student Assistance Forms Appx. D.5.10

ADDITIONAL INFORMATION ABOUT YOUR LOAN

If any information on this Notice is incorrect, please contact the Direct Loan Servicing Center (DLSC).

The DLSC was created to assist you with all matters regarding your Direct Loan(s). Please call us from 8:00 AM to 8:30 PM Eastern Time, Monday through Friday toll-free at 1-800-848-0979. Hearing-impaired individuals with access to a TDD (Telecommunications Device for the Deaf) can call 1-800-848-0983.

You can access our Direct Loan web site at: **www.dl.ed.gov**

Send any correspondence to:

**U.S. Department of Education
Direct Loan Servicing Center
P.O. Box 5609
Greenville, TX 75403-5609**

Please advise us of any changes in name, social security number (SSN), address, or telephone number. Additionally, you are required to immediately report any change in enrollment status and expected student graduation date directly to the school's financial aid office. If you transfer to another school, please request that the new school inform us immediately. This information can affect the status of your loan.

120-DAY LOAN CANCELLATION PROVISION

If you decide you no longer need the funds after your loan money has been disbursed to you, you can cancel all or part of your loan(s) by following the instructions below.

Within 120 days of the date your school disbursed your loan money (by crediting the loan money to your student account, paying it to you directly, or both), you may return all or part of your loan(s) to the U.S. Department of Education. Call the DLSC for guidance on how and where to return your loan money.

You do not have to pay interest or the loan fee on the part of your loan(s) that you return within 120 days of the date your loan(s) is disbursed. If you received an up-front interest rebate on your loan(s), the rebate does not apply to the part of your loan(s) that you return. Your loan(s) will be adjusted to eliminate any interest, loan fee, and rebate amount that applies to the amount of the loan(s) that you return.

Notice to Customers Making Payment by Check

If you send us a check, it will be converted into an electronic funds transfer (EFT). This means we will copy your check and use the account information to electronically debit your account for the amount of the check. The debit from your account will usually occur within 24 hours and will be shown on your regular account statement from your financial institution.

You will not receive your original check back. We will destroy your original check but will keep a copy of it. If the EFT cannot be processed for technical reasons, you authorize us to process the copy in place of your original check. If the EFT cannot be completed because of insufficient funds, we may try to make the transfer one additional time.

Appx. D.5.11   *Student Loan Law*

D.5.11 Perkins Master Promissory Note

FEDERAL PERKINS LOAN MASTER PROMISSORY NOTE
OMB No. 1845-0074 Form Approved Expiration Date 08/31/2012

Section A: Borrower Section

1. Name (last, first, middle initial) and Permanent Address (street, city, state, zip code)	2. Social Security Number
	3. Date of Birth (mm/dd/yyyy)
	4. Home Area Code/Telephone Number
	5. Driver's License Number (List state abbreviation first)

Section B: School Section

6. School Name & Address (street, city, state, zip code)	7. Annual Interest Rate 5%

[Any bracketed clause or paragraph may be included at option of institution]

Terms and Conditions: (Note: Additional Terms and Conditions follow on subsequent pages)

APPLICABLE LAW - The terms of this Federal Perkins Loan Master Promissory Note (hereinafter called the Note) and any disbursements made under this Note shall be interpreted in accordance with Part E of Title IV of the Higher Education Act of 1965, as amended (hereinafter called the Act), as well as Federal regulations issued under the Act. All sums advanced under this Note are subject to the Act and Federal regulations issued under the Act.

REPAYMENT - I am obligated to repay the principal and the interest that accrues on my loan(s) to the above-named institution (hereinafter called the School) over a period beginning 9 months (or sooner if I am a Less-Than-Half-Time Borrower) after the date I cease to be at least a half-time student at an institution of higher education or a comparable School outside the United States approved by the United States Department of Education (hereinafter called the Department) and ending 10 years later, unless I request in writing that my repayment period begin sooner. I understand that the School will report the amount of my installment payments, along with the amount of this loan to at least one national credit bureau. Interest on this loan shall accrue from the beginning of the repayment period. My repayment period may be shorter than 10 years if I am required by my School to make minimum monthly payments. My repayment period may be extended during periods of deferment, hardship, or forbearance and I may make graduated installments in accordance with a schedule approved by the Department. I will make my installment payments in equal monthly, bimonthly, or quarterly installments as determined by the School. The School may round my installment payment to the next highest multiple of $5. [I will make a minimum monthly repayment of $40 (or $30 if I have outstanding Federal Perkins Loans made before October 1, 1992 that included the $30 minimum payment option or outstanding National Direct Student Loans) in accordance with the Minimum Monthly Payment Section of the Terms and Conditions contained on the reverse side of this document.]

LATE CHARGES - The School may impose late charges if I do not make a scheduled payment when due or if I fail to submit to the School on or before the due date of the payment, a properly documented request for any of the forbearance, deferment, or cancellation benefits as described below. No late charges may exceed 20 percent of my monthly, bimonthly, or quarterly payment. The School may add the late charges to principal the day after the scheduled payment was due or include it with the next scheduled payment after I have received notice of the charge, and such notice is sent before the next installment is due.

FORBEARANCE, DEFERMENT, OR CANCELLATION - I may apply for a forbearance, deferment, or cancellation on my loan. During an approved forbearance period, payments of principal and interest, or principal only, may be postponed or reduced. Interest continues to accrue while my loan is in forbearance. During an approved deferment period, I am not required to make scheduled installment payments on my loan. I am not liable for any interest that might otherwise accrue while my loan is in deferment. If I meet the eligibility requirements for a cancellation of my loan, the institution may cancel up to 100 percent of the outstanding principal loan amount. Information on eligibility and application requirements for forbearances, deferments, and cancellations is provided on pages 2 through 4 of this Note. I am responsible for submitting the appropriate requests on time, and I may lose my benefits if I fail to file my request on time.

DEFAULT - The School may, at its option, declare my loan to be in default if (1) I fail to make a scheduled payment when due; (2) I fail to submit to the School, on or before the due date of a scheduled payment, documentation that I qualify for a forbearance, deferment, or cancellation; or (3) I fail to comply with the terms and conditions of this Note or written repayment agreement. The School may assign a defaulted loan to the Department for collection. I will be ineligible for any further federal student financial assistance authorized under the Act until I make arrangements that are satisfactory to the School or the Department to repay my loan. The School or the Department shall disclose to credit bureau organizations that I have defaulted and all other relevant loan information. I will lose my right to defer payments and my right to forbearance if I default on my loan. The School or the Department may accelerate my defaulted loan. Acceleration means that the School or the Department demands immediate payment of the entire unpaid balance of the loan, including principal, interest, late charges, and collection costs. I will lose my right to receive cancellation benefits for service that is performed after the date the School or the Department accelerated the loan.

CHANGE OF STATUS - I will inform the School of any change in my name, address, telephone number, Social Security Number, or driver's license number.

AUTHORIZATION: - I authorize the School, the Department, and their respective agents and contractors to contact me regarding my loan request or my loan(s), including repayment of my loan(s), at the current or any future number that I provide for my cellular phone or other wireless device using automated telephone dialing equipment or artificial or pre-recorded voice or text messages.

PROMISE TO PAY: I promise to pay the School, or a subsequent holder of the Note, all sums disbursed under the terms of this Note, plus interest and other fees which may become due as provided in this Note. **I understand that multiple loans may be made to me under this Note.** I understand that by accepting any disbursements issued at any time under this Note, I agree to repay the loans. I understand that each loan is separately enforceable based on a true and exact copy of this Note. I understand that I may cancel or reduce the amount of any loan by not accepting or by returning all or a portion of any disbursement that is issued. If I do not make any payment on any loan under this Note when it is due, I promise to pay all reasonable collection costs, including attorney fees, court costs, and other fees. I will not sign this Note before reading the entire Note, even if I am told that I am not required to read it. I am entitled to an exact copy of this Note. This loan has been made to me without security or endorsement. My signature certifies I have read, understand, and agree to the terms and conditions of this Note.

I UNDERSTAND THAT I MAY RECEIVE ONE OR MORE LOANS UNDER THIS MASTER PROMISSORY NOTE AND THAT I MUST REPAY SUCH LOANS.

_____   _____
Borrower's Signature   Date

Terms and Conditions (cont.)

DISCLOSURE OF LOAN TERMS - I understand that under this Note, the principal amount that I owe, and am required to repay, will be the sum of all disbursements issued unless I reduce or cancel any disbursements. The School will determine whether to make any loan under this Note after my loan eligibility is determined. At or before the time of first disbursement for each loan, a disclosure statement will be provided to me identifying the amount of the loan and any additional terms of the loan. I may decline a loan or request a lower amount by contacting the School. Any disclosure statement I receive in connection with any loan under this Note is hereby incorporated into this Note.

LOAN REHABILITATION - If I default on my Federal Perkins Loan, and that loan has not been reduced to a judgment as a result of litigation against me, I may rehabilitate my defaulted loan by requesting the rehabilitation and by making a voluntary, on-time, monthly payment, as determined by the School, each month for nine consecutive months. If I successfully rehabilitate my defaulted Federal Perkins Loan, I will again be subject to the terms and conditions and qualify for any remaining benefits and privileges of this Note and the default will be removed from my credit history. **I understand that I may rehabilitate a defaulted Federal Perkins Loan only once.** After my loan is rehabilitated, collection costs on the loan may not exceed 24 percent of the unpaid principal and accrued interest as of the date following the application of the ninth consecutive payment. If I default on my rehabilitated loan, the cap on collection costs is removed.

ASSIGNMENT - A loan made under this Note may be assigned by the School only to the United States, as represented by the United States Department of Education. Upon assignment, the provisions of this Note that relate to the School will, where appropriate, relate to the Department.

HARDSHIP REPAYMENT OPTIONS - Upon my written request, the School may extend my repayment period (1) for up to an additional 10 years if I qualify as a low-income individual during the repayment period; or (2) for the period necessary beyond my 10 year repayment period if, in the School's opinion, prolonged illness or unemployment prevent me from making the scheduled repayments. Interest will continue to accrue during any extension of a repayment period.

If I am required by the School to make a minimum monthly payment on my loan, the School may also permit me to pay less than the minimum monthly payment amount for a period of not more than one year at a time if I experience a period of prolonged illness or unemployment. However, such action may not extend the repayment period beyond 10 years.

GRACE PERIODS - Unless I am a Less-Than-Half-Time Borrower, I will receive an initial nine-month grace period before the first payment of my Federal Perkins Loan must be made. After the close of an authorized deferment period, I will receive a post-deferment grace period of 6 months before my payments resume. Interest does not accrue during the initial grace period or during the post-deferment grace period. The nine-month initial grace period for Federal Perkins Loans does not include any period up to three years during which I am called or ordered to active duty for more than 30 days from a reserve component of the Armed Forces of the United States, including the period necessary for me to resume enrollment at the next available enrollment period. I must notify the school that made my loan of the beginning and ending dates of my service, and the date I resume enrollment. If I am in my initial grace period when called or ordered to active duty, I am entitled to a new nine-month initial grace period upon completion of the excluded period.

If I am a Less-Than-Half-Time Borrower with outstanding Federal Perkins Loans, my repayment period begins when the next scheduled installment of my outstanding loan is due. If I am a Less-Than-Half-Time Borrower with no other outstanding Federal Perkins Loans, my repayment begins the earlier of: 9 months from the date my loan was made, or 9 months from the date I became a less-than-half-time student, even if I received the loan after I became a less-than-half-time student.

PREPAYMENT - I may prepay all or any part of my unpaid loan balance, plus any accrued interest, at any time without penalty. Amounts I repay in the academic year in which the loan was made and before the initial grace period has ended will be used to reduce the amount of the loan and will not be considered a prepayment. If I repay amounts during the academic year in which the loan was made and the initial grace period has ended, only those amounts in excess of the amount due for any repayment period shall be considered a prepayment. If, in an academic year other than the academic year in which the loan was made, I repay more than the amount due for an installment, the excess funds will be used to repay principal unless I designate it as an advance payment of the next regular installment.

MINIMUM MONTHLY PAYMENT - If required by the School, I will make a minimum monthly payment in the amount of $40 (or $30 if I have outstanding Federal Perkins Loans made before October 1, 1992 that included the $30 minimum payment option or outstanding National Direct Student Loans) or its bimonthly or quarterly equivalent. If the total monthly payment amount on this loan and any outstanding Federal Perkins Loans I may have is less than the minimum monthly payment amount established by the School, the School may still require a minimum monthly payment amount. A minimum monthly payment amount will combine my obligation on this and all my outstanding Federal Perkins Loans, unless I have received loans with different grace periods and deferments. At my request and if I am eligible, the school may combine this minimum monthly payment amount with all my outstanding Federal Perkins Loans including those made at other schools. Under these circumstances the portions of the minimum monthly payment that will be applied to this loan will be the difference between the minimum monthly payment amount and the total amounts owed on a monthly basis on my other Federal Perkins Loans. If each school holding my outstanding Federal Perkins Loans exercises the minimum monthly payment amount option, the minimum monthly payment amount will be divided among the Schools in proportion to the loan amount advanced by each school if I request this treatment from each School.

FORBEARANCE - Upon making a properly documented written or oral request to the School, I am entitled to forbearance of principal and interest or principal only, renewable at intervals of up to 12 months for periods that collectively do not exceed three years, under the following conditions: If my monthly Title IV loan debt burden equals or exceeds 20 percent of my total monthly gross income; if the Department authorizes a period of forbearance due to a national military mobilization or other national emergency; or if the School determines that I qualify due to poor health or for other reasons, including service in AmeriCorps. Interest accrues during any period of forbearance.

DEFERMENTS - To apply for a deferment, I must request the deferment from the school. My request does not have to be in writing, but the School may require that I submit supporting documentation to prove my eligibility for a deferment. I may defer making scheduled installment payments and will not be liable for any interest that might otherwise accrue (1) during any period that I am enrolled and attending as a regular student in at least a half-time course of study at an eligible School (if the School obtains student enrollment information showing that I qualify for this deferment, the School may grant the deferment without my request providing the School notifies me and gives me the option to cancel the deferment); (2) during any period that I am enrolled and attending as a regular student in a graduate fellowship program approved by the Department; engaged in graduate or post-graduate fellowship-supported study outside the US; enrolled and attending a rehabilitation training program for disabled individuals approved by the Department; or engaged in public service that qualifies me to have part or all of my loan canceled; (3) for a period not to exceed three years during which I am seeking but unable to find full-time employment; (4) for a period not to exceed three years, for up to one year at a time, during which I am experiencing an economic hardship as determined by the School. I may qualify for an economic-hardship deferment for my Federal Perkins Loan if I provide my school with documentation showing that I have been granted such a deferment under the William D. Ford Federal Direct Loan or Federal Family Education Loan program for the period of time for which I am requesting an economic hardship deferment for my Federal Perkins Loan. If I am serving as a volunteer in the Peace Corps, I am eligible for an economic hardship deferment for my full term of service. An economic hardship deferment based on service as a Peace Corps volunteer may not exceed the lesser of three years or my remaining period of economic hardship eligibility; (5), during any period when I am serving on active duty during a war or other military operation or national emergency, or performing qualifying National Guard duty during a war or other military operation or national emergency (as these terms are defined in 34 CFR 674.34(h) of the Perkins Loan Program regulations) and, if my active duty service includes October 1, 2007 or begins on or after that date, for an additional 180-day period following the demobilization date for my service; and (6) if I am serving on active duty military service on October 1, 2007, or begin serving on or after that date, for at least a 30-day period, for up to 13 months following the conclusion of my active duty military

Terms and Conditions (cont.)

service and initial grace period or until I return to enrolled student status, whichever is earlier, if I am a member of the National Guard or other reserve component of the Armed Forces of the United States or a member of such forces in retired status (as these terms are defined in 34 CFR 674.34(i)(2)) and I was enrolled in a program of instruction at the time I was called to active duty, or within six months prior to the time I was called to active duty. Active duty does not include active duty for training or attendance at a service school or employment in a full-time, permanent position in the National Guard unless I am reassigned from that position to another form of active duty service.

I may continue to defer making scheduled installment payments and will not be liable for any interest that might otherwise accrue for a six-month period immediately following the expiration of any deferment period described in this section.

I am not eligible for a deferment while serving in a medical internship or residency program.

CANCELLATIONS - Upon making a properly documented written request to the School, I am entitled to have up to 100 percent of the original principal loan amount of this loan canceled if I perform qualifying service in the areas listed in paragraphs A through K below. Other cancellation percentages apply if I perform qualifying service in the areas listed in paragraphs L and M, as explained in those paragraphs. Qualifying service must be performed after the enrollment period covered by the loan.

A. Teaching • a full-time teacher in a public or other nonprofit elementary or secondary school or in a school or location operated by an educational service agency that has been designated by the Department in accordance with the provisions of section 465(a)(2) of the Act as a school with a high concentration of students from low-income families. An official Directory of designated low-income schools and locations operated by educational service agencies is published annually by the Department. • a full-time special education teacher in a public or nonprofit elementary or secondary school system, including a system administered by an educational service agency; or • a full-time teacher, in a public or other nonprofit elementary or secondary school system who teaches mathematics, science, foreign languages, bilingual education, or any other field of expertise that is determined by the State Department of Education to have a shortage of qualified teachers in that State.

B. Early Intervention Services • a full-time qualified professional provider of early intervention services in a public or other nonprofit program under public supervision by a lead agency as authorized by section 632(5) of the Individuals with Disabilities Education Act. Early intervention services are provided to infants and toddlers with disabilities.

C. Law Enforcement or Corrections Officer • a full-time law enforcement officer for an eligible local, State, or Federal law enforcement agency; or • a full-time corrections officer for an eligible local, State, or Federal corrections agency.

D. Nurse or Medical Technician • a full-time nurse providing health care services; or • a full-time medical technician providing health care services.

E. Child or Family Service Agency • a full-time employee of an eligible public or private non-profit child or family service agency who is directly providing or supervising the provision of services to high-risk children who are from low-income communities and the families of such children.

F. Attorneys Employed in a Defender Organization • a full-time attorney employed in a defender organization established in accordance with section 3006(g)(2) of title 18, U.S.C.

G. Firefighters • a full-time firefighter for a local, State or Federal fire department or fire district.

H. Tribal College or University Faculty • a full-time faculty member at a Tribal College or University, as that term is defined in section 316 of title 20, U.S.C.

I. Librarian • a full-time librarian who has a master's degree in library science and is employed in an elementary or secondary school that is eligible for assistance under part A of title I of the Elementary and Secondary Education Act of 1965, or who is employed in a public library that serves a geographic area that contains one or more such schools.

J. Speech-Language Pathologist • a full-time speech-language pathologist who has a master's degree and who is working exclusively with schools that are eligible for assistance under title I of the Elementary and Secondary Education Act of 1965.

K. Service in an Early Childhood Education Program • a full-time staff member in the educational component of a Head Start program, or a full-time staff member in a pre-kindergarten or child care program that is licensed or regulated by the State. The program must be operated for a period comparable to a full School year and must pay a salary comparable to an employee of a local educational agency.

Cancellation Rates - For each completed year of service under paragraphs A, B, C, D, E, F, G, H, I, and J a portion of this loan will be canceled at the following rates:

• 15 percent of the original principal loan amount for each of the first and second years; • 20 percent of the original principal loan amount for each of the third and fourth years; and • 30 percent of the original principal loan amount for the fifth year.

For each completed year of service under paragraph K (Service in an Early Childhood Education Program), a portion of this loan will be canceled at the rate of 15 percent of the original principal loan amount .

L. Military Cancellation - Upon making a properly documented written request to the School, I am entitled to have up to 50 percent of the principal amount of this loan canceled for qualifying service that ended before August 14, 2008, and up to 100 percent cancelled for qualifying service that began on or after August 14, 2008, as: • a member of the Armed Forces of the United States in an area of hostilities that qualifies for special pay under section 310 of Title 37 of the United States Code.

Cancellation Rate - For each completed year of service under the Military Cancellation provision that ended before August 14, 2008, this loan will be canceled at the rate of 12½ percent of the original principal loan amount.

For qualifying service that began on or after August 14, 2008, this loan will be canceled at the following rates: • 15 percent of the original principal loan amount for each of the first and second years; • 20 percent of the original principal loan amount for each of the third and fourth years; and • 30 percent of the original principal loan amount for the fifth year.

M. Volunteer Service Cancellation - Upon making a properly documented written request to the School, I am entitled to have up to 70 percent of the original principal loan amount of this loan canceled for qualifying service performed after the enrollment period covered by the loan as: • a volunteer under the Peace Corps Act; • a volunteer under the Domestic Volunteer Service Act of 1973 (ACTION programs).

Cancellation Rate - For each completed year of service under the Volunteer Service Cancellation provision, a portion of this loan will be canceled at the following rates:

• 15 percent of the original principal loan amount for each of the first and second 12-month periods of service; and • 20 percent of the original principal loan amount for each of the third and fourth 12-month periods of service.

DISCHARGES - My obligation to repay this loan may be partially or totally discharged for the reasons specified in paragraphs A, B, C, and D below.

A. Death - In the event of my death, the School will discharge the total amount owed on this loan.

B. Total and Permanent Disability - Upon making a properly documented written request to the School, the total amount owed on this loan may be discharged if the U.S. Department of Education determines that I am totally and permanently disabled as defined in the Act and I meet certain other requirements.

Terms and Conditions (cont.)

C. School Closure - Under certain conditions, my total liability will be discharged, including refunding any amounts I have already paid on the loan, if I was unable to complete the program in which I was enrolled because my School closed.

D. Bankruptcy - Under certain conditions, my loan may be discharged in bankruptcy. In order to discharge a loan in bankruptcy, I must prove undue hardship in an adversary proceeding before the bankruptcy court.

Disclosure of Information

STUDENT LOAN OMBUDSMAN - If I dispute the terms of my Federal Perkins Loan in writing to my School, and my School and I are unable to resolve the dispute, I may seek the assistance of the Department of Education's Student Loan Ombudsman. The Student Loan Ombudsman will review and attempt to informally resolve the dispute.

Notice About Subsequent Loans Made Under This Master Promissory Note

This Note authorizes the School to disburse multiple loans during the multi-year term of this Note upon my request and upon the School's determination of my loan eligibility.

Subsequent loans may be made under this Note for the same or subsequent periods of enrollment at this School. The School, however, may, at its discretion, close this Note at any time and require me to sign a new Note for additional disbursements. I understand that if my School chooses to make subsequent loans under this Note, no such loans will be made after the earliest of the following dates: (i) the date the School receives my written notice that no further loans may be disbursed under this Note; (ii) twelve months after the date of my signature on this Note if no disbursement is made during such twelve-month period; or (iii) ten years after the date of my signature on this Note, or the date the School receives this Note.

Any amendment to the Act governs the terms of any loans disbursed on or after the effective date of such amendment, and such amended terms are hereby incorporated into this Note.

Important Notices

Privacy Act Notice

The Privacy Act of 1974 (5 U.S.C. 552a) requires that the following notice be provided to you:
The authority for collecting the requested information from and about you is §461 et seq. of the Higher Education Act (HEA) of 1965, as amended (20 U.S.C. 1087aa et seq.) and the authorities for collecting and using your Social Security Number (SSN) are §484(a)(4) of the HEA (20 U.S.C. 1091(a)(4)) and 31 U.S.C. 7701(b). Participating in the Federal Perkins Loan (Perkins) Program and giving us your SSN are voluntary, but you must provide the requested information, including your SSN, to participate.

The principal purposes for collecting the information on this form, including your SSN, are to verify your identity, to determine your eligibility to receive a loan or a benefit on a loan (such as a deferment, forbearance, discharge, or forgiveness) under the Perkins Program, to permit the servicing of your loan(s), and, if it becomes necessary, to locate you and to collect and report on your loan(s) if your loan(s) become delinquent or in default. We also use your SSN as an account identifier and to permit you to access your account information electronically.

The information in your file may be disclosed, on a case by case basis or under a computer matching program, to third parties as authorized under routine uses in the appropriate systems of records notices. The routine uses of this information include, but are not limited to, its disclosure to federal, state, or local agencies, to private parties such as relatives, present and former employers, business and personal associates, to consumer reporting agencies, to financial and educational institutions, and to guaranty agencies in order to verify your identity, to determine your eligibility to receive a loan or a benefit on a loan, to permit the servicing or collection of your loan(s), to enforce the terms of the loan(s), to investigate possible fraud and to verify compliance with federal student financial aid program regulations, or to locate you if you become delinquent in your loan payments or if you default. To provide default rate calculations, disclosures may be made to guaranty agencies, to financial and educational institutions, or to state agencies. To provide financial aid history information, disclosures may be made to educational institutions. To assist program administrators with tracking refunds and cancellations, disclosures may be made to guaranty agencies, to financial and educational institutions, or to federal or state agencies. To provide a standardized method for educational institutions efficiently to submit student enrollment status, disclosures may be made to guaranty agencies or to financial and educational institutions. To counsel you in repayment efforts, disclosures may be made to guaranty agencies, to financial and educational institutions, or to federal, state, or local agencies.

In the event of litigation, we may send records to the Department of Justice, a court, adjudicative body, counsel, party, or witness if the disclosure is relevant and necessary to the litigation. If this information, either alone or with other information, indicates a potential violation of law, we may send it to the appropriate authority for action. We may send information to members of Congress if you ask them to help you with federal student aid questions. In circumstances involving employment complaints, grievances, or disciplinary actions, we may disclose relevant records to adjudicate or investigate the issues. If provided for by a collective bargaining agreement, we may disclose records to a labor organization recognized under 5 U.S.C. Chapter 71. Disclosures may be made to our contractors for the purpose of performing any programmatic function that requires disclosure of records. Before making any such disclosure, we will require the contractor to maintain Privacy Act safeguards. Disclosures may also be made to qualified researchers under Privacy Act safeguards.

Financial Privacy Act Notice

Under the Right to Financial Privacy Act of 1978 (12 U.S.C. 3401-3421), the U.S. Department of Education will have access to financial records in your student loan file maintained by the lender in compliance with the administration of the Federal Perkins Loan Program.

Paperwork Reduction Notice

According to the Paperwork Reduction Act of 1995, no persons are required to respond to a collection of information unless it displays a currently valid OMB control number. The valid OMB control number for this information collection is 1845-0074. The time required to complete this information is estimated to average 0.5 hours (30 minutes) per response, including the time to review instructions, search existing data resources, gather and maintain the data needed, and complete and review the information collection. **If you have any comments concerning the accuracy of the time estimate(s) or suggestions for improving this form, please write to:**

U.S. Department of Education
Washington, DC 20202-4537

If you have any comments or concerns regarding the status of your individual submission of this form, write directly to the lender.

ADDENDUM

The College Cost Reduction and Access Act (Pub. L. 110-84), signed into law on September 27, 2007, and the Higher Education Opportunity Act (Pub. L. 108-315), signed into law on August 14, 2008, changed the terms of loans made under the Federal Perkins Loan Program authorized by Part E of the Higher Education Act of 1965, as amended.

CHANGES AFFECTING FEDERAL PERKINS LOANS

LOAN REHABILITATION

If you default on your Federal Perkins Loan, you may rehabilitate your defaulted loan under the terms and conditions specified in your promissory note by making nine on-time, consecutive, monthly payments, as determined by the loan holder. After your loan is rehabilitated, collection costs on the loan may not exceed 24% of the unpaid principal and accrued interest as of the date following the application of the ninth consecutive payment.

FORBEARANCE

Upon making a properly documented request to the holder of your loan, orally or in writing, you are entitled to forbearance of principal and interest, or principal only, renewable at intervals of up to 12 months for periods that collectively do not exceed three years, under the terms and conditions specified in your promissory note.

DEFERMENT

As of October 1, 2007, you may defer making scheduled installment payments, and will not be liable for any interest that might otherwise accrue on your Federal Perkins Loans, for an unlimited period during which you are serving on active duty during a war or other military operation or national emergency, or performing qualifying National Guard duty during a war or other military operation or national emergency, (as these terms are defined in 34 CFR §674.34(h) of the Perkins Loan Program regulations) and, if your active duty service includes October 1, 2007 or begins on or after that date, the 180-day period following the demobilization date for your service.

As of October 1, 2007, if you are serving on active duty military service on that date, or begin serving on or after that date for at least a 30-day period, you may defer making scheduled installment payments, and will not be liable for any interest that might otherwise accrue on your Federal Perkins Loans, for up to 13 months following the conclusion of your service and initial grace period if you are a member of the National Guard or other reserve component of the Armed Forces of the United States or a member of such forces in retired status (as these terms are defined in 34 CFR §674.34(i)(2)) and you were enrolled in a program of instruction at the time, or within six months prior to the time you were called to active duty. Active duty does not include active duty for training or attendance at a service school or employment in a full-time, permanent position in the National Guard unless you are reassigned from that position to another form of active duty service.

CANCELLATION FOR TEACHING SERVICE

Upon making a properly documented written request to the holder of your loan, you are entitled to have up to 100% of the original principal loan amount of your Federal Perkins Loan cancelled for qualifying teaching service that includes August 14, 2008, or begins on or after that date, in a school or location, operated by an educational service agency, that has been determined to have a high concentration of students from low-income families. An official Directory of designated low-income schools and locations operated by educational service agencies is published annually by the Department.

CANCELLATION FOR PRE-KINDERGARTEN OR CHILD CARE PROGRAM

Upon making a properly documented written request to the holder of your loan, you are entitled to have up to 100% of the original principal loan amount cancelled for qualifying service that includes August 14, 2008, or begins on or after that date, as a full-time staff member in a pre-kindergarten or child care program that is licensed or regulated by the State and that is operated for a period comparable to a full school year in the locality if your salary is not more than the salary of a comparable employee of the local educational agency.

CANCELLATION FOR ATTORNEYS EMPLOYED IN A DEFENDER ORGANIZATION

Upon making a properly documented written request to the holder of your loan, you are entitled to have up to 100% of the original principal loan amount cancelled for qualifying full-time service that includes August 14, 2008, or begins on or after that date, as an attorney employed in a defender organization established in accordance with section 3006(g)(2) of title 18, U.S.C.

CANCELLATION FOR FIREFIGHTERS

Upon making a properly documented written request to the holder of your loan, you are entitled to have up to 100% of the original principal loan amount cancelled for qualifying service that includes August 14, 2008, or begins on or after that date, as a full-time firefighter for a local, State or Federal fire department or fire district.

CANCELLATION FOR FACULTY OF A TRIBAL COLLEGE OR UNIVERSITY

Upon making a properly documented written request to the holder of your loan, you are entitled to have up to 100% of the original principal loan amount cancelled for qualifying full-time service that includes August 14, 2008, or begins on or after that date, as a faculty member at a Tribal College or University, as that term is defined in section 316 of title 20, U.S.C.

CANCELLATION FOR SERVICE AS A LIBRARIAN

Upon making a properly documented written request to the holder of your loan, you are entitled to have up to 100% of the original principal loan amount cancelled for qualifying full-time service that includes August 14, 2008, or begins on or after that date, as a librarian, if you have a master's degree in library science and you are employed in an elementary or secondary school that is eligible for assistance under part A of title I of the elementary and Secondary Education Act of 1965, or you are employed in a public library that serves a geographic area that contains one or more of such schools.

CANCELLATION FOR SERVICE AS A SPEECH-LANGUAGE PATHOLOGIST
Upon making a properly documented written request to the holder of your loan, you are entitled to have up to 100% of the original principal loan amount cancelled for qualifying full-time service that includes August 14, 2008, or begins on or after that date, as a full-time speech-language pathologist if you have a master's degree and if you are working exclusively with schools that are eligible for assistance under title I of the Elementary and Secondary Education Act of 1965.

CANCELLATION FOR MILITARY SERVICE IN AN AREA OF HOSTILITY
Upon making a properly documented written request to the holder of your loan, you are entitled to have up to 100% of the original principal loan amount cancelled for qualifying full-time service that includes August 14, 2008, or begins on or after that date, as a member of the Armed Forces of the United States in an area of hostility that qualifies for special pay under section 310 of title 37 of the U.S. Code.

CANCELLATION RATES
For each complete year of service under the Teaching Service, Attorneys Employed in a Defender Organization, Firefighter, Faculty of a Tribal College or University, Librarian, Speech-Language Pathologist and Military Service Cancellation provisions, a portion of your loan will be canceled at the rate of 15% of the original principal loan amount for the first and second years of service; 20% of the original principal amount for the third and fourth years of service; and 30% of the original principal loan amount for the fifth year of service. The complete year of qualifying service must be performed after the enrollment period covered by the loan.

For each complete year of service under the Pre-Kindergarten or Child Care Program Cancellation provision, your loan will be cancelled at a rate of 15% of the original principal loan amount. The complete year of qualifying service must be performed after the enrollment period covered by the loan.

TOTAL AND PERMANENT DISABILITY DISCHARGE
Upon making a properly documented written request to the school on or after July 1, 2008, you are entitled to a discharge of the total amount owed on your Federal Perkins Loan if the Department of Veterans Affairs determines that you are unemployable due to a service-connected disability.

YOU ARE RECEIVING A LOAN THAT MUST BE REPAID

D.6 Private Loan Disclosures and Forms

The Federal Reserve Board issued final rules for private student loan disclosures in August 2009 (74 Fed. Reg. 41194, August 14, 2009). Mandatory compliance began on February 14, 2010. Sample disclosures are reprinted below.

D.6.1 Application and Solicitation Model Form

H-18 Private Education Loan Application and Solicitation Model Form

Page 1 of 2

[Creditor Name]
[Creditor Address]
[Creditor Phone Number]

Loan Interest Rate & Fees

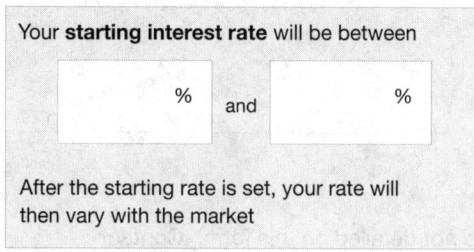

Your **starting interest rate** will be between

____ % and ____ %

After the starting rate is set, your rate will then vary with the market

Your Starting Interest Rate (upon approval)
The starting interest rate you pay will be determined after you apply. [Description of how starting rate is determined]. If approved, we will notify you of the rate you qualify for within the stated range.

Your Interest Rate during the life of the loan
Your rate is variable. This means that your rate could move lower or higher than the rates on this form. The variable rate is based upon the [Index] Rate (as published in the [source of index]). For more information on this rate, see the reference notes.

[Indication of **maximum rate** or **lack thereof**]

Loan Fees

[Itemization of fees]

Loan Cost Examples

The total amount you will pay for this loan will vary depending upon when you start to repay it. This example provides estimates based upon [number of repayment options] repayment options available to you while enrolled in school.

Repayment Option (while enrolled in school)	Amount Provided (amount provided directly to you or your school)	Interest Rate (highest possible starting rate)	Loan Term (how long you have to pay off the loan)	Total Paid over [term of loan] (includes associated fees)
1. [REPAYMENT OPTION] [Description]	$10,000	[Rate]	[Loan Term] [description of when repayment begins]	[Total Cost]
2. [REPAYMENT OPTION] [Description]	$10,000	[Rate]	[Loan Term] [description of when repayment begins]	[Total Cost]
3. [REPAYMENT OPTION] [Description]	$10,000	[Rate]	[Loan Term] [description of when repayment begins]	[Total Cost]

About this example
[Description of example assumptions]
[Description of other loan terms, if applicable]

Federal Loan Alternatives

Loan program	Current Interest Rates by Program Type	
PERKINS for Students	[Rate] fixed	
STAFFORD for Students	[Rate] fixed	Undergraduate subsidized
	[Rate] fixed	Undergraduate unsubsidized & Graduate
PLUS for Parents and Graduate / Professional Students	[Rate] fixed	Federal Family Education Loan
	[Rate] fixed	Federal Direct Loan

You may qualify for Federal education loans.

For additional information, **contact your school's financial aid office or the Department of Education at:**

www.federalstudentaid.ed.gov

Next Steps

1. **Find Out About Other Loan Options.**
   Some schools have school-specific student loan benefits and terms not detailed on this form. Contact your school's financial aid office or visit the Department of Education's web site at: www.federalstudentaid.ed.gov for more information about other loans.

2. **To Apply for this Loan, Complete the Application and the Self-Certification Form.**
   You may get the certification form from your school's financial aid office. If you are approved for this loan, the loan terms will be available for 30 days (terms will not change during this period, except as permitted by law and the variable interest rate may change based on the market).

REFERENCE NOTES

Variable Interest Rate
- [Variable interest rate information, if applicable]

Eligibility Criteria
- [Description of eligibility criteria]

Bankruptcy Limitations
- If you file for bankruptcy you may still be required to pay back this loan.

More information about loan eligibility and repayment deferral or forbearance options is available in your loan application and loan agreement.

Student Assistance Forms   Appx. D.6.2

D.6.2 Loan Approval Model Form

H-19 Private Education Loan Approval Model Form

Page 1 of 2

BORROWER:
[Borrower Name]
[Borrower Address]

CREDITOR:
[Creditor Name]
[Creditor Address]

Loan Rates & Estimated Total Costs

Total Loan Amount	Interest Rate	Finance Charge	Total of Payments
The total amount you are borrowing.	Your current interest rate.	The estimated dollar amount the credit will cost you.	The estimated amount you will have paid when you have made all payments.

ITEMIZATION OF AMOUNT FINANCED

Amount paid to you	[Amount]
Amount paid to others on your Behalf: • [Institution Name]	+ [Amount]
Amount Financed [Description]	= [Amount]
Initial finance charges (total) • [Charge Type], [Amount] • [Charge Type], [Amount]	+ [Amount]
Total Loan Amount	= [Amount]

ABOUT YOUR INTEREST RATE

- **Your rate is variable.** This means that your actual rate varies with the market and could be lower or higher than the rate on this form. The variable rate is based upon the [Index] Rate (as published in the [source of index]). For more information on this rate, see reference notes.

- Although your rate will vary, **it will never exceed [maximum interest rate]** (the maximum allowable [by law] for this loan).

- Your **Annual Percentage Rate (APR) is [Rate]**. The APR is typically different than the Interest Rate since it considers fees and reflects the cost of your loan as a yearly rate. For more information about the APR, see reference notes.

FEES
- [Itemization of Fees, if applicable]

Estimated Repayment Schedule & Terms

[LOAN TERM]	[PAYMENT PERIOD, e.g. MONTHLY PAYMENTS]		
	at [Interest Rate]% the current interest rate of your loan	at [Maximum Rate]% the maximum interest rate possible for your loan	◄ The estimated **Total of Payments** at the Maximum Rate of Interest would be [Total Payment Amount].
[Dates of Deferment Period, if applicable] deferment period	No payment required ([Amount of accrued interest] interest will accrue during this time)	No payment required (Interest will accrue during this time)	
[Payment Due Dates] [number of monthly payments] monthly payments	[Payment Amount]	[Payment Amount]	
[Payment Due Dates] [number of monthly payments] monthly payments	[Payment Amount]	[Payment Amount]	

Federal Loan Alternatives

Loan program	Current Interest Rates by Program Type	
PERKINS for Students	[Rate] fixed	
STAFFORD for Students	[Rate] fixed	Undergraduate subsidized
	[Rate] fixed	Undergraduate unsubsidized & Graduate
PLUS for Parents and Graduate / Professional Students	[Rate] fixed	Federal Family Education Loan
	[Rate] fixed	Federal Direct Loan

You may qualify for Federal education loans.

For additional information, **contact your school's financial aid office or the Department of Education at:**

www.federalstudentaid.ed.gov

Next Steps & Terms of Acceptance

This offer is good until:

[Date of Acceptance Deadline]

1. **Find Out About Other Loan Options.**
   Contact your school's financial aid office for more information.

2. **You Have Until [Date of Acceptance Deadline] to Accept this Offer**
   The terms of this offer will not change except as permitted by law and the variable interest rate may change based on the market.

   To Accept the Terms of this loan,
   [Description of method of acceptance]

REFERENCE NOTES

Variable Interest Rate:
- Your loan has a variable Interest Rate that is based on a publicly available index, the [Index Name], which is currently [Rate]. Your rate is calculated each month by adding a margin of [Margin Rate] to the [Index].
- The Interest Rate may be higher or lower than your Annual Percentage Rate (APR) because the APR considers certain fees you pay to obtain this loan, the Interest Rate, and whether you defer (postpone) payments while in school.
- [Description of effect of an increase]

Bankruptcy Limitations
- If you file for bankruptcy you may still be required to pay back this loan.

Repayment Options:
- [Description of deferment options, if applicable]

Prepayments:
- [Prepayment disclosure]

Security
- You are giving a security interest in [description, if applicable]

See your loan agreement for any additional information about nonpayment, default, any required repayment in full before the scheduled date, and prepayment refunds and penalties.

Student Assistance Forms   Appx. D.6.3

D.6.3 Final Disclosure Model Form

H-20 Private Education Loan Final Model Form

Page 1 of 2

BORROWER:	**CREDITOR:**
[Borrower Name]	[Creditor Name]
[Borrower Address]	[Creditor Address]

RIGHT TO CANCEL

You have a right to cancel this transaction, without penalty, by midnight on [deadline for cancellation]. No funds will be disbursed to you or to your school until after this time. You may cancel by calling us at [Creditor Phone Number].

Loan Rates & Estimated Total Costs

Total Loan Amount	Interest Rate	Finance Charge	Total of Payments
The total amount you are borrowing.	Your current interest rate.	The estimated dollar amount the credit will cost you.	The estimated amount you will have paid when you have made all payments.

ITEMIZATION OF AMOUNT FINANCED

Amount paid to you	[Amount]
Amount paid to others on your Behalf: • [Institution Name]	+ [Amount]
Amount Financed [Description]	= [Amount]
Initial finance charges (total) • [Charge Type], [Amount] • [Charge Type], [Amount]	+ [Amount]
Total Loan Amount	= [Amount]

ABOUT YOUR INTEREST RATE

- **Your rate is variable.** This means that your actual rate varies with the market and could be lower or higher than the rate on this form. The variable rate is based upon the [Index] Rate (as published in the [source of index]). For more information on this rate, see reference notes.

- There **is no limit on the amount the interest rate can increase.**

- Your **Annual Percentage Rate (APR) is [Rate].** The APR is typically different than the Interest Rate since it considers fees and reflects the cost of your loan as a yearly rate. For more information about the APR, see reference notes.

FEES
- [Itemization of Fees, if applicable]

Estimated Repayment Schedule & Terms

[LOAN TERM]	[PAYMENT PERIOD, e.g. MONTHLY PAYMENTS]		
	at [Interest Rate]% the current interest rate of your loan	No Maximum Rate example at 25%	
[Dates of Deferment Period, if applicable] deferment period	No payment required ([Amount of accrued interest] interest will accrue during this time)	No payment required (Interest will accrue during this time)	◀ Though your loan does not have a maximum interest rate, **an example rate of 25% has been used for** comparative purposes.
[Payment Due Dates] [number of monthly payments] monthly payments	[Payment Amount]	[Payment Amount] (your payments will be higher if the rate increases above 25%)	The estimated **Total of Payments** if your rate rises to 25% would be **[Total Payment Amount].** Your Total of Payments will be higher if rate increases above 25%.
[Payment Due Dates] [number of monthly payments] monthly payments	[Payment Amount]	[Payment Amount] (your payments will be higher if the rate increases above 25%)	

REFERENCE NOTES

Variable Interest Rate:
- Your loan has a variable Interest Rate that is based on a publicly available index, the [Index Name], which is currently [Rate]. Your rate is calculated each month by adding a margin of [Margin Rate] to the [Index].
- The Interest Rate may be higher or lower than your Annual Percentage Rate (APR) because the APR considers certain fees you pay to obtain this loan, the Interest Rate, and whether you defer (postpone) payments while in school.
- [Description of effect of an increase]

Bankruptcy Limitations
- If you file for bankruptcy you may still be required to pay back this loan.

Repayment Options:
- [Description of deferment options, if applicable]

Prepayments:
- [Prepayment disclosure]

Security
- You are giving a security interest in [description, if applicable]

See your loan agreement for any additional information about nonpayment, default, any required repayment in full before the scheduled date, and prepayment refunds and penalties.

Student Assistance Forms   Appx. D.6.4

D.6.4 Private Education Loan Applicant Self-Certification Form

Private Education Loan
Applicant Self-Certification

OMB No. 1845-0101
Form Approved
Exp. Date 02-28-2013

Important: Pursuant to Section 155 of the Higher Education Act of 1965, as amended, (HEA) and to satisfy the requirements of Section 128(e)(3) of the Truth in Lending Act, a lender must obtain a self-certification signed by the applicant before disbursing a private education loan. The school is required on request to provide this form or the required information only for students admitted or enrolled at the school. Throughout this Applicant Self-Certification, "you" and "your" refer to the applicant who is applying for the loan. The applicant and the student may be the same person.

Instructions: Before signing, carefully read the entire form, including the definitions and other information on the following page. Submit the signed form to your lender.

SECTION 1: NOTICES TO APPLICANT

- Free or lower-cost Title IV federal, state, or school student financial aid may be available in place of, or in addition to, a private education loan. To apply for Title IV federal grants, loans and work-study, submit a Free Application for Federal Student Aid (FAFSA) available at www.fafsa.ed.gov, or by calling 1-800-4-FED-AID, or from the school's financial aid office.
- A private education loan may reduce eligibility for free or lower-cost federal, state, or school student financial aid.
- You are strongly encouraged to pursue the availability of free or lower-cost financial aid with the school's financial aid office.
- The financial information required to complete this form can be obtained from the school's financial aid office. If the lender has provided this information, you should contact your school's financial aid office to verify this information and to discuss your financing options.

SECTION 2: COST OF ATTENDANCE AND ESTIMATED FINANCIAL ASSISTANCE

If information is not already entered below, obtain the needed information from the school's financial aid office and enter it on the appropriate line. Sign and date where indicated.

A. Student's cost of attendance for the period of enrollment covered by the loan $_____
B. Estimated financial assistance for the period of enrollment covered by the loan $_____
C. Difference between amounts A and B $_____
   WARNING: If you borrow more than the amount on line C, you risk reducing your eligibility for free or lower-cost federal, state, or school financial aid.

SECTION 3: APPLICANT INFORMATION

Enter or correct the information below.

Full Name and Address of School _____

Applicant Name (last, first, MI) _____   Date of Birth (mm/dd/yyyy) ___/___/___

Permanent Street Address _____

City, State, Zip Code _____ _____

Area Code / Telephone Number   Home ( ) _____   Other ( ) _____

E-mail Address _____

Period of Enrollment Covered by the Loan (mm/dd/yyyy)   From ___/___/_____ to ___/___/_____

If the student is **not** the applicant, provide the student's name and date of birth.

Student Name (last, first, MI) _____   Student Date of Birth (mm/dd/yyyy) ___/___/___

SECTION 4: APPLICANT SIGNATURE

I certify that I have read and understood the notices in Section 1 and, that to the best of my knowledge, the information provided on this form is true and correct.

Signature of Applicant _____   Date (mm/dd/yyyy) _____

2/12/2010

SECTION 5: DEFINITIONS

Cost of attendance is an estimate of tuition and fees, room and board, transportation, and other costs for the period of enrollment covered by the loan, as determined by the school. A student's cost of attendance may be obtained from the school's financial aid office.

Estimated financial assistance is all federal, state, institutional (school), private, and other sources of assistance used in determining eligibility for most Title IV student financial aid, including amounts of financial assistance used to replace the expected family contribution. The student's estimated financial assistance is determined by the school and may be obtained from the school's financial aid office.

A **lender is** a private education lender as defined in Section 140 of the Truth in Lending Act and any other person engaged in the business of securing, making, or extending private education loans on behalf of the lender.

A **period of enrollment** is the academic year, academic term (such as semester, trimester, or quarter), or the number of weeks of instructional time for which the applicant is requesting the loan.

A **private education loan** is a loan provided by a private education lender that is not a Title IV loan and that is issued expressly for postsecondary education expenses, regardless of whether the loan is provided through the school that the student attends or directly to the borrower from the private education lender. A private education loan does not include **(1)** An extension of credit under an open-end consumer credit plan, a reverse mortgage transaction, a residential mortgage transaction, or any other loan that is secured by real property or a dwelling; or **(2)** An extension of credit in which the school is the lender if the term of the extension of credit is 90 days or less or an interest rate will not be applied to the credit balance and the term of the extension of credit is one year or less, even if the credit is payable in more than four installments.

Title IV student financial aid includes the Federal Pell Grant Program, the Academic Competitiveness Grant (ACG) Program, the Federal Supplemental Educational Opportunity Grant (FSEOG) Program, the Leveraging Educational Assistance Partnership (LEAP) Program, the Federal Family Education Loan Program (FFELP), the Federal Work-Study (FWS) Program, the William D. Ford Federal Direct Loan (Direct Loan) Program, the Federal Perkins Loan Program, the National Science and Mathematics Access to Retain Talent Grant (National SMART Grant) Program, and the Teacher Education Assistance for College and Higher Education (TEACH) Grant Program. To apply for Title IV federal grants, loans, and work-study, submit a Free Application for Federal Student Aid (FAFSA), which is available at www.fafsa.gov, by calling 1-800-4-FED-AID, or from the school's financial aid office.

SECTION 6: PAPERWORK REDUCTION NOTICE

Paperwork Reduction Notice: According to the Paperwork Reduction Act of 1995, no persons are required to respond to a collection of information unless it displays a currently valid OMB control number. The valid OMB control number for this information collection is 1845-0101. The time required to complete this information collection is estimated to average 0.25 hours (15 minutes) per response, including the time to review instructions, search existing data resources, gather and maintain the data needed and complete and review the information collection.

If you have any comments concerning the accuracy of the time estimate(s) or suggestions for improving this form, please write to: U.S. Department of Education, Washington, DC 20202-4651.

If you have any comments or concerns regarding the status of your individual submission of this form, contact your lender.

2/12/2010

Appendix E   Sample Pleadings and Letters

The sample pleadings and letters in this appendix can also be found on the companion website to this manual.

E.1 Sample Letter and Request for Relief

Date

U.S. Department of Education
Attn: Federal Offset Review Unit
P.O. Box 618064
Chicago, IL 60661-8064

CERTIFIED MAIL
RETURN RECEIPT REQUESTED

Dear Offset Review Unit:

I am writing to request a reduction in the amount currently being offset from my Social Security payments. [*Editor's Note*: Borrowers may also object on hardship grounds to collection of debt against other federal payments and income tax refunds. In the case of Social Security offsets only, the Department will consider a reduction or suspension of the offset due to hardship even before the offset begins. See chapter 5.]

I am 75 years old. My sole source of income is Social Security. Until recently, I was able to supplement my Social Security income with a small amount of money my husband earned from a part-time job. However, my husband passed away last year. I never worked outside my home and my sole source of income is his Social Security survivor's benefits of $900/month. This income is not enough to pay my expenses. I have included a detailed list of expenses below.

The main reason that I am writing to you now is because my situation has become very severe since my husband died. After he died last year, I needed to make some home repairs. We had not been able to afford these repairs while my husband was sick. I needed to get a loan to pay for the repairs. I used a company that came to my door and said that they would get me the best deal. It turned out that they gave me a very expensive loan and never even completed the repairs. I was not able to make the loan payments. Just a few months ago, I lost my home to foreclosure. I am now renting an apartment. It is very important to me to live near my old house because I have lived in this neighborhood for almost 50 years. I tried to find the least expensive rental situation, but it is still $550/month. This leaves me only $350 each month to pay all of my other expenses, including the prescription drugs that are not covered by Medicare, utilities, transportation, food.

Based on the detailed list of income and expenses enclosed with this letter, I am requesting that you reduce the offset from $150/month to $50/month. [*Editor's Note*: Borrowers may also request a complete suspension of offset.]

Enclosed please find the following information to support this request:

1. **Treasury's Offset Notification letter**

2. **Completed financial statement, form (N33)**

3. **Proof of my annual Social Security income and most recent tax returns.**

4. **A copy of the final notice when my house was foreclosed and my current rental agreement**.

Thank you for your prompt attention to this request.

Sincerely,

E.2 Discharge-Related Pleadings

E.2.1 Request for Discharge of All Students

REQUEST FOR DOE DETERMINATION OF ATB FRAUD
BY CAMBRIDGE TECHNICAL INSTITUTE, INC.
FOR USE IN STUDENT LOAN DISCHARGE
APPLICATIONS

I. INTRODUCTION

This memorandum provides the basis for the U.S. Department of Education (DOE) to rule that Cambridge Technical Institute, Inc., a for-profit, proprietary vocational school formerly operating four campuses in Ohio, committed such pervasive fraud and unlawful actions in its determination of students' ability to benefit (ATB) from Cambridge's courses, that all applications for a loan discharge, based on improper ATB determination, will be granted to otherwise-eligible Cambridge students, without independent evidence of ATB fraud. This request for DOE's decision as to Cambridge's improper determination of ATB status for students is being submitted pursuant to DOE's "Dear Colleague" letter GEN-95-42, Section 10. Included herewith are: 1) previous decisions of DOE on former Cambridge students' ATB discharge applications, 2) deposition and affidavit testimony by former students and employees of Cambridge, 3) findings by the Ohio Attorney General's Office, 4) a sample of Cambridge's ATB admissions scores compared with the requirements established by DOE, the accreditation agency for Cambridge, and the ATB test publisher, 5) findings by the Ohio State Board of Proprietary School Registration, and 6) generalized evidence of the widespread fraudulent and unlawful business practices of Cambridge, as set forth in various newspaper articles over the years.

The Legal Aid Society of Cincinnati represented students in a class-action lawsuit against Cambridge in the late 1980s. That lawsuit resulted in a consent decree whereby Cambridge agreed to close its Cincinnati campus as of October, 1990. Following that, the murder of Cambridge's president, and the criminal indictment of one of Cambridge's other officers (who ultimately pleaded guilty), the other three campuses (in Middletown, Dayton, and Cleveland) were also closed or sold. As a result, Cambridge long ago closed its doors in Ohio. Nevertheless, hundreds of students who were lured into Cambridge's classrooms with a promise of a good education and a good job, are now in a worse position than they were when they first heard about Cambridge. Many of them have had their self-esteem harmed and their credit records ruined, and they continue to be dunned for thousands of dollars allegedly owed on their defaulted student loans. Many of those students never should have attended Cambridge to begin with, given their inability to benefit from what Cambridge offered them. DOE now should facilitate the loan discharge process for them by issuing an administrative decision whereby it declares Cambridge's ATB testing and admissions procedures so pervasively fraudulent as to provide across-the-board proof that any applicant for a student loan discharge, based on ATB fraud, will have his or her application granted, provided he or she is otherwise eligible.

II. NUMEROUS FORMER STUDENTS ALREADY HAVE RECEIVED A DISCHARGE OF THEIR LOANS BASED ON CAMBRIDGE'S FALSE CERTIFICATION OF THEIR ABILITY TO BENEFIT.

The U.S. Department of Education already has granted a discharge of student loans to numerous former Cambridge students, based on Cambridge's false certification of their ability to benefit. The following is a partial list of former Cambridge students who have had their loans discharged based on such false certification. See the series A exhibits, attached hereto [*not reprinted herein*].

1. [*Student 1*]: He did not possess a high school diploma or a GED. He was given a ten-question admissions test, which is not consistent with Wonderlic's (the test developer's) test manual procedures. (Wonderlic ATB tests contain 24 or 50 questions). According to Mr. Muntz, "everyone" he heard of passed the exam. After completing the Cambridge course, he could not get a job because of his extensive criminal record.
2. [*Student 2*]: She did not have a high school diploma or a GED. She took a test, but she did not answer many questions. At the time of enrollment, she was suffering from the side effects of brain surgery.
3. [*Student 3*]: He was not given any admissions test, even though he did not have a high school diploma or a GED.
4. [*Student 4*]: She was not given any admissions test, even though she had no high school diploma or GED.
5. [*Student 5*]: He had three different Cambridge loans (all discharged). He did not have a high school diploma or a GED, yet was not given an admissions test. [*Student 5*] was 67 years old, had a glass eye and back problems, and weighed about 100 pounds when he was enrolled for the private security course at Cambridge.
6. [*Student 6*]: She stated that she took the test with a group and they all were told they had passed the test even before it was graded. She did not have a high school diploma or a GED.
7. [*Student 7*]: She had no high school diploma or GED. She was given an admissions test in a room with several other students also taking the test. The person giving the test left the room once the test started, and there was no time limit imposed.
8. [*Student 8*]: He was not given an admissions test nor did he possess a high school diploma or a GED. He also had an extensive criminal record of theft and drug abuse.
9. [*Student 9*]: She did not have a high school diploma or a GED, and was not given an admissions test before enrolling.
10. [*Student 10*]: He was not given an admissions test, nor did he have a high school diploma or a GED.
11. [*Student 11*]: She had neither a high school diploma nor a GED when she enrolled. She had only the equivalent of a fifth grade education and did not take an admissions test.
12. [*Student 12*]: She was not given an admissions test, nor did she have a high school diploma or a GED.

See the enclosed Request for Discharge (False Certification of Ability to Benefit) applications and decisions, Exhibits A-1 through A-12 [*not reprinted herein*].

III. SWORN TESTIMONY OF NUMEROUS FORMER CAMBRIDGE STUDENTS SHOWS A PATTERN OF TESTING AND ADMISSIONS FRAUD.

In the course of litigating *Brown, et al. v. Cambridge Technical Institute, Inc., et al.*, substantial pre-trial discovery took place. Depositions were taken of former students, and affidavits were obtained from others. Although the lawsuit did not raise directly the ability-to-benefit issue, information given by former students to the attorneys shows that Cambridge's test procedures were very lax and, at times, unlawful or fraudulent. The following are summaries of the ATB problems revealed through depositions and/or affidavits given by the listed individuals. See the series B exhibits, attached hereto [*not reprinted herein*].

1. [*Former Student 1*] (a former student and named plaintiff in the lawsuit): She could not read. She could not spell much, including her address. When she took the admissions test, a lady from Cambridge had to read the questions to her. [*Former Student 1*] was taking medication (Cogentin and Prolixin) for her nerves at that time and was being followed by a case manager at the Mental Health Services West office. Although the application form for [*Former Student 1*] states that she went to Taft High School, she did not; she did go to West High. She did not graduate from West High School or any high school. Her last years in school were spent at Gilford School (a school for developmentally delayed students). [*Former Student 1*] is not good at math and numbers. [*Former Student 1*] has a guardian, but she could not remember her name. [*Former Student 1*] does not know the difference between a positive experience and a negative experience. Of all the questions on the Wonderlic admissions test, [*Former Student 1*] completed only six of them. She does not know who filled in the other blanks. When she handed in her test, there were only six answers given by her on her paper. She does not know what happened after that. [*Former Stu-

dent 1] was admitted to Cambridge after the test, and enrolled for custodial maintenance, electronics, and computers. After she attended school for a few days, she stopped going.
2. [*Former Student 2*] (a former student and former employee of Cambridge): [*Former Student 2*] states: "At the Cambridge Admissions Office, I was told that I would have to take an admissions test. When I told [the Cambridge person] that I didn't have time to take the test, he said he would take it for me, and he proceeded to do that."
3. [*Former Student 3*] (a former student): While attending Cambridge, she met another student filling out loan papers. This other student had been enrolled for private security, but had only one leg and had a deformed left hand with only two fingers on it. [*Former Student 3*] also heard another student boasting, in a serious way, that she had given birth last week to a baby which was going to be stuck "back up inside her like all her other babies." This person did not "seem to know where she was." Another student [*Former Student 3*] met seemed very slow or retarded. He would sit near the back window and stare into space. The instructors stated that he flunked every test.
4. [*Former Student 4*] (a former student): [*Former Student 4*] was given the admissions test. The woman at Cambridge giving the test gave [*Former Student 4*] "the answers to the first five questions."

See the enclosed deposition excerpts and affidavits, Exhibits B-1 through B-4 [*not reprinted herein*].

IV. THE OHIO ATTORNEY GENERAL FOUND EVIDENCE OF ADMISSIONS TEST FRAUD BY CAMBRIDGE.

The Ohio Attorney General also filed a separate lawsuit against Cambridge for its operations at the Cleveland "campus." In its investigation of Cambridge's practices at that campus, the Ohio Attorney General's office determined that serious admissions test fraud had occurred. See the series C exhibits, attached hereto [*not reprinted herein*].

In responding to civil discovery requests propounded by Cambridge's attorneys, the Ohio Attorney General stated the following in response to one of the interrogatories regarding admissions testing: "The defendants [Cambridge] administered the test without supervision to students en masse. The test was an altered and simplified version of a valid test. Students were allowed to discuss the test with each other. The test was written, but illiterate students passed the test. The test was administered without time constraint."

Additionally, in this same litigation, the Ohio Attorney General filed a memorandum with the court opposing Cambridge's motion to dismiss the lawsuit. Attached as exhibits to that memorandum were excerpts from depositions of Cambridge officials and affidavits from various other people. The depositions of the Cambridge officials discussed examples of Cambridge enrolling students who obviously could not benefit from instruction. One discussion involved the enrollment of a student when, by Cambridge's own admission, it was "obvious the student should not have been enrolled." The Cambridge official went on to testify that the student was "extremely childlike, he did not seem to be able to carry through in conversation, communication skills were very poor." The student's "mannerisms and inability to communicate and comprehend in general conversation" were acknowledged, as well as the fact that the student, when asked a question, would not respond or would talk about something that was totally different and unrelated to the conversation. Another example testified to in deposition involved a Cambridge instructor reporting a second-quarter student whom the instructor had by then determined "could not read his text books and could not read or comprehend the content of the mid-term examination."

The Attorney General also submitted affidavits executed by two former students of the Cleveland branch of Cambridge. Each details improper testing procedures, including administering the test in a crowded room of other students, giving no explanation of the exam or test procedures, and allowing students to receive assistance on the test.

See the enclosed excerpts from the Attorney General's Supplemental Answers to Defendant's Interrogatories and Appendix thereto, with attachments, and excerpts from the Attorney General's court memorandum, with attachments, and affidavits (note: the above information has been "highlighted" for easy reference), Exhibits C-1 through C-2 [*not reprinted herein*].[1]

V. CAMBRIDGE'S OWN TESTING DOCUMENTS SHOW ABILITY-TO-BENEFIT FRAUD AND OTHER IRREGULARITIES.

Even a cursory review of Cambridge's admissions testing, taken from individual Cambridge files of former students, shows significant violations of the proper test procedures, scoring requirements, and remedial instruction options permitted by DOE and Cambridge's accreditation agency. See the series D exhibits, attached hereto [*not reprinted herein*].

In the 1980s, DOE promulgated regulations regarding the ability-to-benefit standards and the testing to be used by schools to determine whether prospective students actually had the ability to benefit from the school's training. The DOE summarized the ATB requirements in its September, 1995 "Dear Colleague" letter, GEN-95-42. Briefly, for enrollment periods from January 1, 1986 through June 30, 1987, a school could determine that a student had an ability to benefit in accordance with DOE regulations by using a fairly simple procedure. The school only had to:

> *develop and consistently apply criteria* to determine if regular students who did not have a high school diploma or GED, and who were beyond the age of compulsory attendance, had the ability to benefit from the school's training. [Emphasis added].

For periods of enrollment from July 1, 1987 through June 30, 1991, the DOE required more stringent evaluation of students.

---

[1] In a separate forum, Cambridge officials of the Cleveland campus admitted that Ernest Hall, the first example of improperly admitted students cited in the deposition, took his admissions test simultaneously with several other individuals and that his sister not only attended the admissions test with him, but actually helped him with the answers. The deposed official also conceded that the testing employee of Cambridge did not notice any of this during the exam (or, apparently, chose not to do anything about it). This is documented in Cambridge's own letter to a media reporter. See the enclosed Cambridge letter of 3/15/88, Exhibit C-3 [*not reprinted herein*].

During this time period, a school had to use standard admissions practices for any applicants without a high school diploma or a GED. These practices required the school to determine the following:

> (1) the student received a GED prior to the student's completion of the program or by the end of the first year of the program, whichever was earlier; (2) the student was counseled prior to admission *and successfully completed the school's program of remedial or developmental education* that did not exceed one academic year or its equivalent; (3) the student passed a nationally recognized, standardized, or industry-developed ATB test, *subject to criteria developed by the school's accrediting association*; or (4) if the student failed the ATB test, he or she *successfully completed the school's program of remedial or developmental education* that did not exceed one academic year or its equivalent. [Emphasis added].

See the enclosed "Dear Colleague" letter GEN-95-42, page 2, Exhibit D-1 [*not reprinted herein*]. See also 34 C.F.R. § 668.7.

After June 30, 1987, DOE required that all ATB tests be used "subject to criteria developed by the institution's nationally recognized accrediting agency or association." 34 C.F.R. § 668.7(b)(1)(i). Cambridge was accredited by the Accrediting Council for Continuing Education and Training (ACCET), in Richmond, Virginia. ACCET standards for its accredited schools required that the admissions policy for all students be "based on the institution's stated objectives; it must be administered for all applicants as written and published." ACCET also required each institution to document each student's ability to benefit from the training offered. Finally, the school "must determine a student's aptitude to complete successfully the . . . education *by following the applicable standards, procedures, and scores established by the publisher*: . . . *No deviation in scoring or testing procedures are allowed without written approval* of the test publisher and written concurrence by the ACCET Accrediting Commission." [Emphasis added]. See the enclosed 2/12/90 ACCET memorandum, with attachments of "Document 32" (June, 1989), p. 1, and "Document 32A" (February, 1990), p. 2, Exhibit D-2 [*not reprinted herein*]. Note that both of these memos state that they provide "clarification" (and thus do not change any policy); their instructions therefore are applicable back to 1986. See Exhibit D-2.

Cambridge published its admissions policy in its Policy and Procedures Manual. It eventually published the policy on a separate document. See Learning to Learn document, Exhibit D-3. This document represented Cambridge's ATB policy, written to comply with DOE's and ACCET's standards. However, the policy failed to use the cut-off scores "established by the publisher." Further, its scores did not "correspond with an appropriate grade level of the materials utilized in the instructional program" because people admitted with scores as low as Cambridge permitted do not learn well from formalized training and often need to be "explicitly taught" through an apprenticeship program rather than from "book-learning." This is explained next.

In determining the threshold scores needed to show an ability to benefit, Cambridge set scores far below the minimum suggested by the test manufacturer, Wonderlic. The following chart shows five programs offered by Cambridge, Cambridge's "conditional" passing scores on the ATB test, Cambridge's "unconditional" passing scores on the ATB test, and the test publisher's (Wonderlic's) minimum passing scores. As explained in Cambridge's admissions policy, prospective students scoring in the "conditional" range would be required to take the Learn to Learn course to gain admission. Those scoring in the "unconditional" range or higher would be admitted without conditions. However, the conditional scores fall below the scores set by Wonderlic in its testing manual:

Program	Cambridge's Conditional Qualifying Score	Cambridge's Unconditional Qualifying Score	Wonderlic's Passing Score
Custodial Maintenance	8	14	12
Data Entry	9	15	12
Law Enforcement/Security	9	15	10
Nursing Assistant	9	15	11
Word Processing	9	15	15

See Exhibit D-3 and the enclosed Wonderlic ATB Test Score Registration Manual, pp. 11, 12, and 17, Exhibit D-4 [*not reprinted herein*]. Further, the test publisher recommends that schools "recruit and select students that score well above the minimum." See the enclosed Wonderlic ATB Test Score Registration Manual, p. 5, Exhibit D-5 [*not reprinted herein*].

The reason for these suggested scores and recommendations are based on Wonderlic's extensive testing and research to demonstrate its tests' validity, correlation, and reliability. Based on this research, including reviews with employers hiring people for various positions, Wonderlic explains that people in the test score ranges being used by Cambridge would not benefit from a formal training setting and would likely not find employment. Students from these ranges of scores need to be "explicitly taught," as with an apprenticeship program rather than attempting to learn through books and classroom training. See the enclosed Wonderlic User's Manual, p. 26, Exhibit D-6 [*not reprinted herein*].

As a result of Cambridge's own cut-off scores for admission, many students admitted did not have the requisite ability to benefit from the programs offered. The following examples are taken from Cambridge's own files.

1. [*Student 1*]: [*Student 1*] was admitted in December, 1986 without having taken any admissions test. His enrollment agreement and application papers show he attended a high school, but the "Highest Grade Completed" and "Grad Date" blanks have no answers. Similar blanks for this information appear on the student's untitled data sheet containing background data with the courses, credit hours, and grades given. No high school diploma or transcript appears in the file.
2. [*Student 2*]. [*Student 2*] enrolled in Cambridge in October, 1987, and received a grade of 10 on the admissions test. Accordingly, she was required to take the Learn to Learn course, but she never did take that course. A review of the file shows no indication, on any document, of her enrolling, much less completing, the remedial learning program offered by Cambridge.[2]

---

[2] With regard to the students who were in the "conditional" range, and thus required to take the Learn to Learn course, it is evident that where a file does not note the Learn to Learn

3. [*Student 3*]: [*Student 3*] had to take the test twice in order to achieve what appears to be a passable score to gain admittance to Cambridge's custodial maintenance program. On his first try, [*Student 3*] scored a 7; on his second attempt he moved up to an 8. However, serious concerns exist as to whether [*Student 3*], himself, actually filled in all of the answers which appear on the second test. [*Student 3*'] handwriting in forming the numbers 1, 2, 3, and 4 can be gleaned from looking at the few answers he provided on the first test and most of the answers he provided on the second test. Comparing that to the two answers appearing in the second test for questions 21 and 22, it is seen that the handwriting is much lighter and the numbers are less "shaky"—those two answers appear to have been written by a person with more graceful writing. Significantly, both of those answers are correct and bring what otherwise would have been a score of 6 (failing) to an 8 (barely within the passing range). Also significant is that this appears on the second, and last, test which [*Student 3*] would be permitted to take.

Further, because the score of 8 was the absolute minimum score, and left [*Student 3*] in the "conditional" range of passing scores, he was required to take the remedial instruction program offered by Cambridge in order to qualify for admission and federal loan assistance. This remedial course, entitled "Learn to Learn," is nowhere noted in [*Student 3*'] file or on the enrollment agreement or test cover sheet. This is in contrast to the next example below, Mr. Duncan, and other student files discussed later in which the Learn to Learn program is clearly documented.

4. [*Student 4*]: [*Student 4*] sought admittance into Cambridge's custodial maintenance program with a score of 8. This is the absolute minimum score for eligibility, and it requires that the student also take the Learn to Learn program. The Learn to Learn program is documented (as "LL"), but only for the second quarter. Inexplicably, [*Student 4*] was not required to enroll in the Learn to Learn program for the first quarter. This violates Cambridge's own policy—promulgated to comply

---

program, the student did not take that course. Included herewith are examples from other student files which do indicate that the student was enrolled in the Learn to Learn program. For example, see the enclosed Cambridge files of Patty Marie Smith and Anthony Adams, Exhibits D-7, D-8 [*not reprinted herein*]. For ease of reference, documents indicating the student was enrolled in Learn to Learn have been highlighted.

It is interesting to note, however, that even when students did take this course, many of them routinely withdrew with a failing grade. Thus, it is clear that Cambridge did not satisfy the requirement for the ability-to-benefit standard set forth in 34 C.F.R. § 668.7(b)(3): "successfully completes a remedial . . . program. . . ." Both Mr. Adams and Ms. Smith, though ostensibly receiving remedial instruction, withdrew from the Learn to Learn course. In fact, they each took the course twice, the second time after already withdrawing from it in an earlier quarter or semester. Neither, however, took a second admissions test, notwithstanding the fact that they were only conditionally eligible and had not satisfactorily completed the Learn to Learn program which they had been required to take in order to be admitted. Again, Cambridge's practices show an across-the-board disregard for DOE's ATB requirements. Even when given the chance to admit students who failed the ATB test, Cambridge played "fast and loose" with the rules.

with DOE and ACCET mandates—which requires the student to take the instruction "in the first quarter of enrollment." The Learn to Learn program is also documented on the test cover sheet itself (as "L&L"), again, in contrast to [*Student 3*'] file.

5. [*Student 5*]: [*Student 5*] was admitted in November, 1988, after scoring only a 7 on his admissions test. A score of 7 does not meet Cambridge's own admission requirements. Nevertheless, [*Student 5*] was admitted into the custodial maintenance program (and apparently required to take Learn to Learn, as documented on the Master Attendance Record appearing in his file).

6. [*Student 6*]: [*Student 6*] scored an 11 on his admissions test, thus requiring that he take the Learn to Learn program in addition to the custodial maintenance courses he wished to attend. However, his Master Attendance Record, which notes the Learn to Learn program, indicates [*Student 6*] would not have to take the remedial course until the following quarter. This violated Cambridge's own policy which requires the student to take the instruction "in the first quarter of enrollment."

7. [*Student 7*]: [*Student 7*] took his admissions exam in December, 1988, and scored only a 6. Nevertheless, he was admitted into the custodial maintenance program for three quarters, beginning January 2, 1989. A score of 6 does not even meet the "conditional" eligibility minimum score set by Cambridge.

See the enclosed student files, Exhibits D-9 through D-15 [*not reprinted herein*].

VI. CAMBRIDGE CONDUCTED ITS OVERALL BUSINESS PRACTICES IN AN UNLAWFUL AND FRAUDULENT MANNER, RESULTING IN REVOCATION OF ITS LICENSE BY THE STATE OF OHIO.

In late 1990, the Ohio State Board of Proprietary School Registration (SBPSR), the licensing and oversight agency for proprietary, for-profit schools in Ohio, revoked the Certificate of Registration for Cambridge and imposed a civil penalty for Cambridge's violations of various sections of the Ohio Revised Code governing proprietary schools. By the time of the license revocation, Cambridge's default rate for mature student loans was an astounding 83.8%. See the enclosed SBPSR letter of 12/5/90, the SBPSR Final Resolution of 1/23/91, and the Higher Education Assistance Foundation letter of 5/12/89, Exhibits E-1 through E-3 [*not reprinted herein*].

VII. CAMBRIDGE, AND ITS OFFICERS, HAVE BEEN INVOLVED IN OTHER FRAUD AND CRIMINAL ACTIVITY.

Over the years, the Cincinnati newspapers and other media have documented numerous incidents of fraud and criminal activity by Cambridge and its employees or officers. See the series F exhibits, attached hereto [*not reprinted herein*]. Timothy Lovejoy, the former president of Cambridge, was reported by CNN as having defrauded the U.S. government out of $5 million. It was alleged that he submitted information to the DOE which falsely represented more students attending Cambridge than was true. It was further alleged that Mr. Lovejoy kept the loan monies of students who had dropped out of Cambridge instead of returning it to the banks and/or DOE. In late 1990, Mr. Lovejoy was murdered in a telephone booth at a local airport before these allegations could be brought to trial. That murder remains unsolved to this day. Pete McCallister, another officer of Cambridge, was indicted on numerous counts of bribery, conspiracy to defraud, and lying to a grand jury, to cover up student aid fraud. Mr. McCallister was tried in federal court and eventually pleaded guilty to one count of conspiracy; he was sentenced to two years in prison. Former Ohio Congressman Donald "Buz" Lukens also was indicted on various federal charges, some related to Cambridge, and was tried in federal court. He was convicted of accepting bribes from Cambridge.

The newspaper also reported that former Cambridge employees falsified student records before DOE investigators arrived at the school to check on various allegations of fraud. These employees also stated that many student records were destroyed. Additionally, numerous students complained over the years of sharp recruitment practices, unqualified teachers, problems with the school equipment, problems with attendance and books, as well as describing their experiences in job-hunting. Many, many students were told by prospective employers that their Cambridge certificates were worthless. Cambridge's high loan repayment default rate can be attributed to its poor educational quality as well as its poor administrative and business practices.

Further, physical violence was used against a former employee who went public with some of the fraudulent practices at Cambridge. Mr. Lovejoy was accused of hiring two people to physically assault [*Employee*] in April, 1990 because [*Employee*] was talking to the media about Cambridge and was aiding the Legal Aid Society of Cincinnati in its litigation against the school. These two men were sentenced to jail for beating [*Employee*]. And, as was explained earlier, the lawsuit filed by the Legal Aid Society was only the first—the Attorney General's Office filed its own. Both lawsuits succeeded in having Cambridge close its doors.

See the enclosed copies of newspaper articles, Exhibits F-1 through F-8 [*not reprinted herein*].

CONCLUSION

As has been demonstrated, Cambridge's admissions practices were fraudulent across the board. The pervasive fraud and unlawful practices included all areas of the mandatory testing of students for their ability to benefit from Cambridge's purported educational programs. DOE already has seen numerous instances of Cambridge's ATB fraud from individual students and thus has granted those students a discharge of their loans. These individual cases are merely representative of Cambridge's broader approach to education, namely enrolling as many students as could be fit into classrooms, with no regard to the students' ability to learn from the programs. The Ohio State Board of Proprietary School Registration and the Ohio Attorney General found numerous instances of ATB fraud by Cambridge. Numerous former students and employees have testified to the same unlawful practices. It is time for DOE to declare Cambridge's admissions and testing practices so pervasively fraudulent and unlawful as to render their ATB certification meaningless for each and every one of its former students. DOE now should consider any application for a school loan discharge based on improper determination of the student's ability to benefit as proven, so long as that former student did not have a high school diploma or a GED at the time of attending Cambridge.

[*Attorney for Plaintiff*]

E.2.2 Class Action Complaint Challenging Department of Education's False Certification Discharge Procedures

UNITED STATES DISTRICT COURT
EASTERN DISTRICT OF NEW YORK

[*PLAINTIFFS*], individually and on behalf of all others similarly situated,

Plaintiffs,

v.

RICHARD W. RILEY, in his official capacity as Secretary of the United States Department of Education, and the UNITED STATES DEPARTMENT OF EDUCATION,

Defendant.

COMPLAINT

PRELIMINARY STATEMENT

1. This is a class action pursuant to the Administrative Procedure Act, 5 U.S.C. § 701 *et seq.*, for declaratory and injunctive relief on behalf of individuals who have been denied discharges of their federally guaranteed student loans arbitrarily, capriciously and in violation of 20 U.S.C. § 1087(c), the Higher Education Act Amendments ("HEAA"). The statute mandates that the defendant Secretary of Education grant discharges of student loans if the schools attended by the students falsely certified that the students had the ability to benefit from the programs for which their loans were taken (hereinafter "ability-to-benefit discharge"). Instead of carefully considering the evidence of false certification presented by the plaintiffs, the defendant Secretary denied their requests for discharges arbitrarily and capriciously, on the basis of unsupported assumptions and inferences.

JURISDICTION

2. This court has jurisdiction under the Administrative Procedure Act 5 U.S.C. § 701 *et seq.*, 28 U.S.C. § 1331, § 1361, and 20 U.S.C. § 1082(a)(2).

3. Venue is proper in this district pursuant to 28 U.S.C. § 1391(e) because the named plaintiffs reside in this district.

PARTIES

4. Plaintiff 1 resides, and at all relevant times has resided, in Brooklyn, New York.

5. Plaintiff 2 resides, and at all relevant times has resided, in Brooklyn, New York.

6. Defendant RICHARD W. RILEY is the Secretary of the United States Department of Education (hereafter "the Secretary" when speaking of Defendant Riley; and "U.S. ED" when referring to the Department), and as such is responsible for administration of the Federal Family Educational Loan program (hereafter "FFEL"), known until 1992 as the Guaranteed Student Loan Program (hereafter "GSLP"). Defendant Riley is sued only in his official capacity.

CLASS ACTION ALLEGATIONS

7. The named plaintiffs 1 and 2, bring this action, pursuant to Rule 23 of the Federal Rules of Civil Procedure, on behalf of themselves and as representatives of all individuals with federally guaranteed student loans obtained to attend for-profit vocational schools licensed by the New York State Department of Education, who have been or will be denied an ability-to-benefit discharge by the Secretary, without consideration of the facts in their individual cases, but rather in reliance upon an absence of findings by oversight agencies about the certification practices of the schools they attended.

8. The class is so numerous that joinder of all members is impracticable.

9. There are questions of law or fact common to the class which predominate over any questions affecting only the individual plaintiffs, including, but not limited to whether the defendant arbitrarily and capriciously relies on information provided by other agencies or on the absence of such information instead of examining the actual facts of the plaintiffs' cases.

10. The claims of the individual named plaintiff as to the legality of the defendant's practices are typical of the claims of all class members, in that each has had her request for an ability-to-benefit discharge denied arbitrarily and capriciously, without examination by the defendant of the individual facts of her case.

11. The named plaintiffs will adequately and fairly protect the interests of all members of the class, because they have the requisite personal interest in the outcome of this action, have no interest antagonistic to others in the class, and they are represented by the Social Justice Project at BLS Legal Services Corp., counsel experienced in class action litigation generally, and specifically including the rights of people with guaranteed student loan debts.

12. The prosecution of separate actions by individual members of the class would create a risk of inconsistent or varying adjudications with respect to the practices at issue in this action. Separate actions would be, as a practical matter, dispositive of the interests of other individual members of the class and would substantially impair their abilities to protect their interests. Defendants have acted on grounds generally applicable to the class in failing to make individual determinations based on the facts in each case in determining plaintiffs' eligibility for loan discharges. A class action is superior to other available methods for the fair and efficient adjudication of this controversy.

STATUTORY SCHEME

13. The Higher Education Act, 20 U.S.C. § 1071, *et seq.*, authorizes the Secretary to administer a federal student financial aid program (formerly known as the Guaranteed Student Loan (GSL) Program, now known as the Federal Family Education Loan (FFEL) Program).

14. Under the FFEL program, lenders make loans for "eligible borrowers" to attend "eligible" post-secondary institutions; state and private guaranty agencies insure the loans; and the Secretary reinsures the agencies. 20 U.S.C. § 1071 *et seq.*.

15. Through the program, a student may obtain guaranteed student loans to attend a proprietary vocational school if the school (1) admits eligible students, (2) is legally authorized to provide vocational training, (3) has been in existence for at least two years, (4) is accredited by an agency approved by the Secretary, and (5) has a cohort default rate less than the statutorily specified threshold. 20 U.S.C. §§ 1002 (b), 1085 (a).

16. To qualify for a guaranteed student loan, a student must meet various requirements, including the "ability-to-benefit" requirement. The specific requirements have changed slightly during the life of the program, but at all times relevant to this case, have required that to be considered to have the ability to benefit from the program of study, the student must have a high school diploma, or a recognized equivalent (GED), or pass a standardized test given by the school prior to admission of the student, or receive a GED prior to graduation from the course of study or before the end of the first year of study, or be enrolled in and successfully complete an institutionally prescribed program of remedial education not to exceed one year. 20 U.S.C. § 1091; 34 C.F.R. § 668.6; § 682.402(e)(13); § 685.214(c).

17. The Higher Education Act Amendments and implementing regulations provide that the Secretary must discharge a student loan (including interest and collection fees) of a borrower who received a loan after January 1, 1986, if a school falsely certified the borrower as having the ability to benefit from the program of study. 20 U.S.C. § 1087(c).

18. Regulations promulgated by the Secretary require guaranty agencies to send discharge applications to all borrowers who, based on information acquired by the Secretary, may be eligible for such discharge. 34 C.F.R. § 682.402 (e) (i).

19. In evaluating the borrower's request for an ability-to-benefit discharge, the agency holding the loan must consider the information and supporting sworn statement provided by the borrower, "in light of information available from the records of the agency and from other sources, including other guaranty agencies, state authorities, and cognizant accrediting associations." 34 C.F.R. § 682.402 (e) (6) (iv).

20. If the agency determines that the borrower satisfies the requirements for an ability-to-benefit discharge, the agency must (1) pay off the loan debt; (2) notify the borrower that her liability has been suspended; (3) refund to the borrower all amounts paid by the borrower to the lender or agency with respect to the discharged amount; and (4) notify the lender that the borrower's liability with respect to the amount of the loan has been discharged. 34 C.F.R. § 682.402(e)(7)(ii).

21. If the guaranty agency decides that the borrower is not entitled to a discharge, a borrower can request a review of that decision by the Secretary. If a borrower does request a review of the guaranty agency's decision, the agency shall forward the borrower's discharge request and all relevant documentation to the Secretary. 34 C.F.R. § 682.402(e)(11)(i).

22. Discharge of a student loan under 20 U.S.C. § 1087(c), entitles the borrower to:
   (a) relief from any existing or past obligation to repay the loan and any charges imposed or cost incurred by the holder with respect to the loan that the borrower is or was otherwise

obligated to pay. 20 U.S.C. § 1087(c)(1).
(b) restoration of the borrower's eligibility to receive federal assistance under Title IV of the Higher Education Act Amendments. 20 U.S.C. § 1087(c)(3)–(4).
(c) correction of all adverse credit reports by reporting to all credit bureaus to which the holder previously reported the delinquent status of the loan that all adverse credit history assigned to the loan should be deleted. 20 U.S.C. § 1087(c)(5).

23. The Administrative Procedure Act ("APA"), 5 U.S.C. § 706(2)(A), specifically creates a cause of action to "hold unlawful and set aside agency action, findings, and conclusions found to be arbitrary and capricious, an abuse of discretion, or otherwise not in accordance with the law."

24. The APA also creates a cause of action to "hold unlawful and set aside agency action, findings, and conclusions found to be in excess of statutory jurisdiction, authority, or limitations, or short of statutory rights." 5 U.S.C. § 706(2)(C).

FACTS PERTAINING TO THE CLASS

25. The Secretary denies ability-to-benefit discharges, without adequate consideration of the facts of individual students, based upon the inference that the absence of recorded findings of improper ability-to-benefit admissions practices by particular schools means the school was not engaged in improper ability-to-benefit practices.

26. The Secretary administers the guaranteed student loan program in part through giving directions to the guaranty agencies that are the first line of insurance of the federally guaranteed student loans. These directions are sent to the guarantee agencies in the form of memoranda referred to as "Dear Colleague" letters.

27. The Secretary has issued several Dear Colleague letters about ability-to-benefit discharges.

28. In September 1995, in Dear Colleague letter Gen-95-42 (attached hereto as Exhibit A), the Secretary advised guaranty agencies about how to evaluate requests for ability-to-benefit discharges, stating that the absence of findings of improper ATB practices by authorities with oversight responsibilities "raises an inference that no improper practices were reported because none were taking place." *Id.* at 4.

29. In his own actions in administering guaranteed student loans held by U.S. ED, the Secretary follows the practices outlined in the Dear Colleague letter.

30. The Secretary supports and relies on such an inference even though Congress created the ability-to-benefit discharge specifically because agencies with oversight responsibilities have failed "to detect and or take action" regarding abuses such as failure to honestly assess students' ability to benefit from vocational programs. *Senate Permanent Subcommittee on Investigations* (hereinafter the "Committee"), *Abuses in Federal Student Aid Programs*, S. Rep. No. 102-58, (1991) (hereinafter "the Nunn Report").

31. Between 1989 and 1991, the United States Senate Permanent Subcommittee on Investigations, chaired by Senator Sam Nunn, studied the rapid increase of defaulted guaranteed student loans obtained for study at vocational schools. S. Rep. No. 102-58, at 23 (1991).

32. The Nunn Report revealed a national epidemic of fraud by proprietary trade schools, including the practice of fraudulently certifying students' ability to benefit from the schools' programs. *See id* at 12.

33. The Nunn Report found that "one of the most widely abused areas of trade school practices was admissions and recruitment, in particular the admission of students who had not finished high school under the so-called "ability-to-benefit" or "ATB" rule. *Id.* at 12.

34. The Nunn Report also found evidence of a failure "by state and federal authorities to detect and or take action" regarding the abuse of GSLP rules and regulations. *Id.* at 23.

35. The Nunn Report stated U.S. ED "has effectively abdicated its GSLP oversight responsibilities to private accrediting bodies, State licensing authorities, and guaranty agencies. Experience has proven that those bodies have neither the motivation nor the capabilities to effectively police the program." *Id.* at 32.

36. The mandate, in the Higher Education Act Amendments, that the Secretary discharge the loans of students who had been admitted into proprietary schools despite their lack of an ability to benefit from the programs, was a response to Congressional findings that "institutions falsely certified the eligibility of students for Federal loans. . . . [S]tudents were left without the skills needed to obtain employment and consequently did not have the means to repay the loans." *Report of the House Committee on Education and Labor*, H. Rep. No. 102-447, at 116 (1992).

FACTS REGARDING NAMED PLAINTIFFS
PLAINTIFF 1

37. Plaintiff 1 was enrolled in the Robert Fiance Hair Design Institute (hereafter "RFHD") branch at [*Address*] (hereafter "[*Address*]").

38. RFHD is a for-profit vocational school.

39. Plaintiff 1 was enrolled in a course that was scheduled to run from March 10, 1988 to December 8, 1988.

40. Plaintiff 1 financed her studies at RFHD by taking out guaranteed student loans under the Guaranteed Student Loan Program.

41. Plaintiff 1 received the proceeds of the disbursement of her loan on March 10, 1988.

42. At the time of her application to RFHD, Plaintiff 1 did not have, and reported to RFHD that she did not have a high school diploma or a GED.

43. RFHD did not require Plaintiff 1 to take an admission test, and did not enroll her in a GED course or other program of remedial education.

44. Plaintiff 1 attended classes at [*Address*] from March 1988 to early fall 1988.

45. Plaintiff 1 did not receive the training and education for which she was contracted due to her inability to benefit from the program.

46. The guaranteed student loans obtained by Plaintiff 1 for her studies at RFHD were placed in default status by U.S. ED.

47. On December 30, 1999, Plaintiff 1 applied to the Secretary for a discharge of her guaranteed student loans based on the school's false certification of her ability to benefit from the program.

48. On April 10, 2000, the Secretary acknowledged the receipt of Plaintiff 1's loan discharge application and stated that Plaintiff 1 was not entitled to an ability-to-benefit loan discharge because authorities with oversight responsibilities had made no findings or adverse reports relating to false certification of ability-to-benefit at RFHD (Letter attached as Exhibit B [*not reprinted herein*]).

PLAINTIFF 2

49. Plaintiff 2 was enrolled at Commercial Programming Unlimited (hereafter CPU), at [*Address*].

50. CPU is a for profit vocational school.

51. Plaintiff 2 financed her education at CPU by taking out guaranteed student loans under the Guaranteed Student Loan Program.

52. At the time of her application to CPU, Plaintiff 2 did not have, and informed CPU that she did not have a high school diploma or a GED.

53. CPU did not require Plaintiff 2 to take an admission test and did not enroll her in a GED course or any other course of remedial education.

54. Plaintiff 2 began taking classes at CPU in August of 1988. She was enrolled in courses for computer programming.

55. Plaintiff 2 attended classes at CPU for approximately two months.

56. Plaintiff 2 discontinued her studies at CPU because of the difficulty of the course material, inadequate teaching, and overcrowded classrooms, and but she did not formally withdraw from CPU.

57. The guaranteed student loans obtained by Plaintiff 2 for her studies at CPU were placed in default status by the Secretary.

58. Plaintiff 2 applied to the Secretary for a discharge of her guaranteed student loans based on the school's false certification of her ability-to-benefit from the program.

59. In a letter dated March 8, 2000, the Secretary acknowledged the receipt of Plaintiff 2 loan discharge application and stated that Plaintiff 2 was not entitled to an ability-to-benefit discharge because authorities with oversight responsibilities had made no findings or adverse reports relating to false certification of ability-to-benefit at CPU. (Letter attached as Exhibit C [*not reprinted herein*]).

FIRST CAUSE OF ACTION

60. Defendant Secretary's adoption of the policy, stated in the September 1995 Dear Colleague letter, that the absence of findings of improper ATB practices by authorities with oversight responsibilities "raises an inference that no improper practices were reported because none were taking place," and his own reliance on that inference in denying requests for ATB discharges, without adequate consideration of the facts presented by students seeking discharges, is arbitrary and capricious and in violation of 5 U.S.C. § 706(2)(A).

SECOND CAUSE OF ACTION

61. Defendant Secretary's adoption of the policy, stated in the September 1995 Dear Colleague letter, that the absence of findings of improper ATB practices by authorities with oversight responsibilities "raises an inference that no improper practices were reported because none were taking place," and his own reliance on that inference in denying requests for ATB discharges, without adequate consideration of the facts presented by students seeking discharges, is in excess of his statutory authority, in violation of 5 U.S.C. § 706(2)(C).

PRAYER FOR RELIEF

WHEREFORE, plaintiffs respectfully request the court to:

1. Enter an order certifying this action as a class action pursuant to Rule 23(b)(2) of the Federal Rules of Civil Procedure, with the class consisting of all individuals with federally guaranteed student loans obtained to attend for-profit vocational schools licensed by the New York State Department of Education, who have been or will be denied an ability-to-benefit discharge by the Secretary, without consideration of the facts in their individual cases, in reliance upon an absence of findings by oversight agencies about the certification practices of the schools they attended.

2. Enter a judgment against the defendant
   a. declaring that the Secretary's practice of denying requests for ability-to-benefit discharges based solely on the absence of findings by oversight agencies of prior wrongdoing by a school, without consideration of the facts of a debtor's individual circumstances, is arbitrary and capricious and not in accordance with the law.
   b. directing the defendant to
      i. Review the facts of each debtor's request for an ability-to-benefit discharge;
      ii. Discontinue the practice of relying on the absence of reports by oversight agencies;
      iii. Provide debtors with the supporting evidence relied upon by the Secretary in determining that they are not entitled to a loan discharge, including but not limited to a copy of the properly administered and nationally recognized ATB exam or evidence of enrollment in a remedial program of education;
      iv. discharge the loans of Plaintiffs 1 and 2;
      v. cease collection efforts on the loans of Plaintiffs 1 and 2;
      vi. correct any reports to credit agencies or eligible institutions that the loans of Plaintiffs 1 or 2 are in default or delinquent;
      vii. return all money paid voluntarily or involuntarily by Plaintiffs 1 and 2;
      viii. provide notice, within a reasonable time not to exceed 90 days from the date of a resolution favorable to the plaintiff, in a form to be agreed upon by the parties, to all student borrowers denied an a false certification of an ability-to-benefit discharge that they may be eligible for a discharge of their student loans; and providing to them all information in the possession of the Secretary relating to their eligibility for discharge, the procedures for requesting a discharge, and a form on which to request such discharge;
      ix. make determinations, and issue written decisions, on all requests for ability-to-benefit discharges, within 60 days of receipt of the requests;
   c. ordering defendant to pay the cost of this action, together with reasonable attorneys' fees pursuant to the Equal Access to Justice Act, 28 U.S.C. § 2412(d)(1)(A), as determined by the court; and
   d. granting such other and further relief as the Court may deem just and proper.

Dated:

Respectfully submitted,

[*Attorney for Plaintiffs*]

E.2.3 Individual Complaint Challenging Disability Discharge Denial

A preliminary injunction motion for this case as well as a similar pleading in another case can be found on the companion website to this manual.

IN THE UNITED STATES DISTRICT COURT
FOR THE SOUTHERN DISTRICT OF GEORGIA
WAYCROSS DIVISION

```
_____  )
[PLAINTIFF],            )
             Plaintiff, )
                        )
v.                      )
                        )
ROD PAIGE, SECRETARY,   )
UNITED STATES           )
DEPARTMENT OF           )
EDUCATION,              )
             Defendant. )
_____  )
```

COMPLAINT

INTRODUCTION

1. Plaintiff brings this action for judicial review of the United States Secretary of Education's decision denying her application for a discharge of her federally-guaranteed student loan. Plaintiff seeks declaratory and injunctive relief against the Department of Education's new ad hoc, unpublished, and unreasonable standards for evaluating requests to discharge student loans based on the borrower's permanent disability.

I. JURISDICTION

2. This court has jurisdiction under 28 U.S.C. § 1331 (federal question), 20 U.S.C. § 1082 (suits against Secretary of Education), and the federal Administrative Procedure Act, 5 U.S.C. §§ 701 *et seq.* With respect to Plaintiff's request for declaratory relief, this Court has jurisdiction under 28 U.S.C. § 2201.

II. PARTIES

3. Plaintiff [*Plaintiff*], an individual who resides at [*Address*] signed up for a federally-guaranteed student loan by the Riley Training Institute in Waycross in February 1981.

4. Defendant Rod Paige, Secretary of the United States Department of Education, is responsible for the administration of the federally-guaranteed student loan program.

5. The United States Department of Education (DOE) is an agency within the meaning of the federal Administrative Procedure Act, 5 U.S.C. §§ 701 *et seq.*

6. The Riley Training Institute in Waycross, Georgia, was a proprietary trade school that was certified as an eligible institution to participate in federal financial aid programs under the Higher Education Act until it closed in May of 1991.

III. STATEMENT OF FACTS

7. Plaintiff [*Plaintiff*] is a 45-year-old single mother of one who resides in [*Address*], Georgia.

8. Plaintiff graduated from high school in 1975 and enrolled at Okefenokee Technical College for a six weeks nurse's aide course.

9. Plaintiff was successfully employed as a nurse's aide for a period of ten years, 1975 until 1985.

10. In 1989 Plaintiff enrolled in Riley Training Institute to study retail sales management.

11. Upon her acceptance at Riley Training Institute also located in Waycross, Georgia, Plaintiff applied for a federally guaranteed loan in February 1989.

12. Plaintiff [*Plaintiff*] received a student loan from Florida Federal Savings in the amount of $2,625.00.

13. Plaintiff attended Riley Training Institute but did not complete her studies.

14. After being successfully gainfully employed for a period of ten years and attending school for a short while, [*Plaintiff*] suffered severe physical and mental impairments.

15. In 1995, Plaintiff applied for Social Security disability and/or Supplemental Security Income (SSI) and was determined to be permanently and totally disabled by the Social Security Administration (hereinafter "SSA").

16. Plaintiff began receiving SSI benefits in the amount of $458.00 in 1995.

17. In 1999, some four years after receipt of SSI benefits, Satilla Community Mental Health, where [*Plaintiff*] sought assistance, recommended her for participation in the SSI work incentive subsidized/supportive employment program.

18. The subsidized work program pays benefits and wages above the amount that [*Plaintiff*] actually earns. She is able to work because she has a job coach and accommodations are made on a daily basis in consideration of both her physical and mental disability.

19. The accommodations made on a daily basis are substantial and include the ability to leave work when necessary, to return home during the day, to work fewer hours than other employees due to fatigue and to have frequent rest periods during the day.

20. On or before December 1999, Plaintiff [*Plaintiff*] began receiving collection notices from the Department of Education indicating that she was in arrears on her student loan payment and directing her to pay her arrearage in full to Defendant's intermediary, Pioneer Credit Recovery, Inc.

21. On or about June 29, 2000, Defendant received notice that Defendant intended to garnish her income if she did not contact Pioneer Credit Recovery, Inc. to make arrangements to pay her student loan arrearage.

22. The Department of Education has demanded from Plaintiff a loan payment in the amount of $6,004.98.

23. In response to said collection notices, Plaintiff [*Plaintiff*] filed an application for student loan discharge due to her disability.

24. The Higher Education Act provides that an individual who is unable to work because of an injury or illness that is expected to continue indefinitely or result in death is entitled to have the federally guaranteed student loan discharged. 20 U.S.C.§ 1087(a).

25. In conjunction with her application for discharge due to a disability, [*Plaintiff*] informed the Department of Education that she was totally and permanently disabled because she has full-blown AIDS and other complicating medical conditions.

26. [*Plaintiff*] also informed the Agency that she received treatment for AIDS and other medical conditions from her primary care physician of many years.

27. [*Plaintiff*] completed the Department of Education form to request a disability discharge, and, additionally, her physician completed the "Physician's Certification of Borrowers and Total Permanent Disability" listing AIDS, insulin-dependent diabetes mellitus, high blood pressure and the side-effects resulting from several AIDS medications as contributing to Plaintiff's inability to work in a genuine work place without accommodations. (*See* attached Exhibit "A" [*not reprinted herein*].])

28. In addition to notifying the Agency in July 2000 that she was disabled and making an application for a loan discharge due to disability, Plaintiff sent in a request for a hearing along with an administrative wage garnishment disclosure form.

29. Plaintiff's request for an application to cancel the school loan obligation was denied. However, a request for a hearing was granted and scheduled for February 13, 2001. The hearing was held by telephone.

30. At the outset of the hearing, Jacqueline Hughley-Leonard, a Department of Education hearing officer, stated that Plaintiff could present her argument but could not qualify for a disability discharge because she was working.

31. Ms. Hughley-Leonard refused to consider evidence of the completed application for discharge due to disability with the attached physician's certification of disability during the hearing.

32. Upon request from counsel for Plaintiff, Ms. Hughley-Leonard recused herself from the hearing because of her refusal as Hearing Officer to even consider [*Plaintiff*]'s evidence. Hearing Officer Irene Ford then joined Ms. Hughley-Leonard in the hearing and allowed [*Plaintiff*]'s counsel to present evidence of her disability.

33. On February 26, Defendant Department of Education denied Plaintiff's application for a disability discharge stating, "Receiving Social Security disability benefits does not automatically qualify a borrower for total and permanent disability cancellations." (*See* decision attached as Exhibit "B" p. 2 [*not reprinted herein*].])

34. Said February 26 opinion also stated, "A borrower is not considered totally and permanently disabled based on a condition that existed before he or she applied for the loan." (*See* Ex. "B" p.2)

35. Said recitation of fact was a factual error and despite Plaintiff's protestation to the Agency, said correction has not been made. (*See* Plaintiff's letter attached as Exhibit "C" [*not reprinted herein*]).

36. Defendant Agency also requested that Plaintiff [*Plaintiff*] provide financial evidence regarding whether or not she had sufficient funds for garnishment.

37. Said final decision (Ex. "B" p. 2) stated the intention of Defendant to garnish [*Plaintiff*]'s income. Defendant's decision stated, however, that it would stay the garnishment for six months because [*Plaintiff*] did not have sufficient monthly income to pay the amount.

38. As a result of an additional collection activity related to this loan, Plaintiff [*Plaintiff*]'s 2000 tax return, of $262.00 and her August 2001 tax rebate in the amount of $300.00 were both intercepted.

39. [*Plaintiff*]'s income has not improved subsequent to the date of Defendant's decision, but has worsened because her tax refund and rebate were intercepted.

40. In addition to her own expenses, the Plaintiff is attempting to provide a minimum amount of income on a monthly basis to her son who is in school.

41. Garnishment of [*Plaintiff*]'s income would render her unable to moderately function on a monthly basis, and would result in her being unable to participate in her subsidized work program.

42. On June 26, 2001, Plaintiff wrote to Defendant submitting her request for reconsideration of her claim asserting that the denial appeared to be based on the mistake of fact among other issues.

43. Defendant refused to clarify or explain his decision. Defendant's decision constituted Agency action that is reviewable under the Administrative Procedure Act.

44. Defendant's decision also stated, "Our findings are conclusive and represent the Department of Education's final decision on your objections. If you disagree with this decision, you may have this decision reviewed by bringing a lawsuit in federal district court." (*See* Ex. "B" p. 1)

45. Defendant's decision denying Plaintiff's application for discharge due to disability is based on no applicable or discernible law, statute or regulation.

46. Additionally, the ad hoc decision does not contain a statement of fact or an analysis of the facts to the regulation or to the applicable law governing and controlling how a disability discharge should be resolved.

47. Defendant's refusal to discharge Plaintiff [*Plaintiff*]'s student loan is arbitrary and capricious and not in accordance with the law. Plaintiff's application for disability discharge met all of the statutory and regulatory provisions found at 34 C.F.R. § 682.402.

48. [*Plaintiff*]'s loan balance approximates Five Thousand, Eight-Hundred Eighty dollars and 64/100 Dollars ($5,880.64).

49. [*Plaintiff*] has no adequate remedy at law.

50. [*Plaintiff*], has already had her tax refund and rebate intercepted and has also been threatened with imminent garnishment against her earnings.

51. Defendant recently contacted counsel for Plaintiff requesting additional financial information so that it could move ahead to start garnishing her monthly benefit amount.

IV. DEFENDANT'S PRACTICES

52. Defendant has stated that its adverse decision dated February 26, 2001 in Plaintiff's case is "conclusive" and "final" (*See* Ex. "B" p. 1), and therefore constitutes final agency action as defined by 5 U.S.C. § 704.

53. Defendant has persisted in its attempts to collect on [*Plaintiff*]'s loan, most recently seizing her year 2000 tax refund and 2001 tax rebate.

54. Defendant's actions have resulted in its applying new, more restrictive standards to [*Plaintiff*]'s request for a disability discharge.

55. On or about June 7, 1999, the Inspector General of the U.S. Department of Education issued a report entitled "Improving the Process for Forgiving Student Loans" (Hereinafter "IG Report"), which included findings that certain individuals who were allegedly not disabled, had received student loan disability discharges. (*See* attached report as Exhibit "D")

56. In response to the IG report, the Defendant began applying stricter criteria to requests for disability discharges, including but not limited to the following changes:

A. Defendant ceased its prior practice of granting a disability discharge on the basis of a properly completed physician's certification of disability submitted on the Defendant's approved form;

B. Defendant notified its employees and agents that physicians should be informed that eligibility for disability benefits under the Social Security Act would not be sufficient basis to establish eligibility for a student loan disability discharge and that the student loan discharge standard for disability was a "higher standard" than the Social Security standard; and,

C. Defendant directed its employees and agents, who have no medical training, to make an independent determination of whether a physician's certification of disability is definitive, or if the diagnosis and prognosis do not appear to reach the standard of total and permanent disability.

57. Some, but not all, of the Defendant's new policies and rules regarding disability discharges were set forth in a "Dear Colleague letter," designated GEN-99-36 (hereinafter the "Dear Colleague letter"). (*See* attached letter as Exhibit "E").

58. The Dear Colleague letter was not published in the Federal Register for notice and comment.

59. The new rules are set forth in the Dear Colleague letter as absolute requirements for eligibility for disability discharges rather than as guidelines to decision-makers.

60. The substantive changes set forth in the Dear Colleague letter are arbitrary and capricious and not in accordance with the law.

61. The Defendant's adverse decision has caused and will continue to cause substantial and irreparable harm to [*Plaintiff*].

V. CLAIMS FOR RELIEF

COUNT I: DEFENDANT'S DECISION VIOLATES THE DISABILITY DISCHARGE PROVISIONS FOUND IN 20 U.S.C.S. § 1087(A)

62. Plaintiff incorporates paragraphs 1 through 61 of her Complaint as if set forth fully herein.

63. The determination that [*Plaintiff*] is permanently and totally disabled was made and certified by a medical doctor, following a personal examination.

64. Defendant's determination that [*Plaintiff*] is not permanently and totally disabled was based solely upon nonmedical considerations.

65. Defendant's determination that [*Plaintiff*] is not permanently and totally disabled was made by nonmedical personnel.

66. Defendant's total failure to consider [*Plaintiff*]'s documented physical disability in determining whether to grant a discharge pursuant to 20 U.S.C.S. § 1087(a) violates the Congressional mandate to provide debt relief to persons who suffer from debilitating and terminal illnesses.

COUNT II: DEFENDANT'S RELIANCE ON A MISTAKE OF FACT RESULTED IN A FINAL DECISION THAT IS ARBITRARY AND CAPRICIOUS AND VIOLATES 5 U.S.C. § 706(2)(A)

67. Plaintiff incorporates paragraphs 1 through 61 of her Complaint as if set forth fully herein.

68. [*Plaintiff*]'s application seeking discharge of her student loan liability was filed under 20 U.S.C.S. § 1087(a), alleging permanent and totally disability.

69. In determining that [*Plaintiff*] was not entitled to a discharge of her student loan obligation, Defendant failed to address any substantive considerations related to [*Plaintiff*]'s disability status.

70. Defendant relied upon a mistake of fact regarding [*Plaintiff*]'s disability onset date when it ruled against [*Plaintiff*].

71. Defendant has been asked to either rectify its mistake or to clarify its holding and has refused to do so, stating that its decision is final.

72. Defendant's adverse decision on [*Plaintiff*]'s application is arbitrary, capricious and not in accordance with law, and, therefore, violates 5 U.S.C. § 706(2)(a).

COUNT III: DEFENDANT FAILED TO FOLLOW ITS OWN REGULATIONS IN MAKING ITS DECISION TO DENY PLAINTIFF'S DISCHARGE APPLICATION AND, THEREFORE, THE DECISION IS UNLAWFUL UNDER 5 U.S.C. § 706.

73. Plaintiff incorporates paragraphs 1 through 61 of her Complaint as if set forth fully herein.

74. Defendant sets forth the procedures that must be followed by which a borrower becomes entitled to a disability discharge in 34 C.F.R. § 682.402.

75. Defendant's above-cited regulations require that a discharge be granted upon written certification of permanent and total disability by a physician, submitted upon a form approved by Defendant.

76. [*Plaintiff*] submitted the required medical certification of her permanent and total disability.

77. Defendant has refused to approve [*Plaintiff*]'s discharge application in contravention of its own regulations.

COUNT IV: BY APPLYING AN UNPUBLISHED STANDARD OF REVIEW ARTICULATED IN A "DEAR COLLEAGUE" LETTER, DEFENDANT VIOLATED THE NOTICE AND COMMENT REQUIREMENTS FOUND IN 5 U.S.C. § 552.

78. Plaintiff incorporates paragraphs 1 through 61 of her Complaint as if set forth fully herein.

79. Defendant sets forth the procedures that must be followed by which a borrower becomes entitled to a disability discharge in 34 C.F.R. § 682.402.

80. [*Plaintiff*] complied with the above-referenced procedures, and should have been entitled to a discharge.

81. In making its adverse decision, Defendant applied a different standard to [*Plaintiff*]'s application than authorized by statute or regulation.

82. Defendant ignored its formal regulations to apply different eligibility rules set forth in a Dear Colleague letter.

83. The above-mentioned letter was not submitted to a negotiated rule-making process, nor was it widely published, which violates the Administrative Procedure Act requirement, 5 U.S.C. § 552 that regulations be published in the Federal Register for notice and comment prior to being applied by federal agencies.

WHEREFORE, Plaintiff respectfully requests that the Court grant the following relief:

1. Assume jurisdiction over this case;

2. Enter an order declaring that Defendant's new more restrictive standards violate 20 U.S.C.S. § 1087(A), 34 C.F.R. § 682.402 and the requirements of the Administrative Procedure Act;

3. Grant a preliminary and permanent injunction enjoining Defendant from implementing its more restrictive disability discharge standards as set forth in unpublished rules and ordering Defendant to reevaluate any discharge requests denied under the new restrictive standard;

4. Grant a preliminary and permanent injunction enjoining Defendant and its agents from intercepting federal income tax refunds and rebates, garnishing wages or bank accounts, or otherwise collecting the balance of the Plaintiff's student loan.

5. That the Court enter an order reversing the Department's action in denying Plaintiff's discharge request;

6. That the Court enter an order directing Defendant to refund with interest all monies withheld, garnished, or unlawfully collected from Plaintiff;

7. That the Court enter an order awarding Plaintiff costs; and

8. That the Court enter an order granting any other and further relief as is just and proper.

[Dated]

Respectfully submitted,

[Attorneys for the Plaintiff]

E.3 Challenge to Student Loan Collection Letters

E.3.1 Complaint

IN THE UNITED STATES DISTRICT COURT FOR THE
MIDDLE DISTRICT OF LOUISIANA

_____)
[PLAINTIFF], on behalf of)
herself and all others similarly)
situated,)
    Plaintiff,)
)
v.)
)
The Premier Collectors, Inc.,)
    Defendant.)
_____)

CLASS ACTION COMPLAINT

Plaintiff [*Plaintiff*], on her own behalf and on behalf of the class defined below, complains as follows against defendant The Premier Collectors, Inc.:

INTRODUCTION

1. This action is brought to remedy defendant's violations of the federal Fair Debt Collection Practices Act, 15 U.S.C. § 1692 *et seq.* ("FDCPA").

JURISDICTION AND VENUE

2. This Court has jurisdiction under 15 U.S.C. § 1692k(d) and 28 U.S.C. § 1331.

PARTIES

3. Plaintiff [*Plaintiff*] is an individual who resides in Baton Rouge, Louisiana. She is a "consumer" as defined by the FDCPA, 15 U.S.C. § 1692a(3).

4. The Premier Collectors, Inc. ("Premier Collectors") is a Delaware corporation registered to do business in the state of Louisiana. Its registered agent and address are AB Corporation Systems, 1000 Main Street, Baton Rouge, Louisiana.

5. Premier Collectors is regularly engaged for profit in the collection of debts allegedly owed by consumers. It is a "debt collector" as defined in the FDCPA, 15 U.S.C. § 1692a(6).

FACTUAL ALLEGATIONS OF MS. JOHNSON

6. On or about August 11, 1993, [*Plaintiff*] was mailed a collection letter from Defendant for $11,417.31 allegedly owing to the U.S. Department of Education. (Attached hereto as *Exhibit A* [*not reprinted herein*]).

7. On or about April 20, 1994, [*Plaintiff*] was mailed a collection letter from Defendant for $10,706.14 allegedly owing to the U.S. Department of Education. (Attached hereto as *Exhibit B* [*not reprinted herein*]).

8. On or about May 5, 1994, [*Plaintiff*] was mailed a collection letter from Defendant for $10,732.65 allegedly owing to creditor U. S. Department of Education. (Attached hereto as *Exhibit C* [*not reprinted herein*]).

9. These collection letters were mailed in an attempt to collect alleged debts arising from transactions primarily for personal, family, or household purposes.

10. Defendant is not affiliated with the U.S. Department of Education.

11. In *Exhibits A-C*, Defendant lists the principal balance as $5650.49, interest varying from $2,242.59 to $1,744.71, and fees and costs varying from $3,524.23 to $3,310.94.

12. Defendant did not and does not determine the course of legal action taken by the U.S. Department of Justice with regard to such debts.

13. Neither Defendant, the U.S. Department of Justice, nor anyone else, has filed suit against [*Plaintiff*] to collect this debt.

DEFENDANT'S PRACTICES

14. Defendant regularly mails, or causes to be mailed, collection letters bearing the name of the U.S. Department of Education to Louisiana residents in an effort to collect consumer debts.

15. Defendant seeks to recover a collection fee of "42.84%," which is neither "reasonable" nor "enforceable."

16. Defendant states in the collection letters "OUR STAFF AND CLIENT WILL DETERMINE THE APPROPRIATE COURSE OF LEGAL ACTION," suggesting that The Premier Collectors, Inc. will participate in directing the initiation of litigation by the U.S. Department of Justice against the consumer.

17. Defendant states in the collection letters that The Premier Collectors, Inc. will conduct an investigation of the plaintiff's income, savings, employment, real estate ownership and personal assets.

18. Defendant states in the collection letter that a suit by the U.S. Department of Justice may result in garnishment, attachment and/or judgment liens without notifying the consumer of the right to be heard and the necessity of entry of judgment prior to such action.

19. Defendant's collection letter implies that it is "vouched for, bonded by, or affiliated with the United States."

20. Defendant places the validation notice and debt collection warning on the back of the collection letters without reference thereto.

DAMAGES SUFFERED

21. As a result of Defendant's practices, Plaintiff and the class are entitled to statutory damages pursuant to the Fair Debt Collection Practices Act.

VIOLATIONS OF FDCPA

22. Defendant violated the FDCPA by mailing collection letter without proper validation notice or debt collection warning, in violation of 15 U.S.C. § 1692g(a)and e(11).

23. Defendant violated the FDCPA by seeking to collect fees of "42.84%," which are neither "reasonable" nor "enforceable," in violation of 15 U.S.C. § 1692e(2)(A) and f(1).

24. Defendant states in the collection letters "OUR STAFF AND CLIENT WILL DETERMINE THE APPROPRIATE COURSE OF LEGAL ACTION," suggesting that The Premier Collectors, Inc. direct the U.S. Department of Justice to file suit against the consumer in violation of 15 U.S.C. § 1692e and f.

25. Defendant states in the collection letters that The Premier Collectors, Inc. will conduct an investigation of the of the consumer's income, savings, employment, real estate ownership and personal assets, in violation of 15 U.S.C. § 1692e(4), (5) and (10).

26. Defendant states in the collection letter that a suit by the U.S. Department of Justice may result in garnishment, attachment and/or judgment liens without notifying the consumer of the right to be heard and the necessity of entry of judgment prior to such action in violation of 15 U.S.C. § 1692e(4), (5) and (10).

27. Defendant's violated 15 U.S.C. § 1692e(1) and (10) by implying that it is "vouched for, bonded by, or affiliated with the United States."

CLASS ALLEGATIONS

28. [*Plaintiff*] brings this action on behalf of a class of all other persons similarly situated. The class consists of all persons who satisfy the following criteria:

All Louisiana residents who received a notice from Defendant similar to *Exhibit A*, *Exhibit B*, or *Exhibit C*, regarding an alleged debt incurred for personal, family, or household purposes, subsequent to one year prior to the filing of the present litigation.

29. On information and belief, based on the fact that a large number of persons are so contacted by Defendant, the class is sufficiently numerous that joinder of all members is impractical.

30. There are questions of law and fact common to the class, which questions predominate over any questions peculiar to individual class members. The common questions include:

a. Whether Defendant is a "debt collector."
b. Whether Defendant's collection notice fails to provide a proper validation notice and debt collection warning.
c. Whether Defendant's collection notices seek to collect an amount which is not owed.
d. Whether Defendant's collection notices threaten action which is not intended to be taken or cannot legally be taken.
e. Whether Defendant's collection notices falsely represent or imply the seizure, garnishment, attachment or sale of the consumer's property which is not lawful or intended to be taken.
f. Whether Defendant's collection notices falsely represents or implies that it is vouched for, bonded by, or affiliated with the United states.

31. [*Plaintiff*] has the same claims as the members of the class. All of the claims are based on the same factual and legal theories.

32. [*Plaintiff*] will fairly and adequately represent the interest of the class members. [*Plaintiff*] has retained counsel experienced in prosecuting class actions and in consumer protection matters. There is no reason why [*Plaintiff*] and her counsel will not vigorously pursue this matter.

33. Certification of a class pursuant to Fed. R. Civ. P. 23(b)(3) is appropriate. A class action is the only appropriate means of resolving this controversy because the class members are not aware of their rights. In the absence of a class action, a failure of justice will result.

WHEREFORE, plaintiff [*Plaintiff*] requests that the Court grant the following relief in her favor and on behalf of the class and against Defendant:

A. The maximum amount of statutory damages provided under 15 U.S.C. § 1692k.
B. Attorney's fees, litigation expenses and costs.
C. Such other and further relief as is appropriate.

JURY DEMAND

Plaintiff [*Plaintiff*] demands trial by jury.

[*Attorney for Plaintiff*]

E.3.2 Motion for Class Certification

IN THE UNITED STATES DISTRICT COURT FOR
THE MIDDLE DISTRICT OF LOUISIANA

[PLAINTIFF], on behalf of)
herself and all others similarly)
situated,)
                Plaintiff,)
)
v.)
)
The Premier Collectors, Inc.,)
                Defendant.)

PLAINTIFF'S MOTION FOR CLASS CERTIFICATION

Plaintiff, [*Plaintiff*] ("[*Plaintiff*]"), respectfully requests that the Court enter an order certifying that this action be allowed to proceed as a class action pursuant to Fed. R. Civ. P. 23. The class is defined as all Louisiana residents who received a notice from defendant, The Premier Collectors, Inc. ("PCI"), similar to *Exhibit*

A, *Exhibit B*, or *Exhibit C* [*not reprinted herein*], regarding an alleged debt incurred for personal, family or household purposes, on or after August 2, 1993.

In support of this motion, [*Plaintiff*] states:

1. Plaintiff filed this class action under the Fair Debt Collection Practices Act, 15 U.S.C § 1692 *et seq.* ("FDCPA"). The complaint alleges that defendant PCI engaged in the following violations of the FDCPA:

   a. PCI sent printed form collection letters without the "validation notice" required by 15 U.S.C. § 1692g(a) or the debt collection warning required by 15 U.S.C. § 1692e(11).

   b. PCI added to the principal amount of the alleged debt collection fees of "42.84%," which are neither "reasonable" nor "enforceable," in violation of 15 U.S.C. §§ 1692e(2)(A) and 1692f(1).

   c. PCI states in its printed form collection letters "OUR STAFF AND CLIENT WILL DETERMINE THE APPROPRIATE COURSE OF LEGAL ACTION." This suggests to unsophisticated consumers that PCI would direct the Government to file suit against the consumer. The suggestion is unfounded, and therefore making it violates 15 U.S.C. §§ 1692e and 1692f.

   d. PCI states in its form collection letters that PCI will conduct an investigation of the consumer's income, savings, employment, real estate ownership and personal assets. This statement is not true, and making it violates 15 U.S.C. § 1692e(4), (5) and (10).

   e. PCI states in its form collection letters that nonpayment may result in garnishment, attachment and/or judgment liens. The consumer is not told that such action must be preceded by the right to be heard and the entry of judgment. By misrepresenting the imminence of garnishment, attachment and liens, PCI violates 15 U.S.C. § 1692e(4), (5) and (10).

   f. PCI violated 15 U.S.C. § 1692e(1) and (10) by implying that it is "vouched for, bonded by, or affiliated with the United States."

2. All requirements of Rule 23 of the Federal Rules of Civil Procedure have been met.

3. The class is so numerous that joinder of all members is impractical. PCI is one of the largest collection agencies in the United States, with $800 million in annual placements. *Collection Agency Directory* (First Detroit Corporation), 1994 ed., p. 15 (*Exhibit D*) [*not reprinted herein*]. Furthermore, student loans, which were the subject of the form letters at issue, are one of four collection specialties of PCI. *Id.* It is therefore reasonable to infer that the number of members of the proposed class exceeds the 20–40 required for certification.

4. There are questions of law and fact common to the class, which predominate over any questions affecting only individual class members. The principal questions presented by this action are:

   a. Whether PCI is a "debt collector."

   b. Whether PCI's form collection notices fail to provide a proper validation notice and debt collection warning.

   c. Whether PCI's form collection notices seek to collect an amount which is not owed.

   d. Whether PCI's form collection notices threaten action which is not intended to be taken or cannot legally be taken.

   e. Whether PCI's form collection notices falsely represent or imply the seizure, garnishment, attachment or sale of the consumer's property, when such action is not lawful or intended to be taken.

   f. Whether PCI's form collection notices falsely represent or imply that PCI is vouched for, bonded by, or affiliated with the United States.

5. There are no individual questions, other than whether a class member was subjected to one or more of the practices complained of, which can be determined by ministerial inspection of PCI's records.

6. [*Plaintiff*] will fairly and adequately protect the interests of the class. She is committed to vigorously litigating this matter.

7. Plaintiff's claim is typical of the claims of the class. All arise from the same operative facts and are based on the same legal theories.

8. A class action is a superior method for the fair and efficient adjudication of this controversy in that:

   a. Congress specifically contemplated FDCPA class actions as a principal means of enforcing the statute. 15 U.S.C. § 1692k.

   b. Most of the consumers who receive the notices undoubtedly believe that they are receiving a letter from the U.S. Department of Justice, and have no knowledge that their rights are being violated by illegal collection practices.

   c. The interest of class members in individually controlling the prosecution of separate claims against defendant is small because the maximum damages in an individual action are $1,000.

   d. Management of this class action is likely to present significantly fewer difficulties than those presented in many class claims, *e.g.*, for securities fraud.

These grounds are further explained and supported by the accompanying memorandum of law.

WHEREFORE, plaintiff requests that this action be certified as a class action.

[*Attorney for Plaintiff*]

E.3.3 Memorandum in Support of Class Certification

IN THE UNITED STATES DISTRICT COURT
FOR THE MIDDLE DISTRICT OF LOUISIANA

```
_____  )
                          )
[PLAINTIFF], on behalf of )
herself and all others similarly  )
situated,                 )
             Plaintiff,   )
                          )
v.                        )
                          )
The Premier Collectors, Inc.,  )
             Defendant.   )
_____  )
```

MEMORANDUM IN SUPPORT OF
PLAINTIFF'S MOTION FOR CLASS CERTIFICATION

I. NATURE OF THE CASE

Plaintiff filed this class action under the Fair Debt Collection

Practices Act, 15 U.S.C. § 1692 et seq. ("the FDCPA"). The complaint seeks redress for a number of illegal practices of defendants in connection with the collection of debts.

Specifically, the complaint alleges that The Premier Collectors, Inc. ("PCI") engages in the following practices through the use of printed form letters:

a. PCI sent printed form collection letters without the "validation notice" required by 15 U.S.C. § 1692g(a) or the debt collection warning required by 15 U.S.C. § 1692e(11).

b. PCI added to the principal amount of the alleged debt collection fees of "42.84%," which are neither "reasonable" nor "enforceable," in violation of 15 U.S.C. §§ 1692e(2)(A) and 1692f(1).

c. PCI states in its printed form collection letters "OUR STAFF AND CLIENT WILL DETERMINE THE APPROPRIATE COURSE OF LEGAL ACTION." This suggests to unsophisticated consumers that PCI would direct the Government to file suit against the consumer. The suggestion is unfounded, and therefore making it violates 15 U.S.C. §§ 1692e and 1692f.

d. PCI states in its form collection letters that PCI will conduct an investigation of the consumer's income, savings, employment, real estate ownership and personal assets. This statement is not true, and making it violates 15 U.S.C. § 1692e(4), (5) and (10).

e. PCI states in its form collection letters that nonpayment may result in garnishment, attachment and/or judgment liens. The consumer is not told that such action must be preceded by the right to be heard and the entry of judgment. By misrepresenting the imminence of garnishment, attachment and liens, PCI violates 15 U.S.C. § 1692e(4), (5) and (10).

f. PCI violated 15 U.S.C. § 1692e(1) and (10) by implying that it is "vouched for, bonded by, or affiliated with the United States."

II. THE FAIR DEBT COLLECTION PRACTICES ACT

The FDCPA states that its purpose, in part, is "to eliminate abusive debt collection practices by debt collectors," 15 U.S.C. § 1692(e). It is designed to protect consumers from unscrupulous collectors, whether or not there is a valid debt. *Baker v. G.C. Services Corp.*, 677 F.2d 775, 777 (9th Cir. 1982). The FDCPA broadly prohibits unfair or unconscionable collection methods; conduct which harasses, oppresses or abuses any debtor; and any false, deceptive or misleading statements, in connection with the collection of a debt. 15 U.S.C. §§ 1692d, 1692e, and 1692f.

Courts have generally held that whether a communication or other conduct violates the FDCPA is to be determined by analyzing it from the perspective of the "least sophisticated consumer" or "least sophisticated debtor." *Clomon v. Jackson*, 988 F.2d 1314, 1318–20 (2d Cir. 1993); *Graziano v. Harrison*, 950 F.2d 107, 111 (3d Cir. 1991); *Swanson v. Southern Oregon Credit Service, Inc.*, 869 F.2d 1222, 1225–26 (9th Cir. 1988); *Jeter v. Credit Bureau, Inc.*, 760 F.2d 1168 (11th Cir. 1985). "The basic purpose of the least-sophisticated-consumer standard is to ensure that the FDCPA protects all consumers, the gullible as well as the shrewd." *Clomon v. Jackson, supra* at 1318.

The violations alleged in this case include the following:

A. IMPROPER VALIDATION NOTICE

PCI's placement of the § 1692g validation notice and § 1692e(11) debt collection warning on the back of the collection letters without proper reference thereto on the front is in violation of 15 U.S.C. §§ 1692g(a) and 1692e(11). Among the decisions holding that similar conduct violates the FDCPA are *Rabideau v. Management Adjustment Bureau*, 805 F. Supp. 1086 (W.D.N.Y. 1992); *Riveria v. MAB Collections, Inc.*, 682 F. Supp. 174 (W.D.N.Y.1988); and *Ost v. Collection Bureau, Inc.*, 493 F. Supp. 701 (D.N.D. 1980).

B. DIRECTING THE COURSE OF LEGAL ACTION

PCI states in the collection letters "OUR STAFF AND CLIENT WILL DETERMINE The APPROPRIATE COURSE OF LEGAL ACTION," suggesting that PCI directs the filing of lawsuits against the consumer. In fact, the U.S. Department of Justice must decide to file suit against the consumer. The false statement that PCI has that authority violates 15 U.S.C. §§ 1692e and 1692f.

Misrepresenting the imminence of and authority to institute legal action against the consumer is a violation of the FDCPA. *Pipiles v. Credit Bureau of Lockport, Inc.*, 886 F.2d 22 (2d Cir. 1989).

C. INVESTIGATION OF THE CONSUMER'S ASSETS

PCI states in the collection letters that it will conduct an investigation of the consumer's income, savings, employment, real estate ownership and personal assets. It doesn't. The false statement is a violation of 15 U.S.C. § 1692e(4), (5) and (10). *Rosa v. Gaynor*, 784 F. Supp. 1, 5 (D. Conn. 1989); *Woolfolk v. Van Ru Credit Corp.*, 783 F. Supp. 724 (D. Conn. 1990); *Cacace v. Lucas*, 775 F. Supp. 502 (D. Conn. 1990).

D. PADDING DEBTS WITH "UNREASONABLE" CHARGES

PCI, in violation of 15 U.S.C. § 1692e(2)(A) and f(1), adds collection fees of "42.84%" to the principal amount of the debt. Such fees are neither "reasonable" nor "enforceable." *Jenkins v. Heintz*, 25 F.3d 536 (7th Cir. 1994); *Strange v. Wexler*, 796 F. Supp. 1117 (N.D. Ill. 1992).

E. GARNISHMENT WITHOUT NOTIFICATION OF RIGHTS

PCI states in its collection letters that a suit by the U.S. Department of Justice may result in garnishment, attachment and/or judgment liens, without notifying the consumer of the right to be heard and the necessity of entry of judgment prior to such action. This is a misrepresentation of the consequences of nonpayment, and violates 15 U.S.C. § 1692e(4), (5) and (10). *Woolfolk v. Van Ru Credit Corp., supra*; *Cacace v. Lucas, supra*; *Rosa v. Gaynor, supra*.

F. IMPLYING AFFILIATION WITH THE UNITED STATES

PCI also violated 15 U.S.C. § 1692e(1) and (10) by implying that it is "vouched for, bonded by or affiliated with the United States." *Gammon v. GC Services*, 27 F.3d 1254 (7th Cir. 1994).

III. STANDARD FOR CLASS CERTIFICATION

In determining whether a class will be certified, the merits of the case are not examined and the substantive allegations of the complaint should be taken as true, except to the extent that they are contradicted by evidence. *Blackie v. Barrack*, 524 F.2d 891, 901 n. 16 (9th Cir. 1975); *Heastie v. Community Bank of Greater Peoria*, 125 F.R.D. 669, 671 n. 2 (N.D. Ill. 1989); *Riordan v. Smith Barney*, 113 F.R.D. 60, 62 (N.D. Ill. 1986). The Seventh Circuit has said that "Rule 23 must be liberally interpreted" and read to "favor maintenance of class actions." *King v. Kansas City Southern Industries*, 519 F.2d 20, 25–26 (7th Cir. 1975).

Class actions are essential to enforce laws protecting consumers. As the Illinois Appellate Court stated in *Eshaghi v. Hanley Dawson Cadillac Co.*, 214 Ill. App. 3d 995, 574 N.E.2d 760 (1st Dist. 1991):

> Even without resort to the relaxed standards of proof envisioned by the Consumer Fraud Act, Illinois has been hospitable to maintenance of class actions and has been willing to recognize that common questions of law and fact predominate in a great many situations. . . . In a large and impersonal society, class actions are often the last barricade of consumer protection. . . . To consumerists, the consumer class action is an inviting procedural device to cope with frauds causing small damages to large groups. The slight loss to the individual, when aggregated in the coffers of the wrongdoer, results in gains which are both handsome and tempting. The alternatives to the class action—private suits or governmental actions—have been so often found wanting in controlling consumer frauds that not even the ardent critics of class actions seriously contend that they are truly effective. The consumer class action, when brought by those who have no other avenue of legal redress, provides restitution to the injured, and deterrence of the wrongdoer. (574 N.E.2d at 764, 766)

Congress expressly recognized the propriety of a class action under the FDCPA by providing special damage provisions and criteria in 15 U.S.C. §§ 1692k(a) and (b) for FDCPA class action cases. *Brewer v. Friedman*, 152 F.R.D. 142 (N.D. Ill. 1993); *Zanni v. Lippold*, 119 F.R.D. 32, 35 (C.D. Ill. 1988); *Beasley v. Blatt* 1994 U.S. Dist. LEXIS 9383 (N.D. Ill., July 14, 1994); *West v. Costen*, 558 F. Supp. 564, 572–573 (W.D. Va. 1983) (FDCPA class certified re unauthorized charges). Plaintiff's counsel also were involved in two FDCPA class actions that were settled. *Cramer v. First of America Bank Corp.*, 93 C 3189 (N.D. Ill.) (*Exhibit E*); *Boddie v. Meyer*, 93 C 2975 (N.D. Ill.) (*Exhibit F*).

IV. THE PROPOSED CLASS MEETS THE REQUIREMENTS FOR CERTIFICATION

A. RULE 23(A)(1)—NUMEROSITY

Fed. R. Civ. P. 23(a)(1) requires that the class be "so numerous that joinder of all members is impracticable." "When the class is large, numbers alone are dispositive. . . ." *Riordan v. Smith Barney*, 113 F.R.D. 60, 62 (N.D. Ill. 1986). Where the class numbers at least 40, joinder is usually impracticable. *Cypress v. Newport News General & Nonsectarian Hosp. Ass'n*, 375 F.2d 648, 653 (4th Cir. 1967) (18 sufficient); *Swanson v. American Consumer Industries*, 415 F.2d 1326, 1333 (7th Cir. 1969) (40 sufficient); *Riordan v. Smith Barney, supra*, 113 F.R.D. 60, 62 (N.D. Ill. 1986) (10–29 sufficient); *Blatt v. Beasley, supra* (25 sufficient in FDCPA case); *Sala v. National Railroad Passenger Corp.*, 120 F.R.D. 494, 497 (E.D. Pa. 1988) (40–50 sufficient); *Scholes v. Stone, McGuire & Benjamin*, 143 F.R.D. 181, 184 (N.D. Ill. 1992) (about 70). It is not necessary that the precise number of class members be known. *McCleery Tire Service, Inc. v. Texaco, Inc.*, 1975-2 Trade Cas. (CCH) ¶60,581 (E.D. Pa. 1975). "A class action may proceed upon estimates as to the size of the proposed class." *In re Alcoholic Beverages Litigation*, 95 F.R.D. 321 (E.D.N.Y. 1982); *Lewis v. Gross*, 663 F. Supp. 1164, 1169 (E.D.N.Y. 1986).

Here, it is reasonable to infer that the numerosity requirement is satisfied because the actions complained of were carried out by one of the largest collection agencies in the United States through the use of standard, preprinted form documents. This fact alone indicates that the numerosity requirement is satisfied. *Swiggett v. Watson*, 441 F. Supp. 254, 256 (D. Del. 1977) (in action challenging transfers of title pursuant to Delaware motor vehicle repairer's lien, fact that Department of Motor Vehicles issued printed form for such transfer in and of itself sufficient to show that numerosity was satisfied). Plaintiff has propounded discovery to determine the exact number of class members (*Exhibit G*).

B. RULE 23(A)(2)—COMMONALITY

Fed. R. Civ. P. 23(a)(2) requires that there be a common question of law *or* fact. Not all factual or legal questions raised in the litigation need be common so long as at least one issue is common to all class members. *Spencer v. Central States Pension Fund*, 778 F. Supp. 985, 989 n.2 (N.D. Ill. 1991). Where a question of law involves "standardized conduct of the defendants toward members of the proposed class, a common nucleus of operative facts is typically presented, and the commonality requirement . . . is usually met." *Franklin v. City of Chicago*, 102 F.R.D. 944, 949 (N.D. Ill. 1984); *Patrykus v. Gomilla*, 121 F.R.D. 357, 361 (N.D. Ill. 1988).

There are common questions of law and fact common to the class, which questions predominate over any questions affecting only individual class members. These questions include:

a. Whether PCI is a "debt collector."
b. Whether PCI's collection notice fails to provide a proper validation notice and debt collection warning.
c. Whether PCI's collection notices seek to collect an amount which is not owed.
d. Whether PCI's collection notices threaten action which is not intended to be taken or cannot legally be taken.
e. Whether PCI's collection notices falsely represent or imply the seizure, garnishment, attachment or sale of the consumer's property which is not lawful or intended to be taken.
f. Whether PCI's collection notices falsely represents or implies that it is vouched for, bonded by, or affiliated with the United States.

Each of these questions is concerned solely with the conduct of PCI. The only individual issue is the identification of the class members affected by each practice.

C. RULE 23(A)(3)—TYPICALITY

The rule requires that the claims of the named plaintiff be typical of the claims of the class:

> A plaintiff's claim is typical if it arises from the same event or practice or course of conduct that gives rise to the claims of other class members and his or her claims are based on the same legal theory. The typicality requirement may be satisfied even if there are factual distinctions between the claims of the named plaintiffs and those of other class members. Thus, similarity of legal theory may control even in the face of differences of fact.

De La Fuente v. Stokely-Van Camp, Inc., 713 F.2d 225, 232 (7th Cir. 1983) (citation omitted); *see also, Rosario v. Livaditis*, 963 F.2d 1013, 1018 (7th Cir. 1992).

In the instant case, typicality is inherent in both of the class definitions. By definition, each of the class members was subjected to the same violations as the named plaintiff. All class members' claims arise from the same practices of PCI's which gave rise to the named plaintiff's claims.

D. RULE 23(A)(4)—ADEQUACY OF REPRESENTATION

The rule also requires that the named plaintiff provide fair and adequate protection for the interests of the class. That protection involves two factors: "(a) the plaintiff's attorney must be qualified, experienced, and generally able to conduct the proposed litigation; and (b) the plaintiff must not have interests antagonistic to those of the class." *Rosario v. Livaditis*, 963 F.2d 1013, 1018 (7th Cir. 1992).

The qualifications of plaintiff's counsel are set forth in *Exhibits H and I*. Mr. Bragg is widely experienced in FDCPA litigation and class actions. He is the co-author of National Consumer Law Center, *Fair Debt Collection* [(6th ed. 2008 and Supp.)]. Mr. Ridge has litigated several FDCPA cases in Louisiana.

The second relevant consideration under Rule 23(a)(4) is whether the interests of the named plaintiff are coincident with the general interests of the class. Both [*Plaintiff*] and the class members seek money damages as the result of PCI's unlawful collection notice. Given the identity of claims between the plaintiff and the class members, there is no potential for conflicting interests in this action. There is no antagonism between the interests of the named plaintiff and those of the class.

E. RULE 23(B)(3)—COMMON QUESTIONS OF LAW OR FACT PREDOMINATE

Rule 23(b)(3) requires that the questions of law or fact common to all members of the class predominate over questions pertaining to individual members. This criterion is normally satisfied when there is an essential common factual link between all class members and the defendants for which the law provides a remedy. *Halverson v. Convenient Food Mart, Inc.*, 69 F.R.D. 331 (N.D. Ill. 1974).

In this case, the "common nucleus of operative fact," *Id.* at 335, is that all class members, by definition, were subjected to the same violations as plaintiff.

Cases dealing with the legality of standardized documents and practices, are generally appropriate for resolution by class action because the document is the focal point of the analysis. *Halverson v. Convenient Food Mart, Inc.*, supra; *Brooks v. Midas-International Corp.*, 47 Ill. App. 3d 266, 361 N.E.2d 815 (1st Dist. 1977) (claim that advertising conveyed meaning that exhaust systems would be replaced free of charge); *Spirek v. State Farm Mut. Auto. Ins. Co.*, 65 Ill. App. 3d 440, 382 N.E.2d 111 (1st Dist. 1978) (propriety of insurer's practice in requiring execution of subrogation agreements before paying medical benefits); *Haynes v. Logan Furniture Mart, Inc.*, 503 F.2d 1161 (7th Cir. 1974) (propriety of disclosure documents under Truth in Lending Act); *Haroco v. American Nat'l Bk. & Tr. Co.*, 121 F.R.D. 664, 669 (N.D. Ill. 1988) (improper computation of interest); *Kleiner v. First Nat'l Bank of Atlanta*, 97 F.R.D. 683 (N.D. Ga. 1983) (same); *Heastie v. Community Bank of Greater Peoria*, 125 F.R.D. 669 (N.D. Ill. 1989) (execution of home improvement financing documents in sequence that evaded consumers' rescission rights). This is true even though the nature and amount of damages may differ among the members of the class. *Heastie v. Community Bank of Greater Peoria*, supra.

An FDCPA claim challenging the propriety of a form letter is similar to a Truth in Lending disclosure claim, which has frequently been certified as a class actions. *Haynes v. Logan Furniture Mart, Inc.*, 503 F.2d 1161 (7th Cir. 1974); *Adiel v. Chase Fed. S. & L. Ass'n*, 810 F.2d 1051 (11th Cir. 1987); *Hughes v. Cardinal Fed. S. & L. Ass'n*, 566 F. Supp. 834 (S.D. Ohio 1983); *Fetta v. Sears, Roebuck & Co.*, 77 F.R.D. 411 (D.R.I. 1977); *Bantolina v. Aloha Motors, Inc.*, 419 F. Supp. 1116, 1122 (D. Haw. 1976); *Jones v. Goodyear Tire & Rubber Co.*, 442 F. Supp. 1157 (E.D. La. 1977); *Simon v. World Omni Leasing*, 146 F.R.D. 197 (S.D. Ala. 1992); *Johnson v. Steven Sims Suburu Leasing*, 1993 U.S. Dist. LEXIS 8078 (N.D. Ill., June 9, 1993) (Magistrate Judge's recommendation).

FDCPA actions have been certified as class actions on several occasions. *Zanni v. Lippold*, 119 F.R.D. 32, 35 (C.D. Ill. 1988); *Brewer v. Friedman*, 152 F.R.D. 142 (N.D. Ill. 1993); *Beasley v. Blatt*, 1994 U.S. Dist. LEXIS 9383 (N.D. Ill., July 14, 1994); *West v. Costen*, 558 F. Supp. 564, 572–73 (W.D. Va.1983).

Because of the standardized nature of the defendant's conduct, common questions predominate. The only individual issue is the identification of the consumers who received the letters, a matter capable of ministerial determination from PCI's records. This is not the kind of problem that is a barrier to class certification. *Heastie v. Community Bank of Greater Peoria*, 125 F.R.D. 669, 678 (N.D. Ill. 1989). The commonality requirement is therefore met.

F. RULE 23(B)(3)—CLASS ACTION IS SUPERIOR TO OTHER AVAILABLE METHODS TO RESOLVE THIS CONTROVERSY.

Efficiency is the primary focus in determining whether the class action is the superior method for resolving the controversy presented. *Eovaldi v. First Nat'l Bank*, 57 F.R.D. 545 (N.D. Ill. 1972). The Court is required to determine the best available method for resolving the controversy in keeping with judicial integrity, convenience, and economy. *Scholes*, supra, 143 F.R.D. at 189; *Hurwitz v. R.B. Jones Corp.*, 76 F.R.D. 149 (W.D. Mo. 1977). It is proper for a court, in deciding the "best" available method, to consider the " . . . inability of the poor or uninformed to enforce their rights, and the improbability that large numbers of class members would possess the initiative to litigate individually."

Haynes v. Logan Furniture Mart, Inc., supra, 503 F.2d 1161 (7th Cir. 1974).

In this case there is no better method available for the adjudication of the claims which might be brought by each individual debtor subjected to PCI's practice. The special efficacy of the consumer class action has been noted by the courts and is applicable to this case:

> A class action permits a large group of claimants to have their claims adjudicated in a single lawsuit. This is particularly important where, as here, a large number of small and medium sized claimants may be involved. In light of the awesome costs of discovery and trial, many of them would not be able to secure relief if class certification were denied....

In re Folding Carton Antitrust Litigation, 75 F.R.D. 727, 732 (N.D. Ill. 1977) (citations omitted). Class certification of a FDCPA damage action will provide an efficient and appropriate resolution of the controversy. *Zanni v. Lippold, supra,* 119 F.R.D. 32, 35–36 (C.D. Ill. 1988); *West v. Costen, supra,* 558 F. Supp. 564, 572–73 (W.D. Va. 1983); *Beasley v. Blatt, supra,* 1994 U.S. Dist. LEXIS 9383 (N.D. Ill., July 14, 1994); *Brewer v. Friedman,* 152 F.R.D. 142 (N.D. Ill. 1993); *Vaughn v. CSC Credit Services, Inc.,* 1994 U.S. Dist. LEXIS 2172 (N.D. Ill., March 1, 1994); *Duran v. Credit Bureau of Yuma, Inc.,* 93 F.R.D. 607 (D. Ariz. 1982); *Boddie v. Meyer, supra,* 93 C 2975 (N.D. Ill.); and *Cramer v. First of America Bank Corporation, supra,* 93 C 3189 (N.D. Ill.).

CONCLUSION

The proposed class meets the requirements of Rules 23(a) and (b)(3). Plaintiff respectfully requests that the Court certify this action as a class action.

[*Attorney for Plaintiff*]

E.3.4 Individual State and Federal Fair Debt Action Challenging Collection Agency's Improper Threats to Garnish SSI

NEW YORK SUPREME COURT
COUNTY OF NEW YORK

[CONSUMER],
    Plaintiff,

-against-

VAN RU CREDIT CORPORATION,
    Defendant

INDEX NO.
VERIFIED COMPLAINT

Plaintiff, by her attorneys at South Brooklyn Legal Services, as and for her Verified Complaint against the Defendant, alleges as follows:

PRELIMINARY STATEMENT

1. This is an action for statutory damages and declaratory and injunctive relief brought by an individual consumer for violations of the Fair Debt Collection Practices Act ("FDCPA"), 15 U.S.C. § 1692 *et seq.,* which prohibits debt collectors from engaging in abusive, deceptive, or unfair practices and the New York State General Business Law which prohibits deceptive acts or practices in the conduct of any business in New York State.

2. Plaintiff's only source of income is Supplemental Security Income (SSI), a need based disability payment which cannot be garnished or taken to satisfy any debt, including a student loan debt.

3. Defendant Van Ru Credit Corporation has three times misrepresented its ability to garnish plaintiff's Supplemental Security Income benefits in an attempt to coerce the plaintiff into using her SSI to pay her student loan debt.

4. In a letter to the plaintiff, Defendant Van Ru offered a "substantial reduction" in the plaintiff's debt if she completed a financial statement that established eligibility for such a reduction.

5. Yet on information and belief, defendant was never authorized to settle the debt for less than the full amount, and in practice, has never substantially reduced the amount owed to other student loan debtors upon review of their financial statements.

6. Rather, the offer is a ruse designed to obtain financial information, such as the location of bank accounts and the names of employers, which the defendant will use to collect the student loan debt.

JURISDICTION AND VENUE

7. This Court has jurisdiction pursuant to the Fair Debt Collection Practices Act (FDCPA), 15 U.S.C. § 1692k(d) and the New York Consumer Protection Law, N.Y. Gen. Bus. Law 349.

8. Venue in this court is proper pursuant to Civil Practice Law and Rules Section 503(c) because defendant, a foreign corporation, lists New York county as its residence in its certificate filed with the Secretary of State.

PARTIES

9. Plaintiff [*Consumer*] is 51 years old and resides at [*Address*].

10. Defendant Van Ru Credit Corporation, (Hereinafter "Van Ru") is a debt collection firm located at 1350 E. Touhy Avenue, Suite 300E, Des Plaines, Illinois 60018.

11. Defendant Van Ru is a foreign corporation licensed to do business in New York State and lists New York County as its residence with the New York State Secretary of State.

12. Defendant Van Ru is a firm engaged in the business of collecting debts. Defendant Van Ru collects such debts regularly and is a "debt collector" as defined by the FDCPA. 15 U.S.C. § 1692a(6). *See also* Woolfolk v. Van Ru Credit Corp. 783 F. Supp. 724 (D. Conn. 1990).

STATUTORY FRAMEWORK

THE FAIR DEBT COLLECTION PRACTICES ACT

13. Congress enacted the Fair Debt Collection Practices Act (FDCPA) to stop "the use of abusive, deceptive and unfair debt collection practices by many debt collectors." 15 U.S.C. § 1692(a).

14. The term "debt collector" does not include "any officer or employee of the United States . . . to the extent that collecting or attempting to collect any debt is in the performance of his official duties." 15 U.S.C. § 1692a(6)(C).

15. However, professional debt collectors with whom the United States contracts to collect its debts are debt collectors covered by the FDCPA.

16. A debt collector many not "use unfair or unconscionable means to collect or attempt to collect any debt." 15 U.S.C. § 1692f.

17. A debt collector is further prohibited from using of any "false, deceptive, or misleading . . . means in connection with the collection of any debt." 15 U.S.C. § 1692e.

18. Prohibited is "the representation or implication that non-payment of any debt will result in the . . . garnishment . . . of any property or wages of any person unless such action is lawful. . . ." 15 U.S.C. § 1692e(4).

19. Also prohibited is "the threat to take any action that cannot legally be taken. . . ." 15 U.S.C. § 1692e(5).

20. Nor may a debt collector "engage in any conduct the natural consequence of which is to harass, oppress, or abuse any person in connection with the collection of a debt." 15 U.S.C. § 1692d.

21. An individual may recover $1000 in statutory damages from a debt collector violating the above provisions. 15 U.S.C. § 1692k(a)(2)(A).

THE NEW YORK CONSUMER PROTECTION LAW

22. New York prohibits "deceptive acts or practices in the conduct of any business, trade or commerce or in the furnishing of any service in this state. . . ." N.Y. Gen. Bus. Law § 349 (a).

23. An individual "injured by reason of any violation of this section may bring an action in his own name to enjoin such unlawful act or practice, an action to recover his actual damages or fifty dollars, whichever is greater, or both such actions." N.Y. Gen. Bus. Law § 349(h).

24. A GBL § 349 damages award may be increased to an amount not to exceed three times the actual damages up to one thousand dollars ($1,000.00), if a court finds the defendant willfully or knowingly violated this section. N.Y. Gen. Bus. Law § 349 (h).

SUPPLEMENTAL SECURITY INCOME

25. The Social Security Administration ("SSA") administers the Supplemental Security Income ("SSI") program which pays monthly cash benefits to those who are disabled or elderly and who live in poverty. 42 U.S.C. § 1381a.

26. Poverty is defined as having less than $2000 in assets and little or no other income. 20 C.F.R. §§ 416.1110, 416.1205.

27. The overarching objective of the Supplemental Security Income system is "to assure a minimum level of income for people who are age 65 or over, or who are blind or disabled and who do not have sufficient income and resources to maintain a standard of living at the established Federal minimum income level." 20 CFR § 416.110.

28. Congress protects SSI payments from debt collection.

29. More specifically, 42 U.S.C. §§ 407(a) and 1383(d)(1) contain an anti-assignment provision ("the right of any person to any future payment under this subchapter shall not be transferable or assignable, at law or in equity . . .") and an anti-alienation provision ("none of the moneys paid or payable . . . under this title shall be subject to execution, levy, attachment, garnishment, or other legal process. . . .").

30. The broad language of § 407(a) reflects the overarching purpose of the Social Security Act, which is "the protection of its beneficiaries from some of the hardships of existence." *United States v. Silk*, 331 U.S. 704, 711 (1947).

31. In 1996, Congress carved-out an exception to 407(a) that enables the U.S. Department of Education to "off-set" up to 15% of a Social Security payment to collect on a defaulted student loan. 31 U.S.C. § 3716, 31 C.F.R. § 285.4(e)ii.

32. To ensure a Social Security recipient has enough income to meet his or her basic needs, the 15% "off-set" cannot reduces the Social Security payment below $750. 31 U.S.C. § 3716; 31 C.F.R. § 285.4(e)iii.

33. No off-set whatsoever can be made against SSI payments. 31 C.F.R. § 285.4.

FACTS RELATED TO THIS ACTION

34. Plaintiff [*Consumer*] is 51 years old and lives alone.

35. [*Consumer*]'s only monthly income is $761 in Supplemental Security Income (SSI) which she receives due to disability.

36. She also receives $149 in Food Stamps each month.

37. Around 1984, [*Consumer*] obtained a student loan to attend the Burk Trade school to learn clerical skills.

38. [*Consumer*] was unable to earn a degree from Burk because she failed too many classes.

39. Thereafter, [*Consumer*] went on public assistance and was unable to repay her student loan.

40. Sometime between 2000 and 2003, [*Consumer*] went on SSI.

41. On October 23, 2008, the defendant Van Ru Credit Corporation, (hereinafter "Van Ru") sent a letter to [*Consumer*] advising her that the U.S. Department of Education had referred account # 165116 to Van Ru for collection, and that she owed $5871.13.

42. The October 23, 2008 letter stated "[t]his communication is from a debt collector attempting to collect a debt. . . ."

VAN RU'S THREE THREATS TO GARNISH [CONSUMER]'S SUPPLEMENTAL SECURITY INCOME.

43. Sometime between October 23, 2008 and November 19, 2008, [*Consumer*] called Van Ru.

44. The Van Ru representative with whom she spoke told her she had to pay the loan even though her only income was from Supplemental Security Income.

45. Distressed, [*Consumer*] spoke with her social worker at CNR Health Care Network, [*Social Worker*].

46. On November 19, 2008, [*Social Worker*] called Van Ru and spoke with [*Supervisor*], who identified himself as a supervisor.

47. [*Social Worker*] informed [*Supervisor*] that [*Consumer*] receives home care services, that [*Consumer*]'s only monthly income was SSI benefits ($724 at the time), and that [*Consumer*]'s basic living expenses consumed the entire amount of her SSI benefits.

48. [*Supervisor*] told [*Social Worker*] that Van Ru could legally garnish [*Consumer*]'s SSI income and that both SSI and Social Security were garnishable.

49. [*Social Worker*] asked to speak with [*Supervisor*]'s super-

visor, and was told by [*Supervisor*] that he was the supervisor.

50. [*Supervisor*] told [*Social Worker*] that [*Consumer*] needed to pay $75 by December 1, 2008.

51. Furthermore, [*Supervisor*] said that due to the Thanksgiving holiday, [*Consumer*] actually needed to pay by Wednesday, November 26, 2008, the day before Thanksgiving.

52. [*Supervisor*] insisted that [*Consumer*] pay with an automatic deduction from a checking account or a credit card.

53. In the alternative, [*Supervisor*] suggested [*Consumer*] should go to a drug store, purchase a pre-paid debit/credit card, deposit money regularly onto the card, and give Van Ru the card information so Van Ru it could make automatic monthly deductions.

54. Thereafter, [*Social Worker*] called South Brooklyn Legal Services for advice and was informed that SSI benefits cannot be garnished for a debt of this type.

55. In early December 2008, Van Ru representative Josh Trevor called [*Consumer*] and told her she must pay $75 per month either through a credit card, a checking account or a prepaid credit card from the drug store which she would have to refill with money every month.

56. [*Supervisor*] told [*Consumer*] that Van Ru could still garnish her SSI money and the lawyer's advice was incorrect.

VAN RU'S DECEPTIVE AND MISLEADING LETTER

57. On November 24, 2008, Van Ru wrote [*Consumer*] and informed her that she had "ignored all previous notices requesting that you honor your obligation to the United States Department of Education."

58. The letter further stated that [*Consumer*] might be entitled to a "substantial reduction in [her] balance."

59. "To determine if you qualify for such a reduction," Van Ru asked [*Consumer*] to complete an attached "financial form."

60. The financial form asked for personal information such as her sources of income, her assets, the account numbers and balances of any savings and checking accounts, and the name, phone numbers and addresses of her and any spouse's employer.

61. [*Consumer*] did not complete or submit the financial form.

62. On information and belief, Van Ru had no authority to reduce the balance owed on the student loan.

63. On information and belief, Van Ru had no rules, policies or guidelines to determine if a person, after submitting a completed financial form, is entitled to a "substantial reduction" of his or her student loan debt.

64. On information and belief, Van Ru had never substantially reduced the balance owed on a student loan after reviewing a financial form completed by a student loan debtor.

65. On information and belief, Van Ru's November 24, 2008 offer to substantially reduce [*Consumer*] student loan balance was simply a guise to obtain financial information with which to collect the student loan debt.

CLAIMS FOR RELIEF

FIRST CLAIM FOR RELIEF—THE THREAT TO GARNISH SSI.

66. Plaintiff repeats and re-alleges and incorporates by reference preceding paragraphs 1–65.

67. 15 U.S.C. § 1692d provides that a "debt collector may not engage in any conduct the natural consequence of which is to harass, oppress, or abuse any person in connection with the collection of a debt."

68. 15 U.S.C. § 1692f provides that "[a] debt collector may not use unfair or unconscionable means to collect or attempt to collect any debt."

69. 15 U.S.C. § 1692e prohibits a debt collector from using of any "false, deceptive, or misleading . . . means in connection with the collection of any debt."

70. 15 U.S.C. § 1692e(4) prohibits "the representation or implication that nonpayment of any debt will result in the . . . garnishment . . . of any property or wages of any person unless such action is lawful. . . ."

71. Defendant violated §§ 1692d, 1692e, 1692e(4) and 1692f when it stated it would garnish [*Consumer*]'s SSI payments unless she entered into a monthly payment plan.

72. As a direct and proximate result of Defendant's violation, Plaintiff is entitled to statutory damages.

SECOND CLAIM FOR RELIEF—THE DECEPTIVE NOTICE.

73. Plaintiff repeats and re-alleges and incorporates by reference preceding paragraphs 1–65.

74. Defendant violated 15 U.S.C. § 1692e's prohibition against the use of any "false, deceptive, or misleading . . . means in connection with the collection of any debt" when it asked for financial information from [*Consumer*] purportedly to determine if she was eligible for a substantial reduction in the her account balance when the defendant lacked any intent or ability to reduce the amount owed, but instead sought the financial information to facilitate collection.

THIRD CLAIM FOR RELIEF—THE STATE DECEPTIVE PRACTICES CLAIM.

75. As enumerated above in paragraphs 66–74, the Defendant violated § 349 of the New York General Business Law by using deceptive acts and practices in the conduct of their business.

76. As a result of these violations of § 349 of the General Business Law, Plaintiff is entitled to an injunction barring Defendant from engaging in the deceptive acts and practices, and to recover fifty dollars in statutory damages.

PRAYER FOR RELIEF

WHEREFORE, plaintiff prays that the Court:

1. Assume jurisdiction of this action;

2. Declare that Defendant's actions violate 15 U.S.C. §§ 1692d, 1692e, 1692e(4) and 1692f and New York General Business Law § 349;

3. Enjoin Defendant from committing similar violations in the future;

4. Award statutory damages to the Plaintiff;

5. Award costs to the Plaintiff; and,

6. Award such other and further relief that seems just and proper.

Dated: June 12, 2009

_____

[*Attorneys for Plaintiff*]

VERIFICATION

STATE OF NEW YORK

COUNTY OF KINGS

[*Consumer*], being duly sworn, deposes and says:

1. I am the plaintiff in the above entitled proceeding.
2. I have read the contents of the foregoing complaint.
3. The factual information stated therein is true to my own knowledge except as to those matters therein stated to be alleged "upon information and belief," and as to those matters,

I believe the information to be true.

_____ [CONSUMER]

Sworn to before me this 12th day of June 2009

_____ NOTARY PUBLIC

E.4 Cases Challenging Trade School Abuses

Numerous individual and class pleadings raising claims of proprietary school abuses are available on the companion web site.

E.5 Raising School's Fraud in Bankruptcy Proceeding

E.5.1 Discussion Complaint Raising School's Fraud

UNITED STATES BANKRUPTCY COURT
EASTERN DISTRICT OF PENNSYLVANIA

```
_____ )
                         )
In re [CONSUMER],        )
                Debtor   )
[CONSUMER],              )
                Plaintiff)
                         )
v.                       )
                         )
PENNSYLVANIA HIGHER      )
EDUCATION ASSISTANCE     )
AGENCY, PHILADELPHIA     )
SAVINGS FUND SOCIETY     )
and LAMAR ALEXANDER,     )
Secretary, United States )
Department of Education, )
                Defendants)
Stephen Raslavich,       )
          Interim Trustee)
_____ )
```

DEBTOR'S COMPLAINT TO DETERMINE DISCHARGEABILITY OF STUDENT LOAN

PRELIMINARY STATEMENT

1. This is an adversary proceeding brought under the Bankruptcy Code, 11 U.S.C. § 523(a)(8), to determine the dischargeability of an educational loan made, insured or guaranteed by a governmental unit. The debtor also raises various claims under applicable nonbankruptcy law against the defendants.

JURISDICTION

2. Jurisdiction of the bankruptcy court in this matter is provided by 28 U.S.C. §§ 1334 and 157 and the Order of the United States District Court for this district dated July 25, 1984.

3. This is a core proceeding.

PARTIES

4. Plaintiff is an adult individual who resides at [*Address*]. She is the debtor in above-captioned chapter 7 case.

5. Defendant Pennsylvania Higher Education Assistance Agency ("PHEAA") is an instrumentality of the Commonwealth of Pennsylvania, doing business at [*Address*].

6. Defendant Philadelphia Savings Fund Society ("PSFS") is a Pennsylvania corporate financial institution whose local student loan operations are located at [*Address*].

7. Defendant Lamar Alexander is the Secretary of the Department of Education ("ED") and as such is the chief executive official of an agency of the United States (hereinafter "the Secretary.")

8. [*Trustee*] is the interim trustee in this bankruptcy case and is a nominal party to this action.

FACTUAL ALLEGATIONS

9. In November, 1988 plaintiff enrolled in a data entry course at a proprietary trade school in Philadelphia named Commercial Programming Unlimited. Plaintiff, who had never graduated high school, was at the time 55 years old. She was induced to enroll by sales representatives of the school who promised her a) that she would obtain job training and a GED diploma at the school, b) that upon graduation she would receive job placement assistance and c) that the entire cost of this service would be financed by federal financial aid programs.

10. The school arranged a financial aid package for plaintiff which totalled $6,225 for a nine-month course. Included in this package were approximately $5,500 in loans provided by PSFS, guaranteed by PHEAA and insured by ED under the Guaranteed Student Loan (GSL) and Supplemental Loan (SLS) programs established by Subchapter IV of the Higher Education Act, 20 U.S.C. § 1077 *et seq.*

11. Plaintiff attended classes at the school for approximately one month, at which time, due to dissatisfaction with the quality of the teaching, she transferred to another trade school in the next building, the Palmer Business School. As with the first school, Palmer representatives assured her of a GED, job training and placement and a financial aid package covering all costs. The second package, like the first, was arranged by the school through PSFS and was guaranteed and insured, respectively, by PHEAA and ED.

12. In the case of all the above-mentioned student loans, plaintiff did not obtain the loans by herself, nor did she have any direct dealings whatsoever with PSFS. On the contrary, PSFS had the schools, among other things, verify plaintiff's identity, complete all the forms ordinarily completed by the lender, explain the transaction to plaintiff, and obtain her signature on all documents relating to the loans.

13. Plaintiff graduated from Palmer in the summer of 1989. She did not receive a GED, and, on the contrary, learned that she had to contact the School District of Philadelphia in order to take the test and to receive whatever additional GED training she needed. At the one job interview Palmer arranged for plaintiff, she discovered that a GED was a requirement for the job. Soon after this interview Palmer went out of business.

14. Plaintiff's present indebtedness on her student loans is approximately $5,524.

CAUSES OF ACTION

COUNT I—UNDUE HARDSHIP

15. Plaintiff-debtor's present income consists of approximately $600/month earned from a small beauty shop she rents. This amount is not even adequate for her to afford the basic necessities of life.

16. She lacks the resources to repay the student loans and any payments she would make would be at a great hardship. Excepting the loans from discharge would impose an undue hardship on her.

17. The above-described student loan debts are dischargeable under 11 U.S.C. § 523(a)(8)(B).

COUNT II—BREACH OF CONTRACT

18. The purpose of the above-described loans, which the two schools arranged, was to finance the costs of a GED course, job training and job placement services purportedly provided by the school. Thus, plaintiff agreed to repay her indebtedness in consideration for the schools' agreement to provide her with the said services.

19. The schools never provided her the said services and, as a result, failed to perform in accordance with the above-described contract and breached said contract.

20. Plaintiff has been injured by this breach by the indebtedness involved in this case.

21. PSFS had an "origination relationship," *see* 34 C.F.R. § 682.200, with each of the two schools plaintiff attended. Therefore, PSFS, PHEAA and the Secretary are subject to plaintiff's claims and defenses.

COUNT III—FRAUD, MISREPRESENTATION AND/OR UNFAIR TRADE PRACTICES

22. Both of the trade schools induced plaintiff to enroll and to continue in these so-called academic programs through a number of misleading, deceptive or fraudulent representations, including but not limited to representations concerning the quality, value and usefulness of the offered training, concerning the qualifications needed to benefit from the training and to obtain employment, concerning the ability to earn a GED after successful completion of the course, concerning the nature and wage levels of possible employment, and concerning the success rate of students completing the training.

23. The debtor relied on these representations, enrolled in the schools and then maintained herself in good standing until graduation.

24. The defendants are subject to plaintiff's claims and defenses as a result of the "origination relationship" that existed between the schools and PSFS.

COUNT IV—VIOLATION OF HIGHER EDUCATION ACT

25. The underlying student loans are void and unenforceable in that, in addition to defrauding students as described above, the schools also violated numerous federal regulatory requirements, including but not limited to, enrolling plaintiff into the program when she did not have the "ability to benefit" from the training as defined by federal law and failing to maintain standards and procedures for determining whether any applicants for admission had such an "ability to benefit."

WHEREFORE, plaintiff-debtor requests the this Court:
1. Assume jurisdiction of this case;
2. Declare the subject student loans dischargeable under 11 U.S.C. § 523(a)(8);
3. Declare the loan void;
4. Award the debtor damages;
5. Award the debtor's counsel reasonable attorney's fees and
6. Grant the debtor any other appropriate relief.

[*Attorney for Plaintiff*]

E.5.2 Complaint to Determine Dischargeability of Student Loan

Form 123 Complaint to Determine Dischargeability of Student Loan[1]

UNITED STATES BANKRUPTCY COURT
_____ District of _____

In re _____,)
Debtor)
) Case No. _____
_____,)
) Chapter _____
Plaintiff)
) Adv. Proc. No. _____
_____)
Defendant)
_____)

---

[1] Both debtors and creditors may seek determinations with respect to the dischargeability of debts, either during or after the bankruptcy (however, there are deadlines for certain creditor complaints. See Fed. R. Bankr. P. 4007(c); 11 U.S.C. § 523(c)). Such determinations must be sought by way of adversary proceedings. Fed. R. Bankr. P. 7001. For a discussion of complaints in adversary proceedings, see National Consumer Law Center, Consumer Bankruptcy Law and Practice Appx. G.10 (9th ed. 2009 and Supp.) (see notes to Form 100).

Debtors may want such determinations to settle an issue likely to be disputed later, or to obtain an explicit court order enjoining a creditor with whom difficulties are anticipated.

COMPLAINT TO DETERMINE DISCHARGEABILITY OF STUDENT LOAN

1. The Debtor filed this case under chapter 7 of the Bankruptcy Code on [Date]. This Court thus has jurisdiction over this action under 28 U.S.C. § 1334. This proceeding is a core proceeding.

2. One of the unsecured debts owing by the Debtor and listed in Schedule F is a student loan owing to Defendant [Creditor].

3. The Defendant [Director] is the executive director of the [Creditor] and is responsible for the overall operation of the guaranteed student loan program.[2]

4. This loan was incurred to pay expenses at [School].

5. Subsequent to beginning coursework at that school, the Debtor learned that the school had lost its accreditation and that none of its recent graduates had obtained the employment for which they were trained due to that loss.

6. The Debtor was unable to transfer to any other educational program, and was also refused any refund of the tuition paid by the student loan.

7. Since that time, the Debtor has been unemployed, and the sole source of income for herself and her two children has been public assistance in the amount of $[Amount], which barely suffices for the necessities of life.

8. The Debtor has no current or anticipated available income or resources with which to pay the aforementioned loan and any payments on that loan could be made only at great hardship to the Debtor and her children.

WHEREFORE, the Debtor prays that this Court enter an Order declaring the student loan debt of the Debtor to be dischargeable in this bankruptcy case.

Date: _____ [signature]
Attorney for Debtor

---

[2] If the student loan creditor is a governmental entity that may claim Eleventh Amendment immunity, it had previously been desirable to sue named individual officials rather than the entity itself. See Ex Parte Young, 209 U.S. 123, 28 S. Ct. 441, 52 L. Ed. 714 (1908). This procedure is no longer necessary as the Supreme Court's decision in Tennessee Student Assistance Corp. v. Hood, 541 U.S. 440, 124 S. Ct. 1905, 158 L. Ed. 2d 764 (2004), now clearly establishes that the debtor may sue the state directly when seeking a dischargeability determination. See National Consumer Law Center, Consumer Bankruptcy Law and Practice § 13.3.2.2 (9th ed. 2009 and Supp.). However, naming the head of the relevant agency may still be useful for other purposes.

E.6 Private Student Loan Cases

E.6.1 Class Action Complaint Against Private Student Loan Servicer, Lender, and Bank

IN THE UNITED STATES DISTRICT COURT
FOR THE EASTERN DISTRICT OF VIRGINIA
RICHMOND DIVISION

[CONSUMER 1] and)
[CONSUMER 2],)
[CONSUMER 3],)
[CONSUMER 4] and)
[CONSUMER 5],)
               Plaintiffs,)
)
v.   ) Civil Action No.
)
SLM FINANCIAL)
CORPORATION, SALLIE)
MAE, INC., and STERLING)
BANK,)
             Defendants.)

COMPLAINT AND DEMAND FOR JURY TRIAL

INTRODUCTION

1. Plaintiffs bring this action for damages to redress the many violations of law made by a loan broker and a bank regarding an educational loan. Plaintiffs obtained an educational loan arranged by a school but the students were not able to complete their courses because the school closed. The school was never licensed to operate as a school and the loan disclosures were not accurate. Even though the terms of the loans require the Defendants to honor all claims and defenses that Plaintiffs have against the school, the Defendants have not cancelled the loan. This Complaint is filed and these proceedings are instituted under the Truth in Lending Act ("the Act"), 15 U.S.C. § 1601, for statutory, actual, and punitive damages, reasonable attorney fees and costs to redress Defendants' violation of this federal consumer protection statute, their violations of the Virginia Consumer Protection Act and the Virginia Credit Service Businesses Act, and their common law conspiracy.

PARTIES

2. The Plaintiffs [Consumer 1] and [Consumer 2] are natural persons and residents of Midlothian, Virginia.

3. The Plaintiff, [Consumer 3] is a natural person and resident of Chester, Virginia.

4. The Plaintiff [Consumer 4] and [Consumer 5] are natural persons. [Consumer 4] is a resident of Maryland and [Consumer 5] is a resident of New Jersey; they obtained the loan for classes in Virginia.

5. Defendant, SLM Financial Corporation (SLM), is a Virginia

corporation and has, as its registered agent, Commonwealth Legal Services Corporation, at [*Address*].

6. Defendant, Sallie Mae, Inc., (Sallie Mae) is a Delaware corporation doing business in Virginia and has, as its registered agent, Commonwealth Legal Services Corporation, at [*Address*].

7. Defendant Sterling Bank is a New Jersey Bank conducting business in Virginia.

8. At all times relevant hereto, in the ordinary course of its business, Sterling Bank regularly extended or offered to extend consumer credit for which a finance charge is or may be imposed or which, by written agreement, is payable in more than four installments, making Defendant a creditor within the meaning of the Act, 15 U.S.C. § 1602(f) and Regulation Z, 12 C.F.R. § 226.2(a)(17).

JURISDICTION

9. This Court has jurisdiction over this action pursuant to 15 U.S.C. § 1640(e) and 28 U.S.C. § 1331 and has supplemental jurisdiction of the state law claims regarding the same transaction and events under 28 U.S.C § 1367(a).

FACTS

[CONSUMERS 1 AND 2] TRANSACTION

10. In September 2001, Plaintiff [*Consumer 1*] wanted to take classes with Solid Computer Decisions, Inc. (Solid Computer).

11. Solid Computer acted as a representative of SLM to obtain an extension of credit to pay for those classes.

12. Solid Computer was not licensed or certified to conduct business as a proprietary school in Virginia as required by Va. Code § 22.1-331 and 332.

13. In addition to providing assistance regarding obtaining an extension of credit, Solid Computer guaranteed employment to [*Consumer 1*] on the condition that he complete the educational program; this promise violated 8VAC20-350-310 of the Virginia Administrative Code.

14. SLM and Solid Computer and Sterling Bank had agreed that Solid Computer would solicit business for SLM and Sterling Bank.

15. As part of that agreement, Solid Computer interacted with consumers on behalf of SLM, including presenting and explaining documents.

16. As part of their agreement, SLM arranged for Sterling Bank to act as the lender for these extensions of credit and SLM would act as servicer.

17. On September 24, 2001, [*Consumer 1*] and [*Consumer 2*] agreed to accept credit from Sterling Bank to pay for tuition at Solid Computer.

18. Solid Computer presented [*Consumer 1*] with loan documents that these Plaintiffs signed.

19. On behalf of Sterling Bank, SLM and Solid Computer presented these Plaintiffs with Truth in Lending disclosures for the credit. (A true and accurate copy is attached as Exhibit A [*not reproduced herein*]).

THE [CONSUMER 3] TRANSACTION

20. On or about January 10, 2002, [*Consumer 3*] was contacted by a representative of Solid Computer.

21. [*Consumer 3*] was informed about employment opportunities at Solid Computer and agreed to come to interview.

22. On January 14, 2002, [*Consumer 3*] interviewed at Solid Computer in Glen Allen, Virginia, and was informed that once he completed the training program he was guaranteed employment.

23. [*Consumer 3*] stated that he only wanted to take certain classes rather than the full training component.

24. The Solid Computer representative, [*Employee 1*], informed him that, because of the arrangement between SLM and Solid Computer, he would be required to take additional classes to meet SLM's funding requirements.

25. On behalf of SLM and Solid Computer, [*Employee 1*] represented that SLM was the lender and that SLM required that he take $11,000.00 of classes.

26. The allegations of Paragraphs 11 through 16 apply equally to [*Consumer 3*]'s transaction as to [*Consumer 1*].

27. To obtain a loan to cover the courses, [*Consumer 3*] agreed to take $11,000.00 of classes from Solid Computer and filled out an application to obtain the student loan.

28. On January 22, 2002, [*Consumer 3*] agreed to accept credit from Sterling Bank to pay for tuition at Solid Computer.

29. Solid Computer presented [*Consumer 3*] with loan documents that he signed.

30. On behalf of Sterling Bank, SLM and Solid Computer presented [*Consumer 3*] with Truth in Lending disclosures for the credit. (A true and accurate copy is attached as Exhibit B [*not reproduced herein*]).

THE [CONSUMER 4] TRANSACTION

31. Like [*Consumer 1*] and [*Consumer 3*], [*Consumer 4*] signed up for a loan to cover courses at Solid Computer Decisions.

32. [*Consumer 4*] was induced to agree to pay the tuition because of the guarantee of employment that was provided by Solid Computer.

33. The allegations of Paragraphs 11 through 16 apply equally to [*Consumer 4*]'s transaction as to [*Consumer 1*].

34. On October 29, 2001, [*Consumer 4*] agreed to accept credit from Sterling Bank to pay for tuition at Solid Computer.

35. Solid Computer presented him with loan documents that he signed.

36. On behalf of Sterling Bank, SLM and Solid Computer presented [*Consumer 4*] with Truth in Lending disclosures for the credit. (A true and accurate copy is attached as Exhibit C [*not reproduced herein*]).

THE PLAINTIFFS RECEIVE NO BENEFIT FOR THE LOANS THEY SIGNED

37. In each transaction, SLM acted as a credit services business, and was required to comply with Virginia's Credit Services Business Act, Va. Code § 59.1-335.1 *et seq.*

38. In each transaction, Solid Computer acted as a credit services business, and was required to comply with Virginia's Credit Services Business Act, Va. Code § 59.1-335.1 *et seq.*

39. Because Solid Computer was not licensed or certified to operate in Virginia, the contracts it created with any students are void and unenforceable under the common law of Virginia and unenforceable under Va. Code § 22.1-335.

40. Neither Solid Computer nor SLM complied with the requirements of Virginia's Credit Services Business Act.

41. Because of the violations of Virginia's Credit Services Business Act, any contract with Solid Computer or with SLM is unenforceable.

42. As part of Sallie Mae, SLM had been previously informed by the Proprietary Schools Unit of the Virginia Department of Education not to create loans for students of unlicensed or uncertified schools.

43. SLM was specifically informed by the Proprietary Schools Unit of the Virginia Department of Education not to create loans for students of Solid Computer because it was not certified to operate.

44. Even after being specifically informed by the Proprietary Schools Unit of the Virginia Department of Education not to create loans for students of Solid Computer, SLM continued to create loans through its arrangement with Sterling Bank and Solid Computer.

45. Solid Computer never obtained any license or certification to operate in Virginia and simply closed down after signing up hundreds of students.

46. The actions of Defendants towards Plaintiffs were not an isolated instance because Solid Computer signed up approximately 160 students in Northern Virginia and 85 in Richmond.

47. Plaintiffs are informed and believe that Sallie Mae purchased the Plaintiffs' loan contracts from Sterling and that SLM Financial and Sallie Mae currently seek repayment of each loan.

48. Sallie Mae, SLM, and Sterling refuse to abide by the terms of the loan contracts that allow each student to raise against a demand for payment all of their claims and defenses against Solid Computer. (A true and accurate copy of [*Consumer 3*]'s Promissory Note is attached as Exhibit D, and each of the Plaintiffs' Notes are the similar form; the pertinent paragraph is in all capitals on the third page [*not reproduced herein*]).

49. Sallie Mae, SLM, and Sterling never intended to abide by the terms of the loan contracts that allow each student to raise against a demand for payment all of their claims and defenses against Solid Computer.

50. As part of the intent to not honor all the claims and defenses, SLM and Sterling Bank placed a term in the Plaintiffs' notes that seeks to waive each Plaintiffs' right to assert these claims and defenses. (See Exhibit D, Paragraph 10 near the top of the third page).

51. Sallie Mae and SLM continue to use that term to contradict consumers' rights to assert against such loan contracts their claims and defenses against Solid Computer Decisions. (See letter from SLM dated August 7, 2002, Exhibit E [*not reproduced herein*]).

52. Plaintiffs were harmed by the Defendants' conduct and each have been saddled with a loan in excess of $11,000.00, for which no benefit was received.

53. The Defendants' actions were in intentional or reckless disregard of Plaintiffs' rights sufficient to justify an award of punitive damages.

54. Each and every term in each loan contract, including any limitation and waiver, is unenforceable and void against the Plaintiffs.

55. The Promissory Note signed by each of the Plaintiffs is not actually an agreement to extend credit but is more in the nature of an application for credit. (See Paragraph 1 of Section XII on the second page.)

56. Pursuant to the terms of the Notes, the Amount Financed shown on Exhibit A, B, and C, is merely an estimate of the amount of the credit that may be provided at some time in the future.

57. For each transaction, the disclosure of the Annual Percentage Rate, the Amount Financed, the Finance Charge, the Total of Payments, and the Schedule of Payments are not accurate.

CLASS ACTION ALLEGATIONS

58. Plaintiffs bring this action on behalf of themselves and on behalf of a class of similarly situated persons pursuant to F.R. Civ. P. 23. The Class is defined as follows:

> Persons who obtained a loan arranged by SLM Financial to pay for courses at Solid Computer Decisions in Virginia where Sterling was identified as the lender.

59. Members of the class are so numerous that joinder of them is impractical.

60. There are numerous questions of law and fact common to the Class. Such common questions include, but are not limited to:

(a) The acts and practices of the defendants in the scheme described in the paragraphs above;

(b) The violation of the Federal Truth in Lending Act by the defendants in a uniform fraudulent and illegal scheme;

(c) The violation of state statutory and common law provisions by the defendants in a uniform fraudulent and illegal scheme; and

(d) Whether exemplary damages should be awarded and the amount of such damages which should be awarded.

61. Plaintiffs are members of the Class, and their claims are typical of other class members' claims in that, like the other class members, the named plaintiffs obtained a loan arranged by SLM with Sterling as the lender for courses at Solid Computer; that Solid Computer was never licensed to offer classes in Virginia; that Sallie Mae and SLM knew that SLM was not licensed; that each loan will contain similar Truth In Lending Act violations; that each loan is unenforceable; and that Sallie Mae and SLM continue to want repayment of each loan.

62. Plaintiffs are adequate representatives of the Class's interests in that they will vigorously pursue this action on behalf of the entire Class, have no conflicts with the Class, and retained experienced counsel to represent them.

63. Questions of law and fact common to the Class, including the legal and factual issues relating to operation of the scheme described herein by the defendants, and the liability and the nature of the relationships among the defendants, predominate over any questions affecting only individual members.

64. A class action is superior to other available methods for the fair and efficient adjudication of this controversy; the Class is readily definable and can easily be identified by examination of the defendants' records; prosecution of this case as a class action will eliminate the possibility of repetitious litigation and duplicative punitive damage awards against the defendants and will provide redress for claims for individuals who otherwise might not be able to retain counsel to pursue their claims; there are no problems which would make this case difficult to manage as a class action.

CLAIMS FOR RELIEF

FIRST CAUSE OF ACTION

Violations of the Truth in Lending Act

65. In each transaction and for each member of the class, Sterling Bank violated the Truth in Lending Act and Regulation Z by failing to deliver accurate disclosures as required by the Truth in Lending Act and Regulation Z, including the following:
   a. by failing to disclose accurately the "finance charge" in violation of 15 U.S.C. § 1638(a)(3), and Regulation Z, 12 C.F.R. § 226.18(d) and 226.4;
   b. by failing to disclose accurately the "amount financed" in violation of 15 U.S.C. § 1638(a)(2) and Regulation Z, 12 C.F.R. § 226.18(b); and
   c. by failing to disclose accurately the "annual percentage" in violation of 15 U.S.C. § 1638(a)(4) and Regulation Z, 12 C.F.R. § 226.18(e).

66. The violations of this Act are apparent on the loan documents assigned to Sallie Mae and on the face of each loan document for the class such that Sallie Mae, and any other assignee, is liable for the Truth in Lending Act violation.

SECOND CAUSE OF ACTION

Violations of the Virginia Consumer Protection Act

67. Each transaction and each transaction in the class was a consumer transaction for the purchase of goods or services, and SLM was a supplier as defined by the Virginia Consumer Protection Act ("the VCPA") Va. Code § 59.1-196, *et. seq.*, at § 59.1-198.

68. In each transaction and in each transaction in the class, SLM violated the prohibitions contained in § 59.1-200(A)(8) against refusing to provide goods on the terms offered and in § 59.1-200(A)(14) against using any other deception, fraud, false pretense, false promise, or misrepresentation in connection with a consumer transaction.

69. In each transaction and in each transaction in the class, SLM's violations of the Credit Services Business Act were also violations of the VCPA.

70. Plaintiffs and each member of the class suffered a loss as a result of the Defendant's violations.

71. Plaintiffs and each member of the class are entitled to recover three times their actual damages, or at minimum $1,000.00, pursuant to Va. Code § 59.1-204, because Defendant's violations were willful.

THIRD CAUSE OF ACTION

Violations of the Virginia Credit Services Business Act

72. In each transaction and in each transaction in the class, SLM engaged in the activities of a "credit services business" under Va. Code § 59.1-335.2, and Plaintiffs were consumers protected by the Virginia Credit Services Business Act.

73. In each transaction and in each transaction in the class, SLM willfully failed to comply with the requirements of the Virginia Credit Services Business Act.

74. Plaintiffs and each member of the class sustained actual damages as a result of those violations.

75. In the alternative of willful failures to comply, SLM was negligent in failing to comply with this Act.

FOURTH CAUSE OF ACTION

Conspiracy

76. SLM and Sterling and Solid Computer conspired together to accomplish the legal objective of financing education through illegal means.

77. SLM and Sterling and Solid Computer conspired together to accomplish the illegal objectives of funding an unlicensed school and of avoiding the requirements of the state and federal laws regulating the transaction.

78. Sallie Mae joined the conspiracy by purchasing the Plaintiffs' loan and by seeking to enforce them with knowledge that each was unenforceable.

79. Plaintiffs and each member of the class were harmed by the Defendants' actions.

WHEREFORE, Plaintiffs respectfully pray that this Court:

1. Assume jurisdiction of this case;
2. Award statutory damages to each set Plaintiffs and each member of the class against Sterling Bank and Sallie Mae of twice the actual finance charge, pursuant to 15 U.S.C. § 1640(a)(2)(A)(i) for the extension of credit;
3. Award to Plaintiffs and each member of the class against SLM three times actual damages, or $1,000.00, whichever is greater, for each of the willful violations of the Virginia Consumer Protection Act pursuant to Va. Code § 59.1-204;
4. Award Plaintiffs and each member of the class one award of actual damages pursuant to their actual damages claims under the Truth in Lending Act, Virginia Consumer Protection Act, Virginia Credit Services Business Act, and conspiracy claims;
5. Assess punitive damages against each Defendant under the conspiracy claim and against SLM under the Credit Services Business Act claim;
6. Declare that the Plaintiffs' loan agreements and each member of the class's loan agreements with Sterling Bank are unenforceable, and require Defendants to remove any negative credit references regarding this transaction from all credit reports;
7. Award Plaintiffs their costs, expenses, and reasonable attorney fees pursuant to the Truth in Lending Act, at 15 U.S.C. § 1640(a)(3), and the Virginia Consumer Protection Act, at Va. Code § 59.1-204; and
8. Award Plaintiffs such other relief as the court deems appropriate.

TRIAL BY JURY IS DEMANDED

Respectfully submitted,

[*Consumer 1*]
[*Consumer 2*]
[*Consumer 3*]
[*Consumer 4*]
[*Consumer 5*]
By Counsel

E.6.2 Private Student Loan Borrower's Complaint Against Proprietary School and Lender

[*Attorneys for Plaintiff*]
[*Address and Phone Number*]

THIS IS AN ARBITRATION MATTER. ASSESSMENT OF DAMAGES IS REQUIRED.

```
_____  )
[CONSUMER]                     )
[ADDRESS]                      )
                    Plaintiff  )
                               )
v.                             )
                               )
CAREER VISION OF               )
PENNSYLVANIA, INC.             )
[Defendant's Address]          )
                               )
KEY BANK USA, NA               )
[ADDRESS]                      )
                   Defendants  )
_____  )
```

COMPLAINT—CIVIL ACTION

I. INTRODUCTION

1. Plaintiff brings this suit against a for-profit trade school and the bank providing financing for its students, seeking declaratory and equitable relief and damages for Defendants' illegal, unfair, and deceptive business practices. Defendant Career Vision canceled the computer networking course in which plaintiff enrolled several months before completion, and refused to refund his tuition, while Defendant Key Bank refused to acknowledge is liability or responsibility for the actions of its business partner.

II. PARTIES

2. Plaintiff [*Consumer*] resides at [*Address*].

3. Defendant, Career Vision of Pennsylvania, Inc., d/b/a Career Vision, is a Pennsylvania corporation with a place of business at 1617 John F. Kennedy Boulevard, Philadelphia, Pennsylvania, 19103, and a place of business at 120 Wood Avenue, Suite 509, Iselin New Jersey, 08830.

4. Defendant Key Bank, USA, NA is a corporation and federally-chartered bank with its principal place of business at m127 Public Square, Cleveland Ohio, 44114.

III. FACTS

5. Defendant Career Vision owns and operates a for-profit trade school licensed by the Pennsylvania Board of Private Licensed Schools, offering courses in computer technology.

6. In May or June of 2003 [*Consumer*] saw a newspaper advertisement placed by Career Vision offering classes in computer networking, with financial aid available for qualified students.

7. [*Consumer*] visited the school in response to the advertisement, and was greeted by a female sales and admissions representative employed by Career Vision.

8. The Career Vision representative told [*Consumer*] that he could enroll in a nine month computer networking course that would qualify him for jobs earning as much as $70,000 per year.

9. The Career Vision representative also assured [*Consumer*] of the high quality of the networking course, mentioning among other things that the school was licensed by the Pennsylvania Education Department, and accredited.

10. The representations regarding the quality of the training and the salary of its graduates were false and misleading.

11. Relying on these representations [*Consumer*] signed a written enrollment agreement for a nine month Networking course for a tuition of $12,000, and paid a $100 registration fee. A copy of the agreement is attached as Exhibit "A".

12. Career Vision's employees presented [*Consumer*] with various documents to sign in order to apply for financial aid. Although represented to him as financial aid documents, the forms were in reality nothing more than an application and promissory Note to borrow $12,000 plus a $600 loan fee from Defendant Key Bank. [*Consumer*] was also required to obtain a cosigner. A copy of the Note is attached as Exhibit "B".

13. Career Vision and Key Bank had a close business relationship according to which Career Vision employees assisted its customers in applying for Key Bank loans and Key Bank directed the loan proceeds to Career Vision in payment of tuition and fees. In particular and without limitation, Career Vision employees regularly and systematically provided loan application forms from Key Bank to [*Consumer*] and its other students, forwarded the applications to Key Bank, assisted students in completing any additional steps to obtain the loans, and arranged for the loan proceeds to be paid directly from Key Bank to Career Vision.

14. The loan provided by Key Bank to fund the training course was *not* guaranteed or insured by any federal or state government program. As a result, [*Consumer*] would not be eligible for deferments, forbearance, loan discharges, consolidation and other programs commonly available to student loan borrowers with government-backed student loans. This aspect of the loan was not disclosed or explained to [*Consumer*].

15. The courses provided to [*Consumer*] were all taught by a single instructor. After about three months, the instructor began arriving late to class, leaving early, and teaching only one to two hours of a scheduled three hour class.

16. By early November the instructor ceased all instruction. Career Vision employees told [*Consumer*] and the other students that they would be notified when they could return to continue their studies. [*Consumer*] was never contacted after that point and was never offered satisfactory arrangements to complete his course.

17. The Career Vision course did not provide [*Consumer*] with any transferable credits usable by him at any other training or educational institution.

18. [*Consumer*] received no benefit from the aborted and partial training course provided by Career Vision.

19. [*Consumer*] filed a complaint with the Pennsylvania Board of Private Licensed Schools, which eventually found Career Vision in violation of its regulations for failure to make tuition refunds.

20. Career Vision never refunded [*Consumer*] any of his tuition or fees.

21. [*Consumer*] notified Key Bank of the failure of Career

Vision to perform its contractual obligations. Nevertheless, Key Bank has continued to insist that he repay the loan used to fund his aborted training course.

22. [*Consumer*] has made payments to Key Bank of $117.08 monthly for principal and interest from June 2003 to the present. Key Bank continues to assert that he remains liable for the remaining balance of the $12,600 loan.

COUNT I: VIOLATION OF PENNSYLVANIA UNFAIR TRADE PRACTICES AND CONSUMER PROTECTION LAW (CPL)73 P.S. § 201-1 ET. SEQ.

23. Plaintiff realleges and incorporate by reference all preceding allegations of law and fact.

24. Plaintiff obtained the student loans at issue primarily for personal, family or household purposes.

25. Career Vision represented to [*Consumer*] that its services had benefits and characteristics that they did not have, including the quality of the instruction and the potential salary of graduates.

26. Career Vision failed to disclose to [*Consumer*] the drawbacks and lack of benefits that resulted from obtaining a private student loan not guaranteed or provided by any government agency. This information would have been highly material to him.

27. Career Vision's failure to provide the services promised, and its continuing representations that it was not required to refund [*Consumer*]'s tuition despite its complete failure to provide him the training course, was unfair and deceptive conduct within the meaning of the CPL.

28. The representation by Key Bank that Career Vision's failure to deliver the training services promised does not affect [*Consumer*]'s liability on the loan was unfair and deceptive within the meaning of the CPL.

29. The loan from Key Bank to Plaintiff was a "purchase money loan" within the meaning of the Federal Trade Commission's regulation on preservation of claims and defenses, 16 C.F.R. 433.

30. Key Bank failed to include in its promissory Note the Notice required by 16 C.F.R. § 433.2, stating that the loan holder is subject to the consumer's claims arising from the sale of services funded by the loan, i.e., the trade school course.

31. Defendants' violation of the FTC Rule and Pennsylvania law constitutes a *per se* unfair or deceptive act or practice, in violation of the CPL.

32. In addition, Defendants' acts described above are unfair acts or deceptive acts or practices, as defined by 73 P.S. § 201-2(4) and 73 P.S. § 201-3, in that the Defendants have:
   a. Caused a likelihood of confusion or misunderstanding as to the source of the loans, and the relationship between the Defendants and the legal consequences thereof, in violation of 73 P.S. § 201-2(4)(ii) and (iii),
   b. Represented that the training services and the loan services had characteristics or benefits that they did not have, in violation of 73 P.S. § 201-2(4)(v),
   c. Represented that services are of a particular quality when they are of another, in violation of 73 P.S. § 201-2(4)(vii),
   d. Failing to comply with the terms of a written guarantee or warranty, namely the enrollment agreement's guarantee of a full refund in the event a program is canceled, in violation of 73 P.S. § 201-2(4)(xiv) and
   e. Engaged in other deceptive conduct which created a likelihood of confusion or of misunderstanding, as defined by 73 P.S. § 201-2(4)(xxi).

33. In addition to the fact that the above-described illegality constitutes *per se* unfair or deceptive trade practices, Plaintiff has relied to his detriment on Defendant's implied misrepresentations concerning the legality of the contract terms and he has suffered an ascertainable loss of money as a result of these unfair or deceptive acts or practices.

34. Defendants' acts were made knowingly, deliberately, and repeatedly, warranting the imposition of an award of treble damages under 73 P.S. § 201-9.2(a).

COUNT II: BREACH OF CONTRACT

35. Plaintiffs reallege and incorporate by reference all preceding allegations of law and fact.

36. Career Vision breached its contract with Plaintiff.

37. The breach was material and complete, in that the partial and incomplete services offered to the Plaintiff were of no value in the absence of a means to complete the course or transfer credits elsewhere.

38. The enrollment agreement and promissory Note constituted a single and unified contract for the purchase and financing of educational services.

39. Due to Career Vision's material breach, Plaintiff is not obligated to pay the price of the educational services that were never provided, or to pay the loan to Key Bank.

40. Due to Career Vision's material breach, Plaintiff is entitled to a refund of all payments made to Career Vision and Key Bank.

COUNT III: DECLARATION OF CONTRACTUAL UNCONSCIONABILITY

41. Plaintiffs reallege and incorporate by reference all preceding allegations of law and fact.

42. As part of Defendant's scheme to evade U.S. and Pennsylvania law, they implemented a plan to try to increase the likelihood that they could escape accountability for their illegal actions by including in their form loan contracts several provisions intended to limit the legal remedies available to borrowers who might wish to challenge the legality of Defendants' practices.

43. In accordance with this plan, all Key Bank USA contracts during the relevant time period failed to include the mandatory Notice of preservation of consumer claims and defenses required by the FTC Rule, and contained provisions that claim to make the contracts governed by Ohio law, and (c) require borrowers to bring any legal action under the contract in Ohio.

44. These provisions are procedurally unconscionable in that Key Bank loan contracts are essentially adhesion contracts. Borrowers lack the bargaining power to negotiate any material changes to the terms imposed by Defendants.

45. These contract provisions are substantively unconscionable in that they function, as a practical matter, as exculpatory clauses that insulate Defendants from legal accountability and deny consumers access to reasonable and appropriate remedies. As a result Key Bank unreasonably and illegally attempts to shift significant risks associated with the trade school contract to the consumer.

46. It would unfair and unconscionable for Defendant Key Bank to be able to insulate itself from the misconduct of its trade school business partner.

47. Because the contractual clauses and absence of the required FTC Rule provisions are procedurally and substantively unconscionable, Plaintiff is entitled to a declaratory judgment that as to these provisions, the contract is unenforceable because it violates public policy.

WHEREFORE, Plaintiff requests judgment in his favor and against defendant, for actual and treble damages, attorney's fees and costs, voiding or reformation of the contract(s), and any other and further relief as the court deems just and proper.

_____
[*Attorney for Plaintiff*]

[*Attorneys for Plaintiff*]
[*Address and Phone Number*]

```
_____  )
[CONSUMER]                    )
[ADDRESS]                     )
                    Plaintiff )
                              )
v.                            )
                              )
CAREER VISION OF              )
PENNSYLVANIA, INC.            )
[ADDRESS]                     )
                              )
KEY BANK USA, NA              )
[Address]                     )
                   Defendants )
_____  )
```

VERIFICATION

I, [*Consumer*], verify under the penalties of 18 Pa. C. S. A. § 4904 relating to unsworn falsification to authorities that I am the plaintiff in this case and that the facts set forth in this pleading are true and correct to the best of my knowledge, information and belief.

Date:_____

[*Consumer*]

Appendix F Sample Discovery and Freedom of Information Act Requests

The pleadings in this appendix are also available in Word and PDF formats on the companion website to this manual.

F.1 Discovery in Student Loan Collection Cases

IN THE UNITED STATES DISTRICT COURT
FOR THE MIDDLE DISTRICT OF LOUISIANA

—————————————)
[*Consumer*], on behalf of herself)
and all others similarly situated,)
                Plaintiff,)
)
v.   )
)
The Premier Collectors, Inc.,)
              Defendant.)
—————————————)

PLAINTIFF'S FIRST DISCOVERY REQUEST

Plaintiff hereby requests that defendant respond to the following requests for admission, interrogatories and document requests. Throughout this request:

A. If defendant's response to any of the requests for admissions submitted herewith is anything other than an unqualified admission, describe in detail the basis for the inability to make such admission.

B. If any document requested in the document requests submitted herewith was but no longer is in defendant's possession, custody or control, state: the date of its disposition; the manner of its disposition (e.g., lost, destroyed, transferred to a third party); and the circumstances surrounding the disposition of the document including the identity of the person who disposed of it, the reason for its disposal, the identity of anyone who may have copies of it, the identity of anyone ordering or requesting its disposal, and whether its disposal was in compliance with defendant's document destruction policies.

C. Unless otherwise specified in a particular paragraph, the "relevant time period" covered by this request is August 1, 1993 to the present.

D. PCI means The Premier Collectors, Inc.

E. These requests are subject to the instructions and definitions attached hereto as *Exhibit 1* [*Editor's note: Reprinted at end of section*].

REQUESTS FOR ADMISSION

PLEASE TAKE NOTICE THAT, pursuant to Federal Rules of Civil Procedure 26 and 36, plaintiff hereby requests that defendant admit or deny the truth of the following matters in writing within 30 days after service of this request.

1. The Premier Collectors, Inc. ("PCI") is regularly engaged for profit in the collection of debts allegedly owed by consumers.
RESPONSE:

2. PCI is a "debt collector" as defined in the Fair Debt Collection Practices Act, 15 U.S.C. § 1692a(6).
RESPONSE:

3. On or about August 11, 1993, PCI mailed to plaintiff a collection letter demanding $11,417.31 allegedly owing to the U.S. Department of Education. *Exhibit A* is a copy of the letter. [*Editor's note: Not reprinted herein.*]
RESPONSE:

4. On or about April 20, 1994, PCI mailed to plaintiff a collection letter demanding $10,706.14 allegedly owing to the U.S. Department of Education. *Exhibit B* is a copy of the letter. [*Editor's note: Not reprinted herein.*]
RESPONSE:

5. On or about May 5, 1994, PCI mailed to plaintiff a collection letter demanding $10,732.65 allegedly owing to the U.S. Department of Education. *Exhibit C* is a copy of the letter. [*Editor's note: Not reprinted herein.*]
RESPONSE:

6. *Exhibit A–C* were mailed in an attempt to collect alleged debts arising from transactions primarily for personal, family, or household purposes, namely, an alleged student loan.
RESPONSE:

7. Defendant is not affiliated with U.S. Department of Education.
RESPONSE:

8. Defendant did not and does not determine the course of legal action, if any, taken by the United States Government with respect to student loans.
RESPONSE:

9. Neither PCI, the U.S. Department of Justice, nor anyone else, has filed suit against plaintiff to collect the alleged debt referred to in *Exhibits A–C*.
RESPONSE:

10. PCI regularly mails, or causes to be mailed, collection letters

bearing the name of the U.S. Department of Education to Louisiana residents in an effort to collect consumer debts.
RESPONSE:

11. Between August 1, 1993 and the present, PCI mailed more than 20 letters prepared on the same form as *Exhibit A* to Louisiana residents in an effort to collect student loans.
RESPONSE:

12. Between August 1, 1993 and the present, PCI mailed more than 20 letters prepared on the same form as *Exhibit B* to Louisiana residents in an effort to collect student loans.
RESPONSE:

13. Between August 1, 1993 and the present, PCI mailed more than 20 letters prepared on the same form as *Exhibit C* to Louisiana residents in an effort to collect student loans.
RESPONSE:

14. Between August 1, 1993 and the present, PCI sought to recover collection fees exceeding 20% of the principal debt from more than 20 Louisiana residents who allegedly owed money on student loans.
RESPONSE:

15. PCI does not in fact conduct an investigation of the income, savings, employment, real estate ownership and personal assets of each person to whom *Exhibit B* is sent.
RESPONSE:

16. PCI has not in fact conducted an investigation of the income, savings, employment, real estate ownership and personal assets of any person to whom *Exhibit B* was sent.
RESPONSE:

17. A suit by the U.S. Department of Justice on a student loan may not result in garnishment, attachment or judgment liens until the consumer is heard in court and a judgment entered against the consumer.
RESPONSE:

INTERROGATORIES

PLEASE TAKE NOTICE THAT, pursuant to Federal Rules of Civil Procedure 26 and 33, plaintiff propounds the following Interrogatories to be answered by defendant under oath, within 30 days of service hereof.

1a. Describe the method, procedure, or general approach which defendant presently uses in the preparation and mailing of collection notices which are eventually sent to persons who allegedly owe money on student loans. Include in your answer a description of all letters or any series of letters that PCI sends to such persons.
ANSWER:

b. State when the method, procedure or general approach described in response to (a) was adopted;
ANSWER:

c. Describe all other methods, procedures or general approaches defendant uses in the preparation of and mailing of collection letters eventually sent to such persons.
ANSWER:

2a. How many notices, using the same form as *Exhibit A*, were sent to Louisiana residents between August 1, 1993 and the present.
ANSWER:

b. State the names and addresses of each such person.
ANSWER:

3a. How many notices, using the same form as *Exhibit B*, were sent to Louisiana residents between August 1, 1993 and the present.
ANSWER:

b. State the names and addresses of each such person.
ANSWER:

4a. How many notices, using the same form as *Exhibit C*, were sent to Louisiana residents between August 1, 1993 and the present.
ANSWER:

b. State the names and addresses of each such person.
ANSWER:

5. Describe all reports, recommendations for action, or other advice provided by PCI to the United States Government with respect to alleged student loan debts which PCI is unable to collect.
ANSWER:

6. Identify all instances in which PCI has filed suit or caused suit to be filed to collect an alleged student loan debt owed to the U. S. Department of Education.
ANSWER:

7. Describe any basis which PCI has in contract, regulation, or otherwise for demanding a 42.84% collection fee from plaintiff, and how the amount of such fee was determined.
ANSWER:

8. State whether any person to whom PCI has ever (before or during the class period) sent a letter using the same form as *Exhibit B* has had their salary garnished, equity or bank accounts attached, or liens placed against their real estate without a judgment being first entered against that person by a court.
ANSWER:

9. Describe all investigations of income, bank accounts, business and employment information, real estate ownership, automobile ownership and personal assets which PCI has conducted of persons who were sent letters using the same form as *Exhibit B*, identifying each person who was investigated:
ANSWER:

REQUESTS FOR PRODUCTION OF DOCUMENTS

PLEASE TAKE NOTICE THAT, pursuant to Federal Rules of Civil Procedure 26 and 34, plaintiff hereby requests that defendant produce to plaintiff's counsel for examination, inspection and copying all of the documents specified herein in its possession, custody or control, within 30 days of service of this request.

1. All documents showing the number of Louisiana residents to whom PCI sent collection letters using the same forms as *Exhibit A–C* during any portion of the period between August 1, 1993 and the present. If no documents showing the number of Louisiana residents exist, produce all documents showing the number of persons to whom PCI sent such letters during such period, without regard to residence.
RESPONSE:

2. All documents showing the names and addresses of Louisiana residents who were sent a collection letter prepared using the same forms as *Exhibit A–C*, during any portion of the period between August 1, 1993 and the present.
RESPONSE:

3. A copy of each form collection letter sent to Louisiana residents by PCI on or after August 1, 1993.
RESPONSE:

4. All documents purporting to authorize or justify the 42.84%

collection fee referred to in *Exhibit C*.
RESPONSE:

5. All reports, recommendations for action, or other advice provided by PCI to the United States Government with respect to alleged student loan debts which PCI is unable to collect.
RESPONSE:

6. All documents relating to any instance in which PCI has filed suit or caused suit to be filed to collect an alleged student loan debt owed to the U. S. Department of Education.
RESPONSE:

7. All documents relating to any instance (before or during the class period) in which a person to whom PCI sent a letter using the same form as *Exhibit B* has had their salary garnished, equity or bank accounts attached, or liens placed against their real estate without a judgment being first entered against that person by a court.
RESPONSE:

8. All documents relating to investigations of income, bank accounts, business and employment information, real estate ownership, automobile ownership and personal assets which PCI has conducted of persons who were sent letters using the same form as *Exhibit B*.
RESPONSE:

9. All documents relied on by PCI in answering any of the accompanying interrogatories or in responding to any of the accompanying requests for admission.
RESPONSE:

[*Attorney for Plaintiff*]

EXHIBIT 1

INSTRUCTIONS AND DEFINITIONS

Instructions

1. All documents within your possession, custody, or control or that of your agents, employees, or attorneys shall be produced. Without limitation of the term "control" as used in the preceding sentence, a document is deemed to be in your control if you have the right to secure the document or a copy thereof from another person having actual possession thereof.

2. To the extent any paragraph is objected to, set forth all reasons for your objection.

3. If you prefer, you may provide legible copies of documents that reflect all markings, notations and highlighting on the originals.

4. Documents to be produced shall be either (1) organized as they are kept in the ordinary course of business or (2) organized and labelled to correspond with the paragraphs of the request for production or interrogatory to which they are responsive.

5. The singular includes the plural number and vice versa.
The masculine includes the feminine and neuter genders. The past tense includes the present tense where the clear meaning is not distorted by change of tense.

6. To the extent that any document cannot be furnished, such documents as are available shall be supplied, together with a description of the documents not furnished and the reason for not furnishing them.

7. "And" as well as "or" are used either disjunctively or conjunctively as necessary to bring information within the scope of the request that might otherwise be outside the scope of the request.

8. Plaintiff requests that documents be produced as they become ready and that defendant does not wait until all documents are ready to start production.

Definitions

1. The term "document" is used in the broadest sense permitted and includes, by way of illustration only and not by way of limitation, the following, whether printed or reproduced by any process, or written or produced by hand: ledgers; notes; correspondence; communications of any nature; telegrams; memoranda; notebooks of any character; summaries or records of personal conversations; diaries; reports; publications; photographs; microfilm, microfiche and similar media; minutes and records of meetings; transcripts of oral testimony and statements; reports and summaries of interviews; reports and summaries of investigations; court papers; brochures; pamphlets; press releases; drafts of, revisions of drafts of and translations of any document; tape recordings; dictation belts; invoices; bills; accounting records; telephone toll records; and disks, tapes and other magnetic or electronic information storage media. Any document or reproduction of a document bearing on any sheet or side thereof any marks, including by way of illustration only and not by way of limitation initials, stamped indicia or any comment or any notation of any character and not a part of the original text, is to be considered a separate document. Where it is uncertain whether something is a document, this definition shall be construed to include it.

2. References to "you" or any named entity or individual include agents, employees and attorneys of that person, whether or not acting within the scope of their authority; all other persons acting on behalf of the person referred to; and in the case of an entity its merged or acquired predecessors.

3. "Person" includes any individual, corporation, partnership, joint venture, firm, association, proprietorship, governmental agency, board, authority, commission and other entity.

4. "Communication" includes every manner or means of disclosure, transfer or exchange of information, whether orally or by document or whether face-to-face, by telephone, mail, personal delivery or otherwise.

5. "Relates," "refers," and "reflects" include constitutes, describes, contains, discusses, reflects, refers to, and logically pertains to.

6. "Identify" or "identification," when used with respect to a document, means to state the general nature of the document (that is, letter, memorandum, etc.); the name of the author or originator; each addressee; all individuals designated on the document to receive a copy or otherwise known to have received a copy; the date, title and general subject matter of the document; the present custodian of each copy thereof and the last known address of each such custodian; and the date of the making of the document.

7. "Identify" or "identification," when used with respect to a communication, means to state the date of the communication; the type of communication (that is, telephone conversation, meeting, etc.); the place where the communication took place; the identification of the person who made the communication; the identification of each person who received the communication and of each person present when it was made; and the subject matter discussed.

8. "Identify" or "identification," when used with respect to a person, means state the name, last known business and home addresses and telephone numbers, occupation, job titles and Social Security Number of the person being identified.

F.2 Discovery Directed to For-Profit/Proprietary Schools

F.2.1 First Interrogatories and Requests for Production of Documents from a School

COURT OF COMMON PLEAS
PHILADELPHIA COUNTY

_____)
[CONSUMER])
)
)
v.)
)
NATIONAL SCHOOL OF)
HEALTH TECHNOLOGY, INC.)
_____)

PLAINTIFF'S FIRST SET OF INTERROGATORIES AND REQUESTS FOR PRODUCTION DIRECTED TO DEFENDANT

Pursuant to Rules 4005, 4006 and 4009, Pa. Rules of Civil Procedure, defendant demands response within thirty (30) days to the following interrogatories and requests for production of documents:

DEFINITIONS

a. "Defendant" or "the school" shall refer to National School of Health Technology, its agents, officers, or employees.

b. "Plaintiff" shall refer to [*Consumer*].

c. "Document" is used in the broadest possible sense permissible under the rules of civil procedure. Such term shall refer to any mechanism of preserving or transmitting any information, whether it be written, printed, photographed, electronically recorded, or otherwise made and maintained. It shall include all tangible items of any nature, both originals and copies, and all attachments and appendices thereto, and all drafts thereof, including but not limited to, agreements, contracts, communications, correspondence, letters, telegrams, faxes, memoranda, records, reports, books, summaries or other records of meetings and conferences, summaries or other records of negotiations, diaries, calendars, statistical data or statements, work papers, charts, accounts, brochures, circulars, press releases, marginal notations, bills, invoices, journals, lists, files and file jackets, printouts, compilations, minutes, checks, envelopes or folders or similar containers, vouchers, transcripts, articles, tape or disc recordings, photographs and including any information contained in a computer, although not yet printed out, within the possession, custody or control of defendant.

d. "Trial" includes arbitration hearings.

e. "State board" means the Pennsylvania Board of Private Licensed Schools.

f. "And" as well as "or" shall be construed either disjunctively or conjunctively as necessary to bring within the scope of the following interrogatories and requests information and documents that might otherwise be construed to be outside their scope; and as used herein the singular shall include the plural and the plural shall include the singular except as the context may otherwise dictate.

INTERROGATORIES

1. State the date of defendant's incorporation, the state(s) in which it is incorporated and the name of the incorporators.
Answer:

2. State the number of outstanding shares of stock and identify the owners of said stock, including the numbers of shares owned by each person.
Answer:

3. Identify by name, home address and occupation all members of defendant's board of directors on a) January 1, 1985, b) January 1, 1987, c) January 1, 1989 and d) January 1, 1991.
Answer:

4. Identify by name, home address and occupation the officers of defendant corporation as of a) January 1, 1985, b) January 1, 1987, c) January 1, 1989 and d) January 1, 1991.
Answer:

5. Identify by name and home address all individuals who have served as the chief administrator of the school between January 1, 1985 and the present, stating for each the time period during which they served and their salaries during that period.
Answer:

6.a. Is defendant the subsidiary of any other corporation?
  b. Does defendant own any subsidiaries?
  c. If the answer to either a. or b. is affirmative, identify and explain.
Answer:

7. Has defendant undergone any ownership changes since 1980? If so, explain such changes and identify the dates and the parties involved.
Answer:

8a. When did the school at 801 Arch Street open its doors?
  b. When did the (i) Nurse's Aide and (ii) Medical Assistant programs begin?
  c. Is the school at 801 Arch Street a branch of some other school? If so, identify the branching institution.
  d. Describe the relationship, if any, between the school at 801 Arch Street and school of the same name in Northeast Philadelphia.
Answer:

9. Identify all institutional accreditations and all program accreditations pertaining to the Nurse's Aide or Medical Assistant programs which defendant has received since 1980, including the commencement and expiration dates and the accrediting agency.
Answer:

10. Have any past or present employees, directors or officers of defendant served on or been associated with an accreditation commission or agency? If so, identify the person, his/her relationship to defendant, the accrediting institution, position held at the accrediting institution and relevant dates.

Answer:

11. List the fee schedules for a) the Nurse's Aide and b) the Medical Assistant programs for each year since 1985, including all components of that schedule, and for each component explain what it is and, where applicable, the reason for increases.

Answer:

12. List the names, home addresses and positions of all employees or representatives of defendant who, during the time period 1988 to the present worked in the marketing, admissions or financial aid component of defendant's organization, and for each specify the particular job responsibilities held and, as to each position held, the time period applicable and the name and position of the individual's immediate supervisor. In addition, identify which, if any, individuals are still associated with defendant.

Answer:

13. State the names, home addresses, and positions of all officials or employees of defendant which had any policy-making responsibility concerning the standards and procedures employed by admissions personnel at the school during the time period 1988 to the present, and as to each, state what, if any, other positions the individual has had in defendant's organization and the relevant dates of such positions.

Answer:

14. State the names and home addresses of all individuals who made decisions or who participated in making decisions during the time period 1988 to the present to admit prospective students under the school's "ability-to-benefit" standards.

Answer:

15. List all academic instructors who taught courses in either the Nurse's Aide or Medical Assistant program during the years 1988 to the present and for each specify:
   a. The courses taught and the applicable time period;
   b. The individual's degrees, certifications and prior teaching experience;
   c. His/her last known address and telephone number.

Answer:

16. State the names, and, if not previously listed, their last known addresses and phone numbers, of all individuals who participated in the development of the curriculum of either the Nurse's Aide or Medical Assistant program and, in addition, as to each of them:
   a. List their academic and professional credentials;
   b. Describe the nature of the participation; and
   c. Specify all positions, with applicable dates, that they have held in defendant's organization.

Answer:

17. Regarding defendant's pleading that "admissions representatives . . . disclose to applicants the range of hourly rates earned by past graduates based upon the school's placement data," Answer ¶ 6(a),
   a. Specify the range of rates which were disclosed to applicants in the Nurse's Aide and Medical Assistant programs during the period 1988 to the present and
   b. Identify the data and the source of such data upon which the said disclosures were based.

Answer:

18. Identify the name and position of all representatives of defendant who interviewed plaintiff prior to her first day of class and specify the dates and purposes of such interviews.

Answer:

19a. Describe defendant's policy(ies) in effect during the years 1987–89 regarding the payment of commissions to sales representatives, financial aid employees or students?
   b. Was any individual paid a commission as a result of plaintiff's enrollment, financial aid award or attendance? If so, identify the person by name and relationship to defendant and explain the terms and amount of such commission.
   c. What documents were examined for purpose of answering "b?".

Answer:

20a. State the dates in which plaintiff actually attended classes at the school.
   b. State the date plaintiff was terminated from the school.
   c. If the date of termination is different from the last date of attendance, explain how defendant determined the date of termination.

Answer:

21a. State the amount defendant refunded to plaintiff.
   b. State the date paid and the method of payment.
   c. Explain how the amount refunded was calculated.

Answer:

22a. Specify the amounts of all financial aid which defendant received on plaintiff's behalf, including the specific aid program under which funds were received, the payor of such funds and the date received.
   b. Specify the amounts of all financial aid funds received on plaintiff's behalf which defendant refunded to a lender, guarantee agency, or the United States government and as to each refund specify the program, the payee and the date payment was sent.

Answer:

23. State the names, positions and, if not previously stated, the home addresses of all individuals who were responsible to assist prospective or enrolled students in obtaining information concerning the matters covered in document request # 17, *infra*, with the relevant dates.

Answer:

24. For years ending December 31, 1986, 1988 and 1990, identify by name and itemized dollar figures the four highest paid employees or officers of defendant, including salary, fees, commissions or any other form of direct compensation and also including any payments for expenses such as automobiles or travel.

Answer:

DOCUMENT REQUESTS

1. Organizational charts for defendant's organization which exhibit the chain of authority and responsibility.

2. Any and all advertisements, mailings and marketing literature employed by defendant during the period 1988 to the present which was targeted either to prospective students or to prospective employees, including the scripts of all television commercials broadcast during said period.

3. All internal memoranda, training manuals, scripts, documents or writings of any kind which pertain to the standards, procedures or marketing tips or strategies employed by the school's admissions personnel or which instruct, advise, set policy, train or

otherwise advise, educate or set guidelines for agents, representatives, officers or employees of defendant, which were in use or which applied to the time period 1987 to the present.

4. All documents involved in, referring to or relating to studies or surveys pertaining to or used in connection with defendant's recruitment of new students.

5. Any and all admissions tests administered by defendant for admission into its Nurse's Aide and Medical Assistant programs during the time period 1988 to the present, and as to each:
   a. Identify the source for the test and
   b. Produce copies of all applicable written criteria or correspondence from the school's accrediting commission pertaining to the school's use of the particular test.

6. The entire contents of plaintiff's admission file, including file jacket and all documents, notes, and other writings contained therein, including, but not limited to, admissions tests, enrollment agreements, "How Our Students Are Doing" disclosures, interview notes, financial aid inquiries and internal memoranda concerning the plaintiff's application or admission and defendant's decision to admit her.

7. The entire contents of plaintiff's academic and disciplinary files including the file jacket and all documents, notes, and other writings contained therein, including, but not limited to, transcripts, evaluations, internal memoranda, letters and notes of conversations.

8. Any and all account cards, ledger sheets or other documents showing debits, credits, and/or a running balance, pertaining to charges, payments, refunds and other financial transactions involving plaintiff.

9. Any and all documents, not covered by another section of this request, that are signed by plaintiff or that relate to the transaction in question.

10a. Course outlines and reading lists for any remedial courses offered by defendant for "ability to benefit" students during the period 1988 to the present.
   b. Names and addresses of all individuals who taught such courses and relevant time periods that they did so.

11. Any and all applications and supporting documents sent to a third-party accrediting agency or commission and all accrediting documents received regarding the defendant's school in general or regarding in particular the Nurse's Aide or Medical Assistant programs.

12. The raw data, regardless of the form in which it is kept, from which defendant reported to the state board its Nurse's Aide or Medical Assistant enrollments, completions, withdrawals and the employment of graduates for years ending June 30, 1987 to the present.

13. Any and all application forms and all supporting documents submitted by defendant to the United States Department of Education and all eligibility notifications received by defendant concerning a) the school's status as an "eligible institution" to participate in federal financial aid program, and b) the school's designation as a participant in individual programs administered by the Department of Education.

14. All applications and supporting documents submitted by defendant to the state board pertaining to the licensing of its Nurse's Aide and Medical Assistant programs and all documents received from the state board pertaining to same.

15. All site visit and monitoring reports concerning any aspect of defendant's operation which was performed by the state board, by an accrediting institution or by the United States Department of Education since 1985.

16. All written policies and all documents pertaining to such policies in effect during the period 1988 to the present regarding the school's definition of satisfactory academic progress and regarding student appeal rights concerning determinations of unsatisfactory progress and for each identify a) all persons (and their positions) who were responsible for developing these policies and b) their effective dates.

17. All written policies and all documents pertaining to such policies in effect at the school during the time period 1988 to the present regarding student refunds and regarding the application of such refunds to appropriate financial aid accounts.

18. All written materials which defendant disseminated to prospective and enrolled students in the Nurse's Aide or Medical Assistant program during the period 1988 to the present regarding a) financial aid eligibility criteria and the criteria and methods employed for making award determinations, b) itemized course costs, c) the refund policy, d) standards for progress, attendance and other student regulations, e) the academic content of and faculty for each program, f) the extent, nature and success rate of the placement service, g) the pass rates of former students, h) the rate of employment by former students, i) completion rates by former students and j) information regarding starting salaries and job availability in relevant fields.

19. For each document produced in response to request #18, identify a) the source for the document, b) the source of all data which would be contained in a form designed to be filled out, d) all individuals who participated in preparing the document and their positions, e) the time period during which it was used and f) all individuals who would have provided any data contained in a completed form.

20. All documents from which the data referred to in interrogatory #17, *supra*, were obtained.

21. Defendant's annual, audited financial reports for years ending December 31, 1986–1990.

22. Any and all professional articles written by present or past employees or officers of defendant.

23. All documents referring or relating to defendant's document retention policy.

24. All court pleadings pertaining to litigation between defendant and a former student or former employee which were filed on behalf of the former student or employee.

25. Any and all documents defendant intends to introduce at trial.

[Attorney for Plaintiff]

F.2.2 Additional Interrogatories and Request for Production of Documents from a School

UNITED STATES DISTRICT COURT
EASTERN DISTRICT OF PENNSYLVANIA

_____)
[CONSUMER], on behalf of)
herself and of others similarly)
situated,)
              Plaintiffs,)
)
v.)
)
NATIONAL SCHOOL OF)
HEALTH TECHNOLOGY,)
INC., UNITED STUDENT AID)
FUNDS and MERITOR)
SAVINGS BANK/PSFS, on)
behalf of themselves and of)
others similarly situated, and)
LAMAR ALEXANDER,)
SECRETARY OF THE)
UNITED STATES)
DEPARTMENT OF)
EDUCATION,)
              Defendants)
_____)

PLAINTIFF'S FIRST SET OF INTERROGATORIES AND REQUESTS FOR PRODUCTION TO DEFENDANTS FRANCE AND ROBERTS

Plaintiff [Consumer], by her undersigned counsel, propounds the following Interrogatories and Requests for Production of Documents to defendants Diane France and Elizabeth Roberts pursuant to Fed. R. Civ. P. 26, 33 and 34. Each Interrogatory must be answered separately and full in writing under oath, and the answers must be signed by the person making them. A copy of defendants' answers, together with any objections, must be served upon plaintiffs no later than thirty (30) days after the service of these Interrogatories and Document Requests. Defendants are requested to produce for inspection and copying, within thirty (30) days from the date of service hereof, at the offices of below-signed counsel, any and all documents described in the Document Requests below.

INSTRUCTIONS

1. In answering, defendants are requested to identify separately and in a manner suitable for use in a subpoena all sources of information (whether human, documentary or other) and all records maintained by them, by National School of Health Technology or any by any other person, entity or organization on which defendants rely in answering the Interrogatories or which pertain or relate to the information called for by the Interrogatories.

2. The Interrogatories and Document Requests are to be considered continuing, and supplemental answers and documents must be filed by defendants upon discovering or becoming aware of additional responsive documents or of information rendering prior answers or any part thereof inaccurate, incomplete or untrue.

3. If any information called for by any Interrogatory is not available in the full detail requested, such Interrogatory shall be deemed to require the setting forth of the information related to the subject matter of the request in such detailed manner as is available.

4. If defendants withhold any requested information or identification and production of any document on the basis of privilege, please so state, and for each such document provide:
   (a) The nature of the privilege(s) claimed;
   (b) The type of document;
   (c) The general subject matter of the document;
   (d) The date of the document; and
   (e) Such other information as is sufficient to identify the document for a subpoena duces tecum including, where appropriate, the author of the document, the addressee of the document, any other recipients of the document and, where not apparent, the relationship of the author addressee and any recipients to one another.

5. If any requested document has been misplaced, destroyed or discarded, or otherwise disposed of, please so state, and for each such document provide:
   (a) Its date;
   (b) The identity of the person(s) who prepared the document;
   (c) The identity of all persons who participated in preparing the document, to whom the document was sent or who have otherwise seen the document;
   (d) The length of the document;
   (e) The subject matter of the document;
   (f) If misplaced, the last time and place it was seen and a description of efforts made to locate the document;
   (g) If disposed of, the date of and reason for disposal, the identity of the person(s) who authorized disposal and the identity of the person who disposed of the document.

6. If defendants are currently without information necessary to respond to any Interrogatory or Document Request, such Interrogatory or Document Request shall be deemed to require a reasonable investigation and any response thereto shall set forth the facts surrounding such investigation, including the identity of other individuals with knowledge.

7. Unless otherwise noted, the time period for the Interrogatories is 1987 through the present.

DEFINITIONS

1. The terms "you" or "your" shall include [Individual 1], [Individual 2] and all individuals who were employees, officers or agents of National School of Health and Technology. Reference to "the school" means National School of Health and Technology.

2. The term "document" is used in the broadest possible sense and means, without limitation, any written, printed, typed, photostated, photographic, computerized, recorded or otherwise reproduced communication or representation, whether comprised of letters, words, numbers, pictures, sounds or symbols, or any combination thereof. This definition includes copies or duplicates of documents contemporaneously or subsequently created that have any non-nonconforming notes or other markings. Without limiting the generality of the foregoing, the term "document" includes, but is not limited to, correspondence, memoranda, notes, records,

letters, envelopes, file folders, telegrams, messages, reports, analyses, contracts, agreements, forms, working papers, summaries, statistical statements, financial statements or work papers, accounts, analytical records, trade letters, press releases, comparisons, books, calendars, diaries, logs, articles, magazines, newspapers, booklets, brochures, pamphlets, circulars, bulletins, notices, drawing, diagrams, instructions, notes or minutes of meetings, reports and/or summaries of investigations, or other communications of any type, including inter and intra-office communications, questionnaires, surveys, charts, graphs, recordings, films, tapes, computer and word processor disks, data cells, drums, print-outs, all other data compilations from which information can be obtained (translated, if necessary, into usable forms), and any preliminary versions, drafts or revisions of any of the foregoing.

3. The term "identify" when used in connection with a natural person means to state his or her:
  (a) Full name and any aliases;
  (b) Last known address and phone number;
  (c) Last known business address and phone number;
  (d) Employment, title, and job description during the time of their employment at the school; and
  (e) Present employment and job description.

4. The term "identify" or "identity" when used in connection with a "document" or "documents" means to state the following:
  (a) Its date;
  (b) The identity of its author;
  (c) The identity of its sender;
  (d) The identity of the person to whom it was addressed;
  (e) The identity of the recipient;
  (f) Its format;
  (g) Its title;
  (h) The number of pages or other measure of length or size; and
  (i) The identity of each person known or believed to have possession, custody, control of or access to any copy of the document having writings, notations, corrections or markings unique to such copy.

5. The phrase "identify the factual basis" for a denial or an Interrogatory answer means to state:
  (a) Each and every fact which you believe supports the denial or Interrogatory answer;
  (b) The identity of each and every person having knowledge of facts which you believe supports the denial or Interrogatory answer, along with a summary of such facts which that person knows; and
  (c) The identity of each and every document which you believe supports the denial or Interrogatory answer.

INTERROGATORIES

1. Do you contend that plaintiff [*Consumer*] had the "ability to benefit" from the school's Medical Assistant course, within the meaning of federal financial aid regulations? If the answer is "yes," identify the factual basis for this contention.

2. Identify all former students of the school who were admitted without a high school or equivalency diploma and on whose behalf the school obtained any federal grants or loans and, for each, also provide the following information:
  a. The date of the enrollment agreement;
  b. The course of study;
  c. Whether or not the student completed the course;
  d. The relevant dates the student withdrew or graduated;
  e. All grants obtained (not counting refunds);
  f. All grant refunds made to the Government;
  g. All loan proceeds obtained (not counting refunds);
  h. All loan refunds made to a lender or guarantee agency; and
  i. If the student was placed in a job related to the course of study, identify the employer and the starting salary paid.

3. As to the individuals identified in response to Interrogatory #1, do you contend that these individuals had "the ability to benefit" from the course you enrolled them in? If the answer is "yes," identify the factual basis for this contention.

4. Identify all "ability to benefit" tests which the school administered to admissions applicants who lacked a high school or GED diploma from 1986 until the closing. As to each test, also provide the following information, and, if different tests or scores were used for different courses of study, provide all relevant information for each:
  a. The dates during which the test was used;
  b. The author of the test (if purchased from a third party, the name of the entity that produced the test);
  c. The cutoff scores used to determine whether an applicant was qualified for admission;
  d. How such cutoff scores were established, including a description of the methodology and identification of those individuals or entities who participated in making the decision to set a particular cutoff;
  e. The name, address and telephone number of every person who was authorized to administer the test, including the relevant time period for each.

5. Did the school ever study or analyze the relationship between performance on an admission test or "ability to benefit test," on the one hand, and academic success and job placement, on the other? If the answer is "yes," describe the method used to study or analyze the relationship, as well as the system employed for maintaining data on this relationship, and identify all documents which pertain to such studies, analyses and data.

6. Identify all individuals who administered "ability to benefit" tests and the relevant time periods for each.

7. For the years ending December 31, 1986, 1988 and 1990, identify the four highest paid employees or officers of the school, and for each itemize the relevant figures for salary, fees, commissions and other form of compensation, including payments for automobiles or other expenses.

8. For the years 1986–92 identify all payments made by the school to [*Individual 2*], including for each year a description of the factual basis for such payments.

9. For the years 1986–92 identify all automobiles owned or leased by the school including for each:
  a. The year, make and model;
  b. The date of acquisition;
  c. The identity of the person who primarily used the vehicle;
  d. The purchase price or monthly lease payment;
  e. A description of any customization which was done and the cost of such customization; and
  f. A description of the disposition of the vehicle including the date and the reason the school lost possession of the vehicle.

10. During the years 1987–91 did the School arrange loans through guarantee agencies and lenders other than United Student Aid Funds and Meritor Savings Bank? If so, identify the entities and the approximate volume of such dealings.

11. Regarding the averment in defendant [*Individual 1*]'s answer to the original complaint (at ¶ 17) that "students were told about the school's placement rate and the range of salaries that recent graduates received."

  a. Describe in detail the system that existed at the school for ensuring that this information was communicated accurately, including, but not limited to, identification of the roles of the various individuals involved, the methods of communication used between school departments and between the school and students, and any procedures used to ensure and monitor the accuracy of the information.

  b. Identify what, if any, statistics or other information the school maintained concerning placement and salary levels of graduates, including, but not limited to identification of the roles of the various individuals involved, the methods used to obtain and record this information and the manner of maintaining such records.

  c. Identify what, if any statistics or other information the school provided to prospective students and which substantiated the accuracy and truthfulness of such claims, including, but not limited to identification of the roles of the various individuals involved and a description of the form, manner and timing of such disclosures.

REQUESTS FOR PRODUCTION OF DOCUMENTS

1. All documents pertaining to the transfer of ownership and control in the School in December, 1986 from [*Individual 2*] to [*Individual 1*] and [*Individual 2*].

2. The most current resumes or personnel data sheets in your possession for the following individuals:

  a. [*Individual 1*];
  b. [*Individual 2*];
  c. [*Individual 3*];
  d. [*Individual 4*];
  e. [*Individual 5*];
  f. [*Individual 6*];
  f.* [*Individual 7*];
  g. [*Individual 8*] and
  h. [*Individual 9*].

3. All "ability to benefit" tests which the school administered to admissions applicants who lacked a high school or GED diploma from 1986 until the closing and all instruction books for each test.

4. All documents pertaining to the selection of particular tests, the procedures used in administering the tests, and the selection by the school of particular cutoff scores used to determine success or failure on the test.

5. All invoices, purchase orders, cancelled checks or other documents pertaining to the purchase of "ability to benefit" tests from vendors or testing companies.

6. All data or records pertaining to the relationship between performance on admission tests and academic/employment success, including, if they exist, summary reports produced by the testing companies.

7. All annual reports to accrediting commissions, including both NATTS and ABHES, for the years 1985–91.

8. All correspondence between the school and its accrediting commissions during the years 1986–1992.

---

* *Editor's note:* Duplicate alphabet in original.

9. Copies of site visit reports, reviews, show-cause orders or audits pertaining to the school, covering the years 1987–91, which were prepared by either an accrediting commission, the State Board of Private Licensed Schools, or the United States Department of Education, and copies of any responses thereto.

10. Copies of the accrediting criteria of NATTS and of ABHES, which were applicable to the accreditation of the school and/or to the school's Medical Assistant course.

11. The school's annual, audited financial reports for the years 1986–90.

[*Attorney for Plaintiff*]

F.2.3 Production of Documents from a School (Transferability of Credits Case)

UNITED STATES DISTRICT COURT
EASTERN DISTRICT OF MICHIGAN

[*PLAINTIFFS*], on behalf of themselves and a class consisting of all those similarly situated,	)))))
Plaintiffs,	)
v.	))
[defendants]ACADEMY OF COURT REPORTING, INC., DELTA CAREER EDUCATION CORPORATION, GRYPHON COLLEGES CORPORATION, and GRYPHON INVESTORS, INC.	) Case No. _____) [*JUDGE*])))))
Defendants.	)

PLAINTIFFS' FIRST REQUEST FOR PRODUCTION
OF DOCUMENTS TO DEFENDANT ACADEMY OF
COURT REPORTING, INC.

Plaintiffs [*Plaintiffs*], by and through their attorneys, The Googasian Firm, P.C., in accordance with LR 26.1 and pursuant to Fed. R. Civ. P. 34, submit this First Request for Production of Documents to Defendant Academy of Court Reporting, Inc. ("the Academy"). Responses, together with responsive documents, shall be produced within 30 days at The Googasian Firm, P.C., [*Address*].

INSTRUCTIONS

A. These discovery requests shall be deemed continuing. Supplemental answers shall be served promptly after information responsive to these interrogatories is discovered at any time prior to trial.

B. These discovery requests are directed to information known to or in the possession of the Academy and any of its subsidiaries, predecessors, successors, affiliates or other related entities as well as any of its partners, officers, employees, or attorneys who are in possession of or may have obtained information or documents on behalf of the Academy.

C. If a discovery request is objected to in whole or in part, set forth all reasons therefor. As to any request for which a privilege or other immunity from disclosure is asserted to apply in whole or in part, specify the precise privilege or immunity asserted and the facts claimed to support the assertions and identify each document.

D. If information responsive to a discovery request cannot be provided because a document apparently has been destroyed, misplaced or is otherwise unavailable, identify the name of the person(s) who authorized its destruction, the names of all persons who witnessed its destruction, the date of its destruction, and any and all reasons for its destruction.

DEFINITIONS

A. "E-mails" means any electronically sent or stored message **or other electronically created or stored document.**

B. "Document" means any printed or recorded material, including, but not limited to, notes, transcripts, records, work papers, charts, letters, correspondence, memoranda, logs, tapes, sketches, and other written, printed, typed, recorded, transcribed, punched, taped, filmed or graphic matter of any kind, including data stored on computer such as "e-mail," in the possession, custody or control of the defendant, any of its subsidiaries, predecessors, successors, affiliates or other related entities as well as any of its board members, officers, agents, employees, representatives, or attorneys.

C. "Or" means and/or.

D. "Relating to" means directly or indirectly referring to, reflecting, constituting, describing, evidencing, containing, embodying, identifying, stating, dealing with or in any manner pertaining to the stated subject matter.

REQUESTS FOR PRODUCTION OF DOCUMENTS

Produce all documents, **specifically including all e-mails and electronically stored documents,** responsive to each request:

1. All documents relating to the Academy's statement that "it offers, and, at all relevant times has offered, students at its Michigan campus the opportunity to transfer credits to an Ohio campus where upon completion of applicable requirements the student can earn an associate degree."

RESPONSE:

2. All documents relating to any "applicable requirements" ever in effect pursuant to which a student at the Academy's Michigan campus, upon completion of the applicable requirements, has purportedly been able to earn an associate degree.

RESPONSE:

3. All documents relating to any approval by any governmental, regulatory or accrediting entity of the granting of associate degrees to students at the Academy's Michigan campus.

RESPONSE:

4. All documents relating to any approval by any governmental, regulatory or accrediting entity of the granting of associate degrees to students from the Academy's Michigan campus who transfer credits to an Ohio campus.

RESPONSE:

5. All documents relating to any communication to students at the Academy's Michigan campus regarding any opportunity to transfer credits to an Ohio campus where upon completion of applicable requirements the student can earn an associate degree.

RESPONSE:

6. All documents relating to each instance in which a student at the Academy's Michigan campus has undertaken to transfer credits to an Ohio campus where upon completion of applicable requirements that student has earned an associate degree.

RESPONSE:

7. All documents purporting to be associate degrees issued to any student who has at any time been enrolled at the Academy's Michigan campus.

RESPONSE:

[Attorney for Plaintiffs]
[Address]

Dated:

F.3 Discovery in Bankruptcy Proceeding to Determine Dischargeability of Student Loan

UNITED STATES BANKRUPTCY COURT
DISTRICT OF NEW JERSEY, CAMDEN VICINAGE

```
_____ )
IN RE [Debtor]           )
                 Debtor  )
[Debtor],                )
              Plaintiff  )
                         )
v.                       )
                         )
United States Department of )
Education                )
              Defendant  )
_____ )
```

PLAINTIFF'S INTERROGATORIES TO DEFENDANT
U.S. DEPARTMENT OF EDUCATION

To: Defendant U.S. Department Of Education
By and through its attorney of record

A. Defendant is hereby required to answer in writing, under oath in accordance with Rule 7033 of the Rules of this court, the interrogatories attached hereto.

B. In answering these interrogatories, furnish all information in the possession of Defendant, its officers, agents and employees and its attorneys and investigators for its attorneys.

C. If Defendant cannot answer the following interrogatories in full after exercising due diligence to secure the information to do so, state the answer to the extent possible specifying your inability to answer the remainder, and state whatever information or knowledge Defendant has concerning the unanswered portion.

D. Each interrogatory is considered continuing, and if Defendant obtains information which renders its answers or one of them, incomplete or inaccurate, Defendant is obligated to serve amended answers on the undersigned.

E. Insofar as may be applicable, and except as otherwise indicated, the term "document" or "documents" shall refer to any and all writings and recorded materials, of any kind whatsoever, that is or has been in the possession, control or custody of Defendant or of which Defendant has knowledge, whether originals or copies, including but not limited to contracts, documents, notes, rough drafts, interoffice memoranda, memoranda for the files, letters, research materials, correspondence, logs, diaries, forms, bank statements, tax returns, card files, books of account, journals, ledgers, invoices, blueprints, diagrams, drawings, computer print-outs or tapes, reports, surveys, statistical computations, studies, pictures, maps, graphs, charts, minutes, manuals, pamphlets, or books of any nature or kind whatsoever; and all other materials handwritten, printed, typed, mimeographed, photocopied or otherwise reproduced; and slides or motion pictures, television tapes; all tape recordings (whether for computer, audio or visual replay) or other written, printed or recorded matter or tangible things on which words, phrases, symbols or information are affixed.

F. A request to "identify" a document is a request to state (insofar as may be applicable):
1. The date of such document.
2. The type of document or written communication it is.
3. The names and present addresses of the person or persons who prepared such document and of the signers, addressors and addressees of such document.
4. The name of any principal whom or which the signers, addressors and preparers of such document were thereby representing.
5. The present location of such document.
6. The name and present address of the person now having custody of the document.
7. Whether you possess or control the original or a copy thereof and if so, the location and name of the custodian of such original or copy.
8. A brief description of the contents of such document.

G. A request to "describe" any oral statement or communication is a request to state:
1. The name and present address of each individual making such statement or communication.
2. The name of any principal or employer whom or which such individual was thereby representing and the position in which such individual was then employed or engaged by such principal or employee.
3. The name and present address of the individual or individuals to whom the oral statement or communication was made, and the name of any principal or employer whom such person or persons were representing at the time of and in connection with such oral statement or communication, as well as the employment position in which they were then employed or engaged.
4. The names and present addresses of any other individuals present when such oral statement or communication was made or who heard or acknowledged hearing the same.
5. The place where such oral statement or communication was made.
6. A brief description of the contents of such oral statement or communication.

H. A request to "cite" portions or provisions of any document is a request to state, insofar as applicable with reference to such portion or provision, the title, date, division, page, sheet, charge order number, and such other information as may be necessary to accurately locate the portion or provision referenced.

I. The term "person" shall include a natural person, partnership, corporation, association, or other group however organized.

J. Whenever a request is made to "identify" a natural person, it shall mean to supply all of the following information:
1. His/her full name.
2. His/her employer and position at the time.
3. The name of any person or entity (natural or artificial) whom she/he is claimed to have represented in connection with the matter to which the interrogatory relates.
4. His/her last known address, telephone number, and employer.
5. His/her present employer.

K. A request to "explain fully" any answer, denial or claim is a request (insofar as may be applicable) to:
1. State fully and specifically each fact and/or contention in support of your answer, denial or claim; and
2. For each such fact or contention, to identify each person who has knowledge relative to that fact or contention, each document that tends to support that fact or contention; and each document that tends to dispute that fact or contention.

L. A request in any of the enclosed interrogatories to "identify" any document is a request to attach said document to answers to these interrogatories. If documents are attached to answers to these interrogatories, they must be marked to identify which interrogatory they refer to. In identifying documents you
   (a) how many hours each loan agent spent under such instruction;
   (b) whether such instruction was mandatory or voluntary;
   (c) the subject matter of the instruction.

INTERROGATORIES

IMPORTANT: All questions containing the terms "document," "documents," "identify," "describe," "cite," "person" or "explain fully" must be answered in accordance with the definitions of those terms contained in the attached instructions.

1. Please identify the person answering each of these interrogatories.

2. Identify each person Defendant may call as a witness in this case.

3. Identify each document which Defendant may introduce into evidence in this case.

4. State the total amount Defendant alleges to be owing as of the date of the filing of this lawsuit.

5. Itemize the total amount Defendant alleges to be owing by unpaid amounts financed, accrued finance charge, and other charges, as applicable.

6. Please identify any and all persons known to Defendant who have personal knowledge concerning the instant loans. Please specify which of these people are agents of Defendant or were agents of Defendant at the time of the instant transaction.

7. State the total amount of dollars in cash that Plaintiff has paid to Defendant. Identify each payment individually and state the date of payment.

8. List separately all persons to whom and charges, fees, or any other amounts were paid in connection with these loans, including the name and address of the payee, the amount disbursed to each, the date of dispersal, and the check number for each dispersal.

9. State whether you received any requests for deferment of loans from Plaintiff. If so, please specify when each request was made.

10. If you identified any requests in interrogatory 9, please provide your response to Plaintiff's requests.

11. State whether you received any requests for forbearance of loans from Plaintiff. If so, please specify when each request was made.

12. If you identified any requests in interrogatory 11, please provide your response to Plaintiff's requests.

13. Identify your procedures for granting of deferment and forbearance of loans at all relevant times.

14. State any policies and/or programs, outside of traditional deferment and forbearance of loans policies, in which plaintiff may have been qualified to participate.

15. If you identified any such policies and/or programs in interrogatory 14, please provide any information relating to Plaintiff's participation.

16. Please state each and every fact which is the basis for your contention in the Second Affirmative Defense of your Answer and Affirmative Defenses that "Debtor has not made a good faith effort to repay the loan and would not qualify for a discharge on the basis of undue hardship," and for each and every fact, please list the name, address, and telephone number of all witnesses with the knowledge relevant to the fact and all documents, giving the document description, date, and custodian, which touches upon or relates to that fact.

17. Please specify all amounts received from Plaintiff, and when such amounts were received, from the total sum identified in your Ninth Affirmative Defense of your Answer and Affirmative Defenses.

18. Please identify all policies relating to deferment and forbearance of loans, utilized by loan guarantors, the [Guaranty Agency].

19. Identify all documents containing information about the instant loans. State which, if any, of the above documents were given to Plaintiff, including where and when each document was given to Plaintiff.

20. Identify each telephone contact made to Plaintiff by Defendant or Defendant's agent regarding the loans. Describe the substance of each such telephone conversation.

21. Identify each document, including each notice, that Defendant mailed or otherwise delivered to Plaintiff concerning the instant loans. For each document, state the address it was mailed to and whether it was received by Plaintiff.

PLEASE TAKE NOTICE that a copy of the answers to the attached interrogatories and the requested documents must be served upon the undersigned within the time allowed by Rule 7033 of the Rules of this Court.

[*Attorney for Plaintiff*]

F.4 Freedom of Information Act Sample Requests

[Date]

Office of the Inspector General
U. S. Department of Education
400 Maryland Avenue, S.W.
Washington, D.C. 20202-1510

Attn: FOIA Request Officer—Inspector General's Office

Dear Sir or Madam:

This is a request for copies of public records under the Freedom of Information Act, 5 U.S.C. § 552 *et seq*. As you know, this Act requires public bodies to make available for inspection and copying all public records, except certain exempt records, within ten working days of receipt of a written request.

Please provide copies of any and all records, reports, forms, writings, letters, memoranda, books, papers, maps, photographs, microfilms, cards, tapes, recordings, electronic data processing records, recorded information and all other documentary material, regardless of physical form or characteristics, having been prepared or having been or being used, received, possessed or under control of the U.S. Department of Education pertaining to **any and all investigations, inquiries, audits, inspections, findings, administrative actions, or other determinations from *1985 to the present* regarding violations of local, state, or federal law, regulations, or guidelines involving** *"ability to benefit" determinations, testing, admissions or the false certification of student eligibility* **for the following school:**

[School]

[Address]

If you determine that any of the information requested is exempt from release, please delete the material which you determine to be exempt and send me copies of the remaining nonexempt material within ten working days. If you do withhold any part of the requested material, please advise me as to which exemption(s) you believe to be applicable.

I am requesting a fee waiver regarding this material. In support of a waiver, I am advising you of the following:

1. The subject of this request concerns the operations or activities of the government, namely, the administration of Title IV by the Department, and in particular the determination of eligibility of institutions which received Title IV funds.

2. The disclosure is likely to contribute to an understanding of the above-mentioned governmental operations and activities both by us and by the indigent clients we represent.

3. The disclosure is likely to contribute to a public understanding of these matters through our work as public interest lawyers for the poor.

4. Neither I nor my office has any commercial interest which would be furthered by disclosure. On the contrary, we are salaried employees of a government-funded program which provides free legal assistance to the poor.

5. The information we obtain will be disseminated and shared with other members of the public. We continue to provide information to other legal aid and community service agencies, as well

as to the general media, on problem schools participating in Title IV financial aid programs. We expect to make some of the materials obtained available through the National Center on Poverty Law, publishers of the Clearinghouse Review, which makes such documents available at no charge to subscribing legal services agencies around the country, as well as to other individuals and organizations, in both paper and computer-readable forms.

If you have any questions concerning this request, I may be reached at (312) 347-8307.

Sincerely,

[*Attorney for Plaintiff*]

[Date]

Freedom of Information Act Officer
U.S. Department of Education
Washington, D.C. 20002

Re: *Freedom of Information Act Request*
School Name: [School]
OPE-ID: [Number]

Dear Sir or Madam:

This is a request pursuant to the Freedom of Information Act, 5 U.S.C. § 552 ("FOIA"). I would like to receive a copy of the following documents (including any original, reproduction or copy of any kind, whether recorded, drafted, printed, written or documentary matters, including without limitation, correspondence, memoranda, reports, records, studies, computer tapes or other computer storage mediums, compilations, and/or summaries of data and other information) and any other written or printed material evidencing, relating to, or commenting upon the following matters at Tri-State Beauty College, referred to hereinafter as the "College," from January 1, 1985 through the present:

1. Pre-admission testing of students who did not have a high school diploma or GED, including efforts to comply with ability-to-benefit requirements promulgated by DOE;

2. Assessments and decisions made regarding students' ability to benefit ("ATB") from the courses and programs offered by the College;

3. Complaints made by any person or organization to DOE, other organization, or the College itself regarding any aspect of the College's admission's process;

4. All inspections, audits, assessments, evaluations, and findings made by any person or organization as to any aspect of the College operations;

5. All litigation or administrative proceedings brought by or against the College;

6. All information regarding College closure dates established by DOE for each branch of the College, including all materials that relate to how each such date was determined;

7. As to student loan closed school discharge applications filed with DOE, the number:

a) granted
b) denied
c) pending

8. As to student loan ability to benefit false certification discharge applications filed with DOE, the number:

a) granted
b) denied
c) pending

9. Default rates of former students and any default reduction plans, programs, and agreements;

10. All applications and documentation submitted by any former student of the College receiving a discharge of a student loan based on false ATB certification by the College; and

11. Any and all "Emergency Action" memoranda relating to the College.

To the extent that you determine that the release of certain requested documents or records would constitute a clearly unwarranted invasion of the personal privacy of third parties, I ask that you proceed according to 5 U.S.C. § 552(b). For each such document or record, please delete or redact the names, addresses, and SSNs of applicants, loan recipients, students and other persons before producing it so as to remove any risk of invading someone's privacy. *See, Norwood v. Federal Aviation Administration*, 993 F.2d 570, 574–576 (Sixth Cir. 1993) (requiring disclosure after names, SSNs, and other information which, by itself, would identify an individual, had been redacted.)

I request a waiver of fees in connection with this request. Disclosure of these records is in the public interest because it will contribute significantly to public understanding of the activities of this proprietary voc-ed College which received federal monies and federally guaranteed loan monies. I will receive no business, commercial, or financial benefit from this request. Release of this information will serve the public interest because it pertains to the operations of the College and the possible discharge of certain student loans. Disclosure of this information also will benefit a large segment of the population, namely those persons in Ohio who attended the College and who have applied or may apply in the future for discharge of their student loans.

The Legal Aid Society of Greater Cincinnati is a federally funded legal services office. As such, it is a non-profit organization that exists to represent low income people both locally and, when appropriate, state-wide in matters such as federally supported education programs. By law, this office represents only clients who cannot afford to pay for legal assistance; they also cannot afford the cost associated with this request. I intend to use the requested information to assist clients.

I look forward to your response within the time frame described in the FOIA. Please contact me at the above number if you have any questions. Thank you for your assistance.

Yours truly,

[*Attorney for Plaintiff*]

Appendix G — Directory of Guaranty Agencies

As discussed in more detail in Chapter 1, *supra*, the FFEL program was eliminated as of July 1, 2010. No new FFEL loans will be made as of this date. Many guaranty agencies, including all those listed below, are still in business mainly in order to service and collect on the outstanding FFEL loans that were made before the program was eliminated. A few of these agencies were also awarded contracts to service the Department's Direct Loan portfolio. As of 2010, Great Lakes Higher Education Corporation and AES/Pennsylvania Higher Education Authority (in addition to Sallie Mae and Nelnet, Inc.) were all named as servicers under the new "performance based" government servicing contract.

The following information may be found at the U.S. Department of Education website at http://wdcrobcolp01.ed.gov/Programs/EROD/org_list.cfm (see under "State Guaranty Agency"). This appendix is also available on the companion website to this manual.

STATES

ALABAMA

Kentucky Higher Education Assistance Authority
P.O. Box 798
Frankfort, KY 40602-0798
Phone: (502) 696-7200
Toll-Free: (800) 928-8926
Fax: (502) 696-7496
E-mail: kragland@kheaa.com
Website: www.kheaa.com
States Served: Alabama, Kentucky

ALASKA

Northwest Education Loan Association
Suite 300
190 Queen Anne Avenue North
Seattle, WA 98109
Phone: (206) 461-5300
Toll-Free: (800) 562-3001
Fax: (206) 461-5434
E-mail: loaninfo@nela.net
Website: www.nela.net
States Served: Alaska, Idaho, Oregon, Washington

ARIZONA

USA Funds
P.O. Box 6028
Indianapolis, IN 46206-6028
Phone: (317) 806-1200
Toll-Free: (866) 329-7673
Fax: (317) 806-1203
E-mail: contact@usafunds.org
Website: www.usafunds.org
States Served: American Samoa, Arizona, Commonwealth of the Northern Mariana Islands, Federated States of Micronesia, Guam, Hawaii, Indiana, Kansas, Maryland, Mississippi, Nevada, Republic of Palau, Republic of the Marshall Islands, Wyoming

ARKANSAS

Student Loan Guarantee Foundation of Arkansas
10 Turtle Creek Lane
Little Rock, AR 72202-1884
Phone: (501) 372-1491
Toll-Free: (800) 622-3446
Fax: (501) 688-7675
E-mail: slgfa@slgfa.org
Website: www.slgfa.org

CALIFORNIA

EdFund
P.O. Box 419045
Rancho Cordova, CA 95741-9045
Phone: (916) 526-7900
Toll-Free: (877) 233-3863
E-mail: mkelly@edfund.org
Website: www.edfund.org

COLORADO

College Assist
Suite 400
3015 South Parker Road
Aurora, CO 80014
Phone: (303) 696-3500
Toll-Free: (800) 727-9834
Fax: (303) 696-3617
E-mail: askops@college-assist.com or florence.lucero@college-assist.com
Website: www.college-assist.com

CONNECTICUT

Connecticut Student Loan Foundation
525 Brook Street
P.O. Box 1009
Rocky Hill, CT 06067
Phone: (860) 257-4001
Toll-Free: (800) 237-9721
Fax: (860) 563-3247
E-mail: mtrombl@mail.cslf.org or kcharry@mail.cslf.org
Website: www.cslf.com

DELAWARE

American Education Services/PHEAA
1200 North Seventh Street
Harrisburg, PA 17102-1444
Toll-Free: (800) 692-7392
Fax: (717) 720-3903
TTY: (800) 654-5988
E-mail: loanhelp@aessuccess.org
Website: www.aessuccess.org
States Served: Delaware, Pennsylvania, West Virginia

DISTRICT OF COLUMBIA

American Student Assistance
Suite 1600
100 Cambridge Street
Boston, MA 02114
Phone: (617) 728-4200
Toll-Free: (800) 999-9080
E-mail: loaninfo@amsa.com
Website: www.amsa.com/index.cfm
States Served: District of Columbia, Massachusetts

FLORIDA

Office of Student Financial Assistance (Florida)
Florida Department of Education
Suite 70
325 West Gaines Street

Suite 1314
Tallahassee, FL 32399-0400
Phone: (850) 410-5200
Toll-Free: (800) 366-3475
Fax: (850) 488-3612
E-mail: osfa@fldoe.org or
Levis.Hughes@fldoe.org
Website: www.floridastudentfinancialaid.org/osfahomepg.htm

GEORGIA
Georgia Student Finance Commission
2082 East Exchange Place
Tucker, GA 30084
Phone: (770) 724-9022
Toll-Free: (800) 505-4732
Fax: (770) 724-9004
E-mail: info@gsfc.org or monetr@gsfc.org
Website: www.gsfc.org

HAWAII
USA Funds
P.O. Box 6028
Indianapolis, IN 46206-6028
Phone: (317) 806-1200
Toll-Free: (866) 329-7673
Fax: (317) 806-1203
E-mail: contact@usafunds.org
Website: www.usafunds.org
States Served: American Samoa, Arizona, Commonwealth of the Northern Mariana Islands, Federated States of Micronesia, Guam, Hawaii, Indiana, Kansas, Maryland, Mississippi, Nevada, Republic of Palau, Republic of the Marshall Islands, Wyoming

IDAHO
Northwest Education Loan Association
Suite 300
190 Queen Anne Avenue North
Seattle, WA 98109
Phone: (206) 461-5300
Toll-Free: (800) 562-3001
Fax: (206) 461-5434
E-mail: loaninfo@nela.net
Website: www.nela.net
States Served: Alaska, Idaho, Oregon, Washington

ILLINOIS
Illinois Student Assistance Commission
1755 Lake Cook Road
Deerfield, IL 60015-5209
Phone: (847) 948-8500
Toll-Free: (800) 899-4722
Fax: (847) 831-8549
TTY: (800) 526-0857
E-mail: collegezone@isac.org
Website: www.collegezone.com

INDIANA
USA Funds
P.O. Box 6028
Indianapolis, IN 46206-6028
Phone: (317) 806-1200
Toll-Free: (866) 329-7673
Fax: (317) 806-1203
E-mail: contact@usafunds.org
Website: www.usafunds.org
States Served: American Samoa, Arizona, Commonwealth of the Northern Mariana Islands, Federated States of Micronesia, Guam, Hawaii, Indiana, Kansas, Maryland, Mississippi, Nevada, Republic of Palau, Republic of the Marshall Islands, Wyoming

IOWA
Iowa College Student Aid Commission
Fourth Floor
200 10th Street
Des Moines, IA 50309-3609
Phone: (515) 725-3400
Toll-Free: (800) 383-4222
Toll-Free Restrictions: IA residents only
Fax: (515) 725-3401
E-mail: info@iowacollegeaid.org or keith.greiner@iowa.gov
Website: www.iowacollegeaid.org

KANSAS
USA Funds
P.O. Box 6028
Indianapolis, IN 46206-6028
Phone: (317) 806-1200
Toll-Free: (866) 329-7673
Fax: (317) 806-1203
E-mail: contact@usafunds.org
Website: www.usafunds.org
States Served: American Samoa, Arizona, Commonwealth of the Northern Mariana Islands, Federated States of Micronesia, Guam, Hawaii, Indiana, Kansas, Maryland, Mississippi, Nevada, Republic of Palau, Republic of the Marshall Islands, Wyoming

KENTUCKY
Kentucky Higher Education Assistance Authority
P.O. Box 798
Frankfort, KY 40602-0798
Phone: (502) 696-7200
Toll-Free: (800) 928-8926
Fax: (502) 696-7496
E-mail: kragland@kheaa.com
Website: www.kheaa.com
States Served: Alabama, Kentucky

LOUISIANA
Louisiana Office of Student Financial Assistance
P.O. Box 91202
Baton Rouge, LA 70821-9202
Phone: (225) 922-1012
Toll-Free: (800) 259-5626 x1012
Fax: (225) 922-0790
E-mail: custserv@osfa.la.gov
Website: www.osfa.la.gov

MAINE
Finance Authority of Maine
Five Community Drive
P.O. Box 949
Augusta, ME 04332-0949
Phone: (207) 623-3263
Toll-Free: (800) 228-3734
Fax: (207) 623-0095
TTY: (207) 626-2717
E-mail: education@famemaine.com
Website: www.famemaine.com

MARYLAND
USA Funds
P.O. Box 6028
Indianapolis, IN 46206-6028
Phone: (317) 806-1200
Toll-Free: (866) 329-7673
Fax: (317) 806-1203
E-mail: contact@usafunds.org
Website: www.usafunds.org
States Served: American Samoa, Arizona, Commonwealth of the Northern Mariana Islands, Federated States of Micronesia, Guam, Hawaii, Indiana, Kansas, Maryland, Mississippi, Nevada, Republic of Palau, Republic of the Marshall Islands, Wyoming

MASSACHUSETTS
American Student Assistance
Suite 1600
100 Cambridge Street
Boston, MA 02114
Phone: (617) 728-4200
Toll-Free: (800) 999-9080
E-mail: loaninfo@amsa.com
Website: www.amsa.com/index.cfm
States Served: District of Columbia, Massachusetts

MICHIGAN
Michigan Guaranty Agency
P.O. Box 30047
Lansing, MI 48909-7547
Toll-Free: (800) 642-5626
Fax: (517) 241-0155
E-mail: mga@michigan.gov
Website: www.MGALOAN.com

MINNESOTA
Great Lakes Higher Education Corporation
2401 International Lane
Madison, WI 53704-3192
Phone: (608) 246-1800
Toll-Free: (800) 236-5900
Fax: (800) 375-5288
E-mail: CollectionSupport@glhec.org
Website: www.mygreatlakes.org
States Served: Minnesota, Ohio, Puerto Rico, Virgin Islands, Wisconsin

MISSISSIPPI
USA Funds
P.O. Box 6028
Indianapolis, IN 46206-6028
Phone: (317) 806-1200
Toll-Free: (866) 329-7673
Fax: (317) 806-1203
E-mail: contact@usafunds.org

Directory of Guaranty Agencies Appx. G-PA

Website: www.usafunds.org
States Served: American Samoa, Arizona, Commonwealth of the Northern Mariana Islands, Federated States of Micronesia, Guam, Hawaii, Indiana, Kansas, Maryland, Mississippi, Nevada, Republic of Palau, Republic of the Marshall Islands, Wyoming

MISSOURI
Missouri Department of Higher Education
3515 Amazonas Drive
Jefferson City, MO 65109
Phone: (573) 751-2361
Toll-Free: (800) 473-6757
Fax: (573) 751-6635
TTY: (800) 735-2966
E-mail: info@dhe.mo.gov
Website: www.dhe.mo.gov

MONTANA
Montana Guaranteed Student Loan Program
P.O. Box 203101
Helena, MT 59620-3101
Phone: (406) 444-6594
Toll-Free: (800) 537-7508
Fax: (406) 444-1869
E-mail: baliperto@mgslp.state.mt.us or rmuffick@mgslp.state.mt.us
Website: www.mgslp.org

NEBRASKA
Nebraska National Student Loan Program
P.O. Box 82507
Lincoln, NE 68501-2507
Phone: (402) 475-8686
Toll-Free: (800) 735-8778
Fax: (402) 479-6658
TTY: (800) 735-8778
E-mail: JillH@nslp.org or RandyH@nslp.org
Website: www.nslp.org

NEVADA
USA Funds
P.O. Box 6028
Indianapolis, IN 46206-6028
Phone: (317) 806-1200
Toll-Free: (866) 329-7673
Fax: (317) 806-1203
E-mail: contact@usafunds.org
Website: www.usafunds.org
States Served: American Samoa, Arizona, Commonwealth of the Northern Mariana Islands, Federated States of Micronesia, Guam, Hawaii, Indiana, Kansas, Maryland, Mississippi, Nevada, Republic of Palau, Republic of the Marshall Islands, Wyoming

NEW HAMPSHIRE
New Hampshire Higher Education Assistance Foundation
P.O. Box 877
Four Barrell Court
Concord, NH 03302-2087
Phone: (603) 225-6612
Toll-Free: (800) 525-2577
Fax: (603) 228-6726
E-mail: info@gsmr.org or collegeplanning@gsmr.org
Website: www.nhheaf.org

NEW JERSEY
Higher Education Student Assistance Authority (New Jersey)
P.O. Box 540
Trenton, NJ 08625-0540
Phone: (609) 588-3211
Toll-Free: (800) 792-8670
Fax: (609) 588-7389
TTY: (609) 588-2526
E-mail: abouse@hesaa.org or tgervasio@hesaa.org
Website: www.hesaa.org

New Jersey After 3, Inc.
Second Floor
391 George Street
New Brunswick, NJ 08901
Phone: (732) 246-7933
E-mail: info@njafter3.org
Website: www.njafter3.org

NEW MEXICO
New Mexico Student Loan Guarantee Corporation
7400 Tiburon NE
P.O. Box 27020
Albuquerque, NM 87109
Phone: (505) 345-3371
Toll-Free: (800) 279-5063
Fax: (505) 344-3631
E-mail: answers@nmstudentloans.org
Website: www.nmslgc.org

NEW YORK
New York State Higher Education Services Corporation
99 Washington Avenue
Albany, NY 12255
Phone: (518) 473-7087
Toll-Free: (888) 697-4372
Fax: (518) 474-2839
TTY: (800) 445-5234
E-mail: hescpublicaffairs@hesc.org or kcrowder@hesc.org
Website: www.hesc.com/content.nsf

NORTH CAROLINA
North Carolina State Education Assistance Authority
P.O. Box 13663
Research Triangle Park, NC 27709
Phone: (919) 549-8614
Toll-Free: (800) 700-1775
Fax: (919) 549-8481
E-mail: robbie@ncseaa.edu or information@ncseaa.edu
Website: www.CFNC.org

NORTH DAKOTA
Student Loans of North Dakota
c/o Bank of North Dakota
P.O. Box 5524
1200 Memorial Highway
Bismarck, ND 58506-5524
Phone: (701) 328-5654
Toll-Free: (800) 472-2166
Fax: (701) 328-5716
TTY: (800) 643-3916
E-mail: werhardt@nd.gov or slndga@nd.gov
Website: http://starthere4loans.nd.gov

OHIO
Great Lakes Higher Education Corporation
2401 International Lane
Madison, WI 53704-3192
Phone: (608) 246-1800
Toll-Free: (800) 236-5900
Fax: (800) 375-5288
E-mail: CollectionSupport@glhec.org
Website: www.mygreatlakes.org
States Served: Minnesota, Ohio, Puerto Rico, Virgin Islands, Wisconsin

OKLAHOMA
Oklahoma Guaranteed Student Loan Program
P.O. Box 3000
Oklahoma City, OK 73101-3000
Phone: (405) 234-4300
Toll-Free: (800) 442-8642
Fax: (405) 234-4390
TTY: (800) 522-8506
E-mail: infobox@ogslp.org or jsmith@ogslp.org
Website: www.ogslp.org

OREGON
Educational Credit Management Corporation (Oregon)
Suite 190
1500 Valley River Drive
Eugene, OR 97401
Phone: (541) 984-2450
Toll-Free: (888) 323-3262
Fax: (541) 984-2468
TTY: (541) 984-2469
E-mail: info@ecmc.org or jkupper@ecmc.org
Website: www.ecmc.org

Northwest Education Loan Association
Suite 300
190 Queen Anne Avenue North
Seattle, WA 98109
Phone: (206) 461-5300
Toll-Free: (800) 562-3001
Fax: (206) 461-5434
E-mail: loaninfo@nela.net
Website: www.nela.net
States Served: Alaska, Idaho, Oregon, Washington

PENNSYLVANIA
American Education Services/PHEAA
1200 North Seventh Street
Harrisburg, PA 17102-1444
Toll-Free: (800) 692-7392
Fax: (717) 720-3903

TTY: (800) 654-5988
E-mail: loanhelp@aessuccess.org
Website: www.aessuccess.org
States Served: Delaware, Pennsylvania, West Virginia

RHODE ISLAND
Rhode Island Higher Education Assistance Authority
560 Jefferson Boulevard
Warwick, RI 02886-1320
Phone: (401) 736-1170
Toll-Free: (800) 922-9855
Fax: (401) 732-3541
TTY: (401) 222-6195
E-mail: grants@riheaa.org or info@riheaa.org
Website: www.riheaa.org

SOUTH CAROLINA
South Carolina Student Loan
P.O. Box 21487
Interstate Center, Suite 210
Columbia, SC 29221
Phone: (803) 798-0916
Toll-Free: (800) 347-2752
Fax: (803) 772-9410
E-mail: mfox@scstudentloan.org
Website: www.scstudentloan.org

SOUTH DAKOTA
Education Assistance Corporation
115 First Avenue SW
Aberdeen, SD 57401
Phone: (605) 225-6423
Toll-Free: (800) 592-1802
Fax: (800) 354-7070
TTY: (800) 752-3949
E-mail: EAC@eac-easci.org
Website: www2.eac-easci.org/welcome.shtml

TENNESSEE
Tennessee Student Assistance Corporation
Suite 1510, Parkway Towers
404 James Robertson Parkway
Nashville, TN 37243-0820
Phone: (615) 741-1346 x139
Toll-Free: (800) 342-1663
Fax: (615) 741-6101
E-mail: stephanie.aylor@state.tn.us or levis.hughes@state.tn.us
Website: www.tn.gov/CollegePays/index.html

TEXAS
TG (Texas Guaranteed Student Loan Corporation)
P.O. Box 83100
Round Rock, TX 78683-3100
Phone: (512) 219-5700
Toll-Free: (800) 845-6267
Fax: (512) 219-4633
TTY: (512) 219-4560
E-mail: cust.assist@tgslc.org
Website: www.tgslc.org

UTAH
Utah Higher Education Assistance Authority
The Board of Regents Building
The Gateway
60 South 400 West
Salt Lake City, UT 84101-1284
Phone: (801) 321-7200
Toll-Free: (800) 418-8757
Fax: (801) 321-7299
TTY: (801) 321-7130
E-mail: uheaa@utahsbr.edu
Website: www.uheaa.org

VERMONT
Vermont Student Assistance Corporation
P.O. Box 2000
10 East Allen Street
Winooski, VT 05404-2601
Phone: (802) 655-9602
Toll-Free: (800) 642-3177
Fax: (802) 654-3765
TTY: (802) 654-3766
E-mail: info@vsac.org
Website: www.vsac.org

VIRGINIA
Educational Credit Management Corporation (Virginia)
Boulders VII
Suite 200
7325 Beaufont Springs Drive
Richmond, VA 23225
Phone: (804) 267-7100
Toll-Free: (888) 775-3262
Fax: (804) 267-7159
TTY: (804) 267-7104
E-mail: response@ecmc.org or mhawkes@ecmc.org
Website: www.ecmc.org

WASHINGTON
Northwest Education Loan Association
Suite 300
190 Queen Anne Avenue North
Seattle, WA 98109
Phone: (206) 461-5300
Toll-Free: (800) 562-3001
Fax: (206) 461-5434
E-mail: loaninfo@nela.net
Website: www.nela.net
States Served: Alaska, Idaho, Oregon, Washington

WEST VIRGINIA
American Education Services/PHEAA
1200 North Seventh Street
Harrisburg, PA 17102-1444
Toll-Free: (800) 692-7392
Fax: (717) 720-3903
TTY: (800) 654-5988
E-mail: loanhelp@aessuccess.org
Website: www.aessuccess.org
States Served: Delaware, Pennsylvania, West Virginia

WISCONSIN
Great Lakes Higher Education Corporation
2401 International Lane
Madison, WI 53704-3192
Phone: (608) 246-1800
Toll-Free: (800) 236-5900
Fax: (800) 375-5288
E-mail: CollectionSupport@glhec.org
Website: www.mygreatlakes.org
States Served: Minnesota, Ohio, Puerto Rico, Virgin Islands, Wisconsin

WYOMING
USA Funds
P.O. Box 6028
Indianapolis, IN 46206-6028
Phone: (317) 806-1200
Toll-Free: (866) 329-7673
Fax: (317) 806-1203
E-mail: contact@usafunds.org
Website: www.usafunds.org
States Served: American Samoa, Arizona, Commonwealth of the Northern Mariana Islands, Federated States of Micronesia, Guam, Hawaii, Indiana, Kansas, Maryland, Mississippi, Nevada, Republic of Palau, Republic of the Marshall Islands, Wyoming

TERRITORIES

AMERICAN SAMOA
USA Funds
P.O. Box 6028
Indianapolis, IN 46206-6028
Phone: (317) 806-1200
Toll-Free: (866) 329-7673
Fax: (317) 806-1203
E-mail: contact@usafunds.org
Website: www.usafunds.org
States Served: American Samoa, Arizona, Commonwealth of the Northern Mariana Islands, Federated States of Micronesia, Guam, Hawaii, Indiana, Kansas, Maryland, Mississippi, Nevada, Republic of Palau, Republic of the Marshall Islands, Wyoming

COMMONWEALTH OF THE NORTHERN MARIANA ISLANDS
USA Funds
P.O. Box 6028
Indianapolis, IN 46206-6028
Phone: (317) 806-1200
Toll-Free: (866) 329-7673
Fax: (317) 806-1203
E-mail: contact@usafunds.org
Website: www.usafunds.org
States Served: American Samoa, Arizona, Commonwealth of the Northern Mariana Islands, Federated States of Micronesia, Guam, Hawaii, Indiana, Kansas, Maryland, Mississippi, Nevada, Republic of Palau, Republic of the Marshall Islands, Wyoming

Directory of Guaranty Agencies   Appx. G-VI

FEDERATED STATES OF MICRONESIA
USA Funds
P.O. Box 6028
Indianapolis, IN 46206-6028
Phone: (317) 806-1200
Toll-Free: (866) 329-7673
Fax: (317) 806-1203
E-mail: contact@usafunds.org
Website: www.usafunds.org
States Served: American Samoa, Arizona, Commonwealth of the Northern Mariana Islands, Federated States of Micronesia, Guam, Hawaii, Indiana, Kansas, Maryland, Mississippi, Nevada, Republic of Palau, Republic of the Marshall Islands, Wyoming

GUAM
USA Funds
P.O. Box 6028
Indianapolis, IN 46206-6028
Phone: (317) 806-1200
Toll-Free: (866) 329-7673
Fax: (317) 806-1203
E-mail: contact@usafunds.org
Website: www.usafunds.org
States Served: American Samoa, Arizona, Commonwealth of the Northern Mariana Islands, Federated States of Micronesia, Guam, Hawaii, Indiana, Kansas, Maryland, Mississippi, Nevada, Republic of Palau, Republic of the Marshall Islands, Wyoming

PUERTO RICO
Great Lakes Higher Education Corporation
2401 International Lane
Madison, WI 53704-3192
Phone: (608) 246-1800
Toll-Free: (800) 236-5900
Fax: (800) 375-5288
E-mail: CollectionSupport@glhec.org
Website: www.mygreatlakes.org
States Served: Minnesota, Ohio, Puerto Rico, Virgin Islands, Wisconsin

REPUBLIC OF PALAU
USA Funds
P.O. Box 6028
Indianapolis, IN 46206-6028
Phone: (317) 806-1200
Toll-Free: (866) 329-7673
Fax: (317) 806-1203
E-mail: contact@usafunds.org
Website: www.usafunds.org
States Served: American Samoa, Arizona, Commonwealth of the Northern Mariana Islands, Federated States of Micronesia, Guam, Hawaii, Indiana, Kansas, Maryland, Mississippi, Nevada, Republic of Palau, Republic of the Marshall Islands, Wyoming

REPUBLIC OF THE MARSHALL ISLANDS
USA Funds
P.O. Box 6028
Indianapolis, IN 46206-6028
Phone: (317) 806-1200
Toll-Free: (866) 329-7673
Fax: (317) 806-1203
E-mail: contact@usafunds.org
Website: www.usafunds.org
States Served: American Samoa, Arizona, Commonwealth of the Northern Mariana Islands, Federated States of Micronesia, Guam, Hawaii, Indiana, Kansas, Maryland, Mississippi, Nevada, Republic of Palau, Republic of the Marshall Islands, Wyoming

VIRGIN ISLANDS
Great Lakes Higher Education Corporation
2401 International Lane
Madison, WI 53704-3192
Phone: (608) 246-1800
Toll-Free: (800) 236-5900
Fax: (800) 375-5288
E-mail: CollectionSupport@glhec.org
Website: www.mygreatlakes.org
States Served: Minnesota, Ohio, Puerto Rico, Virgin Islands, Wisconsin

Appendix H — Student Loan Collection Agencies

The Department of Education contracts with collection agencies to administer certain collection activities. According to the Department, only those accounts that fail to establish and adhere to a repayment arrangement are subject to assignment to a collection agency. The list of collection agencies is posted on the Department's website and reprinted below. It is current as of July 2010. The list can also be found on the companion website to this manual. Future supplements will include any changes that are posted on the Department's website. Advocates may also check the site on their own at www.ed.gov/offices/OSFAP/DCS/collection.agencies.html.

Account Control Technology, Inc.
P.O. Box 11750
Bakersfield, CA 93380-1750
(866) 887-2800

Allied Interstate, Inc.
P.O. Box 26190
Minneapolis, MN 55426
(800) 715-0395

Coast Professional, Inc.
P.O. Box 2899
West Monroe, LA 71294
(888) 869-1170

CollectCorp
P.O. Box 960
Phoenix, Arizona 85001
(877) 719-7015

Collection Technology, Inc.
P.O. Box 2036
Monterey Park, CA 91754
(800) 620-4284

Collecto, Inc. D.b.a. Collection Company of America
P.O. Box 5369
Norwell, MA 02061-5369
(800) 896-0282

ConServe
P.O. Box 190
Fairport, NY 14450-0190
(866) 804-1700

Delta Management Associates, Inc.
P.O. Box 9192
Chelsea, MA 02150-9192
(866) 441-1957

Diversified Collection Services, Inc.
P.O. Box 9049
Pleasanton, CA 94566-9049
(888) 335-6267

Enterprise Recovery Systems, Inc.
P.O. Box 5288
Oak Brook, IL 60522
(888) 377-5000

Financial Asset Management Systems, INC. (FAMS)
P.O. Box 451109
Atlanta, GA 31145-9109
(888) 668-6925

FMS Investment Corp.
P.O. Box 1423
Elk Grove Village, IL 60009-1423
(800) 889-6321

GC Services
P.O. Box 27323
Knoxville, TN 37927
(866) 846-9964

Immediate Credit Recovery Inc.
P.O. Box 965363
Marietta, GA 30066
(866) 401-7190

National Recoveries
P.O. Box 48367
Minneapolis, MN 55448
(877) 221-9729

NCO
P.O. Box 4929
Trenton, NJ 08650-4929
(888) 475-6741

Pioneer Credit Recovery, Inc.
P.O. Box 99
Arcade, NY 14009
(888) 287-0571

Premiere Credit of North America, L.L.C.
P.O. Box 19289
Indianapolis, IN 46219
(866) 808-7286

Progressive Financial Services
P.O. Box 24098
Tempe, AZ 85285
(800) 745-2345

The CBE Group, Inc.
P.O. Box 930
Waterloo IA 50704-0930
(800) 410-8089

West Asset Management, Inc.
P.O. Box 105646
Atlanta, GA 30348
(800) 270-1022

Windham Professionals, Inc.
P.O. Box 400
East Aurora, NY 14052
(877) 719-4440

Van Ru Credit Corporation
P.O. Box 1027
Skokie, IL 60076-8027
(888) 337-8331

Appendix I   Federal Student Financial Assistance: Frequently Asked Questions

This appendix contains frequently asked questions regarding federal student financial assistance. The questions and answers are provided by NCLC. Additional information may be found at NCLC's Student Loan Borrower Assistance website, www.studentloanborrowerassistance.org. This appendix can also be found on the companion website to this manual.

1. Is Everyone Eligible for Federal Student Assistance?

No. There are a number of requirements to get federal aid. The first requirement is that you must be a student pursuing higher education. You must also be enrolled in a degree, certificate, or other approved program at an eligible higher education school. You must be a U.S. citizen or eligible non-citizen. In addition, you must have a valid Social Security number and register with the Selective Service if required. Also, your eligibility for federal student aid is suspended if you have a conviction for sale or possession of illegal drugs. The period of ineligibility based on drug conviction varies.

2. Must I Have a High School Diploma?

No. You are eligible for financial aid even if you don't have a high school diploma, but the school must certify that you can benefit from the instruction by giving you a valid "ability-to-benefit" (ATB) test. You must pass this test if you don't have a high school diploma or equivalency at the time of admission. You may also be able to meet the "ability to benefit" standard by completing a minimum level of coursework at the institution of higher education.

3. Is Assistance Based on Financial Need?

In most cases, yes. Most federal financial aid is awarded on the basis of financial need. There are a couple of important exceptions. You can get an unsubsidized Stafford loan without having to demonstrate financial need. PLUS loans are also unsubsidized and not dependent on financial need. Interest is charged on unsubsidized loans from the time the loan is disbursed until it's paid in full. In contrast, interest on subsidized loans is not charged until repayment begins. The government pays while the borrower is in school and during grace and deferment periods.

4. Can Parents Borrow to Finance Their Children's Education?

Yes. Parents can apply for the PLUS loan program to help pay education expenses for dependent undergraduate students. Parents have to pass a credit check to qualify. (PLUS loans are also available for graduate and professional students.)

5. What Are the Different Types of Student Loans and What's the Difference Between Them?

As of July 1, 2010, nearly all federal loans will be made by the government through the Direct Loans program. The Family Education Loan program (FFEL) is eliminated as of this date. FFEL loans were made by private lenders and guaranteed by the government.

Perkins loans are still being made. These loans are low-interest loans for both undergraduate and graduate students with exceptional financial need. Perkins loans are originated and serviced by participating schools and repaid to the schools.

These are the main federal financial loan programs. There are also federal grant programs, such as the Federal Pell Grant Program, as well as many state financial assistance programs. In addition, there are many private lenders that offer student loans.

6. What Happens After I Finish School? Do I Have to Pay My Loans Back Right Away?

In most cases, no. The repayment date varies depending on the type of loan you have. Stafford loan repayment generally begins six months after graduation. The time before you have to start repaying is called a grace period. You don't have to pay any principal on the loan and you won't be charged interest during the grace period if you have a subsidized loan. During the grace period on an unsubsidized loan, you don't have to pay any principal, but you will be charged interest. You can choose to pay the interest during the grace period. Perkins loan repayment usually begins nine months after graduation. PLUS loans generally must be paid back within sixty days after the final loan disbursement. However, since July 1, 2008, student PLUS loan borrowers can defer repayment until six months after school. Parent PLUS loan borrowers with these loans can defer repayment while the student on whose behalf the loan was taken is in school and for six months after school. Parents must request this deferment. Because PLUS loans are unsubsidized, interest will accrue during the deferment period.

7. What Happens If I Drop Out? Do I Still Have to Pay Back My Loans?

You may cancel all or a portion of your loan if you inform the school within fourteen days after the school sends you notice that it is crediting your account. If you withdraw later than that, there is a formula that schools must use to determine the amount of assistance you have earned up until your withdrawal date. If you received more assistance than you earned, the excess funds must be returned. If you received excess funds, your school should help explain what portion needs to be returned.

The amount of financial assistance you've earned is calculated on a pro-rata basis. For example, if you completed 30% of the payment period or period of enrollment, you earned 30% of the assistance you were originally scheduled to receive. Once you've completed more than 60% of the payment period or period of enrollment, you earn all of your assistance. You are generally responsible for paying back the assistance you have earned.

8. Do I Have to Pay Back My Loans If the School Didn't Provide Quality Instruction?

Probably. However, you may have some options particularly if the school deceived you by promising something that it didn't deliver. You may be able to raise deception or fraud as a defense if you are later sued for collection. The problem is that it is very difficult to get the lender on the hook for problems caused by the school. You should be eligible to cancel your loan if the school closed while you were in attendance or within ninety days of when you withdrew (see question # 11 below). Be sure to send complaints about the school to both the state and federal departments of education. The sooner you complain, the more likely you can get help.

9. What Can I Do If I Can't Pay Back My Loans?

The answer depends first on whether you are already in default. You have a lot more options if you haven't yet defaulted. In general, you will be in default if you haven't made your payments for nine months.

One way to stay out of trouble before default is to change your payment plan to a more affordable plan. Although the options vary depending on the type of loan you have, every program gives you choices beyond the standard ten-year repayment plan. Both the FFEL and Direct Loan programs have payment plan options for low-income borrowers. Since July 1, 2009, both programs offer income-based repayment to eligible borrowers. The Direct Loan program also has a separate income-contingent repayment plan (ICRP) and the FFEL program has a separate income-sensitive repayment plan (ISRP). Under these plans, your monthly loan payment is based on your annual income, family size, and loan amount.

You can also postpone (or defer) your payments if you are not yet in default (see #10 below). Additionally, you should be able to apply for forbearance whether you are in default or not. Forbearance is a temporary stoppage of payments, extension of time to make payments, or acceptance of smaller payments. Unlike deferments, interest continues to accrue while you are in a forbearance period.

10. What Types of Deferments Are Available?

The deferments are somewhat different depending on the type of loan you have. The following deferments are available for most loans disbursed after July 1993:

- Student deferments for at least half-time study;
- Graduate fellowship deferments;
- Rehabilitation training program deferments;
- Unemployment deferments not to exceed three years;
- Economic hardship deferments, granted one year at a time for a maximum of three years; or
- Military service and post-active-duty deferments.

11. What Types of Cancellations Are Available?

Cancellations vary by type of loan. In particular, the Perkins loan program has many more options than other loan programs. The key cancellation options for all federal loan programs are:

- Closed school (the school closed while you were enrolled or close to the time you withdrew);
- False certification (the school falsely certified your eligibility, usually because you were not a high school graduate and there was a problem with the ability-to-benefit test. There are other grounds for false certification cancellations, including if your loan was forged or if you were a victim of identity theft);
- Borrower's permanent and total disability;
- Borrower's death;
- Unpaid refund (partial or full cancellation if the school failed to pay a refund owed);
- Public service cancellations for borrowers with Direct Loans who have balances remaining after ten years of repayment; or
- Limited cancellations for teachers working in certain designated low-income areas or teaching high-need subjects such as math and science.

You should always check first to see whether you are eligible for a cancellation. This is the most complete way to get out of trouble. If you apply and qualify, your loan will be cancelled, any money you paid voluntarily or involuntarily should be returned, and your credit report should be cleared up.

12. How Do I Apply for a Cancellation?

You usually have to apply in writing. There are different forms for different types of cancellations. The forms are available on the Department of Education website (www.ed.gov) or by calling the Federal Student Aid Line, 1-800-4-FED-AID. The forms are also reprinted in the National Consumer Law Center's publication, *Student Loan Law* (4th ed. 2010).

13. What Can the Government Do to Collect from Me If I Can't Repay My Loans?

The government has collection powers far beyond those of most private creditors. Once you are in default, they can try to collect from you in the following ways:

- Seizing your tax return;
- Garnishing a portion of your wages;
- Taking a portion of certain federal benefits such as Social Security retirement; or
- Suing you in court.

Like most creditors, the government will also report delinquencies and defaults to credit reporting bureaus. Even before you are in default, if you stop paying back your loans, you will begin to receive collection letters and phone calls informing you of the various powers the government can use to collect from you.

14. Doesn't the Government Have to Sue Me First Before Garnishing My Wages, Seizing My Tax Return, or Taking My Federal Benefits?

No.

15. Does the Government Have a Time Limit When They Have to Stop Collecting from Me?

In general, there is no statute of limitations for student loan collections.

16. Can I Go Back to School If I Already Have an Outstanding Student Loan?

You can go back to school, but you are not eligible for new financial assistance if you are in default on previous federal loans. You can become eligible again if you can get out of default.

17. Can I Discharge My Student Loan in Bankruptcy?

Only in very limited circumstances. You must show that repaying your student loan will cause "undue hardship." You can find out more about this standard in the National Consumer Law Center's publication, *Student Loan Law* (4th ed. 2010). This heightened standard applies to both federal and private loans.

18. What Is Loan Consolidation?

Loan consolidation generally allows you to lower monthly payments by combining several loans into one packaged loan and extending your repayment period. It is similar to refinancing a mortgage loan. You can even consolidate just one loan. As of July 1, 2010, all government consolidation loans will be made through the Direct Loan Program. You can find out about the Department of Education's Direct Loan consolidation program by calling 1-800-557-7392 or going on-line at www.loanconsolidation.ed.gov.

19. What Are the Best Ways to Get Out of Default?

The most complete solution is to cancel your loan (see question # 11 above). The problem is that cancellations are available only in very limited circumstances.

You can renew eligibility, but not necessarily get out of default, by requesting a "reasonable and affordable payment plan" and making six on-time consecutive payments under this plan. It is critical not to enter into a repayment plan that you can't afford. If you stop making payments after renewing eligibility through a reasonable and affordable repayment plan, you won't automatically have this option again.

If you make nine consecutive on-time payments in a ten-month period and jump through a few other hoops, you will be eligible to "rehabilitate" your loan. Successful rehabilitation will get you out of default. You are allowed only one rehabilitation per loan.

Loan consolidation (see question # 18 above) is another option. Consolidation eliminates the old loans on which you were in default in favor of a new consolidation loan, with new terms and a new payment schedule. There are some limits to how many times you can consolidate as a way out of default.

In some cases, you can also get out of default by paying a lump sum to the Department of Education or requesting the Department to compromise your loan.

20. Where Can I Go for More Information?

You can find a lot of information on the National Consumer Law Center's Student Loan Borrower Assistance Project's website at www.studentloanborrowerassistance.org. The Department of Education's website is at www.ed.gov. You can also call the Department of Education toll-free at the Federal Student Aid Information Center, 1-800-4-FED-AID (1-800-433-3243). The number for TTY users is 1-800-730-8913. You can get information about the Direct Consolidation Loan program by calling 1-800-557-7392 (TTY: 1-800-557-7395). If you already have a student loan and are having a problem, you should consider contacting the Student Loan Ombudsman toll-free at 1-877-557-2575 or on-line at http://ombudsman.ed.gov. You should first try to resolve the problem on your own before calling the Ombudsman.

The Department of Education publishes very useful guides, including *Funding Education Beyond High School* and *Repaying Your Student Loans*. These guides are available on the Department's website at www.ed.gov. The National Consumer Law Center publishes *Student Loan Law* (4th ed. 2010), a guide for advocates representing clients with student loan problems. See www.consumerlaw.org or call National Consumer Law Center Publications 617-542-9595, extension 1, for more information.

Appendix J NCLC's Student Loan Borrower Assistance Website

NCLC's Student Loan Borrower Assistance (SLBA) website can be found at www.studentloanborrowerassistance.org. The website contains extensive information in a consumer-friendly format. NCLC staff updates the site regularly by posting new advocacy reports, announcements from the Department of Education, and relevant changes to the student loan laws.

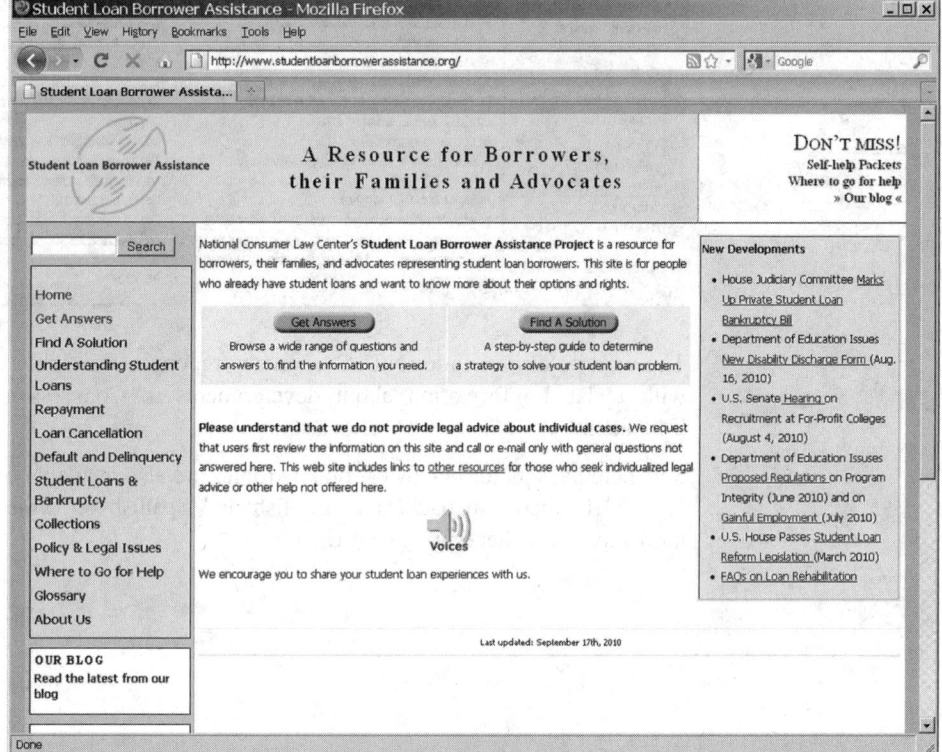

The most frequently used sections of the website include an extensive "Get Answers" section, information about bankruptcy and default, and the "Where to Go for Help" section.

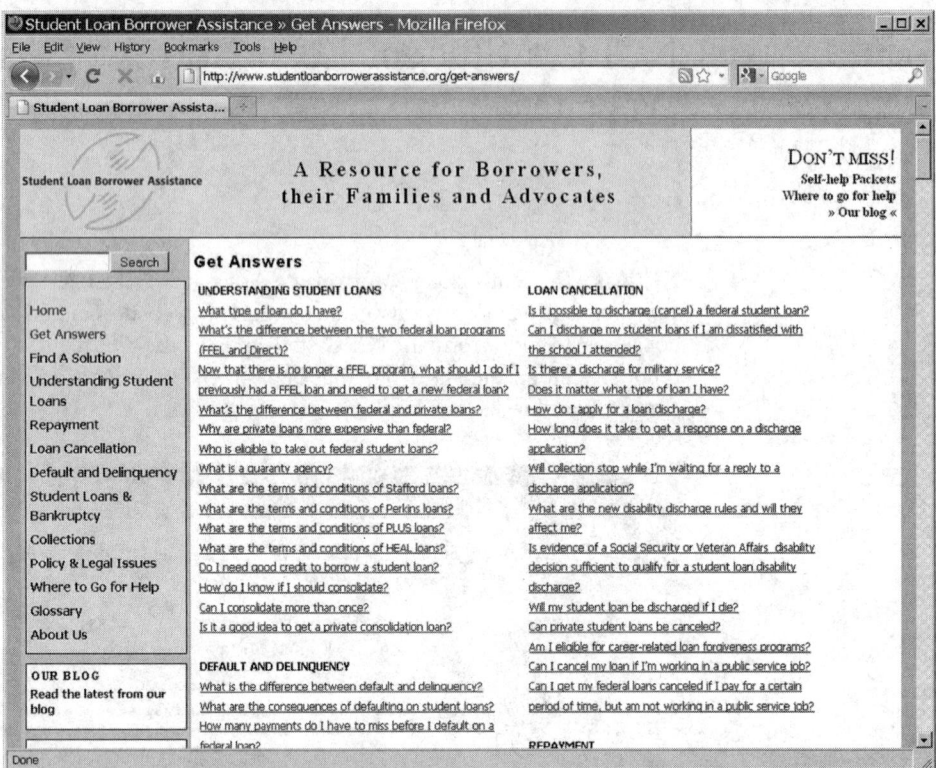

The website also includes NCLC advocacy reports and a "policy and legal issues" section with updated information about developments in Congress and in the Department of Education.

Self-help packets for borrowers on key topics are also available on the SLBA website. As of July 2010, there are packets in English and Spanish on disability discharges, economic hardship, and collection agency rights.

Appendix K Finding Pleadings, Primary Sources on the Companion Website

Student Loan Law includes free access to its companion website, which remains free with continued subscription to this title. The companion websites includes all appendices found in *Student Loan Law* plus approximately fifty sample pleadings and 180 primary source documents—statutes, regulations, agency interpretations, forms, pleadings, handbooks, reports, and much more—all easily located with flexible, powerful search tools. Documents are in PDF format and the pleadings are also in Word format.

This appendix describes the documents found on the companion website, how to access and print them, and how to download them onto your computer or copy-paste them into a word processing file.

K.1 Pleadings and Primary Sources Found on the Companion Website

The *Student Loan Law* companion website is packed with up-to-date information, including key federal statutes and regulations, such as the College Cost Reduction Act of 2007, and Department of Education forms and policy guidance letters, many of which are newly updated for 2010. The site also includes dozens of letters, complaints, and discovery pleadings useful in collection abuse, garnishment, and fraud cases. Numerous reports and helpful student guides are also available.

The website does *not* contain the full text of the manual chapters. See K.5, *infra*, about using Internet-based keyword searches to pinpoint page numbers in the manual where topics are discussed.

K.2 How to Access the Website

One-time registration is required to access the companion website. Once registered, a user subsequently logging in will be granted immediate access to all the websites he or she is authorized to use. For example, one username and password allows a subscriber to four NCLC titles to access all four companion websites.

To register for the first time, go to **www.consumerlaw.org/webaccess** and click on the "New users click here to register" link. Enter the Companion Website Registration Number found on the packing statement or invoice accompanying this publication. Then enter the requested information and click on "Login." An e-mail address may be used for the username or a different username may be chosen.

Subscribers do *not* need to register more than once. If subscribers purchase additional NCLC titles later, they will automatically be given access to the corresponding companion websites. Registering a second time with the same registration number overrides a prior username and password. (Note that, if users allow all their subscriptions to lapse and then subsequently purchase a manual, they will have to register again.)

Once registered, click on the log-in link at **www.consumerlaw.org/webaccess**, enter the username and password, and select the *Student Loan Law* website from the list of authorized websites.

An alternate log-in method may be particularly useful for libraries, legal aid offices, or law firms that subscribe to the entire set of NCLC manuals. Simply e-mail publications@nclc.org with a list or range of static IP addresses for which access should be permitted. Users from those addresses can then go to www.consumerlaw.org/ipaccess to be granted access *without* entering a username and password.

Once logged in, users can click the "My Account" link on the left toolbar to change their personal information. We also encourage users who find any mistakes to notify us using the "Report Errors" button, also on the left toolbar. At minimum, **use of the companion websites with Internet Explorer requires Adobe Reader 7.0 or Adobe Acrobat 7.0 (or later versions of the software). Users of other browsers, or those experiencing problems with the websites, should download the latest version of the free Adobe Reader (currently 9.4) from Adobe's website at www.adobe.com.** A link to Adobe's site is provided on the NCLC companion website log-in page.

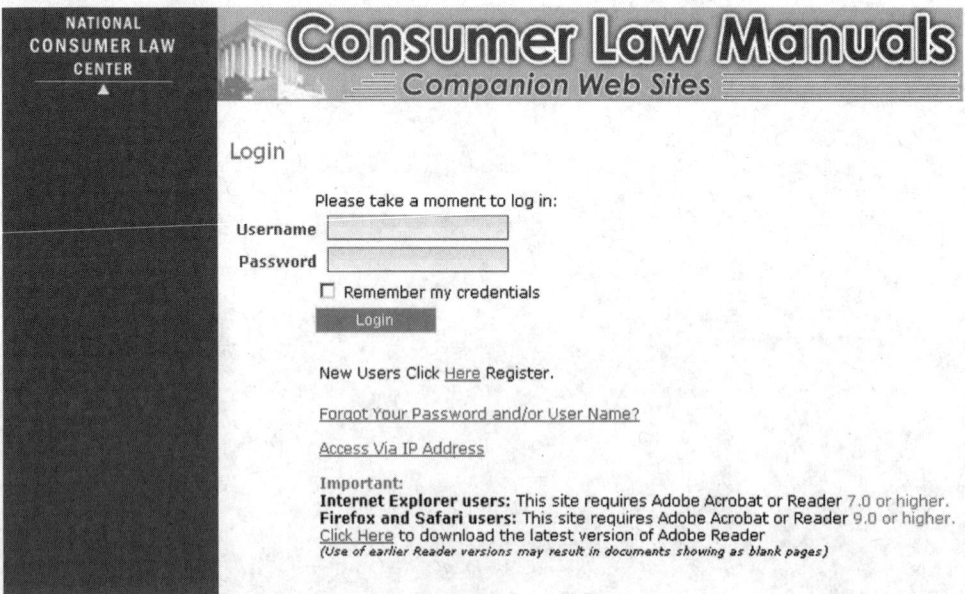

K.3 Locating Documents on the Website

The companion website provides three options to locate documents.

1. The search page (the home page) uses keyword searches to find documents—full text searches of all documents on the website or searches just on the documents' titles.

- Narrow the search to documents of a certain type (such as federal regulations or pleadings) by making a selection from the "Document Type" menu, and then perform a full text or document title search.
- To locate a specific appendix section, select the appendix section number (for example, "A.2.3") or a partial identifier (for example, "A") in the search page's "Appendix" drop-down fields.
- Click on the "Search Hints" link for a quick reference to special search operators, wildcards, shortcuts, and complex searches. Read this closely, as syntax and search operators may be slightly different from those of other websites.

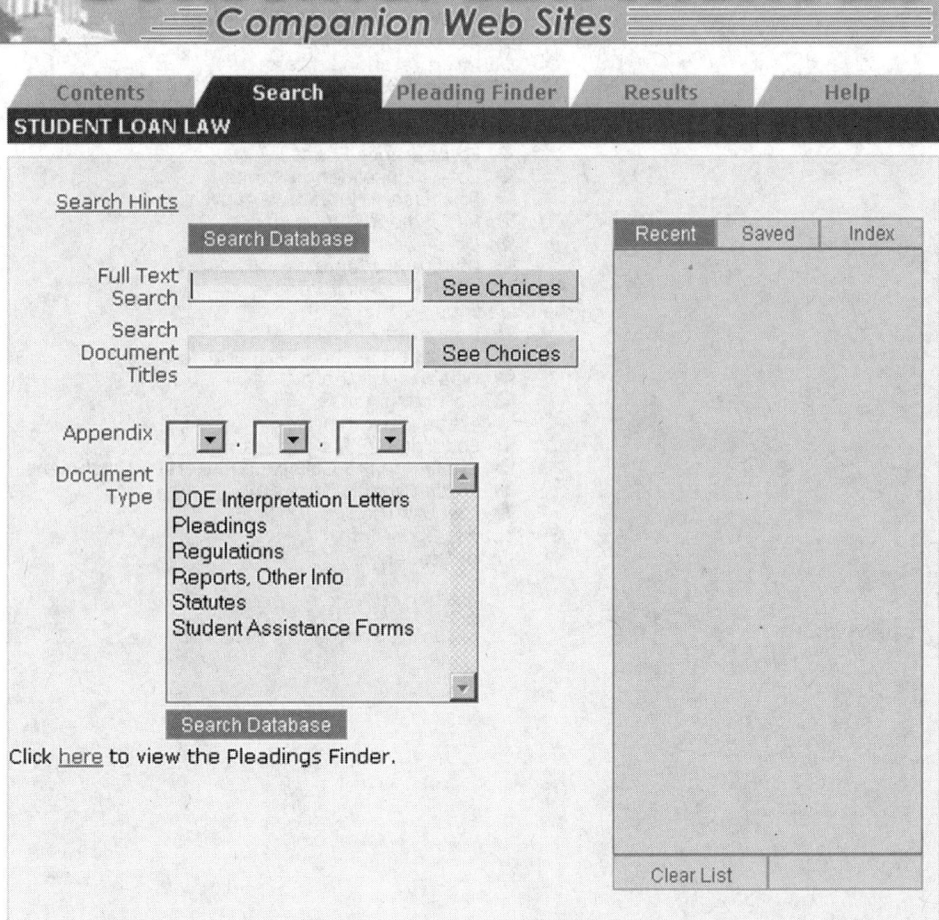

Appx. K.3 *Student Loan Law*

2. The contents page (click on the "Contents" tab at the top of the page) is a traditional "branching" table of contents. Click a branch to expand it into a list of sub-branches or documents. Each document appears once on this contents tree.

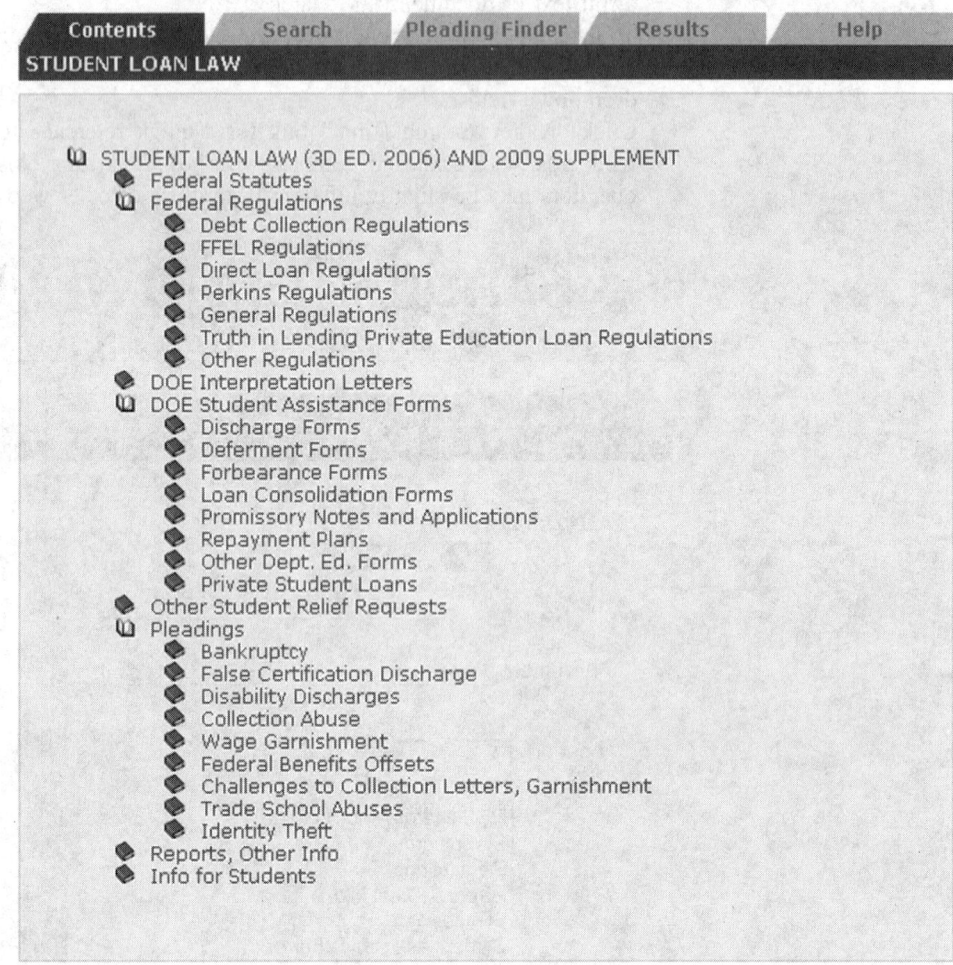

3. The pleading finder page (click on the "Pleading Finder" tab at the top of the page) allows pleadings to be located using one or more menus, such as "Type of Pleading—General" or "Subject." For many users, this will be the preferred method of finding a pleading. More than one item can be selected from a menu using the *Ctrl* key. For example, make one selection from "Type of Pleading—General," one from "Subject," and three from "Legal Claim" to locate all pleadings of that type and subject that contain one or more of the three legal claims selected. If this search produces insufficient results, deselect "Subject" and/or "Legal Claim" to find pleadings of that type in any subject area or based upon any legal claim.

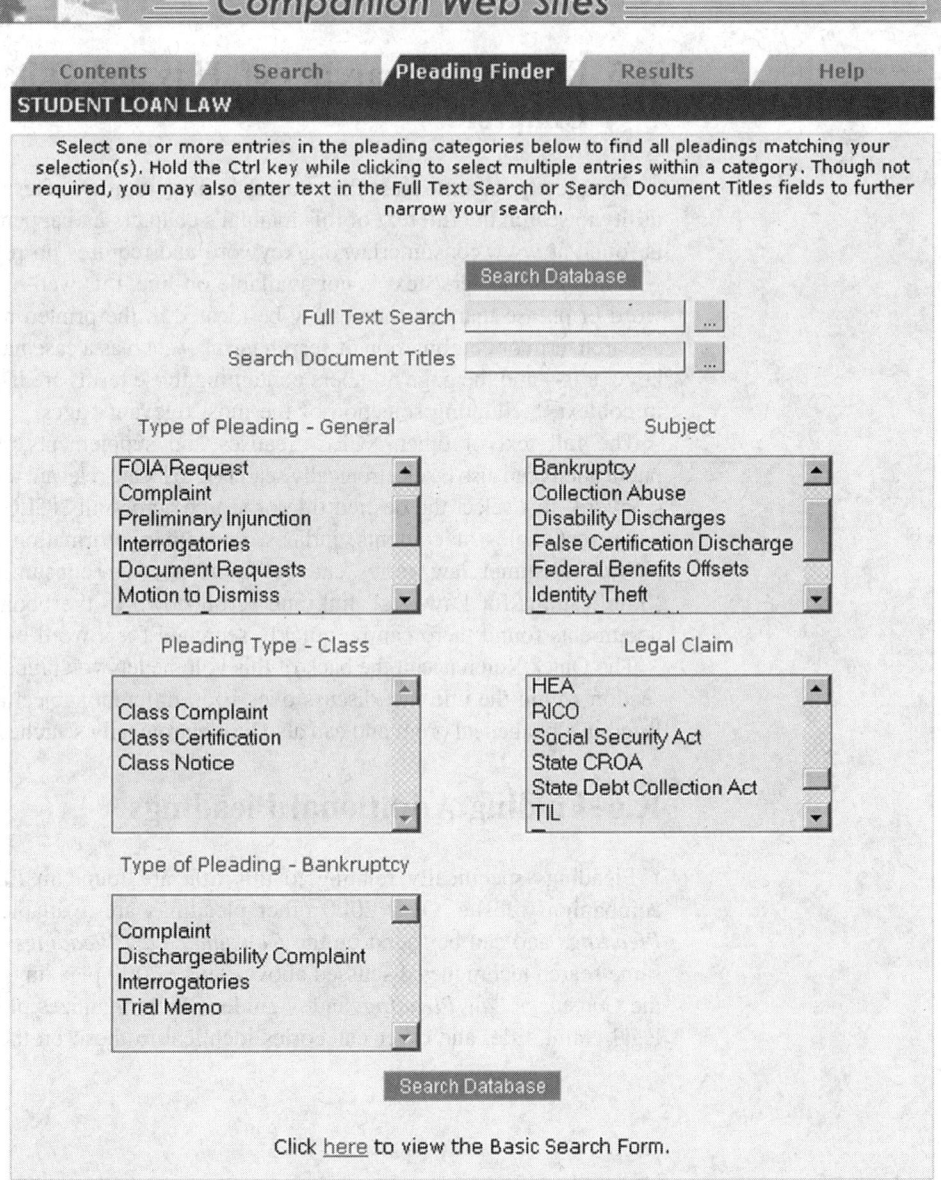

K.4 How to Use the Documents, Find Word Versions, and Locate Additional Features

All documents on the website are in PDF format and can be printed, downloaded onto your computer, or cut and pasted into a word processing document. Pleadings and certain other documents also are available in Word format, facilitating the opening of entire documents in a word processor. After opening the selected PDF file, click on the "Word Version, if available" link at the top of the page. If a Word version is listed as available, click on the "DOC Download Document" link to save the Word file to your computer.

Links on the left hand toolbar bring you to credit math software, search tips, other websites, tables of contents and indices of all NCLC manuals, and other practice aids. Links to especially important new developments will be placed toward the bottom of the "Search" page.

K.5 Electronic Searches of This and Other NCLC Titles' Chapters

Completely separate from the manuals' companion websites, NCLC offers a handy on-line utility to search the full text of this manual's chapters and appendices. This free search utility is found at www.consumerlaw.org/keyword and requires no registration or log-in.

While the chapters' text is not available on-line, this web-based search engine will find a word or phrase that can then easily be located in the printed manual. Select this title, enter a search term or combination of search terms—such as a case name, a regulation cite, or other keywords—and the page numbers containing those terms are listed. Search results are shown in context, facilitating selection of the most relevant pages.

The full text of other NCLC treatises and supplements, *NCLC REPORTS*, and other publications can also be electronically searched to locate relevant topics at www.consumerlaw.org/keyword. Just select the desired title or search across all NCLC titles.

Current tables of contents, indices, and other information for all eighteen titles in the NCLC consumer law series can be found at www.consumerlaw.org/shop. Click on the "Publications for Lawyers" link and scroll down to the book you want. The PDF-format documents found there can be quickly searched for a word or phrase.

The Quick Reference at the back of this volume lets you pinpoint the correct NCLC title and section within the title that discuss over 1000 different subject areas. These subject areas are listed in alphabetical order and can also be electronically searched at www.consumerlaw.org/qr.

K.6 Finding Additional Pleadings

Pleadings specifically relating to this title are found in PDF and Word format on the companion website. Over 2000 other pleadings are available at NCLC's *Consumer Law Pleadings* and can be found on the *Consumer Law Pleadings* companion website using the same search techniques discussed above. These 2000 pleadings can also be pinpointed using the *Consumer Law Pleadings* index guide, which organizes pleadings by type, subject area, legal claim, title, and other categories identical to those on the website.

Appendix L Student Loans on the Web

This appendix can also be found on the companion website to this manual.

Consumer/Borrower Websites

National Consumer Law Center's Student Loan Borrower Assistance Project: www.studentloanborrowerassistance.org

Americans for Fairness in Lending: www.affil.org

Project on Student Debt/The Institute for College Access and Success: www.projectonstudentdebt.org

U.S. PIRG Higher Education Project: www.uspirg.org/higher-education

U.S. Students Association: www.usstudents.org

U.S. Government Agency Websites

Department of Education

General: www.ed.gov
Direct Loans (general): www.ed.gov/offices/OSFAP/DirectLoan/index.html
Direct Loan Consolidation: www.loanconsolidation.ed.gov
Direct Loan Servicing: www.dl.ed.gov/borrower/BorrowerWelcomePage.jsp
Federal Student Aid: www.fsahelp.ed.gov
Federal Student Aid Collections: www.fsacollections.ed.gov/contractors/default.htm (The Department of Education took much of this information off-line in the spring of 2010. Advocates should check to see if and when the site is back on-line).
Information for Financial Aid Professionals: www.ifap.ed.gov/ifap
Information for Financial Aid Professionals Disability Discharge: http://ifap.ed.gov/disabilitydischarge/main.html
National Center for Education Statistics: http://nces.ed.gov
National Student Loan Data System: www.nslds.ed.gov/nslds_SA
Ombudsman: www.ombudsman.ed.gov
Policy Guidance (including Dear Colleague letters): www.ed.gov/policy/highered/guid/edpicks.jhtml?src=ln
Student Aid on the Web: www.studentaid.ed.gov

Department of Treasury Financial Management Service: http://fms.treas.gov

Federal Trade Commission: www.ftc.gov

Government Accountability Office: www.gao.gov

Student Loan Press Websites

Chronicle of Higher Education: www.chronicle.com

Inside Higher Ed: www.insidehighered.com

New America Higher Education Watch Blog: www.newamerica.net/blog/higher_ed_watch

Private Websites

FinAid: www.Finaid.org

Student Lending Analytics: www.studentlendinganalytics.com

Trade Association Websites

Consumer Bankers Association: www.cbanet.org

National Association of State Administrators and Supervisors of Private Schools: www.nasasps.org

National Association of Student Financial Aid Administrators: www.nasfaa.org

National Council of Higher Education Loan Programs: www.nchelp.org

Research and Academic Websites

American Council on Education: www.acenet.edu

College Board: www.collegeboard.com

Education Sector: www.educationsector.org

Lumina Foundation: www.luminafoundation.org

National Center for Education Statistics: http://nces.ed.gov

National Center for Public Policy and Higher Education: www.highereducation.org

Index

ABILITY-TO-BENEFIT (ATB) CERTIFICATION
see also FALSE CERTIFICATION DISCHARGE
ability-to-benefit tests
   approved tests, 9.4.2.1
   language of test, 9.4.2.1
   requirement for student aid, 9.4.2.1
falsification, 9.4.2
   defined, 9.4.2.1
   information on specific schools, 9.4.2.2.5
   investigatory files, 9.4.2.2.2
   school files, 9.4.2.2.3
   testing company information, 9.4.2.2.4

ABUSIVE CONDUCT
collection activities, 7.4
proprietary schools, *see* SCHOOL-RELATED CLAIMS AND DEFENSES

ACADEMIC COMPETITIVENESS GRANTS
see also GRANTS
expiration of program, 1.4.2.4
overview of program, 1.4.2.4

ACADEMIC REQUIREMENTS
student loan eligibility, 1.6.1
   satisfactory academic progress, 1.6.2

ACCOMMODATION PARTIES
bankruptcy discharge, 10.3.2
parental plus loans, *see* PLUS LOANS

ACCREDITING AGENCIES
see also PROPRIETARY SCHOOLS
claims against, 12.6.2.2
concerns with, 12.2.2
recognized accrediting agencies, 12.6.2.2
role of, 12.2.1, 12.2.2, 12.6.2.2

ACTIONS
class actions, *see* CLASS ACTIONS
collection actions, *see* COLLECTION ACTIONS
damages, *see* DAMAGES
defenses, *see* DEFENSES
fraud claims, *see* FRAUD
negligence claims, *see* NEGLIGENCE CLAIMS
private loan lenders, against, 11.10
RICO, *see* RICO CLAIMS
school-related claims, *see* SCHOOL-RELATED CLAIMS AND DEFENSES
UDAP, *see* UDAP CLAIMS

ADMINISTRATIVE GARNISHMENT
see WAGE GARNISHMENTS

ADMINISTRATIVE OFFSETS
federal benefits, *see* FEDERAL BENEFITS OFFSETS
federal salary, *see* FEDERAL SALARY OFFSETS
selected regulations, Appx. B.5.1
student assistance funds, 8.7
tax refunds, *see* TAX REFUND OFFSETS

ADMINISTRATIVE PROCEDURES ACT
claims against DOE, 12.6.2.1

ADMINISTRATIVE REVIEW
due process challenges, 8.2.6, 8.3.5
prior to federal benefit offset, 8.4.3.1
prior to professional license suspension, 8.6
prior to tax refund offset, 8.2.5
prior to wage garnishment, 8.3.2.5, 8.3.3.2
   DOE forms, Appx. D.4.1, Appx. D.4.2

ADVERSARY PROCEEDINGS (BANKRUPTCY)
dischargeability determination
   chapter 13, 10.7.2
   procedures, 10.7.1
   state agencies, involving, 10.8

APPEALS
see also JUDICIAL REVIEW
cohort default rate sanctions, 1.7.4.2.2
discharge denials, 9.15
   closed schools, 9.3.6.4
   disability discharges, 9.7.4.1
   false certification, 9.4.7
   unpaid refunds, 9.5.4
guaranty agency reviews
   tax refund offsets, 8.2.7
   wage garnishments, 8.3.5

APPLICATION FOR STUDENT AID
dependent and independent students, 1.5.2
eligibility criteria, 1.5.1, 1.6, Appx. C.4
forms, Appx. D.1
free on-line application, Appx. D.1.1
private loan disclosures, 11.4.1.4.1
procedure, 1.5.1

ARMED FORCES SERVICE
see MILITARY PERSONNEL

ASSET SEIZURES
see SEIZURE OF PROPERTY AND ASSETS

ASSISTANCE FOR BORROWERS
Department of Education, 1.12.2
   policy guidance letters, Appx. C.3
for-profit counselors, 1.12.4
frequently asked questions, Appx. I

ASSISTANCE FOR BORROWERS (*cont.*)
FSAIC, *see* FEDERAL STUDENT AID INFORMATION CENTER
NCLC Student Loan Borrower Assistance Project, 1.12.3, Appx. J
NSLDS, *see* NATIONAL STUDENT LOAN DATA SYSTEM (NSLDS)
ombudsman programs
    federal ombudsman, *see* STUDENT LOAN OMBUDSMAN
    other programs for federal loans, 1.12.1.2
    private student loans, 1.12.1.3, 11.7.4
type of loan, determination, 1.9

ATB
see ABILITY-TO-BENEFIT (ATB) CERTIFICATION

ATTORNEY FEES AND COSTS
see also ATTORNEYS; COLLECTION FEES
collection actions, 10.9.3
collection fees, inclusion, 7.3.2.1

ATTORNEYS
see also ATTORNEY FEES AND COSTS
FDCPA, application, 7.4.3.2
public service attorneys, cancellation of loans, 9.11
    Perkins loans, 9.12

BANKRUPT SCHOOLS
claims against, 12.6.2.4

BANKRUPTCY DISCHARGE
availability, 10.2
chapter 13 advantages when loan not dischargeable, 10.9
    co-debtor stay, 10.9.2
    raising defenses, 10.9.3
    separate classification, 10.9.1
dischargeability determination, 10.3.1, 10.7
    adversary proceedings, 10.7.1, 10.7.2
    change in circumstances, effect, 10.7.1
    chapter 13 plan provisions, 10.7.2
    older standards, use, 10.7.3
    procedure, 10.7.1
    sample complaint, Appx. E.5.1
    sample discovery, Appx. F.3
    state agencies, involving, 10.8
    subsequent to bankruptcy proceeding, 10.7.1, 10.7.3
effect, 10.11
    credit record, on, 7.2.4.3
exceptions to nondischargeability, 10.2.2
    burden of proof, 10.3.1
    co-obligors, application, 10.3.2
    declaration of status, obtaining, 10.3.1
    pre-BAPCPA covered loans, 10.2.2.4
    private student loans, 10.2.2.1
    refinanced student loans, 10.2.2.3
    some education debts, 10.2.2.2
filing of proceedings
    automatic stay, 10.1.2
    considerations, 10.1
    fees, 10.1.1
    forbearances, 4.4.3
    tax refund offsets, effect, 8.2.9
guaranteed-loan status lost, 7.5.4.3
HEALs, 10.6
means test, 10.10
old loans, 10.2.2.4, 10.2.2.5
overview, 10.1.1

partial discharges, 10.5
raising school's fraud, Appx. E.5
reopening bankruptcy cases, 10.7.1
repayment plans, effect, 10.4.2.3.2
restrictions, 10.2.1, 10.2.2
rights after discharge, 10.11
seven-year rule, 10.2.2.5
tax issues, 9.14
undue hardship requirement, 10.2.1, 10.4

BANKS
FTC Holder Rule violations, 11.9.2.4
guaranteed loans, *see* FFELs
private loans, *see* PRIVATE STUDENT LOANS

BASIC EDUCATIONAL OPPORTUNITY GRANTS (BEOG)
see PELL GRANTS

BORROWER ASSISTANCE
see ASSISTANCE FOR BORROWERS

BORROWERS
see STUDENTS

BUSINESS SCHOOLS
see VOCATIONAL SCHOOLS

CANCELLATION OF LOAN
see also COMPROMISES; FORBEARANCE; STATUTORY DISCHARGES
checklist, 1.11.2
federal loans by student, time, 2.7
income-tied repayment plans
    IBR, 3.1.3.2.5
    ICR, 3.1.3.3.3
overview, 9.1
Perkins loans, 9.12
private loans, 11.4.1.6, 11.7.3
profession-related
    generally, 9.9.1
    other professions, 9.12
    public service cancellation, 9.9.2
    teachers, 9.10
September 11 program, 9.13
tax issues, 9.14

CHECKLISTS
challenging collection, 1.11.5
first steps, 1.11.1
loan cancellation, 1.11.2
postponing payment, 1.11.3
repayment options, 1.11.4

CHECKS
student loan funds, endorsement, 7.5.4.1

CHILD CARE PROVIDERS
cancellation of loans, 9.11
    Perkins loans, 9.12

CITIZENSHIP REQUIREMENTS
student loan eligibility, 1.6.3

CIVIL RIGHTS CLAIMS
collection practices, 7.4.5.1

CLASS ACTIONS
advantages and disadvantages, 12.6.3
proprietary school abuses, 12.6.3

References are to sections

CLASS ACTIONS (*cont.*)
sample pleadings
   collection procedures, Appx. E.3
   DOE discharge procedures, Appx. E.2.2
   private student loans, Appx. E.6.1

CLEARINGHOUSE CITATIONS
see also SARGENT SHRIVER NATIONAL CENTER ON POVERTY LAW
unreported cases, 1.2.2

CLOSED-SCHOOL DISCHARGE
see also STATUTORY DISCHARGES
closure date
   official closure date, 9.3.2
   timing, 9.3.1
correspondence schools, 9.3.3
effect, 9.3.5
eligible loans, 9.2
FISLs, 9.3.7
form, Appx. D.3.1
guaranteed-loan status lost, 7.5.4.3
obtaining, 9.3.6
   appeals, 9.3.6.4, 9.15
   generally, 9.3.6.1
   oral applications, 9.3.6.3
   time limits, 9.3.6.4
   written application, 9.3.6.2
older FFELs, 9.3.7
overview, 9.3.1
Perkins Loans, 9.3.7
relationship to other discharges, 9.6
relief available, 9.3.5
revocation, 9.3.5
Stafford Loans, 9.3.7
teach-out bar, 9.3.4
tuition recovery funds, interrelationship, 12.8.2

CO-DEBTOR STAY
chapter 13 bankruptcy plans, 10.9.2

COHORT DEFAULT RATES
calculation, 5.1.3
causes of default, 5.1.2
"default management" companies, 1.12.4
default triggers, 5.1.4
low-income rate, 1.7.4.2.2
manipulation of rates, 5.1.3
proprietary schools, 5.1.1, 12.3.3.1
school sanctions, 1.7.4.2, 5.1.3
   appeals, 1.7.4.2.2
   generally, 1.7.4.2.1
skyrocketing rates, 5.1.1

COLLECTION ACTIONS
see also COLLECTIONS
bankruptcy stay, 10.1.2
declaratory relief, 12.6.2.1, 12.6.2.4
defenses, *see* DEFENSES
DOE
   alternative powers, 8.1
   attorney fee claims, 10.9.3
FFELs without guaranty status, 7.5.4.3
guaranty agencies, 12.6.2.1
injunctive relief, 12.6.2.1
judgments, *see* JUDGMENTS
private loans, 11.8, 11.9
school-related claims, raising
   see also SCHOOL-RELATED CLAIMS AND DEFENSES
   defense, as, 12.7
   DOE, against, 12.6.2.1, 12.7.2.2
   private loans, 11.9
   procedural issues, 7.5.2
   recoupment claims, 12.6.2.4
   schools and owners, against, 12.6.2.4, 12.7.2.1
statute of limitations, 7.5.3

COLLECTION AGENCIES
see also COLLECTIONS; COLLECTORS
closed-school discharge applications, effect, 9.3.6.1
common collection abuses, 7.4.2
complaints regarding, 7.2.1, 7.4.5.2
   form, Appx. D.4.4
directory of, Appx. H
DOE, use by, 7.2.1, 7.4.1
employee incentives, 6.3.4
factors fostering abuse, 7.4.1
   commission structure, 7.4.1.2
   generally, 7.4.1.1
FDCPA application, 7.4.3.2, 7.4.3.5
   prohibited practices, 7.4.2.2
fees, 7.3
   avoiding, 7.3.3
   calculation, 7.3.2
   generally, 7.3.1
guaranty agencies, use by, 7.2.1, 7.4.1
HEA due diligence rules, 7.4.3.2
standing, 7.5.2
state law, application, 7.4.4
wage garnishment process, participation, 8.3.4

COLLECTION FEES
see also COLLECTIONS
avoiding, 7.3.3
calculation, 7.3.2
challenging in bankruptcy proceedings, 10.9.3
consolidation loans, 6.2.5, 6.4, 7.3.2.2
federal regulations, selected text, Appx. B.5.4
guaranty agencies, 7.3.1
other fees and penalties, 7.3.4
overview, 7.3.1
Perkins loans, 7.3.2.3
rehabilitation of loans, 6.4, 7.3.2.2
waiver, 6.6

COLLECTION LETTERS
see also COLLECTIONS
delinquent loans, 7.2.2
determining sender, 7.4.3.3
sample challenges to
   discovery, Appx. F.1
   pleadings, Appx. E.3

COLLECTIONS
see also COLLECTORS
actions, *see* COLLECTION ACTIONS
agencies, *see* COLLECTION AGENCIES
bankruptcy stay, 10.1.2
checklist, 1.11.5
collector, determining, 7.2.1
credit bureau reporting, 7.2.3, 7.2.4

COLLECTIONS (*cont.*)
deceptive and abusive tactics, 7.4
  common abuses, 7.4.2
  complaints, 7.4.5.2
  factors that foster, 7.4.1
  FDCPA, application, 7.4.3, 12.5.2.4
  federal claims, 7.4.5.1
  sample discovery, Appx. F.1
  sample pleadings, Appx. E.3
  state law, application, 7.4.4
delinquent loans, 7.2.2
demand letters, *see* COLLECTION LETTERS
discharge applications, effect
  closed schools, 9.3.6.1
  disability discharge, 9.7.4.1
  false certification, 9.4.7
  unpaid refunds, 9.5.4
DOE collection and supervision, 7.2.1
federal powers
  see also DEPARTMENT OF EDUCATION (DOE)
  federal benefits offsets, *see* FEDERAL BENEFITS OFFSETS
  generally, 7.1, 7.2, 8.1
  selected regulations, Appx. B.5
  selected statutory provisions, Appx. A.5
  tax refund offsets, *see* TAX REFUND OFFSETS
  wage garnishments, *see* WAGE GARNISHMENTS
fees and penalties, *see* COLLECTION FEES
FFELs, 7.2.3, 7.5.4.3
forbearances, effect, 4.4.1
generally, 7.1, 8.1
guaranteed-loan status lost, 7.5.4.3
guaranty agencies, 7.2.1, 7.2.3, 8.3.3
overview of process, 7.2
post-default collections, 7.2.3
  rehabilitation agreements, effect, 6.3.3
  repayment plans in lieu, *see* REPAYMENT PLANS
pre-default collections, 7.2.2
private student loans, 5.2.3, 11.6.3
school-held loans, 7.2.1
school-related claims, raising, 12.6
state law, application, 7.4.4
statute of limitations, 7.5.3, 8.4.3.3

COLLECTORS
see also COLLECTION AGENCIES; COLLECTIONS
deceptive and abusive tactics, 7.4
  complaints regarding, 7.4.5.2
  FDCPA violations, 7.4.2.2
determining collector, 7.2.1
DOE as, 7.2.1
fees, 7.3
guaranty agency as, 7.2.1, 7.2.3
state law, application, 7.4.4
wage garnishment process, participation, 8.3.4

COLLEGE WORK STUDY PROGRAM (CWS)
see also GRANTS
federal program, 1.4.2.1

COMMON LAW CLAIMS AND DEFENSES
contract law, *see* CONTRACT CLAIMS AND DEFENSES
private lenders, 11.8.1, 11.8.2, 11.10
proprietary school abuses, 12.5.4
  agency theories, 12.7.3.2
  contract claims, 12.5.4.2
  contract defenses, 7.5.4
  fiduciary duty breach, 12.5.4.3
  fraud claims, 12.5.4.1
  misrepresentation, 12.7.3.2
  negligence claims, 12.5.4.1

COMPLAINTS
collection abuses, 7.4.5.2
  complaint form, Appx. D.4.4
Ombudsman programs, *see* OMBUDSMAN PROGRAMS
sample pleadings, Appx. E

COMPROMISES
see also CANCELLATION OF LOAN
Direct loans, authority, Appx. D.5.2
DOE policy on, 6.6, Appx. D.5.1
federal regulations, selected text, Appx. B.5.5
FFELs, 6.6, Appx. D.5.1
Perkins Loans, 6.6

CONSOLIDATION LOANS
see also FEDERAL STUDENT ASSISTANCE
advantages and disadvantages, 1.4.1.3.3, 6.4
applying for, 6.2.5
  application form, Appx. D.1.2
availability, 1.4.1.3.1
bankruptcy discharge, 10.2.2.3, 10.7.1
checklist, 1.11.4
collection abuses, 7.4.1.2
collection fees, 7.3.2.2
counseling requirement, 6.2.2
default of consolidation loan, 6.2.4
defaulted loans, 6.2
deferment rights, 4.3.2, 4.3.5.1
disclosure requirements, 2.5.3
DOE policy guidance letters, Appx. C.2
eligibility, 1.4.1.3.1, 6.2.4, 10.4.2.3.2
forbearances pending, 4.4.3
generally, 6.2.1
IBRPs
  see also INCOME-BASED REPAYMENT (IBR) PLANS
  eligibility, 3.1.3.2.1, 6.2.1
  selecting, 6.2.3, 6.2.5
ICRPs
  see also INCOME-CONTINGENT REPAYMENT (ICR) PLANS
  eligibility, 3.1.3.3.1, 6.2.1
  monthly payments, 3.1.3.3.2
  selecting, 6.2.5
interest rates, 2.3.5
joint consolidation loans, 9.2, 9.7.2
origination fees, 2.4.1
overview, 1.4.1.3
pros and cons, 1.4.1.3.3
public service cancellation, 9.9.2
reconsolidation, 1.4.1.3.2, 6.2.4, 10.4.2.3.2
refinancing through, 6.2.1
school-related defenses, raising after, 7.5.4.4
statutory discharges
  see also STATUTORY DISCHARGES
  death discharge, 9.8
  disability discharge, 9.7.2
  eligibility, 9.2

CONSUMER FINANCIAL PROTECTION BUREAU (CFPB)
private loan oversight, 11.3, 11.10

Index — References are to sections

CONSUMER REPORTS
see CREDIT REPORTS

CONTRACT CLAIMS AND DEFENSES
see also SCHOOL-RELATED CLAIMS AND DEFENSES
availability, 7.5.4.1, 12.5.4.2
DOE, against, 12.6.2.1
overview, 7.5.4.1
private loans, 11.8.1
   direct claims, 11.10
   infancy, 11.8.2
statutory discharges, interrelationship, 7.5.4.2

CONVICTS
eligibility for student aid, 1.6.5, 1.6.6

CORRECTIONS OFFICERS
deferment eligibility, 4.3.8

CORRESPONDENCE COURSES
see also DISTANCE EDUCATION PROGRAMS;
   PROPRIETARY INSTITUTIONS
claims regarding, see SCHOOL-RELATED CLAIMS AND
   DEFENSES
closed-school discharge, 9.3.3
definition, 1.7.1.4
diploma mills, 12.4.2
eligibility for student aid, 1.7.1.4, 12.3.3.6
FTC guides, 12.5.2.3
history of abuses, 12.3.1

COSIGNERS
see ACCOMMODATION PARTIES

COUNSELING
federal loans, requirements, 2.9
   consolidation loans, 6.2.2
for-profit counselors, 1.12.4

CREDIT REPORTS
bankruptcy discharge, effect, 7.2.4.3
defaulted loans, 7.2.4
   cleaning up credit record, 7.2.4.3
   consolidation, 6.4
   expiry, 7.2.4.2
   HEA requirements, 7.2.4.1
   rehabilitated loans, 6.3.5, 6.3.7, 6.4
   reporting of information, 7.2.4.1
discharges
   closed-school discharge, 9.3.5
   false-certification discharge, 9.4.6
   unpaid-refund discharge, 9.5.5
   updating records, 7.2.4.3
identity theft, effect, 9.4.5
inaccurate reports, 7.2.4.3
Metro 2 reporting format, 7.2.4.1
obsolete information, 7.2.4.2, 7.2.4.3
PLUS borrowers, 1.4.1.2
rehabilitated loans
   FFELs, 6.3.5
   generally, 6.4, 7.2.4.3
   Perkins loans, 6.3.7

CREDITORS
see LENDERS

DAMAGES
school-related claims, 12.6.5

DEATH
discharges, 9.8
   eligible loans, 9.2
   tax issues, 9.14
forbearances, 4.4.3

DEBT COLLECTION
see COLLECTIONS

DEBT COLLECTION ACT
selected text, Appx. A.5

DEBT COLLECTION IMPROVEMENT ACT (DCIA)
non-judicial wage garnishments, 8.3.1
statute of limitations, application to student loans, 8.4.3.3

DECEPTIVE CONDUCT
collection activities, 7.4
FTC guides, 12.5.2.3
private lenders, 11.10
proprietary schools, 12.3
UDAP claims, see UDAP CLAIMS

DECLARATORY RELIEF
bankruptcy dischargeability, status, 10.3.1
school-related claims, 7.5.2, 12.6.2.1, 12.7.3.1

DEFAULT JUDGMENTS
setting aside, 7.6

DEFAULT RATES
federal loans, see COHORT DEFAULT RATES
private loans, 5.1.1, 5.2.1

DEFAULT RESOLUTION GROUP (DOE)
see also COLLECTIONS; DEPARTMENT OF EDUCATION
   (DOE)
regional offices, 7.2.1

DEFAULTED LOANS
administrative review, see ADMINISTRATIVE REVIEW
assignment to guaranty agency, 7.2.3
bankruptcy option, see BANKRUPTCY DISCHARGE
causes of default, 5.1.2
checklist, 1.11.3
cohort default rates, see COHORT DEFAULT RATES
collection procedures
   see also COLLECTIONS
   defenses, see DEFENSES
   federal benefits offsets, see FEDERAL BENEFITS OFFSETS
   federal loans, 7.2
   private loans, 5.2.3, 11.6.3
   tax refund offsets, see TAX REFUND OFFSETS
   wage garnishments, see WAGE GARNISHMENTS
compromise and write-off, 6.6
consequences of loan default, 1.1
   federal loans, 5.1.5
   future aid, 1.6.6
   private loans, 5.2.3
consolidated loans, 6.2.4
consolidation of, 6.2
credit reports, 7.2.4
   cleaning up credit record, 7.2.4.3
   generally, 7.2.4.1
   limitations, 7.2.4.2
deferment eligibility, 4.3.2
defined, 5.1.4, 7.4.3.4
delinquency distinguished, 4.3.2

DEFAULTED LOANS (cont.)
discharges, see BANKRUPTCY DISCHARGE; STATUTORY DISCHARGES
forbearances, see FORBEARANCE
for-profit counselors, 1.12.4
low-income rate, 1.7.4.2.2
private student loans, 5.2, 11.6
problem of
   federal loans, 5.1
   private loans, 5.2.1
professional license suspension or revocation, 8.6
reconsolidation, 1.4.1.3.2, 6.2.4, 10.4.2.3.2
records, right to inspect, 7.2.3, 8.2.5
reduced to judgment
   see also JUDGMENTS
   consolidation, 6.2.4
   rehabilitation, 6.3.6
   satisfactory repayment, 6.5
rehabilitation, see REHABILITATION OF LOANS
renewal of eligibility
   consolidation loans, 6.2.1
   loan rehabilitation, 6.3.1
   reasonable and affordable payments, 6.2.2, 6.3.4, 6.5
repayment strategies, 6
   see also REPAYMENT OF LOANS
   compromise or write-off, 6.6
   consolidation loans, see CONSOLIDATION LOANS
   generally, 6.1
   loan rehabilitation, see REHABILITATION OF LOANS
   renewing eligibility, 6.5
   repayment plans, see REPAYMENT PLANS
statute of limitations, 7.5.3
triggers
   federal loans, 5.1.4
   private loans, 5.2.2, 11.6.2

DEFENDANTS
school-related claims, 12.6.2
   bankrupt or insolvent schools, 12.6.2.4
   closed schools, 12.6.2.4
   DOE, 12.5.2.4, 12.6.2.1
   private accrediting agencies, 12.6.2.2
   state licensing agencies, 12.6.2.3

DEFENSES
checklist, 1.11.5
consolidation, effect, 7.5.4.4
contract defenses, 7.5.4.1, 11.8.1, 12.5.4.2
death of borrower, 9.8
equitable defenses, 7.5.3.3.1
infancy, 11.8.2
laches, 7.5.3.3
private loans, 11.8
procedural defenses, 7.5.2
school-related defenses, 12.7
   see also SCHOOL-RELATED CLAIMS AND DEFENSES
   chapter 13 bankruptcy, raising, 10.9.3
   clear situations, 12.7.2
   consolidated loans, 7.5.4.4
   less clear situations, 12.7.3
   private loans, 11.8
   school closure, 9.3.7
   school misconduct, 9.4.1
service members, 7.5.4.5, 11.8.4
standing, 7.5.2

statute of limitations, 7.5.3.1, 11.8.3
statutory discharges, relationship, 7.5.4.2
tax refund offsets, 8.2.3
unpaid refunds, 9.5
wage garnishments, 8.3.2.3, 8.3.3.1

DEFERMENT
accrued interest, 4.3.1
applying for, 4.3.4
available deferments, 4.3.5.1
benefits, 4.3.1
checklist, 1.11.3
defaulted loans, 4.3.2
economic hardship deferments, 4.3.5.2
   forms, Appx. D.2.1
eligibility
   current or delinquent loans, 4.3.2
   general requirements, 4.3.3
forms, Appx. D.2
grounds
   consolidation loans, 4.3.5
   Direct loans, 4.3.5
   economic hardship, 4.3.5.2
   FFELs, 4.3.5, 4.3.7
   generally, 4.3.5.1
   military service, 4.3.5.4, 4.3.5.5
   Perkins loans, 4.3.8
   PLUS loans, 4.3.6
   post-July 1, 1993 loans, 4.3.5, 4.3.8
   pre-July 1, 1993 loans, 4.3.7
   unemployment, 4.3.5.3
military deferment
   active duty, 4.3.5.4
   form, Appx. D.2.3
   post-active duty, 4.3.5.5
parent PLUS borrower deferment, 4.3.6
   form, Appx. D.2.4
private loans, 11.7.2
recertification requirements, 4.3.3
time limits, 4.3.3, 4.3.5.1
   post-active duty deferment, 4.3.5.5
   unemployment deferment, 4.3.5.3
unemployment deferment, 4.3.5.3
   form, Appx. D.2.2

DEFINITIONS
ATB falsification, 9.4.2.1
correspondence courses, 1.7.1.4
debt, 7.4.3.1
debt collector, 7.4.3.1, 7.4.3.5
default, 5.1.4, 7.4.3.4
diploma mill, 12.4.2
discretionary income, 3.1.3.3.2
disposable pay, 8.3.2.1
distance education, 1.7.1.4
eligible institution, 1.7.1.1
family size, 4.3.5.2
gainful employment, 1.7.1.2, 12.3.3.3
incentive compensation, 1.7.2.3
income, 4.3.5.2
low-income rate, 1.7.4.2.2
national emergency, 4.3.5.4, 4.3.5.5
origination relationship, 12.7.3.5
private education loan, 11.4.1.2
private educational lender, 11.4.1.2

DEFINITIONS (cont.)
qualified education loan, 10.2.2.3
teach-out agreement, 9.3.4
total and permanent disability, 9.7.3

DELINQUENT LOANS
collection procedures, 7.2.2
default distinguished, 4.3.2
deferment eligibility, 4.3.2
late charges, 2.4.2

DEMAND LETTERS
see COLLECTION LETTERS

DEPARTMENT OF EDUCATION (DOE)
see also FEDERAL STUDENT ASSISTANCE
assistance within, 1.12.2
central database, see NATIONAL STUDENT LOAN DATA SYSTEM (NSLDS)
claims against, 12.5.2.4, 12.6.2.1
collection agencies, use, 7.2.1, 8.3.4
   complaints, 7.4.5.2, Appx. D.4.4
   factors fostering abuse, 7.4.1
collection procedures, 7.2
   complaints regarding, 7.2.1, 7.4.5.2
   Department-held loans, 7.2.1, 8.1
   FDCPA application, 7.4.3.3
   federal benefits offsets, see FEDERAL BENEFITS OFFSETS
   federal salary offsets, 8.5
   fees, 7.3.1, 7.3.2
   hearings, see ADMINISTRATIVE REVIEW
   injunctive relief, 12.6.2.1
   non-Department loans, 7.2.1
   role of department, 7.2.1
   seizure of student assistance funds, 8.7
   selected regulations, Appx. B.5
   selected statutory provisions, Appx. A.5
   supervisory role, 7.2.1
   tax refund offsets, see TAX REFUND OFFSETS
   wage garnishments, see WAGE GARNISHMENTS
declaratory relief against, 12.6.2.1
Default Resolution Group, see DEFAULT RESOLUTION GROUP (DOE)
defaulted loans
   administrative review, see ADMINISTRATIVE REVIEW
   collection fees, 7.3.1, 7.3.2
   collection procedures, 7.2
   other fees and penalties, 7.3.4
   reporting to credit bureaus, 7.2.4
direct loans from, see DIRECT LOANS
discharge denials, judicial review, 9.15
discharge grants, sample letters, Appx. D.3.5, Appx. D.3.8.2
financial assistance to students, see FEDERAL STUDENT ASSISTANCE
forms, Appx. D
guaranty agencies, supervision, 7.2.1
   policy guidance letters, Appx. C
injunctive relief against, 12.6.2.1
investigatory files, obtaining, 9.4.2.2.2
oversight of schools, 12.2
   gaps, 12.2.3
   inadequate, claims regarding, 12.5.2.4
policy guidance letters, Appx. C
   borrower assistance, Appx. C.3
   consolidation loans, Appx. C.2
   discharges, Appx. C.1
   eligibility for aid, Appx. C.4
Program Participation Agreements, 1.7.2
release of information, Appx. D.5.4
resources, 1.12.2
school misconduct, liability for
   claims regarding, 12.5.2.4, 12.6.2.1
   Direct Loans, 12.7.2.2
   FFELs, 7.5.4.3, 12.7.3
   FISLs, 12.7.2.4
student guides, 1.12.2
Student Loan Ombudsman, see STUDENT LOAN OMBUDSMAN
tort claims against, 12.5.2.4
website, 1.12.2
   see also WEB RESOURCES
   closed-school list, 9.3.2
   default rates available on, 5.1.1
   defaulted loans, information on, 7.2.1
   forms available on, Appx. D
   policy guidance letters available on, Appx. C

DIPLOMA MILLS
concerns, 12.4.2

DIRECT CONSOLIDATION LOANS
see CONSOLIDATION LOANS

DIRECT LOAN SERVICING CENTER
see also DIRECT LOANS; SERVICING AGENCIES
defaulted loans, information, 7.2.1

DIRECT LOANS
see also FEDERAL STUDENT ASSISTANCE
bankruptcy discharge, 10.2.1
cancellation by DOE, see CANCELLATION OF LOAN
cancellation by student, 2.7
cohort default rate, 1.7.4.2.1
collections, see COLLECTIONS
compromise authority, Appx. D.5.2
   see also COMPROMISES
consolidation loans, see CONSOLIDATION LOANS
counseling requirements, 2.9
default triggers, 5.1.4
defaulted loans
   see also COLLECTIONS
   collection costs, 7.3.1
   collection information, 7.2.1
   defined, 5.1.4
   school-related defenses, raising, 12.7.2.2
deferment rights
   see also DEFERMENT
   economic deferments, 4.3.5.2, Appx. D.2.1.2
   grounds, 4.3.5
   military deferments, 4.3.5.4, 4.3.5.5, Appx. D.2.3
   time limits, 4.3.3
   unemployment deferments, 4.3.5.3, Appx. D.2.2
delinquent loans, 7.2.2
disbursement of funds, 2.6
   sample notice, Appx. D.5.10
disclosure requirements, 2.5
   plain language disclosure, Appx. D.5.9
   sample disclosure statement, Appx. D.5.8
forbearances, 4.4.3, Appx. D.2.5
FTC Holder Notice, 12.7.2.5
history of program, 1.3.1

DIRECT LOANS (cont.)
interest rates, 2.3.1
loan servicing, 3.2
master promissory note, see MASTER PROMISSORY NOTE
origination fees, 2.4.1
PLUS Loans, see PLUS LOANS
rehabilitation of loan, 6.3
repayment after withdrawal, 2.7
repayment plans, 3.1, 6.3.2
   IBRPs, 3.1.3.2
   ICRPs, 3.1.3.3
   reasonable and affordable, 6.3.4
school-related defenses, raising, 12.7.2.2
servicing center, see DIRECT LOAN SERVICING CENTER
Stafford Loans, see STAFFORD LOANS (GSLs)
statutory discharges
   see also STATUTORY DISCHARGES
   death discharge, 9.8
   disability discharge, 9.7.2
   eligibility, 9.2
   false-certification discharge, 9.4.1
   unpaid-refund discharge, 9.5
statutory provisions, selected text, Appx. A.1
   regulations, Appx. B.1
switch to, 1.3.2

DISABILITY DISCHARGE
see also STATUTORY DISCHARGES
allowable earnings, 9.7.5.1, 9.7.6
appeals, 9.7.4.1, Appx. E.2.3
application process, 9.7.4
   form, Appx. D.3.8.1
effect of final discharge, 9.7.7
eligible loans, 9.2, 9.7.2
new loans, restrictions, 9.7.5.1, 9.7.7
overview, 9.7.1
paid-in-full loans, 9.3.5
potential roadblocks, 9.7.8
reinstatement of loan, 9.7.5
   generally, 9.7.5.1
   notice, 9.7.5.2
sample DOE letter, Appx. D.3.8.2
servicing center, 9.7.8
tax issues, 9.14
total and permanent disability, 9.7.3
   allowable work, 9.7.6
   veterans, 9.7.4.2

DISABLED PERSONS
benefits offsets, 8.4.1
deferment eligibility
   Perkins Loans, 4.3.8
   pre-July 1, 1993 FFELs, 4.3.7
   rehabilitation training program, 4.3.5.1, 4.3.7
discharges, see DISABILITY DISCHARGE
forbearances, 4.4.3
total and permanent disability, defined, 9.7.3
   veterans, 9.7.4.2

DISASTER SITUATIONS
consolidation loans, 6.2.2
institutional eligibility, 1.7.1.4
rehabilitation of loans, 6.3.2
September 11, 9.13
special forbearance guidelines, 4.4.4

DISCHARGES
see also CANCELLATION OF LOAN
bankruptcy, see BANKRUPTCY DISCHARGE
statutory discharges, see STATUTORY DISCHARGES

DISCLOSURES
consumer information requirements, 1.7.3, 12.3.3.4
federal loans, 2.5
   consolidation loans, 2.5.3
   generally, 2.5.1
   master promissory note, 2.8
   plain language disclosure, Appx. D.5.9
   requirements, 2.5.2
   sample disclosure statement, Appx. D.5.8
HEA, 2.5.1, 11.4.2
private loans, 11.4
   HEA, 11.4.2
   model form, Appx. D.6.3
   TILA, 11.4.1

DISCOVERY
sample discoveries
   bankruptcy proceedings, Appx. F.3
   collection abuses, Appx. F.1
   proprietary school abuses, Appx. F.2

DISCRIMINATION
bankruptcy discharge, prohibition, 10.11
private loans, 11.10

DISTANCE EDUCATION PROGRAMS
see also PROPRIETARY INSTITUTIONS
abuses, 12.3.3.6
correspondence schools distinguished, 1.7.1.4
definition, 1.7.1.4
eligibility for student aid, 1.7.1.4, 12.3.3.6
FTC guides, 12.5.2.3

DOE
see DEPARTMENT OF EDUCATION (DOE)

DRUG CONVICTIONS
effect on eligibility for student aid, 1.6.4

DUE PROCESS CHALLENGES
administrative review process, 8.2.6, 8.3.5
collection practices, 7.4.5.1
federal benefits offsets, 8.4.3.4
statute of limitations elimination, 7.5.3.1
tax refund offsets, 8.2.6
wage garnishments, 8.3.5

EARNED INCOME TAX CREDITS (EITC)
offsets, avoiding, 8.2.8
   bankruptcy filing, 8.2.9

ECONOMIC HARDSHIP
see also UNEMPLOYMENT
bankruptcy discharge, undue hardship, 10.4
deferment eligibility, 4.3.5.2
   Perkins Loans, 4.3.8
   post-July 1, 1993 loans, 4.3.5.1, 4.3.5.2
   pre-July 1, 1993 loans, 4.3.7
   time limits, 4.3.3
forbearances, 4.4.4
   Perkins Loans, 4.4.5
forms
   deferments, Appx. D.2.1
   financial disclosure, Appx. D.4.2, Appx. D.4.3

ECONOMIC HARDSHIP (cont.)
IRB repayment alternative, 4.3.5.2
offset reduction, 8.4.3.2
sample request for reduction, Appx. E.1
wage garnishment defense, 8.3.2.3, 8.3.3.1

EDUCATION LOANS
see STUDENT LOANS

EDUCATIONAL BENEFITS
see FEDERAL STUDENT ASSISTANCE; GRANTS

EDUCATIONAL INSTITUTIONS
see SCHOOLS

EDUCATIONAL MALPRACTICE
claims, 12.5.4.2

EMPLOYMENT PROSPECTS
gainful employment, 1.7.1.2, 12.3.3.3
job placement rates, 1.7.3, 12.3.3.4

EQUAL CREDIT OPPORTUNITY ACT (ECOA)
private loan violations, 11.10

EVIDENCE
school malfeasance, 12.6.4
   ATB falsification, 9.4.2.2

EXPECTED FAMILY CONTRIBUTION (EFC)
federal student loans, 1.5.1

FAIR CREDIT REPORTING ACT (FCRA)
student loans, application, 12.5.2.4

FAIR DEBT COLLECTION PRACTICES ACT (FDCPA)
HEA, conflicts, 7.4.3.2
illegal activities under, 7.4.2.2
student loan collections, application, 7.4.3, 12.5.2.4

FALSE CERTIFICATION DISCHARGE
see also STATUTORY DISCHARGES
ability-to-benefit (ATB) falsification, 9.4.2
   defined, 9.4.2.1
   form, Appx. D.3.2
   group discharges, 9.4.2.3
   proving, 9.4.2.2
applying for, 9.4.7
contract defenses, interrelationship, 7.5.4.1, 7.5.4.2
disqualifying status of student, 9.4.3
   form, Appx. D.3.3
effect, 9.4.6
eligible loans, 9.2
forgery, 9.4.4
   form, Appx. D.3.4
forms, Appx. D.3.2–Appx. D.3.4
generally, 9.4.1
guaranteed-loan status lost, 7.5.4.3
identity theft, 9.4.5
   cooperation agreement, Appx. D.3.6
   form, Appx. D.3.4
procedures, challenging, Appx. E.2.2
relationship to other discharges, 9.6
relief available, 9.4.6
revocation, 9.4.6
sample letter granting, Appx. D.3.5
tuition recovery funds, interrelationship, 12.8.2

FALSE CLAIMS ACT
claims under, 12.5.2.2

FEDERAL BENEFITS OFFSETS
amount of offset, 8.4.2
challenging, 8.4.3, 12.6.2.1
   due process challenges, 8.4.3.4
collection abuses, 7.4.2.1
collection fees, 7.3.3
exempt benefits, 8.4.1
hardship reductions, 8.4.3.2
hearing rights, 8.4.3.1
notice, 8.4.3.1
   sample notice, Appx. D.4.5
overview, 8.4.1
state payments and debts, 8.4.1
statute of limitations, 7.5.3.1, 8.4.3.3
statutory provisions, selected text, Appx. A.5
   regulations, Appx. B.5.1
student loan funds, 8.4.1, 8.7

FEDERAL DIRECT LOANS
see DIRECT LOANS

FEDERAL FAMILY EDUCATION LOANS (FFELs)
see FFELs

FEDERAL GUARANTEED STUDENT LOAN PROGRAM (GSLs)
see STAFFORD LOANS (GSLs)

FEDERAL INSURED STUDENT LOAN PROGRAM (FISLs)
see also FFELs
closed-school discharge, 9.3.7
consolidation, 6.2.4
history of, 1.3.1
laches doctrine, application, 7.5.3.3.3
older loans, 1.4.1.5
school-related defenses, raising, 12.7.2.4

FEDERAL LOANS
see FEDERAL STUDENT ASSISTANCE

FEDERAL PREEMPTION
common law agency, 12.7.3.2
contract claims, 12.5.4.2
disclosure requirements, 2.5.1
fraud claims, 12.5.4.1
HEA, generally, 12.5.3.4
lender liability statutes, 12.7.3.3
National Bank Act, 11.9.2.4
respondeat superior claims, 12.7.3.2
student loan collections, 7.4.4
UDAP and other state claims, 12.5.3.4
usury laws, 2.3.1

FEDERAL SALARY OFFSETS
overview, 8.5

FEDERAL STUDENT AID INFORMATION CENTER
assistance, 1.9
loan information, 7.2.1
student loan guides available from, 1.12.2

FEDERAL STUDENT ASSISTANCE
see also GRANTS; STUDENT LOANS
Academic Competitiveness Grants, see ACADEMIC COMPETITIVENESS GRANTS
administration by guaranty agencies, 1.3.1
administrative capability of school, 1.7.4

FEDERAL STUDENT ASSISTANCE (*cont.*)
admissions standards, 1.7.1.3, 12.3.3.8
applying for, 1.5
　see also APPLICATION FOR STUDENT AID
　forms, Appx. D.1
basic terms and conditions, 2
　cancellations, 2.7
　disbursement of funds, 2.6
　disclosure requirements, 2.5
　interest rates, 2.3
　loan fees, 2.4
　loan limits, 2.2
　master promissory notes, 2.8
　return of funds, 2.7
borrower assistance, *see* ASSISTANCE FOR BORROWERS
cancellation rights, 2.7
central database, *see* NATIONAL STUDENT LOAN DATA SYSTEM (NSLDS)
cohort default rate sanctions, 1.7.4.2, 5.1.3
collection procedures, *see* COLLECTIONS
consolidation loans, *see* CONSOLIDATION LOANS
consumer information requirements, 1.7.3
correspondence courses, 1.7.1.4
counseling requirements, 2.9
default consequences, 5.1.5
default triggers, 5.1.4
defaulted loans, *see* DEFAULTED LOANS
deferments, *see* DEFERMENT
delinquent loans, *see* DELINQUENT LOANS
determining loan type, 1.9
direct loans
　consolidation loans, *see* CONSOLIDATION LOANS
　DOE, *see* DIRECT LOANS
　schools, *see* PERKINS LOANS
disbursement of funds, 2.6
disclosure requirements, 2.5
distance education programs, 1.7.1.4, 12.3.3.6
eligibility criteria
　individual eligibility, 1.6, Appx. C.4
　institutional eligibility, 1.7.1, Appx. B.4.1
expected family contribution (EFC), 1.5.1
Federal Direct Loans, *see* DIRECT LOANS
Federal Family Education Loans (FFELs), *see* FFELs
FISLs, *see* FEDERAL INSURED STUDENT LOAN PROGRAM (FISLs)
forbearances, *see* FORBEARANCE
forms, Appx. D
frequently asked questions, Appx. I
garnishment of funds, 1.4.3, 8.7
GSLs, *see* STAFFORD LOANS (GSLs)
guaranty agencies, *see* GUARANTY AGENCIES
history of, 1.3.1
interest rates, 2.3
job placement and completion statistics, 12.3.3.4
loan fees, 2.4
　late charges, 2.4.2
　origination fees, 2.4.1
loan limits, 2.2
loan verification certificates, 6.2.5
master promissory note, *see* MASTER PROMISSORY NOTE
NSLDS listing, 11.2.2
older loans, 1.4.1.5
overview, 1.4, 2.1
　grants, 1.4.2

　loans, 1.4.1
Pell Grants, *see* PELL GRANTS
percentage restrictions, 1.7.2.2, 12.3.3.5
Perkins Loans, *see* PERKINS LOANS
PLUS Loans, *see* PLUS LOANS
private loans compared, 11.2.1, 11.2.2
Program Participation Agreements, 1.7.2
proprietary schools, reliance on, 12.3.3.5
renewing eligibility, 6.5
　consolidation, 6.2.1
　rehabilitation, 6.3.1
repayment, *see* REPAYMENT OF LOANS
return of funds, 2.7
seizure of funds, 1.4.3, 8.7
SLSs, *see* SUPPLEMENTAL LOANS FOR STUDENTS (SLSs)
SMART Grants, *see* NATIONAL SMART GRANTS
Stafford Loans, *see* STAFFORD LOANS (GSLs)
statutory provisions, selected text, Appx. A
　regulations, Appx. B
TEACH Grants, *see* TEACH GRANTS
third party consent form, Appx. D.5.6
types of assistance, 1.4

FEDERAL STUDENT LOAN OMBUDSMAN
see STUDENT LOAN OMBUDSMAN

FEDERAL TRADE COMMISSION (FTC)
Guides for Private Vocational and Distance Education Schools, 12.5.2.3
Holder Notice
　bank violations, 11.9.2.4
　failure to provide, 12.7.3.4, 11.9.2.3
　FFELs, 12.7.2.3, 12.7.3.1, 12.7.3.4
　private loans, 11.9.2, 12.7.2.5

FEES AND PENALTIES
collection fees, *see* COLLECTION FEES
late fees, *see* LATE CHARGES
origination fees, *see* ORIGINATION FEES
other fees and penalties, DOE collections, 7.3.4

FFELs
see also FEDERAL STUDENT ASSISTANCE
cohort default rate, 1.7.4.2.1
compromise or write-off, 6.6
　procedures for guaranty agencies, Appx. D.5.1
consolidation, 1.4.1.3.1, 1.4.1.3.2, 6.2.4
default triggers, 5.1.4
defaulted loans
　collection costs, 7.3.1
　collection procedures, 7.2.1, 7.2.3
　defined, 5.1.4
　school-related defenses, raising, 7.5.4.3, 12.7.2.3, 12.7.3
deferment rights
　see also DEFERMENT
　economic hardship, 4.3.5.2, Appx. D.2.1.1
　military deferments, 4.3.5.4, 4.3.5.5, Appx. D.2.3
　post-July 1, 1993, 4.3.5
　pre-July 1, 1993, 4.3.7
　time limits, 4.3.3
　unemployment deferments, 4.3.2, 4.3.5.3
delinquent loans, collection procedures, 7.2.2
disclosure requirements, 2.5.2
discontinuation of program, 1.3.2
forbearances, 4.4.3
FTC Holder Notice, 12.7.2.3, 12.7.3.1, 12.7.3.4

FFELs (*cont.*)
  guaranteed status lost, effect, 7.5.4.3
  history of program, 1.3.1
  interest rates, 2.3.1
  loan servicing, 3.2
  origination fees, 2.4.1
  profession-related cancellations
    child care workers, 9.11
    teachers, 9.10
  referral relationship, 12.7.2.3
  rehabilitation of loan, 6.3
    loan sale, 6.3.5
  repayment plans, 3.1, 6.3.2
    IBRPs, 3.1.3.2
    ISRPs, 3.1.3.5
    reasonable and affordable, 6.3.4
  school-related defenses, raising
    newer loans, 12.7.2.3
    older loans, 12.7.3
    when guaranteed status lost, 7.5.4.3
  SLSs, *see* SUPPLEMENTAL LOANS FOR STUDENTS (SLSs)
  Stafford Loans, *see* STAFFORD LOANS (GSLs)
  statutory discharges
    see also STATUTORY DISCHARGES
    disability discharge, 9.7.2
    eligibility, 9.2
    false-certification discharge, 9.4.1
  statutory provisions, selected text, Appx. A.2
    regulations, Appx. B.2

FINANCIAL HARDSHIP
see ECONOMIC HARDSHIP

FORBEARANCE
administrative forbearances, 4.4.3, 4.4.4
  PLUS loans, 4.3.6
applying for, 4.4.2
  form, Appx. D.2.5
checklist, 1.11.3
defaulted loans, 4.4.1, 4.4.4
discretionary forbearances, 4.4.3
effect, 4.4.1
generally, 4.4.1
mandatory forbearances, 4.4.4
  military service, 4.3.5.5, 4.4.4
pending discharge
  closed-school discharge, 9.3.6.4
  pending disability discharge, 9.7.4.1
Perkins Loans, 4.4.5
private loans, 11.7.2
sample request, Appx. D.2.5
verbal forbearances, 4.4.2

FORGERY
see also IDENTITY THEFT
defense to loan enforceability, 7.5.4.1
false-certification discharge
  form, Appx. D.3.4
  grounds, 9.4.4

FORGIVENESS OF LOANS
see CANCELLATION OF LOAN

FORMS
additional forms, Appx. D.5
application forms, Appx. D.1
deferment forms, Appx. D.2
discharge forms, Appx. D.3
forbearance request, Appx. D.2.5
hearing forms, Appx. D.4
private loan model forms, Appx. D.6

FRAUD
see also FALSE CERTIFICATION DISCHARGE
defense to loan enforceability, 7.5.4.1
proprietary schools
  see also SCHOOL-RELATED CLAIMS AND DEFENSES
  accrediting agencies, 12.6.2.2
  common law claims, 12.5.4.1
  False Claims Act, 12.5.2.2
  federal claims, 12.5.2
  history of, 12.3.1
  raising in bankruptcy proceedings, Appx. E.5
  sample pleadings, Appx. E.4, Appx. E.5
  state claims, 12.5.3, 12.5.4.1
  tuition recovery funds, 12.8
scholarship scams, 12.4.1

FREEDOM OF INFORMATION ACT REQUESTS
DOE investigatory files, 9.4.2.2.2
sample request, Appx. F.4

FTC
see FEDERAL TRADE COMMISSION (FTC)

GARNISHMENTS
student assistance funds, 1.4.3, 8.7
wages, *see* WAGE GARNISHMENTS

GOVERNMENT LOANS
see FEDERAL STUDENT ASSISTANCE

GRACE PERIODS
prior to repayment, 4.2

GRADUATE STUDENTS
see also STUDENTS
deferment eligibility, 4.3.5.1
Perkins Loans, 1.4.1.4
PLUS loans, 1.4.1.2
Stafford loans, 1.4.1.1

GRANTS
see also FEDERAL STUDENT ASSISTANCE; SCHOLARSHIPS
ACG, *see* ACADEMIC COMPETITIVENESS GRANTS
Basic Educational Opportunity Grants (BEOG), *see* PELL GRANTS
discharge of prior loans, effect
  bankruptcy discharge, 10.11
  closed-school discharge, 9.3.5
  false-certification discharge, 9.4.6
finder-fee companies, scams, 12.4.1
FSEOG, *see* SUPPLEMENTAL EDUCATIONAL OPPORTUNITY GRANTS (FSEOG)
garnishment of funds, 1.4.3, 8.7
National Science and Mathematics Access to Retain Talent Grants, *see* NATIONAL SMART GRANTS
overpayments, 1.4.2.2.2, 1.6.6
  bankruptcy discharge, 10.2.1
overview of federal programs, 1.4.2
repayment unnecessary, 1.4.2.1
return of funds upon withdrawal, 2.7
seizure of funds, 1.4.3, 8.7

GRANTS (*cont.*)
TEACH Grants, *see* TEACH GRANTS

GUARANTEED STUDENT LOANS (GSLs)
see STAFFORD LOANS (GSLs)

GUARANTY AGENCIES
bankruptcy dischargeability
   contesting, 10.7.1
   sovereign immunity issues, 10.8
collection abuses, complaining to, 7.2.1, 7.4.5.2
collection actions by
   injunctive relief, 12.6.2.1
   joinder of school-related claims, 7.5.2
collection agencies, use, 7.2.1
   complaints, 7.4.5.2, Appx. D.4.4
   factors fostering abuse, 7.4.1
collection fees, 7.3.1, 7.3.2
collection procedures
   FDCPA, application, 7.4.3.5
   generally, 7.2.1
   post-default, 7.2.3
   pre-default, 7.2.2
compromise and write-off procedures, 6.6, Appx. D.5.1
defaulted loans
   administrative review, 8.2.5
   collection procedures, 7.2.1, 7.2.3
   reporting to credit bureaus, 7.2.3, 7.2.4
directory of, Appx. GS
discharge requests, responding to
   closed schools, 9.3.6.4
   false certification, 9.4.7
forbearances, granting, 4.4.1
function, 1.3.1
judicial review of actions, 8.3.3.1, 8.3.5, 9.15
loan servicing, 3.2
ombudsman programs, 1.12.1.2
rehabilitated loans, sale, 6.3.5
school misconduct, liability for, 12.7.3
supervision by DOE
   collections, 7.2.1
   compromise and write-off, Appx. D.5.1
   policy guidance letters, Appx. C
tax refund offsets, 8.2.1
wage garnishments, 8.3.3

HARDSHIP DEFENSE
see ECONOMIC HARDSHIP

HEALTH CARE WORKERS
Perkins loan cancellation, 9.12
public service cancellation, 9.9.2

HEALTH EDUCATION ASSISTANCE LOANS (HEALs)
bankruptcy dischargeability, 10.6
consolidation, 6.2.4
disability discharge, 9.7.2

HEARINGS
defaulted loans, *see* ADMINISTRATIVE REVIEW

HIGHER EDUCATION ACT (HEA)
claims under, 12.5.2.1
disclosure requirements
   federal loans, 2.5
   private loans, 11.4.2
FDCPA, conflicts, 7.4.3.2

history of, 1.3.1
misrepresentation regulations, 1.7.2.6, 12.5.2.1
preemption of state law
   common law claims, 12.5.4.1, 12.5.4.2
   debt collection laws, 7.4.4
   UDAP and other claims, 12.5.3.4

HOLDER RULE (FTC)
FFELs, application, 12.7.2.3, 12.7.3.1, 12.7.3.4
private loans, application, 11.9.2, 12.7.2.5
violations, remedies, 11.9.2.3, 12.7.3.4
   bank violations, 11.9.2.4

IDENTITY THEFT
see also FORGERY
defense to loan enforceability, 7.5.4.1
false-certification discharge, 8.3.4
   cooperation agreement, Appx. D.3.6
   form, Appx. D.3.5
forbearances, 4.4.3

INCARCERATED STUDENTS
eligibility for assistance, 1.6.5

INCOME-BASED REPAYMENT (IBR) PLANS
see also REPAYMENT PLANS
alternative to economic hardship deferment, 4.3.5.2
applying for, 3.1.3.2.3
   forms, Appx. D.1.4, Appx. D.1.5
consolidation loans, 6.2.2, 6.2.3, 6.2.5
Direct Loans, 3.1.3.1
   consolidation loans, 3.1.3.2.1
eligibility, 3.1.3.2.1
FFELs, 3.1.3.1
generally, 3.1.3.1
ICRP compared, 3.1.3.4
leaving plan, 3.1.3.2.4
loan forgiveness, 3.1.3.2.5
repayment formula, 3.1.3.2.2

INCOME-CONTINGENT REPAYMENT (ICR) PLANS
see also REPAYMENT PLANS
applying for, forms, Appx. D.1.4, Appx. D.1.5
consolidation loans, 6.2.2, 6.2.5
Direct Loans, 3.1.3.1
   consolidation loans, 3.1.3.2.1
eligibility, 3.1.3.3.1
generally, 3.1.3.1
IBRP compared, 3.1.3.4
loan forgiveness, 3.1.3.3.3
monthly payments, 3.1.3.3.2

INCOME-SENSITIVE REPAYMENT (ISR) PLANS
see also REPAYMENT PLANS
FFELs, 3.1.3.1, 3.1.3.5

INCOME TAX ISSUES
see TAX ISSUES

INCOME TAX OFFSETS
see TAX REFUND OFFSETS

INFANCY
availability as defense, 7.5.4.1

INFORMATION
see also DISCLOSURES
release form, Appx. D.5.4

References are to sections

INJUNCTIVE RELIEF
collection activities, 12.6.2.1
DOE, against, 12.6.2.1

INSTITUTIONS
see PROPRIETARY INSTITUTIONS; SCHOOLS

INTEGRATED POSTSECONDARY EDUCATION DATA SYSTEM (IPEDS)
information source, 12.6.4

INTEREST
capitalization, 2.3.2
   deferments, 4.3.1
   ICRPs, 3.1.3.3.3
consolidation loans, 2.3.5
federal interest rates, 2.3
income tax deductions, 1.10
military personnel, 2.3.1
Perkins loans, 2.3.4
PLUS loans, 2.3.4
private loans, 2.3.1
Stafford loans, 2.3.3
usury limits, 2.3.1
waiver, 6.6

INTERROGATORIES
see DISCOVERY

JOINDER
school-related claims, 7.5.2

JOINT DEBTORS
discharges
   death, 9.8
   disability, 9.7.2
   joint consolidation loans, 9.2
forbearances, 4.4.3

JUDGMENTS
consolidation of loan after, 6.2.4
disability discharge after, 9.7.2
rehabilitation of loan after, 6.3.6
repayment of loan after, 6.5
vacating collection judgments, 7.6

JUDICIAL REVIEW
discharge denial, 9.15
tax refund offsets, 8.2.7
wage garnishments, 8.3.5

LACHES
application to student loan cases, 7.5.3.3
elements of defense, 7.5.3.3.2
exceptions to the rule barring, 7.5.3.3.2
FISL collections, 7.5.3.3.3

LANGUAGE
ability-to-benefit tests, 9.4.2.1

LATE CHARGES
federal loans, 2.4.2

LAW ENFORCEMENT OFFICERS
deferment eligibility, 4.3.8

LEAVE OF ABSENCE
approved leave, 9.3.1

LENDERS
actions against, see ACTIONS
banks, see BANKS
collections
   collection fees, 7.3.1
   mandatory requirements, 7.2.2, 7.2.4.1
DOE direct loans, see DEPARTMENT OF EDUCATION (DOE)
FDCPA, application, 7.4.3.4
loan verification certificates, 6.2.5
origination relationships, 12.7.3.5
private education loans, see PRIVATE STUDENT LOANS
prohibited inducements, 1.7.2.4
referral relationship with school, 12.7.2.3
   school preferred-lender lists, 1.7.2.4
school as lender
   federally funded loans, see PERKINS LOANS
   private loans, see PRIVATE STUDENT LOANS
school misconduct, liability for
   agency theories, 12.7.3.2
   consolidated loans, 7.5.4.4
   FTC Holder Notice, 12.7.2.5, 12.7.3.4
   guaranteed-status lost loans, 7.5.4.3
   origination theories, 12.7.3.5
   private loans, 11.9
   state law, 12.7.3.3
secondary market lenders, see SECONDARY MARKET LENDERS
servicing agencies, see SERVICING AGENCIES
student loan specialist, see STUDENT LOAN MARKETING ASSOCIATION (SALLIE MAE)

LICENSES
suspension or revocation of professional licenses, 8.6

LICENSING AGENCIES (STATE)
see also ACCREDITING AGENCIES
proprietary schools
   claims against regarding abuses by, 12.6.2.3
   requirements, 12.2.1

LIMITATIONS
see also STATUTE OF LIMITATIONS
credit reports, defaulted loans, 7.2.4.2

LOAN SERVICING
see SERVICING AGENCIES

LOAN VERIFICATION CERTIFICATES
provision, time, 6.2.5

MALPRACTICE
educational malpractice claims, 12.5.4.2

MASTER PROMISSORY NOTE
federal loans, 2.8
   counseling requirements, 2.9
   Perkins loans, Appx. D.5.11
   sample note, Appx. D.5.7

MILITARY PERSONNEL
cancellation of loans, 9.9.2
   Perkins loans, 9.12
collection proceedings, stay, 8.3.2.3
consolidation loans, 6.2.2
defenses for service members, 7.5.4.5
   private loans, 11.8.4
deferments
   active duty, 4.3.5.4
   applying for, 4.3.4, Appx. D.2.3
   Perkins loans, 4.3.8

MILITARY PERSONNEL (*cont.*)
deferments (*cont.*)
   post-active duty, 4.3.5.5
   pre-July 1, 1993 FFELs, 4.3.7
disability discharge, 9.7.4.2
educational benefits for service members, 1.4.4
   other protections and programs, 1.4.4.2
   post-9/11 G.I. bill, 1.4.4.1
forbearances
   mandatory forbearance, 4.3.5.5, 4.4.4
   Perkins loans, 4.4.5
grant repayment, 2.7
interest rate protections, 2.3.1
rehabilitation of loans, 6.3.2
repayment grace period, 4.2
Servicemember Civil Relief Act, 7.5.4.5, 11.8.4
wage garnishment restrictions, 8.3.2.3

MISREPRESENTATIONS
HEA claims, 12.5.2.1
proprietary schools, 12.3.3.4, 12.7.3.2
school eligibility, 1.7.2.6

MISTAKE
defense to loan enforceability, 7.5.4.1

MOTHERS
FFELs deferments, 4.3.7

NATIONAL CENTER FOR EDUCATION STATISTICS (NCES)
information source, 12.6.4

NATIONAL CLEARINGHOUSE FOR LEGAL SERVICES
see SARGENT SHRIVER NATIONAL CENTER ON POVERTY LAW

NATIONAL CONSUMER LAW CENTER STUDENT LOAN BORROWER ASSISTANCE PROJECT
see STUDENT LOAN BORROWER ASSISTANCE PROJECT (NCLC)

NATIONAL DEFENSE STUDENT LOANS
see PERKINS LOANS

NATIONAL DIRECT STUDENT LOANS
see PERKINS LOANS

NATIONAL SMART GRANTS
see also GRANTS
expiration of program, 1.4.2.4
overview of program, 1.4.2.4

NATIONAL STUDENT LOAN DATA SYSTEM (NSLDS)
listing of federal loans, 11.2.2
using, 1.9

NATURAL DISASTERS
see DISASTER SITUATIONS

NEGATIVE AMORTIZATION
ICRPs, 3.1.3.3.2
loan rehabilitation, 6.3.4

NEGLIGENCE CLAIMS
proprietary school abuses, 12.5.4.1
   accrediting agencies, 12.6.2.2
   DOE, 12.5.2.4

NOTICE
defaulted loans
   assignment to guaranty agency, 7.2.3
   prior to credit reporting, 7.2.4.1
   prior to federal benefits offsets, 8.4.3.1
   prior to tax refund offset, 8.2.2
   prior to wage garnishment, 8.3.2.2, 8.3.3.1
deferred interest, 4.3.1
delinquent loans, 7.2.2
disability discharges
   denial, 9.7.4.1
   reinstatement, 9.7.5.2
disbursement of funds, sample notice, Appx. D.5.10
FTC Holder Rule, FFELs, 12.7.2.3, 12.7.3.4
   failure to provide, 12.7.3.4
offset notice, Appx. D.4.5

OFFSETS
federal benefits, *see* FEDERAL BENEFIT OFFSETS
federal salary, *see* FEDERAL SALARY OFFSETS
tax refunds, *see* TAX REFUND OFFSETS

OMBUDSMAN PROGRAMS
federal ombudsman, *see* STUDENT LOAN OMBUDSMAN
guaranty agencies, 1.12.1.2
private loans, 1.12.1.3, 11.7.4
Sallie Mae, 1.12.1.2

ORIGINATION FEES
federal loans, 2.4.1

ORIGINATION RELATIONSHIP
lender and school, 12.7.3.5

OVERPAYMENTS
bankruptcy discharge, 10.2.1
effect on future aid, 1.6.6
Pell Grants, 1.4.2.2.2

PARENTAL LEAVE
see also UNEMPLOYMENT
FFEL deferments, 4.3.7

PARENTAL (PLUS) LOANS
see PLUS LOANS

PARENTS
see ACCOMMODATION PARTIES

PAYMENTS
see REPAYMENT OF LOANS

PEACE CORPS SERVICE
deferment eligibility, 4.3.5.2, 4.3.8
Perkins cancellations, 9.12

PELL GRANTS
see also GRANTS
overpayments, 1.4.2.2.2
overview of program, 1.4.2.2.1
repayment unnecessary, 1.4.2.1

PENALTIES
see COLLECTION FEES

PERKINS LOANS
see also FEDERAL STUDENT ASSISTANCE
administration of, 1.4.1.4
bankruptcy discharge, 10.2.1
   dischargeability, contesting by school, 10.7.1
cancellation of loans, 9.12
cohort default rate, 1.7.4.2.1

PERKINS LOANS (cont.)
collections
   assignment to DOE, 7.2.1
   collection fees, 7.3.2.3
compromise and write-off, 6.6
consolidation, 6.2.4
credit reports, 7.2.4.2
default triggers, 5.1.4
defenses
   false-certification, 9.4.1
   unpaid refunds, 9.5
deferment rights
   grounds, generally, 4.3.8
   military deferment, 4.3.5.4, 4.3.5.5, 4.3.8
disclosure requirements, 2.5.2
forbearances, 4.4.5
interest rates, 2.3.4
loan limits, 2.2.4
master promissory note, 2.8
   sample note, Appx. D.5.11
origination fees, 2.4.1
overview, 1.4.1.4
rehabilitation of loan, 6.3.7
   sample agreement, Appx. D.5.3.2
repayment grace period, 4.2
repayment plans, 3.1.4
school-related defenses, raising, 12.7.2.1
statutory discharges
   see also STATUTORY DISCHARGES
   closed-school discharge, 9.3.7
   death discharge, 9.8
   disability discharge, 9.7.2
   eligibility, 9.2
statutory provision, text, Appx. A.3
   regulations, Appx. B.3

PERSONAL IDENTIFICATION NUMBER (PIN)
federal student aid programs, use, 1.9

PLEADINGS
additional pleadings, Appx. K.6
companion website, Appx. K
sample pleadings, Appx. E

PLUS LOANS
see also DIRECT LOANS
bankruptcy discharge, 10.2.1
   prior bankruptcy, effect, 10.11
consolidation, 6.2.4
counseling requirements, 2.9
deferments, 4.3.6, Appx. D.2.4
disclosure requirements, 2.5.2
IBRP eligibility, 3.1.3.2.1
ICRP eligibility, 3.1.3.3.1
interest rates, 2.3.4
loan limits, 2.2.3
origination fees, 2.4.1
overview, 1.4.1.2
public service cancellation, 9.9.2
repayment grace period, 4.2
statutory discharge
   see also STATUTORY DISCHARGES
   death discharge, 9.8
   disability discharge, 9.7.2
   eligibility, 9.2

unpaid-refund discharge, 9.5

PRACTICE TIPS
ATB falsification, obtaining evidence, 9.4.2.2
checklist for handling student loan issues, 1.11
frequently asked questions, Appx. I
resource aids, *see* RESOURCE AIDS
sample discovery, Appx. F
sample pleadings and letters, Appx. E
school abuses, developing a case, 12.6.4

PREEMPTION
see FEDERAL PREEMPTION

PREFERRED LENDER LISTS
prohibited inducements, 1.7.2.4

PRIVACY
information release form, Appx. D.5.4
Ombudsman privacy release statement, Appx. D.5.5

PRIVATE ACCREDITING AGENCIES
see ACCREDITING AGENCIES

PRIVATE STUDENT LOANS
bankruptcy discharge, 10.2.2.1
cancellation rights, 11.4.1.6, 11.7.3
default and delinquency, 5.2, 11.6
   collections, 5.2.3, 11.6.3
   default triggers, 5.2.2, 11.6.2
   high rate of, 5.2.1, 11.6.1
defenses in collection actions
   contract defenses, 11.8.1
   infancy, 11.8.2
   limitations period, 11.8.3
   service members, 11.8.4
deferments, 11.7.2
direct claims against lenders, 11.10
disclosure requirements, 11.4
   HEA, 11.4.2
   model form, Appx. D.6.3
   TILA, 11.4.1
fair billing issues, 11.5
FTC Holder Notice, 11.9.2, 12.7.2.5
federal loans compared, 11.2.1
forbearances, 11.7.2
guaranteed status lost loans as, 7.5.4.3
how to tell a private loan, 11.2.2
interest rates, 2.3.1
model forms, Appx. D.6
ombudsman, 1.12.1.3, 11.7.4
oversight, 11.3
overview of market, 11.1
   generally, 11.1.1
   school products, 11.1.3
   state products, 11.1.2
   types of borrowers, 11.1.4
overview of problems, 1.8, 5.2.1, 11.6.1
relief for borrowers, 11.7
   deferments, 11.7.2
   direct claims, 11.10
   forbearances, 11.7.2
   generally, 11.7.1
sample pleadings, Appx. E.6
school-related claims and defenses, 11.9, 12.1
   FTC Holder Rule, 11.9.2, 12.7.2.5
   generally, 11.9.1, 12.7.1

PRIVATE STUDENT LOANS (cont.)
self-certification form, 1.7.2.5, 11.4.1.5
  sample form, Appx. D.6.4
servicing issues, 11.5
statutory provisions, selected text, Appx. A.6
  regulations, Appx. B.6
terms and conditions, 11.2
TILA disclosures, 11.4.1
  application disclosures, 11.4.1.4.1
  approval disclosures, 11.4.1.4.2
  final disclosures, 11.4.1.4.3
  form and content, 11.4.1.4
  remedies, 11.4.1.7
  scope, 11.4.1.2
  self-certification, 11.4.1.5
  timing, 11.4.1.3
  waiting period, 11.4.1.6

PRODUCTION OF DOCUMENTS
see DISCOVERY

PROFESSIONAL DISCHARGES
loan cancellation for certain professions, 9.9
  generally, 9.9.1
  other professions, 9.11
  Perkins loans, 9.12
  public service, 9.9.2
  September 11 program, 9.13
  tax issues, 9.14
  teachers, 9.10

PROFESSIONAL LICENSES
suspension or revocation for default, 8.6

PROFESSIONAL STUDENTS
see GRADUATE STUDENTS

PROGRAM PARTICIPATION AGREEMENTS
code of conduct, 1.7.2.4
general requirements, 1.7.2.1
incentive compensation limits, 1.7.2.3
misrepresentation regulations, 1.7.2.6, 12.5.2.1
private education loan certification, 1.7.2.5
prohibited inducement requirements, 1.7.2.4
proprietary schools, 1.7.2.2

PROMISSORY NOTE
see MASTER PROMISSORY NOTE

PROPERTY SEIZURES
see SEIZURE OF PROPERTY AND ASSETS

PROPRIETARY INSTITUTIONS
see also SCHOOLS
abuses
  see also SCHOOL-RELATED CLAIMS AND DEFENSES
  common abuses, 12.3.3
  common law claims, 12.5.4
  federal claims, 12.5.2
  history of, 12.3.1
  private loans, 11.9.1
  sample discovery, Appx. F.2
  sample pleadings, Appx. E.4
  state claims, 12.5.3
accreditation, 12.2, 12.6.2.2
administrative capability, 1.7.4
aggressive marketing, 12.3.3.2
closures, 9.3

cohort default rate
  excessive rates, 5.1.1, 12.3.3.1
  manipulation of rates, 5.1.3
  sanctions, 1.7.4.2
completion rates, 1.7.3, 12.3.3.4
  resource data, 12.6.4
consumer information requirements, 1.7.3
correspondence courses, see CORRESPONDENCE COURSES
definition, 1.7.1.1
diploma mills, 12.4.2
distance education programs, see DISTANCE EDUCATION PROGRAMS
false certification, 9.4
federal student aid eligibility, 1.7
  "90/10" rule, 1.7.2.2, 12.3.3.5
  admissions standards, 1.7.1.3, 12.3.3.8
  criteria, 1.7.1.1
  distance education, 1.7.1.4, 12.3.3.6
  gainful employment, 1.7.1.2, 12.3.3.3
  misrepresentations, 1.7.2.6, 12.5.2.1
  private education certification forms, 1.7.2.5
  regulations, selected text, Appx. B.4.1
fiduciary duty, 12.5.4.3
FTC guides, 12.5.2.3
growth of, 12.3.2
job placement rates, 1.7.3, 12.3.3.4
  resource data, 12.6.4
lender-referral, 12.7.2.3
  preferred-lender lists, 1.7.2.4
private loan products, 11.1.3
  default rates, 5.2.1
Program Participation Agreements, 1.7.2
recruiters, see RECRUITERS
regulation of, 12.2
  oversight gaps, 12.2.3
reliance on federal aid, 12.3.3.5
school as lender
  federally funded loans, see PERKINS LOANS
  private loans, 11.1.3
self-certification form, 1.7.2.5, 11.4.1.5
  sample form, Appx. D.6.4
unpaid refunds, 9.5

PUBLIC ASSISTANCE BENEFITS
deferment eligibility, 4.3.5.2
offsets, see FEDERAL BENEFITS OFFSETS

PUBLIC SERVICE CANCELLATION
see also CANCELLATION OF LOAN
application process, 9.9.2.4
eligible borrowers, 9.9.2.2
eligible jobs, 9.9.2.3
eligible loans, 9.2
generally, 9.9.1, 9.9.2.1
Perkins loans, 9.12
September 11 program, 9.13
tax issues, 9.14
teachers, 9.10

QUALIFIED STUDENT LOANS
income tax purposes, 1.10

RACKETEERING INFLUENCED AND CORRUPT ORGANIZATIONS ACT (RICO)
see RICO CLAIMS

References are to sections

RECORDS
defaulted loans, right to inspect, 7.2.3, 8.2.5
school records and files, obtaining, 9.4.2.2.3
transcripts, *see* TRANSCRIPTS

RECOUPMENT CLAIMS
school-related claims, 12.6.2.4

RECRUITERS
abuses by, 12.3.3.2
   incentive compensation limits, 1.7.2.3, 12.3.3.2

REFINANCED LOANS
see CONSOLIDATION LOANS

REFUNDS
see also UNPAID REFUNDS DISCHARGE
paid-in-full discharged loans, 9.3.5

REHABILITATION OF LOANS
advantages and disadvantages, 6.4
"balance sensitive rehabilitations," 6.3.4
checklist, 1.11.4
collection abuses, 7.4.1.2
collection fees, 7.3.2.2
credit record, effect, 7.2.4.3
formal agreement, 6.3.3
generally, 6.3.1
limits on, 6.3.6
   Perkins loans, 6.3.7
loan sale, 6.3.5
payment requirements, 6.3.2
   reasonable and affordable, 6.3.4
Perkins loans, 6.3.7
   sample agreement, Appx. D.5.3.2
sample agreements, Appx. D.5.3

REHABILITATION TRAINING PROGRAMS
deferment eligibility, 4.3.5.1, 4.3.7

REPAYMENT OF LOANS
allocation of payments, 3.1.5
   IBRPs, 3.1.3.2.2
checklist, 1.11.4
collection procedures, *see* COLLECTIONS
credit reporting, 7.2.4.1, 7.2.4.3
grace periods, 4.2
loan forgiveness, *see* CANCELLATION OF LOAN
loan servicing, 3.2
   performance-based system, 3.2.1
   servicing requirements, 3.2.2
post-default
   consolidation, *see* CONSOLIDATION LOANS
   reasonable and affordable payments, 6.2.2, 6.3.4
   rehabilitation, *see* REHABILITATION OF LOANS
   repayment plans, *see* REPAYMENT PLANS
postponement
   deferment, *see* DEFERMENT
   forbearance, *see* FORBEARANCE
   grace periods, 4.2
pre-default, *see* REPAYMENT PLANS
statute of limitations, *see* STATUTE OF LIMITATIONS

REPAYMENT PLANS
see also REPAYMENT OF LOANS
bankruptcy discharge, effect, 10.4.2.3.2
chapter 13 bankruptcies, *see* BANKRUPTCY DISCHARGE
checklist, 1.11.4
credit record, effect, 7.2.4.3
IBRP, *see* INCOME-BASED REPAYMENT (IBR) PLANS
ICRP, *see* INCOME-CONTINGENT REPAYMENT (ICR) PLANS
ISRP, *see* INCOME-SENSITIVE REPAYMENT (IRS) PLANS
post-default plans
   consolidation loans, 6.2.2
   loan rehabilitation, 6.3.2, 6.3.4
   prior to federal benefit offset, 8.4.3.1
   prior to tax refund offset, 8.2.4
   prior to wage garnishment, 8.3.2.4
pre-default plans
   allocation of payments, 3.1.3.2.2, 3.1.5
   comparing IBR and ICR, 3.1.3.4
   extended plans, 3.1.2
   generally, 3.1.1
   graduated plans, 3.1.2
   income-based repayment, 3.1.3.2
   income-contingent repayment, 3.1.3.3
   income-sensitive repayment, 3.1.3.5
   income-tied plans, generally, 3.1.3.1
   Perkins Loans, 3.1.4
   standard plans, 3.1.2
selection form, Appx. D.1.3

REQUESTS FOR ADMISSIONS
see DISCOVERY

RESOURCE AIDS
Clearinghouse citations, 1.2.2
Department of Education, 1.12.2
loan type determination, 1.9
NCLC borrower assistance project, 1.12.3, Appx. J
NCLC manual, 1.2.1
   companion website, 1.2.1, Appx. K
   web-based text searching, 1.2.3, Appx. K.5
ombudsman programs, 1.12.1.2
pleadings, Appx. K
web resources, *see* WEB RESOURCES

RICO CLAIMS
private student loans, 11
proprietary school abuses
   federal claims, 12.5.2.1
   state claims, 12.5.3.3

SALLIE MAE
see STUDENT LOAN MARKETING ASSOCIATION (SALLIE MAE)

SARGENT SHRIVER NATIONAL CENTER ON POVERTY LAW
see also CLEARINGHOUSE CITATIONS
Clearinghouse documents, obtaining, 1.2.2

SCHOLARSHIPS
see also GRANTS
finder-fee companies, scams, 12.4.1

SCHOOL AS LENDER
federally funded loans, *see* PERKINS LOANS
private loans, *see* PRIVATE STUDENT LOANS

SCHOOL-RELATED CLAIMS AND DEFENSES
see also DEFENSES
accrediting agencies, claims against, 12.6.2.2
actual damages, 12.6.5

673

SCHOOLS

SCHOOL-RELATED CLAIMS AND DEFENSES (*cont.*)
affirmative litigation, 12.6
   class actions, 12.6.3
   common law claims, 12.5.4
   declaratory relief, 12.6.2.1, 7.5.2
   developing the case, 12.6.4
   federal claims, 12.5.2
   injunctive relief, 12.6.2.1
   potential defendants, 12.6.2
   proving damages, 12.6.5
   state claims, 12.5.3
bankrupt schools, 12.6.2.4
chapter 13 bankruptcy, raising, 10.9.3
class actions, *see* CLASS ACTIONS
closed schools, 12.6.2.4
common abuses, 12.3.3
common law claims, 12.5.4
   contracts, 12.5.4.2
   fiduciary duty, 12.5.4.3
   generally, 12.5.4.1
consolidation loans, raising after, 7.5.4.4
contract claims and defenses, 7.5.4, 12.5.4.2
credit reports, correcting, 7.2.4.3
defending collection actions, 7.5, 12.7
   consolidated loans, 7.5.4.4
   contract defenses, 7.5.4
   Direct loans, 12.7.2.2
   federal loans, 7.5
   FFELs, 7.5.4.3, 12.7.2.3, 12.7.3
   FISLs, 7.5.3.3.3, 12.7.2.4
   generally, 7.5.1, 12.7.1
   Perkins loans, 12.7.2.1
   procedural issues, 7.5.2
   service members, 7.5.4.5
diploma mills, 12.4.2
Direct Loans, 12.7.2.2
DOE, claims against, 12.5.2.4, 12.6.2.1
evidence, obtaining, 12.6.4
false certification, 9.4
federal claims, 12.5.2
   False Claims Act, 12.5.2.2
   HEA, 12.5.2.1
   other claims, 12.5.2.4
   RICO, 12.5.2.1
FFELs, 7.5.4.3, 12.7.2.3, 12.7.3
fiduciary duty, 12.5.4.3
FISLs, 12.7.2.4
FTC Holder Rule, 11.9.2
guaranteed status lost, effect, 7.5.4.3
ineligible schools, 7.5.4.3
insolvent schools, 12.6.2.4
joinder, 7.5.2
legal theories and strategies, 12.5
   agency, 12.7.3.2
   common law claims, 12.5.4
   contract claims and defenses, 7.5.4, 12.5.4.2
   education laws, 12.5.2.1, 12.5.3.2
   False Claims Act, 12.5.2.2
   federal claims, 12.5.2
   fraud claims, 12.5.4.1
   misrepresentation, 12.7.3.2
   negligence claims, 12.5.2.4, 12.5.4.1
   RICO, 12.5.2.1, 12.5.3.3
   state claims, 12.5.3
   statutory discharge, 12.5.2.5
   UDAP claims, 12.5.3.1
lender liability for, 12.7
   agency theories, 12.7.3.2
   DOE, 12.5.2.4, 12.7.2.2, 12.7.2.4
   FFELs, 12.7.2.3, 12.7.3
   FTC Holder Notice, 12.7.2.5, 12.7.3.4
   generally, 12.5.1, 12.7.1
   non-guaranteed loans, 7.5.4.3
   origination theories, 12.7.3.5
   private loans, 11
   school as lender, 12.7.2.1
   state law, 12.7.3.3
overview
   abuses, 12.3.3
   claims, 12.5.1
Perkins Loans, 12.7.2.1
private loans, 11.9
raising, 12.1, 12.7.1
recoupment claims, 12.6.2.4
sample discovery, Appx. F.2
sample pleadings, Appx. E.4
scholarship scams, 12.4.1
school closure, 9.3.7
state claims, 12.5.3
   education laws, 12.5.3.2
   other claims, 12.5.3.3
   preemption, 12.5.3.4
   UDAP theories, 12.5.3.1
state licensing agencies, claims against, 12.6.2.3
statutory discharge
   alternative, 7.5.4.1, 12.5.2.5
   interrelationship, 7.5.4.2
tuition recovery funds, 12.8
types of school misconduct, 9.4.1, 12.3.3
UDAP claims, *see* UDAP CLAIMS

SCHOOLS
administrative capability, 1.7.4
admission standards, 1.7.1.3, 12.3.3.8
bankrupt or insolvent schools, 12.6.2.4
claims against, *see* SCHOOL-RELATED CLAIMS AND
   DEFENSES
closed-school discharge, 9.3
code of conduct, 1.7.2.4
cohort default rate sanctions, 1.7.4.2
   appeals, 1.7.4.2.2
   manipulation of rates, 5.1.3
consumer information requirements, 1.7.3
correspondence courses, *see* CORRESPONDENCE COURSES
counseling requirements, 2.9
diploma mills, 12.4.2
distance education programs, *see* DISTANCE EDUCATION
   PROGRAMS
DOE files on, obtaining, 9.4.2.2.2
"eligible institutions," 1.7
   criteria, 1.7.1
   misrepresentations, 1.7.2.6, 12.3.3.4
   regulation and oversight, 12.2
   regulations, selected text, Appx. B.4.1
falsification discharge, 9.4
FDCPA, application, 7.4.3.4
federal grant programs, administration, 1.4.1.1
federal regulations, selected text, Appx. B.4

SCHOOLS (*cont.*)
federal student aid percentages, 1.7.2.2, 12.3.3.5
files and records, obtaining, 9.4.2.2.3
lender-referral, 12.7.2.3
   preferred-lender lists, 1.7.2.4
loans directly from
   collection fees, 7.3.1
   Perkins Loans, *see* PERKINS LOANS
   private loans, 11.1.3
origination relationships, 12.7.3.5
Pell Grant overpayments, 1.4.2.2.2
Program Participation Agreements, 1.7.2
proprietary schools, *see* PROPRIETARY INSTITUTIONS
recruiters, *see* RECRUITERS
scholarship scams, 12.4.1
self-certification form, 1.7.2.5, 11.4.1.5
   sample form, Appx. D.6.4
transcripts, *see* TRANSCRIPTS
types of schools, 1.7.1.1
unpaid refunds, 9.5
vocational schools, *see* VOCATIONAL SCHOOLS

SECONDARY MARKET LENDERS
see also LENDERS
FDCPA, application, 7.4.3.4
Sallie Mae, *see* STUDENT LOAN MARKETING ASSOCIATION (SALLIE MAE)

SECRETARY OF EDUCATION
see DEPARTMENT OF EDUCATION (DOE)

SEIZURE OF PROPERTY AND ASSETS
federal benefits, *see* FEDERAL BENEFITS OFFSETS
federal salary, *see* FEDERAL SALARY OFFSETS
generally, 8.1
student assistance funds, 1.4.3, 8.7
tax refunds, *see* TAX REFUND OFFSETS
wage garnishments, *see* WAGE GARNISHMENTS

SELF-CERTIFICATION FORM
private education loans, 1.7.2.5, 11.4.1.5
   sample form, Appx. D.6.4

SERVICEMEMBER CIVIL RELIEF ACT
see also MILITARY PERSONNEL
protections, 7.5.4.5, 11.8.4
   interest rates, 2.3.1

SERVICING AGENCIES
see also GUARANTY AGENCIES
Direct Loans, *see* DIRECT LOAN SERVICING CENTER
FDCPA, application, 7.4.3.4
generally, 3.2
loan verification certificates, provision, 6.2.5
performance-based system, 3.2.1
private loan requirements, 11.5
Sallie Mae, *see* STUDENT LOAN MARKETING ASSOCIATION (SALLIE MAE)
servicing requirements, 3.2.2

SLSs
see SUPPLEMENTAL LOANS FOR STUDENTS (SLSs)

SMART GRANTS
see NATIONAL SMART GRANTS

SOCIAL SECURITY BENEFITS
see also SUPPLEMENTAL SECURITY INCOME (SSI)

deferment eligibility, 4.3.5.2
offsets, *see* FEDERAL BENEFITS OFFSETS

SOCIAL WORKERS
Perkins loan cancellation, 9.12
public service cancellation, 9.9.2

SOVEREIGN IMMUNITY
laches doctrine, application, 7.5.3.3.1
state agencies, bankruptcy dischargeability proceedings and, 10.8

SPOUSES
consolidation of loans, 1.4.1.3.1
repayment plans, income considerations
   IBRPs, 3.1.3.2.1
   ICRPs, 3.1.3.3.2
tax refund offsets, rights, 8.2.10
temporary disability, FFEL deferment, 4.3.7

STAFFORD LOANS (GSLs)
see also DIRECT LOANS
bankruptcy discharge, 10.2.1
consolidation, 6.2.4
disbursement of funds, 2.6
disclosure requirements, 2.5.2
interest rates, 2.3.3
loan limits, 2.2.2
origination fees, 2.4.1
overview, 1.4.1.1
public service cancellation, 9.9.2
repayment grace period, 4.2
statutory discharges
   see also STATUTORY DISCHARGES
   closed-school discharge, 9.3.7
   death discharge, 9.8
   unpaid-refund discharge, 9.5

STATE AGENCIES
bankruptcy dischargeability proceedings, 10.8
complaints to regarding collection abuses, 7.4.5.2
FOIA requests, 12.6.4
guaranty agencies, *see* GUARANTY AGENCIES
licensing agencies, *see* LICENSING AGENCIES (STATE)
private loan oversight, 11.3
private loan products, 11.1.2
state debts, offsets, 8.4.1

STATE LAW
collection laws, application to student loans, 7.4.4
   garnishment restrictions, 8.3.1
lender liability statutes, 12.7.3.3
loan enforceability, application, 7.5.4.1
preemption, *see* FEDERAL PREEMPTION
private student loans, application, 11.9.2.4, 11.10
professional license suspension for default, 8.6
proprietary school abuses, 12.5.3
   education statutes, 12.5.3.2
   RICO claims, 12.5.3.3
   UDAP claims, *see* UDAP CLAIMS
usury limits, 2.3.1

STATE LICENSING AGENCIES
see LICENSING AGENCIES

STATE TUITION RECOVERY FUNDS
see STUDENT TUITION RECOVERY FUNDS

STATUTE OF LIMITATIONS
appeals of agency decisions, 9.15
federal benefits offsets, 8.4.3.3
federal student loans, elimination, 7.5.3, 11.8.3
   equitable defenses, application, 7.5.3.3.1
   generally, 7.5.3.1
   scope, 7.5.3.2
private student loans, 11.8.3

STATUTORY DISCHARGES
administrative not judicial process, 7.5.4.2
appeals, 9.15
closed-school discharge, *see* CLOSED-SCHOOL DISCHARGE
consolidation loans, 9.2
contract defense alternative, 7.5.4.1
   interrelationship, 7.5.4.2
credit record, cleaning up, 7.2.4.3
death discharge, 9.8
disability discharge, *see* DISABILITY DISCHARGE
DOE policy guidance letters, Appx. C.1
effect on future loans
   bankruptcy discharge, 10.11
   closed-school discharge, 9.3.5
   disability discharge, 9.7.5.1, 9.7.7
   false-certification discharge, 9.4.6
eligible loans, 9.2
false-certification discharge, *see* FALSE-CERTIFICATION DISCHARGE
forbearances pending, 4.4.3
forms, Appx. D.3
guaranteed status lost loans, 7.5.4.3
interrelationship, 9.6
joint consolidation loans, 9.2
judicial review, 9.15
loans reduced to judgment, 9.7.2
multiple discharges, 9.6
overview, 9.1
paid-in-full loans, 9.3.5, 9.7.2
Perkins discharges, 9.12
profession-related loan cancellations, 9.9
   other cancellations, 9.11
   public service discharge, 9.9.2
   teachers, 9.10
relief from school-related abuses, 12.5.2.5
sample pleadings, Appx. E.2
September 11th related, 9.13
tax issues, 9.14
tuition recovery funds, interrelationship, 12.8.2
unpaid refund discharge, *see* UNPAID REFUND DISCHARGE

STUDENT GUIDES
DOE publications, 1.12.2

STUDENT LOAN BORROWER ASSISTANCE PROJECT (NCLC)
see also ASSISTANCE FOR BORROWERS
overview, 1.12.3
   website, Appx. J

STUDENT LOAN MARKETING ASSOCIATION (SALLIE MAE)
FDCPA, application, 7.4.3.4
function, 1.3.1
ombudsman program, 1.12.1.2
private loans, 11.1.1, 11.3

STUDENT LOAN OMBUDSMAN
contacting, 1.12.1.1
   collection abuse complaints, 7.2.1, 7.4.5.2
function, 1.12.1.1
privacy release statement, Appx. D.5.5

STUDENT LOANS
applying for, 1.5
   see also APPLICATION FOR STUDENT AID
   application forms, Appx. D.1
assistance for borrowers, *see* ASSISTANCE FOR BORROWERS
bankruptcy discharge, *see* BANKRUPTCY DISCHARGE
cancellation, *see* CANCELLATION OF LOAN
checklist, 1.11
collections, *see* COLLECTIONS
comparison of federal and private loans
   how to tell difference, 11.2.2
   terms and conditions, 1.2.1
compromises, *see* COMPROMISES
debt rate, problems with, 1.1, 5.1.5
default consequences
   federal loans, 5.1.5
   private loans, 5.2.3
default rates, *see* COHORT DEFAULT RATES
default triggers
   federal loans, 5.1.4
   private loans, 5.2.2, 11.6.2
defaulted loans, *see* DEFAULTED LOANS
deferments, *see* DEFERMENT
delinquent loans, *see* DELINQUENT LOANS
determining loan type, 1.9, 11.2.2
discharges, *see* BANKRUPTCY DISCHARGE; STATUTORY DISCHARGES
disclosure requirements, *see* DISCLOSURES
DOE central database, *see* NATIONAL STUDENT LOAN DATA SYSTEM (NSLDS)
FTC Holder Notice, 11.9.2, 12.7.2.5, 12.7.3.4
federal loans, *see* FEDERAL STUDENT ASSISTANCE
forbearances, *see* FORBEARANCE
forgiveness, *see* CANCELLATION OF LOAN
garnishment of funds, 1.4.3, 8.7
government loans, *see* FEDERAL STUDENT ASSISTANCE
interest on, *see* INTEREST
Internet resources, *see* WEB RESOURCES
intro, 1.1
litigation, *see* SCHOOL-RELATED CLAIMS AND DEFENSES
military personnel, *see* MILITARY PERSONNEL
NCLC manual, using, 1.2
overview, 1.4.1
   federal loans, 2.1
pre-default repayment, *see* PRE-DEFAULT REPAYMENT OPTIONS
private loans, *see* PRIVATE STUDENT LOANS
"qualified loans," 1.10
rehabilitation, *see* REHABILITATION OF LOANS
repayment, *see* REPAYMENT OF LOANS
resource aids, *see* RESOURCE AIDS
school direct loans, *see* PERKINS LOANS
seizure of funds, 1.4.3, 8.7
servicing agencies, *see* SERVICING AGENCIES
statute of limitations, *see* STATUTE OF LIMITATIONS
statutory discharges, *see* STATUTORY DISCHARGES
tax deductions, 1.10

References are to sections

STUDENT TUITION RECOVERY FUNDS
relief for defrauded students, 12.8.1
statutory discharges, interrelationship, 12.8.2

STUDENTS
ability-to-benefit tests, language, 9.4.2.1
approved leaves of absence, 9.3.1
assistance with loans, *see* ASSISTANCE TO BORROWERS
consumer information requirements, 1.7.3
deferment eligibility
   Perkins Loans, 4.3.8
   post-July 1, 1993 loans, 4.3.5.1
   pre-July 1, 1993 FFELs, 4.3.7
eligibility for federal assistance, 1.6, Appx. C.4
federal assistance, generally, *see* FEDERAL STUDENT ASSISTANCE
financial status form, Appx. D.4.3
loans to, generally, *see* STUDENT LOANS
private borrowing, reasons for, 11.1.4
   see also PRIVATE STUDENT LOANS

SUITS
see ACTIONS

SUPPLEMENTAL EDUCATIONAL OPPORTUNITY GRANTS (FSEOG)
see also GRANTS
repayment unnecessary, 1.4.2.1

SUPPLEMENTAL LOANS FOR STUDENTS (SLSs)
see also STAFFORD LOANS (GSLs)
bankruptcy discharge, 10.2.1
consolidation, 6.2.4
death discharge, 9.8
elimination of program, 1.4.1.5
unpaid-refund discharge, 9.5

SUPPLEMENTAL SECURITY INCOME (SSI)
see also SOCIAL SECURITY BENEFITS
offset exemption, 8.4.1
   collection abuses, 7.4.2.1

TAX ISSUES
cancellation of loan, 9.14
   IBR forgiveness, 3.1.3.2.5
income tax deductions and credits, 1.10

TAX REFUND OFFSETS
advantages to borrower, 8.2.8
challenging
   administrative review of loan, 8.2.5
   due process challenges, 8.2.6
   grounds, 8.2.3
   post-offset challenges, 8.2.7
collection fee exemption, 7.3.3
non-obligated spouses, rights, 8.2.10
notice requirements, 8.2.2
   sample notice, Appx. D.4.5
overview, 8.2.1
preventing, 8.2.8
   bankruptcy filing, 8.2.9
repayment plan in lieu, 8.2.4
school-related claims, raising, 12.6.2.1, 12.7.3.1
statute of limitations, 7.5.3.1
statutory provisions, selected text, Appx. A.5
   regulations, Appx. B.5.2

TEACHERS
see also TEACH GRANTS
cancellation of loans, 9.10
   generally, 9.9.1
   Perkins loans, 9.12
   tax issues, 9.14
deferment eligibility, 4.3.8
forbearances, 4.4.3, 4.4.4

TEACH GRANTS
overview, 1.4.2.3

TEACH-OUTS
closed-school discharge, 9.3.4

TECHNICAL SCHOOLS
see VOCATIONAL SCHOOLS

TELEPHONE CONTACTS
defaulted loans, 7.2.3
delinquent loans, 7.2.2

TESTS
ATB certification, 9.4.2

TORT CLAIMS
DOE, against, 12.5.2.4
fraud, *see* FRAUD
negligence, *see* NEGLIGENCE CLAIMS

TRADE SCHOOLS
see PROPRIETARY SCHOOLS; VOCATIONAL SCHOOLS

TRANSCRIPTS
withholding after bankruptcy filing, 10.11

TRUTH IN LENDING ACT (TILA)
application to student loans, 12.5.2.4
   government loans, 2.5.1
   private loans, 11.4, 11.10
violations, 11.10

TUITION RECOVERY FUNDS
see STUDENT TUITION RECOVERY FUNDS

UDAP CLAIMS
federal preemption, 12.5.3.4
FTC Holder Rule violations, 12.7.3.4
private loans, 11
proprietary school abuses, 12.5.3.1
   FTC guides, 12.5.2.3

UNDUE HARDSHIP
see also ECONOMIC HARDSHIP
bankruptcy discharge determination, 10.4
   applying *Brunner* test, 10.4.2
   Brunner test, 10.4.1
   chapter 13 plan provisions, 10.7.2
   other factors, 10.4.3

UNEMPLOYMENT
see also ECONOMIC HARDSHIP
deferment eligibility
   economic hardship deferment, 4.3.5.2, Appx. D.2.1
   FFELs, 4.3.2, Appx. D.2.1.1
   Perkins Loans, 4.3.8
   post-July 1, 1993 loans, 4.3.5.1
   pre-July 1, 1993 FFELs, 4.3.7
   unemployment deferment, 4.3.5.3, Appx. D.2.2
deferment form, Appx. D.2.2

UNEMPLOYMENT (*cont.*)
forbearances, 4.4.4
　sample request, Appx. D.2.5
wage garnishment restrictions
　DCIA, 8.3.2.3
　HEA, 8.3.3.1

UNFAIR PRACTICES
FTC guides, 12.5.2.3
proprietary schools, 12.3
UDAP claims, *see* UDAP CLAIMS

UNPAID REFUND DISCHARGE
see also STATUTORY DISCHARGES
amount, determination, 9.5.3
applying for, 9.5.4
criteria, 9.5.2
effect, 9.5.5
eligible loans, 9.2
form, Appx. D.3.7
generally, 9.5.1
relationship to other discharges, 9.6
relief available, 9.5.5
tuition recovery funds, interrelationship, 12.8.2

USURY LIMITS
interest rates, 2.3.1

VOCATIONAL LICENSES
suspension or revocation for default, 8.6

VOCATIONAL SCHOOLS
see also SCHOOLS
administrative capability, 1.7.4
claims against, *see* SCHOOL-RELATED CLAIMS AND
　　DEFENSES
completion rates, 1.7.3, 12.3.3.4
consumer information requirements, 1.7.3
correspondence courses, *see* CORRESPONDENCE COURSES
distance education, *see* DISTANCE EDUCATION PROGRAMS
eligibility for federal student assistance, 1.7.1
　admissions standards, 1.7.1.3, 12.3.3.8
　gainful employment, 1.7.1.2, 12.3.3.3
　generally, 1.7.1.1
　misrepresentations, 1.7.2.6, 12.5.2.1
　regulations, selected text, Appx. B.4.1
FTC guides, 12.5.2.3
job placement rates, 1.7.3, 12.3.3.4
Program Participation Agreements, 1.7.2
proprietary trade schools, *see* PROPRIETARY SCHOOLS
recruiters, *see* RECRUITERS
regulation and oversight, 12.2
school as lender
　federally funded loans, *see* PERKINS LOANS
　private loans, *see* PRIVATE LOANS

VOLUNTEER SERVICE
see also PUBLIC SERVICE CANCELLATION
deferment eligibility, 4.3.5.2, 4.3.8
Perkins loan cancellations, 9.12

WAGE GARNISHMENTS
see also COLLECTIONS
collection agencies, participation, 8.3.4
consolidation loans, effect, 6.2.4
DOE, DCIA garnishment, 8.3.2
　defenses, 8.3.2.3
　hearing forms, Appx. D.4.1, Appx. D.4.2
　hearing rights, 8.3.2.5
　maximum amount, 8.3.2.1
　notice, 8.3.2.2
　repayment in lieu, 8.3.2.4
DOE policy, 8.3.4
due process challenges, 8.3.5
guaranty agencies, HEA program, 8.3.3
　differences with DCIA, 8.3.3.1
　hearing rights, 8.3.3.2
loan rehabilitation, effect, 6.3.6
school-related claims, raising, 8.3.2.3, 12.6.2.1, 12.7.3.1
statute of limitations, 7.5.3.1
statutory provisions, selected text, Appx. A.5
　regulations, Appx. B.5.3

WAIVERS
defenses, consolidation loan as, 7.5.4.4
federal benefits offsets, 8.4.3.2
loan obligations, *see* COMPROMISES

WEB RESOURCES
closed-school list, 9.3.2
DOE forms, Appx. DS
DOE policy guidance letters, Appx. C
DOE website, 1.12.2
NCLC companion website, 1.2.1, Appx. K
NCLC Student Loan Borrower Assistance Project, 1.12.3, Appx. J
NCLC web-based text searches, 1.2.3, Appx. K.5
NSLDS, 1.9
pleadings, Appx. K
proprietary school abuses, 12.6.4
Sargent Shriver National Center on Poverty Law, 1.2.2
Student Loan Ombudsman, 1.12.1.1
student loan websites, Appx. L
type of loan, determination, 1.9

WONDERLIC TESTS
ATB testing, 9.4.2.2.4

WRITE-OFFS
see COMPROMISES

Quick Reference to the Consumer Credit and Sales Legal Practice Series

References are to sections in *all* manuals in NCLC's Consumer Credit and Sales Legal Practice Series. References followed by "S" appear only in a Supplement.

Readers should also consider another search option available at *www.consumerlaw.org/keyword*. There, users can search all eighteen NCLC treatises for a case name, party name, statutory or regulatory citation, or *any* other word, phrase, or combination of terms. The search engine provides the title, page number and context of every occurrence of that word or phrase within each of the NCLC treatises. Further search instructions and tips are provided on the website.

The Quick Reference to the Consumer Credit and Sales Legal Practice Series pinpoints where to find specific topics analyzed in the NCLC treatises. References are to individual treatise or supplement sections. For more information on these volumes, see *What Your Library Should Contain* at the beginning of this volume, or go to www.consumerlaw.org.

This Quick Reference is a speedy means to locate key terms in the appropriate NCLC treatise. More detailed indexes are found at the end of the individual NCLC volumes. Both the detailed contents pages and the detailed indexes for each treatise are also available on NCLC's website, www.consumerlaw.org.

NCLC *strongly recommends*, when searching for PLEADINGS on a particular subject, that users refer to the *Index Guide* accompanying *Consumer Law Pleadings*, and *not* to this Quick Reference. Another option is to search for pleadings directly on the *Consumer Law Pleadings* website, using the finding tools that are provided there.

The finding tools found on NCLC's companion websites are also an effective means to find statutes, regulations, agency interpretations, legislative history, and other primary source material found in manual appendices and on NCLC's companion websites. Other search options are detailed at page ix, *supra*: *About the Companion Website, Other Search Options*.

Abbreviations

AUS	=	Access to Utility Service (4th ed. 2008 and 2010 Supp.)
Auto	=	Automobile Fraud (3d ed. 2007 and 2010 Supp.)
Arbit	=	Consumer Arbitration Agreements (5th ed. 2007 and 2010 Supp.)
Coll	=	Collection Actions (2008 and 2010 Supp.)
CBPL	=	Consumer Banking and Payments Law (4th ed. 2009 and 2010 Supp.)
Bankr	=	Consumer Bankruptcy Law and Practice (9th ed. 2009 and 2010 Supp.)
CCA	=	Consumer Class Actions (7th ed. 2010)
CLP	=	Consumer Law Pleadings, Numbers 1 Through 16 (2010)
COC	=	The Cost of Credit (4th ed. 2009 and 2010 Supp.)
CD	=	Credit Discrimination (5th ed. 2009 and 2010 Supp.)
FCR	=	Fair Credit Reporting (7th ed. 2010)
FDC	=	Fair Debt Collection (6th ed. 2008 and 2010 Supp.)
Fore	=	Foreclosures (3d ed. 2010)
Repo	=	Repossessions (7th ed. 2010)
Stud	=	Student Loan Law (4th ed. 2010)
TIL	=	Truth in Lending (7th ed. 2010)
UDAP	=	Unfair and Deceptive Acts and Practices (7th ed. 2008 and 2010 Supp.)
Warr	=	Consumer Warranty Law (4th ed. 2010)

Quick Reference to the Consumer Credit and Sales Legal Practice Series

References are to sections in *all* manuals in NCLC's Consumer Credit and Sales Legal Practice Series

Abandonment of Apartment Building in Bankruptcy—Bankr § 18.8.2
Abbreviations Commonly Used by Debt Collectors—FDC App F.4
Abuse of Process—UDAP § 6.10.9; FDC § 10.6
Acceleration—COC §§ 5.6.2, 5.7.1; Repo § 4.1
Accessions—Repo § 3.5.3.2
Accord and Satisfaction—CBPL §§ 2.9, 3.3.1
Account Aggregation—CBPL § 4.14
Account Stated—Coll § 4.7
Accountants—UDAP § 10.4.6
Accrediting Agencies, Student Loans—Stud § 12.6.2.2
Accurate Information in Consumer Reports—FCR Ch. 4
Actuarial Rebates—COC § 5.6.3.4
Adhesion Contracts—UDAP § 5.6.3
Adjustable Rate Mortgages—TIL § 5.13; COC § 4.3.6
Administration of Lawsuit, Class Action—CCA Ch 15
Admissibility of Other Bad Acts—Auto § 9.8.1
Admissions, Requests for—CCA § 8.1.4; Repo App E.5; Fore App. I.8.3; CLP; COC App N; FDC App H.3; Auto App F.1.4; Coll § 4.2.2.
Advertising Credit Terms—TIL §§ 6.4, 13.4
Affordability Programs, Utilities—AUS Ch 9, App E
After-Acquired Property—Repo § 3.4.5.2
Age Discrimination re Credit—CD § 3.4.2
Airbags—Auto §§ 2.8S, 6.3bS
Airline Fare Advertising—UDAP §§ 2.5, 10.2.1
Alteration of Checks—CBPL § 2.5.1.4
Alimony Discharged in Bankruptcy—Bankr § 15.4.3.5
Alimony, Protected Source under ECOA—CD §§ 3.4.1, 5.5.5.3
Alternative Dispute Mechanisms—Arbit; Coll ch 8
American Arbitration Association—Arbit App B.1
Americans With Disabilities Act—CD § 1.6
Amortization Explained—COC § 4.3.1
Amortization Negative—COC § 4.3.1.2
Amount Financed—TIL § 5.3
Annihilating Damages—CCA § 10.5.2.5.5
Annual Percentage Rate—TIL §§ 5.5, 6.6.5; COC § 4.4
Annual Percentage Rate for Variable Rate Loans—TIL § 5.5.6.3
Answer and Counterclaims—Repo Apps D.1, D.2; Fore App. I; COC App N; CLP
Antecedent Debt Clauses—Repo § 3.9
Anti-Competitive Conduct as UDAP Violation—UDAP § 5.8
Anti-Deficiency Statutes—Repo § 12.6.3
Apartment Buildings Abandoned in Bankruptcy—Bankr § 18.8.2
Apartment Leases—Bankr § 12.9; UDAP §§ 2.2.6, 8.2
Appeal of Order Requiring Arbitration—Arbit § 2.6
Applications for Credit—CD § 5.4
Appraisal Fraud—COC § 11.6.6
Appraisals, Right to a Copy—CD § 10.11
APR—*See* Annual Percentage Rate
Arbitration—Arbit; Bankr § 13.3.2.5; COC § 10.6.11; FDC § 15.4; TIL § 12.7; Warr § 13.4
Arbitration and Class Actions—Arbit ch. 10; CCA Ch 3;
Arbitration & Collection Actions – Coll Ch. 8
Arbitration Fees—Arbit §§ 4.4, 6.5.2
Arbitration Forum Unavailable—Arbit § 6.6a
As Is—Warr Ch 5; Auto § 7.8.2
Assignee Liability—UDAP § 11.6; TIL § 12.3
Assignment of Tax Refunds—COC § 7.5.4
Assistance for the Payment of Utility Service—AUS Ch 9
Assisted Living Facilities—UDAP § 10.3.4
Assistive Device Lemon Laws—Warr Ch 16
ATM Cards—CBPL Ch 4
ATM Machines, Bank Liability for Robberies at—CBPL § 4.5.4

ATM Machine Payments—CBPL Ch 4
ATM Machines, Access for Disabled—CBPL § 8.9
Attorney as Debt Collector—FDC §§ 4.2.8, 11.5.3
Attorney Fees—TIL § 11.9; Bankr Ch 16; Auto §§ 5.8.4, 9.12; CD § 11.7.6; FCR § 11.13; FDC §§ 6.8, 11.2.5, 11.3.6; UDAP § 13.8; Warr §§ 2.7.6, 10.7; Coll § 14.1
Attorney Fees, Class Actions—CCA Ch 18, App E
Attorney Fees for Creditors—COC § 7.3.3; Coll Ch. 6
Attorney Fees, Pleadings—Auto App L; FDC App J
Attorney General Enforcement—UDAP Ch 15
Attorneys Liable Under FDCPA—FDC §§ 4.2.8, 4.6.9
Attorneys Liable Under UDAP—UDAP §§ 2.3.9, 10.4.1
Auctions—Repo §§ 10.7.2, 10.10.6; Auto §§ 2.5.4, 2.6.4
Authorization to Represent—CCA App E
Authorization to Sue—CCA § 1.2.4
Authorized Users—Coll § 5.3.3
Automated Clearing House for Electronic Transfer—CBPL Ch4
Automatic Stay—Bankr Ch 9
Automobile Accessories—UDAP § 7.9
Automobile Auctions—*See* Auctions
Automobile Dealer Files—UDAP § 7.1
Automobile Dealer Licensing—Auto § 6.4, App F
Automobile Dealers, Bonding Requirement—Auto § 9.13.4, App C
Automobile Dealers, Investigation of—Auto Ch 2
Automobile Dealers, Registration with Auction—Auto App E.3
Automobile Fraud—Auto
Automobile Insurance, Force-Placed—*See* Force-Placed Auto Insurance
Automobile Leases, Article 9 Coverage—Repo § 14.2.1
Automobile Leases, Default and Early Termination—TIL Ch 13; UDAP § 7.6.3; Repo § 14.2
Automobile Leases, Misrepresentation—UDAP § 7.6
Automobile Leases, Odometer Rollbacks—Auto §§ 4.6.6.5, 5.2.6
Automobile Leases, Sublease Scams—UDAP § 7.8.2
Automobile Leases, Unconscionability—UDAP § 7.6.5
Automobile Pawn Transactions—Bankr § 11.9; COC § 7.5.2.3; Repo § 3.5.5
Automobile Rentals—UDAP § 7.7
Automobile Repairs—Warr Ch 19; UDAP § 7.10
Automobile Repossession—*See* Repossessions
Automobile Safety Inspection Laws—Warr § 15.4.6
Automobile Sales—Warr Chs 14, 15; UDAP §§ 7.1, 7.4, 7.5
Automobile Service—Warr § 19.9; § 10.5.4.2
Automobile Sublease Scams—UDAP § 7.8.2
Automobile, Theft Prevention, Federal Statutes & Regulations—Auto App B.2
Automobile Title—Auto §§ 2.3, 2.4, Apps. D, E; UDAP § 7.3.9; Warr § 15.2
Automobile Valuation—Bankr § 11.2.2.3.2
Automobile Yo-Yo Abuses—UDAP § 7.3.9; Repo § 4.6; TIL §4.5.6
Back Office Conversion—CBPL § 4.7.5
Bad Checks—FDC §§ 5.6.4, 15.3
Bail (i.e. replevin)—Repo Ch 5
Bait and Switch—UDAP § 5.3.1
Balance Billing—Coll § 10.3.6
Balloon Payments—COC § 4.6.2, Ch 5; TIL § 2.2.4.2.3
Bank Accounts, Attachment—Coll Ch 12, CBPL Ch 10
Bank Accounts, Closing—CBPL § 2.8.3
Bank Account Garnishment—CBPL § 10.3, Coll Ch 12
Bank Accounts, Joint—Coll § 12.7
Bank Accounts, Set-Off—CBPL § 10.4
Bank Fees—CBPL § 4.14.5
Bank Accounts, Unfair Practices—UDAP §§ 4.4.9, 6.9

Quick Reference to the Consumer Credit and Sales Legal Practice Series

References are to sections in *all* manuals in NCLC's Consumer Credit and Sales Legal Practice Series

Bankruptcy Abuse Prevention and Consumer Protection Act—Bankr; Stud § 10.2.
Bankruptcy and Debt Collection—FDC §§ 2.2, 9.11; Bankr § 9.4.3
Bankruptcy and Security Interests—Repo Ch 8
Bankruptcy and Utility Service—AUS §§ 12.1, 14.1; Bankr § 9.8
Bankruptcy, Claims Against Landlords in—Bankr § 18.8
Bankruptcy, Claims Against Creditors, Merchants in—Bankr Ch 18; UDAP § 11.8
Bankruptcy Code, Text—Bankr App A
Bankruptcy, Consumer Reports of—FCR Chs 4, §§ 5.2.3.8, 12.6.8
Bankruptcy Court as Litigation Forum—Bankr Ch 14
Bankruptcy Discharge of Student Loans—Stud Ch 10
Bankruptcy Forms—Bankr Apps D, E, G
Bankruptcy Petition Preparers—Bankr § 16.6
Benefit Overpayments and Bankruptcy—Bankr § 15.5.5.4
Bibliography—Bankr
Billing Errors—FDC § 5.7; Fore § 8.2.2
Billing Error Procedures, Credit Cards—CBPL § 6.3S; TIL § 7.9
Bill Stuffers—Arbit § 5.7
Binding Arbitration—Arbit
Blanket Security Interests—Repo § 3.4.5.2.2
Bond, Claims Against Seller's—UDAP § 11.8; Auto § 9.13.4, App C
Bonding Statutes—Auto App C
Book-of-the-Month Clubs—UDAP § 9.5
Bounced Checks—CBPL § 2.7
Breach of Contract—UDAP § 5.6.5
Breach of the Peace and Repossession—Repo § 6.4
Breach of Warranties—Warr; UDAP § 5.6.7.1
Briefs, Class Action—CCA Ch 10
Broadband, National Plan—AUS § 2.1S
Broker Fees—COC §§ 7.4.2, 11.6.4
Brokers, Auto—UDAP § 7.8.2
Brokers, Loan—*See* Loan Brokers
Brokers, Real Estate—*See* Real Estate Brokers
Budget Payment Plans—AUS § 6.4
Burglar Alarm Systems—UDAP § 8.7.1
Business Credit, Discrimination re—CD § 2.2.6.4
Business Opportunities—UDAP §§ 2.2.9.2, 10.6.1
Buy Here, Pay Here Car Sales—UDAP § 7.4.14
Buy Rate—UDAP § 7.5.6
Buying Clubs—UDAP § 10.1.6
Calculating Interest Rates—COC Ch 4
Campground Resort Memberships—UDAP §§ 2.2.8, 10.1.5
Cancellation Rights—TIL Ch 10; UDAP §§ 5.6.6, 9.2
Cardholders' Defenses—TIL §§ 7.9, 7.10, 7.11
Carfax—Auto § 2.3.2, App E.2
Cars—*See* Automobile
Case Selection—CCA § 1.2
Case Summaries, FDCPA—FDC App K
Cash Discounts—TIL § 7.14.4
Cashier's Checks—CBPL § Ch 5
Chapter 7 Bankruptcy—Bankr Ch 3
Chapter 11 Bankruptcy—Bankr §§ 6.3.4, 18.7
Chapter 12 Bankruptcy—Bankr Ch 17
Chapter 13 Bankruptcy—Bankr Ch 4
Charge Cards—TIL § 6.2.4.3
Charitable Contributions—Bankr § 1.1.2.6
Charitable Solicitations—UDAP § 10.6.5
Check 21—CBPL §§ 2.6, App B
Check Advancement Loans—*See* Payday Loans
Check Approval Companies—FCR § 2.6.2.2
Check Cashing Services—UDAP §§ 6.9
Check Cashing Regulation—CBPL § 3.6
Check Collection Agencies Working for DA's—FDC § 1.4.3.10S

Check Guarantee Companies—FDC § 4.2.3
Checklist, Automobile Fraud Litigation—Auto § 1.4
Checklist, Debt Collection—FDC App G
Checklist, Truth in Lending—TIL §§ 1.7, 3.11
Checklist, Usury—COC § 1.6
Checks—CBPL Ch 2
Checks, Bad—FDC §§ 5.6.4, Coll ch. 9, CBPL § 2.7
Checks, Preauthorized Draft—UDAP §§ 6.9, CBPL § 2.5.5
Child Support, Credit Reports—FCR § 7.4.2
Child Support Discharged in Bankruptcy—Bankr § 15.4.3.5
Children in Household, Discrimination Based On—CD § 3.5.1
Choice of Laws—COC § 9.2.9; Repo § 2.6
Churning Repossession Schemes—Repo § 10.11
Civil Rights Act—CD § 1.5
Class Actions Fairness Act of 2005—CCA § 2.4, 13.7, 13.8
Class Actions—CCA; Auto § 9.7, App H; FCR § 11.2.2; FDC §§ 6.2.1.3, 6.6; TIL §§ 10.9.9, 11.8; UDAP § 13.5
Class Actions and Arbitration—Arbit ch 10; CCA Ch 3
Class Actions and Diversity Jurisdiction—CCA §§ 2.3, 2.4
Class Actions Guidelines for Settlement, NACA—CCA App D
Class Actions in Bankruptcy Court—Bankr §§ 13.7, 18.4.2
Class Actions, Removal to Federal Court—CCA § 2.7
Class Arbitration—Arbit ch. 10
Class Certification Motions, Sample—CCA App P; CLP
Class Definitions—CCA Ch 4
Class Notices—CCA Ch 12, Apps S, V
Client Authorization to Represent—CCA App E
Client Authorization to Sue—CCA § 1.2.4
Client Contacts with Other Parties—CCA §§ 1.2.6, 6.3
Client Handout on Bankruptcy—Bankr App K
Client Handout on Credit Discrimination—CD App I
Client Handout on Credit Reporting—FCR App L
Client Interview Checklist, Bankruptcy—Bankr App F
Client Interview Checklist, Debt Collection Harassment—FDC App F
Client Retainer Forms, Sample—CLP
Closed-End Auto Leases—TIL Ch 13; Repo § 14.2
Closed-End Credit—TIL Chs 4, 5
Closed School Discharge—Stud § 9.3
Closing Arguments, Sample—Auto App I
Coercive Sales Techniques—UDAP § 5.5
Collateral—Repo
Collateral Estoppel—CCA ch. 17
Collection Agency Collection of Federal Taxes—FDC § 4.2.9
Collection Fees—Coll § 6.6; Stud § 7.3
Collection Lawsuits—Coll
Collection of Student Loans—Stud Ch 7
Collection via Arbitration—Arbit Ch 12
College Cost Reduction and Access Act of 2007—Stud
Colleges and Credit Cards—TIL § 7.6.3
College Transcripts and Bankruptcy—Bankr §§ 9.4.3, 15.5.5.2
Collision Damage Waiver (CDW)—UDAP § 7.7
Common Law Fraud, Misrepresentation—Warr § 11.4; Auto Ch 7
Common Law Right to Utility Service—AUS § 3.1
Common Law Violations and Credit Reporting—FCR § 10.4
Common Law Warranties—Warr § 19.4
Communications to Client from Other Attorney—CCA § 6.3; FDC § 5.3.3
Community Reinvestment Act—CD § 1.9
Compensating Balances—COC § 7.4.4
Complaint Drafting, Class Actions—CCA Ch 5
Complaints—Auto App G; CD App G; CCA App F; COC App N; FCR App J.3; FDC App G; Repo Apps D.3, D.4; Fore App I; Warr App J; TIL Apps D, E; CLP

Quick Reference to the Consumer Credit and Sales Legal Practice Series

References are to sections in *all* manuals in NCLC's Consumer Credit and Sales Legal Practice Series

Compound Interest—COC § 4.6.1
Computers, Sale of—UDAP § 8.9.3
Condominiums—UDAP § 8.3.10
Condominium Warranties—Warr Ch 18
Consignment—Repo § 9.6.3.3
Consolidation Loan—Stud § 6.2
Conspiracy in Odometer Case—Auto § 4.7
Constitutionality of Arbitration Agreement—Arbit Ch 9
Contract Formation of Arbitration Agreement—Arbit Ch 5
Constructive Strict Foreclosure—Repo §§ 10.5.2, 12.5
Consumer Class Actions—CCA
Consumer Credit Reporting Reform Act of 1996—FCR § 1.4.6
Consumer Guide to Credit Reporting—FCR App L
Consumer Leasing Act—TIL Ch 13, App H.1
Consumer Recovery Funds—Auto § 9.13.5
Consumer Reporting Agencies—FCR
Consumer Reporting Agency List and Addresses—FCR App N
Consumer Reporting Agencies, Enforcement Agreements—FCR App K
Consumer Reports, Disputing—FCR Ch 4
Consumer Reports, Keeping Credit Disputes Out of—FCR § 12.4
Consumer Reports for Business Transactions—FCR §§ 2.3.6.2, 2.3.6.8, 7.2.8
Consumer Reports for Employment Purposes—FCR §§ 2.3.6.4, 7.2.4
Consumer Reports for Government Benefits—FCR §§ 2.3.6.6, 7.2.6
Consumer Reports for Insurance Purposes—FCR §§ 2.3.6.5, 7.2.5
Consumer Reports from Non-Reporting Agencies—FCR § 8.12.1
Consumer/Seller Liability under Odometer Act—Auto § 4.8.13
Contests—UDAP §§ 5.3.6, 10.6.4
Contractual Misrepresentations—UDAP § 5.6.4
Cooling Off Periods—*See* Cancellation
Correspondence Schools—Stud Ch 12
Cosigners—Bankr § 9.4.4; CD § 5.4; Repo § 12.9; TIL §§ 2.2.2.2, 11.2.2; UDAP § 6.11.9
Counseling the Debtor—Bankr Ch 6
Counterclaims—Coll § 5.5
Coupon Settlement, Class Actions—CCA § 13.8
Cramming—AUS § 2.7.5
Credit Abuses—COC; UDAP § 2.2.1, Ch. 6
Credit Accident and Health Insurance—COC § 8.3.1.3; TIL §§ 3.7.9, 3.9.4
Credit Balances—TIL § 7.14.3; UDAP § 6.8.4
Credit CARD Act—TIL chs. 6, 7, 8
Credit Card Change in Terms—TIL §§ 7.2, 7.3
Credit Card Finders—UDAP § 6.8.2
Credit Card Issuers, Raising Seller-Related Claims Against—UDAP § 11.6, TIL § 7.11; CBPL § 6.5S
Credit Card Issuer's Security Interest in Goods Purchased—Repo § 3.6
Credit Card Payment Protections—TIL § 7.7
Credit Card Penalty Fees—TIL § 7.5
Credit Card Surcharges—TIL § 7.14.4
Credit Card Unauthorized Use—TIL § 7.10
Credit Cards—TIL Chs 6, 7 ; CBPL Ch 6; UDAP § 6.8; FDC § 4.2.3
Credit Cards, Reporting Services for Lost—UDAP § 6.4.5
Credit Charges—COC Ch 5; UDAP § 5.1.6
Credit Denial, Notice—CD § 10.5; FCR § 8.5
Credit Disability Insurance—COC §§ 8.3.1.3, 8.5.2.3; Fore § 5.3.3; TIL §§ 3.7.9, 3.9.4
Credit Evaluation—CD §§ 6.2, 6.3
Credit File, Disputing and Right to See—FCR Chs 3, 4

Credit Insurance—COC Ch 8; TIL §§ 3.7.9, 3.9.4; Repo § 4.2.1; UDAP § 10.5.9
Credit Life Insurance—COC §§ 8.3.1.2, 8.5.3.1.2; TIL §§ 3.7.9, 3.9.4
Credit Math—COC Ch 4
Credit Property Insurance—COC §§ 8.3.1.5, 8.5.3.1.4, 8.5.3.4, 8.5.4.4; TIL §§ 3.9.4.4, 3.9.4.6
Credit Rating, Injury to—FCR § 11.11.2.3; FDC §§ 5.5.2.12, 8.3.8; UDAP § 13.3.3.6
Credit Regulation, History of—COC Ch 2
Credit Repair Organizations—FCR Ch 15; UDAP § 6.15.1
Credit Reporting Agencies, Contacting—FCR Ch. 3
Credit Reporting Sample Forms—FCR App I
Credit Reports—FCR; TIL § 7.9.6.5S; AUS § 3.7.4aS
Credit Reports, Affiliate Sharing—FCR §§ 2.4.3, 3.3.1.3.3, 8.12.1
Credit Reports, Furnishers of Information Obligations—FCR Ch 6
Credit Reports, Keeping Credit Disputes Out of—FCR § 12.4
Credit Reports from Non-Reporting Agencies—FCR § 8.12.1
Credit Scams—UDAP Ch 6
Credit Scoring—CD § 6.4; FCR Ch. 14; AUS § 3.7.4aS
Credit Terms—COC; UDAP § 6.4, 6.6
Creditor Remedies—Coll Ch 12; UDAP § 6.10
Creditors, Types of—COC Chs 2, 9
Creditors Filing Bankruptcy—Bankr Ch 18
Creditworthiness—Bankr § 6.2.2.3
Criminal Prosecution Threats—Coll Ch 9
Cross-Collateral—Repo § 3.7.2
Cross Metering, Utility Service—AUS § 5.2
Cruise Line Port Charges—UDAP § 10.2.2
Cure of Default—Repo §§ 4.5, 13.2.4.4
Cy Pres—CCA § 13.9
Daily Accrual Accounting—COC § 4.6.9
Damages—FDC §§ 2.5.2, 6.3, Ch 10; FCR Ch 11; Repo Ch 13; TIL Ch 11; UDAP § 13.3; Warr §§ 10.3–10.5
Damage to Credit Rating—UDAP § 13.3.3.6
Dance Studios—UDAP § 10.1.4
Daubert Doctrine—Warr § 13.8.4
Dealer's Only Auto Auctions—Repo § 10.10.4
Debit Cards—CBPL Ch 4
Debt Buyers—FDC § 1.5.4.1; Coll § 1.4
Debt Cancellation Agreements—TIL §§ 3.7.10, 3.9.4.7
Debt Collection—FDC; Coll; UDAP §§ 2.2.2, 6.10
Debt Collection and Bankruptcy—FDC § 2.2.5
Debt Collection by Arbitration—Coll Ch 8; Arbit Ch. 12
Debt Collection Case Preparation—FDC Ch 2
Debt Collection Improvement Act—Coll App E.1
Debt Collection Procedures Act—Coll § 11.3
Debt Collectors—FDC § 1.2, Ch 4
Debt Collector's Common Abbreviations—FDC App F.4
Debt Harassment, How to Stop—FDC § 2.3
Debtor in Possession under Chapter 12—Bankr § 17.3
Debtor's Examination—Coll § 12.11
Debt Pooling—FDC § 1.10.5
Deceit—Warr § 11.4
Deception—UDAP § 4.2; FDC § 5.5
Deceptive Practices Statutes—*See* UDAP
Deceptive Pricing—UDAP § 5.3.3
Defamation—FDC § 10.5; FCR § 10.5.2
Deeds-in-Lieu of Foreclosure–Fore § 2.5.2
Defamatory Use of Mail—FDC § 9.1
Default—Repo Ch 4
Default Insurance—TIL § 3.7.7
Default Judgments, Setting Aside—Coll § 13.2
Defective Automobile Title—Auto

682

Quick Reference to the Consumer Credit and Sales Legal Practice Series
References are to sections in *all* manuals in NCLC's Consumer Credit and Sales Legal Practice Series

Defenses as Grounds for Nonpayment—Repo § 4.4; Coll
Defenses to Credit Card Charges—CBPL § 6.5S; TIL §§ 7.9, 7.10, 7.11; UDAP § 11.6.5.5; Coll
Deferment of Student Loan—Stud § 4.3
Deferral Charges—COC § 4.8.2
Deferred Payment Plans—AUS § 6.6
Deficiency Actions—Repo Ch 12, App C.1
Deficiency Judgments—Fore § 14.3
Delay—UDAP § 5.7.2
Delaying Tactics, Opposing—CCA Ch 7
Delinquency Charges—*See* Late Charges
Deliverable Fuels—AUS § 1.5
Demonstrator Vehicles—Auto §§ 1.4.9, 2.1.7
Denial of Credit, Notice—FCR § 8.5
Department of Housing and Urban Development (HUD)—CD § 12.3.1, App D; Fore Chs 2, 4, § 3.2
Department of Motor Vehicles—Auto App D
Deposit, Consumer's Right to Return When Seller Files Bankruptcy—Bankr § 18.5
Depositions in Class Actions—CCA § 8.1.3.4, Ch 9
Deposition Notice, Sample—CLP
Deposition Questions, Sample—Auto § 9.5.6; CLP
Deposition Questions and Answers, Sample—CLP
Depository Creditors—COC Ch 2; Coll Ch 12
Deregulation of Utilities—AUS Ch 1
Detinue—Repo Ch 5
Digital Divide—CD § 3.8.2
Direct Deposits—CBPL Ch 9
Direct Express Cards—CBPL § 7.10.2
Disabilities, Discrimination Based On—CD § 3.5.2
Disability Discharge—Stud § 9.7
Disabled Access to ATM machines—CBPL § 8.9
Discharge in Bankruptcy—Bankr Ch 15
Discharge of Indebtedness Income—Fore § 14.6.3
Discharging Student Loan Obligations—Stud Ch 9, § 10.2
Disclaimers, Warranties—Warr Ch 5
Disclosure and UDAP—UDAP § 4.2.14
Disclosure of Credit Terms—TIL
Disconnection of Utility Service—AUS Chs 11, 14
Discovery—Auto § 9.5, App H; *see also* Interrogatories; Document Requests
Discovery, Arbitration—Arbit § 2.4, App C
Discovery, Class Actions—CCA Ch 8, App I
Discovery, Motions to Compel—CCA Apps J, K
Discrimination in Collection Tactics—FDC § 9.8
Discrimination re Credit—CD
Disposition of Repo Collateral—Repo Chs 9, 10
Dispute Resolution Mechanisms—Warr §§ 2.8, 14.2.9
Disputing Information in Consumer Report—FCR Ch. 4
District Attorneys Hiring Check Collection Agencies—FDC § 1.5.8.2
Document Preparation Fees—TIL § 3.9.6.2.3; UDAP § 7.2.8
Document Production Requests, Sample—Arbit App C; Auto App F; CCA App I; CD App H; FDC App H.2; Repo Apps E.2; Fore App. I.10; TIL App F.3; Warr App K.3; CLP
Document Requests, Sample Objection to—CCA App M.4
Dodd-Frank and preemption—UDAP § 2.5
Dodd-Frank and TILA—TIL § 1.2.11, 1.3; Ch. 9.
D'Oench, Duhme Doctrine—COC § 10.7; Repo § 12.10; Fore § 5.14.4; UDAP § 11.7.5
Door-to-Door Sales—UDAP § 9.2
Double Cycle Billing—TIL § 7.4
Dragnet Clauses—Repo § 3.9
Driver Privacy Protection Act—Auto § 2.2.4, App A.2

Driver's Licenses and Bankruptcy—Bankr §§ 15.5.4, 15.5.5.1
Drunk Driving Debts in Bankruptcy—Bankr § 15.4.3.9
Due on Sale Clauses—Fore § 4.9.5
Due Process—Fore § 3.1.2.2, 4.7
Dunning, How to Stop with Sample Letters—FDC § 2.3
Duress—AUS § 6.1.9
Duty of Good Faith and Fair Dealing—COC § 12.8
Early Termination Penalties in Auto Leases—TIL § 13.5
Earned Income Tax Credit—Bankr § 2.5.5
EBT—CBPL Ch 8
E-Commerce, Jurisdiction—COC § 9.2.9.4
Educational Loans—*See* Student Loans
EFT 99—CBPL Ch 9
Election of Remedy Statutes—Repo § 12.4
Electric Service—AUS § 1.2.2; UDAP § 8.5.2
Electronic Banking—CBPL Ch 4
Electronic Benefit Transfers—CBPL Ch 8
Electronic Check Conversion—CBPL Ch 4
Electronic Check Images—CBPL § 2.6.1
Electronic Credit Transactions—COC § 9.2.10
Electronic Disclosure—TIL §§ 4.3, 6.3.5, 9.6.7; UDAP § 4.2.14.3.9
Electronic Fund Transfers—CBPL Chs 4, 9
Electronic Repossession—Repo § 6.6
Electronic Check Representment—CBPL § 2.7.4
Electronic Signatures and Records—CBPL Ch 11
Electronic Transaction Fraud—UDAP § 9.6.4; CBPL Ch 4
Electronic Transfer Account (ETA)—CBPL § 9.5
Employer Bankruptcy—Bankr § 18.7.12
Employment Agencies—UDAP § 10.6.2
Encyclopedia Sales—UDAP § 8.9.9
Endorsements—UDAP § 5.4.8
Energy Savings Claims—UDAP § 8.9.1
Enforceability of Arbitration Clause—Arbit
Equal Credit Opportunity Act—CD; AUS § 3.7.2
Equal Credit Opportunity Act Regulations—CD App B
E-Sign—CBPL Ch 11; COC § 9.2.10
ETAs (Electronic Transfer Accounts)—CBPL § 9.5
Ethnic Discrimination—CD § 3.3.3
Evictions—AUS § 11.8; UDAP § 8.2.8; FDC § 1.10.2
Evidence Spoilation—Warr § 13.2.5
Evidentiary Issues in Automobile Litigation—Auto § 9.8
Exempt Benefits and Bankruptcy—Bankr § 10.2.2.11
Exempting Interest Rates—COC Ch 3
Exemption Laws, Liberal Construction—Coll § 12.2.1
Exemption Planning—Bankr § 10.4.1
Exemptions, Benefits, Earnings, Due Process Protections—Coll Ch 12
Exemption Statutes—Coll Apps C, F
Expert Inspection—Warr § 13.6.1
Experts, Attorney Fee Award for—UDAP § 13.8.7.3
Expert Witnesses—FDC § 2.4.14; Warr § 13.8
Expert Witnesses, Sample Questions—Auto App I
Exportation of Interest Rates—COC Ch 3
Express Warranties—Warr Ch 3
Expressio Unius Est Exclusio Alterius—COC § 9.3.2
Extended Warranties—*See* Service Contracts
Extortionate Collection—FDC § 9.5
FACT Act—FCR
FACT Act Regulations—FCR App B
Fair Credit Billing Act—CBPL § 6.3S; TIL § 7.9; FCR § 12.4.2.; AUS § 11.3.5
Fair Credit Reporting Act—FCR; FDC § 9.6
Fair Debt Collection Practices Act—FDC Chs 3–7, Apps A, B, K
Fair Housing Act—CD

Quick Reference to the Consumer Credit and Sales Legal Practice Series

References are to sections in *all* manuals in NCLC's Consumer Credit and Sales Legal Practice Series

Fair Housing Act Regulations—CD App D
False Certification Discharge—Stud § 9.4
False Pretenses, Obtaining Consumer Reports—FCR § 7.7
Family Expense Laws—Coll § 10.6; CD § 9.3
Farm Reorganizations, Bankruptcy—Bankr Ch 17
Farmworker Camps—UDAP §§ 2.2.7, 8.2.9
Faxes, Junk—UDAP § 9.6.2.2
Federal Agency Collection Actions—Coll Ch 11
Federal Arbitration Act—Arbit Ch 3, App A
Federal Benefit Payments, Electronic—CBPL Ch 9
Federal Civil Rights Acts—CD; AUS § 3.7.1
Federal Direct Deposit of Benefits—CBPL Ch 9
Federal Direct Student Loans—Stud
Federal Employee Salary Offset Statute—Coll App E.2
Federal Energy Regulatory Commission (FERC)—AUS § 1.2.2.2
Federal False Claims Act—UDAP § 14.5
Federal Exemptions—Coll App C
Federal Family Education Loans—Stud
Federal Preemption—FDC §§ 2.2, 6.14; UDAP § 2.5
Federal Preemption of State Usury Laws—COC Ch 3
Federal Racketeering Statute—*See* RICO
Federal Reserve Board—*See* FRB
Federal Tax Collections and Collection Agencies—FDC § 4.2.9
Federal Trade Commission—*See* FTC
Fee Harvester Credit Cards—TIL § 7.8; FDC § 1.5.10.3S
Fees—TIL § 3.7; COC § 7.2.1; FDC § 15.2
FHA Mortgage Foreclosure—Fore Ch 3
Fiduciary Duty—COC §§ 8.7.2, 12.9
Fifth Amendment Privilege—Auto § 9.8.6.7
Filed Rate Doctrine—UDAP § 8.5.3.1
Film Developing Packages—UDAP § 8.9.10
Finance Charge—TIL Ch 3; COC § 4.4
Finance Charges, Hidden—COC Ch 7; TIL § 3.10
Finance Companies—COC Ch 2; UDAP §§ 2.2.1, 6.4
Flipping—COC § 6.1; UDAP § 6.4
Flipping of Property—COC 11.6.6
Flood Damage to Vehicle—Auto § 2.1.3
Food Advertising—UDAP § 10.3.2
Food Stamps, Electronic Payment—CBPL Ch 8
Forbearance of Student Loans—Stud § 4.4
Forbearance Plans, Mortgage Loans—Fore § 2. 4.3
Force-Placed Auto Insurance—UDAP § 10.5.10; COC § 8.3.1.4; TIL § 3.9.4.4.3
Foreclosure—Fore
Foreclosure, False Threat—Repo Ch 6
Foreclosure, Government-Held Mortgages—Fore Ch 3
Foreclosure Mediation—Fore § 4.11
Foreclosure, Preventing Through Bankruptcy—Bankr Ch 9, §§ 10.4.2.6.4, 11.5, 11.6; Fore Ch 9
Foreclosure, Preventing Through Refinancing—COC § 6.5; Fore § 2.3.2
Foreclosure, Preventing Through Rescission—TIL Ch 10; Fore § 5.6.1
Foreclosure, Preventing Through Workouts—Fore Ch 2
Foreclosure, Rescue Scams—Fore ch 15; TIL § 6.8.5, 9.9.3
Foreclosure, Setting Aside—Fore § 14.2
Foreclosure, Summary of State Laws—Fore App E
Foreclosures and UDAP—UDAP § 6.13; Fore § 5.4
Forged Signatures, Indorsements—CBPL § 2.5.1.3
Franchises—UDAP §§ 2.2.9.2, 10.6.1
Fraud—UDAP; Warr § 11.4
Fraud and Arbitration—Arbit Ch 6
FRB Official Staff Commentary on Reg. B—CD App C
FRB Official Staff Commentary on Reg. M—TIL App H.3

FRB Official Staff Commentary on Reg. Z—TIL App C
Free Offers—UDAP § 5.3.4
Freezer Meats—UDAP § 8.9.4
FTC (Federal Trade Commission)—UDAP
FTC Act, No Private Action Under—UDAP § 14.1
FTC Cooling Off Period Rule—UDAP § 9.2, App B.3
FTC Credit Practices Rule—Repo § 3.4.2; UDAP § 6.11, App B.1; FDC § 8.4; Coll App D
FTC Debt Collection Law—FDC Ch 8
FTC FCR Enforcement Actions—FCR App K
FTC FCR Official Staff Commentary—FCR App D
FTC FDCPA Official Staff Commentary—FDC § 3.2.6, App C
FTC Funeral Rule—UDAP § 10.3.5, App B.5
FTC Holder Rule—UDAP § 11.6, App B.2
FTC Mail or Telephone Order Merchandise Rule—UDAP § 9.6.5, App B.4
FTC Staff Letters on FCR—FCR App E
FTC Staff Letters on FDCPA—FDC § 3.2.5, App B
FTC Telemarketing Sales Rule—UDAP App D.2.1
FTC Telephone and Dispute Resolution Rule—UDAP App D.2.2
FTC Used Car Rule—UDAP § 7.2.2, App B.6; Warr § 15.8, App D
Funds Availability—CBPL § 3.4
Funerals—UDAP § 10.3.5
Furniture Sales—UDAP § 8.9.5
Future Advance Clauses—Repo § 3.9
Future Service Contracts—UDAP § 10.1
GAP Insurance—TIL §§ 3.7.10, 3.9.4.7
Garnishment—FDC § 5.5.7; Coll Ch 12, App B
Garnishment of Bank Account—CBPL § 10.3
Garnishment to Repay Student Loans—Stud § 8.3, App B.5.1
Gas Service—AUS § 1.2.1; UDAP § 8.5.2
Gasoline, Price Gouging—UDAP § 8.5.1.5
Gift Cards—UDAP § 6.9.6
Government Benefits—FCR §§ 2.3.6.6, 7.2.6
Government Checks—CBPL Ch 9
Government Collection Practices—Coll Ch 11; Stud Chs 7, 8
GPS Devices—UDAP § 7.7.5
Gramm-Leach-Bliley Act—COC §§ 3.10, 8.4.1.5.2; FCR § 16.4.1
Gray Market Sales—Auto § 1.4.12; Warr § 14.7
Guaranteed Student Loans—Stud
Guarantees—UDAP § 5.6.7.3
Guarantors—*See* Cosigners
Hague Convention—Warr § 13.3.10
HAMP—Fore § 2.8; Bankr. 11.6.1.5S
HARP—Fore § 2.9
Handguns—UDAP § 8.9.8
Handicapped, Discrimination Against—CD § 3.5.2
Handouts for Client—*See* Client Handouts
Health Care Bills—Coll Ch 10; Bankr § 6.2.2.4.1
Health Care Plans, Misrepresentations—UDAP § 10.3.6
Health Care Treatment, Discrimination In—CD § 2.2.2.6
Health Cures, Misrepresentations—UDAP § 10.3
Health Spas—UDAP § 10.1.3
Hearing Aids—UDAP § 10.3.1
Heating Fuel—AUS §§ 1.2, 1.5; UDAP § 8.5
HELOC—TIL Ch. 8
Hidden Interest—COC Ch 7; TIL § 3.10
High Cost Loans, State Laws—COC Ch 7
High Pressure Sales—UDAP § 5.5
Hill-Burton Act Compliance—UDAP § 10.3.5
Holder in Due Course—UDAP § 11.6; COC §§ 10.6.1
Home Builders—UDAP § 8.3.2
Home Equity Lines of Credit—TIL Ch. 8
Home Equity Loans—TIL Ch 9

Quick Reference to the Consumer Credit and Sales Legal Practice Series

References are to sections in *all* manuals in NCLC's Consumer Credit and Sales Legal Practice Series

Home Foreclosure—*See* Foreclosure
Home Heating Fuel—AUS §§ 1.2, 1.5; UDAP § 8.5
Home Improvement Practices—TIL § 10.5.3; UDAP § 8.4; Warr § 19.7, App J.4
Home Mortgage Disclosure Act—CD § 4.4.5, Appxs E, J
Home Mortgage, Rescission of—TIL Ch 10, App E.3
Home Owners' Loan Act—COC § 3.5
Home Ownership & Equity Protection Act—TIL Ch 9, App E.2.3; Fore § 5.8.1
Homes and UDAP—UDAP §§ 2.2.5, 8.3
Homes, Warranties—Warr Ch. 18
Homestead Exemptions, Bankruptcy—Bankr § 10.2.2.2
Hope for Homeowners—Fore § 2.10.1
HOPE NOW—Fore § 2.10.2
Horizontal Privity—Warr § 6.3
Hospital Bills—Coll Ch 10
House Warranties—Warr Ch 18
Household Goods, Bankruptcy Exemption—Bankr §§ 10.2.2.4, 10.4.2.4
Household Goods Security Interest—Repo § 3.4; UDAP § 6.11; TIL § 5.8
Household Goods Security Interest, Credit Property Insurance on—COC § 8.5.4.4
Houses and UDAP—UDAP §§ 2.2.5, Ch. 8
HUD—*See* Department of Housing and Urban Development
Identity Theft—FCR Ch. 9; Coll § 5.3.2
Illegal Conduct—UDAP § 4.3.9
Immigrant Consultants, Deceptive Practices—UDAP § 10.4.2
Immigrant Status, Discrimination Based On—CD § 3.3.3.3
Implied Warranties—Warr Ch 4
Imprisonment for Debt—Coll § 12.10
Improvident Extension of Credit—TIL § 7.6S; Ch. 9; UDAP § 6.3
Incapacity as a Defense—Coll § 5.4.1
Income Verification for Mortgage—TIL § 9.3.3
Incomplete Information in Consumer Reports—FCR Ch 4
Inconvenient Venue—*See* Venue
Indian Tribal Law, Bankruptcy Exemptions—Bankr § 10.2.3.1
Industrial Loan Laws—COC Ch 2
Infancy—*See* Minority
Infliction of Emotional Distress—FDC § 10.2
In Forma Pauperis Filings in Bankruptcy—Bankr §§ 14.6, 17.6
Informal Dispute Resolution—Warr § 2.8
Injunctions—UDAP § 13.6; FDC §§ 6.12
Insecurity Clauses—Repo § 4.2.2
Inspection by Experts—Warr § 13.6.1
Installment Sales Laws—COC §§ 2.3.3.4, 9.3.1.1
Insurance and Arbitration—Arbit § 3.3.4
Insurance and UDAP—UDAP §§ 2.3.1, 10.5
Insurance Consumer Reports—FCR §§ 2.3.6.5, 2.6.8, 7.2.5
Insurance, Credit—COC Ch 8; TIL §§ 3.7.9, 3.9.4; UDAP § 10.5.9
Insurance, Illusory Coverage—UDAP § 10.5.5
Insurance Packing—COC § 8.5.4; UDAP § 10.5.11
Insurance Redlining—CD § 7.3
Insurance, Refusal to Pay Claim—UDAP § 10.5.3
Intentional Infliction of Emotional Distress—FDC § 10.2
Intentional Interference with Employment Relationships—FDC § 10.4
Interest Calculations—COC §§ 4.2, 4.3
Interest, Hidden—COC Ch 7; TIL § 3.10
Interest Rates, Federal Preemption of—COC Ch 3
Interference with Employment Relationships—FDC § 10.4
Interim Bankruptcy Rules–Bankr App B
International Driving Permits–UDAP § 10.2.5
International Money Orders and Wires—CBPL Ch 5

Internet Banking—CBPL Ch 4
Internet, Fraudulent Schemes—UDAP § 9.8
Internet, Invasion of Privacy—UDAP § 5.9
Internet Service Providers—UDAP § 8.5.3.9
Internet Payment Systems—CBPL §§ 4.9, 4.12
Interrogatories—Arbit App C; Auto App F; CCA App E; CD App H; COC App N; FCR App J.4; FDC App I.1; Repo App E; Fore Apps I.8, I.10; Warr App K; TIL App F.2; CLP
Interstate Banking and Rate Exportation—COC § 3.4.5
Interview Checklist for Debt Collection—FDC App F
Interview Form, Bankruptcy—Bankr App F
Invasion of Privacy—FCR §§ 10.5.3, 16.3; FDC § 10.3
Investigative Reports—FCR Ch 13
Investments—UDAP §§ 2.2.9, 10.6
Involuntary Bankruptcy Cases—Bankr §§ 14.8, 17.1.2
JAMS—Arbit App B.3
Joint Bank Accounts, Seizure—Coll § 12.7
Joint Checking Accounts—CBPL §§ 2.8.3, 10.4.6.1
Judicial Liens, Avoiding in Bankruptcy—Bankr § 10.4.2.3
Jury, Disclosure to, that Damages Will Be Trebled—UDAP § 13.4.2.8; Auto § 9.9.10
Jury Instructions, Sample—CCA Ch 16; Auto App G; FDC App I.2; FCR App J.9; TIL App G
Jury Trial, Class Action—CCA Ch 16
Jury Trial, Preparing FDCPA Case—FDC § 2.5.7
Land Installment Sales Contract (aka "Contract for Deed")– Fore Ch. 12
Land Sales—UDAP §§ 2.2.5, 8.3
Land Trusts—TIL §§ 2.2.1.1, 2.4.3
Landlord Evictions—FDC § 1.10.2.2
Landlord Foreclosure's Effect on Tenants—Fore § 14.7
Landlord's Removal of Evicted Tenant's Property—Repo § 15.7.4; FDC § 1.5.2.4
Landlord's Requested Disconnection of Utility Service—AUS § 11.8
Landlord's Termination of Utility Service—AUS § 12.2
Landlord-Tenant—Bankr §§ 12.9, 18.8; UDAP §§ 2.2.6, 8.2; FDC § 1.10.2
Landownership, Utility Service Conditioned on—AUS Ch 4
Late Charges—COC §§ 4.8, 7.2.4; TIL §§ 3.9.3, 5.9.7; UDAP §§ 6.11.8; 6.5
Late Charges, Utility Bills—AUS §§ 6.2, 6.3
Late Posting of Payments and Interest Calculation—COC § 4.6.4.5
Law, Unauthorized Practice of—FDC §§ 4.2.8.7.3, 11.5; Bankr § 16.6
Lawyer—*See* Attorney
Layaway Plans—UDAP § 5.7.1
Lease-Back of Home—COC § 7.5.2.1; TIL § 10.2.5
Leases—Repo Ch 14; TIL §§ 2.2.4.2, Ch 13; UDAP §§ 2.2.6, 7.6, 8.2; Warr Ch 21; Auto §§ 4.6.2.3, 4.6.6.5, 5.2.6; Bankr § 12.9; CD § 2.2.2.2; COC § 7.5.3; *see also* Rent to Own
Lease Terms for Residence—UDAP §§ 8.2.3, 8.2.4
Leased Vehicle Damages—Auto § 9.10.4
Legal Rights, Misrepresentation of—UDAP § 5.6.8
Lemon Cars Being Resold—Auto §§ 1.4.7, 2.1.6, 2.4.5.5, 6.3, App C; Warr § 15.7.3; UDAP § 7.4.7
Lemon Laws—Warr § 14.2, App F
Lender Liability—UDAP Ch 11
Letter to Debt Collector, Sample—FDC § 2.3
Liability of Agents, Principals, Owners—UDAP Ch 11; FDC § 2.8
Licenses to Drive and Bankruptcy—Bankr § 15.5.5.1
Liens—Repo Ch 15
Life Care Homes—UDAP § 10.3.3
Life Insurance, Excessive Premiums for—UDAP § 10.5.7

Quick Reference to the Consumer Credit and Sales Legal Practice Series

References are to sections in *all* manuals in NCLC's Consumer Credit and Sales Legal Practice Series

Lifeline Assistance Programs—AUS § 2.3.2
LIHEAP—AUS Ch 7, App C
Limitation of Remedies Clauses—Warr Ch 9
Live Check Solicitations–UDAP § 6.9.5
Living Trusts—UDAP § 10.4.3
Loan Brokers—UDAP §§ 2.2.1, 6.2; COC § 7.3.2
Loan Flipping—*See* Flipping
Loan Modification—Fore Ch2; Bankr 11.1.6.5S
Loan Rehabilitation—Stud § 6.3
Loans, High Cost—COC Ch7
Long Arm Jurisdiction—COC § 9.2.9.6; UDAP § 12.6.2
Loss Mitigation, Foreclosures—Fore Ch 2
Lost Checks—CBPL §§ 2.10, 3.2
Lost Credit Card Reporting Services—UDAP § 6.4.5
Low Balling—UDAP § 5.3.5
Low Income Home Energy Assistance Program—AUS Ch 7, App C
Magazine Sales—UDAP § 8.9.9
Magnuson-Moss Warranty Act—Warr Ch 2, Apps A, B; Auto § 8.2.11.2
Magnuson-Moss Warranty Act Relation to Federal Arbitration Act—Arbit § 4.2.2, App G
Mail Fraud—UDAP § 14.2.2; FDC § 9.1
Mail Order Sales—UDAP § 9.2
Making Home Affordable Modification Program—Fore § 2.8
Malicious Prosecution—FDC § 10.6.2
Managed Care, Misrepresentations—UDAP § 10.3.6
Manufactured Home Defects—Warr § 17.1.3
Manufactured Home Foreclosure—Fore Ch 11
Manufactured Home Parks—UDAP §§ 2.2.6, 8.1.2
Manufactured Homes, Federal Statutes—Warr App C
Manufactured Homes and Interstate Rate Deregulation—COC Ch 3
Manufactured Homes and Repossession—Repo §§ 2.4.1, 3.5, 4.8.3, 5.2, 6.3.3, 7.1
Manufactured Homes, Sale by Consumer—Repo § 9.6.3
Manufactured Homes and UDAP—UDAP §§ 2.2.5, 8.1.1
Manufactured Homes, Utility Service—AUS Ch 13
Manufactured Homes, Warranties—Warr Ch 17
Manufacturer Rebates—UDAP § 5.3.3
Marital Status Discrimination—CD § 3.4.1
Mass Action—CCA § 2.4.4.3
Master Metering—AUS § 5.5
Math, Credit—COC Ch 4
MBNA Use of Collection via NAF Arbitration—Arbit Ch 12
McCarran-Ferguson Act—Arbit § 3.3.4; COC § 8.5.2.7; TIL § 2.4.9.5.4
Means Testing—Bankr
Mechanical Breakdown Insurance—*See* Service Contracts
Mediation—Auto § 9.11.1.3
Medical—*See* Health Care
Mental Anguish Damages—FDC §§ 2.5, 6.3, 10.2
Mental Incompetence—Coll § 5.4.1.3
MERS—Fore § 4.6
Meter Tampering—AUS Ch 5
Migrant Farmworker Camps—UDAP §§ 2.2.7, 8.2.9
Mileage Disclosure—Auto §§ 2.4.5.8, 4.6.6
Military Personnel and Credit Protection—Coll ch. 7; FCR § 5.7.1; Repo § 6.3.5.1; Fore § 4.12; COC § 7.5.5.6
Military Student Loan Deferment—Stud § 4.3.5.4
Mini-FTC Laws—*See* UDAP
Minority—Coll § 5.4.1.2
Misrepresentation—UDAP § 4.2; Warr § 11.4; Auto § 8.4
Mistaken Undercharges, Utility Bills—AUS § 5.1.2
Mobile Homes—See Manufactured Homes

Model Pleadings—*See* Complaints, Interrogatories, Document Requests, etc.
Modification of Mortgage Loans—Fore § 2. 4.6
Money Orders—CBPL Ch 5
Moratorium on Foreclosures—Fore § 2.13.2
Mortgage Assistance Scams—UDAP § 6.14.2; Fore Ch. 15
Mortgage Assistance, State Programs—Fore § 2.3.3
Mortgage Disclosure of Credit Terms—TIL § 5.7
Mortgage Disclosure Improvement Act—TIL
Mortgage Electronic Registration System (MERS)—Fore § 4.3.4.3
Mortgage Escrow—TIL § 9.5.3.2
Mortgage Fees—TIL § 3.9.6; COC Ch 7
Mortgage Loans—UDAP § 6.4
Mortgage Loan Modification Scams—Fore ch. 15
Mortgage Modification—Fore Ch 2
Mortgage Originator Compensation—TIL § 9.3.2
Mortgage Servicers—Fore § 1.3.3.5, Chs 6, 7; TIL § 9.4.3
Mortgage Servicing, Summary of State Laws—Fore App D
Mortgage Steering—TIL § 9.3.2
Most Favored Lender—COC § 3.4.3
Motion in Limine, Sample—Auto App I; FDC App I.5
Motions for Class Certification—*See* Class Certification Motions
Motor Homes—Warr § 14.8.5
Motor Vehicle Information and Cost Savings Act—Auto Chs 4, 5, App A.1
Motor Vehicle Installment Sales Act—COC § 2.3.3.5; Repo § 2.2
Multiple Damages—UDAP § 13.4.2; Auto § 5.8.1
Municipal Utilities (MUNIs)—AUS Ch.14
NACA Revised Class Actions Guidelines for Settlement—CCA App D
NACHA—CBPL §§ 1.3.3, 4.1.5
National Arbitration Forum—Arbit §§ 1.6, 6.6.aS, App B.2, App H, App I
National Origin Discrimination—CD § 3.3.3
"Nationwide" Reporting Agencies—FCR § 2.6.1
Native Americans and Repossession—Repo § 6.3.5.2
Natural Disasters—Fore § 2.13
Navaho Law and Repossessions—Repo § 12.6.7
Necessities Laws—Coll § 10.6; CD § 9.3
Negative Equity—COC § 11.7.3; Repo § 3.4.6S
Negative Option Plans—UDAP § 9.5
Negligence—Warr Ch 12; FCR § 10.5.4; FDC §§ 10.2, 10.7
Negotiations, Class Actions—CCA Ch 13
Net Present Value Analysis—Fore § 2.8.2.2
New Car Lemon Laws—Warr § 14.2, App F
New Cars, Sales—Warr Ch 14; UDAP § 7.5
New Cars, Undisclosed Damage to—Auto §§ 1.4.6, 6.2.3
New House Warranties—Warr Ch 18
900 Numbers—UDAP §§ 9.7, 11.10, Apps D, E
Nonattorney Legal Service Providers, Deceptive Practices—UDAP § 10.4.2
Nondisclosure and UDAP—UDAP § 4.2.14
Non-English Speaking—UDAP § 5.6.1
Nonfiling Insurance—COC § 8.5.4.5
Nonpayment of Loans, When Excused—Repo § 4.4
Non-Signatories Rights and Obligations—Arbit § 7.4
Notario Fraud—UDAP § 10.4.2
Notice Consumer Deducting Damages From Outstanding Balance—*See* Warr App I.3
Notice of Rescission—*See* Rescission Notice
Notice of Revocation—Warr App I.2
Notice to Class—CCA Ch 12
Notice to Quit, Deceptive—UDAP § 8.2.8.1

Quick Reference to the Consumer Credit and Sales Legal Practice Series

References are to sections in *all* manuals in NCLC's Consumer Credit and Sales Legal Practice Series

Not Sufficient Funds (NSF) Checks—CBPL § 2.7
Nursing Homes, Deceptive Practices—UDAP § 10.3.3
Obsolete Information in Consumer Reports—FCR § 5.2
Odometers—Auto; Warr § 15.7.2; UDAP § 7.4.5
Odometer Tampering—Auto §§ 4.3, 4.4
Offer of Judgment—FDC § 2.4.13; CCA § 7.3.2
Official Bankruptcy Forms—Bankr App D
Oil, Home Heating—AUS § 1.5; UDAP § 8.5
On Account—Coll § 4.6
On-Line Fraud—UDAP § 9.8
On-Line Disclosures—UDAP § 4.2.14.3.9
Open-End Credit—TIL Chs 6, 7, 8; COC § 2.3.2.3; Coll § 4.6
Open-End Credit, Spurious—TIL § 6.2.3
Opening Statement, Sample—Auto App I
Outdated Information in Consumer Reports—FCR § 5.2
Overcharges by Creditor in Bankruptcy—Bankr § 14.4.3.3
Overdraft Loans—TIL § 3.9.3.3, COC § 7.5.6
Overdraft Opt-In for Debit Cards—CBPL § 4.2.4.5S
Pain and Suffering Damages—FDC § 2.5; UDAP § 13.3.3.9
Paralegals, Attorney Fees for—UDAP §§ 13.6.11.6, 13.8.7.2
Parol Evidence—UDAP § 4.2.19.3; Warr § 3.7
Partial Prepayment—COC § 8.2
Pattern and Practice Evidence—Auto § 9.8
Payroll Cards—CBPL § 7.9
Pawnbrokers—COC §§ 2.3.3.9, 7.5.2.3; UDAP § 6.13.5
Payday Loans—COC § 7.5.5
Payment Holidays for Interest-Bearing Loans—COC § 4.8.3
Payment Packing—COC § 11.7.4
Payment Plans, Utility Bills—AUS Ch 6
Pay Phones—AUS § 2.6
Pensions in Bankruptcy—Bankr §§ 2.5.2, 10.2.2.11
Percentage of Income Payment Plans—AUS § 9.2.3
Perkins Loans—Stud
Personal Injury Suits—UDAP § 2.2.11
Personal Property Seized with Repo—Repo Ch 7
Pest Control Services—UDAP § 8.7.2
Petroleum Products, Price Gouging—UDAP § 8.5.1.5
Photoprocessing Packages—UDAP § 8.9.10
Plain English—UDAP § 5.6.
Pleadings—*See* Complaints, Interrogatories, Document Requests, etc.
Point of Sale (POS) Electronic Transfers—CBPL Ch 4
Points—COC §§ 4.7, 6.4.1.3, 7.2.1, 8.3.1.2; TIL § 3.7.5
Postal Money Order—CBPL Ch 5
Postdated Checks—CBPL § 2.8.1
Preauthorized Drafts—CBPL § 2.5.5
Precomputed Interest—COC § 4.5
Precut Housing—UDAP § 8.3.8
Preemption of State Usury Laws—COC Ch 3
Preemption and State Chartered Banks—COC Ch3
Preexisting Debt Clauses—Repo § 3.9
Prepayment—TIL § 5.9.6; COC Ch 5
Prepayment Penalties—COC § 5.8
Prescreening Lists—FCR § 7.3
Preservation of Documents, Class Actions—CCA § 6.2
Price Gouging in an Emergency—UDAP § 4.3.11
Pricing—UDAP § 5.3
Privacy, Invasion of—FCR §§ 10.5.3, 16.3; FDC § 10.3
Privacy, Restrictions on Use of Consumer Reports—FCR § Ch 7, § 12.2
Private Mortgage Insurance (PMI)—COC § 8.3.2.1; UDAP § 10.5.12
Private Sale of Collateral—Repo § 10.5.7
Privity—Warr Ch 6; UDAP § 4.2.193
Prizes—UDAP § 10.6.4

Procedural Unconscionability—Warr § 11.2; COC § 12.7
Proceeds—Repo § 3.3.2
Process Servers—FDC § 1.6.6S
Progress Payments—COC § 4.9
Project Lifeline—Fore § 2.10.3
Propane—AUS § 1.5; UDAP § 8.5
Property Flipping—COC § 11.6.6; Fore § 5.3.4
Proprietary Schools—Stud Ch 12; UDAP § 10.1.7
Protective Orders—CCA § 6.2, Apps L, N
Public Assistance Status, Discrimination Based on—CD § 3.4.3
Public Housing, UDAP Coverage—UDAP §§ 2.3.3.3, 2.3.6
Public Housing, Utility Service—AUS Ch 8
Public Records—FCR
Public Sale of Collateral—Repo § 10.7
Public Utilities—AUS
Public Utility Credit—TIL § 2.4.6
Punitive Damages—Auto § 7.10; CD § 11.7.4; FCR § 11.12; FDC § 2.6, Ch 10; UDAP § 13.4.3
Punitive Damages & Arbitration—Arb § 11.7
Pyramid Sales—UDAP § 10.6.3
Pyramiding Late Charges—COC § 7.2.4.3; AUS § 6.2.6
Qualified Written Request—Fore App H.2.2
Quantum Meruit—Coll § 4.8
Race Discrimination re Credit—CD § 3.3.1
Racketeering Statute—*See* RICO
Reachback Periods—Bankr § 6.5.3.4
Reaffirmations and Bankruptcy—Bankr § 15.5.2
Real Estate—UDAP §§ 2.2.5, 8.3
Real Estate Settlement Procedures Act—*See* RESPA
Real Estate Tax Abatement Laws—Fore App F
Real Party in Interest—Fore § 4. 4
Reassembled Cars from Parts—Auto §§ 1.4.3, 2.1.4; UDAP § 7.4.6
Rebates from Manufacturer—UDAP § 5.3.3.2; TIL § 3.7.5.2
Rebates of Interest—COC Ch 5, §§ 6.3, 6.4; TIL § 3.7.2.3
Recoupment Claims—TIL §§ 10.3.3, 12.2.5; Bankr § 14.3.2.4
Redemption and Repo—Repo § 9.3
Redemption, Foreclosures—Fore §§ 4.2.6, 14.1.2
Redlining—CD §§ 7.1, 7.2
Referral Sales—UDAP § 9.3
Refinancings—COC Ch 6; Repo § 3.8; TIL § 5.15.3; UDAP § 6.4
Refund Anticipation Loans—COC § 7.5.4
Refunds—UDAP § 5.6.6
Regulation B, Text—CD App B
Regulation C, Text—CD App E.2
Regulation E—CBPL Ch 4, App D
Regulation M, Text—TIL App H.2
Regulation Z, Text—TIL App B
Regulation CC—CBPL § 3.4, App B
Regulation DD—CBPL § 2.4.4, App E
Rejection—Warr Ch 8
Reliance—TIL §§ 11.5.3.2, 11.5.4.6; UDAP § 4.2.12
Religious Discrimination re Credit—CD § 3.3.2
Remittances—UDAP § 6.9.4
Rent and Bankruptcy—Bankr §§ 12.9, 15.5.5.3, 18.8
Rent to Own—UDAP § 8.8; Bankr § 11.8; COC § 7.5.3; Repo § 14.3
Rent, Utility Service—AUS Chs 4, 8
Rental Cars—UDAP § 7.7; Auto § 2.4.5.6
Rental Housing, Substandard—UDAP §§ 8.2.5.1, 8.2.5.2
Repairs—UDAP § 5.7.6
Repairs, Automobile—Warr § 19.9; UDAP § 7.10
Repayment Plan for Student Loans—Stud § 6.5
Replevin—Repo Ch 5
Reporting Agencies—FCR

Quick Reference to the Consumer Credit and Sales Legal Practice Series

References are to sections in *all* manuals in NCLC's Consumer Credit and Sales Legal Practice Series

Repossessions—Repo; UDAP § 6.13; FDC § 4.2.6
Repossessions, Stopping—Bankr Ch 9
Resale of Utility Service—AUS § 5.5, Ch. 13
Rescission—TIL Ch 10, App E.2.2; Auto § 7.11; Fore § 5.6.1; UDAP §§ 13.7
Rescission by Recoupment—TIL § 10.3.3
Rescission Notice, Sample—TIL App D
Resisting Repossession, Liability for—Repo § 6.2.4.3
Res Judicata—CCA ch. 17
RESPA—COC § 12.2.2; Fore Ch 8; TIL §§ 4.1.1, 4.4.7
Retail Installment Sales Acts (RISA)—COC § 2.3.3.5; Repo § 2.5.2
Retail Sellers—COC §§ 2.3.1.3.3, 9.2.3.2
Retaliation for Exercise of TIL, CCPA Rights—CD § 3.4.4
Retroactive Statutes—UDAP § 12.4; COC § 9.3.4
Reverse Metering—AUS § 5.1
Reverse Mortgages—Fore § 5.3.7.2
Reverse Redlining—CD § 8.4
Review of Arbitration Decision—Arbit Ch 11
Revised Uniform Arbitration Act – Arbit Ch. 11
Revocation of Acceptance—Warr Ch 8
Revolving Repossessions—Repo § 10.11
RHS—*See* Rural Housing Service
RICO—UDAP §§ 14.2, 14.3, App C.1.1; COC § 12.6; FDC § 9.5; Auto § 8.5
Right to Cure Default—Repo § 4.5, App B; Bankr § 11.6.2
Right to See Consumer Reports—FCR § 3.3
Right to Utility Service—AUS Ch 3
RISA—COC § 2.3.3.5; Repo § 2.5.2
Rooker Feldman—FDC § 7.4.4
RTO Contracts—*See* Rent to Own
Rule of 78—COC § 5.6.3.3; TIL § 3.7.2.; Repo § 11.3.2.2.2
Rural Electric Cooperatives (RECs)—AUS Ch. 14
RHS—*See* Rural Housing Service
Rural Housing Service—Fore § 3.4
Rustproofing—UDAP § 7.2.3
Safety—UDAP § 5.4.4
Sale and Lease-Back—COC § 7.5.2.1; TIL § 10.2.5
Sale of Collateral—Repo Ch 10
Salvage Auctions—Auto § 2.6.4.2
Salvage Vehicles, Sale of—Auto §§ 1.4.3, 2.1.4, 2.4.5.4, 6.2.1; Warr § 15.7.4
Salvaged Parts—UDAP § 7.4.6
Sample Answer and Counterclaims—*See* Answer and Counterclaims
Sample Attorney Fee Pleadings—*See* Attorney Fee Pleadings
Sample Client Retainer Forms— *See* Client Retainer Forms
Sample Closing Arguments—*See* Closing Arguments
Sample Complaints—*See* Complaints
Sample Deposition Questions—*See* Deposition Questions
Sample Discovery—*See* Interrogatories; Document Requests
Sample Document Production Requests—*See* Document Production Requests
Sample Forms, Bankruptcy—*See* Bankruptcy Forms
Sample Interrogatories—*See* Interrogatories
Sample Jury Instructions—*See* Jury Instructions
Sample Motion in Limine—*See* Motion in Limine
Sample Motions for Class Certification—*See* Class Certification Motions
Sample Notice for Rescission—*See* Rescission Notice
Sample Notice of Deposition—*See* Deposition Notice
Sample Notice of Revocation—*See* Notice of Revocation
Sample Objection to Document Requests—*See* Document Requests, Sample Objection to
Sample Opening and Closing Statement—*See* Opening Statement; Closing Argument
Sample Pleadings—*See* Complaint, Interrogatories, Document Requests, etc.
Sample Requests for Admissions—*See* Admission Requests
Sample Trial Brief—*See* Trial Brief
Sample Trial Documents—*See* Trial Documents
Sample Voir Dire—*See* Voir Dire
School-Related Defenses to Student Loans—Stud § 12.7
Schools, Vocational—Stud Ch 12
Scope of Arbitration Agreement—Arbit Ch 7
Scrip Settlements, Class Actions—CCA § 13.8; CLP
Second Mortgage, Rescission of—TIL Ch 10
Secret Warranties—UDAP § 7.5.10.2; Warr § 14.5.3
Securitization of Consumer Paper—COC § 2.4.2
Security Deposits, Consumer's Rights to Reform Where Seller in Bankruptcy—Bankr § 18.8.4
Security Deposits, Tenant's—UDAP §§ 8.2.3, 8.2.4; FDC § 1.10.2.5
Security Deposits, Utility § 3.7
Security Interest Charges—TIL § 3.9
Security Interests—Repo Ch 3; TIL § 5.8
Security Interests, Avoiding in Bankruptcy—Bankr § 10.4.2.4, Ch 11
Security Systems—UDAP § 8.7.1
Seizure of Collateral—Repo
Self-Help Repossession—Repo Ch 6
Service Contracts—Warr Ch 20, App G; UDAP §§ 5.6.7.2, 7.2.5; Auto §§ 2.5.11, 2.6.2.11
Service Contracts, When Hidden Interest—COC §§ 7.2.3, 7.3.1; TIL § 3.6.5
Servicemembers Civil Relief Act—-Coll Ch 7; App A; Fore § 4.12; FCR 5.7.1; Repo 6.3.5.1
Service of Process—Warr § 13.3.10
Servicer Abuses—Fore Ch 6
Services and Warranties—Warr Ch 19
Set Off, Banker's—CBPL § 10.4
Set-Offs—TIL §§ 7.13; FDC § 12.6.7
Setting Aside Default Judgments—Coll § 13.2
Settlement, Auto Case—Auto § 9.11; Warr § 13.7
Settlement, Class Actions—CCA Ch 13, Apps U, W, X
Settlement, Class Actions, Objections—CCA § 14.4, App Y
Settlement, Individual Prior to Class Action—CCA § 1.2
Settlements and Consumer Reports—FCR § 12.6.4
Sewer Service—AUS § 1.2.3
Sex Discrimination re Credit—CD § 3.3.4
Sexual Orientation, Discrimination Based On—CD § 3.7
Shell Homes—UDAP § 8.3.8
Single Document Rule—COC § 11.7.8
Slamming, Telephone Service—AUS § 2.7.5.1; UDAP § 8.5.4
Small Loan Laws—COC § 2.3.3.2
Smart Cards—CBPL § 7.1
SMART Grants—Stud § 1.4.2.4
SNAP, Electronic Payment—CBPL Ch 8
Social Security Benefit Offset to Repay Student Loan—Stud § 8.4
Social Security Payments, Electronic—CBPL Ch 9
Soldiers' and Sailors' Civil Relief Act—-*See* Servicemembers' Civil Relief Act
Spendthrift Trusts in Bankruptcy—Bankr § 2.5.2
Spoilation of Evidence—Warr § 13.2.5
Spot Delivery of Automobiles—Auto Ch 3aS; UDAP § 7.3.9; Repo § 4.6; TIL § 4.4.6; COC § 11.7.5
Spouses, Consumer Reports on—FCR § 5.6.1
Spreader Clauses—TIL § 5.8.6

Quick Reference to the Consumer Credit and Sales Legal Practice Series

References are to sections in *all* manuals in NCLC's Consumer Credit and Sales Legal Practice Series

Spurious Open-End Credit—TIL § 6.2.3
Stafford Loans—Stud
Standard Form Contracts, Unfair—UDAP § 5.6.3
Standing to Collect a Debt—Coll § 4.3
Standing to Foreclose—Fore § 4.4
State Arbitration Law—Arbit Ch 3
State Bonding Laws—Auto App C
State Chartered Banks and Preemption—COC Ch 3
State Cosigner Statutes—Repo § 12.9.6.2
State Credit Discrimination Laws—CD § 1.6, App F
State Credit Repair Laws—FCR App H
State Credit Reporting Laws—FCR § 10.6, App H
State Debt Collection Statutes—FDC § 11.2, App E
State Exemption Laws—Coll App F
State Foreclosure Laws—Fore App E
State High Cost Loan Laws—COC Ch 7
State Home Improvement Statutes and Regs—Warr § 19.8.4
State Leasing Disclosure Statutes—TIL § 13.5.2.2
State Lemon Buyback Disclosure Laws—Auto App C
State Lemon Laws—Warr § 14.2, App F
State Lending Statutes—COC App A
State 900 Number Laws—UDAP App E
State Odometer Statutes—Auto App C
State Real Estate Tax Abatement Laws—Fore App F
State RICO Statutes—UDAP § 14.3, App C.2
State Right to Cure, Reinstate and Redeem Statutes—Repo App B
State Salvage Laws—Auto App C
State Service Contract Laws—Warr App G
State Telemarketing Laws—UDAP App E
State TIL Laws—TIL § 2.6
State Title Transfer Laws—Auto § 6.7, App C
State UDAP Statutes—UDAP App A
State Usury Statutes—COC App A
Statute of Limitations—TIL § 12.2; Coll § 3.7; FCR § 4.5
Statute of Limitations as Consumer Defense to Collection Action—Repo § 12.7; Coll § 3.7
Statutory Damages—TIL § 11.6; FDC §§ 6.4, 11.2; Repo § 13.2; UDAP § 13.4.1
Statutory Liens—Repo Ch 15
Statutory Liens, Avoiding in Bankruptcy—Bankr § 10.4.2.6.3
Staying Foreclosure—Bankr Ch 9
Stolen Checks—CBPL §§ 2.10, 3.2
Stolen Vehicles—Auto §§ 1.4.11, 2.1.8, 8.2.2
Stop Payment on Checks, Credit and Debit Cards—CBPL §§ 2.8.2, 6.5S, Ch 4
Storage of Evicted Tenant's Property—Repo § 15.7.4; UDAP § 8.2.5.2
Stored Value Cards—CBPL Ch 7, App G
Straight Bankruptcy—Bankr Ch 3
Strict Liability in Tort—Warr Ch 12
Student Loan Collection Abuse—Stud Ch 7
Student Loan Repayment Plans—Stud Ch 6
Student Loan Regulations—Stud App B
Student Loans—Bankr § 15.4.3.8; FCR § 12.6.5; Stud; TIL §§ 2.4.5, 5.14
Student Loans and Bankruptcy—Stud Ch 10
Student Loans, Reinstating Eligibility—Stud Ch 6
Subprime Credit Cards—*See* Fee Harvester Cards
Summary Judgment Briefs, Sample—FDC App I.1; CLP
Surety for Consumer Debtor—Repo § 12.9
Surety Liability for Seller's Actions—Auto § 9.13.4
Survey Evidence—FDC § 2.9.3
Surveys, Use in Litigation—CCA § 8.1.3.2.4
Target Marketing Lists—FCR § 7.3.4

Tax Abatement Laws, State Property, Summaries—Fore App F
Tax Collections—FDC §§ 4.2.9; Coll § 11.2
Tax Consequences, Bankruptcy Discharge—Bankr § 15.6
Tax Form 1099-C—CCA § 13.7.3.3.4.6
Tax Implications of Damage Award—CCA § 13.7.3.3.4
Tax Implications to Client of Attorney Fees—CCA § 18.5
Tax Liens—Fore Ch 13
Tax Refund Intercepts—Stud § 8.2; Coll § 11.2.7; Bankr § 9.4.3
Tax Refunds—COC § 7.5.4
Tax Refunds in Bankruptcy—Bankr § 2.5.5
Tax Sales—Fore Ch 13
Taxis, Undisclosed Sale of—Auto § 2.4.5.6
TEACH Grants—Stud § 1.4.2.3
Telechecks—UDAP §§ 6.9
Telecommunications Act of 1996—AUS Ch 2, App B
Telemarketing, Payment—CBPL §§ 2.5.5, 4.8
Telemarketing Fraud—UDAP § 9.6; FCR § 15.4
Telemarketing Fraud, Federal Statutes—UDAP App D
Telephone Cards, Prepaid—CBPL Ch 7
Telephone Companies as Credit Reporting Agencies—FCR § 2.7.9
Telephone Harassment—FDC § 9.3
Telephone Inside Wiring Maintenance Agreements—UDAP §§ 5.6.7.2, 8.5.3.7
Telephone Rates, Service—AUS Ch 2, App B
Telephone Service Contracts—UDAP §§ 5.6.7.2, 8.5.3
Telephone Slamming—AUS § 2.7.5.1; UDAP § 8.5.3.3
Teller's Checks—CBPL Ch 5
Tenant Approval Companies—FCR §§ 2.6.2.2, 3.2.4
Tenant Ownership in Chapter 7 Liquidation—Bankr § 18.8.2
Tenant's Property Removed with Eviction—Repo § 15.7.4
Tenant's Rights When Landlord Files Bankruptcy—Bankr § 18.8; AUS § 12.2
Tenant's Rights When Landlord Foreclosed Upon—Fore § 14.7
Termination of Utility Service—AUS Ch 11
Termite Control Services—UDAP § 8.7.2
Testers, Fair Housing—CD §§ 4.4.4, 11.2.2
Theft at ATM Machines, Bank Liability—CBPL § 4.5.4
Theft of Identity—FCR § 9.2
Third Party Liability Issues—AUS §§ 11.4, 11.5
Threats of Criminal Prosecution—Coll Ch 9
Tie-In Sale Between Manufactured Home and Park Space—UDAP § 8.1.2.2
TIL—*See* Truth in Lending
Time Shares—UDAP § 8.3.10
Timing of TIL Disclosures—TIL § 4.4
Tire Identification—Auto § 2.2.3
Title, Automobile—Auto §§ 2.3, 2.4, Ch 3, Apps. D, E; UDAP § 7.3.9; Warr § 15.4.4
Tobacco—UDAP § 10.3.7
Tort Liability—FDC Ch 11
Tort Liability, Strict—Warr Ch 12
Tort Remedies, Unlawful Disconnections—AUS § 11.7.2
Tort Remedies, Wrongful Repossessions—Repo § 13.6
Towing—UDAP § 7.10.8; Repo Ch 15
Trade-in Cars—UDAP § 7.3.4
Trade Schools—Stud Ch 12; UDAP § 10.1.7
Trading Posts—UDAP § 6.13.5
Transcripts and Bankruptcy—Bankr § 15.5.5.2
Traveler's Checks—CBPL Ch 5, UDAP § 2.2.1.3
Travel Fraud—UDAP § 10.2
Treble Damages—UDAP § 13.4.2
Trebled, Disclosure to Jury that Damages Will Be—UDAP § 13.4.2.7.3
Trial Brief, Sample—FDC App I.4

Quick Reference to the Consumer Credit and Sales Legal Practice Series

References are to sections in *all* manuals in NCLC's Consumer Credit and Sales Legal Practice Series

Trial Documents, Sample—*See* Auto App I; FDC App I; Warr App L
Trustees in Bankruptcy—Bankr §§ 2.6, 2.7, 17.4.1, 18.7
Truth in Lending—TIL; COC §§ 2.3.4, 4.4.1; FDC § 9.4
Truth in Mileage Act—Auto Chs 3, 4, 5
Truth in Savings—CBPL § 2.4.4, Ch 4, App E.1
Tuition Recovery Funds—Stud § 12.8
Typing Services—Bankr § 16.6
UCC Article 2—Warr
UCC Article 2 and Comments Reprinted—Warr App E
UCC Article 2A—Repo §§ 2.5.1.1, 14.1.3.1; Warr Ch 21, App E.4; UDAP § 7.6.5
UCC Articles 3 and 4—CBPL Chs 1, 2, App A
UCC Article 9—Repo
UCC Article 9, Revised—Repo App A
UCC Article 9 and Comments Reprinted—Repo App A
UDAP—UDAP; AUS § 1.6.2; Auto § 8.4; COC §§ 8.5.2.6, 12.5; FDC § 11.3; FCR § 10.6.2; Repo §§ 2.5.3.1, 13.4.3; Warr § 11.1
Unauthorized Practice of Law—FDC §§ 4.2.8.7, 5.6.2, 11.5; Bankr § 16.6; UDAP § 10.4.2
Unauthorized Use of Checks, Credit and Debit Cards—CBPL §§ 2.5, 4.3, 6.4S; TIL § 6.10; Coll § 5.3.2
Unauthorized Use of Utility Service—AUS § 5.3
Unavailability of Advertised Items—UDAP § 5.3.2
Unconscionability—Warr §§ 11.2, 21.2.6; COC §§ 8.7.5, 12.7; UDAP §§ 4.4, 7.4.5; Auto § 8.7
Unconscionability of Arbitration Clauses—Arbit ch. 6
Unearned Interest—COC Ch 5
Unemployment Insurance—COC § 8.3.1.4
Unfair Insurance Practices Statutes—UDAP § 10.5; COC § 8.4.1.4
Unfair Practices Statutes—*See* UDAP
Unfairness—UDAP § 4.3
Uniform Arbitration Act – Arbit. Ch. 11
Uniform Commercial Code—*See* UCC
United States Trustee—Bankr §§ 2.7, 18.7.2
Universal Telephone Service—AUS Ch 2
Unlicensed Activities—COC § 9.2.4.5
Unpaid Refund Discharge of Student Loan—Stud § 9.5
Unsolicited Credit Cards—TIL § 7.12.5
Unsolicited Goods—UDAP § 9.4; FDC § 9.2
Unsubstantiated Claims—UDAP § 5.2
Used as New—UDAP § 5.7.4
Used Car Lemon Laws—Warr § 15.4.5
Used Car Rule—Warr § 15.8, App D; UDAP § 7.4.2, App B.6
Used Cars—Auto; Warr Ch 15, App J.3, App K.4; UDAP § 7.4
Used Cars, Assembled from Salvaged Parts—Auto §§ 1.4.3, 2.1.4
Used Cars, Financing—COC § 11.7
Used Cars, Undisclosed Sale of Wrecked Cars—Auto §§ 1.4.5, 2.1.4
Users of Consumer and Credit Reports—FCR Ch 7
Usury, Trying a Case—COC Ch 10
Utilities—AUS; CD §§ 2.2.2.3, 2.2.6.2; TIL § 2.4.6; UDAP §§ 2.3.2.1, 8.5.2

Utilities and Bankruptcy—AUS §§ 12.1, 12.2; Bankr § 9.8
Utilities as Credit Reporting Agencies—FCR § 2.7.9
Utility Commission Regulation—AUS § 1.3, App A
Utility Service Terminated by a Landlord—AUS § 11.8
Utility Subsidies in Subsidized Housing—AUS Ch 8
Utility Termination, Remedies—AUS § 11.7; UDAP § 8.5.2.1; FDC § 1.10.6
Utility Terminations, Stopping—AUS Ch 11; Bankr Ch 9
VA Mortgage Foreclosures and Workouts—Fore §§ 2.12.2, 3.3
Variable Rate Disclosures—TIL ch. 5
Variable Rates, Calculation—COC § 4.3.6
Vehicle Identification Number—Auto § 2.2.4
Venue, Inconvenient—FDC §§ 6.12.2, 8.3.7, 10.6.3, 11.7; UDAP § 6.10.9
Vertical Privity—Warr § 6.2
Vocational Schools—Stud Ch 12
Voir Dire, Sample Questions—FDC App I.2
Voluntary Payment Doctrine—UDAP § 4.2.19.5; COC § 10.6.6
Wage Earner Plans—Bankr Ch 4
Wage Garnishment—Coll Ch 12, App B
Waiver of Default—Repo § 4.3
Waiver of Right to Enforce Arbitration Clause—Arbit Ch 8
Wage Garnishment of Student Loans—Stud § 8.3, App B.5.1
Warehouseman's Lien—Repo § 15.7.4
Warranties—Warr; Auto § 8.2; UDAP § 5.6.7
Warranties, Secret—Warr § 14.5.3; UDAP § 7.5.10.2
Warranty Disclaimers—Warr Ch 5
Warranty of Habitability, Utility Service—AUS § 4.4.1
Water Affordability—AUS §§ 9.6, 9.7
Water Quality Improvement Systems—UDAP § 8.7.3
Water Service—AUS § 1.2.3; UDAP § 8.5.4
Weatherization Assistance—AUS Ch 10
Web Sites, Consumer Advocacy—UDAP § 1.4
Welfare Benefits, Bankruptcy—Bankr §§ 10.2.2.11, 15.5.5
Welfare Benefits, Credit Discrimination—CD §§ 3.4.3, 5.5.2.5
Welfare Benefits, Credit Reporting—FCR §§ 2.3.6.6, 7.2.2
Welfare Benefits, Exemptions—Coll § 12.5.5
"Wheelchair" Lemon Laws—Warr Ch 16
Wire Fraud—UDAP § 14.2.2.3.5
Wires—CBPL Ch 5
Withholding Credit Payments—Repo § 4.4.3; Warr § 8.5
Women's Business Ownership Act of 1988—CD § 1.3.2.4
Workers Compensation and Bankruptcy—Bankr § 10.2.2.1
Workout Agreements—TIL § 5.15.7
Workout Agreements, Foreclosures—Fore Ch 2
Wraparound Mortgages—COC § 7.4.3
Writ of Replevin—Repo Ch 5
Yield Spread Premiums—CD § 8.5; COC §§ 4.7.2, 7.3.2, 11.2.1.4.3, 11.2.2.6; UDAP §§ 6.2.3, 7.2.4
Young Consumers and Credit Cards—TIL § 7.6.3
Yo-Yo Delivery of Automobiles—Auto Ch 3aS; UDAP § 7.3.9; Repo § 4.6; TIL §4.4.6; COC § 11.2.2.5; CD § 10.4.2

NOTES

NOTES

NOTES

NCLC REPORTS

Consumer Credit and Usury / Deceptive Practices and Warranties Editions

Volume 29
July/August 2010

Developments and Ideas For the Practice of Consumer Law

Special Double Issue on the Dodd-Frank Financial Reform Bill

President Signs Financial Reform Bill

a section or provision, then the section or provision takes effect on the date that the final regulations take effect.[4] A rule required by the mortgage title must be prescribed in final form within 18 months of the transfer date and must take effect within 12 months of the rule's promulgation. If regulations have not been issued [covered by overlay] comes effective at that [covered] and July 21, 2013).[5]

[Much of the left and center text is obscured by an overlaid advertisement flyer reading:]

The Inside Scoop . . . from the Experts 24 times a year

This four page report not only keeps you current, but can help win cases and revolutionize your practice, with novel ideas, key insights, and game-changing tactics.

Recent Issues Cover:

- 7 ways to challenge a foreclosure on standing grounds and taking on MERS
- 13 ways to use loan broker or originator's misconduct to defend a foreclosure
- Special double issue on Dodd-Frank's dramatic changes to TILA, RESPA, FCRA and preemption law
- Using TIL rescission to save homes
- New FDCPA challenges to debt buyer collection and litigation practices
- 10 stunning practice implications of NAF withdrawal from all consumer arbitrations
- 10 creative uses of your state UDAP statute
- 15 things every attorney should know about reverse mortgages
- 8 tips on recovering attorney fees.

$175
24 issues a year with a *free* 3-ring binder

Or subscribe for $60 to only one subject area (6 issues a year):
- BANKRUPTCY & FORECLOSURES
- DEBT COLLECTION & REPOSSESSIONS
- CONSUMER CREDIT & USURY
- DECEPTIVE PRACTICES & WARRANTIES

Prices subject to change

For more information or to start subscribing, visit **www.consumerlaw.org/nr** or call (617) 542-9595

[Footnotes partially visible:]

[1] Pub. L. No. 111-203, 124 Stat. 1376 [Dodd-Frank].
[2] Contact jhiemenz@nclc.org to join... for the 2010 schedule and downloads of past webinars.
[3] Dodd-Frank § 1062.
[10] Id. § 1100E(b), to be codified at 15 U.S.C. § 1603
[11] Id. § 1416, *to be codified at* 15 U.S.C. § 1640(a)(2)(A)(ii).
[12] Id. § 1416, *to be codified at* 15 U.S.C. § 1640(a)(2)(B).